HORNBOOK ON TORTS

Second Edition

Dan B. Dobbs

Regents Professor and
Rosenstiel Distinguished Professor of Law Emeritus
University of Arizona

Paul T. Hayden

Thomas V. Girardi Professor of Consumer Protection Law
Loyola Law School, Los Angeles

Ellen M. Bublick

Dan B. Dobbs Professor of Law
University of Arizona

HORNBOOK SERIES®

WEST
ACADEMIC
PUBLISHING

Hornbook Series is a trademark registered in the U.S. Patent and Trademark Office.

COPYRIGHT © 2000 By WEST GROUP
© 2016 LEG, Inc. d/b/a West Academic
    444 Cedar Street, Suite 700
    St. Paul, MN 55101
    1-877-888-1330

West, West Academic Publishing, and West Academic are trademarks of West Publishing Corporation, used under license.

Printed in the United States of America

ISBN: 978-1-62810-147-8

To all my family—Patsy Waterfall, Anne Butterfield, Kate Ariel, Jean Fonvielle and George, Becky, Hannah, Tim and Ben Dobbs.

– D.B.D.

To Diane, Olivia, Dorothy and Rose.

– P.T.H.

To Daniel, Harrison and David, with love and admiration.

– E.M.B.

Preface

This hornbook is intended to provide a single-volume overview of contemporary tort law. It covers all of the traditional ground of tort law as well as a number of wholly new legal issues, including the fast-growing economic torts. Our aim is to help readers understand the general rules and flavor of contemporary American tort law through recent cases, statutes, and illustrations. While the approach is comprehensive, it is also judicious. Readers who prefer a more exhaustive examination of the topics and a fuller list of citations in support of various rules can turn to our four-volume treatise, Dan B. Dobbs, Paul T. Hayden & Ellen M. Bublick, The Law of Torts (2d ed. 2011 & Supp.).

This edition presents the second iteration of this one-volume hornbook. For the first edition, Professor Dobbs originally intended to write a new version of the Prosser & Keeton treatise, of which he was a co-author. However, the law had changed so much since that hornbook was last edited in 1984, he decided the revision game was not worth the candle; it was better instead to write an entirely new book from the ground up. His efforts became the first edition of this book.

Changes in tort law between the last edition of the Prosser & Keeton hornbook in 1984 and the first edition of this book in 2000 were immense, and certainly included changes in attitudes of judges and legislators. From the first volume of this hornbook in 2000 to the work today, changes have been more incremental, but also pervasive and important. For example, in intentional torts, the Restatement Third of Torts: Intentional Torts to Persons created a new tort of purposeful infliction of bodily harm. Whether courts will embrace the new tort, and with what limitations, is a matter for coming legal development, and lawyers are well-advised to be alert to the new possibilities. Moreover, all-or-nothing doctrines such as assumption of the risk have continued to fade away, and are increasingly discarded as separate defenses and instead incorporated into comparative fault defenses. While legislatures continue to limit the liabilities of many favored groups, common law duties of care are expanding in a number of areas. The areas of duty to protect third persons from harm, and duty to take precautions against emotional harm, are but two examples. The apportionment of liability landscape also has continued to evolve, not only in terms of how liability is divided amongst multiple actors, but also in terms of the way in which liability is envisioned as an initial matter once courts adopt a framework of divisible liability. On the economic torts side, questions about the role and scope of an economic loss rule or rules have dominated the scene.

Throughout all of these issues, this book does not consciously attempt to advance any particular approach to, or theory of, torts. It attempts, instead, to point to overriding policy goals, economic analysis, and concerns of accountability, as well as to practical problems in administering tort law. But the book is not *about* any of those things. It is *about* today's tort law. If we have a view about economic analysis vs. corrective justice or utilitarianism vs. some "moral" approach, it is probably that all of these approaches and their variations have offered, and will offer, a good deal to courts and advocates alike.

On the other hand, this book does occasionally offer comments or assessments of particular cases or legal rules, in the belief that any position taken offers students and lawyers a beginning point for their own analysis.

Conventions

"Defendant" and *"actor."* This book uses several conventions. Like the Restatement, it sometimes uses the term "actor" to refer to the person whose acts are in issue. But more often it uses the term defendant. "Actor" is admittedly more accurate because "actor" covers the case in which the plaintiff's acts are in issue as well as the case in which we are concerned with the defendant's act. Nevertheless, "actor" is often confusing, and professional usage makes it easy to understand that "defendant" can include other actors if the context demands.

"He" and *"she."* The pronouns he and she can be distributed more or less equally by using "she" for all plaintiffs and "he" for all defendants, and that is what we have done here. If it creates a sense that women are always plaintiffs and men always tortfeasor defendants, it is unfortunate, inaccurate and not our aim. But the practice aids clarity. So intending no implications about anyone's character, we typically use she in referring to plaintiffs, and he (or "it" with corporations) in referring to defendants.

Citations and *quotations*. Interior quotation marks are almost always omitted as are case citations appearing without a quotation. The denial of certiorari by the United States Supreme Court does not connote approval of the decision, and thus denial is not noted. Short forms of repeated citations are sometimes used as follows:

Restatement Second of Torts (1965–1977): Restatement Second.

Restatement Third of Torts (project title X): Restatement Third or Restatement Third of X.

W. Page Keeton, Dan B. Dobbs, Robert E. Keeton, & David G. Owen, Prosser & Keeton on Torts (5th ed. 1984): Prosser & Keeton.

Fowler V. Harper, Fleming James, Jr. & Oscar S. Gray, The Law of Torts (2d ed. 1986): Harper, James & Gray.

Dan B. Dobbs, Paul T. Hayden, and Ellen M. Bublick, The Law of Torts (2011 & Supp.): (volume number) Dobbs, Hayden & Bublick, The Law of Torts (section) (2d ed. 2011 & Supp.).

Acknowledgments

This book could not have been published without the dedicated work of many, many people, to whom we are deeply indebted. First and foremost, thanks are due to David Jacobs and Rose Hayden for their exhaustive review and edits of this full work. Thanks too to our fine colleagues at West Academic, who are a delight to work with, and make the whole process of writing and publishing a pleasure.

Professor Hayden adds thanks to all the research librarians at Loyola Law School, under the leadership of Professor Dan Martin, and all the administrative assistants in faculty support, under the leadership of Pam Buckles.

For excellent help with many facets of research, editing, revising and cite-checking, Professor Bublick would like to thank John Salvatore, Nick Lucie, Jana Sutton, Tyler Broker, Brooke Bedrick and Matt Mittlestadt. Thanks also to the James E. Rogers College of Law library, under the Directorship of Mike Chirorazzi, and the assistance of top reference librarian Maureen Garmon. Finally, many thanks to the hard work and professionalism of the Arizona Law Review, particularly, Raisa Ahmad, Alexis Brooks, Margo Casselman, Adam Cirzan, Creighton Dixon, Brett Gilmore, Lindsey Huang, Dan Roberts, Elizabeth Robertson, Christopher Sloot, and Mitch Turbenson, for their able and speedy assistance with hundreds of pages of proofs. No teachers are as lucky as we for the talent, vitality and energy of their students. Finally, thanks to Dean Marc Miller and Associate Dean Chris Robertson for their support of research at the college and of this book in particular.

Summary of Contents

Page

PREFACE V

ACKNOWLEDGMENTS VII

PART I. INTRODUCING TORT LAW

CHAPTER 1. DEFINING TORT LAW 3

CHAPTER 2. AIMS, POLICIES, HISTORY AND METHODS OF TORT LAW ... 15
A. Aims and Policies of Tort Law 15
B. History, Methods and Procedures of Tort Law 27

CHAPTER 3. TORT LAW IN PRACTICE 33
A. Adjudication of Tort Cases 33
B. Fundamental Operating Conceptions 38
C. The Background Conditions of Tort Law 43

PART II. INTENTIONAL TORTS TO PERSONS OR PROPERTY

CHAPTER 4. DIRECT AND INTENTIONAL INTERFERENCE WITH THE
PERSON 53
A. Scope of the Chapter 53
B. Intent and Related Concepts 55
C. Battery 60
D. Assault 69
E. False Imprisonment 73
F. Extended Liability and Damages 79

CHAPTER 5. INTENTIONAL INTERFERENCE WITH REAL PROPERTY:
TRESPASS TO LAND 85

CHAPTER 6. INTENTIONAL INTERFERENCE WITH TANGIBLE
PERSONAL PROPERTY: TRESPASS TO CHATTELS AND
CONVERSION 103

CHAPTER 7. DEFENSES TO INTENTIONAL TORTS 131
A. Self-Defense and Defense of Others 131
B. Discipline 138
C. Defense and Recovery of Property 139
D. Privileges to Detain or Arrest 153
E. Necessity 157

CHAPTER 8. CONSENT 163

PART III. NEGLIGENT PHYSICAL HARMS TO PERSONS OR PROPERTY

SUBPART A. THE PRIMA FACIE CASE

CHAPTER 9. THE NEGLIGENCE ACTION: AN INTRODUCTION **187**
A. Characteristics 187
B. Development 190
C. Fundamentals of Negligence Liability 197

CHAPTER 10. DUTY AND THE ORDINARY STANDARD OF REASONABLE CARE UNDER THE CIRCUMSTANCES **203**
A. The Existence of Duty 203
B. The Ordinary Standard of Reasonable Care 213
C. Particular Circumstances Related to the Standard of Care 218
D. The Standard of Care for Children 233
E. Other Standards of Care 237

CHAPTER 11. IMPORTING STATUTORY STANDARDS OF CARE: NEGLIGENCE PER SE **243**

CHAPTER 12. BREACH OF DUTY **263**
A. Negligent Conduct 263
B. Foreseeability and Risk-Utility 264
C. Custom 281
D. Statutory Compliance 289

CHAPTER 13. PROVING NEGLIGENCE CLAIMS **291**
A. Judge and Jury 291
B. Substitutes for Factual Evidence: Res Ipsa Loquitur 297

CHAPTER 14. ACTUAL HARM & FACTUAL CAUSE **311**
A. Actual Harm 311
B. The Factual Cause Requirement 312
C. The But-For Test of Causation 317
D. Problems with and Alternatives to the But-For Test: The Substantial Factor Test and Tests Aggregating Conduct 321
E. Proving Causation 324
F. Proving Which Defendant's Negligence Caused Harm 327
G. Special Problems: What Harm Was Caused? 331

CHAPTER 15. SCOPE OF LIABILITY (PROXIMATE CAUSE) **337**
A. Rules, Rationales and Context 337
B. The General Rules of Foreseeability 354
C. Intervening Acts or Forces 361
D. Alternatives 375

SUBPART B. DEFENSES

CHAPTER 16. FAULT OF THE PLAINTIFF 379
A.   General Rules 379
B.   Comparative Fault 384
C.   Related Doctrines and Special Cases 401

CHAPTER 17. ASSUMPTION OF THE RISK 409
A.   Express Assumption of Risk 409
B.   Implied Assumption of Risk 414

CHAPTER 18. STATUTES OF LIMITATION AND FEDERAL
     PREEMPTION 427
A.   Statutes of Limitation 427
B.   Federal Preemption 441

PART IV. EXPANDED OR LIMITED DUTIES OF CARE IN
PHYSICAL HARM CASES

CHAPTER 19. EXPANDED DUTIES OF CARE: CARRIERS, INNKEEPERS
     AND FIDUCIARIES 447

CHAPTER 20. PREMISES LIABILITY 459
A.   Duties to Those on the Premises 459
B.   Duties to Those Outside the Premises 483
C.   Duties of Vendors and Lessors 487

CHAPTER 21. LIABILITY OF HEALTH CARE PROVIDERS 493
A.   Medical Malpractice 494
B.   Hospitals and Managed Care Organizations 529
C.   Nursing Homes and Residential Facilities 537

CHAPTER 22. LIABILITY OF GOVERNMENT ENTITIES, OFFICERS AND
     EMPLOYEES 549
A.   Government Entities 549
B.   Individual Government Agents 576
C.   Civil Rights Claims 582

CHAPTER 23. FAMILY MEMBERS AND CHARITIES 591
A.   Family Members 591
B.   Charities 596

CHAPTER 24. PROFESSIONAL RISK-TAKERS 603

CHAPTER 25. LIMITING LIABILITY FOR NON-ACTION 615
A.   The General Rules of Non-Action 615
B.   General Duties to Act Affirmatively to Rescue or Assist 619

CHAPTER 26. DUTY TO PROTECT FROM THIRD PERSONS AND FROM
     SELF-HARM 633
A.   The No-Duty Rule 633

B.   Duty Based on Defendant's Relationship to Plaintiff 637
C.   Duty Based on Defendant's Relationship to a Dangerous Person 651

PART V. SPECIAL TYPES OF HARM

CHAPTER 27. PRENATAL AND BIRTH-RELATED INJURY 669
A.   Prenatal or Preconception Injury 669
B.   Wrongful Birth, Conception or Life 677

CHAPTER 28. WRONGFUL DEATH AND SURVIVAL ACTIONS 685

CHAPTER 29. EMOTIONAL HARM 699
A.   Introduction to Emotional Harm 699
B.   Intentional or Reckless Infliction of Emotional Distress 705
C.   Negligent Infliction of Emotional Harm 713

CHAPTER 30. NUISANCE 733

PART VI. VICARIOUS LIABILITY, STRICT LIABILITY, AND PRODUCTS LIABILITY

CHAPTER 31. VICARIOUS LIABILITY FOR PHYSICAL HARMS 753

CHAPTER 32. STRICT LIABILITY FOR ANIMALS AND ABNORMALLY DANGEROUS ACTIVITIES 777
A.   Introduction 777
B.   Strict Liability for Animals 778
C.   Strict Liability for Abnormally Dangerous Activities 784
D.   Limitations and Defenses 792

CHAPTER 33. PRODUCTS LIABILITY 797
A.   Delineating the Field 797
B.   Tort Liability for Defective Products 804
C.   Defenses 834

PART VII. DAMAGES, APPORTIONMENT, AND ALTERNATIVE SYSTEMS

CHAPTER 34. DAMAGES 851
A.   Compensatory Damages 851
B.   Punitive Damages 861

CHAPTER 35. APPORTIONMENT OF LIABILITY AMONG PARTIES 877
A.   Introduction: Joint and Several Liability and Several Liability 877
B.   Persons and Conduct Subject to Apportionment 888
C.   Standards 893
D.   Special Cases for Apportionment 895
E.   Other Apportionment Systems 901

CHAPTER 36. ALTERNATIVE SYSTEMS FOR COMPENSATING INJURY.. **905**
A.   Criticism of Tort 905
B.   Workers' Compensation 911
C.   Other Injury Systems..922

PART VIII. DIGNITARY AND ECONOMIC TORTS

SUBPART A. DIGNITARY TORTS

CHAPTER 37. DEFAMATION **935**
A.   Introducing Defamation...936
B.   Common Law Requirements 938
C.   Defenses 965
D.   Constitutional Limitations on Recovery 986
E.   Remedies 998

CHAPTER 38. PRIVACY... **1005**

CHAPTER 39. MISUSING JUDICIAL PROCESS **1023**
A.   Introduction: Tortious Use of the Legal Process 1023
B.   Malicious Prosecution 1026
C.   Wrongful Civil Litigation...1036
D.   Abuse of Process 1042
E.   Reforms and New Directions 1046

CHAPTER 40. INTERFERENCE WITH FAMILY RELATIONSHIPS............. **1049**

SUBPART B. ECONOMIC TORTS

CHAPTER 41. ECONOMIC TORTS AND ECONOMIC LOSS RULES **1059**
A.   Economic Loss: An Introduction..1059
B.   Negligent Economic Loss in the Stranger Context 1065
C.   Negligent Economic Loss and Contracting Parties......................1077
D.   Scope and Exceptions 1083

CHAPTER 42. INTERFERENCE WITH CONTRACT AND ECONOMIC INTERESTS **1089**
A.   The Core Rules of Intentional Interference with Contract...........1089
B.   Improper Interference 1098
C.   Intentional Interference with Economic Opportunity 1106
D.   The Prima Facie Tort 1110
E.   Negligent Interference with Contract and Opportunity 1112

CHAPTER 43. MISREPRESENTATION AND FALSEHOODS........................ **1113**
A.   Injurious Falsehood..1113
B.   Fraudulent Misrepresentations 1115
C.   Negligent Misrepresentation..1123
D.   Innocent Misrepresentation..1127
E.   Major Issues..1129

F. Economic Harms in Special Relationships 1143

CHAPTER 44. ECONOMIC HARM TO INTANGIBLE INTERESTS BY CONVERSION OR SPOLIATION **1151**
A. Conversion of Intangible Economic Interests...1151
B. Spoliation of Evidence..1157

CHAPTER 45. LEGAL MALPRACTICE **1163**
A. Malpractice in Civil Matters: Prima Facie Case 1163
B. Malpractice in Civil Matters: Defenses..1177
C. Malpractice in Civil Matters: Damages 1182
D. Malpractice in Criminal Cases 1186

CHAPTER 46. UNFAIR COMPETITION: TRADEMARKS, TRADE SECRETS AND PUBLICITY RIGHTS **1193**

TABLE OF CASES 1211

INDEX..1295

Table of Contents

Page

PREFACE V

ACKNOWLEDGMENTS VII

PART I. INTRODUCING TORT LAW

CHAPTER 1. DEFINING TORT LAW 3
§ 1.1   Defining Torts 3
§ 1.2   Bases of Tort Liability 4
§ 1.3   Types of Interests Protected 5
§ 1.4   Torts and Crimes 6
§ 1.5   Torts and Contracts 7
§ 1.6   Torts and Property 9
§ 1.7   Torts and Regulatory Control 10
§ 1.8   Torts and Personal Injury Law 11
§ 1.9   The Coherence of Tort Law 12

CHAPTER 2. AIMS, POLICIES, HISTORY AND METHODS OF TORT LAW ... 15
A.   Aims and Policies of Tort Law 15
§ 2.1   Justice, Policy, and Process Aims in Summary 15
§ 2.2   Corrective Justice, Distributive Justice, and Policy 17
§ 2.3   Fault and Other Normative Bases for Liability 19
§ 2.4   Compensation, Risk Distribution, and Fault 21
§ 2.5   Deterrence 23
§ 2.6   Alternative Compensation Systems 24
§ 2.7   Process Values in Tort Law 25
B.   History, Methods and Procedures of Tort Law 27
§ 2.8   Historical Development of Tort Law 27
§ 2.9   Common-Law Analysis and the Doctrine of Precedent 30
§ 2.10   Tort Rules and What They Do 31

CHAPTER 3. TORT LAW IN PRACTICE 33
A.   Adjudication of Tort Cases 33
§ 3.1   Trials and Appeals 33
§ 3.2   Judge, Jury, and Community Values 35
B.   Fundamental Operating Conceptions 38
§ 3.3   The Prima Facie Case and the Burden of Proof 38
§ 3.4   Affirmative Defenses 40
§ 3.5   Privilege, Justification, Excuse and Immunity 41
C.   The Background Conditions of Tort Law 43
§ 3.6   Remedies and Attorney's Fees 43
§ 3.7   Sources of Tort Law 44
§ 3.8   Liability Insurance 47

PART II. INTENTIONAL TORTS TO PERSONS OR PROPERTY

CHAPTER 4. DIRECT AND INTENTIONAL INTERFERENCE WITH THE PERSON **53**
- A.   Scope of the Chapter..53
- § 4.1   Scope of the Chapter..53
- B.   Intent and Related Concepts 55
- § 4.2   The Meaning of Intent..55
- § 4.3   Intent and Motive 57
- § 4.4   Intent and Negligence 58
- § 4.5   Intent and Reckless or Wanton Misconduct................................59
- C.   Battery..60
- § 4.6   Simple Battery 60
- § 4.7   Harm or Offense Required to Establish Simple Battery..............62
- § 4.8   Nature of Intent Required to Establish Simple Battery 64
- § 4.9   The Bodily Contact Required to Establish Simple Battery 67
- § 4.10   Battery and Other Torts: Acts and Omissions............................68
- D.   Assault..69
- § 4.11   Simple Assault 69
- § 4.12   Anticipation of Imminent Touching..70
- § 4.13   Assault, Crime, and Other Torts 72
- E.   False Imprisonment 73
- § 4.14   Simple False Imprisonment 73
- § 4.15   Methods of Confinement...74
- § 4.16   Duty to Release from Confinement..77
- § 4.17   False Imprisonment and Other Torts..78
- F.   Extended Liability and Damages 79
- § 4.18   Extended Liability or Transferred Intent 79
- § 4.19   Extended Liability: The Pros and Cons..80
- § 4.20   Damages for Trespassory Torts to the Person 82
- § 4.21   Infliction of Emotional Distress 83

CHAPTER 5. INTENTIONAL INTERFERENCE WITH REAL PROPERTY: TRESPASS TO LAND **85**
- § 5.1   Elements and Terminology 85
- § 5.2   Intent Required...86
- § 5.3   Distinguishing Trespass from Nuisance 89
- § 5.4   Protecting Interests in Possession and Physical Integrity 90
- § 5.5   Tangible Entry 92
- § 5.6   Entries Above the Surface..93
- § 5.7   Entries Below the Surface..95
- § 5.8   Remedies..96
- § 5.9   Temporary or Continuing Trespass vs. Permanent or Completed Trespass..98
- § 5.10   Extended Liability 101

CHAPTER 6. INTENTIONAL INTERFERENCE WITH TANGIBLE PERSONAL PROPERTY: TRESPASS TO CHATTELS AND CONVERSION 103

§ 6.1   Development of Liability for Interference with Chattels 103
§ 6.2   Trespass to Chattels 105
§ 6.3   Conversion of Chattels—Elements and Issues 107
§ 6.4   Conversion: Intent Required 109
§ 6.5   Property Subject to Conversion 110
§ 6.6   Dominion or Control Required 112
§ 6.7   Methods of Committing Conversion—Generally 113
§ 6.8   Conversion by Creditors 115
§ 6.9   Conversion by Bailees 116
§ 6.10   Contract and Tort: Conversion and the Bailment Contract 118
§ 6.11   The Bailor's Option to Sue "In Tort" or "In Contract" and the Economic Loss Rule 120
§ 6.12   The Bona Fide Purchaser of Converted Tangible Goods 122
§ 6.13   The Bona Fide Purchaser of Converted Money or Checks 124
§ 6.14   Remedies for Conversion 125
§ 6.15   Statutes of Limitation in Conversion 127

CHAPTER 7. DEFENSES TO INTENTIONAL TORTS 131

A.   Self-Defense and Defense of Others 131
§ 7.1   General Rule 131
§ 7.2   When Retreat Is Required 133
§ 7.3   Objective vs. Subjective Perceptions of Threat 135
§ 7.4   Types of Harm Appropriate for Self-Defense 136
§ 7.5   Defending Another Person from Apparent Attack 137
B.   Discipline 138
§ 7.6   Parental Privileges to Discipline Children 138
§ 7.7   Discipline by Non-Parents in Charge of Minors 139
C.   Defense and Recovery of Property 139
§ 7.8   Defending Possession of Land or Chattels: General Rule 139
§ 7.9   Qualifying and Explaining the General Rule 140
§ 7.10   Deadly Traps in Defense of Property: Spring Guns 142
§ 7.11   Qualifying and Considering the Deadly-Trap Rules 144
§ 7.12   Types of "Traps" and Negligence Law 146
§ 7.13   Repossession of Land 147
§ 7.14   Repossession of Chattels: General Rules 150
§ 7.15   The Repossessing Seller 151
§ 7.16   Entering Another's Land to Recapture Chattels 152
D.   Privileges to Detain or Arrest 153
§ 7.17   The Merchant's Privilege to Detain for Investigation 153
§ 7.18   Privileged Arrests 155
E.   Necessity 157
§ 7.19   Private Necessity 157
§ 7.20   Public Necessity 158
§ 7.21   Public Entities: Necessity, Police Power, and "Taking" 159

CHAPTER 8. CONSENT **163**
§ 8.1   General Principles 163
§ 8.2   Manifestation of Consent 165
§ 8.3   Unmanifested Consent 168
§ 8.4   Scope of Consent 169
§ 8.5   Revocation or Termination of Consent 170
§ 8.6   Incapacity to Give Consent 171
§ 8.7   Consent on Behalf of Another 173
§ 8.8   Mistake or Misrepresentation Negating Consent........................175
§ 8.9   Consent Obtained by Duress or Coercion....................................177
§ 8.10   Consent Obtained by Abuse of Power or Position........................178
§ 8.11   Medical Battery and Informed Consent 181
§ 8.12   Emergency as a Substitute for Consent 182
§ 8.13   Consent to Crime 183

PART III. NEGLIGENT PHYSICAL HARMS TO PERSONS OR PROPERTY

SUBPART A. THE PRIMA FACIE CASE

CHAPTER 9. THE NEGLIGENCE ACTION: AN INTRODUCTION **187**
A.   Characteristics...187
§ 9.1   Characteristics of the Negligence Case 187
B.   Development 190
§ 9.2   Negligence: The Common Law Background 190
§ 9.3   Negligence: Courts Adopt a General Principle of Liability for Fault 193
§ 9.4   Negligence: After Adoption of the Fault Principle......................195
C.   Fundamentals of Negligence Liability 197
§ 9.5   Elements of the Prima Facie Case for Negligence.......................197
§ 9.6   The Elements: Meaning and Terminology 198
§ 9.7   Negligence as Conduct, Not State of Mind..................................200

**CHAPTER 10. DUTY AND THE ORDINARY STANDARD OF REASONABLE
CARE UNDER THE CIRCUMSTANCES** **203**
A.   The Existence of Duty 203
§ 10.1   General Rules of Duty 203
§ 10.2   Duty vs. Breach Confusion..205
§ 10.3   Determining the Existence of Duty 208
§ 10.4   Foreseeability and Duty Determinations.....................................211
B.   The Ordinary Standard of Reasonable Care................................213
§ 10.5   The Objective Reasonable Person Standard 213
§ 10.6   Circumstances as Part of the Standard: Special Danger 216
C.   Particular Circumstances Related to the Standard of Care 218
§ 10.7   Emergency and Unavoidable Accident 218
§ 10.8   Objective and Subjective Features of the Standard 222
§ 10.9   Physical Characteristics 223
§ 10.10   Mental Capacity..225
§ 10.11   Bases for and Alternatives to the Mental Capacity Rules 227
§ 10.12   Knowledge, Perception, Memory, Experience, and Skills..............229

§ 10.13	Intoxication	231
D.	The Standard of Care for Children	233
§ 10.14	The General Standard of Care for Children	233
§ 10.15	Rationales for the Child Standard	235
§ 10.16	Holding Children to an Adult Standard	236
E.	Other Standards of Care	237
§ 10.17	Alternative Standards	237
§ 10.18	Gross Negligence, Recklessness, and Wanton Misconduct	239

CHAPTER 11. IMPORTING STATUTORY STANDARDS OF CARE: NEGLIGENCE PER SE 243

§ 11.1	The Rule of Negligence Per Se	243
§ 11.2	Statutes Creating a Standard of Care	245
§ 11.3	Negligence Per Se vs. Private Right of Action	246
§ 11.4	Alternatives to Negligence Per Se: Evidence of Negligence	249
§ 11.5	Rationales for Negligence Per Se	250
§ 11.6	Type of Harm Prevented by the Statute	253
§ 11.7	Class of Persons Protected Under the Statute	255
§ 11.8	Interpreting the Scope of Risk	256
§ 11.9	Excused and Unexcused Violations	257

CHAPTER 12. BREACH OF DUTY 263

A.	Negligent Conduct	263
§ 12.1	Specific Negligent Acts	263
B.	Foreseeability and Risk-Utility	264
§ 12.2	Foreseeability of Harm in Breach	264
§ 12.3	Unstructured Weighing of Reasonableness	267
§ 12.4	Structured Weighing of Risks and Utilities	271
§ 12.5	Supporting and Criticizing Structured Risk-Utility Assessments	275
C.	Custom	281
§ 12.6	Custom or Practice: General Rules	281
§ 12.7	Limitations on the Use of Custom and Practice	284
§ 12.8	Private Standards: Defendant's Own "Customs" or Practices	287
§ 12.9	Entering Transactions in Light of Custom	288
D.	Statutory Compliance	289
§ 12.10	Compliance with Statute	289

CHAPTER 13. PROVING NEGLIGENCE CLAIMS 291

A.	Judge and Jury	291
§ 13.1	Roles of the Judge and Jury in Negligence Cases	291
§ 13.2	Burden of Proof and Types of Evidence: Basic Information	293
B.	Substitutes for Factual Evidence: Res Ipsa Loquitur	297
§ 13.3	Res Ipsa Loquitur: General Rules	297
§ 13.4	Inferences Permitted, Required or Unpermitted	299
§ 13.5	Estimating Probabilities of Negligence	301
§ 13.6	Res Ipsa Cases: Illustrations	304
§ 13.7	Attributing Fault to the Defendant	306

CHAPTER 14. ACTUAL HARM & FACTUAL CAUSE.............................. 311
  A.   Actual Harm..311
§ 14.1   The Requirement of Actual Harm 311
  B.   The Factual Cause Requirement...................................312
§ 14.2   Factual Cause and Four Forms of Common Issues.....................312
§ 14.3   Terminology and Structure: Factual Cause and Scope of Liability
      (Proximate Cause)..316
  C.   The But-For Test of Causation 317
§ 14.4   The But-For Test of Factual Cause 317
§ 14.5   But-For Analysis and the Hypothetical Alternative Case 319
  D.   Problems with and Alternatives to the But-For Test..................321
§ 14.6   Alternate Tests When But-For Analysis Fails: The Substantial Factor
      Test and Tests Aggregating Conduct 321
  E.   Proving Causation 324
§ 14.7   Connecting Negligence and Harm 324
§ 14.8   Evidence and Inferences of But-For Causation 326
  F.   Proving Which Defendant's Negligence Caused Harm 327
§ 14.9   Alternative Causes and the Shifted Burden of Proof 327
§ 14.10   Statistical Substitutes for Causation: Market Share Liability...................330
  G.   Special Problems: What Harm Was Caused? 331
§ 14.11   The Lost Chance of Recovery 331

CHAPTER 15. SCOPE OF LIABILITY (PROXIMATE CAUSE) 337
  A.   Rules, Rationales and Context......................................337
§ 15.1   Introduction...337
§ 15.2   Reasons for Scope of Liability Limitations...........................339
§ 15.3   Relation to Factual Cause 342
§ 15.4   Relation to Negligence (Breach of Duty) 342
§ 15.5   Relation to Duty..343
§ 15.6   Patterns and Formal Tests of Scope of Liability......................345
§ 15.7   The Direct-Cause Pattern and Foreseeable Harms......................346
§ 15.8   The Direct-Cause Pattern and Unforeseeable Harms....................350
§ 15.9   The Intervening Cause Pattern and Superseding Cause Analysis 351
  B.   The General Rules of Foreseeability 354
§ 15.10   Foreseeability Terminology: Scope of Risk............................354
§ 15.11   Foreseeability Required: Extent of Harm 355
§ 15.12   Foreseeability Required: Manner of Harm 356
§ 15.13   Injury Remote in Time or Distance 360
  C.   Intervening Acts or Forces..361
§ 15.14   Intervening Intentional or Criminal Acts 361
§ 15.15   Intervening Forces of Nature.......................................364
§ 15.16   Foreseeable Intervening Negligent Acts 365
§ 15.17   Unforeseeable Intervening Acts.....................................369
§ 15.18   Using "Proximate Cause" as a No-Duty Rule 371
§ 15.19   Plaintiff's Own Acts as a Superseding Cause 373
  D.   Alternatives...375
§ 15.20   Joint and Several Liability and Comparative Fault......................375
§ 15.21   Abolishing Superseding Cause Analysis 376

SUBPART B. DEFENSES

CHAPTER 16. FAULT OF THE PLAINTIFF **379**
    A.   General Rules 379
§ 16.1   Effects of Plaintiff Fault 379
§ 16.2   The Parallel Analysis of Plaintiff and Defendant Fault 381
    B.   Comparative Fault 384
§ 16.3   Comparative Fault 384
§ 16.4   Assigning Shares of Fault or Responsibility to the Plaintiff 386
§ 16.5   All-or-Nothing Judgments After Comparative Fault 389
§ 16.6   Allocating Full Responsibility to the Defendant in the Interests of
            Policy or Justice: Plaintiff No-Duty Rules 391
§ 16.7   Traditional Exceptions to the Contributory Negligence Bar and Their
            Status Today 397
    C.   Related Doctrines and Special Cases 401
§ 16.8   Effect of Plaintiff's Illegal Acts 401
§ 16.9   Distinguishing Avoidable Consequences 403
§ 16.10   The Role of Avoidable Consequences in Comparative Fault Regimes 404
§ 16.11   Comparative Fault or Avoidable Consequences in Seatbelt and Other
            Safety Precaution Cases 406

CHAPTER 17. ASSUMPTION OF THE RISK **409**
    A.   Express Assumption of Risk 409
§ 17.1   Shifting Responsibility by Agreement 409
§ 17.2   Contractual Limitations 410
§ 17.3   Public Policy Limitations 412
    B.   Implied Assumption of Risk 414
§ 17.4   The Traditional Rule: Assumption of Risk as a Complete Bar 414
§ 17.5   Development of Constraining Rules 417
§ 17.6   Discarding the Defense of Implied Assumption of Risk 418
§ 17.7   Primary and Secondary Assumption of Risk 420
§ 17.8   Sports Cases 422

**CHAPTER 18. STATUTES OF LIMITATION AND FEDERAL
    PREEMPTION** **427**
    A.   Statutes of Limitation 427
§ 18.1   Foundational Principles and Rationales 427
§ 18.2   The Accrual Rule 429
§ 18.3   The Discovery Rule 429
§ 18.4   Statutes of Repose 432
§ 18.5   Continuing Negligence 435
§ 18.6   Tolling, Grace Periods, and Postponed Accrual 436
§ 18.7   Accrued Claims with Latent Harm 439
    B.   Federal Preemption 441
§ 18.8   Federal Preemption 441

PART IV. EXPANDED OR LIMITED DUTIES OF CARE
IN PHYSICAL HARM CASES

CHAPTER 19. EXPANDED DUTIES OF CARE: CARRIERS, INNKEEPERS AND FIDUCIARIES 447

§ 19.1   Duty of Common Carriers in Personal-Injury Cases 447
§ 19.2   Who Counts as a Common Carrier or Passenger 448
§ 19.3   Protecting Passengers of Common Carriers from Third Persons and Other External Risks 451
§ 19.4   Duty of Innkeepers in Personal-Injury Cases 452
§ 19.5   Duty of Fiduciaries in Personal-Injury Cases 454
§ 19.6   Fiduciary Relationship Imposing an Affirmative Duty to Protect from Others 455

CHAPTER 20. PREMISES LIABILITY 459

A.   Duties to Those on the Premises 459
§ 20.1   Common-Law Classification of Entrants on Land 459
§ 20.2   Duty Owed to Trespassers: Traditional Rule 460
§ 20.3   The Discovered-Trespasser Exception 460
§ 20.4   Licensees: The Classification 462
§ 20.5   Duty Owed to Licensees: Traditional Rule 463
§ 20.6   Invitees: The Classification 465
§ 20.7   Duty Owed to Invitees 468
§ 20.8   Children on the Land 473
§ 20.9   Changing Duties and Categories: Extending the Duty of Reasonable Care to Entrants Other than Invitees 478
§ 20.10   Recreational Use Statutes 479
B.   Duties to Those Outside the Premises 483
§ 20.11   Natural Conditions on the Land 483
§ 20.12   Active Conduct and Artificial Conditions on the Land 485
C.   Duties of Vendors and Lessors 487
§ 20.13   Vendors of Land 487
§ 20.14   Traditional Common Law Duties of Lessors 488
§ 20.15   The Implied Warranty of Habitability 491

CHAPTER 21. LIABILITY OF HEALTH CARE PROVIDERS 493

A.   Medical Malpractice 494
          1. Summary and Context 494
§ 21.1   Malpractice Rules in Summary 494
§ 21.2   Professional Status and Its Significance 495
          2. Duty and the Doctor-Patient Relationship 497
§ 21.3   General Rule and Exceptions 497
§ 21.4   Duties to Non-Patients 500
          3. Standards of Care and Attendant Proof Requirements 503
§ 21.5   The Traditional Medical Standard of Care 503
§ 21.6   The Reasonable Care Standard 506
§ 21.7   The Relevant Geographical Community 508
§ 21.8   The Expert Testimony Requirement 509
          4. Informed Consent 513

§ 21.9   Informed Consent: Underlying Principle and Elements 513
§ 21.10   General Standards of Disclosure 516
§ 21.11   Particular Types of Information to Be Disclosed 518
§ 21.12   The Causation Requirement in Informed Consent Cases 520
           5.   Defenses and Statutory Limits on Liability....................................523
§ 21.13   Good Samaritan Statutes..523
§ 21.14   The "Malpractice Crisis" Statutes 524
§ 21.15   Patient's Contributory Negligence..527
    B.   Hospitals and Managed Care Organizations...529
§ 21.16   Common-Law Responsibility of Hospitals 529
§ 21.17   Mandatory Hospital Screening and Treatment: EMTALA........................531
§ 21.18   Managed Care Organizations 533
    C.   Nursing Homes and Residential Facilities 537
§ 21.19   Injuries in Nursing Homes and Other Care Facilities 537
§ 21.20   Standard of Care for Nursing Homes 538
§ 21.21   Common-Law Claims Against Nursing Homes 542
§ 21.22   Statutory Claims Against Nursing Homes 544

CHAPTER 22. LIABILITY OF GOVERNMENT ENTITIES, OFFICERS AND EMPLOYEES **549**
    A.   Government Entities 549
           1.   Introduction: Traditional Immunities 549
§ 22.1   Traditional Immunities and Their Passing...549
           2.   Federal Government Liability Under the FTCA 551
§ 22.2   The Plan of Federal Government Tort Liability 551
§ 22.3   The Discretionary Immunity..553
§ 22.4   The *Feres* Rule: Tort Claims by Military Personnel 558
§ 22.5   Other Statutory Exceptions to FTCA Liability...562
           3.   Immunities and Liabilities of State and Local Entities..........563
§ 22.6   State Sovereign Immunity and Its Waiver 563
§ 22.7   Local Public-Entity Immunity and Its Waiver 565
§ 22.8   Discretionary Immunity of State and Local Entities 568
§ 22.9   The Public Duty Doctrine...569
§ 22.10   Excluding Liability for Police and Fire Protection 574
§ 22.11   Excluding Liability for Release of Dangerous Persons................................575
    B.   Individual Government Agents 576
§ 22.12   State and Local Officers and Employees...576
§ 22.13   Federal Officers and Employees 580
    C.   Civil Rights Claims...582
§ 22.14   Federal Civil Rights Claims: § 1983 582
§ 22.15   Section 1983 Claims Against State and Local Officials 584
§ 22.16   Section 1983 Claims Against State and Local Entities................................586

CHAPTER 23. FAMILY MEMBERS AND CHARITIES.. **591**
    A.   Family Members 591
§ 23.1   Spousal Immunity...591
§ 23.2   Parental Immunity 593
    B.   Charities..596
§ 23.3   Charitable Immunity..596

§ 23.4   Individual Immunities 599

CHAPTER 24. PROFESSIONAL RISK-TAKERS **603**
§ 24.1   Shifting Responsibility to Professional Risk-Takers 603
§ 24.2   Limited Duties to Professional Risk-Takers: The Firefighters' Rule 605
§ 24.3   Risks Covered by the Risk-Takers Rule 608
§ 24.4   Persons Covered by the Risk-Takers Rule 611

CHAPTER 25. LIMITING LIABILITY FOR NON-ACTION **615**
        A.   The General Rules of Non-Action 615
§ 25.1   The No-Duty-to-Rescue Rule and Exceptions 615
§ 25.2   Scope of the Rule Protecting Non-Action 618
        B.   General Duties to Act Affirmatively to Rescue or Assist 619
§ 25.3   Innocently Harming or Creating a Risk of Harm 619
§ 25.4   Special Relationship Between Plaintiff and Defendant 620
§ 25.5   Beginning to Rescue or Assist 622
§ 25.6   Undertaking Creating a Duty to the Plaintiff 623
§ 25.7   Undertaking Creating a Duty to Third Persons 627

**CHAPTER 26. DUTY TO PROTECT FROM THIRD PERSONS AND FROM
        SELF-HARM** **633**
        A.   The No-Duty Rule 633
§ 26.1   No Duty to Control Others 633
§ 26.2   Actively Creating Risk of Injury by Third Person 634
        B.   Duty Based on Defendant's Relationship to Plaintiff 637
§ 26.3   Types of Relationships Recognized 637
§ 26.4   Landowner's Duty to Protect Lawful Entrants 638
§ 26.5   Landlord's Duty to Protect Tenants and Their Guests 643
§ 26.6   Custodian's and School's State-Law Duty to Protect Wards or Students 645
§ 26.7   Federal Civil Rights Claims 649
§ 26.8   Employer's Duty to Protect Employees 650
        C.   Duty Based on Defendant's Relationship to a Dangerous Person 651
§ 26.9   Relationships Recognized 651
§ 26.10   Negligent Entrustment 653
§ 26.11   Control and Other Means of Protecting from Dangerous Persons 656
§ 26.12   Enhancing Dangers: Providers of Alcohol 661

PART V. SPECIAL TYPES OF HARM

CHAPTER 27. PRENATAL AND BIRTH-RELATED INJURY **669**
        A.   Prenatal or Preconception Injury 669
§ 27.1   Prenatal Injury 669
§ 27.2   Toxic Injuries and Parental Liability 672
§ 27.3   Preconception Negligence 675
        B.   Wrongful Birth, Conception or Life 677
§ 27.4   Negligent Interference with Mother's Opportunity to Avoid or Terminate
              a Pregnancy 677
§ 27.5   Special Damages Rules 680

CHAPTER 28. WRONGFUL DEATH AND SURVIVAL ACTIONS 685
§ 28.1   Wrongful Death and Survival Actions 685
§ 28.2   Survival Actions—Scope and Damages 687
§ 28.3   Wrongful Death Actions: Pecuniary Loss Damages 688
§ 28.4   Wrongful Death Actions: Non-Pecuniary Damages 691
§ 28.5   Procedure, Distribution, Defenses and Damages 694

CHAPTER 29. EMOTIONAL HARM 699
    A.   Introduction to Emotional Harm 699
§ 29.1   Introduction to Emotional Distress and Harm in Tort Law 699
§ 29.2   Stand-Alone Emotional Distress as a Tort in Itself: Policy Concerns 700
§ 29.3   Stand-Alone Emotional Distress as a Tort in Itself: Historical
          Development 703
    B.   Intentional or Reckless Infliction of Emotional Distress 705
§ 29.4   Overlapping or Duplicating Claims for Emotional Distress 705
§ 29.5   Intentional Infliction of Emotional Distress: Rules of Liability 706
§ 29.6   Common Characteristics of Extreme and Outrageous Conduct 707
§ 29.7   The Severe Distress Requirement 710
§ 29.8   Intentional Infliction and Emotional Distress of Third Persons 711
    C.   Negligent Infliction of Emotional Harm 713
§ 29.9   Negligent Infliction of Emotional Harm: General Rules of Liability 713
§ 29.10   Emotional Harm Arising from Risks or Harms to Others 714
§ 29.11   Loss of Consortium 718
§ 29.12   Emotional Distress Arising from Direct Risks of Physical Harm 721
§ 29.13   Toxic Exposures: Fear of Future Harm 725
§ 29.14   Emotional Distress from False or Erroneous Information 726
§ 29.15   Duties of Care to Protect Emotional Well-Being Independent of Physical
          Risks 728
§ 29.16   Sensitive Plaintiffs 731

CHAPTER 30. NUISANCE 733
§ 30.1   Introducing Nuisance Law 733
§ 30.2   Defining and Illustrating Private Nuisance 734
§ 30.3   Intent, Negligence and Strict Liability 736
§ 30.4   Substantial and Unreasonable Interference 738
§ 30.5   Non-Invasive Nuisances 742
§ 30.6   Public Nuisance 744
§ 30.7   Remedies 747

PART VI. VICARIOUS LIABILITY, STRICT LIABILITY, AND PRODUCTS LIABILITY

CHAPTER 31. VICARIOUS LIABILITY FOR PHYSICAL HARMS 753
§ 31.1   Vicarious Liability Generally 753
§ 31.2   Rationales for Respondeat Superior Liability 755
§ 31.3   Scope of Employment: General Principles 757
§ 31.4   Limits on Scope of Employment 758
§ 31.5   Independent Contractors: General Rules 764
§ 31.6   Independent Contractors Performing Nondelegable Duties 766

§ 31.7   Apparent Agency and Agency by Estoppel...770
§ 31.8   Borrowed Servants..773

**CHAPTER 32. STRICT LIABILITY FOR ANIMALS AND ABNORMALLY
      DANGEROUS ACTIVITIES.. 777**
      A.   Introduction 777
§ 32.1   Pockets of Strict Liability in a Fault-Based System.................................777
      B.   Strict Liability for Animals..778
§ 32.2   Trespassing Animals 778
§ 32.3   Abnormally Dangerous Domestic Animals 779
§ 32.4   Wild Animals...782
      C.   Strict Liability for Abnormally Dangerous Activities 784
§ 32.5   Historical Context: From *Rylands* to the Restatement.......................784
§ 32.6   Contemporary Abnormal-Danger Cases 786
§ 32.7   Rationales for Abnormal-Danger Strict Liability 789
      D.   Limitations and Defenses 792
§ 32.8   Limitations on Strict Liability 792
§ 32.9   Defenses to Strict Liability..793

CHAPTER 33. PRODUCTS LIABILITY 797
      A.   Delineating the Field..797
§ 33.1   Theories of Recovery 797
§ 33.2   History, Rationales, and Decline of Strict Liability 799
§ 33.3   The Economic Loss Rule: Stand-Alone Economic Harm 803
      B.   Tort Liability for Defective Products..804
            1.   The Modern Typology of Defect 804
§ 33.4   The Defect Requirement...804
§ 33.5   Summary of Types of Defect...805
            2.   Manufacturing and Design Defects...808
§ 33.6   The Consumer Expectations Test 808
§ 33.7   Proving Manufacturing Defects 810
§ 33.8   Problems with the Consumer Expectations Test: Open and Obvious
            Dangers and Other Difficulties 812
§ 33.9   The Risk-Utility Test for Design Defects 814
§ 33.10   Proving a Design's Risks and Utilities 816
§ 33.11   Reasonable Alternative Design...820
§ 33.12   Shifting the Burden of Proof in Design Defect Cases 824
            3.   Marketing Defects 825
§ 33.13   The Warnings Requirement 825
§ 33.14   Adequacy of Warnings..828
§ 33.15   Learned Intermediaries and Sophisticated Users 830
§ 33.16   Causation in Failure-to-Warn Cases 832
      C.   Defenses 834
§ 33.17   Contributory Negligence and Assumption of Risk 834
§ 33.18   Unforeseeable Misuse, Alteration and Modification 838
§ 33.19   Statutory Defenses..842
§ 33.20   Compliance with Statute and Preemption 844
§ 33.21   Statutes of Limitation...847

PART VII. DAMAGES, APPORTIONMENT, AND ALTERNATIVE SYSTEMS

CHAPTER 34. DAMAGES.. **851**
    A.   Compensatory Damages...851
§ 34.1   Basic Compensatory Damages for Personal Injury 851
§ 34.2   Damages for Harms to Property 856
§ 34.3   Adjustments in Basic Compensatory Damages 858
    B.   Punitive Damages..861
§ 34.4   Punitive Damages and Their Bases.......................................861
§ 34.5   Common Law Factors in Determining the Amount of Punitive Damages 865
§ 34.6   Constitutional Requirements Governing the Award of Punitive Damages 867
§ 34.7   "Tort Reform" Statutes Affecting Compensatory and Punitive Damages.....873

CHAPTER 35. APPORTIONMENT OF LIABILITY AMONG PARTIES............ **877**
    A.   Introduction: Joint and Several Liability and Several Liability 877
§ 35.1   Apportionment of Liability: An Overview 877
§ 35.2   Traditional Rules and Joint and Several Liability 881
§ 35.3   Joint and Several Liability vs. Several Liability Systems 883
§ 35.4   Several Liability Systems..884
§ 35.5   General Effects of Adopting Several Liability Systems 886
    B.   Persons and Conduct Subject to Apportionment............................888
§ 35.6   Immune and Nonparty Tortfeasors 888
§ 35.7   Types of Actionable Conduct Subject to Apportionment 891
    C.   Standards 893
§ 35.8   Apportionment Standards 893
    D.   Special Cases for Apportionment 895
§ 35.9   Defendants Who Negligently Risk Another Tortfeasor's Intentional Harm..895
§ 35.10   Defendants Who Are Under a Duty to Protect Plaintiff from Another's Negligence 898
    E.   Other Apportionment Systems 901
§ 35.11   Joint and Several Liability with Reallocation 901
§ 35.12   Hybrid Systems: Joint and Several Liability Based on Threshold Percentages or Type of Damages 902

CHAPTER 36. ALTERNATIVE SYSTEMS FOR COMPENSATING INJURY.. **905**
    A.   Criticism of Tort..905
§ 36.1   Criticisms of the Tort System 905
    B.   Workers' Compensation 911
§ 36.2   The Workers' Compensation System......................................911
§ 36.3   Workers' Compensation: Injury Arising Out of and In the Course of Employment 914
§ 36.4   Workers' Compensation: Accident vs. Disease............................915
§ 36.5   Workers' Compensation: Exclusive Remedy and Third Parties 918

    C.   Other Injury Systems 922
§ 36.6   Social Security Disability 922
§ 36.7   The Private Insurance Alternative...925
§ 36.8   Government Compensation Funds 927
§ 36.9   Taxing Industry to Create Compensation Funds 929

PART VIII. DIGNITARY AND ECONOMIC TORTS

SUBPART A. DIGNITARY TORTS

CHAPTER 37. DEFAMATION **935**
    A.   Introducing Defamation 936
§ 37.1   Defamation: Scope 936
§ 37.2   Historical Development of Defamation Law 936
    B.   Common Law Requirements..938
§ 37.3   Elements of Defamation—Common Law and Constitution 938
§ 37.4   Requirement of Publication Generally 940
§ 37.5   The Requirement of Defamatory Content and Its Test..........943
§ 37.6   Interpreting Meaning and Effect 948
§ 37.7   Defamation of and Concerning the Plaintiff 951
§ 37.8   The Requirement of Falsity vs. "The Truth Defense" 954
§ 37.9   Special Slander Rules 958
§ 37.10   Libel Per Quod 962
    C.   Defenses 965
§ 37.11   Absolute Privileges and Common Law Qualified Privileges.......965
§ 37.12   Abuse or Loss of Privilege 980
§ 37.13   Revising Privileges After the Constitutional Cases 982
§ 37.14   The Anti-SLAPP Statutes 984
    D.   Constitutional Limitations on Recovery 986
§ 37.15   Constitutional Limitations on Recovery................................986
§ 37.16   Who Are Public Officials...991
§ 37.17   Who Are Public Figures..992
§ 37.18   Proving Constitutional Levels of Fault 994
§ 37.19   Opinion Statements—Constitutional Protections 996
    E.   Remedies 998
§ 37.20   Remedies—Damages 998
§ 37.21   Non-Damages Remedies Including Money Disgorgement 1002

CHAPTER 38. PRIVACY... **1005**
§ 38.1   Privacy Torts: An Introduction 1005
§ 38.2   Appropriation of the Plaintiff's Personality 1005
§ 38.3   Intrusion: Private Life and Information................................1008
§ 38.4   Publicizing Private Life 1013
§ 38.5   False Light 1019

CHAPTER 39. MISUSING JUDICIAL PROCESS **1023**
    A.   Introduction: Tortious Use of the Legal Process 1023
§ 39.1   Scope, Policies and Immunities 1023
    B.   Malicious Prosecution..1026
§ 39.2   Elements..1026

§ 39.3   Instigating or Continuing the Criminal Proceeding......................1027
§ 39.4   Absence of Probable Cause..1028
§ 39.5   Improper Purpose or "Malice" 1032
§ 39.6   Favorable Termination of the Prosecution................................1033
§ 39.7   Special Defenses..1035
    C.   Wrongful Civil Litigation 1036
§ 39.8   Elements..1036
§ 39.9   Probable Cause in Wrongful Civil Litigation 1038
§ 39.10   Malice or Improper Purpose..1039
§ 39.11   Favorable Termination of Former Civil Suit 1040
§ 39.12   Special-Injury or Special-Grievance Requirement 1041
    D.   Abuse of Process 1042
§ 39.13   Elements..1042
§ 39.14   The Meaning of "Process" and Examples of Abuse....................1043
§ 39.15   Collateral Advantage and the "Act After" Requirement 1045
    E.   Reforms and New Directions 1046
§ 39.16   SLAPP Suits, Sanctions, and Counterclaims............................1046

CHAPTER 40. INTERFERENCE WITH FAMILY RELATIONSHIPS.............. 1049
§ 40.1   Alienation of Affections and Criminal Conversation..................1049
§ 40.2   Interference with Parental Custody and Other Rights in Children...........1053
§ 40.3   Alienation of a Parent's or Child's Affections 1056

SUBPART B. ECONOMIC TORTS

CHAPTER 41. ECONOMIC TORTS AND ECONOMIC LOSS RULES 1059
    A.   Economic Loss: An Introduction 1059
§ 41.1   Economic Loss 1059
§ 41.2   Specific Economic Torts vs. General Negligence Claims for Economic
       Loss 1060
§ 41.3   The Core Economic Loss Rules: Contracting Parties and Strangers 1061
§ 41.4   Categories of Economic Torts..1063
    B.   Negligent Economic Loss in the Stranger Context.....................1065
§ 41.5   Strangers: Negligence Toward a Third Person Causing Economic Loss to
       the Plaintiff 1065
§ 41.6   Strangers: General Nonliability for Negligently Caused Stand-Alone
       Economic Harm..1068
§ 41.7   Strangers: Policies or Rationales for Limiting Liability 1071
§ 41.8   Strangers: Exceptions...1073
    C.   Negligent Economic Loss and Contracting Parties....................1077
§ 41.9   Contracting Parties: The Economic Loss Rule Generally 1077
§ 41.10   Contracting Parties: Rationales and Policies for the Economic Loss
       Rule..1080
    D.   Scope and Exceptions 1083
§ 41.11   Scope of and Exceptions to the No-Duty Economic Loss Rule....................1083

**CHAPTER 42. INTERFERENCE WITH CONTRACT AND ECONOMIC
    INTERESTS 1089**
    A.   The Core Rules of Intentional Interference with Contract..........1089

§ 42.1   The Intentional Interference Tort 1089
§ 42.2   Interference with Economic Relations by Committing Other Torts 1091
§ 42.3   General Rules of Intentional Interference Claims 1093
§ 42.4   Elements of the Interference Claims 1095
   B.   Improper Interference 1098
§ 42.5   The Improper Interference Requirement 1098
§ 42.6   Improper Motive or Purpose as a Basis for Liability 1099
§ 42.7   Improper Means or Effects—Independently Tortious Acts, Crimes or
          Violation of Statutes 1102
§ 42.8   Specific Rules or Principles Protecting Interference, Including Right of
          Competition, Advice, and Truth 1103
   C.   Intentional Interference with Economic Opportunity 1106
§ 42.9   Intentional Interference with Economic Opportunity: General Rules 1106
   D.   The Prima Facie Tort 1110
§ 42.10   The Prima Facie Tort 1110
   E.   Negligent Interference with Contract and Opportunity 1112
§ 42.11   General Rule Inhibition Against Recovery for Negligently Caused
          Economic Harm 1112

CHAPTER 43. MISREPRESENTATION AND FALSEHOODS 1113
   A.   Injurious Falsehood 1113
§ 43.1   Falsehoods Published to Others Causing Plaintiff's Economic Harm 1113
   B.   Fraudulent Misrepresentations 1115
§ 43.2   Misrepresentation Torts: An Overview 1115
§ 43.3   Misrepresentation as a Fact vs. a Tort 1117
§ 43.4   Fraudulent Misrepresentation 1118
   C.   Negligent Misrepresentation 1123
§ 43.5   Negligent Misrepresentation 1123
   D.   Innocent Misrepresentation 1127
§ 43.6   Innocent Misrepresentation 1127
   E.   Major Issues 1129
§ 43.7   Reliance 1129
§ 43.8   Factual Representations: Opinion, Law and Prediction 1132
§ 43.9   Defenses and Remedies 1136
   F.   Economic Harms in Special Relationships 1143
§ 43.10   Breach of Fiduciary Duty, Bad Faith, Wrongful Discharge and Economic
          Duress 1143

CHAPTER 44. ECONOMIC HARM TO INTANGIBLE INTERESTS BY
   CONVERSION OR SPOLIATION 1151
   A.   Conversion of Intangible Economic Interests 1151
§ 44.1   Expanding the Traditional Conversion Action 1151
§ 44.2   Conversion of Money and Accounts 1153
§ 44.3   Conversion and Contract 1155
   B.   Spoliation of Evidence 1157
§ 44.4   Intentional Spoliation by a Party to Litigation 1157
§ 44.5   Intentional Spoliation by a Non-Party 1159
§ 44.6   Negligent Spoliation of Evidence 1160
§ 44.7   Factual Causation in Spoliation Cases 1161

CHAPTER 45. LEGAL MALPRACTICE **1163**
    A. Malpractice in Civil Matters: Prima Facie Case 1163
§ 45.1 Scope, Duties, and Elements..1163
§ 45.2 Duty: Establishing a Client-Lawyer Relationship..............1165
§ 45.3 The Professional Standard of Care....................................1168
§ 45.4 Breach of Duty 1169
§ 45.5 Causation of Harm: General Rules....................................1172
§ 45.6 Causation: The Case Within a Case 1173
§ 45.7 Liability to Non-Clients 1175
    B. Malpractice in Civil Matters: Defenses..........................1177
§ 45.8 Contributory Negligence/Comparative Fault....................1177
§ 45.9 *In Pari Delicto* and Quasi-Judicial Immunity..................1178
§ 45.10 Statute of Limitations..1179
    C. Malpractice in Civil Matters: Damages 1182
§ 45.11 Compensatory Damages Generally 1182
§ 45.12 Compensatory Damages in the Case-Within-a-Case Suit..........1184
    D. Malpractice in Criminal Cases 1186
§ 45.13 Criminal Malpractice: Prima Facie Case 1186
§ 45.14 Criminal Malpractice: Defenses and Immunities.............1190

CHAPTER 46. UNFAIR COMPETITION: TRADEMARKS, TRADE SECRETS AND PUBLICITY RIGHTS **1193**
§ 46.1 Unfair Competition and Trademark Infringement 1193
§ 46.2 Sponsorship Confusion and Dilution in Trademark Law 1196
§ 46.3 False Advertising and § 43(a) of the Lanham Act 1198
§ 46.4 Product Design, Trade Dress, and Functional Features...........1201
§ 46.5 Ideas and Trade Secrets 1203
§ 46.6 Rights in Personality and Publicity.................................1206

TABLE OF CASES 1211

INDEX...1295

HORNBOOK ON TORTS

Second Edition

Part I

INTRODUCING TORT LAW

Chapter 1

DEFINING TORT LAW

Analysis

§ 1.1   Defining Torts
§ 1.2   Bases of Tort Liability
§ 1.3   Types of Interests Protected
§ 1.4   Torts and Crimes
§ 1.5   Torts and Contracts
§ 1.6   Torts and Property
§ 1.7   Torts and Regulatory Control
§ 1.8   Torts and Personal Injury Law
§ 1.9   The Coherence of Tort Law

§ 1.1   Defining Torts

A tort is conduct that constitutes a legal wrong and causes harm for which courts will impose civil liability.[1] The essence of tort is the defendant's potential for civil liability to the victim for harmful wrongdoing and the victim's corresponding potential for compensation or other relief.

Tort law is predominantly common law. That is, judges rather than legislatures usually define what counts as an actionable wrong and thus as a tort; they also determine how compensation is to be measured and what defenses may defeat the tort claim. Nevertheless, statutes[2] or even state[3] or federal constitutions[4] may make certain conduct legally wrongful and may permit recovery of damages for such conduct. So violation of statute or constitution, alone or interacting with common law principles,[5] is sometimes a tort for which the violator is subject to liability. In limited circumstances, international law may affect tort issues and even form a basis for tort liability.[6]

Examples of torts can be found everywhere. In the absence of some defense or special facts, it is a tort to punch another in the nose, to negligently run an automobile into another, or to negligently perform a medical operation. It may be a tort to sell a defective product that causes harm. Some torts cause no physical harm at all but are nonetheless actionable. For example, it is tortious to maliciously prosecute a person without probable cause, to damage reputation by libel, to interfere intentionally with a

---

[1]   See Vigil v. Franklin, 103 P.3d 322 (Colo. 2004); Buchanan v. Doe, 246 Va. 67, 431 S.E.2d 289 (1993).

[2]   Fandrey ex rel. Connell v. American Family Mut. Ins. Co., 272 Wis.2d 46, 680 N.W.2d 345 (2004).

[3]   E.g., Dorwart v. Caraway, 312 Mont. 1, 58 P.3d 128 (2002).

[4]   See Chapter 22.

[5]   See Smith v. Wade, 461 U.S. 30, 103 S.Ct. 1625 (1983) (reflecting a constitutional tort claim pursued under a civil rights statute which in turn was interpreted to permit recovery of punitive damages in light of common law acceptance of such damages); Martinez v. California, 444 U.S. 277, 62 L.Ed.2d 481, 100 S.Ct. 553 (1980) (rejecting constitutional tort claim on grounds of remoteness similar to common law proximate cause principles).

[6]   See, e.g., § 19.1 (Warsaw and Montreal Conventions governing international flights).

contract, or to mislead a person by misrepresenting material facts in connection with a sale. Many other torts can be described or named, and in fact courts are free not only to prescribe limits on tort actions but to recognize variations and even "new torts."[7]

Tort law is primarily intended to redress legally recognized harms by rendering a money judgment against the wrongdoer, or "tortfeasor."[8] This award is usually a money award called "damages," and it is usually intended as a kind of compensation for the harm suffered. In some cases, a punitive damages award may be added to compensatory damages to deter further misconduct. Other remedies that are infrequently available include restitution, which forces the tortfeasor to disgorge gains he wrongfully obtained by tort,[9] and injunction, which compels him to cease his tortious conduct.[10] In the great majority of tort cases, however, a favorable judgment for the victim means an award of money as compensation for harm caused.[11]

§ 1.2   Bases of Tort Liability

Tort liability can be defined in part by the grounds on which it is invoked. The term "tort" is derived from Latin roots meaning "twisted," as if to say tortious conduct is twisted conduct, conduct that departs from the existing norm. As the word itself suggests, torts are traditionally associated with wrongdoing in some moral sense. In the great majority of cases today, tort liability is grounded in the conclusion that the wrongdoer was at fault in a legally cognizable way. It is not ordinarily enough to impose liability that the defendant has merely caused harm by accident or happenstance; he must also be at fault. This fault approach is often associated with ideals of freedom; you are free to act without liability, so long as you are not at fault in your actions.

There are many kinds of fault that have no legal significance at all. It is a fault to be lazy or to use the salad fork for a meat dish, but neither fault is a tort. Faulty conduct that is legally important can be described in many ways, but legal fault in the law of torts is usually sorted into two main categories: (1) intentional wrongs or (2) negligent wrongs.[12]

Intentional torts. Intentional wrongs entail at least an intent on the part of the defendant to engage in conduct that the law regards as wrongful. The intentional tort feasor is usually consciously aware of his wrongdoing. Even if he is not, however, he is always aware of his *act*, and that may be sufficient to impose liability if the act is one that is proscribed by common law or statute.

Negligence. Negligent wrongs entail unreasonably risky behavior that actually causes harm. The defendant in the negligence case is sometimes aware that he is taking unreasonable risks; he is always in violation of reasonableness standards whether he is consciously aware of that fact or not.

---

[7]   E.g., Rizzuto v. Davidson Ladders, Inc., 280 Conn. 225, 905 A.2d 1165 (2006). Most "new" torts, however, are developed from the common law fabric of general principles.

[8]   See Chapter 40.

[9]   See Dan B. Dobbs, The Law of Remedies § 4.1(1) (2d ed. 1993) (noting that restitution in money may exceed the more common award of "damages").

[10]   See Id., § 2.1(2) (distinguishing and illustrating different types of injunctions).

[11]   See Chapter 34.

[12]   Sometimes courts recognize a third category, placed between the first two. A willful or wanton wrong is a species of negligence because the wanton defendant does not intend an invasion of the plaintiff's rights. At the same time, it has some resemblance to an intentional wrong because the defendant has an anti-social state of mind; he is conscious of creating a high risk of harm. See § 4.5.

Expanding and limiting liability for fault. Although fault of some kind is commonly found in tort cases, courts may at times seem to expand liability beyond the limits of fault. Sometimes this occurs when courts seem to define fault to include fairly ordinary conduct. At other times, even faulty behavior does not result in liability. Several reasons explain these apparent departures from the fault principle. For instance, courts do not ordinarily impose tort liability for negligence unless the negligence causes harm. And courts may refuse to impose liability for wrongful conduct that in fact causes harm that is remote or <u>fortuitous</u>. These and some other instances may qualify or limit the fault principle. Nevertheless, fault remains the basis of tort liability and a marker of its limits in the overwhelming number of cases.

Fortuitous
(By
Accident
or
Chance)

Strict liability. In a few instances tort law imposes strict liability. Strict liability is liability without proof of fault. Apart from these few instances, an accidentally caused harm is ordinarily not a tort at all; there is no general strict liability. In contrast, intentional or negligent infliction of physical harm is almost always tortious, even if it is subject to defenses in a particular case. The two best-known instances of common law strict liability are cases in which the defendant engages in some abnormally dangerous activity[13] and those in which the defendant manufactures a defective product.[14] In both of those cases, liability may be imposed as a matter of legal policy irrespective of the defendant's fault. In many instances of strict liability, however, the defendant may be at fault in fact, even if the plaintiff has not proved it.

§ 1.3　Types of Interests Protected

Tort liability can be defined in part by the types of interests or values it protects. Tort law recognizes three broad categories of legal interests that deserve protection against wrongdoing. These interests are a person's interest in (1) primary autonomy, physical security and physical liberty; (2) emotional security and other intangible interests such as privacy and reputation; and (3) economic security and opportunity.

Security of person and property. Legal rules give the greatest protection to physical security of persons and property. Intentional and negligent physical interference with persons are both ordinarily tortious in the absence of a good justification. The negligent driver who unintentionally strikes a pedestrian is liable in tort just as the intentional bully who sexually harasses his victim. When the defendant physically interferes with the plaintiff's person or the plaintiff's property in a way that counts as a tort, the plaintiff can recover for all her reasonably connected damages, including reasonable damages for emotional harm and for economic losses.

Emotional security and related interests. When it comes to intangible harm without physical interference or physical harm, courts are much more reluctant to impose tort liability. One form of intangible harm is pure emotional harm. For example, one might intentionally or negligently cause distress to the plaintiff by the use of unpleasant words. In such cases the plaintiff may suffer emotional injury but no physical interference with her person. Some conduct that causes only intangible harm is tortious and some is not, but courts often demonstrate great caution about imposing liability for intangible harm

---

[13]　See Chapter 32.
[14]　See Chapter 33.

unless the defendant has physically interfered with the plaintiff's person or property[15] or violated specific rights such as the right to reputation[16] or privacy.[17]

Economic harms. Very similar statements can be made about pure economic harm, that is, pocketbook harms that do not result from physical interference with person or property. The sign-carrying protester or religious speaker who posts himself outside the plaintiff's shop may drive the plaintiff's customers away. This is stand-alone economic harm—harm that is not the result of physical interference with person or property. Some intentional harms of this kind may be actionable torts, but many negligent economic harms are not.[18] In this particular example, the right we all have to comment honestly and truthfully would be most significant. In other economic harm cases, cases that do not necessarily involve free speech issues, different reasons may lead to the same result, sometimes because courts prefer to leave economic relations to the realm of contract law. There are assuredly economic torts that will result in liability; the point here is that courts are more cautious in protecting the economic interest, as distinct from the physical security interest.

§ 1.4   Torts and Crimes

The relationship between tort law and criminal law is largely explained by their respective purposes. The purpose of criminal punishment is primarily to vindicate the state's interests in deterring crime and imposing justice. The purpose of tort liability is in no way inconsistent, but its emphasis is different—it is primarily to vindicate the individual victim and the victim's rights[19] and secondarily to confirm and reinforce public standards of behavior. Tort law thus shares with criminal law the goal of deterring wrongful conduct, but tort law uses methods aimed at securing compensation of the individual victim.

American common law, including tort law, grew out of English common law. In the development of early English law, tort law in turn grew out of criminal law. Judges who imposed punishment upon lawbreakers also occasionally imposed civil liability. Judges and lawyers gradually perceived that criminal punishment and civil liability had related but distinct purposes. Tort law developed into a separate field in itself, aimed at providing distinctly civil remedies.

Today, a single act might constitute both a crime and a tort. For example, if a defendant beats a person, he is almost certainly committing a crime for which the state can prosecute and punish. He is also committing a tort, for which the injured individual may sue and recover compensation, whether or not the crime is prosecuted.

In tort cases, courts will often take notice of the fact that the defendant's conduct amounted to a crime and will give weight to this fact in determining whether the conduct also amounted to a tort. But this does not work the other way around. Crime is usually

---

[15]   See Chapters 4 to 6.

[16]   See Chapter 37.

[17]   See Chapter 38.

[18]   See Chapter 41.

[19]   Thus courts emphasize that one "purpose of tort law is to make an injured person whole," see Teschendorf v. State Farm Ins. Companies, 293 Wis.2d 123, 717 N.W.2d 258, 273 (2006), by shifting the losses suffered to the faulty person, see Hanks v. Powder Ridge Restaurant Corp., 276 Conn. 314, 885 A.2d 734, 742 (2005).

defined by statute; whether the defendant's conduct is a tort is not important in determining whether conduct violates criminal law.

Substantive comparisons: intent and harm. Substantively speaking, there is no necessary correlation between tort and crime. The most fundamental basis for criminal liability is intent, often very specific intent. Some kind of intent is also required for some torts, but more commonly mere negligence coupled with actual harm will suffice for liability. A second important difference in the two fields can be seen in the different ways in which actual harm is treated. Criminal law redresses the state's interests in the security of society. It may punish conduct that threatens those interests even when no harm has been done. Speeding increases risks to others and so may be punished criminally. Tort law, aimed at protection of individuals, would never impose liability for speeding alone; tort law would impose liability only if harm results.

Procedural comparisons. On the procedural side, tort and crime differ enormously. Criminal prosecutions ordinarily must be initiated and pursued by the government; tort suits may be brought by an aggrieved individual, who decides (usually with a lawyer's assistance) whether to assert a claim and whether and when to settle. Another distinction is that criminal prosecutions can succeed only if the proof shows guilt beyond a reasonable doubt; most tort suits use a more-likely-than-not standard.

§ 1.5   Torts and Contracts

Breach of contract is not in itself a tort. The conventional view goes further. It holds that the fields of tort and contract are entirely distinct because contract duties are created by the promises of the parties, while tort duties are created by the courts and imposed as rules of law. On this view, the province of torts is rights and wrongs and the province of contract is agreements or promises. This perception is that the fields of tort and contract hardly touch each other, much less overlap. Another conventional view supports the same conclusion. It asserts that contracts are largely about economic matters such as buying and selling, whereas torts typically involve physical harms.

A third point is not so often mentioned, but it is important. Contract law is at least formally strict liability law. Most of tort law, on the other hand, is at least formally fault-based. Specifically, a person is often liable for a contract breach even if he is not at fault and made every effort to perform the contract as promised. But a person is not ordinarily liable under tort law even for conduct that causes horrible injuries unless he is at fault in some way. The reasoning and the formal themes of tort law thus differ enormously from those of contract law.

Finally, in the actual practice of law, lawyers who negotiate and draft contracts are seldom focused on litigation. Tort law, with its emphasis on compensation after the fact rather than on planning, is preeminently a law of litigation and litigators. Most cases are settled, but they are settled on the basis of expected litigation outcomes.

Some of the conventional views stated above are partly correct, but they do not furnish a complete picture. The fields of tort and contract do in fact overlap and share many of the same premises.

First, it is usually true that rules of law govern tort cases, while the parties' agreement determines contract liabilities; but the parties' agreement controls their rights only because courts accept a rule of law that says so. For this reason, a rule of law ultimately lies behind both tort and contract. Second, contractual promises sometimes create or underlie tort duties, so that what begins as contract ends as tort if one of the parties is injured.[20] For example, suppose I promise to provide you a safety net for your work as a roofer, but the net I provide will not hold when you fall into it. You do fall into it, it gives way, and you are injured. Courts are likely to hold me liable in tort even though I would not be responsible to provide a net unless I had contracted to do so.[21] A third area of overlap occurs when tort law is invoked to protect contract rights. If I intentionally interfere with your contract with another person so you cannot reap its benefits, I may be liable to you in tort.[22]

Perhaps most importantly, much of tort law is shaped by the expectations of the parties, even when those expectations are not explicitly made part of any contract. Expectations in a relationship have some consensual qualities, in that respect resembling a contract. As the New Jersey Court said, when a person is in a consensual relationship, courts judge the reasonableness of his conduct by reference to his "consent and mutual understanding" and by the "common expectations that serve to identify what conduct is acceptable" among people in the relationship.[23] When the parties stand in some particular relationship, like that of lawyer and client or bailor and bailee, or seller and buyer, courts historically constructed the tort duties out of the parties' expectations, or at least out of what the courts thought their expectations were. Finally, tort duties may at times be limited by the parties' expectations, undertakings, or tacit agreements. So the contract cousins, consent and expectation, play a very large role indeed in shaping tort duties.

A more radical view is that the distinction between tort and contract is entirely manipulative; courts might characterize a case as a contract case when they wish to focus exclusively on the promises of the parties and their enforceability but characterize a case as a tort case when they wish to focus on or emphasize public policy or rules imposed by courts that do not necessarily vindicate the parties' promises. In this view, the distinction between tort and contract does not represent any underlying legal reality; it is merely instead a distinction invoked to facilitate the court's analysis and conclusions.

A more moderate view is that in some cases, the distinctions between tort and contract may be distinctions of degree rather than kind, or they may reflect only factual setting or professional habit. Further than that, contract cases always involve promises. Tort cases often involve expectations of the parties, but only occasionally do they involve explicit promises. Numerous tort cases are characteristically disputes between strangers, that is, people who have no special relationship marked by contract. Such cases cannot be thought of as involving any contract law or any overlap with the field of contracts.

But if the basic division between tort and contract continues to dominate legal thinking and research, that fact should not obscure the importance of contract, informal understandings, and even relationships between the parties in determining duties under the rules of tort law. When a contract is in the picture, tort law almost always treats the contract as important and worth examining; when purely economic interests are

---

[20]   See Shadday v. Omni Hotels Management Corp., 477 F.3d 511, 512 (7th Cir. 2007).

[21]   See Chapters 25 (defendant's undertaking as a basis for tort liability) & 33 (products liability in tort and warranty).

[22]   See Chapter 42.

[23]   Crawn v. Campo, 136 N.J. 494, 507, 643 A.2d 600, 606 (1994).

involved, they often give the contract precedence, allowing the agreement, rather than the rules of tort law, to control.[24]

§ 1.6   Torts and Property

Crime, Tort, Contract and Property designate the traditional great fields of the common law. The preceding sections have indicated that tort law has affinities with both the law of crimes and the law of contracts. Tort law also has affinities with the law of property.

Property law aims at defining rights of people with respect to things rather than with respect to other people. The things at issue in property law can be intangible as well as tangible; one can own a patent or copyright as well as a farm called Blackacre. Property law is fundamentally concerned with establishing ownership of property, with the incidents of ownership, and with the means by which ownership can be changed. The incidents of ownership may include the right to physical integrity of property, the right to exclusive possession of property, and the right to reasonable enjoyment of property.

Because tort law is necessarily centered on conduct of persons, or at least on the results of that conduct, it does not seem at first glance to be concerned at all with static ownership. On this ground it is clearly distinguishable from property law. In addition, property law resembles contract law in that transfers or divisions of ownership are largely a matter of consensual agreements and in that lawyers engaged in property practice are likely to be drafters, negotiators, planners, and facilitators rather than litigators.

Yet ownership of property underlies many torts, and some tort actions are expressly brought for the purpose of establishing or confirming rights in property, while others are brought to vindicate or protect those rights. The ancient action of trespass was a tort action brought to assess damages for invasion of the plaintiff's real property (and later for trespass to chattels as well). In this kind of case, tort law can be viewed as a kind of helper or action arm for property law.

In defining the tort of trespass, the courts necessarily define something of the incidents of ownership of real property. If I enter your land in good faith and in the reasonable belief that it is my own, courts may nevertheless declare that I am a trespasser and liable to you for damages. In so saying, courts in the tort suit determine important incidents of your ownership. By this tort law rule, courts are saying that you have rights to exclusive possession even against a person who enters in good faith, not merely against those who know the land is yours. In the same way, if courts hold that my factory smoke is a nuisance that prevents your reasonable use and enjoyment of land, they have not only defined the legal limits of my conduct; they have also defined the incidents of your land ownership.

So tort law blends with property law just as it does with contract law. Sometimes the only viable issue in a tort case is truly an issue of property rights. At other times the issue will emphasize the defendant's conduct and its possible wrongful character. Differences must often be described in terms of emphasis or focus rather than in terms of essentialities. As a practical matter, however, when the issue is mainly about underlying property rights rather than about the wrongfulness of the defendant's conduct, this book will leave the matter to the law of property.

---

[24]   See Chapter 41.

§ 1.7   Torts and Regulatory Control

Another way to help define the scope of tort law is to contrast it with governmental regulation, which is not a field of law but a different mechanism for enforcing rules. The reason for making the contrast is that both institutions—tort law and regulation—can be seen as means of imposing a degree of social control by preventing injury or compensating it.

Government regulation (of dangerous activities, for example) is always derived ultimately from legislation. A statute passed by Congress or a state legislature might specifically forbid some dangerous activities. Or it might set standards for safety and create an administrative agency to enforce those standards. The federal Occupational Safety and Health Act ("OSHA") and state analogs are examples. These statutes require employers to observe certain levels of safety and empower an agency (a) to make concrete standards by promulgating regulations, (b) to inspect, and (c) to enforce the standards. The administrative agency might, for example, prescribe the amount and design of bracing required to protect workers in trenches from cave-ins.[25]

Regulatory systems govern many important activities in society; they are not limited to regulating health and safety risks. Extensive statutes and regulations govern the way in which securities like stocks and bonds are sold and the kind of information that must be provided to prospective buyers. This is economic, not safety regulation. But like safety regulation, it differs enormously from tort law, yet has its tort law counterparts.

What are the important differences between a tort law way and the regulatory way of trying to control conduct and make compensation? First, regulators look forward: regulation is always formulated in advance. If four-by-four timbers must be used to shore up a trench, the regulation will say so in advance. Tort cases look backward: they decide that conduct that has already taken place was wrongful.

In part this difference derives from another. Regulation is often quite specific and detailed (about the size of the timbers, for example). Tort law standards are usually broad and general until a specific case is decided. Tort law standards are never likely to provide for the use of four-by-four timbers. Instead, tort law standards are likely to provide that the contractor constructing a trench should exercise reasonable care; it is for a jury to decide whether the contractor's shoring-up methods were reasonable. Once the tort case is decided, however, it has precedential effect, and as precedent it looks forward in time just as regulation does. Some jurists once thought that accumulated precedents would eventually provide a kind of catalog of rules or answers, but tort precedents do not work this way; each case is likely to be a little different and rules made for one case may not be well adapted to solution of a slightly different case.[26]

---

[25]   29 C.F.R. § 1926.652 prescribes details about slopes, soil types, shoring systems, and shield systems. An appendix gives details on shoring construction.

[26]   Holmes leaned toward the idea of collecting precedents for everything, leaving little for the jury to decide. See Baltimore & O.R. Co. v. Goodman, 275 U.S. 66, 48 S.Ct. 24 (1927) (holding that a jury could not find that a man was reasonable in crossing railroad tracks without visually assuring himself that no train was coming, by getting out of his car and surveying the terrain if necessary; "when the standard is clear it should be laid down once for all by the Courts"). Nevertheless, Holmes saw the dangers of such an approach when it suited him to do so. Lorenzo v. Wirth, 170 Mass. 596, 49 N.E. 1010 (1898) ("Too broadly generalized conceptions are a constant source of fallacy.").

A signal difference between regulation and tort law is that regulation does not ordinarily aim at compensation. The goal of OSHA regulation on trenches, for example, is to prevent injury, not to compensate an injured worker. If an employer violates an OSHA regulation, the government might ultimately enforce a civil penalty, but that penalty will not go to an injured person. This demonstrates a close analogy between regulatory control and criminal law. Tort law, in contrast, aims specifically at compensating the victim of a wrong by awarding damages. Only occasionally do courts apply tort law to prevent injury in advance by issuing an injunction. However, tort law may reduce the number of injuries in a general way because many people will act with reasonable care to avoid paying the compensation that tort law would require.[27]

Many lawyers distinguishing regulation from tort law would perhaps think first of the procedural incidents of the two systems. Tort law is court law. The victim of a wrong sues. The victim does not rely on others to enforce rights. The suit is in a court (usually nearby) that is open to all individuals. Most notably, the facts in the suit are decided by a jury if either party requests it, not by a judge or an administrator.

Probably no practicing lawyers would think that tort law and regulatory law systems are alike. Yet for all their differences, they are not located in impenetrable compartments. Courts in tort cases may adopt administrative regulations as guidelines for tort law. And courts as well as administrative agencies sometimes provide rules in advance by issuing injunctions. Sometimes the injunction will be just as specific and detailed as an administrative regulation.

§ 1.8   Torts and Personal Injury Law

Many people think of personal injury cases when they think of tort law. But tort law is more than injury law because it includes rules for wrongs that cause economic and emotional injury even when no physical harm of any kind has been done. Tort law is also less than personal injury law. Other social institutions, in addition to tort law, attempt to control and compensate personal injury. Tort law is, in fact, only one of a number of ways in contemporary American society aimed at creating incentives for safety or at providing compensation for loss or both.

The alternative institutions are not even the institutions of the common law, much less of tort law. Yet they account for most of the compensation paid for injury. Tort law cannot be meaningfully understood without understanding that such alternative systems exist. Alternative non-tort systems include social security support for totally disabled persons, medical benefits derived from social security or otherwise, workers' compensation benefits for those injured on the job, no-fault automobile injury systems operating under insurance plans, and others. In some cases dangerous products are subjected to special taxes, which are then used as a fund to pay for injuries those products cause. Mass torts claims, in which hundreds of thousands of people are injured by a product such as asbestos, begin with tort law but are so large and complex that they have generated unique adaptive behaviors within the law. Global settlements of these claims may prescribe more definitions and rules than an administrative agency administering, say, workers' compensation.[28]

---

[27] See § 2.5.

[28] See Peter H. Schuck, Mass Torts: an Institutional Evolutionist Perspective, 80 Cornell L. Rev. 941 (1995).

Alternative, non-tort systems seek to compensate for injury even when injury is not caused by wrongdoing. In that sense they are strict liability systems. So the element of fault that is so prominent in most of tort law is almost wholly missing in the alternative systems. Non-tort systems usually attempt to resolve the injury-compensation question outside of court; although the administrators may hold some court-like hearings, there will be no jury. They also almost always reject or limit recovery for the victim's pain and suffering. These alternative systems often seem more concerned with distributive rather than corrective justice, or with public welfare rather than just deserts or deterrence of wrongdoing. But for lawyers dealing with personal injury cases, torts does not cover all of their work; they must also work with alternative systems.[29]

§ 1.9   The Coherence of Tort Law

The boundaries of tort law staked loosely in the preceding sections may suggest that torts cannot be a coherent field. It is not only large in itself, including all kinds of wrongs of which there are many if not infinite varieties; it also has family ties to criminal, contract, property, and regulatory law, not to mention alternative compensation schemes. The size and diversity of tort law is emphasized by the fact that lawyers do not specialize in tort law but only in some patch of it. Probably no lawyer could be said to "specialize" in a field so diverse that it includes medical malpractice, products liability, interference with contract, libel, privacy, sexual harassment, civil rights, malicious prosecution, and other torts. If size and diversity of tort law threatens to render it incoherent, so does the fact that tort law is always changing.

The unity in tort law, if there is any, does not lie in factual similarities among the different torts. The common threads in tort law may not be satisfying, especially to a beginning student of the field, but they are real even if they sometimes break.

First, tort law attempts to recognize personal responsibility and accountability for harms done to others. It does so primarily by allocating some or all responsibility to those who are at fault. The issue of fault thus dominates most of tort law. Although fault may be defined quite differently according to the factual setting and relationships of the parties, courts are deeply involved with defining fault in a large proportion of all tort cases. The fact that fault is not always properly defined, or is defined with policy problems as well as with justice in mind, does not reflect a rejection of the fault standard, only a difference of opinion about how it should be applied. Where courts have deviated from the fault principle, either in their formal rules or in their unconscious applications of it, they have nevertheless struggled hard to articulate a meaningful basis for legal responsibility that matches in at least some degree the community's sense of justice. Fault, or some aspect of fault, often finds its way into the case by the back door when it is denied entry at the front.

Second, tort litigation has developed and continues to develop a cluster of analytical tools or ways of thinking that are special to tort cases. They say that the defendant's conduct must have in fact caused the plaintiff's harm, and more than that, the defendant's conduct must be a significant or proximate cause of the harm. Those and other concepts used in analysis are not unique to tort law, but they are uniquely important in tort law.

Third, the process of lawyering tort claims is, overall, enormously different from the process of, say, contract drafting or estate planning. Part of that difference lies in the

---

[29]   See Chapter 36.

fact that tort law is litigation law. Tort litigation usually entails a jury, so the members of the public are present to participate and view the professional judges and lawyers at work. The public presence transforms the private world of legal professionals and affects the way they think of themselves and the proceedings, so that the culture of decision-making in American tort law is indeed quite special. The jury's role has made judges and lawyers especially sensitive in tort cases not only to procedures and remedies, but also to the problems of proof and evidence. One of the enduring concerns of the tort law process in the United States is the role of the jury in relation to the role of the judge. Other process differences are generated through a cluster of tort law institutions, including the contingent percentage fee and the prevalence of liability insurance as well as the special role of the jury.

If tort law is a coherent field, its coherence is thus not derived from the factual unity of the cases it determines, but from its focus on wrongdoing, its increased emphasis on certain analytical tools, and its virtually unique process of lawyering and deciding cases.

Chapter 2

AIMS, POLICIES, HISTORY AND METHODS OF TORT LAW

Analysis

A. AIMS AND POLICIES OF TORT LAW

§ 2.1   Justice, Policy, and Process Aims in Summary
§ 2.2   Corrective Justice, Distributive Justice, and Policy
§ 2.3   Fault and Other Normative Bases for Liability
§ 2.4   Compensation, Risk Distribution, and Fault
§ 2.5   Deterrence
§ 2.6   Alternative Compensation Systems
§ 2.7   Process Values in Tort Law

B. HISTORY, METHODS AND PROCEDURES OF TORT LAW

§ 2.8   Historical Development of Tort Law
§ 2.9   Common-Law Analysis and the Doctrine of Precedent
§ 2.10   Tort Rules and What They Do

A. AIMS AND POLICIES OF TORT LAW

§ 2.1   Justice, Policy, and Process Aims in Summary

What policies and aims do judges consciously articulate when they create, choose, or apply tort rules? Because judges are humans and can fall prey to bias and cultural assumptions, their decisions will no doubt often reflect social or personal attitudes, attitudes that may hold rational persuasion at bay. The question here, though, is not what judges do as fate- or culture-determined creatures, but what judges do when they are at their best, consciously acting and rationally explaining their decisions. Put differently, what kinds of arguments of justice or policy, as distinct from arguments of self-interest or bias, can lawyers make to judges who are faced with a choice between conflicting tort rules or a choice about how to apply a tort rule to a particular case?

In medieval England, the law of torts, like the law of crimes, had modest aims, principally to discourage violence and revenge. Today's tort law has much grander aims. All of the aims are laudable, but sometimes one of them will conflict with another. The most commonly mentioned aims of tort law are (1) to compensate injured persons and (2) to deter undesirable behavior. Both of these aims, however, are subsumed in whole or part under even broader goals.

Morality or corrective justice. Particular aims of tort law are usually erected under one of two large systems of thought.[1] The first bases tort law on moral responsibility or

---

[1]   There are many variations in tort theories, particularly in determining what counts as a legal wrong. See, e.g., John C.P. Goldberg & Benjamin C. Zipursky, The Moral of MacPherson, 146 U. Pa. L. Rev. 1733 (1998) (emphasizing relationships of the parties to tort litigation); Mark Geistfeld, Negligence, Compensation,

at least on some idea that the defendant has in some important way wronged the plaintiff. It attempts to hold defendants liable for harms they wrongfully caused and no others. Good social effects may result when courts act to right the wrongs done by defendants, but in this system of thought, that is not the point of imposing liability. Liability is imposed instead when and only when it is "right" to do so.[2]

Social utility or public policy. The second large system of thought reverses the emphasis; it bases tort law on social policy or a good-for-all-of-us view. Social policy may coincide with justice in particular cases, but the dominant concern is not to achieve individualized justice; it is to provide a system of rules that, overall, works toward the good of society.

Process. One kind of utility or social policy is inward-looking. Rules must be made with the legal process itself in mind. They must be the kind of rules judges and juries can understand and apply in a practical way, and they must not leave too much to the judge's or the jury's discretion. These and a host of similar considerations focus on the litigation process itself as a good to be preserved rather than on the abstract ideal of justice or social utility.

Potential conflicts. The first two ways of looking at tort law are usually regarded as antithetical to each other.[3] Although justice and policy often point to the same result, they do not always do so, and when they do not, one of these views must prevail or both must be compromised. The legal process view might also conflict with the aims of justice or those of policy.

Suppose a city, facing a raging and spreading fire, attempts to create a firebreak by blowing up a row of houses. Because time is critical, the city insists upon doing so before the plaintiff, who owns one of the houses, can remove his furniture. When the whole thing is over, the plaintiff claims damages from the city for the value of the furniture he could have saved. The city has acted for the good of its residents generally, but the plaintiff is the one who pays the costs. If the city's action is to be judged by a standard of social policy, some jurists might say the city should not be liable. On the other hand, if it is judged by corrective justice standards, the city should pay for the damage it caused in blowing up the houses. Otherwise, the city would get the advantage of its action (whatever that advantage might be) but would pay none of the costs. There are more subtle examples, but this one is enough to suggest the potential conflict between a decision based upon (supposed) social policy and one based upon justice to the individual.

Some of the goals summarized in this section are discussed in many, many tort cases. These goals influence results and they also stand as measures for evaluating cases and making arguments. They are central in the practice as well as the theory of tort law.

---

and the Coherence of Tort Law, 91 Geo. L.J. 585 (2003); Mark A. Geistfeld, Social Value as a Policy Based Limitation of the Ordinary Duty To Exercise Reasonable Care, 44 Wake Forest L. Rev. 899 (2009) (emphasizing the primacy of personal security).

  [2] See Fairchild v. Glenhaven Funeral Servs., [2002] 3 All E.R. 305, [2002] 3 All. E.R. 305, 2002 WL 820081 (H.L. 2002) ("The overall object of tort law is to define cases in which the law may justly hold one party liable to compensate another.").

  [3] See Kenneth W. Simons, Tort Negligence, Cost-Benefit Analysis, and Tradeoffs: A Closer Look at the Controversy, 41 Loyola L.A.L.Rev. 1171 (2008); George P. Fletcher, Corrective Justice for Moderns, 106 Harv. L. Rev. 1658 (1993) (Reviewing Jules Coleman, Risks and Wrongs). Some writers have tried to find some middle ground in which both morality and social utility are given appropriate room for operation. See Izhak Englard, The Philosophy of Tort Law (1993).

They also play a large part in evaluating subsidiary aims such as compensation and deterrence discussed in the sections that follow.

§ 2.2   Corrective Justice, Distributive Justice, and Policy

Corrective Justice

Tort law is at least partly rights-based. That is, it is at least partly based on ideals of corrective justice, ideals of righting wrongs, or (somewhat relatedly) ideals about accountability or personal responsibility for harm-causing conduct. Every claim is unique because it is about individual human beings, or at least individual corporations acting in particular circumstances.[4] This means that from a corrective justice perspective, claims are not about advancing socially desirable programs but about doing justice in particular cases.

To right wrongs sounds uncontroversial, but the idea is significant for the very reason that courts sometimes reject it, as they do on occasion when they deny recovery to a victim because they believe that justice to the victim would entail high social costs.

Philosophers and political scientists have found a great deal to be said as they have developed detailed disputations about righting wrongs and they have offered differing versions of the whole idea, often in an effort to describe tort law at a high level of abstraction.[5] However, an aim to right wrongs or to administer corrective justice ideals does not by itself directly decide cases. Instead, that aim asks the question, did the defendant wrong the plaintiff? This is not necessarily a detailed set of normative rules that will generate a resulting judgment. Courts usually determine that question by asking whether the defendant was at fault in a way that caused the plaintiff's harm. So the focus in the cases is not about definitions of wrongs, but about some aspect of the more immediate question of fault and causation of harm.[6]

Judges and practicing lawyers use the terminology of corrective justice only occasionally. When they do, it is often only to associate corrective justice with fairness or accountability for fault[7] or to contrast decisions made on grounds of practicality or policy rather than principle or justice.[8] Judges have also used corrective justice to describe basic principles of justice, such as the principle that justice cannot depend upon a person's status, but must depend upon the wrong he has committed.[9] Judges in tort cases usually decide tort cases with a very general view to doing justice by righting wrongs, not, say, by redistributing goods or by protecting businesses from high insurance costs. But, as indicated below, sometimes they are concerned with protecting businesses from what the judges perceive to be high insurance or other costs.

---

[4]   See Kenneth S. Abraham, What Is a Tort Claim? An Interpretation of Contemporary Tort Reform, 51 Md. L. Rev. 172 (1992).

[5]   Many books and articles, often by authors trained in philosophy or political science, are devoted to ideas about corrective justice. See, e.g., Robert L. Rabin, Law for Law's Sake, 105 Yale L. J. 2261 (1996); Jane Stapleton, Evaluating Goldberg and Zipursky's Civil Recourse Theory, 75 Fordham L. Rev. 1529 (2006); Steven Walt, Eliminating Corrective Justice, 92 Va. L. Rev. 1311 (2006); Benjamin C. Zipursky, Civil Recourse, Not Corrective Justice, 91 Geo. L. J. 695 (2003).

[6]   Kenneth W. Simons, Negligence, 16 Social Philosophy & Policy 2 52, 91 (1999).

[7]   United States v. Cannons Eng'g Corp., 899 F.2d 79, 87 (1st Cir. 1990) ("Substantive fairness introduces into the equation concepts of corrective justice and accountability: a party should bear the cost of the harm for which it is legally responsible.").

[8]   Migliori v. Airborne Freight Corp., 426 Mass. 629 690 N.E.2d 413 (1998).

[9]   Mathias v. Accor Econ. Lodging, Inc., 347 F.3d 672 (7th Cir. 2003).

Distributive Justice

Distributive justice distinguished. The idea that courts should right wrongs done by one party to the other disclaims any intent to effect *distributive* justice.[10] Distributive justice ideals consider the question, "How should goods in society be distributed among people?" If you worry that some people do not have enough to eat and think that children should not starve even if their parents do not work, then you might think the basic goods of life are not justly distributed. The most traditional elements of tort law do not in fact aim at a redistribution of goods but are instead concerned with corrective justice or some other form of righting wrongs.[11]

Policy and Utility

As already indicated, corrective justice ideals or standards are also distinguished from ideals or standards based on policy or utility. Tort law often takes policy and utility into account as well as rights or fairness or corrective justice. Policy and utility questions ask what is good for society as a whole. Those questions definitely do not address issues of right and wrong in individual cases. For instance, defendants sometimes argue that they should not be required to pay full damages for harms they cause, because that would drive up the costs of insurance and might even cause some defendants to go out of business. The public in general, they say, would be the loser. This kind of argument is based on policy or utility, one that attempts to establish ideals of public good, not ideals of justice between two individuals. A justice approach in contrast asks whether the defendant wronged the plaintiff and how to right that wrong, even if righting the wrong turns out to cost more than the plaintiff lost.

Both plaintiffs and defendants present policy arguments. Plaintiffs often argue that the defendant as a business enterprise can better "distribute the risk" or "distribute the loss" that results from accidental injury. Even if the defendant is not at fault, they argue, the defendant can better absorb the costs of injuries associated with its enterprise, or even pass those losses on to others, by raising its prices. In certain areas, this kind of argument, associated with the phrase "enterprise liability" or "collective liability,"[12] has sometimes, but not always, been effective. Arguments for liabilities divorced from rights might also have a special place in mass tort litigation where hundreds of thousands of people have been injured by products like asbestos or the Dalkon Shield.[13] Such arguments, however, are not about justice—righting wrongs—but rather about finding effective ways of dealing with injury.

Policy judgments may be very broad or very narrow. Judges seldom have data necessary for broad-based policy judgments, say, judgments about the long term social effects of imposing liability for wrongs. Judges who predict that if wrongs are righted an entire pharmaceutical industry might be destroyed are making broad policy judgments that may be hard to justify in the absence of data.[14] Broad policy judgments may risk

---

[10]   See Ernest J. Weinrib, Corrective Justice, 77 Iowa L. Rev. 403 (1992). An opposite view is that corrective justice has no independent moral force; everything is distributive justice. See Steven Walt, Eliminating Corrective Justice, 92 Va. L. Rev. 1311 (2006) (discussing various views).

[11]   See John G. Cullhane, Tort, Compensation, and Two Kinds of Justice, 55 Rutgers L. Rev. 1027 (2003) (discussing the compensation system for 9/11 victims).

[12]   See Robert L. Rabin, Some Thoughts on the Ideology of Enterprise Liability, 55 Md. L. Rev. 1190 (1996).

[13]   See Francis E. McGovern, Resolving Mature Mass Tort Litigation, 69 B. U. L. Rev. 659 (1989).

[14]   See Potter v. Firestone Tire & Rubber Co., 6 Cal. 4th 965, 25 Cal. Rptr. 2d 550, 863 P.2d 795 (1993).

compromising the judicial process by injecting the judges' ideological views or susceptibility to political propaganda. All cases risk that, but large, undefined policy questions run greater risks to the judicial system than other kinds of judgment.

Narrow policy questions may differ not only in degree but in kind. Narrow policies are focused on the facts of the particular case and not on a social agenda or ideology. Narrow policy questions at times deal with cases in which fairness to all is simply impossible. For instance, if you buy a watch that turns out to have been stolen from the plaintiff, the plaintiff can claim that justice requires that you return it. You, on the other hand, can claim that after all you paid for it in good faith and that it is unjust to force the loss on you when it is not your fault. There may be several ways to resolve this conflict, but one of two innocent people must take a loss and in that situation a narrow policy judgment may be justified when broad policy judgments without data are not. Such a policy judgment might be "property rights are more important in this situation than unfettered exchange of goods" or vice versa.[15] Such policy judgments may be unavoidable and in any event are manageable.

Judges' Choices

Although torts traditionally may emphasize justice or fairness far more than policy or utility,[16] the two goals are in harmony in many cases. It is just that the wrongdoer must pay compensation for his wrong, and it is also good policy to deter wrongdoing. When policy goals are at odds with justice to individuals, different views have been advanced,[17] and courts have sometimes emphasized justice, sometimes policy. For lawyers arguing cases, the question is not likely to be whether judges must wholly exclude policy or wholly exclude justice. Instead, advocacy requires lawyers to show judges why one approach or the other is most appropriate for the particular case. In that respect, at least, the particular individuals before the court with their particular complaints and defenses can be heard.

§ 2.3   Fault and Other Normative Bases for Liability

Fault and justice. Tort law imposes liability upon defendants for conduct the law treats as wrong. In most instances, the conduct adjudged as wrong can be viewed as morally faulty conduct: it is intentional misconduct or at least unreasonably risky conduct likely to cause harm to others. In these cases, tort law seems to be commensurate in a general way with corrective justice ideals. The defendant's fault is a wrong that has harmed the plaintiff in some legally cognizable way; tort law, by subjecting the wrongdoer to a judgment that can be enforced against his assets,[18] can put right the accounts between the parties.

---

[15]   See § 6.12.

[16]   See David A. Fischer, Successive Causes and the Enigma of Duplicated Harm, 66 Tenn. L. Rev. 1127 (1999) (concluding that courts generally choose fairness when forced to choose between the two goals).

[17]   Differing views about justice vs. deterrence (or moral vs. economic analysis) are discussed in many articles, among them Gary T. Schwartz, Mixed Theories of Tort Law: Affirming Both Deterrence and Corrective Justice, 75 Tex. L. Rev. 1801 (1997); William E. Nelson, From Fairness to Efficiency: the Transformation of Tort Law in New York, 1920–1980, 47 Buff. L. Rev. 117 (1999).

[18]   It may be argued that if anyone, wrongdoer or not, compensates the plaintiff, corrective justice has been done. In this view, the state or an insurance company could compensate victims in the interests of corrective justice. Others have emphasized that corrective justice is not merely compensation, but compensation *from* the wrongdoer; that is, it requires a demonstration of "public respect for rights and public recognition of the transgressor's fault by requiring something important to be given up on one side and received

Conversely, it can be argued that in a corrective justice scheme, it would be wrong to impose liability upon a defendant who is not at fault in causing the plaintiff's harm. Society may wish to compensate injured people by the use of public funds, but it cannot justly force one innocent individual to compensate another.

These views emphasize individual accountability for fault, accompanied by individual freedom to act without fault. They are consistent with an ideal of social responsibility for victims. They do not, however, speak against government compensation for victims when the defendant is not at fault, only against compensation by the faultless defendant.

Strict liability and corrective justice. When tort law imposes liability without fault, does it go beyond the principle of justice? At least *some* strict liability seems commensurate with justice. For example, suppose that an established custom in the neighborhood permits any neighbor to borrow garden equipment from any other neighbor, but requires the borrower to pay for any damage done while the equipment is in the borrower's possession. Suppose that Smith borrows Brown's lawnmower, which is damaged when a truck backs over it in Smith's driveway, without any fault on Smith's part. A rule that imposes liability upon Smith would be a strict liability rule because Smith was not at fault, but would seem to accord with justice so long as Smith and Brown both know of the custom.

Uniting the potential for gains and losses. Some thinkers have advocated a general regime of strict liability on the ground that strict liability is a morally based system and is therefore within principles of justice. One idea behind this view is that when a person makes choices about conduct, he is entitled to the gains that may result from that conduct (including personal pleasure), and should also take responsibility for losses caused by that conduct.[19] If a person chooses to hang-glide off a mountainside, either for personal pleasure or as part of a demonstration that brings him profit, then he should pay any for any damages caused when he cannot control the glider and lands on another person's vegetable garden.[20] This line of thought works best when an active person causes harm to a person or thing at rest. When two hang-gliders (or car drivers) crash into each other without fault, it is much harder to work out a system of strict liability that is also based on corrective justice, and in fact strict liability is not imposed upon car drivers who crash into one another.[21]

Nonreciprocal risks. A different view about the justice basis for strict liability is that strict liability can justly be imposed when the defendant imposes nonreciprocal risks on the plaintiff. For example, an airplane pilot imposes only small and quite reasonable risks to people on the ground, since crashes are extremely rare. Nevertheless, the pilot imposes some risks to people below while they impose no similar risks upon him. If

---

on the other, even if there is no equivalence of value possible." Margaret Jane Radin, Compensation and Commensurability, 43 Duke L. J. 56 (1993).

[19]   A most elaborate theory of strict liability based on corrective justice was presented many years ago by Richard Epstein in A Theory of Strict Liability (1980).

[20]   This idea can be viewed as a moral idea and hence a part of justice reasoning, but it has affinities with an economic idea that says an enterprise should not be permitted to externalize its costs. See § 2.5. Both forms of the idea are attractive but both raise additional questions. What costs should be regarded as part of the potential costs or losses that go with hang-gliding? If the answer is "foreseeable harms to others," then the argument sounds like an argument for negligence liability, not strict liability, because the judgment that a defendant has taken unreasonable risks is based on the conclusion that the risks were foreseeable.

[21]   See §§ 32.5 & 32.8 (no strict liability for activities that are common and no strict liability when plaintiff participates in the dangerous activity).

reciprocity is a moral test of liability, then strict liability should be imposed upon the pilot, and such liability would be commensurate with justice reasoning.[22]

Community standards. A third view might emphasize community standards as the basis for corrective justice liability. Community standards might be embodied in an explicit custom, like the neighborhood custom in the lawnmower example above. Or they might be embodied only in the views of the jury that decides the case. If the jury is representative of the community as a whole, its verdict is likely to reflect the implicit standards of fault and liability that already exist at that time and that place. This, too, is a view of corrective justice.[23] Presumably it would permit strict liability where the community standard called for it, perhaps in cases like that of the borrowed lawnmower.

Fault again. Although innovative thinkers have sought to justify strict liability within a corrective justice framework, many of the cases considered seem to be cases of special kinds of fault, for example, fault as judged by the fairness of imposing non-reciprocal risks or as judged by deviations from community-accepted norms. Whatever is to be said of strict liability theories of justice, the great majority of tort cases turn on some kind of perception that the defendant is at fault in a significant way. At least for those cases, tort law begins with ideals of justice, even if those ideals may be modified by considerations of process, pragmatism or policy in particular cases.

§ 2.4   Compensation, Risk Distribution, and Fault

Compensation of persons injured by wrongdoing is one of the generally accepted aims of tort law. If a person has been wronged by a defendant, it is good and just that the defendant make compensation.[24] Compensation is also socially desirable, for otherwise the uncompensated injured persons will trigger further costs and problems for society. A tort system based solely on social policy might conceivably seek to exact compensation from defendants who have caused harms by accident but not by wrongdoing. Alternatively, such a system might provide a social system of insurance for everyone. However, a system of tort law based on justice will ordinarily compensate only those who are injured by some conduct that can be called a wrong.

Injury costs are socially as well as individually significant; the annual cost of unintended injuries, including medical costs and wage losses, exceeds half a trillion dollars.[25] Compensation for injury may actually help reduce personal injury costs. Appropriate medical attention, for example, may allow an injured person to return to work sooner. Injury also has ripple effects, especially when it promotes economic hardship. Children and others within a family stressed by serious injury and consequent economic difficulty may reflect that stress by inflicting still further economic costs upon society, for example, by abusing alcohol or drugs.

---

[22]   George Fletcher, Fairness and Utility in Tort Theory, 85 Harv. L. Rev. 537 (1972), developed the reciprocity idea. Later, Fletcher modified his views a little to speak of "dominance" as ground for liability in contrast to "failed cooperation" which calls for dividing liability between the parties. George Fletcher, Corrective Justice for Moderns, 106 Harv. L. Rev. 1658 (1993) (reviewing Jules Coleman, Risks and Wrongs).

[23]   Catherine Wells, Tort Law as Corrective Justice: A Pragmatic Justification for Jury Adjudication, 88 Mich. L. Rev. 2348 (1990).

[24]   What counts as "compensation" is in part the subject matter of remedies. Conceivably corrective justice might accept some response from the wrongdoer-defendant that is not measured by money losses. See Margaret Jane Radin, Compensation and Commensurability, 43 Duke L. J. 56 (1993).

[25]   See National Safety Council, Injury Facts, published annually and available at www.nsc.org.

Based on these and other considerations, some commentators have argued that tort liability should be strict (or more expansive) in order to secure compensation for more injured persons. Some defendants (if not all) may be seen as good "risk distributors" who should be liable for any harms they cause regardless of fault because they can "distribute" the costs of paying compensation; for example, manufacturers could pay compensation for injuries they cause and then recoup some or all of those costs by raising the price of their products. In this view, each individual purchaser of these products will pay a tiny fraction of the costs of injuries inflicted by those products, and the injured person will not be compelled to bear the entire cost alone.[26] Loss would thus cause less social dislocation. At the same time, an enterprise would be forced to internalize losses typically caused by the business itself.

However, judges have not generally adopted the view that compensation is more important than justice or that tort liability should be strict. Distribution arguments and strict liability have gone hand in hand, but only in certain kinds of cases.[27] They have not supplanted fault as the most common basis for tort liability.

Since compensation *is* indeed important and one of the goals of tort law, why is it that courts do not adopt strict liability across the board and order compensation in every case in which the defendant causes harm? The most obvious possibility is that judges feel heavily committed to a system of justice; they turn to social policy mainly when they feel social policy and corrective justice coincide at least in part. It is also quite possible that even though compensation is a significant and important policy, other social policies counsel only limited compensation through the tort system. It may also be true that risk-distribution arguments are best addressed to legislators rather than to judges; in fact, some legislation (such as workers' compensation statutes) in effect adopts such arguments.

A second reason is that an invariable award of compensation that must be paid by a defendant may eliminate any deterrent effect that the award would have if it were confined to cases of fault. A third reason is that the tort system is an extremely expensive system to operate. If compensation is the most important goal, the tort system is a poor way to accomplish it because other means are cheaper. For instance, workers' compensation insurance is usually more efficient than liability insurance used to pay tort judgments. Relatedly, the tort system is not in *fact* the source of most compensation for injury. Private insurance, such as the injured person's medical insurance, and public assistance programs provide most of the compensation that goes for injury.[28] Fourth, the injured person often bears some of the responsibility for her own injury, and in addition the parties may be equally good at "distributing" the risk by purchasing their own insurance. Still another consideration is that if defendants must pay compensation even

---

[26]   See Escola v. Coca Cola Bottling Co. of Fresno, 24 Cal.2d 453, 462, 150 P.2d 436, 441 (1944) (Traynor, J., concurring); George L. Priest, The Invention of Enterprise Liability: A Critical History of the Intellectual Foundations of Modern Tort Law, 14 J. Leg. Stud. 461 (1985); Virginia E. Nolan & Edmund Ursin, Understanding Enterprise Liability 168 (1995).

[27]   See Gary T. Schwartz, The Beginning and the Possible End of the Rise of Modern American Tort Law, 26 Ga. L. Rev. 601(1992).

[28]   Deborah R. Hensler, et al., Compensation for Accidental Injuries in the United States (RAND 1991). This study concludes that only 10% of all persons who are compensated for injuries receive payments under the tort system, that is, from the tortfeasor or his insurer. These payments amount to even less: 7% of the compensation dollar. The tort system plays a greater role, however, when it comes to auto cases.

when they are not at fault, many such defendants might soon be bankrupted—ultimately defeating compensation for other injured persons.[29]

§ 2.5   Deterrence

Courts and writers almost always recognize that another aim of tort law is to deter certain kinds of conduct by imposing liability when that conduct causes harm. The idea of deterrence is not so much that an individual, having been held liable for a tort, would thereafter conduct himself better. It is rather the idea that all persons, recognizing potential tort liability, would tend to avoid conduct that could lead to tort liability. They might sometimes engage in the conduct in question, but only if they would get more out of it than the tort liability would cost. Some critics believe that tort law fails to provide systematic deterrence.[30] Even if the failure is not pervasive, it is certainly true that tort law fails to provide appropriate deterrence at least on occasion.[31]

Both systems of thought that emphasize justice and those that emphasize social policy goals can agree that deterrence is acceptable, but the two approaches might call for deterring quite different conduct. If you focus on conduct that is wrongful in the sense of being unjust to an individual, you might regard any given act as wrongful even though it is economically useful in society. If you focus on social policy, you might want to forgive defendants who cause harms by their socially useful activities.

Suppose for example that there are two methods of constructing a building the defendant intends to build. One is quick, easy, and cheap. The other is slow and expensive. The trouble is that the quick, easy, cheap building is also a little more dangerous to build, so that, overall, more injuries occur in construction of the cheaper buildings than in construction of the more expensive ones that are slower to build. Not surprisingly, the defendant chooses to build the cheaper, quicker version. Suppose he builds it with care, but, as will inevitably happen sooner or later, someone is injured in a construction accident. Should the injured person have a claim against the builder?

As the example suggests, one particular kind of social policy consideration is economic. If economics is defined broadly enough to include a consideration of all human wants and desires, then perhaps all social policies are in a sense economic.

Economic analysis of the personal injury part of tort law may suggest that deterrence is undesirable in some injury cases. One line of economic thought is that courts should respect the defendant's freedom to act, at least in some cases, more than they respect the plaintiff's physical security. Under this view, people in general ought to be free to build buildings, including cheaper ones, if they do so carefully; the law wants to protect their freedom and indeed encourage the enterprise because economically sound decisions are good for the community as a whole. This line of thought suggests that in deciding the builder's tort liability, the costs of injury should be weighed, but so should the social (economic) utility of the cheaper building.[32] Depending on how much

---

[29] See Mark Geistfeld, Negligence, Compensation, and the Coherence of Tort Law, 91 Geo. L.J. 585 (2003).

[30] See, with different arguments, Stephen D. Sugarman, Doing Away with Personal Injury Law 7–9 (1989); Daniel Shuman, The Psychology of Deterrence in Tort Law, 42 Kan. L. Rev. 115 (1993).

[31] For example, some of the limitations on punitive damages adopted by the Supreme Court under the Due Process Clause, which are not focused on the profit made by the defendant from his tortious activity but on other factors altogether, may eliminate deterrence in some instances. See § 34.6.

[32] See §§ 12.3 to 12.5.

the builder saved and how high the injury costs were, a court might thus deny any recovery against the builder. In the actual cases, this line of economic thought is illustrated and supported by the outcomes, but the judges do not so often explicate these results in economic terms.

A different line of economic/public policy thinking might assert that if it is statistically likely that more injuries occur when the cheaper building is constructed, then the costs of those injuries should be regarded as a part of the builder's costs of doing business. Even if he is not regarded as being at fault, nevertheless, he chose the riskier method and got its benefits (less investment in the building), so should take the disadvantages as well. In economic terms, he should not be permitted to externalize his costs. This line of reasoning might lead to the conclusion that the builder should be held liable for the injuries caused.[33]

Tort law has tended to resolve many disputes in a way consistent with the first line of economic analysis. This means that in determining whether the defendant may be at fault, courts often take into account the benefits and costs of a particular activity. If the benefits are high and the injuries are small or rare, courts will often say that the defendant is not at fault and that he has committed no tort.[34] The second line of economic thought can be seen in some instances, however. Workers' compensation and some other alternatives to tort law, or example, hold the defendant liable even without fault.[35] It may also be seen in the rule that employers who are not personally at fault are generally liable for the torts of their employees who are acting within the scope of their employment.[36]

§ 2.6   Alternative Compensation Systems

Some of the large differences in approach sketched in the preceding sections can be understood in terms of the constant tension in our society between individual accountability and social responsibility. We are all individuals and we are all members of society. That duality shapes our dilemma with many issues beyond tort law.

Part of the tension between personal accountability and social responsibility is minimized or resolved when an individual injured by an innocent defendant can seek compensation from public sources rather than from the defendant. Such an approach treats innocently caused injury as a social responsibility rather than a matter of the defendant's personal accountability. The argument is that when both the plaintiff and defendant are innocent, there is no justice in shifting the plaintiff's suffering to the equally innocent defendant, but there might be a point in alleviating the plaintiff's suffering through some kind of insurance or public benefit system.

Plans like workers' compensation, which requires employers to pay compensation for workers' injuries even when employers are not at fault, may be rationalized on the ground that injury is a regular cost of business to be borne by the business itself. If injury is seen to be as much a part of the worker's life as a part of the business, however, that explanation becomes less convincing. A different explanation for workers' compensation

---

[33]   Cf. Guido Calabresi, The Costs of Accidents (1970) (suggesting that if the activity bears the costs of accidents associated with that activity, the costs of the activity will rise and accidents will be reduced either because people will seek alternate ways of avoiding the higher costs or ways of making the activity safer).

[34]   See §§ 12.3 to 12.5.

[35]   See Chapter 36.

[36]   See Chapter 31.

plans is that the employer is held liable without fault because he can pass on the costs of employee injury to the public who buys his product or services. In this view, the employer is not himself ultimately responsible for worker injuries; rather he is a conduit for a semi-public liability.

Although alternative compensation systems help fulfill a sense of social responsibility or help solve a social problem, they may raise doubts about whether they give enough weight to individual accountability for wrongs, with the possibility of deterrence and justice that such accountability implies. The workers' compensation system, for example, substitutes limited compensation obligations for tort liability, so that the negligent employer escapes any obligation to make full tort payment to a wronged individual. From the employer's point of view, this reduction in tort liability may be balanced by the employer's obligation to pay other workers even when the employer is not at fault, but even so, the employer's incentive for safety is reduced.

Justice and accountability go hand in hand with the individualization that has been characteristic of the traditional legal system. The plaintiff in a tort case tells her own story, the individual facts of injury and grievance. The plaintiff speaks for herself, not as a representative of asbestos victims, or workers, or some other class. The defendant's story is also his own. Traditional tort law is not about workers against employers or about claimants who demand a supportive share of a state's treasury, but rather about Mary Smith's particular grievance against John Jones.[37] The advent of mass tort litigation, and bureaucratic systems of compensation such as those found in social security disability cases, however, has put the individual claimant far from the center of the torts universe.

§ 2.7   Process Values in Tort Law

Judges of course wish to formulate and apply rules to obtain both justice and public policy goals. They also rightly wish to promote and protect process values. Process values are values we attach to the legal process itself, in particular, the process of deciding disputes and formulating legal rules. Jury trial rights are one part of the dispute resolution process, but there are others. Many process values are represented in procedural codes and in constitutional prescriptions. Due process is a prized right, even if it is not precisely formulated: we should hold the trial before the verdict; each party should be entitled to know what the other claims; disputing parties must be able to present their side of the dispute.

Procedural specifications do not cover all considerations of process. Judges consider process values in choosing, formulating, and applying rules of tort law. A judge might justly award damages to an injured plaintiff even if there were no rules at all, but the process of adjudication would then itself be suspect and in a sense unjust. So rules adopted must be rules that can be seen, understood, and applied, at least by the professionals involved in litigation. Judges striving to formulate or apply tort rules attempt to meet this modest concern for the litigation process itself, which sometimes may trump considerations of both justice and other social policies.

Process goals. No authoritative list of process values guides judges, so lawyers can argue that any given rule is undesirable because it does not appropriately respect process

---

[37] See Kenneth S. Abraham, What Is A Tort Claim? An Interpretation of Contemporary Tort Reform, 51 Md. L. Rev. 172 (1992); Glen O. Robinson & Kenneth S. Abraham, Collective Justice in Tort Law, 78 Va. L. Rev. 1481 (1992).

concerns. Broadly phrased, the legal process should be designed not only to get good results in accord with justice, policy and the relevant facts, but also to leave participants with a sense of humane participation in the process.[38] That might include the felt need to tell one's side of the story and relate a sense of injustice. It might also include a sense that justice is not only done but seen to be done. There is also a practical side to process. Rules should be structured to permit efficient decision making—no litigant should be compelled to spend weeks getting a decision that could have been made just as well in a day. Many specific process goals are ordinarily taken for granted. Some system must be in place for gathering facts and insuring that all relevant points of view are heard. To insure even-handedness, a measure of respect must be accorded to precedent in closely similar cases. And to insure that the rule of law prevails instead of pure bias, rules themselves must be reasonably clear, even though they cannot provide perfect certainty.

Loose rule formulation that diminishes judicial accountability. These broadly phrased ideas suggest many more specific concerns. If rules are too abstract, they may fail to constrain the judge or the jury, effectively permitting the decision makers to do as they like. Rules like this can undermine the process of justice because lawyers and other observers cannot confidently say whether the judge or jury applied the law or not. A rule that merely told people "be good" has at least two process defects. First, it fails to point to evidence a lawyer could adduce or arguments that could be made. Second, the rule is so undefined that it fails to constrain the judge in appropriate ways. If their decisions are not subject to professional scrutiny because the rules are so uncertain that anything goes, judges are likely to become, in time, more arbitrary and ultimately less just.[39]

Tight rule formulation that eliminates needed flexibility. Conversely, however, precise rules may overly constrain the decision makers, leaving no room for justly deciding the individual's case which is at the heart of our concept of justice. A rule that says "be good" violates the process interest in having understandable, reasonably precise rules. At the other extreme, a rule that says "never, ever, drive more than 40 miles per hour in this zone" may leave too little flexibility for the case of the driver rushing his child to the emergency room. Evaluating process arguments thus requires both judgment and balance.

Rules guiding lawyers' investigation and arguments. Although some rules are actually read and understood by the people whose conduct they regulate, many tort rules are not. Rules often attempt to reflect the way people should behave even if they have not read the statutes and the cases. Thus, many tort rules are mainly read and understood by lawyers. Judges formulating tort rules must have in mind that lawyers use rules in very practical ways, to know what arguments and what facts are relevant so that investigation can proceed accordingly. Rules devalue the process when they fail to point to arguments and facts that are relevant to the litigation. That was one of the objections to a rule that simply commanded people to be good. The rule gives no hint as to what facts might impress the judge on the goodness scale or what arguments might be structured in favor of one side or the other.

---

[38] See Robert S. Summers, Evaluating and Improving Legal Processes—A Plea for "Process Values", 60 Cornell L. Rev. 1 (1974).

[39] James Henderson, Process Constraints in Tort, 67 Cornell L. Rev. 901 (1982), contains an excellent and well-known discussion of similar ideas. Professor Henderson, however, argues a step further: rules requiring a balance and evaluation of a number of factors detract from legal process partly because they turn judges into intuitive decision-makers, or managers, or planners, (or, one might fear, autocrats).

Rules failing to specify provable facts. Rules also detract from good process when they call for facts that cannot be proved with reasonable confidence or proved within a reasonable length of time. Suppose that it is normally a tort to touch someone who has not consented to being touched, but that it is not a tort to touch someone who has consented. If the plaintiff plays in a game of tag or football, consent seems apparent even if it is not expressed. If judges were to say that anyone touching the plaintiff is liable unless the plaintiff actually, subjectively consents to the touching, the rule would not point to evidence that can be reached by the defendant's lawyer, since no one can produce evidence about the plaintiff's state of mind except so far as it is outwardly or objectively expressed. That may or may not lead to unjust results, but it leads to process concerns because we cannot be very sure of our basis for judging the question of subjective consent if we are not permitted to consider the outward signs.

Deciding by avoiding decision. In some situations, judges believe that their basis for judging is too limited to permit them to act at all. Sometimes this feeling leads to rules that reject tort law solutions altogether. For example, no judge wishes to condone parental abuse of children, but few judges want to tell parents that they cannot punish their children in ways accepted in the community. So if a child were to sue her parent, claiming that punishment was unjust or harmful, some judges might fear their ability to discriminate between abuse and punishment. They might refuse to entertain the case altogether, or if they entertained it, they might demand especially clear proof from the child. Judges might have other reasons besides those related to the legal process for reaching such a decision. Official interference with family life is a troubling and dangerous matter. Nevertheless, inability to decide in a way that can be rationally understood by citizens and lawyers is one of the reasons why judges may refuse to recognize a tort or, if they recognize it, to apply the rules with great caution.

On the other hand, resolution of human disputes cannot await the certainty of a long-term scientific study. Judges must be (and are) prepared to tolerate a degree of uncertainty in many claims. The amount of acceptable uncertainty in proof depends a lot on the judge's assessment of the net cost of error.

Process value arguments as judgment, not logic. Process value arguments probably should be taken as important factors in deciding what rules to formulate and how to apply them, but they probably should not be taken as sovereign commands. They appeal to judgment, not to a sense of inexorable logic. They should be evaluated, too, with the possibility in mind that they tend to favor defendants, for example, by demanding clarity in rules that cannot always be supplied, or by insisting upon certainty of evidence or logic that is seldom available.

B. HISTORY, METHODS AND PROCEDURES OF TORT LAW

§ 2.8   Historical Development of Tort Law

Tort law's traits can often be understood through its history. This section reflects only a small part of that history that bears on some specific tools of thought that sometimes still affect our resolution of cases.

Common Law Writs of Trespass and Case

The early common law was based upon decisions by judges developed gradually in England after the Norman Conquest. Local lords or the courts they controlled decided some cases, but the medieval English King as the chief feudal lord claimed the right to decide cases involving property rights and the "King's peace." Gradually a procedure developed under which the King, through his Chancellor, would issue a "writ" which had the effect of conferring jurisdiction on the King's courts to hear a particular dispute.

The writ of trespass. The writs were stylized documents or forms containing certain words that remained more or less the same from case to case. Lawyers and judges naturally called these writs by a short name based on that commonly used language. Certain early writs, all in Latin, asserted a claim that the defendant had "transgressed" by force and violence. An English word for transgress was trespass, so these writs were called writs of trespass. The trespass writ developed several sub-forms. For instance, one version asserted that the defendant acted *vi et armis*, that is, by use of force. Another asserted that the defendant "broke the close," that is, invaded land and disrupted the plaintiff's rightful possession of it.

The characteristic instance for which an aggrieved person might obtain the writ of *trespass* was one in which the defendant applied direct force to the plaintiff's interests: he rode onto the plaintiff's land or he struck the plaintiff with a stick. The *trespass* action was not so much about land as about direct physical force. You could have trespass to persons, chattels, or land.[40]

The writ of trespass on the case. Over time, the king's agents began to issue new writs, covering instances in which the force applied by the defendant was not direct. The defendant throws a log which strikes the plaintiff. A claim on those facts calls for the writ of *trespass*. The defendant throws a log in the plaintiff's path and he trips over it after it has come to rest. A claim on those facts does not justify the use of the writ of *trespass*.[41] Nevertheless, the claim might appeal to one's sense of justice and in the late 14th century the Chancellor began to issue writs to cover such indirect injuries.[42] The new kind of writ was called *trespass on the case*. As this writ became common, legal professionals began to refer to the new writ simply as *case* and the plaintiff was said to bring an action *on the case*.

Strict liability under the writ of trespass. The writ of *trespass* was based on direct force, which sounds like intentional wrongdoing. However, if we understand the obscure history of this action, intentional wrongdoing was not a required part of the trespass claim. If the defendant threw a log that hit the plaintiff, the defendant was liable even if he had never intended to strike the plaintiff. So, at least according to the dominant view, *trespass* was initially a kind of strict liability tort.[43] Perhaps this was so because trespassory torts were likely in earlier culture to promote revenge and blood feuds, and

---

[40] Judge Arnold collected many early cases of trespass, only a few of which involved trespass to land alone. See Morris Arnold, Select Cases of Trespass from the King's Courts—1307–1399 (1985).

[41] "[I]f a man throws a log into the highway, and in that act it hits me, I may maintain trespass, because it is an immediate wrong; but if as it lies there I tumble over it and receive an injury, I must bring an action upon the case, because it is only prejudicial in consequence. . . ." Reynolds v. Clarke, 1 Str. 634, 93 Eng.Rep. 747, 748 (K.B. 1726) (Forescue, J.).

[42] Before that time, the Royal courts did entertain some indirect injury suits under the Trespass writ. See M.J. Prichard, *Scott v. Shepherd* (1773) and the Emergence of the Tort of Negligence 5, 13 ff. (1976).

[43] Some scholars are skeptical. See Gary Schwartz, Tort Law and the Economy in Nineteenth-Century America: A Reinterpretation, 90 Yale L. J. 1717 (1981); cf. Stephen Young, Reconceptualizing Accountability in the Early Nineteenth Century: How the Tort of Negligence Appeared, 21 Conn. L. Rev. 197 (1989).

because, from very early times, the law sought to substitute payment for the continuing violence that would erupt without it.[44]

Recovery without harm under the writ of trespass. In addition, if *trespass* were the appropriate writ, the plaintiff could recover without proving any actual pecuniary loss. For example, if the defendant directly entered upon the plaintiff's land without a justification, he would be liable for at least nominal damages, even if no harm was done. In the case of more violent torts this rule may also demonstrate the connection between trespass as a tort and trespass as a criminal or quasi-criminal action. As a kind of deterrent, the action inflicted a cost upon the defendant even if the plaintiff suffered no loss.

Fault under the writ of case. The writ of *case*, on the other hand, was associated with fault such as intent or negligence on the part of the defendant. If the plaintiff tripped over the log the defendant had left on the path, the defendant would not be liable unless he was guilty of wrongful intent or negligence.

Damages under the writ of case. Furthermore, where *case* was the appropriate writ, the plaintiff could not recover unless he proved, in addition to fault, some legally recognizable harm such as physical injury or pecuniary loss. If the defendant negligently cut a tree so that it would narrowly miss striking the plaintiff as it fell, the plaintiff would have no claim for this fault unless he could show harm to himself. This rule is still the ordinary rule today: a negligence action lies only if the plaintiff has suffered in a way the courts will recognize as legal harm.

Coming to America

The Spanish conquerors of Mexico and settlers in what is now the American West left a legacy of the civil or code-oriented law. The French version of civil law likewise came to those areas settled by the French. The English colonists in the East brought with them common law assumptions. But colonial institutions did not quite match those of England. No chancellor was there to issue writs even if Americans assumed that the writs matched some more or less immutable form of thinking about law.

The strict liability elements of the *trespass* writ were eroded in the 19th century. In the United States, the year 1850 brought a leading decision of the Massachusetts Court in Brown v. Kendall.[45] A man striking at fighting dogs with a stick raised the stick over his shoulder and in so doing unintentionally struck the plaintiff. The case fit the model of the *trespass* writ because the injury was both direct and forcible, so strict liability might have been imposed under the older rules. But the court rejected that approach and substituted a fault standard instead.

From that time on, courts tended to assume that some kind of fault—negligence or intentional wrong—was required to establish tort liability in most cases. Yet the appeal of strict liability for special cases remained, and courts began to find new occasions to impose liability without fault. Brown v. Kendall made fault the dominant approach to resolution of tort disputes, but it also opened up the courts to new kinds of strict liability, not based on the writs or forms of action at all, but on some sense of justice or policy.

---

[44] On the *bot* or fixed payment that could be demanded for each kind of affront and the blood-feud basis for this procedure, see 2 Sir Frederick Pollock & Frederic William Maitland, History of English Law 451, 525 (1952).

[45] Brown v. Kendall, 60 Mass. (6 Cush.) 292 (1850).

Brown v. Kendall signaled the acceptance of new kinds of reasoning in tort cases, a reasoning that left the formal writs behind.

§ 2.9   Common-Law Analysis and the Doctrine of Precedent

Roman legal principles were stated in the form of a code. Many countries today initially state tort law as general principles arranged in a code of laws. These are the civil law countries, including Mexico, the countries of western Europe, Japan and others. Common law countries—those which, like Canada and the United States, took their early legal thought from England—did not begin with a set of principles but began by deciding cases. Gradually, decisions in individual cases came to be seen as operating on certain principles or rules, which were then taken as the basis for future decisions on similar facts. American tort law, though now often supplemented by statutory law, initially developed from common law decisions and those decisions still constitute the main source to which judges turn for guidance in deciding new cases.

In spite of the preeminent importance of case decision in the common law of torts, many statutes affect tort law today. Statutes may indirectly affect tort law by setting some standard that courts adopt; they may directly affect tort law by creating some claim or defense that would not otherwise be recognized or enforced by the judges. Even ordinances or administrative rules may have some effect in the tort process. Since about 1960, the United States Constitution, too, has been instrumental in creating tort rights by way of a federal statute recognizing civil rights torts. So statutory instruments today are part of tort law. Statutes in the United States, however, often differ from codes in that they do not attempt to provide a complete and coherent set of rules or principles. Instead, they prescribe very particular rules for particular situations.

When statutes do not wholly govern a tort claim, how do appellate judges go about deciding a case? Besides considering the particular facts of the case, judges today are likely to consider logic, public policy, and justice. Most of these considerations will be expressed in terms of rules, principles or policies derived from earlier case decisions. Under the doctrine of precedent, judges are "bound" to follow the rules previously adopted by the same court or a higher court in the same judicial system.

In the United States, the court of one state is not ordinarily required to consider the precedents of another state court. Indeed, precedents of federal courts can be ignored by state courts unless the issue before the state court is an issue of federal law. However, different courts in the United States are staffed with judges who received similar legal training and who know at least a little about the common law background of the cases they decide. So quite frequently the courts of one state will consider decisions of another state to be persuasive. By the same token, if the state has no precedent on point, its courts will frequently look to general principles of common law or to the opinions of commentators or respected professional groups like the American Law Institute.

In the United States today, precedents are usually regarded as important guides, to be taken seriously but not necessarily slavishly followed. If the precedent was decided in a feudal society, it may not be apt to govern disputes in a highly mechanized society. Perhaps just as important, social values change over time. A precedent that is now perceived as unfairly discriminatory is likely to be overruled. Precedents may also be modified because, with time and experience, judges come to perceive that the precedent was stated too broadly or too narrowly, or that when the precedential case was decided, its logical or social implications were not fully grasped.

Application of precedent to new cases is sometimes rather mechanical, but mostly it is not. Lawyers do not litigate clear cases. Unless the lawyers are very bad or the parties very angry, clear cases are settled because lawyers can determine from precedent what the result will be. Sometimes the law is the clearest thing in the case; it is the facts or the inferences to be drawn from the facts that are disputed. Facts are usually resolved by the time the case reaches an appellate court. If a case is on appeal, there is usually a dispute about legal rules. Does a certain rule exist at all, and if so, should it be overruled? If it does exist, should it be applied to the facts of the particular case? How, exactly, should the rule be worded?

Uncertainty. Many beginning students are surprised to learn that after hundreds of years of common law development, so much remains that can be disputed. Part of that surprise is due to some distortion in the picture. Cases reaching the appellate courts are not necessarily representative of the many thousands of other cases that are readily resolved by settlement because the law is clear. But part of the surprise is accurately grounded. Tort law is very much litigation law; it is often somewhat indeterminate or uncertain until the particular case is actually decided. In one way that is unfortunate. In another, it is not. A society with a precise rule for every possible human act and every configuration of circumstances would probably be a society with a great deal of injustice and very little freedom. Change is part of the nature of tort law.

§ 2.10 Tort Rules and What They Do

Tort law is better understood when its limits are appreciated. Law cannot effectively solve all problems. Even issues capable of legal resolution are sometimes resolved outside the law by community standards and practices that do not depend heavily upon formal tort law.[46] In many other instances, however, tort law tends to articulate and reinforce community standards and to provide a framework for discussion and argument about their application.

Some tort rules or principles may be precise enough and well-known enough to guide conduct, at least in a general way. This may be especially so in the case of defendants who act repeatedly and plan their conduct to avoid legal liability. Manufacturers know that dangerous products can lead to tort liability, even if they do not know detailed rules.

Many of the technical or professional rules of tort law, the rules that affect litigation outcomes, however, are not known or understood by people in general. Even if they were known, the tort rules seldom determine outcomes of litigation by themselves. That is, the technical tort rules are almost never detailed enough to lead inexorably to a given conclusion except in extreme cases. Tort law directs people to use reasonable care under the circumstances, but it does not attempt to define in advance what counts as reasonable care in all possible circumstances.

Some tort rules are not even about conduct at all, but about how to interpret its effects. Rules about how to judge whether the defendant's conduct caused harm would almost never guide anyone's actual conduct even if the rules were precise and well-understood.

Why have tort rules at all if people do not know them and cannot use them to guide their conduct?

---

[46]   See Robert C. Ellickson, Order without Law (1991).

First, the traditional tort rules governing conduct to a large extent reflect social values and norms already in existence in the culture. They do not create new standards imposed by authoritarian judges; they merely enforce what society already believes. This view also explains why tort rules can be announced after the dispute arises; they do not invent a new standard and impose it on past conduct, but instead resolve disputes about events in the past in the light of standards we generally share may not have not fully articulated. So we do not expect all tort rules to directly shape conduct. Rather, it is often the case that the tort rule confirms or articulates preexisting social ideals and perhaps reinforces them by imposing liability.

Second, even if tort rules had no effect at all on actual conduct, they are professional tools. They alert lawyers to issues in a dispute that judges and others can recognize as legitimate issues. They tell lawyers what kind of evidence to look for and introduce in court. They help lawyers formulate the terms and structure of their arguments. For example, if a rule says that people must use reasonable care in the circumstances, and that custom of the relevant community is to be considered in judging reasonable care, you would not know from the rule alone what conduct is or is not acceptable. You would know, however, that you could look for evidence of community custom, introduce it in evidence, and construct your argument on the basis of that custom. Rules are thus tools for practical and moral discourse and for legal argumentation. As tools, they work in a setting that not only includes the facts of particular cases but social facts and institutional environment as well.

Chapter 3

TORT LAW IN PRACTICE

Analysis

A. ADJUDICATION OF TORT CASES

§ 3.1   Trials and Appeals
§ 3.2   Judge, Jury, and Community Values

B. FUNDAMENTAL OPERATING CONCEPTIONS

§ 3.3   The Prima Facie Case and the Burden of Proof
§ 3.4   Affirmative Defenses
§ 3.5   Privilege, Justification, Excuse and Immunity

C. THE BACKGROUND CONDITIONS OF TORT LAW

§ 3.6   Remedies and Attorney's Fees
§ 3.7   Sources of Tort Law
§ 3.8   Liability Insurance

A. ADJUDICATION OF TORT CASES

§ 3.1   Trials and Appeals

Tort law as practiced by professionals operates in settings and under conditions that determine much about the impact the formal rules will have on the parties. The characteristics of trials and appeals are among those conditions, and several traits of the trial and appeal system directly affect the way tort law works.

Determining law. Disputes in trials are often either about the facts of the case—what happened—or about the law applicable to the case. Disputes about law commonly include issues of interpretation and application. The parties may interpret earlier decisions of the court in a different way; or one of them may argue that precedent does not apply because the particular facts of the case differ from those in earlier decisions. Disputes about law are decided by the judge.

Determining facts. Factual disputes arise when the parties or witnesses contradict one another and when there are gaps in the evidence that might be filled by different inferences of fact. There is no guarantee that any witnesses will be found, or that they will have good memories, or that they will be reputable and convincing, so some of the disputes are about the trustworthiness of the evidence presented. Factual disputes are decided by the trier of fact ("the trier"), which is the jury if there is one. The parties may in effect waive the jury and permit the judge to step aside from his role as interpreter of the law to determine the facts in particular cases.

Evaluating facts in the light of the law. A third kind of dispute is about how conduct is evaluated. If the trier determines that the defendant drove his car 60 miles per hour, and the judge determines that the law required the defendant to exercise reasonable care under the circumstances, someone must still evaluate the defendant's conduct by applying the legal rule of reasonable care to the facts. Sometimes 60 miles per hour is unreasonable (around children playing, for example) and sometimes not (on an interstate highway, for example). This third or evaluative kind of dispute is frequently decided by the jury, but sometimes judges make a rule of law to cover the particular evaluation.

Adversary presentation. The adversary system of the common law permits and requires the parties to present their respective cases. The plaintiff must initiate a case by filing a complaint summarizing the main facts on which her claim is based and by serving the defendant with a copy. The defendant must ordinarily file an answer summarizing defenses. At trial, the plaintiff must present her evidence, subject to the defendant's cross examination. In turn, the defendant must present his evidence, subject to the plaintiff's cross examination. The judge may ask questions of a witness but seldom does so. Almost never does the judge direct any investigation of facts.

Trials and appeals. All three kinds of disputes are initially decided in the trial court, where the parties present their evidence, usually in the form of witnesses' testimony. The trial judge must decide all issues of law that arise and instruct the jury about the law it is to apply in evaluating the parties' conduct. Appeals are quite different. Judges in the appeals court only determine issues or rules of law; they do not weigh evidence or substitute their own evaluations for those of the jury.[1]

Expense. Trial of a substantial tort claim is expensive. Preparation for trial consumes large amounts of lawyer time. It may entail many expenses, too, such as expenses of finding experts, learning from them, and planning how to present their testimony. If the parties do not settle the case and trial actually takes place, additional costs will be incurred. The parties may dispute both the facts and the application of law to the case. If the amounts in issue are large, both parties will have some incentive to settle to avoid a total loss. Most cases are in fact settled.

Credible threats. The strategy of both parties in tort litigation is to create a credible threat to the other party. The plaintiff makes a credible threat by asserting a claim for damages that the law recognizes as a valid claim, and by asserting facts that support the claim. The defendant makes a credible threat by asserting a defense the law recognizes, along with supporting facts. If the law does not clearly support the plaintiff's claim, the claim is less threatening than if the law clearly favored the plaintiff. In that case, the defendant would either refuse to settle or offer only a relatively small settlement. And vice versa; the weaker the defendant's facts and arguments, the more the defendant would tend to pay in settlement. However, even a weak claim with only a 10% chance of success may become threatening if the plaintiff can plausibly assert that her injuries are very great and her damages thus very high.

Non-objective claims. Claims for pain, suffering, and emotional distress as well as claims for punitive damages are more threatening in many cases than claims for wage loss or medical expenses. The claim for damages for pain or the like is an open-ended, non-objective claim, without any measurement. So it is a potential threat for large sums of money. Such a claim adds magnitude to the threat and tends to encourage the defendant to think of settling the claim.

Motion to dismiss. Two important procedural devices can be used before trial to exclude claims that are not legally justified. The first is a motion to dismiss (called a

---

[1]   Judges do review for sufficiency of evidence, but not its weight. See § 3.2.

general demurrer under earlier common law procedure). The relevant kind of motion to dismiss asserts that the adversary's claim or defense is not legally valid even if all the facts are exactly as claimed by the adversary. This motion is not about facts at all, but about the legal validity of the claim or defense, assuming the alleged facts are true.

Summary judgment. The other major procedure or device used to exclude claims or defenses is the motion for summary judgment. This motion also attempts to interdict a claim or defense before trial, but it is made after the parties have completed discovery. The process of discovery permits the parties to question witnesses under oath to discover what their testimony will be, or to obtain their testimony in written form. Written records of discovered material can be filed with the court. The motion for summary judgment asks the court to consider the *undisputed* testimony as shown in discovery documents and to dismiss a claim or defense on the basis of undisputed testimony if that testimony shows the claim or defense to be legally invalid. Unlike the motion to dismiss, the summary judgment motion permits the judge to consider facts (as shown in the discovery documents) to determine whether there really is a factual dispute. But the summary judgment motion does not permit the judge to decide any disputed fact; disputed facts and factual inferences are issues to be resolved at trial after the trier hears live witnesses.

Other procedures to establish or eliminate threats. Even if the parties are unable to settle and thus are forced to try the case, they will continue to attempt to interdict threatening claims. Partly this is to reduce the danger that the jury will make an unfavorable award and partly it is to continue to create a climate for favorable settlement. In the trial itself, parties argue legal rules (1) to exclude or admit evidence and (2) to support or avoid instructions to the jury according to whether the evidence or instruction is favorable. Finally, the defendant will routinely move for a directed verdict (now often called a motion for judgment as a matter of law or JML) when the evidence is all before the jury. This motion is addressed to the judge and says that the evidence is not sufficient to establish the plaintiff's claim, even if the evidence is taken to be true. If the judge agrees, the motion will be granted and the case dismissed. The jury will have no say in the decision if the evidence is legally insufficient.

Even a very superficial discussion of trial strategies affecting legal rules shows how difficult it is to translate abstract ideals of tort law into practice. Whatever the aims of tort law—justice, compensation, deterrence—they are not likely to be fully realized in all cases. A good claim may founder on an unimpressive or confused witness. Or a doubtful claim combined with expenses of trial and risks of loss may induce a settlement justified only by the expense, not by the merits of the claim. This may be an unavoidable part of human limitations. If so, it is also true that tort goals will be realized only in some cases, not all.

§ 3.2   Judge, Jury, and Community Values

Judge and Jury

The role of the jury is central in tort litigation in the United States. In most cases, a jury trial is available as a matter of right. Jury trial is traditionally almost invariable in substantial tort cases, though the actual use of juries overall is declining.[2]

---

[2]   See Valerie P. Hans & Stephanie Albertson, Empirical Research and Civil Jury Reform, 78 Notre Dame L. Rev. 1497 (2003).

The jury's function is to determine and evaluate the facts.[3] When the judge is designated to act as trier of fact ("the trier"), the judge does the same. The jury as trier will decide whether a witness is speaking truthfully and without mistake. The jury will decide what factual inferences are to be drawn from the evidence. When reasonable people could differ based on the evidence, juries also *evaluate* the conduct at issue. For instance, a jury might determine on the evidence the *fact* that the defendant was driving at 60 miles per hour when he crashed into the plaintiff and then might *evaluate* his conduct by determining that it was unreasonably risky and amounted to negligence.[4] In so doing, jurors bring their own knowledge of "social facts" to bear on the case.[5] Finally, the jury will determine the amount of damages, subject to the judge's instructions about the legal rules for measuring damages.[6]

The trial judge has considerable power to affect the jury's determinations.[7] The judge in the first instance will submit to the jury only those claims for which there is sufficient evidence adduced at the trial. If the plaintiff says she was injured when struck by the defendant's car, but presents no other facts showing how the injury occurred, the trial judge may not submit the claim to the jury at all. The claim is consistent with the idea that the defendant is at fault but also consistent with the idea that the plaintiff is at fault. So the judge might direct a verdict, telling the jury it must find for the defendant. In this extreme kind of case, the judge is not weighing testimony or evidence but is considering its logical or rational sufficiency to establish the plaintiff's claim. Evaluative decisions by the jury are treated similarly. If reasonable people could differ, the claim will be decided by the jury; if not, the judge will direct a verdict for the defendant.[8] Appellate judges may address the same issue on the basis of written transcripts of the testimony. Judges can also control jury determinations to some extent by excluding testimony that is irrelevant or prejudicial.

Judges may minimize or eliminate the jury's role in a different way by making a rule of law that demands a precise result or that casts the judge in the role of decision maker. For example, the traditional rule of law was that trespassers could not recover damages for injuries suffered by conditions negligently created by the landowner on his own land.[9] If the trespasser were a neighboring Girl Scout taking a short cut across the defendant's land, the jury might think the defendant was negligent in creating a dangerous, life-threatening condition. But under this rule, if a trespasser asserted a claim against the landowner, there would be literally nothing for the jury to decide, and

---

[3]   See § 13.1.

[4]   See Godfrey v. Iverson, 559 F.3d 569 (D.C. Cir. 2009); Brooks v. Lewin Realty III, Inc., 378 Md. 70, 835 A.2d 616 (2003) ("The trier of fact must then evaluate whether the actions taken by the defendant were reasonable under all the circumstances."); Restatement Third of Torts: Liability for Physical and Emotional Harm § 8(b) (2010).

[5]   Where the defendant's conduct involves risks the jury cannot evaluate, courts will not permit the jury to make an evaluation of the defendant's conduct unless expert or other testimony is introduced at trial to give the jury a basis for its conclusion. Thus medical malpractice claims often require expert testimony to permit a jury to conclude that the defendant's choice of medical procedures could be evaluated as unreasonable. E.g., Smith v. Andrews, 289 Conn. 61, 959 A.2d 597 (2008).

[6]   See Averyt v. Wal-Mart Stores, Inc., 265 P.3d 456 (Colo. 2011) (while judge has discretion to grant a new trial because of excessive or inadequate damages, "the amount of damages is within the sole province of the jury, and an award will not be disturbed unless it is completely unsupported by the record or if it is so excessive as to indicate that the jury acted out of passion, prejudice, or corruption").

[7]   For more detailed discussion of the trial judge's role, see § 13.1.

[8]   See Restatement Third of Torts: Liability for Physical and Emotional Harm § 8(b) (2010).

[9]   See Chapter 20.

the judge would direct a verdict. The effect is to eliminate any role for the jury in evaluating the defendant's conduct.

For some, civil juries embody democratic values and represent the community's ability to resist harsh rules handed down from above.[10] Supporters also think that civil juries also serve a separation of powers function within the judicial system, contribute to political stability through citizen-participation, and, because of their transitory nature, resist bribery and intimidation.[11] For others, juries are perceived as an almost lawless threat, bent on exercising their prejudices and inflicting undeserved losses upon unpopular defendants. Juries in individual cases can no doubt fit either view, but actual studies, as distinct from anecdotes about particular cases, show that juries take their duties seriously and perform their roles responsibly. For example, they usually get the same outcome that the judge would get, and in some cases actually favor defendants more than judges do.[12] The evidence is that jurors do not favor plaintiffs over corporate defendants.[13] They find for plaintiffs in personal injury tort cases in only just about half the cases on average,[14] and in medical malpractice cases in only around one-third or one-fourth of the cases.[15]

If the defendant is no more at risk when a jury decides the case than when the judge does so, the judge's decision to permit the jury to be the decision maker in a given case still has strategic impact. A judge's decision to reject a defendant's motion for summary judgment, for example, helps to make the plaintiff's claim a more credible threat and hence may increase pressure on the defendant to settle in a way favorable to the plaintiff. This effect may occur even before the judge makes an actual decision. Because litigators are like chess players, thinking at least several moves in advance, the defendants' lawyers will also be inclined to settle when they believe that the judge will leave the case to the jury at the end of the trial.

The Jury as Meliorator and Repository of Community Values

One view of juries sees them as an institution for meliorating the rigors of the law when it applies too harshly in particular cases. In this respect juries could be compared to the chancellor sitting in the old separate equity courts and using discretion rather than law to obtain fair results.[16] Like the chancellor, the jury decides a particular case;

---

[10]   Stephan Landsman, The Civil Jury in America: Scenes from an Unappreciated History, 44 Hastings L. J. 579 (1993), and others see political values in the jury as well as "equity."

[11]   Paul D. Carrington, The Civil Jury and American Democracy, 13 Duke J. Comp. & Int. L. 79 (2003).

[12]   Juries are by no means always better for plaintiffs than judges. See Kevin Clermont & Theodore Eisenberg, Trial by Jury or Judge: Transcending Empiricism, 77 Cornell L. Rev. 1124 (1992); Michael J. Saks, Public Opinion about the Civil Jury: Can Reality Be Found in the Illusions?, 48 DePaul L. Rev. 221 (1998); Leon Green, Judge and Jury 406 (1930). Another study shows that judges and juries make punitive damages awards at similar rates. Theodore Eisenberg, Neil LaFountain, Brian Ostrom, David Rottman & Martin T. Wells, Juries, Judges, and Punitive Damages: an Empirical Study, 87 Cornell L. Rev. 743 (2002).

[13]   Nor do jurors generally disfavor corporate defendants. See Valerie P. Hans, The Illusions and Realities of Jurors' Treatment of Corporate Defendants, 48 DePaul L. Rev. 327 (1998).

[14]   See Valerie P. Hans & Stephanie Albertson, Empirical Research and Civil Jury Reform, 78 Notre Dame L. Rev. 1497 (2003) (reflecting a 52% win rate in 75 large counties in one year and a 49% win rate four years later).

[15]   See Shari Seidman Diamond, Beyond Fantasy and Nightmare: a Portrait of the Jury, 54 Buffalo L. Rev. 717, 730 (2006). A well-known study in Ohio showed medical malpractice claimants losing over two-thirds of the claims taken to court. Deborah Jones Merritt & Kathryn Ann Barry, Is the Tort System in Crisis? New Empirical Evidence, 60 Ohio St. L.J. 315 (1999).

[16]   1 Dan B. Dobbs, Law of Remedies § 2.4 (7) (1993).

it does not make law.[17] Perhaps this gives juries the freedom to act in accord with the community conscience when a judge, who is bound to make a record of the legal rulings and who acts in the sight of lawyers and appellate judges, may feel more constrained.

At any rate, the view of the jury as meliorator of harshness or dispenser of equity is related to the idea that the jury represents the community and its values. And if the jury is drawn from all members of society at random, it will in some sense represent the community. In many tort cases, community values form the basis for moral judgment about the parties' fault and justifications. In those cases, a significant role for the jury may be especially desirable.[18]

On the other hand, one might believe that one's *rights* should not be subject to a judge's or jury's discretionary veto. If the plaintiff has a right not to be discriminated against on the job or subjected to sexual harassment, a judge or jury should not undermine that right by a discretionary refusal to enforce it. When the law seeks to uphold a right that does not fully conform to community feelings, courts are likely to reduce the jury's role for the very reason that it *does* represent working values in the community. In libel cases, for example, courts fear that the jury may lose sight of the value of free speech when faced with derogatory statements about the plaintiff. Accordingly, legal rules constrain liability and give the judges more power in certain libel cases.[19]

Because juries (like judges) both protect community values and undermine them, judges in tort cases play out a considerable ambivalence, sometimes relying heavily on the jury, sometimes manipulating rules and judgments to sideline it. Many of the tort rules and practices seen in this book can be understood as taking one side or another about the jury's appropriate role.

B. FUNDAMENTAL OPERATING CONCEPTIONS

§ 3.3   The Prima Facie Case and the Burden of Proof

Tort law operates with a number of fundamental conceptions in deciding rights of the parties to a dispute. Most of these, such as the concept of negligence, are developed in the substantive chapters of this book; they help define the relevant tort. This section and the next focus instead on conceptions about the gross structure of the tort case, particularly on the non-technical ways courts think about the elements of tort claims and about defenses.

"Elements." The plaintiff cannot prevail in any tort claim without providing evidence of facts that show certain specific elements or features of the claim. The elements differ according to the tort claimed. For instance, the plaintiff who sues for false imprisonment must prove that the defendant confined her; that is one of the elements of that particular claim. The plaintiff who sues for battery need not prove confinement at all, but must prove that the defendant wrongfully touched her. Sometimes the elements to be proved are generalized very broadly; nevertheless, when

---

[17] The chancellor's theory was that he only acted to compel the particular defendant to act in accordance with conscience; he did not make law.

[18] Michael Wells, Scientific Policymaking and the Torts Revolution: The Revenge of the Ordinary Observer, 26 Ga. L. Rev. 725 (1992); Patrick Kelley, Who Decides? Community Safety Conventions at the Heart of Tort Liability, 38 Clev. St. L. Rev. 315 (1990); Catharine Wells, Tort Law as Corrective Justice: A Pragmatic Justification for Jury Adjudication, 88 Mich. L. Rev. 2348 (1990).

[19] See §§ 37.15 to 37.17.

the plaintiff knows all the elements she must prove to avoid losing, she has at least a general idea, maybe a specific one, about the kind of evidence she needs.

The prima facie case. When the plaintiff provides testimony about facts that show all the elements necessary for the tort she claims, she has made a prima facie case. This is an important concept. What this means is best understood by noticing that we cannot say the plaintiff *wins* when she offers testimony on all the elements of the claim. First, the jury might disbelieve her evidence on some essential element. Second, the defendant may have a valid defense. When the plaintiff has made out a prima facie case she qualifies as a starter in the race, and her case goes to the jury.

The burden of proof. "Prima facie" case implies a second important rule. It implies that the plaintiff has the burden of producing evidence and persuading the trier on each of the elements of her case. The term "burden of proof" is itself a troublesome one. Agonizing details can be left for later,[20] but the burden of proof rules are too important in tort litigation to ignore even in a brief introduction to tort law. The term burden of proof means at least two things. First, if nothing is proven on a point, the point must be decided against the party with the burden of proof. If the plaintiff must prove confinement to prove a false imprisonment, but fails to do so, the plaintiff has not met her burden of proving the elements of the claim and she will lose. Second, even if the plaintiff has presented testimony, but the jury is not sure it is convinced by it, the burden of proof rules tell the jury what to do. A juror whose mind is evenly balanced on the issue, not sure that the testimony is true or untrue, must vote against the plaintiff because she has the burden of convincing jurors by the weight of the evidence.[21]

Preponderance of the evidence or probability. The doubtful juror problem is related to the idea that the plaintiff's burden is not merely to offer testimony, but to persuade the jury by a preponderance of the evidence.[22] Preponderance means only "greater weight" of the evidence.[23] Contemporary thinking usually expresses the rule in terms of probabilities. The plaintiff need not prove that each fact necessary for her prima facie case is certainly true or true beyond a doubt. Instead, she must prove that each material fact is more probable or more likely than not.[24]

Plaintiff or defendant as the source of evidence. To say a party has the burden of proof on a given point is *not* to say that the evidence must originate with that party. It is rather a way of describing who will suffer if sufficient evidence does not appear. Suppose the plaintiff in a medical malpractice case has the burden of proving that the defendant physician was negligent, but that the only evidence of his negligence came when the defendant himself admitted under oath that he failed to follow the medical standard of care. Even though the plaintiff herself did not produce that piece of testimony, it is still evidence and will satisfy the plaintiff's burden of proof. When we say that the plaintiff has the burden of proof, then, we mean that if the evidence on an

---

[20] See §§ 13.2 & 13.4.

[21] See, e.g., 1 Ohio Jury Instructions 3.50 (2006) ("If the weight of the evidence is equally balanced, or if you are unable to determine which side of an issue has the preponderance, the party who has the burden of proof has not established such issue by a preponderance of the evidence.").

[22] There are some very limited qualifications to this rule. See § 14.11 (causation); § 37.18 (defamation) & § 43.4 (fraud).

[23] See Rose v. Jaques, 268 Va. 137, 597 S.E.2d 64 (2004).

[24] See Hanks v. Entergy Corp., 944 So.2d 564, 578 (La. 2006). Expressed statistically, this means that the plaintiff must persuade the trier that the likelihood exceeds 50% that each material fact is true.

element (and accompanying persuasion) is absent, the plaintiff will not get her case to the jury at all; the judge will ultimately dismiss it.

Significance of burden of proof rules. Burden of proof rules are enormously important in deciding tort cases and in preparing them as well. They tell lawyers which side has the burden of finding and producing evidence on the elements of the claims and defenses, and what will happen if the burden is not met—that the claim will be lost or the defense will fail. Burden of proof rules then go on to decide many cases. If the plaintiff proves that there is a mere chance that the defendant was negligent, the proof standard will require dismissal of the claim because the plaintiff must prove the claim by a more-likely-than-not standard. There is secondary fallout, too. Courts will rarely direct a verdict *in favor* of the party with the burden of proof, because the jury is ordinarily free to weigh the evidence and to conclude that the evidence does not really show a necessary fact by the more-likely-than-not standard.[25] And a judgment for one party may be reversed simply because the trial judge failed to clearly instruct on the burden of proof.[26]

§ 3.4 Affirmative Defenses

Burden of proof. Although the plaintiff has the burden of proving the elements of her prima facie case by the greater weight of the evidence, it is the defendant who must carry the burden of proof on affirmative defenses. Facts showing affirmative defenses, if believed by the trier of fact, will exculpate the defendant or at least reduce the damages he must pay. The plaintiff's own fault in causing harm is a common affirmative defense in a negligence case.[27] The important point is that the burden is on the defendant when it comes to affirmative defenses. If the defendant asserts self-defense, but proves nothing about it, the jury cannot properly relieve the defendant of liability. Likewise, if the defendant offers testimony to show that the plaintiff was at fault, but the juror's mind is evenly balanced whether the testimony is true or not, the jury must reject the defense.

Nature of affirmative defenses. Affirmative defenses can logically admit that the plaintiff has presented a prima facie case, yet offer a new and independent reason to deny or limit the plaintiff's recovery of damages. For instance, the plaintiff may prove that the defendant intentionally struck her and that she suffered a broken nose as a result, but the defendant may still prevail on the affirmative defense that the statute of limitations has run, even though the plaintiff made out a prima facie case. On this as on all affirmative defenses the defendant will have the burden of proof.

Confusion in colloquial use of "defense." Sometimes lawyers and even appellate judges speak inaccurately of "defenses" when they mean something quite different. Take the plaintiff's claim that the defendant struck her and caused her broken nose. Suppose that instead of pleading the statute of limitations (an affirmative defense), the defendant responds by pleading that (1) he did not in fact strike the plaintiff and (2) the plaintiff's nose was broken before she ever walked into the bar. In a colloquial sense, you could say that the defendant's response asserted two "defenses." However, legally speaking, such

---

[25] Burton v. R.J. Reynolds Tobacco Co., 397 F.3d 906 (10th Cir. 2005); Christenson v. Bergeson, 688 N.W.2d 421 (S.D.2004).

[26] See Barber v. LaFromboise, 908 A.2d 436 (Vt. 2006) ("Few issues in a lawsuit of any nature are more essential than burden of proof.").

[27] E.g., Barber v. LaFromboise, 908 A.2d 436 (Vt. 2006). The affirmative defense may be complete, barring the plaintiff's claim entirely, or it may be partial, reducing the damages that the plaintiff may otherwise recover. Some states still make the plaintiff's fault a complete defense, while others use the plaintiff's fault merely to reduce damages. See Chapter 19.

a description is not only literally inaccurate; it is also likely to lead to legal mistakes or ambiguity.

What the defendant is asserting in those two responses is not something independent of the elements the plaintiff must prove. Nor does the defendant have the burden of proving that he did not strike the plaintiff or cause her harm. He is in fact asserting that the plaintiff has failed to carry her own burden of proof. It is true that the defendant might present facts showing he did not strike the plaintiff, but those facts would tend to negate the plaintiff's prima facie case, rather than establishing some independent ground for denying the plaintiff's claim. Perhaps more importantly, the burden rests with the plaintiff on these issues, not with the defendant.

These difficult ideas can be put differently. Affirmative defenses are relevant only if the plaintiff has made a prima facie case by providing testimony to show all the required elements and if the jury believes that testimony. If the plaintiff has not offered evidence of some element in her case, the trial judge will direct a verdict against her. If she offered evidence but the jury does not believe it, the jury will find against her for failing to sustain her burden. Only if the jury believes the plaintiff's evidence does the question of a defense logically enter into the picture. So rejection of the defendant's defense does not necessarily mean the plaintiff will prevail; the jury might also reject the plaintiff's testimony or conclude that the plaintiff has failed to sustain her burden of proof. If so, there is no tort to begin with and the defendant will prevail for that reason, even if his affirmative defense is invalid.[28]

§ 3.5   Privilege, Justification, Excuse and Immunity

Privileges defeat claims. One kind of affirmative defense is often called a privilege. Although the initial evidence from the plaintiff may show that the defendant has acted tortiously—say, by striking the plaintiff with intent to harm him—nevertheless the defendant may have been justified in doing so if he acted in self-defense. If so, the privilege defeats the plaintiff's claim. Privileges are limited by the justification that gives rise to them. You can defend yourself, but you can't take the occasion to beat the attacker to a pulp.[29] Some privileges, like self-defense, are well-established, but courts may recognize new privileges whenever they believe the defendant's conduct was justified.[30]

Justification and excuse. The concept of justification is that people in general can rightly act as the defendant did in the circumstances. Justifications tend to invoke objective standards of reasonableness to modify the flat rules of intentional and some other nominate torts like libel. *Excuses* differ from justifications. They do not assert that the defendant's act was rightful and that others should act in the same way. They rather assert that the defendant's conduct was understandable given his personal condition and that he is not personally blameworthy for matters not within his control. Excuses focus on subjective mental or psychological characteristics of the actor; they include mental disability, mistake, and infancy (meaning status as a minor).

---

[28]   See the discussion of no-tort below, § 3.5.

[29]   See §§ 7.1 & 7.4.

[30]   See, e.g., Peterson v. Sorlien, 299 N.W.2d 123, 11 A.L.R.4th 208 (1980).

Excuses generally do not defeat tort liability. In general, however, excuses do not furnish defenses to intentional tort claims,[31] but justifications do. As a trespasser on another's land, you are a tortfeasor, even if you mistakenly believed the land was your own.[32] A minor or mentally disabled person may remain liable for tortious conduct.[33] These excuse rules reinforce the idea that the tort systems tends to work with objective, not subjective, standards of liability. However, sometimes tort liability depends upon intent to cause a particular harm. In those cases, the defendant's mistake or mental disability might not show a defense, but might show instead that the defendant lacked any tortious intent in the first place, so that he would not be a tortfeasor at all.[34]

Defeating liability on other grounds. The plaintiff who makes out a prima facie case may be defeated on grounds quite distinct from the justification invoked when a privilege is pleaded. For example, the statute of limitations is a defense, but not a justification. An *immunity* may also permit the defendant to escape liability for tortious conduct. Immunity represents a broad policy that allows the defendant to escape responsibility for wrongs, not, like privilege, a claim that the defendant acted rightfully in the particular circumstances. The immunity of government that allows governmental entities to escape liability in many instances is an example.[35]

The "privilege" way of thinking. Privilege analysis may be invoked when the elements of the tort have been firmly defined by specifying forbidden actions. In such torts, the plaintiff can sometimes make out a prima facie case for liability without proving that the defendant's acts were unreasonable. By invoking a privilege, the defendant injects issues of his reasonableness into the case. Showing that he struck the plaintiff in justified self-defense is one example. If he convinces the trier that he acted on a reasonable belief that self-defense was necessary, and that he used a reasonable amount of force, then he will escape liability.[36]

The "no-tort" way of thinking. Some torts are structured in such a way as to make the reasonableness of the defendant's conduct an issue on the prima facie case. This means that the plaintiff must prove unreasonable conduct to begin with, instead of putting the burden on the defendant to raise a privilege and to assert that his conduct was reasonable. The tort generally called negligence is like this. The plaintiff must prove, among other things, that the defendant took unreasonable risks which caused the plaintiff harm. Since the plaintiff has the burden of proving unreasonable conduct to begin with, the defendant need not raise a privilege asserting that his conduct was reasonable. Instead, he simply points to the plaintiff's burden of proof and says that the plaintiff has not proved unreasonableness. This is the no-tort argument, and it grows out of the fact that in such cases the plaintiff has the burden of proof. The defendant in making the no-tort argument is not asserting an affirmative defense; he is saying the

---

[31] Personal disabilities are important in tort law, but not always because they are defenses. For instance, the plaintiff's infancy or mental disability or ignorance-mistake is very likely to "excuse" delay in bringing suit.

[32] Restatement Second of Torts § 164 (1965); See § 5.2.

[33] See § 4.3. Very young children may be exempted, however. See §§ 10.14 to 10.16.

[34] White v. Muniz, 999 P.2d 814 (Colo. 2000) (one whose mental condition prevents forming an intent to harm or offend by physical touching has not committed battery); Adams v. National Bank of Detroit, 444 Mich. 329, 508 N.W.2d 464 (1993) (a defendant who honestly but mistakenly identifies the plaintiff as the person who committed a crime is not liable for intentional infliction of mental distress; to say that the defendant was honestly mistaken is to say that the defendant lacked the requisite intent to inflict distress).

[35] See Chapter 22.

[36] See §§ 7.1 to 7.4.

plaintiff has not met her burden of proving her claim. This no-tort argument can also apply to some other issues. For example, as already pointed out, the defendant's mental disability is not itself a defense. Even so, a mentally disabled defendant may lack the kind of intent necessary to show a particular kind of tort. The defendant's lawyer in such a case cannot assert that mental disability is a defense, but he can assert that the mental disability negated the intent necessary to show a tort in the first place. This is the no-tort argument as well, in effect saying that the intent element of the plaintiff's prima facie case does not exist.

C. THE BACKGROUND CONDITIONS OF TORT LAW

§ 3.6   Remedies and Attorney's Fees

Three interrelated rules of remedies and attorney compensation fundamentally affect the way tort law is practiced and, indirectly, the operation of tort rules. Tort law cannot be assessed or well understood without grasping these background rules.

The American rule on attorney's fees. The "American rule" about attorney's fees is that the losing party is not required to pay the winning party's fees. Regardless of who wins the case, each party pays its own attorney's fees. There are exceptions,[37] but in the overwhelming number of common law tort cases, this is the rule. One result of this rule is that the plaintiff who prevails in the litigation may not be fully compensated after she deducts the costs of attorney's fees and other litigation expense.

Contingent percentage fees. Second, plaintiffs' lawyers accept most tort cases on a contingent, percentage fee. If the plaintiff does not recover, the attorney is not paid at all. If the plaintiff does recover, the attorney's fee is a percentage of the recovery. The percentage is fixed or limited in some kinds of cases in some states. It may vary from a low of around 25% to a high of about 50%; most are probably between these figures. This practice, combined with the American rule, means that a plaintiff who fully recovers from the defendant may still be uncompensated for anywhere from one-fourth to one-half of her loss. It should not be assumed that a high-percentage fee overcompensates lawyers. Since they are not paid at all when a client does not recover, the percentage fee must pay for the time spent in losing cases as well as in winning them. Defendants' lawyers usually charge an hourly rate. They usually represent liability insurers or businesses that are self-insured.

Non-objective awards. Third, in personal injury tort cases, pain and suffering can be enormous and can extend over years. The verdicts for pain and suffering damage are often quite substantial, even when they are modest in comparison to the injury suffered. Punitive damages awards, when they are made at all, can also be very large. These two kinds of damages have something in common: they cannot be measured by any presently used objective criterion. Consequently, the jury's award may be quite difficult to challenge on appeal. In the case of some intangible harms, such as reputation harm in libel cases, traditional rules permit juries to make a similar award, that is, one that is not limited by pecuniary loss or measurable in any objective way.[38] Although experienced

---

[37] The largest number of cases in which a losing party must pay a prevailing party's reasonable attorney's fees are based on a specific statute authorizing a fee recovery. Federal civil rights cases are a major example. See 1 Dan B. Dobbs, Law of Remedies § 3.10 (2d ed. 1993). A less common exception is that a particular tort like malicious prosecution may be aimed at recovery of attorney's fees. See § 39.1.

[38] See § 37.3. Constitutional and other changes impact this traditional rule but do not entirely eliminate it.

lawyers can often estimate the potential range of jury awards with great accuracy, uncertainty creates a threat that is difficult for defendants to deal with. Two arbitrary methods have been introduced in recent years to limit the uncertainty. Some states have passed damages caps, limiting pain and suffering damages or even damages for needed medical attention resulting from the defendant's tort.[39] And the Supreme Court of the United States has mandated several procedures designed to limit punitive damages, coupled with a strong suggestion that an arbitrary limit on those damages will ordinarily be constitutionally compelled.[40]

One characteristic of non-objective awards has already been noted—that the risk of such awards can create substantial threats to defendants,[41] because if defendants' lawyers believe the facts warrant an award of $500,000, they know that in the absence of objective criteria, jurors might possibly award $1 million instead. This risk in turn incentivizes the defendant to pay more in in settlement than the estimated value of $500,000. A different characteristic is equally important. Non-objective awards, such as damages for pain, provide a fund from which the prevailing plaintiff can pay her attorney's fees and still get her actual out-of-pocket losses paid by the tort recovery.

In the light of these rules and practices, it is easy to understand why plaintiffs' lawyers find it important to assert non-objective damages claims. Besides whatever pressure such claims exert upon defendants and their lawyers, they also increase the chance that the plaintiff will receive full compensation for her actual economic losses. There may be other justifications and needs for such non-objective claims, but these reasons show why they are almost imperative. If the "American rule" on attorney's fees is eventually displaced by a loser-pay rule, non-objective damages will find much less obvious justification.[42]

§ 3.7   Sources of Tort Law

The common law of torts is almost exclusively state law. The federal government is circumscribed, having only those powers specifically provided for by the federal Constitution. States, on the other hand, enjoy plenary power except as limited by the Constitution. These understandings leave the federal courts with almost no admitted common law work to do. Instead, they interpret and enforce federal statutes and the federal Constitution.

Federal statutes. Federal statutes have not adopted any general tort law, and if they attempted to do so they would be constitutionally questioned. Federal statutes create or deeply affect tort law only when they are related to some field constitutionally placed in the hands of the federal government, rather than the states. For example, the Congress has created statutory tort law for the protection of constitutional and other federal rights.[43] Federal statutes also grant—and limit—tort claims against the federal government itself.[44] These statutes are peculiar because they contain federally imposed

---

[39] See § 34.7.

[40] See § 34.6.

[41] See § 3.1.

[42] See Joseph H. King, Jr., Pain and Suffering, Noneconomic Damages, and the Goals of Tort Law, 57 S.M.U. L. Rev. 163, 207–208 (2004).

[43] One statute of very general application is 42 U.S.C.A. § 1983, creating a tort claim for violation of federal rights. Other statutes go further, adding new rules or procedures to implement federal constitutional rights. See, e.g., 42 U.S.C.A. § 2000e ("Title VII").

[44] The Federal Tort Claims Act (FTCA), principally found in 28 U.S.C.A §§ 2671 to 2680.

limits on the tort liability of the federal government, yet otherwise rely upon state law to prescribe the tort rules.[45]

Another field for Congressional action is interstate commerce. Congress can regulate matters affecting commerce and on this ground has enacted tort statutes creating claims for interstate railroad and maritime workers.[46] These statutes are favorable to the workers' claims, providing more expansive rights than would be granted under state law, which of course is displaced by the federal statutes.

Federal environmental statutes supplement the common law tort of nuisance and the common law of strict liability for abnormal danger, sometimes creating surprising liabilities in connection with the release of hazardous substances.[47] The federal trademark statute creates rights in trademarks and in practice it has largely displaced the common law of trademark.[48] Under other constitutional provisions, Congress has enacted patent[49] and copyright[50] statutes. These in effect define certain intellectual property interests and set up tort claims for their infringement. A number of federal statutes create claims in particular settings, for example, claims for misrepresentation in the sale of securities[51] and claims for certain kinds of acts that state tort law would classify as privacy invasions.[52]

Preemption. Sometimes Congress does not actually create a claim in tort but does set a standard of some kind. Congress and its regulatory agencies set safety standards for automobile manufacturers, for example, by requiring seat-belts or airbags. If a manufacturer complies with federal standards, but the product is nevertheless unsafe and causes harm, can state tort law hold the manufacturer liable? The question peels open a new layer of tort issues that in turn opens into the federal system itself.

Since the federal system is supreme (within its constitutional powers), Congress could provide for preemption or displacement of state tort law as it has done with the copyright statute. Even if it does not do so explicitly, its legislation might still imply such a preemption. Or preemption might be thought necessary to carry out the federal scheme of things. On one or more such grounds, courts have found that various federal statutes displaced or preempted state tort law.[53] For instance, a tobacco manufacturer who complies with the warning prescribed by federal statute cannot be held liable under state tort law for failure to give a better warning.[54] The effect is to make the federal standard the only standard and to relieve the defendant who has complied with that standard,

---

[45]   See § 22.2.

[46]   See 45 U.S.C.A. § 51 (FELA, interstate railroad workers); 46 App. U.S.C.A. § 688 (Jones Act, maritime workers).

[47]   See, e.g., 42 U.S.C.A. §§ 9607 et seq. (CERCLA, creating liability for contamination of lands).

[48]   15 U.S.C.A. §§ 1051 et seq. See Chapter 46.

[49]   35 U.S.C.A. §§ 101 et seq.

[50]   17 U.S.C.A. § 101.

[51]   E.g., 15 U.S.C.A. §§ 77k & 77l; 15 U.S.C.A. § 78j (securities); 15 U.S.C.A. §§ 1701 et seq. (interstate land sales); 15 U.S.C.A. §§ 1601 et seq. (certain disclosures to consumers).

[52]   29 U.S.C.A. §§ 2001 et seq. (lie detector tests by employers forbidden, tort claim created); 18 U.S.C.A. §§ 2510 to 2520 (wiretapping, claim created).

[53]   CSX Transportation, Inc. v. Easterwood, 507 U.S. 658, 113 S.Ct. 1732, 123 L.Ed.2d 367 (1993) (federal speed limits for trains, preemption); see §§ 12.10 & 33.20.

[54]   Cipollone v. Liggett Group, Inc., 112 S.Ct. 2608, 120 L.Ed.2d 407 (1992) (but leaving certain other claims available); see § 33.20.

even if, by state law, that defendant was guilty of negligence or other tortious conduct. This is the opposite effect of federal legislation creating a claim for railroad workers.

Constitutional defenses or limits on state tort law. Because federal law, within its sphere, is supreme, states may not impose tort liability in a way that violates the United States Constitution. The Supreme Court seldom strikes down an ordinary state-law tort claim on constitutional grounds, but it is possible. Suits for libel, quintessentially state-law tort claims, are now limited in several ways by the Constitution's free speech provisions, so that, for example, state law may not impose strict liability for derogatory speech published by defendants in discussing issues of public concern.[55]

Federal claims in state courts. In some instances, federal legislation not only preempts state-law claims but also gives federal courts exclusive jurisdiction to hear the claims. For example, patent and copyright claims must be tried in federal courts, not state courts. In other instances, however, federal claims can be tried in either state or federal courts, as the plaintiff wishes. One example is the general federal civil rights claim.[56] When federal claims are enforced in state courts, the states are of course compelled to follow the federal law for those claims, although they may follow their own trial procedures.

State claims in federal court. In a few cases state-law tort claims may be tried in federal courts. Sometimes this is because the state-law claim is so closely related to a purely federal claim that the two should be tried together. At other times this is because Congress has permitted federal jurisdiction over certain claims when the parties are of diverse citizenship, the plaintiff a citizen of one state and the defendant a citizen of another.[57] When state-law tort claims are tried in federal courts, they are still state-law claims and federal courts must apply the state law rules for those claims, even though they follow their own federal procedural rules.[58]

Scope of federal supremacy. Federal law is supreme and must prevail when it conflicts with state law. However, in many instances a federal rule applies only to a federal claim or a federal statute; it has no application at all to a state-law claim. In such cases, even if the federal and state rules are different, they are not in conflict because they do not deal with the same thing. For instance, federal decisions determine the incidents of a tort claim under a federal tort statute like the Federal Employers Liability Act, and state courts trying such cases must follow federal decisions as well as the federal statute. But the federal rules apply only to the tort claims created under that statute, not to similar tort claims brought under state law.

Similarly, a federal rule may set a minimum standard, but may at the same time permit states to set a higher one. The Supreme Court, to protect free speech rights, requires that in most libel actions, the plaintiff must prove at least some degree of fault on the defendant's part to justify a recovery.[59] But states may provide even more protection for free speech by requiring a high degree of fault as a prerequisite to

---

[55] Critics of public officials and public figures can be held liable only for knowing or reckless falsehoods, while critics of private persons on matters of public concern can be held liable for any fault. See § 37.15.

[56] 42 U.S.C.A § 1983.

[57] 28 U.S.C.A § 1332.

[58] The point was established in Erie Railroad v. Tompkins, 304 U.S. 64, 58 S.Ct. 817, 82 L.Ed. 1188 (1938). A long line of federal decisions has explained the details and applied the rule.

[59] Gertz v. Robert Welch, Inc., 418 U.S. 323, 94 S.Ct. 2997, 41 L.Ed.2d 789 (1974). See § 37.13.

liability.[60] In the same way, the fact that a state law does not violate the federal constitution does not mean that it meets the demands of the state's own constitution, and the state courts are of course free to strike down their own rules on state law grounds, even if those rules have been upheld as valid under the United States Constitution.[61]

The relationship of state law to federal law and to the law of other states is the topic of treatises on federal jurisdiction[62] and conflicts of law.[63] The points sketched in this section show that tort law today operates in a complex environment. Lawyers are required not only to take into account the interaction of statutes and common law decisions, but the interaction of state and federal law as well.

§ 3.8　　Liability Insurance

No one can understand tort law in the United States without recognizing that liability insurance fuels the system, limits its capacity for compensation and deterrence, shapes the litigation, and affects the costs and choices in the system as a whole.

Insurer's obligations. Liability insurance protects the insured against tort liability by paying the insured's tort victims. Liability insurance is not health or accident insurance; it pays only when the insured is legally liable to pay because of his tort. Once a claim covered by the policy is asserted against the insured, the liability insurer is obliged to defend the claim and to pay any judgment rendered against the insured, subject to the limits of the policy.

The insurer's/insured's attorney. The insurer has the right and sometimes the duty to settle with the claimant as a way of protecting the insured. As part of the insurer's obligation to defend the insured, it provides an attorney who must, at least in some major degree, represent the individual insured. Although in most states the insurer is not a party to the lawsuit, it stands responsible for almost everything that happens on the defense side of the case.

Social function of insurance and individual veto. Liability insurance fuels a large number of tort cases, especially automobile cases. It does so because many individuals who cause harm do not have sufficient assets to pay for the harm they do and because the chief assets, such as one's home, may be protected by law. In fact, Professor Gilles has demonstrated that the barriers to actual collection of judgments against tortfeasors, including bankruptcy, virtually nullify tort law when the tortfeasor is uninsured.[64] The existence of insurance and its amount become central practical issues for the tort lawyers on both sides. If the insured defendant does not have a sufficient amount of insurance, the plaintiff can be only partly compensated. States now make some effort to require liability insurance to cover automobile drivers, but the amounts of insurance required

---

[60]　E.g., Chang v. Michiana Telecasting Corp., 900 F.2d 1085 (7th Cir. 1990).

[61]　For instance, guest statutes limiting the tort claims that could be brought by automobile passengers have sometimes been stricken as unconstitutional under state law, as in Brown v. Merlo, 8 Cal.3d 855, 106 Cal.Rptr. 388, 506 P.2d 212 (1973), even though guest statutes had been held valid under the federal constitution. Silver v. Silver, 280 U.S. 117, 50 S.Ct. 57, 74 L.Ed. 221 (1929).

[62]　Charles Alan Wright & Arthur R. Miller, Mary Kay Kane, Edward H. Cooper, Kenneth W. Graham, Jr., Victor J. Gold, & Michael H. Graham, Federal Practice & Procedure (available on Westlaw).

[63]　Eugene F. Scoles, Peter Hay, Patrick J. Borchers & Symeon Symeonides (4th ed. 2004); Robert Leflar, Luther McDougal & Robert Felix, American Conflicts Law (4th ed. 1986); Russell Weintraub, Commentary on the Conflict of Laws (5th ed. 2006).

[64]　Stephen G. Gilles, The Judgment-Proof Society, 63 Wash. & Lee L. Rev. 603 (2006).

are quite limited in comparison to the amount of harm that may be inflicted, and drivers may routinely evade insurance requirements.[65] Outside the field of motor vehicles, the decision to purchase insurance, and the decision about its limits, is often up to the individual policyholder, leaving large areas in which violent actors are virtually immune from tort law simply because they are uninsured.[66]

The individual veto on insurance and the lack of compulsory coverage in significant amounts frustrates the tort goals of compensation, deterrence and accountability. On the other hand, it may be argued that the *presence* of insurance, not its absence, undermines deterrence and accountability, since a fully insured individual is protected from any personal payout, at least for harms not caused by intentional acts.[67] However, in many instances, insured drivers may be more aware of and responsive to the potential increase in insurance premiums than they are to relatively remote and uncertain tort liability, although premium adjustments in the case of injury caused by the insured do not fully correlate with the insured's risk-taking conduct.[68] At the very least, insurance costs serve as a periodic reminder that unsafe conduct can have serious consequences.

With some torts, insurance costs may have a dramatic effect on the care exercised. That may be the case with professional malpractice. And if tort law is less a matter of deterrence and more a matter of reinforcing values that the community and the defendant already accept, insurance probably does not undermine tort law's effects. These and other reasons suggest that tort law may retain a residual effect on conduct even in a system dominated by liability insurance. But anyone can justifiably entertain the suspicion that the more insurance serves the goal of compensation, the less it will serve the goal of deterrence.

Insurance affecting decisions on liability? It is probably fair to say that tort law expanded the rights of injured persons during much of the 20th century at various rates of expansion until around 1980. The expansion of accountability for fault occurred in part by changing tort rules to make liability possible in areas where defendants had been previously protected from liability.[69] The expansion, at least in motor vehicle cases, was probably also due in part to the perception of courts and juries that an insurer, not the individual defendant, would pay the judgment in the case.

Ironically, expanded liability tends to drive up insurance costs, which in turn may lead some people to reduce or eliminate their insurance, thus reducing the funds

---

[65] See Gary T. Schwartz, Auto No-Fault and First-Party Insurance: Advantages and Problems, 73 S. Cal. L. Rev. 611, 624 (2000).

[66] See Jennifer Wriggins, Domestic Violence Torts 75 S. Cal. L. Rev. 121 (2001).

[67] See Admiral Ins. Co. v. Price-Williams, 129 So.3d 991 (Ala. 2013); see also Gary T. Schwartz, Reality in the Economic Analysis of Tort Law: Does Tort Law Really Deter?, 42 U.C.L.A. L. Rev. 377, 382 (1994).

[68] See Stephen D. Sugarman, Doing Away with Personal Injury Law 13–14 (1989). And in some areas, as in medical malpractice cases, insurance is not "risk-rated," so the dangerous actor does not risk paying higher premiums. David A. Hyman, Medical Malpractice and the Tort System: What Do We Know and What (If Anything) Should We Do About It?, 80 Tex. L. Rev. 1639 (2002).

[69] In terms of doctrine, which is readily identifiable if not fully reliable, consider these examples: (1) Specific protections for landowners have been restricted in a number of states; (2) immunities of the federal government, state government, and local governments were substantially reduced, mostly in the second half of the 20th century, although thereafter large amounts of immunity were restored by legislation; (3) family immunities have been substantially reduced or abolished; (4) civil rights torts, which hardly existed before about 1960, have become a major field; (5) environmental torts, in the modern sense largely statutory, are even more recent; (6) contributory negligence and assumed risk defenses, which once barred negligence claims, are now considered only in determining the plaintiff's damages, again a liberalization that has occurred almost entirely after 1960. The full list is much longer.

available to make compensation. Alternatively, increased insurance costs have led some groups to seek exemption from tort liability or at least a limitation on the amount of damages they must pay. As this pressure increases, some courts seem inclined to restrict liability in order to protect those funds from excessive demands, resulting in less overall compensation for injury.

Insurance affects more aspects of tort law than can be readily summarized. What has been said, however, should be enough to indicate that tort law does not operate in a sterile laboratory. Its hope for compensation and its hopes for deterrence, for corrective justice and for social utility, are all among the aspects of tort law affected by the presence of liability insurance.

Part II

INTENTIONAL TORTS TO PERSONS OR PROPERTY

Chapter 4

DIRECT AND INTENTIONAL INTERFERENCE WITH THE PERSON

Analysis

A. SCOPE OF THE CHAPTER

§ 4.1   Scope of the Chapter

B. INTENT AND RELATED CONCEPTS

§ 4.2   The Meaning of Intent
§ 4.3   Intent and Motive
§ 4.4   Intent and Negligence
§ 4.5   Intent and Reckless or Wanton Misconduct

C. BATTERY

§ 4.6   Simple Battery
§ 4.7   Harm or Offense Required to Establish Simple Battery
§ 4.8   Nature of Intent Required to Establish Simple Battery
§ 4.9   The Bodily Contact Required to Establish Simple Battery
§ 4.10   Battery and Other Torts: Acts and Omissions

D. ASSAULT

§ 4.11   Simple Assault
§ 4.12   Anticipation of Imminent Touching
§ 4.13   Assault, Crime, and Other Torts

E. FALSE IMPRISONMENT

§ 4.14   Simple False Imprisonment
§ 4.15   Methods of Confinement
§ 4.16   Duty to Release from Confinement
§ 4.17   False Imprisonment and Other Torts

F. EXTENDED LIABILITY AND DAMAGES

§ 4.18   Extended Liability or Transferred Intent
§ 4.19   Extended Liability: The Pros and Cons
§ 4.20   Damages for Trespassory Torts to the Person
§ 4.21   Infliction of Emotional Distress

A. SCOPE OF THE CHAPTER

§ 4.1   Scope of the Chapter

Trespassory torts. This chapter addresses the elements of one group of intentional torts to individual persons, part of a group anciently called "trespassory" torts. Similar torts to property are covered in the next chapter and defenses to these torts in the chapter after that. Trespassory torts are accomplished through the use of physical force,

53

rather than, say, the use of words. Torts like libel and misrepresentation are not trespassory torts, for they are not accomplished by force, and they are accordingly covered much later. Liability for trespassory torts to the person is based upon the defendant's intent to commit some particular act, not upon some generalized assessment of the defendant's behavior. The acts that count as torts in this chapter impact the plaintiff's need for physical security. They also impair the plaintiff's freedom rights, that is, the plaintiff's rights of autonomy and self-determination.

Absence of physical harm requirement. All of these torts are actionable even if the plaintiff has no proven physical harm. Perhaps courts assume that the plaintiff suing for a trespassory tort has some kind of emotional harm, but if so, the plaintiff is not required to prove it. Put differently, these trespassory torts are regarded as harmful in themselves, and in this respect they differ fundamentally from claims for negligence, which always require proof of actual harm.

Other consequences of the categorization as an intentional tort. Intentional torts "are categorically distinct from other torts such as negligence or strict liability."[1] The intentional tort finding has a number of significant legal consequences. Fault of the plaintiff may not be available as a defense. In addition, the defendant may face a broader scope of liability for actions that count as an intentional tort. Categorization as an intentional tort may also matter to some consequences external to tort law itself. For instance, insurance may exclude coverage for some intentional torts. Moreover, workers' compensation exclusive-remedy provisions may not apply to intentional torts. The Restatement Third of Intentional Torts makes clear, however, that intent need not be defined identically in these varied tort and collateral contexts.[2]

Overlapping actions. The trespassory torts are a cluster of specific, though related, causes of action. A given set of conduct may be actionable under several of these causes of action. For example, an employer's "private waterboarding" of an employee may give rise to a cause of action for assault, battery and intentional infliction of emotional distress (and perhaps false imprisonment too).[3] Similarly, a sexual assault may be actionable under a number of trespassory tort claims.[4]

Umbrella liability for intentional physical harm. The Restatement Third of Torts takes a step beyond the traditional trespassory tort rules and establishes an umbrella rule of liability under which, "An actor who intentionally causes physical harm is subject to liability for that harm."[5] This umbrella rule overlaps, but is not entirely coextensive with, the existing trespassory torts.[6]

The new tort of purposeful infliction. To effectuate the umbrella rule, the Restatement Third of Intentional Torts recently creates a new cause of action for

---

[1]   Restatement Third of Torts (Intentional Torts to Persons) Scope note (Tentative Draft No. 1, Apr 8, 2015).

[2]   Id.

[3]   Hudgens v. Prosper, Inc., 243 P.3d 1275 (Utah 2010).

[4]   Lickteig v. Kolar, 782 N.W.2d 810 (Minn. 2010) (when a jurisdiction has enacted a special statute of limitations for "sexual assault," that statute governs, however the underlying cause of action is not a new tort of sexual assault but rather battery, assault, and other torts).

[5]   Restatement Third of Torts (Liability for Physical Harm) § 5 (2005).

[6]   See Kenneth W. Simons, A Restatement (Third) of Intentional Torts?, 48 Ariz. L. Rev. 1063–64 (2006) ("this claim, that the umbrella concept [of the Restatement Third] literally encompasses certain other torts, is false or at least misleading"); Ellen Bublick, A Restatement (Third) of Torts: Liability for Intentional Harm to Persons—Thoughts, 44 Wake Forest L. Rev. 1335 (2009) (examining ways in which the Restatement's umbrella rule is both broader and narrower than the existing trespassory torts).

"purposeful infliction of bodily harm."[7] The purposeful infliction tort may be most useful when an actor purposefully causes physical harm without the physical contact required for a battery cause of action. For example, if a person intentionally snatches a phone from the hand of a dying bedridden man who is calling 911, causing his death, that action may well count as a battery.[8] But if the person instead snatches the phone away before the dying man can even reach it, purposefully causing the man's death without a physical contact, that conduct would be actionable as purposeful infliction.[9]

Scope of the new tort. While the purposeful infliction rule makes sense in many contexts—if negligently caused physical harm is presumptively tortious, intentionally caused physical harm seems an even better candidate for liability—the purposeful infliction tort raises some special difficulties. Negligence requires some objectively unreasonable conduct. However, the purposeful infliction tort can be applied quite broadly so that even an innocuous act that happens to cause harm can become tortious solely because of the actor's bad intent. For example, according to the Restatement Third, moving a chair out of an employee's office could be purposeful infliction if the defendant moved the chair with the purpose of causing the employee to suffer back pain.[10] Whether courts will want to litigate the case of the moved chair to see if the mover's intent was nefarious or not is a matter for legal development. Whether it makes sense to rest a cause of action on the actor's tortious intent raises questions akin to those that arise in the tortious interference context. In tortious interference, some courts hold a claimant need only plead improper purpose, yet others require that improper purpose be coupled with an improper act. As in tortious interference, some courts may elect to impose additional restrictions on the purposeful infliction tort, such as requiring an improper, perhaps negligent, act as well as an improper purpose. In addition, the Restatement takes no position on whether this new purposeful infliction tort should be a gap-filler or available even when the plaintiff has other viable causes of action.[11] This is an issue to follow in courts in the coming years.

B.   INTENT AND RELATED CONCEPTS

§ 4.2   The Meaning of Intent

Non-tortious intent. Intent itself is a neutral word that does not imply wrong. This is so first because intent by itself is never a tort and second because many intents are perfectly honorable. Your intent to pet your dog or paint your house is not a tortious intent; if carried out, no tort is committed. Which intents are tortious are determined by the rules of particular torts such as battery. (In the case of battery, the relevant intent is to touch another person in a way not consented to.)[12]

State of mind showing intent. What is the state of mind required for an intent? The defendant has an intent to achieve a specified result when either (1) the defendant has

---

[7]   Restatement Third of Torts (Intentional Torts to Persons) §104 (Tentative Draft No. 1, Apr 8, 2015).

[8]   Id. § 101 illus. 1.

[9]   Id. § 104 illus. 7.

[10]   Id. § 104 illus. 3.

[11]   Id. § 104 rptr. note.

[12]   Yoder v. Cotton, 276 Neb. 954, 758 N.W.2d 630, 632 (2008) ("The tort of battery requires actual infliction of unconsented injury upon or unconsented contact with another").

a purpose to accomplish that result or (2) the defendant lacks such a purpose but knows to a substantial certainty that his actions will bring about the result.[13]

The purpose test. To illustrate the purpose clause, suppose the defendant attempts to hit a target by firing a rifle from a great distance. It may be unlikely that he can do so, but it is his purpose to do so if he can. Under the first clause, he has intent to hit the target because he has a purpose to do so. The intent is not necessarily tortious or wrong; to see whether the defendant has committed a tort will require other steps in proof and reasoning. The illustration given merely shows the intent element in what may or may not turn out to be a tort.

The substantial certainty test. To see the certainty clause in operation, suppose that the defendant puts sleeping pills in the food served by the cafeteria at a summer camp. His purpose is limited: he knows X will eat the food and wishes to put X to sleep. By the purpose clause, the defendant does not intend to put others to sleep at all. However, if he knows that others will also be eating the cafeteria food at the same time, he must know to a substantial or virtual certainty that they, too, will be affected. Under the certainty clause of the intent definition, the defendant intends to affect others who eat the same cafeteria food at the same time. Mere risk, however, even a very high risk, is not enough to show substantial certainty.[14]

The focused viewpoint of substantial certainty. The substantial certainty test is focused on the plaintiff (or a particular group of plaintiffs) and on the source of the harm and a particular time and place. It will not suffice to say that the defendant maintains a dangerous condition on his land that, over a period of years, is almost certain to cause injury to someone. That might be negligence, but it is not an intent to harm or to commit any trespassory tort.[15]

Deviations. Courts occasionally ignore the substantial certainty test of intent, seemingly to obtain results that could better be explained on other grounds. One case, for example, insisted that smokers did not intend to touch the plaintiff with their second-hand smoke, even though they allegedly knew their smoke was not only touching the plaintiff but also causing her harm.[16] Such a case implicitly rejects the substantial certainty test, but it might better be understood as establishing a privilege or insisting that a more material touching is required to establish a battery.

Intent is specific. Intent is not a general state of mind. One has a purpose to accomplish, or a substantial certainty of accomplishing one or more specific objectives. The defendant might intend to touch and also intend his touching to have harmful

---

[13] Restatement Third of Torts (Liability for Physical Harm) § 1 (2005); Curtis v. Porter, 784 A.2d 18, 23 (Me. 2001) ("a person acts intentionally if he subjectively wants or subjectively foresees that harm to another will almost certainly result from his actions"); Frey v. Kouf, 484 N.W.2d 864 (S.D. 1992); Garratt v. Dailey, 46 Wash. 2d 197, 279 P.2d 1091 (1955); Restatement Second of Torts § 8A (1965).

[14] See Eddy v. Virgin Islands Water & Power Auth., 369 F.3d 227 (3d Cir. 2004); Tomeo v. Thomas Whitesell Constr. Co., 176 N.J. 366, 371, 823 A.2d 769, 772 (2003) (deliberate risk falls short of intent to harm with substantial certainty).

[15] Restatement Third of Torts (Liability for Physical Harm) § 1 cmt. e (2005). Cf. Brown v. Diversified Hospitality Group, Inc., 600 So.2d 902, 906 (La. Ct. App. 1992) (deliberate decision to use inadequate staff increased the risk of robbery and thus of injury to the plaintiff-employee but this is not substantial certainty); but cf. Bradley v. American Smelting & Refining Co., 104 Wash.2d 677, 683, 709 P.2d 782, 786 (1985) (operator of copper smelter had substantial certainty intent that the law of gravity would visit known microscopic particles in its gases "upon someone, somewhere").

[16] Pechan v. Dynapro, Inc., 622 N.E.2d 108 (Ill. App. Ct. 1993).

effects. These are two different intents. Quite possibly one is tortious and the other is not. Consequently, analysis of intent must be quite specific.

Intent is subjective. Since intent is a state of mind, it is necessarily subjective.[17] That is, the relevant state of mind is that of the person whose intent is in question. This differs from negligence, which is judged by an objective standard. Thus a defendant is negligent if he departs from the standard of care expected of people generally, but he is not necessarily acting intentionally merely because other people acting in like circumstances would harbor an intent.

Evidence of intent is objective. Although the relevant intent is subjective, the trier of fact does not have a mind reading machine to determine that subjective intent. One's subjective intent is necessarily determined from external or objective evidence. If the defendant pushes the plaintiff into a room, locks the door and throws away the key, the trier of fact is entitled to infer that the defendant intends to confine the plaintiff, at least for a time. So evidence that the defendant intended any given act may be good evidence that he also intended results that tend to follow such an act.

Defining intent in context. What constitutes intent may vary based on the context. Torts can define intent for the purpose of common law actions differently than they do in the insurance context[18] or the context of workers' compensation.[19] The Restatement of Intentional Torts to Persons specifically encourages courts to consider the "specific policies and principles governing the relevant context."[20] Having done so, tort doctrine and collateral legal rules on intentional torts "might significantly differ."[21]

§ 4.3   Intent and Motive

Motive. A bad motive is occasionally important in determining tort liability, especially in cases involving certain economic torts[22] and claims for punitive damages.[23] But the concept of intent is not the same as the concept of motive. A defendant whose conduct is intentional is not necessarily a defendant who has a bad motive or who is conscious that he is committing a legal wrong.

The difference between intent and motive is illustrated by the case of the physician who forces treatment on an unwilling patient. He may act from the motive of good will and in the belief that his treatment will be best for the patient; he might even believe that he is right to force the treatment upon the patient. But neither his good motive nor his erroneous belief that he is acting rightfully will excuse his intended touching of the

---

[17]   Restatement Third of Torts (Intentional Torts to Persons) §102 cmt. a (Tentative Draft No. 1, Apr 8, 2015).

[18]   For example, in the insurance context, courts interpreting an intentional act exclusion may not employ the substantial certainty test. See Allstate Ins. v. Campbell, 942 N.E.2d 1090 (Ohio 2010).

[19]   Some cases alter the rules of intent in order to avoid the exclusive remedy provisions of workers' compensation statutes and to permit recovery for "intentional" torts. See § 36.5.

[20]   Restatement Third of Torts (Intentional Torts to Persons) Scope note 2 Introduction (Tentative Draft No. 1, Apr 8, 2015).

[21]   Id.

[22]   As in the case of interference with business opportunity without physical threat or harm. See Chapter 42.

[23]   See § 34.4.

patient against the patient's will.[24] Intent, not motive, is the basis of liability for the torts discussed in this chapter.

Capacity: children and mentally disabled persons. In most jurisdictions,[25] neither infancy nor mental disability provides any general immunity from tort liability.[26] Both children[27] and mentally disabled persons[28] may be held responsible for intentional torts. The real question in intentional tort claims against them is the same as in other suits, that is, whether they in fact entertained the intent required to establish a particular tort. Very small children or babies may lack the capacity to entertain an intent, and perhaps some mentally disabled persons lack capacity as well. If they have the requisite intent, however, they do not escape liability because of their age or disability.

§ 4.4   Intent and Negligence

Intent and negligence distinguished. Intent and negligence are different concepts. Negligence entails unreasonably risky conduct; the emphasis is on risk as it would be perceived by a reasonable person, not on the defendant's purpose or on the certainty required to show intent. The defendant may create risks of harm without having either a purpose or a certainty that harm will result.[29] Indeed, negligence does not require a state of mind at all but focuses instead on outward conduct. Even if the defendant recognizes the risk and deliberately decides to chance it without having purpose or certainty required for intent, he is not liable for an intentional tort, only for negligence.[30]

Intent and negligence as mutually exclusive? The traditional thought was that any given act may be intentional or it may be negligent, but it cannot be both. Intent and negligence have been regarded as mutually exclusive grounds for liability.[31] As the saying goes, there is no such thing as a negligent battery, since battery is defined to require an intentional touching without consent not a negligent one.[32] So under traditional conceptions, there was no overlap between intentional and negligent torts.[33] However, the Restatement Third has taken a different view.[34] Taking an approach focused on principle and policy, the Restatement counsels "it should not simply be

---

[24]   Shuler v. Garrett, 743 F.3d 170 (6th Cir. 2014) (patient was given heparin injections despite her objections; battery claim stated). The prankster cases rest on a similar principle. If the prankster's conduct otherwise amounts to a tort and is not consented to, his jocular motives will not assist him. See Fuerschbach v. Southwest Airlines Co., 439 F.3d 1197 (10th Cir. 2006) (arrest as a friendly joke).

[25]   A few jurisdictions protect certain minors. See Horton v. Hinely, 261 Ga. 863, 413 S.E.2d 199 (1992) (nine-year-old boys allegedly set fire to a seven-year-old; minors under 13 were immune).

[26]   Restatement Third of Torts (Liability for Physical and Emotional Harm) § 10 (infants) & § 11 (mentally disabled persons) (2012).

[27]   Farm Bureau Mut. Ins. Co. of Ark. v. Henley, 275 Ark. 122, 628 S.W.2d 301 (1982); Bailey v. C.S., 12 S.W.3d 159 (Tex. App. 2000) (4-year-old hit babysitter in the throat, crushing larynx).

[28]   Polmatier v. Russ, 206 Conn. 229, 537 A.2d 468 (1988); Williams v. Kearbey, 13 Kan.App.2d 564, 775 P.2d 670 (1989).

[29]   E.g., Spivey v. Battaglia, 258 So.2d 815 (Fla. 1972); Frey v. Kouf, 484 N.W.2d 864 (S.D. 1992).

[30]   Thus where a defendant does not know he was infected with HIV but infects his wife, he may not be liable for battery; if he should have known of his infection, he may be liable for negligence, but not for battery. Endres v. Endres, 968 A.2d 336, 338 (Vt. 2008) (affirming summary judgment for defendant because no evidence suggested he either knew or should have known).

[31]   Dormu v. District of Columbia, 795 F.Supp.2d 7, 30 (D.D.C. 2011).

[32]   See District of Columbia v. Chinn, 839 A.2d 701 (D.D.C. 2003).

[33]   American Nat'l Fire Ins. Co. v. Schuss, 221 Conn. 768, 607 A.2d 418 (1992). Statutes on particular topics may blur negligence and intent. See Central Pathology Serv. Med. Clinic, Inc. v. Superior Court, 3 Cal.4th 181, 10 Cal. Rptr. 208, 832 P.2d 924 (1992).

[34]   Restatement Third of Torts (Intentional Torts to Persons) Scope note 2 Introduction (Tentative Draft No. 1, Apr 8, 2015).

presumed that the intentional-tort characterization should always preempt the negligence characterization."[35] Instead, courts should carefully consider whether one cause of action should preempt the other.

Categorizing conduct. In terms of intent and negligence, it is sometimes difficult to discern whether a given set of conduct falls in one category or another. The evidence offered in a case may permit the trier to draw different inferences, so that some jurors would conclude that a defendant acted intentionally, while others would conclude that he acted only negligently. If the evidence warrants either a finding that the defendant acted with substantial certainty or that he took an unreasonable risk, the jury might be permitted to find either negligence or intent.[36] On the other hand, a plaintiff may not generally convert an intentional tort into a negligence claim, for example to escape a shorter statute of limitations or to recover under an insurance policy.[37]

§ 4.5   Intent and Reckless or Wanton Misconduct

Courts often recognize a kind of third category of fault that is distinguishable both from intent and from negligence. This category is called recklessness or willful or wanton misconduct.[38] Not surprisingly, reckless conduct resembles both intentional conduct and negligence, so this category adds a degree of confusion or uncertainty.

Elements. In civil cases, courts find conduct to be reckless, willful or wanton when two elements concur. First, the conduct must not only create an unreasonable risk of harm to others, it must create a high degree of risk or a risk of very serious harm, or, if a lesser risk or less probable risk, then one that is easily avoided.[39] Second, the defendant must be conscious of the risk and proceed without concern for the safety of others.[40] Driving while voluntarily intoxicated and drag racing on the public highway are examples.[41] Sometimes authorities say that the defendant need not actually be aware of the risk if it is obvious. However, obviousness of the risk is probably not the test of recklessness. Instead, obviousness is only evidence about the defendant's probable state

---

[35]   Id.

[36]   In spite of what may be broader language, this may be the idea behind Ghassemieh v. Scafer, 52 Md.App. 31, 447 A.2d 84 (1982).

[37]   Baska v. Scherzer, 283 Kan. 750, 156 P.3d 617, 627 (2007) but cf. Brown v. Robishaw, 282 Conn. 628, 922 A.2d 1086 (2007).

[38]   Courts often attempt to distinguish between wanton and reckless conduct and even between willful and wanton. See, e.g., Anderson v. Massillon, 983 N.E.2d 266, 273 (Ohio 2012) ("Willful misconduct implies an intentional deviation from a clear duty or from a definite rule of conduct, a deliberate purpose not to discharge some duty necessary to safety, or purposefully doing wrongful acts with knowledge or appreciation of the likelihood of resulting injury. Wanton misconduct is the failure to exercise any care toward those to whom a duty of care is owed in circumstances in which there is a great possibility that harm will result. Reckless conduct is characterized by the conscious disregard of or indifference to a known or obvious risk of harm to another that is unreasonable under the circumstances and is substantially greater than negligent conduct." (internal citations omitted)). However well the distinctions can be mapped in the mind, pointing them out on the ground is almost impossible and in any event serves no purpose. As the Connecticut Supreme Court said: "While we have attempted to draw definitional distinctions between the terms willful, wanton or reckless, in practice the three terms have been treated as meaning the same thing." Dubay v. Irish, 542 A.2d 711, 719 (Conn. 1988).

[39]   See Restatement Third of Torts (Liability for Physical Harm) § 2 cmt. e (2005).

[40]   Blakely v. Austin-Weston Ctr. for Cosmetic Surgery LLC, 348 F.Supp.2d 673, 679 (E.D. Va. 2004). The Restatement Third of Torts (Liability for Physical Harm) § 2 cmt. a (2005) says "When a person's conduct creates a known risk that can be reduced by relatively modest precautions, to state that the person displays a reckless disregard for risk is equivalent to stating that the person's conduct is reckless."

[41]   Booker, Inc. v. Morrill, 639 N.E.2d 358, 361 (Ind. Ct. App. 1994) (intoxicated driving is wanton misconduct); Lewis v. Miller, 374 Pa.Super. 515, 521, 543 A.2d 590, 592 (1988) (drinking and drag racing).

of mind. If the risk is obvious enough, the trier can infer that the defendant was in fact conscious of it,[42] and if it is also a serious risk of substantial harm, the trier can find recklessness, willful or wanton misconduct, or "deliberate indifference."[43]

Relation to intent and to negligence. Both elements of recklessness—high risk and consciousness of the risk—bear some relationship to intent, but both fall somewhat short of intent. Conduct that imposes only a moderate risk of harm to others is clearly at most only negligent conduct. As the risk becomes greater it may tend to approach virtual certainty and thus become a species of intent. In the case of recklessness, the risk is very high (or very grave), but it is somewhat short of the certainty required to justify a finding that the defendant was acting with intent to cause harm.

Consciousness of risk or indifference to it also bears some resemblance to intent. In fact, the defendant harbors one kind of intent, namely, an intent to take a risk. An intent to take a risk, however, is far short of an intent to inflict an actual harm or an invasion of the plaintiff's rights, so intentional risk-taking is not itself the basis for finding an intentional tort.

Relevance of recklessness in determining liability. In the overwhelming number of tort cases, the defendant's liability turns on intent or negligence, so that recklessness is irrelevant except perhaps to show grounds for punitive damages. In a few instances, however, recklessness is important when mere negligence is not a sufficient ground for liability.[44]

C. BATTERY

§ 4.6   Simple Battery

Intent. The defendant is subject to liability for a simple battery when he intentionally causes bodily contact[45] to the plaintiff in a way not justified by the

---

[42]   See Farmer v. Brennan, 511 U.S. 825, 114 S.Ct. 1970, 128 L.Ed.2d 811 (1994).

[43]   The deliberate indifference standard used in certain civil rights cases is congruent with the definition of recklessness given in this book. See Farmer v. Brennen, id.

[44]   *Examples:* (1) Some statutes make parents liable (usually in limited amounts) for certain reckless or malicious acts of their children, but in the absence of an agency relationship, not for merely negligent acts. E.g., Conn. Gen. Stat. Ann. § 52–572 (West 2009). See Walker v. Kelly, 314 A.2d 785 (Conn. Cir. Ct. 1973). (2) Guest statutes, now almost entirely obsolete in American law, protected automobile drivers from liability to their passengers for ordinary negligence but held them liable for some higher degree of fault such as wanton or reckless misconduct. E.g., Ala. Code § 32–1–2 (2009). (3) The common law tort of intentional infliction of emotional distress requires either intent or recklessness on the defendant's part. See Chapter 29.5. (4) Some common law rules for the liability of landowners to visitors on the land impose liability under standards similar to a recklessness standard. See Chapter 20. (5) Some civil rights liabilities are imposed only in cases of deliberate indifference, which appears to be a species of recklessness or wanton misconduct. (6) Contributory negligence of a plaintiff was no defense if the defendant was guilty of wanton misconduct. See §§ 16.7, 17.4. (7) In some states, statutory damages caps on non-economic damages (see § 34.7) do not apply if the defendant has engaged in willful or reckless misconduct. See Carrillo v. Boise Tire Co., Inc., 152 Idaho 741, 751, 274 P.3d 1256, 1266 (2012) (applying Idaho Code § 6–1603(4), holding that plaintiffs adequately pleaded reckless misconduct against defendant tire service that allegedly rotated tires improperly, resulting in death of passenger). (8) Some state governmental immunity statutes (see Chapter 22) provide a political subdivision or its employees with a complete defense to a negligence case, but remove that immunity if the acts are committed in a wanton or reckless manner. See Anderson v. Massillon, 983 N.E.2d 266, 273–74 (Ohio 2012) (applying Ohio Rev. Code § 2744.02, holding that the terms "willful," "wanton" and "reckless" are not interchangeable and describe different and distinct degrees of culpability).

[45]   Occasionally courts speak of bodily harm, not merely bodily contact, as in Vandervelden v. Victoria, 177 Wis.2d 243, 249, 502 N.W.2d 276, 278 (Ct. App. 1993). This implies a rejection of the offensive battery, but sometimes "bodily harm" is merely loose language and not intended to be such a rejection.

plaintiff's apparent wishes or by a privilege,[46] and the contact is in fact either harmful or simply against the plaintiff's will.[47] An accidental touching may count as negligence, but it is not a battery.[48]

Harm or offense. Many batteries represent intentional harm, as where one spouse beats or shoots another.[49] Harm usually refers to physical harm—that is some impairment, however small, of the human body.[50] An intent to cause such actual harm is a sufficient intent, but not a necessary one.[51] It is enough that the defendant intends bodily contact that is "offensive,"[52] which is to say a bodily contact that does not appear acceptable to the plaintiff and that is not permitted by a rule of law or a privilege. Any touching that violates ordinary social usages may thus be a battery unless the plaintiff has given signs that it is acceptable. So an aggressive shove that causes no physical harm is a battery.[53] Violence or ill will is not required. A caress, for example, is a battery unless circumstances indicate that it is acceptable.[54] Even medical treatment that involves a touching is a battery if the health care provider has no reason to believe the treatment is consented to.[55] Some opinions get results that are often in accord with these statements, but say that the only intent required is intent to make bodily contact.[56]

Direct vs. indirect harm. In early common law, battery claims were pursued by an action for trespass to the person and thus fell under the rule that trespass actions would lie only if the harm was done directly.[57] If the defendant dug a hole intending the plaintiff to fall into it in the dark, that would not have been a direct harm and hence the trespass claim would not lie. With the abolition of the forms of action, the distinction is meaningless or confusing. In any event, it has been subsumed by the intent rules: if the defendant acts on an intention to inflict a harmful or offensive bodily contact, and he succeeds, he is liable for the battery whether the harm is direct or not.

Damages. Once a battery is established, the defendant becomes liable for the harms resulting, including unintended ones. He may intend only an offensive touching, but he is liable for any actual harm that results. Recovery is permitted for trespassory torts

---

[46]   As to privileges, see Chapters 7 and 8. Even when the defendant is privileged to touch the plaintiff, as where the defendant is privileged to make a lawful arrest, the touching may exceed the privilege because it is excessively forceful or unnecessary. Jackson v. District of Columbia, 412 A.2d 948, 955 (D.C. 1980).

[47]   Compare Restatement Third of Torts (Intentional Torts to Persons) §101 (Tentative Draft No. 1, Apr 8, 2015), with Restatement Second of Torts § 13 (1965). See Marchbanks v. Borum, 806 So.2d 278, 288 (Miss. Ct. App. 2001) ("One commits a battery by the very touching of another without his consent. Mississippi adheres to the basic belief that a patient is 'master of his/her own body.' " (emphasis added)).

[48]   Janelsins v. Button, 102 Md.App. 30, 648 A.2d 1039, 1045 (1994). Under traditional rules, there is no such thing as a negligent battery.

[49]   Cain v. McKinnon, 552 So.2d 91 (Miss. 1989); Noble v. Noble, 761 P.2d 1369 (Utah 1988).

[50]   See Restatement Third of Torts (Liability for Physical Harm) § 4 (2005).

[51]   Frey v. Kouf, 484 N.W.2d 864 (S.D. 1992). As to sufficiency of intent to cause physical harm, see Restatement Third of Torts (Liability for Physical Harm) § 5 (2005).

[52]   Restatement Third of Torts (Intentional Torts to Persons) §§ 101 & 103 (Tentative Draft No. 1, Apr 8, 2015); § 4.7.

[53]   Whitley v. Andersen, 37 Colo.App. 486, 551 P.2d 1083 (1976), aff'd, 194 Colo. 87, 570 P.2d 525 (1977).

[54]   Johnson v. Ramsey County, 424 N.W.2d 800 (Minn. Ct. App. 1988) (kiss implanted by employer); Rogers v. Loews L'Enfant Plaza Hotel, 526 F.Supp. 523 (D.D.C. 1981) (male superior on the job, unwanted touching of the plaintiff's hair).

[55]   See Taylor v. Johnston, 985 P.2d 460 (Alaska 1999); Mims v. Boland, 110 Ga.App. 477, 138 S.E.2d 902 (1964).

[56]   See § 4.8.

[57]   See §§ 2.8 and 5.1.

without proof of pecuniary loss or actual physical harm.[58] The defendant is of course liable for physical harms resulting from the battery, but he is also liable for impermissible touchings that are not physically harmful.

Policy. The law of battery, an outgrowth of the old trespass writ, was originally conceived solely in terms of force and violence.[59] Like much other early law, it served to substitute a legal recovery for revenge and to discourage actual violence. Tort law today of course shares those goals; but as the rules show, it adopts more subtle ones as well. Battery today vindicates the plaintiff's rights of autonomy and self-determination, her right to decide for herself how her body will be treated by others, and her right to exclude their invasions as a matter of personal preference, whether physical harm is done or not.[60]

§ 4.7   Harm or Offense Required to Establish Simple Battery

The central core. The central core of the battery rules is simple. Subject only to the most limited exception, the defendant must respect the plaintiff's apparent wishes to avoid intentional bodily contact. Hostile, aggressive, or harmful touchings are batteries because the plaintiff wishes to avoid them. But the plaintiff's right to avoid unwanted intentional contact does not depend upon the defendant's hostile intent or even upon the reasonableness of the plaintiff's wishes. A person is entitled to refuse well-intentioned medical treatment[61] as well as the bumptious grapplings of an unwelcome swain.[62] In a world full of uncontrollable events, all persons are at least entitled to prohibit unwanted intentional touchings of any kind.[63]

Formulating a rule: the Second Restatement's "harmful or offensive" test. How is this central policy to be formulated in a rule? The Second Restatement attempted to convey the policy by saying that the defendant is subject to liability for causing bodily contact that is either (a) harmful or (b) "offensive." The Restatement did not use "offense" in the sense that a person might be huffy or irritable. Rather, an offensive touching infringes a reasonable sense of personal dignity.[64] More broadly put, a touching is "offensive" if it infringes upon the plaintiff's actual and apparent wishes to avoid it. Although liability may be imposed for harmful attacks, liability does not depend upon harm[65] or even upon

---

[58]   See § 4.20.

[59]   Cole v. Turner, 6 Mod.Rep. 149, 90 Eng.Rep. 958 (Nisi Prius 1704) ("the least touching of another in anger is a battery If any of them use violence against the other . . . it is a battery").

[60]   In the Interest of Baby Boy Doe v. Doe, 260 Ill.App.3d 392, 401, 632 N.E.2d 326, 332 (1994) (right to refuse medical treatment includes right to refuse cesarian operation that might improve chances of fetus or child); James Henderson, Why Vosburg Comes First, 1992 Wis. L. Rev. 853, 859.

[61]   Taylor v. Johnston, 985 P.2d 460 (Alaska 1999); Anderson v. St. Francis-St. George Hosp., 83 OhioApp.3d 221, 614 N.E.2d 841 (1992), rev'd on other grounds, 77 Ohio St.3d 82, 671 N.E.2d 225 (1996) (if life-saving treatment was given against the plaintiff's will, the plaintiff had a battery claim).

[62]   Stockett v. Tolin, 791 F.Supp. 1536 (S.D. Fla. 1992) (employer touched employee's breasts, licked her); Johnson v. Ramsey County, 424 N.W.2d 800 (Minn. Ct. App. 1988) (kissing battery).

[63]   See Conte v. Girard Orthopaedic Surgeons Med. Group, 107 Cal.App.4th 1260, 132 Cal.Rptr.2d 855 (2003).

[64]   Restatement Second of Torts § 19 (1965); cf. Goff v. Clarke, 302 A.D.2d 725, 726, 755 N.Y.S.2d 493, 495 (2003).

[65]   E.g., Whitley v. Andersen, 37 Colo.App. 486, 551 P.2d 1083 (1976), aff'd, 194 Colo. 87, 570 P.2d 525 (1977); Selmeczki v. New Mexico Dep't of Corrections, 139 N.M. 122, 129 P.3d 158 (Ct. App. 2006).

emotional distress[66] to the plaintiff; it depends upon violating the plaintiff's right to decide for herself what touchings of her body are acceptable.

Harm or offense in the Restatement Third. The Restatement Third also bars conduct that causes "bodily harm" or "is offensive."[67] As in the prior Restatement, "contact that offends a reasonable sense of personal dignity" is barred.[68] The Restatement Third is more explicit that contact "highly offensive to the other's unusually sensitive sense of personal dignity" is also actionable if the actor has a purpose to offend the other.[69] However, the Restatement Third specifies that courts should not impose liability for an unusually sensitive sense of dignity if the tort liability would "violate public policy" or be "unduly burdensome."[70] For example, if a person refuses to be touched by a nurse because of the nurse's race, a court could decide that anti-discrimination policy renders compliance with this unusual sensitivity unenforceable through battery liability.

Plaintiff's apparent consent as the central issue. The gist of the battery action is that the plaintiff has been touched, intentionally, in a way that she has not even apparently consented to and that is not justified by some generally recognized privilege or defense.[71] The same idea may apply when the defendant has consent to touch but goes beyond the consent in some particular way. For instance, the surgeon who has consent to remove one organ does not necessarily have consent, even implicit consent, to remove another.[72]

Plaintiff consent and defendant intent to harm or offend. What counts as an apparent consent is an important topic considered later. The central point to note here is that the plaintiff's apparent consent shows that the defendant is not intending to touch in an offensive way and that no right of the plaintiff has been invaded by permitted touchings, even if it turns out to be unintentionally harmful.[73]

The case of social usage and conflicting rights. In one narrow kind of case a defendant may escape liability for an intentional touching even when he knows that the plaintiff wishes to avoid it. A plaintiff who rides the subway may implicitly consent to a certain amount of intentional jostling as other riders leave the car, and if so, the touching would not transgress the plaintiff's rights; in the Restatement Second's words, it would not be offensive.[74] Suppose, however, the subway rider makes it plain to all passengers that she must not be touched by others as they attempt to exit the crowded car. Would

---

[66] This is congruent with the rule for certain kinds of sexual harassment claims under some federal statutes: an abusive or hostile environment is required, but not emotional distress. See Harris v. Forklift Systems, Inc., 114 S.Ct. 367, 371 126 L.Ed.2d 295, 510 U.S. 17, 22 (1993).

[67] Restatement Third of Torts (Intentional Torts to Persons) §101 (Tentative Draft No. 1, Apr 8, 2015).

[68] Id § 103 (a).

[69] Id § 103(b) as subsequently modified.

[70] Id.

[71] See Dubbs v. Head Start, Inc., 336 F.3d 1194, 1219 (10th Cir. 2003) ("Presumably, what makes such contact offensive . . . is the fact that the procedure is performed without consent"); Cohen v. Smith, 269 Ill.App.3d 1087, 1090 648 N.E.2d 329, 332 (1995) ("Liability for battery emphasizes the plaintiff's lack of consent to the touching"); Messina v. Matarasso, 284 A.D.2d 32, 35, 729 N.Y.S.2d 4, 7 (2001) ("Lack of consent is considered in determining whether the contact was offensive").

[72] Mohr v. Williams, 95 Minn. 261, 104 N.W. 12 (1905) (consent to operate on right ear, actual operation on left ear, held a battery, but benefits of the operation are to be considered in fixing damages), overruled on other grounds by Genzel v. Halvorson, 248 Minn. 527, 80 N.W.2d 854 (1957); see Cobbs v. Grant, 8 Cal. 3d 229, 239, 502 P.2d 1, 7, 104 Cal. Rptr. 505, 511 (1972).

[73] Wulf v. Kunnath, 285 Neb. 472, 827 N.W.2d 248 (2013) (consent, actual or apparent, destroys "the wrongfulness of the conduct between the consenting parties"); Hellriegel v. Tholl, 69 Wash.2d 97, 417 P.2d 362 (1966).

[74] Cf. See, e.g., Balas v. Huntington Ingalls Industries, Inc., 711 F.3d 401 (4th Cir. 2013) (supervisor's hug was not objectively offensive given the context).

other riders be liable for a battery if they must push through the throng to reach the exit? Presumably not. Not only are such jostlings socially accepted, they are necessary to protect the rights of others who must also live in an unpleasantly crowded world. The plaintiff's right to avoid bodily contact is important, but so is the defendant's right to take the subway and get to work. The plaintiff cannot preempt the subway space for herself alone.[75] It is more straightforward, however, to deal with this kind of case by recognizing that the defendants are privileged to make their exit by reasonable means rather than by manipulating concepts of consent.[76]

§ 4.8   Nature of Intent Required to Establish Simple Battery

Intent to . . . Intent has been defined to include either a purpose to effect some result or a substantial certainty that the result will follow from the defendant's actions.[77] What results must the defendant intend to establish a simple battery?

The Restatement Second's formula. The Restatement Second's formula is that the defendant must intend a "harmful or offensive contact." An intent to touch in a way the defendant understands is not consented to is sufficient. So is an actual intent to harm. The question is whether the plaintiff shows intent by showing merely an intent to touch that turned out to be offensive or harmful, or whether she must show that the harm or offense was also intended. On this point the Restatement and some of the cases are ambiguous.[78]

Ambiguity illustrated. Suppose the defendant intends to touch the plaintiff but he intends the touching to be friendly and comforting, not either harmful or offensive. That is, he believes the touching is consented to. In this state of mind, he hugs the plaintiff, but the plaintiff is unexpectedly harmed by the hug or revolted by it. Some authority phrases the rule in a way that suggests the defendant will be liable merely because he intended a bodily contact if it in fact caused harm or offense,[79] the so-called single intent rule. Other courts seem to think that the defendant must intend not only a touching but

---

[75]   Restatement Third of Torts (Intentional Torts to Persons) §103 (Tentative Draft No. 1, Apr 8, 2015). Cf. McCracken v. O.B. Sloan, 40 N.C.App. 214, 252 S.E.2d 250 (1979) (plaintiff touched by smoke).

[76]   Perhaps this is what some New York courts have in mind when they say that contact is offensive when it is "wrongful under all the circumstances," as in Goff v. Clarke, 302 A.D.2d 725, 726, 755 N.Y.S.2d 493, 495 (2003).

[77]   Restatement Third of Torts (Intentional Torts to Persons) §102 cmt.(a) (Tentative Draft No. 1, Apr 8, 2015).

[78]   Vitale v. Henchey, 24 S.W.3d 651 (Ky. 2000), might be read to authorize recovery for an innocent touching, one not intended either to harm or to offend. But that was a case in which the defendant in fact knew that the touching was not consented to, so liability is quite appropriate under the intent to harm or offend standard. Other cases sometimes tell us what proof is insufficient—the plaintiff cannot prevail without proving intended bodily contact—but probably should not be construed to mean that when such proof is made it is also sufficient without proof of intent to harm or to violate the plaintiff's wishes. See Laurie Marie M. v. Jeffrey T.M., 159 A.D.2d 52, 559 N.Y.S.2d 336 (1990), aff'd, 77 N.Y.2d 981, 575 N.E.2d 393, 571 N.Y.S.2d 907 (1991).

[79]   Wagner v. State, 122 P.3d 599 (Utah 2005) (state not liable if attack by mentally-limited ward in its care was a battery, and it was, whether the ward intended harm or not); Hunt v. State Dep't of Safety & Homeland Sec., 69 A.3d 360 (Del. 2013) (intent necessary for battery is intent to make contact with the person, not the intent to cause harm, but no battery because no actual harm or offense); Sutton v. Tacoma Sch. Dist. No. 10, 324 P.3d 763 (Wash. Ct. App. 2014) ("the requisite intent for battery is the intent to cause the contact, not the intent to cause injury"). Cf. White v. University of Idaho, 118 Idaho 400, 401, 797 P.2d 108, 109 (1990) (intent to "act" required but not either intent to harm or to offend). In White, a professor and piano enthusiast touched the plaintiff's back with his hands as if playing a piano. The plaintiff was a social acquaintance and fellow enthusiast; neither harm nor offense was intended. An unexpected injury occurred. The victim sued the professor's employer, a state university, which might be held liable for an employee's negligence but not the employee's battery. The court held that the professor's act was a battery so that the university was not liable. In other words, the result of the court's expansive conception of battery is not liability but non-liability.

also must intend it to be harmful or offensive—offensive in the sense that no permission has been given for it, even by implication.[80] The latter rule is sometimes called the dual intent rule because it limits liability to cases in which the defendant intends both touching and harm or offense.

The fault principle argument. The Second Restatement's formula is perhaps ambiguous, but it probably means intent to harm or offend as well as an intent to touch is required. This is in line with the fault principle and also with the freedom to act encouraged by that principle.[81] To see this, suppose that in the illustrative example, the defendant is a wife who hugs her husband, but the hug unexpectedly causes a bone spur to break off and impinge upon a nerve in her husband's spine. If the wife intended neither harm nor any violation of the husband's implicit consent to friendly physical contact, the intent is not tortious or faulty. Except under a general regime of strict liability that is inconsistent with the fault principle, the physical contact alone seems to furnish no ground for liability.

The strict liability arguments. One argument for prima facie strict liability based on intent to contact without an intent to harm or offend is rooted in some particular circumstances. Some insensitive defendants may honestly believe that the plaintiff will welcome their sexual touchings and some abusive defendants will certainly claim so. Should a defendant who fondles strangers be permitted to escape liability if the jury believes that he really thought his attentions were welcome?

One answer is that the jury is free to and presumably would reject such a preposterous claim. A second solution is more subtle. Even if the jury believes that the defendant had no intent to offend, it might find him to be negligent and liable on that ground if he causes actual harm. A third solution is to impose strict liability, holding all defendants liable for the offenses or harms resulting from an intended touching, even if it was apparently consented to. The best solution, however, may be to recognize that the plaintiff's apparent lack of consent must be judged objectively. If the plaintiff says, in words or deeds, "Don't touch me," and the defendant intentionally touches the plaintiff anyway, the defendant, not the plaintiff, must bear the cost of the defendant's foolish belief that no means yes. These solutions do not, however, suggest that the wife who hugs her husband should be liable for an unexpected harm.

Professor Simons, one of the Reporters of the Restatement Third, has presented several vigorous arguments in favor of the single intent rule—permitting liability without any culpable intent, only the intent to touch another person.[82] They are detailed and complex but only two will be mentioned here. First, he has argued that doctors are

---

[80] White v. Muniz, 999 P.2d 814 (Colo. 2000) (full discussion and clear holding); Mullins v. Parkview Hosp., 865 N.E.2d 608 (Ind. 2007) (no battery claim is stated where there is no allegation that the defendant had "the intent to cause harm"); Baska v. Scherzer, 283 Kan. 750, 756, 156 P.3d 617, 622 (2007) ("The gravamen of a civil assault and battery is grounded upon the actor's intention to inflict injury."); Caudle v. Betts, 512 So.2d 389, 390 (La. 1987); Nelson v. Carroll, 355 Md. 593, 600, 735 A.2d 1096, 1099 (1999); Carlsen v. Koivumaki, 227 Cal.App.4th 879 (2014) (requiring proof that "the defendant touched the plaintiff, or caused the plaintiff to be touched, with the intent to harm or offend the plaintiff").

[81] For a thoughtful defense of the dual intent position, see Nancy J. Moore, Intent and Consent in the Tort of Battery: Confusion and Controversy, 61 Am. U. L. Rev. 1585 (2012). For a thoughtful discussion about balancing harms regulated and costs imposed in the intentional tort framework, see Keith N. Hylton, Intent in Tort Law, 44 Val. U. L. Rev. 1217 (2010) ("The intent rules of tort law function as a pricing mechanism that ensures optimal regulation of injury-causing activity. Optimal regulation avoids underdeterrence of harmful conduct and overdeterrence of beneficial activities.").

[82] Kenneth W. Simons, A Restatement (Third) of Intentional Torts?, 48 Ariz. L. Rev. 1061 (2006). He makes similar arguments based on his belief that practical jokers are liable without intent to harm or offend.

liable for exceeding the scope of the patient's consent even when they intend neither harm nor offense, and that such liability shows that an intent to touch suffices for liability if harm or offense results in fact.[83] However, the absence of apparent consent is itself the marker of offense.[84] The physician who knows he exceeds consent has intent to "offend" in this sense and is appropriately held liable. On the other hand, the physician should not be liable if the consent expressed by the patient reasonably appears to authorize the touching. To be sure, the physician is not saved by intentions to do what is best for the patient if he knows that the touching is not consented to, but strict liability of the physician for apparently non-offensive acts is a different matter.

Professor Simons also argues that if intent to harm or offend is required, the apparent consent defense is superfluous.[85] That may be true in most battery cases, but that is only to say that apparent consent—as distinct from actual but unexpressed consent[86]—in battery cases is really not an affirmative defense but a negation of any intent to offend, as some torts teachers try to show students.

Comment. If the plaintiff's consent is apparent, the defendant lacks intent to offend and should not be prima facie liable unless prima facie liability without fault is deemed desirable. There is nothing faulty in the bare act of touching another human being. The fault arises only when the touching exceeds any applicable privilege and the apparent consent (often established by custom, socially accepted practices, and other nonverbal behavior).

If single intent is adopted, and in the case in which the wife hugs her husband with the unexpected result that, without fault, she causes a broken bone,[87] a court says that the husband has made out a prima facie case for battery, the court will force resolution of the case on an affirmative defense. In the affirmative defense, the wife must prove that, by their course of affectionate conduct, the husband consented to the touching. But to resolve the case on the basis of such an affirmative defense, instead of requiring allegations of intentional harm or offense in the complaint,[88] may require extended legal proceedings. If the husband cannot assert in his complaint that a normal domestic activity like his wife's embrace was somehow unconsented to, casting the issue as an affirmative defense seems expensive to the system and needlessly costly to the wife. The single intent rule would thus seem either to impose prima facie strict liability or force the case into an overelaborate and costly "defense" or both.

Single intent in the Restatement Third. Pursuant to Professor Simons' arguments, the Restatement Third has embraced a single intent requirement. Specifically the Restatement provides: "The intent required for battery is the intent to cause a contact

---

[83]   Id. at 1067–68.

[84]   See § 4.7.

[85]   Kenneth W. Simons, supra n. 82, at 1069.

[86]   Actual but unexpressed consent would necessarily be an affirmative defense in the rare case in which it could be established, since that consent would be unknown to the defendant and the defendant's touchings where no consent is known would have to be judged to be offensive.

[87]   Cf. Spivey v. Battaglia, 258 So.2d 815 (Fla. 1972) (friendly, unsolicited hug caused unintended and unexpected paralysis, no liability for battery, but potential liability for negligence).

[88]   In some jurisdictions, the plaintiff may be permitted to allege conclusory allegations that the touching was not permitted or, the same thing, that it was not apparently consented to. See Shugar v. Guill, 304 N.C. 332, 283 S.E.2d 507 (1981). In others, courts may dismiss a complaint if it fails to assert something more than a legal conclusion. See Caldwell v. CVS Corp., 443 F.Supp.2d 654 (D.N.J. 2006). If the plaintiff had not consented or presented the appearance of consent, she should be able to so allege in one form or another in a verified complaint. It is important to recognize that this is not an onerous requirement.

with the person of another. The actor need not intend to cause harm or offense to the other."[89] In many cases, the single intent requirement will produce the same outcome as the dual intent requirement.[90] However, the single intent rule is more likely to impose liability on young children and adults with mental disabilities barring some additional limitation.[91] It is also more likely to make tortious, inoffensive physical contacts that produce unexpected physical harm.[92]

Managing single intent. Because requiring only an intent to contact without requiring any culpable intent to harm or offend can sweep into the prima facie case for battery many completely innocent contacts, such a requirement places more work on other limitations such as apparent consent.[93] It also renders the category of battery actions larger and more diverse than it would otherwise be. Accordingly, rules that make sense for some batteries may not make sense for others. For instance, a court may bar comparative fault as a defense to a battery in which the defendant intended to harm the plaintiff, yet allow comparative fault when the defendant intended only contact but not harm.[94]

§ 4.9   The Bodily Contact Required to Establish Simple Battery

Material touching. The size of the object that touches the plaintiff does not matter. The plaintiff is of course touched if she is struck by a bullet, but she is also touched if she drinks poison put in her cup by the defendant.[95] On the other hand, odors, smokes, or gases have been traditionally treated as intangibles, even though they do have a physical presence.[96] Whether a touching by second-hand tobacco smoke would count as a battery under some circumstances is perhaps uncertain.[97] However, several decisions have found a battery resulting from tobacco smoke, with the qualification that the defendant must have a purpose to harm or offend and is not liable merely for substantial certainty touchings.[98] A little authority supports a battery claim when the defendant intentionally exposes the plaintiff to dangerous radiation or industrial fumes.[99]

---

[89]   Restatement Third of Torts (Intentional Torts to Persons) §102 (Tentative Draft No. 1, Apr 8, 2015).

[90]   Id. § 102 cmt. a.

[91]   Id. § 102 cmt. b.

[92]   Id. § 102 cmt. b illus 3 (touching the back as though it is a piano keyboard, inadvertently causing nerve pain). Compare White v. University of Idaho, 118 Idaho 400, 401, 797 P.2d 108, 109 (1990).

[93]   Id. § 102 cmt. a illus. 5 (one can assume there is apparent consent to a tap on the shoulder in a movie theatre). Cf. Balas v. Huntington Ingalls Industries, Inc., 711 F.3d 401 (4th Cir. 2013) (applying Virginia law: supervisor's hug of female employee was not objectively offensive despite employee's testimony that she was offended, where the employee had just given Christmas cookies to the supervisor, and the supervisor had thanked her and told her that "she never ceased to amaze him"; touching was not unwarranted based on the social usages prevalent at the time and place).

[94]   Id. at Scope note.

[95]   Snouffer v. Snouffer, 621 N.E.2d 879 (Ohio. Ct. App. 1993) (administering poison is a battery).

[96]   This distinction is one of the factual bases for the traditional legal difference between trespass to land (physical, tangible entry) and nuisance (intangible invasions affecting enjoyment but not possession).

[97]   See McCracken v. O.B. Sloan, 40 N.C.App. 214, 252 S.E.2d 250 (1979) (upholding smokers' rights and refusing to find battery); see Renee Vintzel Loridas, Annotation, Secondary Smoke as Battery, 46 A.L.R.5th 813 (1997).

[98]   Richardson v. Hennly, 209 Ga. App. 868, 434 S.E.2d 772 (1993), rev'd on other grounds, 264 Ga. 355, 444 S.E.2d 317 (1994); Leichtman v. WLW Jacor Commc'ns, Inc., 92 Ohio App.3d 232, 634 N.E.2d 697 (1994). See David Ezra, Smoker Battery: An Antidote to Second-Hand Smoke, 63 S. Cal. L. Rev. 1061 (1990) (canvassing theories for claims against smokers).

[99]   Swope v. Columbian Chems. Co., 281 F.3d 185 (5th Cir. 2002) (ozone fumes); Field v. Philadelphia Elec. Co., 388 Pa.Super. 400, 417, 565 A.2d 1170, 1178 (1989) (radiation).

Extended personality. The plaintiff is also touched if the defendant touches some intimate extension of the plaintiff's person,[100] as when the defendant jerks a plate from the plaintiff's hand, even if the hand itself is not touched.[101]

Causing a touching by other objects or by other persons. Touching is not limited to physical contact between the defendant's body and the plaintiff's. The defendant who wears gloves to slap the plaintiff is no less guilty of a battery than one who strikes the plaintiff bare-handed. An unpermitted touching of clothes worn by the plaintiff falls under the same rule.[102] More than that, the plaintiff is touched and a battery committed if the defendant intentionally pulls the chair from under the plaintiff as she sits, with the result that she falls to the ground.[103] Finally, the defendant may be responsible for a battery if he directly causes other persons to effectuate or complete the harmful or offensive bodily contact with the plaintiff.[104]

§ 4.10 Battery and Other Torts: Acts and Omissions

Acts distinguished from involuntary motion and intent. Both versions of the Restatement structure analysis of battery and other trespassory torts by requiring an "act" of the defendant.[105] An act in the Restatement Second's terminology is an external manifestation of will, a voluntary contraction of muscles, nothing more.[106] The "voluntary-act requirement is a minimal one."[107] Involuntary muscle spasms, convulsions, bodily movements during sleep are thus not acts. On the other hand, an instantaneous response to emergency, as where the defendant grabs the plaintiff to avoid falling, constitutes an act.[108] The term "act" does not equate with fault or intent. The defendant "acts" when he strikes another even if he is prompted by insane impulses.[109]

Act distinguished from inaction. The term "act" is also used to emphasize a distinction between affirmative deeds on the one hand and omissions or passive behavior on the other. Battery normally results from the defendant's affirmative acts or deeds: the defendant strikes the plaintiff or spits on him or poisons his drink. Can a defendant be liable for a battery when the defendant does nothing to stop another's bodily contact with the plaintiff? Analogies from negligence law suggest that the defendant who has no

---

[100] Espinoza v. Thomas, 189 Mich.App. 110, 472 N.W.2d 16 (1991) (group of strikers blocking, rocking, and beating on the car plaintiff was driving is a battery); Picard v. Barry Pontiac-Buick, Inc., 654 A.2d 690 (R.I. 1995).

[101] Fisher v. Carrousel Motor Hotel, Inc., 424 S.W.2d 627 (Tex. 1967).

[102] Selmeczki v. New Mexico Dep't of Corrections, 139 N.M. 122, 129 P.3d 158 (Ct. App. 2006).

[103] Garratt v. Dailey, 46 Wash.2d 197, 279 P.2d 1091 (1955).

[104] Richardson v. Hennly, 209 Ga.App. 868, 434 S.E.2d 772 (1993), rev'd on other grounds, 264 Ga. 355, 444 S.E.2d 317 (1994) (it is enough that defendant sets a force in motion that touches the plaintiff, quoting Prosser & Keeton on Torts § 9); Wilder v. Gardner, 147 S.E. 911 (Ga. Ct. App. 1929) ("One who by advice, counsel, or command procures another to commit a wrong" is equally liable); Mock v. Polley, 116 Ind. App. 580, 589, 66 N.E.2d 78, 81–82 (1946) (one aiding and abetting or encouraging battery is "equally guilty" and liable in tort); Leichtman v. WLW Jacor Commc'ns, Inc., 92 Ohio App. 3d 232, 236, 634 N.E.2d 697, 699 (1994) ("one who is present and encourages or incites commission of a battery . . . can be equally liable as a principal"). See similarly Mullins v. Parkview Hosp., 865 N.E.2d 608 (Ind. 2007).

[105] E.g., Restatement Third of Torts (Intentional Torts to Persons) §101 cmt. c (Tentative Draft No. 1, Apr 8, 2015) (actor's conduct must be a voluntary act or course of activity); Restatement Second of Torts § 13 (1965) (liability for harmful battery requires act, intention, and harmful contact).

[106] Restatement Second of Torts § 2 (1965).

[107] Restatement Third of Torts (Intentional Torts to Persons) §101 rptr. note cmt. c (Tentative Draft No. 1, Apr 8, 2015).

[108] Id. Restatement Second of Torts § 2 cmt. b (1965).

[109] Polmatier v. Russ, 206 Conn. 229, 537 A.2d 468 (1988).

special relationship with the plaintiff or her attacker would not be liable for a battery if he merely failed to prevent the attacker from hitting the plaintiff.[110]

Duty to protect the plaintiff from others' batteries? On the other hand, the defendant might be under a duty to protect the plaintiff. Employers, for example, are under a duty to protect employees from sexual batteries (and other forms of sexual harassment). If an employer knows that an employee is being sexually battered by another employee, it is not implausible to say that the employer is also guilty of a battery, though he has not committed any "act" and in some instances the battery claim might be advantageous to the employer.[111] Similarly, a hospital is under a duty to protect patients from attack, and a knowing failure to do so might be thought of as a battery by inaction. In practice, however, courts are likely to think of both kinds of claims as negligence claims turning on reasonableness rather than battery claims turning upon intent.[112] The Restatement Third concurs. "One can imagine cases in which battery or assault liability for an omission to rescue or protect another seems defensible. . . . However, judicial support for such liability is sparse."[113] That is not necessarily the plaintiff's loss, since the defendant's liability insurance may cover negligence but not battery. The upshot is that an affirmative act is at least ordinarily if not invariably required to establish a battery. In addition, liability may be imposed under other theories such as vicarious liability for actions within the scope of employment.[114]

D. ASSAULT

§ 4.11   Simple Assault

Nature of the tort. Newspapers and even judges and lawyers sometimes use the term assault to mean a battery.[115] Technically, assault is a quite different tort, although it often precedes a battery. An assault is an act that is intended to and does place the plaintiff in apprehension of an immediate unconsented-to touching that would amount to a battery.[116] The Restatement Third retains the same basic concepts but swaps the term "apprehension" for the more accurate term "anticipation."[117] The plaintiff's subjective recognition or anticipation that she is about to be touched in an impermissible way is at the core of the assault claim. No actual physical harm or even actual touching

---

[110] Cf. Price v. City of Seattle, 106 Wash. App. 647, 660 24 P.3d 1098 (2001) (defendant's failure to prevent landslides on upper property from damaging the plaintiffs' lower property was not a trespass because failure to act is not an act).

[111] Employers are generally protected from negligence claims under workers' compensation laws, but sometimes not for intentional tort claims. See generally Jean Love, Actions for Nonphysical Harm: The Relationship Between the Tort System and No-Fault Compensation (With an Emphasis on Workers' Compensation), 73 Cal. L. Rev. 857 (1985).

[112] *Employers liable for negligence:* E.g., Ford v. Revlon, Inc., 153 Ariz. 38, 734 P.2d 580 (1987). *Hospital liable for negligence:* Sumblin v. Craven Cnty. Hosp. Corp., 86 N.C.App. 358, 357 S.E.2d 376 (1987). See Ellen Bublick, A Restatement (Third) of Torts: Liability for Intentional Harm to Persons—Thoughts, 44 Wake Forest L. Rev. 1335 (2009) (discussing a hypothetical case in which a lifeguard fails to rescue a person for the purpose of causing harm).

[113] Restatement Third of Torts (Intentional Torts to Persons) § 101 cmt. c (Tentative Draft No. 1, Apr 8, 2015).

[114] See Chapter 31 on vicarious liability generally.

[115] Saucier v. McDonald's Restaurants of Mont., 342 Mont. 29, 47, 179 P.3d 481, 494 (2008) (tort claim referred to conduct as "sexual assault and battery," however plaintiff cited evidence to support battery claim but not separate claim of assault).

[116] Restatement Second of Torts §§ 21 & 32 (1965).

[117] Restatement Third of Torts (Intentional Torts to Persons) §105 (Tentative Draft No. 1, Apr 8, 2015).

is required to complete this tort.[118] And if the plaintiff anticipates that she is about to be battered, her assault claim is in no way diminished by the fact that the battery was completed and that she also has a claim for that.[119] On the other hand, if the plaintiff never anticipated that a battery was forthcoming, the defendant may be liable for a battery but not an assault.[120]

Intent and transferred intent. As in other cases, intent may be based either on the defendant's purpose or on his substantial certainty that a trespassory tort will occur. A mere risk that the plaintiff will be touched or put in apprehension does not qualify as substantial certainty and it forms no basis for liability based on intent. However, under transferred intent, if a defendant intends a battery but not assault, he may yet be liable for assault if the plaintiff does in fact apprehend the imminent blow. In another version of assault using the principle of transferred intent, the defendant may be held liable if his misconduct is directed at a third person but miscarries so that it is the plaintiff who apprehends the immediate or "imminent" touching.[121]

Examples of simple assault. An example of an intended battery that actually culminates only in an assault is the case of the defendant who attempts to strike the plaintiff from behind. If the plaintiff turns in time to see the blow about to be delivered and escapes it, there is no battery since there is no touching. But if the plaintiff anticipateded an imminent touching from the blow, the defendant is liable for an assault.[122] If the plaintiff is not aware of the impending blow, there is no assault at all, although if the blow is actually delivered there will be a battery.[123]

In some instances, the defendant's whole purpose is to convince the plaintiff that a battery is imminent even though the defendant never intends to deliver the threatened blow. In the absence of a privilege, the defendant is liable for assault in such cases as well, so long as he intends to put the plaintiff in apprehension of a battery. For example, the defendant may shoot a pistol at the plaintiff with the intent to frighten but not to touch. Again, if the plaintiff apprehends an imminent battery, the defendant is liable for the assault.

Damages. Since assault is a tort that is historically derived from the writ of trespass, the tort carries with it a right to a damages award even when no physical harm is done.[124]

§ 4.12   Anticipation of Imminent Touching

Apprehension vs. fear. Given the traditional use of the term apprehension, courts often define assault in terms of the plaintiff's fear of an imminent touching, but they probably do not literally mean fear, as much as a recognition that a touching is

---

[118]   Bowie v. Murphy, 271 Va. 127, 624 S.E.2d 74 (2006).

[119]   Id.

[120]   Restatement Third of Torts (Intentional Torts to Persons) §105 illus. 2–4 (Tentative Draft No. 1, Apr 8, 2015); Broadley v. State, 939 A.2d 1016 (R.I. 2008) (severely disabled woman who resided in state-financed facility and had severe bruise had no assault claim because of the lack of evidence that she was placed in fear of physical harm); Koffman v. Garnett, 265 Va. 12, 574 S.E.2d 258 (2003).

[121]   See § 4.18.

[122]   Etherton v. Doe, 597 S.E.2d 87, 89 (Va. 2004).

[123]   Restatement Third of Torts (Intentional Torts to Persons) §105 illus. 2–4 (Tentative Draft No. 1, Apr 8, 2015); McCraney v. Flanagan, 47 N.C.App. 498, 267 S.E.2d 404 (1980) (when plaintiff awoke, she found that defendant had had sexual intercourse with her, but as she had not been aware of an imminent sexual touching, she had no assault claim).

[124]   See § 4.20.

threatened.[125] The courageous plaintiff who fears nothing or is sure he can avoid the threatened touch is entitled to recover for assault if he is aware that the defendant is attempting to land a blow or to shoot him.[126]

Anticipation: reasonableness, words alone. Many opinions have asserted that the plaintiff's apprehension must be reasonable or well-founded,[127] that the defendant must have the apparent present ability to complete the battery,[128] and that words alone, without accompanying action, cannot count as an assault.[129] These rules are sometimes criticized as too restrictive.[130] For example, in one sense there is no such thing as a "words alone" case; all words occur in a social context and that context may reinforce and add substance to the verbal threat.[131] The apparent reality of the threat, not its form, is what counts. The Restatement Third adopts a subjective standard for determining whether a person anticipated imminent harmful or offensive contact unless the "claim stems primarily from the actor's words" or the contact anticipated would not be legally defined as offensive.[132]

Imminence. Although the plaintiff need not suffer fear, she must in fact conclude that the threatened battery is imminent, meaning that it will occur without delay unless an intervening force prevents it or the plaintiff is able to flee. Future danger,[133] or a threatening atmosphere without reason to expect some immediate touching,[134] in other words, is not enough. On the other hand, the threat of imminent touching need not be explicit or verbal. If an angry crowd of men block, rock, and beat on the plaintiff's car, the plaintiff may justly feel apprehension of a battery even if none is expressly threatened.[135] Where a defendant "aggressively and rapidly advanced on the plaintiff with clenched fists, piercing eyes, beet-red face, popping veins, and screaming and

---

[125] Lamb v. State, 93 Md. App. 422, 438, 613 A.2d 402, 409 (1993) (words like fear are sometimes used loosely as shorthand for the traditional term apprehension, but fear is not literally required, citing Prosser & Keeton on Torts § 10).

[126] Restatement Third of Torts (Intentional Torts to Persons) §105 illus. 1 (Tentative Draft No. 1, Apr 8, 2015); Restatement Second of Torts § 24 cmt. b & illus. 1 & 2 (1965).

[127] Allen v. Walker, 569 So.2d 350, 351 (Ala. 1990) ("well-founded fear of an imminent battery, coupled with the apparent present ability to effectuate the attempt, if not prevented"); Espinoza v. Thomas, 189 Mich. App. 110, 472 N.W.2d 16 (1991).

[128] Muslow v. A.G. Edwards & Sons, Inc., 509 So.2d 1012, 1021 (La. Ct. App. 1987) ("reasonable apprehension" based on "present ability"); Hawkins v. Hawkins, 101 N.C.App. 529, 400 S.E.2d 472 (1991), aff'd, 331 N.C. 743, 417 S.E.2d 447 (1992) ("reasonable apprehension, apparent ability").

[129] Webbier v. Thoroughbred Racing Protective Bureau, Inc., 105 R.I. 605, 614, 254 A.2d 285, 290 (1969) ("Words alone are never a sufficient basis for a finding for assault"). However, words-alone cases now tend to recognize that words must be interpreted in light of circumstances and may, in that light, count as an assault. See Muslow v. A.G. Edwards & Sons, Inc., 509 So.2d 1012, 1020 (La. Ct. App. 1987); Johnson v. Bollinger, 86 N.C.App. 1, 356 S.E.2d 378 (1987); Restatement Third of Torts (Intentional Torts to Persons) §105 cmt. g (Tentative Draft No. 1, Apr 8, 2015); Restatement Second of Torts § 31 (1965).

[130] Restatement Second of Torts § 27 (1965).

[131] Words that do not threaten a battery in one setting may do so in another. In Cullison v. Medley, 570 N.E.2d 27 (Ind.1991), the defendants entered the plaintiff's home at night after he had gone to bed. They accused him of bothering a young woman in their family and berated him extensively. One of them kept slapping at a gun he wore on his thigh, but did not draw it. The court held that these facts would support a claim for assault. See also Johnson v. Bollinger, 86 N.C.App. 1, 356 S.E.2d 378 (1987).

[132] Restatement Third of Torts (Intentional Torts to Persons) §105 cmt. d (Tentative Draft No. 1, Apr 8, 2015).

[133] Dickens v. Puryear, 302 N.C. 437, 276 S.E.2d 325 (1981); cf. Johnson v. Brooks, 567 So.2d 34, 35 (Fla. Dist. Ct. App. 1990) (numerous threatening telephone calls not "acts," at most they are statements of intention to act).

[134] Vietnamese Fishermen's Ass'n v. Knights of the Ku Klux Klan, 518 F.Supp. 993 (S.D.Tex. 1981); State Rubbish Collectors Ass'n v. Siliznoff, 38 Cal.2d 330, 240 P.2d 282 (1952).

[135] Espinoza v. Thomas, 189 Mich.App. 110, 472 N.W.2d 16 (1991).

swearing at him," backing plaintiff up against a wall, the plaintiff's belief that he was going to be struck is reasonable, even where no blow was actually attempted.[136]

Conditional threats. The defendant cannot defeat the plaintiff's assault claim on the ground that he gave the plaintiff an unprivileged alternative to the threatened battery. The robber who points a gun and says "your money or your life" is guilty of an assault because he has no right to take either.[137] The rule is different, however, if the defendant has a privilege to insist upon the alternative. "Leave my property or I'll carry you off myself" may be a threat of battery that the defendant is entitled to make in the protection of his property.[138]

§ 4.13 Assault, Crime, and Other Torts

Tort and crime. Assault may be a crime as well as a tort, but criminal law definitions of assault sometimes emphasize the intent to injure and the risk of escalating violence rather than the victim's apprehension of a battery,[139] so criminal assault cases are not necessarily sound authority in the tort setting. Unlike criminal law in which victim awareness may be unimportant, tort law emphasizes and demands the plaintiff's awareness of the threat.

Assault and emotional distress. The law of assault represents a narrow segment in the spectrum of emotional harms.[140] Because of its narrow definition, it is not a very important segment in itself. Lawyers may thus find it more relevant to consider the broader topic of emotional distress in Chapter 29. As that chapter shows, claims that may fail as assault claims may succeed under the rubric of some other tort that also protects interests in emotional security. For instance, some forms of sexual harassment may fall short of a battery or an assault but may be actionable as an intentional infliction of emotional distress,[141] or an invasion of privacy,[142] or as a violation of constitutional[143] or statutory rights.[144] Under the Freedom of Access to Clinics Act,[145] threats of future harm to deter legally rightful abortions are actionable, even though such threats would

---

[136] Raess v. Doescher, 883 N.E.2d 790 (Ind. 2008).

[137] See Gouin v. Gouin, 249 F.Supp.2d 62, 70 (D. Mass. 2003) ("During this altercation involving a dispute over their son, Dori alleges that Gouin told her: 'You can either do it my way or I can beat you half to death'. . . . These allegations are sufficient to state a claim for assault").

[138] Restatement Third of Torts (Intentional Torts to Persons) §105 cmt. h (Tentative Draft No. 1, Apr 8, 2015); Restatement Second of Torts § 30 illus. 1 (1965).

[139] See Wayne LaFave & Austin Scott, Jr., Criminal Law 7.16 (1986) (discussing two types of assault statutes, those that make attempted battery an assault and those that make intentional scaring of the victim an assault).

[140] For this reason, there has been some suggestion that assault might be properly situated in a framework that addresses liability for other types of emotional harms. See Ellen Bublick, A Restatement (Third) of Torts: Liability for Intentional Harm to Persons—Thoughts, 44 Wake Forest L. Rev. 1335 (2009); Robert L. Rabin, Emotional Distress in Tort Law: Themes of Constraint, 44 Wake Forest L. Rev. 1197, 1210 (2009).

[141] E.g., Ford v. Revlon, Inc., 153 Ariz. 38, 734 P.2d 580 (1987).

[142] Phillips v. Smalley Maint. Servs., Inc., 435 So.2d 705 (Ala. 1983) (sexual demands in employment treated as privacy suit).

[143] Assault-like behavior might sometimes count as excessive force prohibited by the Fourth or Eighth Amendments and made actionable by civil rights statutes. See Northington v. Jackson, 973 F.2d 1518 (10th Cir. 1992).

[144] 42 U.S.C.A. § 2000e (2015).

[145] 18 U.S.C.A. § 248 (2015).

not constitute assaults.[146] Similarly, stalking, and the harassment of victims by following, calling, and otherwise pursuing them,[147] may be addressed in criminal[148] or civil statutes.[149]

E. FALSE IMPRISONMENT

§ 4.14 Simple False Imprisonment

Elements of the tort. Courts protect personal freedom of movement by imposing liability for false imprisonment. False imprisonment in its simple form is established by proof that the defendant intentionally[150] confined[151] or instigated[152] the confinement of the plaintiff. Confinement implies that the plaintiff is constrained against her will.[153] A third element, according to the Restatement and some authority, is that the plaintiff must have been aware of the confinement at the time or harmed by it.[154]

"False arrest." False arrest is a term that describes the setting for false imprisonment when it is committed by an officer or by one who claims the power to make an arrest. Although false arrest is not essentially different from false imprisonment,[155] detention by an officer or one acting under color of law may also amount to a civil rights violation.[156]

Motive and duration. Bad motive or hostility to the plaintiff is not required to establish false imprisonment; an intent to confine plus actual confinement is sufficient.[157] Nor need the plaintiff show confinement for a substantial length of time.

---

[146] See Planned Parenthood of Columbia/Willamette, Inc. v. American Coalition of Life Activists, 290 F.3d 1058 (9th Cir. 2002) (exploring constitutional free speech rights but concluding that if posters threatened abortion providers with murder, the speech was not constitutionally protected).

[147] See Silvija Strikis, Stopping Stalking, 81 Geo. L. J. 2771 (1993).

[148] E.g., People v. Borrelli, 77 Cal.App.4th 703, 91 Cal.Rptr.2d 851 (2000); Ariz. Rev. Stat. § 13–2921 ("harassment").

[149] E.g., Cal. Civ. Code § 1708.7. The California statute creates a statutory tort called stalking based on a pattern of conduct the "intent of which was to follow, alarm, or harass the plaintiff," with resulting reasonable fear by the plaintiff for herself or an immediate family member. In addition, the defendant must either make a credible threat or violate a restraining order. See also Or. Rev. Stat. § 30.866.

[150] See Adams v. Wal-Mart Stores, Inc., 324 F.3d 935, 941 (7th Cir. 2003) ("accidentally" confining the plaintiff in a locked room does not meet the intent requirement).

[151] Restatement Second of Torts § 35 (1965). Confinement, detention, restraint are all terms used; they appear to refer to the same underlying idea.

[152] Deadman v. Valley Nat'l Bank of Ariz., 154 Ariz. 452, 743 P.2d 961 (Ct. App. 1987); Desai v. SSM Health Care, 865 S.W.2d 833 (Mo. Ct. App. 1993); Restatement Second of Torts § 45A (1965). This rule explains why a physician who testifies that he examined the plaintiff and found her mentally ill when in fact he never examined her at all may be held for the plaintiff's false imprisonment when she is later confined as a mentally ill person. See Crouch v. Cameron, 414 S.W.2d 408, 30 A.L.R.3d 520 (Ky. 1967).

[153] A plaintiff who voluntarily accepts apparent confinement is not confined if she can leave at any time. See Pounders v. Trinity Court Nursing Home, 265 Ark. 1, 576 S.W.2d 934, 4 A.L.R.4th 442 (1979). In other cases the plaintiff consents in advance to a confinement from which she cannot escape, in which case the confinement is real but the consent is a defense until it is properly revoked. See Day v. Providence Hosp., 622 So.2d 1273 (Ala. 1993) (consent to stay overnight in locked psychiatric ward).

[154] Restatement Second of Torts §§ 35, 42 (1965). The Restatement Third of Intentionnal Torts to Persons is ongoing and has not yet addressed the tort of false imprisonment. See also Douthit v. Jones, 619 F.2d 527 (5th Cir. 1980); Parvi v. City of Kingston, 41 N.Y.2d 553, 362 N.E.2d 960, 394 N.Y.S.2d 161 (1977).

[155] See, e.g., Enders v. District of Columbia, 4 A.3d 457, 461 (D.C. 2010) ("'false arrest' is indistinguishable as a practical matter from the common law tort of 'false imprisonment'"); Asgari v. City of Los Angeles, 15 Cal.4th 744, 937 P.2d 273, 63 Cal.Rptr.2d 842 (1997).

[156] See 1 Dobbs, Hayden & Bublick, The Law of Torts §§ 75–79 (2d ed. 2011 & Supp.).

[157] Fuerschbach v. Southwest Airlines Co., 439 F.3d 1197 (10th Cir. 2006); Fair Oaks Hosp. v. Pocrass, 266 N.J.Super. 140, 628 A.2d 829 (1993).

Unless the defendant is privileged, a confinement for "any appreciable time, however short" is actionable.[158] However, the role of privilege is quite significant in false imprisonment cases, and where the defendant claims a privilege to detain the plaintiff, both his motive in detaining and the duration of the detention may become important in determining whether the defendant exceeded his privilege.[159]

Confinement. Confinement means that the plaintiff is not permitted to go beyond boundaries fixed by the defendant. The plaintiff whose road is obstructed is not confined and neither is the plaintiff who is excluded from a place of public accommodation, although in both instances the plaintiff may have some other kind of tort claim.[160] One court has held that confinement within the country of Taiwan is not confinement for false imprisonment purposes.[161] On the other hand, the boundaries of the plaintiff's confinement may be much less precise than four walls. The plaintiff who is detained on the street by a gang may be confined even if the gang does not specify the exact limits of her free movement. One is not confined at all if there is a reasonable means of egress.[162]

Examples of false imprisonment. False imprisonment is effected in many ways and in diverse social settings, but not surprisingly it most frequently involves a relatively powerful defendant. A storekeeper detains a customer or employee suspected of theft, sometimes by physical restraint and sometimes by threat;[163] a hospital, nursing home, or substance abuse center holds a patient against her will;[164] a driver refuses to stop his car so a passenger can get out;[165] a police officer lacking a warrant and lacking probable cause nevertheless detains or jails an individual.[166] In all these cases the main question in the first place is whether the plaintiff was in fact confined against her will and in the second whether the defendant was privileged to detain her.

§ 4.15 Methods of Confinement

Methods of confinement—physical restraint of person or property. The most obvious kind of confinement is that imposed by a physical barrier or physical force. For example, the defendant may lock the plaintiff in a room,[167] or physically restrain the plaintiff from

---

[158] Fuerschbach v. Southwest Airlines Co., 439 F.3d 1197, 1208 (10th Cir. 2006) ("brief time" sufficient).

[159] Cf. Taylor v. Super Discount Mkt., Inc., 212 Ga.App. 155, 441 S.E.2d 433 (1994) (implicitly a privilege case; store clerk briefly retained the plaintiff's $20 bill to investigate whether it was counterfeit, no false imprisonment); Thornhill v. Wilson, 504 So.2d 1205 (Miss. 1987) (officers' defense to false imprisonment claim where their detention of plaintiff in the course of crime investigation was reasonable).

[160] Obstruction of a public road may be a public nuisance for which a seriously affected individual may have a private right of action. See § 30.6. Refusal to admit the plaintiff to a place of public accommodation may violate civil rights laws and at least permit an injunction. See 42 U.S.C.A. § 2000a–5(a) (2015).

[161] Shen v. Leo A. Daly Co., 222 F.3d 472, 478 (8th Cir. 2000).

[162] Restatement Second of Torts § 36 cmt. a (1965); Krochalis v. Insurance Co. of N. Am., 629 F.Supp. 1360 (E.D. Pa. 1985). To be reasonable, the means of egress must be (a) readily knowable and (b) reasonably safe and appropriate. See Noguchi v. Nakamura, 2 Haw.App. 655, 638 P.2d 1383 (1982) (egress from moving car not reasonable).

[163] See § 7.17.

[164] Collins v. Straight, Inc., 748 F.2d 916 (4th Cir. 1984); Geddes v. Daughters of Charity of St. Vincent de Paul, Inc., 348 F.2d 144 (5th Cir. 1965); see generally Annotation, False Imprisonment in Connection with Confinement in Nursing Home or Hospital, 4 A.L.R.4th 449 (1981).

[165] Noguchi v. Nakamura, 2 Haw.App. 655, 638 P.2d 1383 (1982) (injury trying to escape, potential liability); Sindle v. New York City Transit Auth., 33 N.Y.2d 293, 352 N.Y.S.2d 183, 307 N.E.2d 245 (1973) (similar).

[166] E.g., Gordon v. Villegas, 1994 WL 86373 (Conn. Super. Ct. 1994) (unpublished).

[167] Geddes v. Daughters of Charity of St. Vincent de Paul, Inc., 348 F.2d 144 (5th Cir. 1965).

moving.[168] Similarly, the plaintiff might be confined by taking her clothes,[169] blocking her automobile[170] or taking her keys when use of the vehicle furnished the only reasonable means of egress[171] or by detaining her property so that she herself is effectively confined if she is to protect or retrieve it.[172]

Submission to legal authority. Short of such physical restraints, an officer may effectuate a confinement merely by asserting authority to do so. If the plaintiff submits to a law enforcement officer's assertion of authority to detain her, she has been confined, and unless the officer enjoys a privilege or an immunity, he is liable for false arrest.[173] But there may be a factual question for the jury about whether the plaintiff submitted to authority or merely acquiesced in the detention to clear her name or to provide assistance.[174] With private persons who do not themselves claim to act under color of law, an assertion that the plaintiff must remain because police are being called is at least a factor to determining whether the plaintiff is confined.[175]

Threats and duress. A number of cases involve confinement effectuated by conduct that expresses or implies a threat that the plaintiff will be restrained or subjected to an offensive touching if she attempts to leave.[176] Intimidation in an isolated or coercive environment may effect a confinement in some instances.[177] Threats of actual bodily harm are not required but they are of course sufficient.[178] Threats of harm to the plaintiff's property or to another person may have the effect of restraining the plaintiff.[179] But of course a threat to do what the defendant is privileged to do, to fire an at-will employee if she leaves work, is not an actionable confinement.[180] When a threat, express

---

[168] E.g., Stockett v. Tolin, 791 F.Supp. 1536 (S.D. Fla. 1992) (among many misdeeds, employer pinned employee to chair for a few moments; false imprisonment and other torts were established).

[169] McDonald's Corp. v. Ogborn, 309 S.W.3d 274 (Ky. Ct. App. 2009).

[170] Schanafelt v. Seaboard Fin. Co., 108 Cal.App.2d 420, 239 P.2d 42 (1951).

[171] Verstraelen v. Kellog, 60 Wash.2d 115, 372 P.2d 543 (1962).

[172] Wallace v. Stringer, 260 Ga. App. 850, 553 S.E.2d 166 (2001) (Wal-Mart allegedly took and held baby blanket, claiming it belonged to the store; dominion over the blanket and refusal to allow the plaintiff to go to the bathroom would be confinement); Burrow v. K-Mart Corp., 166 Ga.App. 284, 304 S.E.2d 460 (1983); Ashland Dry Goods Co. v. Wages, 302 Ky. 577, 195 S.W.2d 312 (1946).

[173] Martin v. Houck, 141 N.C. 317, 54 S.E. 291 (1906); Restatement Second of Torts § 41 (1965) (if plaintiff believes authority is valid or is in doubt about its validity and submits to it).

[174] Covell v. McCarthy, 123 Vt. 472, 194 A.2d 394 (1963) (after using a siren and flashing lights to pull driver over, officer asked, "will you come with me to the station?"; the driver accompanied the officer; held, a factual question whether this was submission to authority and therefore a false arrest).

[175] See McCann v. Wal-Mart Stores, Inc., 210 F.3d 51 (1st Cir. 2000) (seemingly considering police call as an important factor in finding confinement of a customer).

[176] Schanafelt v. Seaboard Fin. Co., 108 Cal.App.2d 420, 423, 239 P.2d 42, 43 (1951); Burrow v. K-Mart Corp., 166 Ga.App. 284, 287, 304 S.E.2d 460, 463 (1983) ("reasonable apprehension that force will be used if the plaintiff does not submit"); Jacques v. Childs Dining Hall Co., 244 Mass. 438, 138 N.E. 843, 26 A.L.R. 1329 (1923).

[177] See Collins v. Straight, Inc., 748 F.2d 916 (4th Cir. 1984) (drug treatment center, six and one-half hours of intimidation with door blocked, false imprisonment verdict upheld).

[178] Cassady v. Tackett, 938 F.2d 693 (6th Cir. 1991) (civil rights claim against jailer whose threats allegedly forced the plaintiff to barricade herself in her office).

[179] Restatement Second of Torts § 40A (1965) (threats to member of plaintiff's immediate family). The Restatement's "immediate family" rule seems unduly restrictive. If the plaintiff would be privileged to defend a third person against the action threatened, it seems logical to say that she could attempt to avoid the threatened action by sacrificing her own freedom of movement.

[180] Miraliakbari v. Pennicooke, 254 Ga.App. 156, 561 S.E.2d 483 (2002) (noting, however, that a public employee with a property interest in her job might present a different case).

or implied, is the basis for claiming confinement, the plaintiff must show, as in assault cases, that there is a reason to believe the threat can be carried out.[181]

Implicit threats effecting a confinement. Sometimes plaintiffs feel implicitly threatened when the defendant has made no overt threat at all. One such case occurs when a retailer's manager or security guards invite a customer or employee to a back room for a discussion of suspected theft. If the customer or employee goes along to clear matters up and not as the result of any express or implied threat, there has been no confinement against the customer's will and no false imprisonment.[182] If the customer wishes to leave but does not attempt to do so for fear that she will be restrained or otherwise harmed if she does, she must demonstrate at least an implicit threat to prevent her exit.

Evidentiary detail matters greatly in presenting this kind of claim. In one case[183] the plaintiff, an 18-year-old employee, was taken to an "office" that consisted of a windowless room with bare light bulbs. It had one door only and any exit required passage through two other rooms. The employee was confronted with several persons who insisted that she admit to a kind of theft and make immediate restitution in cash. Their voices, she said, were not soft. She made no effort to leave and testified that she believed she would not be permitted to do so. In this and similar cases[184] courts have held that the evidence sufficed to permit the jury to infer that the plaintiff was confined by implicit threats found in the circumstances.

A threat may be implied in the fact that the plaintiff is isolated and outnumbered,[185] confronted by figures of authority or power, or subjected to hostility and verbal abuse. Other evidence of a threat might include the relative ages, independence, education, and power of the parties. A ten-year-old might feel intimidated when a 28-year-old lawyer would not.[186] When such factors do not weigh in favor of the plaintiff, however, there is no confinement merely because the defendant asserts that the plaintiff must stay,[187] much less because the defendant requests the plaintiff's assistance.[188]

---

[181] Herbst v. Wuennenberg, 83 Wis.2d 768, 266 N.W.2d 391 (1978).

[182] E.g., Hardy v. LaBelle's Distrib. Co., 203 Mont. 263, 661 P.2d 35 (1983); cf. Pounders v. Trinity Court Nursing Home, 265 Ark. 1, 576 S.W.2d 934, 4 A.L.R.4th 442 (1979) (although nursing home told resident that she could not leave and even had her shoes, she was not confined because she had consented to being there initially and could walk out [barefooted?] at any time).

[183] Black v. Kroger Co., 527 S.W.2d 794 (Tex. Civ. App. 1975).

[184] DeAngelis v. Jamesway Dep't Store, 205 N.J. Super. 519, 501 A.2d 561 (1985) (17-year-old employee, shouting, verbal refusal to permit her to leave or talk to parents); Dupler v. Seubert, 69 Wis.2d 373, 230 N.W.2d 626 (1975) (one man stood at the door and another demanded the plaintiff sit down when she attempted to leave).

[185] Compare Dupler v. Seubert, 69 Wis.2d 373, 230 N.W.2d 626 (1975) (plaintiff outnumbered, evidence of threats sufficient), with Herbst v. Wuennenberg, 83 Wis.2d 768, 266 N.W.2d 391 (1978) (three male plaintiffs claimed to have been confined by woman who stood in the doorway, evidence insufficient). See also Collins v. Straight, Inc., 748 F.2d 916 (4th Cir. 1984) (drug treatment center, to induce the plaintiff to accept treatment/confinement used more than one staff member to intimidate the plaintiff for hours in an isolated, windowless room).

[186] Drabek v. Sabley, 31 Wis.2d 184, 142 N.W.2d 798, 20 A.L.R.3d 1435 (1966).

[187] E.g., Pounders v. Trinity Court Nursing Home, 265 Ark. 1, 576 S.W.2d 934, 4 A.L.R.4th 442 (1979); Herbst v. Wuennenberg, 83 Wis.2d 768, 266 N.W.2d 391 (1978).

[188] The Limited Stores, Inc. v. Wilson-Robinson, 317 Ark. 80, 876 S.W.2d 248 (1994) (when the store's alarm went off as plaintiff left the store, employees asked plaintiff if she would return to the store, and when she did, then established that she carried a calculator that might have set off the alarm; no false imprisonment).

Undue influence: affecting the plaintiff's will. Conceivably, the concept of confinement could be expanded to permit liability not only when the plaintiff is physically restrained or threatened but also when the defendant's conduct destroys the capacity of the plaintiff to exert her own will. For instance, a nursing home patient may lose her ability for independent action when she is removed from friends and social support and made dependent on the staff, so that she submits to their assertion of authority to confine her. It has been argued in such cases that the assertion of authority against the vulnerable patient should itself count as false imprisonment or at least that little more should be required.[189] When the defendant systematically uses techniques calculated to destroy the plaintiff's ability to act as an independent human being and then asserts that the plaintiff may not leave, the claim for false imprisonment becomes almost compelling.[190] This kind of issue has arisen when a religious group isolates the plaintiff and subjects her to sleep deprivation and other techniques that critics call brainwashing.[191]

§ 4.16 Duty to Release from Confinement

The ordinary false imprisonment case is one in which the defendant has acted in some affirmative way to effect the plaintiff's confinement, directly or indirectly. If the plaintiff is confined, but not as a result of the defendant's act, does the defendant ever owe a duty to assist in the plaintiff's release?

Custodians. Jailers, at least, owe a duty to release a prisoner when her sentence is up,[192] and no doubt analogous rules apply to other custodians such as psychiatric hospitals to which a person may be committed for a limited period only.[193] Similarly, once a custodian knows or should know that a person was arrested under a mistake of identity, the custodian is under a duty to release and liable for failure to do so.[194]

Promise to release. A defendant who induces a person to accept confinement in reliance on a promise or implicit promise to end the confinement on demand may be obliged to take affirmative action to effect the release when it is demanded. In one well-known case[195] the defendant induced the plaintiff to board his yacht on the promise that he would release her at any time she desired. But while the yacht was anchored offshore, the defendant refused to provide a boat to shore demanded by the plaintiff. The court found a false imprisonment on the basis of the promise or implicit promise that a boat

---

[189] Cathrael Kazin, "Nowhere to Go and Chose to Stay": Using the Tort of False Imprisonment to Redress Involuntary Confinement of the Elderly in Nursing Homes and Hospitals, 137 U. Pa. L. Rev. 903, 904 (1989), criticizing Pounders v. Trinity Court Nursing Home, 265 Ark. 1, 576 S.W.2d 934, 4 A.L.R.4th 442 (1979) (concluding, over dissents, that plaintiff "voluntarily" remained in nursing home).

[190] Cf. Collins v. Straight, Inc., 748 F.2d 916 (4th Cir. 1984) (drug treatment center, intimidation in what reads like the brainwashing pattern); Candy H. v. Redemption Ranch, Inc., 563 F.Supp. 505 (M.D. Ala. 1983) (unwed, pregnant young woman allegedly held incommunicado at "redemption" home, facts alleged would establish common law false imprisonment or civil rights tort).

[191] Laura Brown, He Who Controls the Mind Controls the Body: False Imprisonment, Religious Cults, and the Destruction of Volitional Capacity, 25 Val. U. L. Rev. 407 (1991). As to the sometimes similar techniques in "deprogramming" alleged cult victims, see Taylor v. Gilmartin, 686 F.2d 1346 (10th Cir. 1982).

[192] Douthit v. Jones, 619 F.2d 527 (5th Cir. 1980); Bennett v. Ohio Dep't of Rehab. & Correction, 60 Ohio St.3d 107, 573 N.E.2d 633 (1991).

[193] Cf. Kowalski v. St. Francis Hosp. & Health Ctrs, 1 N.Y.3d 480 (2013) (hospital had no right to force a severely intoxicated patient to remain in the hospital and therefore no duty to do so).

[194] Stalter v. State, 86 P.3d 1159 (Wash. 2004) (but also holding that there is no affirmative duty imposed upon a jailer to investigate identity of persons properly arrested).

[195] Whittaker v. Sandford, 110 Me. 77, 85 A. 399 (1912).

would be made available. In a similar vein, automobile drivers might be expected to make reasonable stops to permit passengers to alight.[196]

Defendant innocently causing imprisonment. Limited authority suggests that the defendant who innocently or under a privilege causes a confinement of the plaintiff has a duty to release the plaintiff or to inform him of an exit he could not otherwise locate once the privilege terminates and release becomes feasible.[197]

Relationship between parties. Perhaps some special relationships between plaintiff and defendant would warrant an extension of the affirmative duty to others,[198] but there seem to be few cases.[199]

§ 4.17 False Imprisonment and Other Torts

Negligence. A defendant who negligently but not intentionally confines the plaintiff is not liable for the intentional tort of false imprisonment, but he may be liable for the tort usually called negligence if all the elements of that tort are proved. However, negligence is not a dignitary tort; it only redresses claims for actual damages. Thus a plaintiff who is negligently but not intentionally confined but who suffers no harms as a result, would have no cause of action.

Civil rights. The common law action for false imprisonment does not stand alone. Confinement imposed by state officials is often privileged, but when it is not, an improperly confined person may also have a federal civil rights claim.[200]

Malicious prosecution. When the confinement takes place as a result of legal process such as a warrant for arrest, the plaintiff will seldom have an actionable claim for false imprisonment, since the legal process ordinarily furnishes a privilege or defense. If the legal proceeding against the plaintiff was itself brought without probable cause and for bad motives, the plaintiff may have a claim for malicious prosecution rather than false imprisonment. The difference, aside from damages measures and potential immunities,[201] is that the malicious prosecution plaintiff must affirmatively prove that the defendant prosecuted without probable cause to do so and prosecuted in bad faith.[202]

Emotional harm claims. False imprisonment is a direct interference with the person and thus a trespassory tort like the others in this chapter. But its effect is not merely to redress physical or pecuniary harms. In most instances, recovery for false imprisonment redresses a dignitary or intangible interest, a species of emotional distress or insult that one feels at the loss of freedom and the subjugation to the will of another. False imprisonment is thus as much part of the universe of emotional harm as it is part of the universe of potential violence associated with trespassory torts. As a practical matter,

---

[196] Cf. Drabek v. Sabley, 31 Wis.2d 184, 142 N.W.2d 798, 20 A.L.R.3d 1435 (1966) (10-year-old child in car being driven to police station); Sindle v. New York City Transit Auth., 33 N.Y.2d 293, 307 N.E.2d 245 (1973) (school bus driver driving boisterous passengers to police station, refusing to stop).

[197] Talcott v. National Exhibition Co., 144 A.D. 337, 128 N.Y.S. 1059 (1911).

[198] Restatement Second of Torts § 45 cmt. a (1965) (store's duty to customer who accidently locks himself in the washroom).

[199] Andrews v. Piedmont Airlines, 297 S.C. 367, 377 S.E.2d 127 (Ct. App. 1989).

[200] See 1 Dobbs, Hayden & Bublick, The Law of Torts § 77 (2d ed. 2011 & Supp.).

[201] Once a formal charge has been made and the plaintiff is confined by judicial order after arraignment, the false imprisonment is terminated and the claim for any remaining damages must ordinarily be one for malicious prosecution. See Asgari v. City of Los Angeles, 15 Cal.4th 744, 937 P.2d 273, 63 Cal. Rptr. 2d 842 (1997).

[202] See Chapter 39.

lawyers considering a false imprisonment suit may also consider asserting not only claims for malicious prosecution, civil rights, and invasion of privacy, but also claims for emotional harm.[203]

F. EXTENDED LIABILITY AND DAMAGES

§ 4.18 Extended Liability or Transferred Intent

Extending liability beyond simple trespassory torts. Courts tend to hold an intentional wrongdoer responsible for an extensive range of consequences, including consequences the wrongdoer never intended, at least in the case of trespassory torts to the person. At least three levels of this extended liability can be demonstrated by examples:

(1) *Offense intended with harm resulting or vice-versa.* Defendant intends to touch the plaintiff in an offensive way, but he intends no harm. The touching actually causes harm to the plaintiff. The defendant is liable for the unintended harm as well as any intended offense.[204] For example, the defendant kisses the plaintiff against her will, but intends no physical harm. In fact, however, the plaintiff suffers an immediate allergic reaction to the defendant's touch. The defendant is liable for the harm as well as for the intended offense. The same principle works to impose liability if the defendant intends a harmful touching but succeeds only in imposing an offensive one.[205]

(2) *Tortious conduct directed at A with resulting invasion of B's rights.* Defendant hurls a stone, intending a harmful battery to A; the stone misses A but strikes B. Defendant is liable for the harm to B although he never intended to touch B at all.[206] The idea might also be applied if the defendant attempts to put A in apprehension of a battery but puts B in apprehension instead,[207] or if defendant intends to imprison A but by mistake or misadventure imprisons B instead.[208]

(3) *One tort intended with another tort resulting.* Defendant fires a pistol intending to put A in apprehension of an immediate and unconsented-to bodily touching but intending no actual touching. Without defendant's fault, the

---

[203] See, e.g., Prince George's Cnty. v. Longtin, 419 Md. 450, 19 A.3d 859 (2011) (affirming jury award of over $5 million for intentional infliction of emotional distress in claim against police department, county, and individual officers for false arrest). See Chapter 29.

[204] Bettel v. Yim, 20 O.R.2d 617, 88 D.L.R.3d 543 (Ont. Co. Ct. 1978); Restatement Second of Torts § 16 (1965).

[205] Restatement Second of Torts §§ 18 & 20 (1965). Because the Restatement Third requires only intent to contact and not intent to harm or offend, this result is implicit. Restatement Third of Torts (Intentional Torts to Persons) § 101 (Tentative Draft No. 1, Apr 8, 2015).

[206] Baska v. Scherzer, 283 Kan. 750, 156 P.3d 617 (2007); Davis v. White, 18 B.R. 246 (Bkrtcy. Va. 1982); Singer v. Marx, 144 Cal.App.2d 637, 301 P.2d 440 (1956); Talmadge v. Smith, 101 Mich. 370, 59 N. W. 656 (1894); Carnes v. Thompson, 48 S.W.2d 903 (Mo. 1932).

[207] Holloway v. Wachovia Bank & Trust Co., 109 N.C.App. 403, 428 S.E.2d 453 (1993), rev'd on other grounds, 339 N.C. 338, 452 S.E.2d 233 (1994).

[208] Du Lac v. Perma Trans Prods., Inc., 103 Cal. App. 3d 937, 163 Cal. Rptr. 335 (1980), overruled on other grounds, Hagberg v. California Fed. Bank FSB, 32 Cal. 4th 350, 81 P.3d 244, 7 Cal. Rptr. 3d 803 (2004); Restatement Second of Torts § 43 (1965).

bullet actually strikes A. Defendant is liable to A for battery although he never intended a battery at all.[209]

Combining the rules. The rules may be combined. For example, if defendant intends to commit a mere assault on A, but actual touching results to B, the defendant is liable to B for the battery.[210] It has been suggested that the doctrine could apply as between any two trespassory torts, including, perhaps, property torts as well as personal torts.[211] The Restatement Third applies the rule only to the torts of battery, assault, false imprisonment and purposeful infliction.[212]

Expressing the principle. The Restatement Second recognized these rules but fragmented the principle of extended liability by building extended liability into the definition of each separate tort.[213] The Restatement Third addresses extended liability in a single provision.[214] Traditional discussion and the Restatement Third express the extended liability doctrine as a result of "transferred intent:" the defendant's intent to harm A is transferred to B, for example. The "transferred" intent expression is merely a metaphor. It may be more accurate to state the rule as an extended liability rule by saying that the defendant, who acts in such a way that the intended injury would be actionable, is liable for all direct consequences even though they are not intended.

Non-tortious or privileged intent. The formulation just suggested makes it clear that the extended liability doctrine properly applies only when the defendant's act would have been a tort if carried out as intended. The defendant who fires a pistol in target practice, intending to hit his own target, has no tortious intent at all. If the bullet strikes the plaintiff instead of the target, then quite possibly the evidence will show that the defendant was negligent, but he has not committed a battery. In the same way, the defendant must not be held liable if his conduct was protected by a privilege and the plaintiff is injured without fault. For example, the defendant may act intentionally in justified self-defense; if his act of self-defense causes injury to a bystander, there is no reason to impose liability unless the defendant was negligent.[215]

§ 4.19 Extended Liability: The Pros and Cons

The rules of extended liability may reflect criminal law doctrine carried over into tort law. Liability for miscarried criminal activity may seem entirely appropriate, since from the state's point of view, the defendant's act justifies punishment whether the harm is done to A or to B. The Restatement finds the concept consistent with the policy of

---

[209] Manning v. Grimsley, 643 F.2d 20 (1st Cir. 1981) (heckled baseball pitcher may have thrown at hecklers protected behind the screen, intending to put them in apprehension of imminent bodily touching; the screen broke and the plaintiff was actually injured); Brown v. Martinez, 68 N.M. 271, 361 P.2d 152 (1961); Restatement Third of Torts (Intentional Torts to Persons) § 106 cmt. b (Tentative Draft No. 1, Apr 8, 2015).

[210] Alteiri v. Colasso, 168 Conn. 329, 362 A.2d 798 (1975) (boy threw a stone intended to scare but not hit A; the stone actually hit B, who was injured; liability). Cf. Sindle v. New York City Transit Auth., 33 N.Y.2d 293, 307 N.E.2d 245 (1973) (bus driver refused to stop to permit rowdy passengers to depart; plaintiff was injured trying to escape).

[211] William Prosser, Transferred Intent, 45 Tex. L. Rev. 650 (1967).

[212] Restatement Third of Torts (Intentional Torts to Persons) § 110(a) (Tentative Draft No. 1, Apr 8, 2015).

[213] The Restatement defines each tort to include cases in which some other tort or harm was intended, and to include as well cases in which the tort was intended to another person. See Restatement Second of Torts §§ 13, 16, 18, 20 & 21 (1965).

[214] Restatement Third of Torts (Intentional Torts to Persons) § 110 (Tentative Draft No. 1, Apr 8, 2015).

[215] Morris v. Platt, 32 Conn. 75 (1864); Moore v. City of Detroit, 128 Mich.App. 491, 340 N.W.2d 640 (1983); William Prosser, Transferred Intent, 45 Tex. L. Rev. 650 (1967).

holding "intentional tortfeasors responsible for a wider range of consequences than negligent tortfeasors."[216] Skeptics might argue, however, that the same justification does not apply when it comes to tort liability.

Consider the case in which the defendant intends a battery to A but causes a battery to B instead. Given that the defendant intended no touching of B, one possibility is that the defendant was nonetheless negligent toward B. If that is the case, the argument against extended liability says that the defendant should be liable to B under the rules for negligence, but not under the rules for battery, since he never intended to batter B. The difference between the two forms of tort liability can be enormous, so the argument is not merely a formal distinction. For example, the defendant might take bankruptcy to escape ultimate responsibility for his negligent torts, but may not be permitted to do so in the case of certain intentional torts.[217] Or a battery claim may be barred by the statute of limitations where a negligence claim is not.[218]

A second possibility in this situation is that the defendant was not negligent towards B; that is, B's presence was unknown and not foreseeable, so a stone hurled at A did not create any recognizable risk to B. In that case, the injury to B is pure accident, and one opposed to the extended liability principle would be compelled to say that B could not recover at all, since, as to him, the defendant intended no tort of any kind and was not negligent.

If these positions against extended liability are plausible, it is because of the broader idea that if tort liability is justly based on intent rather than on strict responsibility, then that liability should not be more extensive than the wrongful intent or the moral fault of the defendant.[219] It is not so clear, however, that the defendant who is held liable for harm to B when he intended only harm to A is being held liable for harms beyond the range of his fault. If his fault lies in his intent and his act rather than in identification of a particular victim, then liability for the intent and the act seems perfectly appropriate even if the particular victim was not the intended one.

Extended liability may be harder to justify in some other kinds of cases. A battery with intent to contact but not harm or offend may be very different than a battery with an intent to harm. Similarly, one might think there really is a significant moral difference between a defendant's intention to put the plaintiff in apprehension of a battery and the defendant's intention to accomplish the battery itself. But even here, the argument against extended liability turns on how you conceive the basis for liability in the first place. If the real basis is intended interference with the plaintiff's autonomy with respect to her own body, then the defendant who batters when he means to assault is properly held liable because the core wrong is the same in either case, namely an infringement of the plaintiff's autonomy. The same can be said with respect to the harm-offense dichotomy.

In addition, it can be said that an intentional aggressor should bear the risk that his aggression will lead to unintended injury or that the aggressor should be subjected

[216] Restatement Third of Torts (Intentional Torts to Persons) § 110 cmt. c (Tentative Draft No. 1, Apr 8, 2015).

[217] See Davis v. White, 18 B.R. 246 (Bkrtcy. Va. 1982).

[218] Baska v. Scherzer, 283 Kan. 750, 156 P.3d 617 (2007) (holding that a plaintiff cannot plead a "transferred intent" battery as negligence in order to avoid a shorter statute of limitations).

[219] It is possible to think of liability in excess of moral fault as a species of strict or absolute liability. In Manning v. Grimsley, 643 F.2d 20 (1st Cir. 1981), the court regarded the transferred intent rules as imposing absolute liability, although the court also thought that to be justified.

to appropriate incentives to deter the aggression.[220] Ironically, sometimes the transferred intent rule advantages the defendant, as where the claim is barred by a shorter statute of limitations because it is classified as an intentional tort.

§ 4.20   Damages for Trespassory Torts to the Person

Physical harm: pecuniary losses. Damages awards usually aim to compensate the plaintiff for the losses resulting from the tort. Rules for compensation of physical harms are the same whether the harm results from a trespassory tort or from ordinary negligence. The plaintiff is entitled, for example, to recover for wage loss and reasonable medical expenses, if any, resulting from a battery, assault, or false imprisonment.[221]

Physical harm: pain, distress, emotional harm. Victims who sustain physical harm are always entitled to recover not only for the consequent pecuniary losses but also for any pain and suffering resulting from that physical harm. In this context, pain and suffering includes mental or emotional suffering, so the plaintiff can also recover for any proven mental distress or emotional harm.[222] Victims are not limited to a recovery for some standard amount of suffering. If they suffer more than most people, they are nevertheless entitled to recover for the suffering they actually undergo; the defendant, it is said, takes his victims as he finds them, with any special vulnerabilities they may have.[223]

Dignitary harm without physical harm. When the trespassory tort causes no physical harm, the traditional tort rule is that the plaintiff can nevertheless recover substantial as distinct from nominal damages. The idea is loosely linked to the idea of mental distress, but no actual proof of mental distress is required. The invasion of the plaintiff's rights is regarded as a harm in itself and subject to an award of damages. If the plaintiff suffers emotional distress as a result of any of these torts, even without physical harm, she is entitled to recover for that emotional distress as a separate element of damages.[224]

Under these rules, the plaintiff who is falsely imprisoned may recover substantial damages even if she suffers neither physical harm nor loss of wages and even if she does not testify to any kind of distress.[225] The circumstances of the imprisonment and its duration will of course affect the amount of damages the trier will be willing to award.[226]

---

[220]   See Manning v. Grimsley, 643 F.2d 20 (1st Cir. 1981) (strong social policy to induce obedience to criminal law by imposing liability); John Fleming, The Law of Torts 25 (8th ed. 1992). Cf. William Prosser, Transferred Intent, 45 Tex. L. Rev. 650 (1967) (as between innocent plaintiff and defendant guilty of moral wrong towards someone, it is better that defendant bear the loss).

[221]   E.g., Caudle v. Betts, 512 So.2d 389 (La. 1987) (nerve damage); Garratt v. Dailey, 46 Wash. 2d 197, 279 P.2d 1091 (1955) (broken bone). Chapter 34 covers damages generally.

[222]   Kennan v. Checker Taxi Co., Inc., 250 Ill. App. 3d 155, 897, 620 N.E.2d 1208, 1214 (1993) ("pain and suffering incurred by the plaintiff as a result of the blows inflicted, and for the humiliation, indignity, and vexation suffered by the plaintiff as a result of his assailant's conduct"); Rosenbloom v. Flygare, 501 N.W.2d 597 (Minn. 1993).

[223]   Stockett v. Tolin, 791 F.Supp. 1536 (S.D. Fla. 1992).

[224]   Raess v. Doescher, 883 N.E.2d 790 (Ind. 2008) (affirming jury award of $325,000 for assault, even where jury rejected plaintiff's intentional infliction of emotional distress claim; plaintiff presented evidence that his major depressive disorder, anxiety and panic disorder was caused by defendant's assault).

[225]   E.g., Kerman v. City of New York, 374 F.3d 93 (2d Cir. 2004) (jury must be instructed that, independent of pain or distress, the falsely imprisoned plaintiff is entitled to substantial compensatory damages for loss of liberty itself, referring to earlier awards of $10,000 for a three-hour detention and $7,500 for a five-hour detention).

[226]   West v. King's Dep't Store, Inc., 321 N.C. 698, 365 S.E.2d 621, 624 (1988) (duration of restraint).

An offensive battery gets similar treatment, so that damages may be awarded without any separate proof of mental distress aside from a preference not to be touched by the defendant.[227] Even beneficial touchings such as medical procedures may warrant damages if they are batteries, although the benefit is no doubt to be considered in determining the appropriate amount of the award.[228] The case of assault is treated in the same way.[229]

Punitive damages. In addition to compensatory damages, most states permit the plaintiff to recover an additional sum as punitive damages when the defendant's conduct and state of mind are especially odious, usually where he acts with malice or oppression, or at least with recklessness. Intentional torts are often candidates for punitive damages where the defendant intends actual harm or serious offense.[230] Punitive damages may be awarded in quite substantial sums, but there are constitutional standards to be met and some states now impose limitations on the amount of punitive damages.[231]

§ 4.21 Infliction of Emotional Distress

Intentional infliction of emotional distress (or mental distress) describes a separate but nontrespassory tort dealt with in Chapter 29. It also describes a possible motive for some intentional trespassory torts. It is worth mentioning here mainly because certain comparisons and contrasts are useful.

The tort was recognized by the Restatement around the middle of the 20th century[232] and courts have widely accepted the Restatement's formulation of the tort. Under this formulation, the defendant's conduct must be (1) extreme and outrageous, (2) based on an intent to cause severe emotional harm or on a reckless disregard of such harm, and (3) in fact a cause of severe emotional harm.[233] Special rules add a recovery for interference with dead bodies[234] and for gross insults by common carriers and utilities.[235]

---

[227] See Beard v. Flying J, Inc., 266 F.3d 792 (8th Cir. 2001); Johnson v. Pankratz, 2 P.3d 1266 (Ariz. Ct. App. 2000) (substantial or presumed damages available even in the absence of evidence as to amount); Johnson v. Ramsey County, 424 N.W.2d 800 (Minn. Ct. App. 1988) (unwanted kiss is actionable); cf. A.R.B. v. Elkin, 98 S.W.3d 99, 104 (Mo. Ct. App. 2003).

[228] Mohr v. Williams, 95 Minn. 261, 104 N.W. 12 (1905), overruled on other grounds by Genzel v. Halvorson, 248 Minn. 527, 80 N.W.2d 854 (1957); McCandless v. State, 3 A.D.2d 600, 162 N.Y.S.2d 570 (1957), aff'd mem., 4 N.Y.2d 797, 173 N.Y.S.2d 30, 149 N.E.2d 530 (1958) (abortion that was less painful than labor and delivery would have been and that improved the plaintiff's mental health, nevertheless warranted $2,000 in compensatory damages).

[229] The traditional case on the whole topic of such damages was an assault case, I de S et ux. v. W de S., Y.B. Lib. Ass. f 99, pl. 60 (1348).

[230] E.g., Beard v. Flying J, Inc., 266 F.3d 792 (8th Cir. 2001); Stockett v. Tolin, 791 F.Supp. 1536 (S.D. Fla. 1992); Kennan v. Checker Taxi Co., Inc., 250 Ill. App. 3d 155, 620 N.E.2d 1208 (1993) (taxi driver battered unsighted passenger; $193,000 punitive award); Carpentier v. Tuthill, 86 A.3d 1006 (Vt. 2013) (affirming $150,000 punitive damage award for trespasory torts based on attempted rape).

[231] See §§ 29.2, 29.3 discussing stand-alone emotional distress as a tort in itself.

[232] Restatement Second of Torts § 46 (1965).

[233] Restatement Third of Torts (Liability for Physical and Emotional Harm) § 46 (2012) ("An actor who by extreme or outrageous conduct intentionally or recklessly causes severe emotional harm to another is subject to liability for that emotional disturbance and, if the emotional disturbance causes bodily harm, also for the bodily harm").

[234] See Cates v. Taylor, 428 So.2d 637 (Ala. 1983).

[235] Restatement Second of Torts § 48 (1965) recognizes the traditional "special liability" of common carriers and public utilities for gross insults to patrons.

To the three elements in the Restatement formulation, some courts are beginning to add a requirement that (4) the distress suffered must be of the kind people in general would suffer and not merely an idiosyncratic reaction.[236] On the other hand, there is no requirement of physical injury resulting from the distress, since the outrageousness of the defendant's conduct is a good guarantee that the emotional harm is real.[237]

Threats of future harm, if they are serious enough, may count as intentional infliction of emotional distress for which the plaintiff can recover, even though they would not threaten the immediate touching required to show an assault.[238] On the other hand, doctrines peculiar to trespassory torts have no application. The defendant is not liable under the extended liability or transferred intent rule for emotional distress,[239] nor is he subject to liability for damages without proof of harm.

When the defendant causes emotional distress by inflicting an unconsented-to and unjustified touching, or by inflicting any trespassory tort, the plaintiff can claim emotional distress damages resulting from that tort, without proving the elements of tort called intentional infliction of emotional distress.[240] Some courts permit the plaintiff to sue for battery or other trespassory tort and also for intentional infliction of emotional distress, raising the possibility that a defense to one of the claims will not defeat the other.[241]

---

[236] 49 Prospect St. Tenants Ass'n v. Sheva Gardens, Inc., 227 N.J. Super. 449, 547 A.2d 1134 (1988).

[237] State Rubbish Collectors Ass'n v. Siliznoff, 38 Cal.2d 330, 240 P.2d 282 (1952).

[238] Id.; Dickens v. Puryear, 302 N.C. 437, 276 S.E.2d 325 (1981).

[239] Restatement Third of Torts (Intentional Torts to Persons) § 110(a) (Tentative Draft No. 1, Apr 8, 2015); Restatement Second of Torts § 46(2) & cmt. l (1965).

[240] Kant v. Altayar, 270 Neb. 501, 704 N.W.2d 537 (2005).

[241] See § 29.4.

Chapter 5

INTENTIONAL INTERFERENCE WITH REAL PROPERTY: TRESPASS TO LAND

Analysis

§ 5.1   Elements and Terminology
§ 5.2   Intent Required
§ 5.3   Distinguishing Trespass from Nuisance
§ 5.4   Protecting Interests in Possession and Physical Integrity
§ 5.5   Tangible Entry
§ 5.6   Entries Above the Surface
§ 5.7   Entries Below the Surface
§ 5.8   Remedies
§ 5.9   Temporary or Continuing Trespass vs. Permanent or Completed Trespass
§ 5.10   Extended Liability

---

§ 5.1   Elements and Terminology

One who intentionally enters or causes tangible entry upon the land in possession of another is a trespasser and liable for the tort of trespass, unless the entry is privileged or consented to.[1] Physical harm to the land is not required.[2] The gist of the tort is intentional interference with rights of exclusive possession; no other harm is required. In modern law, the defendant is a trespasser not only if he intentionally enters or causes entry, but also if he refuses to leave or remove his goods from the land when he is under an obligation to do so; hence a refusal to leave is equivalent to entry for this purpose.[3] One who has consent to be on the land may become a trespasser by exceeding the consent.[4] One who enters above[5] or below[6] the surface may also be a trespasser.

The term *trespass* is confusing because legal professionals use it in at least three quite different ways. First, the term refers to the tort, made up of facts and a set of rules. One commits the tort of trespass only when in addition to an entry or its equivalent, one has an intent to enter. To use the term trespass in this sense is to say that the trespass set of rules applies to determine the case and not, say, the set of rules invoked if the claim is for negligence or nuisance.

---

[1]   Consent will vitiate a claim for trespass. See, e.g., Lee v. Konrad, 337 P.3d 510 (Alaska 2014); N.L.R.B. v. Calkins, 187 F.3d 1080 (9th Cir. 1999). On consent generally, see Chapter 8.

[2]   See § 5.8.

[3]   Crawford v. French, 633 P.2d 524 (Colo. App. 1981) (refusal to remove materials); Suggs v. Carroll, 76 N.C. App. 420, 333 S.E.2d 510 (1985) (refusal to leave); Restatement Second of Torts § 158 (1965).

[4]   Brown v. Dellinger, 355 S.W.2d 742 (Tex. Civ. App. 1962); Restatement Second of Torts § 168 (1965). Consent might be restricted or conditional as to the area or as to activities on the land.

[5]   See § 5.6.

[6]   See § 5.7.

Second, the term sometimes refers only to the *fact* of entry on or harm to land rather than to the legal effect of an entry or the set of rules that attends the trespass theory. One can enter land without committing the tort of trespass, but it is possible, using the term in this second and more limited sense, to say the defendant trespassed on the plaintiff's land even when the tort of trespass was not committed. This explains why, confusing and unfortunate as it is, courts occasionally refer to a negligent trespass, meaning only a negligent entry.[7]

Third, the term trespass can refer to the form of action by the same name, the old writ of *Trespass* used in the earlier common law. The modern tort claim for trespass originated in that writ. Under its rules the plaintiff is not required to prove actual harm to the land or to persons or things on it;[8] interference with possession is itself an injury for which the plaintiff can recover at least nominal damages.[9] These rules still hold.

Trespass: the writ or form of action. Forms of the writ of *Trespass* were used for all claims resulting from direct use of force.[10] The form of the *Trespass* writ or the declaration used for trespass to land was known as *Trespass Quare Clausem Fregit*,[11] because it demanded that the defendant answer to the court wherefore he broke the close, that is, whether or why he entered the plaintiff's land, which was fictionally treated as if it were enclosed.

§ 5.2 Intent Required

The intent required to show a trespass to land is the intent[12] to enter[13] or to commit the equivalent of an entry. To cause an entry upon the land by another[14] or by an object,[15]

---

[7] For example, in this sentence the term trespass does not mean the tort of trespass to land but merely entry that is legally actionable on *any* ground: "A trespass may arise from an intrusion upon plaintiffs' land which is either intentional, negligent or the result of ultrahazardous conduct." Lunda v. Matthews, 46 Or. App. 701, 613 P.2d 63, 66 (1980). Although one may be liable for negligent harm to land, the set of rules that determine liability are quite different from those that determine trespass liability.

[8] Restatement Second of Torts § 163 (1965).

[9] Gross v. Capital Electric Line Builders, 253 Kan. 798, 861 P.2d 1326 (1993); Snow v. City of Columbia, 305 S.C. 544, 409 S.E.2d 797, 802 (Ct. App. 1991) ("Thus, for example if one . . . walks upon it, or casts a twig upon it, or pours a bucket of water upon it, he commits a trespass by the very act of breaking the enclosure. . . . The mere entry entitles the party in possession at least to nominal damages.").

[10] The old common law writ called *Trespass* directly or indirectly generated six torts—battery, assault, and false imprisonment on the personal side, trespass to land, conversion, and trespass to chattels on the property side. All of those torts entailed a direct application of force; that is, they invaded or threatened to invade the plaintiff's physical security of person or property. See § 2.8.

[11] Joseph Koffler & Alison Reppy, Common Law Pleading 155 (1969) (defendant "with force and arms broke and entered the close of the said [plaintiff] . . . and with his feet, in walking, trod down, trampled upon, consumed, and spoiled the grass and herbage . . . there growing, and being of great value, and other wrongs to the said [plaintiff] there did, to the damages of said [plaintiff] and against the peace of our lord the now king.").

[12] See Snow v. City of Columbia, 305 S.C. 544, 553, 409 S.E.2d 797, 802 (Ct. App. 1991) ("Although neither deliberation, purpose, motive, nor malice are necessary elements of intent, the defendant must intend the act which in law constitutes the invasion of the plaintiff's right. Trespass is an intentional tort; and while the trespasser, to be liable, need not intend or expect the damaging consequence of his entry, he must intend the act which constitutes the unwarranted entry on another's land.").

[13] Taft v. Ball, Ball & Brosamer, Inc., 169 Ariz. 173, 818 P.2d 158 (Ct. App. 1991); Restatement Second of Torts § 158 (1965). Early common law envisioned the plaintiff's land as an enclosed parcel and required an entry that "broke the close."

[14] E.g., Houston Lighting and Power Co. v. Sue, 644 S.W.2d 835 (Tex.App. 1982); Prahl v. Brosamle, 98 Wis.2d 130, 295 N.W.2d 768 (1980).

[15] Armitage v. Decker, 218 Cal.App.3d 887, 267 Cal.Rptr. 399 (1990); see also Ondovchik Family Ltd. P'ship v. Agency of Transp., 187 Vt. 556, 996 A.2d 1179 (2010) (moving snow onto another's land without consent can constitute trespass, but defendant was privileged to move snow off highway onto plaintiff's land).

to remain upon the land after a privilege to be there has terminated,[16] to exceed the permitted use of the land,[17] and to refuse to remove goods or materials left there[18] are all equivalent to entry under modern law.

Intent to harm not required. Since intent to enter is sufficient, the plaintiff need not show an intent to cause harm or even to invade the plaintiff's possessory rights.[19] Thus one who intends to and does enter a parcel of land in the mistaken belief that it is his own land or that he has a right to be there is nonetheless a technical trespasser and liable for nominal damages[20] and any actual harm done.[21] Even a child can be a trespasser if he has the intent to enter another's land, or a part of the land not permitted to him.[22]

Harm without intent. The intent rule, however, does not subject the plaintiff to liability for unintended harm when he is rightfully on the land. The negative import of the intent rule is that the defendant is not liable for trespass when he enters by negligence, by accident, or without an act of his own.[23] For example, if he is carried onto the land against his will,[24] if his car goes out of control and runs onto the land,[25] or if his golf game is bad and he slices a ball into the plaintiff's house,[26] the defendant is no trespasser.[27] In such cases, the defendant will be liable only if he is shown to have been negligent in causing the harm.

Scope of the intent requirement. The requirement of intent applies only to the trespass claim; the plaintiff is still free to prove, if she can, that the defendant who lacked

---

[16] Metromedia Co. v. WCBM Maryland, Inc., 327 Md. 514, 610 A.2d 791 (1992) ("An occupancy rightful because permissive becomes tortious when a proper demand to vacate is ignored and it is then the occupants become trespassers and damages for their wrongful occupancy begin to accrue.").

[17] For example, grazing cattle on public lands in excess of the permitted use is viewed as a "trespass." See John S. Harbison, Hohfeld and Herefords: The Concept of Property and the Law of the Range, 22 N.M. L. Rev. 459 (1992).

[18] See Hector v. Metro Centers, Inc., 498 N.W.2d 113 (N.D. 1993); Crawford v. French, 633 P.2d 524 (Colo.App. 1981).

[19] See, e.g., Baugh v. CBS, Inc., 828 F. Supp. 745, 756 (N.D Cal. 1993).

[20] See § 5.8.

[21] Miller v. National Broadcasting Co., 187 Cal.App.3d 1463, 232 Cal.Rptr. 668, 69 A.L.R.4th 1027 (1986) (trial court erred in exonerating intrusive NBC camera crew because it had no malice; intent to enter is enough); Kopka v. Bell Telephone Co. of Pa., 371 Pa. 444, 91 A.2d 232 (1952); Restatement Second of Torts § 164 (1965). The Restatement recognizes other mistakes as well and takes the position that none of them affect the defendant's liability if he entered the land intentionally. Good faith of the trespasser usually operates (a) to exclude punitive damages, see § 5.8, and (b) in the mining context to prevent use of harsh measures of damages. See Reynolds v. Pardee & Curtin Lumber Co., 172 W.Va. 804, 310 S.E.2d 870 (1983).

[22] Farm Bureau Mutual Ins. Co. of Arkansas, Inc. v. Henley, 275 Ark. 122, 628 S.W.2d 301 (1982) (two 6-year-olds); Brown v. Dellinger, 355 S.W.2d 742 (Tex.Civ.App. 1962) (7- and 8-year-olds); Cleveland Park Club v. Perry, 165 A.2d 485 (D.C.Munc.Ct.App. 1960) (9-year-old).

[23] Phillips v. Sun Oil Co., 307 N.Y. 328, 121 N.E.2d 249 (1954). Inaction, though allegedly certain to lead to landslides from defendant's property that would damage homes below, was not enough to count as an act in Price v. City of Seattle, 106 Wash.App. 647, 24 P.3d 1098 (2001).

[24] Smith v. Stone, Style 65, 82 Eng. Rep. 533 (K.B. 1647).

[25] Hawke v. Maus, 141 Ind. App. 126, 226 N.E.2d 713 (1967); Smith v. Pate, 246 N.C. 63, 97 S.E.2d 457 (1957).

[26] Malouf v. Dallas Athletic Country Club, 837 S.W.2d 674 (Tex.App. 1992).

[27] He may intrude upon the land and since "trespass" can be used nontechnically to mean intrusion as a matter of fact, it is possible to say that one negligently trespasses. But such a one is not a trespasser in the legal sense that the trespass rules apply. The negligent intruder, for example, is liable only if he causes harm, while the trespasser is liable whether harm results or not. See Restatement Second of Torts § 165 (1965).

intent to enter was nevertheless negligent in causing a harmful entry,[28] or else that he is subject to strict liability for abnormally dangerous activities.[29] However, if the plaintiff must rely upon a negligence or abnormal danger theory rather than upon a trespass theory, she must prove not only that the defendant was in fact negligent, but also that the plaintiff suffered actual damages, not merely an interference with technical possession.

The term intent in trespass to land cases means what it means in other torts.[30] The defendant intends an entry if it is his purpose to enter. He also intends an entry if he knows that his actions make entry substantially certain.[31] The defendant who releases his hounds for the fox hunt adjacent to the plaintiff's croplands may know to a virtual certainty that they will run on the plaintiff's land; if so, the defendant has the requisite intent and is liable as a trespasser.[32]

Strict liability for trespass. Since the intent required to show a trespass is only an intent to enter land, and since that intent might be wholly innocent, the rules may sometimes impose a limited kind of strict liability. But this appearance may be somewhat misleading.

One possible case of theoretical strict liability is that of the innocent trespasser who enters the land in the reasonable belief that he has a right to be there. But in today's world, suit is unlikely to be brought at all if the defendant is a casual trespasser rather than one who claims a right to be on the land. On the other hand, if the trespasser claims the land as his own, his liability may still be nominal and it may serve to establish the plaintiff's title or right to possession at a cost to the defendant essentially no different from the cost he would incur if a declaratory judgment or some other suit were brought to obtain a judicial determination of the parties' rights. If this is strict liability, not much is to be made of it.

A second possible case of theoretical strict liability occurs if the trespasser exploits the land or its resources in the innocent and reasonable belief that he is entitled to do so. But in that case the trespasser himself has made a gain from the trespass and liability for that enrichment derived from another's property is appropriate, quite apart from tort law and regardless of his innocence.

A third kind of case that might impose strict liability for trespass to land involves harms to land caused by the defendant's use of explosives or other high energy sources, as where the defendant's blasting with dynamite throws stones or debris onto the plaintiff's land. Strict liability was once imposed in such cases, sometimes on a trespass theory.[33] Strict liability is still imposed on the same facts, but the cases are no longer

---

[28]   E.g, Pennsylvania R. Co. v. City of Pittsburgh, 335 Pa. 449, 6 A.2d 907 (1939). Since the term trespass is sometimes used loosely to mean an entry upon land or a harm to it, courts occasionally speak of a negligent trespass, meaning only a negligent entry upon land that causes harm. The phrase is nonsensical when the term trespass is defined to require intent.

[29]   See Chapter 32.

[30]   See §§ 4.2 to 4.5.

[31]   See City of Bristol v. Tilcon Minerals, Inc., 284 Conn. 55, 931 A.2d 237 (2007); Cover v. Phillips Pipe Line Co., 454 S.W.2d 507 (Mo. 1970).

[32]   Pegg v. Gray, 240 N.C. 548, 82 S.E.2d 757 (1954). Note that the defendant might be liable for negligence if he merely took a risk that the hounds would enter the plaintiff's lands and if actual harm were inflicted. Cf. Ream v. Keen, 314 Or. 370, 838 P.2d 1073 (1992) (defendant would be liable for trespass where he knew smoke from burning field would drift onto the plaintiff's property).

[33]   E.g., Green v. General Petroleum Corp., 205 Cal. 328, 270 P.2d 952, 60 A.L.R. 475 (1928); Mulchanock v. Whitehall Cement Mfg. Co., 253 Pa. 262, 98 A. 554 (1916).

perceived as trespass to land cases. Instead, trespass is seen as an accidental or unimportant feature in the cases, which are viewed as turning on the defendant's abnormally dangerous activity.[34] Liability is strict whether the resulting harm is a trespass to land or an injury to the person.[35] The result is that trespass itself generates little or no strict liability.[36]

§ 5.3   Distinguishing Trespass from Nuisance

Trespass is one of the two major tort claims that aim to protect plaintiffs from interference with interests in land; the other is nuisance.[37] The topic of nuisance is worthy of separate treatment and gets a chapter of its own in this treatise.[38] But it can be difficult to explain modern trespass law without references to nuisance, and many cases implicate both claims. Accordingly, a brief exploration of some of the differences and similarities between the two causes of action follows here, and references to nuisance appear at several points in succeeding sections of this chapter.

Trespass and nuisance are different causes of action with different elements, but they are not mutually exclusive.[39] That is, a single act of the defendant could be both a trespass and a nuisance.[40] On the other hand, a trespass is not always a nuisance and vice versa.[41] The clearest way to draw the distinction is to focus on the different interests protected by each tort; the nature of the interest or interests invaded will thus determine whether the defendant can be liable on a trespass theory or a nuisance theory, or both.[42]

As is more fully delineated below, trespass protects a plaintiff's right to *exclusive possession* of land. Nuisance, on the other hand, protects a plaintiff's *use and enjoyment* of land.[43] To invoke the law of nuisance is to invoke a regime of accommodation between conflicting land uses. The noise from your radio bothers me, but it is not a trespass

---

[34]   See § 32.6.

[35]   Even the older cases extend strict liability to personal injuries on a public highway when they resulted from blasting. Sullivan v. Durham, 161 N.Y. 290, 55 N.E. 923 (1900).

[36]   The most significant possibility for strict liability based on trespass (as distinct from that based on grounds of abnormally dangerous activity) arises under the extended liability rule discussed in § 58.

[37]   Other tort rules affecting rights in real property include ejectment (which gives the plaintiff possession of the land from a trespasser who has gone into possession and allows for recovery of *mesne profits*, see 1 Dan B. Dobbs, Law of Remedies §§ 4.2(2), 5.8(2), 5.10(1) (2d ed. 1993)), negligence, and federal civil rights laws (where the trespass is committed under color of state law), see Monroe v. Pape, 365 U.S. 167, 81 S.Ct. 473, 5 L.Ed.2d 492 (1961), *overruled on other grounds,* Monell v. Dep't of Soc. Servs. of City of N.Y., 436 U.S. 658, 98 S.Ct. 2018, 56 L.Ed.2d 611 (1978).

[38]   See Chapter 30.

[39]   See Restatement Second of Torts § 821D, cmt. e (1979); Cook v. DeSoto Fuels, Inc., 169 S.W.3d 94 (Mo. App. 2005) ("[W]hile there are differences between a trespass and a nuisance cause of action, the two are neither mutually exclusive nor inconsistent. Thus where the elements of both actions are fully present, plaintiffs may choose to proceed upon one or both theories."); Traver Lakes Community Maintenance Ass'n v. Douglas Co., 224 Mich.App. 335, 568 N.W.2d 847 (1997) ("claims of trespass and nuisance are difficult to distinguish and include overlapping concepts").

[40]   E.g., Canton v. Graniteville Fire Dist. No. 4, 171 Vt. 551, 762 A.2d 808 (2000) (release of water from quarry onto landowner's property both a trespass and a nuisance).

[41]   E.g., Wilson v. Interlake Steel Co., 32 Cal.3d 229, 649 P.2d 922, 185 Cal.Rptr. 280 (1982) (intrusion of noise waves not a trespass but might be a nuisance).

[42]   Martin v. Reynolds Metals Co., 221 Or. 86, 342 P.2d 790 (1959) ("The same conduct on the part of a defendant may and often does result in the actionable invasion of both of these interests" and thus constitutes both a nuisance and a trespass); Rancho Viejo, LLC v. Tres Amigos Viejos, LLC, 100 Cal.App.4th 550, 123 Cal.Rptr.2d 479 (2002) ("Thus, many activities will give rise to liability both as trespass and a nuisance, if they result in the violation of a person's right of exclusive possession of the land, and also constitute an unreasonable and substantial interference with the use and enjoyment of land.").

[43]   See Babb v. Lee Cnty. Landfill SC, LLC, 405 S.C. 129, 747 S.E.2d 468 (2014).

because it does not interfere with my possession. Courts seek accommodation in such cases by considering the reasonableness and amount of the intrusion. If the noise is too loud or too long, it may be a nuisance, otherwise not. On the other hand, the law of trespass is a law of rights that does not depend upon reasonableness except with certain defenses. Trespass is not traditionally a matter of a lot or a little; it is a yes-or-no kind of tort. If the defendant has committed an act equivalent to an intentional entry and the plaintiff is a possessor, then, prima facie, a trespass has occurred.

Another oft-cited distinction between trespass and nuisance is that trespass deals with *tangible* interferences,[44] whereas nuisance deals primarily with *intangible* ones.[45] Thus in the radio example above, another reason why the defendant's annoying blare is not a trespass is because it is not a tangible interference with my property rights.[46] This distinction perhaps follows logically from the more fundamental idea that while tangible entries onto land may interfere with possession, intangible entries seldom do.

The trespass to land rules are clear and work well in the simple paradigm on which they were built: the defendant walks or rides onto the plaintiff's land. The trespass to land rules are also clear when the variations on that paradigm are insubstantial: the defendant drives his cattle onto the land. But trespass rules may become too inflexible or difficult to apply when the entry is by smoke or pollution,[47] the migration of underground liquids, the growth of tree roots, or high overflights by aircraft.[48] In all those cases, courts have often put aside the trespass theory and analyzed the case on different terms, usually as a potential nuisance.

The line between nuisance and trespass has never been precisely marked, and some modern cases have blurred it further by characterizing the intrusion of harmful microscopic particles as trespasses rather than as nuisances and then by using some of the techniques of nuisance law to weigh the amount and reasonableness of the intrusion.[49]

§ 5.4 Protecting Interests in Possession and Physical Integrity

Interests protected. The common law recognizes and protects two major kinds of rights or interests in land from direct invasion by physical forces: (1) The right to exclusive possession of land; that is, the right to exclude others from the land,[50] somewhat analogous to the right of a person to prohibit touchings by others. (2) The right of physical integrity of the land itself; that is, the right to prevent others from doing physical harm to or taking any part of the land, such as trees or minerals.[51]

---

[44]   See § 5.5.

[45]   Some tangible entries, such as those by water, may be actionable as nuisances where they interfere with use and enjoyment of land. See § 5.5 and Chapter 30.

[46]   See Wilson v. Interlake Steel Co., 32 Cal.3d 229, 649 P.2d 922, 185 Cal.Rptr. 280 (1982) ("noise waves that are merely bothersome and not damaging . . . must be dealt with as a nuisance" and cannot constitute a trespass because it is an intangible intrusion).

[47]   See § 5.5.

[48]   See § 5.6.

[49]   See §§ 5.5 & 30.2. Indeed, some courts have asserted that on such facts the "law of trespass and the law of nuisance come very close to merging." Martin v. Reynolds Metals Co., 221 Or. 86, 342 P.2d 790 (1959).

[50]   E.g., Allred v. Harris, 14 Cal.App.4th 1386, 1390, 18 Cal.Rptr.2d 530, 533 (1993).

[51]   The main issue in many cases, including trespass cases, is the measure of damages for physical harm to land or severance of minerals or timber. E.g., Dethloff v. Zeigler Coal Co., 82 Ill.2d 393, 412 N.E.2d 526 (1980) (coal).

Protecting possession. The right to sue for the tort of trespass was originally conceived as a means of protecting the exclusive possession of one on the land. Accordingly, courts today hold that in order to maintain a suit for trespass, the plaintiff must either have had legal title to the land, or legal possession of the land, when the trespass occurred.[52] The plaintiff need not be an owner in fee; any legal, possessory interest will suffice. For instance, a tenant in possession has a claim for a trespassory entry.[53] Even an adverse possessor of the land might have a claim against a mere trespasser.[54] The owner of vacant land is accounted the possessor and hence has standing to sue the trespasser.[55] However, the owner of an easement—who has only a right to use the land, not a possessory interest in it—has no claim for trespass interfering with possession.[56]

Protecting physical integrity of the land; the owner's reversionary interests. If the entry also causes harm to the land's physical integrity that reduces the value of the owner's interests as well as the possessor's, today's law will also allow the owner to recover for any actual damages he will ultimately suffer. For instance, if the trespasser enters a tenant's apartment, the tenant has an action for trespass; if the trespasser rips the door off, the landlord who must repair it has an action for the damages resulting whether the theory is one of *trespass* or of *case*.[57]

To say that the owner's claim is in *case* rather than *trespass* implies three things: (1) The owner, as distinct from the possessor, will have an action only if the trespass causes actual harm to the owner's interest. Mere interference with possession is not itself enough. (2) The owner would be required to prove fault with respect to the damages he claims. That might mean that the trespasser's intent to enter, if innocent, would not support the owner's claim for actual damages. That result is consistent with the argument that "transferred intent" should not apply in the absence of fault.[58] (3) The trespass statute of limitations is inappropriate so that some other, possibly shorter statute would apply.[59]

Wrongful possessor's suit against the owner. As will appear,[60] a landowner who is in possession of the land is privileged to use reasonable force to defend the land against trespass by others. When another person has come into possession of the land, however, the landowner's use of force to regain possession has long been proscribed by statute[61] in the belief that even reasonable force asserted by the owner will beget violence. It is thus theoretically possible for a wrongful possessor to recover from the true owner who

---

[52]   City of Bristol v. Tilcon Minerals, Inc., 284 Conn. 55, 931 A.2d 237 (2007).

[53]   Indian Bayou Hunting Club, Inc. v. Taylor, 261 So.2d 669 (La. App. 1972); Neilan v. Braun, 354 N.W.2d 856 (Minn. App. 1984).

[54]   Spring Valley Estates, Inc. v. Cunningham, 181 Colo. 435, 438, 510 P.2d 336, 338 (1973) ("from the beginning of his possession period, an adverse possessor has an interest in a given piece of property enforceable against everyone *except* the owner or one claiming through the owner."); Myrick v. Bishop, 8 N.C. 485, 486 (1821).

[55]   E.g., Waters v. Dennis Simmons Lumber Co., 154 N.C. 232, 70 S.E. 284 (1911).

[56]   See P & A Construction, Inc. v. Hackensack Water Co., 115 N.J. Super. 550, 280 A.2d 497 (1971); see also Greenpeace, Inc. v. Dow Chemical Co., 97 A.3d 1053 (D.C. 2014) (plaintiff had no possessory interest in common trash and recycling areas of office building in which it was a tenant and thus could not maintain a trespass claim).

[57]   Smith v. Cap Concrete, 133 Cal.App.3d 769, 184 Cal.Rptr. 308 (1982).

[58]   See § 5.10.

[59]   See AmSouth Bank, N.A. v. City of Mobile, 500 So.2d 1072 (Ala. 1986).

[60]   See § 7.8.

[61]   Since 1381, with the statute of 5 Richard II, c. 8.

attempts to recover the property by force. The scope of this rule depends primarily upon the owner's privilege, or lack thereof, to retake the property.[62]

§ 5.5   Tangible Entry

Intrusion. Entry upon the land, or the equivalent to entry upon land, is definitionally essential to the tort of trespass. Actions outside the land that do not cause intrusions upon it may sometimes warrant liability, as where the adjoining landowner's excavation of his own soil allows the plaintiff's soil to subside.[63] But they are not trespasses because no intrusion has taken place. Courts sometimes speak loosely in such cases, using the term trespass to refer to any case of harms to land rather than to cases that would be actionable only because intent and entry are shown.[64]

Tangible intrusion. Because the action for trespass was conceived as a means of protecting possession, a tangible entry upon the land has been traditionally required. Anything less than a tangible entry, such as penetration of the land by smoke, noise, or light, might affect use and enjoyment (thus constituting nuisance), but it would not affect possession.[65] If the defendant who caused air pollution was guilty of any tort at all, it was not the tort of trespass.[66]

The rule requiring tangible entry for a trespass remains sound today, and reflects ancient history reinforced by contemporary policy. Pollution, noise, gases, unpleasant sights, and dangerous conditions such as stored explosives can all reduce one's enjoyment of land, but courts have been unwilling to say that a landowner would have a claim for damages any time she heard a noise or smelled burning leaves. The policy view is that the law of trespass with its automatic responsibility for any purposeful or certain entry would produce too much liability.[67] It provides no mechanism for limiting liability to serious or substantial invasions. If smoke drifting onto the plaintiff's land were held to be a trespass, even a little smoke would count. The law of nuisance is therefore better suited to such cases.[68]

Waters and liquids. Trespass law has also proved too inflexible in many cases involving intruding waters. States differ in their formal rules about liability for surface waters cast upon the plaintiff's land, but, whether on a nuisance theory or not, the courts'

---

[62]   See § 7.13.

[63]   Removal of lateral or subjacent support subjects the defendant to strict liability as well as to liability for negligence. See Restatement Second of Torts §§ 817 to 821 (1979).

[64]   Nida v. American Rock Crusher Co., 253 Kan. 230, 855 P.2d 81 (1993).

[65]   See, e.g., Babb v. Lee Cnty. Landfill SC, LLC, 405 S.C. 129, 747 S.E.2d 468 (2013). The "intrusion" of airborne particulates onto land has caused something of a split among courts with respect to classification of the claim. Compare, e.g., Johnson v. Paynesville Farmers Union Co-op. Oil Co., 817 N.W.2d 693 (Minn. 2012) (pesticide drift did not constitute a trespass, because trespass requires an intrusion by "people or tangible objects") with Borland v. Sanders Lead Co., 369 So.2d 523 (Ala. 1979) (allowing trespass claim where intangible invasion causes substantial damage to plaintiff's property).

[66]   San Diego Gas & Elec. Co. v. Superior Court, 13 Cal.4th 893, 920 P.2d 669, 55 Cal.Rptr.2d 724 (1996) (to permit trespass as distinct from nuisance action, there must be a "deposit of particulate matter upon the plaintiffs' property or an actual physical damage thereto," hence intrusion of electrical fields without damage is not a trespass).

[67]   Public Service Co. of Colorado v. Van Wyk, 27 P.3d 377 (Colo. 2001), gave this as one reason for insisting that intangible invasions would be actionable as trespasses only if they produced harm to the land, not merely interference with use and enjoyment. Accord, Larkin v. Marceau, 184 Vt. 207, 959 A.2d 551 (2008).

[68]   See Chapter 30. Under the law of nuisance, courts could reject liability for, say, smoke that blows across the plaintiff's land, if the smoke did not much interfere with the plaintiff's enjoyment and if it would be costly or difficult for the defendant to avoid it; at the same time, it could impose liability if the smoke operated as a substantial and serious interference.

tendency is to permit both parties maximum reasonable use so that an intrusion of waters is actionable when it is unreasonable or when independent grounds for strict liability exist, otherwise not.[69] If the defendant's dam breaks, causing downstream flooding, the defendant may be liable for trespass if he intentionally caused the waters to enter the plaintiff's property.[70] Otherwise, his liability is for negligence or nuisance.[71]

Similarly, courts are likely to hold that the trespass theory invokes the wrong set of rules for riparian flooding. They instead incline toward nuisance or negligence theories to invoke rules requiring proof of unreasonable actions by the defendant or separate grounds for strict liability.[72]

Underground liquids that seep into the plaintiff's soil and cause harm represent still another category. Although courts sometimes speak of "trespass" in the underground pollution cases,[73] their actual approach often more closely resembles the reasonableness approach of nuisance law in which the courts see maximum freedom for the legitimate interests of both landowners.[74] Nuisance or negligence rather than trespass is definitely the approach courts take when liquids percolate underground to enter the plaintiff's land beneath the surface.[75]

§ 5.6   Entries Above the Surface

Possessory interests are not limited to the surface of the land. Possessory interests may include chattels, structures, and growth on the land. They also include the right to exclusive possession of reasonably usable airspace above the ground[76] as well as space below the surface.[77] It is a trespass to intrude upon non-navigable waters upon the land,[78] to fire a bullet across it,[79] to maintain a utility line above it,[80] or even to extend an arm into the airspace.[81] Put the other way around, the owner has the right to the

---

[69] Pendergrast v. Aiken, 293 N.C. 201, 236 S.E.2d 787 (1977). States use three different formal doctrines. (1) The common enemy rule treats unwanted surface waters as a common enemy, so that each landowner is free to dispose of them as best he can. (2) The civil law rule is largely the reverse; no landowner is free to alter natural drainage. These two rules are often modified in practice and at times tend to resemble (3) the reasonable use rule under which landowners are free to alter their own natural drainage to the plaintiff's detriment until that alteration causes unreasonable interference. See Janet Fairchild, Annotation, Modern status of rules governing interference with drainage of surface waters, 93 A.L.R.3d 1193 (1979).

[70] Cf. Canton v. Graniteville Fire Dist. No. 4, 171 Vt. 551, 762 A.2d 808 (2000) (an upper property owner who intentionally changes the flow of surface water passing onto lower lands may be found liable for trespass in a suit by the lower landowner).

[71] See Cooper v. Horn, 248 Va. 417, 448 S.E.2d 403 (1994).

[72] Ellis v. Alabama Power Co., 431 So.2d 1242 (Ala. 1983) (dam operator discharging waters in accord with Corps of Engineers flood control plan; liability for release of water must be predicated upon negligence, not trespass); Kunz v. Utah Power & Light Co., 117 Idaho 901, 792 P.2d 926 (1990).

[73] E.g., Cassinos v. Union Oil Co. of California, 14 Cal.App.4th 1770, 18 Cal.Rptr.2d 574 (1993).

[74] The Restatement treats interference with the flow of surface waters as a nuisance issue, not a trespass issue. Restatement Second of Torts § 833 (1979). Interference with one's rights to *use* water of course raises an entirely different issue. See Id. §§ 850–864. Water rights are now an important form of property law and subject to considerable regulation.

[75] See, e.g., Norman v. Greenland Drilling Co., 403 P.2d 507 (Okla. 1965).

[76] See generally Robert R. Wright, The Law of Airspace (1968).

[77] Restatement Second of Torts § 159 (1965).

[78] Steel Creek Development Corp. v. James, 58 N.C.App. 506, 294 S.E.2d 23 (1982).

[79] Whittaker v. Stangvick, 100 Minn. 386, 111 N.W. 295 (1907).

[80] United States v. Gates of the Mountains Lakeshore Homes, Inc., 732 F.2d 1411 (9th Cir. 1984).

[81] Kenney v. Barna, 215 Neb. 863, 341 N.W.2d 901 (1983).

exclusive use of the airspace. She may simply enjoy possession of the space, or, unless zoning rules or covenants prohibit it, she may erect tall buildings or sell the airspace.[82]

Qualifications. Ownership of airspace is qualified by the traditional rule that intangible intrusions like smoke are not trespassory.[83] It is also qualified somewhat by the practice of courts to treat natural intrusions of tree limbs or roots under rules like those for nuisance rather than under the rules of trespass. The victim of a leafy intrusion may usually lop off the leaf and branch at the property line, but she has no action for damages based on the intrusion alone.[84]

The development of aircraft, especially powered aircraft, raised substantial questions about airspace rights. The traditional view of land ownership was expressed as a maxim, *cujus est solum ejus est utque ad coelum*, one who owns the surface owns "up to the heavens." The statement is a literary view of the law and the cosmos, not a technical one. No one "possesses" the upper reaches of airspace, of course, but the maxim clouded all analysis of the problem. The expansive terms of the maxim herded thought into two channels: first, the rights of the owner extended infinitely upward; second, the problem was one of ownership and trespass law. Neither proposition seems sound. Very low overflights can interfere with possession; some of them may be close to the simple trespass paradigm. Sometimes trespass liability has been imposed or recognized in such cases, at least where the flights actually interfere with existing possession.[85] But most of the problems lie with higher flights, with the special problems of airport takeoffs and landings, or with low flights over unoccupied land that interferes with nothing. For these problem cases, many different versions of a trespass rule have been developed, but no firm rule has emerged.[86]

For most problem flights, the known or foreseeable harm done to the plaintiff is a better index to the justice of the case than the mere entry into a column of air. Thus nuisance law, which explicitly limits the landowner's rights to reasonable use and enjoyment,[87] is likely to provide better access to appropriate considerations of justice and policy. A pure trespass analysis would merely ask whether the plane intruded in the airspace, while nuisance law is concerned with a reasonable accommodation of the conflicting interests. Under nuisance rules, some noisy flights might be actionable even if they don't actually overfly the plaintiff's land, while some less troublesome flights might be permissible even if they do. Nuisance rules likewise permit degrees of accommodation, for example, by limiting the number of flights over the plaintiff's land rather than barring all of them.[88]

The Second Restatement purports to address the problem as one of trespass, but in fact invokes some ideas of nuisance law. It provides that overflights are trespasses if (a) they are in the "immediate reaches" of the land *and* (b) they interfere with use and

---

[82] The fee in land may be divided by the owner, who can sell airspace above it or interests in minerals below the surface. See Cheape v. Town of Chapel Hill, 320 N.C. 549, 359 S.E.2d 792 (1987) (air rights).

[83] See § 5.5.

[84] The remedy is usually limited to self-help of the limb-lopping variety, although there may be liability for nuisance where actual harm is proved. See Lane v. W.J. Curry & Sons, 92 S.W.3d 355 (Tenn. 2002).

[85] Hinman v. Pacific Air Lines Transport, 84 F.2d 755 (9th Cir. 1936); United States v. Gaidys, 194 F.2d 762 (10th Cir. 1952).

[86] See Colin Cahoon, Comment, Low Altitude Airspace: A Property Rights No-Man's Land, 56 J. Air L. & Com. 157 (1990) (summarizing several theories).

[87] See Chapter 30.

[88] See Atkinson v. Bernard, Inc., 223 Or. 624, 355 P.2d 229 (1960).

enjoyment.[89] By substituting use and enjoyment for possession, the Restatement in effect tacitly supports at least a partial nuisance analysis.[90] Nuisance analysis may also conform better to federal regulations, which define navigable airspace for aviation purposes and which may be inconsistent with liability for a mere technical trespass, but consistent with liability for actual interference with use and enjoyment.[91]

§ 5.7   Entries Below the Surface

Subsurface trespass. According to the traditional maxim, the landowner owns to the depths as well as to the heavens. Just as intrusions in the immediate airspace above land are trespasses, so are intrusions immediately below its surface, so long as they are intended and without permission. If the defendant mines beneath the plaintiff's land, he is clearly a trespasser.[92] He is also a trespasser if the foundation of his house projects into the plaintiff's land below the surface,[93] or his television cable or his sewer lies beneath the plaintiff's land.[94] In one well-known case, a natural cave lay beneath the land of both the plaintiff and the defendant. The only entrance, however, was on the defendant's land, so that the plaintiff could not have used the cave at all. Nevertheless, the defendant was held liable when he used that part of the cave below the plaintiff's land.[95]

Percolation of liquids underground. Subsurface pollution of water or oil reserves may be regarded as a trespass in some cases. In a California case,[96] the defendant disposed of waste water in a way that contaminated the plaintiff's underground oil. This was regarded as a trespass and actionable on that ground. But migration or percolation of wastes beneath the surface is often considered to be in the domain of nuisance law rather than the domain of trespass.[97] Tree roots that penetrate a neighbor's soil have also been accorded treatment more in line with the milder demands of nuisance law.[98]

Remote intrusions. Remote entries, far underground or far above it, have become technologically feasible. That feasibility challenges the traditional rule which suggests infinite extension of possessory rights above and below the ground just as the airplane challenged the corresponding rule above ground. It seems likely that courts will respond pragmatically. A tunnel hundreds of feet below the surface that does not affect the value

---

[89]   Restatement Second of Torts § 159 (1965).

[90]   Courts in fact have often seemed to confuse the concepts and the rules attached to each. See Robert R. Wright, The Law of Airspace 164 (1968).

[91]   See Jack L. Litwin, Annotation, Airport operations or flight of aircraft as nuisance, 79 A.L.R.3d 253 (1977).

[92]   Killam v. Texas Oil & Gas Corp., 303 Ark. 547, 798 S.W.2d 419 (1990); Maye v. Yappen, 23 Cal. 306 (1863) (gold mine). Rights in underground waters, petroleum, and gas are now frequently regulated by statute in ways that change the traditional rights, often in favor of conservation for mutual advantage.

[93]   509 Sixth Avenue Corp. v. New York City Transit Authority, 15 N.Y.2d 48, 203 N.E.2d 486, 255 N.Y.S.2d 89, 12 A.L.R.3d 1258 (1964).

[94]   Neely v. Coffey, 81 Ill.2d 439, 410 N.E.2d 839 (1980).

[95]   Edwards v. Lee's Adm'r, 265 Ky. 418, 96 S.W.2d 1028 (1936) (defendant made commercial use of the cave; the plaintiff was permitted to recover the profits resulting from the underground trespass). As to profits award, the case was overruled or limited in Triple Elkhorn Min. Co. v. Anderson, 646 S.W.2d 725 (Ky. 1983).

[96]   Cassinos v. Union Oil Co. of California, 14 Cal.App.4th 1770, 18 Cal.Rptr.2d 574 (1993).

[97]   Cambridge Water Co. Ltd. v. Eastern Counties Leather, [1994] 2 W.L.R. 53, [1994] 1 All ER 53 (H.L.) (migration of chemical wastes from a tannery polluted the plaintiff's water wells many miles away; this was regarded as a potential nuisance, although no liability was imposed).

[98]   Cannon v. Dunn, 145 Ariz. 115, 700 P.2d 502 (Ct. App. 1985); Garcia v. Sanchez, 108 N.M. 388, 772 P.2d 1311 (Ct. App. 1989); see also Lane v. W.J. Curry & Sons, 92 S.W.3d 355 (Tenn. 2002) (holding that the remedy was not limited to self-help where a nuisance is established by proof of harm or imminent harm).

of the land or remove minerals probably should not be regarded as a trespass.[99] In one case where the defendant injected industrial wastes far below the surface of its land and they migrated to a position below the surface of the plaintiff's land, the Ohio Supreme Court denied the plaintiff's trespass claim, saying that "ownership rights in today's world are not so clear-cut as they were before the advent of airplanes and injection wells."[100]

§ 5.8   Remedies

Injunctive Relief

Injunctive relief. Courts will issue injunctions to prevent trespasses that threaten to continue or to be repeated. Thus an owner or possessor of property may be able to obtain an injunction to stop trespassing picketers[101] or to force a trespasser to remove a thing or a substance tortiously placed on the land.[102] A person who constructs a building that encroaches on the plaintiff's property may be subject to an injunction ordering him to remove it.[103] As is true with most claims, the plaintiff in a trespass case must generally prove that the legal remedy of damages is inadequate in order to obtain an injunction.[104]

Damages

General principles. More commonly, however, the trespasser is liable for damages. A plaintiff need not allege a physical harm to state a trespass claim.[105] That means that a trespasser is always liable to the possessor for at least nominal damages for the intrusion upon possession.[106] So far as he occupies the land, he is liable for the rental value of its use;[107] somewhat similarly, he may be held for gains he makes directly from use of the land or its resources.[108] He is, of course, liable for other torts he commits in the course of a trespass.

Harm to rights of physical integrity. For any actual harm done to the land, or to things or people upon the land, he is also liable to the possessor or the owner as their interests appear. In the usual case, his liability is measured by the diminution in value of the land resulting from the trespass,[109] or, in some cases, by the reasonable costs of making repairs or restoring the land.

The general principle is that "damages may cover the loss or injury sustained and no more."[110] This means that courts typically will not allow recovery of the diminution

---

[99]   Cf. Application of Gillespie, 173 Misc. 591, 17 N.Y.S.2d 560 (Sup. Ct. 1940) (tunnel 500 feet below ground, nominal damages only).

[100]   Chance v. BP Chemicals, 77 Ohio St.3d 17, 670 N.E.2d 985 (1996). The court used the language of trespass but it required the kind of substantial injury usually associated with nuisance claims.

[101]   E.g., Church of Christ in Hollywood v. Superior Court, 99 Cal.App.4th 1244, 121 Cal.Rptr.2d 810 (2002); Charleston Joint Venture v. McPherson, 308 S.C. 145, 417 S.E.2d 544 (1992).

[102]   E.g., West Town Plaza Assocs. v. Wal-Mart Stores, Inc., 619 So.2d 1290 (Ala. 1993); Walsh v. Johnston, 608 A.2d 776 (Me. 1992).

[103]   Rose Nulman Park Foundation v. Four Twenty Corp., 93 A.3d 25 (R.I. 2014).

[104]   See, e.g., Lambert v. Holmberg, 271 Neb. 443, 712 N.W.2d 268 (2006).

[105]   E.g., College of Charleston Foundation v. Ham, 585 F.Supp.2d 737 (D.S.C. 2008).

[106]   Neely v. Coffey, 81 Ill.2d 439, 410 N.E.2d 839 (1980); Gross v. Capital Electric Line Builders, Inc., 253 Kan. 798, 861 P.2d 1326 (1993). Nominal damages are damages in name only, usually $1 or six cents, but such an award likely makes the plaintiff a "prevailing party" entitled to recover statutory costs.

[107]   Scribner v. Summers, 138 F.3d 471 (2d Cir. 1998).

[108]   1 Dan B. Dobbs, Law of Remedies § 5.9 (2d ed. 1993).

[109]   See Id., § 5.2; Smith v. Carbide and Chem. Corp., 226 S.W.3d 52 (Ky. 2007).

[110]   Estate of De Laveaga, 50 Cal.2d 480, 326 P.2d 129 (1958).

in value if the cost of repairing the property and restoring it to its original condition amounts to less than that diminution.[111] Courts are equally reluctant to approve recovery for repairs or restoration when costs exceed the amount by which the land's value has been diminished.[112] But sometimes the excess-repair-cost recovery is justified, as it usually is in cases of environmental damage,[113] since in those cases the defendant's tort has caused harm to others besides the plaintiff and is likely to continue in the future unless abated.[114]

Lost use and emotional distress. Damages for trespass can always include damages for loss of use and for discomfort and annoyance resulting from the trespass.[115] In some cases, the plaintiff will be entitled to have more general forms of emotional distress considered in fixing his damages.[116] Courts sometimes begin analysis by stating a "general rule" against recovery for distress in the absence of physical impact or harm to the plaintiff's person,[117] but then quickly turn to "exceptions" broad enough to permit awards in any cases in which emotional distress is reasonably foreseeable.[118] At the other end of the spectrum, some courts have declared without qualification that emotional distress damages may be recovered for the trespass.[119]

The actual results in the cases suggest, however, that courts neither routinely grant nor routinely deny emotional harm damages in trespass cases. Emotional harm damages are awarded generally only when the trespass is more than a transient passage.[120] Courts have approved such damages when the trespass is repeated or continuing,[121] when it threatens physical harm or is a deliberate or hostile infringement of the plaintiff's rights,[122] when it physically alters or destroys property of aesthetic value[123] or afflicts some personal sensibility,[124] or when it is accompanied by some other tort.[125]

---

[111] See Starrh and Starrh Cotton Growers v. Aera Energy LLC, 153 Cal.App.4th 583, 63 Cal.Rptr.3d 165 (2007); but see Gilbert Wheeler, Inc. v. Enbridge Piplelines (East Texas), L.P., 449 S.W.3d 474 (Tex. 2014) (allowing recovery of intrinsic value of trees cut by defendant where the diminution of market value was de mimimis).

[112] Id. See also Poffenbarger v. Merit Energy Co., 972 So.2d 792 (Ala. 2007).

[113] E.g., Davey Compressor Co. v. City of Delray Beach, 639 So.2d 595 (Fla. 1994).

[114] See Dan B. Dobbs, Law of Remedies § 5.2(5) (2d ed. 1993).

[115] Restatement Second of Torts § 929(1)(c) (1979).

[116] Britt Builders, Inc. v. Brister, 618 So.2d 899 (La.App. 1993) ("Anguish, humiliation, and embarrassment are appropriate considerations.").

[117] E.g., Valley Development Co. v. Weeks, 147 Colo. 591, 364 P.2d 730 (1961).

[118] Indeed, the "exception" stated is often only the requirement that the harms claimed be the natural or foreseeable result of the trespass. E.g., Douglas v. Humble Oil & Refining Co., 251 Or. 310, 445 P.2d 590 (1968).

[119] Mest v. Cabot Corp., 449 F.3d 502 (3d Cir. 2006); Armitage v. Decker, 218 Cal.App.3d 887, 267 Cal.Rptr. 399 (1990).

[120] In fact, lawyers often attempt to claim emotional distress damages in trespass to land cases by alleging an independent tort, such as intentional or negligent infliction of mental distress.

[121] E.g., McGregor v. Barton Sand & Gravel, Inc., 62 Or.App. 24, 660 P.2d 175 (1983) (spillage of pond water onto plaintiff's lower land and threat of landslides over a long period of time).

[122] E.g., Tran v. General Motors Acceptance Corp., 1989 WL 64564 (E.D. Pa. 1989) (aggressive effort to repossess a car).

[123] Pearce v. L.J. Earnest, Inc., 411 So.2d 1276 (La. App. 1982) (ornamental trees); Phillips v. Town of Many, 538 So.2d 745 (La. App. 1989) (road crew altered plaintiff's property over her repeated protests).

[124] Jefferies v. Bush, 608 So.2d 361 (Ala. 1992) ("Unless the trespass is attended with words or acts of insult or contumely, damages for mental anguish are not recoverable.").

[125] See, e.g., Cullison v. Medley, 570 N.E.2d 27 (Ind. 1991) (trespass accompanied by intimidating conduct and an assault).

Punitive damages.[126] Punitive damages may generally be awarded by the trier of fact only when the defendant has been guilty of some very serious wrongdoing, often described as malice, oppression, or wanton misconduct. Casual, transient trespass cases without other wrongdoing will seldom meet standards for punitive awards. But deliberate and known trespass, coupled with factors such as repetition, destruction or taking of property, or other aggravating elements,[127] warrant substantial punitive awards.[128] Statutes sometimes prescribe double or treble damages where timber or minerals are taken.[129]

§ 5.9   Temporary or Continuing Trespass vs. Permanent or Completed Trespass

If the defendant's trespass or nuisance[130] continues to cause harm to the plaintiff's interests in land, courts usually begin by classifying the invasion as either permanent (completed) or temporary (continuing).[131]

This sounds simple enough. Yet persisting invasions of land create varied and difficult legal problems that cannot be solved just by labeling the trespass or nuisance as either temporary or permanent.[132] For instance, if an embankment on the defendant's land periodically causes floods on the plaintiff's land, one question will be whether to permit or require the plaintiff to sue for each flooding, or whether to say the plaintiff can or must sue for all future damages at once. Conflicting decisions and factual variety make statement of a general rule perilous.[133]

Damages-rules effects of permanent (or completed) classification. If the invasion is permanent, courts award damages only once and assess all future damages in one lawsuit. The permanent or future damages measure is usually the diminished value of the land resulting from the invasion.[134] Once the defendant has paid permanent damages, he will not be liable again for the continuance of the same invasion.

---

[126] On punitive damages generally, see § 34.4; 1 Dan B. Dobbs, Law of Remedies § 3.11 (2d ed 1993).

[127] See Sebra v. Wentworth, 990 A.2d 538 (Me. 2010) (punitive damages award affirmed where defendants continued to traverse plaintiff's property despite a court ruling that they had no easement).

[128] E.g., Hamilton Development Co. v. Broad Rock Club, Inc., 248 Va. 40, 445 S.E.2d 140 (1994) (defendant's blatant recklessness in seizing a neighbor's land, clearing it, grading it, and appropriating it for its own use warranted punitive damages of $200,000).

[129] See 1 Dan B. Dobbs, Law of Remedies § 5.3(3) (2d ed. 1993).

[130] For nuisance cases, see § 404 (discussing remedies).

[131] See Hoery v. United States, 64 P.3d 214 (Colo. 2003); Town of Oyster Bay v. Lizzo Indus., Inc., 22 N.Y.3d 1024 (2013); Restatement Second of Torts § 930 (1979).

[132] Determining the proper measure of damages is the main issue. Other matters that may be determined by the classification include: (1) whether the statute of limitations has run on the entire claim or only on the claims for harms done outside the statutory period, see, e.g, Cook v. DeSoto Fuels, Inc., 169 S.W.3d 94 (Mo.App. 2005); (2) whether more than one suit can be brought (res judicata issues); (3) whether the plaintiff as a purchaser of the land has standing to sue for the invasion or whether the owner at the time of the invasion has standing instead. See, e.g., Vaughn v. Missouri Public Service Co., 616 S.W.2d 540 (Mo.App. 1981).

[133] Courts do not appear to agree even on the definition of the terms. Some authority insists that only the defendant's *act*, not the *harm*, is to be considered in determining "temporary" vs. "permanent," at least in determining when the statute of limitations begins to run. See, e.g., Brandt v. Cnty. of Pennington, 827 N.W.2d 871 (S.D. 2013). Under this view, categorization as temporary or permanent does not determine the outcome; the categorization merely expresses the fact that a series of individual acts of trespass has taken place ("continuing") or that the trespass has ceased ("permanent"). See Breiggar Properties, L.C. v. H.E. Davis & Sons, Inc., 52 P.3d 1133 (Utah 2002).

[134] Starrh and Starrh Cotton Growers v. Aera Energy LLC, 153 Cal.App.4th 583, 63 Cal.Rptr.3d 165 (2007); Mel Foster Co. Properties, Inc. v. American Oil Co., 427 N.W.2d 171 (Iowa 1988).

If the *defendant* is the party successfully demanding that damages be measured by the permanent measure, he is in effect forcing the plaintiff to make a sale of an interest in the land. If the *plaintiff* is the party successfully demanding damages measured by the permanent measure, she is in effect forcing the defendant to make a purchase of an interest in the plaintiff's land.[135]

Damages-rules effects of temporary (or continuing) classification. If the invasion is temporary or continuing, it is treated as if it were renewed daily, with a new trespass or nuisance each day. The plaintiff may sue for all harms that have occurred to the time of suit or trial, but may not sue for future harms that would be incurred only if the trespass continues; that is so because harm linked directly to continued trespass may terminate at any time and may never be incurred at all.[136] This measure of damages contemplates the possibility of successive suits.[137] After the plaintiff recovers once, she may sue again for damages that have occurred since the first suit.[138]

Classification of an invasion as temporary or continuing does not give the defendant any permanent rights to continue the invasion. For that reason, a decision to classify the invasion as temporary can provide the defendant an incentive to eliminate the invasion, since if he does so, he will not be liable for damages in the future.

Example of a permanent invasion. While it is not easy to find harmony in the case results, some courts would classify an invasion as permanent, with a single one-time recovery, on facts similar to this: a city with the power of eminent domain erects a dam, one effect of which is that water periodically floods parts of the plaintiff's land and will continue to do so indefinitely into the future. The dam is durable. Its physical or factual permanence, together with the city's power to condemn a flooding easement in the plaintiff's land, suggests that the case should be treated as a kind of taking of property. The city should be liable to pay all the damages the plaintiff will ever suffer in one suit. If the value of the land is worth $10,000 less because of the prospects of flooding, the city will be liable for that, but never liable again for the same kind of invasive flooding resulting from the dam.[139]

Example of a temporary invasion. A temporary or continuing invasion might take several forms. One might look like this: defendant parks his truck on the plaintiff's land and never moves it. The plaintiff can sue at any time and, having recovered, can sue again for further damages accruing later. The damages for temporary or continuing nuisance will not give the plaintiff the diminished value of the land. That measure assumes that the land could never recover from the parked truck, but that is absurd. Instead, the plaintiff could recover damages measured by the harm suffered up to suit or trial. In this illustration, that is probably the rental value of the land for truck-parking purposes. When the invasion is caused, not by a structure, but by the defendant's method

---

[135] The effect is to force a sale of a limited interest in the land, the right to pollute or continue a trespass. Subject to this limit, it is analogous to the remedy in conversion. See § 6.14.

[136] E.g., City of Bristol v. Tilcon Minerals, Inc., 284 Conn. 55, 931 A.2d 237 (2007); Baker v. Burbank-Glendale-Pasadena Airport Authority, 39 Cal.3d 862, 705 P.2d 866, 218 Cal.Rptr. 293 (1985); Webb v. Virginia-Carolina Chemical Co., 170 N.C. 662, 87 S.E. 633 (1916).

[137] The need to bring successive actions may be seen as rendering the legal remedy of damages inadequate, thus allowing injunctive relief. See, e.g., Lambert v. Holmberg, 271 Neb. 443, 712 N.W.2d 268 (2006).

[138] E.g., City of Holdenville v. Kiser, 195 Okla. 189, 156 P.2d 363 (1945).

[139] Town of Troy v. Cheshire R.R., 23 N.H. 83 (1851).

of operation, courts usually treat the invasion as temporary.[140] The fact that the invasion can be abated is central, but not exclusive, in making that determination.[141]

Many cases are less clear than these models. A person who constructs a part of his building on your property may be compelled to remove it, in which case the trespass is clearly temporary or continuing.[142] But equally, the court might decide that removal is too costly or wasteful and allow him to keep the structure there, paying permanent damages.[143]

Basis for classification. Classification as permanent or temporary is partly a matter of fact and partly a matter of policy seemingly governed by a number of factors. The most significant factors favoring a classification as temporary seem to be:

(1)   The invasion can in fact be terminated or abated;[144]

(2)   The cost of termination is not wasteful or oppressive;[145]

(3)   No privilege or public policy favors a continuation of the invasion;[146]

(4)   An incentive to abate the invasion can be provided by permitting repeated suits for damages as they accrue;[147]

(5)   The plaintiff prefers temporary damages;[148] and

(6)   Overall, it is not just to permit the defendant to acquire the permanent right to invade the plaintiff's interests in land by paying market price for that right against the plaintiff's wishes.[149]

---

[140]   E.g., Ryan v. City of Emmetsburg, 232 Iowa 600, 4 N.W.2d 435 (1942); Webb v. Virginia-Carolina Chemical Co., 170 N.C. 662, 87 S.E. 633 (1916).

[141]   See Spar v. Pacific Bell, 235 Cal.App.3d 1480, 1 Cal.Rptr.2d 480 (1991); Mel Foster Co. Properties, Inc. v. American Oil Co., 427 N.W.2d 171 (Iowa 1988).

[142]   See Rose Nulman Park Foundation v. Four Twenty Corp., 93 A.3d 25 (R.I. 2014).

[143]   See Kratze v. Independent Order of Oddfellows, Garden City Lodge No. 11, 442 Mich. 136, 500 N.W.2d 115 (1993).

[144]   E.g., Mangini v. Aerojet-General Corp., 12 Cal.4th 1087, 912 P.2d 1220, 51 Cal. Rptr. 2d 272 (1996); Knight v. City of Missoula, 252 Mont. 232, 827 P.2d 1270 (1992).

[145]   If the defendant can efficiently terminate the invasion it is not unfair to expect him to do so or to be liable in successive actions as long as he permits the invasion to continue. Where the converse is true, and abatement of the invasion and the harm is extremely costly compared to alternatives, the defendant may in effect be permitted to purchase the right to continue the invasion by paying permanent damages. See Kratze v. Independent Order of Oddfellows, Garden City Lodge No. 11, 442 Mich. 136, 500 N.W.2d 115 (1993).

[146]   When the invasion could be considered the exercise of eminent domain power, the invasion can be considered to be an informal taking by the defendant, who is entitled by statute to acquire the right by paying its value. See Spaulding v. Cameron, 38 Cal.2d 265, 239 P.2d 625 (1952). If a defendant who lacks the power of eminent domain purposefully tries to acquire rights in the plaintiff's land by the invasion (rather than by bargaining), courts are more likely to issue an injunction to require termination of the invasion and hence more likely to treat the invasion as temporary.

[147]   See Mangini v. Aerojet-General Corp., 12 Cal.4th 1087, 1103, 912 P.2d 1220, 1229, 51 Cal.Rptr.2d 272, 281 (1996). Temporary damages do not invariably furnish incentives for avoiding further harm. Where they are not, this factor does not counsel classification as a temporary nuisance.

[148]   When it is the defendant's preference for temporary damages, other factors may counsel holding for the defendant, but not the defendant's preference alone. When it is the *plaintiff's* preference for temporary damages, that is a strong factor in favor of the temporary measure simply because the plaintiff is the victim, not the perpetrator of the tort. This is equivalent to saying that the plaintiff should usually have the power to elect a temporary damages measure. If the defendant has a power of eminent domain with respect to the interest involved, or wasteful costs would be imposed by temporary damages, the plaintiff's preference might be disregarded.

[149]   This factor in effect imports the factors used in conversion cases, where the issue is quite similar. In those cases, the defendant who interferes with possession of the plaintiff's chattel is or is not required to "buy"

§ 5.10 Extended Liability

Doctrine has it that the trespasser is liable for all physical harms directly caused by his trespass, not merely those he caused intentionally or negligently. The Restatement Second says that the trespasser is subject to liability for harms caused by acts done and conditions he created on the land, even if he would not have been liable for such harms had he not been a trespasser.[150] And the trespasser's liability extends not only to the possessor of land but also to members of her household. The rule of extended liability for trespass appears to be the general form of the rule from which the "transferred intent" rule is logically derived.

Under the extended liability rule, the trespasser may be held liable for a personal injury innocently caused in the course of a trespass, as where a trespasser's truck runs over a child,[151] or where his trespass opens a door which allows a mentally disabled but apparently normal person to leave and suffer injury,[152] or where his chemicals cause an allergic reaction.[153] Or he may be held responsible for a fire innocently caused in the course of a trespass.[154] Other cases impose a similar liability.[155]

In line with the common law rules for trespassory torts generally, courts may distinguish direct from indirect injuries, allocating the latter to an action on the case. In this view, liability for trespass would not extend to indirect injuries that were also unintended and unforeseeable.[156] However, some courts have held the trespasser responsible even for unintended injuries that are also "indirect."[157]

As between a conscious wrongdoer on the one hand and an innocent possessor or her family on the other, courts are fully justified in imposing the unexpected loss upon

---

the chattel, depending ultimately upon the justice of forcing him to do so under the circumstances. This is turn is analyzed by considering a number of factors, such as the extent of interference and the defendant's consciousness of wrongdoing. See § 6.6 .

[150] Restatement Second of Torts § 162 (1965).

[151] St. Petersburg Coca-Cola Bottling Co. v. Cuccinello, 44 So.2d 670 (Fla. 1950) (child struck by trespasser's truck; lack of fault no defense since he was a trespasser).

[152] Keesecker v. G.M. McKelvey Co., 141 Ohio St. 162, 47 N.E.2d 211 (1943) (defendant's agent delivered a package at the wrong house; his entry allowed a mentally disabled but apparently normal child to get out and be injured).

[153] Cf. Brabazon v. Joannes Bros., 231 Wis. 426, 286 N.W. 21 (1939) (demonstrating fly spray over the plaintiff's objection, plaintiff became ill from it).

[154] Wyant v. Crouse, 127 Mich. 158, 86 N.W. 527 (1901); Lee v. Stewart, 218 N.C. 287, 10 S.E.2d 804 (1940); cf. Brown v. Dellinger, 355 S.W.2d 742 (Tex.Civ.App. 1962) (7–8 year-old boys intentionally started fire in charcoal grill; the fire got out of hand and burned the garage and house; since the boys were trespassers, they were liable for $28,000 in damages resulting from the unintended spread of the fire).

[155] See Williams v. River Lakes Ranch Development Corporation, 41 Cal.App.3d 496, 116 Cal.Rptr. 200 (1974) (strict liability for cattle trespass and also liability for cattle's "foreseeable" injury to owner); Beavers v. West Penn Power Co., 436 F.2d 869 (3d Cir. 1971) (poles carrying high tension wires tilted over the years and may have hung over the land of another; if the defendant's wires were trespassing objects, the defendant would be liable for death of a child who came in contract with the wires).

[156] Connolley v. Omaha Pub. Power District, 185 Neb. 501, 177 N.W.2d 492 (1970); cf. Wawanesa Mutual Insurance Co. v. Matlock, 60 Cal.App.4th 583, 70 Cal.Rptr.2d 512 (1997) (one smoking and trespassing teenager accidentally set a fire; his fellow trespasser, who had furnished the cigarette, was not liable).

[157] Kopka v. Bell Telephone Co. of Pa., 371 Pa. 444, 91 A.2d 232 (1952) (telephone company was responsible for a hole dug on the plaintiff's land; the plaintiff, hearing of the hole, went looking for it and fell in; the defendant was held liable). The *Kopka* court recognized a limitation, however: "[I]f the owner or possessor of the land, willfully, voluntarily, or by negligence, himself brings about the injury to his person, such an injury cannot be said to be consequent upon the trespass to the land, and in that event the trespasser would not be liable therefor."

the wrongdoer; that result is not obviously correct in the case of the trespasser who is innocently mistaken in believing the land is his or that he has permission to enter it.

Chapter 6

INTENTIONAL INTERFERENCE WITH TANGIBLE PERSONAL PROPERTY: TRESPASS TO CHATTELS AND CONVERSION

Analysis

§ 6.1   Development of Liability for Interference with Chattels
§ 6.2   Trespass to Chattels
§ 6.3   Conversion of Chattels—Elements and Issues
§ 6.4   Conversion: Intent Required
§ 6.5   Property Subject to Conversion
§ 6.6   Dominion or Control Required
§ 6.7   Methods of Committing Conversion—Generally
§ 6.8   Conversion by Creditors
§ 6.9   Conversion by Bailees
§ 6.10   Contract and Tort: Conversion and the Bailment Contract
§ 6.11   The Bailor's Option to Sue "In Tort" or "In Contract" and the Economic Loss Rule
§ 6.12   The Bona Fide Purchaser of Converted Tangible Goods
§ 6.13   The Bona Fide Purchaser of Converted Money or Checks
§ 6.14   Remedies for Conversion
§ 6.15   Statutes of Limitation in Conversion

§ 6.1   Development of Liability for Interference with Chattels

Two sets of variables were important in the early development of liability for interference with chattels.

(a) Taking vs. retention. On one axis of the common law rules lay the case of a defendant who wrongfully took a chattel from the plaintiff who was entitled to it. On an entirely different axis lay the case of a defendant who had rightful possession of the plaintiff's chattel, say a horse the defendant had agreed to feed, but refused to return the chattel on demand. To early common lawyers these two cases were quite different.

(b) Transitory vs. substantial. The common law also drew a distinction between a transitory and inconsequential harm or taking, and a permanent or substantial deprivation of the plaintiff's rights on the other—that is, between the case of a defendant who pets your horse although you have forbidden it and the case of the defendant who steals your horse and rides him to exhaustion. This distinction remains of importance today.

The Trespass writ. These variables—taking vs. keeping on the one hand, and minor vs. substantial interference on the other—led to the use of different common law writs depending on the facts of the case. The simplest case was an intentional taking or damage to a chattel. Because the taking was physical ("forcible") and direct, the writ of *Trespass* could be used to recover damages.[1] This form of trespass was called *Trespass de bonis asportatis*, that is, for the taking of goods.

The Detinue background. However, the defendant might not *take* the chattel at all. He might be a bailee—a person who rightfully possessed the chattel but did not own it. A borrower is a bailee; so is someone who is paid to care for the chattel. If the bailee refused to return the chattel upon demand, he was not guilty of a trespass because he had not wrongfully taken it. In this situation the plaintiff could use *Detinue*. But *Detinue* had attributes different from *Trespass*. In *Detinue* the defendant had the option of either paying for the chattel or returning it.[2] So if he had damaged the chattel he could return it and thus escape liability. The plaintiff could not recover the damages by then invoking *Trespass*, so *Detinue* might prove to be quite inadequate for the plaintiff. A second disadvantage in *Detinue* was that the defendant could also opt to have the case tried by *wager of law*. This meant that the defendant could defeat the claim altogether if he could produce a specific number of oath-helpers, that is, persons who would swear that the defendant was generally a truthful person.[3]

Action on the Case for Trover develops. Because neither *Trespass* nor *Detinue* was a wholly satisfactory solution for the plaintiff, and left gaps in which no remedy at all was found, plaintiffs' lawyers eventually succeeded in developing an action of *Trespass on the Case for Trover*. *Trover* was a word that had been earlier used in certain *Detinue* cases. The allegation in the new *Trover* action was that the defendant had found the goods belonging to the plaintiff. The allegation of a finding was a happy fiction. It negated both trespass and bailment and hence left the way open for an action on the case,[4] because the bare allegation of finding was enough and the plaintiff was never required to prove it.[5] The allegation went on to say that the defendant, having found the goods, "converted them to his own use," that is, kept them or altered them or sold them and retained the money.[6]

Trespassory and non-trespassory claims combined in one action. With the advent of the action on the case for trover, both the taking and wrongful detention cases could be redressed by the single tort we today call conversion. Conversion's parentage—part

---

[1]   Originally, a complete dispossession was required, and even that did not suffice if the chattel was taken by way of *Distress*, that is, by a lord who has (wrongfully) seized the chattel as security for rent. In that case the plaintiff had to proceed by an action called *Replevin*. See J.B. Ames, The History of Trover, 11 Harv. L. Rev. 277, 286 (1897).

[2]   The writ of *Replevin* allowed specific recovery of the chattels, but it originally lay only for chattels wrongfully distrained by the lord as security for the tenant's rent due. See Id. at 287.

[3]   ". . . with a dozen or half-a-dozen ruffians he might swear an honest man out of his goods." Bereford, C.J., in a Yearbook case quoted in C.H.S. Fifoot, History and Sources of the Common Law 29 (1949). Milsom thinks that in the local courts the procedure might not have been so bad, although when the trial was in the central courts and the defendant used hired compurgators it was obviously undesirable to say the least. See S.F.C. Milsom, Historical Foundations of the Common Law 67 (2d ed. 1981).

[4]   To use *Case* the plaintiff had to show that no other writ was appropriate to the facts. That meant that the plaintiff had to claim that neither *Trespass* nor *Detinue* fit the facts alleged. The allegation of a finding and the allegation that the goods were converted to the defendant's own use both played a significant part in showing that *Trespass* and *Detinue* could not apply. The rule that the allegation of finding could not be denied then left the plaintiff almost completely free to use *Case* for *Trover* in lieu of the earlier actions. See, recounting the details and the gaps, A.W.B. Simpson, The Introduction of the Action on the Case for Conversion, 75 L. Q. Rev. 364 (1959).

[5]   J.B. Ames, The History of Trover, 11 Harv. L. Rev. 277 (1897).

[6]   The phrase does not imply, however, that the defendant actually used the goods or that he gained from having them. Thakkar v. St. Ives Country Club, 250 Ga. App. 893, 553 S.E.2d 181 (2001).

Trespass, part *Case*—helps explain the fact that it sometimes seems trespassory and sometimes not. Although there is now one tort of conversion rather than several writs, the two major settings for that tort remain important. Failure-to-return cases—the second setting—raise problems that are not much like the problems raised in the taking cases. The writs are gone, but the factual skeleton on which they once hung still remains.

Substantial vs. insubstantial interference. What of the distinction between substantial and insubstantial interferences? On this point, the development of *Trover* also had its effects. *Trespass* had originally been dedicated to the physical taking cases, but at least by the 1840s, *Trespass* had become the repository for claims of less substantial interference or damage.[7] Substantial interference cases were redressed in *Trover*, that is, by the tort known as conversion. The difference was that *Trespass* permitted the plaintiff to recover actual damages, but *Trover* allowed the plaintiff to recover the full value of the chattel; it was in effect a forced sale. That remains the law today.

§ 6.2   Trespass to Chattels

The tort of trespass to chattels is committed by intentionally interfering with the plaintiff's possession in a way that causes legally cognizable harm. The defendant may interfere with the chattel by interfering with the plaintiff's access or use[8] or by causing actual harm to the chattel.[9] As the term chattel implies, the tort aims to protect interests in tangible property. Some recent cases have extended the tort to protect computer systems from electronic invasions by way of unsolicited bulk email or the like, or hacking into a computer.[10]

The intent required to establish the tort of trespass to chattels is familiar from the trespass to land and conversion cases. It is enough if the defendant had an intent to act upon the property; if his interference is substantial enough, he is liable even though he had no intent to harm or even to invade another's interests.[11] On the other hand, he is not liable for trespass to chattels if he never intended to touch or affect it at all and does so only accidently, as where a contractor excavating land strikes a buried telephone cable.[12]

Direct vs. indirect interference. Trespass was the proper form of action under earlier common law only when the interference with land, chattel, or person was direct and physical. Under this rule, the defendant who locked the door to a room where the plaintiff's goods were located might not be guilty of a trespass, although he might be liable in an action on the case for the intentional interference.[13] The forms of action have long since been abolished, so the distinction between trespass and case (as forms of action) are no longer important. The defendant who places poisoned meat before the plaintiff's dog, intending that the dog will eat it, is no doubt liable if the dog does eat, even though he does not put the meat in the dog's mouth or otherwise touch the dog.

---

[7]   See Fouldes v. Willoughby, 8 M. & W. 540, 151 Eng. Rep. 1153 (1841).

[8]   See Poff v. Hayes, 763 So.2d 234 (Ala. 2000) (taking and photocopying private papers); Zaslow v. Kroenert, 29 Cal.2d 541, 176 P.2d 1 (1946) (removing co-tenant's goods and putting them in storage).

[9]   See Restatement Second of Torts § 218 (1965).

[10]   See § 44.1.

[11]   Restatement Second of Torts § 217, cmt. c (1965).

[12]   Mountain States Tel. & Tel. Co. v. Horn Tower Const. Co., 147 Colo. 166, 363 P.2d 175 (1961); Southwestern Bell Tel. Co. v. M.H. Burton Construction Co., 549 P.2d 1214 (Okla. 1976).

[13]   Restatement Second of Torts § 217, cmt. d (1965).

With the abolition of the forms of action, it is not confusing to call the defendant's tort a trespass where he has caused physical harm or physical interference with the owner's rights.[14] Although the "direct" nature of the interference no longer seems important, the physical nature of the interference remains important. In the absence of physical interference or effects, the plaintiff will normally only suffer pure economic loss, and in that case, the economic loss rules may bar the tort claim, at least where the parties are in a contractual relationship.[15]

Possession. Trespass to chattels parallels trespass to land on some issues and not on others. Although physical interference is required, direct harm has become less important and so has possession. So if the defendant intentionally harms a chattel that the owner has loaned or leased to someone else, the owner is not in possession, but he has an action if his interests in the chattel are adversely affected.[16] In this respect the trespass to chattel rules resemble those for trespass to land.

Harm or dispossession required. Trespass to chattels differs from trespass to land in one important respect. An intended entry upon land is a trespass whether it is harmful or not. An intended touching of a chattel is not. To establish liability for trespass to chattels, the possessor must show legally cognizable harm.[17]

Types of cognizable harm. Three kinds of harm are sufficient to make a trespass to chattel claim actionable. These are: (1) actual dispossession, which implies that the plaintiff's access to the chattel is barred or substantially limited for something more than a few moments;[18] (2) physical harm to the chattel; or (3) physical harm to the plaintiff or to someone or something in which the plaintiff had a legal interest.[19] Intrusion by unwanted commercial calls has been held insufficient to meet criteria like these.[20] Nor does the plaintiff's emotional distress count as physical harm for this purpose; a trespass to chattels does not become actionable merely because it causes emotional distress,[21] although infliction of emotional distress may sometimes be actionable as some other tort.[22] Similarly, use of data about the plaintiff may interfere with the plaintiff's right of privacy or justify an unjust enrichment claim, but is not a conversion of the information under traditional rules.[23] However, some courts have permitted conversion actions for using or broadcasting the plaintiff's information.[24]

Consequential damages. Any of the three types of recognized harm that trigger the trespass to chattel action may cause additional harmful consequences such as business

---

[14] See Restatement Third of Torts (Liability for Physical and Emotional Harm) § 5(2) (2010) ("An actor who intentionally causes physical harm is subject to liability for that harm.").

[15] See Chapter 41.

[16] Restatement Second of Torts § 220 (1965).

[17] Glidden v. Szybiak, 95 N.H. 318, 63 A.2d 233 (1949) (not a trespass to pull dog's ears since dog was not hurt).

[18] See Koepnick v. Sears Roebuck & Co., 158 Ariz. 322, 762 P.2d 609 (Ct. App.1988).

[19] Restatement Second of Torts § 218 (1965).

[20] "J. Doe No. 1" v. CBS Broadcasting Inc., 24 A.D.3d 215, 806 N.Y.S.2d 38 (2005).

[21] Morrow v. First Interstate Bank of Oregon, 118 Or. App. 164, 847 P.2d 411 (1993). Where a chattel's value lies in highly personal attachment, as in the case of pets or family photos, there are difficult problems in determining damages, but even so courts have usually excluded recovery of emotional distress or "sentimental" value in such cases. E.g., Mieske v. Bartell Drug Co., 92 Wash.2d 40, 593 P.2d 1308 (1979).

[22] Torts to redress emotional distress as a stand-alone tort (not as damages for torts like trespass to chattels) are usually limited by elaborate rules. See Chapter 29.

[23] In re JetBlue Airways Corp. Privacy Litigation, 379 F.Supp.2d 299 (E.D. N.Y. 2005).

[24] See § 44.1.

losses that occur before the chattel can be recovered or replaced. In the absence of dispossession or physical harm, business losses would not qualify as harms that would suffice to trigger the trespass to chattels action. However, if dispossession or physical harm is demonstrated, there is no reason to deny the plaintiff recovery of economic losses as consequential damages, provided the damages are adequately proven and causation is shown. Although some courts were traditionally negative about full recovery of losses in conversion cases,[25] where consequential or "special" damages are foreseeable, adequately proven and can be assessed without duplicating awards, there is no reason today to reject such damages if the cause of action itself is established.[26] Courts now in fact approve such awards.[27]

Substantial interference. If the defendant's interference with the chattel is substantial, amounting to an exercise of ownership rights or "dominion" over the chattel, the plaintiff may have an option to claim either trespass to chattels or conversion.[28] As the following sections indicate, however, the interference must be quite substantial to justify the conversion claim, which in effect forces the defendant to buy the chattel.

§ 6.3   Conversion of Chattels—Elements and Issues

The basic conversion case. The tort of conversion, derived from the writ of *Trover*,[29] redresses the plaintiff's possessory rights in personal property when the defendant intentionally exercises a substantial dominion over the property, interfering seriously with the plaintiff's rights.[30] Although the defendant need not act in bad faith, he must intentionally exercise control over the property; transient interference does not qualify. On the other hand, the defendant who exercises significant control over the property is a converter even though he himself gains nothing from the property or his control over it.[31] The property itself must be tangible or at least the legal equivalent of tangible property, as where tangible property is tightly controlled by documents of title or other legal instruments.[32] If conversion is established, the defendant is subject to liability for the value of the chattel converted unless the plaintiff accepts its return.[33]

Examples. (1) White steals Green's watch, worth $500 at the time. He later sells it. White is a converter and liable for the $500. (2) Jones steals Smith's watch, but wears the watch for a year before Smith discovers the facts. Jones is a converter. A sale of the watch is not necessary to establish conversion. (3) Moore takes Lester's watch, intending to use it without Lester's knowledge to impress a potential employer and then return it the next day. However, Moore is in a motor vehicle accident and the watch is damaged beyond repair. Moore is a converter; although he did not intend permanent deprivation

---

[25]   See, e.g., East Coast Novelty Co., Inc. v. City of New York, 842 F.Supp. 117, 124 (S.D.N.Y. 1994).

[26]   See 1 Dan B. Dobbs, The Law of Remedies § 5.15 (2d ed. 1993) (lost profits and other consequential damages).

[27]   E.g., Rajeev Sindhwani, M.D., PLLC v. Coe Business Service, Inc., 52 A.D.3d 674, 861 N.Y.S.2d 705 (2008); see § 6.14.

[28]   Vines v. Branch, 244 Va. 185, 418 S.E.2d 890, 894–895 (1992).

[29]   See § 6.1.

[30]   Shaeffer v. Poellnitz, 154 So.3d 979 (Ala. 2014): P.F. Jurgs & Co. v. O'Brien, 160 Vt. 294, 629 A.2d 325 (1993).

[31]   Wilkinson v. United States, 564 F.3d 927 (8th Cir. 2009).

[32]   See §§ 6.5 & 44.1 to 44.3.

[33]   See § 6.14.

or any damages, he did intend to interfere, and his interference actually caused permanent loss.

Glimpsing beyond the core. Beyond the core case, any form of interference with another's chattel can count as a conversion, provided the interference is substantial enough to warrant a forced sale to the defendant. If the interference with the plaintiff's possession is serious enough and the defendant enjoys no privilege, the defendant is a converter if he dispossesses the plaintiff and likewise if he transfers title or possession and if he fails to return the chattel on demand.[34] He is a converter even if he acquires title to the chattel in good faith from a thief who stole it from the defendant.[35]

Possession. The conversion rules, like those of trespass to land, traditionally protected possessory rights.[36] So a bailee who had no title to the chattel could sue if the defendant seized or destroyed the chattel.[37] Today the owner who is not in possession can also sue to the extent her interests are adversely affected by the conversion.[38]

Substantial interference. Everyone agrees that conversion requires more than intermeddling or interference; it requires very substantial exercise of control or dominion inconsistent with the plaintiff's rights. Jurists have found it impossible to define with precision the amount of control that will count as a conversion. Perhaps the best approach is to ask, with the Restatement, whether the defendant exercised so much control over the chattel that courts can justly require him to pay its full value.[39]

Insubstantial interference. If the defendant's dominion over the chattel was limited, as where he takes the plaintiff's car for a one-block joy ride, the court is unlikely to find a conversion. In that case, the defendant may be liable for the tort of trespass to chattels.[40] But in that case the defendant will not be liable for the entire value of the car, only for actual damages caused.

Alternatives to conversion. The plaintiff who cannot prevail on a conversion claim may have a number of alternatives. The defendant who has committed no conversion may still be liable for a trespass to chattels or for negligent harm to the chattel.[41] If interference occurs through use of the judicial process, the plaintiff's claim may be for malicious prosecution or the like.[42] Statutes may create claims that redress interference with chattels under a set of rules different from those used in conversion cases. When the property in question is purely intangible, a congregation of economic tort claims stands ready for such cases.[43]

Property and tort issues. Two radically different kinds of problems arise in conversion cases. In many cases, the broad issue is whether or not the plaintiff's property interest prevails over the defendant's. In such cases, the focus of inquiry is not on the

---

[34]   See § 6.7.

[35]   See § 6.13.

[36]   E.g., Car Transportation v. Garden Spot Distributors, 305 Ark. 82, 805 S.W.2d 632 (1991).

[37]   See Lawrence v. State, 231 Ga. App. 739, 501 S.E.2d 254 (1998); Priority Finishing Corp. v. LAL Const. Co., Inc., 40 Mass. App. Ct. 719, 667 N.E.2d 290 (1996).

[38]   Restatement Second of Torts § 243 (1965).

[39]   Restatement Second of Torts § 222A (1965). See § 6.6.

[40]   See § 6.2.

[41]   The most common tort case of all is such a case—negligent damage to an automobile. The ordinary rules of negligence law apply in such cases.

[42]   Chapter 39.

[43]   See Chapters 44 & 46 ("conversion" of economic rights and unfair competition and intellectual property respectively).

defendant's conduct but on the plaintiff's property rights. For example, a creditor who loans money to a farmer to buy cows may take a mortgage or other security interest in the cows, even though the farmer keeps them on the farm. If the farmer sells the cows to defendant, contrary to a provision of the mortgage, the defendant will be a converter if the plaintiff's mortgage is a property interest superior to the defendant's. That issue is resolved by rules about the rights or property interests of creditors; tort law is merely the vehicle for enforcing those underlying property rights.[44] So many conversion cases turn primarily on the law of personal property ownership, or on the law of secured transactions, warehouse receipts, or other rules under the Uniform Commercial Code ("UCC"), where the rules attempt to delineate the interests held by adverse parties rather than to prescribe conduct.

In other cases the plaintiff's property interest is clear and the question is whether the defendant's conduct should count as a substantial interference with that interest. If Tom drives Jane's car without her permission, but only take it across the street, the question whether Tom is a converter focuses heavily on his conduct, not on Jane's property interest.

It is true that a court indirectly determines something about your property rights when it decides that my conduct did or did not violate those rights, but conduct is the central focus of the inquiry. So in a sense, the two kinds of cases cannot be wholly separated. Yet the first kind of case, with its concern for determining conflicting interests in property, must be mainly understood through the law of personal property and the Uniform Commercial Code, not through the law of torts.

The tort issues in conversion cases. The main tort issues to be considered in conversion cases fall into three groups:

(1) Did the defendant have the requisite intent? Put the other way around, can the defendant escape liability if he acted in good faith?[45]

(2) Did the defendant exercise sufficient control to be counted as a converter?[46] Or is he, perhaps, guilty only of a trespass to chattels?

(3) What kind of property is subject to conversion?[47]

§ 6.4 Conversion: Intent Required

Intent required. Conversion is an intentional tort; there is no such thing as a conversion by accident. The defendant may accidently damage property and may be liable for doing so if he is negligent or if the facts warrant imposition of strict liability, but negligent damage, destruction, or taking without an intent to affect the chattel at all is not a conversion.[48]

The intent required is the defendant's intent to exercise control of or dominion over the goods, no more.[49] As in other cases, intent is shown either by the defendant's purpose

---

[44] See Production Credit Assn of Madison v. Nowatzski, 90 Wis.2d 344, 280 N.W.2d 118 (1979) (secured creditor who file papers in the proper office under UCC rules had conversion action against the buyer of the goods).

[45] See § 6.4.

[46] See § 6.6.

[47] See § 6.5.

[48] Collin v. American Empire Ins. Co., 21 Cal. App. 4th 787, 26 Cal. Rptr. 2d 391 (1994).

[49] Restatement Second of Torts § 217, cmt. c (1965); Northeast Bank of Lewiston and Auburn v. Murphy, 512 A.2d 344 (Me. 1986).

to affect the goods in question, or by his knowledge that it is substantially certain that they will be affected.[50] For example, the defendant who intentionally seizes the plaintiff's automobile must be substantially certain that in taking the car he will also take the contents. Such a defendant thus intends to seize its contents, even if his only purpose is to repossess the car.[51]

The intent required to show conversion is exactly analogous to the intent required to prove a trespass to land. In neither case is the defendant's bad motive or good faith ordinarily relevant, except on the question of punitive damages. The defendant might believe the goods are his and that he has every right to deal with them, but, even so, he harbors the requisite intent if he intends to act upon the goods.[52] For example, if John mistakenly picks up Jane's casebook from a library table, intending to pick up his own book, and then sells Jane's book on a used-book website—still believing that the book is his—John is a converter. In the same way, an innocent agent who negotiates a sale of goods on behalf of his principal is liable for conversion when it turns out that the principal had no right to the goods and that they belong to the plaintiff instead.[53]

Where the defendant does not benefit from the conversion. The intent rule would be easy to understand if the defendant intending to treat goods as his own always retained the benefit of those goods. If I take your book by mistake, it is not harsh to require me to pay for it if I am then allowed to have title to the book. Conversion law is a kind of informal forced sale, and I do indeed have a right to the book once I have paid you for it.[54] The rule in conversion, however, does not limit liability to cases in which the defendant has himself received or retained a benefit.[55] As applied to the book example, this rule means that I would remain liable for conversion of your book even if I had later lost the book or it had been destroyed in a fire without my fault.

One stringent example of the intent rule occurs when a thief converts your watch, then sells it to an innocent purchaser who reasonably believed that the thief was the owner. Although some innocent purchasers are protected from liability by special rules, the innocent purchaser in the case just described is not.[56] His intent to deal with the goods as owner is a sufficient basis for liability. The effect is that the good faith buyer pays twice, once when he paid the thief and once when he pays the conversion judgment. Economically, then, he is a no-benefit defendant, financially in the same position as the defendant who is held for conversion even though he no longer has the converted goods.

§ 6.5   Property Subject to Conversion

Under the traditional common law rule, only tangible personal property could be converted. This meant three things.

---

[50]   Restatement Second of Torts § 217, cmt. c (1965).

[51]   See Darcars Motors of Silver Springs, Inc. v. Borzym, 379 Md. 249, 841 A.2d 828 (2004).

[52]   Car Transportation v. Garden Spot Distributors, 305 Ark. 82, 805 S.W.2d 632 (1991); P.F. Jurgs & Co. v. O'Brien, 160 Vt. 294, 629 A.2d 325 (1993); Restatement Second of Torts § 244 (1965).

[53]   Kelley v. LaForce, 288 F.3d 1 (1st Cir. 2002); Ensminger v. Burton, 805 S.W.2d 207 (Mo. App. 1991); Restatement Second of Torts § 233 (1965).

[54]   See O'Keeffe v. Snyder, 83 N.J. 478, 416 A.2d 862, 873–74 (1980).

[55]   Kelley v. LaForce, 288 F.3d 1 (1st Cir. 2002); Reed v. Hamilton, 315 Ark. 56, 864 S.W.2d 845 (1993).

[56]   See § 6.13.

First, no action for conversion would lie for dispossession of an interest in real property or damage to it.[57] If timber, minerals, or soil were severed from the land, they became personal property and subject to conversion,[58] but if I occupied your land, you could not effect a forced sale by claiming a conversion.[59]

Second, no action for conversion would lie for interference with intangible rights such as choses in action[60] or trade secrets[61] or other information.[62] Interference with economic rights unattached to specific property may be actionable, but, under the traditional rule, not as "conversion."[63]

Third, no action for conversion would lie for interference with rights that do not count as property rights. In each case, other actions might conceivably lie, but if so they would not have the characteristics of conversion, such as a forced sale or liability for intended but good faith interference.

Modern expansion. Although real property as such has not generally been subject to a conversion claim, contemporary cases sometimes ignore or reject the traditional rules by permitting a conversion action for some kinds of intangible rights.[64] The most common example is that courts may allow the action for the taking of documents that are not merely evidence of a right to recovery but are instead conceived as an embodiment of that right, on the formal theory that in such cases tangible goods are "merged" into documents that represent them,[65] or more accurately on the ground that in such cases the documents actually control access to the tangible goods, at least in the practice of the business community.[66] Paper money and negotiable instruments such as promissory notes and bonds are good examples of the kind of intangible right than can now be converted under some circumstances.[67]

One traditional limitation continues to be applied without exception. Courts recognize a conversion only when the defendant interferes with personal property[68] and the plaintiff has a possessory interest in that property.[69] Modern courts have held that

---

[57] Emerick v. Mutual Benefit Life Ins. Co., 756 S.W.2d 513 (Mo. 1988) (no conversion of leasehold interests).

[58] Pan American Petroleum Corporation v. Long, 340 F.2d 211 (5th Cir. 1964); Hamlet at Willow Creek Development Co., LLC v. Northeast Land Development Corp., 878 N.Y.S.2d 97 (App. Div. 2009).

[59] Rowe v. Barrup, 95 Idaho 747, 518 P.2d 1386 (1974). The same rule applies where the defendant takes a purported title from someone who has no right to convey land.

[60] E.g., Famology.Com Inc. v. Perot Systems Corp., 158 F.Supp. 2d 589 (E.D. Pa. 2001) (web domain name cannot be converted).

[61] See, e.g., Mortgage Specialists, Inc. v. Davey, 904 A.2d 652 (N.H. 2006) (action for conversion of employer's information is preempted or displaced by trade secret law, even if the information turned out not to be a trade secret).

[62] Coyne's & Co., Inc. v. Enesco, LLC, 565 F.Supp. 2d 1027 (D.Minn. 2008); Pestco, Inc. v. Associated Products, Inc., 880 A.2d 700 (Pa. Super. 2005).

[63] See Chapter 44.

[64] See Chapter 44 (conversion of intangible economic values and spoliation of evidence).

[65] Hutchison v. Ross, 262 N.Y. 381, 390, 187 N.E. 65, 69 (1933).

[66] Ayres v. French, 41 Conn. 142 (1874); Agar v. Orda, 264 N.Y. 248, 190 N.E. 479 (1934).

[67] E.g., Lappe and Associates, Inc. v. Palmen, 811 S.W.2d 468 (Mo. App. 1991); Manufacturers Trust Co. v. Nelson, 221 Or. 45, 350 P.2d 169 (1960) (bill of lading); see Tyrone Pac. Intern., Inc. v. MV Eurychili, 658 F.2d 664 (9th Cir. 1981).

[68] H.J., Inc. v. International Telephone & Telegraph Corp., 867 F.2d 1531, 1547 (8th Cir. 1989); Equity Group Ltd. v. Painewebber Incorporated, 839 F.Supp. 930, 933 (D.C.Cir. 1993); see also Ananda Church of Self Realization v. Massachusetts Bay Ins. Co., 95 Cal. App. 4th 1273, 116 Cal. Rptr. 2d 370 (2002) (abandoned property, including document placed in outdoor trash barrel, is no longer "property," no conversion).

[69] Blackford v. Prairie Meadows Racetrack and Casino, Inc., 778 N.W.2d 184 (Iowa 2010).

the donee of a kidney for transplant, having no property right in that kidney, has no cause of action for conversion when the transplant team directs the kidney to a different recipient.[70] Much more significantly, the California Supreme Court has held that taking unique body cells of a patient for use in developing a commercially valuable product is not a conversion.[71] Similarly, intentional interference with dead bodies may constitute a tort to living relatives, but it seems less than helpful to say that the claim arises because relatives have a property interest in the body. The claim of relatives that a body was mishandled is not a claim for the market value of the body, but rather for the relative's emotional distress. Thus such a claim is not about the body as property but the body as the physical remains of a loved one. Conversion is thus the wrong theory for such a case.[72] However, lawyers sometimes invoke the conversion theory anyway and courts sometimes take it seriously.[73]

§ 6.6   Dominion or Control Required

Early torts scholar Thomas M. Cooley defined conversion as "[a]ny distinct act of dominion, wrongfully exerted over one's property in denial of his right or inconsistent with it."[74] Many courts have stated this formula or some variation on it.[75] The plaintiff's consent to the defendant's conduct of course negates a conversion, because where the defendant is acting with the plaintiff's consent, he cannot be acting inconsistently with the plaintiff's rights; much less can he be doing so in a way that counts as "dominion."[76]

The Restatement's test: justice of a forced sale. The Restatement rule requires dominion over the plaintiff's chattel that is so extensive that it will be just to force the defendant to pay full value of the chattel.[77] The conversion action in effect results in a judicially forced sale of the goods to the defendant; this forced sale is the action's most significant feature.[78] A conversion will be found when, but only when, the facts justify such an extreme remedy—when the defendant exercised quite extensive dominion over the chattel. The Restatement's rule does not eliminate judgment calls, but it does tell lawyers and judges what kind of judgment must be made.

The Restatement's factors. The Restatement attempts to provide more specific bases for developing evidence, formulating arguments, and making decisions. It lists six factors that courts should consider in determining whether the defendant's interference with the chattel is serious enough to justify a finding of conversion. The list provides a

[70] Colavito v. New York Organ Donor Network, Inc., 8 N.Y.2d 43, 860 N.E.2d 713, 827 N.Y.S.2d 96 (2006) (at least in this context, the donee had no property right in the kidney).

[71] Moore v. Regents of the University of California, 51 Cal.3d 120, 271 Cal. Rptr. 146, 793 P.2d 479 (1990).

[72] Culpepper v. Pearl St. Bldg., Inc., 877 P.2d 877 (Colo. 1994); Boorman v. Nevada Mem. Cremation Soc'y, Inc., 236 P.3d 4 (Nev. 2010).

[73] See, e.g., Spates v. Dameron Hospital Ass'n, 114 Cal. App. 4th 208, 7 Cal. Rptr. 3d 597 (2003) (conversion claim against a hospital which turned the patient's dead body over to the coroner when family members could not be found; held, the defendant did not intentionally interfere with plaintiff's right of possession and hence was not a converter).

[74] Thomas M. Cooley, Law of Torts 448 (1878). Courts picked up Cooley's definition from various editions.

[75] E.g., Collin v. American Empire Ins. Co., 21 Cal. App. 4th 787, 26 Cal. Rptr. 2d 391 (1994); Darcars Motors of Silver Springs, Inc. v. Borzym, 379 Md. 249, 841 A.2d 828 (2004).

[76] See Jones v. DCH Health Care Authority, 621 So.2d 1322, 1324 (Ala. 1993).

[77] Restatement Second of Torts § 222A(1) (1965); see Montgomery v. Devoid, 181 Vt. 154, 915 A.2d 270 (2006)

[78] Pearson v. Dodd, 410 F.2d 701, 706 (D.C. Cir. 1969); Louisiana State Bar Association v. Hinrichs, 486 So.2d 116 (La. 1986).

convenient evidentiary template, suggesting that evidence on the following points will be helpful to a decision:

(1)   The extent and duration of the defendant's dominion or control;

(2)   The defendant's intent to assert a right in the goods that is inconsistent with the plaintiff's ownership;

(3)   The defendant's good faith;

(4)   The amount of actual interference with the plaintiff's right to use the chattel;

(5)   Any harm done; and

(6)   The inconvenience or expense caused.[79]

An example. Suppose that by happenstance the defendant's car key fits the plaintiff's identical car and the defendant mistakenly takes the wrong car from a parking lot but discovers his mistake and returns the car two hours later with apologies. He has not harmed the car. The first factor tells the lawyer to inquire about the length of time the defendant had the car; it was not long, so that factor perhaps favors the defendant. The second and third factors tell lawyers to consider the defendant's state of mind; and since he did not intend to assert ownership and acted in good faith, those factors also favor the defendant. The fourth factor suggests that lawyers should find out whether the plaintiff was actually inconvenienced by loss of the car's use. For example, if the plaintiff did not actually attempt to use the car and did not even know of its absence, her abstract right to possession has been invaded but she has suffered no actual interference at all. The fifth factor, harm done, and the sixth, actual expense caused, both seem to work for the defendant in this example. The conclusion almost certainly is that the defendant should be liable for trespass to chattels for any harm actually done but should not be compelled to purchase the car by way of a conversion action.[80]

§ 6.7   Methods of Committing Conversion—Generally

Dispossession

As the Restatement recognizes, conversion can be committed in many different ways.[81] A taking of the chattel by a thief is a simple and core example. But the defendant can commit conversion by any act that counts as intentional dominion over the chattel and that is not privileged[82] or protected by law.[83] Dispossessing the plaintiff,[84] or

---

[79]   Restatement Second of Torts § 222A(2) (1965); see, applying these factors, Montgomery v. Devoid, 181 Vt. 154, 915 A.2d 270 (2006).

[80]   Cf. Johnson v. Weedman, 5 Ill. 495 (1843) (holding in accord with the argument by A. Lincoln for the defendant that a bailee's wrongful riding of the bailed horse was not a conversion); LaPlace v. Briere, 404 N.J. Super. 585, 962 A.2d 1139 (2009) (under the Restatement's factors, an individual's unauthorized exercise of the plaintiff's boarded horse, where exercise of horses was routinely provided was not a conversion even though the horse suddenly died; the horse's death was not shown to be a result of the exercise).

[81]   Restatement Second of Torts § 223 (1965) lists seven ways in which conversion can be committed. These include (1) dispossession, (2) destruction or alteration, (3) using a chattel, (4) receiving it, (5) disposing of it, (6) delivering it to the wrong person, or (7) refusing to surrender it to the owner. All of course require intent to deal with the chattel and a substantial interference.

[82]   E.g., attaching an immobilizing boot to a trespassing car, as in Kirschbaum v. McLaurin Parking Co., 188 N.C.App. 782, 656 S.E.2d 683 (2008). On privileges generally, see Chapter 7.

[83]   When the defendant has resorted to the courts to gain possession, the rules of malicious prosecution or similar torts may be used instead of conversion rules. See Chapter 39.

[84]   Restatement Second of Torts § 223 (1965).

preventing the plaintiff's possession when she is entitled to it,[85] is a common form of conversion, so long as the interference with the plaintiff's interests is substantial. For example, even the sheriff who tows away the plaintiff's tractor in the good faith belief that it is stolen property may be liable for conversion.[86]

Seriousness of dispossession. Whether the dispossession is serious enough to count as a conversion is largely a matter of degree, but the defendant's intent or lack of intent to assert a right in the property is also significant. Driving the plaintiff's car across the street without permission is conceivably a dispossession, but if the plaintiff can recover the car by crossing the street, it is not a conversion;[87] taking the car from Mississippi to Kansas, on the other hand, is easily a conversion.[88]

Destruction, Alteration, or Damage

Intentional destruction, major alteration, or serious damage are often extreme cases of dispossession and count as a conversion.[89] For example, the defendant who throws away the plaintiff's possessions is exercising complete dominion over them and is liable for conversion.[90] Destruction or serious damage may also amount to a conversion in a rather different way. If the defendant intermeddles with a chattel, without intent to cause harm to it but substantial harm or destruction nevertheless occurs, the defendant becomes a converter liable for the destruction.[91]

Use or Interference Short of Dispossession

When the defendant uses the plaintiff's chattel or interferes with it but does not damage it or dispossess the plaintiff for any significant time, rules provide little assistance. If the use or interference is substantial enough, the court may find a conversion. If it is not, the court will reject a conversion approach[92] and the defendant will be liable at most for a trespass to chattels. In this setting the defendant's intent or bad faith becomes important,[93] along with the duration of the interference. The defendant who uses your desk to write a letter is probably not a converter even if you have told him not to do so; if he uses it for months and claims ownership, he probably is.[94]

As already indicated, even a minor trespass may warrant liability for conversion if, in the course of the trespass, substantial though unintended harm results to the chattel.

---

[85]   Hartford Financial Corp. v. Burns, 96 Cal. App. 3d 591, 158 Cal. Rptr. 169 (1979); Darcars Motors of Silver Springs, Inc. v. Borzym, 379 Md. 249, 841 A.2d 828 (2004).

[86]   E.J. Strickland Construction, Inc. v. Department of Agriculture and Consumer Services of Florida, 515 So.2d 1331 (Fla.App. 1987).

[87]   Zaslow v. Kroenert, 29 Cal.2d 541, 176 P.2d 1 (1946).

[88]   Cf. Paccar Financial Corp. v. Howard, 615 So.2d 583 (Miss. 1993) (defendant repossessed the plaintiff's 18-wheeler; the plaintiff intentionally left goods in the truck intending to get them later, but the defendant moved the truck from Mississippi to Kansas and did not help get the goods back to the plaintiff; held, conversion of the plaintiff's personal items).

[89]   Snead v. Society for Prevention of Cruelty to Animals of Pennsylvania, 929 A.2d 1169 (Pa. Super. 2007); Iemma v. Adventure RV Rentals, Inc., 632 N.E.2d 1178 (Ind. App. 1994); Restatement Second of Torts § 226 (1965).

[90]   Bowler v. Joyner, 562 A.2d 1210 (D.C. 1989).

[91]   Restatement Second of Torts § 228 (1965).

[92]   Johnson v. Weedman, 5 Ill. 495 (1843); Fouldes v. Willoughby, 8 M. & W. 540, 151 Eng. Rep. 1143 (1841).

[93]   See Veeco Instruments, Inc. v. Candido, 70 Misc.2d 333, 334 N.Y.S.2d 321, 324 (Sup.Ct. 1972) ("a conscious and determined act"); Restatement Second of Torts § 222A(2)(b) & (c) (1965).

[94]   Restatement Second of Torts § 227, illus. 1 to 4 (1965).

This rule is a manifestation of the extended liability rule seen in other intentional torts such as trespass to land and battery.[95]

Acquiring or transferring possession, ownership, or security interests

One who transfers possession of the plaintiff's chattel is ordinarily exercising dominion over it and may thus be liable for conversion.[96] Subject to the special rule for agents stated below, one who acquires possession of a chattel often exercises substantial dominion over the chattel merely by acquiring possession, title, a claim to title, or a security interest in it.[97]

All acquisitions are not conversions, of course; one who acquires possession with appropriate consent of the owner is not a converter, nor is one who acquires transient possession that does not interfere substantially with the plaintiff's rights in the chattel. On the other hand, the plaintiff who purchases a chattel is surely asserting ownership and the right of dominion, and if this is inconsistent with the rights of the plaintiff, then it is a conversion. In particular, the good faith purchaser from a thief is a converter even though he purchases in utter good faith.[98]

Agent receiving goods innocently. A thief steals your computer, then has it stored in the ABC Warehouse, which knew nothing of the theft. The thief has converted your computer and is liable to you. If recovery against the thief is not possible, can you recover for conversion against the ABC Warehouse? The answer is no. The warehouse can be viewed as an agent or bailee of the thief. An agent or bailee who receives goods for storage, safekeeping, or transport is not a converter merely because he acquires possession.[99] The rule is supported by policy; it is commercially convenient to permit storage and transport. It is also supported by the fact that a bailment by itself seldom puts the goods beyond the owner's reach, so that there is relatively little to be gained by imposing liability upon the innocent bailee.

The protective rule for agents and bailees does not extend to those who accept the goods when they knew or had reason to know of the plaintiff's rights. Nor does it extend to those who take an active role in negotiating for their principals' a transfer or sale[100] on the one hand or a purchase or receipt of the goods on the other.[101]

§ 6.8   Conversion by Creditors

A number of dispossession cases arise in the context of creditors' efforts to recover a debt or the property allocated to secure that debt. The defendant's mere assertion of a lien or security interest against the plaintiff's property is not necessarily a conversion of the property even though the defendant has no right to a lien on it.[102] But a creditor-

---

[95] See §§ 4.18 & 5.10.

[96] Sale or misdelivery of chattels often occurs in bailment cases where a bailee sells or misdelivers the plaintiff's personal property. See § 6.9.

[97] See, e.g., Maloney v. Stone, 195 A.D.2d 1065, 601 N.Y.S.2d 731 (1993) (bank knowingly accepted a pledge of securities to secure a trustee's individual obligation); Ocean National Bank of Kennebunk v. Diment, 462 A.2d 35 (Me. 1983) (accepting stock as collateral for a loan).

[98] See § 6.13.

[99] Foreign Car Ctr., Inc. v. Essex Process Serv. Inc., 62 Mass. App. Ct. 806, 821 N.E.2d 483 (2005); Restatement Second of Torts § 230 (1965).

[100] Ensminger v. Burton, 805 S.W.2d 207 (Mo. App. 1991); Restatement Second of Torts § 233 (1965).

[101] Restatement Second of Torts § 231 (1965).

[102] Prewitt v. Branham, 643 S.W.2d 122 (Tex. 1982).

lienor who sells property not subject to its lien is guilty of conversion[103] and so is a sheriff who enforces a judgment by seizing property of the wrong person.[104] So is a creditor who wrongfully repossesses the debtor's car,[105] and one who conducts a sale of it that is not commercially reasonable.[106]

A creditor who can rightfully take possession of mortgaged chattels cannot rightfully seize unmortgaged chattels as well, or if he does, he must make prompt and reasonable efforts to identify and return those not mortgaged.[107] Even if a creditor is entitled to repossess the chattel in an honest and peaceable way, he may be a converter if he repossesses by a breach of the peace,[108] or in some states if he does so by fraud or trickery.[109]

So far as the creditor's interference results from a judicial proceeding, the plaintiff's grievance may not rest on conversion but on malicious prosecution or even on a civil rights tort instead.[110]

§ 6.9   Conversion by Bailees

Bailee's Sale, Disposal, or Transfer of Possession

The defendant's unauthorized transfer of an interest in the plaintiff's property is ordinarily a substantial exercise of dominion over that property and a conversion.[111] This kind of conversion is ordinarily accomplished by bailees. For example, a jeweler who holds the plaintiff's rubies for appraisal is not a converter by the mere act of holding them, but he becomes one if he sells them. Even the jeweler's innocent employee, who believes the jewels to be part of the stock in trade, may be a converter if he negotiates a sale of the rubies and delivers possession of them.[112] Similarly, one who holds property pledged to secure payment of a debt is a converter of the pledge if he sells it in violation of any of the terms of the pledge or after the underlying debt has been paid.[113]

A transfer of possession without an actual sale and without gain to the defendant may still operate as a conversion. For example, a bailee of goods who rebails them to another warehouse in violation of his contract to hold them himself may be a converter,

---

[103]   Central GMC, Inc. v. Helms, 303 Md. 266, 492 A.2d 1313 (1985).

[104]   See Lake Philgas Service v. Valley Bank & Trust Co., 845 P.2d 951 (Utah App. 1993); Curtis v. Carey, 393 S.W.2d 185 (Tex.Civ.App. 1965). Not every seizure is actionable, because it might be privileged. When the sheriff executes upon property of the plaintiff rather than property of the judgment debtor, a statute may provide the exclusive remedy. See the remarkable tribulations of almost everyone in Elliott v. Denton & Denton, 109 Nev. 979, 860 P.2d 725 (1993).

[105]   E.g., Wiley v. General Motors Acceptance Corp., 624 So.2d 518 (Ala. 1993); Entriken v. Motor Coach Federal Credit Union, 256 Mont. 85, 845 P.2d 93 (1992).

[106]   E.g., Klooster v. North Iowa State Bank, 404 N.W.2d 564 (Iowa 1987).

[107]   See Boisdore v. International City Bank & Trust Co., 361 So.2d 925 (La. App. 1978).

[108]   Ivy v. General Motors Acceptance Corp., 612 So.2d 1108 (Miss. 1992); McCall v. Owens, 820 S.W.2d 748 (Tenn. App. 1991). UCC § 9–503 provides for repossession of collateral security if it "can be done without breach of the peace."

[109]   See Ford Motor Credit Co. v. Byrd, 351 So.2d 557 (Ala. 1977).

[110]   As to creditors' unconstitutional use of legal process see § 6.14; 1 Dan B. Dobbs, Law of Remedies § 5.17(2) (2d ed. 1993); as to malicious prosecution see Chapter 39.

[111]   Northeast Bank of Lewiston and Auburn v. Murphy, 512 A.2d 344 (Me. 1986); Kenyon v. Abel, 36 P.3d 1161 (Wyo. 2001).

[112]   Restatement Second of Torts § 233(1) (1965).

[113]   Hartford v. State Bar of California, 50 Cal.3d 1139, 791 P.2d 598, 270 Cal.Rptr. 12 (1990).

at least if the transfer leads to the loss of the goods.[114] A warehouse or other bailee who holds the plaintiff's goods must deliver them only to the plaintiff or to persons the plaintiff designates. If the bailee misdelivers the goods to the wrong person, even by honest mistake, he is a converter and liable for the value of the goods.[115] For instance, the jeweler who does not sell the plaintiff's rubies but mistakenly delivers them to another customer is a converter.[116]

In a classic case,[117] the bailor instructed the bailee to return bailed goods by shipping them Railway Express. The bailee packed the goods and addressed them to the plaintiff, then gave them to a person dressed in an appropriate uniform and who represented that he was from the express agency. But the person was an imposter and the plaintiff never got the goods. Although the bailee was both innocent and reasonable in delivering the goods to the apparent employee of the express company, and although he was a gratuitous bailee and not one for hire, he was held for conversion.

Bailee's nondelivery or withholding possession

When demand and refusal is required. Somewhat strangely, a bailee's non-delivery may be treated more leniently than misdelivery. A bailee who is under an obligation to return goods when a specific event occurs may be liable as a converter when the event occurs and he fails to return the goods, whether or not the plaintiff demands them.[118] But when the plaintiff bails goods for an indefinite time, the bailee is not a converter until the plaintiff has made a demand for their return, unless the bailee commits some affirmative act of dominion by asserting ownership, disposing of or damaging the goods. The rule requiring a demand has even been applied when the defendant is a third person who acquired the goods in good faith from the bailee and who asserts title to them.[119] The date of the demand or refusal may be significant in starting the statute of limitations clock running or in assessing damages.[120] The demand and refusal requirement has a basis in law and good sense when it is applied to defendants who are, at least initially, in rightful possession of the chattel. However, some courts, without appearing to notice the difference, have stated demand and refusal as a general requirement for establishing conversion. Requiring a demand for return would hardly be justified if the defendant has deliberately converted the plaintiff's car by theft or has deliberately destroyed it, so it is easy to see that the demand requirement should be confined to bailment and other rightful possession cases.[121]

What counts as refusal. When a demand is required, the defendant becomes a converter only if he refuses to return the property after the demand is made or if he engages in conduct equivalent to a refusal. "Refusal" is a shorthand term in this context. Once the demand has been made, any conduct of the defendant that is inconsistent with

---

[114] Fotos v. Firemen's Ins. Co. of Washington, D.C., 533 A.2d 1264, 76 A.L.R.4th 875 (D.C. 1987); Johnson v. Johnson, 849 P.2d 1361 (Alaska 1993).

[115] S/M Industries, Inc. v. Hapag-Lloyd A.G., 586 So. 2d 876 (Ala. 1991).

[116] Rensch v. Riddle's Diamonds of Rapid City, Inc., 393 N.W.2d 269 (S.D. 1986).

[117] Baer v. Slater, 261 Mass. 153, 158 N.E. 328 (1927).

[118] Albrecht v. Zwaanshoek Holding en Financiering, B.V., 816 P.2d 808 (Wyo. 1991).

[119] Lawrence v. Meloni, 163 A.D.2d 827, 558 N.Y.S.2d 360 (1990); Lowney v. Knott, 84 R.I. 425, 125 A.2d 98, 57 A.L.R.2d 1042 (1956).

[120] See § 6.15.

[121] See, e.g., Horne v. TGM Assocs., L.P., 56 So.3d 615 (Ala. 2010) (no demand required "where there has been a wrongful taking or an exercise of dominion and control over the property inconsistent with the rights of the owner"); State v. Seventh Regiment Fund, Inc., 98 N.Y.2d 249, 774 N.E.2d 702 (2002) (where "the defendant knows it has no right to the goods, demand is not required").

the plaintiff's rights in the property counts as a refusal or its legal equivalent. The defendant who continues to withhold the plaintiff's goods is a converter if he denies that the goods belong to the plaintiff or that he himself holds them,[122] or refuses to respond to the plaintiff's repeated letters and telephone demands,[123] or demands payment of charges he has no legal right to.[124] Express verbal refusal is not required; an unreasonable delay in returning the property[125] or giving access[126] to it after a demand might be enough to make a jury question on this point. Of course, a bailee might have legitimate reasons for refusing to return goods immediately, and a conditional refusal of delivery, based on reasonable grounds and done in good faith, will not be actionable.[127]

Bailee's burden of proving his innocence. Once the plaintiff has made a demand upon the bailee and the bailee has refused to deliver the goods, the picture becomes a little more complicated. Suitors who claim that a bailee has failed to return the bailed goods often assert both a breach of the bailment contract and a conversion.[128] The bailee's liability for failure to return the plaintiff's goods arises only if he is negligent or is intentionally withholding the goods because of misdelivery or otherwise. However, in most states[129] the bailee must prove his innocence in failing to deliver the goods.[130] Carriers and innkeepers are subject to similar rules.[131] If he fails to prove his innocence, he is either presumptively negligent or has presumptively misdelivered the property, and thus has either breached the bailment contract or is guilty of a conversion.

§ 6.10 Contract and Tort: Conversion and the Bailment Contract

Convergence of tort, contract and property in bailment cases. Contract, negligence, and conversion are theoretically separable bases of liability. A warehouse that fails to redeliver goods to the person entitled to their return upon a proper demand, at times may be held liable for negligence or liable for conversion, depending upon the circumstances.[132] At other times, the plaintiff might have an action for breach of contract.[133] The negligence/conversion/contract theories are often rolled up together. For example, a court may say that breach of the bailment contract *is* a conversion.[134]

---

[122] Driver v. Hice, 618 So.2d 129 (Ala.App. 1993).

[123] McKinley v. Flaherty, 390 N.W.2d 30 (Minn.App. 1986).

[124] Car Transportation v. Garden Spot Distributors, 305 Ark. 82, 805 S.W.2d 632 (1991).

[125] Willis v. Midland Finance Co., 97 Ga. App. 443, 103 S.E.2d 185 (1958) (delay of "days"); see Schroeder v. Auto Driveaway Company, 11 Cal. 3d 908, 523 P.2d 662, 114 Cal. Rptr. 622 (1974).

[126] Russell-Vaughn Ford, Inc. v. Rouse, 281 Ala. 567, 206 So.2d 371 (1968) (refusal to return car keys a conversion of the car).

[127] E.g., White v. Drivas, 954 So.2d 1119, 1123 (Ala. Ct. Civ. App. 2006) ("A limited or qualified refusal to surrender the property is not per se a conversion. But the refusal must be a reasonable qualification or requirement and stated in good faith.").

[128] See §§ 6.10 & 6.11.

[129] The UCC section covering the warehouseman's liability for nondelivery permits states to adopt an alternative which puts the burden on the plaintiff to show the negligence, and some states have done so.

[130] E.g., Kearns v. McNeill Brothers Moving and Storage Company, 509 A.2d 1132 (D.C. 1986); Procter & Gamble Distributing Co. v. Lawrence American Field Warehousing Corp., 16 N.Y.2d 344, 213 N.E.2d 873, 266 N.Y.S.2d 785, 21 A.L.R.3d 1320 (1965).

[131] See 2 Dobbs, Hayden & Bublick, The Law of Torts §§ 260 & 261 (2d ed. 2011 & Supp.).

[132] I.C.C. Metals v. Municipal Warehouse Co., 50 N.Y.2d 657, 662, 409 N.E.2d 849, 852, 431 N.Y.S.2d 372, 376 (1980).

[133] See, e.g., W.E. Stephens Mfg. Co. v. Goldberg, 225 S.W.3d 77 (Tex. App. 2005).

[134] Fotos v. Firemen's Ins. Co. of Washington, D.C., 533 A.2d 1264, 1267 (D.C. 1987).

Not only do the formal theories converge in bailment cases; the underlying concerns of tort law, contract law and property law do so as well. The bailor owns the chattel bailed, or at least has a right to immediate possession. Tort law traditionally respects his possession-ownership rights in permitting him to recover against a bailee who negligently damages the goods and against one who converts them by non-return or otherwise. It also permits the bailor to recover the goods themselves, thus respecting his property interest. Contract, express or implied, however, is the foundation of the bailment. Even a brief account of conversion in bailment cases must thus consider the effects of the bailment contract on the tort recovery and the protection of the bailor's property interests.

Contract-related transactions. Contracts, express or implied, may be significant in various transactions involving the transfer of possession of personal property. Sales of goods with payments to be made over time coupled with a right of the seller to repossess have already been mentioned.[135] Many other transactions are bailments in various forms—transactions in which the bailee accepts possession of personal property with the obligation to return it in accord with agreed terms.[136] These include pledges of property as security for loans; leases and loans of the property; delivery of the property to a carrier for transport of goods or to a warehouseman for safekeeping; and delivery to a bailee who is to perform work on the personal property.

In the absence of an overriding statute, the bailment contract, whether express or implied, normally establishes the bailee's duties. For example, the parties may understand that the obligation to return is conditioned on some event. The bailee need not return goods pledged to him as security for a debt until that debt is paid; he may instead sell the goods to secure his payment.[137] In the same way, the bailee need not return the goods in unaltered condition if the point of the bailment was that the bailee would alter or repair the goods. If the agreement is that the bailee is to grind wheat into flour, he is not a converter by his act of grinding the wheat; he satisfies his obligation if he returns the flour it produced as provided by the express or implied agreement. Another instance in which the bailee is permitted to return different goods is the case of fungible goods, where the obligation is to return goods of like kind, quality, and amount rather than the identical goods.[138] The upshot is that while the bailee must by law use reasonable care in performing his duties, those duties are set by any implied or express contract provisions on point, so that he is not guilty of conversion or any tort if he complies with those contractual duties.

When the bailee, on the contrary, does not comply with the duty to return the goods under the contractual terms, two additional considerations arise: the effect of

---

[135] See § 6.8.

[136] Courts have defined bailment in various degrees of formality and detail. They generally emphasize the delivery of personal property for a specific purpose, pursuant to an express or implied contract to fulfill that purpose and to return the property when the purpose is fulfilled or on demand, *in accord with the terms of the contract.* See, e.g., Grosso v. Monfalcone, Inc., 13 Cal. App. 2d 405, 56 P.2d 1266 (1936); Hadfield v. Gilchrist, 343 S.C. 88, 538 S.E.2d 268, 272 (2000). Whether there is a formal contract behind the bailment or not, the transaction is necessarily a consensual one and the parties' valid expectations to a large extent determine the scope of tort duties.

[137] Restatement of Security § 48 (1941).

[138] See Pub. Serv. Elec. & Gas Co. v. Federal Power Com'n, 371 F.2d 1 (3d Cir. 1967); Mohoff v. Northrup King & Co., 234 Or. 174, 380 P.2d 983 (1963).

exculpatory or damages limiting clauses, and whether the bailee is liable in tort or only in contract.[139]

Contractual provisions protecting the bailee. The underlying duties of the bailee—to hold, to repair, and to transport, for example—are created by the consensual undertaking that creates and limits[140] the duties owed. Two other kinds of contract provisions that might affect liability are quite different, because they do not limit the duty owed or deny its breach. The first limits liability by limiting the damages recoverable; the second attempts to exculpate the bailee entirely by providing he is not liable even for his tortious acts. Cases and statutes usually support agreements that merely limit the amount of the bailee's liability, where such clauses are properly presented and unambiguous.[141] Exculpatory clauses are viewed less charitably. Courts have often thought that clauses completely exempting the bailees for hire from all liability are void or ineffective to relieve the bailee and certain others from liability in tort.[142] This rule developed in an era of "manifest judicial hostility toward release-from-negligence contracts."[143] Some courts today may lean toward the other pole of public policy, freedom of contract, with the result that contracts fully exempting the tortious defendant may be enforced so long as the transaction does not too closely resemble a bailment or one otherwise heavily affected with the public interest.[144]

Other forms of contractual control over liability. Two other contractual limitations are prominent. First, the bailee may contractually prescribe some of the underlying obligations he undertakes. Where statutes do not prescribe otherwise, carriers can restrict the scope of their duties, for example by promising one-week delivery instead of next-day delivery. Second, the defendant may contractually position himself to avoid bailee status altogether, for example by leasing space for storage or parking without accepting possession or control over the goods.[145]

§ 6.11   The Bailor's Option to Sue "In Tort" or "In Contract" and the Economic Loss Rule

Because the bailee's obligation is to return the goods as provided or implied in the contract, a bailee's return of the goods in accord with the contract forecloses a bailor's suit in conversion as well a suit on the bailment contract. The core objective—to respect the valid contract—is thus achieved regardless of whether the claim is conceptualized as being in contract or in tort. So long as the bailee complies with the contract provisions as to the condition of goods on return and the timing of return, he cannot be a converter

---

[139]   See § 6.11.

[140]   See § 6.10.

[141]   See, e.g., Calvin Klein Ltd. v. Trylon Trucking Corp., 892 F.2d 191 (2d Cir. 1989) (New York law). Liability limits are perceived as an integral part of the bailee's charges or rates, a *quid pro quo* or tradeoff that permits lower rates because the bailee's risk of damages is limited, at least where the bailor has an opportunity to bargain for full liability at a greater cost. See Union Pac. R.R. v. Burke, 255 U.S. 317, 41 S.Ct. 283, 65 L.Ed. 656 (1921); ABN AMRO Verzekeringen BV v. Geologistics Americas, Inc., 253 F.Supp. 2d 757 (S.D. N.Y. 2003).

[142]   Agricultural Ins. v. Constantine, 144 Ohio St. 275, 58 N.E.2d 658, 29 O.O. 426 (1944) ("It is now apparently well settled that a bailee for hire cannot, by contract, exempt himself from liability for his own negligence"). Statutes may so provide. E.g., 46 U.S.C.A. § 30704 (carriage of goods by sea).

[143]   Bisso v. Inland Waterways Corp., 349 U.S. 85, 89, 75 S.Ct. 629, 631, 99 L.Ed. 911 (1955).

[144]   Sander v. Alexander Richardson Investments, 334 F.3d 712 (8th Cir. 2003).

[145]   See, e.g., Allright Phoenix Parking, Inc. v. Shabala, 6 Ariz. App. 21, 429 P.2d 513 (1967) (parking in space in defendant's parking lot while owner kept the car keys was not a bailment).

because in such a case he would not have exercised dominion over the goods at variance with the bailor's rights. And in that case, he has not breached the contract, either.

Noncompliance with bailment terms—the plaintiff's traditional option to sue in tort or contract. In the reverse situation, when the bailee does not return the goods either in the original condition or in the condition called for by the bailment, at least three possible claims can be asserted against the bailee—contract, conversion, and negligence. Significantly, courts have said repeatedly that the bailee has the option of suing on the contract or in tort[146] or for restitution.[147] This necessarily means that the existence of a contract right does not traditionally compel a suit in contract, but permits a conversion action (or in some instances a negligence action) if the plaintiff so chooses. Whether the tort claim is for negligence or for conversion depends on whether the facts show conversion and not something less. In one instance, the tort action may be inappropriate. Nonfeasance that does not damage the goods does not look like a conversion. For instance, if the bailee is expected to paint a bailed automobile, but returns it unpainted, he does not look like a converter. The bailor's claim, if he has one, should be exclusively on the contract in such a case.

Limiting the plaintiff's claim to contract actions—the economic loss rules. In recent decades, courts have increasingly been developing rules or doctrines often collectively or separately referred to as economic loss rules.[148] The rules, which eliminate tort claims, can apply where the defendant's wrong, whatever it is, does not cause physical harm or interference with person or property. A common example is a sales case: defendant contracts to deliver to plaintiff a truck suitable for hauling plaintiff's goods to customers. The truck that defendant provides is defective, and plaintiff suffers lost sales because he cannot make delivery to customers. Defendant has caused an economic harm in such a case, but no physical harm to plaintiff or plaintiff's property. One version of the economic loss doctrine holds that, where the parties are in a contractual relationship like the buyer and seller in the example, the defendant's negligence is not actionable as a tort in the absence of physical harm to person or property. Instead, the plaintiff must sue on the contract or not at all. By eliminating the tort claim, this version of the economic loss rule bars recovery altogether if for any reason the plaintiff cannot prevail in contract.

The economic loss doctrine in bailment cases. As generally understood, the economic loss doctrine has no application to cases of interference with tangible property—in bailment cases, the plaintiff can sue in tort or in contract. However, some courts have applied the rules for pure economic loss cases to ordinary conversions of tangible property, without acknowledging either the plaintiff's traditional option to sue in tort or the enormous difference in the approach taken in the pure economic tort cases.[149] Under this view, the plaintiff is compelled to sue in contract if she sues at all, even though the claim rests on interference with tangible property. If the contract contained a liquidated damages clause or the statute of limitations had run on the contract, the plaintiff might even be denied recovery of her own property by way of an action for detinue or replevin.[150]

---

[146] See, e.g., Celanese Corp. of America v. Mayor and Council of Wilmington, 46 Del. 114, 78 A.2d 249 (1950); Vandeventer v. Vandeventer, 132 Ohio App. 3d 762, 726 N.E.2d 534 (1999).

[147] E.g., Rock-Ola Mfg. Corp. v. Music & Television Corp., 339 Mass. 416, 159 N.E.2d 417 (1959).

[148] See Chapter 41.

[149] Command Cinema Corp. v. VCA Labs, Inc., 464 F.Supp. 2d 191 (S.D. N.Y. 2006) (bailed films or tapes not returned); Exxon Mobil Corp. v. Kinder Morgan Operating L.P., 192 S.W.3d 120 (Tex. App. 2006).

[150] See Dan B. Dobbs, The Law of Remedies § 4.2(3) (2d ed. 1993) (replevin as a means to recover converted property).

That in turn would mean that the defendant could simply appropriate the property for himself by paying contract damages, or by paying nothing at all if the contract statute of limitations had run.

Broad statement of the economic loss rule. Some courts may have made overly broad statements on this topic, perhaps without considering the specific bailment situation where the plaintiff traditionally has the option to sue in tort and where exculpatory clauses are often rejected.[151] Or broad pronouncements may be made without adverting to the traditional limits of the economic loss rule. However, it may be possible to restructure the economic loss doctrine into a general preference for contract over tort.[152] If that were to be done, the law of bailment and conversion of tangible goods will be radically altered. But there are reasons not to go so far. In the case of a bailment contract, denial of the tort remedy for non-return of the goods implicates the plaintiff's property rights in the goods. A rule that limited the plaintiff's claim to contract when the defendant failed to perform its duty to return the goods gives the defendant the right to take the plaintiff's property at a price. Perhaps this would be acceptable to some judges, but it seems justifiable only if judges are quite certain that the contract objectively meant to provide for such a forfeiture of property—a quite remote possibility in the case of a bailment.

§ 6.12   The Bona Fide Purchaser of Converted Tangible Goods

Suppose that Oscar is the owner of a valuable watch. Theo gains possession of the watch by theft or fraud, or as a merchant dealing in watches who promises to repair it. Having gained possession, Theo then sells the watch to the defendant who purchases in the good faith belief that Theo is the owner. Is the defendant a converter who is liable to Oscar?

(1)   A bona fide purchaser who buys from a thief-converter, including a converter who takes property by mistake,[153] is fully liable for conversion. The thief got no title and cannot pass title to a purchaser.

(2)   A bona fide purchaser who buys from one who has voidable title is not a converter. One who obtains the plaintiff's property by fraud has voidable title and can pass title to the purchaser if he does so before a legal or equitable action by the owner actually avoids the title.

(3)   Under the UCC, where an owner entrusts goods to a merchant who deals in goods of that kind (for repair, perhaps), a bona fide purchaser who buys such goods from the merchant making an unauthorized sale gets good title and is not a converter.

(4)   One who does not pay value—a donee, for example—is not a bona fide purchaser and is subject to liability for conversion.

Traditional rule of liability. Under the traditional common law rule, one who purchases converted goods from one who has no title is himself a converter by the very act of purchase. The purchaser may be wholly innocent, he may pay value for the goods

---

[151]   See § 6.10.

[152]   See Grynberg v. Questar Pipeline Co., 70 P.3d 1, 43 (Utah 2003) ("All contract duties, and all breaches of those duties—no matter how intentional—must be enforced pursuant to contract law.").

[153]   Kenyon v. Abel, 36 P.3d 1161 (Wyo. 2001).

and he may act in good faith. He is nevertheless a converter.[154] As already shown, good faith is sometimes said to be a factor in determining whether a brief interference with the goods is sufficiently serious to warrant liability for conversion.[155] However, that rule has no application to the case of a purchaser from one who, like a thief, has no title. In the purchaser's case, the act of purchase with its concomitant assertion of a right to the goods is by itself sufficiently serious and always counts as a conversion. If the purchaser is held liable to the owner, he has a claim against the person who sold him the goods, but this claim is seldom of any value to the innocent purchaser, who is usually sued only because the converter cannot be found or has no funds.

The innocent-purchaser rule is usually derived by reasoning in this way: a thief who converts goods does not get title to the goods by converting them. Title to the goods thus remains in the original owner even after the conversion. Since the thief-converter has no title, he cannot pass title to a purchaser, and this is true whether the purchaser is innocent or not. The rationale stands on two well-accepted rules about conversion: first, intent to deal with the goods is enough and bad faith is not required; and second, a purchase of goods is sufficient exercise of dominion or control to count as a conversion.

Traditional rule of non-liability: the bona fide purchaser from one who has voidable title. Conversion is only one of the methods by which a wrongdoer can separate victims from their property. Some others include fraud and duress. If the wrongdoer does not steal the plaintiff's property or obtain it by mistake but instead uses fraudulent representations to induce the plaintiff to give it to him, the wrongdoer acquires a voidable title. When the plaintiff discovers the fraud, she might decide to leave the property with the defendant and to recover damages for the fraud. Or she might decide to avoid the transfer because it was tainted with fraud. This right to avoid the fraudulent deal and get the property back is usually thought of as an equitable right or an "equity."

The victim who loses her property because of a wrongdoer's fraud may pursue either the damages remedy or the avoidance remedy, but unless and until she avoids the transaction, the wrongdoer still has title. He is therefore not in the same position as the ordinary converter. Since he has title, he can pass that title to a bona fide purchaser who pays value for the goods and who has no notice of the wrongdoing.[156] The bona fide purchaser who takes title from the wrongdoer is thus not a converter and not liable to the victim. In the traditional view, a bona fide purchase "cuts off equities" like the owner's right to avoid the fraudulent deal,[157] even though it does not cut off rights based on legal title.

The Uniform Commercial Code rule. The UCC, adopted in almost all states, adds a third rule about innocent purchasers that partly addresses the criticisms above. It provides that if a person entrusts his goods to a "merchant who deals in goods of that kind," then the merchant has a "power" to transfer all the title the entruster had.[158]

---

[154] Kahn v. Quintana, 811 P.2d 458 (Colo. App. 1991); O'Keefe v. Snyder, 83 N.J. 478, 416 A.2d 862 (1980).

[155] See § 6.6.

[156] UCC § 2–403 (1); see Jernigan v. Ham, 691 S.W.2d 553 (Tenn. App. 1984). If title is obtained other than by the owner's voluntary transfer, however, the title is void, not merely voidable. See Inmi-Etti v. Aluisi, 63 Md.App. 293, 492 A.2d 917 (1985).

[157] Western Idaho Production Credit Ass'n v. Simplot Feed Lots, Inc., 106 Idaho 260, 678 P.2d 52 (1984).

[158] UCC § 2–403 (2) ("Any entrusting of goods to a merchant that deals in goods of that kind gives the merchant power to transfer all of the entruster's rights to the goods and to transfer the goods free of any interest of the entruster to a buyer in ordinary course of business.").

For example, Brenda leaves her bicycle for repairs at a shop that sells bikes. The merhant repairs her bike, then sells it to you. You do not know that the bike is Brenda's, so you are a bona fide purchaser. Under the traditional rule you would still be liable as a converter because the merchant did not have any title to pass to you. Under the UCC provision, however, the merchant had power to pass you all the title that Brenda had in the bike.[159] So you own the bike, and you are therefore not a converter. The merchant definitely is a converter, however; he had a *power* to pass title in a way that protects you as the purchaser; but he had no title himself and no *right* to pass title. He would thus be liable to Brenda for the conversion of her bike.

§ 6.13 The Bona Fide Purchaser of Converted Money or Checks

Money and negotiable instruments such as checks are treated differently from tangible chattels. Nonpayment of a debt is of course not a conversion of the amount owed.[160] The traditional common law rule went far beyond that to hold that conversion did not lie even for the taking of paper money, except where it was specifically identified and described with particularity.[161] The plaintiff in such a case, however, had an action of some kind[162] and today the action may well be called one for conversion and entertained when the facts warrant.[163] Whatever the action is called, special rules apply to protect innocent persons to whom the stolen money is paid. The rule is that the person who innocently accepts money from a thief or embezzler is not a converter at all and not liable to the original owner.[164]

An example makes it clear why the rule is all but inevitable. Suppose a thief steals the plaintiff's money, then buys a loaf of bread from the baker. The baker has no knowledge of the money's provenance. If money were treated like a tangible chattel, the baker would be liable to the plaintiff who could make appropriate proof of the facts. But if the baker were liable, he would want to make inquiries about the source of monies offered him by customers, or perhaps he would only sell to customers known to him, or to those who could put up collateral security. Perhaps instead he would raise all prices to cover the costs of potential liability. In any event, trade would be slower or goods would be more costly; some customers might find it difficult to buy goods at all. The legal policy is to avoid the unimaginable inconvenience, commercial lethargy, higher costs, and perhaps discrimination that would result if the baker could not accept currency without inquiry into their source. Hence the rule protects those who receive money innocently, even if the money was in fact stolen from the plaintiff.

The policy to permit free passage of money in trade applies as well to negotiable instruments like checks and negotiable promissory notes.[165] In *Hinkle v. Cornwell Quality Tool Co.*,[166] Zelnar embezzled $57,000 from Hinkle. When discovered, she agreed to repay Hinkle. To that end, she embezzled sufficient sums from Cornwell, deposited them in her bank account, and then wrote checks to Hinkle for $57,000. Hinkle cashed

---

[159] See, e.g., Lindholm v. Brant, 283 Conn. 65, 925 A.2d 1048 (2007).

[160] See § 44.3.

[161] Taylor v. McNichols, 243 P.3d 2010 (Idaho 2010); see § 44.2.

[162] Assumpsit or a debt claim would suffice. Constructive trusts could be applied when the owner could trace the actual funds. See 1 Dan B. Dobbs, Law of Remedies §§ 4.3(2) & 6.1 (2d ed. 1993).

[163] See § 44.2.

[164] Kelley Kar Company v. Maryland Casualty Co., 142 Cal. App. 2d 263, 298 P.2d 590 (1956); City of Portland v. Berry, 86 Or. App. 376, 739 P.2d 1041 (1987).

[165] See, e.g., Federal Ins. Co. I.C. v. Banco de Ponce, 751 F.2d 38 (1st Cir. 1984).

[166] Hinkle v. Cornwell Quality Tool Co., 40 Ohio App. 3d 162, 532 N.E.2d 772 (1987).

the checks and was thus fully repaid. At that point Cornwell discovered that Hinkle had been paid with funds embezzled from Cornwell. Cornwell sued Hinkle. The court refused to permit Cornwell to recover.

Other and more complex doctrines may explain cases like *Hinkle*,[167] and in any event special rules and terminology of negotiable instrument law are codified in the UCC. However, the underlying policy is essentially the same as the policy towards money, with the result that those who are holders in due course of negotiable instruments are protected in much the same way as those who innocently accept money from a thief.

§ 6.14 Remedies for Conversion

Damages

The normal remedy for conversion is an award of damages. The traditional measure of damages (aside from loss-of-use damages) is the market value of the chattel at the time and place of conversion,[168] subject to limitations on liability the parties have validly contracted for.[169] In three different settings the recovery may be measured differently.

(1) Recovery of trespass damages instead. The plaintiff may treat the conversion as a trespass to chattels and sue for her actual damages rather than for the value of the chattel.[170] Where the defendant takes the chattel under a privilege, which he subsequently abuses, he may be no converter at all, and in that case the damages are limited to harm caused by the subsequent abuse.[171]

(2) Restitution—recovery of defendant's gain. The plaintiff may "waive the tort and sue in assumpsit," meaning that the plaintiff can have a restitutionary recovery for the gains the defendant made by converting the chattel. For example, if the chattel was worth $10 when it was converted by the defendant, and he later sells it for $20, the plaintiff would choose this option.[172]

(3) Recovery of a later price increase. When the value of the converted goods tends to fluctuate, as with commodities and with shares of corporate stock, some states permit the plaintiff to recover the value of the chattel at some time after conversion. For instance, if the plaintiff's wheat is worth $1 per bushel in November when it is converted, but the plaintiff only discovers the conversion the following May when wheat is selling for $2 a bushel, it seems obviously wrong to limit the plaintiff to the $1; had the wheat not been converted the plaintiff could have sold it at the $2 price. Even if the plaintiff discovers the conversion immediately, the price may rise before she can effectuate a replacement, so a recovery of the value of the wheat at the time of conversion would not fully compensate.[173]

---

[167] See 1 Dan B. Dobbs, Law of Remedies §§ 4.7(1) & 4.7(2) (2d ed. 1993).

[168] See, e.g., Trustees of Univ. of D.C. v. Vossoughi, 963 A.2d 1162 (D.C. 2009); C.A.R. Transp. Brokerage Co., Inc. v. Seay, 369 Ark. 354, 255 S.W.3d 445 (2007).

[169] See § 6.10.

[170] Vines v. Branch, 244 Va. 185, 418 S.E.2d 890 (1992).

[171] Foreign Car Ctr., Inc. v. Essex Process Serv. Inc., 62 Mass. App. Ct. 806, 821 N.E.2d 483 (2005).

[172] Cross v. Berg Lumber Co., 7 P.3d 922 (Wyo. 2000). The "waiver of tort rule," its peculiar terminology, and its practical effects are explained in 1 Dan B. Dobbs, Law of Remedies § 5.18 (2d ed. 1993).

[173] Some states cope with this problem by allowing the plaintiff the highest price or market value of the goods between conversion and the time of trial. See, e.g., Brown v. Campbell, 536 So.2d 920 (Ala. 1988). This may permit the plaintiff to speculate at the defendant's expense by delaying trial. New York gives the plaintiff the highest value of the goods between the time of conversion and a reasonable time for replacing them, which

Measuring loss-of-use damages. The traditional rule viewed interest from the time of conversion until judgment as an adequate compensation for loss of use, and such interest is undoubtedly recoverable today.[174] However, where the plaintiff needs the chattel or a temporary replacement, the more appropriate measure is the rental value of the converted chattel, or the actual costs of renting a reasonable substitute, or even profits unavoidably lost.[175] When the rental value or profit lost during the relevant period is awarded, no interest should be awarded for the same time period.[176]

Other consequential damages. A plaintiff may suffer additional losses, often called special or consequential damages, in addition to consequential damages for loss of use. For example, the plaintiff may be required to expend monies in trying to find the chattel or in providing a substitute.[177] In general, the plaintiff may recover reasonably proven consequential damages that could not have been reasonably avoided.[178] However, courts usually do not permit a recovery for emotional distress resulting solely from the conversion of a chattel.[179] When the chattel is not an item of value in the marketplace, courts offer a woolly rule that gives the jury a little leeway but not too much: the plaintiff can recover the value to the owner herself rather than market value, but may not get anything for sentimental attachment.[180]

Nominal damages. Courts have said that nominal damages, such as $1 or six cents, may be recovered in conversion actions where there are no provable actual damages.[181]

Punitive damages. Generally speaking, punitive damages are permissible only when the defendant has engaged in serious misconduct coupled with a reckless or malicious state of mind.[182] Some conversion cases fall into this category and permit the award of punitive damages.[183] For example, when the defendant has no honest claim of right to the plaintiff's goods, retention of the goods after a demand for their return would be evidence of malice that supports a punitive damages award, even if the initial taking of the goods was innocent.[184] Punitive damages awards are now subjected to

---

seems to offer a better chance for compensation without speculation. See Ahles v. Aztec Enterprises, Inc., 120 A.D.2d 903, 502 N.Y.S.2d 821 (1986).

[174] E.g., Florida Farm Bureau Casualty Ins. Co. v. Patterson, 611 So.2d 558 (Fla. Dist. Ct. App. 1992).

[175] Dan B. Dobbs, The Law of Remedies § 5.15 (2d ed. 1993)

[176] See Id.

[177] E.g., Veeco Instruments, Inc. v. Candido, 70 Misc.2d 333, 334 N.Y.S.2d 321, 324 (Sup. Ct. 1972) (computer program materials converted, plaintiff recovered costs of reprogramming).

[178] To the extent the conversion prevents operation of a profitable business, the plaintiff may be permitted to recover reasonably proven loss of profits during the period reasonably necessary to find substitute chattels. Newbury v. Virgin, 802 A.2d 413 (Me. 2002); Potter v. Washington State Patrol, 165 Wash. 2d 67, 85, 196 P.3d 691, 700 (2008).

[179] Lance Productions, Inc. v. Commerce Union Bank, 764 S.W.2d 207 (Tenn. App. 1988) (in the absence of malicious acts by the defendant, no emotional distress damages in conversion).

[180] Some courts allow recovery of value to the owner when that amount exceeds the chattel's market value. See, e.g., Trustees of University of Dist. of Columbia v. Vossoughi, 963 A.2d 1162 (D.C. 2009).

[181] MacGuire v. Elometa Corp., 189 A.D.2d 708, 592 N.Y.S.2d 730 (1993).

[182] See § 34.4.

[183] See, e.g., Schroeder v. Auto Driveaway Co., 11 Cal. 3d 908, 523 P.2d 662, 114 Cal. Rptr. 622 (1974) (conversion coupled with fraud); Craig & Bishop, Inc. v. Piles, 247 S.W.3d 897 (Ky. 2008) (when conversion is especially reprehensible); Newbury v. Virgin, 802 A.2d 413 (Me. 2002) (evidence of animosity and egregious misbehavior).

[184] See Darcars Motors of Silver Springs, Inc. v. Borzym, 379 Md. 249, 841 A.2d 828 (2004) (coupled with verbal taunting and the like).

constitutional constraints under the Due Process Clause, so that careful review is required, especially as to the amount awarded.[185]

Recovery of the Chattel—Replevin

If the plaintiff can identify the specific chattel converted by the defendant, the plaintiff usually has the option to recover the chattel itself, together with damages for any harms or losses resulting from its taking. Common law actions to recover the chattel[186] gave way in the United States to statutory actions often called replevin actions after one of their common law predecessors. In the traditional statutory replevin action, the sheriff seized the disputed property. If the plaintiff had posted a bond or other security, the sheriff could turn the property over to the plaintiff before trial. The plaintiff's bond guaranteed a return of the property or payment for it if it turned out after trial that the plaintiff was not entitled to it after all.

Pre-trial seizure of property obviously runs serious risks of error and abuse. In a series of cases, the Supreme Court of the United States has held that some kind of hearing ordinarily[187] must be held before a pre-trial seizure will be constitutional.[188] In response to these decisions, some jurisdictions have modified their statutes to require a brief adversary hearing before the property is seized. In some instances, the statute now authorizes a more straightforward procedure under which the judge, like the old equity judge, orders the defendant to deliver the property to the plaintiff or to deposit it in court.

§ 6.15 Statutes of Limitation in Conversion

The period in which suit must be brought for conversion is the period specified by statute, but even so, the period may turn out to be indefinite or uncertain because several rules have the effect of shifting the prescriptive period or the way it is computed.

Multiple statutes of limitation governing different conversions. States may have two or more statutes of limitation on conversion. These include the general statute of limitations[189] and a special statute under the UCC for conversion of commercial instruments.[190] In addition, some states have still other limitation periods for special cases of conversion.[191] The prescriptive period in a state's general statute and the period

---

[185] See § 34.6.

[186] The common law rights to recover the chattel grew out of the writs of *Detinue* and *Replevin* each circumscribed in particular ways. See 1 Dan B. Dobbs, Law of Remedies § 4.2(2) (2d ed. 1993).

[187] Mitchell v. W. T. Grant Co., 416 U.S. 600, 94 S. Ct. 1895, 40 L.Ed.2d 406 (1974), took a more lenient view where a lienholder sequestered property without notice, but where there was judicial supervision and a factual rather than a conclusory affidavit.

[188] Sniadach v. Family Finance Corp. of Bay View, 395 U.S. 337, 89 S.Ct. 1820, 23 L.Ed.2d 349 (1969) (garnishment of wages without notice or hearing violates due process); Fuentes v. Shevin, 407 U.S. 67, 92 S. Ct. 1983, 32 L.Ed.2d 556 (1972) (provisional relief under replevin statutes without a hearing before seizure violates due process); North Georgia Finishing, Inc. v. Di-Chem, Inc., 419 U.S. 601, 95 S.Ct. 719, 42 L.Ed.2d 751 (1975) (garnishment of corporate bank account without hearing, with no provision for early hearing after garnishment violates due process).

[189] E.g., N.Y. CPLR § 214 (three years for "an action to recover a chattel or damages for the taking or detaining of a chattel").

[190] UCC § 3–118 (action for conversion "of an instrument, for money had and received, or like action based on conversion, . . . must be commenced within three years after the [cause of action] accrues").

[191] E.g., Mont. Code Ann. § 27–2–304 (prescribing special time computation for property taken after death of owner and before letters of administration are issued); N.Y. CPLR § 213 (actions by state for misappropriation of state property, six years).

in the UCC or other special statute may not be the same.[192] This difference sets up the potential for arguments that one of the statutes applies and the other does not.

Shifting the legal conception of the plaintiff's cause of action. In many instances, the facts supporting the plaintiff's claim for conversion can be equally or better conceptualized as a claim for breach of contract, fraud, or some other action. If the statutory periods of limitation are different for each of those causes of action, the court's characterization of the claim will determine the applicable period. So a court may think that the gist or gravamen of a claim is contract rather than conversion, and therefore apply the shorter statute or other rules for contract.[193] Likewise, a court may think that the gist of the action is conversion rather than breach of contract and so apply the shorter statute for conversion.[194] The method for determining the gist or gravamen is vague at best; courts often decide the "gist" of the action without any reference to the policy of honoring the contract. Courts need not make this "gist" determination where the plaintiff has waived the tort and has sued in assumpsit. In such a situation the plaintiff has elected to treat the conversion as a breach of contract and recover restitution,[195] and courts routinely treat the case as one with the attributes of contract,[196] applying the statute of limitations for contract, not for conversion.[197]

Accrual: time of conversion or discovery. In the case of conversion of ordinary chattels, the older rule starts the statute of limitations running at the time of conversion, not at the time the conversion was or should have been discovered.[198] However, a number of courts, sometimes under the impetus of a statute, have supported the discovery rule, holding that the cause of action accrues only when the owner discovered or should have discovered the conversion.[199] When the conversion is accomplished by negotiation or conversion of negotiable instrument, most courts have continued to apply the time-of-conversion rule. For example, if the defendant bank converts the plaintiff's bank account by honoring a forged check, the statute begins to run at the time the account is charged.[200] In these commercial instrument cases, courts emphasize the need for commercial certainty, the importance of free negotiability, and the need for uniform commercial rules across the nation.

—Time of demand. When the defendant rightfully comes into possession of property, for instance when he borrows property or stores it for the owner, he is not a converter merely because he holds the property in accord with the terms of the bailment. He may become a converter, however, if he destroys or sells the property, if a return becomes

---

[192] For instance, the general statute may prescribe a period of two years, as in 12 Okla. Stat. Ann. § 95, while the UCC prescribes three years. UCC § 3–118.

[193] French-Tex Cleaners, Inc. v. Cafaro Co., 893 N.E.2d 1156 (Ind. App. 2008); cf. Klein v. Gutman, 12 A.D.3d 417, 419, 784 N.Y.S.2d 581, 584 (2004) ("The gravamen of the complaint sounds wholly in fraud, not conversion.").

[194] Ernest F. Loewer, Jr. Farms, Inc. v. National Bank of Arkansas, 316 Ark. 54, 870 S.W.2d 726 (1994).

[195] See 1 Dan B. Dobbs, The Law of Remedies § 4–2(3) (2d. ed. 1993).

[196] Id.

[197] H. Russell Taylor's Fire Prevention Serv., Inc. v. Coca Cola Bottling Corp., 99 Cal. App. 3d 711, 160 Cal. Rptr. 411 (1979); Dentists' Supply Co. of N.Y. v. Cornelius, 281 A.D. 306, 119 N.Y.S.2d 570 (1953).

[198] See, e.g., Davis v. Monahan, 832 So.2d 708 (Fla. 2002); State v. Seventh Regiment Fund, Inc., 98 N.Y.2d 249, 774 N.E.2d 702, 746 N.Y.S.2d 637 (2002).

[199] Bemis v. Estate of Bemis, 967 P.2d 437 (Nev. 1998); Investors REIT One v. Jacobs, 46 Ohio St. 3d 176, 546 N.E.2d 206 (1989); Kordis v. Kordis, 37 P.3d 866 (Okla. 2001); Cross v. Berg Lumber Co., 7 P.3d 922 (Wyo. 2000).

[200] Husker News Co. v. Mahaska State Bank, 460 N.W.2d 476 (Iowa 1990); Yarbro, Ltd. v. Missoula Fed. Credit Union, 50 P.3d 158 (Mont. 2002).

impossible and a demand for it useless, or if he fails to return it at the time agreed upon.[201] Otherwise, he becomes a converter only when he refuses to honor a demand by the plaintiff for the property's return. In the case of such bailees, then, the cause of action does not accrue until a demand is made and the defendant withholds the property.[202]

—*Serial conversions.* It is possible to start the statute of limitations running at the time when the plaintiff discovered or should have discovered the theft (or possibly when the plaintiff should have located the possessor of the goods). A "should have discovered" rule has been applied to complicated problem of recovering Nazi-looted art.[203] At the same time, the substantive rules of conversion make it clear that a series of conversions of the same chattel can take place over a period of time. For example, Abel may steal the property, then sell it to Baker. In such a case, both Abel and Baker are converters and liable to the owner in a timely suit. Without a discovery rule, the statute of limitations begins to run in Abel's favor at the time of his theft. Since he has already converted the chattel, his sale of the property to Baker need not be regarded as a new conversion that starts the statute running all over again.[204] On the other hand, Baker's purchase normally counts as a conversion by Baker, and we might expect that, in a suit against Baker, the statute would start running at the time of his purchase or the discovery of the cause of action against him where the discovery rule applies. The upshot is that serial conversions may call for separate statutes of limitation for each converter or at least give the plaintiff the benefit of such a rule or the discovery rule, whichever is more favorable. In the absence of a discovery rule, then, it is quite possible that by the time the plaintiff sues, the statute will have run as to converter Abel but not as to converter Baker.

However, a major qualification is likely to apply. Suppose the statute of limitations has run on the claim against Abel *before* Baker makes his purchase. In that instance, it looks as if Abel, who can no longer be sued, has become the owner. As owner he can pass good title to Baker, who would thus not be a converter at all. The New Jersey Court has said something like this in the case of a theft of a painting by the famous artist, Georgia O'Keeffe.[205]

---

[201] See Zimmerman v. Firstier Bank, 585 N.W.2d 445 (Neb. 1998) (demand not necessary when it would be futile or unavailing); Pecoraro v. M & T Bank Corp., 11 A.D.3d 950, 782 N.Y.S.2d 481 (2004) (bank's conversion occurred upon its destruction of plaintiff's safe deposit box, not at later date of plaintiff's demand).

[202] E.g., Kornegay v. Thompson, 157 Ga. App. 558, 278 S.E.2d 140 (1981); see Annotation, When statute of limitations starts to run against bailor's action for recovery, or for damages for conversion or detention of property deposited for an indefinite time, 57 A.L.R.2d 1044 (1958).

[203] von Saher v. Norton Simon Museum of Art as Pasadena, 592 F.3d 954 (9th Cir. 2010) (rejecting special protections for owners of Nazi-looted art as inconsistent with federal law and applying California's discovery rule instead).

[204] See Harpending v. Meyer, 55 Cal. 555 (1880) (pawnbroker accepted the pawn of the plaintiff's jewelry from Baux, then, when it was not redeemed, sold it much later; the statute runs from the time he accepted the pawn).

[205] O'Keeffe v. Snyder, 83 N.J. 478, 416 A.2d 862 (1980). According to the *O'Keeffe* court, the discovery rule would determine whether the statute had run in the first place. If the statute had run under that rule, then title would pass to the thief, just as it would have passed under the adverse possession rules.

Chapter 7

DEFENSES TO INTENTIONAL TORTS

Analysis

A. SELF-DEFENSE AND DEFENSE OF OTHERS

§ 7.1   General Rule
§ 7.2   When Retreat is Required
§ 7.3   Objective vs. Subjective Perceptions of Threat
§ 7.4   Types of Harm Appropriate for Self-Defense
§ 7.5   Defending Another Person from Apparent Attack

B. DISCIPLINE

§ 7.6   Parental Privileges to Discipline Children
§ 7.7   Discipline by Non-Parents in Charge of Minors

C. DEFENSE AND RECOVERY OF PROPERTY

§ 7.8   Defending Possession of Land or Chattels: General Rule
§ 7.9   Qualifying and Explaining the General Rule
§ 7.10   Deadly Traps in Defense of Property: Spring Guns
§ 7.11   Qualifying and Considering the Deadly-Trap Rules
§ 7.12   Types of "Traps" and Negligence Law
§ 7.13   Repossession of Land
§ 7.14   Repossession of Chattels: General Rules
§ 7.15   The Repossessing Seller
§ 7.16   Entering Another's Land to Recapture Chattels

D. PRIVILEGES TO DETAIN OR ARREST

§ 7.17   The Merchant's Privilege to Detain for Investigation
§ 7.18   Privileged Arrests

E. NECESSITY

§ 7.19   Private Necessity
§ 7.20   Public Necessity
§ 7.21   Public Entities: Necessity, Police Power, and "Taking"

A. SELF-DEFENSE AND DEFENSE OF OTHERS

§ 7.1   General Rule

A person is privileged to use reasonable force to defend himself against unprivileged acts that he reasonably believes will cause him bodily harm, offensive bodily contact, or confinement. The privilege exists even though his use of reasonable force would otherwise amount to a tort such as a battery or assault, but limits are imposed upon the use of deadly force or force likely to cause grave bodily injury. Similar rules grant a privilege to protect other persons from harm.[1] These privileges to defend self or others are affirmative defenses, on which the defendant ordinarily has the burden of proof.[2]

Timing of the use of force. The privilege of self-defense is a privilege to avoid or minimize harm to oneself. It is not a privilege to retaliate or avenge harm already inflicted.[3] Likewise, it is a privilege based on immediate need to prevent an imminent invasion of one's person,[4] or at least on an immediate necessity to prevent a future harm.[5] If the danger reasonably appears to be imminent, the defendant need not await the first blow before asserting himself. On the other hand, the privilege of self-defense cannot be invoked to justify a preemptive strike against someone who threatens no immediate harm merely on the ground that he might attack in the future.[6]

Reasonable force. The force used by the defendant in the exercise of his privilege must be reasonable under the circumstances as they reasonably appeared to the defendant, based on the actual knowledge possessed by the defendant. If the circumstances warrant, the defendant may commit acts that would otherwise constitute a battery, an assault, or a false imprisonment.[7] A technical assault, being a mere threat of battery, may be privileged even when a battery itself would constitute excessive force.[8] The degree of force that is reasonable depends in large measure upon the harm threatened and in some measure on the whole circumstances of the case, including the alternatives that were available to the defendant. In judging reasonableness of the force, courts do not expect the defendant to make a "microscopic analysis" of the situation, only to act reasonably considering the emergency.[9] But deadly force, or force threatening grave bodily harm, is excessive except as a last resort, when the defendant reasonably believes himself to be attacked by such force.[10]

Liability for unreasonable force. If he uses excessive force, the defendant himself becomes, to that extent, a tortfeasor and he will himself be liable for harms caused by the excess.[11] In that case, the original attacker is privileged to defend against the excess force,[12] once the original attacker has attempted to withdraw from his aggressive posture

---

[1] See § 7.5.

[2] E.g., Boyer v. Waples, 206 Cal.App.2d 725, 24 Cal.Rptr. 192 (1962); Winn v. Inman, 119 Ill.App.3d 836, 457 N.E.2d 141 (1983). When the plaintiff claims excessive force by an arresting officer, however, the plaintiff may be required to prove excessive force as part of his prima facie case.

[3] Restatement Second of Torts § 63, cmt. g (1965).

[4] E.g., Martin v. Estrella, 107 R.I. 247, 266 A.2d 41 (1970). Imminent, impending, and "then and there" are phrases used in most of the definitions. Courts sometimes emphasize that the privilege depends upon the fact that resort to courts is impractical.

[5] See Robert Schopp, Barbara Sturgis & Megan Sullivan, Battered Woman Syndrome, Expert Testimony, and the Distinction between Justification and Excuse, 1994 U. Ill. L. Rev. 45, 66 ff. (1994).

[6] Restatement Second of Torts § 63, cmt. g (1965).

[7] Id. § 70.

[8] Id. § 70(2).

[9] In re Paul F., 543 A.2d 255, 257 (R.I. 1988) ("Rather we should view the disruptive and emotional furor that was created by Addison as the events must have appeared to Paul at the time.").

[10] Martin v. Yeoham, 419 S.W.2d 937, 950 (Mo. App. 1967) (to justify deadly force "[t]here must be reasonable cause of apprehension of imminent danger of death or great bodily harm").

[11] E.g., Jahner v. Jacob, 233 N.W.2d 791 (N.D. 1975). One who inflicts bodily harm or offense by using more force than permitted by the privilege is liable for a battery, whether the force is used in self-defense or in the exercise of some other privilege, such as the privilege to make an arrest. Schumann v. McGinn, 307 Minn. 446, 240 N.W.2d 525 (1976).

[12] Fraguglia v. Sala, 17 Cal.App.2d 738, 62 P.2d 783 (1936); Restatement Second of Torts § 71 (1965).

and no longer poses a threat.[13] The defendant is only liable for the excess, not for the privileged force, but if he has caused an indivisible harm, one that cannot practically be separated, he is liable for the entire harm.[14]

Unreasonable force as intentional tort. When a defendant uses excessive force in defense, or uses force where no force at all was reasonable, he is liable for an intentional tort. This is so even where the defendant is merely mistaken about the need for force, or the amount of force needed, in which case his actions closely resemble negligence. Unless some distinct act of negligence is identified, the question in such a situation is whether the defendant exceeded his privilege and thus committed an intentional tort, not whether he was negligent.[15]

Criminal law self-defense rules. The common law self-defense rules are often elaborated from the rules used in criminal prosecutions, which in turn are usually derived from statutes. Sometimes these criminal statutes expressly apply to civil cases as well;[16] other criminal provisions may be expressly incorporated into civil statutes.[17] Even where the connection is not explicit in a statute, criminal precedents are often good guides to the tort law rule. In some instances, however, criminal statutes may contain provisions at odds with the common law tort rules, and the concerns of both policy and justice in criminal cases may be sufficiently different to call for different results in particular instances. Thus criminal statutes and cases should be consulted in tort cases, but analogies must be drawn with care.

§ 7.2　　When Retreat Is Required

Avoidance or retreat generally. In the usual case, the defendant may defend himself from harm by using non-deadly force, even if he could avoid injury by retreating or by complying with some improper demand asserted by the plaintiff and even if his self-defense will inflict harm on the plaintiff.[18] This is also the rule in criminal law.[19]

Negligently threatened harm. But if the harm threatened is unintentional, merely the result of the plaintiff's negligence, the defendant should reasonably avoid the harm if possible, rather than inflict harm upon the negligent plaintiff.[20] In many imaginable cases, this rule may represent only a specific instance of the more general rule that only reasonable force should be used. The plaintiff should not avoid harm to himself by derailing the negligently driven trolley if he can avoid harm by stepping off the track.

Evasion or retreat to avoid the use of deadly force. If the attacker is threatening immediate use of force that reasonably appears likely to cause death or serious bodily harm, the defendant may respond with deadly force if that is the only safe alternative.[21]

---

[13]　Gortarez v. Smitty's Super Valu, Inc., 140 Ariz. 97, 680 P.2d 807 (1984); Jelly v. Dabney, 581 P.2d 622 (Wyo. 1978).

[14]　Restatement Second of Torts § 71, cmt. b (1965).

[15]　District of Columbia v. Chinn, 839 A.2d 701 (D.C. 2003) (on this reasoning, holding it was error to submit both a battery and a negligence theory to the jury.).

[16]　E.g., Ala. Code § 13A–3–23(d) (immunizing person using deadly force in self-defense in some circumstances from both criminal prosecution and civil action); Iowa Code Ann. § 707.6.

[17]　See, e.g., Tex. Civ. Prac. & Remedies Code § 83.001 (2007) (expressly incorporating Penal Code § 9.42 provision that allows the use of deadly force in defense in particular circumstances).

[18]　Restatement Second of Torts § 63 (1965).

[19]　2 Wayne R. LaFave, Substantive Criminal Law 142, 155 (2d ed. 2003).

[20]　Restatement Second of Torts § 64 (1965).

[21]　Id. § 65(1).

But if the defendant can avoid the use of deadly force and harm to himself by a retreat, authorities are divided. The Restatement Second of Torts, speaking only to tort claims and not to criminal prosecutions, has it that one must retreat to avoid inflicting deadly force, provided the retreat can be effected in complete safety.[22] Likewise, if the defendant can avoid the use of deadly force and protect himself adequately by relinquishing some privilege, he must do that.[23]

Many courts, usually said to be a majority, traditionally permit the use of deadly force to counter deadly force without any general requirement of retreat. Such courts might require some kind of retreat to show withdrawal by one who was initially the aggressor, but otherwise allow the defendant to defend himself with deadly force so long as such force was otherwise a reasonable response to an apparent threat.[24]

Most of the cases involve criminal prosecutions, not tort claims, so the legal ideas on this subject are principally generated in the criminal process, which as noted above[25] may be largely based on criminal statutes.[26] As criminal statutes are amended or recodified, they may require a retreat when it can be made safely.[27] This process of change in criminal statutes is likely to encourage courts to adopt a corresponding rule for self-defense in tort cases. Consequently the tort rule on retreat in a given jurisdiction may be discovered lurking in the implications of criminal statutes.

Reasons for a retreat requirement. Reasons given for a retreat requirement usually emphasize the value of human life, as well as the danger of an escalating affray. However, it is quite possible that courts also have in mind a number of practical dangers. History is written by the winners and lethal self-defense may leave few or no independent witnesses to contradict the easy claim of self-defense. In many cases the risk of error on the whole question of self-defense is quite high because the sudden unfolding of events and the shifting behaviors of the antagonists baffle attempts to determine who, at any given moment, is actually the aggressor. Because the risk of error in determining whether the defendant is standing his ground or acting on a license to kill is potentially so high, a requirement of retreat might seem better protection than some alteration of the proof burdens.

Exceptions to the retreat requirement. Even under the rule that a safe retreat is preferable to use of deadly force, the defendant is not required to retreat when he is already in his own home or dwelling place.[28] Nor need the defendant abandon an attempt at a lawful arrest to avoid using deadly force in self-defense.[29] That is not to say, of

---

[22] Id. § 65.

[23] Id. § 65(3). But he need not relinquish his dwelling place or the privilege of making a lawful arrest. Nor of course need he sacrifice his own body to some physical attack. Id., § 65(1)(b).

[24] E.g., People v. Willner, 879 P.2d 19 (Colo. 1994).

[25] See § 7.1.

[26] See, e.g., Tex. Penal Code § 9.32 (c) & (d).

[27] E.g., Conn. Gen. Stats. Ann. § 53a–19(b) (defendant required to retreat before using deadly force, with some exceptions).

[28] E.g., Hanauer v. Coscia, 157 Conn. 49, 54, 244 A.2d 611, 614 (1968) ("Where a person, without fault, is assaulted in his home, he is not required to retreat from his assailant but may resist even to the extent of seriously injuring his adversary when it becomes necessary."); State v. Johnson, 261 N.C. 727, 136 S.E.2d 84 (1964).

[29] Fields v. Dailey, 68 Ohio App.3d 33, 587 N.E.2d 400 (1990); Restatement Second of Torts § 65(2)(c) (1965).

course, that deadly force can always be used to effect an arrest, only that it can be used in self-defense against deadly force.[30]

§ 7.3   Objective vs. Subjective Perceptions of Threat

Appearance of attack: objective standards. The defendant can claim the privilege of self-defense only if he in fact or subjectively believes that the defense was needed because of harm about to occur.[31] But, with only a little authority to the contrary,[32] a mere subjective belief is not sufficient to invoke the privilege. The defendant must also entertain an objectively warranted basis for belief that defense is required. That is, he may use force only if reasonable people in the same situation would perceive the need for force.[33] The amount of force used comes under the same objective standard: it is justified only to the extent that it is reasonable in light of the apparent need.[34]

Objective judgment about subjectively known facts. The tort law standard is objective in the sense that it refuses to justify the use of force on the basis of bizarre perceptions. A chipper "good morning" from an acquaintance would not be perceived by a reasonable person as a harbinger of an imminent attack; thus a defendant who tries to use self-defense to justify a punch in the greeter's nose would not succeed on that argument. But while the tort-law standard requires objective reasonableness, the facts actually known to the defendant are taken into account. Thus if the attacker knew that this seemingly friendly acquaintance had earlier threatened to stab him at their next meeting, the picture changes entirely and the defensive punch might be seen as entirely reasonable. A similar conclusion would follow if the attacker knew that this acquaintance has in the past exploded in violence after smiling and saying, "Good morning." That is, the facts known to the defendant and all the perceptions of events that reasonably grow out of those facts are taken into account in determining the reasonableness of the defendant's actions. Applying this rule, cases have held that if the defendant knows that his attacker has violent propensities,[35] or if he has been hostile to the defendant in the past,[36] he may reasonably perceive an attack, even though bystanders who lack such information would not recognize the need for defense.

Unjustified use of force. The objective standard means that the defendant's irrational fears, or a belief that attack is imminent when there is no evidence of it, do not justify an attack on another, much less an attack with deadly force.[37] Although the facts subjectively known to the defendant are accepted as a basis for action, the action

---

[30]   See Tennessee v. Garner, 471 U.S. 1, 105 S.Ct. 1694, 85 L.Ed.2d 1 (1985).

[31]   E.g., McCoy v. Taylor Tire Co., 254 S.W.2d 923, 924 (Ky. 1953); Tatman v. Cordingly, 672 P.2d 1286 (Wyo. 1983).

[32]   See Moor v. Licciardello, 463 A.2d 268 (Del. 1983) (applying in civil cases a purely subjective standard for self-defense contained in a criminal statute).

[33]   Crabtree v. Dawson, 119 Ky. 148, 83 S.W. 557 (1904) (defendant, believing that one Noble was about to attack him with bricks, and that the plaintiff was Noble, struck the plaintiff and knocked him down a flight of stairs; the defendant could rely on reasonable appearances even though he struck the wrong person); Jahner v. Jacob, 233 N.W.2d 791 (N.D. 1975); Restatement Second of Torts § 63, cmt. i (1965).

[34]   See Boyer v. Waples, 206 Cal.App.2d 725, 727, 24 Cal.Rptr. 192 (1962).

[35]   See Martin v. Estrella, 107 R.I. 247, 266 A.2d 41 (1970) (defendant's knowledge of plaintiff's reputation for violence was admissible); Villines v. Tomerlin, 206 Cal.App.2d 448, 452, 23 Cal.Rptr. 617 (1962) (defendant could "offer evidence of prior specific acts of violence or prior threats of violence to show that plaintiff is a turbulent and dangerous man and the defendant's knowledge thereof").

[36]   Bradley v. Hunter, 413 So.2d 674 (La. App. 1982) (woman's past trouble with man who approached her cursing and threatening; a shot in the head was self-defense, though the man appeared to have no weapon); Maichle v. Jonovic, 69 Wis.2d 622, 230 N.W.2d 789 (1975) (course of attacks by two boys).

[37]   Tatman v. Cordingly, 672 P.2d 1286, 1290 (Wyo. 1983).

itself must reasonably grow out of those facts, or out of appearances that would be shared by other reasonable people, not out of idiosyncratic fears or biases.

This application of the objective standard is sometimes meliorated in practice, however, by the recognition that even the hypothetical reasonable person cannot make a perfectly cool judgment about the force needed in an emergency such as a burglary or a robbery.[38]

Justified use of force. The objective standard leaves the honest but irrational defendant subject to tort liability. But it also excuses the honest and rational response even if that response is mistaken. The defendant is privileged to respond to an apparent threat of attack by the plaintiff, even if it turns out later that the plaintiff never intended to attack at all. So, although mistake itself is not a defense, the defendant's mistaken perception of an attack will warrant reasonable use of force in response, so long as reasonable people in possession of the facts known to the defendant would have perceived the plaintiff's conduct as a threat warranting the response.[39]

§ 7.4   Types of Harm Appropriate for Self-Defense

Self-help. In some instances the law permits a person to remedy past wrongs by self-help and in so doing, to protect himself against future wrongs. Within limits, for example, a person harmed by a nuisance might be privileged to abate it, just as a landowner might be privileged to remove a trespassing object. Self-help is closely analogous to self-defense but may be broader.

Self-defense against physical harms. The self-defense privilege as such is usually raised when the defendant is subjected to physical threat—assault, battery, or false imprisonment. The usual case is a threatened harmful battery. The plaintiff advances upon the defendant with a pitchfork; the defendant responds with a whip. But self-defense is equally warranted against the elevator cowboy's furtive gropings that threaten only offensive, not harmful, batteries.[40] The defendant may also be privileged to defend himself against negligently caused harm by committing acts that would otherwise amount to a trespassory tort such as battery.[41]

Self-defense against words. But the provocative words of an antagonist do not justify a battery to silence the antagonist's utterances.[42] Verbal provocation is no defense, although it does bear on the propriety of punitive damages.[43]

Self-defense against false imprisonment. The defendant who is about to be subjected to confinement, or reasonably appears to be, is ordinarily entitled to use reasonable force to protect himself against such confinement.[44] When the confinement is threatened by an officer, however, special rules may apply.

Self-defense against an officer's unlawful arrest. Courts do not agree about whether the privilege to resist confinement extends to the case of an unlawful arrest by an officer. A number of courts hold that even though an officer's arrest is unlawful, the victim of

---

[38] See, e.g., Bennett v. Dunn, 507 So.2d 451 (Ala. 1987).

[39] Hanauer v. Coscia, 157 Conn. 49, 54, 244 A.2d 611, 614 (1968); Restatement Second of Torts § 63, cmts. h & i (1965).

[40] Restatement Second of Torts § 63(1) (1965) (privilege extends to offensive as well as harmful contact).

[41] Id.

[42] Crotteau v. Karlgaard, 48 Wis.2d 245, 179 N.W.2d 797 (1970).

[43] Manning v. Michael, 188 Conn. 607, 616, 452 A.2d 1157, 1162 (1982).

[44] Restatement Second of Torts § 68 (1965).

that arrest has no privilege to resist.[45] For this view it is said that resistance to an officer's arrest encourages expanding violence and that the victim of such an arrest today enjoys a good probability that bail will be available so that he can promptly be released, that illegally obtained evidence will be excluded from any trial, and that he will have a damages action to redress the wrong.[46]

Some courts, however, still maintain the contrary view,[47] which has a degree of appeal in tort suits. The officer who has attempted an unlawful arrest meets resistance that causes him harm, then sues the citizen he wrongfully attacked, so that the citizen might understandably perceive himself to be twice victimized by the officer. In such cases the policy of minimizing the risk of expanding violence conflicts directly with the demands of justice. Although the choice is no easy matter, the victim's opportunity for redress in the courts at a later date suggests that a rule against a right to resist might substantially satisfy both the desire for peace and the desire for justice.

§ 7.5   Defending Another Person from Apparent Attack

A person is privileged not only to defend himself but also to defend others from an attack that appears to threaten imminent harm to them. Defense of others follows the same analysis as defense of one's own person. The defendant who intervenes to defend another must believe that the victim would have the privilege of self-defense, that is, that the attack makes defense necessary to avoid imminent harm. Reasonable appearances must also justify that belief, and the force used by the defendant must be reasonable in light of the threat. Under such conditions, one is privileged to defend another as well as himself.[48]

Two views once restricted the intervener's privilege. The first was that only family members or those with a special duty of protection enjoyed the privilege. This now seems to be obsolete.[49] A second restriction was that the intervener stood in the shoes of the apparent victim of the attack and had no more privilege than the "victim" had. So if the intervener came to the defense of a "victim" who in fact was an aggressor or who was being lawfully arrested by an officer, he would be liable civilly or to criminal prosecution. Put differently, the good Samaritan who intervened to assist the victim of an attack took the risk that appearances might be deceiving.[50]

At the middle of the twentieth century, the view just stated may have been the common one, so that the privilege for protection of third persons was limited to interveners who correctly perceived the need for protection. However, many states have now enacted criminal statutes that specifically permit the defense of third persons based on apparent need for such a defense.[51] Accordingly, in criminal prosecutions, the

---

[45]   Rhiner v. City of Clive, 373 N.W.2d 466 (Iowa 1985); State v. Haas, 134 N.H. 480, 596 A.2d 127 (1991); State v. Hobson, 218 Wis.2d 350, 577 N.W.2d 825 (1998).

[46]   See State v. Hatton, 116 Ariz. 142, 568 P.2d 1040 (1977).

[47]   White v. Morris, 345 So.2d 461, 466 (La. 1977) ("we cannot abrogate our citizens' time-honored right to resist an unlawful arrest"); State v. Wiegmann, 350 Md. 585, 714 A.2d 841 (1998).

[48]   Restatement Second of Torts § 76 (1965).

[49]   See Gortarez v. Smitty's Super Valu, Inc., 140 Ariz. 97, 680 P.2d 807 (1984); Hartley v. Oidtman, 410 S.W.2d 537 (Mo. App. 1966).

[50]   People v. Young, 11 N.Y.2d 274, 183 N.E.2d 319, 229 N.Y.S.2d 1 (1962).

[51]   E.g., N.Y. Penal Law § 35.15; Conn. Gen. Stats. Ann § 53a–19. See also Danny Veilleux, Annotation, Construction and Application of Statutes Justifying the Use of Force to Prevent the Use of Force Against Another, 71 A.L.R.4th 940 (1989).

reasonably mistaken intervener may be fully protected.[52] Most criminal statutes do not by their terms prescribe a tort-law rule,[53] but at a minimum they reflect an attitude and a policy that will presumably carry over easily to protect the reasonably mistaken intervener in tort cases.

B. DISCIPLINE

§ 7.6   Parental Privileges to Discipline Children

The state has a general duty to protect children and it may remove children from the custody of abusive or neglectful parents. It may also criminally prosecute parents who abuse their children. As to the civil liability of parents under tort law, parents are still generally immune from liability in tort to their children in some states.[54] Where the parental tort immunity has been abolished or limited, parents may still be privileged to carry out specific acts that, but for the privilege, would count as a tort. In particular, parents and those who act in the place of parents, are privileged to apply a degree of force or to impose confinement upon their minor children,[55] a rule largely correlative with the parents' duty to provide for their children.

Although the amount and kind of force that is privileged is obviously limited, it is difficult to formulate a standard describing the limit. An appropriate standard would establish limits but would also recognize the wide cultural and personal differences among parents about methods of child-rearing.[56] The Restatement attempts to solve the problem by saying that the parents may apply the force or impose the confinement that they reasonably believe is necessary for controlling or training their children.[57] Presumably this standard excludes liability for child spanking even though many people oppose such punishment, but at the same time would not exclude liability for burning a child with cigarettes or locking her in a closet for days without food.

Perhaps recognizing that its standard cannot readily be applied, the Restatement adds a series of factors to be considered in determining whether the punishment inflicted is reasonable and administered for the control or training of the child. Factors bearing on the question include the age and condition of the child, the nature of the child's offense, the possibility of an example to other children in the family, whether the punishment inflicted is "necessary and appropriate" to compel obedience, and whether it is disproportionate, unnecessarily degrading or likely to cause serious or permanent harm.[58]

---

[52]   See People v. Smith, 19 Ill.App.3d 704, 312 N.E.2d 355 (1974). The Model Penal Code § 3.05 provides for full protection of the mistaken intervener if "under the circumstances as the actor believes them to be, the person whom he seeks to protect would be justified in using such protective force."

[53]   Some state criminal codes do contain provisions covering civil liability. E.g., Iowa Code Ann. § 707.6 ("No person who injures the aggressor through application of reasonable force in defense of a second person may be held civilly liable for such injury.").

[54]   See Chapter 23.

[55]   Restatement Second of Torts § 147 (1965).

[56]   Cf. Holodook v. Spencer, 36 N.Y.2d 35, 324 N.E.2d 338, 364 N.Y.S.2d 859 (1974) (emphasizing different economic, education, cultural, ethnic and religious attitudes toward child-rearing that make it difficult to judge parental negligence toward a child).

[57]   Restatement Second of Torts § 147 (1965).

[58]   Id. § 150.

§ 7.7   Discipline by Non-Parents in Charge of Minors

The parents' privilege to discipline children is extended to persons who are properly in charge of children but who are not actually parents of the children.[59] This may include schools and teachers, school bus drivers, child-care attendants, surrogate parents and others similarly situated. Persons who take the role of parents, temporarily or permanently, are also accorded a privilege to discipline the child. However, in some cases at least, the parent may impose restrictions on the privilege, for example, by forbidding the babysitter to spank a child.[60] In addition, the amount of force that is acceptable when applied by a parent may be found to be unreasonable when applied by a person only temporarily in charge of a child.[61]

School systems today often regulate the power of teachers and administrators to impose corporal punishment. Where the school system itself does not acknowledge the parents' right to forbid such punishment, parents usually have no common law power to restrict it.[62] Thus teachers or school administrators are generally permitted to impose corporal punishment when it is otherwise within the broad "reasonableness" limits, unless a statute or school regulation provides otherwise.[63] Excessive force, wrongful purpose, or a disproportionate response to the problem are all grounds for concluding that the teacher has exceeded the privilege and loses protection.[64]

C. DEFENSE AND RECOVERY OF PROPERTY

§ 7.8   Defending Possession of Land or Chattels: General Rule

The possessor of land or chattels is privileged to use reasonable force when necessary to defend possession of land or chattels against intrusion, taking, harm, or continuing trespass. A place of business, for example, may remove an unruly customer if the customer will not leave voluntarily, even though the act of touching the customer would otherwise amount to a battery.[65] Or the possessor of land may remove a trespassing chattel left on his land, even though the act of doing so would otherwise amount to a conversion or a trespass to chattels.[66] Similar rules give a privilege of one in possession of a chattel to use reasonable force to prevent a person from harming or carrying it away,[67] and even deadly force against an animal to prevent its destruction of the defendant's property, at least where the defendant's property is more valuable.[68]

---

[59]   See id. § 147(2).

[60]   See id. § 153.

[61]   See id. § 150(a).

[62]   Ingraham v. Wright, 430 U.S. 651, 662, 97 S.Ct. 1401, 1407, 51 L.Ed.2d 711 (1977); Restatement Second of Torts § 153(2) (1965).

[63]   See Rinehart v. Western Local School Dist. Bd. of Education, 87 Ohio App.3d 214, 621 N.E.2d 1365 (1993); see also R.D. Hursh, Annotation, Teacher's civil liability for administering corporal punishment to pupil, 43 A.L.R.2d 469 (1955). The result is similar under federal civil rights laws. See Ingraham v. Wright, 430 U.S. 651, 97 S.Ct. 1401, 51 L.Ed.2d 711 (1977) (use of force that would be privileged as reasonable under common law rules does not violate students' constitutional rights).

[64]   E.g., Thomas v. Bedford, 389 So.2d 405 (La. App. 1980).

[65]   Griego v. Wilson, 91 N.M. 74, 570 P.2d 612 (Ct. App. 1977).

[66]   Restatement Second of Torts § 260 (1965).

[67]   Vacanti v. Master Electronics Corp., 245 Neb. 586, 514 N.W.2d 319 (1994); Restatement Second of Torts §§ 77 & 260 (1965). Some statutes so provide. See, e.g., Iowa Code Ann. § 707.6.

[68]   Grabenstein v. Sunsted, 237 Mont. 254, 772 P.2d 865 (1989) (shooting a dog was privileged where dog was killing defendant's chickens).

Courts usually distinguish between defense of property and its recovery. Once an owner completely loses possession of the land or the chattel the privilege of defense is exhausted; to recover the property he must resort to the courts.[69]

§ 7.9 Qualifying and Explaining the General Rule

Reasonable force. For the possessor of land or chattels to escape liability on the basis of this privilege, it must reasonably appear that any force used to defend possession is needed, adapted, and proportioned to the protection of the possessor's interest in preventing the intrusion or ousting the intruder.[70] The defendant is not ordinarily expected to resort to the courts in the face of an attempted intrusion or dispossession, but he might be required to do so if the only alternative is to use force that is clearly disproportionate to the interests he seeks to protect. For example, if the plaintiff's underground telephone cable trespasses on the defendant's land without interfering with the land's use, a destruction of the cable might be disproportionate to the harm suffered by the defendant. In such a case, the defendant might be well advised to seek the aid of the courts rather than to destroy the cable.[71]

The defendant must limit the force applied to meet the apparent need for it. If the defendant uses excess force, he has exceeded his privilege and will be liable for harms caused by the excess force.[72] As long as there is room for reasonable people to differ in applying the standards, the question of excessive force is one for the jury.[73]

The force justified for the defense of property interests alone is relatively limited, but if the conflict escalates, self-defense or other privileges may be invoked and greater force may become appropriate.[74] Most commonly, the defendant's force will be the kind that counts as a battery, but in appropriate circumstances, a mere threat of a battery (an assault) or a confinement of the intruder may also be appropriate.[75]

Deadly force. Deadly force, including force likely to cause grave bodily harm, may not be used against an apparently peaceable intruder.[76] Even a demonstration of deadly force as a threat might be excessive. But under many criminal statutes, such force may be used, if otherwise reasonable, to defend possession of a home.[77] Some criminal statutes go further, permitting deadly force to protect personal property under some

---

[69] See §§ 7.13 & 7.14.

[70] Person v. Children's Hospital National Medical Center, 562 A.2d 648 (D.C. 1989); Restatement Second of Torts § 77 (1965).

[71] See State v. Patch, 145 Vt. 344, 488 A.2d 755 (1985).

[72] E.g., Terrell v. Hester, 182 Ga.App. 160, 355 S.E.2d 97 (1987).

[73] See Vancherie v. Siperly, 243 Md. 366, 221 A.2d 356 (1966); Fields v. State, 21 So.2d 412 (Miss. 1945).

[74] See Restatement Second of Torts § 79 (1965) (deadly force if intruder appears to threaten serious bodily harm).

[75] Id. § 80. The Restatement expressly recognizes that an assault may be privileged even if it threatens harm that would, if actually inflicted, be excessive. Restatement Second of Torts § 81(2) (1965); State v. Lord, 617 A.2d 536 (Me. 1992) ("A threat to use deadly force is the equivalent of nondeadly force."). Not all assaults are privileged, of course; the reasonableness of the force used must be determined on a case-by-case basis. See, e.g., Appelgren v. Walsh, 136 Ill.App.3d 700, 483 N.E.2d 686 (1985) (threat of shooting was excessive under the circumstances); Scheufele v. Newman, 187 Or. 263, 210 P.2d 573 (1949) (firing a rifle away from the plaintiff but a spot ten feet away from him was excessive force for ejecting a peaceable trespasser).

[76] Restatement Second of Torts § 79 (1965).

[77] E.g., Fla. Stat. Ann. § 782.02. Statutes sometimes provide protection indirectly by calling for a presumption that force used inside a dwelling is used for self-defense, thus invoking whatever privilege exists to use deadly force in self-defense. E.g., Cal.Penal Code § 198.5.

circumstances, especially in carjacking cases.[78] Quite possibly these statutes would guide the rule to be applied in tort cases as well. Indeed, some civil statutes expressly incorporate the provisions of a criminal statute.[79] Deadly force may also be used, under the rules for self-defense and defense of third persons, if the intruder's attack itself appears to threaten a person with deadly force.[80]

Least force that will be effective. Reasonable force is ordinarily the least force that is reasonably likely to be effective in defense of the property interests. If the intruder is peaceable, the defendant must first request the intruder to depart[81] or must otherwise give him a chance to leave peaceably, unless it is apparent that such a request is futile or dangerous. If the intruder enters forcibly, immediate resistance, without a polite request, may be reasonable, but if deadly force is contemplated, a warning would be necessary if it is safe to give one.

Intruder's superior privilege. The intruder's privilege to enter or remain in cases of necessity to save herself from death or grave bodily harm will be superior to the possessor's privilege, at least for a reasonable period of time.[82] Put otherwise, the possessor may not eject the intruder from a fast-moving train.[83] Other privileges of an intruder, such as the privilege to arrest under a warrant or legal authority, will likewise supersede or override the possessor's privilege.[84]

Mistake; appearances. The rule governing mistakes in the exercise of a privilege against an apparent attacker must be stated in a series of switchbacks, as follows:

(a) Reasonable appearances, not hidden actualities, determine the existence and scope of the privilege. If it reasonably appears to the possessor that an intruder is breaking into the house, the possessor may be justified in using force even if the intruder turns out to be a paper boy.[85]

(b) The rule in paragraph (a) is qualified by the rule that if the intruder is acting in the exercise of his superior privilege, the defendant's mistake as to the extent or nature of the intruder's privilege is no defense.[86] For instance, the possessor presumably has no privilege to use force to defend his property against a lawful search or seizure.[87]

(c) The rule in paragraph (b) is also qualified. If the intruder misleads the defendant or causes the defendant's mistake of facts, the defendant is entitled to act on the reasonable appearances induced by the intruder. For example, in a Florida case, testimony was that a number of police officers in possession of a warrant did not knock or announce their warrant, but instead cut the power lines, broke open the door with a sledge hammer, and appeared in plain clothes with ski masks to raid a poker game. In such circumstances, the defendant might reasonably mistake his masked visitors for violent attackers, not

---

[78]   See La. Rev. Stat. Ann. § 14:20 (4); Tex. Penal Code § 9.42.

[79]   See, e.g., Tex. Civ. Prac. & Remedies Code § 83.001 (2007) (incorporating Penal Code § 9.42).

[80]   Restatement Second of Torts § 79 (1965).

[81]   MacDonald v. Hees, 46 D.L.R. 3d 720 (N.S. 1974); Restatement Second of Torts § 77(c) & cmt. j (1965).

[82]   E.g., Depue v. Flatau, 100 Minn. 299, 111 N.W. 1 (1907); see § 7.19.

[83]   See Restatement Second of Torts § 77, cmt. i and Ill. 10 (1965).

[84]   State v. Haas, 134 N.H. 480, 596 A.2d 127 (1991).

[85]   Smith v. Delery, 238 La. 180, 114 So.2d 857 (1959).

[86]   Magnuson v. Billmayer, 189 Mont. 458, 616 P.2d 368 (1980) (easement rights).

[87]   See Restatement Second of Torts § 77(a) & cmt. d (1965).

guardians of order. Their superior privilege based on the warrant was nullified because they actively created a misimpression.[88]

Protecting other people. The Restatement recognizes that the defendant may act to protect the property interests of others, or at least those of family members. The defendant must reasonably believe that the facts would justify the possessor's use of force and must use force proportioned to the facts as they reasonably appear.[89] It would seem that the privilege to protect family members' property would include the privilege to use reasonable force to remove trespassing chattels under the same conditions that he could do so on his own behalf.

Injury to third persons. As in the case of self-defense, an energetic defense of property may unintentionally cause injury to an innocent third person who is in no way involved. So long as the force used by the defendant against the intruder is reasonable and privileged force, the defendant is not liable for an intentional tort, even to the innocent bystander who is injured. In such a case, he may be liable for negligence if he creates an unreasonable risk to the bystander,[90] but he is not liable otherwise.[91]

§ 7.10 Deadly Traps in Defense of Property: Spring Guns

Possessors of land sometimes attempt to protect their property by unattended devices capable of producing deadly force, that is, force likely to include either death or grave bodily harm. Such unattended devices can be called deadly traps. One example is the spring gun, a weapon rigged with trip wires to fire upon intruders, sometimes at very close range. Discussion here focuses on that example. Some other cases that might count as deadly traps are mentioned elsewhere,[92] as are some potential qualifications to the rules.[93]

The Restatement's formulation. The Restatement Second provides that a spring gun or other deadly trap is permissible only when the facts are such that the defendant could have used such force in person.[94] The rule can be criticized as infeasible or even as logically impossible in some cases. For instance, if the defendant were physically present when the plaintiff attempted to enter the property, the defendant would ordinarily be required to warn the plaintiff off before using force and certainly before using deadly force. No such warning could be given by the traditional spring gun, so the comparison to a situation in which the defendant is personally present will at best provide only partial guidance. However, the Restatement's ideas, when picked out in detail, work out to be somewhat similar to the specific rules set out next.

Formulating particular rules. Lacunae in the cases create uncertainties about the precise rules, but a reasonable approximation of the overall tendency of the courts can be expressed as follows.

---

[88]   State v. White, 642 So.2d 842 (Fla. App. 1994). The common law "knock and announce" requirement is part of the reasonableness rule of the Fourth Amendment. Wilson v. Arkansas, 514 U.S. 927, 115 S.Ct. 1914, 131 L.Ed.2d 976 (1995).

[89]   Restatement Second of Torts § 86 (1965) (defendant must reasonably believe that the facts are such that the possessor would have a privilege to use force in defense of the property).

[90]   E.g., Passovoy v. Nordstrom, Inc., 52 Wash.App. 166, 758 P.2d 524 (1988).

[91]   Polando v. Vizzini, 97 N.E.2d 59 (Ohio App. 1949); Restatement Second of Torts § 83 (1965).

[92]   See § 7.12.

[93]   See § 7.11.

[94]   Restatement Second of Torts § 85 (1965). A number of cases make a similar statement. E.g., Allison v. Fiscus, 156 Ohio St. 120, 100 N.E.2d 237, 44 A.L.R.2d 369 (1951).

(1) Self-defense. The defendant is privileged to use deadly traps to protect the persons of himself and others against deadly force if the use of such traps is otherwise reasonable under the rules for self-defense, but except as stated in the next paragraph, there is no independent privilege to protect property interests by deadly traps.

(2) Protection of dwelling place against felonious entry. (a) Unless criminal statutes provide or imply otherwise, the defendant may protect his dwelling place by deadly traps against intruders who are in fact entering or attempting to enter in the course of a felony or attempted felony, provided deadly traps are otherwise reasonable.[95] In some states, this privilege may be extended to permit protection of other buildings against serious depredation.[96] But it seems that the defendant uses a deadly trap at his peril, so that if the spring gun harms or kills a straying child who is not in fact attempting felonious entry, the privilege is no protection.[97] (b) Criminal statutes forbidding any use of spring guns or other deadly traps may be construed to modify or eliminate the rule stated in subparagraph (a).[98] (c) Criminal statutes permitting or refusing to permit the use of deadly force to repel a felony or entry into a dwelling place may be construed to modify or reinforce the rule stated in (a).[99]

(3) Mere trespassers and non-felonious intruders. The defendant has no privilege to use deadly traps to defend against mere trespassers or those committing minor crimes outside the dwelling place. The defendant is liable to such trespassers if they are injured by the defendant's deadly trap.[100]

(4) Unintended harm; negligence. When the defendant creates a condition on his land that may be dangerous to trespassers but is not created for the purpose of causing them harm, the defendant is liable, if at all, only for negligence.[101]

General disapproval of spring guns and deadly traps. Courts express dislike for and concern at the use of spring guns and other deadly traps or "engines of destruction."[102] But cases that reflect general disapproval of spring guns often do not state precise rules governing their use or misuse. Many of these cases are ordinary negligence cases that do not involve spring guns or even intentional torts. They collaterally condemn the use of spring guns against trespassers only on their way to saying that the landowner is not liable for a negligently inflicted injury to a trespasser.[103] Cases in this group provide

---

[95] This is the implication but not the specific holding in a number of cases. E.g., Scheuerman v. Scharfenberg, 163 Ala. 337, 50 So. 335 (1909); Allison v. Fiscus, 156 Ohio St. 120, 100 N.E.2d 237, 44 A.L.R.2d 369 (1951); cf. Katko v. Briney, 183 N.W.2d 657 (Iowa 1971) (if the trespasser is committing a "felony of violence" or one punishable by death).

[96] Scheuerman v. Scharfenberg, 163 Ala. 337, 50 So. 335 (1909).

[97] See Allison v. Fiscus, 156 Ohio St. 120, 100 N.E.2d 237, 44 A.L.R.2d 369 (1951) ("[O]ne who sets a spring gun or trap does so at his peril."); Restatement Second of Torts § 85, cmt. d (1965).

[98] See § 7.11.

[99] E.g., Fla. Stat. Ann. § 782.02.

[100] McKinsey v. Wade, 136 Ga.App. 109, 220 S.E.2d 30 (1975); Katko v. Briney, 183 N.W.2d 657 (Iowa 1971).

[101] The rules of negligence law that hold a landowner liable to a trespasser if the landowner's acts, or the condition he tolerates on the land, amounts to willful or wanton misconduct are closely analogous to the rules that hold the landowner has exceeded his privilege if he uses unreasonable force to repel a trespasser. Under one view, a trap would represent "willful and wanton" misconduct on the landowner's part. See, e.g., Harper v. Kampschaefer, 549 N.E.2d 1067 (Ind. App. 1990).

[102] See Annotation, J.D. Perovich, Use of Set Gun, Trap, or Similar Device on Defendant's Own Property, 47 A.L.R.3d 646 (1973).

[103] E.g., Fox v. Warner-Quinlan Asphalt Co., 204 N.Y. 240, 97 N.E. 497 (1912); Weitzmann v. A.L. Barber Asphalt Co., 190 N.Y. 452, 83 N.E. 477 (1908); Gramlich v. Wurst, 86 Pa. 74 (1878).

little guidance on the question of the possessor's justification for using such force in defense of property, except that they sometimes cite the leading English case with approval.

Bird v. Holbrook. The major English case that has influenced American law on this point is *Bird v. Holbrook*,[104] from 1828. The defendant set a spring gun in his walled garden because he had previously suffered theft of some of the tulips he raised there. A neighbor's peahen escaped and got into the garden. The plaintiff offered to get it. The plaintiff climbed the wall and called out for the occupant, but, getting no answer, jumped into the garden to retrieve the hen. The spring gun was triggered and the plaintiff was seriously wounded.

The *Bird v. Holbrook* court found the defendant liable. Distinguishing earlier authority, one of the judges emphasized that the defendant had not only failed to give notice that the gun was there but had tried to keep it secret in order to wound the thief. Another judge emphasized that if the spring gun were justified, it would be so only at night when the thief might come. *Bird* is clear about the defendant's liability on the facts, but uncertain about the defendant's potential liability to an actual burglar.

Katko v. Briney. The most famous American case is quite different. In *Katko v. Briney*,[105] one of the defendants had inherited an unoccupied farm house. For ten years, a series a housebreaking events repeatedly caused damages. The defendants boarded the windows and posted no trespassing signs. Eventually they set a spring gun, a shotgun rigged with a wire from the doorknob in one of the rooms to the gun's trigger. No signs or other warnings about the gun were given.

The *Katko* plaintiff was a man who was looking for old bottles and jars. He had been there before a shotgun had been set up. This time, however, when he opened the door, the gun was triggered and the blast blew part of his tibia away. He suffered considerable injury and was criminally punished by a fine of $50 and a 60-day jail sentence (from which he was paroled).

Although the plaintiff in this case entered the premises with a minor criminal purpose, he was allowed to recover. The court rejected the defense that spring guns were permissible means of defending property on the ground given in the Restatement, that human life and limb are more important than property interests. The court appeared to approve the Restatement's rule formulation. Some other cases allow recovery by the thief (or his estate), so long as he is not entering a dwelling place.[106]

§ 7.11 Qualifying and Considering the Deadly-Trap Rules

Property vs. Life

Most discussions of deadly force, by traps or otherwise, emphasize the importance of human life. Human life undoubtedly represents the single most important factor to be considered. However, the suggestion that deadly force is invariably unacceptable because property interests are always small in comparison to human life is rhetorically appealing but analytically weak, as is the suggestion that the landowner can always buy insurance to protect property interests.

---

[104] Bird v. Holbrook, 4 Bing. 628, 130 Eng. Rep. 911 (C.P. 1828).

[105] Katko v. Briney, 183 N.W.2d 657 (Iowa 1971).

[106] McKinsey v. Wade, 136 Ga.App. 109, 220 S.E.2d 30 (1975) (young man breaking into vending machine killed when dynamite bomb went off, liability).

First, not all property interests are alike. A storehouse of goods is not like a home. Property in the form of a home, for those lucky enough to have such property, represents fundamental human needs and satisfactions, a very personal refuge, the violation of which is harmful not merely to "property" but to human beings. Second, the defense of property by deadly force is usually not a simple exchange of life for property as the rhetoric suggests, but a risk of life balanced against a certain invasion. Third, if the mentally competent intruder is fully informed of the specific risk that entry is likely to result in a shotgun or dynamite blast but proceeds anyway, human life is surely at risk, but it is the intruder's choice. These considerations suggest that the courts may well be right to imply that defense of a dwelling place by deadly force, including deadly traps, might be justified, although defense of other property is not.

It does not follow, however, that deadly traps are always reasonable, even inside a dwelling place. A trap to impede entrance into a bedroom in the nighttime when people are present might be reasonable if the threat is great, but a stick of dynamite that blows up anyone who rings the front door bell in the daytime is not. Nor is a deadly trap reasonable if the risk of burglars is nil, but the risk of a stray child is high.

Warnings

The risk of grave injury or death to relatively innocent intruders suggests that an advance warning, by signs or pictographs or otherwise, should ordinarily be required. The Restatement does not directly require a notice,[107] but some cases may imply that the spring gun might be justified only if such a notice or warning were given and conversely may imply that if a notice is given then the spring gun would be justified.[108] It is true, of course, that a locked door warns the trespasser that he is not wanted,[109] but it hardly serves to warn him that he faces death by a dynamite explosion. If the Restatement is right in suggesting that the possessor cannot do indirectly by deadly traps what he cannot do in person, then either an actually communicated warning or at least a good faith effort to communicate one would be required. Given the ease and low cost with which a warning can usually be provided, and the fact that a warning might even further the landowner's interests by dissuading some trespassers, perhaps any privilege should be limited to cases in which the landowner has reasonably attempted to provide such a warning.[110] Although this does not sound controversial, some decisions have attributed no significance to a warning and have thus permitted the landowner to create deadly hidden conditions on the land to repel trespassers.[111]

Criminal Statutes

The common law rules for deadly traps, at least in the form of spring guns, may be modified indirectly because a number of statutes proscribe the use of spring guns

---

[107] The Restatement seems to say that no warning is required, but provides that giving a warning is not enough if the force is otherwise unjusitifed. Restatement Second of Torts § 85, cmt. c (1965).

[108] Larmore v. Crown Point Iron Co., 101 N.Y. 391, 394, 4 N.E. 752, 754 (1886) ("he cannot, without giving any warning, place thereon spring-guns or dangerous traps"). Similarly, some cases refer to the "hidden" character of "engines of destruction" like spring guns. Mendelowitz v. Neisner, 258 N.Y. 181, 179 N.E. 378 (1932).

[109] Allison v. Fiscus, 156 Ohio St. 120, 128, 100 N.E.2d 237, 241, 44 A.L.R.2d 369 (1951).

[110] See Richard A. Posner, Killing or Wounding to Protect a Property Interest, 14 J. Law. & Econ. 201, 214 ff. (1971).

[111] Doehring v. Wagner, 80 Md.App. 237, 562 A.2d 762 (1989) (cable stretched across private road to deter motorcyclists).

altogether, with a provision of criminal penalties for a violation.[112] While criminal-law rules do not automatically carry over into tort law, they often do. Criminal statutes against spring guns might be construed to abolish any privilege to use such guns, although that reading might leave other deadly mechanical devices available to the landowner under common law rules.

§ 7.12 Types of "Traps" and Negligence Law

Other deadly traps. The preceding sections have focused on spring guns as the prime example of a deadly trap, but other unattended devices, animate or not, could function in much the same way as a spring gun and could be governed by the same rules. Vicious dogs or poisonous ponds of toxic waste might fall into this category. Conceivably, deep pits[113] or electrified objects on the land,[114] or chains or wires that might not be visible to a motorcyclist or snowmobiler,[115] might all be deadly traps placed to exclude trespassers, although in most instances they are more likely to represent negligence than intentional harm.[116]

Non-deadly traps. Some unattended devices might count as traps without being deadly or likely to cause serious bodily harm. Some of these are undoubtedly permissible, first because they are customary in the community and thus expected, and second because they serve useful purposes for the landowner that have nothing to do with the exclusion of trespassers. A barbed-wire fence, for example, would normally be a privileged means of attempting to exclude trespassers as well as a good means for keeping cattle in.[117]

Relation to negligence law. Courts considering injuries to a trespasser will often think of the case as a negligence case rather than as an intentional tort case with a privilege defense. If the landowner digs an excavation in order to construct a building, for example, his purpose is not to trap the trespasser but to exploit his land. In such a case, the question will be resolved under the rules of negligence law.

As will be seen in the discussions of landowner negligence,[118] landowners may leave dangerous conditions on their property that may *function* like a trap even if their purpose is not to exclude trespassers. In those cases, too, courts are likely to consider the case under the negligence rules. Those rules correlate closely with the privilege rules. In general, landowners are not traditionally required to exercise care for the benefit of trespassers, but they are not to willfully injure or entrap them, and if they do they are liable for the harm done.

What counts as a trap or as willful misconduct may thus become central to resolution of many trespasser-injury cases. Although some courts expressly analogize a

---

[112] 720 Ill.Comp. Stat. 5/24–1(a)(5); Iowa Code Ann. § 708.9; Mich. Comp. L. Ann. § 750.236; Minn. Stat. Ann. § 609.205.

[113] Gramlich v. Wurst, 86 Pa. 74 (1878) (decedent, attempting to rescue another, was an innocent trespasser who fell in pit and was killed; no recovery, seemingly because the landowner had no intent to harm and was not negligent).

[114] Cf. Miller v. General Motors Corp., 207 Ill.App.3d 148, 565 N.E.2d 687 (1990) (trespasser injured in touching electrical object on the land, but since his presence could not have been anticipated, the landowner was not liable for negligence).

[115] Cf. Harper v. Kampschaefer, 549 N.E.2d 1067 (Ind. 1990) (cable across road killed ATV operator).

[116] See § 20.2.

[117] See Restatement Second of Torts § 84 (1965).

[118] See Chapter 20.

vicious dog kept to guard the perimeter of a house as a trap like a spring gun,[119] others seemingly do not.[120] Whether the case is regarded as an intentional tort with a privilege defense, a negligence case, or a strict liability case, the most important consideration is whether the court perceives the dog (or other condition) as a trap or as a product of willful behavior.[121] The significant features of a trap are that it is unexpected and unknown, and can't distinguish between, say, a straying child and a vicious burglar. These are the features that make it an unreasonable form of force to protect against a simple trespass, and which also make the conduct of setting a trap willful if the case is argued as one involving mere negligence.

§ 7.13 Repossession of Land

Summary

Claimants, squatters, and tenants. Conflicts over possession of land arise in several materially different settings. A person who moves into wrongful possession might be a person who believes she has title, or she might be a squatter or a tenant whose possession is wrongful because her lease has terminated for nonpayment of rent. The last is the most common situation. Can the rightful owner of land use reasonable force to oust the wrongful possessor?

Defense vs. recovery. Legal rules distinguish between defense of property on the one hand and its recovery or repossession on the other. The owner-possessor of land may use reasonable force to defend possession and other interests in the land. The privilege continues as long as the owner continues to resist the intruder and contest his right to be there, even if, for the moment, the owner is literally off the land. In such a case, the intruder has not acquired a peaceable possession; she is a mere trespasser or has only "scrambling possession."[122] In this situation, the owner is viewed as defending his own possession; if he uses no more force than necessary and reasonable,[123] he is privileged and not subject to liability.

Once the owner loses possession to another person, however, the owner has no possession to defend and his self-help privilege is at an end. He may not use force to oust the trespasser who is in peaceable possession. Although a mere roomer may be subject to the landlord's self-help eviction,[124] the landowner must ordinarily resort to judicial process if he is to eject a person in firm possession of the land. As will be seen, this rule leads to the possibility that if the owner uses force to repossess his own property, the wrongful possessor may have a tort claim.

---

[119] Brewer v. Furtwangler, 171 Wash. 617, 18 P.2d 837 (1933) (allowing inadvertent trespasser to recover for injuries caused by vicious dog attack).

[120] See Bramble v. Thompson, 264 Md. 518, 287 A.2d 265, 64 A.L.R.3d 1031 (1972) (refusing to impose liability upon a landowner whose allegedly vicious dog attacked an inadvertent trespasser, on the ground that keeping vicious dog would not "be willful or wanton misconduct or entrapment").

[121] *Compare* Brewer v. Furtwangler, 171 Wash. 617, 18 P.2d 837 (1933), *with* Bramble v. Thompson, 264 Md. 518, 287 A.2d 265, 64 A.L.R.3d 1031 (1972), *and* Harper v. Kampschaefer, 549 N.E.2d 1067 (Ind. 1990), *with* Doehring v. Wagner, 80 Md.App. 237, 562 A.2d 762 (1989).

[122] See National Garment Co. v. City of Paris, Missouri, 655 S.W.2d 515 (Mo. 1983).

[123] Schwinn v. Perkins, 79 N.J.L. 515, 78 A. 19 (1910).

[124] Harkins v. Win Corp., 771 A.2d 1025, *on rehearing*, 777 A.2d 800 (D.C. 2001). Similarly, hotel guests are not tenants and do not get the benefit of the forcible entry statutes. See Young v. Harrison, 284 F.3d 863 (8th Cir. 2002).

Forcible Entry Statutes

The underlying rule was developed from a 14th century English statute that forbade forcible repossession by the owner[125] and from American Forcible Entry statutes that do the same.[126] The perception and the policy attributed to these statutes is that forcible repossession creates a risk of a violent response and that the risk of violence should be minimized by forbidding even reasonable force.

Forcible entry and detainer statutes attempt to encourage the owner to use judicial process by offering a carrot and threatening a stick. The carrot is a provision for a relatively speedy and informal trial that will put the owner in possession. The stick is a criminal penalty for resort to force. Many of the statutes are vague about what counts as "forcible" and wholly ambiguous in their implications about a private cause of action in favor of the wrongful possessor.

Tort Actions Against the Rightful Owner for Repossession

Does the statute forbidding forcible reentry mean that the wrongful possessor should have a tort claim against the owner who enters with no more force than required to oust the wrongdoer? No single rule is likely to produce results that are invariably satisfactory.

No action when owner uses reasonable force. While courts are divided, quite a few cases have said that the wrongful possessor has no claim against the repossessing owner, so long as the owner uses no more force than reasonably necessary to evict.[127]

Action allowed against owner who uses reasonable force. A large group of courts, usually said to be the majority,[128] permit the wrongful possessor to recover from the owner who violates the statute by using force to reenter, even though the amount of force used is no more than that made necessary by the possessor's resistance.[129]

Action allowed against owner for peaceable repossession. Some statutes go further and forbid *any* self-help remedy for the owner out of possession, at least when that owner is a landlord. In line with this, some cases actually impose liability upon the owner who repossesses without using force against the occupant or her goods. One example of liability for a peaceable retaking is the case of a landlord's self-help eviction: the landlord locks the tenant out when the rent is not paid and becomes liable for doing so, at least where a speedy remedy in the courts is available.[130] Many cases involve tenants who wrongfully hold over after the lease has expired.

---

[125] 5 Richard II c. 7.

[126] E.g., Cal. Civ. Proc. Code § 1159; N.Y. Real Prop. Acts § 853. Many of these statutes are poorly drafted.

[127] E.g., Watson v. Brown, 67 Haw. 252, 686 P.2d 12 (1984); Shorter v. Shelton, 183 Va. 819, 33 S.E.2d 643 (1945).

[128] See Annotation, Right of Landlord Legally Entitled to Possession to Dispossess Tenant without Legal Process, 6 A.L.R.3d 177 (1966). The majority may be made up at least partly of cases in which actual personal injury or harm to chattels was the result of the entry.

[129] See Daluiso v. Boone, 71 Cal.2d 484, 455 P.2d 811, 78 Cal.Rptr. 707 (1969); Tatro v. Lehouiller, 147 Vt. 151, 153, 513 A.2d 610, 611 (1986).

[130] Berg v. Wiley, 264 N.W.2d 145 (Minn. 1978) (adopting the "modern trend" on this point).

Types of Harm to Be Redressed

Liability of the true owner for retaking his own property is complicated further by the fact that at least three distinct kinds of cases can arise. Courts and writers do not always carefully distinguish among them in counting majorities.

First, the owner-defendant's forcible entry could cause actual harm to the wrongful possessor, a physical injury or the like, even if he uses only reasonable force.[131] In most cases, physical injury betokens a breach of the peace and in any event it is plausible to say that the owner who wishes to use self-help must accept liability for any actual injuries, intended or not. If he wishes to avoid that risk, he must resort to judicial process. So when the wrongful occupant is actually injured, liability is relatively easy to justify.

Second, the owner's forcible entry could cause harm that would be legally cognizable in the absence of a privilege, such as a technical battery that is merely offensive but not harmful. Neither this claim nor the first one is about the wrongful possessor's rights to possession as such, so in an important way they are not about traditional trespass claims at all.[132]

Third, the wrongful possessor might suffer injury only in the sense that he lost possession of property to which he was not entitled and whatever inconvenience or hardship that might entail.[133] This claim sounds like a claim to a property right because it is based solely upon dispossession. Yet the wrongful possessor has no right to possession, so the claim is hardly a property right in the ordinary sense and it seems unjust if not inane to put him back in possession.[134]

Policy

Danger of violence vs. welfare policy. The policy claim for the rule against forcible repossession by the owner has been that, were the rule otherwise, violent confrontations would be likely and that it is better to preserve the government's "monopoly on force" than to permit this form of self-help. The fact that riotous behavior sometimes results from unpopular arrests suggest that there might be some basis in fact for the claim that retaking property could lead to bloodshed. In fact, however, in the landlord-tenant cases, the holdover tenant is almost always quite vulnerable and seldom in a position to generate an affray. Perhaps the policy today is not based so much upon the fear that widespread violence would occur when the landlord repossesses but upon the humane concern that the tenant would be left homeless.[135]

Limits appropriate to welfare policy. If courts allow a suit by a wrongful occupant out of fear that landlords in particular are in a position to oppress or impose hardships,

---

[131] E.g., Daluiso v. Boone, 71 Cal.2d 484, 455 P.2d 811, 78 Cal.Rptr. 707 (1969) (confrontation caused distress and heart problems).

[132] Hemmings v. Stoke Poges Golf Club, [1920] 1 K.B. 720, [1981] All E.R. 798 (C.A. 1919) (plaintiff as wrongful occupant was led gently by the hand off the premises; his wife would not budge from her chair, and she and the chair were carried out).

[133] Freeway Park Buildings, Inc. v. Western States Wholesale Supply, 22 Utah 2d 266, 451 P.2d 778 (1969).

[134] Cf. Schwinn v. Perkins, 79 N.J.L. 515, 516, 78 A. 19 (1910) (courts have observed "the seeming injustice of a judgment restoring the possession of property to one not rightfully entitled thereto").

[135] See Randy G. Gerchick, Comment, No Easy Way Out: Making the Summary Eviction Process a Fairer and More Efficient Alternative to Landlord Self-Help, 41 U.C.L.A. L.Rev. 759 (1994).

they must be thinking especially of residential tenants.[136] If the policy is about this kind of welfare rather than about violence, the tort action might appropriately be allowed to, say, residential tenants, but not to commercial tenants or squatters. Courts have sometimes recognized this by allowing the commercial landlord but not the residential landlord to use reasonable self-help remedies to repossess the land peaceably where the lease so provides.[137]

Tenant's process rights. A third policy judgment in support of liability for a peaceable retaking of the land is that the plaintiff-possessor is entitled to be heard in defense of her possession. Her claim is not for the loss of property or possession itself, but for the denial of fair judicial process.

Some judges seem to be leaning toward the view that the possessor is almost always entitled to judicial process and that if the owner uses a self-help remedy he is committing a tort analogous to the denial of due process.[138] Computation of damages for denial of a process right, as distinct from a right to possession, however, is likely to be problematical.[139] In any event, under this analysis, the tort (if any) to the plaintiff is not an ordinary trespass to real property at all, but rather a highly personal claim to an intangible right.

§ 7.14 Repossession of Chattels: General Rules

No privilege to use force after possession is lost. As already indicated, the privilege to defend one's possession of chattels by reasonable force[140] does not generally include a privilege to recover possession by force[141] or threats of force,[142] or by an arrest without a warrant.[143] Once possession is clearly lost, the owner must resort to the courts to recover the chattel if a peaceable recovery is not possible. Put otherwise, the law favors the rights of actual possession until the courts can actually determine the rights of the matter.[144]

Defending rightful possession and fresh pursuit. A momentary loss of control during a scuffle is not a loss of possession as long as the parties are still contending for the chattel. As long as the scramble continues, the owner or original possessor can use force in defense of the possession so long as the amount of force is reasonable and the use of force reasonably appears to be necessary to defend possession.[145] The original possessor

---

[136] City of Evanston v. O'Leary, 244 Ill.App.3d 190, 614 N.E.2d 114 (1993) ("[T]here is discernible a certain public policy, based upon humane considerations of the wrong, oppression and hardships which might ensue, if families, in any kind of weather, at any time of day or night, might be thus forcibly ejected from their homes with all their effects without notice or warning.").

[137] Rucker v. Wynn, 212 Ga.App. 69, 441 S.E.2d 417 (1994); Craig Wrecking Co. v. S.G. Loewendick & Sons, Inc., 38 Ohio App.3d 79, 526 N.E.2d 321 (1987).

[138] Friends of Yelverton, Inc. v. 163rd Street Improvement Council, Inc., 135 Misc.2d 275, 514 N.Y.S.2d 841 (1986) (specific analogy to due process).

[139] In Carey v. Piphus, 435 U.S. 247, 98 S.Ct. 1042, 55 L.Ed.2d 252 (1978), a schoolboy was suspended without a due process hearing, but he would have been suspended had a hearing been held as well. So proper process would have changed nothing in the ultimate result. The Court limited recovery to nominal damages in the absence of any proven harms.

[140] See §§ 7.8 to 7.12.

[141] Bobb v. Bosworth, 16 Ky. 81 (1808) (violence may not be used to regain possession once lost).

[142] Barnes v. Martin, 15 Wis. 263 (1840) (approaching with a knife to regain chattel).

[143] A shopkeeper may, however, enjoy a privilege to detain briefly for investigation. See § 7.17. As to the law of arrest without a warrant, see § 7.18.

[144] See Adams v. Department of Motor Vehicles, 11 Cal.3d 146, 520 P.2d 961, 113 Cal.Rptr. 145 (1974).

[145] McLean v. Colf, 179 Cal. 237, 176 P. 169 (1918); Spelina v. Sporry, 279 Ill. App. 376 (1935).

may even use reasonable force if needed to recover the chattel in the course of or at the end of a fresh pursuit.[146]

Mistake. But the original possessor must be in the right. If the facts did not justify force, or the amount of force used, he has no privilege even if he acted under a reasonable mistake.[147] Thus the seller who mistakenly believes that payments are in arrears and that he has a right to retake the chattel is liable for a conversion if he takes it,[148] the same rule that applies to any other case of conversion.[149]

Fraudulent taking. Even where the plaintiff obtained the chattel by fraudulent means (and is therefore a wrongdoer) he is entitled to the privilege to use reasonable force to maintain that possession; he is the rightful possessor until found otherwise.[150]

The rules imply that the true owner who has lost possession will be liable for any tort committed in retaking the chattel by force. The more ironic implication of the rules is such an owner may not use force to regain it, but the wrongdoer in possession is privileged to use all the force reasonably necessary to defend the wrongful possession. Juries intent on short-term justice may dislike the irony and disregard the legal rule; but judges intent on long-term peace may in their turn disregard the jury's justice.[151]

§ 7.15   The Repossessing Seller

Peaceable repossession. The problem of repossession often arises when chattels are sold on credit, under a conditional sales contract or the like. When the buyer fails to make payments as due, the seller is ordinarily entitled by the terms of the sales documents to repossess the chattel. The Uniform Commercial Code, which governs rights and remedies in chattel sale cases, provides that the seller may retake possession if he does so "without breach of the peace;"[152] but if the seller uses force, he exceeds that privilege and he is liable for harms done.[153]

Repossession against purchaser's consent. "Breach of the peace" as used in the Code and in the pre-Code cases is a vague term. Although some courts find a breach of peace only when the seller uses substantial force, others treat repossession as a breach of the peace when it goes beyond the express or implied consent of the buyer-debtor. So the debtor's actual resistance to repossession is enough to convert the seller's otherwise peaceful efforts into a breach of the peace.[154] The seller is even considered to be in breach

---

[146] See State v. Elliot, 11 N.H. 540 (1841); Restatement Second of Torts § 103 (1965) (one may chase down the converter of chattels upon timely discovery of the wrong, even if that is hours later).

[147] See Gortarez v. Smitty's Super Valu, Inc., 140 Ariz. 97, 680 P.2d 807 (1984); Restatement Second of Torts § 100, cmt. d (1965).

[148] E.g., Binder v. General Motors Acceptance Corp., 222 N.C. 512, 23 S.E.2d 894 (1943).

[149] See § 6.4.

[150] Hodgeden v. Hubbard, 18 Vt. 504 (1846), *overruled on other grounds*, Loverin v. Wedge, 102 Vt. 138, 146 A. 248 (1929).

[151] See Barnes v. Martin, 15 Wis. 263 (1862) (jury gave a handsome verdict to one Barbara, who came brandishing a knife to the defendant's land to retrieve her wandering cow; reversed).

[152] UCC § 9–503. See 2 James J. White & Robert S. Summers, Uniform Commercial Code § 14.3 (5th ed. 2002).

[153] Even if the breach of the peace is caused, not by the seller, but by the seller's independent contractor, the seller may be held liable on the theory that peaceable repossession is a nondelegable duty. MBank El Paso, N.A. v. Sanchez, 836 S.W.2d 151 (Tex. 1992). As to liabilities of those who employ independent contractors, see §§ 431 & 432.

[154] See Nixon v. Halpin, 620 So.2d 796, 798 (Fla. Dist. Ct. App. 1993) ("A secured party who insists on taking possession after resistance by the debtor faces the consequences of its use of force. . . . He acts at his peril, and exposes himself to severe potential liability. . . .").

of the peace if he continues after a face-to-face demand from the debtor that he desist and depart.[155]

Intrusion in private quarters. Even if the debtor is not physically present and resisting or objecting, the seller may be in breach of the peace because of the intrusive methods of repossession or abusive behavior. For example, a seller who enters the buyer's enclosed areas without consent may be in breach of the peace merely by that entry if the quarters are not normally open to the public or casual users,[156] and even more clearly so if he breaks or picks locks to enter.[157] Privacy expectations count here, so that even entrance into an open but secluded ranch yard might create a "possibility of immediate violence" that would count as a breach of the peace.[158]

Liability for unprivileged repossession. If the repossessor breaches the peace in repossessing, he becomes liable for harms done, including physical harm to the plaintiff by way of battery or otherwise,[159] for damages to other property,[160] and even for conversion of the property he repossesses.[161] Punitive damages may be awarded when the creditor's behavior is wrongful in a sufficiently serious way.[162]

§ 7.16 Entering Another's Land to Recapture Chattels

Sellers governed by the UCC frequently repossess chattels from defaulting buyers by entering upon the buyer's land to obtain the chattel. Unless the seller breaks in, intrudes in a building, or invades privacy interests, courts often make no special point of the fact that entry upon land was required.[163] The common law rule is in accord. It permits a defendant who is entitled to immediate possession to recover the goods from another's land (a) if the defendant did not cause the intrusion of the goods in the first place and (b) if entry is reasonable as to both time and manner.[164]

In some cases, the plaintiff-landowner bears some responsibility for the fact that the goods are on his land, and in such cases the defendant entitled to possession easily has a right to enter, demand the goods, and take them without excessive force.[165] In other cases, the goods have arrived upon the defendant's land through neutral forces, washed up by a flood, for example, or carried upon the land by third persons. Here again, the defendant is privileged to enter and to take the goods, but in these cases the

---

[155] Smith v. John Deere Company, 83 Ohio App.3d 398, 614 N.E.2d 1148 (1993).

[156] E.g., Bloomquist v. First National Bank of Elk River, 378 N.W.2d 81 (Minn. App. 1985) (bank's agents removed broken window to enter garage, then opened garage door from the inside and repossessed the debtor's tools; the debtor was not present but the bank knew that he objected).

[157] Cf. Berg v. Wiley, 264 N.W.2d 145. (Minn. 1978) (landlord's lockout of tenant to repossess premises)

[158] Salisbury Livestock Co. v. Colorado Central Credit Union, 793 P.2d 470 (Wyo. 1990).

[159] Smith v. John Deere Company, 83 Ohio App.3d 398, 614 N.E.2d 1148 (1993).

[160] E.g., Star Bank, N.A. v. Laker, 637 N.E.2d 805 (Ind. 1994); Giese v. NCNB Texas Forney Banking Center, 881 S.W.2d 776 (Tex. App. 1994).

[161] Henderson v. Security National Bank, 72 Cal.App.3d 764, 140 Cal.Rptr. 388 (1977); Bloomquist v. First National Bank of Elk River, 378 N.W.2d 81 (Minn. App. 1985) (apparently intending a full recovery of market value of the goods).

[162] Star Bank, N.A. v. Laker, 637 N.E.2d 805 (Ind. 1994).

[163] See, e.g., Salisbury Livestock Co. v. Colorado Central Credit Union, 793 P.2d 470 (Wyo. 1990) (trespass action might lie in favor of the plaintiff, but only if the entry could count as a breach of the peace).

[164] See Arlowski v. Foglio, 105 Conn. 342, 135 A. 397, 53 A.L.R. 481 (1926); Shehyn v. United States, 256 A.2d 404 (D.C. 1969).

[165] In Wheelden v. Lowell, 50 Me. 499 (1862), the landowner had fraudulently induced the defendant to sell a horse. Upon discovery of the fraud, the defendant rescinded and entered the land to get the horse. This was held to be no trespass. The court heavily emphasized the fault of the plaintiff landowner.

defendant must pay for damage done in the process.[166] Such a case seems indistinguishable from the case of necessity, which requires just such a payment.[167]

Authorities say that if the defendant's chattel comes onto the plaintiff's land by the defendant's own fault, the defendant has no privilege to remove it except by the peaceful agreement of the possessor, unless public or private necessity can be shown.[168] So phrased, the rule might impose liability upon a defendant whose negligently parked car rolls onto the plaintiff's land, not only for the damage done but also for the separate act of "trespass" in recovering the car. Unless the land possessor is entitled to a lien upon the car for some reason, however, it seems useless to suggest that the car owner must pay nominal damages for a peaceable retaking of his car and downright bad policy to suggest that the landowner could properly use force to prevent retrieval of the car. Perhaps it is no problem. The possessor of the land will often agree to a peaceable re-taking of the chattel if no harm has been done, since if he does not agree, he might be held liable for a conversion.[169]

D. PRIVILEGES TO DETAIN OR ARREST

§ 7.17 The Merchant's Privilege to Detain for Investigation

Traditional rule. The traditional common law recognized no privilege of private persons to detain for investigation. The merchant who suspected shoplifting could make an arrest, but only if the shopper was in fact guilty of a felony, or if a felony had in fact been committed and the shopper was reasonably suspected.[170] These privileges provided little protection, since individual thefts might never reach the felony level and since in any event the merchant might be mistaken about whether a theft took place. The limited privilege to arrest for a misdemeanor[171] would not ordinarily apply, since shoplifting does not normally induce breach of the peace.[172] Nor would the privilege to recapture wrongfully taken chattels help if the merchant was mistaken.[173]

Judicial creation of special privileges for merchants. As shoplifting became a major source of losses to merchants, some courts created a privilege more protective than the traditional one. Under this more protective privilege, a merchant who reasonably believes that a person has committed a theft or has attempted a theft may detain the person for a limited period of time and for the limited purpose of investigating the facts.[174] The Restatement endorses this privilege.[175]

---

[166] Wippert v. Burlington Northern Inc., 397 F.Supp. 73 (D. Mont. 1975) (defendant's railroad train derailed because of high winds; entry upon the plaintiff's property to reclaim the train was not a trespass, but defendant was liable for actual damages caused); Restatement Second of Torts § 198(2) (1965).

[167] See § 7.19.

[168] Restatement Second of Torts § 200 (1965).

[169] Id. § 237 liability for failing to surrender posession to one entitled to it, when demand is made).

[170] See Florida v. Jones, 461 So.2d 97, 99 (Fla. 1984) ("The harsh corollary of the common-law rule was that, if the suspicion of theft or interference proved to be erroneous, the detention was per se unreasonable and not warranted by the circumstances.").

[171] See § 7.18.

[172] Gortarez v. Smitty's Super Valu, Inc., 140 Ariz. 97, 680 P.2d 807 (1984).

[173] Great Atlantic & Pacific Tea Co. v. Paul, 256 Md. 643, 261 A.2d 731 (1970); see § 7.14.

[174] Collyer v. S.H. Kress Co., 5 Cal.2d 175, 54 P.2d 20 (1936). The privilege was recognized earlier in the exactly analogous case of a restaurant patron suspected of attempting to leave without paying for a meal. Jacques v. Childs Dining Hall Co., 244 Mass. 438, 138 N.E. 843, 26 A.L.R. 1329 (1923).

[175] Restatement Second of Torts § 120A (1965).

Limited scope of the privilege. In the leading case, a detention of twenty minutes was held to be a justified exercise of the privilege.[176] The defendant is "entitled to use a reasonable amount of compulsion in order to effect that restraint."[177] But the defendant loses the privilege if he detains the plaintiff either for an unreasonable time or in an unreasonable manner.[178] In other words, the defendant's probable cause[179] to believe in the plaintiff's guilt does not justify an improper method of questioning. Thus the defendant who unnecessarily handcuffs the plaintiff or makes an exhibit of her in the presence of other customers may lose the privilege.[180]

Statutory privileges for merchants. Most states have enacted statutory versions of the merchant's privilege, and the contemporary cases are often based on the statute rather on the common law.[181] Some of the statutes reflect a purpose to protect other repeat-theft victims such as farmers, libraries and museums.[182]

Triggering the statutory privilege. The statutory privilege is normally triggered only if the merchant has probable cause to believe a theft has occurred or is being attempted. Since the theft would not normally be completed until the shoplifter has actually passed the checkout counter or left the store, some statutes specifically provide that the privilege to detain for investigation is triggered if the suspect conceals goods[183] or removes anti-theft tags.[184] Others appear to erect the privilege only if the merchant reasonably believes an actual theft has been completed.[185] Some courts have said that the statute must be strictly construed, so that, for example, the merchant may be privileged to detain a suspected thief but not a suspected counterfeiter.[186]

Limiting the statutory privilege. As with the Restatement's privilege, the statutory privilege is usually limited both in duration and in scope. The merchant can investigate, or under some statutes can summon police officers when he has probable cause,[187] but he has no privilege to exact a punishment.[188] And the merchant may detain the suspected shoplifter for a reasonable time to accomplish the investigation or perhaps to await the arrival of officers, but may not detain for longer than a brief or "reasonable" period[189] or by improper or unnecessary force.[190] Some authority has permitted an actual search of

---

[176] Collyer v. S.H. Kress Co., 5 Cal.2d 175, 54 P.2d 20 (1936).

[177] Id.

[178] Jacques v. Childs Dining Hall Co., 244 Mass. 438, 138 N.E. 843, 26 A.L.R. 1329 (1923).

[179] See § 7.18.

[180] See Dillard Dep't Stores, Inc. v. Silva, 148 S.W.3d 370 (Tex. 2004) (security guard forced shopper to the floor, handcuffed him and questioned him in that position; privilege exceeded).

[181] E.g., Gortarez v. Smitty's Super Valu, Inc., 140 Ariz. 97, 680 P.2d 807 (1984); Lerner Shops of Nevada, Inc. v. Marin, 83 Nev. 75, 423 P.2d 398 (1967). See Annotation, Robert A. Brazener, Construction and effect, in false imprisonment action, of statute providing for detention of suspected shoplifters, 47 A.L.R.3d 998 (1973).

[182] E.g., Fla. Stat. Ann. § 812.015 (farmers).

[183] E.g., Iowa Code Ann. § 808.12.

[184] E.g., 11 Del. Code Ann. § 840.

[185] Md. Cts. & Jud. Proc. Code § 5–402.

[186] Taylor v. Super Discount Market, Inc., 212 Ga.App. 155, 441 S.E.2d 433 (1994).

[187] Ariz. Rev. Stats. § 13–1805; 11 Del. Code Ann. § 840.

[188] Ariz. Rev. Stats. § 13–1805; Cal. Penal Code § 490.5(b)(1); Colo. Rev. Stats. § 18–4–407.

[189] E.g., Mass. Gen. L. Ann. 231 § 94B. However, some statutes, if read literally, would appear to authorize a full scale arrest of the suspected shoplifter. Ala. Code § 15–10–14.

[190] Wal-Mart Stores, Inc. v. Mitchell, 877 S.W.2d 616, 618 (Ky. 1994) ("statute does not provide the merchant or its employees with a license to manhandle or browbeat a child in an attempt to discover if he has unlawfully taken merchandise"); K-Mart Corp. v. Washington, 109 Nev. 1180, 866 P.2d 274 (1993).

the plaintiff's person and objects within her immediate control, subject only to a reasonableness limitation,[191] and some statutes expressly allow searches.[192] In determining whether the detention was carried out in a reasonable manner, some courts have permitted the plaintiff to introduce evidence of the merchant's own training or policy manuals.[193]

Issues in the merchant detention cases. Under the common law or a statute, two distinct questions can arise when the merchant claims a privilege to detain. In the first place, no arrest or detention is justified unless the merchant has probable cause[194] to believe that the plaintiff has stolen or has attempted to steal something. But once probable cause is established, the second question is whether the merchant's acts exceed the privilege. As to this second question, the presence of probable cause matters not at all. These two issues dominate most of the cases, but in some cases, the issue may be seen to be less about the privilege than about the plaintiff's consent to questioning, or even more fundamentally about the lack of any real detention. If the defendant merely questions the plaintiff without any implied force or threat, the defendant may not have detained the plaintiff at all—and if not, there is no tort.[195]

§ 7.18 Privileged Arrests

Scope of privilege. An arrest takes a person into custody for the very particular purpose of bringing the person before a court or similar body administering the law.[196] To claim the privilege of arrest, the defendant must be acting in line with such a purpose. A confinement for the purpose of extorting a settlement is not an arrest;[197] nor is confinement for the purpose of holding a witness who is not charged with crime,[198] with some exceptions.[199] Some brief stops or detentions, made for the purpose of investigation rather than bringing a charge, may be privileged under separate rules.[200]

Private persons. Private persons are privileged to effect an arrest for criminal offenses in limited circumstances. This privilege permits a private defendant to arrest the plaintiff when (1) the plaintiff has in fact committed the felony for which he is

---

[191] See Wal-Mart Stores, Inc. v. Cockrell, 61 S.W.3d 774 (Tex. App. 2001) (Wal-Mart's requirement that shopper lift the bandage on his liver-transplant wound was unreasonable and beyond the scope of the privilege). Many states do not allow the merchant to search the detained person. E.g., Gau v. Smitty's Super Valu, Inc., 183 Ariz. 107, 901 P.2d 455 (Ct. App. 1995); Johnson v. K-Mart Enterprises, Inc., 98 Wis.2d 533, 297 N.W.2d 74 (Ct. App. 1980).

[192] See Wal-Mart Stores, Inc. v. Bathe, 715 N.E.2d 954 (Ind. App. 1999) (discussing such statutes).

[193] K-Mart Corp. v. Washington, 109 Nev. 1180, 866 P.2d 274 (1993) (manual was not the standard or test of liability, but was evidence on the question of reasonableness); see also D. A. Johns, Annotation, Admissibility of Defendant's Rules or Instruction for Dealing with Shoplifters, in Action for False Imprisonment or Malcious Prosecution, 31 A.L.R.3d 705 (1970).

[194] See § 7.18.

[195] See Taylor v. Super Discount Market, Inc., 212 Ga.App. 155, 441 S.E.2d 433 (1994) (questions about suspected counterfeit bill not "unlawful"); Sweeney v. F.W. Woolworth Co., 247 Mass. 277, 142 N.E. 50, 31 A.L.R. 311 (1924); see also §§ 4.14 & 4.15 (confinement requirement in false imprisonment claim).

[196] Restatement Second of Torts § 127 (1965).

[197] Cf. § 39.14 (liability for abuse of process).

[198] Illinois v. Lidster, 540 U.S. 419, 124 S.Ct. 885, 157 L.Ed.2d 843 (2004) (detention of witnesses must be confined to basic stops that "interfere only minimally with liberty").

[199] See e.g., 18 U.S.C.A. § 3144 (the federal material witness statute, allowing arrest of recalcitrant witnesses to secure their testimony in criminal proceedings).

[200] Terry v. Ohio, 392 U.S. 1, 88 S.Ct. 1868, 20 L.Ed.2d 889 (1968).

arrested, or (2) someone has committed that felony[201] and the defendant reasonably suspects the plaintiff as the person responsible, or (3) the plaintiff has committed a breach of the peace in the presence of the defendant.[202] Beyond this, the private defendant has a limited privilege to effect an arrest to prevent an attempted felony in his presence.[203] These citizens' arrests, like their official counterparts, are protected only so long as they are made without unreasonable and excessive force.[204]

Police officers and warrantless arrests. Police officers enjoy the same privilege to effect an arrest as private persons, and in addition may arrest without a warrant on reasonable suspicion of a felony even if it turns out that no felony has actually been committed.[205] No warrantless arrest is privileged, however, unless the defendant has probable cause, that is, reasonable objective grounds to believe that a crime was committed and that the plaintiff committed it.[206] Officers may be permitted by statute to arrest for misdemeanors committed in their presence even though no breach of the peace is threatened.

Arrests by officers with warrants. Peace officers are not liable in tort for properly executing a facially valid,[207] lawfully issued warrant[208] or other judicial process according to its terms, even where the arrested person turns out to be innocent. The protection is lost if the warrant is clearly invalid on its face—that is, if its invalidity can be determined simply by reading it.[209] A warrant authorizing the arrest of the plaintiff for investigation does not charge a crime and is not valid on its face; the officer who arrests the plaintiff on such a warrant will be liable for false arrest. And even a valid warrant does not shield officers from liability for excessive force or other unreasonable means of acting under the warrant; an arrest warrant for traffic violations would not ordinarily justify the use of deadly force.[210]

Harm from manner of seizure or from subsequent acts. A warrant fair on its face protects against tort liability for the arrest or seizure it authorizes, but not for any post-arrest or post-seizure torts. For instance, once an arrest is made, the arrested person cannot be held indefinitely without trial; someone, whether the arresting officer or another, must provide a trial or release the detainee.[211] Similarly, an officer who seizes

---

[201] If no felony has actually been committed by anyone, even the reasonably mistaken citizen arrester loses the privilege. Restatement Second of Torts § 119 (1965).

[202] By analogy to rules for officer-arrests, the Iowa court has held that knowledge of one citizen is imputed to those who act in concert with him to effect the arrest, noting that "in the presence" has been liberally construed. Rife v. D. T. Corner, Inc., 641 N.W.2d 761 (Iowa 2002).

[203] Cal. Penal Code § 837; Gortarez v. Smitty's Super Valu, Inc., 140 Ariz. 97, 680 P.2d 807 (1984); Restatement Second of Torts § 119 (1965) (summarizing all the situations).

[204] Whitten v. Cox, 799 So.2d 1 (Miss. 2000); Restatement Second of Torts § 131 (1965).

[205] Restatement Second of Torts § 121 (1965).

[206] See 1 Dobbs, Hayden & Bublick, The Law of Torts § 95 (2d ed. 2011 & Supp.).

[207] Thomas v. Marion County, 652 N.W.2d 183 (Iowa 2002) (protecting officer who arrested the father of the actual suspect, when father's name was mistakenly written on the warrant); Restatement Second of Torts §§ 122 & 124 (1965). The same rule applies to other forms of judicial process. See, e.g., Rock v. Antoine's, Inc., 57 Del. 164, 197 A.2d 737 (1964) (writ of replevin).

[208] A warrant is a writing directing seizure of a person or goods; it must be issued by a court having authority to issue warrants. See Restatement Second of Torts § 113 (1965).

[209] E.g., Allison v. Cnty. of Ventura, 68 Cal.App.3d 689, 137 Cal.Rptr. 542 (1977).

[210] Restatement Second of Torts § 131 (1965) (deadly force authorized if the warrant charges treason or felony and the officer reasonably believes that the arrest cannot be effected without such force).

[211] Cf. Baker v. McCollan, 443 U.S. 137, 144, 99 S.Ct. 2689, 2694, 61 L.Ed.2d 433 (1979) (arrested person "could not be detained indefinitely in the face of repeated protests of innocence even though the warrant under

the plaintiff's property under a facially valid writ is not liable for the seizure, but may become liable for harm resulting to the property because of his failure to protect it while it is in his custody.[212] In the same way, the officer is liable for improper methods of seizure, for instance, in negligently causing damage to property seized,[213] and of course in going beyond the authority of the writ.

E. NECESSITY

§ 7.19 Private Necessity

In a limited group of situations, partial or complete privileges protect defendants whose acts in emergencies would otherwise count as trespass to land or chattels or as conversion. The emergency and the privilege it generates are both called "necessity." The rules recognize two distinct privileges, private necessity and public necessity.

Rule and example. A commonly cited example of private necessity is the case of a sudden storm on a lake that justifies the defendant in putting his small boat ashore on the plaintiff's property to avoid serious threat to his life or property. He is privileged to enter for such a purpose. That privilege means: (a) he is not liable for damages when no harm is no done, (b) he is under no civil disability that attaches to "trespassers,"[214] and (c) the landowner has no privilege to push him back into the lake.[215] If the emergency or necessity arises from the defendant's own fault, it seems probable that he would lose the immunity from liability,[216] but still retain the privilege of shelter on the land so long as the alternatives were unsafe.[217]

Serious and imminent threat required to invoke the privilege. The privilege can only be invoked when the defendant is threatened, or reasonably appears to be threatened, with serious harm and the response is reasonable in the light of the threat.[218] Courts have not suggested that homeless persons could occupy private property on the ground that they have no home of their own.[219] And the harm threatened must not only be imminent but harm that is legally cognizable. For instance, abortion protestors who enter a clinic cannot claim a necessity defense on the ground that their trespasses are necessary to prevent perfectly legal abortions.[220] For the same reason, a homeowner has

---

which he was arrested and detained met the standards of the Fourth Amendment. For the Constitution likewise guarantees an accused the right to a speedy trial.").

[212] Yeager v. Hurt, 433 So.2d 1176, 1180 (Ala. 1983).

[213] See Jeffres v. Countryside Homes of Lincoln, Inc., 214 Neb. 104, 333 N.W.2d 754 (1983).

[214] See Rossi v. DelDuca, 344 Mass. 66, 181 N.E.2d 591 (1962) (child entered defendant's land to escape a dog in the street only to be attacked by the defendant's dog; under the statute she was not entitled to recover if she was a trespasser, but under the necessity privilege she was not a trespasser and could recover).

[215] Ploof v. Putnam, 81 Vt. 471, 71 A. 188 (1908) (on facts similar to those in the text).

[216] Thus where the defendant knew a danger might arise and could have arranged to avoid it he cannot claim the necessity privilege. Currie v. Silvernale, 142 Minn. 254, 171 N.W. 782 (1919).

[217] Cf. Depue v. Flateau, 100 Minn. 299, 111 N.W. 1 (1907) (when supper guest became ill in very cold weather, landowner could not refuse to allow him to stay the night; *semble*, this would hold true even if the guest was voluntarily intoxicated).

[218] Lange v. Fisher Real Estate Dev. Corp., 358 Ill.App.3d 962, 832 N.E.2d 274 (2005).

[219] See London Borough of Southwark v. Williams, [1971] 1 Ch. 734, [1971] 2 All.E.R. 175. Cf. Tobe v. City of Santa Ana, 9 Cal.4th 1069, 40 Cal.Rptr.2d 402, 892 P.2d 1145 (1995) (upholding an ordinance prohibiting various kinds of "camping" on open public property).

[220] Cyr v. State, 887 S.W.2d 203 (Tex. App. 1994). Other protestors have also failed in their assertion of necessity and related defenses. E.g., Commonwealth v. Hood, 389 Mass. 581, 452 N.E.2d 188 (1983) (trespassing to distribute leaflets against nuclear arms race).

no privilege to enter the plaintiff's land to stop the perfectly legal drainage of plaintiff's water upon the defendant's land.[221]

Limits of the privilege: liability for actual harm. The private necessity privilege is "incomplete"[222] because it protects against liability for technical trespass and deprives the landowner of his usual counter-privilege to rebuff the trespasser, but it does not protect the defendant against liability for actual harm done.[223] The skier who is lost in a snow storm may enter your cabin for shelter without liability. But if he burns the furniture to stay warm he must pay for its destruction.

The Vincent case. The leading case establishing liability for actual harm is *Vincent v. Lake Erie Transportation Co.*[224] In *Vincent*, a ship had been tied at the plaintiff's dock unloading goods in Duluth, Minnesota. A violent storm arose. The captain prudently determined that it was unsafe to put out into the lake. He renewed the lines that held the ship at the dock, although this meant that by action of the waves, the ship repeatedly struck the dock and damaged it, a fact of which the captain was aware. Although the dock owner would have no privilege to defend his possession or property by casting the ship off, the dock owner was allowed to recover for actual harm to the dock. The case generates a lot of discussion because the result might be explicable on different grounds and because the scope of the principle is perhaps debatable.[225] But the simplest explanation is that if the captain was a trespasser, he is liable for actual harm done in spite of his incomplete privilege to trespass.

§ 7.20 Public Necessity

In the traditional view of public necessity, a defendant who damages, destroys, or uses the plaintiff's property in the reasonable belief that by so doing he can avoid or minimize serious and immediate harm to the public is protected against liability for intentional torts by a complete privilege.[226] Sometimes the privilege is claimed by a public official acting in the public interest, but even a private individual enjoys its protection.[227]

To invoke the privilege the actor must show that (a) public rather than private interests are involved, (b) he was reasonable in believing that action was needed, and (c) the action he took was a reasonable response to that need.[228] In contrast to the privilege of private necessity, the public necessity privilege is complete because it protects against liability for actual harm inflicted and not merely against liability for technical trespass.

---

[221] Grant v. Allen, 41 Conn. 156 (1874).

[222] Francis Bohlen, Incomplete Privilege to Inflict Intentional Invasions of Interests of Property and Personality, 39 Harv. L. Rev. 307 (1926).

[223] Currie v. Silvernale, 142 Minn. 254, 171 N.W.2d 782 (1919); Vincent v. Lake Erie Transportation Co., 109 Minn. 456, 124 N.W. 221 (1910); Ruiz v. Forman, 514 S.W.2d 817 (Tex. App. 1974); Restatement Second of Torts § 197(2) (1965).

[224] Vincent v. Lake Erie Transportation Co., 109 Minn. 456, 124 N.W. 221 (1910).

[225] A broader possible basis for *Vincent* is that one who acts obtains the benefits of his action and therefore should pay the costs he inflicts upon others. See Richard Epstein, A Theory of Strict Liability, 2 J. Legal Stud. 151, 157–160 (1973).

[226] Restatement Second of Torts §§ 196 (land) & 263 (chattels) (1965). The Restatement uses the term "imminent public disaster." Some courts insist that the public necessity defense requires proof of an "imminent danger" and an "actual emergency." Brewer v. State, 341 P.3d 1107 (Alaska 2014).

[227] Restatement Second of Torts § 196, cmt. e (1965).

[228] Beach v. Trudgain, 43 Va. 345 (1845) (defendants could not justify destruction of plaintiff's house as a firebreak if spread of fire could have been avoided otherwise).

Examples. A time-honored example of the public necessity privilege is the case of the defendant who destroys the plaintiff's house to prevent the spread of fire that would otherwise engulf a whole city. The defendant who reasonably perceives the need for such action cannot be held liable, even for actual harm inflicted.[229] Similarly, the plaintiff's property may be destroyed to prevent the spread of disease[230] or to prevent its use as an agent of destruction by the public enemy such as an invading army.[231]

Private individuals pleading public necessity. The rule of nonliability is easy to understand when it is applied to protect individuals as distinct from public entities. The individual defendant acting in an emergency is not likely to take action to protect against dire public loss if he will be personally liable for the losses that will certainly be inflicted. His interests in such a case may be largely divorced from those of the public at large, so immunity from liability is perhaps needed to induce his beneficial action. Perhaps more importantly, it would be unjust to make a single individual bear the loss reasonably incurred for the benefit of the entire public. This explains why the rule is otherwise in the usual case of private necessity, where the actor has incentive enough to protect his own life and needs no immunity to encourage him.

Injustice to property owner. The public necessity rule recognizes that it would be unjust to impose the costs of saving the city upon its benefactor by making him pay for the destruction of the plaintiff's property. But if it is unjust to make the actor pay the costs of securing the city's safety, is it equally unjust to make the private property owner sacrifice his property for the benefit of other citizens?

In two kinds of cases the uncompensated destruction of the plaintiff's property to protect the public seems fully justified. *First*, the property destroyed for the public benefit might have been lost in any event. To create a firebreak by destroying a house in the path of the fire is only to hasten a loss that seemed inevitable in any event. In a sense, the destruction causes no appreciable loss at all.[232] *Second*, destruction of property without compensation is justified when the property itself threatens others. So a building about to fall upon a city street could be removed, or a diseased herd of cattle could be killed,[233] or infected bedding burned[234] to prevent contagion.

§ 7.21 Public Entities: Necessity, Police Power, and "Taking"

Arguments for public liability. If the destruction of the plaintiff's property actually saves the city, or avoids a substantial risk to it, the plaintiff can plausibly argue that the

---

[229] Surocco v. Geary, 3 Cal. 69 (1853); American Print Works v. Lawrence, 23 N.J.L. 9 (1850), *aff'd*, 23 N.J.L. 590 (1851).

[230] Seavey v. Preble, 64 Me. 120 (1874) (removing wallpaper from smallpox sick room justified); South Dakota Dep't of Health v. Heim, 357 N.W.2d 522 (S.D. 1984) (destruction of diseased herd justified); State v. Mayor and Aldermen of Knoxville, 80 Tenn. 146 (1883) (nuisance created by smoke from repeated burnings of smallpox tainted goods was justified).

[231] United States v. Caltex, Inc., 344 U.S. 149, 73 S.Ct. 200, 97 L.Ed 157 (1952) (destruction of oil and oil terminal as invading troops were entering the city of Manila); Harrison v. Wisdom, 54 Tenn. 99, 116 (1872) (destruction of whiskey as federal troops approached; in determining necessity jury could "consider the rapid advance of a hostile army known to be undisciplined and licentious, and whose occupation of captured places in the line of march was known to be accompanied by acts of besotted vandalism").

[232] In United States v. Caltex, Inc., 344 U.S. 149, 73 S.Ct. 200, 97 L.Ed 157 (1952), if the plaintiff's oil facilities not been destroyed, the enemy army would have seized them, and would probably have destroyed the facilities when the fortunes of war were reversed to prevent the facilities' return to the United States.

[233] South Dakota Dep't of Health v. Heim, 357 N.W.2d 522 (S.D. 1984).

[234] Mayor of Savannah v. Mulligan, 95 Ga. 323, 22 S.E. 621, 622 (1895) ("To destroy property because it is a dangerous nuisance is not to appropriate it to a public use. . . .").

city should pay for the benefit it received at the plaintiff's expense. Such a claim sounds like one for restitution to prevent unjust enrichment or something very close to it.[235] If the city was not in fact saved but the plaintiff's property was intentionally damaged or destroyed by a city's agent, it is still right that the public as a whole bear the costs of harms inflicted to serve public purposes rather than that the individual be forced to sacrifice his property for the good of others.[236] The Restatement's formulation of the public necessity privilege protects the individual actor but leaves open the possibility of public entity liability.[237]

Constitutional compensation requirements. Public entities are constitutionally required to pay just compensation for property they take.[238] For example, if a city wants to create a park or a firebreak, it can take the land of private landowners for such public purposes, but it must pay for what it takes.

Police power. Although a public entity is liable for a taking of the plaintiff's property, courts have said it is not liable for harms resulting from the exercise of police or regulatory power[239] and not liable for destruction as a matter of public necessity.[240] When the destroyed property presented no dangers to others and would not have been destroyed anyway, it is hard to see the difference between cases of "taking" for which compensation must be paid and cases of public necessity (or police power) for which no compensation is due.

Law enforcement damaging private property. The problem is presented when law enforcement officers break into the plaintiff's home or business to capture a felon who has barricaded himself there without the plaintiff's connivance or permission. Capturing the felon is surely a public good that is at least analogous to public necessity; certainly one can think of the officer's action in damaging property as "police power." But it is just

---

[235] Restitution is measured by the value of what the defendant received, not by the loss of the plaintiff. In this context, however, the value received by the defendant would not be the entire value of all property saved but what reasonable people would pay for the right to destroy the plaintiff's property (under eminent domain or otherwise). See 1 Dan B. Dobbs, Law of Remedies § 4.5(1) (2d ed. 1993).

[236] "The . . . guarantee that private property shall not be taken for a public use without just compensation was designed to bar Government from forcing some people alone to bear public burdens which, in all fairness and justice, should be borne by the public as a whole." Armstrong v. United States, 364 U.S. 40, 49, 80 S.Ct. 1563, 1569, 4 L.Ed.2d 1554 (1960). "[I]f it was an act done by the officers having competent authority . . . and especially if the act was done with an honest view to obtain for the public some lawful benefit or advantage, reason and justice obviously require that the city, in its corporate capacity, should be liable to make good the damages sustained by an individual in consequence of the acts thus done." Thayer v. Boston, 36 Mass. 511 (1837). In Owen v. City of Independence, 445 U.S. 622, 100 S.Ct. 1398, 63 L.Ed.2d 673 (1980), the Court quoted the language above from *Thayer* and added that it would be uniquely amiss if government "were permitted to disavow liability for the injury it has begotten." These arguments can be phrased to apply to private defendants: "[I]t seems simply unconscionable to exact that subsidy from the individual victims of serious accidents by depriving them of their right to compensation from the enterprises responsible for their injuries." Gary T. Schwartz, Tort Law and the Economy in Nineteenth-Century America: A Reinterpretation, 90 Yale L. J. 1717 (1981).

[237] Restatement Second of Torts § 196, cmts. e & h (1965).

[238] U.S. Const. Amend. V ("nor shall private property be taken for public use, without just compensation"); U.S. Const. Amend. XIV ("nor shall any State deprive any person of life, liberty, or property, without due process of law"). State constitutions contain similar provisions, which must be construed by each state high court. See, e.g., Dunn v. City of Milwaukie, 355 Or. 339, 328 P.3d 1261 (2014) ("taking" requires intent); City of San Antonio v. Pollock, 284 S.W.3d 809 (Tex. 2009) (same).

[239] Farmers Ins. Exchange v. State, 175 Cal.App.3d 494, 221 Cal.Rptr. 225 (1985). The police power locution is likely to be used when the plaintiff's claim is grounded explicitly on the constitutional right to just compensation for taking of property, while the language of necessity is likely to be used when the plaintiff's claim is grounded in common law tort.

[240] See Brewer v. State, 341 P.3d 1107 (Alaska 2014) (landowners had no constitutional right to compensation if state's actions were justified by public necessity).

as easy to say that the officer's action is a kind of taking or damage of property for which the public entity ought to pay. Minnesota, whose constitution requires payment for property "taken, destroyed or damaged for public use," has said that in this kind of case the entity must pay for the harm to private property of an innocent bystander,[241] although not for damage inflicted in the course of a proper arrest or detention of the property owner himself.[242] There is a little support for the idea elsewhere.[243] But other courts have rejected the inverse condemnation or just compensation claim, holding that police entries upon private land are proper law enforcement activities and either privileged under the public necessity rule or protected as an exercise of legitimate police power. These holdings say the entity is not liable under the just compensation clause for damage to or destruction of property caused by officers incident to a proper arrest or a person[244] or seizure of property[245] or even for damage done in a search for evidence.[246]

Necessity vs. other emergencies. The necessity issue in these cases arises only when acts on behalf of a public entity would, if not privileged, amount to an intentional trespassory tort. If the person acting for public does not intend an invasion of the plaintiff's interests,[247] then the case will be analyzed in terms of negligence or possibly as a civil rights violation, not as an intentional tort with a possible necessity defense. In such cases any emergency faced by the defendant is relevant, but it bears on whether the defendant has committed a tort at all.[248]

Claims against one benefitted by the plaintiff's loss in other settings. The idea that a defendant might be liable for benefits he gained as a result of the losses imposed on the plaintiff is a broad one, not limited to necessity cases. But the language in which the idea is considered and the particular rules applied are enormously different when the defendant commits no intentional invasion of the plaintiff's interest. High-speed police chases may represent emergencies and may risk harm to innocent bystanders for the public good, but such harm is not normally intended; when it is not, the innocent victim must prove negligence[249] or civil rights violations[250] and must face any defenses

---

[241] Wegner v. Milwaukee Mutual Ins. Co., 479 N.W.2d 38, 23 A.L.R.5th 954 (Minn. 1991).

[242] Dokman v. Cnty. of Hennepin, 637 N.W.2d 286 (Minn. App. 2002).

[243] Steele v. City of Houston, 603 S.W.2d 786 (Tex. 1980).

[244] Customer Co. v. City of Sacramento, 10 Cal.4th 368, 895 P.2d 900, 41 Cal.Rptr.2d 658 (1995) (state Constitution requiring compensation for property taken or damaged cannot be read literally to cover law enforcement activities; the law of necessity and corresponding police power confirms that narrow reading of the constitutional provision); Kelley v. Story County Sheriff, 611 N.W.2d 475 (Iowa 2000) (valid forced entry and arrest of man visiting tenant in plaintiff's building, no taking and immunity barred tort claim); Sullivant v. City of Oklahoma City, 940 P.2d 220 (Okla. 1997) (entry of tenant's premises under a warrant, landlord could not recover under the takings clause, but might have a tort recovery if warrant was executed illegally).

[245] Emery v. State, 297 Or. 755, 688 P.2d 72, 44 A.L.R.4th 341 (1984) (seizing and dismantling truck as evidence on murder charge, no obligation to restore truck).

[246] McCoy v. Sanders, 113 Ga.App. 565, 148 S.E.2d 902 (1966) (damage done in draining pond to search for body on the plaintiff's property, no public entity liability for exercise of police power grounded in necessity); Gillmor v. Salt Lake City, 32 Utah 180, 89 P. 714 (1907) (searching for body in river, officers trampled the plaintiff's property; no tort liability for acts done for public benefit).

[247] See § 4.2.

[248] See § 10.7.

[249] Cairl v. City of St. Paul, 268 N.W.2d 908, 100 A.L.R.3d 807 (Minn. 1978), rejected strict liability for damage done in high-speed chases. A ridiculous, cartoon-like chase is described in City of Pinellas Park v. Brown, 604 So.2d 1222 (Fla. 1992) (upholding the plaintiff's allegations of police negligence).

[250] Scott v. Harris, 550 U.S. 372, 127 S.Ct. 1769, 167 L.Ed.2d 686 (2007) (deputy acted reasonably in high-speed chase, thus not violating innocent motorist's Fourth Amendment rights); see generally §§ 22.14 to 22.16.

appropriate to such cases.[251] The concern that innocent individuals should not be made to sacrifice for others' benefit can be reflected in the imposition of strict liability on a defendant who can force all beneficiaries to share the costs, but such liability is imposed only in special cases and it is not addressed by the necessity rules appropriate to intentional torts.[252]

---

[251] California, for example, provides blanket immunities in this situation. See Hernandez v. City of Pomona, 46 Cal.4th 501, 94 Cal.Rptr.3d 1 (2009). In federal civil rights cases, a police officer may mount a powerful qualified immunity defense. See, e.g., Lytle v. Bexar County, Tex., 560 F.3d 404 (5th Cir. 2009); Pasco ex rel. Pasco v. Knoblauch, 566 F.3d 572 (5th Cir. 2009). For more detailed explorations of the qualified immunity, see §§ 22.14 & 22.15.

[252] Strict liability could be imposed in such cases as a means of indirectly requiring benefitted persons to share in the idiosyncratic loss, but this does not require any discussion of necessity.

Chapter 8

CONSENT

Analysis

§ 8.1   General Principles

§ 8.2   Manifestation of Consent

§ 8.3   Unmanifested Consent

§ 8.4   Scope of Consent

§ 8.5   Revocation or Termination of Consent

§ 8.6   Incapacity to Give Consent

§ 8.7   Consent on Behalf of Another

§ 8.8   Mistake or Misrepresentation Negating Consent

§ 8.9   Consent Obtained by Duress or Coercion

§ 8.10   Consent Obtained by Abuse of Power or Position

§ 8.11   Medical Battery and Informed Consent

§ 8.12   Emergency as a Substitute for Consent

§ 8.13   Consent to Crime

§ 8.1   General Principles

A person who consents or apparently consents, by words or conduct, to acts that would otherwise count as an intentional tort[1] cannot recover damages for those acts. Consent is sometimes treated as an affirmative defense, with the defendant bearing the burden to prove that the plaintiff consented, or apparently consented, to the defendant's acts.[2] Other courts regard the absence of consent as a fact that must be proved as part of the plaintiff's prima facie case.[3] While who bears the burden of proof may appear rather muddled in the case law, it is quite clear that in many cases, consent marks a deficiency in the plaintiff's prima facie case at the most fundamental level: where the plaintiff consents, the defendant's act is simply not tortious.[4] For example, the defendant does not intend an offensive battery when he touches the plaintiff with the plaintiff's

---

[1]   Materials in this chapter focus on consent as a bar to an intentional tort claim. The negligence-based "informed consent" claim is discussed most fully in the chapter on medical malpractice. See §§ 21.9 to 21.12.

[2]   See, e.g., Hernandez v. K-Mart Corp., 497 So.2d 1259 (Fla. Dist. Ct. App. 1986) (defendant in false imprisonment case has the burden of proving that the plaintiff consented to detention); Anderson v. Low Rent Housing Com'n of Muscatine, 304 N.W.2d 239 (Iowa 1981) (discussing consent as an affirmative defense in case alleging libel and invasion of privacy); Restatement Second of Torts § 167, cmt. c (1965) (burden of proof is on defendant to establish that a possessor of land consented to an entry).

[3]   See, e.g., Ten Broeck Dupont, Inc. v. Brooks, 283 S.W.3d 705 (Ky. 2009) (plaintiff in battery case must prove she did not consent to touching); Landry v. Bellanger, 851 So.2d 943 (La. 2003) (same); Bennett v. Ohio Dep't of Rehab. & Correction, 60 Ohio St.3d 107, 573 N.E.2d 633 (1991) (plaintiff's case of false imprisonment requires proof that confinement was "against his consent"). Note that a plaintiff in a medical malpractice case alleging breach of the duty to provide sufficient information to obtain informed consent quite clearly bears the burden of proving that the doctor failed to obtain informed consent. See, e.g., Gouse v. Cassel, 532 Pa. 197, 615 A.2d 331 (1992); § 21.9.

[4]   See, e.g., Smith v. Calvary Christian Church, 462 Mich. 679, 614 N.W.2d 590 (2000) ("[N]o wrong is done to one who consents. Without a wrong, plaintiff has no compensable claim.").

consent; such consent negates any tortious intent, so the plaintiff fails in one element of her proof on the prima facie case.

Among the trespassory and intentional torts, consent defeats the claim for battery,[5] for false imprisonment,[6] and for trespass to land or chattels[7] or conversion.[8] For example, a sexual touching would be a battery if it is not effectively consented to, but if the plaintiff effectively consents to the touching, there is no battery.[9] Similarly, if the plaintiff consents to a friendly wrestling match with the defendant, the plaintiff cannot recover for injuries sustained in that match.[10] The same principle applies when the plaintiff consents to practical jokes or other sportive play.[11] An analogous rule applies in some but not all negligence cases under the name of assumption of risk.[12]

The consent principle is general in its scope, firm in its acceptance, and central in its significance. It makes the plaintiff's right of autonomy the centerpiece of the law on intentional torts and to some extent other torts as well. Nevertheless, a cluster of subsidiary rules and definitions both enlarge and constrain its application:

(1) *Objective, manifested, or apparent consent.* The plaintiff effectively consents if appearances created by her words or acts lead the defendant reasonably to believe she consented, even if the plaintiff did not subjectively intend to consent.[13] The plaintiff likewise effectively consents if the she actually or subjectively consents to the defendant's conduct, even if that consent is not otherwise expressed or manifested.[14]

(2) *Consent to conduct, not harm.* The plaintiff who has consented or apparently consented to conduct cannot recover damages for harm resulting from that conduct, even though the plaintiff did not expect harm to result and did not consent to harm.[15]

(3) *Scope and termination of consent.* Neither consent nor apparent consent will not bar a claim for tortious conduct that is outside the scope of that consent, or for any tortious conduct that occurs after consent has been revoked.[16]

(4) *Incapacity and "substituted consent."* Neither the plaintiff's consent nor apparent consent is effective to bar recovery if the plaintiff lacked capacity to give consent due to her minority or mental disability and if the defendant

---

[5]   Houston v. Kinder-Care Learning Centers, Inc., 208 Ga.App. 235, 430 S.E.2d 24 (1993).

[6]   E.g., Lolley v. Charter Woods Hosp. Inc., 572 So.2d 1223 (Ala. 1990).

[7]   See In re IDC Clambakes, Inc., 727 F.3d 58 (1st Cir. 2013).

[8]   See L & W Engineering Co., Inc. v. Hogan, 858 S.W.2d 847 (Mo. App. 1993); Michel v. Melgren, 70 Wash.App. 373, 853 P.2d 940 (1993).

[9]   E.g., Schieffer v. Catholic Archdiocese of Omaha, 244 Neb. 715, 508 N.W.2d 907 (1993).

[10]   Cf. Hellriegel v. Tholl, 69 Wash.2d 97, 417 P.2d 362 (1966) (horseplay). The same principle is of course applicable when the plaintiff consents to practical jokes or other sportive play. Fuerschbach v. Southwest Airlines Co., 439 F.3d 1197 (10th Cir. 2006).

[11]   See Fuerschbach v. Southwest Airlines Co., 439 F.3d 1197 (10th Cir. 2006).

[12]   See Chapter 17.

[13]   See § 8.2.

[14]   See § 8.3.

[15]   See § 8.4.

[16]   See §§ 8.4 & 8.5.

knew or should have known it.[17] Where a person lacks the capacity to consent, others may be empowered to consent on her behalf.[18]

(5) Misrepresentation, duress, and mistake. Consent or apparent consent will be ineffective when the plaintiff is induced to profess consent as a result of the defendant's misrepresentation[19] or duress,[20] or as a result of a mistake of which the defendant knew or should have known.[21] However, the plaintiff's mistake, including a mistake induced by a misrepresentation, does not vitiate her consent if the mistake is only about a "collateral" matter not going to the essential nature of the transaction.[22]

(6) Consent obtained by abuse of power. When employers or psychiatrists use their special power or authority to obtain sexual favors from employees or patients, purported consent by the employee or patient may be ineffective even if these abuses of power fall short of duress. The same principle may apply in some degree to others such as lawyers, physicians, or members of the clergy.[23]

(7) Informed consent. Some defendants, because of their relationship to the plaintiff, are under an affirmative obligation to provide appropriate information to the plaintiff to permit an informed consent, and are subject to liability if they fail to do so and harm results.[24] In many cases, however, the existence of a serious emergency may obviate the need to obtain consent.[25]

(8) Consent to crime. Neither consent nor apparent consent will generally bar an intentional tort claim even where the activity to which the plaintiff consented also constitutes a criminal act. This rule is subject to some qualifications, however, most notably where the statute criminalizing the activity is intended to protect the plaintiff from her own professed consent, such as statutory-rape laws.[26]

§ 8.2   Manifestation of Consent

Manifested or Objectively-Determinable Consent

Actual consent to an act is a subjective willingness for the act to occur. Apparent consent is conduct, including words, that are reasonably understood by another as a reflection of consent.[27] Either actual or apparent consent is effective to relieve the actor of responsibility for the acts addressed.[28]

---

[17] See § 8.6.

[18] See § 8.7.

[19] See § 8.8.

[20] See § 8.9.

[21] See § 8.8.

[22] Id.

[23] See § 8.10.

[24] See § 8.11. For fuller treatment of the negligence claim for a medical professional's breach of the duty to obtain a patient's informed consent, see §§ 21.9 to 21.12.

[25] See § 8.12.

[26] See § 8.13.

[27] Restatement Second of Torts § 892 (1979).

[28] E.g., Smith v. VonCannon, 283 N.C. 656, 661, 197 S.E.2d 524, 529 (1973) ("An apparent consent is sufficient if brought about by acts of the [plaintiff]."); Carr v. Mobile Video Tapes, Inc., 893 S.W.2d 613 (Tex.

Because the appearance of consent is effective if it leads the defendant reasonably to believe consent is actual, a plaintiff's private and uncommunicated reservation does not subject the defendant to liability. The defendant is entitled to rely in good faith upon the reasonable appearance of consent created by the plaintiff. In a well-known case, the plaintiff was in a line of immigrants on board a ship and awaiting a vaccination needed to enter the country. She held up her arm as others did and received the vaccination. She suffered some harm from it and brought suit, but the court held that even if she did not subjectively consent, her conduct gave the appearance of consent and that the defendant was entitled to rely upon the appearance even if the plaintiff never subjectively meant to consent at all.[29] It might be possible to interpret the facts differently. Perhaps the plaintiff's upraised arm was a protest, not a consent.[30] The question is whether the defendant reasonably believed that the plaintiff's words or conduct reflected a genuine consent.

Consent Implied by Conduct

Effective consent can be manifested by the plaintiff's nonverbal conduct. It can be shown by actions, by a course of conduct, by social conventions applicable to the setting, or by a relationship between the parties. Perhaps most real-life consent is implied rather than expressed. We join a game of tag; we consent to being touched.[31] We engage in a course of practical jokes with a friend; we consent to the kind of touchings or confinements those jokes lead us to expect.[32] Body language communicates many feelings or attitudes, including consents. If you go home after a long hard day and slump in the chair, your partner or friend might take that as a consent to have your neck rubbed. Indeed, your relationship with a partner might itself demonstrate a general consent to friendly touchings.

Many false imprisonment cases require judges and juries to interpret conduct. A customer, suspected of shoplifting, is asked to follow a guard and does so. She is taken to a room and interrogated by several store employees. The store employees' nonverbal conduct and demeanor may count as an implicit threat to confine the plaintiff if she attempts to leave. On the other hand, her conduct in remaining there without protest may suggest consent. When the plaintiff merely goes along without protest, courts usually find that the plaintiff was not confined, since she remained voluntarily.[33]

Whether the plaintiff has communicated an apparent consent by conduct rather than by words turns on the interpretation of facts, not on rules. Conduct that might amount to an implied consent must be understood fairly and realistically. Courts are

---

App. 1994) (apparent consent by someone with authority to give it); Restatement Second of Torts §892(2) (1979).

[29]   O'Brien v. Cunard S.S. Co., 154 Mass. 272, 28 N.E. 266 (1891).

[30]   See Symposium, Five Approaches to Legal Reasoning in the Classroom: Contrasting Perspectives on O'Brien v. Cunard S.S. Co. Ltd., 57 Mo. L. Rev. 346 (1992).

[31]   See Avila v. Citrus Community College Dist., 38 Cal. 4th 148, 131 P.3d 383, 41 Cal. Rptr. 3d 299 (2006) ("One who enters into a sport, game or contest may be taken to consent to physical contacts consistent with the understood rules of the game. . . . [H]ere, the baseball player who steps to the plate consents to the possibility the opposing pitcher may throw near or at him"; holding that consent extends to intentional torts as long as those torts are "inherent" in the game).

[32]   Fuerschbach v. Southwest Airlines Co., 439 F.3d 1197 (10th Cir. 2006) (but whether the apparent consent to a workplace prank included consent to arrest by real law officers was a jury question).

[33]   E.g., Reicheneder v. Skaggs Drug Center, 421 F.2d 307 (5th Cir. 1970); Hardy v. LaBelle's Distrib. Co., 203 Mont. 263, 661 P.2d 35 (1983).

charged with the obligation to reject spurious assertions that the plaintiff consented when she obviously did not.

Probably no single act, segregated from its social or relational context, can evince consent. Holding your arm up may signify consent to a vaccination if you are standing in the vaccination line, but it signifies no such thing if you are sitting in class and the teacher is asking questions. The act takes its meaning from the context. What is true of actions is also true of silence. If the plaintiff watches the doctor approach with a syringe and says nothing when the doctor says "I'm going to vaccinate you now," silence may suggest consent even if the plaintiff makes no move at all. But a general rule about silence is not warranted, because situations, relationships, social customs and expectations color the interpretation of acts and silences.

Consent Implied by Custom

A special form of consent by silence arises in the case of social custom, as distinct from overt conduct of the plaintiff. For example, in a given area it may be customary to permit hunting or fishing on unenclosed rural lands, so that unless the landowner posts a notice to the contrary, no one is a trespasser who enters such land to fish.[34]

Qualifications can be illustrated by the door-to-door solicitor case. Suppose social custom permits door-to-door salespersons to knock on your door and offer their wares. Such an entry upon your land is a technical trespass unless you have consented. But if you say nothing to show your dissent from this custom, your silence might reasonably be taken as consent for the door-to-door salesperson to knock on your door.[35]

The salesperson example reflects three important limits. First, you could reasonably be expected to know of the custom to permit unannounced callers to enter without liability for trespass. Second, you have an opportunity, at low cost, to express your dissent from the custom. You could post a sign forbidding salespeople to enter. Third, a harmless entry that does not include entering your home is in accord with the limits of the apparent consent. In the light of these facts, the salesperson can reasonably believe he may enter for the limited purpose of offering goods for sale.

Why Manifested Consent Is a Bar

Why should the plaintiff be barred from recovery on the basis of manifested consent when she has not actually consented? In the usual case, the main reason is that the defendant who acts on a reasonable understanding of appearances is simply not a wrongdoer. The consent does not relieve him of liability for a tort; he is not a tortfeasor at all.[36]

To see this point, suppose the plaintiff and defendant are married to each other and the plaintiff manifests a consent to a loving embrace. Neither plaintiff nor defendant is aware that the plaintiff has a particularly fragile vertebrae. When the defendant embraces the plaintiff in an ordinary way, the bone is broken. In this case the defendant

---

[34]   Marsh v. Colby, 39 Mich. 626 (1878).

[35]   Prior v. White, 132 Fla. 1, 180 So. 347, 116 A.L.R. 1176 (1938) (concluding that such a custom existed and giving the further illustration of a retail business, which implicitly invites people to enter); Smith v. VonCannon, 283 N.C. 656, 663, 197 S.E.2d 524, 529 (1973) ("In the absence of notice to the contrary, a stranger to the occupant of a house is entitled to assume that he may walk to the front door thereof . . . without being sued for trespass.").

[36]   E.g., Janelsins v. Button, 102 Md.App. 30, 648 A.2d 1039 (1994); Schieffer v. Catholic Archdiocese of Omaha, 244 Neb. 715, 508 N.W.2d 907 (1993).

has intentionally touched the plaintiff, but not intentionally harmed her. Intentional touching suffices to show a battery if the touching is intended to be offensive. If the defendant had intended an unconsented—to touching, an intent to offend could be inferred. In that case, the defendant would be liable for all actual harm resulting. But in the hug example, the defendant cannot be seen to intend offense by the embrace; given the appearance of consent, the embrace seems inoffensive and therefore not wrongful.

More generally, any other rule would oppose the freedom and autonomy of both parties, either by imposing liability or making it more difficult for them to obtain what they both want. Suppose you would like to fish in Jay's farm pond and Jay would like you to do so because the pond is woefully overstocked. Jay manifests consent. If you can rely on that manifestation, you and Jay are both be better off; you'll catch the fish you want and Jay will get the stock reduced. A rule that says you cannot rely on the appearance of consent would allow Jay to sue you after you have taken Jay at his word and improved his pond. If that were the law you might well refuse to rely on appearances. The objective-appearance rule fosters both freedom and autonomy.[37]

The downside of the objective rule is that appearances may be misleading. When the people involved differ in gender, ethnicity, or culture, and especially when the conduct in question touches intimate or sensitive matters such as sexual relations, the defendant must not presume too quickly to interpret conduct, custom, or even words as consent.[38] In particular, defendants who possess power or authority over others must be wary of the possibility that appearance of consent is misleading. For example, employers, psychiatrists, and priests must recognize that employees, patients, and parishioners do not necessarily feel free to reject sexual advances and that the appearance of consent is the result of other forces.[39]

§ 8.3   Unmanifested Consent

The usual case is one in which the plaintiff manifests consent to the defendant's act, whether or not the manifestation represents the plaintiff's subjective state of mind. In the reverse situation, the plaintiff does not outwardly manifest consent but does in fact subjectively or secretly consent to the defendant's act. The consensus seems to be that a subjective or "real" consent is a bar to recovery even though the defendant was unaware of such consent.[40]

It seems easy enough to see why a defendant is not a wrongdoer when he reasonably believes he is acting in accord with the plaintiff's wishes; that is the case of manifested consent. The plaintiff's private and unexpressed consent, however, gives the defendant no basis for claiming innocence; by hypothesis, he knows nothing of the plaintiff's consent. Suppose the defendant enters upon the plaintiff's land to fish in the plaintiff's pond, but believes he is unwelcome. In such a case, he is, prima facie, a technical trespasser because he has the intent to enter and he does enter. (He also has an antisocial state of mind, but that is not required to show trespass.) If the plaintiff later brings suit for the trespass and the defendant learns that the plaintiff had in fact written

---

[37]   See, discussing some values of objective approaches in negligence law, Gregory C. Keating, Reasonableness and Rationality in Negligence Theory, 48 Stan. L. Rev. 311, 371 ff. (1996).

[38]   See Judee K. Burgoon, Laura K. Guerrero & Kory Floyd, Nonverbal Communication (2009) (discussing gender, cultural and subcultural differences in nonverbal communication).

[39]   See § 8.10.

[40]   Restatement Second of Torts § 892(1) (1979).

but not mailed a note to say he was welcome, why should the plaintiff's private and unexpressed consent operate to bar the claim?

If such a subjective, unmanifested consent is a bar to the plaintiff's claim it must be because she has suffered no injury when the defendant acted in accordance with her will, even if, later on, she changed her mind about what she wanted. It is not that the defendant is no wrongdoer as it is in the case of manifested consent, but that the plaintiff has suffered no harm when her wishes are met.

While manifested consent indicates that the defendant is not a tortfeasor in the first place, unmanifested consent seems like a true affirmative defense, at least in the pond illustration. Why is that so? It is so because the plaintiff can prove a prima facie case by showing entry and intent to enter. The defendant must then sustain the burden of showing consent.

§ 8.4   Scope of Consent

Consent does not bar the plaintiff's claim for any tortious conduct that is outside the scope of her consent or apparent consent. The plaintiff may limit her consent as she likes, consenting to one act but not to another, or to acts at one time but not at another, or to acts under some conditions but not under others.[41] The scope of the defendant's protection is the scope of the consent. If his conduct would be tortious except for consent and his conduct goes beyond the consent or its conditions, he is subject to liability.[42] Conversely, if the defendant's touching of the plaintiff is within the scope of the plaintiff's consent, the touching is not an actionable battery.[43]

Determining the scope. The scope of consent is often clear. A patient who consents to removal of excess skin is not consenting to a breast augmentation,[44] and a patient who forbids all sedatives in a medical procedure except Demerol is not consenting to some other sedative.[45] But the scope of the consent may itself be subject to dispute, because the scope of consent, like its existence, depends heavily upon implications and the interpretation of circumstances. Consent to shoot rabbits in the landowner's woods is almost certainly not consent to shoot them in the landowner's front yard,[46] yet circumstances, including customs of the parties, might produce a different conclusion. Possibly also a consent to operate on the right ear is not consent to operate upon the left one,[47] but it is not impossible to believe that a patient about to undergo an operation

---

[41]   See Restatement Second of Torts § 892A(3) (1979).

[42]   E.g., Conte v. Girard Orthopaedic Surgeons Medical Group, Inc., 107 Cal.App.4th 1260, 132 Cal.Rptr.2d 855 (2003) ("A typical medical battery case is where a plaintiff has consented to a particular treatment, but the doctor performs a treatment that goes beyond the consent.").

[43]   See, e.g., Christman v. Davis, 179 Vt. 99, 889 A.2d 746 (2005).

[44]   See Perry v. Shaw, 88 Cal. App.4th 658, 106 Cal. Rptr. 2d 70 (2001).

[45]   Duncan v. Scottsdale Med. Imaging, Ltd., 205 Ariz. 306, 70 P.3d 435 (2003).

[46]   But see Florida Publishing Co. v. Fletcher, 340 So.2d 914 (Fla. 1976) (ignoring the difference between consent-by-custom to enter land and consent for a stranger to enter a dwelling place in the owner's absence).

[47]   Mohr v. Williams, 95 Minn. 261, 104 N.W. 12 (1905), *overruled in part*, Genzel v. Halvorson, 248 Minn. 527, 80 N.W.2d 854 (1957). Cf. Kaplan v. Mamelak, 162 Cal.App.4th 637, 75 Cal.Rptr.3d 861 (2008) (jury question whether plaintiff consented to an operation on the wrong disk, just a few inches from the "correct" disk; patient sued doctor for battery).

consents by implication to extensions of the operation that become medically desirable[48] and certainly to extensions needed because of medical emergency.[49]

Consent to act as consent to consequences. Consent to the defendant's acts is not consent to injury resulting from those acts. Nevertheless, the defendant is not liable for an intentional tort so long as his acts are those consented to, even if harmful consequences result.[50] In *Hellriegel v. Tholl*,[51] the plaintiff and other boys were engaged in horseplay. Several boys picked up the plaintiff and threw him into the water. These acts seem to have been tacitly consented to because they were part of the activities engaged in by all the boys. The plaintiff suffered a terrible and unexpected injury. Although he never consented to injury, he did consent to the acts that caused it and that was enough to bar his claim. Put differently, a consent is not normally interpreted to contain an implicit condition, "I consent provided I am not hurt." There are express and implicit conditions to consents, however, and they are traditionally effective if communicated or understood.[52]

§ 8.5   Revocation or Termination of Consent

Power to revoke and effect of revocation. Consent does not bar a plaintiff's claim for an injury caused by any tortious conduct occurring after consent has been effectively revoked and the defendant has a reasonable opportunity to avoid that conduct. A plaintiff who gives consent may terminate or revoke it at any time by communicating the revocation to those who may act upon the consent.[53] Actions speak louder than words, so if a competent patient who has consented to hospitalization later attempts to leave, such an action probably should be taken as a revocation of the consent.[54] A communicated revocation withdraws the defendant's privilege; once the consent is withdrawn he becomes liable for any act that would be tortious without consent. For example, if a patient, about to be operated upon, revokes her consent, the surgeon commits a battery if he proceeds with the operation and becomes liable even if he carried out the operation with skill.[55] If a landowner revokes her consent to a visitor's presence, the visitor becomes a trespasser if he does not leave.[56]

Defendant's reasonable opportunity. The defendant must, however, be permitted a reasonable opportunity to discontinue his conduct. For example, if the plaintiff has permitted the defendant to store his car on the plaintiff's land, the defendant must remove the car when the consent is revoked, but at the same time he is given a

---

[48]   Kennedy v. Parrott, 243 N.C. 355, 90 S.E.2d 754 (1956). When the patient signs a consent form leaving the physician free to perform any procedure that becomes medically necessary, this may override the patient's earlier rejection of a particular procedure. See Hoofnel v. Segal, 199 S.W.3d 147 (Ky. 2006).

[49]   See § 8.12.

[50]   See Janelsins v. Button, 102 Md.App. 30, 38, 648 A.2d 1039, 1043 (1994) ("Where the plaintiff consented to the battery itself, the consent extends to ordinary consequences stemming from it.").

[51]   Hellriegel v. Tholl, 69 Wash.2d 97, 417 P.2d 362 (1966).

[52]   Duncan v. Scottsdale Med. Imaging, Ltd., 205 Ariz. 306, 70 P.3d 435 (2003) (consent to receive sedative, but only if it is morphine or demerol, does not bar battery claim when nurse injected a different sedative); Ashcraft v. King, 228 Cal.App.3d 604, 610, 278 Cal.Rptr. 900 (1991) (consent to a transfusion, but only with family-donated blood; doctor would commit a battery if the condition was not honored).

[53]   Restatement Second of Torts § 892A(5) & cmt. i (1979).

[54]   Cf. Morgan v. Greenwaldt, 786 So.2d 1037 (Miss. 2001) (self-committed psychiatric patient consented to ordinary treatment and could not complain of false imprisonment because she had not revoked her consent or attempted to leave the hospital).

[55]   Pugsley v. Privette, 220 Va. 892, 263 S.E.2d 69 (1980).

[56]   Hector v. Metro Centers, Inc., 498 N.W.2d 113 (N.D. 1993).

reasonable opportunity to do so.[57] Similarly, the physician carrying out a medical procedure when consent to it is revoked must be permitted to discontinue the procedure in a medically safe way.[58]

Automatic termination. A consent may be terminated in accordance with a condition established in the consent itself. Suppose that A gives B permission to move B's house trailer onto A's land and to keep it there for the rest of B's life. By its own conditions, the consent terminates when B dies. B's personal representative becomes a trespasser if he does not remove the trailer within a reasonable time thereafter.[59]

§ 8.6   Incapacity to Give Consent

Effects of Incapacity

Incapacity known to the defendant. Minors, intoxicated persons, insane persons and others similarly situated may lack capacity to give actual consent. A professed consent is not effective to bar the plaintiff's claim if the plaintiff lacked capacity to give consent and the defendant knew or should have known of the plaintiff's incapacity.[60] For instance, if the defendant knows he is dealing with a child or an insane person, he must know that the child cannot effectively consent and he is held liable for torts to the child even if the child professed a consent.[61] The rule ultimately turns on appearances to the defendant rather than on the plaintiff's secret status as a legally incompetent person, and is thus merely an example of the objective-manifestation requirement.

Incapacity not known to the defendant. Incapacity negates actual consent, but when the plaintiff gives the appearance of capacity and the appearance of consent, the defendant is not acting tortiously at all when he acts in accord with appearances. It may be, however, that some defendants, because of their relationship to the plaintiff, are under a duty to take extra precautions to be sure that the plaintiff's consent is based upon adequate understanding of the relevant facts.[62]

Determining Capacity

Adults generally. The competency of adults is a matter of fact to be determined in each case. The plaintiff who wishes to escape the normal consequences of consent must sustain the burden of proving incapacity and that the defendant knew or should have known of the incapacity.[63]

Courts determine mental incapacity in a number of diverse contexts and by somewhat different tests. Capacity is relevant to the validity of a contract or will, to civil commitment, to criminal punishment and to the operation of the statute of limitations. In the law of civil commitment, incapacity is often judged by determining whether a person is a threat to herself or to others.[64] In other situations, courts usually judge

---

[57]   Restatement Second of Torts § 177 (1965).

[58]   Mims v. Boland, 110 Ga.App. 477, 138 S.E.2d 902 (1964).

[59]   Steiger v. Burroughs, 878 P.2d 131 (Colo. App. 1994); Restatement Second of Torts §177 (1965).

[60]   See Reavis v. Slominski, 250 Neb. 711, 551 N.W.2d 528 (1996).

[61]   E.g., United States v. McCabe, 812 F.2d 1060 (8th Cir. 1987) (small child could not consent to his own kidnapping); Commonwealth v. Nickerson, 87 Mass. 518 (1862) (similar).

[62]   As to informed consent, see §§ 21.9 to 21.12.

[63]   Grannum v. Berard, 70 Wash.2d 304, 422 P.2d 812 (1967).

[64]   See Michael Perlin, Law and Mental Disability §1.02 (1994) (reflecting this and other tests in the civil commitment setting).

capacity of adults by asking whether they can manage their own daily affairs[65] or can understand their rights and the nature and effect of their acts.[66]

This means that mental limitations are not equivalent to incapacity. A person is not necessarily incapable of giving consent merely because he has extremely low intelligence.[67] Even a person who suffers from delusions or other mental disabilities may be competent for some purposes and may thus have the capacity to consent to things unaffected by the delusion.[68] So one's ability to pay bills and obtain daily necessities may show sufficient capacity for at least some decisions.

Minors. It is usually said that minors as a class lack legal capacity. Consequently, minors cannot consent to, say, medical procedures. Instead, parents or guardians must consent on their behalf.[69] Nevertheless, minors are obviously competent to make many decisions, and their capacity to do so expands to cover increasingly complex decisions as they mature. In spite of broad language about incapacity, courts do in fact recognize that many minors can consent to some touchings that would be actionable in the absence of consent. Even a small child might effectively consent to a benign handshake, older minors to games that entail touchings,[70] and teenagers or mature minors to at least some medical procedures.[71] In addition, and within limits, mature teenage females have a constitutional right to decide for themselves to have an abortion and hence the power to give or withhold consent to that procedure.[72]

Statutes traditionally criminalized sexual relations with minors under a stated age, in effect depriving those minors of the power to consent. Courts carried these criminal statutes over into tort law, holding that the seducer of an under-age minor would be liable in tort, since the consent would be ineffective.[73] It is said that these statutes are

---

[65] In re Guardianship of Jackson, 61 Mass.App.Ct. 768, 814 N.E.2d 393 (2004); Matter of Estate of Frisch, 250 N.J. Super. 438, 594 A.2d 1367 (1991); McCarthy v. Volkswagen of America, Inc., 55 N.Y.2d 543, 435 N.E.2d 1072, 450 N.Y.S.2d 457 (1982).

[66] Ayuluk v. Red Oaks Assisted Living, Inc., 201 P.3d 1183, 1196 (Alaska 2009); Landmark Medical Center v. Gauthier, 635 A.2d 1145 (R.I. 1994).

[67] State v. Singleton, 1994 WL 772861 (Tenn. Crim. App. 1995) (IQ of 74, consent to search that turned up body in the freezer was valid).

[68] See Matter of Gordy, 658 A.2d 613, 617 (Del. Ch. 1994) ("We all have mental incapacities of various types. Some of us are able to learn foreign languages; for others it seems too difficult; for some calculus (or quantum physics) is beyond us. In some sense mental incapacity is simply the human condition."); Matter of Estate of Zielinski, 208 A.D.2d 275, 623 N.Y.S.2d 653 (1995) (discussing testamentary capacity).

[69] See § 8.7.

[70] Cf. Hellriegel v. Tholl, 69 Wash.2d 97, 417 P.2d 362 (1966) (teenager consenting to roughhouse play could not recover for injury). When the plaintiff pursues such claims on a negligence rather than a battery theory, the consent defense becomes an assumption of risk defense; minors may assume the risk exactly as they may consent. Frazier v. Norton, 334 N.W.2d 865 (S.D. 1983).

[71] In re E.G., 133 Ill.2d 98, 549 N.E.2d 322 (1989) (minor, found to be mature by clear and convincing evidence, was competent to refuse life-saving treatment); Cardwell v. Bechtol, 724 S.W.2d 739, 67 A.L.R.4th 479 (Tenn. 1987) (17-year-old could consent to osteopath's manipulative treatment of her spine, no action for battery when the treatments appeared to produce serious harm).

[72] E.g., Ohio v. Akron Center for Reproductive Health, 497 U.S. 502, 110 S.Ct. 2972, 111 L.Ed.2d 405 (1990); Hodgson v. Minnesota, 497 U.S. 417, 110 S.Ct. 2926, 111 L.Ed.2d 344 (1990).

[73] E.g., Glover v. Callahan, 299 Mass. 55, 12 N.E.2d 194 (1937). Cf. Bjerke v. Johnson, 742 N.W.2d 660 (Minn. 2007) (consent cannot form the basis of an affirmative defense of primary assumption of risk in a civil case alleging negligence in preventing sexual abuse by another).

only sporadically enforced[74] and certainly they have not been the basis for major tort litigation for a long time.

The problem of consent by minors is partly factual, just as it is with arguably incompetent adults. That is, courts want to know whether, as a matter of fact, the individual minor has the experience and intelligence to make the decision in question. The minor's capacity may differ according to the transaction involved. A minor's consent to a touching by another minor might be well within her capacity when consent to touching by an older person might not.[75] Or a child might have capacity to consent to a friendly hug but, even apart from statutes, no capacity to consent to sexual fondling.

Courts are also concerned about preserving a decision-making role for parents or guardians as well. To say that a minor is not legally competent to give consent, then, may be to say either (a) that the minor lacks sufficient maturity to make rational decisions informed by experience or (b) that whatever the minor's practical wisdom, the parents rather than the minor should have the power to decide the particular question. This point shows up when one parent has custody of the child and the other does not. The non-custodial parent cannot avoid liability for kidnapping on the ground that the child consented, even though we may suspect that the child herself may be wise enough to know what she wants.[76] So some consent-by-minors issues are less about protecting minors than about asserting parental rights to govern the minor, or about the right of one parent against another.

§ 8.7   Consent on Behalf of Another

Parents of minors. When a minor lacks capacity to give consent, parents usually have the power to give and withhold consent on the minor's behalf. The common example is that parents are required to consent for a serious or substantial medical procedure to be performed upon a minor,[77] but the rule applies to other invasions of the child's person as well[78] or even to confinement of the child.[79] There are limits, however, to the parent's power to give effective consent.[80] Court approval may be required for seriously invasive procedures like organ donations by an incompetent person, or for decisions to withdraw life support. Similarly, the state's duty to protect the best interests of infants may sometimes lead the state to say that parents cannot withhold consent for a potentially

---

[74]   Michelle Oberman, Turning Girls into Women: Re-Evaluating Modern Statutory Rape Law, 85 J.Crim. L. & Criminology 15, 36 (1994).

[75]   "In some cases consent between minors may be a valid defense where, for example, they are of the same peer group and of equal maturity." Matter of A.B., 556 A.2d 645, 649 (D.C. 1989). Age-of-consent statutes now often reflect such thinking because they criminalize sexual activity with mature minors as statutory rape only in the case of an older person who has sexual relations with the minor. E.g., Vernon's Ann. Mo. Stat., § 566.034 (person over 21 years of age having intercourse with a person less than 17 years of age).

[76]   See Commonwealth v. Nickerson, 87 Mass. 518 (1862).

[77]   Doerr v. Movius, 154 Mont. 346, 463 P.2d 477 (1970).

[78]   Parents may consent on the child's behalf, for example, to discipline in a private kindergarten. Houston v. Kinder-Care Learning Centers, Inc., 208 Ga.App. 235, 239, 430 S.E.2d 24, 27 (1993).

[79]   R.J.D. v. Vaughan Clinic, P.C., 572 So.2d 1225 (Ala. 1990).

[80]   Absent statutory authorization, parents generally lack authority to waive or release a child's tort claim in advance, for example. See, e.g., Kirton v. Fields, 997 So.2d 359 (Fla. 2008) (holding such releases invalid in the context of "commercial activities"); Smith v. YMCA of Benton Harbor/St. Joseph, 216 Mich. App. 552, 550 N.W.2d 262 (1996) (parents have no authority to comprise a child's tort claim). Contra, Sharon v. City of Newton, 437 Mass. 99, 769 N.E.2d 738 (2002) (parents may release child's tort claim in the non-profit setting). See § 17.3.

life-saving medical procedure and that healthcare providers are thus free to impose that treatment upon an infant against the parents' wishes.[81]

Mentally incompetent persons. An agent or guardian may give consent on behalf of an incapacitated adult when the act in question is arguably for the benefit of the incompetent person. The usual case is one in which an incompetent person may need medical treatment or surgery. In the case of one who is temporarily incapacitated because of anesthetic, courts have suggested that an adult family member could consent to a desirable extension of a medical procedure.[82] In the case of one who is more or less permanently incapacitated, a formal guardian might be appointed to make medical decisions. In some cases the guardian has been permitted to refuse consent to life-saving treatments[83] or to withdraw existing treatments necessary to sustain life,[84] provided the guardian follows the standards set by the court for making that decision.

The "best interests" standard. In general, guardians or parents are expected to act in the best interests of their wards or children. Thus neither parents nor guardians could effectively consent to harvesting organs from children or wards merely to sell the organs to strangers. Neither, perhaps, could they consent to experiments upon their children if experiments posed more than minimal health risks and if there were no direct potential health benefits.[85] The best-interests standard asks whether the invasive procedure at issue would be in the best interests of the ward or child. If the answer is no, the procedure may not be used.[86] But when the stakes are high, as when the guardian proposes to withdraw life support from a comatose ward, or a parent proposes to harvest an organ from a child to benefit a sibling, courts have sometimes departed from the best-interest test or have interpreted it in unusual ways.[87]

The "substituted judgment" standard. The substituted-judgment standard, by contrast, asks what decision the ward or child herself would make were she competent to make it. If the ward were the same person except that she was competent and would consent to the procedure, the procedure would be permissible under the substituted-judgment test, but not if the ward would refuse consent.[88] If the ward had clearly stated preferences before she became incompetent, this test might work well. In other cases, the substituted-judgment standard whimsically invites judges to imagine what the ward would be if she were not herself, an approach that seems unusable at best.[89]

---

[81] See Miller v. HCA, Inc., 118 S.W.3d 758 (Tex. 2003).

[82] See Tabor v. Scobee, 254 S.W.2d 474 (Ky. 1951) (20-year old woman under anesthesia, defendants should have obtained consent of mother who was in the hospital before removing fallopian tubes).

[83] Matter of Gordy, 658 A.2d 613 (Del.Ch. 1994).

[84] DeGrella v. Elston, 858 S.W.2d 698 (Ky. 1993).

[85] See Grimes v. Kennedy Krieger Institute, Inc., 366 Md. 29, 782 A.2d 807 (2001). See also Lainie Friedman Ross, In Defense of the Hopkins Lead Abatement Studies, 30 J.L. Med. & Ethics 50 (2002) (criticizing *Grimes*).

[86] Curran v. Bosze, 141 Ill.2d 473, 566 N.E.2d 1319, 4 A.L.R.5th 1163 (1990) (holding that permission to take bone marrow from child under 4 years old would be denied under the best interests standard, even though the bone marrow might save the life of a half-sibling).

[87] See Lisa K. Gregory, Annotation, Propriety of Surgically Invading Incompetent or Minor for Benefit of Third Party, 4 A.L.R.5th 1000 (1993); Strunk v. Strunk, 445 S.W.2d 145, 35 A.L.R.3d 683 (Ky. 1969).

[88] In re Martin, 450 Mich. 204, 538 N.W.2d 399 (1995).

[89] See William Krais, The Incompetent Developmentally Disabled Person's Right of Self-Determination: Right-to-Die, Sterilization and Institutionalization, 15 Am. J. L. & Med. 333 (1989). Much worse things have been said about it because it "allows the state to invade the bodily integrity of the

Limits of both standards. On the other hand, the best-interests standard may not always be meaningful, either. Perhaps it is not meaningful when the question is whether to terminate extraordinary medical life support for a patient in an irreversible coma.[90] The best-interests test could also ignore the ward's known preferences, expressed at a time she was wholly competent.[91] Both tests have the potential for invading the patient's autonomy interests, but if the patient is indeed incompetent, those interests have scant scope in any event and a truly neutral test that does not assume one choice to be better than another is perhaps impossible to find. These difficult cases, perhaps as much as any others, reflect something of the limits of law's ability to resolve real problems in morally acceptable ways.

§ 8.8   Mistake or Misrepresentation Negating Consent

The plaintiff's purported consent is ineffective to bar her claim if it is induced by misrepresentation[92] or is given under a material mistake of which the defendant is or should be aware.[93] The mistake is often induced by the defendant's fraud or misrepresentation. Many cases decided in many settings summarize the point by saying that "fraud vitiates consent"[94] or that consent is ineffective if given as a result of fraud,[95] meaning that the plaintiff in such a case can recover.

Relation to the manifested-consent rule. These rules are often instances of the more general principle that effectiveness of a consent is determined by appearances presented to the defendant.[96] The defendant who misrepresents the nature of the transaction, or who knows that the plaintiff is mistaken about it, knows that the plaintiff is not consenting to the defendant's acts. For instance, suppose the defendant offers the plaintiff a cup of coffee he knows to be contaminated with a poison or a deadly virus. The plaintiff takes the cup with no reason to know it is contaminated. The plaintiff's acceptance of the coffee manifests consent to take the cup and to drink coffee, but not consent to drink poison. Whether this is viewed as a mistake by the plaintiff or a

---

incompetent without having to justify the invasion." Louise Harmon, Falling Off the Vine: Legal Fictions and the Doctrine of Substituted Judgment, 100 Yale. L. J. 1, 61 (1990).

[90]   The decision to remove life support represents a different context from the decision to harvest an organ. On the problems of removing life support, see John Hodson, Annotation, Judicial Power to Order Discontinuance of Life Sustaining Treatment, 48 A.L.R.4th 67 (1966).

[91]   This appeared to be the case in Application of President and Directors of Georgetown College, Inc., 331 F.2d 1000 (D.C. Cir. 1964).

[92]   Alexander v. DeAngelo, 329 F.3d 912 (7th Cir. 2003) (as part of a sting operation, police may have used fraud to obtain the plaintiff's consent to sex with the target, "and if so that was a battery"); Moran v. Selig, 447 F.3d 748 (9th Cir. 2006) (where patient is affirmatively misled and consents to a procedure that is "substantially different" from that which was performed, the doctor may be liable for battery); Duncan v. Scottsdale Med. Imaging, Ltd., 205 Ariz. 306, 70 P.3d 435 (2003) (health care provider who obtained consent to medication by misrepresentation would be subject to liability for battery); Restatement Second of Torts §892B (1979).

[93]   Restatement Second of Torts §49 (1965) & §892B (1979).

[94]   Neal v. Neal, 125 Idaho 617, 873 P.2d 871 (1994); Slawek v. Stroh, 62 Wis.2d 295, 215 N.W.2d 9 (1974) (consent to injections on the misrepresentation that they would not cause miscarriage).

[95]   Janelsins v. Button, 102 Md.App. 30, 648 A.2d 1039 (1994); Micari v. Mann, 126 Misc.2d 422, 481 N.Y.S.2d 967 (1984) (acting teacher represented that students' sexual acts were needed as part of their drama training); see also Taylor v. Johnston, 985 P.2d 460 (Alaska 1999) (if patient had relied upon a physician's representation that physician was licensed when he was not, a medical procedure involving a touching would have been a battery).

[96]   See § 8.2.

misrepresentation by the defendant, the important point is that the defendant cannot believe the plaintiff is consenting to the poison.

Types of Mistake That Will Negate Consent

Misrepresentations and mistakes as to collateral matters. The plaintiff's mistake, whether induced by misrepresentation or not, must be material if it is to vitiate consent. More than that, the mistake must be about the nature of the transaction to which the plaintiff purportedly consents, not merely about some collateral matter of such as the transaction's value, cash cost, or method of payment.[97]

Collateral mistakes. To see a collateral mistake, suppose that a professor wishes to conduct experiments to determine whether people can distinguish between different stimuli applied to their shoulders and agrees to pay the plaintiff "the university rate." The plaintiff consents to be part of the experiment in the belief the rate is $20 an hour when in fact it is only $10. The Restatement suggests that this mistake is collateral only and not a ground for ignoring the plaintiff's consent.[98] So the professor would not be liable for battery although the plaintiff might be permitted to rescind the contract.

Mistakes about the nature of the transaction. The plaintiff is mistaken about the nature or character of the transaction when she is mistaken about a major feature of the transaction. Battery claims provide good examples. For instance, the plaintiff who consents to manipulation of her body in the belief that it is for medical purposes, when in fact it is only for the sexual gratification of the defendant, is mistaken about the nature of the touching, not merely about some collateral matter.[99] The same is true if the plaintiff consents to physical violence by her psychiatrist in the belief that this treatment is therapeutic.[100] A sexual seduction induced by misrepresentation such as the defendant's assertion of an intent to marry is understandable in the same way, as a battery in which fraud has vitiated the consent.[101]

Other plaintiffs who are mistaken about the nature of the transaction include those who consent to sexual relations in the mistaken belief that the defendant is free of infection or that he cannot cause pregnancy. In such cases, if the defendant knows of the plaintiff's mistake or has induced it by a misrepresentation, he becomes liable for a battery, at least if disease or pregnancy actually results.[102] On the other hand, and quite

---

[97]   Restatement Second of Torts §§ 57 (1965) & 892, cmt. g (1979).

[98]   See id. § 892B, Ill. 9 & § 57, Ill. 1.

[99]   Bartell v. State, 106 Wis. 342, 82 N.W. 142 (1900) (nude massage by "magnetic healer" ostensibly for medical purposes).

[100]   Rains v. Superior Court (The Center Foundation), 150 Cal.App.3d 933, 198 Cal.Rptr. 249 (1984).

[101]   See Piggott v. Miller, 557 S.W.2d 692 (Mo. App. 1977). Jane E. Larson, "Women Understand So Little, They Call My Good Nature 'Deceit:'" A Feminist Rethinking of Seduction, 93 Colum. L. Rev. 374 (1993), proposes a much expanded liability to be imposed not only when consent is secured by misrepresentation but also when it is secured by manipulation. The original common law tort for seduction was maintainable only by the father of a minor female and was based upon loss of her services resulting from the seduction.

[102]   Kathleen K. v. Robert B., 150 Cal. App. 3d 992, 198 Cal. Rptr. 273, 40 A.L.R.4th 1083 (1984) (contracting herpes); Hogan v. Tavzel, 660 So.2d 350 (Fla. Dist. Ct. App. 1995) (genital warts not revealed); Crowell v. Crowell, 180 N.C. 516, 105 S.E.2d 206 (1920) (it was an "assault [battery] for the husband to communicate to his wife, while concealing from her the fact that he was infected therewith, a foul and loathsome disease"); Restatement Second of Torts § 892B, Ill. 5 (1979).

apart from the plaintiff's consent, the defendant lacks the intent necessary for a battery if he neither knows nor should know that he is infected.[103]

The point is not limited to battery cases. In a Minnesota case,[104] a homeowner consented to the entry of a woman who identified herself as a student but who in fact was there to videotape scenes for a television station. The homeowner's consent to her entrance did not bar the trespass claim. Commonly held values suggest that the transaction consented to—entrance by a student—would be viewed as radically different in nature from the transaction that actually took place—invasion by a journalist with a video camera. And in another case,[105] the defendants presented an invalid subpoena to an Internet Service Provider, who, believing it to be valid, yielded up copies of the plaintiff's private emails. The ISP's mistake was about the essential nature of the transaction and hence its agreement to provide the emails in its possession was not a consent that barred the plaintiffs' recovery. However, some important cases have held that a landowner effectively consents to entry upon the land by investigative reporters, even when those reporters fraudulently represent their identities and purposes,[106] or have held that even if the reporters are liable for the trespass, they are not liable for publication of information that results from it.[107]

§ 8.9   Consent Obtained by Duress or Coercion

Physical and unlawful threats. Duress includes physical coercion and threats of it, that is, force or coercive threats that are intended to and do prevent the plaintiff's free choice.[108] The defendant cannot arrest the plaintiff at gunpoint and then assert that the plaintiff consented to the arrest because the plaintiff voluntarily chose confinement in preference to a bullet. Threats of physical force or confinement are commonly the basis for false imprisonment claims. That is, confinement may be achieved not only by locking the plaintiff in a room but by indicating that she will be physically halted if she attempts to leave or that she will be subjected to worse forms of imprisonment.[109] Similarly, if the defendant threatens to deprive the plaintiff of her children unless she has her tubes tied to prevent further conception, this is duress or coercion and it cannot be said that the plaintiff has consented to the operation.[110] On the other hand, threats to do acts that are not themselves illegal or tortious seldom render consent ineffective.

Economic threats to produce purely economic gains. Economic threats that induce consent to economic transactions generally do not count as duress or improper coercion.

---

[103] Endres v. Endres, 185 Vt. 63, 968 A.2d 336 (2008); McPherson v. McPherson, 712 A.2d 1043 (Me. 1998).

[104] Copeland v. Hubbard Broadcasting, Inc., 526 N.W.2d 402 (Minn. App. 1995).

[105] Theofel v. Farey-Jones, 359 F.3d 1066 (9th Cir. 2004).

[106] Desnick v. American Broad. Cos., Inc., 44 F.3d 1345 (7th Cir. 1994).

[107] Food Lion, Inc. v. Capital Cities/ABC, Inc., 194 F.3d 505 (4th Cir. 1999); American Transmission, Inc. v. Channel 7 of Detroit, Inc., 239 Mich.App. 695, 609 N.W.2d 607 (2000).

[108] Terms like free will, free choice, genuineness of consent and similar expressions are conventional in discussions of duress, but they may not be the best terms. What is perhaps objectionable is that the plaintiff is forced to make any choice at all, or the choice between the alternatives presented. See John Dalzell, Duress by Economic Pressure, Part I, 20 N.C.L.Rev. 237, 238 (1942).

[109] See Marcus v. Liebman, 59 Ill.App.3d 337, 375 N.E.2d 486 (1978) (threat to involuntarily commit a voluntary psychiatric patient who wanted to leave was a false imprisonment).

[110] See Vaughn v. Ruoff, 253 F.3d 1124 (8th Cir. 2001) (child protective agency removed the plaintiff's two children from her home, then, just before birth of a third child, told her she'd have a good chance of getting the children back if she had her tubes tied; a jury could find her consent coerced and her constitutional rights violated).

For example, transactions involving buying and selling are based on implicit or express threats. The buyer who refuses to pay more than $25,000 for an automobile is in effect threatening not to buy at all unless the seller lowers the price. If the seller consents to sell at that price even though the car is worth more, the seller cannot later recover for conversion of the chattel on the ground that his consent was produced by duress. Similarly, the employer may threaten to discharge an unproductive employee unless her job performance improves. These threats are economic on both sides—they threaten to impose economic loss in order to obtain economic gain.

Objectively non-coercive threats without abuse of power. The difficult cases of duress or coercion lie in the middle ground between threats of physical force or illegal action on the one hand and simple threats of economic self-interest on the other. Many of the everyday bargains by which we arrange our relationships are grounded in implicit or explicit threats. In the Restatement's example,[111] a friend says to you, "if you are not still here when I get back, our friendship is over." You remain in confinement because you value the friendship. You cannot recover for false imprisonment on the ground that your consent was obtained by duress or coercion.

Coercive threats. Many threats or implicit threats are legitimate, and others simply are not the basis for any legal response. There is a general formula for determining which threats count as sufficiently coercive to negate consent: duress is a threat of unlawful conduct that is intended to and does prevent the plaintiff, as a person of ordinary firmness, from exercising free will or choice.[112] The formula seems almost useless in practice and most cases in fact involve contracts or avoidance of transactions rather than claims for trespassory torts like battery or trespass to land.

§ 8.10 Consent Obtained by Abuse of Power or Position

Some threats are viewed either as inherently coercive or as an abuse of power or position, or both. If the threats are coercive, the "consent" is not genuine as a matter of fact and must be given no legal effect. If the threats are an abuse of power, a profession of consent, whether genuine or not, might be denied any legal effect as a matter of policy. The possibility that consent should be disregarded for either of these reasons is not limited to any particular group of cases, because that possibility turns on the facts of the individual case. But the issue may be raised whenever the plaintiff has allegedly consented to sexual relations with an employer, psychotherapist, doctor, lawyer, or religious leader, because of the abuse or potential for abuse of such a special relationship. Other relationships, such as those between student and teacher[113] or jailer and prisoner,[114] could raise the same kind of issue.

Job threats and sexual harassment. Demands for sexual favors by employers or supervisors may be implicitly threatening because of the power of employers to affect jobs and job benefits. Such threats present the employee with choices she should not be

---

[111] Restatement Second of Torts § 892B, cmt. j (1979).

[112] Id. § 871, cmt. f.

[113] Cf. Micari v. Mann, 126 Misc. 2d 422, 481 N.Y.S.2d 967 (1984) (acting teacher induced students to engage in a variety of sexual acts as part of their drama training, held actionable).

[114] Grager v. Schudar, 770 N.W.2d 692 (N.D. 2009) (sexual act with jailer, who asserted consent as a defense; court noted that "consent" procured by jailer's abuse of power would be ineffective); but cf. Graham v. Sheriff v. Logan County, 741 F.3d 1118 (10th Cir. 2013) (in case alleging Eighth Amendment violation, allowing consent defense by guards in county jail who had sex with a female prisoner, because the prisoner never denied she consented "to almost all of the sexual acts that occurred").

required to make. Although an employer may properly make implicit or explicit economic threats to gain economic performance, the employer must not suggest that the job or its benefits in any way depend upon the employee's agreement to sexual relations with the employer. To do so counts as *quid pro quo* sexual harassment under federal job discrimination statutes.[115] Even a simple invitation by an employer or supervisor to engage in sexually related contact may imply a quid pro quo demand or threat and constitute harassment.

Psychotherapists and counselors. Consent, especially consent to physical touching and sexual activity, is often induced by respect, affection, or dependence. Such a consent is of course perfectly effective, and one who consents to sexual activity normally has no claim based on that activity. However, in some cases the defendant owes the plaintiff a duty to avoid a potentially harmful sexual contact even if the plaintiff consents or professes consent. This is most notably the case of psychiatrists and other therapists who routinely confront troubled and vulnerable patients.

The patient's consent in such cases may be the result of diminished capacity or possibly the result of forces outside the patient's control, but even if such a consent is as real as any other, it is usually assumed and always claimed that a patient's sexual behavior with the therapist is ultimately harmful to the patient's recovery and development. If that is in fact so, the therapist who engages in sexual activity with the patient is actually breaching the professional duty of care which includes a duty to avoid the risk of further emotional harm, even if the patient knowingly consents to it. For this reason, and because given the patient's vulnerability, the "consent" is highly suspect, courts[116] and legislatures[117] hold or provide that the therapist is liable in spite of the patient's professed consent.[118]

The plaintiff in these cases often asserts the claim on a theory of negligence, no doubt because the therapist's liability insurance will cover negligence but not intended torts.[119] Some cases have suggested that the therapist is liable for breach of fiduciary duty.[120] In none of these cases is the patient's consent a bar to the claim.

Physicians and attorneys. Medical doctors treating patients for medical conditions ordinarily have little role in providing for the patient's mental health. A physician who engages in sexual activity with a patient is thus not in the same position as a therapist. Courts have said that a medical doctor, having no duty to protect the patient from her own consent or even to avoid risk of emotional harm that can result from sexual activities, can rely on the patient's consent in the absence of fraud or duress by the

---

[115] 42 U.S.C.A. § 2000e ("Title VII").

[116] See, e.g., Simmons v. United States, 805 F.2d 1363 (9th Cir. 1986).

[117] Cal. Civ. Code § 43.93 (b) (patient may recover if there is therapeutic deception); Ill.Comp.Stat. 140/2 (patient may recover if the patient was emotionally dependent or the therapist practiced deception); Minn. Stat. § 148A.02 (similar); Tex. Civ. Prac. & Rem. Code Ann. § 81.002 (patient may recover regardless of emotional dependence or deception); Wis. Stat. Ann. § 895.70 (similar).

[118] A substantial number of states criminalize such conduct by therapists. See Timothy E. Allen, Note, The Foreseeability of Transference: Extending Employer Liability Under Washington Law for Therapist Sexual Exploitation of Patients, 78 Wash. L. Rev. 525, 533 n.65 (2003) (listing statutes)..

[119] See, e.g., Zipkin v. Freeman, 436 S.W.2d 753 (Mo. 1968).

[120] Roy v. Hartogs, 81 Misc. 2d 350, 366 N.Y.S.2d 297 (1975) ("This case involves a fiduciary relationship between psychiatrist and patient and is analogous to the guardian-ward relationship. . . . 'Consent obtained under such circumstances is no consent, and should stand for naught.' ").

physician or known incapacity on the part of the patient.[121] Lawyers are presumably in a similar position. They may find themselves disciplined for violation of ethical rules if they engage in sexual relations with clients,[122] but the clients, not relying upon lawyers for emotional protection from themselves, are free to consent to sexual activities.[123]

The rules about lawyers and medical doctors, however, do not reflect privileges based upon status or profession. They reflect the professional roles undertaken. If a lawyer or medical doctor were to initiate sexual relations as a form of treatment,[124] or to engage in counseling or therapy, then liability would become appropriate.[125] Similarly, if these doctors or lawyers were to demand sexual favors as a condition of providing their best professional services,[126] or to exact a profession of consent by duress,[127] it seems reasonably clear that the professed consent would present no bar to the plaintiff's claim.

Clergy. When pastors or priests abuse minors, courts have sometimes imposed liability,[128] although even in the child abuse cases courts have sometimes invoked immunities to protect the religious organization from liability.[129] When a pastor or priest sexually exploits an adult, such as a member of the congregation or parish who seeks religious counseling, courts have sometimes insisted that the adult's consent is a bar,[130] and when the claim is based upon negligence, they have concluded that there is no tort of "clergy malpractice."[131] Such cases obviously reject the analogy to the abusive therapist,[132] even though in most instances the clergy's sexual abuse originates in counseling situations in which confidence is reposed and authority is respected by the victim. While the cases are not numerous, and may not represent broadly held views,[133]

---

[121] Atienza v. Taub, 194 Cal.App.3d 388, 239 Cal.Rptr. 454 (1987); Odegard v. Finne, 500 N.W.2d 140 (Minn. 1993); Iwanski v. Gomes, 259 Neb. 632, 611 N.W.2d 607 (2000). Claims against therapists are often treated as malpractice claims, while those against physicians are not because the scope of their professional undertaking is different. See McCracken v. Walls-Kaufman, 717 A.2d 346 (D.C. 1998).

[122] See ABA Model Rules of Prof. Conduct 1.8(j); Cal. Rules of Prof. Conduct 3–110; In re Rinella, 175 Ill.2d 504, 677 N.E.2d 909, 222 Ill.Dec. 375 (1997) (lawyer suspended for 3 years).

[123] Suppressed v. Suppressed, 206 Ill. App.3d 918, 565 N.E.2d 101, 105 (1990).

[124] See Atienza v. Taub, 194 Cal.App.3d 388, 239 Cal.Rptr. 454 (1987).

[125] Dillon v. Callaway, 609 N.E.2d 424 (Ind. App. 1993).

[126] McDaniel v. Gile, 230 Cal.App.3d 363, 281 Cal.Rptr. 242 (1991).

[127] See Doe v. Roe, 756 F.Supp. 353 (N.D. Ill. 1991), *aff'd*, 958 F.2d 763 (7th Cir. 1992) (threats of bodily injury unless fee was paid).

[128] See Martinelli v. Bridgeport Roman Catholic Diocesan Corp., 196 F.3d 409 (2d Cir. 1999) (recognizing claim for diocese's breach of fiduciary duty to boy parishioner, but remanding for error in instruction on the statute of limitations); Fontaine v. Roman Catholic Church of Archdiocese of New Orleans, 625 So.2d 548 (La. App. 1993) (priest allegedly sexually abused a 17-year-old and later published photographs in a magazine and circulated video tapes; held, these allegations state a privacy invasion claim); Mrozka v. Archdiocese of St. Paul & Minneapolis, 482 N.W.2d 806 (Minn. App. 1992).

[129] See Schultz v. Roman Catholic Archdiocese of Newark, 95 N.J. 530, 472 A.2d 531 (1984) (forcible sexual acts against a member of priest's Boy Scout group, resulting in boy's suicide; held, the Archdiocese is a charity and thus immune from tort liability for its negligence in failing to prevent such things).

[130] Jacqueline R. v. Household of Faith Family Church, Inc., 97 Cal.App.4th 198, 118 Cal.Rptr.2d 264 (2002) (reasoning also that the plaintiff's consent to touching demonstrates that is was not "offensive" to her, thus negating an element of battery); Schieffer v. Catholic Archdiocese of Omaha, 244 Neb. 715, 718, 508 N.W.2d 907, 911 (1993). When the adult is not in counseling with the minister, the "consenting adults" rule is clearly applicable. See Bladen v. First Presbyterian Church of Sallisaw, 857 P.2d 789 (Okla. 1993).

[131] See 2 Dobbs, Hayden & Bublick, The Law of Torts §330 (2d ed. 2011 & Supp.).

[132] See Hertel v. Sullivan, 261 Ill.App.3d 156, 160, 633 N.E.2d 36, 39 (1994).

[133] See John Wagner, Jr., Annotation, Cause of Action for Clergy Malpractice, 75 A.L.R.4th 750 (1990).

some limited authority supports holding clergy members, or their religious organization or superiors, liable for battery or breach of fiduciary duty.[134]

§ 8.11 Medical Battery and Informed Consent

As already shown, the plaintiff's consent to an invasion is ineffective to bar a claim if the plaintiff is mistaken about the nature of the invasion and the defendant knows it.[135] In some cases, however, the plaintiff is not so much mistaken about the nature of the proposed invasion as ignorant about its potential risks or consequences; in those cases such a mistake does not vitiate the plaintiff's consent.

Medical operations and procedures often involve this point. At one time it was thought that when a surgeon operated upon a plaintiff who did not know and had not been informed of the risks of the operation, the plaintiff might have a claim for battery because the consent would be ineffective. Such a claim would be a good one no matter how well the operation was performed or what benefits it conferred. It is clearly right to treat the operation as unconsented to if the plaintiff was mistaken about the nature of the operation and the defendant knew it. But the plaintiff's ignorance of the risks does not necessarily mean the plaintiff was mistaken about the nature of the operation.

Why is it that the plaintiff who is ignorant of the risks of a medical procedure may not be mistaken about its nature? First, the patient is not mistaken at all if she knows that operations have risks and knows also that she does not know what they are. Mistake is a state of mind not in accord with the facts. A person who knows she does not know a fact is not mistaken about that fact at all.[136] Second, the plaintiff might erroneously believe she knows the risks when she does not; in that case, she is indeed mistaken, but not necessarily about the nature of the operation. The risks of a procedure and safer alternatives might not go to the nature of the operation, only to collateral matters of value. These points indicate some of the reasons why ignorance is not always the equivalent of a mistake that will vitiate consent.

Even if the plaintiff is not mistaken, however, her consent to a medical procedure might be ineffective to bar her suit for other reasons. Courts can impose upon the surgeon or physician a duty to use reasonable care to inform the plaintiff of the important or material risks or at least of risks that other doctors would explain to a patient. That is what courts have come to hold under the rules of negligence law and under the specific rubric of informed consent.[137]

The result is that in most courts, battery claims against the surgeon would be entertained only if the surgeon has exceeded the consent by performing an operation not consented to at all[138] or by operating with knowledge that the plaintiff was mistaken

---

[134] See Moses v. Diocese of Colorado, 863 P.2d 310 (Colo. 1993) (no separate tort of clergy malpractice but church might be liable for negligent hiring, negligent supervision, and breach of fiduciary duty when it neither sought to prevent nor to ameliorate the effects of priestly sexual behavior with vulnerable parishioners); Destefano v. Grabrian, 763 P.2d 275 (Colo. 1988) (clergyperson giving marriage counseling to husband and wife and having sexual intercourse with one of them); F.G. v. MacDonell, 150 N.J. 550, 696 A.2d 697 (1997) (fiduciary duty); contra, e.g., Petrell v. Shaw, 453 Mass. 377, 901 N.E.2d 401 (2009) (church diocese and bishops owe no fiduciary duty to members of parish to protect them from sexual exploitation by rectors).

[135] See § 8.8.

[136] See 2 Dan B. Dobbs, Law of Remedies § 11.2 (2d ed. 1993).

[137] See §§ 21.9 & 21.10.

[138] E.g., Gerety v. Demers, 92 N.M. 396, 589 P.2d 180 (1978); Washburn v. Klara, 263 Va. 586, 561 S.E.2d 682 (2002); Saxena v. Goffney, 159 Cal.App.4th 316, 71 Cal.Rptr.3d 469 (2008).

(not merely ignorant) about the nature of the operation. If the surgeon's fault is that he failed to provide information that should have been provided, the plaintiff's consent holds good to bar the battery claim. In that case, the surgeon's liability, if any, must be based on a showing that he was negligent, either in failing to disclose material facts or in performing the operation itself.[139]

§ 8.12   Emergency as a Substitute for Consent

A health care provider may deliver appropriate emergency care when neither the patient nor an appropriate agent is able to make a decision about that care.[140] This might occur, for example, if the patient was unconscious and would die without immediate treatment, and no family member or guardian was reachable.

The term "emergency" implies both that the plaintiff's health is in jeopardy so that immediate medical attention is required, and that a person authorized to consent is not available to make the requisite decision.[141] In such cases the physician may take medically indicated steps that do not risk more harm than they are likely to avoid, provided that the physician has no reason to think the plaintiff would refuse consent.[142] The effect of these rules is that a true emergency is ordinarily a substitute for the patient's consent where the patient is in fact unable to give or withhold consent.

It is sometimes suggested that the emergency rules are grounded in some kind of implied consent by the patient.[143] But as the patient is unconscious or mentally compromised when the issue arises, it is more accurate to say that the rule is a rule of law rather than a rule of consent. Although the rule is based upon what judges believe people would generally want to happen, it is not based on some implicit communication from the particular patient.

The emergency rule is not intended to permit providers to overrule or avoid confronting the patient's wishes. If the plaintiff is conscious, the physician must inform her of the proposed treatment and its risks.[144] "A physician must respect the refusal of treatment by a patient who is capable of providing consent, even in an emergency."[145] If the patient, while competent, has reliably expressed her opposition to a particular medical procedure, her wishes are not to be overridden when she falls unconscious and death is imminent.[146]

---

[139] See § 21.9.

[140] E.g., Miller v. Rhode Island Hospital, 625 A.2d 778 (R.I. 1993), relying heavily on Canterbury v. Spence, 464 F.2d 772 (D.C.Cir. 1972); Restatement Second of Torts §892D (1979).

[141] E.g., Pizzalotto v. Wilson, 437 So.2d 859 (La. App. 1983).

[142] In re Estate of Allen, 365 Ill. App.3d 378, 848 N.E.2d 202, 302 Ill. Dec. 202 (2006); Restatement Second of Torts §892D (1979). But see Harvey v. Strickland, 350 S.C. 303, 566 S.E.2d 529 (2002) (in spite of patient's pre-surgery categorical refusal to accept a blood transfusion, a jury could find that his alleged statement that he would consider a transfusion could be taken by the surgeon as an implied consent that permitted his mother to consent to the transfusion while he was unconscious).

[143] E.g., Traxler v. Varady, 12 Cal.App.4th 1321, 16 Cal.Rptr.2d 297 (1993); Leach v. Shapiro, 13 Ohio.App.3d 393, 469 N.E.2d 1047 (1984).

[144] Cunningham v. Yankton Clinic, 262 N.W.2d 508 (S.D. 1978); see § 21.9.

[145] Shine v. Vega, 429 Mass. 456, 709 N.E.2d 58 (1999).

[146] Rodriguez v. Pino, 634 So.2d 681 (Fla. Dist. Ct. App. 1994); Estate of Leach v. Shapiro, 13 Ohio. App.3d 393, 469 N.E.2d 1047 (1984).

§ 8.13 Consent to Crime

When the plaintiff is injured in the course of a criminal act to which she has consented, courts can seldom find entirely satisfactory rules. Suppose the plaintiff consents to fight in an illegal boxing match with the defendant. The defendant strikes a forceful blow that injures the plaintiff quite seriously. If the plaintiff's consent is a bar to his claim, the defendant is relieved of liability for his illegal acts. Some courts so hold, not only in the case of illegal fights but in the case of other consensual but illegal activities as well.[147] On the other hand, if the plaintiff's consent is not a bar, the plaintiff recovers in spite of her illegal conduct. Furthermore, the defendant is also entitled to recover for blows he receives. This might be viewed as "rewarding" the illegal conduct or at least as failing to punish it, or perhaps as wasting judicial resources to set off the two claims against one another. But some courts have said a recovery by both is permitted, the consent being no bar.[148]

Neither rule is apt. The obvious solution, and the one adopted by the Second Restatement,[149] is that deterrence and punishment for the illegality is to be left to the criminal law; tort law may thus proceed under its ordinary rules, which means that the plaintiff's consent is a bar just as it is in any other case, subject to two qualifications.

The first qualification is that when the statute makes conduct illegal in order to protect the plaintiff from her own professed consent, her consent is no bar. Age-of-consent or statutory rape statutes, for example, provide that intercourse with a minor under a specified age is a crime regardless of the minor's consent.[150] The second qualification is that consent to an illegal act does not ordinarily make the plaintiff an outlaw. The plaintiff's consent should bar a claim for what she consented to, but no more. Consent to an illegal abortion, for example, is not consent to negligent infliction of harm or death.[151] To bar the plaintiff in such a case is not to enforce her consent but to permit infliction of harm she never consented to.

---

[147] Goldnamer v. O'Brien, 33 S.W. 831 (Ky. 1896) (consent to illegal abortion is a bar to recover for inducing the abortion). The plaintiff is sometimes barred on the basis of a wider rule that selectively refuses to permit the plaintiff to recover if she has participated in an illegal act. See § 16.8.

[148] See Brown v. Patterson, 214 Ala. 351, 108 So. 16 (1926); Annotation, 47 A.L.R. 1093 (1927).

[149] Restatement Second of Torts § 892C (1979).

[150] Vernon's Ann. Mo. Stat., § 566.034.

[151] In Castronovo v. Murawsky, 3 Ill.App.2d 168, 120 N.E.2d 871 (1954), the victim consented to an illegal abortion, and died because it was negligently performed. Nevertheless, the court denied recovery.

Part III

NEGLIGENT PHYSICAL HARMS TO PERSONS OR PROPERTY

Subpart A

THE PRIMA FACIE CASE

Chapter 9

THE NEGLIGENCE ACTION: AN INTRODUCTION

Analysis

A. CHARACTERISTICS
§ 9.1   Characteristics of the Negligence Case

B. DEVELOPMENT
§ 9.2   Negligence: The Common Law Background
§ 9.3   Negligence: Courts Adopt a General Principle of Liability for Fault
§ 9.4   Negligence: After Adoption of the Fault Principle

C. FUNDAMENTALS OF NEGLIGENCE LIABILITY
§ 9.5   Elements of the Prima Facie Case for Negligence
§ 9.6   The Elements: Meaning and Terminology
§ 9.7   Negligence as Conduct, Not State of Mind

A. CHARACTERISTICS

§ 9.1   Characteristics of the Negligence Case

Negligence as one type of fault. A person who negligently causes personal injury or property damage is subject to liability in tort. Negligence liability is liability for one particular kind of fault—typically, failure to use reasonable care under the circumstances. It is contrasted with liability for intentional torts and with strict liability.

Varied negligence claims. Negligence claims represent the great majority of tort claims presented, brought, or tried today. In part, this reflects the large number of injuries resulting from the use of automobiles—which are often used negligently. Negligence claims are not, of course, limited to automobile cases. A wide range of human misery is produced by negligence. Negligence law, on the whole, controls suits for injuries suffered by patients at the hands of doctors,[1] tenants by landlords,[2] and customers by businesses.[3] People are negligently shot, burned, drowned, or poisoned. Less commonly,

---

[1]   See Chapter 21.
[2]   See Chapter 20.
[3]   See Chapters 19 and 20.

people may suffer and die from a negligently transmitted disease[4] or from negligently inflicted genetic harm.[5]

Specific negligent conduct. Conduct can include large scale activities like driving automobiles or operating railroads. These activities certainly impose substantial risks of harm to others. However, such general activities will almost never be negligent in themselves because the value of travel by automobile and the operation of railroads outweighs the risks.[6] So negligent conduct is almost always some specific act such as driving too fast or some omission such as failing to keep a proper lookout. Specific negligent conduct may be found in a wide variety of circumstances. Negligence may consist in failure to apply appropriate tests or to discover danger to others and to avoid it. Building, installing, or maintaining a dangerous structure, safety device, or other condition is often the basis for a negligence action.[7] Providing a dangerous person with instruments of harm, for instance, giving a drunken person keys to a car to drive, can count as negligence.[8] So can failure to protect the plaintiff against attacks by others.[9]

Negligent communication. Communication may be negligent, too. The defendant may give inaccurate information to one who is imperiled by acting upon it,[10] or may give completely accurate information to a person who is likely to use it dangerously.[11] A special case of communicative negligence occurs when the defendant creates a misleading appearance of safety.[12] The concept of negligence and the sets of rules that go with that concept dominate the law of torts.

In terms of broad legal structure, the negligence case can be characterized by a few points:

1.   *Open-ended claims.* The structure of the negligence case allows the plaintiff to claim that any given conduct was negligent. The argument is that the defendant should not have indulged in that conduct at all or should have carried it out more safely. This differs from the traditional rules for the intentional trespassory torts. The trespassory torts described particular conduct that counted as a tort—a harmful or offensive touching, a confinement, an entry upon land. Negligence law in contrast is open-ended.

---

[4]   John B. v. Superior Court, 38 Cal.4th 1177, 137 P.3d 153, 45 Cal.Rptr.3d 316 (2006); S.A.V. v. K.G.V., 708 S.W.2d 651 (Mo. 1986) (negligent transmission of herpes to wife); DiMarco v. Lynch Homes-Chester County, Inc., 525 Pa. 558, 583 A.2d 422 (1990) (negligent medical advice led to plaintiff's contracting hepatitis).

[5]   See Castillo v. E.I. Du Pont de Nemours & Co., Inc., 854 So.2d 1264 (Fla. 2003) (product causing genetic harm).

[6]   Alternatively expressed, courts may not have the institutional competence to weigh the risks of driving automobiles in general against the harms careful driving produces. See Restatement Third of Torts (Liability for Physical and Emotional Harm) § 7 cmt. f (2010).

[7]   Much of products liability law is in this category, see Chapter 33, as is premises liability law, see Chapter 20.

[8]   § 26.10.

[9]   Restatement Third of Torts (Liability for Physical and Emotional Harm) §§ 19, 39 to 44 (2010 and 2012); see generally Chapter 25.

[10]   For instance, by signaling the driver behind that the way ahead is clear for passing. See Joseph B. Conder, Annotation, Motorist's Liability for Signaling Other Vehicle or Pedestrian to Proceed, or to Pass Signaling Vehicle, 14 A.L.R.5th 193 (1993); § 26.2.

[11]   See Remsburg v. Docusearch, Inc., 816 A.2d 1001 (N.H. 2003), on potential liability for negligently providing an unknown person—who turned out to be a killer—with the workplace address of his victim.

[12]   See Killebrew v. Sun Trust Banks, Inc., 221 Ga.App. 679, 472 S.E.2d 504 (1996) (bank stationed employee appearing to be a guard in parking lot near ATM; the employee was no guard and was only there to keep customers of nearby business from parking in the bank lot; hence summary judgment for bank in claim by patron injured by attacker at ATM was error).

The plaintiff can assert that *any* conduct counts as negligence.[13] The plaintiff must, of course, convince the trier of fact of her assertions, but no pre-existing rules require her to prove a particular act.

2.   *Jury roles.* There are many important rules governing negligence cases. Nevertheless, because the negligence claim is open-ended and requires evaluation case-by-case, rules do not always have an enormous direct impact on the ultimate result. The decision maker at trial, on the other hand, has a great impact on the ultimate result of the case. Judge and jury share the role of decision maker. Some of the rules in tort cases bear on allocation of power between the judge, as a trained professional, and the jury, as a representative of the community. Overall, juries are a highly significant force in deciding negligence and are subject to fewer restrictions than in some other kinds of tort cases.

3.   *Actual harm requirement.* A third characteristic of negligence cases can be seen in the rule that no claim for negligence will be recognized unless the plaintiff suffers actual harm.[14] There is no such thing as a negligence suit for nominal damages, much less one for presumed damages.[15] Here again, the trespassory torts were quite different. A trespass to land, for example, always justified at least the recovery of nominal damages.[16] Similar rules applied to the other trespassory torts. The negligence claim is different. No matter how offended or distressed the plaintiff might be when the defendant drives at 100 mph in a school zone, the defendant is not liable for negligence if he causes no harm. What counts as actual harm may be debated or uncertain in the case of toxic exposures that affect the body's structure but have not yet caused pain or loss of function;[17] but the underlying rule that harm is required has not been doubted.

4.   *Preoccupation with bodily harm and property damage.* Courts impose especially restrictive rules on claims that negligence has caused emotional distress alone and deny recovery in many of these cases.[18] Some of the same reluctance to recognize negligence liability for stand-alone emotional harm carries over to other intangible injuries. In the area of financial injuries in which no physical harm is done to the plaintiff, sometimes called "pure economic loss," negligence rules usually limit the cases in which the plaintiff can recover.[19] The upshot is that the core of negligence law is about physical injury to persons and to tangible property.

5.   *Damages when a negligence claim is established.* When the plaintiff succeeds in establishing a negligence claim against the defendant, courts award damages for a wide range of injuries, including damages for emotional harm and financial loss. At first glance, this statement seems to contradict those in the immediately preceding paragraph. But there is no contradiction. The preceding paragraph indicated that there is seldom a tort claim for stand-alone emotional or financial harm based on simple negligence. But once a negligence claim is established by showing that the defendant

---

[13]   This characteristic is limited by no-duty and immunity rules. See Chapter 12.

[14]   E.g., Reardon v. Larkin, 3 A.3d 376 (Me. 2010) (parties stipulated to liability, but no claim was proved where the evidence showed that the plaintiff was not harmed in any way by the defendant's conduct; there was evidence that all of the plaintiff's injuries either existed before the accident, or were caused by things other than the accident).

[15]   Right v. Breen, 277 Conn. 364, 890 A.2d 1287 (2006).

[16]   E.g., Gross v. Capital Elec. Line Builders, Inc., 253 Kan. 798, 861 P.2d 1326 (1993).

[17]   See § 14.1.

[18]   See Chapter 29.

[19]   See Chapter 41.

negligently caused property damage or bodily injury, the victim can recover all damages that are reasonably foreseeable, including damages for such intangibles as pain, a sense of lost enjoyment of life, and emotional distress. Financial loss resulting from injury or property damage, such as lost wages or the costs of medical attention, is likewise recoverable, as are all proven future losses.

B. DEVELOPMENT

§ 9.2 Negligence: The Common Law Background

Strict liability for trespassory torts? In the law of torts, the word negligence is old but its current content is relatively new. Although the concept of fault was important in the old action on the case, negligence did not appear as a somewhat general system for resolving personal injury and property damage claims until the 19th century, mostly after the American Civil War. The English common law of tort as it stood in the 14th century was very largely the law of trespassory torts.[20] The traditional view is that strict liability was imposed when the writ of Trespass could be used.[21] That included cases of direct and immediate harm from the unauthorized use of physical force. Under this view, the defendant might be liable for an accidental shooting, even if the defendant was not negligent.[22]

Action on the case for indirect harms. By the direct harm test in Trespass cases, an ordinary vehicular collision might result in strict liability. But if that was the logic of the old Trespass action, it was never applied to such facts in America. Instead, negligence law developed from the action on the Case.[23] The action on the Case was proper (a) when the defendant inflicted injury that was not immediate and direct,[24] (b) when injury arose out of consented-to invasions that were carried out badly, as where a veterinarian undertakes to cure the plaintiff's horse and fails as a result of his negligence or neglect;[25] and (c) when the defendant's fault lay in his failure to act rather than in some affirmative misconduct.[26] In the action on the Case, the plaintiff was required to prove both the

---

[20] See S.F.C. Milsom, Historical Foundations of the Common Law 305 (2d ed 1981).

[21] Some scholars have challenged this view. See Gary Schwartz, Tort Law and the Economy in Nineteenth-Century America: A Reinterpretation, 9 Yale L.J. 1717 (1981); Gary Schwartz, The Character of Early American Tort Law, 26 U.C.L.A. L. Rev. 641 (1989); Stephen Young, Reconceptualizing Accountability in the Early Nineteenth Century: How the Tort of Negligence Appeared, 21 Conn. L. Rev. 197 (1989).

[22] Weaver v. Ward, Hob. 134, 80 Eng. Rep. 284 (K.B. 1616).

[23] See S.F.C. Milsom, Historical Foundations of the Common Law 283 (2d ed 1981).

[24] The classic and much quoted example of the distinction between Trespass and Case: if you throw a log and strike the plaintiff, he has an action in Trespass, but if you leave a log in the road and the plaintiff falls over it in the dark, the plaintiff has an action on the Case. Reynolds v. Clarke, 1 Str. 634, 93 Eng.Rep. 747 (K.B. 1726). The direct-indirect test for distinguishing Trespass and Case is consistent with earlier decisions, but the explicit formulation of the test is not found until around 1700. See M.J. Prichard, *Scott v. Shepherd* (1773) and the Emergence of the Tort of Negligence 5, 13 ff. (1976).

[25] Waldon v. Marshall, Y.B. Mich., 43 Ed. 3, f. 33, pl. 38 (1370), *printed and translated in* C.H.S. Fifoot, History and Sources of the Common Law: Tort and Contract 81 (1949).

[26] C.H.S. Fifoot, History and Sources of the Common Law: Tort and Contract 66 (1949). See Steinson v. Heath, 3 Lev. 400, 83 Eng. Rep. 750 (K.B. 1694) ("case lies for non-feasance, against my shepherd for negligent keeping my sheep, against my carter for negligent keeping my horses, and for not repairing a bridge by which I am to pass, . . . against a chaplain, for not reading prayers, against an innkeeper, who refuses to lodge me . . ."). One writer went so far as to say that the "primary meaning" of negligence in the early American cases was "nonfeasance," that is, neglect of some positive duty imposed by law. Morton Horwitz, The Transformation of American Law, 1780–1860 86 (1977). A late example of this association of Case and nonfeasance or nonaction was Ogle v. Barnes, 101 Eng.Rep. 1338 (K.B. 1799).

defendant's fault and actual harm. Those instances all invoke the negligence action today.

Relationship of parties in actions on the Case. The action on the Case originally involved parties who had a relationship with each other by contract or status.[27] That setting differed from the Trespass setting, which often involved strangers whose duties did not depend upon a relationship between the parties. In Case, for example, the defendant would be an innkeeper,[28] the plaintiff a guest; or the defendant a surgeon, the plaintiff a patient.[29]

Significance of parties' relationship. The contract or relationship of the parties was doubly important in such cases. *First,* the relationship of the parties is important because that relationship may require the defendant to take affirmative steps to avoid harm to the plaintiff; hence the word neglect (the root for negligence) appears in these cases in the sense that the defendant should be liable for a failure to act.

Second, the standard of care or duty owed by the defendant was implicitly set by accepted community practices and expectations as incorporated in the contract or relationship itself; the defendant who holds himself out as an artificer of any kind implicitly says he will follow the standards of such artificers. The defendant who undertakes to move casks of brandy safely will be liable for spilling the brandy because that is a failure to perform as promised.[30] Equally, the parties' explicit or implicit expectations may relieve the defendant of liability; the guest may undertake to protect his own property and thus relieve the innkeeper of liability when it is stolen.[31]

Particularization of duties in action on the Case. Given that duties in Case tended to find their source in community custom and conduct of the parties, courts naturally did not impose any universal principles of responsibility. They imposed liabilities they thought proportioned to the parties' own contract or expectation. Doctors were to use the care of doctors, farriers the care of farriers and so on. Bailees who without charge accepted temporary custody of another's property owed a duty to care for that property that was considerably different from the duty owed by a bailee who was paid to care for the property.[32] In some categories, the duty could be strict. Common carriers and innkeepers might be charged with loss of the guest's property even if the carrier or

---

[27]   See S.F.C. Milsom, Historical Foundations of the Common Law 393 (2d ed 1981); Percy Winfield, The History of Negligence in the Law of Torts, 42 L. Q. Rev. 184 (1926).

[28]   The Innkeeper's Case, Y.B. Easter, 42 Ed. 3, f. 11, pl. 13 (1369), *printed and translated in* C.H.S. Fifoot, History and Sources of the Common Law: Tort and Contract (1949); Burgess v. Clements, 4 M. & S. 306, 105 Eng.Rep. 848 (K.B. 1815).

[29]   Dr. Groenvelt's Case, 1 Ld. Raym. 213, 91 Eng. Rep. 1038 (1697) (dictum that case would lie against a surgeon for "mala praxis," "his ill practice upon the body of J.S.").

[30]   Coggs v. Bernard, 2 Ld. Raym. 909, 92 Eng. Rep. 107 (1703) (a case actually pleaded as an action on the case with the language of "assumpsit" or undertaking, which was also the language of a contract claim).

[31]   In Burgess v. Clements, 4 M. & S. 306, 105 Eng. Rep. 848 (K.B. 1815), the innkeeper set up the guest in a special show room, giving him a key. The guest left his sample case in the room without locking the door. Lord Ellenborough wanted to bar the guest in part because the property was lost through the guest's own fault. But LeBlanc, J., had a different reason for barring the plaintiff. He thought the parties prescribed their own terms by their conduct, and that in accepting the key, the plaintiff discharged the innkeeper of responsibility.

[32]   See Thomas M. Cooley, The Law of Torts 628–33 (1879). Cooley repeated the supposed rule requiring extreme care, ordinary care, or slight care, depending upon whether the bailment was for the benefit of the bailee, mutual benefit, or the benefit of the bailor only, but he also attempts to fit this to the general formula of ordinary care by treating the benefit issue as part of the circumstances, and he recognizes, too, that the understanding of the parties is what ultimately governs.

innkeeper was not at fault.[33] So defendants might argue that they were not in any recognized category such as a common carrier and hence that they owed no duty of care at all.[34]

Stranger cases. But things were changing by 1700. Defendants who are not in a contractual relation with the plaintiff—strangers they are called—were beginning to cause serious harms. The stranger who caused a collision on the road was still liable in trespass in 1700 and for a long time afterwards,[35] but plaintiffs were beginning to bring suit in Case against strangers who caused indirect or mediate harms.[36] Because the parties were strangers, not in a contractual relationship, the defendant's negligence was understood in a general, or at least undefined sense. By the 1800s, there was nothing unusual about suing a stranger in Case rather than Trespass and the negligence standard necessarily ceased to arise from the parties' relationship. At some point, too, the plaintiff was given an option: he could sue in Case even if injury was direct, so long as he could actually prove negligence and actual harm.[37] The net result is that by 1800, plaintiffs sued in Case for road accident injuries. The older connection of Case (and negligence) to particular occupations and particular duties is no longer required. So negligence had already become a general idea even though its standards had not been articulated.

Coming to America. A great deal of the common law of tort migrated to America with colonization. Even as the American Revolution was being launched, English judges were still debating tort cases by debating the direct vs. indirect distinction.[38] After Independence, the Constitution allocated Admiralty jurisdiction,[39] with its potential for covering maritime torts, to the federal government. Otherwise, tort law was the province of the states, which usually[40] made formal provision for reception of the English common

---

[33]   See Calye's Case, 8 Co. Rep. 32a, 77 Eng.Rep. 520 (K.B. 1584) (if the guest's goods are stolen, the innkeeper is liable); see Chapter 19.

[34]   Lovett v. Hobbs, 2 Show. 127, 89 Eng.Rep. 836 (K.B. 1680). The actual words were "the action lay not," against a coachman who damaged or lost goods because the coachman was not a common carrier. The argument was rejected because the coachman was like a waterman who carries men and goods as a common carrier.

[35]   Leame v. Bray, 2 East. 593, 102 Eng.Rep. 724 (K.B. 1803).

[36]   A master improvidently sends his servant to train ungovernable horses in a crowded place; they cause injury to the plaintiff, who successfully brings an action on the Case. (Harm was considered indirect when the defendant acted through an agent or servant.) Michael v. Alestree, 2 Lev. 172, 83 Eng.Rep. 504 (1676). Or the defendant leaves a pile of lime in the street; the wind blows the lime, which startles the horse, which breaks the chaise in its frightened dash. Lord Mansfield tells the jury to decide whether the defendant was guilty of "blameable negligence." Flower v. Adam, 2 Taunt. 314, 127 Eng.Rep. 1098 (C.P. 1810). See M.J. Prichard, *Scott v. Shepherd* (1773) and the Emergence of the Tort of Negligence 15 ff. (1976) (noting a few "straws in the wind" from earlier times but identifying the late 17th century as the beginning of "non-relationship" negligence cases).

[37]   Williams v. Holland, 10 Bing. 112, 131 Eng. Rep. 848 (C.P. 1833). This view was also followed in America. Dalton v. Favour, 3 N.H. 465 (1826). See E.F. Roberts, Negligence: Blackstone to Shaw To ?: An Intellectual Escapade in a Tory Vein, 50 Cornell L. Rev. 191, 201 (1965).

[38]   Scott v. Shepard, 2 Wm. Bl. 892, 96 Eng.Rep. 525 (1773) (Blackstone, J. dissenting at the court's allowance of Trespass against a defendant who tossed a lighted squib at A, who batted it away towards B, who batted it towards the plaintiff, who lost sight of an eye as a result). If, however, the plaintiff showed both fault and actual harm, at least when harm was not intended, courts sustained the action on the case. Slater v. Baker, 2 Wils. 359, 95 Eng.Rep. 860 (K.B. 1767) (surgeon's treatment of broken leg, plaintiff not required to sue vi et armis).

[39]   1 Thomas Schoenbaum, Admiralty and Maritime Law §§ 1–6 & 3–1 (4th ed. 2003 to 2009).

[40]   Later, Florida, Louisiana, California and some southwestern states were brought into the union with varying degrees of Spanish, or Spanish-French civil rather than common law background. See Lawrence Friedman, A History of American Law 169, 171–76, 364–65 (2d ed. 1985).

law as the basis of their own legal systems.[41] The sparse American authority on torts in the generation or so after adoption of the Constitution seems to indicate that courts were routinely thinking primarily in terms of fault or negligence.[42] Nevertheless, in the early 1800s, negligence seemed not to have become a widespread or general system of adjudication.

§ 9.3 Negligence: Courts Adopt a General Principle of Liability for Fault

Growing into modern tort law. The older tort law, based on a distinction between Trespass with its direct invasion and Case with its indirect invasion, differed from modern tort law in three important ways. *First,* strict liability was or may have been imposed in the Trespass/direct harm cases. *Second,* the liabilities imposed in Case, although based on fault of some kind, were not originally adjudicated under a general fault standard applicable to everyone, but rather under standards set by the particular profession or calling of the defendant. *Third,* the lineaments of negligence itself had not been drawn clearly; what would count as fault in any general system of fault was undetermined. All three of these things began to be altered significantly in the 19th century, mostly after 1850.

(1) Eliminating or limiting the role of strict liability. If strict liability was imposed for direct injuries, such liability was limited or eliminated in favor of a fault-based system. By around 1800 lawyers began arguing that a distinction existed between intentional or willful torts on the one hand and merely negligent torts on the other.[43] The distinction was not immediately developed, but in another generation we find courts beginning to distinguish negligence from intent[44] or at least to show a dislike of the Trespass rule that imposed liability for non-faulty direct harm.[45]

---

[41] E.g., Colo. Rev. Stat. Ann. §§ 2–4–211; 5 ILCS 50/1. See Lawrence Friedman, A History of American Law 107 ff. (2d ed. 1985). Less obviously but more importantly, what the states really adopted, at least over time, was the common law process, not merely rules of particular cases. The common law process contemplates continued development. See, e.g., Wright v. Grove Sun Newspaper Co., Inc., 873 P.2d 983 (Okla. 1994).

[42] See Gary Schwartz, Tort Law and the Economy in Nineteenth-Century America: A Reinterpretation, 9 Yale L.J. 1717 (1981). Many of the early cases seemed to involve indirect injury, so their discussion of negligence is no surprise. E.g., Colt v. M'Mechen, 6 Johns. 160 (N.Y. Sup. Ct. 1810) (considering whether common carrier's loss of goods resulted from negligence as opposed to Act of God); Foot and Reynolds v. Wiswall, 14 Johns. 304 (N.Y. 1817) (jury charge in terms of negligence with the burden upon the defendant to exonerate himself by proving freedom from fault); Vincent v. Stinehour, 7 Vt. 62 (1835) (judgment upheld for the defendant on the ground that "no one can be made responsible, in an action of trespass, for consequences, where he could not have prevented those consequences by prudence and care"). In some other cases the setting involved indirect injury but the facts might have been thought to suggest strict liability in a later generation; yet liability was limited by the fault principle. In Livingston v. Adams, 8 Cow. 175 (N.Y. 1828), an upper riparian owner's dam broke, leading to damages of the lower owner's property. The court considered the case in terms of negligence, not strict liability.

[43] Ogle v. Barnes, 8 T.R. 188, 101 Eng. Rep. 1338 (K.B. 1799); E.F. Roberts, Negligence: Blackstone to Shaw to ? An Intellectual Escapade in a Tory Vein, 50 Cornell L. Q. 191, 199 (1965).

[44] E.F. Roberts, Negligence: Blackstone to Shaw to ? An Intellectual Escapade in a Tory Vein, 50 Cornell L. Rev. 191, 200 (1965).

[45] Ever since Weaver v. Ward, Hob. 134, 80 Eng. Rep. 284 (K.B. 1616), which imposed strict liability but left a safety valve, courts had recognized that the defendant was not liable, even for direct harm resulting from some kinds of "inevitable accidents" in which the defendant was "utterly without fault," provided the defendant shouldered the burden of proving that defense. "Utterly without fault" in Weaver v. Ward seems to have meant that the defendant did not act at all or perhaps that the immediate cause of harm was an intervening act. The idea that liability was inappropriate if the defendant was "utterly without fault" was gradually transmuted. By 1835, the Vermont Court was saying that the defendant would not be liable if the injury was inevitable, which in turn meant that the defendant was not negligent. Vincent v. Stinehour, 7 Vt. 62 (1835).

In 1850, in *Brown v. Kendall*,[46] the Massachusetts Court abolished the rule that a direct physical injury entailed strict liability. The court held that a defendant who attempted to beat a dog but unintentionally struck the plaintiff instead would not be liable for battery in spite of the direct force applied. Instead, the defendant would be liable for battery only if he intended to strike the plaintiff or if he was at fault in striking him. This would seem to mean that other direct applications of force, such as would occur in railroad accidents or industrial injuries, would not automatically subject the defendant to the threat of liability; instead, the plaintiff would be required to prove fault.[47]

(2) Creating a principle of general application. In the 19th century, it looks as if courts began to develop general or "universal" principles. They began to feel, in particular, that in cases of physical harms to persons or property, fault was the general basis for liability and a limit of liability as well. Instead of judging cases by imposing particular duties upon particular callings, courts could simply treat negligence as the basis of liability in all or a large universe of cases. Many observers thought that is what *Brown v. Kendall* did. Intentional invasion, not direct invasion, became the basis for liability in the trespassory tort. Negligence became the basis of liability otherwise. Negligence was no longer focused upon parties who stood in some special or contractual relationship;[48] "neglect," was no longer a matter of a particular duty of a vet to the farmer or innkeeper to a guest, but a general duty of all to all.[49] This generality made it possible for negligence law to cover virtually any kind of case not exempted by statute or some special rule.

There were, of course, qualifications, both because some strict liability was retained or developed and because some faulty defendants escaped liability. No duty and immunity rules might protect landowners or governmental entities from liability for negligence, for example. In any event, negligence thinking, though far less than universal, became the dominant or default mode of thinking about tort suits between strangers in the years after the Civil War.

(3) Developing the negligence concept. Negligence as a general principle that could apply to suits among non-contracting parties or strangers—railroad crossing accidents for example—would require courts to set up some kind of meaningful standard about what would constitute fault or negligence. *Brown v. Kendall*[50] set the general standard for negligence law: the defendant should use ordinary care, or more particularly, the care of a reasonable and prudent person. The actual conduct that would count as ordinary care would vary with circumstances, since a reasonable person would exercise more care when danger is greater.[51]

---

[46]   Brown v. Kendall, 60 Mass. 292 (1850).

[47]   See § 9.4.

[48]   Brown v. Kendall was not the first case to impose a negligence standard among parties who had no contractual relationship. See, e.g., Livingston v. Adams, 8 Cow. 175 (N.Y. 1828).

[49]   See G. Edward White, Tort Law in America 16 (1980); Robert J. Kaczorowski, The Common-Law Background of Nineteenth-Century Tort Law, 51 Ohio St. L. J. 1127 (1990).

[50]   60 Mass. 292 (1850).

[51]   "[W]hat constitutes ordinary care will vary with the circumstances. . . . In general, is means that kind and degree of care, which prudent and cautious men would use, such as it required by the exigency of the case. . . ." Brown v. Kendall, 60 Mass. 292 (1850).

Adopting negligence analysis as the basis of tort law. With the decision in *Brown v. Kendall*, the profession began to perceive torts as a separate subject of the law[52] and came to perceive the defendant's fault as its core.[53] This meant that liability ordinarily required either the defendant's intentional invasion of the plaintiff's rights or a negligent invasion. After the Civil War, jurists began to puzzle out the contours of the negligence action as railroad trains and other machines churned up injuries on a new scale.[54] The ordinary care formula in *Brown v. Kendall* and its minor variations became the basis for an enormous body of modern negligence law.

§ 9.4   Negligence: After Adoption of the Fault Principle

Strangers and privies. Brown v. Kendall[55] explicitly adopted a general principle of fault as the basis of tort liability in 1850,[56] but the implications of a general principle of negligence were not immediately apparent. For a period, courts sometimes continued to think of particular duties owed by a defendant in a particular relationship to the plaintiff. The carrier owed one duty; the gratuitous bailee another, and so on. It remains true today that in spite of the broad negligence principle, many decisions focus on the particular duty or standard of care owed by a particular class of defendant rather than by people generally.[57]

Fleshing out the negligence concept. Adoption of a fault system did not complete the work of creating negligence law. The reasonable and prudent person standard, though beautifully general in its formulation and probably quite useful to many juries, is painfully imprecise as a guide for appellate review of particular cases.[58] It provides a common set of ideals or terms to permit professional discussion, but does not point that discussion in any particular direction. It remained for succeeding generations to develop a series of ideas that tended to make the negligence concept more precise.

Justice Holmes. In his 1881 book, *The Common Law*, Holmes emphasized that the negligence standard was objective, based on abilities of the reasonable person rather than on the actual abilities of the individual defendant.[59] He went on to add something just as important to the simple reasonable person standard. He recognized that there would be no liability for negligence unless the defendant's conduct presented a "threat" of harm, what we would today call a risk. Further than that, liability would not be imposed unless a reasonable person in the defendant's position could have recognized

---

[52]   The first torts book was Francis Hilliard, The Law of Torts (1859). See G. Edward White, Tort Law in America 16 (1980). Most of Hilliard's book was devoted to topics other than negligence—libel, malicious prosecution, and nuisance, for example.

[53]   See O.W. Holmes, The Common Law 77 (1881).

[54]   Lawrence Friedman, A History of American Law 468 (2d ed. 1985) (in the 19th century, railroad law and tort law "grew up together" and were much the same).

[55]   60 Mass. 292 (1850).

[56]   See generally § Friedman, supra n. 54.

[57]   See especially Chapters 19 to 24. E.g., Iemma v. Adventure RV Rentals, Inc., 632 N.E.2d 1178, 1182 (Ind. Ct. App. 1994) ("The bailee must use slight care when the bailment is for the sole benefit of the bailor, great care when the bailment is for the sole benefit of the bailee, and ordinary care when the bailment is for the mutual benefit of the bailor and bailee").

[58]   O.W. Holmes, The Common Law 111 (1881) called the standard a "featureless generality" and thought that with experience, statutes and judicial decisions would make it more precise.

[59]   Id. at 108 (if "a man is born hasty and awkward, is always having accidents and hurting himself or his neighbors, no doubt his congenital defects will be allowed for in the courts of Heaven, but his slips are no less troublesome to his neighbors than if they sprang from guilty neglect. His neighbors accordingly require him . . . to come up to their standard and the courts which they establish decline to take his personal equation into account").

the risk that harm might follow from his conduct, often expressed in abbreviated form by saying harm must be reasonably foreseeable.[60] Reasonable foreseeability of harm became one of the important ways of evaluating the reasonableness of the defendant's conduct.[61]

Professor Terry. By 1915 lawyers were developing the idea that negligence was not only "unreasonable" conduct, but conduct that involves unreasonable risks. Henry Terry proposed to recognize explicitly that unreasonableness of risk turned on a balance of several factors. How risky was the conduct? What values were at risk? What were the hoped-for gains to be derived from the conduct?[62] Terry's ideas of balancing risks of conduct against its utility were to become part of the mainstream thought about negligence law.

The First Restatement. By the 1920s, lawyers and legal scholars were preparing for the First Restatement of Torts. They worked out the physical, mental and "moral" characteristics of the reasonable person whose conduct set the standard of care along lines that are now generally accepted as background.[63] By that time, too, liability insurance had become readily available in its modern and useful form. Details remained to be worked out or altered or given new emphasis—the effect of custom[64] and the effect of statutes[65] and the analysis of risks in a negligence case,[66] for example. But the main conceptions of contemporary negligence law were in place.

Boundaries and exceptions. The new general concept of negligence also required boundaries. Duties of care were limited so as to exclude liability for many purely emotional harms[67] and to limit the care required by, say, landowners to trespassers.[68] Causal rules were worked up; the defendant would not be liable unless he in fact caused actual harm to the plaintiff[69] and even then would not be liable unless the harm was significantly related to his unreasonably risky conduct.[70] The plaintiff's own fault had to be worked into the case somehow,[71] and so did the plaintiff's consent to face the risks imposed by the defendant.[72] Courts also had to think out a way to deal with cases in which several different people were at fault.[73] These and other problems were approached mainly in the 20th or the very late 19th century.

---

[60]   Id. at 96. Contrast the earlier view stated in Thomas G. Shearman & Amasa A. Redfield, Law of Negligence § 7 (1869), that "It is not an essential element of culpable negligence that the defendant should have anticipated, or have had reason to anticipate, that his carelessness would injure another person. It is enough that he did not use the care and skill usual in similar circumstances."

[61]   See Patrick J. Kelley, Who Decides? Community Safety Conventions at the Heart of Tort Liability, 38 Clev. St. L. Rev. 315, 345 (1990). Kelley concludes that before Holmes, "foreseeability" was only relevant on proximate cause issues or was subordinated to the question what a reasonable person would do.

[62]   Henry Terry, Negligence, 29 Harv. L. Rev. 40 (1915). Terry had his own nomenclature and system of explanation, somewhat more complex than the summary here.

[63]   See Warren A. Seavey, Negligence—Subjective or Objective?, 41 Harv. L. Rev. 1 (1927).

[64]   See §§ 12.6 to 12.9.

[65]   See§ Chapter 11.

[66]   See §§ 12.3 to 12.5.

[67]   See Chapter 29.

[68]   See Chapter 20.

[69]   See Chapter 14.

[70]   See Chapter 15.

[71]   See Chapter 16.

[72]   See Chapter 17.

[73]   See § Chapter 35.

Leaving a place for strict liability. Although negligence law came to dominate tort thinking, courts were unwilling to abolish all strict liability after Brown v. Kendall. They retained strict liability or semi-strict liability in a number of cases associated with certain nuisances,[74] certain trespassory acts,[75] and certain especially dangerous or abnormal activities.[76] In the 20th century they added strict liability for defective products to the list.[77] Statutes in recent years have gone on to add liabilities for certain environmental harms.[78]

Disenchantments and alternatives. Negligence law does not necessarily work well in all cases. Many plans have been offered or adopted to make special provisions for particular classes of cases, or in some cases, to supplement negligence law. For example, workers' compensation, which has been adopted everywhere, imposes strict liability upon employers for on-the-job injuries to workers, but the compensation is limited. The Keeton-O'Connell no-fault plan, some form of which has been adopted in many states, requires auto owners to provide for their own minor injuries through special insurance, reserving the negligence claim for cases of more serious injury.[79] In spite of these developments, however, negligence law remains at the center of personal injury and property damage claims in tort.

C. FUNDAMENTALS OF NEGLIGENCE LIABILITY

§ 9.5   Elements of the Prima Facie Case for Negligence

Negligence and the Negligence Case

Negligence as risky conduct. In modern law, the term negligence in its primary meaning merely describes conduct. In that sense it has come to mean conduct that is unreasonably risky, such as driving a car at a high rate of speed. A good deal of tort law is devoted to deciding what counts as an unreasonable risk and to deciding as well whether the judge or the jury is the decision maker in particular cases.

Negligence as a type of case. The term negligence is also used in a different way to refer to the claim or cause of action. That is, the term negligence may refer to the bundle of rules and procedures that govern the negligence case or lawsuit rather than to the defendant's conduct itself.

Elements of the case. The rules for the negligence case impose upon the plaintiff the burden of establishing each of the following elements by proof of facts and persuasion:

> 1.   The defendant owed the plaintiff a duty to exercise some degree of care for the plaintiff's safety;
>
> 2.   The defendant breached that duty by his unreasonably risky conduct;
>
> 3.   The defendant's conduct in fact caused harm to the plaintiff;

---

[74]   See Chapter 30.

[75]   Intentional entry upon land in the reasonably mistaken belief that it is one's own land might be considered semi-strict liability. See § 5.2.

[76]   See Chapter 32.

[77]   See Chapter 33.

[78]   E.g., United States v. Northeastern Pharm. & Chem. Co., 810 F.2d 726 (8th Cir. 1986) (strict liability under CERCLA statutes); United States v. West of England Shipowner's Mut. Prot. & Indem. Ass'n, 872 F.2d 1192 (5th Cir. 1989) (strict liability under Federal Water Pollution Control Act). See Allan J. Topol & Rebecca Snow, Superfund Law and Procedure §§ 1.2, 4.4 (1992).

[79]   Robert Keeton & Jeffrey O'Connell, Basic Protection for the Traffic Victim (1965).

4.   The defendant's conduct was not only a cause in fact of the plaintiff's harm, but also a "proximate cause," meaning that the defendant's conduct is perceived to have a significant relationship to the harm suffered by the plaintiff; in particular, that the harm caused was the general kind of harm the defendant negligently risked; and

5.   The existence and amount of damages, based on actual harm of a legally recognized kind such as physical injury to person or property.

The general formula. The prima facie case for negligence is broad and general. It resolves no cases. Instead, it points to issues and sets the terms in which lawyers will argue the case. The plaintiff must establish each of the elements named by proof or persuasion, but she need not show any others.[80] Each of these elements receives substantial discussion in this book.

Affirmative defenses. The plaintiff who proves her prima facie case will not necessarily prevail because the defendant may succeed in presenting affirmative defenses that will wholly or partly defeat the plaintiff's claim. Common defenses include (1) the plaintiff's fault, which in most states today will reduce the plaintiff's damages but not necessarily defeat her claim; (2) the plaintiff's assumption of the risk, although this defense is increasingly being discarded at least with respect to implied assumption of the risk, and (3) the statute of limitations. In addition to such defenses, whole areas of liability are excluded on the ground that the defendant is immune or owes no duty to the plaintiff.

§ 9.6   The Elements: Meaning and Terminology

Duty or Standard of Care

Duty v. standard of care. There are cases in which the defendant owes the plaintiff no duty to exercise care to prevent the harm suffered.[81] In the ordinary case, however, the defendant does owe a duty of care.[82] The only question about the duty in such cases is whether the care owed is some especially high kind of care or whether it is more modest. This phase of the duty issue is usually discussed in terms of the "standard of care." The duty or standard imposed in most cases is the duty of reasonable care under the circumstances. Equivalent shorthand terms are due care and ordinary care. Judges, not juries, ordinarily determine whether a duty exists and the standard it imposes.[83]

Misusing duty terminology. It is possible to use the term duty in a radical way by speaking of duties that do not involve standards of care at all. Instead of saying that the defendant is under a duty of reasonable care, a judge could say the defendant is under a duty to keep a lookout or to drive so that he could stop within the range of his vision. This kind of usage really refers to something else, often the breach question. In this book, the term duty is used in the first sense, as stating a legal standard by which the defendant's conduct is to be judged.

Breach of Duty: Negligence

Negligence as risk. When the defendant owes a duty of reasonable care, the defendant breaches that duty by conduct that falls short of such care, that is, by conduct

---

[80]   See Restatement Third of Torts (Liability for Physical and Emotional Harm) §§ 3, 6 (2010).
[81]   See Chapters 22, 25, 26.
[82]   See § Chapter 10.
[83]   See § 10.1.

that is unreasonably risky.[84] Juries, not judges, decide whether the defendant was negligent unless the question is too clear to permit different evaluations by reasonable people.

Actual Harm

Actual harm requirement. Negligence law grew out of the old common law action on the Case and carried over its requirement that the plaintiff cannot recover without showing actual harm resulting from the defendant's conduct.[85] Sometimes this is referred to as a requirement that the plaintiff must prove actual damages and sometimes as a part of a requirement that the plaintiff must prove causation in fact.[86]

Factual Cause

Tests of factual cause. The traditional view is that the plaintiff's injury is caused by the defendant's conduct if, but for the defendant's conduct, the plaintiff would have escaped the injury. However, causation turns out to be a complex business, and this but-for test is not always suitable. Sometimes courts tweak the test or abandon it in favor of a softer evaluation of causation. Some jurists believe courts have also abandoned the causation requirement altogether in one line of cases.[87] If that is correct, then the element that must be proved by the plaintiff here is not necessarily causation but causation or a legally recognized substitute for causation. For the great majority of cases, however, the plaintiff must prove that the defendant's tortious conduct caused actual harm, even if courts sometimes use milder tests of causation.[88]

Scope of Liability—"Proximate Cause"

The requirement. In addition to proving causation in fact, the plaintiff must prove that the defendant's conduct was a "proximate cause" of the plaintiff's harm, meaning that the harm that occurred was the general kind that was unreasonably risked by the defendant, the kind of harm the defendant should have been more careful to avoid.[89] Making sense of this idea will require a substantial analysis.[90] But it is important to note at least that the scope of liability analysis excludes liability for fortuitous, unforeseeable harms.[91] Moreover, although some courts speak of "proximate cause" in reference to both factual causation and to scope of risk or scope of liability issues, such usage can be confusing.[92] Accordingly, this book avoids the use of "proximate cause" to include factual causation.

---

[84] Restatement Third of Torts (Liability for Physical and Emotional Harm) § 3 (2010). See Chapters 12 to 16.

[85] See Copeland v. Compton, 914 S.W.2d 378 (Mo. Ct. App. 1996). This rule is important not only in excluding claims in which no legally recognized harm has occurred, but also in determining whether a tort occurred within the period covered by a liability insurance policy, see American Guarantee & Liab. Ins. Co. v. 1906 Company, 273 F.3d 605 (5th Cir. 2001), and in determining when the statute of limitations begins to run.

[86] See, e.g., Reardon v. Larkin, 3 A.3d 376 (Me. 2010) (parties stipulated to liability, but no claim was proved where the evidence showed that the plaintiff was not harmed in any way by the defendant's conduct; court said the plaintiff had failed to prove "the elements of causation and damages").

[87] Where the plaintiff is allowed to recover for the loss of a chance of a better outcome. Lost chance recoveries can be conceptualized in ways consistent with the factual cause requirement. See §§ 14.11.

[88] See Chapter 14.

[89] Cf. Restatement Third of Torts (Liability for Physical and Emotional Harm) § 29 (2010).

[90] See Chapter 15.

[91] Cf. Restatement Third of Torts (Liability for Physical and Emotional Harm) § 30 (2010).

[92] See § 15.3.

§ 9.7   Negligence as Conduct, Not State of Mind

Negligence as risk. Negligence is conduct that creates or fails to avoid unreasonable risks of foreseeable harm to others.[93] That is the specific meaning of the general statement that negligence is a failure to exercise care that is reasonable under the circumstances.[94]

Negligence as conduct, not state of mind. Because the emphasis in negligence cases is on unreasonably risky conduct, a bad state of mind is neither necessary nor sufficient to show negligence.[95] Conduct is everything. One who drives at a dangerous speed is negligent even if he is not aware of his speed and is using his best efforts to drive carefully. Conversely, a person who drives without the slightest care for the safety of others is not negligent unless he drives in some way that is unreasonably risky.[96] State of mind, including knowledge and belief, may motivate or shape conduct, and sometimes may be relevant to the issue of reasonableness, but it is not in itself an actionable tort. The legal concept of negligence as unduly risky conduct distinct from state of mind reflects the law's strong commitment to an objective standard of behavior.

Intentional conduct that creates risk: the relation of negligence and intentional torts. A defendant is not guilty of an intentional tort merely because he knows of a risk from his conduct. Intent to commit a battery, for example, requires either a purpose or a substantial certainty that a harmful or offensive contact will be made. Intentionally taking a *risk* of contact is not the same as a purpose or a certainty that such contact will result. So intentional conduct and even intentional risk-taking is analyzed under negligence rules unless the defendant has a purpose to invade the plaintiff's legally protected interests or a certainty that such an invasion will occur. Moreover, the defendant who intentionally takes a risk may or may not be negligent; negligence will depend upon the seriousness of the risk and the reasons for taking it.

Examples of intentionally risky conduct. To see these points in an example, suppose the batter in a softball game knows the batted ball might conceivably break a window outside the park and across the street, but also knows that it is unlikely. He is intentionally taking a risk when he attempts to bat; but the risk is small, far short of a substantial certainty. By definition, the batter, though intentionally taking a risk, is not intentionally causing the softball to enter another's land. Consequently the batter is not liable for an intentional tort if he hits the ball over the fence. Is the batter then chargeable with negligence if not intent? That depends upon whether the risk was an unreasonable one. If the damaged house is very close even though outside the park,

---

[93]   See Henry Terry, Negligence, 29 Harv. L. Rev. 40 (1915).

[94]   Reasonable person terminology is used in definitions and in jury instructions as a simple and general way of conveying the idea, since reasonable persons will not take unjustified risks. Judicial analysis of negligence claims, however, usually moves to the more specific question of unjustified risk. Professor Simons has shown that reasonable person and unjustified risk are at least theoretically distinct conceptions, see Kenneth W. Simons, Negligence, 16 Soc. Phil. & Pol'y 2, 52 (1999). However, courts analyze the justification for risks in appellate decisions and give the reasonable person instruction at trial with no apparent sense of conflict, so the reasonable person test seems to be the simple or shorthand way of talking about unjustified risks.

[95]   See Beck v. Dobrowski, 559 F.3d 680, 682 (7th Cir. 2009) ("negligence is not a state of mind; it is a failure . . . to come up to the specified standard of care"); Restatement Second of Torts § 282 (1979); Restatement Third of Torts (Liability for Physical and Emotional Harm) §§ 3 ("conduct") & 12 cmt. B (bad judgment irrelevant) (2010).

[96]   See City of Little Rock v. Cameron, 320 Ark. 444, 897 S.W.2d 562 (1995) (defendant, who had been drinking alcohol, ran into and destroyed a traffic light pole; drinking does not prove he committed an act of negligence).

maybe the batter is negligent, but if the risk of a broken window from a batted ball is a very small risk, batting the ball may not be negligent either.

Chapter 10

DUTY AND THE ORDINARY STANDARD OF REASONABLE CARE UNDER THE CIRCUMSTANCES

Analysis

A. THE EXISTENCE OF DUTY

§ 10.1   General Rules of Duty
§ 10.2   Duty vs. Breach Confusion
§ 10.3   Determining the Existence of Duty
§ 10.4   Foreseeability and Duty Determinations

B. THE ORDINARY STANDARD OF REASONABLE CARE

§ 10.5   The Objective Reasonable Person Standard
§ 10.6   Circumstances as Part of the Standard: Special Danger

C. PARTICULAR CIRCUMSTANCES RELATED TO THE STANDARD OF CARE

§ 10.7   Emergency and Unavoidable Accident
§ 10.8   Objective and Subjective Features of the Standard
§ 10.9   Physical Characteristics
§ 10.10   Mental Capacity
§ 10.11   Bases for and Alternatives to the Mental Capacity Rules
§ 10.12   Knowledge, Perception, Memory, Experience, and Skills
§ 10.13   Intoxication

D. THE STANDARD OF CARE FOR CHILDREN

§ 10.14   The General Standard of Care for Children
§ 10.15   Rationales for the Child Standard
§ 10.16   Holding Children to an Adult Standard

E. STANDARDS OTHER THAN REASONABLE CARE

§ 10.17   Alternative Standards
§ 10.18   Gross Negligence, Recklessness, and Wanton Misconduct

---

A. THE EXISTENCE OF DUTY

§ 10.1 General Rules of Duty

Duty: an introduction. Although it was not required in early English law, in order to establish a negligence cause of action today, the plaintiff must show that the defendant owes her a duty of care.[1] "A duty, in negligence cases, may be defined as an

---

[1]   Prosser & Keeton on Torts § 53, p. 356. Romain v. Frankenmuth Mut. Ins. Co., 483 Mich. 18, 762 N.W.2d 911 (2009); Lahm v. Farrington, 90 A.3d 620 (N.H. 2014); MacGregor v. Walker, 322 P.3d 706 (Utah

obligation, to which the law will give recognition and effect, to conform to a particular standard of conduct toward another."[2] A discussion of the subject of duty always begins with Dean Prosser's famous observation that duty "is not sacrosanct in itself, but is only an expression of the sum total of those considerations of policy which lead the law to say that the plaintiff is entitled to protection."[3] A duty may arise "based upon the existence of a contract, a statute, or the common law, or when the relationship of the parties is such that the law imposes an obligation on the defendant to act reasonably for the protection of the plaintiff."[4] Under the common law, the Restatement Third creates a general duty when an actor's conduct creates a risk of physical harm, and in certain contexts of affirmative duty.[5]

Duty and the court. A defendant who is under no duty to use care is, in effect, exempted from the ordinary rules of negligence law, and avoids all accountability for harm inflicted.[6] Whether the defendant owes a duty is determined by judges, not juries.[7] On the other hand, juries determine all other elements of the negligence case unless the answer is so clear that reasonable people cannot differ.[8]

Duty as a preliminary question. Because duty is a question for the judge, a defendant can raise the issue in a motion to dismiss. The defendant need not wait for trial to argue that he was under no duty of care. If the defendant's no-duty argument prevails with the judge, the defendant will escape liability without need of any trial.

General rules: duty and risk of physical harm. In general, when an actor's conduct, creates, maintains, or continues a risk of physical harm, he ordinarily has a duty of care. When such a duty is owed, the standard of care to be applied is ordinarily reasonable

---

2014). The same point is commonly established by the numerous cases that list duty as an element of the negligence claim. E.g., Giggers v. Memphis Hous. Auth., 277 S.W.3d 359 (Tenn. 2008).

    [2]   Prosser & Keeton § 53, p. 356.

    [3]   Id. § 53, p. 358.

    [4]   Lucero v. Holbrook, 288 P.3d 1228, 1232 (Wyo. 2012).

    [5]   Restatement Third of Torts (Liability for Physical and Emotional Harm) §§ 7 and 37 (2010).

    [6]   Gipson v. Kasey, 214 Ariz. 141, 142–43, 150 P.3d 228, 230–31 (2007) ("A conclusion that no duty exists is equivalent to a rule that, for certain categories of cases, defendants may not be held accountable for damages they carelessly cause, no matter how unreasonable their conduct.").

    [7]   Beacon Residential Cmty. Ass'n v. Skidmore, Owings & Merrill LLP, 59 Cal.4th 568, 327 P.3d 850, 173 Cal.Rptr.3d 752 (2014); Forsythe v. Clark USA, Inc., 224 Ill. 2d 274, 864 N.E.2d 227, 309 Ill. Dec. 361 (2007); Commerce Ins. Co. v. Ultimate Livery Serv., Inc., 452 Mass. 639, 897 N.E.2d 50 (2008).

    [8]   E.g., Kane v. Lamothe,182 Vt. 241, 936 A.2d 1303 (2007); Ranger Ins. Co. v. Pierce Cty., 164 Wash.2d 545, 192 P.3d 886 (2008); Restatement Third of Torts (Liability for Physical and Emotional Harm) § 7 cmt. i (2010).

care under the circumstances.[9] This is the approach of the cases,[10] as well as the understanding of major commentators[11] and the Restatement Third of Torts.[12]

No duty and affirmative duties. On the other hand, when the actor does not create or continue a risk of harm, an actor generally has no duty of care.[13] However, quite a number of affirmative duties stand as exceptions to the general rule.[14]

The importance of principle and policy. With respect to both duties and affirmative duties, courts may either deny, limit, create, or expand the duty based on articulated principle or policy factors.[15]

Although these rules are straightforward, judicial application of the rules and different uses of the duty terminology are less so. The cases create some confusion and unpredictability.

§ 10.2 Duty vs. Breach Confusion

Varied ways of discussing duty. In spite of the fundamental importance of duty, lawyers and judges have used the term in a variety of different ways, not always with the same meaning.[16] The orthodox and most useful way to use the term *duty* is to refer to a general standard or obligation. In this sense, a duty is an obligation created by law, usually the common law, to comply with a general standard of care. A judge might say, for example, that the defendant owes a duty to use reasonable care under the circumstances.

Duty that shades into breach. Sometimes, however, judges use the term *duty* as a conclusion about whether the defendant's particular act or omission should be actionable in the particular case, irrespective of any general standard. In that narrow sense, a judge might say that the defendant had *no duty* to stop and look before proceeding into an intersection.[17] Such specific duty determinations in effect put the judge in the jury role,

---

[9]   E.g., United States v. Stevens, 994 So.2d 1062 (Fla. 2008); Werne v. Exec. Women's Golf Ass'n, 158 N.H. 373, 969 A.2d 346 (2009).

[10]   See, e.g., Gipson v. Kasey, 214 Ariz. 141, 142–43, 150 P.3d 228, 230–31 (2007); John B. v. Sup. Ct., 38 Cal. 4th 1177, 137 P.3d 153, 45 Cal. Rptr. 3d 316 (2006); Jupin v. Kask, 447 Mass. 141, 147, 849 N.E.2d 829, 835 (2006) (recognizing "a general principle of tort law, every actor has a duty to exercise reasonable care to avoid physical harm to others"); A.W. v. Lancaster Cty. Sch. Dist., 250 Neb. 205, 784 N.W.2d 907 (2010); Iglehart v. Bd. of Cty. Comm'rs of Rogers County, 60 P.3d 497 (Okla. 2002); Giggers v. Memphis Hous. Auth., 277 S.W.3d 359, 364 (Tenn. 2008).

[11]   See W. Jonathan Cardi & Michael D. Green, Duty Wars, 81 S. Cal. L. Rev. 671 (2008); W. Jonathan Cardi, Purging Foreseeability, 58 Vand. L. Rev. 739 (2005); Aaron Twerski, The Cleaver, the Violin, and the Scalpel: Duty and the Restatement (Third) of Torts, 60 Hastings L.J. 1 (2008) (expressing general agreement with the Restatement). Two commentators in particular have opposed the Restatement view in a number of articles, e.g., John C.P. Goldberg & Benjamin C. Zipursky, Shielding Duty: How Attending to Assumption of Risk, Attractive Nuisance, and Other "Quaint" Doctrines Can Improve Decisionmaking in Negligence Cases, 79 S. Cal. L. Rev. 329 (2006), based on their earlier theory that tort duty is based on relationships. See John C.P. Goldberg & Benjamin C. Zipursky, The Moral of MacPherson, 146 U. Pa. L. Rev. 1733 (1998).

[12]   Restatement Third of Torts (Liability for Physical and Emotional Harm) § 7 (2010).

[13]   Id. § 37.

[14]   Id. §§ 38–44. See Chapter 21 (health care providers).

[15]   Id. § 7(b) and § 37 cmt. g.

[16]   See Marshall v. Burger King Corp., 222 Ill. 2d 422, 856 N.E.2d 1048, 305 Ill. Dec. 897 (2006) ("Much confusion over duty stems from courts' tendency to attribute a variety of different meanings to the term.").

[17]   Alternatively, especially on the issue of contributory negligence, judges may say that the defendant had a specific duty, such as the duty to stop at a railroad track.

whether the rule is for or against a duty of care.[18] In many such cases the words may be the words of duty, but the process of good decision-making requires a jury determination about what counts as ordinary care under the circumstances—the question of breach, not duty.[19]

Duty to follow the standard of reasonable care. Similarly, judges sometimes say that as danger increases, so does the *duty*.[20] But judges do not mean by this that a duty of reasonable care suddenly becomes a duty of excessive or heightened care. Instead, they are using *duty* in the sense of specific conduct and mean only that the duty remains the same—reasonable care under the circumstances—while circumstances of special danger show that reasonable care may be deemed by the trier of fact to require more precautions.[21]

Duty as an obligation to act in accordance with a general standard. The use of the term *duty* to refer to specific conduct produces confusion and often interferes with the jury's role. The most coherent way of using duty states a rule or standard of law rather than a conclusion about the defendant's breach of duty on the particular facts.[22] No-duty rulings are expressions of "global" positions of policy or justice rather than evaluations of specific facts of the case.[23] Because they are rules of law having the quality of generality,[24] they should not merely mask decisions that the defendant was not guilty of negligence or breach of duty.

Distinguishing duty and breach. Thus duty is whether the defendant is under an obligation to use care to avoid injury to others. Breach, in contrast, is whether the defendant did in fact use appropriate care. The duty issue is whether there is a standard the defendant must meet in his conduct; the breach issue is whether the defendant violated that standard.[25] The issue of duty, then, is not, as the Illinois Supreme Court

---

[18]   Dilan A. Esper & Gregory C. Keating, Putting "Duty" in Its Place: A Reply to Professors Goldberg and Zipursky, 41 Loy. L.A. L. Rev. 1225 (2008) (discussing duty as an articulation of a legal rule, not a "retail" judgment about particular cases).

[19]   Courts may translate their own talk of specific "no-duty" rules back into analysis of breach. For example, in Tagle v. Jakob, 97 N.Y.2d 165, 763 N.E.2d 107, 737 N.Y.S.2d 331 (2001), the court expressed its conclusion as a rule that "Jakob had no duty to warn the tenant of that hazard." But in its analysis the court looked to the facts of the case and concluded that the danger was obvious to the tenant so that "as a matter of law, Jakob [the landlord] had no reason to expect that the tenant would not observe the hazard or any conceivable risk associated with it." That seems indistinguishable from a conclusion that, as a matter of law, reasonable people could not find negligence (breach). Likewise, when working through an analysis that is ostensibly based on "duty" rather than breach, the court may more or less explicitly recognize that the issue in the particular case is essentially the negligence (breach) issue. See Happel v. Wal-Mart Stores, Inc., 199 Ill. 2d 179, 262 Ill. Dec. 815 (2002) ("Wal-Mart had a duty to warn and that this duty is encompassed within the pharmacist's duty of ordinary care.").

[20]   E.g., United States v. Stevens, 994 So.2d 1062 (Fla. 2008).

[21]   See Stewart v. Motts, 539 Pa. 596, 654 A.2d 535 (1995) ("There is but one standard of care to be applied to negligence actions involving dangerous instrumentalities in this Commonwealth. This standard of care is 'reasonable care.' ").

[22]   Dilan A. Esper & Gregory C. Keating, Putting "Duty" in Its Place: A Reply to Professors Goldberg and Zipursky, 41 Loy. L.A. L. Rev. 1225 (2008) (discussing duty as an articulation of a legal rule, not a "retail" judgment about particular cases); Mark P. Gergen, The Jury's Role in Deciding Normative Issues in The American Common Law, 68 Fordham L. Rev. 407, 431–39 (1999); Restatement Third of Torts (Liability for Physical and Emotional Harm) § 7 cmt. a (2010).

[23]   See Stephen D. Sugarman, Assumption of Risk, 31 Val. U. L. Rev. 833, 843 (1997) (a clear and lively explanation of the difference between no-duty and no-breach analyses).

[24]   See Dilan A. Esper & Gregory C. Keating, Abusing "Duty," 79 S. Cal. L. Rev. 265 (2006).

[25]   See Lumbermens Mut. Cas. Co. v. Thornton, 92 S.W.3d 259 (Mo. Ct. App. 2002) ("If there is a general duty to exercise some type of care to the plaintiff and the next question one asks is whether the defendant

eloquently wrote, "whether defendants had a duty to install protective poles, or a duty to prevent a car from entering the restaurant, or some such other fact-specific formulation. [The defendants] owed the decedent a duty of reasonable care. The issue is whether, in light of the particular circumstances of this case, defendants *breached* that duty."[26] Similarly, since drivers on the highway owe a duty of reasonable care, it is error for a lower court to rule that a driver has no duty to pull over on the shoulder when confronted with an obstacle to avoid a stop in the lane of traffic; the duty of care is not suspended and the question is whether a failure to pull over is a breach of that duty.[27]

Harms that result when "no-breach" decisions are expressed as "no-duty" rules. To express "no-breach" decisions as "no-duty" rules causes two harms. First, it displaces the jury, which is the decision-maker on issues of breach unless the conclusion is so clear that reasonable people simply could not differ.[28] Second, no-duty rules should be invoked only when all cases they cover fall substantially within the reason that frees the defendant of responsibility for his fault.[29] Elevating a decision about particular facts to a no-duty rule will almost always violate this principle by excluding liability not only in the particular case but also in others that are quite different on their facts and may call for a different result.

Example: foliage cases. In a number of cases, landowners fail to trim foliage at the edge of their land, resulting in a blind intersection where cross-traffic is hidden by the landowner's vegetation. Many cases involving collisions in such circumstances say that the landowner owes no duty to trim the foliage.[30] This means that regardless of how cheap and easy it is to trim the foliage or how dangerous the intersection, the owner is free to be negligent. These cases look like decisions on the breach issue that have been generalized to decisions against duty, that is, decisions in which the court is making determinations about costs and benefits and foreseeability in the particular case, displacing the jury's role in the process.

Some courts have rejected the no-duty rule in the foliage cases. One reason is that rules of law should not ordinarily define specific acts that are exempted from ordinary care. Instead, judges must follow the reasonable care standard, leaving it to juries to apply the reasonable person standard to particular conduct like failure to trim bushes.[31] Facts or data will tell a factfinder how risky the intersection might be and similarly the costs of clearing it; this is not a matter to be decided as a rule of law covering all intersections, at all times, and at all costs.[32] Other judges have made a similar point outside the foliage context.[33]

---

should or should not have acted in a particular way (or refrained from acting), the analysis is evaluative based on the facts of the case and this determination would almost invariably be an issue for the jury.").

[26] Marshall v. Burger King Corp., 222 Ill. 2d 422, 305 Ill. Dec. 897 (2006) (emphasis added).

[27] Hesse v. McClintic, 176 P.3d 759 (Colo. 2008).

[28] This and other criticisms have also been raised against the use of many "factors" in determining the existence or non-existence of a duty. See § 10.3.

[29] Marshall v. Burger King Corp., 222 Ill. 2d 422, 305 Ill. Dec. 897 (2006) (specifically accepting this principle); see Gipson v. Kasey, 214 Ariz. 141, 147, 150 P.3d 228, 234 (2007) (Hurwitz, J., concurring).

[30] See William J. Appel, Annotation, Liability of Private Landowner for Vegetation Obscuring View at Highway or Street Intersection, 69 A.L.R.4th 1092 (1990).

[31] Coburn v. City of Tucson, 143 Ariz. 50, 691 P.2d 1078 (1984); Donaca v. Curry Cnty., 303 Or. 30, 734 P.2d 1339 (1987).

[32] Donaca v. Curry Cnty., 303 Or. 30, 734 P.2d 1339 (1987).

[33] See, e.g., M.A. v. United States, 951 P.2d 851 (Alaska 1998) (responding to the defendant's argument that a physician had no duty to diagnose pregnancy accurately: "The existence of a duty turns not on the

Duty issues. The main issues about duty go to its existence, and its measure. Did the defendant owe any duty to the plaintiff? And if the defendant owed a duty, what was that duty, expressed as a standard of care?

§ 10.3 Determining the Existence of Duty

Determining duty from policy, justice and relationships. How do courts go about determining whether to impose a duty of care? As courts have said, the existence of a duty is not a discoverable fact of nature,[34] but then no legal concept is. To say that the defendant is under a legal duty is merely a conclusion that the defendant should be subject to potential liability in the type of case in question. One of Prosser's most quoted passages had it that "duty is not sacrosanct in itself, but is only an expression of the sum total of those considerations of policy which lead the law to say that the plaintiff is entitled to protection."[35] Or as one court put it, "the question of whether a duty should be imposed in a particular case is essentially one of fairness under contemporary standards—whether reasonable persons would recognize a duty and agree that it exists."[36] These are assertions that duty should be constructed by courts from building blocks of policy and justice[37] with due regard for the relationship between the plaintiff and defendant.[38] And in terms of the trial process, a decision that the defendant is exempt from a duty of reasonable care can be appropriate only where those same issues of policy and justice cannot be considered by the trier of fact on the breach rather than the duty issue.

Prior formulations of factors to determine duty. By about 1960 courts were beginning to formulate some considerations of policy relevant to establishing or rejecting a duty of care. The California Supreme Court said it would consider (1) the extent to which the transaction was intended to affect the plaintiff, (2) the foreseeability of harm to him, (3) the degree of certainty that the plaintiff suffered injury, (4) the closeness of the connection between the defendant's conduct and the injury suffered, (5) the moral blame attached to the defendant's conduct, (6) the policy of preventing future harm by deterrence, and (7) administrative factors, including the feasibility of administering a

---

particularized facts of a given case, but rather on the basic nature of the relationship between the parties . . ."); Martinez v. Woodmar IV Condo. Homeowners Ass'n, 189 Ariz. 206, 941 P.2d 218 (1997) ("[W]e disapprove of attempts to equate the concepts of duty with specific details of conduct."); Marshall v. Burger King Corp., 222 Ill. 2d 422, 305 Ill. Dec. 897 (2006) (rejecting defendant's argument that defendant had no duty to erect posts protecting diners in its restaurant from intrusion by automobiles; defendant had a duty of care, whether posts were required to satisfy that duty is an issue about breach of that duty and for the jury).

[34] See Tarasoff v. Regents of the Univ. of Cal., 17 Cal.3d 425, 434, 551 P.2d 334, 342, 131 Cal.Rptr. 14, 22, 83 A.L.R.3d 1166 (1976) ("[L]egal duties are not discoverable facts of nature, but merely conclusory expressions that, in cases of a particular type, liability should be imposed for damage done."); Marshall v. Burger King Corp., 222 Ill. 2d 422, 305 Ill. Dec. 897 (2006).

[35] Prosser & Keeton on Torts § 54, at 358 (5th ed. 1984).

[36] Casebolt v. Cowan, 829 P.2d 352, 356 (Colo. 1992) (quoting).

[37] E.g., Remy v. MacDonald, 440 Mass. 675, 677, 801 N.E.2d 260, 262 (2004) ("Whether a duty exists is a question of common law, to be determined by 'reference to existing social values and customs and appropriate social policy.'").

[38] Marshall v. Burger King Corp., 222 Ill. 2d 422, 305 Ill. Dec. 897 (2006) (recognizing that duty is a policy issue and that policies are identified through relationship of the parties, foreseeability, and costs of imposing a duty). See John C.P. Goldberg & Benjamin C. Zipursky, The Moral of McPherson, 146 U. Pa. L. Rev. 1733 (1998) (emphasizing relationships of the parties, regarding that as distinct from policy).

rule that imposed a duty.[39] To this list can be added (8) the relationship of the parties[40] and the customs to which they jointly subscribe.[41] New York has named other factors, including expectations of the parties—presumably somewhat different from mere foreseeability.[42] Other courts have considered various other factors.[43]

Widespread criticism of vague factors in duty determinations. As these factors imply, the fact that harm is readily foreseeable to reasonable people is not necessarily sufficient to establish a duty.[44] But these factors are so numerous and so broadly stated that they can lead to almost any conclusion.[45] The factors reflect opinion and value judgments. And since courts do not assign relative weights to the policies or require any evidence to support the factual claims that lie behind them,[46] the vague general factors can simply cover the bias or political preferences of the judge who relies on them.

—Denigrating judicial process. The factors may have had negative effects on the judicial process, because they only furnish an outline for structuring judicial opinions in

---

[39] Amaya v. Home Ice, Fuel & Supply Co., 59 Cal.2d 295, 379 P.2d 513, 29 Cal.Rptr. 33 (1963), overruled in Dillon v. Legg, 68 Cal. 2d 728, 441 P.2d 912, 69 Cal. Rptr. 72 (1968), on its precise holding but not on its methodology. Dillon itself has been modified on its substantive point, without affecting the Amaya factors. Most of the Amaya factors were derived from Biakanja v. Irving, 49 Cal.2d 647, 320 P.2d 16, 65 A.L.R.2d 1358 (1958), not a personal injury case. Biakanja in turn derived them from treatises by Prosser and Harper & James. Perhaps because this history is cluttered, California courts and some writers sometimes simply attribute the factors to Rowland v. Christian, 69 Cal. 2d 108, 70 Cal. Rptr. 97, 443 P. 2d 561 (1968). See Ma v. City & Cty. of San Francisco, 95 Cal. App. 4th 488, 115 Cal. Rptr. 2d 544 (2002). A number of other states have adopted the California list with little or no revision. See, e.g., Rice v. Collins Commc'n, Inc., 236 P.3d 1009 (Wyo. 2010). Rowland was itself modified by West's Ann.Cal.Civ.Code § 847 in the case of certain felon trespassers.

[40] See, e.g., Marshall v. Burger King Corp., 222 Ill. 2d 422, 305 Ill. Dec. 897 (2006) (relationship of invitor-invitee established duty of reasonable care, and while other considerations may affect the existence of a duty, they did not create an exemption from duty once such a relationship was established); Griesi v. Atlantic Gen. Hosp. Corp., 360 Md. 1, 756 A.2d 548 (2000) (two major assessments in determining existence of a duty are "the nature of legal relationship between the parties and the likely harm that results from a party's failure to exercise reasonable care within that relationship"); Lough by Lough v. Rolla Women's Clinic, Inc., 866 S.W.2d 851 (Mo. 1993); Fu v. State, 263 Neb. 848, 643 N.W.2d 659 (2002) (reciting Nebraska's list, similar to California's, but including relationship of parties as the second factor). The existence of a relationship between defendant and plaintiff is usually one of the key grounds for imposing a duty of reasonable care, but the absence of a relationship is usually not a ground for ruling out a duty of care in ordinary physical harm cases. For example, one driving a motor vehicle owes a duty of care to strangers on the road. However, courts occasionally reject a duty of care even in active negligence cases in part on the ground that there is no relationship between the parties. See Doe v. Pharmacia & Upjohn Co., Inc., 388 Md. 407, 879 A.2d 1088 (2005).

[41] See Richard Epstein, The Path to the T.J. Hooper: The Theory and History of Custom in the Law of Tort, 21 J. Leg. Studies 1 (1992) (especially helpful on the question of who is to be bound by a custom).

[42] 532 Madison Ave. Gourmet Foods, Inc. v. Finlandia Ctr., Inc., 96 N.Y.2d 280, 288, 750 N.E.2d 1097, 1101, 727 N.Y.S.2d 49, 53 (2001) ("the reasonable expectations of parties and society generally, the proliferation of claims, the likelihood of unlimited or insurer-like liability, disproportionate risk and reparation allocation, and public policies affecting the expansion or limitation of new channels of liability").

[43] See Cleveland v. Rotman, 297 F.3d 569 (7th Cir. 2002) ("foreseeability, its likelihood, the magnitude of the burden of guarding against it, and the potential consequences of placing that burden on [defendant]"); Stephenson v. Universal Metrics, Inc., 251 Wis.2d 171, 641 N.W.2d 158 (2002) (whether "(1) the injury is too remote from the negligence; (2) the injury is too wholly out of proportion to the tortfeasor's culpability; (3) in retrospect it appears too highly extraordinary that the negligence should have brought about the harm; (4) allowing recovery would place too unreasonable a burden upon the tortfeasor; (5) allowing recovery would be too likely to open the way to fraudulent claims; or (6) allowing recovery would have no sensible or just stopping point").

[44] See, e.g., Cohen v. Cabrini Med. Ctr., 94 N.Y.2d 639, 730 N.E.2d 949, 709 N.Y.S.2d 151 (2000).

[45] See Stephenson v. Universal Metrics, Inc., 251 Wis.2d 171, 641 N.W.2d 158 (2002) (Abrahamson, C.J., dissenting) ("I apply the same six public policy considerations to the facts of the present case and conclude that none of them points to relieving Kreuser of liability in this case.").

[46] See W. Jonathan Cardi, A Pluralistic Analysis of the Therapist/Physician Duty to Warn Third Parties, 44 Wake Forest L. Rev. 877 (2009) (no hierarchy of value and few cases give empirical data).

the direction judges feel appropriate without actual analysis of policy or even the legal process implications.[47]

—Invading jury province. The factors used by the judges are often the very same factors that determine the negligence question. Yet when the question is phrased as a question of duty, the judge, not the jury, may become the decision-maker, evaluating risks created by the defendant, costs of avoiding them, and other such quintessential jury issues as foreseeability. Some courts recognize that they must not invade the jury's province, yet without explanation continue to determine the existence or non-existence of a duty by using factors the jury would consider on the breach issue.[48] Alternatively, the judge may attempt to avoid conflict with the jury's role by declaring that when a factor is relevant both to duty and to negligence or breach, something more is required to establish the duty. For example, it has been said that the moral blame factor on the duty issue requires more than negligence.[49] If that were true, there could never be a duty to exercise reasonable care, because the defendant would always have to be more blameworthy than that. Concomitantly, if the judge found moral blame on the duty issue, that finding of "more than negligence" would leave nothing for the jury to decide on the negligence issue. This would make a shambles of the whole trial process.

The Restatement Third's reaction against the multi-factor approach. The Third Restatement tackles the free-wheeling use of vague factors by three important provisions. First, the default rule, to be applied in all but the most exceptional cases of physical harm, is that everyone owes a duty of care not to create unreasonable risks to others.[50] This sidelines the vague policy factors by sidelining the duty issue itself in most injury cases. Second, foreseeability of harm is not a factor to be considered on the duty issue; it is considered where it has traditionally been considered, on the breach issue, normally by the jury.[51] This minimizes the risk that the court will simply declare its conclusion that harm was not foreseeable without appropriate respect for the trial process. Third, in exceptional cases, courts may consider several specific policy matters in determining whether to impose a duty of care, but these factors are quite different from the factors discussed above.

The Restatement's policy considerations. The Restatement recommends that courts take policy into account when deciding whether to immunize defendants from a duty of reasonable care. But the Restatement's policy considerations tend to channel analysis in specific points capable of articulation.[52] The Restatement rule makes it appropriate to consider exempting the defendant from the duty of reasonable care in five contexts. These are: (1) where a duty of care would conflict with social norms, as many courts seem to think would be the case if liability were imposed upon social hosts for providing alcohol to drunken guests who will leave driving vehicles;[53] (2) where a duty of care conflicts

---

[47]   Id. at 886 ("The typical opinion lists, or at best sketches, the relevant considerations and then simply announces a conclusion.").

[48]   E.g., Satterfield v. Breeding Insulation Co., 266 S.W.3d 347 (Tenn. 2008). However, the use of factors to *establish* duty rather than to *reject* it, as in Satterfield, does not invade the jury's province because the result is to leave the breach issue fully to the jury.

[49]   Ma v. City & Cty. of San Francisco, 95 Cal. App. 4th 488, 506, 115 Cal. Rptr. 2d 544, 557 (2002).

[50]   Restatement Third of Torts (Liability for Physical and Emotional Harm) § 7(a) (2010).

[51]   Id. § 7 cmt. j.

[52]   Id. § 7(b).

[53]   Id. § 7 cmt. c. It may be that the absence of public agreement on social norms is really more of an explanation than a conflict. At the time of the early seat belt cases, the public was quite divided about the seat belt requirement. The same may be true with social host liability for serving to drunken guests who will drive.

with another domain of law, as where economic torts should be dealt with under contract rules, not under negligence rules;[54] (3) where a duty of care would conflict with the relationship between plaintiff and defendant or perhaps with the defendant's other recognized rights;[55] (4) where a duty of care would engage the courts beyond their institutional competence, as where the plaintiff asserts that it is negligent to make motor vehicles at all;[56] and (5) where a duty of care would fail to defer to another branch of government.[57]

Support for the Restatement. Most commentators have expressed concerns and even distress at courts' multi-factored approach. The Restatement, in contrast, has garnered major support in its default duty approach coupled with its use of very pointed factors for exceptional cases.[58] Even those that take issue with particular aspects of the Restatement do not propose a return to the unstructured and vague factors for determining duty, but instead argue for less attention to the factors,[59] or for a principle that considers only narrower factors such as the autonomy interests of the parties and those that will be affected by a duty decision.[60]

Support for an ordinary duty of reasonable care. A general duty of *reasonable* care is by definition not burdensome. Nor does it leave juries free to bring in irrational verdicts, because the judge remains free to direct a verdict when, on the facts of a particular case, reasonable people could not differ. In the great majority of injury cases, the elaborate efforts to describe particular duties are both unnecessary and undesirable.

§ 10.4　Foreseeability and Duty Determinations

Foreseeability as a jury issue. A defendant whose conduct causes harm to another is not ordinarily responsible in tort unless a reasonable person in his position would have recognized the risk of harm. This means that liability is not imposed unless harm would have been foreseeable to a reasonable person—and not only foreseeable but recognizable as unreasonably probable. However, this foreseeability rule is a rule about what counts as breach, not a rule about duty to use reasonable care. Accordingly, foreseeability is addressed by juries on the negligence issue.

The judge's role. Judges have a supervisory role in this issue as on others: they determine whether the evidence presented at trial on the issue of foreseeability is sufficient for reasonable jurors to make a finding of foreseeability. If the judge concludes that reasonable people could not find foreseeability of harm, then the judge directs a verdict or otherwise removes the case from the jury's consideration, ultimately

---

The absence of general social agreement or at least acceptance suggests that juries would be likely to obtain diverse results—not depending on factual difference in the cases, but rather upon the accidental dominance of one norm over the other in particular juries.

[54]　Id. § 7 cmt. d.

[55]　Id. § 7 cmt. e.

[56]　Id. § 7 cmt. f.

[57]　Id. § 7 cmt. g.

[58]　See W. Jonathan Cardi & Michael D. Green, Duty Wars, 81 S. Cal. L. Rev. 671, 678 (2008); Aaron Twerski, The Cleaver, the Violin, and the Scalpel: Duty and the Restatement (Third) of Torts, 60 Hastings L.J. 1, 22–23 (2008); see also Gipson v. Kasey, 214 Ariz. 141, 150 P.3d 228 (2007).

[59]　John C.P. Goldberg & Benjamin C. Zipursky, Shielding Duty: How Attending to Assumption of Risk, Attractive Nuisance, and Other "Quaint" Doctrines Can Improve Decisionmaking in Negligence Cases, 79 S. Cal. L. Rev. 329 (2006).

[60]　Mark A. Geistfeld, Social Value as a Policy Based Limitation of the Ordinary Duty to Exercise Reasonable Care, 44 Wake Forest L. Rev. 899 (2009).

dismissing the claim because the defendant's negligence has not been established. This process does not yield a rule of law about duty or no duty; it merely determines that the evidence in the particular case was insufficient on the matter of breach.

Judge and jury. The distinction between adjudication of a case and announcing a general rule of law is important in marking the appropriate power of judge and jury. Yet some courts have imported considerations of foreseeability into the process of deciding whether a defendant has a duty to exercise care. The effect is to allow judges, who decide all issues of duty, to decide foreseeability,[61] bypassing the jury and short-circuiting full analysis of the case. The Restatement explicitly disapproves the use of foreseeability as a factor in determining the existence of a duty of care.[62] The Restatement's convincing argument, based on Professor Cardi's analysis,[63] was supported in some older cases[64] and has been quickly gaining acceptance in others in the few years since the Restatement Third was adopted.[65]

What are the objections to determining duty by deciding foreseeability of harm? Among the most important are these:

(1) Meaningful no-duty decisions by a court are always about broad categories of cases, not about particular facts of the case before the court. Foreseeability on particular facts is necessarily fact specific, and hence does not fit with the broad assessments of policy necessary for category-wide rulings.

(2) If foreseeability is injected into the duty decision, it is apt to shift the focus away from policies that arguably should or should not control the whole category without reference to individual assessment of negligence.[66]

(3) Foreseeability will be a critical issue in the case, but it will be considered under the negligence and "proximate cause" or scope of risk issues, so at the very best, the determination of foreseeability on the duty issue is duplicative.

(4) If the judges decide foreseeability and conclude it does not exist, they take over the role assigned by our jurisprudence to the jury.

(5) To dodge these objections, courts might attempt to claim that the foreseeability decided by judges is somehow different from the foreseeability

---

[61] Thus the California Supreme Court flatly announced: "Foreseeability, when analyzed to determine the existence or scope of a duty, is a question of law to be decided by the court." Ann M. v. Pacific Plaza Shopping Ctr., 6 Cal. 4th 666, 678, 25 Cal. Rptr. 2d 137, 145, 863 P.2d 207, 215 (1993), overruled on other grounds, Reid v. Google, Inc., 50 Cal. 4th 512, 522, 235 P.3d 988, 995 (2010). Some other courts agree. See Jupin v. Kask, 447 Mass. 141, 849 N.E.2d 829 (2006).

[62] Restatement Third of Torts (Liability for Physical and Emotional Harm) § 7 cmt. j (2010).

[63] W. Jonathan Cardi, Purging Foreseeability, 58 Vand. L. Rev. 739 (2005).

[64] See Staples v. CBL & Assocs., Inc., 15 S.W.3d 83 (Tenn. 2000) (Holder, J., concurring).

[65] Gipson v. Kasey, 214 Ariz. 141, 144, 150 P.3d 228, 231 (2007) ("Whether an injury to a particular plaintiff was foreseeable by a particular defendant necessarily involves an inquiry into the specific facts of an individual case.... The jury's fact-finding role could be undermined if courts assess foreseeability in determining the existence of duty as a threshold legal issue."); Thompson v. Kaczinski, 774 N.W.2d 829 (Iowa 2009); A.W. v. Lancaster Cty. Sch. Dist., 250 Neb. 205, 784 N.W.2d 907 (2010); Behrendt v. Gulf Underwriters Ins., 318 Wis.2d 622, 768 N.W.2d 568 (2009).

[66] See Restatement Third of Torts (Liability for Physical and Emotional Harm) § 7 cmt. j (2010) (policies for exempting actors from the usual duty of reasonable care should be explained without "obscuring references to foreseeability").

decided by juries, so that there is foreseeability[67] for the court and foreseeability for the jury.[68] This injection of wholly new conceptions, even if they can be made meaningful, is likely to carry unnecessary complications and deep confusions.

(6)   Courts' use of foreseeability to reject a duty of ordinary care actually undermines the rule of law, because it is used as a "cover" for discretion or bias; by seating foreseeability in the breach issue decided by the jury, judges' decisions will become more transparent.[69]

All this supports the Restatement view that judges should have very good reasons to exempt a category of people from the ordinary duty of reasonable care and should be able to state what those reasons are without determining matters like foreseeability that depend on the particular facts of one case.

B.   THE ORDINARY STANDARD OF REASONABLE CARE

§ 10.5   The Objective Reasonable Person Standard

Standard of care. In negligence law, when a duty is owed, the standard of conduct to which the defendant must conform is typically the standard of a reasonable person under the circumstances to avoid physical harms to others.[70] However, in some cases the standard of conduct may be different. For example, traditionally a common carrier was obliged to exercise the highest degree of care, and a landowner owed a licensee an obligation less than reasonable care. Judges are the ones who determine both whether a duty of care is owed and what standard of care should be applied.[71]

Generality of the reasonable care standard. In the latter half of the 19th century, courts began to develop a general standard of care describing the duty of all persons to exercise ordinary care, meaning the care of a reasonable person, for the benefit of other persons, not merely the particular duties of, say, a veterinarian to a farmer. The standard for determining negligence purports to apply unvaryingly to almost all negligence cases[72] except where courts consciously limit the duty or standard of care to protect certain classes of defendants.[73] It has been argued that the reasonable person standard is a product of people's fair expectations about how disputes will be resolved in

---

[67]   Some courts have said that foreseeability in the duty context is distinct from foreseeability in the context of breach or scope of liability, in that it is a more generalized inquiry on the duty issue. See, e.g., Mirjavadi v. Vakilzadeh, 310 Conn. 176, 74 A.3d 1278 (2013) (in the duty context, foreseeability is about whether an ordinary person in defendant's position "would anticipate that harm of the general nature of that suffered was likely to result," whereas foreseeability in the scope of liability determination is more specific); Whitt v. Silverman, 788 So.2d 210 (Fla. 2001) (distinguishing duty question based upon "general" foreseeability from breach and proximate cause questions, which turn on specific facts of the case); Robinson v. Vivirito, 217 N.J. 199, 86 A.3d 119 (2014) ("Foreseeability as a determinant of a duty to exercise care to another is distinguishable . . . from foreseeability as a determinant of whether a breach of duty proximately caused an injury.").

[68]   See, e.g., Clohesy v. Food Circus Supermarkets, Inc. 149 N.J. 496, 694 A.2d 1017 (1997); Stahlecker v. Ford Motor Co., 266 Neb. 601, 667 N.W.2d 244 (2003).

[69]   See W. Jonathan Cardi, Purging Foreseeability, 58 Vand. L. Rev. 739, 790–94 (2005).

[70]   Restatement Third of Torts (Liability for Physical and Emotional Harm) § 7 (2010)

[71]   See § 10.1.

[72]   E.g., Fox v. City & Cty. of San Francisco, 47 Cal. App. 3d 164, 120 Cal. Rptr. 779 (1975) ("[T]he standard of care is always the same—ordinary care under the circumstances"); Stewart v. Motts, 539 Pa. 596, 654 A.2d 535 (1995) ("[T]here is but one standard of care to be applied to negligence actions involving dangerous instrumentalities in this Commonwealth. This standard of care is 'reasonable care.' ").

[73]   See §§ 10.7 to 10.16.

tortious situations and that allowing these expectations to shape tort law tends to maximize social utility.[74]

More specific standards. It may be more accurate to say that the general duty or standard of ordinary care is a default rule,[75] a standard applied when there is no other more specific standard addressed to the particular parties or their particular situation and when the defendant has not undertaken some different level of care. The default standard of reasonable care yields to the law's lesser standard for children, for instance, and in medical malpractice cases the standard yields to the standard implicitly undertaken by the physician and based upon the custom of the medical community.[76] Nevertheless, for a great mass of cases, the general standard of ordinary or reasonable care is the standard courts apply.

Stating the general standard of care. The duty owed by all people generally—the standard of care—is the duty to exercise the care that would be exercised by a reasonable and prudent person[77] under the same or similar circumstances to avoid or minimize risks of harm to others.[78] Because no one tries to avoid risks that cannot be identified or harms that cannot be foreseen as a possibility, the reasonable person exercises care only about the kinds of harm that are foreseeable to reasonable people who have any extra knowledge the defendant has.[79] Even then, he uses care only to avoid inflicting risks that are sufficiently great to require precaution.[80] The reasonable person or due care standard applies also when the issue is the plaintiff's contributory negligence.[81]

A reasonable class member? Sometimes the "prudent person" is given an identity as a member of a class. For example, courts have come to say that the defendant must behave as a reasonable prudent physician, engineer, ship captain, plumber, or dog owner when he acts in one of those roles.[82] Such formulations combine a statement of the

---

[74]   David G. Owen, Expectations in Tort, 43 Ariz. St. L.J. 1287 (2011).

[75]   Andersen v. Two Dot Ranch, Inc., 49 P.3d 1011 (Wyo. 2002); see Restatement Third of Torts (Liability for Physical and Emotional Harm) § 7 (2010).

[76]   See Chapter 21.

[77]   Lugtu v. Cal. Highway Patrol, 26 Cal.4th 703, 110 Cal.Rptr.2d 528, 28 P.3d 249 (2001) ("Under general negligence principles, of course, a person ordinarily is obligated to exercise due care in his or her own actions so as not to create an unreasonable risk of injury to others."). Until quite recently, this standard was expressed as the standard of the reasonable man. With the effort to use gender-neutral phrases, that statement of the standard is in the process of being abandoned. In some cases, gender might matter in assessing foreseeable risks and where it does, it may (or may not) be considered as part of the circumstances based on policy considerations.

[78]   E.g., Mansfield v. Circle K. Corp., 877 P.2d 1130 (Okla. 1994) ("[T]he standard of conduct is that of a reasonably prudent person under the same or similar circumstances."); Gossett v. Jackson, 249 Va. 549, 457 S.E.2d 97 (1995) (negligence is "the failure to exercise 'that degree of care which an ordinarily prudent person would exercise under the same or similar circumstances to avoid injury to another' ").

[79]   Mobile Gas Serv. Corp. v. Robinson, 20 So.3d 770 (Ala. 2009); Mirjavadi v. Vakilzadeh, 74 A.3d 1278 (Conn. 2013) (foreseeability in the duty context is about whether an ordinary person in the position of the defendant would anticipate harm "of a general nature"). See § 12.2.

[80]   See §§ 12.3 & 12.4.

[81]   See § 16.2.

[82]   S.K. Whitty & Co. v. Laurence L. Lambert & Assocs., 576 So. 2d 599 (La. Ct. App. 1991) (engineer); Butcher v. Gay, 29 Cal. App. 4th 388, 34 Cal. Rptr. 2d 771 (1994) (dog owner); Fu v. State, 263 Neb. 848, 643 N.W.2d 659 (2002) ("reasonably prudent graduate student with [plaintiff's] level of education and experience"); Greenberg v. Giddings, 127 Vt. 242, 246 A.2d 832 (1968) (plumber); Pryal v. Mardesich, 51 Wash.2d 663, 321 P.2d 269 (1958) (captain); cf. Cerny v. Cedar Bluffs Junior/Senior Pub. Sch., 262 Neb. 66, 628 N.W.2d 697 (2001) (standard for high school sports coach holding certificate was that of a reasonable person holding such a certificate), on appeal after remand, 267 Neb. 958, 679 N.W.2d 198 (2004). Similarly, the reasonable care standard in employment is usually expressed by saying that an employer generally owes employees and contractors a reasonably safe place to work. E.g., Blair v. Campbell, 924 S.W.2d 75 (Tenn. 1996).

standard with an application of it to the facts. Although the standard for physicians and some other professionals has widely been regarded as a standard that differs from the reasonable person standard,[83] it seems fairly certain that not all such formulations are intended to represent a departure from the reasonable person standard. To speak of the reasonable dog owner is to speak of the reasonable person. One of the circumstances is that the defendant owns a dog with all the risks that dog ownership entails, so it is convenient to speak of the reasonable dog owner, and no harm is done by such a locution as long as no one thinks dog owners are relieved of the reasonable person standard or that canine ownership is the only circumstance of significance.

Terminology. The reasonable and prudent person standard of care is often described as the standard of ordinary care, due care, or reasonable care and the term unreasonable risk refers to a breach of that standard.[84] It may also be referred to as the reasonable person or prudent person standard. The terms are interchangeable, and they all refer to external conduct that would be dictated by "care" or "prudence," not to the prudent or careful state of mind. These terms are largely the terms of jury instructions and with only slight variations in expression, they are accepted everywhere.[85] The idea is that the jury would be able to say (for example) that 60 mph was faster than a reasonable prudent person would drive under the particular circumstances and therefore that the defendant who drove that speed was negligent.

Non-technical usages of "proving a standard." The term "standard" (or "duty") sometimes creeps into judicial discussions in a way that is informal at best and potentially confusing. Judges sometimes speak of "proving" a standard of care, for example, but since a standard is by definition set by the judge in the first place, there is never a question of proving the standard itself. Sometimes in locutions like this, judges mean that the plaintiff should prove facts that invoke one standard rather than another as being proper for the case. Or that the plaintiff must prove facts that show a *breach* or *violation* of the standard. It cannot be too often repeated that the standard itself is a general duty prescribed by law.[86]

Relation of reasonable person standard to risk. Courts project the reasonable person as an ideal to help themselves and juries estimate whether the defendant's harm-causing conduct was too risky. Apart from the risk of harms to others, courts are not interested in whether the defendant was unreasonable. The defendant may unreasonably invest in bags of fortune cookies in the belief that they predict the future, but such unreasonable

---

[83] See Chapter 21.

[84] United Blood Servs. v. Quintana, 827 P.2d 509 (Colo. 1992); Stewart v. Motts, 539 Pa. 596, 654 A.2d 535 (1995); Furman v. Rural Elec. Co., 869 P.2d 136 (Wyo. 1994); Restatement Third of Torts (Liability for Physical and Emotional Harm) § 3 cmt. A (2010). "Ordinary" care is not a reference to the statistical occurrence but to a value judgment. See Clarence Morris, Custom and Negligence, 42 Colum. L. Rev. 1147, 1157 (1942). That point can be logically verified by noting that custom (the ordinary practice) is not the standard of care. See §§ 12.6 to 12.9.

[85] Some judges have charged juries in some variation on the language of Baron Alderson in Blyth v. Birmingham Waterworks Co., 11 Ex. 781, 156 Eng.Rep. 1047 (1856): "Negligence is the omission to do something which a reasonable man, guided upon those considerations which ordinarily regulate the conduct of human affairs, would do, or doing something which a prudent and reasonable man would not do." Frequently this kind of language will be combined with both the reasonable person and due care or ordinary care language in a single instruction. E.g., Caliri v. State Dep't of Transp., 136 N.H. 606, 620 A.2d 1028 (1993) (quoting New Hampshire's standard negligence instruction).

[86] Cerny v. Cedar Bluffs Junior/Senior Pub. Sch., 262 Neb. 66, 628 N.W.2d 697 (2001), on appeal after remand, 267 Neb. 958, 679 N.W.2d 198 (2004).

behavior is not negligent because it creates no risks of harm to other people. So the reasonable person standard is always applied to judgments about risky behavior.

Making the reasonable care standard more specific. The legal system has developed a few ways to make the reasonable person standard a little more specific. First, courts invest the imaginary reasonable person with certain mental and physical characteristics. Second, courts may sidestep the effort to apply general standards by adopting specific rules about specific kinds of conduct such as speeding, condemning that conduct as at least prima facie negligence.[87] As a factual truth, courts sometimes make the standard of care more specific by assessing elements of breach such as weighing costs and benefits. However, factors related to breach fall within the province of the jury and an evaluation of those factors by the court in it's analysis of the standard of care supplants the jury's role, unless reasonable people could not differ.[88]

§ 10.6 Circumstances as Part of the Standard: Special Danger

The invariant standard. A defendant is actionably negligent only if he fails to use the care of a reasonable person under the circumstances to avoid known or foreseeable harm.[89] The standard does not change even if the situation is fraught with danger. The circumstances clause allows courts to take into account the fact that the danger is great or small as well as other factors bearing on reasonableness of the defendant's conduct.[90] But the standard itself remains the same—reasonable care commensurate with known and reasonably foreseeable danger and other circumstances.[91]

The firearm illustration. Firearm cases illustrate how the reasonable person standard calls for the right amount of care in a dangerous situation. Suppose the defendant is handling a firearm. Instead of saying that because of its deadly potential, the defendant must meet some higher standard of care, courts only demand that the defendant act as a reasonable person under the circumstances.[92] One of those circumstances is the fact that weapons can kill and cause grave injury. So the *conduct* of a reasonable person handling such a firearm will differ from the conduct he would use if he were handling a fish. The *standard* of care is the same in either case, but the amount of attention or energy called for by that standard will vary with the circumstance of heightened danger. In short, the reasonable person standard requires the defendant to

---

[87] See Chapter 9.

[88] See, e.g., Brokaw v. Winfield-Mt. Union Cmty. Sch. Dist., 788 N.W.2d 386 (Iowa 2010) (because reasonable minds could disagree with respect to factual questions, issue of whether basketball coach should have foreseen that basketball player would strike opposing team player should be left to jury decision); Restatement Third of Torts (Liability for Physical and Emotional Harm) § 3 (2010).

[89] Vazquez-Filippetti v. Banco Popular de Puerto Rico, 504 F.3d 43 (1st Cir. 2007); Boyd v. Moore, 184 Ohio App.3d 16, 919 N.E.2d 283 (2009).

[90] Danger, magnitude of the potential harm and the probability of that harm are key factors in determining reasonable care. These are considered in Chapter 12.

[91] Coburn v. City of Tucson, 143 Ariz. 50, 52, 691 P.2d 1078, 1080 (1984) ("[T]he duty remains constant, while the conduct necessary to fulfill it varies with the circumstances"); Sansonni v. Jefferson Par. Sch. Bd., 344 So. 2d 42 (La. Ct. App. 1977); Stewart v. Motts, 539 Pa. 596, 654 A.2d 535 (1995); Restatement Second of Torts § 298 cmt. b (1965).

[92] Purtle v. Shelton, 251 Ark. 519, 474 S.W.2d 123, 47 A.L.R.3d 609 (1971); Tucker v. Lombardo, 47 Cal. 2d 457, 303 P.2d 1041 (1956); Mikula v. Duliba, 94 A.D.2d 503, 464 N.Y.S.2d 910 (1983).

use ordinary care commensurate with dangers and harms known to him or foreseeable to a reasonable person.[93]

Commensurate care in other cases. These rules of care apply to all kinds of cases. They most obviously apply in cases of heightened danger, as where the defendant is handling toxic substances[94] or firearms, or supplying gas or electricity.[95] But it is not limited to especially dangerous substances. The driver who sees children playing near the road must exercise care commensurate with the recognized danger that children may dart out into the road,[96] and the driver who knows he cannot detect a train on an obstructed track must take his own ignorance into account.[97] The owner of a dog must act on the possibility that the dog will escape,[98] and the operator of a swimming pool must use care proportioned to the risks that arise when non-swimmers are allowed in the pool,[99] and when young children are swimming, the care required of the pool operator may be greater.[100] The risk of a customer's fall in a retail store is small, but if an area of the store has a high volume of customer traffic, the retailer must take that risk into account and act with commensurate care.[101] What counts as care commensurate with the risks is the essential question of breach, sometimes called the negligence question. That question is determined by the facts; even if danger is great, it may be that a warning to the plaintiff will suffice to show reasonable care.[102]

Expressions requiring extraordinary care. When the defendant confronts heightened danger, it may seem easier to say that he must exercise the highest care than to explain the full meaning of the reasonable person standard. Perhaps for this reason, courts have often said they required the utmost care, or extraordinary care, or the highest care when it comes to handling a firearm, or supplying gas or electricity.[103] Opinions that speak in

---

[93] Doe v. Andujar, 297 Ga.App. 696, 678 S.E.2d 163 (2009) (care commensurate with the reasonably foreseeable risk of harm); Anderson v. Nashua Corp., 246 Neb. 420, 519 N.W.2d 275 (1994); Stewart v. Motts, 539 Pa. 596, 654 A.2d 535 (1995).

[94] Imperial Distrib. Servs., Inc. v. Forrest, 741 P.2d 1251 (Colo. 1987); United States v. Stevens, 994 So. 2d 1062 (Fla. 2008) (lab handling anthrax).

[95] Schultz v. Consumers Power Co., 443 Mich. 445, 506 N.W.2d 175 (1993).

[96] Thomas v. Newman, 262 Ark. 42, 553 S.W.2d 459 (1977); Finch v. Christensen, 84 S.D. 420, 172 N.W.2d 571 (1969); cf. Aycock v. Wilmington & W. R. Co., 51 N.C. 231 (1858) (cattle on or near railroad track, engineer should reduce speed and prepare for an emergency stop).

[97] Moore v. Burlington N. R.R., 41 P.3d 1029 (Okla. Civ. App. 2001).

[98] DeRobertis ex rel. DeRobertis v. Randazzo, 94 N.J. 144, 462 A.2d 1260 (1983).

[99] Johnson ex rel. Johnson v. Young Men's Christian Ass'n of Great Falls, 201 Mont. 36, 651 P.2d 1245 (1982).

[100] Chavez v. Cedar Fair, LP, 450 S.W.3d 291, 294 (Mo. 2014), as modified on denial of reh'g (Dec. 23, 2014) (while the facts underlying each situation "may not alter the legal standard of care required to avoid an accident," the underlying facts "often multiply the precautions that must be observed to comply with the standard").

[101] See Jones v. Brookshire Grocery Co., 847 So.2d 43 (La. Ct. App. 2003) ("[T]he degree of vigilance must be commensurate with the risk involved, as determined by the overall volume of business, the time of day, the section of the store and other relevant considerations").

[102] Thus in Hopkins v. Miss. Valley Gas Co., 866 So.2d 514 (Miss. Ct. App. 2004), a gas company reconnecting the plaintiff's hot water heater removed a container of gasoline near the heater and warned the plaintiff against storing it in the same room. This was sufficient care.

[103] E.g., Lee v. Hartwig, 848 S.W.2d 496 (Mo. Ct. App. 1992) (firearms); Blueflame Gas, Inc. v. Van Hoose, 679 P.2d 579 (Colo. 1984) (propane gas); Valiant Ins. v. City of LaFayette, 574 So.2d 505 (La. Ct. App. 1991) (electricity); Wood v. Groh, 269 Kan. 420, 7 P.3d 1163 (2000) (firearm; instruction on higher care required); Kimberlin v. PM Transport, 563 S.E.2d 665 (Va. 2002) (regulation required truck drivers to use "extreme caution" in fog and where traction is diminished, treated as creating an "expanded duty"); cf. J. D. Cousins & Sons, Inc. v. Hartford Steam Boiler Inspection & Ins., 341 F.3d 149 (2d Cir. 2003) (saying that the standard of care increases as the risk increases); United States v. Stevens, 994 So.2d 1062 (Fla. 2008) ("[T]he

such language probably mean only what has already been said, that the defendant must act as a reasonable person under the circumstances and that a reasonable person will normally conduct himself in accordance with the dangers reasonably to be perceived.[104] This is borne out by the fact that when courts actually focus on the issue, they tend to say that the reasonable care standard sufficiently covers the case[105] and that instructions on a higher standard of care would be error.[106]

Most instructions and discussions of commensurate care emphasize the added effort needed when danger is especially prominent, but the underlying point is much broader. Special danger is one, but only one circumstance bearing on the reasonableness of any given risk. The circumstance that safety is especially costly, or that it runs risks to other persons, is also an important circumstance. The relationship of the parties might be another. So the care required is not strictly the care commensurate with danger alone, but care commensurate with all the circumstances, including the probabilities that harm will result.

C. PARTICULAR CIRCUMSTANCES RELATED TO THE STANDARD OF CARE

§ 10.7 Emergency and Unavoidable Accident

Emergency as a circumstance to be considered. When an unforeseeable danger arises and alternative action is possible but requires quick judgment, courts often refer to the "emergency doctrine."[107] If an actor is confronted with a sudden and unforeseeable emergency not of the actor's own making, the jury is permitted to consider the emergency as one of the circumstances relevant in determining whether the actor behaved reasonably.[108] Put differently, even reasonable persons may conduct themselves in response to an emergency in ways that would not be reasonable if time permitted more thoughtful decision-making.[109] Legal issues arise mainly because defendants frequently ask the trial judge to give an instruction specifically authorizing the jury to consider the emergency in determining negligence, or the related instruction that the defendant is not liable for unavoidable accident.

Rationale. Although it is convenient to refer to this idea as the emergency doctrine, it is not, properly speaking, a doctrine at all. It is instead merely an application of the

---

greater the risk of harm to others that is created by a person's chosen activity, the greater the burden or duty to avoid injury to others becomes.").

[104] See Tucker v. Lombardo, 47 Cal. 2d 457, 303 P.2d 1041 (1956); Mikula v. Duliba, 94 A.D.2d 503, 464 N.Y.S.2d 910 (1983).

[105] E.g., Adams v. N. Ill. Gas Co., 211 Ill. 2d 32, 809 N.E.2d 1248, 1258, 284 Ill. Dec. 302, 312 (2004); First Assembly of God, Inc. v. Tex. Utils. Elec. Co., 52 S.W.3d 482 (Tex. App. 2001) ("[A] public utility has a duty to exercise ordinary and reasonable care, but the degree of care required must be commensurate with the danger. This 'commensurate with the danger' standard does not impose a higher duty of care; rather, it more fully defines what is ordinary care under the facts presented.").

[106] Stewart v. Motts, 539 Pa. 596, 605, 654 A.2d 535, 539 (1995).

[107] See Henson v. Klein, 319 S.W.3d 413 (Ky. 2010); Scott ex rel. Scott v. Iverson, 120 Or. App. 538, 853 P.2d 302 (1992).

[108] Willis v. Westerfield, 839 N.E.2d 1179 (Ind. 2006); Regenstreif v. Phelps, 142 S.W.3d 1 (Ky. 2004); Kreidt v. Burlington N. R.R., 615 N.W.2d 153 (N.D. 2000) ("The sudden emergency doctrine is not so much a doctrine as an illustration of how negligence law is applied in a specific situation."); Restatement Second of Torts § 296(1) (1965).

[109] Restatement Third of Torts (Liability for Physical and Emotional Harm) § 9 cmt. b (2010), suggests that emergency be defined functionally—as an event that prevents reasonable persons from exercising the good judgment they ordinarily exercise.

reasonable person under the circumstances standard, with the emergency as one of the circumstances.[110] That necessarily means that if the facts show grounds on which reasonable jurors could differ, the existence of an emergency is a jury question.[111] It also means that since emergency is merely a fact bearing on the reasonable person's care in the circumstance, the emergency doctrine is not a defense and the burden of proof does not shift.[112]

Departing from the rationale. Some courts have complicated the generally accepted understanding of emergency doctrine by saying that it is a defense[113] or that it lowers the standard of care.[114] It has also been called an "excuse."[115] And the whole idea was once explained, not on principle at all, but on the ground that it could be applied on the contributory negligence issue to assist plaintiffs who might otherwise be barred entirely.[116] Sometimes it is difficult to determine whether courts so expressing themselves are merely using loose shorthand language or whether they are seriously postulating a rule inconsistent with the general standard of reasonable care.

Examples. Although sudden and unforeseen emergencies can arise in almost any context,[117] most of the emergency instruction cases involve motor vehicle collisions. The defendant driver is confronted with a sudden threat from another vehicle—it veers into his lane, or suddenly begins backing toward him, or suddenly blocks the defendant's lane of traffic.[118] Or the defendant encounters unforeseeable ice on the road,[119] or suffers a stroke.[120] There are as many variations as there are unexpected dangers. In each case, the defendant steers his own vehicle to avoid the danger, but in doing so he collides with the plaintiff's car or perhaps overturns his own vehicle causing injury to a passenger.

---

[110] See, e.g., Hagenow v. Schmidt, 842 N.W.2d 661, 673 (Iowa 2014) ("Unlike the doctrine of legal excuse—which exonerates a party from liability for negligence per se—the sudden emergency doctrine is merely an expression of the reasonably prudent person standard of care."). See also Regenstreif v. Phelps, 142 S.W.3d 1 (Ky. 2004); Caristo v. Sanzone, 96 N.Y.2d 172, 750 N.E.2d 36, 726 N.Y.S.2d 334 (2001); Restatement Third of Torts (Liability for Physical and Emotional Harm) § 9 (2010).

[111] Hesse v. McClintic, 176 P.3d 759 (Colo. 2008); White v. Taylor Distrib. Co., 482 Mich. 136, 753 N.W.2d 591 (2008); Maglioli v. J.P. Noonan Transp., Inc., 869 A.2d 71 (R.I. 2005).

[112] Vahdat v. Holland, 274 Va. 417, 424, 649 S.E.2d 691, 695 (2007).

[113] Potochnick v. Perry, 861 A.2d 277 (Pa. Super. Ct. 2004) (instruction told jury that burden of proof of emergency was on the defendant, but it does not appear that defendant objected to the instruction on that ground). In Willis v. Westerfield, 839 N.E.2d 1179 (Ind. 2006), the court emphasized that the sudden emergency doctrine was merely a recognition that "emergency is . . . one of the circumstances to be considered in determining whether the actor's conduct was reasonable under all of the circumstances," and consequently that it was not an affirmative defense that the defendant was required to plead. At the same time, however, the court said that a party asserting the sudden emergency doctrine "bears the burden of proof."

[114] See, e.g., Hargrove v. McGinley, 766 A.2d 587 (Me. 2001) (unchallenged assertion that one confronted with an emergency "is not to be held to the same standard of conduct normally applied to one who is in no such situation").

[115] See Totsky v. Riteway Bus Serv., Inc., 233 Wis.2d 371, 607 N.W.2d 637 (2000).

[116] See Moran v. Atha Trucking, 540 S.E.2d 903 (W. Va. 1997).

[117] *Aviation*: Bolick v. Sunbird Airlines, 96 N.C. App. 443, 386 S.E.2d 76 (1989) aff'd per curiam, 327 N.C. 464, 396 S.E.2d 323 (1990); *Medical needs*: Doe v. State, 588 N.Y.S.2d 698 (Ct. Cl. 1992).

[118] Wilson v. Sibert, 535 P.2d 1034 (Alaska 1975); Thomson v. Littlefield, 319 Ark. 648, 893 S.W.2d 788 (1995).

[119] E.g., Regenstreif v. Phelps, 142 S.W.3d 1 (Ky. 2004); Posas v. Horton, 228 P.3d 457 (Nev. 2010); Sullivan v. Fairmont Homes, Inc., 543 N.E.2d 1130 (Ind. Ct. App. 1989).

[120] Hagenow v. Schmidt, 842 N.W.2d 661, 673 (Iowa 2014).

The emergency doctrine contemplates that the actor has only a limited time for decisions and actions.[121]

Negligence in causing or failing to prevent emergency. More broadly, emergency does not explain the defendant's conduct that occurred before the emergency. The defendant who negligently creates an emergency does not escape liability on the ground that, once the emergency occurred, he behaved reasonably.[122] So the emergency instruction may be inappropriate when the emergency is created in whole or part by the defendant's negligence.[123]

Foreseeable dangers. An emergency is by definition unexpected. If a danger is foreseeable and can be prepared for, its arrival is no emergency at all. For example, a driver who encounters ice on the road has notice of danger and he does not face an emergency when he encounters more ice a few minutes later.[124] Even without specific notice, a driver can anticipate that cars ahead may stop suddenly,[125] and that, near a playground, children may run into the street as the car approaches.[126] If those things happen, the driver cannot claim emergency. He is not necessarily negligent in such a case, but the question of his negligence is to be judged with the expectation that he would be prepared for such events, not with the expectation that he would be unable to cope with them. The same thing is true with a physician or surgeon suddenly confronted with complications in the course of a medical procedure; if they are complications that he should reasonably be prepared for, there is no emergency in the legal sense.[127]

Contemporary limitation on emergency instructions. Many courts are now concerned that emergency instructions themselves are both unnecessary and undesirable.[128] A number have consequently held that trial judges should no longer give instructions on

---

[121] See Petefish ex rel. v. Dawe, 137 Ariz. 570, 672 P.2d 914 (1983); Restatement Third of Torts (Liability for Physical and Emotional Harm) § 9 (2010).

[122] Howell v. Cahoon, 236 Va. 3, 372 S.E.2d 363 (1988); Restatement Second of Torts § 296(2) (1965).

[123] E.g., Posas v. Horton, 228 P.3d 457 (Nev. 2010); Brown v. Spokane Cty. Fire Prot. Dist. No. 1, 100 Wash.2d 188, 668 P.2d 571 (1983). Restatement Third of Torts (Liability for Physical and Emotional Harm) § 9 cmt. d (2010).

[124] Caristo v. Sanzone, 96 N.Y.2d 172, 750 N.E.2d 36, 726 N.Y.S.2d 334 (2001); Daly v. McFarland, 812 N.W.2d 113 (Minn. 2012) (snowdrift was "a normal hazard of snowmobiling," and therefore could not create an "emergency situation"); Lifson v. City of Syracuse, 17 N.Y.3d 492, 934 N.Y.S.2d 38, 958 N.E.2d 72 (2011) (sun glare that temporarily blinded motorist was not a "sudden and unexpected circumstance," thus the giving of an emergency instruction was error); Herr v. Wheeler, 634 S.E.2d 317 (Va. 2006) (in rainstorm sheets of water that could lead to hydroplaning are foreseeable, hence no emergency).

[125] E.g., Beyer v. Todd, 601 N.W.2d 35 (Iowa 1999); Posas v. Horton, 228 P.3d 457 (Nev. 2010) (driver who was following too closely rear-ended the car in front of her when it stopped suddenly to avoid hitting a jaywalking woman pushing a stroller); Chodorov v. Eley, 239 Va. 528, 391 S.E.2d 68 (1990).

[126] Cf. Weiss v. Bal, 501 N.W.2d 478 (Iowa 1993) (to one driving through school parking lot after basketball game, the appearance of pedestrians crossing the traveled way to reach their cars was not uncommon and not an emergency).

[127] Mertsaris v. 73rd Corp., 105 A.D.2d 67, 482 N.Y.S.2d 792 (1984); Olinger v. Univ. Med. Ctr., 269 S.W.3d 560 (Tenn. Ct. App. 2008) ("because of a physician's training and background, the sudden emergency doctrine has a limited application in medical malpractice cases;" but the doctrine applies when the medical events present a sudden difficulty which the physician could not have anticipated and for which physicians are not trained).

[128] Bedor v. Johnson, 202 P.3d 924 (Colo. 2013) (reviewing all of the arguments against emergency instructions, and abolishing their use; "the instruction's diminished utility in light of the comparative negligence statute is greatly outweighed by its potential to mislead the jury").

emergency,[129] unavoidable accident,[130] or mere happening,[131] or that if such instructions are given, that they should be used rarely or with caution.[132] Short of this, courts may simply uphold a trial judge's refusal to give the instruction on the ground that the general negligence instruction with its fault standard is sufficient to permit all the jury arguments that would be made under an emergency instruction.[133]

Rationales for rejecting the instructions. The tradition of giving some or all of the instructions probably reflected the view that juries should be channeled as narrowly as possible by specific rules. The reluctance some judges now feel about those instructions may reflect the opposite view that juries can work fairly with guiding principles and rules in light of counsels' argument on both sides.

Statutes creating defenses or immunities in quasi-emergencies. Statutes have created rules that go beyond the emergency doctrine for at least two specific situations involving urgent demands that would not necessarily qualify for the emergency doctrine. One kind of statute makes a special provision for emergency vehicles such as ambulances, fire engines, or police vehicles. Some of these statutes require reasonable care under the circumstances,[134] but others do not, with the result that the operator of an emergency vehicle is not only privileged to disobey traffic rules but also to drive negligently; he is liable only if he goes beyond negligence and acts recklessly.[135] Under these latter decisions, the statutory provisions in effect provide a lower standard of care. States have also adopted statutes providing special protections to doctors and sometimes

[129] Lyons v. Midnight Sun Transp. Servs., Inc., 928 P.2d 1202 (Alaska 1996); Wiles v. Webb, 329 Ark. 108, 946 S.W.2d 685 (1997); Knapp v. Stanford, 392 So.2d 196 (Miss. 1980); Simonson v. White, 220 Mont. 14, 713 P.2d 983 (1986), Bjorndal v. Weitman, 344 Or. 470, 480–81, 184 P.3d 1115, 1121 (2008) ("at least as used in vehicle accident cases . . . it should not be given"). See also Fla. Standard Jury Instructions in Civil Cases 4.8 (Comment); Ill. Pattern Jury Instructions (Civ.3d) 12.02.; Mo. Approved Instructions (MAI) 1.04 ("No 'sudden emergency' instructions may be given.").

[130] Butigan v. Yellow Cab Co. of Cal., 49 Cal.2d 652, 320 P.2d 500, 65 A.L.R.2d 1 (1958); Tolbert v. Duckworth, 262 Ga. 622, 423 S.E.2d 229, 21 A.L.R.5th 852 (1992); Fry v. Carter, 375 Md. 341, 825 A.2d 1042 (2003); Hancock-Underwood v. Knight, 277 Va. 127, 670 S.E.2d 720 (2009).

[131] Kennelly v. Burgess, 337 Md. 562, 654 A.2d 1335 (1995). In medical malpractice cases, closely analogous instructions are to the effect that the doctor is not liable for an honest mistake or that he is not a guarantor or insurer of good results. Some courts have rejected such instructions, as in, e.g., Riggins v. Mauriello, D.O., 603 A.2d 827 (Del. 1992); Nestorowich v. Ricotta, 767 N.E.2d 125, 740 N.Y.S.2d 668 (2002); Pleasants v. Alliance Corp., 209 W.Va. 39, 543 S.E.2d 320 (2001); but others maintain them, e.g., Nowatske v. Osterloh, 198 Wis.2d 419, 543 N.W.2d 265 (1996), modified as to the test of harmless error, Nommensen v. American Cont'l Ins., 246 Wis.3d 132, 629 N.W.2d 301 (2001).

[132] Myhaver v. Knutson, 189 Ariz. 286, 942 P.2d 445 (1997) (emergency; good review of authorities); Vahdat v. Holland, 274 Va. 417, 649 S.E.2d 691 (2007) ("Whether the circuit court erred by giving any jury instruction on the sudden emergency doctrine is not before us. Nonetheless, we reiterate, the grant of a sudden emergency instruction is rarely appropriate.").

[133] Kreidt v. Burlington N. R.R., 615 N.W.2d 153 (N.D. 2000).

[134] Torres v. City of Los Angeles, 58 Cal. 2d 35, 372 P.2d 906, 22 Cal.Rptr. 866 (1962); Frazier v. Commonwealth, 845 A.2d 253, 260 (Pa. Commw. Ct. 2004) ("[W]hile drivers of emergency vehicles are granted conditional privileges to operate in a manner inconsistent with the Vehicle Code, they must still drive with due regard under the circumstances."); cf. Eklund v. Trost, 151 P.3d 870 (Mont. 2006) (high-speed police chase; in requiring due care, the emergency vehicle statute created a special duty to the narrow class of persons who might be in such chases, so the public duty doctrine did not eliminate the defendant's duty of care).

[135] Saarinen v. Kerr, 84 N.Y.2d 494, 620 N.Y.S.2d 297, 644 N.E.2d 988 (1994); Robbins v. City of Wichita, 285 Kan. 455, 172 P.3d 1187 (2007) (listing many cases on both sides of the issue and considering other issues under the statutes as well). Louisiana has held that the plaintiff must prove reckless disregard when the driver of the emergency vehicle has met all the conditions of the statute (audible signals, responding to emergency rather than returning and others); but the reasonable care standard applies when the driver has not met all the statutory conditions. Lenard v. Dilley, 805 So.2d 175 (La. 2002).

others who provide care in certain emergencies. The statues usually eliminate liability for negligence altogether, leaving liability only for reckless or gross derelictions.[136]

§ 10.8 Objective and Subjective Features of the Standard

Standard as objective. The reasonable person care standard is very largely but not entirely objective. The first clause in the standard demands the safety efforts that a reasonable person would make. The standard applies to cases generally, and it is objective because it demands conduct that might be easy enough for the hypothetical reasonable person but that might be difficult for the real and particular defendant. The standard holds the actual defendant mainly to the standards of the ideal reasonable person rather than to the real-life defendant's own best judgment or ability.

Characteristics of reasonable people. When we ask about the characteristics of the reasonable person against whom the defendant is judged, we find that the standard is in part objective. The reasonable person whose standards the defendant must meet is said to have reasonable prudence as well as these attributes:

(1) normal intelligence;[137] and

(2) normal perception, memory, and at least a minimum of standard knowledge.[138]

However, the standard is also in part, subjective. The reasonable person also has these attributes:

(1) all the additional intelligence, skill, or knowledge actually possessed by the individual actor; and[139]

(2) the physical attributes of the actor himself.[140]

Semi-subjective components. The first set of attributes in effect insists on the objective standard. The defendant whose intelligence is less than normal, for instance, is still held to the objective reasonable person standard. He cannot escape liability by doing his own, personal or subjective best. On the other hand, the second set of attributes could be seen as subjective standards because they refer us to the defendant's own special intelligence or skills and his own special physical characteristics. Even these latter items, however, call for a kind of objective judgment. The objective reasonable person would surely use any special physical or mental abilities he might have to avoid unreasonable risks to others, and would take into account any physical limitations or gifts he might have for the same purposes. So in an important practical sense, all of these attributes of the reasonable person ask us to judge the defendant's conduct by a largely objective standard.

Circumstances alter cases. The other clause in the standard "reasonable care under the circumstances" emphasizes the particular facts of the particular case—the circumstances. This is not necessarily a subjective standard; it does not ask whether the defendant is to be excused because he was having a bad day or held to an especially high standard because he had a good night's sleep. Instead, it tells us that what counts as

---

[136] E.g., Cal. Bus. & Prof. Code § 1627.5 (2015) (excuses liability altogether as long as the doctor was in good faith).

[137] See § 10.10.

[138] See § 10.12.

[139] Id.

[140] See § 10.9.

reasonable care will vary with the risks presented. The reasonable person will exercise care commensurate with the danger.[141] Perhaps, for example, a reasonable person would slow down when driving near a group of playing children, but not when driving past a pile of cardboard boxes.

Flexibility from consideration of circumstances. The circumstances clause also has a forgiving aspect. For example, if the defendant was required to act in an emergency not of his own creation, he might react differently than would be reasonable if he had greater time for contemplation. Measuring the defendant's conduct against that of the hypothetical reasonable person under the circumstances, including the circumstance of emergency, we may think the defendant not negligent, even though such a reaction time might be counted as negligence if there were no emergency at all.[142] The circumstances clause brings flexibility and common sense to the standard.

Adding content to the reasonable person. All this is very well, but exceedingly abstract. For practical judgments about negligence, judges and jurors need considerably more than to be told to demand reasonableness. A degree of concrete content can be added to the reasonable person formula by specifying the kinds of mental or physical abilities the defendant must use to avoid creating unreasonable risks to others. This is conventionally done by saying that the reasonable person has certain attributes of mind and body and that he uses them in certain ways. The next sections discuss the attributes of the hypothetical reasonable person.

§ 10.9   Physical Characteristics

Physical disabilities. The reasonable person standard becomes partly subjective when it comes to physical attributes of the defendant. Except in the case of voluntary intoxication in which the actor's limitations are ignored,[143] one with physical illness or other physical disability is held to the standard of a reasonable person having such a disability, not to a standard of some ideal or average physical capacity.[144] A short or unsighted person is not expected to see and avoid danger that could only be perceived by a taller or sighted person. One with a hearing loss is not expected to hear approaching danger.[145] The same idea applies to other physical disabilities or limitations.[146]

Protective aspects of the rule for disabled persons. (a) Known physical traits. Sometimes this rule is discussed as if it were especially protective of persons with

---

[141] E.g., Sheehan v. Roche Bros. Supermarkets, 448 Mass. 780, 863 N.E.2d 1276 (2007) (recognizing rule); Hojnowski v. Vans Skate Park, 187 N.J. 323, 901 A.2d 381 (2006) ("care commensurate with the nature of the risk, foreseeability of injury, and fairness in the circumstances"); Mobile Gas Serv. Corp. v. Robinson, 20 So.3d 770 (Ala. 2009) ("[C]are commensurate with the dangers involved . . . is the same degree of care and vigilance which persons of skill and prudence observe under like circumstances."); see 1 Dobbs, Hayden & Bublick, The Law of Torts § 141 (2d ed. 2011 & Supp.).

[142] See 1 Dobbs, Hayden & Bublick, The Law of Torts § 142 (2d ed. 2011 & Supp.).

[143] See id. § 133.

[144] Muse v. Page, 125 Conn. 219, 4 A.2d 329 (1939); Mem'l Hosp. of S. Bend, Inc. v. Scott, 261 Ind. 27, 300 N.E.2d 50 (1973); Restatement Third of Torts (Liability for Physical and Emotional Harm) § 11(a) (2010); Restatement Second of Torts § 283C (1965).

[145] Fink v. City of New York, 206 Misc. 79, 132 N.Y.S.2d 172 (Sup. Ct. 1954) ("deaf mute" could not hear siren of approaching fire truck, but used his eyes in reliance on a stop light; held, he was not guilty of contributory negligence).

[146] Advanced age is not itself a disability, but courts have sometimes treated age as correlative with or evidence of some kinds of physical limitation. See Plunkett v. Brooklyn Heights R.R., 129 App. Div. 572, 114 N.Y.S. 276 (1908), aff'd per curiam, 198 N.Y. 568, 92 N.E.2d 1098 (1910); cf. Stewart v. Gibson Prods. Co. of Natchitoches Par, 300 So.2d 870 (La. Ct. App. 1974) (court treated age as correlative with frailty).

disabilities or physical limitations.[147] Sometimes that is true. The rule says in effect that an unsighted person is not to be considered negligent merely by going out into the world.[148] The rule forestalls the specious argument that an unsighted person would be negligent in crossing the street because the standard reasonable person would not close his eyes while crossing.[149]

(b) Unknown physical traits, sudden incapacity. The rule also helps protect the defendant who is reasonably unaware of a physical limitation or disability until it results in harm. The defendant who is suddenly and unforeseeably incapacitated while driving, as the result of a heart attack or seizure may lose substantial control of his vehicle and inflict great harm, but even if his movements count as action and not merely as a reflex, he is not in violation of the reasonable person standard and not liable for the harm done, so long as the physical seizure was in fact unforeseeable.[150] This has sometimes been referred to as an affirmative defense,[151] but it actually rests on the proposition that the defendant is judged by his own physical capacity and is simply not negligent unless he knows or should know that he may become incapacitated.

The demanding side of the rule for disabled persons. The physical disability rule is not always protective of disabled persons. First, a disability does not necessarily prevent a person from acting to secure reasonable safety and if it does not, it is irrelevant to the negligence issue.[152]

More importantly, a person with physical disabilities or limitations must still act as a reasonable person with those limitations in mind. To the extent that a reasonable person with similar limitations would do so, a disabled person must adjust for limitations by using other senses or by altering conduct to minimize the risks created by the disability.[153] For example, one who is of small stature and cannot reach the brake pedals, may be negligent in driving a car not equipped with hand controls; a reasonable person of such stature would not drive without being able to stop the car.[154] A person with failing vision may be expected to take special precautions to meet the standard of reasonable

---

[147] Prosser saw the rule as reflecting the disabled person's entitlement "to live in the world." Prosser & Keeton § 32, p. 176.

[148] See Harris v. Uebelhoer, 75 N.Y. 169 (1878) (we are all blind on a dark night; we are not required to stay at home but to exercise reasonable care when we go out); Knoxville Optical Supply, Inc. v. Thomas, 1993 WL 574 (Tenn. Ct. App. 1993).

[149] Warren A. Seavey, Negligence—Subjective or Objective?, 41 Harv. L. Rev. 1, 14, n. 14 (1927), poses this example. The blindfold example is specious in any event; the suggested comparison is not a parallel case because the blindfolded actor would not be using all the senses reasonably available, while the unsighted person would be.

[150] E.g., Baker v. Joyal, 4 A.D.3d 596, 771 N.Y.S.2d 269 (2004) (defendant driver rendered unconscious when he was struck by A); Hancock-Underwood v. Knight, 670 S.E.2d 720 (Va. 2009); Restatement Third of Torts (Liability for Physical and Emotional Harm) § 11(b) (2010).

[151] Thornton v. Lees, 2008 WL 4544408 (E.D. Ky. 2008); Roman v. Estate of Gobbo, 99 Ohio St.3d 260, 791 N.E.2d 422 (2003) (regarding the driver whose vehicle crossed the center line and caused collisions as a result of an unforeseeable heart attack as violating a traffic statute, but holding that, as an affirmative defense, his violation was excused).

[152] See McCartney v. Pawtucket Mut. Ins., 1994 WL 723056 (Conn. Super. Ct. 1994) (elderly woman, house-bound and in a wheelchair, could still have arranged for heating oil to prevent frozen pipes).

[153] E.g., Mahan v. State, 172 Md. 373, 191 A. 575 (1937) (driver whose small stature made vision difficult expected to exercise "greater watchfulness"); Rosser v. Smith, 260 N.C. 647, 133 S.E.2d 499 (1963) (hearing impaired person should have compensated for the impairment by wearing her hearing aid or alternatively by keeping better lookout).

[154] Cf. Sanders v. Walden, 214 Ark. 523, 217 S.W.2d 357, 9 A.L.R.2d 1040 (1949) (one entrusting car to man who might not be able to brake it was negligent, inferentially the driver himself was as well).

care,[155] or even to avoid altogether an activity like driving (at least until autonomous vehicles are on the road).[156]

In the same way, one who knows or can reasonably foresee that he is subject to seizures that prevent safe driving may be negligent in driving if those seizures cannot be controlled.[157] One who has previously undergone hip surgeries may be negligent for hiking alone on a difficult trail in inclement weather.[158] And one who recognizes the onset of an insulin reaction, drowsiness, or fatigue may be unreasonable in continuing to drive or operate machinery.[159]

Contributory negligence. The same general standards apply when the issue is contributory negligence of the plaintiff instead of negligence of the defendant.[160]

Physical prowess. It seems probable that the defendant will be expected to act reasonably in the light of any special physical abilities he might have. If a strong swimmer attempts to save a drowning person; he would almost certainly be expected to use whatever added strength and stamina he has and would not readily be exonerated for giving up the effort merely because he had reached the limits of endurance that could be attributed to the hypothetical reasonable person.

§ 10.10 Mental Capacity

Liability of mentally disabled. In the United States, persons suffering mental disability are liable both for their intentional[161] and negligent torts.[162] The Restatement Third took a position, consistent with the Restatement Second, that "[a]n actor's mental or emotional disability is not considered in determining whether conduct is negligent, unless the actor is a child."[163]

Only limited and somewhat peculiar authority qualifies the general rule of liability. Wisconsin has held that one cannot be liable for acts committed as a result of a sudden onset of an unforeseeable insanity.[164] New York once seemed to hold that liability would

---

[155] Bennett v. State, 503 So.2d 1022 (La. Ct. App. 1987) (driver must turn his head to compensate for poor peripheral vision); Poyner v. Loftus, 694 A.2d 69 (D.C. 1997) ("[I]n the exercise of common prudence one of defective eyesight must usually as a matter of general knowledge take more care and employ keener watchfulness in walking upon the streets and avoiding obstructions than the same person with good eyesight, in order to reach the standard established by the law for all persons alike, whether they be weak or strong, sound or deficient.").

[156] Restatement Third of Torts (Liability for Physical and Emotional Harm) § 11 cmt. a (2010).

[157] E.g., Goodrich v. Blair, 132 Ariz. 459, 646 P.2d 890 (1982) (driver subject to heart attacks); Lutzkovitz v. Murray, 339 A.2d 64, 93 A.L.R.3d 321 (Del. 1975) (risk of blackout); Storjohn v. Fay, 246 Neb. 454, 519 N.W.2d 521 (1994).

[158] N. H. Fish & Game Dep't v. Bacon, 116 A.3d 1060, 1065 (N.H. 2015) (defendant who had undergone multiple hip surgeries, and had an artificial hip that had dislocated five times, was negligent under statute that provided for repayment for rescue operation).

[159] Keller v. DeLong, 108 N.H. 212, 231 A.2d 633 (1967); Howle v. PYA/Monarch, Inc., 288 S.C. 586, 344 S.E.2d 157 (1986).

[160] E.g., Tomey v. Dyson, 76 Cal. App. 2d 212, 172 P.2d 739 (1946); Moore v. Kitsmiller, 201 S.W.3d 147 (Tex. App. 2006); Allen v. Bos. & M. R.R., 245 Mass. 139, 139 N.E. 511 (1923); § 16.2.

[161] See § 4.3.

[162] Restatement Third of Torts (Liability for Physical and Emotional Harm) § 11(c) (2010); Restatement Second of Torts § 895J (1979).

[163] Id.

[164] See Breunig v. American Family Ins., 45 Wis.2d 536, 173 N.W.2d 619, 49 A.L.R.3d 179 (1970) (one who is suddenly overcome by a mental disability without forewarning is to be treated like a person who suffers a sudden heart attack or seizure, which is to say that such a person need not comply with some external standard).

not be imposed for harm caused by a person who became insane as a result of extraordinary efforts to protect the plaintiff.[165] Otherwise, however, the rule that mentally impaired persons are liable for their torts seems to be accepted within the United States, though other countries have rules to the contrary.[166] Moreover, persuasive arguments have been advanced for adjusting the standard of care for people with mental limitations.[167]

Standard of care. The standard of care applied to an adult suffering mental impairment or psychological disturbance remains the standard of the reasonable prudent person of normal intelligence, judgment and rationality. Consequently, defendants who suffer from bad judgment or mental deficiency,[168] insanity[169] or antisocial penchants for abusing children[170] are held to the objective or "external" standard of the reasonable prudent person. The same is true with one who is voluntarily intoxicated.[171] Put differently, if the defendant's conduct, carried out by sane or sober people, would count as negligence, the defendant cannot escape liability on the ground that he behaved as a reasonable and prudent person afflicted with insanity or drunkenness. This objective standard of care does not necessarily mean that a person with diminished capacity will be held liable in every case. It is quite possible that an Alzheimer's patient could escape liability for harms he negligently inflicts upon his own caregivers; in such a setting, the duty of care is a one way street, the caregiver owing a duty to the patient, not the patient to the caregiver.[172]

Fault of the plaintiff. Similar rules or standards may apply to the plaintiff who is charged with contributory negligence or comparative fault.[173] But some courts have resisted this view, preferring to apply a subjective standard to plaintiffs who suffer mental limitations.[174] Some courts have also distinguished complete insanity from some lesser mental impairment, holding that the plaintiff is not to be charged with

---

[165] Williams v. Hays, 157 N.Y. 541, 52 N.E. 589 (1899) (a case difficult to interpret, however).

[166] See, e.g., German Civil Code § 827 (excluding civil responsibility for one who is unable to exercise free will).

[167] Jacob E. McKnite, When Reasonable Care is Unreasonable: Rethinking the Negligence Liability of Adults with Mental Retardation, 38 Wm. Mitchell L. Rev. 1375 (2012).

[168] Vaughan v. Menlove, 3 Bing. (N.C.) 468, 132 Eng. Rep. 490 (C.P. 1837) (rejecting the defendant's argument that he should not be liable if he acted honestly and to the best of his own judgment); see Restatement Third of Torts (Liability for Physical and Emotional Harm) § 12 cmt. b (2010).

[169] Johnson v. Lambotte, 147 Colo. 203, 363 P.2d 165 (1961); Creasy v. Rusk, 730 N.E.2d 659 (Ind. 2000); Restatement Second of Torts §§ 283B & 895J (1965).

[170] C.T.W. v. B.C.G. & D.T.G., 809 S.W.2d 788 (Tex. App. 1991) (one with "pedophilic disorder" must nevertheless meet the standards of the person of ordinary prudence).

[171] See 1 Dobbs, Hayden & Bublick, The Law of Torts § 133 (2d ed. 2011 & Supp.).

[172] See Gregory v. Cott, 59 Cal. 4th 996, 1000, 331 P.3d 179, 181 (2014) ("Alzheimer's patients are are not liable for injuries to caregivers in institutional settings. We conclude that the same rule applies to in-home caregivers."); Berberian v. Lynn, 179 N.J. 290, 845 A.2d 122 (2004) ("We hold that a mentally disabled patient, who does not have the capacity to control his or her conduct, does not owe his or her caregiver a duty of care" and "the professional caregiver may not recover for the conduct of a patient when this conduct is, in part, the reason for the caregiver's role.").

[173] Galindo v. TMT Transp., Inc., 152 Ariz. 434, 733 P.2d 631 (Ct. App. 1986); Fox v. City & Cty. of San Francisco, 47 Cal.App.3d 164, 120 Cal.Rptr. 779 (1975); Restatement Third of Torts (Liability for Physical and Emotional Harm) § 3 cmt. b (2010); Restatement Third of Torts (Apportionment of Liability) § 3 cmt. a (2000).

[174] Mochen v. State, 43 A.D.2d 484, 352 N.Y.S.2d 290 (1974); Stacy v. Jedco Constr., Inc., 119 N.C. App. 115, 457 S.E.2d 875 (1995); Birkner v. Salt Lake Cty., 771 P.2d 1053 (Utah 1989).

contributory negligence or comparative fault if she has no ability for self care,[175] or is under the care of others.[176]

In some cases there are probably better explanations for allowing a mentally impaired plaintiff to recover in spite of conduct that objectively appears to count as contributory negligence. In many instances, the defendant is under a duty to protect the plaintiff from her own fault, as where the defendant is the plaintiff's custodian.[177] A similar approach explains the defendant's liability in the case of jailers who fail to protect intoxicated or suicidal prisoners[178] and in other cases in which the defendant is aware of the plaintiff's disability.[179]

§ 10.11   Bases for and Alternatives to the Mental Capacity Rules

Civil law alternatives. In a sense, courts impose a kind of strict liability when they hold a person responsible for harms he did not have the mental capacity to avoid. A different approach would be to regard the mentally incompetent person as a force of nature, like lightning, and leave it to all other individuals to insure themselves or provide their own protection.[180] Some civil law countries, in fact, have immunized the insane person from tort liability, at least in certain circumstances.[181]

Justifications for the objective standard. A number of justifications have been advanced in support of the objective standard.[182]

(1) Role of objective standards in judicial process. One justification for objective standards in law generally is that they are essential if the judicial process is to remain transparent, accessible and accountable. Lawyers and litigants cannot evaluate judges or the legal process itself if judges can decide the standard in each case, without reference to a fixed standard that lawyers can understand, discuss and argue. If the standard were subjective, it would be difficult (though not impossible) to adduce evidence that the

---

[175] Dodson v. S.D. Dep't of Human Servs., 703 N.W.2d 353, 359 (S.D. 2005) ("If the patient's capacity for self-care is so diminished by mental illness that it is lacking . . . an allocation of fault is not appropriate. In making the fault comparison, the factfinder should always take into account the extent of the patient's diminished mental capacity to care for his own safety.").

[176] Hofflander v. St. Catherine's Hosp., Inc., 262 Wis.2d 539, 566, 664 N.W.2d 545, 558 (2003) ("A person who is mentally disabled is held to the same standard of care as one who has normal mentality" except in some situations "when a mentally disabled person is under the protective custody and control of another.").

[177] Bramlette v. Charter-Medical-Columbia, 302 S.C. 68, 393 S.E.2d 914 (1990); cf. Cowan v. Doering, 215 N.J. Super. 484, 522 A.2d 444 (1987), aff'd, 111 N.J. 451, 545 A.2d 159 (1988).

[178] Myers v. Cty. of Lake, 30 F.3d 847, 853 (7th Cir. 1994) ("A duty to prevent someone from acting in a particular way logically cannot be defeated by the very action sought to be avoided"); Wilson v. Kotzebue, 627 P.2d 623 (Alaska 1981) (intoxication of prisoner); Sandborg v. Blue Earth Cty., 615 N.W.2d 61 (Minn. 2000).

[179] E.g., Stacy v. Jedco Constr., 119 N.C. App. 115, 457 S.E.2d 875 (1995); Higgins v. E. Valley Sch. Dist., 41 Wash. App. 281, 704 P.2d 630 (1985); see Jankee v. Clark Cty., 235 Wis. 2d 700, 746, 612 N.W.2d 297, 315 (2000) ("The subjective standard is well suited for situations in which a tortfeasor is aware of the plaintiff's diminished mental capacity and can take precautions against the disability.").

[180] See Yancey v. Maestri, 155 So. 509 (La. Ct. App. 1934) (under civil law view, insane person's "acts are looked upon as inevitable accidents").

[181] See German Civil Code § 827 (excluding civil responsibility for one who is unable to exercise free will, except where he brought on temporary disability by use of alcohol or similar means). Not all civil law countries today follow this view. In Mexico, the Codigo Civil para el Districto Federal § 1911 provides that the incompetent person is liable unless some other person such as a guardian is liable; for others, see Torts—Liability for One's Own Act § 215, in XI Int. Encyc. Comp. L. (A. Tunc, ed., 1979).

[182] See William J. Curran, Tort Liability of the Mentally Ill and Mentally Deficient, 21 Ohio St. L.J. 52 (1960); Restatement Second of Torts § 283B (1965).

defendant did or did not do his best given his impairment, but even more difficult to know whether the judge or jury made a justifiable decision.

(2) Difficulty of distinguishing incapacity from poor capacity. It may be impossible to distinguish insanity that should exonerate an individual from all the other determinants that shape an actor's conduct. No one is responsible for choosing his or her own genetic makeup, life experience, body chemistry or mental ability. So far as conduct is determined by those things, it can be said that no one is responsible. A person who causes harm through impatience, awkwardness or stupidity in this sense is not morally responsible for his actions. But neither law nor society could survive a rule that exonerated every such fault.[183] The immunity suggested by such reasoning could be pared down by drawing a distinction between stupidity and mental deficiency, but that distinction is difficult to draw as a practical matter and perhaps morally unjustified as well. Similarly, the distinction between mental disability and a propensity for bad behavior may be difficult to maintain. For example, the difference between someone who sexually abuses children and someone who suffers a "pedophilic disorder" is in the mind of the observer.[184]

(3) Difficulty of making causal judgments and setting an appropriate subjective standard. Mental impairments do not necessarily prevent safe behavior; even a person suffering from schizophrenia may drive well. Any rule exonerating insane persons would necessarily force courts to not only decide what counts as insanity but also determine whether the particular insanity on the particular occasion caused the defendant's negligent conduct. And, since some insane persons can do some things safely, courts would be obliged to impose some kind of standard, so that the defendant would remain liable for those harms he could reasonably avoid. This might come uncomfortably close to saying that an insane person would be held to the standard of a reasonable and prudent insane person with the defendant's particular insanity.

(4) Choosing between innocent parties. Tort liability is not a criminal conviction or a badge of infamy. The insane defendant will be obliged to pay a tort judgment, but only if he has the money to do so. The loss must fall somewhere, and as between the injured victim and an insane defendant with insurance or sufficient funds to pay, the loss may appropriately fall upon the defendant who caused the harm. While courts at times adopt this reasoning, courts often reject this same reasoning in contexts in which negligence as judged by an objective view is absent.

(5) Incentives. Finally, some authorities have suggested that tort liability will provide proper incentives to those "in charge" of the insane person to control his conduct. This point does not seem quite right. If one in charge is negligent in failing to control the insane person, he will be liable for his own negligence. If incentive is obtainable in the law of negligence, liability of the caretaker for his own negligence should be more effective than liability of the insane person himself. If the caretaker is not negligent but on the contrary has exercised optimum care to control the insane person, there is no reason to give him incentives to do more.

---

[183] Cf. David E. Seidelson, Reasonable Expectations and Subjective Standards in Negligence Law: The Minor, The Mentally Impaired, and the Mentally Incompetent, 50 Geo. Wash. L. Rev. 17 (1981) (if doing one's best were the standard, universal immunity would result).

[184] In C.T.W. v. B.C.G., 809 S.W.2d 788 (Tex. App. 1991), the defendant sexually abused his step grandchildren. He sought to defend against tort liability on the ground that this sexual abuse was the result of a "pedophilic disorder." The court rejected the argument that the defendant should be held only to the standard of "an ordinary prudent person with the mental illness of pedophilia."

§ 10.12 Knowledge, Perception, Memory, Experience, and Skills

Reasonable person standard as to knowledge and memory. Ordinary care requires one to act in a way that would be reasonable given the knowledge or information that would be possessed by a reasonable person under the circumstances.[185] Relatedly, one must also exercise senses reasonably for the perception of danger,[186] and to fix and retain significant information in memory for a reasonable period of time.[187] Forgetfulness is usually forgiven only when there is a specific reason for it, such as distraction or emergency.[188]

Knowledge possessed by a reasonable person. The reasonable person has some general knowledge in common with others in the community. Knowledge in this sense means systematic information capable of generalization and use in various situations. If you know that dropped objects fall, you will probably perceive a risk that others might be harmed if you were to drop a torts book off a tall building. Speaking of knowledge in this sense, the Restatement has it that the knowledge of a reasonable person is the knowledge that is common in the community generally.[189] The rule means that the defendant is expected to act in a way consistent with knowledge of commonly understood dangers, for example, that high electrical voltages can kill, gas can explode when combined with fire, that children have a propensity for darting into the street, and that a snarling dog can inflict wounds by biting.[190] On the other hand, the defendant is not expected to have specialized knowledge, for example, knowledge that gasoline fumes are heavier than air,[191] or, possibly, that small babies are more likely to die if allowed to sleep on their stomachs.[192]

Variation in knowledge over time. The knowledge held by reasonable people changes over time and varies with place. At one time people knew little or nothing about the dangers of tobacco or asbestos. An architect who specified asbestos in a building in the 1930s would not be expected to know that it could cause serious injury, but almost everyone today knows otherwise. Because of this variation in knowledge from time to time and place to place, the question of appropriate knowledge is often submitted to the jury, subsumed in the broader question whether the defendant conducted himself in an

---

[185] Restatement Third of Torts (Liability for Physical and Emotional Harm) § 12 (2010); Restatement Second of Torts § 290 (1965).

[186] Dobson v. La. Power & Light Co., 567 So.2d 569 (La. 1990); Restatement Second of Torts § 289 cmt. e (1965).

[187] See Jackson v. Axelrad, 221 S.W.3d 650, 656 (Tex. 2007).

[188] See, e.g., Tomlinson v. Wilson & Toomer Fertilizer Co., 165 So.2d 801 (Fla. Dist. Ct. App. 1964); Conner v. Farmers & Merchs. Bank, 243 S.C. 132, 132 S.E.2d 385 (1963). A number of memory cases are analyzed in Mark F. Grady, Why Are People Negligent? Technology, Non Durable Precautions, and the Medical Malpractice Explosion, 82 Nw. U. L. Rev. 293 (1988).

[189] Restatement Third of Torts (Liability for Physical and Emotional Harm) § 12 (2010) (ignoring a person's below average knowledge except in the case of learners or beginners); Restatement Second of Torts § 290 (1965).

[190] See Dorit Rubinstein Reiss, Compensating the Victims of Failure to Vaccinate: What are the Options?, 23 Cornell J.L. & Pub. Pol'y 595 (2014) (discussing potential tort liability of parents who fail to vaccinate their children when their child is the cause of outbreak to students who did vaccinate).

[191] Blakes v. Blakes, 517 So.2d 444 (La. Ct. App. 1987).

[192] LePage v. Horne, 262 Conn. 116, 809 A.2d 505 (2002) (requiring expert testimony rather than letting jury say what knowledge reasonable people in the community have).

unreasonably risky way. There are, however, some decisions that require the plaintiff to prove what knowledge a reasonable person would have had.[193]

Information vs. knowledge. Information, in the sense of isolated facts of transient importance, is different from knowledge that can be generalized. We all know objects fall, but we do not all know the same particular facts. For instance, you know, but others do not, that a pot is on the range and the burner is on. Information of this kind differs from knowledge because this information cannot be generalized; it is both ephemeral and peculiar to circumstances. We might expect everyone in the community to have the knowledge that gunpowder can burn or explode, but we might not expect everyone who sees "sand" in a jar to have the information that the sand is actually gunpowder.[194] Although we cannot standardize the particular information that a reasonable person will possess, we can say that a reasonable person would always use the information that he has acquired or should have acquired in particular circumstances. If the defendant knows or should know that his car's brakes have ceased to work, he must act on that information.

Knowledge of one's own ignorance; failure to acquire information. In some instances the actor knows or should know that he is ignorant of facts that might prove important in estimating a risk. If a reasonable person finds herself in a strange place confronted with a bottle that says "Drink Me," she may know nothing about the bottle's contents, but she surely knows of her own ignorance. Reasonable care may require her to find out something about the bottle's contents or provenance before she imbibes. This is not because she is expected to know the bottle's contents but because what she does know tells her that more information should be sought.[195]

Superior or specialized knowledge or skill. A reasonable person will act in the light of (a) knowledge shared by the community generally and also (b) information, knowledge and skill that he himself has that is not generally known and that reasonable people would not ordinarily have.[196] The Restatement Second put this by saying that the standard is the standard of the reasonable person with the superior knowledge, skill, and other qualities of the defendant.[197] The newer Physical Harms Restatement uses a slightly different formulation—the special skills or knowledge of the actor are "circumstances to be taken into account in determining whether the actor has behaved as a reasonably careful person."[198] The rule applies not only to knowledge in the broad sense, but to transient, particularized information; one who knows that the floor is wet and slippery must use care commensurate with that circumstance.[199]

Professionals. The superior knowledge rule has obvious application to professionals like physicians and surgeons, who are held to possess the skill and knowledge of others

---

[193] Id. (ordering directed verdict for the defendant daycare center because plaintiff failed to prove by expert testimony that operator should have known of risk of death associated with allowing baby to sleep on her stomach, even though operator admitted she knew of the risks associated with stomach sleeping).

[194] The example is from Warren A. Seavey, Negligence—Subjective or Objective?, 41 Harv. L. Rev. 1 (1927).

[195] See, e.g., Cramer v. Hous. Opportunities Comm'n of Montgomery Cty., 304 Md. 705, 501 A.2d 35 (1985); Wilson v. City of Eagan, 297 N.W.2d 146, 8 A.L.R.4th 1277 (Minn. 1980).

[196] Jackson v. Axelrad, 221 S.W.3d 650 (Tex. 2007).

[197] Restatement Second of Torts § 289 (1965) (superior knowledge in recognizing a risk); id. § 299 cmt. f (superior competence in both recognizing and dealing with risk); id. § 290 cmt. f (similar).

[198] Restatement Third of Torts (Liability for Physical and Emotional Harm) § 12 (2010).

[199] Krombein v. Gali Serv. Indus., 317 F.Supp.2d 14 (D.D.C. 2004).

in good standing in their profession.[200] A physician who knows more than a layman must use that additional knowledge in the practice of medicine. But the point reaches even further. A physician who knows more than other physicians is also expected to use that special knowledge. Physicians who know more must not stop short of appropriate treatment on the ground that other physicians would have done no better.[201] The principle applies equally to any kind of skill or experience. A person with special knowledge about the operation of earth scrapers is expected to use that knowledge to avoid injury to others.[202] And a person issued a commercial driver's license to drive a semi-trailer truck must use his special knowledge of driving those vehicles.[203]

Reasonable person standard and superior knowledge. The superior knowledge rule can be explained by saying that the actor's superior knowledge is one of the "circumstances" that a reasonable person would take into account[204] or by saying that a reasonable person will use all the knowledge he actually has in dealing with a recognizable risk. Either way, the standard of care, that of the reasonable person under the same or similar circumstances, remains the same.[205] So it is right to tell a jury that a reasonable person will use the relevant special knowledge he has,[206] but not right to tell the jury that he is held to a higher standard of care.[207] However, courts sometimes find it easier to express the idea as a standard or duty. For example, the Nebraska Supreme Court has said that the standard applied to a certified high school sports coach is that of a reasonable person holding the certificate.[208]

§ 10.13 Intoxication

Sober person standard vs. risk of drinking. A voluntarily intoxicated person[209] is in effect held to the standard of a reasonably sober person.[210] This seems to contradict the rule that the reasonable person has the physical attributes of the actor. The seeming contradiction is ameliorated by the fact that the decision to ingest alcohol or drugs itself creates a risk that the actor's physical (as well as mental) capacities will be diminished. One who drinks knowing he will soon drive a car, for example, may be negligent or contributorily negligent in choosing to drink under those circumstances. Liability might

---

[200] On medical malpractice and its standard of care generally see § 21.5.

[201] Toth v. Comty. Hosp. at Glen Cove, 22 N.Y.2d 255, 239 N.E.2d 368, 292 N.Y.S.2d 440 (1968); Jackson v. Axelrad, 221 S.W.3d 650 (Tex. 2007) (applying the rule to contributory negligence issue where the plaintiff was a physician).

[202] Hill v. Sparks, 546 S.W.2d 473 (Mo. Ct. App. 1976); cf. Dobson v. La. Power & Light Co., 567 So.2d 569 (La. 1990) (tree trimming); Sandella v. Dick Corp., 1995 WL 348192 (Conn. Super. Ct. 1995) (actor was informed of hazard occurring when catatonic polymers and water were combined and was required to act on that knowledge).

[203] Dakter v. Cavallino, 866 N.W.2d 656 (Wisc. 2015).

[204] See Sinai v. Polinger Co., 498 A.2d 520 (D.C. 1985).

[205] LaVine v. Clear Creek Skiing Corp., 557 F.2d 730 (10th Cir. 1977); Cervelli v. Graves, 661 P.2d 1032 (Wyo. 1983).

[206] Cf. Hill v. Sparks, 546 S.W.2d 473 (Mo. Ct. App. 1976).

[207] Fredericks v. Castora, 241 Pa. Super. 211, 360 A.2d 696 (1976); Cervelli v. Graves, 661 P.2d 1032 (Wyo. 1983); see Sinai v. Polinger Co., 498 A.2d 520 (D.C. 1985).

[208] Cerny v. Cedar Bluffs Junior/Senior Pub. Sch., 262 Neb. 66, 628 N.W.2d 697 (2001), on appeal after remand, 267 Neb. 958, 679 N.W.2d 198 (2004).

[209] One who is involuntarily intoxicated, forcibly drugged by another, for example, is not held to an external standard with respect to physical conditions or traits. Davies v. Butler, 95 Nev. 763, 602 P.2d 605 (1979); Restatement Third of Torts (Liability for Physical and Emotional Harm) § 12 cmt. c (2010); Restatement Second of Torts § 283C cmt. d (1965).

[210] Townsend v. Jones, 183 Kan. 543, 331 P.2d 890 (1958); Remmenga v. Selk, 150 Neb. 401, 34 N.W.2d 757, 763 (1948).

then be imposed less because the sober person standard is applied and more because the defendant took unreasonable risks in drinking at all.

Overt conduct required to establish negligence. Intoxication cases raise another problem. Negligence consists of harm-causing conduct.[211] Neither the defendant's state of mind nor his physical condition are in themselves negligence. Consequently, the mere fact that a person's mental or physical faculties are affected by alcohol, does not necessarily lead to the conclusion that the person was negligent if his overt conduct was blameless. On the other hand, if the person was driving and drove too fast, or failed to keep a lookout, or drove in the wrong lane of traffic or violated acceptable blood-alcohol levels in a drunk driving statute, his conduct shows a departure from the reasonable person standard, and liability is appropriate, but because his conduct was faulty, not simply because he was intoxicated.[212]

Statutes. Statutes make intoxication particularly relevant in certain kinds of cases. For example, statutes prohibit driving while intoxicated or under the influence of alcohol. Some courts say that violation of such statutes is negligence per se, that is, negligence in itself.[213] But since the defendant's intoxication must lead to specific negligent conduct, such as an improper lookout or driving on the wrong side of the road,[214] and must be a "proximate cause" of the plaintiff's harm,[215] some states refuse to characterize violation of the statute as negligence per se.[216]

Fault of the plaintiff. What's sauce for the goose is sauce for the gander and the intoxicated plaintiff charged with contributory negligence would normally come under the same rules as the intoxicated defendant.[217] But courts have sometimes excused the plaintiff on the theory that at some point drinking may become involuntary or that the plaintiff's drinking was not a proximate cause of her injury.[218] And in some cases, the defendant may be under a duty to protect an underage plaintiff from her own intoxication—if underage drinking is the very risk the defendant is obliged to guard against.[219]

---

[211] See § 9.1.

[212] See Alan H. McCoid, Intoxication and Its Effect upon Civil Responsibility, 42 Iowa L. Rev. 38 (1956). Thus a decedent who crashed into the rear of another vehicle and had 0.14 blood alcohol could be found negligent. See Dagley v. Thompson, 156 S.W.3d 589 (Tex. App. 2003). In such a case, the act of crashing into another vehicle tends to suggest negligence, and the intoxication tends to strengthen the inference that the crash was a result of driving too fast or failing to keep a reasonable lookout.

[213] Smith v. Chapman, 115 Ariz. 211, 564 P.2d 900 (1977); Hasson v. Hale, 555 So.2d 1014 (Miss. 1990); Cook ex rel. Uithoven v. Spinnaker's of Rivergate, Inc., 878 S.W.2d 934 (Tenn. 1994).

[214] See Yost v. Miner, 163 N.W.2d 557 (Iowa 1968).

[215] Anderson v. Morgan, 73 Ariz. 344, 241 P.2d 786 (1952); King v. Allred, 309 N.C. 113, 305 S.E.2d 554 (1983).

[216] Yost v. Miner, 163 N.W.2d 557, 561 (Iowa 1968) ("The act of driving an automobile while intoxicated is a violation of [statute]. However, it is not negligence per se."); cf. Loevsky v. Carter, 70 Haw. 419, 773 P.2d 1120 (1989) (under Hawaii rule, violation is evidence of negligence only, not negligence per se).

[217] E.g., Stewart v. Manhattan & Bronx Surface Transit Operating Auth., 875 N.Y.S.2d 26 (App. Div. 2009) (evidence of pedestrian's intoxication under the facts warranted jury's apportion of high percentage of fault to the pedestrian); cf. Del E. Webb Corp. v. Super. Ct., 151 Ariz. 164, 726 P.2d 580 (1986) (patron's contributory negligence or assumed risk available as defense in suit against alcohol provider).

[218] See, e.g., Davies v. Butler, 95 Nev. 763, 602 P.2d 605 (1979); Ballou v. Sigma Nu Gen. Fraternity, 291 S.C. 140, 352 S.E.2d 488 (1986); Cook ex rel. Uithoven v. Spinnaker's of Rivergate, Inc., 878 S.W.2d 934 (Tenn. 1994).

[219] See Loeb v. Rasmussen, 822 P.2d 914 (Alaska 1991) (duty to protect minor from her own drinking); McMahon v. N.Y.C., N.H. & H.R. Co., 136 Conn. 372, 71 A.2d 557 (1950); cf. Anderson v. American Family Mut. Ins.., 267 Wis.2d 121, 671 N.W.2d 651 (2003).

D. THE STANDARD OF CARE FOR CHILDREN

§ 10.14 The General Standard of Care for Children

Liability of children. Very young children—usually those under about four or five years of age—are generally thought to be incapable of negligence.[220] Under the "rule of sevens," followed in a few states, children up to the age of seven are protected from tort liability, and children from ages seven to fourteen are presumptively incapable of negligence.[221] Otherwise, children are not immune from tort liability merely by virtue of their status as children.[222] However, the standard of care expected of children is another matter.

Subjective standard generally. With some exceptions, children are not subjected to the reasonable person standard but are instead held to a standard that is largely subjective. A minor, even an older one, is not required to conduct himself as a reasonable adult or even as a reasonable child of similar age.[223] The minor is instead required to conduct himself only with the care of a minor of his own age, intelligence, and experience in similar circumstances[224] and juries are so instructed.[225] In line with this, a minor's violation of a statute is usually not considered as negligence per se.[226]

The child standard for child plaintiffs and defendants. Many of the cases articulating the subjective child standard are concerned with the contributory negligence of the child plaintiff. But child defendants as well as child plaintiffs may escape liability because they acted reasonably in light of their own limited capacity.[227] The rule is not an immunity, though, and if a child fails to use his own intelligence and experience reasonably, he may be liable as a defendant[228] or find his action barred[229] or damages

---

[220] Mastland, Inc. v. Evans Furniture, Inc., 498 N.W.2d 682 (Iowa 1993); Price v. Kitsap Transit, 125 Wash.2d 456, 886 P.2d 556 (1994). See Oscar Gray, The Standard of Care for Children Revisited, 45 Mo. L. Rev. 597 (1980); Restatement Third of Torts (Liability for Physical and Emotional Harm) § 10(b) (2010) (children under five incapable of negligence). Georgia, by construction of a statute, has immunized all children under the age of 13 years. Horton v. Hinely, 261 Ga. 863, 413 S.E.2d 199 (1992) (two nine-year-olds poured gasoline on a seven-year-old and set him afire, no liability).

[221] Savage Indus. v. Duke, 598 So.2d 856 (Ala. 1992); Queen Ins. v. Hammond, 374 Mich. 655, 132 N.W.2d 792 (1965); Steele v. Holiday Inns, Inc., 626 So.2d 593 (Miss. 1993).

[222] Restatement Third of Torts (Liability for Physical and Emotional Harm) § 10 (2010); Restatement Second of Torts § 895I (1979).

[223] There are occasional lapses in which courts may speak of the "average" child or the like. See Fire Ins. Exch. v. Diehl, 206 Mich.App. 108, 520 N.W.2d 675 (1994). It is improbable that these casual statements are intended to alter the usual rule.

[224] See, e.g., First Nat'l Bank of Ariz. v. Dupree, 136 Ariz. 296, 665 P.2d 1018 (Ct. App. 1983); Lehmuth v. Long Beach Unified Sch. Dist., 53 Cal.2d 544, 348 P.2d 887, 2 Cal.Rptr. 279 (1960); Restatement Third of Torts (Liability for Physical and Emotional Harm § 10 (a) (2010); Restatement Second of Torts § 283A (1965).

[225] Frazier ex rel. Frazier v. Norton, 334 N.W.2d 865 (S.D. 1983); Bauman ex rel. Chapman v. Crawford, 104 Wash.2d 241, 704 P.2d 1181 (1985).

[226] Alley v. Siepman, 87 S.D. 670, 214 N.W.2d 7 (1974).

[227] E.g., Lafayette Par. Sch. Bd. v. Cormier ex rel. Cormier, 901 So.2d 1197 (La. Ct. App. 2005) (11-year-old pointing a toy gun); Hudson-Connor v. Putney, 192 Or. App. 488, 86 P.3d 106 (2004) (child defendant allowing another child to operate golf cart).

[228] See e.g., McGregor v. Marini, 256 So.2d 542 (Fla. Dist. Ct. App. 1972) (third-grade boys playing with matches in empty house caused a fire, liability potential if capacity is proven); Deliso v. Cangialosi, 117 Misc. 2d 105, 457 N.Y.S.2d 396 (1982) (11-year-old).

[229] Choate v. Ind. Harbor Belt R.R., 980 N.E.2d 58, 66 (Ill. 2012) ("a landowner has no duty to remedy a dangerous condition if it presents obvious risks that children generally of the plaintiff's age would be expected to appreciate and avoid"; 12-year-old should have appreciated dangers of jumping on a moving train).

reduced as a plaintiff, unless the defendant owes him a duty to protect him against his own negligence.[230]

Factual settings for the rule. Although children may be held to the adult standard in the operation of motor vehicles,[231] the child standard is readily invoked to protect children against legal responsibility for their acts in the course of ordinary childhood games[232] and common childhood activities like bicycle riding[233] or dashing for the ice cream truck.[234] But it also protects children from responsibility for injuries resulting from activities, like playing with fire, that are in no way innocent.[235]

Standard: objective in form, subjective in fact. The child standard of care is cast in an objective form, referring as it does to a hypothetical child. However, the standard is actually subjective because it ultimately refers back to the individual child himself. He is to act as a person with all of his own important qualities, that is, as a person of his age, his experience, and his intelligence. In other words, in spite of its form, the standard is quite literally subjective.[236]

Children with limitations or special abilities. The child with mental limitations is not expected to conduct himself with the care of the ordinary child, but only with the care his mental abilities and experience permit.[237] Conversely, a child whose intelligence and experience give him the capacities of an adult will be expected to act with the same care as a reasonable person.[238] And, since age often correlates with capacity, conduct that is negligent in a 17-year-old may not be negligent in a 14-year-old.[239]

Holding children responsible. In a sense, the child standard is almost no standard at all; it holds the child to whatever he can reasonably do. However, if the child appears to have normal capacity for his age, the conduct and capacity of real-life children of the same age may provide evidence as to the child's probable capacity.[240] Courts have thus held in particular cases that evidence was sufficient to make a jury issue on the minor's negligence or contributory negligence.[241]

---

[230] Boyer v. Johnson, 360 So.2d 1164 (La. 1978).

[231] See § 10.16.

[232] First Nat'l Bank of Ariz. v. Dupree, 136 Ariz. 296, 665 P.2d 1018 (Ct. App. 1983); Hoyt v. Rosenberg, 80 Cal.App. 2d 500, 182 P.2d 234, 238, 173 A.L.R. 883 (1947).

[233] Roberts v. Fisher, 169 Colo. 288, 455 P.2d 871 (1969); King v. Casad, 122 Ill.App.3d 566, 461 N.E.2d 685 (1984).

[234] Neal v. Shiels, Inc., 166 Conn. 3, 347 A.2d 102 (1974) (contributory negligence issue).

[235] Farm Bureau Ins. v. Phillips, 116 Mich.App. 544, 323 N.W.2d 477 (1982).

[236] See, e.g., Hudson v. Old Guard Ins., 3 A.3d 246 (Del. 2010) ("[W]e hold minors to the standard of conduct expected of a reasonable child of similar age and situation"; "The maturity and capacity of the child, [his] ability to understand and appreciate the danger, [his] familiarity with the surroundings, together with the circumstances under which the accident occurred, must all be taken into consideration").

[237] Lafayette Par. Sch. Bd. v. Cormier ex rel. Cormier, 901 So.2d 1197 (La. Ct. App. 2005) (special education student held only to the standard of "the reasonably prudent 11-year-old boy who has the same exceptionalities that Jade possesses"); see Camerlinck v. Thomas, 209 Neb. 843, 312 N.W.2d 260, 27 A.L.R.4th 1 (1981) (stating that mental limitations as well as special mental powers of a child are taken into account).

[238] Dorais v. Paquin, 113 N.H. 187, 304 A.2d 369 (1973).

[239] See Dimond v. Kling, 221 N.W.2d 86, 91 (N.D. 1974).

[240] Oscar Gray, The Standard of Care for Children Revisited, 45 Mo. L. Rev. 597, 602 (1980).

[241] Dorrin v. Union Elec. Co., 581 S.W.2d 852 (Mo. 1979); Camerlinck v. Thomas, 209 Neb. 843, 312 N.W.2d 260, 27 A.L.R.4th 1 (1981); Deliso v. Cangialosi, 117 Misc.2d 105, 457 N.Y.S.2d 396 (1982) (11-year-old playing Monkey-in-the-Middle and tossing keys, which struck plaintiff's car, negligence found).

§ 10.15 Rationales for the Child Standard

Incapacity. Prosser suggested that the child standard is appropriate because children cannot meet an adult standard.[242] This seems to be no rationale at all. The same could be said of insane persons for whom no similar protection is provided. Prosser also suggested that children differ from adults with limited intelligence because the limitations of children are normal to the whole class.[243] The distinction may be sound, but it does not support the subjective standard for children that courts profess to follow. It supports instead only an objective standard based upon a reasonable child of similar age.[244] Perhaps that is in fact how juries interpret the standard.

Protecting children from their contributory negligence. Part of the motivation for adopting a child standard, as distinct from the rationales, no doubt turned on a desire to protect the child from the effects of her own contributory negligence when she was injured by the defendant. Under the original contributory negligence doctrine, a plaintiff guilty of failure to exercise care for her own safety was simply barred, even if the defendant was far more faulty.[245] In the latter half of the 20th century, however, almost all states in the United States had adopted some form of comparative negligence rule under which a plaintiff can recover from the negligent defendant in spite of the plaintiff's own contributory fault, with an appropriate reduction in damages awarded.[246] Perhaps more importantly, however, courts now perceive the possibility that when the plaintiff's minority is known to the defendant, the defendant's duty of reasonable care will require him to protect the plaintiff from his own immaturity so far as that can be done reasonably.

Encouraging child development. What has been called the welfare rationale[247] asserts that children must be permitted to gain experience by acting in the world in order to mature, to learn by doing, and to become socialized by interacting with others. The implicit argument of this rationale may be that tort liability would discourage daily activities of children.

Fairness of protection of child defendants. The welfare rationale may merge with the "fairness" rationale if it is based upon the idea that it would be particularly inappropriate to tax a child defendant with tort liability that might cloud his whole adult life when the child is in fact incapable of taking greater care.

Doubt about these rationales had led at least one commentator to suggest a fundamentally different scheme of child liability.[248] In this structure, carefree or childhood activities of children are distinguished from more dangerous ones. The child standard would be used only for the former, presumably, for example, the games of younger children. For activities that are not of the carefree kind needed for child development, that is to say, dangerous activities, an adult standard would apply. The

---

[242] Prosser & Keeton § 32, p. 179.

[243] The "normal" statement was made in Charbonneau v. MacRury, 84 N.H. 501, 153 A. 457, 73 A.L.R. 1266 (1931).

[244] Prosser & Keeton gave another reason that also suggests an objective child standard, namely that the community has sufficient experience to form a judgment about what could be expected of children. The premise seems correct, but, again, it suggests an objective child standard.

[245] See § 16.1.

[246] See § 15.6.

[247] Caroline Forell, Reassessing the Negligence Standard of Care for Minors, 15 N.M. L. Rev. 485, 498 (1985).

[248] Id.

Restatement and some courts have already imposed an adult standard upon older children for a limited number "of adult activities."[249]

§ 10.16 Holding Children to an Adult Standard

Adult standard of care. Most courts that have considered the question now say that children engaged in certain activities are held to the adult reasonable person standard of care.[250] Most of the cases have held so when a child was operating a motorized vehicle,[251] boat,[252] plane, snowmobile,[253] or machine[254] and most have gone no further. Quite possibly, courts would refuse to impose the adult standard on very young children, even when they operate motorized vehicles.[255]

The adult standard has not usually been applied to minors who handle firearms,[256] although their use is dangerous. The adult standard has likewise been rejected when it comes to children setting fires.[257] The emphasis on the operation of motorized vehicles leads to some odd results: while a 12-year-old is held to an adult standard in operating a motor boat,[258] a 16-year-old is held only to the "child" standard while skiing[259] or attempting to climb out the window of a moving truck.[260]

Generalizations as to activities covered. The Restatement Second applied the adult standard to those activities as those normally undertaken by only adults, and for which adult qualifications are required.[261] The Restatement Third says that the adult standard applies "when the child is engaging in a dangerous activity that is characteristically undertaken by adults."[262]

---

[249] Restatement Third of Torts (Liability for Physical and Emotional Harm) § 10 (2010) ("When children choose to engage in dangerous activities characteristically engaged in by adults, no account is taken of their childhood.").

[250] Restatement Third of Torts (Liability for Physical and Emotional Harm) § 10 (2010); Mahon v. Heim, 165 Conn. 251, 332 A.2d 69 (1973).

[251] Pritchard v. Veterans Cab Co., 63 Cal.2d 727, 408 P.2d 360, 47 Cal.Rptr. 904 (1965); Perricone v. DiBartolo, 14 Ill.App.3d 514, 520, 302 N.E.2d 637 (1973) (gasoline-powered minibike); Ardinger v. Hummell, 982 P.2d 727 (Alaska 1999) (14-year-old allegedly entrusted her mother's car to a 15-year-old companion), appeal after new trial, Crosby v. Hummell, 63 P.3d 1022 (Alaska 2003).

[252] Dellwo v. Pearson, 259 Minn. 452, 107 N.W.2d 859, 97 A.L.R. 2d 866 (1961).

[253] Robinson v. Lindsay, 92 Wash.2d 410, 598 P.2d 392 (1979); Ryan v. Hickson, 55 D.L.R.3d 196 (Ontario H.C. 1974).

[254] E.g., Jackson v. McCuiston, 247 Ark. 862, 448 S.W.2d 33 (1969) (tractor propelled bush hog or stalk cutter); Goodfellow v. Coggburn, 98 Idaho 202, 203–04, 560 P.2d 873 (1977) (tractor).

[255] See DePerno v. Hans, 18 Misc.3d 1119(A), 856 N.Y.S.2d 497 (Sup. Ct. 2007) (noting that court found no case applying the adult standard to an eight-year-old); Restatement Third of Torts (Liability for Physical and Emotional Harm) § 10 cmt. g (2010).

[256] Purtle v. Shelton, 251 Ark. 519, 474 S.W.2d 123, 47 A.L.R.3d 609 (1971) (deer hunting); Thomas v. Inman, 282 Or. 279, 578 P.2d 399 (1978). See Caroline Forell, Reassessing the Negligence Standard of Care for Minors, 15 N.M. L. Rev. 485, 487 (1985). But see Goss v. Allen, 70 N.J. 442, 360 A.2d 388 (1976) (dictum that hunting would normally entail an adult standard); Huebner ex rel. Lane v. Koelfgren, 519 N.W.2d 488 (Minn. Ct. App. 1994) (14 ½-year-old boy handling a BB gun, adult standard).

[257] Farm Bureau Ins. v. Phillips, 116 Mich.App. 544, 323 N.W.2d 477 (1982); Strehlke v. Camenzind, 111 D.L.R.3d 319 (Q.B.Alberta 1980).

[258] Dellwo v. Pearson, 259 Minn. 452, 107 N.W.2d 859, 97 A.L.R.2d 866 (1961).

[259] Goss v. Allen, 70 N.J. 442, 360 A.2d 388 (1976) (17-year-old skiing).

[260] Strait v. Crary, 173 Wis.2d 377, 496 N.W.2d 634 (Ct. App. 1992) (16-year-old drinking passenger attempting to climb out the window of a moving truck fell out and suffered a broken leg; he was entitled to an instruction on the child standard of care).

[261] Restatement Second of Torts § 283A (1965).

[262] Restatement Third of Torts (Liability for Physical and Emotional Harm) § 10 (c) (2010). See Hudson-Connor v. Putney, 192 Or.App. 488, 86 P.3d 106 (2004) (holding that a minor who allowed another minor to

Insurance. Courts have probably been moved to apply the adult standard by several different feelings. They are almost certainly influenced by the fact that liability insurance can and usually does cover activities in motorized vehicles, so that if a minor is held liable there is a good chance that he will not find himself saddled with a heavy debt at the beginning of his adult life.

Reasonable expectations of the other party. Reasonable expectations of others provides a reason for and a limitation to extending the adult standard to children. In an early leading case, the court in *Dellwo v. Pearson* reasoned that while one observing children at play may anticipate risky conduct, those at risk from motor vehicles usually cannot recognize that they are dealing with minors.[263] Other drivers' expect that all vehicle drivers will exercise an adult level of safety. That expectation undermines the other drivers' ability to forestall danger in the case of a minor with whom they do not deal face to face. So when the older minor creates risk to others who cannot identify the actor as a minor or protect themselves, the adult standard seems the most appropriate one for protecting the reasonable expectations of the other party and indeed of the community at large.[264] However, the reasonable expectation rationale implies a limitation as well as an expansion of the adult standard. When the plaintiff knows she is dealing with a minor-defendant and has opportunities to protect herself, the reasonable expectation rationale offers no occasion to apply the adult standard.

E. OTHER STANDARDS OF CARE

§ 10.17 Alternative Standards

The general standard and alternatives. The general standard of care, the duty of the reasonable person under the circumstances, could conceivably be applied in all cases, leaving it to the jury to determine whether, on the facts, the defendant breached that duty by his negligence. However, courts and legislatures do, in fact, impose different standards in particular categories of cases. Such standards may require the defendant to exercise greater care, notably where the defendant is a common carrier obliged to exercise the highest degree of care.[265] More often, they create a lower standard which relieves the defendant of a duty to exercise ordinary care, as in the case of guest statutes.

Different standards of care. In the past, focusing on the status, relationship, or undertakings of the parties, courts held that landowners owed only the duty to not wantonly or intentionally injure trespassers and licensees;[266] that health care providers owed the duty of care established by their peers, which was sometimes of the highest

---

operate a golf cart would be held only to the child standard of care, because (1) there was no evidence that adult skills were required and (2) there was no evidence that golf carts were normally operated only by adults).

[263] "[O]ne cannot know whether the operator of an approaching automobile, airplane, or powerboat is a minor or an adult, and usually cannot protect himself against youthful imprudence even if warned." Dellwo v. Pearson, 259 Minn. 452, 107 N.W.2d 859, 863, 97 A.L.R. 2d 866 (1961).

[264] See David E. Seidelson, Reasonable Expectations and Subjective Standards in Negligence Law: The Minor, The Mentally Impaired, and the Mentally Incompetent, 50 Geo. Wash. L. Rev. 17 (1981); Allen Linden, Canadian Tort Law 132 (5th ed. 1993); Restatement Third of Torts (Liability for Physical and Emotional Harm) § 10 (c) cmt. f (2010).

[265] See § 19.1. There are also a few situations in which strict liability is imposed, but this is outside the negligence regime. See Chapters 32 & 33.

[266] See §§ 20.2 & 20.5.

quality but sometimes woefully unsafe;[267] and that governmental entities,[268] charities,[269] and parents[270] were immune to suits by citizens, beneficiaries, or children, respectively. Courts also once held that no one owed a duty of care to a fetus[271] or a duty of care to avoid killing a person[272] or causing her emotional harm.[273] Nor was a duty of reasonable care owed to take any affirmative steps to aid a person in danger.[274] Courts have gradually altered the limited duty rules in most of these categories, which are discussed at greater length in Part IV. In almost no instance, not even in the case of government immunities, is the defendant without some residual obligation of care, however circumscribed it may be.

More and less negligent acts. To say that there are different potential standards of care is not to say that a different standard of care is required just because breaches of a single standard of care are not equivalent. Although negligence is ordinarily determined by the care of a reasonable person under the circumstances, some negligent acts deviate enormously from that standard while others deviate only slightly. If it is unreasonably risky to drive at 70 mph under given conditions, then it is more risky to drive at 90, and more risky still to do so when children are playing nearby and likely to dart into the street. If the probability or magnitude of harm is higher, we can think of the defendant as "more" negligent. Similarly, if the utility of the defendant's conduct diminishes, even the same risk becomes less justified, which makes his conduct more aggravated. To recognize this point is not to displace the reasonable person standard but to uphold it. The reasonable person recognizes that greater risks call for increased caution, or, as the courts say, care commensurate with the risks.

An older view: degrees of negligence. This line of thought suggests that there is one standard of care but many degrees of negligence in violating that standard. An early 18th century judge, however, came up with the idea that all negligence could be classified in three degrees—slight, ordinary, and gross.[275] The idea was that a person might be guilty of slight negligence if he failed to exercise extraordinary care or guilty of gross negligence if he failed to exercise even slight care. This tripartite division of care happened to fit neatly into the judge's ideas about the kind of care required in bailment cases. He thought you would be obliged to exercise only slight care if you held another's property as a favor, and hence you'd be liable only for gross negligence. On the other hand, if you held another's property for your own benefit, you'd be obliged to exercise extraordinary care and would be liable for slight negligence. If the bailment was for mutual benefit, ordinary care would be required and you would be liable for ordinary negligence. This little schematic picture has not been needed since 1850 when courts

---

[267] See Chapter 21.

[268] See Chapter 22.

[269] See § 23.3.

[270] See § 23.2.

[271] See Chapter 27.

[272] See Chapter 28.

[273] See Chapter 29.

[274] See Chapter 25.

[275] Coggs v. Bernard, 2 Ld. Raym. 909, 92 Eng. Rep. 107 (1703) (addressing the duties of a bailee to care for the bailed goods).

began to recognize that the single standard of care took all the circumstances into account, but is still sometimes the basis for decisions in bailment cases.[276]

Should have known vs. reason to know. In a few specific instances, courts say the defendant owes no duty of care to act on the basis of what the defendant should have known but only on the basis of what he actually knows or *has reason to know.*[277] Under the Third Restatement, a duty to warn is said to be so limited.[278] The "reason to know" test has also been used in some cases of employer liability,[279] and to buttress the special protections afforded landowners.[280] The distinction between the foreseeability standard of the "should have known" test and more demanding requirement of the "had reason to know" test has been recognized by courts in some other contexts.[281] If there is a principle behind the reason to know rule, it is not necessarily apparent. Nor is it entirely clear that the distinction between what a person should have known and what he had reason to know is always a workable difference. The "reason to know" standard may slightly limit liability when harm was foreseeable but the actor had no reason to know of it. But the distinction has not proved significant in the great mass of cases. The ordinary foreseeability or should have known rule is usually adequate to assess care without the "reason to know" complication.[282]

§ 10.18 Gross Negligence, Recklessness, and Wanton Misconduct

Gross negligence under statutes. The gross negligence standard is not often accepted as a common law standard.[283] It is more frequently adopted in statutes to limit defendants' liability. Such statutes include the now almost-extinct guest statutes,[284] and those offering special protections to preferred defendants such as charities[285] or

---

[276] E.g., Coachmen Indus. v. Crown Steel Co., 577 N.E.2d 602 (Ind. Ct. App. 1991) ("Because Coachmen, as bailee, received no benefit from this arrangement, it was obligated to exercise only slight care in protecting the material from injury.").

[277] The reason to know concept is described in Restatement Second of Torts § 12 (1965). The terminology is also used in the Restatement Third of Agency § 1.04(4) (2006) ("A person has notice of a fact if the person knows the fact, has reason to know the fact, has received an effective notification of the fact, or should know the fact to fulfill a duty owed to another person.").

[278] Restatement Third of Torts (Liability for Physical and Emotional Harm) § 18 (2010).

[279] E.g., Schovanec v. Archdiocese of Okla. City, 188 P.3d 158 (Okla. 2008). Many cases quote the Restatement Second of Agency § 213 (1957) on this point.

[280] E.g., Laster v. Norfolk S. Ry. Co., 13 So.3d 922 (Ala. 2009) (child trespasser, landowner must have at least reason to know of child's likely trespass and danger); Foss v. Kincade, 766 N.W.2d 317 (Minn. 2009) (same).

[281] John B. v. Super. Ct., 38 Cal.4th 1177, 137 P.3d 153, 45 Cal.Rptr. 3d 316 (2006) (an infected person's liability for transmitting HIV does not require that he actually know he has the infection; liability "would extend at least to those situations where the actor, under the totality of the circumstances, has *reason to know* of the infection"); Jones v. Mid-Atlantic Funding Co., 362 Md. 661, 766 A.2d 617 (2001) (plaintiff-tenant established that landlord-defendant had reason to know of flaking lead paint and its danger to children).

[282] Thus the Restatement Third drops the "reason to know" test in favor of the ordinary negligence rule in some instances. See Restatement Third of Torts (Liability for Physical and Emotional Harm) § 41, Reporters' Note to Comment c (2010) ("The Second Restatement imposed a duty on parents and employers to control the conduct of minor children and employees only if they knew or had reason to know of their ability to control and knew or had reason to know of the necessity and opportunity of control. In this [Third] Restatement, those conditions are subsumed within the analysis of reasonable care; they are not prerequisites for the existence of a duty."). See also Elizabeth G. Porter, Tort Liability in the Age of the Helicopter Parent, 64 Ala. L. Rev. 533 (2013) (advocating, in general, the Restatement Third reasonable care approach).

[283] It is still sometimes used in bailment cases, however. Waterton v. Linden Motor Inc., 11 Misc.3d 836, 810 N.Y.S.2d 319 (2006) (slight care).

[284] Davis v. Landis Outboard Motor Co., 179 Neb. 391, 138 N.W.2d 474 (1965).

[285] See Ola v. YMCA of Southhampton Rds., Inc., 270 Va. 550, 621 S.E.2d 70 (2005). This protection for charities is no longer so common. See § 23.3.

governmental officers or agencies,[286] as well as specialized statutory instruments,[287] all of which may protect defendants from liability for ordinary negligence. "Gross negligence" is an important term in the Oil Pollution Act, and a significant amount of liability in the Gulf oil spill will turn on interpretation of the term.[288]

Gross negligence defined. The term gross negligence can be used to mean what it says—a high, though unspecified degree of negligence, or as courts sometimes say, the failure to use even slight care.[289] This means conduct that is a more serious departure from safety norms than ordinary negligence, either because the risk itself is more substantial or because the risky conduct produces less compensating benefits. Used in core sense, the term "gross negligence" would not require any particular state of mind so long as the conduct itself creates an extremely unjustified risk.[290] Many courts, however, have defined gross negligence in particular cases as requiring a bad state of mind as well as extreme fault.[291] When they do so, they usually give gross negligence the same definition as willful and wanton misconduct, so that in such cases gross negligence has no distinct meaning of its own.

Reckless, willful or wanton conduct—common law. As a standard of care, recklessness or wanton misconduct is only occasionally found in the common law of torts.[292] One notable instance is that under traditional rules, landowners owe only a limited duty of care to many persons on the land and are sometimes liable only for reckless or wanton conduct or the like.[293] Another is the contemporary rule followed in many courts that sports participants are not responsible for negligent injuries but only those recklessly or wantonly caused.[294] On the matter of damages, punitive damages can be awarded when the defendant is guilty of malice, and some courts also permit recovery of punitive damages when the defendant is guilty of willful or wanton misconduct.[295]

---

[286] See Costa v. Cmty. Emergency Med. Servs., Inc., 475 Mich. 403, 716 N.W.2d 236 (2006). Although some government agencies and officers are subject to liability for gross negligence, in many instances such defendants are entirely immune. See Chapter 22.

[287] Cf. Food Pageant, Inc. v. Consol. Edison Co., Inc., 54 N.Y.2d 167, 429 N.E.2d 738, 445 N.Y.S.2d 60 (1981) (public utility rate schedule limited liability to gross negligence).

[288] See Patrick H. Martin, The BP Spill and the Meaning of "Gross Negligence or Willful Misconduct," 71 La. L. Rev. 957 (2011).

[289] Davis v. Landis Outboard Motor Co., 179 Neb. 391, 138 N.W.2d 474 (1965).

[290] Thus, for example, gross negligence, in its core meaning signifying extreme fault without a bad state of mind, is not a sufficient basis for an award of punitive damages, which requires a state of mind as well. Paiz v. State Farm Fire & Cas. Co., 118 N.M. 203, 880 P.2d 300 (1994).

[291] E.g., Franklin Corp. v. Tedford, 18 So.3d 215, 240 (Miss. 2009) (where "gross negligence . . . evidences a willful, wanton or reckless disregard for the safety of others," a statutory formulation); U-Haul Int'l, Inc. v. Waldrip, 380 S.W.3d 118 (Tex. 2012) (interpreting a statute: gross negligence contains both an objective component—an extreme degree of risk, meaning a likelihood of the plaintiff's serious injury—and a subjective component—defendant's demonstrated indifference to the consequences of its acts, in the face of actual knowledge of the risk); Cowan v. Hospice Support Care, Inc., 268 Va. 482, 603 S.E.2d 916 (2004) (combining "indifference" state of mind with subjective effect on the observer, which must be shocking to fair-minded persons).

[292] Kimble v. Carey, 691 S.E.2d 790 (Iowa 2010) (in a rescuer case the question was whether the rescuer was "rash and reckless").

[293] See Cavillo-Silva v. Home Grocery, 19 Cal.4th 714, 968 P.2d 65, 80 Cal.Rptr. 2d 506 (1998), overruled on other grounds, Aguilar v. Atl. Richfield Co., 25 Cal. 4th 826 (2001); Chapter 20 generally.

[294] See Feld v. Borkowski, 790 N.W.2d 72 (Iowa 2010) (if first baseman who was hit by a bat that flew out of batter's hands could show recklessness rather than mere negligence, liability might attach); Angland v. Mountain Creek Resort, Inc., 213 N.J. 573, 66 A.3d 1252 (2013) (snowboarders; recklessness standard). See also § 17.8 (participants and spectators).

[295] See e.g., Tackett v. State Farm Fire & Cas. Ins., 653 A.2d 254, 265 (Del. 1995) ("Mere inadvertence, mistake or errors of judgment which constitute mere negligence will not suffice. It is not enough that a decision

Reckless, willful or wanton conduct—use in statutes. The reckless/wanton standard, like the gross negligence standard, is largely a statutory limitation on duty governing particular classes of cases, not a common law rule.[296] The Good Samaritan statutes relieve health care professionals of any responsibility for negligence in medical emergencies, generally imposing liability only for reckless or wanton misconduct.[297] Statutes also often provide that operators of emergency vehicles like fire engines are liable only for reckless or wanton misconduct.[298] Similarly, statutes may limit the liability of public entities to cases of wanton misconduct.[299] Some of the old guest statutes provided that the driver of an automobile was liable to a nonpaying guest only for gross negligence, but others limited liability to cases of willful, wanton, or reckless conduct.[300]

Elements of reckless, willful or wanton conduct. Two elements are required to show reckless or willful and wanton misconduct.

a) The risk-utility balance must strongly disfavor the defendant's conduct—the risk must have been high, or very serious harm must have been threatened, or the cost of avoiding the danger must have been very low.[301] Courts sometimes state that the danger must be great[302] or that the harm must be highly probable,[303] but these may be regarded as a short form of the more accurate statement that the risk must be high considering the ease of avoiding it or the seriousness of harm threatened—the net unjustified risk.[304]

b) Courts have often said that reckless, willful or wanton misconduct also entails a mental element. The defendant must know or have reason to know of the risk[305] and must proceed without concern for the safety of others, a rule often expressed as requiring conscious indifference to the rights of others as a condition of liability.[306]

---

be wrong. It must result from a conscious indifference to the decision's foreseeable effect."). On punitive damages, see §§ 34.4 to 34.7.

[296] Delfino v. Griffo, 257 P.3d 917 (N.M. 2010) (social host liability when provision of drinks was reckless).

[297] See § 21.13. There are some differences in the statutory terms and applications.

[298] E.g., Saarinen v. Kerr, 84 N.Y.2d 494, 644 N.E.2d 988, 620 N.Y.S.2d 297 (1994); Estate of Graves v. City of Circleville, 922 N.E.2d 201 (Ohio 2010) (wanton or reckless conduct).

[299] See Calloway v. Kinkelaar, 168 Ill.2d 312, 659 N.E.2d 1322 (1995); cf. Grimm v. Ariz. Bd. of Pardons & Paroles, 115 Ariz. 260, 564 P.2d 1227 (1977) (parole board's release of dangerous prisoner, gross negligence).

[300] See, e.g., Scott v. Villegas, 723 So.2d 642 (Ala. 1998) (quoting and discussing Alabama's guest statute, which requires wanton misconduct, defined to require conscious culpability). Most of these statutes have been repealed or held unconstitutional, as in Brown v. Merlo, 8 Cal.3d 855, 106 Cal.Rptr. 388, 506 P.2d 212 (1973).

[301] Restatement Third of Torts (Liability for Physical and Emotional Harm) § 2 cmt. d (2010).

[302] See Schick v. Ferolito, 167 N.J. 7, 767 A.2d 962 (2001) (relying on Prosser & Keeton, "Reckless conduct is an extreme departure from ordinary care, in a situation in which a high degree of danger is apparent").

[303] Morris v. Leaf, 534 N.W.2d 388 (Iowa 1995) ("in disregard of a risk known to or so obvious that he must be taken to have been aware of it, and so great as to make it highly probable that harm would follow"); Campbell v. City of Elmira, 84 N.Y.2d 505, 644 N.E.2d 993, 620 N.Y.S.2d 302 (1994) (harm highly probable coupled with conscious indifference to the outcome).

[304] See Restatement Third of Torts (Liability for Physical and Emotional Harm) § 2 cmt. d (2010).

[305] Id. cmt. a.

[306] E.g., Estate of Rae v. Murphy, 956 A.2d 1266 (Del. 2008) ("[f]or a defendant's conduct to be found willful or wanton, the conduct must reflect a 'conscious indifference' or 'I don't care' attitude"; negligently failing to notice a red light is insufficient); Doe v. Ortega-Piron, 213 Ill.2d 19, 820 N.E.2d 418, 289 Ill.Dec. 642 (2004). Some courts use a form of "indifference" to define "gross negligence," and thus seem to conflate recklessness and gross negligence, at least for some purposes. See, e.g., Howard v. Chimps, Inc., 251 Or.App. 636, 284 P.3d 1181 (2012) ("To establish gross negligence, plaintiff needed to show that defendant acted with reckless disregard of safety or indifference to the probable consequences of its acts.").

Known risk permitting inference of conscious indifference. Some authority relaxes the conscious indifference element, finding recklessness under an "objective standard" when the defendant knows or has reason to know of the risk and a reasonable person would recognize that it was a very serious risk.[307] The Restatement Third came up with a slightly different approach to the mental component. It provides that recklessness can be found when the defendant has reason to know the risk and his failure to adopt precautions amounts to a "demonstration of [his] indifference to the risk."[308]

Special treatments of willful and wanton. By any definition, recklessness is not the same as intentional harm, but courts sometimes treat "willful" and "wanton" misconduct more like an intentional tort than a negligent one,[309] though at other times these words are treated essentially like recklessness.[310]

---

[307] Boyd v. Nat'l R.R. Passenger Corp., 446 Mass. 540, 845 N.E.2d 356 (2006); Restatement Second of Torts § 500 cmt. a (1965).

[308] Restatement Third or Torts (Liability for Physical and Emotional Harm) § 2 cmt. a (2010).

[309] See Ziarko v. Soo Line R.R., 161 Ill.2d 267, 641 N.E.2d 402 (1994) (sometimes more like negligence, sometimes more like intent); Lennon v. Metro. Life Ins., 504 F.3d 617, 621 (6th Cir. 2008); cf. Doe 1 ex rel. Doe 1 v. Roman Catholic Diocese of Nashville, 154 S.W.3d 22, 38 (Tenn. 2005) (dealing with the claim of reckless infliction of emotional distress; "recklessness contains an awareness component similar to intentional conduct which is not demanded of negligence").

[310] See Restatement Third of Torts (Liability for Physical and Emotional Harm) § 2, Reporters' Note Comment a (2010).

Chapter 11

IMPORTING STATUTORY STANDARDS OF CARE: NEGLIGENCE PER SE

Analysis

§ 11.1　The Rule of Negligence Per Se
§ 11.2　Statutes Creating a Standard of Care
§ 11.3　Negligence Per Se vs. Private Right of Action
§ 11.4　Alternatives to Negligence Per Se: Evidence of Negligence
§ 11.5　Rationales for Negligence Per Se
§ 11.6　Type of Harm Prevented by the Statute
§ 11.7　Class of Persons Protected Under the Statute
§ 11.8　Interpreting the Scope of Risk
§ 11.9　Excused and Unexcused Violations

§ 11.1　The Rule of Negligence Per Se

The negligence per se rule. The negligence per se rule holds that a violation of statute is negligence in itself if the statutory violation causes the type of harm the statute was intended to avoid,[1] to a person within the class of persons the statute was intended to protect.[2] In the absence of a valid excuse,[3] violation of the statute conclusively shows negligence.[4] The Restatement Third echoes this understanding.[5] Violation of statute by a plaintiff equally proves the plaintiff's contributory negligence or comparative fault in appropriate cases.[6]

Examples of negligence per se statutes. The negligence per se rule has been applied to a wide variety of statutory violations. Statutes governing traffic safety are perhaps the most common statutes for application of the negligence per se rule.[7] Violation of a speed limit typically subjects the violator to a criminal misdemeanor prosecution, but courts adopt the speed limit as a tort rule. Many other statutes are adopted by the courts as a standard of care—for example, statutes requiring swimming pool owners to have

---

[1]　Cf. Cullip v. Domann, 266 Kan. 550, 972 P.2d 776 (1999) (boy violated statute by hunting without safety certificate, but was not carrying the gun that discharged and harmed the plaintiff).

[2]　§§ 11.6 to 11.7.

[3]　See § 11.9.

[4]　Rong Yao Zhou v. Jennifer Mall Restaurant, Inc., 534 A.2d 1268 (D.C. 1987); Duphily v. Delaware Elec. Co-op., Inc., 662 A.2d 821 (Del. 1995); Restatement Third of Torts (Liability for Physical and Emotional Harm) § 14 (2010). The rules may be codified in some statutes. See West's Ann. Cal. Evid. Code § 669.

[5]　Restatement Third of Torts (Liability for Physical and Emotional Harm) § 14 (2010) ("An actor is negligent if, without excuse, the actor violates a statute that is designed to protect against the type of accident the actor's conduct causes, and the accident victim is within the class of persons the statute is designed to protect.").

[6]　E.g., Donaldson v. Indianapolis Pub. Transp. Corp., 632 N.E.2d 1167 (Ind. Ct. App. 1994); Adams v. Mills, 312 N.C. 181, 322 S.E.2d 164 (1984).

[7]　E.g., Thomas v. Commerford, 168 Conn. 64, 357 A.2d 476 (1975) (unsignalled turn); Martin v. Herzog, 228 N.Y. 164, 126 N.E. 814 (1920) (lights).

lifeguards,[8] businesses to observe fire safety regulations,[9] landlords to keep premises in safe condition[10] or to provide locks to protect tenants,[11] and building codes that impose safety standards.[12] A statute may require lights on a ship, buildings constructed to specific requirements, safety devices for protection of construction workers, or smoke detectors for the protection of tenants. Violation can be negligence per se.[13] Statutes regulating sales or dispensation of dangerous items like guns,[14] alcohol[15] or prescription drugs[16] may also sometimes furnish grounds for a negligence claim by persons injured as a result of the sale. Statutes regulating economic relations of the parties, such as those requiring disclosure of specific information, have been held to be the basis of a negligence per se claim.[17] Courts might even choose to adopt duties set in an internationally recognized instrument such as the Nuremberg Code as appropriate guides to state tort law.[18]

Statutes from outside tort law. The rule of negligence per se is applied when the statute in question does not prescribe a tort law effect at all. These statutes prescribe nothing about tort law, not even by implication, though they may impose criminal liability or administrative penalties. For that reason, we will refer to these as "nonprescriptive" statutes. Yet courts regularly adopt nonprescriptive statutory rules for specific conduct as rules creating a standard for tort law. In most states, but not all,[19]

---

[8]   Lucas v. Hesperia Golf & Country Club, 255 Cal.App. 2d 241, 63 Cal.Rptr. 189 (1967) (either lifeguard or warning that one was not present required, violation was negligence per se).

[9]   See Camden Oil Co., LLC v. Jackson, 270 Ga.App. 837, 609 S.E.2d 356 (2004); Simpson v. Boyd, 880 So.2d 1047 (Miss. 2004) (statutes requiring fire exits covered any emergent need to escape).

[10]   E.g., Robinson v. Bates, 112 Ohio St. 3d 17, 857 N.E.2d 1195 (2006).

[11]   Brock v. Watts Realty Co., Inc., 582 So.2d 438, 43 A.L.R.5th 839 (Ala. 1991) (common law did not recognize a duty of care to protect tenant against intruders, but ordinance created a duty with respect to locks); Grant v. Thornton, 49 So.2d 529 (Fla. Dist. Ct. App. 1999) (landlord's door locks required key for exit, tenant who could not reach key in a fire injured escaping through a window).

[12]   Pierce v. ALSC Architects, P.S., 270 Mont. 97, 890 P.2d 1254 (1995); Vega v. Eastern Courtyard Assocs., 117 Nev. 436, 24 P.3d 219 (2001) McGuire v. Hodges, 639 S.E.2d 284 (Va. 2007); contra, Mayle v. Ohio Dep't of Rehab. & Corr., 2010 WL 2433119 (Ohio Ct. App. 2010) (building code was administrative rule and thus violation was not to be given the negligence per se effect, only evidence of negligence).

[13]   Kernan v. American Dredging Co., 355 U.S. 426, 78 S.Ct. 394, 2 L.Ed.2d 382 (1958) (ship lights); Haft v. Lone Palm Hotel, 3 Cal.3d 756, 478 P.2d 465, 91 Cal.Rptr. 745 (1970) (lifeguard); Alderman's Inc. v. Shanks, 536 N.W.2d 4 (Minn. 1995) (building, fire door); Barnaby v. A. & C. Properties, 188 A.D.2d 958, 592 N.Y.S.2d 98 (1992) (workers, scaffolding act); Reed v. Phillips, 192 W.Va. 392, 452 S.E.2d 708 (1994).

[14]   E.g., Coker v. Wal-Mart Stores, Inc., 642 So.2d 774 (Fla. Dist. Ct. App. 1994); but cf. Williams ex rel. Raymond v. Wal-Mart Stores East, L.P., 99 So. 3d 112 (Miss. 2012) (store's sale of ammunition to a minor, in violation of a federal statute, was negligent per se, but store was not liable because the store's negligence was not a proximate cause of the death of the victim who was shot by the minor with that ammunition); Rains v. Bend of the River, 124 S.W.3d 580 (Tenn. Ct. App. 2003).

[15]   E.g., Loeb v. Rasmussen, 822 P.2d 914 (Alaska 1991), superseded by statute, Sowinski v. Walker, 198 P.3d 1134, 1140 (Alaska 2008).

[16]   Gipson v. Kasey, 214 Ariz. 141, 150 P.3d 228 (2007).

[17]   Alaface v. Nat'l Investment Co., 181 Ariz. 586, 892 P.2d 1375 (Ct. App. 1994).

[18]   See Grimes v. Kennedy Krieger Inst., Inc., 366 Md. 29, 782 A.2d 807 (2001) (court treats the "Nuremberg Code," standards set by the war crimes tribunals in trials of Nazi doctors for their human experiments as important guideline if not a firm standard in human subjects case).

[19]   E.g., Griglione v. Martin, 525 N.W.2d 810 (Iowa 1994); Elliott v. City of New York, 95 N.Y.2d 730, 747 N.E.2d 760, 724 N.Y.S.2d 397 (2001); Lang v. Holly Hill Motel, Inc., 122 Ohio St.3d 120, 909 N.E.2d 120 (2009) (violation of administrative regulation is evidence of negligence only).

the per se rule can apply not only to statutes but also to violation of some ordinances[20] and administrative regulations.[21]

§ 11.2   Statutes Creating a Standard of Care

Relation to the ordinary negligence claim. The plaintiff who claims that the defendant was negligent per se in violating a safety statute is not claiming a new species of tort but asserting an ordinary negligence claim. The negligence per se rule simply recognizes that negligence is proved by showing the violation of statute aimed at protecting the plaintiff from the kinds of harms she suffered. Because the negligence per se claim is a claim of ordinary negligence, the plaintiff must prove the other elements of negligence: duty, breach, and factual causation of actual harm that is within the scope of the risk, and she will lose if she fails to do so.[22]

Standard of care vs. duty. The statutes applied in negligence per se characteristically are used to supply standards of care for tort law purposes. However, they do not necessarily create a duty of care on the part of the defendant.

Statutes typically create a standard. Courts typically adopt specific statutory standards only when the common law itself imposes a duty to exercise care, or, possibly, when the statute creates a special relationship that becomes the basis for a common law duty of care.[23] The statute's usual function, then, is to specify what particular acts are required to fulfill the common law duty of care. When the statute imposes a new duty unknown to the common law, courts may or may not use the statute to recognize a tort claim.

Illustration; statutory violation as relevant to duty but not dispositive. The Restatement Third makes clear that violation of statute is "relevant to a duty analysis, even though the violation does not signify duty per se."[24] The Restatement Third uses the example of a state court that has ruled that pharmacists have no common law duty to warn their customers of medication side effects. If a state agency then imposes a duty to warn, the court can take this consideration into account when deciding whether to adopt a tort duty. However, "the regulation does not require that the courts now recognize a tort duty."[25]

---

[20]   E.g., Parker Bldg. Servs. Co., Inc. v. Lightsey ex rel. Lightsey, 925 So.2d 927, 931 (Ala. 2005); Fresno Traction Co. v. Atchison, T. & S. F. Ry, 175 Cal. 358, 165 P. 1013 (1917); Nettleton v. Thompson, 117 Idaho 308, 787 P.2d 294 (1990); Vega v. Eastern Courtyard Assocs., 117 Nev. 436, 24 P.3d 219 (2001) (building code adopted by county ordinance).

[21]   Davis v. Marathon Oil Co., 64 Ill. 2d 380, 356 N.E.2d 93, 1 Ill. Dec. 93 (1976); contra, Mayle v. Ohio Dep't of Rehab. & Corr., 2010 WL 2433119 (Ohio Ct. App. 2010) ("an administrative rule violation" but is only evidence of negligence).

[22]   See, e.g., Haft v. Lone Palm Hotel, 3 Cal.3d 756, 478 P.2d 465, 91 Cal.Rptr. 745 (1970); Joseph v. Bozzuto Mgmt. Co., 173 Md. App. 305, 918 A.2d 1230 (2007).

[23]   Kaho'ohanohano v. Department of Human Servs., State of Haw. 117 Haw. 262, 291, 178 P.3d 538, 567 (2008) (a statute calling for immediate action by the child protective agency once an abuse report is received "underscores the recognition of a special relationship between [the agency] and the alleged endangered child and a duty on the part of [the agency] and its social workers to protect that child"); Nelson v. Driscoll, 295 Mont. 363, 371, 983 P.2d 972, 978 (1999) ("A special relationship can be established . . . by a statute intended to protect a specific class of persons of which the plaintiff is a member from a particular type of harm.").

[24]   Restatement Third of Torts (Liability for Physical and Emotional Harm) § 14 cmt. i (2010).

[25]   Id.

Explanation. That is because violation of the statutory standard might prove negligence, but violation does not prove the other elements of the case.[26] In particular, violation of the statute does not prove duty, factual causation, or "proximate cause." As Judge Posner explained:[27]

> [I]f a statute defines what is due care in some activity, the violation of the statute either conclusively or . . . presumptively establishes that the violator failed to exercise due care. But the statutory definition does not come into play unless the tort plaintiff establishes that the defendant owes a duty of care to the person he injured . . . because tort liability depends on the violation of a duty of care to the person injured by the defendant's wrongful conduct. . . . [A]lthough the legislature can and sometimes does create a duty of care to a new class of injured persons, the mere fact that a statute *defines* due care does not in and of itself create a duty enforceable by tort law.

Other thoughtful discussions make the same point in various turns of phrase.[28]

A confusion: negligence per se requires duty and breach. It is sometimes said that negligence per se establishes duty and breach.[29] However, as explained, the defendant must be under a duty to use reasonable care; if he is not, violation of the statute cannot not prove breach of duty,[30] though statutes themselves may sometimes create a duty of care.[31] Furthermore, although the statute provides a standard that frames the breach question, if the statute was not violated at all, there is no breach.[32]

§ 11.3 Negligence Per Se vs. Private Right of Action

Statutes used as per se negligence and those that create private rights of action. It is important to keep in mind that negligence per se "presupposes a statute that declares conduct unlawful but is silent as to civil liability" and "cannot be readily interpreted as

---

[26] See Pile v. City of Brandenburg, 215 S.W.3d 36 (Ky. 2006) ("negligence per se is merely a negligence claim with a statutory standard of care substituted for the common law standard of care"); McGuire v. Hodges, 639 S.E.2d 284 (Va. 2007) (party showing violation of statute need go no further to establish negligence, but still must show proximate cause and other elements).

[27] Cuyler v. U.S., 362 F.3d 949, 952 (7th Cir. 2004).

[28] Marquay v. Eno, 139 N.H. 708, 713–14, 662 A.2d 272, 277 (1995) (The doctrine of negligence per se on the other "provides that where a cause of action does exist at common law, the standard of conduct to which a defendant will be held may be defined as that required by statute, rather than as the usual reasonable person standard. The doctrine of negligence per se, however, plays no role in the creation of common law causes of action. Thus, in many cases, the common law may fail to recognize liability for failure to perform affirmative duties that are imposed by statute."); see also Quiroz v. Seventh Ave. Ctr., 140 Cal.App.4th 1256, 1285, 45 Cal.Rptr.3d 222, 244 (2006); Varela ex rel. Nelson v. St. Elizabeth's Hosp. of Chicago, Inc., 372 Ill.App. 3d 714, 867 N.E.2d 1, 310 Ill.Dec. 688 (2007).

[29] E.g., Olson v. Shumaker Trucking & Excavating Contractors, Inc., 347 Mont. 1, 18, 196 P.3d 1265, 1277 (2008) ("Establishing the existence of negligence per se settles only the questions of duty and breach"); Lang v. Holly Hill Motel, Inc., 122 Ohio St.3d 120, 909 N.E.2d 120 (2009). However, these cases appear to mean only that the statute prescribes the specific means of satisfying an existing duty of reasonable care.

[30] See, e.g., Estate of Johnson ex rel. Johnson v. Badger Acquisition of Tampa LLC, 983 So.2d 1175 (Fla. Dist. Ct. App. 2008) ("violation of a statute may be evidence of negligence, but such evidence only becomes relevant to a breach of a standard of care after the law has imposed a duty of care").

[31] Restatement Third of Torts (Liability for Physical and Emotional Harm) § 14 cmt. i (2010) (violation of a statute can be relevant to a duty analysis).

[32] See Young v. U-Haul Co. of D.C., 11 A.3d 247 (D.C. 2011) (ordinance prohibiting owner of motor vehicle from authorizing or knowingly permitting motor vehicle to be driven by an unauthorized person could not be used as basis for negligence per se where rental company did not know at the time of the rental that the renter's driver's license had been suspended); Hopper v. Swinnerton, 317 P.3d 698 (Idaho 2013) (plaintiffs failed to prove that defendants violated the statute).

impliedly creating a private right of action."[33] Thus in negligence per se cases, courts, under their authority to develop the common law, import non-tort statutes to determine the tort law standards. This differs from simply creating a private tort right of action under a statute.

Negligence per se: statutes creating criminal sanctions but not tort rules. Statutes used to create common law tort standards are typically those that do not to address tort law at all but can nevertheless have tort law effects. These statutes frequently impose criminal or administrative sanction upon defendants who fail to follow a specific safety requirement; but, significantly, these statutes do not attempt to create a tort cause of action or specify tort rules. Traffic safety statutes such as those prescribing speed limits or lights at night are examples.[34] Statutes like this make traffic violations a minor crime but ordinarily say nothing, not even impliedly, about tort rules. Yet courts may adopt the statutory speed limit as a good guide to what is reasonable care under the circumstances in the ordinary common law action. In so doing, they will often say that violation of the criminal statute is negligence per se, that is, violation is itself proof of negligence in a tort case.[35] Less commonly, they may say that violation of the statute is evidence of negligence, but is not conclusive on the issue. Both versions have in common the idea that the court, under no compulsion to do so, has voluntarily accepted the statutory standard for common law tort purposes.

Private rights of action: statutes explicitly or impliedly creating tort rules or actions. Statutes that create private rights of action expressly or implicitly address tort law. A statute that addresses tort law is enforced by the courts according to its express or implied terms, so long as the statute's provisions are constitutional.[36] The Federal Employers Liability Act (FELA) can be viewed in this light. FELA creates a federal claim on behalf of railroad workers injured on the job. The statute abolishes the defenses of contributory negligence and assumed risk[37] and has sometimes been interpreted to impose a liberal view of fault and causation that makes recovery relatively easy.[38] Were there no such statutes, the railroad employees would ordinarily be limited to state tort law claims for workers' compensation payments for on the job injury or would be subject to defenses like contributory negligence and assumed risk. Although FELA cases are still negligence cases in the sense that negligence is an issue, some of the rules of conduct and litigation are different. Many other statutes are like FELA in providing a new set of

---

[33] Restatement Third of Torts (Liability for Physical and Emotional Harm) § 14 cmt. c (2010).

[34] Martin v. Herzog, 228 N.Y. 164, 126 N.E. 814 (1920). Cf. Woods v. Burlington N. & Santa Fe Ry., 324 Mont. 151, 104 P.3d 1037 (2004) (railroad's violation of federal regulation was negligence per se in suit under federal FELA statute).

[35] E.g., Getchell v. Lodge, 65 P.3d 50 (Alaska 2003).

[36] See, e.g., McCormick v. Carrier, 487 Mich. 180, 795 N.W.2d 517 (2010) (Michigan's No-Fault Act); Beggs v. State, Dep't of Soc. & Health Servs., 171 Wash.2d 69, 247 P.3d 421 (2011) (mandatory child abuse reporting statute held to imply cause of action against a mandatory reporter who failed to report suspected abuse).

[37] Federal Employers Liability Act (FELA), 45 U.S.C.A § 51.

[38] See Kernan v. American Dredging Co., 355 U.S. 426, 78 S.Ct. 394, 2 L.Ed.2d 382 (1958); CSX Transp., Inc. v. McBride, 131 S.Ct. 2630, 180 L.Ed.2d 637, 32 I.E.R. Cas. (BNA) 609, 2011 A.M.C. 1521 (2011) (in an FELA case normal rules of proximate causation do not apply; rather, a plaintiff need only show that the railroad's negligence played a part, no matter how small, in bringing about the injury).

rules, even though the case may still fit within the general scheme of negligence law.[39] Even the United States Constitution itself may implicitly create a tort claim.[40]

Losing the distinction. Courts are not always rigorous in distinguishing the two kinds of statutes.[41] When the statute prescribes tort rules, the appropriate judicial response is to simply follow the commands of the statute, whether they are expressed or implied. Yet courts may speak of "negligence per se" even when applying statutes that seem intended to prescribe tort rules.[42] Some other courts seem to treat the negligence per se doctrine as identical with the private cause of action.[43] A Wisconsin court seems to have consciously eliminated the traditional negligence per se liability by refusing to give the statute any effect in tort law unless the statute at least impliedly recognizes a private right of action.[44]

Maintaining the distinction—judicial freedom. The distinction between these two kinds of statutes is important. On the one hand, courts are required to recognize a tort action when the statute creates the action; they are bound to follow a valid statute. On the other hand, if a statute provides nothing about tort law one way or the other, courts are free to either reject the statutory standard for tort law purposes, or to import the statutory standard into the common law of torts and to hold that violation of the standard is either negligence per se or evidence of negligence.

Private rights of action and common law actions. Some statutes create a tort cause of action and limit the duties imposed, damages recoverable, or procedures available for enforcement.[45] That leaves open the possibility that the judges might both recognize the private right of action and create a common law action that does not impose the same limits. If the statute does not explicitly or implicitly exclude common law development, it is quite possible that both a statutory right of action and a common law action will exist side by side but with different duties, defenses, or procedures.[46]

---

[39]   Some important federal statutes like this include the Jones Act, 46 U.S.C.A. § 688 (some FELA rules applied to injured seafaring employees); Federal Tort Claims Act, 28 U.S.C.A. §§ 2671 to 2680 (creating rights against government for certain torts); the Emergency Medical Treatment Act, 42 U.S.C.A. § 1395dd (rights to emergency screening and treatment at certain hospitals); various civil rights acts, including 42 U.S.C.A. § 1983 (denial of federal right under of color of law is actionable); 42 U.S.C.A. § 2000e (certain employment discrimination actionable after procedural prerequisites); Americans with Disability Act, 42 U.S.C.A. §§ 12101 et seq.; Comprehensive Environmental Response, Compensation and Liability Act (CERCLA) (Superfund Act), 42 U.S.C.A. §§ 9607 et seq. In the states, statutes creating a claim for elder abuse are in this category. See, e.g., Wash. Rev. Code § 74.34.200.

[40]   Bivens v. Six Unknown Named Agents of Fed. Bur. of Narcotics, 403 U.S. 388, 91 S.Ct. 1999, 29 L.Ed.2d 619 (1971) (federal officers can be sued for constitutional violations).

[41]   See Marquay v. Eno, 662 A.2d 272 (N.H. 1995) (drawing the distinction to resolve confusion in two seemingly contradictory lines of cases).

[42]   See Robinson v. Bates, 112 Ohio St.3d 17, 857 N.E.2d 1195 (2006) (a statute construed to mean that the open and obvious danger doctrine was abolished and a tort cause of action was created separate from the common law action; referred to as "negligence per se").

[43]   O'Neill v. Dunham, 203 P.3d 68 (Kan. Ct. App. 2009) (referring to private cause of action for negligence per se); Doe v. Marion, 373 S.C. 390, 645 S.E.2d 245 (2007) (similar).

[44]   See Raymaker v. American Family Mut. Ins. Co., 293 Wis.2d 392, 718 N.W.2d 154 (Ct. App. 2006) (asserting that "negligence per se" can be invoked only when "there is some expression of legislative intent that the statute become a basis for the imposition of civil liability").

[45]   See M.W. v. Dep't of Soc. & Health Servs., 149 Wash. 2d 589, 70 P.3d 954 (2003).

[46]   See Craig v. Driscoll, 262 Conn. 312, 813 A.2d 1003 (2003) (statute imposing certain limited liabilities on seller of alcohol to intoxicated person does not foreclose common law action, the statute did not show a legislative intent to occupy the field). The statute was amended after the Craig decision, apparently making the statute exclusive. See Conn. Gen. Stat. Ann § 30–102. See also Hairston v. General Pipeline Constr., Inc., 226 W.Va. 663, 704 S.E.2d 663 (2010) (state statute prohibited excavation, removal or destruction of burial

Statutes disclaiming tort law effects. Legislatures sometimes provide that statutory rules or standards are *not* to be given any tort law effects but are to be enforced solely by criminal law or administrative sanctions. The federal and state Occupational Safety and Health Acts (OSHA) and the accompanying regulations provide detailed rules for safety conditions in many industries.[47] But the statute may be read to say that it is to be enforced by regulatory agencies, not by tort law.[48] Since the legislature is supreme so long as it acts within the scope of its constitutional powers, courts are obliged to follow the statutory directive. They are not free to adopt the safety regulations as tort rules or standards if the legislature has said that the safety regulations are not to affect tort law.[49]

§ 11.4 Alternatives to Negligence Per Se: Evidence of Negligence

Evidence of negligence rule generally. A number of courts reject the per se rule and treat violation of statute as, at most, merely some evidence of negligence[50] or as "guidelines for civil liability."[51] This rule permits the jury to conclude that a statute violator behaved in a reasonable way even though he violated the statute and in so doing caused harm to persons the statute was intended to protect, of the type the statute was intended to prevent.

Special cases for the evidence of negligence rule. Other courts may use the evidence of negligence rule when they believe the per se rule is too inflexible or too demanding[52] or when they believe that the particular statute is better suited to an evidence rule than a per se rule.[53] When the per se rule is rejected because the harm suffered is not the kind at which the statute was aimed or the plaintiff is not within the class to be protected, some courts nevertheless treat violation of the statute as some evidence of negligence.[54] Similarly, a building code requirement passed after the defendant's construction was

---

grounds or unmarked graves without a permit, and preempted common law with respect to those specific matters, but statute did not bar plaintiff's common law claim for grave desecration).

[47]   29 U.S.C.A. §§ 651 et seq.

[48]   The exact provision in the federal statute: "Nothing in this chapter shall be construed to supersede or in any manner affect any workmen's compensation law or to enlarge or diminish or affect in any other manner the common law or statutory rights, duties, or liabilities of employers and employees under any law with respect to injuries, diseases, or death of employees arising out of, or in the course of, employment." 29 U.S.C.A § 653(b)(4).

[49]   A number of courts have refused to treat violation of the OSHA statute as negligence. Ries v. National R.R. Passenger Corp., 960 F.2d 1156 (3d Cir. 1992); Canape v. Petersen, 897 P.2d 762 (Colo. 1995). Others have used violation of the statute as negligence per se. Pratico v. Portland Terminal Co., 783 F.2d 255 (1st Cir. 1985). Others have strived for a middle ground, treating violation of the statute as evidence of negligence, but not negligence in itself. Scott v. Matlack, Inc., 39 P.3d 1160 (Colo. 2002).

[50]   Ridley v. Safety Kleen Corp., 693 So.2d 934 (Fla. 1996); Absolon v. Dollahite, 376 Md. 547, 831 A.2d 6 (2003); Guinan v. Famous Players-Lasky Corp., 267 Mass. 501, 167 N.E. 235 (1929); Praus v. Mack, 626 N.W.2d 239 (N.D. 2001). Statutes may prescribe the evidence of negligence rule. Wash. Rev. Code § 5.40.050.

[51]   Galloway v. State, 654 So.2d 1345 (La. 1995). Wyoming gives the trial judge discretion whether to instruct the jury under the per se or the evidence of negligence rule and reviews for abuse of discretion. Frost v. Allred, 148 P.3d 17 (Wyo. 2006).

[52]   Ferrell v. Baxter, 484 P.2d 250 (Alaska 1971).

[53]   Sawyer v. Food Lion, Inc., 144 N.C.App. 398, 549 S.E.2d 867 (2001) (OSHA regulation). Legislation sometimes provides that violation of a particular statutes has no effect or at most is evidence of negligence. E.g., Cal. Vehicle Code § 27315; N.C. Gen. Stat. § 20–141.

[54]   Koll v. Manatt's Transp. Co., 253 N.W.2d 265 (Iowa 1977); Manchack v. Willamette Indus., Inc., 621 So.2d 649 (La. Ct. App. 1993).

complete has no technical application to the defendant, but may nevertheless be good evidence of a feasible safety standard.[55]

Prima facie or presumption rule. Because certain limited excuses for violation of statute are recognized, some courts describe their rule as a presumption of negligence rule[56] or a prima facie negligence rule.[57] This may be merely a different way of expressing the negligence per se rule, since both recognize excuses. However, taken literally, the presumption of negligence rule can be read as a strong expression of the evidence rule— the plaintiff is guaranteed access to the jury because proof of statutory violation makes her prima facie case. And like the evidence rule, it permits the jury to find that, in spite of the statutory violation, the defendant was not negligent.[58]

§ 11.5 Rationales for Negligence Per Se

Rationales for negligence per se. The history of the negligence per se rule is not familiar,[59] but it appears to have grown up without careful, explicit consideration,[60] and commentators have offered several explanations for this seemingly strange result. One argument was that the legislature intended to provide for tort liability but forgot to do so. Another was that reasonable people always obey statutes.[61] The argument that the legislature invariably forgets what it was aiming to do, while perhaps tempting to a satirist of the political process, seems to provide no basis for a responsible development of rules by the judiciary.

Comity. The Restatement suggests that imposition of the negligence per se rule may be justified because institutional comity requires courts to defer to the legislative standard.[62] However, it seems doubtful that judicial respect for the legislature requires courts to create statutory terms the legislature itself chose not to include. That is an

---

[55] Considine v. City of Waterbury, 279 Conn. 830, 905 A.2d 70 (2006).

[56] Cal. Evid. Code § 669 specifies that certain statutory violations create a presumption of negligence, rebuttable by a showing, among other things, that "The person violating the statute, ordinance, or regulation did what might reasonably be expected of a person of ordinary prudence, acting under similar circumstances, who desired to comply with the law."

[57] See, e.g., Waugh v. Traxler, 186 W.Va. 355, 412 S.E.2d 756 (1991). "Presumption" and "prima facie" are equated in the language of some judges. See Kizer v. Harper, 211 W.Va. 47, 561 S.E.2d 368, 374 (2001).

[58] For instance, some courts might mean that the defendant could rebut the finding of negligence simply by persuading the jury that his conduct was reasonable in spite of the violation. See Childs v. Purll, 882 A.2d 227 (D.C. 2005) (violation of statute creates a presumption of negligence, but if defendant offers evidence to show he acted reasonably in spite of the violation, then violation is merely evidence of negligence); Kalata v. Anheuser-Busch Cos., Inc., 144 Ill.2d 425, 581 N.E.2d 656, 163 Ill.Dec. 502 (1991); Polakoff v. Turner, 385 Md. 467, 869 A.2d 837 (2005). The District of Columbia has elsewhere been more direct: "Ordinarily, while the violation of a statute or a regulation having the force of law may be evidence of negligence, it does not constitute negligence per se." Liu v. Allen, 894 A.2d 453, 459 (D.C. 2006).

[59] In a 2009 article attacking the negligence per se rule, however, Professor Blomquist devoted almost 20 pages to reviewing and quoting cases from 1841 to Cardozo's opinion in Martin v. Herzog. Robert F. Blomquist, The Trouble with Negligence Per Se, 61 S.C. L. Rev. 221 (2009).

[60] The problem runs back as far as the 14th century with the enactment of a statute on repossession of land by forcible entry. 5 Richard II c. 7. Courts have struggled over the years with the question whether that statute created a tort claim and if so what it looked like. As late as 1860 the New York Court of Appeals was rejecting the idea that a criminal statute would have tort law effect. Brown v. Buffalo & State Line R.R., 22 N.Y. 191 (1860). Some 19th century statutes did provide expressly for tort liability and some courts may have moved unthinkingly from those statutes to the now-common statutes that provide nothing of the sort. Another line of 19th century cases involved an element of social reform. Important statutes reflected legislative efforts to protect people from railroads, purveyors of dangerously bad food, unlabeled poisons, and employers of child labor.

[61] See Thayer, Public Wrong and Private Action, 27 Harv. L. Rev. 317 (1913); Prosser & Keeton § 36.

[62] Restatement Third of Torts (Liability for Physical and Emotional Harm) § 14 cmt. c (2010).

especially cogent consideration because the legislature might well have been willing to impose criminal liability, especially for a limited fine typical in many traffic ordinances, but not unlimited civil liability. And it might have been willing to impose liability when guilt is established beyond a reasonable doubt as required in some criminal cases, but not upon merely a preponderance of evidence, the standard in civil cases.

Consistency. A better argument may be that in recurring situations, a flat rule of law that covers every single case is more just than a varied response by different juries.[63] But even this argument has its weakness: it denies the uniqueness of each set of facts and the essential character of justice that it is focused on the individual case, not on patterns.

Judicial borrowing. Contemporary thought recognizes that as courts create common-law tort law rules, they can adopt and import rules from statutes if they wish to do so. The statutory rule, as a Wisconsin Court said, is a "judicial transplant."[64] Colorado has said that statutes, like industry customs, may be "borrowed" to show appropriate safety standards.[65] The Restatement, although advancing some of the older arguments outlined above, accepts this adoption theory[66] and a number of courts have supported it explicitly[67] or by clear implication.[68] Others simply reflect the theory without mentioning it by applying some statutes in tort cases and not applying others.

Judicial policy judgments. A court's acceptance or rejection of a statutory standard necessarily reflects its attitudes about justice and policy. Courts refused for a long time to impose liability upon sellers of alcohol who sold in violation of statutory restrictions. They simply rejected the statutory standard as inappropriate.[69] As public and judicial attitudes changed, courts began to adopt the statutory standards for liquor sellers and to impose tort liability for their violation when, for example, the seller provides alcohol to a minor or an intoxicated person who then causes harm as a result of the intoxication.[70] There are many examples of statutes that are rejected as grounds for tort liability on very broad grounds of policy or attitude, including, for example, statutes that would, if utilized in tort litigation, impose liability upon governmental agencies or

---

[63]   Id.

[64]   Olson v. Ratzel, 89 Wis.2d 227, 278 N.W.2d 238 (Ct. App. 1979).

[65]   Scott v. Matlack, Inc., 39 P.3d 1160 (Colo. 2002).

[66]   Restatement Third of Torts (Liability for Physical and Emotional Harm) § 14 cmt. c (2010).

[67]   Talley v. Danek Med., Inc., 179 F.3d 154 (4th Cir. 1999); Ferrell v. Baxter, 484 P.2d 250 (Alaska 1971); Clinkscales v. Carver, 22 Cal.2d 72, 136 P.2d 777 (1943); Rong Yao Zhou v. Jennifer Mall Restaurant, Inc., 534 A.2d 1268 (D.C. 1987); Mansfield v. Circle K. Corp., 877 P.2d 1130 (Okla. 1994); Rains v. Bend of the River, 124 S.W.3d 580 (Tenn. Ct. App. 2003); Rudes v. Gottschalk, 159 Tex. 552, 324 S.W.2d 201 (1959); see Frost v. Allred, 148 P.3d 17, 22 (Wyo. 2006) (trial judges have "discretion" to adopt the standard as negligence per se or to limit its use to evidence of negligence, reviewable for abuse of discretion).

[68]   See Marquay v. Eno, 139 N.H. 708, 662 A.2d 272 (1995). A number of courts have implicitly accepted the adoption theory in quoting with approval from Restatement sections that express the theory. E.g., Zeni v. Anderson, 397 Mich. 117, 243 N.W.2d 270 (1976); Barrett v. Lucky Seven Saloon, Inc., 96 P.3d 386 (Wash. 2004).

[69]   E.g., Stachniewicz v. Mar-Cam Corp., 259 Or. 583, 488 P.2d 436 (1971), overruled by Davis v. Billy's Con-Teena, Inc., 284 Or. 351, 587 P.2d 75 (1978); Garcia v. Hargrove, 52 Wis.2d 289, 190 N.W.2d 181 (1971), superseded by statute as explained in Meier ex rel. Meier v. Champ's Sport Bar & Grill, Inc., 241 Wis.2d 605, 623 N.W.2d 94 (2001).

[70]   Rong Yao Zhou v. Jennifer Mall Restaurant, Inc., 534 A.2d 1268 (D.C. 1987); Sorensen v. Jarvis, 199 Wis.2d 627, 350 N.W.2d 108 (1984). Legislatures sometimes erected an immunity in favor of the alcohol provider, however, as in Wis. Stat. Ann. § 125.035.

officers. So far, however, courts and commentators have not advanced any systematic principles for determining when to adopt and when to reject a nonprescriptive statute.[71]

Adoption of federal statutes. If state courts are free to make any given common law rule, then they are equally free to adopt that same rule from a federal statute's provisions. Courts could equally use international statutory instruments as an expression of their own law.[72] The rule so adopted is a common law rule, whatever the source of the norms it borrows. Courts have sometimes concluded that a federal statute sets a standard to be incorporated by the state courts into the state's common law.[73] Even federal Medicaid regulations of nursing homes have been adopted to define what counts as abuse or neglect under state law.[74]

Application of statutes beyond the legislative command. Because common law courts are free to create judge-made law, in the negligence per se realm they can adapt, as well as adopt, statutes. In particular, courts might adopt a statutory rule and give it any scope appropriate under the common law, even if the legislature had a much more restricted scope in mind for the statute's criminal law applications.[75] So even if legislation for factory safety were directed only at protection of employees, a court might logically decide that the factory safety standards should apply for the benefit of all persons who might foreseeably be endangered by the statute's violation, including, say, business visitors in the factory. The Colorado Court adopted exactly such a position in receiving evidence that the defendant violated a federal workplace safety statute. The statute itself applied to protect workers, but the court borrowed its regulations as helpful evidence of negligence in a common law claim brought by an independent contractor who was not within the class of persons the statute itself sought to protect.[76]

Unsuitable statutes. However, there are several groups of nonprescriptive statutes that are often regarded as unsuitable for use in tort cases. Courts may reject statutes that do not provide a meaningful standard to apply—for example, statutes that require reasonableness or the like but do not specify the particular conduct required,[77] although

---

[71]   See, proposing a systematic analysis for determining when to adopt a statutory standard, Robert F. Blomquist, The Trouble with Negligence Per Se, 61 S.C. L. Rev. 221 (2009).

[72]   See Grimes v. Kennedy Krieger Inst., Inc., 366 Md. 29, 782 A.2d 807 (2001) (Nuremberg Code might create or confirm a duty of human experimenter to obtain fully informed consent of subject).

[73]   *Americans with Disabilities Act:* Smith v. Wal-Mart Stores, Inc., 167 F.3d 286 (6th Cir. 1999). *Federal gun control statutes:* Franco v. Bunyard, 261 Ark. 144, 547 S.W.2d 91 (1977) (violation of federal statute requiring information to be given before selling a gun is evidence of negligence under Arkansas' evidence-of-negligence rule); Rubin v. Johnson, 550 N.E.2d 324 (Ind. 1990) (one who violates state gun control statute by selling gun to person of unsound mind would be guilty of negligence per se). *Federal safety standard*: Grey's Ex'r v. Mobile Trade Co., 55 Ala. 387 (1876). *Federal regulations:* Price v. Blood Bank of Del., Inc., 790 A.2d 1203 (Del. 2002) (violation of federal regulation designed to protect recipients of blood transfusions from disease bearing blood would be negligence per se); Howard v. Zimmer, Inc., 299 P.3d 463 (Okla. 2013) (federal regulations under the Medical Device Amendments to the FDCA may be given per se effect).

[74]   Conservatorship of Gregory, 80 Cal.App.4th 514, 95 Cal.Rptr. 2d 336 (2000).

[75]   Cf. Rudes v. Gottschalk, 159 Tex. 552, 324 S.W.2d 201 (1959) ("As the power of adopting or rejecting standards rests with the civil courts, we may accept or reject the criminal statute or use such part thereof as may be deemed appropriate for our purpose . . . we still retain the test of foreseeability of harm before liability is imposed under the doctrine of negligence per se.").

[76]   Scott v. Matlack, Inc., 39 P.3d 1160 (Colo. 2002).

[77]   E.g., Chadbourne, III v. Kappaz, 779 A.2d 293 (D.C. 2001) ("No owner of an animal shall allow the animal to go at large"; the term "allow" invokes ordinary negligence judgments, so no negligence per se instruction is appropriate against the dog owner); Wallace v. Ohio Dep't of Commerce, 96 Ohio St. 3d 266, 773 N.E.2d 1018 (2002) (when the statutory duty is defined "only in abstract or general terms, leaving to the jury the ascertainment and determination of reasonableness and correctness of acts and conduct under the proven conditions and circumstances, the phrase negligence *per se* has no application"); cf. Restatement Third of Torts (Liability for Physical and Emotional Harm) § 14 cmt. e (2010) (statutes that duplicate the common law rule).

some fairly abstract statutes are sometimes given the negligence per se effect.[78] Many cases, but not all,[79] discard licensing statutes[80] and some analogues[81] as well. Particular statutes might be rejected on the ground that their use in tort cases would be impractical or difficult—for example, because they might raise unwieldy questions of causation.[82]

Statutes imposing duties to the public but not individuals. Under the public duty doctrine, courts do not adopt the statutory standard to govern tort cases where they believe the statute creates only a "public duty" rather than a duty to a particular class of persons.[83] For example, ordinances may require landowners to remove natural accumulations of snow and ice from abutting public walks. Courts often hold that such ordinances impose a duty to the public, but not a duty to individuals injured by reason of the violation. The result is that the landowner is not liable for injuries resulting from his violation of the ordinance.[84] In many states, the public duty doctrine is only a rule that, subject to exceptions, reflects the discretionary immunity of public entities.[85]

§ 11.6 Type of Harm Prevented by the Statute

When courts will not apply statutes as per se negligence. There are a number of standard limits on application of statutory standards as negligence per se. First, courts usually refuse to adopt statutory standards that were not aimed at protecting against harms of the kind suffered by the plaintiff or at protecting groups that included the plaintiff.[86] Second, courts often excuse the violation of statutes when the violation does not necessarily bespeak negligence. For example, courts routinely refuse to apply the

---

[78] Kimberlin v. PM Transp., 563 S.E.2d 665 (Va. 2002) (regulation required truck drivers to use "extreme caution" in fog and where traction is diminished treated as creating an "expanded duty," although the effect was the same as saying that reasonable care required caution in the face of reduced visibility).

[79] Duty v. East Coast Tender Serv., Inc., 660 F.2d 933 (4th Cir. 1981) (operation of vessel without licensed operator required by Coast Guard regulation); Mundy v. Pirie-Slaughter Motor Co., 146 Tex. 314, 206 S.W.2d 587 (1947) (one who knowingly permits another to drive without a license is guilty of negligence per se); cf. Corgan v. Muehling, 143 Ill.2d 296, 574 N.E.2d 602, 158 Ill.Dec. 489 (1991) (violation of statute requiring psychologist's registration creates an implied private right of action in favor of harmed patient). In Kizer v. Harper, 211 W. Va. 47, 561 S.E.2d 368 (2001), an electrician's work was held to be prima facie negligent because the electrician did not have the license required by statute.

[80] Brown v. Shyne, 242 N.Y. 176, 151 N.E. 197, 44 A.L.R. 1407 (1926) (one holding himself out to practice medicine but who has no license and who injures the would-be patient is not guilty of negligence per se merely because of his breach of the licensing statute); see Keenan v. Hill, 190 Ga. App. 108, 378 S.E.2d 344 (1989) (rule stated, but contrary instruction was not prejudicial on the facts); Gregory, Breach of Criminal Licensing Statutes in Civil Litigation, 36 Cornell L. Rev. 622 (1951).

[81] See Horstmeyer v. Golden Eagle Fireworks, 534 N.W.2d 835 (N.D. 1995); cf. Lingle v. Dion, 776 So.2d 1073 (Fla. Dist. Ct. App. 2001) (statute required surgeon doing outpatient surgery to have hospital privileges for equivalent surgery; held "not a negligence per se statute" so violation is not negligence).

[82] Stanchiewicz v. Mar-Cam Corp., 259 Or. 583, 488 P.2d 436 (1971); Olson v. Ratzel, 89 Wis.2d 227, 278 N.W.2d 238, 4 A.L.R.4th 313 (Ct. App. 1979).

[83] In Pace v. State, 425 Md. 145, 38 A.3d 418, 278 Ed. Law Rep. 444 (2012), the mother of a student who suffered a severe allergic reaction to a peanut butter sandwich served as part of a school lunch program sued various state-government defendants, claiming they breached a duty of care under the National School Lunch Act. The court held that the NSLA did not impose any duty on the state to protect students with food allergies, because its language was insufficiently specific to impose a tort duty and because it was "not designed to protect a particular subset of students, . . . but rather, to serve the needs of all eligible school-aged children."

[84] E.g., Lopatkovich v. City of Tiffin, 28 Ohio St.3d 204, 503 N.E.2d 154 (1986) (duty to municipality only, not to those who might be injured; "snow and ice are part of wintertime life in Ohio"); Martin v. Altman, 568 A.2d 1031 (R.I. 1990) (public duty only).

[85] See Morales v. Town of Johnston, 895 A.2d 721 (R.I. 2006).

[86] Restatement Third of Torts (Liability for Physical and Emotional Harm) § 14 (the per se rule applies if the statute "is designed to protect against the type of accident the actor's conduct causes, and if the accident victim is within the class of persons the statute is designed to protect"); Restatement Second of Torts § 286 (1965); §§ 11.6–11.7.

statutory standard to children.[87] Third, courts sometimes reject statutes on the ground that the statute was intended to protect the public without protecting any individual.[88]

Type of harm and class of persons protected. The first category of limitations encompasses two separate constraints. First, violation of statute is not negligence (or contributory negligence) per se unless the statute is construed to protect against the type of risk or type of harm[89] that actually occurred. Stated in more general times, violation is not negligence per se unless the statute was intended to protect against the "type of accident" that occurred.[90] Second, violation is not negligence or contributory negligence per se unless the statute is construed to protect a class of people that includes the plaintiff.[91]

Type of harm. Suppose a statute forbids poisons in restaurant kitchens. The defendant violates the statute by placing rat poison near a stove in the restaurant's kitchen. The poison causes an explosion in which the plaintiff is injured. One reasonable way to analyze the case is to say that the kind of *harm* the statute is intended to avoid is poisoning, not burns or explosive trauma. Not surprisingly, the Oklahoma Court held that violation of such a statute was not negligence per se in an explosion case.[92]

Room for discretion: level of generality. The rule does not automatically resolve cases. Types of harm or risk can be understood in either very specific or very general terms. If the court generalizes the type of harm, many variants will be covered by the statutory standards. In an Idaho case,[93] regulations required that access to publicly operated landfills had to be controlled by fences or otherwise. By simply walking in, children entered a public landfill on a day when no workers were present. The wall of the landfill collapsed and crushed them. A court could read the regulations as intended to prevent dumping of hazardous wastes, or to prevent injuries to entrants from exposure to hazardous wastes or moving machinery. That reading would make the regulations irrelevant to a claim for injuries resulting from the structural danger of a wall. A divided court, however, generalized the risks by referring to risks to "human health" and by saying that the risks of a falling wall were similar to the risks of earth-moving machinery the statute was intended to prevent.

Type of risk, means, or instrumentality. In some cases the statute might be construed as intended to prevent the very kind of *harm* that occurred, but only when the harm is inflicted by certain means. In a case from Illinois,[94] one "Allen" purchased a small quantity of gasoline from a service station, placing it in a pint-sized insecticide

---

[87]   § 11.9.

[88]   1 Dobbs, Hayden & Bublick, The Law of Torts § 158 (2d ed. 2011 & Supp.).

[89]   E.g., Lopez v. Baca, 98 Cal.App.4th 1008, 120 Cal.Rptr.2d 281 (2002) (statute prohibiting bars from employing persons to solicit the purchase of drinks was a morals statute and injuries in altercation following customer's refusal to pay inflated price was not type of harm statutes were intended to prevent); Lewis v. B & R Corp., 56 S.W.3d 432 (Ky. Ct. App. 2001) (federal regulations intended to provide persons under a disability with safe access to public buildings not intended to prevent risk that driver would back across parking lot, down an embankment, across a road and into a river); Busby v. Quail Creek Golf & Country Club, 885 P.2d 1326 (Okla. 1994).

[90]   "Type of accident" is the language of the Restatement Third. Restatement Third of Torts (Liability for Physical and Emotional Harm) § 14 (2010).

[91]   Ramirez v. Nelson, 44 Cal.4th 908, 188 P.3d 659, 80 Cal.Rptr. 3d 728 (2008); Wright v. Brown, 167 Conn. 464, 356 A.2d 176 (1975); Long v. Daly, 156 P.3d 994 (Wyo. 2007).

[92]   Larrimore v. American Nat'l Ins. Co., 184 Okla. 614, 89 P.2d 340 (1939).

[93]   O'Guin v. Bingham County, 142 Idaho 49, 122 P.3d 308 (2005).

[94]   Stafford v. Borden, 252 Ill. App. 3d 254, 625 N.E.2d 12 (1993).

can. The service station made the sale in violation of a statute that required delivery only to containers that were labeled for gasoline and that met certain other conditions. Allen used the gasoline to start a fire at an apartment building. Four people died in the fire. In a tort suit for their death brought against the service station, the plaintiffs argued that the court should use the statute's provision as a basis for liability. The court refused to do so, even though the statute undoubtedly meant to protect people from fire dangers.

Risks created by the violation. One way to view the facts is to say that the statute intended to protect against fire and burning, but only to the extent that labeling proper containers would tend to increase fire safety. The labeling rule would seldom if ever reduce arson risks, so the statute might have been intended to cover the general *type* of harm suffered—fire—but not the risk of harm by means of arson. This kind of analysis suggests that courts need a rule like the type of risk rule that focuses in part on how the injury came about, as well as a type of harm rule that focuses on the end result alone.

Type of risk overlapping type of harm rule and different interests. The type of risk and type of harm rules can in fact overlap substantially or totally, depending on how broadly the court defines risk and harm. In fact, the Restatement Second subdivided the type of harm/risk rule even further and said that a court should not adopt a statutory rule where the statute was not intended to protect the interest that was in fact harmed.[95] For instance, if a statute was intended to protect bodily security it should not be used as a standard for a case in which economic interests were harmed. Suppose a case in which the defendant violates rules about the safety of building structures with the result that the building collapses. The statute was no doubt intended to protect workers from physical injury, but not intended to protect them from purely economic losses resulting from the fact that they cannot work while the building is being repaired. So the defendant is not liable to workers who are not injured but who lose wages because their employer's place of business is destroyed.

Describing the harm. Inevitably, to describe the harm is to describe at least a little about how the harm comes about. The ability to shift from type of harm to type of risk by slight shifts in linguistic usages and the inability to describe one without implications about the other suggests that the distinction is not so much one found in nature as it is in courtrooms and classrooms. The same may be true of differences in interests. If the distinction is meaningful in practice, it is not because of its intrinsic merit but because courts can bring to it a sense of justice and balance.

§ 11.7   Class of Persons Protected Under the Statute

Class of persons protected. The class of persons rule is very similar to the type of harm, type of risk, or type of accident rule. The idea is that even if the plaintiff suffers the type of harm covered by the statute, she cannot claim negligence per se unless she is within the class or group of people the statute was intended to protect.[96] However, a description of the risk of harm and type of accident often implicitly describe the class of persons as well. So, in many cases, courts could get the same result whether they used the type of harm/type of risk rule or the class of person rule.

---

[95]   Restatement Second of Torts § 286(c) (1965).

[96]   Universal Coops., Inc. v. AAC Flying Serv., Inc., 710 F.3d 790 (8th Cir. 2013); Maurer v. Speedway, LLC, 774 F.3d 1132 (7th Cir. 2014).

Example. In a Mississippi case,[97] the defendant pulled her car over and parked on the left side of the street to chat with a friend. When the visit was completed, the defendant looked in all directions, saw no one, and started driving off. She immediately struck a small child, who had not been visible. The court refused to hold that the defendant's violation of the right-side-of-the-street statute was negligence per se, saying that the class of persons to be protected by that traffic rule was pedestrians and drivers acting in reliance upon the orderly flow of traffic.

Foreseeability of increased harm to the class from the rule violation. The result seems correct. It would be no less correct if the court had said that the statute was aimed at preventing harms that would be more likely to occur from being on the wrong side of the road. If the defendant had gone around the block so as to face the right direction, the risk to children under a bumper would not have been lessened. So the case can be analyzed either in terms of the class of persons or the class of risk involved.

§ 11.8   Interpreting the Scope of Risk

Interpreting scope of risk. Statutes do not always clearly indicate what class of persons and risks they are intended to protect against. That is understandable enough, since the nonprescriptive statutes under discussion make no provision at all for tort liability or tort standards. How, then, are courts to apply the type of accident and class of person rules to statutes that neither call for tort liability nor specify the scope of their protections?

Foreseeable types of harm and protected persons. Given that courts adopt the rules of nonprescriptive statutes as they seem fitted for tort law, one entirely appropriate solution is to treat the statute as encompassing all persons and harms that would foreseeably be safer if the statute were obeyed. Conversely, that solution would treat the statute as encompassing no persons or harms that would not be foreseeably safer if the statute were obeyed.[98]

An example. For example, statutes often regulate driving safety by requiring brakes, limiting speed, or prohibiting intoxicated driving or specific kinds of vehicular movements. Such statutes are obviously for the protection of others using the streets and highways, but since it is foreseeable that bad brakes, excessive speed, intoxicated driving, dangerous vehicular movement, or even overweight vehicles can also cause harms to persons or property off the highway, courts have every reason to say that the statutory rule applies for the benefit of persons off the road as well.[99]

Unforeseeable risks. On the other hand, if you park your car in a zone designated by ordinance for loading commercial vehicles, you are in violation of the statute; but your violation creates no more risk that a child will dart into the street from behind your car than if you had parked in the some other location. If it is a matter of legislative intent, courts can suppose that the legislature never created loading zones as child safety statutes but only as a convenience for merchants, so that violation of the statute is irrelevant. If it is a matter of judicial fairness or policy, the same limitation applies

---

[97]   Haver v. Hinson, 385 So.2d 605 (Miss. 1980).

[98]   Torres v. State, 119 N.M. 609, 894 P.2d 386 (1995).

[99]   Castro v. Hernandez-Davila, 694 S.W.2d 575 (Tex. App. 1985) (intoxicated driver who drove into apartment building, causing a wall to collapse; negligence per se); Sigrist v. Love, 510 P.2d 456 (Colo. Ct. App. 1973) (left turn in violation of statute led to injury off the highway; negligence per se); but cf. Erickson v. Kongsli, 40 Wash.2d 79, 240 P.2d 1209 (1952) (property owners off the road were not within class protected by right of way rules for vehicles).

because the harm risked from illegal parking in the loading zone is not injury to children but delay of persons making a delivery.

Statutory language. Sometimes, however, courts attempt to give the statute's standard a narrow scope because of narrow words used in the statute itself. A statute that requires covering or fencing elevator shafts in workplaces might be titled "An Act to Protect Workers." This or similar language could lead a court to say that only workers are within the class protected, so that if a firefighter or a person making a delivery to the premises falls into an open shaft, he enjoys none of the statute's protections. Courts have actually so held.[100]

Avoiding unjust distinctions. The rule is not working well in cases like this. Although the legislature might properly refuse to impose the costs of fencing a shaft solely for the benefit of odd visitors, a fence guarding an open shaft costs the same whether it protects one worker or ten firefighters who are properly in the building. When the class of persons/risk rules are used in this way, they can lead to invidious differences in protection. Since courts are not required to adopt the statutory rule in the first place, they are not required to adopt its limitation either. So courts are free to avoid making unjust distinctions like those in the shaft cases.

Using a tort foreseeability principle. The best way to do this is by adhering to the foreseeability principle that runs through common law torts: protect all persons who would naturally and foreseeably be injured by a violation of the statute and protect them against risks that are foreseeable from its violation. This is a class of risk and class of person rule, but it judges the scope of the risk and the size of the class by what is foreseeable, not by the preoccupation of the legislature with a particular constituency. The standard is also familiar to judges and lawyers from the analogous cases of "proximate cause."

§ 11.9 Excused and Unexcused Violations

Adoption of statutory standards and relation to excused violation. In the excuse cases, courts accept the statutory rule as the usual standard but reject it for certain instances when the rule appears undesirable or unjust because of the particular facts of the case. In these cases, courts say they "excuse" violation of the statute and that an excused violation is not negligence.[101] The jurisprudence of excuses gives courts a degree of guidance in determining whether to give a statute effect as negligence per se or evidence of negligence. Yet it should be remembered that where the statute does not specify the standard for tort law purposes, courts retain the power to reject the statutory standard for any reason of justice or policy consonant with the common law traditions without regard to formal excuses.[102]

Unexcused violations. The Restatement notes that courts do not excuse violations of the statute merely because the defendant was ignorant of the law or misunderstood it, because people customarily violate the statute, or because the defendant sincerely

---

[100] Kelly v. Henry Muhs Co., 71 N.J.L. 358, 59 A. 23 (1904) (firefighter); cf. DiCaprio v. New York Cent. R.R., 231 N.Y. 94, 131 N.E. 746 (1921) (mandate to railroad to fence out cattle did not protect small child who wandered onto the track).

[101] See, e.g., Gore v. People's Sav. Bank, 235 Conn. 360, 665 A.2d 1341 (1995) ("defendant ordinarily may avoid liability upon proof of a valid excuse or justification"); Restatement Third of Torts (Liability for Physical and Emotional Harm) § 15 (2010).

[102] 1 Dobbs, Hayden & Bublick, The Law of Torts § 150 (2d ed. 2011 & Supp.).

believes the law to be unwise.[103] Nor is mental incapacity of adult an excuse for statutory violation.[104] The rules are slightly nuanced, however. Ignorance of the law is no excuse, but justifiable ignorance of facts calling for care is. And if ignorance of the law arises because a statute is obscure or not well known, a court might be persuaded to reject the per se rule and treat violation only as evidence of negligence.[105] Similarly, a court might reject a confusing, ambiguous criminal statute as a tort standard.[106] And though custom to violate the law is no excuse, customs may help interpret the facts, including the meaning of traffic directions that are allegedly violated.[107] In addition, a known custom of drivers to violate a statute may be relevant to show that an injured pedestrian was chargeable with comparative fault for failure to protect herself against such a known special danger.[108]

Categories of excuses. Excused violation cases are generally those in which the defendant does not appear to be negligent even if he is assumed to have violated the statute. The excuse doctrine helps courts avoid turning statutory commands into a general system of strict liability. The generally recognized excuses,[109] to which others may be added, are as follows:

(1) Childhood or physical disability. Either the statute does not apply to children[110] or the child's violation of statute is excused.[111] *For example*, a child runs into the street chasing a ball, violating the statute by failing to look in both directions.[112] In line with this excuse and this example, courts commonly let the jury consider a minor's conduct under the traditional child standard of care or some variation of it rather than under the strict per se rule.[113] Similarly, one whose physical incapacity prevents compliance with the statute is excused,[114] although he may be liable for antecedent negligence in creating a situation he could not physically cope with.[115]

(2) The actor does not know and could not reasonably discover the occasion for compliance with the statute.[116] *For example*, the nighttime driver

---

[103] Restatement Third of Torts (Liability for Physical and Emotional Harm) § 15 cmt. a (2010).

[104] Id.

[105] See Frost v. Allred, 148 P.3d 17, 22 (Wyo. 2006) (so stating).

[106] Restatement Third of Torts (Liability for Physical and Emotional Harm) § 15 cmt. e (2010).

[107] See Johnson v. Garnand, 18 Ariz. App. 191, 501 P.2d 32 (1972).

[108] See Elliott v. Callan, 255 Or. 256, 466 P.2d 600 (1970) (holding that a custom of violating a speed statute could not excuse the defendant, but that a known custom to violate a safety statute might work against a plaintiff on the issue of contributory negligence if she failed to take the danger into account and also that a such a custom might show negligence of a defendant who motioned a plaintiff to cross the street where drivers customarily violated safety standards).

[109] Restatement Third of Torts (Liability for Physical and Emotional Harm) § 15 (2010).

[110] See Busby v. Quail Creek Golf & Country Club, 885 P.2d 1326, 1331–32 (Okla. 1994); cf. Rudes v. Gottschalk, 159 Tex. 552, 324 S.W.2d 201 (1959) (common law child standard applies).

[111] Bauman v. Crawford, 104 Wash.2d 241, 704 P.2d 1181 (1985).

[112] Cf. Ranard v. O'Neil, 166 Mont. 177, 531 P.2d 1000 (1975) (contributory negligence of 8-year-old dashing into street excused if he lacked capacity for compliance with statute).

[113] E.g., Burgbacher v. Lazar, 97 A.D.2d 496, 468 N.Y.S.2d 14 (1983); Alley v. Siepman, 87 S.D. 670, 214 N.W.2d 7 (1974); Rudes v. Gottschalk, 159 Tex. 552, 324 S.W.2d 201 (1959) (child standard of care rather than child's ability to understand the statute). A few courts have applied the negligence per se rules to children. D'Ambrosio v. Philadelphia, 354 Pa. 403, 47 A.2d 256 (1946).

[114] Hout v. Johnson, 281 Or. 435, 446 P.2d 99 (1968).

[115] E.g., Storjohn v. Fay, 519 N.W.2d 521 (Neb. 1994).

[116] See, e.g., Sabolik v. HGG Chestnut Lake Ltd. P'ship, 180 Ohio App.3d 576, 906 N.E.2d 488 (2009) (landlord excused if he neither knew nor should have known that tenants could be scalded by bath water);

is required by statute to display lights in the rear of his vehicle, but does not know his rear lights have burned out and has no means of anticipating or discovering the fact.[117] This rule does not excuse ignorance of the law, only a reasonable ignorance of facts that would invoke the law.[118] But ignorance of the facts would not be an excuse if the statute requires investigation and knowledge.[119]

(3)   Violation of statute is safer for the actor or others than compliance.[120] On occasion, the only safe thing to do is to violate the literal words of the statue. For example, a driver deliberately crosses to the wrong side of the highway to avoid hitting a child.[121] The Third Restatement eliminates the separate excuse for emergency,[122] relying on this safer-than-compliance excuse instead.[123] The classic and more dubious basis for the supposed rule that excuses violations that are safer arose when the plaintiffs walked on the right side of the highway instead of the left, claiming it was safer.[124] This excuse requires courts to determine whether violation was in fact safer than compliance, or at least whether it would so appear to a reasonable person under the circumstances. This inquiry, like all of the excuse jurisprudence, eliminates the certainty that is the claimed advantage of statutory standards.

(4)   The actor exercised reasonable care in attempting to comply with the statute.[125] The excuse that the actor exercised reasonable care to comply with the statute may be expressed by saying the actor is excused if "he did what might reasonably be expected of a person of ordinary prudence, acting under similar circumstances, who desired to comply with the law"[126] or if he

---

Heath v. La Mariana Apartments, 143 N.M. 657, 661, 180 P.3d 664, 668 n.2 (2008) (he neither knows nor should know of the occasion for compliance); Restatement Third of Torts (Liability for Physical and Emotional Harm) § 15(c) (2010); Restatement Second of Torts § 288A(2)(b) (1965).

[117] Leiken v. Wilson, 445 A.2d 993 (D.C. 1982); Brotherton v. Day & Night Fuel Co., 192 Wash. 362, 73 P.2d 788 (1937).

[118] Hudson v. Old Guard Ins. Co., 3 A.3d 246 (Del. 2010) (statute required driver to sound horn before collision but driver could not anticipate collision); Nettleton v. Thompson, 117 Idaho 308, 787 P.2d 294 (Ct. App. 1990) (Burnett, J., concurring) ("exception might exist where a defendant has no actual or imputed knowledge of the facts invoking application of a legislative standard"); see Juarez ex rel. Juarez v. Wavecrest Mgmt. Team, Ltd., 88 N.Y.2d 628, 649 N.Y.S.2d 115, 672 N.E.2d 135 (1996) (statutory duty of landlords to remove lead paint where child lived in premises did not impose a duty to find out whether a child was there).

[119] Smith v. Owen, 841 S.W.2d 828 (Tenn. Ct. App. 1992) (ordinance imposed upon landlord a duty to inspect wiring in leased premises, hence landlord's lack of knowledge of defect is no defense).

[120] Restatement Third of Torts (Liability for Physical and Emotional Harm) § 15(c); Restatement Second of Torts § 288A(2)(e) (1965).

[121] Cf. See Jones v. Blair, 387 N.W.2d 349 (Iowa 1986) (recognizing principle); Cowell v. Thompson, 713 S.W.2d 52 (Mo. Ct. App. 1986) (driver lost control when another driver pulled out in front, crossed into opposing lane of traffic and collided with car in which plaintiff was a passenger; violation of the right-side-of the-road statute could be excused).

[122] However some courts retain the emergency excuse. See Hagenow v. Schmidt, 842 N.W.2d 661 (Iowa 2014).

[123] See Restatement Third of Torts (Liability for Physical and Emotional Harm) § 15 cmt. f (2010).

[124] A famous example, based on Tedla v. Ellman, 280 N.Y. 124, 19 N.E.2d 987 (1939).

[125] Restatement Third of Torts (Liability for Physical and Emotional Harm) § 15(b) (2010). The Second Restatement used unnecessarily strong language: "he is unable after reasonable diligence or care to comply." Restatement Second of Torts § 288A(c) (1965).

[126] Alarid v. Vanier, 50 Cal.2d 617, 624, 327 P.2d 897, 900 (1958); Waugh v. Traxler, 186 W.Va. 355, 412 S.E.2d 756 (1991); see Lepucki v. Lake County Sheriff's Dep't, 801 N.E.2d 636 (Ind. Ct. App. 2004) (presumption of negligence from violation of safety statute "may be overcome by evidence that [the violator] acted as a reasonable prudent person would act under the circumstances").

"exercised reasonable care in an effort to comply."[127] *For example,* the defendant's car is struck by another, so that the steering mechanisms are damaged; the defendant cannot prevent his car from moving into another lane in front of an oncoming motorcyclist, the plaintiff.[128] This excuse is more general than the others and can be regarded as the principle on which most specific excuses are built. By its terms, however, it is limited to cases in which the actor's conduct would be reasonable for one who is attempting to comply with the statutory standard.

Construing the Statute to Eliminate Violation. Excuse is not the only formal way in which the defendant can avoid a negligence per se condemnation. In some cases, the defendant can plausibly argue that he simply did not violate the statute at all.

One kind of no-violation decision is a purely factual determination; if the plaintiff claims that the defendant ran a stop light in violation of a statute, the jury must determine whether the defendant in fact ran the light.[129] The appellate courts will have little role in such determinations.

The second kind turns on the court's determination of the meaning of statutory language. For instance, statutes almost always require some degree of fault or some intended conduct. If a driver suffers unconsciousness or death from an unforeseeable stroke or seizure, his unguided vehicle may cross the center line and cause a collision, but the driver himself has not acted at all, so the best solution to the negligence per se puzzle on those facts may be to conclude that the statute was not violated. To construe the statute otherwise violates both the tort traditions of liability for fault and the ordinary understanding of language at the same time.

Refusing to accept excuses: strict liability under statutes. Courts are not required to recognize excuses. They can choose instead to impose strict liability so that even if the defendant has acted with every possible effort to comply with the statute, he could be held liable.[130] A few states, for example, hold that a driver is not excused if his vehicle strikes a hidden and unforeseeable patch of ice, goes into a slide that cannot be controlled, and causes a collision on the wrong side of the road,[131] even though it is clear that he is not negligent.[132] In such a case he is said to have violated a statute requiring him to stay on the right side of the road.

Proscribing results rather than conduct. Statutes like the right side of the road statutes do not prescribe conduct, only an ideal result to aim for or achieve. If courts create a tort cause of action based on these statutes, they should recognize that they are

---

[127] Arms v. Halsey, 43 A.D.3d 1419, 842 N.Y.S.2d 847 (2007).

[128] Giancarlo v. Karabanowski, 124 Conn. 223, 198 A. 752 (1938).

[129] See e.g., Pond v. Leslein, 72 Ohio St. 3d 50, 647 N.E.2d 477 (1995).

[130] O'Donnell v. Elgin, J. & E. Ry., 338 U.S. 384, 70 S.Ct. 200, 94 L.Ed. 187 (1949) (under Federal Safety Appliance Act governing certain railroad safety equipment for workers, railroad's reasonable care is irrelevant to liability); cf. Sanatass v. Consolidated Investing Co., 10 N.Y.3d 333, 887 N.E.2d 1125, 858 N.Y.S.2d 67 (2008) (liability for violation of state scaffold law referred to as strict liability).

[131] E.g., Teply v. Lincoln, 125 Idaho 773, 874 P.2d 584 (Ct. App. 1994).

[132] He would not be negligent if the ice could not be anticipated and he faced a sudden emergency, which is a reason given in some courts for excusing wrong-side-of-the-road slides on ice. E.g., Young v. Flood, 182 Mich. App. 538, 452 N.W.2d 869 (1990). He would also not be negligent if he found it impossible to steer once he hit the unforeseeable ice.

imposing strict liability and should spell out justifications for such selective strict liability or return to the fault principle.

Chapter 12

BREACH OF DUTY

Analysis

A.   NEGLIGENT CONDUCT
§ 12.1   Specific Negligent Acts

B.   FORESEEABILITY AND RISK-UTILITY
§ 12.2   Foreseeability of Harm in Breach
§ 12.3   Unstructured Weighing of Reasonableness
§ 12.4   Structured Weighing of Risks and Utilities
§ 12.5   Supporting and Criticizing Structured Risk-Utility Assessments

C.   CUSTOM
§ 12.6   Custom or Practice: General Rules
§ 12.7   Limitations on the Use of Custom and Practice
§ 12.8   Private Standards: Defendant's Own "Customs" or Practices
§ 12.9   Entering Transactions in Light of Custom

D.   STATUTORY COMPLIANCE
§ 12.10   Compliance with Statute

A.   NEGLIGENT CONDUCT

§ 12.1   Specific Negligent Acts

Scope. This chapter focuses on the main rules and concepts used to determine the second element in the negligence case—the defendant's breach of duty, which is to say the defendant's negligence.[1] The general rule is that a person is negligent if he fails to exercise reasonable care under the circumstances to protect against risks of harms.[2] Accordingly, breach is generally a failure to exercise reasonable care under the circumstances. Main tests of whether a party has failed to use reasonable care include an unstructured weighing of risks and utilities, Judge Learned Hand's more structured weighing of risks and utilities,[3] evidence of the custom in the community, and the party's compliance with statute. Of course, as discussed in the previous chapter, violation of statute is also an important consideration. If the standard of care is supplied by statute, as in negligence per se, failure to comply with the statute establishes breach. In special types of cases, additional tests such as notice and opportunity to cure and res ipsa loquitur (letting the accident itself speak to the issue of breach) may also apply.

---

[1]   The elements are summarized in § 9.5. The breach question is often referred to as "the negligence question." Thus the term "negligence" is used to describe both the full cause of action and the single element of breach.

[2]   Restatement Third of Torts (Liability for Physical and Emotional Harms) § 3 (2010).

[3]   See § 12.4.

The specific conduct requirement. Negligence itself is not a historical fact. Negligence represents an evaluation of facts. In general, plaintiff cannot prevail by saying that the defendant drove his car so negligently that he injured the plaintiff. Instead, the plaintiff must point to a particular way in which that conduct could have been made safer. What we need to know is what precise physical actions the plaintiff claims the defendant should have done differently to present less risk. In automobile cases, for example, the plaintiffs commonly attempt to prove that the defendant failed to keep a proper lookout,[4] drove at an excessive speed,[5] followed too closely,[6] or otherwise engaged in specific dangerous acts, not merely that the defendant was negligent in some unspecified way. The plaintiff must show, directly or by a reasonable inference, precisely what the defendant did or didn't do.[7]

Purpose of specificity requirement. Why the requirement of such specificity? One important reason is that only when you know specific conduct can you estimate the risks and utilities of that conduct, a process normally implicit in finding negligence. It is impossible to estimate reasonable care in general or risks and utilities of the defendant's conduct in particular unless specific conduct is identified. If, instead of judging conduct by risks and utilities, you attempt to judge it by community custom or by legislative standards, the same problem arises; you must know the conduct you are judging.

Negligence for engaging in a general activity. It is, of course, possible for a plaintiff to claim that the defendant is negligent by engaging at all in some general activity like driving cars or running hotels. But it would be almost impossible to successfully contend that reasonable people never drive cars or operate hotels, because the utility of such activities is very high.[8] As a practical matter, then, the plaintiff must ordinarily attempt to prove some specific way in which the car was driven or the hotel was maintained that could reasonably have been made safer.

Other purposes. There are some other reasons why specific conduct must be identified in order to claim negligence. It would be impossible to conclude that the defendant's conduct was a cause of the plaintiff's harm or that the harm was within the scope of the risk unless you know what the risk was; to know that, you must know the specific conduct claimed to be negligent.

B. FORESEEABILITY AND RISK-UTILITY

§ 12.2 Foreseeability of Harm in Breach

Negligence entails an unreasonable risk of foreseeable harm. A person is not necessarily negligent merely because he can foresee the possibility of harm resulting

---

[4] E.g., Serio v. Merrell, Inc., 941 So.2d 960 (Ala. 2006) (contributory negligence of plaintiff for failing to keep proper lookout); Tadros v. City of Omaha, 269 Neb. 528, 694 N.W.2d 180 (2005).

[5] E.g., Mississippi Dep't of Pub. Safety v. Durn, 918 So.2d 672 (Miss. 2005).

[6] E.g., Davidson v. Lindsey, 104 S.W.3d 483 (Tenn. 2003).

[7] McQuaig v. Tarrant, 269 Ga.App. 236, 603 S.E.2d 751 (2004) ("the mere fact that an accident happened and the plaintiff may have sustained injuries or damages affords no basis for recovery against a particular defendant unless the plaintiff carries the burden of proof and shows that such accident and damages were caused by specific acts of negligence on the part of that defendant"); Santiago v. First Student, Inc., 839 A.2d 550 (R.I. 2004) (passenger in school bus injured when bus collided with car at an intersection, but no evidence showed any particular actions of the driver; summary judgment for the defendant affirmed).

[8] See Restatement Third of Torts (Liability for Physical and Emotional Harm) § 3 cmt. j (2010) (elaborating this point with other examples and comments).

from his acts; some risks are acceptable.[9] However, foreseeability of harm, though not sufficient, is necessary to show negligence. No actor can be counted as negligent unless he either actually foresaw, or a reasonable person in a similar position would have foreseen a risk of harm.[10] What is foreseeable depends in large part on what facts the defendant actually knew or those he should have known, based on his obligation to know and act as a reasonable person.[11] The language of foreseeability arises in literally thousands of cases where courts attempt to determine negligence and related issues.[12]

Refining foreseeability language: risk. When the language of foreseeability is used instead of the language of risk, it is all too easy to over- or under-state responsibility in tort. Thus a court may easily slip into saying that negligence can be established when harm is foreseeable,[13] although it is clear that foreseeability of harm, though necessary, is not sufficient.[14] For this and other reasons, the foreseeability rules are actually more accurately captured in the language of risk. Thus an actor is negligent when he creates or continues unreasonable risks of foreseeable harm, not merely when harm is foreseeable to him. And he is not unreasonable and not negligent unless he either knew of the risk of foreseeable harm or should have known of it.[15] Statement of the rule in terms of risk permits the rule to describe when negligence can be established as well as when it cannot be.

Refining foreseeability language: foreseeability as unjustified risk. Courts speaking of foreseeable harms often use the term to mean not merely that harm is a foreseeable possibility, but that harm is too likely to occur to justify risking it without added precautions.[16] Even a highly improbable harm may still be too likely to justify a risk of it, as where the foreseeable harm is very serious even though the probability of its occurrence is small.[17]

Lack of forseeability and justified risk. Courts also use foreseeability as a reference to probability in making the negative statement that harm was not foreseeable in a

---

[9]   See, e.g., Parsons v. Crown Disposal Co., 15 Cal.4th 456, 936 P.2d 70, 63 Cal.Rptr. 2d 291 (1997) (foreseeability alone is not enough; court must determine whether conduct at issue is sufficiently likely to result in the kind of harm inflicted); Lowery v. Echostar Satellite Corp., 160 P.3d 959 (Okla. 2007) (similar).

[10]   Rallis v. Demoulas Super Mkts., Inc., 159 N.H. 95, 101, 977 A.2d 527, 532 (2009) (plaintiff must "show that the defendant's conduct created a foreseeable risk of harm; in other words, it was reasonably foreseeable that an injury might occur because of the defendant's actions or inactions"). See also Restatement Third of Torts (Liability for Physical and Emotional Harm) §§ 3 & 7 (2010); Restatement Second of Torts § 291 (1965).

[11]   See § 10.12 (knowledge of a reasonable person).

[12]   Emanuel v. Great Falls Sch. Dist., 351 Mont. 56, 209 P.3d 244 (2009) ("[i]f a reasonably prudent defendant can foresee neither any danger of direct injury nor any risk from an intervening cause he is simply not negligent"); Miller v. David Grace, Inc, 212 P.3d 1223 (Okla. 2009) (foreseeability an element of negligence); Behrendt v. Gulf Underwriters Ins. Co., 318 Wis.2d 622, 768 N.W.2d 568 (2009) ("lack of foreseeable risk," no negligence).

[13]   Smith v. Finch, 285 Ga. 709, 681 S.E.2d 147 (2009) ("negligence may be established where it is shown that by exercise of reasonable care, the defendant might have foreseen that some injury would result from his act or omission, or that consequences of a generally injurious nature might have been expected").

[14]   See n. 9, supra.

[15]   Wal-Mart Stores, Inc. v. Spates, 186 S.W.3d 566 (Tex. 2006).

[16]   Jutzi-Johnson v. United States, 263 F.3d 753, 756 (7th Cir. 2001) ("foreseeable, in the sense of probable"); Edwards v. Honeywell, Inc., 50 F.3d 484, 491 (7th Cir. 1995) ("too unusual, too uncertain, too unreckonable to make it feasible or worthwhile to take precautions against"); Ethyl Corp. v. Johnson, 345 Ark. 476, 49 S.W3d 644 (2001); Healthone v. Rodriguez, 50 P.3d 879 (Colo. 2002) (similar); Doe Parents No. 1 v. State Dep't of Educ., 100 Haw. 34, 58 P.3d 545 (2002).

[17]   Smith v. Finch, 285 Ga. 709, 681 S.E.2d 147 (2009) (reasonable care "often requires the consideration of unlikely but serious consequences").

particular case. In such cases, they may mean that although harm was actually foreseeable on the facts of the case, a reasonable person would not have taken action to prevent it because the risk of harm was low and harm was so improbable that a reasonable person would not have taken safety precautions.[18]

Imprecision from expansive use of the term. Courts that speak of foreseeability in the sense of probability are often collapsing several different inquiries into one statement about foreseeability. The conclusion that harm would have been foreseeable to a reasonable person is entirely distinct from the conclusion that probability of harm was great enough to require care; and both these things are distinct from the conclusion that the actor's conduct was unreasonable in light of all the relevant factors. Clarity requires separation of those issues and the term foreseeability alone is not up to the job.

Should have known and foreseeability. What the actor should have foreseen often depends a great deal on the knowledge and information he has or should have as a reasonable person. The term *should have known,* sometimes discussed in terms of constructive negligence or constructive notice,[19] is one way of saying that the reasonable person standard governs the question of unreasonable risk and foreseeability, so the actor's subjective inability to appreciate a risk is immaterial. Negligence of a plaintiff is judged in the same way, except that with contributory negligence the plaintiff often risks harm to herself rather than to others.

An example: knew or should have known. Suppose you have stored your goods with me and I know that a flood is likely to occur. Given that knowledge, a reasonable person should recognize a risk to your goods and take appropriate action for their safety. If I do not know that a flood is on its way, but merely that my warehouse lies in the flood plain, I may still know enough to about potential harm to require reasonable steps to inform myself by listening to weather reports, in which case courts can say I should have known of the flood risk or that it was reasonably foreseeable. If I know neither of the approaching flood nor the endangered position of the warehouse but a reasonable person would know them, I am still required to act on the basis of the risks that would have been recognized by a reasonable person in my position, and I am liable for the flood damage if I do not do so. Thus, when we speak of foreseeability of harm, it is either harm subjectively foreseeable to the actor or harm foreseeable to a reasonable person that is determinative.

Intentional torts distinguished. Liability for unreasonably risky conduct that causes harm differs from liability for intent, partly in that intentional wrongdoing is based upon conduct that is coupled with either a purpose that is legally wrong or a certainty that

[18]   In Romine v. Village of Irving, 336 Ill.App.3d 624, 783 N.E.2d 1064, 270 Ill. Dec. 764 (2003), the court said that police officers could not foresee criminal acts in general and in particular drunken driving by intoxicated persons they ejected from a fair. Since police are in the business of dealing with criminal activity, and the court itself noted that intoxicated driving was all too common, the court was presumably using the "foreseeability" locution to mean only that probability of harm was remote or even that policy rather than foreseeability reasons counseled against liability. In A.H. v. Rockingham Publ'g Co., Inc., 255 Va. 216, 495 S.E.2d 482 (1998), a young teen paper boy was sexually assaulted in early morning hours while delivering papers. His employer, the newspaper knew of three other similar sexual assaults on its carriers in a town of 30,000, but the court said that such assaults were nevertheless unforeseeable. In such uses of the term, it seems impossible to think that "unforeseeable" is a literal psychological description. It seems instead to mean that the court believed, rightly or wrongly, that the risk or probability was small enough to justify the newspaper's failure to protect the boy, even by a warning.

[19]   See Machado v. City of Hartford, 292 Conn. 364, 972 A.2d 724 (2009) (defects of which town "should be aware" equated with town's "actual or constructive knowledge" of defect); Rallis v. Demoulas Super Mkts., Inc., 159 N.H. 95, 977 A.2d 527 (2009) (equating constructive notice danger and "should have known").

legally cognizable harm will result. Negligence, in contrast, is based upon a reasonably foreseeable harm, not a certain or purposeful one. That is to say, negligence entails a recognizable chance or risk—an unreasonable likelihood—but not a certainty of harm.

Scope of foreseeable harm: breach. Risks or foreseeable harms can be described at different levels of abstraction, that is, broadly or narrowly. If we tried to describe all the particular risks or foreseeable harms that speeding would create, the list would be long, and we might still not think of some particular kinds of harm. But without identifying all the possible versions of speed-related harm, we can surely foresee broad categories of risks and harms to persons and property resulting because the driver might lose control. So if a speeding driver crashes into your living room, the fact that a reasonable person would not have specifically recognized a risk of harm to your favorite easy chair will not operate to avoid the driver's liability.[20] It is one of the cluster of harms in a generally foreseeable category, and that is enough. In the breach area, the foreseeability question is phrased broadly—should the actor have foreseen some harm to someone from the conduct. In contrast, in the proximate cause inquiry, the foreseeability issue is phrased more narrowly—should the actor have foreseen the type of harm that actually occurred to the plaintiff.[21]

Foreseeability as a jury question. Foreseeability is seldom if ever a pure fact. You cannot determine whether a reasonable person would recognize a risk of harm in the way you can determine whether a traffic signal is red. Reasonable foreseeability of harm is instead a judgment call. In some cases it is a call that is easy to make and is so clear that courts will brook no argument. When the issue is negligence,[22] the question of what is or is not foreseeable to a reasonable person in the position of the defendant is normally a jury question, part of its overall evaluation of the defendant's conduct unless the answer is so clear that reasonable people cannot differ.[23]

§ 12.3 Unstructured Weighing of Reasonableness

Accepting useful risks. Tort law recognizes that maximum safety is not always desirable. It is not negligent to maintain bathtubs, although people do fall in them. Risky acts are therefore not always negligent acts, even when harm is foreseeable.[24] An important line of thought on these points is that conduct is not negligent when the usefulness of conduct outweighs the risks it imposes upon others. If the benefit or "utility" of conduct is enough, some degree of risk or foreseeable harm is acceptable.[25]

---

[20] E.g., Castro v. Hernandez-Davila, 694 S.W.2d 575 (Tex. App. 1985) (intoxicated driver who drove into apartment building, causing a wall to collapse).

[21] C.H. v. Los Lunas Schools Bd. Of Educ., 852 F. Supp.2d 1344 (D.N.M. 2012) (foreseeability in the duty/breach context is "a minimal threshold legal requirement," while in the proximate cause context is a "much more specific factual requirement"). See also B.R. & C.R. v. West, 275 P.3d 228 (Utah 2012).

[22] For courts that have imported foreseeability questions into the duty issue, judges may take control of the issue.

[23] Ballard v. Uribe, 41 Cal. 3d 564, 715 P.2d 624 (1986); Pulawa v. GTE Hawaiian Tel., 112 Haw. 3, 143 P.3d 1205 (2006); Brokaw v. Winfield-Mt. Union Cmty. Sch. Dist., 788 N.W.2d 386 (Iowa 2010); Fresco v. 157 E. 72nd St. Condo., 2 A.D.3d 326, 769 N.Y.S.2d 536 (2003).

[24] Barnes v. U.S., 485 F.3d 341 (6th Cir. 2007) (TSA not negligent for not providing a chair for an airline passenger who fell while taking off her shoes in a security area; court stressed the "apparently small likelihood and gravity of the potential harm"); Lowery v. Echostar Satellite Corp., 160 P.3d 959 (Okla. 2007) (even though risk of harm was foreseeable, the defendant is not liable unless its conduct unreasonably endangered the plaintiff); see Restatement Third of Torts (Liability for Physical and Emotional Harm) § 3 (2010).

[25] Many cases exemplify or state the point. In Clark v. St. Dominic-Jackson Mem'l Hosp., 660 So.2d 970 (Miss. 1995), the court stated succinctly that although taking unnecessary chances might be negligence, "[t]aking a 1% chance when necessary might be exemplary. . . ."

This comparison of risks with utilities is justified at least when utility of the dangerous conduct takes the form of increased human safety.[26] Perhaps, as many thinkers believe, the risk-utility comparison is even broader, reflecting the possibility of weighing economic utilities against human safety.[27] This section and those immediately following focus on approaches that, formally or informally, weigh risks against utilities of the defendant's conduct.

The main factors. In determining whether a jury can reasonably find the defendant's conduct to be negligent, the relationship of the parties is important, but courts most commonly consider relationships on the issue of duty.[28] When it comes to negligence, courts routinely engage in an informal assessment of three factors, although in a particular case they often refer only to the factor that has been singled out as determinative for that case.[29] The factors informally weighed are: (1) the foreseeable likelihood that the person's conduct will result in harm, (2) the foreseeable severity of any harm that may ensue, and (3) the burden of precautions to eliminate or reduce the risk of harm.[30]

Expressed differently but meaning the same thing, courts consider the *likelihood* that the defendant's conduct will cause harm and the *amount* of harm it will cause if harm indeed results; and they will weigh these considerations against the *usefulness* of the conduct and the cost of making it safer.[31] For example, a failure to warn is a basic form of negligence[32] because it usually costs little to give a warning so that a warning might be required even when the risk of harm is small.[33] These factors are often explicit in products liability cases.[34]

---

[26]   See Gregory C. Keating, Reasonableness and Rationality in Negligence Theory, 48 Stan. L. Rev. 311, 383 (1996).

[27]   Richard A. Posner, A Theory of Negligence, 1 J. Leg. Studies 29, 32 (1972).

[28]   For instance, courts traditionally said that landowners owed only limited duties to trespassers, such as the duty not to set a trap or wantonly injure them. Some courts have now said that landowners owe a duty of reasonable care to everyone, including trespassers. Under that rule, it may be that the trespasser-landowner relationship is still important in determining what safety precautions are reasonably required. See Scurti v. City of New York, 40 N.Y.2d 433, 387 N.Y.S.2d 55, 354 N.E.2d 794 (1976).

[29]   Chambers v. Village of Moreauville, 85 So.3d 593 (La. 2012) (noting on issue of negligence in failing to repair a sidewalk that "the utility of the sidewalk is high," "the risk of harm created by the deviation is low," and "it would be fiscally exorbitant to require municipalities to correct all sidewalk deviations of one-and-one-quarter to one-and-one-half inches").

[30]   See Doe Parents No. 1 v. State Dep't of Educ., 100 Haw. 34, 58 P.3d 545 (2002) ("Against this probability, and gravity, of the risk, must be balanced in every case the utility of the type of conduct in question."); Dauzat v. Curnest Guillot Logging Inc., 995 So.2d 1184, 1186–87 (La. 2008) (in determining unreasonable risk the courts consider: "(1) the utility of the complained-of condition; (2) the likelihood and magnitude of harm, which includes the obviousness and apparentness of the condition; (3) the cost of preventing the harm; and (4) the nature of the plaintiff's activities in terms of its social utility, or whether it is dangerous by nature"); Gilhooley v. Star Mkt. Co., Inc., 400 Mass. 205, 508 N.E.2d 609 (1987) ("likelihood of injury to others, the seriousness of the injury, and the burden of avoiding the risk"); Gaudreau v. Clinton Irrigation Dist., 30 P.3d 1070, 1074 (Mont. 2001); see Restatement Third of Torts (Liability for Physical and Emotional Harm) § 3 (2010); Restatement Second of Torts § 91 (negligence if magnitude of the risk outweighs the utility of the defendant's act).

[31]   Giant Food, Inc. v. Mitchell, 334 Md. 633, 640 A.2d 1134 (1994) (risk of harm weighed against protection of property). The usefulness or utility of conduct actually includes the costs saved by not adopting some other course of conduct, but it is sometimes clearer if utility and cost of greater safety are stated separately.

[32]   See Restatement Third of Torts (Liability for Physical and Emotional Harm) § 18 cmt. a (2010).

[33]   See Happel v. Wal-Mart Stores, Inc., 199 Ill.2d 179, 766 N.E.2d 1118, 262 Ill.Dec. 815 (2002) (burden on pharmacist to warn that prescription is contraindicated is small, duty exists).

[34]   E.g., Ritchie v. Glidden Co., 242 F.3d 713 (7th Cir. 2001).

General use of risk-utility. Courts depart from this weighing of risks and utilities in a few cases, where they permit industries to set their own standards of care, as in the case of physicians.[35] Otherwise, however, appellate courts have routinely considered these factors in assessing evidence of negligence since the early years of the negligence era.[36] In many instances, courts weigh risks against utilities, costs against benefits, without formally identifying these factors, but, formally or informally, courts do compare costs and benefits or risks and utilities of conduct in evaluating evidence of negligence.[37]

Example. The most ordinary kinds of negligence cases involve such an analysis. Driving cars is risky, as the statistics show, but it is also useful, so you would be negligent for driving a car only if you add to the normal risks of cars by, say, driving fast.[38] But even fast driving is useful on occasion. If you are driving fast because you are transporting a dangerously wounded person to the hospital, there is some extra utility or usefulness in your conduct that justifies some extra risks. If you continue to drive fast although a herd of sheep approaches, maybe you are still justified, since the harm you might do to the herd is still small in comparison to the life of your wounded passenger. But if instead of a herd of sheep you encounter a street full of soccer-playing children, the harm threatened by your speed is now so great that you'll probably be negligent if you don't slow down. Courts routinely follow this kind of reasoned but unquantified weighing of risks and utilities or costs and benefits.

Probability and amount of harm. The case of the fast driver shows that estimating the importance of a risk involves two things. First, you must estimate probability. How *likely* is it that harm will occur?[39] Second, and quite differently, how *much* harm will occur if the risk does in fact eventuate in harm?[40] A person who fires a rifle in an apparently empty meadow runs only a small risk of hitting some unseen person, but if that risk eventuates, the harm potential for serious injury or death is great. On the other

---

[35] Cf. Blue v. Environmental Eng'g, Inc., 215 Ill.2d 78, 828 N.E.2d 1128, 293 Ill.Dec. 630 (2005) (design defect case; custom of the industry).

[36] Many opinions, including contemporary ones, are focused on whichever factor was relevant in the particular dispute, so that some discuss probability, while others discuss the small injury expected or the burden of avoiding it or the advantages of the risky conduct. E.g., Beatty v. Central Iowa Ry. Co., 58 Iowa 242, 12 N.W. 332 (1882) (railroad constructed almost parallel to road created risks that horses would bolt and injure their riders, but "All persons must accept the advantages of this mode of intercommunication with the danger and inconveniences which necessarily attend it"); Chicago, B & Q Ry. Co. v. Krayenbuhl, 65 Neb. 889, 903, 91 N.W. 880, 882 (1902) (weighing danger of machinery against its benefits).

[37] Indiana Consol. Ins. Co. v. Mathew, 402 N.E.2d 1000 (Ind. Ct. App. 1980) (defendant fled when mower caught fire in the plaintiff's garage, instead of pushing it out; the garage burned, but the defendant was not negligent because the expected harm to the garage was less than the expected harm to the defendant); Hoffman v. Union Elec. Co., 176 S.W.3d 706 (Mo. 2005) (public utility did not advise potential rescuers that downed line was de-energized so that rescuers might save person trapped in a car entangled with the line; but danger of line's being re-energized justified utility's silence; conceiving the issue as one of duty rather than negligence); Sergent v. City of Charleston, 209 W.Va. 437, 549 S.E.2d 311 (2001) (police chase was not negligent in light of the costs (dangers) of not apprehending serious felons who had already fired weapons).

[38] Restatement Third of Torts (Liability for Physical and Emotional Harm) § 3 cmt. j (2010), notes that general activities—driving, building railroads, selling products are examples—can seldom count as negligence. The burden of proving that the railroads should not be operated at all would be extremely difficult and might present administratively imposing tasks for the courts. Consequently, the focus in most cases is on the defendant's ability to reduce risks of the activity without bringing it to a halt.

[39] For example, in Lee v. GNLV Corp., 117 Nev. 291, 22 P.3d 209 (2001), the court thought that a restaurant would not be negligent for failing to train its staff in the Heimlich maneuver because of the low probability that diners would choke on a regular basis. Courts sometimes address this probability issue by saying that harm was not very foreseeable. That locution is infelicitous, but its point seems to be that harm may not be sufficiently probable to warrant safety measures.

[40] John B. v. Sup. Ct., 38 Cal.4th 1177, 137 P.3d 153, 45 Cal.Rptr. 3d 316 (2006) ("the gravity of the harm from HIV infection is a justification for imposing a *greater* duty of care on those who are infected").

hand, a person who fires a gun that shoots ping-pong balls into a crowded street creates a very high risk of very small harm. These cases suggest why the trier must consider both the likelihood of harm and its extent.

Utility of defendant's conduct to third persons or society. The risk of harm must be weighed against the usefulness of the defendant's conduct.[41] The defendant's conduct might be useful in several different kinds of ways. In the example of the wounded passenger, the driver seems selfless—the wounded person, not the driver, will benefit from the expedited medical attention. Utility is often like this. The defendant's conduct is a risk to one person, but the same conduct has great utility to another or to society at large.[42] In this situation, if the defendant changes his conduct to make things safer for A, B will pay the cost of that change by facing a greater risk. The trier must determine whether increasing the risk to B is reasonable because the same conduct reduces the risk to A.

Utility of defendant's conduct to himself. Frequently, the utility of the defendant's conduct is a utility mainly or most obviously to himself and beneficial to society only because society's well-being is composed (at least in part) of aggregate individual benefits. I operate a factory that occasionally permits escape of gases that cause small damage to your adjacent property. I can avoid occasional leaks only by expending large sums of money. For me, there is some utility in continuing to permit occasional leaks; it saves me the cost of avoiding them. That kind of cost-saving utility may also be one basis for risk-utility or cost-benefit comparisons. That is partly because the utility to the defendant is seldom if ever utility to him alone; costs to the defendant will be passed on to customers or workers in the form of higher prices or lower wages. It is also partly because plaintiffs and defendants are treated equally so that the utilities to each are properly considered whether they are important to others or not.

Comparing dollar costs. So far, risk-utility balancing has been presented as an unstructured set of considerations, each of which is important in some not-very-defined way, or as Harper, James & Gray express it, the "tone" of the discussion is "more moral than economic."[43] Indeed, from a moral viewpoint, it may be that risks and utilities should be weighed and offset only in very narrow ways. It has been argued that a money cost of safety should not by itself suffice to justify serious risks of human death, for example. In this view, freedom to act might be weighed against personal security from harm, but not against financial costs alone.[44]

---

[41] Cf. Parsons v. Crown Disposal Co., 15 Cal.4th 456, 936 P.2d 70, 63 Cal.Rptr.2d 291 (1997) (noise of a garbage truck frightened nearby horse, which threw its rider; a defendant is not negligent "merely by causing a machine to produce noises or emissions that are necessary to the regular operation of the machine there shall be no liability for fright to a horse and consequent damages . . . when all that the plaintiff can point to is that a socially beneficial machine . . . properly was used in the manner for which it is designed").

[42] Cf. Gooden v. City of Talladega, 966 So.2d 232 (Ala. 2007) (police officer not negligent for conducting high-speed chase in which fleeing motorist was killed, where motorist's reckless driving presented a substantial threat to others on the roadway).

[43] Harper, James & Gray § 16.9, pp. 477–78.

[44] Among the writings discussing this or similar ideas, see Mark A. Geistfeld, Social Value as a Policy Based Limitation of the Ordinary Duty to Exercise Reasonable Care, 44 Wake Forest L. Rev. 900 (2009); Gregory C. Keating, Reasonableness and Rationality in Negligence Theory, 48 Stan. L. Rev. 311, 383 (1996) (offering a detailed theory for measuring "reasonableness", based on ideas of reciprocity and cooperation among free and equal individuals, rather than "rationality", based on maximizing aggregate human values as expressed in dollars); Richard Wright, The Standards of Care in Negligence Law in Philosophical Foundations of Tort Law 249 (David G. Owen, ed. 1995). Professor Simons describes a number of ways in which one could weigh risks and utilities, for example, by saying that risk-taking is justified only if the utility of the risk is very

Some important thinkers, however, have shaped the risk-utility analysis into a more structured model for decision and one that can be based on economic analysis and dollar comparisons between the costs to the defendant of avoiding harm and the cost to the plaintiff of suffering that harm. In the escaping gas example, the more structured approach might hold that I am not negligent if it would cost me more to avoid the gas leaks than those leaks cost you and others in property damage. The next section considers this form of analysis.

§ 12.4　Structured Weighing of Risks and Utilities

A structured approach. Courts routinely apply some form of risk-utility weighing as a means of determining whether conduct was negligent. Some courts have gone further by explicitly approving a form of risk-utility weighing that may be more rigorous or at least more structured[45] than the free-form estimate of risks and costs sketched in the immediately preceding section.[46]

Judge Hand's decision in Carroll Towing. The structured model is usually traced to an opinion written by an impressive judge, Judge Learned Hand, and in fact is often referred to as the Hand formula or as the *Carroll Towing* doctrine after the case in which Hand advanced his ideas. *United States v. Carroll Towing*[47] was an admiralty case. A barge in a busy harbor broke loose and caused damage. Harm could have been avoided if a caretaker or bargee had been on board at all times, but he was not. The question was whether it was negligent not to have a 24-hour bargee on board.

The Hand formula. Judge Hand recognized the traditional idea that a weighing of risks and utilities was necessary. He said, "[T]he owner's duty . . . to provide against resulting injuries is a function of three variables: (1) The probability that [the barge] will break away; (2) the gravity of the resulting injury, if she does; (3) the burden of adequate precautions." This language summed up the experience of many cases, but Hand then went on. He identified the burden of precaution as B, gravity of the loss as L, and probability of harm as P, then stated his famous formula:

> [L]iability depends upon whether B is less than L multiplied by P:
> i.e., whether $B < PL$.

Injury or harm that could not have been foreseen or avoided. Any given act has potential for injury. But the Hand formula only directs us to consider injury or harm that would have been avoided by appropriate care and only those harms that are foreseeable and within the scope of the defendant's duty of care. A defendant who fails to lock up his handguns risks theft and misuse, quite possibly a killing inflicted by the thief. If locking up the guns would not have prevented a theft, or if death is not a foreseeable consequence of the gun theft, the risk of death is not considered in applying

---

much greater than the harm, although he disapproves this approach. See Kenneth W. Simons, Negligence, 16 Soc. Phil. & Pol'y 2, 52, 78–80 (1999).

[45]　Emphasizing the rigor, structure, or form, see Michael D. Green, The Schizophrenia of Risk-Benefit Analysis in Design Defect Litigation, 48 Vand. L. Rev. 609 (1995); Barbara Ann White, Risk-utility Analysis and the Learned Hand Formula: A Hand that Helps or a Hand that Hides?, 32 Ariz. L. Rev. 77 (1990).

[46]　Among the cases expressly recognizing the structured approach embodied in the Hand formula discussed below, see, e.g., Levi v. Southwest La. Elec. Membership Coop., 542 So.2d 1081 (La. 1989); Chicago Title Ins. Co. v. Allfirst Bank, 394 Md. 270, 291, 905 A.2d 366, 378 (2006) (multiply magnitude of potential harm by probability of harm and weigh the result against the burden of exercising care). For a survey of cases and citations to many of them, see Stephen G. Gilles, The Invisible Hand Formula, 80 Va. L. Rev. 1015, 1016 n. 4 (1994).

[47]　United States v. Carroll Towing Co., 159 F.2d 169 (2d Cir. 1947).

the Hand formula[48] If the court concludes that a gun owner owes no duty at all to lock up guns, the negligence issue and the Hand formula is never even reached, for the case will be dismissed on no-duty grounds.

Injury or harm to the defendant himself. Suppose the defendant risks harm to others by driving at 60 mph and also risks harm to himself. Considering risks of harm to others alone, though, 60 mph might be a reasonable speed under all the circumstances. However, if we consider risks of harm to others plus risks of harm to the defendant himself, we might conclude that a speed of 60 mph is negligent. Should a court or jury consider both the risk of harm to others and the risks of harm to one's self in applying the Hand formula? The traditional formulation and the actual practice in the courts suggests that only the risks of harm to others have been considered. Perhaps this is the case less by explicit reasoning and more by virtue of an assumption that the defendant's risk to himself is the defendant's own business.[49] In any event, important economic thinkers have challenged the practice, arguing that in weighing the burdens of precaution against risks, the total foreseeable and avoidable risks, including risks to the defendant himself, should be weighed.[50] Such an approach, they argue, would encourage defendants to take appropriate precautions by undertaking the burden of precaution when the total risk of harm exceeded the cost of that burden. Their approach, if accepted, would apply to contributory or comparative negligence of plaintiffs as well as to negligence of defendants.

Precaution as a burden to third persons or society. The burden of precaution in Judge Hand's formula includes any cost the defendant might have to incur to make things safe enough, but it also includes costs that would be inflicted upon others or upon society at large. For instance, cars often strike telephone or light poles. If the pole gives way and falls on impact, the passengers in the car may be safer than if they had collided with an immovable object. On the other hand, falling poles may strike pedestrians or others. To make things safer for pedestrians may be to make them riskier for car passengers and vice versa. So if the telephone company installs stronger poles to protect the pedestrian, part of the cost of doing so will be borne by car passengers who suffer injury as a result.[51] The burden of greater safety for pedestrians includes a cost in the increased risk to car passengers and, under Judge's Hand's formula, that must be weighed.

Precaution as a burden to defendant. In *Carroll Towing* itself, the burden of precaution was simple: the increased or marginal cost to the defendant of keeping a bargee on board 24 hours a day. Suppose that cost was, say, $30,000 a year in increased wages, and that breakaways averaged one a year with an average damage to other vessels of $20,000. In that scenario, the barge owner would not be negligent in failing to

---

[48] The scope of risk rules (often called rules of proximate cause or legal cause or intervening cause) bar claims that are not considered within the risk created by the defendant's negligence. The degree of risk or magnitude of potential harm is irrelevant if the defendant's act is not considered to be a proximate cause.

[49] See Restatement Second of Torts § 291 (1965) ("risk of harm to another").

[50] Robert Cooter & Ariel Porat, Does Risk to Oneself Increase the Care Owed to Others? Law and Economics in Conflict, 29 J. Leg. Stud. 19 (2000). Restatement Third of Torts (Liability for Physical and Emotional Harm) § 3 cmt. b (2010) supports this view.

[51] See Bernier v. Boston Edison Co., 380 Mass. 372, 403 N.E.2d 391 (1980) (concluding that risks to pedestrians might be greater and hence that the defendant could be found to be negligent in constructing pole that would fall on slight impact).

keep a 24-hour bargee because the cost to prevent a $20,000 loss would be a $30,000 expenditure, a result usually condemned as economically inefficient.[52]

Net burden to the defendant? In assessing the burden of precaution to the defendant do you consider his net burden after taking into account any advantage he gains from precautionary expenditures? Suppose the defendant's added expenditure of $30,000 to keep a bargee on board at all times would save $20,000 in costs to others and also $20,000 in costs to the barge owner himself, since his property as well as that of others is at risk. In that case you could conclude that the net burden of precaution to the barge owner would be only $10,000, because his expenditure of $30,000 would save him $20,000 as well as saving similar losses to others. Although expressed as a net burden, such an approach works out to be the same as saying that you must consider risks of harms to the defendant as well as risks to others.[53] So far, courts have not ordinarily taken into account the benefits the defendant gets from taking precautions.[54]

The firm analogy. The Hand test treats the two parties as if they were partners in a firm. It says the firm would be foolish to spend $30,000 in one department to avoid a $20,000 loss in another department. A firm that does that regularly will soon be out of business. Although the plaintiff and defendant are not in fact members of the same private firm, they are members of the same society. That society is a very large firm that will be poorer if one of its citizens must spend $30 to save another $20.

Putting costs and benefits on the same scale. Thinking about the problem in terms of the *Carroll Towing* formula, a judge or juror[55] can compare benefits with costs because they have now been put on a common scale. Better safety is achieved at a cost of $30,000, but the safety benefit is only $20,000. The same point can be made by saying that the utility or benefit to the defendant in *not* having a bargee is $30,000 a year saved, but that the utility or benefit to injured parties that will result from having a 24-hour bargee is $20,000. By reducing all the costs and benefits to dollar terms, we can make such comparisons, and that is a great advantage. The great disadvantage of reducing the risks, costs, and benefits to dollar terms is that we might be treating quite incommensurate risks alike.[56]

Evidence and arguments suggested by the formula. On the illustrative facts above, the dollar comparison of utilities favors the defendant, but the test can just as easily work the other way around. If the defendant's cost of preventing the harm is less than

---

[52]   See Richard Posner, A Theory of Negligence, 1 J. Leg. Stud. 29 (1972). Posner used examples similar to those given here.

[53]   See Cooter & Porat, supra n. 50 at 28.

[54]   But see Johnson v. City of Milwaukee, 41 F.Supp. 2d 917 (D. Wis. 1999) (discussed in Cooter & Porat, supra n. 50) (reasonableness of officer's decision to draw a gun which later discharged to be judged in part by increased safety for officer as well as for suspect if gun was not drawn under the particular circumstances).

[55]   The formula is mainly used by judges reviewing evidence to determine a directed verdict or motion for summary judgment, and only then when one party makes an argument based on the formula or some part of it. Juries are routinely instructed in the reasonable person standard without explanation about risk-utility balancing. See Stephen G. Gilles, The Invisible Hand Formula, 80 Va. L. Rev. 1015 (1994) (concluding that the Hand formula is "underenforced" because of omissions to instruct the jury in its terms). Juries are instructed on probability (under the rubric of foreseeability) and on commensurate care, a notion that embodies part of the risk-utility weighing. Juries may also hear lawyers' arguments about costs and benefits of the defendant's conduct and understand the relevance of evidence on those issues, such as evidence that the defendant could have achieved safety by a small expenditure.

[56]   See Gregory C. Keating, Reasonableness and Rationality in Negligence Theory, 48 Stan. L. Rev. 311, 342 (1996) (people have "diverse and incommensurable conceptions of the good," and those at risk generally do not value the injurer's aims and benefits as the injurer does, a theme that appears in several places).

the expected value of the harm itself, he is definitely negligent and liable under the Hand formula, as was the case in *Carroll Towing* itself. Indeed, one function of the formula may be to permit a recovery that would otherwise be barred by a rule of law.[57] Another, maybe the most important, is to direct lawyers to helpful kinds of evidence. Plaintiffs' lawyers may be thus led by the Hand formula to claim that the defendant failed to use cheaper means of achieving safety. For instance, a plaintiff's lawyer might try to prove that the defendant could have avoided the breakaway in *Carroll Towing* by making a one-time capital investment in better tie-down technology that would be far less costly than either the full-time bargee or the potential harm from breakaways.[58] Similarly, the formula suggests and supports jury argument. The plaintiff who can show that by spending $1 the defendant could have avoided serious injury or injuries to many people has a ready-made and appealing jury argument. The Hand formula may not work as well for defendants' jury arguments; they may not wish to argue that it would have been costly to a large corporation to avoid paralyzing the plaintiff. But even defendants may find it possible to introduce evidence and to make arguments based on the Hand formula in appellate courts.

Probability and average. To speak of probability is to speak of foreseeability, but the language of probability is more precise in its structure. We can think of probability in terms of odds or percentages—a probability of .9 or a probability of .5 for example—but it sounds foolish to speak of .9 or 90% foreseeability. In the examples used above, probability is reflected in the averaging. If untended barges break away an average of ten times in a ten year period, doing damage each time, we know something about the probability of breakaways—one a year. If the untended barges break way twenty times in a 10-year period, the average is no longer one a year but two a year, and the probability is correspondingly twice as high as our first estimate. The same kind of thinking applies to the amount of harm factor. Some injuries might be small, while others are large, but it is the average that best expresses the total amount of harm for the time period involved.

Discounting to reflect probability. Part of the impact of Judge Hand's test comes from the fact that it literally discounts the plaintiff's damages as a part of getting the average. Probability can be expressed as a percentage or chance. If a given harm is certain to occur, the probability would be 1.00, but if the chance of its occurrence is only 50–50, the probability would be 0.50. So if the defendant's conduct created a risk of $100 damage, but the probability of harm was 0.50, the Hand formula tells us that we treat the damage in issue as $50 instead of $100 for purposes of comparing the defendant's cost. That is because we discount or multiply probability times harm to get the average. 0.50 x $100 gives us an average $50 damage.

Amount of plaintiff's recovery unaffected by discount. Although probability is used to discount the damage when the point is to determine the defendant's negligence, probability is not used to reduce the plaintiff's actual recovery. If the defendant is found to be negligent by application of these rules, he is liable for all of the plaintiff's injury,

---

[57]   In Ritchie v. Glidden Co., 242 F.3d 713 (7th Cir. 2001), the court refused to apply the sophisticated user rule that would relieve a manufacturer of providing a warning directly to endangered users of its products; instead, the court invoked the risk-utility approach and left it to the jury to consider whether the manufacturer should have provided a warning in the light of the low cost on the one hand and the danger on the other.

[58]   The cost of a capital investment may be hard to figure not only because it may avoid many injuries during its effective life but also because the defendant's expenditure is a cost for which the defendant receives some compensating gain in the form of increased capital assets.

whether it is $50, $100, or many times those amounts. The discount applies only as a way of determining the total risk imposed by the defendant's conduct.

Averaging. Averaging, or the use of the probability discount, is important if the defendant is to estimate the appropriate overall amount to invest in safety. Any particular injured individual might suffer damages much less than the defendant's cost to avoid the harm but still recover because the average harm would exceed that cost. And vice versa: the injured individual might suffer much greater harm than the defendant's cost of avoidance and yet be denied recovery because the cost of avoidance was too high compared to the average or probable overall harms. Indeed, one of the criticisms of the Hand formula, at least as it might be rigorously applied, is that it may do social good without doing individual justice. The next section summarizes some of the criticisms.

§ 12.5 Supporting and Criticizing Structured Risk-Utility Assessments

Exceptions to risk utility and the general rule. In some negligence claims based on alleged medical malpractice and a few others, courts may bypass the risk-utility assessment altogether. In those cases, the custom of the profession may furnish the standard of care, so that even very risky procedures may not be counted as negligence if the profession customarily engages in such procedures. Otherwise, however, courts do routinely attempt to weigh risks and utilities to determine whether the defendant was negligent.

Rigor. The Hand formula is often seen to be more rigorous than a free-form weighing of costs and benefits. Part of the rigor lies in the fact that the Hand formula places risks and utilities on a common scale of dollars so that they can be fully compared. Another part lies in the fact that the formula sets up precise relationships among probability, gravity of harm, and cost of safety. These characteristics represent both strengths and weaknesses of the formula.

Justifications and Limits

Economic justifications. Under an economic interpretation of the Hand formula, the purpose of weighing of costs and benefits of the defendant's conduct is to generate a rule of liability that gives actors incentives to invest an appropriate amount in safety. Since virtually all conduct carries some risk, a world of perfect safety would eliminate or fantastically transform almost all conduct. The Hand model of risk-utility weighing is often supported as an economic analysis intended to impose liability for economically inefficient risk-taking, but to protect conduct that is efficient in the sense that the risks involved are worth taking. Risks that are worth taking produce more gains than losses, to the benefit of society as a whole by maximizing wealth (as a measure of human preferences). Judge Posner has provided some of the clearest arguments along these lines.[59]

Other advantages. Although commentators most often discuss economic justifications of the Hand formula, other justifications might be advanced. The Hand approach may be better at protecting everyone's rights and freedoms to act in the world than a more intuitive approach. At the same time, it sets limits on those rights.

---

[59] See Richard Posner, A Theory of Negligence, 1 J. Leg. Stud. 29 (1972); Richard Posner, Economic Analysis of Law 163 ff. (4th ed. 1992).

Moreover, it provides lawyers with a guide that is helpful in knowing what kind of evidence to produce. Finally, it constrains judges to explain their conclusions about negligence, not merely as an unfathomable exercise of power or discretion, but in terms that can be judged by professionals in the field.

Criticizing the Hand Formula

Incentives. Some criticisms of the Hand approach do not attack the underlying ideas of the formula so much as the claim that it promotes efficiency and appropriate safety incentives. In this group, some criticisms offer more or less technical variations or improvements on the formula.[60] Others deny that tort law provides incentives at all and hence suggest that the Hand formula might be irrelevant unless it serves other purposes.[61]

Inability to provide quantified data. A different kind of criticism is based on a misunderstanding of the formula, and it should be disposed of quickly. That criticism is essentially that the data required by the formula will not be available or that lawyers should not have to be mathematicians. But the formula does not require mathematical proof. For instance, the formula does not require lawyers to introduce evidence of probability expressed in mathematical terms or even evidence about dollar costs of safety precautions.

Use of estimates. It is true, of course, that the plaintiff must prove her case somehow, and in some instances she may be unable to make a convincing case without showing some reliable evidence that the defendant's conduct created a substantial probability of harm[62] or that the defendant could have taken safety precautions at a low dollar cost.[63] But the Hand formula does not itself require numerical evidence, although it illuminates the ways in which such evidence is useful. In the great majority of cases, including Hand's own decision in *Carroll Towing*, the formula is applied to rough estimates derived from practical everyday evidence.

A guide to evidence. Like many other legal rules, it may represent less a guide to conduct than a guide for lawyers about the kind of evidence that will be useful, whether or not that evidence is quantified. A plaintiff's lawyer, for example, can attempt to demonstrate that the defendant could easily have provided better safety without demonstrating the exact cost of doing so, or that harm was highly probable because it had often occurred in similar circumstances, even if the probability cannot be expressed in a percentage. The formula also provides a meaningful model for analysis by judges, even if judges must use estimates of probabilities, costs, and benefits.[64]

---

[60]   See Mark Grady, A New Positive Economic Theory of Negligence, 92 Yale L. J. 799 (1983) (since injurers cannot always know what level of precaution courts will find acceptable, the formula must be applied in a different way).

[61]   E.g., Daniel Shuman, The Psychology of Deterrence in Tort Law, 42 Kan. L. Rev. 115 (1993).

[62]   E.g., Turpin v. Merrell Dow Pharms., Inc., 959 F.2d 1349 (6th Cir. 1992) (statistical evidence on probability that Bendectin caused fetal limb-reduction was inadequate).

[63]   McCarty v. Phesant Run, Inc., 826 F.2d 1554 (7th Cir. 1987) (plaintiff claimed hotel should have provided better locks, but put on no evidence as to costs). In contrast, in Grimshaw v. Ford Motor Co., 119 Cal.App.3d 757, 174 Cal. Rptr. 348 (1981), the plaintiff was able to show exact dollar costs of improvements that would have prevented the Pinto car from engulfing its occupants in flames. The evidence was highly effective and the plaintiffs recovered. In addition to direct cost evidence, the plaintiff's lawyer might be able to produce evidence of customary precautions. Such evidence tends to show both foreseeability of harm and the relative feasibility of a safety precaution.

[64]   Levi v. Southwest La. Elec. Membership Coop., 542 So.2d 1081 (La. 1989); see David G. Owen, Defectiveness Restated: Exploding the "Strict" Products Liability Myth, 1996 U. Ill. L. Rev. 743 (1996) ("This

Individual justice. One of the most fundamental criticisms generated by rigorous application of the *Carroll Towing* test is that it emphasizes social good too much and individual justice or moral choice too little.[65] It makes the rights of the individual plaintiff depend in part upon what is good for society as a whole. In one form or another, this is the most central argument against Hand's formula. Although the Hand formula does not call for use of actual numbers like those used in the illustrations, and a complete set of such numbers could seldom be produced in court, the formula does definitely emphasize the importance of estimating social advantage or wealth maximization in society at large by insisting that no one should be required to spend more on safety than the sums saved by those expenditures. Some thinkers may fear that weighing risks and utilities turns "moral analysis into a bloodless form of calculation" that simply involves plugging in numbers.[66]

Incommensurables. Another characteristic of the Hand test has found disfavor in some quarters. At least as it has been developed in economic theory, the Hand test asks us to reduce the utilities of both parties to a common scale of dollars. The common scale is important, because it permits comparison. However, the result is that a broken leg is valued like a commodity; its worth is expressed in dollars in the jury's assessment of value based on medical costs, wage loss, and pain. If that total value is only $10,000 but the cost to the defendant to avoid the injury is $15,000, the defendant is not negligent. But if the death of a human being is intractably incommensurate with dollar costs of safer conduct, the common scale, however elegant, is exactly the wrong scale.[67] To some extent, this criticism is meliorated by the fact that the jury is allowed to decide the value of intangibles like pain and loss of enjoyment, even though the jury must necessarily reduce those values to dollar damages. It might also be meliorated by a "hybrid" approach, as where qualitative values could be considered to constrain the use of a pure dollar scale.[68]

Unworkable in some cases. Still another criticism is that some kinds of cases seem to lend themselves only poorly to a rigorous risk-utility analysis. For instance, when the defendant is charged with a moment's inattention or negligently forgetting to do something necessary for safety, it is quite difficult to analyze the costs to achieve better safety. What are the costs of remembering?[69] One scholar has put the point more strongly

---

type of 'cost-benefit' or 'risk-utility' analysis may be problematic if relied upon excessively as a mechanical device for producing automatic 'right' answers, but it nicely describes the decisional calculus that lies at the heart of products liability law in particular and accident law in general.").

[65] See, e.g., Bamford v. Turnley, 3 B.&S. 67, 122 Eng.Rep. 27 (Exch. Ch. 1862) (Judgment of Bramwell B.) (arguing that defendant must use the gains from his activities to pay the costs of harms inflicted on others); Gregory C. Keating, Reasonableness and Rationality in Reasonableness and Rationality in Negligence Theory, 48 Stan. L. Rev. 311 (1996); George P. Fletcher, Fairness and Utility in Tort Theory, 85 Harv. L. Rev. 537 (1972).

[66] See Kenneth W. Simons, Negligence, 16 Soc. Phil. & Pol'y 2, 52, 80 (1999) (but suggesting that "qualitative" balancing without using dollar costs would avoid this problem).

[67] See Barbara Ann White, Risk-utility Analysis and the Learned Hand Formula: A Hand that Helps or a Hand That Hides?, 32 Ariz. L. Rev. 77, 111 n. 192 (1990); Michael D. Green, The Schizophrenia of Risk-Benefit Analysis in Design Defect Litigation, 48 Vand. L. Rev. 609 (1995) (emphasizing incommensurability and the impracticability of making a jury argument that human lives are worth less than the cost of a safety feature on an automobile); Richard Wright, The Standards of Care in Negligence Law in Philosophical Foundations of Tort Law 249 (David G. Owen, ed. 1995).

[68] Kenneth W. Simons, Negligence, 16 Soc. Phil. & Pol'y 2, 52, 86 (1999) (suggesting that under the Hand test, a value must be placed on human life when it is at risk, but that if the risk is death by fire, the trier could also consider whether such a death is particularly dreaded).

[69] See Izhak Englard, The System Builders: A Critical Appraisal of Modern American Tort Theory, 9 J. Leg. Stud. 27 (1980); Mark Grady, Why Are People Negligent? Technology, Non-Durable Precautions, and the

by saying that where repeated safety efforts are required—as where a driver must constantly keep a lookout—even reasonable people will occasionally lapse, but that in such cases courts routinely impose liability.[70] The implication is that the risk-utility balance cannot explain this liability and thus that the risk-utility balance applies only to "durable precautions" such as designs, plans, or systems for dealing with hazards.

Precautions against unknown risk. A different kind of unworkability argument is that in some cases the defendant knows there is some kind of risk but does not know its extent or what will reduce the risk. In such a case, how much money should he spend to get more information? Without knowing the magnitude or severity of the risks, it will be difficult indeed to know how much to invest in getting more information. This is routinely a problem for manufacturers of new drugs, which usually carry risks the extent of which may never be known.[71]

Perspectives for Evaluating the Hand Formula

(1)   Although the Hand formula in *Carroll Towing* is usually analyzed in economic terms, part of its operation can be viewed as a moral proposition that you should treat others as you would treat yourself.[72] If you can save $100 of your own by spending $50, you should and would do so. If you can save $100 of your own only by spending $200, you would not make the expenditure. Only if you should treat others better than you would treat yourself is there reason to think you are wrong in failing to take the $200 precaution.[73] Sometimes defendants are indeed under an obligation to treat the plaintiff with special care arising from an undertaking or special relationship. But where the defendant is not guilty of misleading, has no special relationship with the plaintiff, and does not owe more care by custom or his own undertaking, the Hand formula can often be seen in moral rather than economic terms. Indeed, utility itself, whether cast in economic terms or not, can be seen to have a moral quality.[74]

(2)   People can reasonably think that both the justifications and the criticisms of the Hand formula are exaggerated. The formula assuredly has its uses in the process of determining negligence, but it may be more useful in some cases than others. Positive statutory law displaces the formula in many cases. Relationships of the parties may dictate duties or defenses in others. Custom may be especially important in still others.

Medical Malpractice Explosion, 82 Nw. U. L. Rev. 293 (1988). Judge Posner himself may have implied the jury could figure a forgetful (or sleepy) person's cost "of schooling herself to greater vigilance." Wassell v. Adams, 865 F.2d 849 (7th Cir. 1989).

[70]   Grady, Res Ipsa Loquitur and Compliance Error, 142 U. Pa. L. Rev. 887 (1994). Restatement Third of Torts (Liability for Physical and Emotional Harm) § 3 cmt. k (2010) addresses the problem arising from the idea that even reasonable persons are fallible on occasion by saying that the trier must focus on the occasion in question, not on fallibility over time.

[71]   David Barnes & Lynn Stout, The Economic Analysis of Tort Law 38 (1992), suggests something like this, reading the Hand formula to mean "victims suffer so that actors may prosper," and suggesting that in non-reciprocal risk cases like the manufacturer-consumer case, using the Hand formula might have "distributional" implications.

[72]   Cf. Kenneth W. Simons, Deontology, Negligence, Tort, and Crime, 76 B.U. L. Rev. 273 (1996).

[73]   Arguing that because willingness to face risks differs legitimately in a plural society, you should indeed treat others according to some standard of reasonableness, not according to your own preferences or according to an economic valuation, see Gregory C. Keating, Reasonableness and Rationality in Negligence Theory, 48 Stan. L. Rev. 311 (1996). Professor Richard Wright thinks that morally speaking, you need not treat others as yourself and in fact a rule requiring you to do so is to treat no one as a distinct person with her own life to lead. See Richard Wright, The Standards of Care in Negligence Law in Philosophical Foundations of Tort Law 249 (David G. Owen, ed. 1995).

[74]   See David G. Owen, The Moral Foundations of Products Liability Law: Toward First Principles, 68 Notre Dame L. Rev. 427 (1993).

The formula can be seen as a default formula, to be used when it is not trumped by something more important.

(3) Judges do in fact use some kind of risk-utility analysis, not necessarily under that name and not necessarily with the rigor that economic analysis would suggest. Most of the objections to the Hand formula seem aimed at its comparison of dollar costs rather than at the underlying idea that some kind of weighing of costs and benefits is necessary.

(4) If all weighing of costs and benefits, risks and utilities, were discarded, courts might be hard pressed to find any generally applicable way of analyzing negligence. A judge's conclusory statements that the defendant did or did not behave reasonably would not be satisfactory and would not much resemble anything we would like to call law. However, it would be possible to weigh costs and benefits, risks and utilities by appealing to the ideals of a reasonable person who considers something besides dollar costs.[75]

Reasonable Expectations About the Care of Others

Jury estimating risks in light of safety efforts of others. Typically the question of breach is a question for the jury. But sometimes it is clear that an act is not risky enough to count as negligence because the defendant could reasonably expect that other people would minimize the risk, thus bringing it within tolerable bounds.[76] That seems especially obvious when the defendant attempts to minimize the risk or shift responsibility by hiring or relying upon a competent person to eliminate it.[77] But the idea is broader. It turns on nothing more than the defendant's reasonable expectations that others will make safety contributions. A driver may not be negligent in driving through an intersection in accordance with a green light, even if the driver cannot see traffic approaching on side streets. There is a risk, but it is small in light of the reasonable expectation that drivers approaching from a blind side street would themselves exercise due care and follow the traffic signal.[78] A physician who leaves town while a patient still requires care may be creating no risk at all if he arranges for a substitute physician.[79] A homeowner who knows that a small child has access to his swimming pool may be reasonable in turning his back if the child is being cared for by her mother.[80] Conversely, if the landowner knows parents are unaware of a risk to children, harm to them is more likely and reasonable care may require a warning.[81] In all of these cases consideration

---

[75] Gregory C. Keating, Reasonableness and Rationality in Negligence Theory, 48 Stan. L. Rev. 311, 342 (1996) (people have "diverse and incommensurable conceptions of the good," and those at risk generally do not value the injurer's aims and benefits as the injurer does, a theme that appears in several places).

[76] See Greycas, Inc. v. Proud, 826 F.2d 1560, 1566 (7th Cir. 1987) ("A pedestrian is not required to exercise a level of care . . . that would be optimal if there were no sanctions against reckless driving. . . . The law normally does not require duplicative precautions unless one is likely to fail or the consequences of failure . . . would be catastrophic." (Posner, J.)).

[77] E.g., Van Hook v. Anderson, 64 Wash.App. 353, 824 P.2d 509 (1992) (surgeon could rely upon nurses to count sponges and he was not negligent in leaving a sponge in the patient's body when he relied on nurses' assurance that sponges were accounted for); cf. Holger v. Irish, 316 Or. 402, 851 P.2d 1122 (1993) (surgeon not vicariously liable for nurse's negligent sponge count).

[78] Many cases state some variation on the rule that a defendant can normally assume that others will exercise reasonable care and can shape his own conduct accordingly. E.g., Morgan v. Braasch, 214 Ga.App. 82, 446 S.E.2d 746 (1994) (intersection collision); Sims v. Huntington, 271 Ind. 368, 393 N.E.2d 135 (1979).

[79] Manno v. McIntosh, 519 N.W.2d 815 (Iowa Ct. App. 1994) (discussed in terms of "abandonment" of the patient).

[80] Padilla v. Rodas, 160 Cal.App.4th 742, 73 Cal.Rptr.3d 114 (2008) (expressing the point as a no-duty rather than as a no-negligence ruling); Herron v. Hollis, 248 Ga.App. 194, 546 S.E.2d 17 (2001).

[81] See Perri v. Furama Rest., Inc., 781 N.E.2d 631, 269 Ill. Dec. 834 (App. Ct. 2002) ("If parents or caregivers are unaware of a particular danger, it is reasonably foreseeable that they will fail to prevent a minor child from encountering that danger. Thus, while defendant was certainly entitled to rely on the adults in

of reasonably expected safety efforts of others is appropriate evidence. However, when reasonable minds could differ, the question is one for the jury.

Jury estimating risks in light of the plaintiff's ability to protect herself. Sometimes the defendant's conduct is not risky enough to count as negligence because the defendant can expect the plaintiff herself to avoid the harm and hence foresees no harm from his actions. This is most commonly so when the defendant creates an open and obvious danger that people can be expected to see and avoid. The risks of a parked car, or a sprinkler head in the lawn, or other obvious dangers,[82] although representing foreseeable harms, are nevertheless sometimes very small risks because most people who might be hurt will see and avoid danger for themselves. Similarly, the owner of a building who hires someone to repair the roof may create a risk by not furnishing safety nets. Although the owner could easily foresee harm from the repairer's fall, the owner might also expect that the repairer would take steps to provide her own safety equipment or at least to ask for it if it is needed.[83] The jury can properly consider, then, the possibility that the defendant's conduct is not unreasonably risky because others, including the plaintiff herself, may reduce the risk. Sometimes courts consider this so clear that they take the issue from the jury and decide for themselves that the defendant was not negligent considering the probability that the plaintiff would avoid a known danger.[84]

Jury estimating risks in light of risks others will add. It is not true, of course, that one never need anticipate the negligence of others. Sometimes that is the very thing the defendant should foresee and protect against. The defendant who creates an obvious risk cannot always expect that it will be avoided; a distracted customer carrying a package might collide with an obstruction that would ordinarily be obvious and avoidable.[85] The defendant who lends a car to an incompetent driver[86] or who gives alcohol to an intoxicated person or a minor[87] creates a risk, perhaps quite unreasonable, that the driver or the drinker will cause harm to others. If the probability of injury is unreasonably high in light of the harm that may result and the relatively low cost of avoiding it, a jury's finding of negligence is entirely appropriate.[88]

Estimation of costs and advantages. Even small risks may be unreasonable and may count as negligence if they can be avoided at little cost. Even large risks might be

plaintiffs' group to protect their children from dangers of which the adults were or should have been aware, defendant is not absolved of its duty . . . simply because Jordan was accompanied by his parents"). Cf. Foss v. Kincaide, 766 N.W.2d 317 (Minn. 2009) (homeowner owed no duty to protect child in home who was under mother's supervision).

[82] See Pomer v. Schoolman, 875 F.2d 1262 (7th Cir. 1989); McFarland v. Kahn, 123 Ariz. 62, 597 P.2d 544 (1979) (sprinkler head); Morse v. Goduti, 777 A.2d 292 (N.H. 2001) (trier to consider whether landowner created unreasonable risk by constructing an unfenced, steep-sided pond or whether risk was reasonable because children could be expected to appreciate and avoid the risk).

[83] Stinnett v. Buchele, 598 S.W.2d 469 (Ky. 1980).

[84] See White v. Georgia Power Co., 265 Ga.App. 664, 595 S.E.2d 353 (2004) (defendants failed to warn boys who could not swim of the dangers of entering a raging river up to their necks; defendants not negligent as a matter of law).

[85] E.g., Ward v. K-Mart Corp., 136 Ill.2d 132, 554 N.E.2d 223 (1990) (customer carrying mirror that blocked his view ran into a dangerously placed obstruction); Urban v. Wait's Supermarket, Inc., 294 N.W.2d 793 (S.D. 1980) (customer distracted by search for cupcake holders fell on watermelons in aisle).

[86] So-called negligent entrustment of a chattel. E.g., Renfro v. Adkins, 323 Ark. 288, 914 S.W.2d 306 (1996).

[87] E.g., Brigance v. Velvet Dove Rest., Inc., 725 P.2d 300 (1986).

[88] See Ransom v. City of Garden City, 113 Idaho 202, 207, 743 P.2d 70, 75 (1987) (quoting Prosser & Keeton).

justified if they carry with them even greater advantages. So the jury must estimate, if it can, something about the costs of greater safety and the advantages of continuing the defendant's conduct as it is. Sometimes evidence can elucidate such issues. Evidence that the defendant repaired premises or changed his way of conducting business after the plaintiff's injury is not usually admissible to show a standard of care, but if the defendant has argued that a safer practice is costly, evidence that the defendant has himself adopted the practice later can fairly be admitted to show that, after all, the practice was in fact feasible and not too costly.[89]

Sometimes it is easy to estimate that costs of greater safety will be low, as where the defendant can make a product safer by including a warning on its label or on a decal.[90] Sometimes it is even possible to obtain rather precise estimates of the cost of greater safety.[91] More commonly, risks cannot be precisely weighed and juries and judges alike are expected to estimate costs in a very broad manner. There are limits: the court's own ball park estimate may convince the court that the case must not be left to the jury at all,[92] or the court may conclude that general experience is not enough to permit a reasonable cost estimate and therefore that the plaintiff must introduce evidence on that subject or suffer a directed verdict.[93] In very many cases, however, the matter of cost, like the matter of risk, is left to the jury's evaluation without a specific requirement of testimony.

C. CUSTOM

§ 12.6 Custom or Practice: General Rules

Custom is significant in the law in a number of ways. This section primarily addresses the relevance of custom in helping the jury determine whether, given a duty to use reasonable care, conduct counts as "negligence."

Custom as evidence of reasonable care. Evidence of customary safety practices is admissible as tending to show that conduct in violation of the customary safety precautions may violate the reasonable person standard of care.[94] Under this rule, custom is only evidence of negligence; it is not conclusive because the standard of care remains that of the reasonable person under the circumstances.[95] Custom itself becomes

[89] See Ray v. American Nat'l Red Cross, 696 A.2d 399 (D.C. 1997).

[90] E.g., Watson v. Navistar Int'l Transp. Corp., 121 Idaho 643, 827 P.2d 656 (1992).

[91] Hunter v. Dep't of Transp. & Dev., 620 So.2d 1149 (La. 1993) (costs of widening median increase safety for left-turn drivers).

[92] In Ramirez v. Plough, Inc., 6 Cal.4th 539, 863 P.2d 167, 25 Cal.Rptr.2d 97 (1993), the court concluded that product warnings for aspirin need not be given in Spanish even though the manufacturer advertised in Spanish to Spanish-speaking consumers. The case turned on several legal doctrines and policies but partly on the court's belief, seemingly not based on actual trial evidence, that costs of adding warnings could be very high.

[93] See McCarty v. Pheasant Run, Inc., 826 F.2d 1554 (7th Cir. 1987).

[94] Texas & Pac. Ry. v. Behymer, 189 U.S. 468, 23 S.Ct. 622, 47 L.Ed.2d 905 (1903); The T.J. Hooper, 60 F.2d 737 (2d Cir. 1932); Mobile Gas Serv. Corp. v. Robinson, 20 So.3d 770 (Ala. 2009) (gas-industry custom to disconnect service when it fed known hazardous appliances is not conclusive but may be considered by jury to determine whether defendant exercised reasonable care in violating the custom); Scott v. Matlack, Inc., 39 P.3d 1160, 1166 (Colo. 2002) ("When the defendant and the plaintiff are part of an industry that conforms to certain well-established safety customs, the jury may consider the customs as non-conclusive evidence of reasonable care the defendant should follow in that industry."); Restatement Third of Torts (Liability for Physical and Emotional Harm) § 13 (2010); Restatement Second of Torts § 295A (1965).

[95] Elkerson v. North Jersey Blood Ctr., 776 A.2d 244 (N.J. Super. Ct. App. Div. 2001) (standard of care applicable to blood bank's allegedly inadequate testing of donated blood was not industry practice but reasonable person standard); Doan v. City of Bismarck, 632 N.W.2d 815, 824 (N.D. 2001) (child trampled by

the standard of care only in specialized situations, mainly involving professional malpractice[96] and negligent sports injuries.[97]

Direct bearing of custom on the negligence issue. Sometimes, custom evidence has a direct bearing on the negligence issue. It is possible to believe that a safety custom reflects the judgment and experience of many people and thus directly suggests how a reasonable person might behave under the circumstances. Customary behavior, the argument goes, is usually not negligent,[98] or, more specifically, such behavior tends to suggest the proper balance of risks and utilities.[99]

The varied uses and functions of safety custom as evidence in negligence analysis. Custom—or even practices that do not rise to the level of custom—might also tend to prove something significant but less global than the ultimate conclusion of negligence.

First, the fact that an industry often takes a particular precaution is excellent evidence that the precaution is feasible and not excessively costly.[100] Thus, the custom points to one of the elements in the risk-utility balance, suggesting that the cost of safety is not disproportionately high compared to potential for injury. The logic of this point holds even if the practice does not count as a custom for some reason and even if the precaution is adopted without a safety purpose in mind. A custom that develops *after* the plaintiff's injury might also show feasibility.[101]

Second, if a common practice is followed for safety purposes, even if irregularly, evidence of that practice shows that harm would be reasonably foreseeable if the practice were not followed. Foreseeability alone does not establish negligence, but it is a necessary step in doing so. Custom can play a significant role in establishing this step, even if it is only a practice followed by the defendant itself or some other actors in the same line of activity. That is true, however, only if the common practice was adopted for safety reasons; otherwise it might show feasibility of the practice but not foreseeability of harm. If the custom is offered to show that a class of people like the plaintiff would foreseeably encounter danger created by the defendant, however, there is no reason to require that the custom be related to safety, but every reason to require evidence that the defendant was aware of the custom.[102]

---

heifer at agricultural show; custom as to training show animals is "evidence of whether conduct meets the general standard of reasonable care under the circumstances").

[96]   See § 21.5.

[97]   See § 17.8.

[98]   See Texas & Pac. Ry. v. Behymer, 189 U.S. 468, 23 S.Ct. 622 (1903) (Holmes, J: "What is usually done may be evidence of what out to be done," though it is only evidence, not the standard of care); The T.J. Hooper, 60 F.2d 737 (2d Cir. 1932) (L. Hand, C.J.: "[I]n most cases reasonable prudence is in fact common prudence").

[99]   Richard A. Posner, Economic Analysis of Law § 6.3 (4th ed. 1992).

[100]   Darling v. Charleston Cmty. Mem. Hosp., 33 Ill.2d 326, 331, 211 N.E.2d 253, 257 (1965) ("Custom is relevant in determining the standard of care [partly] because it illustrates what is feasible," citing the classic article, Clarence Morris, Custom and Negligence, 42 Colum. L. Rev. 1147 (1942)). The point continues to be recognized. See, e.g., Dominick Vetri, Order Out of Chaos: Products Liability Design-Defect Law, 43 U. Rich. L. Rev. 1373, 1454 n. 513 (2009) ("custom evidence is very relevant" in proving existence of feasible, safer design in products cases).

[101]   Subsequent product improvements are admissible at least to show feasibility of a safer product. See Cover v. Cohen, 61 N.Y.2d 261, 461 N.E.2d 864, 473 N.Y.S.2d 378 (1984); D.L. v. Huebner, 110 Wis.2d 581, 329 N.W.2d 890 (1983).

[102]   Otis Elevator Co. v. Melott, 281 P.2d 408 (Okla. 1955), is a case involving the plaintiff's customs, knowledge of which would apprise the defendant of dangers to the plaintiff.

Custom as a sword. Evidence of a custom may be used either as a sword by the plaintiff or a shield by the defendant.[103] Used as a sword, the plaintiff can show the defendant's violation of a safety custom as some evidence that the defendant failed to act as a reasonable person under the circumstances.[104] For example, if a landlord uses ordinary glass as a shower enclosure when the custom of landlords generally is to use tempered glass, the existence of the custom is admissible in a suit by a tenant injured by the broken glass and that evidence may help persuade the trier that the landlord was negligent.[105]

In some cases, evidence of the custom is presented by an expert,[106] and the custom rule can also apply if the custom is institutionalized in even advisory standards of the relevant industrial association.[107]

Custom as a shield. As a shield, the defendant can show his compliance with custom as evidence that his conduct was that of a reasonable person.[108] Where the cost of better safety is low compared to the danger, however, the custom of an industry or line of business to ignore safety precautions is likely to be unpersuasive.[109] Similarly, the plaintiff who is charged with fault is permitted to show that what he did was in accordance with custom and hence arguably, but not conclusively, evidence that he exercised due care.[110]

Custom and duty. A safety custom is most commonly important in assisting the jury's evaluation of the defendant's conduct as negligent or not negligent, and courts have sometimes broadly generalized this fact to say that custom does not establish a duty where none exists otherwise.[111] However, in some instances custom can bear directly on the question of the defendant's duty. Judges do recognize that customs, expectations of the parties, and social values can be important in determining whether to recognize a duty of care or not. For example, the defendant ordinarily owes no duty to

---

[103] Restatement Third of Torts (Liability for Physical and Emotional Harm) § 13(a) & (b) (2010) (violation of custom and compliance with custom are both inconclusive evidence of negligence and no negligence respectively).

[104] McComish v. DeSoi, 42 N.J. 274, 200 A.2d 116 (1964) (testimony based on safety manuals of industry to show what experienced people do as evidence of what should be done); Besette v. Enderlin Sch. Dist. No. 22, 310 N.W.2d 759 (N.D. 1981) (school child injured in fall from slide, evidence that other schools had safer playground surfaces admissible as a custom); Kaiser v. Cook, 67 Wis.2d 460, 227 N.W.2d 50 (1975) (evidence that other race tracks prohibited spectators at the dangerous number 3 and 4 turns sufficient to get the plaintiff to the jury). It should go without saying that the plaintiff must show violation of the custom as well as its existence. Guldy v. Pyramid Corp., 222 A.D.2d 815, 634 N.Y.S.2d 788 (1995).

[105] Trimarco v. Klein, 56 N.Y.2d 98, 436 N.E.2d 502, 451 N.Y.S.2d 52 (1982).

[106] E.g., Doe v. Dominion Bank of Washington, 963 F.2d 1552 (D.C. Cir. 1992) (expert testified as to security customs of commercial landlords; this was sufficient to sustain plaintiff's burden in suit against landlord for rape in the building).

[107] E.g., Hansen v. Abrasive Eng'g & Mfg., Inc., 317 Or. 378, 856 P.2d 625 (1993) (ANSI advisory standard admissible but not conclusive).

[108] The T.J. Hooper, 60 F.2d 737 (2d Cir. 1932); LaVallee v. Vermont Motor Inns, Inc., 153 Vt. 80, 569 A.2d 1073 (1989).

[109] The T.J. Hooper, 60 F.2d 737 (2d Cir. 1932), is the leading case. There, failure of a tug's operator to have a cheap radio on board to receive weather reports that would have allowed him to put into a safe harbor with his string of barges when a storm approached was negligence even though the tugboat industry generally did not carry radios on board.

[110] E.g., Wanner v. Getter Trucking, 466 N.W.2d 833 (N.D. 1991).

[111] See Canal Barge Co., Inc. v. Torco Oil Co., 220 F.3d 370 (5th Cir. 2000) (dictum); Diaz v. Phoenix Lubrication Serv., Inc., 224 Ariz. 335, 230 P.3d 718 (Ct. App. 2010); L.A. Fitness Int'l., LLC v. Mayer, 980 So.2d 550, 558 (Fla. Dist. Ct. App. 2008) ("Although the custom and practice of an industry can help define a standard of care a party must exercise after it has undertaken a duty, industry standards do not give rise to an independent legal duty.").

take positive action to assist a plaintiff,[112] but if parties enter into a transaction in light of industry customs, those customs may impose a duty on one of them that would not exist without the custom. And a custom usually followed by the defendant itself may show that the defendant assumed a duty of care and is bound by it. For example, in the absence of regulation, a natural gas supplier might conceivably owe no duty to odorize its gas for safety, even though smell would be an indication of dangerous gas leaks. Yet, if it has no duty but customarily does odorize the gas, users may come to rely on the custom, and once it is in place, the company would be under a duty to continue the practice until adequate notice of discontinuance is given.[113] The defendant's custom may also indirectly alter the plaintiff's status and thus create a duty, as where the defendant customarily permits persons like the plaintiff to use his land so that they are no longer classed as trespassers who have no rights.[114] Similarly, courts may consider social customs, or what they believe to be social customs, in determining whether there is a duty to protect the plaintiff from third persons.[115]

§ 12.7 Limitations on the Use of Custom and Practice

Customary violation of statute. A custom to provide less care than required by the statute ordinarily cannot be relied upon by the defendant to avoid the statutory standard or to excuse violation.[116] In the case of a minor's violation of statute, however, the courts themselves often reject the statutory standard in favor of the common law protective standard for minors. Consequently courts may permit the minor to rely upon a statute-violating custom.[117] When the custom requires greater care than is required by statute, custom is presumably admissible on the issue of negligence because the statutory standard is usually a minimum, not a maximum.[118]

Custom to provide less care than that dictated by risk-utility. When courts say that custom is not conclusive on the negligence issue, they necessarily mean that custom is trumped by the ordinary care standard, which in turn is often assessed by reference to the risk-utility balance. So if a universal custom were highly risky and likely to cause great harm but could be avoided by an expenditure of $1, the jury would be permitted to find negligence in spite of the exculpatory custom.

Custom to provide more care than that dictated by risk-utility. When a custom clearly calls for *more* care than would be dictated by the risk-utility balance, there is

---

[112] See Rhodes v. Illinois Cent. Gulf R.R., 172 Ill.2d 213, 665 N.Ed.2d 1260 (1996) (no duty to aid trespasser who was injured, but not by the defendant; and internal rules do not create a duty); Buczkowski v. McKay, 441 Mich. 96, 490 N.W.2d 330 (1992) (no duty to protect plaintiff from another person, defendant's internal policies create no such duty). On the general no-duty rule, see Chapters 25 & 26.

[113] See Roberts v. Indiana Gas & Water Co., 140 Ind.App. 409, 218 N.E.2d 556 (1966) (where reliance is foreseeable, omission of the customary precaution may be negligence "in itself").

[114] See Wieghmink v. Harrington, 274 Mich. 409, 413, 264 N.W. 845, 847 (1936) (recognizing that jury could have found defendant's custom constituted the plaintiff an implied invitee, but holding that even if the jury found otherwise, the custom put the defendant on notice that the plaintiff would be in a position of danger so that he was not barred under the trespasser-no-duty rule).

[115] Husband v. Dubose, 6 Mass.App.Ct. 667, 531 N.E.2d 600 (1988) (the "obligations [a host] assume[s are] those which, considering customs and accepted social norms, one would reasonably expect [the host] to fulfill, no more and no less" (quoting)).

[116] Smith v. Aaron, 256 Ark. 414, 508 S.W.2d 320 (1974); Sanchez v. J. Barron Rice, Inc., 77 N.M. 717, 427 P.2d 240 (1967).

[117] Alley v. Siepman, 87 S.D. 670, 214 N.W.2d 7 (1974).

[118] See Duncan v. Corbetta, 178 A.D.2d 459, 577 N.Y.S.2d 129 (1991) (custom to use pressure-treated wood in stair construction, although ordinance permitted use of ordinary lumber; trial judge should have admitted evidence of custom).

some confusion. Although a company's internal policies—which represent a species of unilateral custom as discussed in the next section—may be admissible as evidence of negligence,[119] the highest court of New York has said that such policies cannot be used as evidence of negligence if they "require a standard that transcends reasonable care."[120] On this, several points must be considered. First, since custom is evidence of what reasonable care requires, it is not easy to say that a custom "requires" more than reasonable care, unless the point is so clear that reasonable jurors could not find otherwise. Second, if custom does somehow suggest that more than reasonable care is "required," the higher care suggested by the custom may still govern parties who bargained with the custom in mind as the governing standard.[121]

Non-safety customs: scope of risk. A custom in the community, no matter how well established, is not necessarily related to safety at all. It may be based upon cultural or other preferences. Many churches do not burn candles, but their reasons for leaving candles out of their services are most likely related to religious and stylistic preferences, not to any fear of burning the church down. Violation of a custom that does not arise from considerations of safety may show something important about negligence, notably feasibility of following the custom. But it does not directly establish negligence nor does it, by itself, show that the harm incurred by the plaintiff was foreseeable. Accordingly, the non-safety custom may be held irrelevant in particular cases.[122]

Ambiguities: characterizing custom and its scope. A custom may be certain and, at the same time, its meaning is doubtful. Suppose that it is customary to include certain safety features in bridges, all of which were designed for public use. Is the feature a custom about bridges, or a custom only about bridges designed for public use? The Iowa Court held that the jury should *not* be instructed to consider customs in public bridge design in determining negligence of a private bridge owner, in the absence of testimony that showed the public bridge custom had also become a custom in private bridge cases.[123] Perhaps this is not a subject suited to simple rules. The meaning of some ambiguous conduct, like the meaning of some ambiguous words, can be sorted out by the jury if reasonable people could differ. So in appropriate cases, evidence of the bridge safety custom might be admissible if it were coupled with evidence that the cost of the safety feature was low, or that it was well-known, or otherwise adaptable to privately owned bridges.

---

[119] See Iannacchino v. Ford Motor Co., 451 Mass. 623, 888 N.E.2d 879 (2008) ("It is well established that . . . evidence of the defendant's violation of a statute, regulation, industry standard, or even internal company standard may be admissible on the question of negligence or defective design."); Joyce v. State, Dep't of Corrections, 155 Wash.2d 306, 119 P.3d 825 (2005).

[120] See Gilson v. Metropolitan Opera, 5 N.Y.3d 574, 577, 841 N.E.2d 747, 749, 807 N.Y.S.2d 588, 590 (2005) ("where [a company's internal rules] require a standard that transcends reasonable care, breach cannot be considered evidence of negligence"). There seems to be some tension between the rule as formulated in Gilson, supra, and AG Capital Funding Partners, L.P. v. State St. Bank & Trust Co., 5 N.Y.3d 582, 842 N.E.2d 471, 808 N.Y.S.2d 573 (2005) (custom can create duty of care between bargaining parties).

[121] Strict liability under the Restatement Second's § 402A, which determined defectiveness of products in part by reference to consumer expectations, was probably an example. Similarly, informed consent cases are rooted in the patient's expectations. Even more clearly, then, expectations of the parties would trump risk-utility balancing when those expectations are based on custom.

[122] See Levine v. Russell Blaine Co., 273 N.Y. 386, 7 N.E.2d 673 (1937).

[123] Simon's Feed Store, Inc. v. Leslein, 478 N.W.2d 598 (Iowa 1991). Cf. Rhine v. Duluth, M & I R.R., 210 Minn. 281, 297 N.W. 852 (1941), overruled in part on other grounds, Wessman v. Scandrett, 217 Minn. 312, 14 N.W.2d 445 (1944) (witnesses had observed many instances in which railroad had set flares at crossing, but the custom might have been to set flares only when the trains were engaged in switching movements, not when they were proceeding in a straightaway movement).

The sometime rule of uniform practice. Some courts have said that custom evidence is not admissible to prove negligence unless the custom is uniform, well-known, widely followed, or notorious.[124] More moderately, it has been said that the alleged custom must be common and not merely a sporadic or occasional practice.[125] These limitations may have had their origin in the belief, no longer followed, that the legal effect of recognizing custom was to create a new standard of care and not merely evidence to be considered. With the adoption of the rule that safety customs are only some evidence of negligence, the widespread usage requirement has become less justifiable. However, even today, the limitation may be appropriate in some cases, as where widespread recognition of a custom is needed to show the defendant's awareness of, or the plaintiff's reliance on the custom.[126]

Uniform practice not always required. The uniform practice rule is not always followed.[127] And, as shown in the next section, the uniform or widespread practice rule is not followed when courts allow the jury to consider the defendant's deviation from its own past practices. In addition, the uniform practice rule has little logical application where an industrial safety practice is introduced in evidence only to show that better safety was feasible. Since feasibility is a matter of cost, not defendant's awareness, there is no reason to require especially widespread custom; adoption of a safety practice by others similarly situated tends to show it is not too costly. A custom not universally adopted also tends to show that the defendant could reasonably have foreseen the danger, since others did so, even if the defendant has never heard of the practice.[128] Much the same can be said when the evidence is produced to show that the plaintiff reasonably and foreseeably relied on the defendant's own practices so that the defendant may have been negligent in discontinuing a safety practice without warning,[129] or that the plaintiff reasonably relied upon the safety practice and hence was not chargeable with assumed risk or comparative fault.[130]

---

[124] Rentz v. Brown, 219 Ga.App. 187, 464 S.E.2d 617 (1995) (custom must be universal); Braden v. Workman, 146 Mich.App. 287, 380 N.W.2d 84 (1985) ("certain, uniform and notorious"); Swindell v. J.A. Tobin Const. Co., 629 S.W.2d 536 (Mo. Ct. App. 1981).

[125] Trimarco v. Klein, 56 N.Y.2d 98, 436 N.E.2d 502, 451 N.Y.S.2d 52 (1982).

[126] Thus strangers who have no legal relationship to each other, may expect that the other will follow rules of the road by driving on the right, even on private land. See Restatement Third of Torts (Liability for Physical and Emotional Harm) § 13 cmt. d (2010).

[127] See Bowan ex rel. Bowan v. Express Med. Transporters, Inc., 135 S.W.3d 452 (Mo. Ct. App. 2004) ("Even when the evidence will not show a uniform general custom, however, it may be 'admissible as a generally followed practice tending to show the standard of care exercised by ordinarily prudent persons' in performing the task at issue.").

[128] See Swindell v. J. A. Tobin Constr. Co., 629 S.W.2d 536, 544 (Mo. Ct. App. 1981) (custom admissible when it was "a well-known and widespread trade custom and not confined to the practice of certain individuals only, and the custom is a definite, uniform, and known practice under certain definite and uniform circumstances"); Wessman v. Scandrett, 217 Minn. 312, 14 N.W.2d 445 (1944) (custom must be uniform and also notorious enough to indicate defendant would know of it). But where the issue is only foreseeability, it is wrong to suggest that the issue is whether the custom is well-known enough that the defendant would know about it. The issue is whether, given that the risk was foreseeable to some persons, it would also be foreseeable to the standard reasonable person.

[129] Fowler v. Key System Transit Lines, 37 Cal.2d 65, 230 P.2d 339 (1951); Roberts v. Indiana Gas & Water Co., 140 Ind.App. 409, 218 N.E.2d 556 (1966) (where reliance is foreseeable, omission of the customary precaution may be negligence "in itself"); Florence v. Goldberg, 44 N.Y.2d 189, 404 N.Y.S.2d 583, 375 N.E.2d 763 (1978).

[130] Cf. Atlanta Enters. v. James, 68 Ga.App. 773, 24 S.E.2d 130 (1943) (repairer's reliance on custom that engineer would relieve gas pressure from machine before repair began showed he did not assume the risk of such pressure); McWilliams v. Parham, 269 N.C. 162, 152 S.E.2d 117 (1967) (custom to cry a forewarning before driving golf ball indicated plaintiff was not guilty of assumed risk in being on the fairway).

§ 12.8 Private Standards: Defendant's Own "Customs" or Practices

Defendant's practices as a sword for the plaintiff. While the defendant's internal rules, procedures or past practices cannot generally be used as a shield for the defendant, those internal rules may be admitted on behalf of the plaintiff to show that the defendant who was under a duty to exercise reasonable care[131] recognized the danger and that customary conduct represented a means of reducing it.[132] The defendant's internal rules may even be introduced as evidence of negligence because they bear on care that a reasonable person would provide.[133] Such rules do not themselves ordinarily count as the standard of care.[134] However, when the defendant's liability is based upon its contract or undertaking to use a given standard of care, as in the case of a hospital treating a patient, the defendant's own rules may reflect the standard of care owed.[135] And the defendant's own rules or practices become a virtual standard when the defendant should foresee that the plaintiff will rely upon continued adherence to those rules and that the plaintiff will be endangered when the rules are ignored.[136] The defendant's past practices may even create contractual expectations that set standards. If the plaintiff contracts to lease premises from a landlord that has provided a security guard in the past, the landlord's withdrawal of that guard may be negligence under the standard impliedly set by the parties themselves.[137]

Strangers to community custom. If custom should have special importance when the plaintiff and defendant have consensually accepted it, it may be unfair to give any weight at all to custom when one party is a stranger to it.[138] A community custom to fire shotguns in the air at midnight on New Year's will hardly assist the defendant whose customary blast brings down a passing balloonist who is in no way privy to the custom. On the other hand, if the plaintiff asserts that the defendant violated a safety custom,

---

[131] When the defendant is under no legal duty to act at all, the defendant's internal rules requiring action do not create a duty unless the plaintiff has relied upon those rules or is contractually entitled to benefit from them. See Rhodes v. Illinois Cent. Gulf R.R., 172 Ill.2d 213, 665 N.Ed.2d 1260 (1996) (no duty to aid trespasser who was injured, but not by the defendant; and internal rules do not create a duty); Buczkowski v. McKay, 441 Mich. 96, 490 N.W.2d 330 (1992) (no duty to protect plaintiff from another person, defendant's internal policies create no such duty).

[132] Thropp v. Bache Halsey Stuart Shields, Inc., 650 F.2d 817 (1981); Ganz v. United States Cycling Fed'n, 273 Mont. 360, 903 P.2d 212 (1995). See Potter v. Firestone Tire & Rubber Co., 6 Cal. 4th 965, 863 P.2d 795, 25 Cal. Rptr. 2d 550 (1993) (relying in part on violation of internal rules); Fielder v. Stonack, 141 N.J. 101, 661 A.2d 231 (1995) (relying on internal rules of defendant to determine willful misconduct).

[133] Calloway v. City of New Orleans, 524 So.2d 182, 6 A.L.R.5th 1108 (La. Ct. App. 1988) (sheriff's policies about when to provide medical attention to pregnant women); Briggs v. Morgan, 70 N.C.App. 57, 318 S.E.2d 878 (1984) (city policy to have back-up bells on its garbage trucks admissible in the same way as defendant's voluntarily adopted safety handbook); Hurd v. Williamsburg County, 363 S.C. 421, 611 S.E.2d 488 (2005).

[134] Wal-Mart Stores, Inc. v. Wright, 774 N.E.2d 891 (Ind. 2002) (instruction suggesting that defendant's rules for cleaning up spills in public areas was a recognition by defendant of appropriate standard was error, although defendant's rules were admissible).

[135] See Pedroza v. Bryant, 101 Wash.2d 226, 677 P.2d 166 (1984). The customary practice of health care providers is often the standard of care, not merely evidence.

[136] E.g., Florence v. Goldberg, 44 N.Y.2d 189, 404 N.Y.S.2d 583, 375 N.E.2d 763 (1978) (practice of furnishing crossing guard for school children).

[137] See Kline v. 1500 Massachusetts Ave. Apt. Corp., 439 F.2d 477, 43 A.L.R.3d 311 (D.C. Cir. 1970).

[138] See Richard A. Epstein, The Path to the T.J. Hooper: The Theory and History of Custom in the Law of Tort, 21 J. Leg. Studies 1 (1992). Cf. Morgan v. Scott, 291 S.W.3d 622 (Ky. 2009) (internal standard of dealership forbidding test drives without a dealership employee in the car; failure to follow own guideline not dispositive).

the violation may be quite relevant, whether or not the plaintiff was a stranger. Suppose the passing balloonist is injured because the defendant's factory explodes when the defendant ignores a customary safety precaution. The balloonist is definitely a stranger, in no consensual or special relationship to the factory owner, but if the balloonist is a person within the risk, the violation of the safety custom is relevant to the issue of the defendant's want of care.

§ 12.9 Entering Transactions in Light of Custom

Reliance. In some instances, parties enter transactions, formally or informally, in the expectation that custom will be followed and the custom may thus become a part of their deal. The informal version of this idea has already been mentioned—the plaintiff may reasonably act in reliance on the defendant's own safety "custom" or practice in some cases, which would make the custom critical in determining negligence.

Bargaining in light of custom. In other cases, too, although not all, the plaintiff and defendant are members of the same community of custom and expect the custom to apply to their conduct. For example, they are both part of the same geographical or business community in which the custom is followed, or they are entering into consensual transactions with each other on the basis of the same industrial custom. In such cases, their reasonable expectations of each other are largely or perhaps wholly dictated by the known custom rather than by reasonable care judged in the abstract; consequently it may be appropriate to give the custom very great weight, so much so that that custom might even delineate a duty to take action where none existed otherwise.[139] If we ship our goods by way of a barge to be towed by your tug, we might be understood to accept the customary care that goes with towing barges unless we contract for a different standard of care. At least that is true where we know the customary standard or if you reasonably believe that we know it. Cases like that are in fact very similar to cases in which the defendant's duty of care is limited because the plaintiff assumes the risk or expanded because of the plaintiff's reliance on the defendant's safety practices.

Bargaining—custom as a sword. Great weight might also be given to custom used as a sword when the parties are both members of the same custom community. As Professor Morris argued, one who contracts for the defendant's services is entitled to expect those services to be delivered with the customary safety.[140] In the same way, known safety customs in the design or manufacture of products may bear heavily on the question of whether those products were defective.[141] Professor Epstein has argued that custom is or ought to be the standard of care and not merely evidence of negligence when the parties have bargained against a background of custom.[142] That goes further than the rule usually stated by the courts, but it is surely true that some consensual

---

[139] See AG Capital Funding Partners, L.P. v. State St. Bank & Trust Co., 5 N.Y.3d 582, 842 N.E.2d 471, 808 N.Y.S.2d 573 (2005) (which party had duty to distribute all critical documents in complex business transaction).

[140] Clarence Morris, Custom and Negligence, 42 Colum. L. Rev. 1147, 1153 (1942).

[141] Consumers are not aware, or expected to be aware, of all safety and risk customs of a manufacturer, so the use of custom by the defendant may be circumscribed. On the other hand, consumers may reasonably assume that the product is made with the customary safety designs or equipment and when it is not, the product may be defective. Industry custom might also show that a reasonable alternative design is possible.

[142] Richard A. Epstein, The Path to the T.J. Hooper: The Theory and History of Custom in the Law of Tort, 21 J. Leg. Studies 1 (1992); cf. Richard A. Posner, Economic Analysis of Law § 6.3 (4th ed. 1992). (suggesting that as between industry and its customers, level of precaution taken by industry is "likely to be efficient" and hence that compliance with that custom should be a defense).

relationships may imply an agreed-upon standard that might be something quite different from the standard of the reasonable prudent person.

D. STATUTORY COMPLIANCE

§ 12.10   Compliance with Statute

General rule: not a defense. The fact that the defendant has complied with a statute does not ordinarily indicate that the defendant was not negligent. The trier of fact may find that, although the defendant complied with the statutory directives, he should have done even more to attain reasonable levels of safety.[143] The point is easy to see when it comes to speed limits. Although the speed limit may be 60 m.p.h., under some circumstances during inclement weather reasonable care requires a speed of no more than 30.

Admissible as evidence. On the other hand, the defendant's compliance with a statute that thoroughly regulates the behavior in question tends to support the defendant's argument that he is not negligent. So the defendant's compliance may be evidence for the trier to consider on the negligence issue, even though it is not conclusive.[144]

Bases for the rules. These rules are a product of our understanding about how statutes work and how they are meant to work. Most statutes and even regulations are relatively permanent and relatively abstract; they cannot take into account the particular concerns of individual cases. They aim at minimum standards but are not meant to establish the outer limits of the defendant's safety responsibilities. When it comes to technological standards, they are quickly outdated with no guarantee that the legislature or regulators will have time or information necessary to update them. Beyond that, many statutes are written in response to lobbying efforts of the industry they purport to regulate, and they are not likely to represent a balanced attempt by neutral parties to achieve appropriate safety. For these reasons and many others, including the practical problems of interpreting and applying statutes, compliance with a statute cannot ordinarily count as a defense.[145]

Exceptional cases. Even so, legislators or regulators can expressly provide that the compliance with a particular statute is a complete defense. And what legislators could provide in express terms, they can also imply. In rare cases, courts may conclude that in spite of the general rule to the contrary, compliance with statutory standards is a complete defense, either because the statute itself so implies or because the court concludes as a matter of law that on the facts of the case compliance necessarily shows reasonable care.[146]

---

[143] Restatement Second of Torts § 288C (1965); Restatement Third of Torts (Liability for Physical and Emotional Harm) § 16 (2010).

[144] Ake v. General Motors Corp., 942 F.Supp. 869 (W.D.N.Y. 1996); Miner v. Long Island Lighting Co., 40 N.Y.2d 372, 353 N.E.2d 805, 386 N.Y.S.2d 842 (1976); Zacher v. Budd Co., 396 N.W.2d 122 (S.D. 1986). The Restatement of Products Liability takes the position in § 4 that compliance with statute should be similarly treated in a products liability case alleging defective design. In Malcolm v. Evenflo Co., Inc., 217 P.3d 514 (Mont. 2009), the court expressed its disagreement with the ALI on this point, and held that in a strict products liability action, evidence of statutory compliance was both irrelevant and more prejudicial than probative.

[145] See Teresa Moran Schwartz, The Role of Federal Safety Regulations in Products Liability Actions, 41 Vand. L. Rev. 1121 (1988).

[146] Ramirez v. Plough, Inc., 6 Cal.4th 539, 25 Cal.Rptr.2d 97, 863 P.2d 167 (1993) (statute requiring product warnings in English implied that warnings need not be in Spanish); cf. Poelstra v. Basin Elec. Power Co-op., 545 N.W.2d 823 (S.D. 1996) (affirming grant of directed verdict for defendant, largely on the basis that defendant's conduct complied with a statute).

Chapter 13

PROVING NEGLIGENCE CLAIMS

Analysis

A. JUDGE AND JURY
§ 13.1   Roles of Judge and Jury in Negligence Cases
§ 13.2   Burden of Proof and Types of Evidence: Basic Information

B. SUBSTITUTES FOR FACTUAL EVIDENCE: RES IPSA LOQUITUR
§ 13.3   Res Ipsa Loquitur: General Rules
§ 13.4   Inferences Permitted, Required or Unpermitted
§ 13.5   Estimating Probabilities of Negligence
§ 13.6   Res Ipsa Cases: Illustrations
§ 13.7   Attributing Fault to the Defendant

A. JUDGE AND JURY

§ 13.1 Roles of the Judge and Jury in Negligence Cases

The importance of process. Much of the legal argument in negligence litigation is directed to questions of legal process. The first question for either the plaintiff's or defendant's lawyer is likely to be, will the case get to the jury? Or will the judge intervene to take the case from the jury by summary judgment or directed verdict? Process of course is always important; it is doubly important when, as in negligence cases, the rules of law do not closely constrain the outcome.

Juries as fact-deciders. The first major role for juries in negligence cases is determination of the facts. Where evidence shows a dispute about historical facts, the jury is almost invariably the decision-maker.[1] Did the engineer blow the whistle at the crossing? Was the light green? Did the doctor warn the patient of the dangers of a proposed operation? These are decisions for the jury, not the judge, so long as the evidence creates dispute.

Juries as conduct evaluators. The second major role for juries in negligence cases is to evaluate the facts to determine whether the defendant was negligent, whether his conduct was a legal cause of the plaintiff's harm, and the amount of damages.[2] The jury must determine both historical facts and value judgments.[3] If the plaintiff claims injury when, on a dark night, she bumped into a face-level box attached to a utility pole, the jury must first determine whether defendant attached such a box to the pole, how high

---

[1]   Darling v. J.B. Expedited Servs., Inc., 2006 WL 2238913 (M.D. Tenn. 2006); Restatement Third of Torts (Liability for Physical and Emotional Harm) § 8(a) (2010) (where reasonable minds can differ).

[2]   Restatement Second of Torts § 328C (1965).

[3]   See Mark P. Gergen, The Jury's Role in Deciding Normative Issues in the American Common Law, 68 Fordham L. Rev. 407 (1999); F. Patrick Hubbard, The Nature and Impact of the "Tort Reform" Movement, 35 Hofstra L. Rev. 437, 454 n.67 (2006) ("juries provide community input on norms of behavior by giving contextual specificity to wrongdoing").

it was, and whether the plaintiff in fact bumped into it. Those are questions of historical fact. Once those historical facts are determined, the jury must go further and decide whether the defendant's conduct amounted to the negligent creation of an unreasonable risk. For this there is no conclusive legal guide except the standard of the reasonable and prudent person under the circumstances. It is the jury's job to make a judgment whether the defendant's conduct met that standard.[4] Because part of the jury's role is to make normative decisions or value judgments, courts do not ordinarily grant summary judgment on negligence issues, even if the facts are undisputed. In other words, the jury must still weigh the risks and utilities associated with the facts that it has determined exist.[5]

Judicial roles: legal duties and standards. Common law judges have several major roles in negligence cases as well. Judges rather than juries determine whether the defendant was under a duty of care at all and if so what standard of care applied. If the judge concludes that the defendant owed no duty at all, the judge will grant a motion to dismiss, a summary judgment, or a directed verdict, whichever is procedurally appropriate. If the judge determines that the defendant owed a duty of care, the judge will instruct the jury as to the proper standard.

Sufficiency of the evidence. Although judges are not empowered to decide the factual disputes in the case, they are definitely empowered to conclude that there is no evidence at all and equally empowered to conclude that the evidence is so weak that reasonable people could not accept it as sufficient to prove the plaintiff's case. If no reasonable person could find the defendant's conduct to be negligent, the judge will direct a verdict for the defendant.[6] On the other hand, if reasonable people, considering the evidence in the light most favorable to the plaintiff,[7] could differ, the issue will be one for the jury to decide.

New trial powers. When a judge feels that a jury has done an injustice, the judge can grant a new trial. In some states the judge is empowered to grant a new trial whenever the judge concludes that the jury's verdict was against the weight of the

---

[4]   Considine v. City of Waterbury, 279 Conn. 830, 905 A.2d 70 (2006); Delmarva Power & Light v. Stout, 380 A.2d 1365 (Del. 1977) (jury to decide whether the known conduct violated the reasonable person standard); Deal v. Bowman, 286 Kan. 853, 188 P.3d 941 (2008) (judging driver's negligence is task for the jury); Hincks v. Walton Ranch Co., 150 P.3d 669 (Wyo. 2007) (jury must determine how a cow escaped and whether the defendant rancher took reasonable precautions to keep the cow from escaping); Restatement Third of Torts (Liability for Physical and Emotional Harm) § 8(b) (2010) (where reasonable minds can differ); cf. Kemper v. Builder's Square, 109 Ohio App. 3d 127, 671 N.E.2d 1104 (1996) (jury to say whether defendant's method of displaying and securing was negligent).

[5]   E.g., Little v. Liquid Air Corp., 952 F.2d 841 (5th Cir. 1992); Lugtu v. California Highway Patrol, 26 Cal.4th 703, 110 Cal.Rptr. 2d 528, 28 P.3d 249 (2001) (jury, not court, would decide whether officer was negligent in pulling speeding car over to the median where it was crashed by a truck rather than onto right shoulder); Doan v. City of Bismarck, 632 N.W.2d 815 (N.D. 2001).

[6]   Peterson v. Eichhorn, 344 Mont. 540, 189 P.3d 615 (2008) (summary judgment for defendant where reasonable minds could not find he was negligent); Montas v. JJC Constr. Corp., 985 N.E.2d 1225 (N.Y. 2013) (affirming directed verdict for defendant); Fultz v. Delhaize Am., Inc., 278 Va. 84, 677 S.E.2d 272 (2009) (issue becomes one for the trial judge when "reasonable minds could not differ about what conclusion could be drawn from the evidence").

[7]   E.g., Abebe v. Benitez, 667 A.2d 834 (D.C. 1995); Botelho v. Caster's, Inc., 970 A.2d 541 (R.I. 2009) (upholding jury verdict where "reasonable minds could differ as to . . . negligence"); cf. Banks v. Beckwith, 762 N.W.2d 149, 153 (Iowa 2009) ("if reasonable minds might differ about whether the injury could result from surgery in the absence of negligence, the court should instruct on res ipsa").

evidence,[8] that the damages awarded were seriously inadequate or excessive[9] or that the verdict was manifestly unjust.[10] More cautious jurisdictions may constrain the judge's new trial power somewhat more, but they still permit judges to grant a new trial even where a directed verdict would be improper.[11] Under the more liberal new trial rules, judges are permitted to weigh the evidence and credibility of witnesses in deciding whether to grant a new trial.[12]

Other roles. Judges also play a critical role in many other decisions. For example, judges, through legal rules, prescribe the types of harm compensable and the damages available. They also constrain or shape the jury's participation by deciding what evidence to admit or exclude from the jury's consideration. In the case of expert testimony, the judge may also exclude the evidence if the expert is deemed not sufficiently qualified or if the testimony does not meet up to standards of the expert's profession.[13] In addition, the judge has the power and duty to instruct the jury on legal rules applicable to the facts.[14]

§ 13.2 Burden of Proof and Types of Evidence: Basic Information

Burden of proving facts showing elements of the claim. The plaintiff has the burden of proving facts to establish each element of her case, meaning that if facts supporting elements of the claim are not adduced at trial, the judge will direct a verdict or enter a judgment as a matter of law for the defendant. In the negligence case, it is not enough to show that the plaintiff suffered an injury in an accident in which the defendant was in some way involved.[15] The plaintiff must provide evidence of facts from which the judge can determine that the defendant was under a duty of care,[16] and facts from which a jury

---

[8]   E.g., Bristow v. Flurry, 320 Ark. 51, 894 S.W.2d 894 (1995) ("when the verdict is clearly against the preponderance of the evidence"); Carr v. Strode, 79 Haw. 475, 904 P.2d 489 (1995) (movant need establish only that "the verdict rendered for its opponent is against the manifest weight of the evidence").

[9]   E.g., Dillon v. Frazer, 678 S.E.2d 251 (S.C. 2009) (holding that trial judge abused his discretion in failing to grant a new trial when jury awarded $6,000 for undisputed damages of at least $30,000 and admitted liability).

[10]   E.g., Malmberg v. Lopez, 208 Conn. 675, 546 A.2d 264 (1988) (duty to set aside the verdict when it is manifestly unjust and that includes inadequate award of damages).

[11]   See Gaston v. Viclo Realty Co., 626 N.Y.S.2d 131 (App. Div. 1995).

[12]   Pocatello Auto Color, Inc. v. Akzo Coatings, Inc., 127 Idaho 41, 896 P.2d 949 (1995) ("Because the trial court evaluates the credibility of the evidence on a motion for a new trial, a trial court may properly grant the motion in cases where there is substantial evidence to support the jury's verdict and a judgment n.o.v. [or directed verdict] would have been inappropriate."); Botelho v. Caster's, Inc., 970 A.2d 541 (R.I. 2009) (trial judge ruling on motion for new trial makes "an independent appraisal of the evidence" and "can weigh the evidence and assess the witnesses' credibility," and "reject some evidence and draw inferences which are reasonable in view of the testimony").

[13]   See Daubert v. Merrell Dow Pharms., Inc., 509 U.S. 579, 113 S.Ct. 2786, 125 L.Ed.2d 469 (1993); Kumho Tire Co., Ltd. v. Carmichael, 526 U.S. 137, 119 S.Ct. 1167, 143 L.Ed.2d 238 (1999).

[14]   Handler Corp. v. Tlapechco, 901 A.2d 737 (Del. 2006) ("A party has an 'unqualified right to have the jury instructed with a correct statement of the substance of the law.' "). Trial judges usually have a good deal of discretion in the formulation of a legally correct instruction. Marsingill v. O'Malley, 128 P.3d 151, 161 (Alaska 2006) ("the test for determining the legitimacy of jury instructions is not whether a 'clearer and [a] more accurate statement of the law' is possible but rather whether 'the trial judge's wording wrongly stated the law or was otherwise likely to have led the jury astray' ").

[15]   E.g., Habershaw v. Michaels Stores, Inc., 42 A.3d 1273 (R.I. 2012) (plaintiff alleged that she slipped on a shiny floor; "the mere occurrence of an accident, without more, does not warrant an inference that a defendant has been negligent"); Brewster v. United States, 542 N.W.2d 524 (Iowa 1996).

[16]   See, e.g., Vasquez v. Wal-Mart Stores, Inc., 913 P.2d 441 (Wyo. 1996). Judges sometimes speak of "proving" a duty or a standard of care, duties or standards are by definition set by the judge in the first place,

could reasonably find negligence,[17] cause in fact,[18] and proximate cause[19] by a greater weight of the evidence. The defendant, on the other hand, has the burden of proving facts to support affirmative defenses such as contributory negligence or comparative fault,[20] or the statute of limitations.

Burden of persuasion: The plaintiff has the burden of persuading the trier of fact that the elements of her case have been proven. To say that the plaintiff has the burden of persuasion is to say that even if the plaintiff has produced evidence that would *permit* a reasonable jury to find the issues in her favor, she must still *persuade* the jury to do so, either by offering more evidence or by making persuasive arguments.

The weight or standard of persuasion. The standard for the great majority of tort cases is that the plaintiff must prove or persuade the trier by a preponderance of the evidence.[21] The preponderance requirement means that the plaintiff must persuade the jury that she has proven facts and conclusions necessary to her case by a probability exceeding 50 percent. That is to say, the jury must believe that the plaintiff's essential assertions are more probably true than not.[22] If the jury thinks the defendant might be negligent, but that it is equally likely that he is not, it must find for the defendant, not the plaintiff.[23] In a few instances, courts require a more demanding standard, such as clear and convincing evidence.[24] And sometimes courts, without formally altering the preponderance standard, note special needs to be cautious in some cases,[25] or conversely, that the facts warrant an *inference* that meets the preponderance burden.

Defendant's burden. The defendant has the burden of proving any affirmative defense. For example, if he wishes to assert that his liability should be reduced because of the plaintiff comparative fault, he must meet the burden of production by offering evidence that the plaintiff was at fault. On that issue he likewise has the burden of persuasion, meaning that the jury is instructed *not* to find comparative fault in the plaintiff unless the defendant has convinced the jury of such negligence by a preponderance of the evidence.

---

there is never a question of "proving" the standard itself as distinct from facts which provide grounds for invoking the duty or facts that show a breach of the duty or standard.

[17]   E.g., Anglin v. Kleeman, 140 N.H. 257, 665 A.2d 747 (1995); Habershaw v. Michaels Stores, Inc., 42 A.3d 1273 (R.I. 2012) (allegation of a slip and fall on a shiny floor was insufficient to defeat the defendant's summary judgment motion; plaintiff must in such a case present enough evidence of some unsafe condition of which the defendant should have been aware).

[18]   E.g., Miller v. Evangeline Parish Police Jury, 663 So.2d 398 (La. Ct. App. 1995).

[19]   E.g., Stewart v. Federated Dep't Stores, Inc., 234 Conn. 597, 662 A.2d 753 (1995) ("the plaintiff must show, by a fair preponderance of the evidence, that harm intentionally caused by a third person is within the scope of the risk created by the defendant's negligent conduct").

[20]   Hill v. City of Lincoln, 249 Neb. 88, 541 N.W.2d 655 (1996).

[21]   E.g., California Jury Instructions (Book of Approved Jury Instructions) 2.60.

[22]   Willis v. Manning, 850 So.2d 983 (La. Ct. App. 2003) ("A preponderance of the evidence exists . . . the fact sought to be proved is more probable than not"); Matsuyama v. Birnbaum, 452 Mass. 1, 890 N.E.2d 819 (2008) (preponderance of the evidence equated with "more likely than not"); Barbie v. Minko Constr., Inc., 766 N.W.2d 458 (N.D. 2009) (equal probability not enough).

[23]   See Barbie v. Minko Constr., Inc., 766 N.W.2d 458 (N.D. 2009) (if it is equally probable that the defendant is negligent and that he is not, "the court must direct the jury that the plaintiff has not established a case" (quoting Prosser & Keeton on Torts)); Pike v. Eubank, 197 Va. 692, 90 S.E.2d 821 (1956); 1 Ohio Jury Instructions 3.50 (2006).

[24]   Some cases require clear and convincing evidence to support claims for punitive damages, libel, or fraud.

[25]   See Ellis County State Bank v. Keever, 888 S.W.2d 790 (Tex. 1994) (malicious prosecution, standard is preponderance of evidence, but because resort to courts is important, trier should be cautious).

Forms of evidence to prove negligence issues. Direct evidence from percipient witnesses is a common way of proving historical facts in a negligence case. For example, a witness testifies that he saw defendant drive through an intersection on a red light. When such direct evidence is not available or not conclusive, other possibilities exist. These are subject to many qualifications under the rules of evidence or otherwise, but they include use of collateral estoppel,[26] in-or out-of-court admissions of the defendant,[27] the defendant's destruction or refusal to produce relevant evidence,[28] expert testimony to reconstruct events,[29] police reports,[30] a plea of guilty[31] or a criminal conviction of a defendant based on the same facts that underlie the tort action,[32] custom,[33] voluntary safety codes,[34] and others. The most common alternative to direct evidence of facts, however, is circumstantial evidence.

Circumstantial evidence. Ordinary circumstantial evidence is evidence of one fact that tends to establish some other fact,[35] or when the term is used loosely, to establish a legal conclusion.[36]

Examples. Evidence that a car driven by the defendant came to a stop only after skidding 500 feet and knocking down a tree 12 inches in diameter tends to establish that the defendant was driving very fast, and the trier of fact may so infer.[37] Evidence that a driver struck a large rock in the road tends to establish that the driver was not keeping a proper lookout or that if he was, he failed to act on the basis of what he saw.[38] And evidence of a driver's drunkenness shortly after a bartender served him alcohol may tend

---

[26]   Kimberlin v. DeLong, 637 N.E.2d 121 (Ind. 1994).

[27]   E.g., Martinez v. New York City Transit Auth., 41 A.D.3d 174, 838 N.Y.S.2d 53 (2007) (plaintiff's admission to emergency medical worker that she slipped exiting the bus admissible against her in her claim that the driver closed the doors on her).

[28]   §§ 44.4 to 44.7 (intentional or negligent spoliation).

[29]   E.g., Lincoln v. Clark Freight Lines, Inc, 285 S.W.3d 79 (Tex. App. 2009) (admitting accident reconstruction expert's conclusion as to which driver ran a red light based on calculation of coefficient of friction and other elements).

[30]   Cf. Scott v. Kass, 48 A.D.3d 785, 851 N.Y.S.2d 649 (2008) (police report reflecting party's admission at scene of accident and presenting diagram of scene made by investigating officer). Police reports may, however, be inadmissible as hearsay, see, e.g., Carignan v. Wheeler, 153 N.H. 465, 898 A.2d 1011 (2006), or because they contained mere opinion of an officer who did not qualify as an accident reconstruction expert. See Pilgrim's Pride Corp. v. Smoak, 134 S.W.3d 880 (Tex. App. 2004).

[31]   See Stumpf v. Nye, 950 A.2d 1032 (Pa. Super. Ct. 2008) (discussing when such a plea is admissible and when not).

[32]   Some states have admitted such evidence, see Scott v. Robertson, 583 P.2d 188 (Alaska 1978); others not.

[33]   See §§ 12.6 to 12.8.

[34]   See Considine v. City of Waterbury, 279 Conn. 830, 905 A.2d 70 (2006) (building code applicable only to future construction was nevertheless evidence of present standard of care and admissible, noting that voluntary safety codes are admissible).

[35]   See, e.g., Rando v. Anco Insulations Inc., 16 So.3d 1065 (La. 2009) ("Circumstantial evidence . . . is evidence of one fact, or of a set of facts, from which the existence of the fact to be determined may reasonably be inferred").

[36]   E.g., Branham v. Ford Motor Co., 390 S.C. 203, 701 S.E.2d 5 (2010) (the fact that a bicycle is not equipped with lights "does not create the inference that the bicycle is defective and unreasonably dangerous," quoting). Res ipsa loquitur aside, this book does not use the term inference to describe ultimate evaluations of conduct or products like the conclusion that an actor is negligent.

[37]   Johnson v. Yates, 31 N.C. App. 358, 229 S.E.2d 309 (1976) (excluding a trooper's opinion testimony about speed because the facts were quite sufficient to permit a determination).

[38]   Kimberlin v. PM Transport, 563 S.E.2d 665 (Va. 2002). This simple inference may be expressed in terms of presumption—the defendant is presumed to have seen an obvious condition he encounters, or to have been negligent in failing to see it. Peschke v. Carroll Coll., 280 Mont. 331, 929 P.2d 874 (1996); Branham v. Loews Orpheum Cinemas, Inc., 31 A.D.3d 319, 819 N.Y.S.2d 250 (2006).

to show that the bartender could have observed his apparent intoxication shortly before.[39] Likewise, when a healthy defendant driving a mechanically sound car manages to rear-end another car in good clear weather, on a smooth road, it is fair to conclude that he was negligent in failing to keep his attention on the road—especially if he falsely denies that his cell phone was operative.[40]

Admissibility and weight generally. Subject to the rules of evidence, circumstantial evidence is admissible at trial and often plays a major role in tort cases. Such evidence must of course be weighed case by case, but in general it is entitled to as much weight as direct evidence.[41] In many instances, circumstantial evidence based on physical facts like skid marks may be more trustworthy than eyewitness testimony; as a class of evidence, it has no less weight than direct testimony as a class.[42] Judges have an important role in making evidentiary decisions about circumstantial evidence, when expert testimony is required to introduce or explain it, and when the evidence as a whole is sufficient to permit reasonable jurors to draw the inferences necessary to establish a claim or defense.[43]

Expert testimony and the ultimate evaluation of negligence. When the plaintiff claims professional negligence such as medical malpractice[44] or negligence that requires technical knowledge to understand, experts may be required as well as permitted to testify about risks and alternatives.[45] They may even be permitted to testify that the defendant's conduct violated governing standards.[46] Otherwise, however, experts are generally not required or even permitted to testify either to matters of common knowledge or to the ultimate conclusion of negligence. The conclusion that a person is negligent is quite different from the conclusion that skid marks on a certain road show the car's speed to be no less than 30 mph.[47] The opinion about speed is mainly one about the probable facts, to which the expert may testify if he is appropriately qualified and if the testimony may assist the jury. In contrast, the opinion that driving 30 mph constitutes negligence is an evaluation of the facts.

---

[39] Faust v. Albertson, 167 Wash.2d 531, 222 P.3d 1208 (2009).

[40] See Foddrill v. Crane, 894 N.E.2d 1070 (Ind. Ct. App. 2008).

[41] Prignano v. Prignano, 934 N.E.2d 89, 343 Ill.Dec. 89 (App. Ct. 2010) ("any fact or issue can be proved by circumstantial evidence" as well as direct evidence and "[c]ircumstantial evidence is entitled to the same consideration as any other type of evidence"); Fitzpatrick v. Natter, 599 Pa. 465, 486, 961 A.2d 1229, 1242 (2008) ("Circumstantial evidence is entitled to as much weight as direct evidence, and is admissible to prove all elements of a negligence claim").

[42] See Fitzpatrick v. Natter, 599 Pa. 465, 486, 961 A.2d 1229, 1242 (2008) ("Circumstantial evidence is entitled to as much weight as direct evidence, and is admissible to prove all elements of a negligence claim" and may be "less likely to be falsely prepared and arranged"); Faust v. Albertson, 167 Wash.2d 531, 222 P.3d 1208 (2009).

[43] See, e.g., Blount v. Bordens, Inc., 910 S.W.2d 931 (Tex. 1995). For a fuller discussion of issues related to circumstantial evidence and presumptions from proof, see 1 Dobbs, Hayden & Bublick, The Law of Torts § 166 (2d ed. 2011 & Supp.)

[44] E.g., Walski v. Tiesenga, 72 Ill.2d 249, 381 N.E.2d 279 (1978).

[45] E.g., Turpin v. Merrell Dow Pharms., Inc., 959 F.2d 1349 (6th Cir. 1992) (expert testimony, based on studies, was inadequate to show that drug Bendectin was dangerous).

[46] See Hirst v. Inverness Hotel Corp., 544 F.3d 221, 227 n.8 (3d Cir. 2008) (although ultimate opinions may now sometimes be admitted, rules also exclude "opinions that are not helpful to the trier of fact, a protection against opinions which would merely tell the jury what result to reach, somewhat in the manner of the oath-helpers of an earlier day"); Webb v. Omni Block, Inc., 216 Ariz. 349, 353, 166 P.3d 140, 144 (Ct. App. 2007) ("opinion testimony on an ultimate issue must still be helpful to the trier of fact and cannot be couched in legal conclusions that simply opine how juries should decide cases;" testimony attributing percentages of fault to various parties should have been excluded under this rule).

[47] Brugh v. Peterson, 183 Neb. 190, 159 N.W.2d 321, 29 A.L.R.3d 236 (1968).

Jury evaluation of negligence. Under the general reasonable person standard of care, juries are generally expected to evaluate negligence on the basis of their own experience and perceptions of the risks involved. Neither expert opinion nor evidence of any special custom is required to permit this evaluation, so long as the kinds of risk involved are within the community's general understanding.[48]

B. SUBSTITUTES FOR FACTUAL EVIDENCE: RES IPSA LOQUITUR

§ 13.3   Res Ipsa Loquitur: General Rules

Meaning. Proof that an accident happened or even that the defendant caused an injury is ordinarily not enough by itself to show negligence. As courts say, negligence is not presumed.[49] Cases that fit the res ipsa loquitur pattern constitute something of an exception. The Latin phrase means that the thing speaks for itself, which is to say, the accident itself is evidence of negligence.

The core rule. The core of the res ipsa loquitur doctrine is simple and straightforward. If the defendant owes the plaintiff a duty of care,[50] the jury is permitted to infer that the defendant was negligent in some unspecified way when, on the evidence adduced, there is a rational basis in common experience or expert testimony for finding (1) that the injury was probably the result of negligence,[51] and (2) that the defendant was at least one of the persons who was probably negligent.[52] Jurists express these two

---

[48] E.g., Downey v. Bob's Discount Furniture Holdings, Inc., 633 F.3d 1, 84 Fed.R.Evid.Serv. 640, 78 Fed.R.Serv.3d 621 (1st Cir. 2011) (No expert testimony was needed at all in a case where plaintiff alleged that the defendant delivered new furniture infected by bedbugs that caused the plaintiffs an injury; "This is not a highly technical or scientific field, but, rather, a mundane occurrence that falls within the realm of common experience. Consequently, no expert testimony was necessary to establish the standard of care."); District of Columbia v. Harris, 770 A.2d 82 (D.C. 2001) (whether police adequately investigated for signs of injury to children could be decided by jury without expert testimony); Allison v. Manetta, 284 Conn. 389, 933 A.2d 1197 (2007) (truck parked so as to partially block road while driver addressed hazardous road condition; no expert testimony was required as the jury could judge negligence); Holcombe v. NationsBanc Fin. Servs. Corp., 248 Va. 445, 450 S.E.2d 158 (1994) (expert not required to establish proper angle for storing partitions that fell on the plaintiff); cf. Snyder v. Injured Patients & Families Comp. Fund, 768 N.W.2d 271 (Wis. Ct. App. 2009) (noting that matters within common knowledge of the jury require no expert testimony, holding that adequacy of psychiatric unit's search for weapons was not a medical issue governed by the special medical malpractice statutes).

[49] E.g., Fedorczyk v. Caribbean Cruise Lines, Ltd., 82 F.3d 69 (3d Cir. 1996); Habershaw v. Michaels Stores, Inc., 42 A.3d 1273 (R.I. 2012).

[50] When the defendant literally owes no duty to the plaintiff, the defendant is free to be negligent, so the inference of negligence is of no assistance to the plaintiff in that case. When the defendant owes a reduced duty, such as a duty only to avoid willful misconduct, the facts might justify an inference of negligence but not an inference of willful or reckless behavior. In such cases, res ipsa loquitur does not aid the plaintiff. See Restatement Second of Torts § 328D cmt. j (1965). Conversely, if the defendant owes especially high duty of care, res ipsa loquitur may apply with special ease. See Irwin v. Pacific Sw. Airlines, 133 Cal.App.3d 709, 184 Cal.Rptr. 228 (1982).

[51] E.g., Brewster v. United States, 542 N.W.2d 524 (Iowa 1996) (evidence should show that on the whole, "it is more likely that the event was caused by negligence than that it was not"); Banks v. Beckwith, 762 N.W.2d 149 (Iowa 2009) ("Banks was not required to refute any other possibilities for the breakage. He was only required to provide substantial evidence that it was more likely than not negligence was the cause of the event. He met this burden.").

[52] Restatement Second of Torts § 328D(1)(b) (defendant's responsibility indicated when evidence sufficiently eliminates other responsible causes); Dickens v. Sahley Realty Co., Inc., 756 S.E.2d 484 (2014) (res ipsa only when "defendant's negligence is the only inference that can reasonably and legitimately be drawn from the circumstances").

requirements in various ways.[53] The first requirement, that negligence must be the more probable explanation for the injury, is often expressed by saying that the injury must be of a kind which ordinarily does not occur in the absence of negligence.[54] The Restatement Third of Torts provides that the trier can infer that the defendant was negligent "when the accident causing the plaintiff's physical harm is a type of accident that ordinarily happens as a result of the negligence of a class of actors of which the defendant is the relevant member."[55] The underlying point of the formulations is much the same—to make a reasonable estimate of probabilities that the defendant was guilty of some unspecified and perhaps unknowable negligence.

The limiting rules. At times American cases have imposed constraining rules, most of which have now either been rejected or subjected to substantial qualifications discussed in later sections. These rules said that the res ipsa loquitur doctrine could not apply unless (a) the defendant was in exclusive control of the harm-causing instrumentality at some relevant time and (b) the plaintiff shows that she was not responsible for, or not an active participant in her own injury. Less importantly, some courts have also said that (c) once specific acts of negligence are pleaded or proved, res ipsa loquitur is no longer available; and that (d) res ipsa loquitur is not available at all unless the defendant has superior access to the evidence.

The leading res ipsa example. The most important ancestor of the res ipsa doctrine is also its best illustration. In *Byrne v. Boadle*,[56] the plaintiff was a pedestrian who was struck by a barrel of flour as he was walking adjacent to the defendant's shop. Although it was a fair inference that the barrel had come from the defendant's shop, the plaintiff was unable to show that the defendant had been negligent in any particular way. Nevertheless, the court thought the happening spoke for itself and that the jury would be permitted to find that the defendant was negligent, albeit in unspecified ways.

Relation to circumstantial evidence and the specific conduct requirement. Res ipsa loquitur is not a cause of action[57] and, absent unusual rules, need not be pleaded as a theory of the case.[58] Rather, as courts and commentators often say, res ipsa loquitur represents a kind of circumstantial evidence. At the same time, res ipsa loquitur cases differ from ordinary circumstantial evidence cases in one major respect. In ordinary cases, the plaintiff's evidence, circumstantial or direct, must point to specific conduct of the defendant, as where long skid marks circumstantially prove that the defendant was

---

[53]   That Restatement criticizes some of the other common formulations including one most like that stated in the text above. See Restatement Third of Torts (Liability for Physical and Emotional Harm) § 17 cmt. b (2010).

[54]   Restatement Third of Torts (Liability for Physical and Emotional Harm) § 17 (2010) puts the point affirmatively, that the accident must be of the type that ordinarily *does* occur as a result of negligence. Restatement Second of Torts § 328D (1965) uses the negative formulation. David Kaye, Probability Theory Meets Res Ipsa Loquitur, 77 Mich L. Rev. 1456, 1476 (1979).

[55]   Restatement Third of Torts (Liability for Physical and Emotional Harm) § 17 (2010).

[56]   Byrne v. Boadle, 2 H. & C. 722, 159 Eng. Rep. 299 (Exch. 1863).

[57]   E.g., Kerns v. Sealy, 496 F.Supp.2d 1306 (S.D. Ala. 2007).

[58]   See Clinkscales v. Nelson Secs., Inc., 697 N.W.2d 836 (Iowa 2005); Ianotta v. Tishman Speyer Props., Inc., 46 A.D.3d 297, 852 N.Y.S.2d 27 (2007) ("neither plaintiff's failure to specifically plead res ipsa loquitur nor the allegation of specific acts of negligence . . . constitutes a bar to the invocation or res ipsa loquitur where the facts warrant its application"); cf. Pete v. Youngblood, 141 P.3d 629 (Utah Ct. App. 2006) (res ipsa loquitur must be pleaded only if the plaintiff also relies on specific acts of negligence in addition to res ipsa loquitur). The plaintiff may be required to plead *facts* that would justify invoking res ipsa loquitur, however. See Heastie v. Roberts, 226 Ill.2d 515, 877 N.E.2d 1064, 315 Ill.Dec. 735 (2007).

speeding. In contrast, res ipsa loquitur cases permit the jury to infer negligence without inferring any particular misconduct at all.

Example. For instance, in *Byrne*, the plaintiff did not prove, either circumstantially or otherwise, that the barrel had been stored on its side instead of standing up, or that a rope holding the barrel had frayed and broken or any other particular acts that could be counted as negligence. The claim was only that the circumstances warranted the belief that the defendant was negligent in a wholly mysterious way.

Invocation of res ipsa loquitur where specific conduct can be inferred. However, res ipsa loquitur is sometimes invoked needlessly and inappropriately. If the trier can infer that the defendant was probably guilty of one of several specific acts of negligence but cannot be sure which act it was, res ipsa is not properly involved. Instead, the trier can simply draw the inference of specific negligence. For example, if a car parked at the curb by the defendant begins to roll downhill in the absence of interference by others, a trier might infer that the defendant either failed to set the brakes or failed to cut the wheels properly against the curb, or failed to put the car in parking gear, or some combination. Although the jury might not be sure which of these negligent omissions occurred, if it can conclude that one or more of them did, then the case is merely one of ordinary circumstantial evidence. Similarly, in rear-end collisions: res ipsa is not needed because the jury can ordinarily infer specific negligence on the part of the rear driver—he was either not keeping a proper lookout or driving too fast or both.[59] When courts speak of res ipsa loquitur in cases like this perhaps no harm is done,[60] but they risk confusing the process of estimating the probability of unknown acts of negligence with the process of inferring specific negligent acts.[61]

§ 13.4 Inferences Permitted, Required or Unpermitted

Roles of judge and jury: permissible inferences. When the plaintiff argues that a res ipsa loquitur inference should be available to establish her claim of negligence, the judge in the first instance determines whether, on the evidence adduced, jurors can reasonably

---

[59] Many of the rear-end decisions ignore res ipsa loquitur terminology and concentrate on inferences of specific negligence, such as the inference that the defendant was following too closely. Garnot v. Johnson, 239 Va. 81, 387 S.E.2d 473 (1990) (following too closely). Or they analyze the case as a statutory violation, again for following too closely. Jones v. Bennett, 306 N.J.Super. 476, 703 A.2d 1008 (1998).

[60] See Sullivan v. Snyder, 374 A.2d 866 (D.C. 1977) (discussing res ipsa loquitur in a rear end collision case where an inference of specific negligence seems more plausible); Lambrecht v. Estate of Kaczmarczyk, 241 Wis. 2d 804, 623 N.W.2d 751 (2001) (court permitted a res ipsa loquitur inference of negligence but in one passage seemed to say that some specific acts of negligence could be inferred and even that failure of the driver to wear a seat-belt might have been negligence contributing to loss of control).

[61] In Morris v. Wal-Mart Stores, Inc., 330 F.3d 854 (6th Cir. 2003), a federal diversity case, strong evidence warranted an inference that the plaintiff slipped on water draining from a freezer the defendant had installed in its store without a plug. Given that inference, the defendant's conduct was known and could be evaluated as negligent or non-negligent without reference to res ipsa loquitur. However, the plaintiff characterized her claim as a res ipsa loquitur case, which led the federal judges to a lengthy dispute over the scope and application of the "control" rule for res ipsa, none of which seems necessary when the circumstances show that the defendant probably created the danger by specific, known conduct, the risks and utilities of which could be evaluated directly. In Quinby v. Plumsteadville Family Practice, Inc., 907 A.2d 1061 (Pa. 2006), health care providers left a quadriplegic man on an exam table unattended and unsecured. He fell to the floor. No one could say with confidence what triggered the fall, since he could not move himself. However, the conduct of the health care providers in leaving him unattended was undisputed. The court said this was a res ipsa loquitur case and also said that the jury would be compelled on these facts to find negligence. The use of res ipsa suggests that there was some unknown negligence other than leaving the helpless patient unattended and insecure, but it seems difficult to say that some other and unknown negligence was probable. On the other hand, if res ipsa loquitur terminology is not used at all, the court could still hold, as it did, that leaving a helpless patient would be negligence as a matter of law.

conclude that the defendant was negligent.[62] If the judge concludes that reasonable persons could not draw an inference of negligence on the facts the jury is entitled to believe, then the jury will not be permitted to rely upon res ipsa loquitur. If the judge concludes that reasonable people could differ, the jury is permitted to draw the res ipsa inference, and may be instructed to that effect.[63] In making the determination whether reasonable people could conclude that negligence is the probable explanation for the injury, the judge considers the same common knowledge, expert testimony, alternative explanations and other matters that the jury would consider. The judge determines only whether reasonable people could differ about the probability of negligence as an explanation. Once the judge determines that reasonable people can conclude on the governing facts that negligence is probable, the jury is permitted to infer negligence but it is not required to do so.[64]

Shifting the burden of persuasion. A few jurisdictions, including California, hold that when res ipsa applies, the defendant must introduce at least some evidence to rebut the inference, and that the jury must find negligence if the defendant fails to do so.[65] However, as the Restatement notes, some decisions are ambiguous if not downright contradictory,[66] perhaps because the presumption rule is too stringent or counterintuitive.

Exceptionally strong inferences under the permissible inference rule. Even under the permissible inference rule, rare cases may call for special treatment. The weight of circumstantial evidence is sometimes great, sometimes weak. The same is true with the res ipsa inference. It is possible to imagine that the plaintiff's evidence creates an inference so strong that, unless the evidence is simply not credited, it should carry the case for the plaintiff in the absence of rebuttal.[67]

Effect of rebuttal evidence. Some forms of rebuttal evidence, if taken as true, may convince the judge that reasonable people could not find negligence. However, the defendant's rebuttal evidence might be disbelieved by the trier, so the judge cannot

---

[62] Restatement Third of Torts (Liability for Physical and Emotional Harm) § 17 cmt. j (2010).

[63] See K-Mart Corp. v. Gipson, 563 N.E.2d 667 (Ind. Ct. App. 1990).

[64] See, e.g., Chapman v. Harner, 339 P.3d 519 (Colo. 2014); Banks v. Beckwith, 762 N.W.2d 149, 152 (Iowa 2009) (res ipsa loquitur permits but does not compel the inference of negligence); Romero v. Brenes, 189 Md.App. 284, 984 A.2d 346 (2009); Khan v. Singh, 200 N.J. 82, 91, 975 A.2d 389, 394 (2009) ("permits the jury to infer negligence . . . effectively reducing the plaintiff's burden of persuasion, but not shifting the burden of proof); Deuel v. Surgical Clinic, PLLC, 2010 WL 3237297 (Tenn. Ct. App. 2010) (res ipsa loquitur "permits, but does not compel, a jury to infer negligence from the circumstances of an injury"; it allows an inference of negligence, but it does not alter burden of proof); Restatement Third of Torts (Liability for Physical and Emotional Harm) § 17 cmt j (2010).

[65] See Schmidt v. Gibbs, 305 Ark. 383, 807 S.W.2d 928 (1991) (stating when a res ipsa loquitur case is made out, that creates "prima facie evidence of negligence and shifts to the defendant the burden of proving that it was not caused through any lack of care on its part"); Brown v. Poway Unified Sch. Dist., 4 Cal.4th 820, 826, 843 P.2d 624, 627, 15 Cal.Rptr. 2d 679, 682 (1993) (by statute, res ipsa loquitur is a presumption affecting the burden of proof and "the burden of producing evidence 'require[s] the trier of fact to assume the existence of the presumed' fact unless the defendant introduces evidence to the contrary").

[66] Restatement Third of Torts (Liability for Physical and Emotional Harm) § 17, Reporters' Notes to Comment j (2010).

[67] De Leon Lopez v. Corporacion Insular de Seguros, 931 F.2d 116 (1st Cir. 1991) (hospital mixed newborn babies of two different mothers and did not discover the mistake for over a year); Quinby v. Plumsteadville Family Practice, Inc., 907 A.2d 1061 (Pa. 2006) (holding that the reasonable people could not do other than to find negligence where health care providers left helpless patient alone and unsecured on table from which he fell); Imig v. Beck, 115 Ill.2d 18, 503 N.E.2d 324 (1986) (recognizing that some inferences may be exceptionally strong and that in some cases strong enough to warrant a directed verdict for the plaintiff, but holding that the facts before the court did not warrant application of such an exceptional rule); Bustillo v. Matturro, 292 A.D.2d 554, 740 N.Y.S.2d 360 (2002) (rear-end collision, summary judgment for the plaintiff).

appropriately remove res ipsa loquitur from the case merely because the defendant has offered alternative explanations or other rebuttal evidence.[68] Rather, the jury's role is to resolve conflicts in testimony and to weigh probabilities of negligence, provided the plaintiff's evidence in the first place is prima facie sufficient to permit the inference that negligence is the probable explanation. Possibly, however, there are exceptionally strong cases of uncontradicted rebuttal that clearly dispel the inference of negligence, in which case the jury might even be compelled to find for the defendant.[69]

Incomplete rebuttal evidence. In some cases, the jury can believe all of the defendant's testimony and still rationally find that the defendant was negligent. For example, if the plaintiff was injured by the malfunctioning equipment at the defendant's factory, the defendant's rebuttal evidence might show that the equipment failed because of manufacturing flaws, but the jury might nevertheless still be permitted to draw the res ipsa inference of negligence because the rebuttal does not exclude the possibility that the defendant should have discovered the flaws.[70] Or the defendant might offer evidence describing all its careful acts, but failing to explain how, given its due care, the injury could occur. In such a case, even if the jury believes the rebutting testimony, the inference of negligence is not necessarily dissipated, and the jury may again be allowed to draw the inference of negligence.[71]

§ 13.5   Estimating Probabilities of Negligence

Estimating probabilities: common knowledge or experience. Some judges express caution about submitting res ipsa loquitur claims to the jury.[72] Certainly they will not submit a res ipsa loquitur claim to the jury unless there is some basis on which the jurors can rationally estimate that negligence of some kind is reasonably probable. Such estimates may be based on either of two grounds: general common knowledge, observation or experience on the one hand or expert testimony on the other.

Common knowledge as a common sense of probability in general. The common knowledge requirement envisions general background knowledge, not knowledge about the particular kind of accident that befell the plaintiff. It does not require knowledge of

---

[68] A strong example is Harder v. F.C. Clinton, Inc., 948 P.2d 298 (Okla. 1997). In Morgan v. Children's Hosp., 18 Ohio St. 3d 185, 190, 480 N.E.2d 464, 467 (1985), the court said: "It is a well-established principle that a court may not refuse as a matter of law to instruct on the doctrine of res ipsa loquitur merely upon the basis that the defendant's evidence sufficiently rebuts the making of such an inference. . . . 'The trial court, in a jury trial, in a case which calls for the application of the rule of res ipsa loquitur, is without authority to declare, as a matter of law, that the inference of negligence which the jury is permitted to draw, has been rebutted or destroyed by an explanation of the circumstances offered by the defendant, and such action on the part of the trial court is an invasion of the province of the jury.' "

[69] E.g., Estate of Hall v. Akron Gen. Med. Ctr., 125 Ohio St. 3d 300, 927 N.E.2d 1112 (2010) (defendant's rebuttal evidence would eliminate the likelihood of negligence established by the plaintiff's evidence); Van Hook v. Anderson, 64 Wash.App. 353, 824 P.2d 509 (1992) (sponge remained in patient's body after operation, doctor showed that nurses had reported to him an erroneous sponge count).

[70] Mobil Chem. Co. v. Bell, 517 S.W.2d 245 (Tex. 1974).

[71] E.g., Reynolds Metals Co. v. Yturbide, 258 F.2d 321 (9th Cir. 1958); Escola v. Coca Cola Bottling Co. of Fresno, 24 Cal.2d 453, 150 P.2d 436 (1944); Kambat v. St. Francis Hosp., 89 N.Y.2d 489, 678 N.E.2d 456, 655 N.Y.S.2d 844 (1997) (18-inch towel discovered in patient after hysterectomy, evidence that all the towels were carefully counted does not necessarily dispel inference of negligence by surgeons or hospital); Goldstein v. Levy, 74 Misc. 463, 132 N.Y.S. 373 (App. Term. 1911).

[72] Hailey v. Otis Elevator Co., 636 A.2d 426 (D.C. 1994) ("Given the power of res ipsa loquitur . . . and the consequent caution with which it should be applied . . . [it] must be based upon a widespread consensus of a common understanding").

statistics or even actual experience indicating probabilities.[73] Thus, common knowledge often sounds more like a common or shared sense of probabilities rather than actual knowledge, and in fact common sense is a term frequently used in the cases.[74] For instance, jurors have been permitted to conclude that when a modern airplane crashes without explanation and no other cause appears likely, that the operator of the plane was negligent, even though the jurors themselves are not pilots and have no actual data on the subject of air-crash negligence.[75] Similarly, people outside the health care professions, may know very little about the technical side medical equipment, but if a patient is burned in an operating room fire[76] or catches fire while immobilized in a treatment room,[77] an inference of negligence is entirely fair under the res ipsa loquitur rules unless other explanations are in evidence. On the other hand, courts refuse to submit cases to the jury on the res ipsa loquitur theory when they conclude that there simply is not enough common observation or experience to justify an estimate of probabilities.[78]

Common knowledge where injury is unusual. The mere fact that injury is unusual under the circumstances of the case does not by itself logically prove that negligence is a reasonably probable cause.[79] What is necessary to show that negligence is probable is that injury is not merely unlikely, but unlikely *in the absence of negligence*,[80] or put affirmatively, that negligence is a reasonably likely explanation. For example, the mere

---

[73] "Could it have been reasonably found by the jury that the accident which occurred in this case is of a kind which more probable than not would not have occurred in the absence of negligence upon the part of Fisher? That is a question which cannot be answered with any precision because we do not have statistical data on the relative probability of the negligence of drivers as a cause of this kind of accident. The determination of where the probabilities lie must, ordinarily, be made upon the basis of past experience as it is seen and appraised by the court. 'These are the judgments of common sense.' " Kaufman v. Fisher, 230 Or. 626, 639, 371 P.2d 948, 954 (1962) (quoting 2 Harper & James, Torts § 15.2, at 879 (1956)).

[74] Kubera v. Barnes & Noble Booksellers, Inc., 2009 WL 862168 (Conn. Super. Ct. 2009); McDougald v. Perry, 716 So.2d 783, 786 (Fla. 1998) ("common sense dictates an inference that both a spare tire carried on a truck and a wheel on a truck's axle will stay with the truck unless there is a failure of reasonable care"); Cleary v. Manning, 884 N.E.2d 335, 338 (Ind. Ct. App. 2008); Winters v. Wright, 869 So.2d 357, 362 (Miss. 2003) (medical malpractice res ipsa loquitur "where a layman can observe and understand the negligence as a matter of common sense and practical experience").

[75] Permitting res ipsa loquitur in airplane crashes: Dunn v. Grand Canyon Airlines, Inc., 66 F.3d 334, unpublished opinion available, 1995 WL 547723 (9th Cir. 1995); Widmyer v. Southeast Skyways, Inc., 584 P.2d 1 (Alaska 1978); Newing v. Cheatham, 15 Cal.3d 351, 540 P.2d 33, 124 Cal.Rptr. 193 (1975). Earlier decisions refused to permit res ipsa in airplane cases, some of which were also private plane cases and are conceivably distinguishable on that ground.

[76] Cleary v. Manning, 884 N.E.2d 335, 338 (Ind. Ct. App. 2008).

[77] Heastie v. Roberts, 226 Ill.2d 515, 877 N.E.2d 1064, 315 Ill.Dec. 735 (2007).

[78] See Toogood v. Rogal, 824 A.2d 1140 (Pa. 2003) (physician injecting nerve block in back punctured lung, not enough information for res ipsa loquitur); Ruiz v. Walgreen Co., 79 S.W.3d 235, 239 (Tex. App. 2002) (pharmacy misfilled a prescription for Magsal with Nizoral; the patient became ill and was hospitalized, but res ipsa loquitur could not apply partly because the plaintiffs did not "explain how laymen would know that substitution in this case was improper").

[79] See Ward v. Mount Calvary Lutheran Church, 178 Ariz. 350, 355, 873 P.2d 688, 694 (Ct. App. 1994); Andrews v. Burke, 55 Wash. App. 622, 628–29, 779 P.2d 740, 744 (1989); Fehrman v. Smirl, 20 Wis.2d 1, 121 N.W.2d 255 (1963).

[80] Siverson v. Weber, 57 Cal.2d 834, 837, 372 P.2d 97, 99 (1962) ("The fact that a particular injury suffered by a patient as the result of an operation is something that rarely occurs does not in itself prove that the injury was probably caused by the negligence of those in charge of the operation."); Fieux v. Cardiovascular & Thoracic Clinic, P.C., 159 Or.App. 637, 978 P.2d 429 (1999) (similar).

fact that a plane passenger suffers ear pain when the plane lands does not by itself prove negligence; injury may have resulted from the passenger's own conditions.[81]

Evidence of alternative explanations or their absence. If the judge believes that other explanations for the injury are as likely as negligence, the case cannot to go to the jury on a res ipsa loquitur theory.[82] For example, if the only evidence is that a tire blows out on a moving vehicle, negligence of the manufacturer does not seem to be a probable explanation, since tires are not expected to last forever and many other causes of blowout are readily imaginable.[83] However, the probability of negligence is increased if the plaintiff can produce additional evidence that tends to exclude innocent, non-negligent causes of the injury. For instance, if the plaintiff shows that wear and tear and external harm to the defendant's product are unlikely explanations of the product's failure, the inference that the product was negligently made or defective is considerably strengthened and the jury may be allowed to draw the inference.[84] To generalize the point, when the evidence permits the trier to find that other causes are unlikely, the inference of negligence becomes strong.[85]

Estimating probabilities: expert testimony. When common knowledge or experience furnishes an inadequate basis for estimating probabilities of negligence, most courts now allow the plaintiff to introduce expert opinion testimony to establish the probability that negligence is the explanation for injury.[86] For example, an expert may be able to estimate the probability that negligence is the explanation when a surgical operation goes horribly wrong. The expert's estimate, however, may be disputed by other experts and may be rejected by the jury.[87]

Estimating probabilities: judicial disagreements. In close cases, judges may be uncertain whether common knowledge suffices to warrant submission of the res ipsa loquitur claim to the jury and may even differ among themselves as to the probability of negligence versus the probability of some innocent explanation. In a Wisconsin case the court was closely divided where a wildly out-of-control vehicle crashed into several cars. No one could be sure whether these events were caused by the driver's unforeseeable

[81] But in Calabretta v. Nat'l Airlines, Inc., 528 F.Supp. 32 (E.D.N.Y. 1981), where the passenger ultimately lost her hearing, the court held that res ipsa loquitur applied because ear problems do not commonly result from flights.

[82] Kramer v. Petroleum Helicopters, Inc., 999 So. 2d 101 (La. Ct. App. 2008) (in an action against helicopter manufacturer, "the circumstances surrounding the crash suggested the possibility of other causes of the crash. The flight was at night, was conducted at an altitude that may have been as low as the tree tops, and in an area with rolling terrain. [S]patial disorientation . . . can prevent a pilot from recognizing that the craft is descending rather than ascending;" res ipsa loquitur did not apply); see Restatement Third of Torts (Liability for Physical and Emotional Harm) § 17 cmt. b (2010).

[83] Goodyear Tire & Rubber Co. v. Hughes Supply, Inc., 358 So.2d 1339 (Fla. 1978).

[84] Coulter v. Michelin Tire Corp., 622 S.W.2d 421 (Mo. Ct. App. 1981) (jury could infer that tire produced by defendant was defective when sold where (a) it was new when it exploded and (b) expert evidence excluded the possibility of external damage); Hofer v. Gap, Inc., 516 F.Supp.2d 161 (D. Mass. 2007) (sandal breaking, causing serious fall on its first use, jury can infer negligence).

[85] E.g., Escola v. Coca Cola Bottling Co., 24 Cal. 2d 453, 150 P.2d 436 (1944); see Restatement Third of Torts (Liability for Physical and Emotional Harm) § 17 cmt. d (2010).

[86] LePage v. Horne, 262 Conn. 116, 809 A.2d 505 (2002) (putting baby to sleep on her stomach, SIDS death); Mireles v. Broderick, 117 N.M. 445, 872 P.2d 863 (1994) (listing authorities); Sides v. St. Anthony's Med. Ctr., 258 S.W.3d 811 (Mo. 2008); States v. Lourdes Hosp., 100 N.Y.2d 208, 792 N.E.2d 151, 762 N.Y.S.2d 1 (2003); Morgan v. Children's Hosp., 18 Ohio St. 3d 185, 480 N. E. 2d 464 (1985). Contra Wright v. United States, 280 F.Supp.2d 472 (M.D.N.C. 2003) (North Carolina law); Butler-Tulio v. Scroggins, 139 Md.App. 122, 774 A.2d 1209 (2001).

[87] See, emphasizing this point, States v. Lourdes Hospital, 100 N.Y.2d 208, 792 N.E.2d 151, 762 N.Y.S.2d 1 (2003).

heart attack (which left him dead) or whether the attack came immediately afterward. It seems difficult to say that anyone could estimate the probabilities of the negligence explanation versus the heart attack explanation, but the majority left it to the jury.[88]

Risk of judicial error. Because in close cases there is no certainty what the "right" ruling would be, Judge Calabresi has suggested that judges may properly consider which party should bear the risk of potential judicial error in ruling on res ipsa loquitur. Would an erroneous decision to let the jury decide the res ipsa loquitur inference be more harmful or less harmful than an erroneous decision to dismiss the res ipsa loquitur claim?[89] But this, too, merely injects another estimate, or perhaps it is, as Judge Calabresi says, only intuition.

Pleading res ipsa loquitur in the alternative. Courts traditionally said that if the plaintiff proves, or offers evidence of the defendant's specific acts of negligence, the case cannot be submitted to the jury on a res ipsa loquitur theory.[90] However, "most modern courts find it inappropriate to penalize the plaintiff" for attempting to prove specific negligence.[91] Under this view, the plaintiff may plead and attempt to prove specific acts of negligence and also argue that she is entitled to a res ipsa loquitur inference if the jury does not believe the specific acts were sufficiently proven.[92] The modern rule appears to be the best starting place for analysis. The plaintiff's attorney often cannot know whether the jury will accept proof of specific facts and it is not wrong to attempt to prove them. However, the res ipsa inference of negligence is negated once the jury accepts testimony that fully explains the occurrence,[93] whether that testimony comes from the plaintiff's effort to prove specific acts of negligence or from the defendant's effort to exonerate himself.

§ 13.6 Res Ipsa Cases: Illustrations

Examples: tangible instruments of harm. Most res ipsa loquitur cases arise when the plaintiff is injured by an identified instrument of harm. Frequently an object that should be contained or stationary in fact escapes, moves, or explodes, becoming an active source of harm. For example, a light fixture falls from the ceiling without apparent cause.[94] There are endless variations—the plaintiff is struck by a falling object,[95] by an

---

[88] Lambrecht v. Estate of Kaczmarczyk, 241 Wis.2d 804, 623 N.W.2d 751 (2001) (with three judges dissenting).

[89] Williams v. KFC Nat'l Mgmt. Co., 391 F.3d 411, 425 (2d Cir. 2004) (Calabresi, J., concurring).

[90] E.g., Haugen v. BioLife Plasma Servs., 714 N.W.2d 841 (N.D. 2006). Courts sometimes phrase this as a rule that "direct evidence precludes use of res ipsa loquitur, presumably meaning evidence" of specific negligent acts that explain the accident. See Yorke v. Novant Health, Inc., 666 S.E.2d 127 (N.C. Ct. App. 2008).

[91] Restatement Third of Torts (Liability for Physical and Emotional Harm) § 17 cmt. g (2010).

[92] Gubbins v. Hurson, 885 A.2d 269, 283 (D.C. 2005) ("This court permits the plaintiff in a proper case to rely upon both res ipsa loquitur and proof of specific acts of negligence."); Clinkscales v. Nelson Sec., Inc., 697 N.W.2d 836 (Iowa 2005) (plaintiff can plead and get to the jury on both res ipsa loquitur and evidence of specific negligence, although jury finding specific negligence cannot entertain res ipsa loquitur); Abbott v. Page Airways, Inc., 23 N.Y.2d 502, 512, 245 N.E.2d 388, 393 (1969) ("there can be no logical or reasonable basis for requiring a plaintiff to choose between Res ipsa and specific evidence of negligence or for precluding him from relying on Res ipsa principles once evidence of negligence had been introduced, unless the two alternate modes of proof are fundamentally or inherently inconsistent. Quite obviously, there is no such inconsistency").

[93] Conner v. Menard, Inc., 705 N.W.2d 318 (Iowa 2005).

[94] E.g., Anderson v. Service Merchandise Co., Inc., 240 Neb. 873, 485 N.W.2d 170 (1992); but see Hagler v. Coastal Farm Holdings, Inc., 309 P.3d 1073 (Or. 2013).

[95] E.g., Cardina v. Kash N' Karry Food Stores, Inc., 663 So.2d 642 (Fla. Dist. Ct. App. 1995) (case of tomatoes falling from stack).

unattended car that somehow has broken loose,[96] by a wheel that flies off a moving vehicle;[97] the defendant's grenade explodes prematurely,[98] or its bottle explodes in the plaintiff's hand;[99] or its chair collapses when the plaintiff sits upon it;[100] high voltage lines fall for no apparent reason,[101] gas lines explode or catch fire,[102] water bursts from its pipes,[103] cattle escape from their pens.[104] Sometimes the instrument of harm is something that is properly moving or active to begin with, but it takes a course that is so unexpected that negligence remains a strong likelihood, as where a car driven along a safe and clear highway suddenly leaves the road and strikes an unsuspecting tree in a field.[105] At other times the instrument of harm is almost definitionally defective, as where food in a sealed container proves to be poisonous or otherwise dangerous to health.[106] Because it is all a matter of appraising evidence, res ipsa loquitur may also be rejected in most of these instances if the facts of a particular case suggest an explanation not based on negligence, or if the defendant was not the negligent person.[107]

Examples: unknown instruments of harm; the caretaker and custodial cases. No formal rule limits res ipsa loquitur to cases in which the instrumentality of harm is known. Suppose the plaintiff suffers an injury while in the defendant's custody. The plaintiff is an infant in a day care center, a patient anesthetized upon an operating table, or a nursing home patient unable to communicate. If the infant is returned from day care with a concussion and damage to the optical nerve that requires surgery,[108] a broken arm,[109] or injuries from being chewed by some animal,[110] it is not implausible to say that the day care center, with its obligation to supervise and protect, was likely negligent, even though the plaintiff cannot prove that the harm was done by a falling barrel or any

---

[96] Housing Auth. of City of Rolla v. Kimmel, 771 S.W.2d 932 (Mo. Ct. App. 1989); Hill v. Thompson, 484 P.2d 513 (Okla. 1971).

[97] Neace v. Laimans, 951 F.2d 139 (7th Cir. 1991); McDougald v. Perry, 716 So.2d 783 (1998).

[98] McGonigal v. Gearhart Indus., Inc., 851 F.2d 774 (10th Cir. 1988).

[99] Escola v. Coca Cola Bottling Co., 24 Cal. 2d 453, 150 P.2d 436 (1944).

[100] E.g., Trujeque v. Service Merchandise Co., 117 N.M. 388, 872 P.2d 361 (1994).

[101] Koch v. Norris Pub. Power Dist., 10 Neb. App. 453, 632 N.W.2d 391 (2001).

[102] Cosgrove v. Commonwealth Edison Co., 315 Ill.App. 3d 651, 734 N.E.2d 155, 248 Ill.Dec. 447 (2000); Harvey v. Metro. Utils. Dist. of Omaha, 246 Neb. 780, 523 N.W.2d 372 (1994) (gas leak at meter controlled by the defendant utility).

[103] State Farm Fire & Cas. Co. v. Municipality of Anchorage, 788 P.2d 726 (Alaska 1990) (underground water pipe); cf. Pikersgill v. City of New York, 642 N.Y.S.2d 469 (Civ. Ct. 1996) (sewer backup).

[104] Roberts v. Weber & Sons, Co., 248 Neb. 243, 533 N.W.2d 664 (1995). Some courts categorically refuse to apply res ipsa to cattle-on-the-highway cases, but at least some of the cases refusing res ipsa are justified in doing so on their particular facts. See Vanderwater v. Hatch, 835 F.2d 239 (10th Cir. 1987).

[105] Aldana v. School City of E. Chicago, 769 N.E.2d 1201 (Ind. Ct. App. 2002) (bus left clear, dry road, fishtailed back onto highway, throwing passengers against seats); Eaton v. Eaton, 119 N.J. 628, 575 A.2d 858 (1990); Porterfield v. Brinegar, 719 S.W.2d 558 (Tex. 1986); cf. Lambrecht v. Estate of Kaczmarczyk, 241 Wis.2d 804, 623 N.W.2d 751 (2001) (driver rear-ended two cars traveling same direction, crossed intersection and T-boned plaintiff's car, res ipsa could be invoked).

[106] E.g., Atlanta Coca-Cola Bottling Co. v. Ergle, 128 Ga.App. 381, 196 S.E.2d 670 (1973).

[107] See Benham v. King, 700 N.W.2d 314 (Iowa 2005) (dental chair collapsed with patient when dentist actuated the gear that raised it, no reason for dentist to inspect chair made for professional use, finding of negligence impermissible).

[108] Fowler v. Seaton, 61 Cal.2d 681, 394 P.2d 697, 39 Cal.Rptr. 881 (1964) (child 3 years and 10 months, unable to talk about injury, suffering serious head injury and eye damage).

[109] Ward v. Forrester Day Care, Inc., 547 So.2d 410 (Ala. 1989) (11-week-old baby returned from day care with broken arm); cf. Persinger v. Step by Step Infant Dev. Ctr., 253 Ga.App. 768, 560 S.E.2d 333 (2002) (infant's broken leg coupled with medical testimony that break was inconsistent with the ordinary fall testified to by defendant's witnesses created fact-question for jury).

[110] Myers v. Moore, 240 Mo.App. 726, 217 S.W.2d 291 (1949) (5-week-old baby, apparently chewed by something, possibly rats, while in defendant's care).

other particular tangible item. The same idea applies to others in the custody of caretakers, such as patients in nursing homes[111] infants in hospital care[112] and those who are anesthetized,[113] but of course only if the injury occurred while the plaintiff was in the defendant's care.[114]

Nonreciprocal risks. Almost all the illustrations of res ipsa loquitur given above, whether involving a tangible instrumentality or not, are cases of nonreciprocal risks. That is, the defendant is in a position to negligently harm the plaintiff, but the plaintiff is not in a position to inflict similar harms upon the defendant, sometimes not even in position to protect herself. It is exemplified by all those cases in which gravity plays a heavy role. The pedestrian on the street is endangered by falling barrels but creates no similar risk to people on the second story, nor is she in good position to protect herself. Even where the defendant does not have literal and total control of the risks, the nonreciprocal feature of res ipsa is often very prominent, as where the plaintiff is injured by an exploding soda bottle or a collapsing chair. The defendant may lack literal control in such cases, but the risk remains a one-way street. The nonreciprocal character of many res ipsa cases is not the function of a rule, but it is a characteristic that often appears and may suggest a moral basis for the inference when otherwise the case might be doubtful.

§ 13.7　Attributing Fault to the Defendant

Negligence must be defendant's. Res ipsa loquitur cannot be applied unless the evidence makes it reasonably probable that the defendant is one of the persons whose negligence caused the accident or injury. Or as the Restatement Third puts it, the doctrine does not apply unless the injury-causing accident ordinarily happens "as a result of the negligence of a class of actors of which the defendant is the relevant member."[115]

Defendant's control is sufficient. Evidence that the defendant had exclusive control of the instrumentality of harm at the time of the accident is usually sufficient to permit

---

[111] Sides v. St. Anthony's Med. Ctr., 258 S.W.3d 811 (Mo. 2008) (unexplained disconnection of immobile quadriplegic patient's oxygen supply resulting in his death); DeCarlo v. Eden Park Health Servs., Inc., 66 A.D.3d 1211, 887 N.Y.S.2d 315 (2009) (non-ambulatory patient had unexplained broken bones; though her bones were delicate, this was a condition the nursing home should have taken into account in its treatment); Harder v. F.C. Clinton, Inc., 948 P.2d 298 (Okla. 1997) (nursing home resident somehow ingested an overdose of a medicine that was not prescribed).

[112] Tierney v. St. Michael's Med. Ctr., 214 N.J.Super. 27, 518 A.2d 242 (1986) (17-month-old infant fell from crib in hospital).

[113] Ybarra v. Spangard, 25 Cal.2d 486, 154 P.2d 687 (1944); but cf. J. E. v. Beth Israel Hosp., 295 A.D.2d 281, 744 N.Y.S.2d 166 (2002) (woman underwent operation in defendant's hospital, and on returning home discovered pain and tenderness later identified as resulting from sexual assault; claim dismissed because court states that assault could have occurred elsewhere). Perhaps the court in J.E. was relying on facts it did not report; the plaintiff's verified complaint seems to imply unavoidably that the injury was not inflicted while she was conscious.

[114] In Lamb v. State, 2002 WL 31319755 (Tenn. Ct. App. 2002), the plaintiff, with severe mental limitations, may have been abused, but although the possible abuse was discovered after a period of custody by a caretaker, it could have occurred at other times. Thus the predicate for res ipsa loquitur was missing.

[115] Restatement Third of Torts (Liability for Physical and Emotional Harm) § 17 (2010). Cf. Winfrey v. GGP Ala Moana LLC, 308 P.3d 891 (Haw. 2013) (insufficient evidence to create inference that mall owner was negligent when patron became stuck in rooftop exhaust duct); Dickens v. Sahley Realty Co., Inc., 756 S.E.2d 484 (W. Va. 2014) (summary judgment properly granted where plaintiffs did not offer sufficient evidence that natural erosion, rather than defendant's negligence, caused a pond to encroach on their property).

an inference that any negligence inferred is probably attributable to the defendant.[116] When a barrel falls on the plaintiff, the probability is that someone was negligent. When it falls from the defendant's warehouse, the probability is that the defendant is that negligent person.

Is defendant's control necessary? Courts have often said that the defendant's exclusive control, directly or through its agents,[117] was not only sufficient to show the defendant's probable connection with the accident, but also a necessary prerequisite for the application of res ipsa loquitur.[118] Although some courts continue to state and apply the control rule without analysis, courts in many cases have found it too overstated to accomplish its purpose, for reasons of overbreadth—evidence may show that the defendant was probably the negligent author of the plaintiff's injury even when the defendant was not in control of a dangerous instrument at the time injury occurred.[119] In light of the overbreadth of the traditional control rule, some courts have found various ways to retain the rule but reformulate its meaning.[120] Other courts have reformulated the rule itself.[121] The Second Restatement eliminated the control rule but recognized and enforced its purpose by providing that the evidence must tend to show that other responsible causes are unlikely, thus pointing to the defendant as a negligent party.[122] The Restatement Third likewise eliminates the control rule while at the same time capturing the underlying idea that evidence must warrant a finding that it was the defendant, not merely others, who negligently caused harm.[123]

---

[116] E.g., Heastie v. Roberts, 226 Ill.2d 515, 877 N.E.2d 1064, 315 Ill.Dec. 735 (2007) (defendant owned hospital room where patient caught fire, patient could not have set the fire; this establishes control sufficient to permit plaintiff to go to jury on res ipsa loquitur).

[117] Potthast v. Metro-North R.R., 400 F.3d 143 (2d Cir. 2005).

[118] See, e.g., Hansen v. City of Pocatello, 145 Idaho 700, 702,184 P.3d 206, 208 (2008); Banks v. Beckwith, 762 N.W.2d 149, 152 (Iowa 2009); Contreras v. Vannoy Heating & Air Conditioning, Inc., 270 Mont. 393, 892 P.2d 557 (1995) (defendant did not have exclusive control over exploding boiler); Ebanks v. New York City Transit Auth., 70 N.Y.2d 621, 512 N.E.2d 297 (1987) (escalator injury).

[119] Escola v. Coca-Cola Bottling Co., 24 Cal.2d 453, 150 P.2d 436 (1944); Anderson v. Service Merch. Co., Inc., 240 Neb. 873, 485 N.W.2d 170 (1992). See Aldana v. School City of E. Chicago, 769 N.E.2d 1201, 1205 (Ind. Ct. App. 2002) (sufficient control if "any reasonably probable causes for the injury were under the control of the defendant," driver need not be in control of the road condition as well as his vehicle); Mireles v. Broderick, 117 N.M. 445, 872 P.2d 863 (1994) ("the meaning of 'exclusive control' in res ipsa loquitur cases is fact specific within any given case"); Dalley v. Utah Valley Reg'l Med. Ctr., 791 P.2d 193 (Utah. 1990).

[120] See Potthast v. Metro-North R.R., 400 F.3d 143, 149 n.7 (2d Cir. 2005) (Calabresi, J.: "The meaning given to exclusive control in the cases, however, is anything but consistent with what the requirement, on its face, would seem to demand").

[121] Foster v. City of Keyser, 202 W.Va. 1, 501 S.E.2d 165 (1997) ("Rather than expound further glosses, caveats and corollaries upon our past formulations of res ipsa loquitur, we determine to make a more substantial change. . . ."; extended exploration of the problems with the control rule); cf. Kambat v. St. Francis Hosp., 89 N.Y.2d 489, 678 N.E.2d 456 (1997) (first requiring exclusive control but then restating the rule to say "It is enough that the evidence supporting the three conditions afford a rational basis for concluding that "it is more likely than not" that the injury was caused by defendant's negligence [A]ll that is required is that the likelihood of other possible causes of the injury "be so reduced that the greater probability lies at defendant's door," quoting 2 Harper and James, Torts § 19.7).

[122] Restatement Second of Torts § 328D(1)(b) (defendant's responsibility indicated when evidence sufficiently eliminates other responsible causes). See also Giles v. City of New Haven, 228 Conn. 441, 636 A.2d 1335 (1994) (quoting the Restatement Second and several other authorities); Bonilla v. University of Mont., 328 Mont. 41, 116 P.3d 823 (2005) (using the other responsible causes approach of Restatement Second but concluding that other causes had not been eliminated); Quinby v. Plumsteadville Family Practice, Inc., 589 Pa. 183, 907 A.2d 1061 (2006) (quoting and applying Restatement Second); Cruz v. DaimlerChrysler Motors Corp., 66 A.3d 446 (R.I. 2013) (expressly adopting Restatement Second).

[123] Restatement Third of Torts (Liability for Physical and Emotional Harm) § 17 (2010). For detailed discussion of formulations of the rule, see id. § 17 cmt. b. Cf. Morris v. Wal-Mart Stores, Inc., 330 F.3d 854 (6th Cir. 2003) ("Exclusive control is merely one fact which establishes the responsibility of the defendant; and if it

Control in cases of multiple actors. Res ipsa is not available unless the plaintiff can provide some kind of evidence to show that the particular defendant was one of the negligent actors. For example, if the plaintiff is injured in an unexplained collision between two moving motor vehicles, res ipsa loquitur will not normally apply.[124] The same is true whenever two or more persons, including the plaintiff herself, participate actively in other injury-causing events, such as a slip-and-fall[125] or a collision between two skiers.[126] When particular facts of the collision are in evidence, however, the case can be quite different. In collisions between moving vehicles, if the negligence of one driver can be excluded, the res ipsa inference may be allowed against the other. Although res ipsa loquitur does not ordinarily assist the plaintiff when two or more defendants are in control of the relevant instrumentality at different times, that is serial or consecutive control,[127] additional evidence may sometimes raise the probability that it was the defendant and not some other actor who was at fault.[128] In the classic exploding bottle case, the plaintiff showed that the bottle had not been mishandled or subjected to pressure or temperature change after it left the hands of the defendant bottler. That evidence, if accepted, eliminated negligence of the distributor and retailer, leaving a probability that the defendant and no one else was at fault.[129] In some cases of serial control, the evidence may even warrant the belief that both actors were negligent, the first in causing a defect and the second in failing to discover it.[130]

Due care requiring protection from other actors: public access cases. Since due care means that instruments made available for public access should be made and maintained in a condition safe for use by many people,[131] the fact that the public has access to them does not necessarily mean that the manufacturer, owner, or servicer is not negligent. A plaintiff who is injured when a chair provided by a place of business[132]

---

can be established otherwise, exclusive control is not essential to a res ipsa loquitur case," quoting from helpful Tennessee cases); Sides v. St. Anthony's Med. Ctr., 258 S.W.3d 811, 821 (Mo. 2008) ("Exclusive control is merely one fact which establishes the responsibility of the defendant; and if it can be established otherwise, exclusive control is not essential to a res ipsa loquitur case.").

[124] See Sheltra v. Rochefort, 667 A.2d 868 (Me. 1995).

[125] Brown v. Poway Unified Sch. Dist., 4 Cal.4th 820, 843 P.2d 624, 15 Cal.Rptr.2d 679 (1993) (slip and fall).

[126] E.g., Dillworth v. Gambardella, 970 F.2d 1113 (2d Cir. 1992).

[127] Novak Heating & Air Conditioning v. Carrier Corp., 622 N.W.2d 495 (Iowa 2001) (plaintiff's new goods arrived damaged after they had been in the hands of shipper and then carrier; held, res ipsa loquitur cannot apply to consecutive control cases).

[128] E.g., Schlanger v. Doe, 53 A.D.3d 827, 861 N.Y.S.2d 499 (2008) (glass shattered on first vehicle, causing following vehicle to take evasive maneuver which led to collision with another; res ipsa could apply against first vehicle operator).

[129] Escola v. Coca-Cola Bottling Co., 24 Cal.2d 453, 150 P.2d 436 (1944). Cf. Anderson v. Service Merchandise Co., Inc., 240 Neb. 873, 485 N.W.2d 170 (1992) (one who worked on lighting fixture earlier excluded not likely to be the person responsible for its fall much later, leaving operator of premises in "exclusive control").

[130] Collins v. Superior Air-Ground Ambulance Serv., Inc., 789 N.E.2d 394 (Ill. App. Ct. 2003). Cf. Brown v. Racquet Club of Bricktown, 95 N.J. 280, 471 A.2d 25 (1984).

[131] Trujeque v. Service Merchandise Co., 117 N.M. 388, 872 P.2d 361 (1994) (should be safe for any number of customers).

[132] Potthast v. Metro-North R.R., 400 F.3d 143, 149 n.7 (2d Cir. 2005) (chair provided by employer for use of many people collapsed, res ipsa loquitur can be applied); Brisbon v. Mount Sinai Hosp., 8 Misc.3d 47, 798 N.Y.S.2d 648 (App. Term. 2005) (defendant's handrail came off in plaintiff's hand, causing fall; although organizations outside defendant's control used the area, it was not open to the general public, so trier could still find that defendant was negligent rather than some vandal); contra Rivera-Emerling v. M. Fortunoff of Westbury Corp., 281 A.D.2d 215, 217, 721 N.Y.S.2d 653, 566 (2001) (chair collapsed with the plaintiff; held, res ipsa loquitur does not apply because "the chair was on an open sales floor to which innumerable shoppers had access. Hence, there was no basis for concluding that defendant had exclusive control of the chair.").

or a wheelchair provided by a hospital collapses,[133] an escalator or elevator malfunctions,[134] an automatic door closes on her,[135] or a public telephone shocks her,[136] may often be permitted to claim res ipsa loquitur negligence, so long as she can exclude herself as the probable cause of the injury. But again, it is a matter of assessing the probabilities in each case.

Special liabilities of multiple defendants. Although courts usually insist that res ipsa loquitur must be grounded in some kind of evidence rationally pointing to the defendant as the wrongdoer, there are several kinds of cases in which courts may impose liability upon defendants who are not likely to have been the wrongdoers. These include liability of several health care professionals engaged in surgery upon an anesthetized patient,[137] or of caretakers who exercise custody of a person unable to care for himself. Many theories have been advanced for accepting the captain of the ship doctrine, which makes the chief surgeon vicariously liable, in these cases.[138]

Commenting on caretaker-custodial cases. The just basis for liability of a hospital or surgeon for injury to a patient that may have been caused by any one of the health care team is grounded in the idea that those who accept custody of a person who is unable to care for himself are implicitly accepting responsibility to guarantee care, or at least to provide information about the causes of harm inflicted. In a sense this is a kind of strict liability, but it is rooted in the implicit terms of the parties' consensual arrangements.[139] The idea might appropriately extend to other custodial cases, such as those in which an institution cares for the infirm, and those in which day-care centers accept the care of very young children.

---

[133] Darrough v. Glendale Heights Cmty. Hosp., 234 Ill.App.3d 1055, 600 N.E.2d 1248, 175 Ill. Dec. 790 (1992). Similarly a chair on business premises open to the public. Trujeque v. Service Merchandise Co., 117 N.M. 388, 872 P.2d 361 (1994).

[134] E.g., Cox v. May Dep't Store Co., 183 Ariz. 361, 903 P.2d 1119 (Ct. App. 1995) (plaintiff's jacket caught in escalator handrail assembly); Rosenberg v. Otis Elevator Co., 366 N.J.Super. 292, 841 A.2d 99 (2003); Qualls v. United States Elevator Corp., 863 P.2d 457 (Okla. 1993) (automatic elevator fell from second floor to basement, res ipsa against installer-maintainer; control is in the person who "assumes responsibility for the fitness of an instrumentality").

[135] Brewster v. United States, 542 N.W.2d 524 (Iowa 1996).

[136] Seeley v. New York Tel. Co., 281 A.D. 285, 120 N.Y.S.2d 262 (1953).

[137] E.g., Dalley v. Utah Valley Reg'l Med. Ctr., 791 P.2d 193 (Utah 1990). Cf. Collins v. Superior Air-Ground Ambulance Serv., Inc., 338 Ill. App.3d 812, 789 N.E.2d 394 (2003) (bedridden nursing home resident of five days, unable to speak, was taken home suffering dehydration and broken leg; court's reasoning supported res ipsa loquitur against both ambulance service who transported resident and the nursing home); Ybarra v. Spangard, 25 Cal.2d 486, 154 P.2d 687 (1944). Judge Calabresi has given special emphasis to the defendant's superior knowledge as a ground or at least a factor in the decision to apply res ipsa loquitur. See Williams v. KFC Nat'l Mgmt. Co, 391 F.3d 411 (2d Cir. 2004) (Calabresi, J., concurring).

[138] For a fuller discussion of joint actors cases and superior knowledge as a rationale in res ipsa loquitor see 1 Dobbs, Hayden & Bublick, The Law of Torts § 174 (2d. ed. 2011 & Supp.).

[139] Seavey long ago noted the close analogy to the bailment rule that when a bailee cannot return the bailed chattel in good condition, the burden shifts to the bailee to explain the loss or damage. Warren A. Seavey, Res Ipsa Loquitur: Tabula in Naufragio, 63 Harv. L. Rev. 643, 647 (1950). The idea is now so strongly associated with res ipsa that the bailment rule itself may be explained as a res ipsa rule. E.g., Kinder v. Fantasy Coachworks, Ltd., 762 S.W.2d 533 (Mo. Ct. App. 1988).

Chapter 14

ACTUAL HARM & FACTUAL CAUSE

Analysis

A. ACTUAL HARM

§ 14.1   The Requirement of Actual Harm

B. THE FACTUAL CAUSE REQUIREMENT

§ 14.2   Factual Cause and Four Forms of Common Issues

§ 14.3   Terminology and Structure: Factual Cause and Scope of Liability (Proximate Cause)

C. THE BUT-FOR TEST OF CAUSATION

§ 14.4   The But-For Test of Factual Cause

§ 14.5   But-For Analysis and the Hypothetical Alternative Case

D. PROBLEMS WITH AND ALTERNATIVES TO
THE BUT-FOR TEST

§ 14.6   Alternate Tests When But-For Analysis Fails: The Substantial Factor Test and Tests Aggregating Conduct

E. PROVING CAUSATION

§ 14.7   Connecting Negligence and Harm

§ 14.8   Evidence and Inferences of But-For Causation

F. PROVING WHICH DEFENDANT'S NEGLIGENCE
CAUSED HARM

§ 14.9   Alternative Causes and the Shifted Burden of Proof

§ 14.10   Statistical Substitutes for Causation: Market Share Liability

G. SPECIAL PROBLEMS: WHAT HARM WAS CAUSED?

§ 14.11   The Lost Chance of Recovery

A. ACTUAL HARM

§ 14.1 The Requirement of Actual Harm

Damages required. In a negligence action, the plaintiff is required to prove that the defendant's conduct caused legally recognized damages. In part, this statement means that damages are not presumed as they are in the case of some intentional torts; the plaintiff who is not harmed by negligence cannot recover even nominal damages.[1] Physical harm satisfies the actual harm requirement. According to the Restatement Third, physical harm means "the physical impairment of the human body ('bodily harm') or of real property or tangible personal property ('property damage')."[2] In turn, bodily harm is defined to include "physical injury, illness, disease, impairment of bodily

---

[1]   E.g., Right v. Breen, 277 Conn. 364, 890 A.2d 1287 (2006); Ponder v. Angel Animal Hosp., Inc., 762 S.W.2d 846 (Mo. Ct. App. 1988) (negligent castration of dog not actionable because castration did not affect dog's market value and actual damages are required to sustain negligence action).

[2]   Restatement Third of Torts (Liability for Physical and Emotional Harm) § 4 (2010).

function, and death."[3] Under these definitions, a scratch, whether to the plaintiff's arm or the paint on her car, satisfy the actual harm requirement. The amount of damage does not matter. Any detrimental change in the physical condition of a person's body or property will do.[4] However, the plaintiff will not recover for bodily changes that do not count as harm by way of pain or some detriment,[5] and when bodily changes or damage cannot be shown.[6]

Non-physical harms. When a plaintiff suffers physical harm to person or property, negligence recovery is appropriate. A number of cases question whether negligence that causes solely emotional or economic harm will support liability. In a number of cases the question is whether bodily changes, not physically harmful in themselves, such as plural thickening from exposure to asbestos, ground a claim for emotional harm.[7] Often, as we will see in later chapters, negligence that causes stand-alone emotional harm or pure economic loss is governed by special rules.

B. THE FACTUAL CAUSE REQUIREMENT

§ 14.2 Factual Cause and Four Forms of Common Issues

Defendant's negligence as the factual cause of plaintiff's damages. The statement that defendant's conduct caused damages means that the plaintiff must prove not merely that she suffered harm sometime after the defendant's negligent act occurred but also that the harm was caused in fact by the defendant's conduct,[8] and that the harm was caused by that part of the defendant's conduct that created unreasonable risks—the defendant's negligence.[9] As with other factual matters, the plaintiff ordinarily has the

---

[3]   Id.

[4]   Id. § 4 cmt. b.

[5]   For bodily changes without pain or other obvious detriment courts appear to have different approaches. Searfoss v. Johnson & Johnson Co., 2004 WL 792789 (Pa. Super. Ct. 2004) (denying recovery where the defendant's drug caused plaintiffs' hearts to have a longer QT or "reset time" for the next heartbeat, but caused neither pain nor symptoms nor permanent harm). But cf. Dailey v. Methodist Med. Ctr., 790 So.2d 903 (Miss. Ct. App. 2001) (the defendant administered a labor inducing drug to a male cancer patient, perhaps with resulting change in blood pressure or heart rate; the court may have rejected the argument that these changes did not constitute injury).

[6]   America v. Sunspray Condo. Ass'n, 61 A.3d 1249 (Me. 2013) (failure to enforce smoking ban; plaintiff failed to allege a legally cognizable injury); Schuman v. Greenbelt Homes, Inc., 69 A.3d 512 (Md. Ct. Spec. App. 2013) (plaintiff failed to establish that secondhand smoke coming from neighbor's patio caused him any harm).

[7]   Exposure that causes detrimental bodily changes has been allowed to serve as the basis for a number of emotional distress claims. See Plummer v. United States, 580 F.2d 72 (3d Cir. 1978) (prisoner was infected with tuberculosis but not suffering from it; since tubercle bacilli were actually in his body the court found sufficient impact to permit an emotional distress claim based on the fear that it would be activated in the future); Herber v. Johns-Manville Corp., 785 F.2d 79 (3d Cir. 1986) (pleural thickening from asbestos exposure that had caused no damage plus anxiety over his fear of developing cancer; pleural thickening would count as an impact that would permit recovery of emotional distress damages based on fear of cancer); but see, Simmons v. Pacor, Inc., 543 Pa. 664, 674 A.2d 232 (1996) (pleural thickening was not "injury" that supports an emotional distress claim). See also James A. Henderson & Aaron D. Twerski, Asbestos Litigation Gone Mad: Exposure-Based Recovery of Increased Risk, Mental Distress, and Medical Monitoring, 53 S.C. L. Rev. 815 (2002). The claim of physical impact grounding an emotional distress claim is weaker when the claim is merely one of exposure to a harmful substance without bodily change. Metro-North Commuter R.R. Co. v. Buckley, 521 U.S. 424, 117 S.Ct. 2113, 138 L.Ed.2d 560 (1997) (mere exposure to asbestos was not harm in itself that would support an emotional distress claim).

[8]   Restatement Third of Torts (Liability for Physical and Emotional Harm) § 26 (2010). For a discussion of the Restatement Reporters' rationale for the causation requirements, see Michael D. Green, Flying Trampolines and Falling Bookcases: Understanding the Restatement of Torts, 37 Wm. Mitchell L. Rev. 1011 (2011).

[9]   Most discussions appear to test cause in fact by asking whether the negligent portion of the conduct was a cause of the harm. See Restatement Third of Torts (Liability for Physical and Emotional Harm) § 26

burden of proof and persuasion and hence must prove that the defendant's negligence was more probably than not the cause of the harm suffered.[10]

Four forms of causation issues. The factual cause requirement is usually viewed as a straightforward issue: did he or didn't he cause harm to the plaintiff? That issue manifests itself for lawyers, however, in at least four distinct forms.

Type 1 causation problem: scientific connection. One kind of factual cause problem centers on scientific doubt, or at least on lay ignorance about the connection between the defendant's acts and the plaintiff's injury. Suppose the plaintiff gets skin cancer after she is in an auto accident.[11] Or that she is born with a birth defect after her mother ingested the defendant's drug during her pregnancy.[12] In such cases the plaintiff must present evidence to prove that auto accidents can cause skin cancer or that the defendant's drug can cause birth defects.

Ability to cause harm generally and to plaintiff. The first question raised in such cases is thus whether the putative source of harm is in fact capable of causing such harm. If the defendant's conduct or product could not cause the harm claimed, perhaps liability should be excluded. The ground stated could be that the defendant was not negligent or that the harm was outside the scope of the risk created by the defendant. However, the usual approach now treats this problem as one of causation. Courts say that when the defendant's conduct is incapable of causing the harm claimed by the plaintiff, the plaintiff has failed to prove general or generic causation.[13] Although such general causation is necessary to the plaintiff's case, it is not sufficient; the plaintiff must then go further and present evidence that causation is not merely scientifically possible, but that it existed in her particular case.[14] For example, a plaintiff claiming harm from a prescription drug must show both that the drug was capable of causing the condition and that the plaintiff suffered from that condition.[15] Likewise, if science can establish causation only when a given fact or condition is present, the plaintiff must establish the existence of that fact or condition.[16]

---

cmt. g (2010) (noting that there may be a dispute "about whether the *tortious aspect* of the actor's conduct was a cause of the harm") (emphasis supplied).

[10]   E.g., Ortega v. K-Mart Corp., 26 Cal.4th 1200, 1205, 36 P.3d 11, 15, 114 Cal.Rptr.2d 470, 475 (2001); Lough v. BNSF Ry. Co., 988 N.E.2d 1090 (Ill. App. Ct. 2013) (affirming summary judgment for defendant where plaintiff failed to produce evidence that an automobile accident caused or aggravated medical conditions that caused the driver's death 22 months later). See Restatement Third of Torts (Liability for Physical and Emotional Harm) § 28 cmt. a (2010) ("preponderance" or greater weight of evidence).

[11]   See Kramer Serv., Inc. v. Wilkins, 184 Miss. 483, 186 So. 625 (1939).

[12]   See, e.g., Turpin v. Merrell Dow Pharms., Inc., 959 F.2d 1349 (6th Cir. 1992).

[13]   In re Hanford Nuclear Reservation Litig., 292 F.3d 1124 (9th Cir. 2002), discusses a number of cases using the term.

[14]   See Green v. Alpharma, 284 S.W.3d 29 (Ark. 2008) (genuine issue of material fact whether exposure to arsenic-laced chicken litter from poultry producer caused child to contract leukemia); Merck & Co., Inc. v. Garza, 347 S.W.3d 256, Prod. Liab. Rep. (CCH) P 18692 (Tex. 2011) (in products liability suit alleging harm from prescription drug Vioxx, "when parties attempt to prove general causation using epidemiological evidence, a threshold requirement of reliability is that the evidence demonstrate a statistically significant doubling of the risk"; the plaintiff must also show that he or she is similar to the subjects in the studies, and that other plausible causes are excluded with reasonable certainty).

[15]   Ranes v. Adams Lab., Inc., 778 N.W.2d 677 (Iowa 2010) (prescription drug consumer failed to establish that the drug Phenylpropanolamine caused vasculitis, or that plaintiff suffered from vasculitis).

[16]   See Perkins v. Entergy Corp., 782 So.2d 606 (La. 2001) (electrical shutdown for which defendants were responsible could have loosened particles in oxygen piping system, leading to explosion and injury, but no evidence showed that particles were in fact loosened by the shutdown). In some cases, however, it may be possible to infer the existence of the necessary fact or condition (such as loosened particles in Perkins) by proving that other potential causes were improbable.

Factual determinations. These causal issues raise questions of fact in the scientific sense. On causal issues of this type, rules of law describe the issue or dictate the evidence needed to address the issues, but the causal issue itself is resolved by determinations of fact, not rules of law.

Issues within common experience. Evidence needed on the question of scientific causation varies with the facts. Sometimes the causal issue is so much within common experience that no testimony is required at all. For example, experience shows that impacts can cause bruises, broken bones, painful muscles, and ruptured organs, so we can readily believe that your fall caused the bruise on your arm.[17] Similarly, a court may not require expert testimony to prove that blasting nearby could cause the cracks or damage to your home a short time later.[18] In these situations, common knowledge and experience suffice to permit the trier to infer a causal relationship between tort and injury.

Scientific evidence. However, when the causation issue is not within ordinary understanding and experience, the question of whether the defendant's conduct *could* cause the plaintiff's harm is resolved by scientific or medical evidence.[19] For example, whether a rise in a patient's sodium levels over a certain period of time can cause a serious medical problem is not a matter within usual experience and thus requires expert testimony.[20] In addition, if symptoms differ materially from the symptoms expected from impact or they appear long after the impact, expert testimony may be required.[21] When expert testimony is required, often the focus will be on the admissibility and sufficiency of the evidence.[22]

---

[17] See Choi v. Anvil, 32 P.3d 1 (Alaska 2001) (no expert testimony required where injury is within common experience or knowledge of jurors—pains following auto collision); Ross v. Housing Auth. of Baltimore City, 63 A.3d 1 (Md. Ct. Spec. App. 2013) (childhood exposure to lead paint); Berten v. Pierce, 818 S.W.2d 685 (Mo. Ct. App. 1991) (back pain following auto-pig collision); State Farm Mut. Auto. Ins. Co. v. Lucas, 2001 WL 802195 (Ohio Ct. App. 2001) (neck pain immediately following accident); Alder v. Bayer Corp., AGFA Div., 61 P.3d 1068 (Utah 2002) (where exposure to substance risks the injury plaintiff suffered, close temporal connection between exposure and symptoms can be compelling).

[18] Dyer v. Maine Drilling & Blasting, Inc., 984 A.2d 210 (Me. 2009) ("A fact-finder could infer that these significant changes [to the home's condition], observed over a short period of time in a home over seventy-years-old, were not likely to have been caused by normal settling.").

[19] Cowart v. Widener, 697 S.E.2d 779 (Ga. 2010). Where causation depends upon medical or technical matters outside the usual knowledge of the trier, and where it is required but not produced, the court may hold that causal proof fails as a matter of law. See Randall v. Benton, 802 A.2d 1211 (N.H. 2002) (evidence insufficient to show that, had psychiatrist complied with standard of care, decedent's suicide would have been prevented). The difficulties of producing acceptable evidence in complex, toxic tort cases, can be substantial. Consequently, it has been suggested that as a matter of policy some relief from the burden would be appropriate in special cases. See Margaret A. Berger, Eliminating General Causation: Notes Towards a New Theory of Justice and Toxic Torts, 97 Colum. L. Rev. 2117 (1997). On the proof required in such cases, see Restatement Third of Torts (Liability for Physical and Emotional Harm) § 28 cmt. c (2010).

[20] Harrison v. Binnion, 214 P.3d 631 (Idaho 2009).

[21] Turner v. Davis, 699 N.E.2d 1217 (Ind. Ct. App. 1998) (after auto accident, plaintiff would often fall asleep and was fired from her job for this reason; close temporal connection of impact and symptoms insufficient); Clarke v. Martucci, 289 A.D.2d 816, 734 N.Y.S.2d 364 (2001) (symptoms delayed); Darnell v. Eastman, 23 Ohio St.2d 13, 261 N.E.2d 114 (1970) (symptoms delayed).

[22] See, e.g., Coombs v. Curnow, 219 P.3d 453 (Idaho 2010) (doctor's expert testimony about cause of child's death from long-term high-dose of sedation was sufficiently reliable to sustain the jury's verdict in medical malpractice action); Ranes v. Adams Lab., Inc., 778 N.W.2d 677 (Iowa 2010) (analyzing expert testimony that prescription drug was responsible for plaintiff's stroke or other physical ailments); Goudrealt v. Kleeman, 965 A.2d 1040 (N.H. 2009) (finding sufficient foundation for expert testimony that surgeon more likely than not caused at least one vascular injury); Gonzalez v. Poplawsky, 2001 WL 984836 (Tex. App. 2001) (disregarding a physician's testimony on causation because it was based upon experience, not on peer reviewed studies). See Fed. R. Evid. 702.

Type 2 causation problem: who or what is a cause of the harm? Another kind of factual cause problem occurs when the plaintiff is definitely injured by someone or something but cannot produce evidence to indicate which person among many was the injurer. In an old New York case, the plaintiff contracted typhoid after exposure to contaminated water for which the defendant was responsible. There were many other sources of typhoid, including the common house fly and infected vegetables. So to show causation, the plaintiff needed evidence to show that the water was more probably the source of the disease than other things. Although medical or scientific evidence is important as background in this kind of case, the critical facts are likely to be more mundane. The plaintiff's repeated drinking of the contaminated water over a period of time no doubt counted heavily in favor of a finding that the water and not some fresh vegetable caused the typhoid.[23] The same is true in modern toxic tort cases. If the plaintiff gets cancer after working around asbestos for many years, the court may have no doubt that asbestos caused the cancer. However, to hold a particular producer of asbestos liable, the plaintiff must prove exposure to that company's asbestos. If she fails, she has not proved that that company was a factual cause of her harm,[24] though there are sometimes special rules to aid the plaintiff.

Type 3 causation problem: would safe behavior have avoided injury? A third kind of factual cause problem is one that generates much academic writing. It cannot be resolved by medical or scientific evidence or by proving which of several defendants was the author of the plaintiff's harm. Suppose the defendant does not check his rear view mirror before backing up and in consequence he backs over a child squatting behind the car. The defendant is negligent—he should have checked the mirror—but the critical point for a factual cause argument is that he would not have avoided the injury by checking the mirror, since that would not have revealed the squatting child. Courts say in this kind of case that the defendant's negligence was not a factual cause of the harm and that he therefore is not liable.[25]

As later sections will indicate, this kind of factual cause question turns heavily upon estimates about what would have happened if the defendant had behaved more carefully and upon the legal tests or standards for judging causation. It is this particular kind of factual cause problem that has led many serious thinkers to penetrating and puzzling analyses.[26]

Type 4 causation problem: what harm was caused? A final factual cause problem is to determine what harm was caused by the defendant's negligent conduct. In some instances it is appropriate to apportion harm to causes, that is, to hold a defendant liable

---

[23]   Stubbs v. City of Rochester, 226 N.Y. 516, 124 N.E. 137 (1919).

[24]   See e.g., Claytor v. Owens-Corning Fiberglas Corp., 662 A.2d 1374 (D.C. 1995); Nolan v. Weil-McLain, 910 N.E.2d 549 (Ill. 2009) (holding that manufacturer of asbestos-containing boilers should have been permitted to admit evidence of worker's exposure to asbestos from other sources); cf. City of St. Louis v. Benjamin Moore & Co., 226 S.W.3d 110 (Mo. 2007) (rejecting liability in lead paint litigation where plaintiff could not identify particular defendant whose paint caused harm).

[25]   The illustrative case and many like it could be analyzed as a scope of risk problem; the risk the defendant negligently created by failure to check his mirror only included the risk he could have discovered by looking.

[26]   E.g., Richard Epstein, A Theory of Strict Liability, 2 J. Leg. Stud. 151 (1973), reprinted in Richard Epstein, A Theory of Strict Liability (1980); Wex Malone, Ruminations on Cause-in-Fact, 9 Stan. L. Rev. 60 (1956), reprinted in Wex Malone, Essays on Torts 160 (1986); Robert N. Strassfeld, If . . . : Counterfactuals in the Law, 60 Geo. Wash. L. Rev. 339 (1992); Richard Wright, Causation in Tort Law, 73 Cal. L. Rev. 1735 (1985); Symposium on Causation in the Law of Torts, 63 Chi.-Kent L. Rev. 397 (1987); Arno Becht & Frank Miller, The Test of Factual Causation (1961).

for a portion of the plaintiff's harm but not all of it. That is most obviously the case when one defendant breaks the plaintiff's arm and another defendant, acting independently, breaks the plaintiff's leg. Apportionment problems turn both on proof of facts—who caused what?—and also on several kinds of legal policy.[27]

§ 14.3 Terminology and Structure: Factual Cause and Scope of Liability (Proximate Cause)

Causation and scope of liability. Long but confusing legal tradition has assigned the term "causation" to two entirely different kinds of legal problems. The first issue is about causation in the sense that term is used in everyday speech: Did the defendant's negligent conduct cause the plaintiff's harm or not? This is the factual cause inquiry. The second issue is about the appropriate scope of the defendant's legal liability for negligent conduct that has in fact caused harm. This scope of liability issue often turns on whether the kind of harm the plaintiff suffered was the same kind the defendant risked by his negligence.

Proximate cause as a reference to both issues. Courts often lump these two distinct issues together under the rubric of "proximate cause."[28] However, even courts that call the two issues by the same name recognize that the issues are quite different from each other and turn on quite different kinds of analysis. Consequently, courts that use a single term are quick to say that proximate cause questions are composed of both factual cause and scope of liability issues.[29]

Factual cause and proximate cause terminology. To avoid confusion, the Third Restatement of Torts deliberately adopts two distinct terms—"factual cause" and "scope of liability"—to more accurately describe the separate issues addressed by these terms.[30] This chapter also employs the terms factual cause and scope of liability. However, given prior professional usage of varied terms, at times quotations or summaries in the chapter refer to the factual cause issue as an issue of "actual cause" or "cause in fact." Similarly, at times the scope of liability issue is referred to in case quotations or summaries as an issue of "proximate cause" or "legal cause."

Factual cause and scope of liability principles. Because factual cause and scope of liability represent different legal concerns and are tested by adverting to different legal rules, it is highly important to illustrate their difference, if only in a preliminary way.[31]

An example of factual cause. Suppose the question is: did Donnie break Margaret's leg when he negligently ran into her, or was her leg already broken? That is one form of a question about the existence of causation; was Donnie's conduct a factual cause of the

---

[27] See Chapter 35.

[28] Fedorczyk v. Caribbean Cruise Lines, Ltd., 82 F.3d 69 (3d Cir. 1996) ("Courts have often conflated cause in fact and legal causation into proximate cause, but the two are conceptually distinct.").

[29] See, e.g., Thompson v. Kaczinski, 774 N.W.2d 829 (Iowa 2009) (noting that "causation has two components: cause in fact and legal cause"); Hertog v. City of Seattle, 138 Wash.2d 265, 979 P.2d 400 (1999) ("proximate cause . . . consists of cause in fact and legal causation").

[30] Restatement Third of Torts (Liability for Physical and Emotional Harm) § 26 cmt. a, and ch. 6 Special Note on Proximate Cause (2010).

[31] The different nature of the two inquiries is thoughtfully addressed in Berte v. Bode, 692 N.W.2d 368 (Iowa 2005). For a helpful discussion of the relationship between scope of liability and factual cause see Hale v. Ostrow, 166 S.W.3d 713 (Tenn. 2005); Restatement Third of Torts (Liability for Physical and Emotional Harm) § 29 cmt. f (2010).

harm? The existence of cause—the factual cause question—is often tested by asking whether, but for the defendant's conduct, the injury would have been avoided.

An example of scope of liability (proximate cause). Now suppose that the question turns on different facts: Dennis negligently left tainted meat in his refrigerator. A thief took the meat and sold it to Penny, who ate it and became ill. Should Dennis be liable for his negligence? That is not a question about the *existence* of causation, for Dennis' conduct surely is one of the factual causes of Penny's harm. We can see that by asking whether Penny would have been harmed if Dennis had properly disposed of the meat. Penny would not have been, so Dennis' conduct is one factual cause. The question whether Dennis should escape liability, then, is about the appropriate scope of Dennis' liability, whether Dennis' conduct is important enough to justify imposing liability. Or you could say it is about the legal *significance* of causation, rather than the existence of causation. This kind of question is usually tested by asking whether the general type of harm, or sometimes the intervening force that brought it about, was foreseeable.

Factual cause as one element of the prima facie case. The chief reason to mention the scope of liability or proximate cause issue in a chapter on factual cause is that in judging factual cause issues, it is important to understand that a finding of factual causation does not determine liability. The plaintiff must not only prove negligence, harm and factual causation but also must persuade the judge and jury that liability is morally and practically justified under scope of liability doctrines. Whenever this point is forgotten, the tendency is to build moral and practical judgments into the factual cause question. Those judgments are important, but the law has separate places for them, namely, in the scope of liability issue. The factual cause question is difficult enough without importing difficulties from the scope of liability/proximate cause analysis.

C. THE BUT-FOR TEST OF CAUSATION

§ 14.4   The But-For Test of Factual Cause

The but-for test. In the great mass of cases, courts apply a but-for test to determine whether the defendant's conduct was a factual cause of the plaintiff's harm,[32] although there are some important exceptions.[33] Under the but-for test, the defendant's conduct is a factual cause of the plaintiff's harm if, but-for the defendant's conduct, that harm would not have occurred.[34] The but-for test also implies a negative. If the plaintiff would have suffered the same harm had the defendant not acted negligently, the defendant's conduct is not a factual cause of the harm.[35] The but-for test requires the plaintiff to persuade the trier that different, non-negligent conduct by the defendant would have avoided harm to the plaintiff. For convenience, all the rule statements and illustrations in this chapter address only the defendant's conduct as a factual cause. However, the causal rules are generally the same for fault of the plaintiff.

---

[32]   See, e.g., Garr v. City of Ottumwa, 846 N.W.2d 865 (Iowa 2014) (city's negligence not a but-for cause of plaintiff's harm); Columbia Med. Ctr. of Las Colinas, Inc. v. Hogue, 271 S.W.3d 238 (Tex. 2009) (holding that patient's failure to inform physician of his prior heart murmur had not been proved by sufficient evidence to have been a cause of his delayed diagnosis and treatment).

[33]   See §§ 14.6 to 14.11.

[34]   E.g., Robinson v. Washington Metro. Transit Auth., 774 F.3d 33 (D.C. Cir. 2014); Friedrich v. Fetterman & Assocs., P.A., 137 S.3d 362 (Fla. 2013); Berte v. Bode, 692 N.W.2d 368 (Iowa 2005); Restatement Third of Torts (Liability for Physical and Emotional Harm) § 26 (2010).

[35]   Akin, Gump, Strauss, Hauer & Feld, LLP v. National Dev. & Research Corp., 299 S.W.3d 106 (Tex. 2010).

Meeting the but-for test. In most cases, causation seems obvious and presents no obstacle to the plaintiff. The defendant negligently crashes his airplane into the plaintiff's apartment. The defendant's conduct is a but-for cause of the harm done to the apartment; but-for his negligent piloting, the apartment would have remained standing. Many cases provide a similarly straightforward application of the but-for test.[36]

Failing the but-for test. In a number of cases, however, the but-for test of factual cause puts the plaintiff out of court, even though the defendant is clearly negligent. For example, suppose a sailor fell overboard and sank like a stone. The ship carried a defective lifeboat and the rescue attempt was futile. But even a good lifeboat would have been of no assistance because the sailor was lost immediately.[37] The defective lifeboat was not a but-for cause of the plaintiff's harm. Although it would be possible for courts to look at these cases in other ways,[38] many such cases are resolved on factual cause/but-for grounds, which may be the most straightforward analysis.[39]

Multiple causes under the but-for rule. It is by no means true that the but-for test reduces everything to a single cause.[40] As courts make clear, "It is not necessary that the defendants' act be the *sole* cause of the plaintiff's injury, only that it be *a* cause."[41] In fact, there are always many causes that meet the but-for test, some represented by negligent conduct, some not. A negligently fells a tree; to get around it, B walks out into the street; C, driving a car, hits his brake to avoid running into B; D, a passenger, is thrown into the windshield. As a pure matter of factual cause the conduct of A, B, and C are all factual causes of D's harm. Without A's conduct, none of this would have occurred and the same can be said of the conduct of the others. If A or C escape liability, it will not be on the ground that they are not factual causes.[42] The but-for test shows that they are all factual causes, and if liability is avoided, it will be on an entirely different ground. However, a special problem arises with a subset of multiple cause cases discussed later.

---

[36] See, e.g., City of Jackson v. Spann, 4 So.3d 1029 (Miss. 2009) (substantial evidence supported conclusion that officers' high speed pursuit into intersection was but-for cause of accident).

[37] Ford v. Trident Fisheries Co., 232 Mass. 400, 122 N.E. 389 (1919). However, rescue at sea cases now show a different spirit, demanding that the vessel maximize the sailor's chances and holding it liable for failure to do so. See § 14.11. Cf. Jordan v. Jordan, 220 Va. 160, 257 S.E.2d 761 (1979) (plaintiff was squatting behind a car, if the defendant had looked in the rear-view mirror he would not have seen him; no actual cause).

[38] An alternative analysis is to say that the defendant's *conduct* considered overall is a factual cause of the plaintiff's harm but that the defendant may escape liability because the harm was outside the scope of the risk negligently created by the defendant. On details of the debate see E. Wayne Thode, The Indefensible Use of the Hypothetical Case to Determine Cause in Fact, 46 Tex. L. Rev. 423 (1968); James Henderson, A Defense of the Use of the Hypothetical Case to Resolve the Causation Issue, 47 Tex. L. Rev. 183 (1969); E. Wayne Thode, A Reply to the Defense, 47 Tex. L. Rev. 1344 (1969).

[39] See, e.g., Harrison v. Binnion, 214 P.3d 631 (Idaho 2009) (even if ER doctor had communicated seriousness of patient's condition, attending doctor would not have done anything differently or would have slightly decreased rate of sodium replacement which might not have made any difference); Kovach v. Caligor Midwest, 913 N.E.2d 193 (Ind. 2009) (even if medicine cup had been designed for more precise measurement, overdose of pain medication to child was not caused by imprecise measurement of medication but by erroneous double dosage).

[40] See, e.g., Parnell v. Peak Oilfield Serv. Co., 174 P.3d 757 (Alaska 2008) (holding that two drivers who simultaneously struck moose whose carcass lay in the road and posed hazard to plaintiff could both have been actual causes of the plaintiff's harm and overturning jury instruction that implied "only one actor could have legally created the hazard"); Spann v. Shuqualak Lumber Co., Inc., 990 So.2d 186 (Miss. 2008) (holding there was a genuine issue of material fact as to whether fog from emissions of lumber drying plant was a cause in fact of a two car collision).

[41] Hale v. Ostrow, 166 S.W.3d 713, 718 (Tenn. 2005) (emphasis in original).

[42] For an incredibly thoughtful discussion of multiple cause cases see Jane Stapleton, Unnecessary Causes, 129 LQR 39 (2013) (endorsing an actual cause finding with both but-for cause and when the negligence made a "positive contribution" to the mechanism by which the harm came about).

§ 14.5 But-For Analysis and the Hypothetical Alternative Case

Comparison with a hypothetical alternative. The but-for test of causation can be applied only by comparing what actually happened with a hypothetical alternative. What would have happened if the defendant had *not* been negligent? Would the plaintiff have been injured in the same way in that case? If so, then the defendant's negligent conduct is not a factual cause of the harm.

Difficulty with the approach. One difficulty with the but-for test is that it requires the judge to imagine an alternative set of events that never occurred.[43] Consequently, any comparison of the hypothetical to the events that actually occurred is only a construction of the intellect and often a speculative one at that, not a fact at all. It is nonetheless a construction required by the rule.

The relevant counterfactual. The relevant counterfactual is what would have happened had the defendant not acted negligently. The counterfactual is not whether defendant's conduct could have been non-negligent under different circumstances. In *Cabral v. Ralphs Grocery Co.*,[44] the driver of a car died in a rear-end collision with a parked tractor-trailer driven by Horn, an employee of the defendant. The decedent's wife sued for negligence, and a jury found for the plaintiff, albeit with a reduction for decedent's comparative negligence. On appeal, the defendant claimed that Horn's negligent act in parking the rig on the side of the road could not be a factual cause of harm, "because the same collision would have occurred had Horn stopped for emergency rather than personal reasons." The court disagreed with this reasoning: "The negligent conduct plaintiff claimed caused her husband's death was Horn's stopping his tractor-trailer rig at the site. The counterfactual question relevant to but-for causation, therefore, is what would have happened if Horn had not stopped his tractor-trailer rig there, not what would have happened if Horn had had a better reason to stop. . . . [S]topping by the side of a freeway for an emergency might be just as dangerous to other motorists as stopping for a snack, but an emergency stop will not create liability because it is justified. While potential liability differs in the two situations (emergency and non-emergency), causation does not."[45]

Answering the hypothetical question: the Salinetro *case.* In *Salinetro v. Nystrom*,[46] the plaintiff, who had been in an automobile accident, presented herself to the doctor for x-rays of her lower back and abdomen. According to the plaintiff, the doctor negligently failed to ask whether she was pregnant. Later, learning that x-rays might have injured her fetus, she terminated her pregnancy and brought suit for negligence. The factual cause problem arose because at the time the x-rays were taken, the plaintiff did not know she was pregnant. So the court thought it knew what the hypothetical alternative scenario would have been. It thought that the doctor would have asked the plaintiff "Are you pregnant?" and she would have said "No." That meant the x-rays would have been taken anyway, with the same result. So in the court's view, the doctor's negligent failure to ask was not a but-for cause of the harm.

Other possible views of the negligent act. If the court was right in its vision of the hypothetical alternative, then the *Salinetro* decision is right. But its imagined

---

43 See Note, Torts—Medical Malpractice—Rejection of "But for" Test, 45 N.C. L. Rev. 799, 804 (1967) ("We might as well ask what an elephant would have been if it had not been an elephant").

44 Cabral v. Ralphs Grocery Co., 51 Cal.4th 764, 122 Cal.Rptr. 3d 313, 248 P.3d 1170 (2011).

45 Id.

46 Salinetro v. Nystrom, 341 So.2d 1059 (Fla. Dist. Ct. App. 1977).

alternative is not the only plausible one for two kinds of reasons. First, the doctor could have avoided negligent conduct in quite a number of ways. For instance, he might have posted signs or handed patients an explanatory pamphlet, or insisted on a pregnancy test, or an accurate record of menstrual periods. Some of those alternative methods of avoiding negligence would probably have led the patient to avoid the x-rays and the loss of her child.

Other possible answers to the doctor's question. Second, even if the doctor had merely asked "Are you pregnant," the plaintiff herself might not have responded as the court imagined she would, by saying she was not.[47] She might have said instead "does it matter?"—which in turn might have led her to get full information and to have a pregnancy test before having the x-rays. It is not hard to imagine a patient who is ignorant of the dangers of x-rays or too trusting of doctors, but who would be alert to avoid harm to her fetus if only she is asked the pregnancy question. The truth is that no one knows what would have happened in the imagined world without the defendant's negligence.

Concerns about speculation. The *Salinetro* case is only one of many cases in which the factual cause determination must be made on the basis of speculation about whether the injury really could have been avoided if the defendant had not been negligent.[48] This speculation and other difficulties with the but-for test have led many writers to struggle for greater clarity,[49] to say that the test only works well when causation is so clear that no test is needed anyway, to urge abolition of the test altogether,[50] or to work from models or paradigms rather than from rules.[51] Still, the test is widely used in the United States and abroad.[52] But while the test is well accepted by courts, they have often found ways to alleviate the plaintiff's difficulty with the but-for rule in special cases and lawyers have some strategies available to adapt the but-for rule by changing their view of the negligence or the harm it caused.

---

[47] The plaintiff made it easy for the court to select its particular alternative because she herself said she would have told the doctor she was not. That testimony should not preclude careful lawyers from arguing that further information was still possible along the lines suggested in the text.

[48] See, e.g., Israel v. Barnwell, 1996 WL 365413 (Conn. Super. Ct. 1996); Sweeney v. Bettendorf, 762 N.W.2d 873 (Iowa 2009) (holding that evidence was not sufficient to conclude that had city provided appropriate number of adults to supervise children at baseball game, supervising adult would have been able to block flying bat that hit child spectator); Thompson v. Tuggle, 486 So.2d 144 (La. Ct. App. 1986) (no witnesses saw the chain saw sever decedent's jugular; did the saw kickback or did decedent fall on it? Would a different design have avoided the kickback?). Imprecision may have the same effect. Cf. Harvey v. Washington, 95 S.W.3d 93 (Mo. 2003) (seemingly implying that a negligent failure by Dr. A to advocate kidney dialysis would not have affected Dr. B's decision to delay dialysis because Doctor B knew of the facts and the need for the treatment, but not actually discussing whether advocacy would have induced Dr. B to proceed sooner with dialysis, which is the but-for question).

[49] See Arno Becht & Frank Miller, The Test of Factual Causation (1961).

[50] See Leon Green, The Causal Relation Issue in Negligence Law, 60 Mich. L. Rev. 543 (1962) (the cause questions asks for judgment that has no component parts).

[51] See Richard Epstein, A Theory of Strict Liability, 2 J. Leg. Stud. 151 (1973).

[52] Edwin Peel & James Goudkamp, Winfield and Jolowicz on Tort 7–007 (2014) ("most generally mentioned by the courts is the so-called "but-for" test, or in Latin, causa (or condition) sine qua non"). See also Ken Oliphant, Uncertain Factual Causation in the Restatement Third: Some Comparative Notes, 37 Wm. Mitchell L. Rev. 1599 (2011) (comparing the Restatement Third causation standards with causation standards used in European countries).

D. PROBLEMS WITH AND ALTERNATIVES TO THE BUT-FOR TEST

§ 14.6 Alternate Tests When But-For Analysis Fails: The Substantial Factor Test and Tests Aggregating Conduct

The Need for an Alternate Test in Some Cases

The but-for test and its use with multiple tortfeasors. Any given event, including an injury, is always the result of many causes.[53] Most causes can be ignored in tort litigation, but quite frequently, courts must focus on two or more causes of an injury. This is not necessarily a problem for the but-for test. The but-for test often permits a finding that the negligent acts of any number of tortfeasors, as well as those of the plaintiff, are all factual causes. When this is the case, ordinary causal rules can be applied and policy issues concerning the appropriate scope and extent of liability can be handled under scope of liability doctrines or through apportionment. This is particularly true in the context of multiple causes which are each necessary but not sufficient to produce a given injury.

Where but-for demonstrates multiple actors are factual causes. Example: A creates risk of harm from B's negligence. For example, suppose that an apartment house manager, A, negligently leaves the plaintiff's door unlocked after checking the apartment. The security guard, B, who is required to check all doors, negligently omits to check this one. The result is that a thief walks in the unlocked door and steals the plaintiff's stereo and jewelry. But-for A's negligence in leaving the door unlocked, the plaintiff would have had no loss. But for B's negligence in failing to check, the plaintiff would have had no loss. Both A and B are but-for causes of the loss (as long as the burglar took advantage of the unlocked door and would not have bashed a locked door in).

Failure of the test: where but-for demonstrates that multiple actors, who together caused the harm, are not factual causes. However, there is a subset of multiple cause cases that pose a problem for the but-for test. When each of two or more causes would be sufficient, standing alone, to cause the plaintiff's harm, a literal and simple version of the but-for test holds that neither of the defendants' acts is a cause of the harm. The classic example is the case of two fires being swept by winds towards the plaintiff's property. Either fire is sufficient to burn the property. Before either fire reaches the property, they combine. The combined fire burns the plaintiff's property. If A negligently set one fire and B negligently set the other, each could claim that he is not a factual cause of the harm under the but-for rule, since, even if he had set no fire, the other fire would have burned the property. Since both A and B could make the same argument, a court that applied the unvarnished but-for test here would effectively bar the victim from any recovery from either of the two negligent defendants whose combined action caused the harm. Another famous case in this pattern is *Landers v. East Texas Salt Water Disposal Company,* in which two defendants negligently caused thousands of barrels of salt water to pour into plaintiff's small lake, killing plaintiff's fish.[54]

Modification. The but-for test in such cases leads to a result that is almost always condemned as violating both an intuitive sense of causation and good legal policy. For

---

[53]   See Delgado v. Interinsurance Exch. of Auto. Club of S. Cal., 47 Cal.4th 302, 315, 211 P.3d 1083, 1091 (2009) (so stating).

[54]   Landers v. East Tex. Salt Water Disposal Co., 248 S.W.2d 731 (Tex. 1952).

cases like the two fire cases and the *Landers* case, cases with two independent causes each sufficient in and of itself to cause the injury, courts have modified the test.[55]

The Substantial Factor Test

Substituting the substantial factor test. When each of two or more causes is sufficient standing alone to cause the plaintiff's harm, courts usually drop the but-for test. The Restatement of Liability for Physical and Emotional Harm merely prescribes the outcome: when each of two or more causes is sufficient to cause the plaintiff's harm—both are factual causes of the plaintiff's harm.[56] However, many courts have used the substantial factor test endorsed by earlier Restatements.[57] That test says that all defendants who are substantial factors in the harm are factual causes.[58]

Substantial factor: applied to duplicative causation[59] cases. In the example of the two fires that combine to burn the plaintiff's property, the substantial factor test allows courts to avoid but-for analysis and to hold that the two tortfeasors who set the two different fires are both causes of the plaintiff's harm, provided only that each fire was sufficient standing alone to cause the same harm.[60] If one fire was set by a tortfeasor and the other by lightning, the trier of fact can still find that the tortfeasor is a factual cause and liable for the damage done.[61] The substantial factor approach may also resolve some problems of multiple polluters.[62] When no one polluter independently releases enough hazardous material into the environment to cause harm, but the entire group of polluters, each acting independently, collectively release an amount sufficient to cause harm, courts may treat each as causal. The substantial factor approach is but one of four grounds on which to reach such a holding.[63]

Justified uses of substantial factor. The courts have reached the right result in cases like the two-fires example, where each cause would be sufficient by itself to cause the harm. In fact, in one view, such cases represent the single most justified use for the

---

[55]   Thomas v. McKeever's Enters. Inc., 388 S.W.3d 206 (Mo. Ct. App. 2012).

[56]   Restatement Third of Torts (Liability for Physical and Emotional Harm) § 27 (2010).

[57]   Restatement First of Torts § 432(2) (1934).

[58]   E.g., Vincent v. Fairbanks Mem'l Hosp., 862 P.2d 847 (Alaska, 1993); Mitchell v. Gonzales, 54 Cal.3d 1041, 1 Cal.Rptr.2d 913, 819 P.2d 872 (1991). See Glover ex rel. Glover v. Jackson State Univ., 968 So.2d 1267, 1277 (Miss. 2007) (recognizing the substantial factor test). *Caution*: the but-for test continues to govern except where each of two or more causes is sufficient by itself to cause the harm complained of, Viner v. Sweet, 30 Cal.4th 1232, 70 P.3d 1046, 135 Cal.Rptr. 2d 629 (2003).

[59]   This is the terminology of Professor Richard Wright in Causation in Tort Law, 73 Cal. L. Rev. 1735 (1985), for cases like the two-fire case.

[60]   See Joshi v. Providence Health Sys. of Or. Corp., 342 Or. 152, 149 P.3d 1164 (2006) (requiring that defendant's conduct must be sufficient to cause harm even under the substantial factor test).

[61]   Anderson v. Minneapolis, St. Paul & Sault Ste. Marie Ry., 146 Minn. 430, 179 N.W. 45 (1920) (negligently set fire combined with fire of unknown origin; negligent firesetter is liable for all damage).

[62]   Cf. Landers v. East Tex. Salt Water Disposal Co., 151 Tex. 251, 248 S.W.2d 731 (1952) (two polluters, either of which would seemingly have been sufficient to kill fish in the plaintiff's lake; both are liable). Velsicol Chem. Corp. v. Rowe, 543 S.W.2d 337 (Tenn. 1976), approves Landers and adopts the single indivisible injury approach.

[63]   The four grounds that may be available, depending on the exact facts include: (a) the substantial factor approach, (b) the single indivisible injury rule; (c) but-for causation, which will yield a finding of causation if the entire group of polluters collectively contributes exactly the number of units of pollution to cause harm, since in that case any one polluter would have avoided the harm by withholding his pollution; and (d) the argument that the group of singly insufficient causes is a variation of the duplicative cause or two fire cases where the total pollution is more than enough to cause harm, the extra pollution being compared to the "extra" fire. By statute, a number of persons may be liable for any given "release" of hazardous materials. See, e.g., the Superfund statute, 42 U.S.C.A. § 9607.

substantial factor test.[64] If either fire alone was sufficient to burn the plaintiff's property, and if the defendant (or all defendants) were negligent, justice and policy both point to the liability of each tortfeasor. The defendant was negligent; he created a risk of burning the plaintiff's property; the property was in fact burned; and the harm was neither worse than nor different from the harm that would have been suffered if no other fire had been set. It would be a windfall to the negligent defendants if they were to escape liability for the harm merely because another tortfeasor's negligence was also sufficient to cause the same harm. It is also possible to construct a neutral, non-policy definition of causation to achieve the same result, the bottom line of which is that duplicative causes are still causes.[65]

Limits of substantial factor; preemptive causation[66] *cases.* The substantial factor test does not suggest unlimited liability. If one of the two fires burns the plaintiff's property to the ground before the other spreads to the scene, the second fire is not a factual cause at all,[67] even though it would have burned the plaintiff's property in the same way. Your acts today cannot in any practical sense cause something that happened in 1939, or even something that happened one second before you acted. Moreover, to say that a defendant may have liability when determined to be a factual cause of the harm, is not to determine the extent of the liability.[68]

Limits of substantial factor; its intuitive nature. The substantial factor test is not so much a test as an incantation. It points neither to any reasoning nor to any facts that will assist courts or lawyers in resolving the question of causation. Put differently, the substantial factor test requires no particular mental operation.[69] It invites the jury's intuition.[70] In one view, that represents a loss of precision in analysis with no corresponding gain.[71]

---

[64]   David W. Robertson, The Common Sense of Cause in Fact, 75 Tex. L. Rev. 1765, 1776 (1997).

[65]   This woefully under-expresses the elaborate analysis of causation provided by Professor Richard Wright. He argues that cause is established if an event is a necessary element of a set of events sufficient to produce the harm. The two fire case represents two sufficient sets under this test. See Richard W. Wright, Causation, Responsibility, Risk, Probability, Naked Statistics, and Proof: Pruning the Bramble Bush by Clarifying the Concepts, 73 Iowa L. Rev. 1001 (1988).

[66]   Preemptive cause is Professor Wright's term, contrasting with duplicative cause. See note 65, supra.

[67]   Saden v. Kirby, 660 So.2d 423 (La. 1995) (flooding by one entity had already peaked before other entity's acts).

[68]   The issue of apportionment of liability on causal and fault grounds is addressed more fully in chapter 35. Gerald W. Boston, Toxic Apportionment: A Causation and Risk Contribution Model, 25 Envtl. L. 549 (1995), explores the possibility of apportioning liability in accordance with the comparative risks introduced by the various parties, so long as those risks were in fact causal.

[69]   David W. Robertson, Williams Powers, Jr., & David A. Anderson, Cases and Materials on Torts 158–59 (1989); see Joseph W. Glannon, The Law of Torts 127 (1995).

[70]   An Iowa jury instruction quoted in Foggia v. Des Moines Bowl-O-Mat, Inc., 543 N.W.2d 889 (Iowa 1996), has it that "[t]he conduct of a party is a proximate cause of damage when it is a substantial factor in producing damage and when the damage would not have happened except for the conduct. 'Substantial' means the party's conduct has such an effect in producing damage as to lead a reasonable person to regard it as a cause. There can be more than one proximate cause of an injury or damage." It may be noticed that this is the equivalent, on the causal issue, of the reasonable person instruction on the negligence issue. However, courts and lawyers use detailed analyses to determine whether the evidence suffices to show unreasonably risky conduct; that is the very thing missing from the substantial factor approach to causation.

[71]   David W. Robertson, The Common Sense of Cause in Fact, 75 Tex. L. Rev. 1765, 1780 (1997). For a critique of the Restatement Second's substantial factor test, see also Geoffrey Rapp, Torts 2.0: The Restatement 3rd and the Architecture of Participation in American Tort Law, 32 Wm. Mitchell L. Rev. 1011 (2011).

Aggregating the Conduct of Multiple Actors

The Restatement's approach. The Restatement of Liability for Physical and Emotional Harm drops the terminology of substantial factor in its blackletter rule. When each of two or more causes is sufficient to cause the plaintiff's harm—the Restatement prescribes that both are factual causes of the plaintiff's harm.[72] In cases that fall short of that criteria, when an actor's tortious conduct is not sufficient to cause the plaintiff's harm, but causes the harm when combined with the tortious conduct from other persons, the Restatement uses the language of multiple sufficient causal sets to aggregate the conduct of multiple actors.[73] Under the Restatement, the conduct of all defendants as a group, once aggregated, is considered as a whole. The but-for test is then applied to their conduct taken as a unit or set. If the combined conduct is a but-for cause of the plaintiff's harm, then cause is established. The combined fires, for instance, taken as a whole, undoubtedly burned the plaintiff's property. The Iowa Court has expressly adopted this test for judging causality.[74]

Criteria for choosing units. This approach, which groups defendants or their conduct together into a set of relevant conduct, is more satisfying than the amorphous substantial factor test, but it depends on a decision to group various acts of various defendants together, and on a decision about what acts should be treated in this collective manner. At least to some extent, the decision to aggregate conduct of different defendants, and the decision to include or exclude specific acts in that aggregate unit, is likely to be a policy decision, or merely an intuitive selection.

The NESS Test. Professor Wright, working from suggestions of earlier legal thinkers, has formulated a detailed definition of causation that also works with the idea that conduct or events can be grouped together into a set.[75] But Wright rejects the aggregate but-for test. He proposes to say that if the entire set of events is sufficient to cause the harm and the defendant's act is a necessary element of the sufficient set, then causation is established.[76] He attempts to define the appropriate set or cluster without resorting to policy or intuitive decisions, by limiting the cluster to causally relevant factors.[77]

E. PROVING CAUSATION

§ 14.7 Connecting Negligence and Harm

Changing the negligence in the but-for test. The but-for test links the defendant's negligent conduct with the plaintiff's harm. Plaintiffs who encounter difficulties in proving causation may find that problems surmounting the but-for test may be avoided by asserting that some different conduct of the defendant was negligent, or that some

---

[72]   Restatement Third of Torts (Liability for Physical and Emotional Harm) § 27 (2010).

[73]   Id. § 27 cmt. f. See also Michael D. Green & William C. Powers, Jr., Conceptual Clarity and Necessary Muddles, 90 Tex. L. Rev. 41 (2011).

[74]   Spaur v. Owens-Corning Fiberglas Corp., 510 N.W.2d 854, 858 (Iowa 1994) ("when the conduct of two or more persons is so related to an event that their combined conduct, viewed as a whole, is a but-for cause of the event, and application of the but-for rule to them individually would absolve all of them, the conduct of each is a cause in fact of the event"). On the multiple sufficient causes see Restatement Third of Torts (Liability for Physical and Emotional Harm) § 27 (2010).

[75]   Richard W. Wright, Causation in Tort Law, 73 Calif. L. Rev. 1735 (1985).

[76]   Id.

[77]   Richard W. Wright, Causation, Responsibility, Risk, Probability, Naked Statistics, and Proof: Pruning the Bramble Bush by Clarifying the Concepts, 73 Iowa L. Rev. 1001 (1988).

different harm was caused by the negligent conduct. In addition, some negligence rules like res ipsa loquitur can make not just negligence but also causation easier to prove.

Specific negligence as a key part of the test. The specific act of negligence claimed by the plaintiff largely determines the hypothetical alternative conduct to be compared. If the plaintiff alleges that the defendant failed to keep a proper lookout, the hypothetical alternative case to be considered is one in which the defendant does keep a proper lookout and the question becomes whether, had he done so, he would have avoided injuring the plaintiff. On the other hand, if the plaintiff's claim is that the defendant drove too fast, the alternative case to be considered in testing causation is not one in which the defendant keeps a better lookout but one in which he drives more slowly. Because the specific negligence claimed points to the alternative conduct to be considered in assessing causation, the plaintiff's case on the negligence issue directly affects her case on the causal issue. For this reason the plaintiff's lawyer may spend a great deal of effort in structuring the negligence claim in order to get a favorable outcome on the causal issue.

Switching the specific act claimed to be negligent. Suppose the plaintiff is injured when a tree on the defendant's land falls during a windstorm. The plaintiff can show that the defendant knew the tree was dangerously likely to fall and that he was negligent in failing to brace the tree. However, the windstorm was so severe that it might have blown down the tree even if it had been braced. On such evidence, the plaintiff's case is in jeopardy; she may be unable to show causation under the but-for rule. By relying on a different claim of negligence, the plaintiff's lawyer can sometimes point to an alternative safer scenario that will meet the but-for rule. Instead of asserting that the defendant should have braced the tree, the plaintiff's lawyer can assert that the defendant should have exercised reasonable care by cutting it down. If the tree had been cut down, it surely would not have blown over on the plaintiff. The failure to cut the tree is thus a factual cause of the plaintiff's harm.

Lawyering strategy. This example points to an important connection between the claim of negligence and the causal issue. Except in res ipsa loquitur cases, the legal system demands proof of very specific acts of negligence, partly because the hypothetical alternative demanded by the but-for test can only be applied to specific acts. The plaintiff's strategy can take advantage of this point by asserting negligence that points to favorable hypothetical alternative scenarios. That is not always easy to do. In the tree case, the plaintiff is more likely to be successful on the causal issue if she claims a negligent failure to cut, but she might find it easier to prevail on the negligence issue by claiming only a failure to brace. Nevertheless, some causal problems for the plaintiff can be solved by claiming the right act of negligence.

Changing the harm. Because factual cause connects the defendant's negligence with the plaintiff's harm, another lawyering strategy to overcome but-for cause problems is to change the nature of the harm alleged. This strategy is seen most prominently in lost chance of recovery cases in which the actual harm alleged becomes not cancer or death, but the lost chance of recovering from cancer or avoiding death. Res ipsa loquitur may also aid the plaintiff on some causation issues.[78]

---

[78]   1 Dobbs, Hayden & Bublick, The Law of Torts § 190 (2d ed. 2011 & Supp.).

§ 14.8 Evidence and Inferences of But-For Causation

Judgments from experience. Courts have often recognized, implicitly or explicitly, that the jury must be permitted to make causal judgments from its ordinary experience without demanding impossible proof about what would have occurred if the defendant had behaved more safely.[79] Even scientific or medical causation might be proven by circumstantial evidence leading to an inference of causation.[80]

Inferring factual cause. In particular, if the defendant's conduct is deemed negligent for the very reason that it creates a core risk of the kind of harm suffered by the plaintiff, then it is often plausible to infer factual causation.[81] When we say that the pharmacist is negligent in doubling the dosage of a prescription we are saying that it is too likely that the patient will suffer serious injuries from the drug, and if she does suffer the kind of injury the drug is capable of producing, the trier can infer causation.[82] If we say that the defendant is negligent because his stairs were poorly lighted we are saying that it is all too likely that someone will fall because of the poor lighting. When someone does in fact fall on the poorly lit stairs it is quite reasonable to infer that bad lighting had something to do with it.[83] Where a plaintiff emerges from a sudden rear-end automobile accident with a hurt neck, it is permissible for the jury to infer that the injury was caused by defendant's negligent driving where there was no evidence of a pre-existing neck injury.[84]

Uncertain causation. Courts are avowedly liberal with such causation issues[85] and many cases have permitted an inference of factual causation along these lines. If the defendant is negligent in failing to provide a fire escape in an apartment building,[86] a

---

[79]　See Restatement Third of Torts (Liability for Physical and Emotional Harm) § 28 cmt. b (2010).

[80]　E.g., Reynolds Metals Co. v. Yturbide, 258 F.2d 321 (9th Cir. 1958) (defendant's plant operations produced fluoride compounds; evidence of heavy amounts of such compounds in the vegetation nearby, with lesser amounts farther away, warranted inference of escape; symptoms of nearby landowners, coupled with lack of other explanations, warranted medical opinion that illness resulted from escape of fluorides from the plant).

[81]　See Kenneth S. Abraham, Self-Proving Causation, 99 Va. L. Rev. 1811 (2013) (breach of duty proof that shows negligence can be self-proving evidence of causation when the breach and associated negligence significantly raises the risk of harm).

[82]　Zuchowicz v. United States, 140 F.3d 381 (2d Cir. 1998). See Liriano v. Hobart Corp., 170 F.3d 264 (2d Cir. 1999) ("When a defendant's negligent act is deemed wrongful precisely because it has a strong propensity to cause the type of injury that ensued, that very causal tendency is evidence enough to establish a prima facie case of cause-in-fact.").

[83]　Reynolds v. Texas & Pac. Ry. Co., 37 La. Ann. 694 (1885). See Zuchowicz v. United States, 140 F.3d 381 (2d Cir. 1998); Restatement Third of Torts (Liability for Physical and Emotional Harm) § 28 cmt. b (2010); cf. Alder v. Bayer Corp., AGFA Div., 61 P.3d 1068 (Utah 2002) (plaintiffs' injuries or symptoms were the kinds known to be risked by chemical exposures for which the defendant was allegedly responsible; this is a sufficient "ruling in" to permit differential diagnosis testimony ruling out other diseases or causes).

[84]　Foddrill v. Crane, 894 N.E.2d 1070 (Ind. Ct. App. 2008) (also holding that plaintiff needed no expert testimony on causation on such facts). Cf. Yount v. Deibert, 147 P.3d 1065 (Kan. 2006) (inference that boys who played with fire caused house fire).

[85]　See Thompson v. Sun City Cmty. Hosp., Inc., 141 Ariz. 597, 688 P.2d 605 (1984). To be sure, cases in which courts take a quite restricted view of causation can also be found. See Spencer v. McClure, 217 W.Va. 442, 618 S.E.2d 451 (2005) (holding that passenger in a multiple-vehicle accident presented insufficient evidence that car that failed to stop before hitting accident vehicles could have been a cause of her back injury).

[86]　E.g., Higgins Invs., Inc. v. Sturgill, 509 S.W.2d 266 (Ky. Ct. App. 1974) (although the fire blocked decedent's exit from his room so that he could not have reached a fire escape outside it, the only place for a fire escape would have been *in* his room, so if one had been provided, he could have escaped; consequently the failure to provide an escape was a cause of his death). See Wex Malone, Ruminations on Cause-in-Fact, 9 Stan. L. Rev. 60 (1956), reprinted in Wex Malone, Essays on Torts 160 (1986).

lifeguard at a hotel swimming pool,[87] or a warning about dangers of a product,[88] the risks are all too great that someone will die in a fire, drown, or suffer product injury, so juries may be permitted in such cases to infer that the defendant's negligent conduct was a factual cause of the harms suffered in each case, even though it is perfectly possible that the precautions required would have availed nothing in the particular case.[89]

Inconsistencies. Assessment of causal evidence requires an estimate of probabilities; for that reason, slight differences in the facts might warrant a finding of causation in some cases and not in other very similar cases. But it is hard to escape the feeling that the but-for rule with its hypothetical alternative case can produce contradictory results[90] because it is applied with a light touch in some cases and quite rigorously in others.[91]

F. PROVING WHICH DEFENDANT'S NEGLIGENCE CAUSED HARM

§ 14.9 Alternative Causes and the Shifted Burden of Proof

Alternative causation rule. In the alternative cause cases, both tortfeasors are negligent, but only one of them has caused the plaintiff's harm. The difficulty is that it is impossible to determine which one is the cause. The doctrine of alternative causation was originally rooted in joint and several liability, but has been adopted even in jurisdictions that have adopted several liability.[92] Indeed, the argument for allowing the alternative causation rule may be stronger when the effect of the rule is not to assign full liability to the negligent defendant but instead to allow the negligent defendant who

---

[87] Haft v. Lone Palm Hotel, 3 Cal.3d 756, 478 P.2d 465, 91 Cal.Rptr. 745 (1970) (hotel pool drowning; hotel was required either to provide guard or post a warning; it did neither, burden of proof shifted to the defendant to absolve itself if it can); cf. Kopera v. Moschella, 400 F.Supp. 131 (S.D. Miss. 1975) (no lifeguard at any time, court does not consider whether, had a lifeguard been employed, he would have been on duty when the drowning occurred); but cf. Jojo's Rests., Inc. v. McFadden, 117 S.W.3d 279 (Tex. App. 2003) (if additional security guards were needed there was still no showing that their presence would have prevented injury to customer).

[88] E.g., Coffman v. Keene Corp., 133 N.J. 581, 628 A.2d 710 (1993).

[89] Mitchell v. Cedar Rapids Cmty. Sch. Dist., 832 N.W.2d 689 (Iowa 2013) (it was up to the jury to decide whether school district's negligence increased the risk that student would be raped by another student); Manley v. Sherer, 992 N.E.2d 670 (Ind. 2013) (genuine issue of material fact as to causation when doctor failed to warn patient not to drive on prescribed medication and patient crashed into another driver).

[90] Compare Nallan v. Helmsley-Spear, Inc., 50 N.Y.2d 507, 429 N.Y.S.2d 606, 407 N.E.2d 451 (1980) (presence of lobby attendant would have deterred shooting), with Saelzler v. Advanced Group 400, 25 Cal.4th 763, 23 P.3d 1143, 107 Cal.Rptr.2d 617 (2001) (better security might not have deterred unknown attackers), and Shaner v. Tucson Airport Auth. Inc., 117 Ariz. 444, 573 P.2d 518 (Ct. App. 1978) (lights in parking lot would not have deterred attack on woman).

[91] Fedorczyk v. Caribbean Cruise Lines, Ltd., 82 F.3d 69 (3d Cir. 1996) (fall in defendant's bathtub, which had inadequate non-slip strips; since plaintiff might have been standing on existing strips when she fell, she could not show that the addition of other strips would have prevented the fall); Saelzler v. Advanced Group, 400, 25 Cal.4th 763, 23 P.3d 1143, 107 Cal.Rptr. 2d 617 (2001) (plaintiff's claim that the defendant was negligent in failing to provide better security was dismissed because better security might still have been unsafe for this particular plaintiff). One of the most interesting cases, but most aggressive use of the actual cause element by the court is Aegis Ins. Servs., Inc. v. 7 World Trade Co., L.P., 737 F.3d 166 (2d Cir. 2013) (despite extensive reconstruction by fire science experts, plaintiff insurer had not proved, for purposes of summary judgment, that alleged negligence in the design and construction of 7 World Trade Center was a factual cause of the building's collapse from fire in the 9/11 terrorist attacks).

[92] See Salica v. Tucson Heart Hosp.-Carondelet, LLC, 224 Ariz. 414, 231 P.3d 946 (Ct. App. 2010) (citing Summers with approval and holding that to avoid the " 'unfairness of denying the injured person redress simply because he cannot prove how much damage each [tortfeasor] did, when it is certain that between them they did all,' tortfeasors are left to apportion damages among themselves when causation is potentially indeterminable").

potentially has a causal role to be counted as one defendant in the broader apportionment.

Summers v. Tice. The leading case in the United States is *Summers v. Tice*,[93] where two hunters, acting independently of each other, negligently fired their guns at the same time. One piece of shot struck the plaintiff in the eye. Both hunters were negligent in risking harm to the plaintiff. But only one of them could have fired the shot that struck the plaintiff's eye.[94] As a matter of probabilities, it is not more likely that A fired the shot, nor more likely that B did so, so the plaintiff would be left without recourse against either negligent hunter. The court concluded that the burden should shift to each defendant to show he was not the cause and if he could not make such a showing, then to stand jointly and severally liable to the plaintiff.

Burden shifting and practical effect. Sometimes the burden shifting in *Summers v. Tice* is given prominence in discussions, as if to suggest that the court was not really imposing liability. However, when a jurisdiction has a rule of joint and several liability for indivisible injuries, the practical effect of the rule is to impose joint and several liability upon each defendant when one defendant cannot show that the other defendant was the cause. Consequently, one actor will be held liable although he caused no harm whatsoever. The common term "alternative liability" is misleading. It is causation that is in the alternative, because one or the other, but not both, tortfeasors are causes of the harm.

Rationale. The opinion in *Summers* did not spell out the reasons for this extraordinary liability in any precise way, perhaps because the result, which has sometimes been reached on other grounds,[95] seems so clearly right on the facts. Beyond the dubious suggestion that defendants might know more than plaintiffs,[96] the court seemed to say that each defendant, by his negligent shot, created the doubt about causation or despoiled the evidence that otherwise would have been available to the plaintiff, so that as a matter of policy, the defendants, rather than the innocent plaintiff, should bear the loss.[97] This rationale has been elaborated by the Canadian Supreme Court.[98] Professor Robertson has given a good account of it in connection with another

---

[93]   Summers v. Tice, 33 Cal.2d 80, 199 P.2d 1 (1948).

[94]   The court treats the case as if only one shot struck the plaintiff and only one tortfeasor could have fired. However, the plaintiff was struck elsewhere by another shot that caused minor harm. That raises the possibility that the case could be handled under an indivisible injury rationale, although Prosser and the Restatement might regard this as a case of two injuries and therefore not to be blessed with the indivisible injury treatment. See Restatement Second of Torts § 433A(1)(a) (1965); Prosser & Keeton on the Law of Torts § 41 (5th ed. 1984).

[95]   See McMillan v. Mahoney, 99 N.C.App. 448, 393 S.E.2d 298 (1990). In Fairchild v. Glenhaven Funeral Servs., [2002] 3 All. E.R. 305, 2002 WL 820081 (H.L. 2002), Lord Bingham of Cornhill concluded that most European countries obtained the same result under specific code provisions or otherwise.

[96]   It seems inherently improbable that either hunter firing at the same target would be able to watch the scattered shot fly through the air to strike the plaintiff. Hymowitz v. Eli Lilly & Co., 73 N.Y.2d 487, 541 N.Y.S.2d 941, 539 N.E.2d 1069 (1989), explicitly stated this rationale, but only for the purpose of finding it inapplicable to a case of many actors.

[97]   For a similar later case see Hellums v. Raber, 853 N.E.2d 143 (Ind. Ct. App. 2006). This theme appears in a number of cases that do not necessarily involve the alternative causation but do involve causal doubts. E.g., Gardner v. National Bulk Carriers, Inc., 310 F.2d 284, 91 A.L.R.2d 1023 (4th Cir. 1962) (the defendant's failure to search for a man overboard "obliterated all possibility of evidence to prove whether a search, if undertaken, would have succeeded or failed").

[98]   Cook v. Lewis, [1952] 1 D.L.R. 1 (1951) was a case similar to Summers v. Tice. In Cook, Rand, J., reasoned that the negligent defendants had "violated not only the victim's substantive right to security, but . . . also culpably impaired the latter's remedial right of establishing liability. By confusing his act with

case.[99] Another possibility is that *Summers* is merely an instance of the more general proposition when the defendant creates an unreasonable risk of a specific kind of harm and that kind of harm in fact occurs, it is often possible to conclude that the defendant's negligence is causal.[100] The issue has been thoughtfully addressed from a philosophical perspective.[101]

Requirement that all defendants be acting wrongfully for alternative liability. The Restatement accepts *Summers*. It would shift the burden to the defendants to exculpate themselves when the conduct of two or more actors is tortious and harm has been caused by one of them.[102] Under this rule, the actors must all be wrongdoers before the burden shifts to them to disprove causation.[103] In this respect, the *Summers* alternative causation rule differs from the concert of action rule that sometimes applies to similar facts.[104]

Courts have accepted the rule,[105] but have usually been reluctant to extend the alternative causation rule any further.[106]

---

environmental conditions, he has, in effect, destroyed the victim's power of proof." Later, in Dow Corning Corp. v. Hollis, 129 D.L.R.4th 609 (1995), the majority appeared to approve of that reasoning.

[99] David W. Robertson, The Common Sense of Cause in Fact, 75 Tex. L. Rev. 1765, 1787 (1997), using this reasoning to explain Saunders Sys. Birmingham Co. v. Adams, 117 So. 72 (Ala. 1928), where the lessor provided a car with no brakes and the driver failed to use them.

[100] See Zuchowicz v. United States, 140 F.3d 381, 390–91 (3d Cir. 1998). However, if the principle described rests on a causal inference, such an inference is not logically possible against two actors where it is known that only one of them could have caused the harm, as in Summers itself.

[101] See Judith Jarvis Thomson, Remarks on Causation and Liability, 13 Phil. & Pub. Aff. 101 (1984) (discussing the defendant's freedom of action as a constraint on liability when the defendant has not causally contributed to the plaintiff's injury).

[102] The Restatement Third of Torts (Liability for Physical and Emotional Harm) § 28 (2010) shifts the burden to the defendant when the plaintiff sues all the tortfeasors who exposed the plaintiff to a risk and proves that one or more caused the harm but that he cannot reasonably prove which of the defendants caused it. Comments (b), (f) and (g) discuss inference and speculation in proving causation and burden shifting.

[103] Cuonzo v. Shore, 958 A.2d 840 (Del. 2008) ("To permit burden shifting, both drivers must have been negligent"); State v. CTL Distrib., Inc., 715 So.2d 262 (Fla. Dist. Ct. App. 1998); Canavan v. Galuski, 2 A.D.3d 1039, 769 N.Y.S.2d 629 (2003); Peck v. Serio, 155 Ohio App. 3d 471, 801 N.E.2d 890 (2003); Pennfield Corp. v. Meadow Valley Elec., Inc., 413 Pa. Super. 187, 604 A.2d 1082 (1992).

[104] At times courts have not distinguished between Summers and true concert of action cases. See Scott v. Rayhrer, 185 Cal.App.4th 1535, 111 Cal.Rptr.3d 36 (2010) (regarding Summers as a concert of action case). In McMillan v. Mahoney, 99 N.C. App. 448, 393 S.E.2d 298 (1990), the complaint alleged that two boys were firing air rifles together, that a pellet from one struck the plaintiff causing brain damage, and that one of the boys was negligent. The court appeared to approve the alternative causation theory, but seemingly decided the case on the ground that the boys acted in concert, since that theory would justify liability of both if either one were negligent. See Lewis v. Lead Indus. Ass'n, Inc., 342 Ill.App.3d 95, 793 N.E.2d 869, 276 Ill.Dec. 110 (2003) (lead pigment manufacturers who failed to warn of lead dangers were conspirators, plaintiffs exposed to lead and undergoing medical monitoring could recover from all; each would be liable for the acts of that one co-conspirator).

[105] Minnich v. Ashland Oil Co., Inc., 15 Ohio St.3d 396, 473 N.E.2d 1199 (1984); accord, as to two manufacturers of heparin, a drug alleged to be defective, Wysocki v. Reed, 222 Ill.App.3d 268, 583 N.E.2d 1139 (1991); Huston v. Konieczny, 52 Ohio St. 3d 214, 556 N.E.2d 505 (1990) (several possible suppliers of beer to underage drinker); Jane Stapleton, Lords a'Leaping Evidentiary Gaps, 10 Tort L.J. 276 (2002).

[106] Gaulding v. Celotex Corp., 772 S.W.2d 66 (Tex. 1989); cf. Doe v. Baxter Healthcare Corp., 380 F.3d 399 (8th Cir. 2004) (plaintiff must prove that non-joined persons did not cause the injury and seemingly must do so by a standard much higher than the preponderance of the evidence standard); Collins v. Eli Lilly Co., 116 Wis.2d 166, 342 N.W.2d 37 (1984).

§ 14.10   Statistical Substitutes for Causation: Market Share Liability

History. Market share liability has a specific beginning. It was proposed in a law review comment to deal with DES cases.[107] DES was a prescription drug manufactured by hundreds of companies. Every manufacturer's version was like every other manufacturer's version. Many pregnant women ingested the drug to help prevent miscarriages. Years later, when their daughters reached adulthood, they discovered that DES caused cancers in the daughters' female reproductive system. Since these cancers did not appear for many years, almost no one had records that could establish which of the manufacturers had produced the specific drug ingested by the individual mothers. Indeed, many of the manufacturers no longer existed.

The market share idea. The market share idea was that if manufacturer A sold 40% of all the DES marketed, it was highly probable that A's DES caused about the same percentage of overall injuries. Although A's version of the drug may have caused no injury at all to a particular plaintiff—no one could ever know for sure—if it caused 40% of all injuries, then holding it liable for 40% of each individual plaintiff's injury would be no injustice. In fact, the totals of liability should come out to about the same dollar amount as if each mother were accurately matched with each dose of DES.

DES. Several courts have adopted some form or another of the market share idea in DES cases.[108] These courts hold that each manufacturer of the drug is responsible to each plaintiff, but never for the plaintiff's entire damages,[109] only for a percentage of the plaintiff's damages equal to that manufacturer's share of the market in the drug. Quite a few other courts, worried over the idea of liability based upon statistical rather than literal causation, have rejected the market share theory, even for the DES cases.[110]

Continuing development. When it comes to products other than DES, courts have mixed views.[111] Given the split among courts about the propriety of market share liability, the Restatement of Products[112] and the Restatement of Liability for Physical Injury[113] have left the issue of whether such a rule should be adopted and in what circumstances "to developing law." In the states that have affirmatively permitted some

---

[107] Comment, DES and a Proposed Theory of Enterprise Liability, 46 Fordham L. Rev. 963 (1978).

[108] Sindell v. Abbott Labs., 26 Cal.3d 588, 163 Cal.Rptr. 132, 607 P.2d 924 (1980) (the original case); Conley v. Boyle Drug Co., 570 So.2d 275 (Fla. 1990); Smith v. Cutter Biological, Inc., 72 Haw. 416, 823 P.2d 717 (1991); Hymowitz v. Eli Lilly & Co., 73 N.Y.2d 487, 541 N.Y.S.2d 941, 539 N.E.2d 1069 (1989); Martin v. Abbott Labs., 102 Wash.2d 581, 689 P.2d 368 (1984); Collins v. Eli Lilly Co., 116 Wis.2d 166, 342 N.W.2d 37 (1984) (liability in proportion to risk imposed, with market share relevant in determining that risk).

[109] The California Court, initiating the whole idea in Sindell, may have been uncertain about joint and several liability, but later cleared that up. See Brown v. Sup. Ct., 44 Cal.3d 1049, 751 P.2d 470, 245 Cal.Rptr. 412 (1988). One court rejected market share liability in favor of an alternative causation theory, which of course does use joint and several liability. Abel v. Eli Lilly & Co., 418 Mich. 311, 343 N.W.2d 164 (1984).

[110] Smith v. Eli Lilly & Co., 137 Ill.2d 222, 560 N.E.2d 324 (1990); Zafft v. Eli Lilly & Co., 676 S.W.2d 241 (Mo. 1984); Gorman v. Abbott Labs., 599 A.2d 1364 (R.I. 1991).

[111] Compare Thomas v. Mallett, 701 N.W.2d 523 (Wis. 2005) (market share liability of manufacturers of lead paint), with City of St. Louis v. Benjamin Moore & Co., 226 S.W.3d 110 (Mo. 2007) (disallowing nuisance claim against lead paint manufacturers because city could not identify which lead paint manufacturers' products were used on which homes that required abatement of lead paint), and Bly v. Tri-Continental Indus., Inc., 663 A.2d 1232 (D.C. 1995) (different levels of benzene in petroleum products one reason to reject market share theory on the facts).

[112] Restatement Third of Torts (Products Liability) § 15 cmt. c (1998).

[113] Restatement Third of Torts (Liability for Physical and Emotional Harm) § 28 cmt. p (2010).

form of market share liability, a number of collateral rules about joinder and definition of the appropriate market have become important.[114]

G. SPECIAL PROBLEMS: WHAT HARM WAS CAUSED?

§ 14.11 The Lost Chance of Recovery

What is the harm caused? When harm is caused by multiple negligent actors, or even multiple negligent factors, a common question is what harm did the actor's negligence cause? One approach, when negligence causes distinct or divisible injuries, as when Defendant A breaks the plaintiff's arm and Defendant B breaks the plaintiff's leg, is to turn to causal apportionment.[115]

Preexisting harm. Difficult problems of causation and apportionment arise when the defendant is negligent toward a plaintiff who is already suffering from a disease or disability or is immediately threatened with probable harm.[116] As in many other cases that permit or require apportionment, concerns of justice or policy may shape the apportionment rules.[117]

The lost chance problem. In some cases the defendant risks harm to a person suffering from a preexisting danger or disability, but it is not likely, much less certain, that the defendant actually caused the harm that resulted. Instead, the harm is more likely to have resulted from the preexisting condition.

Example: physician's untimely treatment or diagnosis. One kind of case that has been much litigated is that of a physician who fails to provide a timely diagnosis or treatment of disease, thereby creating a risk that the treatment will come too late. In such cases, the evidence may show that even if diagnosis and treatment had been timely, the patient might have had only a 40% chance of living. On those facts, the plaintiff definitely could not prove by a preponderance of the evidence that the defendant caused the patient's death. Indeed, the heavy preponderance of the evidence is the other way, for the probability is 60% that the defendant did *not* cause the death in spite of his negligence. In these cases, plaintiffs sometimes seek to redefine the harm caused as, not the death itself, but plaintiff's lost chance of recovery.

Denial of all liability. Some courts have insisted that on facts like the delayed treatment example no one can recover for the patient's death, since the plaintiff has failed to establish causation by a preponderance of the evidence.[118] Courts have also

---

[114] 1 Dobbs, Hayden & Bublick, The Law of Torts § 194 (2d ed. 2011 & Supp.).

[115] Id. § 192.

[116] See also CSX Transp., Inc. v. Miller, 46 So.3d 434 (Ala. 2010) (defendant's tortious harm combined with preexisting injury to create indivisible injury; defendant may be liable for full injury); Perius v. Nodak Mut. Ins. Co., 782 N.W.2d 255 (N.D. 2010) (defendant must compensate the victim for the aggravation, but not for the preexisting injury itself); Harris v. ShopKo Stores, Inc., 308 P.3d 449 (Utah 2013).

[117] 1 Dobbs, Hayden & Bublick, The Law of Torts § 195 (2d ed. 2011 & Supp.).

[118] Dumas v. Cooney, 235 Cal.App.3d 1593, 1 Cal.Rptr.2d 584 (1991); Grant v. American Nat'l Red Cross, 745 A.2d 316 (D.C. 2000); Gooding v. University Hosp. Bldg., Inc., 445 So.2d 1015 (Fla. 1984); Fennell v. Southern Md. Hosp. Ctr., Inc., 320 Md. 776, 580 A.2d 206 (1990); Joshi v. Providence Health Sys. of Or. Corp., 342 Or. 152, 149 P.3d 1164 (2006) (death action for malpractice that deprived decedent of a 30% chance could not succeed under death statute's requirement of causation; the but-for test must be used except in the case of multiple tortfeasors each of which is sufficient by itself to cause the harm complained of); Jones v. Owings, 456 S.E.2d 371 (S.C. 1995) (lost chance doctrine contrary to the most basic standards); Kilpatrick v. Bryant, 868 S.W.2d 594 (Tenn. 1993); Columbia Rio Grande Healthcare, L.P. v. Hawley, 284 S.W.3d 851 (Tex. 2009) (finding error when jurors were not told that patient must have had a greater than 50% chance of surviving

raised policy issues, particularly related to the potential financial burden of expanded liability, as a reason to deny lost-chance liability.[119] Some legislation calls for denial of liability in lost chance cases at least where the context is medical malpractice.[120]

Recognizing lost chance of recovery. Although a significant number of states have specifically rejected the lost chance approach, an even larger number has embraced it. A recent article places the count at 16 states against the doctrine and 22 in favor.[121] Most of the courts that have permitted the specific claim that loss of a chance is itself an item of damages for which recovery is appropriate, have permitted recovery in one of two ways.

Liability for all harm or relaxed requirement of causation. When the plaintiff shows loss of a chance, but a chance of only 50% or less, one group of courts permits the jury to find causation and make an award for the whole of the loss, disregarding the fact that the patient was likely to die even if the physician had not been negligent.[122] Not all the cases that permit a full recovery are explicit about the reasoning. The clearest of them reason somewhat along these lines, with which other cases are consistent: (i) The defendant doctor's negligence increased the risk of death; (ii) that increased risk combined with the risk from the existing illness to cause a single indivisible injury, much as the negligently set fire combined with the innocent fire in the two-fire cases. (iii) Consequently, if the doctor's negligence was a substantial factor in producing harm, the doctor is liable for the entire harm unless he can show a basis for apportionment.[123]

Liability for value of the lost chance. A second method of permitting recovery recognizes that the defendant may not have caused death, but did cause the loss of the plaintiff's *chance* to live. The same idea can apply to a living plaintiff who suffers a reduction in life expectancy[124] or the loss of a chance for a better medical outcome.[125] This view was developed by Professor King in an article that is now usually cited in discussions of the topic.[126] The idea is that the plaintiff's chance of survival itself has value for which compensation is due.[127] Confronted with a risk of death, a patient would pay for even a small chance to live.[128] Indeed, a patient retains a physician for that very

---

cancer in order to recover in medical malpractice case); Smith v. Parrott, 833 A.2d 843 (Vt. 2003) (construing statute to codify the common law rules of causation).

[119] See Kemper v. Gordon, 272 S.W.3d 146 (Ky. 2009).

[120] Mich. Comp. Laws Ann. § 609.2912a(2). However, what exactly the statute requires is a subject of dispute. See Stone v. Williamson, 753 N.W.2d 106 (Mich. 2008) (examining the Michigan statute and the lost chance claim).

[121] Steven R. Koch, Whose Loss Is It Anyway? Effects of the "Lost-Chance" Doctrine on Civil Litigation and Medical Malpractice Insurance, 88 N.C. L. Rev. 595 (2010) (arguing that adopting lost-chance claims has no significant impact on state malpractice costs).

[122] Thompson v. Sun City Cmty. Hosp., Inc., 141 Ariz. 597, 688 P.2d 605 (1984); Mayhue v. Sparkman, 653 N.E.2d 1384 (Ind. 1995).

[123] Hamil v. Bashline, 481 Pa. 256, 392 A.2d 1280 (1978). If a court perceives a basis for apportionment, the same reasoning supports the more limited value of the chance award. See Scafidi v. Seiler, 119 N.J. 93, 574 A.2d 398 (1990).

[124] Alexander v. Scheid, 726 N.E.2d 272 (Ind. 2000).

[125] Lord v. Lovett, 770 A.2d 1103 (N.H. 2001); Joseph H. King, Jr., "Reduction of Likelihood" Reformulation and Other Retrofitting of the Loss-of-a-Chance Doctrine, 28 U. Mem. L. Rev. 492 (1998).

[126] Joseph H. King, Jr., Causation, Valuation and Chance in Personal Injury Torts, 90 Yale L. J. 1353 (1981).

[127] See Mohr v. Grantham, 172 Wash.2d 844, 262 P.3d 490 (2011) ("the loss of chance is the compensable injury"; "the injury is the lost chance").

[128] See Murrey v. United States, 73 F.3d 1448 (7th Cir. 1995) ("No doubt Murrey would have paid a lot (if he had had a lot to pay) for a 5 percent chance of survival if the alternative was a certainty of immediate death. This shows that he lost something by being deprived of that chance"); Wollen v. DePaul Health Ctr.,

reason, to maximize his chances of health and survival or a better outcome. In this view, if the plaintiff can sustain the burden of proving that the defendant negligently deprived her of a chance[129] of a better outcome, the defendant should be liable for the value of the chance he has negligently destroyed.[130] This approach is backed, in degrees that vary from case to case, by considerations of fairness, deterrence, and protection of the plaintiff's autonomy interests,[131] but artificial limits on lost chance recoveries are possible.[132]

Amount of recovery. The damages awarded are quite different from the traditional all-or-nothing recovery.[133] Under the value of the chance rule, the plaintiff recovers, but only an amount representing the value of the chance destroyed by the defendant's negligence. The Massachusetts Supreme Judicial Court recently detailed the specific computations required of its courts.[134] Other courts have discussed calculations,[135] which can be done in different ways.[136] One commentator has specifically addressed

---

828 S.W.2d 681 (Mo. 1992) (patient "would pay to have a choice between three unmarked doors—behind two of which were death, with life the third option"); McMackin v. Johnson County Healthcare Ctr., 73 P.3d 1094 (Wyo. 2003), sustained on rehearing, 88 P.3d 491 (2004) ("Much of the American health care dollar is spent on such treatments, aimed at improving the odds"); Joseph H. King, Jr., "Reduction of Likelihood" Reformulation and Other Retrofitting of the Loss-of-a-Chance Doctrine, 28 Mem. St. U. L. Rev. 492, 540 (1998).

[129] See Holton v. Memorial Hosp., 176 Ill.2d 95, 118, 679 N.E.2d 1202, 1212, 223 Ill. Dec. 429, 439 (1997) ("To the extent a plaintiff's chance of recovery or survival is lessened by the malpractice, he or she should be able to present evidence to a jury that the defendant's malpractice, to a reasonable degree of medical certainty, proximately caused the increased risk of harm or lost chance of recovery.").

[130] Alexander v. Scheid, 726 N.E.2d 272, 279 (Ind. 2000) ("We think that loss of chance is better understood as a description of the injury than as either a term for a separate cause of action or a surrogate for the causation element of a negligence claim. If a plaintiff seeks recovery specifically for what the plaintiff alleges the doctor to have caused, i.e., a decrease in the patient's probability of recovery, rather than for the ultimate outcome, causation is no longer debatable. Rather, the problem becomes one of identification and valuation or quantification of that injury."); McMackin v. Johnson County Healthcare Ctr., 73 P.3d 1094 (Wyo. 2003), sustained on rehearing, 88 P.3d 491 (2004).

[131] See Dickhoff v. Green, 836 N.W.2d 321 (Minn. 2013); David A. Fischer, Tort Recovery for Loss of a Chance, 36 Wake Forest L. Rev. 605 (2001).

[132] Connecticut has said that the lost chance recovery will not be permitted unless the plaintiff's chance was greater than 50% to begin with. Boone v. William W. Backus Hosp., 272 Conn. 551, 574, 864 A.2d 1, 18 (2005) ("in order to satisfy the elements of a lost chance claim, the plaintiff must [first] prove that *prior to* the defendant's alleged negligence, the [decedent] had a chance of survival of at least 51 percent," relying on lower court decisions from the same state).

[133] Kivland v. Columbia Orthopaedic Group, LLP, 331 S.W.3d 299 (Mo. 2011) (where plaintiffs can establish that decedent died as a result of the defendants' negligence, the recovery is based on the wrongful death statutes and the loss of chance theory has no application).

[134] Matsuyama v. Birnbaum, 890 N.E.2d 819 (Mass. 2008).

[135] Falcon v. Memorial Hosp., 436 Mich. 443, 462 N.W.2d 44, 52 (1990) ("37.5 percent times the damages recoverable for wrongful death") (now limited by legislation in medical malpractice cases); Scafidi v. Seiler, 119 N.J. 93, 574 A.2d 398 (1990) (jury to determine chance in percentage terms); Perez v. Las Vegas Med. Ctr., 107 Nev. 1, 805 P.2d 589 (1991); Alberts v. Schultz, 126 N.M. 807, 815, 975 P.2d 1279, 1287 (1999) ("the value of a plaintiff's twenty-percent chance of saving a limb is twenty percent of the value of the entire limb"); Roberts v. Ohio Permanente Med. Group, Inc., 76 Ohio St.3d 483, 668 N.E.2d 480 (1996); McKellips v. Saint Francis Hosp., Inc., 741 P.2d 467, 476 (Okla. 1987) ("The amount of damages recoverable is equal to the percent of chance lost multiplied by the total amount of damages which are ordinarily allowed in a wrongful death action").

[136] See Sawlani v. Mills, 830 N.E.2d 932 (Ind. Ct. App. 2005). Sawlani recognizes two formulations used in Indiana cases. In one, damages are calculated by "subtracting the decedent's postnegligence chance of survival from the prenegligence chance of survival," then using the resulting percentage figure to multiply "the total amount of damages which are ordinarily allowed in a wrongful death action." In the other, "damages . . . should be based upon 'the reduction of the patient's expectancy from her pre-negligence expectancy' and the jury must 'attach a monetary amount' to the patient's loss of life expectancy." The court regarded these formulations as calling for different measurements of damages.

computational difficulties.[137] A more subjective approach, taken by one state, might avoid some of these issues, though raise others.[138] Another possibility is suggested by a Michigan case: the plaintiff might recover for present physical injury and emotional harms resulting from the diminished chance, but not for loss of the chance itself.[139]

Increased risk of future harm. In many of the lost chance of recovery cases, the defendant negligently risks harm to the patient and that very harm in fact comes about. Those cases are not necessarily good precedent for liability when the defendant creates a risk of future harm that has not yet in fact occurred and that may never do so.[140] Courts have often denied claims for proportional recovery based on an increased risk of future harm that is not more probable than not to occur[141] and that is entirely separable from the harm that has already occurred.[142] Some courts have recognized an exception by allowing the plaintiff who is subjected to a risk of future harm like cancer to recover immediately for costs of medical monitoring.[143] And if the defendant has inflicted some harm, which in turn may shorten the plaintiff's life, some authority permits the plaintiff to recover for the diminished chance of living out her life expectancy.[144] Illinois has now gone beyond these exceptions, allowing a recovery against the patient's physician for negligently increasing the risk that she will have future harm, with damages proportioned to the probability that such harm will occur.[145]

Further issues. When recovery should be allowed in increased risk and lost chance cases, when full versus partial recoveries should be awarded, whether the doctrines

[137] See Lars Noah, An Inventory of Mathematical Blunders in Applying the Loss-of-a-Chance Doctrine, 24 Rev. Litig. 369 (2005).

[138] Smith v. State, 676 So.2d 543 (La. 1996).

[139] Wickens v. Oakwood Healthcare Sys., 465 Mich. 53, 61, 631 N.W.2d 686, 691 (2001) (plaintiff whose chance of long term survival was reduced by 40% (as interpreted by the court), could not recover for lost chance, but could recover for "(1) the more invasive medical treatments caused by the one-year delay in her diagnosis, (2) the emotional trauma attributable to her unnecessarily worsened physical condition, and (3) the pain and suffering attributable to her unnecessarily worsened physical condition").

[140] See David A. Fischer, Proportional Liability: Statistical Evidence and the Probability Paradox, 46 Vand. L. Rev. 1201 (1993) (distinguishing proportional damage recovery from proportional risk recovery and both from the creation of a fund proportioned to risks but set aside to be paid only when the risk eventuates); Joseph H. King, Jr., "Reduction of Likelihood" Reformulation and Other Retrofitting of the Loss-of-a-Chance Doctrine, 28 Mem. St. U. L. Rev. 492, 560 (1998).

[141] Herber v. Johns-Manville Corp., 785 F.2d 79 (3d Cir. 1986) (distinguishing lost chance cases where harm has actually occurred); Hagerty v. L & L Marine Servs., Inc., 788 F.2d 315 (5th Cir. 1986); Williams v. Manchester, 888 N.E.2d 1 (Ill. 2008) (driver's collision with pregnant mother which required x-rays and increased risk of fetal damage was not a present injury to the fetus for which recovery would be granted); Mauro v. Raymark Indus., Inc., 116 N.J. 126, 138, 561 A.2d 257, 264 (1989).

[142] See James A. Henderson, Jr. & Aaron D. Twerski, Asbestos Litigation Gone Mad: Exposure-Based Recovery for Increased Risk, Mental Distress, and Medical Monitoring, 53 S.C. L. Rev. 815 (2002); cf. See Joseph H. King, Jr., "Reduction of Likelihood" Reformulation and Other Retrofitting of the Loss-of-a-Chance Doctrine, 28 Mem. St. U. L. Rev. 492, 510 (1998) (recovery more likely if future harm is considered part of present injury).

[143] See, e.g., Donovan v. Philip Morris, 914 N.E.2d 891 (Mass. 2009) (permitting cigarette smokers' suit for medical monitoring based on present injury to lung tissue and increased future risk of lung cancer); Simmons v. Pacor, Inc., 543 Pa. 664, 674 A.2d 232 (1996).

[144] Alexander v. Scheid, 726 N.E.2d 272 (Ind. 2000) (cancer progressed substantially when doctor failed to follow up x-ray showing lung spot; it was in remission at time of suit; a reduction in life expectancy is a recoverable item). *Contra:* Wickens v. Oakwood Healthcare Sys., 465 Mich. 53, 631 N.W.2d 686 (2001) (recovery denied under statute but recovery for emotional harms inflicted is permitted).

[145] Dillon v. Evanston Hosp., 771 N.E.2d 357 (Ill. 2002).

should apply beyond the doctor-patient context in which they began, and how to resolve evidentiary disputes are important issues not fully addressed here.[146]

---

[146] 1 Dobbs, Hayden & Bublick, The Law of Torts § 190 (2d ed. 2011 & Supp.).

Chapter 15

SCOPE OF LIABILITY (PROXIMATE CAUSE)

Analysis

A. RULES, RATIONALES AND CONTEXT

§ 15.1   Introduction
§ 15.2   Reasons for Scope of Liability Limitations
§ 15.3   Relation to Factual Cause
§ 15.4   Relation to Negligence (Breach of Duty)
§ 15.5   Relation to Duty
§ 15.6   Patterns and Formal Tests of Scope of Liability
§ 15.7   The Direct-Cause Pattern and Foreseeable Harms
§ 15.8   The Direct-Cause Pattern and Unforeseeable Harms
§ 15.9   The Intervening Cause Pattern and Superseding Cause Analysis

B. THE GENERAL RULES OF FORESEEABILITY

§ 15.10 Foreseeability Terminology: Scope of Risk
§ 15.11 Foreseeability Required: Extent of Harm
§ 15.12 Foreseeability Required: Manner of Harm
§ 15.13 Injury Remote in Time or Distance

C. INTERVENING ACTS OR FORCES

§ 15.14 Intervening Intentional or Criminal Acts
§ 15.15 Intervening Forces of Nature
§ 15.16 Foreseeable Intervening Negligent Acts
§ 15.17 Unforeseeable Intervening Acts
§ 15.18 Using "Proximate Cause" as a No-Duty Rule
§ 15.19 Plaintiff's Own Acts as a Superseding Cause

D. ALTERNATIVES

§ 15.20 Joint and Several Liability and Comparative Fault
§ 15.21 Abolishing Superseding Cause Analysis

A. RULES, RATIONALES AND CONTEXT

§ 15.1   Introduction

To prevail in a negligence action, the plaintiff must bear the burden of showing that the harm she suffered is within the defendant's scope of liability—in other words, that the harm resulted from the risks that made the defendant's conduct tortious in the first place.[1] As the Third Restatement points out, while scope of liability is an element of the prima facie case, "facts beyond those established for other elements of the tort are almost never involved," because usually the plaintiff's harm is within the scope of defendant's

---

[1]   See Restatement Third of Torts (Liability for Physical and Emotional Harm) § 29 (2010).

liability "and requires no further attention."[2] This means that the element operates "more like an affirmative defense, although formally it is not one."[3]

Terminology. This requirement is commonly known as proximate cause, although that well-worn term has been justly criticized for years as inaccurate, misleading, and confusing, and has been rejected by the Third Restatement of Torts, as it was in the Second.[4] This book, following the lead of the Third Restatement, employs the term *scope of liability* where it will aid understanding, but falls back on the still-commonly used term *proximate cause* where use of a different term would itself produce confusion. Factual cause[5] is an entirely separate element.[6]

Function in limiting scope of responsibility. As the newer terminology indicates, proximate cause rules are among those rules that seek to determine the appropriate scope of a negligent defendant's liability.[7] The central goal of this requirement is to limit the defendant's liability to the kinds of harms he risked by his negligent conduct.[8] Judicial decisions about proximate cause rules thus attempt to discern whether, in the particular case before the court, the harm that resulted from the defendant's negligence is so clearly outside the risks he created that it would be unjust or at least impractical to impose liability.[9] The so-called proximate cause issue is not about causation at all but about the appropriate scope of legal responsibility.[10] The issue does not arise until negligence and factual cause have been proven.[11]

Illustrating the issue. Two examples illustrate the idea that a negligent defendant who is a factual cause of harm should nevertheless sometimes escape liability. First, suppose that a surgeon negligently performs a vasectomy. Because the surgery was negligently performed, the patient fathers a child. The child, at the age of 13, sets fire to the plaintiff's barn. Is the surgeon liable for the loss of the barn? He was negligent in performing the vasectomy, and his negligence is a factual cause of the loss of the barn. Almost everyone will agree, however, that while the surgeon might be liable for

---

[2]　Id. cmt. a.

[3]　Id. Courts have recognized that shorthand expressions referring to the "proximate cause defense" are not to be taken literally. See Korando v. Uniroyal Goodrich Tire Co., 159 Ill.2d 335, 637 N.E.2d 1020, 202 Ill.Dec. 284 (1994).

[4]　The Second Restatement substituted the term "legal cause", but that usage never met with wide acceptance in courts. See Restatement Third of Torts (Liability for Physical and Emotional Harm) Chapter 6, Special Note on Proximate Cause (2010) (describing the history of the terminology).

[5]　Chapter 14.

[6]　A number of courts say that "proximate cause" consists of two elements, factual cause and foreseeability (or scope of risk, or something similar). We avoid this usage, while recognizing that others may not. See § 15.3.

[7]　See, e.g., Pittway Corp. v. Collins, 409 Md. 218, 973 A.2d 771 (2009) ("Legal causation is a policy-oriented doctrine designed to be a method for limiting liability after cause-in-fact has been established."). Other rules, those limiting the duty owed by defendants, also seek to impose limits on liability for conduct that would otherwise be considered negligent. Scope of liability or proximate cause rules exclude liability for damages, either all damages suffered or damages for particular items of loss. Thus, where the plaintiff need not prove damages, as in the case of intentional trespassory torts, scope of liability limitations may not apply, or not apply in the same way. See § 4.18.

[8]　Thompson v. Kaczinski, 774 N.W.2d 829 (Iowa 2009); Restatement Third of Torts (Liability for Physical and Emotional Harm) § 29 (2010).

[9]　See, e.g., Goldberg v. Florida Power & Light Co., 899 So.2d 1105 (Fla. 2005) ("The law does not impose liability for freak injuries that were utterly unpredictable in light of human experience.") (quoting McCain v. Florida Power Corp., 593 So.2d 500 (Fla. 1992)).

[10]　See § 15.2.

[11]　See Berte v. Bode, 692 N.W.2d 368 (Iowa 2005); Puckett v. Mt. Carmel Regional Medical Center, 290 Kan. 406, 228 P.3d 1048 (2010).

something, he is surely not liable for the loss of the plaintiff's barn. Courts are likely in such a case to say that the surgeon's negligence is not a proximate cause of the harm, by which they mean that the harm was not within the scope of risks the defendant created. The risk he created was that the child's father would have a child against his wishes, but not that the child would be more likely than other children to set fire to barns.

Second, suppose that the defendant negligently manufactures a vacuum cleaner so that it does not have good suction. After several frustrating days using the cleaner, the purchaser takes it to the repair shop. On her way to the shop, the purchaser is struck by a car and suffers injury. The manufacturer was negligent. The manufacturer's negligence was one of the many factual causes leading to the purchaser's harm—but for the manufacturer's negligence, the purchaser would have stayed home safely cleaning carpets and would not have been struck by a car. Yet here again, legal professionals are likely to agree that the manufacturer's conduct in making the poor vacuum was not a proximate cause of the plaintiff's injury, because the defendant's negligence did not create or increase the risk of injury in a vehicular collision.

Foreseeability tests. The most general and pervasive approach to scope of liability or proximate cause holds that a negligent defendant is liable for all the general kinds of harms he foreseeably risked by his negligent conduct and to the class of persons he put at risk by that conduct. Conversely, in the common parlance, he is not a proximate cause of, and therefore not liable for, injuries that were unforeseeable. This does not mean that the defendant's conduct must be the *only* proximate cause of the plaintiff's injury.[12] On the contrary, several wrongdoers are frequently proximate causes of harm.[13] Put differently, a single harm may be within the scope of liability of several different tortfeasors. In that case, are all liable to the plaintiff, either jointly and severally or on the basis of their comparative fault shares.

On the other hand, if a second person or a new force unforeseeably intervenes to substantially alter or enhance the risk of harm the defendant created, responsibility for the injury may fall solely upon the second actor.[14] The second actor's unforeseeable conduct in such a case will often be called a superseding cause. In these intervening cause cases, courts may phrase the foreseeability test somewhat narrowly, by asking whether the intervening cause itself was foreseeable rather than by asking whether the general type of harm was foreseeable. Under either version of the foreseeability test, courts appear to be working toward the same central idea, that the defendant's liability is limited to those harms risked by his negligence, so that he escapes liability altogether for those harms that were not reasonably foreseeable at the time he acted.[15]

§ 15.2 Reasons for Scope of Liability Limitations

Practical concerns. Why is a defendant, whose negligent act has caused harm, allowed to avoid liability under the scope of liability rules? Courts and writers often

---

[12]   Ehrgott v. City of N.Y., 96 N.Y. 264 (1884); Travis v. City of Mesquite, 830 S.W.2d 94 (Tex. 1992). Although the point is well-settled and logically inescapable, courts often speak of "the" proximate cause, presumably without meaning to attack the settled rule. Use of the phrase "sole proximate cause" perhaps implies that there can be only one proximate cause of harm; this incorrect implication is one reason the Third Restatement suggests that "sole proximate cause" is "a term best avoided." Restatement Third of Torts (Liability for Physical and Emotional Harm) § 34, cmt. f (2010).

[13]   See Pearson v. Tippmann Pneumatics, Inc., 281 Ga. 740, 642 S.E.2d 691 (2007); Holmes v. Levine, 273 Va. 150, 639 S.E.2d 235 (2007).

[14]   See §§ 15.16 & 15.20.

[15]   See § 15.21 on some courts' abolition of the superseding cause approach.

suggest that the proximate cause limitation is imposed primarily for practical reasons.[16] Without such a limit, liability, they say, would go on forever, one harm leading endlessly to others. The negligently made vacuum requires a trip to the repair shop, which leads the user to an auto accident, which leads to medical attention, which leads to another injury, which leads to loss of a job, and so on, more or less without end. The argument is that the line against liability must be drawn somewhere and that the scope of liability or proximate cause rules reflect the effort courts make to draw that line.

Principled limitations. The reasons for so-called proximate cause limitations on liability are principled as well as practical. Judgments about proximate cause are not precise, but, at least roughly speaking, they reflect the ideas of justice as well as practicality.[17] In particular, the rules of proximate cause or scope of liability attempt to limit liability to the reasons for imposing liability in the first place.[18] For instance, if the defendant is considered to be negligent only because it makes a vacuum cleaner that does not clean well, it should not be held liable when the purchaser is in an automobile accident while taking the cleaner to be repaired. The defendant in such a case negligently created a risk that the cleaner was not worth its price or that carpets would remain dirty. If the defendant is liable at all, those are the kinds of harms to which liability extends. But equally, the defendant's liability should be limited to such harms, for those are the ones that led us to say the defendant was negligent.[19] Proximate cause rules, which may dictate these results, can be seen as limiting liability to its reasons.

As a corollary to negligence rules. Scope of liability or proximate cause concerns are not limited to negligence cases.[20] Where negligence cases are concerned, however, a rule limiting liability to the scope of the risk may be viewed as a corollary to or even a part of the basic rule of negligence.[21] Negligence rules say that the defendant is free to ignore risks (foreseeable harms) that a reasonable person would ignore. This might be the case because the risks are small or because the costs of avoiding the risks are too high. If the

---

[16] See Palsgraf v. Long Island R.R., 248 N.Y. 339, 162 N.E. 99, 59 A.L.R. 1253 (1928) (Andrews, J., dissenting) ("What we do mean by the word proximate is that, because of convenience, of public policy, of a rough sense of justice, the law arbitrarily declines to trace a series of events beyond a certain point. This is not logic. It is practical politics."); see also Staelens v. Dobert, 318 F.3d 77 (1st Cir. 2003) (without proximate cause limits, "liability would extend endlessly, one harm leading inevitably to others."); Poskus v. Lombardo's of Randolph, Inc., 670 N.E.2d 383, 423 Mass. 637 (1996) ("There must be limits to the scope or definition of reasonable foreseeability based on considerations of policy and pragmatic judgment."). These cases notwithstanding, policy limitations on liability that are independent of foreseeability are now usually imposed on the ground that the defendant's duty was limited, not on proximate cause grounds.

[17] See Zaza v. Marquess and Nell, Inc., 144 N.J. 34, 675 A.2d 620 (1996) (quoting Caputzal v. Lindsay Co., 48 N.J. 69, 222 A.2d 513 (1966)) ("[Proximate cause doctrine is] an instrument of fairness and policy, although the conclusion is frequently expressed in the confusing language of causation, foreseeability and natural and probable consequences The determination of proximate cause by a court is to be based upon mixed considerations of logic, common sense, justice, policy and precedent.").

[18] See Restatement Third of Torts (Liability for Physical and Emotional Harm) § 29 (2010).

[19] Cf. Lodge v. Arett Sales Corp., 246 Conn. 563, 717 A.2d 215 (1988) (fire engine on way to deal with what turned out to be a false alarm crashed when brakes failed; company that negligently sent the alarm is not liable for the injuries incurred; they were not among the risks generated by a false alarm).

[20] Proximate cause rules or some close analog have been applied, for example, in some strict liability cases, e.g., Fandrey ex rel. Connell v. American Family Mut. Ins. Co., 272 Wis.2d 46, 680 N.W.2d 345 (2004), and in civil rights cases, see Powers v. Hamilton Public Defenders Com'n, 501 F.3d 592 (6th Cir. 2007). Notably, however, scope of risk or proximate cause rules are generally inapplicable in cases where the defendant acted intentionally or recklessly. See Restatement Third of Torts (Liability for Physical and Emotional Harm) § 33 (2010).

[21] See Mark F. Grady, Proximate Cause and the Law of Negligence, 69 Iowa L. Rev. 363 (1984).

scope of liability were not limited to the scope of the risk, the defendant would not, after all, be free to ignore small risks or risks that should be taken.

For example, suppose the defendant parks his car on the street, parallel to the curb, in a no-parking zone. This conduct is negligent because it runs the risk that traffic will be impeded, but leaving a car parked in a no-parking zone does not negligently create a risk of injury to an able-bodied pedestrian. Courts are likely to say that the driver is not a proximate cause of the pedestrian's harm from walking into the car, even though other risks made it negligent to park the car in such a way.

As this illustration suggests, the risk rule of proximate cause and the ordinary rule of negligence are perhaps two aspects of the same underlying idea. With suitable adaptations to the facts of particular cases, this principle, or something very close to it, furnishes a guide to "proximate cause" limitations on liability.

The language of foreseeability and risk. Professional usage almost always reduces proximate cause issues to the question of foreseeability. The defendant must have been reasonably able to foresee the kind of harm that was actually suffered by the plaintiff (or in some cases to foresee that the harm might come about through intervention of others). For the ordinary case, the principles behind scope of liability limitations can be implemented quite well by use of this language. However, the term foreseeability is itself a kind of shorthand. The defendant is not liable merely because he could foresee harm; the harm must be the kind that he should have avoided by acting more carefully. That is what is meant by saying that the harm suffered by the plaintiff must have been within the scope of the risk the defendant negligently created. Risks that the defendant could foresee but that are risks reasonably taken are no more a basis for finding "proximate cause" than for finding negligence.

Limited functions and capacities of "proximate cause" rules. The function of proximate cause rules is to facilitate or express a value judgment about the appropriate scope of liability of a defendant who is negligent and whose negligence in fact causes harm. (Recognition of this point is, of course, behind the drive to change the basic terminology from "proximate cause" to "scope of liability.") The rules and definitions are not primarily aimed at guiding the defendant's conduct but at guiding or expressing judgment about that conduct on the basis of existing social norms. The scope of liability or proximate cause rules give us the language of argument and direct the thought that is brought to bear when the connection between the defendant's negligence and the plaintiff's injury seems tenuous. The rules call for judgments, not juggernauts of logic. In consequence, no version of the rules can be expected to assure any given answer in a particular case,[22] and scope of liability or proximate cause issues must always be determined by the jury on the particular facts of the case[23] unless no reasonable jury could disagree on the issue.[24]

---

[22]   See § 15.5.

[23]   Rascher v. Friend, 279 Va. 370, 689 S.E.2d 661 (2010) ("[W]hether an act was a proximate cause of an event is best determined by a jury. This is so simply because the particular facts of each case are critical to that determination."); see also, e.g., Anselmo v. Tuck, 325 Ark. 211, 924 S.W.2d 798 (1996); Cramer v. Slater, 146 Idaho 868, 204 P.3d 508 (2009); Osborne v. Twin Town Bowl, Inc., 749 N.W.2d 367 (Minn. 2008); Foote v. Simek, 139 P.3d 455 (Wyo. 2006). A few states insist that proximate cause is a question of law for the court. See, e.g., Kim v. Budget Rent A Car Systems, Inc., 143 Wash. 2d 190, 15 P.3d 1283 (2001).

[24]   E.g., Virden v. Betts and Beer Const. Co., 656 N.W.2d 805 (Iowa 2003).

§ 15.3   Relation to Factual Cause

Conflating "proximate cause" and factual cause issues. One major source of confusion about "proximate cause"—and thus another aspect of the pesky terminology problem—lies in the fact that many courts define the term in a way that gives it two distinct meanings. In one form or another, courts often say that the plaintiff, to prove proximate cause, must show (a) factual cause[25] and (b) that the general type of harm was foreseeable.[26] The effect of this definition is that two distinct legal issues can be called by the same name. It is quite correct to say that the plaintiff must normally prove factual cause and that if the plaintiff fails to do so, she will lose. However, factual cause has little or nothing to do with the scope of liability function, turning largely on issues of foreseeability and scope of the risk, to which the so-called proximate cause rules are otherwise directed.[27] When courts conflate the two issues or group them together under the rubric of "proximate cause," lawyers cannot always be sure whether the judge is talking about factual cause or scope of liability problems. Indeed, judges sometimes seem to shift the meanings of the term without realizing it.

§ 15.4   Relation to Negligence (Breach of Duty)

Negligence foreseeability vs. "proximate cause" foreseeability. The issue of scope of liability or proximate cause does not arise at all unless the defendant is negligent in a way that can be identified. If the defendant is negligent, that necessarily means he should have foreseen some harm, of some kind, to some person or property, and that a reasonable person would have taken precautions against such harm. The foreseeability question left to be determined under the proximate cause rules is whether he should have foreseen the kind of harm or the kind of risk that in fact resulted and whether the plaintiff was within the class of persons to whom such harm might foreseeably befall.

Examples: negligence issues only. Although the difference between foreseeability on the negligence issue and foreseeability on the scope of liability (proximate cause) issue seems obvious, it is easy to overlook. When the only negligence alleged is conduct creating a foreseeable risk of the kind of harm that in fact occurred, the court's decision that negligence has been shown rules out any argument that it was not a proximate cause of the harm. Keys-in-the-car cases are good examples. If you leave the keys in the ignition of your parked car, you may be foolish, but not necessarily negligent. You would be negligent only if a reasonable person under the circumstances would foresee that some dangerous use of the car might follow, perhaps because a thief takes the car and drives it negligently. Suppose the plaintiff is injured when a thief speeds from the scene.

---

[25] E.g., Pittway Corp. v. Collins, 409 Md. 218, 973 A.2d 771 (2009). This is the meaning of the statement that a cause of harm must lead in continuous or natural sequence to the harm and in addition must be a cause without which the injury would not have occurred. See Addy v. Jenkins, 969 A.2d 935 (Me. 2009); Anderson v. Nebraska Dep't of Social Services, 248 Neb. 651, 538 N.W.2d 732 (1995); Delbrel v. Doenges Bros. Ford, Inc., 913 P.2d 1318 (Okla. 1996).

[26] E.g., Cramer v. Slater, 146 Idaho 868, 204 P.3d 508 (2009) ("Proximate cause consists of actual cause and true proximate cause, which is also referred to as legal cause."); City of Chicago v. Berretta U.S.A. Corp., 213 Ill.3d 351, 290 Ill.Dec. 525, 821 N.E.2d 1099 (2004) ("The term 'proximate cause' encompasses two distinct requirements: cause in fact and legal cause."); Sibbing v. Cave, 922 N.E.2d 594 (Ind. 2010); Puckett v. Mt. Carmel Regional Medical Center, 290 Kan. 406, 228 P.3d 1048 (2010) ("The traditional conception of proximate cause incorporates concepts that fall into two categories: cause-in-fact and legal causation."); Skinner v. Square D Co., 445 Mich. 153, 516 N.W.2d 475 (1994). On the terminology of proximate cause and factual cause, see § 14.3. The formulas and their interpretation are considered in § 15.6.

[27] See Scott v. Watson, 278 Md. 160, 359 A.2d 548 (1976) ("The determination of proximate cause is subject to considerations of fairness and social policy as well as mere [factual] causation.").

In that case, the trier's decision that you were negligent is a decision that also answers any proximate cause issue, because the finding of negligence means that you should have foreseen the thief and his reckless driving. On the other hand, if a reasonable person would not be expected to foresee a thief's negligent driving, then it is hard to see how you are negligent at all in leaving the keys in the car, since the worst that could happen would be your loss, not injury to another.[28] In cases like this, no substantial issue of scope of liability (proximate cause) arises. The issue is instead about negligence. The distinction can become important in many factual settings[29] and of course applies when the plaintiff's conduct rather than the defendant's is in issue under comparative negligence rules.[30]

Example: when scope of liability or proximate cause issue arises. None of this is to deny that scope of liability or proximate cause issues appropriately arise in many cases. If the thief who finds the owner's keys in the car drives safely away, sells the car to a dealer, who sells it to a retired lawyer, most courts will undoubtedly conclude that the owner's leaving the key in the ignition did not proximately cause the plaintiff's harm. The foreseeability issue in this example is about scope of liability, not about negligence, and its answer is that the defendant is not a "proximate cause" of the harm resulting from the lawyer's driving.

§ 15.5   Relation to Duty

Using no-duty or limited-duty rules to limit liability. Courts sometimes limit the liability of a negligent defendant by holding that the defendant owes no duty to the plaintiff, or that the defendant owes only a duty not to be grossly or wantonly negligent.[31] Scope of liability or proximate cause rules also protect negligent defendants, so the limited duty rules and the "proximate cause" rules have something in common. In fact, some courts will use the language of proximate cause to resolve some cases that other courts might resolve in the language of duty. The duty and scope of liability analyses are not, however, usefully interchangeable, even though either might get the other's result.[32] First, whether a duty is owed is a question of law, while the scope of liability issue is for the jury.[33] Second, duty rules are classically categorical and abstract; they cover a class or category of cases,[34] where scope of liability or proximate cause decisions are quite fact-specific rather than categorical.[35]

---

[28]   See Lucero v. Holbrook, 2012 WY 152, 288 P.3d 1228 (Wyo. 2012).

[29]   For example, in Estate of Heck v. Stoffer, 786 N.E.2d 265 (Ind. 2003), the defendant left his gun, insecure, in his home, though he knew that a fleeing felon had keys to the house and motive to use the gun. The felon did so, killing Officer Heck. The court, answering the defendant's no-duty argument, concluded that a jury could find the theft and killing foreseeable. The defendant then argued that the thief's conduct was a supervening cause. But once the court had permitted a finding of foreseeability, there was no viable proximate cause argument left. "[A] gun owner's duty to safely store and keep his/her firearm protects against the very result the trial court ruled was an intervening act—that a third party would obtain the firearm and use it in the commission of a crime. Denying recovery because the very act protected against occurred would make the duty a nullity."

[30]   See, e.g., Lamp v. Reynolds, 249 Mich. App. 591, 645 N.W.2d 311 (2002).

[31]   See Chapter 10.

[32]   See W. Jonathan Cardi, Purging Foreseeability, 58 Vand. L. Rev. 739 (2005).

[33]   See Jupin v. Kask, 447 Mass. 141, 849 N.E.2d 829 (2006).

[34]   See § 10.2.

[35]   See Zwiren v. Thompson, 276 Ga. 498, 578 S.E.2d 862 (2003) (proximate cause "is always to be determined on the facts of each case upon mixed considerations of logic, common sense, justice, policy, and precedent").

Duty or scope of liability: type of policy concerns involved. Finally, while policy concerns about liability can often be expressed either in the language of "proximate cause" or the language of duty, scope of liability or proximate cause is most centrally concerned with one particular policy or justice issue. It is concerned with limiting liability to risks the defendant negligently created. Duty issues are much broader. Courts may have many reasons, good or bad, for limiting liability. While some courts continue to discuss foreseeability on duty issues,[36] some reasons behind a conclusion that there either is or is not a duty relate not at all to foreseeability, which is central in "proximate cause" cases. For instance, courts may hold that social hosts may continue to serve alcohol to a guest long after his intoxication is apparent and in spite of the fact that he will foreseeability attempt to drive a car and thus impose risks of harm to others.[37] Because it was foreseeable that the drinker would drive negligently and cause injuries, it seems preposterous to say that the alcohol server was not a proximate cause of the victim's injury. If he is not liable, the reason lies elsewhere. Consequently, many decisions once cast in terms of proximate cause are now discussed in terms of duty, where policy concerns completely alien to foreseeability can be analyzed.

Simplification by excluding duty issues. Most issues that can now be seen as issues about the existence of a defendant's duty rather than issues primarily about foreseeability of harm are excluded from this chapter and left for coverage in the chapters on duty.[38] For example, courts treat stand-alone emotional distress quite differently from ordinary physical injuries.[39] In doing so, they have sometimes used the language of proximate cause. In spite of this, their real concerns have not been about foreseeability at all but about the appropriate scope of duty or responsibility for emotional conditions. Leaving these and other similar cases to be resolved under the duty concept permits a coherent view of proximate cause presented in this chapter.

The duty vs. proximate cause debate. Is it better to limit liability by saying that the defendant was under no duty, or by saying that the defendant was not a "proximate cause" of the harm? This is a long-standing and worthwhile question. When the court wishes to make a categorical rule and one not dependent on foreseeability, the issue can usefully be characterized as one of duty rather than one of scope of liability or proximate cause. Be that as it may, however, the debate about appropriate terminology is not always the same as the debate about the appropriate substantive limitations on liability. The famous *Palsgraf* case[40] complicated the lives of generations of law students by tying the terminology question to the substantive question. Judge Cardozo and the majority insisted that the issue should be cast in the terminology of duty and that the substantive rule should relieve the defendant of liability if harm to the plaintiff was unforeseeable. Judge Andrews and the dissenters thought that the issue should be cast in the terminology of proximate cause and that as a matter of substantive law, foreseeability should *not* be determinative. In contemporary law, the terminology distinction has become unimportant whenever the court concludes that the harm inflicted was unforeseeable as a matter of law. Most courts today agree that, whether the issue is cast as one of duty or of proximate cause, the defendant is not liable for unforeseeable kinds

---

[36] See David G. Owen, Figuring Foreseeability, 44 Wake Forest L. Rev. 1277 (2009) (discussing the continued importance of foreseeability in duty determinations).

[37] See § 26.12.

[38] See Chapter 10.

[39] See Chapter 29.

[40] Palsgraf v. Long Island Railroad Co., 248 N.Y. 339, 162 N.E.2d 99 (1928), discussed in § 15.7.

of harm.[41] The distinction remains important, however, when courts wish to limit liability for reasons unrelated to foreseeability.

§ 15.6 Patterns and Formal Tests of Scope of Liability

Courts perceive scope of liability or proximate cause issues in two distinct patterns. Although they ultimately concern themselves with foreseeability in both patterns, the formal language of discussion and the kind of foreseeability involved may depend upon which pattern is involved.

Direct-harm pattern and example. In the first pattern, the defendant negligently creates a risk of a harm—call it Harm A—but an entirely different harm—Harm B—results. For example, the defendant negligently drops a banana peel on the walk, creating a foreseeable risk that someone will slip on it. The plaintiff does not slip on the banana peel but hurts her back when she bends over to pick it up. In this kind of situation most courts simply ask whether the harm that occurred was foreseeable, that is, whether it was one of the general kinds of harm that was unreasonably risked by the defendant's negligence.

Intervening cause pattern and example. In the second situation, the defendant creates a risk of harm but the immediate trigger for the harm is some other force or person. For example, the defendant negligently drops the banana peel and the plaintiff slips on it, but only because a purse snatcher pushes her as he grabs her purse. In this situation courts are also concerned with foreseeability, but they typically use more complicated language to formulate their inquiries, asking whether the purse snatcher may have been a new cause that superseded the negligence of the banana peel dropper.

Substantial identity of issues. In a strictly literal sense, perhaps all cases belong in the intervening cause category. The plaintiff who injured her back in bending over to pick up the banana peel could herself be viewed as an intervening cause. Almost inevitably, something, if only the movement of air, must intervene between the defendant's act and the plaintiff's injury. But it is also true that the intervening cause cases all entail questions about the scope of the risk, so they can be resolved without a mention of intervening or superseding causes.[42] The distinction between direct and indirect causes could very well be abolished, leaving courts merely to ask whether the injury that occurred was within the risk created by the defendant. Indeed, the cases as a whole may have that effect. Nevertheless, in some cases, courts selectively ignore intervening cause analysis while in others they reach out for it. If the result is the same overall, the language of the opinions is not, so the distinction cannot be wholly ignored.

Formal tests. The term *proximate cause* by itself explains nothing, not even the kind of evidence to be considered. In an effort to define the term, courts have at various times

---

[41] See, e.g., Foss v. Kincade, 766 N.W.2d 317 (Minn. 2009); Lucero v. Holbrook, 288 P.3d 1228 (Wyo. 2012).

[42] E.g., Sharp v. Town of Highland, 665 N.E.2d 610 (Ind. App. 1996). Two leading cases, Overseas Tankship (U.K.), Limited v. Morts Dock & Engineering Co., Limited (The Wagon Mound), [1961] A.C. 388 (Privy Council 1961), and Palsgraf v. Long Island Railroad Co., 248 N.Y. 339, 162 N.E. 99 (1928), could have been resolved by discussing intervening causes, but both courts went straight to the foreseeability issue without first discussing intervening cause. For a discussion of the approach some modern courts have taken in rejecting intervening cause analysis, see § 15.21.

invoked a litany of equally impenetrable phrases, some of them simply opaque, others actively misleading.[43]

With slight variations in the words, courts usually instruct juries or begin their own appellate discussions with a formal definition asserting that a proximate cause of an injury is one which, in a natural and continuous sequence, without any efficient intervening cause, produces the injury.[44] Sometimes courts define *proximate* by saying that the defendant is liable only for the "natural and probable consequences" of his acts,[45] a test that arguably might be read to put slightly less emphasis on the sequence of events because it is quickly reduced nowadays to a foreseeability test.[46] In either case, if the plaintiff's injury is triggered by a new or intervening cause—one arising after the defendant's negligent act—courts may conclude that the new cause is a superseding cause and that the defendant is relieved of liability.

The emphasis on sequence and intervening causes seems to depart from a foreseeability rule. But analysis, and most actual decisions as well, indicate that the test ultimately asks judges or juries to consider the reasonable foreseeability of the harm caused or the forces involved in causing it. Judges considering the first or direct harm pattern of cases usually want to know whether the general type of harm is foreseeable, while judges considering the second or intervening cause pattern may want to know whether the intervening actor or the force he represents is foreseeable.

§ 15.7   The Direct-Cause Pattern and Foreseeable Harms

The basic issue. In the direct-cause pattern, the defendant negligently risks one kind of harm but an entirely different kind of harm befalls the plaintiff. The problem in such cases is not that some new cause supersedes the defendant's liability, although courts often try to impose a superseding cause analysis upon such cases. The only problem is whether to impose liability for unforeseeable kinds of harm.

Liability for foreseeable harms. The great majority of cases hold negligent defendants liable only for harm of the same general kind that they should have reasonably foreseen and should have acted to avoid.[47] The phrase, "should have acted to avoid" is a necessary part of the rule; many harms are foreseeable but not risky enough

---

[43]   To take one noteworthy example, some authorities said that to be a proximate cause, the defendant's conduct must be a substantial factor in causing the plaintiff's harm. That term explains nothing about what to look for and runs the risk of confusing factual cause issues, to which it is sometimes applied in lieu of the but-for test. See David W. Robertson, The Common Sense of Cause in Fact, 75 Tex. L. Rev. 1765 (1997).

[44]   Milwaukee & St. P. R. Co. v. Kellogg, 94 U.S. 469, 24 L.Ed. 256 (1876) (the facts must "constitute a continuous succession of events, so linked together as to make a natural whole" without a "new and independent cause intervening between the wrong and the injury"); Anselmo v. Tuck, 325 Ark. 211, 924 S.W.2d 798 (1996); Hale v. Brown, 287 Kan. 320, 197 P.3d 438 (2008); CSX Transp., Inc. v. Continental Ins. Co., 343 Md. 216, 680 A.2d 1082 (1996) ("cause which, in a natural and continuous sequence, unbroken by any efficient intervening cause, logically and probably produces the injury"); Kellermann v. McDonough, 278 Va. 478, 684 S.E.2d 786 (2009).

[45]   E.g., Gilmore v. Shell Oil Co., 613 So.2d 1272 (Ala. 1993).

[46]   See, e.g., Ross v. Nutt, 177 Ohio St. 113, 203 N.E.2d 118 (1964) ("To find that an injury was the natural and probable consequence of an act, it must appear that the injury complained of could have been foreseen or reasonably anticipated from the alleged negligent act.").

[47]   E.g., Tetro v. Town of Stratford, 189 Conn. 601, 458 A.2d 5 (1983) ("The test for finding proximate cause 'is whether the harm which occurred was of the same general nature as the foreseeable risk created by the defendant's negligence.' . . . The foreseeable risk may include the acts of the plaintiff and of third parties."); Thompson v. Kaczinski, 774 N.W.2d 829 (Iowa 2009); Leavitt v. Brockton Hospital, Inc., 454 Mass. 37, 907 N.E.2d 213 (2009); J.T. Baggerly v. CSX Transp., Inc., 370 S.C. 362, 635 S.E.2d 97 (2006). The foreseeability rule may be stated as a rule that the defendant owes no duty or is not negligent except as to foreseeable risks. Di Ponzio v. Riordan, 89 N.Y.2d 578, 679 N.E.2d 616, 657 N.Y.S.2d 377 (1997).

to require greater care.[48] Liability attaches when the defendant not only should have foreseen the type of harm but also should have done something better to avoid it. Literal foreseeability by itself is not enough. The same principle holds defendants liable only to plaintiffs who are in the same general class of people who were at risk from his negligence.[49] These rules make liability congruent with risk or foreseeability. Affirmatively, the defendant is liable for the types of harm he unreasonably risked. Negatively, the defendant is not liable for types of harm that he could not reasonably foresee or those that were foreseeable but were risked by non-negligent, reasonably safe conduct.

The foreseeability rule does not allow a negligent defendant to avoid liability merely because a reasonable person would not have foreseen specific details about the injury or how it happened. It is enough for liability that the kinds of risks, harms, or classes of person were foreseeable in a general way.[50] Similarly, the negligent defendant does not avoid liability merely because the extent of injury is far greater than he could reasonably have foreseen.[51]

The Wagon Mound illustration: type of harm risked. Since the 1960s, an English case has provided a basic model for the foreseeability or risk rule. A ship known as the Wagon Mound, which gives its name to the case,[52] was anchored in the harbor at Sydney, Australia. The ship negligently discharged oil into the water, but, strange to say, the oil created no discernible risk of fire because its composition required very high heat to ignite it.[53] Although the oil created no foreseeable risk of fire, it did create some other risks, most notably the risk that docks in the area would be fouled. To everyone's surprise—a phrase that can almost always announce a proximate cause issue—an improbable concatenation of events led to a fire after all. A piece of debris was floating on the water just under the oil. On the debris a piece of cotton was supported, all apparently by chance. A welder's torch gave off sparks that struck the cotton. The cotton smoldered long enough to acquire sufficient heat to ignite the oil, and the plaintiff's dock was burned.

Under English authority existing up until that time, it would have been possible to reason that the defendant should be liable for the fire because there were no new independent causes of it; the defendant was a direct cause and that would have been enough for liability.[54] But the Privy Council adopted the risk rule instead. It held that liability for negligence was to be coextensive with the negligence. If the defendant negligently created a risk of harm A, but harm B resulted instead, the defendant would not be liable for harm B. The Privy Council thought that since the only harm foreseeable from negligent discharge of the oil was harm in the nature of fouled docks, the defendant should not be liable for the entirely unforeseeable harm caused by fire. One way to express the idea is to say that, as to the fire, the defendant created no unreasonable risk and hence as to the fire, the defendant was not negligent at all. American cases are

---

[48]   See Lodge v. Arett Sales Corp., 246 Conn. 563, 717 A.2d 215 (1998).

[49]   E.g., Splendorio v. Bilray Demolition Co., 682 A.2d 461 (R.I. 1996). Cf. Fisher v. Swift Transp. Co., 342 Mont. 335, 181 P.3d 601 (2008) (duty owed only to foreseeable plaintiffs).

[50]   See § 15.12.

[51]   See § 15.11.

[52]   Overseas Tankship (U.K.), Ltd. v. Morts Dock & Engineering Co., Limited (The Wagon Mound), [1961] A.C. 388 (Privy Council 1961).

[53]   For purposes of the decision, the House of Lords accepted the finding that fire was not foreseeable. Later evidence might cast the finding in doubt, but for purposes of the case, it must be taken as true.

[54]   See § 15.8.

overwhelmingly consistent with this rule, although their manner of expression is often slightly different.

The *Wagon Mound* case should not be misunderstood. If the risk of fire had been small but foreseeable and the defendant had had a good reason to discharge the oil, the balance of risks and utilities might indicate that the defendant was not negligent at all and hence not liable. On the other hand, if the defendant had no good reason for discharging the oil, even a small risk of fire might be enough to justify a finding that the defendant was negligent. In that case, the fact that fire was foreseeable would indicate that the defendant should be liable for fire damage, even though the risk was small.[55]

The Palsgraf illustration: class of persons at risk. The most famous American case on proximate cause (or almost anything) is grounded in the same basic idea that liability should be limited to risks created by the defendant's negligent conduct. In *Palsgraf v. Long Island Railroad Co.*,[56] railroad employees helping a passenger onto a moving train may have negligently jostled his arm, causing him to drop a package. If the employees were negligent at all, it must have been because they created a risk of harm to the passenger, to his package, or by a stretch of imagination to someone very close by. What happened in fact was that the innocent looking package contained fireworks, which exploded when the package fell. As a result of the explosion, some scales at the other end of the platform fell on Mrs. Palsgraf.

Since the unreasonable risk created by the defendant was a risk to the passenger, or at most to a very small circle of persons who might have been close enough to be injured if he fell, it created no recognizable risk at all to Mrs. Palsgraf. As Judge Cardozo said, "Relatively to her it was not negligence at all,"[57] so the defendant was not liable. Although Cardozo did not express this result as a rule of proximate cause, the outcome it dictates is the outcome of a proximate cause rule based on foreseeability of risk. "[T]he orbit of the danger as disclosed to the eye of reasonable vigilance" marked the scope of liability.[58]

Rescuers. Rescuer cases raise issues about the scope of the Palsgraf class-of-persons rule. In a leading case, *Wagner v. International Railway*,[59] the defendant caused A to fall from a train into a gorge. B went in search of the body. Then B himself fell into the chasm. The trial court held that the defendant's negligence toward A would not support a claim for injury to B. This sounds like the *Palsgraf* rule, but on appeal, Judge Cardozo held that B could recover. Unfortunately, Judge Cardozo did not make it clear whether he regarded liability as an exception to *Palsgraf* or whether he believed that, since "[d]anger invites rescue," the rescue and hence the rescuer was within the scope of the foreseeable risk.

---

[55] This was essentially the proof in another round of the same case, Wagon Mound II, Overseas Tankship (U.K.), Ltd. v. Miller Steamship Co., [1967] 1 A.C. 617 (Privy Council 1966).

[56] Palsgraf v. Long Island Railroad, 248 N.Y. 339, 162 N.E.2d 99 (1928).

[57] Id. A number of courts see the "foreseeable plaintiff" issue as going to duty, not to proximate cause. See, e.g., Fisher v. Swift Transp. Co., 342 Mont. 335, 181 P.3d 601 (2008).

[58] Cardozo expressed the rule as a rule that the defendant was not negligent toward Mrs. Palsgraf and also as a rule that it owed her no duty. The dissent by Judge Andrews insisted that the issue was not about negligence or scope of duty but about proximate cause. On their different views and on the "duty" approach to scope of liability issues, see § 15.5. For present purposes, nomenclature is not the point.

[59] Wagner v. International Ry., 232 N.Y. 176, 133 N.E. 437 (1921).

In any event, courts usually recognize that the defendant who is negligent to A may be liable to an injured rescuer,[60] B, so long as B's actions are not wholly abnormal or hopeless.[61] The result, as most courts say, is that the defendant's negligence is a proximate cause of the rescuer's injury and the rescuer's natural heroism is not a superseding cause.[62] To invoke this rule, the rescue generally need not be spontaneous or immediate,[63] although some courts have said otherwise.[64] It has been held that B may recover for injury incurred in a reasonable rescue attempt if the defendant negligently created an appearance that rescue was needed when it was not.[65] Even when the defendant puts only himself in danger, courts have held him liable for injury to his own rescuer suffered in the course of a rescue attempt.[66] Professional rescuers like firefighters and police officers, however, may be barred from recovery under special rules often applied to them.[67]

Classes of persons and classes of risks. Palsgraf differs from *Wagon Mound* in detail but not in fundamental thrust. The fundamental thrust is that liability for negligence is limited to the risks negligently created by the defendant. The difference in detail is that the risk at issue in *Wagon Mound* could be described as a risk of a certain type or class of harm, while the risk at issue in *Palsgraf* could be described as a risk to a certain class of persons. Many, many common law cases are consistent with the scope of risk rules both in the language of foreseeability[68] and in their results.[69]

Risks to particular interests. It is possible to conceptualize different categories of legal interests or entitlements, such as one's interest in personal security as contrasted with the interest in security of one's property. With categories like this in mind, it would be possible to say that under the foreseeability or risk rules, a defendant who negligently risks harm to the plaintiff's property should not be liable if his negligent acts result in harm to the person instead. In fact, however, courts have not drawn a distinction between interests in bodily security and security of one's property.[70] Physical risks of harm to property are in the same general category as risks of physical harm to persons.

---

[60]   E.g., Solomon v. Shuell, 435 Mich. 104, 457 N.W.2d 669 (1990); Tri-State Wholesale Associated Grocers, Inc. v. Barrera, 917 S.W.2d 391(Tex. App. 1996); Restatement Third of Torts (Liability for Physical and Emotional Harm) § 32 (2010); Restatement Second of Torts § 445 (1965).

[61]   In order for the rescue doctrine to apply at all, the rescuer must have had a reasonable belief that the victim was in peril. See Rasmussen v. State Farm Mut. Auto. Ins. Co., 278 Neb. 289, 770 N.W.2d 619 (2009). The rescue doctrine has been applied, however, where the victim was not in actual danger. See Solomon v. Shuell, 435 Mich. 104, 457 N.W.2d 669 (1990). It has also been applied to rescuers of property, not just rescuers of other persons. See Restatement Third of Torts (Liability for Physical and Emotional Harm) § 32 cmt. b (2010). Since rescue is socially useful, some degree of risk-taking by rescuers is reasonable and not at all negligent.

[62]   Clinkscales v. Nelson Securities, Inc., 697 N.W.2d 836 (Iowa 2005).

[63]   See Hollingsworth v. Schminkey, 553 N.W.2d 591, 598 (Iowa 1996).

[64]   See Star Transport, Inc. v. Byard, 891 N.E.2d 1099 (Ind. App. 2008).

[65]   See Clinkscales v. Nelson Securities, Inc., 697 N.W.2d 836 (Iowa 2005); Solomon v. Shuell, 435 Mich. 104, 457 N.W.2d 669 (1990).

[66]   E.g., Sears v. Morrison, 76 Cal.App.4th 577, 90 Cal.Rptr.2d 528 (1999) (thoroughly reviewing the authorities).

[67]   See Chapter 24.

[68]   E.g., Hammerstein v. Jean Development West, 111 Nev. 1471, 907 P.2d 975 (1995).

[69]   E.g., Di Ponzio v. Riordan, 89 N.Y.2d 578, 679 N.E.2d 616, 657 N.Y.S.2d 377 (1997) (gas station negligently allowed motorist to pump gas with engine running, but was not liable when the car rolled backward and injured the plaintiff; running the engine created a fire risk, not a risk of rolling).

[70]   A prominent example of the fact that courts treat these interests as identical is found in the products liability rule that applies strict liability to physical harms of either person or property but does not apply it to stand-alone economic harm. See § 33.3.

If a man negligently sets fire to your house, he is properly held liable for harm to its occupants, even if he had every assurance that the house was empty at the time.[71] Put differently, injury to persons by forces negligently unleashed is not a different kind of injury from injury to property.

§ 15.8 The Direct-Cause Pattern and Unforeseeable Harms

Purported liability for unforeseeable harms. Language used by a few courts suggests they will impose liability upon a negligent defendant for harms that are different in kind from the harms he could have reasonably foreseen.[72] Those courts sometimes seem to say that, given duty, negligence, and factual cause, it is enough that the harm occurred directly, without the intervention of a new actor. It is very doubtful that liability unlimited by foreseeability has much contemporary support.

The Polemis Case. Polemis[73] was a leading case for the rule that the defendant would be liable for all harms directly caused, whether they were foreseeable or not. A stevedore aboard a vessel placed planks across a hatchway. A sling dislodged one of the planks; it fell into the ship's hold. Flames immediately erupted and consumed the ship. The sling operator could surely foresee that if the plank were dislodged, someone below might be struck by it, but no one who has tried making a fire by rubbing pieces of wood together could expect a flame. It was an entirely unexpected result, but because it was "direct," the English Court of Appeal held that the defendants responsible for the plank's fall were liable.

Three groups of cases. Polemis itself was effectively overruled by the *Wagon Mound* decision.[74] Three narrow groups of cases might be understood to support a kind of *Polemis*/direct harm liability unlimited by foreseeability rules. (1) In the rescue cases, the defendant creates a risk to A; he is held liable not only to A for any harm done to him but also to rescuers who come to his aid.[75] These cases do not seem necessarily counter to the foreseeability rule. Injury to a rescuer from the forces set in motion by the defendant's negligence seems to fall easily enough within the scope of the risks created by the defendant. (2) The second group of cases involves a plaintiff who is unusually susceptible to injury and who, for that reason, suffers more harm than an ordinary person as a result of the defendant's negligence. Consistent with the foreseeability or scope of risk approach, these cases can be understood to reflect the general rule that the defendant is liable for the general type of harm he foreseeably put at risk, even if that harm is greater in degree than could be expected.[76] (3) A third group of cases once held that if a carrier of goods negligently delayed delivery to the consignee, it would be liable for any harm that befell the delayed goods, even if that harm resulted from an unforeseeable force of nature over which the carrier had no control. As explained elsewhere, these cases probably have little contemporary effect.[77] In addition, both the

---

[71] Cf. Railway Exp. Agency, Inc. v. Brabham, 62 So.2d 713 (Fla. 1952) (truck running over a box; issue avoided by saying that driver could have reasonably foreseen that a small boy would be in the box).

[72] Busta v. Columbus Hosp. Corp., 276 Mont. 342, 916 P.2d 122 (1996); Rockweit v. Senecal, 197 Wis.2d 409, 541 N.W.2d 742 (1995).

[73] In re Arbitration between Polemis and Furness, Withy & Co., Ltd., [1921] 3 K.B. 560 (C.A. 1921).

[74] See § 15.7.

[75] Id.

[76] See § 15.11.

[77] See § 15.15.

rescue and susceptible plaintiff cases are generally accepted in jurisdictions that clearly limit liability to foreseeable harms.

Reasons to doubt that liability is imposed beyond the risk. Several reasons suggest caution in interpreting cases that purport to impose liability beyond foreseeable harms. Some cases that verbally reject foreseeability as a test of proximate cause in fact limit liability to foreseeable harms under a duty or negligence analysis. In other words, they do not reject the use of foreseeability to limit liability but merely insist that it is to be considered under the heading of duty rather than proximate cause.[78]

Still another reason for uncertainty about cases purporting to impose liability beyond the risk is that, in some formulations, they may stand for no more than the accepted rule that the defendant does not escape liability merely because he could not foresee the exact manner or extent of harm.[79] If they mean no more than this, they are not minority cases at all, but firmly within the mainstream of the foreseeability rule.[80]

Finally, courts that purport to ignore foreseeability on the scope of liability or proximate cause issue are quite willing, like other courts, to make foreseeability controlling as soon as an intervening cause is perceived.[81] The upshot is that less than a handful of courts purport to apply the kind of strict liability entailed in imposing liability beyond the risk the defendant unreasonably created, and even those may covertly or sporadically introduce foreseeability into the liability equation.

It remains to be said that while few cases seem to impose liability for unforeseeable harms, some cases may move in the other direction by rejecting liability even for harms that are entirely foreseeable. This was always the potential under the Polemis direct harm test and some courts have said, at least in certain commercial harm cases, that the harm must be *both* foreseeable and direct, dismissing the claim for foreseeable harm if the harm was not also "direct."[82]

§ 15.9   The Intervening Cause Pattern and Superseding Cause Analysis

In the intervening cause cases, the defendant negligently creates risks of harm, but the immediate trigger of the harm is another person or a force of nature.[83] That by itself presents no impediment to relief. If the first actor negligently creates a risk of harm and the second actor negligently triggers the risk, both actors are tortfeasors, both are causes in fact of the harm, and both are commonly held liable to the plaintiff under the rules of joint and several liability or comparative fault shares.[84] However, in some instances, the second actor causes a harm that may be unforeseeable—outside the scope of the risk originally created by the first. Courts frequently discuss such cases by asking whether the second actor is a "superseding cause" so that the negligence of the first actor is ignored and he escapes all liability. Such cases are simply subsets or particular examples of the basic scope of the risk problem and can be resolved under ordinary foreseeability

---

[78]   E.g., Busta v. Columbus Hosp. Corp., 276 Mont. 342, 916 P.2d 122 (1996) (using a direct-cause test of proximate cause but invoking foreseeability to limit liability).

[79]   See §§ 15.11 & 15.12.

[80]   See Petition of Kinsman Transit Co., 338 F.2d 708 (2d Cir. 1964).

[81]   E.g., LaFaso v. LaFaso, 126 Vt. 90, 223 A.2d 814 (1966).

[82]   Owens Corning v. R.J. Reynolds Tobacco Co., 868 So.2d 331 (Miss. 2004).

[83]   See §§ 15.14 to 15.19.

[84]   See generally Chapter 35.

rules without any intervening cause or superseding cause language at all.[85] A few courts have in fact abandoned the superseding cause analysis, partly on the ground that it is duplicative of the basic scope of risk analysis and confusing to boot.[86] However, the focus on temporal sequences in the superseding cause analysis tends to detract from the essential foreseeability analysis it purports to follow.[87]

Identifying intervening acts and forces. The courts' verbal approach in these cases is built on a rickety scaffold of terms and definitions. First, the issue does not arise at all unless a new force qualifies as an intervening cause. An intervening cause is a new cause that comes into play after the defendant's negligent conduct. If the intervening force is in operation at the time the defendant acted, it is not an intervening cause at all.[88] For instance, if the defendant sets a fire when the wind is blowing, he cannot avoid liability when the wind carries the fire to the plaintiff's house. The wind, as a force in operation when the defendant acted, is not an intervening cause.[89] In many routine cases, causes are deemed legally concurrent rather than intervening. Suppose drivers of two cars both negligently contribute to a collision or a series of collisions that harm the plaintiff. Such cases are almost always treated as cases of concurring negligence, even if the negligence of one driver occurred later than the negligence of the other.[90] The effect is that both are liable for at least a share of the plaintiff's damages and neither can claim the other as a superseding cause.

Superseding causes. If courts perceive an intervening act or force as triggering injury, the defendant's original negligence is still one of the proximate causes of harm if the defendant's conduct led to the plaintiff's injury in a continuous sequence, uninterrupted by an efficient or independent intervening cause.[91] On the other hand, if the judge or the trier of fact believes that the intervening cause is the *only* proximate cause because it is the efficient or immediate cause, then the intervening cause will be called a superseding cause and the defendant will not be liable.[92]

For example, if the defendant left a dangerous open cellar or excavation and an intervening actor pushed the plaintiff into it, some courts, at least at one time, concluded that the intervening actor was an efficient, independent, or superseding cause of the plaintiff's harm. The result was that the defendant, who made the danger available in the first place, was not liable at all.[93] Sometimes the idea is expressed by saying, somewhat argumentatively, that the defendant only passively created a condition or

---

[85]   See People v. Brady, 129 Cal. App.4th 1314, 1333, 29 Cal. Rptr. 3d 286, 302 (2005); Berte v. Bode, 692 N.W.2d 368, 374 (Iowa 2005) (describing superseding cause issues as subsets of the proximate cause issue); Restatement Third of Torts (Liability for Physical and Emotional Harm) § 34 (2010). A few courts place the burden on the defendant to prove a superseding cause, regarding it as an affirmative defense. E.g., Mengwasser v. Anthony Kempker Trucking, Inc., 312 S.W.3d 368 (Mo. App. 2010).

[86]   See § 15.21.

[87]   Cf. Restatement Third of Torts (Liability for Physical and Emotional Harm) § 34 cmt. a (2010) (noting that "were it not for the long history of intervening and superseding causes playing a significant role in limiting liability, this Section would not be necessary" since it tracks the basic and more general scope of liability rule).

[88]   Farr v. NC Machinery Co., 186 F.3d 1165 (9th Cir. 1999) ("A superseding cause generally has to happen after the negligence of the defendant."); Regan v. Stromberg, 285 N.W.2d 97 (Minn. 1979).

[89]   See Chamberland v. Roswell Osteopathic Clinic, Inc., 130 N.M. 532, 27 P.3d 1019 (Ct. App. 2001).

[90]   See, e.g., Watts v. Smith, 375 Mich. 120, 134 N.W.2d 194 (1965).

[91]   See § 15.6 (stating the formal rule).

[92]   E.g., Malolepszy v. State, 273 Neb. 313, 729 N.W.2d 669 (2007).

[93]   See, e.g., Loftus v. Dehail, 133 Cal. 214, 65 P. 379 (1901), and Miller v. Bahmmuller, 124 A.D. 558, 108 N.Y.S. 924 (1908), cases relied upon by the Restatement Second's § 442B in support of its illustration 7.

occasion that made harm possible but that he was not a cause.[94] All of these statements express conclusions, but none of them offers either reasons or guidance to lawyers. Such statements add one more layer of confusion to the analysis.[95] In any event, the propriety of the result in cases like these depends first upon the facts of each case, second upon judicial ideas about the appropriate scope of liability (ideas that have arguably changed over the years), and third upon available alternatives, which now include joint and several liability and comparative fault shares of liability.[96]

Foreseeable intervening causes. A ruling that an intervening actor is a superseding cause embodies the dual conclusion that the intervening actor should be responsible and that the original actor, in spite of his causal negligence, should not. The intervening cause terminology makes the issue look as if it were only concerned about the sequence of events and unrelated to issues of responsibility, foreseeability, or scope of risk. But in contemporary law, when courts then ask what counts as a superseding cause, they return to some form of the foreseeability inquiry. The rule is that if the intervening cause itself is part of the risk negligently created by the defendant,[97] or if it is reasonably foreseeable at the time of the defendant's negligent conduct,[98] then it is not a superseding cause at all. In that case, the defendant is not relieved of liability merely because some other person or force triggered the injury. The wordy labels—superseding, intervening, efficient, independent—although almost always invoked, turn out to be surplusage. The ultimate inquiry on scope of the defendant's liability is merely whether the intervening cause is foreseeable or whether the injury is within the scope of the risk negligently created by the defendant.[99]

Example. In a leading New York case,[100] the plaintiff was working for a company that sealed gas mains with boiling enamel. The contractor responsible for the project required the plaintiff to work at one end of a street excavation where he was exposed to oncoming traffic and protected only by a quite inadequate barricade. This put the plaintiff at risk that the plaintiff or the boiling enamel or both might be struck by a negligent driver. A driver suffered a seizure and ran through the barricade and into the excavation, causing severe injury to the plaintiff. Because the driver had failed to take his anti-seizure medication, the contractor argued that the driver was a superseding cause of the plaintiff's injury. The argument failed. One reason was that the main outlines of the risk to the plaintiff through intervening negligence were foreseeable, even if the driver's seizure itself was not.[101] Put more generally, an intervening cause does not

---

[94]   E.g., Graham v. Keuchel, 847 P.2d 342 (Okla. 1993).

[95]   See Marshall v. Nugent, 222 F.2d 604 (1st Cir. 1955); Duncavage v. Allen, 147 Ill.App.3d 88, 497 N.E.2d 433, 100 Ill.Dec. 455 (1986) (noting that the cause-condition distinction has been discredited).

[96]   As to the intervening criminal acts vs. intervening negligent acts, see § 15.14 & 15.16.

[97]   See, e.g., Goldberg v. Florida Power & Light Co., 899 So.2d 1105, 1116 (Fla. 2005).

[98]   Winschel v. Brown, 171 P.3d 142 (Alaska 2007); Latzel v. Bartek, 846 N.W.2d 153 (Neb. 2014); Johnson v. Hillcrest Health Ctr., Inc., 70 P.3d 811 (Okla. 2003).

[99]   E.g., Bailey v. Lewis Farm, Inc., 343 Or. 276, 171 P.3d 336 (2007).

[100] Derdiarian v. Felix Contracting Corp., 51 N.Y.2d 308, 434 N.Y.S.2d 166, 414 N.E.2d 666 (1980).

[101] In J.T. Baggerly v. CSX Transp., Inc., 370 S.C. 362, 635 S.E.2d 97 (2006), defendants responsible for the condition of railroad tracks failed to keep ballast at the proper level, risking misalignment of tracks and derailment of a train. The tracks so maintained were struck by a street sweeper manned by a driver who had fallen asleep. The blow evidently threw the tracks into misalignment, and the next train, running on the track a few minutes later, derailed, injuring the plaintiff. Proper ballast would have caused the sweeper to ride up over the tracks and not to cause their misalignment. Defendants were subjected to a jury decision on proximate cause; they could foresee misalignment and derailment from some blow, even if they could not foresee that the driver of a sweeper would fall asleep.

supersede the defendant's negligence when it reflects the same general kind of risk which rendered the defendant negligent.

Unforeseeable intervening causes outside the scope of risk. Courts usually say that if an intervening act (or force) is not reasonably foreseeable, then the intervening event is a superseding cause and the defendant as the original actor is relieved of liability.[102] This statement seems to imply that the intervening force itself, not merely the general kind of harm, must have been reasonably foreseeable when the defendant acted. That is not invariably true, however.

B. THE GENERAL RULES OF FORESEEABILITY

§ 15.10 Foreseeability Terminology: Scope of Risk

As the preceding sections show, courts usually reduce the tests of scope of liability or proximate cause, both in direct and in intervening cause cases, to a question of foreseeability. To some extent, the language of foreseeability is simply a shorthand expression intended to say that the scope of the defendant's liability is determined by the scope of the risk he negligently created.[103] Foreseeability correlates with this idea in most cases, but it can be misleading in others. Some harms that are entirely foreseeable are nevertheless not harms a reasonable and prudent person would seek to avoid. The point of limiting the defendant's liability under so-called proximate cause rules is to make the defendant's liability coextensive with his negligence. Consequently, the defendant is not liable even for foreseeable harms if he was not negligent in failing to minimize those harms. A more accurate statement would be that the defendant is not liable for foreseeable harms unless the risk of such harms was one of the reasons for judging him to be negligent in the first place.[104]

Perhaps the easiest illustration is the kind of case in which the defendant is negligent in driving a vehicle at high speed and because of the speed arrives at a spot just in time to be struck by a large tree that falls or an airplane that crashes. An injured passenger can certainly assert that falling trees or crashing airplanes are foreseeable. Nevertheless, the defendant's speed does nothing to create or increase the risk of such an incident. Falling trees are foreseeable, but not a greater risk to those who drive fast than to those who drive slowly. Consequently, the defendant is not liable for injuries resulting in this manner.[105] When courts say that such a risk is unforeseeable what they mean is that it is not a risk enhanced or created by the defendant's conduct.

A carrier's delay in delivering goods can create exactly the same kind of problem. The delay may be negligent because it runs the risk that the shipper or the consignee will suffer economic losses if the goods are not delivered on time. If, because of the delay, the goods aboard a carrier are subjected to an unforeseeable flood or other force of nature,

---

[102] E.g., Duphily v. Delaware Elec. Co-op., Inc., 662 A.2d 821, 829 (Del. 1995) ("If the intervening negligence of a third party was reasonably foreseeable, the original tortfeasor is liable for his negligence because the causal connection between the original tortious act and the resulting injury remains unbroken. If, however, the intervening negligence was not reasonably foreseeable, the intervening act supersedes and becomes the sole proximate cause of the plaintiff's injuries, thus relieving the original tortfeasor of liability.").

[103] See People v. Brady, 129 Cal. App. 4th 1314, 1333, 29 Cal. Rptr. 3d 286, 302 (2005).

[104] See Mitchell v. Cedar Rapids Community School Dist., 832 N.W.2d 689 (Iowa 2013); Restatement Third of Torts (Liability for Physical and Emotional Harm) § 29, cmts. d & j (2010). Cf. Leavitt v. Brockton Hosp., Inc., 454 Mass. 37, 907 N.E.2d 213 (2009) ("resulting injury [must be] within the scope of foreseeable risk arising from the negligent conduct").

[105] Berry v. Sugar Notch Borough, 191 Pa. 345, 43 A. 240 (1899).

loss of or damage to the goods is fortuitous. Although we all know that floods occur and are in that sense foreseeable, reasonable persons do not act on the remote possibility of flooding. For that reason, a carrier does not create an unreasonable risk of flood damage to goods by its delay unless some immediate danger would be apparent. The carrier in such a case is negligent, but not negligent with respect to risks of flooding, so the carrier's negligence is not a "proximate cause" of the flood damage—in other words, the flood damage was not one of the risks the defendant created by its delay. That is all that courts mean by saying that the flood was unforeseeable or that it was an intervening act of God.[106]

§ 15.11   Foreseeability Required: Extent of Harm

General rule. Courts assume a radical distinction between the *nature* of a harm and its *extent*. The foreseeability or risk rule holds the defendant subject to liability if he could reasonably foresee the nature of the harm done, even if the total amount of harm turned out to be quite unforeseeably large.[107] For example, suppose the defendant negligently operates his power boat so that he could foresee that the plaintiff's stamp collection is washed overboard and lost or ruined. If that happens, the defendant is liable for the loss of the collection, even if the defendant thought it was worth only $100 when in fact it was worth $1 million. The defendant was negligent in creating a risk of loss of the collection; he knew or should have known the nature of the risk, even if he could not have guessed the value of the collection.

The thin-skull or eggshell-skull rule. The rule that holds the defendant liable for foreseeable harms even when the amount of harm is not foreseeable finds a special expression in the thin-skull or eggshell-skull rule, as it is usually known. The label derives from an imagined case in which the plaintiff has an unusually thin skull. The defendant, having no reason to know of the plaintiff's peculiar susceptibility, negligently injures the plaintiff's head. The blow would be uncomfortable to normal people, but to the plaintiff it causes a fractured skull and serious injury. It seems to be agreed that the plaintiff is entitled to recover for all the harm done, even though a fractured skull was definitely not foreseeable.[108] The defendant, courts say, takes the plaintiff as he finds her.[109] A variant of the rule is that the defendant is liable for aggravation of preexisting injuries or conditions.[110]

It is easy to misunderstand the thin-skull rule. First, it does not make the defendant liable for the plaintiff's preexisting condition itself. The defendant's negligence today is not a cause in fact of a condition the plaintiff had yesterday. The thin-skull rule merely holds that the defendant is liable for the unforeseeable aggravation of that preexisting condition, not the condition itself.[111] Second, the rule applies only to the scope of liability

---

[106] See § 15.15.

[107] Restatement Second of Torts § 435(1) (1965).

[108] Chicago City Ry. Co. v. Saxby, 213 Ill. 274, 72 N.E. 755 (1904); Cf. Hammerstein v. Jean Development West, 111 Nev. 1471, 907 P.2d 975 (1995) (plaintiff suffered diabetes and was thus more susceptible to gangrene in case of injury to extremity; negligent fire alarm company was liable for that when the plaintiff turned his ankle attempting to escape a hotel when the alarm falsely signaled a fire).

[109] E.g., Gibson v. County of Washoe, Nevada, 290 F.3d 1175 (9th Cir. 2002); David v. DeLeon, 250 Neb. 109, 547 N.W.2d 726 (1996).

[110] These rules are distinguished in Rowe v. Munye, 702 N.W.2d 729 (Minn. 2005).

[111] When the defendant is held liable for the preexisting condition itself and not merely for aggravation of it, it is not because of the thin-skull rule but the indivisible injury rule. See 1 Dobbs, Hayden & Bublick, The Law of Torts § 192 (2d ed. 2011 & Supp.).

issue, not to the negligence issue. It does not require the defendant to exercise special care for an unforeseeably vulnerable plaintiff. The defendant only need exercise ordinary care to prevent foreseeable harms. The thin-skull rule comes into play only when the defendant's conduct would put normal people at risk.[112] Once the defendant does that, the rule provides that he is liable for all the personal injuries actually caused, although they may be greater than those that would be suffered by a normal person.[113] Sometimes, however, courts seem to have taken the rule down different paths, possibly with the unintended effect of imposing liability without fault and even without factual cause.[114]

The fire cases. When the defendant negligently sets a fire that spreads to the plaintiff's property, New York courts developed a unique rule that permitted recovery only by the first person to whose property the fire spread.[115] Other courts have allowed recovery even though the fire has spread substantial distances, or jumped creeks and ridges to reach the plaintiff's property. Perhaps these cases can be explained on the ground that the spread of fire is foreseeable and that no one can count on fires to stop at obvious barriers. However, at least some of the cases seem to illustrate and support the rule that the defendant does not escape liability merely because the harm done is more extensive than the defendant could have foreseen. The defendant who negligently sets a fire might reasonably believe beforehand that if it spread, it would certainly go no farther than the nearest road. If it somehow leaps the road, however, and continues to burn the other side, some cases hold that the defendant is nevertheless liable.[116]

§ 15.12 Foreseeability Required: Manner of Harm

Manner of Injury Generally

Precise manner of injury rule. The defendant is liable for harms he negligently caused so long as a reasonable person in his position should have recognized or foreseen the general kind of harm the plaintiff suffered.[117] He is not ordinarily relieved of liability merely because the precise manner of injury was unforeseeable.[118] On the same principle, the defendant is not relieved of liability merely because he cannot foresee the

---

[112] See, e.g., Rowe v. Munye, 702 N.W.2d 729 (Minn. 2005). If the defendant knows or should know of the plaintiff's peculiar susceptibility, he is of course obliged to exercise ordinary care with that susceptibility in mind and is liable for injuries caused if he does not. But that liability does not invoke the thin-skull rule.

[113] See Vaughn v. Nissan Motor Corporation in U.S.A., Inc., 77 F.3d 736, 738 (4th Cir. 1996); Restatement Third of Torts (Liability for Physical and Emotional Harm) § 31 (2010).

[114] See, e.g., Alder v. Bayer Corp., AGFA Div., 61 P.3d 1068 (Utah 2002).

[115] See Homac Corporation v. Sun Oil Co., 258 N.Y. 462, 180 N.E. 172 (1932).

[116] Atchison, T. & S. F. R. Co. v. Stanford, 12 Kan. 354 (1874) (three and one-half to four miles); Silver Falls Timber Co. v. Eastern & Western Lumber Co., 149 Or. 126, 40 P.2d 703 (1935) (apparently burning for miles, crossing two creeks and a green ridge of timber).

[117] Craig v. Driscoll, 262 Conn. 312, 813 A.2d 1003 (2003) (harm must be of the "same general nature as the foreseeable risk created by the defendant's negligence").

[118] Alcorn v. Union Pacific R.R. Co., 50 S.W.3d 226 (Mo. 2001), *overruled on other grounds*, Badahman v. Catering St. Louis, 395 S.W.3d 29 (Mo. 2013); see also, e.g., Stodola v. Grunwald Mechanical Contractors, Inc., 228 Neb. 301, 305, 422 N.W.2d 341, 344 (1988) ("The law does not require precision in foreseeing the exact hazard or consequence which happens. It is sufficient if what occurs is one of the kind of consequences which might reasonably be foreseen."); Lee Lewis Const. v. Harrison, 70 S.W.3d 778 (Tex. 2002) ("Foreseeability does not require an actor to anticipate the precise manner in which the injury will occur; instead, the injury need only be of a general character that the actor might reasonably anticipate.").

time when injury will occur; if the defendant negligently arms a bomb, he is liable for injuries it causes whether it explodes the next day or two years later.[119]

Examples. If the defendant negligently leaves kerosene where it might be ignited and burn the plaintiff, the fact that ignition unforeseeably triggered an explosion rather than a burning is of no consequence. The general type of accident was foreseeable, and from a known source of harm; the explosion is a mere "variant of the foreseeable."[120] Similarly, the defendant who negligently drives a bus onto a railroad track as the train approaches puts passengers at risk if for any reason the bus is delayed in clearing the track. When the train strikes the bus, the bus driver does not escape liability merely because the delay in getting the bus off the track arose from an unforeseeable obstruction, because some kind of delay and the general type of accident were foreseeable even if the particular obstruction was not. In a South Carolina case,[121] the defendants maintained railroad tracks with insufficient ballast, risking a derailment. The tracks were struck by a street sweeper whose driver had fallen asleep. Shortly thereafter a train derailed, causing injury to the plaintiff. Had the ballast level been proper, the sweeper would have ridden over the tracks without dislocating them or leaving them misaligned. Although a sleeping street sweeper might not have been foreseeable, some kind of dislocation was and that was enough to permit a finding that the defendants were one of the proximate causes.

Risks from forces likely to cause unpredictable and diverse harms. The manner of injury rule is especially applicable when the defendant negligently creates risks of harm that are quite definite in their results but tend to come about in unpredictable ways. When the defendant unleashes large physical forces such as those associated with automobiles, trains, large ships broken loose from their moorings, and other powerful instruments, he creates risks that injury could be caused in diverse ways, too numerous and particular to foresee in detail. For example, if I drive too fast, I create the general risk of causing personal injury and property damage to those on the road and sometimes even to those who are off the road. I probably cannot foresee all the ways in which that general risk might actually come about, but I do know that injury might come about in many particular ways resulting from my speed, including some so bizarre that I might not ever be able to imagine them in advance.[122] In this kind of case, the risk rule does not readily relieve me of liability. The case calls for the rule that if I foresee the risk in general, I need not foresee the details. Consequently, if my speeding causes me to lose control and drive my car into someone's living room, I am liable for the damage done, even if no one would have ever said in advance that the risk of living-room damage is a reason not to speed.[123]

---

[119] Cf. Hembree v. State, 2001 WL 575561 (Tenn. Ct. App. 2001) (negligent release of criminally dangerous mentally ill person, injury two and a half years later; "Peavyhouse was a time bomb waiting to explode").

[120] Hughes v. Lord Advocate, [1963] A.C. 837 (H.L. 1963) (Lord Reid emphasizing "known source" among other things; Lord Guest emphasizing "same type of accident"; and Lord Pearce using the "variant" language).

[121] J.T. Baggerly v. CSX Transp., Inc., 370 S.C. 362, 635 S.E.2d 97 (2006).

[122] See Washington & G. R. Co. v. Hickey, 166 U.S. 521, 17 S.Ct. 661, 41 L.Ed. 1101 (1897) (a delay was to be foreseen as a danger, and a "delay might be occasioned . . . by an almost infinite number of causes. The horses might stumble. The harness might give way. The car might jump the track. A hundred different things might happen which would lead to a delay, and hence to the probability of an accident. It was not necessary that the driver should foresee the very thing itself which did cause the delay.").

[123] See Castro v. Hernandez-Davila, 694 S.W.2d 575 (Tex. App. 1985) (intoxicated driver who drove into apartment building, causing a wall to collapse).

Chain-collision cases and many others attest to the foreseeability of a billiard ball effect when powerful forces operating at great speed strike objects. It is certainly not unforeseeable that the first object struck is sometimes propelled into another. The billiard ball effect is more dramatic or bizarre if a train strikes a horse which is then propelled through the air until it strikes a person, but the general kind of harm from the same kinds of forces is entirely foreseeable even if the details are not. So here again a rule of law against liability is inappropriate. Equally, when a large ship is allowed to break loose from its moorings in a fast-running river, a variety of harms associated with such a large force can be classed together, so that even if no one would have considered that a loose ship might cause upstream flooding because it could crash into a bridge and dam the river, such harm is nevertheless closely associated with the foreseeable forces— ships and heavy waters—so that scope of liability is again an appropriate question for the trier of fact and not to be precluded by a rule of law.

Where manner of harm is integral part of the risk. In contrast to the case of many diverse risks that might result from large forces, defendants sometimes create narrow risks that can foreseeably occur in a limited number of ways. If liability is to be limited to the risks the defendant unreasonably created, in such a case the defendant would not be liable when the injury comes about in an unforeseeable way. In the *Derdiarian* case,[124] the defendant posted the plaintiff in a position of danger from oncoming traffic. The plaintiff was struck by an oncoming car. Such an injury was foreseeable, even though it was not foreseeable that the driver would lose control because he had a seizure. The details, the manner of occurrence, did not matter in that case. But if the plaintiff had been struck by a falling aircraft, the manner of occurrence would have been very important indeed. The defendant created a risk of injury from surface traffic only. Posting the plaintiff at a different location would not have created any predictable risk of aircraft injury. Most often courts can rightly ignore the details about the manner of injury, because the defendant's negligence is broad enough to cover a variety of sequences, motives and events. However, the problem is not resolvable by a rule of law. If the facts of a particular case show that the risk of harm was limited to a very specific kind of accident, the manner in which harm was inflicted will be relevant.

Whether the risk negligently created by the defendant is a narrow one and focused on a particular manner of occurrence requires adjudication rather than rules. In one case,[125] the plaintiff and others were working around a vat of molten liquid at 800 ° centigrade. A worker knocked a cover into the vat, risking the possibility of a splash of molten metal on the plaintiff. That did not happen, but a few moments later, the vat cover, then immersed in the liquid, underwent a chemical change as a result of the intense heat. The chemical change produced a drop of water, which immediately turned to steam and caused an eruption of the molten liquid. The molten liquid struck and injured the plaintiff. The chemical reaction had been completely unknown up until that time, so the eruption by this means was entirely unforeseeable.

As a matter of argumentation, it always serves the defendant to describe the risk as precisely as possible and the plaintiff to describe it as abstractly as possible. The plaintiff can argue that eruption of the molten metal was foreseeable; it was the risk the defendant created. Such an abstract description of the risk includes eruption from chemical reactions as well as from mechanical action of the lid. If accepted, this

---

[124] See § 15.9.
[125] Doughty v. Turner Manufacturing Co., [1964] 1 Q.B. 518 (C.A. 1963).

description of the risk would show proximate cause. The defendant's technique is to characterize the risk at a lower level of abstraction, as a risk of splashing, which implies that the risk was only a risk of mechanical action of the lid's striking the metal, not a risk of chemical reaction at all. If this description of the risk is accepted, then the injury suffered was outside the risk, and thus outside the scope of defendant's liability.

It is not usually possible to say that only one description of the risk is the right one, so the question calls for judgment. Although that judgment is ordinarily left to the jury, sometimes judges feel that the matter is too clear for debate. In the case of the lid falling into the vat of molten metal, the court thought the risk of eruption from a totally unforeseeable chemical change was not anything like the known risk of mechanical action that was risked by knocking the lid into the vat. So, as a matter of law, the plaintiff could not prevail. This result seems understandable when the only foreseeable risk is specifically related to a particular mechanism and that mechanism is not known to create unpredictable results.

Intervening Act Cases

Conflict between intervening act rules and manner of injury rules. Although the courts have often shown that liability is not to be avoided merely because the defendant could not reasonably have foreseen the manner in which injury comes about, they have also said that the defendant will escape liability if the injury comes about through an unforeseeable intervening cause. The two statements seem to be in conflict. If courts relieve the defendant of liability for foreseeable types of harm merely because he could not reasonably have foreseen that the harm would be triggered by an intervening actor, they are in fact saying that the manner of harm (by way of an intervening act) must be foreseeable.

Resolving the conflict. Two approaches help harmonize the manner-of-harm rules with the tendency to focus on intervening causes. First, courts may hold, with the Second Restatement,[126] that intervening causes are not superseding causes if the defendant should have foreseen and avoided the general type of harm that resulted, even though the intervening causes were themselves unforeseeable. Second, courts may declare that an intervening cause is foreseeable if it represents a general type of foreseeable intervention, even though it could not have been specifically anticipated.

Johnson v. Kosmos Portland Cement Co.[127] is a striking and well-known example of the first approach. The defendants negligently failed to clean the hold of a barge to eliminate the possibility of gases accumulating there from the residue of petroleum cargoes. Accumulated gases could explode if an acetylene torch were used or a match inadvertently lit. Neither of these events occurred but lightning struck the barge instead. That caused an explosion of the gases and killed two men. Considering the lightning strike to be an unforeseeable intervening cause, the court nevertheless held that the defendant could appropriately be held responsible because the result or type of harm that occurred—explosion and death or injury by explosion—was foreseeable and that foreseeability of the general type of harm or result was enough.

---

[126] Restatement Second of Torts § 442B (1965). See also Restatement Third of Torts (Liability for Physical and Emotional Harm) § 34 cmt. d (2010) ("When an actor is found negligent precisely because of the failure to adopt adequate precaution against the risk of harm created by another's acts or omissions, or by an extraordinary force of nature, there is no scope-of liability limitation on the actor's liability.").

[127] Johnson v. Kosmos Portland Cement Co., 64 F.2d 193 (6th Cir. 1933).

The second approach can also be illustrated by the *Johnson* facts. Although it might not be foreseeable that lightning would strike the barge and ignite the gases, it was foreseeable that some intervening incendiary force could ignite them. Lightning is merely a particular instance of incendiary forces that could do so. It is enough that the defendant should recognize danger from a set or category of forces to which lightning belongs, without identifying all the possible forces in the set. If the defendant should have foreseen dangers from one of the forces in the category or from the same general kinds of forces, the liability is appropriate even if the particular intervening cause was not foreseeable.[128]

§ 15.13   Injury Remote in Time or Distance

Courts sometimes use short phrases to express ideas about "proximate cause." They may say or imply that a cause of harm is not "proximate" if it is insignificant, remote, or logically unrelated to the harm that follows. These phrases point in the right direction, but they are incomplete. The word *proximate* means near or next or most immediate, and taken literally it suggests that only the most immediate trigger of harm can be the proximate cause. That simply is not the law. As pointed out above, several tortfeasors may all be proximate causes of a single harm;[129] the first tortfeasor in a sequence of events as well as the last is often a legally responsible cause. And the defendant's misconduct is not too remote for liability merely because time[130] or distance[131] separates the defendant's act from the plaintiff's harm. A manufacturer whose negligent construction leads to the explosion of a space ship is no doubt a "proximate cause" of the resulting death and destruction even if the explosion occurs millions of miles away. A doctor who negligently withdraws a psychotic patient's medication may be liable for the patient's murderous acts months later.[132] Nor is the defendant's negligent conduct legally insignificant merely because it is not very bad. In countless cases, defendants are held responsible for injuries inflicted in a moment's inattentiveness at the wheel of a car. The test, once again, turns on some version of reasonable foreseeability, not on mechanics.

Physical distance or the passage of time between the defendant's conduct and the ensuing injury is not, as such, determinative, but may be relevant in several specific ways. For example, in emotional harm claims based upon injury to another person, courts frequently require the plaintiff to be nearby and to witness the injury before the plaintiff can recover for emotional distress.[133] Also, distance between tortious conduct and injury may tend to prove that the injury was not foreseeable where the force negligently launched by the defendant should be foreseen to have only a limited geographical potential for harm, for example, where the defendant negligently trips one person whose fall triggers an unforeseeable series of events that causes injury to another person far away.[134] Distance or the passage of time may be a surrogate or shorthand

---

[128] See Gibson v. Garcia, 96 Cal.App.2d 681, 216 P.2d 119 (1950) (precise form of intervening force need not be foreseeable); Restatement Second of Torts § 435 (1965).

[129] See § 15.1.

[130] See, e.g., Stephenson v. Air Products & Chemicals, Inc., 114 Ill. App. 2d 124, 252 N.E.2d 366 (1969) (as a result of injury caused by defendant, plaintiff suffered a second injury five years later).

[131] Delaware, Lackawanna and Western R. Co. v. Salmon, 39 N.J.L. 299 (1877) (proximate cause refers to "closeness of causal connection, and not nearness in time or distance").

[132] Estates of Morgan v. Fairfield Family Counseling Center, 77 Ohio St. 3d 284, 673 N.E.2d 1311 (1997).

[133] See § 29.10.

[134] See Palsgraf v. Long Island R.R., 248 N.Y. 339, 162 N.E. 99, 59 A.L.R. 1253 (1928).

expression referring to some other rule such as termination of the risk.[135] For example, where the plaintiff trips over a piece of equipment brought to an accident scene by an investigator hours after the defendant's negligence caused the accident, the court may stress the passage of time as tending to prove that the effects of the defendant's negligence had "come to rest."[136]

Sometimes judges characterize the foreseeable geographical zone of risk narrowly, thus excluding liability for distant injuries even when forces launched by the defendant have a known capacity for distant harm. Yet even here, the court that mentions distance may be more influenced by completely different factors. Cases in which a motorist strikes a utility pole, thereby causing a power outage at the plaintiff's home or business with resulting physical harm, illustrate narrow conceptions of foreseeability in which distance plays some part, although probably a minor one. In an Indiana case,[137] a motorist negligently collided with utility pole causing power outage in the plaintiff's plant two miles away. The court said that the zone of foreseeable danger in an automobile accident "encompasses the area immediately surrounding the accident scene. This includes those areas which are unsafe because of downed power lines or the property which may have been directly damaged by an electric utility pole falling upon it," but not a power loss miles away. However, the court seemed less influenced by distance than by the expressed belief that the plaintiff was in a better position to protect against the risk by having back-up power supplies for its business.[138]

C. INTERVENING ACTS OR FORCES

§ 15.14   Intervening Intentional or Criminal Acts

General rule. If an intervening and unforeseeable intentional harm or criminal act triggers the injury to the plaintiff, the criminal act is ordinarily called a superseding cause, with the result that the defendant who negligently creates the opportunity for such acts escapes liability.[139]

As in other superseding cause cases,[140] the real reason to relieve the defendant of liability is not merely that a new cause has intervened but rather that the risk represented by the intentional or criminal act is not one that the defendant negligently created. Suppose the lessor of an automobile would be negligent if it failed to check the driving records of a prospective lessee and that it in fact leases a car to A without checking his records. A properly loans the car to B who improperly loans it to C, who has a bad record for driving while intoxicated and who injures the plaintiff by his intoxicated driving of the leased car. Courts find it very easy to say that C's criminal act is a

---

[135] See § 15.17.

[136] Staelens v. Dobert, 318 F.3d 77 (1st Cir. 2003).

[137] Hammock v. Red Gold, Inc., 784 N.E.2d 495 (Ind. App. 2003).

[138] Id.

[139] E.g., Alston v. Advanced Brands and Importing Co., 494 F.3d 562 (6th Cir. 2007); Ex parte Wild West Social Club, Inc., 806 So.2d 1235 (Ala. 2001); Williams ex rel. Raymond v. Wal-Mart Stores East, L.P., 99 So.3d 112 (Miss. 2012); Phan Son Van v. Pena, 990 S.W.2d 751 (Tex. 1999). The federal statute immunizing licensed gun and ammunition manufacturers and dealers from negligence liability where the plaintiff's injury was caused by the criminal act of a third person explicitly embodies the "sole proximate cause" rule. See Adames v. Sheahan, 233 Ill.3d 276, 909 N.E.2d 742, 330 Ill.Dec. 720 (2009) (applying 15 U.S.C.A. § 7903(5)(A)(v) (2006), which provides that a criminal offense "shall be considered the sole proximate cause of any resulting death, personal injuries or property damage" in a suit against a covered defendant).

[140] See § 15.9.

superseding cause and that the lessor is not liable,[141] but the result is more simply understood as a product of the general rule that the defendant is liable only for injuries that were within the scope of the risk he negligently created. The lessor's failure to inquire of A's driving record was negligent because that failure ran the risk that A would prove to be a dangerous driver; it was not negligent at all about the danger that C, of whom the lessor knew nothing, would drive badly. If the harm caused by an intervening actor's criminal act is within the risk negligently created by the defendant, foreseeability of the criminal act itself seems unimportant.[142]

The backside of the general rule that insulates the defendant from liability in cases of unforeseeable intervening criminal acts is that if a criminal or intentional intervening act is foreseeable,[143] or is part of the original risk negligently created by the defendant in the first place,[144] then the harm is not outside the scope of the defendant's liability— or as most courts still put it, the criminal or intentional act is not a superseding cause.[145] The rule has been applied in civil rights claims as well as in common law tort claims.[146]

Older authorities: unforeseeability as a matter of law. In an earlier era, courts tended to hold that intervening criminal acts were unforeseeable as a matter of law. For example, the defendant negligently spills a tank car full of gasoline, into which the intervening actor throws a lighted match, injuring the plaintiff in the explosion.[147] Or the defendant leaves unguarded a dangerous excavation into which the intervening actor pushes the plaintiff.[148] Or the defendant negligently leaves dynamite where boys might find and steal it. Boys do so; another boy is killed in the explosion that follows.[149]

The earlier cases were prone to declare, contrary to human experience, that criminal acts simply could not be anticipated, or at least that the defendant was under no obligation to anticipate them. Some contemporary cases come close to saying the same thing.[150] This attitude explains why courts at one time held that negligent sellers of alcohol to intoxicated drivers were never responsible; in spite of the fact that there can be many proximate causes, they said it was the drinker, not the seller, who was "the" proximate cause.[151] In the same way, no matter what a defendant did to drive someone to suicide, suicide was the responsibility of the victim, not the defendant.[152] In the most extreme form, the idea was that the last human wrongdoer or last culpable will counts as the "sole proximate cause,"[153] so that intervening criminal acts would always relieve the defendant of liability.

---

[141] See Alamo Rent-A-Car, Inc. v. Hamilton, 216 Ga.App. 659, 455 S.E.2d 366 (1995).

[142] See Restatement Second of Torts § 449 (1965).

[143] Poskus v. Lombardo's of Randolph, Inc., 423 Mass. 637, 670 N.E.2d 383 (1996).

[144] Restatement Third of Torts (Liability for Physical and Emotional Harm) § 34 cmt. d (2010).

[145] Craig v. Driscoll, 262 Conn. 312, 813 A.2d 1003 (2003); Tenney v. Atlantic Associates, 594 N.W.2d 11 (Iowa 1999); Restatement Second of Torts § 449 (1965).

[146] See Harris v. Roderick, 126 F.3d 1189 (9th Cir. 1997).

[147] Watson v. Kentucky & Indiana Bridge & Railroad Co., 137 Ky. 619, 126 S.W. 146 (1910).

[148] See, e.g., Loftus v. Dehail, 133 Cal. 214, 65 P. 379 (1901); Miller v. Bahmmuller, 124 A.D. 558, 108 N.Y.S. 924 (1908).

[149] Perry v. Rochester Lime Co., 219 N.Y. 60, 113 N.E. 529 (1916).

[150] See Estate of Strever v. Cline, 278 Mont. 165, 924 P.2d 666 (1996); Doe v. Linder Const. Co., 845 S.W.2d 173 (Tenn. 1992).

[151] See §§ 15.18 & 26.12.

[152] See § 15.18.

[153] See Patrick J. Kelley, Proximate Cause in Negligence Law: History, Theory, and the Present Darkness, 69 Wash. U. L. Q. 49, 78–81 (1991).

Rejection of the older rule: jury questions. "This archaic doctrine has been rejected everywhere."[154] Today's courts usually recognize that foreseeability, in the nature of things, is fact-specific, so they now often permit juries to find that a criminal act was foreseeable and not a superseding cause.[155] There are, of course, cases that declare a particular criminal act in a particular case to have been unforeseeable as a matter of law.[156] Some of these matter-of-law holdings seem to be out of step and dubious at best,[157] but in any event courts have increasingly recognized that the question is not to be decided categorically but on the facts of each case.[158]

In one group of cases, a driver leaves keys in the ignition of the car. A thief steals the car and causes injury in making his escape. Courts have had difficulty with this one. A number of older cases held as a matter of law that the driver's act of leaving the key available was not a proximate cause of the harm because theft was not foreseeable, or that if it was, then negligence of the thief was not.[159] But circumstances vary and times change. Courts have sometimes had to reject the categorical rule against responsibility and to say that in particular cases the car theft and the thief's negligence were both all too foreseeable in particular cases, or that a jury could so find.[160] In general, the courts have moved away from rule-of-law decisions about broad categories of cases like these and have examined the facts of particular cases to determine whether intervening criminal acts are foreseeable even when the issue is conceived as one of foreseeability on the duty issue rather than foreseeability on the scope of liability or proximate cause issue.[161]

Unforeseeable intervening act causing a foreseeable result. Even if the intervening cause is not foreseeable, the intervening actor may trigger the very kind of harm the defendant's negligence risked. In that case, the general rule of foreseeability would seem

---

[154] Britton v. Wooten, 817 S.W.2d 443, 449 (Ky. 1991). See also Petition of Kinsman Transit Co., 338 F.2d 708, 719 (2d Cir. 1964) ("[T]he discredited notion that only the last wrongful act can be a cause [is] a notion as faulty in logic as it is wanting in fairness.").

[155] Mitchell v. Cedar Rapids Community School Dist., 832 N.W.2d 689 (Iowa 2013); Glover v. Jackson State University, 968 So.2d 1267 (Miss. 2007); McLean v. Kirby Co., a Div. of Scott Fetzer Co., 490 N.W.2d 229 (N.D. 1992); Travis v. City of Mesquite, 830 S.W.2d 94, 98 (Tex. 1992); Cruz v. Middlekauff Lincoln-Mercury, Inc., 909 P.2d 1252 (Utah 1996).

[156] See, e.g., Bower v. Harrah's Laughlin, Inc., 125 Nev. 37, 215 P.3d 709 (2009) (actions of police department in handcuffing, detaining and otherwise roughing up the plaintiffs constituted a superseding cause of plaintiffs' injuries as a matter of law in suit against casino arising out of a brawl between biker gangs).

[157] E.g., Doe v. Linder Const. Co., 845 S.W.2d 173 (Tenn. 1992) (finding defendant not liable as a matter of law for leaving plaintiff's keys accessible to workmen, one of whom raped her, on the ground that the rape was a superseding cause).

[158] However, although California makes case-by-case determinations of foreseeability under the rubric of "duty," at the same time it holds that greater foreseeability or higher probability of harm is required when the injury occurs through a criminal act of a third person. See Wiener v. Southcoast Childcare Centers, Inc., 32 Cal. 4th 1138, 88 P.3d 517, 12 Cal. Rptr. 3d 615 (2004). On duty to protect against acts of third persons generally, see Chapter 26.

[159] E.g., Ross v. Nutt, 177 Ohio St. 113, 203 N.E.2d 118 (1964). If the thief's negligence is not foreseeable, it would seem that the issue is one of negligence, not proximate cause; no harm to others being foreseeable, the defendant simply is not negligent at all. See William H. Danne, Jr., Annotation, Liability of Motorist Who Left Key in Ignition for Damage or Injury Caused by Stranger Operating the Vehicle, 45 A.L.R.3d 787 (1972).

[160] See Palma v. U.S. Industrial Fasteners, Inc., 36 Cal.3d 171, 681 P.2d 893, 203 Cal. Rptr. 626 (1984); Poskus v. Lombardo's of Randolph, Inc., 423 Mass. 637, 670 N.E.2d 383 (1996); Kozicki v. Dragon, 255 Neb. 248, 583 N.W.2d 336 (1998); Herrera v. Quality Pontiac, 134 N.M. 43, 73 P.3d 181 (2003); McClenahan v. Cooley, 806 S.W.2d 767 (Tenn. 1991).

[161] See In re September 11 Litig., 280 F.Supp.2d 279 (S.D.N.Y. 2003) (9–11 terrorists getting control of defendant's plane, defendants were under a duty of reasonable care, since terrorists and injury to victims on the ground were foreseeable).

to call for liability.[162] In a number of cases the defendant has negligently created a danger of fire, or a danger that if fire occurred, victims would not be able to escape promptly. Danger of fire is what makes the defendant negligent. If fire does occur and people are injured by it, courts appropriately hold the defendant liable. His liability in such a case is coextensive with negligence because foreseeability of fire is an ingredient in his negligence. Even if arson is not itself foreseeable, injury from fire is, and that should be enough. Some of the arson cases seem to support this view,[163] and others are at least are consistent with it in subjecting the defendant to liability.[164] However, the principle supporting liability for foreseeable types of harms resulting from foreseeable forces seems to have been rejected by the California Supreme Court, where a defendant who failed to protect small children from the danger of vehicles running onto its inadequately guarded playground escaped liability when the vehicle that killed the children was driven onto the playground intentionally.[165]

No-duty rules. The problem of intervening criminal acts is largely a problem of duty, not scope of liability. Courts have said in many contemporary cases that in the absence of a special relationship, the defendant simply owes no duty to take affirmative action to protect the plaintiff from a third person.[166] If a driver is murdered because Firestone negligently made defective tires that tore up on the road and left the driver alone, stranded, and susceptible to attack, Firestone might nevertheless escape liability because its duty to make safe tires was not a duty to do so for protection against murderers.[167] In the older cases, courts enforced that idea by asserting that, as a matter of law, intervening criminal conduct was not foreseeable. Because intervening criminal acts are quite often entirely foreseeable, that assertion seems strange, but it can now be understood as less about foreseeability itself than about the courts' notion about the appropriate scope of duty, which may turn largely on other matters altogether. Today, once courts decide that a defendant should use reasonable care to protect the plaintiff from crimes, foreseeability of crime has become an issue of fact, not a rule of law. Thus, if a duty of care is owed, taverns providing the alcohol that fuels criminal automobile driving, institutions releasing dangerous persons into the community, landlords leaving locks in disrepair, schools failing to protect students from attackers, and many others are now potentially subject to liability for harmful criminal behavior. But there is no blanket duty any more than there is a blanket immunity. Consequently, such cases must be considered in connection with the rules limiting duty.[168]

§ 15.15 Intervening Forces of Nature

Forces of nature play a role in many negligence cases. Unforeseeable natural forces are still sometimes called acts of God.[169] Courts often speak of natural forces as if special

---

[162] See Gallara v. Koskovich, 364 N.J.Super. 418, 836 A.2d 840 (2003) (plaintiff not required to prove that ultimate harm was foreseeable if the same type of harm caused by intervening act was foreseeable).

[163] Concord Florida, Inc. v. Lewin, 341 So.2d 242, 245 (Fla. Dist. Ct. App. 1976) ("the risk created here was not that of an arsonist or madman setting fire to a building, per se, but rather, the risk of fire, itself").

[164] See, e.g., d'Hedouville v. Pioneer Hotel Co., 552 F.2d 886 (9th Cir. 1977); Britton v. Wooten, 817 S.W.2d 443 (Ky. 1991).

[165] Wiener v. Southcoast Childcare Centers, Inc., 32 Cal. 4th 1138, 88 P.3d 517, 12 Cal. Rptr. 3d 615 (2004) (duty rather than proximate cause analysis).

[166] See § 26.1.

[167] Stahlecker v. Ford Motor Co., 266 Neb. 601, 667 N.W.2d 244 (2003).

[168] See Chapters 25 & 26.

[169] Courts sometimes speak of the act of God "defense", e.g., Eli Investments, LLC v. Silver Slipper Casino Venture, LLC, 118 So.3d 151 (Miss. 2013); Tel Oil Co. v. City of Schenectady, 303 A.D.2d 868, 757

rules are needed in those cases, but with the exception of certain statutory claims and a few common law cases now of little significance, the decisions comport with the general rules of negligence and proximate cause. It is thus entirely possible to drop terms like "act of God" altogether.[170] And again with one exception, natural forces almost never create issues of scope of liability as distinct from issues of factual cause.[171]

First, the defendant who acts in the presence of a natural force such as a high wind cannot plausibly claim that the wind is an intervening cause at all; it does not intervene if it is already in operation when the defendant acts. Second, the defendant who can reasonably be expected to foresee and act upon the danger of a natural force is negligent if he fails to take that force into account.[172] Third, the defendant who cannot reasonably be expected to foresee that a dangerous natural force will appear is usually simply not negligent at all, because no harm of any kind is a foreseeable result of his acts. If no flood is foreseeable, the defendant is not negligent in failing to sandbag the river.[173] Such a result has nothing whatever to do with scope of liability or proximate cause, which is an issue that can only arise when the defendant is negligent and his negligence can be identified as creating specified risks.

§ 15.16   Foreseeable Intervening Negligent Acts

General Rule

Although older cases sometimes took a narrower view, the defendant's responsibility for negligence today is not ordinarily superseded by an intervening cause if he could foresee such an intervening cause or a similar one.[174] Because precise foreseeability is not the test, and because negligence of others is often readily foreseeable, intervening negligent acts can seldom properly count as superseding causes. That is to say that in many cases, the scope of the risk created by the defendant encompasses negligent acts of others that subsequently cause harm, and his scope of liability thus includes harms so caused.[175] The rule is no different when the intervening actor is guilty of negligence per se in violating a statute.[176] The result is that, for the great majority of cases, the negligent original defendant and the negligent intervening actor are both liable for the harm they have together inflicted, under the rules for joint and several liability or comparative fault.

N.Y.S.2d 121 (2003); Lang v. Wonnenberg, 455 N.W.2d 832 (N.D. 1990). Yet the point seems to be only that the defendant was not negligent, which goes to negate the plaintiff's prima facie case but that is not a matter on which the defendant must carry ordinarily the burden of proof. However, when statutes put the burden on the defendant to justify a loss, act of God may be a true affirmative defense.

[170] See Denis Binder, Act of God? Or Act of Man?: A Reappraisal of the Act of God Defense in Tort Law, 15 Rev. Litig. 1 (1996).

[171] "Act of God" often turns out to be about factual cause rather than about intervening forces or scope of liability. Thus intervening forces of nature are said to bar the plaintiff's claim only when the injury would have occurred even without the defendant's activity. See Trotter v. Callens, 89 N.M. 19, 546 P.2d 867 (Ct. App. 1976). That means the defendant's activity was not a factual cause under the but-for rule.

[172] E.g., Keystone Elec. Mfg. Co. v. City of Des Moines, 586 N.W.2d 340 (Iowa 1998); see also Bradford v. Universal Const. Co., 644 So.2d 864 (Ala. 1994) (if high winds were foreseeable, defendant might have been negligent in leaving unweighted plywood sheets where wind might blow them into the plaintiff); Lanz v. Pearson, 475 N.W.2d 601 (Iowa 1991) (icy or obscured condition on highway).

[173] E.g., Rocky Mountain Thrift Stores, Inc. v. Salt Lake City Corp., 887 P.2d 848 (Utah 1994) ("no duty" to protect against unforeseeable flooding, hence no negligence).

[174] See Puckett v. Mt. Carmel Regional Medical Center, 290 Kan. 406, 228 P.3d 1048 (2010); Wilke v. Woodhouse Ford, Inc., 278 Neb. 800, 774 N.W.2d 370 (2009).

[175] See Goldberg v. Florida Power & Light Co., 899 So.2d 1105, 1116 (Fla. 2005).

[176] Austermiller v. Dosick, 146 Ohio App.3d 728, 767 N.E.2d 1248 (2002).

When Intervening Act Is Within the Risk Defendant Negligently Created

Principle. The most obvious case for rejecting a superseding cause argument is one in which the trier's finding of negligence logically includes a finding that an intervening cause was foreseeable. Put otherwise, "intervening causes which lie within the scope of the foreseeable risk . . . are not superseding causes which relieve the initial tortfeasor from liability."[177]

Applications: injury in minimizing or escaping risk defendant created. When the defendant creates a risk of harm to the plaintiff or others, the risk often includes a risk of injury to those attempting to escape or minimize harm. Consequently, the plaintiff who escapes injury from the defendant's negligently driven truck may recover for injuries incurred in the attempt to escape or to minimize risks to others. For instance, if her car is forced off the road by a negligent defendant, she can recover from that defendant for injury suffered when she is struck by another motorist while trying to minimize risks by flagging other motorists.[178] In such cases, the analogy to the rescue doctrine is sufficiently clear.[179] Thus the defendant who negligently causes a collision may be liable not only to those immediately injured, but also to a rescuer who is injured by a second collision in the course of a rescue attempt.[180]

Applications: foreseeable intervening natural forces. The intervention of natural forces is the simplest illustration. Defendant starts a fire in his field. The wind rises and spreads the fire to plaintiff's house. If defendant was negligent at all, it must have been because he could foresee the spread of the fire. A jury's finding that he is negligent must entail a finding that the wind and the spread of fire was foreseeable. That being so, the intervention of the wind is of no consequence whatever; defendant is liable for harm done by the wind-spread fire.[181] Similarly, if a physician fails to warn a patient that his disease is contagious, the doctor can foresee that the disease may spread to others, and cannot avoid liability to those others on the ground that the intervening growth of virus or bacteria is a superseding cause.[182]

Applications: static conditions and intervening acts. A defendant who creates or maintains any kind of static condition is simply not negligent unless he can foresee some intervening act or force that would tend to cause injury. A slippery floor in an empty world presents no risks at all; only if the defendant can foresee that someone may attempt to walk on the floor will he be negligent. Consequently, if the defendant negligently maintains a slippery floor, a dangerous step, an unguarded shaft or excavation, or an obstruction that blocks vision at an intersection, he cannot reasonably argue that the victim's own act was an unforeseeable superseding cause.[183] The victim

[177] Morris v. Farley Enterprises, Inc., 661 P.2d 167, 170 (Alaska 1983); Lugtu v. California Highway Patrol, 26 Cal.4th 703, 110 Cal.Rptr.2d 528, 28 P.3d 249 (2001).

[178] Marshall v. Nugent, 222 F.2d 604 (1st Cir. 1955). But cf. Staelens v. Dobert, 318 F.3d 77 (1st Cir. 2003) (driver of tanker, not injured in impact with negligent defendant, suffered injury when he fell on equipment used by state investigators who came to the scene later, held, summary judgment for defendant affirmed because the fall was unforeseeable).

[179] See § 15.7.

[180] See, e.g., Espinoza v. Schulenburg, 212 Ariz. 215, 109 P.3d 937 (2006).

[181] New York's rule is uniquely different. See § 15.11.

[182] See DiMarco v. Lynch Homes-Chester County, Inc., 525 Pa. 558, 583 A.2d 422 (1990); Bradshaw v. Daniel, 854 S.W.2d 865 (Tenn. 1993).

[183] See, e.g., McKenna v. Wolkswagenwerk Aktiengesellschaft, 57 Haw. 460, 558 P.2d 1018 (1977) (car ran off onto negligently maintained shoulder then went out of control, causing collision; jury could find that negligence of driver was foreseeable, so that city could not escape liability on proximate cause argument);

might be chargeable with contributory negligence in some cases and might for that reason find her damages reduced, but the negligent defendant will not be able to invoke superseding cause rules to escape liability altogether,[184] because the harm is within the scope of the risk negligently created by the defendant.

It is of course possible that the defendant, foreseeing no harm, is not negligent at all and will escape liability for that reason. In addition, a third person may sometimes substantially enhance the risk of harm from a static condition. If so, and if such enhanced risk is not foreseeable and not part of the original risk, the enhanced risk may count as a superseding cause. If enhancement of the risk by third persons is itself foreseeable or is the very danger created by the defendant in the first place, the defendant remains liable.[185] For instance, if the defendant negligently leaves a hole in the roadway and the plaintiff's car, striking it, is immobilized, it is foreseeable that the plaintiff may be struck by another motorist, and the defendant cannot avoid liability on the ground that the motorist is a superseding cause.[186]

Applications: intervening active negligence; negligent entrustment. The very reason for holding a defendant responsible for entrusting a vehicle to an incompetent driver or a gun to a mentally disturbed person is that the driver may drive dangerously or the disturbed person may fire upon others. If the driver causes an injury without driving dangerously, the entrusting defendant would not be responsible, since the risk he unreasonably created was the risk of dangerous driving, not the risk of safe driving.[187] On the other hand, if the driver's dangerous management of the vehicle causes harm, the defendant who entrusted the vehicle to a foreseeably dangerous driver cannot escape liability on the ground that the driver's negligence intervened to cause the harm, because the driver's negligence is the very danger he should have foreseen.[188]

The same is true when it comes to entrustment of a dangerous weapon.[189] And negligently permitting an unsafe user to have access to a dangerous instrumentality is obviously just a variation on the same point.[190] In that case, too, the defendant's negligence consists in creating the foreseeable danger that another person will intervene to misuse the instrumentality in a dangerous way.[191]

Applications: intervening active negligence; high-speed police chases. Contemporary cases involving high-speed police chases also illustrate the principle that when the

---

Atlantic Mut. Ins. Co. v. Kenney, 323 Md. 116, 591 A.2d 507 (1991) (truck parked so as to obstruct drivers' view at intersection).

[184] See Ward v. K-Mart Corp., 136 Ill.2d 132, 554 N.E.2d 223 (1990); Simmers v. Bentley Const. Co., 64 Ohio St.3d 642, 597 N.E.2d 504 (1992). On the plaintiff's fault as a proximate cause rather than comparative fault issue, see § 15.19.

[185] See, e.g., Dew v. Crown Derrick Erectors, Inc., 208 S.W.3d 448 (Tex. 2006).

[186] Cruz v. City of New York, 218 A.D.2d 546, 630 N.Y.S. 523 (1995); cf. Bigbee v. Pac. Tel. & Tel. Co., 34 Cal.3d 49, 665 P.2d 947, 192 Cal.Rptr. 857 (1983) (defective telephone booth at an intersection; plaintiff could not get out when he saw a car coming at him; a jury question whether the telephone company can escape liability on superseding cause grounds).

[187] See, e.g., Keller v. Kiedinger, 389 So.2d 129 (Ala. 1980).

[188] E.g., Jamar v. Patterson, 910 S.W.2d 118 (Tex. App. 1995). On negligent entrustment generally, see § 26.10.

[189] See Ross v. Glaser, 220 Mich. App. 183, 559 N.W.2d 331 (1996) (discussing foreseeability mostly in terms of duty of the entrustor).

[190] Kuhns v. Brugger, 390 Pa. 331, 135 A.2d 395, 68 A.L.R.2d 761 (1957); Annotation, Liability of Person Permitting Child to Have Gun, or Leaving Gun Accessible to Child, for Injury Inflicted by the Latter, 68 A.L.R.2d 782 (1959). See § 26.10.

[191] Moore v. Myers, 161 Md. App. 349, 868 A.2d 954 (2005).

intervening acts are themselves within the risk created by the defendant, they are not superseding causes. Police in pursuit of a law violator may enjoy an immunity from liability or they may not be negligent at all.[192] But if they have no immunity and they are in fact negligent, the risk they create is that some person will be harmed by the negligent high-speed driving of the police or their quarry. If the quarry collides with bystanders, the quarry's negligence cannot logically count as a superseding cause, since, by hypothesis, the police, if negligent at all, must have been negligent because they could foresee that the high-speed chase might injure someone. The quarry's negligence was not only foreseeable, but was the very risk that made the officers negligent. Most courts therefore hold that when injury occurs before the chase ends, it is for the jury to determine whether the quarry's negligence is a superseding cause.[193]

Other applications. In many other cases, the finding of negligence implies that an intervening act is foreseeable and thus eliminates the superseding cause argument. Suppose the state builds a road with a sharp and deep drop at the edge. If this is negligent, it must be because a driver may foreseeably go off the road and lose control with ensuing harm. To find negligence in such a case is to find that a negligent driver's "intervening" act is foreseeable, so once again, that driver's negligence is not a superseding cause.[194] Or a defendant leaves a large industrial cable spool weighing half a ton near a school yard. Children find it, try to ride it and are crushed when they fall under it. The children's play with the spool is not a superseding cause.[195] Indeed, if their play and danger is not foreseeable, it is hard to imagine in what way the defendant was negligent in leaving the spool available.

Similarly, when someone is injured by a product whose manufacturer negligently omitted safety devices, the manufacturer cannot automatically escape liability on the ground that the purchaser's negligence in using the product without the safety device was a superseding cause.[196] If you are negligent in failing to provide safety devices, you must necessarily foresee that injury could result; otherwise, no safety device would be needed, and you would not be negligent at all.

When Intervening Act Is Foreseeable—Aggravated and Second Injuries

Intervening negligent act foreseeable. In many other cases, the intervening negligence does not seem to be so much a part of the original risk but it is deemed foreseeable or at least arguable enough to permit a jury to so find. Under the approaches already discussed, the defendant today does not usually escape liability merely because he could not foresee the specific manner of injury or the specific kind of intervening act that occurred.[197] Juries are allowed to find that intervening causes are foreseeable and thus to hold the original actor responsible even when the intervening act occurs much

---

[192] See § 22.10.

[193] E.g., Tetro v. Town of Stratford, 189 Conn. 601, 458 A.2d 5 (1983); Jones v. Ahlberg, 489 N.W.2d 576 (N.D. 1992); Haynes v. Hamilton County, 883 S.W.2d 606 (Tenn. 1994).

[194] Maresh v. State, 241 Neb. 496, 489 N.W.2d 298 (1992).

[195] Baltimore Gas & Elec. Co. v. Lane, 338 Md. 34, 656 A.2d 307 (1995), *overruled in part*, Baltimore Gas & Elec. Co. v. Flippo, 348 Md. 680, 705 A.2d 1144 (1998); cf. City of Cedar Falls v. Cedar Falls Community School Dist., 617 N.W.2d 11 (Iowa 2000) (golf cart left in presence in many kindergarten children with predictable results, jury could find their intervention foreseeable).

[196] Leibreich v. A.J. Refrigeration, Inc., 67 Ohio St.3d 266, 617 N.E.2d 1068 (1993).

[197] See § 15.12.

later in time.[198] The original actor may be liable, for example, not only for the harm he directly causes, but also for the additional harm inflicted by negligent transportation to the hospital for treatment of the first injury[199] or by negligent medical treatment of that injury.[200] Even a later injury, resulting in part because the plaintiff is still operating under a residual disability from the first injury, may be within the scope of the original risk.[201] In such cases, the jury may find that the second injury was foreseeable, and the defendant who caused the original harm may be liable.

§ 15.17 Unforeseeable Intervening Acts

Injury Outside the Risk

Intervening negligent act as superseding cause. An intervening act is regarded as a superseding cause when it is outside the scope of the risk the defendant negligently created. This idea is usually expressed in shorthand by saying that if the intervening act is itself unforeseeable, then it may become a superseding cause.[202] The shorthand is misleading when the defendant negligently creates a broad risk of harm that may come about through a variety of means. In those cases, foreseeability of the precise intervening act itself is not important.[203] On the other hand, when the defendant creates a narrow risk likely to come about only through a particular kind of intervening act or in a particular sequence, injury that comes about through any other means is not within the risk. These are the unforeseeable intervening act cases, and in these cases liability is inappropriate whether or not the superseding cause language is used. Foreseeability is ordinarily a jury question where reasonable people could differ.[204] Although that proposition is generally accepted, courts often simply declare for themselves—"as a matter of law," as the saying goes—that some intervening act is unforeseeable, thus terminating the plaintiff's claim.[205]

Examples. An example is *Sheehan v. City of New York*.[206] In that case, a bus stopped at an intersection to permit passengers to board or alight, but, in violation of traffic regulations, did not pull over to the curb. While the bus was stopped, it was struck from behind by a sanitation truck in which the brakes had failed. A passenger on the bus was injured. Although the bus driver, by stopping at the intersection in a lane of traffic and

---

[198] E.g., Columbia Rio Grande Healthcare, L.P. v. Hawley, 284 S.W.3d 851 (Tex. 2009) (jury could find that doctor's alleged malpractice occurring 11 months after the defendant hospital's negligent misdiagnosis was not a superseding cause of plaintiff's harm).

[199] Anaya v. Superior Court, 78 Cal.App.4th 971, 93 Cal.Rptr.2d 228 (2000); Atherton v. Devine, 602 P.2d 634 (Okla. 1979).

[200] E.g., Convit v. Wilson, 980 A.2d 1104 (D.C. 2009); Cramer v. Slater, 146 Idaho 868, 204 P.3d 508 (2009); Sibbing v. Cave, 922 N.E.2d 594 (Ind. 2010); Puckett v. Mt Carmel Regional Medical Center, 290 Kan. 406, 228 P.3d 1048 (2010); see V. Woerner, Annotation, Civil liability of one causing personal injury for consequences of negligence, mistake, or lack of skill of physician or surgeon,100 A.L.R.2d 808 (1965); Restatement Third of Torts (Liability for Physical and Emotional Harm) § 35 (2010).

[201] E.g., Miyamoto v. Lum, 104 Hawai'i 1, 84 P.3d 509 (2004); D. Richard Joslyn, Annotation, Proximate Cause: Liability of Tortfeasor for Injured Person's Subsequent Injury or Reinjury, 31 A.L.R.3d 1000 (1970).

[202] E.g., Duphily v. Delaware Elec. Co-op., Inc., 662 A.2d 821 (Del. 1995); Latzel v. Bartek, 846 N.W.2d 153 (Neb. 2014).

[203] See § 15.12.

[204] See Peters v. Calhoun County Com'n, 669 So.2d 847 (Ala. 1995) ("While the issue of foreseeability in the context of an intervening cause may be decided as a matter of law, it is more commonly a question for the trier of fact."); Volpe v. Gallagher, 821 A.2d 699 (R.I. 2003) (characterizing issue as one of duty to exercise care, to be determined by foreseeability, which in turn is usually a jury question).

[205] See § 15.11.

[206] Sheehan v. City of New York, 40 N.Y.2d 496, 387 N.Y.S.2d 92, 354 N.E.2d 832 (1976).

not at the curb, created risks of injury to passengers who might be boarding or alighting, he did not create any special risk to passengers on board the bus; vehicles must frequently stop in traffic lanes, and especially at intersections. The general risk rule would exclude liability. The result can also be expressed by saying that the operation of the sanitation truck was a superseding cause.

In a South Carolina case,[207] a signal at a railroad crossing was out of order, constantly signaling the imminent arrival of a train that was not approaching. The defendant, responsible for maintaining the signal, was negligent in allowing this condition to persist because it was foreseeable that some individuals would learn of the malfunction and ignore the signal at a time when a train really was approaching. That did not happen. Instead, the plaintiff, a driver who did not know of the malfunction, came to a stop at the crossing. The driver behind her failed to stop and the plaintiff was seriously injured. As the court saw it, nothing like this was within the scope of the risk, which was focused on one particular kind of event, a driver's injury from a train resulting because he discounted the signal. Given that view, the defendant should not be liable and that was the court's holding. However, the outcome was expressed, as it usually is, as a product of the superseding cause rules: the second driver's negligence was a superseding cause.

As these cases show, when the superseding cause determination is properly used, it is merely a specific instance of, and a way of talking about, the fundamental rule that liability is limited to the risks that the defendant has negligently imposed. The language of superseding cause itself adds nothing but a layer of language likely to get in the way of clear analysis, and consequently some courts have dropped the superseding cause language.[208]

Termination of the Risk

The same fundamental scope-of-risk idea applies when the defendant creates a risk from particular forces and those forces have been spent, so that lawyers can conceptualize the case as a risk that has "terminated." But this, too, looks like an indirect but potentially misleading way of assessing the scope of the risk the defendant created.

For example, suppose that the defendant negligently drives into the plaintiff's vehicle, leaving it disabled in the eastbound lane of traffic. One risk of the defendant's negligence—impact with the plaintiff's car—has actually eventuated. But other risks remain. In particular, the disabled car might be in danger of being struck from behind by a car traveling in the same direction. If that happens, the defendant will not escape liability merely because some of the injury he risked has already come about.[209] But if the plaintiff's disabled car is struck by a falling airplane, or a car proceeding in the opposite direction that crosses the center line to strike the plaintiff's car, the injury resulting from *that* impact is unforeseeable and not one of the risks the defendant negligently created. In that case, the plaintiff's stopped car is no more at risk from a sudden chance movement of an oncoming car than if the plaintiff had been driving her car in the same lane, and liability is inappropriate.[210] Similarly, as Judge Magruder

[207] Newton v. South Carolina Public Railways Com'n, 319 S.C. 430, 462 S.E.2d 266 (1995).
[208] See § 15.21.
[209] Hairston v. Alexander Tank and Equipment Co., 310 N.C. 227, 311 S.E.2d 559 (1984).
[210] Copple v. Warner, 260 N.C. 727, 133 S.E.2d 641 (1963).

suggested, once the impact is over and the plaintiff drives on down the highway, it is possible to think of the risk as being terminated and the situation stabilized.[211]

The terminology of risk-termination, like a good deal of terminology in so-called proximate cause cases, is superfluous. The underlying idea is that the injury that occurred—a second impact not made more likely by the first—is outside the risk negligently created by the defendant. This is not a mechanical rule. In some cases, the first impact very definitely does create risks of further injuries, and the tortfeasor is liable for them if they occur. For example, a tortfeasor may be liable for injuries inflicted by a health care provider in treating the first injury and also for second injuries resulting because of weakness caused by the first injury.[212]

§ 15.18 Using "Proximate Cause" as a No-Duty Rule

Courts today agree that scope of liability is to be determined on a case-by-case basis, that it is a jury question in all but the most extreme cases, and that it turns on foreseeability in some form. Yet at times courts have disregarded all three of these rules in several kinds of cases, excluding liability for certain categories of injuries as a matter of law. The anomaly is gradually being resolved as courts come to treat the problems raised in these cases as duty problems rather than scope of liability or proximate cause problems.

(1) Alcohol providers. Courts once said that in the absence of a statute specifically imposing tort liability, a bartender who continues to serve alcohol to a minor or to an intoxicated drinker is not liable to the drinker's victims when he drunkenly runs down innocent people, not even if the bartender knows the drinker will drive. The drinker, not the seller of the alcohol, was regarded as the sole proximate cause of the death or injury to others.[213] This could hardly be an application of the proximate cause rules as understood in contemporary thought, since if any harm is foreseeable it is intoxicated driving and its frequent and terrible results. The rule also departed from the usual practice of examining facts of each case to determine foreseeability. Instead, courts made a categorical rule of non-liability for all alcohol providers. To a substantial extent, these rules have changed as courts have come to recognize that the issue is not one of scope of liability or proximate cause at all, but one of duty.[214] The contemporary alcohol cases are considered further in a later chapter.[215]

(2) Suicide/failure to protect the plaintiff from herself. Courts also often hold that a person who committed suicide was the "sole proximate cause" of his own death, and that a defendant whose negligence led to the suicide is therefore categorically excused

---

[211] Marshall v. Nugent, 222 F.2d 604 (1st Cir. 1955). See also Exxon Co., U.S.A. v. Sofec, Inc., 517 U.S. 830, 116 S.Ct. 1813, 135 L.Ed.2d 113 (1996); Staelens v. Dobert, 318 F.3d 77 (1st Cir. 2003) (stressing the passage of 3 to 5 hours between the defendant's negligence and the plaintiff's injury, caused by his tripping over a piece of equipment brought to the scene by an accident investigator; original defendant's act was not a proximate cause because the risks created by that act "had come to rest"); Hale v. Brown, 287 Kan. 320, 197 P.3d 438 (2008) (stressing that the length of time between the first tortfeasor's negligence and the second tortfeasor's negligence was a major factor in the conclusion that the first tortfeasor's act was not a proximate cause as a matter of law).

[212] See § 15.16.

[213] Fleckner v. Dionne, 94 Cal.App.2d 246, 210 P.2d 530 (1949); Parsons v. Jow, 480 P.2d 396. (Wyo. 1971).

[214] This is not to say that the result always changes. See, e.g., Rodriguez v. Primadonna Co., LLC, 216 P.3d 793 (Nev. 2009) (hotel owed no duty to person injured by underage drinking guest who was evicted by the hotel for disorderly conduct).

[215] See § 26.12.

from any liability.[216] Here again, the rule does not resemble the usual scope of liability or proximate cause rule, since at least some suicides would be the foreseeable result of the defendant's negligence, as for example, where the defendant provided heavy doses of depressing drugs.[217] Courts do apply an exception: the negligent defendant would be liable for suicide if the defendant's negligence caused insanity in the victim, who then committed suicide as a result of that insanity.[218] Courts now recognize that at least in some cases a person may have a duty to help prevent suicide, as in the case of a hospital or jail with a known suicidal patient or prisoners.[219] So the most fundamental issue is one of duty.[220] This means that where a duty of care exists, the old categorical rule against liability disappears and the courts consider negligence and scope of liability (proximate cause) in the light of the facts of the particular case.[221] This shift does not mean that liability is inevitable, even if negligence is proved. In some cases, suicide is truly unforeseeable or outside the risk created by the defendant,[222] as in the case of a client who commits suicide because his lawyer negligently lost a case.[223] In addition, courts may impose demanding rules of foreseeability. For example, in one case, the defendant locksmith picked a trigger lock to make a gun available for use by a person he knew to be a minor. The minor used the gun to commit suicide. Instead of asking whether harm from a gunshot was foreseeable, as it surely was, the court asked whether suicide was foreseeable and found that it was not, absolving the locksmith.[224]

A court may rest its conclusion on facts showing that time and other actors intervened to break the causal chain between the defendant's negligence and the suicide. In another Texas case, the defendant hospital and physician discharged a 21-year-old patient from the emergency room after treating him for a failed suicide attempt but without performing a comprehensive risk assessment for suicide. The discharged patient committed suicide 33 hours later. Reversing a jury verdict for the plaintiffs (decedent's estate and his parents), the court held that the suicide was "too attenuated for proximate cause" because the evidence showed that neither the decedent nor his family wanted him to be hospitalized further; the evidence failed to show that hospitalization would have prevented his suicide at a later time; and during the 33 hours between discharge and his

[216] Rollins v. Wackenhut Services, Inc., 703 F.3d 122 (D.C. Cir. 2012) (applying D.C. law).

[217] Cf. Runyon v. Reid, 510 P.2d 943 (Okla. 1973) (providing drugs without a prescription in violation of statute, suicide an independent intervening act); Scott v. Greenville Pharmacy, 212 S.C. 485, 48 S.E.2d 324 (1948) (allegations that pharmacy illegally provided drugs without prescription and that the decedent committed suicide under their influence; addiction but not suicide was foreseeable).

[218] Johnson v. Wal-Mart Stores, Inc., 588 F.3d 439 (7th Cir. 2009) (applying Illinois law); Prill v. Marrone, 23 So.3d 1 (Ala. 2009); McLaughlin v. Sullivan, 123 N.H. 335, 461 A.2d 123 (1983); Clift v. Narragansett Television L.P., 688 A.2d 805 (R.I. 1996); Cook v. Shoshone Nat'l Bank, 126 P.3d 886 (Wyo. 2006). See Gregory G. Sarno, Annotation, Liability of One Causing Physical Injuries as a Result of which Injured Party Attempts or Commits Suicide, 77 A.L.R.3d 311 (1977).

[219] See Joseph v. State, 26 P.3d 459 (Alaska 2001); Hickey v. Zezulka, 439 Mich. 408, 487 N.W.2d 106 (1992); Cowan v. Doering, 111 N.J. 451, 545 A.2d 159 (1988).

[220] See generally Chapter 26.

[221] E.g., Kivland v. Columbia Orthopaedic Group, LLP, 331 S.W.3d 299 (Mo. 2011) (widow was required to show that her husband's suicide was a natural and probable result of the pain caused by surgery negligently performed by defendant doctor); Cramer v. Slater, 146 Idaho 868, 204 P.3d 508 (2009) (question of fact whether defendant's negligent misdiagnosis of HIV status was a proximate cause of patient's suicide; suicide would be a superseding cause only if not reasonably foreseeable); Delaney v. Reynolds, 63 Mass. App.Ct. 239, 825 N.E.2d 554 (2005) (rejecting the application of any "ironclad rule" of scope of liability in suicide cases, applying instead a general foreseeability test).

[222] See Jutzi-Johnson v. United States, 263 F.3d 753 (7th Cir. 2001); Rains v. Bend of the River, 124 S.W.3d 580 (Tenn. App. 2003).

[223] McLaughlin v. Sullivan, 123 N.H. 335, 461 A.2d 123 (1983).

[224] Perez v. Lopez, 74 S.W.3d 60 (Tex. App. 2002).

suicide he was watched "carefully" by his mother.[225] Such reasoning appears to blur the lines unnecessarily between factual cause and scope of liability; if the decedent would have committed suicide even if the defendants had not been negligent, then the defendants' negligence is simply not a but-for cause of the harm and defendants should have prevailed on that ground.

(3)   Emotional harm. Courts have long treated stand-alone emotional harm claims quite differently from physical injury claims.[226] The difference has frequently been explained on the grounds that emotional harm is not a "proximate" result of the defendant's negligence. It may be true that different rules of liability ought to be employed when the plaintiff claims emotional harm independent of physical injury, but it is most definitely not true that there is anything unforeseeable about the emotional harm of a mother who sees her child seriously and continuously hurt by the defendant's negligence. Nor could scope of liability or proximate cause rules explain a categorical rule circumscribing emotional harm recoveries. So the older proximate cause explanations have been gradually giving way to the understanding that if liability for emotional harm is to be limited, the limits turn on issues of practicality, policy, and justice and not on bare foreseeability alone. These rules, too, must be treated outside the framework of scope of liability.[227]

(4)   Economic harm. Stand-alone economic harm, like stand-alone emotional harm, has often been subjected to special rules.[228] For instance, the defendant might negligently cut off a supply of electricity to a factory, with the result that workers there lose a day's wages while the electricity is restored.[229] Courts frequently conclude that negligence is no basis at all for recovery when the plaintiff suffers such economic harm and no personal injury or property damage. Sometimes they have used the language of proximate cause—the injury is too remote or indirect. That is no longer the usual explanation, nor should it be.[230] Courts today more commonly recognize that in many situations the defendant owes no duty to use care to prevent pure economic harm, as distinct from personal injury or property damage.[231] The rule is not universal, but where it applies it bars recovery for reasons quite unrelated to foreseeability.

§ 15.19   Plaintiff's Own Acts as a Superseding Cause

Plaintiff's fault as superseding cause. When the defendant negligently injures the plaintiff, the plaintiff's own fault is normally relevant only under the rules of contributory negligence or comparative fault. In many instances, the plaintiff's fault would be ground for reducing the recovery of damages, but would not exclude recovery altogether. On the other hand, some cases hold that the plaintiff's fault may sometimes count as a superseding cause, or, as courts often say, the "sole proximate cause" of the plaintiff's own harm.[232] If so, the plaintiff does not merely suffer a reduction in damages

---

[225]   Providence Health Center v. Dowell, 262 S.W.3d 324 (Tex. 2008).

[226]   See Chapter 29.

[227]   Id.

[228]   See Chapter 41.

[229]   See Stevenson v. East Ohio Gas Co., 73 N.E.2d 200 (Ohio App.1946).

[230]   See, e.g., Aikens v. Debow, 208 W.Va. 486, 541 S.E.2d 576 (2000) (discussing many cases, focusing on economic rationales for denying purely economic losses in negligence cases).

[231]   See Chapter 41.

[232]   See, e.g., Exxon Company, U.S.A. v. Sofec, Inc., 517 U.S. 530, 116 S.Ct. 1813, 135 L.Ed.2d 113 (1996); General Motors Corp. v. Wolhar, 686 A.2d 170 (Del. 1996); Standard Havens Products, Inc. v. Benitez, 648 So.2d 1192 (Fla. 1994); Komlodi v. Picciano, 217 N.J. 387, 89 A.3d 1234 (2014); Boltax v. Joy Day Camp, 67

but is barred completely. Similarly, under the avoidable consequences rules for minimizing damages, the plaintiff is regarded as the "sole proximate cause" of damages suffered because she failed to mitigate damages once injury occurred.[233] As to those damages, the plaintiff cannot recover at all.

Rejecting superseding cause analysis for plaintiff fault. Although the abstract scope-of-risk test of superseding cause is the same for both negligence of the defendant and the comparative fault of the plaintiff,[234] the superseding cause line of reasoning must be accepted with caution. If it were widely applied, it would undermine the comparative negligence system of fault allocation. For this reason, a number of courts have rejected the possibility that the plaintiff's fault can ever be a superseding cause.[235]

Middle ground. If the rhetoric of "sole proximate cause" and superseding cause is dropped, a middle ground becomes apparent. In some cases, the defendant's negligence simply does not create a risk of the kind of harm that the plaintiff suffered. In such a case, the important thing is not that the plaintiff is at fault, or that the plaintiff's fault was a superseding cause, but rather that the harm was outside the scope of the defendant's liability, or, to put it differently, that the risk created by the defendant had terminated. In *Exxon v. Sofec*,[236] a tanker ship broke away from the defendants' moorings. The defendants may have been responsible. The ship's captain managed to get the breakaway tanker past a number of perils and safely out to sea. Once he reached safety, however, he neglected to get a fix on his position and he ran aground. Exxon was denied a recovery against the defendants. The Court reasoned that the captain's negligence was a superseding cause.

The superseding cause language might suggest heavy reliance on the captain's fault, and if that were the case, it would be plausible to argue that the decision undermines the comparative fault system.[237] But as often is the case, the superseding cause language appears to obscure the more fundamental point that the harm that befell the tanker was simply not one of the risks of negligently managed moorings.

The upshot is that if the harm done is outside the risk negligently created by the defendant, then of course the defendant is not to be held liable. On the other hand, if the

---

N.Y.2d 617, 499 N.Y.S.2d 660, 490 N.E.2d 527 (1986); Buckley v. Bell, 703 P. 2d 1089 (Wyo. 1985). In those few jurisdictions retaining contributory negligence as a complete bar to recovery, a plaintiff's contributory negligence must still be found to have proximately caused her own harm. See Rascher v. Friend, 279 Va. 370, 689 S.E.2d 661 (2010).

[233] See §§ 16.10 to 16.11.

[234] Cf. Norfolk S. Ry. Co. v. Sorrell, 549 U.S. 158, 127 S.Ct. 799, 166 L.Ed.2d 638 (2007) (so stating, but not clearly distinguishing actual cause from proximate cause in the sense of scope-of-risk rules).

[235] See Von der Heide v. Com., Dep't of Transp., 553 Pa. 120, 718 A.2d 286 (1998). Some decisions, often quoting the Restatement Second of Torts § 440, have defined superseding cause as an act of a third person or outside force. E.g., Com., Transp. Cabinet, Dep't of Highways v. Babbitt, 172 S.W.3d 786 (Ky. 2005); Hickey v. Zezulka, 439 Mich. 408, 487 N.W.2d 106 (1992); Vilas v. Steavenson, 242 Neb. 801, 496 N.W.2d 543 (1993). If that definition is adhered to, the plaintiff's own conduct would never count as a superseding cause. If that is the right result, it probably should be achieved through policy analysis rather than through the accident of a definition. See Paul T. Hayden, Butterfield Rides Again: Plaintiff's Negligence as Superseding or Sole Proximate Cause in Systems of Pure Comparative Responsibility, 33 Loy. L.A. L. Rev. 887 (2000).

[236] Exxon Company, U.S.A. v. Sofec, Inc., 517 U.S. 830, 116 S.Ct. 1813, 135 L.Ed.2d 113 (1996).

[237] It may also be that the Court used the superseding cause notion to avoid holding a slightly-negligent defendant liable for a large damages award; other courts appear to have done so.

court focuses on the plaintiff's fault rather than the scope of the risk, the case looks like one for comparative fault rules rather than the Draconian "proximate cause" rules.[238]

In addition, there is one small class of cases in which the defendant's responsibility is to protect the plaintiff from his own actions. If police officers, having an intoxicated person in custody, haul him to the edge of town and deposit him on a dangerous highway where he is struck by a car, they cannot defend a suit on the ground that his intoxication was an intervening cause. To countenance that argument "would be to negate the very duty imposed on the police officers when they took [the plaintiffs] into custody. It would be to march up the hill only to march down again."[239]

D. ALTERNATIVES

§ 15.20 Joint and Several Liability and Comparative Fault

Scope of liability (proximate cause) rules allocate responsibility among tortfeasors. In intervening cause cases, the all-or-nothing rule is no longer the only method for allocating responsibility among the various negligent actors. Another method already discussed is to limit the duty of care owed by defendants in special categories of cases.[240] Even more flexibly, it is now possible and even common to impose joint and several liability upon all the actors in a sequence of wrongdoing that culminates in the plaintiff's harm.[241] Modern procedures for contribution and indemnity permit courts to allocate a portion of responsibility to each of several defendants.[242] With the advent of comparative fault, responsibility can be allocated in different percentages to each defendant. And, where joint and several liability is deemed offensive, each defendant can be held liable for his share of the total fault and no more.[243]

These modern procedures were not all widely available until the latter half of the 20th century, some not until its last quarter. Now that they are in place, they show intervening cause issues in a new light. Before these procedures were available, a judge might perceive that relatively little fault was attributable to A, while much fault was attributable to B. Sometimes the only method for obtaining some kind of rough justice as between A and B was to invoke the all-or-nothing proximate cause rule, letting A go without any liability and imposing all liability upon B. This result was not necessarily justified, because, while it might achieve a rough justice between A and B, it did so at the expense of the innocent plaintiff. Such extremes are no longer necessary. A court can now say, as courts often do, that both tortfeasor A and tortfeasor B are proximate causes

---

[238] See Gunnell v. Arizona Public Service Co., 202 Ariz. 388, 46 P.3d 399 (2002) (noting that where negligence of both parties cause the plaintiff's harm, the state's system for jury determination of comparative fault should not be evaded by casting the issue as one of sole cause rather than as one of negligence); Soto v. New York City Transit Authority, 6 N.Y.3d 487, 846 N.E.2d 1211, 813 N.Y.S.2d 701 (2006) (plaintiff was reckless in running along catwalk beside a subway track, but subway operator was also negligent and the plaintiff's fault "was not so egregious or unforeseeable that it must be deemed a superseding cause of the accident absolving defendant of liability").

[239] Parvi v. City of Kingston, 41 N.Y.2d 553, 560, 362 N.E.2d 960, 965, 394 N.Y.S.2d 161, 166 (1977). Cf. Bexiga v. Havir Manufacturing Corp., 60 N.J. 402, 290 A.2d 281 (1972) (plaintiff's negligence not a defense where defendant owed a duty to protect him from that very negligence).

[240] See § 15.18.

[241] See § 14.6.

[242] See 3 Dobbs, Hayden & Bublick, The Law of Torts §§ 489 & 490 (2d ed. 2011 & Supp.).

[243] See §§ 35.3 to 35.5. Thus, even in that system of apportionment, the all-or-nothing conclusion that the first actor is not a proximate cause is no longer so common.

and impose liability, either jointly and severally or according to their comparative fault share.[244]

Something similar is true in those cases in which the defendant argues that the plaintiff's fault was a superseding cause, or the "sole proximate cause," of her own harm.[245] In the days when states almost always barred the plaintiff for even slight contributory fault, it made little difference whether courts said the plaintiff was guilty of contributory negligence or that her negligence was the sole proximate cause. Either way, the plaintiff would be barred. Now that comparative fault rules have been adopted in most states, the plaintiff who is guilty of comparative fault is not necessarily barred; she may simply find her damages award against the defendant reduced to reflect her fault. Under this system, courts will seldom be justified in resorting to all-or-nothing proximate cause rules that would bar the plaintiff on the ground that her fault was the sole proximate cause.[246]

§ 15.21 Abolishing Superseding Cause Analysis

Relying in part on the contemporary ability to allocate liability among tortfeasors in proportion to their fault,[247] several courts have wholly or partly abolished the separate superseding cause type of analysis but have retained the scope of liability or proximate cause limitation based on foreseeability or scope of risk.[248] Short of that, a court may refuse to apply superseding cause analysis in a particular case, partly because it could undermine comparative-fault apportionment.[249]

Several lines of thought lie behind this movement. The narrowest is that superseding cause analysis was developed to assist plaintiffs whose fault in the old regime of contributory negligence would have completely barred recovery, and that with the coming of comparative fault allocations, this is no longer necessary. This would lead courts to hold that the plaintiff's own fault cannot be a superseding cause.[250] However,

---

[244] Some courts have also curbed the superseding cause analysis in favor of more emphasis on comparative responsibility. See § 15.21.

[245] See § 215. The Restatement Third criticizes the term "sole proximate" cause as particularly confusing and misleading, and counsels against using it at all. See Restatement Third of Torts (Liability for Physical and Emotional Harm) § 34, cmt. f (2010).

[246] See, e.g., Godesky v. Provo City Corp., 690 P.2d 541 (Utah 1984) (noting comparative fault options) & § 215. Some courts have found a plaintiff's negligence to be a superseding or sole proximate cause of harm in pure comparative jurisdictions, apparently as a kind of safety valve to protect a slightly-negligent (comparatively) defendant from a large damages award. Such a safety valve is not needed in a modified comparative jurisdiction. See Paul T. Hayden, Butterfield Rides Again: Plaintiff's Negligence as Superseding or Sole Proximate cause in Systems of Pure Comparative Responsibility, 33 Loy. L.A. L. Rev. 887 (2000). The Restatement Third deals with this problem by suggesting that where an actor's negligence is only a "trivial contribution to a causal set that is a factual cause of harm," then that harm is not within the scope of the actor's liability. Restatement Third of Torts (Liability for Physical and Emotional Harm) § 36 (2010).

[247] See § 15.20.

[248] Barry v. Quality Steel Products, Inc., 263 Conn. 424, 820 A.2d 258 (2003); Archambault v. Soneco/Northeastern, Inc., 287 Conn. 20, 946 A.2d 839 (2008) (holding that "*Barry* clearly establishes that the doctrine of superseding cause is limited to situations in which an unforeseeable intentional tort, force of nature or criminal event supersedes the defendant's tortious conduct"); Control Techniques, Inc. v. Johnson, 762 N.E.2d 104 (Ind. 2002); Torres v. El Paso Elec. Co., 127 N.M. 729, 987 P.2d 386 (1999), *overruled on other grounds*, Herrera v. Quality Pontiac, 134 N.M. 43, 73 P.3d 181 (2003).

[249] Gunnell v. Arizona Public Service Co., 202 Ariz. 388, 46 P.3d 399 (2002); Com., Transp. Cabinet, Dep't of Highways v. Babbitt, 172 S.W.3d 786 (Ky. 2005) (noting that "the rationale for the doctrine of superseding cause has been substantially diminished by the adoption of comparative negligence," citing Restatement Third of Torts (Liability for Physical and Emotional Harm) § 34 cmt. a (2010)); Soto v. New York City Transit Authority, 6 N.Y.3d 487, 846 N.E.2d 1211, 813 N.Y.S.2d 701 (2006).

[250] See § 15.19.

the courts have not stopped with such a limited holding. Recognizing that the underlying issue is scope of the risk and that a separate superseding cause analysis pursues a foreseeability determination already made in assessing the scope of the risk the defendant negligently created, courts have concluded that instructions about superseding cause are both duplicative and confusing.[251] Consequently, the issue in intervening cause cases, like the issue in others involving the scope of the defendant's liability, is whether the general type of harm inflicted was foreseeable and thus within the scope of risks created by the defendant's negligent conduct.

---

[251] See Barry v. Quality Steel Products, Inc., 263 Conn. 424, 820 A.2d 258 (2003); Control Techniques, Inc. v. Johnson, 762 N.E.2d 104 (Ind. 2002).

Subpart B

DEFENSES

Chapter 16

FAULT OF THE PLAINTIFF

Analysis

A. GENERAL RULES

§ 16.1   Effects of Plaintiff Fault
§ 16.2   The Parallel Analysis of Plaintiff and Defendant Fault

B. COMPARATIVE FAULT

§ 16.3   Comparative Fault
§ 16.4   Assigning Shares of Fault or Responsibility to the Plaintiff
§ 16.5   All-or-Nothing Judgments After Comparative Fault
§ 16.6   Allocating Full Responsibility to the Defendant in the Interests of Policy or Justice: Plaintiff No-Duty Rules
§ 16.7   Traditional Exceptions to the Contributory Negligence Bar and Their Status Today

C. RELATED DOCTRINES AND SPECIAL CASES

§ 16.8   Effect of Plaintiff's Illegal Acts
§ 16.9   Distinguishing Avoidable Consequences
§ 16.10 The Role of Avoidable Consequences in Comparative Fault Regimes
§ 16.11 Comparative Fault or Avoidable Consequences in Seatbelt and Other Safety Precaution Cases

---

A. GENERAL RULES

§ 16.1 Effects of Plaintiff Fault

Traditional and Contemporary Rules

Plaintiff fault as a complete bar. The traditional rule held that contributory negligence of a plaintiff was generally a complete bar to the claim.[1] Similarly, the contributory negligence of the person from whom the plaintiff derived her claim was also a complete bar.[2] As contemporary courts have observed in criticizing this older rule, the

---

[1]   Butterfield v. Forrester, 11 East. 59, 103 Eng. Rep. 926 (1809). See, explaining some interpretations, Dan B. Dobbs, Accountability and Comparative Fault, 47 La. L. Rev. 939 (1987); Wex S. Malone, Comment on Maki v. Frelk, 21 Vand. L. Rev. 930 (1968).

[2]   See Restatement Second of Torts § 494 (1965). The spouse of an injured person, for example, may have a claim for loss of consortium or society, but it is commonly regarded as derivative and barred to the extent the injured person herself would be barred. For a discussion of negligence imputed to the plaintiff on

379

plaintiff who was guilty of only slight or trivial negligence was completely barred from any recovery, even if the defendant was guilty of quite serious negligence.[3] No satisfactory reasoning has ever explained the rule. It departed seriously from ideals of accountability and deterrence because it completely relieved the defendant from liability even if he was by far the most negligent actor.[4]

Plaintiff fault allowing recovery with reduced damages. In most states, plaintiffs who are chargeable with fault are no longer barred from recovery against defendants who would otherwise be liable. Instead, damages are reduced in proportion to the plaintiff's fault or responsibility. Thus, shares of the harm are borne by both plaintiffs and defendants.[5]

The Terminology Problem

The term "contributory negligence." Many terms are used to describe the fault of the plaintiff in a proportionate share system. The term "contributory negligence" can still be used to describe the conduct of the plaintiff even when the effect of that conduct is no longer to bar the claim in most states. Indeed, the Restatement Third of Torts uses the term "contributory negligence" in precisely this way.[6] However, use of the term "contributory negligence" sometimes falls flat with lawyers and judges because of the term's historic association not only with the plaintiff's misconduct but also with the older all-or-nothing effect.

Terms used by courts. The term "comparative negligence" suggests not only fault of the plaintiff, but also the proportionate effect of the ruling. The term "comparative fault" is similar to the term "comparative negligence," but at times can be construed more broadly to include causes of action in addition to negligence. The term "comparative responsibility" typically implies a system that includes more than just negligence. Because causes of action like strict liability do not have a fault basis to compare, it is sometimes said that when comparing strict liability and negligence, "responsibility," rather than "fault," is compared.

Terms used in this chapter. This chapter focuses on fault of the plaintiff in the various apportionment systems. Typically, the plaintiff's fault is negligence. Whether plaintiff negligence is an available defense also may depend on the nature of the claim against the defendant. Again, the typical comparison is with the defendant's negligent conduct. However, plaintiff fault as a defense to strict liability or reckless or intentional misconduct is addressed in specific sections too. Although cases and authorities cited in this chapter use a wide range of terms for the fault of the plaintiff, this chapter chiefly employs the term "comparative negligence" or "comparative fault" when discussing the negligence of the plaintiff in a proportionate share system.

---

derivative claims under comparative fault, see Restatement Third of Torts (Apportionment of Liability) § 6 (2010).

[3] E.g., McSwane v. Bloomington Hosp. & Healthcare Sys., 916 N.E.2d 906 (Ind. 2009) (patient who was killed on her way home from hospital by her ex-husband was guilty of contributory negligence as a matter of law for leaving the hospital with abusive former husband); Dunleavy v. Miller, 116 N.M. 353, 862 P.2d 1212 (1993).

[4] See Dan B. Dobbs, Accountability and Comparative Fault, 47 La. L. Rev. 939, 943 (1987).

[5] Restatement Third of Torts (Apportionment of Liability) § 17 at 151–59 (2000).

[6] Restatement Third of Torts (Liability for Physical and Emotional Harm) § 3 (2010).

§ 16.2   The Parallel Analysis of Plaintiff and Defendant Fault

Parallels on the negligence issue. There is some debate about how similar the concepts of plaintiff negligence and defendant negligence are to each other. Traditionally, contributory negligence was a term of art. It meant negligence of the plaintiff in failing to exercise care for herself that was one of the causes of her harm.[7] Under that definition, negligence of the plaintiff differs from negligence of the defendant, which is a failure to exercise reasonable care for others. However, in many ways analysis of the plaintiff's negligence parallels analysis of the defendant's negligence.[8]

Plaintiff's duty. It may be awkward to say that the plaintiff owes the defendant a duty to take reasonable care of herself,[9] but the duty terminology is useful and is embraced by the Restatement Third.[10] In addition to duty, evidence of breach by the plaintiff must also be shown to present the contributory negligence issue to the jury. If the plaintiff's conduct is not negligent, there can be no comparative negligence defense.[11] Thus if a reasonable plaintiff would not have foreseen a risk or taken steps to reduce it, courts will reject the comparative fault defense.[12]

In determining negligence of a plaintiff, as in determining negligence of a defendant, the reasonable person standard of care generally applies.[13] The balance of risks and utilities[14] and other means of assessing fault[15] also apply to the plaintiff as well as to the defendant. A plaintiff may not be guilty of comparative fault when she subjects herself to risks in the course of rescuing another person, because the value of saving another

---

[7]   Restatement Second of Torts § 463 (1965).

[8]   See Restatement Third of Torts (Liability for Physical and Emotional Harm) § 3 cmt. b (2010); Restatement Third of Torts (Apportionment of Liability) § 3 cmt. a (2000).

[9]   Traditionally, a duty is enforceable by a legal action. The defendant has no legal action for breach of a plaintiff's duty to care for herself. Nevertheless, it may be convenient to use the duty locution. You can say (a) that in general, the plaintiff owes a duty to use reasonable care for her own safety, a duty enforceable by a reduction in or a bar to her damages recovery; and (b) in some cases, parallel to negligence analysis, the plaintiff owes "no duty" to protect herself. The latter cases can be addressed by saying that the plaintiff has a right or liberty to rely entirely upon the defendant for care in some instances. Plaintiff "no duty" can be seen as a way of talking about the scope of the defendant's duty to protect the plaintiff against her own risky conduct or a way of asserting that the plaintiff has a correspondingly broad right. These cases are discussed in §§ 16.6–16.7.

[10]   See Restatement Third of Torts (Liability for Physical and Emotional Harm) § 7 cmt. h (2010) ("[C]ases arise in which courts hold that a plaintiff's recovery should not be affected by the plaintiff's own negligent conduct. Just as special problems of policy may support a no-duty determination for a defendant, similar concerns may support a no-duty determination for plaintiff negligence"); Restatement Third of Torts (Apportionment of Liability) § 3 cmt. d (2000).

[11]   See Larchick v. Diocese of Great Falls-Billings, 208 P.3d 836 (Mont. 2009) (no evidence that hit with lacrosse stick was anything other than incidental conduct during a P.E. activity); Harmon v. Washburn, 751 N.W.2d 297 (S.D. 2008) (as a matter of law plaintiff was not negligent to pass another car on a bridge in a legal passing zone, so trial court should not have permitted comparative fault); RGR, LLC v. Settle, 764 S.E.2d 8 (Va. 2014) (plaintiff not contributorily negligent as a matter of law where alleged alternative conduct would have placed him in even greater peril).

[12]   Phillips v. United States, 743 F.Supp. 681, 686–87 (E.D. Mo. 1990) (holding that evidence regarding plaintiff's attempts to merge into heavy traffic was insufficient to warrant jury instruction on contributory negligence); Marple v. Sears, Roebuck & Co., 505 N.W.2d 715, 717–18 (Neb. 1993).

[13]   See, e.g., Basham v. Hunt, 332 Ill. App. 3d 980, 773 N.E.2d 1213 (2002) ("A plaintiff is contributorily negligent when he acts without that degree of care which a reasonably prudent person would have used for his own safety under like circumstances"); Pleiss v. Barnes, 260 Neb. 770, 619 N.W.2d 825 (2000); Sawyer v. Comerci, 264 Va. 68, 563 S.E.2d 748 (2002).

[14]   See Restatement Third of Torts (Liability for Physical and Emotional Harm) § 3 cmt. b (2010).

[15] Richard Wright, Negligence in the Courts: Introduction and Commentary, 77 Chi.-Kent L. Rev. 425 (2002).

makes the risks reasonable.[16] Such holdings are referred to as the second version of the rescue doctrine, but perhaps they don't reflect an independent rule, only the ordinary balance of risks and utilities familiar in negligence cases.[17] Other features of the negligence analysis, such as the emergency doctrine,[18] the negligence per se rules,[19] and even no-duty rules[20] apply to the comparative negligence issue.

Parallels in factual cause and scope of liability issues. Parallels between defendants and plaintiffs can also be seen with respect to issues of factual cause and scope of liability. In terms of factual cause, plaintiff's negligence that is not the but-for cause of harm is rightly disregarded.[21] Moreover, if the harm that occurred as a result of the plaintiff's negligence is different from the type of harm the plaintiff risked, comparative fault will be inappropriate under scope of liability rules.[22] The Restatement Third of Torts specifically provides that liability is not to be assigned to the plaintiff if "the risks posed by the plaintiff's negligence are different from the type of risk that produced the plaintiff's harm."[23]

Parallels in procedural issues. Comparative negligence of the plaintiff is also like the defendant's negligence in terms of a number of procedural issues. For example, the existence of comparative negligence is one for the trier of fact to decide unless the matter is so clear that reasonable persons could not differ.[24] The facts, inference, and essential value-judgments about the reasonableness of plaintiff's conduct are ordinarily for the trier.[25] In particular cases, a court may conclude either that reasonable persons would

---

[16]   Brock v. Peabody Coop. Equity Exch., 186 Kan. 657, 352 P.2d 37 (1960); Kimble v. Carey, 279 Va. 652, 691 S.E.2d 790 (2010). Restatement Third of Torts (Liability for Physical and Emotional Harm) § 32 cmt. d (2010).

[17]   Some courts, however, treat the rescue doctrine as a partial immunity that entirely relieves the plaintiff of responsibility for her own fault unless the plaintiff's actions are in bad faith or willful or wanton. See Ouellette v. Carde, 612 A.2d 687 (R.I. 1990); Kimble v. Carey, 279 Va. 652, 691 S.E.2d 790 (2010).

[18]   See Lyons v. Midnight Sun Transp. Servs., Inc., 928 P.2d 1202 (Alaska 1996); Henson v. Klein, 319 S.W.3d 413 (Ky. 2010).

[19]   E.g., Russell v. Mathis, 686 So. 2d 241 (Ala. 1996) (plaintiff's violation of statute contributory negligence per se). Restatement Third of Torts (Liability for Physical and Emotional Harm) § 14 (2010) (applying negligence per se rules to "an actor" whether plaintiff or defendant, and using both parties in comment illustrations).

[20]   See § 16.6.

[21]   See Brandon v. County of Richardson, 624 N.W.2d 604, 627 (Neb. 2001); Townsend v. Legere, 688 A.2d 77 (N.H. 1997); Rascher v. Friend, 279 Va. 370, 689 S.E.2d 661 (2010) (issue of whether the plaintiff could have avoided the accident if he had not looked down at his speedometer was one for the jury). See also Restatement Third of Torts (Liability for Physical and Emotional Harm) § 26 cmt. m (2010) ("The same rules for factual cause that apply to defendants' tortious conduct also apply to determine whether a plaintiff's contributory negligence is a factual cause of harm suffered by the plaintiff.").

[22]   See Skinner v. Ogallala Pub. Sch. Dist., 631 N.W.2d 510, 526 (Neb. 2001) (upholding lower court ruling against comparative fault in a case in which plaintiff failed to turn on the lights but defendant left open a trap door in a school classroom); Dan B. Dobbs, Accountability and Comparative Fault, 47 La. L. Rev. 939, 956 (1987) (positing a similar scenario); Restatement Third of Torts (Apportionment of Liability) § 4 (2000) ("[T]he defendant also has the burden to prove that the plaintiff's negligence, if any, was a legal cause of the plaintiff's damages.").

[23]   See Restatement Third of Torts (Liability for Physical and Emotional Harm) § 29 cmt. m (2010) ("The rules contained in this Section regarding the scope of liability for tortious conduct are the same for determining when a plaintiff's contributory negligence will reduce the recovery based on comparative responsibility.").

[24]   Botelho v. Caster's, Inc., 970 A.2d 541 (R.I. 2009); Johnson v. Matthew J. Batchelder Co., 779 N.W.2d 690 (S.D. 2010).

[25]   See Martishius v. Carolco Studios, Inc., 355 N.C. 465, 562 S.E.2d 887 (2002); Estate of Moses ex rel. Moses v. Sw. Va. Transit Mgmt. Co., 273 Va. 672, 643 S.E.2d 156 (2007); Louk v. Isuzu Motors, Inc., 198 W.Va. 250, 479 S.E.2d 911 (1996).

necessarily find contributory negligence,[26] or that the plaintiff's comparative negligence is so great, that as a matter of law a directed verdict or summary judgment for the defendant is granted.[27] Courts also sometimes hold that the trier *cannot* attribute fault to the plaintiff because the defendant has presented inadequate evidence to support the assertion of negligence.[28]

Departing from the parallels: the positional difference between plaintiffs and defendants. Although the issue of plaintiff negligence is ordinarily parallel to the issue of defendant negligence, in a few cases the differences between the two issues may be important. One who exposes himself to risks does not necessarily stand in the same moral position as one who exposes others to the same risks.[29] For this reason, some commentators have encouraged use of a semi-subjective standard or other limits on plaintiff negligence determinations that involve self-risk.[30] Even under an objective reasonable person standard, it is possible that a reasonable person would expose himself to risks that he could not reasonably inflict upon others. You might be reasonable, for example, if you dropped into a vat of poison gas to save your child, in spite of the terrible risks;[31] but you could not reasonably push another person into the vat for the same purposes. In addition, the plaintiff is not guilty of either negligence or comparative negligence if responsibility has been allocated solely to the defendant, which is usually the case with the driver of a car, whose passenger is not expected to keep a lookout at all or exercise control over the driving.[32]

Departing from the parallels: mental disability. Cases involving negligence or comparative negligence of children also suggest that there are occasional practical differences between the two concepts. Many of the cases that give children the benefit of a more forgiving standard of care are in fact decisions in which the allegedly negligent child is a plaintiff and the issue is one of comparative negligence.[33] This fact suggests that at least in some cases, the difference between exercising care for one's self and exercising care for others might be important. Some other cases, such as those involving plaintiffs with mental limitations, particularly when a defendant knew or should have

---

[26] E.g., Phillips v. Fujitec Am., Inc., 3 A.3d 324 (D.C. 2010) (summary judgment on issue of contributory negligence when plaintiff who was stuck in an elevator tried to get out between floors although she was told she should stay put and that help was on the way).

[27] Mangold v. Ind. Dep't of Nat'l Res., 756 N.E.2d 970 (Ind. 2001) (12-year-old striking shotgun shell after allegedly misleading or inadequate explanation of shells by defendants); Niskanen v. Giant Eagle, Inc., 122 Ohio St.3d 486, 912 N.E.2d 595 (2009) (fault of patron who shoplifted groceries was greater than fault of grocery store that failed to train employees adequately and killed patron in struggle); Peters v. Menard, Inc., 589 N.W.2d 395 (Wis 1999).

[28] Phillips v. Seward, 51 So.3d 1019 (Ala. 2010); Hayes v. Price, 313 S.W.3d 645 (Mo. 2010) ("[N]o evidence that a reasonable driver could or should have seen any indication of a danger at a time that would allow him to have the means and ability to use an evasive action to avoid the collision" and therefore reversing 20% assignment of fault to plaintiff.); Klutman v. Sioux Falls Storm, 769 N.W.2d 440 (S.D. 2009).

[29] See Gary T. Schwartz, Mixed Theories of Tort Law: Affirming Both Deterrence and Corrective Justice, 75 Tex. L. Rev. 1801, 1828 (1997) (noting that harms to self do not give rise to the same moral indignation as harms to others).

[30] For the semi-subjective standard, see Richard Wright, *The Standards of Care in Negligence Law* in Philosophical Foundations of Tort Law 249 (David G. Owen ed., 1997). For the idea that risks to self should be given more latitude, see Ellen M. Bublick, Comparative Fault to the Limits, 56 Vand. L. Rev. 977, 1029–34 (2003); Gary T. Schwartz, Contributory and Comparative Negligence: A Reappraisal, 87 Yale L.J. 697 (1978).

[31] Cf. Brock v. Peabody Coop. Equity Exch., 186 Kan. 657, 352 P.2d 37 (1960) (mother attempting to enter vat-like warehouse filled with cyanide to rescue child was not necessarily guilty of contributory fault).

[32] E.g., Boomer v. Frank, 993 P.2d 456, 460 (Ariz. Ct. App. 1999); Brawner v. Richardson, 57 Or. App. 178, 643 P.2d 1365 (1982); Thompson v. Michael, 433 S.E.2d 853 (S.C. 1993).

[33] See § 10.14.

known of them,[34] can be interpreted as similarly imposing a less demanding standard upon plaintiffs who put themselves, but not others, at risk.[35]

B. COMPARATIVE FAULT

§ 16.3 Comparative Fault

Development of Comparative Fault

History of comparative fault. Some kinds of comparative fault systems, which reduced the plaintiff's damages but did not bar the claim altogether, have been around on a limited scale for a long time. One earlier experiment allowed the negligent plaintiff to recover if the plaintiff's negligence was slight and the defendant's gross.[36] Admiralty law, in ship collision cases, at one time divided damages fifty-fifty.[37]

Modern comparative fault. Modern comparative negligence law works differently, reducing the plaintiff's recovery in proportion to the plaintiff's fault. The idea got its start in 1908 with the Federal Employers Liability Act (FELA), which governs suits by railroad employees against their employers.[38] A few other federal statutes made similar provisions for limited groups of plaintiffs.[39] In 1910, Mississippi enacted a general comparative negligence statute, followed by Wisconsin in 1931 and Arkansas in 1955.[40] After this slow beginning, change came rather quickly in the 1960s and 1970s. Most of the change came through legislation, but after 1973, a number of states followed Florida's lead[41] by judicially adopting comparative negligence. By the 1980s, only the District of Columbia[42] and four states—Alabama,[43] Maryland,[44] North Carolina,[45] and

---

[34] See Madison by Bryant v. Babcock Ctr., Inc., 638 S.E.2d 650 (S.C. 2006) (plaintiff with mental capacity of 10-year-old to be judged by "behavior to be expected of a person of like age, intelligence, and experience under like circumstances," apparently on the question of determining whether the defendant caregiver exercised due care); Dodson v. S.D. Dep't of Human Servs., 703 N.W.2d 353 (S.D. 2005) (patient of defendant mental health care providers committed suicide, reversing judgment on jury verdict that found defendants negligent in failing to prevent suicide but barring the plaintiff for contributory negligence).

[35] Dan B. Dobbs, Accountability and Comparative Fault, 47 La. L. Rev. 939 (1987).

[36] See Henry Woods & Beth Deere, Comparative Fault § 4.5 (3d ed. 1996). South Dakota still has a statutory variation on this scheme.

[37] See Thomas J. Schoenbaum, Admiralty and Maritime Law, § 14–1 (4th ed. 2004). Admiralty now allocates liability in proportion to fault. United States v. Reliable Transfer Co., 421 U.S. 397, 95 S.Ct. 1708, 44 L.Ed.2d 251 (1975).

[38] 45 U.S.C. § 53 (2012). The plaintiff's negligence still reduces rather than bars a worker's recovery under the FELA. See CSX Transp., Inc. v. Begley, 313 S.W.3d 52 (Ky. 2010).

[39] E.g., the Jones Act, 46 U.S.C. § 30104 (2012) (adopting rule of FELA for seamen).

[40] Victor E. Schwartz, Comparative Negligence § 1.04(b) (4th ed. 2002).

[41] Hoffman v. Jones, 280 So. 2d 431, 78 A.L.R.3d 321 (Fla. 1973).

[42] See Jarrett v. Woodward Bros., Inc., 751 A.2d 972 (D.C. 2000) (recognizing contributory negligence as a complete defense but not in cases where the defendant violated a statute aimed at protecting the plaintiff from his own fault).

[43] See, e.g., QORE, Inc. v. Bradford Bldg. Co., 25 So.3d 1116, 1126 (Ala. 2009) ("A plaintiff who negligently contributes to his own injury cannot recover in a negligence action, notwithstanding a showing that the defendant was also negligent.").

[44] See Coleman v. Soccer Ass'n of Columbia, 69 A.3d 1149 (Md. 2013) (preserving all-or-nothing contributory negligence rule in light of legislative failure to pass bills modifying it); Warsham v. James Muscatello, Inc., 189 Md.App. 620, 985 A.2d 156, 167 (2009) ("[C]ontributory negligence, if proved, is a complete defense that bars a plaintiff's recovery in a negligence action.").

[45] See, e.g., Crawford v. Mintz, 673 S.E.2d 746, 749 (N.C. Ct. App. 2009) ("In North Carolina, a finding of contributory negligence poses a complete bar to a plaintiff's negligence claim.").

Virginia[46]—had retained contributory negligence rules,[47] although a few other states apply contributory negligence in a subset of cases.[48] Proportionate reduction of damage awards in the case of plaintiff fault is now the norm in the U.S. and in many other common law[49] and civil law countries.[50]

Pure vs. Modified Systems of Comparative Fault

The pure or complete system. Two different and mutually exclusive systems of comparative fault are in use. The first, called the complete or pure comparative fault system, applies comparative fault to all plaintiffs in all negligence cases.[51] Under this system, no plaintiff is completely barred from recovery because of her contributory negligence. Fifteen to twenty states as well as the major federal statutes adopt this system.[52]

The modified or incomplete system. The second system of comparative fault, called the modified or incomplete system, continues to use the complete bar rule when the plaintiff's fault reaches a specified breakpoint. The incomplete system itself has two slightly variant versions. In one, the "greater-than" version, the plaintiff is completely barred if her fault exceeds that of the defendant.[53] In the other, the "equal to" version, the plaintiff is completely barred if her fault, though not exceeding the defendant's, is at least equal to it.[54]

Pure vs. modified comparative fault: an example. In simple two-party cases, the examples are straightforward. Suppose the jury finds the plaintiff to be chargeable with 60% of the negligence, the defendant 40%. The plaintiff's damages are $10,000. In a pure comparative fault system, the defendant is liable for only 40% or $4,000; the plaintiff must bear 60% or $6,000 of her own loss. Under modified comparative fault, however, the plaintiff would recover nothing whatsoever; the rules would bar all recovery because plaintiff's negligence is not only equal to but also greater than the defendant's.[55]

---

[46] E.g., O'Neill v. Windshire-Copeland Assocs., L.P., 267 Va. 605, 595 S.E.2d 281 (2004) (contributory negligence a complete defense even though defendant violated building code).

[47] See Victor E. Schwartz, Comparative Negligence § 1.05(e)(3) (4th ed. 2002).

[48] In Indiana, contributory rather than comparative negligence still applies to recovery against government actors and medical malpractice cases. See Clay City Consol. Sch. Corp. v. Timberman, 918 N.E.2d 292 (Ind. 2009); Bruce D. Jones, Unfair and Harsh Results of Contributory Negligence Lives in Indiana: The Indiana Medical Malpractice System and the Indiana Comparative Fault Act, 6 Ind. Health L. Rev. 107 (2009).

[49] Canada: Allen M. Linden & Bruce Feldthusen, Canadian Tort Law, 493–94 (8th ed. 2006); England: See W.V.H. Rogers, Winfield & Jolowicz on Tort 363–64 (18th ed. 2010).

[50] A.M. Honoré, *Causation and Remoteness of Damage*, in XI International Encyclopedia of Comparative Law, Torts, ch. 7, § 146 (1985), reflects variations. For detailed case studies of contributory negligence in Europe, see European Centre for Tort and Insurance Law, Research Unit for Europe, Unification of Tort Law: Contributory Negligence (2004).

[51] As to the inclusion of torts other than negligence, see Chapter 35.

[52] Restatement Third of Torts (Apportionment of Liability) § 17 at 151 to 159 (2000); Victor E. Schwartz, Comparative Negligence § 2.01(a) (4th ed. 2002); Henry Woods & Beth Deere, Comparative Fault § 1.11 (3d ed. 1996).

[53] E.g., N.H. Stats. Ann. § 507:7–d (plaintiff can recover if her negligence is "not greater than the fault of the defendant").

[54] E.g., Ark. Code Ann. § 16–64–122.

[55] Lake v. D & L Langley Trucking, Inc., 233 P.3d 589 (Wyo. 2010). Appellate decisions and practical experience both reveal that jurors do not shy away from attributing high percentages of negligence to plaintiffs in many cases in spite of terrible injuries. E.g., Wassell v. Adams, 865 F.2d 849 (7th Cir. 1989) (victim of rape at under-secured motel, jury charged plaintiff with 97% of the negligence); Hamilton v. Oppen, 653 N.W.2d 678 (N.D. 2002) (plaintiff slipped into auger, which ground his leg to "hamburger," jury finding that he was chargeable with 60% of the negligence barred his claim).

Evaluating systems. The pure or complete system has been favored by thoughtful commentators including Dean Prosser,[56] by a number of courts,[57] and in the federal statutes such as the FELA.[58] Legislators, on the other hand, have tended to favor the modified system.[59] The pure system of comparative fault often strikes casual observers as unfair because in that system, a plaintiff guilty of 90% of the negligence could recover damages from the defendant who is guilty of only 10% of the negligence.[60] In evaluating the complete system of comparative negligence, however, it is important to remember that each party bears his or her proportionate share of the damages. The plaintiff guilty of 90% of the negligence would, after all, bear 90% of her loss. It is also important to remember that if the defendant is also injured, as often is the case in automobile collisions, the same plaintiff would bear 90% of the defendant's loss.

A cutoff's dramatic effect. Moreover, under the incomplete systems, the plaintiff who is charged with 49% of the negligence would recover 51% of her damages, while the plaintiff charged with 51% would recover nothing at all. Yet it is hard to justify absolving a defendant of all liability when he was guilty of 49% of the negligence.[61] In addition, questions arise as to whether the jury should be told of the extreme difference in effect between these two seemingly similar sets of percentages.[62] As the Michigan Court said, the incomplete systems do not eliminate the traditional bar of contributory negligence, they only "lower the barrier."[63]

§ 16.4 Assigning Shares of Fault or Responsibility to the Plaintiff

Comparing unjustified risks. Typically, for comparative fault, juries compare the plaintiff's causally related negligence alongside the defendant's causally related negligence.[64] That is, juries can compare the relevant unjustified risks taken by the plaintiff with the relevant unjustified risks taken by the deendant.[65] Evaluation of risks

---

[56]   William L. Prosser, Comparative Negligence, 41 Cal. L. Rev. 1, 25 (1953).

[57]   Kaatz v. State, 540 P.2d 1037 (Alaska 1975); Li v. Yellow Cab Co. of Cal., 13 Cal. 3d 804, 532 P.2d 1226, 119 Cal. Rptr. 858 (1975); Hoffman v. Jones, 280 So. 2d 431 (Fla. 1973); Placek v. City of Sterling Heights, 405 Mich. 638, 275 N.W.2d 511 (1979). See also United States v. Reliable Transfer Co, Inc., 421 U.S. 397, 95 S.Ct. 1708, 44 L.Ed.2d 251 (1975) (admiralty damages to be allocated in proportion to fault).

[58]   45 U.S.C.A. § 53.

[59]   Restatement Third of Torts (Apportionment of Liability) § 17 rptr.nt. (2000).

[60]   Such extreme findings are rare, but in Wassell v. Adams, 865 F.2d 849 (7th Cir. 1989), the jury attributed 97% of the negligence to the plaintiff. Under the complete comparative negligence system then controlling in Illinois, the plaintiff recovered $25,500 out of her $850,000 damages. See also Cabral v. Ralphs Grocery Co., 51 Cal. 4th 764, 122 Cal. Rptr. 3d 313, 248 P.3d 1170 (2011) (affirming jury verdict that fixed 90% of responsibility on plaintiff and 10% on defendant); Mulhern v. Catholic Health Initiatives, 799 N.W.2d 104 (Iowa 2011) (affirming a judgment where jury fixed 90% of the fault on plaintiff and 10% on defendant).

[61]   See Alvis v. Ribar, 85 Ill. 2d 1, 421 N.E.2d 886 (1981) (advocating a pure system which was later supplanted by legislation).

[62]   Compare Baudanza v. Comcast of Mass. I, Inc., 454 Mass. 622, 912 N.E.2d 458 (2009) (court has discretion about whether to tell jurors about consequences of assignment of percentages of comparative negligence), with Sollin v. Wangler, 627 N.W.2d 159 (N.D. 2001) (jury should be informed about consequences of its verdict).

[63]   Placek v. City of Sterling Heights, 405 Mich. 638, 661, 275 N.W.2d 511, 519 (1979). See also Li v. Yellow Cab Co. of Cal., 13 Cal. 3d 804, 827, 532 P.2d 1226, 1242, 119 Cal. Rptr. 858, 875, 78 A.L.R.3d 393 (1975) (similar).

[64]   Prosser and Keeton on Torts § 65 at 453–54 (5th ed. 1984). Arguing contra, Richard A. Epstein, Plaintiff's Conduct in Products Liability Actions: Comparative Negligence, Automatic Division and Multiple Parties, 45 J. Air L. & Com. 87 (1979).

[65]   See David W. Robertson, Eschewing Ersatz Percentages: A Simplified Vocabulary of Comparative Fault, 45 St. Louis U. L.J. 831 (2001).

taken by the plaintiff and defendant should ordinarily be well within the traditional capacities of the jury.

Example. Suppose there is a collision between a vehicle operated by the defendant at 100 mph and a vehicle operated by the plaintiff at 70 mph. The trier concludes that both drivers were negligent in that speeding unreasonably increased the risk of collision and serious damages. Possibly the risk of collision created by the two drivers would be similar, but the defendant almost certainly created a greater likelihood of greater harm by driving at 100 mph. If the defendant created unjustified risks of collision that far exceeded the unjustified risks created by the plaintiff, it becomes easy to say he was comparatively "more negligent" than the plaintiff. How much more is an estimate based on degree of risk. If the trier believes that driving 100 mph created about three times the risk of driving negligently at 70 mph, the apportionment could be 75–25%. The 75–25 apportionment is only a rough estimate of comparative fault, but it has usually seemed better than no effort to estimate it at all.[66]

In a few cases, defendants may be subject to a standard of care (or duty) different from the standard or duty owed by a reasonable person, as when the defendant owes only a duty to avoid gross negligence. In such cases the standard of care for the plaintiff and that for the defendant may differ, a point that would affect estimates of their respective fault.[67]

Excluding justified and irrelevant risks. A comparison of negligence is a comparison of unjustified risks. No comparison is to be made of risks that are justified, that is, of non-negligent conduct. Suppose the plaintiff speeds at 75 mph in a 55 mph zone because she is rushing her injured child to the hospital. She may not be negligent at all, because the risk may be justified by the prospect of aiding the child. Suppose, however, the jury believes that, considering the nature of the child's injury, 75 mph is much too fast, and that, given the risk to others and to herself, the plaintiff should not have driven more than 65 mph. Some of the risk created by the plaintiff in that case would be justified, that is, non-negligent. The jury would compare only the risk created by increasing the speed from 65 to 75. The point is not that the jury knows how much risk is created by the added speed, but that its estimate should be about that unjustified risk and not about another. Similarly, risks of harm to different classes of people and risks of radically different kinds of harm should be excluded from the comparison. If the defendant's speed not only ran the risk of collision but also the risk that the engine would be damaged by the speed itself, the engine-damage risk probably should not be piled on top of the collision risk in estimating the defendant's fault.[68]

---

[66] See Kaatz v. State, 540 P.2d 1037, 1048 (Alaska 1975) (allocations under comparative fault more accurate than the traditional all-or-nothing rule). Maine, however, has adopted a radically different system, which essentially tells the jury to do justice without regard to relative degree of fault, so a defendant whose fault was more than 50% might nevertheless be called on to pay only a small fraction, say 20% of the damages. See Pelletier v. Fort Kent Golf Club, 662 A.2d 220 (Me. 1995).

[67] See Aguallo v. City of Scottsbluff, 267 Neb. 801, 678 N.W.2d 82 (2004) (recognizing that a difference in standards of care is highly relevant in the allocation of responsibility to each party).

[68] This is not to say that the trier should not consider all risks of the same general kind, whether to self or others. See Robert Cooter & Ariel Porat, Does Risk to Oneself Increase the Care Owed to Others? Law and Economics in Conflict, 29 J. Leg. Stud. 19 (2000); Kenneth W. Simons, The Puzzling Doctrine of Contributory Negligence, 16 Cardozo L. Rev. 1693, 1725–26 (1995).

Comparing fault. Although the fault is not relevant if it is not a cause of the harm, courts in negligence cases ordinarily compare fault, not causation,[69] although causal comparisons do come into play in apportionments with some other causes of action.[70]

"Factors" Bearing on Comparison of Fault

Specifying factors bearing on the negligence issue. Some authorities suggest that relative fault judgments will be improved if a number of important "factors" guide the assignment of relative fault. For example, it has been suggested that the jury should be told to consider the reasonableness of a party's conduct in confronting a risk, the existence of a sudden emergency, and whether the conduct might be justified because it was aimed at saving a life.[71] These particular factors are merely familiar instances of the fundamental negligence analysis.

Comparing conduct; not state of mind. The orthodox view is that negligence is conduct, not a state of mind. That view comports with the equally orthodox holding that conduct is judged by the standard of the reasonable and prudent person, not by the subjective capacities of the individual actor. However, the actor's state of mind is relevant in judging the unreasonable risks created by his conduct when his state of mind bears upon the utility of his conduct. His purpose in speeding to save a child's life may show that his speeding has some utility. His purpose to gratify his own ill-will and spite by frightening others shows just the contrary.[72] The Restatement of Apportionment proposes to take into account "each person's actual awareness, intent, or indifference with respect to the risks created by the conduct."[73] These considerations are difficult to formulate, but presumably they do not justify liability that turns on evaluations of the actor's moral worth rather than upon unreasonable risky conduct. Undue emphasis upon mental capacity in comparing fault may also undermine substantive rules. One case[74] suggested that personal capacities of the actor, including age, maturity, and education should be considered in allocating fault. These are indeed factors that might traditionally be considered for child actors,[75] but not adults. If they are considered for adults, the result would be that the substantive rule of tort law holds an adult liable for risky

---

[69] Professor Robertson, listing five misunderstandings about damages apportionment under comparative fault, put at the head of his list the erroneous view that the defendant who is 30% at fault has caused only 30% of the damages. See David W. Robertson, Eschewing Ersatz Percentages: A Simplified Vocabulary of Comparative Fault, 45 St. Louis U. L.J. 831, 838 (2001).

[70] Restatement Third of Torts (Apportionment of Liability) § 8 (2000).

[71] Eaton v. McLain, 891 S.W.2d 587, 592 (Tenn. 1994). The Eaton Court listed these factors: "(1) the relative closeness of the causal relationship between the conduct of the defendant and the injury to the plaintiff; (2) the reasonableness of the party's conduct in confronting a risk, such as whether the party knew of the risk, or should have known of it; (3) the extent to which the defendant failed to reasonably utilize an existing opportunity to avoid the injury to the plaintiff; (4) the existence of a sudden emergency requiring a hasty decision; (5) the significance of what the party was attempting to accomplish by the conduct, such as an attempt to save another's life; and (6) the party's particular capacities, such as age, maturity, training, education, and so forth." Cf. Purvis v. Grant Parish Sch. Bd., 144 So.3d 922 (La. 2014) (setting forth five specific factors to be considered in allocating fault).

[72] See Gregory C. Keating, Reasonableness and Rationality in Negligence Theory, 48 Stan. L. Rev. 311, 369 (1996).

[73] Restatement Third of Torts (Apportionment of Liability) § 8(b) (2000).

[74] Eaton v. McLain, 891 S.W.2d 587 (Tenn. 1994).

[75] See § 10.14. Some authority favors considering the child's age, experience, and intelligence not only on the issue of liability but also on the issue of apportionment. See Hanson v. Binder, 260 Wis. 464, 50 N.W.2d 676 (1952). Judge Woods concluded that most other decisions assumed that these subjective factors bore on liability but had no effect upon apportionment. See Henry Woods & Beth Deere, Comparative Fault 12:3—12:4 (3d ed. 1996).

behavior by an objective standard, but that the apportionment rule could allow a trier of fact to excuse him for substandard conduct.

Comparative Responsibility

Comparing negligence. The orthodox view in negligence cases is that comparative negligence is just what it sounds like—a comparison of the negligence or culpability of each party, an idea easily understood as a comparison of the unjustified risks taken by each actor. The only negligence to be compared is negligence that is, as affirmed by the Restatement Third, conduct that "is relevant for determining percentage shares of responsibility only when it caused the harm and when the harm is within the scope of the person's liability."[76]

Comparing responsibility. An issue discussed at greater length in the apportionment chapter is the recent suggestion that in comparative apportionment systems, responsibility rather than fault should be compared. Some cases[77] and authorities[78] use terminology that suggests that the trier of fact, in weighing comparative fault, could also weigh the causal importance of the parties' respective fault.[79] Suppose a court says that the jury coming up with a comparative negligence figure should consider "the relative closeness of the causal relationship between the conduct of the defendant and the injury to the plaintiff."[80] That sounds like an invitation to make some kind of judgment about comparative proximate cause, perhaps an invitation to conclude that although both parties negligently contributed to an indivisible injury, and both were equally at fault, the negligence of one was more proximate or more important than the other. Or perhaps it is an invitation to compare factual cause. There is some ambiguity about the meaning of this criterion. If the language is intended to add a comparison of causal significance to the ordinary negligence case, it looks very much as if a whole new conceptual apparatus will be needed.

§ 16.5 All-or-Nothing Judgments After Comparative Fault

Distinguishing Cases of No Defendant Negligence

Locating plaintiff fault in the prima facie case and defenses. The old regime of contributory negligence as a complete bar began with a looming ambiguity. Was the defendant relieved of liability because some separate principle barred the plaintiff who was at fault? Or only because the defendant could reasonably rely upon the plaintiff to protect herself and was thus simply not negligent? The ambiguity had little practical significance in the old system, because, either way, the defendant escaped liability. Comparative negligence changes that. If the plaintiff's fault establishes her negligence, she may still recover with reduced damages. On the other hand, if the defendant owes

---

[76]   Restatement Third of Torts (Apportionment of Liability) § 8 cmt. b (2000).

[77]   See Eaton v. McLain, 891 S.W.2d 587, 592 (Tenn. 1994) ("the relative closeness of the causal relationship between the conduct of the defendant and the injury to the plaintiff" is one factor in assessing percentages).

[78]   According to the Restatement Third of Torts, the factors for assigning liability are both fault and "the strength of the causal connection between the person's risk-creating conduct and the harm." Restatement Third of Torts (Apportionment of Liability) § 8 (2000).

[79]   See the excellent discussion in Victor Schwartz, Comparative Negligence § 17.01(a) (4th ed. 2002).

[80]   Eaton v. McLain, 891 S.W.2d 587 (Tenn. 1994).

no duty of care or if he is not negligent because he could reasonably expect the plaintiff to protect herself, he is not liable at all.[81]

An illustration of the overlap. Negligence on the part of the plaintiff and lack of negligence on the part of the defendant are easily confused in these circumstances.[82] In a number of contexts it may be said that conduct on the part of the plaintiff relates to the negligence of the defendant.[83] For example, if the patient, a medical expert, fails to give the defendant-doctor information needed to make an accurate diagnosis, the defendant may have acted reasonably in light of his expectation that the patient would provide full information. In such a case, the plaintiff's fault might allow a reduced recovery, but not if the defendant simply was not negligent at all.[84]

Plaintiff Conduct That Is Not a Factual Cause of the Harm

No comparative fault defense when plaintiff is not a factual cause. In some cases, the plaintiff may retain full recovery despite the ordinary rule of comparative fault. For example, the plaintiff's comparative negligence is a defense only if the plaintiff's negligence is one of the but-for causes of the plaintiff's harm or a substantial factor in causing that harm, as both case law[85] and authorities note.[86]

Plaintiff Conduct That Causes Harm Outside the Scope of Liability

No comparative fault defense when the harm falls outside plaintiff's scope of liability. The same rules of scope of liability that apply on the issue of defendant's negligence also apply on the issue of plaintiff's fault.[87] For example, if the plaintiff is thought to be negligent in mounting a slippery platform because she risks a slip and a fall, that negligence does not bar recovery when the defendant negligently causes a brick wall to fall on the plaintiff.[88] The risk of slip and fall created by the plaintiff is not the risk that eventuated, and therefore her fault is not within the scope of liability and no bar to her recovery. On occasion the reverse situation has been found: the plaintiff's negligence is

---

[81] See Wex S. Malone, Some Ruminations on Contributory Negligence, 1981 Utah L. Rev. 91, reprinted in Wex S. Malone, Essays on Torts 197 (1986); Wex S. Malone, Comment on Maki v. Frelk, 21 Vand. L. Rev. 930 (1968).

[82] Afarian v. Massachusetts Elec. Co., 449 Mass. 257, 866 N.E.2d 901 (2007) (utility company owed no duty to position utility pole so that it would not be struck by a drunk driver who veered off the road); Lowery v. Echostar Satellite Corp., 160 P.3d 959 (Okla. 2007) (plaintiff attempted to install satellite dish on roof; defendant owed no duty to protect her from the obvious danger).

[83] Solanki v. Ervin, 21 So.3d 552 (Miss. 2009) (plaintiff stopped her car after it stalled in the middle of the highway rather than on the median and defendant ran into it).

[84] Juchniewcz v. Bridgeport Hosp., 914 A.2d 511 (Conn. 2007).

[85] See Brandon v. County of Richardson, 261 Neb. 636, 624 N.W.2d 604 (2001) (any negligence of the deceased was not a cause in fact of death, no damages reduction for supposed comparative fault); Pavlou v. City of N.Y., 868 N.E.2d 186 (N.Y. 2006) (worker operated crane with an excess load, but a crack in the crane made it unsafe to operate with any load).

[86] Some courts once said that the plaintiff's contributory negligence will bar her recovery if it makes the "slightest contribution" to the resulting harm. E.g., Crane v. Neal, 389 Pa. 329, 132 A.2d 675 (1957). If that language meant to ignore the usual causal rules, it has now been rejected. See McCay v. Philadelphia Elec. Co., 447 Pa. 490, 291 A.2d 759 (1972). In general, causal rules on the issue of the plaintiff's fault are the same as the rules on the defendant's negligence. Restatement Third of Torts: Apportionment of Liability § 4 (2010); Restatement Third of Torts (Liability for Physical and Emotional Harm) § 26 cmt. m (2010).

[87] See Control Techniques, Inc. v. Johnson, 762 N.E.2d 104 (Ind. 2002); Estate of Moses ex. rel. Moses v. Southwestern Va. Transit Mgmt. Co., 643 S.E.2d 156 (Va. 2007); Restatement Second of Torts § 468 (1965).

[88] Smithwick v. Hall & Upson Co., 59 Conn. 261, 21 A. 924 (1890); see Lamp v. Reynolds, 249 Mich. App. 591, 645 N.W.2d 211 (2002) (plaintiff could not have foreseen that in riding just off the edge of defendant's motocross raceway he would strike a hidden stump, so any negligence in doing so was not a proximate cause of his harm; no reduction in damages).

considered a superseding cause so that the defendant is not liable at all.[89] Commentators have taken different views of the propriety of this sort of ruling in comparative negligence systems.[90]

Torts Not Subject to Comparative Fault

No comparative fault defense based on the tort cause of action. Another way in which comparative fault might be avoided between plaintiff and defendant is that a court may conceptualize the case as one about some tort such as fraud for which comparative fault rules may not apply.[91] Conceptualizing the case as a non-negligence case might result in bypassing the comparative negligence analysis, though some other torts may adopt more stringent rules against the plaintiff.[92]

§ 16.6 Allocating Full Responsibility to the Defendant in the Interests of Policy or Justice: Plaintiff No-Duty Rules

Risk-taking plaintiff's recovery not always reduced. Under today's comparative fault regimes, the risk-taking plaintiff does not always suffer a reduction in damages. This is the case if the plaintiff cannot reasonably foresee harm, or foresees harm but takes reasonable steps to avoid it, or if the plaintiff is negligent but her negligence is not a cause in fact of the harm, or the harm is not within the scope of liability. In such cases, the plaintiff can recover full damages because she is not negligent or has caused none of her own harm.

Specific rules barring plaintiff fault defenses. Sometimes, courts go further and erect rules of law that the plaintiff is not chargeable with fault in particular situations. For instance, it has been held that seamen cannot be charged with comparative fault for obeying a work order or answering a specific call for help aboard ship[93] and that minors cannot be charged with comparative fault for failing to protect themselves against sexual abuse.[94]

Restatement "plaintiff no-duty rules." The Restatement Third of Torts endorses the idea of policy and principle limits on comparative fault defenses and leaves the category to common law development,[95] while also outlining some categories of cases in which limits are particularly appropriate.[96] These categories are addressed in this section, with the exception of plaintiffs injured by intentional tortfeasors, which is addressed

---

[89]   See Exxon Co., U.S.A. v. Sofec, Inc., 517 U.S. 830, 116 S.Ct. 1813, 135 L.Ed.2d 113 (1996); Wright v. N.Y.C. Transit Auth., 633 N.Y.S.2d 393 (App. Div. 1995). Cf. Ala. Power Co. v. Moore, 899 So.2d 975 (Ala. 2004).

[90]   Compare Michael D. Green, The Unanticipated Ripples of Comparative Negligence: Superseding Cause in Products Liability and Beyond, 53 S.C. L. Rev. 1103 (2002); with Paul T. Hayden, Butterfield Rides Again: Plaintiff's Negligence as a Superseding or Sole Proximate Cause in Systems of Pure Comparative Responsibility, 33 Loyola L.A. L. Rev. 887 (2000).

[91]   However, some comparative fault acts are so broad that comparative fault may be a defense to fraud. See WFND, LLC v. Fargo Marc, LLC, 730 N.W.2d 841 (N.D. 2007) (statute including all acts or omissions "that subject a person to liability").

[92]   See Doe v. Dilling, 228 Ill.2d 324, 888 N.E.2d 24 (2008).

[93]   Simeonoff v. Hiner, 249 F.3d 883 (9th Cir. 2001).

[94]   Christensen v. Royal Sch. Dist. No. 160, 124 P.3d 283 (Wash. 2005).

[95]   See Restatement Third of Torts (Liability for Physical and Emotional Harm) § 7 cmt. h (2010) ("[C]ases arise in which courts hold that a plaintiff's recovery should not be affected by the plaintiff's own negligent conduct. Just as special problems of policy may support a no-duty determination for a defendant, similar concerns may support a no-duty determination for plaintiff negligence."); Restatement Third of Torts (Apportionment of Liability) § 3 cmt. d (2000).

[96]   Restatement Third of Torts (Liability for Physical and Emotional Harm) § 7 cmt. h (2010).

separately because of its long historical roots. Rules that relieve the plaintiff of an obligation for reasonable self-care can be referred to as "no-duty rules," in an analogy to no-duty rules that are well understood in the context of defendants.[97]

No-duty rules as the exception. Although principle and policy reasons to limit comparative fault defenses may arise in a number of different circumstances, they are still exceptions to the general rule that the fault of the plaintiff is typically an issue for the jury to resolve, particularly after the shift from contributory to comparative.[98] Moreover, while no-duty rules always aid a defendant, plaintiff no-duty rules or other restrictions on the comparative negligence defense may or may not assist a plaintiff. That is so because when comparative fault cannot be assigned, the jury may allow the plaintiff full recovery, or may provide her with none at all.

Risks Allocated in Whole or in Part to Defendant

Principles and policies that may limit comparative fault defenses. Although the term "plaintiff no-duty rules" is quite new, first coming into general use with the Restatement Third of Torts, judicial recognition of limits on plaintiff fault defenses is not new. Commentators have noted some consistent and identifiable principles or policies that have shaped limits to defenses based on plaintiff fault.[99]

Plaintiff's limited capacity. One factor that has sometimes limited plaintiff fault defenses is the plaintiff's incapacity for self-care. For example, it would be unacceptable to say that a 14-month-old who has not strapped himself into a safety seat[100] or a two-year-old who eats lead paint chips[101] is guilty of comparative fault. Although this conduct departs from an objective standard of reasonable care, the departures are consistent with the limited abilities of children.[102] For this reason, the Restatement Third of Torts adopts a rule precluding comparative negligence of a child under age five and endorses a semi-subjective standard of care for other children.[103] Limits might also be appropriate for plaintiffs with other demonstrated indicia of lack of capacity to care for themselves as with the institutionalized elderly.[104]

Defendant's superior knowledge or experience. Courts may also limit comparative fault defenses when the parties are in a special relationship and there are differentials in experience, knowledge or control such that the defendant can take better care of the plaintiff's interests than can the plaintiff herself. For example, a parent, if he owes a duty of care at all, should owe a duty to protect the child against dangers arising from the child's own foolishness or mental limitations.[105] A common carrier might owe a

---

[97]   Id.

[98]   See Del Lago Partners, Inc. v. Smith, 307 S.W.3d 762 (Tex. 2010) (discussing the importance of leaving comparative negligence issue to the jury in light of the Restatement Third of Torts).

[99]   See generally Ellen M. Bublick, Comparative Fault to the Limits, 56 Vand. L. Rev. 977 (2003).

[100]   Rider v. Speaker, 692 N.Y.S.2d 920 (App. Div. 1999).

[101]   Lopez v. No Kit. Realty Co., 679 N.Y.S.2d 115 (App. Div. 1998).

[102]   Chu v. Bowers, 656 N.E.2d 436 (Ill. App. Ct. 1995).

[103]   Restatement Third of Torts (Apportionment of Liability) § 10 cmt. e (2000).

[104]   Fields v. Senior Citizens Ctr., Inc., 528 So. 2d 573, 581 (La. Ct. App. 1988).

[105]   Cf. Lynch v. Rosenthal, 396 S.W.2d 272 (Mo. Ct. App. 1965) (adult plaintiff of very low mental ability injured in farm machinery while living with farmer; plaintiff not necessarily chargeable with contributory fault).

special duty of care to protect a passenger from the effects of her own known disabilities.[106]

Experience differentials: children and adult activities. In terms of experience differentials, children are not expected to know how to handle adult sexuality, but adults are. Consequently, a church that is negligent in retaining a sexually abusive priest cannot claim the comparative fault of the child who does not end the abusive relationship.[107] Nor can a teacher who has sexual contact with a minor student plead the comparative negligence of the minor, and this limit also applies to school officials who fail to use care in selecting or supervising the teacher.[108] Along the same lines, when a defendant creates a risk that a child will take part in adult activities that put the child herself at risk, the defendant owes care to protect her.[109]

Knowledge differentials: doctors and patients. A special relationship in which knowledge differentials are a factor in the defendant's superior ability to care for the plaintiff's interests is well illustrated by the relationship between doctors and patients. Doctors may owe a duty to provide patients with material information about the need for and risks of proposed operations. Given the doctor's duty and the patient's corresponding right to rely upon the doctor's care, the doctor who advises a mastectomy can hardly be permitted to defend his actions on the ground that his patient was unreasonable in relying upon his advice.[110] However, while a patient may not be required to evaluate medical advice, a patient can be held negligent for other sorts of failures, for example, failing to provide accurate information[111] or failing to take medicine as prescribed.[112]

Control of safety-related systems. Comparative fault defenses at times may be limited in special relationship cases when defendants have a greater ability to control systemic safety-related decisions such that they are expected to guard against plaintiff lapses. So a manufacturer of a punch press machine may be negligent in failing to provide safety devices to prevent workers from carelessly putting their hands under the press as it descends. Since workers' predictable negligence in carrying out repetitive tasks is the very thing the manufacturer should have protected against, to apply the contributory negligence bar would be to negate the manufacturer's duty. Hence, some courts removed the contributory negligence bar in such cases.[113] It remains to be seen whether restrictions on the plaintiff fault defense will apply when comparative fault

---

[106] See McMahon v. N.Y., N.H. & H.R. Co., 136 Conn. 372, 71 A.2d 557 (1950) (intoxicated passenger); Vaughn v. Nw. Airlines, Inc., 558 N.W.2d 736 (Minn. 1997) (passenger injured in handling own luggage).

[107] Hutchison v. Luddy, 763 A.2d 826, 847 (Pa. Super. Ct. 2001), vacating disallowance of punitive damages claim at Hutchison ex rel. Hutchison v. Luddy, 870 A.2d 766 (Pa. 2005).

[108] Christensen v. Royal Sch. Dist. No. 160, 124 P.3d 283 (Wash. 2005).

[109] See Ellen M. Bublick, Comparative Fault to the Limits, 56 Vand. L. Rev. 977, 1004–07 (2003).

[110] Brown v. Dibbell, 227 Wis.2d 28, 595 N.W.2d 358 (1999) (patient claimed doctor failed to advise fully on whether mastectomy was needed; if true, negligence of patient in undergoing operation would be no defense). Distinguish McCrystal v. Trumbull Mem'l Hosp., 115 Ohio App.3d 73, 684 N.E.2d 721 (1996), where the *plaintiff* sought and was entitled to a comparative negligence instruction because evidence might have suggested to the jury that she was at fault in relying on the defendant's medical advice.

[111] Brown v. Dibbell, 227 Wis.2d 28, 595 N.W.2d 358 (1999) (patient provided doctor with false information about her family history of breast cancer); Son v. Ashland Cmty. Healthcare Servs., 239 Or. App. 495, 244 P.3d 835 (2010) (child's failure to tell treating doctors of her consumption of drugs that led to her hospitalization was negligence question for the jury).

[112] Shinholster v. Annapolis Hosp., 685 N.W.2d 275 (Mich. 2004).

[113] Tulkku v. Mackworth Rees Div. of Avis Indus., Inc., 281 N.W.2d 291 (Mich. 1979); Bexiga v. Havir Mfg. Corp., 290 A.2d 281 (N.J. 1972).

diminishes rather than denies the plaintiff's recovery.[114] When the defendant is negligent because of violation of a statute meant to protect the plaintiff from her own negligence or incapacity, for example child labor acts or employee protection statutes, many courts have not allowed a contributory negligence defense.[115] Similarly, plaintiffs may not be charged with comparative fault for failing to discover a product's defect.[116] And a pharmacist who negligently dispenses the wrong prescription may not be able to defend on the ground that plaintiff should have been able to find the mistake by knowing the name of the prescription[117] or the look of the medication.[118] However, some courts now deal with similar matters, such as a doctor's wrongful prescription of drugs to an addicted adult or teen, through comparative negligence.[119] And though it might be said that bans on the sale of alcohol to minors are for the protection of underage drinkers, some courts now permit the underage drinker's use of alcohol to count as comparative fault.[120] This may reflect the shift to comparative negligence or perhaps the fact that the minor's misconduct in these cases is typically more than just negligent.

Custom or understanding. Customary practices, the relationship of the parties, or their implicit understandings, may operate to allocate some risks entirely to the defendant. A pedestrian is not expected to wear a helmet against the possibility that a driver may run him down. "The law normally does not require duplicative precautions" in such a case,[121] but instead expects drivers to keep their vehicles off the sidewalk. Likewise, if an employer owes a duty to provide a safe place to work, the employee's conduct should be evaluated in the light of that expectation.[122]

Defendant's duty to protect plaintiff from herself. At times, the idea is expressed that the defendant's duty is to protect the plaintiff from her own negligence. A mental hospital that accepts a suicidal patient suffering from emotional or mental problems should exercise care to prevent suicide, and if it does not, may not be able to defeat a claim for the patient's death by suicide by asserting that the patient was at fault,[123] at least where the patient is in the hospital's physical custody.[124] In such a case, the hospital has

---

[114] See Hardy v. Monsanto Enviro-Chem Sys. Inc., 323 N.W.2d 270 (Mich. 1982) (holding that the rule in Tulkku, supra n. 113, does not apply after the shift to comparative negligence).

[115] See § 16.7 (protecting vulnerable classes).

[116] See 2 Dobbs, Hayden & Bublick, The Law of Torts § 470 (2011 & Supp.).

[117] Walter v. Wal-Mart Stores, Inc., 748 A.2d 961, 969–72 (Me. 2000).

[118] Olson v. Walgreen Co., 1992 WL 322054 (Minn. Ct. App. 1992).

[119] Weaver v. Lentz, 561 S.E.2d 360 (S.C. Ct. App. 2002) (reducing recovery by 50% for estate of deceased who overdosed on drugs recklessly prescribed by defendant in spite of high risk of patient's abuse) (not citing Bramlette, supra n. 33, from the same jurisdiction). Contra Argus v. Scheppegrell, 472 So. 2d 573 (La. 1985) (doctor who was under a duty not to prescribe drugs for addicted teenager could not rely upon her contributory negligence to defeat a claim for her death from overdose). However, the rule in Argus no longer applies after comparative fault. See Scheidt v. Denney, 644 So. 2d 813 (La. Ct. App. 1994).

[120] Baxter v. Noce, 752 P.2d 240 (N.M. 1988). Minnesota holds that an underage drinker's purchase of alcohol can be "complicity" which operates as a complete bar to recovery akin to contributory negligence. Spragg v. Shuster, 398 N.W.2d 683 (Minn. Ct. App. 1987). This approach would seem to negate the defendant's duty to use any protection for the child. But see Slager v. HWA Corp., 435 N.W.2d 349 (Iowa 1989) (comparative fault does not apply to dramshop act).

[121] Greycas, Inc. v. Proud, 826 F.2d 1560, 1566 (7th Cir. 1987).

[122] See Vendetto v. Sonat Offshore Drilling Co., 725 So. 2d 474, 479 (La. 1999).

[123] E.g., McNamara v. Honeyman, 406 Mass. 43, 546 N.E.2d 139 (1989); Tomfohr v. Mayo Found., 450 N.W.2d 121(Minn. 1990); Cowan v. Doering, 111 N.J. 451, 545 A.2d 159 (1988); Bramlette v. Charter-Medical-Columbia, 302 S.C. 68, 393 S.E.2d 914 (1990) ("[T]he very act which the defendant has a duty to prevent cannot constitute contributory negligence or assumption of the risk as a matter of law.").

[124] Where the decedent was an out-patient, some cases have allowed the jury to compare the patient's fault in committing suicide with the defendant's fault in failing to protect her from her own suicidal tendencies.

assumed the patient's duty of self-care and, logically, cannot thrust it back upon the disabled patient. The rule is not based upon statute, or upon strict liability, but upon the principle that the defendant has assumed a duty to protect the plaintiff from her own dangerous propensities. While courts have also found that a jailer who has custody of prisoners may owe them a duty to protect against suicide as well as against others' harms,[125] the comparative fault defense may be allowed more readily in this setting.[126]

Defendant's professional role and antecedent plaintiff fault. At times the policies that commend the need for defendant care for negligent plaintiffs stem from social or contractual understandings about the defendant's professional role. For example, if the defendant is obliged to care for an injured plaintiff, the fact that the plaintiff herself negligently caused her own initial injury or need for treatment does not reduce the defendant's liability for his later negligent treatment and this is as true under comparative fault as it was under contributory negligence.[127] So even if the plaintiff needed treatment because he caused the accident that occasioned the need for treatment, the physician cannot reduce his responsibility for negligent treatment of the patient's injury on the ground that the injury he undertook to treat came about in the first place through the patient's fault.[128] This result can be explained on the ground that the defendant has undertaken a duty to use care in spite of the plaintiff's (earlier) negligence and injury. The Restatement Third of Torts expressly takes this view.[129]

See Hobart v. Shin, 185 Ill.2d 283, 705 N.E.2d 907, 235 Ill. Dec. 724 (1998); Mulhern v. Catholic Health Initiatives, 799 N.W.2d 104 (Iowa 2011). Cf. Maunz v. Perales, 276 Kan. 313, 76 P.3d 1027 (2003) (rejecting the rule for a suicidal outpatient, but at the same time using a subjective standard for judging the patient's fault in the light of his mental limitations).

[125] See Hickey v. Zezulka, 439 Mich. 408, 487 N.W.2d 106 (1992) (superceded by statute); Sandborg v. Blue Earth Cty., 615 N.W.2d 61 (Minn. 2000) (jail suicide; when jailer assumed duty of protecting one in custody, arrestee's duty of self-care was shifted to the jailer; arrestee "is relieved of his duty in these extraordinary circumstances, he can have no fault to be compared"); Gregoire v. City of Oak Harbor, 244 P.3d 924 (Wash. 2010) (city could not assert contributory negligence or assumption of risk as affirmative defense in wrongful death action concerning inmate who committed suicide).

[126] See Joseph v. State, 26 P.3d 459 (Alaska 2001) (holding suicide is not superseding cause where defendant is under a duty of care to prevent it, but seemingly contemplating that jury could reduce damages by allocating some fault to the person who committed suicide); Tufo v. Township of Old Bridge, 147 N.J. 90, 685 A.2d 1267 (1996) (police had duty of care to arrestee in custody, but arrestee's pre-arrest negligence in consuming drugs could count as comparative fault to reduce municipality's liability; distinguishing health care cases and asserting a "strong public policy of this State to make such arrestees legally accountable for violating the drug laws").

[127] Harvey v. Mid-Coast Hosp., 36 F.Supp.2d 32 (D. Me. 1999) (attempted suicide merely furnished the occasion for medical treatment and does not reduce liability for the subsequent causal negligence of the treating physician); DeMoss v. Hamilton, 644 N.W.2d 302 (Iowa 2002) (error to give comparative fault instruction based upon plaintiff's behavior before consulting physician); Fritts v. McKinne, 934 P.2d 371 (Okla. Civ. App. 1996); Eiss v. Lillis, 233 Va. 545, 357 S.E.2d 539 (1987) (the plaintiff's self-caused condition was "merely a factor that the doctor had to take into consideration" in providing treatment); Rowe v. Sisters of the Pallottine Missionary Soc'y, 211 W.Va. 16, 560 S.E.2d 491 (2001) (plaintiffs who negligently injure themselves are entitled to subsequent, non-negligent medical treatment, so liability of the plaintiff's doctor for malpractice is not reduced by plaintiff's negligence in causing the injury for which he sought treatment).

[128] Cavens v. Zaberdac, 849 N.E.2d 526 (Ind. 2006) (asthmatic used excessive medication and delayed treatment, but fault which occurred prior to presentation at emergency room did not amount to contributory negligence); Son v. Ashland Cmty. Healthcare Servs., 239 Or. App. 495, 244 P.3d 835 (2010) (child's consumption of drugs that led to her hospitalization could not be used as an affirmative defense for fault-allocation purposes in action against treating physicians); Mercer v. Vanderbilt Univ., Inc., 134 S.W.3d 121 (Tenn. 2004) (a patient's negligent conduct that occurs prior to a health care provider's negligent treatment and provides only the occasion for the health care provider's subsequent negligence may not be compared to the negligence of the health care provider; citing many cases).

[129] Restatement Third of Torts (Apportionment of Liability) § 7 cmt. m (2000) ("[I]n a case involving negligent rendition of a service, including medical services, a factfinder does not consider any plaintiff's conduct that created the condition the service was employed to remedy.").

Plaintiff in the exercise of her rights. In other cases, the plaintiff is not to be charged with comparative fault. This can be true when plaintiff is doing what she has a right to do. In the leading case, the plaintiff was a landowner who stacked goods on his land near a railroad track. The railroad negligently caused a fire and, when sued for damage, argued that the plaintiff should be barred because he could have stacked his goods farther from the track. This argument was of no avail because the plaintiff's risky conduct was conduct he had a right to pursue.[130]

Autonomy and fundamental rights. Such cases can be viewed as cases in which the plaintiff's autonomy or citizenship rights permit her to ignore reasonable self-care. These cases are limited. As Professor Epstein points out, loss prevention efforts on both sides are now commonly required.[131] But some cases warrant a recognition of the plaintiff's overriding rights. It is surely unacceptable to say that women are guilty of contributory negligence if they venture out at night because they might be raped,[132] or that a homeowner is at fault if he lives near a golf course where a negligent duffer can slice a ball into his eye.[133] Similarly, based on recognition of fundamental rights, a court might not permit a woman to be assigned comparative fault for refusing to undergo an abortion,[134] or for living in a first-floor apartment as a single female.[135]

Prudential limits and normative clarity. Some comparative fault defenses may be curbed because of prudential limits, for example where litigant welfare might be harmed by blaming a child victim for his sexual abuse.[136] A related concern is that in certain instances, clear normative statements may be desirable and yet impaired by a percentage allocation of relative fault. This is not only true in intentional tort cases, but also in more mundane cases. For example, a court may be understandably reluctant to allow a defense that a plaintiff, hit by a defendant who runs a light, is to any degree negligent for going on green.[137] Limits placed on comparative fault defenses in the

---

[130] Leroy Fibre Co. v. Chicago, Milwaukee & St. Paul Ry. Co., 232 U.S. 340, 34 S.Ct. 415, 58 L.Ed. 631 (1914). Perhaps the rule in this case is affected by the difference between property rights, which are more absolute, and tort rules, which require reasonableness. See William Powers, Border Wars, 72 Tex. L. Rev. 1209 (1994).

[131] Richard A. Epstein, Torts § 8.2.1 (1999).

[132] See Ellen Bublick, Citizen No-Duty Rules: Rape Victims and Comparative Fault, 99 Colum. L. Rev. 1413 (1999).

[133] Hennessey v. Pyne, 694 A.2d 691 (R.I. 1997) (homeowner does not assume the risk by living near golf course). Distinguish the sometime-defense based on coming to the nuisance. Lewis v. Puget Sound Power & Light Co., 29 P.3d 1028 (Mont. 2001), seems to have held that the plaintiff might herself be negligent in purchasing property that might be damaged by the defendant in the future. The court may have had coming to the nuisance in mind, because it seems to suggest that the plaintiff might have been "paid" for future damage in getting a reduced purchase price.

[134] Lovelace Med. Ctr. v. Mendez, 805 P.2d 603, 604 (N.M. 1991).

[135] Despite obvious equality concerns with the defense, in Jackson v. Post Props., Inc., 513 S.E.2d 259, 261–62 (Ga. Ct. App. 1999), a civil liability action stemming from rape, the issue of a woman's comparative negligence for living in a first-floor apartment was permitted to be submitted to a jury.

[136] Landreneau v. Fruge, 676 So.2d 701, 707 (La. Ct. App. 1996); Christensen v. Royal Sch. Dist. No. 160, 124 P.3d 283 (Wash. 2005); but see Buel v. ASSE Int'l, Inc., 233 F.3d 441, 450–51 (7th Cir. 2000) (upholding jury assignment of 41% of responsibility for repeated rape by father of host family to teenaged foreign exchange student from Germany). See also Shelley Murphy, Judge Raps US over Bulger Civil Trial: Says Victims, Families Were Unfairly Blamed, Boston Globe, September 25, 2010 (ordering the U.S. government to pay $5000 each to families of murder victims who had to respond to the government's attempt to unfairly blame the victims for their deaths, a process which embarrassed the victims' families).

[137] See Hayes v. Price, 313 S.W.3d 645 (Mo. 2010) ("a driver is entitled to assume a car going in the opposite direction will yield the right of way to oncoming traffic before turning," reversing 20% assignment of fault to plaintiff); Olson v. Parchen, 816 P.2d 423, 426–27 (Mont. 1991); Springer v. Bohling, 643 N.W.2d 386, 392–94 (Neb. 2002).

conduct of a defendant guilty of an intentional or reckless tort are separately discussed below as a traditional exception.

§ 16.7   Traditional Exceptions to the Contributory Negligence Bar and Their Status Today

Exceptions and their current status. The regime of contributory negligence which barred the negligent plaintiff's recovery altogether recognized at least three major exceptions to the rule. Contributory negligence was not a defense i) when the defendant had the last clear chance to avoid the injury or had discovered plaintiff's peril, ii) when the defendant committed an intentional or reckless tort, and iii) when the defendant was under a duty to protect the plaintiff, as discussed in the prior section. The main question asked in most jurisdictions today is whether and to what extent these exceptions survive the shift to comparative fault.

Last clear chance. A complicated exception to the contributory negligence defense was called the last clear chance doctrine. In these cases, the plaintiff negligently put herself in danger from which she could not escape. The defendant then negligently caused harm to the helpless plaintiff. The salient fact was that the plaintiff could do nothing to save herself once she had put herself in danger, but that the defendant could have avoided injury by ordinary care.[138] In such cases, the plaintiff's earlier contributory negligence would be no bar.[139] The original case involved a plaintiff who had tied his donkey in the road, where it stood eating grass when the defendant negligently ran into it. The plaintiff was not on hand to free the animal and it could not escape. The plaintiff's negligence was no bar to recovery because the defendant had the "last clear chance" to prevent the accident.[140]

Discovered peril. Some jurisdictions modified the last clear chance exception, applying a version known as the discovered peril rule. The discovered peril rule held that the exception would not apply unless the defendant actually discovered the plaintiff's helpless condition and was negligent thereafter in failing to avoid injury.[141] The difference between this rule and the last clear chance version is that under the latter, the exception can be invoked not only when the defendant actually discovered the danger but also when he should have done so in the exercise of reasonable care.

Dropping last clear chance and discovered peril in comparative fault regimes. Although some recent analysis focuses on care in sequential decisions to reach optimal levels of precaution,[142] the last clear chance doctrine has been widely regarded as a judicial effort to ameliorate the harsh bar of contributory negligence. Given that view, it is no surprise that once comparative negligence systems were adopted, the last clear chance doctrine was almost always discarded,[143] either legislatively[144] or judicially.[145]

---

[138] Dominguez v. Manhattan & Bronx Surface Transit Operating Auth., 46 N.Y.2d 528, 388 N.E.2d 1221, 415 N.Y.S.2d 634 (1979); Restatement Second of Torts § 479 (1965).

[139] E.g., Robinson v. District of Columbia, 580 A.2d 1255 (D.C. 1990).

[140] Davies v. Mann, 10 M. & W. 547, 152 Eng. Rep. 588 (Exch. 1842).

[141] E.g., Walker v. Spokane, Portland & Seattle Ry., 262 Or. 606, 500 P.2d 1039 (1972).

[142] See Giuseppe Dari-Mattiacci & Nuno Garoupa, Least-Cost Avoidance: The Tragedy of Common Safety, 25 J.L. Econ. & Org. 235 (2009) (finding that the last clear chance rule may prevent accidents but is not efficient).

[143] Henry Woods & Beth Deere, Comparative Fault § 8.3 (3d ed. 1996).

[144] E.g., Conn. Gen. Stat. Ann. § 52–572h (*l*); Minn. Stat. Ann. § 604.01; Ore. Rev. Stat. § 31.620.

[145] E.g., Spahn v. Town of Port Royal, 330 S.C. 168, 499 S.E.2d 205 (1998); Del Lago Partners, Inc. v. Smith, 307 S.W.3d 762 (Tex. 2010); cf. Penn Harris Madison Sch. Corp. v. Howard, 861 N.E.2d 1190 (Ind. 2007)

The Restatement Third of Torts has also taken the position that the rule should be abolished in comparative fault systems.[146]

Contributory negligence not a defense to intentional or reckless tort. Contributory negligence of a plaintiff was never a defense to claims for intentionally inflicted harm.[147] By extension, courts came to hold that negligence of the plaintiff was no defense if the defendant was guilty of willful or wanton or reckless misconduct.[148] However, if the plaintiff, as well as the defendant, was guilty of reckless or wanton misconduct, the plaintiff's claim was barred.[149]

Reasons for the rule. Many intentional torts involve an intent to harm, or at least offend. Reckless torts involve "utter indifference to or conscious disregard for the safety of others." Reckless torts border on intentional wrongdoing because they involve a bad state of mind, as well as risky conduct. Contributory negligence was not allowed because it would seem to justify in part that wrongdoing. To say, as one court did, that a gang rape was in part attributable to the rapists intentional tort and in part attributable to a 13 year old's willingness to go with the boys to drink beer is to shift responsibility for rape from rapist to rape victim.[150] The same would be true with contributory fault in other intentional and reckless torts.

Reasons for retaining the rule under comparative fault. It is morally appealing to think that each person should bear some accountability for his or her own fault, whether that fault is grounded in intent or in negligence. Yet the measure of liability should not be divorced from the basis for that liability and the rules must apply the fault comparison in ways that can be rationally evaluated by reviewing judges. Although it has been argued that negligence and other kinds of fault are not truly different except in degree and that negligence can thus be compared with other kinds of fault,[151] the similarity between negligence and intentional wrongdoing seems to appear mainly at high levels of abstraction. In negligence claims, risks and utilities may be difficult to estimate, but we know what we are estimating. Intent—its clarity and intensity, its moral quality, and its roots in personal failure, tragedy, misapprehensions, or cultural ideals—would be very hard to weigh on a scale comparable to the risk-utility scale in negligence cases. Such difficulties open the door to highly subjective and variable judgments. Biased judgments would be difficult or impossible to detect and review on appeal in the absence of a firm standard for comparison.

Right to engage in conduct. Moreover, the risk-taking plaintiff may have some sort of privilege or right. For example, the plaintiff has a right to walk on the street, even if there is a constant danger that she will be attacked by an intentional wrongdoer. In such

---

(noting decline of last clear chance doctrine with the advent of comparative fault, but holding it still applicable to a case in which contributory negligence rules applied).

[146] Restatement Third of Torts (Apportionment of Liability) § 3 cmt. b (2000) (No last-clear-chance rule categorically forgives a plaintiff for conduct that would otherwise constitute negligence").

[147] E.g., Lambrecht v. Schreyer, 129 Minn. 271, 152 N.W. 645 (1915); Galveston, H. & S.A. Ry. v. Zantzinger, 92 Tex. 365, 48 S.W. 563 (1898).

[148] E.g., Sparks v. Ala. Power Co., 679 So. 2d 678 (Ala. 1996); Wolfe v. Baube, 241 Va. 462, 403 S.E.2d 338 (1991); Murray v. Chi. Youth Ctr., 224 Ill.2d 213, 864 N.E.2d 176 (2007); Zeroulis v. Hamilton Am. Legion Assocs., 705 N.E.2d 1164, 1166 (Mass. Ct. App. 1999).

[149] Harlow v. Connelly, 548 S.W.2d 143 (Ky. Ct. App. 1977); Sorrells v. M.Y.B. Hospitality Ventures of Asheville, 423 S.E.2d 72 (N.C. 1992).

[150] Morris v. Yogi Bear's Jellystone Park Camp Resort, 539 So.2d 70 (La. Ct. App. 1989).

[151] Gail D. Hollister, Using Comparative Fault to Replace the All-or-Nothing Lottery Imposed in Intentional Torts Suits in Which Both Plaintiff and Defendant Are at Fault, 46 Vand. L. Rev. 121 (1993).

cases, an attacker could scarcely hope to reduce the plaintiff's recovery on the ground that she should have remained locked in her house.[152] Courts may find that the plaintiff in particular cases had no duty to protect herself against an intentional tort.[153]

Current status of the defense. Most courts dealing with the question of plaintiff negligence as a defense to intentional torts have carried the ban on the defense over to the regime of comparative negligence, holding or assuming that the plaintiff's comparative fault cannot be used to reduce the liability of an intentional tortfeasor.[154] Statutes in some states with comparative apportionment codify the common law rule so that the plaintiff's damages are not reduced when the defendant's liability is based on either recklessness or an intentional tort.[155] Under this view, if the defendant batters the plaintiff, the plaintiff's negligence in taunting the defendant does not reduce the plaintiff's damages.[156] In fact, few cases so far seem to have reduced a personal injury defendant's liability for his own intentional wrongdoing merely because the plaintiff was guilty of contributory negligence.[157] The Restatement Third suggests that in jurisdictions that permit apportionment of liability, a plaintiff "no-duty rule could be the basis for eliminating the victim's carelessness from consideration" in a suit against the intentional tortfeasor.[158] If the defense of comparative fault were permitted as a defense

---

[152] See Restatement Third of Torts (Apportionment of Liability) § 3 rptr. n. d (2000).

[153] Restatement Third of Torts (Liability for Physical Harm) § 7 cmt. h (2010); Ellen Bublick, Citizen No-Duty Rules: Rape Victims and Comparative Fault, 99 Colum. L. Rev. 1413 (1999).

[154] E.g., Gates v. Navy, 274 Ga. App. 180, 617 S.E.2d 163 (2005); Cartwright v. Equitable Life Assurance Soc'y, 276 Mont. 1, 914 P.2d 976 (1996); Wightman v. Consolidated Rail Corp., 86 Ohio St. 3d 431, 715 N.E.2d 546 (1999) (acts committed with actual malice); Shin v. Sunriver Prep. Sch., Inc., 199 Or. App. 352, 111 P.3d 762 (2003); Christensen v. Royal Sch. Dist. No. 160, 124 P.3d 283 (Wash. 2005) (neither teacher who was guilty of intentional sexual contact with his 13-year-old student, nor negligent supervisors of the teacher could assert student's consent as comparative fault); Ellen M. Bublick, The End Game of Tort Reform: Comparative Apportionment and Intentional Torts, 78 Notre Dame L. Rev. 355, 367–68 (2003); Henry Woods & Beth Deere, Comparative Fault § 7.1 (3d ed. 1996); Allan L. Schwartz, Annotation, Applicability of Comparative Negligence Principles to Intentional Torts, 18 A.L.R.5th 525 (1995).

[155] See Matthiessen v. Vanech, 266 Conn. 822, 836 A.2d 394 (2003) (applying Conn. Gen. Stat. § 52–572h (o)); Ezzell v. Miranne, 4 So.3d 641 (La. Ct. App. 2011) (the defendant punched plaintiff in the face after plaintiff called him an "A-----e," as the court delicately put it; it was improper to allow the jury to reduce plaintiff's damages for plaintiff fault); La. Civ. Code Ann. art. 2323 (c) ("if a person suffers injury, death, or loss as a result partly of his own negligence and partly as a result of the fault of an intentional tortfeasor, his claim for recovery of damages shall not be reduced").

[156] Whitlock v. Smith, 297 Ark. 399, 762 S.W.2d 782 (1989). See also Landry v. Bellanger, 851 So.2d 943 (La. 2003) (under statute, plaintiff who negligently provokes intentional tort attack recovers damages without reduction, but damages are reduced if plaintiff is herself guilty of an intentional tort provoking the attack). Louisiana had been the one state to allow provocation to limit the damages recovery in a battery case.

[157] Thus neither the school teacher who intentionally has sexual contact with his own 13-year-old student, nor the school that may have been negligent with respect to the child, can claim her "consent" or other conduct as comparative fault. Christensen v. Royal Sch. Dist. No. 160, 124 P.3d 283 (Wash. 2005). Comeau v. Lucas, 90 A.D.2d 674, 455 N.Y.S.2d 871 (1982), may have been a case permitting an intentional tortfeasor to reduce liability for the plaintiff's comparative fault. The court there approved a comparative negligence instruction, but whether it went only to the claim of negligent supervision or to the claim against the intentional tortfeasor is unclear from the report.

[158] Restatement Third of Torts (Liability for Physical and Emotional Harm) § 7 cmt. h (2010); see also Restatement Third of Torts (Apportionment of Liability) § 3, cmt. d (2000).

to an intentional tort, low culpability intentional torts[159] or high-culpability plaintiff fault would seem the most innocuous areas for comparison.[160]

Defendant recklessness and plaintiff fault. There is somewhat more ambiguity concerning plaintiff fault as a defense to recklessness. The Uniform Comparative Fault Act required comparison of the plaintiff's negligence with the defendant's reckless or wanton misconduct, so long as that misconduct fell short of an intentional tort.[161] Some cases agree,[162] at least where the facts of the particular case make the reckless conduct more like negligence than intent.[163] But some cases go the other way, allowing an unreduced recovery by the plaintiff when the defendant is chargeable with reckless or wanton misconduct.[164]

Defendant's duty to protect against plaintiff's risky conduct. In some cases, either by statute or common law, the defendant is under a duty to use reasonable care to protect the plaintiff from her own weakness, incapacity, or fault. When the plaintiff is harmed because the defendant breaches that duty of care, the defendant cannot defend on the ground of contributory negligence, since that was the very thing he was obliged to prevent. Another way to state essentially the same idea is to say that what counts as contributory negligence is determined largely by the scope of the defendant's duty.

Statutes. One group of cases derives from a statutory duty to protect the plaintiff. Contributory negligence is no defense at all if the defendant violates a statute intended to protect the plaintiff from his own negligence or incapacity. Courts sometimes say that such statutes impose strict liability.[165] Child labor acts are good examples. If a minor is injured while employed in violation of such a statute, his claim is not to be defeated by his contributory negligence, becausethe purpose of the statute is to protect him from the risks of his own incapacity and negligence.[166]

---

[159] Some intentional torts like trespass are artificially defined to impose liability even though harm is not intended. Intentional torts committed by low culpability intentional tortfeasors like children is another area in which commentators suggest some comparison might be appropriate. See William J. McNichols, Should Comparative Responsibility Ever Apply to Intentional Torts?, 37 Okla. L. Rev. 641, 644–46 (1984) (using illustrations of intentional torts committed by young children). Shields v. Cape Fox Corp., 42 P.3d 1083, 1088 (Alaska 2002); Jake Dear & Steven E. Zipperstein, Comparative Fault and Intentional Torts: Doctrinal Barriers and Policy Considerations, 24 Santa Clara L. Rev. 1, 32–38 (1984) (suggesting plaintiff fault as a defense to nuisance).

[160] Kenneth W. Simons, A Restatement (Third) of Intentional Torts? 48 Ariz. L. Rev. 1061 (2006); Ellen M. Bublick, The End Game of Tort Reform: Comparative Apportionment and Intentional Torts, 78 Notre Dame L. Rev. 355, 368–69 (2003). At least part of the reason for applying comparative fault principles in Bonpua v. Fagan, 253 N.J. Super. 475, 602 A.2d 287 (1992), was that there were intentional physical attacks by both plaintiff and defendant.

[161] Unif. Comparative Responsibility Act § 1 (2002) (" 'Fault' includes acts or omissions that are in any measure negligent or reckless toward the person or property of the actor or others.").

[162] E.g., Yerkes v. Asberry, 938 S.W.2d 307 (Mo. Ct. App. 1997); Cartwright v. Equitable Life Assurance Soc'y, 276 Mont. 1, 914 P.2d 976 (1996); Weaver v. Lentz, 348 S.C. 672, 561 S.E.2d 360 (Ct. App. 2002).

[163] Poole v. City of Rolling Meadows, 167 Ill.2d 41, 656 N.E.2d 768 (1995); see Annotation, Application of Comparative Negligence in Action Based on Gross Negligence, Recklessness, or the Like, 10 A.L.R.4th 946 (1981).

[164] E.g., Davies v. Butler, 95 Nev. 763, 602 P.2d 605 (1979); see also Zeroulias v. Hamilton Am. Legion Assocs., Inc., 705 N.E.2d 1164 (Mass. App. Ct. 1999) ("If conduct is negligent it cannot also be intentional [or willful, wanton, or reckless]. Similarly, a finding of intentional [or willful, wanton, or reckless] conduct precludes a finding that the same conduct was negligent.").

[165] E.g., Van Gaasbeck v. Webatuck Cent. Sch. Dist., No. 1, 21 N.Y.2d 239, 287 N.Y.S.2d 77, 234 N.E.2d 243 (1967).

[166] E.g., Strain v. Christians, 483 N.W.2d 783 (S.D. 1992); D.L. by Friederichs v. Huebner, 110 Wis.2d 581, 329 N.W.2d 890 (1983).

Protecting vulnerable classes. The rule depends upon construction of individual statutes as intended to protect "persons from their own inexperience, lack of judgment, inability to protect themselves or to resist pressure, or tendency toward negligence." The most likely candidates are perhaps those statutes aimed at protecting children, and others under a disability,[167] and those aimed at protecting workers from on-the-job risks they cannot avoid.[168] Statutes prohibiting the sale of dangerous articles like guns,[169] alcohol,[170] or drugs[171] have sometimes been treated in the same way, so that the buyer may be allowed, in some instances, to recover from the seller in spite of the buyer's own contributory fault. These holdings may[172] or may not[173] survive the adoption of comparative fault and several liability.

Common law. In the absence of statute, courts are of course free to impose duties that require defendants to protect vulnerable, incapacitated, or minor plaintiffs from their own inability to protect themselves. One excellent example is the case of a plaintiff who, because of mental or physical disability is under the defendant's care. For example, a suicidal patient suffering from emotional or mental problems may expect a hospital to use reasonable care to prevent her suicide, and if it does not, it may not be able to defeat the patient estate's claim by asserting that the patient was negligent.[174] In this setting too, the question of whether the holdings survive comparative fault is unclear.

C. RELATED DOCTRINES AND SPECIAL CASES

§ 16.8 Effect of Plaintiff's Illegal Acts

Principle of the rule. People should not profit from their own wrongs. Courts in scores and scores of cases have said that this is a basic principle of law. Although its roots reach into restitutionary law, its principle has been invoked in a variety of cases, but selectively.[175] Many cases that invoke the principle would be decided the same way, even if no such principle existed. The robber and the burglar cannot complain if they are

---

[167] Del E. Webb Corp. v. Superior Court, 151 Ariz. 164, 726 P.2d 580 (1986); Van Gaasbeck v. Webatuck Cent. Sch. Dist., No. 1, 21 N.Y.2d 239, 287 N.Y.S.2d 77, 234 N.E.2d 243 (1967).

[168] CSX Transp., Inc. v. Miller, 46 So.3d 434 (Ala. 2010) (Locomotive Inspection Act); Wilson v. Vukasin, 277 Mont. 423, 922 P.2d 531 (1996) (under version of statute in effect at the time of injury); Gordon v. Eastern Ry. Supply, Inc., 82 N.Y.2d 555, 626 N.E.2d 912, 606 N.Y.S.2d 127 (1993).

[169] Tamiami Gun Shop v. Klein, 116 So.2d 421 (Fla. 1959).

[170] See, refusing to set aside contributory or comparative negligence rules, Lee v. Kiku Restaurant, 127 N.J. 170, 603 A.2d 503 (1991).

[171] Zerby v. Warren, 297 Minn. 134, 210 N.W.2d 58 (1973) (glue sold to minor who died after sniffing).

[172] Magna Trust Co. v. Illinois Cent. R.R., 728 N.E.2d 797 (Ill. App. Ct. 2000) (barring a comparative fault claim to the Safety Appliances Act).

[173] See Sowinski v. Walker, 198 P.3d 1134 (Alaska 2008) (holding that one of Alaska's earlier rulings on the issue did not survive the statutory adoption of pure several liability); Spragg v. Shuster, 398 N.W.2d 683 (Minn. Ct. App. 1987) (suggesting that Zerby v. Warren would not apply after comparative fault; not leaving fault of the underage drinker plaintiffs to a comparative fault determination, but finding "complicity" by the plaintiff that operated as a complete bar akin to contributory negligence).

[174] E.g., McNamara v. Honeyman, 406 Mass. 43, 546 N.E.2d 139 (1989); Tomfohr v. Mayo Found., 450 N.W.2d 121 (Minn. 1990); Cowan v. Doering, 111 N.J. 451, 545 A.2d 159 (1988); Bramlette v. Charter-Medical-Columbia, 302 S.C. 68, 393 S.E.2d 914 (1990) ("[T]he very act which the defendant has a duty to prevent cannot constitute contributory negligence or assumption of the risk as a matter of law.").

[175] See, criticizing the serious misconduct bar on this and other grounds, Joseph H. King, Jr., Outlaws and Outlier Doctrines: the Serious Misconduct Bar in Tort Law, 43 Wm. & Mary L. Rev. 1011 (2002).

harmed when the victim reasonably defends himself, but the victim's privilege suffices to explain that result without resort to any special privilege or immunity.[176]

The doctrine. In some cases, courts have extended the principle that people should not profit from their wrongs to mean that a plaintiff who suffers a tortious injury as a result of her own seriously[177] illegal or immoral act cannot recover from the tortfeasor who owes her a duty of care.[178] A similar idea can be found in a number of cases in which courts conclude that as a matter of law, the negligence of the plaintiff is greater than that of the defendant.[179]

Tension between an all-or-nothing bar and comparative fault. Before the adoption of comparative negligence systems, it would not have mattered whether the court invoked the immoral plaintiff principle or the contributory negligence bar, because both would have barred the plaintiff's recovery. After the adoption of comparative negligence, however, a rule that bars the claim of the immoral plaintiff is in tension with comparative negligence, which would only reduce damages.[180] The immoral acts rule may be rejected on this basis.

An example. In *Barker v. Kallash*,[181] the 15-year-old plaintiff was making a pipe bomb with ingredients furnished by the defendant. The bomb exploded, causing injury to the plaintiff. Instead of reducing the plaintiff's recovery under comparative negligence rules, the court denied recovery altogether. It concluded that when "the plaintiff's injury is a direct result of his knowing and intentional participation in a criminal act he cannot seek compensation for the loss, if the criminal act is judged to be so serious an offense as to warrant denial of recovery. . . . Thus a burglar who breaks his leg while descending the cellar stairs, due to the failure of the owner to replace a missing step cannot recover compensation from his victims." Although the comparative negligence statute on its face seemed to govern and to permit the plaintiff to proceed subject to a reduction in damages, the court thought that the immoral plaintiff principle required dismissal of the claim altogether. Similarly, Michigan has held that one injured by drugs obtained from a

---

[176] Cf. Calvillo-Silva v. Home Grocery, 19 Cal. 4th 714, 968 P.2d 65, 80 Cal. Rptr. 2d 506 (1998) (statutory immunity from liability to one injured in the commission of a felony, but immunity for use of deadly force ultimately turned on common law justification), overruled on other grounds as stated in Powerhouse Motorsports Grp., Inc. v. Yamaha Motor Corp., 221 Cal. App. 4th 867, 887, 164 Cal. Rptr. 3d 811, 827 (2013). Statutes that not only recognize a privilege of defending one's self or property but also provide immunity to defendants whose acts are outside the scope of the privilege, may raise constitutional questions. See Sonoran Desert Investigations v. Miller, 213 Ariz. 274, 141 P.3d 754 (2006) (statute unconstitutional under state Constitution).

[177] See Winschel v. Brown, 171 P.3d 142 (Alaska 2007) (plaintiff's violation of a bike-path regulation was not the kind of "serious criminal conduct" that bars a negligence claim); Ardinger v. Hummell, 982 P.2d 727 (Alaska 1999) (public policy rationale for barring all recovery in a comparative fault system is limited to "cases involving serious criminal conduct that intentionally threatened the safety of others, such as homicide, rape, and arson"); O'Brien v. Bruscato, 289 Ga. 739, 715 S.E.2d 120 (2011) (reversing summary judgment for psychiatrist in malpractice case brought by patient who killed his mother after being taken off his medication by the defendant, on the ground that there was a contested issue of fact on whether the patient "knowingly" committed the criminal act, given his mental disability). Some courts have been less cautious, however. See Martin v. Ziherl, 269 Va. 35, 607 S.E.2d 367 (2005) (premarital sexual activity enough to bar the plaintiff).

[178] Cole v. Taylor, 301 N.W.2d 766, 768 (Iowa 1981).

[179] See Peters v. Menard, 589 N.W.2d 395 (Wis. 1999).

[180] Duggar v. Arredondo, 408 S.W.3d 825 (Tex. 2013) (comparative responsibility statute abrogates "unlawful acts" doctrine).

[181] Barker v. Kallash, 63 N.Y.2d 19, 468 N.E.2d 39 (1984). The case was not a sympathetic one for the plaintiff: the defendant was a nine-year-old boy who had furnished firecracker powder. The court's language and the principle it invokes, however, would seem to apply equally if a terrorist had paid the plaintiff to make bombs. In that case, the principle would seem to benefit a party whose acts are probably morally more reprehensible.

pharmacist without a valid prescription has no claim against the pharmacist for injuries that follow.[182]

Reliance on reprehensibility. These cases rest on the idea that courts can identify some particularly reprehensible conduct that ought to outlaw the plaintiff who commits it, even if such a ruling protects a person who has negligently harmed the plaintiff. Some cases deserve to be dealt with in that way, but perhaps not cases in which the defendant is as much at fault as the plaintiff.[183] A number of cases limit the immoral plaintiff principle.[184]

Statutory version. The immoral plaintiff rule may be approximated by statute.[185] In an Arizona case, a statute provided that the defendant would not be liable for harms he caused by his negligence or even his gross negligence while the plaintiff was committing a crime.[186] The court concluded that the statute was equivalent to a provision that the criminal plaintiff was assuming the risk of negligence as a matter of law and held that it violated the state's constitutional provision leaving assumed risk and contributory negligence to the jury in all cases.[187] Thereafter, the state's constitutional law was amended by referendum.[188]

§ 16.9 Distinguishing Avoidable Consequences

The avoidable consequences/mitigation of damages rule. The main rule of avoidable consequences denies the plaintiff a recovery for negligently inflicted damages that she could have avoided or minimized by reasonable care or expenditure.[189] Another important rule is that the plaintiff can recover the reasonable costs she incurs in seeking to minimize damages.[190] As with other defenses, the burden is on the defendant to prove that the plaintiff failed to mitigate damages.[191]

An example. An example of the avoidable consequences rule is that the plaintiff who unreasonably delays in obtaining medical attention for her injury, or who unreasonably refuses to follow medical advice, cannot recover for exacerbation of the injury caused by her own delay or refusal.[192] The defendant must prove not only that the plaintiff's post-injury[193] conduct was unreasonable, but also that such conduct was a cause-in-fact of

[182] Orzel v. Scott Drug Co., 449 Mich. 550, 537 N.W.2d 208 (1995).

[183] See Paul T. Hayden, Butterfield Rides Again: Plaintiff's Negligence as Superseding or Sole Proximate Cause in Systems of Pure Comparative Responsibility, 33 Loy. L.A. L. Rev. 887 (2000).

[184] Alami v. Volkswagen of Am., Inc., 97 N.Y.2d 281, 766 N.E.2d 574 (2002).

[185] To similar effect, a New Jersey statute bars an uninsured motorist from maintaining a personal injury action for damages. The statute was applied in Aronberg v. Tolbert, 207 N.J. 587, 25 A.3d 1121 (2011), to bar a mother's wrongful death action where her son was uninsured. The court suggested that it disagreed with the legislature's policy choice, but found no constitutional infirmity standing in the way of enforcing the statute.

[186] The statute provided the same for both felonies and misdemeanors, but only the misdemeanor provision was under review. Ariz. Rev. Stat. § 12–717.

[187] Sonoran Desert Investigations, Inc. v. Miller, 213 Ariz. 274, 141 P.3d 754 (Ct. App. 2006).

[188] Ariz. Const. art. 18, § 6.

[189] See, e.g., Willis v. Westerfield, 839 N.E.2d 1179 (Ind. 2006). The rule is not limited to tort cases. See 3 Dan B. Dobbs, Law of Remedies § 12.6 (2d ed. 1993).

[190] See Borley Storage & Transfer Co. v. Whitted, 271 Neb. 84, 710 N.W.2d 71 (2006). For the other rules of avoidable consequences or "mitigation," see 1 Dan B. Dobbs, Law of Remedies § 3.9 (2d ed. 1993).

[191] Tibbetts v. Dairyland Ins. 999 A.2d 930 (Me. 2010).

[192] Preston v. Keith, 217 Conn. 12, 584 A.2d 439 (1991); Bryant v. Calantone, 286 N.J. Super. 362, 669 A.2d 286 (1996).

[193] Avoidable consequences comes into play after a legal wrong has occurred but while some damages can still be averted. Trustees of Univ. of D.C. v. Vossoughi, 963 A.2d 1162 (D.C. 2009) (professor's pre-injury

harm that otherwise would have been avoided,[194] and sometimes proof of actual cause requires expert testimony.[195] When unreasonable conduct that caused harm is proved, the plaintiff's recovery is reduced by the damages she could reasonably have avoided, but the plaintiff's claim itself is not barred.[196] For example, if the plaintiff unreasonably failed to take antibiotics after the defendant caused her injury, and her failure to do so necessitated four weeks of hospital care that otherwise would not have been required, the avoidable consequences rule would relieve the defendant of all liability for the added hospitalization.[197]

Application of the two systems. The avoidable consequences approach to apportionment does not yield the same results as the comparative negligence apportionment except by happenstance. Suppose that the plaintiff's damages were $100,000 and that the plaintiff's fault was 5% of the total. Under a comparative fault approach, the plaintiff's award would be reduced by 5% so that she would recover $95,000. Now suppose that the plaintiff's only fault was her failure to take antibiotics after the injury was inflicted and that this failure aggravated her injury and necessitated additional hospitalization costing $10,000. If we think of the plaintiff's fault as comparative negligence amounting to 5%, she will recover $95,000. But if we think of it as a failure to minimize damages, the avoidable consequences rule will allow her to recover only $90,000.

§ 16.10 The Role of Avoidable Consequences in Comparative Fault Regimes

Which rule applies? With the adoption of comparative fault regimes in most states, the remaining role of the avoidable consequences or mitigation of damages approach has been called into question. In many instances, it is not possible to identify distinct avoidable consequences, so that no causal apportionment is possible, and comparative fault represents the only possible method for apportionment. For example, it is seldom possible in highway accidents to say that the plaintiff's broken leg is a result of the defendant's fault, but that the plaintiff alone is responsible for her broken arm. Comparative fault apportionment is particularly well suited when causal apportionment is not possible.

The options. When causal apportionment is possible, as where the plaintiff's failure to follow medical advice makes her injuries worse, adoption of comparative fault rules leaves courts with several basic options, on which complex variations can be imagined.

---

failure to protect property was not proper defense to conversion and trespass to chattels claim against university that cleaned out his research lab without his knowledge).

[194] Willis v. Westerfield, 839 N.E.2d 1179 (Ind. 2006); Morgan v. Scott, 291 S.W.3d 622 (Ky. 2009) (defendant did not present adequate evidence that plaintiff's smoking and obesity caused bone fracture healing difficulties); Borley Storage & Transfer Co. v. Whitted, 271 Neb. 84, 96, 710 N.W.2d 71, 81 (2006) (the trial judge's instruction No. 2 appeared to approve the mitigation defense without proof that efforts to mitigate would have reduced the plaintiff's damages; a later and more accurate instruction probably cured the error).

[195] Willis v. Westerfield, 839 N.E.2d 1179 (Ind. 2006) ("on medical matters which are within the common experience, observation, or knowledge of laymen, no expert testimony is required to permit a conclusion on causation"); Cartier v. Northwestern Elec., Inc., 777 N.W.2d 866 (N.D. 2010) (plaintiff failed to preserve causal issue for appeal).

[196] See Borley Storage & Transfer Co. v. Whitted, 271 Neb. 84, 95, 710 N.W.2d 71, 80 (2006).

[197] See Keans v. Bottiarelli, 35 Conn. App. 239, 645 A.2d 1029 (1994).

(1) Comparative negligence principles absorb the avoidable consequences rule. If the plaintiff and defendant are both culpable causes of the plaintiff's injury,[198] apportionment of responsibility is made entirely under comparative fault rules; mitigation or avoidable consequences rules are dropped altogether. Some courts may take this approach.[199] Statutes,[200] including the Uniform Apportionment of Tort Responsibility Act,[201] may lend support for this approach by defining fault to include failure to minimize damages.

The total comparative fault approach has some problems. First, the percentage of overall fault the jury allocates to the plaintiff might not correspond with the discrete portion of harm she caused. Second, when the plaintiff is chargeable with fault in causing an indivisible harm and also with fault in causing some divisible and isolated item of harm, the complexities become quite difficult.[202] A third possible problem results from the fact that by combining the plaintiff's fault in causing the accident with her fault in failing to minimize damages, the court may be required to bar the plaintiff's claim altogether under the modified systems of comparative fault.

(2) Applying avoidable consequences rule to post-injury conduct. Some courts hold that the plaintiff's negligence is counted as comparative negligence if it contributed to the initial injury. But these courts go on to hold that the plaintiff's failure to minimize damages *after* the injury has occurred is a matter of the avoidable consequences rule, to be causally apportioned where possible.[203] Under this rule, the plaintiff who fails to use a safety device like a seatbelt is not chargeable with comparative negligence, because failure to use the seatbelt did not cause the accident. Equally, she is not subject to the mitigation rules because the failure to use the seatbelt occurred before rather than after injury.[204]

This solution may be criticized on the ground that at least on some occasions the plaintiff's pre-injury fault can cause a separate and identifiable element of harm. Indeed, when continuing conduct is involved, it may not even be reasonably possible to know what is "before" and what is "after."[205] The picture is also more complicated when injury

---

[198] See Baker v. Morrison, 309 Ark. 457, 829 S.W.2d 421 (1992) (requiring causation to invoke comparative negligence apportionment in failure to minimize cases); Waterson v. General Motors Corp., 111 N.J. 238, 544 A.2d 357 (1988).

[199] E.g., Ridley v. Safety Kleen Corp., 693 So.2d 934 (Fla. 1996); McKay's Family Dodge v. Hardrives, 480 N.W.2d 141 (Minn. Ct. App. 1992); Business Men's Assurance Co. of Am. v. Graham, 891 S.W.2d 438 (Mo. Ct. App. 1994).

[200] E.g., Minn. Stat. Ann. § 604.01 (" 'Fault' includes . . . unreasonable failure to avoid an injury or to mitigate damages.").

[201] Unif. Apportionment of Tort Responsibility Act § 2 (2002).

[202] See Paul A. LeBel, Reducing the Recovery of Avoidable "Seat-belt Damages": a Cure for The Defects of Waterson v. General Motors Corporation, 22 Seton Hall L. Rev. 4 (1991). In Ridley v. Safety Kleen Corp., 693 So.2d 934 (Fla. 1996), the court attempted to simplify the computation by requiring the jury to make a single finding of fault that included both the plaintiff's negligence that contributed to impact and her negligence that merely aggravated injury, but it remains to be seen whether that simplification generates difficulties of its own.

[203] Kocher v. Getz, 824 N.E.2d 671 (Ind. 2005); Shuette v. Beazer Homes Holdings Corp., 124 P.3d 530 (Nev. 2005); Russo Farms, Inc. v. Vineland Bd. of Educ., 144 N.J. 84, 675 A.2d 1077 (1996); Ostrowski v. Azzara, 111 N.J. 429, 545 A.2d 148 (1988). This was the view of the Restatement Second. See Restatement Second of Torts § 918 (1979) ("after the commission of a tort").

[204] See 1 Dobbs, Hayden & Bublick, The Law of Tort § 231 (2011 & Supp.).

[205] See the court's struggle in Cipollone v. Liggett Group, Inc., 893 F.2d 541 (3d Cir. 1990), aff'd in part and rev'd in part on other grounds, 505 U.S. 504 (1992). When nonaction is negligent, it may "begin" before the defendant's negligence and continue afterwards. See Del Tufo v. Township of Old Bridge, 147 N.J. 90, 685 A.2d

occurs long after the defendant's negligent conduct, as may be the case with either medical malpractice or defective products.[206]

(3) Applying avoidable consequences rule to discrete items of harm. Some courts reject the first two approaches. They apply comparative fault apportionment unless the plaintiff's pre-injury fault caused some particular item of damage to which causal apportionment principles could be applied.[207] Under the view of these cases, if the plaintiff suffers added injury in an auto collision because she failed to wear a seatbelt, these courts invoke the avoidable consequences or mitigation of damages rule to bar recovery for the added injuries. They do so even though the plaintiff's fault occurred before rather than after the injury. In such cases, the defendant must prove that the plaintiff was at fault and that some identifiable items or amounts of harm resulted from that fault. In addition, it must appear that the separate items of harm should justly be borne entirely by the plaintiff rather than apportioned between the parties. If the defendant cannot identify separate items of harm, then the avoidable consequences rule is inappropriate.[208]

(4) Restatement of apportionment. The Restatement of Apportionment supports a combination rule. First, the defendant is fully liable without reduction for all injuries that he alone caused. Second, injury resulting both from the defendant's negligence and the plaintiff's failure to mitigate is seen to be itself an indivisible injury which must be apportioned on the rules of comparative fault rather than the rules of avoidable consequences.[209] For example, the defendant negligently breaks the plaintiff's leg without any fault of the plaintiff. For that, the defendant is fully responsible. If the plaintiff then has an additional medical expense because she failed to take antibiotics prescribed, that additional expense is a result of the combined fault of the defendant, whose negligence created the need for antibiotics, and the plaintiff, for failure to take her medication. As to the additional medical expense, comparative fault apportionment is used.[210] The seatbelt cases discussed in the next section raise similar possibilities.

§ 16.11 Comparative Fault or Avoidable Consequences in Seatbelt and Other Safety Precaution Cases

Seatbelts and contributory or comparative negligence. In the light of safety factors involved, the plaintiff's failure to wear an available seatbelt or safety harness may be quite unreasonable. Today, with pervasive seatbelt use and statutes requiring it, failure

---

1267 (1996) (arrestee's continuing negligence in failing to inform police that he had taken overdose of cocaine treated as contributory negligence, not avoidable consequences).

[206] See Lynch v. Scheininger, 162 N.J. 209, 744 A.2d 113 (2000), discussing both the avoidable consequences rule and superseding cause where a doctor's negligence alleged put a mother at risk for bearing a child suffering severe abnormalities. The mother's decision to conceive in spite of the risk might reduce damages under the former or bar recovery under the latter.

[207] Spier v. Barker, 35 N.Y.2d 444, 323 N.E.2d 164 (1974) (failure to wear seatbelt), codified in N.Y. Veh. & Traf. Code § 1229–c8; Halvorson v. Voeller, 336 N.W.2d 118 (N.D. 1983) (cyclist's failure to wear helmet).

[208] The defendant generally bears the burden of proving the amount of harm that would have been avoided. See Caiazzo v. Volkswagenwerk, 647 F.2d 241 (2d Cir. 1981) (defendant had burden of proving the "consequences of the Caiazzos' failure to wear seat belts"); Business Men's Assurance Co. of Am. v. Graham, 891 S.W.2d 438 (Mo. Ct. App. 1994). However, in a number of cases courts have assigned percentages of damages to the plaintiff on the basis that a consequence was avoidable. See Karczmit v. State, 155 Misc.2d 486, 588 N.Y.S.2d 963 (N.Y. Ct. Cl. 1992) (25%).

[209] See Restatement Third of Torts (Apportionment of Liability) § 3 cmt. b (2000) (plaintiff's "failure to mitigate damages should no longer constitute a bar to recovering those damages," but rather is "a factor to consider when assigning percentages of responsibility").

[210] See id. § 3 cmt. b, illus. 4.

to wear a seatbelt certainly could count as comparative fault.[211] However, this result is barred by many state statutes.[212] Historically, courts mostly held that failure to wear a seatbelt did not count as contributory negligence to bar the entire claim.[213] In part, this holding was based on the fact that failure to use a seatbelt does not normally cause injuries in the initial impact, only injury from a "second collision" when the unbelted plaintiff is thrown out of the car or against an object in the car.

Seatbelts: avoidable consequences and comparative negligence. When comparative fault is not allowed, other methods for reducing the plaintiff's damages have been permitted in seatbelt cases. One method for reduction is to use the avoidable consequences or mitigation of damages rule, eliminating altogether the portion of the plaintiff's damages that the defendant proves could reasonably have been avoided by use of a seatbelt, but otherwise allowing the plaintiff's claim. A fair number of courts have authorized such reductions in the plaintiff's damages[214] based upon the avoidable consequences[215] or comparative fault rules.[216]

Capped reduction. One solution to the comparative negligence complexities might be an arbitrary statutory reduction at a fixed percentage. Several states have authorized a comparative negligence reduction with an arbitrary limit providing that the reduction may not exceed a specified small percentage figure, such as 5%.[217] Another legislative approach admits seatbelt non-use evidence to mitigate pain and suffering damages but not others.[218]

---

[211] Green v. Ford Motor Co., 942 N.E.2d 791, Prod. Liab. Rep. (CCH) P 18571 (Ind. 2011) (jury could apportion fault to plaintiff motorist for failure to wear seatbelt if plaintiff's actions were a proximate cause of his enhanced injuries); Barnes v. Paulin, 73 A.D.3d 1107, 900 N.Y.S.2d 886 (2010) (damage reduction based on seat belt nonuse); Restatement Third of Torts (Apportionment of Liability) § 3 cmt. b illus. 3 (2000) (counting failure to wear a seatbelt as a factor in apportionment of liability absent a statute to the contrary); Kelly H. Foos, Toward a Rational Seat Belt Policy in Kansas, 56 U. Kan. L. Rev. 1005 (2008) (citing data that suggest that seatbelt nonuse is unreasonable and arguing that defense of comparative negligence should be permitted for failure to wear a seat belt).

[212] See Ala. Code § 32–5B–7; 75 Pa. Cons. Stat. Ann. § 4581(e) ("In no event shall a violation or alleged violation of this subchapter be used as evidence in a trial of any civil action").

[213] See Leonard Schwartz, The Seat Belt Defense and Mandatory Seat Belt Usage: Law, Ethics, and Economics, 24 Idaho L. Rev. 275 (1988).

[214] See Christopher Hall, Annotation, Nonuse of Seatbelt as Reducing Amount of Damages Recoverable, 62 A.L.R.5th 537 (1998).

[215] Spier v. Barker, 35 N.Y.2d 444, 323 N.E.2d 164 (1974) (failure to wear seat belt), codified in N.Y. Veh. & Traf. Code § 1229–c8; Halvorson v. Voeller, 336 N.W.2d 118 (N.D. 1983) (cyclist's failure to wear helmet).

[216] Hutchins v. Schwartz, 724 P.2d 1194 (Alaska 1986); Ridley v. Safety Kleen Corp., 693 So.2d 934 (Fla. 1996); Tetrick v. Frashure, 119 S.W.3d 89 (Ky. Ct. App. 2003) (absent statutory duty, court should define the duty of care in general terms and leave it to the jury to determine whether failure to wear a seat belt was a breach of the duty of care); Waterson v. General Motors Corp., 111 N.J. 238, 544 A.2d 357 (1988). Wisconsin has adopted different systems for dealing with seatbelt negligence and helmet negligence, but both systems entail a reduction in the plaintiff's recovery. Stehlik v. Rhoads, 253 Wis.2d 477, 645 N.W.2d 889 (2002). Some statutes authorize the reduction. E.g., Cal. Veh. Code § 27315 (i); Ohio Rev. Code Ann. § 4513.263 (F) ("shall be considered by the trier . . . as contributory negligence" and may diminish the recovery).

[217] E.g., Vredeveld v. Clark, 504 N.W.2d 292 (Neb. 1993) (5% but some evidence must be presented that injuries would have been less with seatbelt); Estep v. Mike Ferrell Ford Lincoln-Mercury, Inc., 672 S.E.2d 345 (W. Va. 2008); Mich. Comp. Laws Ann. § 257.710e; Mo. Ann. Stat. § 307.178 (4) (not to exceed 1%).

[218] See Anderson v. Watson, 953 P.2d 1284, 62 A.L.R.5th 877 (Colo. 1998) (applying the Colorado statute to this effect); Pringle v. Valdez, 171 P.3d 624 (Colo. 2007) (holding that the statute does not encompass physical impairment and disfigurement damages).

Barring all reduction. Judges have held in many states that the award is not to be reduced either under comparative fault or avoidable consequences rules[219] and legislation now so provides in most states. Indeed, some of the statutes broadly exclude admission of evidence about seatbelt non-use for any purpose,[220] and some even relieve adults of liability to a child when the adult negligently fails to utilize child restraint systems.[221] However, courts applying these absolute exclusions do not necessarily view them as just.[222] Difficulties are particularly salient in automobile design defect cases,[223] and some states allow evidence of seatbelt non-use in products liability actions.[224] At times, jurisdictions also allow evidence regarding non-use of a seatbelt for some types of purposes other than comparative fault or mitigation of damages.[225]

Other pre-injury safety precautions. Many non-seatbelt cases fit the seatbelt pattern and may involve similar issues.[226] For example, the virtually identical problem of the cyclist who fails to wear a helmet has already arisen and been treated to the same split of common law authority that governs seatbelts.[227] Many other cases could exhibit the same essential characteristics of a pre-injury failure of care that causes discrete, divisible harm.[228]

---

[219] E.g., Amend v. Bell, 89 Wash.2d 124, 570 P.2d 138 (1977); see Christopher Hall, Annotation, Nonuse of Seatbelt as Reducing Amount of Damages Recoverable, 62 A.L.R.5th 537 (1998).

[220] About 30 statutes in three groups provide that evidence of failure to wear a seatbelt (1) is not evidence of contributory negligence, or (2) "shall not be admissible into evidence in a civil action," with specified exceptions, or (3) is not admissible and no exceptions are recognized. See Olson v. Ford Motor Co., 558 N.W.2d 491 (Minn. 1997) (plaintiff could not prove that defective seatbelt caused his injury); contra: Bridgestone/Firestone, Inc. v. Glyn-Jones, 878 S.W.2d 132 (Tex. 1994).

[221] E.g., Iowa Code Ann., § 321–446 (operator's failure to comply with requirements for use of a child restraint system "does not constitute negligence"); cf. Gaertner v. Holcka, 219 Wis.2d 436, 580 N.W.2d 271 (1998) (no contribution claim will lie against person who violated statute requiring children be secured with seatbelts).

[222] See Gaudio v. Ford Motor Co., 976 A.2d 524 (Pa. 2009) (excluding seatbelt evidence in airbag defect case because statutory language required it, whether or not the result was "unjust").

[223] Estep v. Mike Ferrell Ford Lincoln-Mercury, 672 S.E.2d 345 (W. Va. 2008) (based on clear language of statute, court cannot permit car maker to introduce evidence of nonuse of seatbelt in case involving nondeployment of air bag).

[224] Ark. Code Ann. § 27–37–703(a)(1) ("The failure of an occupant to wear a properly adjusted and fastened seat belt shall not be admissible into evidence in a civil action," but allowing the defense in some products liability cases).

[225] See Rougeau v. Hyundai Motor Am., 805 So.2d 147 (La. 2002) (adopting a version of the Mississippi rule: "Such evidence is only admissible in a product liability action if: (1) it has probative value for some purpose other than as evidence of negligence, such as to show that the overall design, or a particular component of the vehicle, was not defective; (2) its probative value is not outweighed by its prejudicial effect or barred by some other rule of evidence; and (3) appropriate limiting instructions are given to the jury, barring the consideration of seat belt non-usage as evidence of comparative negligence or to mitigate damages").

[226] See Shantigar Found. v. Bear Mountain Builders, 441 Mass. 131, 804 N.E.2d 324 (2004) (plaintiff's barn burned down due in part to the defendant's negligence; admission of evidence that the plaintiff should have had sprinkler systems installed held proper; the jury found the plaintiff chargeable with 60% of the fault); Acculog, Inc. v. Peterson, 692 P.2d 728 (Utah 1984) (failure to have fire extinguisher to protect valuable equipment could not be considered as contributory fault, withholding a ruling on avoidable consequences).

[227] E.g., Dare v. Sobule, 674 P.2d 960 (Colo. 1984) (evidence of failure to wear helmet inadmissible to show negligence or reduce damages under mitigation doctrine); Halvorson v. Voeller, 336 N.W.2d 118 (N.D. 1983) (failure to wear helmet goes to reduce damages caused by that failure). See Stehlik v. Rhoads, 253 Wis.2d 477, 645 N.W.2d 889 (2002) (following a rule similar to but not identical with Wisconsin's seatbelt rule).

[228] 1 Dobbs, Hayden & Bublick, The Law of Torts § 231 (2011 & Supp.) (for a discussion of these cases as well as policy rationales suggested by courts).

Chapter 17

ASSUMPTION OF THE RISK

Analysis

A. EXPRESS ASSUMPTION OF RISK

§ 17.1   Shifting Responsibility by Agreement
§ 17.2   Contractual Limitations
§ 17.3   Public Policy Limitations

B. IMPLIED ASSUMPTION OF RISK

§ 17.4   The Traditional Rule: Assumption of Risk as a Complete Bar
§ 17.5   Development of Constraining Rules
§ 17.6   Discarding the Defense of Implied Assumption of Risk
§ 17.7   Primary and Secondary Assumption of Risk
§ 17.8   Sports Cases

A. EXPRESS ASSUMPTION OF RISK

§ 17.1 Shifting Responsibility by Agreement

Exculpatory clauses disfavored. Assumption of the risk, in all of its forms, is a disfavored doctrine. Nevertheless, in appropriate situations, the parties to a transaction can agree, by contract, as to which of them should bear the risk of injury. This agreement may include the risk of being injured, in person or property, by another person's negligence. A person may expressly assume the risk by accepting a valid disclaimer of responsibility or by giving a valid release or other exculpatory agreement in advance of injury.[1] If the plaintiff is injured by one of the risks covered by the agreement and sues the defendant with whom the agreement was made, the plaintiff's claim will be entirely barred unless the agreement is unenforceable for reasons of contract law,[2] public policy,[3] or other state law.[4]

---

[1]   See K.A. Drechsler, Annotation, Validity of contractual provision by one other than carrier or employer for exemption from liability, or indemnification, for consequences of own negligence, 175 A.L.R. 8 (1948) (containing an exhaustive collection of cases).

[2]   Pearce v. Utah Athletic Found., 179 P.3d 760 (Utah 2008) (express assumption of the risk is a contract subject to ordinary rules of contract interpretation and will not be upheld if it is unclear or ambiguous).

[3]   Restatement Third of Torts (Apportionment of Liability) § 2 (2000); Restatement Second of Torts § 496B (1965). Some courts limit the enforceability of releases to particular types of activity and hold releases in other contexts void for public policy reasons. See, e.g., Vodopest v. MacGregor, 128 Wash.2d 840, 913 P.2d 779 (1996) (releases generally valid only in the context of "adult high-risk sports activities"). Others have taken the opposite approach and have struck down releases in particular contexts, leaving them potentially enforceable outside those settings. See, e.g., Hanks v. Powder Ridge Restaurant Corp., 276 Conn. 314, 885 A.2d 734 (2005) (even well-drafted releases void in the recreational-activity setting).

[4]   See Phelps v. Firebird Raceway, Inc., 210 Ariz. 403, 111 P.3d 1003 (2005) (recognizing that a release of liability in advance is a form of assumption of risk; under the state constitution, provision leaving assumption of risk to the jury in all cases would apply).

Express assumption of risk by contract. The plaintiff can expressly assume the risk in writing, or orally as permitted by contract law.[5] An express assumption of risk ordinarily will relieve the defendant of the duty that otherwise existed.[6] Alternatively, it will establish that he has breached no duty.[7]

Examples of potentially valid exculpatory clauses. For example, those who contract for the privilege of engaging in dangerous activities like racing or sky-diving are often required to release the provider from all liability in advance.[8] Likewise, a patient might oppose blood transfusions and consent to only a surgery without them.[9]

What may not be waived: gross negligence and recklessness. Defendants assert express assumption of risk most commonly in negligence cases. Indeed, many states disallow releases that purport to go further and attempt to waive liability for grossly negligent, reckless, or intentional behavior.[10] Other states have enforced releases to bar claims based on reckless or grossly negligent behavior, where the release clearly expressed the parties' intention and was not the product of overreaching or grossly unequal bargaining power.[11]

§ 17.2 Contractual Limitations

Limitations stemming from contract. Any assumption of risk in its express form is a contract, and is thus subject to the laws of contract enforceability and interpretation.[12]

---

[5] E.g., Davis v. Sun Valley Ski Educ. Found., Inc., 130 Idaho 400, 941 P.2d 1301 (1997); Siglow v. Smart, 43 Ohio App.3d 55, 539 N.E.2d 636 (1987) ("Express assumption of risk is either oral or written consent to a dangerous activity or condition.").

[6] E.g., Deuley v. DynCorp Int'l, Inc., 8 A.3d 1156, 31 I.E.R. Cas. (BNA) 1849 (Del. 2010), cert. denied, 131 S. Ct. 2119, 179 L. Ed. 2d 894, 32 I.E.R. Cas. (BNA) 128 (2011) (liability clause in employment contract clearly and unambiguously released the employer from any liability for employees' deaths or injuries, thus barring a wrongful death claim by employee's survivors); Thompson v. Hi Tech Motor Sports, Inc., 183 Vt. 218, 945 A.2d 368 (2008) (but not waiving negligent misrepresentation claim); Moore v. Waller, 930 A.2d 176 (D.C. 2007); Boyle v. Revici, 961 F.2d 1060 (2d Cir. 1992); Restatement Third of Torts (Apportionment of Liability) § 2 (2000).

[7] Many courts simply say that a valid release bars the plaintiff's claims. See, e.g., Howard v. Chimps, Inc., 251 Or. App. 636, 284 P.3d 1181 (2012) (upholding release to bar claims based on negligence and strict liability against operator of chimpanzee sanctuary).

[8] E.g., Moore v. Hartley Motors, Inc., 36 P.3d 628 (Alaska 2001) (release signed by all-terrain vehicle rider); Jones v. Dressel, 623 P.2d 370 (Colo. 1981) (sky-diving); Plant v. Wilbur, 345 Ark. 487, 47 S.W.3d 889 (2001) (release signed by pit crew).

[9] Shorter v. Drury, 103 Wash.2d 645, 695 P.2d 116 (1985) (patient religiously opposed to blood transfusions specifically released surgeon in advance of operation); cf. Estate of Reinen v. Northern Ariz. Orthopedics, Ltd., 198 Ariz. 283, 9 P.3d 314 (2000) (treating patient's religious refusal of blood transfusions as issue of contributory negligence or assumption of risk, which, under Arizona's constitution, was for the jury).

[10] E.g., Tayar v. Camelback Ski Corp., Inc., 47 A.3d 1190 (Pa. 2012) (against public policy for a pre-injury release to relieve a party of liability for reckless conduct); Pearce v. Utah Athletic Found., 179 P.3d 760 (Utah 2008); Laeroc Waikiki Parkside, LLC v. K.S.K. (Oahu) Ltd. P'ship, 115 Haw. 201, 166 P.3d 961 (2007) (declaring unenforceable any releases that purport to cover "intentional or reckless conduct"); cf. City of Santa Barbara v. Superior Court, 41 Cal.4th 747, 161 P.3d 1095, 62 Cal.Rptr.3d 527 (2007) (release invalid to the extent it purported to apply to future gross negligence of operators of city-sponsored recreational program for developmentally disabled children).

[11] See, e.g., Murphy v. North Am. River Runners, Inc., 186 W.Va.310, 412 S.E.2d 504 (1991); see also Restatement Second of Torts § 496B & cmt. b (1965) (allowing express waivers of "negligent or reckless conduct"). The Restatement Third would go one step further and accept a release of "intentional or reckless conduct" and even "an intentional tort." Restatement Third of Torts (Apportionment of Liability) § 2 cmts. g & f (2000). It seems unlikely that many, if any courts, will extend acceptance of exculpatory clauses this far, at least when the intentional tort involves an intent to harm.

[12] Cohen v. Five Brooks Stable, 159 Cal.App.4th 1476, 72 Cal.Rptr.3d 471 (2008) ("Contract principles apply when interpreting a release, and normally the meaning of contract language, including a release, is a legal question."). A number of courts have stressed "freedom of contract" as fundamental to the general rule

For example, ambiguities are construed against the drafter, usually the party attempting to assert the express assumption of risk as a defense in later litigation.[13] Beyond this, because of the nature of express assumption of risk—that it represents the advance waiver of a legal right to sue for a tortiously caused injury to person or property—courts have long given them stricter scrutiny than would be given to more benign contracts.[14] For example, some authority holds that exculpatory provisions must be expressed in unmistakable language.[15] More authority, in line with the Apportionment Restatement, requires that exculpatory contracts must meet "higher standards for clarity than other agreements."[16] Releases that are drafted too broadly, purporting to waive all of a defendant's liability, are often held unenforceable.[17] Not surprisingly, parties often litigate over how clear the language of a release really is.[18] Many courts also require that any written waiver be "conspicuous," alerting the signer to the nature and significance of what is being signed.[19] Moreover, if the waiver purports to exclude liability for negligence, that fact must be mentioned explicitly.[20]

Scope of the release. An express assumption of risk is enforceable (if at all) only to the extent that reflects the plaintiff's voluntary agreement to free the defendant from liability in advance.[21] Thus, even where a release is otherwise properly enforceable, that is, untainted by any contractual or public policy problems, a question may still remain whether the scope of the release covers the claim being asserted by the injured plaintiff.[22] Of course, the question of the scope of the release and the question of whether the release is sufficiently clear are not unrelated. A court may well determine that a particular

---

enforcing such agreements. See, e.g., Morrison v. Northwest Nazarene Univ., 152 Idaho 660, 273 P.3d 1253, 278 Ed. Law Rep. 625, 34 I.E.R. Cas. (BNA) 1077 (2012).

[13] Zipusch v. LA Workout, Inc., 155 Cal.App.4th 1281, 66 Cal.Rptr.3d 704 (2007) (ambiguities construed against drafter; "voiding the purported release").

[14] See, e.g., Hanks v. Powder Ridge Rest. Corp., 276 Conn. 314, 885 A.2d 734 (2005) (justifying stricter scrutiny because "exculpatory provisions undermine the policy considerations governing our tort system"); Plant v. Wilbur, 345 Ark. 487, 47 S.W.3d 889 (2001) (exculpatory contracts are "strictly construed against the party relying on them" because of the "public policy concern encouraging the exercise of care"); Fujimoto v. Au, 95 Haw. 116, 19 P.3d 699 (2001) ("Exculpatory contracts are not favored by the law because they tend to allow conduct below the acceptable standard of care.").

[15] Gross v. Sweet, 49 N.Y.2d 102, 424 N.Y.S.2d 365, 400 N.E.2d 306 (1979); Sweeney v. City of Bettendorf, 762 N.W.2d 873 (Iowa 2009); Cohen v. Five Brooks Stable, 159 Cal.App.4th 1476, 72 Cal.Rptr.3d 471 (2008).

[16] Provoncha v. Vermont Motocross Ass'n, 964 A.2d 1261 (Vt. 2009) (citing Restatement Third of Torts (Apportionment of Liability) § 2 cmts. d & e (2000)).

[17] See, e.g., Richards v. Richards, 181 Wis.2d 1007, 513 N.W.2d 118 (1994) (quoting: "This court will not favor an exculpatory contract that is broad and general in its terms."); Jesse v. Lindsley, 149 Idaho 70, 233 P.3d 1 (2008) (release in residential lease voided for overbreadth). But see, e.g., Booth v. Santa Barbara Biplanes, LLC, 158 Cal.App.4th 1173, 70 Cal.Rptr.3d 660 (2008), upholding a clearly-drafted but very broad release.

[18] See, e.g., Atkins v. Swimwest Family Fitness Ctr., 691 N.W.2d 334 (Wis. 2005).

[19] E.g., Littlefield v. Schaefer, 955 S.W.2d 272 (Tex. 1997); Yauger v. Skiing Enters., Inc., 206 Wis.2d 76, 557 N.W.2d 60 (1996); Vodopest v. MacGregor, 128 Wash.2d 840, 913 P.2d 779 (1996).

[20] Donahue v. Ledgends, Inc., 331 P.2d 342 (Alaska 2014); Layden v. Plante, 101 A.D.3d 1540, 957 N.Y.S.2d 458 (2012) ("[a]n agreement that seeks to release a defendant from the consequences of his or her own negligence must 'plainly and precisely' state that it extends this far," and holding that because the release at issue in the case "makes no unequivocal reference to any negligence or fault" of the defendant, it does not bar the plaintiff's negligence claim).

[21] E.g., McGrath v. SNH Dev., Inc., 158 N.H. 540, 969 A.2d 392 (2009) (negligence claim held to fall within the terms of a liability release).

[22] E.g., Cohen v. Five Brooks Stable, 159 Cal.App.4th, 72 Cal.Rptr.3d 471 (2008); Moore v. Hartley Motors, Inc., 36 P.3d 628 (Alaska 2001).

release does not cover the plaintiff's injury because it does not *clearly* do so, as required by law.[23]

§ 17.3 Public Policy Limitations

Limitations stemming from public policy. State courts frequently strike down pre-injury releases on a number of different public policy grounds.[24] In many cases, courts decide that a party cannot waive its duty of reasonable care despite the agreement.[25] Courts seeking to identify appropriate public policy limits frequently begin their analysis with the California Supreme Court's influential *Tunkl* case.[26] In *Tunkl*, the defendant-hospital would admit patients only if the patients signed a release relieving the hospital of all liability. The California Supreme Court believed that such a release was void as against public policy, partly because the patients did not truly acquiesce voluntarily to relieve the defendants of liability, and partly because medical services were themselves so important.[27] In its opinion, the court identified factors for determining whether an exculpatory clause should be invalidated.

The Tunkl factors. The *Tunkl* court identified six different factors relevant for determining whether a release violates public policy, with the caveat that not all six factors need be present to invalidate a release:

> [1] [The exculpatory contract] concerns a business of a type generally thought suitable for public regulation. [2] The party seeking exculpation is engaged in performing a service of great importance to the public, which is often a matter of practical necessity for some members of the public. [3] The party holds himself out as willing to perform this service for any member of the public who seeks it. . . . [4] As a result of the essential nature of the service, in the economic setting of the transaction, the party invoking exculpation possesses a decisive advantage of bargaining strength against any member of the public who seeks his services. [5] In exercising superior bargaining power, the party confronts the public with a standardized adhesion contract of exculpation, and makes no provision whereby a purchaser may pay additional reasonable fees and obtain protection against negligence. [6] Finally, as a result of the transaction, the person or property of the purchaser is placed under the control of the seller, subject to the risk of carelessness by the seller or his agents.

---

[23] E.g., Hargis v. Baize, 168 S.W.3d 36 (Ky. 2005) (holding that a wrongful death claim was not barred by an exculpatory clause, noting that the agreement was ambiguous and "could reasonably be construed" to release defendant only from a limited subset of potential legal claims).

[24] Not infrequently, courts incorporate contract-law limitations into their public policy conceptions, saying that a release void for contract-law reasons such as bargaining-power disparity or overbreadth is unenforceable as a matter of public policy. See, e.g., McGrath v. SNH Dev., Inc., 158 N.H. 540, 969 A.2d 392 (2009); Yauger v. Skiing Enters., Inc., 206 Wis.2d 76, 557 N.W.2d 60 (1996). Other courts more clearly separate the contract analysis from the public policy one. See, e.g., Thompson v. Hi Tech Motor Sports, Inc., 183 Vt. 218, 945 A.2d 368 (2008); Moore v. Hartley Motors, Inc., 36 P.3d 628 (Alaska 2001).

[25] Cf. Langemo v. Montana Rail Link, Inc., 38 P.2d 782 (Mont. 2001) (indemnity agreement under which plaintiff, injured in collision with a train at a private crossing on defendant's railroad, had agreed to indemnify the railroad would not exempt railroad from liability for its own proportionate share of the negligence).

[26] Tunkl v. Regents of the Univ. of Cal., 60 Cal.2d 92, 32 Cal.Rptr. 33, 383 P.2d 441, 6 A.L.R.3d 693 (1963).

[27] Tunkl, 60 Cal.2d at 98–101.

A large number of states have adopted these factors or have developed similar variants.[28] The Restatement Third draws on these factors in devising a similar list.[29]

Examples of exculpatory clauses invalidated based on public policy. Products manufacturers and distributors cannot use disclaimers or exculpatory agreements to avoid liability for personal injury resulting from dangerous products.[30] Similarly, releases in cases of medical research upon human beings—experimentation as distinct from treatment—may be void.[31] Public agencies like schools may not be allowed to condition a student's participation rights on a general release of all liability for negligence.[32] Caregivers, such as child care centers[33] and nursing homes,[34] having undertaken care, can hardly be permitted to undermine their promise by a clause that release them from a duty of care. Historically, businesses affected with a public interest, including some professional bailees,[35] carriers,[36] and public utilities,[37] could not contractually avoid liability for their own negligence. Although many courts have refused to extend this kind of thinking to nonessential recreational activity,[38] a few have done so, holding that a release-in-advance will not absolve a recreation-provider from liability for its own negligence.[39] And courts have declared it against public policy for employers

---

[28] See, e.g., Provoncha v. Vermont Motocross Ass'n, Inc., 974 A.2d 1261 (Vt. 2009); Hanks v. Powder Ridge Rest. Corp., 276 Conn. 314, 885 A.2d 734 (2005) (listing and classifying several jurisdictional variations).

[29] Restatement Third of Torts (Apportionment of Liability) § 2 cmt. e (2000).

[30] See § 33.17.

[31] Vodopest v. MacGregor, 128 Wash.2d 840, 913 P.2d 779 (1996). Federal regulations governing research on human subjects require informed consent without either exculpatory language or a release of the researcher. 45 C.F.R. § 46.116.

[32] Wagenblast v. Odessa Sch. Dist. No. 105–157–166J, 110 Wash.2d 845, 758 P.2d 968 (1988); see also Kyriazis v. Univ. of W. Va., 192 W.Va. 60, 450 S.E.2d 649 (1994) (state university sponsored club rugby a "public service;" release therefore void as a matter of public policy). But cf. Joseph H. King, Jr., Exculpatory Agreements for Volunteers in Youth Activities—The Alternative to "Nerf®" Tiddlywinks, 53 Ohio St. L.J. 683 (1992) (favoring effective exculpatory agreement for volunteers and sponsoring entities in youth activities).

[33] Gavin W. v. YMCA of Metro. Los Angeles, 106 Cal.App.4th 662, 131 Cal.Rptr.2d 168 (2003) ("To permit a child care provider to contract away its duty to exercise ordinary care is, in any event, antithetical to the very nature of child care services").

[34] Covenant Health & Rehab. of Picayune, LP v. Estate of Moulds, 14 So.3d 695 (Miss. 2009).

[35] E.g., Berrios v. United Parcel Serv., 265 N.J.Super. 436, 627 A.2d 701 (1992), aff'd per curiam, 265 N.J.Super. 368, 627 A.2d 665 (1993) (parking lot owners cannot exempt themselves from liability for negligent care to vehicle owner).

[36] Interstate carriers subject to federal control are permitted to limit liability under specified circumstances. See, e.g., 49 U.S.C.A. § 11706 (c) (provisions for limits by rail carriers).

[37] E.g., Southwestern Pub. Serv. Co. v. Artesia Alfalfa Growers' Ass'n, 67 N.M. 108, 353 P.2d 62 (1960).

[38] Lloyd v. Sugarloaf Mtn. Corp., 833 A.2d 1(Me. 2003) (organizer of bike race); McCune v. Myrtle Beach Indoor Shooting Range, Inc., 364 S.C. 242, 612 S.E.2d 462 (Ct. App. 2005) (paintball game provider); Lewis Operating Corp. v. Superior Court, 200 Cal.App.4th 940, 132 Cal.Rptr.3d 849 (2011) (apartment complex's tenant-only exercise facility waiver was valid but clause related to basic or essential common areas would not be).

[39] Hanks v. Powder Ridge Rest. Corp., 276 Conn. 314, 885 A.2d 734 (2005) (customer's advance release of snowtubing facility for its negligence is against public policy and ineffective); Reardon v. Windswept Farm, LLC., 280 Conn. 153, 905 A.2d 1156 (2006) (extending Hanks to horseback riding); Berlangieri v. Running Elk Corp., 134 N.M. 341, 76 P.3d 1098 (2003) (statute expressed policy that equine operators should be held accountable for their negligence, release to the contrary violated public policy); Bagley v. Mt. Bachelor, Inc., 340 P.3d 27 (Or. 2014) (safety of patrons of ski area was a matter of broad social concern; enforcing exculpatory clause would be unacceptable); Dalury v. S-K-I, Ltd., 164 Vt. 329, 670 A.2d 795 (1995) (ski resort's general exculpatory agreement invalid). Factors emphasized in the Connecticut cases as grounds for disregarding the release in advance, include these: "(1) the societal expectation that family oriented activities will be reasonably safe; (2) the illogic of relieving the party with greater expertise and information concerning the dangers associated with the activity from the burden of proper maintenance of the snowtubing run; and (3) the fact that the release at issue was a standardized adhesion contract, lacking equal bargaining power between the

to use the contract of employment to extract a release of liability for their own negligence.[40]

Parental waivers. Somewhat differently, but to similar effect, the vast majority of states that have made a decision on the issue have held that parents have no authority to release their minor children's potential claims in advance of an injury in connection with a commercial activity, and that accompanying indemnity agreements that would shift liability to the parents are also void.[41] In the community-run and school-sponsored activity setting, some waivers have been invalidated,[42] but others upheld.[43] To some extent, the decisions about whether to uphold the waiver seem to reflect the extent of unreasonable conduct that led to injury. *Galloway*, for example, invalidated the releases for a community sponsored program in which young children were told to cross a highway without supervision.[44]

Waivers of precaution required by statute. Statutory liability schemes may also influence the enforceability of releases. For example, a statute might set forth safety standards for a particular industry. If an exculpatory clause purports to release an industry member from liability for violating those standards, the clause will not be enforceable.[45] Even a statute that immunizes an industry from a certain range of claims may lead a court to conclude that a release cannot go further without violating public policy.[46]

B. IMPLIED ASSUMPTION OF RISK

§ 17.4 The Traditional Rule: Assumption of Risk as a Complete Bar

Traditional rule no longer valid. Most agreements in everyday life are tacit, not expressed. No logical reason prevents parties from tacitly or impliedly consenting or agreeing to a shift of responsibility to the plaintiff. The traditional assumption of risk

---

parties, and offered to the plaintiff on a take it or leave it basis." See Reardon, 280 Conn. at 161, 905 A.2d at 1161.

[40] See Brown v. Soh, 280 Conn. 494, 909 A.2d 43 (2006); Edgin v. Entergy Operations, Inc., 331 Ark. 162, 961 S.W.2d 724 (1998); Lakube v. Cohen, 304 Mass. 156, 23 N.E.2d 144 (1939); Pittsburgh, C. C. & St. L. Ry. v. Kinney, 95 Ohio St. 64, 115 N.E. 505 (1916).

[41] Sweeney v. City of Bettendorf, 762 N.W.2d 873 (Iowa 2009); Kirton v. Fields, 997 So.2d 349 (Fla. 2008); Hojnowski v. Vans Skate Park, 187 N.J. 323, 901 A.2d 381 (2006); Woodman v. Kera, LLC, 280 Mich.App. 125, 760 N.W.2d 641 (2008) (Michigan "strictly adheres to the common-law preclusion of parental authority in these situations, recognizing only very limited and specific statutory exceptions").

[42] Galloway v. State, 790 N.W.2d 252, 261 Ed. Law Rep. 819 (Iowa 2010) (14-year-old student on educational field trip organized by university and state).

[43] BJ's Wholesale Club, Inc. v. Rosen, 80 A.3d 345 (Md. 2013) (child injured in play area); Sharon v. City of Newton, 437 Mass. 99, 769 N.E.2d 738 (2002) (voluntary high-school cheerleading program); Zivich v. Mentor Soccer Club, Inc., 82 Ohio St.3d 367, 696 N.E.2d 201 (1998); Hohe v. San Diego Unified Sch. Dist., 224 Cal.App.3d 1559, 274 Cal.Rptr. 647 (1990) (school-sponsored event).

[44] Galloway v. State, 790 N.W.2d 252, 261 Ed. Law Rep. 819 (Iowa 2010).

[45] See Martin County Coal Corp. v. Universal Underwriters Ins. Co., 727 F.3d 589 (6th Cir. 2013) (can't contract away liability where liability rests on mine-safety statute); Hargis v. Baize, 168 S.W.3d 36 (Ky. 2005) ("A party cannot contract away liability for damages caused by that party's failure to comply with a duty imposed by a safety statute."); Finch v. Inspectech, LLC, 229 W.Va. 147, 727 S.E.2d 823 (2012) (home inspection statute). See also Marcinczyk v. State of N.J. Police Training Comm'n, 203 N.J. 586, 5 A.3d 785, 31 I.E.R. Cas. (BNA) 745 (2010) (training at county police academy).

[46] See, e.g., Rothstein v. Snowbird Corp., 175 P.3d 560 (Utah 2007) (release purporting to waive all claims against ski resort unenforceable as contrary to public policy in light of statute that immunizes ski operators from liability for inherent risks); but see Penunuri v. Sundance Partners, Ltd., 301 P.3d 984 (Utah 2013).

rules found such tacit consent when the plaintiff, knowing of the risk and appreciating its quality, voluntarily chose to confront it. If these facts were shown, then the plaintiff's claim for negligently caused injury was completely barred. A few states continue to follow this traditional "complete bar" rule.[47] Most states do not. The Restatement Third has generally done away with the concept of implied assumption of the risk.[48]

Consent. The traditional assumption of risk rule was sometimes expressed in terms of the maxim *volenti non fit injuria* or under the name of incurred risk. However formulated, the essential idea was that the plaintiff assumed the risk whenever she impliedly did so by words or conduct, just as would be true if she did so expressly. Children as well as adults could assume the risk and if they did, their claims would be barred.[49] Courts began to think that conduct implied consent whenever the plaintiff had specific knowledge of the risk posed by the defendant's negligence, appreciated its nature, and proceeded voluntarily to encounter it nonetheless.[50] By focusing on the plaintiff's knowledge of the risk as if that were an agreement to relieve the defendant of liability, courts sometimes allowed the negligent defendant to escape all responsibility for his misconduct even though the plaintiff acted quite reasonably and never signaled any intent to relieve the defendant from responsibility.[51] The Second Restatement and more modern theory added that the risk was assumed only if the plaintiff's conduct in encountering the risk manifested the plaintiff's willingness to accept responsibility for the risk.[52]

The connection to contributory negligence. In spite of the doctrine's grounding in the plaintiff's actual or apparent consent to accept responsibility for a risk, courts often applied the doctrine without inquiring whether the plaintiff's conduct could reasonably be interpreted as any kind of consent at all.[53] Instead, they treated the plaintiff's voluntary encounter with the risk as sufficient to raise the bar of assumption of risk, even though in many instances such conduct would not bespeak consent at all.[54]

---

[47] See, e.g., Thomas v. Panco Mgmt. of Md., LLC, 423 Md. 387, 31 A.3d 583 (2011) (continuing to apply the traditional implied assumption of risk rule; state also continues to follow complete bar version of contributory negligence, and the two defenses often overlap).

[48] Restatement Third of Torts (Apportionment of Liability) § 2 cmt. i (2000).

[49] Tucker v. Lombardo, 47 Cal.2d 457, 303 P.2d 1041 (1956) (12-year-old working on skeet shooting range); Greaves v. Galchutt, 289 Minn. 335, 184 N.W.2d 26 (1971) (11- and 12-year-old boys playing with gun they thought unloaded).

[50] See H.R.H. Metals, Inc. v. Miller, 833 So.2d 18 (Ala. 2002) (subjective standard for assumption of risk); Myers v. Boleman, 151 Ga.App. 506, 260 S.E.2d 359 (1979) (assumption of risk "applies only where the plaintiff, with full appreciation of the danger involved and without restriction from his freedom of choice . . . deliberately chooses an obviously perilous course of conduct"); Duda v. Phatty McGees, 758 N.W.2d 754 (S.D. 2008).

[51] Crews v. Hollenbach, 358 Md. 627, 751 A.2d 481 (2000) (plaintiff who worked for gas company was severely injured in an explosion during a repair; claim asserting negligence of contractor who was working on an underground cable and broke a hole in the gas line barred).

[52] Restatement Second of Torts § 496C (1965). Even those who wish to retain the formal language of assumption of risk for a narrow class of implied assumption of the risk cases agree that knowing confrontation of a risk is not equivalent to a consent that should bar the plaintiff. See Kenneth W. Simons, Reflections on Assumption of Risk, 50 U.C.L.A. L. Rev. 481 (2002).

[53] See Crews v. Hollenbach, 358 Md. 627, 751 A.2d 481 (2000). Another example is Curtis v. Traders Nat'l Bank, 314 Ky. 765, 237 S.W.2d 76 (1951) (customer entering a bank during a rainstorm tried to walk carefully through water accumulated on the marble floor but slipped; court held that she assumed the risk).

[54] Spahn v. Town of Port Royal, 326 S.C. 632, 486 S.E.2d 507 (Ct. App. 1997), aff'd on other grounds, 330 S.C. 168, 499 S.E. 205 (1998) (plaintiff attempted to move a boat that had fallen onto the highway; jury can evaluate assumption of risk, although plaintiff was not consenting to driver's negligence).

Assumption of risk took on a life of its own, reflecting policies or biases of the time rather than the plaintiff's actual or apparent consent.[55]

The no-duty or no-negligence connection. In another set of cases, courts used the term assumption of risk to express the view that the defendant should not be liable, but the reasons for nonliability did not lie in the plaintiff's consent or in her culpability. These were cases in which courts themselves, for reasons not much connected to the plaintiff's conduct or consent, narrowed or eliminated the defendant's duty, or else concluded that the defendant simply was not negligent.

No duty of landowners. For instance, courts have often held that landowners are free to leave dangerous conditions on their land, so long as those conditions are not hidden. If someone is injured by a dangerous but obvious condition on the land, the landowner is frequently not liable.[56] Courts often expressed this rule by saying that the plaintiff assumed the risk of open dangers on the land or those of which she knew.[57] However, the use of assumption of risk terminology in such cases added greatly to the existing confusion, because in these cases, assumption of risk did not mean either consent or contributory negligence. Ultimately, it was not even based on the plaintiff's conduct, but upon judicial policy to free the landowner from a duty of care. The assumption of risk terminology in cases like these thus serves mainly to distract courts from considering whether the defendant *should* owe a duty of care, or whether no duty was breached as a matter of law.[58]

"Consent" to employment risks. The early law of implied assumption of risk which arose in the nineteenth century was devoted to liabilities of employers for injury to employees.[59] Courts seldom inquired about the employee's real or even apparent consent to accept employment risks. Instead, courts conclusively "presumed" that, by accepting employment, the employee assumed the ordinary risks of employment and in addition assumed risks of specific employer negligence when he was made aware of those risks.[60] Since accepting employment could hardly count as contributory negligence and since it would seldom reflect either actual or apparent consent to employer negligence, these cases seem in reality to reflect a judicial policy or bias, not a decision about the plaintiff's

---

[55]   See Peter H. Schuck, Rethinking Informed Consent, 103 Yale L.J. 899, 912 (1994) (assumption of risk as a "culturally constructed and highly normative doctrine" rather than a "fact").

[56]   The details and qualifications to this traditional idea are covered in Chapter 20.

[57]   See DeAmiches v. Popczun, 35 Ohio St.2d 180, 299 N.E.2d 265 (1973) (plaintiff returning to her rented home in icy weather could not see unrepaired hole under snow; assumption of the risk for fall although it was not unreasonable to return home). See also Morgan State Univ. v. Walker, 397 Md. 509, 919 A.2d 21 (2007) (plaintiff was visiting her daughter at the university in order to bring her money she needed slipped on the ice and broke her leg; she assumed the risk of injury by walking on ice).

[58]   See, e.g., Beninati v. Black Rock City, LLC, 175 Cal.App.4th 650, 96 Cal.Rptr.3d 105 (2009) (holding that a festival promoter owed no duty to an attendee who walked directly into an area of burning embers, where the risk was obvious).

[59]   For a succinct history, see Dilan A. Esper & Gregory C. Keating, Abusing "Duty," 79 S. Cal. L. Rev. 265, 291–95 (2006). See also Perez v. McConkey, 872 S.W.2d 897 (Tenn. 1994) (tracing history of assumption of risk back to Roman times and recounting nineteenth-century development in England).

[60]   See, e.g., Wilson v. Lindamood Farms, Inc., 675 S.W.2d 187 (Tenn. Ct. App. 1984) ("ordinary risks are assumed by an employee whether he is actually aware of them or not; for the dangers and risks that are normally or necessarily incident to his occupation are presumably taken into account in fixing his rate of wages"); Grant v. Nihill, 64 Mont. 420, 210 P. 914 (1922) ("A servant by the act of entering the service of his master assumes all the usual and ordinary risks attendant upon his employment, not including risks arising from the negligence of the master, and he assumes the latter as well if he knows of the defects from which they arise and appreciates the dangers which flow from such defects."); Lamson v. American Axe & Tool Co., 58 N.E. 585 (Mass. 1900) (barring worker from suing his employer for on-the-job injury on the ground that he knew of the particular danger yet "stayed, and took the risk").

conduct at all. Holdings like this gave the doctrine of implied assumption of risk a bad name, and most courts gradually moved away from them.[61]

The fellow-servant rule and its abolition. The early employment cases also developed the fellow-servant rule, which asserted that a worker always assumed the risk of the negligence of fellow employees. An employee of a railroad, for example, could not recover from the railroad when the railroad's engineer negligently derailed a train and caused injury to other employees.[62] Twentieth century statutes abolished assumption of risk defenses in the employment context,[63] but not before the doctrine had spread beyond the employer-employee setting in most states.

§ 17.5 Development of Constraining Rules

Developing limits to the harsh traditional rule. The traditional rule of implied assumption of risk acted as a complete bar to a plaintiff's recovery and thus could work as harshly in application as the traditional rule of contributory negligence. However, courts began to develop some constraining rules to soften these harsh all-or-nothing applications.

Voluntariness; reasonable alternatives. One such constraining rule was that the plaintiff's confrontation of the risk had to be voluntary, which was to say that the plaintiff had to have a reasonable alternative course of action.[64] For example, if passengers in a car discover that their driver is dangerous and voluntarily remain in the car, they assume the risk of the dangers they have discovered. But if they are by then in an unfamiliar area, on a cold night, without any alternative transport to their homes or jobs, their continued exposure to the risk "is not in a true sense voluntary" and their claim for injury at the driver's hands is not barred.[65]

Knowledge of the risk itself. Another rule to avoid the harsh results of the implied assumption of risk doctrine held that the plaintiff did not assume the risk unless she knew of the risk itself as well as the facts that gave rise to it and "really" assumed the risk.[66] The plaintiff's subjective consent was required.[67]

---

[61] See Siragusa v. Swedish Hosp., 60 Wash.2d 310, 373 P.2d 767 (1962).

[62] E.g., Murray v. South Carolina R.R., 11 S.C.L. (2 McMul. 166) (S.C. 1841). The idea originated in Priestly v. Fowler, 3 M. & W. 1 (Exch. 1837), where Lord Abinger argued that the employee was in the best position to protect himself from co-workers and should bear the risk for that reason.

[63] Assumption of risk as a complete defense was abrogated by the Federal Employers' Liability Act (FELA) as to interstate railroad employees. 45 U.S.C.A. § 53.

[64] Courts that continue to use implied assumption of risk to bar a claim entirely adhere to this rule. See Thomas v. Panco Mgmt. of Md., LLC, 423 Md. 387, 31 A.3d 583 (2011) (finding contested issue of fact as to whether tenant had a reasonably safe alternative path to the one taken, when she slipped on ice when exiting her apartment).

[65] Ridgway v. Yenny, 223 Ind. 16, 57 N.E.2d 581 (1944). Cf. Pettry v. Rapid City Area Sch. Dist., 630 N.W.2d 705 (S.D. 2001) ("the alternatives confronting her on the night of her fall were to park in the dark, icy street and walk a block or more to the gymnasium or to park in the dark, icy playground and walk only a few steps to the gymnasium").

[66] Some states accomplished this by statute. See, e.g., Patch v. Hillerich & Bradsby Co., 361 Mont. 241, 257 P.3d 383, Prod. Liab. Rep. (CCH) P 18669 (2011) (applying Mont. Code Ann. § 27–1–719(5)(a), which allows a product manufacturer to use assumption of risk as a complete defense if the "consumer of the product discovered the defect or the defect was open and obvious," construing it to apply only when "the victim actually knew he or she would suffer serious injury or death," a subjective standard of knowledge).

[67] See Get-N-Go, Inc. v. Markins, 544 N.E.2d 484 (Ind. 1989); see also Poole v. Coakley & Williams Constr., Inc., 423 Md. 91, 31 A.3d 212 (2011); Duda v. Phatty McGees, Inc., 758 N.W.2d 754 (S.D. 2008); Jay v. Moog Auto., Inc., 264 Neb. 875, 652 N.W.2d 872 (2002) (defendant manufacturer produced no evidence of "subjective, conscious choice on [plaintiff's] part to voluntarily expose himself to the risk").

Problems with implying consent from conduct: Prosser's jaywalker. The real problem in these cases is not reached by rules about voluntariness or subjective consent. The problem lies in the courts' tendency to equate confrontation of known risks with a manifestation of consent. A plaintiff who knows of a risk, understands it, and decides to take it anyway may be negligent in some cases, but a defendant could seldom reasonably understand the plaintiff's conduct to mean that she agreed to accept all risks of the defendant's negligence. As Prosser pointed out, the driver of an automobile cannot reasonably believe that the jaywalking plaintiff is consenting to the driver's negligence.[68] The jaywalker assuredly confronts a known risk and does so voluntarily, but voluntary confrontation of the risk does not communicate any release of the driver from the duties of ordinary care. Instead, the jaywalker is simply negligent. His negligence is to be judged under comparative fault rules. Moreover, court findings of consent when the plaintiff confronts a known risk in a reasonable way limits the plaintiff's freedom to act reasonably.

§ 17.6 Discarding the Defense of Implied Assumption of Risk

Abolishing implied assumption of the risk. "[W]hen we are tempted to say 'assumption of risk' we should instead say something else."[69] As early as the 1950s, some courts began to recognize that implied assumption of risk rules had no separate status or function and could be usefully abolished.[70] Since assumption of risk always seemed to be a way of talking about some other established legal doctrine, a number of courts found that implied assumption of risk could be better expressed by discussing the basic concepts of duty, negligence, or contributory negligence.

Resolving assumption of the risk questions through other doctrines. The insight that implied assumption of risk is a superfluous and unnecessarily confusing doctrine has spread inexorably.[71] Reflecting this evolution in judicial thinking, assumption of risk today is increasingly discarded as a separate defense, except in its express form. Cases formerly resolved under assumption of risk rationales can now be resolved by (1) applying the comparative fault rules, (2) holding that the defendant had no duty of care, or (3) holding that the defendant did not breach a duty. Which resolution is appropriate depends upon the facts of the case.[72]

Merging assumption of the risk into comparative negligence. After the advent of comparative negligence, courts found it logically or morally difficult to maintain a dual system in which the plaintiff's fault only reduced damages if it was called contributory negligence, while it barred the plaintiff entirely if it was called assumption of risk. Consequently, most comparative negligence states, by statutory provision[73] or judicial

[68] Prosser & Keeton on Torts § 68, at 490 (5th ed. 1984).

[69] Stephen D. Sugarman, Assumption of Risk, 31 Val. U. L. Rev. 833, 835 (1997).

[70] See, e.g., Gilson v. Drees Bros., 19 Wis.2d 252, 120 N.W.2d 63 (1963); Williamson v. Smith, 83 N.M. 336, 491 P.2d 1147 (1971); Arnold v. City of Cedar Rapids, Iowa, 443 N.W.2d 332 (Iowa 1989); Perez v. McConkey, 872 S.W.2d 897 (Tenn. 1994). Meistrich v. Casino Arena Attractions, Inc., 31 N.J. 44, 155 A.2d 90, 82 A.L.R.2d 1208 (1959), initiated the trend towards this view.

[71] The arguments for the abolition of assumption of risk as a separate defense are thrashed out in a Symposium, 22 La. L. Rev. 1 (1961).

[72] John Diamond, Assumption of Risk after Comparative Negligence: Integrating Contract Theory into Tort Doctrine, 52 Ohio St. L.J. 717 (1991), is very helpful on the translation of old assumption of risk into contemporary doctrines of limited duty and comparative fault.

[73] Ind. Code § 34–6–2–45 (fault defined to include certain types of assumption of risk); Mass Gen. L. Ann. ch. 231, § 85 (defense abolished).

decision,[74] simply "merge" assumption of risk into comparative negligence in many routine cases. Regrettably, some courts receptive to the idea that assumption of risk is merely an alternative expression for other concepts still use the language of assumption of risk.[75]

Assumed risk as plaintiff fault. Many cases are amenable to resolution under the comparative negligence rules. The hitchhiker who falls asleep on the highway's edge is not assuming the risk of being run over by a negligent driver; he is merely negligent and accordingly may suffer a defeat or a reduction in damages under comparative negligence rules.[76] The same is true for the customer who falls in her attempt to enter a business in spite of water on its floor.

The contemporary view. Contemporary courts usually say that implied assumption of risk does not survive the adoption of comparative negligence.[77] They sometimes add that *express* assumption of the risk survives the adoption of comparative negligence.[78] This view is in line with the Third Restatement.[79] Some commentators have counseled that there is a small subset of cases concerning full preference for risk in which the doctrine of implied assumption of the risk should be retained—as when a plaintiff would rather jump out of a plane with a potentially defective parachute than a sound one.[80] But given the history of overbroad uses of implied assumption of the risk, many courts are justifiably reluctant to accommodate this narrow category of preferred risk by restarting the game of determining when the plaintiff consents to the negligence itself. When this view is adopted, assumption of the risk is absorbed into three other elements: defendant duty, defendant negligence, and plaintiff comparative fault.

Assumption of risk as consent to relieve the defendant of a duty of care. Where assumption of risk is a matter of the plaintiff's apparent consent to accept risks generated by the defendant, sometimes referred to as "primary" assumption of the risk, the defendant may have no duty of care.[81] For example, the nurse hired to care for and restrain combative Alzheimer's patients may impliedly assume the risk that one of her patients will harm her, or put otherwise, the patient is not liable for harm to the nurse

---

[74] See, e.g., Rountree v. Boise Baseball, LLC, 296 P.3d 373 (Idaho 2013); Knight v. Jewett, 3 Cal.4th 296, 11 Cal.Rptr.2d 2, 834 P.2d 696 (1992); Green v. Mid Dakota Clinic, 673 N.W.2d 257 (N.D. 2004); Hale v. Beckstead, 116 P.3d 263 (Utah 2005); King v. Kayak Mfg. Corp., 182 W.Va. 276, 387 S.E.2d 511 (1989); Anderson v. Ceccardi, 6 Ohio St.3d 110, 451 N.E.2d 780 (1983).

[75] See, e.g., Patterson Enters. Inc. v. Johnson, 272 P.3d 93 (Mont. 2012) (using the old assumption of the risk terminology but awarding damages in line with comparative fault); Morgan v. State, 90 N.Y.2d 471, 685 N.E.2d 202 (1997) (using both assumption of risk and limited-duty language).

[76] Simmons v. Frazier, 277 Ark. 452, 642 S.W.2d 314 (1982).

[77] Rountree v. Boise Baseball, LLC, 296 P.3d 373 (Idaho 2013) (implied assumption of risk, whether in its "primary" or "secondary" form, is no longer a valid defense; to allow it is "inconsistent with our comparative negligence system"); Simmons v. Porter, 312 P.3d 345 (Kan. 2013) (implied assumption of risk no longer viable after comparative fault).

[78] E.g., Shorter v. Drury, 103 Wash.2d 645, 695 P.2d 116 (1985).

[79] Restatement Third of Torts (Apportionment of Liability) § 2 cmt. (2000).

[80] Assumption of Risk and Consent in the Law of Torts: A Theory of Full Preference, 67 B.U. L. Rev. 213 (1987).

[81] See, e.g., Turcotte v. Fell, 68 N.Y.2d 432, 510 N.Y.S.2d 49, 502 N.E.2d 964 (1986); King v. Kayak Mfg. Corp., 182 W.Va. 276, 387 S.E.2d 511 (1989). In some cases it is possible to think of the plaintiff's consent or agreement to the defendant's conduct as a kind of equitable estoppel that bars the plaintiff's claim. See Geddes v. Mill Creek Country Club, Inc., 196 Ill.2d 302, 751 N.E.2d 1150, 256 Ill.Dec. 313 (2001) (plaintiff agreed to layout of golf course on adjoining land, now suffers thousands of golf balls, but since defendant built in reliance, the plaintiff is equitably estopped to complain).

even though he may be liable if he harms strangers.[82] The outcome today is often expressed either in terms of assumption of risk or a rule that the defendant owes no duty.

Assumption of risk showing no negligence on defendant's part. In other cases, the plaintiff's consent to accept a risk simply shows that the defendant was not negligent. For example, suppose a seriously ill patient, losing confidence in ordinary medical treatment, asks her doctor for an experimental treatment that is also dangerous. When the risky experimental treatment causes harm or fails to cure, the patient cannot recover on the theory that following her wishes was negligent.[83] Some courts might explain this outcome by saying that the patient's consent relieved the doctor of a duty of care, but that seems to be the wrong explanation. The physician undoubtedly owes his patient a duty of reasonable care and the real question on these facts is whether he breached that duty, that is, whether he was negligent. The patient's consent determines that issue. Where the physician administered only the care to which the patient consented, he was rendering appropriate care and thus fulfilled his duty, making him not negligent.[84] Indeed, the physician would violate the patient's rights if he administered a traditional treatment after agreeing not to.

Assumption of risk as comparative fault. Finally, as with Prosser's jaywalker, what was once termed assumption of the risk actually may now be used to show that the plaintiff is at fault.[85] A person who crosses the street in the middle of the road, although not consenting to the negligence of a driver, may have liability apportioned to her under principles of comparative fault.

§ 17.7 Primary and Secondary Assumption of Risk

Types of implied assumption of risk. In a perfect world, we would speak no more of "implied assumption of risk." As discussed above, the existing rules of plaintiff negligence, defendant duty, and defendant negligence render the separate existence of assumption of the risk entirely superfluous and potentially confusing. But in a significant number of states, the terminology doggedly persists, albeit in a somewhat modified form. In these states, the term "primary assumption of risk" is used to indicate a no-duty or no-breach conception; and the term "secondary assumption of risk" is used to indicate the plaintiff negligence conception.[86] This "primary" and "secondary" terminology developed in the twentieth century mainly in response to the adoption of comparative negligence, which made it imperative to decide whether all forms of implied

---

[82]   See Berberian v. Lynn, 179 N.J. 290, 845 A.2d 122 (2004); Creasy v. Rusk, 730 N.E.2d 659 (Ind. 2000) (nurse had duty to patient, not the other way around); Gregory v. Cott, 331 P.3d 179 (Cal. 2014); Anicet v. Gant, 580 So.2d 273 (Fla. Dist. Ct. App. 1991); Gould v. American Family Mut. Ins. Co., 543 N.W.2d 282 (Wis. 1996).

[83]   She might, of course, recover on different grounds where the physician committed some independent act of negligence, or where the physician induced her to accept experimental treatments by fraud. See Heinrich v. Sweet, 308 F.3d 48 (1st Cir. 2002) (plaintiff's informed consent to experimental treatment barred medical malpractice claim based on choice of treatment, although it would not bar a malpractice claim based upon independent negligence, as where surgeon leaves scalpel in the plaintiff's body).

[84]   E.g., Boyle v. Revici, 961 F.2d 1060 (2d Cir. 1992) (on very similar facts, jury could find assumption of risk).

[85]   Prosser & Keeton on Torts § 68, at 490 (5th ed. 1984).

[86]   E.g., Sunday v. Stratton Corp., 136 Vt. 293, 390 A.2d 398 (1978); Turcotte v. Fell, 68 N.Y.2d 432, 502 N.E.2d 964 (1986); Knight v. Jewett, 3 Cal.4th 296, 11 Cal.Rptr.2d 2, 834 P.2d 696 (1992); Leonard v. Behrens, 601 N.W.2d 76 (Iowa 1999); Sullivan-Coughlin v. Palos Country Club, Inc., 349 Ill.App.3d 553, 812 N.E.2d 496, 285 Ill.Dec.676 (2004); Yoneda v. Tom, 110 Haw. 367, 133 P.3d 796 (2006).

assumption of risk were properly subsumed within that system, or whether some forms should completely bar a plaintiff's recovery.[87]

Problems with primary and secondary terminology. As descriptive terminology, there is nothing at all remarkable here. Implied assumption of risk does appear, when unpacked to its essentials, to be divisible into either a no-duty/no-breach conception or a contributory negligence conception. However, continued use of the primary/secondary terminology is ill-advised for a number of reasons. First, the distinction tends to muddle the issue of who has the burden of proof. If the issue is no duty or no negligence, placing the burden of proving assumption of risk on the defendant in essence forces a defendant to prove that an element of the plaintiff's prima facie case (duty or breach) has not been proved.[88] Another problem is that the usage sometimes invites confusion over the proper roles of judge and jury. Many courts hold that assumption of risk in any form is a jury issue;[89] some state constitutions so require.[90] Many other courts say that once the defense is presented in its "primary" form—in its "no-duty" form—it is a legal question, for the judge.[91] Finally, the "primary" and "secondary" implied assumption of risk usage is needlessly redundant in its most common form. If "primary assumption of risk" is synonymous with "no duty" or "no negligence," then why retain an additional term for those well-established concepts?

Abandoning the implied assumption of risk term. Judges have perceptively noted that the application of the doctrine of implied assumption of risk "has been somewhat tangled"[92] and has spawned "confusion and complications" in the law.[93] Using "assumption of risk" terminology at all is the real culprit here, because courts must then recognize that that one term harbors at least three different meanings. Such a task is not easy for busy judges to keep straight, especially if confronted by lawyers whose briefs and arguments are focused mostly on older precedent that takes no account of contemporary analysis. Courts would do better to abandon the term entirely and to more transparently address the issues of duty, negligence and contributory negligence that are raised by the arcane assertion of the "assumption of risk defense."

---

[87] See Allen v. Dover Co-Recreational Softball League, 148 N.H. 407, 807 A.2d 1274 (2002) (giving history of assumption of risk, including primary and secondary forms, citing many cases from various states). See also Dilan A. Esper & Gregory C. Keating, Abusing "Duty," 79 S. Cal. L. Rev. 265, 292 (2006) (analyzing development of "primary" and "secondary" terminology). Torts scholar Fleming James appears to have invented the terminology as a matter of bringing some coherence to the law by distinguishing contributory negligence from the absence of duty, long before the widespread adoption of comparative fault principles. See Fleming James, Jr., Contributory Negligence, 62 Yale L.J. 691 (1953).

[88] See Spar v. Cha, 907 N.E.2d 974 (Ind. 2009) (holding that primary assumption of risk "may not require pleading as an affirmative defense" under local Trial Rule because it "negate[s] an element of the claim"); Bennett v. Hidden Valley Golf & Ski, Inc., 318 F.3d 868 (8th Cir. 2003) (Mo. law) ("Because the doctrine of implied assumption of risk focuses on whether the defendant owed a duty to the plaintiff with respect to the risk in question, it is not strictly an affirmative defense.").

[89] E.g., Schneider v. Erickson, 654 N.W.2d 144 (Minn. Ct. App. 2002) (both primary and secondary assumption of risk "usually a question for the jury, unless the evidence is conclusive").

[90] See, e.g., Phelps v. Firebird Raceway, Inc., 210 Ariz. 403, 111 P.3d 1003 (2005). Even in the face of such a provision, a court may find that primary assumption of risk remains a question of law for the judge because it goes to duty. See Tucker v. ADG, Inc., 102 P.3d 660 (Okla. 2004).

[91] Turner v. Mandalay Sports Entm't, LLC, 180 P.3d 1172 (Nev. 2008); Gallagher v. Cleveland Browns Football Co., 74 Ohio St.3d 427, 659 N.E.2d 1232 (1996).

[92] Neighbarger v. Irwin Indus., Inc., 8 Cal.4th 532, 882 P.2d 347, 34 Cal.Rptr.2d 630 (1994) (Mosk, J.).

[93] Perez v. McConkey, 872 S.W.2d 897 (Tenn. 1994). See also Tiller v. Atlantic Coast Line R.R., 318 U.S. 54, 63 S.Ct. 444, 87 L.Ed. 610 (1943) (Frankfurter, J., concurring).

§ 17.8 Sports Cases

The sports cases. While there is no formal category of implied assumption of the risk that is specific to sports-related injuries, this setting is a frequent context of assumption of risk questions. Most of these issues concern primary assumption of the risk—the defendant no-duty or no-negligence conception.

Spectators: limited duty not to increase inherent risks. Before the adoption of comparative negligence, courts concluded that spectators at sporting events such as baseball games assumed the risk of being struck by wayward balls or the like. A more current version of the idea might say that the defendant sports arena owed no duty to them for inherent risks of the sport.[94] So a sports operator may have a duty to provide some reasonably safe accommodations, for example, to provide screening in the most dangerous areas sufficient to protect the number of people who can be expected to wish such protection on ordinary occasions.[95] However, if the plaintiff has the option of a safer seat and sits in an unprotected area, if she is injured by a foul or mis-thrown ball or an errant hockey puck, she simply has no claim.[96] Put more broadly, the operator of sports enterprises "has no duty to protect an invitee against the ordinary hazards of the sports activity,"[97] or more accurately, to protect against the inherent risks that remain after due care is exercised.[98]

The duty of care. These rules do not mean that the sports enterprise never owes a duty of care, much less that it never breaches the duty. For instance, the enterprise might provide a defective screen behind home plate, or bleachers that collapse. If so, it is quite likely to be held liable for its negligence.[99] In the collapsing bleachers example, it would be hard to assert that the sports enterprise owed no duty of care to provide reasonably safe bleachers.

Defining inherent risks. Which risks are inherent and which risks should be avoided through reasonable care is a subject of continued litigation.[100] Moreover, the doctrinal

---

[94] Edward C. v. City of Albuquerque, 148 N.M. 646, 241 P.3d 1086 (2010) (reviewing many jurisdictional approaches, concluding that a jury question is presented on whether the limited duty is breached upon a showing that the defendant stadium owner or occupant "has done something to increase the risks beyond those necessary or inherent to the game, or to impede a fan's ability to protect himself or herself"), overruled on other grounds, Rodriguez v. Del Sol Shopping Ctr. Assocs., L.P., 326 P.3d 465, 468 (N.M. 2014); Creel v. L & L, Inc., 287 P.3d 729 (Wyo. 2012) (duty of golf tournament official was only to not increase the risks to spectators, beyond the inherent risk that spectators would be struck by a golf ball; fact issues on that issue precluded summary judgment); Sciarrotta v. Global Spectrum, 194 N.J. 345, 944 A.2d 630 (2008); Hurst v. East Coast Hockey League, Inc., 371 S.C. 33, 637 S.E.2d 560 (2006); Tucker v. ADG, Inc., 102 P.3d 660 (Okla. 2004); McGarry v. Sax, 158 Cal.App.4th 983, 70 Cal.Rptr.3d 519 (2008).

[95] Arnold v. City of Cedar Rapids, Iowa, 443 N.W.2d 332 (Iowa 1989); Akins v. Glens Falls City Sch. Dist., 53 N.Y.2d 325, 424 N.E.2d 531, 441 N.Y.S.2d 644 (1981). See also, criticizing the rule as removing the incentive for stadium owners to update safety measures as sports and technology change, David Horton, Comment, Rethinking Assumption of Risk and Sports Spectators, 51 U.C.L.A. L. Rev. 339 (2003).

[96] Lawson v. Salt Lake Trappers, Inc., 901 P.2d 1013 (Utah 1995) (foul ball); Gilchrist v. City of Troy, 67 N.Y.2d 1034, 494 N.E.2d 1382, 503 N.Y.S.2d 717 (1986) (puck). But see South Shore Baseball, LLC v. DeJesus, 11 N.E.3d 903 (Ind. 2014) (suggesting that no sport, even baseball, merits its own special rule of liability).

[97] King v. Kayak Mfg. Corp., 182 W.Va. 276, 387 S.E.2d 511 (1989).

[98] Hurst v. East Coast Hockey League, Inc., 371 S.C. 33, 637 S.E.2d 560 (2006) (quoting; also noting that assumption of risk in this sense is not an affirmative defense but a conclusion that the defendant owes no duty or is not negligent with respect to risks that cannot be reduced by further care).

[99] As in, e.g., Boyer v. Iowa High Sch. Athletic Ass'n, 260 Iowa 1061, 152 N.W.2d 293 (1967) (collapsing bleachers, res ipsa loquitur applicable).

[100] Coomer v. Kansas City Royals Baseball Corp., 437 S.W.3d 184 (Mo. 2014) (en banc) (risk of injury from being struck by hot dog thrown into the stands by team mascot was not an inherent risk of watching

development of the baseball spectator cases themselves shows the extent to which the risks considered inherent in an activity are a social construct that changes over time. Requirements for providing screening or alternate seating have increased since the earlier cases.[101]

Sports participants: general rule. Participants in organized and even private sporting activities are governed by rules similar to those that apply to spectators. In the old language of assumption of risk, participants impliedly "assume the risk" of all the dangers inherent in the sport and thus have no claim arising out of such dangers. In newer terminology, it might be said that the defendant has breached no duty to sporting participants when it does not protect them from inherent risks of the game.

Inherent dangers distinguished from negligently created dangers. In many sporting activities, dangers inherent in the sport would never include the defendant's negligence. In the old language of assumption of the risk, this case of no negligence is expressed by saying that a skier impliedly assumes only the risks of dangers inherent in skiing, but does not assume the risk of dangers hidden below the snow as a result of the slope operator's negligence. In such cases, the operator's negligence is by no means inherent in the sport.[102] Similarly, a horseback rider assumes the risk of being thrown, but the rider assumes only the inherent risk, not the added risk incurred by reason of the stables' negligence.[103] Put the other way around, unless policy dictates otherwise, the defendant does not avoid liability for negligence that adds either new risks to a dangerous activity or substantially increases the risks that are inherent in the activity.[104] However, courts sometimes describe seemingly nonessential and avoidable dangers as "inherent," and thus protect the defendant.[105]

Risks of negligence assumed. Participants in active, competitive sporting contests—football and ice hockey, for example—often must expect negligently caused physical injury. A number of courts have accordingly held that in such cases the duty of other

---

baseball); FCH1, LLC v. Rodriguez, 335 P.3d 183 (Nev. 2014) (being injured when a patron in a sports bar dove for a tossed souvenir was not an inherent risk of watching a television game in a sports bar).

[101] Jones v. Three Rivers Mgmt. Corp., 483 Pa. 75, 394 A.2d 546 (1978) (baseball stadium so designed that patron was at risk from batted balls while she was walking on an interior concourse; this design is not an inherent, ordinary, or expected risk of baseball, so the no-duty rule did not apply).

[102] See Sunday v. Stratton, 136 Vt. 293, 390 A.2d 398 (1978). The ski industry has prevailed upon legislatures to enact protective statutes which, in some states, provide that the skier assumes risks inherent in the sport. Some other businesses have secured similar legislation intended to offer protection. See Derricotte v. United Skates of Am., 350 N.J. Super. 227, 794 A.2d 867 (2002) (reflecting a roller skating statute and adoption of similar statutes in a number of states). The statutes may offer less protection than intended, since "an inherent risk is one that cannot be removed through the exercise of due care." Brett v. Great Am. Recreations, Inc., 144 N.J. 479, 499, 677 A.2d 705, 715 (1996). But some statutes appear to force individuals to assume risks of hidden dangers that could have been corrected by the operators' reasonable care. See Utah Code Ann. § 78–27–51.

[103] Halpern v. Wheeldon, 890 P.2d 562 (Wyo. 1995). A number of states have now passed equine recreation statutes which, like the ski statutes, are aimed at limiting liability.

[104] Cohen v. Five Brooks Stable, 159 Cal.App.4th 1476, 72 Cal.Rptr.3d 471 (2008) (no duty to reduce risks of harm inherent in sport, but reckless conduct of trail guide is not an inherent risk of horse riding); Luna v. Vela, 169 Cal.App.4th 102, 86 Cal.Rptr.3d 588 (2008) (host of volleyball match owed a duty only to not increase the inherent risks of the sport).

[105] See Barrett v. Mt. Brighton, Inc., 474 Mich. 1087, 712 N.W.2d 154 (2006) (describing a snowboarding rail as an inherent risk of skiing, which was defined broadly in the governing statute, with dissents arguing to the contrary); Rayeski v. Gunstock Area/Gunstock Area Comm'n, 776 A.2d 1265 (N.H. 2001) (concluding that the dangers of an unpadded light pole to late-afternoon skiers was inherent in skiing); Avila v. Citrus Cmty. Coll. Dist., 38 Cal.4th 148, 162, 131 P.3d 383, 392, 41 Cal.Rptr. 3d 299, 309 (2006) (opining that intentionally pitching a ball to hit the batter in the head in a community college game would be an inherent risk of the sport).

participants is only a duty to avoid intentional or reckless injury.[106] Some states have statutes to this effect.[107] The rule apparently does not protect non-participants such as the owner of premises whose negligence increased the risk to the players.[108]

Intentional harms as inherent danger. California has gone further, holding that even an intentional tort may be an inherent risk of the game, so that a willing participant in the game cannot recover for such an "inherent" risk.[109] California applied that rule to eliminate a claim by a batter who was injured when the pitcher intentionally struck him in the head with a pitched ball. In some of these cases, it looks as if courts are treating *foreseeable* misconduct in sports as if such misconduct were *inherent* in the sport. This rationale seems unsound—the court opined that intentionally hitting a batter in the head as a retaliatory measure would be accepted in the sport without taking any evidence from college coaches or players from the region—and its theory has not been adopted by other courts.

Rationale. The limited duty (or standard of care) is derived directly from the plaintiff's limited expectations of safety.[110] The limited-duty approach makes it clear that even violation of a rule of the game does not in itself result in liability; the defendant will be liable only if he is reckless or intends harm.[111]

Applications. The limited-duty rule has been applied to organized sports like pro football[112] and college hockey,[113] and to professional horse racing.[114] Quite arguably it is best confined to professional sports.[115] But the limited-duty rule has also been applied to

---

[106] Karas v. Strevell, 227 Ill.2d 440, 884 N.E.2d 122, 318 Ill.Dec. 567 (2008); Knight v. Jewett, 3 Cal.4th 296, 11 Cal.Rptr.2d 2, 834 P.2d 696 (1992) (conduct must be so reckless "as to be totally outside the range of the ordinary activity involved in the sport"); Nabozny v. Barnhill, 31 Ill.App.3d 212, 334 N.E.2d 258, 77 A.L.R.3d 1294 (1975) (soccer; deliberate prohibited kick could be actionable); Horvath v. Ish, 134 Ohio St. 3d 48, 979 N.E.2d 1246 (2012) (plaintiff skier injured in a collision with a snowboarder had to prove that the snowboarder acted recklessly or intentionally).

[107] See Noffke v. Bakke, 315 Wis.2d 350, 760 N.W.2d 156 (2009) (applying Wisc. Stat. Ann. § 895.525(4m)(a), which immunizes participants in "contact sports" from negligence claims, to bar a negligence suit by one high-school cheerleader against another).

[108] See also Sherry v. East Suburban Football League, 292 Mich.App. 23, 807 N.W.2d 859 (2011) (ordinary care standard applied, rather than reckless-misconduct "co-participant" standard, in suit by injured cheerleader against franchise member of football league, league, cheerleading coach, and cheerleading coordinator; none of the defendants were co-participants in the recreational activity of cheerleading).

[109] Avila v. Citrus Cmty. Coll. Dist., 38 Cal.4th 148, 162, 131 P.3d 383, 392, 41 Cal.Rptr. 3d 299, 309 (2006). Although the negligence claim was considered in "no duty" terms, the potential battery claim was defeated on the ground that the batter consented to the pitcher's intentional act of hitting him in the head with a "bean ball." Cf. Distefano v. Forester, 85 Cal.App.4th 1249, 102 Cal.Rptr.2d 813 (2001) (off-roading, collision atop a blind hill, defendant's violation of speed statute is not a breach of duty owed, since, even if reckless, the defendant did not act totally outside the range of ordinary activity in the sport).

[110] See Turcotte v. Fell, 68 N.Y.2d 432, 510 N.Y.S.2d 49, 502 N.E.2d 964 (1986). Some states have statutes that define the "inherent risks" of particular sports. See Jackson Hole Mountain Resort Corp. v. Rohrman, 150 P.3d 167 (Wyo. 2006) (looking at other states' statutes on inherent risks of skiing and as guide to a common-law determination).

[111] Gauvin v. Clark, 404 Mass. 450, 537 N.E.2d 94 (1989); Turcotte v. Fell, 68 N.Y.2d 432, 510 N.Y.S.2d 49, 502 N.E.2d 964 (1986).

[112] Hackbart v. Cincinnati Bengals, Inc., 601 F.2d 516 (10th Cir. 1979).

[113] Gauvin v. Clark, 404 Mass. 450, 537 N.E.2d 94 (1989).

[114] Turcotte v. Fell, 68 N.Y.2d 432, 510 N.Y.S.2d 49, 502 N.E.2d 964 (1986).

[115] See Stephen D. Sugarman, Assumption of the Risk, 31 Val. U. L. Rev. 833 (1997).

recreational games of football,[116] soccer,[117] softball,[118] paintball,[119] and even to games that seem to be little more than horseplay in which the rules are constructed on the fly[120] and to children's activities that are not really games at all.[121]

Consent and parties' expectations as foundations for the duty of care. If the underlying point is the one rooted in the consent type of implied assumption of risk, that is, the reasonable expectations of the parties involved, a more cautious formulation is required. To say that professional football players must expect some rather serious misbehavior is not to say that ping pong players should expect to be blinded by a thrown paddle.[122] If the limited-duty rule is true to its consensual heritage, the reasonable expectations of the parties must be taken into account, so that the particular facts of the cases and the particular kind of sporting activity and expectations of players involved will be important.[123] Hunters, for example, presumably know that they are at risk from other hunters, but given the seriousness of potential injury, those who participate should not be viewed as consenting to being shot by negligent gunners. Consequently, the cases so far have required hunters to exercise the care of reasonable and prudent persons.[124] And Connecticut has said that the expectations of skiers, considering the dangers of the sport, is that other skiers will follow the rules and exercise care, with the result that skiers owe each other a duty of reasonable care undiminished by any supposed assumption of risk.[125] Expectations of care may govern with respect to playful activities as well.[126]

Limiting duty based on policy rather than consent or expectations. It may be that some courts are in the process of creating a freestanding limited-duty rule, divorced from

---

[116] Knight v. Jewett, 3 Cal.4th 296, 11 Cal.Rptr.2d 2, 834 P.2d 696 (1992).

[117] Jaworski v. Kiernan, 241 Conn. 399, 696 A.2d 332 (1997).

[118] Crawn v. Campo, 136 N.J. 494, 643 A.2d 600 (1994); Chrisman v. Brown, 246 S.W.3d 102 (Tex. App. 2007).

[119] Leonard v. Behrens, 601 N.W.2d 76 (Iowa 1999); cf. Schneider v. Erickson, 654 N.W.2d 144 (Minn. Ct. App. 2002) (paintball-game participant held to have primarily assumed the risk of being shot in the eye).

[120] Pfister v. Shusta, 167 Ill.2d 417, 657 N.E.2d 1013, 212 Ill.Dec. 668 (1995) (kicking a crushed can in dormitory lobby); Marchetti v. Kalish, 53 Ohio St. 3d 95, 559 N.E.2d 699 (1990) (child's game of kick-the-can); but cf. Yount v. Johnson, 121 N.M. 585, 915 P.2d 341 (Ct. App. 1996) (limited duty rule inapplicable to horseplay between teenaged young men).

[121] Gentry v. Craycraft, 101 Ohio St. 3d 141, 802 N.E.2d 1116 (2004) (limited-duty rule applied to bar a child who was participating with other children in the activity of pounding nails into wood).

[122] See Bangert v. Shaffner, 848 S.W.2d 353 (Tex. App. 1993) (parasail harnessed upside down with disastrous results, ordinary care standard applied).

[123] See, e.g., Feld v. Borkowski, 790 N.W.2d 72 (Iowa 2010) (limited-duty rule applies only to "contact sports"; in such sports, the participants know and understand the inherent risks of injury, including injuries that result from improper execution of an activity contemplated by the sport; issue of fact in the case whether a softball batter who allowed the bat to fly out of his hands, striking the plaintiff who was playing first base, was acting recklessly).

[124] See Hendricks v. Broderick, 284 N.W.2d 209 (Iowa 1979) (decided when Iowa was still using the assumption of risk terminology; no assumption of the risk of another hunter's negligence); Knight v. Jewett, 3 Cal.4th 296, 11 Cal.Rptr. 2d 2, 834 P.2d 696 (1992) (cautioning that the sports rule might not apply to less active sports and pointing out that the reasonable care standard was routinely applied to hunters).

[125] Jagger v. Mohawk Mountain Ski Area, Inc., 269 Conn. 672, 849 A.2d 813 (2004).

[126] Custodi v. Town of Amherst, 20 N.Y.3d 83, 957 N.Y.S.2d 268, 980 N.E.2d 933 (2012) (refusing to extend the application of primary assumption of risk to a case in which the plaintiff fell while rollerblading in her residential neighborhood; to recognize the primary assumption of risk in this case, the court said, "would create an unwarranted diminution of the general duty of landowners—both public and private—to maintain their premises in a reasonably safe condition.").

its foundation in the parties' expectations.[127] The opinions suggest that the duty should be limited because of the danger of a flood of litigation, and because of a supposed policy of encouraging vigorous physical competition.[128] Both these reasons are potentially at odds with the parties' expectations. Where the parties reasonably expect that a game rule will be followed by other players, it would seem that the parties' expectations should control. Ordinary care under the circumstances should be the standard unless the plaintiff has clear notice that she is entitled to lesser protection. Moreover, when a court sets rules about parties' reasonable expectations, it not only reflects those expectations, it generates future expectations. As such, policies regarding care can also be important when deciding whether to limit ordinary care standards.

Rejecting the exculpatory rules. A few courts in recent years have insisted on the ordinary negligence standard for sports participants.[129] Quite possibly that standard would yield the same results in most cases, since reasonable care takes circumstances, including the customs and expectations of the parties, into account.

---

[127] Pfister v. Shusta, 167 Ill.2d 417, 657 N.E.2d 1013, 212 Ill.Dec. 668 (1995) (applying the limited duty rule and rejecting, semble, inquiry into scope of plaintiff's consent in a spontaneous game without rules).

[128] Karas v. Strevell, 227 Ill.2d 440, 884 N.E.2d 122, 318 Ill.Dec. 567 (2008); Gentry v. Craycraft, 101 Ohio St. 3d 141, 802 N.E.2d 1116 (2004) (concern with "open[ing] the floodgates to a myriad of lawsuits involving the backyard games of children"); Kahn v. East Side Union High Sch. Dist., 31 Cal.4th 990, 4 Cal.Rptr.3d 103, 75 P.3d 30 (2003); Leonard v. Behrens, 601 N.W.2d 76 (Iowa 1999); Jaworski v. Kiernan, 241 Conn. 399, 696 A.2d 332 (1997).

[129] Pfenning v. Lineman, 947 N.E.2d 392 (Ind. 2011) (golf, but holding that any limited duty rules for sports participants would violate the statutory comparative fault act); American Powerlifting Ass'n v. Cotillo, 401 Md. 658, 934 A.2d 27 (2007) (powerlifting); Allen v. Dover Co-Recreational Softball League, 148 N.H. 407, 807 A.2d 1274 (2002) (softball); Auckenthaler v. Grundmeyer, 110 Nev. 682, 877 P.2d 1039 (1994) (horse and dog event); Lestina v. West Bend Mut. Ins. Co., 176 Wis.2d 901, 501 N.W.2d 28 (1993) (recreational soccer). But see Stehlik v. Rhoads, 253 Wis.2d 477, 645 N.W.2d 889 (2002) (landowner had no duty to insist on helmet for users of his ATV).

Chapter 18

STATUTES OF LIMITATION
AND FEDERAL PREEMPTION

Analysis

A. STATUTES OF LIMITATION

§ 18.1   Foundational Principles and Rationales
§ 18.2   The Accrual Rule
§ 18.3   The Discovery Rule
§ 18.4   Statutes of Repose
§ 18.5   Continuing Negligence
§ 18.6   Tolling, Grace Periods, and Postponed Accrual
§ 18.7   Accrued Claims with Latent Harm

B. FEDERAL PREEMPTION

§ 18.8   Federal Preemption

A. STATUTES OF LIMITATION

§ 18.1 Foundational Principles and Rationales

Basic information. Statutes of limitation almost invariably prescribe the period of time in which the plaintiff must bring a given kind of claim, and sometimes counterclaim. The structure of statutes of limitation, and the periods they prescribe, vary from state to state and vary as well according to the kind of claim asserted. In negligence cases, statutes often require the plaintiff to commence her action within two or three years. Commencement of the action is defined differently in different systems.[1]

As an affirmative defense. The statute of limitations, in contrast, attempts to state a bright-line rule barring claims within the named class after the period specified in the statute. In most instances, the defendant has the burden of pleading the statute of limitations as a defense and the burden of proving facts that show it has run.[2] If the defendant does not plead the statute in a timely way, the defense is waived.[3]

---

[1]   See N.D. R. Civ. P. 3 (at service of process); Cal. Civ. Proc. Code § 350 (at filing of complaint). The federal approach is under Rules 3 and 4 of the Federal Rules of Civil Procedure.

[2]   Overton v. Grillo, 896 N.E.2d 499 (Ind. 2008); Public Serv. Co. of Okla. v. Allen, 876 P.2d 680 (Okla. 1994). Because the defendant must plead and prove the defense, it cannot be raised by motion to dismiss unless the time bar appears on the face of the complaint or prior pleading by which the plaintiff is bound. Pontier v. Wolfson, 637 So.2d 39 (Fla. Dist. Ct. App. 1994).

[3]   E.g., Reddell v. Johnson, 942 P.2d 200 (Okla. 1997); Feldman v. Gogos, 628 A.2d 103 (D.C. 1993). See also Roe v. Gelineau, 794 A.2d 476 (R.I. 2002) (plaintiff's failure to argue at trial level that statute of limitation was tolled during his minority was a waiver of the issue); Pratcher v. Methodist Healthcare Memphis Hosps., 407 S.W.3d 727 (Tenn. 2013).

Reasons for adopting a limitation system. Courts and writers usually give a variety of reasons for the statute of limitations.[4] Sometimes courts suggest that the plaintiff might have "waived" her claim by her delay in bringing suit,[5] but more often they emphasize justice and process concerns, including those that follow:

(1)   Evidence will deteriorate as memories fade or even become distorted in ways that cannot be convincingly tested, so "stale claims" should be barred.

(2)   Renewal of an ancient grievance in court may initiate more conflicts than it resolves; and in any event society should not use its judicial resources to reignite a conflict that had been quieted by time.

(3)   The defendant, who may not in fact have been a wrongdoer, is entitled at some point in time to peace of mind that comes from knowing the potential conflict has burned out.

(4)   The defendant's ability to manage business or personal affairs is clouded by a potential law suit; for instance, he may be unable to borrow money or make business commitments until claims are resolved; if he does not in fact know of the potential claims, he may make financial commitments that prove disastrous in the light of a late-asserted claim.

(5)   For similar reasons, insurers find it costly to insure against a defendant's liability for an indefinite time into the future; these costs represent real costs to society (in the form of increased premiums for insurance or increased costs of goods); if these costs can reasonably be avoided by requiring a prompt suit, society in general is better off.

(6)   In some cases, stability of transactions or relationships has other important social values; a consent to adoption of a child should not be subject to revocation or attack long after the child has established a relationship with adoptive parents, for example.[6] In greater or lesser degree, the same stability or security interests affect many other potential litigations as well.

(7)   Over time, society's expectations and standards change, sometimes in ways that society itself does not perceive immediately; without a limitation, judges or juries might unjustly impose today's standards on events that took place twenty, thirty, or fifty years ago.

Inflexibility. Although these reasons are convincing, none of them points to any particular time limit. It would be possible to imagine a system in which judges attempt to estimate, in each case, whether the plaintiff had waited too long to bring suit. Other alternatives could include financial disincentives for delayed filings. Part of the value of the statute is that it provides a bright-line rule.[7] Such a rule excludes a suit brought one

---

[4]   An excellent statement of the reasons for statutes of limitations is found in Institute of Law Research and Reform, Limitations (Report Discussion No. 4, Edmonton, 1986).

[5]   E.g., Davis v. Provo City Corp., 193 P.3d 86 (Utah 2008), *quoting* Lee v. Gaufin, 867 P.2d 572 (Utah 1993).

[6]   See In re Joseph B., 258 Ill.App.3d 954, 630 N.E.2d 1180 (1994).

[7]   Laches, the old defense originating in the once-separate equity courts and still applied mainly in cases where equitable relief is sought, was not a bright-line approach to the bar. Laches allowed judges to decide in each case whether the plaintiff had unreasonably delayed in bringing suit and whether the defendant was prejudiced by the delay. See 1 Dan B. Dobbs, Law of Remedies § 2.4(4) (2d ed. 1993). The ordinary statute of limitations approach is not comparable. However, courts occasionally do suggest that the trial court has a

day late as well as a claim that is twenty years old.[8] So, in spite of its value, the application of the statute can seem arbitrary or unjust at times.

Flexibility. Although old claims may be unjust claims, the general policy of courts is to decide cases on their merits; courts, not time, should generally decide whether the claim is unjust or not. Courts infuse a degree of flexibility in applying statutes of limitation, principally but not exclusively by their control over the starting time for the statutory clock and by their control over time-outs or tolling. Sometimes courts can also choose which of several statutes applies to the case. How flexibly a court applies a statute of limitations often depends on the underlying claim and the particular statute of limitations involved.[9]

§ 18.2 The Accrual Rule

Starting the clock: accrual of the claim. The prescriptive period traditionally began—the statutory clock started to run—when the plaintiff's claim accrued. In negligence claims, unlike some others, the claim did not accrue until (a) the defendant had committed a negligent act and (b) it had caused legally cognizable harm.[10]

Act vs. harm. Sometimes, contrary to the rule stated above, courts say that the claim accrues when the defendant commits the negligent act. Special statutes aimed at protecting particular groups may so provide.[11] Such a provision could bar the claim before the plaintiff could sue. If the defendant negligently gives the plaintiff a dangerous medication in January, but it does not cause harm until three years later, a two-year statute that begins to run at the time of the defendant's act rather than at the time of the plaintiff's harm would have run long before the plaintiff had a cause of action. The traditional view avoids that result by holding that the claim accrues when damage is done and the plaintiff can sue.

§ 18.3 The Discovery Rule

Undiscovered injury. Under the accrual rule, the plaintiff's claim was barred unless she commenced suit within the statutory time period, even if she was not aware of either harm or negligence during that period.[12] The problem of undiscovered harm is especially acute when the plaintiff is subjected to toxins that cause harm slowly over long periods

---

range of discretion in determining when the claim accrues in doubtful cases. See Lindsay Mfg. Co. v. Universal Surety Co., 246 Neb. 495, 519 N.W.2d 530 (1994).

[8]   E.g., State v. Johnson, 19 Kan.App.2d 315, 868 P.2d 555 (1994) (one day late); see also, e.g., Williams v. Medical Coll. of Pa., 381 Pa.Super. 418, 554 A.2d 72 (1989) (claim barred where limitations period ended on a Friday and suit was not filed until the following Tuesday).

[9]   John R. Sand & Gravel Co. v. United States, 128 S.Ct. 750, 169 L.Ed.2d 591 (2008).

[10]   Restatement Second of Torts § 899 cmt. c (1979); Stuard v. Jorgenson, 150 Idaho 701, 249 P.3d 1156 (2011) (statute of limitations began to run on the date that the surgeon performed surgery and caused "some damage" that was objectively ascertainable on that date, even though patient had no symptoms or knowledge of the doctor's negligence until over two years later). See also Crosslin v. Health Care Auth. of City of Huntsville, 5 So.3d 1193 (Ala. 2008) (under statute that starts the clock on a statute of repose in medical malpractice cases at the time the act complained of causes "legal injury," a failure to diagnose a tumor was not the legal injury where the tumor later caused him to lose vision in both eyes).

[11]   Herron v. Anigbo, 897 N.E.2d 444 (Ind. 2008) (statutory limitations period for medical malpractice cases, which fixed accrual at the date of the act of malpractice, is unconstitutional if applied to a plaintiff who "despite exercise of reasonable diligence does not learn of the injury or malpractice before the period expires").

[12]   E.g., Shearin v. Lloyd, 246 N.C. 363, 98 S.E.2d 508 (1957).

of time. Accordingly, many modern statutes[13] and case decisions[14] postpone the accrual date until the plaintiff discovers or should discover some of the relevant facts. A few medical malpractice statutes limit the discovery rule to cases in which the defendant surgeon has left a foreign object in the patient's body.[15]

Facts that must be discovered to start the clock. The overriding discovery rule principle is that the statute begins to run when a person of reasonable diligence discovers or should have discovered facts that would show she has a reasonable claim, or facts that would lead a reasonable person to investigate further.[16] A number of decisions, without formulating definitive rules, have specified particular facts that would put the plaintiff on notice to sue or investigate. Given some latitude for differences in the exact wording, the usual idea seems to be that the statute will not begin to run until:

(a)   all the elements of the tort are present; *and*

(b)   the plaintiff discovers, or as a reasonable person should have discovered,

(i)   that she is injured;[17] and

(ii) that the defendant, or the defendant's product or instrumentality, had a causal role in the injury,[18] or that there was enough chance that defendant was connected with the injury to require further investigation that in turn would have revealed the defendant's connection;[19] and

(iii) according to some authority, that the defendant may have been negligent or otherwise legally responsible, or that there was enough chance that defendant was legally responsible that a reasonably diligent person would further investigate the facts showing the defendant's responsibility.[20] Other authority, however, starts the

---

[13]   E.g., 42 U.S.C.A. § 9658 (certain toxic torts cases); Ill. Comp. Stat. Ann. § 13–212 (a).

[14]   United States v. Kubrick, 444 U.S. 111, 100 S.Ct. 352, 62 L.Ed.2d 259 (1979) (Federal Tort Claims Act); Urie v. Thompson, 337 U.S. 163, 69 S.Ct. 1018, 93 L.Ed. 1282, 11 A.L.R.2d 252 (1949); Genereux v. Am. Beryllia Corp., 577 F.3d 350 (1st Cir. 2009) (Mass. law); Gerdau Ameristeel, Inc. v. Ratliff, 368 S.W.3d 503 (Tenn. 2012) (discovery rule applies to workers' compensation claim; claim does not accrue "until a plaintiff discovers or, in the exercise of reasonable diligence, should have discovered that he has a claim").

[15]   A little authority holds this parsimonious use of the discovery rule to be unconstitutional. See Austin v. Litvak, 682 P.2d 41 (Colo. 1984); Frohs v. Greene, 253 Or. 1, 452 P.2d 564 (1969). Where the statutes are constitutional, litigation erupts over what counts as a foreign body. E.g., Meadors v. Still, 344 Ark. 307, 40 S.W.3d 294 (2001) (breast implant not a foreign object). See Sara L. Johnson, Annotation, Medical malpractice: applicability of "foreign object" exception in medical malpractice statutes of limitations, 50 A.L.R.4th 250 (1987).

[16]   E.g., Fox v. Ethicon Endo-Surgery, Inc., 35 Cal.4th 797, 27 Cal.Rptr.3d 661, 110 P.3d 914 (2005); Barrett v. Montesano, 269 Conn. 787, 849 A.2d 839 (2004).

[17]   Barnes v. Koppers, 534 F.3d 357 (5th Cir. 2008); Murtha v. Cahalan, 745 N.W.2d 711 (Iowa 2008); Aebischer v. Stryker Corp., 535 F.3d 732 (7th Cir. 2008). Some courts have also said that discovery of temporary injury is not enough to start the statute if in fact the injury is permanent. Schiele v. Hobart Corp., 284 Or. 483, 587 P.2d 1010 (1978).

[18]   See Rathje v. Mercy Hosp., 745 N.W.2d 443 (Iowa 2008) (citing cases from many jurisdictions, stressing that knowledge or imputed knowledge of "both the injury and its cause in fact" are necessary "to put a reasonably diligent plaintiff on notice to investigate" who actually caused the harm); Harrinton v. Costello, 7 N.E.3d 449 (Mass. 2014).

[19]   E.g., T.R. v. Boy Scouts of Am., 344 Or. 282, 181 P.3d 758 (2008); Rathje v. Mercy Hosp., 745 N.W.2d 443 (Iowa 2008); Colosimo v. Roman Catholic Bishop of Salt Lake City, 156 P.3d 806 (Utah 2007); Grunwald v. Bronkesh, 131 N.J. 483, 621 A.2d 459 (1993); Schiele v. Hobart Corp., 284 Or. 483, 587 P.2d 1010 (1978).

[20]   McRae v. Group Health Plan, Inc., 753 N.W.2d 711 (Minn. 2008). See also Norgard v. Brushwellman, Inc., 95 Ohio St.3d 165, 766 N.E.2d 977 (2002) ("when the employee discovers, or by the exercise of reasonable

statute running upon discovery of injury and causation without
discovery of facts suggesting the defendant's fault.[21]

Discovery of facts and consequences. Some cases emphasize that the discovery rule
does not depend upon discovery of legal rights as distinct from discovery of facts; if the
plaintiff discovers the facts, her ignorance of legal rules that give her a claim has no
effect to postpone running of the statute.[22] Perhaps less debatably, courts have also said
that the rule does not depend upon discovery of all the consequences of the injury or the
full extent of damages.[23] If the plaintiff discovers the injury and its connection to the
defendant, the statute begins to run even if some of its injurious consequences are not
discovered until much later.[24] However, if the plaintiff suffered two distinct injuries,
discovery of one does not start the statute running on the other.[25]

Not discovering defendant's connection. If the plaintiff reasonably believes the
injury is not caused by the defendant, and is not chargeable with knowledge of the
defendant's identity, mere knowledge of the injury alone is not enough to start the
clock.[26] But case law[27] or statutory language may dictate a different result.[28]

---

diligence should have discovered, the workplace injury and the wrongful conduct of the employer"); Anthony
v. Abbott Labs., 490 A.2d 43 (R.I. 1985) (prescription drug products liability action); Caravaggio v. D'Agostini,
166 N.J. 237, 765 A.2d 182 (2001) (medical malpractice claim; plaintiff knew of her injury and possible fault of
medical device manufacturer, but had no knowledge that her surgeon might have been negligent).

[21] See Poole v. Coakley & Williams Constr., Inc., 423 Md. 91, 31 A.3d 212 (2011) (statute of limitations
accrued on the date that plaintiff fell on black ice, which gave him sufficient notice of the "nature and cause of
his injury"; he was thus under a duty "to acquire the identities of all potential defendants before the running
of the limitations period").

[22] See United States v. Kubrick, 444 U.S. 111, 100 S.Ct. 352, 62 L.Ed.2d 259 (1979); Jolly v. Eli Lilly &
Co., 44 Cal.3d 1103, 751 P.2d 923, 245 Cal.Rptr. 658 (1988).

[23] E.g., Larson & Larson, P.A. v. TSE Indus., Inc., 22 So.3d 36 (Fla. 2009).

[24] In re World Trade Ctr. Lower Manhattan Disaster Site Litig., 758 F.3d 202 (2d Cir. 2014) (under
New York law, only the discovery of manifestations or symptoms of the latent disease is required for accrual
of a claim based on exposure to toxins); Moll v. Abbott Labs., 444 Mich. 1, 506 N.W.2d 816 (1993); Highland
Indus. Park, Inc. v. BEI Defense Sys. Co., 357 F.3d 794 (8th Cir. 2004) ("[W]e know of no state whatever in
which an injured party must know the full extent of damages that it may recover before the statute of
limitations begins to run on its claim.").

[25] See Larson v. Johns-Manville Sales Corp., 427 Mich. 301, 399 N.W.2d 1 (1987); Grisham v. Philip
Morris U.S.A., Inc., 40 Cal.4th 623, 151 P.3d 1151, 54 Cal.Rptr.3d 735 (2007) (cause of action based on personal
injury accrued when plaintiff discovered her tobacco-related illness, not earlier when she discovered her
economic injury).

[26] Winbun v. Moore, 143 Wash.2d 206, 18 P.3d 576 (2001); Harris v. Jones, 209 W.Va. 557, 550 S.E.2d
93 (2001) (quoting earlier authority, when the plaintiff knows or should know injury, wrongdoer's identity, and
causal relation).

[27] See, e.g., Rathje v. Mercy Hosp., 745 N.W.2d 443 (Iowa 2008) (medical malpractice statute begins to
run when the patient knew or should have known of the injury, even though the patient did not know that the
physician had negligently caused the injury); Lincoln Elec. Co. v. McLemore, 54 So. 3d 833 (Miss. 2010) ("a
plaintiff's cause of action accrues at the point at which he discovered, or by reasonable diligence should have
discovered, the injury" and "knowledge of the cause of an injury is irrelevant to the analysis," relying on Angle
v. Koppers, Inc., 42 So.3d 1, 70 Env't. Rep. Cas. (BNA) 1910 (Miss. 2010)).

[28] Jolly v. Eli Lilly & Co., 44 Cal.3d 1103, 751 P.2d 923, 245 Cal.Rptr. 658 (1988) (general rule is that
"ignorance of the identity of the defendant does not affect the statute of limitations"); Fuller v. Tucker, 84
Cal.App.4th 1163, 101 Cal.Rptr.2d 776 (2000) (noting that the statute of limitations in such a situation can be
effectively met by filing a Doe complaint and amending to include the named defendant when he is identified);
Rawlinson v. Cheyenne Bd. of Pub. Utils., 17 P.3d 13 (Wyo. 2001); see also Moriarty v. Garden Sanctuary
Church of God, 341 S.C. 320, 534 S.E.2d 672 (2000).

Statutory provisions. The governing statute of limitations may itself determine what must be discovered.[29] For instance, a Massachusetts environmental statute starts the limitations period running when the plaintiff discovers or should have discovered that the defendant "is a person liable"—seemingly a rule that does not start the clock on discovery of damage alone.[30] Mississippi has a statute of limitations specifically for actions involving "latent injury or disease" that begins the clock when "the plaintiff has discovered, or by reasonable diligence, should have discovered, the injury."[31]

Issues of fact. When reasonable people may differ as to whether or when the plaintiff actually discovered relevant facts or should have discovered them, the question may be left to the jury to determine.[32] In that kind of case, the statute of limitations defense is not a threshold defense at all, but instead is tried along with the merits of the case. There are, however, a number of cases in which the undisputed facts allow the court to say as a matter of law that the plaintiff actually discovered the relevant facts or that reasonable people could only conclude that she should have done so.[33]

An objective test. The "should have discovered" portion of the rule is important. The test seems to be objective, that is, what a reasonable person in the plaintiff's position would have discovered.[34] That is, if known facts would lead a reasonable person to investigate, the statute will begin to run when such an investigation would have led to discovery of injury and its cause, unless the plaintiff is for some reason relieved of the duty to investigate.[35]

§ 18.4 Statutes of Repose

Statutes of ultimate repose. Statutes of ultimate repose provide a counter-rule to the accrual-discovery rule by adding an alternative prescriptive period which begins running at the time of the defendant's act rather than at the time harm was inflicted or discovered. For example, the traditional accrual statute might provide that suits must be brought within three years from the time harm occurred or should have been discovered. The repose statute might add that in no event can suits be commenced more than ten years after the defendant's negligent act. In the case of injury by a manufactured product, the repose statute might provide that suit must be brought no more than ten years after the product was sold by the defendant.[36] In such a case, the

---

[29]   Libby v. Eighth Judicial Dist. Court, 325 P.3d 1276 (Nev. 2014) (applying medical malpractice statute).

[30]   See Taygeta Corp. v. Varian Assocs., Inc., 436 Mass. 217, 763 N.E.2d 1053 (2002).

[31]   Miss. Code Ann. § 15–1–49(2) (Rev. 2003); Phillips 66 Co. v. Lofton, 94 So. 3d 1051 (Miss. 2012).

[32]   E.g., Wilson v. El-Daief, 600 Pa. 161, 964 A.2d 354 (2009); Herron v. Anigbo, 897 N.E.2d 444 (Ind. 2008); Huss v. Gayden, 991 So.2d 162 (Miss. 2008); Mohr v. Commonwealth, 421 Mass. 147, 653 N.E.2d 1104 (1995).

[33]   E.g., Alaface v. National Inv. Co., 181 Ariz. 586, 892 P.2d 1375 (Ct. App. 1994); Ridenour v. Boehringer Ingelheim Pharms., Inc., 679 F.3d 1062, Prod. Liab. Rep. (CCH) P 18854 (8th Cir. 2012) (holding that as a matter of law plaintiff's cause of action accrued when he saw a television advertisement that suggested a link between the defendant's drug and the symptoms plaintiff was exhibiting).

[34]   Hanson v. Singsen, 898 A.2d 1244 (R.I. 2006) (medical malpractice case); see also BASF Corp. v. Symington, 512 N.W.2d 692 (N.D. 1994) (test is objective even if the plaintiff is mentally disabled).

[35]   Taygeta Corp. v. Varian Assocs., Inc., 436 Mass. 217, 763 N.E.2d 1053 (2002) (environmental damage statute put burden wholly upon defendant to notify neighbors of contamination, so neighbor, though put on suspicion, had no duty to investigate possible contamination of its land).

[36]   E.g., Conn. Gen. Stat. § 52–577a (10 years from date defendant parted with possession of the product); 735 Ill. Comp. Stat. 5/13–213(b) (12 years from first sale or 10 years from sale to first purchaser,

plaintiff gets the benefit of the accrual and discovery rules, but only during the first ten years after the defendant sold the product.

Affected groups. These statutes, usually considered to be a part of the "tort reform" legislation of the 1970s and 1980s,[37] were constructed for the protection of particular groups that have lobbied for them,[38] notably products manufacturers, architects and builders, health care professionals, and governmental entities.[39] Until the middle of the twentieth century or even later, all these groups enjoyed the protection of special substantive rules or practices, such as the privity rule that protected manufacturers and builders. So to some extent, the statutes of repose substitute some new special protections that courts had removed.

Trigger dates. In the case of architects, engineers, and builders on real property, the trigger date for starting the repose period is usually the date on which the improvements on real property were "completed."[40] Health care providers' repose statutes begin to run with the doctor's last act or completion of the treatment, even if harm does not occur or become apparent until later.[41] Government entities often benefit from special notice-of-claim statutes requiring the plaintiff to assert a claim administratively or give notice of the claim within a relatively short time of its accrual.[42]

Construction of statutes. Statutes of repose require judicial construction of their operative terms, just as any other statutes do. For example, statutes of repose that trigger accrual in property-improvement cases at the date of substantial completion of an improvement have spawned litigation over what counts as substantial completion and what counts as an improvement.[43] The medical malpractice statutes likewise require construction to determine whether the claim is a malpractice claim or not. For instance,

---

whichever is shorter, in strict product liability actions), held unconstitutional as not severable in Best v. Taylor Mach. Works, 179 Ill.2d 367, 689 N.E.2d 1057 (1997).

[37] Some rules of ultimate repose antedated the tort reform era. See Collins v. Scenic Homes, Inc., 38 So.3d 28 (Ala. 2009) (reviewing history of Alabama common-law rule establishing a 20-year "rule of repose" for all claims, dating to 1888); Owens-Illinois, Inc. v. Wells, 50 So.3d 413 (Ala. 2010) (holding that a claim does not accrue under the 20-year statute of repose until the plaintiff suffers some "manifest present injury," so that plaintiffs were not barred by the statute when they sued more than 20 years after exposure to asbestos manufactured by defendant).

[38] See Irish v. Gimbel, 691 A.2d 664 (Me. 1997) (plaintiff's counsel could properly cross-examine defendant's expert medical witness about his lobbying efforts for tort reform); In re Dow Corning Corp., 142 F.3d 433 (6th Cir. 1998) (unpublished) (lawyers for plaintiffs pursuing defendant who was in bankruptcy were not authorized to lobby to counter defendant's lobbying efforts).

[39] E.g., Noll v. Harrisburg Area YMCA, 537 Pa. 274, 643 A.2d 81 (1994) (statute protecting improvers of real property); Whitlow v. Board of Educ. of Kanawha County, 190 W.Va. 223, 438 S.E.2d 15 (1993) (but holding the preference for governmental defendants to be unconstitutional as applied to claims of minors).

[40] E.g., Cal. Civ. Proc. Code § 337.15 (10 years after the substantial completion of the development or improvement); Vernon's Ann. Mo. Stat. § 516.097 (10 years after improvement is completed); 42 Pa. Cons. Stat. Ann. § 5536 (12 years after completion of construction or improvement); Horning v. Penrose Plumbing & Heating Inc., 336 P.3d 151 (Wyo. 2014); cf. Ala. Code § 6–5–221 (13 years after action accrued or would have accrued).

[41] See Fla. Stat. Ann. § 95.11 (4); Mich. Comp. L. Ann. § 600.5838a; Vernon's Ann. Mo. Stat. § 516.105.

[42] E.g., Rev. Code Wash. § 4.92.110.

[43] Noll v. Harrisburg Area YMCA, 537 Pa. 274, 643 A.2d 81 (1994) (with chattels added, permanent addition is the test, taking into account the law of fixtures plus objective intent of parties controls; easily removable diving blocks were not fixtures, hence not covered by the statute). See William D. Bremer, Annotation, What Constitutes "Improvement to Real Property" for Purposes of Statute of Repose or Statute of Limitations, 122 A.L.R.5th 1 (2004).

some courts confer the protections of the malpractice repose statutes upon suppliers of allegedly defective blood products,[44] while other courts do not.[45]

Statute of repose effects. When a statute of repose governs the case, the plaintiff might be barred before she discovers her injury. Beyond that, the plaintiff might be barred before any harm at all has occurred.[46] For instance, if the statue of repose uses a twelve-year period of time and the plaintiff suffers injury from a product that was sold in defective condition thirteen years earlier, the statute of repose would have barred her claim a year before she was injured at all. This was never possible under the traditional statute of limitations.

Extreme cases. A particularly stringent form of "repose" bars a young minor's claim before majority and possibly before the claim accrues.[47] Other extraordinary effects are using the repose statute to bar a medical malpractice claim even if the claim was fraudulently concealed by the surgeon-defendant.[48] And protecting a defendant products manufacturer whose failure to correct a defect might seem to be a continuing tort.[49]

Constitutional challenges. Some decided cases have upheld the constitutionality of statutes of repose against attacks by adult plaintiffs based on the claim that the statutes violate due process, equal protection, or state constitutional guarantees.[50] A different and substantial group of jurists have roundly condemned the statutes for barring the claim before it accrues.[51] A number of courts have held some version of the statutes to

---

[44]   Smith v. Paslode Corp., 7 F.3d 116 (8th Cir. 1993) (Red Cross was health care provider for statute of limitations purposes); Bradway v. American Nat'l Red Cross, 263 Ga. 19, 426 S.E.2d 849 (1993).

[45]   Silva v. Southwest Fla. Blood Bank, Inc., 601 So.2d 1184 (Fla. 1992) (supplier of blood contaminated with HIV virus was not engaged in diagnosis, treatment, or care and hence did not get the protection of the medical statute); Swanigan v. American Nat'l Red Cross, 313 S.C. 416, 438 S.E.2d 251 (1993); Doe v. American Nat'l Red Cross, 176 Wis.2d 610, 500 N.W.2d 264 (1993).

[46]   See Blazevska v. Raytheon Aircraft Co., 522 F.3d 948 (9th Cir. 2008) (18-year statute of repose of the General Aviation Revitalization Act of 1994 bars products liability claims by survivors of passengers killed in airplane crash); Land v. Yamaha Motor Corp., 272 F.3d 514 (7th Cir. 2001) (boat known to be dangerous by its manufacturer exploded more than ten years after delivery to consumer, ten year repose statute barred claim; the claim was not resuscitated by a post-sale failure to warn).

[47]   E.g., Kaminer v. Canas, 282 Ga. 830, 653 S.E.2d 691 (2007) (applying statute to bar child's claim for negligent misdiagnosis of AIDS). Some courts have struck down such statutes on state constitutional grounds. See, e.g., Sands ex rel. Sands v. Green, 156 P.3d 1130 (Alaska 2007) (statute that tolled statute of limitations for personal injury claims by minors injured before their eighth birthdays only until they reached the age of eight violated due process rights); Lee v. Gaufin, 867 P.2d 572 (Utah 1993) (statute that treated minor medical malpractice victims differently violated state constitution).

[48]   Horn v. Citizens Hosp., 425 So.2d 1065 (Ala. 1982).

[49]   See Spilker v. City of Lincoln, 238 Neb. 188, 469 N.W.2d 546 (1991) (Westinghouse sold electrical switchgear with an instruction book that directed workers making a repair to use a specified receptacle, an action that in fact would subject the victim to high voltage burns and ultimate death; the product and deadly instruction had been delivered 22 years earlier, so the statute barred the claim). Whether the manufacturer's failure to correct a deadly instruction is a continuing tort would depend upon whether the manufacturer was under a duty to give a post-sale warning. See Patton v. Hutchinson Wil-Rich Mfg. Co., 253 Kan. 741, 861 P.2d 1299 (1993).

[50]   E.g., Yarbro v. Hilton Hotels Corp., 655 P.2d 822 (Colo. 1982) (equal protection, due process, and state constitutional attacks); Zapata v. Burns, 207 Conn. 496, 542 A.2d 700 (1988) (equal protection); Harlfinger v. Martin, 435 Mass. 38, 754 N.E.2d 63 (2001) (though it cuts off rights of minors, statute does not violate either due process or equal protection rights; rational basis test); 1518–1525 Lakeview Blvd. Condo. Ass'n v. Apartment Sales Corp., 144 Wash.2d 570, 29 P.3d 1249 (2001) (violates neither equal protection nor state access to courts provisions); Josephine Herring Hicks, The Constitutionality of Statutes of Repose: Federalism Reigns, 38 Vand. L. Rev. 627 (1985).

[51]   "Except in topsy-turvy land you can't die before you are conceived, or be divorced before ever you marry, or harvest a crop never planted, or burn down a house never built, or miss a train running on a non-existent railroad. For substantially similar reasons, it has always heretofore been accepted, as a sort of legal

be unconstitutional, frequently under state constitutional provisions that require open courts or that guarantee a remedy.[52] Professor McGovern found no less than 17 different types of state constitutional provisions involved in the constitutional arguments.[53] Some of the major arguments included these elements: (1) Victims of the statute's preferred defendants are treated differently from victims of other defendants. (2) The repose statute denies due process of law by a rule that potentially bars a claim before it arises. (3) The statutes are designed to provide a benefit to one group at the expense of another. They benefit the preferred defendants by reducing their exposure to liability and thus indirectly reducing their insurance costs. Similarly they may benefit the public by reducing costs of services or goods from the preferred defendants. Yet these benefits are not paid for by those who receive them, but by their victims. (4) The statutes deny a remedy to one who has suffered a wrong or close the doors of courts in violation of a state constitutional provision.

Minors. When the statutes seek to abrogate the rights of minors for the benefit of the preferred defendants, courts have frequently found the statutes to be unconstitutional on the ground that they denied equal protection or analogous provisions of state constitutions.[54]

§ 18.5   Continuing Negligence

Defendant's continuing acts. When the defendant's act rather than the plaintiff's discovery starts the statute running, the defendant's continuing intentional harms[55] or continuing negligence presents a difficult problem. His continuing failure to act can be even more puzzling. For example, suppose that the defendant, by polluting ground water or air, subjects the plaintiff to toxic exposures every day over a long period of time. His original act of dumping toxic materials may have been completed long ago, but in a sense he continues to be at fault because he could clean up the pollution at any time, as recently as yesterday.

'axiom,' that a statute of limitations does not begin to run against a cause of action before that cause of action exists, i.e., before a judicial remedy is available to the plaintiff." Dincher v. Marlin Firearms Co., 198 F.2d 821, 823 (2d Cir. 1952) (Frank, J., dissenting). Another locution of some popularity is that the legislatures that pass such statutes are attempting "to declare the bread stale before it is baked." See Moll v. Abbott Labs., 444 Mich. 1, 506 N.W.2d 816 (1993), *quoting* Fleishman v. Eli Lilly & Co., 96 A.D.2d 825, 826, 465 N.Y.S.2d 735 (1983) (Gibbons, J., concurring in part and dissenting in part).

[52] E.g., Hazine v. Montgomery Elevator Co., 176 Ariz. 340, 861 P.2d 625 (1993); Perkins v. Northeastern Log Homes, 808 S.W.2d 809 (Ky. 1991); Horton v. Goldminer's Daughter, 785 P.2d 1087 (Utah 1989); cf. DeYoung v. Providence Med. Ctr., 136 Wash.2d 136, 960 P.2d 919 (1998) (statute provided privileges not equally available to all and was not rationally related to purpose); Turner Constr. Co. v. Scales, 752 P.2d 467 (Alaska 1988) (equal protection). The legislature's reiteration of a repose statute already declared unconstitutional was firmly rejected in State ex rel. Ohio Academy of Trial Lawyers v. Sheward, 86 Ohio St.3d 451, 715 N.E.2d 1062 (1999).

[53] See Francis E. McGovern, The Variety, Policy and Constitutionality of Product Liability Statutes of Repose, 30 Am. U. L. Rev. 579, 600 ff. (1981).

[54] See Green v. Lewis Truck Lines, 433 S.E.2d 844 (S.C. 1993); Lee v. Gaufin, 867 P.2d 572 (Utah 1993); Whitlow v. Board of Educ. of Kanawha County, 190 W.Va. 223, 438 S.E.2d 15 (1993); but cf., Kumar v. Hall, 262 Ga. 639, 423 S.E.2d 653 (1992) (comatose, brain damaged person had no "standing" to assert unconstitutionality of repose statute because he was in fact represented by a guardian).

[55] See Feltmeier v. Feltmeier, 207 Ill.2d 263, 798 N.E.2d 75 (2003) (former husband's infliction of emotional distress by a pattern of repeated abuse over eleven years of marriage constituted one large continuing tort, so that the statute of limitations did not begin to run until after the last act of abuse or last injury suffered, which occurred after dissolution of the marriage); Pugiese v. Superior Court, 146 Cal.App.4th 1444, 53 Cal.Rptr.3d 681 (2007).

Continuing relationship. A different example involves a relationship between plaintiff and defendant, with the added possibility here that the statute should not begin to run before the relationship is terminated, at least as it relates to the particular condition or problem at hand.[56] The case of the physician who negligently fails to diagnose or treat the patient is in this category, as are legal malpractice cases[57] and perhaps any others in which the defendant is a professional in whom the plaintiff has placed her trust.[58] As long as the patient remains in his care, she could reasonably expect a correction of the diagnosis or treatment, so again, the defendant in a sense continues to be negligent. In such cases it is sometimes possible to say that the statute should not begin to run until the negligent conduct has ceased. Fairness dictates that the statute should be tolled until the relationship with respect to the particular ailment or problem is terminated, but it does not suggest that termination itself should start the statute running when the plaintiff does not and could not discover the injury until some time after termination.

Major variables. At least two variables seem important. First, the continuing negligence might produce either a series of separately identifiable harms or it might produce only a single indivisible injury. Second, defendants may owe a duty to take affirmative steps to minimize harm to the plaintiff or they may not. When the defendant owes a duty to the plaintiff to act affirmatively and fails to do so, and when that failure produces a single harm, or a series of harms that cannot be segregated one from another, the defendant's negligence is continuing and the statute does not begin to run until some definitive event occurs.[59] What counts as continuing medical treatment or continuing medical negligence is a particularly important issue in the medical liability context.[60]

§ 18.6   Tolling, Grace Periods, and Postponed Accrual

Grounds for tolling or time-out. In the case of a true statute of limitations, the statute is tolled or under certain conditions stated in the statute itself or judicially imposed by courts. Typically the statute is tolled because of some impediment to the plaintiff's pursuit of her claim—she is a minor;[61] she is mentally disabled;[62] she is in

---

[56]   See Zielinski v. Kotsoris, 279 Conn. 312, 901 A.2d 1207 (2006) (continuous treatment rule may be invoked where treatment for a "particular injury or malady" continues); Watkins v. Fromm, 108 A.D.2d 233, 488 N.Y.S.2d 768 (1985) (continuous "treatment doctrine applies only to treatment for the same or related illnesses or injuries" rather than to the "mere continuity of a general physician-patient relationship").

[57]   Legal malpractice cases usually say that the continuous representation ends for statute of limitations purposes at the end of the lawyer's representation of the client on the particular matter that is the subject of the malpractice claim. E.g., Shumsky v. Eisenstein, 96 N.Y.2d 164, 726 N.Y.S.2d 365, 750 N.E.2d 67 (2001).

[58]   See Williamson ex rel. Lipper Convertibles, L.P. v. PriceWaterhouse Coopers LLP, 9 N.Y.3d 1, 840 N.Y.S. 730 (2007) (noting that "continuous representation doctrine" applies to all such cases, but declining to apply it on the facts of the particular accountant-malpractice case before the court).

[59]   Alston v. Hormel Foods Corp., 273 Neb. 422, 730 N.W.2d 376 (2007) (applying "continuing tort" rule to a claim by an employee against an employer for failing to provide a safe workplace over a long period of time); John Doe 1 v. Archdiocese of Milwaukee, 303 Wis.2d 34, 734 N.W.2d 827 (2007) (holding that claims of negligent supervision of an abusive priest accrued on the date of the last incident in a series of sexual molestations); Page v. United States, 729 F.2d 818, 822–23 ("To us it seems unrealistic to regard each prescription of drugs as the cause of a separate injury, or as a separate tortious act triggering a new limitation period."); Meadows v. Union Carbide Corp., 710 F.Supp. 1163 (N.D. Ill. 1989).

[60]   1 Dobbs, Hayden & Bublick, The Law of Torts § 245 (2d ed. 2011 & Supp.).

[61]   E.g., N.Y. C.P.L.R. § 208; Kordus v. Montes, 337 P.3d 1138 (Wyo. 2014) (unconstitutional to apply two-year statute of limitations to case of a minor patient who lacks capacity to sue).

[62]   E.g., Va. Code § 8.01-229. Courts emphasize that practical ability to manage one's affairs precludes a finding of mental disability or "unsound mind." E.g., Sherrill v. Souder, 325 S.W.3d 584 (Tenn. 2010); Ellis v. Estate of Ellis, 169 P.3d 441 (Utah 2007) (tolling for mental incompetency is designed to "relieve from the

prison[63] or in the armed forces;[64] some other suit or claim is pending on the same subject matter;[65] or she was compelled to use part of the period in an administrative proceeding as a prerequisite to suit.[66]

Postponed accrual. Another form of the general idea is that courts might postpone accrual of the claim or the start of the prescriptive period. For example, a number of courts say they postpone accrual of the claim by a client against a lawyer until the termination of the lawyer's representation of the client on the matter at issue.[67]

Contemporary statutory schemes. Legislatures have now written complex tolling statutes in line with the statutes of repose. Many limitations are severe and include one or more of these provisions:

(1) Tolling for some disabilities may be eliminated altogether. For example, Michigan provides that for medical malpractice injuries to the reproductive system of a child under thirteen years of age, suit must be brought before the child's fifteenth birthday.[68] But in some states, the traditional tolling for minority is a protected constitutional right, so that a minor's claim accrues only when she reaches majority.[69]

(2) Instead of truly tolling the statute of limitations, legislatures may now afford the plaintiff only a short grace period for suit after her disability has terminated. Instead of having two or three years in which to bring suit as provided under a basic limitation period, the minor plaintiff may be allowed only six months or a year to sue after reaching majority.[70]

(3) Legislatures have now sometimes provided that there is an outerlimit to tolling just as there is an outer limit to the discovery rule.[71] That means that plaintiffs who suffer injury as very young minors might be barred by the outer-limit or repose provision long before they reach maturity.[72]

---

strict time restrictions people who are unable to protect their legal rights because of an overall inability to function in society").

[63]   Ala. Code § 6–2–8; 12 Vt. Stat. Ann. § 551 (a) (at the time the cause of action accrues).

[64]   50 App. U.S.C.A. § 526.

[65]   Norris v. Bell Helicopter-Textron, Inc., 712 F.2d 171 (5th Cir. 1983); Stevens v. Novartis Pharms. Corp., 358 Mont. 474, 247 P.3d 244, Prod. Liab. Rep. (CCH) P 18553 (2010), cert. denied, 131 S. Ct. 2938, 180 L. Ed. 2d 226 (2011) (statute of limitations on patient's failure to warn case against drug manufacturer was tolled by the filing of a separate class action suit by others alleging the same defect).

[66]   New Hampshire Div. of Human Servs. v. Allard, 138 N.H. 604, 644 A.2d 70 (1994).

[67]   Black v. Power, 955 A.2d 712 (D.C. 2008); Shipman v. Kruck, 593 S.E.2d 319 (Va. 2004); Shumsky v. Eisenstein, 96 N.Y.2d 164, 726 N.Y.S.2d 365, 750 N.E.2d 67 (2001); Murphy v. Smith, 411 Mass. 133, 579 N.E.2d 165 (1991); Bjorgen v. Kinsey, 466 N.W.2d 553 (N.D. 1991); Neilsen v. Beck, 157 Cal.App.4th 1041, 69 Cal.Rptr.3d 435 (2007).

[68]   Mich. Comp. L. Ann. § 600.5851(8).

[69]   Piselli v. 75th St. Med., 371 Md. 188, 808 A.2d 508 (Md. 2002).

[70]   See Mich. Comp. L. Ann. § 600.5851(1).

[71]   E.g., S.D.C.L. § 15–2–22 (limiting tolling to a maximum of five years, or "no longer than one year after the disability ceases").

[72]   Oregon's statute of limitations for medical negligence actions extends the usual two-year period by five years if the plaintiff is a child, and provides that the claim accrues on the date of medical treatment. Thus a child injured as an infant will have to sue before reaching age six, even where the parents have no reason to suspect negligence. Christiansen v. Providence Health Sys. of Or. Corp., 344 Or. 445, 184 P.3d 1121 (2008) (barring a claim on this ground, and upholding the statute against constitutional attack). In Barrio v. San Manuel Div. Hosp. For Magma Copper Co., 143 Ariz. 101, 692 P. 2d 280 (1984), a statute barred small children

(4) Legislatures have sometimes set up tolling-repose rules that vary, depending upon the point in the tolling period when injury is inflicted or discovered. For instance, Michigan's provision for reproductive injury to children by medical malpractice provides that for younger minors, suit must be brought no later than before the fifteenth birthday, while for older minors suffering the same injury, the general malpractice statute applies.[73]

Tolling rules have thus become quite complex. Within whatever constitutional constraints courts are willing to impose, legislatures are free to limit tolling as they wish, so statutes of individual states must be consulted.

Judicial or "equitable" tolling. Courts can impose tolling rules of their own if they are not in conflict with the statutory rules.[74] Where the statute itself specifies exclusive grounds for tolling, however, courts must apply it absent some constitutional infirmity.[75] Due process or equal protection principles may indeed require the court to impose a tolling rule when the statute fails to provide one.[76] In particular cases, courts may also allow the plaintiff to pursue an untimely claim based on misrepresentations by the defendant.[77] In such cases courts may say that the defendant is estopped to plead the statute of limitations defense. Estoppel applies only if the plaintiff delayed filing suit in reliance upon the defendant's acts or representations.[78] Even without an estoppel, however, courts may decide that, as a matter of equity, the statute should be tolled because of the defendant's unfair conduct that prejudiced the plaintiff's timely suit,[79] or for other equitable reasons.[80]

Fraudulent concealment. The defendant's fraudulent concealment of facts that would reveal plaintiff's injury or her rights can provide grounds for equitable tolling of the statute[81] or can be viewed as merely an appealing instance for treating the claim as accruing upon discovery.[82] Either way, if established, the concealment will extend the plaintiff's time for bringing suit.[83] If fraudulent concealment is viewed as an independent ground for tolling the statute, some courts say the plaintiff must ordinarily prove

from suits for medical malpractice by the time they were ten years old. This was held unconstitutional under a state constitutional provision.

[73] Mich. Comp. L. Ann. § 600.5851(8).

[74] But see Casey v. Merck & Co., Inc., 283 Va. 411, 722 S.E.2d 842, Prod. Liab. Rep. (CCH) P 18788 (2012) (court may not toll a statute of limitations in the absence of a clear statutory enactment to that effect).

[75] Larson & Larson, P.A. v. TSE Indus., Inc., 22 So.3d 36 (Fla. 2009).

[76] Adamsky v. Buckeye Local Sch. Dist., 73 Ohio St. 3d 360, 653 N.E.2d 212 (1995), held that a two year statute of limitations with no tolling provision discriminated against minors and in so doing violated the state's equal protection provision.

[77] E.g., Brown Transp. Corp. v. James, 243 Ga. 701, 257 S.E.2d 242 (1979); Hagen v. Faherty, 133 N.M. 605, 66 P.3d 974 (Ct. App. 2003).

[78] E.g., DeLuna v. Burciaga, 223 Ill.2d 49, 306 Ill.Dec. 136, 857 N.E.2d 229 (2006); Stalberg v. Western Title Ins. Co., 27 Cal.App.4th 925, 32 Cal.Rptr.2d 750 (1994); Redwing v. Catholic Bishop for Diocese of Memphis, 363 S.W.3d 436 (Tenn. 2012).

[79] Thus in Bowen v. City of New York, 476 U.S. 467, 106 S.Ct. 2022, 90 L.Ed.2d 462 (1986), a federal limitation period was tolled because the very policy being attacked by the class-action plaintiffs had been a secret policy as well as an illegal one.

[80] See Stalberg v. Western Title Ins. Co., 27 Cal.App.4th 925, 32 Cal.Rptr.2d 750 (1994).

[81] See Bowen v. City of New York, 476 U.S. 467, 106 S.Ct. 2022, 90 L.Ed.2d 462 (1986); Emberton v. GMRI, Inc., 299 S.W.3d 565 (Ky. 2009); Florida Dep't of Health & Rehab. Servs. v. S.A.P., 835 So.2d 1091 (Fla. 2002); Doe v. Bishop of Charleston, 754 S.E.2d 494 (S.C. 2014); Detwiler v. Bristol-Myers Squibb Co., 884 F.Supp. 117 (S.D.N.Y. 1995).

[82] Erdelyi v. Lott, 326 P.3d 165 (Wyo. 2014).

[83] See Walk v. Ring, 202 Ariz. 310, 44 P.3d 990 (2002); Woods v. Schmitt, 439 N.W.2d 855 (Iowa 1989).

affirmative acts other than the original negligence itself.[84] Many courts appear to require that the act of concealment be "active," such as by making an actual misrepresentation of fact as opposed to simply remaining silent.[85] However, if the defendant is regarded as a fiduciary, as might be the case if the defendant is the plaintiff's physician, a knowing nondisclosure might count as concealment that postpones the statute of limitations.[86]

Childhood sexual abuse: statutes. A number of claims raise limitations questions concerning childhood sexual abuse. Suit has been delayed so long in these cases that the tolling provisions for minors are often of no aid to the plaintiff. Consequently, nothing else appearing, such suits are dismissed on orthodox grounds.[87] However, when the plaintiff has repressed memories of abuse, some courts have held that the discovery rule could be applied,[88] provided the proven facts warranted it.[89] A number of states have now enacted statutes addressed to delayed claims of childhood sexual abuse, permitting the victim to sue within a specified time after "discovery" of the abuse or the injury or emotional condition resulting from it.[90]

§ 18.7   Accrued Claims with Latent Harm

Present injuries that also threaten future harm. When the defendant negligently causes small harm to the plaintiff—say through exposure to a toxin or failure to make a timely diagnosis that results in immediate harm—the statute of limitations is a potential problem. The plaintiff must sue within the statutory period for the small harm done and also (under rules against splitting a cause of action) for all future harm.[91] The trouble is that the plaintiff may be unable to show a likelihood of future damages. If she sues at

---

[84] Langner v. Simpson, 533 N.W.2d 511 (Iowa 1995); Redwing v. Catholic Bishop for Diocese of Memphis, 363 S.W.3d 436 (Tenn. 2012). Cf. Meadors v. Still, 344 Ark. 307, 40 S.W.3d 294 (2001) ("some positive act of fraud, something so furtively planned and secretly executed as to keep the plaintiff's cause of action concealed, or perpetrated in a way that it conceals itself").

[85] See Emberton v. GMRI, Inc., 299 S.W.3d 565 (Ky. 2009); Ryan v. Roman Catholic Bishop of Providence, 941 A.2d 174 (R.I. 2008); Florida Dep't of Health & Rehab. Servs. v. S.A.P., 835 So.2d 1091 (Fla. 2003).

[86] Walk v. Ring, 202 Ariz. 310, 44 P.3d 990 (2002) ("fraudulent concealment occurs with nondisclosure of the facts pertaining to negligence"; "if Defendant thought he may have been negligent in his treatment of Plaintiff, his fiduciary duty to disclose required him to explain that to her"). See also Redwing v. Catholic Bishop for Diocese of Memphis, 363 S.W.3d 436 (Tenn. 2012).

[87] E.g., Colosimo v. Roman Catholic Bishop of Salt Lake City, 153 P.3d 806 (Utah 2007); Kopalchick v. Catholic Diocese of Richmond, 274 Va. 332, 645 S.E.2d 439 (2007); Doe v. Archdiocese of Cincinnati, 109 Ohio St.3d 491, 849 N.E.2d 268 (2006); McAfee v. Cole, 637 A.2d 463 (Me. 1994); Snyder v. Boy Scouts of Am., Inc., 205 Cal.App.3d 1318, 253 Cal.Rptr. 156 (1988) (now covered by statute).

[88] Hearndon v. Graham, 767 So.2d 1179 (Fla. 2000); Logerquist v. Danforth, 188 Ariz. 16, 932 P.2d 281 (1997); McCollum v. D'Arcy, 138 N.H. 285, 638 A.2d 797 (1994); Olsen v. Hooley, 865 P.2d 1345 (Utah 1993); Johnson v. Johnson, 701 F.Supp. 1363 (N.D. Ill. 1988). But see Doe v. Archdiocese of Milwaukee, 211 Wis.2d 312, 565 N.W.2d 94 (1997); Travis v. Ziter, 681 So.2d 1348 (Ala. 1996); Lemmerman v. Fealk, 449 Mich. 56, 534 N.W.2d 695 (1995). Cf. Maness v. Gordon, 325 P.3d 522 (Alaska 2014) (claim of repressed memory syndrome could not be used absent expert testimony).

[89] Cf. Rigazio v. Archdiocese of Louisville, 853 S.W.2d 295 (Ky. Ct. App. 1993) (plaintiff knew of abuse, then repressed his knowledge, then recovered it; discovery rule did not assist him).

[90] 10 Del. Code § 8145; Alaska Stat. § 09.55.650; Conn. Gen. Stat. Ann. § 52–577d (17 years from age of majority is maximum time); Iowa Code Ann. § 614.8A; Kan. Stat. Ann. § 60–523; Mass. Gen. L. Ann. c. 260, § 4C; 14 Me. Rev. Stat. Ann. § 752–C; Mont. Code Ann. § 27–2–216; N.J. Stat. Ann. § 2A:61B–1; N.M. Stat. Ann. § 37–1–30; R.I. Gen. L. Ann. § 9–1–51; Rev. Code Wash. Ann. § 4.16.340. Distinguish statutes addressed to sexual abuse by therapists, which may also cover some child abuse cases. See, e.g., Wis. Stat. Ann. § 893.585.

[91] See Medved v. Glenn, 125 P.3d 913 (Utah 2005) (plaintiff who allegedly was required to undergo mastectomy and suffered other harms due to the defendant's negligence is permitted to claim damages for increased risk of recurrence, emphasizing the rule against splitting a cause of action and reversing courts below).

all, res judicata rules traditionally prevented a later suit brought after injury actually resulted. If she did not sue, the statute of limitations would eventually run because once she suffered some degree of harm, her cause of action accrued.

An example. In *Hagerty v. L & L Marine Services, Inc.*,[92] the plaintiff was thoroughly drenched with a known carcinogen, dripolene. He knew that the substance was carcinogenic and he showered off, but he had some immediate symptoms including cramping, dizziness, and stinging in his extremities. His claim for tort was complete because he suffered damages. But, although cancer was a distinct possibility in his future, he did not have cancer at that time. He could not postpone suit to await events, since his claim had accrued.

Possible solutions. In situations like this, several possible options are available, perhaps none very satisfactory. One might be to permit the plaintiff to sue within the time permitted by the statute of limitations and to retain jurisdiction over the case for a long period, with or without medical monitoring damages.[93] This solution runs counter to established habits and might defeat the purpose of the statute of limitations.

A second option is to allow the plaintiff damages for his fear of future cancer, but nothing for the cancer itself, should it occur, because only one claim arises from a single set of facts.[94]

A third option is to allow the plaintiff to recover for the increased risk of harm, or put the other way around, for the value of his lost chance of a healthy life. If he had a 40% chance of getting cancer, this approach might allow him to recover 40% of the damages that would be appropriate if he actually suffered cancer. Although some courts have approved lost chance recoveries in certain cases,[95] in most of the lost chance cases, no future event can make causation or loss clear.[96] A little authority supports recovery for increased risk of future but improbable harm.[97]

The solution in Hagerty. To the *Hagerty* court it seemed wrong to bar the plaintiff from recovery for a devastating disease caused by the defendant merely because he has suffered some minor harm much earlier. It also seemed wrong to allow a recovery for a cancer he might never have.[98] So the court concluded that Hagerty could recover now for injuries suffered so far and for his emotional harm based on fear of the cancer but that if cancer occurred later, he should be permitted to bring a separate suit for that.[99]

---

[92]   788 F.2d 315 (5th Cir.), modified on other grounds on denial of rehearing en banc, 797 F.2d 256 (5th Cir. 1986).

[93]   On medical monitoring damages and funds, see § 29.13.

[94]   Fear of future harm is a recoverable element of damages once a tort is established, see § 29.1.

[95]   See § 14.11.

[96]   For instance, if the defendant physician fails to correctly diagnose cancer in January but does diagnose it in September, the delay is likely to reduce the patient's chances of survival, but if the patient dies, no one can be sure whether the physician's failure actually made a difference or not.

[97]   Dillon v. Evanston Hosp., 199 Ill.2d 483, 771 N.E.2d 357, 264 Ill.Dec. 653 (2002); see Joseph H. King, Jr., "Reduction of Likelihood" Reformulation and Other Retrofitting of the Loss-of-A-Chance Doctrine, 28 U. Mem. L. Rev. 491 (1998).

[98]   See also Eagle-Picher Indus., Inc. v. Cox, 481 So.2d 517, 525 (Fla. Dist. Ct. App. 1985).

[99]   "[T]he disease of cancer should be treated as a separate cause of action for all purposes. . . . A prior but distinct disease, though the tortfeasor may have paid reparations, should not affect the cause of action and damages for the subsequent disease." Hagerty v. L & L Marine Servs., Inc., 788 F.2d 315, 320 (5th Cir.), modified on other grounds on denial of rehearing en banc, 797 F.2d 256 (5th Cir. 1986).

Two distinct injuries. In the toxic torts setting, many courts have endorsed Hagerty with enthusiasm.[100] A much-cited Florida decision took a similar view, saying that if the plaintiff's exposure to asbestos had not yet caused cancer, the plaintiff would be permitted to sue later when and if cancer occurred.[101] The idea is that the plaintiff suffers two distinct injuries from the defendant's wrongdoing, not merely one injury with latent or late-developing harm.[102] In such a case, the claim for the second injury will not be barred either by a judgment in the first suit or by the plaintiff's failure to sue on the first injury within the limitation period.[103] This follows the approach generally taken in release cases. In those cases the courts hold that a broadly worded release bars claims for unknown damages resulting from a known injury but not claims for an unknown injury that neither the plaintiff nor the defendant believed was involved.[104]

B. FEDERAL PREEMPTION

§ 18.8 Federal Preemption

The defense. Federal statutes are sometimes construed to preempt or displace state law, including state tort law. For instance, federal statutes can specify the warnings to be placed upon poisons or dangerous substances like tobacco products. At the same time, the federal statute may preempt tort law so that if the defendant who sells poisons prints the warning prescribed by the federal statute, state courts, even though they believe the warning is dangerously inadequate, cannot impose tort liability.[105] When preemption

---

[100] Ayers v. Jackson Twp., 106 N.J. 557, 525 A.2d 287 (1987). Even commentators who vehemently oppose other claims based upon exposure believe that allowing a second action is the enlightened position. See James A. Henderson, Jr. & Aaron D. Twerski, Asbestos Litigation Gone Mad: Exposure-Based Recovery for Increased Risk, Mental Distress, and Medical Monitoring, 53 S.C. L. Rev. 815 (2002) (listing many cases in support).

[101] Eagle-Picher Indus., Inc. v. Cox, 481 So.2d 517 (Fla. Dist. Ct. App. 1985). The court noted that the rule against splitting a cause of action was correlative with the rule that allowed the plaintiff to recover all (future) damages in one suit. If the plaintiff could not recover the future harm damages, then the rule against splitting the cause of action had no application.

[102] See, e.g., Pooshs v. Philip Morris USA, Inc., 51 Cal.4th 788, 123 Cal.Rptr.3d 578, 250 P.3d 181, Prod. Liab. Rep. (CCH) P 18626 (2011) (earlier-discovered disease—COPD—does not trigger the statute of limitations on a suit based on a later-discovered separate latent disease—lung cancer-caused by the same tobacco use); Daley v. A.W. Chesterton, Inc., 37 A.3d 1175, Prod. Liab. Rep. (CCH) P 18792 (Pa. 2012) ("separate disease" rule allowed cancer patient to bring separate lawsuits for more than one malignant disease that resulted from the same exposure to asbestos; the second action—for mesothelioma—was not barred by res judicata).

[103] Carroll v. Owens-Corning Fiberglas Corp., 37 S.W.3d 699 (Ky. 2000) (action for cancer accrues on date of cancer diagnosis, not on date of earlier diagnosis of asbestosis); Pustejovsky v. Rapid-American Corp., 35 S.W.3d 643 (Tex. 2000); Hamilton v. Asbestos Corp., 22 Cal.4th 1127, 95 Cal.Rptr.2d 701, 998 P.2d 403 (2000); Sopha v. Owens-Corning Fiberglas Corp., 230 Wis.2d 212, 601 N.W.2d 627 (1999); Miller v. Armstrong World Indus., Inc., 817 P.2d 111 (Colo. 1991).

[104] 2 Dan B. Dobbs, Law of Remedies § 11.9 (2d ed. 1993).

[105] See CSX Transp., Inc. v. Easterwood, 507 U.S. 658, 113 S.Ct. 1732, 123 L.Ed.2d 387 (1993); Cipollone v. Liggett Group, Inc., 505 U.S. 504, 112 S.Ct. 2608, 120 L.Ed.2d 407 (1992). There is a continuing, divisive, and wide-ranging jurisprudence of preemption, which sometimes leads to the conclusion that tort law has not been displaced and that the claim can proceed. E.g., Wyeth v. Levine, 555 U.S. 555, 129 S.Ct. 1187 (2009). In a single case, a federal statute may be found to preempt some of the plaintiff's state tort claims, but not others. See, e.g., Elam v. Kansas City S. Ry. Co., 635 F.3d 796 (5th Cir. 2011) (Interstate Commerce Commission Termination Act preempts plaintiffs' negligence per se claim based on a state statute, but not their ordinary negligence claim in which they alleged that the railroad negligently failed to provide adequate warning of a train's presence at a crossing). A statute may also be found to preempt claims by certain plaintiffs but not others. See, e.g., Vreeland v. Ferrer, 71 So. 3d 70 (Fla. 2011), cert. denied, 132 S.Ct. 1557 (2012) (federal aircraft owner/lessor liability statute limits liability to people who are physically on the ground or in the water when harmed, and therefore does not preempt a state-law tort claim by passengers or airline crew).

occurs, the defendant's compliance with a preemptive federal statute leaves the plaintiff nowhere to turn.[106] The effect is that compliance with a federal preemptive statute is a complete defense.[107]

Forms of preemption. Federal preemption of state law springs from the Supremacy Clause of the United States Constitution, which makes federal law "the supreme law of the land . . . any Thing in the Constitution or Laws of any State to the Contrary notwithstanding."[108] Federal preemption may be either "express" or "implied." The express form occurs when Congress explicitly, in the text of a law, displaces state law (usually in a preemption clause).[109] The implied form turns on a court's deducing of Congressional intent from a statute's broader purpose. In each case, the ultimate touchstone of a preemption analysis is deducing Congressional intent.[110]

Implied preemption. Implied preemption itself takes two forms: (1) field preemption, in which federal regulation of a particular field is so "pervasive as to make reasonable the inference that Congress left no room for the States to supplement it,"[111] or where the "federal interest" in the field is "dominant";[112] and (2) conflict preemption, where federal and state law either directly or indirectly conflict.[113] No matter which type of preemption is found, when a federal law is held to preempt state law, the effect is to bar completely the state-law claim.

Illustrations. As noted above, federal preemption occurs in a number of tort-law settings. For example, federal regulations govern the speed of railroad trains under some circumstances. These regulations have been construed to preempt state law. So the plaintiff injured by a fast-moving train is defeated when the railroad can show that the speed of the train complied with the limits set by the federal government, regardless of whether the speed was unreasonable in the given locality.[114] Similarly, a plaintiff hit by a train at a railroad crossing who claims that the railroad was negligent for failing to install adequate warning signs at a railroad crossing will lose completely on preemption grounds if the court finds that federal regulations specified the kinds of warnings that

[106] Noncompliance with a preemptive federal statute bars the state-law claim but may leave the defendant subject to federal criminal or administrative penalties that do not assist the injured plaintiff. In Buckman Co. v. Plaintiffs' Legal Committee, 531 U.S. 341, 121 S.Ct. 1012, 148 L.Ed.2d 854 (2001), the plaintiffs injured by the defendant's medical product alleged that the defendant had secured permission to market the product by fraud on the federal regulatory agency, the FDA. The Court held that the tort claim was preempted because it would conflict with administration of the law by the federal agency, noting that the FDA itself could impose civil penalties, pursue criminal sanctions, or seize the products.

[107] For a succinct description and analysis of federal preemption, see David G. Owen, Products Liability Law § 14.4 (2d ed. 2008).

[108] U.S. Const., art. VI, cl. 2.

[109] See, e.g., Northwest, Inc. v. Ginsberg, 134 S.Ct. 1422, 188 L.Ed.2d 538 (2014) (airline deregulation act); Roth v. Norfalco LLC, 651 F.3d 367 (3d Cir. 2011) (Hazardous Materials Transportation Act).

[110] Wyeth v. Levine, 555 U.S. 555, 129 S.Ct. 1187, 173 L.Ed.2d 51 (2009).

[111] Rice v. Santa Fe Elevator Corp., 331 U.S. 218, 230 (1947); see also United States v. Locke, 529 U.S. 89, 120 S.Ct. 1135, 146 L.Ed. 69 (2000) (field preemption occurs when "Congress [] left no room for state regulation of these matters").

[112] Rice v. Santa Fe Elevator Corp., 331 U.S. 218, 230 (1947).

[113] See English v. General Elec. Co., 496 U.S. 72, 110 S.Ct. 2270, 110 L.Ed.2d 65 (1990) (conflict preemption occurs when it is "impossible for a private party to comply with both state and federal requirements); Hines v. Davidowitz, 312 U.S. 52, 61 S.Ct. 399, 85 L.Ed.2d 581 (1941) (conflict preemption also occurs where state law "stands as an obstacle to the accomplishment and execution" of Congressional purposes and objectives).

[114] See CSX Transp. v. Easterwood, 507 U.S. 658, 113 S.Ct. 1732, 123 L.Ed.2d 387 (1993); cf. Norfolk S. Ry. v. Shanklin, 529 U.S. 344, 120 S.Ct. 1467, 146 L.Ed.2d 374 (2000) (crossing warnings, preemption).

should be installed, at least where federal funds were used as well, and the defendant did install such warnings.[115] Preemption has been a major issue in the field of products liability, and gets longer and separate treatment in a later chapter.[116]

---

[115] Missouri Pac. R.R. Co. v. Limmer, 299 S.W.3d 78 (Tex. 2009), cert. denied, 562 U.S. 829, 131 S.Ct. 75, 178 L.Ed.2d 25 (2010). See also Elam v. Kansas City S. Ry. Co., 635 F.3d 796 (5th Cir. 2011) (Interstate Commerce Commission Termination Act completely preempted plaintiffs' negligence per se claim based on a Mississippi state statute that purported to manage a railroad's switching operations, including its decisions as to train speed, length and scheduling).

[116] See § 33.20.

Part IV

EXPANDED OR LIMITED DUTIES OF CARE IN PHYSICAL HARM CASES

Chapter 19

EXPANDED DUTIES OF CARE: CARRIERS, INNKEEPERS AND FIDUCIARIES

Analysis

§ 19.1   Duty of Common Carriers in Personal-Injury Cases

§ 19.2   Who Counts as a Common Carrier or Passenger

§ 19.3   Protecting Passengers of Common Carriers from Third Persons and Other External Risks

§ 19.4   Duty of Innkeepers in Personal-Injury Cases

§ 19.5   Duty of Fiduciaries in Personal-Injury Cases

§ 19.6   Fiduciary Relationship Imposing an Affirmative Duty to Protect from Others

§ 19.1 Duty of Common Carriers in Personal-Injury Cases

The general duty of highest care. Some species of strict liability may be imposed on common carriers for the safekeeping of goods belonging to the passengers.[1] But except under the Warsaw Convention,[2] proof of carrier negligence is required when the same passengers suffer personal injury or death.[3] Under traditional rules, however, the duty owed is expanded in the sense that it is measured by a high standard. Passengers necessarily put their well-being completely in the hands of the carrier, are totally dependent upon the carrier, and will often lack access to evidence about the carrier's behavior.[4] Largely for these reasons, most courts say that common carriers are required to exercise an elevated level of care, not merely reasonable care, for the safety of fare-paying passengers.[5] Thus courts usually say the common carrier owes the utmost[6] care

---

[1]   See, e.g., Booth v. Quality Carriers, Inc., 276 Ga.App. 406, 623 S.E.2d 244 (2005); see also 2 Dobbs, Hayden & Bublick, The Law of Torts § 260 (2d ed. 2011 & Supp.).

[2]   The Warsaw Convention (now the Montreal Convention) provides for strict liability for accidents causing injury aboard an international air carrier, but only for approximately the first $135,000 in damages. Above that sum, carriers can avoid liability by proving that they were not negligent. See Edward C. Bresee, Jr., and Sirce Elliott, Recent Developments in Aviation Law, 71 J. Air L. & Com. 101, 170 (2006).

[3]   Robert J. Kaczorowski, The Common-law Background of Nineteenth-Century Tort Law, 51 Ohio St. L. J. 1127, 1158 (1990), explains the difference: passengers and guests are not inanimate objects but can instead help take care of themselves.

[4]   In Nalwa v. Cedar Fair, L.P., 55 Cal. 4th 1148, 150 Cal. Rptr. 3d 551, 290 P.3d 1158 (2012), the court held that the owner of a bumper car ride at an amusement park was not held to the higher duties of a common carrier. The court distinguished its earlier decision in Gomez v. Superior Court, 35 Cal. 4th 1125, 29 Cal. Rptr. 3d 352, 113 P.3d 41 (2005), which had held the operator of a roller coaster ride to the higher common carrier duty, on the ground that in the bumper car ride, "patrons exercise independent control over the steering and acceleration of the cars," and "do not surrender their freedom of movement and actions" to the operator. In short, said the court, unlike the situation with the roller coaster, riders on the bumper car ride "are not passively carried or transported from one place to another."

[5]   If the intending passenger rightfully enters the premises or the conveyance itself, she is entitled to the utmost care, even though the fare was not actually paid before injury occurred. See Greater Richmond Transit Co. v. Wilkerson, 242 Va. 65, 406 S.E.2d 28 (1991).

[6]   Fairchild v. The California Stage Co., 13 Cal. 599 (1859), *codified in* Cal.Civ. Code § 2100 ("carrier of persons for reward must use the utmost care and diligence for their safe carriage"); Markwell v. Whinery's Real Estate, Inc., 869 P.2d 840 (Okla. 1994).

or the highest care,[7] or the highest care consistent with operation of the business,[8] or some variant of these terms.[9] The different verbalizations are probably not intended to state different standards, although they might differ in their impact on the jury. Under the heightened duty, the carrier owes not only the highest care in the transport itself, but also owes passengers a safe means of boarding and exiting the conveyance.[10] And in discharging the passenger, the carrier is bound to do so at a reasonably safe place.[11] Special care may likewise be required if the carrier knows or should know that the passenger has a disability.[12]

Rejecting the expanded duty. Several courts have rejected or discarded the expanded duty in favor of a reasonable care standard, on the theory that the duty of reasonable care, which always considers circumstances in determining reasonableness, can adequately accommodate all cases.[13]

Practical differences. It has been suggested that the expanded duty of common carriers is not really a greater duty at all because the duty of reasonable care would permit the jury to consider any special dangers encountered on public conveyances and because the jury would be unimpressed with the supposed duty of utmost care.[14] However, systematically instructing the jury on the duty to use the highest care seems on its face likely to sway juries in closer cases—and swaying even one juror might be enough in many instances. In fact, judges themselves have constructed grounds for liability derived from the higher duty of care and have affirmed or reversed cases accordingly.[15] In addition, the higher duty of care may give rise to subsidiary doctrines favorable to some plaintiffs.[16]

§ 19.2 Who Counts as a Common Carrier or Passenger

Common carriers vs. private carriers. The utmost care duty imposed upon common carriers does not usually apply to non-carriers such as amusement rides[17] or to private

---

[7]   Aliotta v. Nat'l R.R. Passenger Corp., 315 F.3d 756 (7th Cir. 2003) (Ill. law); Doser v. Interstate Power Co., 173 N.W.2d 556 (Iowa 1970); Todd v. Mass Transit Administration, 373 Md. 149, 816 A.2d 930 (Md. 2003).

[8]   Gomez v. Superior Court, 35 Cal. 4th 1125, 1130, 113 P.3d 41, 44, 29 Cal. Rptr. 3d 352, 356 (2005) ("the degree of care and diligence which they must exercise is only such as can reasonably be exercised consistent with the character and mode of conveyance adopted and the practical operation of the business of the carrier").

[9]   Gleeson v. Virginia Midland Ry. Co., 140 U.S. 435, 11 S.Ct. 859, 35 L.Ed. 458 (1891) (utmost care and diligence "as far as human care and foresight will go"); Burton v. Des Moines Metro. Transit Auth., 530 N.W.2d 696 (Iowa 1995) ("duty to protect passengers as far as human care and foresight will go").

[10]   Washington Metro. Area Transit Auth. v. Reading, 109 Md.App. 89, 674 A.2d 44 (1996).

[11]   See Burton v. Des Moines Metro. Transit Auth., 530 N.W.2d 696 (Iowa 1995); Hines v. Garrett, 131 Va. 125, 108 S.E. 690 (1921) ("A carrier, in the discharge of the very high duty which it owes to its passengers, is bound to know the character of the place at which it wrongfully discharges them; and if the defendant wrongfully required the plaintiff to get off at a dangerous place without knowing it, it did so at its peril.").

[12]   See, e.g., Montgomery v. Midkiff, 770 S.W.2d 689 (Ky. Ct. App. 1989) (jury question whether failure to provide seat belts in bus for disabled passengers was negligence).

[13]   Nunez v. Professional Transit Management of Tucson, Inc., 229 Ariz. 117, 271 P.3d 1104 (2012); Union Traction Co. of Indiana v. Berry, 188 Ind. 514, 121 N.E. 655 (1919); Bethel v. New York City Transit Authority, 92 N.Y.2d 348, 703 N.E.2d 201, 681 N.Y.S.2d 201 (1998).

[14]   See 3 Harper, James & Gray, The Law of Torts 509 (2d ed. 1986).

[15]   See Capital Transit Co. v. Jackson, 149 F.2d 839 (1945); Plumb v. Richmond Light & R.R., 233 N.Y. 285, 135 N.E. 504 (1922).

[16]   See 2 Dobbs, Hayden & Bublick, The Law of Torts § 265 (2d ed. 2011 & Supp.).

[17]   E.g., Nalwa v. Cedar Fair, L.P., 55 Cal. 4th 1148, 150 Cal. Rptr. 3d 551, 290 P.3d 1158 (2012) (bumper car ride); Chavez v. Cedar Fair, LP, 450 S.W.3d 291 (Mo. 2014); but see Gomez v. Superior Court, 35 Cal. 4th 1125, 29 Cal. Rptr. 3d 352, 113 P.3d 41 (2005) (operator of a roller coaster ride held to the higher common

carriers,[18] who are held only to the standard of reasonable care unless some special reason induces courts in particular cases to impose a different standard.[19] As a result, courts ordinarily distinguish common carriers from private or contract carriers.[20]

Common carriers. A common carrier is one who undertakes to, or does, transport all persons indiscriminately,[21] or at least contracts to transport all persons within a definite class.[22] Some courts emphasize that an operator counts as a common carrier only if he is in the business of carrying passengers, the carriage of passengers is a primary function of that business,[23] and that the carriage is "for hire" and not gratuitous.[24]

Private carriers. In contrast, a private carrier, sometimes called a contract carrier, merely transports people under specific contracts, and reserves the right to reject any given passenger. For example, the operator of passenger ship is a common carrier,[25] but a fishing boat captain who picks and chooses those to whom he charters the boat is not;[26] a passenger railroad is a common carrier,[27] but a construction company running a train merely to transport its workers to the job site is not, even if it carries an occasional

---

carrier duty). The California court in *Nalwa* distinguished *Gomez* on the ground that in the bumper car ride, "patrons exercise independent control over the steering and acceleration of the cars," and "do not surrender their freedom of movement and actions" to the operator. In short, said the court, unlike the situation with the roller coaster in *Gomez*, riders on the bumper car ride "are not passively carried or transported from one place to another."

[18]   McClure v. Johnson, 50 Ariz. 76, 69 P.2d 573 (1937); Hammerlind v. Clear Lake Star Factory Skydiver's Club, 258 N.W.2d 590 (Minn. 1977).

[19]   Thus school bus operators are not usually common carriers, but some courts say that such operators owe the highest duty of care nonetheless.

[20]   The distinction may also be significant in interpretation of regulatory or licensing statutes and in determining insurance coverage. This chapter does not address those concerns.

[21]   Shoemaker v. Kingsbury, 79 U.S. 369, 20 L.Ed. 432 (1870) (common carriers "undertake, for hire, to carry all persons indifferently who apply for passage"); Doe v. Rockdale Sch. Dist. No. 84, 287 Ill. App. 3d 791, 679 N.E.2d 771, 223 Ill. Dec. 320 (1997) ("A common carrier undertakes for hire to carry all persons indifferently, who may apply for passage so long as there is room and there is no legal excuse for refusal."); Wright v. Midwest Old Settlers and Threshers Assn., 556 N.W.2d 808 (Iowa 1996) ("the distinctive characteristic of a common carrier is that it holds itself out as ready to engage in the transportation of goods or persons for hire, as public employment, and not as a casual occupation"). The undertaking to accept all passengers can be and is conditioned on availability of space and on the absence of a legal excuse for refusal, such as the passenger's drunkenness.

[22]   See Woolsey v. Nat'l Transp. Safety Bd., 993 F.2d 516 (5th Cir. 1993) (operator can be a common carrier if it "held itself out to the public or to a definable segment of the public as being willing to transport for hire, indiscriminately;" operator here "held itself out as being willing to serve all members of the music industry who were able to pay for its services").

[23]   Jones v. Dressel, 623 P.2d 370 (Colo. 1981) (air service for parachute drops was not primarily engaged in carriage of passengers and not a carrier); Wright v. Midwest Old Settlers and Threshers Assn., 556 N.W.2d 808 (Iowa 1996) (casual transport excluded); Mount Pleasant Independent Sch. Dist. v. Estate of Lindburg, 766 S.W.2d 208 (Tex. 1989) (school district operating school buses was not in the business of carrying passengers).

[24]   Thus in railroad free-pass cases, the railroad could exempt itself from liability to the passenger traveling wholly without payment or other consideration. See Walther v. Southern Pac. Co., 159 Cal. 769, 116 P. 51 (1911).

[25]   Hennigan v. Nantasket Boat Line, Inc., 329 Mass. 690, 110 N.E.2d 323 (1953). Even a cruise ship is a common carrier. Nadeau v. Costley, 634 So.2d 649 (Fla. Dist. Ct. App. 1994).

[26]   Semon v. Royal Indemn. Co., 279 F.2d 737 (5th Cir. 1960).

[27]   Carter v. Kurn, 127 F.2d 415 (8th Cir. 1942).

passenger;[28] the operator of a taxicab is a common carrier,[29] but a car rental agency is not.[30]

Similarly, courts have said that operators of school buses are not common carriers,[31] although even if such operators are only private carriers, they may owe special care proportioned to the children's "inability to foresee and avoid the perils which they may encounter."[32] Likewise, ambulance operators have been held to be private carriers only.[33] However, the rationale for the utmost care duty—that passengers have no ability to protect themselves when the carrier is in complete control—may cast doubt on the distinction between private and common carriers in the context of carriers like school buses and ambulances.[34]

Modes of conveyance that count as carriers; amusement vs. carriage. As already indicated, common carriers include those who undertake transport for the public by bus,[35] railroad,[36] airplane,[37] taxicab,[38] passenger ship,[39] and ferry[40] and other similar public transport.[41] However, some courts have gone beyond these obvious cases and have treated as common carriers those who operate elevators,[42] escalators[43] chair lifts at ski resorts,[44] and even amusement park rides.[45] But for other courts, transport in connection with amusement and recreational activities may be treated as remote from or incidental to the business of carrying passengers, with the result that operators of air transport for

---

[28]   Shoemaker v. Kingsbury, 79 U.S. 369, 20 L.Ed. 432 (1870).

[29]   George v. Estate of Baker, 724 N.W.2d 1 (Minn. 2006).

[30]   Dymond Cab Co. v. Branson, 191 Okla. 604, 131 P.2d 1007 (1942). Arguably the rental agency is not any kind of carrier when the lessee is in control of the vehicle.

[31]   Hancock v. Bryan County Bd. of Educ., 240 Ga. App. 622, 522 S.E.2d 661(Ga. App. 1999) (a school bus is not a common carrier because it was used "solely in transporting schoolchildren and teachers to and from public schools"); Mount Pleasant Independent Sch. Dist. v. Estate of Lindburg, 766 S.W.2d 208 (Tex. 1989) (emphasizing that school district was not in the business of carrying passengers and did not undertake to provide transport for the public generally).

[32]   Grace v. Kumalaa, 47 Haw. 281, 386 P.2d 872 (1963).

[33]   Hollander v. Smith & Smith, 10 N.J.Super. 82, 76 A.2d 697 (1950) (ambulance company did not hold itself out as public or common carrier, hence was a private carrier). Ambulance personnel performing professional services are governed by the professional standard of care rather than by the common carrier rule. Bondy v. Allen, 635 N.W.2d 244 (Minn. App. 2001).

[34]   Bricks v. Metro Ambulance Serv., Inc., 177 Ga.App. 62, 338 S.E.2d 438 (1985) ("No individual is more at the mercy of a carrier than a person dying, or ill or injured enough to require carriage. In holding that this kind of ambulance is a common carrier, we decline to discriminate against such person merely because the ambulance he is forced to ride in was not forced to take him.").

[35]   E.g., O'Dee v. Tri-County Metropolitan Transp. Dist. of Oregon, 212 Or. App. 456, 157 P.3d 1272 (2007).

[36]   E.g., Aliotta v. Nat'l R.R. Passenger Corp., 315 F.3d 756 (7th Cir. 2003).

[37]   See D. E. Buckner, Annotation, Air Carrier as Common or Private Carrier, and Resulting Duties as to Passenger's Safety, 73 A.L.R.2d 346.

[38]   Ingham v. Luxor Cab Co., 93 Cal. App. 4th 1045, 113 Cal. Rptr. 2d 587 (2002) (as common carrier, taxi operator has duty to deliver passenger to her destination and is liable for wrongful ejectment).

[39]   Hennigan v. Nantasket Boat Line, Inc., 329 Mass. 690, 110 N.E.2d 323 (1953).

[40]   E.g., Henderson v. Taylor, 315 S.W.2d 777 (Mo. 1958) (but ferryman was not negligent on the facts).

[41]   Martin v. Chicago Transit Authority, 128 Ill. App. 3d 837, 471 N.E.2d 544, 84 Ill. Dec. 15 (1984) (elevated train); Reardon v. Boston Elevated Ry. Co., 311 Mass. 228, 40 N.E.2d 865 (1942) (subway).

[42]   E.g., Cash v. Otis Elevator Co., 684 P.2d 1041 (Mont. 1984).

[43]   Vandagriff v. J.C. Penney Co., 228 Cal.App.2d 579, 39 Cal.Rptr. 671 (1964).

[44]   Platzer v. Mammoth Mountain Ski Area, 104 Cal.App.4th 1253, 128 Cal.Rptr.2d 885 (2002); cf. Bayer v. Crested Butte Mountain Resort, Inc., 960 P.2d 70 (Colo. 1998) (ski lift operator owes duty of a common carrier even though he is not characterized as a carrier).

[45]   See Gomez v. Superior Court, 35 Cal.4th 1125, 113 P.3d 41, 29 Cal.Rptr.3d 352 (2005) (roller coaster).

the purpose of recreational parachuting,[46] or thrill rides on a speed boat,[47] are not carriers at all. These courts apply the duty of ordinary care in such cases. The outcome is in line not only with the general duty of care but also with amusement-ride cases in particular.[48]

Who counts as a passenger. The carrier's duty of utmost care is owed only to those who count as passengers, not to strangers such as pedestrians or drivers of other vehicles. However, a person who has not yet purchased a ticket may be a passenger entitled to the utmost care if he intends to take passage within a reasonable time and is in a place such as a boarding platform that the carrier has provided for passengers.[49] At least this has been the rule with respect to injury from the carrier's moving vehicles.[50] With respect to premises defects not involving transport vehicles—for example, an ordinary slip-and-fall in a waiting room or passage—many courts treat the plaintiff as a non-passenger or say that he is entitled only to ordinary care.[51] Other courts may obtain the same result by limiting the utmost care duty to cases in which the passenger is in the act of boarding, riding, or alighting[52] or is otherwise injured in some way by the carrier's vehicle or transport.[53] At the other end of the journey, one remains a passenger until she is discharged in a place of reasonable safety.[54] Finally, one using the carrier's vehicle or machinery for some purpose other than carriage may not be a passenger to whom the heightened duty of care is owed.[55]

§ 19.3 Protecting Passengers of Common Carriers from Third Persons and Other External Risks

Protecting passengers from third persons. Courts have generally been reluctant to impose liability upon defendants for failing to protect the plaintiff from attacks by others. However, a defendant may owe a duty of care to protect the plaintiff from herself or others in several circumstances—when the defendant's actions enhance the risk of

---

[46] Jones v. Dressel, 623 P.2d 370 (Colo. 1981).

[47] Speed Boat Leasing, Inc. v. Elmer, 124 S.W.3d 210 (Tex. 2003).

[48] Chavez v. Cedar Fair, LP, 450 S.W.3d 291 (Mo. 2014); Dockery v. World of Mirth Shows, Inc., 264 N.C. 406, 142 S.E.2d 29 (1965). Amusement operations of course also owe the duty of ordinary or reasonable care as to acts and conditions that are distinct from rides. Dahna v. Clay County Fair Ass'n, 232 Iowa 984, 6 N.W.2d 843 (1942).

[49] See Skelton v. Chicago Transit Auth., 214 Ill. App. 3d 554, 573 N.E.2d 1315, 158 Ill. Dec. 130 (1991).

[50] Aliotta v. Nat'l R.R. Passenger Corp., 315 F.3d 756 (7th Cir. 2003).

[51] Orr v. Pacific Southwest Airlines, 208 Cal. App. 3d 1467, 257 Cal. Rptr. 18 (1989); Davis v. South Side Elevated R.R., 292 Ill. 378, 127 N.E. 66 (1920). Distinguish falls in boarding or alighting; as to these, the utmost-care rule applies. E.g., Saltis v. A.B.B. Daimler Benz, 243 Ga. App. 603, 533 S.E.2d 772 (2000) (automated train doors closed on passenger).

[52] See Trevino v. Flash Cab Co., 272 Ill. App. 3d 1022, 651 N.E.2d 723, 209 Ill. Dec. 545 (1995).

[53] Some cases both extend and limit the utmost-care duty to any sphere of carrier activity that constitutes "a mobile or animated hazard to the passenger." See Orr v. Pacific Southwest Airlines, 208 Cal. App.3d 1467, 257 Cal. Rptr. 18 (1989).

[54] See Louisville & J. Ferry Co. v. Nolan, 135 Ind. 60, 34 N.E. 710 (1893) ("It is bound to exercise the strictest of diligence, not only in carrying them to their destination, but also in setting them down safely, if human care and foresight can do so."); Hines v. Garrett, 131 Va. 125, 108 S.E. 690 (1921). Although the carrier cannot properly discharge the passenger into a position of peril—"for example allowing a drunk to exit onto a busy highway at night"—unforeseeable harms that otherwise occur after a passenger is discharged in a safe place are not the carrier's responsibility. See Mastriano v. Blyer, 779 A.2d 951 (Me. 2001); Jay M. Zitter, Annotation, Liability of Motorbus Carrier or Driver for Death Of, or Injury To, Discharged Passenger Struck by Other Vehicle, 16 A.L.R.5th 1 (1993).

[55] Takashi Kataoka v. May Dep't Stores Co., 60 Cal.App.2d 177, 140 P.2d 467 (1943) (small child, not riding escalator but testing escalator with his hand, was not a passenger).

attacks, when the defendant undertakes protection, and when the defendant is in a special relationship with the plaintiff or the attacker.[56] The relationship of common carrier and passenger is one of the special relationships that generate a duty to use care in protecting the plaintiff from herself or others.[57] And, in some cases, at least, the carrier may be required to use the utmost or highest care in dealing with third person attacks.[58] Liability, however, is only imposed when the duty is breached by negligence of the carrier.[59]

Risks after carriage is completed. The carrier is not responsible for passengers' injuries after they have left the conveyance[60] unless the carrier has negligently[61] discharged the passengers at an unsafe place.[62]

§ 19.4 Duty of Innkeepers in Personal-Injury Cases

General rule. Innkeepers owe a strict liability duty to prevent loss or damage to goods brought into the hotel by a guest,[63] but most cases say, with only limited qualifications, that innkeepers owe only a duty of ordinary reasonable care for the guest's personal safety and not an expanded duty at all.[64] A very small group of cases hold otherwise, imposing a heightened duty of care upon innkeepers, analogous to the special duty imposed upon carriers.[65]

The innkeeper cases arise in several distinct settings, including injuries arising from conditions of the premises, acts or omissions of the innkeeper, and from attacks by third parties.

---

[56] See generally Chapter 26.

[57] Kenny v. Southeastern Pennsylvania Transportation Authority, 581 F.2d 351 (3d Cir. 1978); Todd v. Mass Transit Administration, 373 Md. 149, 816 A.2d 930 (2003) (carrier subject to liability for passenger injury resulting from attack by fellow passengers if "it knew or should have known of the imminent harm with adequate time and available resources to have prevented or mitigated it"); La Sota v. Philadelphia Transp. Co., 421 Pa. 386, 219 A.2d 296 (1966).

[58] McPherson v. Tamiami Trail Tours, Inc., 383 F.2d 527 (5th Cir. 1967) (seemingly a racially motivated attack on bus; carrier required to use "extraordinary care and diligence to protect its passengers in transit from violence or injury by third persons"); Quigley v. Wilson Line of Mass., 338 Mass. 125, 154 N.E.2d 77 (1958) ("a common carrier owes to its passengers the highest degree of care in the anticipation and prevention of violence from its employees, other passengers, and even strangers, as is consistent with the nature and operation of its business. The test is foreseeability of harm"); *contra,* Rodriguez v. New Orleans Pub. Serv., Inc., 400 So.2d 884 (La. 1981) (standard of care is not that of a carrier but that of a business, because attacks on public conveyance are not risks of transportation).

[59] See, e.g., Lopez v. Southern California Rapid Transit Dist., 40 Cal.3d 780, 710 P.2d 907, 221 Cal. Rptr. 840 (1985).

[60] E.g., Parlato v. Connecticut Transit, 181 Conn. 66, 434 A.2d 322 (1980) (passenger fell in a hole covered with leaves after alighting, no negligence); Hurd v. Williamsburg County, 363 S.C. 421, 611 S.E.2d 488 (2005) (for injury after passenger safely alights, ordinary care is the standard; passenger discharged from bus in the dark, and on the shoulder of a road known to be dangerous, was injured attempting to cross behind the bus; jury question whether defendant was negligent).

[61] Forminio v. City of New York, 68 A.D.3d 924, 892 N.Y.S.2d 134 (2009).

[62] E.g., Locke v. Ford, 54 Ga. App. 322, 187 S.E. 715 (1936) (driver of taxicab allegedly deposited four-year-old child between crossing streets in the center of a heavily traveled city street).

[63] See, e.g., Paraskevaides v. Four Seasons Washington, 272 F.3d 886 (D.C. Cir. 2002) (theft of guest's jewelry). State statutes often protect innkeepers from strict liability. See, e.g., Cal. Civ. Code § 1960.

[64] Hassan v. Stafford, 472 F.2d 88 (3d Cir. 1973) (death in a fire; negligence alleged was failure to take certain fire precautions); John Q. Hammons, Inc. v. Poletis, 954 P.2d 1353 (Wyo. 1998) (defective bathtub fixture led to fall).

[65] Hollander v. Days Inn Motel, 705 So.2d 1126 (La. App. 1998); Taboada v. Daly Seven, Inc., 271 Va. 313, 626 S.E.2d 428 (2006) ("utmost care").

Static conditions on the premises. First, with respect to conditions on the premises, the guest is an invitee[66] and is entitled to the same duty of reasonable care as other invitees,[67] including those who are invited to the premises by the guest himself[68] and those who are there to communicate with the guest.[69] And since the care owed derives from invitee status, the innkeeper may owe only the duty not to willfully or wantonly injure him if the guest enters private portions of the hotel where he is not expected to go and where his status is no longer that of an invitee.[70] In jurisdictions that no longer distinguish invitees from licensees and trespassers, the innkeeper would owe the duty of reasonable care to those on the premises regardless of invitee status.[71]

Applying negligence and cause rules. Given the general duty of reasonable care, the ordinary rules for establishing breach of the duty and causation apply. For example, res ipsa loquitur seldom applies in slip-and-fall cases, but some injury-producing conditions on the premises will warrant application of res ipsa loquitur to show a breach of the duty of care.[72] And violation of a fire safety statute by the innkeeper may subject him to liability under the negligence per se rules.[73]

Natural accumulations of ice. In a few cases, the innkeeper's duty may be less than the duty to use reasonable care. Some jurisdictions may shield land occupiers, including innkeepers, from liability for negligent failure to clear natural accumulations of ice and snow,[74] although that rule seems particularly inappropriate given the relationship of innkeeper and guest.

Innkeeper as carrier. In one situation, the innkeeper's duty may be greater than the duty of reasonable care. As shown in discussing common carriers, some jurisdictions say that one who operates elevators or escalators is a common carrier owing a heightened duty of care with respect to that conveyance.[75] In those jurisdictions, the innkeeper, in his capacity as a common carrier but not otherwise, would presumably be subject to that special duty or standard of care.[76]

Active negligence and active forces causing harm. Innkeepers are also under a duty of reasonable care to avoid creating risks of harm to guests from active forces. And of

---

[66]   Woodty v. West's Lamplighter Motels, 171 Ariz. 265, 830 P.2d 477 (Ct. App. 1992)

[67]   Smith v. Otis Elevator Co., 217 F.Supp. 2d 105 (D. Me. 2002) (guest died after he was trapped between two elevator doors); John Q. Hammons, Inc. v. Poletis, 954 P.2d 1353 (Wyo. 1998) (towel bar in guest's room pulled loose, leading guest to fall in the tub). As to invitees generally, see § 20.7.

[68]   Woodty v. West's Lamplighter Motels, 171 Ariz. 265, 830 P.2d 477 (Ct. App. 1992); Corinaldi v. Columbia Courtyard, Inc., 162 Md. App. 207, 873 A.2d 483 (2005).

[69]   Steinberg v. Irwin Operating Co., 90 So.2d 460 (Fla. 1956).

[70]   See Jones v. Bland, 182 N.C. 70, 108 S.E. 344 (1921) (invitee status is lost when visitor to guest goes to some "remote portion of the premises . . . and where there is no reason to expect him to go"). This is an application of the general rule of premises liability. See Chapter 20.

[71]   See § 20.9. As reflected there, some jurisdictions have abolished the distinction between invitees and licensees, but have retained the old limited duty rules for trespassers. Under any system of analysis, the innkeeper would continue to owe a guest the duty of reasonable care.

[72]   Marx v. Huron Little Rock, 88 Ark.App. 284, 198 S.W.3d 127 (2004) (guest thrown to floor when toilet seat slipped off toilet).

[73]   Herberg v. Swartz, 89 Wash.2d 916, 578 P.2d 17 (1978).

[74]   Morin v. Traveler's Restat Motel, Inc., 704 A.2d 1085 (Pa. Super. 1997). Some snow and ice cases turn, not on the limited duty, but on the absence of negligence, as where the innkeeper does not have time to clear the snow or ice. E.g. Mangieri v. Prime Hospitality Corp., 251 A.D.2d 632, 676 N.Y.S.2d 207 (1998).

[75]   See § 19.10 & 19.11.

[76]   Smith v. Otis Elevator Co., 217 F.Supp.2d 105 (D. Me. 2002) (innkeeper owed only a duty of reasonable care with respect to elevator safety).

course they must make reasonable efforts to prevent harm when the risk arises. Exemplifying both points is *Knott Corp. v. Furman*,[77] where the innkeeper was held responsible for negligence in storing combustibles, which started a fire, then in leaving doors open so as to permit spread of smoke into guest rooms, and finally in failing to warn guests and to notify the fire department in a timely manner.

Protection from third persons. In one narrow respect the duty of innkeepers is expanded by comparison to the duty people generally owe to strangers. The usual rule that one owes no duty to take positive steps to assist another who is in danger even when assistance would be reasonable and safe.[78] When a special relationship exists between the plaintiff and defendant, however, the parties are no longer strangers and the defendant owes a duty of care, which, if breached, can result in liability. The relationship of innkeeper and guest is such a special relationship, giving rise to a duty of care and to potential liability on the part of the innkeeper for attacks on the guest by others.[79] In these cases, the general duty of care is not a duty to use more than reasonable care under the circumstances, but it is nonetheless a duty greater than the duty strangers owe.

§ 19.5 Duty of Fiduciaries in Personal-Injury Cases

Fiduciary duties are most often determinative in economic harm cases,[80] but fiduciary duties also sometimes play a critical role in analysis of ordinary negligence cases involving physical or emotional harm. This is so because a fiduciary, including one in a confidential relationship with the plaintiff, owes a series of special duties to his beneficiary. A breach of any of those duties is a tort and is actionable by the beneficiary, provided the harm caused is within the scope of the fiduciary duty.

Nature of fiduciary's duty. The fiduciary's overall duty is one of loyalty to the beneficiary.[81] The duty of loyalty ordinarily requires the fiduciary to put his beneficiary's interests ahead of his own. And notably, the fiduciary may be obliged to act in a positive way to protect the beneficiary, meaning that the general rule of nonliability for "doing nothing" offers little protection for the fiduciary.

Who is a fiduciary? Courts attach fiduciary duties to many named special relationships, such as the relationship of trustee to beneficiary, agent to principal, lawyers to clients, doctors to patients, personal representatives to the estates they represent.[82] Some other fiduciary relationships, often called confidential relationships, are less formalized. These are ad hoc relationships, built on implicit or explicit undertakings of loyalty of a particular person and confidence reposed in him by the beneficiary.[83] Ordinary contract or business relationships entail no fiduciary duties; in those cases, the parties are said to deal as adversary bargainers or "at arms-length."

---

[77] Knott Corp. v. Furman, 163 F.2d 199 (4th Cir. 1947).

[78] See Chapters 25 & 26.

[79] Restatement Second of Torts § 314A (1965).

[80] See 3 Dobbs, Hayden & Bublick, The Law of Torts §§ 696 to 699 (2d ed. & Supp.).

[81] See Deborah A. DeMott, Breach of Fiduciary Duty: On Justifiable Expectations of Loyalty and Their Consequences, 48 Ariz. L. Rev. 925 (2006).

[82] E.g., Stafford v. Shultz, 42 Cal.2d 767, 777, 270 P.2d, 7 (1954) ("the existence of the relationship between the parties of physician and patient, which in contemplation of law is a fiduciary one").

[83] E.g., Mabus v. St. James Episcopal Church, 884 So.2d 747 (Miss. 2004) (no fiduciary relationship between Episcopal priest and parishioner absent a showing that parishioner reposed special trust and confidence in priest).

Breach and type of harm. Breach of fiduciary duty is often intentional in the sense that the fiduciary often knows his intended breach of duty is harming the beneficiary, but in other cases, the breach of fiduciary duty is caused by negligence.[84] The types of harm that result from fiduciary breach may also vary from case to case. They are often purely economic harms. There are, however, a few cases that implicate the fiduciary's duty in physical and emotional harm cases, including cases that implicate the fiduciary's duty to make full disclosure[85] and those arising from a claim of clergy sexual abuse or exploitation.[86] The claim is also sometimes asserted in cases of patient abuse by a psychiatrist, psychologist, or marriage counselor.[87] Sexual abuse or exploitation of a person who does not appear to consent or to have the capacity to consent would be a tort regardless of any fiduciary duty. For that reason, the claim that such abuse violated a fiduciary duty might seem at first glance to add nothing to the abuser's duty. However, a fiduciary duty may expand the ordinary reasonable care duty in several situations.

§ 19.6 Fiduciary Relationship Imposing an Affirmative Duty to Protect from Others

A fiduciary relationship is a kind of "special relationship" that functions to impose a duty to take positive reasonable steps to protect a beneficiary. Under the nonfeasance rule, strangers who know of a priest's sexual abuse of a minor may have no duty at all to do anything about it,[88] but if the diocese knows its priests are abusing children with whom it has a special relationship, general rules impose a duty to take reasonable action for their protection.[89] That is equally so if the special relationship is a fiduciary one. In such cases, the fiduciary such as a church organization is called upon to take positive steps of reasonable care to protect children from the priests, a duty not required of strangers.[90]

Finding fiduciary duty: clergy child abusers. Although parishioners and congregation members might all place their trust in the church not to act in ways antagonistic to their interests, courts have been reluctant to find that religious leaders and organizations are fiduciaries to every person they are supposed to serve.[91] However, when the religious institution engages in a relationship focused on individuals or particular groups within the religious body, inviting their trust and confidence, the case for a fiduciary duty seems especially strong and has been recognized in the courts.[92] In

---

[84]   See § 696. If the fiduciary intends a breach of his duty but harm is neither substantially certain nor intended, his intentional act is merely creating a risk. Intentional *risk-taking* is a negligent tort, not an "intentional" one. See § 9.7.

[85]   See 2 Dobbs, Hayden & Bublick, The Law of Torts § 269 (2d ed. 2011 & Supp.).

[86]   See id. § 268. As to clergy malpractice generally, see id. §§ 329 to 332.

[87]   See id. §§ 268 & 269.

[88]   See §§ 25.1 & 26.1.

[89]   See §§ 26.3 & 26.9.

[90]   The priest himself is presumably a fiduciary, too, but to describe him by that label may add little in many cases; having taken positive actions, he could not hide behind the nonfeasance rule in any event.

[91]   Mabus v. St. James Episcopal Church, 884 So.2d 747 (Miss. 2004); Berry v. Watchtower Bible and Tract Soc'y of New York, 152 N.H. 407, 879 A.2d 1124 (2005).

[92]   See Martinelli v. Bridgeport Roman Catholic Diocesan Corp., 196 F.3d 409 (2d Cir. 1999) (emphasizing priest's relationship with abused boy in special groups, field trips and the like); Sanders v. Casa View Baptist Church, 134 F.3d 331 (5th Cir. 1998) (emphasizing jury instruction that "the primary relationship between a minister and a parishioner is not a fiduciary one, and that Baucum could not be held liable for breaching his fiduciary duties unless he 'acquired and abused' influence and 'betrayed' confidences learned in a 'relationship of trust' "); F.G. v. MacDonell, 150 N.J. 550, 696 A.2d 697 (1997).

this light, a fiduciary relationship can be found when an altar boy submits to the priest,[93] a minor with a potential church career is molested by his priest-mentor,[94] a church member is individually pressured by the church to act against her own interests or those of her family,[95] or a couple trusts the priest in marriage or other counseling.[96] Secular therapy or counseling, of course, also entails a fiduciary relationship.[97] In these cases, the religious organization or other employer of an abuser is itself a fiduciary, and will be liable for its own fiduciary breach. If it knows or should know that abuse is a risk, or if it ratifies the abuse or aids and abets it, or if it is guilty of doing nothing after the priest's predatory nature is discovered, liability may follow.[98]

Whether fiduciary relationship is necessary to the duty. While a fiduciary relationship is *sufficient* to invoke a duty of the religious organization to protect the beneficiary, it is not so clear that fiduciary relation is *necessary* to invoke that duty. Any relationship the court is willing to recognize as a special relationship will suffice to impose a duty to use reasonable care for the beneficiary's protection.[99] Negligently hiring, retaining or supervising a known dangerous priest, or placing him in a position to prey on children, might also furnish ground for relief.[100] And so might the diocese's control over the perpetrators.[101] In this light, the claim of a fiduciary relationship appears to add little to the duty, although it may affect collateral issues.[102]

First Amendment defenses for clergy and religious organizations. First Amendment protections for exercise of religion and prohibitions against establishment of religion raise questions entirely separate from the question whether a state-law fiduciary duty exists. The constitutional question is therefore outside the scope of this chapter on the duty issue.[103] However, there is a perception among some observers that First Amendment religious freedom defenses are more likely to fail once the court recognizes a fiduciary duty.[104] As shown above, a number of cases have recognized a fiduciary duty,

---

[93]   Fortin v. The Roman Catholic Bishop of Portland, 871 A.2d 1208 (Me. 2005).

[94]   Doe v. Liberatore, 478 F.Supp.2d 742 (M.D. Pa. 2007).

[95]   Cf. Berry v. Watchtower Bible and Tract Soc'y of New York, 152 N.H. 407, 879 A.2d 1124 (2005) (church did not report child abuse and allegedly counseled mother of child to keep the matter within the church; no fiduciary duty was shown because "the plaintiffs did not allege that the elders acquired influence over them or that their confidence had been reposed in the elders").

[96]   Destefano v. Grabrian, 763 P.2d 275 (Colo. 1988); Doe v. Evans, 814 So.2d 370 (Fla. 2002) (diocese had fiduciary duty to take reasonable steps to control sexually predatory priests who counsel vulnerable individuals); F.G. v. MacDonell, 150 N.J. 550, 696 A.2d 697 (1997).

[97]   See, e.g., Purdy v. Fleming, 655 N.W.2d 424 (S.D. 2002) (secular counseling).

[98]   See, rejecting vicarious liability of the priests' employers but imposing liability upon them for their own breach of fiduciary duty, Doe v. Liberatore, 478 F.Supp. 2d 742 (M.D. Pa. 2007); Moses v. Diocese of Colorado, 863 P.2d 310, 322 (Colo. 1993).

[99]   See Fortin v. The Roman Catholic Bishop of Portland, 871 A.2d 1208 (Me. 2005) (presenting fiduciary duty as one form of special relationship that triggers a duty to take positive steps toward reasonable care); see §§ 26.3 & 26.9.

[100]   The duty to use reasonable care in hiring, retaining, or placing an employee who foreseeably may injure others is generally accepted independent of any fiduciary duty and independent of clergy sexual abuse. See, e.g., Underberg v. Southern Alarm, Inc., 284 Ga. App. 108, 110, 112, 643 S.E.2d 374, 377, 378 (2007); J. v. Victory Tabernacle Baptist Church, 236 Va. 206, 372 S.E.2d 391 (1988). See § 423 (general principle). As to clergy liability, see 2 Dobbs, Hayden & Bublick, The Law of Torts §§ 329 to 332 (2d ed. 2011 & Supp.).

[101]   See Fortin v. The Roman Catholic Bishop of Portland, 871 A.2d 1208 (Me. 2005) (control over priests as one ground for church's duty).

[102]   See 2 Dobbs, Hayden & Bublick, The Law of Torts § 270 (2d ed. 2011 & Supp.).

[103]   See id., §§ 329 to 332.

[104]   Diana L. Grimes, Practice What You Preach: How Restorative Justice Could Solve the Judicial Problems in Clergy Sexual Abuse Cases, 63 Wash. & Lee L. Rev. 1693, 1721 (2006).

breach of which would be actionable. But that is not to say that court barring a negligent supervision claim on First Amendment grounds would uphold the claim on the same facts once a fiduciary relationship is found to exist. The cases do not say so.[105] Some cases even expressly hold that the First Amendment bars fiduciary breach claims for clergy sexual abuse.[106] In any event, for practical reasons, it should be recognized that some courts have avoided the duty issue by concluding that the First Amendment prohibits courts from considering clergy abuse and its tacit approval by religious organizations where the plaintiff claims that the abusive clergy were negligently hired or retained or that they were chargeable with negligent counseling.[107]

---

[105] However, some authority, having condemned claims for clergy malpractice, has purported to distinguish fiduciary breach claims, which are actionable. See Moses v. Diocese of Colorado, 863 P.2d 310, 321 n.13 (Colo. 1993).

[106] Dausch v. Rykse, 52 F.3d 1425 (7th Cir. 1994); H.R.B. v. J.L.G., 913 S.W.2d 92 (Mo. App. 1995) (recognizing such actions would "inevitably entangle civil courts in religious matters"); Schieffer v. Catholic Archdiocese of Omaha, 244 Neb. 715, 508 N.W.2d 907 (1993).

[107] E.g., Franco v. The Church of Jesus Christ of Latter-Day Saints, 21 P.3d 198 (Utah 2001); §§ 329 & 332 (clergy malpractice); Marjorie A. Shields, Annotation, Liability of Church or Religious Organization for Negligent Hiring, Retention, or Supervision of Priest, Minister, or Other Clergy Based on Sexual Misconduct, 101 A.L.R.5th 1 (2002) (canvassing cases going both ways).

Chapter 20

PREMISES LIABILITY

Analysis

A. DUTIES TO THOSE ON THE PREMISES

§ 20.1   Common-Law Classification of Entrants on Land
§ 20.2   Duty Owed to Trespassers: Traditional Rule
§ 20.3   The Discovered-Trespasser Exception
§ 20.4   Licensees: The Classification
§ 20.5   Duty Owed to Licensees: Traditional Rule
§ 20.6   Invitees: The Classification
§ 20.7   Duty Owed to Invitees
§ 20.8   Children on the Land
§ 20.9   Changing Duties and Categories: Extending the Duty of Reasonable Care to Entrants Other than Invitees
§ 20.10   Recreational Use Statutes

B. DUTIES TO THOSE OUTSIDE THE PREMISES

§ 20.11   Natural Conditions on the Land
§ 20.12   Active Conduct and Artificial Conditions on the Land

C. DUTIES OF VENDORS AND LESSORS

§ 20.13   Vendors of Land
§ 20.14   Traditional Common Law Duties of Lessors
§ 20.15   The Implied Warranty of Habitability

A. DUTIES TO THOSE ON THE PREMISES

§ 20.1   Common-Law Classification of Entrants on Land

The traditional common law classifies entrants on land as either trespassers, licensees, or invitees, classifications that abound with subtleties and sub-classifications.[1] Under this traditional categorization approach, landowners—a term that includes possessors of land and those who stand in their shoes[2]—owe different duties to each class, although the duty to trespassers and licensees is closely similar. The standard duty of care, that of the reasonable and prudent person under the same of similar circumstances, is owed only to invitees; a lesser duty is owed to those in either of the

---

[1]   Some courts subdivide the traditional categories. E.g., Ryals v. U.S. Steel Corp., 562 So.2d 192 (Ala. 1990) ("mere" trespassers and those who enter with intent to commit a crime); Baltimore Gas & Elec. Co. v. Flippo, 348 Md. 680, 705 A.2d 1144 (1998) (noting licensee by invitation and bare licensee subcategories). The Restatement Third subdivides the trespasser category into "flagrant" and non-flagrant, with a lesser dutiy of care owed only to the former. See Restatement Third of Torts (Liability for Physical and Emotional Harm) § 52(a) & cmt. a (2012).

[2]   Persons in actual occupancy of land and exercising control over it, as well as members of the possessor's household, may take advantage of these limited-duty rules. See Restatement Second of Torts §§ 328E, 382 (1965).

other categories. Most courts continue to begin the analysis of landowner duties to entrants by classifying the entrant using the traditional categories, although a substantial number have now held that the duty of ordinary care extends to licensees or even trespassers, as well as to invitees.[3]

§ 20.2   Duty Owed to Trespassers: Traditional Rule

The trespasser category includes anyone[4] who enters another's land without the owner's express or implied consent. The category is thus broader than simply the group of entrants who might be sued for the tort of trespass. For example, a person who was carried unconscious onto the land by others might be a trespasser for the purpose of determining the landowner's duty of care.[5] The category is fluid; persons who were invitees or licensees in one part of the premises might become trespassers when they enter areas to which no permission extends.[6]

No duty of reasonable care to trespassers. In the traditional scheme, the landowner does not owe a duty of reasonable care to trespassers.[7] Instead, the duty is merely not to cause intentional injury, to set a trap, or to cause wanton injury.[8] A statute regulating the landowner's conduct might[9] or might not[10] have any effect on this common-law rule. The rule severely limiting duties of care to trespassers is slightly less harsh that it might sound, because in many cases to which it would apply, the landowner probably was not negligent even under an ordinary care standard. In addition, modern courts have modified the rule substantially both by way of definitions and by way of exceptions.

§ 20.3   The Discovered-Trespasser Exception

Even a trespasser is not an outlaw.[11] In most states, once the landowner has discovered the trespasser's presence on the land in circumstances that suggest he might encounter danger, the landowner comes under a duty of ordinary care.[12] Under the

---

[3]   See § 20.9.

[4]   Under some circumstances, excluding some children. See § 20.8.

[5]   Copeland v. Baltimore & Ohio R. Co., 416 A.2d 1 (D.C. 1980); cf. Gladon v. Greater Cleveland Regional Transit Auth., 75 Ohio St.3d 312, 662 N.E.2d 287 (1996) (man who was invitee on train platform because either a trespasser or a licensee when he fell or was pushed by criminals onto the tracks). Frederick v. Philadelphia Rapid Transit Co., 337 Pa. 136, 10 A.2d 576 (1940) (man who fell on tracks was treated as if he were a trespasser).

[6]   Handy v. Nejam, 111 So.3d 610 (Miss. 2013). An entrant's status may pose a difficult issue of fact under these circumstances. E.g., Boyrie v. E & G Property Services, 58 A.3d 475 (D.C. 2013).

[7]   This idea is sometimes expressed in the saying that trespassers take the land at their own risk and as they find it. See Gaboury v. Ireland Road Grace Brethern, Inc., 446 N.E.2d 1310 (Ind. 1983).

[8]   E.g., Ryals v. U.S. Steel Corp., 562 So.2d 192 (Ala. 1990); Alexander v. Medical Assocs. Clinic, 646 N.W.2d 74 (Iowa 2002); Taylor v. Mississippian Ry., Inc., 826 So.2d 742 (Miss. 2002) (wanton injury, which requires "conscious disregard of a known and serious danger").

[9]   See, e.g., O'Guin v. Bingham County, 142 Idaho 49, 122 P.3d 308 (2005) (statute requiring landfills to bar access by unauthorized persons construed to impose a duty of reasonable care to trespassers).

[10]   See § 11.1 & 11.2.

[11]   See Antoniewicz v. Reszcynski, 70 Wis.2d 836, 236 N.W.2d 1 (1975) (unless he is in fact on the premises for illegal purposes). Some states provide landowners an immunity from claims by persons injured in the act of committing a felony. See Cal. Civ. Code § 847.

[12]   See Aluminum Company of American v. Guthrie, 303 Ark. 177, 793 S.W.2d 785 (1990) (duty "to exercise ordinary care under the circumstances to avoid injury to him after discovering his peril"); Lee v. Chicago Transit Authority, 152 Ill.2d 432, 605 N.E.2d 493, 178 Ill.Dec. 699 (1992).

Second Restatement's view, foreseeability of a trespasser is not enough; the landowner must know or have reason to know that he is actually present.[13]

Some jurists regard the known-trespasser rule as an exception to the general willful-wanton standard.[14] Others think that it is an application of the general willful and wanton test because failure to exercise ordinary care after discovery of a human being in danger is regarded as willful and wanton misconduct for which landowners are always liable.[15] Either way, the possessor is under a duty of reasonable care once he knows or is on notice of both the trespasser's presence and the impending danger.

Breach of duty. With the duty of care so established, the plaintiff still has the burden of showing that it was violated by failure to act as a reasonable person under the circumstances. In many cases a warning from the landowner that the trespasser is about to walk into danger suffices to fulfill his duty. If the danger is one that the trespasser could reasonably be expected to see and avoid, even a warning may not be required.

Affirmative action to save trapped trespasser. If the landowner has breached no duty to a trespasser, but discovers that the trespasser is trapped, or is injured and helpless, it would seem that the landowner must then exercise reasonable care to provide affirmative assistance, even though the landowner did not cause harm in the first place.[16] This is in line with the rule in other circumstances that requires reasonable care when the defendant's instrumentality innocently causes harm.[17]

Foreseeability tests. For the Second Restatement, foreseeability of trespassers was enough to trigger a duty only if the trespassers were "constantly" trespassing on a limited area.[18] Otherwise, the duty to trespassers would be triggered only if the landowner actually knew or had reason to know that the trespasser was about to encounter a danger. "Have reason to know" was a term of art. It did not mean foreseeability but specific knowledge that leads to the inference that the trespasser is actually present.[19] However, some courts have departed from the Restatement's scheme by treating foreseeable trespassers as if they were "known" trespassers.

The result for these courts is that if a trespasser's presence and encounter with danger is reasonably foreseeable, the landowner does owe a duty of reasonable care. For example, where a landowner places an unmarked cable in a wooded area where horseback riders, snowmobilers, motorcyclists and others foreseeably would be harmed,

---

[13] Restatement Second of Torts §§ 337 & 338 (1965). The Third Restatement, in a comment, is largely in accord on this point, requiring that a landowner be "aware of the existence and plight of a flagrant trespasser" before a duty of reasonable care arises. Restatement Third of Torts (Liability for Physical and Emotional Harm) § 52(b), cmt. g (2012).

[14] McVicar v. W.R. Arthur & Co., 312 S.W.2d 805 (Mo. 1958).

[15] Frederick v. Philadelphia Rapid Transit Co., 337 Pa. 136, 10 A.2d 576 (1940) ("[I]t is wanton negligence, within the meaning of the law, to fail to use ordinary and reasonable care to avoid injury to a trespasser after his presence has been ascertained."); see Ryals v. U.S. Steel Corp., 562 So.2d 192 (Ala. 1990) ("Wantonness may arise after discovery of actual peril, by conscious failure to use preventive means at hand.").

[16] Pridgen v. Boston Housing Authority, 364 Mass. 696, 308 N.E.2d 467, 70 A.L.R.3d 1106 (1974). Distinguish Rhodes v. Illinois Cent. Gulf R.R., 172 Ill.2d 213, 665 N.E.2d 1260, 216 Ill.Dec. 703 (1996) (injured intoxicated person on premises, but injury did not result from landowner's premises or acts, no duty). Liability, if any, is of course limited to harms resulting from the landowner's negligent failure to provide assistance.

[17] See § 25.3.

[18] Restatement Second of Torts §§ 334 & 335 (1965).

[19] Restatement Second of Torts § 12 (1965) defines "reason to know" to mean that the actor had information that would lead a reasonable person to infer the existence of the fact in issue. This is definitely not the same as recognizing a risk or probability that the fact exists."

the landowner cannot escape under the no-duty rule; he owes a duty of reasonable care.[20] Some courts get the same results on the theory that the landowner, by failing to make the cable reasonably visible, has acted willfully or wantonly.[21] Either way, the total picture of duties to trespassers is very different from the one presented by the general no-duty rule.

§ 20.4 Licensees: The Classification

Licensees are those on the land with the landowner's express or implied consent[22] but who are there for their own purposes.[23] They do not qualify for invitee status because they are not on land open to the public generally, and not present for any potential economic transaction with or benefit to the landowner.[24] One who is an invitee on one portion of the land may be a licensee on another.[25]

The traditional definition of licensees has the effect of saying that even social guests are licensees, not invitees, because, although the owner's invitation is consent to their presence, they are not potentially engaged in direct economic transactions with the owner.[26] Quite a few other people fit the definition of a licensee. For examples, people who are hunting or fishing on the land with at least the tacit or implied permission of the landowner are licensees,[27] as are those permissibly on the land to look for their pet,[28] take a short cut,[29] sell goods or distribute advertising[30] or religious literature[31] or to solicit contributions.[32] So are people who are on the premises to help friends or relatives

---

[20] E.g., Webster v. Culbertson, 158 Ariz. 159, 761 P.2d 1063 (1988) (relying in part on Restatement Second of Torts § 337 (1965) as to known trespassers, but applying it, in line with § 335 to a case of a trespasser who was merely foreseeable). Accord, Lee v. Chicago Transit Authority, 152 Ill. 2d 432, 605 N.E.2d 493, 178 Ill. Dec. 699 (1992) (man electrocuted on "third rail"; foreseeability, *semble*, is equivalent to reason to know; it is not necessary to show that the defendant foresaw anyone "about" to encounter danger).

[21] Seeholzer v. Kellstone, Inc., 80 Ohio App.3d 726, 610 N.E.2d 594 (1992).

[22] Restatement Second of Torts § 330 (1965). Those privileged to be on the land for reasons other than the occupier's consent—notably firefighters and police officers—do not fit this definition. See Chapter 24.

[23] Porto v. Carlyle Plaza, Inc., 971 So.2d 940 (Fla. Dist. Ct. App. 2007); Skinner v. Ogallala Pub. Sch. Dist. No. 1, 262 Neb. 387, 631 N.W.2d 510 (2001); Vogt v. Murraywood Swim and Racquet Club, 357 S.C. 506, 593 S.E.2d 617 (2004).

[24] See Johnson v. Investment Co. of the South, LLC, 869 So.2d 1156 (Ala. Civ. App. 2003) (former tenant injured while moving out of her apartment was a licensee, not an invitee, because her moving out did not confer any material or commercial benefit on the landowner); Slavin v. Plumbers & Steamfitters Local 29, 91 Ark. App. 43, 207 S.W.3d 586 (2005) (union member who was injured doing volunteer maintenance work at union hall was a licensee; land not open to the public, and plaintiff was "really there for his own benefit" given the unique nature of unions); Hudson v. Courtesy Motors, Inc., 794 So.2d 999 (Miss. 2001) (person who came on defendant's car lot, not as a potential customer but rather to see an independent seller, was not an invitee of the defendant).

[25] See § 20.6.

[26] Chapman v. Chapman, 147 Idaho 756, 215 P.3d 476 (2009); Carter v. Kinney, 896 S.W.2d 926 (Mo. 1995); Parker v. Rogers, 176 N.J. 491, 825 A.2d 1128 (2003).

[27] Douglas v. Bergland, 216 Mich. 380, 185 N.W.2d 819 (1921) (fisherman); Waller v. Smith, 116 Wash. 645, 200 P. 95 (1921) (hunter), *overruled on other grounds*, Laudermilk v. Carpenter, 78 Wash.2d 92, 457 P.2d 1024 (1969).

[28] French v. Sunburst Properties, 521 N.E.2d 1355 (Ind. App. 1988).

[29] Cochran v. Burger King Corp., 937 S.W.2d 358 (Mo. App. 1996) ("gratuitous licensee").

[30] E.g., Malatesta v. Lowry, 130 So.2d 785 (1961); Stacy v. Shapiro, 212 A.D. 723, 209 N.Y.S. 305 (1925).

[31] Perry v. Williamson, 824 S.W.2d 869 (Ky. 1992); Singleton v. Jackson, 85 Wash.App. 835, 935 P.2d 644 (1997) (Jehovah's Witness, on premises to make "religious solicitation," was implicitly permitted to make contact by way of front door, but was not an invitee).

[32] See Reilly v. Spiegelhalter, 100 N.J. Super. 276, 241 A.2d 665 (1968) (conceded to be at least a licensee); Singleton v. Jackson, 85 Wash.App. 835, 935 P.2d 644 (1997) ("religious solicitation").

with work around the house[33] or to help with a Girl Scout troop[34] or to study the Bible with an owner who does not make a business of such things.[35] Likewise, family members at the defendant's home for no better reason than that the defendant enjoys their company are of course only licensees.[36]

§ 20.5 Duty Owed to Licensees: Traditional Rule

Courts applying the traditional common law classification system have repeatedly said that the duty owed to licensees is the same or substantially the same as the duty owed to trespassers.[37] In the absence of special circumstances, courts do not regard the landowner's permission to enter, or even his invitation to a social guest, as an assurance that the premises will be made safe.[38] Hence, the landowner is under no general duty of reasonable care with respect to conditions on the land, but owes only the duty not to intentionally, willfully, or wantonly injure the licensee.[39] This means, subject to the exceptions below, that the landowner need not inspect the land or correct unsafe conditions for the licensee's benefit.[40] As with trespassers, a duty of reasonable care is imposed once the landowner actually knows or has notice of the licensee's presence and knows or has notice of the danger the licensee is about to encounter.[41]

Conditions on the land. The duty to licensees may go beyond the duty to trespassers both as to passive conditions on the land and as to active negligence. As to conditions, the landowner is under a duty at least to warn when he knows, or has reason to know[42] both (1) the existence of a danger and (2) the plaintiff's presence in a place where she might encounter it. This is the same rule used for trespassers. The question is whether, in the case of licensees, the duty is imposed more readily.

It would be possible to say that a "should have known" test is applied to both factors. Alternatively, it would be possible to say that such a test is applied to one factor, but as to the other the landowner must have actually known or had reason to know. The Restatement says the defendant must either know or "have reason to know" of the first factor, danger.[43] This means that the landowner who should have known of the danger,

---

[33]   Young v. Paxton, 316 Ark. 655, 873 S.W.2d 546 (1994); but cf. Pinnell v. Bates, 838 So.2d 198 (Miss. 2002) (guest helping host unpack items in new home may have been an invitee; issue of fact for jury).

[34]   Zuther v. Schild, 224 Kan. 528, 581 P.2d 385 (1978). The classification in *Zuther* is now obsolete in Kansas with its adoption of a general reasonable care standard. Jones v. Hansen, 254 Kan. 499, 867 P.2d 303 (1994). See § 20.9.

[35]   Carter v. Kinney, 896 S.W.2d 926 (Mo. 1995).

[36]   See Reicheneker v. Reicheneker, 264 Neb. 682, 651 N.W.2d 224 (2002) (grandmother babysitting three-year-old without pay because she enjoyed spending time with him, not an invitee).

[37]   E.g., Waddell v. New River Co., 141 W.Va. 880, 93 S.E.2d 473 (1956).

[38]   See, e.g., Vogt v. Murraywood Swim and Racquet Club, 357 S.C. 506, 593 S.E.2d 617 (2004) (guest of club member was a licensee).

[39]   E.g., Nucor Corp. v. Kilman, 358 Ark. 107, 186 S.W.3d 720 (2004); Illinois Central R. v. White, 610 So.2d 308, 316 (Miss. 1992) ("The duty owed to a licensee and trespasser is the same, i.e., not to willfully or wantonly injure him.").

[40]   E.g., Furstein v. Hill, 218 Conn. 610, 590 A.2d 939 (1991).

[41]   See Chapman v. Chapman, 147 Idaho 756, 215 P.3d 476 (2009); Illinois Central R. v. White, 610 So.2d 308 (Miss. 1992). As with trespassers, courts sometimes say that it is willful or wanton not to use reasonable care after the licensee's presence is or should be known. Cooper v. Corporate Property Investors, 220 Ga.App. 889, 470 S.E.2d 689 (1996). As applied to leased premises, the landlord and tenant who know of the dangerous condition both owe a duty to warn the tenant's social guest. Rittenour v. Gibson, 656 N.W.2d 691 (N.D. 2003).

[42]   See § 20.3.

[43]   Restatement Second of Torts § 342 (1965).

but did not, would have no duty to a licensee whose presence was known.[44] Sometimes, however, courts say that the landowner must make the premises "as safe as they appear to be," a statement that can be read abstractly to imply that the landowner is responsible even if he did not actually know of the danger.[45]

As to the second factor, the licensee's presence, the Restatement makes no clear and explicit statement. Perhaps it is enough that the presence of the licensee could be reasonably foreseen, that is, that the landowner should have known the licensee was or might be present. Some cases seem to take this view,[46] while others seem to require actual knowledge of the licensee's presence.[47] For instance, in an Arkansas case, the owner knew that friends of farm employees sometimes came to the farm and shared the employees' work until their work day was done. Knowing that and also knowing the dangers of specialized machinery, the landowner owed a duty of reasonable warning to the licensee-visitors.[48]

Activities on the land. Courts have imposed duties of reasonable care with respect to activities as distinct from mere conditions on the land[49] when the landowner should foresee the risk of harm.[50] So if a landowner is engaged in active operations on the land, for example by driving vehicles, operating cranes, or constructing buildings, he must keep a reasonable lookout for licensees who have permission to be present and must govern his operations by the standards of reasonable care.[51]

The remaining negligence issue. The warning required in all duty cases applies here: to establish a duty of care is not to prove its breach. The landowner who is required to keep a reasonable lookout is not necessarily required to keep a constant lookout for a licensee who is unlikely to appear.[52] Equally, if the landowner reasonably believes that the licensee knows of the danger or would discover the danger and protect herself, the landowner is not negligent, although courts may express this notion by saying that the landowner is under no duty of care with respect to such dangers.[53] This is not a question

---

[44] See Parks v. Rogers, 176 N.J. 491, 825 A.2d 1128 (2003) ("the social guest is at least entitled to the same knowledge possessed by the host").

[45] Holzheimer v. Johannsen, 125 Idaho 397, 871 P.2d 814 (1994) ("A landowner is only required to share with the licensee knowledge of dangerous conditions or activities on the land."); Scifres v. Kraft, 916 S.W.2d 779, 781 (Ky.App. 1996) ("A possessor of land owes a licensee the duty of reasonable care either to make the land as safe as it appears, or to disclose the fact that it is as dangerous as he knows it to be.").

[46] Cooper v. Corporate Property Investors, 220 Ga.App. 889, 891, 470 S.E.2d 689, 691 (1996) ("[A]s to a licensee, ordinary care and diligence must be used to prevent injuring him after his presence is known or reasonably should be anticipated.").

[47] See Nunez v. Spino, 14 So.3d 82 (Miss. App. 2009).

[48] Dorton v. Francisco, 309 Ark. 472, 833 S.W.2d 362 (1992).

[49] Morin v. Bell Court Condominium Ass'n, 223 Conn. 323, 612 A.2d 1197 (1992); Lipham v. Federated Dep't Stores, Inc., 263 Ga. 865, 440 S.E.2d 193 (1994) (host negligently bumped into guest); Hoffman v. Planters Gin Co., 358 So.2d 1008 (Miss. 1978) (plaintiff's leg amputated by operating auger in a cotton gin).

[50] E.g., Saucier v. Biloxi Regional Medical Center, 708 So.2d 1351 (Miss. 1998).

[51] Jeffries v. Potomac Development Corp., 822 F.2d 87 (D.C. Cir. 1987) (licensee by invitation, duty of reasonable care as to affirmative acts); Ragnone v. Portland School Dist. No. 1J, 291 Or. 617, 633 P.2d 1287 (1981) ("As to activities on the land, the occupier has a duty to exercise reasonable care for the protection of a licensee.").

[52] Cf. Lane v. Gilbert Const. Co., 383 S.C. 590, 681 S.E.2d 879 (2009) (duty owed to licensee includes using reasonable care to discover the licensee).

[53] Young v. Paxton, 316 Ark. 655, 873 S.W.2d 546 (1994); Dorr v. Big Creek Wood Products, Inc., 84 Wash.App. 420, 927 P.2d 1148 (1996); see Restatement Second of Torts §§ 341 to 342 (1965). Section 342 puts both an objective and a subjective test. The landowner is not liable if he reasonably believes that the licensee will discover the danger and protect herself. Id. § 342(a). The landowner is also not liable if the licensee does in fact know or have reason to know of the danger. Id. § 342(c). This second or subjective test seems to be an

of the licensee's contributory negligence in failing to avoid the danger, which is a matter entirely distinct from the question of the landowner's duty and breach. Courts typically speak as if the fact that the danger is obvious or open is enough in itself to eliminate any duty by the landowner to warn of the danger.[54] However, the fact that a danger is obvious is good, but not necessarily conclusive, evidence that the licensee can be expected to avoid the danger without a warning by the landowner.[55]

§ 20.6 Invitees: The Classification

Entrants are in the invitee classification if they are either (a) "public invitees" who are expressly or impliedly invited to enter the land as a member of the public, or (b) "business invitees," who are invited to enter the land in connection with some business dealing with the landowner or occupier.[56] Landowners ordinarily owe a duty of reasonable care to their invitees.[57]

An "invitation" is an essential element under both the public invitee and business invitee tests, although it is not sufficient to confer invitee status.[58] A person who is on the land under an official privilege—a firefighter, for example—is not an invitee at all.[59] The word "invitation" is itself a term of art. In few cases does the invitee have a personal, formal, and express invitation. The invitation is found in the fact that the premises are held open to the public as in the case of retail stores, airports, and public parks, or in the fact that the landowner has arranged for the plaintiff to be on the land, as in the case of a contractor hired to haul out garbage. Any conduct that communicates the idea that the entrant's presence is desired will do.[60] On the other hand, the landowner who merely permits a hunter to use his land has not issued any invitation at all, even implicitly.

Perhaps the focus should be less on invitation than on the underlying principle. The real point is that anyone who receives implicit or explicit assurance of safety is entitled to the invitee status and the reasonable care that goes with it.[61] The public invitee and business visitor categories only represent efforts to find objective correlatives to this underlying principle.

---

inappropriate importation of contributory negligence rules. So far as duty and negligence are concerned, the test is logically about what the landowner could reasonably expect of the licensee.

[54] See Scott v. Archon Group, L.P., 191 P.3d 1207 (Okla. 2008).

[55] See Bagnana v. Wolfinger, 385 N.J.Super. 1, 10, 895 A.2d 1180, 1186 (2006); cf. Tincani v. Inland Empire Zoological Soc'y, 124 Wash.2d 121, 875 P.2d 621 (1994) (defining open and apparent danger as one of which the licensee knows or has reason to know). The topic is discussed in more detail in § 20.7.

[56] Restatement Second of Torts § 332 (1965).

[57] See § 20.7.

[58] See Cole v. Fairchild, 198 W.Va. 736, 482 S.E.2d 913 (1996).

[59] The upshot is that firefighters and police officers are treated more or less like licensees in many cases, although the theory has become more complicated. See Chapter 24.

[60] Cole v. Fairchild, 198 W.Va. 736, 482 S.E.2d 913 (1996) ("An 'invitation' occurs when a possessor of certain premises exhibits conduct which makes others believe the possessor wants them to be on the premises.").

[61] See Blair v. Ohio Dep't of Rehab. & Corr., 61 Ohio Misc.2d 649, 582 N.E.2d 673 (Ct. Cl. 1989) ("the basis for invitee status is the implied assurance of safety conveyed to the visitor"). Scores of cases have quoted or paraphrased the assertion that the invitee enters upon the representation or assurance that the land has been prepared and made safe for his reception. See Restatement Second of Torts § 343, cmt. b (1965). That statement implies something about the nature of the landowner duty, but also something about who counts as an invitee—one who receives assurances, often implicit, that the land is reasonably safe for her entry.

Who is included in the invitee category. Customers and prospective customers on the premises of any business open to sell goods,[62] provide services,[63] entertainment[64] or recreation[65] are easily invitees by any definition. So are employees,[66] independent contractors,[67] and the employees of independent contractors[68] who have been expressly or impliedly invited to the land. So are people who are invited to private portions of the premises, if they are invited for potential economic benefit of the landowner.[69] When consistent with the purpose for which the invitation is implicitly or explicitly issued, those who accompany the invitee are themselves invitees.[70] Visitors to invitees are also invitees in some cases. For example, visitors to patients in a hospital[71] and visitors to inmates in a correctional institution[72] are invitees, as are those who enter a cemetery to visit a grave.[73]

When courts thought of invitees solely as "business visitors," it was hard to explain many of the actual decisions, which are now entirely understandable on the ground that invitees include every person on land open to the public, as long as his presence is consistent with the public invitation. So you are an invitee in a store at the airport even if you enter only to kill time between flights and have no intention of buying anything.[74] If you have children in tow, they, too are invitees.[75] If you are at the airport to see a

---

[62]   E.g., Hose v. Winn-Dixie Montgomery, Inc., 658 So.2d 403 (Ala. 1995); Clohesy v. Food Circus Supermarkets, Inc. 149 N.J. 496, 694 A.2d 1017 (1997); Hoover v. Broome, 324 S.C. 531, 479 S.E.2d 62 (Ct. App. 1997); Janis v. Nash Finch Co., 780 N.W.2d 497 (S.D. 2010).

[63]   See Boren v. Worthen Nat'l Bank of Arkansas, 324 Ark. 416, 921 S.W.2d 934 (1996) (bank customer); Branks v. Kern, 320 N.C. 621, 359 S.E.2d 780, 68 A.L.R.4th 817 (1987) (pet owner in veterinarian's office), *abrogated on other grounds by* Nelson v. Freeland, 349 N.C. 615, 507 S.E.2d 882 (1998) (modifying common-law entrant-classification scheme). When the service itself rather than a condition of the land is the source of harm, the service provider may be held to a duty appropriate to the type of service. A health care provider, for example, would be held to that special standard in the provision of those services. See Chapter 21.

[64]   Martin v. City of Washington, Mo., 848 S.W.2d 487 (Mo. 1993) (high school football game, bleachers gave way with the plaintiff, who was classified as a public invitee); Mostert v. CBL & Associates, 741 P.2d 1090 (Wyo. 1987) (movie patron invitee and entitled to warning of off-premises flash flooding due to storms during movie).

[65]   E.g., Hylazewski v. Wet 'N Wild, Inc., 432 So.2d 1371 (Fla. App. 1983) (swimming pool, artificial waves); Peterson v. Summit Fitness, Inc., 920 S.W.2d 928 (Mo. App. 1996) (fitness center, swimming pool).

[66]   Afoa v. Port of Seattle, 176 Wash.2d 460, 296 P.3d 800 (2013).

[67]   See Lane v. Groetz, 108 N.H. 173, 230 A.2d 741 (1967); Dawson v. Bunker Hill Plaza Associates, 289 N.J.Super. 309, 673 A.2d 847 (1996). This category includes those who by invitation make delivery of goods, e.g., Busy Fee Buffet v. Ferrell, 82 Ariz. 192, 310 P.2d 817 (1957), and those who haul trash or garbage out. Hull v. Bishop-Stoddard Cafeteria, 238 Iowa 650, 26 N.W.2d 429 (1947).

[68]   Montes v. Indian Cliffs Ranch, Inc., 946 S.W.2d 103 (Tex. App. 1997).

[69]   Cf. Landry v. Hilton Head Plantation Property Owners Ass'n, 317 S.C. 200, 452 S.E.2d 619 (1994) (resident of gated community an invitee while in common areas of the community, since resident's presence conferred economic benefit on owners).

[70]   This is true of children, for example, but not only children. See Morris v. De La Torre, 36 Cal. 4th 260, 113 P.3d 1182, 30 Cal. Rptr. 3d 173 (2005) (plaintiff was an invitee when he accompanied friends to the defendant's restaurant, although he did not intend to eat); but see Vogt v. Murraywood Swim and Racquet Club, 357 S.C. 506, 593 S.E.2d 617 (2004) (guest invited onto club premises by member of club was a licensee).

[71]   Wieseler v. Sisters of Mercy Health Corp., 540 N.W.2d 445 (Iowa 1995); Sutherland v. Saint Francis Hospital, Inc., 595 P.2d 780 (Okla. 1979).

[72]   Blair v. Ohio Dep't of Rehab. & Corr., 61 Ohio Misc.2d 649, 582 N.E.2d 673 (Ct. Cl. 1989).

[73]   Gaita v. Laurel Grove Cemetery Co., 323 N.J. Super. 89, 731 A.2d 1245 (1998); see Thomas J. Goger, Annotation, Liability in Action Based upon Negligence, for Injury to, or Death of, Person Going upon Cemetery Premises, 63 A.L.R.3d 1252 (1975) (also reflecting some cases holding visitors to be licensees).

[74]   Cf. Hoover v. Broome, 324 S.C. 531, 479 S.E.2d 62 (App. 1997) (entering service station to ask directions).

[75]   E.g., Orr v. First Nat'l Stores, Inc., 280 A.2d 785 (Me. 1971).

friend off, you are still an invitee, and so is the photographer taking pictures of deplaning passengers.[76] It is no longer necessary to justify such holdings with farfetched suggestions that the visitor who buys nothing today might do so at some indefinite time in the future. The public invitee category can cover these examples quite easily, as well as the case in which you enter a public park or national forest where no economic transaction is even possible.[77]

The tests also explain why salespersons calling at a residence can be classified in different ways. A salesperson who comes uninvited to your home is not an invitee, for she has no invitation of any kind.[78] The salesperson who comes in response to an implicit or explicit invitation is a business invitee, for that person has an invitation to be there and is dealing with you in a potential economic exchange.[79] Similarly, a delivery person who comes to your door with a package, even though you did not order it, may be a business invitee where the you had accepted such deliveries for years, on a theory that such deliveries provide you with a material benefit.[80] Finally, the salesperson who enters a place open to the public should qualify as a public invitee.

Scope of invitation. The scope of the invitation or assurance of safety may be limited. For this reason, a person may be an invitee on one portion of the premises but not on another.[81] For instance, the plaintiff at a shopping mall may be an invitee on the parking lot, but not while taking a shortcut through the flower bed.[82] And a person may be an invitee at one time but not another.[83] For instance, a restaurant customer is an invitee when she parks and retrieves her car during serving hours,[84] but not when she leaves her car there and returns for it after the restaurant is closed.[85] The nature of the invitation and its purposes, custom, and reasonable expectations of the invitee are usually a clear guide. The layout of the premises may also be instructive. A customer in search of a public restroom on the premises is still an invitee if she reasonably enters a storeroom by mistake.[86] Courts have also held that an invitation to enter for one purpose

---

[76] Cf. Mathias v. Denver Union Terminal Ry. Co., 137 Colo. 224, 323 P.2d 624 (1958) (photographer making photographs at train station was invitee so long as he was in area intended for public use).

[77] Smith v. United States, 117 F.Supp. 525 (N.D. Cal. 1953) (public campground in National Forest owned by United States).

[78] Stacy v. Shapiro, 212 A.D. 723, 209 N.Y.S. 305 (1925); Bidiman v. Gehrts, 133 Or.App. 145, 890 P.2d 436 (1995) (insurance agent had previously contacted the defendant for policy renewal at defendant's business, not at home; no implicit invitation); cf. Edmunds v. Copeland, 197 Ga.App. 292, 398 S.E.2d 280 (1990) (invitation not established, insurance sales agent was a licensee only); Singleton v. Jackson, 85 Wash.App. 835, 935 P.2d 644 (1997) (entrance to make religious solicitation was by implicit permission, but not by invitation, hence solicitor was licensee only).

[79] Handleman v. Cox, 39 N.J. 95, 187 A.2d 708 (1963) (salespersons on portion of premises not open to the public, but prior dealings of the parties would support a jury finding of invitation to be there).

[80] Johnson v. Short, 213 Or. App. 255, 160 P.3d 1004 (2007).

[81] E.g., Handy v. Nejam, 111 So.3d 610 (Miss. 2013); Mathias v. Denver Union Terminal Ry. Co., 137 Colo. 224, 323 P.2d 624 (1958); Gladon v. Greater Cleveland Regional Transit Auth., 75 Ohio St.3d 312, 662 N.E.2d 287 (1996); Egede-Nissen v. Crystal Mountain, Inc., 93 Wash.2d 127, 606 P.2d 1214 (1980).

[82] Cf. Nicoletti v. Westcor, Inc., 131 Ariz. 140, 639 P.2d 330 (1982) (short cut through plantings).

[83] Restatement Second of Torts § 332, cmt. l (1965).

[84] Morris v. De La Torre, 36 Cal. 4th 260, 113 P.3d 1182, 30 Cal. Rptr. 3d 173 (2005) (attack on plaintiff in restaurant parking lot, plaintiff who was an invitee inside the restaurant was still an invitee and owed a duty of care).

[85] Savage v. Flagler Company, 185 Ga.App. 334, 364 S.E.2d 52 (1987), *modified on other grounds,* Flagler Company v. Savage, 258 Ga. 335, 368 S.E.2d 504 (1988).

[86] Miniken v. Carr, 71 Wash.2d 325, 428 P.2d 716 (1967).

may not carry with it an assurance of safety when the entrant uses the land for an inconsistent purpose.[87]

§ 20.7 Duty Owed to Invitees

General duties of care. The landowner owes to the invitee a non-delegable[88] duty of care to make conditions on the land reasonably safe[89] and to conduct his active operations with reasonable care for the invitee whose presence is known or reasonably foreseeable.[90] In addition, building codes may impose structural requirements, and, under the usual rules,[91] violation of a code's safety provision can establish negligence per se[92] or at least furnish evidence of negligence.[93] Even apart from statute, reasonable care under the circumstances sometimes requires an inspection of the premises and active steps to make the premises safe.[94] But sometimes reasonable care does not suggest that inspection is needed. Where conditions appear to be safe, the landowner is not negligent in failing to inspect for dangers.[95] In other cases, the landowner may satisfy his duty of reasonable care by providing an adequate warning of dangerous conditions.[96] Under limited circumstances, the landowner also owes a duty of care to protect the invitee from other persons or from animals.[97] Given the duty of reasonable care, the invitee's suit is an ordinary negligence case and the ordinary rules of negligence apply, so that the

---

[87]   Markle v. Hacienda Mexican Restaurant, 570 N.E.2d 969 (Ind. 1991) (plaintiff drove into shopping center to eat at a restaurant there, saw a friend, and was transferring an item from his vehicle to his friend's when he fell in a pothole; jury question whether this was within the scope of the invitation); cf. Chapman v. Willey, 134 P.3d 568 (Colo. App. 2006) (man with landowner's permission to visit his wife at motel was a trespasser when he went there to fight with another man).

[88]   See Backiel v. Citibank, N.A., 299 A.D.2d 504, 751 N.Y.S.2d 492 (2002) (duty of landowner to keep entryways and common passages safe is nondelegable); Thomas v. E-Z Mart Stores, Inc., 102 P.3d 133 (Okla. 2004) (store owed invitee a nondelegable duty to act reasonably to assure that floor mats supplied by another company at store's entrance were safe).

[89]   Mensink v. American Grain, 564 N.W.2d 376 (Iowa 1997); Janis v. Nash Finch Co., 780 N.W.2d 497 (S.D. 2010); Adkins v. Chevron, USA, Inc., 199 W.Va. 518, 485 S.E.2d 687 (1997); Restatement Second of Torts § 343 (1965).

[90]   E.g., New York Cent. R. v. Wyatt, 135 Ind.App. 205, 184 N.E.2d 657 (1962). See Glen Weissenberger & Barbara B. McFarland, The Law of Premises Liability § 4.10 (4th ed. 2014). When active operations or negligent delivery of services are involved, courts often proceed directly to discussion of ordinary negligence without classifying the plaintiff.

[91]   See Chapter 11.

[92]   Vega v. Eastern Courtyard Associates, 24 P.3d 219 (Nev. 2001); cf. Pierce v. ALSC Architects, P.S., 270 Mont. 97, 890 P.2d 1254 (1995) (architect negligent per se for design in violation of code).

[93]   Chambers v. St. Mary's School, 82 Ohio St.3d 563, 697 N.E.2d 198 (1998) (under state's rule that violation of administrative codes is not negligence per se); Elliott v. City of New York, 95 N.Y.2d 730, 747 N.E.2d 760, 724 N.Y.S.2d 397 (2001) (under state's rule that violation of ordinances is evidence of negligence only).

[94]   See Mensink v. American Grain, 564 N.W.2d 376 (Iowa 1997).

[95]   See Benham v. King, 700 N.W.2d 314 (Iowa 2005) (dentist was not negligent in failing to inspect dental chair where manufacturer had not suggested any form of maintenance).

[96]   Providing an inadequate warning will not, of course, satisfy the duty. See TXI Operations, L.P. v. Perry, 278 S.W.3d 763 (Tex. 2009) (a 15 mile-per-hour speed limit sign was inadequate as a matter of law to warn of a massive pothole in defendant's road).

[97]   Restatement Second of Torts § 344 (1965); see Chapter 26 (on protecting from third persons). But see Luoni v. Berube, 431 Mass. 729, 729 N.E.2d 1108 (2000) (landowner owed no duty to social guests to protect them from fireworks brought and used by other guests, since the risk did not arise from the guests' use of the defendant's land or chattels); Smaxwell v. Bayard, 274 Wis.2d 278, 682 N.W.2d 923 (2004) (landowner not liable to protect persons lawfully on the land from known dangers of dogs, where the landowner was not the owner or keeper of the dogs).

plaintiff must prove actual and proximate cause as well as negligence by the defendant in creating or maintaining an unreasonably dangerous condition.[98]

Slip-and-fall cases. Slip-and-fall cases and their variants[99] are quite common.[100] The duty of reasonable care is routinely played out in three ways:

(a) The defendant negligently creates the dangerous condition or an unreasonable risk of it. Such a defendant may be subjected to liability for injuries suffered in the invitee's fall. The clear cases are those in which the defendant's employees themselves create the condition, as where a grocery clerk spills a slippery substance on the floor, or the defendant negligently waxes the floor.[101]

(b) The landowner's mode of operation is negligent, as where he negligently markets goods in such a way that they are likely to be dislodged by other customers with resulting injury to the plaintiff.[102] Once an inference of negligence arises in these "mode of operation" cases, most courts shift the burden of producing evidence of non-negligence to the defendant.[103]

(c) Some unknown person creates a condition of danger, by dropping a substance on the floor for example. The store defendant is not negligent in creating the danger but may be negligent in failing to inspect periodically for such mishaps.[104]

---

[98] Harradon v. Schlamadinger, 913 N.E.2d 297 (Ind. App. 2009) (soft sofa on which a sleeping baby suffocated was not an "unreasonably dangerous condition" on land).

[99] As where merchandise falls on a customer, or a customer carrying parcels collides with an object in the aisle. See Linda A. Sharp, Annotation, Liability for Injury to Customer from Object Projecting into Aisle or Passageway in Store, 40 A.L.R.5th 135 (1996); Michael P. Sullivan, Annotation, Liability for Injury to Customer or Other Invitee of Retail Store by Falling of Displayed, Stored, or Piled Objects, 61 A.L.R.4th 27 (1989).

[100] Many are reviewed in annotations. See, e.g., Sonja A. Soehnel, Annotation, Liability of Operator of Grocery Store to Invitee Slipping on Spilled Liquid or Semiliquid Substance, 24 A.L.R.4th 696 (1981)

[101] Morris v. Wal-Mart Stores, Inc., 330 F.3d 854 (6th Cir. 2003) (by inference, defendant installed a freezer without a plug, permitting it to drain water into area where shoppers pushing carts could slip); Getchell v. Rogers Jewelry, 203 Cal. App. 4th 381, 136 Cal. Rptr. 3d 641 (2012) (cleaning solution on floor; where plaintiff produces evidence from which a reasonable inference can be drawn that the dangerous condition was created by the defendant, the defendant is charged with notice of that condition); Finan v. Atria East Associates, 230 A.D.2d 707, 646 N.Y.S.2d 164 (1996) (claim of negligently waxed floor); Smith v. Wal-Mart Stores, Inc., 314 S.C. 248, 442 S.E.2d 606 (1994) (same).

[102] The mode of operation rule should not apply generally to all accidents in self-service retail establishments, but only to those accidents that result from particular hazards that either occur regularly or are inherently foreseeable due to the particular mode of operation employed on the premises. Fisher v. Big Y Foods, Inc., 298 Conn. 414, 3 A.3d 919 (2010). See also FGA, Inc. v. Giglio, 278 P.3d 490 (Nev. 2012) (mode of operation instruction is proper only where there is evidence that the defendant created an increased risk of a potentially hazardous condition by having its customers perform tasks traditionally carried out by employees).

[103] E.g., Kelly v. Stop and Shop, Inc., 281 Conn. 768, 918 A.2d 249 (2007); Markowitz v. Helen Homes of Kendall Corp., 826 So.2d 256 (Fla. 2002); Sheehan v. Roche Bros. Supermarkets, Inc., 448 Mass. 780, 863 N.E.2d 1276 (2007); Nisivoccia v. Glass Gardens, Inc., 175 N.J. 559, 818 A.2d 314 (2003); Blair v. West Town Mall, 130 S.W.3d 761 (Tenn. 2004); Owens v. Redd, 215 Va. 13, 205 S.E.2d 669 (1974); Malaney v. Hannaford Bros. Co., 177 Vt. 123, 861 A.2d 1069 (2004). See Glen Weissenberger & Barbara B. McFarland, The Law of Premises Liability § 7.06 (4th ed. 2014).

[104] Courts often say in these cases that the defendant must have actual or constructive knowledge of the danger. See, e.g., American Multi-Cinema, Inc. v. Brown, 285 Ga. 442, 679 S.E.2d 25 (2009). This expression is merely another way of saying that the plaintiff must prove that the defendant either knew or should have known of the danger. See, e.g., Thoma v. Cracker Barrel Old Country Store, Inc., 649 So.2d 277 (Fla. App. 1995); Jones v. Imperial Palace of Mississippi, LLC, 147 So.3d 318 (Miss. 2014). Some courts view this not as

In this last scenario, courts tend to say that if the substance has been present for a long period of time, the trier can infer that the store was negligent in failing to inspect or discover.[105] California has said that failure to inspect for a long time warrants an inference that the substance has been present for a long time.[106] Sometimes the reasoning in cases is so stylized that the results look almost like a kind of strict liability.[107] On the other hand, courts usually refuse to apply res ipsa loquitur to slip and fall cases,[108] and if no evidence supports an inference that the condition has been present for a substantial period, the jury has no basis for concluding that the defendant was negligent.[109]

Traditional rule for obvious dangers. Following the First Restatement, courts often said, and some still say, that the landowner owed no duty to his invitees to make the premises safe or to warn of dangers known or obvious to invitees.[110] That was equivalent to saying that if the danger was open or obvious, then the defendant was under no duty at all, even if he could expect that invitees would not learn enough to protect themselves. Some states have held that where the injury to the invitee arises from a condition on land, the plaintiff must prove that the landowner had "superior knowledge" of the danger.[111] When the danger is equally obvious to both the entrant and the landowner, that fact will obviously be unprovable.

Traditional rule for natural accumulations. Courts have also sometimes said that the landowner was not liable to invitees for injuries resulting from natural accumulations of snow or ice. But some of the cases cited for this proposition seem to involve injuries on the public sidewalk adjacent to the land rather than on the land itself; others seem to be applications of the open-and-obvious danger rule.[112] The accumulations rule, as applied on the land itself, would therefore presumably be modified when the open-and-obvious danger rule is modified.[113]

---

a requirement but rather as a factor in the negligence analysis. See, e.g., Edenshaw v. Safeway, Inc., 186 P.3d 568 (Alaska 2008).

[105] E.g., J. Weingarten, Inc. v. Thompson, 251 Ark. 914, 475 S.W.2d 697 (1972) (from discoloration of old, black-looking leaf, far from vegetable display, an inference that it had been present two days in spite of regular cleanups).

[106] Ortega v. K-Mart Corp., 26 Cal.4th 1200, 36 P.3d 11, 114 Cal.Rptr.2d 470 (2001).

[107] In Sokolowski v. Medi Mart, Inc., 24 Conn.App. 276, 587 A.2d 1056 (1991), the plaintiff slipped on a substance on the floor, perhaps a lotion. Workers were standing nearby for 15 minutes and had not heard a bottle break. Hence, the court reasoned, the substance might have been on the floor more than 15 minutes and that was sufficient time for a reasonable store to discover the condition and make it safe. Similarly, in Kenney v. Kroger Co., 569 So.2d 357 (Ala. 1990), the fact that a bottle of liquid was open on the shelf and a large amount of liquid had spilled or dripped to the floor was said to support an inference that the condition had been present a long time.

[108] See, e.g., Ex parte Harold L. Martin Distributing Co., 769 So.2d 313 (Ala. 2000); contra, Morris v. Wal-Mart Stores, Inc., 330 F.3d 854 (6th Cir. 2003) (applying Tennessee law).

[109] E.g., Gulycz v. Stop and Shop Companies, 29 Conn. App. 519, 615 A.2d 1087 (1992); Hartley v. Waldbaum, Inc., 69 A.D.3d 902, 893 N.Y.S.2d 272 (2010); Wal-Mart Stores, Inc. v. Spates, 186 S.W.3d 566 (Tex. 2006).

[110] E.g., Wood v. RIH Acquisitions MS II, LLC, 556 F.3d 274 (5th Cir. 2009) (applying Mississippi law); Dolgencorp, Inc. v. Taylor, 28 So. 3d 737 (Ala. 2009); Armstrong v. Best Buy Co., 99 Ohio St.3d 79, 788 N.E.2d 1088 (2003); Griebler v. Doughboy Recreational, Inc., 160 Wis.2d 547, 466 N.W.2d 897 (1991).

[111] E.g., Warner v. Simmons, 288 Neb. 472, 849 N.W.2d 475 (2014).

[112] See Brandert v. Scottsbluff Nat'l Bank & Trust Co., 194 Neb. 777, 235 N.W.2d 864 (1975); Wilden v. Neumann, 344 Mont. 407, 189 P.3d 610 (2008) (landlord owed no duty to keep adjacent city-owned alley free of ice and snow).

[113] See Iwai v. State, 129 Wash.2d 84, 915 P.2d 1089 (1996); see also Papadopoulos v. Target Corp., 457 Mass. 368, 930 N.E.2d 142 (2010) (citing the earlier modification to the open-and-obvious rule, holding that

The Restatement rule for obvious dangers. The Second Restatement, in line with general negligence law, adopted a more cautious view. It provided that when the allegedly dangerous condition is open and obvious, the landowner is not liable to invitees for harm from known or obvious dangers except where the landowner should anticipate harm in spite of the knowledge or obviousness.[114] The Third Restatement is in accord, except it extends this rule not only to invitees but to all entrants onto land, except non-flagrant trespassers.[115] Putting this rule other way around, the landowner is subject to liability if he can foresee harm in spite of the fact that the danger was obvious. In recent years, this view has commanded substantial acceptance where it has been expressly considered.[116] Whether a defendant should have foreseen the plaintiff's encounter with a particular "obvious" hazard will present a jury issue where reasonable people can differ.[117]

Basis for the Restatement rule. For the Restatement and its adherents, the basis of the rule is that the landowner is not negligent at all if he can foresee no harm, and that is the case if he can reasonably believe that the invitee will (a) know or see the danger and (b) avoid it.[118] On the other hand, he is indeed negligent if he can foresee that the plaintiff will encounter the danger in spite of its obvious character and fails to take reasonable steps to protect the plaintiff from that danger.[119] As the Utah court said, the old no-duty version of the open and obvious danger rule in effect excused the defendant's negligence, while the Restatement's rule defines it, yoking it firmly to the ordinary foreseeability test.[120]

Where plaintiff's encounter with obvious danger is foreseeable. Landowners can foresee that the invitee will encounter an obvious danger for several reasons. First, in some cases the plaintiff's only reasonable choice is to encounter the danger. A tenant in an apartment building, for example, may be required to cross a floor maintained by the

---

there is no distinction between natural and unnatural accumulations of snow and ice for purposes of a premises liability claim).

[114]   Restatement Second of Torts § 343A(1) (1965).

[115]   Restatement Third of Torts (Liability for Physical and Emotional Harm) § 51, cmt. k (2012). See Foster v. Costco Wholesale Corp., 291 P.3d 150 (Nev. 2012) (open and obvious character of hazard does not automatically relieve the landowner of a duty of due care, but rather bears on the assessment of whether reasonable care was exercised).

[116]   See, e.g., DeBusscher v. Sam's East, Inc., 505 F.3d 475 (6th Cir. 2007) (Michigan law); Shelton v. Kentucky Easter Seals Soc., Inc., 413 S.W.3d 901 (Ky. 2013); O'Sullivan v. Shaw, 431 Mass. 201, 726 N.E.2d 951 (2000); Warner v. Simmons, 288 Neb. 472, 849 N.W.2d 475 (2014); Foster v. Costco Wholesale Corp., 291 P.3d 150 (Nev. 2012). See also Ernest H. Schopler, Annotation, Modern Status of the Rule Absolving a Possessor of Land of Liability to Those Coming Thereon for Harm Caused by Dangerous Physical Conditions of Which the Injured Party Knew and Realized the Risk, 35 A.L.R.3d 230 (1971).

[117]   See, e.g., Lombard v. Colorado Outdoor Educ. Center, Inc., 187 P.3d 565 (Colo. 2008); Shelton v. Kentucky Easter Seals Soc., Inc., 413 S.W.3d 901 (Ky. 2013); Dos Santos v. Coleta, 465 Mass. 148, 987 N.E.2d 1187 (2013); Grolean v. Bjornson Oil Co., 676 N.W.2d 763 (N.D. 2004).

[118]   See Lugo v. Ameritech Corp., Inc., 464 Mich. 512, 629 N.W.2d 384 (2001); General Elec. Co. v. Moritz, 257 S.W.3d 211 (Tex. 2008); Restatement Third of Torts (Liability for Physical and Emotional Harm) § 51, cmt. k (2012) ("Known or obvious risks pose a reduced risk compared to comparable latent dangers because those exposed can take precautions to protect themselves."). Whether a dangerous condition is "open and obvious" at all may present a jury question. See Bruns v. City of Centralia, 21 N.E.3d 684 (Ill. 2014).

[119]   Even where the defendant owes a duty to protect the plaintiff from an obvious risk, that duty is not breached where the defendant takes adequate precautions. See Payne v. United States, 359 F.3d 132 (2d Cir. 2004) (New York law).

[120]   Hale v. Beckstead, 116 P.3d 263 (Utah 2005) ("Though the distinction between excusing acknowledged negligence and defining a narrow duty of care may be subtle, we find it nonetheless important. Where there is no duty, there is no fault to compare or distribute under the comparative fault scheme.").

landlord that has become dangerously slippery from waxing, or to cross ice on the steps in order to reach her apartment. Even if she knows the danger, a decision to encounter it is more reasonable than a decision to never enter her apartment. The plaintiff's decision to encounter a known danger will often be reasonable when the plaintiff is exercising a right like the tenant's right to reach her own apartment through a common passageway, or the right of a member of the public to use public land or to reach a public utility.[121] Similarly, the plaintiff's decision to encounter a known risk is sometimes reasonable when the plaintiff must take the risk to fulfill an obligation or to carry out employment obligations.[122]

A second kind of case in which the plaintiff's encounter with obvious danger is foreseeable is one in which the plaintiff is foreseeably distracted,[123] or acts under emergency or pressing need. A grocery store owner who puts watermelons down in a crowded aisle may be able to foresee that a distracted shopper will take a step backward and fall.[124] The operator of a pharmacy that remains open in spite of ice covering its parking lot and entrance must surely hope and foresee that people will attempt to enter, and must surely foresee that one of them might be injured in a fall.[125] In such cases, the result would turn on the plaintiff's possible contributory negligence, not on the defendant's lack of duty.[126]

A third kind of case is that of the rescuer who attempts to save people or property endangered by the defendant's negligence. In such cases, the rescuer almost always confronts an open and obvious danger, so that the well-recognized liability to a rescuer[127] could not be established if the open-and-obvious danger rule were applied—as some defendants have argued. But the rule is not applied in such cases, and the rescuer whose conduct is foreseeable in facing an obvious danger remains a hero, not an outcast.[128]

Distinguishing contributory negligence. In spite of the relative clarity of the Restatement, good analysis of obvious-danger cases is prey to at least two levels of

[121] Iwai v. State, 129 Wash.2d 84, 915 P.2d 1089 (1996); Restatement Second of Torts § 343A(2) (1965).

[122] See Osborn v. Mission Ready Mix, 224 Cal.App.3d 104, 273 Cal.Rptr. 457 (1990); Steichen v. Talcott Properties, LLC, 368 Mont. 169, 292 P.3d 458 (2013). Cf. Wood v. Mercedes-Benz of Oklahoma City, 336 P3d 457 (Okla. 2014) (car dealership had duty to protect employee of catering service from slipping on accumulated ice on premises; court noted that dealership knew of the ice and that the employee would encounter it in furtherance of her employment).

[123] See, e.g., Duffy v. Togher, 382 Ill.App.3d 1, 887 N.E.2d 535, 320 Ill.Dec. 391 (2008) (issue of fact whether homeowners had reason to suspect that intoxicated invitee would be distracted and not recognize the danger of diving into a pool); Gilmore v. Walgreen Co., 759 N.W.2d 433 (Minn. App. 2009) (issue of fact whether employees of drug store could have anticipated a customer tripping over a pallet); Luther v. City of Winner, 674 N.W.2d 339 (S.D. 2004) (fact issue whether step in public sidewalk was unreasonably dangerous where plaintiff testified to being distracted).

[124] Urban v. Wait's Supermarket, Inc., 294 N.W.2d 793 (S.D. 1980); see also Tennant v. Shoppers Food Warehouse Md. Corp., 115 Md.App. 381, 693 A.2d 370 (1997) ("The storekeeper expects and intends that his customers shall look not at the floor but at the goods which he displays. . . . He at least ought not to complain, if they look at the goods displayed instead of at the floor to discover possible pitfalls, obstructions, or other dangers, or if their purchases so encumber them as to prevent them from seeing dangers which might otherwise be apparent. Patrons are entitled therefore to rely to some extent at least upon the presumption that the proprietor will see that the passage ways provided for their use are unobstructed and reasonably safe.").

[125] Dawson v. Payless for Drugs, 248 Or. 334, 433 P.2d 1019 (1967).

[126] See Restatement Third of Torts (Liability for Physical and Emotional Harm) § 51, cmt. k (2012) ("An entrant who encounters an obviously dangerous condition and who fails to exercise reasonable self-protective care is contributorily negligent.").

[127] See § 15.7 (rescuer's acts not a superseding cause) & § 16.2 (rescuer's confrontation with danger not contributory fault).

[128] Clinkscales v. Nelson Securities, Inc., 697 N.W.2d 836 (Iowa 2005).

confusion. One level of potential confusion arises because evidence that a condition is open or obvious to observers is good evidence about two distinct things. First it might suggest that the plaintiff was chargeable with contributory negligence.[129] Second, it might suggest that the defendant was not negligent—he could perhaps rely on the plaintiff to avoid obvious danger and thus avoid injury.[130] These two points are entirely different. In most courts, if the jury concluded that the plaintiff was guilty of contributory negligence in failing to avoid an obvious danger, the result might be merely to reduce the damages award under the rules of comparative negligence.[131] If the jury found the defendant not negligent on the ground that, since the plaintiff could be expected to avoid the danger, harm was not foreseeable, the plaintiff could not recover at all.

Case analysis vs. rule of law. Another level of potential confusion in open and obvious danger cases arises because it is all too easy to confuse a finding for the defendant on the facts of a particular case with a rule of law for all cases. In some particular cases, the obviousness of danger is compelling, so that the court might take the case from the jury by directed verdict or summary judgment.[132] The court might conclude that the defendant was not negligent at all because he could expect the plaintiff to avoid the danger and thus avoid injury, and further that reasonable jurors could not reach a contrary conclusion. Such a conclusion would be plausible if, for example, the plaintiff injured herself by walking into the checkout counter at a grocery store. Holding that the particular defendant was not negligent would not be a rule of law that an obvious danger always bars recovery, but rather an analysis of the evidence in the particular case.

§ 20.8　Children on the Land

Invitees and Licensees

Children as well as adults are subject to the traditional entrant-classification scheme in those states that still use it,[133] and except as explained below, their rights are determined by the classification in the same way as adults' rights.

---

[129] In Steigman v. Outrigger Enterprises, Inc., 126 Haw. 133, 267 P.3d 1238 (2011), the court held that the "known or obvious danger defense was no longer a complete defense" to a premises liability claim, and instead any known or obvious characteristics of the danger should be considered "as factors in the larger comparative negligence analysis," finding the all-or-nothing rule inconsistent with the legislative adoption of comparative negligence.

[130] In many states today, assumption of risk need not be a third complication, because it would be covered either in the contributory negligence analysis or in the no-negligence analysis. See § 237. Some states do allow assumption of risk as a complete defense in an entrant's suit against a landowner. See Werne v. Exec. Women's Golf Ass'n, 158 N.H. 373, 969 A.2d 346 (2009) (golfer assumed the risk of being struck by a golf ball on defendant's golf course). Where assumption of risk remains as a theoretically separate concept, the confusion is both formidable and depressing. See the discussion of the problem in Parker v. Highland Park, Inc., 565 S.W.2d 512 (Tex. 1978).

[131] See, e.g., Fulmer v. Timber Inn Restaurant and Lounge, Inc., 330 Or. 413, 9 P.3d 710 (2000) (defendant serving alcohol at the top of dangerous, unguarded stairs, predictably risking injury; defendant owed plaintiff a duty but plaintiff's recovery might be reduced for comparative fault).

[132] See Bufkin v. Felipe's Louisiana, LLC, 171 So.3d 851 (La. 2014) (visual obstruction was "obvious and apparent, and reasonably safe for persons exercising ordinary care and prudence"; no duty); Tagle v. Jakob, 97 N.Y.2d 165, 763 N.E.2d 107, 737 N.Y.S.2d 331 (2001) (no duty where on the particular facts, no harm was foreseeable because danger would be seen and avoided).

[133] Where the entrant categories have been abolished and in favor of the general rule of reasonable care, see § 20.9, the rule applies to protect children on the land as well as others. Silva v. Union Pacific R.R. Co., 85 Cal.App.4th 1024, 102 Cal.Rptr.2d 668 (2000); Morse v. Goduti, 146 N.H. 697, 777 A.2d 292 (2001).

When adults are classed as invitees, the children who accompany them onto the land are properly categorized in the same way unless the entrance of children is inconsistent with the express or implied limits of the invitation.[134] Children can of course also be invitees in their own right, as where they enter a retail store.[135] The duty owed to child invitees is the same as that owed the adult invitee, namely, the duty of reasonable care.[136] However, what counts as reasonable care with a child invitee may be different, since children may overlook dangers that adults would avoid.[137] This also means that what is open and obvious to an adult may not be open an obvious to a child.[138] Of course, some dangers are so obvious that even a child can be expected to recognize and avoid them, such as fire, water, and falling from heights.[139] Nonetheless, where a landowner knows that children continue to encounter an open danger despite being warned, public policy may impose a duty to take reasonable actions to prevent injury.[140]

Children, like adults, may be licensees, as for example where they are social guests or with adults who are social guests.[141] In such cases, they are ordinarily owed only the care owed to adult licensees.[142] However, where the defendant owes a duty of care to child trespassers under the rules stated below, he owes the same duty to child licensees.[143] In addition to the limitation on duty implied in the licensee category, some authority holds that with children of tender years who are accompanied by parents, responsibility for their safety shifts to the parents, at least if the parents know of the danger.[144] On the other hand, if the landowner (or anyone else) has been entrusted with

---

[134] E.g., Wal-Mart Stores, Inc. v. Lerma, 749 S.W.2d 572 (Tex. App. 1988) (child injured in store while swinging on clothing rack as mother shopped; store liable).

[135] Orr v. First National Stores, Inc., 280 A.2d 785, 50 A.L.R.3d 1202 (Me. 1971).

[136] E.g., Bae v. Dragoo & Assoc., Inc., 156 Ohio App.3d 103, 804 N.E.2d 1007 (2004) (finding no breach of duty by landowner in maintaining pool in which child invitee drowned).

[137] See Johnson v. Pettigrew, 595 N.E.2d 747 (Ind.App. 1992).

[138] E.g., Quereshi v. Ahmed, 394 Ill.App.3d 883, 916 N.E.2d 1153, 334 Ill.Dec. 265 (2009) (child playing on treadmill). Where reasonable people can differ on the obviousness point, it presents a jury issue. See Kopczynski v. Barger, 887 N.E.2d 928 (Ind. 2008) (child jumping on neighbor's trampoline). Where a landowner knows of a particular child's inability to appreciate risk, and knows the child might be present, this may create a question of fact as to whether the landowner should have foreseen that a "patent" danger was nonetheless unreasonably risky to that child. Morse v. Goduti, 146 N.H. 697, 777 A.2d 292 (2001).

[139] See, e.g., Ahmed v. Pickwick Place Owners' Ass'n, 385 Ill.App.3d 874, 896 N.E.2d 854 (2008) (landowners do not owe children a duty to warn them of the hazards of drowning in water, thus defendants owed no duty to a 7-year-old resident of its apartment complex to provide a warning of the dangers presented by a retention pool in which the child drowned). Cf. Restatement Second of Torts § 339, cmt. j (1965) (discussing trespassing children).

[140] E.g., Grant v. South Roxana Dad's Club, 381 Ill.App.3d 665, 886 N.E.2d 543, 319 Ill.Dec. 780 (2008) (eight-year-old child injured when attempting to become airborne on his bicycle, using a four-foot pile of dirt in playground operated by defendant). Illinois has adopted a rule that absolves a landowner of a duty to a child who is harmed by an obvious danger while under parental supervision, or when the parent knew of the existence of the dangerous condition. See Harlin v. Sears Roebuck & Co., 369 Ill.App.3d 27, 307 Ill.Dec. 825, 860 N.E.2d 479 (2006) (two-year-old child hit head on display stand in defendant's store while mother was shopping; no liability).

[141] E.g., Bradford v. Feeback, 149 Mich.App. 67, 385 N.W.2d 729 (1986).

[142] Robles v. Severyn, 19 Ariz.App. 61, 504 P.2d 1284 (1973).

[143] Restatement Second of Torts § 343B (1965).

[144] Padilla v. Rodas, 160 Cal.App.4th 742, 73 Cal.Rptr.3d 114 (2008) (homeowner owed no duty to care to two-year-old child while mother was supervising him, where child drowned in backyard pool); Foss v. Kincade, 746 N.W.2d 912 (Minn. App. 2008) (homeowner owed no duty to protect a three-year-old visitor who was under the supervision of his mother, where an empty bookcase fell on the child as he tried to climb it).

and accepted responsibility for supervising a child, he owes a duty of reasonable care to provide supervision regardless of the child's status on the land.[145]

Child Trespassers

The problem. Children may be and often are trespassers to whom the landowner owes no more duties than he owes to adult trespassers. But child trespassers are not for that reason alone evil-doers or even negligent actors and they are almost always more vulnerable to harm because they fail to understand danger or its seriousness. Many of these trespassers are small children: a three-year-old trespasser wanders into a neighbor's backyard, falls into the unfenced pool and drowns;[146] a seven-year-old deliberately enters a garbage dump to look for comic books and is horribly burned when the crust gives way and he sinks into burning embers.[147]

Contemporary general rule. If the landowner in such cases could foresee that children might enter and be harmed because, given their age and experience, they might fail to appreciate the danger, and if the landowner could have avoided such serious risks with a relatively small expense, courts today generally recognize a duty of care to the child and liability for negligence.[148] Where the landowner owes such a duty to a trespassing child, he owes no less to the child licensee or invitee.[149] The child's adult rescuer is given the status of the child and comes under the same protection.[150] The child-trespasser rules are subject to some qualification or at least explanation, and a few courts reject them altogether, treating the child trespasser like any other.[151]

Origin of the special rule. The idea originated around 1875. A seven-year-old child played on a revolving turntable, a heavy piece of machinery used to rotate railroad engines. Caught between the surface and the wall, he lost a leg. The railroad asserted that it owed no duties to this trespasser. The Minnesota Court, noting that the turntable appealed to the "natural instincts" of children and at the same time was highly dangerous to them, argued that the child was "induced" to use the turntable by its very attractiveness. The court compared the allure of the turntable to strong-scented meat

---

[145] Johnson v. Pettigrew, 595 N.E.2d 747 (Ind. App. 1992). But the duty to supervise does not arise unless the defendant has accepted responsibility by word or deed. Bradley v. Welch, 94 Ark.App. 171, 228 S.W.3d 559 (2006).

[146] Giacona v. Tapley, 5 Ariz. App. 494, 428 P.2d 439 (1967) (five-year-old, liability recognized); Goodwin v. Jackson, 484 So.2d 1041 (Miss. 1986) (three-year-old, liability denied).

[147] Rush v. Plains Tp., 371 Pa. 117, 89 A.2d 200 (1952) (no liability); cf. Dehn v. S. Brand Coal & Oil Co., 241 Minn. 237, 63 N.W.2d 6 (1954) (similar facts but stronger evidence that landowner knew of fires, liability).

[148] See Glen Weissenberger & Barbara B. McFarland, The Law of Premises Liability § 2.07 (4th ed. 2014).

[149] See S.W. v. Towers Boat Club, Inc., 315 P.3d 1257 (Colo. 2013) (attractive nuisance doctrine applies to all children, not simply trespassing children); Mason v. City of Mt. Sterling, 122 S.W.3d 500, 509 (Ky. 2003) (same); but see Uddin v. Embassy Suites Hotel, 165 Ohio App.3d 699, 848 N.E.2d 519 (2005) (attractive nuisance doctrine inapplicable to child who is not a trespasser).

[150] Bennett v. Stanley, 92 Ohio St.3d 35, 748 N.E.2d 41 (2001); see Whipple v. American Fork Irrigation Co., 910 P.2d 1218, 1221 (Utah 1996) (defendant did not challenge the rule giving rescuer the child's status).

[151] E.g., Osterman v. Peters, 260 Md. 313, 272 A.2d 21 (1971); Anderson v. Claiborne County Recreation Club, Inc., 812 So.2d 965 (Miss. 2002) (only duty owed to a child trespasser is not to willfully or wantonly harm). The Third Restatement provides that all entrants on land are owed a duty of reasonable care, except for "flagrant trespassers." See Restatement Third of Torts (Liability for Physical and Emotional Harm) § 52 (a) & cmt. b (2012). Child trespassers are subject to no special rules in the Third Restatement. If they are "flagrant trespassers," then they are owed a lesser duty; if they are merely non-flagrant trespassers, as many children will undoubtedly be, then they are owed a duty of reasonable care. See Id. § 51, cmt. l.

used to attract and trap dogs.[152] For this reason the trespass was to be forgiven and the child treated as an invitee.

"Attractive nuisance" vs. foreseeability. The earliest cases were based on the theory that the child was lured to the land by some special attraction like the railroad's turntable. For this reason, courts often called the special rule for child trespasses the "attractive nuisance" doctrine. The idea that the child had to be lured to the land by something attractive to children led Justice Holmes to hold that the doctrine had no application unless the child was attracted to the land by the very thing that injured her.[153] Technically, Holmes may not have been overruled,[154] but in any event his view is now usually rejected in mainstream tort law.[155] What is now required instead of allure is that a reasonable landowner would know, have reason to know, or at least foresee, that children are likely to trespass and because of their youth will be at unreasonable risk for serious injury.[156] For this reason, "attractive nuisance" is no longer a good description of the doctrine.

Foreseeability vs. "reason to know." The Second Restatement says the landowner must *know or have reason to know*[157] both that child trespassers are likely, and that a condition on the land may endanger them. That seems to be an obscure way of saying that the landowner need not investigate to discover the condition or the possibility of trespassers.[158] If the point were reformulated to say that the landowner owes a duty of reasonable care to foreseeable child trespassers, the outcome of cases would ordinarily be the same, because ordinary care would not require investigation about the prospect of trespassers unless some fact suggested the need to inspect or investigate.

Yet a small effort toward investigation or inspection is warranted in some cases. It would not be fearsomely burdensome to hold that if a railroad is going to install a turntable it might inquire whether children play nearby. If the Restatement's formula rejects liability on such facts, it is questionable at best. If the formula accepts liability on such facts, it would be simpler to say that the landowner owes a duty of reasonable

---

[152] Keffe v. Milwaukee & St. Paul Ry., 21 Minn. 207 (1875). The Supreme Court had held for the plaintiff in a similar case two years earlier in Sioux City & Pacific R.R. v. Stout, 84 U.S. 657 (1873).

[153] United Zinc & Chemical Co. v. Britt, 258 U.S. 268, 66 L.Ed. 615, 42 S.Ct. 299 (1922).

[154] See McGettigan v. National Bank of Washington, 320 F.2d 703, 706 (D.C. Cir. 1963). Holmes' decision in *Britt* was rendered in the days before Erie R.R. v. Tompkins, 304 U.S. 64, 82 L.Ed. 1188, 58 S.Ct. 817 (1938). After the decision in *Erie*, the federal common law of torts more or less ceased to exist, so it would now be difficult for the Court directly to overrule the *Britt* case.

[155] E.g., Henson ex rel. Hunt v. Intern. Paper Co., 374 S.C. 375, 650 S.E.2d 74 (2007) (attractive nuisance doctrine does not require that the injured child was attracted to the property by the very temptation that caused the injury); Banker v. McLaughlin, 146 Tex. 434, 208 S.W.2d 843 (1948) ("The element of attraction is important only in so far as it may mean that the presence of children was to be anticipated."); Kessler v. Mortenson, 16 P.3d 1225 (Utah 2000). Contra, Nelson v. City of Rupert, 128 Idaho 199, 911 P.2d 1111 (Idaho 1996) (child trespasser must be attracted by the injury-causing condition).

[156] E.g., Kahn v. James Burton Company, 5 Ill.2d 614, 126 N.E.2d 836 (1955) ("The element of attraction is significant only in so far as it indicates that the trespass should be anticipated, the true basis of liability being the foreseeability of harm to the child.").

[157] Restatement Second of Torts § 339 (1965). See, e.g., Croaker v. Mackenhausen, 592 N.W.2d 857 (Minn. 2009) (applying the "reason to know" test, finding defendant had no reason to know of child's trespass). "Reason to know" is not necessarily actual knowledge of the fact in question, but it is knowledge of specific facts that would lead to an inference of such a fact. See Restatement Second of Torts § 12 (1965).

[158] See Restatement Second of Torts § 339, cmts. g & h (1965).

care under the circumstances.[159] Some of the decisions approve the Restatement's six-paragraph rule *in toto* without necessarily focusing on the "reason to know" formula.[160] Other courts have definitely used a *should know* or foreseeability formulation in place of the *reason to know* phrase.[161] Sometimes the same court will use both terms,[162] a fact that may suggest a minuscule difference in practice between the two formulations.

Harmful potential. The attractive nuisance doctrine is largely an application of ordinary negligence law. This means in part that the defendant who is under a duty of care is nevertheless not liable for harms done to anyone on his land, trespasser or not, unless he fails to act with ordinary care. If, on the facts, a reasonable person would perceive no unreasonable risk, then the landowner is not negligent and not liable. The landowner must be on notice of (or be able, as a reasonable person, to foresee) both the dangerous condition[163] on the land and the likelihood of child trespassers[164] who because of their youth and inexperience will not protect themselves.[165]

Balance of risks and utilities. Even if harm is foreseeable, the risk may be small compared with the cost of removing it. The ordinary negligence rule invites juries to compare the risks of injury with the utility to the defendant of keeping the risks as they are. So if the cost or burden of eliminating or reducing the risk is great, and the foreseeable risk is small, the defendant is not negligent and not liable at all. The same rule is applied in the trespassing child case.[166] A large rotating auger that could dismember a human being may have great utility in unloading a railroad car, but at

---

[159] Mathis v. Massachusetts Elec. Co., 409 Mass. 256, 565 N.E.2d 1180 (1991) (child trespasser rules reflect national trend toward uniform standard of care); McGettigan v. National Bank of Washington, 320 F.2d 703 (D.C. Cir. 1963) (favoring an ordinary negligence approach).

[160] Porter v. Delmarva Power & Light Co., 547 A.2d 124 (Del. 1988); Hofer v. Meyer, 295 N.W.2d 333 (S.D. 1980); Texas Utilities Elec. Co. v. Timmons, 947 S.W.2d 191 (Tex. 1997) (quoting the formula, seemingly not recognizing that it had stated a foreseeability test decades earlier in Banker v. McLaughlin, 146 Tex. 434, 208 S.W.2d 843 (1948)); Thunder Hawk ex rel. Jensen v. Union Pacific R. Co., 844 P.2d 1045 (Wyo. 1992).

[161] E.g., Gregory v. Johnson, 249 Ga. 151, 289 S.E.2d 232 (1982) (reasonable foreseeability); Mt. Zion State Bank & Trust v. Consolidated Communications, Inc., 169 Ill.2d 110, 214 Ill. Dec. 156, 660 N.E.2d 863 (1995) (but holding that harm from obvious danger was not foreseeable); Mason v. City of Mt. Sterling, 122 S.W.3d 500 (Ky. 2003) (landowner may be liable for any artificial condition "which the possessor realizes, or should realize, creates an unreasonable risk" to young children); Mathis v. Massachusetts Electric Co., 409 Mass. 256, 565 N.E.2d 1180 (1991) (foreseeable child trespassers); Banker v. McLaughlin, 146 Tex. 434, 208 S.W.2d 843, 8 A.L.R.2d 1231 (1948).

[162] Anderson v. Cahill, 485 S.W.2d 76 (Mo. 1972); Bateman v. Mello, 617 A.2d 877 (R.I. 1992).

[163] Restatement Second of Torts § 339(b) (1965).

[164] Id. § 339(a). See, e.g., Laster v. Norfolk Southern Ry. Co., 13 So.3d 922 (Ala. 2009) (landowner must have at least reason to know of child's likely trespass and danger); Foss v. Kincade, 766 N.W.2d 317 (Minn. 2009) (same).

[165] See, e.g., Fields v. Henrich, 208 S.W.3d 353 (Mo. App. 2006) (plaintiff failed to prove that defendant landowners knew or had reason to know that children too young to appreciate the danger presented by a sewage pond were likely to trespass on their land); Restatement Second of Torts § 339 cmt. i (1965). Illinois has come up with a stringent rule that appears to allow the defendant to invariably shift responsibility for the trespassing child to the parents who "bear the primary responsibility for safety of their children" whenever the danger is "obvious." In effect the defendant is allowed to assume that if the child is out alone, he has capacity to appreciate dangers. Mt. Zion State Bank & Trust v. Consolidated Communications, Inc., 169 Ill.2d 110, 214 Ill. Dec. 156, 660 N.E.2d 863 (1995).

[166] Bateman v. Mello, 617 A.2d 877 (R.I. 1992) (liability on the facts would pose "devastating implications for landowners"); Banker v. McLaughlin, 146 Tex. 434, 208 S.W.2d 843, 8 A.L.R.2d 1231 (1948) (dangerous pit was easily filled and served no useful purpose); Restatement Second of Torts § 339(d) (1965) (the special rule for trespassing children does not apply unless "the utility to the possessor of maintaining the condition and the burden of eliminating the danger are slight as compared with the risk to children").

relatively small cost, it can be covered to protect children, so a jury could appropriately find negligence if the landowner could foresee that children may play nearby.[167]

§ 20.9 Changing Duties and Categories: Extending the Duty of Reasonable Care to Entrants Other than Invitees

A number of state courts have now held that a duty of reasonable care is owed not only to invitees, but also to licensees, while retaining a lesser duty with respect to trespassers.[168] Another group of courts has applied the reasonable care standard to all entrants, essentially abolishing the categories entirely.[169] The Third Restatement, admittedly without stating either a majority or a plurality rule on the topic, suggests a duty of reasonable care to all entrants on land with the exception of "flagrant trespassers."[170] Continued reform at the state level seems probable, while uniformity seems largely out of reach even among states that respond favorably to the Third Restatement's moderate reform invitation.

Just how earth-shaking is this reform? Perhaps less than appears at first glance. Reasonable care does not require actions to protect or warn visitors whose coming is not known or reasonably foreseeable.[171] Since trespassers and licensees are often unforeseeable visitors, the standard of reasonable care under the circumstances will not often result in any new liability, even where a duty of reasonable care is owed to all entrants. Courts sometimes say explicitly that the status of the visitor remains relevant on the issue of the foreseeability of the harm or the landowner's reasonable expectations.[172] That is a shorthand expression; it is not the status itself that is relevant but some of the facts that establish status.[173]

---

[167] Spur Feeding Co. v. Fernandez, 106 Ariz. 143, 472 P.2d 12, 49 A.L.R.3d 925 (1970).

[168] The tally includes Iowa, Kansas, Maine, Massachusetts, Minnesota, Nebraska, New Mexico, North Carolina, North Dakota, Rhode Island, Tennessee, Vermont, West Virginia, Wisconsin, and Wyoming. Illinois abolished the licensee-invitee distinction by statute. The list may be expanded to include those states that define invitees to include social guests but otherwise retain the licensee category. Florida and Indiana are in this category. The U.S. Supreme Court rejected the common-law classification approach in Admiralty cases in Kermarec v. Compagnie Generale Transatlantique, 358 U.S. 625, 3 L.Ed.2d 550, 79 S.Ct. 406 (1959).

[169] Alaska, California, Colorado, District of Columbia, Hawaii, Louisiana, Montana, Nevada, New Hampshire, and New York. Legislation in Colorado has since intervened to restore much of the common law approach. Colo. Rev. Stats. § 13–21–115. The trend began in the states with Rowland v. Christian, 69 Cal.2d 108, 70 Cal.Rptr. 97, 443 P.2d 561 (1968). This was once seen by many as an inexorable tide, but as the Arkansas court put it twenty years after *Rowland*, the complete-abolition movement may have "lost its steam." Baldwin v. Mosley, 295 Ark. 285, 748 S.W.2d 146 (1988).

[170] Restatement Third of Torts (Liability for Physical and Emotional Harm) §§ 51 & 52 (2012).

[171] See Webb v. City and Borough of Sitka, 561 P.2d 731 (Alaska 1977) ("the foreseeability of her presence determines in part (a) the likelihood of injury to her, and (b) the extent to which the City must take action or the interest it must sacrifice to avoid the risk of injury"), *superseded by statute as stated in* Univ. of Alaska v. Shanti, 835 P.2d 1225 (Alaska 1992); Marioenzi v. DiPonte, Inc., 114 R.I. 294, 333 A.2d 127 (1975), *overruled on other grounds,* Tantimonico v. Allendale Mutual Ins. Co., 637 A.2d 1056 (R.I. 1994); Hudson v. Gaitan, 675 S.W.2d 699 (Tenn. 1984) ("foreseeability of the presence of the visitor and the likelihood of harm to him being one of the principal factors in assessing liability"), *abrogated on other grounds,* McIntyre v. Balentine, 853 S.W.2d 52 (Tenn. 1992).

[172] See Boycher v. Livingston Parish School Board, 716 So.2d 187 (La. App. 1998) ("Although the common law classifications of invitee-licensee-trespasser are not determinative of liability, the plaintiff's status has a bearing on the question of liability."); Peterson v. Balach, 294 Minn. 161, 199 N.W.2d 639 (1972); Scurti v. City of New York, 40 N.Y.2d 433, 387 N.Y.S.2d 55, 354 N.E.2d 794 (1976); Demag v. Better Power Equip., Inc., 102 A.3d 1101, 2014 VT 78 (2014).

[173] See Smith v. Arbaugh's Restaurant, Inc., 469 F.2d 97 (D.C. Cir. 1972) ("Foreseeability of the visitor's presence determines in part the likelihood of injury to him, and the extent of the interest which must be sacrificed to avoid the risk of injury."); Basso v. Miller, 40 N.Y.2d 233, 386 N.Y.S.2d 564, 352 N.E.2d 868 (1976)

§ 20.10   Recreational Use Statutes

Statutory Protections

All or virtually all states have enacted recreational use statutes.[174] The gist of these statutes is to immunize landowners or occupiers from liability for most non-willful harms to persons who are permitted to use the land for recreational purposes without a fee or charge, or who pay relatively small charges for the use of the land.[175] The stated purpose of the statutes is to encourage landowners to open private lands for recreational use in an increasingly crowded society with inadequate public recreational space.[176] This purpose is sometimes determinative in construing the statute. Some states tack on various additional provisions, such as special protections for farmer-landowners[177] or educational uses.[178]

The statutes are couched in stringent terms. For instance, they may say that the permitted but non-paying user has neither invitee nor licensee status[179] or that he is to be treated as a trespasser.[180] The statutes commonly provide that no duty of care is owed to make the premises safe for non-paying recreational users. Such provisions have the effect of restoring the common-law trespasser or licensee categories. They sometimes grant landowners even broader protections than they would get under contemporary common law categories. That is certainly the case with the recreational user who is on land open to the public. The common law rule would treat such a person as a public invitee, to whom the landowner owes a duty of reasonable care.[181] Under the recreational use statute, however, the landowner owes only the duty to avoid willful or malicious injury,[182] or sometimes gross negligence.[183] Some statutes provide that the owner owes

---

(adopting a single standard of reasonable care for all entrants, and quoting *Smith*); see also O'Leary v. Coenen, 251 N.W.2d 746 (N.D. 1977) ("We hold only that the status of an entrant [as] a licensee, or an invitee is no longer solely determinative of the duty of care. . . . The circumstances of a visitor's entry will continue to have a direct relationship to the question of landowner liability."); Cf. Foss v. Kincade, 766 N.W.2d 317 (Minn. 2009) ("in any premises liability negligence case, . . . the landowner's duty of reasonable care is modified according to the expected use of the land").

[174] See Glen Weissenberger & Barbara B. McFarland, The Law of Premises Liability §§ 5.07–5.12 (4th ed. 2014); Robin Cheryl Miller, Annotation, Effect of Statute Limiting Landowner's Liability For Personal Injury to Recreational User, 47 A.L.R.4th 262 (1987).

[175] None of the statutes protect landowners who accept a fee for the use of their land. See Coleman v. Oregon Parks and Recreation Dept., 347 Or. 94, 217 P.3d 651 (2009) (even where state did not charge a fee to campers who entered park, state's imposition of fees to use particular facilities within park removed the immunity provided by the recreational use statute). Merely charging for parking will not usually convert the entrant into a "paying" guest, however. See, e.g., Stone Mountain Mem'l Ass'n v. Herrington, 225 Ga. 746, 171 S.E.2d 521 (1969); Garreans v. City of Omaha, 216 Neb. 487, 345 N.W.2d 309 (1984), *overruled on other grounds*, Bronsen v. Dawes County, 272 Neb. 320, 722 N.W.2d 17 (2006); Cole v. South Carolina Elec. and Gas, Inc., 355 S.C. 183, 584 S.E.2d 405 (App. 2003).

[176] This purpose is often expressed in the statute itself. E.g., Fla. Stat. Ann. § 375.251.

[177] Mich. Comp. L. Ann. § 324.73301.

[178] N.C. Gen. Stats. § 38A–4.

[179] E.g., Cal. Civ. Code § 846.

[180] N.C. Gen. Stat. § 38A–4; see Howard v. East Texas Baptist Univ., 122 S.W.3d 407 (Tex. App. 2003) (the recreational use statute would apply the standard of care owed by a landowner to a trespasser).

[181] See § 20.6.

[182] Cal. Civ. Code § 846 ("willful or malicious failure to guard or warn"); N.Y. Gen. Oblig. L. § 9–103. As always, courts must interpret the operative statutory terms. See, e.g., Roeder v. United States, 432 S.W.3d 627 (Ark. 2014) ("malicious" in statute includes "conduct in reckless disregard of the consequences from which malice may be inferred") (answering certified question).

[183] Mich. Comp. L. Ann. § 324.73301; S.C. Code § 27–3–60.

no duty to warn as to dangerous activities,[184] which could conceivably mean that the owner is not liable for an activity negligently carried on. Others, however, track the traditional premises liability rules in protecting against liability for conditions on the land but not necessarily protecting against liability for active negligence.[185]

Known dangers. Some of the statutes affirmatively provide that liability may be imposed when the landowner actually knows of a danger.[186] However, other statutes make no such provision. Most do not directly recognize the common law distinctions between known and unknown dangers, between known and unknown users, or between natural and artificial conditions. Such statutes raise the possibility that the landowner would be immune from liability even when he fails to warn a known user who is about to encounter a known danger.[187] It seems quite possible that such statutes would actually leave the permissive land user worse off than she would be under the contemporary liberal rules for liability to known or foreseeable trespassers.

Attractive nuisance. The statutes may also relieve the landowner of common law duties recognized under the attractive nuisance or child-trespasser rules. Although some statutes specifically recognize the ongoing validity of the attractive nuisance rules,[188] others say nothing at all about the child trespasser. When the statute says nothing on the subject, some courts have read in an exception so that the landowner remains responsible for his negligent harm to foreseeable child trespassers who could not be expected to discover the dangers on the land for themselves.[189] But some courts have held that the recreational use statutes, giving landowners special benefits without exception, in effect supersede the attractive nuisance rules.[190] This puts the child who is subjected to foreseeable dangers in a worse position than many adult trespassers under the common law rules.[191]

Statutory Coverage

Owners; recreational use. Much of the litigation under recreational use statutes deals with their coverage. The statutes do not apply at all unless the defendant is an owner or occupant as defined in the statute.[192] Nor do they apply when the plaintiff's use of the land is not for a recreational purpose as defined in the statute.[193] Some statutes

---

[184] E.g., Idaho Code § 36–1604.

[185] See Klein v. United States, 50 Cal.4th 68, 112 Cal.Rptr.3d 722 (2010) (recreational use statute does not shield landowner from his negligent driving of a vehicle on the property); Dickinson v. Clark, 767 A.2d 303 (Me. 2001) (negligent supervision of minor-guest's use of log-splitter not protected by statute).

[186] Ala. Code § 35–15–24 (landowner knows of danger and of user's presence); Rev. Code Wash. Ann. § 4.24.210 ("known dangerous artificial latent condition for which warning signs have not been conspicuously posted").

[187] For example, where the defendant strings a steel cable across a trail, knowing that cyclists ride there. See Wirth v. Ehly, 93 Wis.2d 433, 287 N.W.2d 140 (1980) (denying recovery under a predecessor of the current statute).

[188] E.g., Ariz. Rev. Stat. § 33–1551; Rev. Code Wash. Ann. § 4.24.210.

[189] Smith v. Crown-Zellerbach, Inc., 638 F.2d 883 (5th Cir. 1981).

[190] E.g., Coursey v. Westvaco Corp., 790 S.W.2d 229 (Ky. 1990).

[191] See § 20.2.

[192] See Stanton v. Lackawanna Energy, Ltd., 584 Pa. 550, 886 A.2d 667 (2005) (easement holder in possession of land was an "owner" entitled to recreational use immunity); Urban v. Grasser, 243 Wis.2d 673, 627 N.W.2d 511 (2001) (injury while traversing easement over defendant's land held by third person, defendant is "owner").

[193] See, e.g., Wilkins v. City of Haverhill, 486 Mass. 86, 8 N.E.3d 753 (2014) (statute applies when member of the public has entered land "for the purposes for which the owner has permitted general access"). Both subjective purpose of the plaintiff and the nature of the activity are sometimes considered in determining

define recreational purpose in general terms,[194] but others present a catalog of recreational activities that might include skateboarding, spelunking, parachuting, and many other specific activities.[195] Where the statute is not precisely determinative, courts may characterize the plaintiff's use broadly in some cases but quite narrowly in others.[196]

Open to the public. The statutes' stated purpose is to encourage use of private land for recreation.[197] However, the landowner need take no steps to qualify for the special protections of the statute. The statutes do not require the landowner to dedicate an easement for public use, to register the land, or even to inform the public by signs or otherwise that it is available. Even the statutes that require that the land be open for public recreational use[198] do not require the landowner to mention the fact to anyone.[199]

Some of the statutes do not even require that the land be open to the public, only that the landowner permit or invite a person to use the land.[200] Such statutes may protect the landowner even if he has tried to exclude all users by erecting barriers and posting *No Trespassing* signs.[201] In consequence, the statutes sometimes reduce the landowner's duty to something considerably less than reasonable care even when the landowner withholds the recreational benefits the statute purports to seek.[202] Some

---

whether the statute applies. See Auman v. School Dist. of Stanley-Boyd, 248 Wis.2d 548, 635 N.W.2d 762 (2001). However, some courts say if the land serves a recreational purpose it does not matter whether the plaintiff was actually involved in recreational activity at the time of injury. E.g., Camicia v. Howard S. Wright Construction Co., 179 Wash.2d 684, 317 P.3d 987 (2014).

[194] E.g., N.C. Gen. Stats. § 38A–2. A user's "subjective intent" may be irrelevant to some courts construing their statutes broadly to cover "recreational users." See Ali v. City of Boston, 441 Mass. 233, 804 N.E.2d 927 (2004) (bicyclist a "recreational user" under the statute even where he was using the park for a non-recreational purpose at the time of his injury; riding a bicycle is an objectively recreational activity).

[195] E.g., Cal. Civ. Code § 846 (listing 20 activities, some of which overlap, but not including skateboarding); Rev. Code Wash. Ann. § 4.24.210 (amended to include skateboarding).

[196] Compare, e.g., Wilson v. Kansas State University, 273 Kan. 584, 44 P. 3d 454 (2002) (burn from unknown substance on toilet seat in football stadium restroom; stadium is recreational, toilets an integral part, statutory immunity applies) and Thompson v. Kyo-Ya Co., Ltd., 112 Hawai'i 472, 146 P.3d 1049 (2006) (permissive use of the defendant's property for access to recreational use elsewhere falls within the protections of the statute), with Liberty v. State Dep't of Transp., 342 Or. 11, 148 P.3d 909 (2006) (defendant's property, not itself used for recreation but only for access to recreation elsewhere, was not covered by the statute); Minnesota Fire & Cas. Ins. Co. v. Paper Recycling of La Crosse, 244 Wis.2d 290, 627 N.W.2d 527 (2001) (boys playing with matches among bales of paper stacked by defendant to create tunnels and "forts" were not engaged in "recreational" activities).

[197] In some cases, however, statutes have been broadened and this feature—central to the originals—has been de-emphasized, leading to judicial doubts whether there is any coherent principle that permits construction of the statute. See Auman v. School Dist. of Stanley-Boyd, 248 Wis.2d 548, 635 N.W.2d 762 (2001) ("We continue to be frustrated in our efforts to state a test that can be applied easily because of the seeming lack of basic underlying principles in the statute.").

[198] E.g., Fla. Stat. Ann. § 375.251; Rev. Code Wash. Ann. § 4.24.210.

[199] See Coursey v. Westvaco Corp., 790 S.W.2d 229 (Ky. 1990) ("a landowner must show he knew and condoned the public making recreational use of his property, and by the landowner's words, actions or lack of action it must be able to be reasonably inferred the landowner intended to permit such use"),

[200] New York, for example, provides that the owner "owes no duty to keep the premises safe for entry or use by others for [stated recreational activities] or to give warning of any hazardous condition or use of or structure or activity on such premises to persons entering for such purposes. . . ." N.Y. Gen. Oblig. L. § 9–103.

[201] E.g., Larini v. Biomass Industries, Inc., 918 F.2d 1046 (2d Cir. 1990); cf. Verdoljak v. Mosinee Paper Corp., 200 Wis.2d 624, 547 N.W.2d 602 (1996) (gate barred entrance; motorcyclist injured in running into the gate, a bar suspended from chains; held, the statute "does not purport to condition that limit to owners who open their land to those who use it for recreational activities.").

[202] Saari v. Winter Sports, Inc., 314 Mont. 212, 64 P.3d 1038 (2003) (statute's purpose "is to encourage landowners to make their property freely available for public use by granting the landowner relief from liability to people gratuitously entering the property for recreational purposes," but in spite of this purpose, the statute reduces the landowner's duty even when premises are not open to the public).

authority goes the other way, withholding the statutory protections when the landowner in fact excludes users.[203] That result seems compelled where the statute actually requires that the land be opened to the public.

Suitability for recreation. The statutes do not by their terms require that the land be suitable for recreation, although some courts have added that requirement.[204] Where courts have not done so, the landowner gets the protection of the statute even if the land is not suited for recreation. In a California case, the plaintiff child was sitting to one side while other children played on stacked pipes. The pipes dislodged and fell on the child. The court thought that the child was a recreational user, even if she was not engaged in playing on the pipes and even if the land was not suited to recreation.[205]

Public land, urban land. Given a purpose to encourage owners to open private lands to the public for recreation, it seems unlikely that the statute would apply to lands already owned by the public, to lands such as parks that are already open to the public, or indeed to urban land generally. Some statutes specifically answer one or more of these questions, for example, by granting the statutory immunities to urban[206] and public lands[207] or sometimes by limiting the statutory favors to private or rural owners.[208]

When the statute is not explicit, courts have divided on such issues. Most courts appear to give public entities[209] and urban landowners[210] the benefit of the statutory protections, but some hold that the statute, intended to encourage opening of private lands, could hardly have been meant to apply to municipalities or other governmental

---

[203] See Crawford v. Tilley, 780 P.2d 1248 (Utah 1989).

[204] See Bragg v. Genesee County Agr. Soc., 84 N.Y.2d 544, 644 N.E.2d 1013 (1994); cf. Sallee v. Stewart, 827 N.W.2d 128 (Iowa 2013) (list of activities in recreational use statute must be interpreted to promote "activities traditionally undertaken outdoors" and "true outdoor activity").

[205] Ornelas v. Randolph, 4 Cal.4th 1095, 847 P.2d 560, 17 Cal.Rptr. 2d 594 (1993).

[206] E.g., La. Stat. Ann.—R.S. 9:2795; Rev. Code Wash. Ann. § 4.24.210.

[207] Ariz. Rev. Stat. § 33–1551 (a public or private owner); 745 Ill. Comp. Stat. 10/3–106 ("neither a local public entity nor a public employee is liable for an injury where the liability is based on the existence of a condition on any public property intended or permitted to be used for recreational purposes" unless the public entity or employee acts willfully or wantonly). In Moore v. Chicago Park Dist., 2012 IL 112788, 365 Ill. Dec. 547, 978 N.E.2d 1050 (Ill. 2012), the court applied this provision to bar a claim by the estate of a pedestrian who died after falling in the parking lot of a city park after slipping on snow and ice, holding that accumulated snow and ice was a "condition." Kan. Stat. Ann. 75–6104(o) (providing exception to governmental liability for claims for injuries resulting from the use of public property "intended or permitted to be used" for recreational purposes. N.H. Rev. Stat. § 508:14, I (statute applies to any "owner, occupant, or lessee of land, including the state or any political subdivision"). The New Hampshire statute was construed broadly in Coan v. New Hampshire Dep't of Environmental Services, 161 N.H. 1, 8 A.3d 109 (2010), to cover an injury on water, where the boys who drowned in the lake "gained access to the water by using land owned by the State"). See also Lane v. Atchison Heritage Conference Center, Inc., 283 Kan. 439, 153 P.3d 541 (2007) (construing recreational provision broadly).

[208] N.C. Gen. Stats. § 38A–2 (defining owner to exclude governmental entities).

[209] E.g., Daniel v. City of Colorado Springs, 327 P.3d 891 (Colo. 2014); Sega v. State, 60 N.Y.2d 183, 456 N.E.2d 1174, 469 N.Y.S.2d 51 (1983); Pauley v. Circleville, 137 Ohio St.3d 212. 998 N.E.2d 1083 (2013).

[210] E.g., Palmer v. United States, 945 F.2d 1134 (9th Cir. 1991) (Hawai'i law); Martin v. City of Gadsden, 584 So.2d 796 (Ala. 1991); Neal v. Wilkes, 470 Mich. 661, 685 N.W.2d 648 (2004); Waggoner v. City of Woodburn, 196 Or.App. 715, 103 P.3d 648 (2004).

entities.[211] Likewise, a few apply the statute only to rural or undeveloped lands.[212] Independent of the recreational use statute, it is of course possible that governmental immunity will immunize a public entity from all liability.[213]

B. DUTIES TO THOSE OUTSIDE THE PREMISES

§ 20.11 Natural Conditions on the Land

Courts traditionally have drawn a major distinction between natural and artificial conditions on the land. The usual statement is that occupiers of land are under no duty to use care to alter the land's natural condition, even when those conditions are dangerous to persons on public ways.[214] So for example, if the plaintiff falls because of natural precipitation on the land, unaffected by negligent human actions,[215] or if naturally occurring surface waters[216] or insects escape[217] from the land and cause harm, the landowner is responsible only if his affirmative acts contributed to those evils.

Even more clearly, the landowner ordinarily has no obligation to remove or make safe naturally occurring snow or ice from sidewalks adjacent to but not a part of his land,[218] although he may be subject to liability for actively making matters worse,[219] for example by artificially and unreasonably draining harmful waters from his own land. Even beginning to clear snow and ice may not produce liability where a plaintiff slips on the remaining natural accumulation.[220]

---

[211] E.g., Delta Farms Reclamation Dist. v. Superior Court, 33 Cal.3d 699, 660 P.2d 1168, 190 Cal. Rptr. 494 (1983); Blonski v. Metropolitan Dist. Com'n, 309 Conn. 282, 71 A.3d 465 (2013); Bronsen v. Dawes County, 272 Neb. 320, 722 N.W.2d 17 (2006) (also assigning other reasons). But see Auman v. School Dist. of Stanley-Boyd, 248 Wis.2d 548, 635 N.W.2d 762 (2001).

[212] See Harrison v. Middlesex Water Co., 80 N.J. 391, 403 A.2d 910 (1979); Stone v. York Haven Power Co., 561 Pa. 189, 749 A.2d 452 (2000) (the statutory immunity, deemed inapplicable to highly developed recreational areas, applied to a lake but not to the dam that created it).

[213] See Anderson v. City of Springfield, 406 Mass. 632, 549 N.E.2d 1127 (1990); Ballard v. Ypsilanti Tp., 457 Mich. 564, 577 N.W.2d 890 (1998).

[214] E.g., Skinner v. South Carolina Dep't of Transp., 383 S.C. 520, 681 S.E.2d 871 (2009) (landowner owed no duty to motorists with respect to naturally-occurring ruts on the shoulder of road that caused car accident); see Restatement Second of Torts § 363 (1965). Cf. Restatement Third of Torts (Liability for Physical and Emotional Harm) § 54(b) (2012) (for natural conditions on land that pose a risk of physical harm to those outside the land, the landowner has a duty of reasonable care if the land is commercial, but otherwise owes such a duty only if the he knows of the risk, or if the risk is obvious to him).

[215] See Anderson v. Fox Hill Village Homeowners Corp., 424 Mass. 365, 676 N.E.2d 821 (1997) ("As a general rule, there is no duty by a landowner to remove a natural accumulation of snow and ice."); Tyrrell v. Investment Associates, Inc., 16 Ohio App.3d 47, 474 N.E.2d 621 (1984) (duty to protect business invitee only from non-natural accumulations of snow and ice).

[216] Ken Cowden Chevrolet, Inc. v. Corts, 112 Mich.App. 570, 316 N.W.2d 259 (1982) (land in natural condition blocked view and caused erosion, no liability for nuisance).

[217] Merriam v. McConnell, 31 Ill.App.2d 241, 175 N.E.2d 293, 83 A.L.R.2d 931 (1961) (trees that hosted insects that then migrated to plaintiff's land not a nuisance); Denison Parking, Inc. v. Davis, 861 N.E.2d 1276 (Ind. App. 2007).

[218] See, e.g., Luchejko v. City of Hoboken, 207 N.J. 191, 23 A.3d 912 (2011). Even when an ordinance compels removal, it is usually interpreted as imposing a duty to assist the city, not a duty to individuals who may be injured. E.g., Lopatkovich v. City of Tiffin, 28 Ohio St.3d 204, 503 N.E.2d 154 (1986).

[219] See Restatement Third of Torts (Liability for Physical and Emotional Harm) § 54 & cmt. c (2012) (a land possessor has no duty with respect to a risk posed by a condition on an adjacent public walkway, as long as the possessor did not create the risk, unless the land is commercial); Wyso v. Full Moon Tide, LLC, 78 A.3d 747 (R.I. 2013).

[220] See Cranshaw v. Cumberland Farms, Inc., 613 F.Supp.2d 147 (D. Mass. 2009) (Massachusetts law).

It follows that the landowner need not alter existing conditions on roads or lands around his own, even to make entrance to his own business safer for customers.[221] The Third Restatement places commercial landowners under a duty of reasonable care for all natural conditions,[222] on the rationale that commercial land "is likely to be in proximity to other property or persons" and thus "will on the whole pose a greater risk to persons off the land than will natural conditions on residential or unimproved land."[223] Some courts have used this distinction to impose duties on owners of commercial property that are not imposed on private residential landowners.[224]

Falling trees. A number of cases have arisen in which naturally growing[225] trees on the defendant's land[226] have become rotten and have fallen upon persons using the adjacent highway or neighboring land. Many courts apply the urban-rural distinction in such cases. In this view, the landowner who is not on notice that the tree is dangerous is under no duty to use care with respect to natural rural trees but must use care with respect to natural urban trees.[227] This view turns the courts' attention to the classification of lands as urban or rural rather than to an adjudication of actual negligence.[228] The debate about falling trees and limbs is mostly about a duty of inspection. If the landowner actually knows that a tree has become a danger to those on the highway, he is obliged to use reasonable care to deal with the risk whether he is urban, rural, or in-between.[229] The debate itself is not always on target, however, because a duty of reasonable care would not invariably require inspection in any event.

Vegetation obscuring vision of highway users. In the case of vegetation on the land that obscures highway dangers and thus indirectly contributes to a collision and injury, awareness of risk has not been a serious consideration. A number of courts have simply said the landowner has no duty to cut vegetation that is dangerous as an impediment to highway users' clear vision.[230] The other view is that no reason counsels departure from

---

[221] See Davis v. Westwood Group, 420 Mass. 739, 652 N.E.2d 567 (1995) (placement of parking lot for business across a dangerous highway; not actionable); A landowner may have some special relationship to the plaintiff, however, that generates some duty of protection outside the land. See Chapter 26.

[222] Restatement Third of Torts (Liability for Physical and Emotional Harm) § 54(b) (2012).

[223] Id., cmt. c.

[224] Compare, e.g., Williams v. Davis, 974 So.2d 1052 (Fla. 2007) (residential property owner has no duty to cut back foliage on his property that obscures drivers' view, unless foliage actually extends into the public right of way and creates a foreseeable hazard to traffic), with Whitt v. Silverman, 788 So.2d 210 (Fla. 2001) (pedestrians were struck and killed when motorist failed to see them because of foliage on defendant's commercial service station property; landowners owed duty to pedestrians to cut foliage on their property to provide a safe egress of vehicles from the premises).

[225] If the trees have been planted, they may come under the rule for artificial rather than natural conditions. See Carver v. Salt River Valley Water Users' Ass'n, 104 Ariz. 513, 456 P.2d 371 (1969); Rosengren v. City of Seattle, 149 Wash. App. 565, 205 P.3d 909 (2009).

[226] On the reverse facts, where the landowner knows that a dangerous tree on adjacent land may fall on visitors on his own land, New York has said the landowner owes no duty to warn his visitors who are in the dangers area. Galindo v. Town of Clarkstown, 2 N.Y.3d 633, 814 N.E.2d 419, 781 N.Y.S.2d 249 (2004).

[227] E.g., Vallinet v. Eskew, 574 N.E.2d 283 (Ind. 1991); Staples v. Duell, 494 S.E.2d 639, 329 S.C. 503 (Ct. App. 1997).

[228] Hensley v. Montgomery County, 25 Md.App. 361, 334 A.2d 542, 94 A.L.R.3d 1148 (1975) (concluding that suburban forest land was more like rural land).

[229] See Lemon v. Edwards, 344 S.W.2d 822 (Ky. 1961). Note, however, that if the landowner is a state or federal government, the defendant may retain an immunity for failure to inspect and remove dead trees from the land. E.g., Com., Transp. Cabinet, Dep't of Highways v. Sexton, 256 S.W.3d 29 (Ky. 2008) (inspection and removal of dead trees a discretionary act, leaving state immune from suit). See generally Chapter 22.

[230] E.g., Driggers v. Locke, 323 Ark. 63, 913 S.W.2d 269 (1996); see generally William J. Appel, Annotation, Liability of Private Landowner for Vegetation Obscuring View at Highway or Street Intersection, 69 A.L.R.4th 1092 (1990). Cf. Hale v. Ostrow, 166 S.W.3d 713 (Tenn. 2005) (overgrown foliage blocked

the duty of ordinary care, so that the question of the landowner's negligence will go to the jury if reasonable people can differ.[231]

§ 20.12 Active Conduct and Artificial Conditions on the Land

Nuisance aside,[232] the occupier of land must use reasonable care for the safety of those outside the land to prevent direct harm resulting from his affirmative activities on the land.[233] For instance, if he negligently allows building materials to fall on persons outside the land, he is subject to liability.[234] The same applies to those persons such as building contractors who are on the land in the right of an occupier. Similarly, except under open-range rules, the owner must use care to prevent horses or cattle from escaping onto the highway where they might cause collisions.[235] The idea also justifies liability for negligently allowing workers on the land to carry dangerous substances like asbestos dust off the land to the injury of others.[236] The landowner who is "present" is under a duty to use reasonable care to control others on his land to prevent them from causing harm to outsiders.[237]

Artificial conditions on the land: general rule. The occupier must also use care with respect to artificial conditions on the land that risk injury to those outside it. If structures on his land cause water to accumulate on the walk, he must use reasonable care to avoid injury to pedestrians who may slip on the ice it forms.[238] Even trees planted in front of the landowner's property may be seen as an artificial condition, placing the landowner under a duty to exercise reasonable care to prevent their branches, roots or trunks from harming pedestrians on the sidewalk.[239] The landowner who makes some special use of an adjacent public way may be subject to liability for negligence, certainly in creating

---

plaintiff's way on adjacent walkway); Williams v. Davis, 974 So.2d 1052 (Fla. 2007) (placing commercial landowners and residential landowners under different duties to trim foliage).

[231] See Coburn v. City of Tucson, 143 Ariz. 50, 691 P.2d 1078 (1984); Whitt v. Silverman, 788 So.2d 210 (Fla. 2001) ("general" foreseeability of risk establishes duty; remaining issues of breach and proximate cause are fact-specific); Inglehart v. Board of County Com'rs of Rogers County, 60 P.3d 497 (Okla. 2002); Donaca v. Curry Cnty., 303 Or. 30, 734 P.2d 1339 (1987).

[232] Landowners and possessors owe a duty to neighboring landowners not to create a nuisance, that is, a serious interference with their use and enjoyment of land by pollution or the like. On the whole, nuisance law addresses risks to the use and enjoyment and economic rights rather than risks of physical harm to individuals. See Chapter 30.

[233] Restatement Second of Torts § 371 (1965); Restatement Third of Torts (Liability for Physical and Emotional Harm) § 54(a) & cmt. b (2012).

[234] Cf. Bradford v. Universal Const. Co., 644 So.2d 864 (Ala. 1994) (plywood sheet blown by heavy wind).

[235] Roberts v. Weber & Sons, Co., 248 Neb. 243, 533 N.W.2d 664 (1995) (applying res ipsa loquitur). Even where fencing-in statutes have been repealed, liability for negligence in allowing livestock to roam the highways is still possible. Klobnak v. Wildwood Hills, Inc., 688 N.W.2d 799 (Iowa 2004). Further, open-range laws themselves may not protect a landowner whose cattle stray onto public highways and remain there because of the landowner's negligence. Larson-Murphy v. Steiner, 303 Mont. 96, 15 P.3d 1205 (2000).

[236] Olivo v. Owens-Illinois, Inc., 186 N.J. 394, 895 A.2d 1143 (2006); Satterfield v. Breeding Insulation Co., 266 S.W.3d 347 (Tenn. 2008). Most states have rejected liability on these facts, however, for a variety of reasons. See, e.g., Martin v. Cincinnati Gas and Elec. Co., 561 F.3d 439 (6th Cir. 2009); Van Fossen v. MidAmerican Energy Co., 777 N.W.2d 689 (Iowa 2009); In re Certified Question from the Fourteenth District Court of Appeals of Texas, 479 Mich. 498, 740 N.W.2d 206 (2007); In re New York City Asbestos Litigation, 5 N.Y.3d 486, 840 N.E.2d 115 (2005).

[237] Volpe v. Gallagher, 821 A.2d 699 (R.I. 2003) (mother as landowner permitting dangerous adult son to live with her and (the jury could find) to store weapons, which he used to shoot a neighbor); Restatement Second of Torts § 318 (1965). On the duty to control others generally, see Chapter 26.

[238] Pritchard v. Mabrey, 358 Mass. 137, 260 N.E.2d 712 (1970).

[239] Rosengren v. City of Seattle, 149 Wash.App. 565, 205 P.3d 909 (2009).

the condition[240] and perhaps even for failure to maintain the "special use" area with reasonable safety.[241] When legitimate activity on the land does not itself cause immediate physical harm but merely distracts motorists on nearby highways with resulting collisions and injuries, courts may assign the entire responsibility to the motorists and none to the landowner.[242]

Reasonable care owed to foreseeable strays from the highway. The land occupier owes not only a duty of reasonable care to protect those on the public way from activities and artificial conditions on his land, but also a duty of care to those who foreseeably stray from the road onto the land itself and are injured by a condition such as an excavation that was put there after the road was built. Many courts say that the motorist's deviation from the roadway is foreseeable where it is a normal incident of travel.[243] The duty of care is owed if the landowner should foresee that a highway user would inadvertently enter the land even if she is exercising due care.[244]

"Reasonably careful" travelers and foreseeable deviations. The rule of foreseeability to straying travelers says is that the risk must be one to travelers who are reasonably careful.[245] It does not say that the plaintiff must herself be without fault in the particular instance if the risk would also be one to reasonably careful people. The fault of the actual plaintiff would thus become a matter of contributory negligence, not a matter of the defendant's duty.[246] It is easy to miss the distinction, and some authority holds that the defendant is under no duty to one who is actually at fault, even if the land's condition was a threat to persons who were faultless as well.[247] But no matter what, harm to someone must be foreseeable and on that point the danger's distance from the road is highly relevant. A pile of construction materials at the road's edge is a great danger even when it is obvious, while a hidden excavation 100 yards from the road is not.[248]

The utility pole cases. A good number of cases involve motorists straying from the highway and hitting utility poles. Utility poles near the road are certainly obvious hazards, but it is often reasonably foreseeable that a motorist might hit one.[249] In many

[240] See Breger v. City of New York, 297 A.D.2d 770, 747 N.Y.S.2d 577 (2002) (creating the danger or causing the defect in the public way through special use such as use of the public way as a driveway to defendant's property).

[241] Rose v. Provo City, 67 P.3d 1017 (Utah. Ct. App. 2003) (even though landowner did not create the danger, use of the dangerous public property as a driveway to owner's parking lot justified imposition of duty).

[242] See Largosa v. Ford Motor Co., 708 N.E.2d 1219, 237 Ill.Dec. 179 (1999) (landowner-operating of commercial bungee jumping business adjacent to the highway not responsible for accidents resulting when motorists gaped at jumpers). Cf. Haymon v. Pettit, 9 N.Y.3d 324, 880 N.E.2d 416, 849 N.Y.S.2d 872 (2007) (baseball park operator owed no duty to warn or protect a non-patron spectator who was hit by a car while chasing a foul ball hit out of the stadium on a public street).

[243] E.g., Military Highway Water Supply Corp. v. Morin, 156 S.W.3d 569 (Tex. 2005) (no duty owed to motorist who hit a horse on the road, then traveled 500 feet off the road, where he was injured by an artificial condition on defendant's land; motorist must be "traveling with reasonable care" and "foreseeably deviating from the highway in the ordinary course of travel" for a duty to arise).

[244] Restatement Second of Torts § 368 (1965).

[245] See, e.g., Witmat Development Corp. v. Dickison, 907 N.E.2d 170 (Ind. App. 2009).

[246] See, e.g., Keller v. City of Spokane, 44 P.3d 845 (Wash. 2002) (city's duty to provide reasonably safe intersection was not limited to fault-free plaintiffs; comparative negligence, not a no-duty rule, would apply to account for highway user's negligence).

[247] See City of McAllen v. De La Garza, 898 S.W.2d 809 (Tex. 1995).

[248] Cf. Restatement Second of Torts § 368, cmt. h (1965).

[249] See Memphis Light, Gas and Water Div. v. Goss, 494 S.W.2d 766 (Tenn. 1973) (question of fact whether position of pole, nine inches from the road, with guy wires less than a foot from the road, was an obstruction unreasonably dangerous to motorists).

cases, the pole has been placed within the highway right of way, although at some distance from the paved portion of the highway. Distance from the road is a factor in these cases,[250] although many courts are reluctant to impose liability even where the distance is very small.[251] The pole cases, as distinct from most excavation cases, may be affected by governmental regulations,[252] and by public policy considerations against imposing liability on utility companies.[253]

C. DUTIES OF VENDORS AND LESSORS

§ 20.13 Vendors of Land

Once the landowner sells the land or leases it to a tenant, his duties to make conditions on the land reasonably safe are limited or nonexistent.[254] The reasons for and effects of the limitation are not like those in landowner cases already covered. In other landowner cases, the question was whether anyone owed a duty of any kind. In cases of vendors and landlords, however, the question is not so much whether a duty is owed but who owes it. It is not the existence of responsibility but the allocation of it. Subject to some qualifications, the traditional common law regarded the transfer of land title as a shift of responsibility[255] for conditions that might cause physical harm to others on the land.

Once the purchaser of land takes title and possession, he becomes responsible for dangers to himself or others on the land; and correspondingly the vendor is freed from responsibility.[256] If the vendor knew of a danger on the land and concealed it, he would remain responsible for harms resulting after transfer to the purchaser, but then only until the purchaser discovered the danger or had reason to know of it, or perhaps until

---

[250] See, e.g., Gouge v. Central Illinois Public Service Co.,144 Ill.2d 535, 582 N.E.2d 108 (1991) (not reasonably foreseeable that an automobile would leave the roadway and strike a pole 15 feet away, causing the pole to fall away from the road and injure the plaintiff).

[251] See, e.g., Coates v. Southern Maryland Co-op., Inc., 354 Md. 499, 731 A.2d 931 (1999) (no liability where utility pole was placed three feet from the road; distance was only one factor in the foreseeability analysis); Board of County Com'rs of Cecil County v. Dorman, 187 Md. App. 443, 979 A.2d 167 (2009) (no liability where pole was two and one-half feet off county road; motorist's striking of pole was nonetheless not reasonably foreseeable, based on evidence that no one had struck that pole in 40 years).

[252] E.g., Turner v. Ohio Bell Tel. Co., 118 Ohio St.3d 215, 887 N.E.2d 1158 (2008) (no liability for pole placed on highway right-of-way where public utility had obtained permits to install the pole there, and pole did not interfere with the usual course of travel). See also Seals v. County of Morris, 210 N.J. 157, 42 A.3d 157 (2012) (private utility was not immune from liability for negligence in placing an electric pole, interpreting governmental immunity statute).

[253] See Coates v. Southern Maryland Coop., Inc., 354 Md. 499, 731 A.2d 931 (1999) ("We do not wish, or intend, to establish a law that provides an absolute immunity for utility companies. . . . Nor, however, are we willing to create the prospect of a damage award against a utility every time someone runs off the road and strikes a pole.").

[254] E.g., Jackson v. Scheible, 902 N.E.2d 807 (Ind. 2009) (vendor owes no duty to protect from a dangerous condition, because vendor no longer controls the condition of the property).

[255] Shifting responsibility: see § 213. The rules are commonly explained by the maxim caveat emptor, let the buyer beware, but so far as liability to third persons is concerned, they seem to represent the expectations of the parties to the sale or lease.

[256] See, e.g., O'Connor v. Altus, 67 N.J. 106, 335 A.2d 545 (1975) (distinguishing a former owner from a former owner who was also a builder); Restatement Second of Torts § 352 (1965); Emile F. Short, Annotation, Liability of Vendor or Grantor of Real Estate for Personal Injury to Purchaser or Third Person Due to Defective Condition of Premises, 48 A.L.R.3d 1027 (1973).

the purchaser has time to make it reasonably safe.[257] The vendor would also escape liability if the purchaser knew of the danger or had reason to know of it.

When the condition creates a danger which causes harms to persons outside the land, the vendor remains responsible for his negligence in creating or maintaining the condition, but again the responsibility would terminate when the purchaser discovers the danger and perhaps until he has reasonable opportunity to make it reasonably safe.[258]

§ 20.14 Traditional Common Law Duties of Lessors

Relevance of the common law framework. The traditional common law duties of landlords[259] may be modified in some instances when the landlord is charged with negligence in failing to protect a tenant from an attacker, or when the landlord is charged with breaching a "warranty" of habitability. The duty to protect the plaintiff from others is a large subject not limited to landlords and it is considered in another chapter.[260] The so-called warranty of habitability is considered in the next section. This modification may require repairs by a landlord that would not be required by the common law rules. On the other hand, some common law rules will require an inspection that would not be required under the warranty of habitability. Further, the warranty of habitability does not apply to all cases. Consequently, the common law rules remain important not only as the starting place for the habitability warranty but also because in a number of instances they are controlling.

Responsibility shifted to tenant. Under the common law with respect to dangerous conditions of leased premises, lessors ordinarily owe the same duties to the tenant and the tenant's guests or others on the premises with the tenant's consent.[261] Under the traditional approach, that is frequently no duty at all. The traditional common law viewed a lease as a sale of land for a period of time. Consequently, when the landowner leased land to a tenant, the tenant was in the role of a land buyer. Like other land buyers, the tenant became responsible for the harms caused by negligently created or maintained conditions of the leased premises; concomitantly, the landlord ceased to be responsible. In the absence of an exception, the landlord was not legally responsible for conditions that arose on the land after he leased it[262] or even for those that existed at the time of the lease.[263]

---

[257] See Restatement Second of Torts § 353 (1965).

[258] Id. § 373 (if the vendor creates or conceals the condition, his responsibility continues until the purchaser both discovers and has opportunity to make the condition safe; if he merely permits a dangerous condition to remain, his responsibility terminates when the purchaser has reasonable opportunity to discover the danger).

[259] On the whole topic, see Jean C. Love, Landlord's Liability for Defective Premises: Caveat Lessee, Negligence, or Strict Liability?, 1975 Wis. L. Rev. 19.

[260] See Chapter 26.

[261] Shump v. First Continental-Robinwood Associates, 71 Ohio St.3d 414, 644 N.E.2d 291 (1994) (breach of duty to tenant would be breach to tenant's guest); Rittenour v. Gibson, 656 N.W.2d 691 (N.D. 2003) (landlord who knows of dangerous condition on leased premises owes duty to warn tenant's guest, and, if tenant does not know of the danger, tenant herself); Ortega v. Flaim, 902 P.2d 199 (Wyo. 1995) (no duty to tenant, no duty to tenant's guest).

[262] Restatement Second of Torts § 355 (1965).

[263] Id. § 356. Thus in the absence of an exception, the landlord has no duty to provide safety features on upper-story windows, even when he leases to families with small children. See Chiu v. City of Portland, 788 A.2d 183 (Me. 2002) (but finding window was in landlord's control).

Concealed or undisclosed conditions. Under an exception to the general common law rule, the landlord remains liable for harms done by an unreasonably dangerous condition[264] of which he knew or had reason to know and which he concealed or failed to disclose, provided it is also a condition that the tenant was not likely to discover and does not in fact discover.[265] The proviso is often expressed by saying that the landlord's responsibility for conditions existing at the time of the lease extends only to latent defects, not patent ones.[266] Once the tenant discovers the danger and had opportunity to remedy it, the landlord's responsibility for concealment terminates; perhaps in some cases it terminates as soon as the tenant *should* have discovered the danger and taken precautions.[267]

Contract to repair. By common law, the landlord is responsible for unreasonably dangerous conditions if he has contracted to repair them and negligently fails to do so after he knows or should know of the danger.[268] At one time this was viewed as a purely contractual matter, so that the landlord would be liable for the cost of making repairs or some similar measure of damages but would not be liable for the injury caused by the disrepair.[269] Today, however, the landlord's contract to repair is treated as creating a duty of reasonable care as well.[270] If he negligently fails to repair an unreasonably dangerous condition, he becomes liable for negligence, so that he is liable for the harms caused by disrepair as well as for the cost of bringing the premises up to the promised standard.[271] Since the landlord is liable only for a negligent failure to comply with the contractual duty, he is not responsible for repairs under this exception unless he is put on notice that they are needed and has a reasonable opportunity to make them.[272]

---

[264] In Rivera v. Nelson Realty, LLC, 7 N.Y.3d 530, 858 N.E.2d 1127, 825 N.Y.S.2d 422 (2006), the court held that a radiator without a cover was not an unreasonably hazardous condition; thus the landlord had no duty to "repair" it by providing a cover.

[265] Restatement Second of Torts § 358 (1965). See, e.g., Heynen v. Fairbanks, 293 P.3d 470 (Alaska 2013). Courts often say that the dangerous condition must have been actually known by the landlord. E.g., Oretga v. Flaim, 902 P.2d 199 (Wyo. 1995). If this is to be taken literally, the landlord's "reason to know" will not be enough. The Restatement Third's position is that a landlord owes a duty to disclose to the lessee any dangerous condition that poses a risk to entrants, exists when the lessee takes possession, is latent and unknown to the lessee, and is "known or should be known" to the landlord. Restatement Third of Torts (Liability for Physical and Emotional Harm) § 53(c) (2012).

[266] See, e.g., Ayala v. B & B Realty Co., 32 Conn. Super. 58, 337 A.2d 330 (1974); Dowler v. Boczkowski, 148 N.J. 512, 691 A.2d 314 (1997); Munzi v. Kennedy, 538 A.2d 1015 (R.I. 1988).

[267] Restatement Second of Torts § 358 (1965) (if the landlord does not actively conceal the condition, his responsibility terminates when the tenant has reasonable opportunity to discover the condition).

[268] Id. § 357. See Meier v. D'Ambose, 419 N.J. Super. 439, 17 A.3d 271 (App. Div. 2011), certification denied, 208 N.J. 370, 29 A.3d 742 (2011) (landlord owed duty to tenant to maintain resident's furnace, and to inspect it periodically for defects, where lease explicitly required landlord to keep the furnace clean). Statutes may impose a duty of reasonable care on the landlord to remedy unsafe conditions upon receipt of notice of such conditions. In Bishop v. TES Realty Trust, 459 Mass. 9, 942 N.E.2d 173 (2011), the court extended the state statute to commercial landlords as well as residential ones, in a case in which ceiling plaster fell on a commercial tenant and injured her.

[269] E.g., Leavitt v. Twin County Rental Co., 222 N.C. 81, 21 S.E.2d 890 (1942).

[270] E.g., Childress v. Bowser, 546 N.E.2d 1221 (Ind. 1989) (covenant to repair could be inferred from landlord's telling tenant not to do anything to the apartment, and later promising to make repairs).

[271] E.g., Markarian v. Simonian, 373 Mass. 669, 369 N.E.2d 718 (1977) (negligent installation of window screens; child fell from window); Restatement Second of Torts § 375 (1965).

[272] See McKenzie v. Egge, 207 Md. 1, 113 A.2d 95 (1955); Juarez v. Wavecrest Management Team Ltd., 88 N.Y.2d 628, 649 N.Y.S.2d 115, 672 N.E.2d 135 (1996) (lead-based paint; stating notice requirement both for contractual and statutory duty of repair); Charette v. Santspree, 68 A.D.3d 1583, 893 N.Y.S.2d 315 (2009) (landlord lacked actual knowledge that lead-based paint was chipping or peeling inside tenant's apartment, but fact issue whether landlords had either actual or constructive knowledge that paint was peeling in common areas).

Repairs negligently made. Even if not contractually obliged to make repairs, the landlord is under a common law duty to use reasonable care when he voluntarily makes repairs on the leased premises after the tenant has taken possession.[273] He is thus subject to liability for actual harm if he negligently repairs a condition so that it was more dangerous, provided the tenant neither knows nor should have known of the increased danger.[274] The condition might be more dangerous either because alterations made it more infirm than before[275] or because the purported alterations gave an appearance of safety upon which the tenant relied.[276]

Land leased for public admission. The lessor who leases the premises for admission of the public owes a duty of reasonable care to discover dangers to the public and to correct them if he has reason to think that the lessee will admit the public before putting the premises in reasonably safe condition.[277] Even when this rule applies, it does not impose strict liability; the lessor's duty is to exercise reasonable care, no more.[278]

Portions of premises over which lessor retains control. In many instances, the lessor retains control over some portion of the premises that various tenants have a right to use. For instance, the landlord controls halls, stairways, and sidewalks that are part of an apartment building or complex of buildings. At the same time, those portions of the premises are intended for the tenants' use. As to such portions, the lessor owes a duty of reasonable care to make the premises safe for the benefit of the tenants and others lawfully upon the land.[279] Reasonable care will require inspection from time to time and reasonable effort to make dangerous situations safe. The landlord must usually have knowledge or constructive knowledge of the defect,[280] but the tenant's actual knowledge of the danger does not relieve the lessor of a duty of care. The tenant's property rights— to enter her apartment, for example, even if the only stairs to it are in dangerous condition—are trumps in this instance.

The rules just discussed are often referred to as the common passageway rules. However, the point is not that tenants are entitled to use the premises but that the landlord has retained control. For that reason, similar rules apply to other parts of the land that are not intended for the tenants' use but that must be safe if the leased

---

[273] Repairs negligently completed before the lease commences will not bring the landlord under this rule. Casey v. Estes, 657 So.2d 845 (Ala. 1995).

[274] See Restatement Second of Torts § 362 (1965).

[275] E.g., Durkin v. Hansen, 313 S.C. 343, 437 S.E.2d 550 (Ct. App. 1993) (landlord's carpet cleaning left slippery soap on the kitchen tile floor with predictable results).

[276] In Ginsberg v. Wineman, 314 Mich. 1, 22 N.W.2d 49 (1946), the landlord's agent purported to make a stair safe but (as the trier could find) actually only reinserted nails in holes that were loose, then told the tenant the stair was repaired. The tenant's employee, who was badly injured when the stair gave way, was allowed to recover.

[277] Restatement Second of Torts § 359 (1965); see Lopez v. Superior Court, 45 Cal.App.4th 705, 52 Cal.Rptr.2d 821 (1996). The Third Restatement places a landlord under a duty of reasonable care for any dangerous condition on the leased premises at the time the lessee takes possession, if the lease is for a purpose that includes admitting the public to the premises and the landlord has reason to believe that the lessee will admit persons onto the premises without rectifying the dangerous condition. Restatement Third of Torts (Liability for Physical and Emotional Harm) § 53(d) (2012).

[278] See Johnson County Sheriff's Posse, Inc. v. Endsley, 926 S.W.2d 284 (Tex. 1996) (lessor of rodeo arena was not negligent in failing to pick all rocks on its dirt floor).

[279] Rodrigue v. Rodrigue, 694 A.2d 924 (Me. 1997); Restatement Second of Torts § 360 (1965); Restatement Third of Torts (Liability for Physical and Emotional Harm) § 53(a) (2012).

[280] E.g., Charette v. Santspree, 68 A.D.3d 1583, 893 N.Y.S.2d 315 (2009) (fact issue whether landlords had either actual or constructive knowledge that lead-based paint was peeling in common areas of apartment).

premises are to be safe.[281] For example, the lessor must not negligently allow the roof to collapse[282] or wiring within the walls to become a fire hazard.[283] So far as a window's safety depends upon fittings installed outside the building rather than in the lease premises themselves, the landlord may be in control and hence owe a duty of care.[284]

A reasonable person standard. Some courts have dropped these special rules limiting landlord liability and have substituted a rule of ordinary care instead.[285] Wisconsin, applying this approach, has held that once a landlord learns that paint is peeling in premises constructed before lead paint was banned, he is under a duty to test for lead paint and take appropriate steps to prevent its harm to a tenant's child.[286]

§ 20.15 The Implied Warranty of Habitability

Most states, by statute or judicial decision, have now recognized an implied warranty of habitability in residential leases,[287] but not commercial ones.[288] Courts say that by leasing the property, the lessor implicitly guarantees that there are no defects, or at least no latent defects, and no housing law violations in facilities vital to the use of the premises, and, in many states, that essential features will remain in such condition during the lease, and that it will remain "habitable."[289] A number of courts take the position that the warranty cannot be "waived" except perhaps in the case of a single-family dwelling.[290]

Strict liability rejected. The implied warranty originally served to give the tenant leverage to insist upon repairs. The tenant might, for example, withhold rent or make repairs and deduct the cost from her rental obligations. Yet the language of implied

---

[281] See Restatement Second of Torts § 361 (1965); Restatement Second of Property § 17.4 (1976).

[282] Restatement Second of Torts § 361 (1965).

[283] Leavitt v. Glick Realty Corp., 362 Mass. 370, 285 N.E.2d 786 (1972) (subtenant died of smoke inhalation from fire caused by wiring in the ceiling of the apartment). Cf. Coleman v. Steinberg, 54 N.J. 58, 253 A.2d 167 (1969) (heating system for all tenants caused harm to child in one apartment).

[284] Chiu v. City of Portland, 788 A.2d 183 (Me. 2002) (jury question as to landlord's control of acrylic window dangerously fitted so that it would easily pop out). But the lessor's "explicit reservation of the authority to enter the premises and to make repairs is insufficient to constitute retention of control"; and "the landlord's making of prior repairs is also insufficient," as is "the landlord's right to approve the air conditioning contractor." Settles v. Redstone Development Corp., 797 A.2d 692 (D.C. 2002).

[285] Pagelsdorf v. Safeco Ins. Co. of America, 91 Wis.2d 734, 284 N.W.2d 55 (1979); Favreau v. Miller, 156 Vt. 222, 591 A.2d 68 (1991). In Tagle v. Jakob, 97 N.Y.2d 165, 763 N.E.2d 107, 737 N.Y.S. 2d 331 (2001), the court approached a claim brought against a landlord by a tenant's guest as part of the reasonable care regime it had adopted for landowners. See § 20.9. The Third Restatement adopts a general duty of reasonable care for lessors, owed to the lessee and all other entrants on the leased premises, with narrow exceptions. See Restatement Third of Torts (Liability for Physical and Emotional Harm) § 53 (2012).

[286] Antwaun A. v. Heritage Mut. Ins. Co., 228 Wis.2d 44, 596 N.W.2d 456 (1999).

[287] E.g., Pole Realty Co. v. Sorrells, 84 Ill.2d 178, 417 N.E.2d 1297, 49 Ill.Dec. 283 (1981) (warranty applies to single-family dwellings as well as to multiple-unit dwelling structures); Scott v. Garfield, 454 Mass. 790, 912 N.E.2d 1000 (2009) (allowing visitor to recover damages caused by landlord's breach of the implied warranty of habitability); Kline v. Burns, 111 N.H. 87, 276 A.2d 248 (1971) (implied warranty of habitability in an apartment rental); see Mark S. Dennison, Cause of Action for Breach of Implied Warranty of Habitability in Residential Lease, 25 Causes of Action 2d 493 (2004); Jonathan M. Purver, Annotation, Modern Status of Rules as to Existence of Implied Warranty of Habitability or Fitness for Use of Leased Premises, 40 A.L.R.3d 646 (1972). Several states have refused to recognize the warranty. E.g., Murphy v. Hendrix, 500 So.2d 8 (Ala. 1986) (concluding that adoption of such a rule is for the legislature); Moglia v. McNeil Co., 270 Neb. 241, 700 N.W.2d 608 (2005); Ortega v. Flaim, 902 P.2d 199 (Wyo. 1995).

[288] See Thomas M. Fleming, Annotation, Implied Warranty of Fitness or Suitability in Commercial Leases—Modern Status, 76 A.L.R.4th 928 (1990).

[289] Estate of Vazquez v. Hepner, 564 N.W.2d 426 (Iowa 1997).

[290] E.g., Green v. Superior Court, 10 Cal.3d 616, 111 Cal.Rptr. 704, 517 P.2d 1168 (1974).

warranty, long associated with strict liability, suggested that the landlord would be liable without fault for personal injuries resulting from dangers on the leased premises. As courts began to consider the implied warranty theory in personal injury claims, however, it has turned out that the landlord was not strictly liable at all.[291] The "warranty" requires only that the landlord keep the premises in reasonable repair when the landlord knows or should know of the defect.[292] The warranty is not a warranty that the lessor has implicitly made, but rather a rule of law imposed by the court.[293]

Statutes. Statutes or ordinances often establish a warranty of habitability or some specific requirement for safety and habitability of the premises, for example, by prohibiting exposed lead paint. Courts have held that these statutes do not impose strict liability, but do impose a duty of reasonable care. Sometimes courts make this point by saying that the landlord's obligation arises only when he has notice of the defect, or when he should have discovered the defect by reasonable care.[294] This means that although negligence in some form is required in order to establish liability, actual notice of the defect is not always necessary.

---

[291] Peterson v. Superior Court, 10 Cal.4th 1185, 899 P.2d 905, 43 Cal.Rptr.2d 836 (1995), *overruling* Becker v. IRM Corp., 38 Cal.3d 454, 213 Cal.Rptr. 213, 698 P.2d 116 (1985); Martin v. Rankin Circle Apartments, 941 So.2d 854 (Miss. App. 2006) (suit on warranty of habitability is essentially a negligence action); Antwaun A. v. Heritage Mut. Ins. Co., 228 Wis.2d 44, 596 N.W.2d 456 (1999). However, defects that threaten personal safety may be actionable, not because injury results but because the premises were worth less due to the defect. In that case, damages would be measured by the difference between the value of the premises as warranted and the value actually received. Williard v. Parsons Hill P'ship, 178 Vt. 300, 313, 882 A.2d 1213, 1222 (2005).

[292] Peterson v. Superior Court, 10 Cal.4th 1185, 899 P.2d 905, 43 Cal.Rptr.2d 836 (1995); Estate of Vazquez v. Hepner, 564 N.W.2d 426 (Iowa 1997); Benik v. Hatcher, 358 Md. 507, 750 A.2d 10 (2000).

[293] See Scott v. Garfield, 454 Mass. 790, 912 N.E.2d 1000 (2009); contra, Johnson v. Scandia Associates, Inc., 717 N.E.2d 24 (Ind. 1999) (implied warranty "is not imposed by law on every residential lease contract, but may be implied in fact in the agreement between landlord and tenant").

[294] E.g., Gore v. People's Sav. Bank, 235 Conn. 360, 665 A. 2d 1341 (1995); Childs v. Purll, 882 A.2d 227 (D.C. 2005) (liability for violation of the statute if landlord reasonably should have known of the condition); Charette v. Santspree, 68 A.D.3d 1583, 893 N.Y.S.2d 315 (2009) (landlord must have either actual or constructive notice that paint was chipping and peeling in common areas of the building to be liable to tenant's child allegedly poisoned by lead paint).

Chapter 21

LIABILITY OF HEALTH CARE PROVIDERS

Analysis

A. MEDICAL MALPRACTICE

    1.   Summary and Context

§ 21.1   Malpractice Rules in Summary

§ 21.2   Professional Status and Its Significance

    2.   Duty and the Doctor-Patient Relationship

§ 21.3   General Rule and Exceptions

§ 21.4   Duties to Non-Patients

    3.   Standards of Care and Attendant Proof Requirements

§ 21.5   The Traditional Medical Standard of Care

§ 21.6   The Reasonable Care Standard

§ 21.7   The Relevant Geographical Community

§ 21.8   The Expert Testimony Requirement

    4.   Informed Consent

§ 21.9   Informed Consent: Underlying Principle and Elements

§ 21.10   General Standards of Disclosure

§ 21.11   Particular Types of Information to Be Disclosed

§ 21.12   The Causation Requirement in Informed Consent Cases

    5.   Defenses and Statutory Limits on Liability

§ 21.13   Good Samaritan Statutes

§ 21.14   The "Malpractice Crisis" Statutes

§ 21.15   Patient's Contributory Negligence

B. HOSPITALS AND MANAGED CARE ORGANIZATIONS

§ 21.16   Common-Law Responsibility of Hospitals

§ 21.17   Mandatory Hospital Screening and Treatment: EMTALA

§ 21.18   Managed Care Organizations

C. NURSING HOMES AND RESIDENTIAL FACILITIES

§ 21.19   Injuries in Nursing Homes and Other Care Facilities

§ 21.20   Standard of Care for Nursing Homes

§ 21.21   Common-Law Claims Against Nursing Homes

§ 21.22   Statutory Claims Against Nursing Homes

A. MEDICAL MALPRACTICE

1. Summary and Context

§ 21.1 Malpractice Rules in Summary

Medical malpractice actions sound in negligence. Thus they are governed by the general negligence elements and are subject to the ordinary negligence defenses such as comparative fault and assumption of risk. Liability of health care providers, however, is often limited because of special standards and proof requirements.

Duty: standard based on medical customs. A doctor-patient relationship is necessary to establish a duty to provide active medical care for the patient, with some exceptions.[1] While some modern courts have departed from it,[2] the traditional duty to patients is not the familiar duty of reasonable care, but rather the duty to comply with medical customs or medical standards that supposedly dictate the exact methods by which a medical procedure is carried out.[3] Because of this rule, expert testimony must be introduced to show the medical standard.

Medical standards of which community? Originally, the relevant medical community that would set the medical standard of care by its custom was the local medical community where the defendant practiced. Most courts now hold that the medical community that sets the standard is broader, either the same community of the defendant or a similar one.[4] Some courts have adopted a national medical community standard.[5] Some special rules may govern the liability of doctors who are hospital residents.[6]

Different schools of thought and specialists. Even within the community of medical doctors, there may be two different schools of thought about how to perform a given procedure. If both views have substantial acceptance, the physician who follows either one is deemed not negligent.[7] Specialists such as orthopedic surgeons are governed by the national standards of their specialty.[8]

Expert testimony requirement. Except where the defendant's negligence is obvious even to a layman or the res ipsa loquitur rules apply,[9] the plaintiff is required to produce expert testimony to prove breach of the standard of care and usually also to prove factual

---

[1]   §§ 21.3 & 21.4.

[2]   § 21.6 (duty of reasonable care).

[3]   § 21.5 & 21.6. In some cases, predetermined guidelines set by a government agency might be adopted as standards. See 2 Dobbs, Hayden & Bublick, The Law of Torts § 295 (2d ed. 2011 & Supp.).

[4]   § 21.7. Non-medical practitioners—chiropractors, for example—are held to similar rules, but their standards are set by the particular kind of health care they profess. Thus if a chiropractor holds himself out as such, he will be held to the standard of other chiropractors in the relevant chiropractic community. See, e.g., Felton v. Lovett, 388 S.W.3d 656 (Tex. 2012). However, if he holds himself out as a podiatrist he is held to the standard of a podiatrist, see, e.g., Creasey v. Hogan, 292 Or. 154, 637 P.2d 114 (1981), and if he claims to be a physician he will be held to that standard, see, e. g., Brown v. Shyne, 242 N.Y. 176, 151 N.E. 197 (1926).

[5]   § 21.7.

[6]   See 2 Dobbs, Hayden & Bublick, The Law of Torts § 301 (2d ed. 2011 & Supp.). Courts have utilized three different broad approaches to the standard of care for licensed residents. See Joseph H. King, The Standard of Care for Residents and Other Medical School Graduates in Training, 55 Am. U. L. Rev. 683 (2006).

[7]   See 2 Dobbs, Hayden & Bublick, The Law of Torts § 296 (2d ed. 2011 & Supp.).

[8]   § 21.7.

[9]   See 2 Dobbs, Hayden & Bublick, The Law of Torts §§ 305 & 306 (2d ed. 2011 & Supp.).

causation.[10] Under the traditional medical standard, the expert's testimony must establish the medical custom or medical standard of care, such as a custom to locate a certain nerve before cutting nearby[11] or the custom to refer to a specialist when the patient has a given condition.[12] If the reasonable care standard applies instead, the expert might be permitted to testify differently, perhaps that the risk of the procedure adopted by the defendant was high and the benefits correspondingly low so as to warrant an inference of negligence without appeal to medical custom.

Informed consent. Informed consent claims are somewhat different. The gist of the informed consent claim is that the physician failed to provide information to the patient, usually about the risk of the proposed procedure or about safer alternatives.[13] In these cases, the patient suffers an injury from a medical procedure, but not because the procedure was negligently performed. The plaintiff's claim is that she, or a reasonable person, would have refused consent to the procedure had she been given appropriate information.[14] Some courts require the physician to disclose all material information, while others say that what the physician must disclose is determined by medical custom, not by what is relevant to the patient's decision-making.[15]

Emergencies. Statutes generally provide that physicians and other health care providers are not liable for negligence when they act in an emergency.[16] Many other statutes, especially those growing out of perceived medical malpractice crises, offer other advantages to doctors and others in the health care industry, such as limits on damages that can prevent seriously injured persons from obtaining full compensation.[17]

§ 21.2 Professional Status and Its Significance

Tort duties are often affected by a defendant's professional status. Under traditional rules, physicians owe a duty of care set by the custom of their profession rather than a duty of reasonable care under the circumstances.[18] Other medical professionals, such as

---

[10] § 21.8.

[11] § 21.5.

[12] Id.

[13] § 21.9.

[14] § 21.12.

[15] §§ 21.10 & 21.11.

[16] § 21.13.

[17] § 21.14.

[18] §§ 21.5 & 21.6.

nurses,[19] physician assistants,[20] pharmacists,[21] physical therapists,[22] dentists,[23] mental health professionals[24] and licensed practitioners like chiropractors and podiatrists[25] have been held to owe a similar professional duty. A number of non-medical professionals, such as architects,[26] engineers,[27] lawyers,[28] social workers[29] and even sports coaches,[30] owe their clients the care provided or generally accepted as the standard by qualified practitioners in the same profession. Some courts are now re-evaluating this "professional duty" rule in favor of a general standard of the reasonable person under the circumstances,[31] which would require physicians to use the knowledge and skill they actually possess as well as the knowledge and skill they should possess, whether or not other physicians in the relevant community of physicians used such skill.

Three important points must be made about the professional status of a defendant.

First, favoritism is not the legal or moral basis for any special and favorable rules that are applied to professionals. If there is a basis for special rules protecting professionals, it lies in the relationship and expectation of the parties, for which professional status is a marker, not in the defendant's elite status in itself.

Second, courts that state limited duties or special standards of care for professionals may really have in mind only a specific application of the general rule that everyone, professional or not, is obliged to use reasonable care under the circumstances. In many instances, the defendant's profession is a relevant "circumstance." For example, a professional physician who is treating a patient, would be expected to use all the special expertise he has as a professional. But the principle is not distinctively applied to professionals; it applies to non-professionals as well. Given a recognized risk, all reasonable persons should use the knowledge and skill at their disposal. In this light, it

[19] See Hill v. Fairfield Nursing & Rehabilitation Center, LLC, 134 So.3d 396 (Ala. 2013); Fein v. Permanente Med. Group, 38 Cal.3d 137, 211 Cal. Rptr. 368, 695 P.2d 665 (1985); Berdyck v. Shinde, 66 Ohio St.3d 573, 613 N.E.2d 1014 (1993).

[20] See Cox v. M.A. Primary and Urgent Care Clinic, 313 S.W.3d 240 (Tenn. 2010). State statutes may require that physician assistants be held to the standard of the supervising physician. See, e.g., Mich. Comp. L. Ann. § 333.17078(2).

[21] See Downing v. Hyland Pharmacy, 194 P.3d 944 (Utah 2008). The professional duty of pharmacists has been undercut in many states by rulings as a matter of law that if the pharmacist accurately fills a physician's prescription, he has no duty to warn the patient that the dosage is too high, or that the drug has special dangers. See, e.g., Springhill Hospitals, Inc. v. Larrimore, 5 So.3d 513 (Ala. 2008); see also David J. Marchitelli, Annotation, Liability of Pharmacist Who Accurately Fills Prescription for Harm Resulting to User, 44 A.L.R.5th 393 (1996). Other states have recognized a pharmacist's duty to warn a patient where the pharmacist actually knows of some problem, such as where the drug prescribed is contraindicated for the patient's condition, see, e.g., Happel v. Wal-Mart Stores, Inc., 199 Ill.2d 179, 766 N.E.2d 1118, 262 Ill.Dec. 815 (2002); Moore v. Memorial Hospital of Gulfport, 825 So.2d 658 (Miss. 2002). Federal and state statutes often place pharmacists under special duties to counsel patients. See, e.g., 42 U.S.C.A. § 1396r–8(g); Cal. Bus. & Prof. Code § 4074.

[22] See Rehabilitative Care System of America v. Davis, 73 S.W.3d 233 (Tex. 2002).

[23] Douglas v. Freeman, 117 Wash.2d 242, 814 P.2d 1160 (1991) (dental clinic).

[24] Stone v. Proctor, 259 N.C. 633, 131 S.E.2d 297 (1963) (psychiatrist, electroshock treatments); Michael L. Perlin, Law and Mental Disability § 3.02 (1994); see Vilcinskas v. Johnson, 252 Neb. 292, 562 N.W.2d 57 (1997) (by implication).

[25] See § 21.7.

[26] E.g., Simon v. Drake Constr. Co., 87 Ohio App.3d 23, 621 N.E.2d 837 (1993).

[27] Affiliated FM Ins. Co. v. LTK Consulting Services, Inc., 170 Wash. 2d 442, 243 P.3d 521 (2010).

[28] See Chapter 45.

[29] District of Columbia v. Hampton, 666 A.2d 30 (D.C. 1995); Advincula v. United Blood Servs., 176 Ill.2d 1, 678 N.E.2d 1009, 223 Ill.Dec. 1 (1996).

[30] Cerny v. Cedar Bluffs Junior/Senior Pub. Sch., 262 Neb. 66, 628 N.W.2d 697 (2001).

[31] See § 21.6.

seems probable that if a court tells us that the dog catcher is obliged to use the care of dog-catchers, it means only to say that reasonable care is required, not to say that a community of negligent dog-catchers can set their own lax standards.

Third, the defendant's professional or expert status, whether as a physician or a dog catcher, is a good flag to warn that technical proof, perhaps by way of qualified experts, may be required to show negligence. That is not because professionals are entitled to escape responsibility for negligent and harmful acts, but because in many instances judges and juries will not know when a professional is negligent unless they hear expert testimony. Except for the sometime need for technical evidence, the ordinary duties of reasonable care could suffice for professionals as well as others. It is possible that some of the decisions are moving in this direction.[32]

2. *Duty and the Doctor-Patient Relationship*

§ 21.3   General Rule and Exceptions

Courts often say that a medical malpractice action does not lie unless the parties are in a doctor-patient relationship; if there is no such relationship, the doctor is under no medical duty to the putative patient,[33] with some qualifications. In the usual case, the doctor-patient relationship is formed by the doctor's undertaking[34] to act for the benefit of the patient[35] or with her express or implied consent or that of her representative. The duty is of course limited by the scope of the undertaking.[36] The same principle means that the physician is not subject to malpractice liability for injury inflicted upon a patient outside the scope of his professional relationship unless an exception applies.[37] In the absence of statute or exception, the same essential principle applies to hospitals that have no relationship to the plaintiff.[38]

Under these rules, when a patient's physician consults another doctor but does not employ him, the consulted doctor who does not see the patient, perform any tests, or

---

[32] E.g., United Blood Servs., Div. of Blood Systems, Inc. v. Quintana, 827 P.2d 509 (Colo. 1992); see § 21.6.

[33] See, e.g., Kananen v. Alfred I. DuPont Inst. of Nemours Found., 796 A.2d 1 (Del. Super.), *aff'd*, 768 A.2d 470 (Del. 2000); Smith v. Pavlovich, 394 Ill.App.3d 458, 466, 914 N.E.2d 1258, 1266 (2009).

[34] Adams v. Via Christi Reg'l Med. Ctr., 270 Kan. 824, 19 P.3d 132 (Kan. 2001); Kelley v. Middle Tennessee Emergency Physicians, P.C., 133 S.W.3d 587, 593 (Tenn. 2004); Didato v. Strehler, 262 Va. 617, 554 S.E.2d 42 (2001); see James L. Rigelhaupt, Jr., Annotation, What Constitutes Physician-Patient Relationship for Malpractice Purposes, 17 A.L.R.4th 132 (1982).

[35] Walters v. Rinker, 520 N.E.2d 468 (Ind. Ct. App. 1988) ("The important fact in determining whether the relationship is a consensual one, however, is not who contracted for the service but whether it was contracted for with the express or implied consent of the patient *or for his benefit*.") (emphasis added); Kelley v. Middle Tennessee Emergency Physicians, P.C., 133 S.W.3d 587, 593 (Tenn. 2004). See also Olson v. Wrenshall, 284 Neb. 445, 822 N.W.2d 336 (2012) (surgeon owed no duty to kidney donor during allegedly negligent treatment in which the kidney was damaged).

[36] See Garcia v. Lifemark Hospitals of Fla., 754 So.2d 48 (Fla. Dist. Ct. App. 1999) (emergency room doctor's duty was to treat the emergency condition, not to test for psychiatric conditions that might lead to suicide).

[37] Iwanski v. Gomes, 259 Neb. 632, 611 N.W.2d 607 (2000) (consensual sexual relationship with patient not medical malpractice; if it is not some other tort, no liability).

[38] See Kananen v. Alfred I. DuPont Institute of Nemours Foundation, 796 A.2d 1 (Del. Super. 2000), *aff'd*, 768 A.2d 470 (Del. 2000) (hospital owes no duty to bystander-parent who fainted while watching treatment of her small child). As to the statutory duty of hospitals to accept emergency patients, see § 21.17.

otherwise act except to give advice he knows will be followed, has no doctor-patient relationship with, and no duty to the patient on whose behalf he was consulted.[39]

However, contemporary ways of delivering health care compel some adjustments in our conception of the doctor-patient relationship. A hospital patient may be treated by whole teams of health care providers, or may be handed off from one to another, raising questions about the duties of each.[40] Telephone or on-line consultations may establish a doctor-patient relationship and hence a duty quite outside the traditional face-to-face encounter.[41] The physician's contract with someone other than the patient, such as a hospital, may count as an undertaking of a physician-patient relationship with persons who appropriately present themselves for hospital care, thus requiring the physician to provide appropriate supervision for patients he has never seen.[42]

When a duty exists without a doctor-patient relationship. On its face, the rule requiring a doctor-patient relationship is merely a specific application of a very general tort principle. Defendants who have neither committed affirmative acts nor caused harm are not compelled to take affirmative steps to protect others unless an exception applies. One exception is that defendants who have undertaken to protect the plaintiff are under a duty to use care to do so in certain circumstances. Another is that defendants who stand in a special relationship with the plaintiff (or with some tortfeasor who inflicts harm upon the plaintiff) are again under a duty to use reasonable care.[43] The physician is thus under a duty of care even to non-patients in three broad categories of cases: (1) when he engages in non-medical conduct that involves no professional judgment, in which case ordinary negligence rules apply;[44] (2) when he undertakes by words or conduct to provide medical advice for or attention to a person not previously his patient;[45] and (3) when he creates an unreasonable risk by positive acts of negligence.[46]

---

[39]   Gilbert v. Miodovnik, 990 A.2d 983 (D.C. 2010) (physician consulting with nurse-midwives unknown to patient, no doctor patient-relationship, no duty); Jennings v. Badgett, 230 P.3d 861 (Okla. 2010) (physician consulting with another physician, no contact with patient, no duty, although consulting physician knew patient's physician would rely on his advice).

[40]   See, e.g., Nold ex rel. Nold v. Binyon, 272 Kan. 87, 31 P.3d 274 (2001).

[41]   See, e.g., Adams v. Via Christi Regional Medical Center, 270 Kan. 824, 19 P.3d 132 (2001) (telephone conversation with mother of adult daughter, with "advice" to take daughter to emergency room if pain became worse, generated a doctor-patient relationship with the daughter); Mozingo v. Pitt County. Memorial Hospital, Inc., 331 N.C. 182, 415 S.E.2d 341 (1992) (noting changing practice and increased reliance on teams of health care providers, some of whom do not see patient); see also Mead v. Legacy Health System, 352 Or. 267, 283 P.3d 904 (2012) (the standard for determining whether a doctor who has not personally seen a patient nonetheless has a doctor-patient relationship with that patient is whether the doctor either knows or should know that he or she is diagnosing the patient's condition or treating the patient; there is no requirement that the doctor must actually intend to participate in such diagnosis or treatment). For a discussion of the duties owed by on-call physicians, who often speak to patients via telephone or email, see 2 Dobbs, Hayden & Bublick, The Law of Torts § 287 (2d ed. 2011 & Supp.). Mainstream cases recognize a duty of care owed to patients triggered by the doctor's acceptance of on-call status. Id.

[42]   See Lam v. Global Med. Sys., Inc., 127 Wash. App. 657, 111 P.3d 1258 (2005) (medical consulting service, contracting with ship operators to provide telephonic medical advice while ship was at sea was under a duty of care to seaman who took ill); Lownsbury v. VanBuren, 94 Ohio St. 3d 231,762 N.E.2d 354 (2002).

[43]   § 25.1.

[44]   See MCG Health, Inc. v. Casey, 269 Ga.App. 125, 603 S.E.2d 438 (2004) ("Administrative, clerical, or routine acts demanding no special expertise fall in the realm of simple negligence. We have previously held that a nurse's failure to activate an alarm, as a doctor ordered, was ordinary negligence"); Sullo v. Greenberg, 68 A.3d 404 (R.I. 2013) (patient fell on entrance ramp of doctor's office; normal landlowner-invitee duty applied, not any special professional duty).

[45]   E.g., Nold ex rel. Nold v. Binyon, 272 Kan. 87, 31 P.3d 274 (2001); Hoover v. Williamson, 236 Md. 250, 203 A.2d 861 (1964); Meinze v. Holmes, 40 Ohio App.3d 143, 532 N.E.2d 170 (1987).

[46]   Healthone v. Rodriguez, 50 P.3d 879 (Colo. 2002); Smith v. Welch, 265 Kan. 868, 967 P.2d 727 (1998).

Medical examinations on behalf of third persons. Doctors are sometimes retained to examine prospective employees, prospective insureds, or litigation claimants for the purpose of reporting to their principals on the examinee's bodily or mental condition. They are not in the usual kind of physician-patient relationship, but they may harm the examined plaintiff (1) by inflicting a dangerous and negligent examination that directly causes harm, (2) by failing to diagnose a serious condition, (3) by failing to advise the plaintiff of a serious condition that was accurately diagnosed, or (4) by reaching an erroneous conclusion that interferes with the examinee's economic prospects in employment, insurance, or litigation.[47]

Liability to patient when third party has retained the doctor. In the first category of cases, courts agree that when harm results from the examination itself, the doctor or other professional, such as a physical therapist, owes a duty of care.[48] However, when the examining physician negligently fails to diagnose a serious condition with resulting harm or death,[49] and sometimes even when he diagnoses the condition but fails to advise the plaintiff,[50] a number of courts have said that the physician is not liable because he is not in a doctor-patient relationship with the plaintiff, and that his sole duty is to the employer or insurer who retained him. This seems unnecessarily stringent. The fact that one person pays the health care provider should not determine whether another person is the patient. The general rule, in fact, is that an undertaking to a third person to act for the safety of the plaintiff is generally sufficient to create a duty to the plaintiff.[51] That rule applies to physicians as well as others.[52] Perhaps the core idea is that the expectations of the plaintiff and undertakings of the defendant should control. In accord with this view, some authority has expressly held that a doctor who actually examines[53] a patient or reads his X-rays owes a duty of reasonable care in making a diagnosis and in notifying the patient of serious medical conditions within the scope of the examination he has undertaken.[54] If the physician has undertaken to provide care to a person or

[47] Courts have usually rejected a duty of care to the examinee for such economic harms. See, e.g., Martinez v. Lewis, 969 P.2d 213 (Colo. 1998); Woodruff v. Gitlow, 91 A.3d 805 (R.I. 2014).

[48] See, e.g., Greenberg v. Perkins, 845 P.2d 530 (Colo. 1993); Dyer v. Trachtman, 470 Mich. 45, 679 N.W.2d 311(2004); Harris v. Kreutzer, 271 Va. 188, 624 S.E.2d 24 (2006).

[49] Lee v. City of New York, 162 A.D.2d 34, 560 N.Y.S.2d 700 (1990) (broadly stating that "[t]he physician-patient relationship does not exist if the physician is retained solely to examine an employee on behalf of an employer" although in fact the claim was for failing to diagnose, not failing to disclose a condition the physician actually discovered).

[50] See Ervin v. American Guardian Life Assurance Co., 376 Pa.Super. 132, 545 A.2d 354 (1988) (physician retained by insurer; physician "owed no duty to the plaintiff's decedent either to discover his heart problem or, having discovered it, to inform the decedent thereof").

[51] See § 25.7.

[52] See Stanley v. McCarver, 208 Ariz. 219, 223, 92 P.3d 849, 853 (2004) (physician contracted with another to interpret plaintiff's X-rays and in so doing "he undertook a professional obligation with respect to Ms. Stanley's physical well-being").

[53] Some of the no-duty cases are actually cases in which the doctor was retained only to screen records and did not examine the patient at all. Judy v. Hanford Envtl. Health Found., 106 Wash.App. 26, 22 P.3d 810 (2001).

[54] Green v. Walker, 910 F.2d 291 (5th Cir. 1990) (doctor conducting exams for employer had "a duty to conduct the requested tests and diagnose the results thereof, exercising the level of care consistent with the doctor's professional training and expertise, and to take reasonable steps to make information available timely to the examinee of any findings that pose an imminent danger to the examinee's . . . well-being"); Stanley v. McCarver, 208 Ariz. 219, 92 P.3d 849 (2004); Reed v. Bojarski, 166 N.J. 89, 764 A.2d 433 (2001).

created a reasonable expectation that he would do so, then delivery of such care should be the order of the day, whether that person is characterized as a patient or not.[55]

§ 21.4 Duties to Non-Patients

Duty to non-patients based on duty to patient. In some instances, a physician's patient may pose a threat of physical or emotional harm to others. Perhaps the strongest case for holding the physician to a duty of care to a third person is the one in which the physician creates unreasonable risks to third persons by negligently risking harm to his own patient.[56] For example, the patient drives a vehicle, but because of the physician prescribed needless or inappropriate medication, the patient loses consciousness and drives into the plaintiff. Some courts have recognized a duty of care to the non-patient in such situations.[57] Similarly, the physician may be liable for negligently failing to diagnose the patient's epilepsy or failing to warn the epileptic or medicated patient against driving,[58] and also when the physician prescribes a drug that is counter-indicated because it would incapacitate the patient-driver.[59]

Liability to non-patients has also been imposed when the physician fails to use reasonable care to discover and reveal that his patient has a contagious disease[60] or a genetic condition that may risk harm to others.[61] The patient herself is entitled to have a proper diagnosis and to know of it so she can minimize risks to herself and others. Some courts simply reject liability to non-patients without recognizing that fulfillment of the physician's duty to his own patient in these cases imposes no additional burden.[62] Others have said that imposing a duty to non-patients would present the physician with a conflict between duties to his patient and duties to non-patients.[63] Such arguments are inapplicable, however, when the physician's duty of care to his own patient calls for exactly the same diagnosis or treatment that would also be safer for members of the

---

[55] Hoover v. Williamson, 236 Md. 250, 203 A.2d 861 (1964) (allegations that physician examining employee for employer actually advised employee wrongly was sufficient to show an undertaking).

[56] See, e.g., B.R. ex rel. Jeffs v. West, 275 P.3d 228 (Utah 2012) (providers prescribed medication to patient that allegedly caused the patient to become violent and shoot and kill his wife).

[57] McKenzie v. Hawai'i Permanente Med. Group, Inc., 98 Hawai'i 296, 47 P.3d 1209 (2002) (recognizing duty to warn); Wilschinsky v. Medina, 108 N.M. 511, 775 P.2d 713 (1989); Kaiser v. Suburban Transp. Sys., 65 Wash.2d 461, 398 P.2d 14 (1965).

[58] Coombes v. Florio, 450 Mass. 182, 877 N.E.2d 567 (2007) (failure to warn medicated patient); Duvall v. Goldin, 139 Mich. App. 342, 362 N.W.2d 275 (1984) (failure to diagnose and failure to warn of epilepsy).

[59] Taylor v. Smith, 892 So.2d 887 (Ala. 2004); Cheeks v. Dorsey, 846 So.2d 1169 (Fla. Dist. Ct. App. 2003) (methadone allegedly given to patient already on drugs, with resulting incapacity that caused vehicular crash, killing the plaintiff's decedent and her daughter).

[60] Reisner v. Regents of Univ. of Cal, 31 Cal. App. 4th 1195, 37 Cal. Rptr. 2d 518 (1995); DiMarco v. Lynch Homes-Chester County, Inc., 525 Pa. 558, 583 A. 2d 422 (1990); Estate of Amos v. Vanderbilt Univ., 62 S.W.3d 133 (Tenn. 2001).

[61] Pate v. Threlkel, 661 So.2d 278 (Fla.1995) (physician's duty to warn patient of genetic condition that might have been passed on to daughter); Renslow v. Mennonite Hosp., 67 Ill. 2d 348, 10 Ill. Dec. 484, 367 N.E.2d 1250, 91 A.L.R.3d 291 (1977) (negligent blood transfusion resulted in harm to child conceived many years later); Molloy v. Meier, 679 N.W.2d 711 (Minn. 2004) (physician treating child had duty to advise child's mother or a surrogate that child's condition was genetically caused so mother could avoid conceiving another child).

[62] Iodice v. United States, 289 F.3d 270 (4th Cir. 2002) (defendants knew patient was an addict to drugs and alcohol but kept overproviding drugs instead of insisting on treating addiction, no duty under North Carolina law).

[63] As in Kolbe v. State, 661 N.W.2d 142 (Iowa 2003). See also Jarmie v. Troncale, 306 Conn. 578, 50 A.3d 802 (2012) (no duty to warn non-patient, in part because of interference with duties owed to patient, in part because of legislative scheme of non-liability to non-patients in medical malpractice cases).

public.[64] In this situation, there is neither a conflict of loyalties nor any additional burden upon the physician; he satisfies his duty to third persons when he satisfies his duty to his patient.

When a direct duty may be owed to non-patients. When a condition of the physician's patient puts others at risk, can the physician be under a duty to use reasonable care for the safety of those others, even when he has fulfilled his duty to his own patient? Some cases have said so.[65] For example, the physician may be under a duty to use care to warn the non-patient of the patient's disease[66] or assaultive purpose[67] or even to control the patient through commitment or otherwise.[68] In the latter two instances, involving physical dangers from a patient's attack on the plaintiff, the defendants are usually mental health providers, but physicians might also owe the same duty.[69] Courts have recognized that imposing a duty might create a confidentiality problem, and some have circumscribed the duty accordingly.[70]

The control rule. When judges perceive the physician's alleged negligence as a failure to control his patient (rather than, say, a failure to warn his patient against driving), they may consider and sometimes invoke the rule that one normally has no duty to control others for the plaintiff's benefit.[71] This rule does not usually dissolve the duty of care owed by the physician when he has a special relationship with either the immediate tortfeasor (such as the patient) or with the plaintiff herself.[72] Thus a therapist who discovers his patient's intent to murder a non-patient owes a duty in many states to warn the non-patient or take some other step for her protection where the therapeutic standard of care would dictate such steps.[73] A few cases, however, hold to the contrary, rejecting the duty altogether.[74] The control rule is grounded in the more general principle

---

[64]   Hardee v. Bio-Medical Apps. of S.C., Inc., 370 S.C. 511, 516, 636 S.E.2d 629, 632 (2006) ("Importantly, this duty owed to third parties is identical to the duty owed to the patient, i.e., a medical provider must warn a patient of the attendant risks and effects of any treatment. Thus, our holding does not hamper the doctor-patient relationship."); see also Coombes v. Florio, 450 Mass. 182, 877 N.E.2d 567 (2007) (opinion of Ireland, J.).

[65]   On the other hand, some have said no such duty should be imposed. See, e.g., McNulty v. City of New York, 100 N.Y.2d 227, 792 N.E.2d 162, 762 N.Y.S.2d 12 (2003) (seeing "the danger that a recognition of a duty would render doctors liable to a prohibitive number of possible plaintiffs," holding that doctor would owe a duty to a non-patient only if the danger arose from his actual treatment of the patient, and that mere failure to warn a person who had no particular relation to the patient would not be actionable).

[66]   Bradshaw v. Daniel, 854 S.W.2d 865 (Tenn. 1993) (warning to wife of husband's Rocky Mountain Spotted Fever and necessity of avoiding ticks which carry it).

[67]   This usually arises when the physician or therapist is treating a patient for a mental disorder or emotional problems. If the patient's threats or other behavior indicates that he may attack others, many states, following the leading case, Tarasoff v. Regents of Univ. of Cal., 17 Cal.3d 425, 131 Cal. Rptr. 14, 551 P.2d 334 (1976), impose a duty to warn those others. See § 26.11.

[68]   Leonard v. State, 491 N.W.2d 508 (Iowa 1992) (institution holding dangerous patient had duty to control, but only for benefit of identified victims).

[69]   See Restatement Third of Torts: Liability for Physical and Emotional Harm § 41, cmt. h (2010).

[70]   See Bellah v. Greenson, 81 Cal.App.3d 614, 146 Cal.Rptr. 535 (1978) (the therapist is under a duty of care to patient to use care to prevent the patient's suicide, but that does not include a duty to warn family members, which would entail breach of confidentiality and might impair therapy).

[71]   Calwell v. Hassan, 260 Kan. 769, 925 P.2d 422 (1996) (treating a failure to warn the patient as a failure to control the patient).

[72]   See § 26.11.

[73]   Tarasoff v. Regents of Univ. of Cal., 17 Cal.3d 425, 131 Cal.Rptr. 14, 551 P.2d 334 (1976); Emerich v. Phila. Ctr. for Human Dev. Inc., 554 Pa. 209, 720 A.2d 1032 (1998). A court recognizing the duty of care for the benefit of potential victims may also hold that it encompasses a duty to make a professionally proper diagnosis of the patient and so to recognize the dangers he poses to others or himself. Schuster v. Altenberg, 144 Wis.2d 223, 424 N.W.2d 159 (1988).

[74]   Thapar v. Zezulka, 994 S.W.2d 635 (Tex. 1999); Nasser v. Parker, 249 Va. 172, 455 S.E.2d 502 (1995).

that, absent an undertaking or special relationship, one is not liable for mere nonfeasance, that is, for doing nothing to prevent harm. But in some of the physician cases, courts have, consciously or not, rejected a duty of reasonable care, even when the physician's alleged negligence consists of an active creation of a risk, not mere nonfeasance.[75]

Outpatients. While courts have seldom invoked blanket no-duty rules to defeat liability to nonpatients, they have sometimes found ways to constrict liability. Some courts have created a special rule of law declaring that a physician or therapist has no "control" over outpatients as distinct from institutionalized patients. They go on to hold that if the physician has no control, he owes no duty to those the outpatient may harm.[76] Control in some of these cases does not seem to be a question about whether the physician could in fact control the outcome or reasonably protect the third person. It rather seems to be a rule of law that forecloses any scrutiny of the actual facts. Not surprisingly, other authority rejects any rule of law excluding duties arising from treatment of outpatients.[77]

Specifically identified plaintiffs. More commonly, cases involving the patient's threat to others turn, not on control itself, but on the rule applied in some courts that a duty to control can be invoked only by a specifically identified victim. On this basis, a court might hold that while a physician may owe a duty to "control" a patient to protect a member of the patient's family, he does not owe the duty to the public at large.[78] Some cases may have applied the identified-victim rule even when the physician's negligence is a failure to warn or to otherwise properly treat his own patient.[79] However, in such cases the issue is not truly about control but about information or about using ordinary care in medical treatment. Applying the rule to cases like that seems to ignore the fundamental point that no added burden is imposed when the physician is held responsible for his failure to treat his own patient properly. The rule as applied in such cases also ignores the plaintiff's claim that a dangerous driver or a murderous psychiatric patient who should have been committed or medicated is a loose cannon who may harm anyone at all, not just family members or named victims.[80] Thus while the identified-victim rule might be justified if the physician is charged with taking on added responsibilities beyond those to his own patient—warning others, for example—it seems at least arguable that it has no sound basis when the physician is asked only to do what reasonable care for his patient requires anyway. In line with these comments, some courts have rejected the identified-victim requirement.[81]

[75] Thus, some courts invoke the control rule when the physician has created a risk by prescribing or injecting medication without appropriate warnings. See Shortnacy v. N. Atlanta Internal Medicine, P.C., 252 Ga. App. 321, 556 S.E.2d 209 (2001) (seemingly the case, although the negligence was not clearly specified).

[76] Calwell v. Hassan, 260 Kan. 769, 925 P.2d 422 (1996).

[77] Estate of Morgan v. Fairfield Family Counseling Center, 77 Ohio St.3d 284, 673 N.E. 2d 1311 (1997), *abrogated in part by* Ohio Rev. Code § 5122.34.

[78] Kirk v. Michael Reese Hosp. and Med. Ctr., 117 Ill.2d 507, 513 N.E.2d 387, 111 Ill.Dec. 944 (1987); Leonard v. State, 491 N.W.2d 508 (Iowa 1992).

[79] Werner v. Varner, Stafford & Seaman, P.A., 659 So.2d 1308 (Fla. Dist. Ct. App. 1995) (failure to warn patient of driving danger, duty only to identified victims; hence no liability for injuries caused in driving); cf. Britton v. Soltes, 205 Ill. App. 3d 943, 563 N.E.2d 910, 150 Ill. Dec. 783 (1990) (physician failed to diagnose patient's TB, neighbor was infected as a result; no relationship that "necessarily" would cause harm); Leonard v. State, 491 N.W.2d 508 (Iowa 1992) (defendants "had a duty to control [the patient's] conduct, or at least not negligently to release him from custody," but the duty does not run to the general public).

[80] See Estate of Amos v. Vanderbilt Univ., 62 S.W.3d 133, 137 (Tenn. 2001).

[81] Estate of Morgan v. Fairfield Family Counseling Center, 77 Ohio St.3d 284, 673 N.E.2d 1311 (1997).

Balancing tests. Finally, some of the decisions rejecting liability on the particular facts do so after considering several broadly formulated factors, such as the relationship of the physician to others involved, foreseeability of harm, and public policy considerations.[82] Where the proposed duty would require the physician to warn nonpatients or pressure him to make extreme treatment choices (like confinement of a dangerous patient), public policy requires a degree of caution lest treatment, assumed to be useful, would be disrupted. Perhaps the most significant policy is that the physician should never be under a duty to third persons that requires him to forego appropriate treatment of his own patient. Perhaps this policy actually covers all the bases; the entire problem could be simplified by saying that the physician (a) never owes care to a third person inconsistent with care owed to his own patient, and (b) always owes a duty to avoid foreseeable and unreasonable risks to third persons when that can be fulfilled by properly treating his own patient and without taking on any additional obligation.

3. *Standards of Care and Attendant Proof Requirements*

§ 21.5 The Traditional Medical Standard of Care

The traditional professional-peer standard. Although some courts have adopted the ordinary reasonable care standard in some medical malpractice cases,[83] the traditional standard for health care practitioners is different, a "medical" standard of care. That standard dictates a rule of proof: the plaintiff must ordinarily[84] present expert evidence[85] detailing the standard. In general, the "standard" bears no resemblance to the usual standard in non-medical cases—the standard of reasonable care under the circumstances. Instead, the "standard" in medical cases is conceived of as the specific procedure or medical conduct that the relevant medical community considered to be acceptable at the time of the alleged negligence[86]—for instance, the specific way to make a cut in a surgical procedure,[87] or the specific dosage of a drug or injection,[88] or the particular precautions to be taken under given conditions.[89] The medical standard may vary with the locality as well as with the work the physician holds himself out as competent to do.[90]

Medical custom and conclusory opinions as the standard. The medical standard is often understood to be the medical custom or practice with respect to the particular act

---

[82] Webb v. Jarvis, 575 N.E.2d 992 (Ind. 1991) (relationship, foreseeability, public policy); J.A.H. v. Wadle & Assocs., P.C., 589 N.W.2d 256 (Iowa 1999) (same).

[83] See § 21.6.

[84] Exceptions include: (1) cases of obvious negligence or res ipsa loquitur; (2) cases of non-medical negligence; and (3) cases of informed consent where expert testimony as to standards is not necessarily required.

[85] On the requirement of expert testimony, see § 21.8.

[86] A standard—such as the reasonable person standard—has generality, does not change, and frequently leaves room for judgment calls. The term "standard" as used in medical claims lacks these characteristics. Thus "[t]here are virtually thousands of standards of care pertaining to health-care services in the United States today." Eleanor D. Kinney, The Brave New World of Medical Standards of Care, 29 J.L. Med. & Ethics 323 (2001).

[87] Walski v. Tiesenga, 72 Ill.2d 249, 21 Ill. Dec. 201, 381 N.E.2d 279 (1978) (requiring expert testimony as to the medically accepted method of cutting in performing a thyroidectomy).

[88] Lake v. McCollum, 295 S.W.3d 529 (Mo. App. 2009) (testimony that in light of patient's condition, administration of specified drugs violated the standard of care).

[89] E.g., Mody v. Ctr. for Women's Health, P.C., 998 A.2d 327 (D.C. 2010).

[90] See § 21.7.

of diagnosis or treatment.[91] However, courts do not ordinarily survey actual behavior or customs of physicians.[92] Instead, the medical standard is often established by conclusory testimony of an expert that specified conduct simply is "the standard."[93] Practically speaking, the standard can be the custom or practice of the relevant medical community, or it can be a qualified expert's opinion that does not refer to custom or practice at all and may not even refer to any source.

Skill and knowledge. The medical standard is sometimes stated by saying that physicians must exercise at least the skill, knowledge, and care normally possessed and exercised by other members of their profession[94] in the same school of practice in the relevant medical community.[95] In spite of the "knowledge and skill phraseology," in practice, the physician's actual *conduct* is what counts, not his possession of abstract knowledge or skill. Thus his failure of a board exam is not important if he has not departed from accepted medical practice in his in diagnosis, technique, or treatment.[96]

Referral. Medical doctors are generally under a duty to use reasonable care to consult with, or to refer a patient to a specialist when the physician knows or should know treatment or diagnosis is beyond his competency or that specialist care is needed.[97] The same is true when diagnosis or treatment requires equipment the first physician does not have available.[98] Consequently, a physician is subject to liability if he should refer the patient to another health care provider for tests, diagnosis, or treatment but fails to do so.[99] Equally he is subject to liability if he refers the patient to a physician he should know is inappropriate for the patient's care.[100] The plaintiff must of course

---

[91]   See Osborn v. Irwin Mem. Blood Bank, 5 Cal. App. 4th 234, 7 Cal. Rptr. 2d 101 (1992) ("professional prudence is defined by actual or accepted practice within a profession, rather than theories about what 'should' have been done"); Palandjian v. Foster, 446 Mass. 100, 105, 842 N.E.2d 916, 921 (2006) ("because the standard of care is determined by the care customarily provided by other physicians, it need not be scientifically tested or proven effective: what the average qualified physician would do in a particular situation *is* the standard of care"). See also Philip G. Peters, Jr., The Role of the Jury in Modern Malpractice Law, 87 Iowa L. Rev. 909 (2002).

[92]   See William Meadow & Cass R. Sunstein, Statistics, Not Experts, 51 Duke L. J. 629 (2001) (advocating generation and use of statistical data about actual practices as opposed to opinion evidence about those practices presented by witnesses); William Meadow, Operationalizing the Standard of Medical Care: Uses and Limitations of Epidemiology to Guide Expert Testimony in Medical Negligence Allegations, 37 Wake Forest L. Rev. 675 (2002) (similar).

[93]   See, e.g., Robinson v. Okla. Nephrology Associates, Inc., 154 P.3d 1250 (2007) (only reported testimony on standard was that defendant "violated acceptable standards when he did not hospitalize Mrs. Robinson as soon as he knew of her critically low blood sodium level"); Bitar v. Rahman, 272 Va. 130, 630 S.E.2d 319 (Va. 2006) ("Dr. Jacobs opined that Dr. Bitar, in planning and performing the abdominoplasty, breached the standard of care because Dr. Bitar pre-determined the amount of tissue to be removed.").

[94]   E.g., Keebler v. Winfield Carraway Hosp., 531 So.2d 841 (Ala. 1988) ("such reasonable care, diligence, and skill as reasonably competent physicians" in the relevant medical community would exercise in the same or similar circumstances); Purtill v. Hess, 111 Ill.2d 229, 489 N.E.2d 867, 95 Ill.Dec. 305 (1986) (knowledge, skill, and care of a reasonably well-qualified physician in the relevant medical community).

[95]   See § 21.7.

[96]   See Marsingill v. O'Malley, 128 P.3d 151, 161 (Alaska 2002).

[97]   Weiss v. Rojanasathit, 975 S.W.2d 113 (Mo. 1998) ("where the doctor knows or should know that a condition exists that requires further medical attention to prevent injurious consequences, the doctor must render such attention or must see to it that some other competent person does so"); King v. Flamm, 442 S.W.2d 679 (Tex. 1969).

[98]   Jorgenson v. Vener, 616 N.W.2d 366 (S.D. 2000), *abrogated on other grounds by* S.D.C.L. § 20–9–1.1.

[99]   King v. Flamm, 442 S.W.2d 679 (Tex. 1969); Vito v. North Medical Family Physicians, P.C., 16 A.D.3d 1039, 791 N.Y.S.2d 797 (2005).

[100]   Rise v. United States, 630 F.2d 1068 (5th Cir. 1980) (also noting that the referring physician may, in some circumstances, owe a duty of care to supervise or review the work of the second physician).

provide evidence that referral would have been reasonably likely to lead to a better outcome, or at least to improve his chances.[101]

Application and scope of professional standard. Medical standards ordinarily require the physician to exercise professional care not only in diagnosis and treatment and referrals to a specialist, but to keep appropriate medical records needed for patient care,[102] and to warn the patient when new developments affect the patient's past care.[103] The medical standard applies only to conduct of health-care providers acting within the ambit of their professional work. The reasonable person standard applies to ordinary non-medical negligence such as a hospital's slippery floors.[104]

Jury instructions. The usual jury instructions state the medical standard of care, making due reference to the defendant's specialty or school of practice and incorporating the locality rule where that rule is still followed. The jury is often told that the physician must "possess and use the care, skill and knowledge ordinarily possessed and used under like circumstances."[105] Consistent with the medical custom standard, the jury may also be told that the physician is negligent only if he failed to follow the medical conduct of other physicians in similar circumstances.[106] Sometimes courts add that the physician must use ordinary care in applying professional skills, knowledge and training.[107]

However, courts very often add a good deal of rhetoric that repeatedly emphasizes instances of non-liability. For instance, the trial judge may tell the jury that the plaintiff has the burden of proving the standard of care and its breach, and then go on to repeat the same point by saying that the law presumes the physician exercised proper care.[108] Other rhetorical instructions are commonly given even where the plaintiff has never asserted the liabilities the instruction negates. For example, trial judges often say that the doctor-defendant is not required to exercise the highest care, only the ordinary care of his profession;[109] that the physician is not liable for a bad result or for a mistake where he acted in good faith; that medicine is an inexact science; or that the physician is not an insurer of the plaintiff's health or a guarantor of her recovery.[110] Such instructions

---

[101] Kardos v. Harrison, 980 A.2d 1014 (Del. 2009) (even under Delaware's rule that lost chance is sufficient, evidence failed to show loss of patient's chance had referral been made); Goldberg v. Horowitz, 73 A.D.2d 691, 901 N.Y.S.2d 95, 98 (2010) (improved chance or better outcome, evidence sufficient); Bryan v. Sherick, 279 S.W.3d 731 (Tex. App. 2007) (failure to refer not actionable without proof that prompt referral would have led to less harm).

[102] See Harris v. Raymond, 715 N.E.2d 388 (Ind. Ct. App. 1999); cf. Robinson v. St. John's Med. Ctr., Joplin, 508 S.W.2d 7 (Mo. 1974) (hospital nurse recorded sponge count erroneously, resulting in sponge left in the operating field).

[103] Cox v. Paul, 828 N.E.2d 907 (Ind. 2005) (reasonable care duty owed to warn patient that FDA had now warned of dangers of the temporomandibular joint replacement the defendant had provided years earlier).

[104] The professional standard is irrelevant to non-professional activities, for example, to slippery floors in a hospital, see Self v. Exec. Comm. Ga. Baptist Convention of Ga., Inc., 245 Ga.548, 266 S.E.2d 168 (1980), or a physician's failure to warn co-workers that a patient is dangerous, see Powell v. Catholic Medical Ctr., 145 N.H. 7, 749 A.2d 301 (2000). Sometimes it is difficult to differentiate bad housekeeping and bad medical care, as where rats in a hospital repeatedly bit a comatose patient. See LeJeune v. Rayne Branch Hosp., 556 So.2d 559 (La. 1990).

[105] Vergara v. Doan, 593 N.E.2d 185 (Ind. 1992); Burns v. Metz, 245 Neb. 428, 513 N.W.2d 505 (1994).

[106] McLaughlin v. Sy, 589 A.2d 448 (Me. 1991).

[107] See Boyanton v. Reif, 798 P.2d 603 (Okla. 1990).

[108] See Beach v. Lipham, 276 Ga. 302, 578 S.E.2d 4092 (2003) (three-way split, majority holding the presumption instruction not error but saying it should be revised, other judges arguing that the presumption instruction should not be mentioned at all).

[109] See Tennant v. Marion Health Care Foundation, Inc., 194 W.Va. 97, 459 S.E.2d 374 (1995).

[110] See Dotson v. Hammerman, 932 S.W.2d 880 (Mo. App. 1996) ("An honest error of judgment in making a diagnosis is insufficient to support liability unless that mistake constitutes negligence"); Donaldson v.

overemphasize the defendant's position, especially when repeated,[111] and are affirmatively misleading. An instruction that tells the jury that the physician is not liable for honest error or good faith mistake injects subjective, good faith issues into the objective negligence test and may lead the jury to think that bad faith, not a departure from professional standards, is the test of liability.[112] Some courts have begun to reconsider the no-guarantee instruction as well, holding that it should not be given when the plaintiff has not actually asserted a guarantee,[113] or that its use should be constrained.[114]

§ 21.6　The Reasonable Care Standard

The medical standard restated. The professional standard of care is not identical to the reasonable person standard used in most negligence cases.[115] The professional standard asks the trier only to determine whether the defendant's specifically identified conduct conformed to the medical standard or medical custom in the relevant community with respect to the particular acts alleged to be negligent.[116] As long as a doctor followed the medical standard or custom, he is not legally negligent under the medical standard, regardless of how risky the custom might be. Conversely, if he failed to follow the medical standard of care, he would be negligent under that standard even in the absence of scientific studies establishing the need for the precaution customarily taken.[117]

Contrasting the reasonable person standard. The reasonable person standard asks the trier to weigh the reasonableness, that is, at least in part, to weigh the risks and utilities of the defendant's conduct[118] as explained by competent expert evidence. It thus appeals to science or evidence-based medicine as the standard. Under the reasonable care test—the normal negligence standard—a physician who ignores an inexpensive and risk-free diagnostic test that might save a patient's sight does not necessarily avoid liability merely because other physicians also ignore the test.[119] Under the medical custom test, in contrast, no physician could be held accountable for ignoring science as long as other physicians also do so.

Criticisms of traditional standard. The ordinary reasonable care standard requires physicians, like others, to exercise any superior knowledge or skill they actually possess,

---

Maffucci, 397 Pa. 548, 156 A.2d 835 (1959); Bryan v. Burt, 486 S.E.2d 536 (Va. 1997) ("A physician is neither an insurer of diagnosis and treatment nor is the physician held to the highest degree of care known to the profession. The mere fact that the physician has failed to effect a cure or that the diagnosis and treatment have been detrimental to the patient's health does not raise a presumption of negligence.").

[111] See Wall v. Stout, 310 N.C. 184, 311 S.E.2d 571 (1984) (jury instructed at least three times that doctor was not a guarantor or insurer).

[112] See Passarello v. Grumbine, 87 A.3d 285 (Pa. 2014) (disapproving such instructions on this ground, and surveying a number of other states).

[113] Bratton v. Bond, 408 N.W.2d 39 (Iowa 1987) (unless, perhaps, where the plaintiff asserts a warranty claim); Wall v. Stout, 310 N.C. 184, 197, 311 S.E.2d 571, 579 (1984) ("an instruction to the effect that a physician is 'not an insurer of results' should not be given when no issue concerning a guarantee has been raised").

[114] Jones v. Porretta, 428 Mich. 132, 405 N.W.2d 863 (1987); Christensen v. Munsen, 123 Wash.2d 234, 867 P.2d 626, 30 A.L.R.5th 822 (1994).

[115] See Harris v. Groth, 99 Wash.2d 438, 663 P.2d 113 (1983).

[116] See David v. McLeod Regional Med. Ctr., 367 S.C. 242, 247–248, 626 S.E.2d 1, 4 (2006).

[117] See Palandjian v. Foster, 446 Mass. 100, 105, 842 N.E.2d 916, 921 (2006).

[118] See §§ 12.3 to 12.5.

[119] See Helling v. Carey, 83 Wash.2d 514, 519 P.2d 981, 67 A.L.R.3d 175 (1974).

even if ordinary people would not be so knowledgeable or skillful.[120] For this reason, the medical standard is not needed to require healthcare providers to exercise the skills they hold themselves out as having. The medical standard thus only changes the ordinary tort law standard by reducing the duty owed when the relevant medical custom calls for less care than is appropriate in light of risks and benefits. Put differently, neither science nor assessments of risks comes in to the picture when applying the traditional medical standard. This departure from the standard of reasonable care normally used in negligence cases has been criticized as giving too much deference to the medical profession to set its own standards[121] and because there is often no "standard" practice, or if there is, it is not really known to other physicians who may testify.[122]

Rejecting medical custom, adopting reasonable care. A number of courts have now said or implied that the standard of care for health care providers is the reasonable care standard applied in negligence law generally.[123] Statutes also sometimes prescribe a reasonable care standard.[124] By definition, adoption of the reasonable care standard is a rejection of the medical custom standard. Medical custom, however, remains relevant as evidence of what might count as reasonable care under the circumstances, although it is not determinative if other evidence shows a lack of reasonable care.

Consequences. Adoption of a reasonable care standard in medical cases logically dictates several distinct and important consequences: (1) New kinds of evidence would be *admissible.* The plaintiff would not be required to adduce expert testimony showing the medical custom, but instead would be permitted to show by any competent evidence that the physician's conduct subjected his patient to unreasonable risks. Courts might even admit conclusory testimony by experts that the physician's treatment of his patient was inappropriate or unreasonable.[125] (2) The *sufficiency* of the evidence of physician negligence would be judged by considering all the competent evidence, not merely by assessing medical custom. (3) Juries would be instructed to evaluate negligence under the reasonable care standard, not the medical custom standard. In each instance, medical custom would presumably represent important but not conclusive evidence of what a reasonable physician would do under the circumstances.

---

[120] Toth v. Cmty. Hosp. at Glen Cove, 22 N.Y.2d 255, 239 N.E.2d 368, 292 N.Y.S.2d 440 (1968); Jackson v. Axelrad, 221 S.W.3d 650 (Tex. 2007); Restatement Third of Torts (Liability for Physical and Emotional Harm) § 12 (2010) ("If an actor has skills or knowledge that exceed those possessed by most others, these skills or knowledge are circumstances to be taken into account in determining whether the actor has behaved as a reasonably careful person.").

[121] See Philip G. Peters, Jr., The Quiet Demise of Deference to Custom: Malpractice Law at the Millennium, 57 Wash. & Lee L. Rev. 163 (2000) (presenting the traditional standard as a special privilege).

[122] Tim Cramm, Arthur J. Hartz, & Michael D. Green, Ascertaining Customary Care in Malpractice Cases: Asking Those Who Know, 37 Wake Forest L. Rev. 699 (2002) (also casting doubt on the reliability of some expert testimony).

[123] The leading case is Helling v. Carey, 83 Wash.2d 514, 519 P.2d 981 (1974), *reaffirmed in* Harris v. Groth, 99 Wash.2d 438, 663 P.2d 113 (1983). See also, e.g., Ray v. American Nat'l Red Cross, 696 A.2d 399 (D.C. 1997); Advincula v. United Blood Services, 176 Ill. 2d 1, 678 N.E.2d 1009, 223 Ill. Dec. 1 (1996).

[124] Ga. Code. Ann. § 51–1–27 (requiring "a reasonable degree of care and skill" and providing for tort liability for "injury resulting from a want of such care and skill"); La. Rev. Stat. Ann. § 9:2794 (couched as a proof requirement; the plaintiff must prove a lack of appropriate skill or that the physician "failed to use reasonable care and diligence, along with his best judgment in the application of that skill").

[125] See Philip G. Peters, Jr., the Quiet Demise of Deference to Custom: Malpractice Law at the Millennium, 57 Wash. & Lee L. Rev. 163, 189 (2002).

§ 21.7 The Relevant Geographical Community

At one time, courts generally held that the professional standard of care for medical doctors was the custom or standard followed or professed by other doctors in the very same locality where the doctor practiced.[126] If a town's six doctors all ignored helpful new drugs for treatment of the plaintiff's condition, none of them would be guilty of medical malpractice for failing to prescribe such a drug when it was needed.

One theory sometimes advanced for this result was that small-town doctors might not have the latest equipment or training and should not be liable merely for that reason. But the locality standard did not necessarily apply to other professionals, and in any event the reason given for it was spurious. Even without a locality rule, the jury could have considered all the circumstances bearing on the reasonableness of the physician's conduct, including limitations on equipment.[127] A physician who lacks equipment or training to treat a given patient need only refer the patient to a more appropriate provider.[128] Under none of the standards is the physician or surgeon held to any level of care he has not undertaken to give. Albert Schweitzer was not committing a tort when he exercised reasonable care in a primitive clinic in equatorial Africa. The rural general practitioner confronted with an emergency requiring the skill of an orthopedic surgeon is not held to the orthopedist's standard of care, but that is not because he practices in a rural rather than an urban community. It is because, like all others, he is held to the standard he professes, not some other.

Besides the faulty rationale for the same locality rule, courts and writers often point out that today's mainstream medical doctors are all trained in the same basic way throughout the country and all have access to continuing education and even to instant computer guidance.[129] Medical and scientific facts are the same everywhere. These considerations, and perhaps a moral revulsion at the idea that a small group of bad practitioners can inflict substandard care on rural communities,[130] have led most states by statute or judicial decision to discard the same locality test of the standard of care,[131] although a few states continue to use that test in some form.[132]

---

[126] The idea seems to have originated in Small v. Howard, 128 Mass. 131 (1880), but courts might have read too much into that case. The defendant there was a village doctor and not a surgeon, but was required to do surgery for the plaintiff. The court emphasized that the village doctor should not be expected to practice at the level of "eminent surgeons" in large cities. The point seems to have been as much that the defendant was not a specialist in surgery as that he was practicing in a village.

[127] Courts adopting a similar- or national-community rule often point out that the local conditions are among the circumstances to be taken into account. E.g., Brune v. Belinkoff, 354 Mass. 102, 235 N.E.2d 793 (1968).

[128] Jorgenson v. Vener, 616 N.W.2d 366 (S.D. 2000) ("Our current medical malpractice regime expects that any physician, rural or urban, who is uncertain about his ability to treat a patient's condition will refer the patient to another who is more skilled or experienced Whether medical care is administered in a rural or urban setting, among the latest technology or with the most primitive of instruments, a patient still has the right to expect competence in his physician's care."), *abrogated on other grounds by* S.D.C.L § 20–9–1.1.

[129] See 1 Barry R. Furrow, Thomas L. Greaney, Sandra H. Johnson, Timothy S. Jost & Robert L. Schwartz, Health Law § 6–2 (2d ed. 2000).

[130] See Pederson v. Dumouchel, 72 Wash. 2d 73, 431 P.2d 973, 31 A.L.R.3d 1100 (1967) ("Negligence cannot be excused on the ground that others in the same locality practice the same kind of negligence. No degree of antiquity can give sanction to usage bad in itself.").

[131] See James O. Pearson, Jr., Annotation, Modern Status of "Locality Rule" in Malpractice Action Against Physician Who Is Not a Specialist, 99 A.L.R.3d 1133 (1980).

[132] See Trindle v. Wheeler, 23 Cal.2d 330, 143 P.2d 932 (1943); Morris v. Thomson, 937 P.2d 1212 (Idaho 1997) (same-locality standard by statute except when local standard cannot be ascertained).

Except as commanded otherwise by a tort-reform statute, most courts now look to the medical community in the same-or-similar localities,[133] in the state,[134] or in the nation as a whole[135] for appropriate standards. In the last category, some courts do not mention geography except to say that the locality might be relevant as a circumstance to be considered in determining whether the doctor exercised reasonable care.[136]

The national standard for specialists. Many medical doctors are specialists who have additional training and experience and who have been examined by a specialty board. For board-certified medical specialists, the standard is usually said to be a single national standard of the specialty involved. Medical training and examination of board-certified specialists is the same without regard to locality. Consequently, even a locality rule would refer ultimately to the national standard when it comes to specialists. Thus one who holds himself out as a specialist is held to the standard of care set by the standards for the specialty, which are in fact uniform and national.[137] The recognition of these different standards has important indirect consequences in determining whether a physician in one specialty may testify about the standard of care appropriate for a physician in another specialty.[138]

§ 21.8 The Expert Testimony Requirement

The standard of care. Where the medical standard of care applies, courts require the plaintiff to establish that standard by expert testimony,[139] unless res ipsa loquitur applies or negligence is obvious.[140] To establish a medical standard, the expert testimony must ordinarily be specific rather than general. Testimony does not state that the medical standard is "high care" or "reasonable care" or "good medical care"; rather, it must state that the particular diagnosis, treatment, or procedure in question did or did not meet the "standards" of the medical community.[141] For example, an expert might testify that the medical community's "standard" called for a diagnostic test that was not administered, or called for the administration of a smaller dosage of an anesthetic.

In many cases of scientifically bad medical judgment, it is difficult to say that there is a customary standard or that anyone knows what it is. If the plaintiff's expert witness can testify only that he was medically trained not to use the procedure used by the defendant, that in his own judgment the defendant's treatment was wrong,[142] that he

---

[133] E.g., Purtill v. Hess, 111 Ill.2d 229, 489 N.E.2d 867, 95 Ill.Dec. 305 (1986); Bahr v. Harper-Grace Hosps., 448 Mich. 135, 528 N.W.2d 170 (1995); Donaldson v. Maffucci, 397 Pa. 548, 156 A.2d 835 (1959); DiFranco v. Klein, 657 A.2d 145 (R.I. 1995). Statutes so provide in some states.

[134] Fitzmaurice v. Flynn, 167 Conn. 609, 617, 356 A.2d 887, 892 (1975) (in Connecticut, the "general neighborhood" standard means the whole state).

[135] Keebler v. Winfield Carraway Hosp., 531 So.2d 841 (Ala. 1988); Sheeley v. Mem. Hosp., 710 A.2d 161 (R.I. 1998); Arbogast v. Mid-Ohio Valley Med. Corp., 214 W.Va. 356, 589 S.E.2d 498 (2003).

[136] Vergara v. Doan, 593 N.E.2d 185 (Ind. 1992); Brune v. Belinkoff, 354 Mass. 102, 235 N.E.2d 793 (1968); Pederson v. Dumouchel, 72 Wash.2d 73, 431 P.2d 973, 31 A.L.R.3d 1100 (1967).

[137] See Heinrich v. Sweet, 308 F.3d 48 (1st Cir. 2002); Smethers v. Campion, 210 Ariz. 167, 171, 108 P.3d 946, 950 (2005); Jordan v. Bogner, 844 P.2d 664 (Colo. 1993); Perin v. Hayne, 210 N.W.2d 609 (Iowa 1973); Rule v. Cheeseman, 181 Kan. 957, 317 P.2d 472 (1957).

[138] See § 21.8.

[139] See, e.g., Love v. Walker, 423 S.W.3d 751 (Ky. 2014).

[140] See, e.g., McGathey v. Brookwood Health Services, Inc., 2013 WL 3958299 (Ala. 2013) (obvious negligence). On res ipsa loquitur in malpractice cases, see 2 Dobbs, Hayden & Bublick, The Law of Torts §§ 305–306 (2d ed. 2011 & Supp.).

[141] See, e.g., Murray v. UNMC Physicians, 282 Neb. 260, 806 N.W.2d 118 (2011).

[142] Walski v. Tiesenga, 72 Ill.2d 249, 21 Ill.Dec. 201, 381 N.E.2d 279 (1978). See also Murray v. UNMC Physicians, 282 Neb. 260, 806 N.W.2d 118 (2011) (testimony of the plaintiff's expert that it was his personal

himself would not have used the procedure or would have used a better one,[143] or that all the doctors he knows agree that the treatment was wrong,[144] his testimony has not necessarily established a standard. In that case, the plaintiff may find her case dismissed. Even if the physician-witness testifies firmly to a medical practice he deems to be the standard of care, his testimony is not necessarily enough. If he adopts a different approach or practice for himself, evidence of that fact may be admissible at least on the issue of his credibility[145] and perhaps even as bearing on the standard of care.[146]

The locality rule and the standard of care. In some cases, the physician-defendant himself testifies to or admits to the standard of care claimed by the plaintiff.[147] When he does not, the plaintiff's lawyer must show that her medical expert is qualified to give an opinion about the medical standard. Under the same-locality rule, if the defendant doctor practiced in Nantucket, any qualified medical expert could testify about medical causation, which is a scientific fact that does not vary with state boundaries. However, only an expert who could state the standard or custom in Nantucket could testify that the defendant's conduct fell short of that the Nantucket standard of care for physicians. The effect of this rule was that the plaintiff suing a Nantucket doctor would usually be required to find another Nantucket doctor who would testify, or at least a non-local physician who somehow could show that he knew the Nantucket standard.[148] In many instances, the plaintiff could obtain quite good evidence, but only from "outsiders" who were not allowed to testify.[149] The effect was that the plaintiff's claim was defeated.

Similar localities and national standards of care. When courts began to hold that the relevant medical community included similar localities or even the nation as a whole, the most immediate practical effect was that physicians from other localities were allowed to testify about the proper standard. However, rules on expert testimony can undercut the adoption of a national or other broader standard. In one national standard jurisdiction, an expert witness testified to a standard, but failed to identify it as a *national* standard. The court in effect assumed that the testimony could have referred to a local rather than a national standard and that the two were different. So the

---

practice to try to work with a patient "to find another way for the patient to get [an expensive] drug" was not about the general standard of care; thus the trial judge was incorrect in granting new trial after a jury verdict for the defendants).

[143] See Clark v. District of Columbia, 708 A.2d 632 (D.C. 1997).

[144] Travers v. District of Columbia, 672 A.2d 566, 569 (D.C.App. 1996) ("It is the consensus of opinion of all the surgeons with which I have worked with and taught with that we do use aspirin when it reaches about two times normal," did not establish standard).

[145] See Smethers v. Campion, 210 Ariz. 167, 108 P.3d 946 (2005).

[146] Condra v. Atlanta Orthopaedic Group, P.C., 285 Ga. 667, 681 S.E.2d 152 (2009) ("[E]vidence regarding an expert witness' personal practices, unless subject to exclusion on other evidentiary grounds, is admissible both as substantive evidence and to impeach the expert's opinion regarding the applicable standard of care.").

[147] E.g., Douglas v. Freeman, 117 Wash. 2d 242, 814 P.2d 1160 (1991).

[148] *Compare* Handa v. Munn, 642 S.E.2d 540 (N.C. App. 2007) (expert testified he knew the Raleigh standard of care, testimony acceptable) *with* Fitts v. Arms, 133 S.W.3d 187 (Tenn.Ct.App. 2003) ("Dr. Megison never states in his affidavit that he is familiar with the recognized standard of professional practice applicable . . . in the locality and at the time in question. This familiarity must be affirmatively established; we may not impute such knowledge to the affiant"; testimony unacceptable).

[149] See, e.g., Holmes v. Elliott, 443 So.2d 825 (Miss. 1983). Mississippi has since gone to a national standard.

plaintiff's case was dismissed.[150] And no matter what standard of care is adopted, tort reform statutes may specifically preclude testimony by experts outside the region.[151]

Testimony by a witness belonging to a different specialty or school of medicine. Can an expert witness testify about the standard of care appropriate for a defendant who practices a different specialty, or even an entirely different kind of school of healing? Courts have not agreed. One view requires the expert witness not merely to *know* the standard applicable to the defendant but to *practice in* a specialty or kind of practice that uses substantially the same standard. Taken literally, this view means that an orthopedic surgeon may not be heard in court on the subject of podiatric standards, even if he knows the standard of care for podiatrists.[152] This approach, which does not merely assess the sufficiency of evidence but excludes it altogether, may become even more rigid under tort reform statutes.[153] Other courts have allowed a doctor to testify as to the standards governing another school of practice when the standards are the same as to the particular procedure in issue,[154] or, more vaguely, when the standards turn on matters that each of the two schools "share in common in terms of education, training and licensure."[155] Still others have permitted the expert to testify about the standard in a different specialty or different community once he establishes his knowledge of that standard.[156] This latter, more liberal, view does not make the differences in specialties irrelevant. It merely refuses to automatically exclude testimony merely because it comes from a physician with a different specialty. The trier of fact might still conclude that the witness was not sufficiently informed to be reliable and might reject his testimony as unpersuasive.

---

[150]　Travers v. District of Columbia, 672 A.2d 566 (D.C. 1996).

[151]　See Legg v. Chopra, 286 F.3d 286 (6th Cir. 2002) (reflecting Tennessee's statute precluding experts not from Tennessee or a contiguous state and holding that it applied in federal court as a substantive rule under Erie); Endorf v. Bohlender, 26 Kan. App. 2d 855, 995 P.2d 896 (2000) (percentage of time practicing in state).

[152]　See Dolan v. Galluzzo, 77 Ill. 2d 279, 396 N.E.2d 13, 32 Ill. Dec. 900 (1979) (stating that to testify about podiatry standards, the witness would have to be a licensed podiatrist); but see Witherell v. Weimer, 515 N.E.2d 68, 113 Ill. Dec. 259, 118 Ill.2d 321 (Ill. 1987) (rejecting the requirement of a licensing and giving weight to the witness's added training and work experience in pharmacology). Statutes may provide something similar. See Wexler v. Hecht, 928 A.2d 973 (Pa. 2007) (podiatrist, not having an unrestricted license to practice medicine, could not testify against one who does). Note that the statutory unrestricted license requirement standing alone would not prevent the medical doctor from testifying against a podiatrist, however.

[153]　See, e.g., Smith v. Fisher, 143 So.3d 110 (Ala. 2013) (interpreting statute: where defendant is a board-certified specialist, only another board-certified specialist in the same field is competent to testify on the standard of care); Woodard v. Custer, 476 Mich. 545, 719 N.W.2d 842 (2006), (similar); Nicholas v. Mynster, 213 N.J. 463, 64 A.3d 536 (2013) (statute not satisfied where defendant is board-certified but expert is only credentialed by hospital).

[154]　Pollard v. Goldsmith, 117 Ariz. 363, 572 P.2d 1201 (1977); Marshall v. Yale Podiatry Group, 5 Conn.App. 5, 496 A.2d 529 (1985); Bennett v. Butlin, 236 Ga. App. 691, 512 S.E.2d 13 (1999) (orthopedist would be permitted to testify against podiatrist where methods of treatment are the same as to particular procedure involved).

[155]　Rosenberg v. Cahill, 99 N.J. 318, 334, 492 A.2d 371, 379 (1985).

[156]　See Bodiford v. Lubitz, 564 So.2d 1390 (Ala. 1990) ("orthopedic surgeon who is familiar with the standard of care for podiatrists may be considered an expert in the area of podiatry"); Melville v. Southward, 791 P.2d 383 (Colo. 1990); Troupe v. McAuley, 955 So.2d 848, 856 (Miss. 2007) (no "per se rule" requiring witness to be in same specialty as defendant, but witness must be familiar with the applicable standards); Creasey v. Hogan, 292 Or. 154, 637 P.2d 114 (1981) (as to different community; possibly a tighter standard as to different specialty); Miller v. Brass Rail Tavern, Inc., 541 Pa. 474, 480 (the "test to be applied when qualifying an expert witness is whether the witness has *any* reasonable pretension to specialized knowledge on the subject under investigation. If he does, he may testify and the weight to be given to such testimony is for the trier of fact to determine.").

Nurses. Given that nurses are subject to the nursing standard of care, it is no surprise that nurses have been permitted to testify as experts on that standard[157] and on hospitals standards, at least so far as those standards are met by nurses.[158] Although doctors have sometimes been allowed to testify to the nursing standard of care,[159] testimony of nurses, no matter how qualified by training and experience, has been held inadmissible or insufficient to establish a standard of care for medical doctors.[160] Testimony of nurses on medical causation is also often rejected.[161]

Experts and factual cause. The plaintiff must always prove that the medical defendant's negligence was a factual cause of the plaintiff's harm, and doing so often requires expert testimony.[162] For example, the trier of fact could not ordinarily find that a psychiatrist's negligent mode of treatment caused his patient to commit suicide, without the aid of expert opinion to that effect.[163] Similarly, without expert testimony on causation, the trier could not find that a physician's failure to notice an abnormal electrocardiogram led to the patient's heart attack.[164] In such cases the absence of expert testimony on causation dooms the plaintiff's claims even though the plaintiff has established negligence.[165] Even with expert testimony, the plaintiff will also lose if that testimony is itself is speculative or inadequate to show causation.[166] Where expert testimony as to medical causation is required, it would seem to be a question of evidence whether any given witness is qualified to give an opinion, but a number of courts have made a blanket rule that nurses cannot give causal testimony in cases against doctors.[167]

Scientific basis of medical testimony. In recent years, federal and some state courts have increasingly excluded a great deal of expert testimony on the ground that it is not

---

[157] E.g., Salter v. Deaconess Family Medicine Center, 267 A.D.2d 976, 701 N.Y.S.2d 586 (1999); Gaines v. Comanche Cnty. Med. Hosp., 143 P.3d 203 (Okla. 2006) (citing many cases).

[158] Mattox v. Life Care Centers of America, Inc., 337 P.3d 627 (Idaho 2014).

[159] Tapp v. Owensboro Medical Health System, Inc., 282 S.W.3d 336 (Ky. App. 2009); Nold ex rel. Nold v. Binyon, 272 Kan. 87, 31 P.3d 274 (2001); contra, Smith v. Pavlovich, 394 Ill.App.3d 458, 914 N.E.2d 1258 (2009) (pediatrician could not testify to standard of care for Advanced Practice Nurse). See also Hankla v. Postell, 293 Ga. 692, 749 S.E.2d 726 (2013) (statute requires that expert and defendant be in the "same profession," which requires that the witness have actual knowledge and experience in the area; physician was not qualified to testify against a nurse midwife because they were not in the same profession and the physician had never supervised a nurse midwife).

[160] Seisinger v. Siebel, 220 Ariz. 85, 203 P.3d 483 (Ariz. 2009); Dombrowski v. Moore, 299 A.D.2d 949, 752 N.Y.S.2d 183 (2002); see also Smith v. Pavlovich, 394 Ill.App.3d 458, 914 N.E.2d 1258 (2009) (nurse working in pediatrics is not "competent to testify to the standard of care applicable to a pediatrician").

[161] See, e.g., Vaughn v. Mississippi Baptist Medical Center, 20 So.3d 645 (Miss. 2009) (recognizing a general rule against nurse testimony on causation). Cf. Williams v. Eight Judicial Dist. Court of State, ex rel. County of Clark, 262 P.3d 360 (Nev. 2011) (nurse not competent to give causation testimony in products liability case against drug manufacturer).

[162] E.g., Milliun v. New Milfort Hospital, 310 Conn. 711, 80 A.3d 887 (2013); Beckles v. Madden, 160 N.H. 118, 993 A.2d 209, 214 (2010). Expert testimony is not required where the connection between the defendant's negligent conduct and the plaintiff's injury or death is understandable by lay persons. Williams v. Lucy Webb Hayes Nat'l Training Sch. for Deaconesses and Missionaries, 924 A.2d 1000 (D.C. 2007); Williamson v. Amrani, 283 Kan. 227, 152 P.3d 60 (2007).

[163] Randall v. Benton, 147 N.H. 786, 802 A.2d 1211 (2002) (evidence insufficient to show that, had psychiatrist complied with standard of care, decedent's suicide would have been prevented).

[164] Rodriguez v. Clark, 400 Md. 39, 926 A.2d 736 (2007).

[165] Snelson v. Kamm, 204 Ill.2d 1, 787 N.E.2d 796, 272 Ill. Dec. 610 (2003); Smith v. Knowles, 281 N.W.2d 653 (Minn. 1979).

[166] E.g., Chakalis v. Elevator Solutions, Inc., 205 Cal. App. 4th 1557, 141 Cal. Rptr. 3d 362 (2012) (expert testimony failed to address whether the conduct caused plaintiff's injuries "within a reasonable medical probability"); Price v. Divita, 224 S.W.3d 331 (Tex. App. 2006).

[167] Vaughn v. Mississippi Baptist Medical Center, 20 So.3d 645 (Miss. 2009); Colwell v. Holy Family Hosp., 104 Wash.App. 606, 15 P.3d 210 (2001).

reliable, sometimes requiring scientific studies or experiments before testimony is admitted at all.[168] This approach has been applied in medical malpractice cases as well.[169] Some courts, however, have given weight to the expert's general experience, even in the absence of others' research on the subject.[170] In addition, some courts may admit a medical expert's testimony without subjecting it to special reliability rules at all if the expert's conclusion is based on application of accepted medical or scientific principles, even though the conclusion itself has not been verified by studies in the field.[171] "Tort reform" statutes may, however, exclude experts on the basis of mechanical criteria not necessarily related to the experts' reliability.[172]

4. *Informed Consent*

§ 21.9   Informed Consent: Underlying Principle and Elements

Courts have recognized that the patient's right of self-determination implies a right to important information about the nature of the medical procedure proposed. For example, patients or their representatives[173] are entitled to information about the risks of the procedure, its necessity, and alternative procedures that might be preferable. This is the general principle of informed consent, the "bedrock of . . . respect for the individual's right."[174] The patient who asserts that she was not given appropriate medical information, such as information about risks of a medical procedure, is asserting that, even if the physician was not negligent in performing the procedure, he is liable for harmful results because the patient would have refused consent and avoided the harm had she been appropriately informed.[175]

Who owes the duty to inform. In consequence of these principles, a duty to inform patients of certain information is usually placed on one or more of the treating[176] healthcare providers, including physicians,[177] surgeons,[178] dentists[179] and

---

[168] See 2 Dobbs, Hayden & Bublick, The Law of Torts § 463 (2d ed. 2011 & Supp.) (excluding expert testimony in products liability cases).

[169] See, Domingo v. T.K., 289 F.3d 600 (9th Cir. 2002) (excluding medical testimony on causation, in part because, under the Ninth Circuit's stringent test, the expert must have done independent research on the issue or else base his opinion on objective evidence such as research done by others).

[170] See Pipitone v. Biomatrix, Inc., 288 F.3d 239 (5th Cir. 2002) (emphasizing that revised Rule 702 expressly permits experience as a foundation for expert opinion and pointing out that the trial judge should address that experience in determining whether to admit the testimony); Miller v. Brass Rail Tavern, Inc., 541 Pa. 474, 664 A.2d 525 (Pa. 1995).

[171] Hayes v. Decker, 263 Conn. 677, 822 A.2d 228 (2003).

[172] See, applying such a statute, Perdieu v. Blackstone Family Practice Center, Inc., 264 Va. 408, 568 S.E.2d 703 (2002).

[173] A mother may consent for a child and if that consent is not informed, the child will have her own informed consent action. Niemiera v. Schneider, 114 N.J. 550, 555 A.2d 1112 (1989); Miller ex rel. Miller v. Dacus, 231 S.W.3d 903 (Tenn. 2007); see § 27.1.

[174] Fox v. Smith, 594 So.2d 596, 604 (Miss. 1992).

[175] Backlund v. Univ. of Washington, 137 Wash.2d 651, 975 P.2d 950 (1999) (the informed consent claim "allows a patient to recover damages from a physician even though the medical diagnosis or treatment was not negligent"). On details of causal rules, see § 21.12.

[176] Referring physicians who do not treat or retain control, are generally not expected to provide the information and secure the consent. See Koapke v. Kerfendal, 660 N.W.2d 206 (N.D. 2003).

[177] Long v. Jaszczak, 688 N.W.2d 173 (N.D. 2004) (physician ordering medical test).

[178] E.g., Quintanilla v. Dunkelman, 133 Cal. App. 4th 95, 34 Cal. Rptr. 3d 557 (2005).

[179] See Degennaro v. Tandon, 89 Conn.App. 183, 873 A.2d 191 (2005); Koapke v. Kerfendal, 660 N.W.2d 206 (N.D. 2003).

chiropractors.[180] Courts have held, however, that a hospital that is not itself involved in securing consent has no duty to inform or to supervise treating physician's efforts to inform.[181] On the other hand, a hospital may undertake an enforceable duty to initiate appropriate discussions.[182] And federal statutes require hospitals participating in experimental studies to secure informed consent.[183]

Battery vs. negligence approaches. On the basis of the informed consent principle, some courts hold that a physician who performs a procedure upon the patient's body without first providing adequate information is subject to liability for battery.[184] On principles of autonomy and self-determination, human beings have the right to determine what can be done to their own bodies.[185] Consequently, a patient's consent to the procedure or medical treatment actually performed by the defendant operates to bar any claim for battery,[186] but equally patients have a right to refuse a recommended medical procedure or treatment,[187] even if it is necessary to save the patient's life.[188] Under these rules, a surgeon who operates without the appearance of consent[189] is by definition prima facie guilty of a battery.[190] Consent procured by misrepresentation of material facts[191] or duress[192] is also ineffective and a medical procedure performed on the basis of such a consent would also be a battery. The same idea applies when the plaintiff consents only to an operation by Dr. A, but it is performed in fact by Dr. B.[193]

---

[180] Hannemann v. Boyson, 282 Wis.2d 664, 698 N.W.2d 714 (2005); Felton v. Lovett, 388 S.W.3d 656 (Tex. 2012).

[181] See Ackerman v. Lerwick, 676 S.W.2d 318 (Mo. App. 1984); Montalvo v. Borkovec, 256 Wis.2d 472, 647 N.W.2d 413 (Ct. App. 2002).

[182] See Bryant v. HCA Health Servs. of No. Tennessee, Inc., 15 S.W.3d 804 (Tenn. 2000).

[183] See Friter v. Iolab Corp., 414 Pa. Super. 622, 607 A.2d 1111 (1992). State statutes may also indirectly impose a duty, at least if the hospital takes part in the consent process. See Rogers v. T. J. Samson Community Hosp., 276 F.3d 228 (6th Cir. 2002).

[184] Montgomery v. Bazaz-Sehgal, 568 Pa. 574, 798 A.2d 742 (2002) (no consent and lack of informed consent are both treated as battery claims).

[185] Schloendorff v. Society of New York Hosp., 211 N.Y. 125, 105 N.E. 92 (1914), *overruled in part by* Bing v. Thunig, 2 N.Y.2d 656, 143 N.E.2d 3, 163 N.Y.2d 3 (1957).

[186] As in Bowling v. Foster, 254 Ga. App. 374, 562 S.E.2d 776 (Ga. App. 2002).

[187] See Miller v. Rhode Island Hosp., 625 A.2d 778, 784 (R.I. 1993) ("[C]entral to the doctrine of informed consent is every competent adult's right to forgo treatment."). Thus the patient can refuse treatment by medication as well as surgery. E.g., Duncan v. Scottsdale Med. Imaging, Ltd., 205 Ariz. 306, 70 P.3d 435 (2003).

[188] See In re A.C., 573 A.2d 1235 (D.C.1990); In re Dubreuil, 629 So.2d 819 (Fla. 1993); Harvey v. Strickland, 350 S.C. 303, 566 S.E.2d 529 (2002).

[189] See §§ 8.6 & 8.12 (consent for those lacking capacity and emergency as a substitute for consent). In Harvey v. Strickland, 350 S.C. 303, 566 S.E.2d 529 (2002) the patient categorically refused a blood transfusion and the doctor knew he was Jehovah's Witness, but the patient allegedly also said he would "consider" a transfusion. While the patient was unconscious and allegedly in need of a transfusion, the defendant surgeon obtained "consent" from the patient's mother. The court held it was a jury question whether the patient had impliedly consented to a substituted consent.

[190] E.g., Gragg v. Calandra, 297 Ill. App. 3d 639, 696 N.E.2d 1282, 231 Ill. Dec. 711 (1998); see § 33. The battery claim—based on the evidence that the plaintiff did not consent to the operation at all—does not require expert testimony to establish the fact of no consent, even though in many courts expert testimony is required to establish the entirely different claim that the patient was given inadequate information. Gouveia v. Phillips, 823 So.2d 215 (Fla. Dist. Ct. App. 2002).

[191] See Duncan v. Scottsdale Med. Imaging, Ltd., 205 Ariz. 306, 70 P.3d 435 (2003) (plaintiff can either claim misrepresentation as a tort or proceed on the battery claim, because misrepresentation vitiates consent); Bloskas v. Murray, 646 P.2d 907, 913 (Colo. 1982).

[192] § 8.9.

[193] Vitale v. Henchey, 24 S.W.3d 651 (Ky. 2000); Perna v. Pirozzi, 92 N.J. 446, 457 A.2d 431 (1983). Damages in such cases, however, may be severely limited unless the plaintiff can show "that the results of the surgery would have been different had it been performed by" the surgeon to whom consent was given. Meyers v. Epstein, 282 F.Supp. 2d 151 (S.D. N.Y. 2003).

Most courts have now held that the patient whose claim is grounded in lack of information has a claim for negligence, not for battery.[194] The negligence in the informed consent claim is not negligence in performing a medical procedure, but rather negligence in failing to explain its risks, alternatives, and other related information.[195] The battery claim is still viable, but only when the patient did not consent at all, or when the treatment administered was different from the one to which the patient consented.[196] Thus under the currently prevailing view, the scope of the consent is critical in determining whether the claim is for battery or for negligence. The patient who consents to an operation on his right toe has a battery action if the surgeon operates on the left toe instead. But the patient who consents to an operation on his right toe without being informed that the operation entails a serious risk that he will lose his leg must make out the informed consent claim for negligent nondisclosure.

Negligence in performing procedure distinguished. Under neither view, however, is the plaintiff required to prove negligence in conducting the operation. If the elements of an informed consent claim are proved under the applicable theory, the surgeon is liable for the harm resulting even if he operated with consummate skill. The wrong done is not a negligent operation but a failure to respect the patient's right of choice. The differences between the claim based upon lack of informed consent and the ordinary medical malpractice claim are striking, but the plaintiff very often presents both claims together, often preferring to prevail on the malpractice claim and using the informed consent claim as a backup. This practice is useful for plaintiffs, but it does run some risks of confusion and reversible error in instructions if the two claims are not clearly separated.[197]

Elements. For many courts, the shift to a negligence theory means that the plaintiff must prove five things: (1) nondisclosure of required information,[198] (2) actual damage (such as loss of a leg), (3) resulting from risks about which the patient was not informed; (4) factual cause, which is to say that the plaintiff would have rejected the medical treatment if she had known the risk,[199] and (5) that reasonable persons, if properly informed, would have rejected the proposed treatment.[200]

---

[194] E.g., Cobbs v. Grant, 8 Cal.3d 229, 502 P.2d 1, 104 Cal.Rptr. 505 (1972); Kennis v. Mercy Hosp. Medical Center, 491 N.W.2d 161 (Iowa 1992); Howard v. Univ. of Med. & Dentistry of New Jersey, 172 N.J. 537, 800 A.2d 73 (2002); Jaskoviak v. Gruver, 638 N.W.2d 1 (N.D. 2002); Blanchard v. Kellum, 975 S.W.2d 522 (Tenn. 1998).

[195] Hayes v. Camel, 283 Conn. 475, 927 A.2d 880 (2007) ("a claim for lack of informed consent focuses not on the level of skill exercised in the performance of the procedure itself but on the adequacy of the explanation given by the physician in obtaining the patient's consent"); see also Spencer v. Goodill, 17 A.3d 552 (Del. 2011) (construing state statute; plaintiff must "prove that defendant's failure to obtain informed consent was a proximate cause of plaintiff's injury").

[196] Shuler v. Garrett, 743 F.3d 170 (6th Cir. 2014) (Tenn. Law); Duncan v. Scottsdale Med. Imaging, Ltd., 205 Ariz. 306, 70 P.3d 435 (2003); Washburn v. Klara, 263 Va. 586, 561 S.E.2d 682 (Va. 2002); Christman v. Davis, 889 A.2d 746 (Vt. 2005); see also O'Brien v. Synnott, 72 A.3d 331 (Vt. 2013) (defendants may be liable for battery where patient consented to a blood draw without knowing that it was for a non-medical, law enforcement purpose).

[197] See Betterton v. Leichtling, 101 Cal. App. 4th 749, 124 Cal. Rptr. 2d 644 (2002)

[198] §§ 21.10 & 21.11.

[199] Tashman v. Gibbs, 263 Va. 65, 556 S.E.2d 772 (2002); § 21.12.

[200] See Aronson v. Harriman, 321 Ark. 359, 901 S.W.2d 832 (1995) (but treating third element as a "factor" to consider); Woolley v. Henderson, 418 A.2d 1123 (Me. 1980); Ashe v. Radiation Oncology Assocs., 9 S.W.3d 119 (1999); § 21.12.

§ 21.10   General Standards of Disclosure

As to what must be disclosed to the patient, the courts are divided into roughly two camps, between a "medical" and a "materiality" standard of disclosure. Tabulating the position of different states is inherently imprecise[201] and may be even more so when, as here, legislatures have intervened to enact specific requirements. For what it is worth, however, a little more than half the states, many under the command of a statute,[202] appear to adopt the medical standard of disclosure as a general rule rather than the materiality standard,[203] or alternatively specify major limitations on the claim that are more demanding than the materiality standard.[204]

The medical standard of disclosure. The older cases, and many statutes, require the plaintiff to prove the medical standard of disclosure. Under that standard, if medical custom[205] requires no disclosure, the doctor, though a fiduciary, owes no duty to divulge information, no matter how critical it might be to the patient.[206] If the medical standard requires disclosure of one risk but not another equally great, the rule entitles the plaintiff to half of the relevant information, not all of it. The medical standard requires expert testimony to establish the standard of disclosure,[207] although possibly testimony by a physician in a related specialty will be sufficient[208] and the defendant may have the burden of showing what the medical standard is.[209] The burden of proof could be decisive, because there may be no real custom of disclosure at all.[210]

The materiality standard of disclosure. Beginning in 1972 when three leading opinions broke with earlier decisions,[211] courts deciding the issue on first impression and independent of statutory commands have tended to favor a duty to disclose all material information, that is, information the physician can reasonably expect a patient would

---

[201] Some state statutes set forth lists of exactly what must be disclosed in certain situations.

[202] E.g., N.Y. CPLR 4401–a & N.Y. Pub. Health L. § 2805–d; N.C. Gen. Stat. § 90–21.13.

[203] E.g., Davis v. Caldwell, 54 N.Y.2d 176, 429 N.E.2d 741, 445 N.Y.S.2d 63 (1981); Ashe v. Radiation Oncology Assocs., 9 S.W.3d 119 (1999). See 1 Barry R. Furrow, Thomas L. Greaney, Sandra H. Johnson, Timothy Stolzfus Jost & Robert L. Schwartz, Health Law § 6–10 (2d ed. 2000) (listing cases and statutes). As to cases, see Laurent B. Frantz, Annotation, Modern Status of Views as to General Measure of Physician's Duty to Inform Patient of Risks of Proposed Treatment, 88 A.L.R.3d 1008 (1978).

[204] See Daniels v. Gamma West Brachytherapy, LLC, 221 P.3d 256 (Utah 2009) (reflecting statutory displacement of common law fiduciary duty claim requiring disclosure of material information).

[205] See § 21.5

[206] Woolley v. Henderson, 418 A.2d 1123 (Me. 1980); Hamilton v. Bares, 267 Neb. 816, 678 N.W.2d 74 (2004) (under statute codifying medical standard, physician must provide "information which would ordinarily be provided to the patient under like circumstances by health care providers" in the relevant community).

[207] E.g., Woolley v. Henderson, 418 A.2d 1123 (Me. 1980); Tashman v. Gibbs, 263 Va. 65, 556 S.E.2d 772 (2002). The testimony may, of course, come from defense witnesses, as in Davis v. Caldwell, 54 N.Y.2d 176, 429 N.E.2d 741, 445 N.Y.S.2d 63 (1981).

[208] In Griffin v. Moseley, 356 Mont. 393, 234 P.3d 869 (2010), the defendant was a neurosurgeon, the witness a neuro-opthalmologist. The court thought the witness could not be permitted to testimony on alleged negligence in the surgery, but could testify as to standards for providing the patient information about alternatives to surgery.

[209] Gorab v. Zook, 943 P.2d 423 (Colo. 1997) (once the plaintiff proves nondisclosure, "the burden then shifts to the physician to go forward with expert testimony showing that the nondisclosure conformed" with medical standards).

[210] See Canterbury v. Spence, 464 F.2d 772 (D.C. Cir. 1972) (doubting the "reality of any discernible custom" as to communication and recognizing "danger that what is in fact no custom at all may be taken as an affirmative custom to maintain silence"); Cobbs v. Grant, 8 Cal.3d 229, 502 P.2d 1, 104 Cal.Rptr. 505 (1972) (standards of disclosure so nebulous that doctors would be vested with "virtual absolute discretion").

[211] Canterbury v. Spence, 464 F.2d 772 (D.C. Cir. 1972); Cobbs v. Grant, 8 Cal. 3d 229, 502 P.2d 1, 104 Cal. Rptr. 505, (1972); Wilkinson v. Vesey, 110 R.I. 606, 295 A.2d 676, 69 A.L.R.3d 1202 (1972).

consider in determining whether to undergo the medical procedure.[212] These courts have insisted that "[r]espect for the patient's right of self-determination . . . demands a standard set by law for physicians rather than one which physicians may or may not impose upon themselves."[213] Further, the patient's right to weigh her subjective fears against the risks disclosed is a personal, not a medical question, and it is "reserved to the patient alone."[214] For this reason, the patient is entitled to an explanation of the different risks associated with the potential medical procedures even if, on balance, medical judgment would clearly favor one procedure over the other.[215]

Expert testimony under the materiality standard. Because a medical standard is not involved in the materiality test, expert testimony is not required. Disclosure is to be made when the information is material to a decision, which is to say that the physician must disclose information a reasonable patient would want to be aware of in determining whether to proceed.[216] Although experts are not required to prove materiality, an expert may be required to show both that material, undisclosed information existed and that the defendant should reasonably have known about it.[217] In other words, the medical standard governs the questions whether a risk existed and the medical alternatives and whether the doctor should have known of the undisclosed risk. On a different plane entirely, expert testimony on the custom of the medical community may be admitted as supplementary information, although not to define the physician's duty.[218]

The therapeutic exception or privilege. Some courts have acknowledged a putative privilege to withhold information for therapeutic reasons. The idea is that in some instances, if a physician told the patient of the risk, the knowledge itself would harm the patient. With this in mind, courts have said they would recognize a therapeutic privilege of nondisclosure if the physician shows that in the patient's particular case, disclosure would be so harmful that it would be against the patient's best interests.[219] Courts have warned themselves to be cautious should such a case actually appear. They have said that the supposed privilege should not be recognized merely because a physician fears that disclosure of risks will lead the patient to make a bad decision. And even if

---

[212] See, e.g., Janusauskas v. Fichman, 264 Conn. 796, 826 A.2d 1066 (2003); Carr v. Strode, 79 Hawai'i 475, 904 P.2d 489 (1995); Spar v. Cha, 907 N.E.2d 974, 979 (Ind. 2009); Harnish v. Children's Hosp. Medical Center, 387 Mass. 152, 439 N.E.2d 240 (1982); Largey v. Rothman, 110 N.J. 204, 540 A.2d 504 (1988); Moure v. Raeuchle, 529 Pa. 394, 604 A.2d 1003 (1992). Some statutes adopt the materiality standard. As to the information to be disclosed, see § 21.11.

[213] Canterbury v. Spence, 464 F.2d 772 (D.C. Cir. 1972).

[214] Cobbs v. Grant, 8 Cal.3d 229, 502 P.2d 1, 104 Cal.Rptr. 505 (1972).

[215] Harrison v. United States, 284 F.3d 293 (1st Cir. 2002).

[216] See Acuna v. Turkish, 192 N.J. 399, 930 A.2d 416 (2007). The physician is also required to disclose information he should recognize the particular patient would want to know. See § 21.11.

[217] Betterton v. Leichtling, 101 Cal. App. 4th 749, 124 Cal. Rptr. 2d 644 (2002) ("Whether to disclose a significant risk is not a matter reserved for expert opinion. Whether a particular risk exists, however, may be a matter beyond the knowledge of lay witnesses, and therefore appropriate for determination based on the testimony of experts"); Harnish v. Children's Hosp. Medical Center, 387 Mass. 152, 439 N.E.2d 240 (1982); Jaskoviak v. Gruver, 638 N.W.2d 1 (N.D. 2002).

[218] Flatt v. Kantak, 687 N.W.2d 208 (N.D. 2004).

[219] See Barcai v. Betwee, 98 Hawai'i 470, 50 P.3d 946 (2002) (emphasizing that a general rule of nondisclosure for a category of patients would not suffice to show the privilege, which must be based on particularized assessment of the individual patient lest the privilege swallow the duty to provide information). See also Felton v. Lovett, 388 S.W.3d 656 (Tex. 2012) ("In sum, a reasonable health care provider must disclose the risks that would influence a reasonable patient in deciding whether to undergo treatment but not those that would be unduly disturbing to an unreasonable patient.").

disclosure by itself could seem to menace the patient's health, the physician may be obliged to make the disclosure to a relative.[220]

§ 21.11   Particular Types of Information to Be Disclosed

What must be disclosed under the medical standard depends on medical evidence in the case. The materiality standard, in contrast, depends mainly on the judge and jury's judgment about what reasonable people want to know before choosing to accept a medical procedure. The materiality standard, not being a medical one, requires no medical testimony to establish. If there is room for debate about materiality the jury determines whether a reasonable person would want to know the information that was withheld.[221] However, plaintiff's attorneys have at times introduced medical opinion on what should be divulged, even in states following the materiality standard.[222] Although medical testimony is not required to show what reasonable people would want to know, it is usually required to show the existence or non-existence of risk, the medical alternatives, and their respective prospects for success.[223] Other kinds of evidence on materiality may be important in specific cases.

Objective and subjective tests of materiality. The patient's subjective attitude toward certain risks or advantages may be determinative on the materiality issue. If the patient attaches special importance to some particular matter and the doctor knows or should know it, that matter is material even if most other people would not be concerned about it.[224] For example, relatively few people object to blood transfusions, but some do, and if the doctor knows that the patient is one of the few, the matter is clearly material to that patient. When the doctor could not be reasonably expected to know of any special concerns the patient might have, materiality is judged by the objective reasonable person standard. Material information is that which "a reasonable patient would consider in deciding whether to undergo the medical procedure,"[225] even if such information is not by itself decisive.

Immaterial items. Medical doctors sometimes caricature the informed consent rules by suggesting that they impose preposterous obligations, such as an explanation about the size of thread used in sutures. But the materiality rule does not require detailed

---

[220] Canterbury v. Spence, 464 F.2d 772 (D.C. Cir. 1972).

[221] Fitzpatrick v. Natter, 599 Pa. 465, 961 A.2d 1229 (2008) ("determination of what risks would be material to the patient's decision is a jury question; however, in making that determination, the jury must be supplied with expert information not only as to the potential harm, but the likelihood of that harm occurring"); Bubb v. Brusky, 321 Wis.2d 1, 768 N.W.2d 903 (2009).

[222] See Wyszomierski v. Siracusa, 290 Conn. 225, 963 A.2d 943 (2009).

[223] Sard v. Hardy, 281 Md. 432, 379 A.2d 1014 (1977). See also University of Maryland Medical System Corp. v. Waldt, 411 Md. 207, 983 A.2d 112 (2009) ("Expert testimony is necessary to establish the material risks and other pertinent information regarding the treatment or procedure."); Fitzpatrick v. Natter, 599 Pa. 465, 961 A.2d 1229 (2008). An expert may also be required to testify that it was more likely than not that the undisclosed risk actually materialized and was a factual cause of the injury. White v. Leimbach, 131 Ohio St. 3d 21, 959 N.E.2d 1033 (2011).

[224] See Cross v. Trapp, 170 W.Va. 459, 294 S.E.2d 446, 468 (1982) ("the disclosure issue is approached from the reasonableness of the physician's disclosure or nondisclosure in terms of what the physician knows or should know to be the patient's informational needs"); Restatement Second of Torts § 538(2)(b) (1977) (knows or has reason to know that the recipient regards the material as important).

[225] Moure v. Raeuchle, 529 Pa. 394, 405, 604 A.2d 1003, 1008 (1992). Variations in wording appear to be aimed at the same idea. See Hondroulis v. Schuhmacher, 553 So.2d 398 (La. 1988) (material information would influence the decision); Restatement Second of Torts § 538(2)(a) (1977) (material information would be important in making a choice).

disclosure of methods unless they are unusual or affect the risks.[226] Certainly the physician owes no obligation to provide the patient a general medical education.[227] Nor need he disclose matters that the patient already knows, or those that the physician reasonably believes she knows.[228]

Items generally to be disclosed. It is sometimes said that the physician should disclose the diagnosis, the general nature of the contemplated procedure, the material risks involved in the procedure, the probability of the procedure's success, the prognosis if the procedure is not carried out, and the existence and risks of any available options for medical treatment.[229] Beyond this, the physician may be required to disclose some information even if there is no immediate medical procedure to be performed, specifically a diagnosis of or test result showing that the plaintiff has a disease.[230] The list is obviously not exclusive.

Material risk. Whether a risk is objectively material depends upon its severity and its likelihood of occurrence.[231] "A very small chance of death or serious disablement may well be significant; a potential disability which dramatically outweighs the potential benefit of therapy or the detriments of the existing malady" may require discussion.[232] The materiality of a risk is ordinarily for the jury,[233] but in some cases the risk is so remote or negligible that a directed verdict or summary judgment is appropriate.[234]

The prognosis or probability of the success of the proposed treatment is highly material in almost any imaginable case. In *Arato v. Avedon*,[235] the court recognized that, and left the issue to the jury under a materiality instruction. However, the court also held that the materiality standard would not govern the duty to reveal information that was not about risks of the procedure itself. For all other information—life expectancy information was in issue in *Arato*—the medical standard of disclosure would govern. So when doctors recommended a painful course of treatment that had no known chance of significantly prolonging the patient's life, the materiality standard did not control at all. Under that view, an informed consent claim could be pursued only if the *medical* standard required doctors to reveal the improbability of success or the fact that it might

---

[226] Masquat v. Maguire, 638 P.2d 1105 (Okla. 1981) (different methods of performing a tubal ligation, no disclosure required).

[227] See Cobbs v. Grant, 8 Cal.3d 229, 502 P.2d 1, 104 Cal.Rptr. 505 (1972).

[228] See, e.g., Sard v. Hardy, 281 Md. 432, 445, 379 A.2d 1014, 1022 (1977).

[229] E.g., Vasa v. Compass Medical, P.C., 456 Mass. 175, 921 N.E.2d 963 (2010) ("Doctors have a duty to inform patients of available options for medical treatment and the material risks that each option entails); Matthies v. Mastromonaco, 160 N.J. 26, 733 A.2d 456 (1999); Hopfauf v. Hieb, 712 N.W.2d 333 (N.D. 2006) (risk and options); Tisdale v. Pruitt, 302 S.C. 238, 394 S.E.2d 857 (1990); Felton v. Lovett, 388 S.W.3d 656 (Tex. 2012) (doctor must disclose the inherent risks of treatment," meaning those risks "which are directly related to the treatment and occur without negligence," including "side effects and reactions, whether likely or only possible, that are directly related to the treatment provided").

[230] See Nold ex rel. Nold v. Binyon, 272 Kan. 87, 31 P.3d 274 (2001) ("Where a communicable disease has been diagnosed in a pregnant woman who desires to continue her pregnancy to term and deliver a healthy baby, we agree with the district court that the woman's physician has an obligation as a matter of law to inform the woman of the diagnosis."). Under the materiality test, a doctor may also owe a duty to inform the patient of the availability of a test that a reasonable patient would want to know about. Jandre v. Wisconsin Injured Patients and Families Compensation Fund, 340 Wis. 2d 31, 813 N.W.2d 627 (2012).

[231] Feeley v. Baer, 424 Mass. 875, 876, 679 N.E.2d 180, 181 (1997) ("materiality of information about a potential injury is a function not only of the severity of the injury, but also of the likelihood that it will occur").

[232] Wilkinson v. Vesey, 110 R.I. 606, 295 A.2d 676, 689, 69 A.L.R.3d 1202 (1972).

[233] Moure v. Raeuchle, 529 Pa. 394, 405, 604 A.2d 1003 (1992).

[234] Feeley v. Baer, 424 Mass. 875, 679 N.E.2d 180 (1997).

[235] Arato v. Avedon, 5 Cal.4th 1172, 23 Cal.Rptr.2d 131, 858 P.2d 598 (1993).

extend life only for several months. Since the medical standard in that case was nondisclosure rather than disclosure, the doctors were not subject to liability. Even the patient's answer to the doctor's questionnaire that he wished to be told the truth did not "heighten the duty of disclosure."[236] A less restrictive view of the physician's obligation is that he must provide relevant medical information, but the information, if material, would not be limited to the precise medical procedure itself.[237]

Disclosure of other information. The law of informed consent traces its origin to battery cases, which necessarily involve a bodily contact. However, with the recognition of the law's autonomy-respecting principle, courts may impose liability for failure to provide certain kinds of information even when no bodily contact results.[238] In particular, physicians may be obliged to properly explain fetal genetic defects to pregnant patients[239] and if a patient refuses to undergo a diagnostic procedure or operation, then to explain to the patient the risks of the refusal.[240] For the same reason, the physician who treats a fracture with bed rest must explain the disadvantage of such treatment, the surgical alternatives, and their risks and advantages.[241] The point in such cases is that the decision belongs to the patient. The doctor is liable for harm done in depriving the patient of that decision, even though no bodily contact has resulted.

Manner of disclosure. Discussions of the disclosure required by informed consent rules usually seem to assume that the doctor holds a face-to-face conversation with the patient. No doubt that has often been true, but there has long been some tendency to formalize the process. There are now on the books a number of informed consent statutes that encourage the doctor to list risks in a written consent form and that provide at least a presumption that full disclosure has been made once the patient signs the form.[242] As with boilerplate in commercial documents, extensive explanation may defeat the informative purpose. Besides the statutes, other forces are at work to mechanize or formalize the disclosure process. Managed care organizations and even individual physicians provide patients with booklets or pamphlets, monthly health magazines, and even night classes in various aspects of health. The efficiency of such organizations may mean that a staff member may casually inform the patient of risks and that the doctor will not. These changes in the practice of medicine are likely to raise new issues about the effectiveness of mass-produced and impersonal disclosures.

§ 21.12 The Causation Requirement in Informed Consent Cases

In most states, informed consent cases require proof of legally cognizable harm resulting from the nondisclosure.[243] The requirement of damages is also, at least in

---

[236] Arato, 5 Cal.4th at 1189, 23 Cal.Rptr.2d at 142, 858 P.2d at 609.

[237] See Acuna v. Turkish, 192 N.J. 399, 930 A.2d 416 (2007).

[238] See McQuitty v. Spangler, 410 Md. 1, 976 A.2d 1020 (Md. 2009) ("[R]equiring a physical invasion to sustain an informed consent claim contravenes the very foundation of the informed consent doctrine—to promote a patient's choice.").

[239] § 27.4 (interference with mother's choice to avoid or terminate pregnancy).

[240] Truman v. Thomas, 27 Cal.3d 285, 165 Cal.Rptr. 308, 611 P.2d 902 (1980); cf. Marsingill v. O'Malley, 58 P.3d 495 (Alaska 2002) (upon hearing patient's symptoms by telephone, physician merely informed patient to go to the emergency room without indicating seriousness of failure to do so; jury should be instructed on the materiality or reasonable patient standard).

[241] Matthies v. Mastromonaco, 160 N.J. 26, 733 A.2d 456 (1999).

[242] See Iowa Code Ann. § 147.137; Tex. Civ. Prac. & Rems. Code §§ 74.105 to 74.106.

[243] See Spencer v. Goodill, 17 A.3d 552 (Del. 2011) (construing state statute to mean that plaintiff must "prove that defendant's failure to obtain informed consent was a proximate cause of plaintiff's injury"); Anderson v. Hollingsworth, 136 Idaho 800, 41 P.3d 228 (2001) ("To establish a claim based on the doctrine of

theory, a requirement of factual causation. Thus a plaintiff may have to prove with expert testimony that it was more likely than not that the undisclosed risk actually materialized and was a but-for cause of her injury.[244] Most commonly, the gist of the plaintiff's claim is that her consent to a medical procedure was procured by nondisclosure of risks or other information the defendant was required to disclose, that the procedure caused harm even if the procedure was skillfully performed, and that the plaintiff would not have undergone the procedure and suffered the harm had she been properly informed. This would establish factual causation—but for the tortious nondisclosure, the plaintiff would have avoided the harm she suffered.

The "subjective" rule of causation. Some courts follow this traditional but-for rule. They hold that evidence that the plaintiff would have refused the harmful operation is necessary to establish causation and that failure to provide such evidence means that causation has not been shown.[245] This is sometimes labeled the subjective rule, but it is in fact the only rule that actually addresses but-for causation.

The objective rule. Most courts have applied what is often called an objective test of causation, saying that the plaintiff cannot prevail unless a reasonable person given the required information would have refused consent to the operation.[246] They reason that the doctor should be protected because the plaintiff's testimony that she would not have consented had she been properly informed might be false.[247] This rule effectively treats the plaintiff's testimony on this point as always false, contrary to the normal rule that credibility is for the jury.[248] The rule is at odds with the inference of causation available when the harm that comes to pass is the very harm the defendant risked.[249] The rule is also at odds with the rule in products liability cases. In those cases, courts hold that when a manufacturer fails to give a warning or other information, they will presume that the victim would have read and acted upon the information.[250]

The objective rule as a non-causal rule of restricted duty. The objective rule, though explained as a rule of causation, is not in fact about causation at all. Causation cannot be proved by showing what would have happened with a purely hypothetical plaintiff. If the full disclosure would have led the plaintiff to refuse the operation, both the

---

informed consent, a patient must prove three basic elements: nondisclosure, causation and injury."); Curran v. Buser, 271 Neb. 332, 711 N.W.2d 562 (2006) (proof required that lack of informed consent proximately caused injury and damages); Scott v. Bradford, 606 P.2d 554 (Okla. 1980) (elements of claim include duty, cause and injury).

[244] See White v. Leimbach, 131 Ohio St. 3d 21, 2011-Ohio-6238, 959 N.E.2d 1033 (2011).

[245] Riedisser v. Nelson, 111 Ariz. 542, 534 P.2d 1052 (1975) ("Furthermore, no damage can be said to have proximately resulted from a failure to disclose unless Mrs. Riedisser would not have had the operation had the disclosures been made."); Scott v. Bradford, 606 P.2d 554 (Okla. 1980) ("The second element, that of causation, requires that plaintiff patient would have chosen no treatment or a different course of treatment had the alternatives and material risks of each been made known to him."). A statute may prescribe this rule. See Alaska Stat. § 09.55.556 (patient must prove failure to inform properly and that "but for that failure the claimant would not have consented to the proposed treatment or procedure").

[246] Spencer v. Goodill, 17 A.3d 552 (Del. 2011); Sard v. Hardy, 281 Md. 432, 379 A.2d 1014 (1977). However, the "reasonable person" for some judges may turn out to have some of the plaintiff's characteristics. If so, this objective standard becomes at least somewhat subjective. See Bernard v. Char, 79 Hawai'i 362, 903 P.2d 667 (1995); Ashe v. Radiation Oncology Assocs., 9 S.W.3d 119 (Tenn. 1999).

[247] See Canterbury v. Spence, 464 F.2d 772 (D.C. Cir. 1972) (the subjective or but-for rule "places the physician in jeopardy of the patient's hindsight and bitterness").

[248] See § 13.1.

[249] See Zuchowicz v. United States, 140 F.3d 381 (2d Cir. 1998); § 191.

[250] See § 33.16.

defendant's breach and its causal role is clearly established.[251] The objective rule is really a further restriction of the physician's duty. While the materiality test requires the doctor to provide information that a reasonable person would wish to know in considering the proposed procedure, the "objective test" further restricts the physician's duty so that he need not provide all relevant information but only information that would actually be *decisive* to a reasonable person. The effect is that the "patient's right of self-determination is irrevocably lost,"[252] unless the plaintiff's own risk tolerance happens to jibe with that of hypothetical reasonable people as the jury imagines them to be.

The dual requirement. Several states have explicitly held that both subjective and objective tests must be met, so that the plaintiff will fail if she would have accepted the medical procedure even when fully informed, and she will also fail if she would have rejected it but a reasonable person would not have.[253] Some of the cases that may be listed as adopting either the subjective or objective test fail to state whether the test adopted is necessary and exclusive or whether it is merely sufficient. For this reason, some of these cases do not clearly rule out the dual demand upon the plaintiff.[254]

In addition, the cases that explain the reasonable person rule as a necessary method of proving what the individual plaintiff would likely have done can be interpreted as implicitly adopting a dual requirement. This can be seen by supposing that a reasonable person would have refused consent had she been given appropriate information but that the plaintiff herself would have consented anyway. If the objective, reasonable person test is the only requirement to show "causation," the plaintiff would recover in those circumstances. Yet it is difficult to believe that such courts, all of which have recognized the ordinary but-for rule, would allow the plaintiff to recover.[255] For this reason, such courts seem to be effectively adopting both the subjective and objective requirements, which is to say that courts adopting the objective test are in reality limiting the physician's duty to disclose material information and also requiring factual causation in the form of the subjective test.

Comparative fault. Although a patient's comparative fault may reduce her damages in medical malpractice cases,[256] some authority takes the view that comparative/contributory fault has no place as a partial or complete defense in informed consent claims.[257] The comparative fault defense is surely inappropriate in jurisdictions that adopt a battery theory of informed consent and also refuse to apply comparative

---

[251] Arena v. Gingrich, 305 Or. 1, 748 P.2d 547 (1988).

[252] Scott v. Bradford, 606 P.2d 554 (Okla. 1979).

[253] Harnish v. Children's Hosp. Medical Center, 387 Mass. 152, 439 N.E.2d 240 (1982).

[254] See Tashman v. Gibbs, 263 Va. 65, 556 S.E.2d 772 (2002) ("Here, [the plaintiff] did not state that she would have decided against having the . . . procedure if Dr. Tashman had informed her of the . . . alternative," hence the plaintiff failed to prove factual cause).

[255] A number of courts have appealed to Canterbury v. Spence, 464 F.2d 772 (D.C. Cir. 1972), in support of the rule that the plaintiff will be barred if a reasonable person would have consented in spite of receiving full information. But *Canterbury*, like some other cases, recognized that the ultimate issue was but-for causation and insisted that "[a] causal connection exists when, but only when, disclosure of significant risks incidental to treatment would have resulted in a decision against it."

[256] See § 21.15.

[257] Keomaka v. Zakaib, 8 Haw.App. 518, 811 P.2d 478 (1991) ("contributory negligence 'has no place in an action for failure to obtain informed consent;' " given the superior knowledge of the doctor "and the generally limited ability of the patient to ascertain the existence of certain risks and dangers that inhere in certain medical treatments, it would be unfair and illogical to impose on the patient the duty of inquiry or other affirmative duty with respect to informed consent").

fault principles in intentional tort cases.[258] It may be difficult to say that no case whatever can possibly arise in which the patient's comparative fault in an informed consent claim should be considered. However, even if comparative fault can be an appropriate plea in informed consent cases, the patient should not be charged with comparative fault merely because he failed to read the physician's written consent form or to ask the physician for more detailed information.[259] Certainly the physician's responsibility should not be reduced on the ground that the plaintiff should have ascertained the required medical information from some other source. On the contrary, the physician's duty to disclose, when it exists, demonstrates the plaintiff's right to rely upon his disclosure.[260]

5. Defenses and Statutory Limits on Liability

§ 21.13 Good Samaritan Statutes

All states, following California's lead, have adopted Good Samaritan statutes that reduce the duty of care otherwise owed by licensed health care providers when they are rendering certain professional assistance at the scene of an emergency occurring outside the professional's regular practice.[261] Under none of the statutes is the provider liable for medical negligence. Although these statutes are potentially unjust in relieving a negligent physician of responsibility for his acts, in some cases they may be invoked only as a convenient if confusing way to protect a doctor who needed no protection. They may be invoked, that is, to protect a physician who was not negligent in the first place and who would not have been held liable under ordinary tort rules.

Some of California's statutes literally eliminate liability even for gross or wanton negligence, so long as the practitioner acts in good faith.[262] "[T]he goodness of the Samaritan is a description of the quality of his or her intention, not the quality of the aid delivered."[263] Other statutes do not go quite so far; they eliminate liability for ordinary negligence, but preserve a duty not to act wantonly or intentionally.[264]

Some statutes apply only if the defendant renders assistance without payment or expectation of payment,[265] and sometimes only he does so at the "scene of an emergency" or outside his ordinary employment or practice.[266] However, unusual decisions have extended statutes to protect surgeons operating in a regular hospital operating room[267]

---

[258] Bey v. Sacks, 789 A.2d 232 (Pa. Super. 2001).

[259] Keomaka v. Zakaib, 8 Haw.App. 518, 811 P.2d 478 (1991).

[260] Brown v. Dibbell, 227 Wis.2d 28, 595 N.W.2d 358 (1999) (but noting that the patient might be chargeable with fault in failing to accurately give her medical history).

[261] David W. Louisell & Harold Williams, Medical Malpractice § 21–10 (2d ed. 2000). See Stewart R. Reuter, Physicians as Good Samaritans, 20 J. Legal Med. 157 (1999); Danny R. Veilleux, Annotation, Construction and Application of "Good Samaritan" Statutes, 68 A.L.R.4th 294 (1989).

[262] E.g., Cal. Bus. & Prof. Code § 1627.5 (dentists).

[263] Perkins v. Howard, 232 Cal. App.3d 708, 283 Cal. Rptr. 764 (1991).

[264] E.g., N.C. Gen. Stat. § 20–166(d).

[265] E.g., Home Star Bank and Financial Services v. Emergency Care and Health Organization, Ltd., 2014 IL 115526, 6 N.E.3d 128, 379 Ill. Dec. 51 (2014) (treatment is not "without fee" for purposes of Good Samaritan Act where the doctor is compensated for his time working, even where patient is not charged).

[266] E.g., Conn. Gen. Stat. Ann. § 52–557b. See Velazquez v. Jiminez, 172 N.J. 240, 798 A.2d 51 (2002) (categorizing statutes, and concluding that the statute should be construed to apply only in cases where equipment, assistance and sanitation were not available, making it inapplicable to doctors working in hospital emergencies).

[267] Perkins v. Howard, 232 Cal. App.3d 708, 283 Cal. Rptr. 764 (1991). Statutes in some states expressly provide an immunity for the provision of medical care in an emergency room. See Johnson v. Omondi, 294 Ga.

and even to operating room cases where no emergency exists and the surgeon only mistakenly believes that it does.[268]

Some states go on to provide similar protections to other specified persons such as ambulance personnel or teachers on school grounds,[269] and even to any person acting in an emergency.[270] Some specifically apply the special protection to medical professionals who volunteer to provide medical services at sports events and who are thus prepared for the emergency that arises but who are not paid for their services.[271]

The purported basis for these statutes was that they were needed to encourage physicians to render assistance in roadside emergencies. The idea was that without the statute's immunity, physicians would refuse to provide medical care for fear of legal liability. In fact, however, suits for negligent medical care rendered in such emergencies are practically non-existent. When such suits are brought, the due care standard or the traditional standard for physicians would afford full protection. Those standards take account of the fact that one acting in an emergency is not necessarily at his best and that equipment and professional assistance may be lacking.[272] When the statute's immunity is extended to cover doctors working in hospital emergencies, the rationale changes from fear of liability to a desire to encourage voluntary medical services in the hospital itself.[273]

Some other statutes do not invariably eliminate liability for negligence but instead require the plaintiff to wage an uphill battle. For instance, a statute may require the plaintiff to prove negligence by clear and convincing evidence rather than by a preponderance of the evidence.[274]

§ 21.14 The "Malpractice Crisis" Statutes

Respected studies have shown that only a small fraction of people who are negligently injured by health care providers actually make claims.[275] Nevertheless, an apparent increase in malpractice litigation has been almost the constant story of medical

---

74, 751 S.E.2d 288 (2013) (construing Ga. Code Ann. 51–1–29.5(c), holding that fact issue remained as to whether the defendant's actions constituted "gross negligence" and were therefore outside the statute's protection).

[268] Pemberton v. Dharmani, 207 Mich. App. 522, 525 N.W.2d 497 (1994).

[269] Conn. Gen. Stat. Ann. § 52–557b (teachers not liable for negligence in administering aid on school grounds); TransCare Maryland, Inc. v. Murray, 431 Md. 225, 64 A.3d 887 (2013) (statute providing immunity to certain members of government-operated or volunteer fire departments, ambulance or rescue squads, or law enforcement agencies, held not to apply to employees of "commercial ambulance services").

[270] See Swenson v. Waseca Mut. Ins. Co., 653 N.W.2d 794 (Minn. App. 2002) (statute protected a stranger-driver who voluntarily picked up a snowmobiler with a dislocated knee, then made a U-turn into the path of a speeding truck as she headed for the hospital, causing the death of the snowmobiler); Certification of a Question of Law from United States District Court, 779 N.W.2d 158 (S.D. 2010) (statute protecting a number of specific persons, including members of any "rescue or emergency squad, or any citizen acting as such as a volunteer, applied to protect a volunteer" firefighter from liability).

[271] Ariz. Rev. Stat. § 32–1472. In these statutes and some others, the theme of the now-discredited guest statutes seems prominent, namely that one who is not paid owes no duty of reasonable care.

[272] See § 10.7 (emergency rules).

[273] See Hirpa v. IHC Hosps., Inc., 948 P.2d 785 (Utah 1997).

[274] Ga. Code Ann. § 51–1–29.5(c) (requiring proof of gross negligence by clear and convincing evidence); see also Ariz. Rev. Stat. § 32–1473 (when negligence is claimed in connection with emergency labor or delivery).

[275] See Paul C. Weiler, Howard H. Hiatt, Joseph P. Newhouse, William G. Johnson, Troyen A. Brennan, & Lucian L. Leape, A Measure of Malpractice (1993) (reflecting, in one study, 27,179 negligent medical injuries with only 3,682 claims). Persons with the best claims often do not sue. See Localio, Lawthers, Brennan, Laird, Hebert, Peterson, Newhouse, Weiler & Hiatt, Relation between Malpractice Claims and Adverse Events Due to Negligence, 325 N. Eng. J. Med. 245 (July 25, 1991).

malpractice since 1840.[276] Many observers have thought that malpractice litigation increased in particular sometime after World War II. By about 1970 the perception of increased litigation was raising concerns among health care professionals to new levels. One undisputed reality was that premiums for medical malpractice insurance rose, probably in part because the insurers' investments of premium income were bringing smaller returns, perhaps in part because the insurance industry was (and is) largely unregulated. In some places, malpractice insurance was difficult to procure at all.

Medical professionals and their representatives called this a "malpractice crisis." They generally blamed lawyers rather than negligent physicians or unregulated insurers, and there are current efforts to limit the fees of plaintiffs' lawyers.[277] In a few states, the term crisis might not have been hyperbole; but considered overall, doctors' incomes increased more in the critical period than the cost of insurance, so that they were actually paying a smaller percentage of their income on premiums.[278] If the crisis was not as clear as it seemed, the effect of litigation in producing it was just as uncertain.[279] Many studies show that there has been little or no increase in medical malpractice recoveries,[280] even though insurers continue to raise premiums.[281]

One theme commonly advanced by supporters of the health care industry is that American juries are biased against doctors and have more or less gone crazy. This notion has been thoroughly disproved. In fact, studies indicate that juries more than doctors tend to forgive medical negligence and find for the defendant doctor far more often than for the plaintiff.[282] Another theme that has now clearly been advanced by health care providers is that individual responsibility or "blame" for medical negligence is unacceptable and that liability should be directed only at institutions and systems.[283] In any event, the health care profession demanded relief from the threat of responsibility in tort and many legislatures responded. Besides statutory provisions intended to guarantee that insurance would be available, legislation, which differed from state to state, often introduced substantive, remedial, or procedural changes.

Substantive changes. In varying combinations, substantive changes at the state level included the following: (1) The standard of care was narrowed to the defendant's own local community in contrast to the increasing common-law acceptance of a similar

---

[276] See Kenneth Allen de Ville, Medical Malpractice in Nineteenth-Century America: Origins and Legacy 3 (1990).

[277] See Casey L. Dwyer, An Empirical Examination of the Equal Protection Challenge to Contingency Fee Restrictions in Medical Malpractice Reform Statutes, 56 Duke L. J. 611 (2006).

[278] See 1 Barry R. Furrow, Thomas L. Greaney, Sandra H. Johnson, Timothy S. Jost, & Robert L. Schwartz, Health Law § 6–20 (2d ed. 2000).

[279] See Id.

[280] See Deborah Jones Merritt & Kathryn Ann Barry, Is the Tort System in Crisis? New Empirical Evidence, 60 Ohio St. L.J. 315 (1999). Another study examined over 1400 closed claims, and concluded that medical errors in fact existed in about 60 of them. Most of the claims not involving medical error found by the investigators were not paid. David M. Studdert, Michelle M. Mello, Atul A. Gawande, Tejal K. Gandhi, Allen Kachalia, Catherine Yoon, Ann Louise Puopolo & Troyen A. Brennan, Claims, Errors, and Compensation Payments in Medical Malpractice Litigation, 354 New Eng. J. Med. 2024 (2006).

[281] See Casey L. Dwyer, An Empirical Examination of the Equal Protection Challenge to Contingency Fee Restrictions in Medical Malpractice Reform Statutes, 56 Duke L. J. 611 (2006) (tabulating premium increases and amounts in all states).

[282] Philip G. Peters, Jr., Doctors & Juries, 105 Mich. L. Rev. 1453 (2007) (reviewing, re-analyzing, and explaining the studies).

[283] See Institute of Medicine, To Err is Human: Building a Safer Healthy System (2000); American Law Institute, Reporter's Study of Enterprise Liability (1991) (proposing to eliminate individual doctors' liability in favor of hospital liability).

community or national community standard.[284] (2) Informed consent claims were limited or discouraged, for instance, by adopting a medical standard of disclosure rather than a materiality standard.[285] Claims for actual battery were sometimes abolished altogether.[286] (3) Res ipsa loquitur was eliminated from medical negligence claims;[287] or was limited to specific lists of cases such as those in which surgical instruments were left within the patient's body.[288] (4) The statute of limitations defense was strengthened in several ways, for example, by restricting the discovery rule[289] and by enacting statutes of repose which could bar some claims before the patient could discover the harm done.[290]

Remedial changes. The most striking crisis legislation capped the damages recoverable in malpractice suits, either by limiting pain and suffering recovery or by limiting the total that could be recovered even for actual money costs of a serious injury.[291] Other provisions tinkered with special damages rules like the collateral source rule, or permitted periodic payment of judgments.[292]

Procedural changes. Legislatures enacted various procedural impediments along the road to suit, including requirements that medical malpractice claims be screened by a panel which may include health care providers. Panel decisions on the merits may lead the parties to a settlement, but if not, the panel decision may be introduced in evidence at trial.[293] Other statutes promoted binding arbitration.[294] Plaintiffs were sometimes required to file special notices before suit could be brought[295] and attorneys were required to personally certify the quality of the claim or to supply an affidavit of a physician. Some statutes imposed severe restrictions on expert testimony, excluding testimony of experienced health care professionals in the community if they had not

---

[284] Idaho Code § 6–1012.

[285] E.g., Ark. Code Ann. § 16–114–206 (physician need only disclose "type of information . . . as would customarily have been given to a patient in the position of the injured person . . . by other medical care providers with similar training and experience" at the same time and in the same or similar locality); N.C. Gen. Stat. § 0–21.13.

[286] In Duncan v. Scottsdale Med. Imaging, Ltd., 205 Ariz. 306, 70 P.3d 435 (2003), the court held that a statute abolishing battery claims against health care providers was in violation of the state constitution's protection of common law actions.

[287] Idaho Code § 6–1012 (in malpractice action, claimant must prove breach of community standard by direct expert testimony); N.H. Rev. Stat. Ann. § 507–C:2 ("In any action for medical injury, the doctrine of res ipsa loquitur shall not apply") (held unconstitutional in Carson v. Maurer, 120 N.H. 925, 424 A.2d 825 (1980), *overruled on other grounds*, Community Resources for Justice, Inc. v. City of Manchester, 154 N.H. 748, 917 A.2d 707 (2007)).

[288] Nev. Rev. Stat. § 41A.100 (five exceptions which codify the pattern of cases, but which leave no room for cases the drafters had not considered); N.D. Cent. Code § 28–01–46.

[289] See, e.g., Schroeder v. Weighall, 179 Wash.2d 566 (2014) (statute that eliminated tolling for minority in medical malpractice actions struck down as unconstitutional).

[290] See § 18.4.

[291] For a thorough discussion of the lack of rationality in using damages caps to address an "alleged medical malpractice insurance crisis," see Estate of McCall v. United States, 134 So.3d 894 (Fla. 2014) (striking down statutory cap on noneconomic damages as violative of equal protection under state constitution). For a discussion of damages caps generally, see § 486.

[292] See § 34.3 (collateral source rule and abolition under tort reform statutes).

[293] E.g., Kan. Stat. Ann. § 60–4904.

[294] See 1 Barry R. Furrow, Thomas L. Greaney, Sandra H. Johnson, Timothy S. Jost, & Robert L. Schwartz, Health Law § 6–21 (2d ed. 2000).

[295] Hillsborough Cnty. Hosp. Authority v. Coffaro, 829 So.2d 862 (2002), illustrates some of the complex effects on statutes of limitations of these pre-suit notice statutes.

engaged in clinical practice of the same or related specialty within one year, whether or not they had knowledge of the standards.[296]

Negligence unrelated to diagnosis, treatment, or care. Because the malpractice crisis statutes may eliminate a claim altogether (under a stringent statute of limitations, for example) or prevent recovery of all the plaintiff's actual damages (under a cap), it is often in the plaintiff's interest to claim that the provider's tort was not "malpractice," but some other kind of negligence.[297] Presumably a slip-and-fall on a hospital floor is purely mechanical, not malpractice at all,[298] yet Ohio applied its health care provider statute to a case in which the plaintiff's wheelchair collapsed.[299] A battery or other intentional tort may escape the terms of a statute capping damages in professional "negligence" cases.[300] Although a nursing home may be obliged to provide nursing diagnosis and evaluation of care by nursing staff, the special demands of the medical malpractice statutes do not necessarily apply to actions for breach of statutory duties under elder-care or nursing-home statutes.[301]

§ 21.15 Patient's Contributory Negligence

Because a medical malpractice action is a specific instance of a negligence claim, the affirmative defenses that apply in ordinary negligence actions also apply in medical malpractice claims, although the different context may have some effects.

In malpractice cases, the patient's negligence bars the claim or reduces the damages according to the rule applicable generally under governing law, provided the plaintiff's fault is a factual and proximate cause of the harm complained of.[302] The patient is completely barred in jurisdictions that reject comparative fault rules generally[303] or for medical malpractice cases in particular.[304] In most states, the patient's own causal fault only reduces his damages, unless, in a modified comparative fault jurisdiction, his fault is equal to or greater than the physician's.[305]

---

[296] See, e.g., Endorf v. Bohlender, 26 Kan. App. 2d 855, 995 P.2d 896 (2000); Perdieu v. Blackstone Family Practice Center, Inc., 264 Va. 408, 568 S.E.2d 703 (2002).

[297] See, e.g., Psychiatric Solutions, Inc. v. Palit, 414 S.W.3d 724 (Tex. 2013); R.K. v. St. Mary's Medical Center, Inc., 229 W. Va. 712, 735 S.E.2d 715 (2012) (patient's claim for unauthorized disclosure of confidential medical information not governed by medical malpractice statute's limitations).

[298] But see Marks v. St. Luke's Episcopal Hosp., 319 S.W.3d 658 (Tex. 2010) (patient's negligence claim based on falling from his bed, alleging that the hospital was negligent in failing to provide a safe environment and in assembling or maintaining the bed, was a "health care liability" claim within the meaning of the Texas Medical Liability statute, and thus properly dismissed for failing to file expert reports).

[299] Rome v. Flower Memorial Hosp., 70 Ohio St.3d14, 635 N.E.2d 1239 (1994) (claim was medical and thus had to be brought within one year); contra, Williamson v. Hosp. Serv. Dist. No. 1 of Jefferson, 888 So.2d 782 (La. 2004) (considering whether the defendant's act involved assessment of the patient's condition and other matters).

[300] Perry v. Shaw, 88 Cal. App. 4th 658, 106 Cal. Rptr. 2d 70 (2001).

[301] Integrated Health Care Servs., Inc. v. Lang-Redway, 840 So. 2d 974 (Fla. 2002).

[302] E.g., Viox v. Weinberg, 169 Ohio App.3d 79, 861 N.E.2d 909 (2006); Zak v. Zifferblatt, 292 Wis.2d 502, 715 N.W.2d 739 (Ct. App. 2006) (patient's delay in returning for care not shown to have caused any harm).

[303] Hall v. Carter, 825 A.2d 954 (D.C. 2003) (patient's contributory negligence a complete bar and, on the facts, the last clear chance doctrine did not apply to save her claim); Dehn v. Edgecombe, 384 Md. 606, 865 A.2d 603 (2005).

[304] Cavens v. Zaberdac, 849 N.E.2d 526 (Ind. 2006) (comparative negligence act did not apply to medical malpractice claims).

[305] E.g., Shea v. Esensten, 622 N.W.2d 130 (Minn. App. 2001) (no error to instruct on comparative fault where patient failed to follow physician's advice to quit smoking, failed to take all medication, and failed to go to the emergency room as instructed).

A patient's failure to follow instructions,[306] to return for further care,[307] and even to accurately report medical history or symptoms[308] have all been counted as plaintiff fault, although a failure to report symptoms or history accurately might in some cases simply show that the physician was not negligent at all because he responded appropriately to the symptoms reported.

In the medical malpractice context, however, the plaintiff is entitled to rely heavily on the physician; the patient is not required to self-diagnose or to report symptoms he has no reason to suspect are relevant,[309] much less to seek a second opinion.[310] More broadly, what counts as contributory fault chargeable against the plaintiff may be limited by the doctor's duty. The patient's act of self-risk may be one the doctor has a duty to prevent. If so, it is logically improper to assert that act as contributory fault.[311]

In some states, plaintiff fault that occurs after the physician's negligent conduct will be treated under the rules of avoidable consequences or minimizing damages rather than under the rules of comparative fault.[312] One effect of this is that even if the plaintiff's post-injury negligence is greater than the physician's, the plaintiff will not be barred completely in a modified comparative fault jurisdiction. Rather, her damages will be reduced to the extent that her post-injury fault caused additional harm. The Restatement view is that comparative fault rules supersede the old minimizing damages approach.[313]

Pre-treatment fault of the patient that caused the injury or condition treated by the physician is logically irrelevant. The physician undertakes to treat the plaintiff as she is. Consequently, an injured person, one who smokes, or one who is overweight is entitled to full care without a reduction because the condition she brought to the doctor for medical attention was her own fault. The courts almost completely agree that pre-treatment fault of the patient does not count as contributory fault, either to bar the plaintiff or reduce her damages.[314]

---

[306] E.g., Harlow v. Chin, 405 Mass. 697, 545 N.E.2d 602 (1989) (if doctor told patient to return if pain intensified, patient could be charged with comparative fault in not returning for an extended period).

[307] Dehn v. Edgecombe, 384 Md. 606, 865 A.2d 603 (2005) (vasectomy patient failed to follow post-op instructions for semen testing, contributory negligence a bar).

[308] Hall v. Carter, 825 A.2d 954 (D.C. 2003) (patient who told surgeon she smoked half a pack of cigarettes a day, but didn't mention that she had smoked two packs a day until recently; this was contributory negligence that barred her claim for malpractice); Elkins v. Ferencz, 694 N.Y.S.2d 27 (App. Div. 1999) (failure to furnish accurate medical history; also patient's use of drugs and delay of treatment).

[309] See Jackson v. Axelrad, 221 S.W.3d 650 (Tex. 2007) ("Doctors are paid for their expertise, so diagnosis will always be primarily their responsibility. Thus, we agree with the court of appeals that in most cases an ordinary patient's failure to report the origin of pain will be no evidence of negligence.").

[310] Brown v. Dibbell, 227 Wis.2d 28, 595 N.W.2d 358 (Wis. 1999).

[311] Argus v. Scheppegrell, 472 So.2d 573 (La. 1985) (doctor could not defend on the ground that an addicted teenager was at fault in taking prescribed drugs, since taking drugs was the very act the doctor was under a duty to prevent by refusing a prescription).

[312] E.g., Keans v. Bottiarelli, 35 Conn. App. 239, 645 A.2d 1029 (1994); Hopkins v. Silber, 141 Md. App. 319, 785 A.2d 806 (2001) (patient's effort to have sexual intercourse soon after penile implants). On the minimizing damages or avoidable consequences rules and comparative fault see §§ 16.10 & 16.11.

[313] See § 16.10.

[314] Cavens v. Zaberdac, 849 N.E.2d 526 (Ind. 2006) ("It is a staple of tort law that the tortfeasor takes her victim as she finds him."); Lambert v. Shearer, 84 Ohio App.3d 266, 616 N.E.2d 965 (1992) (plaintiff fault does not count against plaintiff unless it is "contemporaneous" with the physician's negligence); Mercer v. Vanderbilt Univ., Inc., 134 S.W.3d 121 (Tenn. 2004); Eiss v. Lillis, 233 Va. 545, 357 S.E.2d 539 (1987); Restatement Third of Torts, Apportionment § 7, cmt. m (2000); Ellen M. Bublick, Comparative Fault to the Limits, 56 Vand. L. Rev. 977, 1017 (2003); contra, Shinholster v. Annapolis Hosp., 471 Mich. 540, 685 N.W.2d 275 (2004).

B. HOSPITALS AND MANAGED CARE ORGANIZATIONS

§ 21.16 Common-Law Responsibility of Hospitals

National or reasonable person standard of care. The conflict between local and national standards of care has never been as intense in the case of hospitals as it has been with individual physicians. The consensus seems to be that, except when the hospital's liability is vicarious and premised on a doctor's negligence,[315] the duty of hospitals toward patients is to act with reasonable care under all the circumstances,[316] or in accordance with the national standard of care for hospitals.[317] One basis for this view is that all hospitals accredited by the Joint Commission must follow national standards set by that accrediting organization in order to get and keep that accreditation. The Joint Commission's standards,[318] the hospital's own bylaws based on national standards,[319] and any statutory requirements are at least evidence of a minimal standard of care.

Immunity. Hospital liability, although now accepted, did not come easily. First, under traditional rules, charitable hospitals, like other charities,[320] were immune to suit for their tortious activities. Similarly, governmentally operated hospitals once shared in governmental immunities.[321] Both the charitable and governmental immunity have generally been abolished or modified, but vestiges remain. In some states, new immunities have been erected[322] or recovery of damages limited,[323] often as part of widespread efforts to reduce legal responsibility for negligence generally.

Practice of medicine. Second, courts once held that corporations—hospitals—could not legally practice medicine and therefore could not control physicians working in the hospital. For that reason, some of the older cases held that, contrary to the ordinary rules of agency law, hospitals could not be vicariously liable for the negligence of physicians, even those actually employed by the hospital.[324] This view has changed radically but not universally. Hospitals and medical corporations that do not enjoy an immunity on other grounds are now generally subjected to liability for the medical negligence of their employees,[325] but the view is not universal.[326]

---

[315] See Advincula v. United Blood Services, 176 Ill.2d 1, 678 N.E.2d 1009, 223 Ill.Dec. 1 (1996).

[316] Shilkret v. Annapolis Emergency Hospital Ass'n, 276 Md. 187, 349 A.2d 245 (1975); Johnson v. Hillcrest Health Ctr., Inc., 70 P.3d 811 (Okla. 2003); Duling v. Bluefield Sanitarium, Inc., 149 W.Va. 567, 142 S.E.2d 754 (1965); see also Pederson v. Dumouchel, 72 Wash.2d 73, 431 P.2d 973 (1967).

[317] Wickliffe v. Sunrise Hospital, Inc., 104 Nev. 777, 766 P.2d 1322 (1988).

[318] E.g., Health Trust, Inc. v. Cantrell, 689 So.2d 822 (Ala. 1997).

[319] Pedroza v. Bryant, 101 Wash. 2d 226, 677 P.2d 166 (1984).

[320] § 23.3.

[321] See Chapter 22 (governmental immunities).

[322] See St. Luke's Episcopal Hospital v. Agbor, 952 S.W.2d 503 (Tex. 1997).

[323] See § 34.7 (tort reform statutes).

[324] Rosane v. Senger, 112 Colo. 363, 149 P.2d 372 (1944) (a view reestablished by statute); see Hamburger v. Cornell University, 240 N.Y. 328, 148 N.E. 539 (N.Y. 1925) (per Cardozo, J., a slightly different formulation getting the same result).

[325] Dias v. Brigham Med. Assocs., Inc., 438 Mass. 317, 780 N.E.2d 447 (2002) (professional corporation employing physician would be liable as employer even if it had no right to control details of his treatment of patient); Bing v. Thunig, 2 N.Y.2d 656, 143 N.E.2d 3, 163 N.Y.S.2d 3 (1957) (overruling cases supporting the earlier view). Statutes sometimes expressly or impliedly permit corporate practice of medicine through individuals who are licensed. E.g., Ariz. Rev. Stats. §§ 10–3301.

[326] See, e.g., Colo. Rev. Stat. Ann. § 13–64–202 (eliminating hospitals' vicarious liability for physician negligence). Similar provisions are sometimes enacted for the benefit of health service plans.

Vicarious liability. Private physicians who attend their own patients in a hospital are independent contractors, not employees of the hospital.[327] Consequently, the hospital is not vicariously responsible for the negligence of such an independent contractor-physician.[328] But the hospital or clinic is now vicariously liable under agency principles for the negligent acts of its own employees if those acts are committed within the scope of employment.[329] For instance, patients can pursue claims against hospitals and clinics for the negligence of its paramedics or emergency medical technicians,[330] physician assistants,[331] paid resident physicians,[332] and nurses it employs.[333]

Ostensible agency. By estoppel or ostensible agency, the hospital may also be liable when it creates or sustains the appearance that an independent physician or surgeon is its employee.[334] So if the hospital contracts with independent physicians for its emergency room work,[335] or X-ray lab,[336] or anesthesia services,[337] but presents those services as part of the routine hospital work, juries are allowed to find that the independent contractor/physician was the ostensible agent of the hospital so that the hospital becomes liable for his negligence. And of course a hospital may actually employ physicians to carry out medical duties, and if so, it is subject to vicarious liability for their torts committed within the scope of their employment.[338]

"Corporate negligence." The claim of corporate negligence is not based upon vicarious liability of the hospital for acts of a physician or surgeon. The leading case is *Darling v. Charleston Community Memorial Hospital,*[339] where a doctor's treatment of a broken leg in the defendant hospital led to gangrene and amputation of the leg. The plaintiff claimed that the hospital (1) should have provided nurses sufficiently trained to recognize the signs of gangrene early enough to have avoided the need for amputation, and (2) should have provided some kind of supervision or review of the doctor's treatment. The court thought that both claims were tenable and supported by the evidence. In line with *Darling*, the cases now generally recognize that the hospital itself owes the patient a non-delegable duty of care.[340] Hospitals are thus subject to liability if

---

[327] See Clark v. St. Dominic-Jackson Memorial Hospital, 660 So.2d 970 (Miss. 1995); Pedroza v. Bryant, 101 Wash. 2d 226, 677 P.2d 166 (1984).

[328] Renown Health, Inc. v. Vanderford, 126 Nev. 24, 235 P.3d 614 (2010).

[329] Statutes may say this explicitly. See Grove v. PeaceHealth St. Joseph's Hospital, 341 P.3d 261 (Wash. 2014) (affirming jury verdict for patient against hospital; statutory definition of "health care provider" includes any "entity" employing physicians, physicians' assistants, or nurses acting in the scope of employment).

[330] Cf. Calloway v. City of New Orleans, 524 So.2d 182 (La. App. 1988) ("corpsman" trained like ambulance attendant).

[331] Cox v. M.A. Primary and Urgent Care Clinic, 313 S.W.3d 240 (Tenn. 2010).

[332] Register v. Wilmington Medical Center, Inc., 377 A.2d 8. (Del. 1977); Moeller v. Hauser, 237 Minn. 368, 54 N.W.2d 639, 57 A.L.R.2d 364 (1952).

[333] See Providence Hospital, Inc. v. Willis, 103 A.3d 533 (D.C. 2014); McMillan v. Durant, 312 S.C. 200, 439 S.E.2d 829 (1993). As to standard of care for nurses, see 2 Dobbs, Hayden & Bublick, The Law of Torts § 301 (2d ed. 2011 & Supp.).

[334] Wilkins v. Marshalltown Medical and Surgical Center, 758 N.W.2d 232 (Iowa 2008); Renown Health, Inc. v. Vanderford, 235 P.3d 614 (Nev. 2010); Clark v. Southview Hosp. & Family Health Center, 68 Ohio St.3d 435, 628 N.E.2d 46, 58 A.L.R.5th 929 (1994).

[335] E.g., Jackson v. Power, 743 P.2d 1376 (Alaska 1987) (now refined by Alaska Stats. § 09.65.096); Simmons v. Tuomey Regional Medical Center, 341 S.C. 32, 533 S.E.2d 312 (2000).

[336] Sampson v. Contillo, 55 A.D.3d 588, 865 N.Y.S.2d 634(2008).

[337] See Seneris v. Haas, 45 Cal.2d 811, 291 P.2d 915 (1955).

[338] See Biddle v. Sartori Memorial Hospital, 518 N.W.2d 795 (Iowa 1994).

[339] Darling v. Charleston Cmty. Mem. Hosp., 33 Ill.2d 326, 211 N.E.2d 253 (1965).

[340] See, e.g., Aidan Ming-Ho Leung v. Verdugo Hills Hosp., 55 Cal. 4th 291, 145 Cal. Rptr. 3d 553, 282 P.3d 1250 (2012).

they fail to provide appropriate facilities, equipment, and staff support,[341] fail to maintain the patient's chart accurately and in a timely manner,[342] and if they negligently select or train employees[343] or negligently review or supervise[344] physicians who are permitted to use the hospital's resources.

Changes. Although the common-law development of hospital liability is somewhat uneven, its general direction seems clear. From the earlier no-liability rules, courts have increasingly recognized that hospitals may be liable for the negligence of their own medical employees, for that of independent contractor-physicians who are identified with the hospital in the public mind, and even for failure to supervise or exclude physicians whose skill is not to be trusted.[345] The direction suggested by these changes perhaps forecast others, such as the studied proposal to impose strict liability[346] and the federal statute prohibiting "patient dumping."[347]

§ 21.17 Mandatory Hospital Screening and Treatment: EMTALA

Common law. The usual common law view is that, subject only to the most limited kinds of exceptions, no individual or entity is legally obliged to aid a person who is ill or injured.[348] Although neither hospitals nor doctors could abandon a person who had been accepted as a patient,[349] neither would be required to accept a patient in the first place. For example, doctors and hospitals could refuse patients who were unable to pay for its services.[350] Some courts developed a limited exception, requiring a hospital to give at least some treatment to a patient who presented an unmistakable medical emergency.[351]

EMTALA statute generally. Protected by the common law rules, some hospitals engaged in "patient dumping," refusing treatment for the impecunious and uninsured. Congress enacted the Emergency Medical Treatment and Active Labor Act (EMTALA) in 1986 to alleviate that problem.[352] That statute requires hospitals that have emergency departments and that are part of the Medicare program to provide medical screening and emergency treatment under specified conditions, but it is not limited to Medicare

---

[341] Register v. Wilmington Medical Center, Inc., 377 A.2d 8. (Del. 1977); Douglas v. Freeman, 117 Wash.2d 242, 814 P.2d 1160 (1991). See Edward L. Raymond, Jr., Annotation, Medical Malpractice: Hospital's Liability For Injury Allegedly Caused by Failure to Have Properly Qualified Staff, 62 A.L.R.4th 692 (1989). Understaffing in hospitals may be actionable if it causes harm to a patient, as it is in nursing home cases. See Staley v. Northern Utah Healthcare Corp., 230 P.3d 1007 (Utah 2010).

[342] Johnson v. Hillcrest Health Ctr., Inc., 70 P.3d 811 (Okla. 2003).

[343] Healthtrust, Inc. v. Cantrell, 689 So.2d 822 (Ala. 1997); Doe v. Guthrie Clinic, Ltd., 22 N.Y.3d 480, 5 N.E.3d 578 (2014).

[344] Oehler v. Humana Inc., 105 Nev. 348, 775 P.2d 1271 (1989); Pedroza v. Bryant, 101 Wash. 2d 226, 677 P.2d 166 (1984). But see Paulino v. QHG of Springdale, Inc., 2012 Ark. 55, 386 S.W.3d 462 (2012) (rejecting a cause of action for negligent credentialing and negligent retention, finding the creation of such a cause of action would be at odds with Arkansas statutes concerning the peer review of health service employees).

[345] See, emphasizing the general historical movement toward increased hospital liability, Clark C. Havighurst, Making Health Plans Accountable for the Quality of Care, 31 Ga. L. Rev. 587 (1997).

[346] See 2 American Law Institute, Reporter's Study of Enterprise Liability for Personal Injury 515 (1991); Paul Weiler, Medical Malpractice on Trial 132–158 (1991).

[347] § 21.17.

[348] § 25.1.

[349] See Lyons v. Grether, 218 Va. 630, 239 S.E.2d 103 (1977).

[350] See Harper v. Baptist Medical Center-Princeton, 341 So.2d 133 (Ala. 1976).

[351] See Walling v. Allstate Ins. Co., 183 Mich. App. 731, 455 N.W.2d 736 (1990).

[352] 42 U.S.C.A. § 1395dd.

patients or even to uninsured or impecunious patients.[353] The statute specifically provides that a civil action may be brought for its violation.[354] By it terms, the statute's civil remedies run only against the covered hospitals, not to physicians.[355]

Duties to screen and stabilize. If an individual "comes to the emergency department" with a medical request, the hospital is potentially subjected to two duties. First, it must provide "appropriate" medical screening within the limits of the hospital's capability.[356] Second, if the hospital "determines" that an individual has an emergency medical condition—which is defined to include active labor[357]—the hospital must ordinarily provide medical attention to stabilize that condition before transferring the patient.[358] In the case of active labor, stabilization means complete delivery. Otherwise, stabilization requires treatment that reasonably assures that no deterioration of the condition would result from transfer to another facility.[359] Liability for failure to stabilize does not require proof that the hospital had a discriminatory or other bad motive.[360]

Role of state-law malpractice. EMTALA is not a general malpractice statute and it does not preempt state tort law claims. A hospital that abandons an accepted patient might thus be liable under state law, even if it is not responsible under the federal statute.[361] State law governs damages,[362] too, and for this reason courts have applied state statutory caps to limit damages recovery under EMTALA if the cap would apply to a state-law claim based upon the same facts.[363]

The EMTALA statute does not set up a standard of care or prohibit negligent medical acts. Instead, it works through specific commands to provide appropriate medical screening and to provide medical treatment needed to assure that the condition is stabilized. Federal courts have striven to constrain the statute so that it does not become a substitute for state malpractice law. Consequently, they have held that the statute's requirement of "appropriate" screening does not create liability for negligent screening, but only screening that the hospital would provide to a paying patient, or patients generally.[364] On this basis it has been held that a hospital's negligent diagnosis and treatment of a patient is not itself actionable under EMTALA. Instead, the hospital that negligently diagnoses or treats an emergency patient is subject to the statutory liability only if it releases or transfers the patient with knowledge of the unstabilized emergency medical condition. As long as the hospital continues to provide screening and

---

[353] Morales v. Sociedad Espanola de Auxilio Mutuo y Beneficencia, 524 F.3d 54 (1st Cir. 2008); Cleland v. Bronson Health Care Group, Inc., 917 F.2d 266, 269 (6th Cir. 1990).

[354] 42 U.S.C.A. § 1395dd(c)(2).

[355] Moses v. Providence Hosp. and Medical Centers, Inc., 561 F.3d 573 (6th Cir. 2009); Cygan v. Kaleida Health, 51 A.D.3d 1373, 857 N.Y.S.2d 869 (2008). Physicians are, however, subject to civil money penalties for negligently violating the statute. 42 U.S.C.A. § 1395dd (c)(1)

[356] 42 U.S.C.A. § 1395dd(a).

[357] 42 U.S.C.A. § 1395dd(e)(1)(B).

[358] 42 U.S.C.A. § 1395dd(b).

[359] 42 U.S.C.A. § 1395dd(e)(3)(A).

[360] Roberts v. Galen of Virginia, Inc., 525 U.S. 249, 119 S.Ct. 685 (1999).

[361] See Bryan v. Rectors and Visitors of the University of Virginia, 95 F.3d 349 (4th Cir. 1996).

[362] 42 U.S.C.A. § 1399dd(d)(2)(A).

[363] Barris v. County of Los Angeles, 20 Cal. 4th 101, 972 P.2d 966, 83 Cal. Rptr. 2d 145 (1999); Godwin v. Memorial Medical Center, 130 N.M. 434, 25 P.3d 273 (2001) (but holding that pre-suit notice provision of state law was preempted).

[364] See Summers v. Baptist Medical Center Arkadelphia, 91 F.3d 1132 (8th Cir. 1996); Cleland v. Bronson Health Care Group, Inc., 917 F.2d 266 (6th Cir. 1990); Power v. Arlington Hospital Ass'n, 42 F.3d 851 (4th Cir. 1994).

treatment to stabilize the patient, it does not violate the EMTALA duty, even if it is negligent.[365] Even so, it would seem that the requirement of "appropriate" screening appeals to some kind of normative standard. For this reason, a failure to meet ordinary hospital standards in screening a patient looks like an inappropriate screening, even if the hospital treats all its patients equally badly. In fact, it has been held that if the hospital does not screen at all or its acts are not calculated to reveal medical emergencies, liability follows.[366]

§ 21.18 Managed Care Organizations

The Managed Care Structure vs. Fee-for-Service

The traditional rules of professional liability originated in a fee-for-service system. Patients paid health care professionals for a service. If patients were insured or covered by statutory programs like Medicare or Medicaid, the insurer or the program paid for the service agreed upon by doctor and patient. Under this system, doctors might prefer to recommend more than optimum diagnosis or treatment, say an X-ray "just to be sure." If they were covered by programs or insurance, patients might insist on more. Whether entirely for these reasons or not, costs soared.

Managed care systems, well on their way to replacing the fee-for-service approach, attempt to achieve cost-effective medical care. The idea is to minimize total costs without reducing overall good medical outcomes. Managed care operates by interposing a third force between doctor and patient, a kind of economically efficient medical conscience that says no to some diagnoses or treatments.

The term Managed Care Organization (or "MCO") refers to any form of managed care structure. A familiar version is the Health Maintenance Organization (or "HMO"). Employers might contract with an HMO to provide comprehensive health care services for all employees, who might in turn contribute to the costs through payroll deductions. The HMO in turn either hires physicians or contracts with organizations of physicians to provide care. The HMO is not merely an insurer; it is actively engaged in managing health care costs by limiting the delivery of medical services unlikely to be helpful.

The amount and perhaps quality of care provided by an HMO is limited by several factors. (1) The contract itself may exclude certain care items such as experimental treatments. (2) The primary physician is usually the first physician to be seen by the patient; that physician acts as a gatekeeper who may have motives besides purely medical ones to limit the patient's access to some kinds of care by refusing a referral to the expensive specialized treatment or hospitalization. The non-medical motives arise from the HMO system for compensating physicians, under which physicians who refer less may be compensated more. (3) The physician is usually paid per capita, which is a specified fee for each patient seen during the coverage period. Repeat visits thus represent a cost to the physician without any increase in income from the HMO.

Inside a hospital, managed care may take the form of utilization review. Utilization review is a system of monitoring hospitalization time and notifying the hospital that the

---

[365] See, e.g., Cruz-Vazquez v. Mennonite General Hospital, Inc., 717 F.3d 63 (1st Cir. 2013) (hospital's own internal screening procedures set the parameters for an appropriate screening that will satisfy EMTALA).

[366] Correa v. Hospital San Francisco, 69 F.3d 1184 (1st Cir. 1995) (delay so egregious that it amounted to a denial of screening).

HMO or insurer will pay only for a specified hospital stay for a given illness or surgery. In the case of publicly funded hospital stays, regulations may perform the same function.

Potential Liability of MCOs

Vicarious responsibility—staff model. The HMO is a fiscal and management organization; it does not itself practice medicine. For this reason, some statutes provide complete immunity to the HMO against liability based on negligence of the person rendering services.[367] However, when the HMO is organized on the "staff model," it actually employs physicians, so that under ordinary agency principles, it would be legally responsible for their negligence within the scope of employment. At one time courts took the view that corporations could not practice medicine so that even if a physician were a corporate employee, the corporation could not exercise significant control and could not be vicariously liable. This view has been largely repudiated in the case of hospitals,[368] and it seems likely that most courts will also apply ordinary vicarious liability rules to HMOs.

Independent-provider model. The Independent Provider Association or IPA model for MCOs is structurally different. Here the MCO contracts with still another organization to provide physicians, or in a variation on that, contracts directly with independent physicians who would traditionally be seen as independent contractors, not employees of the HMO. Because the physicians in this situation usually appear to be independent contractors, the HMO is not vicariously responsible for their acts unless the plaintiff can show an exception to the rule.[369]

One set of exceptions holds the employer of independent contractors vicariously liable on an ostensible agency, apparent authority, or agency by estoppel theory.[370] In the case of hospitals, for example, the hospital may be liable for independent contractors who operate the hospital emergency room, since patients reasonably think that going to the emergency room is "going to the hospital;" they do not think they are consulting an unnamed independent contractor.[371] Although authority is sparse, some cases have carried over this idea to impose vicarious liability upon an IPA type MCO[372] or upon a staff type MCO who employs an independent consultant.[373]

The second exception is really an assertion that, in spite of appearance to the contrary, the physician is not an independent contractor because the MCO exercises pervasive control over his work and is thus in the role of a "master" who is vicariously liable. MCOs do in fact exercise a good deal of control—that is how cost containment works—but it is more likely to relate to the provision of expensive services rather than, say, a simple bad diagnosis. Not surprisingly, then, some courts have found the control

---

[367] 215 Ill. Comp. Stats, 165/26; Vernon's Ann. Mo. Stats. § 354.125. A statute in this form does not appear to address the question of liability for cost-savings decisions.

[368] § 21.16.

[369] Chase v. Independent Practice Ass'n, Inc., 31 Mass.App.Ct. 661, 583 N.E.2d 251 (1991). As to independent contractors and ostensible agency rules, see Petrovich v. Share Health Plan of Illinois, Inc., 188 Ill.2d 17, 241 Ill.Dec. 627, 719 N.E.2d 756 (1999).

[370] On the distinctions, see § 31.7.

[371] § 21.16 (ostensible agency in emergency department situations); § 31.7 (apparent authority or ostensible agency generally).

[372] Boyd v. Albert Einstein Medical Center, 377 Pa. Super. 609, 547 A.2d 1229 (1988).

[373] See Schleier v. Kaiser Found. Health Plan of the Mid-Atlantic States, Inc., 876 F.2d 174 (D.C.Cir. 1989).

not to be extensive enough to warrant vicarious liability.[374] But the question turns heavily upon details of evidence as well as argumentation in particular cases, and some authority has recognized that vicarious liability may be imposed under this exception.[375]

Direct liability—negligent selection or retention of physicians. Unless federal law preempts them, at least two kinds of claims might plausibly be asserted against an MCO that are not based on vicarious liability but on its own primary negligence. First, the analogy to hospital liability suggests that MCOs might well owe a duty of care in selecting and monitoring physicians and hospitals. If so, the MCO would be liable directly for its negligence in selecting or retaining an unsuitable physician, even when it would not be vicariously liable and some cases have so held.[376]

Cost-containment devices creating risks. Second, the cost-containment methods used by MCOs may undercut appropriate care in particular instances. If a cost-containment method such as utilization review effectively denies the patient her rights under the insurance or MCO plan and also counts as bad medical care, liability in tort or contract or both seems entirely appropriate.[377] The design of contractually valid cost-containment systems itself may create undue risks. The incentive system created by the compensation plans often provides the physician with more compensation if he uses fewer expensive tests and referrals. This may actually put the physician in a conflict of interest when medical needs might dictate a referral that would represent a dollar cost to the physician.[378] Other cost-containment features may involve the MCOs' dictation of drug and hospital choices that could conceivably be against the patient's interests.[379]

Informed consent or duty to provide information. The role of MCOs in providing important information to patients is a special problem. In some respects, the advent of managed care creates new risks, particularly risks associated with financial incentives and the absence of coverage for some treatments.[380] It is quite possible that courts will eventually impose a common law duty upon MCOs to provide certain important information to the subscriber-patient, perhaps including information about the

---

[374] E.g., Raglin v. HMO Illinois, Inc., 230 Ill.App.3d 642, 595 N.E.2d 153, 172 Ill.Dec. 90 (1992), overruled as to apparent authority, Petrovich v. Share Health Plan of Illinois, Inc., 188 Ill.2d 17, 241 Ill.Dec. 627, 719 N.E.2d 756 (1999).

[375] Schleier v. Kaiser Foundation Health Plan of the Mid-Atlantic States, Inc., 876 F.2d 174 (D.C. Cir. 1989) (staff model HMO hiring independent consultant); Villazon v. Prudential Health Care Plan, Inc., 843 So.2d 842 (Fla. 2003) (emphasizing right to control the "contractor" and the totality of circumstances).

[376] McClellan v. Health Maintenance Org. of Pa., 413 Pa. Super. 128, 604 A.2d 1053 (1992).

[377] See Mintz v. Blue Cross of California, 172 Cal.App.4th 1594, 92 Cal.Rptr.3d 422, 435 (2009) ("administrator of a health care plan owes a duty to plan members to exercise due care to protect them from physical injury caused by its negligence in making benefit determinations under the plan"); McEvoy v. Group Health Cooperative of Eau Claire, 213 Wis.2d 507, 570 N.W.2d 397 (1997) (HMO that refused, for cost-containment reasons, to approve continued "out of network" treatment needed by a patient and to which patient was entitled would be liable for bad faith breach of contract); Kathleen J. McKee, Annotation, Liability of Third-Party Health-Care Payor for Injury Arising from Failure to Authorize Required Treatment, 56 A.L.R.5th 737 (1998).

[378] See Neade v. Portes, 193 Ill. 2d 433, 739 N.E.2d 496, 250 Ill. Dec. 733 (2000).

[379] McKenzie v. Hawai'i Permanente Med. Group, Inc., 98 Hawai'i 296, 47 P.3d 1209 (2002) (rejecting HMO liability on the ground that health care decisions should be made by "stakeholders" such as physicians and professionals, not by courts).

[380] See Susan M. Wolf, Toward a Systemic Theory of Informed Consent in Managed Care, 35 Hous. L. Rev. 1631 (1999) (advocating "systemic analysis" and pointing to the need for information from MCOs and even employers who provide health plans); Joan H. Krause, Reconceptualizing Informed Consent in an Era of Health Care Cost Containment, 85 Iowa L. Rev. 261 (1999) (suggesting statutes and professional disciplinary approaches on the problem of information about non-covered treatment).

individual physician's record of success or failure.[381] However, the Supreme Court has held that the ERISA statute does not impose a fiduciary duty upon the MCO to reveal financial incentives adverse to the patient-subscriber.[382]

ERISA Preemption. The most serious impediment for many patients injured by managed care organizations is the prospect of federal preemption, which may leave the plaintiff without meaningful redress. The problem arises under the Employee Retirement Income Security Act (ERISA),[383] a federal statute intended to set uniform standards for employee benefit and retirement plans. The statute covers medical benefits provided through employment, and hence covers most managed care systems. By its terms, it "supersedes" state laws and court decisions that may "relate to any employee benefit plan" covered.[384] Where this provision applies, the covered employee (meaning a patient in the context of medical benefits) may sue under the federal statute itself to recover benefits denied.[385] But the patient may not sue for negligence that caused harms to her body when needed and covered medical care was denied.[386]

Sometimes preemption is a deadly vacuum, leaving the injured patient nothing, but the claim is not always "completely preempted."[387] Using various terminology, courts have sought to distinguish between an HMO's coverage or "eligibility" decisions, which are preempted, and its medical or treatment decisions, which are not, although the difference if any can be hard to spot.[388] If the claim against an HMO is based on the assertion of ordinary malpractice and vicarious liability, not based upon the denial of coverage or benefits, it is simply not preempted.[389] On the other hand, if the claim is that the plan wrongly denied benefits such as hospitalization, then that would be a benefits-denied case and thus preempted,[390] even if the coverage decision was made negligently.[391] Federal regulations attempt to control abusive denials of coverage, but an HMO's violation does not create any tort rights for the victim.[392]

---

[381] Aaron D. Twerski & Neil B. Cohen, The Second Revolution in Informed Consent: Comparing Physicians to Each Other, 94 Nw. U. L. Rev. 1 (1999); Lynn M. LoPucki, Twerski and Cohen's Second Revolution: A Systems/Strategic Perspective, 94 Nw. U. L. Rev. 55 (1999) (recognizing some possible adverse effects of such information but supporting disclosure nonetheless).

[382] Pegram v. Herdrich, 530 U.S. 211, 120 S.Ct. 2143, 147 L.Ed.2d 164 (2000).

[383] 29 U.S.C.A. §§ 1001 to 1461.

[384] 29 U.S.C.A. § 1144(a) & (c).

[385] "A civil action may be brought (1) by a participant or beneficiary . . . to recover benefits due to him under the terms of his plan, to enforce his rights under the terms of the plan, or to clarify his rights to future benefits under the terms of the plan. . . ." 29 U.S.C.A § 1132 (a).

[386] See Aetna Health Inc. v. Davila, 542 U.S. 200, 124 S.Ct. 2488 (2004).

[387] Dukes v. U.S. Healthcare, Inc., 57 F.3d 350 (3d Cir. 1995).

[388] See Pryzbowski v. U. S. Healthcare, Inc., 245 F.3d 266 (3d Cir. 2001) (HMO's long delay in approving needed services of a specialist was "administration of benefits," not a medical decision, hence the plaintiff was left "without effective relief"); Jennifer Arlen & W. Bentley MacLeod, Malpractice Liability for Physicians and Managed Care Organizations, 78 N.Y.U. L. Rev. 1929, 1947 (2003) ("MCO insurers can . . . deny coverage for any treatment that they conclude is either not medically necessary or experimental. This authority over insurance coverage effectively grants MCOs authority to determine the treatment their patients receive in certain circumstances.").

[389] Pacificare of Oklahoma, Inc. v. Burrage, 59 F.3d 151 (10th Cir. 1995) (also reflecting the split of authority on this point among lower courts); Villazon v. Prudential Health Care Plan, Inc., 843 So.2d 842 (Fla. 2003) (emphasizing right to control the "independent contractor" and the totality of circumstances).

[390] See Corcoran v. United Healthcare, Inc., 965 F.2d 1321 (5th Cir. 1992); Jass v. Prudential Health Care Plan, Inc., 88 F.3d 1482 (7th Cir. 1996).

[391] See Aetna Health Inc. v. Davila, 542 U.S. 200, 124 S.Ct. 2488 (2004).

[392] See 29 C.F.R. § 2560.503–1(c) & (*l*) (respectively dealing with delays in determining rights under the plan and providing that violation gives the patient a right to sue for benefits under the act (not tort damages)).

C. NURSING HOMES AND RESIDENTIAL FACILITIES

§ 21.19 Injuries in Nursing Homes and Other Care Facilities

The liability of nursing homes for residents' injuries is a subset of the larger topic of elder abuse.[393] Some other adult care homes may raise similar legal problems. Injuries to often-helpless nursing home residents are numerous, serious, painful, and often horrifying, disgusting and deadly. Gross estimates suggest that as many as five million seniors are abused each year.[394] Most residents suffer from serious physical and mental limitations that prevent them from revealing abuse or neglect, even if they are aware of what causes their pain and misery.

Surveys of nursing homes show that large numbers of them are deficient in standard care requirements. Not all deficiencies are serious, but the GAO concluded in 2002 that one-fourth of all nursing homes have deficiencies—substandard care—"that harmed residents or placed them at risk of death or serious injury."[395] Given that nursing homes are largely closed societies where injuries and bad practices may never be discovered, it is a safe bet that injury rates are much higher than these percentages suggest.

In one sense, most nursing home claims are like other tort claims—nursing homes may be sued for negligence in the same way hospitals can, and the plaintiff must show duty, breach, factual cause, proximate cause, and damages.[396] Similarly, apportionment of responsibility among several tortfeasors follows the state's apportionment rules as applied in other actions. Yet nursing home injury is a complex subject, and tort suits are difficult to pursue. At the same time, physicians who serve in nursing homes feel especially vulnerable to suit, although this feeling is often out of line with reality[397] and physicians' fear of liability may result in better care of nursing home residents.[398]

One difficulty is that the topic is relatively new and some fundamental conceptions are unsettled. Another is that nursing home conduct causing injuries ranges over a wide spectrum, some resembling professional malpractice and some resembling ordinary negligence. More significantly, the topic is conceptually clouded and imperfectly coherent because the conceptions and terminology in state and federal statutes and regulations come from a legal culture of regulation and administration in which protection is expected to come from state inspections and civil fines, not primarily from tort suits that enforce individual rights. At the same time, the regulatory agencies seek to maintain nursing homes at an operating level and to funnel Medicaid money to them, so there is

---

[393] Family and community abuse seems to be substantial. See Sieniarecki v. State, 756 So.2d 68 (Fla. 2000).

[394] See John B. Breaux & Orrin G. Hatch, Confronting Elder Abuse, Neglect, and Exploitation: The Need for Elder Justice Legislation, 11 Elder L.J. 207 (2003). There are almost no reliable data on the actual numbers.

[395] General Accounting Office, Nursing Home: More Can Be Done to Protect Residents from Abuse 2 (March 2002), available at www.gao.gov with search for GAO-02-312 (reviewing an earlier study). Deficiencies listed in official reports may be understated. See General Accounting Office, Many Shortcomings Exist in Efforts to Protect Nursing Home Residents from Abuse 9 (March 2002), available at www.gao.gov with search for GAO 02–448T (recognizing "the difficulty of estimating the extent of resident abuse using nursing home inspection data").

[396] See, e.g., Rachou v. Cornerstone Village Inc., 819 So.2d 473 (La. App. 2002); Hendrickson v. Genesis Health Venture, Inc., 151 N.C.App. 139, 565 S.E.2d 254 (2002).

[397] See Marshall B. Kapp, The Liability Environment for Physicians Providing Nursing Home Medical Care: Does It Make a Difference for Residents?, 16 Elder L. J. 249, 262–263 (2009).

[398] Id. at 273–274.

little disposition to use regulatory power to force bad violators to make corrections or leave the business.

The result is that tort suits are a badly needed corrective. Yet tort suits are difficult to mount. This is true at one level because the nursing home industry has engaged in several practices to make suit useless. Some nursing homes restructure their business so that their property, which produces large income, is owned by a separate corporation from the one that runs the nursing home with little cash, in effect creating an immunity for the only substantial assets the business has. Some go without liability insurance or only buy inadequate insurance.[399] Both moves can mean that efforts to impose accountability for the nursing home's wrong is useless. Compelled arbitration may likewise displace accountability in tort.[400]

At another level, tort suits are difficult to pursue because nursing home residents are often so mentally or physically incapacitated that they cannot report the harms done to them, much less arrange for a law suit. If a suit is brought, several factors can operate to limit damages so severely that most lawyers simply cannot afford to engage in the complex task of preparing for suit. For example, an 87-year-old resident may die of abuse or neglect, but she has lost no income, and no dependents have lost support. Unless damages for pain and suffering are very high, or remedies are enhanced by statute,[401] or punitive damages are recoverable,[402] the case may promise a recovery too small to fund a reasonable attorney's fee under the contingent fee system. Tort reform legislation can force the same result. According to one view, this has virtually eliminated nursing home suits (and therefore the rights of nursing home victims) in some states.[403]

§ 21.20 Standard of Care for Nursing Homes

Nursing homes, having undertaken the care of their residents, owe them a duty, including a duty to use care to protect them from their own infirmities[404] and from attacks by others.[405] However, it is not always clear at first glance what standard of care is owed, or even whether health care statutes apply to nursing homes. If courts think the

---

[399] See, recounting some of these tactics, Marshall B. Kapp, The Liability Environment for Physicians Providing Nursing Home Medical Care: Does It Make a Difference for Residents?, 16 Elder L. J. 249, 261 (2009).

[400] A state may not prohibit all pre-dispute agreements to arbitrate personal injury or wrongful death claims against nursing homes, because such a prohibition would violate the Federal Arbitration Act. Marmet Health Care Center, Inc. v. Brown, 132 S. Ct. 1201, 182 L. Ed. 2d 42 (2012). Post-*Marmet* decisions have upheld arbitration agreements, see, e.g., Entrekin v. Internal Medicine Associates of Dothan, P.A., 689 F.3d 1248 (11th Cir. 2012), even while recognizing that an arbitration agreement may be invalidated by a state-law contract defense of general applicability, such as fraud, duress, or unconscionability, without running afoul of the FAA. See Carter v. SSC Odin Operating Co., LLC, 2012 IL 113204, 364 Ill. Dec. 66, 976 N.E.2d 344 (2012).

[401] See § 21.22 (state nursing home statutes).

[402] When the facts can be uncovered, punitive damages are justified in many cases of nursing home neglect. See, e.g., Montgomery Health Care Facility, Inc. v. Ballard, 565 So.2d 221 (Ala. 1996) ($2 million); Advocat, Inc. v. Sauer, 353 Ark. 29, 111 S.W.3d 346 (2003) ($21 million); Horizon/CMS Healthcare Corp. v. Auld, 34 S.W.3d 887 (Tex. 2000) ($9.5 million).

[403] See Michael L. Rustad, Neglecting the Neglected: the Impact of Noneconomic Damage Caps on Meritorious Nursing Home Lawsuits, 14 Elder L. J. 331, 333, 374–75 (2006).

[404] Elder residents are particularly prone to injuries from falling and entitled to reasonable care to protect them from this infirmity. E.g., Owens v. DeKalb Med. Ctr., Inc., 253 Ga.App. 19, 557 S.E.2d 404 (2001). Others, often confused, tend to wander off into danger; they are entitled to care to prevent such wandering. E.g., Bailey v. Rose Care Ctr. Div. of C.A.R.E., Inc., 307 Ark. 14, 817 S.W.2d 412 (1991).

[405] See Juhnke v. Evangelical Lutheran Good Samaritan Soc'y, 6 Kan. App. 2d 744, 634 P.2d 1132 (1981) (attack by fellow patient known by nursing home to be dangerous); Limbaugh v. Coffee Med. Ctr., 59 S.W.3d 73 (Tenn. 2001) (attack by nursing assistant).

claim against a nursing home is "medical," the plaintiff will ordinarily be required to prove the medical standard of care, or an analogy to it—the care used by other nursing homes—rather than the reasonable person standard of ordinary negligence.[406] Unless the nursing home's negligence is obvious or within the common knowledge of jurors,[407] the plaintiff will need expert witnesses who can testify to the standard.[408] The same is true when the plaintiff sues a physician whose care of the nursing home resident is alleged to be negligent.[409] Distinctly but relatedly, if the claim is for a medical error rather than for custodial negligence, it may fall within the purview of the tort reform statutes that provide special and significant protections for health care providers such as physicians. Those protections are effective and eliminate many claims,[410] and under some statutes may limit even non-medical claims against nursing homes.[411]

Applying a single approach to all nursing home activities? Some courts seem to have lumped together all nursing home activities, treating them all alike and subject to the same standards, and asserting generally that nursing homes owe residents a duty of ordinary care, commensurate with the resident's mental and physical needs.[412] Others have said that nursing homes are subject to a medical standard or the standard set by other nursing homes in the same community.[413] Such statements assume that the standard is determined by the nature of the defendant as a nursing home or healthcare unit regardless of the kind negligence that inflicted harm. Consequently, they may look for evidence of a standard of care to govern defendants with the status of nursing homes rather than the standard to govern the act that caused harm.[414] This status-oriented view of the standard could lead a court to shield nursing homes under the health care statutes, even when the nursing home has committed acts that do not seem to be medical at all, as when it knowingly committed acts of abuse or violated statutory directives.[415]

---

[406] E.g., Mattox v. Life Care Centers of America, Inc., 337 P.3d 627 (Idaho 2014) (plaintiff's expert produced sufficient evidence on the medical standard of care to defeat summary judgment).

[407] In Juhnke v. Evangelical Lutheran Good Samaritan Soc'y, 6 Kan. App. 2d 744, 634 P.2d 1132 (1981), the court thought no expert testimony was required to support a finding of negligence where the plaintiff was attacked by a fellow patient, known by the nursing home to have violent proclivities.

[408] See, e.g., Perdieu v. Blackstone Family Prac. Ctr., Inc., 264 Va. 408, 568 S.E.2d 703 (2002) (claim that the nursing home failed to prevent patient's falls required expert testimony, which could not be provided by a hospital nurse); Ayuluk v. Red Oaks Assisted Living, Inc., 201 P.3d 1183 (Alaska 2009) (R.N. and former nursing home investigator allowed to testify as experts in sexual abuse claim). Hospital nurses are usually qualified to give opinions as to the standard of care for hospitals in preventing bedsores or decubitus ulcers, which are common and preventable injuries in nursing homes. E.g., Gaines v. Comanche County Med. Hosp., 143 P.3d 203 (Okla. 2006).

[409] Carraway v. Kurtts, 987 So.2d 512 (Ala. 2007).

[410] See Michael L. Rustad, Neglecting the Neglected: the Impact of Noneconomic Damage Caps on Meritorious Nursing Home Lawsuits, 14 Elder L. J. 331, 333, 374–375 (2006) (claims eliminated by caps on non-economic damages because resulting verdicts for actual economic loss of elderly are too small to pay attorneys).

[411] See Tex. Civ. Prac. & Rems. Code § 74.301(b) & (c) (claims against nursing homes capped not only when negligence was medical malpractice but also when it related "healthcare" and "safety").

[412] Regions Bank & Trust v. Stone County Skilled Nursing Facility, Inc., 345 Ark. 555, 563, 49 S.W.3d 109, 112 (2001); Harder v. F.C. Clinton, Inc., 948 P.2d 298 (Okla. 1997).

[413] E.g., Richards v. Broadview Heights Harborside Healthcare, 150 Ohio App. 3d 537, 782 N.E.2d 609 (2002).

[414] See Rosemont v. Marshall, 481 So.2d 1126, 1130 (Ala. 1986) ("the standard of care applicable to intermediate nursing care facilities such as Rosemont").

[415] See Shaw v. BMW Healthcare, Inc., 100 S.W.3d 8 (Tex. App. 2002) (claim that nursing home overdosed resident on medicines and did so for the illicit purpose of staff convenience was merely a medical malpractice claim); Alphin v. Huguley Nursing Center, 109 S.W.3d 574 (Tex. App. 2003) (allegations of "civil

Custodial nature of nursing home care and the standard of care. However, an invariant rule that either applies or rejects the medical standard overlooks two important facts. First, most nursing home operations are truly custodial, not medical; they are not even authorized to deliver medical care and they do not do so. Second, most of the primary care is in fact given, not by registered nurses or even LPNs, but by unlicensed nurses' aides or "certified nursing assistants."[416] Neither of these groups is qualified to exercise medical judgment. Consequently, many nursing home operations— providing food, hydration and hygiene, for example—are simply not medical at all, so that a medical standard would be grossly out of line. Something similar can be said about the protective healthcare statutes; they may classify nursing homes as healthcare providers, but some of those statutes are intended to provide protection only for acts "related to medical treatment"[417] or at least for acts requiring some kind of medical judgment. For example, a surgeon is a healthcare provider, yet it is certain that if he runs over a child in a crosswalk, the healthcare statute has no application at all. In the same way, if nursing homes are permitted to and do make purely medical judgments, the protective statutes would apply, but there is no occasion to apply their protections to merely custodial conduct such as providing or failing to provide food.

Abuse. Abuse of a resident is clearly outside the realm of medical or health care treatment. No one needs to hear testimony about a medical-professional standard to know that abuse such as physical attacks by staff,[418] sexual abuse or rape,[419] and forced treatment[420] are tortious. If the nursing home fails to protect the patient from abuse, no medical or professional judgment seems to be involved, although some states define health care to include issues of physical safety from attacks by others and thus go on to apply the statutory limitations on redress for negligence.[421] Nursing home residents, however helpless, are free men and women, not prisoners. By federal law, restraints, chemical or physical, are forbidden when imposed for the convenience of the staff.[422] Frequently, it would be equally easy to know without medical testimony that a restraint upon residents is unnecessary[423] and an abuse in violation of this standard.

---

conspiracy", and fraud due to a "knowing violation" of the nursing home statute was a medical malpractice claim).

[416] "In nursing homes, the primary caregivers are nurse aides." General Accounting Office, Nursing Home: More Can Be Done to Protect Residents from Abuse 7 (March 2002), available at www.gao.gov with search for GAO-02-312.

[417] Richard v. Louisiana Extended Care Ctrs., Inc., 835 So.2d 460 (La. 2003).

[418] As in Limbaugh v. Coffee Med. Ctr., 59 S.W.3d 73 (Tenn. 2001).

[419] Doe v. Westfall Health Care Ctr., Inc., 303 A.D.2d 102, 755 N.Y.S.2d 769 (2002) (staff member raped resident who had been in vegetative state for years, resident became pregnant and gave birth to a child); Healthcare Ctrs. of Texas, Inc. v. Rigby, 97 S.W.3d 610 (Tex. 2003) (rape or attempted rape by resident who was not properly controlled by staff in spite of many instances that gave warning of his danger to others); Niece v. Elmview Group Home, 929 P.2d 420 (Wash. 1997) (child in home for developmentally disabled sexually assaulted by staff member).

[420] Roberson v. Provident House, 576 So.2d 992 (La. 1991).

[421] Diversicare General Partner, Inc. v. Rubio, 185 S.W.3d 842 (Tex. 2005). The statute was amended after the events in Diversicare, which led a different Texas court to conclude that "safety" claims, as distinct from treatment and health claims, would be covered by the statute only if they were "directly related to health care." Valley Baptist Med. Ctr. v. Stradley, 210 S.W.3d 770 (Tex. App. 2006).

[422] 42 U.S.C.A. § 1396r(c)(1)(A)(ii) ("right to be free from physical or mental abuse, corporal punishment, involuntary seclusion, and any physical or chemical restraints imposed for purposes of discipline or convenience and not required to treat the resident's medical symptoms").

[423] See Clites v. State, 322 N.W.2d 917 (Iowa 1982).

Neglect. Neglect includes negligent mistreatment and also failure to provide rudimentary care in cleaning patients[424] and in turning them to prevent bedsores that leave the flesh rotting to the bone in some cases.[425] It also includes failure to provide medicines, food, and water[426] and failures to provide trained personnel for feeding those in danger of choking[427] as well as all forms of active negligence, such as provision of wrong medications[428] or overdoses.[429] In cases like these, the standard of care can be viewed as the ordinary reasonable care standard, easy enough to apply without expert testimony detailing the practices of other nursing homes,[430] which is only to say that it would be tortious to refuse food to a helpless resident even if all nursing homes followed that practice. Another way to make the same point is to recognize that statutes and regulations set specific standards (for feeding, nutrition, and bedsores, for example),[431] so testimony about standards should be unnecessary or even impermissible if the testimony proposes standards that vary from the standard set by law. Similarly, no medical judgment is involved when a nursing facility fails to supervise a patient who is known to be dangerous to herself.[432] Equally, active custodial mistreatment—bathing a helpless resident in scalding water, for example—is hardly a medical decision and ordinary reasonable care standards can be applied to such cases.

Premises conditions, institutional management decisions. Some of the harms to residents arise only remotely from the application of health care itself, although the risks may be more threatening because of the residents' disabilities. A nursing home's management decisions—decisions to save money by understaffing, or by permitting dangerous conditions on the premises—almost by definition entail business or managerial judgment, not professional care-giving judgments. Good management, not good medicine, exterminates fire ants so that they do not attack residents in their beds.[433] Much the same can be said about conditions of the premises dangerous to residents who suffer from dementia and tend to wander. If the premises give access to upper-story windows, a fall is foreseeable,[434] and if the premises are sited on an unfenced

[424] The complaint is often heard that residents who cannot control bowel movements are left lying in their own feces. E.g., Advocat, Inc. v. Sauer, 353 Ark. 29, 111 S.W.3d 346 (2003).

[425] E.g., DeLaney v. Baker, 20 Cal.4th 23, 971 P.2d 986, 82 Cal.Rptr.2d 610 (1999); Horizon/CMS Healthcare Corp. v. Auld, 985 S.W.2d 216 (Tex. App. 1999), aff'd, Horizon/CMS Healthcare Corp. v. Auld, 34 S.W.3d 887 (Tex. 2000).

[426] See Texas Health Enters., Inc. v. Geisler, 9 S.W.3d 163 (Tex. App. 1999) (low levels of medications ingested caused seizures); Julie A. Braun & Elizabeth A. Capezuti, A Medico-legal Evaluation of Dehydration and Malnutrition among Nursing Home Residents, 8 Elder L. J. 239, 247 (2000).

[427] Crowne Investments, Inc. v. Reid, 740 So.2d 400 (Ala. 1999).

[428] See Marshall B. Kapp, Resident Safety and Medical Errors in Nursing Homes, 24 J. Legal Med. 51, 57 (reporting studies showing a high incidence of serious, often preventable adverse drug events).

[429] As claimed in Shaw v. BMW Healthcare, Inc., 100 S.W.3d 8 (Tex. App. 2002) (claim dismissed for failing to comply with special requirements for medical malpractice suits).

[430] Bailey v. Rose Care Ctr., Div. of C.A.R.E., Inc., 307 Ark. 14, 817 S.W.2d 412 (1991).

[431] Nutrition, hydration, and turning to prevent bedsores are not only custodial rather than medical, they are specifically required by federal law. See, respectively, 42 C.F.R. §§ 483.25(i), 483.25(j), 483.25(c). The presence of lawful standards eliminates any contention that medical judgment is involved. State regulations may independently specify some such elementary requirements. E.g., Ariz. Admin. Code R9–10–912 (detailed dietary rules).

[432] See Taylor v. Vencor, Inc., 525 S.E.2d 201 (N.C. App. 2000) (defendant failed to supervise resident properly, with the result that the resident caused a fire from which she suffered deadly burns, this is ordinary negligence, not medical malpractice); Virginia S. v. Salt Lake Care Ctr., 741 P.2d 969 (Utah Ct. App. 1987) ("[C]ases require that supervision be tailored to the known needs of the patients.").

[433] Rein v. Benchmark Construction Co., 865 So.2d 1134 (Miss. 2004).

[434] Richards v. Broadview Heights Harborside Healthcare, 150 Ohio App.3d 537, 782 N.E.2d 609 (2002).

canal, drowning is the danger to be avoided by supervision or fencing.[435] If the trier of fact can conclude that open upper windows are dangerous to children,[436] it seems equally appropriate to permit the trier to draw similar conclusions about premises safety in health care institutions as a matter of ordinary negligence law without medical overtones. The claim that personal restraints should have been imposed to protect wandering residents, however, differs from a claim of danger resulting from premises designs or defects, from negligent supervision, and from needlessly risky management decisions. There are serious concerns about undue personal restraints, so the mere absence of a restraint without more does not necessarily permit an inference of negligence.[437] However, an alarm that alerts the staff when an unable resident attempts to get out of bed is an alternative to bed rails and intrusive restraints.[438] Supervision of exits is another alternative to prevent wandering into danger outside the home.[439]

§ 21.21 Common-Law Claims Against Nursing Homes

Apart from statutory actions,[440] a number of major claims for nursing home injury are possible.

Suits against staff members. Suits against staff members who physically attack or sexually abuse a resident easily fit the definition of battery,[441] and suits against staff members for restraint of the resident by unnecessary physical or chemical constraints, may fit either false imprisonment or negligence theories.[442] Conceivably, a staff member who is not himself an abuser would have a duty to report abuse caused by others, and would be potentially liable for failing to do so. Suits against such a staff member, however, are practically unlikely to produce an enforceable judgment against the individual.

Nursing homes' vicarious liability for intentional abuse by staff. The nursing home may itself be liable for abuse by its servants, purely as a matter of vicarious liability. Some courts take a narrow view of vicarious liability that might exclude vicarious

---

[435] Selvin v. DMC Regency Residence, Ltd., 807 So.2d 676 (Fla. Dist. Ct. App. 2001).

[436] As in Chiu v. City of Portland, 788 A.2d 183 (Me. 2002) (landlord might be liable for fall of child from upper window if landlord retained control).

[437] See Palmer v. Intermed, Inc., 270 Ark. 538, 606 S.W.2d 87 (1980) (hip broken, no evidence of where or how, no evidence of defendant's control or assumed duty, res ipsa loquitur rejected); Ivy Manor Nursing Home, Inc. v. Brown, 488 P.2d 246 (Colo. App. 1971) (fall in the bathroom, nursing home negligence not the more likely explanation); Murphy v. Allstate Ins. Co., 295 So.2d 29 (La. App. 1974) (dementia resident wandered off into traffic, res ipsa loquitur not warranted).

[438] See Julie A. Braun & Elizabeth A. Capezuti, The Legal and Medical Aspects of Physical Restraints and Bed Siderails and Their Relationship to Falls and Fall-Related Injuries in Nursing Homes, 4 DePaul J. Health Care L. 1 (2000).

[439] In Daniels v. Twin Oaks Nursing Home, 692 F.2d 1321 (11th Cir. 1982), the resident, known to be a persistent wanderer, had to walk past a nurses station to exit the building; the court thought this permitted an inference that the home was negligent in supervising the exit, though the plaintiff lost on other grounds.

[440] See § 21.22.

[441] See Roberson v. Provident House, 576 So.2d 992 (La. 1991) (insertion of catheter over objection of quadriplegic resident, nursing home held liable). Any unprivileged touching that is not consented to, or apparently consented to, is a battery. See § 4.6.

[442] Courts and lawyers have tended to think chemical restraint as negligence rather than false imprisonment. See Clites v. State, 322 N.W.2d 917 (Iowa 1982) (long-term administration of tranquilizers in substandard way causing harm to resident of state facility for the "mentally retarded," affirming judgment for the plaintiff); Shaw v. BMW Healthcare, Inc., 100 S.W.3d 8 (Tex. App. 2002) (allegedly, defendant dosed the resident to prevent wandering for the convenience of nursing staff, a violation of statute; although plaintiff claimed an unspecified "intentional tort," the court regarded the claim as a mere recasting of a negligence claim).

liability in the case of a staff rape of a resident,[443] but it is not true that rape is necessarily outside the scope of employment. Where the employment enhances a risk of intentional harms, or provides the impetus or particular opportunity for such harms, as where the job gives the rapist a great deal of power over his victim, vicarious liability, even for so personal a tort as rape has been imposed.[444] The description exactly fits institutional care settings and a little authority has recognized vicarious liability for sexual attacks on institutionalized persons.[445]

Negligent hiring, retention, or supervision of an employee. The nursing home may be liable for its own negligence in hiring, retaining, or supervising dangerous or incompetent staff members that put residents at risk. For example, it is liable for an aid's sexual assault if it negligently failed to check the aid's criminal background and if a reasonable investigation would have revealed that he was dangerous or could not be licensed.[446] Even if the nursing home is not negligent in hiring, it may be negligent in failing to discharge, discipline, or supervise a staff member whose behavior has given notice that he may be dangerous.[447]

Negligent protection of residents from employees and others. A defendant's duty to protect the plaintiff may arise either because of his relationship with the dangerous person or because of his relationship with the plaintiff.[448] The nursing home does not breach its duty of care arising from a relationship with a dangerous employee unless it knows, or in the exercise of ordinary care should know of the danger. If the home has investigated the employee's background and found no criminal record and his work has not given reason for concern, the home is not negligent in hiring or retaining the employee, but may be in breach of its duty arising from its relationship with the resident.[449] In the same way, if reasonable care requires constant supervision of a helpless resident, the nursing home may be held liable for an unknown assailant's rape of the patient, whether he was an employee or not.[450]

Understaffing. One of the most common complaints is that some nursing homes systematically understaff the institution, a major cost-saving for nursing home chains.[451] Understaffing is indeed the most obvious explanation for failure to provide adequate food

---

[443] See §§ 31.3 & 31.4. In Doe v. Westfall Health Care Ctr., Inc., 303 A.D.2d 102, 755 N.Y. S.2d 769 (2002), the court suggested that the plaintiff would have difficulty with the scope of employment issue in a common law suit against a nursing home for rape by a staff member, but that the claim would be actionable under a nursing home statute.

[444] The vicarious liability rule has been applied in other contexts, as well. Costos v. Coconut Island Corp., 137 F.3d 46 (1st Cir. 1998) (rape by manager of inn where the plaintiff was staying); Mary M. v. City of Los Angeles, 54 Cal.3d 202, 285 Cal.Rptr. 99, 814 P.2d 1341 (1991) (employer of police officer vicariously liable for officer's rape of a woman he detained; job gave officer much coercive power over citizen and that is potential for abuse).

[445] Stropes v. Heritage House Childrens Ctr. of Shelbyville, Inc., 547 N.E.2d 244 (Ind. 1989) (vicarious liability for sexual abuse of institutionalized child with mental ability of a baby); Samuels v. Southern Baptist Hosp., 594 So.2d 571 (La. App. 1992) (rape of teenager committed to a psychiatric unit).

[446] See Deerings West Nursing Center v. Scott, 787 S.W.2d 494 (Tex. App. 1990) (negligently hiring unlicensed male nurse who later allegedly struck 80-year-old visitor; licensing process would have revealed 56 convictions of moral turpitude, affirming judgment for $35,000 actual and $200,000 punitive damages).

[447] See Limbaugh v. Coffee Med. Ctr., 59 S.W.3d 73 (Tenn. 2001).

[448] See § 25.4.

[449] Regions Bank & Trust v. Stone County Skilled Nursing Facility, Inc., 345 Ark. 555, 49 S.W.3d 107 (2001).

[450] Virginia S. v. Salt Lake Care Ctr., 741 P.2d 969 (Utah Ct. App. 1987).

[451] See Victoria Vron, Using Rico to Fight Understaffing in Nursing Homes: How Federal Prosecution Using RICO Can Reduce Abuse and Neglect of the Elderly, 71 Geo. Wash. L. Rev. 1025 (2003).

and hydration[452] and for advanced bedsores, which almost never occur unless the staff fails to periodically reposition the immobilized resident. Some appellate cases have upheld liabilities imposed in whole or part for injuries or death resulting ultimately from understaffing.[453] Federal statutes mandate some rudimentary staffing levels—one nurse, for example[454]—but these are not proportioned to the number of residents. In some of the cases, the injuries are so egregious that understaffing seems almost impossible to deny, and federal officials do attempt to enforce a degree of accountability through administrative procedures.[455] In closer cases, however, plaintiffs may encounter difficulties in proving a staffing standard to which the residents are entitled and also in proving factual causation.

Particular acts of negligence. Understaffing and poor training are the root causes of many particular acts of negligence. However, in many suits, the plaintiff may concentrate on the immediate and specific cause, such as failure to provide prescribed medications, failure to feed, failure to turn the immobile resident to prevent ulcerations, many acts and omissions causing falls, and failures in supervision and security that permit disoriented residents to wander into the nearest street or canal.[456] In addition, nursing homes are expected to observe the condition of residents and provide a nursing diagnosis. Failure to notify the resident's physician when the resident's condition changes or calls for medical attention is another likely source of complaint.[457]

§ 21.22 Statutory Claims Against Nursing Homes

Statutes and their subsidiary regulations are a major presence in nursing home operation and litigation. At a minimum, they are part of the regulatory structure under which government agencies attempt both to finance nursing care and to bring that care up to minimal standards. The structure, the concepts, and the language of the statutes are heavily influenced by the regulatory culture out of which they grew, sometimes leading to imperfect coherence as documents of tort law. Statutes may create a private right of action; may be given negligence per se effect; or may restrict or revise remedies or impose procedural obstacles.

Federal Nursing Home Statutes

Aims. The dual aim of federal statutes is to finance nursing home construction and operation by paying directly or indirectly for Medicare or Medicaid residents and to

---

[452] See Julie A. Braun & Elizabeth A. Capezuti, A Medico-Legal Evaluation of Dehydration and Malnutrition among Nursing Home Residents, 8 Elder L. J. 239, 247 (2000).

[453] See Advocat, Inc. v. Sauer, 353 Ark. 29, 111 S.W.3d 346 (2003) (consistent understaffing leading to dehydration, malnutrition; an incontinent patient was left in her feces; punitive award (remitted to $21 Million) justified partly on understaffing evidence); Miller v. Levering Regional Health Care Center, LLC, 202 S.W.3d 614 (Mo. Ct. App. 2006); Texas Health Enters., Inc. v. Geisler, 9 S.W.3d 163 (Tex. App. 1999) (understaffing apparently the basis for finding negligence and awarding punitive damages); Manor Care, Inc. v. Douglas, 763 S.E.2d 73 (W.Va. 2014) (affirming punitive damages award of $32 million were chronic understaffing of nursing home resulted in resident's death from dehydration).

[454] 42 U.S.C.A. § 1939i–3(b)(4)(C)(i)

[455] See, e.g., Richard P. Kusserow & Thomas E. Herrmann, More Health Care Executive and Board Accountability on the Way, 12No. 4 J. Health Care Compliance 41 (July/August 2010) (reporting the Inspector General's efforts to deal with particular instances of chronic understaffing).

[456] Where the plaintiff cannot identify specific acts of negligence, reliance on res ipsa loquitur might be appropriate. See, g., Ward v. Forrester Day Care, Inc., 547 So.2d 410 (Ala. 1989).

[457] Unless grounds for notifying the physician are obvious, the plaintiff will presumably be required to prove either a statutory obligation to notify or a standard of care determining that notification is required under conditions present in the case. See Rosemont v. Marshall, 481 So.2d 1126 (Ala. 1985); Norman v. Life Care Ctrs. of America, Inc., 107 Cal. App. 4th 1233, 132 Cal. Rptr. 2d 765 (2003).

require a minimum quality of care. The quality is required by conditioning payment upon meeting statutory standards.

Federal standards and required results. Many of the standards spelled out in the statutes or their subsidiary regulations could resolve issues in tort litigation against nursing homes. Unlike some of the state Resident Rights statutes that do not address rights to care, the federal statutes provide some minimal rules against neglect and abuse.[458] The general principle is that the facility "must care for its residents in such a manner and in such an environment as will promote maintenance or enhancement of the quality of life of each resident." Beyond that, however, the federal statutes include a few specific standards or rules, including, for example, a requirement that the nursing home make an assessment of each individual resident and provide a care plan appropriate to her condition.[459] Nutrition and other services must be provided in accord with the patient's condition.[460] Regulations are more specific. For example, one regulation flatly provides that the nursing home must ensure that a resident who enters without pressure sores does not develop them in the nursing home, barring some unavoidable reason—seemingly a mandatory result, not a direction for specific acts of care.[461]

A private right of action? The federal nursing home statutes do not expressly create a private right of action, and courts have said that they create no implied right of action either.[462] However, it has been held that the most notable section of the nursing home statutes[463] does vest specific rights in individual nursing home residents and does mandate their observance by the nursing homes, with the result that violation of those rights can be redressed in a civil rights claim against those acting under color of state law.[464]

Use of federal standards in state law. Since there is no federal system of common law tort responsibility, the absence of a private right of action under the federal statutes usually dooms federal-law claims, with the possible exception of civil rights claims. However, that does not rule out the possibility that state courts will choose to adopt federal standards as their own, treating violation of the federal standards as negligence per se or at least as evidence of negligence. State court adoption of federal standards for tort litigation is theoretically sound and not uncommon,[465] so it is no surprise that courts have incorporated federal nursing home standards into state law.[466] State statutes themselves may indicate a desire to comport with federal standards.[467] However, in line

---

[458] See 42 U.S.C.A. § 1395i–3; 42 U.S.C.A. § 1396r; 42 C.F.R. § 483.25(c). The statutes list a number of "resident rights," but these are mainly intended to protect against financial exploitation, invasion of privacy, interference with communication and the like, not rights to care. Care rights are presented as standards the nursing home must meet.

[459] 42 U.S.C.A. § 1395i–3(b)(3).

[460] 42 U.S.C.A. § 1395i–3(b)(4)(A)(iv).

[461] See, e.g., 42 C.F.R. § 483.25(c).

[462] Stewart v. Bernstein, 769 F.2d 1088 (5th Cir. 1985); Nichols v. St. Luke Center of Hyde Park, 800 F.Supp. 1564 (S.D. Ohio 1992).

[463] 42 U.S.C.A. § 1396r.

[464] Grammer v. John J. Kane Regional Centers-Glen Hazel, 570 F.3d 520 (3d Cir. 2009).

[465] See § 11.1.

[466] Conservatorship of Gregory, 80 Cal. App. 4th 514, 95 Cal. Rptr. 2d 336 (2000); McLain v. Mariner Health Care, Inc., 279 Ga.App. 410, 631 S.E.2d 435 (2006).

[467] As in Conn. Gen. Stat. Ann. § 19a–550; Ga. Code Ann., § 31–8–108(a)(2) (requiring compliance with "applicable laws and regulations"); N.C. Gen. Stats. § 131E–117.

with the general rule,[468] statutes or regulations cannot be used to establish negligence per se when they merely state an abstract general principle or goal without specifying particular conduct required. A federal statute or regulation that merely requires appropriate care would surely be in this category.[469]

State Nursing Home Statutes

Statutes creating standards of care or not. Most states have enacted statutes affecting nursing homes, either as part of a more general elder protection law or as a direct regulation of nursing homes and sometimes other long-term care institutions. Some statutes are the Residents' Bill of Rights type. These protect residents against financial exploitation and create a host of specific rights related to discrimination, communication, privacy, and informed consent. This type of statute standing alone may profess a general condemnation of abuse or neglect, but usually does not directly specify particular rules or the nursing homes' standard of care for the residents' physical and mental well-being.[470] Other statutes, however, appear to adopt general or specific standards of care intended to protect residents against both abuse and neglect.[471] A statute may even create a private right of action for violation of any right of a resident created by any other statutes, state and federal.[472] Even so, the regulatory, non-tort focus of many statutes is reflected in the fact that some statutes may create "a private right of action" without including standards of care for physical well-being that are specific and meaningful enough to guide the jury or substitute for expert testimony.[473]

Adding remedies. Statutes that go beyond the Residents' Bill of Rights may create a new cause of action for nursing home abuse or neglect, or at least add new remedies and remove limitations and impediments to suit. Permitting the prevailing plaintiff's attorney to recover a reasonable attorney fee, for example, tends to encourage representation in notoriously difficult nursing home claims where the damages may be small and the contingent fee limited. Some statutes have expressly mandated an award of attorney's fees by the prevailing plaintiff,[474] but within that group of statutes one sees some additional restrictions on fee awards.[475] Some statutes permit but do not require

---

[468]   See §§ 11.2 & 11.6.

[469]   Conley v. Life Care Centers of America, Inc., 236 S.W.3d 713, 733 (Tenn. Ct. App. 2007).

[470]   Conn. Gen. Stat. Ann. § 19a–550; N.C. Gen. Stats. Ann. § 131E–117.

[471]   See Brogdon v. National Healthcare Corp., 103 F.Supp.2d 1322 (N.D. Ga. 2000) (Georgia statute "imposes enforceable duties upon operators of long-term care facilities").

[472]   N.Y. Pub. Health L. § 2801–d. By its terms, this statute is "cumulative," adding to any other remedy the resident might have. See Kash v. Jewish Home and Infirmary of Rochester, N.Y., Inc., 873 N.Y.S.2d 819 (App. Div. 2009).

[473]   Thus the Missouri statute creates a private right of action, see Bachtel v. Miller County Nursing Home Dist., 110 S.W.3d 799 (Mo. 2003), but the definition of neglect that might be the basis for the cause of action for physical harm specifies no acts or omissions that are forbidden, only the requirement of "services which are reasonable and necessary to maintain the physical and mental health of the resident, when such failure presents either an imminent danger to the health, safety or welfare of the resident or a substantial probability that death or serious physical harm would result." Mo. Rev. Stats. § 198.006 (defining neglect); Mo. Rev. Stats. § 198.088 (listing general rights of residents). This generality would almost certainly leave the plaintiff with a need to show by proof extrinsic to the statute what was reasonable and necessary, perhaps exactly the same proof that would be required without a statute.

[474]   210 ILCS 45/3–602 ("The licensee shall pay the actual damages and costs and attorney's fees to a facility resident whose rights, as specified in . . . this Act, are violated"); N.J. Stat. Ann. § 30:13–8 ("Any plaintiff who prevails in any such action shall be entitled to recover reasonable attorney's fees and costs of the action"); Rev. Code Wash. § 74.34.200(3) (a plaintiff who prevails in asserting statutory rights, "shall be awarded his or her actual damages, together with the costs of the suit, including a reasonable attorney's fee").

[475]   Cal. Welf. & Inst. Code § 15657 (fee award only if the plaintiff proves nursing home conduct that is reckless or worse, by clear and convincing evidence).

an award of fees to the prevailing plaintiff, making the attorney's prospect for adequate payment chancy.[476] Others expressly exclude recovery of attorney's fees.[477]

Removing impediments to suit. A few statutes, especially those that are regarded as creating a new cause of action, may remove impediments that otherwise might impair the ability of nursing home victims to pursue claims. California's statute is perhaps best known. It leaves California's damages caps in place, but allows the estate of a deceased resident to claim pain and suffering damages that are otherwise rejected in claims by a decedent's estate.[478] Florida's statute exempts the nursing home claimant from the strictures of the statutes that offer special protections for malpractice defendants,[479] and it has been held that contracts with prospective nursing home residents for limiting damages may be avoided under the policy established by the state's protective statutes.[480]

Statutory shift of proof burden, statutory res ipsa loquitur or semi-strict liability. State statutes may expressly shift the burden of proof or persuasion, so that the nursing home defendant must show, as an affirmative defense, that it exercised "all care reasonably necessary" to prevent the resident's injury or deprivation.[481] Other statutes specify results to be achieved or injuries to be avoided rather than acts to be carried out. For instance, a California provision defines neglect of an elder in terms of negligence law, but adds that failure to prevent malnutrition or dehydration also count as neglect.[482] If this dehydration and other forbidden conditions are actionable in themselves,[483] the plaintiff would not be required to prove any particular misconduct, only the injury— malnutrition or dehydration. Liability based on proof of malnutrition, dehydration, or the like, occurring after the resident enters the nursing home, would not be radical; the same result might be justified under the common law rules of res ipsa loquitur.[484]

Conflict with protective medical malpractice statutes. Nursing home statutes aim at better protection for nursing home residents. They are potentially in conflict with the aims of the protective medical malpractice statutes already mentioned—those that seek to minimize exposure of physicians, surgeons, hospitals and other health care providers.[485] Courts have reacted somewhat variously to this problem. Some courts believe that nursing homes are health care providers and that the medical malpractice rules and standards govern in all cases, regardless of the kind of negligence or injury.[486] Other courts have struggled to find ways of defining what claims against nursing homes fall within the plaintiff-favorable nursing home statutes and what claims fall within the

---

[476]   Ariz. Rev. Stat. § 46–455; Mo. Rev. Stats. § 198.093; N.Y. Pub. Health L. § 2801–d(6).

[477]   Ark. Code. Ann. § 20–10–1209(a)(5).

[478]   Cal. Code Civ. Pro. § 377.34 provides that damages in survival type actions—suits that the decedent could have pursued had she lived—do not include recovery for pain and suffering. Cal. Welf. & Inst. Code § 15567(b) provides that these limitations do not apply when the plaintiff can recover under the elder protection law embodied in that section.

[479]   Fla. Stat. Ann. § 400.023(1).

[480]   Alterra Healthcare Corp. v. Bryant, 937 So.2d 263 (Fla. Dist. Ct. App. 2006).

[481]   N.Y. Pub. Health L. §§ 2801–d (1) & (2). See, recognizing that reasonable care is an affirmative defense, Doe v. Westfall Health Care Ctr., Inc., 303 A.D.2d 102, 755 N.Y.S.2d 769 (2002).

[482]   Cal. Welf. & Inst. Code § 15610.57(b)(4).

[483]   The California statute makes neglect actionable and includes attorney fees where the neglect is reckless or worse. See Cal. Welf. & Inst. Code § 15657.

[484]   See §§ 13.3 to 13.7.

[485]   As to these statutes, see § 21.14.

[486]   See Makas v. Hillhaven, Inc., 589 F.Supp. 736 (M.D. N.C. 1984).

defendant-favorable protective statutes for medical malpractice.[487] One way to determine whether the protective statutes apply is to examine the nature of the alleged negligent acts; if they are "medical" acts or omissions, the protective statutes apply, otherwise they do not.[488]

---

[487] See DeLaney v. Baker, 20 Cal. 4th 23, 971 P.2d 986, 82 Cal. Rptr. 2d 610 (1999); Estate of McGill v. Albrecht, 57 P.3d 384 (Ariz. 2002).

[488] Richard v. Louisiana Extended Care Ctrs., Inc., 835 So.2d 460 (La. 2003) (many violations of statute could never be characterized as medical malpractice). Fla. Stat. Ann. § 400.023(1) (exempting nursing home plaintiffs from the statutes that give special protections to medical malpractice defendants).

Chapter 22

LIABILITY OF GOVERNMENT ENTITIES, OFFICERS AND EMPLOYEES

Analysis

A. GOVERNMENT ENTITIES

1. Introduction: Traditional Immunities

§ 22.1 Traditional Immunities and Their Passing

2. Federal Government Liability Under the FTCA

§ 22.2 The Plan of Federal Government Tort Liability

§ 22.3 The Discretionary Immunity

§ 22.4 The *Feres* Rule: Tort Claims by Military Personnel

§ 22.5 Other Statutory Exceptions to FTCA Liability

3. Immunities and Liabilities of State and Local Entities

§ 22.6 State Sovereign Immunity and Its Waiver

§ 22.7 Local Public-Entity Immunity and Its Waiver

§ 22.8 Discretionary Immunity of State and Local Entities

§ 22.9 The Public Duty Doctrine

§ 22.10 Excluding Liability for Police and Fire Protection

§ 22.11 Excluding Liability for the Release of Dangerous Persons

B. INDIVIDUAL GOVERNMENT AGENTS

§ 22.12 State and Local Officers and Employees

§ 22.13 Federal Officers and Employees

C. CIVIL RIGHTS CLAIMS

§ 22.14 Federal Civil Rights Claims: § 1983

§ 22.15 Section 1983 Claims Against State and Local Officials

§ 22.16 Section 1983 Claims Against State and Local Entities

A. GOVERNMENT ENTITIES

1. *Introduction: Traditional Immunities*

§ 22.1 Traditional Immunities and Their Passing

History of sovereign immunity. As a matter of sheer power, the medieval kings of England simply did not permit suits against themselves in their own courts, much less in the courts of feudal barons. Eventually, this power was cloaked with a theory or ideal: kings could not be sued because kings were governed by "divine right" and because "The King can do no wrong." As the state took over functions of the monarch, it inherited the monarch's immunity.

Federal and state government immunity. The thoroughly undemocratic ideas that underlay the king's immunity continued to prosper after the American Revolution,[1] so that both federal and state governments enjoyed a complete immunity from suit except so far as they consented to suit or waived the immunity. The state and federal immunity within the United States covered all the departments and agencies of the respective governments. Constitutions created one partial exception to the general immunity by providing that governments could not take private property for public use without paying just compensation.[2]

Municipal immunity. Municipalities and local public entities also enjoyed governmental immunities, but municipalities were not sovereigns and their immunity historically grew out of an entirely different idea: that they were not "entities" at all, just collections of people.[3] Municipalities have long since been chartered by the state and are usually recognized today as corporate entities. Nevertheless, the immunity remained long after the historical reason disappeared.

Officers and employees. The immunity of sovereigns and municipalities did not extend to officers or employees of public entities. At one time, it was said that public officers were in fact generally liable for their torts, even if the public entity they served was immune. Today, however, a web of immunities, some absolute, some qualified, may protect public officers in many instances.[4]

Abolishing immunities. Over the years, legislators found reasons, not for the blanket protection of government wrongdoing, but for limited immunities. First and most broadly, some kind of immunity was required to preserve the independence of each branch of government, so that the judicial branch could not intrude upon the appropriate functions of the legislative and executive branches by adjudicating tort suits. Second, some governmental decisions could not be measured against a standard of care. Otherwise, it is now usually accepted that government, instituted to protect and foster the well-being of citizens, should be obliged to make good on the losses it causes by misconduct.

Although all members of the public suffer a cost in some theoretical sense when governmental funds are paid to injured individuals, other members of the public—the injured persons—will suffer in the same amount if the public takes the benefits of governmental activity without also paying its costs. Even if governmental liability does not expose wrongdoing or provide incentives for better government, at least some liabilities have come to seem appropriate on these grounds and others like them.

Consequently, the traditional blanket immunities of sovereigns and municipalities have been abolished or substantially modified at both the federal and state levels. Nevertheless, some kind of immunity, or unique constraints on duties of governmental entities, remains everywhere. In fact, many courts construe the statutes waiving

---

[1]   See Osborn v. Bank of United States, 22 U.S. 738, 6 L.Ed. 204 (1824).

[2]   The Constitution creates one partial exception to the general immunity by providing that government cannot could not take private property for public use without paying just compensation. See U.S. Const. Amend. V (just compensation required) and Amendment XIV § 1 (property not to be taken without due process). Such takings are redressed, although not on a tort theory, even when the governmental immunity is otherwise maintained.

[3]   Russell v. Men of Devon, 2 Term Rep. 667, 100 Eng.Rep. 359 (1798).

[4]   See §§ 22.12 & 22.13.

immunity in favor of immunity rather than in favor of governmental accountability,[5] although some take the opposite view, favoring adjudication on the merits when the statute does not clearly grant immunity.[6]

2. *Federal Government Liability Under the FTCA*

§ 22.2 The Plan of Federal Government Tort Liability

In 1887, Congress authorized courts to entertain contract suits—but not tort suits—against the United States.[7] At various times, however, Congress consented to tort suits against the government in particular instances,[8] sometimes simply by providing that a federal agency could sue or be sued.[9] In addition, Congress dealt with many individual cases by private legislation that appropriated funds directly to the victim.[10] Such a procedure became a burden to Congress. Finally, in 1946, it enacted the Federal Tort Claims Act (FTCA), which gave a general consent to suit against the United States in federal courts, subject to a number of specific limitations.[11]

Procedural requirements. Procedurally, no suit may be brought until a claim has first been presented to the appropriate federal agency.[12] The statute itself contains a two-year statute of limitations.[13] After the agency has denied the claim, or has delayed more than six months in determining the claim, the plaintiff may sue. Suit must be brought in federal court.[14] No jury trial is permitted in FTCA claims.[15] Under the statute as it now stands, the only proper party is the government, or the agency involved; governmental employees who commit torts in the scope of their employment are not liable at all under the FTCA.[16]

Governing substantive law. Although the claim must be brought in federal court, state tort law governs the rights and duties of the parties. The FTCA requires the court

---

[5]   Library of Congress v. Shaw, 478 U.S. 310, 106 S.Ct. 2957, 92 L.Ed.2d 250 (1986) (superseded by statute on other grounds); Trout v. Sec'y of Navy, 317 F.3d 206 (D.C. Cir. 2003).

[6]   Springer v. City and County of Denver, 13 P.3d 794 (Colo. 2000); Smith v. Burdette, 211 W.Va. 477, 566 S.E.2d 614 (2002).

[7]   24 Stat. 505. Jurisdiction for most contract disputes is in the United States Court of Federal Claims. 28 U.S.C.A. § 1491.

[8]   Government immunity for maritime torts is waived by the Suits in Admiralty Act, 46 U.S.C.A. §§ 741 to 752, and the Public Vessels Act, 781 to 790; substantive issues of liability are then determined by federal maritime law. See generally Thomas J. Schoenbaum, Admiralty and Maritime Law § 20–1 (4th ed. 2004).

[9]   E.g., Federal Deposit Insurance Corp. v. Meyer, 510 U.S. 471, 114 S.Ct. 996, 127 L.Ed.2d 308 (1994).

[10]   See Dalehite v. United States, 346 U.S. 15, 73 S.Ct. 956, 97 L.Ed. 1427 (1953) ("the private bill device was notoriously clumsy" so Congress substituted simple access to federal courts).

[11]   60 Stat. 843. The provisions are scattered through the United States Code. Jurisdiction is granted in 28 U.S.C.A. § 1346. The main substantive provisions are cited in the discussion of particular provisions.

[12]   28 U.S.C.A. § 2875. This requirement is usually said to be jurisdictional, that is, failure to comply with the presentment requirement will result in dismissal for want of subject-matter jurisdiction. See Mader v. U.S., 654 F.3d 794 (8th Cir. 2011) (discussing the issue at length).

[13]   28 U.S.C.A. § 2401(b) (tort claim "shall be forever barred unless it is presented in writing to the appropriate Federal agency within two years after such claim accrues). Federal law governs when the claim accrues and whether equitable tolling may apply. See A.Q.C. ex rel. Castillo v. U.S., 656 F.3d 135 (2d Cir. 2011); Santos v. United States, 559 F.3d 189 (3d Cir. 2009).

[14]   28 U.S.C.A. § 1346 (b) (exclusive jurisdiction in federal court).

[15]   28 U.S.C.A. § 2402.

[16]   See § 22.13. Also, the government itself "may not be held responsible for negligent acts or omissions committed by employees of government contractors whose daily operations are not closely supervised by United States officials—in essence, eliminating vicarious liability as a theory of recovery against the federal government." Carroll v. U.S., 661 F.3d 87 (1st Cir. 2011) (citing U. S. v. Orleans, 425 U.S. 807, 96 S. Ct. 1971, 48 L. Ed. 2d 390 (1976)).

to follow the law of the state in which the government's negligent act or omission occurred.[17] The statute makes it clear that liability for a negligent act or omission depends upon a showing that the employee was acting within the scope of his government employment.[18] Federal law governs the question whether the entity in question is a federal agency, but the law of the appropriate state determines whether the employee is acting within the scope of his government employment.[19] State law also governs the ordinary substantive tort law questions—the rules of causation and comparative fault, for example,[20] and all the rules limiting duties, such as those governing suits against health care providers or landowners.[21] In some instances, state law might recognize a state-law tort duty arising out of a federal statute and if so, the government's violation of such a statute may furnish the basis for federal governmental liability.[22]

Governing remedial law. Since state law control the rights and duties of the parties, it also controls the determination of damages, which is a practical reflection of the state-law right.[23] The FTCA itself, however, limits that general rule in two respects. First, the plaintiff in an FTCA case cannot recover punitive damages, and second, interest on the amounts due does not begin to accrue until judgment is entered.[24]

Comparable private-person liability. The main substantive directive of the statute provides that the government is to be liable under the appropriate state law when a private person would be liable under like circumstances.[25] The thrust of this provision is simply to apply the substantive law of the appropriate state without regard to the government's historic immunity. It only requires that general legal principles would dictate liability[26] or its limits[27] if a private person were sued for similar acts or omissions. For example, only the government inspects mines, but private persons carry on non-

---

[17]   28 U.S.C.A. § 1346(b)(1). If government negligence occurs in State A but harm results in State B, State A's law controls; but that includes State A's choice of law rule, which is likely to refer to the law of State B, where harm occurred. If so, the FTCA claim ultimately looks to State B's law. Richards v. United States, 369 U.S. 1, 82 S.Ct. 585, 7 L.Ed.2d 492 (1962).

[18]   28 U.S.C.A. § 1346(b).

[19]   See, e.g., Fowler v. U.S., 647 F.3d 1232 (10th Cir. 2011).

[20]   E.g., Wojciechowicz v. United States, 582 F.3d 57 (1st Cir. 2009) (no liability for government where air traffic controller did not breach a duty and his acts did not cause air crash).

[21]   See, e.g., Lomando v. U.S., 667 F.3d 363 (3d Cir. 2011) (applying New Jersey substantive law on medical malpractice and charitable immunity). The legal effect of state statutes as negligence per se or evidence of negligence, for example, is determined by state, not federal, law. E.g., Jackson v. United States, 156 F.3d 230 (1st Cir. 1998).

[22]   See Lambertson v. United States, 528 F.2d 441, 444 (2d Cir. 1976). However, if federal employees violate a federal law that is not incorporated into the law of the state, the government is not liable. Williams v. United States, 242 F.3d 169 (4th Cir. 2001).

[23]   E.g., Williams v. United States, 435 F.2d 804 (1st Cir. 1970) (wrongful death damages measures); Trevino v. United States, 804 F.2d 1512 (9th Cir. 1986) (issue of excessiveness).

[24]   28 U.S.C.A. § 2674.

[25]   Id.

[26]   Thus in Indian Towing Co. v. United States, 350 U.S. 61, 76 S.Ct. 122, 100 L.Ed. 48 (1955), the government's negligent operation of a lighthouse was actionable although private persons do not operate lighthouses. Likewise, the government could not claim the immunity of municipalities operating lighthouses, but was liable as if it were a private person.

[27]   This means, for example, that if a private person would be immune under state law for the same actions, the government will be as well. See In re FEMA Trailer Formaldehyde Products Liability Litigation (Mississippi Plaintiffs), 668 F.3d 281 (5th Cir. 2012) (because Mississippi and Alabama "emergency statutes" immunize private persons who voluntarily and without compensation allow their property or premises to be used as shelter in a natural disaster, the federal government's voluntary provision of emergency housing units to hurricane victims was also immunized conduct under the FTCA).

governmental safety inspections and can be liable for their negligence in doing so; consequently, the government can be liable for negligent mine inspections.[28]

Limitations. Although the FTCA begins with a general rule that government is liable for torts in much the same way a private person would be, the Act then carves out exceptions, withholding jurisdiction from courts when the government's alleged tort is the enforcement of a statute or the exercise of a discretionary function,[29] and also in a number of very particular instances listed in the statute.[30] Beyond this, the Supreme Court itself has concluded that the government cannot be held strictly liable[31] and that the government cannot be liable for its torts to members of the armed forces.[32]

Civil rights claims against the federal government. The FTCA relies, at least formally, on the relevant state's law of torts. It does not authorize a suit against the federal government for violation of constitutional or other federally guaranteed rights. Constitutional civil rights claims based upon federal actions must be asserted, if at all, against the individual officers responsible, not against the government.[33]

§ 22.3   The Discretionary Immunity

Protecting Discretion

Enforcement or nonenforcement of statutes. The FTCA retains sovereign immunity in two major and related instances. The courts have no jurisdiction to hear claims based simply upon the government's enforcement of a statute or regulation, even if the statute or regulation turns out to be invalid.[34] This is a corollary to the idea that under the separation-of-powers principle, courts cannot force Congress to pass a statute or to repeal one, because the power to adopt or reject a statute is legislative in nature, not judicial.[35] The FTCA recognizes that the government may be liable for negligent acts committed while enforcing a statute—an agent's negligent driving while enforcing a statute, for example—but not for the mere fact of enforcement itself.

Enactment or failure to enact regulation. Even more clearly, the government cannot be held for failing to enact a statute or a set of regulations, or for adopting a statute or regulations that cause harm. The fact that the plaintiff's injury could have been avoided if a government agency had adopted a reasonable set of regulations establishes no claim at all.[36] Equally, the government is free to adopt a public-works project, such as a flood control program that causes the plaintiff harm, without liability in tort.[37]

---

[28] United States v. Olson, 546 U.S. 43, 126 S.Ct. 510, 163 L.Ed.2d 306 (2005).

[29] See OSI, Inc. v. United States, 285 F.3d 947 (11th Cir. 2002) (once the government asserts a discretionary immunity, the "burden is on the plaintiff to prove that jurisdiction exists").

[30] 28 U.S.C.A. § 2680.

[31] Laird v. Nelms, 406 U.S. 797, 92 S.Ct. 1899, 32 L.Ed.2d 499 (1972) (sonic boom).

[32] See § 22.4.

[33] See § 22.13.

[34] "The provisions of this chapter and section 1346(b) of this title shall not apply to—(a) Any claim based upon an act or omission of an employee of the Government, exercising due care, in the execution of a statute or regulation, whether or not such statute or regulation be valid. . . ." 28 U.S.C.A. § 2680(a).

[35] See Dalehite v. United States, 346 U.S. 15, 73 S.Ct. 956, 97 L.Ed. 1427 (1953).

[36] E.g., Loge v. United States, 662 F.2d 1268 (8th Cir. 1981).

[37] Coates v. United States, 181 F.2d 816 (8th Cir. 1950).

Discretionary immunity. The statute likewise retains sovereign immunity for governmental performance or nonperformance of a discretionary function.[38] For instance, an agency's decision to regulate a financial institution,[39] to carry out safety inspections,[40] to interdict foreign fruit suspected of containing poisons,[41] to issue or deny a grazing permit,[42] to fire employees,[43] to delegate hazardous waste disposal to an independent contractor,[44] or to parole a prisoner,[45] are all protected activities for which liability cannot be imposed, so long as the activities are generally or specifically authorized by statute.[46] In such cases, the fact that the governmental agency has acted negligently or even abused its discretion is irrelevant, for the government is immune.

Justification. The chief justification for this hiatus in governmental responsibility lies in the separation-of-powers concept.[47] Other reasons support a degree of protection in particular cases. Many administrative decisions cannot be measured against a standard of care. Others may be like judicial decisions, best left to be redressed by internal review rather than by liability. The problem in all cases has been to determine what counts as a discretionary decision that must not be reviewed by courts and what, on the contrary, counts as simply tortious conduct.

Operational-planning distinction. In the first generation after the enactment of the FTCA, the Court worked with a distinction between planning decisions and operational decisions. The first case referred to the "level" of the decision,[48] but later cases seemed more concerned with the nature of the decision.[49] If it was a planning decision, involving a broad issue of social or political policy, it was discretionary. The Coast Guard's decision to operate a lighthouse might be a planning decision and protected, but its failure to maintain the light, with a resulting shipwreck, would be merely operational negligence for which liability would be appropriate.[50] Later decisions of the Supreme Court, however, have shifted focus and perhaps have eliminated the planning-operational terminology.

---

[38] "The provisions of this chapter and section 1346(b) of this title shall not apply to—(a) Any claim . . . based upon the exercise or performance or the failure to exercise or perform a discretionary function or duty on the part of a federal agency or an employee of the Government, whether or not the discretion involved be abused." 28 U.S.C.A. § 2680(a). See generally 2 Lester S. Jayson & Robert C. Longstreth, Handling Federal Tort Claims, Chapter 12 (2007 & Supp.).

[39] United States v. Gaubert, 499 U.S. 315, 111 S.Ct. 1267, 113 L.Ed.2d 335 (1991).

[40] United States v. S.A. Empresa de Viacao Aerea Rio Grandense, 467 U.S. 797, 104 S.Ct. 2755, 81 L.Ed.2d 660 (1984).

[41] Fisher Bros. Sales, Inc. v. United States, 46 F.3d 279 (3d Cir. 1995).

[42] See United States v. Morrell, 331 F.2d 498 (10th Cir. 1964).

[43] Sydnes v. United States, 523 F.3d 1179 (10th Cir. 2008).

[44] Andrews v. United States, 121 F.3d 1430 (11th Cir. 1997).

[45] Payton v. United States, 679 F.2d 475 (5th Cir. 1982).

[46] The discretion is lost if a statute mandates a different action. For instance, issuance of a license or permit may be authorized and thus discretionary in some cases, but in others regulations may mandate a refusal of a license until certain conditions are met. In that case, the regulation removes the discretion. See Berkovitz by Berkovitz v. United States, 486 U.S. 531, 108 S.Ct. 1954, 100 L.Ed.2d 531 (1988).

[47] See Harold J. Krent, Preserving Discretion without Sacrificing Deterrence: Federal Governmental Liability in Tort, 38 U.C.L.A. L. Rev. 871 (1991).

[48] Dalehite v. United States, 346 U.S. 15, 73 S.Ct. 956, 97 L.Ed. 1427 (1953).

[49] See S.A. Empresa de Viacao Aerea Rio Grandense, 467 U.S. 797, 104 S.Ct. 2755, 81 L.Ed.2d 660 (1984).

[50] Indian Towing Co. v. United States, 350 U.S. 61, 76 S.Ct. 122, 100 L.Ed. 48 (1955).

The Berkovitz case: room for choice and a decision grounded in social or political policy. In the *Berkovitz* case,[51] one of the plaintiff's allegations was that a government agency licensed the manufacture of a polio vaccine. The vaccine caused harm to the plaintiff. The government agency allegedly issued the license without receiving data required by regulation to show that the manufacturer's product was safe. The agency had no rightful choice about this matter. It could not rightfully violate the statute or regulation. For this reason it had no discretion and no discretionary immunity.

The Court in *Berkovitz* envisioned a kind of two-part test for the discretionary immunity. (1) Did the government have room for choice? (2) If so, did the choice depend upon "decisions grounded in social, economic, and political policy?" If the answer to either question is "no," the discretionary immunity does not protect the government (although some other rule may do so). The first part of the test asks whether any discretion at all is involved. If the government had no choice because constitutional, statutory, or regulatory rules compelled a given decision, no discretion was involved at all.[52] The second part of the test asks whether the discretion is the kind that is protected— discretion in decision making that involves social, economic, or political "policy judgment." Although the planning-operational terminology is subordinated to these tests, governmental acts in implementing policy, as distinct from forming policy, usually will not involve policy judgment and thus will usually not be protected.[53]

United States v. Gaubert: low-level decisions susceptible of policy analysis. Although the Supreme Court clearly adopted the principle that a decision on social, economic, or political issues is required to establish discretionary immunity, the Court in *Gaubert*[54] also established some rules that tend to undermine that principle. First, *Gaubert* held that a discretionary decision can be made at any level of the government, as long as it was "susceptible to policy analysis."[55] The Court also held that the immunity for discretion stands to bar a claim even if the government did not *actually* consider any policy issues at all, at least when the discretion finds its source in "established governmental policy, as expressed or implied by statute, regulation, or agency guidelines."[56] Both rules have been criticized as providing excessive protection for negligent governmental decisions that cause harm.[57]

Applications and Examples

Regulatory activity and public-benefit programs. Regulatory activity (or inactivity) may be the obvious case for protection under the discretionary immunity. Even if the FAA is required to inspect airplanes for safety, it may decide on spot-checks rather than complete strip-down inspections of all planes.[58] Regulation of financial institutions may in the end cost investors millions, but it is no surprise to find that such regulation, even

---

[51]   Berkovitz by Berkovitz v. United States, 486 U.S. 531, 108 S.Ct. 1954, 100 L.Ed.2d 531 (1988).

[52]   Accord, Loge v. United States, 662 F.2d 1268 (8th Cir. 1981); Myers v. U.S., 652 F.3d 1021 (9th Cir. 2011); Miles v. Naval Aviation Museum Found., Inc., 289 F.3d 715 (11th Cir. 2002).

[53]   See Whisnant v. United States, 400 F.3d 1177, 1181 (9th Cir. 2005) ("[W]e have generally held that the *design* of a course of governmental action is shielded by the discretionary function exception, whereas the *implementation* of that course of action is not.").

[54]   United States v. Gaubert, 499 U.S. 315, 111 S.Ct. 1267, 113 L.Ed.2d 335 (1991).

[55]   Gaubert, 499 U.S. at 325, 111 S.Ct. at 1275.

[56]   Id.

[57]   Bruce A. Peterson & Mark E. Van der Weide, Susceptible to Faulty Analysis: United States v. Gaubert and the Resurrection of Federal Sovereign Immunity, 72 Notre Dame L. Rev. 447, 486 ff. (1997).

[58]   United States v. S.A. Empresa de Viacao Aerea Rio Grandense, 467 U.S. 797, 104 S.Ct. 2755, 81 L.Ed.2d 660 (1984).

in its details, is discretionary and protected.[59] Governmental decisions involving distribution of benefits through large public programs are presumably in the same category. For instance, a governmental decision to implement or reject flood control programs may affect lives and property of many persons, but unless statute or regulation is violated, such decisions are at the core of discretionary immunity.[60] Even without the discretionary immunity, courts might be forced to reach the same result because the government would ordinarily have no duty to disburse public benefits and it is hard to imagine a standard of care that could be applied to many regulatory decisions apart from statutory directives themselves.

Nondeliberative decisions. Governmental decisions that are not in fact based on deliberation or consideration of policy do not sound like policy decisions. As already indicated, *Gaubert* held that a decision might be discretionary and protected even if government agents made the decision without considering policy, as long as the decision was "susceptible to policy analysis." However, even if *Gaubert* applies outside the regulatory case, the discretionary immunity only protects policy decisions "based on the purposes that the regulatory regime seeks to accomplish." Driving a motor vehicle "requires the constant exercise of discretion" but negligent driving is not protected because the discretion in driving is not "grounded in regulatory policy."[61]

Policy choices made pursuant to standards. Beyond this, a discretionary decision must be one that is potentially based on something that could be called policy, and it must be a policy about social, economic, or political issues. Many choices involving balancing of costs and benefits might not be *policy* choices at all because they are choices made pursuant to safety standards or goals. So the government has rightly been held subject to liability for negligent operation of motor vehicles,[62] airport control towers,[63] and lighthouses,[64] as well as for negligence in treatment of prisoners[65] and in maintenance of government property.[66] Indeed, in most of these cases the discretionary immunity is not even asserted.

Professional, scientific, or technical decisions. Similarly, when the objective is to follow a scientific, technical, or safety standard, the government agent may have many choices. The agent may be required to balance many diverse considerations, but the

[59]   United States v. Gaubert, 499 U.S. 315, 111 S.Ct. 1267, 1274, 113 L.Ed.2d 335 (1991).

[60]   See A.O. Smith Corp. v. United States, 774 F.3d 359 (6th Cir. 2014) (claim that Army Corps of Engineers failed to follow flood-control protocols barred by discretionary immunity); National Union Fire Ins. v. United States, 115 F.3d 1415 (9th Cir. 1997) (decision to postpone raising breakwater in a harbor while the corps studied even larger improvements led to millions in flood damage but was discretionary). There is also a specific statute. "No liability of any kind shall attach to or rest upon the United States for any damage from or by floods or flood waters at any place. . . ." 33 U.S.C.A. § 702c.

[61]   United States v. Gaubert, 499 U.S. 315, 111 S.Ct. 1267, 113 L.Ed.2d 335 (1991).

[62]   E.g., Hetzel v. United States, 343 F.3d 1500 (D.C. Cir. 1995).

[63]   E.g., Daley v. United States, 792 F.2d 1081 (11th Cir. 1986); contrast Collins v. United States, 564 F.3d 833 (7th Cir. 2009) (holding that the government's decision to allocate its limited funds to provide different levels of safety systems to different airports was discretionary).

[64]   Indian Towing Co. v. United States, 350 U.S. 61, 76 S.Ct. 122, 100 L.Ed. 48 (1955).

[65]   See United States v. Muniz, 374 U.S. 150, 83 S.Ct. 1850, 10 L.Ed.2d 805 (1963).

[66]   See, e.g., Young v. United States, 769 F.3d 1047 (9th Cir. 2014); Buscaglia v. United States, 25 F.3d 530 (7th Cir. 1994). However, even maintenance of property may sometimes "involve considerable discretion that invokes policy judgment," Terbush v. United States, 516 F.3d 1125 (9th Cir. 2008), especially where the decision whether and how to maintain the property is connected to judgments about how to use funds. See Cope v. Scott, 45 F.3d 445 (D.C. Cir. 1995).

choices are not often choices of policy.[67] Medical decisions by government doctors are in this category. Even if regulations provide that the Veterans' Administration "may" admit or reject a patient, when the VA refuses admission on the basis of a negligent medical judgment, the government may be liable for the harm done.[68] An agency's negligence in releasing a dangerous vaccine is in the same category if the decision is scientific or technical rather than governmental.[69] Indeed, the presence of a preexisting safety standard, or any appropriate standard governing the activity, should tend to displace discretion.[70]

Expansive reading of the immunity. In spite of the cases just mentioned, federal courts have tended to read the discretionary immunity quite broadly.[71] Sometimes they treat routine governmental decisions as decisions of "policy." Sometimes they ignore the policy element and treat any choice as sufficient without considering whether it involves a policy choice on a social or economic matter.[72] Surely no policy judgment is involved when a government driver operates a vehicle in a way to cause a deadly accident. Yet, without finding any policy element at all, the Tenth Circuit invoked the discretionary immunity in such a case.[73] Another Tenth Circuit case expressly found that a park ranger's actions in unsuccessfully guiding a park visitor around a hostile moose were matters of government "policy."[74] Building bridges with defective guardrails seems even less a matter of policy. But the Fourth Circuit, by no means alone, thinks it is a matter of policy because it is likely to entail an allocation of resources.[75] Such a conception of policy encompasses virtually all human acts and certainly all safety measures, few of which can be cost-free.[76]

---

[67] See Whisnant v. United States, 400 F.3d 1177, 1181 (9th Cir. 2005) ("matters of scientific and professional judgment—particularly judgments concerning safety—are rarely considered to be susceptible to social, economic, or political policy").

[68] Collazo v. United States, 850 F.2d 1 (1st Cir. 1988).

[69] E.g., Deasy v. United States, 99 F.3d 354 (10th Cir. 1996).

[70] See, e.g., Navarette v. United States, 500 F.3d 914 (9th Cir. 2007).

[71] See, e.g., criticizing the Court's interpretation of the FTCA as "producing an immunity essentially identical to that applicable before the law was passed," Mark C. Niles, "Nothing But Mischief": The Federal Tort Claims Act and the Scope of Discretionary Immunity, 54 Admin. L. Rev. 1275 (2002).

[72] See, e.g., C.R.S. v. United States, 11 F.3d 791 (8th Cir. 1993) (Army's negligent screening of blood donations entailed a "policy" judgment so that the government was not responsible for the Army's communication of AIDS to soldiers through transfusion of contaminated blood).

[73] Flynn v. United States, 902 F.2d 1524 (10th Cir. 1990).

[74] Tippett v. United States, 108 F.3d 1194 (10th Cir. 1997).

[75] Baum v. United States, 986 F.2d 716 (4th Cir. 1993) ("The question of what materials to use in such a project is also fundamentally described as a question of how to allocate limited resources among competing needs. Considered in this light, . . . the Park Service's decision in this regard plainly was one bound up in economic and political policy considerations."); see also Collins v. United States, 564 F.3d 833 (7th Cir. 2009) (noting in airport-safety case that "The prioritization of demands for government money is quintessentially a discretionary function."); Merando v. United States, 517 F.3d 160 (3d Cir. 2008) (immunizing government decisions in connection with tree-management plan in National Forest, on the ground that the decisions involved consideration of how to allocate limited resources); Hughes v. United States, 110 F.3d 765 (11th Cir. 1997) (postal service's decision to provide inadequate lighting of parking lot, coupled with hedges and other hiding places and a lack of security guards allegedly made the lot dangerous for those rightfully obtaining mail and led to attack on the plaintiff, but these were decisions about resources and thus protected by the discretionary immunity exception); Cope v. Scott, 45 F.3d 445 (D.C. Cir. 1995) (decision whether to repair a road required park service to "establish priorities for the accomplishment of its policy objectives against such practical considerations as staffing and funding").

[76] Some authority, however, rejects the view that allocation of resources is necessarily a policy matter. See, e.g., O'Toole v. United States, 295 F.3d 1029 (9th Cir. 2002) (agency did not allocate funds to maintenance of irrigation system in its control, with result waters backed up and damaged the plaintiff's nearby land; decision to risk harm to others is not a policy decision).

Criticism of broad "policy" formulations. When federal courts use the discretionary immunity to protect all governmental decisions involving costs and benefits or allocation of resources, their logic could foreclose all possibility of governmental liability for negligence. That is so because negligence invariably entails some estimate about the reasonableness of the costs and benefits of the defendant's conduct. It seems plain, then, that some courts have too quickly equated cost-benefit decisions with the discretionary immunity. Excessive reliance on the discretionary immunity to resolve FTCA cases also tends to displace state tort law, which, by statute, is controlling on the substantive issues. It is true that discretion itself is a federal, not a state, issue. But as courts increasingly rely on federal statutes and regulations defining employee's duties, they increasingly displace state tort law, using their analysis of discretion as a substitute for analysis of duty or negligence issues. Finally, legal incentives should not be set perversely to discourage governmental concern with the kind of safety that other institutions are expected to consider. If Ford produces a dangerous car that tends to explode upon a rear impact, consumers will sooner or later get the information and seek alternatives. In addition, Ford is encouraged to avoid such designs by tort rules that allow victims to recover. But if the federal government chooses dangerously bad materials for bridge railings, highway users will be unlikely to hear of it—and even if they do they cannot turn to another government for safer highways. A more circumspect application of the discretionary immunity would help ensure that the government is held to reasonable safety standards analogous to those found in the private sector.

§ 22.4 The *Feres* Rule: Tort Claims by Military Personnel

Combatant activity, foreign country claims. The FTCA provides a number of specific exceptions to the waiver of immunity, one of which retains the immunity for all claims "arising out of the combatant activities of the military or naval forces, or the Coast Guard, during time of war."[77] Another exception that can apply even to protect non combatant military operations is the immunity for claims "arising in a foreign country."[78] Other particular exceptions may also apply if the military action comes within their terms.

The Feres "incident to service" rule. The largest protection against liability for torts of a military origin is not to be found in the statute, however, but was created entirely by the Supreme Court in *Feres v. United States.*[79] In that case, a soldier on active duty perished in a barracks fire, allegedly because of the Army's negligence. The soldier's executrix sued. In companion cases, soldiers sued for Army negligence in performing surgery. The Court concluded that, although the statute contained no language protecting the government from such liabilities, the government should nevertheless be protected against suits "for injuries to servicemen where the injuries arise out of or are in the course of activity incident to service." The *Feres* rule, initially applied to suits against the government under the FTCA, has been carried over to civil rights cases against government agents.[80]

---

[77] 28 U.S.C.A. § 2680(j).
[78] 28 U.S.C.A. § 2680(k).
[79] Feres v. United States, 340 U.S. 135, 71 S.Ct. 153, 95 L.Ed. 152 (1950).
[80] As to suits against individual tortfeasors instead of the government, see §§ 22.12 & 22.13; on civil rights grounds, §§ 22.14 & 22.15.

Rationales for Feres. By ordinary standards of statutory construction, the decision has seemed wrong to most observers[81] and the Supreme Court's applications of it have created a "troubled doctrine,"[82] the meaning of which is uncertain decades after its genesis.[83] Most of the original rationales for the *Feres* rule have been undermined, altered, or applied erratically in later decisions of the Supreme Court. The *Feres* Court's first rationale, that there are no comparable private liabilities because private persons do not have armies and because the Army was not historically liable for torts, has been quietly shelved.[84] The second rationale, that military service members should not recover in tort because they are entitled to military benefits for injury or death,[85] has been undermined by decisions that grant recovery to others in the same position, including discharged veterans,[86] and by decisions that deny recovery even to those who have no such benefits.[87] The last *Feres* rationale, that service members stand in a distinctive relationship to the government so that federal law should control, was at best a strange argument to raise against a statute that neither exempted military negligence nor provided for the application of federal law, and has been incrementally altered in a series of subsequent cases. It now appears as an entirely different idea: the courts must not adjudicate tort claims because to do so "might" interfere with military discipline.[88] Although the military-discipline rationale has some affinity with the discretionary immunity,[89] the *Feres* rule it is intended to support is far, far broader, because the rule excludes liability for all injuries "incident to service," whether command or discretionary decisions are involved or not.[90] Thus for example, an ordinary case of medical malpractice, such as negligent prenatal care for a soldier, does not usually invoke the discretionary immunity but does invoke the *Feres* immunity.

Including off-duty service members. Although the *Feres* rule does not ordinarily bar claims of service members who are injured while they are on furlough,[91] the Supreme Court ruled out a claim for death of a furloughed solider who was kidnapped and murdered by another service man, allegedly because the Army failed to control the killer,

---

[81]   See, e.g., United States v. Johnson, 481 U.S. 681, 107 S.Ct. 2063, 95 L.Ed.2d 648 (1987) (Scalia, J., dissenting); Taber v. Maine, 67 F.3d 1029 (2d Cir. 1995) (Calabresi, J.). See also 2 Dobbs, Hayden & Bublick, The Law of Torts § 340 (2d ed. 2011 & Supp.).

[82]   Estate of McAllister v. United States, 942 F.2d 1473 (9th Cir. 1991).

[83]   Taber v. Maine, 67 F.3d 1029 (2d Cir. 1995).

[84]   See Indian Towing Co. v. United States, 350 U.S. 61, 76 S.Ct. 122, 100 L.Ed. 48 (1955) (government liability for negligent management of lighthouse, although a municipality would be immune); United States v. Muniz, 374 U.S. 150, 83 S.Ct. 1850, 10 L.Ed.2d 805 (1963) (government liability for negligent injury to federal prisoner; *Feres* is inapplicable partly because "the Government's liability is no longer restricted to circumstances in which government bodies have traditionally been responsible for misconduct of their employees"); United States v. Olson, 546 U.S. 43, 126 S.Ct. 510, 163 L.Ed.2d 306 (2005).

[85]   Where a workers' compensation statute applies, the benefits provided are ordinarily exclusive, so that the injured worker has no tort claim. This is the rule for federal as well as for private employees. See 5 U.S.C.A. § 8116.

[86]   United States v. Brown, 348 U.S. 110, 75 S.Ct. 141, 99 L.Ed. 139 (1954); United States v. Muniz, 374 U.S. 150, 83 S.Ct. 1850, 10 L.Ed.2d 805 (1963).

[87]   Stencel Aero Eng'g Corp. v. United States, 431 U.S. 666, 97 S.Ct. 2054, 52 L.Ed.2d 665 (1977).

[88]   United States v. Brown, 348 U.S. 110, 75 S.Ct. 141, 99 L.Ed. 139 (1954); United States v. Muniz, 374 U.S. 150, 83 S.Ct. 1850, 10 L.Ed.2d 805 (1963) ("*Feres* seems best explained" by the discipline rationale); Stencel Aero Engineering Corp. v. United States, 431 U.S. 666, 97 S.Ct. 2054, 52 L.Ed.2d 665 (1977); United States v. Shearer, 473 U.S. 52, 105 S.Ct. 3039, 87 L.Ed.2d 38 (1985).

[89]   See Chappell v. Wallace, 462 U.S. 296, 103 S.Ct. 2362, 76 L.Ed.2d 586 (1983) ("complex, subtle, and professional decisions . . . are essentially professional military judgments").

[90]   See United States v. Stanley, 483 U.S. 669, 107 S.Ct. 3054, 97 L.Ed.2d 550 (1987).

[91]   Brooks v. United States, 337 U.S. 49, 69 S.Ct. 918, 93 L.Ed. 1200 (1949).

whose propensity for violence was known. To permit such a suit, the Court thought, would implicate military discipline in the sense that commanding officers would have to defend their decisions to a civilian court.[92] The *Feres* incident-to-service rule was thus subordinated to the concern over military discipline,[93] which in turn has become a concern to avoid judicial intrusion on decisions of the armed services.

Including claims based on civilian negligence. The Court has gradually expanded its concept of military discipline. In *United States v. Johnson*,[94] a U.S. Coast Guard pilot died in a crash allegedly caused by the negligence of a civilian FAA controller. Although the plaintiff did not charge negligence against any branch of the armed forces, Justice Powell argued that military discipline included "duty and loyalty to one's service and to one's country." He thought that suits by service members against the government for negligence in any branch "could undermine the commitment essential to effective service and thus have the potential to disrupt military discipline in the broadest sense of the word." The Court has also held that whether the *particular* suit would undermine discipline was irrelevant. If injury was incident to service, no suit would be permitted.[95]

Injury after discharge, or during furloughs. The *Feres* rule bars claims by members of the armed services, including reservists on active duty,[96] members of the National Guard,[97] and ROTC cadets,[98] but only those claims that arise "incident to service." If government negligence occurs when the plaintiff has no active connection with the military, the *Feres* rule does not protect the government against liability. A soldier on furlough struck by a jeep on a civilian highway,[99] an Air Force sergeant on a weekend pass injured when an Air Force plane crashed into his house,[100] a discharged veteran who is given negligent treatment at a VA hospital[101]—none has sustained injury "incident to service." Accordingly, each may proceed with suit.

In active service but off duty. Courts have usually thought that a service member injured while on active duty is barred by *Feres* even if she is in a sense "off duty" at the moment of injury.[102] Nevertheless, courts may be reluctant to extend the *Feres* rule to

---

[92]   United States v. Shearer, 473 U.S. 52, 105 S.Ct. 3039, 87 L.Ed.2d 38 (1985).

[93]   However, the Court later, without explaining *Shearer*, insisted that "incident to service" remained the test and that the military status of the plaintiff, not the tortfeasor, was the critical issue. United States v. Johnson, 481 U.S. 681, 107 S.Ct. 2063, 95 L.Ed.2d 648 (1987).

[94]   United States v. Johnson, 481 U.S. 681, 107 S.Ct. 2063, 95 L.Ed.2d 648 (1987).

[95]   See United States v. Stanley, 483 U.S. 669, 107 S.Ct. 3054, 97 L.Ed.2d 550 (1987) (civil rights claim subject to *Feres* rules; *held*, judicial inquiry into extent of disruption of discipline would itself be too intrusive, thus no suit permissible for human experiments on unknowing members of the service, even if chain of command was not implicated).

[96]   Jackson v. United States, 110 F.3d 1484 (9th Cir. 1997).

[97]   Zaputil v. Cowgill, 335 F.3d 885 (9th Cir. 2003).

[98]   Lovely v. United States, 570 F.3d 778 (6th Cir. 2009).

[99]   Brooks v. United States, 337 U.S. 49, 69 S.Ct. 918, 93 L.Ed. 1200 (1949); cf. Schoenfeld v. Quamme, 492 F.3d 1016 (9th Cir. 2007) (soldier on liberty heading off-base when injured in car crash on road partially open to the public).

[100]   Snyder v. United States, 118 F.Supp. 585 (D. Md. 1953), *judgment reinstated*, 350 U.S. 906, 76 S.Ct. 191, 100 L.Ed. 796 (1955); cf. Taber v. Maine, 67 F.3d 1029 (2d Cir. 1995) (Seabee on weekend liberty).

[101]   United States v. Brown, 348 U.S. 110, 75 S.Ct. 141, 99 L.Ed. 139 (1954); Brown v. United States, 451 F.3d 411 (6th Cir. 2006); cf. Bradley v. United States, 161 F.3d 777 (4th Cir. 1998) (service woman given disability rating and removed from activity service; claim for negligent medical treatment causing death not *Feres*-barred).

[102]   Skees v. United States, 107 F.3d 421 (6th Cir. 1997) (suicide by off-duty member of the service, allegedly as a result of medical negligence, is incident to service); Jones v. United States, 112 F.3d 299 (7th Cir. 1997) (serviceman trying out for Military Olympics allegedly injured by medical negligence; injury was

bar a claim by an off-duty service member who is not involved in any military errand, and is injured off the base.[103]

Broad interpretation of incident-to-service test. As the cases demonstrate, courts have usually interpreted "incident" to service quite broadly.[104] Although peacetime medical treatment does not seem particularly military, the service member who is injured or killed by military surgery[105] or misdiagnosis[106] or negligent prenatal care[107] is barred by *Feres*. So is one who dies in a barracks fire although the connection to military discipline is only that the dead soldier was sleeping in assigned quarters.[108] An enlisted woman who suffers sexual harassment has no claim because such harassment is incident to service.[109] A recruit who dies because a brutal "trainer" holds his head under water dies incident to service.[110] Enlisted men who are victims of damaging human experimentation by the armed forces are suffering "incident to service" and are *Feres*-barred,[111] as are obedient soldiers who suffer genetic damage because they were deliberately exposed to dangerous doses of radioactivity.[112]

Claims by service members' families. A survivor's claim for wrongful death of a service member killed incident to service is treated as a derivative claim and stands on no better ground than a direct claim by the service member had she lived; *Feres* itself was a wrongful death claim. Similarly, a spouse's loss of consortium claim based upon a service member's injury incident to service is barred along with the main claim for the injury itself.[113] The same is true if the claim is for emotional injury to the spouse; that, too, has its genesis in the service-connected injury.[114] On the other hand, family members may conceivably have independent claims of their own. When dependents of service members are directly injured, as by negligent medical treatment, *Feres* does not bar their claims and is often not even mentioned in the decisions.[115] However, a number of cases have held that if the service member was exposed to some toxin incident to service, the family member who suffers injury through genetic damage to the parent has no claim, often on the argument that military discipline would be disrupted even though the claim does not depend upon injury to the service member.[116]

---

incident to service); Costo v. United States, 248 F.3d 863 (9th Cir. 2001) (off duty, participating in military-sponsored recreational rafting, Feres bars claim). Some courts reach this result by weighing various factors.

[103] See Taber v. Maine, 67 F.3d 1029 (2d Cir. 1995).

[104] See Major v. United States, 835 F.2d 641 (6th Cir. 1987) ("[T]he Court has embarked on a course dedicated to broadening the *Feres* doctrine to encompass, at a minimum, all injuries suffered by military personnel that are even remotely related to the individual's status as a member of the military. . . .").

[105] Feres v. United States, 340 U.S. 135, 71 S.Ct. 153, 95 L.Ed. 152 (1950).

[106] Cutshall v. United States, 75 F.3d 426 (8th Cir. 1996).

[107] Del Rio v. United States, 833 F.2d 282 (11th Cir. 1987).

[108] See Feres v. United States, 340 U.S. 135, 71 S.Ct. 153, 95 L.Ed. 152 (1950) (death in a barracks fire).

[109] Stubbs v. United States, 744 F.2d 58 (8th Cir. 1984).

[110] Kitowski v. United States, 931 F.2d 1526 (11th Cir. 1991).

[111] United States v. Stanley, 483 U.S. 669, 107 S.Ct. 3054, 97 L.Ed.2d 550 (1987).

[112] See Hinkie v. United States, 715 F.2d 96 (3d Cir. 1983).

[113] E.g., Skees v. United States, 107 F.3d 421 (6th Cir. 1997).

[114] Lombard v. United States, 690 F.2d 215, 69 A.L.R. Fed. 921 (D.C. Cir. 1982).

[115] E.g., Williams v. United States, 435 F.2d 804 (1st Cir. 1970); see 1 Lester S. Jayson & Robert C. Longstreth, Handling Federal Tort Claims § 5A.09 (2007, with Supp.).

[116] Lombard v. United States, 690 F.2d 215, 69 A.L.R.Fed. 921 (D.C. Cir. 1982); Hinkie v. United States, 715 F.2d 96 (3d Cir. 1983) (exposure to radioactivity); Mondelli v. United States, 711 F.2d 567 (3d Cir. 1983) (genetic damage by service member's exposure to nuclear explosion, causing cancer to child); Monaco v. United

§ 22.5 Other Statutory Exceptions to FTCA Liability

Specific conduct excepted. Besides the very broad discretionary immunity, the statute creates a number of very specific exceptions to governmental liability. For example, no claim will be recognized for negligent transmission or loss of mail,[117] tax assessments or collections,[118] or claims arising in foreign countries.[119] A number of others are in the statutory list.

Specific torts excepted. One group of exceptions deals with specific torts. Subject to some qualification, § 2680(h) exempts the government from liability if the claim "arises out of" (1) assault, (2) battery, (3) false imprisonment and false arrest, (4) malicious prosecution, (5) abuse of process, (6) libel and slander, (7) misrepresentation and deceit,[120] and (8) interference with contract rights.[121]

Scope of the exceptions. Sometimes writers refer to this statutory list as creating an intentional tort exception, but that is inaccurate, for not all intentional torts are named in the list and some torts named are not necessarily based upon intent. The list notably omits such traditional intentional torts as trespass to land[122] and conversion of personal property,[123] and such newer torts as intentional infliction of emotional distress[124] and privacy invasion.[125] Consequently, the statute does not preclude suit for those torts unless the conduct relied upon to establish them amounts to one of the excepted torts or falls within another area of retained immunity. For example, a plaintiff may recover for intentional infliction of emotional distress accomplished by way of sexual harassment if the harassment was carried out without a bodily touching that would count as a battery. But the battery exception will bar her claim if it is based on a bodily touching.[126] In the same way, if the facts the plaintiff must rely upon amount to a false imprisonment, the plaintiff is barred, even though the facts also show an invasion of privacy or an intentional infliction of emotional harm.[127]

Exceptions to the exceptions. The main statutory qualification is that, after all, the government is liable for assault, battery, false imprisonment, false arrest, abuse of process, or malicious prosecution where the tort is committed by investigative or law

---

States, 661 F.2d 129 (9th Cir. 1981); Minns v. United States, 155 F.3d 445 (4th Cir. 1998) (gulf war toxins, family members have no claim).

[117] 28 U.S.C.A. § 2680(b). In Dolan v. United States Postal Serv., 546 U.S. 481, 126 S.Ct. 1252, 163 L.Ed.2d 1079 (2006), the plaintiff allegedly tripped over mail negligently left on her porch. The Court held that the exception for transmission of mail was not applicable because it was intended to retain immunity "only for injuries arising, directly or consequentially, because mail either fails to arrive at all or arrives late, in damaged condition, or at the wrong address." By the same token, the mail exception does not immunize the postal service in auto accident cases. Id.

[118] 28 U.S.C.A. § 2680(c). Other statutes, however, regulate suits to recover overpayment of taxes.

[119] 28 U.S.C.A. § 2680(k). The exception applies even where command decisions that authorize tortious activities in foreign countries are made in the United States. Sosa v. Alvarez-Machain, 542 U.S. 692, 124 S.Ct. 2739, 159 L.Ed.2d 718 (2004).

[120] See United States v. Neustadt, 366 U.S. 696, 81 S.Ct. 1294, 6 L.Ed.2d 614 (1961); Block v. Neal, 460 U.S. 289, 103 S.Ct. 1089, 75 L.Ed.2d 67 (1983).

[121] 28 U.S.C.A. § 2680(h).

[122] See Hatahley v. United States, 351 U.S. 173, 76 S.Ct. 745, 100 L.Ed. 1065 (1956); United States v. Gaidys, 194 F.2d 762 (10th Cir. 1952).

[123] See CHoPP Computer Corporation, Inc. v. United States, 5 F.3d 1344 (9th Cir. 1993).

[124] See Limone v. United States, 579 F.3d 79 (1st Cir. 2009).

[125] Birnbaum v. United States, 588 F.2d 319 (2d Cir. 1978).

[126] Truman v. United States, 26 F.3d 592 (5th Cir. 1994).

[127] Metz v. United States, 788 F.2d 1528 (11th Cir. 1986).

enforcement officers of the United States. So a battery, say, would be actionable against the government if it were committed by an officer who is "empowered by law to execute searches, to seize evidence, or to make arrests for violations of Federal law."[128] Separate statutes have also provided that military and VA medical batteries—operations without consent—remain actionable.[129] A battery by other federal employees, on the other hand, is not ordinarily actionable.

Negligently permitting battery by non-employees. In one group of cases, the plaintiff is injured by a battery that the government could have prevented by the exercise of reasonable care. For instance, prison authorities may be negligent in failing to prevent a group of prisoners from beating another prisoner. The Supreme Court has recognized liability in such a case.[130] Because the United States would not be liable for batteries of non-employees (or off-duty employees), the exception applies only to batteries committed by employees of the government acting within the scope of employment.[131] Batteries by prisoners or off-duty service members are not within the exception. So if the plaintiff can prove negligence of the government in permitting or risking a battery by non-employees or off-duty employees, the battery exception is irrelevant and the claim may proceed as a simple negligence claim.

Negligently permitting battery by federal employees. That leaves a major group of cases in which the government negligently permits a battery by a federal employee.[132] For instance, the government may negligently hire or supervise a dangerous child molester or a violent worker. If the worker molests children or attacks citizens with acid, the plaintiff's claim is based on the government's negligence. Nevertheless, the plaintiff must ultimately prove the battery in order to show damages. For this reason, some courts have held that the battery exception applies to bar the plaintiff's claims.[133] However, the Ninth Circuit has held that the battery immunity does not relieve the government of liability when its negligent supervision is a proximate cause of a battery.[134] And, more broadly, the immunity will fail if the government assumed a duty to the plaintiff prior to the battery and independent of it, while the immunity will remain if the government's negligence arises only at the time of and because of the battery.[135]

3. *Immunities and Liabilities of State and Local Entities*

§ 22.6 State Sovereign Immunity and Its Waiver

Traditional immunity. Subject to limits imposed by the federal constitution, the American states are sovereigns. The states and their departments and agencies are

---

[128] 28 U.S.C.A. § 2680(h). See Nguyen v. United States, 556 F.3d 1244 (11th Cir. 2009).

[129] 10 U.S.C.A. § 1089(e) (armed forces); 38 U.S.C.A. § 7316 (Veterans' Administration).

[130] United States v. Muniz, 374 U.S. 150, 83 S.Ct. 1850, 10 L.Ed.2d 805 (1963).

[131] Sheridan v. United States, 487 U.S. 392, 108 S.Ct. 2449, 101 L.Ed.2d 352 (1988).

[132] See Kathleen M. Dorr, Annotation, Construction and application of Federal Tort Claims Act provision excepting from coverage claims arising out of assault and battery (28 U.S.C.A. § 2680(h)), 88 A.L.R. Fed. 7 (1988).

[133] See Leleux v. United States, 178 F.3d 750 (5th Cir. 1999); (sexual battery by Navy officer on female recruit); Johnson v. United States, 788 F.2d 845 (2d Cir. 1986) (molestation by letter carrier); Miele v. United States, 800 F.2d 50 (2d Cir. 1986) (soldier threw acid in child's face).

[134] Brock v. United States, 64 F.3d 1421 (9th Cir. 1995) (rape of Forest Service employee by supervisor); Bennett v. United States, 803 F.2d 1502 (9th Cir. 1986) (kidnaping and rape of children by person hired by government to teach them).

[135] LM ex rel. KM v. United States, 344 F.3d 695 (7th Cir. 2003) (child molestation by letter carrier).

constitutionally obliged to pay for property taken for public purposes.[136] Otherwise, the state public entities can claim the traditional sovereign immunity from suit. States also enjoy a kind of jurisdictional immunity, because under the Eleventh Amendment to the United States Constitution[137] they ordinarily cannot be sued for damages in federal court.[138] The immunity of the states and their agencies as sovereigns differs from the immunities enjoyed by state officers and by purely local governments.

Abolition of blanket immunity. Almost all states have now enacted tort claims statutes waiving the blanket common law immunity of the state and its agencies. Other statutes may affect immunities in particular cases. As a matter of structure, about thirty states abolish the tort immunity generally, but retain it in specified circumstances.[139] A second group works in reverse, retaining the immunity generally, but abolishing it for a list of cases in which liability is permitted.[140] In several states, a tort claim against the state must be presented to an administrative body instead of to a court.[141] Some states set up a separate court of claims for hearing tort claims against the state.[142] A very small number of states appear to retain a very broad immunity.[143]

Cases for liability. States in the second group list specific instances in which liability is permitted.[144] They usually include motor vehicle accidents[145] and injuries on negligently maintained state property, dangerous roads and highways,[146] but the list may include other instances, such as medical malpractice in state schools or hospitals.[147]

---

[136] See Chicago, Burlington & Quincy R.R. Co. v. Chicago, 166 U.S. 226, 17 S.Ct. 581, 41 L.Ed.2d 979 (1897).

[137] "The judicial power of the United States shall not be construed to extend to any suit in law or equity, commenced or prosecuted against one of the United States by citizens of another state, or by citizens or subjects of any foreign state." U.S. Const. Amend. XI.

[138] See Hans v. Louisiana, 134 U.S. 1, 10 S.Ct. 504, 33 L.Ed. 842 (1890). Federal courts may issue injunctions against state officials but may not use such injunctions to reach the state's treasury for past obligations. See Edelman v. Jordan, 415 U.S. 651, 94 S.Ct. 1347, 39 L.Ed.2d 662 (1974). States may also be sued in federal court under the Fourteenth Amendment where Congress has so provided. See Quern v. Jordan, 440 U.S. 332, 99 S.Ct. 1139, 59 L.Ed.2d 358 (1979).

[139] E.g., Alaska Stats. § 09.50.250; Ga. Code § 50–21–23.

[140] E.g., Colo. Rev. Stats. Ann. § 24–10–106; Tex. Civ. Prac. & Rem. Code § 101.021. This form of immunity waiver probably operates to impose governmental responsibility in fewer cases. For example, it may automatically leave all common law immunity-related doctrines, such as the public duty doctrine, standing as a bar. See Ezell v. Cockrell, 902 S.W.2d 394 (Tenn. 1995).

[141] E.g., Ark. Code Ann. § 19–10–204; Conn. Gen. Stat. § 4–160.

[142] E.g., 705 ILCS 505/8.

[143] See Ala. Const. Art I, § 14 (the state "shall never be made a defendant in any court of law or equity"); S.D. Cod. L. § 21–32–16 (but liability insurance coverage waives immunity); Wis. Stat. Ann. § 895.104.

[144] California's statute specifically and broadly provides for public entity liability for failure to discharge a mandatory duty. See Guzman v. County of Monterey, 46 Cal.4th 887, 209 P.3d 89, 95 Cal.Rptr.3d 183 (2009) (interpreting Cal. Govt. Code § 815.6).

[145] E.g., Ohio Rev. Code § 2744.02 (B)(1). See Doe v. Marlington Local School Dist. Board of Educ., 122 Ohio St.3d 12, 907 N.E.2d 706 (2009) (exception did not apply to a school bus driver's alleged failure to supervise children on a bus, as opposed to negligence in the actual driving of the bus).

[146] See, e.g., 14 Me. Rev. Stats. Ann. § 8104–A; Mich. Comp. L. Ann. § 691.1407; N.J. Stat. Ann. 59:4–2; Wyo. Stats. § 1–39–104. Neither acts by third persons on state property, nor activities by the entity itself, necessarily count as conditions of the property as to which immunity is waived. See, e.g., Zelig v. County of Los Angeles, 27 Cal.4th 1112, 45 P.3d 1171, 119 Cal.Rptr.2d 709 (2002); Lightfoot v. School Administrative Dist. No. 35, 816 A.2d 63 (Me. 2003). Insofar as the government's property is dangerous because it is negligently and unsafely designed, some courts might find a discretionary immunity to design badly if the designers actually considered costs and benefits of the dangerous design, even if they did so negligently. See Garrison v. Deschutes County, 334 Or. 264, 48 P.3d 807 (2002).

[147] See Pa. Consol. Stats. Ann. § 8522; Tenn. Code Ann. § 9–8–307 (perhaps the most detailed list).

Cases for no liability—exceptions to the waiver of immunity. In the largest group of states, the state waives immunity generally, but retains it or otherwise excludes liability in a number of specified instances. Many of these statutes are similar to the FTCA in providing for liability like that of a private person in similar circumstances,[148] then carving out an immunity for discretionary decisions[149] together with a number of rather specific exclusions from liability. Some statutes are phrased to waive immunity only for cases of personal injury, property damage, or death, thus impliedly retaining the immunity for economic and dignitary torts that do not fall in one of these categories.[150] Strict liability is routinely excluded.[151]

Not infrequently, the pattern of retained immunity or excluded liability is much like that in the FTCA. For instance, statutes may exclude liability for intentional torts like assault, battery, and false imprisonment[152] and for claims resulting from tax assessment or collection.[153] No summary can capture all the exceptions, some of which are quite narrow. Several states, for example, exempt the state from liability for certain injuries resulting from snow and ice conditions.[154] Some specific immunities may be waived to the extent that the public entity is covered by liability insurance.[155]

Substantial areas of immunity remain even under the most liberal statutes. But even that is not the whole picture. In some states, the plaintiff whose claim against the state is defeated by immunity may nevertheless be able to recover against the tortious officer. The state may then indirectly pay by indemnifying the officer and providing for the costs of his defense.[156]

Procedural and remedial limitations. Statutes almost always impose some special procedural rules for claims against the state, for example, a requirement of notice before suit. Many states cap recovery for compensatory damages[157] and punitive damages are denied altogether.[158]

§ 22.7 Local Public-Entity Immunity and Its Waiver

Common-law rule. Municipalities are corporations chartered by the state, not sovereigns. Nevertheless, a peculiar history[159] led courts to recognize a distinct

---

[148] E.g., Kan. Stat. Ann. § 75–6103; Mass. Gen. L. Ann. ch. 158, § 2.

[149] E.g., Iowa Code Ann. § 669.14; Mass. Gen. L. Ann. ch. 258, § 10; Nev. Rev. Stats. § 41.032. New Jersey is a little more detailed on this. N.J. Stats. Ann. § 59:2–3. Several states do not rely upon the discretionary immunity concept, substituting traditional tort rules about duty limitations instead. See N.M. Stats. Ann. § 41–4–2 B.

[150] E.g., Fla. Stat. Ann. § 768.28 (1) (personal injury, property damage, death); Texas Civ. Prac. & Rem. Code § 101.021(1).

[151] E.g., Colo. Rev. Stats. Ann. § 24–10–106.5. That may be the implication of statutes requiring a negligence or wrongful act, too. E.g., Idaho Code § 6–903.

[152] E.g., Idaho Code § 6–904; Hawai'i Rev. Code § 662–15.

[153] E.g., Minn. Stat. Ann. § 3.736; Or. Rev. Stats. § 30.265.

[154] E.g., 51 Okla. Stats. Ann. § 155.

[155] See 12 Vt. Stats. Ann. § 5601.

[156] See §§ 22.12 & 22.13.

[157] Fla. Stat. Ann. § 768.28 (5) ($200,000 per person); Ind. Code 34–13–3–4 ($700,000); Kan. Stat. Ann. § 75–6105 ($500,000); 14 Me. Rev. Stats. Ann. § 8105 ($400,000).

[158] E.g., Cal. Gov. Code § 818; Fla. Stat. Ann. § 768.28 (5); Hawai'i Rev. Stats. § 662–2.

[159] See Borchard, Government Liability in Tort, 34 Yale L. J. 129, 132–133 (1924). The immunity originated with Russell v. Men of Devon, 2 Term. Rep. 667, 100 Eng.Rep. 359 (1798), where there was no municipal entity at all and no treasure from which to pay the claim, which, in effect, was against the population as individuals.

municipal immunity as a matter of common law. While many states have adopted statutes that modify the common law approach, a number have retained it. As a matter of general common law, municipalities are immune from tort liability, except for (1) torts committed in a proprietary rather than governmental capacity, and (2) nuisance committed by the municipality. Liability may also extend to cases of (3) negligently maintained municipal property[160] and (4) negligently maintained roads, streets, and sewers.[161]

Governmental vs. proprietary. Courts have conceived of the municipal government as operating in several different capacities. If it causes harm while acting in a purely governmental capacity, say in police activities,[162] it enjoys the immunity.[163] But many courts say that the municipality has no immunity for its torts when it operates in a corporate or proprietary capacity.[164] For example, a municipality will be subject to liability for torts inflicted in the operation of a municipal electric or water utility.[165]

Courts do not agree on a test for determining whether an activity is proprietary. Courts have variously held that an activity is or tends to be proprietary (1) if it is carried on for profit,[166] (2) if a fee is paid,[167] (3) if the activity relates to public service, whether or not a fee is paid,[168] (4) if the city is under no duty to carry it out,[169] or (5) if the activity is historically one carried out by private enterprise.[170]

Application of governmental-proprietary test. The governmental-proprietary distinction can produce some surprising case outcomes. A city's operation of an automotive repair garage for its police vehicles has been considered proprietary, for

---

[160] E.g., Hensley v. Jackson County, 227 S.W.3d 491 (Mo. 2007) (stop sign); Pohl v. County of Furnas, 682 F.3d 745 (8th Cir. 2012) (road sign; Neb. law); Connelly v. City of Omaha, 284 Neb. 131, 816 N.W.2d 742 (2012) (trees in city park).

[161] Woods v. Town of Marion, 245 Va. 44, 425 S.E.2d 487 (1993) (waterworks).

[162] E.g., Mosby v. Moore, 716 So.2d 551 (Miss. 1998) (city's establishment of police force was "governmental function" making city immune from liability for injuries caused by high-speed chase); see § 22.10.

[163] E.g., Caneyville Volunteer Fire Department v. Green's Motorcycle Salvage, Inc., 286 S.W.3d 790 (Ky. 2009) (reviewing law of many states, concluding that in determining immunity Kentucky places "greater weight on the extent to which the entity engages in an essential government function," finding a city volunteer fire department immune).

[164] E.g., Wittorf v. City of New York, 23 N.Y.3d 473, 15 N.E.2d 333, 991 N.Y.S.2d 578 (2014) (keeping roads and highways in reasonably safe condition a proprietary function, no immunity).

[165] E.g., Ranells v. City of Cleveland, 41 Ohio St.2d 1, 321 N.E.2d 885 (1975) (water department operation); contra, Fisk v. City of Kirkland, 164 Wash.2d 891, 194 P.3d 984 (2008) (city-run water company owed no legally-enforceable duty to maintain adequate water pressure in fire hydrants, where such a failure resulted in fire damage to plaintiff's RV).

[166] See Town of Brunswick v. Hyatt, 91 Md. App. 555, 605 A.2d 620 (1992) (struggling with cases that seemed to say so); cf. Considine v. City of Waterbury, 279 Conn. 830, 905 A.2d 70 (2006) (revenue in excess of costs is one factor in immunity analysis, though not controlling).

[167] Schulz v. City of Brentwood, 725 S.W.2d 157 (Mo.App. 1987) (city day-care center and preschool).

[168] See City of Atlanta v. Chambers, 205 Ga.App. 834, 424 S.E.2d 19 (1992); Richardson v. City of St. Louis, 293 S.W.3d 133 (Mo. App. 2009).

[169] E.g., Blue Fox Bar, Inc. v. City of Yankton, 424 N.W.2d 915 (S.D. 1988).

[170] Considine v. City of Waterbury, 279 Conn. 830, 905 A.2d 70 (2006) (similarity to private enterprise activity is one test or factor; leasing city property to private enterprise was proprietary); Waters v. Biesecker, 60 N.C. App. 253, 298 S.E.2d 746 (1983) (Board's operation of alcoholic beverage store).

example.[171] On the other hand, some courts treat public parks or swimming pools as proprietary[172] while others do not.[173]

Statutory structures. Many legislatures have replaced the blanket immunity with a list of very specific immunities[174] or with a list of instances in which public entities may be subjected to tort rules. As with sovereign immunity of the state itself, some legislatures have reversed this approach, asserting that the local entity is immune except so far as the statute creates a specific exception.[175] Immunity may be waived to the extent that the public entity is covered by liability insurance.[176] Nevertheless, extensive protection may remain by way of affirmative defenses or otherwise. As a matter of legislature structure, some states subject all public entities to more or less the same rules of immunity and liability, so that one statute applies both to states and other public entities such as municipal corporations. Other states treat local public entities under separate statutes.[177]

Another structural difference in approaches can be seen in the way public officers and employees are treated. In some instances, the immunity of the employee and the municipality are coextensive, so that if the employee is immune, the municipality is likewise protected.[178] In others, the employee may be exposed to liability when the municipality is not.[179] In either case, the employee who is held liable to the plaintiff may have a right of indemnity against the municipality.[180] The effect of the indemnity is that whether the municipality is formally immune or not, it ultimately pays and thus becomes liable through its obligation to indemnify the individual employee.

Finally, some statutes create an entirely new scheme of liability and immunity, while others adopt one or more of the common law rules, such as the rule based upon the governmental-proprietary distinction, for particular situations.[181] The recovery of damages and prejudgment interest is limited in many states, and punitive damages barred altogether. Under any of these systems, lawyers must consult the general statutory provisions for immunity and liability and frequently must also find narrowly drawn statutes providing immunities for very particular activities, such as the system for 911 emergency calls[182] or the operation of airports.[183]

---

[171] E.g., Thomas v. Hilburn, 654 So.2d 898 (Miss. 1995).

[172] Morgan v. City of Ruleville, 627 So.2d 275 (Miss. 1993) "Proprietary activities are those which, while beneficial to the community and very important, are not vital to a City's functioning. (Zoo, football stadium.)"

[173] E.g., Town of Brunswick v. Hyatt, 91 Md.App. 555, 605 A.2d 620 (1992).

[174] See § 22.6.

[175] As in 42 Pa.C.S. §§ 8541.

[176] E.g., N.C. Gen. Stat. § 153A–435.

[177] For example, Chapter 745 of the Illinois Statutes contains separate subdivisions for states, local entities, schools, officers and a number of other immunities.

[178] E.g., 745 ILCS 10/2–109 ("A local public entity is not liable for an injury resulting from an act or omission of its employee where the employee is not liable."); Sletten v. Ramsey County, 675 N.W.2d 291 (Minn. 2004) (applying the rule that the county enjoys "vicarious official immunity" where the employee is immune by virtue of engaging in a discretionary function).

[179] E.g., Ex parte City of Tuskegee, 932 So.2d 895 (Ala. 2005) (city liable where employee acts negligently, but the city is immune and only the employee is liable where he acts in bad faith or with malice).

[180] E.g., Wiehagen v. Borough of North Braddock, 527 Pa. 517, 594 A.2d 303 (1991).

[181] Ohio Rev. Code § 2744.02(B)(3).

[182] Alaska Stats. § 29.35.133; N.J. Stat. Ann. 52:17C–10(D).

[183] Ala. Code § 4–4–4.

§ 22.8 Discretionary Immunity of State and Local Entities

Policy basis. Perhaps the chief immunity or defense remaining after statutory restructuring of state- and local-entity liability is the immunity for decisions of discretion or basic policy.[184] Judicial and legislative decisions are easily included in this category, but so are some executive-branch decisions and action. As explained in connection with the FTCA, the idea is that social and economic policy is to be fixed by legislative and executive branches of the government, not the judiciary, and that the judicial branch must not intrude on those basic decisions.[185] In some instances, this same policy is advanced by the separate rule called the public duty doctrine.[186] The policy dictates that public entities must not be held liable for passing or failing to pass legislation, even if that legislation is wise and would have avoided injury to the plaintiff.[187] Judicial decisions and some executive branch decisions, such as decisions about the level of security for juvenile detainees,[188] are sufficiently analogous to come within the same immunity. But courts sometimes go beyond this by characterizing rather minor and routine decisions of a governmental agency as decisions of social, economic and political policy, and thus barring trial to discover whether the agency's acts were negligent.[189]

Limits. The policy behind the discretionary immunity is sound, but it has limits. To hold a public entity liable for a negligent course of conduct in the administration of programs by the executive branch is not invariably an inappropriate intrusion. Liability for negligent operation of a city bus or even of a police department does not mean that the negligent conduct is forbidden. Liability only means that if the entity chooses a dangerous course of conduct, it should pay its way, as private businesses must do. Besides that, since costs of many governmental decisions and actions represent a real loss or expense to someone in the polity—either the individual victim or the public entity—judges must not defer too readily to misconduct in another branch of government.

Where governmental function is to exercise care. Application of the discretionary immunity is largely a matter of policy perceptions. The immunity is defined by the courts' "pragmatic assessment" of the need for it.[190] Perhaps the immunity is not needed when the entity undertakes activities that can be judged under ordinary standards of care. The function of a public entity's officer is frequently to use due care. A child-care worker exercises discretion at almost every moment, but his function is ultimately to exercise due care for the children; thus judges do not intrude upon the executive branch if they hold him to the care his function requires.[191] A department of transportation may be in charge of highway safety and appropriately held liable if it negligently fails to maintain reasonably safe highway conditions.[192] A therapist assuredly exercises professional

---

[184] Often by statute, as in e.g., Kan. Stat. Ann. § 75–6104.

[185] See, e.g., Terwilliger v. Hennepin County, 561 N.W.2d 909 (Minn. 1997). The federal cases on the same general rule under the Federal Tort Claims Act are discussed in § 336.

[186] See § 22.9.

[187] Cf. Hill v. Alderman of City of Charlotte, 72 N.C. 55 (1875) (injury when city suspended anti-fireworks ordinance, no liability).

[188] Jarboe v. Board of County Comn'rs of Sedgwick County, 262 Kan. 615, 938 P.2d 1293 (1997).

[189] See Shelton v. State, 644 N.W.2d 27 (Iowa 2002); Schroeder v. St. Louis County, 708 N.W.2d 497 (Minn. 2006).

[190] Defoor v. Evesque, 694 So.2d 1302 (Ala. 1997).

[191] See Bell v. Chisom, 421 So.2d 1239 (Ala. 1982).

[192] See Reynolds v. Kansas Dep't of Trans., 43 P.3d 799 (Kan. 2002); but see Steward v. State, 322 P.3d 860 (Alaska 2014) (decision not to reinstall a removed guardrail was discretionary); Truman v. Griese, 762

judgment and in that sense exercises discretion, but his function as a doctor provided by a public entity is to professionally treat patients. If the professional standard of care constrains his choice of treatment or diagnosis, there is no logical occasion to immunize his unprofessional decisions.[193] Essentially the same idea is expressed by saying that the discretionary immunity only applies when a high degree of discretion is required and when it is applied, not merely to routine matters but to "basic policy decisions."[194]

Conscious-choice rule. Be that as it may, courts' perceptions of the need for immunity differ by shades, so the line between immunity and responsibility is one of the law's ghostlier demarcations. Some state cases refuse to grant the immunity unless the governmental entity made a conscious choice of conduct,[195] For example, under the conscious-choice rule, if the public entity fails to erect a guardrail on public property where ordinary care would require one, the entity may be liable to an injured person under ordinary negligence rules unless it chose to omit the rail for some reason of policy.[196] The alternative would be to follow the federal approach,[197] immunizing the public entity if there was room for policy choice, even if the entity did not actually make a choice. Under this approach, the entity will be immune if the court can imagine policy choices that could have been made, even if the entity did not act for any of the imagined policy reasons or make any conscious choice at all.[198]

Planning vs. operational. Some states also utilize the distinction between planning and operational decisions, limiting the immunity to cases of "planning" and excluding it for actual operations or execution of decisions.[199] Similarly, state cases have often drawn a distinction between discretionary, legislative, or judicial acts on the one hand, and ministerial acts on the other, with immunity for the former only.[200] These distinctions are phrased as if they were tools used to discover the answer to immunity questions. In fact, however, they are usually labels applied after the decision on immunity is reached, so they have not been immensely helpful.

§ 22.9 The Public Duty Doctrine

Even if no immunity protects a public entity, the entity may escape liability because it owes no duty to the plaintiff. For example, if a fire safety ordinance requires smoke alarms in all new housing but does not require the city to inspect for compliance,

---

N.W.2d 75 (S.D. 2009) (state department of transportation's decision on the placement of warning signs at an intersection was discretionary).

[193] See Terwilliger v. Hennepin County, 561 N.W.2d 909 (Minn. 1997).

[194] See, e.g., Graber v. City of Ankeny, 56 N.W.2d 157 (Iowa 2003) (no immunity for decisions about traffic light timing); Mahan v. New Hampshire Dep't of Administrative Services, 141 N.H. 747, 693 A.2d 79 (1997).

[195] Johnson v. State, 69 Cal.2d 782, 447 P.2d 352, 73 Cal.Rptr. 240 (1968) ("[T]o be entitled to immunity the state must make a showing that such a policy decision, consciously balancing risks and advantages, took place."); Thompson v. Newark Housing Authority, 108 N.J. 525, 531 A.2d 734 (1987).

[196] Creech v. South Carolina Wildlife and Marine Resources Dept., 491 S.E.2d 571 (S.C. 1997).

[197] E.g., Anderson v. State, 692 N.W.2d 360 (Iowa 2005); Martinez v. Maruszczak, 123 Nev. 433, 168 P.3d 720 (2007). See § 22.3.

[198] See, e.g., Rosebush v. United States, 119 F.3d 438 (6th Cir. 1997); Bowman v. United States, 820 F.2d 1393 (4th Cir. 1987).

[199] E.g., Kohl v. City of Phoenix, 215 Ariz. 291, 160 P.3d 170 (2007); Wallace v. Dean, 3 So.3d 1035 (Fla. 2009); S.W. v. Spring Lake Park School Dist. No. 16, 580 N.W.2d 19 (Minn. 1998); Giggers v. Memphis Hous. Auth., 363 S.W.3d 500 (Tenn. 2012).

[200] See Defoor v. Evesque, 694 So.2d 1302 (Ala. 1997); Commonwealth, Trans. Cabinet, Dep't of Highways v. Sexton, 256 S.W.3d 29 (Ky. 2008); Umansky v. ABC Ins. Co., 319 Wis.2d 622, 769 N.W.2d 1 (2009).

ordinary tort rules place no responsibility upon the public entity.[201] Most courts go much further by holding that when a statute imposes upon a public entity a duty to the public at large, and not a duty to a particular class of individuals, the duty is not enforceable in tort.[202] Under this view, as the saying is, a duty to all is a duty to none.

Public duty rule and nonfeasance. In the classic case for invoking the public duty doctrine, the duty is imposed by a statute[203] that requires the defendant to act affirmatively, and the defendant's wrongdoing is a *failure* to take positive action for the protection of the plaintiff. If the entity undertakes to act or enters into action for the plaintiff's protection, liability may be warranted for breach of common law duties rather than the statute. As so described, the public duty rule could apply to any defendant whose only wrong is noncompliance with a statutory directive that requires positive action. In fact, however, many courts treat the public duty doctrine as a rule of public-entity immunity and not as a rule about the existence of a duty.[204]

Examples. Under the public duty rule a police officer is free to ignore dangerous and illegal conduct committed in his presence; victims injured by such conduct have no claim for his nonfeasance.[205] City inspectors can ignore inspection and such matters as building codes and fire safety standards.[206] A county may be under a statutory duty to maintain a 911 system adequately, but the duty may be seen as running to the public at large, not to any individual citizen, thus barring a claim even for wanton conduct.[207] The public duty doctrine may be invoked to bar relief for police failure to protect citizens even when no statute is involved and sometimes even when the police seem to have committed affirmative acts of negligence.[208]

Scope; special duty created by statute. The public duty doctrine has no application when the court concludes that a statute or court order has created a special tort duty or specific obligation to a particular class of persons rather than to the public at large.[209] A child who is injured as a result of a governmental agency's failure to enforce a court's protective order,[210] or its breach of a statutory duty to investigate child abuse,[211] may be

---

[201] See § 11.1 & 11.2. Courts may invoke the public duty doctrine in such a situation even though a simple holding that the statute imposed no duty at all might seem less complicated. E.g., Benson v. Kutsch, 181 W.Va. 1, 7, 380 S.E.2d 36, 42 (1989).

[202] See Kolbe v. State, 625 N.W.2d 721 (Iowa 2001); Lauer v. City of New York, 95 N.Y.2d 95, 711 N.Y.S.2d 112, 733 N.E.2d 184 (2000); Morris v. Anderson County, 564 S.E.2d 649 (S.C. 2002); Osborn v. Mason County, 157 Wash.2d 18, 134 P.3d 197 (2006).

[203] See Madison ex rel. Bryant v. Babcock Center, Inc., 371 S.C. 123, 638 S.E.2d 650 (2006) (public duty rule relieves public entity of a duty of care "only when an action is founded upon a statutory duty").

[204] See Varner v. District of Columbia, 891 A.2d 260 (D.C. 2006); Kunzie v. City of Olivette, 184 S.W.3d 570 (Mo. 2006); Morales v. Town of Johnston, 895 A.2d 721 (R.I. 2006).

[205] Massengill v. Yuma County, 104 Ariz. 518, 456 P.2d 376, 41 A.L.R.3d 692 (1969), overruled, along with the public duty doctrine itself, in Ryan v. State, 134 Ariz. 308, 656 P.2d 597, 38 A.L.R.4th 1188 (1982).

[206] E.g., Ware v. City of Chicago, 375 Ill.App.3d 574, 873 N.E.2d 944, 314 Ill.Dec. 14 (2007); Rakowski v. Sarb, 269 Mich.App. 619, 713 N.W.2d 787 (2006); Torres v. Damicis, 853 A.2d 1233 (R.I. 2004).

[207] Donovan v. Village of Ohio, 397 Ill.App.3d 844, 921 N.E.2d 1238, 337 Ill.Dec. 100 (2010). However, if the 911 operator expressly makes promises and assurances that are not fulfilled, liability is possible. See Munich v. Skagit Emergency Communication Center, 175 Wash. 2d 871, 288 P.3d 328 (2012).

[208] See, on both counts, Varner v. District of Columbia, 891 A.2d 260 (D.C. 2006).

[209] Eklund v. Trost, 335 Mont. 112, 151 P.3d 870 (2006) (statute authorizing emergency vehicles to violate traffic laws).

[210] Sorichetti v. City of New York, 65 N.Y.2d 461, 492 N.Y.S.2d 591, 482 N.E.2d 70 (1985); Nearing v. Weaver, 295 Or. 702, 670 P.2d 137 (1983).

[211] Brodie v. Summit County Children Services Board, 51 Ohio St.3d 112, 554 N.E.2d 1301 (1990); Gagnon v. State, 570 A.2d 656 (R.I. 1990); Sabia v. State, 164 Vt. 293, 669 A.2d 1187 (1995).

permitted to present evidence of negligence and to recover if negligence and causation is proven, provided the court thinks the statute sufficiently narrows the duty to a particular class.[212] But whether a statutory duty is public or special is largely in the eye of the beholder. Some courts permit the agency charged with protecting children to ignore inspection requirements and leave the injured child without a claim.[213] Most courts have concluded that a child-abuse reporting statute does not create a private right of action,[214] often on a public duty rationale when the defendant is a public entity or employee.[215] And even if the statute creates a special duty to a narrow class, no action will lie if the legislative scheme envisions only administrative or regulatory enforcement that excludes tort liability.[216]

Exceptions and qualifications. Some courts have said that the public duty doctrine will not apply to protect the entity when it is guilty of egregious misconduct,[217] intentional wrongdoing, malice, or recklessness.[218] More significantly, the public duty doctrine eliminates the tort claim based upon a statutory duty but it does not necessarily forbid an action based upon common law duties.[219]

Triggers of duty. Although some states impose special conditions limiting the public entity's duty of care,[220] apart from immunities, the public entity ordinarily has a duty to take reasonable affirmative steps to protect the plaintiff, in any of the following instances: (1) the public entity undertakes to provide assistance by promise or conduct which induces the plaintiff to rely upon action by the public entity;[221] (2) the public entity

---

[212] Ducote v. State, Dep't of Social and Health Services, 167 Wash.2d 697, 222 P.3d 785 (2009)

[213] See, e.g., P.W. and R.W. v. Kansas Dep't of Social and Rehabilitation Services, 255 Kan. 827, 877 P.2d 430 (1994); see Danny R. Veilleux, Annotation, Governmental Liability For Negligence in Licensing, Regulating, or Supervising Private Day-care Home in Which Child Is Injured, 68 A.L.R.4th 266 (1989).

[214] See, e.g., Cuyler v. United States, 362 F.3d 949 (7th Cir. 2004).

[215] See, e.g., Doe v. Marion, 373 S.C. 390, 645 S.E.2d 245 (App. 2007) (citing cases from many jurisdictions); Barbina v. Curry, 650 S.E.2d 140 (W.Va. 2007); Danny R. Veilleux, Annotation, Validity, Construction, and Application of State Statute Requiring Doctor or Other Person to Report Child Abuse, 73 A.L.R.4th 782 (1990). A small number of cases go the other way, see, e.g., Landeros v. Flood, 17 Cal.3d 399, 131 Cal.Rptr. 69, 551 P.2d 389, 97 A.L.R.3d 324 (1976). States may also restrict the scope of duty created by such statutes. O'Toole v. Denihan, 118 Ohio St.3d 374, 889 N.E.2d 505 (2008) (no duty under child abuse reporting statute to report to law enforcement).

[216] See Pelaez v. Seide, 2 N.Y.3d 186, 810 N.E.2d 393, 778 N.Y.S.2d 111 (2004) (lead paint in rental housing).

[217] Tedesco v. Connors, 871 A.2d 920 (R.I. 2005).

[218] Estate of Graves, 124 Ohio St. 3d 339, 922 N.E.2d 201 (2010) (wanton or reckless conduct); Ezell v. Cockrell, 902 S.W.2d 394 (Tenn. 1995).

[219] See Marquay v. Eno, 139 N.H. 708, 662 A.2d 272 (1995) (common law duty based on relationship of parties); Edwards v. Lexington County Sheriff's Dept., 386 S.C. 285, 688 S.E.2d 125 (2010) (county and sheriff's department owed common law duty of care to plaintiff based on creation of risk of harm); Benson v. Kutsch, 181 W.Va. 1, 7, 380 S.E.2d 36, 42 (1989) (local public entity would still be liable for negligent conduct in its proprietary capacity). Common law duties to take affirmative action are considered principally in Chapter 25.

[220] See Gleason v. Peters, 568 N.W.2d 482 (S.D. 1997) (plaintiff must show some combination of "(1) actual knowledge of the dangerous condition; (2) reasonable reliance by persons on official representations and conduct; (3) an ordinance or statute setting forth mandatory acts clearly for the protection of a particular class of persons rather than the general public; and (4) failure to use due care to avoid increasing the risk of harm").

[221] See, e.g., Florence v. Goldberg, 44 N.Y.2d 189, 404 N.Y.S.2d 583, 375 N.E.2d 763 (1978) (duty to provide school crossing guards; city's conduct induced reliance). If the city has not engaged on reliance-inducing conduct, the plaintiff must show a promise, see, e.g., McLean v. City of New York, 12 N.Y.3d 194, 905 N.E.2d 1167, 878 N.Y.S.2d 238 (2009) (city did not have sufficient contact with mother whose child was harmed in city day-care center to be deemed to have "promised" anything, on which the plaintiff could reasonably rely, see Braswell v. Braswell, 330 N.C. 363, 410 S.E.2d 897 (1991) (sheriff's general assurances of safety not sufficient); Babcock v. Mason County Fire Dist. No. 6, 144 Wash.2d 774, 30 P.3d 1261 (2001) (homeowners could not justifiably rely on firefighter's statement that their property would be protected).

stands in a special relationship either to the plaintiff or to a person causing harm;[222] or (3) the public entity is guilty of negligent action rather than inaction.[223]

911 operators. A city whose dispatcher for the 911 emergency call system may be regarded as acting affirmatively, or as undertaking a duty not imposed upon it by statute, or as entering into a special relationship with the victim, and on any of those grounds may be held responsible for negligence even though no statute by its terms imposes a special duty to that victim.[224]

Rejection of the doctrine. A number of contemporary courts have broadly rejected the public duty doctrine.[225] Some have restricted it to special cases. For example, some states use the public duty doctrine only to exclude liability for failure of police protection;[226] others use the term "public duty" to describe discretionary immunity.[227] Where the common-law public duty doctrine is rejected or limited by judicial decision, statutes sometimes add immunities in particular cases to get results like those obtained under the public duty rule. For instance, the statute may exclude liability for failure to make an arrest.[228] Even without such statutes, rejection of the doctrine does not automatically result in liability. The plaintiff must establish a duty under ordinary tort principles, and then prove all other elements of a negligence claim, as in any other case.

The logic of the orthodox public duty rule is formally different from the logic of immunity. It is that the statute creates no duty to act and hence, regardless of immunity, the public entity cannot be liable.[229] Which statutes create a tort duty and which do not? Courts talk as if the answer lay in statutory construction. If the statutory duty is narrowed to protect a particular class of persons, it may create a tort duty, otherwise

---

[222] Special relationships that generate a duty to take positive acts of reasonable care include the familiar categorical relationships like landowner-invitee, see Raas v. State, 729 N.W.2d 444 (Iowa 2007), or custodian-ward, see Jackson v. City of Kansas City, 263 Kan. 143, 947 P.2d 31 (1997) (handcuffed man). Informal or ad hoc relationships may also trigger a duty. See, e.g., Schuster v. City of New York, 5 N.Y.2d 75, 154 N.E.2d 534, 180 N.Y.S.2d 265 (1958) (police informant); Edwards v. Lexington County Sheriff's Dept., 386 S.C. 285, 688 S.E.2d 125 (2010) (where police had arranged a hearing for a domestic-violence victim). Prior contact with a plaintiff might produce a special duty simply on the idea that such contact makes injury to that particular plaintiff foreseeable. See St. James Condominium Ass'n v. Lokey, 676 A.2d 1343 (R.I. 2006) (town inspectors had earlier conducted allegedly negligent inspection of plaintiff's condominium).

[223] Thus where police have engaged in a high-speed chase resulting in harm to an innocent person, the public duty doctrine will not usually bar the claim. See Williams v. Mayor & City Council of Baltimore, 359 Md. 101, 753 A.2d 41 (2000); Seide v. State, 875 A.2d 1259 (R.I. 2005); but see Southers v. City of Farmington, 263 S.W.3d 603 (Mo. 2008) (using public duty doctrine to immunize police chief and supervising officer in high-speed chase case). For more on high-speed chases, see § 22.10.

[224] See Hutcherson v. City of Phoenix, 192 Ariz. 51, 961 P.2d 449 (1998); De Long v. County of Erie, 60 N.Y.2d 296, 469 N.Y.S.2d 611, 457 N.E.2d 717 (1983); Munich v. Skagit Emergency Communication Center, 175 Wash. 2d 871, 288 P.3d 328 (2012).

[225] E.g., Commercial Carrier Corp. v. Indian River County, 371 So.2d 1010 (Fla. 1979); Jean W. v. Commonwealth, 414 Mass. 496, 610 N.E.2d 305 (1993); Southers v. City of Farmington, 263 S.W.3d 603 (Mo. 2008); Ficek v. Morken, 685 N.W.2d 98 (N.D. 2004); Wallace v. Ohio Dep't of Commerce, 96 Ohio St. 3d 266, 773 N.E.2d 1018 (2002). In some states, statutory schemes of immunity have affected these holdings.

[226] Gregory v. Clive, 282 Ga. 476, 651 S.E.2d 709 (2007); Beaudrie v. Henderson, 631 N.W.2d 308 (Mich. 2001); Lovelace v. City of Shelby, 526 S.E.2d 652 (N.C. 2000); E.P. v. Riley, 604 N.W.2d 7 (S.D. 1999). In contrast, Muthukumarana v. Montgomery County, 370 Md. 447, 805 A.2d 372 (2002), applies the doctrine to at least some other employees.

[227] O'Gara v. Ferrante, 690 A.2d 1354 (R.I. 1997) (doctrine "shields the state and its political subdivisions from tort liability arising out of discretionary governmental actions that by their nature are not ordinarily performed by private persons").

[228] E.g., Ariz. Rev. Stats. § 12–820.02 A 1 (unless grossly negligent); Mass. Gen. L. Ann. ch. 258 § 10(h).

[229] See, e.g., Holsten v. Massey, 200 W.Va. 775, 490 S.E.2d 864 (1997) ("The public duty doctrine . . . is not based on immunity from existing liability. Instead, it is based on the absence of duty in the first instance.").

not.[230] Little statutory construction is possible in most cases and courts sometimes implicitly admit that it is less a matter of construction than a matter of judicial policy. They have thus suggested numerous reasons to exempt public entities from the obligations apparently imposed by statutes.

One argument is essentially the same one presented for the discretionary immunity. Expressed in various ways, the core proposition is that courts should leave allocation of resources to the legislature or to the executive.[231] The argument is persuasive in some cases, but not all cases involve allocation of substantial resources. Some involve simply bad mistakes or horrendous negligence. The officer who simply watches a drunk driver go through dangerous antics for a substantial period without attempting to deal with the situation is not allocating resources; he is behaving very negligently indeed. The resources argument is puzzling, too, when compared to the same argument on the issue of discretionary immunity. A statutory directive to act in a particular way—to investigate reports of child abuse, for example—seems to remove all discretion. Yet the public duty doctrine is intended to foster and protect discretion in the very case where statutes seem to have removed it.

Another argument seems to be predicated upon a deep distrust of the judicial system itself. This argument implicitly asserts that courts cannot formulate and administer an appropriate rule about the scope of liability. An officer should have no duty to arrest a drunk driver he encounters, one court said, because if he tries "to avoid liability by removing from the road all persons who pose any potential hazard, he may find himself liable in many instances for false arrest."[232] It is hard to believe that courts would administer the reasonable care rule of negligence law to require the arrest of every hazardous driver on the road in the first place. If courts did such an unprecedented thing, they could hardly impose liability for doing what they required.

Although the arguments do not seem broad enough to support a public duty rule, they rightly point to particular instances in which liability is inappropriate. For instance, if an officer must choose when to arrest a dangerous person, appropriate caution may counsel delay. If so, he cannot be found negligent. In the same way, a busy precinct may have no officers to spare for the protection of every person within its jurisdiction. If not, it cannot be found negligent. Ordinary negligence rules appropriately exclude liability in such cases, but they leave open the possibility of liability when police officers unprofessionally shirk their duty and when administrative bumbling sends officers to the wrong place. The public duty doctrine, in contrast, excludes liability in all cases in which agencies fail to enforce or obey a statutory directive that is deemed to create a duty to the public at large.

---

[230] Distinguish negligence per se, which allows a statute to set the standard of care if the statute is designed to protect a class of persons the plaintiff is in against a type of harm that occurred. See Chapter 11.

[231] E.g., Tipton v. Town of Tabor, 567 N.W.2d 351 (1997).

[232] See Shore v. Town of Stonington, 187 Conn. 147, 156, 444 A.2d 1379, 1383 (1982); see also Remet Corp. v. City of Chicago, 509 F.3d 816 (7th Cir. 2007) ("[I]f a municipality were required to meet every allegation of negligence, enormous public resources would be diverted from the provision of governmental services to the defense of litigation and payment of judgments."); Prosser v. Kennedy Enterprises, Inc., 342 Mont. 209, 179 P.3d 1178 (2008) ("The public duty doctrine prevents individual members of the public from using tort liability to constrain unduly a municipality's discretion to use its limited resources to promote the general welfare.").

§ 22.10   Excluding Liability for Police and Fire Protection

The usual rule is that public entities are free of all liability for failure to provide police or fire protection, even if that failure was negligent. Similarly, statutes and judicial decisions usually exclude liability for failure to arrest a dangerous person who later harms or kills others.[233] However, unless statutes dictate otherwise, liability may be imposed for failure to protect a specific person if the police create a special relationship with that person by undertaking protection and then carrying it out negligently.

For example, if police attempt to answer a 911 call but negligently go to the wrong address, liability may be imposed because the police have themselves allocated resources.[234] Similarly, unless a statute specifically provides otherwise, courts have imposed liability when a fire department negligently uses dangerous or inadequate methods of fighting a fire.[235] But when the city does nothing to address the particular crime or fire, no liability is the usual rule. The city is not liable if a police officer does nothing at all upon learning that a woman has been kidnapped, even though the officer could have saved her by making a phone call.[236] A city is not liable when its police fail to arrest a man known to be dangerous, even after a warrant had issued.[237] Nor is it liable when it fails to respond to a fire call,[238] fails to enforce fire-safety regulations,[239] or fails to provide adequate water,[240] although there are a few decisions to the contrary.[241] Even when a special relationship is established by police investigation and promises of protection, liability is sometimes rejected.[242] Some authority has gone far beyond these immunities for failure to act by shielding the local public entity even for affirmative acts of negligence in operating a police department.[243]

Negligent police chases. One special category of police activity is the high-speed chase that ends in injury or death, sometimes because the person pursued runs down a bystander, sometimes because the police driver does so, and sometimes because the pursued person is himself killed or injured. These cases are not like those in which the police simply fail to act at all. Rather, they involve affirmatively dangerous conduct that creates risks to the plaintiff. So it is possible to resolve such cases under ordinary negligence rules, holding the public entity subject to liability when the dangers of the chase outweigh the advantages of capturing a suspect, as where as many as twenty police

---

[233] South v. Maryland, 59 U.S. 396, 15 L.Ed. 433 (1855); Ezell v. Cockrell, 902 S.W.2d 394 (Tenn. 1995).

[234] De Long v. County of Erie, 60 N.Y.2d 296, 469 N.Y.S.2d 611, 457 N.E.2d 717 (1983). In such cases, police may not only have allocated resources, thereby undertaking a duty of care, but may also have lost any immunity for discretionary activities, because once a known and present danger is encountered, reasonable rescue action becomes a ministerial task. See, expounding this doctrine, but rejecting its application to the facts, Lodl v. Progressive Northern Ins. Co., 253 Wis.2d 323, 646 N.W.2d 314 (2002).

[235] Harry Stoller and Co. v. City of Lowell, 412 Mass. 139, 587 N.E.2d 780 (1992); Invest Cast, Inc. v. City of Blaine, 471 N.W.2d 368 (Minn. 1991). *Contra,* City of Daytona Beach v. Palmer, 469 So.2d 121 (Fla. 1985) (decisions on how to fight a fire involve discretionary judgments).

[236] See Kircher v. City of Jamestown, 74 N.Y.2d 251, 544 N.Y.S.2d 995, 543 N.E.2d 443 (1989).

[237] Dore v. City of Fairbanks, 31 P.3d 788 (Alaska 2001).

[238] Frye v. Clark County, 97 Nev. 632, 637 P.2d 1215 (1981).

[239] Motyka v. City of Amsterdam, 15 N.Y.2d 134, 204 N.E.2d 635, 256 N.Y.S.2d 595 (1965). See Kan. Stats. Ann. 75–6104(n); Mass. Gen. L. Ann. ch. 258 § 10(g).

[240] E.g., Remet Corp. v. City of Chicago, 509 F.3d 816 (7th Cir. 2007) (Illinois law); Westbrook v. City of Jackson, 665 So.2d 833 (Miss. 1995); Fisk v. City of Kirkland, 164 Wash.2d 891, 194 P.3d 984 (2008).

[241] Ziegler v. City of Millbrook, 514 So.2d 1275 (1987); Adams v. State, 555 P.2d 235 (Alaska 1976) (fire hazards actually discovered in hotel). These cases implicate the public duty doctrine, see § 22.9.

[242] Barillari v. City of Milwaukee, 194 Wis.2d 247, 533 N.W.2d 759 (1995).

[243] Niese v. City of Alexandria, 264 Va. 230, 564 S.E.2d 127 (2002).

vehicles pursued a traffic violator for 25 miles through densely populated urban areas, with resulting death to bystanders.[244] Such decisions, like many other negligence cases, call for a balancing of risks and utilities, so if the pursuer is a dangerous criminal and the risks to innocent people are low, the chase may not be negligent at all.[245] A variation on this approach might reduce the standard of care for emergency vehicles[246] or might limit the care owed to the person being pursued while maintaining the negligence standard for bystanders.[247]

Some courts, however, tend to think that balancing risks and utilities requires an immunity rather than a simple negligence analysis. Thus some courts resolve the high-speed chase cases on immunity grounds because risks must be weighed.[248] The result of the immunity approach is that it eliminates the capacity to distinguish good cases for liability from bad ones; all chase claims are treated substantially the same. So pursuit of a known violent criminal and pursuit of a traffic violator can equally call for intense risks to the public. Some states extend this immunity to negligence use of firearms by police.[249]

A third approach demands that the public entity itself prescribe a balancing of risks and utilities in its policies for police officers. If the entity provides an adequate policy, then it is immune. If not, liability is imposed for negligence in failing to prescribe the policy.[250]

§ 22.11 Excluding Liability for Release of Dangerous Persons

Courts tend to deny recovery by victims of dangerous prisoners, mental patients, and others who have been negligently released from custody[251] or who have escaped. Although public entities owe a duty of reasonable care to those in custody, and also a duty of reasonable care to control dangerous persons in custody,[252] public entities often avoid responsibility for their negligence in authorizing parole or permitting escape,[253] either because statutes specifically say so,[254] because courts invoke discretionary

---

[244] See City of Caddo Valley v. George, 340 Ark. 203, 9 S.W.3d 481 (2000); City of Pinellas Park v. Brown, 604 So.2d 1222 (Fla. 1992).

[245] See Sergent v. City of Charleston, 549 S.E.2d 311 (W. Va. 2001); cf. Gooden v. City of Talladega, 966 So.2d 232 (Ala. 2007) (police not negligent for engaging in high-speed chase where the fleeing driver's attempts to evade arrest posed an immediate threat to other motorists).

[246] It is increasingly common for statutes to be construed to limit the standard of care for emergency vehicles, so that liability for high-speed chases is imposed only for reckless or similar exaggerated fault. See, e.g., Robbins v. City of Wichita, 285 Kan. 455, 172 P.3d 1187 (2007); Saarinen v. Kerr, 84 N.Y.2d 494, 620 N.Y.S.2d 297, 644 N.E.2d 988 (1994); Seide v. State, 875 A.2d 1259 (R.I. 2005); City of Amarillo v. Martin, 971 S.W.2d 426 (Tex. 1998); Rochon v. State, 177 Vt. 144, 862 A.2d 801 (2004).

[247] See Estate of Day v. Willis, 897 P.2d 78 (Alaska 1995); Robinson v. City of Detroit, 462 Mich. 439, 613 N.W.2d 307 (2000); Lindstrom v. City of Corry, 563 Pa. 579, 763 A.2d 394 (2000).

[248] E.g., Pletan v. Gaines, 494 N.W.2d 38 (Minn. 1992); Mosby v. Moore, 716 So.2d 551 (Miss. 1998); Southers v. City of Farmington, 263 S.W.3d 603 (Mo. 2008); McBride v. Bennett, 764 S.E.2d 44 (Va. 2014).

[249] See Alston v. City of Camden, 168 N.J. 170, 773 A.2d 693 (2001) (under statute).

[250] See Alcala v. City of Corcoran, 147 Cal.App.4th 666, 53 Cal.Rptr.3d 908 (2007); Estate of Cavanaugh v. Andrade, 202 Wis.2d 290, 550 N.W.2d 103 (1996).

[251] See generally Janet Boeth Jones, Annotation, Governmental Tort Liability For Injuries Caused by Negligently Released Individual, 6 A.L.R.4th 1155 (1981).

[252] See §§ 26.9 & 26.11.

[253] See, e.g., S.C. Code § 15–78–60 (21); Don F. Vaccaro, Annotation, Liability of Public Officer or Body For Harm Done by Prisoner Permitted to Escape, 44 A.L.R.3d 899 (1973).

[254] E.g., N.J. Stats. Ann. § 59:5–2 (parole or escape); 51 Okla. St. Ann. § 155; S.C. Code § 15–78–60.

immunity,[255] or because they apply the public duty rule[256] or some other immunity.[257] Sometimes courts simply say the state owed no duty to foster safety for its citizens by warning or by supervision of a parolee.[258] But the tendency is not universal; a few cases have imposed responsibility upon public entities for negligently permitting a prisoner's escape[259] or for the release of dangerous persons.[260] Some states impose liability if the public employee was willful or wanton in permitting escape,[261] and a few statutes contemplate liability for gross negligence in releasing a dangerous person.[262] The decision to release may be distinguished from negligent supervision by a parole officer,[263] and from a failure to warn persons endangered by the release[264] Even when a state-employed therapist did not have physical custody of a dangerous person but knew of his threats to a specific individual, the state could be liable if he unreasonably failed either to seek commitment or to provide a warning to the potential victim.[265] Some courts impose a duty to warn whenever a reasonable person would provide a warning.[266] Perhaps the question ought to be, not whether the victim is identifiable, but whether an effective warning could reasonably have been given to someone who would have prevented the harm.[267]

B. INDIVIDUAL GOVERNMENT AGENTS

§ 22.12 State and Local Officers and Employees

Employee immunity and indemnity. Employees and officers of public entities are often immune from liability for harms they cause in the scope of their public

---

[255] E.g., State, Dep't of Corrections v. Cowles, 151 P.3d 353 (Alaska 2006).

[256] E.g., Parkulo v. West Virginia Board of Probation and Parole, 199 W.Va. 161, 483 S.E.2d 507 (1996) (public duty rule and discretionary immunity); Leonard v. State, 491 N.W.2d 508 (Iowa 1992).

[257] Board of Regents of the University System of Georgia v. Riddle, 229 Ga.App. 15, 493 S.E.2d 208 (1997) (statutory assault-and-battery immunity).

[258] Schmidt v. HTG, Inc., 265 Kan. 372, 961 P.2d 677 (1998).

[259] E.g., Natrona County v. Blake, 81 P.3d 948 (Wyo. 2003) (county owed duty of care to prevent escape of known dangerous criminal and is potentially liable for his murder of an unrelated victim in another state).

[260] See Grimm v. Arizona Board of Pardons & Paroles, 115 Ariz. 260, 564 P.2d 1227 (1977).

[261] See Shepherd v. Washington County, 331 Ark. 480, 962 S.W.2d 779 (2998).

[262] Mass. Gen. L. Ann. ch. 258 § 10(i) (gross negligence standard); see Ariz. Rev. Stats. § 12–820.02.

[263] Faile v. South Carolina Dep't of Juvenile Justice, 350 S.C. 315, 566 S.E.2d 536 (2002) (no immunity; gross negligence); Hertog v. City of Seattle, 138 Wash.2d 265, 979 P.2d 400 (1999) (imposing duty of reasonable supervision).

[264] Johnson v. State, 69 Cal.2d 782, 447 P.2d 352, 73 Cal.Rptr. 240 (1968) (no immunity); *accord,* Anderson v. Nebraska Dep't of Social Services, 248 Neb. 651, 538 N.W.2d 732 (1995).

[265] Tarasoff v. Regents of Univ. of Cal., 17 Cal.3d 425, 131 Cal.Rptr. 14, 551 P.2d 334, 83 A.L.R.3d 1166 (1976). See § 26.11. However, the same court took the view that no warning was required when the authorities released a young man who threatened to molest and murder an unnamed child, and then did so, on the ground that the release did not create a specific threat to a particular child. Thompson v. County of Alameda, 27 Cal.3d 741, 167 Cal.Rptr. 70, 614 P.2d 728, 12 A.L.R.4th 701 (1980); accord, Schmidt v. HTG, Inc., 265 Kan. 372, 961 P.2d 677 (1998).

[266] Hamman v. County of Maricopa, 161 Ariz. 58, 775 P.2d 1122 (1989); Schuster v. Altenberg, 144 Wis.2d 223, 424 N.W.2d 159 (1988). When the plaintiff claims negligence on some ground other than failure to warn, the absence of an identifiable victim is not controlling. See Estates of Morgan v. Fairfield Family Counseling Center, 77 Ohio St. 3d 284, 673 N.E.2d 1311 (1997).

[267] See Anderson v. Nebraska Dep't of Social Services, 248 Neb. 651, 538 N.W.2d 732 (1995).

employment.[268] Although civil rights cases are discussed in separate sections,[269] they, too, allow for immunities. The supposition is that immunity is required in at least some cases to assure that the ardor of public officials for performing their tasks will not be dampened.[270] Courts usually assume that official ardor is desirable. They also assume it can be dampened unduly. The first point is a question of values; the second is a question of data. Neither point is demonstrated in most of the case discussions. The Supreme Court has also suggested that unfounded lawsuits entail social costs, including expenses of litigation and diversion of official energies.[271] That argument, however, seems wide of the mark, since the result of immunity is to avoid the trial that could tell us whether the suit was unfounded or not. Not surprisingly in this state of affairs, exact agreement on the application of immunities is not to be found.

The justifications advanced for employee immunity show that it is distinct from the immunity of public entities. In fact, some plaintiffs who would be defeated by the entity's immunity might prevail in a suit against an individual officer. In some states, however, statutes provide that the public entity's liability depends upon the liability of the employee whose acts caused harm. In those states, the plaintiff can recover against both the officer and the entity or against neither.[272] In still others, the officer has a very broad immunity and the plaintiff's claim is only a non-jury claim against the state.[273] By statute in some states, the public entity must or may defend the employee who is sued for acts committed within the scope of his employment. Likewise, the public entity may be permitted or required to indemnify the employee if he is held liable.[274] When that procedure is applied, it effectively circumvents the entity's immunity and also absolves the employee of any personal responsibility, much as if the employee were covered by liability insurance. From the public employee's point of view, immunity and a right or likelihood of indemnity are both protective devices. From the victim's point of view, any immunity will operate to bar the claim, while existence of indemnity for the employee is often desirable as an indirect contribution to payment of the claim. An approach that achieves similar results is to grant a very broad immunity to the public employee and permit the plaintiff to assert against the public entity whatever claims would otherwise have been available against the employee.[275]

Judicial and quasi-judicial functions. Judges and legislators are usually said to be "absolutely privileged" or absolutely immune from suit based on acts within the scope of

---

[268] See, e.g., Ohio Rev. Code 2744.03(A)(6)(b); Murray v. Plainfield Rescue Squad, 210 N.J. 581, 46 A.3d 1262 (2012) (statute grants an immunity to individual members of city rescue squad, but the immunity does not extend to the rescue squad as an entity).

[269] See §§ 22.14 to 22.16. The protections provided by state statutes may be overridden by federal civil rights liability. Id.

[270] See, e.g., Harlow v. Fitzgerald, 457 U.S. 800, 102 S.Ct. 2727, 73 L.Ed.2d 396 (1982).

[271] Id.

[272] Cal. Gov't Code § 815.2 ("Except as otherwise provided by statute, a public entity is not liable for an injury resulting from an act or omission of an employee of the public entity where the employee is immune from liability."). See Thomas v. City of Richmond, 9 Cal.4th 1154, 892 P.2d 1185, 40 Cal.Rptr.2d 442 (1995) (recognizing limited exceptions).

[273] See Martin v. Brady, 261 Conn. 372, 802 A.2d 814 (2002) (allegedly illegal search and physical attack by officer not shown to be made with requisite malice, plaintiff left only with a claim to be filed with claims commissioner).

[274] E.g., Me. Rev. Stats. Ann. § 8112 ("A governmental entity, with the consent of the employee, shall assume the defense of and, in its discretion, may indemnify any employee against a claim which arises out of an act or omission occurring within the course and scope of employment and for which the governmental entity is not liable"); Minn. Stat. Ann. § 3.736, subd. 9.

[275] See Martin v. Brady, 261 Conn. 372, 802 A.2d 814 (2002) (outlining such a procedure).

their judicial or legislative duties. The term "absolute" reflects the rule that immunity will not be lost even if the defendant acted maliciously, in bad faith, or recklessly.[276] A judge acting within his subject matter jurisdiction, for example, is not liable to a litigant for a malicious ruling.[277] A judge retains absolute immunity from civil suit even where the conduct is criminal, such as accepting bribes,[278] although the judge may be subject to criminal liability just as any other citizen would be.[279]

The immunity embraces all those appropriately engaged in the task. It is most obviously applied, not to personal injury suits, but to defamation claims and other dignitary and economic-harm claims.[280] So witnesses and lawyers as well as judges are immune from suit based on their words in court.[281] Prosecutors share the absolute judicial immunity from suit based on prosecutorial decisions within the scope of their jurisdiction and traditional powers,[282] and so do experts appointed by the judge to render quasi-judicial evaluations.[283] Non-judicial work of the same persons, however, is another matter.[284] In hiring and discharging employees, for example, a judge is performing executive rather than judicial functions and in that case loses the absolute privilege.[285] State social workers making recommendations to the court furnish another example. These state employee may enjoy absolute judicial or quasi-judicial immunity in making recommendations to the court for placement of a child in foster care, but not in their later management of foster care for the child.[286]

Legislative-branch officials. Legislators, too, are immune from suit based upon their official votes and generally from suits based upon speech in the legislature and on related matters.[287] Some states extend the absolute immunity to city councils[288] and other similar rulemaking bodies.[289]

Executive officers and employees. Public employees of the executive branch— everyone who is not in the legislative or judicial branches—were originally liable for

---

[276] See Pierson v. Ray, 386 U.S. 547, 87 S.Ct. 1213, 18 L.Ed.2d 288 (1967).

[277] See, e.g., K.D. v. Bozarth, 313 N.J.Super. 561, 713 A.2d 546 (1998).

[278] E.g., Sherman v. Almeida, 747 A.2d 470 (R.I. 2000).

[279] Ex parte Virginia, 100 U.S. (10 Otto) 339, 25 L.Ed. 676 (1880).

[280] See § 37.11.

[281] See, e.g., Hawkins v. Harris, 141 N.J. 207, 661 A.2d 284 (1995); Restatement Second of Torts §§ 585 to 589 (1977). The privilege has reached far beyond official and governmental functions; it may be extended protect not only witnesses in courts, but individuals involved in preparing for trial and even those reporting a suspected crime. See § 37.11. See also Rehberg v. Paulk, 132 S. Ct. 1497, 182 L. Ed. 2d 593 (2012) (in § 1983 actions, grand jury witness is entitled to same absolute immunity as a trial witness).

[282] See Imbler v. Pachtman, 424 U.S. 409, 96 S.Ct. 984, 47 L.Ed.2d 128 (1976); Slater v. Clarke, 700 F.3d 1200 (9th Cir. 2012). If the prosecutor goes beyond the traditional role, he may lose his immunity. See Doe v. Phillips, 81 F.3d 1204 (2d Cir. 1996) (prosecutor demanded that criminal defendant swear an oath on the Bible in church as a condition to dismissal of charge; no immunity). Some states have extended the absolute immunity to public defenders. See Bradshaw v. Joseph, 164 Vt. 154, 666 A.2d 1175 (1995).

[283] See LaLonde v. Eissner, 405 Mass. 207, 539 N.E.2d 538 (1989). Guardians ad litem, appointed by a court to represent another's interests in litigation, are often granted an absolute immunity for acts done within the scope of their official duties. See § 727.

[284] See, e.g., Burns v. Reed, 500 U.S. 478, 111 S.Ct. 1934, 114 L.Ed.2d 547 (1991) (state prosecutor absolutely immune from liability for damages under § 1983 for participating in a probable cause hearing, but not entitled to absolute immunity for giving legal advice to the police).

[285] See Forrester v. White, 484 U.S. 219, 108 S.Ct. 538, 98 L.Ed.2d 555 (1988).

[286] State v. Second Judicial District Court, County of Washoe, 55 P.3d 420 (Nev. 2002).

[287] See Bogan v. Scott-Harris, 523 U.S. 44, 118 S.Ct. 966, 140 L.Ed.2d 79 (1998) (civil rights claim).

[288] See Butler v. Town of Argo, 871 So.2d 1 (Ala. 2003); Sanchez v. Coxon, 175 Ariz. 93, 854 P.2d 126 (1993); Voelbel v. Town of Bridgewater, 144 N.H. 599, 747 A.2d 252 (1999).

[289] Noble v. Ternyik, 273 Or. 39, 539 P.2d 658 (1975) (members of local port commission).

their torts[290] and certainly for those committed in excess of their authority. In the twentieth century, state courts developed immunities for officers and employees of public entities. One solution holds state officers liable only for gross negligence or for specified misconduct.[291] A little authority even provides an absolute immunity to higher-level state officers, at least as to defamation[292] or as to matters in which it is especially important for high-level officers to feel unhampered by possible legal actions.[293] One state statutory technique is like that now employed for suits against federal employees;[294] the employee is simply immune to claims for negligence committed within the scope of his employment. In such states, the suit must be against the public entity, to stand or fall as the rules for public entities dictate.[295]

More generally, officers and employees enjoy qualified immunity for discretionary acts, but not for ministerial acts.[296] Ministerial acts are those acts the officer has no discretion to avoid.[297] Some courts apply the discretionary-ministerial rule in a roundabout way by classifying public servants as either officers or employees, and, at least prima facie, attributing discretion to officers and ministerial duties to employees, with the result that officers are immune and employees are not.[298] As with the discretionary immunity for state and federal public entities, some courts may treat almost any choice as "discretionary," while others may emphasize that only policy choices are protected.[299] The discretionary immunity is qualified or conditional because it is usually lost if the officer is guilty of bad faith, malice, corruption, wanton misconduct or the like.[300]

Whether an act is treated as ministerial or discretionary probably depends in part on the how the court feels about the risks of error in the judicial decision. Since application of immunity tends to foreclose trial on the merits, it risks excluding some claims that are meritorious and would be allowed if judges had a fully developed record of the facts. Judicial preference may be either to minimize the risk of error that may harm officials or to minimize the risk of error that may harm citizens. If it is the latter,

---

[290] See Restatement Second of Torts § 895D, cmt. a (1979).

[291] See Maiden v. Rozwood, 461 Mich. 109, 597 N.W.2d 817 (1999) (applying statute).

[292] Bauer v. State, 511 N.W.2d 447 (Minn. 1994); Restatement Second of Torts § 591(b) (1977).

[293] See Thoma v. Hickel, 947 P.2d 816 (Alaska 1997).

[294] See § 22.13.

[295] S.C. Code § 15–78–70; 12 Vt. Stats. Ann. § 5602.

[296] Estate of Logusak v. City of Togiak, 185 P.3d 103 (Alaska 2008); DiPino v. Davis, 354 Md. 18, 729 A.2d 354 (1999); Southers v. City of Farmington, 263 S.W.3d 603 (Mo. 2008).

[297] Courts state the definition of a ministerial act stringently: "The duty is ministerial when it is absolute, certain, and imperative, involving merely execution of a specific duty arising from fixed and designated facts." Faile v. South Carolina Dep't of Juvenile Justice, 350 S.C. 315, 566 S.E.2d 536 (2002). For instance, if a statute requires the officer to perform a specific task and gives him no option, the duty is ministerial. See Gregor v. Argenot Great Central Ins. Co., 851 So.2d 959 (La. 2003).

[298] E.g., Meyer v. Walls, 347 N.C. 97, 489 S.E.2d 880 (1997). On the face of it, the officer-employee distinction tends to limit the immunity to persons exercising significant state power. See Muthukumarana v. Montgomery County, 370 Md. 447, 805 A.2d 372 (2002) (911 operator not an officer, partly because operator did not exercise "sovereign power of the state").

[299] Compare Merrow v. Hawkins, 266 Ga. 390, 467 S.E.2d 336 (1996) (jailer's decision to give car keys to inmate so he could wash a car led to theft of the car and damage to others; giving the keys is "discretionary") *with* Morway v. Trombly, 789 A.2d 965 (Vt. 2001) (operating a snow plow is ministerial)

[300] See City of Lancaster v. Chambers, 883 S.W.2d 650 (Tex. 1994). As in federal civil rights cases, "good faith" may turn out to be something of a reasonableness rule. See, e.g., Telthorster v. Tennell, 92 S.W.3d 457 (Tex. 2002) ("[T]o establish his good faith for official-immunity purposes [the officer] must show that a reasonably prudent officer, under the same or similar circumstances, could have believed that his conduct was justified based on the information he possessed.").

the immunity will be applied more narrowly and more acts recognized as ministerial. The Restatement has suggested various factors that judges are likely to consider in characterizing the actions of officials as ministerial or discretionary. These include the nature of the injury claimed, the availability of alternative remedies, the ability of courts to judge fault without unduly invading the executive officer's function, and the importance of protecting particular kinds of official acts.[301] Even if the officer's act is ministerial, however, he may be entitled to some specific statutory immunity.[302]

§ 22.13   Federal Officers and Employees

Federal officers and employees[303] often enjoy substantial immunity from civil lawsuits. Sometimes this immunity is provided by statute, and at other times by the Constitution itself.

Employees. The Federal Tort Claims Act did not originally immunize all federal employees. Congress has now provided that the claim against the government authorized by the FTCA is the exclusive remedy for anyone injured by a federal employee.[304] Except for constitutional and specific statutory violations by the employee,[305] he is granted complete immunity for torts committed within the scope of his employment.[306] If suit is brought against a federal employee, the Attorney General may certify that he was acting within the scope of his employment. Unless the Attorney General's certification is overturned, the court must substitute the government as the sole defendant and dismiss the claim against the individual government employee.[307]

Where the action against the federal employee has been filed in state court, the Attorney General's certification requires removal to federal court and the substitution of the United States as the sole defendant. At that point the federal court has exclusive competence to adjudicate the case and may not remand the suit to state court even if the federal court believes the Attorney General's certification was unwarranted, absent a specific determination that the employee in fact engaged in conduct beyond the scope of

---

[301]   Restatement Second of Torts § 895D, cmt. f (1979).

[302]   E.g., Brown Eyes v. South Dakota Dep't of Social Services, 630 N.W.2d 501 (S.D. 2001) (social workers' placement of child in foster home was ministerial but social workers were protected by statutory good faith immunity).

[303]   Government contractors may enjoy immunity as well. See 2 Dobbs, Hayden & Bublick, The Law of Torts § 352 (2d ed. 2011 & Supp.). The leading case is Boyle v. United Technologies Corp., 487 U.S. 500, 108 S. Ct. 2510, 101 L. Ed. 2d 442 (1988).

[304]   28 U.S.C.A. § 2679. The statute which is the basis of this code section was enacted in response to Westfall v. Erwin, 484 U.S. 292, 108 S.Ct. 580, 98 L.Ed.2d 619 (1988), and is consequently often referred to as the Westfall Act.

[305]   The statute leaves a remedy against the employee in claims for violation of the constitution or a federal statute "under which such action against an individual is otherwise authorized." 28 U.S.C.A. § 2679 (b)(2)(A) & (B). As to civil rights claims against federal officers, see § 22.14; 2 Dobbs, Hayden & Bublick, The Law of Torts § 356 (2d ed. 2011 & Supp.).

[306]   E.g., Wuterich v. Murtha, 562 F.3d 375 (D.C. Cir. 2009) (Congressman not acting outside the scope of employment when he uttered allegedly defamatory statements about the plaintiff, thus Congressman is immune from suit). Whether an employee was acting within the scope of employment is determined by applying the law of the state in which the accident occurred. Fowler v. U.S., 647 F.3d 1232 (10th Cir. 2011).

[307]   28 U.S.C.A. § 2679 (d). The statute provides that the attorney general's certification is "conclusive," but the Court has held that it is judicially reviewable. Gutierrez de Martinez v. Lamagno, 515 U.S. 417, 115 S.Ct. 2227, 132 L.Ed.2d 375 (1995).

his employment.[308] Under this provision, the plaintiff may have no remedy even for an admitted wrong.[309]

Legislative officers and employees. An explicit Constitutional provision, the Speech and Debate Clause, grants members of Congress and Senators absolute immunity from civil suits based on their statements made within either House of Congress.[310] The Court has extended that beyond the literal walls of Congress, but the privilege is narrowly construed and "does not extend beyond what is necessary to preserve the integrity of the legislative process."[311] When it does apply, it protects not only members of Congress themselves, but also their staff members, consultants and investigators who have assisted in the legislative process.[312] The constitutional immunity does not extend, however, to the republication of defamatory statements even if they were originally made within the halls of Congress.[313] However, even if the Speech and Debate Clause does not apply, a member of Congress may be immune from a suit for defamation on the ground that his statements were made in the course of his official duties under the Westfall Act.[314]

Executive officers. The President of the United States enjoys absolute immunity from damages liability for his official acts,[315] although such immunity does not extend to liability for acts allegedly done before he took office.[316] Other executive-branch officials may be sued directly under the Constitution in what is called a *Bivens* action, but they enjoy a qualified privilege for those claims.[317]

Judicial officers and those working within the judicial system. Federal judges are absolutely immune from civil lawsuits based on their statements or actions made in connection with their judicial function.[318] Federal prosecutors are also absolutely immune from suits that are based on words and conduct undertaken within the scope of their duties as part of the judicial function.[319] Federal public defenders are not absolutely immune from civil suits, however,[320] unlike some of their state counterparts.[321]

---

[308]   Osborn v. Haley, 549 U.S. 225, 127 S.Ct. 881, 166 L.Ed.2d 819 (2007).

[309]   See United States v. Smith, 499 U.S. 160, 111 S.Ct. 1180, 113 L.Ed.2d 134 (1991).

[310]   U. S. Const. Art. I, § 6 (". . . for any Speech or Debate in either House, they shall not be questioned in any other Place").

[311]   United States v. Brewster, 408 U.S. 501, 92 S.Ct. 2531, 35 L.Ed.2d 507 (1972) (criminal prosecution for accepting a bribe is not barred by the Speech and Debate Clause).

[312]   Doe v. McMillan, 412 U.S. 306, 93 S.Ct. 2018, 36 L.Ed.2d 912 (1973).

[313]   Hutchinson v. Proxmire, 443 U.S. 111, 99 S.Ct. 2675, 61 L.Ed.2d 411 (1979) (U.S. Senator was subject to suit for defamation based on newsletters and news releases).

[314]   See Wuterich v. Murtha, 562 F.3d 375 (D.C. Cir. 2009).

[315]   See Nixon v. Fitzgerald, 457 U.S. 731, 102 S.Ct. 2690, 73 L.Ed.2d 349 (1982).

[316]   Clinton v. Jones, 520 U.S. 681, 117 S.Ct. 1636, 137 L.Ed.2d 945 (1997).

[317]   Butz v. Economou, 438 U. S. 478, 98 S.Ct. 2894, 57 L.Ed.2d 895 (1978) (rejecting argument that officials of the Department of Agriculture are entitled to absolute immunity).

[318]   Mullis v. U.S. Bankruptcy Court for Dist. of Nevada, 828 F.2d 1385 (9th Cir. 1987). This immunity extends to administrative law judges as well. Butz v. Economou, 438 U. S. 478, 98 S.Ct. 2894, 57 L.Ed.2d 895 (1978)

[319]   Yarelli v. Goff, 275 U.S. 503, 48 S.Ct. 255, 72 L.Ed. 395 (1927).

[320]   Ferri v. Ackerman, 444 U.S. 193, 100 S.Ct. 402, 62 L.Ed.2d 355 (1979).

[321]   See § 22.12.

C. CIVIL RIGHTS CLAIMS

§ 22.14   Federal Civil Rights Claims: § 1983

Context. Civil rights violations are torts.[322] They have generated an important specialty,[323] in which the courts often look to common law tort rules as models.[324] Civil rights litigation covers a broad spectrum. Much of it deals with wrongful acts such as discrimination that does not directly produce physical harms. For instance, state officials might remove students from a religious boarding school, violating the religious-freedom rights of the students and their parents.[325] Or officials might interfere with a family's custody of a child without due process.[326] A large number of civil rights cases involve physical harms, producing a substantial and growing body of case law.

Section 1983. The most prominent single federal civil rights statute is 42 U.S.C.A. § 1983.[327] Section 1983 authorizes tort claims for deprivation of federal rights under color of state law.[328] The defendants are usually state or local officials or local governments, although the victim may also assert a claim against a private individual who uses state law to violate federal rights. (Against *federal* officials, the victim can claim directly under the constitution for violation of constitutional rights.)[329] The prevailing party in a § 1983 suit is entitled to recover reasonable attorney's fees.[330] Suit may be brought in either federal or state court.[331]

Major constitutional bases for § 1983 claims. Section 1983 " 'is not itself a source of substantive rights,' but merely provides 'a method for vindicating federal rights

---

[322] Imbler v. Pachtman, 424 U.S. 409, 417, 96 S.Ct. 984, 988, 47 L.Ed.2d 128 (1976).

[323] Among the books see Martin A. Schwartz, Section 1983 Litigation: Claims and Defenses (4th ed. 2003, 4 vols. & Supp.); Rodney A. Smolla, Federal Civil Rights Acts (3d ed. 1994, 2 vols. & Supp.); Sheldon Nahmod, Civil Rights and Civil Liberties Litigation: the Law of Section 1983 (4th Ed. 1997).

[324] See Hartman v. Moore, 126 S.Ct. 1695, 164 L.Ed.2d 441 (2006) (civil rights torts have their own special elements, but the common law is "a source of inspired examples"); Heck v. Humphrey, 512 U.S. 477, 114 S.Ct. 2364, 129 L.Ed.2d 383 (1994).

[325] Heartland Academy Community Church v. Waddle, 595 F.3d 798 (8th Cir. 2010).

[326] Swipies v. Kofka, 419 F.3d 709 (8th Cir. 2005).

[327] "Every person who, under color of any statute, ordinance, regulation, custom, or usage, of any State or Territory or the District of Columbia, subjects, or causes to be subjected, any citizen of the United States or other person within the jurisdiction thereof to the deprivation of any rights, privileges, or immunities secured by the Constitution and laws, shall be liable to the party injured in an action at law, suit in equity, or other proper proceeding for redress. . . ." 42 U.S.C.A. § 1983.

[328] A person acts under the color of state law when he exercises power "possessed by virtue of state law and made possible only because [of] the authority of state law. . . ." See West v. Atkins, 487 U.S. 42, 108 S.Ct. 2250, 101 L.Ed.2d 40 (1988). Private individuals ordinarily do not act under color of state law, but may do so at times. See Adickes v. Kress & Co., 398 U.S. 144, 90 S.Ct. 1598, 26 L.Ed.2d 142 (1970); Fabrikant v. French, 691 F.3d 193 (2d Cir. 2012). Courts have said that a private person is not a state actor—not acting under color of law—unless he is performing a traditional state function or the state is significantly involved in his activity. See Wilson v. Price, 624 F.3d 389 (7th Cir. 2010).

[329] Bivens v. Six Unknown Named Agents of Federal Bureau of Narcotics, 403 U.S. 388, 91 S.Ct. 1999, 29 L.Ed.2d 619 (1971). The *Bivens* claim is analogous to the § 1983 claim against state officials, and subject to the same immunities. See 2 Dobbs, Hayden & Bublick, The Law of Torts § 356 (2d ed. 2011 & Supp.).

[330] See 42 U.S.C.A. § 1988. The statute has produced litigation over who is a "prevailing" party. See, e.g., Lefemine v. Wideman, 133 S.Ct. 9, 184 L.Ed.2d 313 (2012) (plaintiff who secured a permanent injunction but no monetary damages was a "prevailing party" entitled to fees); Farrar v. Hobby, 506 U.S. 103, 113 S. Ct. 566, 121 L. Ed. 2d 494 (1992) (plaintiff "prevails" when "actual relief on the merits of his claim materially alters the legal relationship between the parties by modifying the defendant's behavior in a way that directly benefits the plaintiff").

[331] See Haywood v. Drown, 129 S.Ct. 2108, 173 L.Ed.2d 920 (2009); Howlett v. Rose, 496 U.S. 356, 110 S.Ct. 2430, 110 L.Ed.2d 332 (1990).

elsewhere conferred.' "[332] Claims may arise out of federal rights created by case law,[333] by statute,[334] or by any provision of the Constitution designed to protect the plaintiff against the harm inflicted. Most § 1983 suits, however, are generated from one of three constitutional provisions. These are: (1) the Fourteenth Amendment's guarantees of substantive and procedural due process of law and equal protection of the laws;[335] (2) the Fourth Amendment's provision against unreasonable searches and seizures,[336] and (3) the Eighth Amendment's provisions against "cruel and unusual punishments."[337]

Common-law tort claims compared to § 1983 claims. Many constitutional torts redressed under § 1983 would also qualify as a prima facie common law tort. Trespassory torts such as battery,[338] false imprisonment,[339] or assault[340] are examples. Certainly some of the misconduct condemned as a civil rights violation is conduct that would constitute a property tort such as conversion[341] or trespass.[342] But no common-law tort analogy is required; in all § 1983 cases, the substantive basis for the claim must be found in the words and history of the federal law that forms the basis for the suit. In Fourteenth Amendment substantive due process cases, the test is whether the defendant's intentional[343] official conduct shocks the conscience of the court.[344] Fourth Amendment violations are objectively judged by a reasonableness standard;[345] neither the officer's malice nor his good faith is important if his objective conduct was reasonable, and

---

[332] Graham v. Connor, 490 U.S. 386, 109 S.Ct. 1865, 104 L.Ed.2d 443 (1989) (quoting Baker v. McCollan, 443 U.S. 137, 99 S.Ct. 2689, 61 L.Ed.2d 433 (1979)).

[333] E.g., Moldowan v. City of Warren, 578 F.3d 351 (6th Cir. 2009) (city may be liable under § 1983 for failing to train its police officers regarding their obligations under Brady v. Maryland, 373 U.S. 83, 83 S.Ct. 1194, 10 L.Ed.2d 215 (1963), to disclose exculpatory evidence to a criminal defendant); Tennison v. City and County of San Francisco, 570 F.3d 1078 (9th Cir. 2009) (affirming trial court's ruling that homicide investigators were not immune from § 1983 liability where they failed to fulfill *Brady* obligations to plaintiffs).

[334] E.g., Grammer v. John J. Kane Regional Centers-Glen Hazel, 570 F.3d 520 (3d Cir. 2009) (federal nursing home statute).

[335] Under the Fourteenth Amendment, states may not deny "equal protection of the laws" to any person, and must not "deprive any person of life, liberty, or property, without due process of law." Similar clauses in the Fifth Amendment apply to the federal government. For § 1983 cases arising under the Fourteenth Amendment, see 2 Dobbs, Hayden & Bublick, The Law of Torts § 76 (2d ed. 2011 & Supp.).

[336] The Fourth Amendment, which limits the powers of the states by way of the Fourteenth Amendment, provides: "The right of the people to be secure in their persons, houses, papers, and effects, against unreasonable searches and seizures, shall not be violated, and no Warrants shall issue, but upon probable cause, supported by Oath or affirmation, and particularly describing the place to be searched, and the persons or things to be seized." For § 1983 cases arising under the Fourth Amendment, see 2 Dobbs, Hayden & Bublick, The Law of Torts §§ 77 & 78 (2d ed. 2011 & Supp.).

[337] For § 1983 cases arising under the Eighth Amendment, see 2 Dobbs, Hayden & Bublick, The Law of Torts § 79 (2d ed. 2011 & Supp.).

[338] Webster v. City of Houston, 689 F.2d 1220 (5th Cir. 1982), *on rehearing en banc,* 739 F.2d 993 (5th Cir. 1984) (police shooting); Cottrell v. Kaysville City, Utah, 994 F.2d 730 (10th Cir. 1993) (strip search)

[339] Harper v. McDonald, 679 F.2d 955 (D.C. Cir. 1982) (detention without warrant or probable cause).

[340] McDonald v. Haskins, 966 F.2d 292 (7th Cir. 1992) (pointing gun at head of 9-year-old-child).

[341] Cf. United States v. Eight Thousand Eight Hundred and Fifty Dollars, 461 U.S. 555, 103 S.Ct. 2005, 76 L.Ed.2d 143 (1983) (customs officers may seize property without a prior hearing but under some circumstances must institute forfeiture proceedings thereafter).

[342] See Monroe v. Pape, 365 U.S. 167, 81 S.Ct. 473, 5 L.Ed.2d 492 (1961), *overruled on other grounds by* Monell v. Dep't of Social Services of the City of N.Y., 436 U.S. 658, 98 S.Ct. 2018 (1978).

[343] The Supreme Court has said that negligence is not enough. See Daniels v. Williams, 474 U.S. 327, 106 S.Ct. 662, 88 L.Ed.2d 662 (1986). In cases of non-action, "willful indifference"—conscious omissions to act— is enough. See, e.g., Tamas v. Dep't of Social & Health Services, 630 F.3d 833 (9th Cir. 2010).

[344] Collins v. City of Harker Heights, Texas, 503 U.S. 115, 112 S.Ct. 1061, 117 L.Ed.2d 261 (1992).

[345] E.g., Phillips v. Community Ins. Corp., 678 F.3d 513 (7th Cir. 2012); McCullough v. Antolini, 559 F.3d 1201 (11th Cir. 2009).

neither is important if he lacks probable cause for the arrest or justification for an investigatory stop.[346]

The operative tests for constitutional violations in Eighth Amendment cases depend on the plaintiff's allegations. Examples of cruel and unusual punishment that count as constitutional torts include (1) cases of excessive force inflicted upon prisoners by prison guards, (2) cases of excessively harsh conditions of confinement, and (3) cases in which necessary medical attention is denied. In excessive-force or harsh-conditions cases, the defendant's conduct must be objectively as well as subjectively wrong,[347] and must violate contemporary standards of decency.[348] Further, in both harsh-conditions and medical-deprivation cases, the official is liable only if he is guilty of "deliberate indifference"[349] to the prisoner's danger or medical needs. In this context,[350] "deliberate indifference" is an explicitly subjective standard,[351] but an objective component appears in both settings. In the harsh-conditions cases, the official has not violated the Eighth Amendment if he provides reasonable protection against the risk, even if it turns out that the protection provided was insufficient and the plaintiff was harmed.[352] Essentially the same idea is re-worded for the medical-deprivation cases: the deprivation must be serious and it must be a denial of "the minimal civilized measures of life's necessities." The Court appears to regard these formulations as addressing an objectively judged risk.[353] If this is correct, then the plaintiff apparently would be required to show both an objectively serious risk and a subjective indifference by the defendants.

The qualified immunity. While state-law immunities will not protect a defendant in a federal civil rights claim,[354] many individual defendants can assert a qualified federal immunity from suit in a § 1983 action.[355] This is a powerful immunity, and through its application many individual state and local officials escape liability.

§ 22.15 Section 1983 Claims Against State and Local Officials

Potential for liability under § 1983. The plaintiff may sue officers in their individual or personal capacity[356] for actions under color of state law,[357] in which case the officer is potentially personally liable for his own unconstitutional actions and for his

---

[346] Graham v. Connor, 490 U.S. 386, 109 S.Ct. 1865, 104 L.Ed.2d 443 (1989); Hopkins v. Bonvicino, 573 F.3d 752 (9th Cir. 2009).

[347] See Wilson v. Seiter, 501 U.S. 294, 111 S.Ct. 2321, 115 L.Ed.2d 271 (1991).

[348] Hudson v. McMillian, 503 U.S. 1, 112 S.Ct. 995, 117 L.Ed.2d 156 (1992).

[349] Wilson v. Seiter, 501 U.S. 294, 111 S.Ct. 2321, 115 L.Ed.2d 271 (1991) (prison conditions); Estelle v. Gamble, 429 U.S. 97, 97 S.Ct. 285, 50 L.Ed.2d 251 (1976) (medical attention in prison).

[350] Deliberate indifference may be an objective standard in some situations. See City of Canton v. Harris, 489 U.S. 378, 109 S.Ct. 1197, 103 L.Ed.2d 412 (1989) (municipal liability for failure to train employees).

[351] Farmer v. Brennan, 511 U.S. 825, 114 S.Ct. 1970, 128 L.Ed.2d 811 (1994); see also Wilson v. Seiter, 501 U.S. 294, 111 S.Ct. 2321, 115 L.Ed.2d 271 (1991).

[352] Farmer v. Brennan, 511 U.S. 825, 114 S.Ct. 1970, 128 L.Ed.2d 811 (1994).

[353] See Wilson v. Seiter, 501 U.S. 294, 298, 111 S.Ct. 2321, 2324, 115 L.Ed.2d 271 (1991); Farmer v. Brennan, 511 U.S. 825, 834, 114 S.Ct. 1970, 1977, 128 L.Ed.2d 811 (1994).

[354] If a defendant is sued not only on federal civil rights grounds, but also on state-law grounds, then state-law immunities can be asserted as to the latter claims. See, e.g., Hagans v. Franklin County Sheriff's Office, 695 F.3d 505 (6th Cir. 2012); Hoyt v. Cooks, 672 F.3d 972 (11th Cir. 2012).

[355] See § 22.15.

[356] If the officer is sued in his "official capacity", the suit is treated as one against the entity. If he is sued in his individual capacity, the suit aims to recover against the officer personally, albeit for actions that were in a sense official. The distinction has created pitfalls. See Kentucky v. Graham, 473 U.S. 159, 105 S.Ct. 3099, 87 L.Ed.2d 114 (1985).

[357] See § 22.14 on "color of state law."

unconstitutional failure to supervise or control subordinates.[358] Even a failure to act may violate rights and subject a defendant to § 1983 liability.[359]

Absolute immunity. The common-law absolute immunity for legislative and judicial acts cases carries over to § 1983 claims as well.[360] The President of the United States is likewise absolutely immune even to suits for constitutional violations.[361]

The qualified immunity. Increasingly, the outcome of § 1983 cases against individual state and local officials depends on the existence of a qualified immunity. The usual analysis of common law tort claims first considers the prima facie case—whether the defendant has a duty and whether it was violated—and then considers affirmative defenses. With civil rights torts, however, the case may begin with the assertion by the defendant of a qualified immunity. When a defendant raises this immunity, often at the pleading stage, the plaintiff bears the heavy burden of proving[362] that (1) the defendant violated a federal right, and (2) that the right was "clearly established" at the time of the defendant's conduct.[363] These issues may be addressed in any order, but both must be established for the immunity to be overcome.[364] The qualified immunity has been said to allow "ample room for mistaken judgments by protecting all but the plainly incompetent or those who knowingly violate the law."[365]

When is a constitutional or other federal right "clearly established" for qualified immunity purposes? The Supreme Court has said that even if reasonable officers would know that the *constitutional right* is established, the defendant retains the immunity unless established law makes it apparent that his *particular conduct* is unconstitutional.[366] For example, a warrantless search of a home is established as unconstitutional unless the officer has probable cause and there are exigent circumstances requiring a search. A reasonable officer should know the rule about warrantless searches, but a reasonable officer would not necessarily know whether information he holds counts as probable cause and whether the circumstances are

---

[358] See Poolaw v. Mercantel, 565 F.3d 721 (10th Cir. 2009); Velazquez v. City of Hialeah, 484 F.3d 1340 (11th Cir. 2007) (finding fact issues on whether police officers failed to intervene to stop others' use of force); Skrtich v. Thornton, 280 F.3d 1295 (11th Cir. 2002) (Eighth Amendment, prison officers who watched an unprivileged beating and subject to liability).

[359] See Clem v. Lomeli, 566 F.3d 1177 (9th Cir. 2009) (failure to prevent attack by plaintiff's cellmate an Eighth Amendment violation).

[360] See e.g., Butz v. Economou, 438 U.S. 478, 98 S.Ct. 2894, 57 L.Ed.2d 895 (1978) (federal administrative law judge carrying out judicial function); Bogan v. Scott-Harris, 523 U.S. 44, 118 S.Ct. 966, 140 L.Ed.2d 79 (1998) (city official); Cousins v. Lockyer, 568 F.3d 1063 (9th Cir. 2009) (California Attorney General absolutely immune from suit under § 1983 based on prosecutorial function). See § 22.12.

[361] Nixon v. Fitzgerald, 457 U.S. 731, 102 S.Ct. 2690, 73 L.Ed.2d 349 (1982).

[362] Kovacic v. Villarreal, 628 F.3d 209 (5th Cir. 2010); Cassady v. Goering, 567 F.3d 628 (10th Cir. 2009) (calling the two-part burden "strict"); Gonzalez v. City of Elgin, 578 F.3d 526 (7th Cir. 2009).

[363] See Pearson v. Callahan, 555 U.S. 223, 129 S.Ct. 808, 172 L. Ed. 2d 565 (2009); Saucier v. Katz, 533 U.S. 194, 121 S.Ct. 2151, 150 L. Ed. 2d 272 (2001).

[364] See Messerschmidt v. Millender, 132 S. Ct. 1235, 182 L. Ed. 2d 47 (2012); Ryburn v. Huff, 132 S. Ct. 987, 181 L. Ed. 2d 966 (2012); Safford Unified School Dist. No. 1 v. Redding, 557 U.S. 364, 129 S. Ct. 2633, 174 L. Ed. 2d 354, 245 Ed. Law Rep. 626 (2009).

[365] Hunter v. Bryant, 502 U.S. 224, 229, 112 S.Ct. 534, 116 L.Ed.2d 589 (1991) (quoting Malley v. Briggs, 475 U.S. 335 (1986)).

[366] See Ashcroft v. al-Kidd,131 S.Ct. 2074, 2083, 179 L.Ed.2d 28 (2011) (plaintiff need not show a case "directly on point, but existing precedent must have placed the statutory or constitutional question beyond debate" in order to prove that the right was "clearly established"); accord, Stanton v. Sims, 134 S.Ct. 3, 187 L.Ed.2d 341 (2013) (per curiam).

sufficiently pressing to justify the search. If a reasonable officer could believe that the search was permissible in spite of the general rule, the immunity remains.[367]

§ 22.16 Section 1983 Claims Against State and Local Entities

States. Section 1983 imposes liability upon "every person" who violates the plaintiff's constitutional or other federal rights. As a matter of historical analysis, the Supreme Court has concluded that states were not considered "persons" and hence cannot be sued at all under § 1983,[368] although they might fall within the proscriptions of some other statutes.

Local public entities subject to liability without immunity. Local public entities are treated as "persons" covered by § 1983, but subject to some special rules. The local entity cannot claim the qualified immunity of its officer,[369] and has no discretion to violate the Constitution.[370]

Requirement of policy, custom, or official decision. Second, local entities are not liable for every constitutional violation, only those that result from a policy, custom, or official decision of the entity.[371] The fact that a police officer used excessive force in making an arrest and thus violated the Fourth Amendment, for example, is enough to make the officer liable, but not the entity. On the contrary, the entity will not be responsible unless its policy, custom, or official decision caused the constitutional violation.[372] The Court sometimes expresses this rule by saying that the entity is not to be held vicariously liable, only liable for its own acts.[373] That is a convenient expression but not a literal one; more accurately, the entity is held vicariously liable for official policy decisions made by policymaking officials.

Single act or decision at policymaking level. Plaintiffs can implicate a public entity in constitutional violations in two basic ways. First, they can prove an ongoing plan, program or practice that is unconstitutional or fosters unconstitutional action. Second, they can prove a single "official decision" that is unconstitutional or fosters unconstitutionality. When the plaintiff claims that a single decision rather than an ongoing plan, practice, or program has violated her constitutional rights, she must show

---

[367] Anderson v. Creighton, 483 U.S. 635, 107 S.Ct. 3034, 97 L.Ed.2d 523 (1987). Similarly, the officer's excessive force, as judged by objective reasonableness, violates the Fourth Amendment, but though an officer must know that rule, he may not know whether a push or a shove is excessive force in particular circumstances. To say that a particular shove establishes a constitutional violation that will govern future conduct is not to say that the officer should have known that the particular shove was unconstitutional at the time. See Saucier v. Katz, 533 U.S. 194, 121 S.Ct. 2151, 150 L.Ed.2d 272 (2001); Youngbey v. March, 676 F.3d 1114 (D.C. Cir. 2012) (reasonable officer could have believed that conducting a nighttime search without knocking would not violate the Fourth Amendment).

[368] Will v. Michigan Dep't of State Police, 491 U.S. 58, 109 S.Ct. 2304, 105 L.Ed.2d 45 (1989). Similarly, a judgment against an individual officer of the state cannot serve as a basis for reaching state funds. See Hafer v. Melo, 502 U.S. 21, 112 S.Ct. 358, 116 L.Ed.2d 301 (1991).

[369] Leatherman v. Tarrant County Narcotics Intelligence and Coordination Unit, 507 U.S. 163, 113 S.Ct. 1160, 122 L.Ed.2d 517 (1993).

[370] Owen v. City of Independence, Mo., 445 U.S. 622, 100 S.Ct. 1398, 63 L.Ed.2d 673 (1980).

[371] Monell v. Dep't of Social Services, 436 U.S. 658, 98 S.Ct. 2018, 56 L.Ed.2d 611 (1978).

[372] E.g., Board of County Comn'rs of Bryant County v. Brown, 520 U.S. 397, 117 S.Ct. 1382, 137 L.Ed.2d 626 (1997); Kelly v. Borough of Carlisle, 622 F.3d 248 (3d Cir. 2010).

[373] Connick v. Thompson, 131 S. Ct. 1350, 179 L. Ed. 2d 417 (2011) (Local governments "are not vicariously liable under § 1983 for their employees' actions.") (quoting Pembaur v. City of Cincinnati, 475 U.S. 469, 106 S. Ct. 1292, 89 L. Ed. 2d 452 (1986)).

that the decision was made by the public entity's policymaker for that issue.[374] The same rule can apply to any single decision as long as it is made by the policymaking official for the issue involved. Thus where a county attorney made decisions that led officers to break into private premises without a warrant, his decision was official and the county could be subjected to liability.[375]

Ongoing plan, practice or custom. When the plaintiff claims that an ongoing plan, policy, or custom of the entity is unconstitutional, the policy might be either formalized and written or simply acted out in a custom or practice. No formal policy is required; a custom or practice is sufficient.[376] For example, if a city refuses to train its police officers in the proper use of force, or regularly delays investigation of complaints about excessive force, the city's practice coupled with the city's notice of the problem may be viewed as a custom or even a policy, even though poor training or delay is not a formal or written part of the system.[377] But perhaps the terms policy and custom are inadequate in this setting. Maybe the important thing is that the custom or practice is carried on over time so that the entity or its policymaker has a fair chance to review and decide whether to alter the practice. A custom or practice that is strong and persistent proves its own acceptance at the policymaking level.

Policies and decisions that only risk constitutional violations by others. Most official decisions and policies of a public entity are not themselves unconstitutional; they merely create a risk of unconstitutional action by others. For example, a city that inadequately trains new police officers runs a risk that some individual officers, lacking training, will act unconstitutionally, perhaps by using excessive and even deadly force, but it is not a certainty and probably not the purpose of a custom not to train. The problem for the plaintiff in such cases may be three-fold. First, negligence by itself, even official negligence, is ordinarily not sufficient to show a violation of due process or equal protection rights when the official rule or policy is not unconstitutional on its face.[378] A policy that *risks* unconstitutional violations but does not dictate or approve them is not unconstitutional on its face and sounds like a policy that is negligent only, so it might be argued that such a policy does not violate the Constitution at all. Second, a practice that risks unconstitutional violations by others might not be considered a custom or policy that violates the Constitution unless the entity's acquiescence in that practice shows deliberate indifference.[379] Third, a policy that is not itself unconstitutional but merely risks constitutional harm by others might be deemed an insufficient basis for liability, either because it does not reflect sufficient fault or because it is causally remote.[380] With

---

[374] Cf. Owen v. City of Independence, Mo., 445 U.S. 622, 100 S.Ct. 1398, 63 L.Ed.2d 673 (1980) (some council members and city manager published accusations, then discharged police chief without a hearing).

[375] Pembaur v. City of Cincinnati, 475 U.S. 469, 106 S.Ct. 1292, 89 L.Ed.2d 452 (1986).

[376] See, e.g., Monell v. Department of Social Services of City of New York, 436 U.S. 658, 690, 98 S.Ct. 2018, 2036, 56 L.Ed.2d 611 (1978); Griffin v. City of Opa-Locka, 261 F.3d 1295 (11th Cir. 2001) (city's indifference to sexual harassment by its city manager).

[377] See, e.g., Moldowan v. City of Warren, 578 F.3d 351 (6th Cir. 2009); Allen v. Muskogee, Oklahoma, 119 F.3d 837 (10th Cir. 1997); see also Connick v. Thompson, 131 S. Ct. 1350, 179 L. Ed. 2d 417 (2011).

[378] Daniels v. Williams, 474 U.S. 327, 106 S.Ct. 662, 88 L.Ed.2d 662 (1986) (due process); Washington v. Davis, 426 U.S. 229, 96 S.Ct. 2040, 48 L.Ed.2d 597 (1976) (equal protection).

[379] See City of Canton, Ohio v. Harris, 489 U.S. 378, 109 S.Ct. 1197, 103 L.Ed.2d 412 (1989).

[380] See Collins v. City of Harker Heights, Texas, 503 U.S. 115, 112 S.Ct. 1061, 117 L.Ed.2d 261 (1992); Board of County Com'rs of Bryan County v. Brown, 520 U.S. 397, 117 S.Ct. 1382, 137 L.Ed.2d 626 (1997).

some of these considerations in mind, the Court has said that the plaintiff in these cases must prove that the entity was guilty of willful indifference.[381]

Willful indifference might be found in some cases of ongoing policies or programs, even in ongoing failures to act, because sooner or later the entity must become aware of the effects and because the unconstitutional action is highly likely over time. Hence, a number of courts have recognized that an entity's failure to train police officers might subject the entity to liability for the untrained officers' use of excessive force,[382] failure to use proper protocols for handling domestic violence complaints,[383] or denial of medical attention.[384] Similarly, a city's do-nothing attitude can be construed as tacit approval of rampant sexual harassment and hence willful indifference.[385] In all of these cases, however, the plaintiff is more likely to lose because deliberate indifference or other quasi-intentional wrongdoing will be difficult to prove.[386]

On the other hand, when a single decision is made that does not set a standard for the future, the policy decision does not reflect intent to harm. It reflects instead only an unreasonable risk of harm, which is to say negligence. So the Court has held that a policymaker's one-time failure to check the background of an officer, although a policy decision, was not one that showed deliberate indifference.[387]

Constitutional violation. A clear policy of deliberate indifference is not by itself enough to prove a § 1983 claim. The plaintiff must also show a violation of a constitutional or other federal right.[388] A city might be deliberately indifferent to the nutritional needs of its residents, but unless the residents have a right to the city's nutritional beneficence, they have no constitutional claim. With limited exceptions, public entities do not owe affirmative duties of protection.[389] Consequently, a public school is not liable under § 1983 when it is deliberately indifferent to the probability that

---

[381] City of Canton, Ohio v. Harris, 489 U.S. 378, 109 S.Ct. 1197, 103 L.Ed.2d 412 (1989).

[382] E.g., Weigel v. Broad, 544 F.3d 1143 (10th Cir. 2008); Flores v. Cameron County, Tex., 92 F.3d 258 (5th Cir. 1996) (remand to determine deliberate indifference after verdict for the plaintiff); Atchinson v. District of Columbia, 73 F.3d 418 (D.C. Cir. 1996) (reversing dismissal of claim). To show causation, the plaintiff must show that proper training would have prevented the constitutional injury. See Pineda v. City of Houston, 291 F.3d 325 (5th Cir. 2002).

[383] Okin v. Village of Cornwall-on-Hudson Police Dept., 577 F.3d 415 (2d Cir. 2009).

[384] City of Canton, Ohio v. Harris, 489 U.S. 378, 109 S.Ct. 1197, 103 L.Ed.2d 412 (1989).

[385] Griffin v. City of Opa-Locka, 261 F.3d 1295 (11th Cir. 2001).

[386] E.g., Soto v. Flores, 103 F.3d 1056 (1st Cir. 1997) (although police officer knew that wife was at risk if he revealed that she had sought police protection from husband's abuse, he told husband, who then killed wife's children and himself, but neither this nor a climate of police disapproval of domestic violence rights sufficed to show discriminatory intent necessary for equal protection claim); Eaglesteon v. Guido, 41 F.3d 865 (2d Cir. 1994) (no showing that failing to protect woman from abusive husband was in furtherance of a purpose to discriminate against women); Ricketts v. City of Columbia, Mo., 36 F.3d 775 (8th Cir. 1994) (failure to arrest abusive husband; no evidence of intentional discrimination, thus no equal protection violation);

[387] Board of County Com'rs of Bryan County v. Brown, 520 U.S. 397, 117 S.Ct. 1382, 137 L.Ed.2d 626 (1997).

[388] County of Sacramento v. Lewis, 523 U.S. 833, 118 S.Ct. 1708, 140 L.Ed.2d 1043 (1998) (high speed chase).

[389] Town of Castle Rock v. Gonzales, 545 U.S. 748, 125 S.Ct. 2796, 162 L.Ed.2d 658 (2005) (victim has no constitutionally-protected property interest in police enforcement of a protective order); DeShaney v. Winnebago County Dep't of Social Services, 489 U.S. 189, 109 S.Ct. 998, 103 L.Ed.2d 249 (1989); Price-Cornelison v. Brooks, 524 F.3d 1103 (10th Cir. 2008) (refusal to enforce protective order did not violate right to equal protection). On the lack of duty to take affirmative action for the protection of others, see Chapters 35 & 36.

a student will commit suicide, because the school owes no constitutional obligation to protect the student.[390]

---

[390] Wyke v. Polk County School Board, 129 F.3d 560 (11th Cir. 1997).

Chapter 23

FAMILY MEMBERS AND CHARITIES

Analysis

A. FAMILY MEMBERS

§ 23.1   Spousal Immunity
§ 23.2   Parental Immunity

B. CHARITIES

§ 23.3   Charitable Immunity
§ 23.4   Individual Immunities

A. FAMILY MEMBERS

§ 23.1 Spousal Immunity

Wives' disabilities at earlier common law. At earlier common law, although a spouse might have claims against an outsider for interference with marital rights,[1] claims by one spouse against the other were almost nonexistent. The earlier common law subjugated wives to their husbands by viewing the marital couple as a single entity. In the legal unity of husband and wife, the husband was in charge. He was entitled to possess and draw the profits from his wife's properties, for example, and even to "discipline" her. In the formal, hobbled reasoning of some common law periods, the couple was regarded as one legal entity, with the result that neither individual could sue the other.[2]

Married Women's Property Acts. Common law rules were improved somewhat in the 19th century by statutes called the Married Women's Property Acts. These acts allowed the wife to maintain a legal action against her husband to vindicate her property interests. For example, she could sue her husband for negligent injury to her property or for its conversion. Courts held that the statutes destroyed the legal identity of the two persons so that wife and husband could sue each other.

Immunities remaining after the statutes. For a long time, however, personal torts fell under the old rule, so that neither spouse could sue the other for negligent or even intentional injury. Courts argued that even though the Married Women's Act had individualized the rights of the two parties to the marriage, immunity stood intact, mainly on the theory that suits between husband and wife would be fictitious and fraudulent and that in any event they would destroy the peace and harmony of the home.[3] Translated into today's language, courts argued that a husband could not be

---

[1]   As to claims against third persons for interference with family relationships, see § 29.11 (loss of consortium) and Chapter 40 (alienation of affection and the like).

[2]   There are many good brief summaries of this abysmal history. See Price v. Price, 732 S.W.2d 316 (Tex. 1987); Restatement Second of Torts § 895F cmts. b and c (1979).

[3]   See Carl Tobias, Interspousal Tort Immunity in America, 23 Ga. L. Rev. 359, 441 (1989) (listing judicial concerns over (1) marital harmony, (2) fraud and collusion, (3) the need to defer to the legislature, (4) excessive and frivolous claims, and (5) the availability of alternative remedies).

challenged in court for beating his wife because the marriage was entitled to "privacy" and freedom from judicial scrutiny.[4]

Rejecting the fraud and family harmony arguments. Courts have now widely rejected or discounted the arguments for immunity. Although some claims between spouses might be fraudulent, fraud is also a possibility with suits among friends. Even strangers on a train could cook up a fictitious claim. So courts gradually recognized that the way to deal with fraudulent spousal claims may be to expose the fraud rather than to bar good claims along with bad ones. The family disruption argument has never seemed very persuasive. In many cases, the peace and harmony of the home that courts sought to protect seems not to have existed, or if it did, was destroyed by the tortious behavior for which the wife sued.

Abolishing the blanket immunity. In the latter half of the 20th century, most courts removed the blanket immunity for spousal suits. A large number of these courts simply apply ordinary tort rules to suits between spouses, at least in personal injury cases and frequently in all cases.[5] The Restatement reflects this approach in its simple provision that no spousal immunity remains.[6]

Some courts have replaced the blanket immunity with a screen that filters out some but not all claims for spousal torts. For instance, some courts initially abolished the immunity only for injuries inflicted by the use of automobiles.[7] But it is hard to draw a rational line at automobile cases, and as the decisions came down, courts gradually moved to a more general abolition of the immunity, so that ordinary tort rules increasingly apply.[8] Thus courts have said that one spouse might be subject to liability to the other for invasion of privacy,[9] or for negligently communicating a sexually transmitted disease,[10] or for negligently causing falls,[11] as well as for causing vehicular injuries. When civil unions were recognized, a "spouse" for purposes of spousal immunity included partners to a civil union as well as well as marital partners.[12]

[4] See Reva B. Siegel, "The Rule of Love": Wife Beating as Prerogative and Privacy, 105 Yale L.J. 2117 (1996).

[5] E.g., Leach v. Leach, 227 Ark. 599, 300 S.W.2d 15 (1957) (relying on Married Women's Property Act); Klein v. Klein, 58 Cal.2d 692, 376 P.2d 70, 26 Cal.Rptr. 102 (1962) (compensation for tort is the fundamental principle in the absence of compelling policy against it); Waite v. Waite, 618 So.2d 1360 (Fla. 1993); Boone v. Boone, 345 S.C. 8, 546 S.E.2d 191 (2001) (immunity was so repugnant that court would refuse to apply its normal choice of law rule to injury that occurred in Georgia, but would apply the South Carolina rule permitting spousal suits instead); Ellis v. Estate of Ellis, 169 P.3d 441 (Utah 2007) (rejecting immunity rationales, and holding that interspousal immunity has been abrogated for all tort claims by Married Women's Act); Price v. Price, 732 S.W.2d 316 (Tex. 1987). Statutes abolish the immunity in some states. E.g., Haw. Rev. Stat. § 572–28; 750 Ill.Comp.Stat. 65/1; N.C. Gen. Stat. § 52–5.

[6] Restatement Second of Torts § 895F(1) (1979).

[7] E.g., Fernandez v. Romo, 132 Ariz. 447, 646 P.2d 878 (1982).

[8] See Brown v. Brown, 381 Mass. 231, 409 N.E.2d 717 (1980); Merenoff v. Merenoff, 76 N.J. 535, 388 A.2d 951 (1978).

[9] Miller v. Brooks, 123 N.C.App. 20, 472 S.E.2d 350 (1996).

[10] S.A.V. v. K.G.V., 708 S.W.2d 651 (Mo. 1986); cf. John B. v. Superior Court, 38 Cal.4th 1177, 137 P.3d 153, 45 Cal.Rptr. 3d 316 (2006). See Kristyn J. Krohse, Note, No Longer Following the Rule of Thumb—What to Do with Domestic Torts and Divorce Claims, 1997 U. Ill. L. Rev. 923, 929 (1997).

[11] Klein v. Klein, 58 Cal.2d 692, 376 P.2d 70, 26 Cal.Rptr. 102 (1962).

[12] Conn. Gen. Stat. § 46b–3800 (2005) ("Wherever in the general statutes the terms 'spouse', 'family', 'immediate family', 'dependent', 'next of kin' or any other term that denotes the spousal relationship are used or defined, a party to a civil union shall be included in such use or definition").

Domestic violence torts. Intentional torts of a spouse, often in the form of domestic violence, easily call for liability.[13] The Seventh Circuit held that an earlier Illinois immunity for intentional torts was unconstitutional since it could not rationally serve the purpose of protecting family harmony to immunize these torts.[14] When the issue has been presented in recent years, state courts have usually abolished the immunity for intentional torts.[15] State domestic violence statutes also sometimes support a claim.[16] Often, victims of domestic violence have little incentive to sue, even after divorce or separation, since intentional torts are usually not covered by an insurance policy and the perpetrator's assets may be hard to reach. This arguably leads to woeful under-enforcement of anything like adequate minimum standards. Dissatisfaction, especially with the position of women under this regime, has led to proposals for some kind of mandatory insurance covering these torts.[17]

§ 23.2 Parental Immunity

Rise and Decline of the Parental Immunity

History of parental immunity. The early common law that ascribed a single legal identity to husband and wife had no application to suits between parents and children. Consequently writers have supposed that children could sue parents, at least for torts to property. In 1891, however, Mississippi decided *Hewlett v. George*,[18] which spawned a general rule in American law that parents and those in *loco parentis*[19] could not be held liable for either intentional or negligent torts to their minor, unemancipated children. The blanket immunity has now been discarded in Mississippi, the state of its origin, and in most others.

Confusion of immunity and privilege. The blanket immunity may have gained its standing from the confusion of immunities with privileges. Immunity depends only upon the status of the parties; privilege depends upon justifications for the defendant's actions. Parents are undoubtedly privileged to discipline their children, for example, but that is hardly a reason to say that parents are free to beat or rape their children.[20]

Exceptions. Over the half century or so after the immunity was introduced, courts gradually seem to have recognized the distinction, because they created a number of exceptions to the immunity. For example, courts allowed a cause of action when the child

---

   [13] See generally Douglas D. Scherer, Tort Remedies for Victims of Domestic Abuse, 43 S.C. L. Rev. 543 (1992).

   [14] Moran v. Beyer, 734 F.2d 1245 (7th Cir. 1984).

   [15] E.g., Stevens v. Stevens, 231 Kan. 726, 647 P.2d 1346 (1982); Lusby v. Lusby, 283 Md. 334, 390 A.2d 77 (1978).

   [16] See N.J. Stat. Ann. § 2C:25–29(b)(4).

   [17] Jennifer Wriggins, Domestic Violence Torts, 75 S. Cal. L. Rev. 121 (2001).

   [18] Hewlett v. George, 68 Miss. 703, 9 So. 885 (1891) (also styled Hewellette v. George), overruled in Glaskox v. Glaskox, 614 So.2d 906 (Miss. 1992).

   [19] Typically full-time caretakers who act in the role of parents. See Queen v. Carey, 210 Ga.App. 41, 435 S.E.2d 264 (1993) (grandparent); McGee v. McGee, 936 S.W.2d 360 (Tex. App. 1996) (step parent); but cf. Zellmer v. Zellmer, 164 Wash.2d 147, 188 P.3d 497 (2008) (in loco parentis status of step parent should not be lightly be inferred; in loco parentis status was a question of fact); Brabant v. Republic Servs., Inc., 800 N.E.2d 200 (Ind. Ct. App. 2003) (immunity is correlative with responsibility; if step parent has not adopted child and thus committed to his care, he does not get the immunity).

   [20] Roller v. Roller, 37 Wash. 242, 79 P. 788 (1905), overruled in part, Borst v. Borst, 41 Wash.2d 642, 251 P.2d 149 (1952) (rejecting Roller's "absolute" immunity; no immunity as to nonparental transactions).

was injured in the course of the parent's business activity[21] or by acts that were tortious to people generally and not merely to the child.[22] Courts also allowed recovery for intentional or willful torts, and even where the immunity otherwise remains, they still do.[23]

Partial abrogation of immunity: The Goller *formula.* In the second half of the twentieth century, most states removed the blanket immunity of parents and children.[24] Some of them addressed only or mainly automobile cases,[25] but others attempted a more general and principled approach. The trend was led by Wisconsin's 1963 decision in *Goller v. White.*[26] The Wisconsin court's abrogation of immunity, however, left immunity standing in two situations. First, parents would be immune whenever the alleged negligent act involved an exercise of parental authority over the child. Second, the immunity would remain where the alleged negligent act involved an exercise of parental discretion with respect to the provision of food, clothing, housing and other care.

A number of other courts adopted the Wisconsin formula retaining the immunity when issues of parental authority and discretion were involved[27] or, as sometimes said, for acts that are inherent in the parent-child relationship.[28] A variation on that rule, especially associated with New York cases, retains immunity for injuries resulting from parental "supervision" or its absence.[29]

These formulas have immunized parents in some fairly horrible cases. For example, an Illinois case held that foster parents' decision to place a three-year-old child in the "upper half of a divided shelf of a wooden cabinet inside a bedroom closet at [their] home with the door closed" with inadequate ventilation and heat fell within the immunity so that there was no liability for the child's death.[30] Such an interpretation of the Wisconsin-type rules leave an enormous fortress of immunity in place.

Complete abrogation of immunity. A number of courts have rejected the reserved immunity and adopted an ordinary negligence test.[31] They take the position that

---

[21]   E.g., Dzenutis v. Dzenutis, 200 Conn. 290, 512 A.2d 130 (1986); Brabant v. Republic Servs., Inc., 800 N.E.2d 200 (Ind. Ct. App. 2003).

[22]   See Grivas v. Grivas, 113 A.D.2d 264, 496 N.Y.S.2d 757 (1985); Hoppe IV v. Hoppe III, 281 A.D.2d 595, 724 N.Y.S.2d 65 (2001).

[23]   Newman v. Cole, 872 So.2d 138 (Ala. 2003); Herzfeld v. Herzfeld, 781 So.2d 1070 (Fla. 2001) (exception for alleged sexual abuse of child); Fager v. Hundt, 610 N.E.2d 246 (Ind. 1993) (a parent has no immunity for sexual abuse of his child under the "intentional felonious conduct" standard); Foldi v. Jeffries, 93 N.J. 533, 461 A.2d 1145 (1983); Connolly v. Holt, 332 N.C. 90, 418 S.E.2d 511 (1992) (repeated rapes and sexual molestation); Pavlick v. Pavlick, 491 S.E.2d 602 (Va. 1997).

[24]   See Lickteig v. Kolar, 782 N.W.2d 810 (Minn. 2010) (discussing state's abrogation of intrafamilial immunity and establishing that the immunity does not apply between siblings).

[25]   See Smith v. Holmes, 921 So.2d 283 (Miss. 2005); Verdier v. Verdier, 219 S.W.3d 143, 364 Ark. 287 (2005) (recognizing the state's exception to parental immunity for "a direct-action suit against a motor vehicle liability insurance carrier for uninsured motorist coverage . . . when insurance benefits are the damages requested," but refusing to create an exception to parental immunity when homeowners insurance is available to cover the loss).

[26]   Goller v. White, 20 Wis.2d 402, 122 N.W.2d 193 (1963).

[27]   Sears, Roebuck & Co. v. Huang, 652 A.2d 568 (Del. 1995); Bonin v. Vannaman, 261 Kan. 199, 929 P.2d 754 (1996); Wagner v. Smith, 340 N.W.2d 255 (Iowa 1983); Broadwell v. Holmes, 871 S.W.2d 471 (Tenn. 1994); Jilani v. Jilani, 767 S.W.2d 671 (Tex. 1988).

[28]   Cates v. Cates, 156 Ill.2d 76, 619 N.E.2d 715 (1993).

[29]   See Holodook v. Spencer, 36 N.Y.2d 35, 364 N.Y.S.2d 859, 324 N.E.2d 338 (1974). Zellmer v. Zellmer, 164 Wash.2d 147, 188 P.3d 497 (2008).

[30]   Commerce Bank v. Augsburger, 288 Ill.App.3d 510, 680 N.E.2d 822, 223 Ill.Dec. 872 (1997).

[31]   Broadbent v. Broadbent, 184 Ariz. 74, 907 P.2d 43 (1995); Gibson v. Gibson, 3 Cal.3d 914, 92 Cal.Rptr. 288, 293, 479 P.2d 648 (1971); Anderson v. Stream, 295 N.W.2d 595 (Minn. 1980); Hartman v.

ordinary negligence rules will provide protections for the parents' rightful authority and discretion because appropriate latitude for parental judgment and authority is built into the reasonable person standard. They say that the supervision immunity and the Wisconsin exceptions are vague and protect arbitrary and harmful parental conduct. In contrast, the "standard of reasonable care under the circumstances is well understood in tort law."[32] Under the ordinary negligence rule, a parent might be liable for brain damage to an infant child left alone in a swimming pool, even though the negligence involved "supervision."[33] However, a number of courts that permit parental liability note concerns about respecting cultural pluralism.[34]

Rationales for immunity: traditional rationales. Courts that still retain a substantial immunity for parents have invoked the historical rationales of domestic tranquility, family harmony, and fraud prevention. They have also said that the immunity is needed to prevent subversion of parental authority or discipline.

Rationales: inheritance and family funds. Courts have also suggested that without the immunity the negligent parent liable for the child's injury might later inherit the child's recovery and that parental liability might deplete family funds needed to foster other interests of the family. Since most suits will be brought when the parent is insured, the depletion of funds may not be so likely.[35] The problem of the possible inheritance by the wrongdoing parent of the child's recovery is a significant one, but can be dealt with directly.[36]

Rationales: parental freedom. The last[37] argument for immunity—or for some kind of legal buffer—is that courts must protect parental freedom to rear children in accordance with their own beliefs and attitudes. This view has led to the partial retention of immunity under the Wisconsin and New York rules, but in fact all courts, including those that have flatly abolished the immunity, agree with the aim.[38] The only question is whether categories like "supervision" or "parental discretion" will help judges focus on policies supporting parental freedom better than the ordinary negligence rules. The negligence rules have the advantage of focusing on the circumstances of the particular case.

Effect of parental liability on the child's recovery from other tortfeasors. Although the effect of abrogating parental immunity is often to permit an injured child to recover against a parent or the parent's insurance policy, with the advent of comparative apportionment, abrogation of parental immunity can also make it more difficult for a child to recover against other tortfeasors. In some circumstances, the child is better able

---

Hartman, 821 S.W.2d 852 (Mo. 1991); Kirchner v. Crystal, 15 Ohio St.3d 326, 474 N.E.2d 275 (1984); Winn v. Gilroy, 296 Or. 718, 681 P.2d 776 (1984).

[32]   E.g., Hartman v. Hartman, supra note 31, 821 S.W.2d at 857.

[33]   Broadbent v. Broadbent, supra note 31.

[34]   Id. (Feldman, J., concurring). Cf. Buono v. Scalia, 358 N.J.Super. 210, 817 A.2d 400 (2003), aff'd, 179 N.J. 131, 843 A.2d 1120 (2004) (court emphasized that in supervision cases the governing policy was "respect for differences in parenting philosophies and for the degree to which parents understand the uniqueness of their own children").

[35]   A joint tortfeasor might implead an uninsured parent for contribution and thus indirectly deplete family coffers. See Holodook v. Spencer, 36 N.Y.2d 35, 364 N.Y.S.2d 859, 324 N.E.2d 338 (1974).

[36]   Broadbent v. Broadbent, 184 Ariz. 74, 907 P.2d 43 (1995).

[37]   Courts have generated longer lists, as in Wagner v. A.O. Smith, 340 N.W.2d 255 (Iowa 1983), but they appear merely to offer alternate labels for essentially similar arguments.

[38]   Broadbent v. Broadbent, 184 Ariz. 74, 907 P.2d 43 (1995) (Feldman, J., concurring).

to recover from other tortfeasors if parents are immune from suit.[39] The extent of parental immunity and the ability of other defendants to invoke parental responsibility need not be identical. In at least one case, a court allowed tortfeasors to assert parental responsibility to diminish liability even though the parent would have been immune from the child's direct suit.[40] A court might more easily embrace the reverse proposition—that parental liability can be asserted by an injured child but not by other parties to the suit.

B. CHARITIES

§ 23.3   Charitable Immunity

General principle. General principles of tort law hold that each person is responsible for the harm he negligently causes. He is not relieved of liability for negligence merely because on other occasions he has behaved with charity and generosity towards others. From time to time, however, courts or legislatures appear to forget these principles and relieve certain defendants of liability for negligently caused harm on the ground that, although their conduct was negligent, the injury was inflicted in the course of kindness or charity. For example, guest statutes once relieved the negligent automobile driver of all liability to his guest. The guest was expected to be so grateful for the ride that the little matter of negligent injury should be forgotten.

Risk-utility balance distinguished. Perhaps the impulse to relieve the good-hearted defendant results from an inadequate understanding of the reasonable person standard. That standard itself gives the defendant full credit for the usefulness of the act that causes harm. It does so by providing that he is not at fault at all (and hence is not liable) when his harm-causing act would be overall more useful than harmful. He should not be deterred merely because his act entails small and unavoidable risks. But that is not the same as saying that the defendant should be relieved of responsibility for reasonably avoidable risks resulting from unreasonable and harmful acts, or that his merit as a good citizen should exempt him from the legal rules. In fact, the risk-utility balance assesses the merits of the case, while the immunity prevents a consideration of the merits. Nevertheless, the idea of affording special privileges to benevolent people for unreasonable behavior becomes law from time to time. The old guest statutes represent one example. The immunities of charities represent another.

Charitable immunity: history. The immunity of charitable organizations was recognized in a 19th century English dictum,[41] then discarded by the House of Lords.[42] The original case did not even involve personal injury, only a claim by a beneficiary of the charity to share in the charity's program. Its logic had no application to corporate charities, as distinct from trusts, but neither its repudiation in England, nor its origin

---

[39]   Sias ex rel. Mabry v. Wal-Mart Stores, Inc., 137 F.Supp.2d 699, 702 (S.D. W.Va. 2001) (after child was injured on a bike purchased at Wal-Mart, parental immunity barred counterclaim for negligent supervision; West Virginia's parental immunity doctrine barred not only claims by a child against a parent for negligence, but also "defensive assertions of contributory negligence against a parent for injuries to a child").

[40]   In Doering ex rel. Barret v. Copper Mountain, Inc., 259 F.3d 1202 (10th Cir. 2001), children on a ski slope while under the supervision of their mother collided with the resort's grooming equipment and suffered injury. Although Colorado courts recognize a qualified immunity doctrine that prevents children from suing parents for simple negligence, this immunity did not prevent the mother from being considered a non-party joint tortfeasor whose alleged contributory negligence could be considered by the jury. See also Landis v. Hearthmark, LLC, 750 S.E.2d 299 (Va. 2014).

[41]   Feoffees of Heriot's Hosp. v. Ross, 8 Eng. Rep. 1508 (H.L. 1846), relying in part on an earlier case.

[42]   Mersey Docks & Harbour Bd. of Trustees v. Gibbs, 111 Eng. Rep. 1500 (1866).

outside the realm of injury law, nor its irrelevance to corporate charities prevented its adoption in America.[43] As a result, a wide range of charities were allowed to pursue their work without reasonable care and without responsibility for the harms caused by their negligence. At various times the immunity has extended to the Boy Scouts,[44] museums of various kinds,[45] a Jewish Community Center,[46] a Confederate Memorial Association,[47] a Little League Baseball organization,[48] and to churches,[49] private schools,[50] and hospitals.[51] Which entities qualify as charities for purposes of charitable immunity is a subject of continued litigation.[52]

Rationales. Courts gave different reasons, or combinations of reasons, for the immunity. They said variously that liability would divert trust funds for purposes inconsistent with the charity and its donor's intent; that ordinary rules of vicarious liability should not apply to impose liability for the acts of employees; that beneficiaries of a charity should not recover from it because they must waive their claims or assume the risk of negligence; and that donations to charities should not be discouraged by imposing liability for fault; and that liabilities might terminate a charity's good works.[53]

Rationales attacked. These reasons were individually deficient, as many judges and other critics have pointed out repeatedly. As to the trust fund argument, most charities are corporations, not trusts. More importantly, two people by contract (or donation in trust) cannot dictate their responsibility for torts to those not a party to their arrangement. The argument that charities were not liable under the doctrine of respondeat superior, on the ground that its employees were working for public good rather than for the charity, seems spurious on its face and certainly illogical in the light of the charity's vicarious liability to strangers.[54] The waiver or assumed risk argument was at best fictional. Worse, it operated to remove protection for those who most needed reasonable care. But even then it did not explain all the cases, because beneficiaries of an individual charity (as opposed to a corporate charity) were allowed to recover for negligence, although they assumed the risk as much as beneficiaries of corporations. Further, the immunity applied even to infants who could not possibly have assumed the

   [43] Beginning with McDonald v. Mass. Gen. Hosp., 120 Mass. 432 (1876), overruled in part by Colby v. Carney Hosp., 254 N.E.2d 407 (Mass. 1969).

   [44] Schultz v. Boy Scouts of Am., Inc., 65 N.Y.2d 189, 480 N.E.2d 679, 491 N.Y.S.2d 90 (1985) (New Jersey law).

   [45] Morales v. N.J. Acad. of Aquatic Sciences., 302 N.J.Super. 50, 694 A.2d 600 (1997) (aquarium).

   [46] Abramson v. Reiss, 334 Md. 193, 638 A.2d 743 (1994).

   [47] Bodenheimer v. Confederate Mem'l Ass'n, 5 F.Supp. 526 (E.D. Va. 1932).

   [48] Pomeroy v. Little League Baseball of Collingswood, 142 N.J.Super. 471, 362 A.2d 39 (1976).

   [49] Rev. Thomas Paprocki, As the Pendulum Swings from Charitable Immunity to Bankruptcy, Bringing it to Rest with Charitable Viability, 48 J. Cath. Legal Stud. 1 (2009).

   [50] E.g., Ettlinger v. Trustees of Randolph-Macon Coll., 31 F.2d 869 (4th Cir. 1929).

   [51] E.g., Howard v. S. Baltimore Gen. Hosp., 191 Md. 617, 62 A.2d 574 (1948).

   [52] Mayfield-Brown v. Sayegh, 667 S.E.2d 785, 276 Va. 555 (2008) (university's medical practice group was not immune from tort liability under doctrine of charitable immunity); Univ. of Va. Health Servs. Found. v. Morris, 657 S.E.2d 512, 275 Va. 319 (2008); Tonelli v. Bd. of Educ. of Twp. of Wycoff, 888 A.2d 433, 185 N.J. 438 (2005) (township school board was not entitled to charitable immunity under state act); Ola v. YMCA of S. Hampton Roads, Inc., 270 Va. 550, 621 S.E.2d 70 (2005) (YMCA recreation center was immune from liability for sexual assault of child in its program based on charitable immunity doctrine).

   [53] For a discussion of state policies which favor charitable immunity and those that oppose it, see P.V. ex. rel. T.V. v. Camp Jaycee, 962 A.2d 453, 197 N.J. 132 (2009). See also Rev. Thomas Paprocki, As the Pendulum Swings from Charitable Immunity to Bankruptcy, Bringing it to Rest with Charitable Viability, 48 J. Cath. Legal Stud. 1 (2009) (outlining the hundreds of millions of dollars paid by the Catholic Church to settle abuse claims and expressing concern about charitable programs lost and effect on religious practice).

   [54] See Miss. Baptist Hosp. v. Holmes, 214 Miss. 906, 933, 55 So.2d 142, 153 (1951).

risk. The "public policy" argument that charities might go out of business if held liable was answered by observing that only the cost of reasonable behavior was entailed. After all, nothing requires a charitable hospital to inflict burns upon a newborn infant in her bassinet.[55] If reasonable care is too much to ask of charities, the cost of insurance is not. Perhaps a more important answer was that if a charity causes so much harm by its negligence that a requirement of reasonable care would drive it out of business, then perhaps it should not be in business at all for in that case it is doing more harm than good.

Doctrine as a subsidy. Beyond the individual defect of each supposed reason for the immunity, all of the reasons were founded directly or indirectly on the policy of subsidizing organizations denominated as charities. Courts accomplished the subsidy by allowing charities to avoid financial responsibility for unreasonable and harmful acts. But these subsidies were not paid by the state; they were paid by the victims whose recovery was denied—through a "coerced donation" of their right of recovery.[56] Not surprisingly, courts ultimately refuted each of the various rationales for the immunity.[57]

Modifications or exceptions to immunity. Courts first developed a large number of exceptions or modifications that varied from state to state. Most adopted one or more of the following rules. They said that charities would be liable (1) to the extent they have assets that form no part of the charitable trust assets, for example, to the extent that liability was covered by insurance, or had assets not part of the charitable funds;[58] (2) for their torts to strangers, that is, to persons who do not receive the benefactions of the charity;[59] (3) for the torts of upper level management, including negligence in hiring or retaining dangerous employees;[60] (4) to beneficiaries of the charity who actually pay for the services that cause harm, at least to the extent that a judgment can be enforced against non-charitable assets,[61] and for gross negligence or willful and wanton negligence.[62]

Rejecting immunity. Most American courts[63] or legislatures[64] have now rejected the immunity. The Restatement simply says no such immunity exists.[65] Many of the

---

[55]   Durney v. St. Francis Hosp., Inc., 46 Del. 350, 83 A.2d 753 (1951).

[56]   Albritton v. Neighborhood Ctrs. Ass'n for Child Dev., 12 Ohio St.3d 210, 466 N.E.2d 867, 871 (1984).

[57]   The classic criticism, which more or less turned immunity thinking around, is President and Directors of Georgetown College v. Hughes, 130 F.2d 810 (D.C. Cir. 1942). One of the best summaries of major arguments against immunity is Note, The Quality of Mercy: 'Charitable Torts' and Their Continuing Immunity, 100 Harv. L. Rev. 1382 (1987).

[58]   See, e.g., Me.Rev.Stat.Ann. tit. 14, § 158 (insurance coverage is a waiver of immunity); Picher v. Roman Catholic Bishop of Portland, 974 A.2d 286 (Me. 2009); cf. Md. Ins. Code § 19–103. Self-insurance, or a reserve for contingencies, may or may not qualify as insurance that waives immunity. Archer v. Sisters of Mercy Health Sys., St. Louis, Inc., 294 S.W.3d 414, 375 Ark. 523 (2009) (does qualify); Ponder v. Fulton-DeKalb Hosp. Auth., 256 Ga. 833, 353 S.E.2d 515 (1987) (does not).

[59]   E.g., Alabama Baptist Hosp. Bd. v. Carter, 226 Ala. 109, 145 So. 443 (1932); Byrd Theatre Found. v. Barnett, 754 S.E.2d 299 (Va. 2014).

[60]   Harrell v. Louis Smith Mem'l Hosp., 197 Ga.App. 189, 397 S.E.2d 746 (1990); J. J. v. Victory Tabernacle Baptist Church, 236 Va. 206, 372 S.E.2d 391 (1988).

[61]   Ponder v. Fulton-DeKalb Hosp. Auth., 256 Ga. 833, 353 S.E.2d 515 (1987).

[62]   Cowan v. Hospice Support Care, Inc., 268 Va. 482, 603 S.E.2d 916 (2004).

[63]   E.g., President & Dirs. of Georgetown Coll. v. Hughes, 130 F.2d 810 (D.C. Cir. 1942) (the leading case); Albritton v. Neighborhood Ctrs. Ass'n for Child Dev., 12 Ohio St.3d 210, 466 N.E.2d 867 (1984). Janet Fairchild, Annotation, Tort Immunity of Nongovernmental Charities—Modern Status, 25 A.L.R.4th 517 (1981).

[64]   Conn. Gen. Stat. § 52–557d.

[65]   Restatement Second of Torts § 895E (1979).

decisions arose out of suits against charitable hospitals, but the reasoning was broad enough to eliminate the immunity for other charitable organizations as well.[66] In addition, some of the states that retain the immunity limit its effect by defining charities with increasing rigor[67] and by removing the immunity to the extent that insurance protects the charity.[68] Because state law regarding immunity differs so substantially between states, which state's law applies can be contested and outcome determinative.[69]

Immunity remnants. Once the courts abolished or rejected the immunity, however, legislatures sometimes reinstated the immunity or some remnant of it for particular cases.[70] Legislatures in a number of states impose a cap on damages recoverable against charitable organizations.[71] In addition, several states retain the immunity with whatever modifications or exceptions have been applied in those states.[72] The rules are so deeply wrinkled that classification is unreliable. Massachusetts, for example, permits a recovery capped at such a low level that for most purposes Massachusetts could be classified as a state retaining the immunity.[73] On the other hand, Maine purports to retain the immunity but defines charities narrowly.[74] And its charitable immunity statute was found to be inapplicable to intentional torts.[75]

§ 23.4 Individual Immunities

Immunities for classes of people. The traditional charitable immunity protected trusts and then charitable or nonprofit corporations. Individuals, however, have never enjoyed general protection from liability merely because they were engaged in charitable work when they negligently caused harm.[76] However, legislatures have often been

---

[66]   See Friend v. Cove Methodist Church, Inc., 65 Wash.2d 174, 396 P.2d 546 (1964); Widell v. Holy Trinity Catholic Church, 19 Wis.2d 648, 121 N.W.2d 249 (1963).

[67]   The organization may not get the immunity if its articles of incorporation fail to reflect a charitable purpose, perhaps even an exclusive one. See Snyder v. Am. Ass'n of Blood Banks, 144 N.J. 269, 676 A.2d 1036 (1996). Likewise, in some states if the charity receives income from sources other than charitable donations. Ouachita Wilderness Inst., Inc. v. Mergen, 329 Ark. 405, 947 S.W.2d 780 (1997) (organization for rehabilitation of juvenile offenders was not a charitable organization in part because it received state funds, hence was not a charity dependent upon donations); Lutheran Hosps. & Homes Soc'y of Am. v. Yepsen, 469 P.2d 409 (Wyo. 1970). Arkansas adopted a flexible definition of charities, using a number of factors. Masterson v. Stambuck, 321 Ark. 391, 902 S.W.2d 803 (1995).

[68]   E.g., Me. Rev. Stat. Ann. tit. 14, § 158. Self-insurance may or may not qualify for this exception. Compare Archer v. Sisters of Mercy Health Sys., St. Louis, Inc., 375 Ark. 523, 294 S.W.3d 414 (2009), with Coulombe v. Salvation Army, 790 A.2d 593 (Me. 2002).

[69]   P.V. ex. rel. T.V. v. Camp Jaycee, 962 A.2d 453, 197 N.J. 132 (2009) (applying choice of law principles in the charitable immunity context).

[70]   For instance, Rhode Island rejected the immunity early on, but the legislature enacted a statutory immunity for charitable hospitals. Later still, however, the legislature recanted and provided for ordinary liability. See, reflecting this history, Hodge v. Osteopathic Gen. Hosp. of R.I., 107 R.I. 135, 265 A.2d 733 (1970); R.I. Gen. Laws § 9–1–26.

[71]   See Md. Code Ann. Cts. & Jud. Proc. § 5–632 (as to hospitals carrying insurance of at least $100,000, that sum is the cap on liability); S.C. Code § 33–56–180 ($250,000); Tex. Civ. Prac. & Rem. Code § 84.006 ($500,000/$1,000,000). The caps do not apply in all cases.

[72]   Hemenway v. Presbyterian Hosp. Ass'n, 161 Colo. 42, 419 P.2d 312 (1966).

[73]   Mass. Gen. Laws Ann. ch. 231, § 85 (2012) ($20,000 plus costs, but for medical malpractice actions up to $100,000).

[74]   Child v. Central Maine Med. Ctr., 575 A.2d 318 (Me. 1990).

[75]   Picher v. Roman Catholic Bishop of Portland, 974 A.2d 286 (Me. 2009) (allowing fraudulent concealment claim against bishop based on child sexual abuse by priest); cf. Hardwicke v. Am. Boychoir Sch., 188 N.J. 69, 902 A.2d 900 (2006) (same; New Jersey). See also Matthew Cobb, A Strange Distinction: Charitable Immunity and Clergy Sexual Abuse in Picher v. Roman Catholic Bishop of Portland, 62 Me. L. Rev. 703 (2010).

[76]   See President & Dirs. Of Georgetown Coll. V. Hughes, 130 F.2d 810, 814 (D.C. Cir. 1942).

prevailed upon to enact immunities or privileges for particular classes of persons. One thread that runs through many statutes is that persons who act in specified charitable ways either deserve protection against legal responsibility or should be given that protection to encourage their charity.

Individual charitable acts. These statutes differ from the traditional common law charitable immunity in several important ways. First, many of them cover only particular charities or acts of charity. Second, they often apply to individuals. Third, not all of the statutes enact a flat immunity; some merely lower the standard of care owed by a charitable individual or organization. One prominent group of statutes is medical Good Samaritan statutes which relieve medical personnel and sometimes others of any obligation of due care in medical emergencies.[77] In addition, recreational use statutes, limiting a landowner's standard of care to those who use the land without charge, have been enacted almost everywhere.[78]

Favored groups. More recently, statutes have either enacted immunities or lowered standards of care for particular groups favored by the legislature, for example emergency-room doctors.[79] Or the statutes protect those who cause harm while acting as a volunteer for particular charities. Volunteers to libraries,[80] athletic programs[81] horseback riding programs[82] and bingo games and raffles[83] are examples. Architects and engineers who provide post-emergency inspections may enjoy special protections.[84] Also, donors of food to non-profit organizations are now receiving protections from liability,[85] and the non-profit organization that distributes food may be similarly protected.[86] Again, the statutes may lower standards of care without conferring a complete immunity.

Broad protection for volunteers. One recent type of legislation protects virtually all volunteers for work in non-profit activities, and sometimes boards of directors as well.[87] Courts may be recognizing similar immunities for individuals.[88] In 1997, Congress enacted a volunteer protection statute that eliminates most potential liability of volunteers for "nonprofit" organizations unless the volunteer is willfully or grossly negligent. The term nonprofit may include a number of organizations such as the Chamber of Commerce that would not necessarily have been regarded as charitable.[89]

---

[77] Discussed in § 21.13.

[78] See § 20.10.

[79] See Fla. Stat. Ann. § 768.13 (reckless disregard standard for doctors providing emergency services).

[80] Vt. Stat. Ann. tit. 12, § 5762.

[81] Mass. Gen. Laws ch. 231, § 85V (immunity from negligence liability for volunteer coaches, umpires, referees and others); Ga. Code Ann. § 51–1–20.1 (immunity from negligence liability for volunteers to sports or safety programs of a non-profit unless insurance coverage is available); 745 Ill. Comp. Stat. § 80/1 (volunteers who coach or umpire in non-profit sports programs; standard of care lowered so that no liability is imposed unless conduct falls "substantially below" standard).

[82] See Jones v. Westernaires, 876 P.2d 50 (Colo. Ct. App. 1993), overruled so far as it provided immunity for organizations as well as individuals, Concerned Parents of Pueblo v. Gilmore, 47 P.3d 311 (Colo. 2002).

[83] Colo. Rev. Stat. Ann § 12–9–111.

[84] Cal. Bus. & Prof. Code § 5536.27 (architects); Cal. Bus. & Prof. Code § 6706 (engineers).

[85] Cal. Civ. Code § 1714.25 (addressing the standard of care).

[86] 745 Ill. Comp. Stat. 50/4.

[87] Colo. Rev. Stat. § 13–21–116; 76 Okla. Stat. § 31.

[88] Moore v. Warren, 250 Va. 421, 463 S.E.2d 459 (1995). The court refused to extend this immunity to the donor of tea and services for an immune religious organization on the ground that the individual who spilled hot tea was not acting for the charity but for the donor. Bhatia v. Mehak, Inc., 262 Va. 544, 551 S.E.2d 358 (2001).

[89] See 26 U.S.C.A. § 501(c).

As broad as this shield is, however, liability remains for most ordinary motor vehicle negligence and for willful misconduct or gross negligence.[90] Congress actually enacted an argument for this statute, asserting that without its protection, volunteers would be discouraged from providing their services to nonprofit organizations because of "unwarranted litigation costs" and other concerns.[91] The statute is thus one of a number that come under the general heading of "tort reform," aimed at overall reduction in liabilities. Although the statute preempts state law, states are permitted to opt out of the statute under certain circumstances.[92]

---

[90] 42 U.S.C.A. § 14503.

[91] 42 U.S.C.A. § 14501(a)(6).

[92] 42 U.S.C.A. § 14503.

Chapter 24

PROFESSIONAL RISK-TAKERS

Analysis

§ 24.1   Shifting Responsibility to Professional Risk-Takers
§ 24.2   Limited Duties to Professional Risk-Takers: The Firefighters' Rule
§ 24.3   Risks Covered by the Risk-Takers Rule
§ 24.4   Persons Covered by the Risk-Takers Rule

§ 24.1 Shifting Responsibility to Professional Risk-Takers

General Rule

Agreement to repair a danger. An employer ordinarily owes a duty of reasonable care to provide workers and contractors a reasonably safe place in which to work.[1] The employer must typically remove, or at least warn of, hidden dangers of which the employer knew or should have known.[2] However, if the employer retains a contractor to repair a dangerous condition which is known to both parties, the employer is not liable merely because he created the danger.[3] In that situation, the parties implicitly or explicitly shift responsibility for repair of the dangerous condition to the contractor, who generally has no complaint if the danger he undertook to repair causes him harm.[4]

Limited duty. This rule of limited duty has been entangled with, or even expressed as, a rule of assumed risk in the sense of no duty or consent.[5] However, the argument has been made that the all-or-nothing result of a limited duty or assumed risk rule is incompatible with more recent trends toward comparative apportionment.[6] That argument is particularly persuasive where the plaintiff did not willingly consent to accept a specific, known risk. The limited duty rule does not preclude recovery for injury

---

[1]   See Hastings v. Mechalske, 336 Md. 663, 650 A.2d 274 (1994).

[2]   Bennett v. Trevecca Nazarene Univ., 216 S.W.3d 293 (Tenn. 2007). Brewster v. Colgate-Palmolive Co., 279 S.W.3d 142 (Ky. 2009) (unknown asbestos).

[3]   See Chance v. Dallas County, Ala., 456 So.2d 295 (Ala. 1984); Hannon v. Hayes-Bickford Lunch Sys., Inc., 336 Mass. 268, 145 N.E.2d 191 (1957).

[4]   State ex rel. Union Elec. Co. v. Dolan, 256 S.W.3d 77 (Mo. 2008); Olivo v. Owens-Illinois, Inc., 186 N.J. 394, 895 A.2d 1143 (2006); Kowalsky v. Conreco Co., Inc., 264 N.Y. 125, 190 N.E. 206 (1934); cf. Dyer v. Superior Court, 56 Cal.App.4th 61, 65 Cal.Rptr.2d 85 (1997) (tow truck driver injured on the highway while responding to call assumed the risks of highway injury and could not recover against driver who failed to maintain his car and thus necessitated the call for a tow).

[5]   This was sometimes called "contractual assumed risk." Courts once applied the idea to virtually any job risks, including those that could have been eliminated by reasonable care or providing a reasonably safe place. E.g., Comer v. Texaco, Inc., 514 F.2d 1243 (5th Cir. 1975) (worker who needed job assumed risk of attack by working in a high crime area even if he could not get a job elsewhere; consequently the employer was not liable); Smith v. Officers & Dirs. of Kart-N-Karry, Inc., 346 So.2d 313 (La. Ct. App. 1977) (similar). This broad approach to assumed risk has largely passed from the picture.

[6]   Compare Brewster v. Colgate-Palmolive Co., 279 S.W.3d 142 (Ky. 2009), with Hale v. Beckstead, 116 P.3d 263 (Utah 2005). In a comparative apportionment system, a jury might be permitted to weigh the responsibility of multiple parties such as general contractor, a subcontractor and its employee. See Coho Res., Inc. v. Chapman, 913 So.2d 899 (Miss. 2005).

resulting from hidden dangers of which the contractor does not know,[7] or from dangers that arose after the work was undertaken.[8] Knowledge of the risk is the watchword[9]— both the knowledge of the employer, and the knowledge of the contractor.[10]

Illustrations. A Tennessee case illustrates the general principle. In that case, the defendant property owner had allowed a roof to become rotten and to leak. The defendant retained a contractor to remove the rotten roof and install a new one. Although the contractor did not know the extent of the rot, he knew he was removing and replacing a roof that was not worth keeping. When the roof collapsed with him, he had no claim against the owner.[11]

Conversely, suppose a chemist hires a local moving company to transport furniture and packages, but does not tell the movers that the boxes contain chemicals which will be dangerous in the heat. If the chemicals explode during the move and injure the moving van's driver, the chemist is subject to liability for failure to take precautions or warn of the danger.[12]

Effect on Third Persons

Shifting responsibility for injuries to third persons. An arrangement under which the contractor assumes the risks of dangers inherent in a job might conceivably affect rights of or against third persons. If the contractor in control of the dangerous instrument makes repairs negligently, or fails to make them, or fails to warn those who are in danger, with resulting injury to some third person, the contractor is subject to liability to the injured person.[13] But in at least some cases, the employer who reasonably relies upon the contractor for safety can escape liability to the victim.[14] The employer may be viewed as having shifted responsibility to the contractor unless the rules of non-delegable duty, contractual or other assumed duty make him liable along with the contractor.[15] The limited liability of the employer is often at issue when the contractor's

---

[7] See, e.g., Kinsman v. Unocal Corp., 37 Cal.4th 659, 123 P.3d 931 (2005) (concealed asbestos hazard; a "landowner cannot effectively delegate to the contractor responsibility for the safety of its employees if it fails to disclose critical information needed to fulfill that responsibility"); General Elec. Co. v. Moritz, 257 S.W.3d 211 (Tex. 2008) (absence of handrails was not a concealed defect); Olivo v. Owens-Illinois, Inc., 186 N.J. 394, 895 A.2d 1143 (2006) (issues of fact concerning whether asbestos exposure was a known risk incidental to the work contractor was hired to perform); Chance v. Dallas County, Ala., 456 So.2d 295 (Ala. 1984).

[8] See, e.g., Bennett v. Trevecca Nazarene Univ., 216 S.W.3d 293 (Tenn. 2007).

[9] Benefield v. Pep Boys-Manny, Moe & Jack, Inc., 291 Ga. App. 79, 661 S.E.2d 214 (2008) (reversing grant of summary judgment when contractor performing work on lighting fixtures had not seen that protective metal shielding the conveyor had been removed).

[10] In Roberts v. NASCO Equip. Co., Inc., 986 So.2d 379 (Ala. 2007), the Alabama Supreme Court wrote, "A party claiming that a duty to warn existed must show: (1) that the defect or danger was hidden; (2) that it was known to the owner; and (3) that it was neither known to the contractor, nor such as he ought to know." See also Jones Food Co., Inc. v. Shipman, 981 So.2d 355 (Ala. 2006) (finding that employer did not have superior knowledge of hazard ladder posed).

[11] Blair v. Campbell, 924 S.W.2d 75 (Tenn. 1996).

[12] Restatement Third of Torts (Liability for Physical and Emotional Harm) § 55 illus. 4 (2012).

[13] Id. § 55 (actor who hires an independent contractor to perform an activity that creates a risk of physical harm is potentially subject to liability).

[14] Id. § 56 (no liability factor has not retained control over that part of the work).

[15] Id. § 57 (vicarious liability of an actor who hires an independent contractor in the case of abnormally dangerous activities, activities posing a peculiar risk, and six additional circumstances). See also Hull v. Baran Telecom, Inc., 242 Fed. Appx. 504, 2007 WL 2007571 (10th Cir. 2007); Farabaugh v. Pennsylvania Turnpike Comm'n, 590 Pa. 46, 911 A.2d 1264 (2006); Handler Corp. v. Tlapechco, 901 A.2d 737 (Del. 2006). Cf. In re World Trade Ctr. Disaster Site Litig., 456 F.Supp.2d 520 (S.D.N.Y. 2006) (granting and denying some defendants' motions to dismiss claims brought by workers who inhaled toxic fumes during restoration of the World Trade Center after the September 11, 2001 attacks).

employee or subcontractor is injured.[16] If the contractor's employee was fully informed of the danger, he is in the same position as the contractor.[17] If the contractor's employee was not fully informed, the employer may nevertheless be reasonable in relying upon the contractor to inform the contractor's employee.[18] In either event, absent a non-delegable duty or other exception, the injured contractor's employee has a claim against the contractor, but not against the employer.[19]

Retained control. The contours of the exceptions in which liability of the employer as well as the independent contractor is recognized vary in different jurisdictions.[20] The Restatement Third hinges direct liability for work entrusted to an independent contractor on retained control.[21] The Restatement also retains vicarious liability for those who hire independent contractors in eight situations, which include work involving abnormally dangerous activities,[22] activity posing a peculiar risk,[23] precautions required by statute or regulation,[24] and several additional circumstances.[25]

§ 24.2 Limited Duties to Professional Risk-Takers: The Firefighters' Rule

General rule. When firefighters,[26] police officers,[27] and perhaps other public safety officers are injured by perils that they have been employed to confront, many courts hold that they ordinarily have no claim against the person who created those perils. For example, if a landowner negligently causes a fire, the firefighter injured by risks inherent in firefighting has no claim against the landowner. The same is true if the fire is caused by a strict liability activity.[28] The rule is known both as the professional rescuers doctrine, and, in spite of its expansion, as the firefighters' rule.[29] This chapter also uses the term public safety officer to include all those to whom the rule applies. The rule says that one has no duty to public safety officers to avoid creating a danger that

---

[16]   E.g., Meadowcraft Indus., Inc., 817 So.2d 702 (Ala. 2001); Whitlow v. Seaboard Air Line R.R. Co., 222 F.2d 57 (4th Cir. 1955); Kowalsky v. Conreco Co., Inc., 264 N.Y. 125, 190 N.E. 206 (1934).

[17]   See Kamla v. Space Needle Corp., 147 Wash.2d 114, 52 P.3d 472 (2002).

[18]   Brewster v. Colgate-Palmolive Co., 279 S.W.3d 142, 144 n.4 (Ky. 2009).

[19]   Helms v. Carmel High Sch. Vocational Bldg. Trades Corp., 854 N.E.2d 345 (Ind. 2006); Franks v. Independent Prod. Co., Inc., 96 P.3d 484 (Wyo. 2004); Shell Oil Co. v. Khan, 138 S.W.3d 288 (Tex. 2004).

[20]   For example, in Delaware, a general contractor has a duty to protect an independent contractor's employees when the general contractor: (1) actively controls the manner and method of performing the contract work; (2) voluntarily undertakes the responsibility for implementing safety measures; or (3) retains possessory control over the work premises during work. Handler Corp. v. Tlapechco, 901 A.2d 737 (Del. 2006).

[21]   Restatement Third of Torts (Liability for Physical and Emotional Harm) § 56 (2012).

[22]   Id. § 58.

[23]   Id. § 59.

[24]   Id. § 63.

[25]   Id. §§ 57–65.

[26]   E.g., Krauth v. Geller, 31 N.J. 270, 157 A.2d 129 (1960) (a leading case on the "firefighters' rule"), superseded by statute as discussed in Roma v. U.S., 344 F.3d 352 (3rd Cir. 2003).

[27]   E.g., Moody v. Delta Western, Inc., 38 P.3d 1139 (Alaska 2002); White v. State, 419 Md. 265, 19 A.3d 369 (2011); Farmer v. B & G Food Enters., Inc., 181 So.2d 1154 (Miss. 2002); Wadler v. City of New York, 14 N.Y.3d 192, 899 N.Y.S.2d 73, 925 N.E.2d 875 (2010); Ellinwood v. Cohen, 87 A.3d 1054 (R.I. 2014). Contra, holding the grounds for the firefighters' rule do not apply to police officers, Cole v. Hubanks, 681 N.W.2d 147 (Wis. 2004).

[28]   See Lipson v. Superior Court of Orange County (Berger), 31 Cal.3d 362, 644 P.2d 822, 182 Cal.Rptr. 629 (1982).

[29]   Older cases called it the fireman's rule and must be searched under that term. It is also sometimes referred to as the professional rescuer's doctrine. See Fordham v. Oldroyd, 171 P.3d 411 (Utah 2007).

requires their services or to protect them against unknown associated dangers.[30] Qualifications almost always follow such Draconian rules, and that is certainly the case with the firefighters' rule.

Landowner cases. The firefighters' rule was originally a product of and justified by the premises liability rules.[31] Perhaps in some states the rule would still be confined to suits against the occupant of the premises.[32] In the premises cases, courts usually treated firefighters as licensees, holding that they took the premises as they found them, so the landowner would not be liable for negligently setting the fire that injured the firefighter, or even for leaving a dangerous condition on the premises.[33] Under the premises liability rules, the injured firefighter could recover in several specific kinds of cases—when the landowner is guilty of active negligence, as distinguished from unsafe conditions of the property itself,[34] when the landowner has violated an ordinance or safety statute aimed at protecting firefighters or officers,[35] when the firefighter's presence is known and the landowner fails to warn of known dangers,[36] and when injury occurs on premises open to the public.[37] But if the safety officer was in a private residence, or on business premises at a place not open to the public, the courts otherwise barred recovery.

Extension beyond landowners. The courts eventually began to divorce the rule from its connection to landowner cases. They began to say that public safety officers in the course of their employment should be denied recovery for injuries inflicted by the defendant's negligence even when injury occurred outside the defendant's land and even when the defendant was not a landowner at all.[38] For example, in a California case, a police officer was injured while attempting to stop a highway speeder. The rule applied to bar the officer's claim against the speeder. That could not represent a landowner's rule.[39] At the same time, a fair number of courts abolished the special landowner rules

---

[30]   Carson v. Headrick, 900 S.W.2d 685, 690 (Tenn. 1995) (using a variant formulation: "a citizen owes no duty of reasonable care to police officers responding to that citizen's call for assistance").

[31]   For a collection of the landowners' cases, see Larry D. Scheafer, Annotation, Liability of Owner or Occupant of Premises to Fireman Coming Thereon in Discharge of His Duty, 11 A.L.R.4th 597 (1981); Richard C. Tinney, Annotation, Liability of Owner or Occupant of Premises to Police Officer Coming Thereon in Discharge of Officer's Duty, 30 A.L.R.4th 81 (1981).

[32]   See Court v. Grzelinski, 72 Ill.2d 141, 379 N.E.2d 281, 19 Ill.Dec. 617 (1978); Knight v. Schneider Nat'l Carriers, Inc., 350 F.Supp.2d 775, 782 (N.D. Ill. 2004).

[33]   E.g., Lee v. Luigi, Inc., 696 A.2d 1371 (D.C. 1997) (police officer responding to burglar alarm when owner was absent slipped on dangerous substance).

[34]   See Buren v. Midwest Indus., Inc., 380 S.W.2d 96 (Ky. 1964).

[35]   E.g., Dini v. Naiditch, 20 Ill.2d 406, 170 N.E.2d 881, 86 A.L.R.2d 1184 (1960).

[36]   See Wright v. Coleman, 148 Wis.2d 897, 436 N.W.2d 864 (1989).

[37]   See Meiers v. Fred Koch Brewery, 229 N.Y. 10, 127 N.E. 491, 13 A.L.R. 633 (1920); Cameron v. Abatiell, 127 Vt. 111, 241 A.2d 310 (1968), overruled by duty Demag v. Better Power Equip., Inc., 197 Vt. 176, 102 A.3d 1101, 1105 (2014) (rejecting the status categories).

[38]   See, e.g., White v. State, 419 Md. 265, 19 A.3d 369 (2011) (firefighters' rule barred police officer's claim against the state for the negligence of a police dispatcher in reporting a shoplifting incident as an armed robbery, causing the officer to engage in a high-speed chase during which he was injured).

[39]   Hubbard v. Boelt, 28 Cal.3d 480, 620 P.2d 156, 169 Cal.Rptr. 706 (1980), superseded by statute limiting application of the firefighter's rule as stated in Gibb v. Stetson, 199 Cal.App.3d 1008, 245 Cal.Rptr. 283 (1988); cf. Moody v. Delta Western, Inc., 38 P.3d 1139 (Alaska 2002) (police officer injured trying to stop stolen vehicle loaded with flammables; recovery against owner who negligently permitted theft is barred by firefighters' rule).

and applied ordinary negligence rules to persons who were injured on the land. These changes and other perceptions required reconsideration of the rationales.[40]

Rationales. Sometimes it is suggested that if landowners were liable for negligence in setting fires, they would delay calling for professional help with potential for the spread of fire to neighbors.[41] Prosser thought this was a preposterous suggestion, but no behavioral data has been offered either for or against that view. Such a rationale would limit the rule to a narrow group of cases.

Foreseeability. Prosser suggested that the "most legitimate" basis for the firefighters' rule was that public safety officers were likely to enter the premises at unforeseeable times and places.[42] If this is the most legitimate rationale for the rule, then the rule has little support indeed. First, it cannot explain use of the rule outside the landowner's cases, as where a police officer is injured in pursuing a criminal. Second, unforeseeability of the officer's presence is a question of fact that differs from case to case; it is not something you can make a rule about.

Public benefits. Some courts suggested that the safety officer would collect workers' compensation or similar benefits from the public employer and that if the negligent defendant were required to pay tort damages, the defendant would pay twice, once indirectly as a taxpayer and again as a tortfeasor.[43] One difficulty with this argument is that it was not applied in other instances of public employee injury. Even in its own terms, it did not work. The public employer who paid compensation benefits to the injured firefighter would in fact recoup some or all of the payments from the tort recovery against the negligent defendant.

Duty and policy. If firefighters and police officers were to be denied recovery whether injury occurred on the defendant's land or not, the most plausible explanation was grounded, not in the landowners' rules, but in a public policy which in turn was based primarily on arguments from assumed risk in the no-duty sense.[44] The argument is that firefighters and police officers are paid to face risks inherent in their work, including, evidently, the risks of negligence by third persons. If salaries of these employees do or should reflect advance payment for taking risks, no other payment is due when injury occurs.[45] So the defendant owes no duty to protect safety officers from risks they are employed to confront. Under this rationale, courts currently tend to

---

[40] In some cases the shift is explicit, as in Hack v. Gillespie, 74 Ohio St.3d 362, 658 N.E.2d 1046, 1049 (1996). For a newer take on rationales that support retaining at least a limited form of the firefighters' rule, see Gerritt De Geest, Who Should Be Immune From Tort Liability?, 41 J. Legal Stud. 291 (2012).

[41] See, e.g., Sallee v. GTE South, Inc., 839 S.W.2d 277 (Ky. 1992).

[42] Prosser & Keeton on Torts § 61, pp. 431–32.

[43] E.g., Farmer v. B & G Food Enters., Inc., 181 So.2d 1154 (Miss. 2002).

[44] See, e.g., Hack v. Gillespie, 74 Ohio St.3d 362, 658 N.E.2d 1046 (1996). Some opinions have sought to avoid the assumed risk expression, but they nevertheless raise the same kind of arguments. See Flowers v. Rock Creek Terrace Ltd. P'ship, 308 Md. 432, 520 A.2d 361 (1987) (public policy derived from fact that firefighters are employed for the very purpose of confronting such risks); Kreski v. Modern Wholesale Elec. Supply Co., 429 Mich. 347, 415 N.W.2d 178 (1987).

[45] See Babes Showclub, Jaba, Inc. v. Lair, 918 N.E.2d 308 (Ind. 2009) ("Many emergencies are caused by the negligence of some party. The public employs firefighters, police officers, and others to respond to emergencies, and these responders knowingly combat the effects of others' negligence."); Krauth v. Geller, 31 N.J. 270, 274, 157 A.2d 129, 131 (1960) ("Hence, for that risk, the fireman should receive appropriate compensation from the public he serves, both in pay which reflects the hazard and in workmen's compensation benefits. . . ."), superseded by statute as discussed in Roma v. U.S., 344 F.3d 352 (3rd Cir. 2003).

analyze the cases by considering the risks which were, or were not, inherent in the professional's work or risks.[46]

Rejections and limitations. Besides the limits implicit in the rule itself, some courts have begun to reject any special rule for firefighters, officers, and others who must confront danger. Where assumed risk has been abolished as a separate doctrine, and where the special landowners' rules have been abolished as well, the formal supports for the doctrine are shaky. The Restatement Third of Torts takes "no position" on the firefighters' rule or its scope, but notes that the Restatement's adoption of a duty of reasonable care owed to licensees undercuts one traditional justification for the rule.[47] Even where the landowners' rules are retained, they offer no support for the firefighters' rule as applied to injuries outside the land. For reasons like these, the Supreme Court of Oregon abolished the rule,[48] while others have never accepted it,[49] or counseled a cautious or narrow use of the rule.[50] The English House of Lords noted the American adoption of the rule and summarily dismissed the whole idea.[51] In some states, the rule does not apply to bar recovery when the defendant violated a fire-safety statute or ordinance.[52] And legislatures have abolished the rule[53] or limited it[54] in some states. It should go without saying, however, that abolishing the special rule of immunity to public safety officers does not necessarily result in liability, which may be defeated by any of the ordinary rules of negligence law.[55]

§ 24.3 Risks Covered by the Risk-Takers Rule

Risks associated with professional employment. Courts may express the firefighters' rule by saying that it prohibits recovery by a professional risk-taker for injuries from

---

[46] Ruffing v. Ada County Paramedics, 145 Idaho 943, 188 P.3d 885 (2008); Beupre v. Pierce County, 161 Wash.2d 568, 166 P.3d 712 (2007). Hart v. Shastri Narayan Swaroop, Inc., 385 Md. 514, 870 A.2d 157 (2005).

[47] See Restatement Third of Torts (Liability for Physical and Emotional Harm) § 51 cmt. m (2010).

[48] Christensen v. Murphy, 296 Or. 610, 620, 678 P.2d 1210, 1217 (1984).

[49] See Mull v. Kerstetter, 373 Pa.Super. 228, 540 A.2d 951 (1988); Minnich v. Med-Waste, Inc., 349 S.C. 567, 564 S.E.2d 98 (2002) ("The more sound public policy—and the one we adopt—is to decline to promulgate a rule singling out police officers and firefighters for discriminatory treatment.").

[50] See Sallee v. GTE South, Inc., 839 S.W.2d 277, 278 (Ky. 1992) ("We narrowly circumscribe the application of such exceptions so as to protect no one from responsibility for the consequences of their wrongdoing except where protecting the public makes it essential to do so."); DeLaire v. Kaskel, 842 A.2d 1052 (R.I. 2004) (refusing to extend rule to animal control officers); Cole v. Hubanks, 681 N.W.2d 147 (Wis. 2004) (refusing to apply the rule to police officers).

[51] Ogwo v. Taylor, 1 A.C. 431 (1987).

[52] See N.Y. Gen. Mun. L. § 205–a.

[53] E.g., Fla. Stat. Ann. § 112.182 (as to property owners; firefighters and police officers classified as invitees when lawfully on the property); 425 Ill. Comp. Stat. 25/9(f) ("The owner or occupier of the premises and his or her agents owe fire fighters . . . duty of reasonable care if the fire fighter is injured due to the lack of maintenance of the premises. . . ."); Minn. Stat. Ann. § 604.06; N.J. Stat. Ann. § 2A:62A–21; N.Y. Gen. Oblig. L. § 11–106. See also Ruiz v. Mero, 189 N.J. 525, 917 A.2d 239 (2007) (holding that the New Jersey statute cited herein did indeed abrogate the firefighters' rule completely).

[54] Cal.Civ. Code § 1714.9; Nev. Rev. Stat. § 41.139. But cf. Mich. Comp. L. Ann. §§ 600.2965 to .2967 (detailed codification with some highly specific rules restricting recovery).

[55] E.g., Lazenby v. Mark's Constr., Inc., 236 Ill.2d 83, 337 Ill.Dec. 884, 923 N.E.2d 735 (2010) (firefighter injured while fighting fire in residence was properly barred from recovery because sufficient evidence supported the jury's finding that the firefighter was more than 50% negligent, thus barring the claim under the modified form of comparative negligence); Leavitt v. Brockton Hosp., Inc., 454 Mass. 37, 907 N.E.2d 213 (2009) (if rescue doctrine rather than firefighters' rule applied, plaintiff police officer still could not recover because his injury was unforeseeable).

"the negligently created risk that was the very reason for his presence on the scene."[56] Put negatively, courts sometimes say that the firefighters' rule does not bar recovery when the defendant's negligence is "independent" of the circumstances that occasioned the professional's presence.[57]

Risks that did not occasion the officer's presence. To say that the officer is barred only when injury results from risks that produced the officer's presence may be to permit recovery in an assortment of cases. One case held that a firefighter could not recover for injuries resulting from a negligently set fire, but could recover for injuries inflicted by the owner's attack dogs, since the officer was responding to the fire but not to attack dogs.[58] A number of cases reflect a similar approach.[59] A firefighter might be denied recovery for burns in an electrical fire for which she was summoned, but she could recover for injuries from the explosion of a gasoline tank on the premises[60] or for injuries from other dangerous conditions on the premises.[61]

Denials for associated risks. However, a number of decisions are not so favorable to the safety officer. These appear to protect defendants not only when the officer is injured by the very risk that necessitated the officer's presence, but also a range of associated risks. Such decisions have denied recovery to a firefighter who falls in an unguarded elevator shaft,[62] to a firefighter injured by an explosion of the defendant's car that occurred after the fire was in progress,[63] and to a police officer who slips on oil while investigating premises for a suspected burglary.[64] The professional's presence was not required by the elevator shaft, the car that exploded, or the slippery oil, but recovery was nevertheless denied. Although these risks did not occasion the officer's presence, they were a part of the bundle of risks associated with the particular operation and that was enough.

Risks not inherent in the dangerous work or heightened by it. Another way of looking at the issue is that the professional risk-taker assumes only those risks that are inherent in the occupation or in the particular operation[65] and perhaps only risks that are

---

[56]   White v. State, 419 Md. 265, 19 A.3d 369 (2011); Flowers v. Rock Creek Terrace Ltd. P'ship, 308 Md. 432, 449, 520 A.2d 361, 368 (1987); Farmer v. B & G Food Enters., Inc., 181 So.2d 1154 (Miss. 2002) (officer is "barred only when the sole negligent act is the same negligent act that necessitated rescue"); Boulter v. Eli & Bessie Cohen Found., 97 A.3d 1127 (N.H. 2014); Wiley v. Redd, 110 Nev. 1310, 885 P.2d 592 (1994); Ruffing v. Ada County Paramedics, 145 Idaho 943, 188 P.3d 885 (2008).

[57]   Harris-Fields v. Syze, 461 Mich. 188, 600 N.W.2d 611 (1999); Lipson v. Superior Court of Orange County (Berger), 31 Cal.3d 362, 644 P.2d 822, 182 Cal.Rptr. 629 (1982).

[58]   Cf. Wiley v. Redd, 110 Nev. 1310, 885 P.2d 592 (1994).

[59]   See, e.g., Lurgio v. Commonwealth Edison Co., 914 N.E.2d 659, 333 Ill.Dec. 240 (App. Ct. 2009) (firefighters' rule did not apply to injured police officer's claim that electric utility company unreasonably delayed shutting off power to downed power line after officer had been deployed to the scene to redirect traffic).

[60]   See Lipson v. Superior Court of Orange County (Berger), 31 Cal.3d 362, 377, 644 P.2d 822, 832, 182 Cal.Rptr. 629, 639 (1982).

[61]   Rennenger v. Pacesetter Co., 558 N.W.2d 419 (Iowa 1997); cf. Paul v. Luigi's, Inc., 557 N.W.2d 895 (Iowa 1997) (similar, police).

[62]   Flowers v. Rock Creek Terrace Ltd. P'ship, 308 Md. 432, 520 A.2d 361 (1987).

[63]   White v. Edmond, 971 F.2d 681 (11th Cir. 1992); cf. Sobanski v. Donahue, 792 A.2d 57 (R.I. 2002).

[64]   Lee v. Luigi, Inc., 696 A.2d 1371 (D.C. 1997). However, when the New Jersey Supreme Court held that the firefighters' rule barred recovery by an officer providing emergency medical assistance when the officer slipped on powdered sugar in the defendant's kitchen, Rosa v. Dunkin' Donuts of Passaic, 122 N.J. 66, 583 A.2d 1129 (1991), the legislature promptly abolished the firefighters' rule. See Ruiz v. Mero, 917 A.2d 239 (N.J. 2007).

[65]   See Maltman v. Sauer, 84 Wash.2d 975, 979, 530 P.2d 254, 257 (1975) (was the risk causing injury "inherently within the ambit of those dangers which are unique to and generally associated with the particular rescue activity").

unique[66] to the occupation or in some significant manner heightened by it.[67] Even then, the worker is not barred unless it is plausible to think that the public employer has paid the worker to relieve negligent persons from liability; the garbage worker may face risks of street injury more than an office worker, but the garbage worker is not paid to assume the risks of injury on the street.[68] The defendant does not escape when the negligence occurs after the firefighter's presence was or should have been discovered,[69] or in any case when he negligently injures the plaintiff through a risk not inherent in the plaintiff's professional work.[70] Put another way, when a risk poses a broad threat to any number of people, "It would be illogical to insulate" the risk creator from liability "simply because the person injured happened to be a police officer or firefighter."[71] Thus an independent contractor who negligently builds a deck stair that collapses as it is climbed, is not insulated from liability because the stair climber happens to be a deputy sheriff investigating the sound of a burglar alarm.[72]

Intentional or reckless torts that occasion the officer's presence. The defendant is liable for certain intentional, reckless or willful torts to the safety officer, but quite possibly not for all. When the defendant's reckless misconduct simply causes a fire, for example, a court may protect the defendant on the ground that the firefighter assumed the risk of fire whether it was set recklessly or negligently.[73] Other courts have taken the opposite view, holding that assumed risk is only one element in the public policy behind the firefighters' rule and that moral culpability of the defendant who willfully or recklessly causes a fire weighs so heavily that recovery should be allowed.[74] In a case from New Mexico, firefighters were allowed to recover against a gas company for intentional infliction of emotional distress suffered in the course of fighting a fire caused by a gas explosion when they saw several victims burned to death.[75] The court held that a firefighter could recover damages if the harm was proximately caused by (1) intentional

---

[66] See id. (unique). The policy rationale seems to support only risks that are peculiar to or of a demonstrably greater magnitude in the plaintiff's professional work. Cf. Woods v. City of Warren, 439 Mich. 186, 193, 482 N.W.2d 696, 699 (1992).

[67] Wadler v. City of New York, 14 N.Y.3d 192, 899 N.Y.S.2d 73, 925 N.E.2d 875 (2010) (firefighters' rule barred police officer's negligence suit against the city for an injury caused by a negligently operated security gate in the parking lot of police headquarters; the security gate "was plainly a risk associated with particular dangers inherent in police work. Ordinary civilians may encounter such devices, but police officers, whose duties may include working in secure areas that are at risk of a terrorist attack, are far more likely to do so."); Ciervo v. City of New York, 240 A.D.2d 693, 659 N.Y.S.2d 320 (1997), aff'd, 93 N.Y.2d 465, 715 N.E.2d 91, 693 N.Y.S.2d 63 (1999) (heightened, not inherent is the test).

[68] Ciervo v. City of New York, 93 N.Y.2d 465, 715 N.E.2d 91, 693 N.Y.S.2d 63 (1999).

[69] See Lurgio v. Commonwealth Edison Co., 914 N.E.2d 659, 333 Ill.Dec. 240 (App. Ct. 2009); Garcia v. City of South Tucson, 131 Ariz. 315, 640 P.2d 1117 (Ct. App. 1982); Cal. Civ. Code § 1714.9.

[70] See Lipson v. Superior Court, supra note 60; Sallee v. GTE South, Inc., 839 S.W.2d 277 (Ky. 1992) (not barred as to injury resulting from risk "different in both kind and character"); Flowers v. Rock Creek Terrace Ltd. P'ship, 308 Md. 432, 520 A.2d 361 (1987) (rule does not apply as to perils not reasonably foreseeable as part of the occupational risk).

[71] Torchik v. Boyce, 121 Ohio St. 3d 440, 905 N.E.2d 179 (2009).

[72] Id.; but see Krajewski v. Bourque, 782 A.2d 650 (R.I. 2001) (firefighters' rule barred recovery for injuries officer sustained when he slipped on ice on the landowner's steep driveway).

[73] Cf. Hubbard v. Boelt, 28 Cal.3d 480, 620 P.2d 156, 169 Cal.Rptr. 706 (1980) (driver whose speed prompted an officer to give chase was not liable for injuries incurred by the officer in the crash that ensued, a result that may be affected by Cal. Civ. Code § 1714.9); Young v. Sherwin-Williams Co., 569 A.2d 1173 (D.C. 1990) (driver's recklessness left him in great danger, firefighter injured in rescue could not recover since the doctrine is based on assumed risk, not culpability of the defendant).

[74] Mahoney v. Carus Chem. Co., Inc., 102 N.J. 564, 510 A.2d 4, 62 A.L.R.4th 703 (1986). Cf. Berko v. Freda, 93 N.J. 81, 459 A.2d 663 (1983) (police officer). Much expanded recovery is now allowed by statute in New Jersey see Ruiz v. Mero, 917 A.2d 239 (N.J. 2007).

[75] Baldonado v. El Paso Natural Gas Co., 143 N.M. 288, 176 P.3d 277 (2008).

conduct, or (2) reckless conduct, "provided that the harm to the firefighters exceeded the scope of risks inherent in the firefighters' professional duties." When the defendant's willful, wanton, or reckless conduct occurs after the occasion has arisen for the safety officer's presence, the case for recovery is particularly strong.

§ 24.4 Persons Covered by the Risk-Takers Rule

Generally. As already indicated, courts now extend the firefighters' rule to police officers and sometimes to other safety officers, with the effect that many public safety officers are denied recovery for injuries that fall within the inherent special risks of their professions.

Volunteers and off-duty officers. Although the rule by its terms does not include private persons who engage in various forms of rescue work, it has sometimes been extended to volunteer firefighters, who may be barred along with others.[76] As to off-duty public safety officers, it is difficult to see why the firefighters' rule should be invoked to protect the negligent defendant, since the off-duty officer is essentially in the role of a private rescuer, and some authority so holds, at least in the absence of evidence that the officer is, by regulation or function, truly on duty.[77] But some cases, involving police officers in particular, have held that the police officer who is off duty and out of uniform is nevertheless always on duty in some sense and thus could be barred by the professional rescuer's rule when he is injured in the course of a "rescue" or emergency involving police-type intervention.[78]

Public building inspectors and others not employed to face risks. The special rule for public safety officers does not apply to many other public officers or employees who are injured by a defendant's negligence. For example, it does not apply to a public sanitation worker[79] or a publicly employed building inspector or postal worker[80] who is injured by the defendant's negligence, even though, like the firefighter and police officer, the inspector will have compensation from public funds. Rhode Island has said public safety officers should be treated differently because the firefighters' rule should be limited to

---

[76] E.g., Waggoner v. Troutman Oil Co., Inc., 320 Ark. 56, 894 S.W.2d 913 (1995); Baker v. Superior Court (Leach), 129 Cal.App.3d 710, 181 Cal.Rptr. 311 (1982); Carpenter v. O'Day, 562 A.2d 595 (Del. Super.), aff'd 553 A.2d 638 (Del. 1988). Contra: Roberts v. Vaughn, 459 Mich. 282, 587 N.W.2d 249 (1998) (criticizing cases barring the volunteer on the ground that the cases did not explain why policy reasons applied to paid firefighter also applied to the unpaid one).

[77] Espinoza v. Schulenburg, 212 Ariz. 215, 129 P.3d 937 (2006) (fully reasoned but succinct opinion); Alessio v. Fire & Ice, Inc., 197 N.J.Super. 22, 484 A.2d 24 (1984) ("the rule depends on a realistic determination of whether, in the particular circumstances, the off-duty officer was acting as a police officer or as a volunteer;" discussing the dangers faced by lone officer out of uniform and recognizing that although such an officer may assume the risk, he is not barred by the firefighters' rule if he is facing greater risks because he lacks backup and is out of uniform); Wadler v. City of New York, 14 N.Y.3d 192, 899 N.Y.S.2d 73, 925 N.E.2d 875 (2010).

[78] Hodges v. Yarian, 53 Cal.App. 4th 973, 62 Cal.Rptr. 2d 130 (1997) (even though officer was off duty, out of uniform, and injured investigating a burglary in progress at his own residence, the firefighters' rule barred a claim against the landlord for inadequate security because his attempt to deal with the intruder was "inherently" part of his job); Levine v. Chemical Bank, 221 A.D.2d 175, 633 N.Y.S.2d 296 (1995); cf. Trammel v. Bradberry, 256 Ga.App. 412, 568 S.E.2d 715 (2002) ("an off-duty officer is always on duty when a crime is committed in his presence," seemingly applicable to the firefighters' rule as well as to the assumed risk issue the court was discussing).

[79] Ciervo v. City of New York, 93 N.Y.2d 465, 715 N.E.2d 91, 693 N.Y.S.2d 63 (1999).

[80] See J.D. Perovich, Annotation, Liability of Owner or Occupant of Premises to Building or Construction Inspector Coming upon Premises in Discharge of Duty, 28 A.L.R.3d 891 (1970); cf. J.D. Perovich., Annotation, Liability of Owner or Operator of Premises for Injury to Meter Reader or Similar Employee of Public Service Corporation Coming to Premises in Course of Duties, 28 A.L.R.3d 1344 (1970).

officers dealing with a crisis or emergency.[81] Perhaps in line with the assumed risk/no duty analysis, it could be said that the other public employees have not been paid to assume any special, identifiable risks, or at least not the risk that caused injury.[82] In other words, a building inspector at a place open to the public or where the landowner expects her to be, is assuming no risks of defective premises.[83]

Conflicting results. In a limited number of cases involving paramedics and the like, courts have sometimes applied the firefighters' rule and sometimes not.[84] Some courts tend to assume that a categorical rule is required for such cases rather than an evaluation of the facts bearing on whether the worker was paid to assume the risk in question. Several have said that EMTs, paramedics, or ambulance drivers and the like are not included in the firefighters' rule,[85] or even that the firefighters' rule is limited to firefighters and police officers and hence automatically excludes all others.[86] On the other hand, some courts have extended the rule to bar EMTs[87] or lifeguards[88] injured in the course of a rescue.

Case-specific evaluation based on inherent risks. Alternatively, courts can treat the question of the paramedic's assumption of risk as a fact question to be decided like other fact questions, case by case. A court might, for example, conclude that the particular risk encountered by a rescue worker was not inherent in the work and hence not a risk the worker assumed, while leaving it open to conclude that some other risk was one the worker was paid to encounter. Under such a case-specific approach, a court might conclude that a paramedic was not employed to confront toxic fumes generated by the defendant,[89] but that an attendant in a mental health facility for dangerous patients was definitely employed to assume the risks of violent patients[90] or a helicopter rescue crew was employed to face the risk, among others, that the helicopter would crash.[91]

Privately employed safety workers. Police, firefighting, and other safety efforts can be thought of in terms of the rescue doctrine. The rescue doctrine has it that a defendant who negligently creates risks to A may be liable to B who is injured in coming to A's rescue. The doctrine applies even if the defendant is the person being rescued.[92] The rescue doctrine most clearly applies to spontaneous rescuers who have no professional stake or duty in effecting a rescue. When the rescuer is a publicly paid professional whose

---

[81] Labrie v. Pace Membership Warehouse, Inc., 678 A.2d 867 (R.I. 1996).

[82] See Ciervo v. City of New York, 93 N.Y.2d 465, 715 N.E.2d 91, 693 N.Y.S.2d 63 (1999).

[83] See Boyer v. Anchor Disposal, 135 N.J. 86, 638 A.2d 135 (1994) (fire inspector did not assume risk of hidden slippery substance).

[84] See Joseph B. Conder, Application of "Firemen's Rule" to Bar Recovery by Emergency Medical Personnel Injured in Responding to, or at Scene of, Emergency, 89 A.L.R.4th 1079 (1992).

[85] Kowalski v. Gratopp, 177 Mich.App. 448, 442 N.W.2d 682 (1989) (paramedic or EMT); Krause v. U.S. Truck Co., Inc., 787 S.W.2d 708 (Mo. 1990) (ambulance driver killed at scene of multi-vehicle collisions on Interstate 70).

[86] Lees v. Lobosco, 265 N.J.Super. 95, 625 A.2d 573 (1993).

[87] Maggard v. Conagra Foods, Inc., 168 S.W.3d 425 (Ky. Ct. App. 2005) (but seemingly going off on the conclusion that, as a matter of law, the defendant simply was not negligent); Pinter v. American Family Mut. Ins. Co., 236 Wis.2d 137, 613 N.W.2d 110 (2000).

[88] City of Oceanside v. Superior Court, 81 Cal.App. 4th 269, 96 Cal.Rptr. 2d 621 (2000).

[89] See Philip Morris, Inc. v. Emerson, 235 Va. 380, 368 S.E.2d 268 (1988).

[90] Anicet v. Gant, 580 So.2d 273 (Fla. Dist. Ct. App. 1991).

[91] Maltman v. Sauer, 84 Wash.2d 975, 530 P.2d 254 (1975).

[92] § 15.7.

duty includes such a rescue, states that apply the firefighters' rule are in effect saying that the rescue doctrine is inapplicable.[93]

Privately employed risk takers. The privately employed risk-taker is neither a spontaneous good citizen nor a public employee, so the question arises whether to apply the firefighters' rule or something closer to the rescue doctrine. The assumed risk/public policy rationale of the firefighters' rule is based on the somewhat plausible view that the public employer is paying wages and compensation benefits to the firefighter to protect citizens from firefighter suits because by so doing the public employer exonerates citizens who are also taxpayers-constituents of that public entity. But it is not equally persuasive to construct such a vision of the private employer's relation to third persons who may be negligent toward its employees. While a privately employed safety officer may know of risks to be confronted, it is quite unlikely that the private employer is paying the officer to forego claims against others. Consequently, courts have refused to apply the firefighters' rule to privately employed professional risk-takers, with the result that the ordinary claims and defenses will determine the case.[94]

Suits against employers. To say that privately employed risk-takers are not subject to the firefighters' rule, however, is not to say that private risk-takers can recover against one who hires them to face the risk. Nurses hired to deal with a mentally disabled patient[95] or veterinarians and kennel workers hired to treat or groom a dog,[96] like the contractors hired to repair a dangerous roof,[97] may find themselves barred from recovery for foreseeable job-related hazards by some version of assumed risk or no-duty reasoning. Similarly, manufacturers of defective or negligently made or designed products are normally responsible for the harms inflicted by those products.[98] When the product causes a fire or makes it worse, however, several courts have held that the firefighters' rule bars recovery by the injured firefighter.[99]

---

[93]   Espinoza v. Schulenburg, 129 P.3d 937 (Ariz. 2006).

[94]   Neighbarger v. Irwin Indus., Inc., 8 Cal.4th 532, 34 Cal.Rptr.2d 630, 882 P.2d 347 (1994); Kowalski v. Gratopp, 177 Mich.App. 448, 442 N.W.2d 682 (1989).

[95]   See Anicet v. Gant, 580 So.2d 273 (Fla. Dist. Ct. App. 1991); Creasy v. Rusk, 730 N.E.2d 659 (Ind. 2000).

[96]   Priebe v. Nelson, 39 Cal.4th 1112, 140 P.3d 848, 47 Cal.Rptr.3d 553 (2006) (holding kennel worker employed by veterinarian was also subject to this bar, but would not be barred if dog owner knew of dangerous propensity and did not reveal it).

[97]   Stinnett v. Buchele, 598 S.W.2d 469 (Ky. Ct. App. 1980).

[98]   Chapter 33.

[99]   White v. Edmond, 971 F.2d 681 (11th Cir. 1992) (Volvo allegedly exploded at scene of fire, causing injuries, manufacturer not liable); Flowers v. Rock Creek Terrace Ltd. P'ship, 308 Md. 432, 520 A.2d 361 (1987) (manufacturer of elevator not liable when firefighter fell twelve stories while fighting fire; such an injury is within the range of anticipated risks); Austin v. City of Buffalo, 179 A.D.2d 1075, 580 N.Y.S.2d 604 (1992); Mahoney v. Carus Chem. Co., Inc., 102 N.J. 564, 510 A.2d 4, 62 A.L.R.4th 703 (1986); Mignone v. Fieldcrest Mills, 556 A.2d 35 (R.I. 1989).

Chapter 25

LIMITING LIABILITY FOR NON-ACTION

Analysis

A. THE GENERAL RULES OF NON-ACTION

§ 25.1   The No-Duty-to-Rescue Rule and Exceptions
§ 25.2   Scope of the Rule Protecting Non-Action

B. GENERAL DUTIES TO ACT AFFIRMATIVELY TO RESCUE OR ASSIST

§ 25.3   Innocently Harming or Creating a Risk of Harm
§ 25.4   Special Relationship Between Plaintiff and Defendant
§ 25.5   Beginning to Rescue or Assist
§ 25.6   Undertaking Creating a Duty to the Plaintiff
§ 25.7   Undertaking Creating a Duty to Third Persons

A. THE GENERAL RULES OF NON-ACTION

§ 25.1 The No-Duty-to-Rescue Rule and Exceptions

General rule. Absent special relationships or particular circumstances or actions, a defendant is not liable in tort for a pure failure to act for the plaintiff's benefit. The starkest form of this no-duty-to-act rule arises where the defendant is sued for failing to rescue or assist the plaintiff, who is in need of such help.[1] This general rule applies even where the defendant foresees harm to a particular individual from his failure to act, and where he could act without placing himself in any peril at all.[2]

To take the Second Restatement's example, suppose the defendant sees an unsighted person about to step in front of an approaching car. The defendant could prevent his injury or death by a word or touch, without endangering or inconveniencing himself, yet he does nothing to prevent injury. The general rule applies to relieve the defendant of any liability.[3] The cases are seldom so dramatic, but they accept and apply the rule.[4] Scholarly commentary on the general no-duty-to-rescue rule goes back more

---

[1]   The no-duty-to-act rule takes on a somewhat different form in the insistence that the defendant is under no duty to protect the plaintiff from harm by a third person. See Chapter 26.

[2]   See, e.g., Williams v. Southern Calif. Gas Co., 176 Cal.App.4th 591, 98 Cal.Rptr.3d 258 (2009) (rule applies "no matter how great the danger in which the other is placed, or how easily he or she could be rescued and even if the actor realizes or should realize that action on his part is necessary for another's aid or protection") (internal citations omitted).

[3]   Restatement Second of Torts § 314, Illus. 1 (1965). See also Restatement Third of Torts (Liability for Physical and Emotional Harm) § 37 & 38 (2010) (covering the same ground, also making it clear that the defendant does not escape liability if he has himself created a risk of physical harm).

[4]   See Yania v. Bigan, 397 Pa. 316, 155 A.2d 343 (1959) (although defendant had challenged a neighbor to jump into a pit of water on the defendant's land, defendant had no duty to save the neighbor when he was drowning); Long v. Patterson, 198 Miss. 554, 22 So.2d 490 (1945) (no duty to warn of dangerous approaching traffic); Cilley v. Lane, 985 A.2d 418 (Me. 2009) (no duty owed by homeowner, whose former boyfriend committed suicide in her house, to render any emergency assistance to him); Krieg v. Massey, 239 Mont. 469, 781 P.2d 277 (1989) (manager of apartment house, who had power to take gun from suicidal tenant, had no

than a century.[5] Now, as then, scholars have differed on the merits of the rule, with some arguing in favor of it[6] and others taking an opposing view in varying degrees.[7]

Exceptions. There are relatively few cases as simple as the above illustration. In the failure-to-rescue cases, litigation is apt to turn not on the existence of the rule, but on its scope and exceptions. In fact, it may be that properly understood exceptions have the effect of creating a duty to act in most instances where a reasonable person would feel compelled to act. The exceptional circumstances in which a defendant may owe a duty of reasonable assistance to a plaintiff include: (1) the defendant or his instrumentalities, innocently or not, have created risks or caused harm to the plaintiff;[8] (2) the defendant is in a special relationship to the plaintiff that is deemed to create a duty of care that encompasses affirmative action;[9] (3) the defendant begins to offer assistance;[10] and (4) the defendant has in some other way assumed a duty of affirmative care by action or promise that evinces such an assumption.[11]

Courts have sometimes gone beyond these categories, or have expanded them substantially, to find a duty to assist.[12] A common denominator in these cases is that the defendant could have assisted with little effort and the effect of non-assistance was deadly; thus the moral blame attached to the defendant's inaction was particularly pronounced. In *Soldano v. O'Daniels,*[13] the plaintiff alleged that a patron of Happy Jack's Saloon went across the street to the Circle Inn and asked the bartender there to call the police or to permit the patron to do so because a man had been threatened in Happy Jack's. The bartender refused to call or to permit the patron to do so. The plaintiff's father was shot and killed in Happy Jack's Saloon, presumably after the patron's failed effort to call the police. In the court's view, Circle Inn "displayed a disregard for human life that can be characterized as morally wrong" and the burden of permitting use of the phone in a public place of business would have been minimal. Under these circumstances, the defendant owed a duty to permit the use of the phone, given the close connection between the defendant's conduct and the injury.[14]

---

duty to do so and is not liable for his death); cf. Rocha v. Faltys, 69 S.W.3d 315 (Tex. App. 2002) (facts very similar to those in *Yania, supra*, with same result on slightly different reasoning).

    [5]   See James Barr Ames, Law and Morals, 22 Harv. L. Rev. 97, 111–13 (1908) (critical of the rule); Francis H. Bohlen, The Moral Duty to Aid Others as a Basis of Tort Liability, 56 U. Pa. L. Rev. 217 (1908) (supporting the rule as reflecting a basic distinction between misfeasance and nonfeasance, which is "founded on that attitude of extreme individualism so typical of Anglo-Saxon legal thought").

    [6]   See Richard Epstein, A Theory of Strict Liability, 2 J. Leg. Studies 151, 198 ff. (1973); Philip W. Romohr, A Right/Duty Perspective on the Legal and Philosophical Foundations of the No-Duty-to-Rescue Rule, 55 Duke L.J. 1025 (2006); James A. Henderson, Jr., Process Constraints in Tort, 67 Cornell L. Rev. 901 (1982); Saul Levmore, Waiting for Rescue: An Essay on the Evolution and Incentive Structure of the Law of Affirmative Obligations, 72 Va.L.Rev. 879, 938 (1986); David A. Hyman, Rescue Without Law: An Empirical Perspective on the Duty to Rescue, 84 Tex. L. Rev. 653 (2006); Marin Roger Scordato, Understanding the Absence of a Duty to Reasonably Rescue in American Tort Law, 82 Tul. L. Rev. 1447 (2008).

    [7]   E.g., Ernest J. Weinrib, The Case for a Duty to Rescue, 90 Yale L. J. 247 (1980); Steven J. Heyman, Foundations of the Duty to Rescue, 47 Vand. L. Rev. 673 (1994); Richard L. Hasen, The Efficient Duty to Rescue, 15 Int'l Rev. L. & Econ. 141 (1995); Amelia H. Ashton, Rescuing the Hero: The Ramifications of Expanding the Duty to Rescue on Society and the Law, 59 Duke L.J. 69 (2009).

    [8]   See § 25.3.

    [9]   See § 25.4.

    [10]   See § 25.5.

    [11]   See §§ 25.6 & 25.7.

    [12]   Duty does not equate to liability, of course; finding a duty is merely a step that permits evaluation of the negligence and causal issues.

    [13]   Soldano v. O'Daniels, 141 Cal. App. 3d 443, 190 Cal. Rptr. 310, 37 A.L.R. 4th 1183 (1983).

    [14]   Soldano, 141 Cal.App.3d at 451–52.

In a more recent case, *Podias v. Mairs*,[15] the plaintiff's decedent, Podias, was injured when his motorcycle was struck at night by a car driven by an intoxicated teenager, Mairs. Two other teenagers were passengers in Mairs' vehicle. The three of them left Podias helpless in the middle of the road and did nothing to assist him; they made numerous cell phone calls, but none to summon help. Shortly thereafter Podias was killed when another car ran over him. Podias's widow sued the three teenagers, among others. Mairs settled prior to trial for over a million dollars,[16] but the trial court granted summary judgment for the two passengers on the ground that they owed no duty to assist. The appeals court reversed, resting its decision primarily on the theory that there was a "concert of action," in that "the defendants acquiesced in the conditions that may have helped create [the initial risk] and subsequently in those conditions that further endangered the victim's safety." The defendants were "far more than innocent bystanders," the court said; rather, they "bear some relationship not only to the primary wrongdoer but to the incident itself." While the court expressly disclaimed that it was creating a rule of general application, it also stressed that "defendants had both the opportunity and ability to help prevent an obviously foreseeable risk of severe and potentially fatal consequence," and that on such facts "the imposition of a duty . . . does not offend notions of fairness and common decency."[17]

Both *Soldano* and *Podias* reflect deep judicial doubt about the rectitude of the basic no-duty rule. Indeed, to the extent they search for an exception to the rule based on ease of assistance and reasonably foreseeable fatal consequences of non-assistance, they run up squarely against the Second Restatement's example, where the defendant could have prevented foreseeable death or serious bodily harm with almost no effort and with absolutely no peril. Perhaps, however, both courts' opinions can be seen as rejecting the general no-duty rule only where the defendant is not simply a "passive bystander," but rather is someone with much more involvement in the incident. Perhaps the result in both cases can be explained in part by the notion that the defendant prevented others from assisting.[18] But just as such failure-to-assist cases are both rare and exceptional, so are the opportunities for any broad judicial condemnation of the general rule itself.

"Bad Samaritan" statutes. A handful of states have adopted statutes that criminalize a failure to rescue or assist, at least under particular circumstances; an even smaller number of these statutes provide for potential civil liability.[19] The oldest such

---

[15]   Podias v. Mairs, 394 N.J.Super. 338, 926 A.2d 859 (App. Div. 2007).

[16]   See Podias v. Mairs, 2008 WL 4763275 (N.J. Super. App. Div. 2008) (unpublished) (after remand).

[17]   Podias v. Mairs, 394 N.J.Super. 338, 351–52, 926 A.2d 859, 866–67 (App. Div. 2007).

[18]   See Soldano v. O'Daniels, 141 Cal. App.3d 443, 452–53, 190 Cal.Rptr. 310 (1983) (stating that the facts "come very nearly" within Restatement Second's § 327, which imposes a duty not to prevent another person from giving aid to another); Podias v. Mairs, 394 N.J.Super. 338, 352, 926 A.2d 859, 867 (App. Div. 2007) ("Even assuming no independent duty to take affirmative action, at the very least defendants were obligated, in our view, not to prevent Mairs from exercising his direct duty of care.").

[19]   While some label these "good Samaritan" statutes, they are more properly called "bad Samaritan" statutes. "Good Samaritan" statutes immunize from negligence liability those defendants who *do* assist a plaintiff in distress; such statutes are most often limited in their scope to medical personnel and the provision of medical assistance. See § 21.13 (medical personnel) & § 25.5 (non-medical personnel). The statutes discussed in this section, by contrast, place a defendant under some form of legal duty to assist and provide for criminal or civil liability for non-assistance. Perhaps the label-confusion is understandable since many of the "bad Samaritan" statutes also have a "good Samaritan" provision—meaning that these statutes both place the defendant under an affirmative duty to assist, then provide for an immunity where the assistance is provided negligently. Most civil-law countries have some form of duty-to-rescue provision, usually in their criminal code. See Damien Schiff, Samaritans: Good, Bad and Ugly: A Comparative Law Analysis, 11 Roger Williams U. L. Rev. 77 (2005); see also Julie A. Davies & Paul T. Hayden, Global Issues in Tort Law 120–29 (2008) (comparing the common law approach to that of France and Germany).

statute, adopted in Vermont in 1967, requires reasonable assistance when the defendant knows that another person is "exposed to grave physical harm" and can assist without danger to himself.[20] Minnesota's statute is similar, making it a petty misdemeanor for a person at the scene of an emergency to fail to provide reasonable assistance, then immunizing a rescuer from civil liability unless the assistance is provided "in a willful and wanton or reckless manner."[21] Rhode Island's criminal statute requires "any person at the scene of an emergency who knows that another person is exposed to, or has suffered, grave physical harm" to give "reasonable assistance" if "he or she can do so without danger or peril to himself or others."[22] Criminal prosecutions under these statutes have been rare to nonexistent,[23] and very few torts cases have applied them in situations where a defendant has allegedly not assisted at all.[24] Another small group of states has narrower "rescue" provisions in their criminal statutes; these usually apply only to persons present at a crime scene, requiring them to notify law enforcement or medical personnel if they can do so without peril to themselves.[25]

§ 25.2 Scope of the Rule Protecting Non-Action

A failure to rescue or assist is classically viewed as an instance of non-action, or "nonfeasance," as it is often called. The meaning of this term may seem self-evident. However, many omissions to act are not regarded as nonfeasance at all but as only a part of some larger action. If, driving your car, you fail to apply your brakes when you approach a person in a crosswalk, you cannot defend his claim for injury by saying you did nothing. In such a case, you drove a car and did it very badly and will be chargeable with a negligent act, not merely with nonfeasance. Similarly, if a contractor acting under public authority digs a hole in the highway, then fails to light it at night, courts do not think that failing to light it is nonfeasance. The failure to light is merely one part of a course of affirmative conduct—digging improperly without lighting or guarding the excavation.[26] With cases like these in mind, courts very often instruct the jury that negligence includes "the omission to do something" a reasonable person would do as well as the doing of something a prudent person would not do.[27]

But no rule has been formulated to prescribe whether courts are to characterize conduct as affirmative action with an embedded omission or as simple non-action. In

---

[20]   Vt.Stat.Ann. tit. 12, § 519(a). Paragraph (b) of the same statute provides that a person who provides such "reasonable assistance" is immune from civil liability "unless his acts constitute gross negligence or unless he will receive or expects to receive remuneration." The net effect, then, is to place a defendant under an affirmative duty to provide assistance if the circumstances described in the statute present themselves (the "bad Samaritan" part), but then to immunize a defendant who begins to assist unless he does so in a "grossly negligent manner" or is paid for his help (the "good Samaritan" part). "Reasonable assistance" refers to "the extent of the rescuer's effort to comply with the statutory duty to render aid, not to the adequacy of the aid actually rendered." Hardingham v. United Counseling Service of Bennington, 164 Vt. 158, 667 A.2d 289 (1995).

[21]   Minn. Stat. § 604A.01

[22]   R.I. Gen. Laws § 11–56–1.

[23]   See David A. Hyman, Rescue without Law: An Empirical Perspective on the Duty to Rescue, 84 Tex. L. Rev. 653, 657 & n.7 (2006) (finding no reported prosecutions under the various statutes).

[24]   See, e.g., Kane v. Lamothe, 182 Vt. 241, 936 A.2d 1303 (2007).

[25]   See Wis. Stat. Ann. § 940.34; Fla. Stat. § 794.027; Mass Gen. Laws ch. 268, § 40; Hawai'i Rev. Stat. § 663–1.6; Wash. Rev. Code § 9A.36.160.

[26]   Newton v. Ellis, 5 El. & Bl. 115, 119 Eng. Rep. 424 (K.B. 1855). Compare Smit v. Anderson, 72 P.3d 369 (Colo. App. 2002) (characterizing a contractor's failure to supervise as misfeasance rather than nonfeasance), with Gilson v. Metropolitan Opera, 5 N.Y.3d 574, 841 N.E.2d 747, 807 N.Y.S.2d 588 (2005) (treating an allegation of failure to light a theater as nonfeasance).

[27]   Many cases have adopted this language from Blyth v. Birmingham Waterworks Co., 11 Ex. 781, 156 Eng.Rep. 1047 (1856).

Jackson v. City of Joliet,[28] an officer encountered a flaming car that had gone off the road. He called the fire department and directed traffic, but did nothing to rescue the occupants of the car or to call an ambulance. One occupant, an expectant mother, died. Quite possibly the officer's actions were reasonable in the light of the risks to himself. However, the court did not even consider whether the officer was negligent or not. It concluded that, at least in a civil rights claim, the officer's conduct had to be viewed as a failure to prevent death, not as an affirmative act causing death.

Since there are no settled criteria for distinguishing pure non-action from conduct that includes a negligent omission, the *Jackson* court may have been right. But it would be just as plausible to say that the officer's failure would be like the contractor's failure to light the excavation, rather than a case of nonfeasance.[29] That view would lead a court to consider whether, under the circumstances, the officer was negligent or not. In contrast, if the no-duty rule applies, courts do not determine whether the defendant's conduct was unreasonably risky or whether it was justified.

Perhaps the cases as a whole would justify the unsurprising and not so helpful conclusion that judges avoid extremes in characterizing conduct. They do not characterize conduct by segregating highly specific omissions (like failing to brake a car) from closely related conduct (like driving). On the other hand, they do not characterize conduct at its most abstract level, either. A water company's failure to provide water to a fire hydrant is not likely to be viewed as a case of running a water company in a negligent way, but rather as a case of mere nonfeasance for which there is no liability in the absence of an exceptional duty.[30]

B. GENERAL DUTIES TO ACT AFFIRMATIVELY TO RESCUE OR ASSIST

§ 25.3 Innocently Harming or Creating a Risk of Harm

Defendant innocently causing harm. The defendant who knows or should know that he has caused physical harm to the plaintiff, even if caused without fault, owes a duty of reasonable care to avoid further harm.[31] If reasonable care requires it, he must act affirmatively to minimize the harm he has innocently caused and he is subject to liability for any additional harm caused by his failure to do so. The defendant is subject to liability for the entire harm done if he was negligent in the first place; but even if he acted innocently in causing the initial harm, he is subject to liability for the added harm he could have avoided by taking reasonable steps.[32] For instance, if the defendant's railroad train runs over the plaintiff and severs a limb, the defendant may not refuse to provide

[28] Jackson v. City of Joliet, 715 F.2d 1200 (7th Cir. 1983).

[29] See, e.g., Pehle v. Farm Bureau Life Ins. Co., Inc., 397 F.3d 897, 902 (10 Cir. 2005) (defendant's failure to notify life insurance applicants that tests indicated HIV-positive status "could be considered a normal part of testing for HIV" rather than nonfeasance); Lugtu v. California Highway Patrol, 26 Cal.4th 703, 110 Cal.Rptr.2d 528, 28 P.3d 249 (2001) (highway patrolman's failure to protect plaintiffs from injury when he pulled them over into the median was not nonfeasance; it was "affirmative conduct" that "created a serious risk of harm").

[30] H.R. Moch Co. v. Rensselaer Water Co., 247 N.Y. 160, 159 N.E. 896 (1928). For a discussion of how *Moch* relates to modern approaches to undertakings, see 2 Dobbs, Hayden & Bublick, The Law of Torts 412 (2d ed. 2011 & Supp.).

[31] Restatement Second of Torts § 322 (1965).

[32] L.S. Ayres & Co. v. Hicks, 220 Ind. 86, 40 N.E.2d 334, 41 N.E.2d 195 (1942) (injury innocently caused by defendant's instrumentality, or by master or invitor); South v. National Railroad Passenger Corp., 290 N.W.2d 819 (N.D. 1980) (railroad employees refused to assist victim of crossing accident, liability).

assistance even if the railroad was not negligent to begin with and even if the plaintiff himself was contributorily negligent.[33] Most states have adopted criminal "hit and run" statutes that provide that a vehicle driver who causes an accident, even non-negligently, cannot flee the scene without rendering reasonable assistance to anyone who is injured.[34]

Defendant innocently risking harm. The same principle has been applied when the defendant knows or should know that he has innocently created a risk to others and the defendant has an opportunity to minimize the risk before harm actually eventuates.[35] For instance, if the defendant, without fault, collides with and kills a horse on the highway, reasonable care may oblige him to take steps to warn others or have the animal removed. If he does not do so and a second driver is later injured in striking the carcass or attempting to avoid it, the defendant is again subject to liability if he failed to exercise reasonable care.[36]

Perhaps neither of these exceptions will apply to aid the plaintiff when the defendant is protected by a no-duty rule based upon policy not associated with the failure-to-act rules.[37] For instance, Massachusetts limits the liability of social hosts to guests who are injured when they become intoxicated by drinking the host's alcohol. The no-duty rule protecting the social host is not altered by the innocent-harm and innocent-risk rules.[38]

§ 25.4 Special Relationship Between Plaintiff and Defendant

Sometimes the defendant is under a duty to use reasonable care to rescue (or to protect) the plaintiff because the defendant stands in a special relationship to the plaintiff or to a person causing harm to the plaintiff.[39] When a legally recognized special relationship exists, the defendant may be under a duty to use reasonable care even when he has neither created the initial risk to the plaintiff nor independently undertaken to rescue or protect the plaintiff.[40]

Categorical relationships. The Second Restatement recognized five kinds of formal relationships that require the defendant to use reasonable care for the plaintiff's safety, including reasonable affirmative efforts to rescue.[41] The Third Restatement's list is longer. According to the Third Restatement, the first person in all these relationships owes a duty of reasonable care for the protection of the second: (1) carrier-passenger;[42] (2) innkeeper-guest;[43] (3) invitor-invitee, or possessor of land open to the public-lawful

---

[33] Maldonado v. Southern Pac. Transp. Co., 129 Ariz. 165, 629 P.2d 1001 (Ct. App. 1981).

[34] See W.J. Dunn, Annotation, Violation of statute requiring one involved in an accident to stop and render aid as affecting civil liability, 80 A.L.R.2d 299 (1961).

[35] Restatement Third of Torts (Liability for Physical and Emotional Harm) § 39 (2010); Restatement Second of Torts § 321(1) (1965).

[36] Pacht v. Morris, 107 Ariz. 392, 489 P.2d 29 (1971).

[37] See Restatement Third of Torts (Liability for Physical and Emotional Harm) § 39, cmt. b (2010).

[38] Panagakos v. Walsh, 434 Mass. 353, 749 N.E.2d 670 (2001).

[39] E.g., Delgado v. Trax Bar & Grill, 36 Cal. 4th 224, 113 P.3d 1159, 30 Cal. Rptr. 3d 145 (2005); see generally Marshall S. Shapo, The Duty to Act: Tort Law, Power & Public Policy (1977).

[40] On whether the special relationship itself is the source of duty, or whether it is merely the language courts may use when they believe a duty should be applied, see W. Jonathan Cardi & Michael D. Green, Duty Wars, 81 S. Cal. L. Rev. 671, 677 n.36 (2008).

[41] Restatement Second of Torts §§ 314A & 314B (1965).

[42] See §§ 19.1 to 19.3 & 26.3.

[43] E.g., Taboada v. Daly Seven, Inc., 271 Va. 313, 626 S.E.2d 428 (2006); see George L. Blum, Annotation, Liability of Hotel or Motel Operator for Injury to Guest Resulting from Assault by Third Party, 17 A.L.R.6th 453 (2006); see also §§ 19.4 & 26.3.

entrant;[44] (4) employer-employee;[45] (5) school-student;[46] (6) landlord-tenant;[47] and (7) custodian-one in custody.[48] The relationship of a parent to a minor child likewise almost certainly imposes an affirmative duty upon the parent to use reasonable care to rescue the child from a known danger.[49] Indeed, anyone who assumes what some courts have called a protective relationship will owe a duty of care appropriate to that relationship.[50]

The list is not necessarily closed, and in any event the duty of reasonable care may be created even in the absence of the categorical relationship if the defendant creates an unreasonable risk in the first place, or undertakes a duty of care. For example, if an employee-seaman goes overboard, the captain is required to conduct a search even if there is little hope.[51] A landowner whose invitee becomes ill may have a duty to summon care or at least to provide shelter until the invitee improves.[52] Under the rubric of custodian and ward, if the operator of a day-care center finds that a child in his care is injured or ill, he is obliged to use reasonable care to obtain appropriate medical attention.[53] Under the same principle, a jailer must secure medical aid and otherwise protect those held in custody. If he fails to do so, he is subject to liability as a matter of common law[54] and also in a civil rights action under the Eighth Amendment.[55] In the absence of custody, however, duties of rescue or protection under civil rights statutes may be quite limited.[56] Another way in which the Restatement list may be incomplete is that highly transient relationships that cannot be categorized may be sufficient to impose a duty.[57]

---

[44]   E.g., Cilley v. Lane, 985 A.2d 481 (Me. 2009) (rejecting a duty to assist on the part of a homeowner where the entrant was a trespasser); see also § 26.4.

[45]   See § 26.8.

[46]   Doe Parents No. 1 v. State Dep't of Educ., 100 Hawai'i 34, 58 P.3d 545 (2002); Mirand v. City of New York, 84 N.Y.2d 44, 614 N.Y.S.2d 372, 637 N.E.2d 263 (1994); see § 418.

[47]   See § 26.5.

[48]   See, e.g., Bell ex rel. Bell v. Dawson, 82 A.3d 827 (Me. 2013) (but duty created by custodial relationship terminates with the ending of the relationship itself); Restatement Third of Torts (Liability for Physical and Emotional Harm) § 40 (2010); see also § 26.6.

[49]   When the issue is protection from third persons, courts often implicitly so recognize. E.g., A.R.H. v. W.H.S., 876 S.W.2d 687 (Mo. App. 1994) (grandmother); Hite v. Brown, 100 Ohio App. 3d 606, 654 N.E.2d 452 (1995) (mother).

[50]   Caulfield v. Kitsap County, 108 Wash.App. 242, 29 P.3d 738 (2001) (social service department and county that took over its duties to monitor home care of the vulnerable plaintiff owed the plaintiff a duty).

[51]   Gardner v. National Bulk Carriers, Inc., 310 F.2d 284, 91 A.L.R.2d 1023 (4th Cir. 1962).

[52]   See Lundy v. Adamar of New Jersey, Inc., 34 F.3d 1173 (3d Cir. 1993).

[53]   See Applebaum v. Nemon, 678 S.W.2d 533 (Tex. App. 1984); Restatement Second of Torts § 314A, Illus. 7 (1965).

[54]   See Brownelli v. McCaughtry, 182 Wis.2d 367, 514 N.W.2d 48 (1994).

[55]   Estelle v. Gamble, 429 U.S. 97, 97 S.Ct. 285, 50 L.Ed.2d 251 (1976).

[56]   See § 26.7.

[57]   Farwell v. Keaton, 396 Mich. 281, 240 N.W.2d 217 (1976) (plaintiff and defendant were "companions on a social venture" with an implicit undertaking to aid one another, sufficient to trigger a duty); Podias v. Mairs, 394 N.J.Super. 338, 352, 926 A.2d 859, 867 (App. Div. 2007) (duty to assist, partly on the ground that two passengers in a car driven by their friend had "some relationship not only to the primary wrongdoer but to the incident itself," in which the driver struck a motorcyclist and all three failed to assist). Restatement Second of Torts § 314A, cmt. b (1965), notes that the law seems to be "working slowly toward a recognition of the duty to aid or protect in any relation of dependence or of mutual dependence." Many courts have been more cautious in recognizing ad hoc relationships as triggers of duty. See, e.g., Fiala v. Rains, 519 N.W.2d 386 (Iowa 1994); Cilley v. Lane, 985 A.2d 481 (Me. 2009); Carter v. Abbyad, 299 S.W.3d 892 (Tex. App. 2009).

§ 25.5   Beginning to Rescue or Assist

When the defendant acts affirmatively to aid a person who is helpless, he must of course act with reasonable care,[58] unless a statute says otherwise. It will not do to lift the stranded plaintiff from an ice gorge in a helicopter and then negligently drop her. Liability for injuries incurred in the drop would appear to be based upon negligent action, not upon any exception to the non-action rule.[59]

The Third Restatement makes it clear that the rescuer who "takes charge" must use reasonable care not to discontinue his aid or protection in a way that leaves the plaintiff in a worse position than existed before the defendant took charge.[60] This duty is frequently perceived to be different from the duty involved in the helicopter rescue illustration in the preceding paragraph. Negligently dropping the person you are rescuing is ordinary negligence, but the discontinuing aid can be conceived of as doing nothing. Under that conception, the Restatement provision is requiring the rescuer to take affirmative acts of care. The rule goes further: the rescuer must not unreasonably discontinue aid even if the imperiled plaintiff is not relying on that aid, as might be the case, for example, if the plaintiff was unconscious at the time.[61]

The Third Restatement's blackletter rule permits the rescuer to discontinue aid if the imperiled plaintiff is left in a no-worse position than if the defendant had not taken charge or undertaken care. That might seem to imply that one could begin towing a drowning swimmer to shore, then give up on the effort when the swimmer is halfway to shore. However, the Restatement provides otherwise by further requiring the rescuer to use reasonable care in terminating rescue efforts if the plaintiff is in imminent peril;[62] it nails down this point by adding that once the rescuer brings the plaintiff to safety, he may not return him to danger, even if the danger is no greater than the plaintiff would have faced without rescue.[63]

To the extent that the rescuer's liability for discontinuing aid depends upon making matters worse than they were before a rescue was begun, it seems fair to say that matters will not be worse for the helpless victim unless someone relies on the appearance of safety or rescue, or the rescue attempt prevents salvation by other means.[64] On this, perhaps courts are willing to accept very sparse evidence of reliance. When a customer became ill, a department store put her in its infirmary for six hours, but provided no medical attention. The court assumed that had the store done nothing, some good-

---

[58]   E.g., Collins v. Thomas, 182 Vt. 250, 938 A.2d 1208 (2007) (driver of pickup truck did not breach a duty of reasonable care after volunteering to drive the intoxicated plaintiff, where he had the plaintiff sit in the bed of the pickup; while he owed a duty of reasonable care, he was entitled to expect that the plaintiff would exercise reasonable caution for his own safety in the back of the truck); see § 414.

[59]   See Restatement Third of Torts (Liability for Physical and Emotional Harm) § 44, cmt. h (2010); Restatement Second of Torts § 324(a) (1965).

[60]   Restatement Third of Torts (Liability for Physical and Emotional Harm) § 44(b) (2010).

[61]   Id. § 44. In this respect, an undertaking to rescue is treated differently from some other undertakings. See § 25.6.

[62]   Restatement Third of Torts (Liability for Physical and Emotional Harm) § 44(b) (2010).

[63]   Id. § 44, cmt. h.

[64]   Indeed, one of the clearest examples of leaving a victim "worse off" than she would have been had aid never commenced is where others who would have assisted do not do so, based on the appearance that the rescuer has taken charge and further assistance is not needed. Restatement Second of Torts § 314A(4) (1965); see Coville v. Liberty Mut. Ins. Co., 57 Conn.App.275, 748 A.2d 875 (2000). It is an even clearer case where the would-be rescuer affirmatively interferes with others' ability to assist. See, e.g., Podias v. Mairs, 394 N.J. Super. 338, 926 A.2d 859 (App. Div. 2007); Restatement Second of Torts § 326 (1965) (intentionally interfering with another person's assistance is actionable).

hearted bystander would have provided an ambulance.[65] When the Coast Guard misread its incoming messages and wrongly informed people that a vessel in distress had arrived safely, its negligence dissuaded a private person from a search by ship, and the court was seemingly willing to assume that the search would have been successful.[66]

Perhaps these cases are best explained by saying that, when it comes to the rescue situation, courts apply a kind of lost-chance reasoning[67]—that is, that loss of a chance will count as worsening the victim's position even if it is less than clear that there was a decent chance of the victim's being saved. To say that loss of a chance of rescue is enough to show worsened position is not, of course, to say that the court must accept loss-of-the-chance or increased-risk reasoning generally.[68]

Good Samaritan statutes. All states have adopted one or more "good Samaritan" statutes, which typically immunize particular classes of people against negligence liability for offering assistance in specified kinds of emergencies; most commonly, these apply to medical personnel.[69] A good number of states, however—over a dozen—extend this protection to "all persons," usually protecting them from negligence liability for providing emergency assistance at the scene of an accident, as long as they have not received payment for their assistance.[70] The purpose of these statutes is to encourage people to provide emergency care or services without fear of negligence liability.[71] Liability under these statutes follows only where the rescuer acts in a grossly negligent way, or as some statutes have it, willfully or wantonly. These statutes have been held to immunize lay people who negligently assisted plaintiffs in need of rescue;[72] where the statute is inapplicable, however, the general rule—that a defendant is liable for negligently assisting—will apply.[73]

§ 25.6 Undertaking Creating a Duty to the Plaintiff

Undertaking or Assuming a Duty

Undertaking as promise or commitment. Special relationships that impose a duty may arise from status, as in the case of parent and child, or jailer and prisoner. Special relationships may also arise from voluntary contracts or undertakings.[74] An undertaking

---

[65] Zelenko v. Gimbel Bros., 158 Misc. 904, 287 N.Y.S.134 (1935), *aff'd per curiam*, 247 A.D. 867, 287 N.Y.S. 136 (1936).

[66] United States v. DeVane, 306 F.2d 182 (5th Cir. 1962); see also Fochtman v. Honolulu Police and Fire Departments, 65 Hawai'i 180, 649 P.2d 1114 (1982) (private person would have investigated frantic flashlight signal if police had not assured him they would check it out).

[67] See § 14.11.

[68] In particular, it is not to say that the Restatement Second's § 323 supports lost chance claims. See Restatement Second of Torts § 319 (1965).

[69] See § 21.13; Danny R. Veilleux, Annotation, Construction and application of "good Samaritan" statutes, 68 A.L.R.4th 294 (1989).

[70] See, e.g., Cal. Health & Safety Code § 1799.102; Ga. Code Ann. § 51–1–29; Minn. Stat. Ann. § 604A.01(2); Nev. Stat. § 41.500; N.J. Stat. Ann. § 2A:62A–1; N.Y. Pub. Health L. § 300–a(1); Tex. Civ. Prac. & Rem. Code § 74.151; Vt. Stat. Ann. § 519(b); Rev. Code Wash. § 4.24.300; Wis. Stat. Ann. § 895.48(1).

[71] In re Certification of a Question of Law from the United States District Court, 779 N.W.2d 158 (S.D. 2010).

[72] See, e.g., In re Certification of a Question of Law from the United States District Court, 779 N.W.2d 158 (S.D. 2010); Swenson v. Waseca Mut. Ins. Co., 653 N.W.2d 794 (Minn. 2002).

[73] See, e.g., Mueller v. McMillian Warner Ins. Co., 290 Wis.2d 571, 714 N.W.2d 183 (2006).

[74] See Grimes v. Kennedy Krieger Institute, Inc., 366 Md. 29, 782 A.2d 807 (2001) (contract between researcher and his human subject could create a special relationship and concomitant duty of care apart from the express terms of the contract). Courts widely recognize that undertakings amounting to the assumption of a duty of reasonable care can create a duty where otherwise none existed, see Davis v. Venture One Const.,

in this sense is a kind of explicit or implicit promise, or at least a commitment,[75] conveyed in words or in conduct. The undertaking may be and usually is entirely gratuitous.[76] The general rule that undertakings can create a duty of care is often expressed by saying one who voluntarily assumes a duty must then perform that duty with reasonable care.[77] Undertakings expressed verbally and those expressed by action or implication may be equally enforceable. Some undertakings may be enforceable as contracts but undertakings relating to physical safety of person or property usually suggest that the rules and policies of tort law should apply.[78]

Duty created by undertaking. Although a defendant's actions as well as words may count as undertakings, some actions by a defendant are negligent and harmful independent of any supposed undertaking. If a defendant leads a child across the street into the path of a vehicle, he has acted negligently and there is no need to discuss "undertakings," only the duty of ordinary care and its breach.[79] On the other hand, if the defendant's words or actions show an undertaking to escort children across the street but the defendant never shows up to do the job and children are struck in crossing alone, courts and writers usually think the defendant has not "acted" at all, so that a source of affirmative duty must be found. The defendant's undertaking is such a source.

A person who undertakes actions that would increase physical safety[80] for the plaintiff is under a duty to use reasonable care to carry out his undertaking, but only if one of two conditions is met. The plaintiff must show either (1) that the defendant's failure to exercise reasonable care increased the risk of harm so that it was more than it would have been with no undertaking,[81] or (2) that the plaintiff relied on the

---

Inc., 568 F.3d 570 (6th Cir. 2009), even against municipalities which are frequently protected by no-duty rules. See Wolfe v. City of Wheeling, 182 W. Va. 253, 387 S.E.2d 307 (1989). However, courts occasionally overlook or ignore the point and insist that an undertaking would be actionable only "in contract" if it is actionable at all. See Lockhart v. Airco Heating & Cooling, Inc., 211 W.Va. 609, 567 S.E.2d 619 (2002); Spengler v. ADT Security Services, Inc., 505 F.3d 456 (6th Cir. 2007) (home alarm company's obligation to dispatch emergency services is enforceable only in a breach of contract action).

[75]   See E. Allan Farnsworth, Decisions, Decisions: Some Binding, Some Not, 28 Suffolk U. L. Rev. 17 (1994). On whether a gratuitous *promise,* where the defendant does nothing toward performance, can create a duty, see 2 Dobbs, Hayden & Bublick, The Law of Torts § 411 (2d ed. 2011 & Supp.); Restatement Third of Torts (Liability for Physical and Emotional Harm) § 42, cmt. e (2010) (gratuitous promises as well as gratuitous actions that reduce danger may be the basis for demanding reasonable care for the plaintiff's physical safety).

[76]   The "takes charge" cases, see § 25.5, may be regarded as a species of commitment expressed in conduct.

[77]   See, e.g., Lokey v. Breuner, 2010 MT 216, 358 Mont. 8, 243 P.3d 384 (2010) (truck driver who waved at motorist approaching from opposite direction, signaling that it was safe for him to turn left, assumed a duty of reasonable care to assure that the parallel lane was clear); Carignan v. New Hampshire Int'l Speedway, Inc., 151 N.H. 409, 858 A.2d 536 (2004) (if defendant posted a man to signal traffic from highway to defendant's establishment, defendant owed a duty of care to persons on the highway); Florence v. Goldberg, 44 N.Y.2d 189, 375 N.E.2d 763, 404 N.Y.S.2d 583 (1978).

[78]   See §§ 25.6 & 25.7.

[79]   Restatement Third of Torts (Liability for Physical and Emotional Harm) § 42, cmt. c & Ill. 2 (2010).

[80]   See, e.g., Landon v. Kroll Laboratory Specialists, Inc., 91 A.D.3d 79, 934 N.Y.S.2d 183 (2d Dep't 2011) (state-licensed laboratory that contracted with county probation department to do drug testing on plaintiff as a condition of probation owed him a duty of reasonable care in doing the test, and could be liable to him for its negligence in reporting a false positive result to county probation officials, despite the lack of any formal contractual relationship between plaintiff and defendant); Restatement Third of Torts (Liability for Physical and Emotional Harm) § 42, cmt. c & Ill. 2 (2010).

[81]   See Belhumeur v. Zilm, 949 A.2d 162 (N.H. 2008); MacGregor v. Walker, 322 P.3d 706 (Utah 2014).

undertaking.[82] At least this is the rule usually advanced, although it may be possible that in some cases the defendant will be held to a duty even if neither condition is met.[83]

The Increased-Risk Avenue

The double relevance of increased risk. Increased risk in an undertaking case is important in two ways. First, an undertaking might actively work to create risks. In that case the undertaking is itself an affirmative act of negligence and it rightly suffices as a basis for liability.[84] For example, if one of two workers at a day-care center assures the other worker he will take a comatose child to the emergency room, his assurance or undertaking creates the risk that the other will not take needed action. In such a case the child at risk does not rely; she is comatose. Nevertheless, the risk to the child is increased as a result of the undertaking and its non-performance, and that is enough.[85]

Second, the increased-risk clause limits liability to harms resulting from the risk that the undertaking was intended or reasonably expected to protect against. A New Jersey case[86] illustrates the point. The plaintiff's band contracted to play at the defendant's place of business and the defendant contracted to provide helpers to unload band equipment. The defendant breached this provision and the plaintiff had to load the equipment himself. While he was doing so, he slipped and suffered injury. The defendant's non-performance of his undertaking to provide helpers to do the loading was a cause in fact of the harm. But the undertaking was not about avoiding falls, and liability grounded on the undertaking was inappropriate.

The Reliance Avenue

Action as undertaking. The Restatement rules also impose a duty to act affirmatively (and with reasonable care) when the defendant undertakes action and the plaintiff relies upon the undertaking.[87] An undertaking assuredly includes an express promise,[88] but it also includes actions that express an intention or commitment to act. If a city always provides crossing guards for children walking to school, that action is an undertaking to continue the protection until notice to the contrary. If a public entity provides 911 emergency service, it is undertaking to exercise reasonable care in its operation, at least when assurances are given to a specific victim who is in significant contact with the system.[89]

---

[82]   Restatement Third of Torts (Liability for Physical and Emotional Harm) § 42 (2010).

[83]   The Third Restatement, finding no pattern of cases, takes no position on this. Restatement Third of Torts (Liability for Physical and Emotional Harm) § 42, cmt. f (2010).

[84]   As the court said in Herrington v. Deloris Gaulden, 294 Ga. 285, 751 S.E.2d 813 (2013), liability does not attach when an undertaking merely fails to decrease the risk of harm.

[85]   Increased risk will often result from the reliance upon the undertaking by the plaintiff or someone acting upon her behalf, as where the city undertook to maintain a fence between a playground and a river and a mother relied upon the integrity of the fence in allowing her child to play. Nelson v. Salt Lake City, 919 P.2d 568 (Utah 1996). The separate provision for increased risk as well as for reliance allows courts to recognize a duty even if the plaintiff herself or her agent did not rely. The Third Restatement specifies that reliance by "another" is sufficient. Restatement Third of Torts (Liability for Physical and Emotional Harm) § 43(c) (2010).

[86]   Coyle v. Englander's, 199 N.J. Super. 212, 488 A.2d 1083 (1985).

[87]   Restatement Third of Torts (Liability for Physical and Emotional Harm) § 42 (2010); Restatement Second of Torts § 323(b) (1965).

[88]   See Bourgonje v. Machev, 841 N.E.2d 96, 112, 298 Ill. Dec. 953, 969 (2005) (landlord's promise of safety); Sabia v. State, 164 Vt. 293, 669 A.2d 1187 (1995) (promise and statutory duties); Restatement Third of Torts (Liability for Physical and Emotional Harm) § 42, cmt. d (2010).

[89]   Hutcherson v. City of Phoenix, 192 Ariz. 51, 961 P.2d 449 (1998) ("The City clearly had a duty to act reasonably in handling emergency calls. By creating a 911 system, it accepted the obligation of attempting to prevent the very kind of harm that occurred here."); but see Washington Cummins v. Lewis County, 156

Reliance by the plaintiff. Under the reliance alternative, as distinct from the increased-risk alternative, the plaintiff must show reliance on the defendant's undertaking or assumed duty.[90] Reliance shows that the defendant's failure to live up to his undertaking was a factual cause of the plaintiff's harm. The probability that the plaintiff relied is a matter of judging human behavior, thus well within the competence of the jury in many cases without the need for expert testimony.[91] Perhaps the reliance must be foreseeable or justified,[92] but at least reliance in fact is required unless perhaps the plaintiff and defendant are in one of the categorical relationships such as carrier and passenger.[93] If a child is struck in an unguarded crosswalk where guards have always been provided before, liability for negligently failing to provide the guard follows if the parents relied on the guard. Reliance is possible only when the parent has knowledge of the undertaking and has a choice whether to provide some other means of protection. Testimony that the parents knew that a guard was regularly provided and would have taken the child to school themselves if they had known that guards would be withdrawn shows reliance and permits recovery.[94]

In the same circumstances, however, the reliance requirement can defeat the claim for the child's injury if the child's parent did not know that guards had been provided. The reliance requirement would also defeat liability if the parent knew of the guards but, because she was working the early shift, could not have taken the child to school herself or found other means of protection. In that case, the parent would have no choice and could hardly be said to have relied on the guard since she could not have changed her actions even if she had known that the guards had been withdrawn. So if two children are struck in the same crosswalk at the same time because the protection of a crossing guard had been discontinued, only the one whose parents could have themselves escorted the child could recover for withdrawal of the guard.[95]

Some authority seems more lenient in finding reliance.[96] There is even the possibility that a person could rely even though she has learned that the defendant is not performing the promise at the time of injury. That might occur, for example, if the plaintiff enters into a lease only because the landlord promises or represents that specific safety devices will be installed. Although the tenant may be aware after she moves in

Wash.2d 844, 133 P.3d 458 (2006) (requiring both "dialog" and assurances of assistance by the 911 operator, plus reliance by the caller or victim); Muthukumarana v. Montgomery County, 370 Md. 447, 805 A.2d 372 (2002) (911 operator had no special relationship with the victim unless the operator's response exceeded "the response generally made to other members of the public"). Some states override tort liability by expressly providing statutory immunity to 911 or other emergency services. See Regester v. County of Chester, 568 Pa. 410, 797 A.2d 898 (2002).

90 E.g., Wiseman v. Hallahan, 113 Nev. 1266, 945 P.2d 945 (1997); (plaintiff who fell on ice on public walk at defendant's building did not rely on defendant's custom of clearing ice and could not recover for the defendant's failure to clear ice that day); Zima v. North Colonie Central School District, 225 A.D.2d 993, 639 N.Y.S.2d 558 (1996) (plaintiff who saw ice could not have relied on defendant's clearing or sanding it).

91 Estate of Long ex rel. Smith v. Broadlawns Med. Ctr., 656 N.W.2d 71 (Iowa 2002).

92 Heard v. City of New York, 82 N.Y.2d 66, 623 N.E.2d 541, 603 N.Y.S.2d 414 (1993).

93 Fried v. Archer, 139 Md. App. 229, 775 A.2d 430 (2001), *aff'd on other grounds*, Muthukumarana v. Montgomery County, 370 Md. 447, 805 A.2d 372 (2002) (in the absence of a categorical relationship, "It is the victim's justifiable reliance on an expectation of assistance that creates the "special relationship" between the victim and the defendant, and in turn, justifies the imposition of a special duty to aid, protect, or rescue that victim.").

94 Florence v. Goldberg, 44 N.Y.2d 189, 196, 375 N.E.2d 763, 767, 404 N.Y.S.2d 583, 587 (1978).

95 New York has applied the reliance requirement stringently, at least when when the claim is asserted against a public entity. See Kircher v. City of Jamestown, 74 N.Y.2d 251, 544 N.Y.S.2d 995, 543 N.E.2d 443 (1989) (also requiring "direct contact" between the plaintiff and the defendant).

96 See Beal v. City of Seattle, 134 Wash.2d 769, 954 P.2d 237 (1998).

that the safety devices are not installed, it can be said that she relied on the promise by executing the lease. In this view, the fact that she remains on the unsafe premises after she learns that they are unsafe does not negate the reliance demonstrated when she signed the lease but instead goes to the issue of comparative fault.[97] Finally, the undertaking itself may be so broad that reliance can easily be found, for example, if the defendant undertakes to care for a small child while the parents are at work.[98]

What duty is undertaken? A number of cases that accept the principles of duty based on undertakings end up concluding that the duty undertaken was not one that would have saved the plaintiff and consequently that the plaintiff cannot recover.[99] For example, in another crossing-guard case, the school provided guards in the afternoons after school, but that was not construed as an undertaking to provide guards when the kindergarten children walked home much earlier, so the school breached no duty to such a kindergartner who was struck at the dangerous and unguarded crossing.[100] Actions without promises are often ambiguous ways of showing an undertaking. Courts sometimes seem to believe that the defendant undertakes only what he actually does, which would mean that the defendant could never be liable because he would always have fulfilled his undertaking.[101] A moderate position determines the scope of the defendant's assumed duty by considering the plaintiff's reasonable expectations of care induced by the defendant's actions,[102] although reliance cannot be required when the plaintiff is unconscious or helpless.[103] Some authority suggests that whether the defendant's actions count as an undertaking depends on an assessment of the defendant's purposes; if it is as likely that he acted for his own purposes as it is that he acted to aid the plaintiff, the plaintiff has not proved that he undertook a duty to her, at least where the plaintiff has not reasonably relied upon appearances to the contrary.[104] The Third Restatement rejects this view, providing that although the defendant must know that his undertaking reduces risk to the plaintiff, the undertaking may be for his own benefit rather than the plaintiff's.[105]

§ 25.7 Undertaking Creating a Duty to Third Persons

Active negligence. The defendant is of course under a duty to exercise reasonable care in his affirmative activities. If his unreasonably risky affirmative acts cause harm,

---

[97] Cf. Bourgonje v. Machev, 841 N.E.2d 96, 112, 298 Ill. Dec. 953, 969 (2005), where the court did not use the term comparative fault but suggested that eventually the plaintiff would be barred.

[98] See O.L. v. R.L., 62 S.W.3d 469 (Mo. App. 2001) (recognizing caretaker's duty to protect small child, parents' reliance not discussed).

[99] E.g., Bourgonje v. Machev, 841 N.E.2d 96, 112, 298 Ill. Dec. 953, 969 (2005) (landlord's undertaking to provide buzzers was not an undertaking to provide them as protection outside the building); Davis v. Westwood Group, 420 Mass. 739, 652 N.E.2d 567 (1995) (racetrack's arrangement for officers to control traffic at the crossing from parking facility was under an undertaking to provide safe crossing, but only to perform the "the discrete task" of traffic direction); Trull v. Town of Conway, 140 N.H. 579, 669 A.2d 807 (1995) (officer's request that another warn highway department of dangerous ice condition was not an undertaking to get the message through).

[100] Jefferson County School District R-1 v. Gilbert, 725 P.2d 774 (Colo. 1986).

[101] Cf. Paulson v. Andicoechea, 926 P.2d 955 (Wyo. 1996) (the defendant had customarily cleared snow but had not done so after the last snowfall; defendant's prior actions in clearing snow only reflected an undertaking to clear snow on the days he actually cleared it).

[102] See Cottam v. CVS Pharmacy, 436 Mass. 316, 764 N.E.2d 814 (2002) (pharmacist's incomplete list of warnings about prescription drug; patient could reasonably understand that the list was complete).

[103] See Wakulich v. Mraz, 203 Ill.2d 223, 785 N.E.2d 843, 271 Ill.Dec. 649 (2003) (citing Restatement Second of Torts § 324 (1965)).

[104] See LM v. United States, 344 F.3d 695 (7th Cir. 2003).

[105] Restatement Third of Torts (Liability for Physical and Emotional Harm) § 42 (2010).

he is subject to liability for that harm. In that case, whether he has undertaken or promised something to a third person is entirely irrelevant; what is relevant is that he did something and did it negligently.[106] The problem addressed in this section is different. It concerns the defendant who, in his dealings with one person, can be perceived as having undertaken actions that will provide safety for a different person, but who has not begun performance of those actions and thus cannot be said to have been engaged in risk-creating conduct. The defendant promises to keep A's brakes in good condition, but never lifts a finger to do so, with the foreseeable result that when A's brakes fail, the others with whom the defendant has not dealt at all are injured. In this third-party nonperformance situation, courts once rejected all liability on the grounds that the plaintiff was not in privity with the defendant[107] and that the defendant was chargeable only with nonfeasance, not affirmative acts of negligence.[108] However, modern tort law makes room for negligence liability under a series of rules.

Contemporary rules. The defendant who makes an undertaking to A may be under a duty of reasonable care to others to perform that undertaking if the defendant should know that his failure to act on his undertaking would increase the risks of physical harm to others, provided that one of three conditions is met: (1) the defendant's breach of the duty undertaken made matters more dangerous for the plaintiff; *or,* (2) the plaintiff or another relied upon the undertaking; *or* (3) the defendant's undertaking was to perform a duty already owed by another person. The duty of care as so described by the Restatements[109] has been widely recognized in the courts.[110] The defendant's undertaking generates a duty of reasonable care whether it is an enforceable promise or merely a gratuitous undertaking.[111] The duty does not extend to stand-alone economic harms, however, but only to those harms that can be considered to be associated with the plaintiff's physical well-being.[112]

Non-performance increasing risk of physical harm. When the defendant, dealing with A, undertakes or contracts to carry out acts that he should know will tend to make B safer from physical harm, every reason supports a duty of care to B to carry out his undertaking unless he arranges to safely withdraw from it. Where the defendant promises a city to repair a malfunctioning traffic signal, his failure to act on the promise creates a definite risk of harm to travelers from readily foreseeable intersection collisions. In such cases courts have imposed a duty to use care to perform the undertaking and have recognized that liability will be appropriate if the plaintiff is

---

[106] Schmeck v. City of Shawnee, 232 Kan. 11, 651 P.2d 585 (1982); Dowis v. Continental Elevator Co., Inc., 241 Neb. 207, 486 N.W.2d 916 (1992); Landon v. Kroll Laboratory Specialists, Inc., 22 N.Y.3d 1, 977 N.Y.S.2d 676, 999 N.E.2d 1121 (2013).

[107] Winterbottom v. Wright, 10 M. & W. 109, 152 Eng.Rep. 402 (Exch. Pl. 1842) (defendant's promise to the owner of a coach to keep it in repair, no duty to the plaintiff who was injured when the coach collapsed).

[108] See H.R. Moch Co. v. Rensselaer Water Co., 247 N.Y. 160, 159 N.E. 896 (1928).

[109] Restatement Third of Torts (Liability for Physical and Emotional Harm) § 43 (2010); Restatement Second of Torts § 324A (1965).

[110] Stanley v. McCarver, 208 Ariz. 219, 92 P.3d 849 (2004) (doctor contracting with A to examine B owed duty to B if B relied on report); Paz v. State of California, 22 Cal.4th 550, 994 P.2d 975, 93 Cal. Rptr. 2d 703 (2000) (reviewing the three conditions); Gazo v. City of Stamford, 255 Conn. 245, 765 A.2d 505 (2001) (contractor undertook to clear snow from sidewalk adjacent to A's building, liability to B who fell on snow or ice there); Louisville Gas & Elec. Co. v. Roberson, 212 S.W.3d 107 (Ky. 2006).

[111] Restatement Third of Torts (Liability for Physical and Emotional Harm) § 43, cmt. a (2010).

[112] Id.

injured by a breach of that duty.[113] The same of course applies to other similar undertakings, such as the undertaking to repair a dangerous elevator.[114]

Some cases, following the Restatement, take the position that there is no increased risk unless the defendant's non-performance made the risk greater than it would have been if the defendant had undertaken nothing at all.[115] Risk to the plaintiff is not compared with the risk the plaintiff would face if the defendant had safely performed his undertaking. Instead, it is compared to the risk the plaintiff would face if the defendant had never made any undertaking at all. In the traffic-signal cases, the fact that the defendant promised to repair a malfunctioning traffic signal does not by itself make the signal more dangerous than it would have been if the defendant had not undertaken repair. Therefore, under this view, such defendants would have no duty to the foreseeable victims unless he was negligent in some affirmative act, or one of the other alternative conditions for liability is met.

Non-performance of undertaking relied upon by another. If the plaintiff or some other person relies on the defendant's undertaking to provide better safety, then that by itself is sufficient to trigger a duty of reasonable care to perform his undertaking or to effect a safe withdrawal from it.[116] Although reliance is enough by itself, reliance will often also show that the undertaking increased the risk, so under the restrictive view of increased risk adopted by the Restatement, reliance will often become the ultimate issue.[117] The plaintiff need not personally rely if someone else does. For example, the Coast Guard's undertaking to rescue someone might induce other potential rescuers to rest on their oars. This is reliance on the Coast Guard's undertaking and it is ground for saying that the Coast Guard is subject to liability for failing to proceed with the rescue it undertook.[118]

Non-performance when defendant undertakes to perform another person's existing duty. When the defendant undertakes with Person A to perform a duty owed by A to the plaintiff, the defendant is then duty-bound to exercise reasonable care for the plaintiff's physical safety in accord with that duty.[119] For example, an employer owes his employees a duty of reasonable care, including a duty to provide a reasonably safe place in which to work. If the employer contracts with the defendant to provide that workplace safety, then the defendant is contracting to fulfill the employer's duty and is obliged to use

---

[113] Rust International Corp. v. Greystone Power Corp., 133 F.3d 1378 (11th Cir. 1998) (Georgia law under Restatement Second § 324A); cf. Clay Elec. Coop., Inc. v. Johnson, 873 So.2d 1182 (Fla. 2004) (contractual obligation to maintain street lights, increased risk and negligence could be found from failure to have regular inspections to discover non-working lights).

[114] Banaghan v. Bay State Elevator Co., 340 Mass. 73, 162 N.E.2d 807 (1959); Dowis v. Continental Elevator Co., Inc., 241 Neb. 207, 486 N.W.2d 916 (1992); Rosenberg v. Otis Elevator Co., 366 N.J.Super. 292, 841 A.2d 99 (2004); Bollin v. Elevator Const. & Repair Co., 361 Pa. 7, 63 A.2d 19, 6 A.L.R.2d 277 (1949).

[115] See Belhumeur v. Zilm, 949 A.2d 162 (N.H. 2008); Thames Shipyard and Repair Co. v. United States, 350 F.3d 247 (1st Cir. 2003); Canipe v. National Loss Control Serv. Corp., 736 F.2d 1055 (5th Cir. 1984); Restatement Third of Torts (Liability for Physical and Emotional Harm) § 43, cmt. d (2010).

[116] Stanley v. McCarver, 208 Ariz. 219, 92 P.3d 849 (2004) (plaintiff should have opportunity to prove reliance upon doctor's promise to third person to examine the plaintiff and report).

[117] See, e.g., Union Park Mem. Chapel v. Hutt, 670 So.2d 64 (Fla. 1996); see also Lindsey v. E & E Automotive & Tire Service, Inc., 241 P.3d 880 (Alaska 2010).

[118] See Thames Shipyard and Repair Co. v. United States, 350 F.3d 247, 261 (1st Cir. 2003). See also Alder v. Bayer Corp., AGFA Div., 61 P.3d 1068 (Utah 2002) (duty created where defendant undertook to vent dangerous fumes in hospital; hospital relied on that undertaking and hence did nothing to protect its employees, who were injured).

[119] Restatement Third of Torts (Liability for Physical and Emotional Harm) § 43(b) (2010); Restatement Second of Torts § 324A(b) (1965).

reasonable care in doing so.[120] The principle can apply to any case in which the defendant accepts responsibility for carrying out the safety duty of another.[121] The defendant who undertakes to perform another's duty of care for the plaintiff's physical safety is subject to liability for breach of that duty even if his undertaking did not increase the risk and even if no reliance on the undertaking is proven.[122] This is clearly right. If Person A owes a duty of care to the plaintiff, A may avoid liability by taking reasonable precautions to protect the plaintiff, including a precaution in the form of a contract with another person to provide the protection needed. So A can normally shift either all or part of the responsibility and be relieved of liability by contracting with the defendant to perform A's duties of care.[123] By the same token, however, the defendant must be held to the duty he has assumed, for otherwise the plaintiff's rights would have been determined by the contract of two other people to which he was not a party.[124] In addition, when the defendant contracts to fulfill A's duty to the plaintiff, the plaintiff may look like a creditor beneficiary entitled to sue for a breach of the contract that leads to her injury.[125]

Policy against recognizing a duty in particular cases. To recognize a duty of care based on the defendant's undertaking is fully consonant with modern tort thinking, but, as always, the duty issue ultimately turns on the courts' sense of policy and justice. Consequently, even if the defendant has undertaken to act for the plaintiff's safety, the court may conclude that a duty of care is unwarranted on the facts of the particular case.[126] In a Massachusetts case, a tenant promised the landlord that the tenant would clear snow and ice from the property. The plaintiff was employed on the property, though not by the tenant. She fell on a patch of ice. Since the tenant owed no common law duty to clear the ice, the plaintiff relied upon the tenant's promise to the landlord. But the defendant's promise to the landlord was not intended for the benefit of third persons and Massachusetts has a strong policy against imposing snow-clearance duties. So not surprisingly, the court refused to permit the tenant's promise to create a tort duty.[127]

---

[120] Canipe v. National Loss Control Serv. Corp., 736 F.2d 1055 (5th Cir. 1984); Palka v. Servicemaster Management Services Corp., 83 N.Y.2d 579, 589, 611 N.Y.S.2d 817, 822, 634 N.E.2d 189, 194 (1994). But see Espinal v. Melville Snow Contractors, Inc., 98 N.Y.2d 136, 773 N.E.2d 485, 746 N.Y.S.2d 120 (2002) (a *comprehensive* assumption of another's duty to the plaintiff is required; a mere contract to plow snow, though it performed one duty of the plaintiff's employer to the plaintiff, was not enough); Alexander v. Mitchell, 930 A.2d 1016 (Me. 2007) (defendant snow-plow company owed no tort duty to the public arising from its snow-plowing contract with the town); Rice v. Collins Commc'n, Inc., 2010 WY 109, 236 P.3d 1009 (Wyo. 2010) (communications companies that supplied emergency communications system for a county did not owe a private property owner a duty of care in operating and maintaining the system).

[121] See Gazo v. City of Stamford, 255 Conn. 245, 765 A.2d 505 (2001) (defendant contractually assumed duty of landowner to clear adjacent sidewalk of ice and snow, tort duty thereby assumed to plaintiff using the walk); Phinney v. Boston Elevated Ry. Co., 201 Mass. 286, 87 N.E. 490 (1909) (railroad contractually assumed city's duty of care and was liable for its failure to act in performance of that duty).

[122] Restatement Third of Torts (Liability for Physical and Emotional Harm) § 43, cmt. g (2010).

[123] On the shifting-responsibility concept, see 1 Dobbs, Hayden & Bublick, The Law of Torts § 213 (2d ed. 2011 & Supp.).

[124] See Palka v. Servicemaster Management Services Corp., 83 N.Y.2d 579, 589, 611 N.Y.S.2d 817, 822, 634 N.E.2d 189, 194 (1994) (liability justified in part because of the "displacement and substitution of a particular safety function designed to protect persons like this plaintiff").

[125] L.A.C. v. Ward Parkway Shopping Ctr. Co., 75 S.W.3d 247 (Mo. 2002) (security company contracting to help fulfill mall owner's duty to protect its invitees owed a contract duty to invitee who was allegedly raped).

[126] Restatement Third of Torts (Liability for Physical and Emotional Harm) § 37, cmt. i (2010) (suggesting that special considerations involved with public entity defendants might sometimes trump the rules of liability based on undertakings).

[127] Anderson v. Fox Hill Village Homeowners Corp., 424 Mass. 365, 676 N.E.2d 821 (1997). Distinguish Gazo v. City of Stamford, 255 Conn. 245, 765 A.2d 505 (2000) (defendant contracted to take over all snow clearing duties of plaintiff's employer, defendant is subject to liability).

Such a result is entirely consistent with a general acceptance of the assumed-duty rules recognized by the Restatement in cases that do not involve the same policies.

Scope of assumed duty or undertaking. The Third Restatement does not limit liability for third-person undertakings to cases in which the defendant intended to provide protection for the plaintiff. If the defendant's undertaking increases the risk or induces reliance or assumes the duty already owed by another, it is enough that the defendant knows or should know that his undertaking will also reduce the risk of physical harm to others.[128] Yet, the scope of the undertaking can matter a great deal if the limitation of the undertaking makes risk or reliance unforeseeable. In such a case, and if the defendant's duty arises solely from his undertaking, the scope of his undertaking can limit the scope of his duty.[129] The trouble is that, as observed in another connection,[130] undertakings in the form of actions rather than words are often ambiguous. An adjuster's inspection of a dangerous building to determine whether damage to the building comes within insurance coverage is not necessarily an undertaking to warn neighbors of dangers that the building may collapse on them, or indeed an undertaking to anyone except the insurer who employed him.[131]

---

[128] Restatement Third of Torts (Liability for Physical and Emotional Harm) § 43, cmt. f (2010).

[129] Bailey v. Edward Hines Lumber Co., 308 Ill. App. 3d 58, 719 N.E.2d 178, 241 Ill. Dec. 317 (1999) ("the duty of care imposed on a defendant is limited to the extent of its undertaking"); Rein v. Benchmark Construction Co., 865 So.2d 1134 (Miss. 2004) (undertaking associated with a service contract terminated when service contract was terminated); Torrington Co. v. Stutzman, 46 S.W.3d 829 (Tex. 2000) ("duty to exercise reasonable care in performing a voluntarily assumed undertaking is limited to that undertaking. When, as here, the facts about the scope of the assumed duty are in dispute, the jury should be instructed to that effect.").

[130] See § 25.6.

[131] Gooch v. Bethel A.M.E. Church, 246 Kan. 663, 792 P.2d 993, 13 A.L.R.5th 974 (1990).

Chapter 26

DUTY TO PROTECT FROM THIRD PERSONS AND FROM SELF-HARM

Analysis

A. THE NO-DUTY RULE

§ 26.1   No Duty to Control Others
§ 26.2   Actively Creating Risk of Injury by Third Person

B. DUTY BASED ON DEFENDANT'S RELATIONSHIP TO PLAINTIFF

§ 26.3   Types of Relationships Recognized
§ 26.4   Landowner's Duty to Protect Lawful Entrants
§ 26.5   Landowner's Duty to Protect Tenants and Their Guests
§ 26.6   Custodian's and School's State-Law Duty to Protect Wards or Students
§ 26.7   Federal Civil Rights Claims
§ 26.8   Employer's Duty to Protect Employees

C. DUTY BASED ON DEFENDANT'S RELATIONSHIP TO A DANGEROUS PERSON

§ 26.9   Relationships Recognized
§ 26.10   Negligent Entrustment
§ 26.11   Control and Other Means of Protecting from Dangerous Persons
§ 26.12   Enhancing Dangers: Providers of Alcohol

A. THE NO-DUTY RULE

§ 26.1 No Duty to Control Others

In many cases, the defendant himself does not directly injure the plaintiff but instead fails to prevent the risk of injury by another person (or by the plaintiff herself). The immediate tortfeasor is sometimes merely negligent but often he carries out a criminal attack on the plaintiff. The question is whether the defendant, who could have prevented the injury by a warning, or by exercising the control he had over the attacker or over the plaintiff herself,[1] or otherwise, is under any duty to do so.[2]

In the usual case, the problem is not rescue of a plaintiff already in peril; it is rather the use of care to prevent harm in the first place. For example, when a newly released parolee with a history of violence toward women does not appear at the halfway house

---

[1]   See Madison ex rel. Bryant v. Babcock Center, Inc., 371 S.C. 123, 638 S.E.2d 650 (2006) (caregiver owes duty to patient with mental disability to control her to protect her from harming herself). For cases involving allegations that a defendant negligently failed to prevent another person's suicide, see §§ 15.18 (superseding cause) & 26.6 (duty).

[2]   Many cases have tried to resolve the matter on scope of liability (proximate cause) grounds, which is problematic. See 2 Dobbs, Hayden & Bublick, The Law of Torts § 413 (2d ed. 2011 & Supp.).

to which he is required to report, the halfway house can minimize the risk that the parolee will commit crimes by warning the prison or the police that he has not appeared as required. Although a phone call by the halfway house does not seem onerous, given the halfway house's effort to direct criminals into a better path, courts have often conceived of this and a variety of other situations narrowly as a question of the defendant's *control over others* rather than as a question of the defendant's *ability to protect* the plaintiff from foreseeable harm by actions that are neither costly nor demanding. They have frequently said that, with certain exceptions, the defendant owes no duty to control the dangerous person and have taken that premise as grounds for refusing relief to the parolee's victims.[3]

In some instances, the defendant has done nothing, so the nonfeasance rule would protect the defendant unless his relationship establishes an affirmative duty to act.[4] However, in many of the cases, the defendant seems to be acting affirmatively and in so doing creating a risk of harm to the plaintiff.[5] Perhaps that is true in the halfway house example, because it is possible to think that the defendant is operating a halfway house and doing a very bad job of it, not merely failing to use the telephone. Although the no-duty-to-control rule logically seems to be an application of the nonfeasance rule,[6] some courts seem to apply the no-duty-to-control rule independently, that is, whether or not the defendant has affirmatively created a risk by his negligent actions. In those courts, the rule can sometimes immunize affirmative risky acts.[7]

In four types of cases, the rule of non-liability for failure to control third persons does not shield the defendant from liability for negligence: (1) Where the defendant's conduct is seen as having actively created an unreasonable risk of injury from such third persons.[8] (2) Where a statute imposes a duty of care, as with statutes requiring state agencies to investigate and deal with reports of suspected child abuse.[9] (3) Where defendant is in a special relationship with the plaintiff that requires the defendant to use reasonable care for the plaintiff's safety.[10] (4) Where the defendant is in a special relationship with the dangerous third person and is in a position to control his tortious behavior, or at least to minimize risks to the plaintiff by some means.[11]

§ 26.2 Actively Creating Risk of Injury by Third Person

The rule that no one owes a duty to control others is a particular instance of the general rule that nonfeasance is not a tort unless there is a duty to act.[12] Consequently,

---

[3] See Johnson v. State, 553 N.W.2d 40 (Minn. 1996). Several courts, however, have held that a parole officer, by virtue of his supervisory relationship with the parolee, is under a duty of reasonable care to victims in a foreseeable class. State, Dep't of Corrections v. Cowles, 151 P.3d 353 (Alaska 2006).

[4] E.g., England v. Brianas, 166 N.H. 369, 97 A.3d 255 (2014) (defendant owed no duty to warn boyfriend of stalking by former boyfriend, who broke into defendant's home and stabbed plaintiff).

[5] See § 26.2. This is clearly the situation in negligent entrustment cases, see § 26.10.

[6] See Restatement Third of Torts (Liability for Physical and Emotional Harm) § 19 & cmt. e (2010); § 25.2.

[7] See §§ 26.2 (perceptions of active negligence vs. nonfeasance) & 26.12 (alcohol providers).

[8] See § 26.2.

[9] See District of Columbia v. Harris, 770 A.2d 82 (D.C. 2001); Rees v. State, Dep't of Health & Welfare, 143 Idaho 10, 137 P.3d 397 (2006); Jensen v. Anderson County Dep't of Social Services, 304 S.C. 195, 403 S.E.2d 615 (1991); Sabia v. State, 164 Vt. 293, 669 A.2d 1187 (1995). See also § 26.6.

[10] See §§ 26.3 to 26.8.

[11] See §§ 26.9 to 26.12. For example, a jailer or other custodian of a dangerous person owes a duty of reasonable care to prevent that person from harming others, see § 26.11.

[12] See Chapter 25.

the no-duty-to-control rule has no logical application when the defendant is affirmatively negligent in creating a risk of harm to the plaintiff through the instrumentality of another or otherwise.[13]

Differing perceptions of active negligence. Sometimes courts, or lawyers arguing the cases, have missed this point, with the result that defendants have been relieved of liability even when they acted affirmatively and negligently to create a risk of harm by third persons.[14] Sometimes, also, courts make broad statements that, taken literally, would eliminate a duty to use care even in cases of positive acts such as driving an automobile, or do not perceive affirmative negligence of the defendant and consequently treat the case as if the defendant did nothing.[15] Although perceptions may differ, it is possible to say that, in accord with the logic of the nonfeasance rule, when courts do in fact perceive the defendant's conduct as actively creating an unreasonable risk of injury by third persons, they usually recognize a duty of care and liability based upon the active exposure to risks. The defendant in these cases is not being required to control others or even to protect them from attacks. On the contrary, he is being required only to take no active steps in creating risks of danger from third persons. In such cases, the no-duty-to-control rule should not protect the defendant.[16]

Creating danger through misleading signals. One way to actively create risks is to give or withhold information, that is, to create the appearance of safety without correcting the deceptive appearance. One simple kind of case of this sort involves the driver who is in a position to see danger and who, by motions or otherwise, indicates to the plaintiff that she can safely proceed, thereby leading her into the path of an oncoming vehicle driven by a third person.[17] In some such cases the plaintiff may be chargeable with contributory negligence or comparative fault,[18] and in others the defendant's signal may be interpreted to mean only that the defendant waives his own right of way, not that he has assessed the safety of the move he invites the plaintiff to make.[19] But even

---

[13]   See, e.g., Domagala v. Rolland, 805 N.W.2d 14 (Minn. 2011); Madison ex rel. Bryant v. Babcock Center, Inc., 371 S.C. 123, 638 S.E.2d 650 (2006); Strahin v. Cleavenger, 216 W.Va. 175, 603 S.E.2d 197 (2004).

[14]   See, e.g., Parish v. Truman, 124 Ariz. 228, 603 P.2d 120 (Ct. App. 1979) (defendant opened door to unknown persons in a dangerous area, held, no duty because there was no special relationship between defendant and plaintiff, who was his social guest); Brewster v. Rush-Presbyterian-St. Luke's Medical Center, 361 Ill.App.3d 32, 836 N.E.2d 635, 296 Ill. Dec. 884 (2005) (defendant alleged worked employee 32 consecutive hours and should have known she was unfit to drive; she fell asleep at the wheel on leaving employment, running into the plaintiff, but employer had no duty to the plaintiff); Fiala v. Rains, 519 N.W.2d 386 (Iowa 1994) (defendant met plaintiff in bar and invited him and others to her house, failing to tell the man that she had another male friend who was extremely jealous; male friend attacked plaintiff; no liability).

[15]   See Johnstone v. City of Albuquerque, 140 N.M. 596, 145 P.3d 76 (Ct. App. 2006) ("Conduct that falls below a standard of care does not alone support liability. To impose a duty, a relationship must exist that legally obligates Defendant to protect Plaintiff's interest.").

[16]   See, e.g., Anderson v. PPCT Management Systems, Inc., 145 P.3d 503 (Alaska 2006) (negligently training a corrections officer who harmed plaintiff); Shepherd v. Washington County, 331 Ark. 480, 962 S.W.2d 779 (1998) (transporting dangerous prisoner to clinic; prisoner attacked plaintiffs); Olivo v. Owens-Illinois, Inc., 186 N.J. 394, 895 A.2d 1143 (2006) (carry-home asbestos); Satterfield v. Breeding Insulation Co., 266 S.W.3d 347 (Tenn. 2008) (same); see also Restatement Third of Torts (Liability for Physical and Emotional Harm) § 19, cmt. e (2010).

[17]   See, e.g., Lokey v. Breuner, 358 Mont. 8, 243 P.3d 384 (2010).

[18]   Hanks v. Melancon, 338 So.2d 1215 (La. App. 1976).

[19]   The apparent ability of the signaling driver to assess safety more accurately than the plaintiff is key evidence in determining whether to interpret the signal as a communication about safety. See Dawson v. Griffin, 249 Kan. 115, 816 P.2d 374 (1991).

if the defendant escapes liability on such grounds, it is not because he owes no duty.[20] And where the plaintiff can reasonably rely upon the defendant's affirmative signal, the defendant is subject to liability for negligently creating a risk of harm by other traffic.[21] A misleading signal may be less direct or more ambiguous. When one deer hunter fires in the direction of the plaintiff, that may signal to his fellow hunters that firing in that direction is safe. If so, the plaintiff who is shot by the second hunter may conceivably have an action against the first on the ground that his firing implied safety and thus triggered the injury-causing shot.[22]

Vouching for qualities of third person. The defendant might also actively create an appearance of safety by explicitly or implicitly vouching for the qualifications of a dangerous person, thus leading others to rely on the appearance of safety and to expose the victim to injury.[23] Presenting a person for treatment without warning of his unusual and extremely violent tendencies looks like an affirmative act that creates a risk, so that liability for the harm done by the person under treatment is entirely appropriate.[24]

Actions facilitating injury by third person. There is no limit on examples of liability for actively creating a risk of harm by third persons. A street vendor may entice small children to cross the street in traffic to obtain his wares, actively subjecting them to the risk of being struck by negligent drivers. Liability does not depend on "control" of the driver in such cases but on the active creation of the risk.[25] In civil rights cases, liability for affirmative misconduct as distinct from nonfeasance is understood as "state-created danger."[26] Similarly, the older rule that one who provided alcohol to an intoxicated person who was expected to drive a vehicle had no duty to third persons who might foreseeably be injured has now been largely displaced by judicial and legislative action.[27]

Fatigued-worker cases. A smaller group of cases involve employees who fall asleep at the wheel on the way home after excessively long work periods. In some cases, these employees have worked 30 hours or more without sleep. Predictably, fatigue leads to a collision that injures or kills others. Some courts have held that the employer who imposes debilitating workloads, and knows the employee will drive home in an unfit condition, may have breached a duty of care to those on the highway who are foreseeably injured by the employee. Those cases require only reasonable care; they do not forbid long hours or overtime. Liability is imposed upon the employer because of the employer's own affirmative creation of a risk by overworking or by not offering rest or alternative

---

[20]   Key v. Hamilton, 963 N.E.2d 573 (Ind. Ct. App. 2012) (driver who signaled motorist through intersection owed duty to injured motorcyclist); contra, Gilmer v. Ellington, 159 Cal.App.4th 190, 70 Cal.Rptr.3d 893 (2008) (gesturing driver owed no duty to injured motorcyclist).

[21]   Frey v. Woodard, 748 F.2d 173 (3d Cir. 1984); Phillips v. Capps, 155 Ariz. 597, 748 P.2d 1221 (1988); Key v. Hamilton, 963 N.E.2d 573 (Ind. Ct. App. 2012). See also Joseph B. Conder, Annotation, Motorist's Liability for Signaling Other Vehicle or Pedestrian to Proceed, or to Pass Signaling Vehicle, 14 A.L.R.5th 193 (1993).

[22]   Hellums v. Raber, 853 N.E.2d 143 (Ind. App. 2006) (on the theory that the first hunter was aiding or encouraging the second).

[23]   E.g., Randi W. v. Muroc Joint Unified Sch. Dist., 14 Cal.4th 1066, 929 P.2d 582, 60 Cal.Rptr.2d 263 (1997) (letter of recommendation created impression that teacher would be safe around children).

[24]   See Fuhrman v. State, 265 Neb. 176, 655 N.W.2d 866 (2003). Cf. Bryson v. Banner Health System, 89 P.3d 800 (Alaska 2004) (group treatment center owed duty to plaintiff who was attacked by co-participant in treatment, where center employees knew of attacker's history of violence yet encouraged plaintiff and others to "support" each other outside the group).

[25]   See § 26.11.

[26]   See § 26.7.

[27]   See § 26.12.

transport to the fatigued employee.[28] The plaintiff in these cases is ordinarily not claiming vicarious liability[29] or even a duty to "control" the employee, as some contrary authority has perhaps implied in rejecting such claims.[30] The claim instead is that the employer affirmatively created the unreasonable risk that came to pass.

Motivating injury by third person. In another group of cases the defendant's act provides the motivation or incentive for a third person to injure or kill a victim. For example, if a person takes out a life insurance policy on the life of someone else and later murders the insured, the insurer may be liable if it issued the policy without doing a reasonable investigation.[31] Because the insurer has affirmatively created the risk by issuing the policy with inadequate checks, the no-duty-to-control rule has no application.

B. DUTY BASED ON DEFENDANT'S RELATIONSHIP TO PLAINTIFF

§ 26.3 Types of Relationships Recognized

The defendant's relationship to the plaintiff has been recognized as a ground for requiring the defendant to take affirmative acts of reasonable care in a substantial body of cases. Courts frequently speak as if duties are generated only within a list of formal relationships such as carrier-passenger, but as already indicated in discussing rescue cases,[32] the list is not closed.[33] In any event, since duty is a question of justice and policy, some less formal or describable relationships may work in the same way. On the other hand, the duty may not be coextensive with all the recognized formal relationships.

Courts recognize several formal relationships between the defendant and the plaintiff as grounds for imposing a duty of reasonable care. Many courts have said that even where there is a special relationship, the risk of harm must be reasonably foreseeable in order to trigger a duty.[34] Satisfying that duty may require the defendant to give warnings to the plaintiff, to provide shelter, to call for help, or to act otherwise as reasonable care may dictate, to prevent harm by others, although the extent of the duty owed is sometimes debated. In general, the categories of relationships include: (1) A

---

[28]   Faverty v. McDonald's Restaurants of Oregon, Inc., 133 Or. App. 514, 892 P.2d 703 (1995); Robertson v. LeMaster, 171 W.Va. 607, 301 S.E.2d 563 (1983).For other cases involving the active creation of a risk of injury by a third person, see § 26.2.

[29]   Employees on their way home are seldom within the scope of employment, see § 428, so vicarious liability is usually out of the question. See Lev v. Beverly Enterprises—Massachusetts, Inc., 457 Mass. 234, 929 N.E.2d 303 (2010).

[30]   E.g., Nabors Drilling, U.S.A., Inc. v. Escoto, 288 S.W.3d 401 (Tex. 2009).

[31]   Liberty Nat'l Life Ins. Co. v. Weldon, 267 Ala. 171, 100 So.2d 696 (1957); Bajwa v. Metropolitan Life Ins. Co., 208 Ill. 2d 414, 804 N.E.2d 519, 281 Ill.Dec. 554 (2004).

[32]   See § 25.4.

[33]   See, e.g., Pipher v. Parsell, 930 A.2d 890 (Del. 2007) (driver of private automobile owed duty to passenger to guard against another passenger's foreseeable interference with safe driving). However, many courts are quite cautious in recognizing a duty based on a "special relationship" that does not fit within a recognized category. See, e.g., Hurn v. Greenway, 293 P.3d 480 (Alaska 2013) (defendant danced provocatively with a woman, while both the woman and her husband were guests on his property; no special relationship between defendant and either the victim or the attacker; attack had nothing to do with land possession and was also unforeseeable); Ouch v. Khea, 963 A.2d 630 (R.I. 2009) (no duty owed by driver to passengers who were members of the same "street gang" to protect them from intentional criminal acts of rival gang members).

[34]   See, e.g., Commonwealth v. Peterson, 749 S.E.2d 307 (Va. 2013) (no duty owed by state to warn Virginia Tech students about the possibility of a shooter on campus, after officials had begun investigating off-campus shooting and believed that shooter had fled the area and posed no danger to others); O'Brien v. Synnott, 72 A.3d 331 (Vt. 2013) (hospital and nurse owed no duty to patient to protect him from alleged attacks by police officers while he was in the hospital, where such attacks were not reasonably foreseeable).

landowner, usually a business enterprise open to the public, and an invitee or other person properly on the premises. This category includes the specific relationships between carrier and passenger; innkeeper and guest; and to some extent, landlord and tenant.[35] (2) Custodian and ward, a category that includes jailers and their prisoners, persons institutionalized with severe mental or physical disabilities, and an indeterminate number of other custodial or caretaker relationships.[36] (3) Schools and students.[37] (4) Spouses, and parents and children.[38] (5) Employers and their employees.[39]

§ 26.4 Landowner's Duty to Protect Lawful Entrants

Recognizing a Duty of Care

Earlier decisions recognized that carriers, innkeepers, theaters, fairs and places of public entertainment owed affirmative duties of reasonable care to protect their customers and sometimes to others rightfully upon their premises. Those duties included the duty to take reasonable steps to protect against acts of third persons[40] and, if reasonable, to provide aid when a customer or passenger is attacked by others.[41] The rule today is usually generalized to include all private landowners who open their land to the public for business[42] and even to colleges with respect to their students.[43] The rule requires such landowners to use reasonable care to protect against both foreseeable negligence[44] and foreseeable criminal acts of third persons.[45] If landowners create dangerous conditions attracting crime, even landowners whose premises are not open to the public may be under a duty of care.[46]

Earlier cases sometimes focused on specific events taking place in the defendant's presence. For example, a tavern that permitted a man to drink all day long and into the night, causing "trouble" from time to time, could be found to have been negligent in failing to deal with the marathon drinker before he finally caused an injury.[47] There are still cases in this pattern.[48] For instance, when one customer hit another in a Taco Bell, then adjourned to the parking lot for a serious beating, Taco Bell was liable because its employees unreasonably failed to call for police.[49] Some courts continue to limit liability

---

[35]   See § 26.5.

[36]   See § 26.6. Some courts have recognized that the relationship between hospital and patient gives rise to a duty of reasonable care to protect the patient from third-party attack, although the contours of such a duty are not clear. See McSwane v. Bloomington Hosp. & Healthcare Sys., 916 N.E.2d 906 (Ind. 2009) (but suggesting no breach of duty, and holding the duty did not extend to protection from off-premises attack).

[37]   See § 26.6.

[38]   Id.

[39]   See § 26.8.

[40]   See Smith v. Cumberland County Agricultural Soc'y, 163 N.C. 346, 79 S.E. 632 (1913) ("fairs, shows and theaters").

[41]   Todd v. Mass Transit Admin., 373 Md. 149, 816 A.2d 930 (2003). See § 408.

[42]   Restatement Second of Torts § 344 (1965).

[43]   Stanton v. University of Maine System, 773 A.2d 1045 (Me. 2001).

[44]   Marshall v. Burger King Corp., 222 Ill. 2d 422, 856 N.E.2d 1048, 305 Ill. Dec. 897 (2006).

[45]   E.g., Nallan v. Helmsley-Spear, Inc., 50 N.Y.2d 507, 429 N.Y.S.2d 606, 407 N.E.2d 451 (1980). See also § 15.14. The victim may still face difficulty in proving factual cause. See Saelzler v. Advanced Group 400, 25 Cal. 4th 763, 23 P.3d 1143, 107 Cal. Rptr.2d 617 (2001) (better security would have made premises safer, but not necessarily for the particular plaintiff, whose attackers might have been able to enter premises and might have eluded patrols). On this problem, see § 14.8.

[46]   See Nixon v. Mr. Property Management Co., 690 S.W.2d 546 (Tex. 1985) (vacant apartment, no lock).

[47]   Greco v. Sumner Tavern, Inc., 333 Mass. 144, 128 N.E.2d 788 (1955).

[48]   E.g., Cullum v. McCool, 432 S.W.3d 829 (Tenn. 2013).

[49]   Gould v. Taco Bell, 239 Kan. 564, 722 P.2d 511 (1986).

to such cases of imminent harm, and to those in which the defendant's method of doing business attracts crime.[50]

Other contemporary decisions go a step beyond these cases by imposing a duty of antecedent care, that is, to use care against harms that are generally foreseeable even when the wrongdoer's presence is not known and the wrongdoer himself not specifically identifiable. In particular, courts have imposed liability upon landowners when crime against patrons is foreseeable and when the landowner could reasonably have prevented shootings,[51] robberies,[52] beatings,[53] rapes,[54] or killings,[55] in office buildings, grocery stores, hospitals and other places of business, or in their parking lots or perimeters.[56] Even courts that limit the landowner's duties to protection from ongoing or imminent crime may extend liability to all foreseeable crimes in the case of a carrier or innkeeper.[57]

Foreseeability of Crime

Totality of circumstances approach. One major issue that has drawn the courts' attention has been whether the defendant's duty is triggered only when he knows or should know of similar incidents of crime on his own property or nearby. On this point the courts are split. One view is that ordinary negligence rules apply, meaning that foreseeability is a question of fact and turns on the evidence, not on a rule requiring specific crimes like the one that resulted in harm to the plaintiff. Similarly, violent incidents in the neighborhood might be enough to alert the defendant that crime could spread to his own property.[58] Indeed, a business might foresee criminal attacks in a dark parking garage even if none had ever occurred there before,[59] and certainly might foresee attacks in a blind spot in its parking lot adjacent to a place where people loitered to drink and where 60 incidents of other kinds of crime had been noted.[60] Even a private homeowner needs no prior incidents to foresee that if she permits a man subject to delusions to live in her home and store weapons there, disaster is around the corner.[61]

---

[50]   Dudas v. Glenwood Golf Club, Inc., 261 Va. 133, 540 S.E.2d 129 (2001).

[51]   Nallan v. Helmsley-Spear, Inc., 50 N.Y.2d 507, 429 N.Y.S.2d 606, 407 N.E.2d 451 (1980).

[52]   Butler v. Acme Markets, Inc., 89 N.J. 270, 445 A.2d 1141 (1982).

[53]   Paragon Family Restaurant v. Bartolini, 799 N.E.2d 1048 (Ind. 2003); Del Lago Partners, Inc. v. Smith, 307 S.W.3d 762 (Tex. 2010) (purporting to apply a general foreseeability test, but noting that the defendant actually knew that the harm to the plaintiff was imminent).

[54]   Madden v. C & K Barbecue Carryout, Inc., 758 S.W.2d 59 (Mo. 1988); Bray v. St. John Health System, Inc., 187 P.3d 721 (Okla. 2008).

[55]   Sharpe v. Peter Pan Bus Lines, Inc., 401 Mass. 788, 519 N.E.2d 1341 (1988).

[56]   The limit of the owner's property is usually the limit of the owner's obligation. See McSwane v. Bloomington Hospital and Health Care System, 916 N.E.2d 906 (Ind. 2009); Simpson v. Big Bear Stores Co., 73 Ohio St.3d 130, 652 N.E.2d 702 (1995); Estate of Desir ex rel. Estiverne v. Vertus, 214 N.J. 303, 69 A.3d 1247 (2013). Some courts decline to draw the boundary line as brightly. See, e.g., Banks v. Hyatt Corp., 722 F.2d 214 (5th Cir. 1984) (maintenance of security patrols off property could enlarge duty-area); Novak v. Capital Management & Development Corp., 432 F.3d 902 (D.C. Cir. 2006) (where defendant made "substantial special use" of an alley, and attack was foreseeable), *after remand,* Novak v. Capital Management & Development Corp., 570 F.3d 305 (D.C. Cir. 2009) (affirming plaintiff's verdict); Reynolds v. CB Sports Bar, Inc., 623 F.3d 1143 (7th Cir. 2010) (duty to protect bar patron from off-premises attack, where the bar's employees knew or should have known that two other patrons were getting the plaintiff intoxicated in the bar for the purpose of sexually exploiting her elsewhere).

[57]   See Taboada v. Daly Seven, Inc., 271 Va. 313, 626 S.E.2d 428 (2006).

[58]   See Isaacs v. Huntington Memorial Hosp., 38 Cal.3d 112, 211 Cal.Rptr. 356, 695 P.2d 653 (1985); Monk v. Temple George Associates, LLC, 273 Conn. 108, 869 A.2d 179 (2005) (but saying that foreseeability alone cannot trigger a duty if public policy cuts against it).

[59]   See Small v. McKennan Hospital, 437 N.W.2d 194 (S.D. 1989).

[60]   Clohesy v. Food Circus Supermarkets, Inc. 149 N.J. 496, 694 A.2d 1017 (1997).

[61]   Volpe v. Gallagher, 821 A.2d 699 (R.I. 2003).

Some courts are now calling this approach the "totality of circumstances" approach. The label may suggest that it reflects a special rule, but as the New Jersey Court said, it is only the ordinary negligence rule, which determines foreseeability by considering "all the factors a reasonably prudent person would consider,"[62] no more, no less.[63]

Specific similar incidents and other requirements. A more conservative view insists that the landowner has no duty of reasonable care to the customer unless similar incidents had occurred. But even this similar-incident requirement does not limit liability to those harms that are identical to those that have previously been inflicted on the property or in the neighborhood.[64] One court, in a case of an alleged rape at a shopping mall, observed that "[f]oreseeability does not require identical crimes in identical locations. Violent crimes against women, particularly, serve sufficient notice to reasonable individuals that other violent crimes, including sexual assault or rape of women, may occur."[65]

Business attracting wrongdoers. Perhaps the most demanding rule of all holds that the defendant is under no duty of care unless his business is operated in a way that actually attracts wrongdoers, or the defendant knows of a presently occurring assault.[66]

Specific similar incidents required when risk is low or cost of safety is high—"the balancing test and beyond." In 1993, California said that when the defendant's supposed negligence lies in the failure to take costly safety precautions such as posting security guards, "a high degree of foreseeability is required" and that this rule would ordinarily require evidence of "prior similar incidents of violent crime on the landowner's premises."[67] As noted in an earlier chapter,[68] locutions that refer to degrees of foreseeability usually mean risk or probability, so the court's statement appears to mean that the foreseeable risk or probability of harm must be high in order to impose a duty that requires an added heavy expense such as a security guard. This is the balancing of probability of harm against the burden of taking effective precautions. And when the attack on the plaintiff is imminent or actually taking place in the landowner's presence, the landowner may owe invitees a duty of reasonable care, because in that case no deep analysis is required to foresee that injury may result.[69] In addition, the limitations on the special-relationship duty would not necessarily apply to a duty based on the landowner's undertaking; that duty would depend on what the landowner undertook to do and whether his action induced reliance or increased the risk of harm.[70]

Some other courts have adopted a "balancing" approach to the threshold issue of duty under which a more onerous burden would be imposed as probability of harm increases, a balance in which prior similar incidents play an important but not

---

[62]   Clohesy v. Food Circus Supermarkets, Inc. 149 N.J. 496, 507, 694 A.2d 1017, 1023 (1997).

[63]   See Boren v. Worthen Nat'l Bank of Arkansas, 324 Ark. 416, 921 S.W.2d 934 (1996) (rejecting the "totality of circumstances" approach on the ground that it "would result in the imposition of a duty to guard against random criminal acts by third parties" and would penalize businesses operating in high-crime areas).

[64]   See Sturbridge Partners, Ltd. v. Walker, 267 Ga. 785, 482 S.E.2d 339 (1997) (landlord's knowledge of several prior burglaries might be enough to show that rape of a tenant was foreseeable).

[65]   L.A.C. v. Ward Parkway Shopping Ctr. Co., 75 S.W.3d 247 (Mo. 2002).

[66]   Burns v. Johnson, 250 Va. 41, 458 S.E.2d 448 (1995).

[67]   Ann M. v. Pacific Plaza Shopping Center, 6 Cal.4th 666, 863 P.2d 207, 25 Cal.Rptr.2d 137 (1993).

[68]   See § 12.2.

[69]   Morris v. De La Torre, 36 Cal. 4th 260, 113 P.3d 1182, 30 Cal. Rptr. 3d 173 (2005).

[70]   Delgado v. Trax Bar & Grill, 36 Cal. 4th 224, 249, 113 P.3d 1159, 1175, 30 Cal. Rptr. 3d 145, 164 (2005). On undertakings, see §§ 25.6 & 25.7.

necessarily a determinative part.[71] Conversely, this view leaves room to say that if the plaintiff claims only that low-cost protection should have been afforded—that a warning should have been given or that the parking lot should have been better lighted or covered with a surveillance camera—prior similar incidents may not be required.[72]

A requirement of prior similar incidents as a precondition to a duty is an application of the usual risk-utility balance in the sense that it weighs costs of safety against the probable harm. It differs from the usual risk-utility balance in two related and important ways. As a precondition to a duty, the balance is performed by judges, not juries, and it is turned into something like a rule of law for all cases rather than a guide to adjudication of particular cases that may arise.

Foreseeable Actions Actuated by Unforeseeable Criminal Intent

In most cases, liability of the landowner has turned on whether the landowner could reasonably have foreseen criminal conduct of the type that caused harm to the plaintiff.[73] But in *Wiener v. Southcoast Childcare Centers, Inc.,*[74] the criminal actor triggered events that were arguably foreseeable, even if the criminality itself was not. One of the defendants operated a child-daycare center, while the other was the landlord. The playground was on a busy intersection virtually at road level and only four feet away from the street. Its fence was allegedly inadequate to prevent motor vehicles from crashing into the playground, and a motor vehicle did so, killing two children.

The vehicle driven into the playground was a Cadillac operated with murderous intent by a man named Abrams. The parties seem to have taken it as a given that Abrams' criminal behavior was so unlikely that, standing alone, the defendant would not be negligent in failing to protect against such a risk. But the risk of traffic incursions by drivers who wish to murder small children arguably did not stand alone. Instead, it could be viewed as a risk subsumed in a much larger and more probable set of risks— those risks of vehicular incursions into the playground resulting from mere negligence of drivers or even from non-negligent accidents. If vehicular incursions are foreseeable, the plaintiff argued, it would not matter that the foreseeable incursion in the particular case was actuated by criminal intent. The same kind of harm resulted, from the same kind of forces that were foreseeable, and the precautions to avoid the harm would be

---

[71]   Hurn v. Greenway, 293 P.3d 480 (Alaska 2013); Posecai v. Wal-Mart Stores, Inc., 752 So.2d 762 (La. 1999); Bass v. Gopal, Inc., 395 S.C. 129, 716 S.E.2d 910 (2011); McClung v. Delta Square Ltd. P'ship, 937 S.W.2d 891, 901 (Tenn.1996). Thus if the plaintiff claims that a business should have maintained expensive security guards, a high probability of criminal injury or death might be required as a matter of law by casting the question as one of duty; but if the plaintiff only claims that lighting should have been better to discourage criminal attacks, the court applying a balancing test may recognize a duty of reasonable care and leave it to the trier to determine whether the business was negligent in failing to have better lighting. See Pinsonneault v. Merchants & Farmers Bank & Trust Co., 816 So.2d 270 (La. 2002).

[72]   The California Supreme Court has continued to apply a requirement of "heightened foreseeability" in the context of third-party criminal acts, see Wiener v. Southcoast Childcare Centers, Inc., 32 Cal. 4th 1138, 1149–1150, 88 P.3d 517, 524, 12 Cal. Rptr. 3d 615, 623 (2004), but has indicated that the "heightened foreseeability" required to impose heavy burdens of precaution is not required to impose a duty of reasonable care that entails only simple or minimal burdens. Delgado v. Trax Bar & Grill, 36 Cal. 4th 224, 145, 113 P.3d 1159, 1172, 30 Cal. Rptr. 3d 145, 161 (2005). See also Sigmund v. Starwood Urban Retail VI, LLC, 617 F.3d 512 (D.C. Cir. 2010) (D.C. law requires "precise proof of a heightened showing of foreseeability" in third-party criminal-attack cases).

[73]   A court may use proximate cause as the vehicle for a defense judgment, on a finding that the intervening criminal act was unforeseeable. See, e.g., Double Quick, Inc. v. Moore, 73 So. 3d 1162 (Miss. 2011).

[74]   Wiener v. Southcoast Childcare Centers, Inc., 32 Cal.4th 1138, 88 P.3d 517, 12 Cal.Rptr.3d 615 (2004).

exactly those that were required anyway in response to the risk of non-criminal incursions.

The court held that the daycare center operator and the landlord were under no duty to the children in their care to protect them from the criminal driver. First, it held that the probability of harm must be especially high to warrant liability for criminal acts and that such probability was not demonstrated on the facts. Second, it held that even if the daycare center could foresee that inadequate fencing would permit deadly vehicular incursions, the defendant would still have no duty to erect a better fence. Instead, the defendant would escape responsibility unless it could foresee that the vehicle entering the playground would be driven by a person with criminal intent.[75] Third, the court appeared to say that in any event even ordinary, non-criminal intrusions were unforeseeable, so the operator would owe no duty to care to protect the child even from accidental automobile injuries, much less a duty to protect them from intentional ones.[76]

The second holding in *Wiener* addressed liability for foreseeable harms resulting from improbable motives. As the court saw it, the motive or criminal intent itself, not merely the forces launched by that intent, had to be foreseeable before the defendant would owe a duty. In so holding, court was in effect rejecting the view that a duty of care arises when the defendant can foresee the same general kind of harm that actually occurred and from the same general kinds of forces that were actually in play.

Limiting Duty or Finding No Negligence

Even when risks are entirely foreseeable, the landowner or business is not necessarily liable for crimes against invitees or others, since the duty is only to exercise reasonable care, not to guarantee safety.[77] If the risk of assault upon customers is small (and not generated by the business itself), good lighting alone may satisfy the duty of reasonable care. In other cases, a reasonable business might be expected to give a warning of danger, or to eliminate hiding places from which an assault might be launched, or even to provide security guards. But a manager's informal patrol of the parking lot every half-hour may readily satisfy the duty of reasonable care in many situations.[78] To a large extent, the issue of whether the duty of care is breached is for the jury to decide if reasonable people could differ.[79]

---

[75] Wiener, 32 Cal. 4th at 1148–1149, 88 P.3d at 525, 12 Cal. Rptr. 3d at 622–623 ("[O]ur cases analyze third party criminal acts differently from ordinary negligence, and require us to apply a heightened sense of foreseeability before we can hold a defendant liable for the criminal acts of third parties.").

[76] "[I]n the present action, the one freak accident involving a runaway mail truck in which no one was injured could have occurred anywhere, at any time. That fact, together with the evidence indicating the physical layout of defendants' fence and the playground had adequately protected the children against all other intrusions, was simply inadequate to make any automobile intrusion through the fence foreseeable." Wiener, 32 Cal. 4th at 1150, 88 P.3d at 524, 12 Cal. Rptr. 3d at 624.

[77] See Monk v. Temple George Associates, LLC, 273 Conn. 108, 869 A.2d 179 (2005) (finding material issues of fact on whether defendant was negligent and whether any negligence was a cause of the harm, in a case involving an attack in defendant's parking garage); Bass v. Gopal, Inc., 395 S.C. 129, 716 S.E.2d 910 (2011) (affirming summary judgment for motel in negligence case brought by guest shot by an assailant on the property; while a duty was owed, plaintiff failed to adduce any evidence that respondent's preventive actions were unreasonable given the degree of risk). See also Double Quick, Inc. v. Moore, 73 So.3d 1162 (Miss. 2011) (reversing trial court's denial of defense motion for summary judgment in premises liability action against convenience store sued for negligence in failing to protect victim from fatal shooting; plaintiff failed to produce evidence that the fatal shooting was reasonably foreseeable, thus case failed on proximate cause grounds).

[78] See Kelly v. Retzer & Retzer, Inc., 417 So.2d 556 (Miss. 1982).

[79] See Draper Mortuary v. Superior Court, 135 Cal. App.3d 533, 185 Cal. Rptr. 396 (1982) (sexual assault on body in mortuary, jury question whether mortuary had exercised reasonable care).

Some cases, however, may be carved out for special treatment. When an armed robber demands funds from a business, noncompliance may endanger patrons, but even so, the Supreme Court of California has said that the business has no duty to give in to the robber's demands, and if its resistance provokes the robber to injure the plaintiff standing nearby, the plaintiff has no complaint.[80] Some other authority has taken a similar position on similar facts.[81] Such cases, however, do not reject the landowner's duty of care wholesale; they simply carve out exceptions.

§ 26.5   Landlord's Duty to Protect Tenants and Their Guests

Affirmatively creating risks. In one class of cases, the duty of landlords and condominium associations to protect tenants and their guests[82] from thefts or from attacks by humans or animals, turns on the fact that the landlord actually helped to create a danger,[83] for example, by leasing to dangerous tenants or failing to restrict their dangerous activities.[84] Perhaps the landlord who stores combustibles in an area where many people are known to toss cigarettes can likewise be seen as creating or cooperating in the creation of unreasonable risk of fire that could harm tenants.[85] Certainly a landlord who allows a dangerous employee to have access to the apartment keys of a tenant has created a foreseeable risk of violent attack on that tenant.[86]

Failing to maintain reasonably safe premises. In a second group of cases, the landlord does not necessarily create the immediate danger but he fails to protect the tenant from an attacker by employing adequate door locks or otherwise. The traditional starting point was that the landlord who did not create the danger owed the tenant no duty to protect the tenant from the criminal acts of third persons, but many courts have now imposed a duty of reasonable care to maintain the physical condition of the premises so as to minimize the risk of criminal attacks.[87] While it might be fair to say that the

---

[80]   Kentucky Fried Chicken of California, Inc. v. Superior Court, 14 Cal.4th 814, 927 P.2d 1260, 59 Cal.Rptr.2d 756 (1997).

[81]   Boyd v. Racine Currency Exchange, Inc., 56 Ill.2d 95, 306 N.E.2d 39 (1973) (robber who demanded that a teller give him money, else he would shoot a customer; the teller didn't and the robber did, killing Boyd; a duty of care on these facts would only benefit criminals, who would then be encouraged to take hostages).

[82]   The duty of landlords and condominiums runs not only to the tenant but to the tenant's guests. Martinez v. Woodmar IV Condominiums Homeowners Ass'n, Inc., 189 Ariz. 206, 941 P.2d 218 (1997); Thomas v. Columbia Group, LLC, 969 So.2d 849 (Miss. 2007).

[83]   Where a person actively creates a risk of harm, a no-duty rule has no logical application. See § 26.2.

[84]   Samson v. Saginaw Professional Bldg., Inc., 393 Mich. 393, 224 N.W.2d 843 (1975) (commercial lease to innocuously named mental health clinic whose major clients were convicted criminals on parole; no warning to other tenants, liability for attack by clinic's criminal client on employee of commercial tenant). Liability for leasing to known gang members is difficult to impose, largely because of anti-discrimination laws that remove many of the landlord's options. Casteneda v. Olsher, 41 Cal.4th 1205, 63 Cal. Rptr. 3d 99, 162 P.3d 610 (2007). Many courts have been reluctant to impose a duty on landlords to control tenants' pets. See e.g., Smaxwell v. Bayard, 274 Wis.2d 278, 682 N.W.2d 923 (2004) (as a matter of public policy, the landlord/landowner who was not an owner or keeper of the pets would not be liable; there would be no sensible stopping place for liability).

[85]   Scully v. Fitzgerald, 179 N.J. 114, 843 A.2d 1110 (2004).

[86]   See Or v. Edwards, 62 Mass. App. Ct. 475, 818 N.E.2d 163 (2004); see also Rowe v. State Bank of Lombard, 125 Ill.2d 203, 531 N.E.2d 1358, 126 Ill. Dec. 519 (1988) (landlord assumed a duty of care by retaining a copy of tenant's key and then allowing it to get into attacker's hands); but cf. Doe v. Linder Const. Co., 845 S.W.2d 173 (Tenn. 1992) (no liability on proximate cause grounds where owner-developer of planned-unit development failed to secure pass-keys to homes and plaintiff, a resident, was raped by a painter-paper hanger employed by defendant).

[87]   See Tracy A. Bateman & Susan Thomas, Annotation, Landlord's Liability For Failure to Protect Tenant From Criminal Acts of Third Person, 43 A.L.R.5th 207 (1996).

landlord always owes care that is reasonable in the light of all the circumstances,[88] what counts as reasonable care will ordinarily depend in part upon the landlord's express or implied undertakings, his representations, and his powers under the lease as well as upon foreseeability of harm.

Common areas. When a tenant has been attacked in common areas of the premises such as entrance halls, the landlord's control of the area together with foreseeable harm may suffice to impose a duty of reasonable care to provide appropriate doors, locks,[89] and lighting.[90] When the tenant is attacked in her apartment, landlords have been held liable for failure to use reasonable care for the tenant's safety for failing to repair locks or windows as required by the lease[91] or by statute,[92] for misrepresenting safety[93] or failing to disclose known dangers,[94] for failing to provide appropriate lighting of dangerous areas,[95] or otherwise maintaining conditions that would attract violent persons,[96] and for mishandling keys to the apartment.[97]

Landlord's undertaking as basis for duty. The landlord's undertaking, express or implied, as a term of the lease or otherwise, is often a basis for the duty to protect the tenant. A leading case[98] was a suit brought by a tenant in a large apartment building after she was attacked by an intruder in the hallway. When she had leased the apartment, the building had been protected by a doorman and other devices. At the time of the attack some years later, the doorman and other protections had been withdrawn, although assaults, larcenies, and robberies in common passages were common. The court held that, in light of the landlord's control over the common passageway, the special character of the modern urban multiple-unit lease, and the notice to the landlord of other attacks, the landlord owed her a duty of care. The acts required of the landlord to fulfill his duty of care, however, was dictated largely by contractual expectations—the landlord was required to provide the degree of protection that he himself had provided when the plaintiff first became a resident.

---

[88]   Sharp v. W.H. Moore, Inc., 118 Idaho 297, 796 P.2d 506 (1990); Tenney v. Atlantic Associates, 594 N.W.2d 11 (Iowa 1999); Nash v. Port Authority of New York and New Jersey, 51 A.D.3d 337, 856 N.Y.S.2d 583 (2008) (owner of World Trade Center had duty to take reasonable action to minimize the risk of harm from 1993 terrorist bombing; landlord's overarching duty is to act as a reasonable person in maintaining property in a reasonable condition in view of all the circumstances); but see Funchess v. Cecil Newman Corp., 632 N.W.2d 666 (Minn. 2001) (invoking no-duty rule).

[89]   Trentacost v. Brussel, 82 N.J. 214, 412 A.2d 436 (1980).

[90]   Duncavage v. Allen, 147 Ill.App.3d 88, 497 N.E.2d 433, 100 Ill.Dec. 455 (1986).

[91]   See Cordes v. Wood, 918 P.2d 76 (Okla. 1996).

[92]   See Brock v. Watts Realty Co., Inc., 582 So.2d 438 (Ala. 1991) (housing code violations).

[93]   See Veazey v. Elmwood Plantation Associates, Ltd., 650 So.2d 712 (La. 1994).

[94]   See O'Hara v. Western Seven Trees Corp., 75 Cal. App.3d 798, 142 Cal.Rptr. 487 (1977).

[95]   Poor lighting or other conditions outside the apartment may increase the tenant's vulnerability in the apartment. See Hemmings v. Pelham Wood Ltd. Liability Partnership, 375 Md. 522, 826 A.2d 443 (2003).

[96]   See Walls v. Oxford Management Co., 137 N.H. 653, 633 A.2d 103 (1993).

[97]   Rowe v. State Bank of Lombard, 125 Ill.2d 203, 531 N.E.2d 1358, 126 Ill. Dec. 519 (1988) (by retaining a copy of key and then allowing it to get into attacker's hands, landlord breached an implicitly assumed duty of care); Tenney v. Atlantic Associates, 594 N.W.2d 11 (Iowa 1999).

[98]   Kline v. 1500 Massachusetts Ave. Apt. Corp., 439 F.2d 477 (D.C. Cir. 1970).

Foreseeability of harm. Apart from the landlord's voluntary undertaking or assumption of a duty,[99] the usual claim depends in part on the foreseeability of harm,[100] and if harm is not foreseeable, no precaution is required.[101] Evidence of prior instances of crime in the general neighborhood is usually sufficient to show that intrusion and assault is foreseeable.[102] But even without incidents of crime, it is reasonable to say that harm is foreseeable when the condition of the landlord's premises or the landlord's careless key management facilitate entry into the tenant's private apartment; thus liability has been imposed in such cases.[103]

Commercial properties. The most common case for liability involves the lease of premises for residential purposes, usually in multi-unit properties, but liability has also been imposed upon landlords of commercial premises. The office worker attacked in an elevator[104] or on a vacant floor,[105] for example, stands in the shoes of the commercial tenant and is entitled to an equal measure of protection.

§ 26.6 Custodian's and School's State-Law Duty to Protect Wards or Students

Anyone who has custody of another owes a duty of reasonable care to protect that person from foreseeable harm.[106] A custodian may thus be held liable for failure to make reasonable efforts to protect a ward from a third person's attack or molestation, and even to protect the ward from his own self-destructive inclinations.

Jailers and custodians of mentally or physically disabled. Custodians include those who actually exercise control over their charges or who have legal authority to control them. One clear example is the jailer who holds prisoners in custody. By reason of his custody, the jailer owes the prisoner a duty of reasonable protection from attack[107] and from suicide.[108] The same point applies to an officer who takes a person into custody.[109]

---

[99] When the landlord undertakes a duty of care, his undertaking, not foreseeability, is the basis for and hence the measure of his responsibility. Thus where a landlord has undertaken to provide reasonable security measures such as exterior lighting, he must maintain such lighting in a reasonable manner. Hemmings v. Pelham Wood Ltd. Liability Partnership, 375 Md. 522, 826 A.2d 443 (2003).

[100] E.g., Trentacost v. Brussel, 82 N.J. 214, 412 A.2d 436 (1980) (75 or more incidents of crime against persons in neighborhood and in apartment house in recent years).

[101] See Timberwalk Apartments, Partners, Inc. v. Cain, 972 S.W.2d 749 (Tex. 1998) (no violent personal crimes in the apartment complex in the previous ten years; no duty to provide additional security).

[102] E.g., Jacqueline S. v. City of New York, 81 N.Y.2d 288, 614 N.E.2d 723, 598 N.Y.S.2d 160 (1993).

[103] Brock v. Watts Realty Co., 582 So.2d 438, 43 A.L.R.5th 839 (Ala. 1991) (statutory duty to keep locks in repair, similar incidents not required); Tenney v. Atlantic Associates, 594 N.W.2d 11 (Iowa 1999) (key management).

[104] Samson v. Saginaw Professional Bldg., Inc., 393 Mich. 393, 224 N.W.2d 843 (1975).

[105] See Doe v. Dominion Bank of Washington, N.A., 963 F.2d 1552 (D.C.Cir. 1992) (extending the principle of Kline v. 1500 Massachusetts Avenue Apartment Corp., 439 F.2d 477, 43 A.L.R.3d 311 (D.C. Cir. 1970), to commercial leases).

[106] See Restatement Second of Torts § 314A(4) (1965).

[107] See, e.g., Mattox v. State Dep't of Corrections, 323 P.3d 23 (Alaska 2014); Giraldo v. California Dep't of Corrections and Rehabilitation, 168 Cal.App.4th 231, 85 Cal.Rptr.3d 371 (2008) (citing cases from many jurisdictions).

[108] Joseph v. State, 26 P.3d 459 (Alaska 2001); Falkenstein v. City of Bismarck, 268 N.W.2d 787 (N.D. 1978).

[109] Jackson v. City of Kansas City, 263 Kan. 143, 947 P.2d 31 (1997) (arrestee attacked by his girlfriend while he was handcuffed). Jailers who fail in their duty might be held liable either under state tort law or under federal civil rights laws. See Estelle v. Gamble, 429 U.S. 97, 97 S.Ct. 285, 50 L.Ed.2d 251 (1976).

What is true of jailers is equally true of those who have custody of or caregiving responsibility for insane or incompetent persons.[110]

Hospitals and patients. Similarly, a hospital may be found to owe a duty of reasonable care to protect a patient from third-party attack and self-destructive acts. For example, a hospital may owe a duty to supervise a non-employee social worker who engaged in an improper sexual relationship with a patient.[111] And a hospital may be placed under a duty to take reasonable measures to protect a patient who presents observable signs of domestic abuse from further harm.[112]

Parents and children. Although the issue has seldom arisen, where parents cannot claim the traditional parental immunity they undoubtedly owe a duty of care to their unemancipated minor children so long as they have custody.[113] Other family members may also take custody of a child and if they do, they assume the protective obligations of custodians.[114] For instance, they may be obliged to protect a child from sexual abuse by others.[115] And a caretaker who does not have full-time custody but has undertaken to provide care for a child owes a duty as a result of the voluntary undertaking.[116]

Schools. Common lore has it that while children are in the charge of a school, the school stands *in loco parentis,* that is, in the role of parents.[117] That would mean that the school, during periods in which it has charge of students, would owe them the same duties as their parents, presumably the duty of reasonable care. Schools may be able to take advantage of parental or statutory immunities.[118] Absent an immunity, a school owes its students a duty of reasonable supervision[119] and other forms of reasonable protection, sometimes likened to that which parents would provide.[120] For breach of such duties, schools may be held responsible for a student's own self-harm or suicide,[121] although many cases have denied such recovery.[122] Schools may likewise be responsible

---

[110] See Niece v. Elmview Group Home, 131 Wash.2d 39, 929 P.2d 420 (1997) (group home for developmentally disabled); Regions Bank & Trust v. Stone County Skilled Nursing Facility, Inc., 345 Ark. 555, 49 S.W.3d 107 (2001) (nursing home); see also Youngberg v. Romeo, 457 U.S. 307, 102 S.Ct. 2452, 73 L.Ed.2d 28 (1982) (federal due process rights; state institution for the mentally retarded).

[111] Dragomir v. Spring Harbor Hospital, 970 A.2d 310 (Me. 2009).

[112] McSwane v. Bloomington Hospital and Healthcare System, 916 N.E.2d 906 (Ind. 2009) (but finding no breach of duty as a matter of law).

[113] See Hite v. Brown, 100 Ohio App.3d 606, 654 N.E.2d 452 (1995).

[114] A.R.H. v. W.H.S., 876 S.W.2d 687 (Mo. App. 1994) (grandmother); Kellermann v. McDonough, 278 Va. 478, 684 S.E.2d 786 (2009) (mother of friend of child who was entrusted by parents with child's welfare during visit to friend's house).

[115] Frideres v. Schiltz, 540 N.W.2d 261 (Iowa 1995); Werre v. David, 275 Mont. 376, 913 P.2d 625 (1996).

[116] See O.L. v. R. L., 62 S.W.3d 469 (Mo. App. 2001).

[117] McLeod v. Grant County School Dist. No. 128, 42 Wash.2d 316, 255 P.2d 360 (1953) ("the protective custody of teachers is mandatorily substituted for that of the parent").

[118] Stiff v. Eastern Illinois Area of Special Educ., 279 Ill. App. 3d 1076, 666 N.E.2d 343, 216 Ill. Dec. 893 (1996) (parental immunity); Henrich v. Libertyville High School, 186 Ill. 2d 381, 712 N.E.2d 298 (1998) (broad statutory immunity); Allan E. Korpela, Annotation, Modern Status of Doctrine of Sovereign Immunity as Applied to Public Schools and Institutions of Higher Learning, 33 A.L.R.3d 703 (1971).

[119] See, e.g., Eric M. v. Cajon Valley Union School Dist., 174 Cal.App.4th 285, 95 Cal.Rptr.3d 428 (2009); Jerkins v. Anderson, 191 N.J. 285, 922 A.2d 1279 (2007).

[120] Lunsford v. Board of Educ. of Prince George's County, 280 Md. 665, 374 A.2d 1162 (1977).

[121] Eisel v. Board of Educ. of Montgomery County, 324 Md. 376, 597 A.2d 447, 17 A.L.R.5th 957 (Ct. App. 1991). Statutes may cover this area. See Carrier v. Lake Pend Oreille School Dist., 142 Idaho 804, 134 P.3d 655 (2006) (construing Idaho Code § 33–512B, which places a teacher or district under a duty to warn of a student's "suicidal tendencies" only when the teacher has "direct knowledge" such tendencies).

[122] See Mikell v. School Admin. Unit No. 33, 158 N.H. 723, 972 A.2d 1050 (2009); see also Rogers v. Christina School Dist., 73 A.3d 1 (Del. 2013) (no liability on general negligence theory, but defendant might be

for a student's injury from attack,[123] harassment,[124] or molestation by outsiders,[125] other students,[126] and, in some cases, by teachers or other school staff.[127] Injury generated outside the school property, outside of curricular or extra-curricular activities, and from sources unconnected to the school,[128] is not likely to be the school's responsibility.[129]

As in most other negligence cases, liability is imposed only if the defendant's negligent conduct caused the harm complained of.[130] And of course the duty imposed under these rules is only a duty of reasonable care, so liability does not follow unless the school breached its duty. If the harm was not reasonably foreseeable, or if the school took reasonable precautions in the light of foreseeable harm, it simply is not negligent and liability cannot be imposed.[131] But harm from third persons may be foreseeable in some situations even if it has not occurred before and if so, reasonable protection is required.[132]

Sexual harassment or abuse in schools. Sexual harassment in schools presents complex legal problems which the common law of tort deals with only in part.[133] If a student is sexually molested by a member of the school staff, she presumably has an ordinary battery claim against her molester. Because a teacher's sexual conduct toward students is often regarded as outside the scope of his employment,[134] liability often must be based upon the school's negligence in hiring or retaining a dangerous person[135] or in

---

negligent per se based on violation of state Education Code). As an alternative to a no-duty ruling, a student's suicide may be held to be a superseding intervening cause. See Corales v. Bennett, 567 F.3d 554 (9th Cir. 2009) (applying California law).

[123] See A.W. v. Lancaster County School Dist. 0001, 280 Neb. 205, 784 N.W.2d 907 (2010).

[124] See, e.g., Zeno v. Pine Plains Cent. School Dist., 702 F.3d 655 (2d Cir. 2012) (affirming jury verdict against school district in case brought under Title VI, where defendant allowed plaintiff's fellow high school students to racially harass him for three and a half years).

[125] Fazzolari v. Portland School Dist. No. 1J, 303 Or. 1, 734 P.2d 1326 (1987).

[126] Jennifer C. v. Los Angeles Unified School Dist., 168 Cal.App.4th 1320, 86 Cal.Rptr.3d 274 (2008); Mirand v. City of New York, 84 N.Y.2d 44, 614 N.Y.S. 2d 372, 637 N.E.2d 263 (1994); McLeod v. Grant County School Dist. No. 128, 42 Wash.2d 316, 255 P.2d 360 (1953).

[127] C.A. v. William S. Hart Union High School Dist., 53 Cal. 4th 861, 138 Cal. Rptr. 3d 1, 270 P.3d 699 (2012); Doe Parents No. 1 v. State, Dep't of Educ., 100 Hawai'i 34, 58 P.3d 545 (2002); Marquay v. Eno, 139 N.H. 708, 662 A.2d 272 (1995). Statutes sometimes grant immunity to teachers for acts and omissions resulting from the supervision, care or discipline of students, as long as the teacher acts in good faith and does not engage in gross negligence or willful misconduct. See, e.g., Va. Code Ann. § 8.01–220.1:2.

[128] Statutes requiring the report of suspected child abuse may require teachers as well as some others to report incidents of abuse, including abuse inflicted by third persons entirely outside the school setting, see Kimberly S.M. v. Bradford Central School, 226 A.D.2d 85, 649 N.Y.S.2d 588 (1996), but many courts have held that violation of these statutes is not negligence per se. See, e.g., Perry v. S.N., 973 S.W.2d 301 (Tex. 1998).

[129] See Stoddart v. Pocatello School Dist. No. L25, 149 Idaho 679, 239 P.3d 784 (2010); Young v. Salt Lake City School Dist., 52 P.3d 1230 (Utah 2002); Edson v. Barre Supervisory Union No. 61, 182 Vt. 157, 933 A.2d 200 (2007); but see Jerkins v. Anderson, 191 N.J. 285, 922 A.2d 1279 (2007) (school's duty of reasonable supervision requires school to create reasonable dismissal policies to protect students as the school day ends).

[130] E.g., Skinner v. Vacaville Unified School Dist., 37 Cal.App.4th 31, 43 Cal.Rptr.2d 384 (1995); Doe A. v. Coffee County Board of Educ., 925 S.W.2d 534 (Tenn. App. 1996).

[131] See Beshears v. United School District No. 305, 261 Kan. 555, 930 P.2d 1376 (1997) (after-school, off-grounds fight was unforeseeable and school is not liable for injuries inflicted; expressed as a no-duty rule).

[132] E.g., Garcia v. City of New York, 222 A.D.2d 192, 646 N.Y.S.2d 508 (1996) (small child allowed to go to bathroom alone in violation of school safety rules was sexually assaulted, judgment for plaintiff affirmed).

[133] L.W. ex rel. L.G. v. Toms River Regional Schools Board of Educ., 189 N.J. 381, 915 A.2d 535 (2007) (applying state Law against Discrimination statute, which creates a cause of action against a school district for student-on-student sexual-orientation harassment).

[134] John R. v. Oakland Unified School Dist., 48 Cal.3d 438, 256 Cal.Rptr. 766, 769 P.2d 948 (1989); P. L. v. Aubert, 545 N.W.2d 666 (Minn. 1996).

[135] See § 26.11; cf. C.A. v. William S. Hart Union High School Dist., 53 Cal. 4th 861, 138 Cal. Rptr. 3d 1, 270 P.3d 699 (2012) (school district vicariously liable for the negligence of school administrators in the supervision of employees who abused student); Randi W. v. Muroc Joint Unified School District, 14 Cal.4th

failing to report or otherwise deal with cases of known or suspected abuse of this kind. Given the purpose of the teacher's vocation and the school's relationship to its students, it is appropriate to impose upon the school a duty of care that includes protection from sexual exploitation and abuse. Reasonable care might, for example, include reasonable supervision of students and teachers; it might also require a report to authorities who can control the abuser's conduct or dismiss him.[136] The duty is only one of reasonable care. If the school has no notice that a teacher is a risk for sexual or other abusive misconduct, the school simply is not negligent and is not liable.[137]

Colleges. Colleges may act in a number of different roles. Either as colleges having a relationship to students, or as landlords of student housing, they may be under a duty to protect their tenants from attack by supplying appropriate door locks or otherwise.[138] A student might also be considered as an invitee and entitled to an invitee's protections.[139] Colleges might, again like others, undertake duties of care by promises or representations.[140] Likewise, a college may be under a duty of care to avoid assigning students to unreasonably dangerous sites for off-campus internships or the like.[141] In each case, the duty is only one of reasonable care, and liability will follow only where all elements of the prima facie case are proved.[142]

Because college students are regarded as independent adults, many courts have refused to impose upon colleges any duty to protect them from the pressures of college life.[143] When the college knows that one of its students poses a serious danger to others, some authority requires the college to exercise reasonable care to protect students who may be victimized.[144] But some courts have been unwilling to require colleges to exercise

---

1066, 60 Cal. Rptr.2d 263, 929 P. 2d 582 (1997) (allegation that defendant, with knowledge of the problem, negligently recommended a sexually dangerous person to a school, with resulting molestation of student at the new school).

[136] See Marquay v. Eno, 139 N.H. 708, 662 A.2d 272 (1995) (distinguishing between school personnel who have relationships to students and owe a duty for that reason and school personnel who have responsibility for hiring and firing; the latter may owe duties of care in selecting teachers and discharging them).

[137] E.g., Moore v. Berkeley County School Dist., 326 S.C. 584, 486 S.E.2d 9 (1997) (school knew that teacher ran a lax classroom but had no notice that she was having sex with students; no liability).

[138] Mullins v. Pine Manor College, 389 Mass. 47, 449 N.E.2d 331 (1983); Miller v. State, 62 N.Y.2d 506, 467 N.E.2d 493, 478 N.Y.S.2d 829 (1984).

[139] Stanton v. University of Maine System, 773 A.2d 1045 (Me. 2001); Nero v. Kansas State University, 253 Kan. 567, 861 P.2d 768 (1993).

[140] George v. University of Idaho, 121 Idaho 30, 822 P.2d 549 (Ct.App. 1991) (faculty-student handbook and customs; university's failure to prevent repeated sexual harassment by law professor); Delaney v. University of Houston, 835 S.W.2d 56 (Tex. 1992) (assurance of security, failure to repair broken lock).

[141] Nova Southeastern University, Inc. v. Gross, 758 So.2d 86 (Fla. 2000).

[142] See Hall v. Board of Supervisors Southern University, 405 So.2d 1125 (La. App. 1991) (no proof of breach or factual cause); Brown v. North Carolina Wesleyan College, 65 N.C. App. 579, 309 S.E.2d 701 (1983) (no breach of duty).

[143] See Jain v. State, 617 N.W.2d 293 (Iowa 2000) (no duty to warn college student's parents that their son had attempted suicide earlier, where university did not have "custody" of student and did nothing to increase the risk of his suicide); Beach v. University of Utah, 726 P.2d 413, 62 A.L.R.4th 67 (Utah 1986).

[144] E.g., Nero v. Kansas State University, 253 Kan. 567, 861 P.2d 768 (1993) but cf. Commonwealth v. Peterson, 749 S.E.2d 307 (Va. 2013) (no duty to warn Virginia Tech students about the possibility of a shooter on campus, after officials had begun investigating off-campus shooting and believed that shooter had fled the area and posed no danger to others).

reasonable care to protect one college student from another,[145] even when the college knows it has admitted a dangerous student.[146]

§ 26.7 Federal Civil Rights Claims

Formal custody has been of controlling importance in the analysis of federal civil rights duties to protect from third persons.[147] The Supreme Court has recognized that the custodial relationship imposes affirmative duties upon a custodian, both in the case of a prisoner[148] and an involuntarily committed mental patient.[149] In the *DeShaney* case,[150] the county department of social services took temporary custody of a small child, Joshua, because of evidence that he was being abused by his father. The department returned the child to his father under an agreement with the father that established the department's right to monitor Joshua's safety. The department in fact regularly sent a caseworker, but in spite of mounting evidence that he was being savagely beaten, the caseworker did nothing to regain control. Joshua's father's beatings finally produced profound brain damage and left Joshua confined for life in an institution for the profoundly retarded. The Court held, however, that the department did not have custody of Joshua even though it had the practical power to obtain custody and had taken a number of inadequate steps to protect him. For the Court, "custody" meant depriving the plaintiff of liberty so that he could no longer protect himself or obtain aid from others. Because Joshua was not in custody in this strict sense, no civil rights action would lie.[151] Although as a matter of ordinary tort law, defendants are often under a duty of care because they voluntarily assumed such a duty by acts or promises, *DeShaney* might be read to mean that such undertakings have no constitutional significance unless state action makes the plaintiff worse off than no state action.[152]

Children in foster homes. The strict custody requirement of the *DeShaney* case does not foreclose a constitutionally based duty of care when the public entity actually takes guardianship of a child and then fails to exercise appropriate custodial supervision, with the result that the child is injured or killed.[153] For instance, the state officers who take charge of a child and then knowingly or indifferently[154] place her in a dangerous foster

---

[145] See Tanja H. v. Regents of Univ. of Cal., 228 Cal.App.3d 434, 278 Cal.Rptr. 918 (1991) (college's failure to enforce its own drinking rules, allegedly resulting in a dormitory sexual assault).

[146] Varner v. District of Columbia, 891 A.2d 260 (D.C. 2006) (dismissing a complaint that university negligently dealt with a dangerous student, who was left free to, and did, murder another student); Eiseman v. State, 70 N.Y.2d 175, 518 N.Y.S.2d 608, 511 N.E.2d 1128 (1987).

[147] Liability does not always turn on custody, however. A public entity that focuses on the plight of particular children at risk for domestic injury has undertaken a duty of care and may become liable for negligence in failing to protect the children. See District of Columbia v. Harris, 770 A.2d 82 (D.C. 2001). Federal constitutional rights may also be violated and a federal civil rights action may lie when state officers affirmatively increase the risk of harm to a discrete group of persons. See Joseph M. Pellicciotti, Annotation on, "State-Created Danger," or Similar Theory, as Basis for Civil Rights Action under 42 U.S.C.A. § 1983, 159 A.L.R. Fed. 37 (2000); Bennett ex rel. Irvine v. City of Philadelphia, 499 F.3d 281 (3d Cir. 2007).

[148] Estelle v. Gamble, 429 U.S. 97, 97 S.Ct. 285, 50 L.Ed.2d 251 (1976) (Eighth Amendment).

[149] Youngberg v. Romeo, 457 U.S. 307, 102 S.Ct. 2452, 73 L.Ed.2d 28 (1982) (due process).

[150] DeShaney v. Winnebago County Dep't of Social Services, 489 U.S. 189, 109 S.Ct. 998, 103 L.Ed.2d 249 (1989).

[151] State tort law may defeat claims like the one in *DeShaney* on the basis of immunity. See Marshall v. Montgomery County Children Services Bd., 92 Ohio St. 3d 348, 750 N.E.2d 549 (2001).

[152] See Brown v. Commonwealth of Pennsylvania, Dep't of Health Emergency Medical Services Training Institute, 318 F.3d 473 (3d Cir. 2003); Wyke v. Polk County School Board, 129 F.3d 560 (11th Cir. 1997).

[153] Camp v. Gregory, 67 F.3d 1286 (7th Cir. 1995).

[154] The constitutional standard for violation of due process is that the defendant's conduct shocks the conscience, often shown by deliberate indifference. A failure to exercise professional judgment in investigating

home environment are subject to liability for depriving the child of due process rights by causing her harm.[155] As Judge Posner put it, "If the fire department rescues you from a fire that would have killed you, this does not give the department a constitutional license to kill you, on the ground that you will be no worse off than if there were no fire department."[156] In addition, the state, having placed a child in a foster home, may be expected to verify that the home continues to be safe for children and may even be held to a standard of professional judgment.[157]

Compulsory schooling and custody. The general view is that compulsory school attendance is not custody, and that short of "custody" the Constitution does not require any school to protect one student from another,[158] from himself,[159] or from intruders.[160] In fact, unless the school maintains a policy or custom supporting abusive teachers, or the school is responsible under Title IX, it may escape responsibility under federal law for its teachers' sexual abuse of minor students.[161]

§ 26.8 Employer's Duty to Protect Employees

Employers owe a general duty of reasonable care to their employees, as well as to independent contractors and their employees. This principle is usually expressed by saying the employer owes a duty of reasonable care to furnish a safe place in which to work.[162] More specifically, the employer may be under a duty to use reasonable care to protect the employee from attacks by third persons. The duty may arise from the employment relationship alone or from the employer's implied undertaking to provide appropriate protection.[163] For instance, the duty of care may require the employer to provide a reasonably safe workplace by providing appropriate lighting and windows so that a night employee in an isolated place can see to protect herself from attack, and the employer who does not do so may properly be found negligent.[164] In some cases the duty might be satisfied by a warning that reveals the danger.[165] Besides providing reasonable protection against third persons, employers whose medical examination of employees

---

foster homes may count as deliberate indifference. See Weatherford ex rel. Michael L. v. State, 206 Ariz. 529, 81 P.3d 320 (2003).

[155] E.g., Meador v. Cabinet for Human Resources, 902 F.2d 474 (6th Cir. 1990); Burton v. Richmond, 276 F.3d 973 (8th Cir. 2002).

[156] K.H. v. Morgan, 914 F.2d 846, 849 (7th Cir. 1990) (Posner, J.).

[157] Kara B. v. Dane County, 205 Wis.2d 140, 555 N.W.2d 630 (1996).

[158] Morrow v. Balaski, 719 F.3d 160 (3d Cir. 2013); Stevens v. Umsted, 131 F.3d 697 (7th Cir. 1997); Patel v. Kent School Dist., 648 F.3d 965 (9th Cir. 2011).

[159] Wyke v. Polk County School Board, 129 F.3d 560 (11th Cir. 1997).

[160] See Johnson v. Dallas Independent School Dist., 38 F.3d 198 (5th Cir. 1994).

[161] See Doe v. Claiborne County, Tennessee, 103 F.3d 495 (6th Cir. 1996).

[162] See Didier v. Ash Grove Cement Co., 272 Neb. 28, 718 N.W.2d 484 (2006) (duty of owner in possession and control of premises includes a duty to provide a safe place for work by a contractor's employee); Olivo v. Owens-Illinois, Inc., 186 N.J. 394, 895 A.2d 1143 (2006) (reasonable care duty owed to invitees, including independent contractor's employees, includes duty to provide a reasonably safe place in which to work).

[163] See Linda A. Sharp, Annotation, Employer's Liability to Employee or Agent for Injury or Death Resulting from Assault or Criminal Attack by Third Person, 40 A.L.R.5th 1 (1996).

[164] Lillie v. Thompson, 332 U.S. 459, 92 L.Ed. 73, 68 S.Ct. 140 (1947).

[165] Pratt v. St. Marie, 45 Or.App. 709, 609 P.2d 411 (1980) (defendant hired plaintiff to help evict tenant but did not warn the plaintiff that the tenant might be violent; defendant potentially liable when tenant shot the plaintiff).

and prospective employees reveals a serious medical condition may be under a duty of care to reveal the condition to the employee or prospective employee.[166]

C. DUTY BASED ON DEFENDANT'S RELATIONSHIP TO A DANGEROUS PERSON

§ 26.9 Relationships Recognized

General rule. A distinct ground for imposing a duty to protect from a third person is that the defendant stands in a special relationship to a dangerous person and is in a position to control that person or limit his capacity for harm. The usual starting point is that the defendant is under no duty to take affirmative steps to control a dangerous person in the absence of an undertaking to do so, or a special relationship, either with the plaintiff or with the dangerous person. For instance, a passenger in an automobile, perceiving that the driver is dangerously intoxicated, owes no duty to anyone other than himself[167] to persuade the driver to stop or relinquish the driving task to others.[168] Frequently, however, actual custodial *control* of a dangerous person is not really the point.[169] Rather, the relationship of the defendant to the dangerous person may be enough to require the defendant to use reasonable means at his disposal to protect the plaintiff or reduce the risk to her, even if control is impossible. Thus the usual statement of the rule in terms of "control" tends to obscure the possibility that a reasonable defendant might save the plaintiff by the most limited efforts, such as a warning.

Recognized relationships to dangerous person. However that may be, several relationships establish a right, authority, and duty to control dangerous persons, which in turn requires the defendant to exercise reasonable care. In particular, the Restatement Second recognizes that the defendant is expected to exercise care to control (1) his minor children,[170] and those in his custody or immediate control,[171] (2) employees

---

[166] See Union Carbide & Carbon Corp. v. Stapleton, 237 F.2d 229, 69 A.L.R.2d 1206 (6th Cir. 1956) (emphasizing employee's reliance, expectation, and the affirmative action of the employer in requiring physical exams); Coffee v. McDonnell-Douglas Corp., 8 Cal. 3d 551, 503 P.2d 1366, 105 Cal. Rptr. 358 (1972) (pre-employment exam, relationship of the parties created when defendant undertook the examination); Dornak v. Lafayette General Hospital, 399 So.2d 168 (La. 1981) (pre-employment exam). As to the physician's personal duty to the pre-employment examinee, see 2 Dobbs, Hayden & Bublick, The Law of Torts § 286 (2d ed. 2011 & Supp.).

[167] See Bouley v. Guidry, 883 So.2d 1099 (La. App. 2004); Halvorsen v. Ford Motor Co., 132 A.D.2d 57, 522 N.Y.S.2d 727 (1987); Taylor v. Coats, 636 S.E.2d 581 (N.C. App. 2006).

[168] Martinson v. Cagle, 454 So.2d 1383 (Ala. 1984); Olson v. Ische, 343 N.W.2d 284 (Minn. 1984); Champion ex rel. Ezzo v. Dunfee, 398 N.J.Super. 112, 939 A.2d 825 (App. Div. 2008). Distinguish the case of a passenger who actively provides alcohol to the driver or encourages him to engage in dangerous behavior. See, e.g., Shelter Mutual Ins. Co. v. White, 930 S.W.2d 1 (Mo.App. 1996).

[169] See Hertog v. City of Seattle, 138 Wash.2d 265, 979 P.2d 400, 408 (1999) ("[C]ustodial control is not required. The relevant inquiry is the relationship of the officer with the parolee."); see also State, Dep't of Corrections v. Cowles, 151 P.3d 353 (Alaska 2006) (parole officer's duty to victims arose from officer's supervisory relationship to parolee).

[170] Restatement Second of Torts § 316 (1965).

[171] Duvall v. Lawrence, 86 S.W.3d 74 (Mo. App. 2002); Gritzner v. Michael R., 235 Wis.2d 781, 611 N.W.2d 906 (2000).

who are using his premises or chattels,[172] (3) dangerous persons in his custody[173] or subject to his authority,[174] and (4) those who are subject to his power because they are licensees on his land or using his chattels.[175] The Third Restatement recognizes similar categories, and also acknowledges the duty of mental health professionals to use reasonable care in protecting others from their dangerous patients.[176]

Parents: specific dangers. Courts have been reluctant to impose liability upon parents for the torts of their children, even when parents know that their child is dangerous and could take steps to prevent harm.[177] In these cases, courts have rejected liability when the parents could foresee that their child would cause harm, but could not reasonably foresee the specific harm or the specific occasion for harm inflicted by the child.[178] In some such instances, the parents may have made reasonable decisions, since teenaged children need experience with freedom as well as control and since courts should interfere with child-rearing decisions only in clear cases. Given parental knowledge of a specific propensity and an imminent danger or occasion for it, however, the parents are liable for negligence in failing to control the child or failing to warn potential victims.[179] But again, negligence is required and courts have recognized that older children, though more dangerous, may also be more difficult to control, and hence have displayed a strong disinclination to impose liability in those cases.[180] When the dangerous child is an adult, the parent is not likely to be held responsible for his foreseeable misconduct absent some unusual element of control, and financial support of such a child is probably insufficient to justify liability of the parent.[181] A parent who

---

[172] Restatement Second of Torts § 317 (1965); Satterfield v. Breeding Insulation Co., 266 S.W.3d 347 (Tenn. 2008) (employer owed duty to employees and their family members who came in contact with asbestos on clothing, picked up at work). Where no risk of harm is foreseeable to the employer, however, no liability can result. See, e.g., Martin v. Cincinnati Gas and Elec. Co., 561 F.3d 439 (6th Cir. 2009) (no liability to family member exposed to asbestos on father's work clothes where it was not reasonably foreseeable that the asbestos would pose a risk of harm to the family member); Simpkins v. CSX Transp., Inc., 2012 IL 110662, 358 Ill. Dec. 613, 965 N.E.2d 1092 (2012) (complaint was insufficient to establish that railroad, allegedly negligent for failing to take precautions to protect wife of employee from take-home asbestos on employee's clothing, although remand for leave to amend was warranted); McGuire v. Curry, 766 N.W.2d 501 (S.D. 2009) (no duty to perform background check before hiring employee where his position did not require frequent contact with the public). On the duty of employers to protect their own workers from third-party attack, see § 26.8. On negligent hiring, supervision or retention of employees who injure others, see § 26.11.

[173] Restatement Second of Torts § 319 (1965).

[174] See Osborn v. Mason County, 157 Wash.2d 18, 134 P.3d 197 (2006) (public entity owes duty to protect against dangerous persons where it has "authority to control" them, "to the extent it has authority to control them").

[175] Restatement Second of Torts § 318 (1965).

[176] Restatement Third of Torts (Liability for Physical and Emotional Harm) § 41 (2010) (stating that the list is not exclusive).

[177] A number of states simply do not recognize a claim for negligent or even wanton supervision of children. See Beddingfield v. Linam, 127 So.3d 1178 (Ala. 2013) (noting that there are "few reported cases, either in Alabama or in other states, that have recognized [such] a claim").

[178] E.g., Dinsmore-Poff v. Alvord, 972 P.2d 978 (Alaska 1999) ("A plaintiff must show that the parent had reason to know with some specificity of a present opportunity and need to restrain the child to prevent some imminently foreseeable harm. General knowledge of past misconduct is, in other words, necessary but not sufficient for liability."); Parsons v. Smithey, 109 Ariz. 49, 504 P.2d 1272 (1973); Doe v. Andujar, 297 Ga.App. 696, 678 S.E.2d 163 (2009).

[179] Wood v. Groh, 269 Kan. 420, 7 P.3d 1163 (2000); Gritzner v. Michael R., 235 Wis.2d 781, 611 N.W.2d 906 (2000).

[180] See, e.g., Williamson v. Daniels, 748 So.2d 754 (Miss. 1999).

[181] Remsburg v. Montgomery, 376 Md. 568, 831 A.2d 18 (2003); Bridges v. Parrish, 366 N.C. 539, 742 S.E.2d 794 (2013). Distinguish Courtney v. Courtney, 186 W.Va. 597, 413 S.E.2d 418 (1991) (mother providing drugs and alcohol to her grown, married son, knowing that these substances make him violent; she is subject to liability to his abused wife).

negligently leaves firearms available to a child or negligently entrusts the child with weapons presents a different issue.[182]

Where defendant's care owed to one person will protect others. In one distinct group of cases, the defendant owes a duty of reasonable care to one person, who becomes dangerous to others only because the defendant has not fulfilled his duty of care. Put differently, the defendant's compliance with his duty of care to A will also tend to protect B and others at no added cost. For example, a landowner owes invitees a duty of reasonable care; if he breaches that duty by exposing them to disease, the breach of duty to the invitee may cause foreseeable communication of that disease to others outside the land.[183] Similarly, a physician who gives a patient medication likely to produce dizziness owes the patient a duty of reasonable care, probably satisfied by a warning not to drive.[184] If he fails to warn, there is a good chance that the patient himself may be injured in driving and may injure third persons as well. In these cases, imposing a duty upon the defendant to those third persons imposes no new burden. If he is held liable it is only because he breached a duty already owed and because his reasonable care would have protected others as well. The ground for liability seem to be near the core of tort law and a number of courts have recognized that breach of a duty of care that risks injuries to others is ground for liability.

§ 26.10　Negligent Entrustment

Control of licensees and negligent entrustment. The defendant's ownership or right to control land and chattels imposes upon him a duty to use reasonable care to control permissive users to prevent them from negligently or intentionally inflicting harm.[185] This obligation is closely related to the owner's responsibility for negligent entrustment of chattels to people who foreseeably might use the chattel in a way dangerous to themselves[186] or others.[187] The typical case is negligent entrustment of an automobile[188] or a weapon[189] to a person whom the defendant knows or should know is apt to use it in

---

[182]　See § 26.10.

[183]　Olivo v. Owens-Illinois, Inc., 186 N.J. 394, 895 A.2d 1143 (2006) (exposure to asbestos on land, carried home); Satterfield v. Breeding Insulation Co., 266 S.W.3d 347 (Tenn. 2008) (same); see § 26.11.

[184]　Hardee v. Bio-Medical Applications of South Carolina, Inc., 370 S.C. 511, 636 S.E.2d 629 (2006).

[185]　Restatement Second of Torts § 318 (1965). See e.g., Volpe v. Gallagher, 821 A.2d 699 (R.I. 2003) (for the benefit of a neighbor, landowner under a duty of care to control dangerous person living in her home and storing weapons there). When one in control of a chattel supplies it to another for use that in some way benefits the supplier, control and benefit together impose a duty of care to provide a safe chattel. See Heinz v. Heinz, 653 N.W.2d 334 (Iowa 2002); Restatement Second of Torts § 390 (1965). As to scope of liability (proximate cause) issues and the non-liability of the entrustor where the entrustee is not at fault, see § 15.16.

[186]　Ardinger v. Hummell, 982 P.2d 727 (Alaska 1999). Entrustment to the plaintiff herself might not be sufficient under Restatement Second § 308, see Stehlik v. Rhoads, 253 Wis.2d 477, 645 N.W.2d 889 (2002). However, the Restatement Third generalizes the principle broadly, to cover entrustments to a plaintiff who is dangerous to herself. See Restatement Third of Torts (Liability for Physical and Emotional Harm) § 19 (2010).

[187]　See, using the "injury to others" formula, Lulay v. Parvin, 359 Ill.App.3d 653, 834 N.E.2d 989, 296 Ill.Dec. 184 (2005); Tart v. Martin, 353 N.C. 252, 540 S.E.2d 332 (2000).

[188]　E.g., LeClaire v. Commercial Siding and Maintenance Co., 308 Ark. 580, 826 S.W.2d 247 (1992) (but atypically involving a sub-entrustment); DeWester v. Watkins, 275 Neb. 173, 745 N.W.2d 330 (Neb. 2008); Green v. Harris, 70 P.3d 866 (Okla. 2003). Cf. Rippy v. Shepard, 80 So. 3d 305 (Fla. 2012) (applying state's "dangerous instrumentality doctrine," holding that vicarious liability is imposed on the owner of a motor vehicle, in this case a farm tractor, who entrusts the vehicle to another person whose negligent operation causes harm to the plaintiff).

[189]　Morin v. Moore, 309 F.3d 316 (5th Cir. 2002); Kitchen v. K-Mart Corp., 697 So.2d 1200 (Fla. 1997) (seller of firearm to intoxicated buyer may be liable to woman he shot with the gun); Bernethy v. Walt Failor's Inc., 97 Wash.2d 929, 653 P.2d 280 (1982) (gun dealer allowed intoxicated man to walk off with rifle); but see Hamilton v. Beretta U.S.A. Corp., 96 N.Y.2d 222, 727 N.Y.S.2d 7, 750 N.E.2d 1055 (2001) (refusing to apply

a dangerous way because of his age and inexperience,[190] physical or mental limitations,[191] his character or habits,[192] or his actual intoxication[193] or perhaps his propensity for it.[194] Some courts have found negligent entrustment, not because the entrustee was dangerous, but because the instrumentality, such as a paint gun[195] or an air rifle,[196] was. The duty of care of course extends to other goods as well, if the defendant should know that entrustment runs an unreasonable risk of harm.[197] One court has even held that selling or facilitating access to gasoline for use by a driver known to be intoxicated can count as a negligent entrustment so that the negligent seller may be held for harms inflicted by the buyer's drunken driving,[198] although others have rejected this and similar claims.[199]

Negligence rules applicable. Once the duty of care is imposed, the negligent-entrustment case is an ordinary negligence case to which all the principles of negligence law apply.[200] The lender who is not negligent when he entrusts an automobile may come under a duty to terminate the entrustment if he later learns that the borrower is using it dangerously; the defendant may even be responsible to the borrower herself where he owes her a duty to protect her from her own incompetence.[201] If no harm is reasonably foreseeable as a result of the entrustment, or if the likelihood of harm is so small that the entrustment is nevertheless reasonable, the defendant is not negligent at all.[202] Conversely, if harm is foreseeable, liability is appropriate not only when the defendant

---

negligent entrustment theory to a claim that manufacturers of handguns negligently marketed their products so as to facilitate illegal use resulting in injury to the plaintiffs, because the manufacturer did not entrust to specific individuals known to be dangerous, only to a class of persons who were perhaps dangerous as a class). The federal statute providing an immunity to many gun sellers and manufacturers where the plaintiff was harmed by a criminal's use of the gun contains an express exception for negligent entrustment claims. 15 U.S.C.A. § 7903(5)(A)(ii).

[190] Ardinger v. Hummell, 982 P.2d 727(Alaska 1999) (entrustment of car to 15-year-old unlicensed driver); DeWester v. Watkins, 275 Neb. 173, 745 N.W.2d 330 (Neb. 2008) (entrustment of a car to a child); Green v. Harris, 70 P.3d 866 (Okla. 2003) (same).

[191] See Sanders v. Walden, 214 Ark. 523, 217 S.W.2d 357 (1949) (lending automobile to man who could not reach brake pedals and had a bad driving record).

[192] Swicegood v. Cooper, 341 N.C. 178, 459 S.E.2d 206 (1995) (bad driving record known to defendant).

[193] E.g., Casebolt v. Cowan, 829 P.2d 352 (Colo. 1992); Hays v. Royer, 384 S.W.3d 330 (Mo. Ct. App. 2012).

[194] See Eagle Motor Lines, Inc. v. Mitchell, 223 Miss. 398, 78 So.2d 482 (1955). Departing from ordinary negligence rules, some cases have required that the defendant have actual knowledge of the entrustee's intoxication or other disability at the time of the entrustment. See Frank J. Wozniak, Annotation, Liability Based on Entrusting Automobile to One Who is Intoxicated or Known to be Excessive User of Intoxicants, 91 A.L.R.5th 1, at § 4[a] (2001).

[195] Danielle A. v. Christopher P., 3 Misc.3d 357, 776 N.Y.S.2d 446 (2004).

[196] Phillips v. D'Amico, 21 So.2d 748 (La. App. 1945), *overruled on other grounds*, Turner v. Bucher, 308 So.2d 270 (La. 1975).

[197] See Moore v. Myers, 161 Md. App. 349, 868 A.2d 954 (2005) (pit bull entrusted to child); Hickle v. Whitney Farms, Inc., 148 Wash. 2d 911, 64 P.3d 1244 (2003) (entrustment of hazardous substances to hauler).

[198] West v. East Tennessee Pioneer Oil Co., 172 S.W.3d 545 (Tenn. 2005).

[199] Fuller v. Standard Stations, Inc., 250 Cal. App.2d 687, 58 Cal. Rptr. 792 (1967); Roberts v. Stop & Go, Inc., 502 So.2d 915 (Fla. Dist. Ct. App. 1986).

[200] See, e.g., Olguin v. City of Burley, 119 Idaho 721, 810 P.2d 255 (1991). Thus negligent entrustment may show contributory negligence as well as negligence itself. Swicegood v. Cooper, 341 N.C. 178, 459 S.E.2d 206 (1995).

[201] Casebolt v. Cowan, 829 P.2d 352 (Colo. 1992); Frain v. State Farm Ins. Co., 421 So.2d 1169 (La. Ct. App. 1982); see Ward Miller, Annotation, Negligent Entrustment: Bailor's Liability to Bailee Injured Through His Own Negligence or Incompetence, 12 A.L.R.4th 1062 (1981).

[202] E.g., Young v. U-Haul Co. of D.C., 11 A.3d 247 (D.C. 2011); Taft v. Jumbo Foods, Inc., 155 Idaho 511, 314 P.3d 193 (2013); Guardianship of Garvin v. Tupelo Furniture Market, Inc., 127 So.3d 197 (Miss. 2013).

intentionally "entrusts" the chattel to a dangerous person, but also when he negligently leaves the chattel at a place where he should expect that a dangerous person is likely to find and use it. A well-known kind of case is one in which a person negligently leaves keys in a vehicle, which is then stolen by a thief who injures the plaintiff with the vehicle. Courts have imposed liability on such facts where the vehicle itself is particularly dangerous.[203] Similarly, liability may follow if a defendant leaves a gun unprotected from children or thieves.[204]

Control of chattel required. The duty of reasonable care is not imposed on negligent-entrustment grounds unless the defendant has the right to control the chattel.[205] A bailee is not required to withhold the automobile from its owner[206] and a police officer is not required to arrest the intoxicated owner so he can take control of the car.[207] Although some authority holds that the defendant must not even sell or donate a car to a known dangerous driver,[208] others say that the defendant who knows the purchaser or donee is dangerous has no responsibility to restrict sales of automobiles.[209] Similarly, the seller of a motorcycle may have no liability for negligent entrustment, even where the buyer was unlicensed, because the seller gave up "control" upon completion of the sale.[210]

Firearms. When it comes to firearms, however, sellers may be required to deliver them only to properly identified buyers who do not appear to be especially dangerous.[211] Because stolen guns are often used in criminal activities leading to serious harm, it would seem that a dealer should exercise care to prevent theft of his handguns, but some courts have disagreed.[212] Some courts have similarly held that a gun owner is under no duty to keep firearms in reasonably safe places to prevent theft and killings,[213] or that theft and illegal use by the thief are not foreseeable.[214] Perhaps some courts do not view the business of selling guns or storing them as affirmative conduct, so that failure to take reasonable steps to guard against theft is assumed to be mere nonfeasance. If a court perceives active conduct, however, the ordinary duty of reasonable care would

---

[203] See Carrera v. Maurice J. Sopp & Son, 177 Cal.App.4th 366, 99 Cal.Rptr.3d 268 (2009) (tow truck; citing cases involving large trucks and bulldozers). Courts have been reluctant to impose liability where the vehicle was an ordinary car or pickup truck. See Richards v. Stanley, 43 Cal.2d 60, 271 P.2d 23 (1954); Lucero v. Holbrook, 288 P.3d 1228 (Wyo. 2012).

[204] E.g., Estate of Heck v. Stoffer, 786 N.E.2d 265 (Ind. 2003); Jupin v. Kask, 447 Mass. 141, 849 N.E.2d 829 (2006); Kuhns v. Brugger, 390 Pa. 331, 135 A.2d 395 (1957). Some courts have rejected liability in such cases, citing unforeseeability of harm or lack of causation on the particular facts.

[205] Ability to control the chattel (rather than mere ownership) is what most courts require, in line with the Restatement Second of Torts § 308 (1965). See Tissicino v. Peterson, 211 Ariz. 416, 121 P.3d 1285 (Ct. App. 2005) (citing cases from many jurisdictions); DeWester v. Watkins, 275 Neb. 173, 745 N.W.2d 330 (Neb. 2008).

[206] E.g., Knighten v. Sam's Parking Valet, 206 Cal.App.3d 69, 253 Cal.Rptr. 365 (1988); Umble v. Sandy McKie and Sons, Inc., 294 Ill.App.3d 449, 698 N.E.2d 157, 228 Ill.Dec. 848 (1998).

[207] Olguin v. City of Burley, 119 Idaho 721, 810 P.2d 255 (1991); but cf. Ransom v. City of Garden City, 113 Idaho 202, 743 P.2d 70 (1987) (once officer had arrested owner and taken keys, he was under a duty not to make keys available to other dangerous drivers).

[208] Vince v. Wilson, 151 Vt. 425, 561 A.2d 103 (1989).

[209] Horne v. Vic Potamkin Chevrolet, Inc., 533 So.2d 261 (Fla. 1988).

[210] Laurel Yamaha, Inc. v. Freeman, 956 So.2d 897 (Miss. 2007).

[211] Kitchen v. K-Mart Corporation, 697 So.2d 1200 (Fla. 1997).

[212] Valentine v. On Target, Inc., 353 Md. 544, 727 A.2d 947 (1999).

[213] McGrane v. Cline, 94 Wash. App. 925, 973 P.2d 1092 (1999).

[214] See Estate of Strever v. Cline, 278 Mont. 165, 924 P.2d 666 (1996).

apply,[215] although liability of gun manufacturers and federally licensed sellers may be cut off in some cases by a federal statute.[216]

§ 26.11   Control and Other Means of Protecting from Dangerous Persons

Control can be sufficient for duty. One in charge of a person who is or should be recognized as dangerous is under a duty of reasonable care to control that person so as to prevent harm.[217] For example, a prison is under a duty of reasonable care not to permit its inmates to escape and do harm;[218] and, if not immune,[219] custodians who release dangerous persons have sometimes been held liable for the death or injury they foreseeably cause.[220] Parole officers may have a sufficient relationship if not "control" over dangerous criminals on parole to require them to exercise care in supervision.[221] Similarly, police may have sufficient control over a dangerous person because they are under a duty to enforce an injunction against an abusive husband or father by arrest if necessary to protect the family.[222]

Neither control nor custody are necessary for duty. Cases have not required anything like "custody" of the dangerous person to trigger the duty of reasonable care to protect the plaintiff. Consequently, it would be more accurate as well as less confounding to recognize that "control" is merely one of the ways in which a defendant might act reasonably to minimize the risk of harm to others.

Examples. The Pied Piper cases supply one example of a defendant who owes a duty of care without having "control." A mobile street vendor selling ice cream by attracting children into the street has no control over dangerous traffic, but the vendor must use reasonable care to protect the small children attracted by his music and his wares and may be liable if a child is struck by a car.[223] Other examples abound. Airlines may owe a duty to screen passengers to exclude terrorists for the safety not only of other passengers but also for the safety of potential victims on the ground.[224] Again without formal custody, or even immediate control, a landlord with a dangerous tenant[225] and a hospital

---

[215] Outside the gun context, the principle seems well established. See, e.g., United States v. Stevens, 994 So.2d 1062 (Fla. 2008) (government owes duty to prevent theft of anthrax it had developed).

[216] 15 U.S.C.A. §§ 7901 to 7903 (but containing an exception to immunity for negligent entrustment).

[217] Restatement Second of Torts § 319 (1965).

[218] Raas v. State, 729 N.W.2d 444 (Iowa 2007); Marceaux v. Gibbs, 699 So.2d 1065 (La. 1997).

[219] Immunity may protect the public entity operating the prison. See § 22.11.

[220] E.g., DeJesus v. U. S. Dep't of Veterans Affairs, 384 F.Supp.2d 780 (E.D.Pa. 2005).

[221] State, Dep't of Corrections v. Cowles, 151 P.3d 353 (Alaska 2006); Hertog v. City of Seattle, 138 Wash.2d 265, 979 P.2d 400 (1999).

[222] See Sorichetti v. City of New York, 65 N.Y.2d 461, 492 N.Y.S.2d 591, 482 N.E.2d 70 (1985); Nearing v. Weaver, 295 Or. 702, 670 P.2d 137 (1983). However, absent an injunctive order or the like, courts usually invoke some version of the public duty doctrine to relieve police from liability for failure to arrest. See § 345.

[223] E.g., Neal v. Shiels, Inc., 166 Conn. 3, 347 A.2d 102 (1974). See David Rand, Jr., Annotation, Civil Liability of Mobile Vendor for Attracting into Street Child Injured by Another's Motor Vehicle, 84 A.L.R.3d 826 (1978).

[224] In re September 11 Litigation, 280 F.Supp.2d 279 (S.D.N.Y. 2003).

[225] Courts may find indirect control in the landlord's ability to exclude dangerous tenants or terminate their tenancy. On this or some similar basis, the landlord may be held responsible for a tenant's dangerous use of firearms, Rosales v. Stewart, 113 Cal. App. 3d 130, 169 Cal. Rptr. 660 (1980), or a tenant's dangerous pets, Giacalone v. Housing Authority of Town of Wallingford, 306 Conn. 399, 51 A.3d 352 (2012); Strunk v. Zoltanski, 62 N.Y.2d 572, 479 N.Y.S.2d 175, 468 N.E.2d 13 (1984). When courts think of control narrowly, however, liability may be denied because the landlord has no control of the premises in the tenant's possession, see, e.g., Stewart v. Aldrich, 788 A.2d 603 (Me. 2002) (landlord's liability for attack by tenant's dog depends upon right of control, which "does not include the incidental control that comes from being able to threaten tenants with

with a dangerous surgeon[226] may be required to exercise care to prevent harm to others if for no other reason than because they are in a position to "terminate the tenancy" or other privileges. Along the same lines, a wife who knows her husband molests children certainly does not have her husband in custody and probably does not control him, but she is under a duty of reasonable care to neighboring children.[227] Such a duty might be satisfied by warning the neighbors, but much less disruptive solutions may be reasonably available; for example, she might arrange to be present when neighbor children visit.[228]

Negligent hiring, retention or supervision of an employee. Employers must exercise reasonable care to "control" their employees,[229] which often translates to a duty to use care in hiring,[230] supervising,[231] or retaining[232] a dangerous person whose job puts him in a position to harm others,[233] even if in harming others he is not acting within scope of employment.[234] Where the public duty doctrine or other immunities do not protect negligent public employers, they too are subject to a duty of care in hiring, supervising

---

nonrenewal of a lease or with eviction"); Frobig v. Gordon, 124 Wash. 2d 732, 881 P.2d 226 (1994) (liability flows from "ownership or direct control"); Englund v. Vital, 2013 S.D. 71, 838 N.W.2d 621 (2013) (landlord owed no duty to protect plaintiff from rock-throwing child of tenants where landlord lacked control over tenants' property). Liability for leasing to illicit drug traffickers has also been difficult to impose. See Muniz v. Flohern, Inc., 77 N.Y.2d 869, 568 N.Y.S.2d 725, 570 N.E.2d 1074 (1991) (commercial landlord owed no duty to person shot during a robbery of the drug-dealing tenant).

[226] Darling v. Charleston Community Memorial Hospital, 33 Ill.2d 326, 211 N.E.2d 253 (1965) (leading case); Strubhart v. Perry Memorial Hospital Trust Authority, 903 P.2d 263 (Okla. 1995).

[227] See Pamela L. v. Farmer, 112 Cal.App.3d 206, 169 Cal.Rptr. 282 (1980).

[228] J.S. v. R.T.H., 155 N.J. 330, 714 A.2d 924 (1998).

[229] Restatement Second of Torts § 317 (1965). This is the case, for example, in many of the "fatigued employee" cases, where the employee causes an accident on the way home because he has worked long hours. E.g., Barclay v. Briscoe, 427 Md. 270, 47 A.3d 560 (2012); Nabors Drilling, U.S.A., Inc. v. Escoto, 288 S.W.3d 401 (Tex. 2009). On the other hand, where the employer has exercised "control" in affirmatively encouraging the employee to drive home drunk, for example, courts have found liability. See Otis Engineering Corp. v. Clark, 668 S.W.2d 307 (Tex. 1983). Such cases may be better analyzed as affirmative risk-creation cases, making the "control" point largely irrelevant. See § 26.2.

[230] See Underberg v. Southern Alarm, Inc., 284 Ga. App. 108, 643 S.E.2d 374 (2007); Ponticas v. K.M.S. Investments, 331 N.W.2d 907, 38 A.L.R.4th 225 (Minn. 1983); J. v. Victory Tabernacle Baptist Church, 236 Va. 206, 372 S.E.2d 391 (1988). Negligent hiring of an independent contractor who causes harm to others may also be actionable, see Schelling v. Humphrey, 123 Ohio St.3d 387, 916 N.E.2d 1029 (2009) (negligent-credentialing claim against hospital for negligently granting staff privileges to a surgeon whose malpractice caused injury to plaintiff), but the hiring employer is usually not liable to the negligently hired independent contractor's employee for on-the-job injury. See Carmago v. Tjaarda Dairy, 25 Cal.4th 1235, 25 P.3d 1096, 108 Cal.Rptr.2d 617 (2001).

[231] Foradori v. Harris, 523 F.3d 477 (5th Cir. 2008); Seguro v. Cummiskey, 82 Conn. App. 186, 844 A.2d 224 (2004); Trahan-Laroche v. Lockheed Sanders, Inc., 139 N.H. 483, 657 A.2d 417 (1995).

[232] E.g., Welsh Mfg., Div. of Textron, Inc. v. Pinkerton's, Inc., 474 A.2d 436, 44 A.L.R.4th 603 (R.I. 1984).

[233] See, e.g., Doe v. Saint Francis Hosp. & Medical Center, 309 Conn. 146, 72 A.3d 929 (2013). Where the employment itself does not foreseeably create the risk of harm that came to fruition, the employer may escape liability for employee-caused injury. E.g., Raleigh v. Performance Plumbing and Heating, Inc., 130 P.3d 1011 (Colo. 2006) (injury caused by defendant's employee as he was driving home from work).

[234] Many courts have held that a claim of negligent hiring, training or supervision may be maintained only where the employee has acted outside the scope of employment. See Diaz v. Carcamo, 51 Cal.4th 1148, 126 Cal.Rptr.3d 443, 253 P.3d 535 (2011) (employer's admission of vicarious liability renders inadmissible any evidence of the employer's negligence); McHaffie v. Bunch, 891 S.W.2d 822 (Mo. 1995); DiCosala v. Kay, 91 N.J. 159, 450 A.2d 508 (1982). Others allow such claims even where respondeat superior liability has been admitted. See Quinonez v. Andersen, 144 Ariz. 193, 696 P.2 1342 (1984); Marquis v. State Farm Fire & Cas. Co., 265 Kan. 317, 961 P.2d 1213 (1998); James v. Kelly Trucking Co., 377 S.C. 628, 661 S.E.2d 329 (2008). Some allow the claims where the employee has acted within the scope of employment only if the employer has been grossly negligent in hiring, training or supervision of the employee. Lockett v. Bi-State Transit Auth., 94 Ill.2d 66, 67 Ill. Dec. 830, 445 N.E.2d 310 (1983); see Annotation, 30 A.L.R.4th 838 (1984).

and retaining.[235] A duty to supervise may even extend to one organization's relationship to another, as where a national fraternal organization failed to supervise the activities of a local chapter and its members, who negligently served alcohol to a minor, leading to the minor's death in an automobile accident.[236] A school district may be vicariously liable for a school administrator's negligent supervision of a school employee who sexually abused a high school student.[237]

Reasonable-care limits. Some but not all cases in which the defendant is asked to protect the plaintiff from dangerous persons raise policy conflicts, and sometimes courts simply refuse to impose a duty.[238] A duty of reasonable care by definition cannot be an undue burden, but it may still be difficult for a hospital to supervise a physician or a wife to chaperone her husband without risking damage to the relationship. Given a duty of care in such cases, liability by no means follows. It might be, for example, that the duty of reasonable care is readily satisfied by a hospital's annual review of a physician's performance. In the same way, a high school may have sufficient control over its students to prevent them from leaving campus during lunch break, but the only duty is the duty of reasonable care to avoid unreasonable risks, not to exercise all the control possible. No special facts appearing, the school creates no unreasonable risks of harm to others in failing to restrict students to campus, even if some students will drive cars with their customary flair and disregard for safety.[239]

The therapist's dangerous patient. The policy conflict in imposing a duty was the strongest argument in one of the famous cases, *Tarasoff v. Regents of the University of California.*[240] In that case, a psychologist concluded that his patient, Poddar, intended to kill Tatiana Tarasoff. He was concerned enough to tell the police, but the police released Poddar after a brief detention. The psychologist and his superiors did not attempt to commit Poddar or even to warn the Tarasoff family. Poddar did in fact kill Tatiana Tarasoff. In a suit against the psychologist for Tatiana's wrongful death, the defendants argued that it was against public policy to impose a duty of care upon therapists because it would force them to breach their confidence and would undermine the essential trust between therapist and patient. The court, however, imposed a duty of reasonable care, at least when a specific, known person was endangered. The therapist is thus required to act only when his own professional judgment indicates that others are in danger.[241] Many states have adopted the *Tarasoff* duty of reasonable care.[242] The same rule may apply as well to school counselors and others less well-trained, but in that case, they are expected only to make a diagnosis that meets their own professional standards.[243] Many courts limit the duty to warn to cases in which specific victims are

---

[235] E.g., Haddock v. City of New York, 140 A.D.2d 91, 532 N.Y.S.2d 379 (1988).

[236] Grand Aerie Fraternal Order of Eagles v. Carneyhan, 169 S.W.3d 840 (Ky. 2005).

[237] C.A. v. William S. Hart Union High School Dist., 53 Cal.4th 861, 138 Cal.Rptr.3d 1, 270 P.3d 699 (2012).

[238] See Hornback v. Archdiocese of Milwaukee, 313 Wis.2d 294, 752 N.W.2d 862 (2008) (recovery against Catholic diocese precluded on policy grounds).

[239] Collette v. Tolleson Unified School Dist. No. 214, 203 Ariz. 359, 54 P.3d 828 (Ct. App. 2002).

[240] Tarasoff v. Regents of Univ. of Cal., 17 Cal.3d 425, 131 Cal.Rptr. 14, 551 P.2d 334 (1976).

[241] Once there is a legal duty in place for a therapist to reveal a patient's threats, the therapist breaches no duty of confidentiality by doing so. See United States v. Auster, 517 F.3d 312 (5th Cir. 2008).

[242] E.g., Hamman v. County of Maricopa, 161 Ariz. 58, 775 P.2d 1122 (1989) (rejecting specific-victim requirement); Schuster v. Altenberg, 144 Wis.2d 223, 424 N.W.2d 159 (1988) (same).

[243] See Eisel v. Board of Educ. of Montgomery County, 324 Md. 376, 597 A.2d 447 (1991).

identified; risks to the general public are not, in their view, sufficient to trigger a duty.[244] Some states have rejected *Tarasoff* on the ground that a psychologist owes no duty to a person other than his patient, absent some particular facts (beyond those presented in *Tarasoff*) creating a special relationship between the doctor and the victim.[245]

Tarasoff statutes. Many states, including California itself,[246] have enacted statutes imposing a *Tarasoff* duty or something very similar.[247] A number of statutes specify that there is no duty to warn except where the patient has communicated an actual threat of physical violence against a reasonably identifiable victim.[248] Some statutes have been interpreted to impose substantial restrictions on recovery, in some cases even eliminating the therapist's duty of care under the professional standard and limiting liability to cases in which the therapist personally believed a patient's serious threat of harm,[249] or immunizing a care facility when the threat is acted out rather than verbal.[250] Other statutes have been construed narrowly, to abrogate a common-law duty of reasonable care only if the precise conditions set forth in the statute are present in the case.[251] Still others, which require mental health centers to report mental patients' material noncompliance with outpatient orders, have been held to create a duty only to the general public and not to any particular individual later harmed by the patient.[252]

Duty to diagnose. In *Tarasoff* itself, the psychologist made a correct diagnosis of the patient and knew of the danger. Some cases impose a duty of care to third persons to make a non-negligent diagnosis in the first place.[253] Other authority takes the view that the duty to diagnose with reasonable care runs only to the patient, so that if the physician never recognizes the danger at all, he is not then responsible for the patient's violence to others.[254] Some states have rejected any duty at all, even a duty to warn of known danger.[255]

---

[244] See, e.g., DeJesus v. U.S. Dep't of Veterans Affairs, 479 F.3d 271 (3d Cir. 2007); Thompson v. County of Alameda, 27 Cal.3d 741, 167 Cal.Rptr. 70, 614 P.2d 728, 12 A.L.R.4th 701 (1980); Munstermann ex rel. Rowe v. Alegent Health-Immanuel Medical Center, 271 Neb. 834, 716 N.W.2d 73 (2006); Emerich v. Philadelphia Center for Human Development, Inc., 554 Pa. 209, 720 A.2d 1032 (1998); Doe v. Marion, 373 S.C. 390, 645 S.E.2d 245 (2007).

[245] See Tedrick v. Community Resource Center, Inc., 235 Ill.2d 155, 920 N.E.2d 220, 336 Ill.Dec. 210 (2009).

[246] Cal. Civ. Code § 43.92.

[247] See Michael L. Perlin, Mental Disability Law: Civil and Criminal (2d ed. 1998; 5 vols. & supps.) (reviewing many statutes).

[248] See, e.g., Utah Code § 78–14a–102a.

[249] See Ewing v. Northridge Hospital Medical Center, 120 Cal. App.4th 1289, 16 Cal. Rptr. 3d 591 (2004); Munstermann v. Alegent Health-Immanuel Medical Center, 271 Neb. 834, 716 N.W.2d 73 (2006).

[250] Campbell v. Ohio State Univ. Medical Center, 108 Ohio St.3d 376, 843 N.E.2d 1194 (2006).

[251] See Dawe v. Dr. Reuven Bar-Levav & Associates, P.C., 485 Mich. 20, 780 N.W.2d 272 (2010); Marshall v. Klebanov, 188 N.J. 23, 902 A.2d 873 (2006).

[252] Adams v. Board of Sedgwick County Com'rs, 289 Kan. 577, P.3d 1173 (2009).

[253] Emerich v. Philadelphia Center for Human Development, Inc., 554 Pa. 209, 720 A.2d 1032 (1998); Schuster v. Altenberg, 144 Wis.2d 223, 424 N.W.2d 159 (1988).

[254] Van Horn v. Chambers, 970 S.W.2d 542 (Tex. 1998). Cf. McKenzie v. Hawai'i Permanente Med. Group, Inc., 98 Hawai'i 296, 47 P.3d 1209 (2002) (prescribing physician under a duty to third persons to warn patient of medication's side effects that make driving dangerous, but not under duty to use care in prescribing safer medication or dosage).

[255] Thapar v. Zezulka, 994 S.W.2d 635 (Tex. 1999); Nasser v. Parker, 249 Va. 172, 455 S.E.2d 502 (1995). However, Texas recognizes a duty of care to *control* a patient in custody to prevent foreseeable and reasonably preventable harms. See Texas Home Management, Inc. v. Peavy, 89 S.W.3d 30 (Tex. 2002).

The contagious or incapacitated patient.[256] Similarly, to protect persons who are not patients,[257] some courts have imposed a duty upon medical doctors to warn their own patients,[258] and non-patients as well,[259] that the patient's diseases are contagious or infectious, or to warn them that prescribed drugs may make driving unsafe for others on the road.[260] So long as the warning is made directly to the patient herself, and for the patient's benefit as well as for the public's benefit, neither the confidentiality nor the privacy issue is implicated. Nor is there any possible conflict of interest on the part of the physician or intrusion in the doctor patient relationship where the only duty is to warn the patient, who can then take appropriate steps to protect both himself and members of the public.[261] There is not even any burden or cost to the physician beyond the burden he undertook to treat the patient with reasonable care. Yet some courts have refused to recognize a doctor's duty to warn the patient herself that she carries an infectious disease or that she is not a safe driver.[262]

Warnings to non-patients. When the plaintiff claims that a warning should have been given to a non-patient, however, stronger reasons appear for denying the duty. In some cases, it will be impossible to know who besides the plaintiff should receive a warning. Even when the doctor could identify the person most at risk from the patient's disease, issues of confidentiality and privacy like those raised in *Tarasoff* will be important. But *Tarasoff*'s answer—requiring a reasonable warning to endangered non-patients—is not necessarily controlling when the patient himself has expressed no intent to harm others. A warning to the patient that she has an infectious disease, or that she cannot safely drive, would ordinarily reduce the risk to harm to non-patients to tolerable proportions. So cases that deny the duty to warn non-patients[263]—or that deny that the duty was breached—often represent intelligible policy decisions. On the other hand,

---

[256] See also § 21.4.

[257] See Tracy A. Bateman, Annotation, Liability of Doctor or Other Health Practitioner to Third Party Contracting Contagious Disease from Doctor's Patient, 3 A.L.R.5th 370 (1992).

[258] See Reisner v. Regents of Univ. of Cal., 31 Cal.App.4th 1195, 37 Cal. Rptr. 2d 518 (1995); C.W. v. Cooper Health System, 388 N.J.Super. 42, 906 A.2d 440 (2006) (positive HIV test); DiMarco v. Lynch Homes-Chester County, Inc., 525 Pa. 558, 583 A.2d 422 (1990); Estate of Amos v. Vanderbilt Univ., 62 S.W.3d 133 (Tenn. 2001) (possible exposure to HIV from blood transfusion).

[259] See, e.g., Davis v. Rodman, 147 Ark. 385, 227 S.W. 612, 13 A.L.R. 1459 (1921) (but denying liability on causal grounds); Bradshaw v. Daniel, 854 S.W.2d 865 (Tenn. 1993).

[260] McKenzie v. Hawai'i Permanente Med. Group, Inc., 98 Hawai'i 296, 47 P.3d 1209 (2002); Coombes v. Florio, 450 Mass. 182, 877 N.E.2d 567 (2007). Courts have rejected claims that a pharmacist owes a duty to third persons in connection with filling prescriptions. See, e.g., Sanchez v. Wal-Mart Stores, Inc., 221 P.3d 1276 (Nev. 2009). This is in line with the rule that the pharmacist typically owes no duty to warn the patient directly of a drug's side-effects where the doctor has prescribed it. See §§ 328 & 466.

[261] Hardee v. Bio-Medical Applications of South Carolina, Inc., 370 S.C. 511, 636 S.E.2d 629 (2006) ("Importantly, this duty owed to third parties is identical to the duty owed to the patient, i.e., a medical provider must warn a patient of the attendant risks and effects of any treatment. Thus, our holding does not hamper the doctor-patient relationship.").

[262] Kirk v. Michael Reese Hosp. and Med. Ctr., 117 Ill.2d 507, 513 N.E.2d 387, 111 Ill.Dec. 944 (1987); Webb v. Jarvis, 575 N.E.2d 992 (Ind. 1991) (based on absence of privity); Kolbe v. State, 661 N.W.2d 142 (Iowa 2003) (suggesting conflict of the physician's duty to patient and duty to public); Lester ex rel. Mavrogenis v. Hall, 126 N.M. 404, 970 P.2d 590 (1998) (discussing lack of control, remoteness of injury, "intrusion" upon the physician's loyalty to patient, and burden on doctor); Estate of Witthoeft v. Kiskaddon, 557 Pa. 340, 733 A.2d 623 (1999) (citing lack of foreseeability and a fear of absolute liability). The general disposition of courts to relieve health care practitioners from a duty to third persons in the absence of special circumstances is consistent with this view. See Dehn v. Edgecombe, 384 Md. 606, 865 A.2d 603 (2005); § 285.

[263] Lemon v. Stewart, 111 Md. App. 511, 682 A.2d 1177 (1996) (AIDS); Seebold v. Prison Health Services, Inc., 57 A.3d 1232 (Pa. 2012) (doctors had no duty to warn corrections officers that inmates had a contagious bacterial infection).

courts sometimes seem inclined to eliminate the doctor's duty of care even when the policy concerns are not present.[264]

§ 26.12   Enhancing Dangers: Providers of Alcohol

Traditional common law rule. Alcohol-impaired driving is a major factor in serious and fatal automobile injuries.[265] The traditional common law rule, however, was that those who provided alcohol to minors and intoxicated persons had no responsibility whatever for injuries inflicted by those drinkers, for example, injuries inflicted by the intoxicated person who drives negligently after consuming the defendant's alcohol. The rule was usually explained on the ground that the consumption of alcohol, not its provision, was "the" proximate cause of the subsequent injury and that injury was "too remote."[266] Since the drinker's intoxication and subsequent negligent acts would be entirely foreseeable, and the risk created by the defendant—intoxicated driving—is exactly the risk that comes about, proximate cause reasoning seems inappropriate at best. For this reason, and because courts made a flat rule of law that did not depend upon circumstances of individual cases, the common-law rule looked like a no-duty rule rather than a proximate cause rule tailored to particular facts. A proximate cause rule, might have inquired, for example, into the foreseeability that the drinker would drive, the time of day and traffic conditions, the time between drinking and the injury, and other such factors. But none of this was relevant; the traditional rule covered all cases in the general model of facts without regard to circumstances.

Effect of regulatory statutes. Three kinds of statutes potentially affected liability of the alcohol provider. First, regulatory statutes usually criminalize the sale of alcohol to intoxicated persons, minors, or habitual drunkards. Regulatory statutes also put the provider's license in jeopardy when he makes such sales. The usual rule that violation of a statute is negligence per se or prima facie negligence, however, was not applied to these statutes, so their violation had no effect at all in the tort suit.[267] That left the victim of an intoxicated driver without rights against the provider who knowingly supplied alcohol to a minor or intoxicated person.

Dram shop or civil damage acts. The second kind of statute was known as a Dram Shop or Civil Damage Act. These statutes, originally enacted in only a small number of states, did not merely regulate the sale of alcohol. Instead, they provided expressly for civil liability of alcohol providers. Dram shop statutes sometimes imposed strict liability upon the provider (and sometimes upon the lessor of the premises where alcohol was sold as well). On the other hand, liability in such cases might be limited to a rather small

---

[264] See, e.g., McNulty v. City of New York, 100 N.Y.2d 227, 792 N.E.2d 162, 762 N.Y.S.2d 12 (2003) (doctor would owe a duty to a non-patient only if the danger arose from his actual treatment; mere failure to warn a person who had no particular relation to the patient would not be actionable).

[265] Annual reports from the National Highway Traffic Safety Administration, available at www.nhtsa. gov, show that about one-third of all highway traffic deaths are alcohol-related.

[266] E.g., Carr v. Turner, 238 Ark. 889, 385 S.W.2d 656 (1965), *overruled in* Shannon v. Wilson, 329 Ark. 143, 947 S.W.2d 349 (1997); Wegleitner v. Sattler, 582 N.W.2d 688 (S.D. 1998) (reflecting a legislative enactment of the traditional view of proximate cause, that drinking, not serving, is "the" proximate cause); Robinson v. Matt Mary Moran, Inc., 259 Va. 412, 525 S.E.2d 559 (2000). Some courts following the traditional rule conclude that any decision about liability is best left to the legislature. Prime v. Beta Gamma Chapter of Pi Kappa Alpha, 47 P.3d 402 (Kan. 2002); Warr v. JMGM Group, LLC, 433 Md. 170, 70 A.3d 347 (2013).

[267] See, e.g., Mills v. City of Overland Park, 251 Kan. 434, 837 P.2d 370 (1992) (statute forbidding sale of liquor to incapacitated persons "was intended to regulate the sale of liquor and was not intended to impose civil liability"); Robinson v. Matt Mary Moran, Inc., 259 Va. 412, 525 S.E.2d 559 (2000) (violation of regulatory statute not a proximate cause of the harm).

sum.[268] Contemporary statutes imposing liability may also impose specific limits and may provide the exclusive remedy, barring any common law claim.[269]

Reversing the common law rule. Dram Shop statutes aside, the courts began reversing themselves about 1960.[270] Legislatures then sometimes took over the issue with a third type of statute, recognizing liability for negligence in some cases but not others.[271] Most courts not constrained by statute now impose a common law duty of reasonable care and impose liability when the licensed seller of alcohol negligently sells to a minor or intoxicated person who, as a result, causes injury to the plaintiff.[272] If the harm is foreseeable, liability is not to be avoided merely because the provider furnished alcohol to a minor indirectly, for instance, by negligently selling to one who is a foreseeable conduit of alcohol to minors,[273] or negligently permitting a theft by minors.[274] The provider's ultimate share of liability to injured third persons may be reduced by the drinker's comparative fault share,[275] or, in joint and several liability jurisdictions, by contribution or indemnity from the drinker.

Negligence. The regime is not one of strict liability; the plaintiff must prove negligence. This ordinarily takes the form of evidence that, in violation of liquor regulations, the defendant negligently provided alcohol to a person whom the seller should have recognized as being a minor or intoxicated.[276] For example, the bartender who serves many drinks to a patron and observes his drunken behavior and incoherent speech has reason to think he is intoxicated. Subsequent blood-alcohol tests may support an inference not only that the patron was intoxicated but that the signs of drunkenness must have been visible to the alcohol provider.[277]

Scope of liability or proximate cause. Ordinarily, the plaintiff must also prove scope of liability (proximate cause) as in other negligence cases. The negligent provider who supplies alcohol to teenagers or intoxicated persons enhances the risk that the drinker

---

[268] Il St Ch 235 § 5/6–21 (liability not limited to serving intoxicated or minor persons; liability limited to $45,000 for injury, $55,000 for death in 1999, with increases thereafter keyed to consumer price index).

[269] See Bauer v. Nesbitt, 198 N.J. 601, 969 A.2d 1122 (2009); Mazzacano v. Estate of Kinnerman, 197 N.J. 307, 962 A.2d 1103 (2009) (recognizing that the Dram Shop Act itself creates a negligence claim against a seller of alcohol); 20801, Inc. v. Parker, 249 S.W.3d 392 (Tex. 2008).

[270] See Rappaport v. Nichols, 31 N.J. 188, 156 A.2d 1, 75 A.L.R.2d 821 (1959).

[271] E.g., Wis. Stat. Ann. § 125.035 (immunizing providers generally but recognizing liability when the provider knew or should have known he was providing alcohol to an underage drinker).

[272] E.g., Ontiveros v. Borak, 136 Ariz. 500, 667 P.2d 200 (1983); Rappaport v. Nichols, 31 N.J. 188, 156 A.2d 1 (1959); Brigance v. Velvet Dove Restaurant, Inc., 725 P.2d 300 (Okla. 1986); Sorensen v. Jarvis, 119 Wis.2d 627, 350 N.W.2d 108 (1984). Contra, retaining the traditional common law rule: Snyder v. Viani, 110 Nev. 1339, 885 P.2d 610 (1994); Wegleitner v. Sattler, 582 N.W.2d 688 (S.D. 1998). See Joel E. Smith, Annotation, Common-law Right of Action For Damage Sustained by Plaintiff in Consequence of Sale or Gift of Intoxicating Liquor or Habit-forming Drug to Another, 97 A.L.R.3d 528 (1980).

[273] Tobin v. Norwood Country Club, Inc., 422 Mass. 126, 661 N.E.2d 627 (1996) ("hand to hand" sale not required, liability for death of non-purchasing minor); Delahoussaye v. Mary Mahoney's, Inc., 783 So.2d 666 (Miss. 2001); Schooley v. Pinch's Deli Market, Inc., 134 Wash.2d 468, 951 P.2d 749 (1998) (similar).

[274] Petolicchio v. Santa Cruz County Fair and Rodeo Ass'n, Inc., 177 Ariz. 256, 866 P.2d 1342 (1994) (one minor foreseeably stole from liquor licensee and foreseeably provided alcohol to driver of car which caused death of decedent).

[275] See Sowinski v. Walker, 198 P.3d 1134 (Alaska 2008); Red Flame, Inc. v. Martinez, 996 P.2d 540 (Utah 2000).

[276] E.g., Flores v. Exprezit! Stores 98-Georgia, LLC, 289 Ga. 466, 713 S.E.2d 368 (2011); Faust v. Alberton, 166 Wash.2d 653, 222 P.3d 1208 (2009). Liability is even easier to find where the alcohol seller actively increases the risk of drunk driving beyond merely providing the alcohol, as by encouraging or assisting a drunk patron to drive away. Simmons v. Homatas, 23 Ill.3d 459, 925 N.E.2d 1089, 338 Ill.Dec. 883 (2010).

[277] Cusenbary v. Mortensen, 296 Mont. 25, 987 P.2d 351 (1999).

will drive dangerously,[278] that the drinker was therefore injure himself or others, and even that close relatives will suffer emotional harm upon seeing injury to the primary victim.[279] Since all these things are foreseeable and within the risk created by the alcohol provider, scope of liability (proximate cause) is established in such cases. But the alcohol provider does not necessarily create a risk that the drinker will set a house afire[280] or commit rape and murder,[281] or jump off a bridge into a river in an attempt to avoid a DWI arrest,[282] and if not, the provision of alcohol is not within the scope of defendant's liability—in other words, not a proximate cause of such harms. But the scope of liability issue, as in other negligence cases, is for the jury where reasonable people could differ. And Dram Shop statutes may be construed to permit liability if factual cause and direct injury from intoxication are proven.[283]

Duty to, and responsibility of, the intoxicated person. With the reversal of the traditional rule, new issues have arisen. The provider's liability to the intoxicated person does not, of course, displace the intoxicated person's own liability to the injured victim. Even so, some courts have held that the alcohol provider is liable to the drinker when the drinker injures himself instead of others.[284] Other courts have rejected any such liability.[285] The same division of opinion prevails under Dram Shop or Civil Damage Acts, where some statutes are interpreted to exclude liability to the drinker himself.[286] Some authority has distinguished between adults and minors, holding that the alcohol provider owes a duty of care to the minor drinker but not to the intoxicated adult.[287]

Duty of social hosts. Social hosts, like anyone else, may undertake a duty of reasonable care to assist or protect guest-drinkers; and if they do so may be held liable for breach of that duty.[288] Social hosts may likewise be in a special relationship to guests, a relationship that calls for reasonable care with respect to dangerous intoxication.[289]

---

[278] It is enough that the drinker's behavior, particularly with automobiles, will be dangerous, even though the specific way in which he will behave is unpredictable. Cusenbary v. Mortensen, 296 Mont. 25, 987 P.2d 351 (1999) (drinker in wheelchair, upon leaving tavern, drove car through tavern's wall).

[279] See Craig v. Driscoll, 262 Conn. 312, 813 A.2d 1003 (2003).

[280] Griesenbeck v. Walker, 199 N.J.Super. 132, 488 A.2d 1038 (1985) (alcohol provider not liable for fire caused by intoxicated smoker).

[281] Phan Son Van v. Pena, 990 S.W.2d 751 (Tex. 1999); cf. Kunza v. Pantze, 531 N.W.2d 839 (Minn. 1995) (intoxicated drinker attacked his wife, who was injured in trying to escape); Cameron v. Murray, 151 Wash.App. 646, 214 P.3d 150 (2009) (high school student killed by unidentified, allegedly drunken student at high-school graduation party for which wholesale beer distributor had provided the alcohol).

[282] Osborne v. Twin Town Bowl, Inc., 749 N.W.2d 367 (Minn. 2008).

[283] Berte v. Bode, 692 N.W.2d 368 (Iowa 2005).

[284] See Ellis v. N.G.N. of Tampa, Inc., 586 So.2d 1042 (Fla. 1991); Nunez v. Carrabba's Italian Grill, Inc., 448 Mass. 170, 859 N.E.2d 801 (2007); Busby v. Quail Creek Golf & Country Club, 885 P.2d 1326 (Okla. 1994); Fulmer v. Timber Inn Restaurant and Lounge, Inc., 33 Or. 413, 9 P.3d 710 (2000).

[285] Panagakos v. Walsh, 434 Mass. 353, 749 N.E.2d 670 (2001) (social host); Bridges v. Park Place Entertainment, 860 So.2d 811 (Miss. 2003) (citing many similar cases).

[286] Jackson v. PKM Corporation, 430 Mich. 262, 422 N.W.2d 657 (1988); Kirchner v. Shooters on the Water, Inc., 167 Ohio St.3d 708, 856 N.E.2d 1026 (Ct. App. 2006); Tobias v. Sports Club, Inc., 332 S.C. 90, 504 S.E.2d 318 (1998); Langle v. Kurkul, 146 Vt. 513, 5120 A.2d 1301 (1986).

[287] See Estate of Kelly v. Falin, 127 Wash.2d 31, 896 P.2d 1245 (1995) (duty owed to minor drinker, but not to adult drinker). A number of statutes also draw this distinction. See Doering v. WEA Ins. Group., 193 Wis.2d 118, 532 N.W.2d 432 (1995) (upholding statute's constitutionality).

[288] Estate of Massad ex rel. Wilson v. Granzow, 886 So.2d 1050 (Fla. Dist. Ct. App. 2004) (no social host liability for furnishing alcohol, but liability based on the fact that host "took charge" of the guest when he was helpless); Wakulich v. Mraz, 322 Ill. App. 3d 768, 751 N.E.2d 1, 255 Ill. Dec. 907 (2000), aff'd, 203 Ill.2d 223, 271 Ill.Dec. 649, 785 N.E.2d 843 (2003) (similar).

[289] Biscan v. Brown, 160 S.W.3d 462 (Tenn. 2005). However, in the absence of an undertaking or special relationship, it has been held that there is no duty to supervise minor guests. Ritchie v. Goodman, 161 S.W.3d

The control that goes with land ownership may also subject the landowner-social host to potential liability for intoxication injuries on principles akin to those that support negligent entrustment.[290] And beyond these special situations, a few cases impose liability on a social host or companion who negligently supplies alcohol to an intoxicated person likely to drive and hence likely to cause injury to others.[291] On the whole, however, courts and legislatures have been reluctant to impose a duty on social hosts based solely on their provision of alcohol to guests.[292] A wide range of disgusting behavior may be brought under the protective mantle of this social-host rule.[293]

A number of factual configurations are involved in the cases, some more likely than others to result in a duty of care. First, the intoxicated person may be either an adult or an underage drinker. Social hosts or companions are generally under no duty to protect adult drinkers[294] or their victims[295] from harms resulting from the host's provision of alcohol. But courts and legislatures have sometimes imposed a duty of care on social hosts or companions to avoid furnishing alcohol to minors, with the result that such a host may be held liable for injury due to a minor guest's intoxication if the host should have known he was providing alcohol to a minor.[296] Some kind of statutory platform is often the point of departure in this cases of liability to a minor guest-drinker. Statutes

---

851 (Mo. Ct. App. 2005). Those who provide dangerous drugs may owe similar duties. Cf. Gipson v. Kasey, 214 Ariz. 141, 150 P.3d 228 (2007) (coworker owed duty of care to decedent not to give her prescription drugs at an employee party).

[290] See Estate of Hernandez v. Arizona Board of Regents, 177 Ariz. 244, 866 P.2d 1330 (1994) ("We perceive little difference in principle between liability for giving a car to an intoxicated youth and liability for giving drinks to a youth with a car."); Huston v. Konieczny, 52 Ohio St. 3d 214, 556 N.E.2d 505 (1990); cf. McGuire v. Curry, 766 N.W.2d 501 (S.D. 2009) (employer/landowner held to owe duty to supervise underage employee to prevent him from becoming intoxicated at work); contra, Ritchie v. Goodman, 161 S.W.3d 851(Mo. Ct. App. 2005) (even if Restatement Second § 318 created a duty in landowner to control guests' intoxicated driving, precedent defeats the claims of victims on the theory that the driving-drinker is "the" proximate cause and the host is not). On negligent entrustment and its variations, see § 26.10.

[291] Kelly v. Gwinnell, 96 N.J. 538, 476 A.2d 1219 (1984) (adult guest; superseded in part by statute); Hart v. Ivey, 332 N.C. 299, 420 S.E.2d 174 (1992) (party, minor drinker; ordinarily principles of the negligence case apply). In some states, a "social host" may be defined as anyone who provides alcohol gratuitously to another person, even if that consists of buying drinks for the drinker in commercial establishments. In Delfino v. Griffo, 150 N.M. 97, 257 P.3d 917 (2011), a state that uses such a definition, the court held that pharmaceutical representatives who bought drinks for a person known to be driving could be liable for the death of a third person killed by the driver, where their provision of drinks to the driver was reckless.

[292] E.g., Burkhart v. Harrod, 110 Wash.2d 381, 755 P.2d 759 (1988) (if social host liability is to be imposed, it should be done by the legislature). Where the social host does not actually furnish alcohol, and the guest brings his own alcohol and consumes it on the premises, the imposition of a duty seems even less likely. See, e.g., Juliano v. Simpson, 461 Mass. 527, 962 N.E.2d 175 (2012).

[293] See, e.g., Wakulich v. Mraz, 322 Ill. App. 3d 768, 751 N.E.2d 1, 255 Ill. Dec. 907 (2000), aff'd, 203 Ill.2d 223, 785 N.E.2d 843, 271 Ill. Dec. 649 (2003) (men who induced a 16-year-old young woman to drink a full quart of 80-proof alcohol were merely social hosts with no duty to help prevent her death).

[294] Sampson v. MacDougall, 60 Mass. App. Ct. 394, 802 N.E.2d 602 (2004) (recognizing potential liability to third persons but rejecting liability to adult guest himself, even though guest was underage).

[295] D'Amico v. Christie, 71 N.Y.2d 76, 518 N.E.2d 896, 524 N.Y.S.2d 1, 62 A.L.R.4th 1 (1987); Willis v. Omar, 954 A.2d 126 (R.I. 2008); Carson v. Adgar, 326 S.C. 212, 486 S.E.2d 3(1997) ("a social host incurs no common law liability to a third party when he serves alcohol to his adult guests"); Smith v. Merritt, 940 S.W.2d 602 (Tex. 1997) (adult drinker injured third party, no liability for serving alcohol to adult). See Edward L. Raymond, Jr., Annotation, Social Host's Liability For Injuries Incurred by Third Parties as a Result of Intoxicated Guest's Negligence, 62 A.L.R.4th 16 (1989).

[296] See Marcum v. Bowdens, 372 S.C. 452, 643 S.E.2d 85 (2007) ("An adult social host who knowingly and intentionally serves, or causes to be served, an alcoholic beverage to a person he knows or reasonably should know is between the ages of 18 and 20 is liable to the person served and to any other person for damages proximately resulting from the host's service of alcohol."); see also, e.g., Ah Mook Sang v. Clark, 130 Hawai'i 282, 308 P.3d 911 (2013); Martin v. Marciano, 871 A.2d 911 (R.I. 2005).

may directly (or indirectly) provide for liability of hosts who furnish alcohol to minors.[297] Still, in the absence of a compelling statutory platform, many courts immunize the host even in the case of minors or underage drinkers.[298]

Second, there may be significant differences between cases of injury to a guest and injury to a third person caused by an intoxicated guest. For example, an intoxicated guest may negligently cause a post-party auto accident that kills a stranger. The latter case opens a potential field of liability not so clearly associated with the host's premises, so the same court that rejects liability to third persons may accept host-liability to the minor guest himself.[299] On the other hand, the injured stranger is not a participant in the intoxication, only a victim, and for that reason might seem especially worthy of protection from the host's negligence.[300]

Legislative reaction. In a number of states, legislatures have amended, modified, or limited the old regulatory statutes.[301] The modified regulatory statutes are now often called Dram Shop statutes, too. Where a true Dram Shop statute has been enacted, the statute is sometimes read to exclude the development of common law liability,[302] though a number of courts hold that it is not the exclusive remedy and hence now also permit an ordinary common law negligence action.[303] Most legislation passed in response to the decisions is restrictive. In particular, a number of statutes limit or abolish liability of social hosts,[304] or abolish their liability to the adult drinker himself.[305] Some impose evidentiary restrictions, limiting liability to cases in which the adult drinker was visibly intoxicated, for example.[306] Others go beyond that, limiting liability to specific situations

---

[297] See, e.g., Wis. Stat. Ann. § 125.035(2) & (4)(b); see Ennabe v. Manosa, 58 Cal.4th 697, 168 Cal.Rptr.3d 440, 319 P.3d 201 (2014) (social host who "sells" alcohol to minor may be liable under statute; charging a fee for a party may constitute "sale"); Rust v. Reyer, 91 N.Y.2d 355, 693 N.E.2d 1074, 670 N.Y.S. 2d 822 (1998) (facts alleged would support social-host liability under statute where host gave permission to have "keg party" at her house, provided storage for the kegs, and negotiated free beer for herself).

[298] E.g., Bankston v. Brennan, 507 So.2d 1385 (Fla. 1987); Bell v. Hutsell, 2011 IL 110724, 353 Ill. Dec. 288, 955 N.E.2d 1099 (2011); Andres v. Alpha Kappa Lambda Fraternity, 730 S.W.2d 547 (Mo. 1987); Reeder v. Daniel, 61 S.W.3d 359 (Tex. 2001). See also Diane Schmauder Kane, Annotation, Social Host's Liability for Death or Injuries Incurred by Person to Whom Alcohol Was Served, 54 A.L.R.5th 313. The host may still be liable for intentional or reckless conduct.

[299] Compare Ferreira v. Strack, 652 A.2d 965 (R.I. 1995) (no liability to third person) *with* Martin v. Marciano, 871 A.2d 911 (R.I. 2005) (liability to minor guest injured through another guest's intoxicated attack); and Reynolds v. Hicks, 134 Wash.2d 491, 951 P.2d 761(1998) (no liability to third person) *with* Hansen v. Friend, 118 Wash.2d 476, 824 P.2d 483 (1992) (liability for wrongful death of minor resulting from provision of alcohol by social host).

[300] See Sampson v. MacDougall, 60 Mass. App. Ct. 394, 802 N.E.2d 602 (2004).

[301] E.g., Ariz. Rev. Stat. § 4–311 (recognizing liability of liquor licensee for dispensing to intoxicated persons and minors).

[302] Ballard v. Hazel's Blue Sky, 653 N.W.2d 609 (Iowa 2002) (holding that statute preempted a common law claim for loss of consortium by parents of a deceased teenaged bar patron); D'Amico v. Christie, 71 N.Y.2d 76, 518 N.E.2d 896, 524 N.Y.S.2d 1, 62 A.L.R.4th 1 (1987) ("As an exception to the common law, the statute must of course be construed narrowly."). The statute itself may so provide. See Tex. Alc. Bev. Code Ann. § 2.03.

[303] E.g., Kowal v. Hofher, 181 Conn. 355, 436 A.2d 1 (1980) (where sale is reckless or wanton); Nunez v. Carrabba's Italian Grill, Inc., 448 Mass. 170, 859 N.E.2d 801 (2007) (dram shop act does not limit liability where sale is to an underage person). The statute itself may so provide, as in Minn. Stat. Ann. § 340A.801.

[304] Ariz. Rev. Stat. § 4–301; Cal. Civ. Code § 1714.

[305] N. J. Stat. Ann. § 2A:15–5.7.

[306] Ga. Code Ann. § 51–1–40.

or to a comparative fault share.[307] The California statute abolishes all liability of alcohol providers except those who furnish alcohol to an obviously intoxicated minor.[308]

---

[307] N.J. Stat. Ann. § 2A:15–5.8.

[308] Cal. Bus. & Prof. Code §§ 25602 & 25602.1. In Ennabe v. Manosa, 58 Cal.4th 697, 168 Cal.Rptr.3d 440, 319 P.3d 201 (2014), the court held that a social host can be liable under this statutory provision, reasoning that the word "sold" does not require commercial gain; thus a cover charge at a party can fit the statutory definition.

Part V

SPECIAL TYPES OF HARM

Chapter 27

PRENATAL AND BIRTH-RELATED INJURY

Analysis

A. PRENATAL OR PRECONCEPTION INJURY

§ 27.1   Prenatal Injury
§ 27.2   Toxic Injuries and Parental Liability
§ 27.3   Preconception Negligence

B. WRONGFUL BIRTH, CONCEPTION OR LIFE

§ 27.4   Negligent Interference with Mother's Opportunity to Avoid or Terminate a Pregnancy
§ 27.5   Special Damages Rules

A. PRENATAL OR PRECONCEPTION INJURY

§ 27.1 Prenatal Injury

The Traditional Rule and Its Demise

The early no-duty rule. Until about the middle of the 20th century, in the United States, a tortfeasor whose impact upon a pregnant woman resulted in harm to the later-born child was protected against liability. Expressed in terms of duty, the tortfeasor owed a duty to the mother, but not to the child. One reason was that the causal connection was difficult to trace. The other was the purely formal argument that the fetus was not a person to whom any duty could be owed.[1]

Rejection of the rule. The causal argument justifies scrutiny of causal proof, which depends upon facts and evidence; but it does not justify a flat rule that prohibits the very proof that would establish causation in particular cases. The formal argument, bereft of either policy or human concern, was just as inadequate if not worse. Both arguments were rejected in 1946 in *Bonbrest v. Kotz*,[2] after which courts reversed course. They now universally hold that no one is to be denied compensation for injury merely because the harm was inflicted before that person's birth.[3] So long as the living plaintiff can prove the elements of a tort claim, the fact that the harm was initially done to a pre-viable fetus does not defeat the claim.[4]

---

[1]   Dietrich v. Northhampton, 138 Mass. 14 (1884) (emphasizing lack of personhood at the time of injury), abrogation recognized by Angelini v. OMD Corp., 575 N.E.2d 41 (Mass. 1991).

[2]   Bonbrest v. Kotz, 65 F.Supp. 138 (D.D.C. 1946). The dissent of Justice Boggs in Allaire v. St. Luke's Hosp., 184 Ill. 359, 56 N.E. 638 (1900), presaged this shift, as did the Canadian decision in Montreal Tramways v. Leveille, [1933] 4 D.L.R. 337 (Sup. Ct. 1933).

[3]   E.g., Amann v. Faidy, 415 Ill. 422, 114 N.E.2d 412 (1953); Woods v. Lancet, 303 N.Y. 349, 102 N.E.2d 691, 27 A.L.R.2d 1250 (1951); Sinkler v. Kneale, 401 Pa. 267, 164 A.2d 93 (1960); Restatement Second of Torts § 869(1) (1979). The reversal was complete by about 1972. See Huskey v. Smith, 289 Ala. 52, 265 So.2d 596 (1972); Roland F. Chase, Annotation, Liability for Prenatal Injuries, 40 A.L.R.3d 1222 (1972).

[4]   Sylvia v. Gobeille, 101 R.I. 76, 220 A.2d 222 (1966) ("we are unable logically to conclude that a claim for an injury inflicted prior to viability is any less meritorious than one sustained after. . . . With us the test will not be viability but causation"). As to harm inflicted before conception, however, see § 27.3.

Wrongful Death Cases

Death claim issues. Death claims for loss of a fetus or for loss of a child injured before birth are more complicated, partly because of the way damages are calculated in death actions, partly because death statutes require the "death" of a "person," and partly because other means may be available to redress the loss to parents. In determining whether injury to a fetus was followed by "death of a person"[5] as required by statute, courts have considered two potentially critical questions: (1) Was the fetus viable at the time of injury or at least sometime before stillbirth? (2) Was the child born alive, with death occurring at some moment after birth?

Fetus not born alive. Some states reject the action altogether in the absence of a live birth.[6] The effect of this rule is that if the defendant does enough damage to terminate the life of the fetus before birth, he simply is not liable in a death action. Another group of states rejects the wrongful death action in the absence of a live birth, but permits the mother or parents to recover for mental anguish or emotional harm.[7] Most courts, however, now recognize that an action lies for wrongful death of a stillborn infant or of a fetus not born alive, at least where the fetus was viable at the time or injury[8] or became viable before stillbirth.[9]

Born alive after pre-viable injury. A different pattern occurs if the fetus is injured before viability, but the child is then born alive. In that case, the child could maintain a personal injury action if it lived, so there seems no objection to a wrongful death claim if the born-alive child dies. A few courts have insisted that viability at injury is also essential to any action.[10] If the reality of a tort-caused loss is the essential question, then this view may be too restrictive. Perhaps, as some authority holds, *either* (a) viability at time of injury *or* (b) live birth (with later death) should suffice as a basis for liability.[11] Consistent with this view, some courts have allowed the claim to proceed if the child is born alive, whether or not injury occurred before the fetus was viable.[12]

---

[5] E.g., Miccolis v. Amica Mut. Ins. Co., 587 A.2d 67 (R.I. 1991).

[6] Peters v. Hospital Auth. of Elbert County, 265 Ga. 487, 458 S.E.2d 628 (1995); Shaw v. Jendzejec, 717 A.2d 367 (Me. 1998). Arkansas originally rejected the claim in Chatelain v. Kelley, 322 Ark. 517, 910 S.W.2d 215 (1995), but in Aka v. Jefferson Hosp. Ass'n, Inc., 344 Ark. 627, 42 S.W.3d 508 (2001), that case was overruled on the ground that an antiabortion amendment to the state's constitution expressed a policy of protecting the life of unborn children to the extent permitted by federal law.

[7] Tanner v. Hartog, 696 So.2d 705 (Fla. 1997); Smith v. Borello, 370 Md. 227, 804 A.2d 1151 (2002); Giardina v. Bennett, 111 N.J. 412, 545 A.2d 139 (1988); Krishnan v. Sepulveda, 916 S.W.2d 478 (Tex. 1995). Cf. Bolin v. Wingert, 764 N.E.2d 201 (Ind. 2002); Jeter v. Mayo Clinic Ariz., 211 Ariz. 386, 121 P.3d 1256 (2005) (wrongful death claim rejected for defendant's loss of pre-implantation, fertilized and cryo-preserved ova, but recognizing a damages claim based on negligent loss, leaving open the question whether emotional harm would be a recoverable item of damages); Spangler v. Bechtel, 958 N.E.2d 458 (Ind. 2011) (special bystander rule allowed recovery where mother was neither harmed nor sufferd a physical impact).

[8] Summerfield v. Superior Court, 144 Ariz. 467, 698 P.2d 712 (1985); Shelton v. DeWitte, 271 Kan. 831, 26 P.3d 650 (2001); Moen v. Hanson, 85 Wash.2d 597, 537 P.2d 266 (1975) (death action); Cavazos v. Franklin, 73 Wash.App. 116, 867 P.2d 674 (1994) (survival action permitted). See Sheldon R. Shapiro, Annotation, Right to Maintain Action or to Recover Damages For Death of Unborn Child, 84 A.L.R.3d 411 (1978). Parvin v. Dean, 7 S.W.2d 264 (Tex. App. 1999), held that it would be unconstitutional to deny recovery for injury to a viable child who was stillborn.

[9] See Pino v. United States, 183 P.3d 1001 (Okla.2008); Nealis v. Baird, 996 P.2d 438 (Okla. 1999).

[10] Miller v. Kirk, 120 N.M. 654, 905 P.2d 194 (1995).

[11] McKinstry v. Valley Obstetrics-Gynecology Clinic, 428 Mich. 167, 405 N.W.2d 88 (1987); Hudak v. Georgy, 535 Pa. 152, 634 A.2d 600 (1993).

[12] Kalafut v. Gruver, 239 Va. 278, 389 S.E.2d 681 (1990); Miccolis v. Amica Mut. Ins. Co., 587 A.2d 67 (R.I. 1991); Gonzales v. Mascarenas, 190 P.3d 826 (Colo. Ct. App. 2008) (when child is born alive, viability does not matter).

Neither viability at injury nor live birth. The most extreme case occurs when injury is inflicted before viability and no live birth occurs. Most courts reject liability in such cases.[13] From one viewpoint, the defendant should not escape liability merely because his acts occurred early rather than late in fetal development, much less because the harm was sufficient to terminate life before birth occurred. With some such view in mind, a few recent decisions have allowed recovery in this situation.[14] This might open the door to wrongful death claims when the mother was pregnant for only a week or a day, or possibly even for a claim of death if an egg fertilized *in vitro* is destroyed before it is ever implanted in the mother, although the latter claim has been expressly rejected.[15]

Tortfeasor's negligence caused need for therapeutic abortion. A particularly difficult issue is when the fetus is not born alive because the mother terminated the pregnancy due to harms caused by the tortfeasor. In one wrongful death case, Williams v. Manchester, the defendant driver collided with the mother, who was severely injured in the accident. Her treatment required x-rays which would expose the fetus to radiation and risk of harm. In addition the mother faced increased risks to her own health if she did not terminate the pregnancy and have immediate pelvic surgery. When she elected to terminate the pregnancy in light of the increased risks to the fetus and herself, the court held that the "voluntary" nature of the termination barred her wrongful death recovery. However, her emotional distress claim was not barred.[16] The result in Williams seems contrary to many comparative fault and minimizing damages cases which hold that the negligent defendant cannot defend its negligence by claiming that the pregnant woman's post-negligence choice (to carry the pregnancy to term) was inappropriate.[17] Often wrongful death claims in which the mother elected to terminate the pregnancy are deeply embroiled with debates over abortion.[18]

What is and is not important. Courts have sometimes emphasized viability of the fetus for purely formal or conceptual reasons that are quite divorced from the purposes of tort law. The idea is that until the fetus is viable, there is no "person" apart from the mother. Any harm done is harm to the mother. In personal injury cases, however, that argument misses the point entirely. Whatever may have been the case when injury was inflicted, it set in motion a chain of events that caused injury to a living and suffering human being. Both compensation and deterrence goals of tort law counsel a rule allowing the child to recover for the tort in personal injury cases and one allowing the parents, or at least the mother, to recover when the fetus does not survive or the child dies of the

---

[13]   See Coveleski v. Bubnis, 535 Pa. 166, 634 A.2d 608 (1993); Crosby v. Glasscock Trucking Co., Inc., 340 S.C. 626, 532 S.E.2d 856 (2000); Baum v. Burrington, 119 Wash.App. 36, 79 P.3d 456 (2003).

[14]   Mack v. Carmack, 79 So. 3d 597 (Ala. 2011) (Wrongful Death Act permits an action for the death of a previable fetus); Wiersma v. Maple Leaf Farms, 543 N.W.2d 787 (S.D.1996); Carranza v. U.S., 267 P.3d 912 (Utah 2011) (wrongful death statute, as it existed before recent amendments, permitted an action for the death of unborn child; reporting that 36 other states have recognized a cause of action for the wrongful death of an unborn child, and three others have recognized a cause of action for the wrongful death of an unborn child, beginning at conception); Farley v. Sartin, 195 W.Va. 671, 466 S.E.2d 522 (1995) (emphasizing, however, that the decision did not necessarily apply to cases of conception outside the mother's body). Some of the cases are based upon construction of the statute.

[15]   Jeter v. Mayo Clinic Ariz., 211 Ariz. 386, 121 P.3d 1256 (2005) (rejecting the wrongful death claim on viability grounds but also recognizing a negligence claim for the defendant's loss of the fertilized cryo-preserved cells).

[16]   Williams v. Manchester, 228 Ill.2d 404, 888 N.E.2d 1 (2008).

[17]   See § 16.6.

[18]   See Acuna v. Turkish, 192 N.J. 399, 930 A.2d 416 (2007).

injury. The status of the fetus at the time of injury has no bearing on the status of the plaintiff, who is a living human being, harmed by the defendant's torts.

Form of recovery. It is not necessarily so, however, that wrongful death actions represent the best way to redress the real loss suffered by the parents. The losses are not much like those at which the traditional death statute was aimed—the loss of pecuniary advantage. Instead, the losses are usually emotional and intangible. An action for emotional harm to parents may be a more manageable and suitable form of redress and may also provide a vehicle for deterrence.

§ 27.2   Toxic Injuries and Parental Liability

Fetal Toxic Harm Cases

Toxic exposures. While traditional fetal injury claims were usually based on physical impact upon the mother, as in automobile collision cases and simple falls,[19] most fetal harms today are likely to be the result of licit and illicit drugs, environmental toxins, workplace exposures, or contaminants in water or food. Courts are now facing claims of fetal injury from some such exposures and no doubt more will follow.

Difficult proof of causation. Toxic torts frequently involve low dosages over time, often with a long latency period before harm appears. Unlike an automobile accident, a medical mishap, or a punch in the nose, no one can see the toxic tort happen. A fetus may be peculiarly susceptible to some toxins which can pass from the mother directly to the fetus.[20] But in the case of fetal injuries, many toxic injuries can be inflicted that are not dramatic enough to be identified immediately or with certainty by the use of existing technology. Studies may show, for example, that carbon monoxide, a well-known danger, is harmful to the fetus, but they may be inconclusive about the nature of the harms when exposure is not great.[21] Some effects remain hidden because they operate on the central nervous system of the fetus and leave behind intelligence and learning ability deficits rather than distorted appendages or chemicals in the urine. For instance, even a mother's moderate ingestion of alcohol during pregnancy may lead to substantial deficits in her child's learning ability,[22] but unless the child is a part of a scientific study, her lifelong learning difficulties may never be understood, much less attributed to her mother's drinking. The same seems to be true if the mother is exposed to lead.[23] For these and associated reasons, lawyers will find it quite difficult—and very expensive—

---

[19]   E.g., Cushing v. Time Saver Stores, Inc., 552 So.2d 730 (La. Ct. App. 1989) (brain damage to child resulting from fetal impact that caused abruption of the placenta).

[20]   A good introduction to the methods by which prenatal toxic harm can occur is Steven S. Paskal, Liability for Prenatal Harm in the Workplace: the Need for Reform, 17 U. Puget Sound L. Rev. 283 (1994). Many potential toxic agents are described in various articles in Gideon Koren (Ed.), Maternal-Fetal Toxicology: A Clinician's Guide (2d ed. 1994); see also Sam Kacew & George H. Lambert, Environmental Toxicology and Pharmacology of Human Development (1997).

[21]   The difficulties of producing a conclusive carbon monoxide study are summarized, along with limited conclusions, in Gideon Koren, Teresa Sharav & Anne Pastuszak, A Multicenter, Prospective Study of Fetal Outcome Following Accidental Carbon Monoxide Poisoning in Pregnancy, in Gideon Koren, supra n. 20, at 253.

[22]   See Ann Pytkowicz Streissguth, Paul D. Sampson, Helen M. Barr, Fred L. Bookstein & Heather Carmichael Olson, The Effects of Prenatal Exposure to Alcohol and Tobacco: Contributions from the Seattle Longitudinal Prospective Student and Implications for Public Policy, in Herbert L. Needleman & David Belligener, Prenatal Exposure to Toxicants—Developmental Consequences 148 (1994). Possibly the father's use of alcohol too. See Gladys Friedler, Developmental Toxicology: Male-mediated Effects, in Maureen Paul, Occupational and Environmental Reproductive Hazards, a Guide for Clinicians 52 (1993).

[23]   See David Bellinger & Herbert L. Needleman, The Neurotoxicity of Prenatal Exposures to Lead: Kinetics, Mechanisms and Expressions, in Herbert L. Needleman & David Bellinger, Prenatal Exposure to Toxicants—Developmental Consequences 89 (1994).

to prove scientific causation.[24] Many authors have proposed rules to make the road easier for the toxic plaintiff,[25] even as others propose to tighten causal rules to provide more protection for defendants.[26]

Workplace Injury to Fetus and the Workers' Compensation Limit

Workers' compensation no bar. When the fetus is exposed to hazardous materials because of the mother's or father's exposure in the workplace, workers' compensation laws are potentially implicated. Those laws generally provide for standardized compensation to workers injured on the job as the exclusive remedy; tort claims are forbidden. When a child asserts a claim that she was injured in utero by her mother's exposure to hazardous materials on the mother's job, the question is whether the child's claim in tort should be barred by the workers' compensation rules. The answer in the handful of cases on point has uniformly been that the claim is not barred by the workers' compensation exclusive remedy rules.[27]

Employer negligence. To eliminate the exclusive remedy rule is not to impose liability upon employers for fetal injury. The child, like anyone else claiming tort damages against the employer, will be required to show negligence or, possibly, abnormally dangerous activities. The fact that an employer's business uses dangerous chemicals does not necessarily mean that the employer is negligent. Only if dangerous chemicals are unnecessary or if feasible precautions against injury are ignored, is negligence established. In addition, federal antidiscrimination law requires employers to allow women equal access to jobs, including jobs that may endanger a fetus.[28] If the employer's only supposed negligence is in permitting a fully informed pregnant woman to work around dangerous materials, the federal antidiscrimination rule probably protects the employer against tort liability.[29]

---

[24] Mass studies showing an increased risk of harm to fetuses from particular substances may still fall short. A good illustration is Turpin v. Merrell Dow Pharms., Inc., 959 F.2d 1349 (6th Cir. 1992). Limitations imposed upon "scientific" testimony in Daubert v. Merrell Dow Pharms., Inc., 509 U.S. 579, 113 S.Ct. 2786, 125 L.Ed.2d 469 (1993), may add to the difficulty. See generally Michael Green, Expert Witnesses and Sufficiency of Evidence in Toxic Substances Litigation: The Legacy of Agent Orange and Bendectin Litigation, 86 Nw. U. L. Rev. 643 (1992). D.H. Kaye, Is Proof of Statistical Significance Relevant?, 61 Wash. L. Rev. 1333 (1986); Neil B. Cohen, Confidence in Probability: Burdens of Persuasion in a World of Imperfect Knowledge, 60 N.Y.U. L. Rev. 385 (1985).

[25] Thus some advocate changes in the requirements of causal evidence in toxic tort cases, see Margaret A. Berger, Eliminating General Causation: Notes Towards a New Theory of Justice and Toxic Torts, 97 Colum. L. Rev. 2117 (1997), while others advocate changes in regulation and compensation systems. See Anita Bernstein, Formed by Thalidomide: Mass Torts as a False Cure For Toxic Exposure, 97 Colum. L. Rev. 2153 (1997).

[26] See James A. Henderson & Theodore Eisenberg, The Quiet Revolution in Products Liability: An Empirical Study of Legal Change, 37 UCLA L. Rev. 479 (1990). Professor Boston proposed a demanding standard for mass tort cases, less for individualized injuries. Gerald W. Boston, A Mass-Exposure Model of Toxic Causation: the Content of Scientific Proof and the Regulatory Experience, 18 Colum. J. Envtl. L. 181 (1993).

[27] Namislo v. Akzo Chems., Inc., 620 So.2d 573 (Ala. 1993); Snyder v. Michael's Stores, Inc., 16 Cal.4th 991, 945 P.2d 781, 68 Cal.Rptr.2d 476 (1997); Pizza Hut of Am., Inc. v. Keefe, 900 P.2d 97 (Colo. 1995); Hitachi Chem. Electro-Products, Inc. v. Burley, 219 Ga.App. 675, 466 S.E.2d 867 (1995). See also Meyer v. Burger King Corp., 26 P.3d 925 (Wash. 2001).

[28] United Auto. Workers v. Johnson Controls, Inc., 499 U.S. 187, 111 S.Ct. 1196, 113 L.Ed.2d 158 (1991).

[29] Id.

Father's exposure. Workplace exposure of the father may also cause fetal harm. Besides the possibility of chromosome damage by radiation,[30] some studies, still at the early stage, indicate that fetal harm or anomalies are often associated positively with the father's occupation.[31] The hypothesis is that toxic agents associated with particular occupations may affect chromosome structure, or that the father may inadvertently carry home toxins on his body or in his clothes, exposing the mother during pregnancy. As with so many potential claims of toxic harm, however, proof of causation may have to await further study.

Product and Environmental Injuries to Fetus

Exposures. A number of substances in the environment or in products may cause fetal harm. Lead is famously dangerous to a developing fetus as well as to children.[32] Second-hand smoke is probably a toxin to the fetus.[33] Some prescription drugs can damage the fetus, and even kill the child.[34] In such a case, if exposure is demonstrated and harm results, liability may be established.[35] As already indicated, however, proof of causation has failed in many claims for prenatal injury against pharmaceutical manufacturers, either on the ground that the evidence of experts was insufficient or on the ground that it was inadmissible altogether as insufficiently accepted among scientists.[36]

Parents' Duty to Fetus

Parents' exposures and fetal harm. A father whose genetic material is injured may pass along serious birth defects from the moment of conception. A mother may intentionally or unintentionally ingest alcohol—the "teratogen of choice" one authority called it[37]—or harmful agents such as cocaine or lead. Use of these and other drugs in

---

[30]   As claimed in cases like Hinkie v. United States, 715 F.2d 96 (3d Cir. 1983) (exposure to radioactivity); Mondelli v. United States, 711 F.2d 567 (3d Cir. , 1983) (genetic damage by service member's exposure to nuclear explosion causing cancer to child); Monaco v. United States, 661 F.2d 129 (9th Cir. 1981).

[31]   Andrew F. Olshan, Kay Teschke & Patricia A. Baird, Paternal Occupation and Congenital Anomalies in Offspring, 20 Am. J. of Indus. Med. 447 (1991).

[32]   E.g., Kim N. Dietrich, Kathleen M. Kraft, Robert L. Bornschein, Paul B. Hammond, Omer Berger, Paul A. Succop & Mariana Bier, Low-Level Lead Exposure Effect on Neurobehavioral Development in Early Infancy, 80 Pediatrics 721 (1987).

[33]   See H. Westley Clark & Meryle Weinstein, Chemical Dependency in Maureen Paul, Occupation and Environmental Reproductive Hazards 344, 347–48 (1993); see also Julie E. Lippert, Comment, Prenatal Injuries from Passive Tobacco Smoke: Establishing a Cause of Action for Negligence, 78 Ky. L.J. 865 (1989/90).

[34]   Mobile OB-GYN, P.C. v. Baggett, 25 So.3d 1129 (Ala. 2009) (medical malpractice liability for prescribing and failing to advise patient to discontinue blood pressure drug Benicar during pregnancy and for failing to appreciate developing signs of fetal damage).

[35]   Sheppard-Mobley ex rel. Mobley v. King, 4 N.Y.3d 627, 830 N.E.2d 301 (2005) (unsuccessful chemical abortion attempt by physician caused severe physical injuries in utero to fetus who was later born alive); Brucker v. Mercola, 227 Ill.2d 502, 886 N.E.2d 306 (2007) (doctor prescribed L-glutamine but dispensed selenium to pregnant woman whose fetus was poisoned when the mother ingested it); Hogle v. Hall, 112 Nev. 599, 916 P.2d 814 (1996) (product Accutane, known to be teratogenic if used during pregnancy, physician liable for prescription). Because the physician is acting on behalf of both mother and fetus, an infant in utero was held to have an informed consent claim against the delivering physician. See Miller ex rel. Miller v. Dacus, 231 S.W.3d 903 (Tenn. 2007).

[36]   See, e.g., Blackwell v. Wyeth, 408 Md. 575, 971 A.2d 235 (2009) (rejecting expert testimony trying to link the preservative thimerisol in vaccines with childhood autism); Merrell Dow Pharms., Inc. v. Havner, 953 S.W.2d 706 (Tex. 1997) (reviewing the sufficiency and admissibility holdings in the Bendectin cases where plaintiffs asserted that children suffered limb reduction defects because of fetal exposure through mothers' ingestion of Bendectin).

[37]   See Ann Pytkowicz Streissguth, et al., supra n. 22 at 174.

pregnancy is quite common and cuts across social and racial lines.[38] Some, perhaps all, of those and other ingested substances may harm the fetus and permanently damage the child. If parents are not protected by an immunity,[39] the question is whether a child has a good claim against her own mother or father for fetal injuries of this kind.

A parent's duty? Few cases deal with the parents' duty to the fetus. In non-toxic cases, one claim consistently denied is the claim for dissatisfied life brought by a child against a parent for causing his birth as an illegitimate child.[40] At least two courts in automobile accident cases refused to entertain a child's action against the mother based upon the mother's negligent driving during pregnancy.[41] Other courts in automobile cases have held that the mother owed reasonable care to a child once it was born, therefore a duty of care should be imposed for the fetus as well.[42] The argument against liability seems most significantly addressed to cases involving the mother's use of substances that could harm the fetus. Liability in substance abuse cases, which could include excessive consumption of coffee or use of tobacco, might conflict with the mother's right of autonomy, bodily integrity, and privacy. Where mother's ingestion is involved, it is plausible to argue that the mother's legal, but dangerous, activities like smoking would entail too much of an intrusion on autonomy. A Texas court has rejected any duty by a pregnant woman that would impose liability for illegal ingestion of cocaine during pregnancy.[43] So far one substance-ingestion case actually recognized a potential liability, but it did not discuss the central issue of the mother's own rights, and its authority is clouded by later decisions.[44] Although the mother-autonomy reasons that animate substance abuse cases do not obviously apply to auto cases, at least one court thought that even a rule permitting the liability of a mother to a child born injured because of the mother's negligent driving would be a dangerous precedent.[45] The problem of a mother's potential responsibility for treatment of her own body, or her fetus mirrors the problem much-debated in the criminal field.[46]

§ 27.3　Preconception Negligence

Preconception negligence. When the plaintiff is injured by negligent acts that occur before the plaintiff was conceived, courts are somewhat divided.[47] Such injuries have

---

[38]　See Ira J. Chasnoff, Harvey J. Landress & Mark E. Barrett, The Prevalence of Illicit Drug or Alcohol Use During Pregnancy, 322 New Eng. J. Med. 1202 (1990).

[39]　See § 23.2.

[40]　E.g., Slawek v. Stroh, 62 Wis.2d 295, 215 N.W.2d 9 (1974).

[41]　Stallman v. Youngquist, 125 Ill.2d 267, 531 N.E.2d 355, 126 Ill.Dec. 60, 78 A.L.R.4th 1071 (1988); Remy v. MacDonald, 440 Mass. 675, 801 N.E.2d 260 (2004).

[42]　Bonte v. Bonte, 136 N.H. 286, 616 A.2d 464 (1992). Accord National Cas. Co. v. Northern Trust Bank of Fla., 807 So.2d 86 (Fla. Dist. Ct. App. 2001) (cautiously supporting liability where the mother is chargeable with negligent driving and recognizing that the answer might be different if issues of the mother's personal privacy or health choices were involved).

[43]　Chenault v. Huie, 989 S.W.2d 474 (Tex. App. 1999) (doubting whether a workable standard of care could be developed; "The 'reasonable person' standard . . . is simply not design to apply to matters involving intimate, private, and personal decisions").

[44]　Grodin v. Grodin, 102 Mich.App. 396, 301 N.W.2d 869 (1980), disagreement recognized by Mickel v. Wilson, 2010 WL 3418897 (Mich. Ct. App. 2010).

[45]　Remy v. MacDonald, 440 Mass. 675, 682, 801 N.E.2d 260, 266 (2004).

[46]　Whitner v. State, 328 S.C. 1, 492 S.E.2d 777 (1997), authorized criminal conviction of a mother who used crack cocaine to the injury of the fetus in the third trimester. In State v. McKnight, 352 S.C. 635, 576 S.E.2d 168 (2003), the court affirmed the homicide conviction of a mother who used cocaine during pregnancy.

[47]　See generally Julie A. Greenberg, Reconceptualizing Preconception Torts, 64 Tenn. L. Rev. 315, 349 ff. (1997); Annotation, Liability for Child's Personal Injuries or Death Resulting from Tort Committed Against Child's Mother Before Child Was Conceived, 91 A.L.R.3d 316 (1980).

occurred in several ways. For example, the defendant might damage genetic material of either parent before the plaintiff was conceived, with resulting genetic defects in the plaintiff once conception and birth took place.[48] Or the defendant may negligently harm the mother before conception, resulting in oxygen deprivation of the fetus much later[49] or early termination of pregnancy and damage to the child.[50] Or health care providers, acting before the plaintiff's conception, may negligently fail to prevent development of antibodies in the mother that would damage the fetus once conception occurs.[51]

Duty of care. About a dozen cases have passed on the defendant's duty when the plaintiff had not been conceived at the time the defendant acted. Most of them expressly or implicitly recognize that the ordinary duty of care does not disappear merely because the child was not conceived at the time of the defendant's negligent conduct. In an analogous situation, if the defendant negligently constructs a balcony so that two years later it falls upon a one year-old child, no one believes that the child should be denied recovery on the ground that she was not in existence when the defendant's negligent acts took place.[52] The defendant will be held liable for foreseeable harms he causes to the later-conceived child.[53] Some other courts, seemingly receptive to the claim, have left the matter open.[54] Most of these cases that recognize a duty of care to an unconceived child are in fact suits against health care professionals who are engaged in treating the mother and who at least implicitly undertake to provide appropriate care for the child as well.[55]

It is possible to imagine that a drug needed by the mother might be harmful to either a fetus already carried or one that might be carried in the future, but a conflict like that is not limited to preconception duties and in any event is usually resolved by giving the mother full information and allowing her to make the choice.[56]

---

[48] Some such claims against the government for harms resulting from exposure to nuclear radiation have been dismissed under the Feres rule. See § 22.4.

[49] Albala v. City of New York, 54 N.Y.2d 269, 445 N.Y.S.2d 108, 429 N.E.2d 786 (1981).

[50] Hegyes v. Unjian Enters., Inc., 234 Cal.App.3d 1103, 286 Cal.Rptr. 85 (1991).

[51] E.g., Walker v. Rinck, 604 N.E.2d 591 (Ind. 1992); Lynch v. Scheininger, 162 N.J. 209, 744 A.2d 113 (2000). Several versions of such cases arise, but all essentially turn on the fact that health care providers either trigger antibodies in the mother's blood by transfusion of incompatible blood or fail to test the mother's blood and administer RhoGAM once the blood has been sensitized. In all these cases, injury to the fetus can be avoided only by preconception care.

[52] See Lough v. Rolla Women's Clinic, Inc., 866 S.W.2d 851 (Mo. 1993) (giving a version of this hypothetical).

[53] Estate of Amos v. Vanderbilt Univ., 62 S.W.3d 133 (Tenn. 2001) (failure to inform mother of risk of HIV from blood transfusion left her unable to take precautions to guard against transmission to her child); Bergstreser v. Mitchell, 577 F.2d 22 (8th Cir. 1978); Jorgensen v. Meade Johnson Lab., Inc., 483 F.2d 237 (10th Cir. 1973); Empire Cas. Co. v. St. Paul Fire & Marine Ins. Co., 764 P.2d 1191 (Colo. 1988); Renslow v. Mennonite Hosp., 67 Ill.2d 348, 10 Ill.Dec. 484, 367 N.E.2d 1250, 91 A.L.R.3d 291 (1977); Walker v. Rinck, 604 N.E.2d 591 (Ind. 1992); Graham v. Keuchel, 847 P.2d 342 (Okla. 1993); Sweeney v. Preston, 642 So.2d 332 (Miss. 1994) (without separate discussion of the preconception issue).

[54] Grover v. Eli Lilly & Co., 63 Ohio St.3d 756, 591 N.E.2d 696 (1992) (child could not recover for injury ultimately due to his grandmother's ingestion of DES 28 years earlier; blanket rule against preconception tort liability not required).

[55] Hegyes v. Unjian Enters., Inc., 234 Cal.App.3d 1103, 286 Cal.Rptr. 85 (1991) (duty might be recognized in professional negligence cases but not in car accident cases three years before conception); Taylor v. Cutler, 306 N.J.Super. 37, 703 A.2d 294 (1997), aff'd without opinion as to this point, 157 N.J. 525, 724 A.2d 793 (1999).

[56] See Julie A. Greenberg, Reconceptualizing Preconception Torts, 64 Tenn. L. Rev. 315, 347 ff. (1997).

While a blanket rule in favor of a duty of care fits well with the usual tort rules—liability for negligence is the norm—courts can find plenty of room to shape duties to their sense of policy and justice without barring all cases.[57]

B. WRONGFUL BIRTH, CONCEPTION OR LIFE

§ 27.4 Negligent Interference with Mother's Opportunity to Avoid or Terminate a Pregnancy

Causes of action. Claims for interference with a mother's opportunity to avoid pregnancy, or to terminate it, have taken three distinct forms.[58] All three forms have in common the assertion that, but for the defendant's negligence, the mother could have avoided giving birth to a child who is either unwanted or who suffers painful birth defects. The claim is typically brought against a physician with the allegation that the physician negligently failed to perform a birth control surgery, or that the physician negligently failed to inform the mother that she was carrying a child with genetic defects, and that, but for the physician's negligence, the mother would have avoided giving birth to the child. As in other medical malpractice cases, the plaintiff must prove that the physician was negligent in violating a medical standard of care or a governing statute or regulation.[59]

The three kinds of claims are usually labeled differently, although some authority discards the labels, emphasizing that the claim is merely a negligence claim subject to the ordinary negligence rules.[60] The labels are used here for convenience in identifying the various claims.

Wrongful life. The wrongful life claim is one asserted by a child suffering birth defects such as a painful and debilitating disease. The claim is definitely not that the physician caused the disease or defect. It is rather that the physician negligently allowed the child to be born at all and that the child has a claim for the suffering he must undergo as a result. Most courts reject this claim altogether,[61] partly because they are unwilling to say that life itself is harm, or that compensation can be measured for the harm of living as compared to never having lived at all.[62]

Recoveries. A few courts have allowed the child to recover on wrongful life claims. These have largely limited the child to recovery for medical expenses.[63] The wrongful life

---

[57] See Restatement Third of Torts (Physical and Emotional Harm) §§ 3, 7 (establishing a baseline duty of reasonable care and a mechanism for courts to create exception based on principle or policy).

[58] Analogous problems arise when the plaintiff bears a child as a result of a rape, see Doe v. Westfall Health Care Ctr., Inc., 303 A.D.2d 102, 755 N.Y.S.2d 769 (2002) (grandparents who adopted child could not recover cost of raising child from caretaker whose staff member raped vegetative patient).

[59] In Galvez v. Frields, 88 Cal.App.4th 1410, 107 Cal.Rptr.2d 50 (2001), the court held it prejudicial error to refuse a negligence per se instruction when evidence supported the claim that, in failing to order a screening test, a physician violated a state regulation.

[60] Bader v. Johnson, 732 N.E.2d 1212 (Ind. 2000).

[61] E.g., Willis v. Wu, 362 S.C. 146, 607 S.E.2d 63 (2004) (rejecting wrongful life claim of eight-year-old born with hydrocephalus); Walker v. Mart, 164 Ariz. 37, 790 P.2d 735 (1990); Cowe v. Forum Group, Inc., 575 N.E.2d 630 (Ind. 1991); Kassama v. Magat, 368 Md. 113, 792 A.2d 1102 (2002) ("an impaired life is *not* worse than non-life, and, for that reason, life is not, and cannot be, an injury"); B.D.H. ex rel. S.K.L. v. Mickelson, 792 N.W.2d 169 (N.D. 2010) (statute precluded "wrongful life" claim).

[62] See Clark v. Children's Mem'l Hosp., 353 Ill.Dec. 254, 955 N.E.2d 1065 (2011) (on public policy grounds, a child born with a genetic or congenital condition does not have a claim for wrongful life because "his life, while burdened by his condition, is as a matter of law, always preferable to nonlife").

[63] Turpin v. Sortini, 31 Cal.3d 220, 182 Cal.Rptr. 337, 643 P.2d 954 (1982); Harbeson v. Parke-Davis, Inc., 98 Wash.2d 460, 656 P.2d 483 (1983); Johnson v. Superior Court, 101 Cal.App.4th 869, 124 Cal.Rptr.2d

claim permits recovery of the extraordinary expenses for the child's entire life expectancy.[64]

Wrongful birth. The wrongful birth claim is asserted by the parent, not the child. The mother typically claims that, but for the defendant's negligence in testing[65] or counseling,[66] the mother would have terminated a pregnancy to avoid birth of a child with serious genetic defects. The claim was initially rejected in 1967,[67] but since a mother's constitutional right to an early-term abortion was recognized,[68] almost all of the courts considering the question have allowed some kind of recovery in these cases.[69] One court has even held that it would violate its public policy to apply the state law rules of a state that does not recognize such a claim.[70] A wrongful birth claim is typically asserted by the mother. Whether a father also has a claim is the subject of differing views.[71] In at least one instance, siblings sought recovery, which was rejected.[72]

A case closely analogous to wrongful birth cases arises when an adoption agency negligently or fraudulently places a child with a genetic illness with adoptive parents, who learn only much later of the difficulty and the expense. Consistent with the wrongful birth cases, courts here again allow parental recovery.[73]

The wrongful birth claim can be viewed as a species of an informed consent claim, protecting essential values of individual choice, autonomy, and self-determination. But there is a difference of sorts. The wrongful birth plaintiff does not recover for the genetic

---

650 (2002) (defendants allegedly supplied defective sperm for artificial insemination knowing that the donor's family had a history of polycystic kidney disease likely to be inherited; Brittany, the child born of this arrangement, suffered the disease as a result. In her suit against these suppliers, the court held that she could not recover for emotional distress because this was essentially a wrongful life claim).

[64] See, e.g., Arche v. United States, 247 Kan. 276, 798 P.2d 477 (1990) (limiting the parents' recovery of damages to the period of the child's minority). Most courts apparently would not impose such a limit. See Smith v. Cote, 128 N.H. 231, 513 A.2d 341 (1986).

[65] In Galvez v. Frields, 88 Cal.App.4th 1410, 107 Cal.Rptr.2d 50 (2001), the court held that negligent testing could be established under the negligence per se rule by showing that the defendant failed to order a screening test required by regulation.

[66] E.g., Burns v. Hanson, 249 Conn. 809, 734 A.2d 964 (1999) (alleged negligence in diagnosis of or advice about pregnancy of severely disabled mother in time to permit abortion of healthy child); Smith v. Cote, 128 N.H. 231, 513 A.2d 341 (1986).

[67] Gleitman v. Cosgrove, 49 N.J. 22, 227 A.2d 689, 22 A.L.R.3d 1411 (1967), abrogation recognized by Hummel v. Reiss, 608 A.2d 1341 (N.J. 1992).

[68] Roe v. Wade, 410 U.S. 113, 93 S.Ct. 705, 35 L.Ed.2d 147 (1973).

[69] E.g., Lininger v. Eisenbaum, 764 P.2d 1202 (Colo. 1988); Hummel v. Reiss, 608 A.2d 1341 (N.J. 1992); Becker v. Schwartz, 46 N.Y.2d 401, 413 N.Y.S.2d 895, 386 N.E.2d 807 (1978); Thibeault v. Larson, 666 A.2d 112 (Me. 1995) (under a statute); cf. Arche v. United States, 247 Kan. 276, 798 P.2d 477 (1990) (claim is cognizable only when the "child has such gross deformities, not medically correctable, that the child will never be able to function as a normal human being").

[70] Laboratory Corp. of Am. v. Hood, 395 Md. 608, 911 A.2d 841 (2006) (analyzing public policy exception to choice of law provisions).

[71] Compare Fruiterman v. Granata, 276 Va. 629, 668 S.E.2d 127 (2008) (husband of pregnant wife was not a patient to whom doctor owed a duty for purposes of wrongful birth claim), with Laboratory Corp. of Am. v. Hood, 395 Md. 608, 911 A.2d 841 (2006) (whether lab that misdiagnosed cystic fibrosis genetic mutation owed a duty to the father as well as the mother was fact-dependent inquiry as "in many cases, especially when the woman is married, that decision [to terminate a pregnancy] is one jointly arrived at by the woman and her husband").

[72] Moscatello v. University of Med. & Dentistry of N.J., 342 N.J.Super. 351, 776 A.2d 874 (2001) (duty did not extend to others who had no right of choice).

[73] See Halper v. Jewish Family & Children's Serv. of Greater Philadelphia, 600 Pa. 145, 963 A.2d 1282 (2009) (accepting the cause of action but finding that its requirements were not met in the case before it); Meracle v. Children's Serv. Soc'y of Wis., 149 Wis. 2d 19, 437 N.W.2d 532 (1989); Burr v. Board of County Comm'rs of Stark County, 23 Ohio St. 3d 69, 491 N.E.2d 1101, 56 A.L.R.4th 357 (1986).

defect itself but for the loss of the choice to terminate the pregnancy and the damages that flow from that loss. It has been held enough, therefore, if the plaintiff proves that given appropriate testing and information,[74] she would have terminated the pregnancy, even if the genetic harm to the child arose from risks separate from those of which she should have been warned.[75]

Rejecting the claim. A small number of courts has denied the wrongful birth claim on the assertion that existence of human life cannot be permitted to count as legal damages,[76] or on the ground that parents would be tempted to perjure themselves to establish their willingness to terminate the pregnancy.[77] In addition, some states have passed statutes as anti-abortion legislation.[78] These statutes, where constitutional,[79] curtail or eliminate the wrongful birth action.[80] Some advocates for the disabled also dislike the wrongful birth action because it perpetuates the "disability hierarchy" of values in which the disabled are regarded as worth less.[81]

Wrongful conception or pregnancy. The claim for wrongful pregnancy or conception typically asserts that the defendant physician was negligent in giving genetic advice[82]

---

[74] What counts as appropriate information has been the subject of some litigation. See Hall v. Dartmouth Hitchcock Med. Ctr., 153 N.H. 388, 899 A.2d 240 (2006).

[75] Pre-conception negligence in genetic counseling suffices if the parent would have avoided conception or terminated pregnancy upon being fully advised. See Didato v. Strehler, 554 S.E.2d 42 (Va. 2001); Canesi v. Wilson, 158 N.J. 490, 730 A.2d 805 (1999).

[76] See Grubbs v. Barbourville Family Health Ctr., P.S.C., 120 S.W.3d 682 (Ky. 2003) (involving pregnancies of 22 and 24 weeks at the time information about fetal condition was acquired; although rejecting the tort action for lack of injury, the court approved a breach of contract action against physicians who breach contract obligations to diagnose and report correctly); Azzolino v. Dingfelder, 315 N.C. 103, 337 S.E.2d 528 (1985). Georgia insists that the claim does not "does not fit within the parameters of traditional tort law" and that only the legislature can recognize it. Etkind v. Suarez, 271 Ga. 352, 519 S.E.2d 210 (1999).

[77] See Wilson v. Kuenzi, 751 S.W.2d 741 (Mo. 1988).

[78] E.g., Idaho Code § 145.424; Minn. Stat. Ann. § 5–334.

[79] Wood v. University of Utah Med. Ctr., 67 P.3d 436 (Utah 2002) (upholding statute); Hickman v. Group Health Plan, Inc., 396 N.W.2d 101 (Minn. 1986) (Minnesota statute did not violate constitutional guarantees); but see Note, Wrongful Birth Actions: The Case against Legislative Curtailment, 100 Harv. L. Rev. 2017 (1987); Julie F. Kowitz, Note, Not Your Garden Variety Tort Reform: Statutes Barring Claims for Wrongful Life and Wrongful Birth Are Unconstitutional under the Purpose Prong of Planned Parenthood v. Casey, 61 Brook. L. Rev. 235 (1995) (arguing that statutes deny the constitutional rights recognized in Roe v. Wade and later cases); Stephanie S. Gold, An Equality Approach to Wrongful Birth Statutes, 65 Fordham L. Rev. 1005 (1996) (arguing the statutes engage in gender discrimination); Julie Gantz, State Statutory Preclusion of Wrongful Birth Relief: A Troubling Re-Writing of a Woman's Right to Choose and the Doctor-Patient Relationship, 4 Va. J. Soc. Pol'y & L. 795 (1997).

[80] After the statutes, actions seeking recovery for harms other than the loss of opportunity to terminate a pregnancy may still be actionable. For example, failures of preconception genetic counseling may be actionable. See Molloy v. Meier, 679 N.W.2d 711 (Minn. 2004) (statute did not preclude malpractice claim in which parents alleged that if their first child had been accurately diagnosed with genetic disorder, their second child would not have been conceived, but rather, would not have been conceived). Similarly, in Vanvooren v. Astin, 141 Idaho 440, 111 P.3d 125 (2005), the court rejected a claim styled as a claim for negligent infliction of emotional distress which essentially sought recovery for the parents' distress as the result of their inability to terminate the pregnancy. However, the court left aside as not properly presented, the plaintiff's deposition claim that the physician's failure to provide accurate information denied her the opportunity to better prepare for the birth.

[81] See Allan H. Macurdy, Disability Ideology and the Law School Curriculum, 4 B.U. Pub. Int. L.J. 443 (1995). See also Jillian T. Stein, Backdoor Eugenics: The Troubling Implication of Certain Damages Awards in Wrongful Birth and Wrongful Life Claims, 40 Seton Hall L. Rev. 1117 (2010).

[82] E.g., Didato v. Strehler, 554 S.E.2d 42 (Va. 2001) (alleged failure to advise parents after first child that future children would likely suffer serious genetic harm); McAllister v. Ha, 347 N.C. 638, 496 S.E.2d 577 (1998).

or performing a medical procedure or dispensing contraceptives to prevent conception[83] and that as a result the mother bore a child, with the added expense of child rearing. If the medical procedure is, like a vasectomy, performed upon the husband rather than the wife, there is the striking possibility that the wife would be a non-patient to whom no duty was owed.[84]

The claim differs from wrongful birth in two important respects. First, it does not rest on a claim that the mother had a right to terminate her pregnancy.[85] The claim thus escapes the bar of those statutes that prohibit suits based upon the mother's loss of opportunity for an abortion.[86] Perhaps partly for this reason, some of the few courts that reject the wrongful birth action actively support the wrongful pregnancy claim.[87]

The wrongful pregnancy claim also differs from the wrongful birth claim because it does not necessarily involve an unhealthy or genetically damaged child. Instead, the mother or the parents had decided against enlarging the family for personal or economic reasons. One or two states reject the wrongful pregnancy action altogether.[88] The great majority now recognize the claim,[89] but subject it to some unusual limitations on damages recoverable discussed in the next section.

§ 27.5 Special Damages Rules

Damage rules. Although wrongful birth and wrongful pregnancy claims are accepted in most courts, they are often limited by unusual damages rules. The normal compensatory damages rules would award damages for emotional harm and economic costs inflicted by the tort. In the case of wrongful birth or pregnancy, that would mean a recovery for emotional harm to the mother, and perhaps to the father, and also the costs of rearing the child—two harms that would have been avoided if the physician had not been negligent. Courts have been struck, however, by the idea that a child, healthy or not, would give the parents pleasure and that the parents' putative pleasure should be

---

[83] E.g., Chaffee v. Seslar, 786 N.E.2d 705 (Ind. 2003) (negligent salpingectomy); Simmerer v. Dabbas, 890 Ohio.St.3d 586, 233 N.E.2d 1169 (2000) (negligent sterilization of mother); Heather A. Weisser, Abolishing the Pharmacist's Veto: An Argument in Support of a Wrongful Conception Cause of Action Against Pharmacists Who Refuse to Provide Emergency Contraception, 80 S. Cal. L. Rev. 865 (2007).

[84] See Doe v. Pharmacia & Upjohn Co., Inc., 388 Md. 407, 879 A.2d 1088 (2005) (seemingly so implying). However, other courts may well take a broader view of the physician's duty, see, e.g., Estate of Amos v. Vanderbilt Univ., 62 S.W.3d 133 (Tenn. 2001).

[85] This must be qualified in cases like Burns v. Hanson, 249 Conn. 809, 734 A.2d 964 (1999), where the plaintiff, a severely disabled person for whom pregnancy was contraindicated, claimed that the doctor failed to advise her of her pregnancy in time to permit an abortion. In such a case, the patient must show that she would have undergone an abortion if she had been given timely information. The trial judge refused to permit the plaintiff to testify that she would have had an abortion, then told the jury that she was required to prove that she would have had one. This was error and judgment for the defendant was reversed on appeal.

[86] E.g., Minn. Stat. Ann. § 145.424 ("No person shall maintain a cause of action or receive an award of damages on the claim that but for the negligent conduct of another, a child would have been aborted," also specifically preserving the wrongful pregnancy claim). See Molloy v. Meier, 679 N.W.2d 711 (Minn. 2004) (statute quoted does not bar claim based on assertion that mother would not have conceived second child had she been properly advised that first child's disability was genetic). A physician's negligent failure to diagnose pregnancy in time to permit termination is closely analogous to the wrongful pregnancy case. See M.A. v. United States, 951 P.2d 851 (Alaska 1998).

[87] Etkind v. Suarez, 271 Ga. 352, 519 S.E.2d 210 (1999); Jackson v. Bumgardner, 318 N.C. 172, 347 S.E.2d 743 (1986).

[88] See Schork v. Huber, 648 S.W.2d 861 (Ky. 1983) (healthy child is not an injury); Thibeault v. Larson, 666 A.2d 112 (Me. 1995).

[89] E.g., Emerson v. Magendantz, 689 A.2d 409 (R.I. 1997) (reviewing the cases).

taken into account.[90] The result has been a series of special rules that do not comport with ordinary rules of damages.

Damages in Wrongful Birth Claims Generally

Expenses of child rearing. Where the claim for wrongful birth is recognized, most courts allow recovery of some, but usually not all the child-rearing expenses that would have been avoided by a timely termination of the pregnancy.[91] The same rule has been applied to claims based upon an adoption agency's misrepresentations of a prospective adoptive child's health.[92] The cases usually permit recovery of less than all of the costs inflicted by the tort by limiting the recovery to the "extraordinary" expenses, those over and above the ordinary expenses of child rearing.[93] A few courts have rejected the extraordinary expenses limitation.[94] A few courts have also limited the recovery to the costs of rearing the child to the age of majority.[95] Another view permits recovery only for costs of the continuation of the pregnancy and rejects all costs of treating and rearing the child.[96]

Emotional harm. Some courts take the rather straightforward view that harms count as personal injury and allow recovery of emotional harm for both parents, or at least for the mother.[97] Varied cases permit this recovery.[98] However, other courts have been unwilling to permit emotional harm damages at all.[99]

Damages in Wrongful Pregnancy or Conception Generally

Child rearing expenses. Wrongful pregnancy cases are usually based upon failed sterilization procedures intended to prevent conception. Most courts have disallowed recovery for cost of rearing a healthy child.[100] Although the financial and sometimes

---

[90]   See Chapter 34.

[91]   Phillips v. United States, 575 F. Supp. 1309 (D.S.C. 1983); Smith v. Cote, 128 N.H. 231, 513 A.2d 341 (1986); Becker v. Schwartz, 46 N.Y.2d 401, 413 N.Y.S.2d 895, 386 N.E.2d 807 (1978); Speck v. Finegold, 497 Pa. 77, 439 A.2d 110 (1981); Naccash v. Burger, 223 Va. 406, 290 S.E.2d 825 (1982); Harbeson v. Parke-Davis, Inc., 98 Wash.2d 460, 656 P.2d 483 (1983); James G. v. Caserta, 332 S.E.2d 872 (W.Va. 1985).

[92]   Meracle v. Children's Serv. Soc'y of Wis., 149 Wis. 2d 19, 437 N.W.2d 532 (1989).

[93]   E.g., Keel v. Banach, 624 So.2d 1022 (Ala. 1993); Arche v. United States, 247 Kan. 276, 798 P.2d 477 (1990). Under the traditional collateral source rule of damages, the claim may be maintained even when government programs pay some of the child's extraordinary expenses. Foote v. Albany Med. Ctr. Hosp., 892 N.Y.S.2d 203 (App. Div. 2009).

[94]   Contra: Robak v. United States, 658 F.2d 471 (7th Cir. 1981).

[95]   Clark v. Children's Mem'l Hosp., 353 Ill.Dec. 254, 955 N.E.2d 1065 (2011) (parents could not recover damages in wrongful birth suit for costs of caring for child during his majority, because parents are not legally obligated to pay an adult child's expenses); Shull v. Reid, 258 P.3d 521 (Okla. 2011) (recovery of damages allowed in wrongful birth action alleging medical malpractice is limited to extraordinary expenses for the period of time of the child's life expectancy or until the child reaches the age of majority, whichever is shorter); but see Arche v. United States, 247 Kan. 276, 798 P.2d 477 (1990) (but noting that the state would be responsible for the disabled child after the child reached adulthood).

[96]   Schirmer v. Mt. Auburn Obstetrics & Gynecological Assocs., Inc., 108 Ohio St.3d 494, 844 N.E.2d 1160 (2006).

[97]   Phillips v. United States, 575 F. Supp. 1309 (D.S.C. 1983); Greco v. United States, 111 Nev. 405, 893 P.2d 345 (1995). See Annotation, Recoverability of Compensatory Damages for Mental Anguish or Emotional Distress for Tortiously Causing Another's Birth, 74 A.L.R.4th 798 (1989).

[98]   Hill v. Mills, 26 So.3d 322 (Miss. 2010).

[99]   Smith v. Cote, 128 N.H. 231, 513 A.2d 341, 348–49 (1986); Becker v. Schwartz, 46 N.Y.2d 401, 413 N.Y.S.2d 895, 386 N.E.2d 807 (1978); Schirmer v. Mt. Auburn Obstetrics & Gynecologic Assocs., 108 Ohio St.3d 494, 844 N.E.2d 1160 (2006), rev'g, 155 Ohio App.3d 640, 802 N.E.2d 723 (2003).

[100]   See Cockrum v. Baumgartner, 95 Ill.2d 193, 69 Ill.Dec. 168, 447 N.E.2d 385 (1983); Chaffee v. Seslar, 786 N.E.2d 705 (Ind. 2003); Schork v. Huber, 648 S.W.2d 861 (Ky. 1983); O'Toole v. Greenberg, 64 N.Y.2d 427, 477 N.E.2d 445, 488 N.Y.S.2d 143 (1985); Johnson v. University Hosps. of Cleveland, 44 Ohio St.3d 49, 540

emotional costs of child rearing can be enormous, some courts say it is no injury, even though the parents sought to avoid those costs by employing the defendant.[101] The "no injury" assertion is, in reality a way of asserting a judicially created policy.[102]

A few courts in important decisions have allowed the jury to award child-rearing costs, at least where the parents sought to avoid having children in part for economic reasons.[103] However, even many of these more liberal courts may reduce the award by imposing offsets.

Emotional and other damages. In the wrongful pregnancy or conception cases, courts have allowed recovery for the mother's pain in delivery of the child and emotional distress at having an unplanned, unwanted, or unaffordable child,[104] the expenses of the negligently performed pregnancy-avoidance procedure,[105] or the cost of repeating the procedure later,[106] pregnancy-related medical expenses, including wages lost because of pregnancy or delivery,[107] and expenses or wages lost in the post-natal period in appropriate cases.[108] The father is entitled to recover for loss of consortium.[109] Perhaps most courts allow recovery of emotional distress damages,[110] but predictably enough, some courts have refused to permit any emotional distress recovery at all,[111] or have limited the recovery of all forms of pain and suffering, including emotional harm, to the period of time from discovery of pregnancy until recovery from childbirth.[112]

Almost all of the limitations on the damages recovery in wrongful birth and wrongful pregnancy actions[113] are derived in part from the idea that if the parents suffer economic and emotional harm as a result of having a child, they also gain offsetting benefits which should somehow be taken into account.

Avoidable Consequences—"Mitigation" of Damages

Abortion not required. The avoidable consequences rule excludes recovery for any damages that could have been reasonably avoided by the plaintiff.[114] This rule has raised the question whether a plaintiff suffering from an unwanted pregnancy as the result of the defendant's negligence must seek an abortion to minimize damages. Although courts

---

N.E.2d 1370 (1989); Smith v. Gore, 728 S.W.2d 738, 751 (Tenn. 1987); James G. v. Caserta, 332 S.E.2d 872 (W. Va. 1985); Beardsley v. Wierdsma, 650 P.2d 288 (Wyo. 1982).

[101] See Burke v. Rivo, 406 Mass. 764, 551 N.E.2d 1 (1990).

[102] See Cf. Michael B. Kelly, The Rightful Position in "Wrongful Life" Actions, 42 Hastings L. J. 505, 525–35 (1991).

[103] University of Ariz. Health Scis. Ctr. v. Superior Court, 136 Ariz. 579, 667 P.2d 1294 (1983); Ochs v. Borrelli, 187 Conn. 253, 445 A.2d 883 (1982); Jones v. Malinowski, 299 Md. 257, 473 A.2d 429 (1984); Burke v. Rivo, 406 Mass. 764, 551 N.E.2d 1 (1990); Lovelace Med. Ctr. v. Mendez, 805 P.2d 603 (N.M. 1991); Zehr v. Haugen, 318 Or. 647, 871 P.2d 1006 (1994); Marciniak v. Lundborg, 153 Wis.2d 59, 450 N.W.2d 243 (1990).

[104] Pitre v. Opelousas Gen. Hosp., 530 So.2d 1151 (La. 1988); Burke v. Rivo, 406 Mass. 764, 551 N.E.2d 1 (1990).

[105] Smith v. Gore, 728 S.W.2d 738, 751 (Tenn. 1987).

[106] Lovelace Med. Ctr. v. Mendez, 805 P.2d 603 (N.M. 1991).

[107] Pitre v. Opelousas Gen. Hosp., 530 So.2d 1151 (La. 1988) (expenses of pregnancy and delivery).

[108] Smith v. Gore, 728 S.W.2d 738, 751 (Tenn. 1987).

[109] Pitre v. Opelousas Gen. Hosp., 530 So.2d 1151, 1161–62 (La. 1988); Burke v. Rivo, 406 Mass. 764, 551 N.E.2d 1 (1990); Smith v. Gore, 728 S.W.2d 738, 751 (Tenn. 1987).

[110] Jackson v. Bumgardner, 318 N.C. 172, 347 S.E.2d 743 (1986).

[111] Lovelace Med. Ctr. v. Mendez, 805 P.2d 603 (N.M. 1991); Emerson v. Magendantz, 689 A.2d 409 (R.I. 1997).

[112] Smith v. Gore, 728 S.W.2d 738, 751 (Tenn. 1987).

[113] See § 27.4.

[114] See 1 Dan B. Dobbs, Remedies § 3.9 and 2 id. § 8.7.

have sometimes played with the idea as an argument for severely limiting the claim or denying it altogether, almost no court seems to have actually applied such an idea.[115] As the Tennessee Court observed, any such requirement might "infringe upon Constitutional rights to privacy in these matters," and in addition would fail the reasonableness test which is built into the avoidable consequences rule.[116]

Adoption not required. In wrongful birth cases, the nature of the case is that there is no opportunity for terminating the pregnancy, but there remains the possibility, also open in wrongful pregnancy cases, that damages could be minimized by relinquishing the child for adoption. Relinquishment might indeed work a sound economic result, but the tort is not exclusively an economic tort. The defendant, having deprived the mother of one choice, has no right to force upon her another choice she does not want to make. With these ideas in mind, it seems unlikely that courts will require a mother to give up her legitimate claim or her child, one or the other.

---

[115] See Lovelace Med. Ctr. v. Mendez, 805 P.2d 603 (N.M. 1991). The possibility of abortion to minimize damages has been suggested as a ground for denying recovery of normal child-rearing expenses. See Robak v. United States, 658 F.2d 471, 479 n. 23 (7th Cir. 1981) ("Because they freely chose not to have an abortion, they should be responsible for the costs of a normal child"); Sorkin v. Lee, 78 A.D.2d 180, 434 N.Y.S.2d 300 (1980). These cases appear to adopt a rule of damages that excludes the normal costs of child-rearing for the very purpose of *avoiding* the issue of minimizing damages and some of the decisions have spelled this point out in detail. See Flowers v. District of Columbia, 478 A.2d 1073 (D.C. 1984). In Hall v. Dartmouth Hitchcock Medical Center, 153 N.H. 388, 899 A.2d 240 (2006), the court did apparently consider the fact that the wrongful-birth-claimant mother could have sought an abortion even at the late date that she was informed of an increased possibility of birth defects.

[116] Smith v. Gore, 728 S.W.2d 738, 751–52 (Tenn. 1987). See also Ochs v. Borrelli, 187 Conn. 253, 445 A.2d 883, 885 (1982); Marciniak v. Lundborg, 153 Wis.2d 59, 450 N.W.2d 243, 247 (1990) (not reasonable under ordinary rules to require abortion to minimize damages); Ellen M. Bublick,Comparative Fault to the Limits, 56 Vand. L. Rev. 977, 1023–24 (2003) (outlining courts' reluctance to allow comparative fault claims based on the plaintiff's exercise of fundamental and sometimes constitutionally-protected rights).

Chapter 28

WRONGFUL DEATH AND SURVIVAL ACTIONS

Analysis

§ 28.1   Wrongful Death and Survival Actions
§ 28.2   Survival Actions—Scope and Damages
§ 28.3   Wrongful Death Actions: Pecuniary Loss Damages
§ 28.4   Wrongful Death Actions: Non-Pecuniary Damages
§ 28.5   Procedure, Distribution, Defenses and Damages

§ 28.1 Wrongful Death and Survival Actions

Common law rules. According to a Latin maxim, personal actions die with the person. The common law followed that maxim, holding that the death of either the tortfeasor or the victim eliminated all tort claims. In particular: (1) If the tort victim died, his cause of action was at an end; his estate had no cause of action.[1] (2) If the tortfeasor himself died, the victim's claim died as well.[2] (3) If the victim died, her survivors had no independent claim of their own against the tortfeasor for their loss of support or for their grief and sorrow.[3] There has never been any good explanation for all these rules.[4] For a brief period, some American authority reversed the English common law rule,[5] but by the middle of the 19th century, American courts had returned to the common law fold, leaving death actions to the legislature.[6]

Adoption of statutes. In the latter half of the 19th century, following the lead of English legislation often known as Lord Campbell's Act,[7] the American states addressed the problem by legislation which remains the source of almost all rights arising out of a person's death.[8]

---

[1]   See Higgins v. Butcher, Yelv. 89, 80 Eng. Rep. 61 (K.B. 1607). Torts to personal property did survive, however. See Percy H. Winfield, Death as Affecting Liability in Tort, 29 Colum. L. Rev. 237, 242–43 (1929).

[2]   See Winfield, supra note 1 at 242; T. A. Smedley, Wrongful Death—Bases of the Common Law Rules, 13 Vand. L. Rev. 605 (1960).

[3]   Baker v. Bolton, 1 Camp. 493, 170 Eng. Rep. 1033 (Nisi Prius 1808).

[4]   However, an historical explanation for some of the rules can be found in primitive English law. The English idea was that there was no private tort action for a felony because the tort action merged in the felony, which was to say that the felon's property was forfeited to the Crown, which was unwilling to share any of the assets with the felon's victim.

[5]   See Malone, The Genesis of Wrongful Death, 17 Stan. L. Rev. 1043 (1965).

[6]   Carey v. Berkshire R.R., 55 Mass. (1 Cush.) 475, 48 Am. Dec. 616 (1848), overruled in part, Gaudette v. Webb, 284 N.E.2d 222 (Mass. 1972). This decision may have been influenced by the fact that the Massachusetts legislature had much earlier created certain rights to recover for death on badly maintained bridges and death caused by boat or railroad. Only limited damages were allowed railroad passengers under these statutes. In the face of these statutes, the Massachusetts Court may have been reluctant to create a general common law right to recover for death without limitation.

[7]   9 & 10 Vict. Ch. 93 (1846).

[8]   A few decisions have said that a common law right of action for death existed in their jurisdictions and consequently that the present death statute should be interpreted in light of the common law action or even as a codification of that cause of action. See LaFage v. Jani, 166 N.J. 412, 766 A.2d 1066 (2001) (flexibility in tolling statute of limitations is permitted because statute codified common law).

Federal statutes. Tort law is usually state law and that is also true with wrongful death statutes. However, a number of important federal statutes have been enacted, among them the Federal Employers' Liability Act (FELA)[9] and the Jones Act,[10] providing rights for railroad workers and seamen respectively. A complex mixture of statutes and decisional law of Admiralty covers some maritime cases.[11] Treaties and protocols deal with death on international air flights.[12] Almost all state and federal legislation deals with death claims in two basic ways or in some combination of those two ways—through survival actions and wrongful death claims.

Survival statutes. Survival statutes provide for the survival of whatever tort cause of action the deceased herself would have had if she had been able to sue at the moment of her death. For example, if at the time of her death the deceased would have been entitled to recover from the tortfeasor for her pain and suffering, loss of wages, and medical expenses between the time of injury and the time of death, a survival statute would enable the deceased's estate to pursue that recovery. The right to sue under the survival statute is subject to claims of the deceased's creditors.

Wrongful death statutes. Wrongful death statutes, by contrast, create a new action in favor of certain beneficiaries who suffer from another's death. All states recognize some kind of claim. Indeed, foreign jurisdictions recognize such claims.[13] Because a wrongful death statute creates a new cause of action and vests that action in the survivors (or their representative), the wrongful death recovery does not go to the deceased's estate and is not subject to claims of the deceased's creditors.

Combining the two. In most states both the wrongful death and the survival claim can be made because they do not duplicate items of damages. Some states combine the features of both kinds of actions in a single statute. Such hybrid statutes may produce different approaches to damages or defenses.

Underlying issues. The underlying substance of the claims in death cases is much the same as in other tort cases. Familiar issues of duty, breach, causation, and proximate cause are basic to all wrongful death and survival actions based on negligence.[14] Likewise, the special problems associated with fetal harm, governmental immunity, federal preemption, medical practice and many other issues arise in death actions.[15]

---

[9]   45 U.S.C.A. § 51.

[10]   46 U.S.C.A. § 30104.

[11]   The Death on the High Seas Act, 46 U.S.C.A. § 30301, covers death from injury one maritime league from shore, but when seamen or longshoremen are the victims, the judge-made law of Admiralty or other statutes may apply. See Miles v. Apex Marine Corp., 498 U.S. 19, 111 S.Ct. 317, 112 L.Ed.2d 275 (1990).

[12]   See Edward C. Bresee, Jr., & Sirce Elliott, Recent Developments in Aviation Law, 71 J. Air L. & Com. 101, 170 (2006).

[13]   See, e.g., Helmut Koziol, Recovery for Economic Loss in the European Union, 48 Ariz. L. Rev. 871, 882 (2006) (noting that cases of relational loss are a frequent situation in which European countries assign liability for economic loss).

[14]   Henry v. Mutual of Omaha Ins. Co., 503 F.3d 425 (5th Cir. 2007) (holding that insurance company's denial of benefits was not "wrongful" and thus not actionable even assuming that the denial was an actual cause of the insured's death); Goldizen v. Grant County Nursing Home, 693 S.E.2d 346 (W. Va. 2010) (holding that cause of death listed on death certificate created issue of factual cause).

[15]   See, e.g., Williams v. Manchester, 228 Ill.2d 404, 888 N.E.2d 1, 320 Ill.Dec. 784 (2008) (mother has no wrongful death action against negligent driver for death of fetus); Mack v. Carmack, 79 So. 3d 597 (Ala. 2011) (Wrongful Death Act permits an action for the death of a pre-viable fetus, overruling prior precedent to the contrary); Carranza v. U.S., 267 P.3d 912 (Utah 2011) (prior to amendment, wrongful death statute permitted action for death of unborn child).

§ 28.2　Survival Actions—Scope and Damages

Nature and purpose of the survival action. The survival action reverses the common law rule that a cause of action abates with the death of either party. In its usual form, the survival action allows the deceased's tort cause of action to continue or survive after his death. For example, if the defendant negligently breaks the victim's leg, resulting in wage loss and medical costs, damages for those items could be recovered by the victim in his lifetime. If the victim dies six months later from other causes without having settled or recovered, the survival statutes permit recovery of the same damages by the victim's estate.

Damages suffered by the decedent before death. The ordinary survival statute is intended to recoup the losses suffered by the decedent up to the time of his death. The usual rule permits the survival action regardless of the cause of death and regardless of whether death was instantaneous,[16] provided only that permissible elements of damages can be shown. Another group of statutes allows the survival action where the injury resulted in death only if death is not instantaneous.[17]

Types of damage allowed. Damages in the survival action are often quite limited. They reflect only the damages the decedent herself could have claimed at the moment of her death.[18] Recovery in the survival action may include damages for the decedent's conscious[19] pain and suffering resulting from the injury.[20] Conscious pain and suffering may include the suffering arising from the deceased's imminent apprehension of death before physical impact.[21] Damages in a survival action may also include medical expenses resulting from the injury,[22] decedent's lost enjoyment of life,[23] any earnings lost between the time of injury and the death,[24] punitive damages against a living

---

[16]　See Cal. Civ. Proc. Code § 377.20.

[17]　Starkenburg v. State, 934 P.2d 1018 (Mont. 1997) (on the ground that there could be no damages for which the decedent could have sued if she died instantly).

[18]　See Meadows v. Blake, 36 So.3d 1225 (Miss. 2010) (widower of decedent, as party to malpractice action and legal representative of decedent, could appeal final judgment of circuit court that was issued before decedent's death).

[19]　Proof must show that there was in fact pain and suffering which in turn requires consciousness for at least a short interval. See, e.g., Smith v. Louisiana Farm Bureau, 35 So. 3d 463 (La. Ct. App. 2010) (other driver heard gurgling sounds coming from decedent's body a few minutes after the accident); Royal Indem. Co. v. Pittsfield Elec. Co., 293 Mass. 4, 199 N.E. 69 (1935).

[20]　See, e.g., Small v. McKennan Hosp., 437 N.W.2d 194 (S.D. 1989).

[21]　DRD Pool Serv., Inc. v. Freed, 416 Md. 46, 5 A.3d 45 (2010) (affirming jury verdict where evidence supported a reasonable inference that a five-year-old boy who drowned was conscious and suffered while he was drowning, despite there being no eyewitnesses; two experts testified that to a reasonable degree of medical certainty, the boy, who did not know how to swim, experienced pain and suffering as he drowned); Nelson v. Dolan, 230 Neb. 848, 434 N.W.2d 25 (1989) (decedent's motorcycle was locked to the defendant's car at high speeds for five seconds before the final impact that caused death; pre-impact fear was a recoverable item); Yowell v. Piper Aircraft Corp., 703 S.W.2d 630 (Tex. 1986) (recovery for pre-impact distress was allowed when decedents' plane broke up and they fell 10,000 feet to an immediate death).

[22]　Warner v. McCaughan, 77 Wash.2d 178, 460 P.2d 272 (1969), superseded by statute as stated in Tait v. Wahl, 987 P.2d 127 (Wash. Ct. App. 1999).

[23]　See Carona de Camargo v. Schon, 278 Neb. 1045, 776 N.W.2d 1 (2009).

[24]　Miles v. Apex Marine Corp., 498 U.S. 19, 111 S.Ct. 317, 112 L.Ed.2d 275 (1990) (under Admiralty powers, Court would limit recovery to losses incurred during the decedent's lifetime); Prunty v. Schwantes, 40 Wis. 2d 418, 162 N.W.2d 34 (1968).

tortfeasor,[25] and funeral expenses,[26] provided such expenses have not been allocated to[27] or actually recovered in the wrongful death action.[28] Some states allow broader recoveries.[29] Particular statutes, however, may exclude some of the listed items of damage. For example, some statutes exclude pain and suffering recoveries,[30] recovery for lost enjoyment of life,[31] or punitive damages.[32]

Actions that survive or do not. Many survival statutes are somewhat narrow because they expressly exclude a number of economic and dignitary torts such as libel, slander, malicious prosecution and the like, leaving those actions to abate upon death of either party under the common law rule.[33] When the scope of the statute is not clear, courts have sometimes interpreted it generously in favor of survival.[34] A few decisions have held that the statute's exclusion of particular causes of action, such as those for defamation, is unwarranted and unconstitutional, with the result that in such a state the libel action survives along with ordinary personal injury claims.[35]

Surviving the tortfeasor's death. The usual case for invoking a survival statute involves the death of the tortfeasor's victim and survival of the claim. However, the common law rule also abated the claim if the tortfeasor himself died before judgment. Most survival acts now appear to be worded broadly enough to permit a suit not only when the tort victim has died but also when the tortfeasor himself has died.[36] When the tortfeasor has died, the survival action is brought against his estate. In that kind of survival action, punitive damages are often denied,[37] though not always so.[38]

§ 28.3 Wrongful Death Actions: Pecuniary Loss Damages

Wrongful death actions. The traditional wrongful death statutes created a whole new cause of action for the benefit of the decedent's survivors. Except in Alabama, which

---

[25] E.g., Quintero v. Rodgers, 221 Ariz. 536, 212 P.3d 874 (Ct. App. 2009); Berenger v. Frink, 314 N.W.2d 388 (Iowa 1982).

[26] E.g., Estate of Kronemeyer v. Meinig, 948 P.2d 119 (Colo. Ct. App. 1997).

[27] Mo. Ann. Stat. § 537.090 specifically lists funeral expenses as recoverable in the death action.

[28] In some instances such expenses are allowed on an either/or basis, with recovery permitted in either the survival or the death action but not in both. E.g., S.C. Code § 15–5–100.

[29] One Nat'l Bank v. Pope, 372 Ark. 208, 272 S.W.3d 98 (2008) (allowing recovery in survival action for "decedent's loss of life," measured by "the value that the decedent would have placed on his or her life").

[30] E.g., Ariz. Rev. Stat. § 14–3110; Wash. Rev. Stat. § 4.20.046.

[31] See Quintero v. Rodgers, 221 Ariz. 536, 212 P.3d 874 (Ct. App. 2009); Otani v. Broudy, 151 Wash.2d 750, 92 P.3d 192 (2004).

[32] E.g., N.Y. Est. Powers & Trusts Law § 11–3.2 (b).

[33] E.g., N.M. Stat. Ann. § 37–2–4; Ohio Rev. Code Ann. § 2311.21; see also William H. Binder, Publicity Rights and Defamation of the Deceased: Resurrection or R.I.P.?, 12 DePaul-LCA J. Art. & Ent. L. 297 (2002) (arguing that publicity actions should be treated in the same way as defamation actions and should not survive the decedent's death).

[34] E.g., Harrison v. Loyal Protective Life Ins. Co., 379 Mass. 212, 396 N.E.2d 987 (1979) (infliction of mental distress is harm to person which survives).

[35] Thompson v. Estate of Petroff, 319 N.W.2d 400 (Minn. 1982) (intentional tort); Moyer v. Phillips, 462 Pa. 395, 341 A.2d 441, 77 A.L.R.3d 1339 (1975) (libel).

[36] E.g., Blakeley v. Shortal's Estate, 236 Iowa 787, 20 N.W.2d 28 (1945) (deceased's tort was that he committed suicide by slitting his throat in the plaintiff's home, causing her emotional distress; the claim survived the deceased's death even though harm was not done until after death).

[37] E.g., Doe v. Colligan, 753 P.2d 144 (Alaska 1988). Statutes may so provide. See Cal. Civ. Proc. Code § 377.42.

[38] Some courts allow punitive damages against the estate. See Haralson v. Fisher Surveying, Inc., 31 P.3d 114 (Ariz. 2001); Bennett v. Gordon, 770 A.2d 517 (Del. Super. Ct. 2001).

has used a punitive measure of damages,[39] recovery was limited to pecuniary harm of the survivors and thus did not originally include any recovery for, say, the emotional distress of a bereaved spouse.[40] The pecuniary harm of the survivors in United States jurisdictions is calculated in a highly individualized manner.[41] Other countries,[42] as well as quasi-tort compensation systems in the United States,[43] have relied on more generalized computations. Under the influence of statutory language, courts have estimated pecuniary harm in two quite different ways: (1) as the loss to dependents, or (2) as the loss to the estate. Both main approaches to pecuniary loss may vary by statutory detail.

Loss to Dependents Measure

Loss of support to dependents as a measure of pecuniary loss. Courts have usually interpreted both state[44] and federal[45] wrongful death statutes to allow recovery of sums necessary to replace the direct or indirect financial support lost by the decedent's dependents.[46] Contributions by the decedent to the dependents' support might take the form of cash, but perhaps more often they take the form of provisions for shelter, food, or services rendered.[47]

Forms of evidence. As a matter of proof, dependents might adduce evidence of the reasonable value of, say, benefits provided by the decedent, such as furnished living quarters. Or the dependents might show the decedent's total income together with evidence about the amounts the decedent would probably spend for his own maintenance and other items that would not go toward support of the plaintiffs. The difference would reflect an estimate of the pecuniary value of the support provided.[48]

---

[39]   See Tatum v. Schering Corp., 523 So.2d 1042 (Ala. 1988). However, Alabama says that its wrongful death damages are punitive in nature but "nonpenal in effect" because the purpose is to preserve life. See Industrial Chem. & Fiberglass Corp. v. Chandler, 547 So. 2d 812 (Ala. 1989). Massachusetts formerly applied a punitive measure in death actions.

[40]   For more detail and additional citations on several points, see 2 Dan B. Dobbs, Law of Remedies § 8.2(4) (2d ed. 1993).

[41]   For a discussion of the way in which an individualized approach historically resulted in racial inequalities in some wrongful death cases, see Martha Chamallas and Jennifer B. Wriggins, The Measure of Injury 58–62 (2010).

[42]   For example, in the People's Republic of China wrongful death damages are generally awarded at twenty times the previous year's average net income in the area in which the court is located or the party is domiciled, whichever is higher. George W. Conk, A New Tort Code Emerges in China: An Introduction to the Discussion with a Translation of Chapter 8—Tort Liability, of the Official Discussion Draft of the Proposed Revised Civil Code of the People's Republic of China, 30 Fordham Int'l L.J. 935 (2007).

[43]   The September 11th Victims Compensation fund relied on compensation tables to determine awards. See Brian Walker, Lessons that Wrongful Death Tort Law Can Learn from the September 11th Victim Compensation Fund, 28 Rev. Litig. 595 (2009) (commending the fund's method of relying on more generalized data for both economic and noneconomic damages).

[44]   E.g., Freeman v. Davidson, 768 P.2d 885 (Nev. 1989); see Comment, 44 N.C. L. Rev. 402 (1966).

[45]   E.g., Death on High Seas Act: Moore-McCormack Lines, Inc. v. Richardson, 295 F.2d 583, 96 A.L.R.2d 1085 (2d Cir. 1961); Jones Act: Van Beeck v. Sabine Towing Co., 300 U.S. 342, 57 S.Ct. 452, 81 L.Ed. 685 (1937).

[46]   E.g., Thomas v. Uzoka, 290 S.W.3d 437, 454 (Tex. App. 2009) ("present value of the benefits, including money and other benefits that could be valued in terms of money, that the beneficiary could reasonably expect to have received from the deceased had he survived").

[47]   See Armantrout v. Carlson, 166 Wash.2d 931, 214 P.3d 914 (2009) (permitting recovery for loss of services provided by deceased adult daughter to mother who was blind and had diabetes).

[48]   See Lorenz v. Air Illinois, Inc., 168 Ill.App.3d 1060, 119 Ill.Dec. 493, 522 N.E.2d 1352 (1988) (considering a standard instruction allowing the jury to consider the amount of "money, goods and services the decedent customarily contributed in the past" and "was likely to have contributed in the future," as well as what he "spent for customary personal expenses"); Elmer Buchta Trucking, Inc. v. Stanley, 744 N.E.2d 939

Prospects of continued support and time period. The fact that support has been provided in the past does not ensure that it will continue in the future, so courts admit evidence of the decedent's affection for the dependents, or the lack of it, as bearing on future probable contributions.[49] The decedent's prospects of gaining greater income in the future is also to be considered.[50] Finally, the time period during which support would probably be provided must be proven.

Decedents not earning or contributing. Measuring loss to dependents may present serious problems when the decedent is a child, a homemaker, or a retired person with no dependents, especially where non-pecuniary damages are not recoverable. In the case of a child or retired person, the pecuniary loss to dependents is likely to be zero or very little at most.[51] The traditional measure for a child-death was the value of the child's services minus the cost of rearing the child.[52] However, some courts now presume that a pecuniary loss is suffered in the case of a child's wrongful death.[53] In the case of a homemaker, services in the home can be valued as a pecuniary contribution,[54] but the sums represented by these services can be relatively small. Another possibility is to compensate for lost earning capacity.[55] In the case of a retired person, substantial recovery is also confounded by the limited life expectancy of older persons. These limits on recovery in the case of people whose lives are valuable but who do not earn money in the labor market can be avoided by permitting awards for mental anguish or the like, by recognizing some measure of welfare loss to the decedent,[56] or, in some cases, by adopting the loss to the estate measure of pecuniary loss.

Loss to the Estate Measure

Loss to the estate as a measure of pecuniary loss. The second approach to measuring pecuniary loss figures a recovery on the basis of accumulations or savings cut short by the decedent's untimely death. Damages under this approach might be measured in slightly different ways, but the main idea is to add up what the decedent would probably have earned[57] in a normal lifetime and award that sum after subtracting something for

---

(Ind. 2001) (emphasizing the propriety of evidence showing decedent's income minus amount for his own support); Johnson v. Manhattan & Bronx Surface Transit Operating Auth., 71 N.Y.2d 198, 524 N.Y.S.2d 415, 519 N.E.2d 326 (1988) (gross income is an admissible beginning even though decedent would have paid taxes).

[49] McDonald v. Price, 80 Cal.App.2d 150, 181 P.2d 115 (1947); McCormick v. Kopmann, 23 Ill.App.2d 189, 161 N.E.2d 720 (1959) ("habits of industry and sobriety"). Similarly, the decedent's character or conduct may suggest that support would not continue. See Dollarhide v. Gunstream, 55 N.M. 353, 233 P.2d 1042 (1951) (husband drank, attacked wife). Or that the decedent was of no value to the dependent. See Quinonez v. Andersen, 144 Ariz. 193, 696 P.2d 1342 (Ct. App. 1984) (death of wife and evidence that surviving husband beat her admitted, ". . . all that Mr. Quinonez lost was a punching bag and a just and fair award for this loss was zero").

[50] E.g., United States v. Furumizo, 381 F.2d 965 (9th Cir. 1967).

[51] See Sanchez v. Schindler, 651 S.W.2d 249, 251 (Tex. 1983) ("If the rule were literally followed, the average child would have a negative worth").

[52] E.g., Missouri Pac. R.R. v. Maxwell, 194 Ark. 938, 109 S.W.2d 1254 (1937).

[53] E.g., Bullard v. Barnes, 102 Ill.2d 505, 82 Ill.Dec. 448, 468 N.E.2d 1228 (1984).

[54] Thorn v. Mercy Mem'l Hosp. Corp., 761 N.W.2d 414 (Mich. Ct. App. 2008) (holding that economic value of household services that decedent would have provided to her children were recoverable economic damages permitted under wrongful death statute).

[55] European Group on Tort Law, Principles of European Tort Law Art. 10:202 cmt. 4 (2005).

[56] See One Nat'l Bank v. Pope, 372 Ark. 208, 272 S.W.3d 98 (2008); Eric A. Posner & Cass R. Sunstein, Dollars and Death, 72 U. Chi. L. Rev. 537 (2005).

[57] The decedent's savings from non-earned income such as inheritance or investments are disregarded in most formulas. E.g., State v. Mayberry, 415 N.W.2d 644 (Iowa 1987) ("present worth or value of the estate which the decedent would reasonably be expected to have saved and accumulated as the result of her efforts between the time of her death and the end of her natural life had she lived").

the costs the decedent would have had to maintain himself.[58] This measure is sometimes called the loss to the estate measure. It ignores loss of support to survivors and concentrates on the potential property loss someone would have had if the decedent had lived out a full lifetime. Inevitably, a certain amount of speculation is permitted in death claims, because the alternative in most instances would be to deny all compensation.[59]

Combined Measures

Adding loss of inheritance to the loss to dependents approach. Some courts have allowed dependents to claim both loss to dependents and loss of inheritance of heirs or presumptive heirs. In *Martin v. Atlantic Coast Line Railroad*,[60] the proof at trial tended to show that at the time of his death, the decedent was making contributions to his spouse, and that he would have increased earnings which would probably have been saved. Under the loss to dependents rule, the spousal contributions would be recoverable; under the loss to the estate measure, the provable lifetime savings would be recoverable. The *Martin* court allowed recovery of both elements, in effect holding the tortfeasor liable for all losses caused.

Statutory adoption. The *Martin* approach, or something similar, has been adopted by statute[61] and by judicial decision[62] in a number of cases, and when not available under the wrongful death act, is nevertheless sometimes allowed under the survival act.[63] Some such approach might be one of the only methods by which recovery could be allowed to survivors like adult children who received no current contributions from the deceased.[64] Some authority, however, has expressly rejected the loss of inheritance claim.[65]

§ 28.4 Wrongful Death Actions: Non-Pecuniary Damages

Traditional rule. Traditionally, a death statute protected only the pecuniary interests of survivors so nothing was recovered for the survivor's mental anguish or

---

[58] E.g., Carrano v. Yale-New Haven Hosp., 279 Conn. 622, 904 A.2d 149 (2006) ("Net earnings are calculated by deducting the decedent's income taxes and personal living expenses from his gross earnings"; plaintiff who presented evidence of gross loss of income but not net could not recover economic damages); State v. Mayberry, 415 N.W.2d 644, 645 (Iowa 1987) ("That measure is the present worth or value of the estate which the decedent would reasonably be expected to have saved and accumulated as the result of her efforts between the time of her death and the end of her natural life had she lived. Relevant factors in this determination are the 'decedent's age and life expectancy, characteristics and habits, health, education or opportunity for education, general ability, other occupational qualifications, industriousness, intelligence, manner of living, sobriety or intemperance, frugality or lavishness, and other personal characteristics that are of assistance in securing business or earning money.' ").

[59] See State v. Mayberry, 415 N.W.2d 644 (Iowa 1987).

[60] Martin v. Atlantic Coast Line R.R. Co., 268 F.2d 397, 91 A.L.R.2d 472 (5th Cir. 1959).

[61] Fla. Stat. Ann. § 768.21 provides for a loss to survivors recovery and in addition for the "Loss of the prospective net accumulations of an estate" if there is a surviving spouse or lineal descendant, and also in some cases where there is no recovery for loss to survivors. See also Ohio Rev. Code Ann. § 2125.02(B) (loss of support, plus loss of prospective inheritance to heirs at law).

[62] E.g., Martin v. Atlantic Coast Line R.R., 268 F.2d 397, 91 A.L.R.2d 472 (5th Cir. 1959) (Federal Employers Liability Act); National Airlines, Inc. v. Stiles, 268 F.2d 400 (5th Cir.), cert. denied, 361 U.S. 926, 80 S.Ct. 157, 4 L.Ed.2d 121 (1959) (Death on High Seas Act); Yowell v. Piper Aircraft Corp., 703 S.W.2d 630 (Tex. 1986); James T. Tucker, Annotation, Wrongful Death Damages For Loss of Expectancy of Inheritance From Decedent, 42 A.L.R.5th 465 (1996).

[63] See Weil v. Seltzer, 873 F.2d 1453 (D.C. Cir. 1989); McClinton v. White, 497 Pa. 610, 444 A.2d 85 (1982); Criscuola v. Andrews, 82 Wash. 2d 68, 507 P.2d 149 (1973); James O. Pearson, Jr., Annotation, Recovery, in action for benefit of decedent's estate in jurisdiction which has both wrongful death and survival statutes, of value of earnings decedent would have made after death, 76 A.L.R.3d 125 (1977).

[64] See Schaefer v. American Family Mut. Ins. Co., 192 Wis.2d 768, 531 N.W.2d 585 (1995).

[65] Pfau v. Comair Holdings, Inc., 15 P.3d 1160 (Idaho 2000).

emotional loss.[66] In the most stringent view, nothing could be recovered for loss of society either, unless that loss of society could be expressed in monetary terms.[67]

Problems with a solely pecuniary focus. As noted, a limitation of damages to pecuniary losses results in virtual denial of recovery when the decedent is a child, a retired person or any person not in the labor market.[68] Even in a case in which the decedent was an active wage earner, pecuniary damages fail to capture the full measure of the loss either to the decedent or to dependents or others. Some distinguished scholars have forcefully argued that state wrongful death damages are too low because they do not adequately take account of the welfare loss of the decedent and dependents.[69]

Current rule on nonpecuniary recovery. Today, many jurisdictions permit nonpecuniary recovery for the survivor's loss of companionship, society, advice and guidance,[70] sometimes on the theory that such elements have a pecuniary value.[71] Indeed, the September 11th Victim Compensation Fund, which was modeled on tort principles, scheduled significant noneconomic benefit awards into its compensation structure.[72] In addition, some states take account of the lost value of life to the decedent,

---

[66] E.g., Nelson v. Dolan, 230 Neb. 848, 434 N.W.2d 25 (1989).

[67] Miles v. Apex Marine Corp., 498 U.S. 19, 111 S.Ct. 317, 112 L.Ed.2d 275 (1990) (statutory beneficiaries in FELA, Jones Act, and general maritime claims can recover pecuniary harms only); In re Air Crash at Belle Harbor, N.Y. on Nov. 12, 2001, 450 F.Supp. 2d 432 (S.D.N.Y. 2006) ("New York law permits recovery in wrongful death cases for fair and just compensation for the pecuniary injuries resulting from the decedent's death to the persons for whose benefit the action is brought. . . . New York law does not permit recovery of loss of consortium, mental anguish, or grief damages.").

[68] In each case, but especially in the case of a homemaker, the value of the service rendered would have pecuniary value and would be recoverable. E.g., Missouri Pac. R.R. Co. v. Maxwell, 194 Ark. 938, 109 S.W.2d 1254 (1937); Siebeking v. Ford, 128 Ind.App. 475, 148 N.E.2d 194 (1958); Oliver v. Morgan, 73 S.W.2d 993 (Mo. 1934). But the sums recovered are not likely to reflect real values or the value of human life. McGowan v. Estate of Wright, 524 So.2d 308 (Miss. 1988) (upholding a jury verdict that awarded only funeral expenses for a man who was killed instantly in a car accident).

[69] Eric A. Posner & Cass R. Sunstein, Dollars and Death, 72 U. Chi. L. Rev. 537 (2005) (arguing that regulatory policy places a much higher value on life than do wrongful death cases and that to account for decedents' welfare losses courts should allow testimony in wrongful death cases about the victim's willingness to pay to avoid the risk in question). See also Gregory C. Keating, Irreparable Injury and Extraordinary Precaution: The Safety and Feasibility Norms in American Accident Law, 4 Theoretical Inquiries L. 1, 4 (2003) ("Because tort accident law stops short of imposing on tortfeasors the full cost of the harms they have inflicted, it falls short in its effort to discourage the accidental infliction of irreparable physical injury.").

[70] Brandon v. County of Richardson, 261 Neb. 636, 624 N.W.2d 604 (2001) (for wrongful death of child, parent can recover for loss of the child's society, comfort, and companionship, which have intrinsic value, and damages are not necessarily dependent on the personal qualities of the child). Lacking a statutory provision on consortium, Montana permits the claim for death of an adult child only if the parent-child relationship had been especially close. Adams v. U.S., 669 F.Supp.2d 1203 (D. Mont. 2009); Hern v. Safeco Ins. Co. of Ill., 125 P.3d 597 (Mont. 2005). Statutes now often provide for loss of society recovery. E.g., Alaska Stat. § 09.55.580(c) ("loss of consortium" and also "loss of assistance or services"); Mass. Gen. Laws Ann. ch. 229, § 2 ("services, protection, care, assistance, society, companionship, comfort, guidance, counsel and advice"). In other cases, courts may regard loss of consortium as being distinct from anguish or grief and may attribute pecuniary value to it. E.g., Krouse v. Graham, 19 Cal.3d 59, 68, 137 Cal.Rptr. 863, 867, 562 P.2d 1022, 1026 (1977); Green v. Bittner, 85 N.J. 1, 424 A.2d 210 (1980).

[71] See Nelson v. Dolan, 230 Neb. 848, 434 N.W.2d 25 (1989); Wilcox v. Vermeulen, 781 N.W.2d 464 (S.D. 2010).

[72] See Robert L. Rabin, The September 11th Victim Compensation Fund: A Circumscribed Response or an Auspicious Model?, 53 DePaul L. Rev. 457 (2003) (noting that noneconomic compensation under the plan was set at $250,000 per victim with an increased benefit of $100,000 per partner or child, so that noneconomic benefits to the spouse of a decedent with two children would have been $550,000).

sometimes termed "hedonic damages," in wrongful death,[73] or survival actions.[74] Additionally, many states permit recovery for emotional harm or anguish in wrongful death actions. Some of the statutes now provide for it directly, usually in addition to the claims for lost companionship, society, guidance and the like.[75] Elsewhere, some courts have expanded liability to include mental anguish recovery through other torts[76] or under statutes that do not specifically authorize it.[77]

Punitive damages. Alabama has a unique approach to wrongful death damages, basing recovery on a purely punitive measure.[78] But traditional death statutes, by limiting damages to pecuniary losses, might appear to exclude punitive damages altogether in the death (but not necessarily the survival) action.[79] Punitive damages could also be excluded on the ground that because the action was statutory, no award could be made unless explicitly authorized by the statute.[80]

Rationale. However, the policies supporting punitive damages apply as much or more in death actions as any other. For this and similar reasons, some courts have allowed punitive damages in spite of the statute's pecuniary loss requirement.[81] In addition, some statutes can be construed to permit punitive damages because they authorize damages that are fair and just,[82] or because they allow modification of the basic damages award for aggravating or mitigating circumstances.[83] Other statutes now explicitly provide for the award of punitive damages.[84] Besides the statutes themselves,

---

[73] See, e.g., Smith v. Ingersoll-Rand Co., 214 F.3d 1235, 1244 (10th Cir. 2000) (applying New Mexico law); Montalvo v. Lapez, 884 P.2d 345, 364 (Haw. 1999); Kennedy v. Ill. Cent. R.R. Co., 30 So.3d 333 (Miss 2010); Marcotte v. Timberlane/ Hampstead Sch. Dist., 733 A.2d 394, 405 (N.H. 1999). See also Dorn v. Burlington N. Santa Fe R.R. Co., 397 F.3d 1183 (9th Cir. 2005). But see Frontier Ins. Co. v. Blaty, 454 F.3d 590 (6th Cir. 2006) (affirming lower court's rejection of hedonic damages).

[74] One Nat'l Bank v. Pope, 372 Ark. 208, 272 S.W.3d 98 (2008); McGee v. A C & S, Inc., 933 So.2d 770 (La. 2006).

[75] E.g., Ark. Code Ann. § 16–62–102; Del. Code Ann. tit. 10, § 3724; N.D. Cent. Code § 32–03.2–04; Ohio Rev. Code Ann. § 2125.02(b). See also Weigel v. Lee, 752 N.W.2d 618 (N.D. 2008). In Shepard v. Capitol Foundry of Virginia, Inc., 262 Va. 715, 554 S.E.2d 72 (2001), the court upheld a jury verdict for $1.7 million for the death of a 67-year-old woman, allocating $1.1 million to the surviving husband and $100,000 for each of six children. The award was evidently based almost entirely on mental anguish and loss of society, companionship, comfort, and guidance.

[76] See Pierce v. Physicians Ins. Co. of Wis., Inc., 692 N.W.2d 558 (Wis. 2005) (holding that after settlement of wrongful death action over stillbirth of infant, mother could pursue separate claim of negligent infliction of emotional distress).

[77] E.g., City of Tucson v. Wondergem, 105 Ariz. 429, 466 P.2d 383 (1970); Hern v. Safeco Ins. Co. of Ill., 125 P.3d 597 (Mont. 2005); Sanchez v. Schindler, 651 S.W.2d 249, 251 (Tex. 1983). See Annotation, Recovery of Damages for Grief or Mental Anguish Resulting from Death of a Child—Modern Cases, 45 A.L.R.4th 234 (1986).

[78] See, e.g., Wood v. Wayman, 47 So.3d 1212 (Ala. 2010) (citing Alabama case law holding that in the "context of a wrongful-death action, a 'personal representative' acts 'as agent by legislative appointment for the effectuation of a legislative policy of the prevention of homicides through the deterrent value of the infliction of punitive damages' "); Killough v. Jahandarfard, 578 So.2d 1041 (Ala. 1991).

[79] See Rubeck v. Huffman, 54 Ohio St.2d 20, 374 N.E.2d 411 (1978).

[80] See Alsenz v. Clark County Sch. Dist., 109 Nev. 1062, 864 P.2d 285 (1993).

[81] Portwood v. Copper Valley Elec. Ass'n, Inc., 785 P.2d 541 (Alaska 1990) (pecuniary injury requirement applies only to compensatory damages).

[82] See Boies v. Cole, 99 Ariz. 198, 407 P.2d 917 (1965); Vickery v. Ballentine, 293 Ark. 54, 732 S.W.2d 160 (1987).

[83] E.g., Mo. Stat. Ann. § 537.090.

[84] N.Y. Est. Powers & Trusts Law § 5–4.3(b); N.C. Gen. Stat. § 28A–18–2(b).

a sizeable number of decisions have now allowed a recovery of punitive damages in death actions or have approved them in principle.[85]

§ 28.5 Procedure, Distribution, Defenses and Damages

Plaintiffs in wrongful death and survival actions. Some statutes permit direct wrongful death action suits by beneficiaries; others provide that the wrongful death suit is to be brought by a representative on the beneficiaries' behalf. Sometimes the representative in the wrongful death case is the personal representative of the estate— the same person who sues under the survival act.[86] However, monies recovered under the survival act are payable to the estate and generally subject to claims of the estate's creditors, while damages recovered for the beneficiaries are payable to the beneficiaries without going through the estate and the death action recovery is typically not subject to claims the creditors might have against the estate itself.[87] The distribution of damages differs from state to state and the governing statutes must always be consulted for determinative detail.[88]

Arbitration clauses. When the decedent had signed an agreement to arbitrate claims, the arbitration clause would seem to apply to the decedent's survival claim but not to the wrongful death action, which belongs to the beneficiaries themselves.[89] However, a number of courts have held that the wrongful death claim itself is subject to arbitration.[90] Precisely which parties and claims are subject to arbitration as a result of the decedent's pre-death agreement is a particularly significant issue in light of a recent narrowing of courts' ability to review arbitration agreements for unconscionability.[91]

Limiting wrongful death recovery to specified family members. All statutes limit the beneficiaries in some way, usually to specified family members such as spouses, children, parents, or heirs.[92] This sort of list is underinclusive because many who receive support or who suffer grief at the deceased's loss may not count as "heirs" or children.[93] Indeed,

---

[85]   Portwood v. Copper Valley Elec. Ass'n, Inc., 785 P.2d 541 (Alaska 1990); Lewis v. Hiatt, 683 So.2d 937 (Miss. 1996); Roach v. Jimmy D. Enters., Ltd., 912 P.2d 852 (Okla. 1996); McCourt v. Abernathy, 318 S.C. 301, 457 S.E.2d 603 (1995); Behrens v. Raleigh Hills Hosp., Inc., 675 P.2d 1179 (Utah 1983) (suggesting that allowance represents a trend); Clymer v. Webster, 156 Vt. 614, 596 A.2d 905 (1991).

[86]   However, in other states the representative is not required to be the estate's administrator or executor. See, e.g., In re Estate of Johnson, 231 P.3d 873 (Wyo. 2010).

[87]   See In re Estate of Maldanado, 117 P.3d 720 (Alaska 2005) ("Survivorship damages may be sought by the personal representative for the benefit of the estate, not for the benefit of any particular survivor"); Antisdel v. Ashby, 688 S.E.2d 163, 167 (Va. 2010).

[88]   Ariz. Rev. Stat. § 12–612 C (distribution "in proportion to their damages"); Kan. Stat. Ann. § 60–1905; see Chang v. State Farm Mut. Auto. Ins. Co., 182 Wis. 2d 549, 514 N.W.2d 399 (1993). See also Arnold v. Turek, 185 W.Va. 400, 407 S.E.2d 706 (1991) (under then existing statute, damages were to include sums for loss of support of various persons but were to be distributed according to the laws of descent and distribution); In re Estate of Bennett, 308 P.3d 63 (Mont. 2013).

[89]   See Lawrence v. Beverly Manor, 273 S.W.3d 525 (Mo. 2009); Ruiz v. Podolsky, 50 Cal.4th 838, 237 P.3d 584 (2010); Woodall v. Avalon Care Center-Federal Way, LLC, 231 P.3d 1252 (Wash. Ct. App. 2010) (holding that wrongful death claims are not bound by arbitration agreements but that survival claims are).

[90]   Briarcliff Nursing Home, Inc. v. Turcotte, 894 So.2d 661 (Ala. 2004); Cleveland v. Mann, 942 So.2d 108 (Miss. 2006); In re Golden Peanut Co., LLC, 298 S.W.3d 629 (Tex. 2009). But see Covenant Health & Rehab. of Picayune, LP v. Estate of Moulds, 14 So.3d 695 (Miss. 2009) (rejecting arbitration clause in nursing home wrongful death case based on unconscionability).

[91]   See Rent-A-Center, West, Inc. v. Jackson, 561 U.S. 63, 130 S.Ct. 2772 (2010).

[92]   E.g., Kan. Stat. Ann. § 60–1902 (heirs).

[93]   See, e.g., Ablin v. Richard O'Brien Plastering Co., 885 P.2d 289 (Colo. Ct. App. 1994) (only surviving relatives were siblings, but siblings were not "heirs" as Colorado understands that term).

at one time illegitimate children were excluded. That is now unconstitutional.[94] But other issues remain.[95] Traditionally, unmarried domestic partners were excluded from claims for emotional distress resulting from injury or death of the other partner, from loss of consortium claims, and from wrongful death claims. Some statutes now permit recovery by a qualified domestic partner for wrongful death of the other partner.[96] Recognition of same sex marriages should lessen, though not alleviate, the problem. California allows some different-sex partners to recover as well.[97] European principles permit compensation beyond formal family members.[98]

Caps on wrongful death damages. Tort reform legislation in a number of states has imposed caps on recoveries in death actions in certain situations. Medical providers are frequent beneficiaries of these statutes.[99] When medical malpractice causes death, some states cap recovery.[100] However, caps are not exclusive to the malpractice context. Caps on noneconomic losses[101] and other items[102] can also limit recoveries in other types of wrongful death cases. Of course, these limits are imposed by particular legislation and many states have no such limits on recoveries or have constitutional or statutory provisions that explicitly disallow them.[103]

---

[94]   As a matter of equal protection, states can no longer refuse a child's recovery merely because the child is illegitimate. Levy v. Louisiana, 391 U.S. 68, 88 S.Ct. 1509, 20 L.Ed.2d 436 (1968). Equally, a parent of an illegitimate child can recover for the child's death. Glona v. American Guarantee & Liab. Ins. Co., 391 U.S. 73, 88 S.Ct. 1515, 20 L.Ed.2d 441 (1968).

[95]   To avoid a problem of excluding a stepchild, the court in Lawson v. Atwood, 42 Ohio St.3d 69, 536 N.E.2d 1167 (1989), came up with the conclusion that the deceased had become the child's parent, even though he had not adopted the child.

[96]   See Cal. Civ. Pro. Code § 377.60 (domestic partner has standing to bring wrongful death action), addressed in Armijo v. Miles, 26 Cal.Rptr.3d 623, 127 Cal.App.4th 1405 (2005) (permitting wrongful death recovery by same-sex partner). See also 15 Vt. Stat. Ann. §§ 1204(a) & 1204(e)(2) (civil union permitted between persons of same sex, generally granting rights of married persons and specifically including right to sue for wrongful death). Cf. Ceja v. Rudolph & Sletten, Inc., 302 P.3d 211 (Cal. 2013) (subjective good faith belief that marriage was valid).

[97]   See Cal. Fam. Code § 297 (defining domestic partners).

[98]   Persons in a similar position to a family member who "had been in fact or would be maintained by the deceased" may also recover for the decedent's wrongful death. European Group on Tort Law, Principles of European Tort Law Art. 10:202 cmt. 2 (2005).

[99]   Hughes v. PeaceHealth, 344 Or. 142, 178 P.3d 225 (2008) (upholding and applying such a cap in the context of a medical provider).

[100]   See Tex. Civ. Prac. & Rem. Code § 74.303 (capping health care liability claims for wrongful death or survival actions at $500,000 per claimant for all damages), applied in In re Columbia Med. Ctr. of Las Colinas, 306 S.W.3d 246 (Tex. 2010); W. Va. Code § 55–7B–8 (capping compensatory damages against health care providers at $500,000 per occurrence for death and certain serious injury claims).

[101]   Alaska Stat. § 09.17.010 (noneconomic damages for wrongful death or personal injury may not exceed $400,000 or $8,000 per year of remaining life expectancy, whichever is higher); Alaska Stat. § 09.55.580 (where decedent has no spouse, children, or dependents, damages are limited to pecuniary losses); Colo. Rev. Stat. § 13–21–203 (capping recovery for noneconomic losses at $250,000 where the decedent does not have certain dependents unless there was a felonious killing); Kan. Stat. Ann. § 60–1903(a) (noneconomic damages capped at $250,000); Wis. Stat. Ann. § 895.04(4) (nonpecuniary damages for wrongful death limited to $500,000 for minors and $350,000 for adults).

[102]   For statutes reducing recovery based on some collateral source payments, see: Colo. Rev. Stat. § 13–21–111.6; Conn. Gen. Stat. § 52–225a; Or. Rev. Stat. § 31.580.

[103]   For examples of constitutional provisions, see Ariz. Const. art. II, § 31 ("No law shall be enacted in this state limiting the amount of damages to be recovered for causing the death or injury of any person"); Ark. Const. art. 5, § 32 (providing for workers compensation laws and providing that "otherwise no law shall be enacted limiting the amount to be recovered for injuries resulting in death or for injuries to persons or property; and in case of death from such injuries the right of action shall survive, and the General Assembly shall prescribe for whose benefit such action shall be prosecuted"); Thompson v. KFB Ins. Co., 850 P.2d 773 (Kan. 1993). For statutes that disclaim limits, see Haw. Rev. Stat. § 431:10C–306 (allowing liability for death actions

Wrongful death actions as independent or derivative: defenses. Wrongful death statutes create a new cause of action for the benefit of survivors; it is not merely a continuance of the deceased's own claim. At the same time, many statutes provide that no new cause of action is created unless the deceased himself would have been able to sue had he lived.[104] The effect of this statutory provision can be conceived as making the death action derivative of the decedent's own claim, not a wholly independent action. Following this thinking, a defense that would have defeated the deceased's claim had he lived may also defeat the wrongful death suit.[105] Of course, not all defenses need be treated in the same way. In wrongful death suits, a statutory beneficiary whose negligence contributed to the deceased's death is usually subject to the contributory or comparative negligence rules.[106]

Survival claims as derivative: defenses. Since survival statutes merely perpetuated the cause of action the decedent himself would have had, a defense that would bar or reduce damages of the deceased would have the same effect on the estate's claim under the survival act.[107] However, a few courts have dealt with the beneficiary's negligence in a different manner.[108] The survival action is prosecuted by the deceased's personal representative and recoveries are paid to the estate. Consequently, in a formal sense, the negligence of a person who inherits from the estate might seem irrelevant, as some courts have held.[109]

Statutes of limitation in wrongful death actions. One of the central statutes of limitation questions in wrongful death actions arises when the tort victim dies long after the injury was inflicted. If she dies after her personal injury claim is barred, can a wrongful death action be brought? The argument for allowing the claim is that the wrongful death action creates a new cause of action in favor of the survivors, and that the survivors or their representative could not bring the action until death occurred,[110] so that the statute of limitations should begin to run at death, not sooner. For this

---

from motor vehicle accidents as an exception to no fault insurance as the exclusive remedy in other circumstances).

[104] E.g., Fla. Stat. Ann. § 768.19 ("When the death of a person is caused by the wrongful act, negligence, default, or breach of contract or warranty of any person . . . and the event would have entitled the person injured to maintain an action and recover damages if death had not ensued. . . ."); Mo. Ann. Stat. § 537.080 (when "the death of a person results from any act, . . . which, if death had not ensued, would have entitled [decedent] to recover damages in respect thereof . . ."); Wy. Stat. 1977 § 1–38–101.

[105] See Griffis v. Wheeler, 18 So.3d 2 (Fla. Dist. Ct. App. 2009) (statutory rule that certain intoxicated persons could not recover for personal injury barred wrongful death suit as well); Cramer v. Slater, 146 Idaho 868, 204 P.3d 508 (2009) (holding that when professionals fail to assess and prevent suicide and patient commits suicide, matter is one of comparative fault and jury is charged with assigning liability).

[106] Winding River Vill. Condo. Ass'n, Inc. v. Barnett, 218 Ga.App. 35, 459 S.E.2d 569 (1995) (beneficiary's contributory negligence would reduce her share of award).

[107] E.g., Allison v. Snelling & Snelling, Inc., 425 Pa. 519, 229 A.2d 861 (1967) (barring both wrongful death and survival claims).

[108] In re Estate of Infant Fontaine, 128 N.H. 695, 519 A.2d 227 (1986); Teeter v. Missouri Highway & Transp. Comm'n, 891 S.W.2d 817 (Mo. 1995) (defendant could claim contribution for the negligence of one of two beneficiaries).

[109] See Byrne v. Schneider's Iron & Metal, Inc., 190 Mich.App. 176, 475 N.W.2d 854 (1991); cf. In re Estate of Infant Fontaine, 128 N.H. 695, 519 A.2d 227 (1986) (death action with survival attributes). It is usually said that this is the majority rule. See Henry Woods & Beth Deere, Comparative Fault 9:4 (3d ed. 1996); 2 Stuart M. Speiser, Charles F. Krause & Juanita M. Madole, Recovery for Wrongful Death and Injury 5:10 (3d ed. Looseleaf).

[110] Martin v. Naik, 300 P.3d 625 (Kan. 2013) (negligent treatment resulting in coma and later death; survival statute did not run for patient because he could not reasonably ascertain that he had a cause of action, and wrongful death statute did not run for survivors because they did not have a cause of action until the patient died).

reason, or because the death statute specifically provides for accrual at the time of death, a good many courts who are not constrained by specific statutory commands have held that the wrongful death suit may be maintained even after the personal injury action on which it is based has expired.[111] The other major view is that, although the wrongful death statute creates a new cause of action for survivors, the claim is to some extent derivative of the deceased's own rights. If he would have had no right to sue had he lived, then the survivors would have no rights.[112] In the same way, if his once-existing right had expired, then the survivors' rights have expired, too.[113]

Prior judgment or release: effect of injured victim's settlement on survival and wrongful death claims. When an injured victim pursues her claim against the tortfeasor to judgment or settles and releases her claim with him, the victim's claim is terminated. Consequently, there is no personal injury claim to survive and no survival action may be brought.[114] The question that has produced division is whether the wrongful death claim is also terminated by the victim's inter vivos settlement or by litigation that goes to judgment. The answer of most courts—in which some legislatures have joined[115]—is that either a settlement by the victim or a judgment for or against him will preclude the wrongful death action where death resulted from the original injury and not from its later aggravation.[116]

[111] Chapman v. Cardiac Pacemakers, Inc., 105 Idaho 785, 673 P.2d 385 (1983); Mummert v. Alizadeh, 77 A.3d 1049 (Md. 2013) (statute of limitations on decedent's claim no bar); Carroll v. W.R. Grace & Co., 252 Mont. 485, 830 P.2d 1253 (1992); Fernandez v. Kozar, 107 Nev. 446, 814 P.2d 68 (1991). Accord Restatement Second of Torts § 899 cmt. c (1979). Tolling may also apply in the case of wrongful concealment. Alldedge v. Good Samaritan Home, Inc., 9 N.E.3d 1257 (Ind. 2014). A variant of this problem is whether a survivor can amend a complaint brought by the plaintiff during his lifetime, against the defendant and in a timely manner, to include a wrongful death claim after the plaintiff's death, where the statute of limitations or a statute of repose has expired by that time. See Sisson v. Lhowe, 460 Mass. 705, 954 N.E.2d 1115 (2011) (allowing the substitution of a wrongful death claim).

[112] Estate of Genrich v. OHIC Ins. Co., 318 Wis.2d 553, 769 N.W.2d 481 (2009).

[113] Henderson v. MeadWestvaco Corp., 23 So.3d 625 (Ala. 2009) (based on statutory language). Russell v. Ingersoll-Rand Co., 841 S.W.2d 343 (Tex. 1992) (asserting that this is the more authoritative position). Accord Nelson v. American Red Cross, 26 F.3d 193 (D.C. Cir. 1994); Brown v. Pine Bluff Nursing Home, 359 Ark. 471, 199 S.W.3d 45 (2004) (original claim for negligence dismissed as untimely; subsequent wrongful death claim, being "derivative," must also be dismissed); Jenkins v. Pensacola Health Trust, Inc., 933 So. 2d 923 (Miss. 2006); Edwards v. Fogarty, 962 P.2d 879 (Wyo. 1998).

[114] Cf. Kronemeyer v. Meinig, 948 P.2d 119 (Colo. Ct. App. 1997) (earlier wrongful death suit and settlement did not bar survival claim).

[115] 740 Ill. Comp. Stat. Ann. § 180/1 (foreclosing death claim if judgment rendered or settlement made in decedent's lifetime); cf. D.C. Code Ann. § 16–2701 (barring suit if victim "recovered damages" in her lifetime).

[116] Hutton v. Davis, 26 Ariz.App. 215, 547 P.2d 486 (1976); Union Bank of Cal., N.A. v. Copeland Lumber Yards, Inc., 213 Or.App. 308, 160 P.3d 1032 (2007); see Vitauts M. Gulbis, Annotation, Judgment in Favor Of, or Adverse To, Person Injured as Barring Action For His Death, 26 A.L.R.4th 1264 (1981).

Chapter 29

EMOTIONAL HARM

Analysis

A. INTRODUCTION TO EMOTIONAL HARM
§ 29.1   Introduction to Emotional Distress and Harm in Tort Law
§ 29.2   Stand-Alone Emotional Distress as a Tort in Itself: Policy Concerns
§ 29.3   Stand-Alone Emotional Distress as a Tort in Itself: Historical Development

B. INTENTIONAL OR RECKLESS INFLICTION OF EMOTIONAL DISTRESS
§ 29.4   Overlapping or Duplicating Claims for Emotional Distress
§ 29.5   Intentional Infliction of Emotional Distress: Rules of Liability
§ 29.6   Common Characteristics of Extreme and Outrageous Conduct
§ 29.7   The Severe Distress Requirement
§ 29.8   Intentional Infliction and Emotional Distress of Third Persons

C. NEGLIGENT INFLICTION OF EMOTIONAL HARM
§ 29.9   Negligent Infliction of Emotional Harm: General Rules of Liability
§ 29.10   Emotional Harm Arising from Risks or Harms to Others
§ 29.11   Loss of Consortium
§ 29.12   Emotional Distress Arising from Direct Risks of Physical Harm
§ 29.13   Toxic Exposures: Fear of Future Harm
§ 29.14   Emotional Distress from False or Erroneous Information
§ 29.15   Duties of Care to Protect Emotional Well-Being Independent of Physical Risks
§ 29.16   Sensitive Plaintiffs

A. INTRODUCTION TO EMOTIONAL HARM

§ 29.1 Introduction to Emotional Distress and Harm in Tort Law

General recognition of emotional distress. Courts have long recognized that tortfeasors should be responsible for causing distress, emotional harm, anxiety, diminished enjoyment, pain, loss of autonomy, and similar intangible harms. The exact form of the intangible harm seldom matters. These harms can be referred to as distress or as emotional harm.

Two radically different approaches to emotional harm. Courts approach emotional distress damages in two radically different ways, depending on whether the emotional harm is considered "parasitic" to another tort or a "stand-alone" emotional harm claim.

Emotional distress as an item of damages in some other tort cause of action. In the first type of claim, emotional distress damages are merely items of damage in the recovery for some other tort. A plaintiff who establishes a right to recover for emotional distress under a tort cause of action such as assault, battery, false imprisonment, libel, malicious prosecution, invasion of privacy, nuisance, or ordinary negligence, can recover full damages for emotional distress without any special limiting rules such as those requiring physical manifestations of emotional distress or serious or severe distress.[1] In cases in which the defendant's tortious conduct has produced some other tort of which distress is a part, the scope of recoverable distress damages can be quite broad.[2]

Parasitic damages for emotional harm are usually rejected in breach of contract claims, at least where the claim is essentially economic in nature,[3] not aimed at protection of emotional well-being.[4] In the same way, recovery of emotional distress damages as an item of damages for infliction of a purely financial tort, where there is no physical harm risked or caused, may be inappropriate.[5]

Stand-alone emotional distress as a tort in itself. In the second type of emotional harm claim, there is no other tort and the plaintiff must claim that infliction of emotional distress is itself a tort. The second kind of claim is usually subject to substantial limitations. Even so, in the second kind of claim the plaintiff may establish a separate tort either for intentional infliction of emotional distress (IIED) or negligent infliction of emotional distress (NIED).[6] At times, the two approaches overlap, or sometimes collide, when a plaintiff claims both that emotional distress is an element of damage, and brings a separate cause of action for intentional or negligent infliction of emotional distress.

§ 29.2 Stand-Alone Emotional Distress as a Tort in Itself: Policy Concerns

Differing views on the stand-alone claim. The problem of stand-alone emotional distress has fascinated many lawyers and judges, who have written about it at length.[7] Legal professionals differ considerably in their attitude toward recovery for emotional

---

[1] Millennium Equity Holdings, LLC v. Mahlowitz, 456 Mass. 627, 925 N.E.2d 513 (2010); Ammondson v. Northwestern Corp., 220 P.3d 1 (Mont. 2009); but see Betsinger v. D.R. Horton, Inc., 232 P.3d 433 (Nev. 2010).

[2] Norfolk & W. Ry. v. Ayers, 538 U.S. 135, 153–54, 123 S.Ct. 1210, 1221–22, 155 L.Ed.2d 261 (2003) ("Once found liable for 'any bodily harm,' a negligent actor is answerable in damages for emotional disturbance 'resulting from the bodily harm or from the conduct which causes it,' " citing Restatement Second of Torts § 456(a) (1965)); Thornton v. Garcini, 928 N.E.2d 804 (Ill. 2010).

[3] See John Hancock Mut. Life Ins. Co. v. Banerji, 447 Mass. 875, 858 N.E.2d 277 (2006); 3 Dan B. Dobbs, The Law of Remedies § 12.5(1) (2d ed. 1993).

[4] In re Hannaford Bros. Co. Customer Data Sec. Breach Litig., 4 A.3d 492 (Me. 2010) (electronic payment data); Murphy v. Implicito, 392 N.J. Super. 245, 266, 920 A.2d 678, 690 (2007) (surgeon allegedly breached contract by using cadaver parts in operation); Larsen v. Banner Health Sys., 81 P.3d 196 (Wyo. 2003) (health care provider switched babies of two mothers at birth). Breach of contracts made to secure physical safety (including warranties) may produce liability for personal injury and pain and emotional suffering damages.

[5] See J. Smith Lanier & Co. v. Se. Forge, Inc., 280 Ga. 508, 630 S.E.2d 404 (2006). See similarly Molina v. Merritt & Furman Ins. Agency, Inc., 207 F.3d 1351 (11th Cir. 2000); Sawyer v. Bank of Am., 83 Cal.App.3d 135, 145 Cal.Rptr. 623 (1978); Stein, Hinkle, Dawe & Assocs., Inc. v. Continental Cas. Co., 313 N.W.2d 299 (Mich. Ct. App. 1981).

[6] McKay v. Wilderness Dev't, LLC, 221 P.3d 1184 (Mont. 2009) (breach of restrictive covenant, independent tort of IIED also could be asserted).

[7] E.g., Francis H. Bohlen, Right to Recover for Injury Resulting from Negligence Without Impact, 50 Am. L.Regs. 141 (1902); Martha Chamallas, Unpacking Emotional Distress: Sexual Exploitation, Reproductive Harm, and Fundamental Rights, 44 Wake Forest L. Rev. 1109 (2009); Fowler V. Harper & Mary Coate McNeely, A Re-Examination of the Basis for Liability for Emotional Ditress, 1938 Wis. L. Rev. 426; Stanley Ingber, Rethinking Intangible Injuries: A Focus on Remedy, 73 Cal. L. Rev. 772 (1985); Gregory C. Keating, Is Negligent Infliction of Emotional Distress a Freestanding Tort?, 44 Wake Forest L. Rev. 1131 (2009); Nancy Levit, Ethereal Torts, 61 Geo. Wash. L. Rev. 136 (1992); Calvert Magruder, Mental and Emotional Disturbance in the Law of Torts, 49 Harv. L. Rev. 1033 (1936); Robert L. Rabin, Emotional Distress in Tort Law: Themes of Constraint, 44 Wake Forest. L. Rev. 1197 (2009).

distress. Some see the claim as trivial, as a disruption of the judicial process, or even as presenting risks of outright fakery.[8] Others, on the contrary, contend that courts, perhaps reflecting society at large, have not only perpetuated an outmoded dualism but have devalued the importance of emotional life by their caution in granting recovery.[9]

Doubts that emotional distress is genuine. It is certainly true that on the whole, courts have been extremely cautious in allowing claims for stand-alone emotional harm.[10] In the past, courts often expressed concerns about the reality of emotional distress, but in most cases the reality or existence of the distress is not in doubt. If you are seriously threatened with future harm by a hostile group of masked men who gather around you in a circle, the rest of us should not doubt that you suffered fear. If your child is crushed by a car, we can believe you suffered anguish. Although stand-alone emotional harm is a real and an important concern, emotional harm does have some special characteristics that call for a degree of caution.

The exhaustion of funds argument. One broadly expressed concern is that defendants who must pay emotional harm damages to the first plaintiff may have no funds left for payment of more serious claims for pain or actual financial costs suffered by later plaintiffs.[11] This problem, however, is not really about emotional harm claims but about equitable distribution to multiple victims when the wrongdoer's funds are inadequate to cover the harms he has inflicted. The problem occurs not only with emotional harm claims but also with punitive damages awarded to an early claimant and even with ordinary economic loss claims paid to the first plaintiff and leaving nothing for claims of the second. It may be that the legal solution should aim at the whole problem and not merely at the isolated instance of it when emotional harm is claimed.[12] More particular concerns are narrower.

Inability to estimate damages. First, emotional harm, as distinct from the financial costs of treatment, cannot ordinarily be represented in dollar awards. We may be confident that the plaintiff suffers distress or some other form of diminished enjoyment in life, but seldom can we give reasons why the distress is worth $100,000 rather than one-tenth as much or ten times as much. That makes us uncertain about the justice and even-handedness of awards. Judicial review is correspondingly difficult. The same difficulty increases risks that the trier will be more influenced by personal feelings or biases for or against the defendant or the plaintiff than by any good estimate of the harm. Problems of this ilk create problems in justice and also in trial strategy and settlement. A defendant who estimates the chance of losing at 50% may offer to settle for something like 50% of the plaintiff's damages. If damage awards for emotional harm are erratic

---

[8]   Richard N. Pearson, Liability to Bystanders for Negligently Inflicted Emotional Harm—A Comment on the Nature of Arbitrary Rules, 34 U. Fla. L. Rev. 477 (1982).

[9]   E.g., Leslie Bender, Feminist (Re)torts: Thoughts on the Liability Crisis, Mass Torts, Power, and Responsibilities, 1990 Duke L.J. 848 (1990); Nancy Levit, Ethereal Torts, 61 Geo. Wash. L. Rev. 136 (1992).

[10]   Robert L. Rabin, Emotional Distress in Tort Law: Themes of Constraint, 44 Wake Forest. L. Rev. 1197 (2009). See also Turley v. ISG Lackawanna, Inc., 774 F.3d 140 (2d Cir. 2014) ("highly disfavored"); Milk v. Federal Home Loan Mortg. Corp., 743 F.3d 149 (6th Cir. 2014) ("standards for this tort are strict"); Hayward v. Cleveland Clinic Found., 759 F.3d 601 (6th Cir. 2014) ("to say that Ohio courts narrowly define 'extreme and outrageous conduct' would be something of an understatement").

[11]   See Norfolk & W. Ry. v. Ayers, 538 U.S. 135, 123 S.Ct. 1210, 155 L.Ed.2d 261 (2003) (Kennedy, J., dissenting).

[12]   Short of bankruptcy, the legal system has provided only crude solutions or none at all, but it would be possible to expand interpleader or otherwise provide for common distribution system when claims exceed assets. See 1 Dan B. Dobbs, The Law of Remedies § 2.9(4), at 238 (2d ed. 1993).

because they have no objective measurement, settlement will be erratic, too, or will depend on extraneous factors. The same point, however, applies to awards for physical pain and suffering, so perhaps it should have little weight as long as courts are willing to award damages for physical pain. Another possibility is to create some presumptive measures of emotional harm compensation.[13]

What should be expected of the plaintiff in mitigation? Second, we may be confident that distress is real but quite uncertain how deep-seated it is and what to expect of the plaintiff herself by way of mitigation. The law is usually compelled to attribute a degree of free will to competent actors. An injured person cannot heal a broken leg by acquiring a better attitude about it. But some persons cope with distress better than others; everyone suffers distress in some measure and most people learn to get over or at least to minimize distress over a period of time. Others nurse their distress and build it up. Even under a thin skull rule, the defendant probably should not be liable for the plaintiff's maladaptive attitudes about distress.[14]

Do awards for distress achieve compensation? Third, we cannot at this juncture be confident about whether awards for distress accomplish compensation. Awards are not likely to approximate what the plaintiff would have paid to avoid the injury or would have accepted to suffer the injury. No matter what the award for emotional distress, the plaintiff may remain distressed. Indeed, it is possible that awarding a person substantial sums for distress will confirm and reinforce the distress and so perpetuate it.[15] Whether this is true or not, it is easy to see that if you recover damages for lost wages, they replace your wage loss, while if you recover damages for pure emotional harm they don't replace your peace of mind.

Overexaction. A more subtle variation on this problem is that if a recovery of damages does in fact provide some solace to the victim, the solace may be small compared to the harm done the defendant. It is true that the defendant was by hypothesis the guilty party and that an award can at least demonstrate society's support for the victim; but an ounce of solace to the plaintiff that costs a pound of pain to the defendant reduces the total happiness in an unhappy world. Perhaps punitive damages would work better than awards for distress if the defendant is truly deserving of punishment, for punitive damages would focus on the defendant's misconduct and guide damages proportionately.

Flood of litigation. Finally, in some situations (but not all) courts do not see any reasonable limit on the number of emotional harm claims that can be brought as the result of a single tort. Not only may some plaintiffs pursue trivial affronts, but a large number of people might suffer some degree of distress as a result of a single tort. A negligent or intentional killing might shock millions who watch it on television or read about it, all of whom might sue. This argument is grounded in deep pessimism about the judiciary's ability to fulfill its function in determining disputes. As Dean Prosser wrote of the flood of litigation concern, "It is the business of the law to remedy wrongs that deserve it, even at the expense of a 'flood of litigation,' and it is a pitiful concession of

---

[13] This was the approach taken by the 9/11 Victim's Compensation Fund. Kenneth R. Feinberg, et al., Final Report of the Special Master for the September 11th Victim Compensation Fund of 2001, at 9 (2004), available at http://www.justice.gov/final_report.pdf, "each claim received a uniform non-economic award of $250,000 for the death of the victim and an additional non-economic award of $100,000 for the spouse and each dependent of the victim").

[14] Guido Calabresi, Toward a Unified Theory of Torts, 1 J. Tort L. 1 (Oct. 2007).

[15] Id.

incompetence on the part of any court of justice to deny relief on such grounds."[16] The argument about large numbers of trivial claims also probably miscalculates plaintiff incentives. Although lawyers may misjudge the merits of their clients' cases, they have little incentive to sue on claims that will not pay off, since their fee will only be generated by a recovery.

What caution suggests. The reasons for caution about emotional distress claims are not reasons to ignore or reject all such claims. Indeed, they provide some guidance for allowing some claims. When common experience tells us that the injury is real and tortiously produced, the reasons for caution suggest that judges can focus on careful assessment of damages rather than on blanket exclusions of stand-alone emotional harm. More radically, it may be suggested that the focus on sudden, shocking events and the dramatic emotional injury that results has distracted attention from chronic emotional harm that may be more devastating—the grief and absence from loss of a loved one rather than the shock at seeing his death.

§ 29.3 Stand-Alone Emotional Distress as a Tort in Itself: Historical Development

Historical development of liability for stand-alone emotional distress claims. Although stand-alone claims for infliction of distress have expanded significantly over the last fifty years, those claims are not without significant historical precedent. Indeed, even one hundred years ago courts permitted claims for some kinds of purely emotional harm.

Carriers and innkeepers. In the earlier law, while damages generally could not be recovered for stand-alone emotional harm, courts recognized an exception by imposing a special duty upon common carriers[17] and innkeepers[18] to exercise civility toward passengers. This traditional exception involved a contractual relationship between the plaintiff and the defendant. Early cases purported to find an implied contract of courteous treatment.[19] Some courts applied the same rule to telegraph companies, who might, for instance, be held liable for emotional distress caused by failing to deliver a death notice or the like.[20] This rule went far beyond a duty to avoid severe emotional harm; it imposed liability for such minor misconduct as insulting or profane language. The special liability was somewhat peculiar and courts today might well conclude that liability for a carrier's insult alone is no longer justified because more finely tuned rules now apply to all defendants.[21] However, the liability of carriers and innkeepers probably played a role in developing a degree of responsibility for emotional harm.

Interference with dead bodies. Courts also allowed recovery of emotional distress in another class of cases—those involving some kind of mishandling of dead bodies.[22] Indeed, the common law action for "tortious interference with a dead body" still survives

---

[16]   W. Page Keeton et.al, Prosser and Keeton on Torts § 12, at 56 (5th ed. 1984).

[17]   See Cole v. Atlanta & W.P.R. Co., 102 Ga. 474, 31 S.E. 107 (1897); Lipman v. Atlantic Coast Line R.R., 108 S.C. 151, 93 S.E. 714 (1917).

[18]   See DeWolf v. Ford, 193 N.Y. 397, 86 N.E. 527 (1908).

[19]   E.g., Chamberlain v. Chandler, 3 Mason. 242, Fed. Cas. No. 2,575 (Cir. Ct. D. Mass. 1823).

[20]   Stuart v. W. Union Tel. Co., 66 Tex. 580, 18 S.W. 351 (1885).

[21]   Cf. Adams v. N.Y.C. Transit Auth., 88 N.Y.2d 116, 666 N.E.2d 216, 643 N.Y.S.2d 511 (1996).

[22]   E.g., Rollins v. Phillips, 554 So.2d 1006 (Ala. 1989) (unauthorized autopsy); see also Restatement Second of Torts § 868 (1979).

in some jurisdictions.[23] In earlier cases, courts purported to find a property or quasi-property interest in the body. Some courts still use quasi-property reasoning.[24] However, the property theory has been generally dismissed as a fiction and displaced in favor of analyzing the claim in terms of emotional distress.[25]

Generalizing liability. Over time, still other cases seemed to demand relief. Courts would sometimes find a battery or other tort so that emotional harm damages could be recovered, if need be by stretching rules to find a physical touching or at least physical harm. In a well-known English case, the defendant deliberately told the plaintiff that her husband had been "smashed up" in an accident and that she must go to him immediately. The victim of this atrocious behavior was seriously distressed and suffered some physical consequences of that distress. The court appeared to think that the physical harm as well as the emotional distress must have been intended and partly on that ground recognized liability.[26]

The First Restatement of Torts. As the exceptions to the rule against liability accumulated, courts and lawyers gradually began to realize that the traditional rule against liability for emotional harm alone no longer accurately stated what courts were doing in fact. In a 1948 Supplement to the First Restatement of Torts, the American Law Institute for the first time recognized a separate tort for intentional infliction of emotional distress. The special rules and exceptional cases are now largely subsumed in this newly recognized tort.

The Second and Third Restatements of Torts. As revised in the Restatement Second, the American Law Institute recognized a cause of action for intentional infliction of emotional distress only when (1) the defendant causes severe emotional distress, (2) intentionally or recklessly, and (3) by extreme and outrageous conduct.[27] Provisions were also enacted for intended emotional harm related to risk of bodily harm and unintended emotional distress that results in bodily harm.[28] The Second Restatement also provided for liability for negligent infliction of emotional disturbance but only to the extent that physical harm resulted.[29] The current scope of stand-alone emotional distress claims under the Restatement Third of Torts and contemporary case law is discussed below.[30] When stand-alone emotional distress as a separate tort, the Restatement Third recognizes two versions of the claim, one for intentional infliction of emotional distress (IIED), the other for negligent infliction (NIED).

---

[23] See Adams v. King Cnty., 164 Wash.2d 640, 192 P.3d 891 (2008) (defendants permitted to remove some brain tissue for experimental purposes, obtained the entire brain and other body samples from the dead body of the plaintiff's son). Cf. Boorman v. Nev. Mem'l Cremation Soc'y, 236 P.3d 4 (Nev. 2010).

[24] E.g., Smialek v. Begay, 104 N.M. 375, 721 P.2d 1306 (1986). Some courts may continue to mention property rights in the body even while grounding liability in the tort of "outrage." See Travelers Ins. Co. v. Smith, 338 Ark. 81, 991 S.W.2d 591 (1999).

[25] See Culpepper v. Pearl St. Bldg., Inc., 877 P.2d 877 (Colo. 1994); Guth v. Freeland, 96 Haw. 147, 28 P.3d 982 (2001). See also Crocker v. Pleasant, 778 So. 2d 978 (Fla. 2001); Lascurain v. City of Newark, 349 N.J. Super. 251, 793 A.2d 731 (2002).

[26] Wilkinson v. Downton, [1897] 2 Q.B. 57.

[27] Restatement Second of Torts § 46 (1965).

[28] Id. §§ 312, 313.

[29] Id. §§ 436, 436A.

[30] See §§ 29.4–29.16.

B. INTENTIONAL OR RECKLESS INFLICTION OF EMOTIONAL DISTRESS

§ 29.4 Overlapping or Duplicating Claims for Emotional Distress

Overlapping causes of action. Given various ways in which tort causes of action can redress emotional distress, a question of both practical and theoretical importance arises—can the plaintiff recover both for stand-alone emotional distress and for other torts that permit a recovery for emotional distress? The question is not whether the plaintiff who is battered or defamed can recover for emotional distress. The question is whether a separate cause of action can be stated for emotional distress on facts that are addressed by the law of some more specific tort like battery or defamation. The answer matters in at least two distinct kinds of cases. In the first, the plaintiff has a viable claim for, say, battery and wishes to claim emotional distress arising in whole or part from that same battery. A second pattern involves an emotional harm claim that may seem to be asserted to avoid some limitation imposed by the rules of the more specific tort.

Reasons to permit dual claims. In the first case, one reason to permit the two claims is that they address somewhat different actionable conduct. The battery claim is limited to the unwanted touching and its effect, while part of the emotional distress may have resulted from a whole sequence of events preceding the battery as well as from the battery itself. To reject the emotional distress claim in those circumstances would be to impose artificial limitations on the plaintiff's recovery. Another reason to permit the claim is to allow for alternate pleading. The plaintiff's lawyer cannot be sure in advance whether the jury would render a favorable verdict on the battery claim and ought not be forced to choose between two claims when the facts are sufficient for both. For these reasons, courts that allow both the battery and the emotional distress claim in these circumstances seem well justified.[31]

Duplicative damage awards. The only obvious reason to forbid the plaintiff from suing on both a battery and an intentional infliction of emotional distress theory is that even well-instructed jurors may tend to feel that two claims means two sets of emotional distress damages. The jury may award emotional distress as an item of damages in the battery claim and again separately in the separate emotional harm claim. Some overlap cases raise puzzling damage problems that are not so readily resolved.[32]

Artful pleading. A second pattern of overlapping claims involves an emotional harm claim that may seem to be asserted to avoid some limitation imposed by the rules of the more specific tort. For instance, the battery statute of limitations may foreclose the battery claim. If a stand-alone claim for emotional distress can be asserted in such a case, it looks very much as if the court is permitting the plaintiff to circumvent the statute. More stringent policy concerns might arise in defamation and false light privacy cases, where constitutional free-speech rules might preclude the defamation and privacy claim altogether. If the plaintiff can simply substitute an emotional distress claim based on the same facts and recover the same damages that would be recoverable for emotional

---

[31] K.M. v. Ala. Dep't of Youth Servs., 360 F.Supp.2d 1253 (M.D. Ala. 2005) (serious sexual battery, but both battery and emotional distress claims allowed); Durban v. Guajardo, 79 S.W.3d 198 (Tex. App. 2002) (extended conflict between two people including some batteries).

[32] Alderson v. Bonner, 142 Idaho 733, 132 P.3d 1261 (Ct. App. 2006).

distress in a defamation or privacy claim, then the plaintiff penetrated the constitution's shield for free speech.[33]

End run versus different underlying policies. It seems axiomatic that rules designed to preclude a claim should not be subverted by renaming it and claiming the same damages on the same facts. Yet it may be difficult to determine when this policy should apply. The rules of assault permit recovery for harm that is essentially a form of emotional distress when the defendant intentionally puts the plaintiff in apprehension of an imminent unwanted touching, but preclude recovery for threats of a touching that lies in the future. A defendant who threatens to castrate the plaintiff at some indefinite time in the future is not committing an assault, and the plaintiff could not recover on an assault theory. The plaintiff, however, should be and has been permitted to claim an intentional infliction of emotional distress on similar facts.[34] That seems right. The emotional distress claim was recognized in part because the limitations of the assault claim were too narrow. There is thus no overarching policy of the law to prevent recovery on these facts. Similarly, a plaintiff who loses a claim for negligent or intentional infliction of emotional distress because her distress is not regarded as sufficiently severe might nevertheless succeed on a privacy claim based on intrusion.[35] Because privacy law protects against intrusions into private matters whether or not they cause severe harm, the difference in outcome seems justified.

Case by case adjudication. In contrast, if the plaintiff could not prevail in the privacy case because the defendant's conduct was a protected report by a news organization, the tort of IIED should also be rejected.[36] This analysis suggests that when facts and damages overlap, case by case assessment is required to determine when the policy of precluding one claim operates to preclude the other as well. Some courts have specifically said that the intentional infliction claim cannot be used to make an end run around the limitations imposed by other torts,[37] or that the intentional infliction claim is a gap filler, to be used only when some other tort like battery or false imprisonment is not established on the facts.[38]

§ 29.5 Intentional Infliction of Emotional Distress: Rules of Liability

Elements under the Restatement Third of Torts. The basic contemporary claim for intentional (or reckless) infliction of emotional disturbance is well stated by the Restatement Third of Torts. That authority provides: "An actor who by extreme and outrageous conduct intentionally or recklessly causes severe emotional harm to another is subject to liability for that emotional harm and, if the emotional harm causes bodily

---

[33] The Supreme Court may have permitted something like this in Time, Inc. v. Firestone, 424 U.S. 448, 96 S.Ct. 958, 47 L.Ed.2d 154 (1976).

[34] See State Rubbish Collectors Ass'n v. Siliznoff, 38 Cal.2d 330, 240 P.2d 282 (1952); Dickens v. Puryear, 302 N.C. 437, 276 S.E.2d 325 (1981). See also, e.g., Smith v. Welch, 265 Kan. 868, 967 P.2d 727 (1998) (IIED claim permitted although battery claim was time barred).

[35] Alderson v. Bonner, 142 Idaho 733, 132 P.3d 1261 (Ct. App. 2006).

[36] Valadez v. Emmis Commc'ns, 229 P.3d 389 (Kan. 2010).

[37] See Uranga v. Federated Pubs. Inc., 138 Idaho 550, 67 P.3d 29 (2003); K.G. v. R.T.R., 918 S.W.2d 795 (Mo. 1996); see also Veilleux v. National Broad. Co., 206 F.3d 92 (1st Cir. 2000).

[38] Banks v. Fritsch, 39 S.W.3d 474 (Ky. Ct. App. 2001); Baliva v. State Farm Mut. Auto. Ins. Co., 286 A.D.2d 953, 730 N.Y.S.2d 655 (2001); GTE Sw., Inc. v. Bruce, 998 S.W.2d 605 (Tex. 1999).

harm, also for the bodily harm."[39] Under this formulation it is said that the intentional infliction of emotional harm tort, also called the tort of "outrage," has three elements (1) extreme and outrageous conduct by the defendant, (2) intent to cause severe distress, or at least recklessness in risking it, and (3) severe distress caused by the conduct.

Intent requirement. As elsewhere in the law of torts, intent can be shown either by evidence that the defendant acted with a purpose or desire to accomplish the harm, or by evidence that such harm was substantially certain to occur.[40] In the Restatement, as in most states, reckless or willful attitude will also suffice to meet the requirement.[41]

Additional elements. Neither intent nor recklessness alone suffice to make out the case; the conduct itself must be both extreme and outrageous. The requirement of extreme and outrageous conduct not only serves to limit the tort, but also to provide strong evidence of intent and evidence that severe harm in fact resulted.[42] Given evidence of severe distress, the plaintiff is not required to show that she suffers physical symptoms or harm.[43] Almost all courts recognize the tort and apply these basic rules.[44]

§ 29.6 Common Characteristics of Extreme and Outrageous Conduct

Distinguishing extreme and outrageous conduct. In the famous parlance of the Restatement Second, conduct was extreme or outrageous if "the case is one in which the recitation of the facts to an average member of the community would arouse his resentment against the actor, and lead him to exclaim, 'Outrageous!' "[45] Such a colorful description of anticipated audience response gives a sense of the moral approbation that underlies the tort and the extent to which the tort is meant to capture "a very small slice of human behavior."[46] Courts often join the Restatement in saying that misconduct causing emotional harm alone is actionable only when it is utterly intolerable and goes beyond all bounds of civilized society.[47] By articulating conduct that is beyond the bounds of human decency, the tort plays an important but difficult role in articulating social norms.[48]

---

[39] Restatement (Third) of Torts: Liability for Physical and Emotional Harm § 46 (2012).

[40] E.g., Alexander v. Bozeman Motors, Inc., 234 P.3d 880 (Mont. 2010); Flizack v. Good News Home for Women, Inc., 346 N.J. Super. 150, 787 A.2d 228 (2001); Jackson v. Sun Oil Co. of Pa., 361 Pa. Super. 54, 521 A.2d 469 (1987); Kjerstad v. Ravellette Pubs., Inc., 517 N.W.2d 419 (S.D. 1994); Restatement (Third) of Torts: Liability for Physical and Emotional Harm § 46 cmt. h (2012). But see Rabideau v. City of Racine, 243 Wis. 2d 486, 627 N.W.2d 795 (2001).

[41] Pollard v. E.I. DuPont De Nemours, Inc., 412 F.3d 657 (6th Cir. 2005); O'Phelan v. Loy, 2010 WL 3779209 (D. Haw. 2010); Walker v. City of Huntsville, 62 So.3d 474 (Ala. 2010); Restatement (Third) of Torts: Liability for Physical and Emotional Harm § 46 cmt. h (2012).

[42] See Traynor, J., in State Rubbish Collectors Ass'n v. Siliznoff, 38 Cal. 2d 330, 240 P.2d 282 (1952). Dickens v. Puryear, 302 N.C. 437, 276 S.E.2d 325 (1981).

[43] See 2 Dobbs, Hayden & Bublick, The Law of Torts § 388 (2d ed. 2011 & Supp.).

[44] E.g., Hac v. University of Haw., 102 Haw. 92, 73 P.3d 46 (2003). But see Goodrich v. Long Island R.R. Co., 654 F.3d 190, 32 I.E.R. Cas. (BNA) 1662 (2d Cir. 2011) (applying "zone of danger" requirement in intentional infliction of emotional distress case brought under the Federal Employers' Liability Act (FELA)).

[45] Restatement Second of Torts § 46 cmt. d (1965).

[46] Restatement (Third) of Torts: Liability for Physical and Emotional Harm § 46 cmt. a (2012).

[47] E.g., White v. Brommer, 747 F.Supp.2d 447 (E.D. Pa. 2010); Hunt ex rel. DeSombre v. State, Dep't of Safety & Homeland Sec., Div. of Del. State Police, 69 A.3d 360 (Del. 2013); Valadez v. Emmis Commc'ns, 229 P.3d 389 (Kan. 2010); Almy v. Grisham, 273 Va. 68, 639 S.E.2d 182 (2007).

[48] See Robert L. Rabin, Emotional Distress in Tort Law: Themes of Constraint, 44 Wake Forest. L. Rev. 1197 (2009).

Function of terms "extreme" and "outrageous." But to say that recovery is reserved for truly outrageous conduct is not to provide anything like a predictable standard. The Restatement Third treats the terms extreme and outrageous as each serving an important definitional role—the "extreme" requirement filtering out poor conduct that is common such as marital infidelity. And the outrageous requirement filtering out atypical conduct that nevertheless lacks sufficient wrongful character to be actionable.[49] Much of the case law that addresses the extreme and outrageous requirements focuses on sifting out ordinary affronts from actionable misconduct. Insult, affront, indignity, trivial annoyance, or the like, are all excluded from the outrage category (although perhaps still sufficient in some common carrier cases).[50] Similarly, defendants are given latitude in pursuing their own legitimate interests, even if they exceed the bounds of good taste, decency, and fairness. This latitude for legitimate self-interest is not a matter of privilege; it rather tends to show that the conduct is not outrageous.[51] Thus employers are not outrageous in evaluating an employee's work, even if the evaluation is unfair and subjects the employee to humiliation.[52] Creditors can bill the plaintiff for debts claimed, even if the timing of the bill is crude or insulting. For example, if a lawyer terminates a sexual or romantic relationship with a former client and then sends her a bill for legal services previously rendered, he adds insult to injury, but his conduct is not actionable; it is only an inappropriate way of pursuing his own interests.[53]

Four markers of outrage. In drawing the line between extreme and outrageous conduct and other conduct, four important markers lend support to a finding of outrage: the defendant (1) abuses power or position, that is, by using a position of dominance;[54] (2) takes advantage of or emotionally harms a plaintiff known by the defendant to be especially vulnerable;[55] (3) repeats or continues undesirable acts,[56] particularly when

---

[49]   Wood v. Neuman, 979 A.2d 64 (D.C. 2009).

[50]   See Ennett v. Cumberland Cnty. Bd. of Educ., 698 F.Supp.2d 557 (E.D. N.C. 2010); Lybrand v. Trask, 31 P.3d 801 (Alaska 2001) (sign painted on the defendant's roof offering several Biblical quotations such as "love thy neighbor" was visible by and addressed to the uphill plaintiffs); Hughes v. Pair, 209 P.3d 963 (Cal. 2009) (sexual advances by a trustee of deceased husband's estate); Hernandez v. Hillsides, Inc., 211 P.3d 1063 (Cal. 2009) (workplace video camera set to go on after plaintiff employees left for the day); Tetrault v. Mahoney, Hawkes & Goldings, 425 Mass. 456, 681 N.E.2d 1189 (1997); Mikell v. School Admin. Unit No. 33, 972 A.2d 1050 (N.H. 2009) (teacher's allegedly false report of student misconduct).

[51]   Ortberg v. Goldman Sachs Group, 64 A.3d 158 (D.C. 2013); Wood v. Neuman, 979 A.2d 64 (D.C. 2009).

[52]   Crowley v. N. Am. Telecomms. Ass'n, 691 A.2d 1169 (D.C. 1997); Taggart v. Drake Univ., 549 N.W.2d 796 (Iowa 1996) (conduct of a dean who loses his temper and refers to the plaintiff faculty member in a "sexist and condescending manner" as a "young woman," is not actionable, even considering the disparity between the parties).

[53]   Gaspard v. Beadle, 36 S.W.3d 229 (Tex. App. 2001).

[54]   Wilkinson v. United States, 564 F.3d 927 (8th Cir. 2009) (Bureau of Indian Affairs' position of power over landowners); Davis v. Pickell, F.Supp.2d 771 (E.D.Mich. 2013) (severe beating by sherriff's deputies); District of Columbia v. Tulin, 994 A.2d 788 (D.C. 2010) (police officer who caused accident and then caused motorist to be falsely arrested for reckless driving); Brandon v. Cnty. of Richardson, 261 Neb. 636, 624 N.W.2d 604 (2001) (sheriff cruely grilling transsexual victim soon after rape); Grager v. Schudar, 770 N.W.2d 692 (N.D. 2009) (jailer who had sex with inmate); Travis v. Alcon Labs., Inc., 504 S.E.2d 419 (W. Va. 1998) (supervisor at work over extended period).

[55]   Liberty Mut. Ins. Co. v. Steadman, 968 So. 2d 592 (Fla. Dist. Ct. App. 2007) (insurer delayed payment for a lung transplant knowing that claimant had limited life expectancy); Doe v. Corporation of President of Church of Jesus Christ of Latter-Day Saints, 141 Wash.App. 407, 167 P.3d 1193 (2007) (bishop of church told teenaged sexual abuse victim that if she reported the abuse she would be responsible for the breakup of her family).

[56]   Hughes v. Pair, 209 P.3d 963 (Cal. 2009) (substantial or enduring quality of acts); Gleason v. Smolinski, 88 A.3d 589 (Conn. 2014) (relentlessly hanging posters near plaintiff's home for the sole purpose of intimidation); Cabaness v. Thomas, 232 P.3d 486 (Utah 2010) (pattern of continuing and ongoing tortious

the plaintiff cannot avoid them;[57] or (4) commits acts of physical violence,[58] or threats of violence to plaintiff,[59] a person,[60] or occasionally property,[61] in which the plaintiff is known to have a special interest. In each of these instances the defendant uses the parties' inequality to inflict emotional harm without regard for the plaintiff's interests.[62] Small children might recover for outrage if they witness the defendant beating their mother, even if the beating occurs only once and no act at all is directed at the children.[63] When the markers are absent or reversed, for example, when the plaintiff is an employee in no position of authority or power over the defendant, it will be difficult indeed to find that the employee's acts were outrageous.[64] However, these markers are not required elements of proof. Moreover, other factors can come into play. For example, the defendant's treatment of the plaintiff in violation of some identifiable public policy may in itself tend to prove outrage.[65] Misuse of positions of trust may also create actionable outrage.[66] Additional examples of conduct judged to be extreme and outrageous, or not, can be instructive.[67] When reasonable people can differ, whether conduct is extreme and outrageous is a jury question.[68]

---

conduct); Travis v. Alcon Labs., Inc., 504 S.E.2d 419 (W. Va. 1998) (duration as well as intensity); Kanzler v. Renner, 937 P.2d 1337 (Wyo. 1997). Federal and state anti-discrimination law recognizes a similar point; a work environment may be hostile and discriminatory if the harassing conduct is "pervasive" as well as when it is "severe." See Meritor Sav. Bank, FSB v. Vinson, 477 U.S. 57, 67, 106 S.Ct. 2399, 2405, 91 L.Ed.2d 49 (1986).

[57] E.g., Contreras v. Crown Zellerbach Corp., 88 Wash.2d 735, 565 P.2d 1173 (1977) (workplace harassment).

[58] E.g., Murphy v. Islamic Republic of Iran, 740 F.Supp.2d 51 (D.D.C. 2010) (acts of terrorism).

[59] Planned Parenthood of Columbia/Willamette, Inc. v. Am. Coal. of Life Activists, 290 F.3d 1058 (9th Cir. 2002), on second appeal, 422 F.3d 949 (9th Cir. 2005) (credible threats to murder abortion providers); Delfino v. Agilent Techs., Inc., 145 Cal.App. 4th 790, 52 Cal.Rptr. 3d 376 (2006) (repeated threats of physical harm in graphic terms).

[60] Plotnik v. Meihaus, 208 Cal.App. 4th 1590, 146 Cal.Rptr. 3d 585 (2012) (threat against homeowner's wife and dog); Nims v. Harrison, 768 So.2d 1198 (Fla. Dist. Ct. App. 2000) (threat to harm children).

[61] See Gordon v. Bank of N.Y. Mellon Corp., 964 F.Supp.2d 937 (N.D. Ind. 2013) (breaking into plaintiff's home); State Rubbish Collectors Ass'n v. Siliznoff, 38 Cal.2d 330, 240 P.2d 282 (1952) (coercive methods to get plaintiff to agree to give up accounts). Threats to companion animals can produce actionable distress. LaPorte v. Associated Indeps., Inc., 163 So.2d 267, 1 A.L.R.3d 992 (Fla. 1964) (malicious destruction of plaintiff's dog in her presence by throwing a garbage can at the animal). But see Scheele v. Dustin, 998 A.2d 697 (Vt. 2010) (denying noneconomic damages in case in which property owner intentionally shot unleashed nonaggressive dog that wandered onto his property; court reasoning focused on negligent rather than intentional infliction cases, however, court also held open the possibility of punitive damages).

[62] See Daniel Givelber, The Right to Minimum Social Decency and the Limits of Evenhandedness: Intentional Infliction of Emotional Distress by Outrageous Conduct, 82 Colum. L. Rev. 42, 43 (1982) (a kind of private due process in dealings among unequals).

[63] See Bevan v. Fix, 42 P.3d 1013 (Wyo. 2002).

[64] Langeslag v. KYMN, Inc., 664 N.W.2d 860 (Minn. 2003) (employee's false reports to police that employer had committed crimes).

[65] Lees v. Sea Breeze Health Care Ctr., Inc., 391 F.Supp.2d 1103 (S.D. Ala. 2005) (employer's alleged retaliation against employee who joined Air Force Reserve, policy set by federal statute); Cabaness v. Thomas, 232 P.3d 486 (Utah 2010) (supervisor committed serious safety violation by ordering crew member to use jackhammer near live electrical wires); but see Lybrand v. Trask, 31 P.3d 801 (Alaska 2001) (a sign painted on the defendant's roof which violated ordinance was nevertheless not outrageous).

[66] See McQuay v. Guntharp, 331 Ark. 466, 963 S.W.2d 583 (1998) (physician fondles patient); Drejza v. Vaccaro, 650 A.2d 1308 (D.C. 1994) (police officer belittled rape victim); Schmidt v. Mt. Angel Abbey, 223 P.3d 399 (Or. 2009) (priest engaged minor seminary student in sexual acts); Doe v. Corporation of President of Church of Jesus Christ of Latter-Day Saints, 141 Wash.App. 407, 167 P.3d 1193 (2007) (church official allegedly counseled teenaged church member not to report sexual abuse by stepfather, telling her that she would be the subject of church gossip, and responsible for her family breaking up, if she did so).

[67] See 2 Dobbs, Hayden & Bublick, The Law of Torts §§ 386–87 (2d ed. 2011 & Supp.).

[68] Bratton v. McDonough, 91 A.3d 1050 (Me. 2014).

Discrimination and words causing emotional harm. In earlier days of the outrage tort, the defendant's conduct was sometimes an act of violence that shocked or frightened a witness, or was an exceedingly cruel prank aimed at a single vulnerable individual such as a delusional older person.[69] Contemporary cases sometimes deal with distress resulting from discrimination, which may take many forms, including the use of words. Quite a few state and federal statutes that bar discrimination on the basis of race, gender, or disability, and permit recovery of emotional distress damages, sometimes as the only substantial ingredient in the claim.[70] Discrimination and harassment of the type prohibited in these statutes can also found a claim of intentional infliction of emotional distress.[71] However, some First Amendment free speech and freedom of religion limits may apply.[72]

§ 29.7 The Severe Distress Requirement

Severe harm required. The tort for intentional infliction of emotional distress requires not only that the defendant intend severe distress, but also that such distress in fact results from the defendant's outrageous conduct. The point is often put emphatically by saying that the distress must be so severe that no reasonable person should be expected to endure it,[73] but sometimes courts have used a subjective test, saying the plaintiff need prove only that she herself experienced severe distress.[74]

Severity judged by outrageousness of the conduct. All courts require some kind of evidence of severe distress. Consequently, when the defendant's conduct is extreme enough that fact tends to prove severe distress,[75] the question of causation and severity of the distress is for the jury.[76] It is, of course, for the court to determine whether the evidence would warrant reasonable people in finding severe distress.[77] When the defendant's conduct is not so extreme, the plaintiff may need proportionately stronger

---

[69]   See Restatement Second of Torts § 46 illus. 9 (1965).

[70]   A refusal to rent to African Americans or to tenants with children, for example, may require an emotional distress award, although no physical harm is inflicted. Johnson v. Hale, 940 F.2d 1192 (9th Cir. 1991) (under federal statute); Human Rights Comm'n v. LaBrie, Inc., 164 Vt. 237, 668 A.2d 659 (1995) (under state statute).

[71]   Ford v. Revlon, Inc., 153 Ariz. 38, 734 P.2d 580 (1987); McQuay v. Guntharp, 336 Ark. 534, 986 S.W.2d 850 (1999) (doctor allegedly fondling patients during physical examination); Hughes v. Pair, 209 P.3d 963 (Cal. 2009); Fisher v. San Pedro Peninsula Hosp., 214 Cal.App.3d 590, 262 Cal.Rptr. 842 (1989); Kerans v. Porter Paint Co., 61 Ohio St.3d 486, 575 N.E.2d 428 (1991) (store manager's touchings, self-exposure and sexual requests); Kanzler v. Renner, 937 P.2d 1337 (Wyo. 1997).

[72]   See, e.g., Snyder v. Phelps, 562 U.S. 443, 131 S.Ct. 1207, 179 L.Ed.2d 172, 39 Media L. Rep. (BNA) 1353 (2011); Citizen Publ'g Co. v. Miller, 210 Ariz. 513, 115 P.3d 107 (2005) (letter to the editor saying that whenever another atrocity is inflicted upon Americans in Iraq, "we" should "proceed to the closest mosque and execute five of the first Muslims we encounter" rejected as IIED on First Amendment grounds); Hustler Magazine v. Falwell, 485 U.S. 46, 108 S.Ct. 876, 99 L.Ed.2d 41 (1988). See generally Paul T. Hayden, Religiously Motivated "Outrageous" Conduct: Intentional Infliction of Emotional Distress as a Weapon against "Other People's Faiths," 34 Wm. & Mary L. Rev. 579 (1993).

[73]   E.g., Hayward v. Cleveland Clinic Found., 759 F.3d 601 (6th Cir. 2014); McQuay v. Guntharp, 331 Ark. 466, 963 S.W.2d 583 (1998).

[74]   Campbell v. State Farm Mut. Auto. Ins. Co., 65 P.3d 1134 (Utah 2001), rev'd on other grounds, State Farm Mut. Auto. Ins. Co. v. Campbell, 538 U.S. 408, 123 S.Ct. 1513, 155 L.Ed.2d 585 (2003).

[75]   Brandon v. Cnty. of Richardson, 261 Neb. 636, 624 N.W.2d 604 (2001).

[76]   See, e.g., Savage v. Boies, 77 Ariz. 355, 272 P.2d 349 (1954).

[77]   Hatch v. State Farm Fire & Cas. Co., 930 P.2d 382 (Wyo. 1997).

evidence that her distress is severe.[78] Medical testimony is not ordinarily required to demonstrate either the severity of the distress or its cause.[79]

Severity; physical impact, harm, symptoms. Neither the Restatement[80] nor most cases require proof of physical symptoms, much less proof of physical harm or impact.[81] Some courts, however, have carried over the requirement of physical manifestation or symptoms from the law of negligent infliction of distress.[82] Some decisions seem to be exceptionally demanding on the severity issue, with the result that a very serious wrongdoer is shielded from responsibility, although he no doubt intended to cause distress and caused it in fact.[83]

§ 29.8 Intentional Infliction and Emotional Distress of Third Persons

Third person injury pattern. A familiar pattern in the law of torts arises when a defendant acts tortiously toward A but in fact harms B. The pattern appears in the intentional infliction of distress cases as well as elsewhere. Suppose that the defendant threatens to kill person A, and makes the threat credible by drawing a pistol. The threatened person may have an action in such a case, possibly one for assault, possibly one for intentional infliction of distress. Now suppose that B is watching the pending murder with increasing fear and apprehension. The question is whether B has an action against the defendant for intentional infliction of emotional distress.

The Restatements' limitations. Under certain circumstances, the Restatement Third permits B, a third person, to recover for severe distress B suffers as a result of the defendant's conduct directed at A. When the defendant has a *purpose* to cause emotional harm to A by falsely reporting the horrible death of a family member, he does not avoid liability because he mistakenly made the false report to A's brother B instead.[84] The Third Restatement imposes limitations, though, in the different case that occurs when the defendant causes emotional distress to A as he intended, and to B. First, the Restatement suggests that B can recover in such a case only if the defendant acts with a purpose or substantial certainty of harming B himself, or is reckless in that regard. Second, recovery is limited to close family members who contemporaneously perceive the defendant's harmful conduct.[85] Consequently, the defendant who inflicts harm upon a

---

[78]   See Kennedy v. Town of Billerica, 617 F.3d 520 (1st Cir. 2010); Stump v. Ashland, Inc., 201 W.Va. 541, 499 S.E.2d 41 (1997); cf. Millington v. Kuba, 532 N.W.2d 787 (Iowa 1995).

[79]   See Thornton v. Garcini, 928 N.E.2d 804 (Ill. 2010); Gamble v. Dollar Gen. Corp., 852 So. 2d 5 (Miss. 2003); Miller v. Willbanks, 8 S.W.3d 607 (Tenn. 1999); Stump v. Ashland, Inc., 201 W.Va. 541, 499 S.E.2d 41 (1997).

[80]   Restatement Second of Torts § 46 (1965); Restatement (Third) of Torts: Liability for Physical and Emotional Harm § 46 cmt. l (2012).

[81]   See Curtis v. Firth, 123 Idaho 598, 601, 850 P.2d 749, 752 (1993); Knierim v. Izzo, 22 Ill.2d 73, 85, 174 N.E.2d 157, 164 (1961); Blakeley v. Shortal's Estate, 236 Iowa 787, 20 N.W.2d 28 (1945); Vicnire v. Ford Motor Credit Co., 401 A.2d 148 (Me. 1979).

[82]   Reedy v. Evanson, 615 F.3d 197 (3rd Cir. 2010); Vallinoto v. DiSandro, 688 A.2d 830 (R.I. 1997).

[83]   Lascurain v. City of Newark, 349 N.J.Super. 251, 793 A.2d 731 (2002); Russo v. White, 241 Va. 23, 400 S.E.2d 160 (1991) (340 hang up calls from a man a woman dated once); Harris v. Jones, 281 Md. 560, 380 A.2d 611, 86 A.L.R.3d 441 (1977) (on-the-job mimicking of a speech impediment); Grantham v. Vanderzyl, 802 So. 2d 1077 (Ala. 2001) (defendant intentionally splashes the plaintiff's face with blood).

[84]   Restatement (Third) of Torts: Liability for Physical and Emotional Harm § 46 cmt. m (2012).

[85]   Id.

mother knowing that her child is present has every reason to know that both will suffer emotional harm.[86]

Widespread harm. Transferred intent would not apply under the Restatement Third to permit recovery where the actor's conduct is "substantially certain to cause emotional disturbance to a large group of individuals."[87] Consequently, even if millions of people might conceivably suffer emotional harm if they watch the torture or murder of a countryman or elected official on television, recovery would not be allowed. The Restatement's line against recovery in this area is grounded in the fear of virtually unlimited liability.

Conduct reckless toward or intended to harm those not present. However, if the defendant's conduct is sufficiently outrageous and intended to inflict severe emotional harm upon a person who is not present, no rule, nor any essential reason of logic or policy prevents liability.[88] The same is true with outrageous conduct that is reckless. Thus courts have recognized a right to recover in a number of cases in which the defendant's conduct seems not to be directed specifically at the absent plaintiff. For instance, family members not present might be allowed to recover against those who financed the 9–11 terrorist attacks,[89] or the Beirut bombing of American servicemen[90] although the attacks were directed at the families only in a very broad sense. Other cases have supported recovery when the defendant tells the plaintiff he will kill her husband and then does so out of her presence,[91] or when the defendant kills himself by slitting his own throat in the plaintiff's kitchen but out of her presence.[92] Likewise, families of those tortured at length outside the United States have been allowed to proceed although they were not present.[93] In *Doe 1 v. Roman Catholic Diocese of Nashville*,[94] a priest of the defendant Diocese sexually abused numerous boys he encountered in his duties and did so for many years. The plaintiff-victims sued the Diocese for reckless infliction of emotional distress, claiming it knew of the priest's behavior but in various ways recklessly failed to prevent further sexual abuse, by warning or otherwise. The Diocese argued that it could not be held responsible because its alleged recklessness was not "directed at" any specific boy. The court rejected that argument. It also rejected the Restatement's special conditions for bystander claims.

Relationship of defendant to plaintiff. When the defendant is in a special relationship with the plaintiff, the relationship rather than the plaintiff's presence may

---

[86]   Bevan v. Fix, 42 P.3d 1013 (Wyo. 2002) (child who watched battery of mother); cf. Kunsler ex rel. Kunsler v. Int'l House of Pancakes, Inc., 799 N.Y.S.2d 863 (N.Y. City Civ. Ct. 2005) (analyzing child emotional distress from allegations of theft against mother in terms of transferred intent).

[87]   Restatement (Third) of Torts: Liability for Physical and Emotional Harm § 46 cmt. i (2012).

[88]   See Hatch v. Davis, 147 P.3d 383 (Utah 2006).

[89]   Burnett v. Al Baraka Inv. & Dev. Corp., 274 F.Supp.2d 86 (D.D.C. 2003). See also Shemenski v. Chapiesky, 2003 WL 21799941 (N.D. Ill. 2003) (false arrest of husband, wife not present could recover).

[90]   Murphy v. Islamic Republic of Iran, 740 F.Supp.2d 51 (D.D.C. 2010).

[91]   Knierim v. Izzo, 22 Ill. 2d 73, 174 N.E.2d 157 (1961).

[92]   Blakeley v. Shortal's Estate, 236 Iowa 787, 20 N.W.2d 28 (1945).

[93]   Burnett v. Al Baraka Inv. & Dev. Corp., 274 F.Supp.2d 86 (D.D.C. 2003); Jenco v. Islamic Republic of Iran, 154 F.Supp.2d 27 (D.D.C. 2001), aff'd, Bettis v. Islamic Republic of Iran, 315 F.3d 325 (D.C. Cir. 2003) (siblings of victim tortured in Iran could recover for intentional infliction of emotional distress but not nieces and nephews, drawing the line as "family members" rather than at "presence").

[94]   Doe 1 v. Roman Catholic Diocese of Nashville, 154 S.W.3d 22 (Tenn. 2005).

best prescribe the limits of liability.[95] Most states have abolished the alienation of affections or criminal conversation actions, and consequently a therapist who seduces his patient has no obligation to the patient's spouse and is not liable for the spouse's emotional injury when the seduction is discovered.[96] But when both spouses are patients of the therapist, the therapist's seduction of one may be an intentional or reckless infliction of distress upon the other in the light of the therapist's undertaking to care for both.[97]

C. NEGLIGENT INFLICTION OF EMOTIONAL HARM

§ 29.9 Negligent Infliction of Emotional Harm: General Rules of Liability

Emotional versus physical harms. It has been said that "An actor ordinarily has a duty to exercise reasonable care when the actor's conduct creates a risk of *physical* harm."[98] But no equivalent proposition ever has been adopted with respect to *emotional* harm. Nor, given the ubiquity of emotional harms, is it likely to be.[99] Instead, the story of liability for negligently inflicted emotional harms is one of ever changing pragmatic liabilities and limitations which continues to elicit new suggestions for analysis and disposition.[100]

Contemporary claims for negligent infliction of distress. When the defendant is negligent and emotional harm is foreseeable and caused in fact by his negligence, most courts today allow recovery for some stand-alone emotional harms.[101] These cases are often grouped into two main categories of tortious conduct—negligent conduct that directly inflicts emotional disturbance on the plaintiff, and negligent infliction of emotional disturbance resulting from bodily harm to a third person.[102]

Limitations. Courts acknowledge liability in these two areas, but they remain deeply concerned to impose limitations. In the direct victim context, courts may restrict recovery to cases in which the plaintiff has been placed in immediate danger of bodily harm,[103] or distress occurs within the confines of particular undertakings or special

---

[95] Cf. Hatch v. Davis, 147 P.3d 383 (Utah 2006) (relationship of target to the plaintiff is one factor to be considered in permitting recovery by an absent plaintiff).

[96] Homer v. Long, 90 Md.App. 1, 599 A.2d 1193 (1992); cf. Argoe v. Three Rivers Behavioral Ctr. & Psychiatric Solutions, 388 S.C. 394, 697 S.E.2d 551 (2010); Moseng v. Frey, 822 N.W.2d 464, 34 I.E.R. Cas. (BNA) 927 (N.D. 2012).

[97] See Horak v. Biris, 130 Ill.App. 3d 140, 474 N.E.2d 13, 85 Ill.Dec. 599 (1985); Rowe v. Bennett, 514 A.2d 802 (Me. 1986). Cf. Destefano v. Grabrian, 763 P.2d 275 (Colo. 1988) (clergy person providing marriage counseling to both spouses); Marlene F. v. Affiliated Psychiatric Med. Clinic, Inc., 48 Cal. 3d 583, 770 P.2d 278, 257 Cal. Rptr. 98 (1989) (negligence case, therapist treating both mother and son who molested son).

[98] E.g., A.W. v. Lancaster Cnty. Sch. Dist. 0001, 784 N.W.2d 907 (Neb. 2010); Restatement (Third) of Torts: Liability for Physical and Emotional Harm § 7 (2010).

[99] It has been argued, however, that the distinction between physical and emotional is not helpful given the physical basis for emotional phenomena. See Oscar Gray, Commentary, 44 Wake Forest L. Rev. 1193 (2009).

[100] E.g., Gregory C. Keating, Is Negligent Infliction of Emotional Distress a Freestanding Tort?, 44 Wake Forest L. Rev. 1131 (2009) (arguing that the rules for negligent infliction of emotional distress are best seen as rules of proximate cause rather than rules of duty).

[101] Restatement (Third) of Torts: Liability for Physical and Emotional Harm §§ 47–48 (2012). A very small number of states continue to resist this trend and reject the stand-alone mental distress claim. See Dowty v. Riggs, 385 S.W.3d 117 (Ark. 2010).

[102] Restatement (Third) of Torts: Liability for Physical and Emotional Harm §§ 47–48 (2012).

[103] Id. § 47 cmt. a (2012).

relationships.[104] In the bystander cases where harm is inflicted on a third person, courts may only permit claims of those who are close family members of the direct victim and who also contemporaneously perceived the harm-causing event.[105] Outside these categories, courts may entirely preclude distress claims. For example, courts tend to reject distress recoveries based upon negligent harm or threat[106] to real[107] or personal property, including companion animals such as dogs.[108] It is perhaps an open question whether courts will permit recovery for emotional harm resulting from the negligent loss of human ova that have been fertilized *in vitro* but not yet implanted.[109]

Limitations: severe distress. With limited exceptions,[110] most courts hold that the plaintiff can recover only if a normally constituted person would suffer,[111] and the plaintiff in fact suffered severe distress.[112] In some instances, courts may require not only severe distress but medical evidence of it[113] or physical manifestation of it.[114] Moreover, courts sometimes demand, not merely that a reasonable person would foresee the general type of harm, but also serious emotional harm in particular.[115] It is fair to say that these rules are not in fact about foreseeability but about pragmatic limits on liability, which are endemic to this area.

§ 29.10   Emotional Harm Arising from Risks or Harms to Others

Bystander cases. Sometimes the plaintiff who suffers emotional distress is a bystander to the physical harm. In bystander cases, the plaintiff's emotional harm results from her awareness that another person is in danger or is actually harmed. A mother might fear for her daughter's life if she sees a speeding car bearing down on the daughter; she might suffer shock if she sees the car strike her daughter or discovers her child's body afterwards.[116]

---

[104] Hedgepeth v. Whitman Walker Clinic, 22 A.3d 789 (D.C. 2011); see Restatement (Third) of Torts: Liability for Physical and Emotional Harm § 47 (2012); Dan B. Dobbs, Undertakings and Special Relationships in Claims for Negligent Infliction of Emotional Distress, 50 Ariz. L. Rev. 49 (2008); §§ 29.14–29.15.

[105] Restatement (Third) of Torts: Liability for Physical and Emotional Harm § 48 (2012); § 29.10.

[106] Cf. Paul v. Providence Health System-Oregon, 351 Or. 587, 273 P.3d 106 (2012) (no recovery based on a future risk of identity theft risked by the theft of digital records).

[107] See Hawkins v. Scituate Oil Co., Inc., 723 A.2d 771 (R.I. 1999) (defendant poured oil down wrong pipe, flooding basement and dispossessing owners; recovery for inconvenience, discomfort, and annoyance). But see In re Air Crash at Belle Harbor, N.Y. on Nov. 12, 2001, 450 F.Supp.2d 432 (S.D.N.Y. 2006).

[108] Nichols v. Sukaro Kennels, 555 N.W.2d 689, 61 A.L.R.5th 883 (Iowa 1996); McDougall v. Lamm, 211 N.J. 203, 48 A.3d 312 (2012) (reviewing many authorities); Petco Animal Supplies v. Schuster, 144 S.W.3d 554 (Tex. App. 2004); Rabideau v. City of Racine, 243 Wis.2d 486, 627 N.W.2d 795 (2001); Scheele v. Dustin, 998 A.2d 697 (Vt. 2010) (although court may accept alternate means of valuing worth of a pet, noneconomic damages are not available).

[109] See Jeter v. Mayo Clinic Ariz., 211 Ariz. 386, 121 P.3d 1256 (2005).

[110] Statutory actions that permit recovery for emotional distress may not require severe distress. See Vortex Fishing Sys., Inc. v. Foss, 38 P.3d 836 (Mont. 2001). It is also possible that severe distress is not required when the distress is evidenced by physical symptoms. Henricksen v. State, 84 P.3d 38 (Mont. 2004).

[111] See, e.g., Spangler v. Bechtel, 931 N.E.2d 387, 393 (Ind. Ct. App. 2010) (damages related to stillbirth of child), rev'd on other grounds, 958 N.E.2d 458 (Ind. 2011).

[112] Feller v. First Interstate Bancsystem, Inc., 299 P.3d 338 (Mont. 2013); Bovsun v. Sanperi, 61 N.Y.2d 219, 461 N.E.2d 843, 473 N.Y.S.2d 357 (1984); Johnson v. Ruark Obstetrics & Gynecology Assocs., P.A., 327 N.C. 283, 304, 395 S.E.2d 85, 97 (1990); Larsen v. Banner Health Sys., 81 P.3d 196 (Wyo. 2003).

[113] See Camper v. Minor, 915 S.W.2d 437 (Tenn. 1996).

[114] See § 29.12.

[115] See Perodeau v. City of Hartford, 259 Conn. 729, 754, 792 A.2d 752, 767 (2002).

[116] Amaya v. Home Ice, Fuel & Supply Co., 59 Cal.2d 295, 379 P.2d 513, 29 Cal.Rptr. 33 (1963), overruled in Dillon v. Legg, 68 Cal.2d 728, 69 Cal.Rptr. 72 441 P.2d 912 (1968).

Zone of danger and fear for one's self. The mother herself could also be physically endangered. If mother and child are both in a crosswalk in the speeder's path, the mother might fear for her own bodily safety as well for that of her child. With the abolition of the old rule requiring an impact,[117] the mother could recover for the fear for her own safety. Given that her cause of action was thus established, she could recover all her damages resulting from the tortious conduct, including damages resulting because she feared for her child. This zone of danger rule found support in the Second Restatement.[118] A number of court decisions support liability under this test as well.[119] For example, the Ninth Circuit allowed the operator of a small fishing vessel threatened by a large freighter to recover negligent infliction based on the fact that he himself was in the zone of danger even though he did not witness the death of the nearby fishing vessel captain who was killed.[120] Under the zone of danger rule courts generally deny recovery to a person who was not in the zone or did not fear for his own safety.[121] The Supreme Court of the United States has adopted the zone of danger rule for claims under the Federal Employers' Liability Act.[122]

Rejecting or supplementing the zone of danger limitation. The zone of danger fear-for-oneself rule was an improvement on the older rule that excluded recovery for emotional distress. But zone of danger rule still excludes recovery for a mother who watches from safety as the tortfeasor runs down and kills her child, or against a hospital responsible for the abduction of the plaintiff's newborn child.[123] In 1968, the California Supreme Court held in *Dillon v. Legg*[124] that, in bystander cases, foreseeability of emotional harm should be the general test of liability. Most states now appear to have joined *Dillon* in adoption of some alternate approach,[125] or permit recovery for bystanders under either the zone of danger or the bystander test,[126] which is also the position of the Restatement Third.[127]

---

[117] See § 29.12.

[118] Restatement Second of Torts § 313(2) (1965).

[119] Keck v. Jackson, 122 Ariz. 114, 593 P.2d 668 (1979); Bovsun v. Sanperi, 61 N.Y.2d 219, 461 N.E.2d 843, 473 N.Y.S.2d 357 (1984); cf. Rickey v. Chicago Transit Auth., 98 Ill.2d 546, 457 N.E.2d 1, 75 Ill.Dec. 211 (1983).

[120] Stacy v. Rederiet Otto Danielsen, A.S., 609 F.3d 1033 (9th Cir. 2010).

[121] E.g., Siegel v. Ridgewells, Inc., 511 F.Supp.2d 188 (D.D.C. 2007); Grube v. Union Pac. R.R., 256 Kan. 519, 886 P.2d 845 (1994) (under FELA); Coleson v. City of New York, 24 N.E.3d 1074 (N.Y. 2014); Leo v. Hillman, 164 Vt. 94, 665 A.2d 572 (1995).

[122] Consolidated Rail Corp. v. Gottshall, 512 U.S. 532, 114 S.Ct. 2396, 129 L.Ed.2d 427 (1994); cf. Goodrich v. Long Island R.R. Co., 654 F.3d 190, 32 I.E.R. Cas. (BNA) 1662 (2d Cir. 2011) (applying "zone of danger" requirement in *intentional* infliction of emotional distress case brought under FELA). The zone of danger test has also been applied in cases brought under federal admiralty law. See Chaparro v. Carnival Corp., 693 F.3d 1333 (11th Cir. 2012).

[123] Johnson v. Jamaica Hosp., 62 N.Y.2d 523, 467 N.E.2d 502, 478 N.Y.S.2d 838 (1984); but cf. Perry-Rogers v. Obasaju, 282 A.D.2d 231, 723 N.Y.S.2d 28 (2001) (embryo containing plaintiffs' genetic material mistakenly implanted in another woman, claim stated).

[124] Dillon v. Legg, 68 Cal.2d 728, 69 Cal.Rptr. 72, 441 P.2d 912 (1968).

[125] E.g., Zell v. Meek, 665 So.2d 1048 (Fla. 1995); Smith v. Toney, 862 N.E.2d 656 (Ind. 2007); Mississippi State Fed'n of Colored Women's Club Housing for Elderly in Clinton, Inc. v. L.R., 62 So.3d 351 (Miss. 2010); St. Onge v. MacDonald, 154 N.H. 768, 917 A.2d 233 (2007). See Dale Joseph Gilsinger, Annotation, Recovery under State Law for Negligent Infliction of Emotional Distress under Rule of Dillon v. Legg, 68 Cal.2d 728, 69 Cal.Rptr. 72, 441 P.2d 912 (1968), or Refinements Thereof, 96 A.L.R.5th 107 (2002).

[126] Catron v. Lewis, 271 Neb. 416, 712 N.W.2d 245 (2006).

[127] Restatement (Third) of Torts: Liability for Physical and Emotional Harm §§ 47–48 (2012).

Foreseeability under Dillon v. Legg. Under *Dillon*, the foreseeability test was to be focused by three guidelines. Foreseeable emotional harm would be more likely if (1) the plaintiff was near the scene at which another was injured or threatened, (2) actually knew of the injury or threat to the other, and (3) was closely related. Under that test, a family member might recover for emotional harm even if she herself was never endangered and even if she did not learn of the injury until after it occurred. For instance, in a New Jersey case, a small boy was trapped between an elevator door and the wall of the shaft.[128] The elevator moved and dragged him. His mother watched rescue efforts for over four hours while he was dying of massive internal hemorrhaging and suffering great pain. Although the zone of danger rule would have barred the mother's claim since she was not in physical danger, under the *Dillon* rule the court allowed recovery.

Contemporaneous and sensory awareness of injury. A guidelines approach to foreseeable emotional distress does not necessarily require the plaintiff to witness the initial injury, but it is not enough that she simply hear about it later. Courts usually agree that the plaintiff must see the injured person before the victim's condition has substantially changed,[129] although they express this essential idea in slightly different ways.[130] Some authority is a little more liberal; Alaska upheld the right of a mother to recover when she rushed to the scene of the accident but saw her injured daughter only later at the hospital.[131] Some cases have insisted that the plaintiff must not only see the victim's suffering or death, but that the event they witness is sudden and traumatic. So families who watch a child's prolonged suffering and death because of a druggist's mis-filled prescription[132] or a doctor's misdiagnosis simply have no claim for bystander emotional distress.[133] On occasion, courts have permitted recovery for a person who did not contemporaneously perceive the event. For example, Hawaii held that a school negligently permitting a teacher to molest grade-school girls is liable to parents for their emotional harm as well as to children.[134]

Restrictive approach to close relationship. Although many relationships may be close, courts have tended to restrict the "close relationship" category.[135] Many cases have denied recovery to strangers who engage in heroic and distressing rescue attempts.[136]

---

[128]   Portee v. Jaffee, 84 N.J. 88, 417 A.2d 521 (1980).

[129]   In re Air Crash at Belle Harbor, N.Y. on Nov. 12, 2001, 450 F.Supp. 2d 432 (S.D.N.Y. 2006); Hegel v. McMahon, 136 Wash.2d 122, 960 P.2d 424 (1998); Bowen v. Lumbermens Mut. Cas. Co., 183 Wis.2d 627, 517 N.W.2d 432 (1994).

[130]   Groves v. Taylor, 729 N.E.2d 569 (Ind. 2000) ("came on the scene soon after the death or severe injury"); Gabaldon v. Jay-Bi Property Mgmt., Inc., 925 P.2d 510 (N.M. 1996) (plaintiff must be a witness "either when the injury occurs or soon after, but before the arrival of emergency medical professionals at the scene"); Eskin v. Bartee, 262 S.W.3d 727 (Tenn. 2008) (observation at the scene of the accident before the scene has been "materially altered"); Colbert v. Mooba Sports, Inc., 163 Wash.2d 43, 176 P.3d 497 (2008) (plaintiff must arrive at scene shortly after the accident happened).

[131]   Beck v. State, 837 P.2d 105 (Alaska 1992).

[132]   Fernandez v. Walgreen Hastings Co., 968 P.2d 774 (N.M. 1998).

[133]   Finnegan ex rel. Skoglind v. Wis. Patients Comp. Fund, 263 Wis.2d 574, 666 N.W.2d 797 (2003).

[134]   Doe Parents No. 1 v. State Dep't of Educ., 100 Haw. 34, 58 P.3d 545 (2002).

[135]   Groves v. Taylor, 729 N.E.2d 569 (Ind. 2000) (relationship must be "analogous to" that of spouse, parent, child, grandparent, grandchild). See also Dale Joseph Gilsinger, Annotation, Relationship Between Victim and Plaintiff-Witness as Affecting Right to Recover under State Law for Negligent Infliction of Emotional Distress Due to Witnessing Injury to Another Where Bystander Plaintiff Is Not Member of Victim's Immediate Family, 98 A.L.R.5th 609 (2002).

[136]   Hislop v. Salt River Project Agric. Improvement & Power Dist., 5 P.3d 267 (Ariz. Ct. App. 2000) (coworker put out flames when coworker was engulfed in fire and got him to the hospital); Michaud v. Great

Similarly, non-family participants who, because of the defendant's negligence, innocently trigger horrifying harms to the victim have also been denied recovery,[137] although English courts may grant recovery on such claims.[138] Even a fiancé who witnessed the death of the man she was engaged to marry was denied recovery.[139] And family members whose relationships were considered not close enough—a son in law,[140] a noncustodial parent,[141] an aunt who raised the child[142]—have seen recovery denied. The rule may exclude recovery for distress resulting from witnessing harm to a companion animal, who necessarily lacks a blood or marital relationship to the plaintiff.[143]

Flexible approach to close relationships. Not all courts are so restrictive, however. Some fiancés[144] and unmarried cohabitants living together as domestic partners[145] may qualify as close family. And more distant family members sometimes may be allowed to recover if relationship with the primary victim was otherwise especially close,[146] particularly in the case of intentional infliction claims.[147] Some courts take a flexible approach in determining which relationships are sufficiently close. New Hampshire considers factors like duration of the relationship, the extent and quality of shared experience and others.[148] Tennessee has said that a number of intimate relationships may suffice.[149]

N. Nekoosa Corp., 715 A.2d 955 (Me. 1998) (diver attempting underwater rescue of trapped coworker saw the worker pulled apart when surface workers attempted to pull him out of trap by a chain); Migliori v. Airborne Freight Corp., 426 Mass. 629, 690 N.E.2d 413 (1998) (bystander gave auto-victim CPR, but saw her bleeding from eyes, nose and elsewhere). The majority in a House of Lords decision likewise refused to treat rescuers differently from other bystanders and accordingly disallowed recovery in White v. Chief Constable of South Yorkshire, [1999] 2 A.C. 455, [1999] 1 All E.R. 1.

[137] See Kallstrom v. United States, 43 P.3d 162 (Alaska 2002); Catron v. Lewis, 271 Neb. 416, 712 N.W.2d 245 (2006); Slaton v. Vansickle, 872 P.2d 929 (Okla. 1994).

[138] M.H. Matthews, Negligent Infliction of Emotional Distress: A View of the Proposed Restatement (Third) Provisions from England, 44 Wake Forest L. Rev. 1177 (2009).

[139] Smith v. Toney, 862 N.E.2d 656 (Ind. 2007); Grotts v. Zahner, 115 Nev. 339, 989 P.2d 415 (1999); Zimmerman v. Dane Cnty., 329 Wis.2d 270, 789 N.W.2d 754 (Ct. App. 2010).

[140] Moon v. Guardian Postacute Servs., Inc., 95 Cal.App. 4th 1005, 116 Cal.Rptr. 2d 218, 98 A.L.R.5th 767 (2002).

[141] Eskin v. Bartee, 262 S.W.3d 727, 740 n.31 (Tenn. 2008).

[142] Trombetta v. Conkling, 82 N.Y.2d 549, 626 N.E.2d 653, 605 N.Y.S.2d 678 (1993).

[143] Thompson v. Lied Animal Shelter, 2009 WL 3303733 (D. Nev. 2009); Rabideau v. City of Racine, 243 Wis.2d 486, 627 N.W.2d 795 (2001); Scheele v. Dustin, 998 A.2d 697 (Vt. 2010) (denying claim for loss of companionship).

[144] Graves v. Estabrook, 818 A.2d 1255 (N.H. 2003); Yovino v. Big Bubba's BBQ, LLC, 896 A.2d 161 (Conn. Super. Ct. 2006).

[145] So provided in Cal. Civ. Code § 1714.01.

[146] See, e.g., Groves v. Taylor, 729 N.E.2d 569 (Ind. 2000); Eskin v. Bartee, 262 S.W.3d 727 (Tenn. 2008).

[147] See Estate of Heiser v. Islamic Republic of Iran, 659 F.Supp.2d 20 (D.D.C. 2009) (non-adoptive stepfathers were "functional equivalent" of fathers and count as closely related family).

[148] The factors are: (1) the duration of the relationship; (2) the degree of mutual dependence; (3) the extent of common contributions to a life together; (4) the extent and quality of shared experience; (5) whether the plaintiff and the victim were members of the same household; (6) their emotional reliance upon each other; (7) the particulars of their day-to-day relationship; and (8) the manner in which they related to each other in attending to life's mundane requirements. See St. Onge v. MacDonald, 154 N.H. 768, 917 A.2d 233 (2007) (applying factors to deny recovery to a woman who was a passenger on a motorcycle driven by her boyfriend of six months, who was killed).

[149] See also Eskin v. Bartee, 262 S.W.3d 727 (Tenn. 2008) (placing the burden on the plaintiff to "prove the existence of the close and intimate personal relationship" and allowing defendant to contest it).

Close relationship when bystander is in the zone of danger. The close relationship issue is most pointed when the bystander-plaintiff is NOT within the zone of danger, because recovery there is perceived as risking many suits, while the zone of danger rule automatically precludes most possible plaintiffs. However, in some instances a state has invoked a relationship rule even though the plaintiff *was* in the zone of danger.[150] Since both the zone of danger rule and the relationship rule are invoked to limit the number of possible plaintiffs, and since the zone of danger rule excludes most of the universe, we might question whether the relationship rule ought to apply at all to a plaintiff who is in the zone of danger.

From guidelines to rules. The California court that had created the *Dillon* rule later substantially modified it. Under the new version, the "guidelines" in *Dillon* became precise rules. Regardless of foreseeable and actual emotional harm to the plaintiff, plaintiff would be denied recovery under the new rule unless she was actually present and witnessed the injury or threat to a close relation.[151] Some courts have accepted this modification of Dillon or approximated it with modifications of their own.[152] The states that have special bystander rules do not all treat claimants in the same way.[153] Needless to say, this a rapidly-changing and tumultuous area of law where generalizations are difficult.

§ 29.11 Loss of Consortium

Loss of consortium and emotional harm. Loss of consortium is a species of emotional harm. When one member of a family is injured or killed, others in the family suffer a loss, particularly with respect to injured person's companionship and society. The loss is obviously different from the shock or fright at witnessing injury of a family member, but it is also obviously similar in that both claims address injuries to emotional well-being from harm to another.

Derivation. As a matter of historical derivation, however, loss of consortium seems little related to the claim for emotional distress. The claim originally asserted that the master was entitled to recover because his servant or apprentice had been enticed away or injured by the defendant, resulting in the master's loss of services. By crude analogy, the husband was then allowed to recover when the defendant caused him to lose the services of his wife or child. Thus when a wife or child was injured by the defendant's negligence, the husband as well as the primary victim would have a recovery for his own losses. Traditionally, no other relationships generated a loss of consortium claim.

---

[150] Keck v. Jackson, 122 Ariz. 114, 593 P.2d 668 (1979); Hislop v. Salt River Project Agric. Improvement & Power Dist., 5 P.3d 267 (Ariz. Ct. App. 2000).

[151] Thing v. La Chusa, 48 Cal.3d 644, 257 Cal.Rptr. 865, 771 P.2d 814 (1989). See also Bird v. Saenz, 28 Cal.4th 910, 123 Cal.Rptr. 2d 465, 51 P.3d 324 (2002). Cf. Ess v. Eskaton Props., Inc., 97 Cal.App.4th 120, 118 Cal.Rptr.2d 240 (2002) (plaintiff not present when sister was sexually attacked by intruder in defendant's nursing home, no recovery for distress).

[152] Clohessy v. Bachelor, 237 Conn. 31, 675 A.2d 852 (1996); Bowen v. Lumbermens Mut. Cas. Co., 183 Wis.2d 627, 517 N.W.2d 432 (1994) (injury to primary victim must be serious or fatal; the plaintiff must witness some extraordinary event, but that might include arriving at the scene of an accident after it had occurred, and the plaintiff must be spouse, parent, child, grandparent or sibling of injured person); Heldreth v. Marrs, 188 W.Va. 481, 425 S.E.2d 157 (1992) (injury to primary victim must be serious or fatal).

[153] New Jersey, for example, follows a Thing-like rule for bystanders, but allows a non-bystander to sue only if she "suffers substantial bodily injury or sickness arising from the plaintiff's location within the zone of risk created by the defendant's negligent conduct." Jablonowska v. Suther, 195 N.J. 91, 948 A.2d 610 (2008).

Contemporary consortium claims. Contemporary loss of consortium claims differ in several important respects.

(1)   The emphasis has shifted from pure loss of service claims to losses of various intangibles, usually described as services, society, and sexual intercourse. It includes "the mutual right of the husband and wife to that affection, solace, comfort, companionship, society, assistance, and sexual relations necessary to a successful marriage."[154]

(2)   The claim is no longer the husband's claim alone; the wife may also sue for loss of her husband's services, society, and sexual attention.[155]

(3)   Although the loss of consortium claim traditionally enforced "marital rights" only of spouses,[156] a similar claim for loss of a parent's society, guidance, and the like is now actionable by children in a substantial number of the states,[157] though not all.[158] At times the right has been extended even to adult children.[159] Occasionally a complementary claim is actionable by parents, usually where the child is severely injured,[160] but many cases disclaim such recoveries.[161] Most courts also continue to reject the loss of consortium claims of siblings,[162] although death statutes frequently permit recovery of these claims.[163] New Mexico has even permitted a grandparent to recover for loss of consortium resulting from injury and death to a grandchild.[164]

(4)   As indicated more fully below, some courts have now made it possible for an unmarried person to claim loss of consortium when her domestic partner is injured.

Limitations. Loss of consortium recovery permits plaintiff to recover not only for loss of companionship and affection through the time of the trial but also for prospective

---

[154]   Martin v. Ohio Cnty. Hosp. Corp., 295 S.W.3d 104 (Ky. 2009); Erickson v. U-Haul Int'l, 767 N.W.2d 765 (Neb. 2009); Wal-Mart Stores, Inc. v. Alexander, 868 S.W.2d 322, 328 (Tex. 1993).

[155]   Millington v. Se. Elevator Co., Inc., 22 N.Y.2d 498, 239 N.E.2d 897, 293 N.Y.S.2d 305 (1968); Blunt v. Medtronic, Inc., 760 N.W.2d 396 (Wis. 2009). However, some courts still do not permit loss of consortium claims brought by husband or wife. See Cardenas v. Muangman, 998 A.2d 303 (D.C. 2010) (Virginia law does not, although D.C. law does).

[156]   Laws v. Griep, 332 N.W.2d 339 (Iowa 1983); Nicholson v. Hugh Chatham Mem. Hosp., Inc., 300 N.C. 295, 266 S.E.2d 818 (1980).

[157]   Children's claims for loss of parental consortium began to be recognized in 1980 with the decision in Ferriter v. Daniel O'Connell's Sons, Inc., 381 Mass. 507, 413 N.E.2d 690, 11 A.L.R.4th 518 (1980), superceded by statute, Sheehan v. Weaver, 7 N.E.3d 459 (Mass. 2014). Other courts gradually accepted the claim throughout the 1980s and 1990s. By 1997, about 16 courts had done so. See Giuliani v. Guiler, 951 S.W.2d 318 (Ky. 1997) (where mother died and a separate wrongful death suit was pending). Wrongful death statutes now frequently permit recoveries for lost consortium. Jean C. Love, Tortious Interference with the Parent-Child Relationship: Loss of an Injured Person's Society and Companionship, 51 Ind. L.J. 591 (1976).

[158]   Mendillo v. Bd. of Educ. of E. Haddam, 246 Conn. 456, 717 A.2d 1177 (1998); Harrington v. Brooks Drugs, Inc., 148 N.H. 101, 808 A.2d 532 (2002); Taylor v. Beard, 104 S.W.3d 507 (Tenn. 2003).

[159]   North Pacific Ins. Co. v. Stucky, 338 P.3d 56 (Mont. 2014); Rolf v. Tri State Motor Transit Co., 91 Ohio St.3d 380, 745 N.E.2d 424 (2001).

[160]   Howard Frank, M.D., P.C. v. Superior Court, 150 Ariz. 228, 722 P.2d 955 (1986) (adult child, severe brain damage); Masaki v. General Motors Corp., 71 Haw. 1, 780 P.2d 566 (1989).

[161]   See Roberts v. Williamson, 111 S.W.3d 113 (Tex. 2003).

[162]   E.g., Elgin v. Bartlett, 994 P.2d 411 (Colo. 1999) (citing cases).

[163]   See Rothstein v. Orange Grove Ctr., Inc., 60 S.W.3d 807 (Tenn. 2001) (filial consortium recoverable under death statute).

[164]   Fernandez v. Walgreen Hastings Co., 126 N.M. 263, 968 P.2d 774 (1998).

damages resulting from the premature death.[165] The life expectancy of the plaintiff and the injured party, whichever is shorter, places an outer limit on the loss of consortium recovery.[166] A spouse cannot claim for loss of consortium based upon injury inflicted upon the other spouse before marriage[167] or after it is dissolved.[168] Although this rule is contested.[169] In addition to these limits, courts usually say that the consortium claim is derivative, that is, that it will fail if the primary victim's claim would fail,[170] and that damages will be reduced under comparative fault rules if the primary victim's damages would be reduced.[171] The claim may also be subject to special statutory restrictions,[172] or defenses personal to the plaintiff.[173] To avoid problems of duplication of damages, courts may require that the consortium claim be joined with the injury claim brought by the primary victim, where joinder is feasible and just.[174]

The unmarried cohabitant. Some of the other limitations on consortium recoveries may be dissolving. Some statutes[175] and cases[176] have now authorized claims for

---

[165]   Boeken v. Philip Morris USA, Inc., 230 P.3d 342 (Cal. 2010).

[166]   Id.; Martin v. Ohio Cnty. Hosp. Corp., 295 S.W.3d 104 (Ky. 2009) (loss of consortium damages do not cease at the death of the injured party).

[167]   Sawyer v. Bailey, 413 A.2d 165 (Me. 1980); Hite v. Brown, 100 Ohio App.3d 606, 654 N.E.2d 452 (1995).

[168]   Doerner v. Swisher Int'l, Inc., 272 F.3d 928 (7th Cir. 2001).

[169]   Leonard v. John Crane, Inc., 206 Cal.App.4th 1274, 142 Cal.Rptr.3d 700 (2012) (allowing loss-of-consortium claim by wife of man whose exposure to asbestos predated their marriage, recognizing a split in authority among other states on the issue).

[170]   Lyons v. Vaughan Reg'l Med. Ctr., LLC, 23 So.3d 23 (Ala. 2009); Voris v. Molinaro, 302 Conn. 791, 31 A.3d 363 (2011) (settlement of the predicate personal injury claim extinguishes the derivative claim for loss of consortium); Murray v. Motorola, Inc., 982 A.2d 764 (D.C. 2009); Erickson v. U-Haul Int'l, 767 N.W.2d 765 (Neb. 2009); Fiorenzano v. Lima, 982 A.2d 585 (R.I. 2009); Blunt v. Medtronic, Inc., 760 N.W.2d 396 (Wis. 2009); contra Beaver v. Grand Prix Karting Ass'n, Inc., 246 F.3d 905 (7th Cir. 2001) (pre-injury release by injured spouse does not bar consortium claim of other spouse; Indiana law).

[171]   Possibly the claim is "derivative" in the sense that it will be affected by the primary victim's contributory negligence or comparative fault but "independent" in the sense that it cannot be released by the primary victim. Compare Kibble v. Weeks Dredging & Constr. Co., 161 N.J. 178, 735 A.2d 1142 (1999), with Tichenor v. Santillo, 218 N.J. Super. 165, 527 A.2d 78 (1987). But see Massengale v. Pitts, 737 A.2d 1029 (D.C. 1999) (defendant must be negligent but spouse's contributory negligence does not bar consortium claim); Feltch v. Gen. Rental Co., 383 Mass. 603, 421 N.E.2d 67 (1981) (refusing to reduce a wife's consortium recovery because of the husband's contributory fault).

[172]   Ruiz v, Podolsky, 50 Cal.4th 838, 237 P.3d 584 (2010) (Medical Injury Compensation Reform Act bound patient's adult children to arbitrate loss of consortium claims); Proctor v. Washington Metro. Area Transit Auth., 990 A.2d 1048 (Md. 2010) (statutory cap on noneconomic damages claim applied to loss of consortium action); Smith v. HCA Health Servs. of N.H., 977 A.2d 534 (N.H. 2009) (expert testimony was required for loss of consortium claim related to hospital's refusal to release patient).

[173]   See Wesche v. Mecosta Cnty. Rd. Comm'n, 267 Mich.App. 274, 705 N.W.2d 136 (2005), overruled so far as it interposed a governmental immunity to bar the consortium claim, Kik v. Sbraccia, 272 Mich.App. 388, 726 N.W.2d 450 (2006).

[174]   Kelley v. Centennial Contractors Enters., 236 P.3d 197 (Wash. 2010) (genuine issue of material fact as to whether joinder of children's loss of consortium claim was feasible); 2 Dan B. Dobbs, The Law of Remedies § 8.1 (5) (1993). Some courts regard joinder as the preferred solution, but do not necessarily require it. See Evans v. Dayton Hudson, 234 Cal.App. 3d 49, 285 Cal.Rptr. 550 (1991).

[175]   Cal. Civ. Code § 1714.01 (negligent infliction of emotional distress may be brought by domestic partner); Cal. Civ. Pro. Code § 377.60 (domestic partner has standing to bring wrongful death action); Vt. Stat. Ann. tit. 15 §§ 1204(a) & 1204(e)(2) (civil union permitted between persons of same sex, generally granting rights of married persons and specifically including right to sue for wrongful death). The California statutes displace Elden v. Sheldon, 46 Cal.3d 267, 250 Cal.Rptr. 254, 758 P.2d 582 (1988), which dismissed an action brought by an unmarried cohabitant.

[176]   Surette v. Islamic Republic of Iran, 231 F.Supp.2d 260 (D.D.C. 2002) ("This result is justified by the nature and closeness of the relationship between Beverly Surette and William Buckley for over twenty years, a bond that was the functional equivalent of a legal marriage. The strength of their 'close emotional relationship,' was recognized by Buckley's family, his colleagues and his employer, and it merits recognition

emotional distress or wrongful death by unmarried domestic partners. New Mexico has specifically recognized a loss of consortium claim in favor of an unmarried cohabitant where there is a committed relationship.[177] Idaho has not.[178]

Absence of special limiting rules. When loss of consortium can be asserted, courts do not concern themselves with zone of danger rules or demands for physical injury or manifestations of emotional harm. They seem willing to assume the reality of injury, at least when the plaintiff testifies to it. Perhaps the disparity between the treatment of consortium and other forms of emotional distress results in part from the severity of injury in many of these cases or the fact that the consortium claim cannot be brought except by a spouse or close family member. Perhaps the difference is that loss of consortium had and still has a modest economic component.[179] Or maybe courts are simply more comfortable with the evidence that supports the consortium claim. Instead of evidence of a plaintiff who is dysfunctional, near an emotional breakdown, or filled with anxiety, they hear evidence of a comfortable homey relationship that has lost its content: one spouse can no longer go dancing,[180] or the injured spouse can no longer recognize the other.[181] The special rules limiting emotional distress recovery do not apply to the consortium claim.[182] Damages awards, however, are difficult to assess[183] and some courts may impose special limitations on the award.[184]

§ 29.12 Emotional Distress Arising from Direct Risks of Physical Harm

The fright or shock pattern. In a famous case from the late 1800s, *Mitchell v. Rochester Railway Co.*, the plaintiff was about to board a railway car when the defendant drove a team of horses at her. By the time the horses were stopped, plaintiff found herself standing between the horses, although they had not touched her. She later suffered a miscarriage as a result. The New York Court of Appeals denied recovery for fright alone in the absence of physical injury.[185] The facts in this case are part of what is sometimes referred to as the "fright or shock" pattern. In this set of cases, the defendant's negligent

---

by this Court"); Mueller v. Tepler, 95 A.3d 1011 (Conn. 2014); Graves v. Estabrook, 149 N.H. 202, 818 A.2d 1255 (2003); Dunphy v. Gregor, 136 N.J. 99, 642 A.2d 372 (1994).

[177] Lozoya v. Sanchez, 66 P.3d 948 (N.M. 2003), overruled on other gorunds, Heath v. La Mariana Apartments, 180 P.3d 664 (N.M. 2008).

[178] But see Connor v. Hodges, 333 P.3d 130 (Idaho 2014) (loss of consortium claim "is predicated on the existence of marriage").

[179] Richardson v. Children's Hosp., 797 N.W.2d 235 (Neb. 2010) (attorney suggested jury consider the $35 per day they were compensated for jury service when determining award for mother of deceased child).

[180] Rutherford v. State, 605 P.2d 16 (Alaska 1979).

[181] Board of Comm'rs v. Nevitt, 448 N.E.2d 333, 344 (Ind. Ct. App. 1983).

[182] E.g., Mealy v. B-Mobile, Inc., 195 Cal.App.4th 1218, 124 Cal.Rptr.3d 804 (2011) (applying bystander rule to plaintiffs' negligent infliction of emotional distress claim, but not to separate loss of consortium claim).

[183] Morgan v. Scott, 291 S.W.3d 622 (Ky. 2009) (upholding $4 million verdict for personal injury and loss of consortium arising out of car accident).

[184] In Arpin v. U.S., 521 F.3d 769 (7th Cir. 2008), Judge Posner imported some of the factors used to limit punitive damages under the Supreme Court's constitutional rulings, including a ratio between compensatory (economic) damages and the consortium award. However, in wrongful death cases such as Arpin itself, such a limitation seems particularly inappropriate because wrongful pecuniary damages in such actions depend mainly upon prospective earnings of the deceased, which bear no standard relationship at all to the loss of the deceased companionship and consortium.

[185] Mitchell v. Rochester Ry. Co., 45 N.E. 354 (N.Y. 1896), overruled by Battalla v. State, 176 N.E.2d 729 (N.Y. 1961).

acts put the plaintiff at immediate risk of physical injury and the plaintiff's reaction to that risk is fright or shock.

Physical impact or injury followed by distress. After *Mitchell*, many courts adopted the "impact" rule, in which a negligently inflicted physical impact to the plaintiff would ordinarily result in enough physical harm to count as a tort in itself, so that emotional harm would be recoverable as parasitic damage. Courts then held that if any impact occurred, emotional distress damages could be recovered.[186] The impact rule would still preclude recovery where runaway horses almost ran down the plaintiff, but stopped inches away, even if the plaintiff suffered subsequent physical harm such as a miscarriage resulting from the emotional distress.[187] The rule did not draw the line against liability at a satisfactory place, and it has now been abolished in most states in favor of quite different limitations,[188] but a few courts retain the impact rule[189] with particular exceptions.[190]

Physical manifestation or symptom of distress. Some jurisdictions adopted a different condition: The plaintiff can only recover if she produces evidence of some bodily harm or physical manifestation of the shock or fright.[191] So if horses had run at the plaintiff and without touching her caused a miscarriage or heart attack, recovery would be permitted. The physical manifestation or symptom of distress need not be so severe. Sometimes, courts that require physical symptoms are ready to find such symptoms in fairly transient physical phenomena, as where one plaintiff, confronted with a shock, lost control of bladder and bowel.[192] Likewise, some courts may recognize a medically diagnosable condition even without objective symptoms.[193] However, not all courts apply such a broad standard. For instance, when a man fired a shotgun in a nightclub, killing and injuring people, the plaintiff attempted to deal with the man and narrowly escaped harm himself. The plaintiff had nightmares, frequent headaches, dizziness, depression, nervousness, weight loss, and poor appetite and was medically diagnosed as suffering

---

[186] See Rickey v. Chicago Transit Auth., 98 Ill.2d 546, 457 N.E.2d 1, 75 Ill.Dec. 211 (1983) (reviewing some of the cases and concluding that in the light of the mechanical or formal application of the rule, impact should not be required).

[187] Mitchell v. Rochester Ry. Co., 151 N.Y. 107, 45 N.E. 354 (1896).

[188] E.g., Battalla v. State, 10 N.Y.2d 237, 176 N.E.2d 729, 219 N.Y.S.2d 34 (1961); Rickey v. Chicago Transit Auth., 98 Ill.2d 546, 457 N.E.2d 1, 75 Ill.Dec. 211 (1983); Osborne v. Keeney, 399 S.W.3d 1 (Ky. 2012).

[189] Chouinard v. Health Ventures, 179 Or.App. 507, 39 P.3d 951 (2002); Patterson v. Ind. Newspapers, Inc., 589 F.3d 357 (7th Cir. 2009); Spangler v. Bechtel, 958 N.E.2d 458 (Ind. 2011); Atlantic Coast Airlines v. Cook, 857 N.E.2d 989 (Ind. 2006) (emotional distress resulting from an out-of-control passenger on a commercial flight not long after 9/11 and even closer in time to the foiled shoe-bomber would not be recoverable; there was no impact from the passenger's thuds in the cabin or his illicit smoking and emotional distress was transient).

[190] E.g., Fla. Dep't of Corr. v. Abril, 969 So.2d 201 (Fla. 2007) (impact generally required, but not when the emotional distress was caused by a clinical laboratory's breach of a statutory duty of confidentiality); Hagan v. Coca-Cola Bottling Co., 804 So.2d 1234 (Fla. 2001) (ingestion of contaminated food or drink; ingestion is impact or alternatively, this is an exception to impact requirement); Tanner v. Hartog, 696 So. 2d 705 (Fla. 1997); Lee v. State Farm Mut. Ins. Co., 533 S.E.2d 82 (Ga. 2000).

[191] Metro-North Commuter R.R. Co. v. Buckley, 521 U.S. 424, 117 S.Ct. 2113, 138 L.Ed.2d 560 (1997) (at least in toxic exposure cases symptoms are required to sustain the action); Keck v. Jackson, 122 Ariz. 114, 593 P.2d 668 (1979); Willis v. Gami Golden Glades, LLC, 967 So.2d 846 (Fla. 2007); Paz v. Brush Engineered Materials, Inc., 949 So. 2d 1 (Miss. 2007) (to recover for negligently-caused emotional distress, plaintiff must prove "a resulting physical illness or assault upon the mind, personality or nervous system of the plaintiff which is medically cognizable and which requires or necessitates treatment by the medical profession").

[192] Armstrong v. Paoli Mem'l Hosp., 430 Pa.Super. 36, 633 A.2d 605 (1993).

[193] Johnson v. Ruark Obstetrics & Gynecology Assocs., 327 N.C. 283, 395 S.E.2d 85 (1990); See Hegel v. McMahon, 136 Wash.2d 122, 134, 960 P.2d 424, 431 (1998).

from a recognized post-traumatic stress disorder. Nevertheless, his emotional harm claim was rejected because he demonstrated no objectively verifiable physical symptoms.[194] At times the limitation has been applied in ways that appear ridiculous.[195]

An alternative limitation: recovery for cases of severe distress. In other jurisdictions, plaintiff can recover for negligently inflicted emotional harm when the plaintiff's evidence shows by a preponderance of the evidence that she in fact suffered serious or severe emotional harm, even if the plaintiff suffered no physical impact and has no physical manifestations or symptoms of the harm. Courts taking this position argue that the requirement of physical symptoms is overinclusive because it allows trivial and transient symptoms to support the emotional harm claim, and underinclusive because it "mechanically denies" convincing claims for emotional distress. They also point out that the nature of the defendant's conduct is often a better guarantee of genuine emotional harm than are mechanical symptoms.

Dropping the physical manifestation requirement. A large number of cases have either dropped the requirement of physical symptoms or manifestations or have held that the requirement does not apply when the facts of the case tend to show the reality of the plaintiff's emotional harm.[196] At times the physical manifestations requirement has been dropped for particular categories of cases, such as bystander cases[197] or direct harm cases.[198] And of course the requirement typically does not apply to parasitic claims of distress.[199] The Restatement Third of Torts directly disavows a requirement of physical manifestations of distress. Instead, the Restatement limits claims to "serious emotional disturbance," whether accompanied by physical manifestations or not.[200]

Abolishing restrictive rules: severe distress that is reasonably foreseeable. A few courts have expressed a desire to eliminate all the restrictive rules in emotional distress cases. In the first, the Montana Supreme Court seemed to hold that the plaintiff could recover for emotional distress incurred when the defendants told authorities that she had stolen goods. The court phrased its new rule broadly: "An independent cause of action for the tort of infliction of emotional distress will arise under circumstances where serious or severe emotional distress to the plaintiff was the reasonably foreseeable

---

[194] Wilson v. Sears, Roebuck & Co., 757 F.2d 948 (8th Cir. 1985).

[195] In a Rhode Island case, the defendant negligently delivered the plaintiff's child, causing the child overwhelming brain damage. Although the mother would live with the burden of caring for a child nearly totally devastated in mind and body, the court insisted that if the mother had no physical symptoms of emotional harm she could not recover because emotional harm is too easy to feign. Reilly v. United States, 547 A.2d 894 (R.I. 1988).

[196] See Culbert v. Sampson's Supermarkets, Inc., 444 A.2d 433 (Me. 1982); Sacco v. High Country Indep. Press, Inc., 271 Mont. 209, 896 P.2d 411 (1995); Folz v. State, 110 N.M. 457, 797 P.2d 246 (1990); Johnson v. State, 37 N.Y.2d 378, 334 N.E.2d 590, 372 N.Y.S.2d 638 (1975); Camper v. Minor, 915 S.W.2d 437 (Tenn. 1996); Hegel v. McMahon, 136 Wash.2d 122, 134, 960 P.2d 424, 431 (1998); Bowen v. Lumbermens Mut. Cas. Co., 183 Wis.2d 627, 517 N.W.2d 432 (1994) (in bystander cases); Gates v. Richardson, 719 P.2d 193 (Wyo. 1986).

[197] Pennsylvania abolished the physical manifestations requirement in Sinn v. Burd, 486 Pa. 146, 404 A.2d 672 (1979), but that turned out to be the rule only for bystander cases. See Simmons v. Pacor, Inc., 543 Pa. 664, 674 A.2d 232 (1995).

[198] Alaska and Illinois eliminated the physical manifestation requirement in direct victim cases only. Chizmar v. Mackie, 896 P.2d 196 (Alaska 1995); Corgan v. Muehling, 143 Ill.2d 296, 574 N.E.2d 602, 158 Ill.Dec. 489 (1991).

[199] When an independent cause of action is shown—invasion of privacy, for example—the requirement of bodily harm is dropped. See, e.g., Fairfax Hosp. v. Curtis, 254 Va. 437, 492 S.E.2d 642 (1997) (medical providers release of plaintiff's confidential records was actionable for emotional harm without physical harm).

[200] Restatement (Third) of Torts: Liability for Physical and Emotional Harm § 47 cmt. j and § 48 cmt. i (2012).

consequence of the defendant's negligent or intentional act or omission. . . ."[201] Because the claim was based in part on a report to authorities that attributed a crime to the plaintiff, the claim would ordinarily be handled under a malicious prosecution theory, with all the special rules that entails. If the negligent infliction claim displaces malicious prosecution (and perhaps other torts), the rules designed to encourage reports to authorities will be substantially undermined (unless imported into the new claim). If general foreseeability becomes sufficient to make an emotional distress claim, it may become important to carve out cases that are subject to special rules that apply in cases for malicious prosecution, defamation, privacy invasion, and the like.

Foreseeability of distress as the test. In 1996 a Tennessee case also abolished special rules for emotional distress. It substituted a general test of foreseeability instead.[202] But that court expressly recognized that the foreseeability test might end up in much the same way as under the restrictive rules. For instance, a plaintiff who was in the zone of danger might be a readily foreseeable victim of emotional distress, while a bystander outside the zone might be required to show some other evidence, such as a close relationship with the injured person that brought her within the range of foreseeability.[203] The court has now added a requirement that the plaintiff support such claims with expert medical or scientific proof.[204] It thus remains to be seen whether adoption of the general foreseeability approach, which treats emotional harm like any other injury, will expand liability or whether it will instead be applied to obtain results similar to those the courts now reach under the various restrictions canvassed above.[205] It also remains to be seen how many jurisdictions will follow suit and use foreseeability and severity of harm as the main guideposts for NIED claims.[206]

Direct emotional harms without sudden injury. As the requirements of reasonably foreseeable severe distress suggest, the scope of liability for emotional distress could be quite a bit larger than that originally stemming from the fright or shock pattern. Emotional harm resulting from direct risk or injury—the fright and shock pattern—is but one pattern of recovery in which the plaintiff is the direct victim of emotional harm. Some courts have begun to recognize recovery for emotional harms that do not result from a sudden event or threat of an impact, for example in the case of toxic exposures, erroneous information, or defendants under a duty to care for the plaintiff's well-being.

---

[201] Sacco v. High Country Indep. Press, Inc., 271 Mont. 209, 220 896 P.2d 411, 418 (1995).

[202] Camper v. Minor, 915 S.W.2d 437 (Tenn. 1996).

[203] See Ramsey v. Beavers, 931 S.W.2d 527 (Tenn. 1996).

[204] See Flax v. DaimlerChrysler Corp., 272 S.W.3d 521 (Tenn. 2008).

[205] See Ennett v. Cumberland Cnty. Bd. of Educ., 698 F.Supp.2d 557 (E.D.N.C. 2010) (applying foreseeability and severity test for NIED to bar claim on the ground that superintendent's conduct, which was intentional, was not extreme and outrageous). For a discussion of Tennessee claims after the shift in standard see Daniel E. Wanat, Infliction of Emotional Injury: The General Negligence Claim within Serious or Severe Injury Limits as Proven by Medical or Scientific Evidence—The Tennessee Common Law Approach, 36 U. Mem. L. Rev. 233 (2006) (citing requirement of proof through medical experts as the problem with Tennessee's approach).

[206] See Hall v. Bergman, 994 A.2d 666 (Conn. 2010) (listing forseeability, severity, causation and negligent risk of emotional distress as the main factors in an NIED claim). See also Osborne v. Keeney, 399 S.W.3d 1 (Ky. 2012) (reversing longstanding precedent: physical impact is not required to recover for claims involving emotional distress; plaintiff must show elements of negligence plus, by presenting expert testimony, a severe or serious emotional injury).

§ 29.13   Toxic Exposures: Fear of Future Harm

Specific incident causing fear of future harm. When the plaintiff is subjected to a specific intangible trauma like excessive x-rays, she may be able to prove by a preponderance of the evidence that some specific harm will eventuate in the future.[207] But even if the plaintiff cannot prove that a disease will result in the future, courts have permitted recovery for reasonable fears that the impact will inflict some future disease. She might fear cancer in the case of excessive x-ray doses[208] or exposure to asbestos that has already actually resulted in some physical harm;[209] she might fear brain damage or paralysis in the case of a head injury that caused loss of cerebral fluid.[210] Even if such harms are not necessarily more probable than not, they are worrisome, and courts have allowed recovery readily enough.[211] Such cases often fit the pattern of parasitic damages—emotional harm results from an initial injury and is recovered as one element of damages for that injury.

Claims for fear of future harm without specific impact. Courts have also allowed some claims of fear about future harm even when no impact has occurred at all and the rule for parasitic damages could not be invoked. For example, as a result of a negligent reading of a pap smear test, it appeared that the plaintiff needed no treatment. The error was discovered much later and the needed treatment was given, but the delay made future cancer more likely. The court upheld the claim for emotional distress.[212] Two factors especially call for relief in such a case. First, as suggested in the next section, the parties are not strangers; on the contrary, the defendant has undertaken to care for the plaintiff professionally and failed to do so. Second, the fear arises from a specific incident rather than, say, gradual environmental exposure.

Reasonable fear of future harm. When the defendant has negligently exposed the plaintiff to a toxic substance like the AIDS virus, plaintiff may fear future harm. Over a period of time, this fear may subside if tests repeatedly prove negative,[213] but at least during the "window of anxiety," until tests can establish the plaintiff's health, the fear seems to be reasonable in the sense that many if not most people in our culture would suffer a similar fear. Courts have often insisted, however, that the plaintiff must prove that her fear was reasonable by showing that (1) the virus was present and (2) there was

---

[207] See § 14.11 on loss of a chance.

[208] Ferrara v. Galluchio, 5 N.Y.2d 16, 152 N.E.2d 249, 176 N.Y.S.2d 996 (1958).

[209] CSX Transp., Inc. v. Hensley, 556 U.S. 838, 129 S.Ct. 2139, 173 L.Ed.2d 1184 (2009); Norfolk & W. Ry. v. Ayers, 538 U.S. 135, 123 S.Ct. 1210, 155 L.Ed.2d 261 (2003) (plaintiff suffering from asbestosis as a result of exposure for which defendant was responsible could recover for fear of future cancer, even if such cancer would not result from the asbestosis injury but from the exposure; the cancer "need not be more likely than not to materialize"); Eagle-Picher Indus., Inc. v. Cox, 481 So. 2d 517 (Fla. Dist. Ct. App. 1985).

[210] Davis v. Graviss, 672 S.W.2d 928 (Ky. 1984).

[211] See David Carl Minneman, Annotation, Future Disease or Condition, or Anxiety Relating Thereto, as Element of Recovery, 50 A.L.R.4th 13 (1987).

[212] Gilliam v. Roche Biomedical Labs., Inc., 989 F.2d 278 (8th Cir. 1993).

[213] In one type of case the plaintiff's distress during the "window of anxiety" period is severe enough to cause permanent or lasting harm that may go on for years. See Chizmar v. Mackie, 896 P.2d 196, 206 (Alaska 1995) (misdiagnosis of AIDS; "we do not foreclose the possibility that a plaintiff may be able to establish, through appropriate expert testimony, long-term emotional trauma proximately related to the defendant's negligent conduct"); cf. Doe v. Arts, 360 N.J. Super. 492, 823 A.2d 855 (2003) (misdiagnosis of AIDS; seemingly approving recovery for long-term harm outside the window of anxiety period where the harm was inflicting during that period); Ornstein v. N.Y.C. Health & Hosp. Corp., 881 N.E.2d 1187 (N.Y. 2008) (permitting nurse to seek damages beyond six months after exposure despite her negative HIV tests).

a scientifically accepted channel for transmission of the disease.[214] For instance, if the plaintiff drinks from a soft drink bottle, then discovers what appears to be a used condom in it, her fear claim cannot succeed unless she shows that there was a virus present and that it could be communicated by drinking contaminated Coca-Cola.[215]

Actual exposure versus reasonable fear of exposure. If the plaintiff is negligently stuck with a used hospital needle which cannot be identified and tested, she might reasonably fear contamination and the possibility of AIDS, but if she cannot show that the needle was in fact contaminated, or that she suffers some immediate physical injury, a number of courts hold that she has no claim for emotional distress even though she sustained a physical impact.[216] Or the plaintiff in an emergency room is seated in a pool of unidentified blood. He cannot recover for his fear of AIDS unless he can show that the blood actually entered his body.[217] Some courts have made this requirement of "actual exposure" quite stringent.[218] Several major decisions have now taken a different view, saying that if the defendant negligently subjected the plaintiff to a reasonable fear of exposure to AIDS, for example, if she is stuck by a needle that cannot be tested, that will be enough to warrant a recovery for the period until testing can reasonably assuage that fear.[219] Some kinds of environmental contamination expose many people to risks of future physical harm. These cases pose special problems.[220]

§ 29.14 Emotional Distress from False or Erroneous Information

Erroneous or inadequate information supplied to the plaintiff. At times the plaintiff has been permitted to recover for distress arising from the defendant's negligent transmission or failure to transmit important information. The classic case was for a telegraphic message wrongly announcing a death.[221] Recovery was permitted even though there was no physical risk or harm to the plaintiff or anyone else. Courts that follow the zone of danger rule sometimes apply it to exclude recovery for emotional harms not based on a physical danger, as where a nursing home provides false information

---

[214] Exxon Mobil Corp. v. Albright, 71 A.3d 30 (Md.), on reconsideration in part, 71 A.3d 50 (Md.), and cert. denied, 134 S.Ct. 648 (2013) (state standard for emotional distress damages for fear of contracting a latent disease because of toxic exposure).

[215] Coca-Cola Bottling Co. v. Hagan, 813 So.2d 167 (Fla. Dist. Ct. App. 2002). See also Laurel v. Prince, 154 So.3d 95 (Ala. 2014).

[216] Majca v. Beekil, 183 Ill.2d 407, 701 N.E.2d 1084, 233 Ill.Dec. 810 (1998); Carroll v. Sisters of Saint Francis Health Servs., Inc., 868 S.W.2d 585 (Tenn. 1993).

[217] Barrett v. Danbury Hosp., 232 Conn. 242, 654 A.2d 748 (1995) (rejecting the actual exposure test but concluding as a matter of law that the plaintiff's fear was not reasonable).

[218] In K.A.C. v. Benson, 527 N.W.2d 553 (Minn. 1995), the plaintiff's physician had lesions on his hands and forearms. He performed gynecological examinations upon the plaintiff and others. He tested positive for HIV (the AIDS virus), so there was a risk to his patients in spite of the fact that he used gloves in performing the examinations. The court imported the zone of danger rule from the fear-for-another setting and held that the plaintiff could not recover for emotional distress at her fear that she might suffer AIDS. She had not demonstrated "actual exposure."

[219] Faya v. Almaraz, 329 Md. 435, 620 A.2d 327 (1993) (doctor's invasive operations on women without informing patient that he was an HIV carrier; recovery for the window of anxiety period); S. Cent. Reg'l Med. Ctr. v. Pickering, 749 So. 2d 95 (Miss. 1999) (unsafe disposal of instruments, rebuttable presumption in favor of the plaintiff); Madrid v. Lincoln Cnty. Med. Ctr., 923 P.2d 1134 (N.M. 1996) (blood containers leaked onto plaintiff's hand; plaintiff had papercuts, but did not know whether blood was infected); Hartwig v. Oregon Trail Eye Clinic, 254 Neb. 777, 580 N.W.2d 86 (1998); Williamson v. Waldman, 150 N.J. 232, 696 A.2d 14 (1997); Fitzgerald v. Tin, 2003 WL 4901 (B.C. S.C. 2003).

[220] E.g., Potter v. Firestone Tire & Rubber Co., 6 Cal.4th 965, 25 Cal.Rptr. 2d 550, 863 P.2d 795 (1993); see 2 Dobbs, Hayden & Bublick, The Law of Torts § 394 (2d ed. 2011 & Supp.).

[221] E.g., Russ v. W. Union Tel. Co., 222 N.C. 504, 23 S.E.2d 681 (1943).

about the health of the plaintiff's mother[222] or a physician fails to provide appropriate information about the genetic defects of a fetus.[223]

Distressing misdiagnosis—split authority. Suppose the defendants tested the plaintiff for AIDS but negligently and erroneously reported to her that she was infected with the disease when she was not. Since AIDS is presently incurable, the diagnosis is bound to be severely distressing, but the diagnosis itself does not place anyone in danger. Some decisions deny any recovery to the victim of this negligent misdiagnosis because the diagnosis does not endanger the victim in a physical way,[224] although others recognize that emotional harm from this kind of misinformation is foreseeable and worthy of redress.[225]

Three characterizations of the claim. The claim for negligent infliction of emotional distress based on information supplied to the plaintiff can take on different legal colors depending how the claim is theorized. Three possibilities of conceptualizing such a claim are illustrated in *Friedman v. Merck & Co.*[226] The plaintiff there was an ethical vegan, a person who refuses to ingest animal products as a matter of personal ethics. He was offered a job contingent on undergoing a TB test. Since the test would put substances in his body, he asked the manufacturer for assurance that it contained no such animal products and was told that it was "vegan friendly." He accepted the test, then discovered that the manufacturer's assurance was false. He claimed emotional harm and physical harms resulting from that emotional harm.

Products warnings. The first possibility, apart from a straightforward claim for negligent infliction of emotional distress, is that the manufacturer should have warned potential users, but the *Friedman* court rejected that claim, coupled with reliance on the requirement that emotional harm must be serious. Since no substantial number of people would both seek to avoid all animal products *and* suffer serious emotional harm from unintended ingestion of them, the manufacturer owed no duty to warn with respect to emotional harm. This ruling turns not merely on foreseeability but foreseeability of substantial numbers of victims, so the outcome might conceivably be different if a manufacturer made assurances to larger or better-defined groups—to Orthodox Jews that the seller's food was kosher or to Jehovah's Witnesses that its medical treatment contained no blood products. Yet if a Jehovah's Witness could recover in such a case, the effect is to protect some more widely held beliefs but not beliefs of small minorities, a position that may sit quite uncomfortably with traditional individualistic values.

Duty undertaken or assumed. The second possibility was that the defendant had undertaken or assumed a duty to the plaintiff, given that it knew plaintiff's beliefs and undertook to state the relevant facts.[227] But the court thought the defendant had not

---

[222] Hart v. Child's Nursing Home Co., Inc., 298 A.D.2d 721, 749 N.Y.S.2d 297 (2002) (alleged misinformation about health of mother confined in the defendant's nursing home did not endanger the plaintiff or fall within any exceptions to requirement that the plaintiff be endangered).

[223] Cauman v. George Washington Univ., 630 A.2d 1104 (D.C. 1993).

[224] R.J. v. Humana of Fla., Inc., 652 So. 2d 360 (Fla. 1995); Heiner v. Moretuzzo, 73 Ohio St. 3d 80, 652 N.E.2d 664 (1995).

[225] Chizmar v. Mackie, 896 P.2d 196 (Alaska 1995) (AIDS misdiagnosis); Doe v. Arts, 360 N.J. Super. 492, 823 A.2d 855 (2003); Brammer v. Dotson, 190 W.Va. 200, 437 S.E.2d 773 (1993).

[226] Friedman v. Merck & Co., 107 Cal.App. 4th 454, 131 Cal.Rptr.2d 885 (2003).

[227] Thompson v. Lied Animal Shelter, 2009 WL 3303733 (D. Nev. 2009) (animal shelter represented to the out-of-town plaintiff that his dog would be kept safe for 13 days, but instead the dog was euthanized without notice before the plaintiff reached the shelter).

assumed a duty with respect to emotional harm; the defendants "did not voluntarily undertake any duty that encompassed plaintiff's emotional tranquility." This point, too, was intertwined with the idea that *serious* emotional harm was not foreseeable.

Negligent misrepresentation on matters of emotional significance. The third possibility may have broader relevance. The plaintiff in *Friedman* asserted that the defendant was chargeable with negligent misrepresentation, a liberalized claim growing out of the old tort of intentional deceit.[228] Fraud and deceit, and their cousin, negligent misrepresentation, are normally seen as economic torts, with no recovery for emotional harm.[229] Yet there are cases in which the representation is mainly about a matter of emotional significance, just as there are contract cases in which the promise is not so much economic in nature as emotional. It should go without saying that such claims are successful where the facts meet all the requirements of a claim for negligent or intentional infliction of emotional distress, and equally that they are often denied when the facts do not show a ground for relief under the emotional harm rules.[230] Such claims are at bottom emotional distress claims with a misrepresentation label. For example, in the "wrongful adoption" cases, parents adopt a child based on an adoption agency's knowing or negligent false representation that the child is mentally and physically healthy, when in fact it turns out after adoption has taken place that the child has the most serious kinds of physical or mental health problems. Some authority directly supports the parents' recovery for emotional distress as well as economic harm in such cases,[231] though some does not.[232]

The *Friedman* court, however, thought that the gist of the vegan plaintiff's claim concerning the TB test was essentially one for emotional harm, and that no pertinent authority supported liability for stand-alone emotional harm based on such misrepresentation, conceived of as a tort separate from negligence.

§ 29.15 Duties of Care to Protect Emotional Well-Being Independent of Physical Risks

Defendant duty to protect plaintiff's emotional well-being. Another situation in which a plaintiff may recover for stand-alone emotional distress is the context in which the defendant has a special relationship to the plaintiff and the defendant has undertaken a duty of care that implicates the plaintiff's emotional well-being.[233] For

---

[228] See § 43.5.

[229] §§ 43.2–43.5. Examples include Cornell v. Wunschel, 408 N.W.2d 369 (Iowa 1997); Fetick v. Am. Cyanamid Co., 38 S.W.3d 415 (Mo. 2001).

[230] See McConkey v. Aon Corp., 354 N.J. Super. 25, 804 A.2d 572 (2002) (suggesting that the severe emotional harm requirement would be applied if argued by attorneys); Bailey v. Searles-Bailey, 746 N.E.2d 1159 (Ohio Ct. App. 2001) (wife's paramour not outrageous in nondisclosure that he was father of husband's putative children).

[231] Dahlin v. Evangelical Child & Family Agency, 2002 WL 31557625 (N.D. Ill. 2002) (suit based on fraud, "negligence," consisting of misrepresentation and concealment, and breach of fiduciary duty; direct duty to parents, hence emotional distress damages recoverable); Burr v. Bd. of Cnty. Comm'rs of Stark Cnty., 23 Ohio St.3d 69, 491 N.E.2d 1101 (1986) (claim of fraud); Price v. State, 114 Wash.App. 65, 57 P.3d 639 (2002) (suit by adoptive parents and adoptive sibling for "negligent failure to disclose information pertinent to an adoption decision" permits parents to recover for emotional distress, although sibling cannot recover at all).

[232] See M.H. v. Caritas Family Servs., 488 N.W.2d 282 (Minn. 1992); Juman v. Louise Wise Servs., 254 A.D.2d 72, 678 N.Y.S.2d 611 (1998).

[233] For a careful examination of this category see Dan B. Dobbs, Undertakings and Special Relationships in Claims for Negligent Infliction of Emotional Distress, 50 Ariz. L. Rev. 49 (2008). See also Restatement (Third) of Torts: Liability for Physical and Emotional Harm § 47(b) (2012) (liability for negligent conduct that causes serious emotional disturbance when the conduct "occurs in the course of specified categories of

example, in some cases of mishandling of dead bodies courts permit negligent infliction of distress claims,[234] although the majority rule probably confines liability to intentional mishandling.[235] In both kinds of mishandling cases, the contractual relationship between the parties and its implicit undertakings undoubtedly play a large part in liability. The duty assumed by a mortuary or other party in custody of the body expressly or impliedly is a duty to take care for the feelings of the survivors. Mishandling a dead body foreseeably affects the welfare of survivors, and warrants a claim for emotional distress.[236] For instance, when a hospital performed a dissection upon a mother's stillborn fetus over her objection but not in her presence, the mother and not the deceased child was the "primary victim."[237] But again, some cases have rejected liability on zone of danger grounds, perhaps because the assumed or independent duty argument was not presented.[238]

Obstetrician's assumed duty of care for mother and child. Another example of a case in which a special relationship or undertaking arises such that recovery is not dependent on special bystander rules is California's decision in *Burgess v. Superior Court*.[239] Burgess obtained prenatal care from Dr. Gupta and others. After Burgess entered labor, Gupta diagnosed a prolapsed cord, meaning the child would not receive sufficient oxygen. For reasons not explained in the opinion, 44 minutes elapsed before the child was taken by Cesarean Section. By that time, the child had suffered severe brain damage from oxygen deprivation. A suit was brought for the child and Burgess brought her own suit for emotional harm. California had repudiated the zone of danger rule, but would still exclude the plaintiff's emotional harm claim unless the plaintiff was contemporaneously aware of the child's injury. Burgess may not have been aware of her child's injury until much later. Nevertheless, the California court thought that the plaintiff could recover. The key point was that the plaintiff and defendant were already in a physician-patient relationship. The physician's duty to the mother was not derivative of some duty to the

---

activities, undertakings, or relationships in which negligent conduct is especially likely to cause serious emotional harm"). This category has been viewed as a particularly important avenue for future development of the tort. See Martha Chamallas, Unpacking Emotional Distress: Sexual Exploitation, Reproductive Harm, and Fundamental Rights, 44 Wake Forest L. Rev. 1109 (2009).

[234] Chesher v. Neyer, 392 F.Supp.2d 939 (S.D. Ohio 2005) ("vile" photographs of dead bodies in county morgue, complete with props, negligent infliction of distress actionable by relatives without proof of physical peril to the plaintiffs); Christensen v. Superior Court (Pasadena Crematorium of Altadena), 54 Cal.3d 868, 820 P.2d 181, 2 Cal.Rptr.2d 79 (1991); Guth v. Freeland, 96 Haw. 147, 28 P.3d 982 (2001) (duty of reasonable care in preparing a body for final disposition; statute forbidding recovery of emotional distress for negligent property damage does not apply to a body); Adams v. King Cnty., 164 Wash.2d 640, 192 P.3d 891 (2008) (reaffirming a separate common law action for "tortious interference with a dead body," which requires willful conduct and "allows recovery for mental suffering derived from willful misuse of a dead body").

[235] See Washington v. John T. Rhines Co., 646 A.2d 345 (D.C. 1994); Lions Eye Bank of Tex. v. Perry, 56 S.W.3d 872 (Tex. App. 2001) (defendant negligently but not intentionally harvested eyes of deceased without permission, but family had no negligence claim in the absence of contract or special relationship; the family did not qualify for recovery under the bystander rules).

[236] Christensen v. Superior Court, 54 Cal.3d 868, 2 Cal.Rptr. 2d 79, 820 P.2d 181 (1991); Boorman v. Nev. Mem'l Cremation Soc'y, 236 P.3d 4 (Nev. 2010). See also Guth v. Freeland, 96 Haw. 147, 28 P.3d 982 (2001).

[237] Janicki v. Hospital of St. Raphael, 744 A.2d 963 (Conn. Super. Ct. 1999); accord, as to autopsy, Kelly v. Brigham & Women's Hosp., 745 N.E.2d 969 (Mass. App. Ct. 2001).

[238] See Washington v. John T. Rhines Co., 646 A.2d 345 (D.C. 1994) (survivors were not in zone of danger from negligent embalming (nobody was), hence could not recover, relying in part on zone of danger cases in which the defendant was a stranger).

[239] Burgess v. Superior Court (Gupta), 2 Cal.4th 1064, 831 P.2d 1197, 9 Cal.Rptr.2d 615 (1992).

child; he owed her a direct duty of care based on the duty he assumed by entering the physician-patient relationship.

Support for the assumed duty to mother and child. The *Burgess* idea is relatively new and seems not to have been argued in a number of cases. Some cases quite similar to *Burgess* on their facts have rejected the mother's claim without mentioning the idea that the physician-patient relationship created a duty of care to her that would not otherwise exist.[240] Where the point has been considered, however, courts have been receptive to the rule or some form of it.[241] Somewhat similarly, decisions in New York[242] and Wisconsin[243] have permitted the mother to recover for her own emotional distress when her physician's negligence resulted in loss of her fetus. Pennsylvania even more recently held on similar facts that where the plaintiff and defendant are in a preexisting special relationship "involving duties that obviously and objectively hold the potential of deep emotional harm in the event of breach," no special rules constrain the claim for negligent infliction of emotional distress.[244]

Support for an assumed or independent duty for plaintiff's emotional well-being in other contexts. Although the childbirth setting is perhaps the most prominent example of the independent duty, the same reasoning can be applied whenever the defendant assumes a duty by contract or otherwise and when that duty encompasses the plaintiff's emotional well-being. A therapist who agrees to treat the plaintiff is assuming a duty to exercise care for the plaintiff's emotional condition; if he instead negligently inflicts emotional harm, he is responsible.[245] Or suppose a hospital negligently switches babies, so that two recent mothers each take home the other's child and upon discovery years later suffer emotional distress. The hospital's negligence ordinarily poses no special physical danger to the parents or children. In light of the obligations the hospital had to the families, however, it is no surprise to find that baby-switching hospitals may be held responsible.[246] The court wrote, "Where a contractual relationship exists for services that carry with them deeply emotional responses in the event of breach, there arises a duty to exercise ordinary care to avoid causing emotional harm."[247] A number of other courts obtain results entirely consistent with the independent duty analysis when they permit recovery for emotional distress from an embryo allegedly implanted in the wrong

---

[240] Cauman v. George Washington Univ., 630 A.2d 1104 (D.C. 1993).

[241] Carey v. Lovett, 132 N.J. 44, 622 A.2d 1279 (1993); Smith v. Borello, 370 Md. 227, 804 A.2d 1151 (2002) (permitting expectant mother to recover for emotional distress resulting from negligently inflicted loss of nonviable fetus).

[242] Broadnax v. Gonzalez, 2 N.Y.3d 148, 809 N.E.2d 645, 777 N.Y.S.2d 416 (2004). The New York Court was unwilling to recognize the same right in the mother when the fetus was injured and born alive. However, the court held that if the mother could prove direct injury to herself, possibly in the form of negligent medical advice to have an abortion, then she could recover for her emotional distress. Sheppard-Mobley v. King, 4 N.Y.3d 627, 830 N.E.2d 301, 797 N.Y.S.2d 403 (2005).

[243] Pierce v. Physicians Ins. Co. of Wis., Inc., 278 Wis.2d 82, 692 N.W.2d 558 (2005) (noting that the mother was a "participant," not merely a bystander).

[244] Toney v. Chester Cnty. Hosp., 36 A.3d 83 (Pa. 2011) (applying the new rule to a claim by a patient against her obstetrician for the emotional distress of seeing her child born with serious birth defects) (citing the Treatise).

[245] Corgan v. Muehling, 143 Ill.2d 296, 574 N.E.2d 602, 158 Ill.Dec. 489 (1991).

[246] Larsen v. Banner Health Sys., 81 P.3d 196 (Wyo. 2003).

[247] Id.

woman,[248] a medical test that caused emotional harm without risking physical injury,[249] a blood transfusion given over plaintiff's objection,[250] and a wedding cancellation of which the engaged couple was given no notice.[251]

Rationale for recognizing liability in assumed and independent duty cases. When the defendant owes an independent duty of care to the plaintiff, there is no risk of unlimited liability to an unlimited number of people. Liability turns solely on relationships accepted by the defendant, usually under a contractual arrangement. Consequently, the duty extends only to those for whom the contract was made.[252] The idea that a contractual or similar relationship can bespeak a duty assumed by the defendant or one imposed by law is itself of respectable lineage. The early allowance of emotional distress damage in suits against carriers, innkeeper, and telegraph companies was based precisely on the consensual relationship between the plaintiff and the defendant.[253] The scope of the independent duty owed by the defendant "directly" to the plaintiff dictates the limits of liability.

§ 29.16   Sensitive Plaintiffs

Severe distress to a reasonable person and plaintiff's special vulnerabilities. Courts sometimes note that the defendant's conduct must have been such that it would have severely distressed a reasonable person who is normally constituted.[254] This requirement that the plaintiff be normally constituted or "reasonable," does not mean that the plaintiff's special vulnerabilities are ignored. If the defendant knows or should know that he deals with an especially sensitive plaintiff that is all the more reason for care. Thus a therapist treating an emotionally distressed patient would know of her special vulnerability and be expected to act with reasonable care for that condition. If he does not, liability for her emotional distress is entirely proper.[255]

Damage of distress that is greater than anticipated. Neither does the reasonable person rule mean that the plaintiff is limited to an amount of damages that would be incurred by a normal person. If the defendant's conduct would subject him to liability for severe distress to a reasonable person, he is also liable for damages to an especially sensitive person, even if those damages are much greater because of the special

---

[248] See Perry-Rogers v. Obasaju, 282 A.D.2d 231, 723 N.Y.S.2d 28 (2001) (plaintiff was entitled to claim damages for emotional harm caused by losing "the opportunity of experiencing pregnancy, prenatal bonding and the birth" of the child).

[249] Curtis v. MRI Imaging Servs., II, 327 Or. 9, 956 P.2d 960 (1998).

[250] Campbell v. Delbridge, 670 N.W.2d 108 (Iowa 2003) (healthcare providers negligently failed to check chart, which would have revealed patient's objection to receiving blood; provider gave him blood after an operation; the providers owed duty of care to patient not to negligently inflict emotional harm regardless of physical injury).

[251] Murphy v. Lord Thompson Manor, Inc., 105 Conn.App. 546, 938 A.2d 1269 (2008).

[252] For a deeper exploration of this theory, its limitations and possible extensions, see Dan B. Dobbs, Undertakings and Special Relationships in Claims for Negligent Infliction of Emotional Distress, 50 Ariz. L. Rev. 49 (2008).

[253] See §§ 19.1–19.3.

[254] E.g., Bailey v. Bayer Cropscience, 563 F.3d 302 (8th Cir. 2009) (employee falsely accused of a homosexual advance reacted with panic attacks and PTSD, a reaction that was not consistent with the reasonable person); Culbert v. Sampson's Supermarkets, Inc., 444 A.2d 433 (Me. 1982); Sinn v. Burd, 486 Pa. 146, 404 A.2d 672 (1979); Restatement (Third) of Torts: Liability for Physical and Emotional Harm § 47 cmt. l (2012) (the stimulus must "cause a reasonable person to suffer serious emotional harm").

[255] As in Corgan v. Muehling, 143 Ill.2d 296, 574 N.E.2d 602, 158 Ill.Dec. 489 (1991).

sensitivity.[256] This rule is merely the familiar thin skull or eggshell skull rule as applied to emotional harm. On the other hand, the reasonable person rule excludes compensation for emotional harm when a reasonable person would suffer no serious emotional harm at all.[257] Such a result seems logical. If only transient distress is foreseeable to a normal person and the defendant neither knows nor should know of the plaintiff's special sensitivity, serious distress is by definition not foreseeable.[258] In some cases, it may be difficult for a particularly sensitive plaintiff to show that the defendant's conduct was the factual cause[259] or proximate cause[260] of the distress.

---

[256] Miley v. Landry, 582 So.2d 833 (La. 1991); Poole v. Copland, Inc., 348 N.C. 260, 498 S.E.2d 602 (1998); see Brackett v. Peters, 11 F.3d 78 (7th Cir. 1993) (envisioning small physical harm triggering serious mental disease); Steinhauser v. Hertz Corp., 421 F.2d 1169 (2d Cir. 1970); cf. Curtis v. MRI Imaging Servs. II, 327 Or. 9, 956 P.2d 960 (1998) (panic attacks, perhaps due to preexisting conditions, allegedly resulting from negligently administered MRI).

[257] Williamson v. Bennett, 251 N.C. 498, 112 S.E.2d 48 (1960) (defendant negligently struck the plaintiff's car; plaintiff went into a terrible emotional state, imagining that she had somehow struck a child on a bicycle; recovery denied); see also McMahon v. Bergeson, 9 Wis.2d 256, 101 N.W.2d 63 (1960).

[258] See Johnson v. Ruark Obstetrics & Gynecology Assocs., P.A., 327 N.C. 283, 395 S.E.2d 85 (1990).

[259] Clemensen v. Providence Alaska Med. Ctr., 203 P.3d 1148 (Alaska 2009) (patient's husband could not maintain an action against hospital on the basis that releasing wife with Alzheimers to daughter rather than husband led to couple's divorce).

[260] Corales v. Bennett, 567 F.3d 554 (9th Cir. 2009) (middle school student's suicide after vice principal's stern lecture not to leave campus without authorization was unforseen); Cramer v. Slater, 204 P.3d 508 (Idaho 2009) (medical center's negligence in handling positive HIV test led to patient suicide; genuine issue of material fact as to whether husband's conduct was superseding cause).

Chapter 30

NUISANCE

Analysis

§ 30.1   Introducing Nuisance Law
§ 30.2   Defining and Illustrating Private Nuisance
§ 30.3   Intent, Negligence and Strict Liability
§ 30.4   Substantial and Unreasonable Interference
§ 30.5   Non-Invasive Nuisances
§ 30.6   Public Nuisance
§ 30.7   Remedies

§ 30.1   Introducing Nuisance Law

Private nuisance law deals primarily with the plaintiff's right to use and enjoy her land free from invasions, which are often intangible and can be loosely called pollution. Private nuisance almost always involves incompatible uses of two parcels of land. The use-and-enjoyment side of nuisance law is now supplemented heavily by zoning and land-use statutes and ordinances, backed by specialized legal literature,[1] which may take lawyers into the law of unconstitutional takings of property by regulation.[2] Sometimes nuisance law and regulation work together, each supplementing the other;[3] at other times regulation displaces nuisance law.[4]

Dean William Prosser once described the law of nuisance as an "impenitrable jungle."[5] This was in part because of the peculiar history of nuisance, but more often for other reasons. Older decisions employed broad, almost meaningless definitions[6] and bewildering terminology that can now be largely discarded.[7] The term *nuisance* itself, which in a lay sense means only annoyance, was applied to a wide assortment of

---

[1]   E.g., Arden H. Rathkopf, Daren Rathkopf & Edward H. Ziegler, Jr., Rathkopf's Law of Zoning and Planning (5 vol. 1995 & Supps.) (available on Westlaw).

[2]   See Tarbell Administrator, Inc. v. City of Concord, 157 N.H. 679, 956 A.2d 322 (2008).

[3]   E.g., State of New York v. Shore Realty Corp., 759 F.2d 1032 (2d Cir. 1985) (CERCLA and nuisance); Freeman v. Grain Processing Corp., 848 N.W.2d 58 (Iowa 2014) (Clean Air Act and nuisance).

[4]   San Diego Gas & Elec. Co. v. Superior Court, 13 Cal.4th 893, 920 P.2d 669, 55 Cal.Rptr.2d 724 (1996).

[5]   Prosser & Keeton on Torts § 86, at 616 (5th ed. 1984).

[6]   See § 30.2.

[7]   *Absolute nuisance* means any interference for which courts would impose liability without regard either to the defendant's fault or to the gravity and unreasonableness of the harm done. Under contemporary rules recognizing negligent, intentional, and strict liability nuisances, the term can be dropped. A *nuisance per se* is an activity or condition that is a nuisance in itself and not permissible under any circumstances. This category mainly, or perhaps, solely consists of uses prohibited by statute or regulation, e.g., Tiegs v. Watts, 135 Wash.2d 1, 954 P.2d 877 (1998), but some courts use the term much more broadly. A lawful business, by definition, is not a nuisance per se. A *nuisance in fact* or *per accidens* is the ordinary private nuisance, an activity or condition that is out of place or is a nuisance because of the particular way it is carried on. Sowers v. Forest Hills Subdivision, 294 P.3d 427 (Nev. 2013) (defining the terminology and holding that a wind turbine in a residential area is a nuisance in fact); see § 30.4.

seemingly unrelated cases.[8] Judges and commentators approached nuisance with different philosophical orientations. Public and private nuisance were not carefully distinguished; neither was the remedial distinction between damages and abatement.[9]

Formal distinctions of an earlier era also make nuisance confusing to contemporary observers. For instance, what might seem like an ordinary trespass by backed up waters or sewage might be called a nuisance in many cases,[10] either because the formalistic thinking of an earlier era would not qualify the unintended entry as a trespass or because description of the act as a nuisance allowed the plaintiff to penetrate the defendant's governmental immunity. To classify a problem as nuisance rather than trespass is to invoke a regime of reasonable accommodation between conflicting uses and to reject absolute rights associated with trespass. So airplane overflights, a trespass under older views, may be analyzed under the nuisance rules under which the landowner's right to enjoy her property is weighed against the defendant's rights.[11]

Quite different kinds of nuisances arise because legislatures that wish to terminate a given land use often declare first that the use is a nuisance. For example, statutes may declare that use of land for prostitution is a nuisance.[12] Still other cases involve interferences with the common right and are said to be "public nuisances," as where a public stream is polluted, a condition that may lead to a private right of action in certain instances.[13] These examples suggest that nuisance could not be clearly defined.

Two increasingly clear perceptions facilitate a reasonably coherent understanding of nuisance law. First, if public and statutory nuisance cases are set aside for separate analysis, some paths can be marked in the remaining private nuisance tort. Second, private nuisance does not describe any particular conduct of the defendant, but rather a type of harm suffered by the plaintiff—impaired enjoyment of rights in land.[14]

§ 30.2 Defining and Illustrating Private Nuisance

Definitions of private nuisance. A private nuisance today is a condition[15] or activity[16] that interferes with the possessor's[17] use and enjoyment of her land, typically by non-trespassory invasions[18] that she cannot reasonably be expected to bear without

---

[8]   See Copart Indus., Inc. v. Consolidated Edison Co. of New York, Inc., 41 N.Y.2d 564, 362 N.E.2d 968, 394 N.Y.S.2d 169 (1977) (discussing the phenomenon).

[9]   See Louise A. Halper, Untangling The Nuisance Knot, 26 B.C. Envtl. Aff. L. Rev. 89 (1998).

[10]   E.g., Fletcher v. City of Independence, 708 S.W.2d 158 (Mo. App. 1986) (sewer backup); Bible Baptist Church v. City of Cleburne, 848 S.W.2d 826 (Tex. App. 1993) (same).

[11]   See Aviation Cadet Museum v. Hammer, 373 Ark. 202, 283 S.W.3d 198 (2008) (overflights held to be a nuisance when the flights were at such a low altitude that they posed a physical threat to people on the neighbor's property); Atkinson v. Bernard, Inc., 223 Or. 624, 355 P.2d 229 (1960).

[12]   E.g., Cal. Penal Code § 11225.

[13]   See § 30.6.

[14]   See Graber v. City of Peoria, 156 Ariz. 553, 753 P.2d 1209 (Ct. App. 1988).

[15]   E.g., Rodrigue v. Copeland, 475 So.2d 1071 (La. 1985) (Christmas display drawing heavy traffic). A condition of purely natural origin cannot be a nuisance, under the traditional common-law rule. Belhumeur v. Zilm, 157 N.H. 233, 949 A.2d 162 (2008) (wild bees in tree; citing numerous cases from other states).

[16]   E.g., Bowers v. Westvaco Corp., 244 Va. 139, 419 S.E.2d 661 (1992) (continual loading and moving of trucks a few feet from the plaintiff's house).

[17]   E.g., a lessee, Nichols v. Mid-Continent Pipe Line Co., 933 P.2d 272 (Okla. 1996); but not a mortgagee, Stevensen v. Goodson, 924 P.2d 339 (Utah 1996).

[18]   Restatement Second of Torts § 821D (1979).

compensation.[19] What the plaintiff can reasonably be expected to bear is often determined by the character of the neighborhood, but the utility of the defendant's activity is also relevant.[20] The interference may cause tangible harm to the land, diminution in its market value, or personal discomfort to its occupants. The interference must be one that would interfere with the normal use and enjoyment of a normal person; the interference is not a nuisance if it interferes only with especially sensitive persons or uses.[21] Proof that the nuisance has resulted in a diminution of the land's market value shows or tends to show that the harm is not merely the result of the plaintiff's sensitivity, since loss of market value necessarily means that potential buyers would also be affected by the nuisance. If a nuisance exists, the defendant is subject to liability only if he intentionally interfered with the plaintiff's use and enjoyment interests, or did so by engaging in strict liability activities, or by conduct that was negligent.

Examples. The issue of nuisance often arises because the defendant's activity causes pollution of air, water, or land by dust or smoke,[22] odors,[23] chemicals,[24] or noise.[25] Heavy traffic in a neighborhood[26] or an intense light shone directly into the plaintiff's bedroom might constitute a nuisance.[27] If the defendant's electromagnetic radiation[28] or stray voltage[29] invades the land, it is a nuisance if it is a tort at all.[30]

Distinguishing trespass: possession vs. enjoyment. A person who enters another's land may be a trespasser, and liable for interference with the landowner's right to possession, even if the land is not harmed.[31] But if the invasion is accomplished with noxious odors or electromagnetic radiation, there is no trespass claim under traditional law, because there is no interference with possession. Instead, liability in such cases is for nuisance, which protects the landowner's interest in the use and enjoyment of the

---

[19] Usually put in short form: the interference must be substantial and unreasonable. E.g., San Diego Gas & Elec. Co. v. Superior Court, 13 Cal.4th 893, 920 P.2d 669, 55 Cal.Rptr.2d 724 (1996); Sowers v. Forest Hills Subdivision, 294 P.3d 427 (Nev. 2013). Nuisance does not, however, require unreasonable actions by the defendant, only that the plaintiff cannot reasonably be expected to bear the harm.

[20] See § 30.4.

[21] Simpson v. Kollasch, 749 N.W.2d 671 (Iowa 2008) (employing a "normal person" standard for whether a nuisance involving personal discomfort or annoyance is significant enough to constitute nuisance); Amphitheaters, Inc. v. Portland Meadows, 184 Or. 336, 198 P.2d 847, 5 A.L.R.2d 690 (1948) (lights from race track interfered with drive-in movie by casting glow on the screen, but outdoor movie represented an abnormally sensitive use, thus no recovery).

[22] Boomer v. Atlantic Cement Co., 26 N.Y.2d 219, 309 N.Y.S.2d 312, 257 N.E.2d 870, 40 A.L.R.3d 590 (1970) (cement dust, remedy limited to damages, however); Smith v. Wallowa County, 145 Or.App. 341, 929 P.2d 1100 (1996) (smoke, dust, odors).

[23] Penland v. Redwood Sanitary Sewer Serv. Dist., 156 Or.App. 311, 965 P.2d 433 (1998).

[24] Scribner v. Summers, 84 F.3d 554 (2d Cir. 1996) (barium); Mel Foster Co. Properties, Inc. v. American Oil Co., 427 N.W.2d 171 (Iowa 1988) (gasoline); Taygeta Corp. v. Varian Assocs., Inc., 436 Mass. 217, 763 N.E.2d 1053 (2002) (untreated chemical waste).

[25] E.g., Rose v. Chaikin, 187 N.J.Super. 210, 453 A.2d 1378, 36 A.L.R.4th 1148 (1982); Mandel v. Geloso, 206 A.D.2d 699, 614 N.Y.S.2d 645 (1994).

[26] Rodrigue v. Copeland, 475 So.2d 1071 (La. 1985).

[27] Green v. Spinning, 48 S.W.2d 51 (Mo. App. 1932).

[28] San Diego Gas & Elec. Co. v. Superior Court, 13 Cal.4th 893, 920 P.2d 669, 55 Cal.Rptr.2d 724 (1996) (common law claim could not be pursued because of regulation of administrative agency).

[29] Vogel v. Grant-Lafayette Elec. Co-op., 201 Wis.2d 416, 548 N.W.2d 829 (1996).

[30] See Kuper v. Lincoln-Union Elec. Co., 557 N.W.2d 748 (S.D. 1996) (stray voltage of a public utility is not a nuisance in the absence of negligence).

[31] See §§ 5.1 & 5.8.

property.[32] Some contemporary cases have been impatient with these distinctions between visible and invisible interferences, and have treated some invasions by polluting particles as micro-trespasses that invade possessory rights.[33] At the same time, they have sometimes used the word *trespass* to describe the tort but have then proceeded to apply at least some of the rules of nuisance.[34]

The significant point, however, is that the terms *trespass* and *nuisance* stand for two different approaches to handling interference with rights in land. To say the case is for trespass is to declare that the rights of the plaintiff landowner brook no interference, not even a little, not even if it is reasonable, not even if it does no physical harm. To say that the case is for nuisance is to insist that with some kinds of interference, liability must be limited not only to cases of actual harm but also to cases in which the harm is unreasonable. The question of where to draw the line between these two regimes is perhaps less important than the realization that courts can consciously adopt one set of rules or the other as the facts demand. The two torts may overlap on some facts.[35]

§ 30.3   Intent, Negligence and Strict Liability

Contemporary cases say a nuisance is actionable only if the defendant creates the nuisance either by strict liability activity, by negligence, or by intentional interference with the plaintiff's enjoyment interests.[36] That being so, the law of private nuisance could be radically restated as liability for substantial and unreasonable interference with the plaintiff's use and enjoyment of her land by negligent or intentional interference, or, more rarely, by strict liability activities.

Negligence. Insofar as a supposed nuisance rests upon proof of the defendant's negligence, the case proceeds largely as would any other negligence case, and the nuisance label adds little or nothing to the analysis.[37] For example, courts have said repeatedly that when the defendant's negligent conduct is the basis for liability in nuisance, the plaintiff's contributory or comparative fault is a defense as in other

---

[32]   Pub. Serv. Co. of Colo. v. Van Wyk, 27 P.3d 377 (Colo. 2001); Adams v. Cleveland-Cliffs Iron Co., 237 Mich. App. 51, 602 N.W.2d 215 (1999).

[33]   Bradley v. American Smelting & Refining Co., 104 Wash.2d 677, 709 P.2d 782 (1985). Other courts have refused to find a trespass "[w]hen particles enter the ambient environment without any demonstrated impact on the land." Larkin v. Marceau, 184 Vt. 207, 959 A.2d 551 (2008) (pesticides sprayed in orchard).

[34]   See Borland v. Sanders Lead Co., Inc., 369 So.2d 523, 2 A.L.R.4th 1042 (Ala. 1979) (invasion of possessory interest is not determined by size of particles, but actual damages must be proven if the trespass is with microscopic particles); Martin v. Reynolds Metals Co., 221 Or. 86, 342 P.2d 790 (1959) (treating microscopic particles as trespass but excluding liability when the harm is *de minimis*); Bradley v. American Smelting & Refining Co., 104 Wash.2d 677, 709 P.2d 782 (1985) (requiring "actual and substantial" damages); but see Stevenson v. E.I. DuPont de Nemours & Co., 327 F.3d 400 (5th Cir. 2003) (under Texas law, the deposit of airborne particulates from the defendant's plant would constitute a trespass to land and the plaintiff would *not* be required to prove substantial damages).

[35]   See Restatement Second of Torts § 821D, cmt. e (1979). But that only means that in some cases courts will allow the plaintiff to have the advantage of the more favorable rules, usually the rules of the trespass regime. The problem of tree branches overhanging the plaintiff's land is a good example. If treated as a trespass, the plaintiff could sue for trivial and even desirable intrusions of foliage or roots. If treated as a problem in nuisance law, the plaintiff would be limited to self-help remedies unless the incursions substantially reduced reasonable use and enjoyment of the plaintiff's land. See §§ 5.6 & 5.7; Fancher v. Fagella, 274 Va. 549, 650 S.E.2d 519 (2007).

[36]   Restatement Second of Torts § 822 (1979).

[37]   See Hocking v. City of Dodgeville, 768 N.W.2d 552 (Wisc. 2009) (analyzing nuisance suit under state's ordinary negligence factors); Milwaukee Metro. Sewerage Dist. v. City of Milwaukee, 277 Wis.2d 635, 648, 691 N.W.2d 658, 665 (2005) ("when a nuisance is predicated on negligence, all the usual rules and defenses applicable to negligence claims apply").

negligence cases.[38] Similarly, compliance with regulations and standards, though not a defense in itself, may be some evidence that the defendant's conduct would not be a nuisance.[39] To put it bluntly, a nuisance claim based on negligence is merely a negligence claim with harm to interests in use and enjoyment. When a public entity creates a nuisance, some courts will reject common law immunities and subject the entity to liability.[40] However, because a nuisance claim based on negligent acts is merely a claim of negligence that causes loss of use and enjoyment of land, the logical result is that immunity depends on whether the defendant's negligent acts called for immunity, not on the nuisance label itself. Thus if a city negligently creates a nuisance but its negligent acts are discretionary, it would enjoy the discretionary immunity.[41] Of course, to the extent that the conduct exceeds the city's immunity, suit will be permitted.[42] Finally, to find a nuisance is to say that the plaintiff can recover for loss of enjoyment, a kind of chronic emotional harm that might be viewed more cautiously if no nuisance is established.[43]

Strict liability. One unusual form of strict liability appears when the landowner is held responsible for abating a nuisance on his land that was created by someone else.[44] In some such cases, the landowner may be at fault, but his fault is not necessarily a requirement, provided abatement is actually feasible. Except for this kind of vicarious responsibility, the Restatement rule imposes strict liability only if the plaintiff can show that the defendant maintained or pursued an abnormally dangerous condition or activity.[45] This view finds support in the cases that deny liability when the defendant unintentionally discharges fumes or the like on a single occasion without knowing of the harm until after it has occurred. If the fumes are not regarded as abnormally dangerous, many such cases require the plaintiff to prove negligence.[46] Some thinkers believe that some strict liability should be imposed more broadly, even when the defendant's activity is not abnormally dangerous,[47] and some cases have stated the same view.[48] Although it does not impose strict liability for a single, unintended escape of substances that are not abnormally dangerous, the Restatement does impose liability upon reasonable and careful defendants who repeatedly or continuously discharge substances that deprive the plaintiff of her rights of use and enjoyment, on a theory of intentional invasion.

---

[38]　See Copart Indus., Inc. v. Consolidated Edison Co. of New York, Inc., 41 N.Y.2d 564, 362 N.E.2d 968, 394 N.Y.S.2d 169 (1977); Vogel v. Grant-Lafayette Elec. Coop., 201 Wis.2d 416, 548 N.W.2d 829 (1996); Restatement Second of Torts § 840B(1) (1979). Coming to the nuisance, though not usually a matter of contributory fault, may defeat the plaintiff for other reasons. See § 30.4.

[39]　Simpson v. Kollasch, 749 N.W.2d 671 (Iowa 2008).

[40]　See § 22.7.

[41]　City of Atlanta v. Kleber, 285 Ga. 413, 677 S.E.2d 134 (2009); Tucci v. District of Columbia, 956 A.2d 684 (D.C. 2008); Milwaukee Metro. Sewerage Dist. v. City of Milwaukee, 277 Wis.2d 635, 691 N.W.2d 658 (2005).

[42]　Tarbell Administrator, Inc. v. City of Concord, 157 N.H. 679, 956 A.2d 322 (2008).

[43]　See § 29.9 (reflecting limitations on emotional harm recoveries).

[44]　New York v. Shore Realty Corp., 759 F.2d 1032 (2d Cir. 1985); Nassr v. Commonwealth, 394 Mass. 767, 477 N.E.2d 987 (1985); Restatement Second of Torts § 839 (1979).

[45]　Restatement Second of Torts § 822 (1979). As to strict liability for abnormal danger, see § 32.6.

[46]　E.g., Wright v. Masonite Corp., 368 F.2d 661 (4th Cir. 1966); Waschak v. Moffat, 379 Pa. 441, 109 A.2d 310 (1954); see William K. Jones, Strict Liability for Hazardous Enterprise, 92 Colum. L. Rev. 1705, 1737 (1992).

[47]　See Robert E. Keeton, Restating Strict Liability and Nuisance, 48 Vand. L. Rev. 595 (1995).

[48]　Washington Suburban Sanitary Comm'n v. CAE-Link Corp., 330 Md. 115, 622 A.2d 745 (1993).

Intent and strict-liability effects. The defendant intends the invasion not only when he has a purpose to invade the plaintiff's land, but also when he is substantially certain that his activities will cause such an invasion.[49] The defendant who attracts indigents to a neighborhood and knows that they continuously invade the neighbors' rights is responsible for the nuisance he has fostered, though his own acts and motives are entirely praiseworthy.[50] An industrial nuisance might begin innocently, but once the defendant is apprised of its effect upon the plaintiff's use and enjoyment, it is intentional if the defendant continues the harmful condition. In such cases, the fact that the defendant exercises care or uses the best technology available does not relieve him of responsibility for activity that unreasonably invades the plaintiff's rights to use and enjoy her land.[51] Although the industrial nuisance can be regarded as an intentional invasion, it works as a soft version of strict liability because even extraordinary care by the defendant does not defeat the claim. It may be, however, that social utility of the defendant's activity and its economic value to the community will protect the defendant from a damages award[52] or an injunction.[53]

§ 30.4 Substantial and Unreasonable Interference

The invasion that affects the plaintiff's use and enjoyment must be unreasonable as well as substantial. "Unreasonable" in nuisance law is not like "unreasonable" in the law of negligence, for it does not refer to risk-creating conduct of the defendant but to the reasonable expectations of a normal person occupying the plaintiff's land. Reasonable expectations must take into account the fact that others, too, have the right to use their land. For this reason, even an intentional invasion is not necessarily a nuisance. The defendant may know that the noise of his church bells or the smells of his baking bread invade the plaintiff's land and are offensive to the plaintiff, but the invasion would seldom be unreasonable.[54] Similarly, the fact that the defendant's activity diminishes the value of the plaintiff's land does not necessarily show that the defendant's activity is a nuisance. In a neighborhood of mansions, a small home may diminish the value of the large homes nearby, but a small home is not in itself a nuisance. What is unreasonable depends upon a number of considerations discussed below.

Character of the neighborhood or social expectations. In the absence of physical harm to the plaintiff's land or person or prohibited activity such as toxic dumping, courts almost always consider, directly or indirectly, the character, custom, and culture of the neighborhood or community in determining whether the defendant's legal activities cause unreasonable and substantial harm and thus count as a nuisance.[55] The obligatory

---

[49] Copart Indus., Inc. v. Consolidated Edison Co. of New York, Inc., 41 N.Y.2d 564, 362 N.E.2d 968, 394 N.Y.S.2d 169 (1977); Jost v. Dairyland Power Coop., 45 Wis.2d 164, 172 N.W.2d 647 (1970); Restatement Second of Torts § 825 (1979).

[50] Armory Park Neighborhood Ass'n v. Episcopal Community Services in Arizona, 148 Ariz. 1, 712 P.2d 914 (1985).

[51] Parker v. Barefoot, 519 S.E.2d 315 (N.C. 1999).

[52] See § 30.4.

[53] See § 30.7.

[54] See Langan v. Bellinger, 203 A.D.2d 857, 611 N.Y.S.2d 59 (1994) (church bells liked by some neighbors were not a nuisance).

[55] See, e.g., Weinhold v. Wolff, 555 N.W.2d 454 (Iowa 1996) (location a major factor); Clinic & Hospital v. McConnell, 241 Mo.App. 223, 236 S.W.2d 384 (1951) (noise exceeding level of neighborhood); Robie v. Lillis, 112 N.H. 492, 299 A.2d 155 (1972) (incompatible with the surrounding neighborhood). In many instances, the character of the neighborhood or locality is a way of summarizing the kinds of reciprocal harms that are

observation is that a nuisance may be the right thing in the wrong place, like a pig in the parlor instead of the barnyard.[56] Noise, odors, or sights that are consistent in nature and extent with the neighborhood's legitimate use patterns are seldom if ever a nuisance, but the same invasions are likely to be nuisances if they are out of character with the neighborhood.[57] A factory in a residential district may well be a nuisance, but a factory in the factory district operating like others usually is not. In line with this, the fact that the defendant is in compliance with a zoning ordinance, although not ordinarily conclusive, is at least a relevant factor in determining a nuisance.[58] Environmental justice advocates might argue that the emphasis on the neighborhood's character tends to distribute environmental burdens unfairly to neighborhoods that are already carrying more than their fair share of pollution.[59] This may suggest that courts will need to work out responsibility for cumulative pollution, but it is also true that a defendant could be held liable under present rules if he causes more harm than is reasonably expected in the neighborhood.

Magnitude, frequency, or duration exceeding neighborhood norms. The defendant's use of his land may be broadly consistent with the uses to which the neighborhood is dedicated, yet because of its magnitude, frequency, or duration, the use may be a nuisance.[60] For example, pigs are part of rural life, but an excessive concentration of them in a small area with inadequate drainage and ventilation may produce a stench that is unbearable and unreasonable even in a farming community.[61] The same is true with the frequency of invasions; an occasional invasion may be tolerated as reasonable and within neighborhood norms but continuous, repeated, or frequent invasions may not be.[62] An understanding of the neighborhood character, customs, and values suffices to determine whether the odor is a nuisance. Even if the defendant's activity has high social

---

acceptable; so long as neighbors impose similar harms upon each other, there is no nuisance. See Bamford v. Turnely, 3 B & S 66, 122 Eng.Rep. 25 (Exch. Ch. 1862) (Judgment of Bramwell, B.).

[56] Village of Euclid, Ohio v. Ambler Realty Co., 272 U.S. 365, 388, 47 S.Ct. 114, 118, 71 L.Ed. 303, 54 A.L.R. 1016 (1926).

[57] E.g., Sowers v. Forest Hills Subdivision, 294 P.3d 427 (Nev. 2013) (proposed wind turbine in a residential area would be a nuisance in fact because of noise, shadow flicker and aesthetic impact; these problems far outweigh any potential utility of the turbine); Burch v. Nedpower Mount Storm, LLC, 220 W.Va. 443, 647 S.E.2d 879 (2007) (wind-power electric generating facility a nuisance because of proximity to residential district, given its "unusual and recurring noise").

[58] E.g., Prah v. Maretti, 108 Wis.2d 223, 321 N.W.2d 182 (1982); Trickett v. Ochs, 176 Vt. 89, 838 A.2d 66 (2003). A California statute requires a finding of unreasonable operation before an industry can be found a nuisance while operating in an expressly permitted zone. Cal. Code Civ. Proc. § 731a. Federal preemption may in effect immunize activities that are in compliance with federal law. See Rushing v. Kansas City Southern Ry. Co., 185 F.3d 496 (5th Cir. 1999) (no nuisance liability for railroad noise levels that do not violate federal standards), *superseded by statute on other grounds*, Mathis v. Exxon Corp., 302 F.3d 448 (5th Cir. 2002).

[59] See Kathy Seward Northern, Battery and Beyond: A Tort Law Response to Environmental Racism, 21 Wm. & Mary Envtl. L. & Pol'y Rev. 485 (1997).

[60] Clinic & Hospital v. McConnell, 241 Mo.App. 223, 236 S.W.2d 384 (1951) ("alleged music" on loudspeaker in business district); Trickett v. Ochs, 176 Vt. 89, 838 A.2d 66 (2003).

[61] Weinhold v. Wolff, 555 N.W.2d 454 (Iowa 1996). Right to farm laws may jeopardize this example as well as the environment generally. See Neil D. Hamilton, Right-to-Farm Laws Reconsidered: Ten Reasons Why Legislative Efforts to Resolve Agricultural Nuisances May Be Ineffective, 3 Drake J. Agric. L. 103 (1998).

[62] See, e.g., Rose v. Chaikin, 187 N.J.Super. 210, 453 A.2d 1378, 36 A.L.R.4th 1148 (1982) (constant noise of windmill in quiet residential neighborhood); Penland v. Redwood Sanitary Sewer Serv. Dist., 156 Or.App. 311, 965 P.2d 433 (1998).

utility and is well-intended, there are some invasions the landowner should not be required to bear.[63]

Priority in time. Courts resolving nuisance disputes consider priority in time as an important factor. The defendant who moves hog production to an established residential neighborhood will need mighty justifications to escape liability. In the reverse situation, when a plaintiff moves her residence to a neighborhood of nonresidential uses such as small factories, the nonresidential uses are not often a nuisance.[64] Prior use in that case has stamped the neighborhood with its character, so that the residents must reasonably expect the kind of factory operations that were present when the residents chose to move in. A second reason for denying relief to one who "came to the nuisance" is that the price the plaintiff paid for the land reflects factory-neighborhood prices, not upscale suburban prices. She has, in a sense, already been paid for the inconvenience she may suffer because that inconvenience is reflected in the reduced purchase price.

Limits on coming to the nuisance rules. Such conclusions are not inevitable, however.[65] First, the factory may substantially change its operation to make it more detrimental, as where a factory begins operating at night after the plaintiff moves to the neighborhood. Second, the factory may accidentally discharge toxic materials that cause personal injury distinct from any nuisance. Liability in that case will turn on ordinary rules of negligence or strict liability. Third, the first landowner to arrive upon the scene should not be permitted to rule out all other uses, in effect unilaterally zoning his neighbor's land for the uses he has adopted on his own. In a dynamic country, a certain amount of change must be expected in many communities and neighborhoods. In one famous case,[66] suburban developments expanded outward until they came close to a cattle feed lot that produced large amounts of manure and attracted flies to the neighborhood. Although the feed lot was there first, the growth of cities must be expected and permitted, so the feed lot was a nuisance in spite of its priority.

Gravity of harm. Character of the neighborhood does not always cast direct light upon the nuisance issue. When the nuisance is invasive and seriously affects the land's physical integrity, as where toxic chemicals contaminate the groundwater, it may be a nuisance as a matter of law, without regard to the neighborhood's character.[67] In many instances, the gravity has been weighed by legislators and administrators under federal or state environmental laws. Statutes or regulations may thus establish that the defendant's chemical pollution is a nuisance or may create a claim independent of common law nuisance. Courts may also consider gravity of harm in determining whether the harms caused by the defendant's activity go beyond those sanctioned by

---

[63]   Jost v. Dairyland Power Cooperative, 45 Wis.2d 164, 172 N.W.2d 647 (1970); see Robert E. Keeton, Restating Strict Liability and Nuisance, 48 Vand. L. Rev. 595 (1995); Restatement Second of Torts § 826(b) (1979) (if the harm is serious and compensation is feasible).

[64]   See Erbrich Products Co., Inc. v. Wills, 509 N.E.2d 850 (Ind. App. 1987) (statutory version of coming-to-nuisance rule).

[65]   Mark v. State ex rel. Dep't of Fish and Wildlife, 191 Or. App. 563, 84 P.3d 155 (2004) (coming to the nuisance did not apply to purchasers of property adjacent to nude beach where they lacked constructive knowledge of land use).

[66]   Spur Industries, Inc. v. Del E. Webb Development Co., 108 Ariz. 178, 494 P.2d 700, 53 A.L.R.3d 861 (1972). Cf. LeRoy Fibre Co. v. Chicago, Milwaukee & St. Paul Ry. Co., 232 U.S. 340, 34 S.Ct. 415, 58 L.Ed. 631 (1914) (railroad was present first, but that did not immunize it from liability to adjacent landowner who stored inflammable flax on his own property near the track).

[67]   E.g., New York v. Shore Realty Corp., 759 F.2d 1032 (2d Cir. 1985).

neighborhood usage, as in the case of excessive odors from a hog farm in a rural area.[68] Courts may well hinge a finding of nuisance on the fact that the defendant's activity creates a physical threat to people on adjoining properties.[69]

Lack of utility of defendant's activity. If the defendant's activity is conducted at an inappropriate location[70] or causes harm that is reasonably avoidable,[71] it can count as a nuisance regardless of its social utility. Even when the defendant's land use is properly conducted and at a proper location, however, the fact that it has little or no social utility compared to the harm it causes classes the activity as a nuisance.[72] That is the case of malicious nuisances such as "spite fences" erected solely to obstruct the plaintiff's view.[73]

Discounting the utility of defendant's activity. The more-debated question deals with the converse situation, when the defendant's socially useful activity causes harm that cannot be eliminated by reasonable care. Should the utility or social value of the activity relieve the defendant of liability? When the harm is severe, the Restatement says not.[74] An important body of opinion supports that view.[75] To find a nuisance even when the social utility of the activity outweighs the harm, courts must first find that the activity would count as a nuisance if its utility is disregarded.[76] The Restatement and some cases imply that the defendant must be able to capture enough of the activity's utility (in profits) to pay damages without going out of business,[77] but even if the defendant's activity is a charity or conducted in the public interest and not for profit, its social utility will not necessarily be enough to justify the harm it causes.[78] The remedy of injunction is a different matter, however; while the useful nuisance may subject the defendant to damages, courts may require payment of damages and allow it to continue.[79]

Counting social utility. In spite of what has just been said, the social utility of the defendant's activity is important at least in the sense that if the activity is useful to the community or to society, the plaintiff might reasonably expect to put up with more annoyance.[80] Consequently, courts as well as the Restatement do attempt to consider the

[68]   Weinhold v. Wolff, 555 N.W.2d 454 (Iowa 1996).

[69]   See, e.g., Aviation Cadet Museum v. Hammer, 373 Ark. 202, 283 S.W.3d 198 (2008) (private airport operated so that low-flying planes posed a risk of serious accidents to people on neighboring properties).

[70]   Restatement Second of Torts §§ 828 & 831 (1979).

[71]   Highview North Apartments v. County of Ramsey, 323 N.W.2d 65 (Minn. 1982) (socially useful sewer system could have been placed to avoid sewage backup harming the plaintiff); Restatement Second of Torts §§ 828 & 830 (1979).

[72]   See Restatement Second of Torts § 829A (1979).

[73]   See Tarlton v. Kaufman, 348 Mont. 178, 199 P.3d 263 (2008); Welsh v. Todd, 260 N.C. 527, 133 S.E.2d 171 (1963). In some states, spite fences are proscribed by statute. Alberino v. Balch, 969 A.2d 61 (Vt. 2008).

[74]   Restatement Second of Torts § 829A (as read with § 826).

[75]   See Jost v. Dairyland Power Cooperative, 45 Wis.2d 164, 172 N.W.2d 647 (1970); Bamford v. Turnley, 3 B & S 66, 122 Eng.Rep. 25 (Exch. Ch. 1862) (Judgment of Bramwell, B.); Restatement Second of Torts §§ 826 (b) & 829 (1979).

[76]   Thus, courts have found no nuisance at all when an industry without negligence accidentally emits a noxious gas on a single occasion and the gas is not abnormally dangerous. See § 30.3.

[77]   Restatement Second of Torts § 826(b) (1979).

[78]   See Armory Park Neighborhood Ass'n v. Episcopal Community Services in Arizona, 148 Ariz. 1, 712 P.2d 914 (1985) (church organization provided free meals to indigents, whose misbehavior became a nuisance to residents); Rose v. Chaikin, 187 N.J.Super. 210, 453 A.2d 1378, 36 A.L.R.4th 1148 (1982) (windmill).

[79]   See § 30.7.

[80]   See Fleming James, Jr., Memorandum: The Element of Fault in Private Nuisance, Appendix, Restatement Second of Torts Tentative Draft No. 16 at 132, 140–141 (1970).

usefulness of the defendant's activity.[81] But the weighing of social utilities does not mean that a plaintiff with a low-value residence will always lose her claim against a defendant whose factory has great economic importance. On the contrary, the high value of the defendant's operation may suggest that the factory should pay damages or buy the plaintiff's property. Beyond this, it is now apparent that the cost of cleaning up toxic wastes produced by some industries is astronomical; so high, in fact, that courts may well be uncertain that a given industry's social value exceeds the harm it causes.

§ 30.5 Non-Invasive Nuisances

The Restatement speaks of private nuisances as "invasions."[82] Courts often speak of nuisances as "interferences."[83] Most private nuisances in fact involve invasion of the plaintiff's land by matter, sound, or light. For example, a light shone upon the plaintiff's property is an invasion that may count as a nuisance.[84] A plume of contamination deep under the plaintiff's land is an invasion, and if permanent and serious enough, can count as a nuisance, even though the landowner cannot directly perceive it and is harmed only because the value of her land is reduced by its presence.[85] In some cases, however, the plaintiff's discomfort arises because light or air is blocked by the defendant's structures, or because the defendant's activities are aesthetically repugnant, or because they generate fear of future harm without any invasion at all. Plaintiffs have fared less well in such cases unless the defendant acts with "malice."

Blocking light, air, view, or other amenities. When the defendant erects a useful structure on his own land, the plaintiff will seldom be able to show a nuisance merely because her view or air is blocked.[86] However, when the defendant's structure interferes with the plaintiff's view, light, or air for no purpose useful either to others or to the defendant himself, many courts have been willing to find a nuisance.[87] Similarly, the defendant who intentionally scares game or uses his own land to fence game off the plaintiff's hunting lands may be subjected to liability.[88]

Aesthetic nuisances. The unsightliness of the defendant's property may be considered in balancing the rights of the parties.[89] But because tastes differ and criteria for aesthetic judgment are deemed unreliable, courts have been reluctant to say that an inappropriate and ugly sight can be a nuisance.[90] So when the one neighbor mounted a

---

[81] See Monks v. City of Rancho Palos Verdes, 167 Cal.App.4th 263, 84 Cal.Rptr.3d 75 (2008) ("The primary test for determining whether the invasion is unreasonable is whether the gravity of harm outweighs the social utility of the defendant's conduct."); Carpenter v. Double R Cattle Co., Inc., 108 Idaho 602, 701 P.2d 222 (1985); Lakey v. Puget Sound Energy, Inc., 176 Wash.2d 909, 296 P.3d 860 (2013).

[82] Restatement Second of Torts § 822 (1979).

[83] E.g., Robie v. Lillis, 112 N.H. 492, 299 A.2d 155 (1972).

[84] Green v. Spinning, 48 S.W.2d 51(Mo. App. 1932); Firth v. Scherzberg, 366 Pa. 443, 77 A.2d 443 (1951) (noise and lights at night); cf. Golen v. Union Corp., U.C.O.-M.B.A., Inc., 718 A.2d 298 (Pa. Super. 1998) (light not invasive but could be a nuisance because it could be seen by a person on the land).

[85] Bradley v. Armstrong Rubber Co., 130 F.3d 168 (5th Cir. 1997).

[86] Tarlton v. Kaufman, 348 Mont. 178, 199 P.3d 263 (2008) (fence); see also Thomas R. Trenkner, Annotation, Zoning Regulations Prohibiting or Limiting Fences, Hedges, or Walls, 1 A.L.R.4th 373 (1981).

[87] Sundowner, Inc. v. King, 95 Idaho 367, 509 P.2d 785 (1973) (listing many authorities); Welsh v. Todd, 260 N.C. 527, 133 S.E.2d 171 (1963).

[88] See Suprise v. Dekock, 84 S.W.3d 378 (Tex. App. 2002).

[89] Robie v. Lillis, 112 N.H. 492, 299 A.2d 155 (1972).

[90] Tarlton v. Kaufman, 348 Mont. 178, 199 P.3d 263 (2008) (allegedly unsightly fence); see Raymond Robert Coletta, The Case for Aesthetic Nuisance: Rethinking Traditional Judicial Attitudes, 48 Ohio St. L.J. 141 (1987).

toilet "seat and its lid on a piece of plywood placed atop a post overlooking his neighbors' land" with a brown spot alleged by the plaintiff to represent human excrement, the victim of this continuing visual assault had no right to abate the nuisance.[91] Vagaries of taste do indeed make it difficult to pass judgment upon outdoor sculptures and architectural disasters, but neighborhood character may permit a court to say with confidence that a front yard full of junked autos[92] or a mortuary[93] can constitute a nuisance where it is wholly inconsistent with the neighborhood's character, even though its impact derives solely from visual perception and distaste.

Recovery for nuisances creating anticipated harm without invasion. Many activities outside the land that threaten future harm are non-invasive.[94] Some cases have been willing to impose liability, as when the defendant's building threatens to harm the plaintiff's nearby building through increased snow-load,[95] when the defendant's stored explosives create a reasonable fear and depreciate the value of the plaintiff's property,[96] when toxic materials contaminate a general area or nearby land,[97] and when a halfway house in a residential neighborhood presents a serious danger that convicted felons on early release will cause harm.[98] When a degree of invasion can be found, the plaintiff may be able to recover parasitically for the accompanying fear, as where the noise of automatic weapon fire next door is itself invasive and also creates anticipation of harm.[99] In addition, contamination of the defendant's land may count as a public nuisance that can be abated by public action even though none of the hazardous materials have escaped.[100]

Denying recovery for anticipated harm without invasion. But many recent cases have denied recovery for conditions that diminish the plaintiff's property value but do not physically invade or physically harm the property. It should go without saying that if the defendant's waste is not the cause of the contamination complained of, the plaintiff's loss in property value is not the defendant's responsibility,[101] but a number of decisions have gone far beyond this by refusing to treat fear-creating activities as a nuisance in the absence of an actual invasion upon the land or physical harm to it. Some have done so even when the activity actually causes depreciation in the plaintiff's land value, so-called stigma damages.[102] Some other opinions, mostly in toxic pollution cases, have asserted broadly that a nuisance exists only when there is an invasion that is

[91] Wernke v. Halas, 600 N.E.2d 117 (Ind. App. 1992).

[92] Foley v. Harris, 223 Va. 20, 286 S.E.2d 186 (1982).

[93] Mitchell v. Bearden, 255 Ark. 888, 503 S.W.2d 904 (1974).

[94] See, e.g., Simpson v. Kollasch, 749 N.W.2d 671 (Iowa 2008).

[95] Omega Chemical Co., Inc. v. United Seeds, Inc., 252 Neb. 137, 560 N.W.2d 820 (1997).

[96] Cumberland Torpedo Co. v. Gaines, 201 Ky. 88, 255 S.W. 1046 (1923) (depreciation of value due to fear, not fear itself, is the basis); Comminge v. Stevenson, 76 Tex. 642, 13 S.W. 556 (1890). Most of the explosives storage cases, however, involve an actual explosion.

[97] Gray v. Westinghouse Elec. Corp., 624 N.E.2d 49 (Ind. App. 1993) (PCBs in adjacent landfill); Allen v. Uni-First Corp., 151 Vt. 229, 558 A.2d 961 (1988).

[98] Arkansas Release Guidance Foundation v. Needler, 252 Ark. 194, 477 S.W.2d 821 (1972).

[99] Cf. Kolstad v. Rankin, 179 Ill.App.3d 1022, 534 N.E.2d 1373, 128 Ill.Dec. 768 (1989) (preliminary injunction issued, to be modified as to scope).

[100] See New York v. Shore Realty Corp., 759 F.2d 1032 (2d Cir. 1985); on public nuisances, § 30.6.

[101] Anglado v. Leaf River Forest Products, Inc., 716 So.2d 543 (Miss. 1998) (rejecting stigma damages where defendant did not produce the contaminating dioxin).

[102] Adkins v. Thomas Solvent Co., 440 Mich. 293, 487 N.W.2d 715 (1992). Perhaps similar thinking has prompted some other decisions that have refused claims of "stigma" damages without clearly stating reasons. See, e.g., Chance v. BP Chemicals, 77 Ohio St.3d 17, 670 N.E.2d 985 (1996).

harmful to the land or its occupants, or at least is perceptible to one on the land.[103] Variations on the theme assert that fear of future harm cannot count as a nuisance[104] and that no nuisance can exist when the land is wholly unmarketable because of adjacent deadly contamination, so long as the plaintiff can actually use the land.[105] Ironically, courts may impose upon the victimized homeowner a duty to reveal the pollution or danger when she attempts to sell to another,[106] thus guaranteeing that the homeowner will realize the loss in market value.

§ 30.6 Public Nuisance

Definitions. A public nuisance, as distinct from a private nuisance, is a substantial and unreasonable interference with a right held in common by the general public, in use of public facilities, in health, safety, and convenience.[107] A wide range of specific activities has been declared to be a public nuisance by criminal statutes. However, in certain cases it may be a matter of statutory interpretation whether the legislature meant not only to prohibit a particular activity but also to provide for a public nuisance action against it.[108] To count as a public nuisance, the condition for which the defendant is responsible[109] must in some way invade a public right. If citizens have a right to store firearms in their homes, for example, then such storage does not invade a public right.[110]

Public-entity suits. A public nuisance may be abated or enjoined by public authorities, even if it is not specifically declared to be a nuisance or a crime by statute.[111] Public as well as private nuisance theories may supplement environmental statutes as a tool for dealing with hazardous wastes and other environmental contaminations.[112] Much of public nuisance law arises in the context of public litigation or in suits about public regulatory activity and its limits.[113] Conditions created by a tortfeasor may require public entities to expend monies for added police, fire, health, or other public services. Although a public entity may be entitled to abate a nuisance and to recover the

---

[103] See Adams v. Star Enterprise, 51 F.3d 417 (4th Cir. 1995); Wilson v. Amoco Corp., 33 F.Supp.2d 981 (D. Wyo. 1998); In re Chicago Flood Litigation, 176 Ill.2d 179, 205, 680 N.E.2d 265, 278, 223 Ill.Dec. 532, 545 (1997).

[104] Koll-Irvine Center Property Owners Ass'n v. County of Orange, 24 Cal.App.4th 1036, 29 Cal.Rptr.2d 664 (1994).

[105] Golen v. Union Corp., U.C.O.-M.B.A., Inc., 718 A.2d 298 (Pa. Super. 1998).

[106] Reed v. King, 145 Cal.App.3d 261, 193 Cal.Rptr. 130 (1983) (home seller required to disclose fact that multiple murders were committed in the house); Strawn v. Canuso, 140 N.J. 43, 657 A.2d 420, 41 A.L.R.5th 859 (1995) (seller must disclose existence of nearby landfill that may affect land's market value).

[107] Restatement Second of Torts § 821B (1979). Sometimes courts emphasize that a public nuisance interferes with the rights of a sizeable number of persons, a formula that may lose the idea of a public right.

[108] See City of New York v. Smokes-Spirits.com, 12 N.Y.3d 616, 911 N.E.2d 834, 883 N.Y.S.2d 772 (2009) (statute barring direct shipment of cigarettes to consumers did not authorize the city to bring a public nuisance claim, at least where the nuisance claim alleged tax evasion rather than harm to public health).

[109] See Sholberg v. Truman, 496 Mich. 1, 852 N.W.2d 89 (2014) (nonpossessory title owners not liable for public nuisance, where they were not in control of the property and did not create the alleged nuisance).

[110] See Jupin v. Kask, 447 Mass. 141, 849 N.E.2d 829 (2006) (rejecting nuisance and strict liability claims against homeowner who permitted storage of firearms, one of which was foreseeably stolen and used to shoot a police officer).

[111] Armory Park Neighborhood Ass'n v. Episcopal Community Services in Arizona, 148 Ariz. 1, 712 P.2d 914 (1985); People v. Gallo, 14 Cal.4th 1090, 929 P.2d 596, 60 Cal.Rptr.2d 277 (1997) (enjoining certain activities of street gangs).

[112] See North Carolina v. Tennessee Valley Authority, 515 F.3d 344 (4th Cir. 2008).

[113] Whether public regulation constitutes a taking of property for which compensation must be made may depend in part upon whether the property could have been regulated as a nuisance. See Louise A. Halper, Untangling The Nuisance Knot, 26 B.C. Envtl. Aff. L. Rev. 89 (1998).

cost of abatement as damages, some courts have not allowed recovery of increased costs of typical public services resulting from the nuisance.[114] Some public nuisance litigation raises issues of manufacturers' liability for the societal costs of their products. For instance, in one case a number of counties sued manufacturers of over-the-counter cold medications containing pseudophedrine for the counties' costs in dealing with the effects of the methamphetamine epidemic; the court denied the public nuisance claim in light of proximate cause considerations.[115]

Private suits; public nuisance causing special harm or private nuisance. In the absence of a statute allowing citizens to enforce the public's rights, those rights are normally enforced only by public authorities. The "private attorney general," welcomed in consumer fraud claims or civil rights litigation, is given little place in protecting public environmental rights. However, a private tort action is available to redress private harm resulting from a public nuisance if (1) the public nuisance is also a private nuisance to the plaintiff because it substantially and unreasonably diminishes her use and enjoyment of her land,[116] or (2) the nuisance is a public nuisance that causes special harm to the plaintiff in the exercise of the public right, and that harm differs in kind from the harm caused to other members of the public generally.[117]

Street obstructions. Traditional examples of a public nuisance involve obstruction of public streets or ways. While the mere presence of an obstruction might be a public nuisance, the fact that the inconvenienced plaintiff used the street more than other people would not give her standing to sue. Her inconvenience might be greater than that suffered by people generally, but it would be of the same general kind. The abortion protester who is dampened by a sprinkler that sprays partly on the public sidewalk thus has no claim based upon public nuisance.[118] Even the retail business owner may be denied relief when the collapse of a building blocks the access of customers in a wide area, since many members of the community will suffer losses similar in kind.[119]

Travelers and abutting owners. In fact, the street-obstruction cases are ordinarily maintained only by abutting owners whose property is denied access to or from the public way.[120] Although courts have sometimes talked of public nuisance in these cases, the relevant right seems to be the plaintiff's own right of access as a property owner, not the public right.[121] If access is made substantially more burdensome, the blockage need not

---

[114] City of Flagstaff v. Atchison, Topeka & Santa Fe Ry., 719 F.2d 322 (9th Cir. 1983). Statutes may also require or permit liability. See Kodiak Island Borough v. Exxon Corp., 991 P.2d 757 (Alaska 1999).

[115] Ashley County, Arkansas v. Pfizer, Inc., 552 F.3d 659 (9th Cir. 2009).

[116] See Armory Park Neighborhood Ass'n v. Episcopal Community Services in Arizona, 148 Ariz. 1, 712 P.2d 914 (1985); Restatement Second of Torts § 821B cmt. h & § 832C cmt. e. (1979) (bawdy house next door to a private residence). When the public nuisance actually substantially interferes with the integrity of the land itself or causes personal injury to its occupants, it would almost always qualify as a private nuisance and also demonstrate special harm different in kind from that suffered by the public generally.

[117] Lower Commerce Ins. Inc. v. Halliday, 636 So.2d 430 (Ala. 1994); Newhall Land & Farming Co. v. Superior Court (Mobil Oil Corporation), 19 Cal.App.4th 334, 23 Cal.Rptr.2d 377 (1993); Hale v. Ward County, 848 N.W.2d 245 (N.D. 2014); Restatement Second of Torts § 821C(1) (1979).

[118] Hartford v. Womens Services, 239 Neb. 540, 477 N.W.2d 161 (1991).

[119] 532 Madison Avenue Gourmet Foods, Inc. v. Finlandia Center, Inc., 96 N.Y.2d 280, 750 N.E.2d 1097, 727 N.Y.S.2d 49 (2001).

[120] E.g., Hall v. Polk, 363 So.2d 300 (Ala. 1978); Brown v. Florida Chautauqua Ass'n, 59 Fla. 447, 52 So. 802 (1910); Shamhart v. Morrison Cafeteria Co., 159 Fla. 629, 32 So.2d 727, 2 A.L.R.2d 429 (1947).

[121] See Powell v. Houston & T.C. R.R., 104 Tex. 219, 135 S.W. 1153 (1911) ("It does not affect [plaintiff's] right to recovery that the owners of property fronting on the same street have been injured in the same manner.").

occur at the property line.[122] However, when a remote street is blocked so that the property owner's access is merely inconvenienced, her claim cannot rest upon her property right but must instead be founded on a public nuisance. Yet as a public nuisance claim it must fail if she suffers mere inconvenience in travel, since that is a harm shared by other members of the public when a street is blocked. Remote obstructions are therefore not likely to be actionable.[123]

Public waters. The same rules apply to public waters. An interference with public waters, if substantial enough, will count as a public nuisance. For example, if the defendant contaminates public waters by chemical spills or the continuous discharge of noxious effluent, he may have created a public nuisance (and may have violated environmental statutes as well). Those who suffer "special harm" different in kind from that suffered by the public generally can recover for the harms suffered in their exercise of the public right. This includes direct users such as those engaged in commercial fishing,[124] but does not include pleasure-users who suffer harm in common with the public generally or even owners of nearby businesses who suffer economic loss when pollution of the waters reduces tourism.[125]

Personal injury. When a land occupant or her family suffers personal injury such as illness from a private nuisance, recoverable damages may include an award for that personal injury. Public nuisances causing personal injury are different. First, legislatures can declare almost any low-grade crime to be a nuisance, and the court holding that violation of such a statute is actionable may adopt the statutory term and declare that the defendant is liable for a nuisance.[126] Second, a public nuisance is actionable under the common law only if the plaintiff's enjoyment of a public right is diminished and her injury differs in kind from injury to the general public.[127] Thus, the defendant who substantially pollutes the air or public waters commits a public nuisance, and is liable if a few people suffer personal injury as a result,[128] but if the defendant's pollution causes respiratory problems for everyone in town, the plaintiff's respiratory harm does not differ in kind from that suffered by others and she cannot recover on a public nuisance theory.[129] Third, talk of public nuisance in personal injury cases can be confusing when the plaintiff claims damages rather than abatement. If the defendant should be liable for the injury, it is because he has intentionally caused personal injury,

---

[122] See Restatement Second of Torts § 821C cmt. f (1979).

[123] See Taylor v. Barnes, 303 Ky. 562, 198 S.W.2d 297 (1946) (distinguishing abutting owner from others); Burrell v. Kirkland, 242 S.C. 201, 130 S.E.2d 470 (1963); see also Hall v. Polk, 363 So.2d 300 (Ala. 1978) (obstruction of the road did not deny plaintiff access from property to public street, but it did obstruct the only convenient access to a nearby river that the plaintiff was entitled to access).

[124] Union Oil Co. v. Oppen, 501 F.2d 558 (9th Cir. 1974); Hampton v. North Carolina Pulp Co., 223 N.C. 535, 27 S.E.2d 538 (1943).

[125] See Louisiana ex rel. Guste v. M/V Testbank, 752 F.2d 1019, 88 A.L.R.Fed. 239 (5th Cir. 1985).

[126] Corgan v. Muehling, 143 Ill.2d 296, 574 N.E.2d 602, 158 Ill.Dec. 489 (1991) (psychologist would be liable if he engaged in sexual activities with patient without holding a current registration as required by "nuisance" statute).

[127] E.g., In re Lead Paint Litigation, 191 N.J. 405, 924 A.2d 484 (2007); State v. Lead Industries Ass'n, Inc., 951 A.2d 428 (R.I. 2008).

[128] Anderson v. W.R. Grace & Co., 628 F.Supp. 1219 (D. Mass. 1986) (leukemia victims of groundwater contamination).

[129] Venuto v. Owens-Corning Fiberglas Corp., 22 Cal.App.3d 116, 99 Cal.Rptr. 350 (1971); cf. In re The Exxon Valdez, 104 F.3d 1196 (9th Cir. 1997) (massive oil spill; "'the right to obtain and share wild food, enjoy uncontaminated nature, and cultivate traditional, cultural, spiritual, and psychological benefits in pristine natural surroundings' is shared by all Alaskans" and hence Native Americans suffered no "special harm").

carried on an abnormally dangerous activity, violated a statute aimed at protecting the plaintiff, or was negligent. To label the case as one of nuisance adds nothing to the clarity of decision-making or policy. Plaintiffs usually assert a public nuisance causing personal injury for strategic reasons, for example, to avoid the effect of their own contributory fault. But as Cardozo said in the leading case, "whenever a nuisance has its origin in negligence, one may not avert the consequence of his own contributory fault by affixing . . . the label of a nuisance."[130] In personal injury cases, the law would be clarified by dropping the public nuisance label and by directly considering the rules and policies of negligence and strict liability.[131]

§ 30.7 Remedies

The remedies potentially available for a private nuisance (or a public nuisance with special harm to the private plaintiff) are (1) compensatory damages, (2) punitive damages in egregious cases, and (3) injunctions abating or modifying the nuisance and (rarely) (4) a "compensated injunction" that abates the nuisance but requires the plaintiff to pay the costs of that abatement. Some of the confusion about nuisance arises when the liability question (is there a nuisance?) is confused with the remedy question (what remedy should be permitted?). The choice among remedies has a good deal of impact, however, and has generated a good deal of analysis.

Injunctive relief: abatement and modification. On the ground that the damages remedy is inadequate to protect property rights, courts often issue injunctions compelling the defendant to abate private or public nuisances.[132] Injunctions may be tailored narrowly to fit the nuisance. If a factory operation is a nuisance because of noise, it may be that an injunction closing the factory is unnecessary and that the nuisance can be remedied by an injunction that bars or limits the noise. Such an approach would properly match the remedy to the wrong.

Denying injunctions. Courts may also limit or even refuse injunctions in private nuisance cases, for a number of reasons. The main one is that if the defendant is carrying on an activity that is socially useful or economically important, then the injunction closing the defendant's operation may do more harm than good. Unavoidable industrial nuisances, for example, may have great value to the public because of the products that result or the jobs they foster. Courts may weigh the good against the harm and conclude that the injunction should be refused but that the defendant must nevertheless pay the plaintiff's damages. In a leading modern case, *Boomer v. Atlantic Cement Co.*,[133] the defendant was a cement plant that constantly produced high levels of cement dust that clogged the homes of neighboring residents. The operation was a nuisance as the courts found, but the defendant employed 300 persons and had invested $45 million in the plant. The total damage to the neighbors was $185,000. The court concluded that the injunction should be denied if the defendant paid the damages, bringing New York law

---

[130] McFarlane v. City of Niagara Falls, 247 N.Y. 340, 160 N.E. 391 (1928).

[131] The use of the nuisance label to evade public entity immunities is more complicated because the immunities are so often overstated in the first place. Ideally, in such cases the nuisance label would be dropped when the plaintiff asserts personal injury, and the immunity reformulated more narrowly.

[132] E.g., Aviation Cadet Museum v. Hammer, 373 Ark. 202, 283 S.W.3d 198 (2008) (upholding lower court decision that operation of airport was a nuisance and could be enjoined); Bishop Processing Co. v. Davis, 213 Md. 465, 132 A.2d 445 (1957) (injunction to avoid escape of noxious gases that interfere with plaintiff's use and enjoyment of property); see 1 Dan B. Dobbs, Law of Remedies § 5.7(2) (2d ed. 1993).

[133] Boomer v. Atlantic Cement Co., 26 N.Y.2d 219, 257 N.E.2d 870, 309 N.Y.S.2d 312 (1970).

into line with the practice in a number of other states.[134] A court may also be reluctant to enjoin an anticipated nuisance if there is evidence that if care is used, the defendant's conduct or facility might not constitute a nuisance.[135] Nor will an injunction issue if the nuisance has abated at the time of trial.[136]

Limiting the injunction to avoid closing a useful business. To deny the injunction is to permit the defendant to take rights in the plaintiff's property at a valuation determined by judges or juries. Even if their valuation is an accurate estimate of the market, it may not represent the price at which the plaintiff would voluntarily sell the property right. The effect is to give the defendant a power much like the power of eminent domain. So denial of injunction is a serious matter. For this reason, the injunction is definitely granted when the defendant harms the plaintiff willfully or when he could reasonably avoid doing so.[137] Courts may find a middle ground by ordering the defendant to minimize or eliminate the nuisance without closing down operations,[138] for example, by reducing the amount of dynamite in any one quarry explosion,[139] or reducing nighttime activities.[140] Courts can also order the defendant to experiment with alternative processes or procedures as potential means of minimizing the harm.[141]

The compensated injunction. One other way of avoiding an injunction that closes the defendant's business but still manages some relief for the plaintiff is most unusual. The compensated injunction is illustrated in a famous Arizona case where suburban development gradually pushed so close to a massive feed lot that life quickly became intolerable to the residents. The developer was granted an injunction forcing the feed lot to move further away from inhabited areas, but only on condition that the costs of the move were borne by the developer.[142]

Damages: permanent nuisance and diminished market value. Because damages are intended to compensate the plaintiff for actual harm done, the award may be measured in different ways according to the evidence.[143] If the harm done by the nuisance will not terminate or be abated, then the nuisance is said to be permanent. In that case, one traditional measure of damages awards the plaintiff the diminished market value of her

---

[134] E.g., Northern Indiana Pub. Serv. Co. v. Vesey, 210 Ind. 338, 200 N.E. 620 (1936); Riter v. Keokuk Electro-Metals Co., 248 Iowa 710, 82 N.W.2d 151 (1957) (factory furnishing work in the community); Madison v. Ducktown Sulphur, Copper & Iron Co., 113 Tenn. 331, 83 S.W. 658 (1904) (jobs in community plus enormous increase in tax assessments in county due to defendants' smelters); see Jonathan M. Purver, Annotation, Modern Status of Rules as to Balance of Convenience or Social Utility as Affecting Relief From Nuisance, 40 A.L.R.3d 601 (1971).

[135] See Simpson v. Kollasch, 749 N.W.2d 671 (Iowa 2008) (refusing to prospectively enjoin construction of a proposed hog-processing facility); but see Sowers v. Forest Hills Subdivision, 294 P.3d 427 (Nev. 2013) (permanent injunction upheld against proposed wind turbine in a residential area, where noise, shadow flicker and aesthetic impact far outweigh the turbine's potential utility).

[136] E.g., Spirit Ridge Mineral Springs, LLC v. Franklin County, 337 P.3d 583 (Idaho 2014) (private nuisance action seeking to enjoin a gun range; any nuisance created by the range had abated in 2008).

[137] See Mobile & O.R. R. v. Zimmern, 206 Ala. 37, 89 So. 475 (1921).

[138] See 1 Dan B. Dobbs, Law of Remedies § 2.4(6) (2d ed. 1993).

[139] Beecher v. Dull, 294 Pa. 17, 143 A. 498 (1928).

[140] Smith v. Stasco Milling Co., 18 F.2d 736 (2d Cir. 1927).

[141] Restatement Second of Torts § 941 cmt. e (1979).

[142] Spur Industries, Inc. v. Del E. Webb Development Co., 108 Ariz. 178, 494 P.2d 700, 53 A.L.R.3d 861 (1972). See Guido Calabresi & A. Douglas Melamed, Property Rules, Liability Rules, and Inalienability: One View of the Cathedral, 85 Harv.L.Rev. 1089 (1972).

[143] On the damages rules for nuisance, see 1 Dan B. Dobbs, Law of Remedies § 5.6(2) (2d ed. 1993).

land.[144] That might be the case if the land is irremediably contaminated for an indefinite time, for example.[145]

Temporary nuisance and loss of rental value or cost of restoring land. On the other hand, if the harm is temporary, the parallel measure of damages would be an award for loss of use, usually based upon the reduction of rental value of the land while the nuisance lasts.[146] With some nuisances, the harm is abated when the defendant's activity is abated. That is true, for example, if the nuisance is noise inflicted upon the plaintiff. When the noise stops, the plaintiff has nothing to repair. But if the nuisance is a toxic contamination of groundwater or land, the harm does not terminate when the defendant stops dumping toxins. In cases like that, the plaintiff is entitled to have her land restored if that is feasible, and if the defendant does not restore it, the plaintiff is entitled to the cost of doing so in addition to her recovery for diminished rental value for the period until the cleanup is completed.[147]

Personal illness or annoyance. Courts have allowed land occupants in nuisance cases to recover damages for loss of quality of life, including physical illness, discomfort, and annoyance.[148] But care should be exercised not to overlap awards if the plaintiff claims diminished value based on conditions that cause discomfort, along with discomfort as a separate item of damages.[149]

To enjoin or not to enjoin: efficiency and externalizing. A great deal of analysis, far more than can be summarized here, has gone into the question of whether courts should always, never, or sometimes enjoin socially useful nuisances.[150] One reason not to weigh social utilities is that accurate weighing may be unlikely or at least expensive. The interest in efficiency may suggest to some that if more value can be generated by keeping the nuisance and paying the damages, the injunction should be denied, but it may be that this should be accomplished by routinely denying the injunction rather than by weighing utilities. On the other hand, if we are sure that the cost of, say, running a rocket laboratory is the disposal of toxic wastes it generates, the rocket facility should not be able to dump the fuel where it will cause harm to others; in doing so, it would be externalizing its costs, forcing others to bear costs of its business.[151]

---

[144] See, e.g., Tri-County Investment Group, Ltd. v. Southern States, Inc., 231 Ga.App. 632, 500 S.E.2d 22 (1998); Smith v. Carbide & Chemicals Corp., 507 F.3d 372 (6th Cir. 2007).

[145] Weinhold v. Wolff, 555 N.W.2d 454 (Iowa 1996); see also Hager v. City of Devils Lake, 773 N.W.2d 420 (N.D. 2009); Schneider Nat'l Carriers, Inc. v. Bates, 147 S.W.3d 264 (Tex. 2004).

[146] E.g., Superior Const. Co. v. Elmo, 204 Md. 1, 102 A.2d 739, 48 A.L.R.2d 932 (1954).

[147] Reeser v. Weaver Bros., Inc., 78 Ohio App.3d 681, 605 N.E.2d 1271 (1992). In the case of a private nuisance without threat of public harm, such as waters backed up onto the plaintiff's land without toxic deposits, recovery of repair or cleanup costs may be limited so that they do not exceed the diminution in value that would occur if the nuisance were allowed to recur. See Stratford Theater, Inc. v. Town of Stratford, 140 Conn. 422, 101 A.2d 279, 41 A.L.R.2d 1060 (1953).

[148] E.g., Woodmen of the World, United Number 3 v. Jordan, 231 Ga.App. 517, 499 S.E.2d 900 (1998); Gorman v. Sabo, 210 Md. 155, 122 A.2d 475 (1956).

[149] See 1 Dan B. Dobbs, Law of Remedies § 3.3(7) (2d ed. 1993).

[150] See, e.g., Robert C. Ellickson, Alternatives to Zoning: Covenants, Nuisance Rules, and Fines as Land Use Controls, 40 U.Chi.L.Rev. 681 (1973); W. Page Keeton & Clarence Morris, Notes on "Balancing the Equities," 18 Tex. L. Rev. 412 (1940); Jeff L. Lewin, Compensated Injunctions and the Evolution of Nuisance Law, 71 Iowa L.Rev. 775 (1986); A. Mitchell Polinsky, Resolving Nuisance Disputes: The Simple Economics of Injunctive and Damages Remedies, 32 Stan.L.Rev. 1075 (1980); Edward Rabin, Nuisance Law: Rethinking Fundamental Assumptions, 63 Va.L.Rev. 1299 (1977). Some of the writings on this subject are discussed in 1 Dan B. Dobbs, Law of Remedies § 5.7(4) (2d ed. 1993).

[151] See Marshall S. Shapo, Principles of Tort Law ¶ 36.04, at 195 (2003).

Strategic behavior. One approach might be to leave the whole matter to party bargaining. If nuisances are not enjoined, the defendant is permitted to buy rights to interfere with the plaintiff's land at a price fixed by courts but not one agreed to by the plaintiff. People who do not commit nuisances are not permitted to take rights in the plaintiff's land except by paying a price the plaintiff will accept, so it is somewhat anomalous that the defendant who commits a nuisance can in effect compel a sale. Yet if nuisances are enjoined, the community may lose enormously, or alternatively the plaintiff may be able to sell the injunction back to the defendant (by agreeing not to enforce it) at an extortionate price that is far in excess of the plaintiff's loss and the plaintiff's own subjective valuation. Extortionate behavior is possible on either side.

Damages measured to provide appropriate incentives. If an injunction is denied and damages are awarded for diminished value of the plaintiff's property, then the defendant will, in effect, have purchased an easement to commit the nuisance forever. In a world of changing technology, some of which might in the future allow the defendant to operate without causing harm to others, it may be unwise to remove the incentive to invest in technology. A better measure of damages in some cases would be the temporary measure (lost rental value), which would allow the plaintiff to sue periodically as long as the nuisance continues. Given accurate damages measures, however, a refusal to enjoin a nuisance like the cement dust may often turn out well even under the permanent or diminished market value measure. If the defendant pays the true loss in value of the plaintiffs' homes, the plaintiffs will be able to sell them to purchasers who, because of the cheaper price, are willing to put up with the nuisance. Alternatively, if the plaintiffs prefer to remain neighbors of the cement plant, they are evidently satisfied with less comfort and more cash. This optimistic view, however, will work only if the court can be confident that its estimate of damages is accurate.

Part VI

VICARIOUS LIABILITY, STRICT LIABILITY, AND PRODUCTS LIABILITY

Chapter 31

VICARIOUS LIABILITY FOR PHYSICAL HARMS

Analysis

§ 31.1   Vicarious Liability Generally
§ 31.2   Rationales for Respondeat Superior Liability
§ 31.3   Scope of Employment: General Principles
§ 31.4   Limits on Scope of Employment
§ 31.5   Independent Contractors: General Rules
§ 31.6   Independent Contractors Performing Nondelegable Duties
§ 31.7   Apparent Agency and Agency by Estoppel
§ 31.8   Borrowed Servants

§ 31.1 Vicarious Liability Generally

Vicarious liability is liability for the tort of another person. Such liability is an important exception to the usual rule that each person is accountable for his own legal fault, but in the absence of such fault is not responsible for the actions of others. The most common kind of vicarious liability is based upon the principle of respondeat superior.[1] Under that principle, private employers[2] are generally jointly and severally liable along with the tortfeasor employee for the torts of employees committed within the scope of employment.[3] The principle does not apply among employees themselves—employees are not liable for the torts of the employer or other employees.[4]

The terminology of respondeat superior, somewhat strange in today's world, sets up some fundamental distinctions. Broadly speaking, employers are *principals* and employees are *agents*.[5] Some employees are only agents in the sense that they can make contracts or sell goods for the employer. As to these agents, the employer may be liable on the contract signed by the agent but not for the agent's torts. Other employees, those who are expected to carry out physical tasks, are called *servants*. The employer of these

---

[1]   Respondeat superior is not the only kind of vicarious liability. Conspirators, those who act in concert, partners, and joint enterprisers are all vicariously liable for the acts of each other committed as part of their agreed-upon activity. See 2 Dobbs, Hayden & Bublick, The Law of Torts § 435 (2d ed. 2011 & Supp.).

[2]   Some public employers are also subject to vicarious liability for employee torts. See, e.g., Mary M. v. City of Los Angeles, 54 Cal.3d 202, 814 P.2d 1341, 285 Cal.Rptr. 99 (1991); Melin-Schilling v. Imm, 149 Wash.App. 588, 205 P.3d 905 (2009). In actions brought under the Federal Tort Claims Act, however, only the government employer is liable for the torts committed by the employee within the scope of employment. See §§ 335 & 351. The same is true under many state tort claims acts. See, e.g., Vaughn v. First Transit, Inc., 346 Or. 128, 206 P.3d 181 (2009). Further, respondeat superior liability of the employer is unavailable when a plaintiff seeks damages from a municipality under federal civil rights laws. Monell v. City of New York, 436 U.S. 658 (1978); see § 22.16.

[3]   Restatement Third of Agency §§ 2.04 & 7.07(1) (2006). See §§ 31.3 & 31.4.

[4]   See Ware v. Timmons, 954 So.2d 545 (Ala. 2006). An employee may be liable for acts of co-employees when they act in concert or in a conspiracy. See Jones v. City of Chicago, 856 F.2d 985 (7th Cir. 1988).

[5]   See Restatement Third of Agency § 1.01 (2006).

servants is called a *master*.[6] The terms distinguish not only between servants and other agents, but also between servants and independent contractors. The master is vicariously liable in tort for the torts of servants committed within the scope of their employment, but the employer is not ordinarily vicariously liable for the torts of independent contractors.[7]

Respondeat superior liability has ancient roots in Roman law and may have been in continuous use in some form more or less since the Norman Conquest of England.[8] The ordinary instances of it today are non-controversial. The bus company's driver negligently drives the company's bus into the plaintiff's car. The negligent driver is of course liable;[9] under the principle of respondeat superior, the bus company itself is treated as a tortfeasor as well. As a practical matter, that means that the plaintiff will be able to collect her judgment against the bus company and will not be left without a remedy merely because the driver himself could not pay.[10]

Distinguishing vicarious liability from primary liability. An employer may be liable to an injured plaintiff because of the employer's own fault. For example, the employer might have negligently provided a vehicle for use by an employee known to be a dangerous driver,[11] or might have negligently hired, trained, or supervised a dangerous employee.[12] In such cases the employer might be liable for his own negligent entrustment or for his negligence in hiring or supervising. Such primary liability—liability for the employer's own fault—is not *vicarious* liability.[13]

Role of fault in vicarious liability. From the employer-defendant's point of view, vicarious liability is strict liability, since he is liable without personal fault. That is not quite the case from the plaintiff's point of view. The plaintiff must prove that the employee committed a tort[14] and was acting within the scope of employment when he did so. In the great majority of cases, then, the plaintiff must thus prove fault, although not necessarily the personal fault of the employer.

---

[6]   The Restatement Third of Agency abandons this terminology, which was used in the Restatement Second of Agency and persists in many judicial decisions. See Id., § 2.04.

[7]   See § 31.5.

[8]   See Oliver Wendell Holmes, Jr., Agency, 4 Harv. L. Rev. 345 (1891). Respondeat superior was probably not a widespread or generalized rule until the 18th century, however.

[9]   Restatement Third of Agency § 7.01 (2006) (unless an applicable statute provides otherwise); Restatement Second of Agency § 343 (1959) (except where agent is exercising a privilege of the principal and in similar cases).

[10]   The employer is given a right of indemnity against the employee, but the right is seldom exercised. See 2 Dobbs, Hayden & Bublick § 425 (2d ed. 2011 & Supp.).

[11]   See Ali v. Fisher, 145 S.W.3d 557 (Tenn. 2004).

[12]   See § 26.11; Restatement Third of Agency § 7.05(1) (2006). Failure to discipline or terminate an employee who has committed a serious wrong can be seen as "ratifying" the tort, leading to liability that is said to be "an alternative theory to respondeat superior." C.R. v. Tenet Healthcare Corp., 169 Cal.App.4th 1094, 87 Cal.Rptr.3d 424 (2009) (sexual harassment case); see also Restatement Third of Agency §§ 4.01, 4.03, 4.06 (2006) (ratification as a trigger of liability).

[13]   A plaintiff can pursue both theories, although double recovery is not permitted. See, e.g., MV Transportation v. Allgeier, 433 S.W.3d 324 (Ky. 2014). Some states hold that a plaintiff cannot pursue a primary-liability claim against the employer where it has admitted vicarious liability. See Diaz v. Carcamo, 51 Cal. 4th 1148, 126 Cal. Rptr. 3d 443, 253 P.3d 535 (2011).

[14]   See, e.g., National Union Fire Ins. Co. of Pittsburgh, Pa. v. Wuerth, 122 Ohio St.3d 594, 913 N.E.2d 939 (2009) ("[A] principal is vicariously liable only when an agent could be held directly liable. . . ."). Relatedly, a settlement with the agent is usually held to extinguish the principal's liability as well. See Doe v. City of Chicago, 360 F.3d 667 (7th Cir. 2004) (Ill. law).

§ 31.2 Rationales for Respondeat Superior Liability

It would not be difficult to justify respondeat superior liability if it only meant that the master was liable for torts committed at his specific direction, as where the master tells the servant to drive faster than the speed limit permits. But respondeat superior liability is much broader. The master is liable for the servant's negligent acts even though master did not command those acts and could not foresee them in any specific way. Sometimes, masters are liable even for torts committed by servants in violation of specific directions or rules.[15]

Tort law is assuredly imperfect, but it usually attempts to hold individuals accountable for their wrongs and only for their wrongs. Although pockets of strict liability exist, such liability is relatively rare. Consequently, vicarious liability under the doctrine of respondeat superior, which is strict in the sense that it holds an employer liable without the employer's personal fault, seems to require some explanation.

Courts have usually defended strict liability by emphasizing either (1) that an innocent person, either the plaintiff or the employer,[16] must bear the loss, (2) that the employer had formal right of control over the employee's work,[17] or (3) that the employer benefits from the employee's work.[18] The first argument is suspect because it is applied selectively, not as a general principle of tort law. To apply it generally would be to adopt a general regime of strict liability. The other two arguments offer attractive implications that responsibility follows control and that one who intentionally reaps the benefits of an activity must bear the burdens as well. But control is doubtful in many cases and the connection between the employee's tort and the employer's benefit is often tenuous.

Commentators have developed some other explanations. One is that deterrence is best achieved by imposing liability on the employer, who will then seek to avoid his own liability by exercising his considerable control over employees to discourage their torts.[19] Economic thinkers have argued that enterprise liability—that is, the strict liability of business enterprises for harms perceived to be recurrently associated with their operation—is justified as economically efficient. By this they mean that such liability will tend to provide optimal deterrence of activities that are harmful.[20] Others, argue that enterprise liability provides appropriate "insurance" against harms that are not worth preventing. The enterprise can raise prices or lower dividends and thus distribute

---

[15] Restatement Third of Agency § 7.07, cmt. c (2006) ("[C]onduct is not outside the scope of employment merely because an employee disregards the employer's instructions.").

[16] See South Carolina Ins. Co. v. James C. Greene and Co., 290 S.C. 171, 348 S.E.2d 617 (Ct. App. 1986) (recounting historical development).

[17] National Convenience Stores, Inc. v. Fantauzzi, 94 Nev. 655, 658, 584 P.2d 689, 691 (1978) ("Nevada's policy rationale for the doctrine of respondeat superior is grounded on the theory of control rather than on the entrepreneur theory."). See also Restatement Third of Agency § 1.01 (2006) (defining agency as a relationship in which a person is "subject to the principal's control") & § 7.07(2) (defining "scope of employment" as turning in part on "the employer's control").

[18] Mary M. v. City of Los Angeles, 54 Cal.3d 202, 814 P.2d 1341, 285 Cal.Rptr. 99 (1991).

[19] Clarence Morris, The Torts of an Independent Contractor, 29 Ill. L. Rev. 339 (1935). See also Restatement Third of Agency § 2.04, cmt. b (2006) ("Respondeat superior creates an incentive for principals to choose employees and structure work within the organization so as to reduce the incidence of tortious conduct.").

[20] See Alan Q. Sykes, The Economics of Vicarious Liability, 93 Yale L.J. 1231 (1984); see also Alan Q. Sykes, The Boundaries of Vicarious Liability: an Economic Analysis of the Scope of Employment Rule and Related Legal Doctrines, 101 Harv. L. Rev. 563 (1988) (emphasizing inefficiencies arising out of the agent's insolvency and those arising from the cost of contracting between principal and agent).

or spread the losses resulting from injury to all those who benefit from its activities.[21] In this way, the injured individual does not bear the whole weight of the loss herself. Since no one person bears the whole loss, the loss is not so disruptive. Perhaps more importantly, those subjected to risks of the enterprise are also those who share in the burdens and benefits of its liability. The consumer pays a small sum more for the products of the enterprise, but in return obtains a degree of protection in the form of liability if she is injured.[22]

Still another justification for respondeat superior liability is that it is fair or just. When risks are created randomly by occasional, infrequent acts of individuals, liability is imposed only if the act causing harm is negligent. When an enterprise, individual or corporation, engages in systematic or repeated activity, however, some risks are more or less typical or characteristic of the activity even when no negligence can be shown. The bus company must expect that sooner or later its buses will cause harm, even if drivers are invariably careful. In this sense, bus companies impose risks that are materially greater than or different from the risks that we all impose upon one another by occasional use of motor vehicles. Although the substantial-certainty definition of intent has not been carried so far, it is nevertheless reasonable to say that the bus company can be statistically certain that bus injuries will be negligently inflicted and in that sense intends them. Although this is not moral fault, the bus company employer should accept the burdens that go with the benefits of its operation and hence should be responsible for the bus driver's negligence as a matter of justice or fairness.[23]

Many decisions either verbalize similar reasoning or obtain results consistent with it.[24] This rationale is also consistent with the rule that the employer remains liable for harms caused by risks of the enterprise even if the employee has a purely personal defense, as where the statute of limitations has run on the plaintiff's suit against the employee but not on the suit against the employer[25] or where the employee enjoys a purely personal immunity but the employer does not.[26] Some authority, however, has refused to consider the "enterprise liability" rationale for respondeat superior liability, but may nonetheless obtain results consistent with that rationale.[27]

---

[21] Young B. Smith, Frolic and Detour, 23 Colum. L. Rev. 444, 456 (1923); see also George L. Priest, The Invention of Enterprise Liability: A Critical History of the Intellectual Foundations of Modern Tort Law, 14 J. Leg. Stud. 461, 47–83 (1985).

[22] See Fruit v. Schreiner, 502 P.2d 133 (Alaska 1972); Warren A. Seavey, Speculations as to "Respondeat Superior," Harvard Legal Essays in Honor of Joseph Henry Beale and Samuel Williston 433, 450–451 (1934).

[23] See Gregory C. Keating, The Idea of Fairness in the Law of Enterprise Liability, 95 Mich. L. Rev. 1266 (1997); see also Ira S. Bushey & Sons, Inc. v. United States, 398 F.2d 167 (2d Cir. 1968) (Friendly, J.) ("[A] business enterprise cannot justly disclaim responsibility for accidents which may fairly be said to be characteristic of its activities.").

[24] E.g., Fahrendorff v. North Homes, Inc., 597 N.W.2d 905 (Minn. 1999) (counselor's sexual contact with group home resident; expert's view that "inappropriate sexual contact or abuse of power in these situations, although infrequent, is a well-known hazard in this field" showed that such abuse was foreseeable risk of the business, which is sufficient for vicarious liability).

[25] Hughes v. Doe, 273 Va. 45, 639 S.E.2d 302 (2007); Cohen v. Alliant Enterprises, Inc., 60 S.W.3d 536 (Ky. 2001); see also Restatement Second of Agency § 180 (1959). The rule is otherwise when the employee's defenses goes to the merits and justifies his actions, as in the case of self-defense.

[26] See Johnson v. LeBonheur Children's Medical Ctr., 74 S.W.3d 338 (Tenn. 2002) (narrowly distinguishing cases that might be understood as contrary to the principle); Restatement Second of Agency § 217 (1959) (noting some contrary authority, but describing the rule stated as a trend).

[27] E.g., Carter v. Reynolds, 175 N.J. 402, 815 A.2d 460 (2003); O'Toole v. Carr, 175 N.J. 421, 815 A.2d 471 (2003).

§ 31.3 Scope of Employment: General Principles

Vicarious liability under the respondeat superior doctrine ordinarily requires an employment relationship or another consensual arrangement under which one person agrees to act under another's control.[28] Thus, apart from statute, parents are not vicariously liable for their children's torts, although they may be responsible for their own negligence in failing to control children.[29] Similarly, someone who merely assists the defendant without submitting to the defendant's right of control is not ordinarily an agent or servant.[30] Employment itself is not enough for vicarious liability, however. With certain exceptions, vicarious liability attaches for physical harms resulting from conduct of an employee only when the employee acts as a "servant" rather than as an independent contractor.[31] Finally, respondeat superior liability is imposed only for acts of the servant committed within the scope of his employment.[32]

General requirements. Under the traditional rules, a servant's conduct is not within the scope of his employment unless it is of the same general kind as authorized or expected, or incidental to such conduct, and the servant was acting within the authorized time and space limits. The Restatement Second of Agency added that the servant's conduct must have been "actuated, at least in part, by a purpose to serve the master,"[33] a requirement echoed in the Restatement Third as well.[34] Some authority accepts this rule more or less literally,[35] but a number of modern courts have rejected it.[36] Even where the Restatement "purpose" limitation has been recognized, it is usually understood as a broad aim rather than as a technical demand.[37] It is also substantially qualified by the

---

[28] See Restatement Third of Agency §§ 1.01 & 7.07(3)(a) (2006); Restatement Second of Agency §§ 1 & 2 (1959); Kavanagh v. Trustees of Boston Univ., 440 Mass. 195, 795 N.E.2d 1170 (2003) (student at university is neither a "servant" nor an employee of the university, no vicarious liability); Glover v. Boy Scouts of America, 923 P.2d 1383 (Utah 1996) (scoutmaster was not an employee of the Scout organization, no vicarious liability).

[29] See § 26.9.

[30] E.g., Austin v. Kaness, 950 P.2d 561 (Wyo. 1997) (adult son feeding cats while parents were away was not agent or servant of parents).

[31] See § 31.5.

[32] Restatement Third of Agency §§ 2.04 & 7.07 (2006).

[33] Restatement Second of Agency § 228(1)(c) (1959).

[34] Restatement Third of Agency § 7.07(2) (2006) ("An employee's act is not within the scope of employment when it occurs within an independent course of conduct not intended by the employee to serve any purpose of the employer.").

[35] See Engler v. Gulf Interstate Engineering, Inc., 230 Ariz. 55, 280 P.3d 599 (2012) (expressly adopting the Restatement Third; driver was not advancing the employer's business purpose at the time he caused a traffic accident); Adames v. Sheahan, 233 Ill.2d 276, 909 N.E.2d 742, 330 Ill.Dec. 720 (2009) (requiring that an employee's act "was motivated, at least in part, by a desire to serve his master," applying the Restatement Second); Mid-States Plastics, Inc. v. Estate of Bryant, 245 S.W.3d 728 (Ky. 2008) (for employer to be held vicariously liable for employee's tort committed against guest who had been invited on business trip by employee, guest's presence had to be for the purpose of furthering the employer's work); Auer v. Paliath, 140 Ohio St.3d 276, 17 N.E.3d 561 (2014) (key question is whether employee "acted or believed himself to have acted, at least in part, in his employer's interest").

[36] See, e.g., Frieler v. Carlson Marketing Group, Inc., 751 N.W.2d 558 (Minn. 2008) (employee's act must be foreseeable, related to, and connected with acts otherwise within the scope of employment); Barnett v. Clark, 889 N.E.2d 281 (Ind. 2008) (employee's act must either be "incidental to the conduct authorized," or it must to an appreciable extent, further the employer's business); Gina Chin & Assoc. v. First Union Bank, 260 Va. 533, 537 S.E.2d 573 (2000) ("[T]he motive of the employee in committing the act complained of is not determinative. . . . Rather, the issue is whether the service itself, in which the tortious act was done, was within the ordinary course of such business."); Doe v. Samaritan Counseling Center, 791 P.2d 344 (Alaska 1990); Marston v. Minneapolis Clinic of Psychiatry and Neurology, 329 N.W.2d 306 (Minn. 1982).

[37] See, e.g., Cooper Clinic, P.A. v. Barnes, 366 Ark. 533, 237 S.W.3d 87 (2006) (employee must be "carrying out the object and purpose of the enterprise"); Baker v. Saint Francis Hosp., 126 P.3d 602 (Okla. 2005) (employee's act must be incidental to and done in furtherance of the business of the employer).

rule that the employer is vicariously liable for the employee's acts outside the scope of employment if his employment aided him in accomplishing the tort.[38]

Determining scope of employment. Courts have provided many examples of the broad approach to scope-of-employment issues. For instance, a cook in a restaurant who is not actually cooking but who is instead talking with a customer and flipping a knife that has nothing to do with his job is within the scope of his employment when the knife accidently strikes the customer.[39] Similarly, an employee-driver does not leave the scope of his employment merely because he acts negligently in violation of his employer's instruction to act with care, or even when he violates his employer's instructions not to take a passenger.[40] Scope of employment questions are usually resolved only by evaluation of many factual details on a case-by-case basis.[41] Not surprisingly, then, the question whether an employee's act is within the scope of employment is for the jury unless the matter is so clear that reasonable people could not differ.[42]

§ 31.4 Limits on Scope of Employment

The Going and Coming Rule

General rule. The master is not vicariously responsible for the acts of a servant before work begins or after it ends. In particular, the going and coming rule holds that in jobs with a situs such as an office or factory, an employee coming to work or going home from it is not in employment.[43] Consequently, the employer is not liable for, say, automobile accidents of employees on their way to work or after they have left work.[44]

Exceptions. The employer may be held vicariously liable if the job is broader and requires travel outside the area or the employee is paid for travel time.[45] The same may be true where an employee who works out of town is paid portal-to-portal or is on call or on duty at all times. In such cases the employee may remain in the course of employment even during travel, although vicarious liability will follow only where his act is found to be within the scope of employment.[46] Similarly, employees like police officers who are always subject to job demands may be acting within the scope of employment even when

---

[38] Costos v. Coconut Island Corp., 137 F.3d 46 (1st Cir. 1998) (employer vicariously liable where manager was aided in accomplishing rape on plaintiff by the agency relationship); Doe v. Forrest, 853 A.2d 48 (Vt. 2004) (employer could be vicariously liable if the plaintiff can show that the employee was aided in accomplishing his intentional sexual assault on her by the existence of the employment relationship); Restatement Second of Agency § 219(2)(d) (1959). The Restatement Third of Agency rejects the Second's § 219(2)(d), as have some courts. See Zsigo v. Hurley Medical Ctr., 475 Mich. 215, 716 N.W.2d 220 (2006).

[39] Riviello v. Waldron, 47 N.Y.2d 297, 391 N.E.2d 1278, 418 N.Y.S.2d 300 (1979).

[40] Perez v. Van Groningen & Sons, Inc., 41 Cal.3d 962, 719 P.2d 676, 227 Cal.Rptr. 106 (1986).

[41] Because factual details count, and because the facts require reasonableness evaluations, summary judgment is often inappropriate on the scope of employment issue. See Pyne v. Witmer, 129 Ill.2d 351, 543 N.E.2d 1304, 135 Ill.Dec. 557 (1989).

[42] See, e.g., Bagent v. Blessing Care Corp., 224 Ill.2d 154, 308 Ill.Dec. 782 (2007); Baker v. Saint Francis Hosp., 126 P.3d 602 (Okla. 2005); Plummer v. Center Psychiatrists, Ltd., 252 Va. 233, 476 S.E.2d 172 (1996).

[43] Restatement Third of Agency § 707, cmt. e (2006).

[44] E.g., Hamm v. United States, 483 F.3d 135 (2d Cir. 2007) (FTCA case); Faul v. Jelco, Inc., 122 Ariz. 490, 595 P.2d 1035 (Ct. App. 1979); Barclay v. Briscoe, 427 Md. 270, 47 A.3d 560 (2012).

[45] Hinman v. Westinghouse Elec. Co., 2 Cal.3d 956, 88 Cal.Rptr. 188, 471 P.2d 988 (1970). See also Bowyer v. Loftus, 346 Mont. 182, 194 P.3d 92 (2008) (no vicarious liability where employee was not being compensated for his mileage during trip).

[46] See Carroll Air Sys., Inc. v. Greenbaum, 629 So.2d 914 (Fla. Dist. Ct. App. 1993); Edgewater Motels, Inc. v. Gatzke, 277 N.W.2d 11 (Minn. 1979).

off duty[47] so long as they are not engaged in purely personal activities.[48] Problems arise with off-duty police officers employed part-time by private businesses. A number of cases conclude that an off-duty officer is still obliged to enforce at least some laws when he is off duty and in such a case he cannot be acting within the scope of his employment for a private employer.[49] Some other courts have rejected this line of reasoning, holding that, following usual agency principles, the officer could be within the scope of his private employment even when enforcing the law or apprehending criminals.[50]

Exceptions to the going and coming rule have also been found when the employee is on a special errand for the employer while on his way to or from work or after regular work hours[51] or otherwise is serving the employer's interests as well as his own (the so-called dual-purpose exception).[52] This may be the case where the employer, by general policy or specific command, directed the employee to carry out some job-related errand during time that would otherwise be off the job.[53] It may also be the case where the employer directed the employee to attend a business conference out of town.[54] An exception to the general going and coming rule may also be found when the employer requires the employee to use the employer's vehicle for commuting, but not necessarily when the employer merely *permits* use of the employer's vehicle for this purpose.[55]

Frolic and Detour

Detours. Employees who have arrived at work and begun their jobs can nevertheless physically remove themselves from the job. Not uncommonly, employees indulge in "detours" for their personal amusement. The office messenger, delivering a message from the tenth floor to the fifth, might stop off to confirm a date with a friend on the ninth floor, for example. If he takes the stairs rather than the elevator because the ninth floor is only one flight away but negligently knocks the plaintiff down before he reaches the landing, he has physically "deviated" from employment only in taking the stairs rather than the elevator; in terms of his intent, he has a dual motive, part of which is to serve the employer, since he is still on his way.[56] As long as the detour is a slight deviation or is usual, expected, or tolerated in the particular employment, the servant is still acting within the general scope of employment and the employer will be vicariously liable for torts committed along the way.[57]

[47] E.g., Osborne v. Lyles, 63 Ohio St.3d 326, 587 N.E.2d 825 (1992); see Alexander C. Black, Annotation, Liability of Municipal Corporation or Other Governmental Entity For Injury or Death Caused by Action or Inaction of Off-Duty Police Officer, 36 A.L.R.5th 1 (1996).

[48] See Russell v. Noullet, 721 So.2d 868 (La. 1998) (attack by off-duty officer).

[49] See Brown v. Dillard's, Inc., 289 S.W.3d 340 (Tex. App. 2009); Bauldock v. Davco Food, Inc., 622 A.2d 28 (D.C. 1993).

[50] Ambling Management Co. v. Miller, 295 Ga. 758, 764 S.E.2d 127 (2014); Lovelace v. Anderson, 785 A.2d 726 (Md. 2001); White v. Revco Discount Drug Centers, Inc., 33 S.W.3d 713 (Tenn. 2001).

[51] See Restatement Third of Agency § 7.07, cmt. e & Illus. 12 to 14 (2006).

[52] See Fackrell v. Marshall, 490 F.3d 997 (8th Cir. 2007) (Mo. law); Carter v. Reynolds, 175 N.J. 402, 815 A.2d 460 (2003).

[53] See Gutierrez de Martinez v. Drug Enforcement Admin., 111 F.3d 1148 (4th Cir. 1997).

[54] See Jeewarat v. Warner Bros. Entertainment, Inc., 177 Cal.App.4th 427, 98 Cal.Rptr.3d 837 (2009) (fact question as to whether employee was still in the scope of employment when he caused a traffic accident while returning home from an out-of-town business trip).

[55] See Ahlstrom v. Salt Lake City Corp., 73 P.3d 315 (Utah 2003).

[56] See Young B. Smith, Frolic & Detour, 23 Colum. L. Rev. 444, 716, 722 ff. (1923).

[57] Pyne v. Witmer, 129 Ill.2d 351, 543 N.E.2d 1304, 135 Ill.Dec. 557 (1989).

Frolics and reentry. On the other hand, if the messenger decides the day is too nice to miss a baseball game and negligently crashes his car into the plaintiff on his way to the ball park, he is almost certainly "on a frolic of his own" and not at all within the scope of employment.[58] When the frolicking employee starts back to work after the game is over, the problem is to determine when he has reentered employment. Reentry into employment occurs only when the employee reaches a point reasonably near the authorized time and space limits of the job and the employee has formed an intent to serve the employer's business.[59] Such cases leave much room for different evaluations by the jury about the extent and expectation of deviation from or return to employment.[60]

Non-work-related tasks. Although frolic-and-detour terminology is often associated with an employee's geographical or temporal deviation from employment, employees may depart from employment without leaving the situs of their work. They may do so by undertaking tasks alien to the work they were employed to do. For example, an employee hired to cut down an elm tree on the employer's property undertakes to cut down an oak on the neighbor's land. That may enhance the employer's view and hence benefit the employer in some sense, but it is outside the scope of employment and the employer will not be vicariously liable for the employee's tort.[61]

An employee's personal acts. Employees may also depart from employment by engaging in purely personal acts during working hours.[62] Employee participation in recreational activities sponsored or permitted by the employer may remain personal and outside the scope of employment, in spite of the fact that the recreation is offered as compensation or for morale, if the recreation serves no specific business purpose and recreation is not a characteristic of the business.[63] On the other hand, activities on the job that serve both personal and business purposes do not necessarily count as a departure from employment.[64] Most acts for personal comfort, such as using the toilet,[65] taking a coffee break,[66] and even smoking[67] or drinking alcohol[68] are now recognized as acts incident to employment, so that the employer is liable when the employee negligently injures another while so engaged.

---

[58]   The terminology of "frolic and detour" comes from Joel v. Morrison, 172 Eng. Rep. 1338 (1834), in which the court said that where "servants, being on their master's business, took a detour to call upon a friend, the master will be responsible . . . but if he was going on a frolic of his own, without being at all on his master's business, the master will not be liable."

[59]   Prince v. Atchison, Topeka & Santa Fe Ry. Co., 76 Ill.App.3d 898, 32 Ill.Dec. 362, 395 N.E.2d 592 (1979); Fiocco v. Carver, 137 N.E. 309 (N.Y. 1922); Restatement Third of Agency § 7.07, cmt. e (2006); Restatement Second of Agency § 237 (1959).

[60]   E.g., Pyne v. Witmer, 129 Ill.2d 351, 543 N.E.2d 1304, 135 Ill.Dec. 557 (1989); Sheffer v. Carolina Forge Co., 306 P.3d 544 (Okla. 2013).

[61]   See Restatement Second of Agency § 229, Ill. 1 (1959).

[62]   Restatement Third of Agency § 7.07, cmt. d (2006).

[63]   See Richard v. Hall, 874 So.2d 131 (La. 2004) (hunting opportunities made available by employer, but not involved in soliciting business or the like; employer not liable for accidental death caused by employee's discharge of gun); Rogers v. Allis-Chalmers Mfg. Co., 153 Ohio St. 513, 92 N.E.2d 677 (1950) (even though employer paid green fees and provided a shirt for employees' participation in a golf league organized by YMCA, golfer was not within scope of employment when he hooked a ball into the plaintiff).

[64]   Hudson v. Muller, 653 So.2d 942 (Ala. 1995).

[65]   Levine v. Peoples Broadcasting Corp., 149 W.Va. 256, 140 S.E.2d 438 (1965).

[66]   Melin-Schilling v. Imm, 149 Wash.App. 588, 205 P.3d 905 (2009) (driving back from coffee break).

[67]   Edgewater Motels, Inc. v. Gatzke, 277 N.W.2d 11 (Minn. 1979).

[68]   Gutierrez de Gutierrez de Martinez v. Drug Enforcement Admin., 111 F.3d 1148 (4th Cir. 1997).

An Employee's Intentional Torts

In many cases, perhaps most, an employee's intentional torts are purely personal acts and thus not within the scope of employment. An employee strikes a customer because of his personal grudge. Nothing more appearing, the tort is the employee's tort and the employer is not liable. In recent years the reported cases have often involved sexual assaults or other sexual behavior of an employee. Intentional sexual torts, like other violent conduct, is often personal to the employee, so that the employer is usually not found liable.[69]

As noted above,[70] both the Second and Third Restatements of Agency provide that the tortfeasor's act must be motivated, at least in part, to serve the employer.[71] Such an approach leaves little room for vicarious liability of an employer whose worker has committed an intentional tort,[72] although such a result is possible, as where a car dealership's employee fired a pistol at the tires of a vehicle in an attempt to repossess it while a customer was driving it.[73]

However, at least since the middle of the last century, a number of courts have rejected the Restatement formulation by recognizing that intentional torts committed by an employee are within the scope of employment when employment furnishes the specific impetus for or increases a general risk of employee misbehavior.[74] Although the precise tortious act itself is not something the servant was employed to do, it is enough for some courts if the general job activity that gave rise to the tortious act was within the scope of employment.[75] The bar bouncer hired to eject unruly patrons may use excessive force and thus become the author of a battery. Even if that occurs because the bouncer loses his temper or is unnecessarily rough because of an argument with the patron, it is nevertheless the very kind of risk that goes with the work, and the bar owner is vicariously liable.[76] The employee who commits assault and battery on a competitor's worker to try to prevent theft of his employer's stored supplies will be found to be acting

---

[69]   E.g., Hansen v. Board of Trustees of Hamilton Southeastern School Corp., 551 F.3d 599 (7th Cir. 2008) (teacher's sexual misconduct with student); Frieler v. Carlson Marketing Group, 751 N.W.2d 588 (Minn. 2008) (supervisor's sexual harassment, accompanied by assault and battery, of fellow employee); Barnett v. Clark, 889 N.E.2d 281 (Ind. 2008) (deputy trustee's rape and false imprisonment of applicant for public assistance); Doe v. Newbury Bible Church, 182 Vt. 174, 933 A.2d 196 (2007) (pastor's sexual misconduct); Zsigo v. Hurley Medical Ctr., 475 Mich. 215, 716 N.W.2d 200 (2006) (employee's sexual assault on patient); Porter v. Harshfield, 329 Ark. 130, 948 S.W.2d 83 (1997) (ultrasound technician sexually assaulted a patient while performing a gallbladder examination); Baumeister v. Plunkett, 673 So.2d 994 (La. 1996) (hospital supervisor sexually assaulted clinical technician in nurse's lounge of hospital during business hours); Lisa M. v. Henry Mayo Newhall Mem. Hosp., 12 Cal.4th 291, 48 Cal.Rptr. 510, 907 P.2d 358 (1995) (ultrasound technician employed by hospital extended the examination in a sexual way).

[70]   See § 31.3.

[71]   Restatement Third of Agency § 7.07 (2006); Restatement Second of Agency § 228(1)(c) (1959).

[72]   See, e.g., Nichols v. Land Transport Corp., 223 F.3d 21 (1st Cir. 2000) (truck driver stabbed motorist in "road rage" incident; no vicarious liability because the act was not motivated by a purpose to serve the master); Davis v. Devereux Foundation, 209 N.J. 269, 37 A.3d 469 (2012) (employee of home for developmentally disabled poured hot water over resident; conduct was "clearly outside the scope of her employment" because "it was not by any measure 'actuated' by a purpose to serve" the employer).

[73]   Patterson v. Blair, 172 S.W.3d 361 (Ky. 2005).

[74]   See Ira S. Bushey & Sons, Inc. v. United States, 398 F.2d 167 (2d Cir. 1968); see also Carr v. Wm. C. Crowell Co., 28 Cal.2d 652, 171 P.2d 5 (1946); Baumeister v. Plunkett, 673 So.2d 994, 996 (La. 1996).

[75]   Plummer v. Center Psychiatrists, Ltd. 252 Va. 233, 476 S.E.2d 172 (1996) (clinical psychologist employed by defendant had sex with patient; court rejected any test based on "motive of the employee"); see also Phillips v. Restaurant Mgmt. of Carolina, L.P., 146 N.C.App. 203, 552 S.E.2d 686 (2001) (restaurant was subject to vicarious liability for customer's distress when the customer discovered that a restaurant employee had spat in his food).

[76]   Mason v. Sportsman's Pub, 305 N.J.Super. 482, 702 A.2d 1301 (1997).

within the scope of employment if his "use of force was foreseeable given his employment and the duties he undertook."[77] The hospital day-care worker who strikes an infant's head on the corner of a shelf to stop the child from crying may leave the hospital vicariously liable unless the worker's action was "so far removed from any work-related endeavor" that it could be seen as "a personal course of conduct unrelated to her work."[78] The bartender who puts a toothpick in a patron's bottle of beer will leave the employer vicariously liable for the patron's injuries, as long as that act was "fairly and naturally incidental to the employer's business, although mistakenly or ill-advisedly done."[79] Still, there are limits even to this broader approach (or set of approaches), and vicarious liability will not be imposed where the employee's acts are fairly seen as "completely personal" or "highly unusual."[80]

Employees in positions of trust and confidence. Counselors, therapists, clergy, youth leaders, and others in a position of trust and confidence often seem to take advantage of innocent or vulnerable patients or parishioners to engage in sexual activity with them, usually to their detriment. Although sexual activity is quintessentially personal, such activity is one of the risks of relationships that generate confidence. Consequently, employers of therapists and clergy have been held subject to vicarious liability in many such cases.[81] The case of outright rape by an employee who is otherwise carrying out employment duties is more difficult, but sometimes even here the employment creates the risk or impetus of the attack, just as it can create the risk of other physical batteries. A police officer's job, for instance, gives him a great deal of coercive power over citizens who might be subject to arrest and inherent in that power is the potential for abuse. Accordingly, the courts have held that the employer was vicariously responsible for a police officer's on-duty rape of a woman he had detained[82] or even a sexual assault on a citizen who is not detained.[83] Even if rape is not an inherent risk of the type of work, vicarious liability is appropriate when, in the particular case, it arises immediately out

---

[77] Kirlin v. Halverson, 758 N.W.2d 436 (S.D. 2008).

[78] Baker v. Saint Francis Hosp., 126 P.3d 602 (Okla. 2005).

[79] Daugherty v. Allee's Sports Bar & Grill, 260 S.W.3d 869 (Mo.App. 2008).

[80] Brown v. Mayor, 167 Md.App. 306, 892 A.2d 1173 (2006) (uniformed police officer not acting within the scope of employment when he murdered a man he suspected of having an affair with his wife). See also Barnett v. Clark, 889 N.E.2d 281 (Ind. 2008) (employee's rape and false imprisonment against client of employer "were not an extension of authorized physical contact" and "not incidental to nor sufficiently associated with [his] authorized duties"); Frieler v. Carlson Marketing Group, 751 N.W.2d 588 (Minn. 2008) (even under a general "foreseeability" test, employer not vicariously liable for supervisor's assault, battery and sexual harassment of another employee, because such acts were entirely personal).

[81] Doe v. Samaritan Counseling Ctr., 791 P.2d 344 (Alaska 1990) (therapist-minister); Marston v. Minneapolis Clinic of Psychiatry and Neurology, Ltd., 329 N.W.2d 306 (Minn. 1982) (psychologist); Fearing v. Bucher, 328 Or. 367, 977 P.2d 1163 (1999) (priest acting as youth pastor, friend and confessor to minor plaintiff and his family; motive to serve employer in actual act of sexual assault not required if priest's general motives included, initially, a desire to serve the Archdiocese); Lourim v. Swensen, 328 Or. 380, 977 P.2d 1157 (1999) (Boy Scout leader); Plummer v. Center Psychiatrists, Ltd. 252 Va. 233, 476 S.E.2d 172 (1996) (psychiatrist; scope of employment a jury question). Contra, Birkner v. Salt Lake County, 771 P.2d 1053 (Utah 1989) (therapist's sexual misconduct with patient in mental health facility not within scope of employment).

[82] Mary M. v. City of Los Angeles, 54 Cal.3d 202, 285 Cal.Rptr. 99, 814 P.2d 1341 (1991); but cf. Lisa M. v. Henry Mayo Newhall Mem. Hosp., 12 Cal. 4th 291, 48 Cal. Rptr. 510, 907 P.2d 358 (1995) (the employment must generate not only the risk of sexual misbehavior but its "motivating emotions" as well).

[83] Doe v. Forrest, 176 Vt. 476, 853 A.2d 48 (2004); but cf. Cockrell v. Pearl River Valley Water Supply Dist., 865 So.2d 357 (Miss. 2004) (patrol officer's attempt to kiss motorist was outside the scope of employment because it was not in furtherance of the employer's business; no discussion of risks associated with the job).

of a conflict generated by the employment[84] and even when it is made peculiarly possible by the employment.[85]

Schools and churches. Some courts take a much narrower view of vicarious liability, at least in cases where the liability of schools and churches is in issue. In a Maryland case, a public school teacher used a ruler to beat a 9-year-old student with Down syndrome who had urinated in his pants, but the court believed that this action was outside the scope of employment because corporal punishment had been forbidden.[86] In a Minnesota case, the court thought a school teacher's sexual activity with a teenaged student represented a risk that was unforeseeable to the school-employer and hence outside the scope of employment, although it occurred in classrooms and at school-related functions.[87] A number of courts have also displayed a determination to relieve churches of liability, often asserting that the First Amendment makes it necessary to do so.[88] It is not clear whether these cases reflect narrow notions of vicarious liability, a preference for the public and religious employers, or merely a lack of information about the kinds of risks associated with the activities involved.

Caretakers. Courts have sporadically recognized that those who undertake the care of people who are helpless to care for themselves may fall under special duties. A day-care center that cares for infants and toddlers would be expected to respond in damages for harms done to such a small child even if the child cannot prove how the harm came about.[89] The special duty of caretakers may be expressed in special rules of respondeat superior as well. In fact, common carriers were once treated as caretakers, because during carriage, their passengers were removed from normal sources of support and relatively helpless.[90] Under this approach, carriers were held responsible for injuries inflicted on passengers by servants who were not in the scope of employment, often on the rationale that an implied contract between carrier and passenger to deliver the passenger safely to her destination creates a nondelegable and strict duty.[91] In an Indiana case,[92] the defendant Children's Center cared for a severely retarded and disabled child of 14, who had the mental capacity of a five-month-old infant. One of its attendants sexually abused the child. In a suit against the Children's Center, the court held that the jury could find these acts sufficiently related to employment to warrant vicarious liability. The court went on to hold, by analogy to the common carrier rule, that the Center's duty to the helpless could not be satisfied by delegating the duty to others.[93]

---

[84] See Lyon v. Carey, 533 F.2d 649 (D.C. Cir. 1976) (truck driver delivering a mattress got into dispute with customer about whether he was to carry it into the apartment, escalating into a rape of the customer).

[85] Costos v. Coconut Island Corp., 137 F.3d 46 (1st Cir. 1998) (rape of guest by manager of inn).

[86] Tall v. Board of School Comn'rs of Baltimore City, 120 Md. App. 236, 706 A.2d 659 (1998).

[87] P.L. v. Aubert, 545 N.W.2d 666 (Minn. 1996).

[88] Doe v. Newbury Bible Church, 182 Vt. 174, 933 A.2d 196 (2007) (stressing that "holding a small church and school vicariously liable" for a pastor's sexual misconduct would not further the policies behind vicarious liability); Destefano v. Grabrian, 763 P.2d 275 (Colo. 1988) (priest, encouraged by church to engage in marriage counseling, also engaged in sexual activity with one of the marital partners he was counseling); Byrd v. Faber, 57 Ohio St. 3d 56, 565 N.E.2d 584, 5 A.L.R.5th 1115 (1991) (similar, rejecting vicarious liability unless the church had hired Faber to rape, seduce or otherwise physically assault congregants).

[89] See § 13.5.

[90] See § 19.1.

[91] See Connell v. Call-A-Cab, Inc., 937 So.2d 71 (Ala. 2006); St. Michelle v. Catania, 252 Md. 647, 250 A.2d 874 (1969); Gilmore v. Acme Taxi Co., 349 Mass. 651, 212 N.E. 235 (1965); Maryland Cas. Co. v. Baker, 304 Ky. 296, 200 S.W.2d 757 (1946); Restatement Third of Agency § 7.06 (2006) (nondelegable duty).

[92] Stropes v. Heritage House Childrens Ctr. of Shelbyville, Inc., 547 N.E.2d 244 (Ind. 1989).

[93] Id.

§ 31.5 Independent Contractors: General Rules

Employers are not vicariously liable for the torts of carefully selected independent contractors,[94] subject to a number of exceptions.[95] Independent contractors are contrasted with the kind of employee traditionally called servants. An independent contractor—say the person hired to paint your car—might be within the scope of employment when he negligently injures someone, but, unless an exception applies, you are not liable for his tort. As the courts see it, it is the contractor's business, the contractor's tort, and the contractor's liability. The employer may be liable in such cases for his own personal negligence if he hires a dangerous contractor or otherwise personally risks harm to the plaintiff, but he is not vicariously liable.[96]

Jurists have found it difficult to formulate a crisp and workable definition of independent contractors, but the concept is easy to understand and in many cases easy to apply as well. Independent contractors are usually persons who are perceived to be operating their own business and hence not subject to the employer's right of control over the manner, means, and details of the work.[97] Instead, the independent contractor's employer has a say-so only about whether the end product is acceptable, not about the exact manner or means used to achieve it.[98] On the other hand, if the employer has a right to control the manner, means, and details of the work, the employee is almost always a servant. Even if the employer does not exercise control over the manner of work but merely has the right to control, the employee is still a servant.[99]

Several kinds of evidence bear on the employer's power to control. The employer's right to discharge the employee; payment of regular wages, taxes, workers' compensation insurance and the like; long-term or permanent employment; and detailed supervision of the work tend to indicate a master-servant relationship. The employee's special skills; the fact that he works for others or is perceived to be in a business of his own; supplies his own tools or instrumentalities; and hires and fires his own employees tend to show that the employee is an independent contractor. Many pieces of subsidiary evidence may be relevant. For instance, the fact that the employer is not in business would tend to show that the employee is an independent contractor operating his own business. All these "factors" in one form or another have been considered in the cases[100] and approved

---

[94]   See, e.g., Patterson v. T.L. Wallace Construction, Inc., 133 So.3d 325 (Miss. 2013); Fifth Club, Inc. v. Ramirez, 196 S.W.3d 788 (Tex. 2006); Sanchez v. Medicorp Health Sys., 270 Va. 299, 618 S.E.2d 331 (2005); Fisher v. Townsends, Inc., 695 A.2d 53 (Del. 1997).

[95]   The two major exceptions: when the employer owes a nondelegable duty of care, see § 31.6, and when the employer creates the appearance that the independent contractor is acting as his servant, see § 31.7.

[96]   The employer may be liable for his own negligence that causes harm to the independent contractor. See, e.g., McKown v. Wal-Mart Stores, Inc., 27 Cal.4th 219, 115 Cal.Rptr.2d 868, 38 P.3d 1094 (2002); Tafoya v. Rael, 145 N.M. 4, 193 P.3d 551 (2008).

[97]   E.g., Mavrikidis v. Petullo, 153 N.J. 117, 707 A.2d 977 (1998); Crocker v. Morales-Santana, 854 N.W.2d 663 (S.D. 2014). Yet some employees who are free to act independently of the employer's control over details of their work nevertheless remain in the category of servant rather than independent contractor. See Dias v. Brigham Med. Assocs., Inc., 438 Mass. 317,780 N.E.2d 447 (2002) (employer of physician may be vicariously liable for torts committed by physician in the scope of his employment).

[98]   See Gaytan v. Wal-Mart, 289 Neb. 49, 853 N.W.2d 181 (2014).

[99]   See, e.g., Sperl v. C.H. Robinson Worldwide, Inc., 408 Ill. App. 3d 1051, 349 Ill. Dec. 269, 946 N.E.2d 463 (2011); McDonald v. Hampton Training School for Nurses, 254 Va. 79, 486 S.E.2d 299 (Va. 1997). If the employer actually exercises control, that fact may be good evidence that he has a right or power to do so.

[100]   E.g., Mavrikidis v. Petullo, 153 N.J. 117, 707 A.2d 977 (1998); Walderbach v. Archdiocese of Dubuque, Inc., 730 N.W.2d 198 (Iowa 2007); Kime v. Hobbs, 252 Neb. 407, 562 N.W.2d 705 (1997).

by both the Second and Third Restatements of Agency.[101] No one factor or piece of evidence is controlling. The employee's special skill tends to indicate that he is an independent contractor, but nowadays even skilled professionals such as doctors may be "servants" of a hospital for vicarious liability purposes if they are subject to the employer's control.[102]

The fact that someone works only for a single employer tends to show that he is a servant of that employer, and not an independent contractor. Thus a full-time house cleaner or janitor is a servant, while one who provides cleaning services to all comers may be viewed as operating his own business as an independent contractor.[103] A weighmaster who works exclusively for one chicken processor may be an employee even though he provides his own trucks and hires his own chicken-catching crews.[104]

The own-business and control rules are hard to apply in close cases. Working relationships are varied and the circumstances emit mixed signals. In addition, courts may differ in their sense of appropriate policy. Patients might be surprised to find that their hospital has hired an independent contractor to operate its emergency room.[105] A foster parent who is paid by the state to care for one or more children usually only works for one person—the state. The foster parent is subject to state inspections and some degree of state control. Yet the control may not extend to small daily tasks, so the foster parent may be considered an independent contractor.[106] The newspaper carrier who delivers papers to your porch may be rousted out of bed by the employer if he is late, but sometimes courts have treated him as an independent contractor even though he is permitted to work only for the newspaper.[107]

When the evidence points in both directions, litigation is likely to be required. That litigation is resolved less by rules than by analysis of the evidence pointing to control, with analogies to factually similar cases. When the evidence is substantially mixed, the question is usually one for the jury. But if the undisputed evidence shows that the employer has little control over the means and manner of work, the court may conclude as a matter of law that the worker is an independent contractor.[108]

Franchisees and licensees. Service stations, motels, fast-food outlets and many other businesses may appear to consumers[109] to be manifestations of a national company with a well-known name. Yet the local operator may be an independent contractor who is a licensee of the franchisor's trademark. At the same time, the licensee or franchisee is usually subject to somewhat intense control by the franchisor. For this reason, it is

---

[101] Restatement Second of Agency § 220 (1959); Restatement Third of Agency § 7.07, cmt. f (2006).

[102] See, e.g., McDonald v. Hampton Training School for Nurses, 254 Va. 79, 486 S.E.2d 299 (Va. 1997).

[103] See, e.g., Shaw v. C.B. & E., Inc., 630 So.2d 401 (Ala. 1993).

[104] Fisher v. Townsends, Inc., 695 A.2d 53 (Del. 1997).

[105] And hospitals have been surprised to find that they are nevertheless liable under doctrines of apparent agency or the like. See § 31.7.

[106] District of Columbia v. Hampton, 666 A.2d 30 (D.C. 1995).

[107] Miami Herald Publishing Co. v. Kendall, 88 So.2d 276 (Fla. 1956); contra, Santiago v. Phoenix Newspapers, Inc., 164 Ariz. 505, 794 P.2d 138 (1990) (analyzing factors in detail); Zirkle v. Winkler, 214 W.Va. 19, 585 S.E.2d 19 (2003) (concluding that the weight of authority in newspaper delivery cases treats the status of the employee as a jury issue); see Mary J. Cavins, Annotation, Newspaper Boy or Other News Carrier as Independent Contractor or Employee for Purposes of Respondeat Superior, 55 A.L.R.3d 1216 (1974).

[108] E.g., Leaf River Forest Products, Inc. v. Harrison, 392 So.2d 1138 (Miss. 1981) (that a logger financed his own operation, used his own equipment, hired and fired his own workers, and was paid by volume produced, not by the hour, meant that there was no rational basis for finding a master-servant relationship).

[109] On apparent agency or agency by estoppel, see § 31.7.

sometimes argued that the local enterprise's appearance as an independent contractor is illusory. Although the parties' intent is a factor in determining their status, the fact that they themselves label the agent as an independent contractor is not determinative.[110] Instead, courts will consider many factual details tending to prove or disprove the employer's right to control, or practical exercise of control, over details of the work. Given the employer's interest in protecting its trademark by setting operating standards, courts may tolerate a degree of control over details and still characterize the local operation as an independent contractor.[111]

The local owner or lessee of the gasoline service station, for example, might be subject to many of the national franchisor's company rules, but if he is free to set prices and hours of operation, and free to choose employees, and free to cancel the arrangement, courts are likely to treat him as an independent contractor unless other evidence shows that the franchisor has the right to control details of operation.[112] Similar holdings can be found for fast-food restaurants[113] and other franchisees.[114] Sometimes, even taxi drivers who "lease" a cab from the franchisor are regarded as independent contractors.[115] Everything turns on the facts, however; if the franchisor exercises sufficiently detailed control, the court will permit the jury to find that the franchisee is a servant, not an independent contractor.[116]

§ 31.6 Independent Contractors Performing Nondelegable Duties

In spite of the general rule to the contrary, courts have recognized that a business enterprise should not always escape responsibility by doing its work through independent contractors. When courts conclude that as a matter of policy the enterprise should be responsible for the torts of independent contractors who are carrying out the work of the enterprise, they say that the enterprise had a "nondelegable duty." What they mean by this is that the enterprise cannot discharge its obligation of reasonable care by hiring independent contractors to fulfill it;[117] they do not mean to say that the independent contractor himself escapes liability.[118] Courts conclude that some duties cannot be transferred or shifted to contractors because the enterprise that employs the

---

[110] Santiago v. Phoenix Newspapers, Inc., 164 Ariz. 505, 794 P.2d 138 (1990); Fisher v. Townsends, Inc., 695 A.2d 53 (Del. 1997).

[111] See Ciup v. Chevron U.S.A., Inc., 122 N.M. 537, 928 P.2d 263 (1996) (service station); Cislaw v. Southland Corp., 4 Cal.App.4th 1284, 6 Cal.Rptr.2d 386 (1992) (convenience store).

[112] E.g., Jamison v. Morris, 385 S.C. 215, 684 S.E.2d 168 (2009); Miller v. Sinclair Ref. Co., 268 F.2d 114 (5th Cir. 1959).

[113] Vandemark v. McDonald's Corp., 153 N.H. 753, 904 A.2d 627 (2006); Kennedy v. Western Sizzlin Corp., 857 So.2d 71 (Ala. 2003); O'Banner v. McDonald's Corp., 173 Ill.2d 208, 218 Ill.Dec. 910, 670 N.E.2d 632 (1996); Hoffnagle v. McDonald's Corp., 522 N.W.2d 808 (Iowa 1994).

[114] E.g., Myszkowski v. Penn Stroud Hotel, Inc., 430 Pa.Super. 315, 634 A.2d 622 (1993) (hotel). Cf. Smith v. Delta Tau Delta, Inc., 9 N.E.3d 154 (Ind. 2014) (national fraternity not vicariously liable for torts of local fraternity).

[115] See Hosein v. Checker Taxi Co., Inc., 95 Ill. App. 3d 150, 50 Ill.Dec. 460, 419 N.E.2d 568 (1981); Thomas v. Checker Cab Co., 66 Mich.App. 152, 238 N.W.2d 558 (1975); R. L. Martyn, Annotation, Owning, Leasing, or Otherwise Engaging in Business of Furnishing Services for Taxicabs as Basis of Tort Liability for Acts of Taxi Driver under Respondeat Superior Doctrine, 8 A.L.R.3d 818 (1967).

[116] J.M. v. Shell Oil Co., 922 S.W.2d 759, 764 (Mo. 1996).

[117] See Restatement Third of Agency § 7.06 (2006) ("A principal required by contract or otherwise by law to protect another cannot avoid liability by delegating performance of the duty. . . .").

[118] Gazo v. City of Stamford, 255 Conn. 245, 765 A.2d 505 (2001).

independent contractor reaps the benefit of his work,[119] and can select competent and financially sound contractors who could bear the costs of their own torts.[120]

Inherent danger. Courts say that the duty of care is nondelegable when the employer engages in activities he knows or has reason to know are inherently or intrinsically dangerous.[121] Such activities are dangerous by nature and not merely because they are carried out in a risky manner.[122] If the enterprise hires an independent contractor to dust crops with poison, it is liable for his negligence in doing so, in spite of the fact that he is undoubtedly a contractor and not a servant.[123] The activity need not be abnormally dangerous or ultrahazardous, which would provide an independent ground of employer strict liability.[124] Any things that are destructive by nature fall under the rule for inherently dangerous activities, for example, poisons, explosives or fireworks,[125] strong acids,[126] or high voltage lines in an area of public accommodation.[127] Even an independent contractor's provision of armed guards as part of a security service may be inherently dangerous, making the employer liable for the guards' negligence in using their weapons.[128] And Florida has held that transport of an 82-ton turbine by road is inherently dangerous, with the result that the person who arranged the transport by an independent contractor is vicariously liable.[129]

Peculiar risk. The idea has been extended to cover not merely inherently risky work but also work that creates a "peculiar" or special risk of substantial harm in the absence of special precautions.[130] To be peculiar, the risk must be somehow "different"[131] but the peculiarity of the risk may lie in the eye of the beholder. Courts have included or allowed juries to include the risk that use of a brush-hog will throw out debris that injures

---

[119] Haseman v. Orman, 680 N.E.2d 531, 535 (Ind. 1997).

[120] Miller v. Westcor Ltd. P'ship, 171 Ariz. 387, 831 P.2d 386 (Ct. App. 1992).

[121] Restatement Second of Torts § 427 (1965); see Francis M. Dougherty, Annotation, Liability of Employer With Regard to Inherently Dangerous Work For Injuries to Employees of Independent Contractor, 34 A.L.R.4th 914 (1981). Nuisance is a related idea. See Mavrikidis v. Petullo, 153 N.J. 117, 707 A.2d 977 (1998).

[122] Fike v. Peace, 964 So.2d 651 (Ala. 2007); King v. Lens Creek Ltd. Partnership, 199 W.Va. 136, 483 S.E.2d 265 (1996).

[123] Boroughs v. Joiner, 337 So.2d 340 (Ala. 1976); see also Brandenburg v. Briarwood Forestry Services, 354 Wis.2d 413, 847 N.W.2d 395 (2014) (spraying herbicide on trees).

[124] Restatement Second of Torts § 427, cmt. c (1965). If the contractor is carrying out an abnormally dangerous activity for which he would be strictly liable, see § 32.6, the enterprise, too, may be strictly liable for harms resulting from the abnormally dangerous character of the operation. Bahrle v. Exxon Corp., 145 N.J. 144, 156, 678 A.2d 225, 231 (1996); Saiz v. Belen Sch. Dist., 113 N.M. 387, 827 P.2d 102 (1992); Restatement Second of Torts § 427A (1965).

[125] Miller v. Westcor Ltd. Partnership, 171 Ariz. 387, 831 P.2d 386 (1991); cf. District of Columbia v. Howell, 607 A.2d 501 (D.C. 1992) (school chemistry experiment that went horribly wrong).

[126] Beck v. Woodward Affiliates, 226 A.D.2d 328, 640 N.Y.S.2d 205 (1996).

[127] Saiz v. Belen School Dist., 113 N.M. 387, 827 P.2d 102 (1992).

[128] Pusey v. Bator, 94 Ohio St. 3d 275, 762 N.E.2d 968 (2002) (merging inherent danger and peculiar risk conceptions: "Work is inherently dangerous when it creates a peculiar risk of harm to others unless special precautions are taken.").

[129] American Home Assurance Co. v. National R.R. Passenger Corp., 908 So.2d 459 (Fla. 2005).

[130] E.g., Cunnington v. Gaub, 335 Mont. 296, 153 P.3d 1 (2007). See Restatement Second of Torts §§ 413 & 416 (1965). Inherent danger and peculiar risk represent the same fundamental idea and courts often treat them interchangeably.

[131] See Huddleston v. Union Rural Elec. Ass'n, 841 P.2d 282, 290 (Colo. 1992) (danger risked by the activity must be "different in kind from the ordinary risks that commonly confront persons in the community"); Saiz v. Belen School Dist., 113 N.M. 387, 396, 827 P.2d 102, 111 (1992) (risk must be normal to the work done but "different from one to which persons commonly are subjected by ordinary forms of negligence").

bystanders,[132] that sprayed paint will spatter a neighbor's property,[133] that cranes used in construction will drop girders weighing many tons,[134] that demolition of buildings in a crowded city will cause them to fall into adjacent buildings,[135] and that door-to-door salesmen, once in a prospect's home to sell vacuum cleaners, will sexually assault the customer.[136] In the usual peculiar risk case, the employer is vicariously liable for the contractor's negligence, but quite distinctly, the employer may be liable for its own negligence in failing to provide in the contract for special precautions or to supervise the contractor's work in cases of special danger.[137]

Beyond this, one who employs a contractor to do work that is likely to involve trespass or creation of a nuisance is liable for the harm resulting from such a trespass or nuisance.[138] Underground coal mining necessarily involves risks that removal of coal will cause the surface to subside to the damage of its owners, so it is appropriate to hold the owner of the mine liable for such harm even if a lessee carried out actual removal of the coal.[139] The same idea has been applied when the work to be done runs substantial risks of harm through breach of the peace or otherwise.[140]

Public danger. Special danger in the work itself is not the only basis for finding a nondelegable duty. Such duties are imposed as well when the enterprise acts through contractors to carry on construction or the like in public places, for example in excavating or maintaining a public highway.[141]

Landowner-employers. Many of those who hire independent contractors are landowners contracting for repair or improvements. The duty of a lessor to maintain leased premises in reasonable safety is said to be nondelegable,[142] as it is the possessor's duty to maintain premises in reasonably safe condition, at least for those rightfully upon the land.[143] That duty includes the duty of care imposed when land is held open to the public.[144] In each of these cases, the landowner-employer is subject to liability for the contractor's negligence. For instance, the hotel owner whose independent plumber misconnects the cold water faucet so that a guest is burned in the shower is responsible as if he had done the work himself.[145]

Statutes. Statutes are sometimes construed to provide nondelegable duties.[146] For example, scaffolding acts or the like provide that certain safety standards must be met

---

[132] Falls v. Scott, 249 Kan. 54, 815 P.2d 1104 (1991).

[133] Benesh v. New Era, Inc., 207 Ill. App. 3d 1049, 566 N.E.2d 779, 152 Ill.Dec. 902 (1991).

[134] LaCount v. Hensel Phelps Const. Co., 79 Cal.App.3d 754, 145 Cal.Rptr. 244 (1978).

[135] Majestic Realty Associates, Inc. v. Toti Contracting Co., 30 N.J. 425, 153 A.2d 321 (1959).

[136] McLean v. Kirby Co., a Div. of Scott Fetzer Co., 490 N.W.2d 229 (N.D. 1992); Read v. Scott Fetzer Co., 990 S.W.2d 732 (Tex. 1998).

[137] Traudt v. Potomac Elec. Power Co., 692 A.2d 1326 (D.C. 1997); Gordon v. Sanders, 692 So.2d 939 (Fla. Dist. Ct. App. 1997); Restatement Second of Torts § 413 (1965).

[138] Restatement Second of Torts § 427B (1965).

[139] Haseman v. Orman, 680 N.E.2d 531 (Ind. 1997).

[140] Hester v. Bandy, 627 So.2d 833, 843 (Miss. 1993) (repossession from a debtor).

[141] Restatement Second of Torts §§ 417 cmt. a & 418 (1965).

[142] Id. §§ 419 to 421.

[143] Otero v. Jordon Restaurant Enters., 119 N.M. 721, 895 P.2d 243 (Ct. App. 1995); Restatement Second of Torts § 422 (1965).

[144] Restatement Second of Torts § 425 (1965). Similarly, one who uses a contractor to maintain safety of a chattel supplied to others in the course of business has a nondelegable duty. Id.

[145] Id. Ill. 2.

[146] See Restatement Second of Torts § 424 (1965).

in structural work and that the landowner who employs a contractor as well as the contractor himself is responsible.[147] But courts have gone further by treating statutory commands as creating nondelegable duties even when the statute itself is not construed to require such a rule.[148] For instance, a creditor who hires a contractor to repossess a delinquent debtor's car is liable if the contractor violates a statute by breaching the peace in making the repossession.[149] A contract between employer and contractor might have the same effect, so that the contractor cannot escape liability to the employer when his subcontractors cause harm.[150]

Although the rule that statutes create a nondelegable duty is sometimes stated broadly,[151] as if to say that the employer is liable for harm resulting from any statutory violation by the contractor, that is not so; there are certainly cases that refuse to make a duty nondelegable merely because it is one imposed by statute.[152] Courts seem to use statutes as a basis for creating a nondelegable duty when the statute coincides with judicial notions of fairness or policy. Banks that hire contractors to repossess cars are very definitely pursuing their enterprise as lenders and should be liable for the predictable breaches of the peace that accompany this method of enforcing a security interest. A statute against breach of the peace adds little or nothing to such a perception. In other statutory-violation cases there is no reason to impose liability upon the contractor's employer. If you take a cab to the airport, you have certainly hired an independent contractor, not a servant; but it is highly improbable that you would be liable to an injured person if the driver causes harm by violating a traffic ordinance.

Collateral negligence. Even when the duty is nondelegable, the employer is not responsible for "collateral negligence" of the independent contractor.[153] Collateral negligence creates a risk that is not a usual or inherent part of the work[154] or is outside the scope of the employer's enterprise.[155] For instance, if the contractor's activity is inherently dangerous because it involves explosives, an injury from explosives is definitely an injury inherent in the risk and the employer of the contractor remains subject to liability.[156] On the other hand, if the injury occurs only because a defective ladder is used in connection with the same work, such an injury is collateral because it is not a result of the inherent danger.[157] Similarly, when the nondelegability rule is based

---

[147] See, e.g., Sanatass v. Consolidated Investing Co., 10 N.Y.3d 333, 887 N.E.2d 1125, 858 N.Y.S.2d 67 (2008); Kennerly v. Shell Oil Co., 13 Ill.2d 431, 150 N.E.2d 134 (1958); Evard v. Southern California Edison, 153 Cal.App.4th 137, 62 Cal.Rptr.3d 479 (2007).

[148] E.g., Miller v. Lambert, 196 W.Va. 24, 467 S.E.2d 165 (1995).

[149] MBank El Paso v. Sanchez, 836 S.W.2d 151 (Tex. 1992); accord, Hester v. Bandy, 627 So.2d 833 (Miss. 1993).

[150] Gordon v. Sanders, 692 So.2d 939 (Fla. Dist. Ct. App. 1997).

[151] See Restatement Second of Torts § 424 (1965) (requiring only that the statute impose "specified safeguards or precautions for the safety of others").

[152] E.g., Pelletier v. Sordona/Skanska Const. Co., 286 Conn. 563, 945 A.2d 388 (2008) (no nondelegable duty under state Building Code to inspect steel welds); Midland Oil Co. v. Thigpen, 4 F.2d 85, 53 A.L.R. 311 (8th Cir. 1925) (no nondelegable duty created by state and federal clean-water regulations).

[153] Loyd v. Herrington, 143 Tex. 135, 182 S.W.2d 1003 (1944) (as a joke, independent contractor's employee attached dynamite cap to car engine expecting it to explode when the car was started; it didn't, but it exploded when an auto mechanic opened the hood; because the injury was collateral to the contract, the prime contractor was not liable for these acts of the independent contractor's employees).

[154] Restatement Second of Torts § 426 (1965).

[155] See Clarence Morris, The Torts of an Independent Contractor, 29 Ill. L. Rev. 339, 352 (1935).

[156] Miller v. Westcor Ltd. Partnership, 171 Ariz. 387, 831 P.2d 386 (Ct. App. 1992).

[157] Cf. Barbera v. Brod-Dugan Co., 770 S.W.2d 318 (Mo. Ct. App. 1989) (great heights made work dangerous, but fall was due to defective equipment, not to special danger of heights).

upon the landowner's duty to provide reasonably safe conditions rather than upon inherent danger, the landowner-employer of a contractor will not be responsible for the contractor's negligence in driving negligently to get supplies, but will be liable for harm caused by defective conditions created by the contractor on the land.[158] The affinity of this line of thought with the scope-of-risk rules of proximate cause seems plain enough.

Retained control: primary and vicarious liability. The independent contractor rule does not relieve employers of liability for their own negligence. For example, employers may be negligent in choosing an incompetent and dangerous contractor, or in failing to exercise appropriate supervision and control.[159] The employer is frequently a landowner upon whose land the contractor is working. If the employer retains possession of the land or otherwise retains a degree of control for other reasons, he must exercise that control with reasonable care for the safety of others.[160] The owner who actively directs a contractor's dangerous construction work on his land may thus be held liable for his own negligence, quite apart from any vicarious liability or nondelegable duty. It is also possible to think of retained control as bearing on the owner's purely vicarious liability, because to the extent control is retained, the putative independent contractor may look more like a servant.[161]

§ 31.7   Apparent Agency and Agency by Estoppel

Apparent agency issues arise in the tort-law context when an employer retains an independent contractor but creates the appearance that the contractor is acting as his servant. If the plaintiff deals with the independent contractor in the reasonable belief, induced by the employer's conduct, that she is dealing with the employer himself or his servants, she is entitled to hold the employer vicariously liable when she suffers physical harm at the hands of the contractor.[162] In effect, the plaintiff can hold the employer to the appearances he has created. Similarly, if the employer creates the appearance that an employee is acting within the scope of his employment or authority when he is not, the plaintiff who reasonably relies upon the appearance can rightly subject the employer to vicarious responsibility.[163] The employer's conduct creating apparent agency may include non-action, as where the employer with opportunity to do so fails to clarify appearances that an agent is acting within the scope of employment.[164]

---

[158] See Otero v. Jordon Restaurant Enterprises, 119 N.M. 721, 895 P.2d 243 (Ct. App. 1995). Collateral negligence is also described as casual negligence or negligence in operational detail rather than in plan or general method of work. The fundamental idea, however, is that the landowner's responsibility extends only to features that are characteristic of the work for which he retained the contractor. See Restatement Second of Torts § 426, cmt. a (1965).

[159] See e.g., Puckrein v. ATI Transport, Inc., 186 N.J. 563, 879 A.2d 1034 (2006) (retaining an independent contractor who lacked the proper permits to perform the job legally); Madison by Bryant v. Babcock Ctr., Inc., 371 S.C. 123, 628 S.E.2d 650 (2006) (liability for negligence in choosing contractor or in failing to deal with contractor once the danger it created was discovered); see Restatement Third of Torts (Liability for Physical and Emotional Harm) § 19 (2010).

[160] See Hammond v. Bechtel Inc., 606 P.2d 1269 (Alaska 1980); see also Lee Lewis Const., Inc. v. Harrison, 70 S.W.3d 778 (Tex. 2001).

[161] Hooker v. Dep't of Transportation, 27 Cal. 4th 198, 38 P.3d 1081, 115 Cal. Rptr. 2d 853 (2002).

[162] See, e.g., Restatement Second of Torts § 429 (1965); Restatement Second of Agency § 267 (1959); Restatement Third of Agency § 2.03 (2006). The rule is well-established but some courts have rejected it. See, e.g., Sanchez v. Medicorp Health Sys., 270 Va. 299, 618 S.E.2d 331 (2005).

[163] See Restatement Third of Agency § 2.05 (2006).

[164] Boren v. Weeks, 251 S.W.3d 426 (Tenn. 2008); Wilkins v. Marshalltown Medical and Surgical Center, 758 N.W.2d 232 (Iowa 2008); Burless v. West Virginia University Hospitals, Inc., 215 W.Va. 765, 601 S.E.2d 85 (2004).

For example, suppose the plaintiff wishes to hire a moving or storage company and finds the name "Bekins" in the Yellow Pages. She recognizes the name and calls the listed number. The phone call is answered "Bekins" and when she retains the company, its employees wear uniforms saying "Bekins." One of the employees negligently sets fire to her house, but upon investigation it appears that the company she hired was merely an independent company permitted to use the Bekins name. In such a case, Bekins is subject to liability, for it has created the appearance that the local company was its agent or servant and not merely a licensee of its trade name.[165]

An issue that has both bedeviled and divided courts in this area is whether a plaintiff must prove reliance on the appearance of agency the defendant has created, and if so, what exactly that means.[166] According to some courts, the Restatement Second of Agency rule for physical harm cases,[167] often called agency by estoppel, requires reliance by the plaintiff. But, the same jurists say, the Restatement Second of Torts rule,[168] often called apparent or ostensible agency, allows recovery without reliance,[169] specifically only a "reasonable belief" that the services are being rendered by the employer.[170]

The two Restatements reflect an even greater difference on another issue. The Restatement Second of Agency—the "estoppel" approach as the courts have labeled it— requires that the employer manifest or create the appearance that the employee is a servant. The Restatement Second of Torts imposes no such requirement. It requires only that the services be accepted in the reasonable belief that they are delivered by the defendant rather than an independent contractor. The plaintiff's reasonable belief will most often arise because of the defendant's acts in creating the appearance of agency. Under the estoppel approach, even the plaintiff who reasonably believes that the independent contractor is the defendant's servant cannot recover without showing that the defendant himself created that belief.[171]

Moving toward resolution. The Restatement Third of Agency, unlike the Second, divides "apparent authority"[172] and "estoppel to deny existence of an agency relationship"[173] into two sections and sets up different rules for each. Apparent authority requires no reliance at all, only that a third party (such as a plaintiff) "reasonably believes the actor has authority to act on behalf of the principal and that belief is traceable to the principal's manifestations."[174] Agency by estoppel, on the other hand, applies when a person "has not made a manifestation" that an actor is an agent; such a person may nonetheless be liable to anyone "who justifiably is induced to make a detrimental change in position" because of a belief in the agency relation, if the defendant has either "intentionally or carelessly caused such belief," or having notice of

[165] Independent Fire Ins. Co. v. Able Moving and Storage Co., 650 So.2d 750 (La. 1995).

[166] See 2 Dobbs, Hayden & Bublick, The Law of Torts § 433 (2d ed. 2011 & Supp.).

[167] Restatement Second of Agency § 267 (1959).

[168] Restatement Second of Torts § 429 (1965).

[169] Jackson v. Power, 743 P.2d 1376 (Alaska 1987). See also Fletcher v. South Peninsula Hosp., 71 P.3d 833 (Alaska 2003) (applying *Jackson*); Osborne v. Adams, 346 S.C. 4, 550 S.E.2d 319 (2001).

[170] The Restatement Second of Agency actually requires only an attenuated kind of reliance, as opposed to the kind of but-for reliance the term itself would imply (i.e., that the plaintiff would not have used the services but for the fact that it was the defendant's service). Both Restatement Seconds, then, which have been widely cited for years on these points, are likely to call for the same result in many tort cases.

[171] Baptist Memorial Hosp. System v. Sampson, 969 S.W.2d 945 (Tex. 1998).

[172] Restatement Third of Agency § 2.03 (2006).

[173] Id. § 2.05.

[174] Id. § 2.03.

it has failed to correct the misapprehension.[175] All of the examples and illustrations in the latter section deal with transactions, not torts, meaning that the Restatement Third of Agency has now staked out the position that reliance is not required in the usual tort case, bringing it in line with the Restatement Second of Torts.[176]

Whatever their differences on the reliance requirement, most courts have invoked apparent or ostensible agency when hospitals farm out some of their routine or "integral"[177] functions to independent physicians.[178] Patients who seek medical assistance in a hospital's regular, full-time emergency room no doubt believe they are getting care provided by the hospital. The hospital, however, may have arranged for physicians' groups to provide emergency-room services as independent contractors. In such cases courts have said that the hospital has created the appearance that the emergency room is part of the hospital itself and hence that it is subject to liability for emergency-room malpractice under an ostensible or apparent agency theory, or at least that the jury could so find from the evidence.[179] The same may be said for other hospital units, so long as the hospital's self-presentation leads the patient reasonably to believe that she is being treated by the hospital and its own physicians.[180] There seems to be no reason to limit the principle to institutions. For this reason, a physician who performs medical procedures in his office but uses the services of a nurse anesthetist who is an independent contractor may be liable for the nurse's negligence under the ostensible-agency rule.[181]

The plaintiff seeking hospital emergency care relies in a loose or attenuated sense on the hospital's care, but almost certainly does not rely in the sense that the patient would have refused care had she known that the physician providing it was an independent contractor.[182] Nevertheless, this reliance—*expectation* might be a more accurate word—has been sufficient in emergency-room cases, if indeed reliance is required at all in the physical harm cases.

Courts may not apply this looser concept of reliance so readily in all cases. Suppose the plaintiff slips and falls in a local McDonald's restaurant. The local restaurant may be owned by an independent contractor, who pays for the privilege of using the McDonald's name and is obliged to follow the franchisor's rules but who is not the servant of the franchisor. Nevertheless, the almost uniform appearance of such restaurants, the use of trademarks and the trade name, the standardized food items and promotions

---

[175]   Id. § 2.05.

[176]   See, applying the rule, Jones v. HealthSouth Treasure Valley Hosp., 147 Idaho 109, 206 P.3d 473 (2009) (hospital could be vicariously liable for the torts of an independent contractor based on apparent authority without any showing of reliance).

[177]   Integral services of the hospital may include radiology and pathology as well as emergency department services. See Jennison v. Providence St. Vincent Medical Ctr., 174 Or. App. 219, 25 P.3d 358 (2001).

[178]   Distinguish "staff physicians" who merely have permission to use hospital facilities but who are retained in the first instance by the patient.

[179]   Jackson v. Power, 743 P.2d 1376 (Alaska 1987) (refined and codified by Alaska Stats. § 09.65.096); Clark v. Southview Hosp. & Family Health Ctr., 68 Ohio St. 3d 435, 628 N.E.2d 46, 58 A.L.R. 5th 929 (1994); Jennison v. Providence St. Vincent Medical Ctr., 174 Or. App. 219, 25 P.3d 358 (2001).

[180]   See Osborne v. Adams, 346 S.C. 4, 550 S.E.2d 319 (2001) (NICU or neonatal intensive care unit presented as part of hospital's excellent facilities).

[181]   Parker v. Freilich, 803 A.2d 738 (Pa. Super. 2002).

[182]   This is essentially the analysis of the issue in York v. Rush-Presbyterian-St. Luke's Medical Ctr., 222 Ill.2d 147, 854 N.E.2d 635, 305 Ill.Dec. 43 (2006). The court, looking at earlier Illinois precedent, concluded that the "reliance" element of apparent authority could be satisfied by a showing that "the plaintiff relies upon *the hospital* to provide medical care, rather than upon a specific physician." (Emphasis in original.)

might all give customers the impression that a single entity operates all local restaurants and that the entity is McDonald's, the franchisor. To this kind of claim some courts have answered that the plaintiff did not rely on the franchisor's care, at least with respect to the injuries suffered in the particular case,[183] although others have denied the apparent-agency claim on the ground that a franchisor does not hold out the franchisee as an agent merely by licensing the trademark to him.[184]

Everything depends upon an assessment of the facts, so in some franchise cases the franchisor is liable because he has created the appearance that the local unit is part of the larger operation.[185] If injury allegedly results from food in a McDonald's restaurant, for example, the fact that the plaintiff patronized a local McDonald's outlet because she had confidence in McDonald's food would suffice to show reliance.[186] Perhaps the hospital cases are stronger cases for vicarious liability, not so much because the holding-out and reliance are different, but because of public policy concerns with health care.[187]

§ 31.8   Borrowed Servants

The problem of the borrowed (or loaned) servant arises when one person directs his servant, as a part of the job, to do work for another. For example, Company M may rent heavy equipment to Company B and furnish the servant as operator. If the servant negligently causes injury to others, the question is whether vicarious liability should be visited upon M as the general employer, or upon B as the special employer, or upon both.

Control test. The answer is such cases usually turns on the familiar control test,[188] perhaps coupled with a sense that "short term cooperation" is not the same thing as a loaned employee.[189] If the general employer retains control, then courts usually say that he and only he is vicariously liable for the loaned servant's tort. On the other hand, if the special employer has the right to direct details of the borrowed servant's conduct, then the special employer is the temporary master and he becomes vicariously liable. In that case, the general employer is not liable under respondeat superior rules.

It is quite possible that the general employer will retain control over some activities of the servant, while the special employer will have control over others, with liability for an act following control, wherever it lies.[190] Although courts say that what counts is control over details, the manner, means, and day-to-day work, control is not a precise concept. In fact, courts may require on-the-spot control over details in one breath, while in the next permitting an "inference" of control based on who pays or furnishes equipment of the employee.[191] In addition, there are usually important ways in which

---

[183] O'Banner v. McDonald's Corporation, 173 Ill.2d 208, 218 Ill.Dec. 910, 670 N.E.2d 632 (1996).

[184] Mobil Oil Corp. v. Bransford, 648 So.2d 119 (Fla. 1995) (service station); Smith v. Foodmaker, Inc., 928 S.W.2d 683 (Tex. App. 1996) (fast-food restaurant).

[185] Crinkley v. Holiday Inns, Inc., 844 F.2d 156 (4th Cir. 1988) (motel bandits at a Holiday Inn franchise, reliance found in part because guest had specifically sought out Holiday Inn).

[186] Miller v. McDonald's Corp., 150 Or.App. 274, 945 P.2d 1107 (1997).

[187] See York v. Rush-Presbyterian-St. Luke's Medical Ctr., 222 Ill.2d 147, 854 N.E.2d 635, 305 Ill.Dec. 43 (2006); Clark v. Southview Hosp. and Family Health Ctr., 68 Ohio St. 3d 435, 628 N.E.2d 46 (1994).

[188] The evidence to show control or its lack is similar to that used to establish the employee's status as a servant in other cases. See § 31.5.

[189] See Frank L. Maraist & Thomas C. Galligan, Jr., The Employer's Tort Immunity: A Case Study in Post-Modern Immunity, 57 La. L. Rev. 467, 487 (1997) (discussing workers' compensation effects of borrowing).

[190] New York Cent. R. Co. v. Northern Indiana Public Service Co., 140 Ind. App. 79, 221 N.E.2d 442 (1966); Restatement Second of Agency § 227, cmt. a (1959).

[191] Galvao v. G.R. Robert Const. Co., 179 N.J. 462, 846 A.2d 1215 (2004).

the general employer retains control at the same time that the special employer has control over some particular acts.[192] Control is thus indeterminate in many cases, so that cases reciting control elements are necessarily decided on the basis of judicial beliefs about appropriate outcomes that are not directly related to control.[193] Because facts bearing on control frequently lead to conflicting conclusions, sometimes courts merely leave the "whose servant" issue to the jury.[194]

Treating both lender and borrower as employers. Given uncertain or conflicting conclusions based upon control, some courts have simply said that both the general and special employers should be treated as masters of the worker, or at least that they could be so treated in particular cases.[195] On the surface, treating both employers as masters offers a common-sense solution to the problem in one setting. Suppose that Simon is the regular employee of Company M, but is loaned to Company B to dig a trench with a backhoe. At B's direction, Simon digs the trench to a dangerous depth. The trench later caves in and injures the plaintiff, who was employed by B to lay pipe in the trench. From the plaintiff's point of view the maximum benefits can be obtained if (a) he can claim workers' compensation from B, his employer and (b) sue M in tort for damages. If both M and B are deemed masters of the loaned servant who dug the ditch, the plaintiff will be able to assert both claims.[196] Those who like this solution may find it less attractive, however, if M's servant Simon is injured while digging the trench for B. If both B and M are masters, each will owe workers' compensation benefits, but neither will be liable in tort under the rule that workers' compensation is the exclusive remedy for a covered employee.[197] If B negligently caused the injury, the effect of treating both employers as masters in this setting is that B acquires an immunity in tort.

Captain-of-the-ship doctrine. One variation on the borrowed-servant theme occurs in a medical malpractice setting when a nurse or resident employed by a hospital is directed to assist an independent surgeon in an operation, and negligently harms the patient. Some courts have said on such facts that the surgeon was "captain of the ship" and temporarily had the right to control the nurse's work, so should be liable for the negligence of hospital employees who assisted him,[198] or that the hospital would not be liable at all because its employee had become the surgeon's servant.

If this doctrine imputes control to the surgeon as a matter of law and without regard to the facts, it is more stringent than the borrowed-servant doctrine because the borrowed-servant doctrine would treat the surgeon's control as a question of fact to be determined case by case. Some courts have rejected the doctrine so far as it automatically holds the surgeon liable, but have left room for ordinary applications of the borrowed-servant rule, so that if the surgeon in fact has control of hospital employees in the

---

[192] See Armoneit v. Elliott Crane Service, Inc., 65 S.W.3d 623 (Tenn. App. 2001) (discussing many cases).

[193] Some courts have attempted to resolve borrowed servant issues by asking which of the two employers benefits, or whose business is furthered by the servant's activity. See, e.g., Franks v. Independent Prod. Co., 96 P.3d 484 (Wyo. 2004) (using a dual "benefit" and "control" test).

[194] E.g., Eastman v. R. Warehousing & Port Services, Inc., 141 So.3d 77 (Ala. 2013); Estate of Himsel v. State, 36 P.3d 35 (Alaska 2001); Weaver v. Brush, 166 Vt. 98, 689 A.2d 439 (1996).

[195] Bright v. Cargill, Inc., 251 Kan. 387, 837 P.2d 348 (1992); Kastner v. Toombs, 611 P.2d 62 (Alaska 1980); Marsh v. Tilley Steel Co., 26 Cal.3d 486, 606 P.2d 366 (1980).

[196] See Kastner v. Toombs, 611 P.2d 62 (Alaska 1980).

[197] See § 36.5.

[198] See McConnell v. Williams, 361 Pa. 355, 65 A.2d 243 (1949) (originating the metaphor); Rudeck v. Wright, 218 Mont. 41, 709 P.2d 621 (Mont. 1985); Ochoa v. Vered, 212 P.3d 963 (Colo. App. 2009).

operating room, he is vicariously liable, otherwise not.[199] When courts automatically impose liability upon the surgeon for acts of hospital personnel, the case appears to be one of a nondelegable duty,[200] perhaps grounded upon the special duties undertaken by those who care for helpless persons[201] rather than upon control. When a court imposes a nondelegable duty as a matter of policy, the law will be clarified by dropping the "captain" terminology.

Such a nondelegable duty may be less compelling than it was when hospitals had the protection of blanket charitable immunities so that they could not be sued for their employees' negligence. But immunities have made a strong if incomplete comeback in the form of damage caps if nothing else.[202] In addition, doctors and hospitals are in a position to contract for indemnity of the surgeon in such cases, so a nondelegable duty, recognized as such or imposed under the captain-of-the-ship doctrine, is not without some purpose to the plaintiff.

---

[199]　E.g., Nazar v. Branham, 291 S.W.3d 599 (Ky. 2009); Starcher v. Byrne, 687 So.2d 737 (Miss. 1997); Harris v. Miller, 335 N.C. 379, 438 S.E.2d 731 (1994).

[200]　See Long v. Hacker, 246 Neb. 547, 520 N.W.2d 195 (1994) (surgeon's liability for radiologist's X-ray interpretation).

[201]　See McConnell v. Williams, 361 Pa. 355, 65 A.2d 243 (1949) (after analogizing the surgeon's control to that of the captain, emphasizing that the unconscious patient was entitled to special protection "by reason of her trust and confidence in, and necessary reliance upon, the surgeon she employed to take care of her and her child when born").

[202]　See § 23.3. In Lewis v. Physicians Ins. Co. of Wisconsin, 627 N.W.2d 484 (Wis. 2001), the court said that the captain of the ship doctrine was developed only because hospitals had charitable immunity, so courts helped the plaintiff by allowing her to recover against the surgeon, but that such judicial assistance was no longer needed after the abolition of charitable immunity. However, in that very case, the hospital was immunized for all liability in excess of $50,000.

Chapter 32

STRICT LIABILITY FOR ANIMALS AND ABNORMALLY DANGEROUS ACTIVITIES

Analysis

A. INTRODUCTION

§ 32.1   Pockets of Strict Liability in a Fault-Based System

B. STRICT LIABILITY FOR ANIMALS

§ 32.2   Trespassing Animals
§ 32.3   Abnormally Dangerous Domestic Animals
§ 32.4   Wild Animals

C. STRICT LIABILITY FOR ABNORMALLY DANGEROUS ACTIVITIES

§ 32.5   Historical Context: From *Rylands* to the Restatement
§ 32.6   Contemporary Abnormal-Danger Cases
§ 32.7   Rationales for Abnormal-Danger Strict Liability

D. LIMITATIONS AND DEFENSES

§ 32.8   Limitations on Strict Liability
§ 32.9   Defenses to Strict Liability

A. INTRODUCTION

§ 32.1 Pockets of Strict Liability in a Fault-Based System

Strict liability is imposed upon a defendant without proof that he was at fault. In other words, when liability is strict, neither negligence nor intent must be shown. Strict liability is routinely imposed for breach of contract, but is not so common in tort law. The liability of a master for torts of a servant, seen in the last chapter and justified either on grounds of fairness or economic analysis, is a species of strict liability so far as the fault-free master is concerned. An even older form was found in early tort law, which, according to traditional views, imposed strict liability for all direct and forcible harms to person or property[1] and perhaps for the spread of fire as well. In the mid-19th century, fault became the normal basis for tort liability,[2] but pockets of strict liability remained.

The cases of strict liability discussed in this chapter have in common the fact that the defendant created or introduced a dangerous condition not commonly accepted or reciprocated in the social unit.[3] The risk introduced is not necessarily a very large one,

---

[1]   See §§ 9.2 & 9.3.

[2]   See Brown v. Kendall, 60 Mass. 292, 6 Cush. 292 (1850) (rejecting strict liability for direct and forcible harms).

[3]   Many states have even today retained isolated pockets of strict liability that have nothing to do with abnormal dangers, but do involve the imposition of non-reciprocal risks. See, e.g., Prete v. Cray, 49 R.I. 209, 141 A. 609 (1928) (landowner removing soil from his own land, causing adjacent lands to subside of their own

but it is always generated by an activity not commonly pursued in the relevant community or neighborhood. The cases fall roughly into two factual settings. In one, the defendant introduces wild or abnormally dangerous domestic animals into a community. In the other, the defendant uses explosives or other forces that are not common in the community, subjecting others to risks that are quite different from the risks the community imposes upon the defendant.

B. STRICT LIABILITY FOR ANIMALS

§ 32.2 Trespassing Animals

In early England, if a cattle owner drove his cattle onto your land so that your crops were trampled, he would easily be liable under the writ of Trespass, since he directly caused an entry onto your land.[4] However, if the cattle merely escaped and wandered onto your land, the entry looks indirect and thus does not sound like an appropriate use of the Trespass writ. When these claims first arose, however, courts had to use the Trespass writ or nothing, because Case, with its idea of negligence, had not yet been invented. The writ of Trespass carried strict liability with it, so that, with some exceptions,[5] the owner of wandering cattle was strictly liable, just as he was strictly liable in other cases where the writ of Trespass was used.[6] The rule stuck even after the writ of Case became available. The rule of strict liability applied to barnyard animals generally.[7] It did not apply to pets like dogs and cats,[8] although the keeper of such animals might be liable for negligently or intentionally causing them to enter the land.[9]

Modern applications. Imposing this form of strict liability put the economic burden upon cattle owners to protect crop-growers, perhaps by building fences to keep cattle in. The Restatement Second imposed strict liability for the trespass, but not for personal injuries caused by the trespassing animals.[10] The Restatement Third expands strict liability for trespassing animals (other than cats and dogs) to any physical injury resulting from animal intrusion that is a characteristic of such intrusion.[11] Many states, especially in the west, substantially reversed the common law strict liability rule by adopting statutes allowing landowners to recover for harm done by trespassing cattle only if the landowner had first erected a fence that met statutory standards—a "fencing

---

weight); Haseman v. Orman, 680 N.E.2d 531 (Ind. 1997) (owner of mineral rights removing support for the surface of plaintiff's land).

[4]   For the rules of the writ of Trespass and the distinction between Trespass and Case see §§ 2.8 & 9.2.

[5]   There were exceptions for cattle being driven along a public way; in that case, liability was imposed only for negligence. See Restatement Second of Torts § 505 (1977).

[6]   This account is based upon L. Glanville Williams, Liability for Animals (1939).

[7]   E.g., Gresham v. Taylor, 51 Ala. 505 (1874) (hogs); Adams Bros. v. Clark, 189 Ky. 279, 224 S.W. 1046, 14 A.L.R. 738 (1920) (chickens); Nixon v. Harris, 15 Ohio St.2d 105, 238 N.Ed.2d 785 (1968) (cow); Morgan v. Hudnell, 52 Ohio.St. 552, 40 N.E.716 (1895) (horse).

[8]   Van Houten v. Pritchard, 315 Ark. 688, 870 S.W.2d 377 (1994) (tomcat running at large, and "spraying" the plaintiff's property, no liability for its bite resulting in multiple surgeries).

[9]   See Pegg v. Gray, 240 N.C. 548, 551, 82 S.E.2d 757, 759 (1954) ("in deference to this natural instinct of dogs . . . [the law allows] a reputable dog a modicum of liberty to follow his roaming instincts without imposing liability on its master," but owner of pack of foxhounds who engaged in a chase adjoining the plaintiff's farm would be liable for the damage they caused if he sent them out knowing they would enter the land); Baker v. Howard County Hunt, 171 Md. 159, 188 A. 223 (1936) (similar).

[10]   See Williams v. Goodwin, 41 Cal.App.3d 496, 116 Cal.Rptr. 200 (1974) (liability for unprovoked attack by bull trespassing in plaintiff's garden; reviewing cases considering whether injuries were a direct result of the trespass); Restatement Second of Torts § 504(2) (1977); James L. Rigelhaupt, Jr., Annotation, Liability for Personal Injury or Death Caused by Trespassing or Intruding Livestock, 49 A.L.R.4th 710 (1987).

[11]   Restatement Third of Torts (Liability for Physical and Emotional Harm) § 21, cmt. g (2010).

out" rule.[12] That left the rancher liable for intentionally driving his cattle upon the land of others, but not strictly liable and not liable for ordinary negligence.[13]

As some areas became more settled and fencing more practical, however, legislatures partly returned to the common law rule by imposing liability upon ranchers for livestock trespasses unless the rancher could show he had built an adequate fence to contain them.[14] Frequently enough, current statutes provide for open range and free grazing without liability for areas where cattle ranching is dominant, but adopt a different rule for other localities or permit a kind of local option.[15] Local control over the issue is also furthered by contracts or easements assigning grazing rights, and—informally—by local customs.[16] However, a great deal of public land owned and managed by the federal government is leased or allotted for grazing. Rights of the government against trespassing graziers are not dependent upon the state rules.[17]

Highway cases. Under any of the rules, injuries inflicted by livestock loose on a public highway represent a different problem. If a motorist is injured in colliding with a cow, there is no trespass to land and hence no strict liability claim. In most instances, the defendant responsible for an animal who strays onto the highway is liable for negligence and only for negligence.[18] Such liability is imposed by some courts even when the defendant is entitled to graze animals on open range.[19] Others have held that open-range rules, perhaps in combination with a scheme of statutory regulation, relieve the owner of any duty of reasonable care to keep livestock off the roads.[20] Some courts have taken the position that the animal owner owes no duty at all to those on the highway and hence is not liable to them in any case, even for negligence.[21]

§ 32.3 Abnormally Dangerous Domestic Animals

Owners and keepers of domestic animals such as dogs and cats are not strictly liable for the animals' trespasses at all, but under limited conditions can be strictly liable for

---

[12] E.g., Colo. Rev. Stat. § 35–46–102. Ellickson concluded that the fencing out rule became the dominant rule in the 19th century and was not limited to western states. Robert C. Ellickson, Of Coase and Cattle: Dispute Resolution among Neighbors in Shasta County, 38 Stan. L. Rev. 623, 660, n. 94 (1986).

[13] Garcia v. Sumrall, 58 Ariz. 526, 121 P.2d 640 (1942) (noting a division of opinion as to what constitutes willful trespass, holding that mere foreseeability is not enough).

[14] See, e.g., Williams v. Goodwin, 41 Cal.App.3d 496, 116 Cal.Rptr. 200 (1974) (recounting history); Cal. Food & Agric. Code § 17122 (limiting victim's rights unless he had a "good and substantial" fence).

[15] E.g., Ariz. Rev. Stats. § 3–1421 (taxpayers may petition to establish a district to reverse the fence-out rule).

[16] See Robert C. Ellickson, Of Coase and Cattle: Dispute Resolution among Neighbors in Shasta County, 38 Stan. L. Rev. 623 (1986).

[17] See John S. Harbison, Hohfeld and Herefords: the Concept of Property and the Law of the Range, 22 N.M. L. Rev. 459, 484 ff. (1992).

[18] E.g., Hastings v. Sauve, 21 N.Y.3d 122, 967 N.Y.S.2d 658, 989 N.E.2d 940 (2013).

[19] Owners and keepers (and others) may be liable for negligently failing to prevent harms inflicted by animals. See, e.g., Klobnak v. Wildwood Hills, Inc., 688 N.W.2d 799 (Iowa 2004); Carrow Co. v. Lusby, 167 Ariz. 18, 804 P.2d 747 (1990).

[20] Andersen v. Two Dot Ranch, Inc., 49 P.3d 1011 (Wyo. 2002).

[21] Douglass v. Dolan, 286 Ill. App. 3d 181, 675 N.E.2d 1012, 221 Ill.Dec. 588 (1997) (no common law duty, but recovery if the plaintiff can bring herself within a statute imposing liability upon those in charge of animal); James L. Rigelhaupt, Jr., Annotation, Liability of Owner of Animal for Damage to Motor Vehicle or Injury to Person Riding Therein Resulting from Collision with Domestic Animal at Large in Street or Highway, 29 A.L.R.4th 431 (1981).

personal injuries inflicted by such animals.[22] Such liability is imposed only when the owner or keeper knows or has reason to know that his animal is abnormally dangerous in some way and injury results from that danger.[23] For example, if a dog owner knows or at least has notice[24] that his dog has an abnormal or vicious propensity to attack and bite, or his horse to kick, he is strictly liable for the dog's biting and the horse's kicking. Of course, some dog bites and horse kicks are entirely normal to the species; strict liability is imposed, if at all, when an animal has an *abnormal* propensity to bite, kick or otherwise cause harm. For example, there is nothing abnormal about an aggressive bull or a frisky horse, and thus the keeper of such animals is not strictly liable for injuries inflicted as a result of those characteristics unless some added and abnormal quality is shown.[25] The rule does not entitle every animal to "one bite"; the owner or keeper may be aware of an animal's abnormally dangerous traits long before it harms anyone.[26]

Strict liability is not absolute liability; the plaintiff must prove that the animal's dangerous propensity is a cause of the plaintiff's harm. The fact that the plaintiff is injured by an abnormally dangerous animal is not relevant if the injury results from some normal trait or from a danger of which the keeper had neither knowledge nor notice.[27] For example, if a dog's keeper knows of its vicious tendency to bite, but not of its tendency to chase bicycles, the keeper is not strictly liable for injuries caused by the dog's chasing a bicycle.[28] However, if the tendency to bite includes the likelihood that the dog will chase its targeted victim in order to bite him, the chase victim's injury from a fall may well be within the risks imposed by the abnormally dangerous animal. Likewise, knowledge of some traits is capable of generalization—a nervous, agitated horse who is known to bite may be equally likely to kick, in which case strict liability is again appropriate.[29]

Negligence claims. Although in some states courts have approached domestic-animal cases using a negligence analysis,[30] the plaintiff is usually permitted to assert

---

[22]   E.g., Allen v. Cox, 285 Conn. 603, 942 A.2d 296 (2008); Holcomb v. Colonial Assocs., LLC, 358 N.C. 501, 597 S.E.2d 710 (2004); Strunk v. Zoltanski, 62 N.Y.2d 572, 468 N.E.2d 13, 479 N.Y.S.2d 175 (1984); Trager v. Thor, 445 Mich. 95, 516 N.W.2d 69 (1994).

[23]   Morgan v. Marquis, 50 A.3d 1 (Me. 2012); Carreiro v. Tobin, 66 A.3d 829 (R.I. 2013); Restatement Second of Torts § 509 (1977); Restatement Third of Torts (Liability for Physical and Emotional Harm) § 23 (2010).

[24]   Although this knowledge or scienter requirement necessarily means that harm is foreseeable in light of the animal's known propensity, this liability differs from ordinary negligence because liability is imposed even if the defendant exercised reasonable care to prevent the harm. See Van Houten v. Pritchard, 315 Ark. 688, 870 S.W.2d 377 (1994).

[25]   Duren v. Kunkel, 814 S.W.2d 935 (Mo. 1991) (bull); Jividen v. Law, 194 W.Va. 705, 461 S.E.2d 451 (1995) (horse).

[26]   See Van Houten v. Pritchard, 315 Ark. 688, 870 S.W.2d 377 (1994) (rejecting a one-bite rule).

[27]   Restatement Second of Torts § 509 cmt. i (1977); Restatement Third of Torts (Liability for Physical and Emotional Harm) § 23, cmt. g (2010).

[28]   McNair v. Jones, 137 Ga.App. 13, 14, 223 S.E.2d 27, 28 (1975) ("[I]t is necessary that he have reason to know of its propensity to do harm of the type which it inflicts.").

[29]   Restatement Second of Torts § 509 cmt. i (1977); see Restatement Third of Torts (Liability for Physical and Emotional Harm) § 23, cmt. g (2010).

[30]   See Martin v. Christman, 99 A.3d 1008 (Vt. 2014) (no strict liability for dog bites; stating that "eighteen or so states" have adopted strict liability for dog bites, most by statute); see also Vendrella v. Astriab Family Limited Partnership, 311 Conn. 301, 87 A.3d 546 (2014) (strict liability for dog bites by statute, but under common law owners of other domestic animals are liable only for negligence).

her claim under either a theory of strict liability or a theory of negligence or both.[31] The plaintiff may of course establish negligence by showing that the keeper of an animal knew of its abnormally dangerous propensities,[32] but negligence might be shown in other ways as well. For example, if a horse's owner encourages small children to play alone with the horse, he may be negligent even though the horse is not abnormally dangerous, because his conduct put the children at risk even from normal behavior of a horse.[33] Or if a shelter designs and operates a "cat lounge" so as to cause an otherwise calm and docile cat to become agitated and attack a child, negligence liability may be imposed.[34]

Dog-bite statutes. Statutes and ordinances often impose broader liability on dog owners and keepers.[35] Some statutes, for example, provide that an owner is liable for a bite if the plaintiff was bitten in a public place, regardless of whether the dog was vicious or known to be vicious.[36] Such statutes have been applied to cities where the city owned the dog that bit the plaintiff.[37] Ordinances and leash laws potentially imposing liability are also common.[38] The dog-bite statutes usually leave room for defenses based upon provocation or trespass by the plaintiff,[39] or sometimes more generally for a plaintiff's contributory negligence.[40] Further, some courts may give the defendant some wiggle-room where imposing strict liability would work a grave injustice.[41] Nonetheless, it is fair to say that unconditional strict liability is often imposed by statute for dog bites.[42]

---

[31]   Jividen v. Law, 194 W.Va. 705, 461 S.E.2d 451 (1995); Trager v. Thor, 445 Mich. 95, 516 N.W.2d 69 (1994); Arnold v. Laird, 94 Wash.2d 867, 621 P.2d 138 (1980); contra, Petrove v. Fernandez, 12 N.Y.3d 546, 910 N.E.2d 993 (2009) (liability for the owners of domestic animals is strict or not at all).

[32]   Cf. Jackson v. Mateus, 70 P.3d 78 (Utah 2003) (no negligence liability where cat attack was not reasonably foreseeable to owners).

[33]   Williams v. Tysinger, 328 N.C. 55, 399 S.E.2d 108 (1991).

[34]   Lieberman v. Powers, 70 Mass.App.Ct. 238, 873 N.E.2d 803 (2007).

[35]   E.g., Pawlowski v. American Family Mutual Ins. Co., 777 N.W.2d 67 (Wis. 2009) (applying Wisconsin's strict liability dog-bite statute to hold a non-owner strictly liable to a person bitten by a dog the defendant was watching in her home, even where the owner himself was present at the time).

[36]   See Borns ex rel. Gannon v. Voss, 70 P.3d 262 (Wyo. 2003) (counting 20 states with such a statute); Cal. Civ. Code § 3342; 510 ILCS 5/16; N.J. Stat. Ann. 4:19–16; S.C. Code § 47–3–110.

[37]   Wilson v. City of Decatur, 389 Ill.App.3d 555, 329 Ill. Dec. 597 (2009) (holding that the city can be strictly liable pursuant to the dog-bite statute's clear language, even where the city was immune from negligence liability). But see Tate v. City of Grand Rapids, 671 N.W.2d 84 (Mich. App. 2003) (rejecting plaintiff's argument that a statute retaining governmental immunity from "tort liability" did not apply to dog bite statute because statute was "strict liability").

[38]   See, e.g., Poznanski v. Horvath, 788 N.E.2d 1255 (Ind. 2003); Clo v. McDermott, 239 A.D.2d 4, 668 N.Y.S.2d 743 (1998) (violation of ordinance requiring dogs to be under control in public places would be evidence of negligence when dog ran in front of bicycling plaintiff, causing a fall).

[39]   See Stroop v. Day, 271 Mont. 314, 896 P.2d 439 (1995) (plaintiff's act of chasing dog four weeks earlier was not provocation, nor was plaintiff's act of leaning on fence where dog was penned).

[40]   See Dougan v. Nunes, 645 F.Supp.2d 319 (D.N.J. 2009) (noting that New Jersey law allows a defense of contributory negligence in strict liability dog-bite cases, but finding the defense not established where the plaintiff neither knew of the animal's viciousness nor provoked it).

[41]   Wisconsin courts, for example, have sometimes utilized "judicial public policy factors" to avoid imposing statutory strict liability on owners and keepers of dogs. See Pawlowski v. American Family Mutual Ins. Co., 777 N.W.2d 67 (2009); see also Augsburger v. Homestead Mut. Ins. Co., 856 N.W.2d 874 (Wis. 2014) (statutory strict liability of dog owners is in derogation of the common law, so should be interpreted narrowly).

[42]   See Ward Miller, Annotation, Modern Status of Rule of Absolute or Strict Liability for Dogbite, 51 A.L.R.4th 446 (1987); Russell G. Donaldson, Validity and Construction of Statutes, Ordinance, or Regulation Applying to Specific Dog Breeds, such as "Pit Bulls" or "Bull Terriers," 80 A.L.R.4th 70 (1990).

§ 32.4 Wild Animals

General rule. Animals wild by nature and by the customary understanding of the community are treated differently from domestic animals.[43] The English rule held that keepers of wild animals were strictly liable for harm caused by such animals.[44] That is, liability is imposed even if the keeper exercised the utmost care to keep the animal confined and safe.[45] The rule has long been recognized by most American decisions[46] and is accepted by the Restatement,[47] although strict liability for animals is sometimes rejected when it comes to public-entity defendants such as public zoos.[48] The strict liability rule applies even if the animal is not known to have vicious or abnormal propensities to cause harm.[49] Strict liability is, however, limited to harm that results from the wild or dangerous character of the animal or from dangerous traits of which the keeper knows or should know.[50]

Keepers and harborers. The Second Restatement extends strict liability to those who harbor as well as those who own, possess, or keep the animal.[51] For instance, a parent who permits a child to keep a lion on the parent's premises may not possess the lion but harbors it nonetheless and is responsible accordingly.[52] The emphasis shifts from possession and control of the animal to possession and control of the premises. But of course this does not mean that a landowner is strictly liable for injuries inflicted by a wild animal that intrudes upon his property. In that case, liability will be imposed only if the landowner was negligent, for example by negligently failing to repel the animal or to protect guests.[53] The Third Restatement drops the "harboring" terminology and imposes strict liability upon owners or possessors of wild animals (or both where the owner has permitted the possession of another). This does not seem to change the basic coverage of the rule, except that landowning itself is of no significance if the defendant owns or possesses the wild animal.[54] Equally, landowning is of no significance if the animal is not owned but merely a wild animal on the land.[55]

---

[43]   See Harper v. Robinson, 263 Ga. App. 727, 589 S.E.2d 295 (2003).

[44]   See W.V.H. Rogers, Winfield & Jolowicz on Tort 799 (18th ed. 2010); cf. May v. Burdett, 9 Q.B. 101 (1846) (liability for monkey known to be of mischievous nature even if defendant exercised due care).

[45]   City of Dallas v. Heard, 252 S.W.3d 98 (Tex. App. 2008); Smith v. Jalbert, 351 Mass. 432, 221 N.E.2d 744 (1966).

[46]   See, e.g., Irvine v. Rare Feline Breeding Ctr., Inc., 685 N.E.2d 120 (Ind. App. 1997); American States Ins. Co. v. Guillermin, 108 Ohio App.3d 547, 671 N.E.2d 317 (1996) (lion); contra, Vaughan v. Miller Bros. "101" Ranch Wild West Show, 109 W.Va. 170, 153 S.E. 289, 69 A.L.R. 497 (1930).

[47]   Restatement Second of Torts § 507(1) (1977); Restatement Third of Torts (Liability for Physical and Emotional Harm) § 22 (2010).

[48]   See William E. Shipley & Sonja A. Soehnel, Annotation, Governmental Liability from Operation of Zoo, 92 A.L.R.3d 832 (1980) (reflecting decisions both ways). The general rule applied in other cases is that public entities are not strictly liable.

[49]   E.g., Smith v. Jalbert, 351 Mass. 432, 221 N.E.2d 744 (1966) (zebra).

[50]   Restatement Second of Torts § 507(2) (1977); Restatement Third of Torts (Liability for Physical and Emotional Harm) § 22, cmt. f (2010).

[51]   Restatement Second of Torts § 514 (1977).

[52]   See American States Ins. Co. v. Guillermin, 108 Ohio App.3d 547, 671 N.E.2d 317 (1996).

[53]   See Woods-Leber v. Hyatt Hotels of Puerto Rico, Inc., 124 F.3d 47 (1st Cir. 1997) (rejecting statutory strict liability where hotel was invaded by a rabid mongoose which bit a sunbathing guest; there was no evidence of negligence); Overstreet v. Gibson Product Co. of Del Rio, 558 S.W.2d 58 (Tex. Civ. App. 1977) (no strict liability where rattlesnake is on premises but not harbored by defendant).

[54]   Restatement Third of Torts (Liability for Physical and Emotional Harm) § 22, cmt. e (2010).

[55]   Id., implying that the landowner is under no obligation to get rid of wild animals on his land merely because he knows they are there, giving rattlesnakes as an instance.

Defining "wild." The list of animals considered by the courts[56] to be wild runs from Ape[57] to Zebra.[58] It obviously includes such animals as lions and tigers and bears,[59] but courts have classified many others animals, such as elephants, snakes and wolves, as wild,[60] although it is possible that some of these might become domesticated.[61]

The term "wild animals" might imply that only violent, highly dangerous animals are included in the category. It might also be thought that strict liability is imposed for such animals only because of their extraordinary danger and to provide the owner an incentive to remove the tiger from his backyard.[62] But great danger does not in fact seem to be a necessary element in this form of strict liability. Probably no one living in Springfield, Massachusetts, would rate zebra danger as one of the major risks of living in that city, but zebras count as wild animals in Massachusetts, and their owners are strictly liable for harms done.[63] Perhaps, however, the wild animal must be dangerous enough that liability would be imposed if the owner intentionally allowed it to roam. The Third Restatement imposes a double requirement by defining wild animals as those not generally domesticated and which are likely to cause personal injury if not restrained.[64] Whether the Massachusetts Zebra would satisfy this definition is not clear.[65]

The theme that runs through the cases and that explains the rule is that these animals and the risks they bring with them are uncommon or abnormal in the community and therefore not mutual or reciprocal. Whether the abnormal quality of risks associated with wild animals is such that strict liability is justified, the theme of abnormality can be seen in the way the wildness of wild animals is determined. An animal is not regarded as wild merely because it is excessively dangerous nor as domesticated because it is generally safe. An animal is instead wild or domesticated according to whether, by local custom, it is devoted to the service of mankind[66] or commonly treated by the community as a tame or domestic animal. An illustration frequently mentioned is the elephant, which may be regarded as a domestic animal in parts of the former British Empire[67] but not in England itself.[68] Bees are wild in the sense that they have not been trained and also in the sense that they can sometimes be

---

[56]   The classification of an animal as wild is an issue of law for the court. Restatement Third of Torts (Liability for Physical and Emotional Harm) § 22, cmt. b (2010).

[57]   Normand v. City of New Orleans, 363 So.2d 1220 (La. Ct. App. 1978).

[58]   Smith v. Jalbert, 351 Mass. 432, 221 N.E.2d 744 (1966).

[59]   Lion: American States Ins. Co. v. Guillermin, 108 Ohio App.3d 547, 671 N.E.2d 317 (1996); tiger: Irvine v. Rare Feline Breeding Ctr., Inc., 685 N.E.2d 120 (Ind. Ct. App. 1997); bear: City of Mangum v. Brownlee, 181 Okla. 515, 75 P.2d 174 (1938).

[60]   Coyotes: Collins v. Otto, 149 Colo. 489, 369 P.2d 564 (1962); deer (bucks): Hudson v. Janesville Conservation Club, 168 Wis.2d 436, 484 N.W.2d 132 (1992); elephants: Filburn v. People's Palace & Aquarium Co., Ltd., 25 Q.B.D. 258 (1890); monkeys: Whitefield v. Stewart, 577 P.2d 1295 (Okla. 1978) (pet wooly monkey was a "tamed wild animal" and by analogy to dog statute, owner would be strictly liable if it bit without provocation); rattlesnakes: Keyser v. Phillips Petroleum Co., 287 So.2d 364 (Fla. Dist. Ct. App. 1973); wolves: Hays v. Miller, 150 Ala. 621, 43 So. 818 (1907).

[61]   Swain v. Tillett, 269 N.C. 46, 152 S.E.2d 297 (1967).

[62]   G.J. Leasing Co., Inc. v. Union Elec. Co., 54 F.3d 379, 386 (7th Cir. 1995) (Posner, J.) (using tiger in the backyard as analogy in asbestos-release case).

[63]   Smith v. Jalbert, 351 Mass. 432, 221 N.E.2d 744 (1966).

[64]   Restatement Third of Torts (Liability for Physical and Emotional Harm) § 22(b) (2010).

[65]   See id. cmt. b (iguanas, pigeons, and manatees are not dangerous and hence not covered).

[66]   Restatement Second of Torts § 506 (1977).

[67]   Maung Kyaw Dun v. Ma Kyin, 2 Upper Burma Rul. 570 (1897).

[68]   Filburn v. People's Palace & Aquarium Co., Ltd., 25 Q.B.D. 258 (1890).

quite dangerous, but beekeeping is commonly practiced almost everywhere and strict liability is not imposed for bee stings.[69]

C. STRICT LIABILITY FOR ABNORMALLY DANGEROUS ACTIVITIES

§ 32.5 Historical Context: From *Rylands* to the Restatement

Strict liability is imposed for activities that are both highly dangerous and not commonly pursued in the community.[70] Courts impose liability without fault, for example, when carefully handled explosives cause harm. The focus is on whether the plaintiff's injuries are caused by abnormally dangerous *activities* of the defendant, not whether they are caused by dangerous *materials*.[71] The idea is not necessarily to deter such activities altogether but to make them "pay their way" by charging them with liability for harms that are more or less inevitably associated with the activity.[72]

The Nuisance Connection: *Rylands v. Fletcher*

The law of strict liability for abnormally dangerous activities seems to have originated in problems between neighbors arising from their incompatible uses of their lands, a central concern of nuisance law.[73] A theme in many nuisance cases is that the defendant has imposed a nonreciprocal or non-mutual harm upon the plaintiff and one that is out of line with the character and customs of the neighborhood. A noisy factory in a residential neighborhood, for example, substantially impedes the residential neighbors in the enjoyment of their property (and their sleep), but the residential neighbors impose no similar limitation upon the factory owner's enjoyment of his factory.

Several years after Baron Bramwell relied on non-reciprocity as a ground for liability in nuisance in the 1863 case of *Bamford v. Turnley*,[74] the House of Lords decided the famous *Rylands v. Fletcher case*.[75] In *Rylands*, the defendant retained an independent contractor to construct a pond in Lancaster, England. Beneath the land were old mine shafts that had long since been filled or covered. Neither the contractor nor the landowner discovered any reason for concern. The ponded water eventually broke through the debris in the shafts and flowed into them, then through horizontal shafts to flood the plaintiff's mine. The House of Lords held that the landowner who was not negligent at all would be strictly liable. On its face, *Rylands* dealt with a nuisance or something very much like it and in any event it adjudicated rights arising from incompatible land uses.

---

[69] See, e.g., Ferreira v. D'Asaro, 152 So.2d 736, 737 (Fla. App. 1963); David B. Harrison, Annotation, Liability For Injury or Damage Caused by Bees, 86 A.L.R.3d 829 (1978).

[70] Restatement Second of Torts §§ 519 to 520 (1977); Restatement Third of Torts (Liability for Physical and Emotional Harm) § 20 (2010) (formulating the rules differently but with much the same thrust).

[71] Selwyn v. Ward, 879 A.2d 882 (R.I. 2005) (rejecting strict liability for a liquor store's sale of grain alcohol to a minor, where another minor ignited it; even if grain alcohol is a dangerous material, selling it is not a dangerous activity).

[72] See Spano v. Perini Corp., 25 N.Y.2d 11, 17, 302 N.Y.S.2d 527, 531, 250 N.E.2d 31, 34 (1969) (liability does not "exclude the defendant from blasting and thus prevent desirable improvements," nor does it mean that blasting is unlawful; it merely determines who should bear the cost of harms it causes). See also Mark Geistfeld, Should Enterprise Liability Rules Replace the Rule of Strict Liability for Abnormally Dangerous Activities?, 45 U.C.L.A. L. Rev. 611 (1998).

[73] See Chapter 30.

[74] Bamford v. Turnley, 3 B & S 66, 122 Eng.Rep. 25 (Exech. Ch. 1862) (Judgment of Bramwell, B.).

[75] Rylands v. Fletcher, L.R. 3 H.L. 330 (1868).

The Lords in *Rylands* may have advanced two strands of thought. One was that a person who introduces something to the land that is not naturally there and likely to do mischief if it escapes must be held strictly liable for foreseeable harms resulting if it does in fact escape.[76] The focus here seemed to be on the natural state of the land itself and its alteration by humans. The second strand of thought could be understood quite differently to focus on non-natural use of the land, that is, a use of the land that was not natural or normal in the community, or an activity that was incompatible with surrounding land use. The focus of this line may have been on the community's usage and custom, not on the natural condition of the land itself. English courts came to accept some such view. Thus strict liability would be imposed only in the case of "some special use bringing with it increased danger"; landowners would be not be liable for "ordinary" uses of the land. Waters and their storage tanks are not on the land in a state of nature, but they are natural in the sense that they reflect ordinary use, so escape of household water of this kind is not a non-natural use.[77]

Although some nineteenth century American courts accepted *Rylands*,[78] others rejected it because they interpreted it to impose liability without fault even when the land use was perfectly normal.[79] However, courts did impose liability for nuisance-type invasions[80] and, on the theory of trespass, for harm done by use of explosives.[81]

The Restatement formulations

First Restatement. The First Restatement of Torts attempted to reconcile the different strands of reasoning in *Rylands* by providing that strict liability would be imposed for harms resulting from "ultrahazardous" activities, that is, activities that were especially dangerous and could not be made safe even by the exercise of the utmost care. Strict liability would be imposed, however, only if the activity in question was not a matter of common usage.[82]

Second Restatement's factors. The Second Restatement characterized the problem as one involving "abnormally dangerous activities" rather than "ultrahazardous activities," and eliminated the elements of strict liability imposed in the First Restatement in favor of factors to be considered.[83] Under this factors approach, strict liability is more likely to be imposed if the defendant's activity (a) creates a high risk, (b)

---

[76] This version (more fully stated) is seen as the rule in Rylands in W.V.H. Rogers, Winfield & Jolowicz on Tort 763–765 (18th ed. 2010).

[77] Rickards v. Lothian, [1913] A.C. 263, 280 (Privy Council).

[78] E.g., Ball v. Nye, 99 Mass. 582 (1868) (percolating filth, seemingly applying substantial-certainty intent).

[79] Brown v. Collins, 53 N.H. 442 (1873) (defendant's horse frightened by a train, knocked down the plaintiff's lamppost); Marshall v. Welwood, 38 N.J. Law 339 (1876) (boiler explosion damaged neighboring property); Losee v. Buchanan, 51 N.Y. 476 (1873) (same); Turner v. Big Lake Oil Co., 128 Tex. 155, 96 S.W.2d 221 (1936) (pond of salt water used in oil well work collapsed and caused damage to neighboring lands). *Rylands* would probably have supported a judgment for the defendant in all these cases.

[80] Ball v. Nye, 99 Mass. 582 (1868).

[81] See Sullivan v. Dunham, 161 N.Y. 290, 55 N.E.923 (1900) (blasting of stumps, one flew through the air and struck and killed decedent, a trespass to the person). As these cases did not involve any intent to enter the land or to harm the person of another, the trespass explanation was either a fiction or a leftover from the days before *Brown v. Kendall* adopted fault as the usual basis of liability.

[82] Restatement First of Torts § 520 (1938). The common usage requirement was criticized as a "subtle tactic" to stifle development of strict liability as a means of loss spreading in Virginia E. Nolan & Edmund Ursin, The Revitalization of Hazardous Activity Strict Liability, 65 N.C. L. Rev. 257, 259, 265 ff. (1987).

[83] The judge, not the jury, weighs these factors to determine whether strict liability applies. Restatement Second of Torts § 520 cmt. l (1977); see, e.g., Selwyn v. Ward, 879 A.2d 882 (R.I. 2005); Bella v. Aurora Air, Inc., 279 Or. 13, 566 P.2d 489 (1977).

with a likelihood of great harm, (c) that cannot be avoided by reasonable care, and if (d) the activity is uncommon and (e) inappropriate at the particular site. Strict liability is less likely to be imposed if (f) the activity has value to the community which outweighs its dangerous attributes.[84]

The high risk of an activity as well as its abnormality in the community are important, but strict liability can be imposed under the Second Restatement's approach even if the activity was not especially risky or uncommon. In addition, these factors look like a poorly disguised negligence regime, balancing such things as the value of the defendant's activity to the community. If strict liability is determined by the same factors that determine negligence cases, this form of strict liability is needless at best and probably should be subjected to Occam's razor. Put the other way around, if strict liability is to be retained, the factors represent a poor way to delineate its contours. It has been said also that the factors cannot be appropriately applied because the Restatement has furnished no intelligible rationale for this form of strict liability[85] and that strict-liability decisions should directly consider the goals of strict liability.[86]

Third Restatement. The Third Restatement comes closer to the first. It provides for strict liability for harms caused by abnormally dangerous activities if (1) the defendant's activity creates a reasonably foreseeable risk of physical harm; (2) the risk is "highly significant"; (3) the risk remains even when reasonable care is exercised; and (4) the activity is not a matter of common usage.[87] If reasonable care by everyone involved (including potential victims) can reduce the risk of the activity to a less-than-significant level, strict liability is rejected.[88] The strongest case for strict liability is one in which the defendant actually knows of the high risk and makes a deliberate choice to carry on the activity in spite of the risk[89] and in which the defendant's activity causes harm without "meaningful contribution" of other actors, as in blasting cases.[90] Once again, however, it must be a case in which negligence liability would be denied, for if care can avoid the risk, the rules of negligence, not strict liability, would apply. The Third Restatement suggests that strict liability is morally or "ethically" right when the defendant knows of the special risks and chooses, for his own purposes, to pursue his activity anyway,[91] and that it may also be right because in certain kinds of cases negligence will escape appropriate detection.[92]

§ 32.6 Contemporary Abnormal-Danger Cases

Courts now have generally accepted the principle that for some activities involving special dangers, especially those not commonly pursued, liability can be imposed without fault. However, aside from a few clear cases, the decisions—especially those based on the Second Restatement's multi-factor approach—do not harmonize pleasantly. Frequently enough, courts reject strict liability in particular cases because the evidence

---

[84] Restatement Second of Torts § 520 (1977).

[85] See Mark Geistfeld, Should Enterprise Liability Replace the Rule of Strict Liability for Abnormally Dangerous Activities?, 45 U.C.L.A. L. Rev. 611 (1998).

[86] Joseph H. King, Jr., A Goals-Oriented Approach to Strict Tort Liability for Abnormally Dangerous Activities, 48 Baylor L. Rev. 341 (1996). As to goals or rationales, see § 32.7.

[87] Restatement Third of Torts (Liability for Physical and Emotional Harm) § 20 (2010).

[88] Id. cmt. h.

[89] Id. cmts. f & i.

[90] Id. cmt. e.

[91] Id. cmt. f.

[92] Id. cmt. b.

does not demonstrate that the activity in issue is highly dangerous or that it cannot be made safe by the exercise of care.[93] Courts also reject strict liability in particular cases on the ground that the activity is one commonly pursued in the community.[94]

Strict liability for explosives and high-energy activities. Strict liability seems most readily imposed when physical harm results from the defendant's use[95] or storage[96] of dynamite or other materials[97] intended to cause explosions. The idea has been extended to the case of an oil well that blew out and showered the plaintiff's home with debris for 24 hours[98] and to explosions of large quantities of gasoline or propane carried as cargo on the highways,[99] on private property,[100] or railroads.[101] One court has even imposed strict liability for fireworks injuries.[102] As courts dropped the older trespass theories of liability for explosions, they recognized that strict liability could be imposed for vibration damage generated by explosives, even when the explosion did not throw objects upon the land or into persons.[103] From here, some courts have gone on to hold that strict liability applies to other large forces causing vibration damage to property, in particular to vibrations caused by testing a large rocket[104] and those caused by pile driving.[105]

---

[93]   E.g., In re Flood Litigation, 216 W.Va. 534, 607 S.E.2d 863 (2004) (removal of natural resources from land that allegedly caused flooding); Valentine v. Pioneer Chlor Alkali Co., Inc., 109 Nev. 1107, 864 P.2d 295 (1993) (chlorine gas); Doundoulakis v. Town of Hempstead, 42 N.Y.2d 440, 368 N.E.2d 24, 398 N.Y.S.2d 401 (1977) (hydraulic dredging and filling with water impounded near the plaintiffs' homes, leading to subsidence).

[94]   E.g., DeNardo v. Corneloup, 163 P.3d 956 (Alaska 2007) (rejecting strict liability for cigarette smoking where secondhand smoke caused harm; "Smoking is a matter of common usage."); Grube v. Daun, 213 Wis.2d 533, 570 N.W.2d 851 (1997) (underground storage tanks for gasoline on farms were common, no strict liability for contaminating leak); Mahowald v. Minnesota Gas Co., 344 N.W.2d 856 (Minn. 1984) (natural gas is common and is valuable to community, no strict liability).

[95]   Dyer v. Maine Drilling & Blasting, Inc., 984 A.2d 219 (Me. 2009) (noting that at least 41 states have adopted strict liability for blasting).

[96]   Yukon Equip. v. Fireman's Fund Ins. Co., 585 P.2d 1206 (Alaska 1978).

[97]   By a federal statute and international law, even goods not intended to cause explosion or fire might come under strict liability rules: the shipper of dangerous goods not so identified to the carrier is strictly liable to the carrier for harm done by those goods during carriage at sea, where both parties were ignorant of the especially dangerous characteristic. Senator Linie Gmbh & Co. Kg v. Sunway Line, Inc., 291 F.3d 145 (2d Cir. 2002) (construing Carriage of Goods by Sea Act § 4(6), 46 U.S.C.A. § 30701 note). If either party knows that the cargo might be hazardous, however, liability must be based on negligence and is not strict. In re M/V DG Harmony, 533 F.3d 83 (2d Cir. 2008).

[98]   Green v. General Petroleum Corp., 205 Cal. 328, 270 P. 952, 60 A.L.R. 475 (1928) (advancing a trespass theory).

[99]   Siegler v. Kuhlman, 81 Wash.2d 448, 502 P.2d 1181 (1972).

[100]   Zero Wholesale Gas Co., Inc. v. Stroud, 264 Ark. 27, 571 S.W.2d 74 (1978) (propane delivery truck at propane depot).

[101]   National Steel Service Ctr. Inc. v. Gibbons, 319 N.W.2d 269, 31 A.L.R.4th 650 (Iowa 1982).

[102]   Klein v. Pyrodyne Corp., 117 Wash.2d 1, 810 P.2d 917 (1991); contra, Cadena v. Chicago Fireworks Mfg. Co., 297 Ill.App.3d 945, 697 N.E.2d 802, 232 Ill.Dec. 60 (1998) (fireworks display not "ultrahazardous" since risk can be controlled and they are in common use). In Beddingfield v. Linam, 127 So.3d 1178 (Ala. 2013), the court distinguished *Klein*, which involved a large public fireworks display being conducted before a large crowd, rejecting strict liability in a case in which three boys were shooting bottle rockets on private property near a lake, which is "not the type of activity that the strict-liability rule was designed to cover"; the fireworks in the case "are commonly used," the court said, and "much of the risk involved with ordinary consumer fireworks can be eliminated by the use of reasonable care."

[103]   Exner v. Sherman Power Constr. Co., 54 F.2d 510, 80 A.L.R. 686 (2d Cir. 1931); Birmingham Coal & Coke Co. v. Johnson, 10 So.2d 993 (Ala. 2008).

[104]   Smith v. Lockheed Propulsion Co., 247 Cal.App.2d 774, 56 Cal.Rptr. 128, 29 A.L.R.3d 538 (1967); Berg v. Reaction Motors Division, 37 N.J. 396, 181 A.2d 487 (1962) (testing of rocket engine).

[105]   Caporale v. C.W. Blakeslee and Sons, Inc., 149 Conn. 79, 175 A.2d 561 (1961); Sachs v. Chiat, 281 Minn. 540, 162 N.W.2d 243 (1968); Vern J. Oja Assocs. v. Washington Park Towers, Inc., 89 Wash.2d 72, 569 P.2d 1141 (1977); contra, Gallagher v. H.V. Pierhomes, LLC, 182 Md.App. 94, 957 A.2d 628 (2008); In re

It is difficult to reconcile all of the decisions, however. Materials such as gasoline, propane, and natural gas have explosive and flammable potential. In line with what has already been said, some authority supports strict liability when such items are stored or accumulated in unusual volume.[106] Many decisions, however, have rejected such liability or applied a negligence standard in the case of explosions resulting from the storage of such materials.[107] Apparently all of them have rejected it for explosions of natural gas in connection with its transmission in mains or pipes.[108] Likewise, strict liability has been rejected when such substances as propane or gas are used as fuel for vehicles, factories, or homes.[109] Transmission of electricity in uninsulated power lines is not regarded as an abnormally dangerous activity.[110] And while the law of products liability may impose strict liability upon manufacturers of dangerous defective products, courts have almost always said that neither manufacturers of handguns nor manufacturers of especially destructive ammunition are strictly liable on an abnormal-danger theory.[111]

Poisons and toxic materials. Strict liability for abnormally dangerous activities has been imposed when the defendant has used toxic materials commercially to kill pests[112] or protect crops.[113] Hazardous materials (often wastes or byproducts of industrial processes) may contaminate lands, water, and air, and may cause death or serious bodily harm, making strict liability for accumulation, escape, percolation, or disposal of such wastes especially appropriate. Some cases do in fact support such liability even when toxic materials cause contamination of land rather than bodily harm.[114] This approach is in line with the strict liability imposed under some state and federal environmental statutes, although the statutes usually deal with contamination and cleanup costs rather than with personal injury or property damage.[115]

On the other hand, when the release of dangerous materials was unintentional, courts have sometimes emphasized that the activity, not merely the substance, must be abnormally dangerous.[116] The idea is that although the substance may be dangerous— asbestos and chlorine gas are examples—some activities dealing with the substance can be carried out with reasonable safety, thereby precluding strict liability.[117] For example,

---

Chicago Flood Litigation, 176 Ill.2d 179, 680 N.E.2d 265, 223 Ill.Dec. 532 (1997); Ted's Master Service, Inc. v. Farina Brothers Co., 343 Mass. 307, 178 N.E.2d 268 (1961).

[106] McLane v. Northwest Natural Gas. Co., 255 Or. 324, 467 P.2d 635 (1970); Siegler v. Kuhlman, 81 Wash.2d 448, 502 P.2d 1181 (1972) (gasoline being hauled in tank truck).

[107] See Barron C. Ricketts, Annotation, Liability in Connection with Fire or Explosion Incident to Bulk Storage, Transportation, Delivery, Loading, or Unloading of Petroleum Products, 32 A.L.R.3d 1169 (1971).

[108] See, e.g., Foster v. City of Keyser, 202 W.Va. 1, 501 S.E.2d 165 (1997).

[109] E.g., Allison v. Ideal Laundry & Cleaners, 215 S.C. 344, 55 S.E.2d 281 (1949); Siegler v. Kuhlman, 81 Wash.2d 448, 502 P.2d 1181 (1972).

[110] Kent v. Gulf States Utils. Co., 418 So.2d 493 (La. 1982).

[111] E.g., Copier v. Smith & Wesson Corp., 138 F.3d 833 (10th Cir. 1998).

[112] Luthringer v. Moore, 31 Cal.2d 489, 190 P.2d 1 (1948); Old Island Fumigation, Inc. v. Barbee, 604 So.2d 1246 (Fla. Dist. Ct. App. 1992).

[113] Loe v. Lenhardt, 227 Or. 242, 362 P.2d 312 (1961); Langan v. Valicopters, Inc., 88 Wash.2d 855, 567 P.2d 218 (1977); see Jonathan M. Purver, Annotation, Liability For Injury Caused by Spraying or Dusting of Crops, 37 A.L.R.3d 833 (1972).

[114] See Yommer v. McKenzie, 255 Md. 220, 257 A.2d 138 (1969) (gasoline percolated through the ground and contaminated the plaintiff's water); T. & E. Indus. Inc. v. Safety Light Corp., 123 N.J. 371, 587 A.2d 1249 (1991) (radium accumulated on the defendant's land); State, Dep't of Environmental Protection v. Ventron, 94 N.J. 473, 468 A.2d 150 (1983) (283 tons of mercury escaped from defendant's property).

[115] See William K. Jones, Strict Liability for Hazardous Enterprise, 92 Colum. L. Rev. 1705, 1742 (1992).

[116] E.g., Valentine v. Pioneer Chlor Alkali Co., Inc., 109 Nev. 1107, 864 P.2d 295 (1993).

[117] G.J. Leasing Co., Inc. v. Union Elec. Co., 54 F.3d 379 (7th Cir. 1995) (sale of building containing asbestos, no strict liability, partly because danger could be "adequately contained by taking care"); Grube v.

Rhode Island refused to apply strict liability rules to inspections of asbestos, although some other asbestos-related activities might well warrant strict liability.[118] Alabama has similarly said that disposal of masses of batteries for recycling, although it raises risks of lead contamination, is not dangerous enough to be an abnormally dangerous activity.[119] Courts may also find it easy to characterize the activity as common and thus to support a conclusion that liability must be based upon fault.[120]

Release or escape of impoundments. Rylands v. Fletcher[121] itself involved escape of water from a mill pond and consequent harm to a neighbor. Building a mill pond hardly sounds like an activity of special hazard like explosives; and whatever may have been true in the mining neighborhood where it was built, it was hardly an uncommon activity in the country as a whole. Not surprisingly, American courts have generally rejected Rylands as a basis for liability for the sudden escape of impounded water.[122] But, on one theory or another, strict liability has sometimes been imposed for escape of toxic substances,[123] for overflow of a natural waterway due to the defendant's obstruction,[124] for percolation of harmful substances[125] and for intentional release of wastes.[126]

§ 32.7 Rationales for Abnormal-Danger Strict Liability

The variety of settings in which strict liability may be imposed for abnormally dangerous activities is matched by the divergence in the holdings. It is somewhat dismaying to read that impoundment of water leads to strict liability in England but not America, and that storage of dynamite may lead to strict liability but that storage of natural gas may not. The variety of factors introduced by the Second Restatement contributed to the differences in decisions and to uncertainty about what strict liability for abnormal dangers is all about. Theorists might explain such differences, but as it turns out theorists and commentators have quite divergent views of their own.

Deterrence. One view is that strict liability can reduce risks of harm and encourage actors engaged in abnormally dangerous activities to find safer methods or at least a safer place for dangerous activities.[127] The suggestion is that there is more room to reduce risk with high-risk activities than with others. But it is not so clear that strict

---

Daun, 213 Wis.2d 533, 570 N.W.2d 851 (1997) (underground gasoline storage tank was common and could be made safe by reasonable care).

[118] Splendorio v. Bilray Demolition Co., 682 A.2d 461 (R.I. 1996).

[119] Thompson v. Mindis Metals, Inc., 692 So.2d 805 (Ala. 1997).

[120] See, e.g., Mahowald v. Minnesota Gas Co., 344 N.W.2d 856 (Minn. 1984); Grube v. Daun, 213 Wis.2d 533, 570 N.W.2d 851 (1997).

[121] Rylands v. Fletcher, L.R. 3 H.L. 330 (1868), discussed in § 32.5.

[122] See Chicago & N.W. Ry. v. Tyler, 482 F.2d 1007 (8th Cir. 1973); Bowling v. City of Oxford, 267 N.C. 552, 148 S.E.2d 624 (1966) (stream dammed, negligence required); cf. Turner v. Big Lake Oil Co., 128 Tex. 155, 96 S.W.2d 221 (1936) (escape of ponded salt water).

[123] See Cities Service Co. v. State, 312 So.2d 799 (Fla. Dist. Ct. App. 1975) (escape of billions of gallons of slime).

[124] See Amish v. Walnut Creek Development, Inc., 631 S.W.2d 866 (Mo. App. 1982); Gossner v. Utah Power & Light, 612 P.2d 337 (Utah 1980).

[125] Branch v. Western Petroleum, Inc., 657 P.2d 267 (Utah 1982) (citing cases).

[126] Atlas Chemical Industries, Inc. v. Anderson, 514 S.W.2d 309 (Tex. Ct. App. 1974), *aff'd*, 524 S.W.2d 681 (Tex. 1975).

[127] See Mark Geistfeld, Should Enterprise Liability Replace the Rule of Strict Liability for Abnormally Dangerous Activities?, 45 U.C.L.A. L. Rev. 611 (1998); cf. G.J. Leasing Co., Inc. v. Union Elec. Co., 54 F.3d 379, 386 (7th Cir. 1995) (Posner, J.: we want the person who keeps a tiger in his backyard to "consider seriously the possibility of getting rid of the tiger altogether").

liability reduces risk,[128] or that it is more important to reduce the small danger of useful high-risk activities like blasting than to reduce the more pervasive risk of activities like automobile driving to which no strict liability attaches. And it may be difficult to know whether risk-reduction by strict liability comes at too high a price, by over-deterring, for example. Furthermore, some risks simply cannot be reduced. Even the repeated suggestion that the defendant might move the activity to a safer location, if that is somehow different from a question of negligence, will not always work. One might give up recreational blasting lest he be held strictly liable, but contractors cannot very well give up blasting for subways, tunnels, and highways, nor can they consider moving the site for those activities. The requirement that the activity be an uncommon or "non-natural" one would be puzzling, too, if deterrence or risk-reduction were the goal.

Risk distribution. The enterprise-liability approach takes a different tack. It is rooted in the belief that even when an enterprise is not at fault, it should "pay its way." This view is often associated with the idea that a business enterprise is a good risk-distributor, meaning that the enterprise can pay for the harms with less dislocation than individuals. It might, for example, pass on the costs to its customers in the form of higher prices, or might absorb some or all of the costs itself as part of the expense of doing business. The idea of the good risk-distributor was very popular at one time and still has ardent supporters.[129] However, it has been argued that life today is not much like life in the Great Depression of the 1930s. Individuals today are often very good risk-distributors because they (or their employers) can purchase their own insurance against some risks more efficiently than enterprises can purchase liability insurance and defend lawsuits.[130] For the many individuals who cannot protect themselves from harms that occur without negligence—including some well above the poverty line—an inadequate but enormous range of social support now exists through both private and public programs.[131] In this setting, use of the judicial system to secure support for victims of non-negligent harms may be less attractive than it once was.

Fairness or justice. Enterprise liability can be justified, however, on different and broader grounds not limited to profit-making business or ability to absorb loss suffered by others. It can be argued that as a matter of fairness or justice an actor ought to pay for the costs that are uniquely or recurrently a result of his acts so long as the community as a whole does not create or tolerate similar risks and the plaintiff himself contributes nothing to it. Activities that are common or "natural" in the community come under the rule of live and let live, so that liability is imposed in those cases only if the activity is carried out negligently.[132] Although such activities may cause harms, they do not represent costs that can be especially identified with the defendant's operations, only with those of the community at large. In contrast, when the defendant carries out some activity that carries with it unique, typical, or recurrent risks, different from those imposed by activities shared by others in the community, strict liability may be fair and

---

[128] See Joseph H. King, Jr., A Goals-Oriented Approach to Strict Tort Liability for Abnormally Dangerous Activities, 48 Baylor L. Rev. 341, 353–354 (1996).

[129] Virginia E. Nolan & Edmund Ursin, The Revitalization of Hazardous Activity Strict Liability, 65 N.C. L. Rev. 257 (1987).

[130] See King, supra n. 128, at 351 (less than half of premium dollars for liability insurance reach victims); Geistfeld, supra n. 127; David G. Owen, the Moral Foundations of Products Liability Law: Toward First Principles, 68 Notre Dame L. Rev. 427, 504 (1993).

[131] See Geistfeld, supra n. 127, at 626–627.

[132] See Bamford v. Turnley, 3 B & S 67, 122 Eng.Rep. 27 (Exch. Ch. 1862); Richard A. Epstein, A Theory of Strict Liability, 2 J. Leg. Stud. 151 (1973); Richard A. Epstein, Nuisance Law: Corrective Justice and Its Utilitarian Constraints, 8 J. Leg. Stud. 49 (1979); George P. Fletcher, Tort Theory, 85 Harv. L. Rev. 537 (1972).

just. In that case the defendant takes the benefit of his activity and must similarly pay the tolls that are regularly associated with that activity.

Fairness rationales, like others, are incomplete or suffer from weak spots. Quite arguably, new technology with its new risks should not automatically produce strict liability and it is noteworthy that when railroads were built, posing new risks unlike any others, the courts created the law of negligence, not the law of strict liability.

Common usage. Whatever its weaknesses and strengths, fairness reasoning shows why common usage is as important as high risk. The risk in *Rylands v. Fletcher* that impounded water will by its weight make the ground below it give way leading to a flood of an unknown mine is surely a very low-order risk. The risk that carefully conducted mining will cause the surface of the land to subside is likewise a small risk. Even storage of dynamite presents a relatively small risk if it is placed in a remote area of Alaska. All these and other cases of not-very-risky activities have invoked strict liability, however. The explosives cases, where liability was originally imposed on entirely different reasoning,[133] led those who tried to synthesize the law to the wrong emphasis. A special hazard requires a greater quantum of care—you handle explosives quite differently from the way you handle flour—but not strict liability. Strict liability is triggered when the risks of the defendant's activity are special to that activity and not common to similar activities carried on generally in the community. A broader formulation would be that risks unilaterally imposed by the defendant entail strict liability, while risks generated by interaction of the plaintiff and defendant on an equal footing do not.[134]

Characterization. All the rationales require more explication than can be given here and all have their own strengths and weaknesses. One problem common to any approach is that courts have no principled method for characterizing the activity in question. Yet their characterization of the activity foreordains the outcome because, depending on how you describe the activity, it may or may not seem to be abnormally dangerous or uncommon. In one claim, the plaintiff asserted that she was exposed to paints containing dangerous heavy metals and other compounds and suffered some injuries as a result. The paints were used by the defendant in his occupation as an artist in his own home. The court characterized the activity as "painting in one's house," which made it a certainty that the activity was a common usage.[135] If the court had characterized the activity as "exposing others to dangerous fumes" the activity might have seemed both hazardous and uncommon.

To some extent these problems in characterization can be minimized if courts shift the inquiry slightly to ask whether the risk was peculiarly identified with the defendant's activity, or was rather the product of an interaction with a plaintiff who had some control over the risks.[136] A one-way risk, imposed by a defendant upon whom similar risks are not imposed by others, would be a good candidate for strict liability.

---

[133] Sullivan v. Dunham, 161 N.Y. 290, 55 N.E.923 (1900); cf. Colton v. Onderdonk, 69 Cal. 155, 10 P. 395 (1886) (trespass theory with talk of intrinsic danger).

[134] William K. Jones, Strict Liability for Hazardous Enterprise, 92 Colum. L. Rev. 1705 (1992).

[135] Humphreys v. Humphreys, 949 F.Supp. 1014 (E.D. N.Y. 1997).

[136] See William K. Jones, Strict Liability for Hazardous Enterprise, 92 Colum. L. Rev. 1705 (1992).

D. LIMITATIONS AND DEFENSES

§ 32.8 Limitations on Strict Liability

Strict liability is not unlimited liability. The defendant's strict-liability activities must be both a factual and "proximate" cause of the plaintiff's harm. In the case of animals known to have mischievous propensities, the latter requirement means that the harm must have resulted from that propensity and not from some other characteristic of the animal. For example, if the defendant's dog has a known propensity to bite house guests, the defendant will be strictly liable for the dog's bites, but not strictly liable when the dog merely gets in the plaintiff's way and causes a fall.[137] Similarly, in the case of abnormally dangerous activities, the harm must result from the characteristic that prompted strict liability in the first place. For example, the defendant will be strictly liable for impacts caused by use of explosives and also for vibration damage, but not for the loss of mink pelts resulting because the noise of explosion drives mother minks to eat their young.[138]

The Second Restatement provides one specific rule as an instance of this principle: the defendant is not strictly liable for harms resulting from abnormally dangerous activities if those harms would not have resulted but for the abnormal sensitivities of the plaintiff's own activities.[139] The case of the mother minks illustrates that particular rule as well as the more general principle.[140]

Intervening acts. What if the defendant is engaging in abnormally dangerous activities, but an act of a third person intervenes to cause the plaintiff's harm? The Third Restatement applies the ordinary scope-of-risk rule to such cases,[141] reflecting the idea that strict liability is appropriate in that context only when the risks that led courts to impose strict liability included risks that third persons would participate in or trigger the harm. Thus if storage of dynamite runs no special risks that others will set it off, the defendant should escape strict liability when a striking worker fires a rifle at the defendant's stored dynamite, causing an explosion that injures the plaintiff.[142] The Second Restatement in effect took the view that intervention of others is always part of the risk of abnormally dangerous activity, at least when the intervening actor is not guilty of intentional harm.[143] Ultimately, it seems that case by case analysis is required

---

[137] See Restatement Second of Torts § 509(2) (1977); Restatement Third of Torts (Liability for Physical and Emotional Harm) § 23, cmt. g (2010) (strict liability limited to risks that are characteristic of the risks posed by abnormally dangerous activities or by animals).

[138] See Foster v. Preston Mill Co., 44 Wash.2d 440, 268 P.2d 645 (1954); Restatement Third of Torts (Liability for Physical and Emotional Harm) § 29, cmt. l (2010).

[139] Restatement Second of Torts § 524A (1977).

[140] The Third Restatement omits the special provision, recognizing that the point is covered by the general scope of risk principle. However, the special sensitivity of the plaintiff suggests that the plaintiff is as much a part of the riskiness as the defendant, a ground for denying strict liability in the first place. See Restatement Third of Torts (Liability for Physical and Emotional Harm) § 29, cmt. l (2010).

[141] Restatement Third of Torts (Liability for Physical and Emotional Harm) § 34, Reporter's Note (2010).

[142] Pecan Shoppe of Springfield, Missouri, Inc. v. Tri-State Motor Transit Co., 573 S.W.2d 431 (Mo. App. 1978).

[143] Restatement Second of Torts § 522 (1977); cf. Yukon Equip. v. Fireman's Fund Ins. Co., 585 P.2d 1206 (Alaska 1978) (because one reason that storage of large amounts of dynamite is abnormally dangerous is that third persons may set it off, defendant was strictly liable for an explosion deliberately set by a third person).

to determine whether the harm is any less characteristic of the activity merely because a third person intervenes.[144]

§ 32.9 Defenses to Strict Liability

Assumption of risk and plaintiff fault. Under the Second Restatement's view, the defendant who was subject to strict liability either because he possessed an animal that caused harm[145] or because he carried on abnormally dangerous activities[146] could not assert ordinary contributory negligence as a defense. For instance, if the plaintiff negligently failed to discover the danger, he was not barred by his fault.[147] However, except where statutes provide otherwise,[148] the defendant could defend on the ground that the plaintiff assumed the risk[149] or was guilty of contributory negligence by knowingly and unreasonably subjecting himself to the risk of harm from the strict liability activity.[150]

The Third Restatement. The Third Restatement now recognizes a plaintiff's contributory fault as grounds for reducing the plaintiff's recovery under comparative responsibility principles.[151] Assumption of risk has no status separate from contributory fault and is subject to the same reduction-of-damages rule.[152] However, strict liability is rejected altogether if the plaintiff seeks contact with the strict-liability risk to secure a benefit of his own,[153] and, indeed, according to some authority, also if the plaintiff participates in the strict-liability activity.[154] Beyond this, when the risk of the activity can be reduced to a modest level by reasonable care of the plaintiff (or anyone), strict liability would not be acceptable under the Third Restatement.[155]

Merits of the rules. The Second Restatement justified recovery by a plaintiff whose own fault contributed to her injury for a purely formal reason. It said that since the strict liability action is not founded on the defendant's fault in the first place, the plaintiff's fault should furnish no defense.[156] The conclusion that contributory negligence is no defense is explained by rephrasing the conclusion as "the policy of the law," but without asserting any reason for the supposed policy. The result is that the person who is at fault in causing the harm recovers from the person who is not at fault in causing it.

The rule seems wrong. If the plaintiff negligently contributes to her own injury, that means she necessarily has some control over the risks. In that case, the risks cannot be

---

[144] See Klein v. Pyrodyne Corp., 117 Wash.2d 1, 17, 810 P.2d 917, 925 (1991), amended, 817 P.2d 1359 (1991) (defendant relieved of liability "only if those acts were unforeseeable in relation to the extraordinary risk created by the activity").

[145] Restatement Second of Torts § 515 (1977).

[146] Id. § 524.

[147] Matkovic v. Shell Oil Co., 218 Mont. 156, 707 P.2d 2 (1985).

[148] Statutes and ordinances often control liability for injuries by dogs and may equally prescribe and limit the defenses available. See Donner v. Arkwright-Boston Mfrs. Mut. Ins. Co., 358 So.2d 21 (Fla. 1978) (error to instruct on assumed risk in dog bite case; only the statutory provocation defense is available).

[149] Restatement Second of Torts § 523 (1977) (assumption of risk as to abnormally dangerous activities).

[150] Id. § 524 (knowing exposure to risk of abnormally dangerous activities) & § 515 (knowing exposure or assumed risk as to animals); cf. Rickrode v. Wistinghausen, 128 Mich. App. 240, 340 N.W.2d 83 (1983) (willful provocation of an animal is a defense).

[151] Restatement Third of Torts (Liability for Physical and Emotional Harm) § 25 (2010).

[152] Id., cmt. e.

[153] Id. § 24(a).

[154] Pullen v. West, 92 P.3d 584 (Kan. 2004).

[155] Restatement Third of Torts (Liability for Physical and Emotional Harm) § 20, cmt. h (2010).

[156] Restatement Second of Torts § 515, cmt. b & § 524, cmt. a (1977).

said to be entirely those fostered by the defendant's activities. Even one who speaks for expanded strict liability might support the use of the contributory negligence defense, at least in the present world of comparative fault,[157] and in the case of strict products liability, many courts have rejected the rule protecting plaintiffs from their own fault.[158]

Although it seems wrong to impose a rule of law that exculpates negligent plaintiffs in all cases, it must be remembered that the plaintiff is not necessarily negligent in relying upon the safety of the defendant's activity. For example, it is not negligent to visit a zoo any more than it is negligent for the defendant to operate one; the risk of escaping animals is simply not an unreasonable one if the zoo is well-maintained. Even the plaintiff who knows of the danger is not necessarily at fault in refusing to move her home or business to avoid it. If she is entitled to be where she is, she is not at fault in being there.[159] Finally, in some rare cases, the defendant may owe a duty to protect the plaintiff from her own fault, in which case the plaintiff's fault is no defense.[160]

An entirely different question arises when the facts show that the plaintiff knowingly and unreasonably encountered the danger. The Second Restatement recognized this as a complete defense.[161] The problem with that analysis, as recognized by the Third Restatement,[162] is that with the general adoption of comparative fault rules in the United States, assumption of risk in negligence cases is now usually treated like contributory negligence, so that it no longer invariably bars recovery but usually only reduces damages. At the same time, however, some cases that were once decided for the defendant on an assumption of risk analysis may now be decided for the defendant on the ground that the defendant owed no duty to the plaintiff or did not breach the duty he owed. The result is that some former assumption of risk cases are now matters of comparative fault with a reduction in recovery, while others are now matters of no duty with a complete denial of all recovery.[163]

The difference in the treatment of the plaintiff who confronts known danger lies largely in the question of contract, consent, or apparent consent. In the context of strict liability, the person who foolishly tries to pet the defendant's tiger is assuredly foolish and her recovery should probably be reduced, but she has almost certainly not consented to accept the risk and to relieve the defendant of all responsibility.[164] In contrast, the plaintiff who accepts employment as trainer of the defendant's wild animals apparently consents to the abnormal risks that entails and hence should not recover on a strict

---

[157] See William K. Jones, Strict Liability for Hazardous Enterprise, 92 Colum. L. Rev. 1705, 1756–1757 (1992).

[158] See § 33.17.

[159] See Leroy Fibre Co. v. Chicago, Milwaukee & St. Paul Ry. Co, 232 U.S. 340, 34 S.Ct. 415, 58 L.Ed. 631 (1914); William K. Jones, Strict Liability for Hazardous Enterprise, 92 Colum. L. Rev. 1705, 1756–1757 (1992); cf. Gary T. Schwartz, Rylands v. Fletcher, Negligence, and Strict Liability in Peter Cane & Jane Stapleton, Essays in Celebration of John Fleming 209, 224 (1998).

[160] See §§ 16.2 & 16.6.

[161] Restatement Second of Torts §§ 515(2) & 524(2) (1977).

[162] Restatement Third of Torts (Liability for Physical and Emotional Harm) § 25, cmt. e.

[163] See §§ 17.6, 17.7 & 33.17.

[164] Cf. Leiner v. First Wythe Ave. Serv. Station, Inc., 121 Misc.2d 559, 468 N.Y.S.2d 302 (1983), aff'd, 127 Misc.2d 794, 492 N.Y.S.2d 708 (N.Y. Sup. App. 1985) (plaintiff's conduct toward vicious dog treated as comparative fault).

liability basis;[165] certainly this is true if she expressly contracts to assume the risk.[166] This kind of case is captured by the Third Restatement in its rejection of strict liability when harm is occasioned by a plaintiff who encounters the activity to secure a benefit for herself.[167]

---

[165] Cf. Peneschi v. National Steel Corp., 170 W.Va. 511, 295 S.E.2d 1 (1982) (acceptance of job dealing with abnormally dangerous activities is assumption of risk barring a strict liability recovery).

[166] See Integrated Waste Services, Inc. v. Akzo Nobel Salt, Inc., 113 F.3d 296 (2d Cir. 1997) (conclusion that defendant owed no duty because contractual allocations of rights between the parties bars strict liability and negligence claims).

[167] Restatement Third of Torts (Liability for Physical and Emotional Harm) § 24(a) (2010).

Chapter 33

PRODUCTS LIABILITY

Analysis

A. DELINEATING THE FIELD

§ 33.1 Theories of Recovery
§ 33.2 History, Rationales, and Decline of Strict Liability
§ 33.3 The Economic Loss Rule: Stand-Alone Economic Harm

B. TORT LIABILITY FOR DEFECTIVE PRODUCTS

1. The Modern Typology of Defect

§ 33.4 The Defect Requirement
§ 33.5 Summary of Types of Defect

2. Manufacturing and Design Defects

§ 33.6 The Consumer Expectations Test
§ 33.7 Proving Manufacturing Defects
§ 33.8 Problems with the Consumer Expectations Test: Open and Obvious Dangers and Other Difficulties
§ 33.9 The Risk-Utility Test for Design Defects
§ 33.10 Proving a Design's Risks and Utilities
§ 33.11 Reasonable Alternative Design
§ 33.12 Shifting the Burden of Proof in Design Defect Cases

3. Marketing Defects

§ 33.13 The Warnings Requirement
§ 33.14 Adequacy of Warnings
§ 33.15 Learned Intermediaries and Sophisticated Users
§ 33.16 Causation in Failure-to-Warn Cases

C. DEFENSES

§ 33.17 Contributory Negligence and Assumption of Risk
§ 33.18 Unforeseeable Misuse, Alteration and Modification
§ 33.19 Statutory Defenses
§ 33.20 Compliance with Statute and Preemption
§ 33.21 Statutes of Limitation

A. DELINEATING THE FIELD

§ 33.1 Theories of Recovery

The law of products liability concerns the bases for, defenses to, and scope of liability of those who are in the business of manufacturing, selling or supplying goods for harms caused by defective tangible products.[1] The field has enjoyed an enormous vogue in legal

---

[1]   With few exceptions, any special products liability rules apply only to manufacturers and those who are in the business of either selling or distributing tangible products. See 2 Dobbs, Hayden & Bublick, The

circles since about 1963, partly because jurists were challenged by the new idea of strict liability that began to be developed about that time.[2] Scores of books,[3] many of them multi-volume treatises,[4] as well as hundreds of law review articles, have argued the theory and the rules.

The focus on defect. The Restatement of Products Liability[5] provides a convenient language for discussion of all products liability claims. No manufacturer or distributor is liable for harm caused by a product unless the product is *defective*. The language of defectiveness encompasses negligence, warranty, and strict tort liability. The Restatement's "defect" analysis makes it possible to discuss the rules of liability without necessarily identifying the negligence or warranty basis for them,[6] although the various liability theories retain their currency for many purposes today.

The main theories. (1) Negligence. As a practical matter the plaintiff has often found it useful to assert negligence in the manufacture or sale of a product.[7] Although the Restatement Second collects more than a dozen rules directed at the liability of chattel suppliers for negligence,[8] the rules reflect general negligence principles and require little separate discussion here. To a very large extent, the negligence claim applies the general rules of negligence in a products setting. Consequently, questions of industry custom[9] and product risks[10] discussed below in connection with product defects are central to the negligence theory as well as to others.

(2) Breach of warranty. So far as the plaintiff claims a breach of express or implied warranty, that claim is often associated with contract liability. Liability for breach of warranty is ordinarily strict liability: liability results from breach even if the defendant used reasonable efforts to perform. To a large extent, the law of implied warranty has gradually merged with strict tort liability. For the purpose of drafting a complaint and presenting alternative theories to the court, warranty theories must be separated from

---

Law of Torts §§ 477 & 478 (2d ed. 2011 & Supp.). Sellers of raw materials and component parts used to manufacture goods are subject to the products liability rules; "casual sellers," those not in the business of selling the goods at issue, are not. Id. § 478.

[2] See § 33.2.

[3] See, e.g., David G. Owen, Products Liability Law (2d Ed. 2008).

[4] See Louis R. Frumer & Melvin I. Friedman, Products Liability (Cary Stewart Sklaven ed. 2008) (11 vols.); David G. Owen & Mary J. Davis, Owen & Davis on Products Liability (4th ed. 2014, updated on Westlaw) (3 vols.); Marshall S. Shapo, The Law of Products Liability (4th ed. 2002, updated on Westlaw) (2 vols.); American Law of Products Liability (Timothy E. Travers ed., 3d ed., updated on Westlaw) (23 vols.).

[5] Restatement Third of Torts (Products Liability) (1998).

[6] See §§ 33.4 & 33.5.

[7] See David G. Owen, Products Liability Law § 2.1, at 60–61 (2d ed. 2008) ("Negligence is the classic products liability claim . . . [and] remains a vital theory of recovery in products liability litigation."); Reis v. Volvo Cars of North America, 24 N.Y.3d 35, 18 N.E.3d 383, 993 N.Y.S.2d 672 (2014) (negligent design defect); Lance v. Wyeth, 85 A.3d 434 (Pa. 2014) (same); 5 Star, Inc. v. Ford Motor Co., 408 S.C. 362, 759 S.E.2d 139 (2014) (same).

[8] Restatement Second of Torts §§ 388 to 402 (1965). A chattel supplier is often not a manufacturer, but an employer or landowner who supplies chattels for some self-benefit, say in employment or in land improvements, or some analogous role. See Heinz v. Heinz, 653 N.W.2d 334 (Iowa 2002) (discussing Restatement Second of Torts § 392 (1965) and requiring a supplier to make reasonable inspections and to warn users of the chattel for the supplier's benefit or to make it safe for them). Another non-manufacturing chattel supplier is the lender.

[9] Industry custom—what is actually done in the industry on safety matters—is at least relevant in establishing negligence. See Morden v. Continental AG, 235 Wis.2d 325, 611 N.W.2d 659 (2000). See generally David G. Owen, Products Liability Law § 2.3 (2d ed. 2008).

[10] See §§ 33.9.

others.[11] For the purpose of outlining contemporary products liability law, the standards for determining merchantability under warranty law and the standard for determining whether a product is defective under tort law are largely interchangeable.[12]

(3) Misrepresentation. The misrepresentation claim is little different. The idea is that the plaintiff relies upon a representation, perhaps on a label. For example, the plaintiff might use a ladder, relying on the label that says it can hold 500 pounds. If the ladder collapses with a load of 200 pounds, the plaintiff has a misrepresentation claim and perhaps a warranty claim.[13] Neither claim requires proof that the defendant was at fault in making or designing the ladder. Even misrepresentations contained in advertisements or press releases, coupled with a course of conduct designed to mislead the public, might suffice.[14] When it comes to nondisclosure of important information, the law of misrepresentation sometimes but not always imposes a duty to speak and liability for nondisclosure.[15] But perhaps there is no need to resort to the fraud cases for precedent; the law of products liability, with its rules requiring warnings of danger, probably has adequate precedent to deal with this problem.[16]

(4) Strict liability in tort. Since the early 1960's, plaintiffs have frequently asserted that the manufacturer or distributor is strictly liable, not as matter of warranty or misrepresentation, but as a matter of tort law. The claim has been that it is enough for liability that the ladder is defective and its defective condition causes harm. It is the strict-liability theory that captured most of the thinking and generated most of the developing jurisprudence after about 1963. One of the issues today is whether, or to what extent, strict liability is actually imposed.

§ 33.2 History, Rationales, and Decline of Strict Liability

Early Development and the Privity Rule

The privity requirement. The steps that brought about a measure of strict liability for defective products have been traced well and often.[17] In brief, they begin with *Winterbottom v. Wright,*[18] a decision of an English court in 1842 holding that a negligent manufacturer was definitely *not* subject to liability for a defective product when the injured victim was not the person who had purchased the product. If the plaintiff was not in contractual privity with the defendant, he had no claim. The privity requirement continued to protect negligent manufacturers until well into the 20th century,[19] with

---

[11] A product manufacturer or distributor can limit implied warranties of merchantability, subject to the Uniform Commercial Code and other statutes. However, a manufacturer cannot disclaim liability for personal injuries, as opposed to commercial loss. See UCC § 2–719(3); Restatement Second of Torts § 402A, cmt. m (1965); Restatement Third of Torts (Products Liability) § 18 (1998); 2 Dobbs, Hayden & Bublick, The Law of Torts § 472 (2d ed. 2011 & Supp.).

[12] Wright v. Brooke Group Ltd., 652 N.W.2d 159 (Iowa 2002) (quoting White & Summers, Uniform Commercial Code § 9.8 (4th ed. 1995)).

[13] See Restatement Second of Torts § 402B (1965).

[14] See Wright v. Brooke Group Ltd., 652 N.W.2d 159 (Iowa 2002).

[15] See § 43.8.

[16] See Wright v. Brooke Group Ltd., 652 N.W.2d 159 (Iowa 2002).

[17] David Owen, Products Liability Law Restated, 49 S.C.L. Rev. 273 (1998); William L. Prosser, The Assault upon the Citadel (Strict Liability to the Consumer), 69 Yale L. J. 1099 (1960); William L. Prosser, The Fall of the Citadel (Strict Liability to the Consumer), 50 Minn. L. Rev. 791 (1966); 1 David G. Owen & Mary J. Davis, Owen & Davis on Products Liability § 5.2 (4th ed. 2014, updated on Westlaw).

[18] Winterbottom v. Wright, 10 M. & W. 109, 152 Eng. Rep. 402 (Exch. Pl. 1842).

[19] See, e.g., Losee v. Clute, 51 N.Y. 494 (1873) (defendant negligently made a boiler and sold it to the plaintiff's neighbor; the plaintiff was injured when it exploded, but the plaintiff had no contractual relationship

exceptions allowing recovery when the manufacturer was guilty of fraud or misrepresentation or dangerous mislabeling and also when the product itself was inherently or intrinsically dangerous.[20]

Judge Cardozo substantially abolished the privity rule for negligence cases in the famous case of *MacPherson v. Buick Motor Co.*,[21] decided in 1916. In that case a wheel on the plaintiff's new car collapsed and the plaintiff was injured. The plaintiff was not in privity with the manufacturer—he had purchased the car from a retailer, not from the manufacturer—but Judge Cardozo permitted his claim against the manufacturer to proceed. Imminent, inherent, or intrinsic danger was no longer required to avoid the privity limitation. "If [the manufacturer] is negligent where danger is to be foreseen, a liability will follow."[22] Over the years, other courts came to accept *MacPherson*.

Development of implied warranties. After *MacPherson*, injured plaintiffs could recover against manufacturers for negligence, but negligence of a manufacturer or even a retailer remained difficult to prove. To avoid this difficulty, plaintiffs sometimes sued for breach of express warranty. If breach were established, the defendant would have been liable in contract without proof of fault. Few manufacturers expressly guarantee that the product will produce no injury, so plaintiffs began to urge that the sale of goods *implied* a warranty. As ultimately codified, a sale of goods impliedly carried a warranty that the goods were merchantable, that is, that they were what they seemed to be and fit for the ordinary purposes for which such goods were sold. Likewise, if the seller knew of particular purposes of the buyer, the seller impliedly warranted them to be fit for those purposes as well. Implied warranties were codified as rules of law in the Uniform Sales Act and later in the Uniform Commercial Code. Since an implied warranty claim suggested that the manufacturer had implicitly contracted to provide a reasonably safe product, the plaintiff was not required to prove fault. On the other hand, the privity rule, which had been abolished by *MacPherson* for negligence cases, still applied to bar the express and implied warranty claims except when the plaintiff sued his immediate seller.

The best of both worlds: avoiding the privity rule. For a period, courts developed special exceptions to the privity rule, allowing the plaintiff who was not in privity to recover on an implied-warranty claim against a manufacturer of deleterious food[23] and sometimes of other products intended for intimate bodily use or considered to be especially dangerous. The Uniform Commercial Code went a little further, eliminating the privity requirement for members of the product purchaser's household, so a daughter could recover on warranty if her mother had purchased the product from the defendant. It also provided more liberal options for expanding warranty liability.[24] Then in 1960, the New Jersey Supreme Court rendered a famous decision in *Henningsen v. Bloomfield Motors*.[25] In that case the plaintiff was injured when the steering failed in a new car. The court held that the implied warranty extended not only to items like food, but to any

---

with the manufacturer-defendant so the privity rule barred recovery); Field v. Empire Case Goods Co., 179 A.D. 253, 166 N.Y.S. 509 (1917) (purchase from a retailer, no privity with manufacturer).

[20] Thomas v. Winchester, 6 N.Y. 397 (1852) (deadly poison mislabeled creating "imminent danger").

[21] MacPherson v. Buick Motor Co., 217 N.Y. 382, 111 N.E. 1050 (1916).

[22] Id.

[23] Davis v. Van Camp Packing Co., 189 Iowa 775, 176 N.W. 382 (1920); Jacob E. Decker & Sons, Inc. v. Capps, 139 Tex. 609, 164 S.W.2d 828 (1942).

[24] UCC § 2–318.

[25] Henningsen v. Bloomfield Motors, Inc., 32 N.J. 358, 161 A.2d 69 (1960).

item. Neither the absence of privity nor the presence of contractual limitations on the manufacturer's responsibility would bar the claim. A new era seemed to be dawning.

Development of Strict Liability in Tort

Strict liability in tort. The chief problems with strict liability under an implied-warranty theory is that the term itself implies a contractual liability with privity limitations. In 1963, this objection was eliminated by the new leading case, *Greenman v. Yuba Power Products.*[26] In *Greenman*, Justice Traynor held that strict liability would be imposed upon manufacturers of defective products. It was to be imposed by courts as a matter of tort law, not by implied warranty as a matter of contract law. Since the claim was now to be perceived as one brought in tort, privity was not required. Furthermore, as it turned out, strict liability in tort also meant that the plaintiff's claim would not be barred by the defendant's contractual disclaimers or limits on liability. Dean Prosser, drafting the Restatement Second of Torts, picked up *Greenman's* idea and incorporated it in a new section, § 402A; that section provided that if a product was defective and the defect caused harm, liability would be imposed upon the product's manufacturer and distributors, regardless of their fault or the existence of privity. Courts widely adopted § 402A and regarded it as their guide, philosopher, and friend.[27]

Rationales for Strict Products Liability

Current thinkers tend to emphasize one of two or three rationales for holding a manufacturer or distributor strictly liable for defective products. The main ones are: (1) enterprise liability, (2) deterrence or economic efficiency, and (3) justified consumer expectations. All have their supporters, and courts have stated these rationales occasionally, along with some doubtful variations.[28]

Compensation, loss spreading, or enterprise liability. This line of reasoning holds that manufacturer liability is socially desirable as a means of spreading losses that would be a hardship upon individuals but that can be passed on by enterprises through insurance and increased prices.[29] A different version emphasizes that strict liability is just in imposing liability for harms that are statistically associated with the enterprise. This view is that the enterprise should "pay its own way." This view is easiest to sustain when safety does not require care by the product user.

Deterrence, greater safety. This view holds that manufacturers will tend to make products safer if strict liability is imposed. This rationale is usually grounded in economic analysis. It is sometimes associated with the idea that liability will require manufacturers of products either to make them safer or to raise prices, and that either

---

[26]   Greenman v. Yuba Power Prods., Inc., 59 Cal.2d 57, 27 Cal.Rptr. 697, 377 P.2d 897 (1963).

[27]   A few retained a kind of implied warranty theory that was regarded as largely coincident and congruent with liability under § 402A. See Ex parte Chevron Chemical Co., 720 So.2d 922 (Ala. 1998); Com. v. Johnson Insulation, 425 Mass. 650, 682 N.E.2d 1323 (1997).

[28]   E.g., Doe v. Miles Laboratories, Inc., Cutter Laboratories Div., 927 F.2d 187, 191 (4th Cir. 1991) ("[T]he fundamental purpose underlying the theory of strict tort liability is to force hazardous products from the market."); Boles v. Sun Ergoline, Inc., 223 P.3d 724 (Colo. 2010) (stressing enterprise liability rationale); Sylvan R. Shemitz Designs, Inc. v. Newark Corp., 291 Conn. 224, 967 A.2d 1188 (2009) (stressing consumer expectations rationale); Sternhagen v. Dow Co., 282 Mont. 168, 935 P.2d 1139 (1997) (adopting both enterprise liability and deterrence rationales, along with some minor ideas); Brooks v. Beech Aircraft Corp., 120 N.M. 372, 902 P.2d 54 (1995) (discussing several rationales); Horst v. Deere & Co., 319 Wis.2d 147, 769 N.W.2d 536 (2009) (same).

[29]   See, e.g., Virgina E. Nolan & Edmund Ursin, Enterprise Liability and the Economic Analysis of Tort Law, 57 Ohio St. L. J. 835 (1996) (one of numerous publications by the authors).

action would promote safety. Higher prices would promote safety because the higher prices would reflect true costs (including losses resulting from injuries) and buyers, to save money, would often seek cheaper substitutes, which would tend to be safer.[30] A related proposition is that the manufacturer is, or sometimes is, in the best position to weigh risks and utilities and is therefore the "cheapest cost avoider."[31] It has also been suggested that the cost of contracting for appropriate safety and the cost of regulation may be so high that it may be efficient to decide after injury whether the defendant should be liable,[32] which of course is the common law method.

Consumer reliance on representations. The rationale here is that manufacturers at least implicitly represent their products as healthy and safe, and consumers are entitled to rely upon that appearance.[33]

Decline of Strict Liability Theory

As the cases worked out the details of strict liability, many observers began to think that strict liability for design defects, as distinct from occasional product flaws, was wrong in principle. Indeed, many came to believe that the courts were often using the language of strict liability but effectively determining liability on negligence standards. Opponents of strict-liability language and strict-liability results, along with perennial defendants, gradually developed a critical mass. In 1973, James A. Henderson, Jr., published a strong attack on any kind of judicially imposed liability for design defects.[34] Others, reinforced by Henderson's stream of articles on products liability, added their criticisms.[35] By 1979 the Commerce Department published a "Model Uniform Product Liability Act" as a potential guide to the states and aimed mainly at clarifying and limiting liability.[36] Principally in the 1980's, many states passed products liability statutes limiting liability in one regard or another.

In 1998, the American Law Institute published the Restatement Third, Torts: Products Liability. The Products Restatement drops all references to strict products liability. Its view is that courts have mostly come to apply negligence standards in determining design and warning defects, even when they maintained the language of strict liability. The effect, although not the language, of the Products Restatement is that strict liability is retained when it comes to manufacturing defects, but negligence or something very much like it is the test of liability for design and warning defects.[37]

---

[30]   See Guido Calabresi, The Costs of Accidents (1970).

[31]   Guido Calabresi & Jon T. Hirschoff, Toward a Test for Strict Liability in Torts, 81 Yale L. J. 1055 (1972).

[32]   See William M. Landes & Richard A. Posner, A Positive Economic Analysis of Products Liability, 14 J. Leg. Studies 535 (1985).

[33]   Marshal S. Shapo, The Law of Products Liability (4th ed. 2002, updated on Westlaw); William L. Prosser, The Assault upon the Citadel (Strict Liability to the Consumer), 69 Yale L. J. 1099, 1123 (1960).

[34]   James A. Henderson, Jr., Judicial Review of Manufacturers' Conscious Design Choices: The Limits of Adjudication, 73 Colum. L. Rev. 1531 (1973).

[35]   E.g., James A. Henderson & Aaron D. Twerski, Doctrinal Collapse in Products Liability: The Empty Shell of Failure to Warn, 65 N.Y.U. L. Rev. 265 (1990); Sheila L. Birnbaum, Unmasking the Test for Design Defect: From Negligence [to Warranty] to Strict Liability to Negligence, 33 Vand. L. Rev. 593 (1980); David A. Fischer, Products Liability—Functionally Imposed Strict Liability, 32 Okl. L. Rev. 93 (1979); Aaron D. Twerski, Seizing the Middle Ground Between Rules and Standards in Design Defect Litigation: Advancing Directed Verdict Practice in Law of Torts, 57 N.Y.U. L. Rev. 521 (1982).

[36]   See 44 Fed. Reg. 62714 (1979).

[37]   See Wright v. Brooke Group Ltd., 652 N.W.2d 159 (Iowa 2002) (expressly adopting Restatement Third approach).

The history is certainly not yet complete. Courts that have developed products liability jurisprudence grounded in strict liability language or theory may continue to use the language and concepts of strict liability, even if they obtain results that are consistent with the Products Restatement's fault-oriented approach.[38] Some courts continue to base their analysis on the Restatement Second of Torts § 402A on which strict liability was erected, sometimes without even citing the newer Restatement.[39] Similarly, a court may follow particular comments of the older Restatement, in spite of a different approach in the newer one.[40] Or again, courts may retain a consumer expectations analysis although it is generally discarded in the Products Restatement.[41] And in some cases, courts that retain strict liability theory may obtain results quite inconsistent with negligence theory, as with statute of limitations or comparative fault issues. Doctrinal complexity of this sort is perhaps unsurprising in an area of such great economic and moral importance.

§ 33.3   The Economic Loss Rule: Stand-Alone Economic Harm

In all but a few states,[42] when a product's defect causes commercial or economic harm without causing physical harms to persons or to property that is not part of the product itself, courts generally exclude tort claims for strict liability and negligence,[43] and perhaps even for fraud.[44] For example, if the product ceases to be usable for its intended purposes[45] or if it sets itself afire,[46] the plaintiff has economic loss, but no physical harm has been done to persons or to other property that is distinct from the product itself. That leaves the plaintiff only with whatever claims she can establish

---

[38]   See generally 1 David G. Owen & Mary J. Davis, Owen & Davis on Products Liability § 5.7 (4th ed. 2014, updated on Westlaw) (discussing current variations on the Restatement Second's § 402A rules).

[39]   E.g., Fuchsgruber v. Custom Accessories, Inc., 244 Wis.2d 758, 628 N.W.2d 833 (2001). A few states retain statutes that embody the language of § 402A, giving courts little or no leeway to make a change themselves. See David G. Owen, Products Liability Law § 8.3, at 504 (2d ed. 2008).

[40]   Vitanza v. Upjohn Co., 257 Conn. 365, 778 A.2d 829 (2001) (invoking Restatement Second Comment k to protect against strict liability for unknowable danger).

[41]   E.g., Karlsson v. Ford Motor Co., 140 Cal.App.4th 1202, 45 Cal.Rptr.3d 265 (2006); Mikolajczyk v. Ford Motor Co., 231 Ill.2d 516, 901 N.E.2d 329, 327 Ill.Dec. 1 (2008); Jackson v. General Motors Corp., 60 S.W.3d 800 (Tenn. 2001); Green v. Smith & Nephew AHP, Inc., 245 Wis.2d 772, 629 N.W.2d 727 (2001). Statutes in some states compel this approach.

[42]   See, rejecting the economic loss rule entirely, La. Rev. Stat. Ann. § 9:2800.53(5) (2009); Farm Bureau Ins. Co. v. Case Corp., 317 Ark. 467, 878 S.W.2d 741 (1994); Thompson v. Nebraska Mobile Homes Corp., 198 Mont. 461, 647 P.2d 334 (1982). Some courts have recognized limited exceptions; the principle one is for asbestos products. See Shooshanian v. Wagner, 672 P.2d 455 (Alaska 1983). Some have withdrawn the protection of the economic loss rule where the defendant was grossly negligent, see Sommer v. Federal Signal Corp., 79 N.Y.2d 540, 593 N.E.2d 1365, 583 N.Y.S.2d 957 (1992), or where the defendant's conduct has risked very serious personal injury, see Lloyd v. General Motors Corp., 397 Md. 108, 916 A.2d 257 (2007).

[43]   East River Steamship Corp. v. Transamerica Delaval, Inc. 476 U.S. 858, 106 S.Ct. 2295, 90 L.Ed.2d 865 (1986); Seely v. White Motor Co., 63 Cal. 2d 9, 45 Cal. Rptr. 17, 403 P.2d 145 (Cal.1965); Giddings & Lewis, Inc. v. Industrial Risk Insurers, 348 S.W.3d 729 (Ky. 2011); Dobrovolny v. Ford Motor Co., 281 Neb. 86, 793 N.W.2d 445 (2011). See generally Jay M. Zitter, Annotation, Strict Products Liability: Recovery for Damage to Product Alone, 72 A.L.R.4th 12 (1989).

[44]   See Digicorp, Inc. v. Ameritech Corp., 262 Wis.2d 32, 662 N.W.2d 652 (2003) (discussing jurisdictional variations on the "fraud exception" to the economic loss rule).

[45]   Moorman Mfg. Co. v. National Tank Co., 91 Ill. 2d 69, 61 Ill. Dec. 746, 435 N.E.2d 443 (1982) (grain storage tank developed crack); Alejandre v. Bull, 159 Wash.2d 674, 153 P.3d 864 (2007) (recognizing the fraud exception but finding that plaintiffs failed to prove fraud; claim thus barred by economic loss rule).

[46]   See Fleetwood Enterprises, Inc. v. Progressive Northern Ins. Co., 749 N.E.2d 492 (Ind. 2001) (mobile home engulfed itself in flames).

under the contract or warranty. If the contract excludes or limits liability,[47] or if the statute of limitations has run on the contract claims,[48] the plaintiff has no viable claim at all.

The economic loss rule does not bar tort recovery for economic losses resulting from harms to persons. For instance, a defective product may cause a consumer's death, leaving her dependents to sue for their loss of support. That is an economic loss, but it is treated under the ordinary personal-injury rules and not excluded by the economic loss rule. The same is true with harm a defective product causes to "other property."[49] If a defective automobile blows itself up, the economic loss rule governs the claim, leaving the owner to sue on warranty or not at all. But if the defective automobile also blows up an adjacent home, the homeowner can claim in tort for the damage to the home, since the home is "other property" and not the product itself.[50]

B. TORT LIABILITY FOR DEFECTIVE PRODUCTS

1. *The Modern Typology of Defect*

§ 33.4 The Defect Requirement

Whether a product is in some way defective remains the most central issue in products liability litigation. Section 402A of the Restatement Second imposes strict liability only for harm caused by products that were defective and unreasonably dangerous.[51] The Restatement of Products Liability agrees that liability, whether or not it is strict, requires a defect in the product.[52]

Under § 402A, the burden is upon the plaintiff to prove that (a) the defendant was in the business of selling products, (b) he sold or otherwise supplied the product in question, (c) the product was expected to and did reach the consumer without substantial change, (d) the product was defective when it left the defendant's hands, and (e) the

---

[47] See Seely v. White Motor Co., 63 Cal. 2d 9, 45 Cal. Rptr. 17, 403 P.2d 145 (Cal.1965) (recognizing that disclaimer of warranty as to economic loss is permitted); Van Lare v. Vogt, Inc., 274 Wis.2d 631, 683 N.W.2d 46 (2004) (economic loss rule particularly appropriate where the parties' contract excludes liability for economic harm). One of the reasons frequently given for the economic loss rule is that it preserves the contract's limitations on liability and other allocations of losses. See, e.g., LAN/STV v. Martin K. Eby Constr. Co., 435 S.W.3d 234 (Tex. 2014).

[48] E.g., Neibarger v. Universal Cooperatives, Inc., 439 Mich. 512, 486 N.W.2d 612 (1992).

[49] What counts as "other property" is sometimes a difficult question. The Products Restatement asks whether the product is an integrated whole. Restatement Third of Torts (Products Liability) § 21, cmt. e (1998). If so, damage to the whole product by a component part is not damage to "other property;" instead, the product is deemed to have damaged itself, leaving the plaintiff to whatever contract rights he had and excluding the tort claims. See Travelers Indem. Co. v. Dammann & Co., 594 F.3d 238 (3d Cir. 2010) (N.J. law); Gunkel v. Renovations, Inc., 822 N.E.2d 150 (Ind. 2005).

[50] E.g., A.J. Decoster Co. v. Westinghouse Elec. Corp., 333 Md. 245, 634 A.2d 1330 (1994) (backup power system manufactured by defendant allegedly did not work, resulting in loss of 140,000 chickens in a power failure; upon proof, the plaintiff can recover its losses).

[51] Restatement Second of Torts § 402A (1965).

[52] Restatement Third of Torts (Products Liability) § 1 (1998).

product's defect was a factual cause[53] of physical harm[54] to the plaintiff[55] and (f) a proximate cause as well.[56] The more recent Restatement of Products Liability does not use the terminology of either strict liability or negligence, but in effect it requires the same essential elements and adds that in the case of claimed design and warning defects, the risks of harm must be foreseeable.[57]

Danger and negligence. Under § 402A, the plaintiff can show a defect in a product without showing negligence of its manufacturer.[58] The focus, as courts have said many times over, is upon the condition of the product, not the conduct of the defendant.[59] Thus the defendant is liable for a defective product even though he is entirely without fault.[60] At the same time, the mere fact that a product is dangerous does not render it defective. Knives are not defective merely because they are sharp, nor guns because they propel projectiles.[61] The Second Restatement tried to capture this idea by saying that the product must be both unreasonably dangerous and defective.[62] The point of requiring unreasonable danger was not to import negligence thinking; it was rather to insist that risky products are not necessarily defective and that a defect is indeed required.

§ 33.5 Summary of Types of Defect

After the promulgation of the Second Restatement's § 402A, courts and writers began to think that three types of product defect should be distinguished from one another. These were (1) manufacturing defects or production flaws,[63] (2) design defects, and (3) information or warning defects, also called "marketing" defects. These categories are now generally recognized and applied in most courts.[64] Courts initially attempted to retain the language of strict liability for all these claims, but they increasingly used

---

[53]   See, e.g., Doomes v. Best Transit Corp., 17 N.Y.3d 594, 935 N.Y.S.2d 268, 958 N.E.2d 1183 (2011); BIC Pen Corp. v. Carter, 346 S.W.3d 533 (Tex. 2011).

[54]   See, e.g., Sinclair v. Merck & Co., 195 N.J. 51, 948 A.2d 587 (2008) (claims of increased risks of health problems do not satisfy the definition of "harm" so as to allow a claim). See also Bylsma v. Burger King Corp., 176 Wash.2d 555, 293 P.3d 1168 (2013) (damages for emotional distress, absent physical injury, are recoverable in products liability action only where distress was "reasonable" and manifested by objective symptomatology).

[55]   The defendant may be subject to liability for harms to users of the product as well as bystanders injured by the product. See 2 Dobbs, Hayden & Bublick, The Law of Torts § 471 (2d ed. 2011 & Supp.).

[56]   See, e.g., Stahlecker v. Ford Motor Co., 266 Neb. 601, 667 N.W.2d 244 (2003) (defective tire causing motorist to be stranded alone and exposing her to murderous attack). To everyone's confusion, proximate cause issues have at times been treated as defenses. See § 33.18.

[57]   Section 1 of the Products Restatement provides for liability of one engaged in the business of selling or distributing products where there has been a sale or distribution. The same section requires a defect. Sections 2 (b) & (c) require foreseeable risks of harm when the claim is for design or warning defects. In a design defect case, § 2 (b) also requires proof of a reasonable alternative design. See § 33.11.

[58]   The Products Restatement also requires a defect, but imposes strict liability in only some of the cases. See § 33.5.

[59]   E.g., Lewis v. Coffing Hoist Div., Duff-Norton Co., 515 Pa. 334, 528 A.2d 590 (1987); Malcolm v. Evenflo Co, 352 Mont. 325, 217 P.3d 514 (2009).

[60]   Restatement Second of Torts § 402A(2) (1965).

[61]   E.g., Moss v. Crosman Corp., 136 F.3d 1169 (7th Cir. 1998); cf. McCarthy v. Olin Corp., 119 F.3d 148 (2d Cir. 1997) (Black Talon bullets designed to bend upon impact in order to inflict maximum harm to organs of a person were intended to be dangerous but were not defective).

[62]   Restatement Second of Torts § 402A, cmt. i (1965). See John W. Wade, On the Nature of Strict Tort Liability for Products, 44 Miss. L. J. 825 (1973). The Products Restatement uses the term "not reasonably safe" instead of "unreasonably dangerous." See Restatement Third of Torts (Products Liability) § 2(c) & (d) (1998).

[63]   The terms are synonymous.

[64]   See David G. Owen, Products Liability Law § 6.2 (2d ed. 2008).

negligence principles and approaches to decide design and warning defects claims, leaving strict liability to cases involving manufacturing defects.

Manufacturing defects. A product has a manufacturing defect when it disappoints consumer expectations by departing from its intended design.[65] A manufacturing defect is usually a random failing or imperfection,[66] because the defect lies in the production or distribution of the particular item, not in the design of the entire product line. Examples of manufacturing defects include the soft-drink bottle that explodes because of a microscopic crack in that particular bottle,[67] a blade of an electric saw that shatters because the metals in the blade are not fully bonded together,[68] and food or drink that is contaminated with foreign or dangerous matter.[69] The manufacturer or other distributor may be held strictly liable in such cases for harm caused by the manufacturing defect. For such claims, the product is tested against the consumer's reasonable safety expectations. For example, consumers reasonably expect that food will not be contaminated, so strict liability is imposed when it is.[70] The manufacturing defect cases justify strict liability most readily because the flawed product violates the intention of both the manufacturer and the consumer to sell and buy a standardized product with standard value, utility, and safety features.[71]

Design defects. In contrast to the manufacturing defect that unintentionally appears in isolated or occasional product items, a design defect occurs when the intended design of the product line itself is inadequate and needlessly dangerous.[72] If an automobile is designed in an unsafe and defective way, the entire product line is defective, so the potential for liability in design defect cases can be very great indeed.[73] "Design" includes chemical formulations and natural, inherent characteristics of a product such as asbestos.[74] Prescription drugs that risk cancer when others drugs could provide the same benefit with less risk are defectively designed.[75] Badly conceived products that carry needless danger are designed defectively. For example, a powered machine furnished

---

[65]　See Restatement Third of Torts (Products Liability) § 2(a) (1998).

[66]　Flaws may occur systematically rather than randomly if the production facility is badly maintained, as where a manufacturing plant is contaminated and permits products to be contaminated. See Torrington Co. v. Stutzman, 46 S.W.3d 829 (Tex. 2000).

[67]　See Welge v. Planters Lifesavers Co., 17 F.3d 209 (7th Cir. 1994) (permitting inference of some such defect when glass jar of peanuts shattered); Lee v. Crookston Coca-Cola Bottling Co., 290 Minn. 321, 188 N.W.2d 426 (1971) (inferring some such defect).

[68]　Van Deusen v. Norton Co., 204 A.D.2d 867, 612 N.Y.S.2d 464 (1994).

[69]　Schafer v. JLC Food Systems, Inc., 695 N.W.2d 570 (Minn. 2005); Restatement Third of Torts (Products Liability) § 7 (1998).

[70]　E.g., Jackson v. Nestle-Beich, Inc., 147 Ill.2d 408, 168 Ill.Dec. 147, 589 N.E.2d 547 (1992). See § 33.6 (consumer expectations test). Strict liability for defects in food is often imposed on a warranty theory rather than on a tort theory. See Jane Massey Draper, Annotation, Liability for injury or death caused by food product containing object related to, but not intended to be present in, product, 2 A.L.R.5th 189 (1992).

[71]　David G. Owen, The Moral Foundations of Products Liability Law: Toward First Principles, 68 Notre Dame L. Rev. 427, 467 (1993).

[72]　See § 33.9.

[73]　See David G. Owen, Design Defects, 73 Mo. L. Rev. 291 (2008) ("[U]nlike a manufacturing defect claim, which implicates merely a single product unit, a design defect claim challenges the integrity of the entire product line and so pierces to the very core of the manufacturer's enterprise. For this reason, design defect claims are of greatest concern to manufacturers[.]").

[74]　E.g., Adkins v. GAF Corp., 923 F.2d 1225 (6th Cir. 1991); Hammond v. North American Asbestos Corp., 97 Ill.2d 195, 454 N.E.2d 210, 73 Ill.Dec. 350, 39 A.L.R.4th 385 (1983).

[75]　E.g., Brochu v. Ortho Pharmaceutical Corp., 642 F.2d 652 (1st Cir. 1981).

without a readily available safety device,[76] an off-road vehicle with a roll-bar that doesn't protect against end-over-end rolls,[77] and an electric pot that cooks liquid hot enough to destroy a child's skin for a lifetime but isn't equipped with a lockable lid[78] are all defectively designed products.

The design defect, like the manufacturing flaw, may result from negligence, but under the rule of Restatement § 402A and many cases that followed it, the liability was said to be strict. The plaintiff was thus not required to prove negligence. As will appear, however, courts have now generally adopted a risk-utility test to determine whether a harmful design is also a defective design.[79] When a risk-utility test is applied, the courts seem to be requiring negligence or at least some similar species of fault. The point is controversial, but the Products Restatement adopts the risk-utility test of defectiveness and discards the strict-liability way of looking at design defects.[80]

Marketing defects—warning and information defects. Some products are reasonably safe and not defective if they are accompanied by a warning of their dangers or by information needed to use them safely. Those same products may become unreasonably dangerous and defective if no information explains their use or warns of their dangers. Such products suffer from information or warning defects. For example, it is perfectly reasonable to market full-strength glucose, but since it is dangerous to babies unless diluted, the manufacturer should not market it in a baby bottle with a nipple, or if it does, must give parents a warning to dilute it.[81]

—express warranty breach. Express warranties and representations of fact set their own standards. If either the warranty or misrepresentation creates a reasonable expectation about the nature or performance of the product and plaintiff is injured because the product does not meet that expectation, the warrantor is subject to liability, either because the product is defective as judged by the seller's own warranty or because no separate defect is required.[82] The plaintiff must rely on the warranty, but not necessarily by purchasing the item; it is enough if he *uses* the product in reliance on the warranty.[83] A warranty may occur in any kind of communication to the buyer, including those in advertisements,[84] in owners' manuals,[85] in the manufacturer's ratings for strength or use[86] and others.[87] The primary questions in express warranty claims are whether the communication is a warranty, whether its scope covered the characteristic that caused injury, whether it was breached, whether the plaintiff relied, and what harm

---

[76]   E.g., Knitz v. Minster Mach. Co., 69 Ohio St. 2d 460, 432 N.E.2d 814 (1982).

[77]   Leichtamer v. American Motors Corp., 67 Ohio St.2d 456, 424 N.E.2d 568 (1981). See also § 33.18.

[78]   Moulton v. Rival Co., 116 F.3d 22 (1st Cir. 1997).

[79]   See § 33.9 (adoption of risk-utility test).

[80]   Restatement Third of Torts (Products Liability) § 2(b) (1998).

[81]   Ross Laboratories, Div. of Abbott Laboratories v. Thies, 725 P.2d 1076 (Alaska 1986).

[82]   The Products Restatement implies that express warranty claims are not based upon a finding of defect. See Restatement Third of Torts (Products Liability) § 2 cmt. n (1998).

[83]   See Caboni v. General Motors Corp., 278 F.3d 448 (5th Cir. 2002) (under Louisiana statute).

[84]   Triple E, Inc. v. Hendrix and Dail, Inc., 344 S.C. 186, 543 S.E.2d 245 (2001); see Tracy Bateman Farrell, Annotation, Products Liability: Statements in Advertisements as Affecting Liability of Manufacturers or Sellers for Injury Caused by Product Other than Tobacco, 93 A.L.R.5th 103 (2001).

[85]   See Caboni v. General Motors Corp., 278 F.3d 448 (5th Cir. 2002) (under Louisiana statute).

[86]   See Sundberg v. Keller Ladder, 189 F.Supp.2d 671 (D. Mich. 2002) (ladder rated for 200 pounds allegedly collapsed with 150-pound plaintiff).

[87]   For other examples see 1 David G. Owen & Mary J. Davis, Owen & Davis on Products Liability § 4:8 (4th ed. 2014, updated on Westlaw).

resulted because the warranty was breached. The fact that the product is not defectively designed or manufactured is irrelevant; the "defect" at issue is its failure to meet the standards expressed in the warranty or representation itself.

2. *Manufacturing and Design Defects*

§ 33.6   The Consumer Expectations Test

Consumer expectations test under § 402A. The test of defectiveness under § 402A is the consumer expectations test. Under that approach, the product is defective if, considering its reasonably foreseeable use, it left the seller's hands in an unreasonably dangerous condition "not contemplated by the ultimate consumer."[88] For example, consumers rightfully expect that food will not be contaminated with foreign matter[89] or even with some inappropriate and dangerous part of the food item such as a shell in pecan candy[90] or a bone in a "boneless" meat dish.[91]

Application. The consumer expectations test reflects the contract side of strict liability, derived from its warranty history.[92] It may also reflect the fact that manufacturers make a good many representations about their products, sometimes directly, and sometimes by the product's appearance or by soothing words designed to inspire confidence.[93] The test has worked especially well in the case of non-obvious product flaws, as distinct from design defects. If the grocer displays cartons of milk, the buyer has every reason to think she is buying milk and not milk with human toes in it. The seller in turn knows the buyer's expectations. Both parties understand that the seller is to provide pure milk, not that he will merely exercise care. Even if the producer could not discover the impurity, liability is appropriate.[94]

Products Restatement's general rejection of the test. The Products Restatement rejects any general use of the consumer expectations test, reserving it only for food[95] and to a limited extent used products;[96] in all other cases, the consumer's expectation is merely one factor to consider in determining whether a product is defective.[97] Some

---

[88]   Restatement Second of Torts § 402A, cmt. g (1965).

[89]   E.g., Schafer v. JLC Food Systems, Inc., 695 N.W.2d 570 (Minn. 2005) (unidentified foreign object in pumpkin muffin); Massey v. ConAgra Foods, Inc., 156 Idaho 476, 328 P.3d 456 (2014) (pot pies contaminated with salmonella); see also Restatement Third of Torts (Products Liability) § 7 (1998). Most courts use the consumer expectations test, or some version of it, in the food-defect cases, although a small number use a "foreign-natural" distinction, in which the plaintiff can prevail on a strict liability theory only where some harmful feature is "foreign" to the particular food product. See Mexicali Rose v. Superior Court, 1 Cal. 4th 617, 4 Cal. Rptr. 2d 145, 822 P.2d 1292 (1992) (one-inch chicken bone in chicken enchilada was "natural" to the product, thus no strict liability).

[90]   Jackson v. Nestle-Beich, Inc., 147 Ill. 2d 408, 168 Ill. Dec. 147, 589 N.E.2d 547 (1992); Restatement Third of Torts (Products Liability) § 7, cmt. b (1998).

[91]   E.g., Estate of Pinkham v. Cargill, Inc., 55 A.3d 1 (Me. 2012) (bone fragment in boneless turkey product); but see Vitello v. Captain Bills Restaurant, 191 A.D.2d 429, 594 N.Y.S.2d 295 (1993) (consumers must reasonably expect fish bones in a fish fillet).

[92]   Under the UCC, the test is comparable. Goods breach the warranty of merchantability unless they are fit for the ordinary purposes for which the goods are used. See UCC § 2–314.

[93]   On the representational background of products liability, see Marshall S. Shapo, The Law of Products Liability § 1.02 and passim (4d ed. 2002, updated on Westlaw).

[94]   Cf. 2 Dobbs, Hayden & Bublick, The Law of Torts § 462 (2d ed. 2011 & Supp.) (unknowable dangers and design defects).

[95]   Restatement Third of Torts (Products Liability) § 7 (1998).

[96]   Id. § 8.

[97]   Id. § 2, cmts. g & h.

commentators have disfavored the Products Restatement on this (and related) points, partly because the consumer expectations test is sometimes regarded as a consumer-favorable test, while its chief rival, the risk-utility test, is regarded as industry-favorable.[98] But as will be seen, either of these tests can assist the plaintiff in some cases and defeat the plaintiff in others.

Many courts have adopted and applied the consumer expectations test in products cases, brought both on breach of warranty[99] and on strict tort liability theories.[100] Despite its shortcomings,[101] a few states retain the consumer expectations test as the exclusive test even in design defect cases,[102] and many others allow its use in conjunction with risk-utility balancing.[103] Some states give the plaintiff the option to use risk-utility balancing if the test aids in determining consumer expectations, or if the consumer expectations test alone does not prove defect.[104] Some allow the plaintiff to use the consumer expectations test where the defect is relatively simple, but force the use of a risk-utility test otherwise.[105] Others use the consumer's expectations, not as a test, but as only one factor among several used to determine a product's defectiveness.[106] Some allow the parties to offer evidence that would support its side of the case on either theory, and hold that the trial judge should instruct the jury on either consumer expectations, or risk-utility balancing, or both, as the parties wish, as long as the evidence supports the test.[107] In short, the consumer expectations test remains widely used, despite its virtual deletion from the Products Restatement.

---

[98] Marshall S. Shapo, In Search of the Law of Products Liability: The ALI Restatement Project, 48 Vand. L. Rev. 631 (1995); Rebecca Korzec, Dashing Consumer Hopes: Strict Products Liability and the Demise of the Consumer Expectations Test, 20 B.C. Int'l & Comp. L. Rev. 227 (1997).

[99] Phillips v. Town of West Springfield, 405 Mass. 411, 540 N.E.2d 1331 (1989) (food case); Denny v. Ford Motor Co., 87 N.Y.2d 248, 662 N.E.2d 730, 639 N.Y.S.2d 250 (1995) (sport-utility vehicle rollover case).

[100] E.g., Potter v. Chicago Pneumatic Tool Co., 241 Conn. 199, 694 A.2d 1319 (1997) (alleged defect in pneumatic hand tools, approving the use of supplemental risk-utility test in some cases).

[101] See § 33.8.

[102] See Godoy ex rel. Grambling v. E.I. DuPont de Nemours and Co., 319 Wis.2d 91, 768 N.W.2d 674 (2009) (Prosser, J., concurring) (listing states).

[103] E.g., Tincher v. Omega Flex, Inc., 104 A.3d 328 (Pa. 2014); Jackson v. General Motors Corp., 60 S.W.3d 800 (Tenn. 2001).

[104] See DeLaney v. Deere and Co., 268 Kan. 769, 999 P.2d 930 (2000) (while consumer expectations remains the controlling test, the risks and utilities of a product may be used as "a guide"); McCathern v. Toyota Motor Corp., 332 Or. 59, 23 P.3d 320 (2001) (consumer expectations is the controlling test; jurors will know those expectations in some cases from common experience; when that is not the case, the plaintiff can offer risk-utility evidence to show reasonable expectations).

[105] E.g., Tran v. Toyota Motor Corp., 420 F.3d 1310 (11th Cir. 2005) (consumer expectations instruction is a basis of liability independent of the risk-utility test "when the product in question is one about which an ordinary consumer could form expectations"; seatbelts are such a product); Soule v. General Motors Corp., 8 Cal. 4th 548, 34 Cal. Rptr.2d 607, 882 P.2d 298 (1994); D'Ascanio v. Toyota Industries Corp., 309 Conn. 663, 72 A.3d 1019 (2013).

[106] Wright v. Brooke Group Ltd., 652 N.W.2d 159 (Iowa 2002); Evans v. Lorillard Tobacco Co., 465 Mass. 411, 990 N.E.2d 997 (2013); American Tobacco Co., Inc. v. Grinnell, 951 S.W.2d 420 (Tex. 1997).

[107] Mikolajczyk v. Ford Motor Co., 231 Ill.2d 516, 327 Ill. Dec. 1, 901 N.E.2d 329 (2008) (characterizing the consumer expectations test and the risk-utility balancing test as "methods of proof" rather than "theories"). *Compare* Show v. Ford Motor Co., 659 F.3d 584 (7th Cir. 2011) (requiring expert testimony in Ford Explorer rollover case "when aspects of a product's design or operation are outside the scope of lay knowledge"), *with* Mansur v. Ford Motor Co., 197 Cal. App. 4th 1365, 129 Cal. Rptr. 3d 200 (2011) (on similar facts, consumer expectations test "is reserved for cases in which the everyday experience of the products' users permits a conclusion that the product's design violated minimum safety assumptions, and 'is defective regardless of expert opinion about the merits of design' " and thus "expert witnesses may not be used to demonstrate what an ordinary consumer should expect").

§ 33.7 Proving Manufacturing Defects

The plaintiff who asserts a manufacturing defect need not prove that the manufacturer or distributor was negligent. However, the plaintiff must prove by a preponderance of the evidence that (a) the product was defective (b) at the time it left the defendant's hands, (c) that it was expected to and did reach the consumer without change, and (d) the product caused harm.

The plaintiff may show a defect by direct evidence that points to the defect and identifies it as a departure from the defendant's intended design.[108] For example, evidence that parts in a tool had measurements outside the tolerance prescribed by the defendant's own specifications shows a manufacturing defect.[109] Similarly, the plaintiff might show that a hand tool or a scaffolding plank had unintended cracks likely to cause it to break, or that food contained dangerous foreign matter. Such evidence of specific, identified defects might be made by direct observation or through expert testimony.

In many cases, however, the plaintiff seeks to prove a defect circumstantially by evidence that the product malfunctioned or miscarried in a way unlikely to occur if the product had been properly made. Sometimes courts say that a mere malfunction does not itself prove a defect.[110] Dozens of other opinions have said that the plaintiff need not prove a specific or identifiable defect but may rely upon circumstantial evidence somewhat analogous to the evidence presented in a good res ipsa loquitur case.[111]

Neither statement is to be taken as a rule of law for all manufacturing defect cases. The effect of a product's malfunction is case-specific, because malfunction sometimes tends to show a defect and sometimes not.[112] Evidence that a product malfunctions is sufficient to show a manufacturing defect when either expert testimony or common experience tells us that, under the circumstances, the malfunction is probably inconsistent with a properly made product.[113] For instance, if a new tire blows out and causes injury when inflated to normal pressure for the first time, the trier can conclude that a defect was the likely explanation.[114] On the other hand, if the product has been subjected to a number of forces that would cause a well-made product to malfunction, the inference of a product defect may disappear altogether.[115] Consequently, the plaintiff

---

[108] Restatement Third of Torts (Products Liability) § 2(a) (1998); Casey v. Toyota Motor Engineering & Mfg. North America, Inc., 770 F.3d 322 (5th Cir. 2014) (Texas has expressly adopted the Restatement Third approach to manufacturing defects; plaintiff's failure to show that "the airbag in this case differs from the airbags that Toyota produced in the same period and installed in other Highlander vehicles" is fatal to the claim).

[109] McKenzie v. S K Hand Tool Corp., 272 Ill.App.3d 1, 650 N.E.2d 612, 208 Ill.Dec. 918 (1995).

[110] E.g., Walker v. General Elec. Co., 968 F.2d 116 (1st Cir. 1992); Burley v. Kytec Innovative Sports Equipment, Inc., 737 N.W.2d 397 (S.D. 2007); Rohde v. Smiths Medical, 165 P.3d 433 (Wyo. 2007).

[111] E.g., Metropolitan Property and Cas. Ins. Co. v. Deere and Co., 302 Conn. 123, 25 A.3d 571 (2011); Lawson v. Mitsubishi Motor Sales of America, Inc., 938 So.2d 35 (La. 2006); Schafer v. JLC Food Systems, Inc., 695 N.W.2d 570 (Minn. 2005); Barnish v. KWI Building Co., 602 Pa. 402, 980 A.2d 535 (2009). See also Restatement Third of Torts (Products Liability) § 3 (1998).

[112] See Christopher H. Hall, Annotation, Strict Products Liability: Product Malfunction or Occurrence of Accident as Evidence of Defect, 65 A.L.R.4th 346 (1989).

[113] See, e.g., Murray v. Farmers Ins. Co., 118 Idaho 224, 796 P.2d 101 (1990); Anderson v. Chrysler Corp., 184 W.Va. 641, 403 S.E.2d 189 (1991).

[114] Colboch v. Uniroyal Tire Co., 108 Ohio App.3d 448, 670 N.E.2d 1366 (1996). Age of the product alone is not conclusive; it is a matter of assessing the likelihood that a defect, not other forces, caused the harm. See Myrlak v. Port Authority of New York and New Jersey, 157 N.J. 84, 723 A.2d 45 (1999).

[115] E.g., Winter v. Brenner Tank, Inc., 926 F.2d 468 (5th Cir. 1991) (ladder welded to truck broke, but it could have been weakened over time by impacts; jury verdict for defendant affirmed).

must ordinarily show not only a malfunction, but must also negate the probability that other forces caused it.[116] The judicial problem is to assess evidence in each case, and close cases can produce results in either direction.[117]

Defect when product left defendant's hands. The plaintiff may need to negate outside forces affecting the product for another reason: to prove that the defect existed at the time the product left the defendant's hands.[118] For example, evidence showing that the plaintiff handled a glass jar of peanuts carefully at all times and that it was stored in a safe place in her home tends to show that when the jar shattered in ordinary use its defect must have been present when the defendant made the jar, and was not introduced later.[119] Evidence that a coffee maker that allegedly caused a fire was packed in a box with styrofoam when it was purchased, and remained in its box until the night before the fire, and appeared to be in good condition when the plaintiff took it out of the box, would lead a reasonable jury to conclude that the product defect that caused the fire already existed when the coffee maker left the manufacturer's hands.[120] Expert evidence may also point to the manufacturing process as the source of the defect.[121]

Causation of harm. The existence of a defect when the product left the hands of the defendant often carries with it the reasonable conviction that the defect also caused the harm of which the plaintiff complains, but causation is analytically a separate item and one not to be overlooked. For example, when an automobile bursts into flames in the plaintiff's garage, the circumstances make it plausible to believe the car was defective. But if the owner claims lung damage from the smoke, the mere fact of the malfunction does not prove that damage, much less the amount.[122] Once again, expert testimony may be helpful in resolving this issue.[123]

---

[116] See Crawford v. Sears Roebuck & Co., 295 F.3d 884 (8th Cir. 2002) (20-year-old ladder buckled, throwing plaintiff to the ground; since plaintiff offered no evidence to exclude other forces that might have affected ladder, there could be no inference of defect at the time ladder left the seller's hands); Parsons v. Ford Motor Co., 85 S.W.3d 323 (Tex. App. 2002) (parked car burst into flames, justifying inference of negligence or defect, but since the probable source of flames was ignition that had been worked on by a dealer, defect could not be attributed to manufacturer).

[117] *Compare* Kerr v. Corning Glass Works, 284 Minn. 115, 169 N.W.2d 587 (1969) (exploding Pyrex plate; problem could have resulted from use) *with* Lee v. Crookston Coca-Cola Bottling Co., 290 Minn. 321, 188 N.W.2d 426 (1971) (exploding soft-drink bottle, inference of defect permissible).

[118] See, e.g., Liberty Northwest Ins. Co. v. Spudnik Equipment Co., 155 Idaho 730, 316 P.3d 646 (2013) (plaintiff must identify which particular conveyor of the many on the job site caused his injury); Barnish v. KWI Building Co., 602 Pa. 402, 980 A.2d 535 (2009) (plaintiff failed to show why sensors suddenly failed after 10 years of proper functioning).

[119] Welge v. Planters Lifesavers Co., 17 F.3d 209 (7th Cir. 1994) ("Chicago is not Los Angeles; there were no earthquakes. . . . Elves may have played ninepins with the jar of peanuts while Welge and Godfrey were sleeping. . . . The plaintiff in a products liability suit is not required to exclude every possibility, however fantastic or remote, that the defect . . . was caused by someone other than one of the defendants.").

[120] Allstate Ins. Co. v. Hamilton Beach/Proctor Silex, Inc., 473 F.3d 450 (2d Cir. 2007) (Vermont law).

[121] Van Deusen v. Norton Co., 204 A.D.2d 867, 612 N.Y.S.2d 464 (1994) (parts of power saw improperly bonded).

[122] Ford Motor Co. v. Reed, 689 N.E.2d 751 (Ind. App. 1997) (but inferring causation largely on the basis of sequence and timing). See also Estate of Pinkham v. Cargill, Inc., 55 A.3d 1 (Me. 2012) (fact issue on whether consumer's perforated esophagus was caused by bone fragment in defendant's boneless turkey product precluded summary judgment for defendant).

[123] Allstate Ins. Co. v. Hamilton Beach/Proctor Silex, Inc., 473 F.3d 450 (2d Cir. 2007) (expert testimony provided sufficient evidence that defect in coffee maker probably caused house fire).

§ 33.8 Problems with the Consumer Expectations Test: Open and Obvious Dangers and Other Difficulties

The consumer expectations test may work best in cases involving manufacturing flaws rather than design defects. Although many courts have approved and continue to use the consumer expectations test even in design defect cases,[124] the test poses special kinds difficulties in those cases.

(1) Vagueness and ambiguity. First, the detailed structure of the consumer expectations test has not been worked out in the cases and to a large extent it is vague or ambiguous where it is most needed.[125] Although the consumer expectations test seems to appeal to a reasonable consumer who might be thought to resemble the objective reasonable person in negligence law, sometimes writers seem to assume that the knowledge of the particular injured person, rather than an objective consumer, is the test. Another uncertainly lies in the level of abstraction by which expectation is judged. Must consumers expect particular safety devices, or, at the other extreme, only expect that the product will be generally safe?

California has held that a general expectation that the product will be reasonably safe is not good enough; some expectation more specific than that may be required.[126] And the consumer expectations test may not work so well when safety depends upon complex, scientific, or technical information.[127] On the other hand, it may work well when widely-shared, well-defined "everyday experience" leads to somewhat specific safety expectations[128] that can be judged by the jury without expert testimony about what consumers might expect.[129] A new bridge should not fall when the first car crosses it, although we need no test at all to tell us that.

(2) Overbreadth. A second problem with the consumer expectations test is that it may be overbroad.[130] If the test means that any injury consumers would not expect—say an unpredictable reaction to a new drug—demonstrates a product defect, liability would

---

[124] See § 33.6.

[125] The consumer expectations test has been criticized as "amorphous or unprincipled," and as a test that provides only "meager and insufficient guidance." See Douglas A. Kysar, The Expectations of Consumers, 103 Colum. L. Rev. 1700, 1705 (2003).

[126] Soule v. General Motors Corp., 8 Cal. 4th 548, 34 Cal. Rptr.2d 607, 882 P.2d 298 (1994); see also McCabe v. American Honda Motor Co., 100 Cal.App.4th 1111, 123 Cal.Rptr.2d 303 (2002) ("If the facts permit an inference that the product at issue is one about which consumers may form minimum safety assumptions in the context of a particular accident, the consumer expectations test may be used."); Mansur v. Ford Motor Co., 197 Cal. App. 4th 1365, 129 Cal. Rptr. 3d 200 (2011) (consumer expectations test "is reserved for cases in which the everyday experience of the products' users permits a conclusion that the product's design violated minimum safety assumptions, and 'is defective regardless of expert opinion about the merits of design' "); D'Ascanio v. Toyota Industries Corp., 309 Conn. 663, 72 A.3d 1019 (2013) (when case involves "complex product design," trier of fact must view consumer expectations in light of various factors that balance utility of design with its risks).

[127] See, e.g., Morson v. Superior Court, 90 Cal. App.4th 775, 109 Cal. Rptr.2d 343 (2001); Biosera, Inc. v. Forma Scientific, Inc., 941 P.2d 284 (Colo. Ct.App. 1996), *aff'd on other grounds*, Forma Scientific, Inc. v. Biosera, 960 P.2d 108 (Colo. 1998); Jackson v. General Motors Corp., 60 S.W.3d 800 (Tenn. 2001).

[128] See Soule v. General Motors Corp., 8 Cal.4th 548, 34 Cal.Rptr.2d 607, 882 P.2d 298 (1994); Ray v. BIC Corp., 925 S.W.2d 527 (Tenn. 1996).

[129] If the consumer expectations must be based on widely shared general knowledge about those expectations, expert testimony to establish those expectations is likely to be excluded, as in Soule v. General Motors Corp., 8 Cal.4th 548, 34 Cal. Rptr. 2d 607, 882 P.2d 298 (1994).

[130] See Prosser & Keeton on Torts § 99, at 698 (5th ed. 1984).

follow from almost all product injuries. Although some advocates prefer this kind of total liability, tort law has never gone that far.

(3) Consumer's knowledge of dangers precluding liability. A third problem is perhaps the most severe: the consumer expectations test can foreclose liability for unnecessarily dangerous products if consumers know of the product's dangerous quality. For example, a cigarette lighter can be made child-resistant, but if consumers do not know that, they at least understand that children might use the lighter and cause fires and burns. The consumer's ignorance of safer designs hardly seems like a good reason to deny liability if a safer design is in fact cheap and useful, but the consumer expectations test has been used in just that way.[131] In the case of tobacco, it is argued that consumers already know that cigarettes are unhealthy, perhaps deadly. Consumers thus do not expect safety, so ordinary cigarettes are not defective under the consumer expectations test.[132] On the same rationale, a cigarette is not defective under the consumer expectations test because it starts a fire when left burning in a chair.[133] Even when the product is not generally known to be dangerous, the product's dangers may be apparent to the consumer when the product is purchased or used. This is most likely the case when the product is badly or dangerously designed, as where it obviously lacks safety devices. In such cases, courts once thought that the product was not defective under the consumer expectations test and some still do.[134]

The open and obvious nature of the danger is no doubt a factor in determining design defect, but not necessarily a conclusive one.[135] It is best applied when the plaintiff can see the nature or structure of the product and that structure is directly related by everyday experience to the danger in question, and the plaintiff has full choice whether to confront it. For example, it might make sense to say that the dangers of a convertible automobile are obvious, at least once the consumer envisions an overturned car,[136] and equally to say that an officer who wears a bullet-resistant vest must recognize the obvious fact that she remains exposed to projectiles in areas not covered by the vest.[137] These are cases in which the consumer need not synthesize information or make a series of deductions in order to perceive the existence and extent of danger, and in which the consumer knows both the nature and extent of the risk.

---

[131] Todd v. Societe Bic, 21 F.3d 1402 (7th Cir. 1994); Calles v. Scripto-Tokai Corp., 224 Ill.2d 247, 864 N.E.2d 249, 309 Ill.Dec. 383 (2007); Hernandez v. Tokai Corp., 2 S.W.3d 251 (Tex. 1999). In the same cases, the risk-utility test would support liability for harms done to children by lighters that feasibly could be child resistant. Perkins v. Wilkinson Sword, Inc., 83 Ohio St.3d 507, 700 N.E.2d 1247 (1998). Similarly, an ordinary negligence claim may be successfully asserted. See Talkington v. Atria Reclamelucifers Fabrieken BV, 152 F.3d 254 (4th Cir. 1998).

[132] American Tobacco Co. v. Grinnell, 951 S.W.2d 420 (Tex. 1997) (ruling as to marketing or warning defects only; but the addictive qualities of tobacco were not necessarily known and the product may be defective for that reason). A Texas statute applicable to later cases appears to eliminate all liability for tobacco products except that based upon manufacturing defects and breach of express warranty. See Tex. Civ. Prac. & Rem. Code § 82.004.

[133] Mercer Mut. Ins. Co. v. Proudman, 396 N.J.Super. 309, 933 A.2d 967 (App. Div. 2007).

[134] Haddix v. Playtex Family Products Corp., 138 F.3d 681(7th Cir. 1998); Lamke v. Futorian Corp., 709 P.2d 684 (Okla. 1985).

[135] See Perkins v. Wilkinson Sword, Inc., 83 Ohio St.3d 507, 700 N.E.2d 1247 (1998).

[136] Delvaux v. Ford Motor Co., 764 F.2d 469 (7th Cir. 1985) (danger of a convertible—as a roofless car—is open and obvious, thus as a matter of law not defective under consumer expectations test).

[137] See Linegar v. Armour of America, Inc., 909 F.2d 1150 (8th Cir. 1990); House v. Armour of America, Inc., 929 P.2d 340, 345 (Utah 1996).

But some courts have thought that the consumer expectations test goes much further. They believe that the test would bar the plaintiff whose work required her to use a machine that lacked a safety device, because it would be "obvious" that the safety device was not present. For instance, some courts have said that the operator of a bulldozer not equipped with a canopy or cage would understand the danger that bulldozed trees might fall upon the operator.[138] Courts have also held that workers who did not purchase the dangerous machine and who had little choice but to face its dangers would have no claim if its dangers were open and obvious to the employer or other purchaser.[139] Similarly, children have been denied recovery if the danger was obvious to their parents or the product was safe for the intended adult use.[140]

When coupled with the open-and-obvious-danger rule, the consumer expectations test can defeat otherwise sound claims for strict liability.[141] In particular, some products are needlessly dangerous and could be made safe quite cheaply. Workers, children, and bystanders who are injured by products may lack any real choice in facing their dangers. Even if all product-injured people had full information, free choice, and the market power to reject dangerous products, the open-and-obvious-danger rule does nothing to encourage the manufacturer to provide safer products, as many courts have observed.[142] For this and similar reasons, most courts have wisely rejected any automatic application of the open-and-obvious-danger rule.[143] Instead, the obviousness of the danger in a design defect claim is merely one factor in determining whether a defect exists. Such a view suggests, however, that consumer expectations are always only part of the test of liability.

§ 33.9   The Risk-Utility Test for Design Defects

Courts and many commentators have recognized for some time that the consumer expectations test covers both too much and too little, potentially imposing liability for sound products and excluding liability for needlessly dangerous products.[144] Largely as a result of the work of Page Keeton[145] and John Wade,[146] many courts came to believe that an additional test of strict liability was required. A number of courts have adopted a risk-utility test of defectiveness, especially where the plaintiff alleged a design defect

---

[138] Orfield v. International Harvester Co., 535 F.2d 959 (6th Cir. 1976).

[139] Gray v. Manitowoc Co., Inc., 771 F.2d 866 (5th Cir. 1985); Spangler v. Kranco, Inc., 481 F.2d 373 (4th Cir. 1973); cf. Sauder Custom Fabrication, Inc. v. Boyd, 967 S.W.2d 349 (Tex. 1998) (where "average user of product" that injured employee would recognize the obviousness of the product's risks, employee's recovery barred even where he had no subjective knowledge of those risks).

[140] Calles v. Scripto-Tokai Corp., 224 Ill.2d 247, 864 N.E.2d 249, 309 Ill.Dec. 383 (2007); cf. Moss v. Crosman Corp., 136 F.3d 1169 (7th Cir. 1998) (judging obvious danger of air gun by appearances to parent)

[141] See David G. Owen, Products Liability Law § 5.6, at 306 (2d ed. 2008) ("[T]he consumer expectations test undesirably bars consumers in virtually every case in which a danger was obvious, even if the manufacturer could easily and cheaply removed a serious danger.").

[142] E.g., Byrns v. Riddell, Inc., 113 Ariz. 264, 550 P.2d 1065 (1976); Camacho v. Honda Motor Co., 741 P.2d 1240 (Colo. 1987) (citing many cases).

[143] Pike v. Frank G. Hough Co., 2 Cal.3d 465, 467 P.2d 229, 85 Cal.Rptr. 629 (1970) (negligent design claim); Camacho v. Honda Motor Co., Ltd., 741 P.2d 1240 (Colo. 1987) (strict liability design defect); Ogletree v. Navistar Intern. Transp. Corp., 269 Ga. 443, 500 S.E.2d 570 (1998) (under risk-utility balancing test).

[144] See §§ 33.6 & 33.8.

[145] Page Keeton, Product Liability and the Meaning of Defect, 5 St. Mary's L. J. 31 (1973); Page Keeton, Manufacturer's Liability: The Meaning of "Defect" in the Manufacture and Design of Products, 20 Syracuse L. Rev. 559 (1969).

[146] John W. Wade, On the Nature of Strict Tort Liability for Products, 44 Miss. L. Rev. 825 (1973).

rather than a manufacturing flaw.[147] Statutes also sometimes prescribe a risk-utility test.[148] The Products Restatement likewise adopts a similar system.[149] Some courts adopt the risk-utility test as one part of a two-part test which allows the plaintiff to show a defect in the product's design if the product fails *either* the risk-utility test *or* the consumer expectations test[150] or as one of a series of factors to be considered in determining whether a product is defective.[151]

Under the risk-utility test, the risks of the product as designed are balanced against the costs of making the product safer; costs of making the product safer include any loss of product utility. Risks of the product include not only the likelihood of harm but also its magnitude. Dean Wade once listed seven factors and courts have often referred to them for guidance: (1) the usefulness and desirability of the product; (2) the probability and magnitude of potential injury; (3) the availability of substitutes; (4) the manufacturer's ability to eliminate the unsafe character; (5) the user's ability to avoid danger; (6) the user's probable awareness of the danger; and (7) the manufacturer's ability to spread the loss.[152] Except for the seventh,[153] these factors are essentially those routinely considered in determining negligence.[154] Given the use of a risk-utility test, nominal strict liability now appears to most observers to be ordinary negligence liability traveling under the name of strict liability.[155]

Risk-utility assessments are often straightforward and simple, and where reasonable people could differ on the evidence, the jury determines the risk-utility balance, just as it does in negligence cases.[156] Suppose a manufacturer produces an industrial press that delivers 60 tons of force. Such a press creates a risk that the operator's hand may be crushed if the press is accidentally activated when the operator is handling material in the press bed. The manufacturer can cheaply eliminate the risk by designing the press so that it can be activated only when the operator presses two separate buttons away from the press area. A jury could easily find that the press is defective under the risk-utility balancing test because a large reduction in risk can be

---

[147] E.g., Barton v. Adams Rental, Inc., 938 P.2d 532 (Colo. 1997); Warner Fruehauf Trailer Co. v. Boston, 654 A.2d 1272 (D.C. 1995); Ogletree v. Navistar Intern. Transp. Corp., 269 Ga. 443, 500 S.E.2d 570 (1998); St. Germain v. Husqvarna Corp., 544 A.2d 1283 (Me. 1988); Voss v. Black & Decker Mfg. Co., 59 N.Y.2d 102, 450 N.E.2d 204, 463 N.Y.S.2d 398 (1983); Knitz v. Minster Mach. Co., 69 Ohio St.2d 460, 432 N.E.2d 814 (1982); Ray v. BIC Corp., 925 S.W.2d 527 (Tenn. 1996). "Danger-utility" and "cost-benefit" are among the terms referring to risk-utility analysis.

[148] N. C. Gen. Stat. § 99B–6 (b) (as with many formulations, listing a number of factors all of which could be subsumed under risk or utility); Ohio Rev. Code Ann. § 2307.7.

[149] See Restatement Third of Torts (Products Liability) § 2, cmt. a & f (1998); David Owen, Products Liability Law Restated, 49 S. C. L. Rev. 273 (1998).

[150] See Barker v. Lull Engineering Co., 20 Cal.3d 413, 143 Cal.Rptr. 225, 573 P.2d 443 (1978); Ontai v. Straub Clinic and Hosp., Inc., 66 Haw. 237, 659 P.2d 734 (1983); Calles v. Scripto-Tokai Corp., 224 Ill.2d 247, 864 N.E.2d 249, 309 Ill.Dec. 383 (2007); Soproni v. Polygon Apartment Partners, 137 Wash.2d 319, 971 P.2d 500 (1999).

[151] Hernandez v. Tokai Corp., 2 S.W.3d 251 (Tex. 1999).

[152] John W. Wade, On the Nature of Strict Tort Liability for Products, 44 Miss. L. Rev. 825, 837 (1973). See Restatement Third of Torts (Products Liability) § 2, cmt. f (1998).

[153] The Products Restatement's discussion of factors, § 2, cmt. f, does not mention the seventh factor.

[154] This is so because they are particular pieces of the risk-utility balance used in negligence cases generally. See §§ 12.2 to 12.5.

[155] Defenses in negligence and strict liability cases may be different, however, and in a few states, the burdens of proof. See § 33.12.

[156] E.g., Bryant v. Hoffmann-La Roche, Inc., 262 Ga.App. 401, 585 S.E.2d 723 (2003); Giunta v. Delta Intern. Machinery, 300 A.D.2d 350, 751 N.Y.S.2d 512 (2002).

achieved at a relatively small cost.[157] Conversely, if the risk were low and the cost of avoiding it high, the product would not be defective, and the defendant would not be liable either on a negligence or a "strict liability" theory.[158]

The Products Restatement and the reasonable alternative design requirement. As noted above,[159] many courts adopting the risk-utility test also retain the consumer expectations test, allowing the plaintiff to recover if a product defect can be shown under either test. The Products Restatement, however, endorses the consumer expectations test only with respect to food[160] and in a limited way with used products.[161] For other cases, the consumer expectations test is merely one factor to consider. In design and warning defect claims, the Products Restatement indirectly requires a kind of risk-utility balancing. With limited exceptions, it also requires the plaintiff to show that the manufacturer could have avoided or reduced the danger of the product by adopting a reasonable alternative design.[162]

Similarity to or identity with negligence. After the adoption of the risk-utility test for design defect cases, liability remains strict for product flaws or manufacturing defects, but looks like ordinary negligence liability in the case of design defects. However, depending upon the precise rules adopted, some differences between products liability and negligence liability might remain. For example, in products cases the burden of proof might be shifted to the defendant,[163] rules of evidence might be different,[164] and defenses that apply to negligence claims might be rejected.[165] Products cases could also differ from ordinary negligence cases if the manufacturer could be held liable for unknowable risks in a design.[166] A few states have adopted one or more of these distinguishing rules,[167] but in the main the courts appear to use the risk-utility balance as they do in ordinary negligence cases.

§ 33.10   Proving a Design's Risks and Utilities

In a design defect case brought on a risk-utility theory, the plaintiff in most states has the burden of proving that the design was defective and that its defective character was both a factual and proximate cause of the plaintiff's injury. The plaintiff's burden on the defect element may be met easily if the product's design is manifestly too risky in the light of its low utility.[168] The plaintiff may also show a defect in the product by

---

[157] E.g., Knitz v. Minster Mach. Co., 69 Ohio St.2d 460, 432 N.E.2d 814 (1982). As this example suggests, the product may be defective under the risk-utility analysis even if the product does not malfunction. Perkins v. Wilkinson Sword, Inc., 83 Ohio St.3d 507, 700 N.E.2d 1247 (1998) (disposable cigarette lighter could have been made child-resistant).

[158] See § 33.10.

[159] See § 33.6.

[160] Restatement Third of Torts (Products Liability) § 7, cmt. b (1998).

[161] Id. § 8.

[162] Id. § 2(b). See § 33.11.

[163] See § 33.12.

[164] The defendant's post-injury remedial measures are admitted in some strict liability cases but not in negligence cases. See, e.g., Caprara v. Chrysler Corp., 52 N.Y.2d 114, 417 N.E.2d 545, 436 N.Y.S.2d 251 (1981).

[165] See § 33.17.

[166] See 2 Dobbs, Hayden & Bublick, The Law of Torts § 462 (2d ed. 2011 & Supp.).

[167] See §§ 33.12.

[168] Restatement Third of Torts (Products Liability) § 2, cmt. e (1998). The defendant may win just as easily if the design's utilities obviously outweigh its risks. E.g., Bravman v. Baxter Healthcare Corp., 984 F.2d 71 (2d Cir. 1993) (heart valve allegedly too noisy).

showing that its design violated a safety statute as to risks the statute aimed to prevent.[169] Sometimes it is said that a product's dangerous malfunction may itself suffice to show a defect, as where the brakes fail on a new car,[170] but more likely such proof will show a defect in manufacture, not in design.[171]

Estimates of risks and utilities. In the great majority of cases, the plaintiff must provide evidence from which the trier can reasonably estimate risks of the product's design and the utilities or advantages that would be lost if it were made safer.[172] That burden does not necessarily mean that the plaintiff must adduce either quantified or expert evidence.[173] Juries will frequently be able to estimate dangers and benefits of a product design based on descriptions of familiar products or familiar kinds of risks. For example, the jury could easily conclude that sharp, protruding, propeller-like blades on a hubcap would be unreasonably dangerous to anyone who might accidentally come into contact with the spinning blades in a vehicular accident or otherwise. Jurors could also conclude that the utility of such blades is virtually zero, at best serving only someone's peculiar aesthetic sense by creating serious risks of harm to others.[174] In such cases, the plaintiff's burden is satisfied without any special testimony about the degree of risk or the lack of utility.

Expert testimony. An expert's quantified or unquantified estimates of the risk, the feasibility of an alternative and safer design,[175] testimony about the benefits of the product, and testimony about costs of obtaining greater safety would all be relevant.[176] An expert's testimony that the defendant's product is unsafe for specific reasons and that safer products are actually available should ordinarily suffice to show a defect.[177] To the extent that the plaintiff must show a feasible alternative design or that the defendant's design was a cause in fact of the plaintiff's harm, expert testimony may be required as a practical matter. In that case, rules that permit judges to exclude expert testimony they consider unreliable may defeat the plaintiff's claim.[178]

Cash costs. Sometimes the cost of greater safety can be spelled out in testimony as cash costs. Evidence showing exceedingly small costs to avoid an occasional horrifying

[169] See, e.g., Orthopedic Equip. Co. v. Eutsler, 276 F.2d 455, 79 A.L.R.2d 390 (4th Cir. 1960); Restatement Third of Torts (Products Liability) § 4 (1998). Industry standards and non-binding governmental standards, though not controlling, may be admissible as evidence bearing on defectiveness, see Hansen v. Abrasive Engineering and Mfg., Inc., 317 Or. 378, 856 P.2d 625 (1993), although not all courts allow such evidence.

[170] E.g., Tweedy v. Wright Ford Sales, Inc., 64 Ill.2d 570, 357 N.E.2d 449, 2 Ill.Dec. 282 (1976).

[171] See Burley v. Kytec Innovative Sports Equipment, Inc., 737 N.W.2d 397 (S.D. 2007) ("It is not within the common experience of a jury to decide merely from an accident and injury that a product was defectively designed.").

[172] Multi-function products may create some challenges in evaluation. In Beard v. Johnson and Johnson, Inc., 41 A.3d 823 (Pa. 2012), the plaintiff sued the manufacturer of a medical instrument that had many functions. The defendant argued that the risk-utility balance must only take account of the particular function or feature actually being used at the time of the injury. The court rejected this argument, holding that the assessment of the risks and utilities of the design of a multi-function product should not be limited to considering only a single use of that product.

[173] Restatement Third of Torts (Products Liability) § 2, cmt. f (1998), recognizes that an expert is not required "in every case," but asserts that an expert will be required in "many" cases.

[174] See Passwaters v. General Motors Corp., 454 F.2d 1270 (8th Cir. 1972).

[175] Garnsey v. Morbark Indus., Inc., 971 F.Supp. 668 (N.D.N.Y. 1997).

[176] See, e.g., Goodner v. Hyundai Motor Co., Ltd., 650 F.3d 1034 (5th Cir. 2011) (reviewing five factors that a jury should weigh "holistically" in determining defect, under Texas law).

[177] Violette v. Smith and Nephew Dyonics, Inc., 62 F.3d 8 (1st Cir. 1995).

[178] See 2 Dobbs, Hayden & Bublick, The Law of Torts § 463 (2d ed. 2011 & Supp.).

injury may suffice to get the plaintiff past a summary judgment or directed verdict. In the Ford Pinto case,[179] the plaintiff was able to show a number of items that could have helped prevent the Pinto's eruption into flames upon a mild impact. Some of the safety improvements would have cost as little as $1.80 per car, and although a number of improvements might have been required to insure safety, the totals seem small in comparison to the terrible death and suffering that Ford risked. In some cases even general testimony that costs of a safety device would have been small has been sufficient.[180] The fact that costs of better safety are small does not establish that the product is defective, because the risk of the product may be even smaller than the costs or the utility of the product may be very great.[181] Testimony about the cost of safety is not the same as testimony about the profits of the manufacturer, which would not normally be admissible except on the issue of punitive damages.[182]

Inferring reasonable costs. Evidence that other products have safer designs should usually suffice to show that a safer design is feasible, at least in the absence of specialized purposes for the defendant's design.[183] In this respect, the use of safer designs by other manufacturers or by the defendant on other models resembles evidence of custom in an ordinary negligence suit. At the very least, a widespread practice tends to show that the customary practice is feasible, even though the custom does not set the standard of care.[184]

Costs in loss of productive utility. Cash costs are not the only costs associated with getting a safer product. If adding a safety feature to a product reduces the product's capacity to function, that also is a cost.[185] A bullet-proof vest for police officers would protect more of the body if it were a full-length coat, but only at a considerable loss of utility because such a design would restrict movement at the very time agility might be most needed.[186] If industrial machinery can be made safer only by slowing it to half speed, the costs in reduced production may be quite high. Similarly, a safety improvement in some products used in the workplace may impose costs for re-training and supervision.[187]

Costs in increased risks to others. Still another kind of cost that might attend a product's improvement is the cost of new risks the improvement would introduce.[188]

---

[179] Grimshaw v. Ford Motor Co., 119 Cal.App.3d 757, 174 Cal.Rptr. 348 (1981).

[180] Soler v. Castmaster, Div. of H.P.M. Corp., 98 N.J. 137, 484 A.2d 1225 (1984).

[181] Riley v. Becton Dickinson Vascular Access, Inc., 913 F.Supp. 879, 889 (E.D. Pa. 1995) (harmful product costs $0.78 per unit, arguably safer product costs $1.40); Beaver v. Howard Miller Clock Co., 852 F.Supp. 631 (W.D. Mich. 1994) (safety strap to stabilize grandfather clock would have cost $1.75 per clock).

[182] See Ake v. General Motors Corp., 942 F.Supp. 869 (W.D. N.Y. 1996).

[183] See, e.g., Goodner v. Hyundai Motor Co., Ltd., 650 F.3d 1034 (5th Cir. 2011) (economic feasibility of an alternative design for the front seats of a car was proved by evidence that the manufacturer used an alternative design for the rear seats of the same car); see also Restatement Third of Torts (Products Liability) § 2, cmt. f (1998) (acknowledging relevance of evidence that an alternative design is already on the market).

[184] See Clarence Morris, Custom and Negligence, 42 Colum. L. Rev. 1147 (1942); §§ 12.6 to 12.9.

[185] E.g., Timpte Industries, Inc. v. Gish, 286 S.W.3d 306 (Tex. 2009) (trailer was not defective in design, because changing the design "would have increased the cost and weight of the trailer while decreasing its utility").

[186] See Linegar v. Armour of America, Inc., 909 F.2d 1150 (8th Cir. 1990).

[187] See Riley v. Becton Dickinson Vascular Access, Inc., 913 F.Supp. 879 (E. D. Pa. 1995).

[188] See Self v. General Motors Corp., 42 Cal.App.3d 1, 8, 116 Cal.Rptr. 575, 579 (1974) ("Protection gained against a head-on collision may be at the expense of protection against one that is broadside, for like an army in battle the vehicle can't be uniformly strong at all points and under all conditions."), *overruled on other grounds*, Soule v. General Motors Corp., 8 Cal.4th 548, 34 Cal.Rptr.2d 607, 882 P.2d 298 (1994).

Suppose the defendant manufactures a drug that saves victims of a certain kind of cancer but risks blindness to one in a million people. The drug could be reformulated to eliminate the risk of blindness, but the reformulation would introduce an even greater risk of total paralysis. In that case, the new drug would be safer with respect to blindness, but at the cost of risking even more injuries to others. Thus present drug, with its small risk of causing blindness, probably has greater utility than the alternative, with its high risk of causing total paralysis. A simpler example, taken from a Texas case, is where defendant manufactured a ladder for use with a trailer, which was also manufactured by defendant. Plaintiff fell from the ladder's top rung and claimed that it should have had the two top rungs removed. But removing those two rungs, while it would have prevented plaintiff's injury, "might also increase the risk of injury to others who might need those rungs as a failsafe handhold" and "could cause the ladder to bend or become unstable under pressure."[189] Given a low risk of injury on the ladder, its design has more utility than the proposed alternative, which adds additional risks.

Proving presence or absence of risks. As in ordinary negligence cases, issues about risk fall into two large categories. The first is associated with probability and foreseeability: how likely is it that the product will cause harm? The second is associated with the magnitude of the harm likely to befall a victim if harm in fact results. A risk that has a low probability of occurrence might nevertheless represent a defect in the product if the harm threatened is devastating bodily injury or death.

Foreseeability of harm and defectiveness. Courts and juries have routinely made judgments about foreseeability of harm in deciding negligence issues, frequently on the basis of ordinary experience in life and without any special evidence. If the product's design does not create any foreseeable risk of harm, or the plaintiff has failed to persuade judges that harm was foreseeable, the product is not defective under the risk-utility test, even if greater safety was in fact possible.[190] Some decisions have clearly demanded evidence about the magnitude of the risk and the utility of proposed alternatives, although quite possibly those decisions are meant to be nothing more than assessment of the evidence in particular cases.[191] But in some cases the risk is demonstrable; anyone can foresee that harm can result when workers must place their hands in or near moving presses that are not equipped with safety devices.

Prior similar injuries. In other cases the plaintiff may sometimes be able to show both the risk and its foreseeability by proving that similar injuries had occurred before and that the manufacturer knew it.[192] Evidence that in one year small objects or toys caused eleven choking deaths in small children does not by itself show high probability that such harm will occur, but it is enough to show that brightly colored blocks less than an inch wide are dangerously defective for small children when slightly larger blocks can easily avoid the risk.[193] In some cases the parties can go further and provide actual

---

[189] Timte Industries, Inc. v. Gish, 286 S.W.3d 306 (Tex. 2009).

[190] Grzanka v. Pfeifer, 301 N.J. Super. 563, 694 A.2d 295 (1997) (traffic signal's control box was vandalized, disabling signal and resulting in collision; vandalism not shown to be foreseeable, even though a better-protected control box was feasible).

[191] Owens v. Allis-Chalmers Corp., 414 Mich. 413, 326 N.W.2d 372 (1982) (forklift without seatbelts turned over and crushed operator; evidence did not reveal magnitude of the risks, judgment for defendant affirmed).

[192] Ryan v. KDI Sylvan Pools, Inc., 121 N.J. 276, 579 A.2d 1241 (1990); Shipler v. General Motors Corp., 271 Neb. 194, 710 N.W.2d 807 (2006).

[193] Metzgar v. Playskool, Inc., 30 F.3d 459 (3d Cir. 1994).

estimates of probability. The risk of a needle-stick injury with a medical catheter may be demonstrably small, the risk of an AIDS infection from a needle stick even smaller.[194] Sometimes, estimates are not quantified in any formal way and courts can only identify factors that tend to reduce or increase risk. For example, the presence of an effective warning may reduce the risk that would otherwise be imposed by a product, but an ineffective one may not.[195] Likewise, danger may be so obvious that users will be likely to protect themselves, leaving only a small net risk.

Obviousness bearing on product's risks. The plaintiff is no longer automatically barred in all cases merely because the product's danger is open and obvious.[196] But obviousness of danger bears on the product's risks because a product that is excessively dangerous when its dangers are hidden may be much less dangerous when its dangers are known.[197] Harm is less likely to eventuate if the user is aware of danger and can protect herself.[198] And equally, if the plaintiff will foreseeably encounter the risk in spite of its obvious character, liability may still be appropriate.[199] The manufacturer's warnings are likewise relevant as bearing on the user's awareness and ability to avoid danger[200] and thus on the likelihood of harm. So if the manufacturer can expect that people will generally recognize the risk and either avoid it or take feasible safety precautions, the risk may be so low that the product is not defective at all. With common everyday objects whose dangers are not only obvious but well known, courts may even conclude as a matter of policy that liability should be rejected.[201]

§ 33.11　Reasonable Alternative Design

In many and perhaps most design defect cases, the plaintiff will have to prove that a safer, reasonable alternative design was available to the defendant, and that the failure to adopt that design would have prevented the plaintiff's harm from occurring.[202] This reasonable alternative design concept, adopted as a rule in the Products Restatement,[203] is perhaps the central core of the risk-utility balancing test as applied

---

[194] Riley v. Becton Dickinson Vascular Access, Inc., 913 F.Supp. 879, 885 (E. D. Pa. 1995).

[195] See Braswell v. Cincinnati Inc., 731 F.3d 1081 (10th Cir. 2013) (press brake machine that injured plaintiff was not defective, in part because warnings on machine covered all salient risks). Presence of adequate warnings may not provide a complete defense to a design defect claim, however. See, e.g., Weigel v. SPX Corp., 729 F.3d 724 (7th Cir. 2013).

[196] See Bourne v. Mary Gilman, Inc., 452 F.3d 632, 636 (7th Cir. 2006) ("[T]he accident magnet is just as obvious to the designer as the user, and the rule should not work just one way.").

[197] See, e.g., Timpte Industries, Inc. v. Gish, 286 S.W.3d 306 (Tex. 2009).

[198] Bourne v. Marty Gilman, Inc., 452 F.3d 632, 637 (7th Cir. 2006) (goal posts that would snap and fall when pulled down by fans after a football game were not unreasonably dangerous because they presented obvious danger; "In some cases, the obviousness of the risk will obviate the need for any further protective measures. . . ."); Braswell v. Cincinnati, Inc., 731 F.3d 1081 (10th Cir. 2013).

[199] See Mesman v. Crane Pro Services, Div. of Konecranes, Inc., 409 F.3d 846 (7th Cir. 2005); Blue v. Environmental Engineering, Inc., 280 Ill. Dec. 957, 803 N.E.2d 187 (App. 2003), *aff'd on other grounds*, 215 Ill. 2d 78, 828 N.E.2d 1128, 293 Ill. Dec. 630 (2005).

[200] See Warner Fruehauf Trailer Co. v. Boston, 654 A.2d 1272 (D.C. 1995).

[201] Kearney v. Philip Morris, Inc., 916 F.Supp. 61 (D. Mass. 1996) (no liability for manufacturer of cigarette that caused fire on plaintiff's upholstered furniture).

[202] See David G. Owen, Products Liability Law § 8.5, at 522 (2d ed. 2008) ("Without affirmative proof of a feasible design alternative, a plaintiff usually cannot establish that product's design is defective.").

[203] Restatement Third of Torts (Products Liability) § 2(b) (1998).

to design defects.[204] Under the risk-utility test, a product is not defective in design unless its design makes harm reasonably foreseeable.[205] Foreseeability of harm, though necessary, is not sufficient; as the Products Restatement puts it, a product is defective in design when the product's "foreseeable risks of harm could have been reduced or avoided by the adoption of a reasonable alternative design" and the failure to adopt the alternative leaves the product "not reasonably safe."[206] While proof of a reasonable alternative design does not necessarily prove that the product is defective,[207] a plaintiff's claim may founder for lack of such proof.[208]

Much controversy surrounded the Product Restatement's adoption of the reasonable alternative design requirement, but many states now require a plaintiff to prove reasonable alternative design, either by statute[209] or by case law.[210] Many other states do not require such proof, but see the existence of a reasonable alternative design as relevant, perhaps highly relevant, to the design-defect inquiry.[211] By treating reasonable alternative design as a factor only and not as determinative in itself, these decisions may imply that such evidence is not required; sometimes courts have expressly said that it is not.[212] Some courts have been more broadly critical.[213] And two small groups of courts necessarily reject any flat requirement that the plaintiff prove a reasonable alternative design: (1) those that apply the consumer expectations test alone in design defect cases,[214] and (2) those that shift the burden of proof to the defendant to justify that the design's utilities outweigh its risks.[215] In any event, evidence of a reasonable alternative

---

[204] See Jones v. NordicTrack, Inc., 274 Ga. 115, 550 S.E.2d 101 (2001) ("The 'heart' of a design defect case is the reasonableness of selecting from among alternative product designs and adopting the safest feasible one.").

[205] See §§ 33.9 & 33.10.

[206] Restatement Third of Torts (Products Liability) § 2(b) (1998).

[207] E.g., Slisze v. Stanley-Bostich, 979 P.2d 317 (Utah 1999) (that the same company produced a safer nailer was not sufficient to show that another one was defective); Brown v. Crown Equipment Corp., 181 S.W.3d 268 (Tenn. 2005).

[208] The Products Restatement acknowledges that a reasonable alternative design need not be shown when a defect is shown by circumstantial evidence, or where the design violates a safety statute or is manifestly unreasonable. See Restatement Third of Torts (Products Liability) § 2, cmts. b & e (1998).

[209] See, e.g., N.J. Stat. Ann. § 2A:58C–3a(1); N.C. Gen. Stat. Ann. § 99B–6(1); Ohio Rev. Code § 2307.75(F); Tex. Civ. Prac. & Rem. Code § 82.005; Wash. Rev. Code § 7.72.030(1)(a), (3).

[210] E.g., Wankier v. Crown Equip. Corp., 353 F.3d 862 (10th Cir. 2003) (Utah law); Guarascio v. Drake Associates Inc., 582 F.Supp.2d 459 (S.D.N.Y. 2008) (New York law); Bagley v. Mazda Motor Corp., 864 So.2d 301 (Ala. 2003); Artis v. Corona Corp. of Japan, 703 A.2d 1214 (D.C. 1997); Parish v. Jumpking, Inc., 719 N.W.2d 540 (Iowa 2006); Toyota Motor Corp. v. Gregory, 126 S.W.3d 35 (Ky. 2004).

[211] E.g., Boerner v. Brown & Williamson Tobacco Corp., 260 F.3d 837 (8th Cir. 2001) (Ark. law); Dart v. Wiebe Mfg., Inc., 147 Ariz. 242, 709 P.2d 876 (1985); Banks v. ICI Americas, Inc., 264 Ga. 732, 736, 450 S.E.2d 671, 674 (1994) (jury "may consider" safer designs); Mikolajczyk v. Ford Motor Co., 231 Ill.2d 516, 901 N.E.2d 329 (2008).

[212] E.g., Osorio v. One World Technologies Inc., 659 F.3d 81 (1st Cir. 2011) (Mass. law); Potter v. Chicago Pneumatic Tool Co., 241 Conn. 199, 694 A.2d 1319 (1997); Mikolajczyk v. Ford Motor Co., 231 Ill.2d 516, 901 N.E.2d 329 (2008); Kallio v. Ford Motor Co., 407 N.W.2d 92 (Minn. 1987); Vautour v. Body Masters Sports Industries, Inc., 147 N.H. 150, 784 A.2d 1178 (2001).

[213] See, e.g., Vautour v. Body Masters Sports Industries, Inc., 147 N.H. 150, 784 A.2d 1178 (2001) (requiring reasonable alternative design tends to limits the inferences that can be drawn from the evidence before the evidence is even presented, and may eliminate just claims); Godoy ex rel. Grambling v. E.I. DuPont de Nemours and Co., 319 Wis.2d 91, 768 N.W.2d 674 (2009) (to adopt such a requirement would "impose an expensive burden and require a battle of experts over competing product designs").

[214] E.g., Delaney v. Deere and Co., 268 Kan. 769, 999 P.2d 930 (2000); Godoy ex rel. Grambling v. E.I. DuPont de Nemours and Co., 319 Wis.2d 91, 768 N.W.2d 674 (2009). See § 33.6.

[215] Those courts place the burden of proving the absence of a reasonable alternative design on the defendant, although they may not make it an essential element of defendant's proof. See, e.g., Caterpillar

design remains extraordinarily important in practice to persuade the trier of fact that a product is defective.[216]

Proof. The Products Restatement says that "the plaintiff is not required to establish with particularity the costs and benefits associated with adoption of the suggested alternative design."[217] In line with this, a number of cases have held the plaintiff's evidence adequate when experts testified, apparently in general terms, that a specific improvement would be safer and could be used without impairing the usefulness of the product or imposing undue costs.[218] Many courts are more demanding, however.[219] The most stringent version of the reasonable alternative design requirement requires the plaintiff to prove, in addition to causation, that the proposed safer design was, at the time the product was sold, (a) technologically feasible, (b) economically feasible,[220] and (c) safer, or at least as safe overall, not merely safer in the particular circumstances causing the plaintiff's injury.[221]

Other product designs as evidence of feasible alternatives. Perhaps the clearest evidence of a reasonable alternative design is evidence that other products already have safer designs. If a car roof is weakly supported and deforms downward into the passenger compartment when a side impact occurs, testimony that other mass-marketed vehicles have stronger roof-supports that would have avoided the injury seems to establish prima facie a reasonable alternative design.[222] The defendant's own use of a safer design for products it distributes in other countries seems equally to show that such a design is cost-feasible.[223]

Expert testimony. The Products Restatement specifically recognizes that a reasonable alternative design can be established without adducing expert testimony and that the plaintiff need not necessarily build a prototype of the proposed alternative. At the same time, however, it suggests that experts will often be required to establish the nature and feasibility of an alternative design.[224] Indeed, some courts have required that the expert must have actually built or tested the alternatively-designed product, a requirement that goes beyond the Product Restatement's more lenient formulation.[225]

Tractor Co. v. Beck, 593 P.3d 871 (Alaska 1979); Barker v. Lull Engineering Co., 20 Cal.3d 413, 143 Cal.Rptr. 225, 573 P.2d 443, 96 A.L.R.3d 1 (1978). See § 33.12.

[216] See David G. Owen, Products Liability Law § 8.5, at 522 (2d ed. 2008) ("[T]here typically is nothing wrong with a product that simply possesses inherent dangers that cannot feasibly be designed away.").

[217] Restatement Third of Torts (Products Liability) § 2, cmt. f (1998). This substantive rule may be defeated by evidentiary requirements imposed in federal courts, and in many state courts. See 2 Dobbs, Hayden & Bublick, The Law of Torts § 463 (2d ed. 2011 & Supp.).

[218] E.g., Soler v. Castmaster, Div. of H.P.M. Corp., 98 N.J. 137, 484 A.2d 1225 (1984).

[219] See Bagley v. Mazda Motor Corp., 864 So.2d 301 (Ala. 2003); Smith v. Keller Ladder Co., 275 N.J. Super. 280, 645 A.2d 1269 (1994).

[220] Artis v. Corona Corp. of Japan, 703 A.2d 1214 (D.C. 1997).

[221] See Quintana-Ruiz v. Hyundai Motor Corp., 303 F.3d 62 (1st Cir. 2002); Honda of America Mfg., Inc. v. Norman, 104 S.W.3d 600 (Tex. App. 2003).

[222] Restatement Third of Torts (Products Liability) § 2, cmt. f (1998) (other products already on the market may serve as reasonable alternatives).

[223] Stallings v. Black and Decker (U.S.), Inc., 342 Ill. App.3d 676, 277 Ill.Dec. 428, 796 N.E.2d 143 (2003); see also Goodner v. Hyundai Motor Co., Ltd., 650 F.3d 1034 (5th Cir. 2011) (economic feasibility of an alternative design was established by evidence that the manufacturer itself used a different design in some of its own vehicles).

[224] Restatement Third of Torts (Products Liability) § 2, cmt. f (1998).

[225] See, e.g., Casey v. Toyota Motor Engineering & Mfg. North America, Inc., 770 F.3d 322 (5th Cir. 2014) (Texas law); Colon ex rel. Molina v. BIC USA, Inc., 199 F.Supp. 2d 53 (S.D.N.Y. 2001); Volpe v. IKO Industries, Ltd., 327 Ill.App.3d 567, 763 N.E.2d 870, 261 Ill.Dec. 621 (2002).

From the plaintiff's point of view, the practical requirement of expert testimony on reasonable alternative design is a serious impediment to recovery. One reason for this is that the cost of expert preparation is likely to drive out smaller claims where the potential recovery is not predictably sufficient to pay the costs of experts. Another is that, in some courts, expert testimony must often be buttressed by scientific study that is not likely to be available when the issue is one of ordinary engineering principles.[226] Finally, the best experts in this area may be already employed by private industry and more likely to be called for the defense, whereas plaintiffs may be forced to go to universities or to private consulting firms where "professional experts" work.[227]

Subsequent design changes or repairs. The defendant's own subsequent design changes might be used to prove that other designs are feasible. Evidence of a defendant's subsequent repairs of a dangerous condition is usually excluded in negligence cases, but some decisions have admitted it in strict liability claims.[228] If a plaintiff must prove a reasonable alternative design, the defendant's own subsequent design change would be highly relevant to show that a design change was feasible.[229]

What counts as an alternative design. One of the objections to the requirement of reasonable alternative design evidence can be meliorated if it we understand "design" broadly to include constant features of the product (and its proffered alternative). The objections can also be meliorated if the court can consider as alternatives not only a modified product but also a substitute product.[230] If a reasonable alternative design means that the product must remain the same except for minor tinkering, there will be few reasonable alternatives, since any substantial modification will result in a new and different, not merely altered, product. On the other hand, if a broad conception of the product is permissible, a wide range of safer functional alternatives or substitutes might be safer than the defendant's product.

For example, in the narrow view, asbestos is asbestos; you can't change its design and hence there is no reasonable alternative. But you don't have to characterize a product by its specific name or its chemical compound.[231] The important design characteristic of asbestos is that it furnishes very good insulation. If you characterize asbestos as insulating material, you can find very good substitutes that can easily count as reasonable alternative designs. The Products Restatement recognizes this point. However, adjudication of this point will present some difficulties. If three-wheeled all-terrain vehicles are unsafe, probably the plaintiff should be permitted to prove that four-

---

[226] See 2 Dobbs, Hayden & Bublick, The Law of Torts § 463 (2d ed. 2011 & Supp.).

[227] See David G. Owen, Products Liability Law § 6.3, at 368–71 (2d ed. 2008).

[228] Ault v. International Harvester Co., 13 Cal.3d 113, 528 P.2d 1148, 117 Cal.Rptr. 812, 74 A.L.R.3d 986 (1974); Forma Scientific, Inc. v. Biosera, Inc., 960 P.2d 108 (Colo. 1998); McFarland v. Bruno Mach. Corp., 68 Ohio St.3d 305, 626 N.E.2d 659 (1994); Caprara v. Chrysler Corp., 52 N.Y.2d 114, 417 N.E.2d 545, 436 N.Y.S.2d 251 (1981) (rejecting blanket exclusion). Federal Rule of Evidence 703 provides that subsequent remedial measures are not admissible to prove "negligence, culpable conduct, a defect in the product's design, or a need for warning or instruction," but contains an exception where the evidence is offered for "another purpose," such as the "feasibility of precautionary measures, if controverted." Many states have similar evidence rules.

[229] See Duchess v. Langston Corp., 564 Pa. 529, 769 A.2d 1131 (2001) (where defendant put feasibility in issue, trial judge may admit evidence of subsequent remedial changes).

[230] Cf. Brown v. Superior Court, 44 Cal.3d 1049, 245 Cal.Rptr. 412, 751 P.2d 470 (1988); Restatement Third of Torts (Products Liability) § 2, cmt. e (1998).

[231] Brown v. Superior Court, 44 Cal.3d 1049, 751 P.2d 470, 245 Cal.Rptr. 412 (1988) ("[D]efendants' attempt to confine the issue to whether there is an 'alternative design' for DES poses the problem in an 'unreasonably narrow' fashion.").

wheeled vehicles could provide a reasonable substitute and would be safer.[232] Courts should be permitted to characterize the product broadly or, much the same thing, to consider substitute products that have similar functions[233] or those that would be accepted by consumers as substitutes.[234]

An alternative: specific-defect proof. Perhaps the plaintiff should be allowed to show a specific defect rather than a reasonable alternative design. Design defect claims are certainly more plausible when the plaintiff can identify the particular defect and less plausible when the plaintiff can only say that the product should somehow have been designed not to cause injury. When the plaintiff can point to specific defects, she can almost always suggest an alternative design. If the claimed defect is that a machine's blades or pulleys keep turning dangerously for minutes after the machine is shut off, the jury does not need evidence to conclude that there is some reasonable way to brake the machine automatically when it is switched off; most people have seen instant braking on kitchen appliances.[235] If an automobile suddenly accelerates at full throttle and cannot be stopped, it is probably fair to infer that there is a defect, since other automobiles do not generally behave in this manner, and fair, for the same reason, to infer that something reasonable can be done to prevent such a defect.[236] Unless the defendant comes forward with convincing evidence that costs or other disutilities are significant, it is reasonable enough to conclude that the brakeless machine is defective. It is not necessary to require the plaintiff to invent a new design for the defendant's business.[237]

§ 33.12　Shifting the Burden of Proof in Design Defect Cases

A small handful of states have shifted the burden to the defendant to justify the design of a product once the plaintiff shows that a design feature caused injury.[238] The leading case is *Barker v. Lull Engineering Co.*[239] The plaintiff there was operating a high-lift industrial loader. The load was high; the loader began to vibrate as if it were about to tip over. The plaintiff scrambled out and was injured by lumber falling from the load. The loader had two design characteristics that made it arguably defective. First, it had no outriggers to steady it; second, it had no protective canopy to shield the operator from objects falling from the load. The court held that the plaintiff could recover if the product was defective under either the consumer expectations or the risk-utility test. Under the risk-utility test the plaintiff gained an added benefit: once the plaintiff proved that "the

---

[232] See Richard L. Cupp, Jr., Defining the Boundaries of "Alternative Design" Under the Restatement (Third) of Torts: the Nature and Role of Substitute Products in Design Defect Analysis, 63 Tenn. L. Rev. 329, 348 (1996).

[233] When a product is purchased chiefly for its aesthetic appeal, that appeal could be considered to be its "function." Toys and games, appealing to senses that are not easily described in terms of function or aesthetics, present special challenges, especially where a degree of danger is part of the attraction for users.

[234] See Richard L. Cupp, Jr., Defining the Boundaries of "Alternative Design" Under the Restatement (Third) of Torts: the Nature and Role of Substitute Products in Design Defect Analysis, 63 Tenn. L. Rev. 329, 365 (1996) ("cross-elasticity of demand").

[235] Garnsey v. Morbark Indus., Inc., 971 F.Supp. 668 (N.D. N.Y. 1997).

[236] Cf. Jarvis v. Ford Motor Co., 283 F.3d 33 (2d Cir. 2002) (evidence sufficed to show negligence in design based largely on the fact of acceleration).

[237] See Frank J. Vandall, The Restatement (Third) of Torts: Products Liability Section 2(b): The Reasonable Alternative Design Requirement, 61 Tenn. L. Rev. 1407, 1423 (1994).

[238] Caterpillar Tractor Co. v. Beck, 593 P.2d 871 (Alaska 1979); Barker v. Lull Engineering Co., 20 Cal.3d 413, 143 Cal.Rptr. 225, 573 P.2d 443 (1978); Ontai v. Straub Clinic and Hosp., Inc., 66 Haw. 237, 659 P.2d 734 (1983). Also Puerto Rico, Quintana-Ruiz v. Hyundai Motor Corp., 303 F.3d 62 (1st Cir. 2002).

[239] Barker v. Lull Engineering Co., 20 Cal.3d 413, 143 Cal.Rptr. 225, 573 P.2d 443 (1978).

product's design proximately caused his injury" the defendant had to prove that the design was justified under a risk-utility approach.[240]

The effect of the *Barker* holding is that the plaintiff does not need to prove that the design could have been made safer at a reasonable cost; instead the defendant must establish that it could not. For example, a plaintiff who fell from her seat to the floor of a public bus made a prima facie case against the bus manufacturer by showing that no hand-hold was within reach of her seat.[241] Where the burden-shifting rule is adopted, strict liability under the risk-utility test does indeed differ from negligence under the same test,[242] because the burden of proof is different. Most courts to consider it have rejected this approach, however,[243] as has the Products Restatement.[244]

3. Marketing Defects

§ 33.13 The Warnings Requirement

A product is defective not only when it suffers from a manufacturing flaw or design defect, but also when its manufacturer or distributor fails to provide a reasonable warning about reasonably foreseeable risks of harm.[245]

Strict Liability vs. Negligence

The jurisprudence of strict liability that developed under the Restatement Second's § 402A conceived of warning failures not merely as negligence but as grounds for strict liability. The theory was that the product itself was not reasonably safe if it could be made safer by the reasonable addition of warnings or instructions. Since only reasonable warnings were required, however, a failure-to-warn-or-instruct claim always had a strong affinity with an ordinary negligence claim. The two theories, strict liability and negligence, would be distinguishable if the manufacturer were required to give warnings about scientifically unknowable dangers, but the cases held overwhelmingly to the contrary.[246] The result is that warning claims gravitated toward a negligence approach even while courts were using the language of strict liability.

---

[240] See Pannu v. Land Rover North America, Inc., 191 Cal. App. 4th 1298, 120 Cal. Rptr. 3d 605 (2011) (affirming plaintiff's verdict, where defendant failed to prove that SUV was not defective in design with respect to its tendency to roll over; evidence showed that the benefits of the design did not outweigh the inherent risks, and that inexpensive modifications could have greatly improved rollover resistance).

[241] Campbell v. General Motors Corp., 32 Cal.3d 112, 184 Cal.Rptr. 891, 649 P.2d 224 (1982).

[242] The plaintiff is of course free to assert negligence with its emphasis on unreasonable risks whether *Barker v. Lull* is adopted or not, see Green v. Smith & Nephew AHP, Inc., 245 Wis.2d 772, 629 N.W.2d 727 (2001), but that would not entail a shift of the burden of proof.

[243] E.g., Ray v. Bic Corp., 925 S.W.2d 527 (Tenn. 1996) (describing the burden shift as an aberration).

[244] See Restatement Third of Torts (Products Liability) § 2(b) & cmts. c, d & f (1998).

[245] Restatement Third of Torts (Products Liability) § 2(c) (1998). A reasonable warning might require a warning about use with other products. For example, a propane supplier might be obliged to warn against storage in old or corroded tanks, even though the supplier does not provide the tanks. See Robles v. Shoreside Petroleum, Inc., 29 P.3d 838 (Alaska 2001). Or a respirator manufacturer could owe a duty to warn of the dangers of asbestos, where the respirators created the danger of exposure to asbestos when they were cleaned and then reused, which was an intended use. See Macias v. Saberhagen Holdings, Inc., 175 Wash. 2d 402, 282 P.3d 1069 (2012).

[246] E.g., Rosa v. Taser Intern., Inc., 684 F.3d 941 (9th Cir. 2012) (manufacturer of taser had no duty to warn of the risk that the application of the taser to a human could cause fatal levels of metabolic acidosis, where that risk was not known or knowable prior to the taser's distribution); Anderson v. Owens-Corning Fiberglas Corp., 53 Cal.3d 987, 810 P.2d 549, 281 Cal.Rptr. 528 (1991); Vassallo v. Baxter Healthcare Corp., 428 Mass. 1, 696 N.E.2d 909 (1998).

Under the Products Restatement, the manufacturer's duty is only to provide reasonable warnings against foreseeable risks of harm. Liability is imposed only if the danger could have been reduced or avoided by the omitted information and if the product without warnings was not reasonably safe.[247] In effect, warning claims are negligence claims,[248] as a number of courts recognize.[249] Some courts continue to apply the terminology of strict liability in warning cases,[250] but even so, the actual evidence and analysis usually invokes negligence principles of reasonableness.[251]

The Role of and Necessity for Warning

The role of warnings and design safety. When a product is unavoidably dangerous, a warning permits the consumer to make informed choices whether to accept the product. When the danger is avoidable, a warning may reduce the risk or magnitude of harm by permitting the consumer to use the product with greater safety.[252]

Some warnings will predictably fail to induce better safety. A warning to a worker not to place hands in the operating area of a machine will predictably fail to protect all workers all of the time because fatigue, repetitious work, and other elements make it almost certain that some workers will be harmed. If a reasonably priced safety device could have been built into the product, the product is defective in design. In such cases, even the very best warning does not remedy the design defect.[253] If no safety device is practicable, on the other hand, a good warning must do the whole job of achieving safety. For example, if an industrial cleaner can be made safer only by substantially reducing its effective cleaning power but users can easily protect themselves by using rubber gloves, an adequate warning may mean that the product is not defective, although a warning would not suffice if the product's danger could be eliminated without cost or loss of utility.

Risk-utility analysis. The Products Restatement subjects warning defect claims to a risk-utility analysis.[254] Under that test, now commonly used in ordinary negligence and in design defect cases, it might seem that warnings would almost always be required, since manufacturers can usually provide them quite cheaply; even a remote risk deserves

---

[247] Restatement Third of Torts (Products Liability) § 2(c) (1998). For two reasons, this formulation of the rule is arguably too narrow. First, even a reasonably safe product might be even safer with a reasonable warning. Second, the warning sometimes provides information analogous to that required of a physician in informed-consent cases, namely, of information that would be *material*. See § 21.11 (informed consent).

[248] See David G. Owen, Defectiveness Restated: Exploding the "Strict" Products Liability Myth, 1996 U. Ill. L. Rev. 743 (1996).

[249] E.g., Olson v. Prosoco, Inc., 522 N.W.2d 284 (Iowa 1994); Georgia Pacific, LLC v. Farrar, 432 Md. 523, 69 A.3d 1028 (2013).

[250] E.g., Carlin v. Superior Court, 13 Cal.4th 1104, 920 P.2d 1347, 56 Cal.Rptr.2d 162 (1996).

[251] See Rohde v. Smiths Medical, 165 P.3d 433 (Wyo. 2007) ("Unlike traditional strict liability claims, a claim for failure to provide adequate warnings incorporates some negligence components in determining whether a warning is necessary and/or whether the warnings provided were adequate.").

[252] A person injured by a product may be found to be a "user" even where he never purchased the product at all; a duty to warn such a person thus may be owed. See Patch v. Hillerich & Bradsby Co., 361 Mont. 241, 257 P.3d 383 (2011) (child was struck by batted ball that came off a bat manufactured by defendant; child was a "user" of the product; jury verdict for plaintiff on failure-to-warn theory affirmed).

[253] E.g., Lewis v. American Cyanamid Co., 155 N.J. 544, 715 A.2d 967 (1998); Uniroyal Goodrich Tire Co. v. Martinez, 977 S.W.2d 328 (Tex. 1998). Since obvious danger furnishes a kind of warning, this rule is exactly parallel to the rule that a product may be defective even if its danger is obvious, as to which see Ogletree v. Navistar Intern. Transp. Corp., 269 Ga. 443, 500 S.E.2d 570 (1998).

[254] See Restatement Third of Torts (Products Liability) § 2, cmt. i (1998) (Subsection (c) on warnings adopts a reasonableness test that parallels Subsection (b), on design defects) and cmt. k (risk-utility balance in allergy cases reflects risk-utility balance used in warnings cases generally).

a line of print on the product label.[255] But it has been argued that there are costs in providing detail in warnings because detail takes time for consumers to read,[256] and because when confronted with too much detail, consumers may ignore all the warnings.[257] If true, that is definitely a cost to be considered, but the information-overload claim does not apply to all warning cases, since added detail is not always necessary to improve a warning or to change its misleading characteristics. Where information-overload is established, however, it raises a genuine risk-utility issue that is quintessentially one that must be determined on the particular facts of individual cases. In most instances a case-by-case decision is required to determine the reasonableness of a warning. Unless the matter is so clear that reasonable people cannot differ, that assessment is for the jury.[258]

Known or obvious risks. One reason a warning may not be required is that the risks involved are either generally known or are obvious to a purchaser or user. One function of a warning is to alert the product user to risks. A warning may not be needed if people already know of the risks,[259] or know of the warning itself, if given by another up the chain of distribution.[260] In this respect, the warning problem differs greatly from the design problem. If a manufacturer can make a press that is safe just as cheaply as it can make one that is dangerous, its choice to manufacture the dangerous version is unjustified and the machine is defective, even if its danger is open and obvious.[261] But if the machine as designed is reasonably safe and its unavoidable dangers are known or obvious, the consumer is already warned by her knowledge so that reasonable care does not ordinarily require the manufacturer to provide a separate warning.[262] In the case of simple products, courts sometimes say that there is no duty to warn of obvious danger.[263] The question of obviousness is for the jury if reasonable people can differ.[264] Nevertheless, courts have sometimes concluded that risks are obvious as a matter of law

---

[255] See Ross Laboratories Div. of Abbott Laboratories v. Thies, 725 P.2d 1076 (Alaska 1986).

[256] See Cotton v. Buckeye Gas Products Co., 840 F.2d 935, 938 (D.C. Cir. 1988).

[257] James A. Henderson, Jr. & Aaron D. Twerski, Doctrinal Collapse in Products Liability: The Empty Shell of Failure to Warn, 65 N.Y.U. L. Rev. 265, 296 (1990); see also Mark Geistfeld, Inadequate Product Warnings and Causation, 30 U. Mich. J.L. Ref. 309 (1997) (supporting risk-utility analysis in warnings cases, with detailed workout on costs and proposed interrogatories to the jury). The information-overload argument has been applied in determining what disclosures are required in securities cases. See TSC Indus., Inc. v. Northway, Inc., 426 U.S. 438, 449, 96 S.Ct. 2126, 2132, 48 L.Ed.2d 757 (1976).

[258] See Restatement Third of Torts (Products Liability) § 2, Illus. 11 (1998). Where the manufacturer has provided no warning at all, whether that failure to warn rendered the product unreasonably dangerous is also for the jury. See, e.g., Moore v. Ford Motor Co., 332 S.W.3d 749 (Mo. 2011).

[259] See, e.g., In re Prempro Products Liab. Litigation, 514 F.3d 825 (8th Cir. 2008); cf. Carrier v. City of Amite, 50 So. 3d 1247 (La. 2010) (retailer of bicycle helmets can safely assume that a customer will ask for particular instructions about fitting if he wants them; there is no duty to volunteer those instructions).

[260] Ford Motor Co. v. Rushford, 868 N.E.2d 806 (Ind. 2007) ("[A]bsent special circumstances, if the manufacturer provides adequate warnings of the danger of its product and the seller passes this warning along to the buyer or consumer, then the seller has no obligation to provide additional warnings.").

[261] See § 33.8.

[262] E.g., Ex parte Chevron Chemical Co., 720 So.2d 922 (Ala. 1998); Caterpillar, Inc. v. Shears, 911 S.W.2d 379 (Tex. 1995); Restatement Third of Torts (Products Liability) § 2, cmt. j (1998).

[263] Mills v. Giant of Maryland, LLC, 508 F.3d 11 (D.C. Cir. 2007) (no duty to warn of dangers of milk to the lactose-intolerant); Glittenberg v. Doughboy Recreational Industries, 441 Mich. 379, 491 N.W.2d 208 (1992) (no duty to warn of dangers of diving headfirst into an above-ground swimming pool).

[264] E.g., Keogh v. W.R. Grasle, Inc., 816 P.2d 1343 (Alaska 1991) (jury found ordinary user would recognize danger of high voltage system, judgment for defendant affirmed); Smith v. Minster Mach. Co., 233 A.D.2d 892, 649 N.Y.S.2d 257 (1996) (obviousness a jury question; summary judgment denied); see also Maneely v. General Motors Corp., 108 F.3d 1176 (9th Cir. 1997) (stating rule; risk of riding in pickup truck bed was obvious as a matter of law).

because rational thinkers would be able to figure them out.[265] Such an approach may too readily relieve manufacturers of warning obligations. Beyond this, warnings may have another function. They may alert the user to safer alternatives that are far from obvious. "Do not use meat grinder without its safety attachment" not only warns of the obvious danger but informs the user that a safety device is available. In such cases, the fact that danger is obvious does not negate the need for a warning.[266]

§ 33.14   Adequacy of Warnings

Whether warnings are defective because they are inadequate is a question for the jury if evidence would permit reasonable people to differ,[267] but judges often conclude as a matter of law that warnings in a particular case are adequate.[268] Warnings can be defective in several distinct ways—in factual content; in lack of clarity of expression or communication; and in the mode of communication, such as words versus pictures.[269]

Adequacy of content and expression. Warnings must contain facts necessary to permit reasonable persons to understand the danger[270] and in some cases how to avoid it.[271] Warnings and instructions for use are not reasonable unless they are of sufficient clarity and also sufficient force and intensity to convey the nature and extent of the risks to a reasonable person.[272] A manufacturer's techniques in promoting the product,[273] inconsistencies or undue qualifications in stating the warning or directions,[274] and depictions of uses that run counter to warnings[275] may each nullify or dilute the warnings provided in printed literature. Unless the warning taken as a whole is so clear and forceful that it overrides the dilutions and inconsistencies, the diluted warning may be quite inadequate.[276] Neither the warning itself nor the marketing style should imply

---

[265] See Maneely v. General Motors Corp., 108 F.3d 1176, 1180 (9th Cir. 1997) (riding in the cargo bed of a pickup); Sollami v. Eaton, 201 Ill.2d 1, 772 N.E.2d 215, 265 Ill.Dec. 177 (2002) ("rocket jumping" on a trampoline; falling from heights is an obvious danger, eliminating any need for warnings).

[266] See Liriano v. Hobart Corp., 170 F.3d 264 (2d Cir. 1999) (Calabresi, J., explaining the two warning functions and why obvious danger does not eliminate the need for the informative warning in certain cases).

[267] E.g., Ford Motor Co. v. Rushford, 868 N.E.2d 806 (Ind. 2007); Bond v. Lincoln Elec. Co., 179 Ohio App.3d 559, 902 N.E.2d 1023 (2008).

[268] E.g., Koruba v. American Honda Motor Co., 396 N.J. Super. 517, 935 A.2d 787 (App. Div. 2007); Town of Bridport v. Sterling Clark Lurton Corp., 166 Vt. 304, 693 A.2d 701 (1997).

[269] Brochu v. Ortho Pharmaceutical Corp., 642 F.2d 652, 657 (1st Cir. 1981); see David G. Owen, Products Liability Law § 9.3, at 597–602 (2d ed. 2008).

[270] See, e.g., Gray v. Badger Mining Corp., 676 N.W.2d 268 (Minn. 2004) (warning must attract the user's attention, explain the "mechanism and mode of injury" and provide instructions for safe use).

[271] See Wood v. Old Trapper Taxi, 286 Mont. 18, 952 P.2d 1375 (1997) (manufacturer of radio tower failed to warn against erecting tower without guy wires).

[272] Martin v. Hacker, 83 N.Y.2d 1, 11, 628 N.E.2d 1308, 1313, 607 N.Y.S.2d 598, 603 (1993) (language of warning must be "direct, unequivocal and sufficiently forceful to convey the risk").

[273] Brown v. Glaxo, Inc., 790 So.2d 35 (La. App. 2000) (evidence that oral warnings were inconsistent with written warnings was sufficient to support a jury finding for plaintiff); Levey v. Yamaha Motor Corp., 361 N.J. Super. 312, 825 A.2d 554 (App. Div. 2003) ("seller vitiated the effectiveness" of written warnings and instructions by demonstrating the product to potential customers in a manner that violated those very instructions).

[274] McFadden v. Haritatos, 86 A.D.2d 761, 448 N.Y.S.2d 79 (1982) (prescription drug; warning was diluted by statement that adverse reactions disappear when drug is discontinued).

[275] Yamaha Motor Co., U.S.A. v. Arnoult, 114 Nev. 233, 955 P.2d 661 (1998) (manufacturer of ATV warned against "jumping" with vehicles but depicted its use in rough desert terrain).

[276] See Martin v. Hacker, 83 N.Y.2d 1, 628 N.E.2d 1308, 607 N.Y.S.2d 598 (1993) (inconsistencies may dilute warning, but whether it is adequate depends upon overall clarity; the force of the warning may be strong enough to outweigh inconsistencies).

a safety that does not exist.[277] The defect in many warnings is that they are not warnings at all, merely directions. A decal on a child's motor bike that says "no passengers" gives no warning that passengers would be burned.[278] Instructions on a high chair to "secure baby with safety straps" does not warn the user of the risk that the baby will be strangled if not properly secured.[279] Unless the warning specifies the risk, it may be wholly ineffective, but this point has been overlooked in some cases.[280] When possible harm is severe, quite specific information may be required.[281] A drug warning about possible blood clotting may disguise rather than reveal the possibility of a stroke.[282]

Adequacy of form, location or display. When the warning is addressed to the user, is should be sufficiently conspicuous and so located as to attract the user's attention.[283] Fine print won't do. Neither will a warning in the wrong place.[284] On the other hand, the mere fact that the warning could be brighter or bigger does not in itself show that it is inadequate.[285]

English-only warnings. Children, illiterate adults, and adults who do not read English cannot be warned by an English-only label. In a California case, an aspirin manufacturer targeted Spanish-speaking groups with its Spanish advertising, but its aspirin contained no Spanish warnings that aspirin could cause small children severe neurological damage, blindness, spastic quadriplegia and mental retardation. The court thought that the legislature, by affirmatively requiring warnings in English, negatively implied that no others could be required.[286] A few other cases have gone the other way, considering that when illiterate users are foreseeable, symbols or pictographs may be necessary in the warning.[287] Others see this as simply requiring a case-by-case inquiry about the reasonableness of the warning, holding that Spanish-language warnings are

---

[277] See Ross Laboratories, a Division of Abbott Laboratories v. Thies, 725 P.2d 1076 (Alaska 1986) (undiluted glucose marketed in baby bottle with nipple). Thus lawn darts that can readily pierce a child's skull and enter the brain should not be marketed as toys. See First National Bank of Dwight v. Regent Sports Corp., 803 F.2d 1431 (7th Cir. 1986). They are now banned altogether. See 16 C.F.R. § 1306.4 and 16 C.F.R. § 1500.18.

[278] Evridge v. American Honda Motor Co., 685 S.W.2d 632 (Tenn. 1985); cf. Benjamin v. Wal-Mart Stores, Inc., 185 Or.App. 444, 61 P.3d 257 (2002) (direction not to use warmer in tent failed to warn that such use could be fatal).

[279] McConnell v. Cosco, 238 F.Supp.2d 970 (S.D. Ohio 2003).

[280] See Davis v. Berwind Corp., 547 Pa. 260, 690 A.2d 186 (1997) (a meat grinder-mixer directed users to keep fingers out of specified areas, but did not warn that the blades continued to revolve for a substantial time after the machine was turned off; the direction to keep fingers out was treated as a full warning, although the plaintiff lost her fingers in attempting to clean the machine after it was off).

[281] See Fyssakis v. Knight Equipment Corp., 108 Nev. 212, 826 P.2d 570 (1992) (corrosive cleaner should warn that blindness can result).

[282] MacDonald v. Ortho Pharmaceutical Corp., 394 Mass. 131, 475 N.E.2d 65 (1985).

[283] Gray v. Badger Mining Corp., 676 N.W.2d 268 (Minn. 2004); Town of Bridport v. Sterling Clark Lurton Corp., 166 Vt. 304, 693 A.2d 701 (1997).

[284] Bloxom v. Bloxom, 512 So.2d 839 (La. 1987) (Pontiac Firebird must be parked on pavement because its exhaust system will ignite leaves or grass, but the only warning was buried in the 100-page owner's manual), *superseded by statute on other grounds*, La. Rev. Stat. § 9:2800.54 (a).

[285] See General Motors Corp. v. Saenz, 873 S.W.2d 353 (Tex. 1993).

[286] Ramirez v. Plough, Inc., 6 Cal.4th 539, 25 Cal.Rptr.2d 97, 863 P.2d 167 (1993).

[287] Hubbard-Hall Chemical Co. v. Silverman, 340 F.2d 402 (1st Cir. 1965) (suggesting skull and crossbones on deadly poison used by agricultural workers); Campos v. Firestone Tire & Rubber Co., 98 N.J. 198, 485 A.2d 305 (1984) ("In view of the unskilled or semi-skilled nature of the work and the existence of many in the work force who do not read English, warnings in the form of symbols might have been appropriate"). See Marjorie A. Caner, Annotation, Products Liability: Failure to Provide Product Warning or Instruction in Foreign Language or to Use Universally Accepted Pictographs or Symbols, 27 A.L.R.5th 697 (1995); David G. Owen, Products Liability Law § 9.3, at 604–09 (2d ed. 2008) (providing pictorial examples of several graphic warnings).

not required unless, for example, the manufacturer specifically markets the product to Spanish speakers.[288]

Statutes. Increasingly, statutes have required warnings and have prescribed either content or expression. Sometimes the statutory requirement is taken to mean that no additional information can be required by reasonable-care rules. When the statute is a valid federal statute, it may impose the same result because it preempts state law altogether and makes federal law the only law on point. The federal statute requiring warnings on cigarette packages is like this. It preempts state tort law that would require a more adequate warning.[289] In broader perspective, the question is whether tort obligations should be decided exclusively by administrative regulations or statutes where they exist.[290]

§ 33.15　Learned Intermediaries and Sophisticated Users

The learned-intermediary doctrine. A manufacturer of prescription drugs or medical devices has an affirmative duty to warn healthcare professionals of the products' dangers, and equally has a strong defense if it has fulfilled that duty. The manufacturer must warn appropriate healthcare professionals such as prescribing physicians or hospital personnel who use its medical devices of substantial dangers in the product.[291] Where the plaintiff proves that the manufacturer's failure to provide an adequate warning to the intermediary caused her harm, the manufacturer may be held liable.[292] On the defensive side, courts almost always hold that a prescription drug manufacturer's warning to the doctor who prescribes a drug is sufficient to warn the doctor's patient as well. If the doctor fails to inform the patient of the risks, the patient has a claim against the doctor, but not against the manufacturer of the drug.[293] This is usually referred to as the learned-intermediary doctrine, and it is usually conceived of as a rule of law rather than a matter of balancing risks and utilities in each case.[294] The rule applies not only to drugs but also to medical devices and bodily implants that are usually accompanied

---

[288] See Farias v. Mr. Heater, Inc., 684 F.3d 1231 (11th Cir. 2012) (applying Florida law; English language and pictorial warnings on box that held propane gas heater accurately and warned even a Spanish-speaking consumer such as the plaintiff of the dangers of using the product inside a home).

[289] Cipollone v. Liggett Group, Inc., 505 U.S. 504, 112 S.Ct. 2608, 120 L.Ed.2d 407 (1992).

[290] See § 33.20.

[291] Section 6 of the Products Restatement limits this duty stringently to cases in which the properly informed healthcare professional would not prescribe the product for "any class" of patients. Hansen v. Baxter Healthcare Corp., 198 Ill.2d 420, 764 N.E.2d 35, 261 Ill.Dec. 744 (2002), imposed a duty to warn without passing on the "any class of patients" limitation.

[292] E.g., Simon v. Wyeth Pharmaceuticals, Inc., 989 A.2d 356 (Pa. Super. 2009) (patient satisfied causation requirement by testifying that she would not have taken hormone-replacement drug had doctor informed her of risks that it would cause cancer); see also Hoffman-LaRoche Inc. v. Mason, 27 So.3d 75 (Fla. Dist. Ct. App. 2009) (plaintiff failed to prove causation where doctor testified that even if he had been adequately warned, he would have prescribed the drug anyway).

[293] E.g., Stone v. Smith, Kline & French Laboratories, 447 So. 2d 1301 (Ala. 1984); Humes v. Clinton, 246 Kan. 590, 792 P.2d 1032 (1990) Restatement Third of Torts (Products Liability) § 6(d) (1998). Although the doctor is not chronologically an intermediary between pharmacist and patient, the doctor is the final and only decision-maker about the choice of drug. Hence the pharmacist is traditionally not liable for failure to warn about a drug's inherent dangers. See Kowalski v. Rose Drugs of Dardanelle, Inc., 2011 Ark. 44, 378 S.W.3d 109 (2011); Klasch v. Walgreen Co., 264 P.3d 1155 (Nev. 2011); Coyle v. Richardson-Merrell, Inc., 526 Pa. 208, 584 A.2d 1383 (1991).

[294] E.g., Centocor, Inc. v. Hamilton, 372 S.W.3d 140 (Tex. 2012) (adopting the rule, exhaustively reviewing the cases from other jurisdictions). See Richard C. Ausness, Learned Intermediaries and Sophisticated Users: Encouraging the Use of Intermediaries to Transmit Product Safety Information, 46 Syracuse L. Rev. 1185 (1996).

by medical advice and supervision.[295] Courts have said that the rule in some way requires them to immunize pharmacies for failure to warn customers of prescription drug dangers,[296] but it has also been held that the pharmacy does not enjoy that immunity when liability is asserted on its own express warranty.[297]

Exceptions. Three main exceptions to the learned-intermediary rule appear in the cases. *First*, a direct warning to the patient, if feasible, is required in the case of mass inoculations and other instances of unsupervised dispensation of prescription drugs. This idea is pretty well accepted.[298] *Second*, when prescription drugs are advertised directly to the consumer, some courts have said that the rule should not protect the manufacturer from liability for failure to warn the consumer directly.[299] New Jersey has so held, with the proviso that if the warning complies with FDA standards it is presumptively adequate.[300] West Virginia, finding that increasingly common direct-to-consumer advertising "obviates each of the premises upon which the doctrine rests," has expressly declined to adopt the learned-intermediary rule at all.[301] *Third*, a number of cases have concluded that the rule applies only to warnings about the general side effects of drugs, not to particular problems known to the pharmacist, which might include particular dangers of the prescription being filled (such as an excessive quantity), or particularized contraindications,[302] or the fact that the FDA has withdrawn the drug from the market.[303] This line of cases essentially recognizes that the learned-intermediary rule does not and should not shield pharmacists from a basic duty of reasonable care in a number of situations.

Warning through sophisticated users. In many cases, the manufacturer or distributor sells goods to people in the trade who work with such goods regularly or who for other reasons can be expected to know their dangers. Because the danger is already known, a warning for the buyer's protection may not be required at all.[304] In many cases, however, the goods, although sold to buyers in the trade, will foreseeably be used by or affect others who may not be knowledgeable. When it is foreseeable that other, less

---

[295] E.g., Morguson v. 3M Co., 857 So.2d 796 (Ala. 2003) (vent tubing used in bypass surgery); Hurley v. Heart Physicians, P.C., 278 Conn. 305, 898 A.2d 777 (2006) (pacemaker); Craft v. Peebles, 78 Haw. 287, 893 P.2d 138 (1995) (breast implant); Rohde v. Smiths Medical, 165 P.3d 433 (Wyo. 2007) (venous access device).

[296] Coyle v. Richardson-Merrell, Inc., 526 Pa. 208, 584 A.2d 1383 (1991); Schaerrer v. Stewart's Plaza Pharmacy, Inc., 79 P.3d 922 (Utah 2003). *Schaerrer*'s scope was limited in Downing v. Hyland Pharmacy, 194 P.3d 944 (Utah 2008), which held that the learned intermediary doctrine could not protect a pharmacist from negligence liability for continuing to fill prescriptions for a drug that had been withdrawn from the market by the FDA, without informing patients of that fact. See also Klasch v. Walgreen Co., 264 P.3d 1155 (Nev. 2011) (citing a number of cases).

[297] Rite Aid Corp. v. Levy-Gray, 391 Md. 608, 894 A.2d 563 (2006) (a warranty found on the basis of the pharmacy-generated advice and directions accompanying the prescription drug).

[298] Restatement Third of Torts (Products Liability), § 6, cmt. e (1998). But cf. Macias v. State of California, 10 Cal.4th 844, 42 Cal.Rptr.2d 592, 897 P.2d 530 (1995) (manufacturers of poison sold to state for widespread spraying by helicopter had no duty to correct state's widely publicized misinformation about dangers).

[299] See Centocor, Inc. v. Hamilton, 310 S.W.3d 476 (Tex. App. 2010) (seeing the need for an exception to the rule in such cases because "the premises underlying the doctrine are unpersuasive when considered in light of direct marketing to patients").

[300] Perez v. Wyeth Laboratories Inc., 161 N.J. 1, 734 A.2d 1245 (1999) (Norplant, a contraceptive drug-implant, advertised directly to potential users).

[301] State ex rel. Johnson & Johnson Corp. v. Karl, 220 W.Va. 463, 647 S.E.2d 899 (2007).

[302] See Klasch v. Walgreen Co., 264 P.3d 1155 (Nev. 2011).

[303] See Downing v. Hyland Pharmacy, 194 P.3d 944 (Utah 2008).

[304] See Johnson v. American Standard, Inc., 43 Cal.4th 56, 179 P.3d 905, 74 Cal.Rptr.3d 108 (2008).

sophisticated users may be endangered, the questions are whether the manufacturer can omit warnings altogether because of the immediate buyer's sophistication, and whether, if a warning is required, it must be made directly to those who will be endangered.[305] The problem is similar to that presented in the learned-intermediary cases, but the analysis may be different in some cases.[306]

Products sold to employers for use by employees or contractors. Frequently, the troubling problem of intermediary warning arises in cases of sales of dangerous goods to employers or to contractors whose work exposes others to risks from the manufacturer's product.[307] Many employers are woefully careless about their employees' safety. Many remove safety devices to enhance production; others actively encourage unsafe practices that violate safety instructions. The prospect that a manufacturer's warnings to the employer will be passed on to employees obviously varies from employer to employer. When neither the employees nor the employer can be expected to know the risks, however, the manufacturer must warn someone and the question is whether a warning to the employer alone will suffice.

§ 33.16 Causation in Failure-to-Warn Cases

At least in theory, the plaintiff has the burden of proving that the product defect was a factual and proximate cause of the harm claimed. In warning cases, the plaintiff must show that, had a proper warning been given, the injury would have been avoided.[308] Presumably the plaintiff must also show that the reason a better warning was needed was to guard against the forces and types of harm that the plaintiff in fact suffered, and that no superseding cause insulates the defendant from liability.[309]

The Heeding Presumption

No warnings. The most common factual cause problem arises with the question of whether the plaintiff would have both read and heeded the warning had it been given, or given adequately. When no warning at all is given, a few courts have said that the plaintiff must prove that she would have read and heeded a warning had it been given.[310] Many more have been willing to presume or infer that the plaintiff would have heeded a warning.[311] Similarly where the defendant fails to warn an intermediary, the

---

[305] See, e.g., First Nat'l Bank and Trust Corp. v. American Eurocopter Corp., 378 F.3d 682 (7th Cir. 2004) (manufacturer owed duty to warn its sophisticated customer of hidden dangers of helicopter rotor blades, but under Indiana law owed no duty to provide a warning directly to the ultimate user of the helicopter, who was killed by the blades).

[306] See Vitanza v. Upjohn Co., 257 Conn. 365, 778 A.2d 829 (2001) (distinguishing between learned intermediaries and sophisticated users).

[307] See Swan v. I.P., Inc., 613 So.2d 846 (Miss. 1993) (manufacturer supplied chemical to contractor; contractor working on a school, seriously injured teacher by exposing her to the product); Randy R. Koenders, Products Liability: Liability of Manufacturer or Seller as Affected by Failure of Subsequent Party in Distribution Chain to Remedy or Warn against Defect of Which He Knew, 45 A.L.R.4th 777 (1987).

[308] E.g., Ford Motor Co. v. Gibson, 283 Ga. 398, 659 S.E.2d 346 (2008); Ford Motor Co. v. Boomer, 285 Va. 141, 736 S.E.2d 724 (2013). Proof of factual causation in an inadequate-warning case may require expert testimony. See, e.g., Nationwide Mut. Ins. Co. v. Barton Solvents Inc., 855 N.W.2d 145 (S.D. 2014).

[309] Superseding cause arguments are often dealt with under the rubric of misuse and modification. As to these, see § 33.18.

[310] E.g., Riley v. American Honda Motor Co., 259 Mont. 128, 856 P.2d 196 (1993).

[311] E.g., In re Prempro Products Liab. Litigation, 586 F.3d 547 (8th Cir. 2009) (applying Arkansas law, noting that the vast majority of states apply this presumption); Thom v. Bristol-Myers Squibb Co., 353 F.3d 848 (10th Cir. 2003) (Wyoming law). See generally Benjamin J. Jones, Annotation, Presumption or Inference,

presumption is that a properly warned intermediary would have passed on a warning to the plaintiff.[312] Either the presumption or the inference would normally get the plaintiff to the jury on the factual cause issue[313] unless other evidence makes it clear that the plaintiff would not in fact have read and heeded an appropriate warning.[314] Perhaps the best ground for invoking the presumption is that the plaintiff could seldom prove convincingly that he would have read a warning, so that the manufacturer's duty to warn would be effectively avoided in almost all cases. In this view, the presumption represents a policy decision to enforce the duty to warn.[315]

Inadequate warnings, read and unread. When a warning is in fact given, but is inadequate in its expression or content, the plaintiff who actually read the warning but did not understand it can plausibly claim that an adequate warning would have protected her. However, if the plaintiff failed to read the content-inadequate warning, it is frequently difficult to see how a more adequate warning would have made any difference in the outcome. In such a case the presumption that the plaintiff would have read and heeded an adequate warning may not arise, or if it arises it may be rebutted by a finding that the plaintiff did not read the warning that was given.[316] Nevertheless, the evidence may warrant the belief that even though the plaintiff did not personally read the label, her employer or co-workers did so, and would have advised the plaintiff of the dangers if those dangers had been adequately set forth.[317]

If the warning's inadequacy lies in its display rather than its content, the story is different. In that case, the plaintiff's whole point is that an adequately displayed warning would have caught her eye and she would have avoided the danger. If such evidence is accepted, courts can apply the presumption in the same way they apply it where no warning at all was given.[318]

Rebutting the presumption. In addition to introducing evidence that the plaintiff did not read the warning that was given, defendants can attempt to show that the plaintiff would not have heeded the warning if it had been read. Evidence that the plaintiff disregarded warnings that he did receive may tend to show that the plaintiff would likewise have disregarded the "missing" warning.[319] Although the fact that the plaintiff already knew of the danger does not necessarily show that a warning would not have

---

in Products Liability Action Based on Failure to Warn, That User of Product Would Have Heeded an Adequate Warning Had One Been Given, 38 A.L.R.5th 683 (1996).

[312] See Eagle-Picher Indus., Inc. v. Balbos, 326 Md. 179, 604 A.2d 445 (1992) (inference); Coffman v. Keene Corp., 133 N.J. 581, 628 A.2d 710 (1993) (presumption that warnings to employer will be heeded, although defendant may show that the employer would not have passed on the warning). The plaintiff may adduce direct testimony on this issue, as in In re Levaquin Products Liability Litigation, 700 F.3d 1161 (8th Cir. 2012) (doctor testified that he would not have prescribed the drug had he been given the warning).

[313] See, e.g., Schilf v. Eli Lilly & Co., 687 F.3d 947 (8th Cir. 2012) (fact issue on whether an adequate warning would have changed doctor's decision to give medication to patient precluded summary judgment).

[314] See, e.g., Evans v. Lorillard, 465 Mass 411, 990 N.E.2d 997 (2013) (defendant failed to rebut presumption).

[315] Coffman v. Keene Corp., 133 N.J. 581, 599, 628 A.2d 710, 718 (1993) ("The heeding presumption thus serves to reinforce the basic duty to warn.").

[316] Daniel v. Ben E. Keith Co., 97 F.3d 1329 (10th Cir. 1996); Bushong v. Garman Co., 311 Ark. 228, 843 S.W.2d 807 (1992) (apparently treating warning as content-inadequate).

[317] Ferebee v. Chevron Chem. Co., 736 F.2d 1529 (D.C. Cir. 1984).

[318] See East Penn Mfg. Co. v. Pineda, 578 A.2d 1113, 1124 (D.C. 1990); Town of Bridport v. Sterling Clark Lurton Corp., 166 Vt. 304, 693 A.2d 701 (1997).

[319] Gosewisch v. American Honda Motor Co., 153 Ariz. 400, 737 P.2d 376 (1987), *overruled on other grounds*, Jimenez v. Sears, Roebuck and Co., 183 Ariz. 399, 904 P.2d 861 (1995).

reminded her, it is at least cogent evidence on the causal issue.[320] When the plaintiff acts out of momentary inadvertence rather than out of ignorance, the court may conclude that a warning would have made no difference at all.[321] Likewise, if a proper warning would have been ineffective because the plaintiff was not aware of conditions that would have made the warning applicable, a failure to warn would not be a factual cause of the harm, and the plaintiff could not recover.[322]

Scope of Risk (Proximate Cause)

Superseding causes[323] can sometimes insulate the defendant from liability for failing to warn.[324] More centrally, the injury suffered must be within the class of injury that the warning requirement was meant to avoid. For example, the plaintiff, if properly warned that asbestos might cause cancer, might have stopped working around asbestos. A failure to give such a warning could result in liability if the plaintiff did develop cancer as a result of asbestos exposure. But the failure to provide such a warning would not result in liability if the plaintiff, not being warned, kept her job and lost a hand in a job-related machine accident. In that example, failure to warn would be a factual cause—the plaintiff would have been elsewhere, not working at the machine, if a proper warning had been given—but it is not a proximate cause. In other words, the plaintiff's harm is not within the risk that a warning was designed to avoid.

C. DEFENSES

§ 33.17 Contributory Negligence and Assumption of Risk

Emerging orthodoxy. Differences among the courts make a statement of the rules of comparative fault and assumption of risk unreasonably complicated. But mainstream thought now seems to be more straightforward. That thought in products liability actions presently holds that (1) conduct amounting to contributory fault reduces the plaintiff's damages under the comparative fault rules, and (2) assumption of risk is now ordinarily regarded as a species of fault also treated under the comparative fault rules, except that (3) some "assumption of risk" may turn out upon analysis to be an obscure way of saying that the product was not defective or that a superseding cause insulates the manufacturer from liability. The history, variations, and debates about these rules and their alternatives provide a more detailed picture.

Comparative fault rules generally applied. The Restatement Second of Torts provides that contributory negligence, in the sense of failure to discover a product's defect, does not bar recovery in a strict liability case, but that "assumption of risk," in the sense of a voluntary and unreasonable exposure to a known danger, does.[325] Some courts, under statutory directives or otherwise, continue to hold that the plaintiff's fault does not bar or reduce damages.[326] With the advent of comparative fault systems in all but a few states, however, courts and legislatures now usually say that the plaintiff's

---

[320] In re Prempro Products Liab. Litigation, 514 F.3d 825 (8th Cir. 2008).

[321] Conti v. Ford Motor Co., 743 F.2d 195 (3d Cir. 1984) (driver inadvertently started standard-transmission car in reverse gear while wife was getting in; warning would not have avoided wife's injury).

[322] See Shelcusky v. Garjulio, 172 N.J. 185, 797 A.2d 138 (2002).

[323] See generally §§ 15.14 to 15.19.

[324] See § 33.18.

[325] Restatement Second of Torts § 402A cmt. n (1965).

[326] Shipler v. General Motors Corp., 271 Neb. 194, 710 N.W.2d 807 (2006).

comparative negligence can be raised as an affirmative defense and applied to reduce damages, both when the plaintiff asserts negligence and when she asserts strict liability.[327] The Products Restatement adopts this position.[328] Not every foible counts as plaintiff fault, however. For instance, workers who have little choice but to work with dangerous machinery on the job are not necessarily guilty of either comparative fault[329] or assumption of risk[330] when they do so.

Assumption of risk. What used to be treated as a separate defense of assumption of risk is now largely subsumed in comparative fault.[331] In products cases, assumption of risk is often defined as a voluntary and unreasonable encounter with a known danger. There is no real reason to distinguish this form of plaintiff-fault from, say, negligently using a product like an automobile. Thus, the driver who negligently crashes his car and is thrown from it may be able to show that the car had a defective door latch, but his damages will be reduced for his fault whether that fault is denominated contributory negligence or assumed risk.[332]

However, some courts still treat assumption of risk as a separate and complete defense, barring the risk-assuming plaintiff entirely.[333] In addition, if the product's danger is objectively obvious, the risk it presents may be a reasonable one because users could reasonably be expected to protect themselves. In that case, the product may not be defective at all and the plaintiff will be denied recovery for that reason.[334] On the other hand, when the manufacturer should reasonably foresee that the user will have little choice but to deal with the risky product, as is usually the case with machinery used in employment, even an obviously dangerous product may be unreasonably dangerous and therefore defective.[335] In that case, no good grounds appear for a complete bar as distinct from a comparative fault reduction in damages.

The known-risk rule. Before the system of comparative fault was generally adopted, most courts refused to recognize the defense of contributory negligence in strict liability actions.[336] Even after the advent of comparative fault, some courts apply a similar rule, so that a voluntary and unreasonable exposure to a known risk can count against the

---

[327] E.g., Smith v. Ingersoll-Rand Co., 14 P.3d 990 (Alaska 2000); Daly v. General Motors Corp., 20 Cal.3d 725, 575 P.2d 1162, 144 Cal.Rptr. 380 (1978); Fuchsgruber v. Custom Accessories, Inc., 244 Wis. 2d 758, 628 N.W.2d 833 (2001). Some statutes specifically prescribe comparative fault reductions in products cases. E.g., Colo. Rev. Stats. § 13–21–406. Where a comparative fault statute by its terms addresses "negligence" cases only, courts must determine whether to judicially supplement the statute at all, and if so whether to do so in "strict liability" cases.

[328] Restatement Third of Torts (Products Liability) § 17 (1998).

[329] See Jurado v. Western Gear Works, 131 N.J. 375, 387, 619 A.2d 1312, 1318 (1993); Theer v. Philip Carey Co., 133 N.J. 610, 622, 628 A.2d 724, 730 (1993).

[330] Carrel v. Allied Prods. Corp., 78 Ohio St.3d 284, 677 N.E.2d 795 (1997); cf. Green v. Edmands Co., 639 F.2d 286 (5th Cir. 1981) (no alternative way to accomplish job task, no assumed risk).

[331] See generally § 17.6.

[332] Cf. Daly v. General Motors Corp., 20 Cal.3d 725, 575 P.2d 1162, 144 Cal.Rptr. 380 (1978) (driver killed, comparative fault rule adopted).

[333] E.g., Wangsness v. Builders Cashway, Inc., 779 N.W.2d 136 (S.D. 2010).

[334] Cases finding no defect because danger was generally known are like this. E.g., Farnham v. Bombardier, Inc., 161 Vt. 619, 640 A.2d 47 (1994) (snowmobile dangers); Elliott v. Brunswick Corp., 903 F.2d 1505 (11th Cir. 1990) (motorboat propeller not defective because dangers were inherent and known).

[335] See Ogletree v. Navistar Intern. Transp. Corp., 269 Ga. 443, 500 S.E.2d 570 (1998); Carrel v. Allied Products Corp., 78 Ohio St.3d 284, 677 N.E.2d 795 (1997).

[336] See Gary D. Spivey, Annotation, Products Liability: Contributory Negligence or Assumption of Risk as Defense Under Doctrine of Strict Liability in Tort, 46 A.L.R.3d 240 (1973).

plaintiff as a bar or in reduction of damages but other forms of plaintiff-fault count for nothing.[337] For brevity, this rule can be called the known-risk rule. The point here is not what does affect the plaintiff's claim but what does not.

An example of the known-risk rule is *Bowling v. Heil Co.*[338] The bed of a dump truck did not return to the down position after the load had been deposited. A worker put his head under the raised truck bed and manipulated a lever, whereupon the truck bed fell, instantly causing his death. Since the jury found that the decedent was chargeable with contributory fault but had not assumed the risk, the court refused to reduce recovery for the defect in the hoist mechanism. On the other hand, if the jury had characterized the decedent's conduct as an assumption of the risk, the claim would have been completely barred.[339] And if the court had characterized the decedent's conduct as a superseding cause, rather than as comparative fault, the claim would have been barred as well.[340]

The failure-to-discover rule. Many courts say that no comparative fault reductions should be made when the plaintiff's only fault is the failure to discover the product's defect.[341] This rule can be called the failure-to-discover rule. This rule may come down to saying that the plaintiff is not at fault in trusting the defendant's product until the plaintiff has notice that requires investigation of it. That is ordinarily correct. The plaintiff who bites into a Mr. Goodbar candy has no reason to inspect its insides for worms and eggs.[342] Consumer expectations, whether a test of product defectiveness or not, are at least relevant to show that the consumer behaved reasonably in accepting the product at face value. Beyond this, it should be said that many less-than-optimal acts by product users do not appear to constitute plaintiff negligence. In one case,[343] a power saw suddenly started up. The startled plaintiff moved his hand in response to this unsuspected event, and in so doing lost his fingers. His movement was not the best response, but in the sudden danger created by the defect, as in an emergency, it would be hard to say that he was negligent.

If all plaintiff fault consists of either failure to discover or voluntary exposure to a known risk, the failure-to-discover rule is merely a negative statement of the known-risk rule. But it is fair to say that between the two categories lies a very large group of cases that do not fit well in either. The plaintiff's fault in failing to wear a safety harness while working on high-rise steel girders does not depend upon either failure to discover a girder defect or upon exposing oneself to it. In such a case, the plaintiff presumably has not in fact discovered the girder's defect that will cause a fall, but his fault does not consist in

---

[337] Bowling v. Heil Co., 31 Ohio St. 3d 277, 511 N.E.2d 373 (1987); Jay v. Moog Automotive, Inc., 264 Neb. 875, 652 N.W.2d 872 (2002); Kimco Development Corp. v. Michael D's Carpet Outlets, 536 Pa. 1, 637 A.2d 603 (1993); Smith v. Smith, 278 N.W.2d 155 (S.D. 1979). In some states, statutes have displaced judicial decisions that once so held.

[338] Bowling v. Heil Co., 31 Ohio St. 3d 277, 511 N.E.2d 373 (1987).

[339] E.g., Krajewski v. Enderes Tool Co., 469 F.3d 705 (8th Cir. 2006) (plaintiff's use of pry bar without wearing goggles constituted an assumption of risk of eye injury, under Nebraska law); Onderko v. Richmond Mfg. Co., 31 Ohio St. 3d 296, 511 N.E.2d 388 (1987) (assumption of risk is a complete bar to strict liability claim but is treated as comparative negligence if the plaintiff sues for negligence). Accord, that assumption of risk is a complete bar, Jimenez v. Sears, Roebuck & Co., 183 Ariz. 399, 904 P.2d 861 (1995).

[340] See Davis v. Berwind Corp., 547 Pa. 260, 690 A.2d 186 (1997).

[341] E.g., Jimenez v. Sears, Roebuck and Co., 183 Ariz. 399, 904 P.2d 861 (1995); Coney v. J.L.G. Indus., Inc., 97 Ill.2d 104, 454 N.E.2d 197, 73 Ill.Dec. 337 (1983); Johansen v. Makita U.S.A., Inc., 128 N.J. 86, 607 A.2d 637 (1992); General Motors Corp. v. Sanchez, 997 S.W.2d 584 (Tex. 1999). Some statutes so provide. E.g., Idaho Code § 6–1305.

[342] Kassouf v. Lee Bros., Inc., 209 Cal.App.2d 568, 26 Cal.Rptr. 276 (1962).

[343] Smith v. Smith, 278 N.W.2d 155 (S.D. 1979).

failure to discover it; it consists in failure to use a safety harness that would protect against a fall, whatever its cause.[344] Similarly, the essence of the plaintiff's fault in driving an automobile while intoxicated does not turn either upon discovery of a defect in the door latch or exposure to known danger. Likewise, the plaintiff who discovers no defect at all may be at fault in failing to follow safety instructions that accompany the product even if the jurisdiction rejects a defense based on contributory fault.[345] In such in-between cases, the plaintiff's fault appropriately reduces recovery.[346]

Rejecting reductions in defective safety device cases. Some courts refuse to reduce the plaintiff's recovery when the product was defective for the very reason that it failed to guard the plaintiff against her own momentary lapse, inattentiveness, or other fault. Many machines expose users to moving parts that can crush a hand, amputate an arm or leg, or even kill. In each case, the user can avoid such terrible injuries by staying away from moving parts. Yet it is entirely foreseeable that eventually almost all users will be too close to the moving machinery; some will do so because of inadvertence, some because of confidence born of past good experience with machinery, some because of job pressures to produce. Given this foreseeable harm, the machine is easily counted as defective if it omits a feasible safety device that would avoid such injuries. These cases illustrate the rule, recognized by some courts, that when the product should have been designed to prevent the act or omission that triggers harm, that act should not count as contributory fault.[347] It is a contradiction to say that the defendant has a duty to provide the safety device but then to say that in all cases where it is needed, the plaintiff is guilty of contributory fault.

Deterrence argument for ignoring plaintiff-fault. Among the arguments for ignoring the plaintiff's comparative fault in strict liability cases, the most common is based on the need to deter the production of defective products. If manufacturers systematically get a reduction in damages because many plaintiffs will be guilty of some degree of fault, manufacturers will lack appropriate incentives to invest in safety.[348] This argument asserts that deterrence operates differentially: when the plaintiff's damages are reduced, defendants will be less careful, but plaintiffs will not be more careful.[349] The net result, in this view, would be an increase in injuries. However, if comparative-fault reductions represent the right way to account for the plaintiff's fault in, say, a case brought for negligent repairs to a building or negligent medical practice, it is not clear why the

---

[344] Cf. Smith v. Ingersoll-Rand Co., 14 P.3d 990 (Alaska 2000) (failure to wear a hard hat, any form of plaintiff fault can be considered under comparative fault statute).

[345] See Jay v. Moog Automotive, Inc., 264 Neb. 875, 652 N.W.2d 872 (2002) ("Failure to follow plain and unambiguous instructions is a misuse of the product," and misuse is a defense).

[346] The Texas Court made this point when a defective parking-gear design permitted a truck to pop out of gear and roll, crushing the owner. While the court held that mere failure to discover a product defect is not contributory fault that will bar or reduce recovery, it also held that the user might be chargeable with fault in parking unsafely, quite independent of the defect; if so, his damages would be reduced accordingly. General Motors v. Sanchez, 997 S.W.2d 584 (Tex. 1999).

[347] Bexiga v. Havir Mfg. Corp., 60 N.J. 402, 412, 290 A.2d 281, 286 (N.J.1972).

[348] Webb v. Navistar Intern. Transp. Corp., 166 Vt. 119, 692 A.2d 343, 356 (1996) (Johnson, J., dissenting); cf. Daly v. General Motors Corp., 20 Cal.3d 725, 760, 575 P.2d 1162, 1183, 144 Cal.Rptr. 380, 401 (1978) (Mosk, J., dissenting) ("The defective product is comparable to a time bomb ready to explode; it maims its victims indiscriminately, the righteous and the evil, the careful and the careless.").

[349] See Howard A. Latin, Problem-Solving Behavior and Theories of Tort Liability, 73 Calif. L. Rev. 677, 732 (1985) (emphasizing that most accidents are due to momentary lapses); Howard Latin, "Good" Warnings, Bad Products, and Cognitive Limitations, 41 U.C.L.A. L. Rev. 1193, 1254 (1994) (people can learn about risks but product engineers can learn better).

plaintiff's fault should be disregarded in product cases merely because the defendant's liability is strict or nominally strict.

Apples and oranges. On a rather different plane, it has been argued that courts cannot compare apples and oranges—the fault of the plaintiff and the non-faulty defect of the defendant's product. The answer has been to treat the objection as a purely practical one and to recognize that juries can come up with some kind of "equitable" (or perhaps intuitive) apportionment of responsibility.[350] An intuitive approach of this kind will make meaningful appellate review quite difficult, but as the Texas Court later said, juries could compare causation rather than fault so that in strict liability cases the rule is comparative causation rather than comparative fault.[351] The idea seems to be that the causal role of the defendant's product can be compared on the same scale as the causal role of the plaintiff in causing harm.[352] The Restatement of Apportionment prefers the vague term "comparative responsibility"[353] and a system that invites the trier of fact to consider virtually anything, including mental states, in assigning responsibility. Under this approach, definitions of negligence built over generations seem to be of little use.

§ 33.18 Unforeseeable Misuse, Alteration and Modification

Sometimes courts speak of "misuse" or the "misuse defense" as though the term refers to a doctrine or rule distinct from the more familiar concepts of tort law. In truth, the term refers to a pattern of facts, not a rule of law. Depending on the facts, evidence of the plaintiff's unforeseeable misuse may tend to show that (a) the product is not defective at all; or (b) the defective product was not a proximate cause of harm; or (c) where the product is defective, that the plaintiff was negligent.[354] Evidence of misuse is not exclusively relevant to any one of these issues alone. Its probative value on any of them depends on the facts. Alterations of a product by the plaintiff can have the effect of misuse. Much the same thing can be said about risk-enhancing alterations of a product by third persons.[355] In the end, analysis would be clearer if the term "misuse" were dropped and courts approached the issues of defectiveness, comparative fault, and proximate cause directly.

---

[350] Daly v. General Motors Corp., 20 Cal.3d 725, 734, 144 Cal.Rptr. 380, 385, 575 P.2d 1162, 1167 (1978); Coney v. J.L.G. Indus., Inc., 97 Ill.2d 104, 454 N.E.2d 197, 73 Ill.Dec. 337 (1983).

[351] Duncan v. Cessna Aircraft Co., 665 S.W.2d 414 (Tex. 1984).

[352] The language is relatively new to the law, and perhaps confusing. It does not refer to factual cause. Perhaps comparative causation is best understood as an effort to rate causal significance. Instead of concluding that one actor's contributions have no causal significance at all, as juries might do in finding "no proximate cause," juries can estimate the importance of each cause—the plaintiff's conduct and the defendant's defective product.

[353] Restatement Third of Torts (Apportionment) § 8, cmt. a (2000).

[354] See Chapman v. Maytag Corp., 297 F.3d 682 (7th Cir. 2002); Jurado v. Western Gear Works, 131 N.J. 375, 619 A.2d 1312 (1993); Restatement Third of Torts (Products Liability) § 2, cmt. p (1998).

[355] See Jurado v. Western Gear Works, 131 N.J. 375, 619 A.2d 1312 (1993); Amatulli v. Delhi Const. Corp., 77 N.Y.2d 525, 571 N.E.2d 645, 569 N.Y.S.2d 337 (1991) (above-ground pool installed in-ground and provided with a deck, giving the appearance of a deeper pool; alteration precluded manufacturer liability); Stark ex rel. Jacobsen v. Ford Motor Co., 365 N.C. 468, 723 S.E.2d 753, Prod. Liab. Rep. (CCH) P 18830 (2012) (modification of seat belt by plaintiff's father, by simply placing the shoulder belt behind the child passenger's chest, provided a defense in a design defect case; interpreting statutory language, the affirmative defense of alternation or modification of the product by a "party" other than the manufacturer applies not only to a party to the action, but to anyone other than the manufacturer or seller).

Misuse Bearing on Product Defect

Unforeseeable misuse. A product is defective in design or warning only if harm is reasonably foreseeable. Hence the product is not defective at all if the plaintiff's unforeseeable misuse is the sole cause of the harm.[356] For instance, if the evidence is that the plaintiff was injured because the tread separated on a tire manufactured by the defendant, a tire defect might be the probable explanation. However, if the defendant can show that the tire was eight years old and had suffered numerous punctures and major patches, the inference that the tire was defective at the time it left the defendant's hands is considerably lessened, perhaps destroyed.[357] The point of misuse in this kind of case is not that the plaintiff or a third person was at fault, but that no defect has been shown. A tire that blows out after its useful life is over simply does not seem to be defective.[358] Whether the evidence is convincing on the issue of defectiveness of course turns on the facts of the particular case. For example, misuse that does not cause or enhance the injury does not ordinarily affect the inference of defect.[359] Since the plaintiff has the burden of proving a defect in the first instance, misuse in this kind of case, including alteration, is not properly speaking a defense at all; it is instead evidence that bears on, and tends to negate, an element of the plaintiff's prima facie case.[360] Consequently, the burden may remain on the plaintiff to show the product was not altered or otherwise misused in order to show that it was defective.[361]

Foreseeable misuse. Some cases say that foreseeable misuse is not "misuse" at all. Whether or not that is a helpful locution, the cases have generally acknowledged that foreseeable misuse does not negate the defectiveness of the product.[362] That is the rule because manufacturers are obliged to design products and give warnings with the realities of use in mind. Put otherwise, the product must be reasonably safe for foreseeable misuses;[363] the plaintiff proves defectiveness by proving that the product was not reasonably safe for normal use, including foreseeable misuse.[364] Children, for example, may be expected to use some products in dangerous ways, and while manufacturers can sometimes rely upon parents to protect children, experience teaches

---

[356] See Matthews v. Remington Arms Co., Inc., 641 F.3d 635 (5th Cir. 2011) (applying Louisiana statute that makes a manufacturer liable only when plaintiff's harm arose from "a reasonably anticipated use of the product by the claimant or another person or entity"; use of a rifle without the bolt-assembly pin was not such a use, affirming verdict for defendant); Payne v. Gardner, 56 So. 3d 229 (La. 2011) (same statute; riding on the moving pendulum of an oil well pump was not a reasonably anticipated use, and thus the plaintiff's claim should have been dismissed with prejudice).

[357] Korando v. Uniroyal Goodrich Tire Co., 159 Ill.2d 335, 637 N.E.2d 1020, 202 Ill.Dec. 284 (1994).

[358] See Jurado v. Western Gear Works, 131 N.J. 375, 388, 619 A.2d 1312, 1318 (1993).

[359] Sears, Roebuck and Co. v. Harris, 630 So.2d 1018, 1027 (Ala. 1993) ("A manufacturer or seller remains liable if the alteration or modification did not in fact cause the injury.").

[360] See Ellsworth v. Sherne Lingerie, Inc., 303 Md. 581, 495 A.2d 348, 52 A.L.R.4th 247 (1985).

[361] See Tober v. Graco Children's Products, Inc., 431 F.3d 572 (7th Cir. 2005) (plaintiff had burden of proving, as one element of the claim, that the product was expected to and did reach the consumer without substantial alteration; statute describing alteration as defense available to defendant did not mean to shift burden to the defendant, but only to permit defendant to controvert the plaintiff's prima facie case).

[362] E.g., Sears, Roebuck and Co. v. Harris, 630 So.2d 1018 (Ala. 1993); Hart-Albin Co. v. McLees Inc., 264 Mont. 1, 870 P.2d 51 (1994); Brown v. U.S. Stove Co., 98 N.J. 155, 484 A.2d 1234 (1984).

[363] E.g., Ellsworth v. Sherne Lingerie, Inc., 303 Md. 581, 495 A.2d 348, 52 A.L.R.4th 247 (1985); Reid v. Spadone Mach. Co., 119 N.H. 457, 404 A.2d 1094 (1979), *overruled on other grounds*, Daigle v. City of Portsmouth, 129 N.H. 561, 534 A.2d 689 (1987).

[364] Reilly v. Dynamic Exploration, Inc., 571 So.2d 140 (La. 1990).

that parents cannot supervise children at all times, so that if a safer design is feasible, the manufacturer should utilize it to protect against a child's foreseeable misuse.[365]

Enhanced injury or crashworthiness cases. An important example of the rule that designs should take reasonable account of foreseeable misuse is the case of the overturned or crashed automobile. Manufacturers do not intend their automobiles to be crashed, but they do foresee that vehicles will be subjected to crashes and rollovers resulting from misuse and otherwise. Consequently the vehicle's design must take such eventualities into account. The vehicle need not be crash-proof but it must use reasonable safety features. If, upon slight impact, a roof collapses, a gas tank spews burning gasoline on the passengers, or a restraint system permits occupants to be thrown from the vehicle, the automobile is not designed reasonably, and it is defective.[366] This rule necessarily means that the manufacturer remains liable for a proven defect even if other causes contribute to or concur in causing the injury.[367] In particular, the fact that the crash was a result of the injured plaintiff's negligence or even his intoxication goes to issues of comparative fault and proximate cause, but does not by itself relieve the defendant of its duty to provide a reasonably safe vehicle.[368]

Burden of proof in enhanced-injury cases. When the defect does not cause the impact itself but only adds to the injury, the manufacturer is subject to liability only for the portion of the injury that would have been avoided by a non-defective product, if that portion can be established by evidence.[369] Who has the burden of proving how much the injury was enhanced by the defect? One group of courts hold that the plaintiff must prove both that the defect caused the enhanced injury and also the amount of that injury.[370] Some others hold that the plaintiff must first prove that the product defect caused enhancement of the injury, but then the defendant has the burden of proving how much of that injury would have occurred even with a non-defective product.[371] The Products Restatement provides that if evidence shows that additional harm did in fact occur, but does not permit the trier to distinguish between increased harm caused by the product and the harm that would have occurred anyway, the defendant is liable for the whole

[365] See Jerry J. Phillips, Products Liability for Personal Injury to Minors, 56 Va. L. Rev. 1223 (1970). But cf. Halliday v. Sturm, Ruger & Co., Inc., 368 Md. 186, 792 A.2d 1145 (2002) (death of small child who found his father's hidden gun which had been sold without safety lock, no liability under consumer expectations test).

[366] See Turner v. General Motors Corp., 584 S.W.2d 844 (Tex. 1979); Slone v. General Motors Corp., 249 Va. 520, 457 S.E.2d 51 (1995).

[367] Malen v. MTD Products, Inc., 628 F.3d 296 (7th Cir. 2010) (Ill. law; the premise of the crashworthiness doctrine "is that some products, although not made for certain purposes—such as accidents—should nevertheless be reasonably designed to minimize the injury-producing effect of an accident"); Collins v. Navistar, Inc., 214 Cal.App.4th 1486, 155 Cal.Rptr.3d 137 (2013) (truck manufacturer could be liable for defective windshield that broke when struck by a chunk of concrete thrown from a freeway overpass; issue for jury was whether a chunk of concrete was a reasonably foreseeable road hazard); Jurado v. Western Gear Works, 131 N.J. 375, 619 A.2d 1312 (1993).

[368] Green v. Ford Motor Co., 942 N.E.2d 791 (Ind. 2011) (jury could apportion fault to motorist who sued manufacturer for enhanced injuries allegedly caused by defective restraint system in vehicle); Alami v. Volkswagen of America, Inc., 97 N.Y.2d 281, 766 N.E.2d 574, 739 N.Y.S.2d 867 (2002) (deceased's intoxication caused crash, but manufacturer's unsafe design allegedly caused deadly injuries; rule that a serious wrongdoing can recover nothing at all has no application to relieve manufacturer of its duty).

[369] Mazda Motor Corp. v. Lindahl, 706 A.2d 526 (Del. 1998); Jensen v. American Suzuki Motor Corp., 136 Idaho 460, 35 P.3d 776 (2001).

[370] See, e.g., Caiazzo v. Volkswagenwerk A.G., 647 F.2d 241 (2d Cir. 1981); Jahn v. Hyundai Motor Co., 773 N.W.2d 550 (Iowa 2009); Egbert v. Nissan Motor Co., 228 P.3d 737 (Utah 2010).

[371] Fox v. Ford Motor Co., 575 F.2d 774 (10th Cir. 1978); Mitchell v. Volkswagenwerk AG, 669 F.2d 1199 (8th Cir. 1982); Polston v. Boomershine Pontiac-GMC Truck, Inc., 262 Ga. 616, 423 S.E.2d 659 (1992).

amount.[372] An alternative to all these solutions is to apportion liability by fault rather than by causation, that is, to estimate the fault of each party rather than to estimate the amount of increased harm caused by the manufacturer's bad design.[373]

Foreseeability does not invariably prove defect. The rule that designs must take foreseeable use into account does not relieve the plaintiff of proving a defect in the product. The defendant must design reasonably with the product's use in mind, but the manufacturer cannot avoid all foreseeable abuses. It is certainly foreseeable that some drinkers will misuse alcohol, but uncontaminated alcoholic beverages have not been regarded as defective.[374] The plaintiff's misuse of alcohol may be foreseeable, but that will not assist the plaintiff unless she can demonstrate that alcohol is defective.

Misuse, Alteration, or Other Conduct as Superseding Cause

The plaintiff's own unforeseeable negligence, misuse, or alteration of the product, if it is one of the causes of her injury, may be a superseding cause that relieves the manufacturer of liability for the defective product, even in states that refuse to reduce recovery for the plaintiff's comparative fault.[375] The same is true with the unforeseeable negligence, misuse, or alteration by others.[376] A common case is an employer's removal of safety devices from machinery used by workers. If the alteration is unforeseeable, the manufacturer is not liable to the injured worker.[377] But if the alteration or misuse is itself foreseeable as a potential increase in the risk of harm, it is not a superseding cause and is not a ground for avoiding liability if the product is defective.[378] As usual, where reasonable people could differ, foreseeability is a jury question.[379] Likewise if the alteration or misuse did not in fact cause the harm, it is of no consequence.[380]

---

[372] Restatement Third of Torts (Products Liability) § 16 (1998). Accord, Trull v. Volkswagen of America, Inc., 145 N.H. 259, 761 A.2d 477 (2000) (where injuries are indivisible, defendant has burden of showing which injuries were caused by initial collision and which by the defect); Johnson v. Ford Motor Co., 45 P.3d 86 (Okla. 2002) (defective seatbelt; jury could find brain injury was single and indivisible; award of $5 million affirmed).

[373] See Hillrichs v. Avco Corp., 514 N.W.2d 94 (Iowa 1994).

[374] See Joseph E. Seagram & Sons, Inc. v. McGuire, 814 S.W.2d 385 (Tex. 1991). Because the risks of alcohol are so well known, courts have also routinely rejected claims that advertisements are misleading in suggesting that alcohol may be safely consumed. See Gawloski v. Miller Brewing Co., 96 Ohio App.3d 160, 644 N.E.2d 731 (1994) (citing cases).

[375] General Motors Corp. v. Wolhar, 686 A.2d 170 (Del. 1996) (seatbelt non-use admissible to show non-use as supervening cause of injury); Monsanto Co. v. Reed, 950 S.W.2d 811 (Ky. 1997). Some statutes, at least in form, prohibit all recovery when the product has been altered even in a foreseeable way. See Ky. Rev. Stats. § 411.320 (1).

[376] E.g., Landis v. Hearthmark, LLC, 232 W.Va. 64, 750 S.E.2d 280 (2013) (defendant could assert as a defense that parents' conduct in leaving a bottle of fire starter near a fireplace and within reach of their child was an intervening cause of child's injuries); Moyer v. United Dominion Industries, Inc., 473 F.3d 532 (3d Cir. 2007) (evidence of long-term misuse and improper maintenance of machine that injured plaintiff was admissible on issue of causation).

[377] E.g., Tanksley v. ProSoft Automation, Inc., 982 So.2d 1046 (Ala. 2007); Davis v. Berwind Corp., 547 Pa. 260, 690 A.2d 186 (1997).

[378] E.g., Witthauer v. Burkhart Roentgen, Inc., 467 N.W.2d 439 (N.D. 1991).

[379] E.g., Horn v. Fadal Machinery Centers, LLC, 972 So.2d 63 (Ala. 2007) (foreseeability of plaintiff's misuse); Chairez v. James Hamiliton Const. Co., 146 N.M. 794, 215 P.3d 732 (Ct. App. 2009) (foreseeability of modification of defendant's rock crusher); see also Collins v. Navistar, Inc., 214 Cal.App.4th 1486, 155 Cal.Rptr.3d 137 (2013) (truck manufacturer could be liable for defective windshield that broke when struck by a chunk of concrete thrown from a freeway overpass; issue for jury was whether a chunk of concrete was a reasonably foreseeable road hazard).

[380] See Johnson v. Niagara Mach. & Tool Works, 555 So.2d 88 (Ala. 1989).

Misuse as Comparative Fault

In some cases a product is defective and its defect is a concurring cause, along with the plaintiff's misuse, of the plaintiff's harm. In these cases, evidence of the plaintiff's misuse may be relevant on the issue of comparative fault, even though it does not negate a defect or causation.[381]

For example, if the product is an automobile, it might be considered a kind of misuse to drive it drunkenly at high speeds, but since such uses are foreseeable, manufacturers must nevertheless include seatbelts and other reasonable crash-protection designs. If they do not do so, the product is defective. If the driver is killed because no protection was available when she crashed the car, the defect was one of the causes of harm. But the driver's fault is also one of the causes of harm, and where comparative fault systems are used in products cases, the plaintiff's conduct warrants a reduction of damages whether the driver's speed is considered to be misuse or some other brand of fault.[382] Treating misuse as comparative fault makes total sense when the misuse is foreseeable. If the misuse is not foreseeable, the product would seem to be objectively safe, and thus not defective at all.

§ 33.19 Statutory Defenses

Most states have enacted statutory limitations on liability for product defects. To a large extent, these statutes provide rules substantially in accord with the rules developed by judicial decision in most states. Such statutes may, for example, provide that damages are to be reduced for plaintiff fault and that unforeseeable alteration which is the proximate cause of the harm relieves the defendant of liability, as do some kinds of product misuse. Special protective statutes of limitation are included as well,[383] and damages caps may be imposed either specially in products actions or as part of broad limitations on recoveries.[384]

One of the important substantive effects of the statutes is to adopt a negligence standard, at least in effect, holding the manufacturer responsible for a design defect if it should reasonably have known of an avoidable risk, but not otherwise. The statutes achieve this result by a variety of provisions ranging from a direct statement that liability is limited to negligence to a provision exculpating the manufacturer if the product met the "state of the art."[385]

Scientific knowability or industry standards? Do the state-of-the-art statutes make industry custom the standard of care, contrary to the general tort rule on the effect of custom?[386] Or do they only mean to foreclose liability for scientifically unknowable risks? Most of the statutes rather clearly foreclose liability for scientifically unknowable risks

---

[381] Chapman v. Maytag Corp., 297 F.3d 682 (7th Cir. 2002) (failure to heed warnings); Jimenez v. Sears, Roebuck and Co., 183 Ariz. 399, 904 P.2d 861 (1995); Coney v. J.L.G. Industries, Inc., 97 Ill.2d 104, 454 N.E.2d 197, 73 Ill.Dec. 337 (1983).

[382] See Daly v. General Motors Corp., 20 Cal.3d 725, 575 P.2d 1162, 144 Cal.Rptr. 380 (1978).

[383] See § 33.21.

[384] E.g., Mich. Comp. Laws Ann. § 600.2946a.

[385] Ariz. Rev. Stat. § 12–683 (state of art); N.C. Gen. Stat. § 99B–1.1, 99B–4 & 99B–6 (no strict liability; state of the art defense for prescription drugs; requirement of feasible alternative design); N.J. Stat. Ann. § 2A:58C–3 (manufacturer not liable if there was no feasible alternative design); Ohio Rev. Code Ann. § 2307.75(A) (invoking risk-benefit test for design defect cases).

[386] See § 12.6.

but definitely do not adopt the industry's own standards as the governing test.[387] Other statutes may allow the industry to set its own standards for its products. One statute presumes the product nondefective if it conformed either to "generally recognized and prevailing standards" *or* to the state of the art, a disjunction that distinguishes prevailing standards from state of the art and exculpates the product if either is established.[388] Others provide that the defendant is not liable if the product design and its method of manufacture, testing and labeling conformed to "the state of the art" at the time.[389] In the absence of a definition or implications to the contrary, such a statute conceivably could mean that the industry's own practices set the limits of the industry's liability. But some such statutes have been construed to establish feasibility rather than the industry's own custom as the standard, even though evidence of industry custom is admissible as tending to show what may be feasible.[390]

Burden of proof. State-of-the-art statutes, including those that do not actually use that term, also raise questions about the burden of proof. Some of them, referring to a "defense," impliedly or perhaps explicitly put the burden on the defendant to show that the product met the state of the art.[391] Others leave the question in doubt.[392] Insofar as the statute merely provides for admissibility of state-of-the-art evidence without prescribing a substantive rule, the statute does not indicate anything about the burden of proof.

Manufacturing defects. The case of manufacturing defects, as distinguished from design and warning defects, is now the core case for strict liability, because if a product's risk is unknowable, the design and warning claims now generally fail. But knowability of risks is logically no part of the manufacturing defect case; product flaws are happenstantial, so the fact that the flaw was not known or reasonably knowable seems to be irrelevant as a common-law matter. But some state-of-the-art statutes can be read to bar strict liability claims for all types of product defect.[393] Other statutes limit the state-of-the-art defense in some way and appear to permit strict liability in manufacturing defect claims.[394] Certainly the fact that a product's design is state of the

---

[387] See, e.g., Ark. Code Ann. § 16–116–104 ("consideration" may be given to industry practice); Colo. Rev. Stat. § 13–21–403(1)(a) (rebuttably presumed that product is nondefective if product conformed to the state of the art "as distinguished from industry standards"); Kan. Stat. Ann. § 60–3307(a) (evidence of industry's improvements inadmissible); N.H. Stat. Ann. § 507:8–g (an affirmative defense if risks were not discoverable using "prevailing research and scientific techniques").

[388] Ky. Rev. Stat. § 411.310(2).

[389] Ariz. Rev. Stat. § 12–683(1); Ind. Code § 34–20–5–1 (rebuttable presumption when product conforms to "generally recognized state of the art").

[390] Hughes v. Massey-Ferguson, Inc., 522 N.W.2d 294 (Iowa 1994).

[391] Ariz. Rev. Stat. § 12–683 ("if the defendant proves"); Mo. Stat. § 537.764(2) ("defense" in warning claims); Iowa Code § 668.12 (no fault assigned to one who pleads and proves state of the art); La. Rev. Stat. § 9:2800.59 ("if the manufacturer proves"); Neb. Rev. Stat. § 25–21,182 ("defense").

[392] Colo. Rev. Stat. Ann. § 13–21–403 (product rebuttably presumed non-defective if it conformed to state of the art). This provision is difficult to interpret, since the product is already "presumed" to be non-defective in the sense that the plaintiff has the burden of production and persuasion.

[393] Iowa Code § 668.12 (design, manufacturing and warning claims all included); Ky. Rev. Stat. § 411.310 (if design, methods of manufacture and testing conformed to prevailing standards, product "presumed" nondefective).

[394] Miss. Code Ann. § 11–1–63 (requiring that the manufacturer should have known danger in warning and design defect case but making no such requirement in manufacturing defect cases); Mo. Stat. § 537.764 (2) (state of the art is a complete defense and relevant evidence in strict liability failure to warn claims); Neb. Rev. Stat. § 25–21,182 (state of art is a defense in action for negligence, defective design, testing or labeling, no mention of manufacturing defect).

art, meaning it could not feasibly be made safer, does not mean its workmanship is also state of the art.[395]

§ 33.20 Compliance with Statute and Preemption

Under the common law, the defendant's compliance with a statute is not in itself a defense to a negligence action.[396] If the defendant is driving only 50 miles per hour in a 55 zone, he may still be negligent in driving too fast for the circumstances. The common-law rule in products cases is the same—evidence of compliance with statute or regulation is relevant to judgments about the product's alleged design or warning defects and hence admissible,[397] but not by any means conclusive.[398]

Some states have enacted statutes attempting to provide some kind of protection for manufacturers whose products could be found defective even when they have complied with federal statutes. A few of these merely provide that evidence of compliance is admissible as tending to show that the product is not defective or negligently made.[399] A few others provide that when compliance is proven, the product is rebuttably "presumed" non-defective.[400] Neither group appears to change much. The plaintiff already has the burden of proving that the product is defective, which is to say that the product is "presumed" non-defective until the plaintiff sustains that burden. Statutes could, however, meaningfully provide that the presumption resulting from compliance is rebutted only by some especially demanding level of proof, such as clear and convincing evidence.[401] A few statutes eliminate punitive damages when compliance with statute or regulation is demonstrated.[402]

Although the state compliance statutes do not appear to have much effect, federal statutes or regulations[403] sometimes preempt or entirely displace state law, including tort law.[404] The effect is that when a manufacturer complies with a federal statute, no tort claim can be pursued, so in that case compliance is a complete defense. As already

[395] Falada v. Trinity Industries, Inc., 642 N.W.2d 247 (Iowa 2002).

[396] See 1 Dobbs, Hayden & Bublick, The Law of Torts § 249 (2d ed. 2011 & Supp.). The rule is the same with respect to a defendant's compliance with industry customs or standards. See Jablonski v. Ford Motor Co., 2011 IL 110096, 353 Ill. Dec. 327, 955 N.E.2d 1138 (2011).

[397] E.g., Dillon v. Nissan Motor Co., 986 F.2d 263 (8th Cir. 1993); Wagner v. Clark Equipment Co., 243 Conn. 168, 700 A.2d 38 (1997). Contra, Malcolm v. Evenflo Co., 352 Mont. 325, 217 P.3d 514 (2009) (evidence that the defendant's child safety seat complied with federal motor vehicle safety standards was inadmissible in a design defect case, expressly rejecting the Products Restatement).

[398] Bammerlin v. Navistar Intern. Transp. Corp., 30 F.3d 898 (7th Cir. 1994); Doyle v. Volkswagenwerk A.G., 267 Ga. 574, 481 S.E.,2d 518 (1997); Estep v. Mike Ferrell Ford Lincoln-Mercury, Inc., 223 W.Va. 209, 672 S.E.2d 345 (2008); Restatement Third of Torts (Products Liability) § 4 (1998).

[399] Ark. Code Ann. § 16–116–105; Rev. Code Wash. § 7.72.050 (1) (but providing a complete defense where the defendant was in compliance with "a specific mandatory government contract specification").

[400] Colo. Rev. Stat. Ann. § 13–21–403(1)(b); Kan. Stat. Ann. 60–3304; Tenn. Code Ann. § 29–28–104; see also Wright v. Ford Motor Co., 508 F.3d 263 (5th Cir. 2007) (applying Tex. Civ. Prac. & Rem. Code § 82.008).

[401] See James A. Henderson, Jr., Manufacturers' Liability for Defective Product Design: A Proposed Statutory Reform, 56 N.C. L. Rev. 625, 632 (1978) (proposing to bar the plaintiff if the product complied with a mandatory standard or regulation unless the plaintiff proved "by clear and convincing evidence" and by "other facts" than already required to prove her case, that the standards were inadequate).

[402] Or. Rev. Stats. § 30.927 (as to regulated prescription drugs).

[403] Federal agency regulations, as well as statutes, can establish federal law having preemptive force. See Fellner v. Tri-Union Seafoods, LLC, 539 F.3d 237 (3d Cir. 2008).

[404] The preemption effect is not limited to products cases. It may include such diverse matters of the safe (or unsafe) operation of railroads and the denial of medical benefits due under employment medical plans. For some examples, see §§ 18.8 & 21.22.

discussed, manufacturers who produce major products to government specifications are often accorded the same protection.[405]

Federal statutes may preempt state law, either expressly or impliedly. Even where Congress has not included an express preemption clause, implied preemption may occur if a federal statute or set of valid regulations either (1) occupies the regulated field ("field preemption") or (2) conflicts with state law ("conflict preemption"). Where preemption is found, the federal law entirely displaces state law. Federal lawmaking culture is oriented to regulation, not to private tort rights, and only a few federal statutes create private tort claims for personal injury.[406] In many instances when state tort rights are displaced, no new comparable federal tort right is substituted. Instead, the manufacturer is subjected to regulation without being subjected to liability. Consequently, a defendant who violates the preemptive federal statute, as well as the defendant who complies with it, may be immunized from all tort liability.[407]

Because preemption requires courts to interpret federal regulatory statutes that are themselves far from clear, preemption issues have bred a good deal of litigation. A given statute may preempt some tort claims but not others. A good example arises under the tobacco labeling act. Congress requires cigarette packages to bear a health-warning label. The statute forbids additional advertising requirements but says nothing about common law tort claims. However, the Supreme Court held that a common law tort claim based on failure to warn would be an additional advertising requirement. Hence no tort claim could be pursued based solely upon the manufacturer's failure to give a better warning than required by Congress. On the other hand, a claim based upon negligent research or upon express warranty would not be preempted.[408] In a later case construing the same tobacco labeling act, the Court held that a plaintiff's state law deceptive-advertising claims against manufacturers of "light" cigarettes were not preempted.[409]

A number of federal statutes set products standards or regulate products, and may include provisions that arguably expressly or impliedly preempt state tort claims. These include, besides the tobacco labeling act, statutes on flammable fabrics,[410] on insecticides and other poisons,[411] on railroad equipment,[412] on hazardous substances, and on motor vehicle safety standards.[413] Food and drugs are regulated heavily, but with no obvious preemptive intent.[414] However, medical devices such as pacemakers and penile implants

---

[405] See 2 Dobbs, Hayden & Bublick, The Law of Torts § 352 (2d ed. 2011 & Supp.).

[406] The Federal Employers Liability Act and its maritime companion are two of the few that eliminate state-law rights and at the same time furnish a federal substitute remedy. See 45 U.S.C.A. § 51; 46 U.S.C.A. § 688.

[407] See Buckman Co. v. Plaintiffs' Legal Committee, 531 U.S. 341, 121 S.Ct. 1012, 148 L.Ed.2d 854 (2001).

[408] Cipollone v. Liggett Group, Inc., 505 U.S. 504, 112 S.Ct. 2608, 120 L.Ed.2d 407 (1992).

[409] Altria Group, Inc. v. Good, 555 U.S. 70, 129 S.Ct. 538, 172 L.Ed.2d 398 (2008).

[410] 15 U.S.C.A. § 1203.

[411] 7 U.S.C.A. § 136v.

[412] 49 U.S.C.A. §§ 20701 et seq. (Locomotive Inspection Act). The Act was held to preempt all state-law duties and standards of care directed to the subject of locomotive equipment in Kurns v. Railroad Friction Products Corp., 132 S. Ct. 1261 (2012), a products liability case brought by a former railroad employee and his wife against the manufacturers of asbestos brake pads and engine valves containing asbestos.

[413] 49 U.S.C.A. § 30103(b) & (e).

[414] See Wyeth v. Levine, 555 U.S. 555, 129 S.Ct. 1187, 173 L.Ed.2d 51 (2009) (state-law failure to warn claims against a drug manufacturer not preempted). Preemption has been found in this area frequently, however. See Bruesewitz v. Wyeth LLC, 131 S. Ct. 1068, 179 L. Ed. 2d 1 (2011) (National Childhood Vaccine Injury Act preempts all design-defect claims against vaccine manufacturers brought by plaintiffs who claimed

are regulated under the same general scheme, and as to these devices the statute contains preemptive language.[415] The Consumer Products Safety Commission Act[416] and the Occupational Safety and Health Act are less likely to generate substantial preemption defenses.[417] Whether a given claim is preempted depends upon statutory language, which itself may emanate contradictory signals.[418]

The result is that a case-by-case analysis is required to determine whether a claim is preempted, not only because statutes themselves may differ from each other, but because some claims under a given statute may be preempted while others are not.[419] And courts disagree among themselves on a number of claims.

The Supreme Court has held that the absence of a regulation on anti-lock brakes is not itself a declaration that manufacturers are free to omit anti-lock brakes. Thus the federal motor vehicle regulations do not preempt a tort claim based on the absence of anti-lock brakes.[420] But the exact words and policy of the statute or regulation matter, and the Supreme Court has also held that a federal regulation requiring airbags on some vehicles but not others left manufacturers of others free to omit that protection, and preempted any state law requirement to the contrary.[421] On the other hand, the Court has held that where a statute expressly preempts local "law or regulation" relating to boat safety, the preemption only applies to positive enactments such as regulations or statutes and does not prevent states from recognizing common law tort liability for unreasonably unsafe boat motors.[422]

---

injury from the side-effects of vaccines); PLIVA, Inc. v. Mensing, 131 S.Ct. 2567, 180 L.Ed.2d 580 (2011) (federal law preempts state laws imposing a duty on generic drug manufacturers to change a drug's label); Mutual Pharmaceutical Co. v. Bartlett, 133 S.Ct. 2466, 186 L.Ed.2d 607 (2013) (federal law that expressly prohibits manufacturers of generic drugs from making any unilateral changes to a drug's label preempts design defect claim under New Hampshire law in which plaintiff argued that generic drug manufacturer failed to warn of the risks of certain diseases).

[415] 21 U.S.C.A. § 360k. Thus many claims of this type are expressly preempted, see, e.g., Wolicki-Gables v. Arrow Intern., Inc., 634 F.3d 1296 (11th Cir. 2011); In re Medtronic, Inc., Sprint Fidelis Leads Products Liability Litigation, 623 F.3d 1200 (8th Cir. 2010). In addition, suppliers of biomedical materials are largely immunized unless they manufacture the implant. See 21 U.S.C.A. § 1604.

[416] 15 U.S.C.A. § 2075(b) by its terms permits more demanding regulation. In BIC Pen Corp. v. Carter, 251 S.W.3d 500 (Tex. 2008), the court held that a design defect claim against a disposable lighter manufacturer was impliedly preempted by Consumer Product Safety Commission regulations, although a manufacturing defect claim was not.

[417] See § 11.3.

[418] See, e.g., Wood v. General Motors Corp., 865 F.2d 395 (1st Cir. 1988); Hernandez-Gomez v. Leonardo (Volkswagen of America, Inc.), 185 Ariz. 509, 917 P.2d 238 (1996).

[419] See, e.g., Hughes v. Boston Scientific Corp., 631 F.3d 762 (5th Cir. 2011) (Medical Device Amendments to the FDC Act expressly preempt state law claims purporting to impose liability despite manufacturer's compliance with FDA specifications for medical devices, but failure to warn claims were neither expressly nor impliedly preempted).

[420] Freightliner Corp. v. Myrick, 514 U.S. 280, 115 S.Ct. 1483, 131 L.Ed.2d 385 (1995). See also MCI Sales and Service, Inc. v. Hinton, 329 S.W.3d 475 (Tex. 2010) (relying on *Freightliner*, holding that claims that a motorbus importer, assembler and seller should have installed seatbelts and laminated glass windows were not preempted: "an agency's mere decision to leave an area unregulated is not enough to preempt state law").

[421] Geier v. American Honda Motor Co., 529 U.S. 861, 120 S.Ct. 1913, 146 L.Ed.2d 914 (2000). See also Williamson v. Mazda Motor of America, Inc., 131 S. Ct. 1131, 179 L. Ed. 2d 75 (2011) (same statute as in *Geier*, which gives manufacturers the choice of installing either simple lap belts or lap-and-shoulder belts, does not preempt state tort suits claiming that manufacturers should have installed lap-and-shoulder belts on rear inner seats; state tort action does not conflict with the federal regulation because the choice given to manufacturers does not further a significant regulatory objective).

[422] Sprietsma v. Mercury Marine, a Div. of Brunswick Corp., 537 U.S. 51, 123 S.Ct. 518, 154 L.Ed.2d 466 (2002).

A similar story, with varying degrees of preemption, can be told of other statutes. In the medical device area, the Supreme Court has held that the Food and Drug Administration's pre-market approval process establishes federal standards for medical devices, and that a patient's state-law claims of negligence, strict products liability and breach of warranty against the manufacturer of a balloon catheter were thus preempted.[423] Earlier the Court had held that a plaintiff's design and warning defect claims in connection with a heart pacemaker were not preempted, where the pacemaker had been approved under a grandfather clause and not actually covered by specific federal regulations.[424] Preemption in the device cases applies only when state law conflicts with the specific federal regulation because compliance with both state and federal rules is impossible, or because compliance with the state law would impede enforcement of the federal.[425] For that reason, preemption is most likely when federal regulation is extensive or specific and when the state law "requirement" is also specific in its conflict.[426]

§ 33.21 Statutes of Limitation

To a large extent, what has already been said about the statute of limitations in negligence cases applies in products liability cases as well.[427] The traditional rule starts the statute of limitations running at the time of injury; the discovery rule starts the statute running only when the plaintiff discovered or should have discovered injury and causation; the new statutes of repose put an outer limit on the discovery rule by providing that after a stated period, the statute bars the claim even if the injury has not yet occurred and even if it could not have been discovered. Products cases, however, tend to highlight several specific considerations.

Time of accrual. The cause of action for strict tort liability is usually treated under the rules applicable to negligence,[428] so accrual begins when injury occurs,[429] subject to the discovery rule[430] and statutes of repose where applicable. The claim for breach of

---

[423] Riegel v. Medtronic, Inc., 552 U.S. 312, 128 S.Ct. 999, 169 L.Ed.2d 892 (2008). See also Bass v. Stryker Corp., 669 F.3d 501 (5th Cir. 2012) (applying *Riegel*, holding that plaintiff's negligent-manufacturing claim and strict liability claim of manufacturing defect, premised on manufacturer's alleged violations of FDA regulations, were not preempted; other claims of failure to warn and breach of warranty were preempted); Walker v. Medtronic, Inc., 670 F.3d 569 (4th Cir. 2012) (applying *Riegel*, FDA regulations preempted negligence, strict liability and warranty claims based on drug-infusion pump manufacturer's alleged failure to adhere to specifications); Cornett v. Johnson & Johnson, 211 N.J. 362, 48 A.3d 1041 (2012) (applying *Riegel*, failure to warn and breach of express warranty claims against manufacturer of arterial stint that had been approved by the FDA as a medical device were partially preempted).

[424] Medtronic, Inv. v. Lohr, 518 U.S. 470, 116 S.Ct. 2240, 135 L.Ed.2d 700 (1997).

[425] See Worthy v. Collagen Corp., 967 S.W.2d 360 (Tex. 1998).

[426] See, e.g., Weston v. Kim's Dollar Store, 399 S.C. 303, 731 S.E.2d 864 (2012) (device-specific FDA requirements preempted plaintiff's claims that would impose common-law requirements "different from, or in addition to" those requirements, but not claims that merely "parallel" the federal requirements).

[427] See §§ 18.1 to 18.7.

[428] See Sheldon R. Shapiro, Annotation, Products Liability: What Statute of Limitations Governs Actions Based on Strict Liability in Tort, 91 A.L.R.3d 455 (1980); E.E. Woods, Annotation, Statute of Limitations: When Cause of Action Arises on Action against Manufacturer or Seller of Products Causing Injury or Death, 4 A.L.R.3d 831 (1966).

[429] See Gladhart v. Oregon Vineyard Supply Co., 332 Or. 226, 26 P.3d 817 (2001); Ogle v. Caterpillar Tractor Co., 716 P.2d 334 (Wyo. 1986); see also Golla v. General Motors Corp., 167 Ill.2d 353, 657 N.E.2d 894, 212 Ill.Dec. 549 (1995) (claim accrued at time of sudden traumatic injury; no need to apply discovery rule).

[430] E.g., Bendix Corp. v. Stagg, 486 A.2d 1150 (Del. 1984) (asbestosis, a disease of long latency; statute begins to run when disease manifested itself and became physically ascertainable); Cornett v. Johnson & Johnson, 211 N.J. 362, 48 A.3d 1041 (2012) (latent injury at site of stent implantation; discovery rule applied under either New Jersey or Kentucky law). Some courts have rejected the discovery rule in products actions.

warranty, however, can arguably accrue at the time the product was sold on the ground that warranty claims are based on contract, which is breached at the time of sale if the product is defective. That rule is especially adapted to commercial or economic loss cases and is accepted by the Uniform Commercial Code.[431] A number of courts have gone further by applying a time-of-sale rule to personal injury cases brought on a warranty theory.[432] Such an approach can bar the claim before injury occurs.[433] Not surprisingly, other courts have rejected this time-of-sale rule. They say that even if the claim for personal injury is constructed on a warranty theory, the claim is essentially one in tort and governed by the tort statute of limitations.[434] Neither the contract nor the tort approach consistently favors one party or the other. The plaintiff who buys a product that immediately causes a known injury will benefit from the longer warranty statute of limitations, although it begins to run immediately.[435] When the state has enacted a specific products liability statute, it may control regardless of the legal theory.[436]

Statutes of repose. Statutes of repose are especially popular in products and related cases. A plaintiff may be injured today by a product manufactured in 1930. Likewise, the plaintiff may be injured today by a product manufactured only last year, but the injury may not become apparent for ten or twenty years, especially with toxic injuries. These possibilities have led to widespread use of statutes of repose in products cases, typically cutting off all liability after an easily ascertainable time, such as six, eight, or ten years after the product was first sold for consumption.[437] The most extreme result would foreclose the plaintiff's claim before she was even injured. A few courts have held that statutes of repose violate their respective state constitutions,[438] but mostly these statutes have been upheld against constitutional attack.[439] The repose rule may be meliorated in narrow circumstances by allowing additional time to sue, as long as the injury itself occurred within the repose period,[440] or by declaring the rule unconstitutional only insofar as it bars the claim before it arises.[441]

See Jane Massey Draper, Annotation, Statute of Limitations: Running of Statute of Limitations on Products Liability Claim Against Manufacturer as Affected by Plaintiff's Lack of Knowledge of Defect Allegedly Causing Personal Injury or Disease, 91 A.L.R.3d 991 (1980).

[431] UCC § 2–725 (2).

[432] Ogle v. Caterpillar Tractor Co., 716 P.2d 334 (Wyo. 1986).

[433] E.g., Rufo v. Bastian-Blessing Co., 417 Pa. 107, 207 A.2d 823 (1965).

[434] Rubino v. Utah Canning Co., 123 Cal.App.2d 18, 266 P.2d 163 (1954).

[435] As in Sinka v. Northern Commercial Co., 491 P.2d 116 (Alaska 1971).

[436] See Oats v. Nissan Motor Corp., 126 Idaho 162, 879 P.2d 1095 (1994) (statute of repose applied to warranty claim, which was regarded as essentially a strict tort liability claim); Kambury v. DaimlerChrysler Corp., 334 Or. 367, 50 P.3d 1163 (2002) (specific products liability statute of limitations governs over more general wrongful death statute of limitations).

[437] Neb. Rev. Stat. § 25–224 (ten years from first sale or lease for consumption); Tenn. Code Ann. § 29–28–103 (six years from injury, ten years from purchase for consumption, one year after anticipated life of product, whichever is shortest). Statutes may also protect those contributing to improvements on real property. N.C. Gen. Stat. § 1–50 (six years for improvement to real property).

[438] E.g., Hazine v. Montgomery Elevator Co., 176 Ariz. 340, 861 P.2d 625 (1993); Groch v. General Motors Corp., 117 Ohio St.3d 192, 883 N.E.2d 377 (2008) (as retroactively applied to certain plaintiffs); see also § 18.4.

[439] E.g., Daily v. New Britain Mach. Co., 200 Conn. 562, 512 A.2d 893 (1986); see Jay M. Zitter, Annotation, Validity and Construction of Statute Terminating Right of Action for Product Caused Injury at Fixed Period after Manufacture, Sales, or Delivery of Product, 30 A.L.R.5th 1 (1995).

[440] See Davis v. Toshiba Machine Co., America, 186 Ill.2d 181, 237 Ill. Dec. 769, 710 N.Ed.2d 399 (1999).

[441] Diamond v. E.R. Squibb and Sons, Inc., 397 So.2d 671 (Fla. 1981).

Part VII

DAMAGES, APPORTIONMENT, AND
ALTERNATIVE SYSTEMS

Chapter 34

DAMAGES

Analysis

A. COMPENSATORY DAMAGES

§ 34.1   Basic Compensatory Damages for Personal Injury
§ 34.2   Damages for Harms to Property
§ 34.3   Adjustments in Basic Compensatory Damages

B. PUNITIVE DAMAGES

§ 34.4   Punitive Damages and Their Bases
§ 34.5   Common Law Factors in Determining the Amount of Punitive Damages
§ 34.6   Constitutional Requirements Governing the Award of Punitive Damages
§ 34.7   "Tort Reform" Statutes Affecting Compensatory and Punitive Damages

A. COMPENSATORY DAMAGES

§ 34.1 Basic Compensatory Damages for Personal Injury[1]

Terms and Elements of Damages

Damages as an element of a claim in negligence but not intentional torts. In cases of intentional torts to the person and property—assault, battery, false imprisonment, for example—the tort itself is regarded as harmful and the plaintiff is always entitled to recover at least nominal damages. In intentional tort cases, plaintiff is often entitled to recover a substantial sum without proof of any specific loss other than the tort itself.[2] In negligence cases, however, damages are an essential element of the plaintiff's claim.[3] Unless she has suffered legally recognized harm, she has no claim at all.[4]

Damages, restitution, and injunction. The term damages refers to the monetary award for legally recognized harm. The damages remedy is distinct from restitution and injunction, both of which are also occasionally available in tort cases. Restitution, when available, requires the defendant to restore any gains he made in a transaction;[5] injunction, when available, forbids threatened actions or requires the defendant to alter harmful conduct or repair its consequences.[6]

---

[1]   Damages in wrongful death and survival actions are considered in Chapter 28. Damages for wrongful pregnancy and wrongful birth are considered in Chapter 27.

[2]   See § 4.20.

[3]   See § 9.5.

[4]   Right v. Breen, 277 Conn. 364, 890 A.2d 1287 (2006); Donovan v. Philip Morris USA, Inc., 455 Mass. 215, 914 N.E.2d 891 (2009).

[5]   See generally 1 Dan B. Dobbs, Law of Remedies §§ 4.1–4.9 (2d ed. 1993). A prominent example is recovery "in assumpsit" for conversion. See id. § 5.18.

[6]   See, e.g., id. §§ 5.7 (relief from nuisances) & 5.10 (injunction to remove encroaching structures); 2 Dobbs §§ 6.4(5) (injunctions against trademark infringement), 7.3(5) (dignitary rights generally), & 7.4(4) (constitutional rights).

Compensatory damages. In personal injury cases the normal remedy is compensatory damages, awarded in a lump-sum, for all losses that have proximately resulted from the tort and all losses that will so result in the future. The plaintiff has the burden of proving both past and future damages by a preponderance of the evidence. Punitive damages may be added in limited cases.[7]

Elements of damages recoverable. Properly proven, the plaintiff is entitled to recover damages under three basic categories. (1) Time losses. The plaintiff can recover loss of wages or the value of any lost time or earning capacity where injuries prevent work. (2) Expenses incurred by reason of the injury.[8] Under one of the avoidable consequences rules, expenses reasonably incurred to minimize damages are recoverable.[9] Expenses recovered in personal injury cases are usually medical expenses and kindred items. (3) Pain and suffering in its various forms, including emotional distress and consciousness of loss of life's pleasures.[10] The basic damages recovery, comprising all these elements of past and future damages, is subject to various adjustments[11] and sometimes to limits on the total award.[12] In the absence of statute, the prevailing plaintiff does not recover for her attorney's fees.

Lost Earnings and Earning Capacity

Lost earnings. If the plaintiff is wholly or partly unable to carry out gainful activity as a result of tortiously inflicted injury, she is entitled to recover for actual wages[13] and fringe benefits[14] that have been lost or that will be lost in the future. Evidence of earnings before and after the injury are relevant, though it is also important to establish that the reduction is a proximate result of the injury.[15] Pre-injury earnings may understate the actual loss. If future wage increases are to be expected, either because of a general increase in industrial productivity or because of the plaintiff's reasonably expected advancement, those increases have also been lost and are thus recoverable as damages.[16]

Lost earning capacity. At least under some circumstances, the plaintiff is entitled to claim lost earning capacity instead of actual or prospective lost earnings. Lost earning capacity reflects the value of work the plaintiff could have done but for the injury. If the plaintiff was not working when injured and had no plans to do so, she has no immediate

---

[7]   See § 34.4.

[8]   Millennium Equity Holdings, LLC v. Mahlowitz, 925 N.E.2d 513 (Mass 2010) (costs incurred in successfully defending abusive lawsuit recoverable as an item of damages in subsequent abuse of process suit).

[9]   See 1 Dan B. Dobbs, Law of Remedies § 3.9 (2d ed. 1993).

[10]   Some courts define pain and suffering more narrowly to exclude mental anguish and loss of enjoyment of life, but then add the excluded categories back as items of damages separate from pain and suffering. See, e.g., Fantozzi v. Sandusky Cement Prods. Corp., 64 Ohio St.3d 601, 597 N.E.2d 474 (1992). Either way, the full range of losses is usually allowable. Similarly, some courts have treated disfigurement and physical impairment as separate items of damages rather than as evidence of other elements.

[11]   See § 34.5–34.7.

[12]   See 1 Dan B. Dobbs, Law of Remedies § 3.10 (2d ed. 1993). Civil rights statutes do often provide for attorneys' fees. See e.g., 42 U.S.C.A. § 1988 (general federal civil rights fee statute).

[13]   E.g., Fuqua v. Aetna Cas. & Sur. Co., 542 So. 2d 1129 (La. Ct. App. 1989).

[14]   E.g., Rivera v. Philadelphia Theological Seminary of St. Charles Borromeo, Inc., 510 Pa. 1, 507 A.2d 1 (1986).

[15]   See Robinson v. Greeley & Hansen, 114 Ill.App.3d 720, 725, 70 Ill.Dec. 376, 380, 449 N.E.2d 250, 254 (1983).

[16]   See Felder v. Physiotherapy Assocs., 215 Ariz. 154, 158 P.3d 877 (Ct. App. 2007); Henry v. National Union Fire Ins. Co., 542 So.2d 102, 107 (La. Ct. App. 1989).

lost income, but her injury nevertheless reduces her earning *capacity*. The most sympathetic case for such a claim is the domestic partner or family member who does not work in the labor market but works without pay in the family business or in the household. Such persons are allowed to recover for their lost capacity to work although they have lost no income and cannot project any future income losses.[17] The same rule applies to religious persons who have taken a vow of poverty[18] and to children and unemployed persons.[19] Lost earning capacity claims are entirely just in many cases; recovery reflects opportunity cost[20] or provides excellent evidence of the value of non-income work. In extreme cases, as where the plaintiff took early retirement the day before injury, courts view lost earning capacity claims with healthy skepticism.[21]

Calculating lost earnings. In calculating lost earnings, the parties generally present projections taking into account factors such as the injured party's age, education, and job status. Calculations traditionally take into account life expectancy and expected earnings. Mortality tables are often admitted for this purpose.[22] However, whether to permit tables that factor in race and gender presents a difficult policy issue. On the one hand, the compensatory purpose of the damages award suggests that liability should be restricted to actual loss and the tables reflect measured differences. However, because the data aggregate differences based on membership in protected groups, use of the categories has been questioned and in some cases rejected.[23]

Medical and Other Expenses

Medical and non-medical expenses. The injured plaintiff is entitled to recover reasonable medical and other expenses proximately resulting from tortious injury and expenses that will probably result in the future.[24] The reasonable charges of health care professionals for relief of pain or for treatment are recoverable, including reasonable charges for diagnostic tests, drugs, medical devices and artificial limbs used.[25] Non-medical expenses are also recoverable if they proximately result from the injury.[26] The traditional measure of recovery is not the cost of services or appliances needed but their

---

[17] E.g., American Nat'l Watermattress Corp. v. Manville, 642 P.2d 1330 (Alaska 1982) (76-year-old woman pinned under waterbed that rolled off its pedestal, lost 48 hours a week working in family business for which she was paid only nominal salary; plaintiff was entitled to recover full lost earning capacity).

[18] McLaughlin v. Chicago, M., St. P. & P. Ry. Co., 31 Wis.2d 378, 143 N.W.2d 32 (1966).

[19] Bishop v. Poore, 475 So.2d 486 (Ala. 1985); cf. Rubio v. Davis, 231 Ga.App. 425, 500 S.E.2d 367 (1998) (three-year-old child's arm amputated, evidence of earning capacity before and after injury not required; damages are in the jury's sound discretion).

[20] See 2 Dan B. Dobbs, Law of Remedies § 8.1(2) (2d ed. 1993).

[21] Cf. Saul Levmore, Self-Assessed Valuation Systems for Tort and Other Law, 68 Va. L. Rev. 771, 803–05 (1982) (expressing doubts about earning capacity recovery).

[22] See 2 Dan B. Dobbs, Law of Remedies § 8.5(2) (2d ed. 1993).

[23] See McMillan v. City of New York, 253 F.R.D. 247 (E.D.N.Y. 2008) (holding race-based statistics inadmissible in estimating life expectancy for purposes of calculating damages, because of unreliability, due process, and equal protection); Martha Chamallas, Civil Rights in Ordinary Tort Cases: Race, Gender, and the Calculation of Economic Loss, 38 Loy. L.A. L. Rev. 1435 (2005); Michael I. Meyerson & William Meyerson, Significant Statistics: The Unwitting Policy Making of Mathematically Ignorant Judges, 37 Pepp. L. Rev. 771 (2010); Jennifer Wriggins, Damages in Tort Litigation: Thoughts on Race and Remedies, 1865–2007, 27 Rev. Litig. 37, 53–57 (2007).

[24] Donovan v. Philip Morris USA, 455 Mass. 215, 914 N.E.2d 891 (2009) (jury may award future damages that are "reasonably probable" to occur, as opposed to those that may only "possibly" occur).

[25] E.g., Atlanta Transit Sys., Inc. v. Nowell, 138 Ga.App. 443, 226 S.E.2d 286 (1976) (diagnosis); Haudrich v. Howmedica, Inc., 169 Ill.2d 525, 662 N.E.2d 1248, 215 Ill.Dec. 108 (1996) (knee replacement); see 2 Dan B. Dobbs, Law of Remedies § 8.1(3) (2d ed. 1993).

[26] Thierrien v. Target Corp., 617 F.3d 1242 (10th Cir. 2010).

reasonable value,[27] and then only if the services are reasonably required as a result of the injury.[28]

Medical surveillance or monitoring. When the plaintiff has been tortiously exposed to a toxic substance that may result in disease after a long latency period, the best way to minimize the harm is to maintain regular periodic medical checkups. Recovery of reasonable monitoring expenses, once a tort has been established, appears to be in accord with the usual rules of personal injury damages for diagnostic expenses and also with the rule that permits recovery of expenses incurred to minimize damages. Some courts have not only allowed for such periodic future monitoring expenses,[29] but, in line with commentators,[30] have sometimes suggested that the defendant might be required to set up a special fund to finance such medical checkups as they arise.[31] Courts have shown caution, however, sometimes establishing a number of conditions to be met before damages can be recovered for monitoring. One sensible condition is that the plaintiff must be at significant risk; other conditions may require proof that monitoring is likely to help discover disease and that early discovery is likely to help.[32] But if the plaintiff has incurred no detectible harm, there is contrary authority denying the recovery of medical monitoring expenses altogether.[33]

Mental and Physical Pain and Suffering

Entitlement to recovery. The plaintiff is entitled to recover for all forms of suffering proximately caused by tortious injury, including future suffering. The pain for which recovery is allowed includes virtually any form of conscious suffering, both emotional[34] and physical.[35] Pain from medical treatments that are themselves required by the injury

---

[27]   See, e.g., Pexa v. Auto Owners Ins. Co., 686 N.W.2d 150 (Iowa 2004); Steinauer v. Sarpy County, 217 Neb. 830, 843, 353 N.W.2d 715, 724 (1984).

[28]   Pexa v. Auto Owners Ins. Co., 686 N.W.2d 150 (Iowa 2004); see also Kempner v. Schulte, 318 Ark. 433, 885 S.W.2d 892 (1994).

[29]   Hagerty v. L & L Marine Servs., Inc., 788 F.2d 315 (5th Cir. 1986); Donovan v. Philip Morris USA, 455 Mass. 215, 914 N.E.2d 891 (2009); Meyer v. Fluor Corp., 220 S.W.3d 712 (Mo. 2007); Ayers v. Jackson Twp., 106 N.J. 557, 525 A.2d 287 (1987); Bower v. Westinghouse Elec. Corp., 206 W.Va. 133, 522 S.E.2d 424 (1999).

[30]   Note, Increased Risk of Disease from Hazardous Waste: A Proposal for Judicial Relief, 60 Wash. L. Rev. 635, 647–52 (1985) (suggesting that the court should use its equitable powers to require the defendant to provide an insurance policy covering the group at risk).

[31]   Friends For All Children, Inc. v. Lockheed Aircraft Corp., 746 F.2d 816, 46 A.L.R.4th 1113 (D.C. Cir. 1984) (preliminary injunction ordered the defendant to fund medical monitoring program); see Ayers v. Jackson Twp., 106 N.J. 557, 525 A.2d 287 (1987) (medical surveillance costs for those exposed to toxic chemicals; courts should encourage use of court-ordered medical surveillance funds, but lump-sum award here because case was tried that way).

[32]   E.g., Perrine v. E.I. du Pont de Nemours & Co., 694 S.E.2d 815, 873 (W.Va. 2010).

[33]   Metro-North Commuter R.R. Co. v. Buckley, 521 U.S. 424, 117 S.Ct. 2113, 138 L.Ed.2d 560 (1997); Wood v. Wyeth-Ayerst Labs., 82 S.W.3d 849 (Ky. 2002); Henry v. Dow Chem. Co., 473 Mich. 63, 701 N.W.2d 684 (2005) (in the absence of present physical injury, negligence rules forbid a tort claim and courts should leave issue to the legislature, especially since impact of the defendant's liability on the business climate of the state is uncertain); Paz v. Brush Engineered Materials, Inc., 949 So.2d 1 (Miss. 2007); Sinclair v. Merck & Co., 195 N.J. 51, 948 A.2d 587 (2008); La. Civ. Code Ann. art. 2315(B).

[34]   E.g., Wood v. Mobil Chem. Co., 50 Ill.App.3d 465, 8 Ill.Dec. 701, 365 N.E.2d 1087 (1977) (anxiety and depression following brain injury); Alphonso v. Charity Hosp. of La. at New Orleans, 413 So.2d 982 (La. Ct. App. 1982) (post-traumatic stress disorder following rape, along with other serious problems).

[35]   E.g. Sears, Roebuck & Co. v. Hartley, 160 F.2d 1019 (9th Cir. 1947) (past pain plus pain of recalling it); Black v. Comer, 38 So.3d 16 (Ala. 2009) (pain from removal of tissue mass in abdomen that turned out to be plaintiff's kidney as well as internal bleeding). See Marcus L. Plant, Damages for Pain and Suffering, 19 Ohio St. L.J. 200 (1958) (discussing purely subjective pain).

is also recoverable, so long as it can be deemed a proximate result of the tort.[36] Expert testimony can address pain, but frequently the physical injury itself and the kind of medical attention needed either permit or require an inference that the plaintiff suffered physically or emotionally.[37] Awards for pain are not easy to evaluate because there is no objective criterion for judgment.

Comparable awards. A number of courts consider awards in comparable cases to be instructive,[38] whereas other courts have prohibited such comparison.[39] If a court approves an award in because prior decisions have approved similar awards on similar facts, perhaps this is only a little more than application of precedent.[40] Judge Posner has insisted that federal trial judges must consider comparable awards, and, seemingly, that federal juries must be apprised of such awards as well.[41] However, an Indiana court took the opposite view, holding that consideration of comparable awards would not ordinarily be permissible, reasoning in part that each plaintiff is entitled to have an individual award by the jury, not an award set by some other trier for some other individual.[42] Courts that do consider comparable cases seemingly only look to awards that were both made by the jury and upheld against challenge[43]—normally awards that have been reported and passed on in appellate cases.

Forms of suffering included. Courts have said that the award of pain and suffering includes the sensation of physical pain itself[44] and the inconvenience, pain, and sense of loss that may be built on physical injury. Loss of a bodily member[45] and loss of bodily functions,[46] for example, are likely to entail considerable further pain and inconvenience, all of which is well within the broad definition of pain and suffering. Compensable

---

[36]   See Abrams v. City of Mattoon, 148 Ill.App.3d 657, 101 Ill.Dec. 780, 499 N.E.2d 147 (1986) (side effects of drugs prescribed as result of injury). Self-inflicted pain may also qualify. Alphonso v. Charity Hosp. of La. at New Orleans, 413 So.2d 982 (La. Ct. App. 1982) (mental patient/rape victim mutilated herself to prevent further attacks).

[37]   Choi v. Anvil, 32 P.3d 1 (Alaska 2001) (so long as jurors' common knowledge or experience would permit an inference that the impact to the plaintiff caused pain, no expert testimony is required, rejecting Nebraska's rule of law that requires expert testimony for purely subjective injury).

[38]   E.g., Meyers v. Wal-Mart Stores, East, Inc., 257 F.3d 625 (6th Cir. 2001) (trial judge properly relied upon comparable case to reduce pain award only slightly); R.J. Reynolds Tobacco Co. v. Webb, 93 So.3d 331 (Fla. Dist. Ct. App.), review denied, 107 So.3d 406 (Fla. 2012) (vacating damages award after reviewing comparable awards for non-economic damages); Bissell v. Town of Amherst, 56 A.D.3d 1144, 867 N.Y.S.2d 582 (2008) (examining prior cases to determine reasonable compensation).

[39]   Velarde v. Illinois Cent. R.R. Co., 354 Ill.App.3d 523, 820 N.E.2d 37, 289 Ill.Dec. 529 (2004); Moteberg v. Johnson, 297 Minn. 28, 210 N.W.2d 27 (1973) ("In considering whether a verdict is excessive, a comparison with previous verdicts is not justified because of the variations in facts and changes in the economy.").

[40]   Prior awards might be used in several distinct ways on the prior court decision as precedent; on prior awards from earlier appellate decisions as data, such non-precedential awards might be accepted as indicating an average range of "good" awards; and at the triers' awards themselves as guidelines, emphasizing averages or ranges.

[41]   Arpin v. United States, 521 F.3d 769 (7th Cir. 2008) (trial judge must consider comparable awards in order to adequately explain his decision). For application of this approach, see Maldonado v. Sinai Med. Group, Inc., 706 F.Supp.2d 882 (N.D. Ill. 2010).

[42]   Ritter v. Stanton, 745 N.E.2d 828 (Ind. Ct. App. 2001).

[43]   Bravo v. United States, 532 F.3d 1154 (11th Cir. 2008) (FTCA case); Graeff v. Baptist Temple of Springfield, 576 S.W.2d 291 (Mo. Ct. App. 1978) ("a comparison of the compensation awarded *and permitted* in cases of comparable injuries" (italics added)).

[44]   Wald v. Grainger, 64 So.3d 1201 (Fla. 2011) (sensitivity and discomfort).

[45]   Mileski v. Long Island R.R., 499 F.2d 1169 (2d Cir. 1974) (eye).

[46]   See, e.g., Foradori v. Harris, 523 F.3d 477 (5th Cir. 2008) (upholding jury award of $10 million for pain and suffering in spinal-cord injury case); Kenton v. Hyatt Hotels Corp., 693 S.W.2d 83 (Mo. 1985) (plaintiff's loss of excretory and sexual functions).

suffering also includes emotional anguish or distress resulting from injury.[47] Any form of unpleasant emotional reactions to the injury or its consequences, so long as it is proximately related to the tort, can be a basis for the pain and suffering recovery. Disfigurement, for example, may cause mental pain or embarrassment. Other unpleasant emotional states are covered by the rule. Terror at an approaching injury,[48] worry about whether a dog bite will lead to rabies, or a burn, to cancer[49] are examples of suffering over the future course of an injury already inflicted. Depression, anxiety, and hysterical or conversion reactions are all covered so long as they proximately result from the tortious injury.[50]

Loss of enjoyment of life. The rules permitting recovery for suffering are easily broad enough to permit recovery for the plaintiff's mental reactions to pain and to her sense of loss. If the plaintiff's injury makes it impossible for her to see a sunset, or hear music, engage in sexual activity, or pursue a chosen vocation, she may have no physical sensation of pain but she may be aware of loss and suffer from it. The same can be true with any loss of function. Almost without exception, loss of enjoyment of life in this sense is as compensable as any other negative emotional state resulting from tortious injury.[51] Older cases that denied the recovery altogether seem to be largely obsolete today.

In current cases, loss of enjoyment damages are often characterized as "hedonic" damages, a term from the Greek referring to pleasure. Three main issues are being litigated. (1) Are damages for loss of enjoyment merely one form of pain and suffering damages? (2) Can loss of enjoyment damages be awarded when the victim is not and cannot be aware of the loss, as where the victim is deceased or in a permanent coma? (3) Is expert value-of-life testimony admissible to show the value of lost enjoyment?[52]

§ 34.2 Damages for Harms to Property

Two basic rules. Harms to property are complex, partly because, besides physical injury to property itself, its owner may suffer loss of use because he is dispossessed, or

---

[47] E.g., Boryla v. Pash, 960 P.2d 123 (Colo. 1998).

[48] E.g., Blum v. Airport Terminal Servs., Inc., 762 S.W.2d 67 (Mo. Ct. App. 1988) (decedent had been aware that plane would crash); Yowell v. Piper Aircraft Corp., 703 S.W.2d 630 (Tex. 1986) (preimpact distress damages allowed when decedents' plane broke up and they fell 10,000 feet to an immediate death).

[49] E.g., Ferrara v. Galluchio, 5 N.Y.2d 16, 176 N.Y.S.2d 996, 152 N.E.2d 249, 71 A.L.R.2d 331 (1958) (worry about cancer).

[50] See Averyt v. Wal-Mart Stores, Inc., 265 P.3d 456 (Colo. 2011) (award of $5.5 million in non-economic damages affirmed where evidence showed that physical injuries to the plaintiff caused "chronic pain and that such pain induces personality changes such as depression, difficulty sleeping, and difficulty concentrating," all of which greatly affected plaintiff's enjoyment of life); see also 2 Dan B. Dobbs, Law of Remedies § 8.1(4) (2d ed. 1993).

[51] E.g., Thompson v. National R.R. Passenger Corp., 621 F.2d 814 (6th Cir. 1980); Averyt v. Wal-Mart Stores, Inc., 265 P.3d 456 (Colo. 2011) (chronic pain and depression caused loss of enjoyment of life; testimony specifically addressed plaintiff's sadness "that she could no longer drive her truck, which she enjoyed doing," and that she could no longer "do the job that she loved and was good at," all resulting in a loss of independence she had in her job as a truck driver); MacDougald v. Garber, 73 N.Y.2d 246, 257, 538 N.Y.S.2d 937, 536 N.E.2d 372, 376 (1989) (as a form of conscious pain and suffering). Some cases emphasize specific lost abilities. See McAlister v. Carl, 233 Md. 446, 197 A.2d 140, 15 A.L.R.3d 496 (1964) (vocation); Kenton v. Hyatt Hotels Corp., 693 S.W.2d 83 (Mo. 1985) (emphasizing plaintiff's loss of ability to play tennis, ski, jog, and carry on other athletic activities). Many others treat loss of functioning in gross as a loss of ability to enjoy life without requiring or emphasizing proof of specific loss, such as a lost ability to play tennis. E.g., Gregory v. Carey, 246 Kan. 504, 791 P.2d 1329 (1990); Banks v. Sunrise Hosp., 102 P.3d 52 (Nev. 2004).

[52] These issues are all discussed at greater length in 3 Dobbs, Hayden & Bublick, The Law of Torts § 479 (2d ed. 2011 & Supp.).

loss of enjoyment because of the defendant's activities outside the property.[53] When the defendant's tort has physically damaged real or personal property without severing and taking any part of it,[54] courts usually measure damages by one of two rules. (1) The first rule is the diminished value rule. It gives the plaintiff the difference between the value of the property immediately before harm was done and the value immediately afterwards.[55] This measures the loss in capital value of the land or chattel. (2) The second rule is the cost rule. It gives the plaintiff the cost of repair or replacement (subject to appropriate adjustments for salvage).[56] This measures the potential cash impact upon the plaintiff. When the property is either converted or totally destroyed by negligence, a special version of the diminished value rule applies; the plaintiff recovers the value of the property at the time it was destroyed or converted,[57] or, in the case of conversion, at a reasonable time thereafter.[58]

Choosing the right rule for the case. Neither the diminished value rule nor the cost rule works well in all cases. If the cost of repair is much higher than the diminished value, sometimes the diminished value should impose a ceiling on recovery because repairs would be economically foolish. For example, if I own a car worth $500 it would be foolish to spend $1,000 on repairs. It would be far better to salvage the car and buy another for something in the neighborhood of $500. However, sometimes the damaged property has such important personal significance or social value that I might be justified in spending more in repair than the property is worth on the market. Where the damaged property is a companion animal, some courts have allowed recovery of the cost of medical treatment that exceeds the fair market value of the animal, typically on the ground that the market value of the pet was quite low, if measurable at all.[59] Costly repair might also be warranted where the defendant has negligently bulldozed shade trees or a vegetable garden,[60] or damaged a church building used for low-income housing.[61] Similarly, if the defendant is contaminating the plaintiff's real property,

---

[53]   See 1 Dan B. Dobbs, Law of Remedies §§ 5.6, 5.8, 5.9 (damages and restitution for loss of exclusive possession of real property) (2d ed. 1993).

[54]   As to severance of minerals, timber or the like, see id. § 5.3.

[55]   E.g., Ross v. A Betterway Rent-A-Car, Inc., 213 Ga.App. 288, 444 S.E.2d 604 (1994); Ken Hood Constr. Co. v. Pacific Coast Constr., Inc., 201 Or.App. 568, 120 P.3d 6 (2005), *modified on other points*, 203 Or.App. 768, 126 P.3d 1254 (2006).

[56]   E.g., Halpin v. Schultz, 917 N.E.2d 436 (Ill. 2009); Falcone v. Perry, 68 Wash.2d 909, 416 P.2d 690 (1966).

[57]   Travis Lumber Co. v. Deichman, 319 S.W.3d 239 (Ark. 2009); Chlopek v. Schmall, 224 Neb. 78, 396 N.W.2d 103 (1986); Daughten v. Fox, 372 Pa.Super. 405, 539 A.2d 858 (1988).

[58]   See 1 Dan B. Dobbs, Law of Remedies § 5.13(2) (2d ed. 1993).

[59]   See Martinez v. Robledo, 210 Cal.App.4th 384, 147 Cal.Rptr.3d 921 (2012), review denied (Jan. 23, 2013) (reversing in two consolidated cases; "a pet owner is not limited to the market value of the pet and may recover the reasonable and necessary costs incurred for the treatment and care of the pet attributable to the injury"); Kimes v. Grosser, 195 Cal.App.4th 1556, 126 Cal.Rptr.3d 581 (2011) (allowing recovery of costs of medical treatment of pet cat shot by defendant, even where those costs exceeded the negligible market value of the cat); Burgess v. Shampooch Pet Indus., Inc., 35 Kan.App.2d 458, 131 P.3d 1248 (2006) (affirming damage award of $1,308.89, representing the cost of the dog's successful hip surgery, on the ground that such a measure of damages was "practical" and accorded with "common sense" where the pet—a 13-year-old terrier—had "no discernable market value"); Zager v. Dimilia, 138 Misc.2d 448, 524 N.Y.S.2d 968 (J. Ct. 1988) (citing cases, holding that "reasonable and necessary costs of reasonable veterinary treatment" was the "proper measure of damages" in a pet-injury case).

[60]   See, e.g., Andersen v. Edwards, 625 P.2d 282, 288 (Alaska 1981); Weitz v. Green, 230 P.3d 743 (Idaho 2010); Restatement Second of Torts § 929 cmt.b (1979); 1 Dan B. Dobbs, Law of Remedies § 5.2(2) (2d ed. 1993).

[61]   Roman Catholic Church of the Archdiocese of New Orleans v. Louisiana Gas Serv. Co., 618 So.2d 874 (La. 1993) (costly repair costs for church-managed property used for low-income housing represented appropriate measure of damages).

damages based on costs of cleanup might be preferable even if they exceed diminished land value, partly because of deterrent effects and partly because of public interests.[62]

Consequential damages. A tort to property may not only harm the property itself but may cause consequential losses if the property cannot be used during repair or replacement period. Consequential damages such as lost profits or other forms of lost use are recoverable in appropriate cases,[63] but the existence and amount must be proven with reasonable certainty and must also be a proximate result of the tort.[64] Courts have generally denied emotional harm resulting from damage or destruction of chattels, even such personal chattels as pets,[65] but intentional harm to a pet might qualify as an intentional infliction of emotional distress, for which emotional harm damages could be recovered.[66] One consequential item is generally recoverable: the reasonable expenditures made to minimize damages.[67]

§ 34.3 Adjustments in Basic Compensatory Damages

Downward adjustments. The basic estimate of compensatory damages is subject to a number of downward adjustments. Comparative negligence rules—including the avoidable consequences rules for minimizing damages—can substantially reduce the recovery.[68] Absolute caps on the recovery or some elements of it simply refuse to permit recovery of actual damages after those damages reach a stated level.[69] The remaining issues about adjusting damages awards are narrower.

Adjustments in Awards for Future Losses

Fixing a loss period. When the plaintiff claims that she will suffer future losses, she must prove by a preponderance of the evidence that those losses will in fact be incurred in the future. She must also prove the duration of those losses. If she will endure pain for the rest of her life, the trier must have some basis for estimating her life expectancy. If her injury is permanent and will never allow her to work, the trier must have some basis for estimating how long the plaintiff would have worked if she had not been injured. Such periods may be very long, easily thirty or forty years in some cases. Mortality and "work-life" tables are often admitted as a baseline for making this determination, and the estimates are adjusted based on individual traits of the injured party. Such tables may cause controversy because of different statistical expectancies by race and gender, yet their general use may be consistent with the concept that the defendant should be obligated to compensate only for the actual loss caused.[70]

---

[62] See 1 Dan B. Dobbs, Law of Remedies § 5.2(2) (2d ed. 1993).

[63] E.g., Tri-G, Inc. v. Burke, Bosselman & Weaver, 222 Ill.2d 218, 856 N.E.2d 389, 305 Ill.Dec. 584 (2006) (lawyer malpractice caused client to lose claim for lost profits against a bank); Walker v. Brown, 501 So.2d 358 (Miss. 1987); Gateway Foam Insulators, Inc. v. Jokerst Paving & Contracting, Inc., 279 S.W.3d 179 (Mo. 2009); Chemical Express Carriers, Inc. v. French, 759 S.W.2d 683 (Tex. App. 1988) (insurance agent's income dropped when he could not use airplane to transport clients).

[64] 1 Dan B. Dobbs, Law of Remedies § 3.4 (2d ed. 1993).

[65] E.g., Nichols v. Sukaro Kennels, 555 N.W.2d 689, 61 A.L.R.5th 883 (Iowa 1996); Scheele v. Dustin, 998 A.2d 697 (Vt. 2010).

[66] Richardson v. Fairbanks N. Star Borough, 705 P.2d 454, 456 (Alaska 1985).

[67] See 1 Dan B. Dobbs, Law of Remedies § 3.9 (2d ed. 1993).

[68] See Chapter 16.

[69] § 34.7.

[70] See generally 2 Dan B. Dobbs, Law of Remedies § 8.5(2) (2d ed. 1993).

Reduction to present value. Courts have said that damages awarded for losses that will occur in the future should be reduced to present value, so as not to overcompensate.[71] No reduction is required for pain and suffering damages.[72] Once the appropriate interest rate and the time of the future losses are determined, the reduction is simply mathematical and made using tables, a formula, or a software program. The most critical element in the reduction is the appropriate discount or interest rate. The "legal rate" of interest is not a good guide here. Courts have said the rate should be what an unsophisticated investor can safely earn in such investments as a savings account or something equally safe.[73] Many issues are also raised concerning prejudgment interest.[74]

Adjusting for inflation. The long period of future losses also implicates the problem of inflation. Courts once refused to make any adjustment for inflation.[75] To avoid under compensation, in the last generation, courts have increasingly been willing to take inflation into account. Courts either: (1) make a straightforward estimate of probable future inflation;[76] (2) use a very low interest rate in computing the reduction to present value but make no separate adjustment for inflation, on the theory that this reflects the "real" rate of interest;[77] or (3) let the present value and inflation adjustment wash each other out. In the last scenario, the judge would make no reduction to present value and no addition for inflation.[78]

Gains or Savings Resulting from Injury

The collateral source rule. In many cases, the injured plaintiff receives some compensation for injuries from sources that have nothing to do with the defendant. The plaintiff's own insurance, job benefits, or donations by friends may all operate to reduce the plaintiff's loss. The traditional rule is that compensation from "collateral sources" is none of the defendant's business and does not reduce the defendant's obligation to pay damages, either in negligence[79] or in strict liability cases.[80] Thus if the plaintiff has an injury causing loss of $100,000 and $50,000 of that injury is covered by the plaintiff's own insurance, the defendant must still pay the full $100,000.

---

[71]   E.g., Monessen Sw. Ry. Co. v. Morgan, 486 U.S. 330, 108 S.Ct. 1837, 100 L.Ed.2d 349 (1988); Green v. General Motors Corp., 310 N.J. Super. 507, 709 A.2d 205 (1998).

[72]   E.g., Cox v. Crown Coco, Inc., 544 N.W.2d 490 (Minn. Ct. App. 1996); Friedman v. C & S Car Servs., 108 N.J. 72, 527 A.2d 871 (1987).

[73]   See Chesapeake & Ohio Ry. v. Kelly, 241 U.S. 485, 490, 36 S.Ct. 630, 632, 60 L.Ed.2d 1117, 1122 (1916).

[74]   See 3 Dobbs, Hayden & Bublick, The Law of Torts § 485 (2d ed. 2011 & Supp.).

[75]   Zaninovich v. American Airlines, Inc., 26 A.D.2d 155, 271 N.Y.S.2d 866 (1966).

[76]   See Schleier v. Kaiser Found. Health Plan, 876 F.2d 174 (D.C. Cir. 1989).

[77]   See Doca v. Marina Mercante Nicaraguense, S.A., 634 F.2d 30, 37 (2d Cir. 1980); Feldman v. Allegheny Airlines, Inc., 524 F.2d 384 (2d Cir. 1975). The Supreme Court thought that some such approach would be permissible. Jones & Laughlin Steel Corp. v. Pfeifer, 462 U.S. 523, 103 S.Ct. 2541, 76 L.Ed.2d 768 (1983).

[78]   See Beaulieu v. Elliott, 434 P.2d 665 (Alaska 1967).

[79]   Helfend v. Southern Cal. Rapid Transit Dist., 2 Cal.3d 1, 84 Cal.Rptr. 173, 465 P.2d 61, 77 A.L.R.3d 398 (1970); Willis v. Foster, 229 Ill.2d 393, 323 Ill.Dec. 26, 892 N.E.2d 1018 (2008); Scott v. Garfield, 454 Mass. 790, 912 N.E.2d 1000 (2009); Mahoney v. Nebraska Methodist Hosp., 251 Neb. 841, 560 N.W.2d 451 (1997) (pension); Kenney v. Liston, 760 S.E.2d 434 (W. Va. 2014); Leitinger v. DBart, Inc., 302 Wis.2d 110, 736 N.W.2d 1 (2007); Restatement Second of Torts §§ 920A & 920 (1979); 2 Dan B. Dobbs, Law of Remedies § 8.6(3) (2d ed. 1993).

[80]   Gypsum Carrier, Inc. v. Handelsman, 307 F.2d 525, 4 A.L.R.3d 517 (9th Cir. 1962); Tebo v. Havlik, 418 Mich. 350, 343 N.W.2d 181 (1984).

Rationales. Perceived overcompensation is often more theoretical than real. In many instances, the collateral source rule only operates to preserve the subrogation rights of an insurer. To the extent an insurer pays the plaintiff under an insurance policy, the insurer acquires the plaintiff's rights to sue. If the collateral source rule were reversed so that payment of the plaintiff's loss by his own insurer eliminated the plaintiff's right to recover damages for such items, the insurer, who stands in the plaintiff's shoes, would lose the right to recover. It is argued without the collateral source rule to protect the insurer's subrogation right, insurance premiums would rise.[81] It is also argued that the plaintiff has, after all, paid for her insurance coverage. When compensation is in the form of donations rather than insurance, it is said that donors do not intend to donate to the defendant but to the plaintiff. Supporters of the rule have also argued that the defendant should not get a windfall.

Concerns. Because first party insurance (the plaintiff's) is usually cheaper than liability insurance (the defendant's), the effect of the collateral source rule is to draw on the most expensive kind of insurance and to add the costs of subrogation suits in the bargain. Considering the matter prospectively rather than after the fact, it may well be that compensation could be more cheaply secured without the collateral source rule.[82]

Abolishing the collateral source rule. As part of a tort reform program, around half of the states have abolished or limited the collateral source rule for specified claims, frequently medical malpractice claims and those against public entities. Some statutes cover all tort actions or even all actions for damages.[83] Others cover claims against favored defendants, such as health care providers or public entities.[84] One approach simply authorizes admission of evidence of collateral benefits;[85] another specifically requires the trier or the judge to deduct collateral benefits from the award.[86] Ideally, the deduction would be allowed only for collateral benefits that matched the items of damages the plaintiff recovered, and it has been so held.[87] When the award is reduced because the plaintiff has received payments from her own insurance company, the plaintiff may be allowed to add back into the award some of the sums she expended in premiums for that insurance.[88] Some states abolishing the collateral source rule reduce the plaintiff's award only if no insurance company is subrogated to the plaintiff's rights. Those states protect the subrogation rights of the plaintiff's insurer by retaining the

---

[81]   Cates v. Wilson, 321 N.C. 1, 361 S.E.2d 734 (1987).

[82]   See Alfred E. Conard, The Economic Treatment of Automobile Injuries, 63 Mich. L. Rev. 279, 311 (1964); 2 Dan B. Dobbs, Law of Remedies § 8.6(3) (2d ed. 1993).

[83]   E.g., Mont. Code Ann. § 27–1–308 (actions for injury or death where total award exceeds $50,000); N.Y. C.P.L.R. § 4545 ("In any action brought to recover damages for personal injury, injury to property or wrongful death").

[84]   E.g., 231 Mass. Gen. Laws Ann. § 60G. Iowa's statute covers only payments received for medical care, so that the plaintiff's disability payments do not reduce recovery. Collins v. King, 545 N.W.2d 310 (Iowa 1996).

[85]   E.g., Ala. Code § 12–21–45.

[86]   E.g., N.Y. C.P.L.R. § 4545; Colo. Rev. Stat. § 13–21–116.6. See also Smith v. Jeppsen, 277 P.3d 224 (Colo. 2012); Wal-Mart Stores, Inc. v. Crossgrove, 276 P.3d 562 (Colo. 2012); Idaho Code Ann. § 6–1606; Carrillo v. Boise Tire Co., Inc., 152 Idaho 741, 274 P.3d 1256 (2012).

[87]   Pikulski v. Waterbury Hosp. Health Ctr., 269 Conn. 1, 848 A.2d 373, 376 (2004) ("only payments specifically corresponding with items of damages included in the jury's verdict [are] to be deducted as collateral sources from the economic damages award"); McMullen v. Ohio State Univ. Hosp., 88 Ohio St.3d 332, 725 N.E.2d 1117 (2000).

[88]   Mont. Code Ann. § 27–1–308 (premiums paid for five years before injury, those paid from injury to judgment, and the value of those to be paid in the next three years).

collateral source rule as to the insurer.[89] A few courts have held these statutes unconstitutional under provisions of state constitutions.[90] Other courts have upheld the statutes.[91]

Tax savings.[92] Under the United States Revenue Code, the personal injury plaintiff pays no taxes on compensatory damages for physical injury.[93] When the injured plaintiff is entitled to recover for loss of wages or earning capacity, the tax gift to the plaintiff raises two questions. First, should the defendant's liability be reduced to reflect the tax savings so that the plaintiff is not overcompensated? Second, if the answer is no and the defendant is liable for full wage loss even though some of that loss is recovered through the tax gift, should the jury be warned not to add anything for taxes? The traditional answer to both questions highly favored the plaintiff. Courts permitted the plaintiff to recover the full wage loss, which replaced taxable wages with untaxable substitute funds.[94] Courts also usually refused to instruct the jury on this topic,[95] which in the view of some courts left a substantial probability that many juries would "add something" because of supposed taxation.[96] In 1980, the Supreme Court rejected the traditional rule, holding that in suits under the Federal Employers Liability Act the basic computation should be reduced to account for the plaintiff's tax savings so that the plaintiff would recover full compensation.[97] So far, however, this holding has not influenced states to change their rules.[98]

B. PUNITIVE DAMAGES

§ 34.4 Punitive Damages and Their Bases

Availability. No cause of action exists for punitive damages as such. In the great majority of states,[99] punitive (or "exemplary") damages may be awarded when the plaintiff has suffered legally recognized harm and the tortfeasor has committed quite serious misconduct with a bad intent or bad state of mind such as malice. Punitive damages represent a monetary award apart from compensatory damages.

---

[89]   Ala. Code § 12–21–45; Mich. Comp. Laws Ann. § 600.6303 (2) & (4).

[90]   Thompson v. KFB Ins. Co., 252 Kan. 1010, 850 P.2d 773 (1993) (discrimination against victims with greater harm); Farley v. Engelken, 241 Kan. 663, 740 P.2d 1058, 74 A.L.R.4th 1 (1987) (discrimination against medical malpractice victims); O'Bryan v. Hedgespeth, 892 S.W.2d 571 (Ky. 1995) (admission of evidence is judicial function, statute violated separation of powers).

[91]   Eastin v. Broomfield, 116 Ariz. 576, 570 P.2d 744 (1977); see James J. Watson, Annotation, Validity and Construction of State Statute Abrogating Collateral Source Rule as to Medical Malpractice Actions, 74 A.L.R.4th 32 (1990).

[92]   See generally 2 Dan B. Dobbs, Law of Remedies § 8.6(4) (2d ed. 1993).

[93]   26 U.S.C.A. § 104 (a). The Code by its terms does not relieve the taxpayer of taxes for non-physical injuries like emotional distress or defamation. See Murphy v. Internal Revenue Serv., 493 F.3d 170 (D.C. Cir. 2007).

[94]   E.g., Marcel v. Placid Oil Co., 11 F.3d 563 (5th Cir. 1994); Johnson v. Manhattan & Bronx Surface Transit Operating Auth., 71 N.Y.2d 198, 524 N.Y.S.2d 415, 519 N.E.2d 326 (1988).

[95]   E.g., Hall v. Chicago & Nw. Ry. Co., 5 Ill.2d 135, 125 N.E.2d 77 (1955).

[96]   See, e.g., Norfolk & W. Ry. v. Liepelt, 444 U.S. 490, 100 S.Ct. 755, 62 L.Ed.2d 689 (1980).

[97]   Norfolk & W. Ry. v. Liepelt, 444 U.S. 490, 100 S.Ct. 755, 62 L.Ed.2d 689 (1980).

[98]   See, e.g., Klawonn v. Mitchell, 105 Ill.2d 450, 86 Ill.Dec. 478, 475 N.E.2d 857 (1985) (there is no evidence that jury would add to the award on the erroneous assumption that it would be heavily taxed); Spencer v. A-1 Crane Serv., Inc., 880 S.W.2d 938 (Tenn. 1994).

[99]   Several states reject or purport to reject punitive damages altogether. E.g., Killebrew v. Abbott Labs., 359 So.2d 1275 (La. 1978); Distinctive Printing & Packaging Co. v. Cox, 443 N.W.2d 566 (Neb. 1989). But some of these smuggle in awards under statutes in particular cases. See 1 Dan B. Dobbs, Law of Remedies § 3.11(1).

Defendant's conduct and state of mind. Courts have traditionally agreed that punitive damages can be awarded only when the tortfeasor causes harm by conduct that is "outrageous"[100] or "that constitutes an extreme departure from lawful conduct"[101] and that is motivated by or evinces an antisocial mental state as well.[102] The exact mode of expressing this requirement has varied somewhat. Some courts insist upon malice, ill-will, intent to injure, evil motive or the like,[103] while others have found it sufficient that the defendant engages in wanton misconduct with a conscious indifference to risk.[104] A great many other terms without much legal or descriptive content have been used to characterize the conduct permitting a punitive award. For instance it has been said that the defendant may be held liable for punitive damages if he is oppressive, evil, wicked, guilty of wanton or morally culpable conduct, or shows flagrant indifference to the safety or rights of others.[105] Perhaps the defendant's abuse of power or of a special relationship is another marker for punitive awards.[106] Some courts have been willing to award punitive damages when the defendant intentionally indulges in serious risk-taking, without requiring an actual intent to inflict harm.[107] The plaintiff has the burden of proving the factual basis for punitive damages by a preponderance of the evidence. Some courts and legislatures have now altered this to require clear and convincing evidence[108] or even proof beyond a reasonable doubt.[109]

Examples. Punitive damages have been approved at least in principle in a wide variety of cases, both against defendants engaged in economic activity (manufacturing

---

[100] Exxon Shipping Co. v. Baker, 554 U.S. 471, 493, 128 S.Ct. 2605, 2621, 171 L.Ed.2d 570 (2008) (quoting Restatement Second of Torts § 908(2)).

[101] David Owen's phrase, see David G. Owen, The Moral Foundations of Punitive Damages, 40 Ala. L. Rev. 705, 730 (1989). The conduct itself, as distinct from the state of mind, is in fact almost always serious. But to some extent, the conduct may seem egregiously bad because of the defendant's bad purpose or bad state of mind. Kolstad v. American Dental Ass'n, 527 U.S. 526, 119 S.Ct. 2118 (1999).

[102] See Smith v. Wade, 461 U.S. 30, 103 S.Ct. 1625, 75 L.Ed.2d 632 (1983).

[103] Owens-Illinois, Inc. v. Zenobia, 325 Md. 420, 601 A.2d 633 (1992); Ross v. Louise Wise Servs., Inc., 8 N.Y.3d 478, 836 N.Y.S.2d 509, 868 N.E.2d 189 (2007).

[104] E.g., Pouzanova v. Morton, 327 P.3d 865 (Alaska 2014) ("reckless disregard of safety of another"); Galaxy Cable, Inc. v. Davis, 58 So.3d 93 (Ala. 2010); Qwest Servs. Corp. v. Blood, 252 P.3d 1071 (Colo. 2011), cert. dismissed, 132 S.Ct. 1087, 181 L.Ed.2d 805 (2012); Hutchison v. Luddy, 896 A.2d 1260 (Pa. Super. Ct. 2006); Johnson v. Rogers, 763 P.2d 771 (Utah 1988); Philip Morris, Inc. v. Emerson, 235 Va. 380, 407, 368 S.E.2d 268, 283 (1988).

[105] E.g., First Nat'l Bank of Pulaski, Tenn. v. Thomas, 453 So. 2d 1313, 1320 (Ala. 1984) ("rudeness, wantonness, recklessness, or an insulting manner, or accompanied by circumstances of fraud and malice, oppression, aggravation, or gross negligence"); Johnson & Johnson v. Superior Court, 192 Cal. App. 4th 757, 121 Cal. Rptr. 3d 640 (2d Dist. 2011) (quoting Cal. Civ. Code 3294 (c)(1), punitive damages may be awarded only upon proof of "despicable conduct . . . carried on by the defendant with a willful and conscious disregard of the rights of safety of others"; also saying that summary judgment was proper "only when no reasonable jury could find the plaintiff's evidence to be clear and convincing proof of malice, fraud or oppression"); Selle v. Tozser, 786 N.W.2d 748 (S.D. 2010) ("presumed malice" for purpose of punitive damages can be shown by a disregard for the rights of others).

[106] See David Owen, Civil Punishment and the Public Good, 56 S. Cal. L. Rev. 103, 104 (1982). Although courts may verbalize the test of punitive liability as involving at least a deliberate indifference, the facts may show abuse of power or special relationship, and may be a good predictor of the court's conclusion. Hutchison v. Luddy, 896 A.2d 1260 (Pa. Super. Ct. 2006).

[107] See Smith v. Wade, 461 U.S. 30, 47–48, 103 S.Ct. 1625, 1636, 75 L.Ed.2d 632, 646 (1983); Countrywide Home Loans, Inc. v. Thitchener, 192 P.3d 243, 252 (Nev. 2008).

[108] E.g., Pouzanova v. Morton, 327 P.3d 865 (Alaska 2014); Linthicum v. Nationwide Life Ins. Co., 150 Ariz. 326, 723 P.2d 675 (1986); Brokaw v. Winfield-Mt. Union Cmty. Sch., 788 N.W.2d 386 (Iowa 2010); Flax v. DaimlerChrysler Corp., 272 S.W.3d 521 (Tenn. 2008); see also Lee R. Russ, Annotation, Standard of Proof as to Conduct Underlying Punitive Damage Awards—Modern Status, 58 A.L.R.4th 878 (1987).

[109] Colo. Rev. Stat. § 13–25–127.

products that cause harm, for example)[110] and against individual defendants who act in anti-social ways for personal gratification. Courts have approved punitive damages in principle in a variety of cases, including those in which the defendant is guilty of battery,[111] failure to care for vulnerable nursing home patients,[112] child molestation,[113] environmental harm,[114] breach of fiduciary duty,[115] fraud,[116] repeated misconduct,[117] or driving a vehicle in an extremely dangerous manner.[118] A deliberate policy of corporate misconduct[119] may suffice. The A.H. Robins Company marketed its Dalkon Shield IUD knowing it was dangerous to women and presumably hoping that profits would exceed liability. Punitive damages were of course appropriate.[120] A number of scandalous cases have turned on corporate concealment of serious danger and efforts to cover-up misconduct.[121]

Purpose. Courts usually emphasize that punitive damages are awarded to punish or deter.[122] The idea of punishment or retribution is that it is just for the defendant to suffer for his misconduct.[123] The idea of deterrence is quite different. It is that a sufficient

---

[110]   E.g., White v. Ford Motor Co., 500 F.3d 963 (9th Cir. 2007).

[111]   E.g., Hough v. Mooningham, 139 Ill.App.3d 1018, 487 N.E.2d 1281, 94 Ill.Dec. 404 (1986) (defendant struck plaintiff with shovel).

[112]   See Horizon/CMS Healthcare Corp. v. Auld, 34 S.W.3d 887 (Tex. 2000).

[113]   See Hutchison v. Luddy, 896 A.2d 1260 (Pa. Super. Ct. 2006) (clergy).

[114]   See Potter v. Firestone Tire & Rubber Co., 6 Cal.4th 965, 863 P.2d 795, 25 Cal.Rptr.2d 550 (1993). By statute punitive damages can be recovered by the United States in certain cases. 42 U.S.C.A. § 9607(c)(3).

[115]   E.g., Coster v. Crookham, 468 N.W.2d 802 (Iowa 1991). If a restitutionary remedy is granted for breach of fiduciary duty or fraud, however, some courts may still refuse punitive damages.

[116]   E.g., Talent Tree Personnel Servs. v. Fleenor, 703 So.2d 917 (Ala. 1997) (either intentional misrepresentation or concealment of facts defendant was obliged to disclose, if oppressive or malicious).

[117]   West v. Western Cas. & Sur. Co., 846 F.2d 387 (7th Cir. 1988); Hutchison v. Luddy, 896 A.2d 1260 (Pa. Super. Ct. 2006) (diocese's pattern and practices in addressing neither the problem of its child-molester priests nor the consequences they caused to parishioners).

[118]   E.g., Campbell v. Van Roekel, 347 N.W.2d 406 (Iowa 1984) (single vehicle accident); Cabe v. Lunich, 70 Ohio St.3d 598, 640 N.E.2d 159 (1994) (evidence that driver had consumed alcohol prior to accident is relevant and bears on malice).

[119]   E.g., Torres v. North Am. Van Lines, Inc., 135 Ariz. 35, 658 P.2d 835 (Ct. App. 1982) (company's failure to monitor driving-time logs of drivers); Loughry v. Lincoln First Bank, 67 N.Y.2d 369, 378, 494 N.E.2d 70, 74–75, 502 N.Y.S.2d 965, 970 (1986) (employer liable for punitive damages if "the wrong was in pursuance of a recognized business system" of the employer). Cf. Qwest Servs. Corp. v. Blood, 252 P.3d 1071 (Colo. 2011), cert. dismissed, 132 S. Ct. 1087, 181 L. Ed. 2d 805 (2012) ($18 million punitive damages award was justified where the evidence showed beyond a reasonable doubt that the telephone utility consciously chose to forgo a periodic wooden-pole inspection program and knew or should have known that the conduct would probably result in injuries, and refused to institute such an inspection program even after a lineman was injured when a pole collapsed).

[120]   Tetuan v. A.H. Robins Co., 241 Kan. 441, 738 P.2d 1210 (1987).

[121]   See, e.g., id. (concealment, cover-up by attempted burning of corporate records); Cynthia R. Mabry, Warning! The Manufacturer of this Product May Have Engaged in Cover-Ups, Lies, and Concealment: Making the Case for Limitless Punitive Awards in Product Liability Lawsuits, 73 Ind. L.J. 187, 216–34 (1997) (detailing Dalkon Shield, asbestos, tobacco and other cases).

[122]   See, e.g., Exxon Shipping Co. v. Baker, 554 U.S. 471, 492, 128 S.Ct 2605, 2621, 171 L.Ed.2d 570 (2008) ("the consensus today is that punitives are aimed not at compensation but principally at retribution and deterring harmful conduct"). Courts have also sometimes considered punitive damages as a source of funds to aid in financing costly litigation, see 1 Dan B. Dobbs, Law of Remedies § 3.11(3) (2d ed. 1993), as an emphatic expression of community values, and as a sum added when it is difficult to be sure that the compensatory award was sufficient and the defendant's conduct has no redeeming value. See Kemezy v. Peters, 79 F.3d 33 (7th Cir. 1996); Haralson v. Fisher Surveying, Inc., 201 Ariz. 1, 31 P.3d 114 (2001).

[123]   This interest is arguably absent when the defendant dies, as some courts have recognized in barring the recovery of punitive damages for personal injuries after the death of the defendant. See Vincent v. Alden-Park Strathmoor, Inc., 241 Ill.2d 495, 350 Ill.Dec. 330, 948 N.E.2d 610 (2011). Wrongful death statutes

sum should be exacted from the defendant to discourage the misconduct or make its repetition unlikely. In some major punitive damages cases, deterrence is necessary because the defendant's activity is profitable or the defendant retains gains even after compensatory damages are paid.[124] Because punishment alone does not adequately describe the bases for such damages, they are sometimes called extracompensatory damages.

Issues. Punitive damages raise unique problems. Sometimes they resemble criminal fines, sometimes civil damages. For instance, vicarious liability of an employer for punitive damages may be allowed, but only in the case of management complicity in or ratification of the actor's misconduct,[125] although a few courts apply ordinary vicarious liability rules to hold the employer punitively liable.[126] Likewise, some authorities hold that liability insurers may cover punitive damages[127] while others hold they may not.[128] Many articles[129] and books[130] have addressed punitive damages. Punitive damages are currently controversial because of claims that they are unpredictable or excessive.[131] Yet empirically, judges and juries award punitive damages in relatively few cases,[132] although still more frequently and in higher amounts in the United States than anywhere else in the world.[133] Moreover, the punitive damages limits embraced by the

---

sometimes alter this result, either explicitly or as interpreted by courts. See 2 Dobbs, Hayden & Bublick, The Law of Torts § 375 (2d ed. 2011 & Supp.).

[124] See, elaborating this idea and constructing a theory for punitive awards and their measure, A. Mitchell Polinsky & Steven Shavell, Punitive Damages: An Economic Analysis, 111 Harv. L. Rev. 869 (1998).

[125] Nev. Rev. Stat. Ann. § 42.007; Restatement Second of Torts § 909 (1979); see also Model Punitive Damages Act § 6; 1 Dan B. Dobbs, Law of Remedies § 3.11(6) (2d ed. 1993).

[126] Haralson v. Fisher Surveying, Inc., 201 Ariz. 1, 31 P.3d 114 (2001); Stroud v. Denny's Rest., Inc., 271 Or. 430, 532 P.2d 790 (1975).

[127] Whalen v. On-Deck, Inc., 514 A.2d 1072, 1074 (Del. 1986); Lunceford v. Peachtree Cas. Ins. Co., 230 Ga.App. 4, 495 S.E.2d 88 (1997); Va. Code Ann. § 38.2–227. See also Ross Neely Sys., Inc. v. Occidental Fire & Cas. Co. of N.C., 196 F.3d 1347 (11th Cir. 1999) (Alabama insurers may include or exclude coverage for punitive damages generally, but must cover punitive damages for wrongful death).

[128] See Flint Hills Rural Elec. Coop. Ass'n v. Federated Rural Elec. Ins. Corp., 262 Kan. 512, 941 P.2d 374 (1997) (not permissible to insure against punitive liability for one's own act, but permissible to insure against vicarious punitive liability).

[129] Among a great many, see Dan B. Dobbs, Ending Punishment in "Punitive" Damages: Deterrence-measured Remedies, 40 Ala. L. Rev. 831, 871–88 (1989); Dorsey D. Ellis, Jr., Fairness and Efficiency in the Law of Punitive Damages, 56 S. Cal. L. Rev. 1 (1982); Thomas C. Galligan, Jr., Foreward: Punitive Damages Today and Tomorrow, 70 La. L. Rev. 421 (2010) (introducing symposium on punitive damages); Dan Markel, How Should Punitive Damages Work?, 157 U. Pa. L. Rev. 1383 (2009); David G. Owen, The Moral Foundations of Punitive Damages, 40 Ala. L. Rev. 705 (1989); A. Mitchell Polinsky & Steven Shavell, Punitive Damages: An Economic Analysis, 111 Harv. L. Rev. 869 (1998); Cass R. Sunstein, et al., Assessing Punitive Damages (With Notes on Cognition and Valuation in Law), 107 Yale L.J. 2071 (1998); Symposium, The Future of Punitive Damages, 1998 Wis. L. Rev. 1 (eleven articles).

[130] John J. Kircher & Christine M. Wiseman, Punitive Damages Law and Practice (2 vols. 2d ed. 2000); Linda L. Schlueter & Kenneth R. Redden, Punitive Damages (2 vols. 4th ed. 2000); see 1 Dan B. Dobbs, Law of Remedies § 3.11 (2d ed. 1993).

[131] Exxon Shipping Co. v. Baker, 554 U.S. 471, 496, 128 S.Ct 2605, 2625, 171 L.Ed.2d 570 (2008).

[132] One large empirical study found that among the cases sampled, punitive damages were awarded in only about 4% of cases won by plaintiffs. Of these, a large proportion consisted of intentional tort and fraud cases. See Theodore Eisenberg, et al., Juries, Judges, and Punitive Damages: An Empirical Study, 87 Cornell L. Rev. 743 (2002). The same study concluded that judges award punitive damages about as often as juries and in about the same ratio to compensatory awards as juries. Id. at 746.

[133] See Exxon Shipping Co. v. Baker, 554 U.S. 471, 496, 128 S.Ct 2605, 2623, 171 L.Ed.2d 570 (2008).

court are largely controversial to the extent that they may thwart the deterrent function of the tort law,[134] and create a variety of other problems.[135]

Handling wealth evidence. The traditional assumption was that although evidence of the defendant's financial condition was admissible, nothing compelled the plaintiff to produce such evidence. California and Wyoming have held that the plaintiff must produce evidence of the defendant's wealth if she is to recover any punitive award.[136] However, this view has been surgically dissected and discarded by Judge Posner.[137] If evidence of the defendant's wealth is admitted, it might induce some jurors to find against the defendant on the more basic issue of liability for compensatory damages. In some states, through judicial decision or statute, the trial of the basic liability issues is held before any evidence of the defendant's wealth is admitted. Only if the defendant is found to have committed a tort is the jury to consider punitive damages, sometimes only after compensatory damages have been determined as well.[138] The procedure that requires two trial segments is called bifurcation.[139]

§ 34.5 Common Law Factors in Determining the Amount of Punitive Damages

Traditional factors—common law. The traditional common law punitive damage awards are open ended, without any particular limit in amount. No objective measure for such damages exists.[140] Courts have tried to provide a framework for assessing punitive damages by considering several factors. In the absence of legislation restricting punitive damages, the main factors in setting the amount of an award of punitive damages have included: (1) the reprehensibility of the defendant's misconduct; (2) the defendant's wealth; (3) the profitability of the misconduct; (4) litigation costs; (5) the aggregate of all civil and criminal sanctions against the defendant; and (6) the ratio between the harm caused, or potentially caused, by the defendant's misconduct and the losses suffered by the plaintiff.[141] The suggestion has been made that, in addition, courts fixing the punitive award could consider the amount of uncompensated loss inflicted by the defendant, at least in some cases.[142]

---

[134] E.g., Jeff Kerr, Exxon Shipping Co. v. Baker: The Perils of Judicial Punitive Damages Reform, 59 Emory L.J. 727 (2010); Leo M. Romero, Punishment for Ecological Disasters: Punitive Damages and/or Criminal Sanctions, 7 U. St. Thomas. L.J. 154 (2009); W. Kip Viscusi, Saving Lives Through Punitive Damages, 83 S. Cal. L. Rev. 229 (2009).

[135] E.g., Doug Redleman, Common Law Punitive Damages: Something for Everyone, 7 U. St. Thomas. L.J. 1 (2009); Catherine M. Sharkey, The Exxon Valdex Litigation Marathon: A Window on Punitive Damages, 7 U. St. Thomas. L.J. 25 (2009).

[136] Adams v. Murakami, 54 Cal. 3d 105, 284 Cal. Rptr. 318, 813 P.2d 1348 (1991); Adel v. Parkhurst, 681 P.2d 886 (Wyo. 1984).

[137] Kemezy v. Peters, 79 F.3d 33 (7th Cir. 1996).

[138] E.g., Campen v. Stone, 635 P.2d 1121, 32 A.L.R.4th 410 (Wyo. 1981); Cal. Civ. Code § 3295 (d); N.C. Gen. Stat. § 1D–30 (jury first determines liability and compensation, then punitive damages); Tex. Civ. Prac. & Rem. Code Ann. § 41.009.

[139] Trifurcation with separate segments for liability, compensation, and punitive awards is also a possibility.

[140] Multiple damages statutes, authorizing, say, treble damages, may have punitive effects but only fortuitously will a fixed multiple reflect either appropriate deterrence levels or appropriate retribution.

[141] Labonte v. Hutchins & Wheeler, 424 Mass. 813, 678 N.E.2d 853 (1997); Garnes v. Fleming Landfill, Inc., 186 W.Va. 656, 413 S.E.2d 897 (1991); see also Model Punitive Damages Act § 7 (listing similar factors and others, including "any adverse effect of the award on innocent persons").

[142] See Mathias v. Accor Econ. Lodging, Inc., 347 F.3d 672 (7th Cir. 2003).

Economic vs. personal gratification activity. One large class of potential punitive damage cases involves defendants engaged in economic activity that causes harm. Firms that cause pollution or produce products that cause harm are examples. A second class involves defendants, usually individuals rather than corporations, who obtain personal gratification from tortious anti-social behavior. Individuals who beat or rape others or who drive while intoxicated are examples.

Ratio rules. As traditionally applied, the ratio factor holds that the punitive award should bear some reasonable (but unspecified) relationship to either: (a) the potential for harm created by the defendant's conduct; or (b) the actual damages suffered by the plaintiff.[143] If the rule addresses the actual harm, as it does in some statements of the rule, it does not seem especially relevant at all. The defendant who fires a bullet at the plaintiff's head but only breaks a cheap pair of glasses has caused little apparent harm, but it makes no sense at all to suggest that the $50 pair of glasses is somehow mathematically related to any purpose of punitive awards, since it does not measure either just punishment or needed deterrence.[144] In those circumstances, the relevant ratio is the relationship between the amount of *potential* harm from the defendant's conduct and the punitive award.[145]

Defendant's financial status. The defendant's financial status is a traditional factor in determining the right amount of punitive damages.[146] The theory is that the trier must know something about the defendant's financial condition in order to inflict a liability that will have an appropriate sting.[147] Proof may show either a wealthy defendant or a poor one.[148] In the case of personal ill-will or evil disposition as where the defendant beats or rapes another person, the defendant's financial condition is obviously of some relevance, since a small punitive award against a very wealthy person may have little effect while a large award against a person with little wealth might fail to deter if all the defendant's assets are exhausted so that he has nothing left to lose. On the other hand, when a tort is committed by income-producing activity—by deliberately selling dangerous products, for example—profitability of the tortious activity is probably more significant for deterrence than wealth.[149]

---

[143] E.g., Palmer v. Ted Stevens Honda, Inc., 193 Cal.App.3d 530, 238 Cal.Rptr. 363 (1987); see generally 1 Dan B. Dobbs, Law of Remedies § 3.11(11) (2d ed. 1993).

[144] Distinguish the use of compensatory damage multiples under the Polinsky-Shavell theory. See n. 124, supra.

[145] TXO Prod. Corp. v. Alliance Res. Corp., 509 U.S. 443, 459, 113 S.Ct. 2711, 125 L.Ed.2d 366 (1993). See also Bowden v. Caldor, 350 Md. 4, 40, 710 A.2d 267, 285 (1998).

[146] See 1 Dan B. Dobbs, Law of Remedies, § 3.11(5) (2d ed. 1993).

[147] See, e.g., Zarcone v. Perry, 572 F.2d 52, 56 (2d Cir. 1978) ("A $60,000 award may bankrupt one person and be a minor annoyance to another"); Thiry v. Armstrong World Indus., 661 P.2d 515 (Okla. 1983). In Mathias v. Accor Econ. Lodging, Inc., 347 F.3d 672 (7th Cir. 2003), Judge Posner commented that the defendant's wealth might permit it to aggressively defend in order to make litigation too costly for the plaintiff to afford.

[148] See Michael v. Cole, 122 Ariz. 450, 595 P.2d 995 (1979); Hardin v. Caldwell, 695 S.W.2d 189 (Tenn. Ct. App. 1985); Bankhead v. ArvinMeritor, Inc., 205 Cal.App. 4th 68, 139 Cal.Rptr.3d 849 (2012), as modified, (Apr. 25, 2012), and review denied (July 11, 2012). See also Sulton v. HealthSouth Corp., 400 S.C. 412, 734 S.E.2d 641 (2012) (hospital's net operating revenue of $2 billion should not have gone to the jury in damages phase; net revenue has no necessary relation to net worth).

[149] See Dan B. Dobbs, Ending Punishment in "Punitive" Damages: Deterrence-measured Remedies, 40 Ala. L. Rev. 831, 871–88 (1989) (proposing punitive damages to equal the amount needed to deter, either the wrongdoer's profits from the tortious activity or where that measure is not feasible, a reasonable attorney's fee for the plaintiff, not limited to a percentage of recovery). See also Johnson v. Ford Motor Co., 35 Cal.4th 1191, 1207–08, 113 P.3d 82, 29 Cal.Rptr.3d 401 (2005).

Aggregate punishment. In some cases punitive damages awards run the risk that the defendant will be punished several times over, perhaps because he is criminally liable and perhaps because he has been or will be subjected to other punitive damages judgments. Punitive damages awards are not subject to the prohibition against double jeopardy,[150] but the aggregate of punishments is a clear and even a constitutional concern in determining the justification for and amount of punitive awards.[151] Balancing these concerns against the relevance of the defendant's repeated similar misconduct is difficult.[152] At trial, a corporate defendant who may be held punitively liable in the future probably does not wish to argue to the jury that others will also punish him. The other extreme would permit only a single punitive award, even though the defendant's reckless or malicious behavior has injured many people.[153] Perhaps the best that can be done is to permit the judges in reviewing a jury verdict of punitive damages to consider past and potential punitive awards, although as to future awards, this is necessarily speculative.

§ 34.6 Constitutional Requirements Governing the Award of Punitive Damages

Constitutional restrictions. The traditional punitive damages regime was perceived as overly subjective and unpredictable.[154] Consequently, the United States Supreme Court has closely examined and largely circumscribed the award of punitive damages, relying primarily on the Due Process Clause.[155] Though binding, the Supreme Court approach itself has been subject to criticism.[156]

Procedural requirements. The Supreme Court has held that awards of punitive damages do not in themselves violate the Eighth Amendment[157] or Due Process requirements.[158] But due process exacts substantial requirements. First, some kind of guidance must be given to the jury about the purpose of punitive damages as retribution or deterrence, perhaps along with an instruction that an award is not required.[159] Second, courts must provide post-trial review of punitive awards.[160] Guidance and

---

[150] John J. Kircher & Christine M. Wiseman, 1 Punitive Damages Law and Practice § 3:2 (2d ed. 2000 & Supps.).

[151] See Pacific Mut. Life Ins. Co. v. Haslip, 499 U.S. 1, 20, 111 S.Ct. 1032, 1045, 113 L.Ed.2d 1, 21 (1991).

[152] See discussion in Johnson v. Ford Motor Co., 35 Cal.4th 1191, 1208–12, 113 P.3d 82, 29 Cal.Rptr.3d 401 (2005).

[153] This was dictated in Ga. Code § 51–12–5.1, held unconstitutional as discriminatory in McBride v. General Motors Corp., 737 F.Supp. 1563 (M.D. Ga. 1990).

[154] See Exxon Shipping Co. v. Baker, 554 U.S. 471, 499, 128 S.Ct 2605, 2625, 171 L.Ed.2d 570 (2008).

[155] Commentators have argued that the response to unpredictability logically should be legislatively enacted guidelines similar to criminal sentencing guidelines, rather than judicially-adopted guidelines to limit awards. See, e.g., id.at 504–05, 128 S.Ct. at 2628–29 (but rejecting notion that federal criminal sentencing guidelines have provided predictability); Mathias v. Accor Econ. Lodging, Inc., 347 F.3d 672, 678 (7th Cir. 2003); Jeffrey L. Fisher, The Exxon Valdez Case and Regularizing Punishment, 26 Alaska L. Rev. 1, 46 (2009).

[156] E.g., W. Kip Viscusi, Saving Lives Through Punitive Damages, 83 S. Cal. L. Rev. 229 (2010) (arguing that Supreme Court's focus on punitive damages ratios rather than total damages needed for deterrence is mistaken).

[157] Browning-Ferris Indus. of Vt., Inc. v. Kelco Disposal, Inc., 492 U.S. 257, 109 S.Ct. 2909, 106 L.Ed.2d 219 (1989).

[158] Pacific Mut. Life Ins. Co. v. Haslip, 499 U.S. 1, 111 S.Ct. 1032, 1043, 113 L.Ed.2d 1 (1991).

[159] Id.

[160] See Honda Motor Co. Ltd. v. Oberg, 512 U.S. 415, 114 S.Ct. 2331, 129 L.Ed2d 336 (1994).

review on the basis of factors already mentioned—reprehensibility of the defendant's conduct being the chief—was initially held to be sufficient.[161]

Prohibition of Excessive Awards

BMW of North America v. Gore.[162] Beginning in 1996, the Supreme Court has taken several steps beyond the question of judicial process. In *BMW*, without placing caps on the punitive award, the Court held that the amount of a punitive award could be so grossly excessive that it would in itself violate due process. In so holding, the Court examined some factors that are not in the traditional list. The facts may have shaped a good deal of the opinion. Gore had purchased from BMW a "new" car, which as it turned out had been damaged while still in BMW's possession, probably from acid rain. BMW repainted the car and sold it as a new car without disclosing the repair. The fact that it had been repainted before being delivered to a customer might have reduced its resale value by $4,000. The jury awarded $4 million in punitive damages. The Alabama Court reduced that to $2 million. The United States Supreme Court struck the award on the ground that it was grossly excessive and a violation of due process.

Extraterritoriality and limits on state sovereignty. The Supreme Court first considered the scope of the state's interests in imposing punitive damages. The state has no interest in imposing sanctions for conduct outside the state or changing the defendant's behavior in other states. Its interest was in its own citizens and its justification for a punitive award was circumscribed accordingly. In other words, a large punitive award could not be justified on the ground that such a large award was necessary to change the defendant's conduct elsewhere. A punitive award that was based in part on extra-state conduct might therefore be constitutionally excessive.

Three "guideposts." The *BMW* Court also insisted that an award of punitive damages could not satisfy the notion of fair notice inherent to due process unless the defendant was on notice of the conduct that was subject to sanction and of the potential severity of the penalty. Consequently, each award must satisfy three "guideposts" against which the defendant, and the trier of fact, may evaluate the defendant's conduct. In the specific case of BMW, those guideposts were: (a) the degree of reprehensibility of the nondisclosure; (b) the disparity between the harm or potential harm suffered by Gore and his punitive damages award;[163] and (c) the difference between this remedy and the civil penalties authorized or imposed in comparable cases. This third guidepost is one that may raise substantial impediments to deterrence-measured punitive awards. In *BMW*, the Court compared the punitive award with statutory fines for similar conduct, with the inevitable result that the punitive award was considered grossly excessive.

De novo review. In 2001, the Court added another layer of control by holding that the amount of punitive awards should be reviewed, not merely for clear error or abuse of discretion, but de novo, that is, without deference to the trial court's decision.[164] The

---

[161] Pacific Mut. Life Ins. Co. v. Haslip, 499 U.S. 1, 20, 111 S.Ct. 1032, 1045, 113 L.Ed.2d 1, 21 (1991). See also TXO Prod. Corp. v. Alliance Res. Corp., 509 U.S. 443, 113 S.Ct. 2711, 125 L.Ed.2d 366 (1993).

[162] BMW of N. Am. v. Gore, 517 U.S. 559, 116 S.Ct. 1589, 134 L.Ed.2d 809 (1996).

[163] In BMW, the Court's language first speaks of the ratio of punitive damages to potential *harm*, id. at 575, 116 S.Ct. at 1598, but later of the ratio of punitive damages to actual *damages*, id. at 580, 116 S.Ct. at 1601. When the Court finally explicates the principle, it returns to the concept of potential harm. Id. at 581, 116 S.Ct. at 1602.

[164] Cooper Indus., Inc. v. Leatherman Tool Group, Inc., 532 U.S. 424, 149 L.Ed. 2d 674, 121 S.Ct. 1678 (2001).

requirement of de novo review also seems to apply to state courts when examining the federal constitutionality of punitive damages awards.[165]

State Farm Mutual Automobile Insurance Company v. Campbell.[166] In 2003, the United States Supreme Court again set aside a punitive award as constitutionally excessive. The defendant insurer had failed to settle within policy limits and used a number of reprehensible tactics in exposing its insured to an excess-of-policy judgment. The plaintiff was able to show that the insurer's practice was part of a larger nefarious scheme carried out in other states as well. Some of the insurer's tactics involved direct mishandling of their own insureds' claims and others concerned indirect harm to their insureds through failing to settle within policy limits. The trial court, reducing a jury's verdict, entered judgment for $1 million compensatory damages and $25 million punitive damages. The Utah Supreme Court reinstated the jury's original punitive verdict of $145 million. The United States Supreme Court held that $145 million was constitutionally excessive.

Ratios. One heavily emphasized concern in *Campbell* was the ratio between harm or potential harm and the punitive damages. However, the Court did not attempt to estimate risks created by the defendant's conduct, that is, *potential* harmful effects. Much less did it attempt to estimate the effects on other State Farm insureds and injured persons. Instead, the Court shifted focus to emphasize the ratio between the punitive award and the actual award of compensatory damages to the particular plaintiff. While the Court said there were no automatic benchmark ratios, it strongly suggested that 4-to-1 would often be the constitutional limit and that in practice, few awards exceeding a single-digit ratio would satisfy due process.[167]

Court reaction. Courts have interpreted the *Campbell* guidelines as sufficiently flexible to permit punitive damages that exceed the Supreme Court's strongly suggested limit.[168] The California Supreme Court has interpreted *Campbell* as establishing a presumption that must be met "absent special justification" such as extreme reprehensibility or unusually small, hard-to-detect or hard-to-measure compensatory damages.[169] The California Court later found a 1-to-1 ratio to be the constitutional maximum in cases with relatively low reprehensibility and a substantial award of noneconomic damages.[170]

---

[165] See Simon v. San Paolo U.S. Holding Co., Inc., 35 Cal.4th 1159, 1172 & n.2, 113 P.3d 63, 29 Cal.Rptr.3d 379 (2005); Groshek v. Trewin, 784 N.W.2d 163 (Wis. 2010). However, a New Mexico court has held that Cooper Industries' de novo review rule is not a constitutional requirement but only a federal procedural standard. Seitzinger v. Trans-Lux Corp., 40 P.3d 1012, 1023 (N.M. Ct. App. 2001).

[166] State Farm Mut. Auto. Ins. Co. v. Campbell, 538 U.S. 408, 123 S.Ct. 1513, 155 L.Ed.2d 585 (2003).

[167] Id. at 424–25; 123 S.Ct. at 1524. See Goddard v. Farmers Ins. Co. of Or., 344 Or. 232, 179 P.3d 645 (2008) (rejecting jury's 16-to-1 award in favor of 4-to-1 award based on "general rule" for economic injuries).

[168] Mitchell, Jr. v. Fortis Ins. Co., 686 S.E.2d 176 (S.C. 2009) (9.2-to-1 ratio in case in which insurer spent no more than 3 minutes on decision for rescission of policy to HIV infected policyholder); Flax v. DaimlerChrysler Corp., 272 S.W.3d 521 (Tenn. 2008) (upholding a 5.35-to-1 ratio award, emphasizing reprehensibility in a wrongful death action). Kemp v. American Tel. & Tel. Co., 393 F.3d 1354 (11th Cir. 2004).

[169] Simon v. San Paolo U.S. Holding Co., Inc., 35 Cal. 4th 1159, 1182, 113 P.3d 63, 77, 29 Cal. Rptr. 3d 379, 395 (2005).

[170] Roby v. McKesson Corp., 47 Cal.4th 686, 718, 219 P.3d 749, 769 (2009) (wrongful discharge and harassment claim). This 1-to-1 ratio has not been seen as an absolute limit where the defendant's conduct was found to be "highly reprehensible," as in Bankhead v. ArvinMeritor, Inc., 205 Cal.App.4th 68, 139 Cal.Rptr.3d 849 (2012), as modified (Apr. 25, 2012), and review denied (July 11, 2012) (affirming a punitive damages award of about 2.4 times the compensatory damages).

Concern with focus on actual compensatory award. Although now seemingly entrenched,[171] the emphasis on the actual compensatory award seems hard to square with the reprehensibility guidepost and hard to square as well with the deterrence function. The risk of harm—meaning both the likelihood of harm and its potential magnitude—bears strongly on the reprehensibility issue, but the actual award to a particular plaintiff does not. Additionally, the emphasis on the compensatory damages award has led some courts to rule that an award of compensatory damages is a necessary prerequisite to an award of punitive damages; otherwise an evaluation of the proportionality of the award would not be possible.[172]

Importance of reprehensibility. Courts applying the Supreme Court's guideposts have focused considerable attention on reprehensibility, at times calling it the most important indicium of the reasonableness of a punitive damages award.[173] Courts have also specified some factors in the evaluation of reprehensibility, for example, whether the harm caused (or threatened) is physical or economic, whether the tortious conduct evinces indifference to or reckless disregard for health and safety, whether the target of the conduct is vulnerable, whether the defendant's conduct involved repeated actions, and whether the harm was the result of malice, trickery or deceit.[174] Courts have also focused on deliberate concealment of wrongdoing and failure to take responsibility for the conduct.[175] The focus on deterring repeated wrongful actions has been interpreted to permit argument that a case is important to wider industry practices beyond the case itself.[176] At the same time, compliance with standards may be evidence tending to show that the conduct was not reprehensible.[177]

Extraterritoriality. The *Campbell* Court also emphasized the plaintiff's use of evidence about State Farm's egregious misconduct in other states. The evidence was offered, not to measure punitive damages but for other purposes, such as to rebut State Farm's claim of inadvertence. The Court recognized that even though the state could not punish lawful out-of-state conduct, a court could admit evidence of such conduct when "it demonstrates the deliberateness and culpability of the defendant's action in the State where it is tortious." Where the out-of-state conduct causes harm to the plaintiffs at their home in the forum state, however, and the conduct is wrongful in both states, there seems to be no reason to exclude punitive damages or impose any special limit on them.[178]

---

[171] See Exxon Shipping Co. v. Baker, 554 U.S. 471, 507, 128 S.Ct 2605, 2629, 171 L.Ed.2d 570 (2008) ("the ratio between compensatory and punitive damages is . . . a central feature in our due process analysis"); Kimble v. Land Concepts, Inc., 845 N.W.2d 395 (Wis.), cert. denied, 135 S.Ct. 359 (2014).

[172] See Perrine v. E.I. du Pont de Nemours & Co., 694 S.E.2d 815, 879 (W.Va. 2010) (rejecting availability of punitive damages in medical monitoring claim); Groshek v. Trewin, 784 N.W.2d 163, 171 (Wis. 2010) (rejecting availability of punitive damages in rescission claim; Chief Justice Abrahamson filied a lengthy dissent).

[173] Mitchell, Jr. v. Fortis Ins. Co, 686 S.E.2d 176 (S.C. 2009).

[174] Id.

[175] Goff v. Elmo Greer & Sons Constr. Co., Inc., 297 S.W.3d 175 (Tenn. 2009) (burying waste tires on property, under 8–9 feet of rock, in violation of agreement with landowners despite repeated reassurances to the contrary).

[176] Weinstein v. Prudential Prop. & Cas. Ins. Co., 233 P.3d 1221 (Idaho 2010).

[177] Malcolm v. Evenflo Co., Inc., 217 P.3d 514 (Mont. 2009).

[178] See Boyd v. Goffoli, 216 W.Va. 552, 608 S.E.2d 169 (2004) (plaintiffs, West Virginia workers, were fraudulently induced to leave jobs in West Virginia and apply for Pennsylvania commercial truck drivers' licenses in a scheme that violated Pennsylvania law and resulted in harm to the plaintiffs at their homes in West Virginia; held, Campbell did not foreclose basing punitive damages in part on the Pennsylvania conduct).

Comparable civil and criminal penalties. The *Campbell* Court also reiterated the idea that criminal and civil penalties for comparable acts serve to indicate how serious the state regards the defendant's wrong, with the idea that the punitive awards should bear some kind of unspecified relationship to those penalties. The Court compared the $145 million punitive damage award to Utah's $10,000 fine for an act of fraud. Because of the immense disparity, the Court failed to specify exactly how to assess the relationship of the punitive damage award to the civil penalty. Courts applying this guidepost discuss it as they must, but some have expressed frustration with the lack of guidance on how to apply it, and ultimately appear to ignore it, particularly when it grossly conflicts with the result suggested by the other two guideposts.[179]

Defendant's wrongs that do not cause the plaintiff's injury. The *Campbell* Court also emphasized that the defendant's wrongdoing unrelated to the plaintiff's claim could not legitimately form the basis for punitive damages. Instead, the plaintiff would be required to show conduct with "a nexus to the specific harm suffered by the plaintiff." In fact, the Court stated what might be an even more demanding standard: "A defendant's dissimilar acts, independent from the acts upon which liability was premised, may not serve as the basis for punitive damages." The Court characterized *Campbell* as a third-party suit, arising because of a claim by the injured person who was not a State Farm insured. Therefore, the Court considered evidence of misconduct in non-third party cases to be dissimilar.[180]

Applying Campbell. Campbell's holding must not be read too broadly. Punitive damages may not be based on *dissimilar* acts that are independent of the acts upon which liability is based,[181] but punitive damages can still be based on post-tort misconduct, such as a manufacturer's cover-up of the facts, even though the cover-up itself did not cause the plaintiff's injury.[182] Some "nexus" is required between the injury or injury-causing conduct and the defendant's other wrongful conduct, but a general requirement of a "nexus" seems to leave a degree of flexibility in striving for fair deterrence-measured punitive awards.[183] One solution is to hold that (a) conduct not causing compensatory damages to the plaintiff may not be used as a *basis* for awarding punitive damages, but (b) such conduct may bear on reprehensibility and hence on the *amount* of punitive damages when punitive damages are otherwise authorized.[184]

---

[179] Flax v. DaimlerChrysler Corp., 272 S.W.3d 521, 539–40 (Tenn. 2008); see also Willow Inn, Inc. v. Public Serv. Mut. Ins. Co., 399 F.3d 224, 237–38 (3d Cir. 2005).

[180] The Court thus appears to apply a very narrow concept of similarity. Although third-party claims are different from first-party claims, the Utah courts believed that the evidence in Campbell showed a larger scheme to systematically cheat its own insureds, regardless of the nature of the claim, and to cover up the evidence. Thus, a common purpose or similar modes of committing two different acts is seemingly not enough to establish similarity when it comes to applying constitutional limits to punitive damages.

[181] The later decision in Philip Morris USA v. Williams, 549 U.S. 346, 127 S.Ct. 1057 (2006), discussed below, appears to support this view.

[182] As to punitive liability for post-injury conduct, see 2 Dobbs, Hayden & Bublick, The Law of Torts § 469 (2d ed. 2011 & Supp.).

[183] See In re Tobacco Litig., 218 W.Va. 301, 624 S.E.2d 738 (2005) (in consolidated cases, allowing a determination of the punitive damages multiplier before assessing individual compensatory damages in a second stage of trial, using a "reasonably related" standard rather than a standard requiring punitive damages must be based on "acts upon which liability was premised").

[184] See BMW of N. Am., Inc. v. Gore, 517 U.S. at 574 n.21, 116 S.Ct. at 1598 n. 21; Johnson v. Ford Motor Co., 35 Cal.4th 1191, 113 P.3d 82, 29 Cal.Rptr.3d 401 (2005); Schwarz v. Philip Morris Inc., 235 P.3d 668 (Or. 2010).

Philip Morris USA v. Williams.[185] Something similar to this last-stated view appears to have been accepted by the Supreme Court in 2007. The defendant was found liable for its sale of cancer-causing cigarettes which were represented as safe. Many people had undoubtedly been harmed and killed over the years the defendant maintained this conduct. The plaintiffs apparently suggested to the jury that jurors could "punish" the defendant for harms inflicted on victims who were not parties. The defendant sought an instruction that would allow the jury to consider harms to non-parties in determining the ratio of punitive to compensatory damages, but that would tell the jury it could not punish Philip Morris for harms done to others. The Court held that the Constitution does not permit direct punishment of a defendant for harms it has inflicted on nonparties. One reason was that the defendant could not defend itself appropriately. Another was that the court regarded such an approach as being without standards because the trial court is not likely to know how many such victims there are or the circumstances of their injuries. However, the Court went on to say that the plaintiff may offer evidence of harm to others on the issue of reprehensibility of the defendant's conduct, which in turn indirectly bears on the amount of the punitive award. The difference between the constitutionally forbidden direct punishment for nonparty injury and the permitted consideration of those same nonparty injuries in determining the amount of punitive liability may be hard to discern in trials where a lawyer's incorrect phrasing in the heat of argument may lead to constitutional objections.

Lessons from Exxon Shipping Company v. Baker.[186] In 2008, although deciding the limits of federal common law, not constitutional limits, on punitive damages awards, the Supreme Court provided insight into the constitutional requirements through Justice Souter's lengthy discussion of the history and perceived problems remaining with punitive damages jurisprudence. The Court held that the "fair upper limit" ratio of punitive damages to compensatory damages in admiralty cases is 1-to-1, and on that basis reduced the award of punitive damages in one of the Exxon Valdez cases to just over $500 million. The Court's holding reinforced concepts from its previous constitutional decisions when it ruled that the 1-to-1 ratio was justified because the compensatory damages in the case were "substantial,"[187] also supporting the argument that courts may more freely exceed lower ratios when the compensatory damages themselves are low.

Deterrence and profitability of wrongdoing. Emphasis on ratios, comparable penalties, and perhaps other guideposts tends to ignore factors that must be considered to provide adequate deterrence, especially against repeat economic offenders. These factors include, notably, profitability of the wrongdoing[188] and the likelihood that the defendant will often escape liability altogether because victims do not identify the defendant as the cause of their injuries or the cost of litigation.[189] Courts have said, however, that while deterrence objectives may be compromised in some cases by the Supreme Court's decisions, the goal of deterring wrongful conduct is still a legitimate one. Thus although the Supreme Court did not list the defendant's wealth as one of the

[185] Philip Morris USA v. Williams, 549 U.S. 346, 127 S.Ct. 1057, 166 L.Ed.2d 940 (2007).

[186] Exxon Shipping Co. v. Baker, 554 U.S. 471, 128 S.Ct. 2605, 171 L.Ed.2d 570 (2008).

[187] See also State Farm Mut. Auto. Ins. Co. v. Campbell, 538 U.S. 408, 425, 123 S.Ct. 1513, 155 L.Ed.2d 585 (2003).

[188] Dan B. Dobbs, Ending Punishment in "Punitive" Damages: Deterrence-Measured Remedies, 40 Ala. L. Rev. 831, 871–88 (1989).

[189] See § 34.5.

guideposts, in appropriate cases profitability and wealth, along with the cost and difficulty of enforcement, can still be factors in measuring the punitive award.[190]

§ 34.7 "Tort Reform" Statutes Affecting Compensatory and Punitive Damages

Tort reform. The drive to restrict tort liability has generally been referred to as "tort reform." Whether reform is needed or desirable is hotly debated.[191] However, tort reform has succeeded in many states by imposing preconditions to suit, shortening statutes of limitations, modifying the collateral source rule, abolishing joint and several liability, raising the plaintiff's burden of proof, and, most directly, limiting compensatory and punitive damages. The last is the topic of this section.

Capping statutes—cases covered. The most severe tort reform statutes put a limit or cap on recovery of compensatory damages. Well over half of the states have enacted some kind of cap on damages recoverable. In some instances the cap applies only to particular kinds of tort claims, such as claims for professional malpractice,[192] suits against public entities,[193] or suits against alcohol providers.[194] A California statute eliminates pain damages suffered by uninsured motorists.[195] For claims arising out of the terrorist attack of September 11, 2001, the federal September 11th Victims' Compensation statute eliminates some suits and caps damages in others.[196] Other statutes cap all tort claims.[197]

What damages are capped; varied amounts. The statutes are diverse in other ways, too, sometimes capping damages but providing the plaintiff with substitute claims against a fund to care for extreme cases.[198] Statutes may impose an absolute cap on all damages[199] or may impose a cap only on "noneconomic" damages like those awarded for pain and suffering.[200] The statutory cap on recovery varies from state to state. Utah says

[190] White v. Ford Motor Co., 500 F.3d 963 (9th Cir. 2007); Mathias v. Accor Econ. Lodging, Inc., 347 F.3d 672 (7th Cir. 2003); Simon v. San Paolo U.S. Holding Co., Inc., 35 Cal. 4th 1159, 113 P.3d 63, 29 Cal. Rptr. 3d 379 (2005); International Union of Operating Eng'rs, Local 150 v. Lowe Excavating Co., 225 Ill.2d 456, 870 N.E.2d 303, 312 Ill. Dec. 238 (2006); Tarr v. Bob Ciasulli's Mack Auto Mall, Inc., 194 N.J. 212, 943 A.2d 866 (2008); Williams v. Philip Morris Inc., 344 Or. 45, 176 P.3d 1255 (2008).

[191] The arguments on both sides are considered in 3 Dobbs, Hayden & Bublick, The Law of Torts § 502 (2d ed. 2011 & Supp.).

[192] E.g., Cal. Civ. Code § 3333.2 (professional negligence).

[193] E.g., Boiter v. South Carolina Dep't of Transp., 393 S.C. 123, 712 S.E.2d 401 (2011); Oliver v. Cleveland Indians Baseball Co. Ltd. P'ship, 915 N.E.2d 1205 (Ohio 2009); Me. Rev. Stat. Ann. tit. 14 § 8105. Or. Rev. Stat. Ann. § 30.270(1), which limited compensatory damages against public bodies, was declared unconstitutional for violating the state constitution's remedy clause in Clarke v. Oregon Health Sciences Univ., 343 Or. 581, 175 P.3d 418 (2007).

[194] E.g., Utah Code Ann. § 32A–14–101(5) ($500,000 cap).

[195] Cal. Civ. Code § 3333.4. See Allen v. Sully-Miller Contracting Co., 28 Cal.4th 222, 47 P.3d 639, 120 Cal.Rptr.2d 795 (2002) (applying the statute to bar a recovery for pain in a suit for a property defect that caused the plaintiff's motorcycle to overturn).

[196] September 11th Victim Compensation Fund of 2001, Pub.L. 107–42 tit. IV, 115 Stat. 230 (2001) (uncodified sections reprinted in the United States Code Annotated notes following 49 U.S.C.A. § 40401).

[197] Md. Code Ann., Cts. & Jud. Proc. § 11–108.

[198] La. Rev. Stat. Ann. § 40:1299.42; see Butler v. Flint Goodrich Hosp., 607 So. 2d 517 (La. 1992).

[199] Colo. Rev. Stat. § 13–64–302; Va. Code § 8.01–581.15 ($1 million cap on total damages against health care provider).

[200] Cal. Civ. Code § 3333.2; Md. Code Ann., Cts. & Jud. Proc. § 11–108; Ohio Rev. Code Ann. § 2315.18 (as amended 2005); Green v. N.B.S, 976 A.2d 279 (Md. 2009) (applying Maryland's statutory cap on noneconomic damages in personal injury actions).

alcohol providers cannot be liable for more than $500,000.[201] California's cap for pain and suffering is $250,000.[202] Kansas permits only $250,000 in recovery for noneconomic harms in death actions, an extreme limit but one that is mitigated in some cases because sums received in settlement do not count against the cap. This means that a plaintiff who settles with one tortfeasor for $100,000 could still recover $100,000 from another tortfeasor.[203] Ohio's statute, revised after being declared unconstitutional, limits noneconomic damages in most tort cases to the greater of (1) $250,000 or (2) three times the economic damages up to a maximum of $350,000, or $500,000 per single occurrence, with a further caveat: these limits do not apply if the plaintiff suffered "permanent and substantial physical deformity, loss of use of a limb, or loss of a bodily organ system," or "permanent physical functional injury that permanently prevents the injured person from being able to independently care for self and perform life-sustaining activities."[204] When multiple tortfeasors and claims are involved, applying the caps raises difficult logistical issues.[205]

Objections to caps. So far as a cap is effective, the punitive award will be calibrated to neither the defendant's aggravated misconduct nor the need for deterrence. And caps do not necessarily accomplish much.[206] They can prevent excessive punitive awards that are also higher than the cap, but they do not address the problem of excess awards at lower levels.[207] In close cases, judges and juries may actually tend to balloon the award to the cap level.[208] Finally, caps on punitive damages, like an outright prohibition of punitive damages, can protect against excessive awards, but the cap necessarily protects those tortfeasors who are perceived by the trier to be guilty of the most aggravated misconduct. In practice, the most central probably is that reduction of damages actually suffered eliminates appropriate compensation and reduces appropriate levels of deterrence. Defendants have supported caps on the theory that by reducing liabilities they can reduce insurance premiums. But if damages were correctly figured before caps were introduced, that argument translates to an argument that seriously injured individuals must suffer without compensation for the benefit of others.[209] It makes A pay so B can save money.

Constitutionality. Plaintiffs have presented several arguments that damages caps are unconstitutional. They have asserted the right to a jury trial, equal protection, due

---

[201] Utah Code Ann. § 32A–14–101(5).

[202] Cal. Civ. Code § 3333.2.

[203] Kan. Stat. Ann. § 60–1903; see Adams v. Via Christi Reg'l Med. Ctr., 19 P.3d 132 (Kan. 2001).

[204] Ohio Rev. Code Ann. § 2315.18(B) (as amended 2005). This portion was upheld against constitutional attack in Arbino v. Johnson & Johnson, 116 Ohio St.3d 468, 880 N.E.2d 420 (2007).

[205] See 3 Dobbs, Hayden & Bublick, The Law of Torts § 485 (2d ed. 2011 & Supp.).

[206] See, e.g., Thomas A. Eaton, et al., The Effects of Seeking Punitive Damages on the Processing of Tort Claims, 34 J. Legal Stud. 343 (2005) (study finding "no statistically significant impact on most phases of the litigation process," except that suits with uncapped punitive damages claims were less likely to settle and more likely to go to trial than suits with capped punitive damages claims).

[207] A cap of, say, $250,000 on punitive damages does not at all touch the median punitive award in many counties. An American Bar Foundation study found that the median punitive award was as low as $10,000 in some counties with a top of $204,000 in San Diego. See Michael L. Rustad, Unraveling Punitive Damages: Current Data and Further Inquiry, 1998 Wis. L. Rev. 15, 20–30.

[208] Cf. Luciano v. Olsten Corp., 110 F.3d 210 (2d Cir. 1996) (the maximum is not the ceiling on a scale, so trier can fix the award at the maximum even if the misconduct is not the worst imaginable).

[209] See Morris v. Savoy, 61 Ohio St.3d 684, 691, 576 N.E.2d 765, 771 (1991) (cap imposes "the cost of the intended benefit to the general public solely upon a class consisting of those most severely injured by medical malpractice").

process, and separation of powers under state constitutional provisions and others. A number of courts have found particular statutes unconstitutional on one ground or another.[210] Other courts have upheld caps. Some of these broadly reject arguments based on due process, equal protection, the right to a jury trial or taking of property,[211] but others have upheld the caps only because the legislature provided the victim with some substitute remedy such as a claim against a Patient Compensation Fund when damages were higher than the cap.[212] In one Oregon case, the court upheld damages caps against constitutional attack in a wrongful death case on the ground that the "remedy" guarantee of the state Constitution applied by its terms to protect remedies in causes of action that were recognized at the time of the drafting of the Constitution in 1857, and that wrongful death claims did not exist at all at common law and were only later authorized by statute.[213]

Limiting pain and suffering damages without caps. The tort reform statutes have so far attempted to limit compensatory damages only through raw caps, but students of the problem have been developing others kinds of limits for pain and suffering damages, not to create a windfall for tortfeasors, but because such damages are inherently difficult to estimate. One kind of limitation would reverse the cap effect and exclude small rather than large claims by imposing a minimum threshold. Much as a collision insurance policy might not cover the first $100 dollars of the loss, this kind of rule would disallow pain and suffering damages that were not significant in amount.[214] The second kind of limitation would ask jurors to compare the case they heard with a set of ten or so other

---

[210] Moore v. Mobile Infirmary Ass'n, 592 So.2d 156 (Ala. 1991) (malpractice noneconomic damage cap denied right to jury trial and equal protection; statute created favored class of defendants); Bayer CropScience LP v. Schafer, 385 S.W.3d 822 (Ark. 2011) (statutory cap on punitive damages unconstitutional under section of Arkansas Constitution prohibiting the legislature from limiting the amount to be recovered for injuries resulting in death or for injuries to persons or property); Smith v. Department of Ins., 507 So.2d 1080 (Fla. 1987); Best v. Taylor Mach. Works, 179 Ill.2d 367, 413, 689 N.E.2d 1057, 1080, 228 Ill.Dec. 636, 659 (1997) (noneconomic damages generally capped at $500,000; the statute "undercuts the power, and obligation, of the judiciary to reduce excessive verdicts" and violates separation of powers provisions); Lewellen v. Franklin, 441 S.W.3d 136 (Mo. 2014) (cap on punitive damages violates state constitutional right to trial by jury); State v. Sheward, 86 Ohio St.3d 451, 715 N.E.2d 1062 (1999) (first-taker rule for punitive damages unconstitutionally deprived plaintiff of jury trial); Morris v. Savoy, 61 Ohio St.3d 684, 576 N.E.2d 765 (1991) (medical malpractice cap was irrational and arbitrary and violates due process); Klutschkowski v. PeaceHealth, 311 P.3d 461 (Or. 2013) (cap on economic damages unconstitutional under jury trial provision of Oregon constitution); Ferdon v. Wisconsin Patients Comp. Fund, 284 Wis. 2d 573, 701 N.W.2d 440 (2005) (noneconomic damage cap of $350,000 in medical malpractice claims violated state constitution's equal protection provision; there was no rational basis for caps that made the worst-injured malpractice victims contribute part of their damages to medical insurers and data showed no basis for thinking that caps would reduce insurance costs).

[211] Patton v. TIC United Corp., 77 F.3d 1235 (10th Cir. 1996); Fein v. Permanente Med. Group, 38 Cal.3d 137, 695 P.2d 665, 211 Cal.Rptr. 368 (1985); Garhart v. Columbia/Healthone, LLC, 95 P.3d 571 (Colo. 2004); Kirkland v. Blaine County Med. Ctr., 4 P.3d 1115 (Idaho 2000); Murphy v. Edmonds, 325 Md. 342, 601 A.2d 102 (1992); Sanders v. Ahmed, 364 S.W.3d 195 (Mo. 2012); Gourley v. Nebraska Methodist Health Sys., Inc., 265 Neb. 918, 663 N.W.2d 43 (2003); Robinson v. Charleston Area Med. Ctr., Inc., 186 W.Va. 720, 414 S.E.2d 877 (1991). Cf. Estate of McCall ex rel. McCall v. U.S., 642 F.3d 944 (11th Cir. 2011).

[212] Univ. of Miami v. Echarte, 618 So.2d 189 (Fla. 1993) (caps apply only when defendant accepts arbitration, regarded as an offsetting benefit); Butler v. Flint Goodrich Hosp., 607 So.2d 517 (La. 1992) (patient compensation fund). See also Miller v. Johnson, 295 Kan. 636, 289 P.3d 1098 (2012) (upholding constitutionality of cap on non-economic damages in medical malpractice cases in part because legislature provided a substitute remedy in the form of a patient compensation fund). Cf. Samples v. Florida Birth-Related Neurological Injury Comp. Ass'n, 114 So.3d 912 (Fla. 2013) (upholding constitutionality of damage caps in case of birth-related neurological injury where statute provides for no-fault insurance via an alternative plan).

[213] Hughes v. PeaceHealth, 344 Or. 142, 178 P.3d 225 (2008).

[214] See II American Law Institute, Reporter's Study, Enterprise Responsibility for Personal Injury 230 (1991).

standardized scenarios ranging from very little injury and pain to the most serious.[215] The law could fix damages for each scenario and the jury's decision that their case was worse than scenario 5 and not as bad as scenario 6 would narrow the available pain and suffering damages. A more complicated version would not assign pre-set values to the scenarios, but rather advise the jury of the national or state average awards for cases similar to each scenario. Several other variations on this approach can be imagined.[216] A narrower and more flexible version of standardized damages for pain has appeared in some of the suits by former hostages or their estates against countries that sponsored abduction and torture. As one court said: "Subject to adjustment for cases deviating from the more common experience of victims, this Court typically has awarded former hostages or their estates roughly $10,000 for each day of captivity." The same court added $1 million "for the portion of that time that [the hostage] faced certain death alone."[217]

Comparative scales. One study came up with a surprising finding.[218] In many mock trials, jurors of diverse wealth, education, gender and ethnicity came to almost complete agreement about punitive damages issues when they were allowed to rate the conduct on a given scale, say one to six. Their agreement disappeared when they tried to convert to dollars. The indication is that a set of scenarios or even a scale of one to ten would increase predictability of awards for both punitive and pain and suffering damages. These studies offer considerable opportunity for eliminating the occasional run-away verdict without imposing caps that make the most injured absorb the costs.

Reallocation of punitive damages. Several states provide for allocation of a portion of the punitive award to a state agency.[219] From the point of view of the plaintiff, this reallocation operates like a cap. From the defendant's point of view, this reallocation does nothing to minimize punitive damages awarded. The defendant's protection from statutes like this comes much earlier. The limitation on punitive damages may cut the funds from which attorneys' fees and litigation costs can be paid, with the result that some suits will not be pursued at all. When suits are not pursued because it is financially infeasible under these statutes, the defendants who most deserve punishment or deterrence may be the ones who escape liability altogether. The most recent cases have upheld the redirection or "forfeiture" of a portion of the punitive award against state constitutional challenges based on guaranteed remedies, substantive due process, jury trial rights, and taking of property without just compensation.[220]

---

[215] Randal R. Bovbjerg, Frank A. Sloan & James F. Blumstein, Valuing Life and Limb in Tort: Scheduling "Pain and Suffering", 83 Nw. U. L. Rev. 908 (1989) (considers variations and details).

[216] See § 36.6 (the grids used in social security claims).

[217] Surette v. Islamic Republic of Iran, 231 F.Supp. 2d 60 (D.D.C. 2002).

[218] Cass R. Sunstein, et al., Assessing Punitive Damages (With Notes on Cognition and Valuation in Law), 107 Yale L.J. 2071 (1998).

[219] Iowa Code Ann. § 668A.1 (75% or more to a state agency except when tort is "directed at" the plaintiff).

[220] See Evans v. State, 56 P.3d 1046 (Alaska 2002) (affirming 2–2 a judgment upholding constitutionality); Cheatham v. Pohle, 789 N.E.2d 467 (Ind. 2002); DeMendoza v. Huffman, 334 Or. 425, 51 P.3d 1232 (2002).

Chapter 35

APPORTIONMENT OF LIABILITY
AMONG PARTIES

Analysis

A. INTRODUCTION: JOINT AND SEVERAL LIABILITY
AND SEVERAL LIABILITY

§ 35.1   Apportionment of Liability: An Overview
§ 35.2   Traditional Rules and Joint and Several Liability
§ 35.3   Joint and Several Liability vs. Several Liability Systems
§ 35.4   Several Liability Systems
§ 35.5   General Effects of Adopting Several Liability Systems

B. PERSONS AND CONDUCT SUBJECT TO APPORTIONMENT

§ 35.6   Immune and Nonparty Tortfeasors
§ 35.7   Types of Actionable Conduct Subject to Apportionment

C. STANDARDS

§ 35.8   Apportionment Standards

D. SPECIAL CASES FOR APPORTIONMENT

§ 35.9   Defendants Who Negligently Risk Another Tortfeasor's Intentional Harm
§ 35.10 Defendants Who Are Under a Duty to Protect Plaintiff from Another's Negligence

E. OTHER APPORTIONMENT SYSTEMS

§ 35.11 Joint and Several Liability with Reallocation
§ 35.12 Hybrid Systems: Joint and Several Liability Based on Threshold Percentages or Type of Damages

---

A.   INTRODUCTION: JOINT AND SEVERAL LIABILITY
AND SEVERAL LIABILITY

§ 35.1 Apportionment of Liability: An Overview

Apportionment basics. When the tortious conduct of multiple parties causes a harm, questions arise about how to divide responsibility for damages among the various actors. This issue of damages division is addressed by the rules of apportionment of liability. There are two basic forms of liability apportionment: causal apportionment and fault or responsibility based apportionment.[1]

---

[1]   When the negligence of various parties was being compared, this was often referred to as comparative "fault." However, now that some jurisdictions compare conduct such as strict liability as well, the term comparative "responsibility" is often used. The term "fault or responsibility based apportionment" is used to denote apportionment that includes the fault or legal responsibility of the party as at least one factor in the apportionment. Restatement (Third) of Torts: Apportionment of Liability § 1 (2000).

Causal apportionment. When two or more tortfeasors cause divisible harms to the plaintiff, most authorities agree that causal apportionment should be employed.[2] For example, if tortfeasor A negligently causes the plaintiff to suffer a broken leg and tortfeasor B negligently causes the plaintiff to suffer a broken arm, each tortfeasor is normally liable for 100% of the damages that the tortfeasor separately caused.[3] Causal apportionment,[4] may also be required when the plaintiff suffers a single injury rather than distinct harms but the single injury is capable of being apportioned in some rational way.[5] The principle of causal apportionment can apply between a plaintiff and a defendant as well as between defendants, as where the defendant's asbestos causes lung damage and the plaintiff's smoking causes a different lung damage, with both contributing to a shortness of breath. If evidence shows a basis for saying that the asbestos caused 90% of the disability, the defendant will be liable only for that portion of the harm. If no evidence shows a basis for causal apportionment, the court may allocate liability in proportion to fault or responsibility instead,[6] unless special considerations of public policy bar fault apportionment.[7]

Fault apportionment. Fault apportionment takes place when a plaintiff has suffered a single indivisible injury at the hands of two or more tortfeasors and the loss cannot be reasonably allocated by causal measures between the two. Instead, the loss is allocated based on percentages of fault. For example, suppose tortfeasor A, who is speeding, crashes into plaintiff's car. Tortfeasor B, who is sending a text message while driving, fails to keep a lookout and hits the plaintiff's car as well. The plaintiff emerges from the near-simultaneous accidents with a serious back injury. Experts attribute the injury to the combined impact of the crashes but cannot segregate the amount of harm caused by each. Because both defendants are factual causes of the plaintiff's single injury and no causal apportionment of the injury is possible, a jury would be asked to apportion liability by assigning a percentage of fault or responsibility to each defendant.

Joint and several liability. Suppose the jury finds that defendant A is chargeable with 60% of the fault and defendant B with 40% of the fault. The jury also finds that the plaintiff has suffered $100,000 in damages: $50,000 in past and future medical expenses and $50,000 in pain and suffering. If joint and several liability applies, each defendant will be liable to the plaintiff for the full $100,000 in damages, subject to the caveat that the plaintiff can only receive one satisfaction of the judgment. Consequently, if the plaintiff recovers the full $100,000 from defendant A, she can recover nothing at all against defendant B. However, defendant A can call upon defendant B for contribution for the $40,000 owed by B.

---

[2]   Id. § 26; Restatement (Third) of Torts: Products Liability § 16 (1998).

[3]   Restatement (Third) of Torts: Apportionment of Liability § 26 (2000).

[4]   For a discussion of several forms of causal apportionment, see Chapter 14. For a discussion of causal apportionment in products liability, see Dobbs, Hayden & Bublick, The Law of Torts § 471 (2d ed. 2011 & Supp.).

[5]   Restatement (Third) of Torts: Apportionment of Liability § 26 cmts. f, h, k (2000).

[6]   On similar facts, but when no evidence permitted causal apportionment, the court upheld a jury award that apportioned 50% of the fault to the defendant as supplier of the asbestos. Owens Corning Fiberglass Corp. v. Parrish, 58 S.W.3d 467 (Ky. 2001).

[7]   For example, because CERCLA maintains joint and several liability, only causal apportionment is appropriate to that context. See Burlington N. & Santa Fe Ry. Co. v. U.S., 556 U.S. 599, 129 S.Ct. 1870 (2009) ("Equitable considerations play no role in the apportionment analysis; rather, apportionment is proper only when the evidence supports the divisibility of the damages jointly caused by the [potentially responsible parties]").

Several liability. If on the other hand, several liability applies, the plaintiff only can call on defendant A for payment of $60,000 and defendant B for payment of $40,000. If either of the two negligent defendants cannot pay, it is the plaintiff who will bear the uncompensated loss.

Other ways to apportion liability; joint and several liability for economic damages. Although joint and several liability and several liability are two prominent options for sharing the loss, they are far from the only options. Some jurisdictions retain joint and several liability, but only for certain elements of the damages such as those based on the economic harm done to the plaintiff. In a jurisdiction like this, not only would defendant A pay the $60,000 liability assigned to A, but also defendant A would be jointly and severally liable for the $20,000 of defendant B's liability to plaintiff for economic losses (40% of the plaintiff's $50,000 economic loss damages). Defendant A would not be jointly and severally liable for the $20,000 of defendant B's share of the judgment that was due to pain and suffering. Similarly, some jurisdictions retain joint and several liability only if the defendant's percentage of responsibility exceeds a certain threshold percentage such as 50%. In a jurisdiction with this rule, defendant A, assigned 60% of the liability, would be jointly and severally liable for defendant B's uncollectible share. However, defendant B, assigned 40% of the total liability, would not be jointly and severally liable if defendant A's share were uncollectible. Other possibilities exist.

Joint and several liability with reallocation. Some jurisdictions have joint and several liability with reallocation. This means that if the plaintiff cannot collect a judgment from one of the parties, that portion of the judgment will be reallocated among the remaining parties on the basis of the remaining parties' fault. In the example with defendant A and B, because the plaintiff was assigned no fault, defendant A would bear the full cost of defendant B's insolvency. However, if instead the plaintiff had been assigned 30% of the fault and defendant A 30% of the fault, defendant B's uncollectible 40% share would be split by defendant A and the plaintiff 1:1—each would bear their assigned shares of the loss plus one-half of B's share.

Varied rules. As the variations in these illustrations suggest, apportionment of liability among multiple actors, once a fairly straightforward topic, has now become increasingly fragmented and complex. In fact, so divided is state law that when the Restatement Third of Torts was published at the start of the millennium, its provisions recognized five alternative "tracks" of liability apportionment that states might employ to address the situation of multiple tortfeasors who create indivisible harms—one for joint and several liability, another for several liability, one for joint and several liability with reallocation, another for hybrid liability based on a threshold percentage of comparative responsibility, and a final chapter on hybrid liability based on the type of damages.[8] And the categories are not mutually exclusive.[9] Indeed, given the varied apportionment-related statutes and case law in existence at the time the Restatement was enacted,[10] no single approach to the issue could have been followed in all

---

[8]   Restatement (Third) of Torts: Apportionment of Liability §§ 17, A18-E21 (2000); Edward J. Kionka, Recent Developments in the Law of Joint and Several Liability and the Impact of Plaintiff's Employer's Fault, 54 La. L. Rev. 1619 (1994). One English commentator has called the tracked sections of the Restatement of Apportionment "a trackless morass, Dismal Swamp, and Desolation of Smaug." Tony Weir, All-or-nothing?, 78 Tul. L. Rev. 511, 534 n.63 (2004).

[9]   Restatement (Third) of Torts: Apportionment of Liability § 17 rptr. note (2000) (noting states that employ multiple systems).

[10]   Restatement (Third) of Torts: Apportionment of Liability § 17 tables at 151 to 159 (2000).

jurisdictions. As is the case whenever statutes pervade and state case law varies, reference to the legislation and precedent of particular jurisdictions is essential. Despite jurisdictional differences, the issue of indivisible injury remains significant across the board. In joint and several liability the defendant is liable for that indivisible injury. In other types of apportionment of liability arrangements, the fact that the plaintiff suffered an indivisible injury remains significant because the defendant's percentage of liability is measured as a portion of the total of plaintiff's indivisible injury damages.[11]

Issues within apportionment systems. Jurisdictional difference concerning joint and several liability and several liability frames the organization of the Restatement and informs the structure of this chapter. However, many additional issues divide and pervade the apportionment landscape. In joint and several liability systems, one of the most important questions is how joint liabilities are divided between multiple tortfeasors through contribution and indemnity. In several liability systems, contribution issues arise much less frequently, but courts have many other issues to resolve. Because several liability systems typically apportion liability into mutually exclusive portions, the key questions in these systems center on (1) which types of conduct and which types of actors can be a part of the apportionment percentages, (2) on what basis percentage apportionments are made, and (3) in what circumstances exceptions to the several liability rule are called for.

Apportionment and policy choices. Courts frequently address apportionment of liability as though the apportionment itself is a neutral issue—the defendant should be accountable for its fair share of responsibility and no more. However, the variation in state answers to the question of what constitutes a fair share of damages for which to hold a defendant to account, highlights just how important a policy question apportionment of liability has become.

Terminology. Unfortunately, there is no uniform nomenclature that marks which types of actionable conduct are included in a jurisdiction's apportionment of liability system. Because strict liability and negligence are types of conduct compared in some jurisdictions, the term comparative "negligence" or even comparative "fault" becomes problematic. When jurisdictions use the term comparative "responsibility," it is typically employed because the comparisons include at least one form of actionable conduct in addition to negligence, such as strict liability. A "comparative fault" system might include comparisons across types of actionable misconduct,[12] or it might not.[13] Comparative "negligence" systems are more likely to focus on negligent acts alone. The term "apportionment of liability" in this chapter is used as an umbrella term to encompass all forms of apportionment.

---

[11] Piner v. Superior Court, 192 Ariz. 182, 962 P.2d 909 (1998); Gross v. Lyons, 763 So. 2d 276 (Fla. 2000). Shifting the burden to the defendants to show apportionment in indivisible injury cases, as in Yount v. Deibert, 147 P.3d 1065 (Kan. 2006), might lead to a similar analysis. This may lead to quite complex calculations if there are multiple parties in two or more separate injuries that lead to an indivisible result.

[12] See, e.g., Hutcherson v. City of Phoenix, 961 P.2d 449 (Ariz. 1998) (holding that plain meaning of the statutory term "fault" included intentional torts); Couch v. Red Roof Inns, Inc., 291 Ga. 359, 729 S.E.2d 378 (2012) (statute calls for the allocation of damages among those at "fault"; intentional assailant was partially at fault for purpose of apportioning damages in premises liability case involving an attack on a guest while staying at hotel).

[13] See, e.g., Welch v. Southland Corp., 952 P.2d 162 (Wash. 1998) (holding that unambiguous definition of "fault" does not include intentional torts).

§ 35.2   Traditional Rules and Joint and Several Liability

The meaning of joint and several liability. Joint and several liability has been recognized since the 1700s,[14] and has been supported by influential torts commentators for some time.[15] When two or more tortfeasors are jointly and severally liable, each defendant is subject to liability for all of the plaintiff's damages.[16] The effect is to provide the plaintiff with more than one source of funds but not more than one complete satisfaction.[17] If tortfeasor A has few assets and is underinsured, or A enjoys an immunity or partial immunity, the plaintiff may be able to enforce the judgment against tortfeasor B.

Three traditional rules. Apart from the rule requiring causal apportionment where possible, three other fundamental rules traditionally governed the apportionment of responsibility among multiple tortfeasors and the plaintiffs.

(1) *Indivisible injury.* If the injury was indivisible in nature (a death or a single broken arm for example), then each tortfeasor who contributed proximately to that injury was liable for the entire judgment, although the plaintiff could not collect more than one full recovery.[18] This is often referred to as a rule for concurrent torts, but concurrence in time is not required. The essence of the rule is that each tortfeasor is liable in full for an indivisible injury.[19] At one time this rule was cluttered with procedural problems in joinder, but all parties can now usually be joined.

(2) *Actions in concert, vicarious liability.* Whether or not the injury was indivisible, if the defendants acted in concert, or one defendant acted tortiously and the other was vicariously liable, each defendant was liable for the entire injury.[20]

(3) *Contribution.* Apportionment is completed under the rule that when one tortfeasor paid more than his appropriate share of liability, he could ordinarily obtain contribution from the other tortfeasors, a rule generally followed in the latter part of the 20th century.

Current joint and several liability rules. In 2000, about 14 states retained substantial joint and several liability rules, and 4 more retained joint and several liability when the plaintiff is not legally responsible for any part of her own injury.[21] The Supreme Court has also retained joint and several liability in Federal Employers

[14] See Merryweather v. Nixan, 101 Eng. Rep. 1337 (1799) (reflecting one tortfeasor's payment of the entire liability).

[15] See, e.g., William Prosser, Joint Torts and Several Liability, 25 Cal. L. Rev. 413 (1937); John Henry Wigmore, Joint-Tortfeasors and Severance of Damages: Making the Innocent Party Suffer Without Redress, 17 Ill. L. Rev. 458 (1923).

[16] Restatement (Third) of Torts: Apportionment of Liability § 27A (2000); John W. Wade, Should Joint and Several Liability of Multiple Tortfeasors Be Abolished?, 10 Am. J. Trial Advoc. 193 (1986).

[17] Complete satisfaction of the claim by one tortfeasor thus bars the plaintiff's claim against another tortfeasor. Underwood-Gary v. Mathews, 366 Md. 660, 785 A.2d 708 (2001).

[18] See also Bridgestone/Firestone North America Tire, LLC v. Naranjo, 206 Ariz. 447, 79 P.3d 1206 (Ct. App. 2003).

[19] See Watts v. Smith, 375 Mich. 120, 134 N.W.2d 194 (1965).

[20] E.g., Biercyznski v. Rogers, 239 A.2d 218 (Del. 1968). This remains the rule today in a number of states. Smith v. Town of Greenwich, 899 A.2d 563 (Conn. App. Ct. 2006); Richards v. Badger Mut. Ins. Co., 309 Wis.2d 541, 749 N.W.2d 581 (2008); Restatement (Third) of Torts: Apportionment of Liability § 24 (2000).

[21] Restatement (Third) of Torts: Apportionment of Liability § 17 at 151–53 (2000).

Liability Act (FELA) cases.[22] Even when jurisdictions apply several liability as the normal rule, joint and several liability sometimes applies.[23]

Contribution and indemnity. Because multiple defendants can be fully liable to the plaintiff under joint and several liability, the division of damages liability between the defendants through contribution or indemnity is an important part of fairly distributing the ultimate liability. The history of contribution and indemnity, the requirements for making such claims, the way in which contribution is measured, and the credits issued are complicated issues only touched on here.[24]

Contribution. Either by statute or judicial decision, a right of contribution is now a generally accepted part of the joint and several liability system[25] except that contribution may still be denied to intentional tortfeasors.[26] Early statutes authorized contribution only when one tortfeasor satisfied a judgment for the plaintiff; the same tortfeasor's settlement with the plaintiff would not support a contribution claim against the other tortfeasors. These statutes have in effect been broadened by judicial decisions creating a contribution right even in cases of settlement, somewhat misleadingly called "equitable indemnity."[27] Other statutes specifically authorize contribution in favor of a tortfeasor who satisfies the plaintiff's claim, whether by paying a judgment or effecting a settlement that releases the other tortfeasors.[28]

Traditional indemnity. Indemnity differs from contribution. While contribution contemplates that two defendants who are liable to the plaintiff in tort will share in the ultimate liability, indemnity contemplates that one of those two will fully repay the other. Suppose A and B are both liable to an injured person and that A pays that person's claim, thus extinguishing B's liability to the victim. A does not ordinarily have a claim for indemnity against B. Rather, indemnity is permitted in only a few situations, where courts have recognized some special duty of B to indemnify A.[29] The special duty to indemnify arises primarily when statutes so provide[30] and in three cases spelled out in the Restatement of Apportionment—essentially when the indemnitee is liable because

---

[22] Norfolk & W. Ry. v. Ayers, 538 U.S. 135, 123 S.Ct. 1210, 155 L.Ed.2d 261 (2003).

[23] See § 35.4.

[24] For a fuller explanation see Dobbs, Hayden & Bublick, The Law of Torts §§ 489–91 (2d ed. 2011 & Supp.).

[25] E.g., Cal. Civ. Proc. Code § 875; 740 Ill. Comp. Stat. § 100/3; Iowa Code Ann. § 668.5; Mich. Stat. Ann. § 600.2925a; Unif. Apportionment of Tort Responsibility Act § 7 (2002).

[26] Hansen v. Anderson, Wilmarth & Van Der Maaten, 630 N.W.2d 818 (Iowa 2001); but see Restatement (Third) of Torts: Apportionment of Liability § 23 cmt. 1 (2000).

[27] See, e.g., American Motorcycle Ass'n v. Superior Court, 20 Cal.3d 578, 146 Cal. Rptr. 182, 578 P.2d 899 (1978); Rancho Niguel Ass'n v. Ahmanson Devs., Inc., 86 Cal.App.4th 1135, 103 Cal.Rptr.2d 895 (2001). California retains joint and several liability as well as contribution for economic damages, see Cal. Civ. Code § 1431.2. However, liability for noneconomic damages is now several only. Cal. Civ. Code § 1432. See also Greyhound Lines, Inc. v. Cobb County, Ga., 681 F.2d 1327 (11th Cir. 1982) (allowing contribution but rejecting the "indemnity" label). Traditional indemnity, in contrast, is not a system for dividing responsibility but for shifting it entirely to one of the tortfeasors.

[28] E.g., Mass. Gen. L. Ann. ch. 231B § 1(a).

[29] See Habco v. L & B Oilfield Serv., Inc., 138 P.3d 1162 (Wyo. 2006).

[30] E.g., Tucson Elec. Power Co. v. Dooley-Jones & Assocs., Inc., 746 P.2d 510 (Ariz. Ct. App. 1987) (statute provided that persons performing certain work in specified proximity to high voltage electrical lines were required to notify power company and to indemnify power company if it is held liable to others for injury; statutory terms, not common law, controls).

of vicarious liability, is an innocent supplier of a product that caused harm to another, or is under a contractual duty to indemnify.[31]

§ 35.3 Joint and Several Liability vs. Several Liability Systems

Criticism of joint and several liability. Until the tort reform movement appeared, joint and several liability was not controversial. Principally in the 1980s, joint and several liability was attacked on the ground that it was inconsistent with the adoption of comparative fault and that it forced one tortfeasor to pay without regard to the degree of his culpability. A third attack suggested that much of the problem lay with immunities enjoyed by many tortfeasors.[32] If the law decided that some tortfeasors should be immune, it would be unfair to saddle solvent tortfeasors with the burden of conduct that the law has in a sense approved.

Responses to the criticism. Perhaps all these points are easily overrated. At best, they apply to some categories of joint and several liability but not others. When the plaintiff is not chargeable with any fault, the adoption of comparative negligence suggests no reason to dispense with the rule of joint and several liability,[33] although it does suggest how contribution among tortfeasors should be measured. If the problem is that immunities of some tortfeasors throw the burden disproportionately upon non-immune defendants under a joint and several liability system, the adoption of several liability merely shifts the burden to the injured plaintiff; and if the problem lies with immunities and other departures from a fault-based liability, the right response is to return to liability based upon fault.

Liability and defendant's fault for damage caused. As to the liability disproportionate to culpability, liability has always attached for actual damages, no matter how high they might be, even when the defendant's fault was quite limited, perhaps a second's distraction. In other words, damages have never been proportioned to fault and to suggest that they must be is to confuse tort liability with the criminal law of proportionate penalties. The criticism of joint and several liability also mistakenly identified *comparative* fault with *degree* of fault. The defendant's fault may be small by comparison to other tortfeasors, especially if the defendant can identify a large number of wrongdoers, but his fault may be extensive nonetheless. In no case is the defendant liable for damages unless (a) his conduct was negligent or otherwise actionable, (b) he was a cause in fact of those damages and (c) he was a proximate or legal cause as well.[34]

Defendant as one cause of full damages. Finally, critics often failed to recognize different categories of joint and several liability. In some types of joint and several liability, the defendant's negligent conduct was sufficient by itself to cause the plaintiff's harm and would have caused it in the same degree even if no other tortfeasor had appeared on the horizon. In cases like this, neither the defendant's fault nor his causal impact is less in any degree merely because other tortfeasors also participated. For example, A and B separately set fire to the plaintiff's house with a blowtorch and a gallon

---

[31] Restatement (Third) of Torts: Apportionment of Liability § 22 (2000).

[32] See Aaron D. Twerski, The Joint Tortfeasor Legislative Revolt: A Rational Response to the Critics, 22 U.C. Davis. L. Rev. 1125 (1989); but see Richard Wright, Throwing Out the Baby with the Bathwater: A Reply to Professor Twerski, 22 U.C. Davis L. Rev. 1147 (1989).

[33] See, e.g., Sitzes v. Anchor Motor Freight, Inc., 169 W.Va. 698, 289 S.E.2d 679 (1982).

[34] See John W. Wade, Should Joint and Several Liability of Multiple Tortfeasors Be Abolished?, 10 Am. J. Trial Advoc. 193 (1986); Richard W. Wright, The Logic and Fairness of Joint and Several Liability, 23 Mem. St. U. L. Rev. 45 (1992).

of gasoline. Either fire would have burned the house down.[35] Similarly, "if two people kill a third, it is not the case that each has half-killed him."[36] In such cases, no logic suggests why the appearance of a second tortfeasor should provide the defendant a windfall; he is no less at fault and he has caused no less harm. In some other cases, something better might be said for abolishing joint and several liability,[37] but the critics have generally lumped all joint and several liability cases together.

§ 35.4 Several Liability Systems

The trend towards several liability. Most states have now altered or abolished joint and several liability rules for certain classes of cases or for certain kinds of damages. They replace it with several liability of each individual actor based on the defendant's apportioned share of the total liability.[38]

Issues in several liability jurisdictions. In several liability systems, issues related to contribution as a result of settlement and satisfaction may still arise,[39] but because shares of liability are typically separate for each defendant, these issues are a rare possibility. However, there are no shortage of new issues that arise in jurisdictions with several liability systems.

Counting fault of many persons. When states have abolished or partially abolished joint and several liability, each tortfeasor is liable for his comparative fault share of an indivisible injury. Where that is the case, the plaintiff's recovery is directly affected by the number of actors whose fault can be counted. One hundred percent is the maximum fault available to share among all the negligent actors, whether there are two or twenty. When only two actors are negligent, the average fault of each tortfeasor is 50%; when twenty actors are negligent, the average fault is 5%. In the absence of joint and several liability, defendants will do better if they can find additional negligent actors to share in the blame. If defendant A can get the court to count the fault of defendants B and C, A's own percentage of fault and therefore percentage of liability is likely to be less. That is true, as the Arkansas court long ago pointed out,[40] even though defendant A's own fault remains exactly what it was before other tortfeasors were discovered.[41]

Included tortious conduct and included parties. Because each party's apportioned share of liability is diminished by the share assigned to other parties, defendants, and sometimes plaintiffs, have a strong incentive to bring in as many other potential defendants as possible. In the process of splitting liability among multiple parties, two key issues about the parties in the apportionment arise. First, for which types of tortious conduct can liability be apportioned—negligent conduct, strict liability, intentional torts?[42] Second, to which types of actors—employers, other immune parties,

---

[35]   Id. at 59.

[36]   Tony Weir, All-or-Nothing?,78 Tul. L. Rev. 511 (2004).

[37]   Supporters of joint and several liability do not necessarily think so. See Richard Wright, supra n.34 at 56–57.

[38]   See, e.g., Ariz. Rev. Stat. § 12–2506, upheld against constitutional attack in State Farm Ins. Cos. v. Premier Manufactured Sys., Inc., 217 Ariz. 222, 172 P.3d 410 (2007); Kan. Stat. Ann., § 60–258a.

[39]   See § Dobbs, Hayden & Bublick, The Law of Torts § 489 (2d ed. 2011 & Supp.).

[40]   Walton v. Tull, 234 Ark. 882, 356 S.W.2d 20, 8 A.L.R.3d 708 (1962).

[41]   But cf. Lyon v. Ranger III, 858 F.2d 22, 25 (1st Cir. 1988) ("We are aware of no legal principle that requires a district court to reduce, perhaps to inconsequential levels, such serious fault, simply because two (or three, or thirty) colleagues also failed to take proper care.").

[42]   See § 35.7.

nonparties—can apportionment percentages be assigned?[43] When the parties to be included in the process have been determined, another issue is the standard that the jury should use for apportioning damages, and the standard of review that appellate courts should apply. Finally, several liability jurisdictions are called on to decide in what circumstances exceptions to the general rule of several liability rule are called for, either by statute or by common law.

Joint and several liability in several liability systems—statutes. Many exceptions to several liability may be expressly created by state statute. Although some states abolished joint and several liability without any explicit exception or qualification,[44] other statutes provide specific exceptions[45] and may retain joint and several liability for tortfeasors whose liability is vicarious and those who act in concert.[46] Some statutes retain joint and several liability in certain types of cases when the plaintiff herself is not at fault.[47] In addition, the abolition statute may implicitly retain joint and several liability for some torts besides personal injury by defining its scope to include only injury, property damage, and death actions, thus leaving the joint and several liability rules intact for economic torts.[48] Moreover, the state statutes do not touch federal contribution rights such as those under environmental statutes.[49]

Joint and several liability in several liability systems—common law. Common law exceptions also may be called for in certain circumstances as well. For example, the Restatement recommends that courts retain joint and several liability when the defendant is an intentional tortfeasor or acting in concert.[50] In addition, the Restatement recommends that joint and several liability be retained when the secondary issue of apportioning liability between defendants may negate the tortfeasor's primary liability. For example, if a jury were permitted to assign vicarious liability to an employer for negligent acts of an employee, but then apportion liability between those two defendants

---

[43]   See § 35.6.

[44]   Ky. Rev. Stat. § 411.182; 12 Vt. Stat. Ann. § 1036.

[45]   E.g., Fla. Stat. Ann. § 768.81 (pollution cases); Or. Rev. Stat. § 31.610 (environmental harm cases of various kinds).

[46]   Ariz. Rev. Stat. § 12–2506; N.Y. C.P.L.R. § 1602; Smith v. Town of Greenwich, 899 A.2d 563 (Conn. App. 2006); Woods v. Cole, 181 Ill. 2d 512, 693 N.E.2d 333, 230 Ill. Dec. 204 (1998); Reilly v. Anderson, 727 N.W.2d 102 (Iowa 2006); Yount v. Deibert, 147 P.3d 1065 (Kan. 2006); Richards v. Badger Mut. Ins. Co., 749 N.W.2d 581 (Wis. 2008); Unif. Apportionment of Tort Responsibility Act § 6 (2002).

[47]   For example, unless the plaintiff is chargeable with at least equal fault, Wisconsin retains joint and several liability in claims of strict product liability. See Fuchsgruber v. Custom Accessories, Inc., 244 Wis. 2d 758, 628 N.W.2d 833 (2001).

[48]   E.g., Mich. Comp. L. Ann. § 600.6304. The Uniform Act, in determining comparative fault of the plaintiff, applies in actions "seeking damages for personal injury or harm to property based on negligence or strict liability" and also to cases in which "the claimant may be subject to a defense in whole or part based on contributory fault." Unif. Apportionment of Tort Responsibility Act § 3 (2002). In providing for the allocation of responsibility to multiple tortfeasors, the Act applies in actions "to recover damages for personal injury or harm to property involving the responsibility of more than one party or a released person." Id. § 4.

[49]   42 U.S.C.A. § 9607 creates liability of various parties for release of hazardous substances, while 42 U.S.C.A. § 9613 authorizes contribution. This is a system of joint and several liability. Niagara Mohawk Power Corp. v. Chevron U.S.A., Inc., 596 F.3d 112 (2d Cir. 2010); Cox v. City of Dallas, 256 F.3d 281 (2001); North Am. Galvanizing & Coatings, Inc. v. Lake River Corp., Inc., 2010 WL 2350588, at *4 (N.D. Ill., Jun 09, 2010) (differentiating CERCLA contribution claims from state-law contribution for state tort environmental damage claims). When evidence supports the divisibility of damages, causal apportionment may be appropriate. Burlington N. & Santa Fe Ry. Co. v. U.S., 556 U.S. 599, 129 S.Ct. 1870 (2009).

[50]   Reilly v. Anderson, 727 N.W.2d 102 (Iowa 2006) (joint and several liability for concerted action applied even after adoption of state comparative fault act); Strahin v. Cleavenger, 216 W.Va. 175, 603 S.E.2d 197 (2004) (joint and several liability of landowner for actions of assailant); Restatement (Third) of Torts: Apportionment of Liability §§ 12, 15 (2000).

so that the negligent employee bore most of the liability, the policy of vicarious liability would be defeated. The same concern applies in the case of a tortfeasor liable for failure to protect the plaintiff from the specific risk of an intentional tort.[51] If, for example, the jury finds a landowner negligent because the landowner's failure to repair a doorlock left the plaintiff vulnerable to physical attack in the lobby, it would negate the landowner's liability to allow a jury to apportion liability between the landowner and the assailant. A similar argument can be made when the defendant is under a duty to protect the plaintiff from another's negligence.[52]

§ 35.5   General Effects of Adopting Several Liability Systems

Comparative fault and several liability. Sometimes discussions of several liability are cast as discussion about proportional responsibility or apportionment. However, not all apportionments have the same effects. Comparative fault systems call for apportionment, but they do not necessarily abolish joint and several liability. It is several liability—the abolition of joint and several liability—that creates a radical change in the responsibility of tortfeasors for their actions. Three distinct effects of apportionment are shown in the illustrationsbelow.

Illustrations.

1) *Apportionment between plaintiff and tortfeasor A.* Plaintiff, chargeable with 10% of the fault for her own damages, recovers from defendant A, who is chargeable with 90% of the fault for plaintiff's damages. This form of apportionment holds plaintiff and defendant accountable for their assigned fault shares.

2) *Apportionment between defendant A and defendant B for contribution only.* Defendant A is chargeable with 60% of the fault and defendant B with 40%. Under rules of joint and several liability or vicarious liability, plaintiff can enforce her judgment for all of her damages against either defendant A or B. The tortfeasor who pays will be entitled to contribution (or, in special circumstances, indemnity) against the other tortfeasor. This is an apportionment, but it does not reduce the plaintiff's recovery except for plaintiff's own fault, if any.

3) *Apportionment between defendants A and B to reduce plaintiff's recovery.* Defendant A is chargeable with 60% of the fault, B with 40%. With no joint and several liability, plaintiff can recover 60% of her damages from defendant A, 40% from defendant B. This apportionment can deprive the plaintiff of compensation. For example, if defendant A is insolvent and uninsured, plaintiff will recover only 40% of her damages (from B). This is true even if defendant B's conduct, standing alone, would have caused all of plaintiff's damages.

Effects of apportionment. Statutes abolishing joint and several liability have no effect on the apportionment in illustration (1), but they abolish the kind of apportionment seen in illustration (2)—apportionment that merely measures contribution rights. In substituting several liability for the traditional joint and several liability, these statutes create a situation in which a defendant's liability is reduced because others were also at fault in producing injury.

---

[51]   Smith v. Town of Greenwich, 899 A.2d 563 (Conn. App. Ct. 2006) (joint and several liability of property owner for claim against snow removal contractor assigned a nondelegable duty); Restatement (Third) of Torts: Apportionment of Liability §§ 13, 14 (2000).

[52]   See § 35.10.

Effect of several liability with two defendants. A routine effect of adopting a several liability system can be illustrated by a case of concurrent tortfeasors whose negligent acts cause a single injury, as in the case of two automobile drivers who cause a collision that injures the plaintiff. If one driver's fault is rated at 10% and the other's at 90%, the plaintiff recovers 10% of her damages from the one and 90% from the other.[53] The same approach may apply to manufacturers whose defective products, in conjunction with another defendant's negligence, cause some or all of the plaintiff's injury,[54] and can be applied to some successive torts, as well. For example, under the traditional rule, a tortfeasor who causes injury is jointly and severally liable for any aggravation caused by a negligent health care provider, but under the several liability regime, the initial tortfeasor is liable only for his comparative fault share.[55] In all such cases, as indicated in the table, if one tortfeasor is immune or uninsured and insolvent, the plaintiff will not be fully compensated. The uninsured tortfeasor will not be appropriately deterred, of course—such tortfeasors seldom are. The tortfeasor who pays only his "proportionate share," say 10% in the first example above, however, may be under-deterred in spite of the language of proportionality.[56] That is so because his liability is reduced based not on his own conduct or the harm that he caused, but because another person (uninsured) was also negligent.

Effects with multiple defendants. A more dramatic effect of several liability and comparative apportionment rules is that if more people were at fault, it is likely that the defendant's comparative share will be less. That is of no great consequence if the plaintiff can identify, sue, and collect from each of the many tortfeasors. However, if the fault of, say, an immune tortfeasor is to be weighed in determining the remaining defendant's comparative share, the plaintiff will collect less from the defendant and nothing at all from the immune tortfeasor. This is sometimes referred to as the "tortfest" critique of several liability.[57] These effects may be magnified by some statutes that cap damages.[58] So defendants have an interest in asserting that all fault must be considered, including the fault of nonparties, the fault of insolvent and immune tortfeasors, and the fault of intentional tortfeasors. Plaintiffs wish to argue that in weighing the comparative significance of the defendant's fault, the court should consider only the fault of parties and persons against whom suit is possible.

---

[53] Lackman v. Rousselle, 257 Neb. 87, 596 N.W.2d 15 (1999); Staab v. Diocese of St. Cloud, 853 N.W.2d 713 (Minn. 2014).

[54] E.g., Restatement (Third) of Torts: Apportionment of Liability § 14 (2000); Restatement (Third) of Torts: Products Liability § 16(b) (1998).

[55] See Henry v. Superior Court, 160 Cal.App.4th 440, 72 Cal.Rptr.3d 808 (2008) (several liability for noneconomic damages pursuant to statute); Dumas v. State, 828 So.2d 530 (La. 2002); Haff v. Hettich, 593 N.W.2d 383 (N.D. 1999).

[56] Mark M. Hager, What's (Not!) In a Restatement? ALI Issue-Dodging on Liability Apportionment, 33 Conn. L. Rev. 77 (2000) (arguing that several liability will provide suboptimal deterrence); Lewis A. Kornhauser & Richard L. Revesz, Sharing Damages Among Multiple Tortfeasors, 98 Yale L.J. 831 (1989) (demonstrating that joint and several liability rules are more likely to produce efficient results); William Landes & Richard Posner, Joint and Multiple Tortfeasors: An Economic Analysis, 9 J. Leg. Stud. 517 (1980).

[57] Richard W. Wright, The Logic and Fairness of Joint and Several Liability, 23 Mem. St. U. L. Rev. 45, 74 (1992).

[58] Especially where the cap is the total limit of recovery against the whole group of defendants. See § 34.7.

B. PERSONS AND CONDUCT SUBJECT TO APPORTIONMENT

§ 35.6 Immune and Nonparty Tortfeasors

Issue and strategy. In the apportionment process, courts must decide whether juries should apportion fault to persons who are not joined as parties, perhaps because they cannot be found or because they are insolvent. Courts must also determine whether fault should be apportioned to persons who are in some sense at fault but who are not liable because of a formally recognized immunity or otherwise.[59] Strategically, the defendant's interest in a several liability system is to assert the negligence of many other persons regardless of immunity. That is because all liabilities are comparative, not absolute. When fault is attributed to other tortfeasors, that attribution reduces the fault that can be attributed to the defendant. The plaintiff's interest, in contrast, is to assert that nonparties and persons who are immune are not in fact at fault.[60]

Only parties' fault compared. Statutes may answer at least some of these questions by limiting the comparison of the negligence to "parties" or "defendants."[61] Sometimes statutes expressly state that the negligence of non-parties is definitely not to be compared.[62] This approach has been supported on the ground that, where joint and several liability is abolished, comparing the fault of non-parties forces the plaintiff to join large numbers of defendants whose liability is doubtful, lest the trier conclude that not all of the negligence is attributable to joined parties.[63] Another variation is a statute construed to compare negligence only of the parties and immune persons.[64] Similarly, the negligence of a settling party may be excluded in some jurisdictions.[65] The 2002 Uniform Act disregards the fault of all nonparties except released persons.[66] When nonparty fault cannot be compared, it may still be possible for the defendant to assert that some divisible portion of the plaintiff's injury was caused by a third party and not

---

[59] Relatedly, crediting the nonsettling tortfeasor in the light of the settling tortfeasor's payment is considered with other apportionment materials in Dobbs, Hayden & Bublick, The Law of Torts § 491 (2d ed. 2011 & Supp.).

[60] Cf. Restatement (Third) of Torts: Apportionment of Liability § 19B cmt. e (2000) (noting that sometimes "immunity" appears in reality to be a case of no-negligence or no duty, in which case the joined defendant cannot attribute part of the negligence to the "immune" person).

[61] See Shantigar Found. v. Bear Mountain Builders, 441 Mass. 131, 804 N.E.2d 324 (2004) (construing statute to compare fault only of the plaintiff and defendants, excluding the fault of a settling non-party tortfeasor); Unif. Apportionment of Tort Responsibility Act (2002).

[62] E.g., Conn. Gen. Stat. § 52–572h (negligence compared is that of "parties" and "released persons," but defendant may implead others not originally joined); cf. Jefferson County Commonwealth Attorney's Office v. Kaplan, 65 S.W.3d 916 (Ky. 2001) (statute required apportionment only among parties and settling tortfeasors).

[63] See Donner v. Kearse, 234 Conn. 660, 662 A.2d 1269 (1995) ("fostering marginal and costly litigation in our courts").

[64] Field v. Boyer Co., 952 P.2d 1078 (Utah. 1998).

[65] See Ready v. United/Goedecke Servs., Inc., 232 Ill.2d 369, 328 Ill.Dec 836 (2008) (excluding settling tortfeasors from apportionment percentages).

[66] See Unif. Apportionment of Tort Responsibility Act, Preface, Apportioning Tort Responsibility in This Act (2002); cf. Fuchsgruber v. Custom Accessories, Inc., 244 Wis.2d 758, 628 N.W.2d 833 (2001).

by the defendant, thus reducing the defendant's liability by causal rather than by a fault apportionment.[67]

Non-parties' fault compared. A different rule, by express statutory requirement,[68] or by judicial construction,[69] is that the trier is to compare all of the fault that is a proximate cause of the harm, whether it is the fault of parties or not. Statutes may also provide specially for considering and comparing the fault of settling tortfeasors.[70] With the exception of an immune tortfeasor, most courts in several liability systems appear to consider the fault of any tortfeasor, whether or not joined as a party.[71]

Relevant non-parties. However, even in jurisdictions that allow the trier to compare the negligence of nonparties, included are only those nonparties the plaintiff has a legal right to sue.[72] Presumably the nonparty must indeed be, prima facie, a tortfeasor who owes a duty to the plaintiff and breached it with proximately resulting harm, and several cases have expressly so held.[73] Similarly, where there is insufficient evidence to put the issue of the negligence of an immune party to the jury, the party may not be included in the apportionment.[74] Other requirements, such as timely notice of the named nonparty at fault may also be required.[75] At least one court has held a legislature's nonparty-fault provision unconstitutional.[76]

Third persons who are legally or practically immune. In many situations, a person who might be considered "at fault" in causing harm is formally or practically immune

---

[67] Truman v. Montana Eleventh Judicial Dist. Ct., 315 Mont. 165, 68 P.3d 654 (2003) (under Montana law, a negligent defendant cannot reduce his liability by *fault* of nonparties, but he can introduce evidence that a divisible portion of the plaintiff's injuries were *caused* by a nonparty).

[68] Colo. Rev. Stat. Ann. § 13–21–111.5 (3)(b) permits the defendant to give formal notice claiming that a nonparty is negligent within 90 days of the suit's commencement, presumably to permit the plaintiff to join that person; Owens Corning Fiberglass Corp. v. Cobb, 754 N.E.2d 905 (Ind. 2001) (by statute, defendant can assert fault of nonparty but has the burden of proof).

[69] See Wells v. Tallahassee Mem'l Reg'l Med. Ctr., Inc., 659 So.2d 249 (Fla. 1995); Couch v. Red Roof Inns, Inc., 291 Ga. 359, 729 S.E.2d 378 (2012) (nonparty assailant had to be given a portion of the responsibility where statute referred apportioning damages according to "fault" of "tortfeasors"); Bode v. Clark Equipment Co., 719 P.2d 824 (Okla. 1986) (in aggregating negligence of tortfeasors to compare with the plaintiff's negligence, trier must consider negligence of immune nonparty tortfeasors as well as negligence of defendant); accord as to identified persons where several liability prevails, Restatement (Third) of Torts: Apportionment of Liability § 29B cmts. d & e (2000). Tennessee compares the negligence of nonparties whom the plaintiff has the right to sue and join. Ridings v. Ralph M. Parsons Co., 914 S.W.2d 79 (Tenn. 1996).

[70] Colo. Rev. Stat. Ann. § 13–21–111.5 (3)(b); Conn. Gen. Stat. § 52–572h.

[71] Ogden v. J.M. Steel Erecting, Inc., 201 Ariz. 32, 31 P.3d 806 (Ct. App. 2001); Wells v. Tallahassee Mem'L Reg'l Med. Ctr. Inc., 659 So.2d 249 (Fla. 1995) (negligence of nonparty considered); Chianese v. Meier, 98 N.Y.2d 270, 746 N.Y.S.2d 657, 774 N.E.2d 722 (2002) (negligence of nonparty intentional attacker considered). Details may vary. West Virginia has held that the negligence of nonparties is to be compared when the plaintiff is guilty of comparative fault, but that the rule of several liability does not apply to permit apportionment between party and nonparty tortfeasors when the plaintiff is innocent of negligence. Rowe v. Sisters of the Pallottine Missionary Soc'y, 211 W.Va. 16, 560 S.E.2d 491 (2001) (explicating earlier authority).

[72] Van Brunt v. Stoddard, 39 P.3d 621 (Idaho 2001) (court found that passenger in defendant's vehicle, who told defendant to turn, triggering a turn into the plaintiff, breached no duty and was not a cause, hence his "fault" need not be counted in comparing fault of plaintiff and defendant); Pepper v. Star Equip., Ltd., 484 N.W.2d 156 (Iowa 1992); Ridings v. Ralph M. Parsons Co., 914 S.W.2d 79 (Tenn. 1996).

[73] See Jones v. Crawforth, 205 P.3d 660 (Idaho 2009); Morgan v. Scott, 291 S.W.3d 622 (Ky. 2009) ("[F]ault may not be properly allocated to a party, a dismissed party or settling nonparty unless the court or the jury first find that the party was at fault; otherwise, the party has no fault to allocate"); Romain v. Frankenmuth Mut. Ins. Co., 762 N.W.2d 911 (Mich. 2009).

[74] See Morgan v. Scott, 291 S.W.3d 622 (Ky. 2009).

[75] Scottsdale Ins. Co. v. Cendejas, 205 P.3d 1128 (Ariz. Ct. App. 2009).

[76] Johnson v. Rockwell Automation, Inc., 308 S.W.3d 135 (Ark. 2009).

from tort liability. From the plaintiff's point of view, that is of no concern in a joint and several liability system if other tortfeasors are solvent. However, where the rule of joint and several liability has been abolished and each defendant is liable only for his comparative fault share, plaintiffs stand to lose significantly if an immune actor's fault is considered, for it will reduce the amount of fault that can be assigned to the defendant and hence will usually reduce the defendant's liability.

Employers. The issue most often arises in the case law in terms of employers. Employers who provide workers' compensation benefits to employees are generally immune to tort liability, so they are not liable in tort even if they negligently injure an employee. The injured employee is still free to sue others, such as product manufacturers who contribute to her harm. The question is whether the fault of such a defendant should be judged in comparison to the fault of the immune employer or whether the fault of the employer should be ignored. The fault of the product manufacturer or other defendant may be relatively small in comparison to that of the employer, but relatively large (or total) if the employer's negligence cannot be considered. Where liability is several only, this issue can be critical. The Uniform Act treats the employer who pays workers' compensation and who is immune under workers' compensation laws as a released person, counting the employer's responsibility in the total and thus reducing the share apportioned to others.[77] Some states have taken this position, holding that the fault of an employer who is immune from liability under workers' compensation laws, must be considered in assessing the fault of the defendant,[78] with the expected result that defendant's percentage share of fault will be less than it would be if only the defendant's fault were considered. However, other jurisdictions oppose apportionment of liability to the immune employer.[79]

Other immune parties. In other instances, courts may reach the same result with when a defendant is immune for other reasons.[80] A few courts, most notably the Supreme Court of Iowa, have held that the immune defendant's fault is to be ignored not only in the case of an employer immune under workers' compensation statutes[81] but also in the case of other immunities as well.[82] The Iowa court said that, to prevent "fault siphoning",

---

[77]   Unif. Apportionment of Tort Responsibility Act § 9 (2002).

[78]   DaFonte v. Up-Right, Inc., 2 Cal.4th 593, 828 P.2d 140, 7 Cal.Rptr.2d 238 (1992); Dietz v. General Elec. Co., 169 Ariz. 505, 821 P.2d 166 (1991); cf. Bode v. Clark Equip. Co., 719 P.2d 824 (Okla. 1986) (fault of immune employer considered to determine whether the fault of all persons exceeded the plaintiff's fault). Unzicker v. Kraft Food Ingredients Corp., 783 N.E.2d 1024 (Ill. 2002), held in accord with the text, but subsequent legislation seems to ignore the employer's negligence, at least for some purposes. See Skaggs v. Senior Servs. of Cent. Ill., Inc., 355 Ill. App. 3d 1120, 823 N.E.2d 1021, 291 Ill. Dec. 435 (2005). See also Andrew R. Klein, Apportionment of Liability in Workplace Injury Cases, 26 Berkeley J. Emp. & Lab. L. 65 (2005).

[79]   See CSX Transp., Inc. v. Miller, 46 So.3d 434 (Ala. 2010) (FELA); Burnett v. Columbus McKinnon Corp., 69 A.D.3d 58, 887 N.Y.S.2d 405 (2009); Troup v. Fischer Steel Corp., 236 S.W.3d 143 (Tenn. 2007); Dresser Indus. v. Lee, 880 S.W.2d 750 (Tex. 1993) (not permitting evidence of employer negligence for percentage apportionment but allowing it for other purposes); Jonathan Cardi, Apportioning Responsibility To Immune Nonparties: An Argument Based on Comparative Responsibility and the Proposed Restatement (Third) of Torts, 82 Iowa L. Rev. 1293, 1314 (1997).

[80]   Y.H. Invs., Inc. v. Godales, 690 So.2d 1273 (Fla. 1997) (on the facts, parent was immune to a claim by her child, but her fault is considered in assessing the defendant's fault and defendant is liable only for his share). But see Mack Trucks, Inc. v. Tackett, 841 So.2d 1107 (Miss. 2003) (distinguishing employers from other immune parties).

[81]   Peterson v. Pittman, 391 N.W.2d 235 (Iowa 1986); Ridings v. Ralph M. Parsons Co., 914 S.W.2d 79 (Tenn. 1996) ("fault may be attributed only to those persons against whom the plaintiff has a cause of action in tort").

[82]   Pepper v. Star Equip., Ltd., 484 N.W.2d 156 (Iowa 1992) (bankrupt's immunity); Schwennen v. Abell, 430 N.W.2d 98 (Iowa 1988) (wife could not recover against husband for husband's negligence in causing injury

the negligence of a nonparty is not to be considered if the plaintiff "has no possibility of obtaining an enforceable judgment" against him.[83]

§ 35.7 Types of Actionable Conduct Subject to Apportionment

Comparative responsibility in negligence cases. A significant issue in comparative responsibility for the last few decades has been the type of actionable conduct that can be compared in apportionment of liability systems. The negligent conduct of multiple actors—whether defendants or plaintiffs—is widely accepted by jurisdictions as appropriate action for comparison. More controversies arise about causes of action other than negligence.

Comparative responsibility in strict liability cases. When one or more of the tortfeasors is strictly liable, it is literally not possible to compare fault.[84] Moreover, concerns have been raised that strict liability—negligence comparisons undermine the policy reasons for imposing strict liability.[85] Yet many states have included strict liability claims in apportionment systems.[86] In these states, responsibility is allocated between strictly liable and negligent defendants in much the same way that states allocate responsibility between negligent defendants so that, for example, one defendant might be chargeable with 80% of the responsibility while the other is chargeable with only 20%.[87] Sometimes it is said that this approach must be comparative causation. The Restatement of Apportionment prefers the term "comparative responsibility."[88] Use of the term "comparative responsibility" typically suggests that a jurisdiction's comparisons include at least one form of actionable conduct in addition to negligence, such as strict liability.

Comparative responsibility in cases of reckless or intentional torts. The most controversial question concerning the types of tortious conduct to be considered in apportionment systems is whether one defendant's intentional tortious activity can and should be compared with another defendant's negligence.[89] Most jurisdictions do not

---

to himself; in wife's suit against third person for loss of consortium, husband's negligence is not to be considered).

[83] Pepper v. Star Equip., Ltd., 484 N.W.2d 156, 158 (Iowa 1992).

[84] See § 33.17 (discussing the argument that comparing strict liability with fault is like comparing apples and oranges).

[85] See, e.g., Mark E. Rozkowski & Robert A. Prentice, Reconciling Comparative Negligence and Strict Liability: A Public Policy Analysis, 33 St. Louis U. L.J. 19 (1988).

[86] See State Farm Ins. Cos. v. Premier Manufactured Sys., Inc., 172 P.3d 410, 418 (Ariz. 2007); William J. McNichols, The Relevance of the Plaintiff's Misconduct in Strict Products Liability, the Advent of Comparative Responsibility, and the Proposed Restatement (Third) of Torts, 47 Okla. L. Rev. 201 (1994).

[87] Safeway Stores, Inc. v. Nest-Kart, 21 Cal.3d 322, 146 Cal.Rptr. 550, 579 P.2d 441 (1978) (Safeway, negligent, was chargeable with 80%, the manufacturer of a product causing injury, strictly liable, chargeable with 20%).

[88] Restatement (Third) of Torts: Apportionment of Liability § 8 cmt. a (2000). This Restatement invites an unweighted consideration of broadly stated factors, including states of mind. It may invite jurors to decide more of their preferences for the parties than their judgment of conduct.

[89] See Ellen M. Bublick, The End Game of Tort Reform: Comparative Apportionment and Intentional Torts, 78 Notre Dame L. Rev. 355 (2003) (finding that in 2003 the majority of states did not compare the responsibility of intentional and negligent tortfeasor defendants but that of the 22 states that had recently considered the issue, 14 were in favor and 8 opposed); Christopher M. Brown & Kirk A. Morgan, Consideration of Intentional Torts in Fault Allocation: Disarming the Duty to Protect Against Intentional Conduct, 2 Wyo. L. Rev. 483 (2002); William J. McNichols, Should Comparative Responsibility Ever Apply to Intentional Torts, 37 Okla. L. Rev. 641 (1984).

make such comparisons.[90] However, the number of states that apportion responsibility between intentional and negligent tortfeasor defendants has grown significantly.[91] Similar issues arise with respect to reckless[92] conduct.

Which causes of action to include as a policy decision. Interpretation of state statutes plays an important role in these divisions as some statutes specifically include or exclude intentional torts from comparative apportionment systems. However, when the issue is a question of common law analysis, courts are quick to rely on causation or coherence arguments, but these arguments are a red herring. To be in the apportionment at all, a defendant's actionable conduct must have been a cause of the plaintiff's full harm.[93] Moreover, excluding intentional torts in apportionment creates one kind of incoherence—between defendants who have a negligent tortfeasor codefendant and those who have an intentional tortfeasor codefendant—while including them creates another—between plaintiffs exposed to risks of a negligent and an intentional tortfeasor as opposed to two forms of negligent harms or a negligent and a nonnegligent harm.[94] Instead, policy issues concerning the effects of apportionment are critical in this context. Thus, while the Restatement of Apportionment adopted apportionment for all bases of liability including intentional torts, it did so only after acknowledging that "intentional torts present special problems of apportionment," and fashioning special rules to address the inclusion of intentional torts.[95] Unfortunately courts that include intentional torts in apportionment of liability systems have not always recognized these special issues or rules.

Contexts in which intentional-negligent comparisons arise. Neither are courts, advocates and commentators always careful to differentiate the context in which the intentional-negligent fault comparison question arises. Intentional-negligent fault comparisons can be applied in at least three quite different apportionment contexts with potentially quite different impacts: (1) The plaintiff is an intentional tortfeasor injured by the negligent defendant.[96] (2) The defendant is an intentional tortfeasor and the plaintiff is merely negligent to himself or others. (3) One of two defendants is negligent, the other is intentional. Subcategories of this last category might include (a) defendants acting independently but causing a single indivisible injury and (b) a negligent defendant who creates a risk of an intentional tort by another.

Negligent defendant and intentional tortfeasor defendant comparison as the paradigm context. The difference in the various contexts counsels for caution in making a category-wide rule that always or never applies to intentional-negligent fault comparisons. When courts say they compare negligent and intentional torts they are typically talking about comparing the negligent and intentional conduct of two

[90]	See, e.g., Brandon v. County of Richardson, 261 Neb. 636 (2001) (rejecting comparisons in light of common law considerations).

[91]	See, e.g., Slack v. Farmers Ins. Exch., 5 P.3d 280 (Colo. 2000); Board of County Comm'rs of Teton County ex rel. Teton County Sheriff's Dep't v. Bassett, 8 P.3d 1079 (Wyo. 2000).

[92]	Jim Hasenfus, The Role of Recklessness in American Systems of Comparative Fault, 43 Ohio St. L.J. 399 (1982).

[93]	David W. Robertson, Eschewing Ersatz Percentages: A Simplified Vocabulary of Comparative Fault, 45 St. Louis U. L.J. 831 (2001). See also § 35.4.

[94]	Ellen M. Bublick, Apportionment and Intentional Torts, 78 Notre Dame L. Rev. 355, 398–402, 408 (2003) (explaining that liability is *not* assigned based on the defendant's own fault or causation per se).

[95]	Restatement (Third) of Torts: Apportionment of Liability § 1 (2000).

[96]	In some cases in this pattern, the intentionally wrongdoing plaintiff is barred completely, in others allowed a full recovery, depending, evidently, upon the strength of the policies involved. See § 16.8.

defendants. Indeed, most of the cases that permit comparisons involve a comparison of one defendant's negligence with another defendant's intentional wrongdoing.[97] Courts frequently do not allow comparisons of intentional and negligent conduct when an intentional tortfeasor is acting as the plaintiff and suing a negligent defendant.[98] Similarly, courts have taken a much narrower view of the comparisons when an intentional tortfeasor defendant asserts the comparative negligence of a plaintiff.[99] Of course, most jurisdictions do not compare even the negligent and intentional torts of defendants. And when courts do, it may turn out that intentional torts should be weighed on the comparative responsibility scale only in some case patterns but not others.[100]

C. STANDARDS

§ 35.8 Apportionment Standards

Standards for assigning responsibility. Once courts have determined which parties and which causes of action should be included in apportionment percentages, they must also determine by what metrics percentage comparisons are assigned and reviewed. In traditional comparative fault systems, the degree of fault attributable to the various parties is the item to be compared. However, there is no accepted metric for comparing intentional torts, recklessness and negligent torts.[101] The American Law Institute has called the endeavor "impossible in theory."[102] And yet, the Restatement and many jurisdictions now call on juries to make these comparisons.

Restatement factors. The factors listed by the Restatement as relevant to assigning shares of responsibility are: "the nature of the person's risk-creating conduct, including any awareness or indifference with respect to the risks created by the conduct and any intent with respect to the harm created by the conduct," and "the strength of the causal connection between the person's risk-creating conduct and the harm."[103] These factors provide little guidance about how to compare and apportion. But the difficulty of defining the standard is perhaps eased by the treatment of the jury's apportionment as a question

---

[97]　E.g., Hutcherson v. City of Phoenix, 192 Ariz. 51, 961 P.2d 449 (1998); Reichert v. Atler, 117 N.M. 623, 875 P.2d 379 (1994); Rodenburg v. Fargo-Moorhead Young Men's Christian Ass'n, 632 N.W.2d 407 (N.D. 2001) ("A negligent tortfeasor's conduct is compared with an intentional tortfeasor's conduct").

[98]　Compare Hutcherson v. City of Phoenix, 192 Ariz. 51, 961 P.2d 449 (1998) (allowing comparison of one defendant's intentional tort with another defendant's negligence), with Williams v. Thude, 934 P.2d 1349 (Ariz. 1997) (disallowing suit by willful and wanton plaintiff against negligent defendant).

[99]　Compare Martin v. United States, 984 F.2d 1033, 1039–40 (9th Cir. 1993) (holding that under California's comparative fault act, intentional and negligent torts of defendants should be compared), with Heiner v. K-Mart Corp., 100 Cal.Rptr.2d 854, 864 (Ct. App. 2000) (refusing to allow batterer to assert plaintiff negligence).

[100]　See Dobbs, Hayden & Bublick, The Law of Torts §§ 222 & 494 (2d ed. 2011 & Supp.) on apportionment problems in multiple tortfeasor cases and in particular § 498 in the kind of case in which A negligently risks B's intentional wrongdoing.

[101]　Kenneth W. Simons, Dimensions of Negligence in Criminal and Tort Law, 3 Theoretical Inquiries L. 283, 329 (2002) (calling the apples to oranges comparisons "treacherous").

[102]　Geoffrey C. Hazard, Jr., Foreword, Restatement Third of Torts (Apportionment of Liability) xii–xiii (Proposed Final Draft (Revised) 1999).

[103]　Restatement (Third) of Torts: Apportionment of Liability § 8 cmt. a (2000).

of fact.[104] Under that formulation, a jury's apportionment is entitled to deference unless it is clearly erroneous[105]—a very lenient standard.[106]

Apportioning more responsibility to a negligent tortfeasor than to an intentional tortfeasor. Still, there are decisions that pose a challenge even to that standard. Perhaps the most difficult apportionment cases are those that allocate a greater share of responsibility to a negligent tortfeasor than to a reckless or intentional tortfeasor.[107] One particularly interesting case that fits this pattern is the 1993 World Trade Center Bombing Litigation. In that case, the jury apportioned 32% of the total responsibility in the case to the terrorists who deliberately planted a bomb in the building's garage, and 68% to the Port Authority of New York and New Jersey which negligently failed to take recommended security precautions to thwart a potential car bomb.[108] Although the allocation seems surprising, the apportionment was upheld on appeal on the basis that the bombing "had actually been foreseen," that the risks were "dire," the cost of precaution "inconsequential," and the decisions not to minimize the risks were "deliberate" ones made by "top management."[109] Moreover, the court found that the intentional wrongdoing "was not simply concurrent with the negligence, but to an unseemly degree flowed from the negligence and was determined by it"—an analysis akin to a determination that the negligent tortfeasor risked the intentional harm.[110] However, the New York Supreme Court ultimatel ruled that the Port Authority had no duty, such that the apportionment question was moot.[111]

Comparative responsibility versus comparative fault. Many other courts have also upheld apportionments that assign a greater responsibility share to the negligent defendant. Courts that take this view often remark that comparative responsibility does not simply compare wrongfulness or reprehensibility.[112] Along with that view, courts can also think of the apportionment of civil responsibility as only one part of the system of legal responsibility, which includes criminal liability as well. Given these attitudes, courts may conclude that the traditional norms of accountability permit apportionment of a greater share of the civil responsibility to negligent tortfeasors than to intentional tortfeasors.[113]

Effect of culpability-based apportionments if intentional tortfeasors are included. Some courts have overturned apportionments that assign greater responsibility to negligent than intentional tortfeasors when the process was viewed as one that primarily

---

[104] Morden v. Continental AG, 235 Wis.2d 325, 611 N.W.2d 659 (2000).

[105] State, Dep't of Health & Soc. Servs. v. Mullins, 328 P.3d 1038 (Alaska 2014) ("plainly unreasonable" finding would be overturned).

[106] See, e.g., Southern Alaska Carpenters Health & Sec. Trust Fund v. Jones, 177 P.3d 844 (Alaska 2008); Fontenot v. Patterson Ins., 23 So.3d 259 (La. 2009) ("the allocation of fault is not an exact science, or the search for one precise ratio, but rather an acceptable range . . . any allocation by the factfinder within that range cannot be clearly wrong").

[107] See, e.g., Paragon Family Restaurant v. Bartolini, 799 N.E.2d 1048 (Ind. 2003); Roman Catholic Diocese of Covington v. Secter, 966 S.W.2d 286 (Ky. 1998).

[108] In re World Trade Ctr. Bombing Litig., 776 N.Y.S.2d 713 (Sup. Ct. 2004).

[109] Nash v. Port Auth. of N.Y. & N.J., 856 N.Y.S.2d 583 (App. Div. 2008).

[110] See § 35.9.

[111] In re World Trade Ctr. Bombing Litigation, 957 N.E.2d 733 (N.Y. 2011).

[112] Hutcherson v. City of Phoenix, 961 P.2d 449 (Ariz. 1998); Weiss v. Hodge, 567 N.W.2d 468 (Mich. 1997).

[113] See Ellen M. Bublick, Upside Down? Terrorists, Proprietors, and Civil Responsibility for Crime Prevention in the Post-9/11 Tort-Reform World, 41 Loy. L.A. L. Rev. 1483 (2008).

compares the parties' relative culpability.[114] Because many intentional tortfeasors are judgment proof, if an intentional tortfeasor must be assigned more than 50% of the total responsibility, a plaintiff will rarely be able to recover more than 50% of her damages in a case involving a negligent and an intentional tortfeasor. Consequently, in jurisdictions that have several liability systems and compare intentional and negligent fault, courts must consider an exception for negligent defendants who negligently risk another tortfeasor's intentional harm if they do not want to erase liability in this area.[115]

Adjustments on appeal. When an appellate court finds that some portion of an apportionment must be overturned on appeal, difficult issues arise with respect to the need for a new trial. At least one court has dealt with this situation by ruling that "after an appellate court finds a 'clearly wrong' apportionment of fault, it should adjust the award, but only to the extent of lowering or raising it to the highest or lowest point respectively which is reasonably within the trier of fact's discretion."[116]

D. SPECIAL CASES FOR APPORTIONMENT

§ 35.9 Defendants Who Negligently Risk Another Tortfeasor's Intentional Harm

Negligently creating a risk of an intentional tort. Should the fault of negligent tortfeasors be compared with the fault of intentional tortfeasors? That issue has already been addressed.[117] What remains is a subset of that problem that occurs when a negligent defendant creates a risk that a second defendant will commit an intentional tort. For example, if A leaves dynamite where children can steal it, the risk is that they will do so and cause injury to others. Older decisions might have disposed of such a case by concluding that A was not liable because the children's act constituted a superseding cause.[118] Contemporary cases tend to say that defendants cannot escape liability for foreseeable risks. Consequently, in a joint and several liability regime today, both A and the children would be liable in many such cases. Perhaps the most notable version of the problem occurs when a landlord or a business fails to use reasonable care to prevent a robbery or a rape of a customer or tenant or when a police officer, owing a citizen a duty of care, fails to protect her from attack.

The concern about comparisons. In the joint and several liability system, the careless handler of dynamite, the business, the landlord, or the police officer would be liable for the plaintiff's damages resulting from the explosion, the robbery or the rape. When joint and several liability has been abolished, the question is whether negligent actors like the landlord who refuses to repair a broken lock can escape full liability when a rapist takes advantage of the disrepair to rape the plaintiff in her unprotected apartment. The issue is critical because the negligence of the landlord, no matter how great, will often be perceived as tiny in comparison to the fault of the rapist, so if a rule of several liability operates, the landlord may be liable for, say, 1% of the damages, the rest being the responsibility of the insolvent rapist. The result is that the plaintiff will

---

[114] See Stevens v. New York City Transit Auth., 797 N.Y.S.2d 542 (App. Div. 2005).

[115] See § 35.9; Restatement (Third) of Torts: Apportionment of Liability § 14 (2000) (adopting an ameliorative rule for all tracks of liability because the secondary issue of apportionment would otherwise endanger the primary issue of imposition of liability in the first place).

[116] Brewer v. J.B. Hunt Transp. Inc., 35 So.3d 230 (La. 2010).

[117] See Dobbs, Hayden & Bublick, The Law of Torts § 227, 498 (2d ed. 2011 & Supp.).

[118] Id. at § 209.

recover virtually nothing. Given the poor prospects of substantial recovery, lawyers for the plaintiff may conclude that it is not economically worth it to sue. The result in that case is both under-deterrence and under-compensation. There are variations on this model set of facts that raise the same essential issue whenever a criminal is one of the tortfeasors.[119] The apportionment question between defendants is quite distinct from the question whether the plaintiff's own comparative negligence should reduce her recovery against an intentional wrongdoer like the rapist.[120] Even so, if joint and several liability is abolished, apportionment between defendants will routinely mean a severe reduction in the plaintiff's recovery.

Divided authority. Some cases hold or imply that the negligent actor's fault is compared with that of the intentional actor. Given that joint and several liability has been abolished, the negligent actor is thus only severally liable for his apportioned share.[121] Other authority refuses to permit the negligent tortfeasor to reduce his liability by comparing the fault of the intentional tortfeasor whose acts he risked.[122] In this view, the negligent tortfeasor is entirely liable to the plaintiff[123] though he might conceivably obtain contribution or indemnity against the intentional tortfeasor. Washington appears to have come up with a unique rule that requires causal apportionment rather than fault apportionment between intentional and negligent tortfeasors, although it is not clear at this juncture how such a rule can work where indivisible harm results.[124]

Modes of full liability in several liability systems. Good policy arguments favor full joint and several liability in cases of those who negligently facilitate torts of others. The landlord who negligently facilitates access of rapists to his tenants' apartments should have an indemnity action against the rapist, but the risk of the rapist's insolvency should fall upon the negligent landlord, not upon the innocent plaintiff. Can such policy be effectuated in states that abolish joint and several liability? At least four lines of authority and legal thought may be invoked to hold the landlord and other facilitators liable for all or a substantial part of the plaintiff's damages (subject always to his right of contribution against the criminal actor).

---

[119] See Lubecki v. City of New York, 304 A.D.2d 224, 758 N.Y.S.2d 610 (2003) (robber took a hostage as a shield, police officers fired, allegedly in contravention of police standards, killing the hostage; police entities may be held jointly and severally if officers acted recklessly). See also Tegman v. Accident & Med. Investigations, Inc., 150 Wash.2d 102, 75 P.3d 497 (2003) (where the negligent tortfeasor was second in point of time and the intentional tortfeasor first; the court applied a unique rule requiring causal apportionment rather than apportionment based on fault).

[120] See Dobbs, Hayden & Bublick, The Law of Torts § 227 (2d ed. 2011 & Supp.)..

[121] Weidenfeller v. Star & Garter, 1 Cal.App.4th 1, 2 Cal.Rptr.2d 14 (1991); Ozaki v. Association of Apartment Owners of Discovery Bay, 87 Haw. 265, 954 P.2d 644 (1998); Steele v. Kerrigan, 148 N.J. 1, 689 A.2d 685 (1997); Barth v. Coleman, 118 N.M. 1, 878 P.2d 319 (1994); Rodenburg v. Fargo-Moorhead Young Men's Christian Ass'n, 632 N.W.2d 407 (N.D. 2001); Board of County Comm'rs of Teton County v. Basset, 8 P.3d 1079 (Wyo. 2000).

[122] See, e.g., Ali v. Fisher, 145 S.W.3d 557 (Tenn. 2004).

[123] Bhinder v. Sun Co., 263 Conn. 358, 819 A.2d 822 (2003) (recognizing a statutory change effecting this result); Kansas State Bank & Trust Co. v. Specialized Transp. Servs., Inc., 249 Kan. 348, 819 P.2d 587 (1991); Brandon v. County of Richardson, 624 N.W.2d 604 (Neb. 2001); Turner v. Jordan, 957 S.W.2d 815 (Tenn. 1997). The court in Brandon construed its statutes to exclude comparison between negligence and intent, but also observed that "it would be irrational to allow a party who negligently fails to discharge a duty to protect to reduce its liability because there is an intervening intentional tort when the intervening intentional tort is exactly what the negligent party had a duty to protect against." Brandon, supra, 624 N.W.2d at 620.

[124] Tegman v. Accident & Med. Investigations, Inc., 150 Wash.2d 102, 75 P.3d 497 (2003).

Specific exceptions. The Restatement creates a specific exception for this circumstance. If the defendant owes a specific duty to protect the plaintiff from an intentional tortfeasor, the defendant remains jointly and severally liable.[125] The Uniform Act similarly retains joint and several liability for one who fails to protect another from causing intentional harm.[126]

Not comparing intentional and negligent conduct when the negligent defendant risked the intentional tort. Second, where the statute does not compel a different answer, courts could refuse to compare intentional harm with negligence.[127] That was the traditional practice on the distinct issue of contributory negligence; the plaintiff was not barred by her contributory fault when she sued an intentional tortfeasor. As already indicated, however, a number of courts now hold that, at least in some situations, the fault of a negligent tortfeasor can be compared to that of an intentional tortfeasor.[128] In the absence of an exception, juries would compare the negligence of the landlord with the intentional crime of rape and on this comparison might find the landlord to be comparatively innocent, so that the landlord's liability would be minuscule and the plaintiff, unlikely to find, identify, and recover from the rapist, would be severely under-compensated.

Assigning responsibility not culpability. Third, it can be argued that some statutes and the Restatement of Apportionment envision an assignment of responsibility rather than a comparison of fault. In that system of thought, even if negligence counts as less fault than an intentional tort, a jury can assign greater civil responsibility to the negligent tortfeasor than to the intentional one.[129] One rational reason for such a view is that when the negligent actor creates a risk of an intentional tort, especially when the foreseeable tortfeasor is likely to escape or to have no assets, his negligence encompasses that tort. Arguably, then, one who facilitates an intentional tort of another should be treated like an employer of an independent contractor who is under a nondelegable duty,[130] and held jointly and severally liable under the usual rule that persons who are vicariously liable remain jointly and severally liable even under the statutes that otherwise abolish joint and several liability.[131] It is too soon to know how courts and juries will handle this argument, but several courts have already recognized that a

---

[125] Restatement (Third) of Torts: Apportionment of Liability § 14 (2000).

[126] Unif. Apportionment of Tort Responsibility Act § 6(1) (2002). Statutes may obliquely address the problem. See N.Y. C.P.L.R. § 1602, leaving joint and several liability standing in actions that require proof of intent and also those in which the target defendant acted recklessly.

[127] See Ellen M. Bublick, The End Game of Tort Reform: Comparative Apportionment and Intentional Torts, 78 Notre Dame L. Rev. 355 (2003).

[128] Id. The Restatement supports the general view that the fault involved in intentional torts is to be compared with the fault in negligent torts, see Restatement (Third) of Torts: Apportionment of Liability § 1 (2000), even though it rejects the rule of several liability where the negligent actor creates a specific risk of intentional harm.

[129] Hutcherson v. City of Phoenix, 192 Ariz. 51, 961 P.2d 449, 452 (1998); Ellen Bublick, Upside Down? Terrorists, Proprietors, and Civil Responsibility for Crime Prevention in the Post-9/11 Tort-Reform World, 41 Loy. L.A. L. Rev. 1483 (2008).

[130] See Dobbs, Hayden & Bublick, The Law of Torts § 432 (2d ed. 2011 & Supp.).

[131] Statues may so provide, e.g., Mich. Comp. L. Ann. § 600.2956. See generally Restatement (Third) of Torts: Apportionment of Liability § 13 (2000). This is especially so in the case of an employer who negligently hires or negligently retains a dangerous employee, even if the dangerous employee is acting outside the scope of his employment.

negligent tortfeasor who risks an intentional tort by another may be assigned more significant responsibility than an intentional tortfeasor.[132]

A broad view of action in concert. Fourth, tortfeasors who create a risk of intentional harm to the plaintiff might be counted as tortfeasors acting in concert or aiding and abetting the intentional tortfeasor. Liability of one who acts in concert is at least partly vicarious. In concerted action cases, joint liability presumably remains even after several liability statutes.[133] If so, the landlord acting in concert with the rapists would be liable for the entire damages. Whether the landlord's negligence can count as concerted action, however, has yet to be adjudicated.

Dealing with the problem by jury instructions. In addition to these four potential rules of law, it is possible to deal with the problem in some degree by instructing the jury to determine apportionment by considering the importance of the facilitator's duty.[134]

§ 35.10 Defendants Who Are Under a Duty to Protect Plaintiff from Another's Negligence

When the defendant's negligence risks the negligence of another. The most dramatic concern where joint and several liability has been abolished is the case in which the defendant creates a risk of intentional harm by another, particularly if degrees of wrongfulness are a part of the responsibility apportionment. But the case in which the defendant creates a risk of negligent harm by another is actually much the same, provided the defendant is under a duty to protect against such harm. For example, if the law assigns an alcohol provider the duty to withhold alcohol from an obviously drunken customer, the major point is to protect citizens who may be injured as a result of the drinker's drunken driving. On much the same rationale that applies in a case in which the landlord would be liable for negligent security that permits a rape, it can be said that the alcohol provider should also be liable for negligent provision of alcohol to a driver whose driving devastates a family.

Differing views. In the case of a negligent alcohol provider, courts are divided about the issue of several liability apportionment between defendants that reduces the plaintiff's recovery. Some opinions have approved several liability apportionment,[135] sometimes even when the opinion recognizes that apportionment dilutes the duty and

---

[132] Hutcherson v. City of Phoenix, 192 Ariz. 51, 961 P.2d 449, 452 (1998) ("jury may apportion fault among defendants and nonparties, without distinguishing between intentional and negligent conduct or requiring that a minimum percentage of responsibility be assigned to the former"); Nash v. Port Auth. of N.Y. & N.J., 856 N.Y.S.2d 583 (App. Div. 2008). Some courts have found allocation of more fault to the negligent facilitator to be unsupported by evidence. E.g., Scott v. County of Los Angeles, 27 Cal.App.4th 125, 32 Cal.Rptr.2d 643 (1994); but cf. Frugis v. Bracigliano, 177 N.J. 250, 827 A.2d 1040 (2003) (listing factors and policies that might justify greater liability on the part of the facilitator).

[133] Woods v. Cole, 181 Ill.2d 512, 693 N.E.2d 333, 230 Ill.Dec. 204 (1998); Reilly v. Anderson, 727 N.W.2d 102 (Iowa 2006); Yount v. Deibert, 147 P.3d 1065 (Kan. 2006) (recognizing that joint and several liability remains for intentional and concerted action, but only when the claim is brought by a third person who was not acting in concert); Jedrziewski v. Smith, 128 P.3d 1146 (Utah 2005); Strahin v. Cleavenger, 216 W.Va. 175, 603 S.E.2d 197 (2004) (taking a broad view of joint tortfeasors in this context); Restatement (Third) of Torts: Apportionment of Liability § 24 (2000). Some of the joint and several liability statutes say so, some do not.

[134] See Frugis v. Bracigliano, 177 N.J. 250, 827 A.2d 1040 (2003), discussed below.

[135] In some instances, statutes specifically abolish joint and several liability in alcohol provider cases. See Peters v. Saft, 597 A.2d 50 (Me. 1991) (liquor liability law made provider severally liable only, held, constitutional); Kavadas v. Lorenzen, 448 N.W.2d 219 (N.D. 1989) (provision of alcohol to one who later injured officer in resisting arrest; statute limiting provider's liability to proportionate responsibility was constitutional under rational basis test as against equal protection challenge).

incentive of the facilitator.[136] Although the statutory system of several or proportionate liability was held to apply in apportioning ultimate responsibility between the provider and the intoxicated patron, the provider's liability to the victims was different. The court thought that liability was partly based on imputed negligence and thus analogous to vicarious liability, as to which the several liability system changed nothing. Consequently, the victim could recover all damages from the provider, who in turn was left to recover, if he could, from the drinker himself.[137] Where the statute imposes liability upon the alcohol provider without requiring fault or causation on his part, the claim that liability is vicarious and hence that liability is joint and several is particularly strong.[138]

Examples of negligence that facilitates other torts. Those who negligently provide alcohol to intoxicated or minor drinkers are among the tortfeasors who facilitate the torts of others.[139] In this same category are employers who negligently hire, train, or retain dangerous employees,[140] and individuals who negligently entrust instrumentalities to persons likely to use them in a harmful way.[141] Comparison of fault and apportionment of responsibility in such cases is not easy to rationalize, since the fault of the direct actor is encompassed in the fault of the facilitator.[142]

Facilitator fault or vicarious liability? Where joint and several liability has been abolished, courts struggling with this problem have sometimes sought to resolve it by determining whether the facilitator's liability is purely based on his own fault or, on the contrary, it is based on a kind of vicarious liability, with the negligence of the actor directly causing harm imputed to the facilitator. When courts conclude that the facilitator's liability is rooted in his personal fault, they require apportionment, meaning that the facilitator is liable only for his comparative share.[143] Apportionment may also be required without reference to the distinction between personal fault and vicarious liability.[144] But other courts have rejected apportionment in this setting, retaining the

---

[136] See Steele v. Kerrigan, 148 N.J. 1, 14, 689 A.2d 685, 691 (1997).

[137] See the very thoughtful dissenting opinion of Chief Justice Jefferson in F.F.P. Operating Partners, L.P. v. Duenez, 237 S.W.3d 680 (Tex. 2007).

[138] William D. Underwood & Michael D. Morrison, Apportioning Responsibility in Cases Involving Claims of Vicarious, Derivative, or Statutory Liability for Harm Directly Caused by the Conduct of Another, 55 Baylor L. Rev. 617, 621 (2003).

[139] Writers have used various terms for this special kind of case, sometimes referring to the facilitator of torts caused by others as enablers, sometimes as sentinels. See William K. Jones, Tort Triad: Slumbering Sentinels, Vicious Assailants, and Victims Variously Vigilant, 30 Hofstra L. Rev. 253 (2001) ("sentinel"); Robert L. Rabin, Enabling Torts, 49 DePaul L. Rev. 435 (1999).

[140] See § 26.2, and specific instances, such as a hospital's liability for admission of incompetent physicians or failure to supervise them, §§ 21.16 & 26.6.

[141] See § 26.10.

[142] See Steele v. Kerrigan, 148 N.J. 1, 14, 689 A.2d 685, 691 (1997) (recognizing but not applying the view that apportionment between tortfeasors is precluded when the duty of one "encompassed the obligation to prevent the specific misconduct of the other"). Other New Jersey cases have also recognized that apportionment in several liability systems dilutes the duty of the facilitator-defendant. See Frugis v. Bracigliano, 177 N.J. 250, 827 A.2d 1040 (2003).

[143] Rausch v. Pocatello Lumber Co., Inc., 135 Idaho 80, 14 P.3d 1074 (2000) (negligent supervision by employer); McCart v. Muir, 230 Kan. 618, 641 P.2d 384 (1982) (negligent entrustment); Ali v. Fisher, 145 S.W.3d 557 (Tenn. 2004) (negligent entrustment).

[144] See Bohrer v. DeHart, 961 P. 2d 472 (Colo. 1998) (negligent hiring and supervision, apportionment of responsibility between employer and employee); cf. Frugis v. Bracigliano, 177 N.J. 250, 827 A.2d 1040 (2003) (apportionment and hence limited liability of school board-employer for employee's sexual misbehavior with students, emphasizing statutory construction).

traditional joint and several liability,[145] sometimes finding that the facilitator's liability is rooted, at least by analogy, in vicarious liability rather than personal fault and at least implicitly deciding that apportionment between a tortfeasor and one vicariously liable is inappropriate.[146]

A policy perspective. The vicarious liability/personal fault distinction may not help to resolve the issue, partly because the policy and statutory issues are not necessarily reached through that distinction and partly because the liability of the facilitating tortfeasor may be viewed as partaking of both personal fault and imputed negligence.[147] The facilitator, such as a negligent entrustor, is not liable unless he himself is negligent; in this way, his liability seems grounded in personal fault, not imputed negligence. On the other hand, the facilitator is not liable even if he is at fault unless the entrustee is negligent; in this way, his liability may bear some comparison to imputed negligence. If the statute leaves the court free on this issue, full liability of facilitating tortfeasors, coupled with a right of contribution or indemnity, seems preferable in part because of the lack of logical or just basis for comparing the encompassing fault of the facilitator with the fault the person whose negligence is the more immediate cause.

Guideline instructions. Where courts feel required by statute to limit each defendant's responsibility to his proportionate share of fault, a pragmatic compromise may still be available in the form of guidelines to the jury that require it to consider broad policy issues favoring heavy responsibility on the part of the facilitator. This approach was taken in a New Jersey case, *Frugis v. Bracigliano*.[148] In that case, an elementary school principal sexually abused students. A victim sued the school board as well as the principal, claiming that the school board negligently hired or retained the principal. The proof was powerful that the school board was negligent. However, the court construed the governing statute to require apportionment of fault between the board and the principal. At the same time, the court was concerned that apportionment might leave the board with such a small share of responsibility that its duty would be diluted and it would not be appropriately encouraged to behave with care for the students. To deal with that, the court specifically required instructions that told the jury to apportion responsibility in light of the board-employer's heightened duty and other similar considerations.[149] Although *Frugis* involved a negligent employer who facilitated an intentional tort, the principle behind guiding instructions seems applicable to cases involving defendants who facilitate negligent torts as well, albeit with adjustment in the instruction to recognize that not every facilitator has the heavy responsibility imposed on school boards. The guideline instruction route has some appeal, but it could take some

---

[145] Mitchell v. Hastings & Koch Enters., Inc., 647 N.E.2d 78 (Mass. App. Ct. 1995); Rosell v. Central W. Motor Stages, Inc., 89 S.W.3d 643 (Tex. Ct. App. 2002) (drawing analogy to vicarious liability (which would impose joint and several liability) because the entrustor, no matter how negligent, is not liable unless the entrustee commits a tort). The same outcome may result as a side effect of a common rule that if employment relation and vicarious liability are admitted, the plaintiff cannot also rely on a negligent entrustment or negligent hiring theory. See McHaffie v. Bunch, 891 S.W.2d 822 (Mo. 1995).

[146] Rosell v. Central W. Motor. Stages, Inc., supra n. 145 (drawing analogy to vicarious liability (which would impose joint and several liability) because the entrustor, no matter how negligent, is not liable unless the entrustee commits a tort).

[147] In F.F.P. Operating Partners, L.P. v. Duenez, 237 S.W.3d 680 (Tex. 2007), the court rejected the argument that an alcohol provider was vicariously liable and also rejected the analogy to negligent entrustment.

[148] Frugis v. Bracigliano, 177 N.J. 250, 827 A.2d 1040 (2003).

[149] Spelling out guidelines governing the jury's apportionment. See id. at 282–83, 827 A.2d at 1059.

plaintiffs into dangerous territory if the actor directly causing harm is fully solvent but the facilitator is not.

E. OTHER APPORTIONMENT SYSTEMS

§ 35.11 Joint and Several Liability with Reallocation

Reapportionment of uncollectible shares. Some jurisdictions find joint and several liability unsatisfying because the system imposes on one defendant the complete burden of the insolvency of another. But the several liability system is no more satisfying because it imposes that burden of insolvency entirely on a plaintiff, who may be completely without fault in occasioning the harm. A compromise provision, and one adopted in the Uniform Apportionment of Tort Responsibility Act passed by the National Commissioners on Uniform State Laws, is a system of liability that permits liability for uncollectible shares to be reapportioned among the plaintiff and any other defendants on the basis of the parties' relative responsibility.

An example. Consider this scenario. Suppose the trier finds that the plaintiff suffered $100,000 in damages and was chargeable with 10% of all the negligence, thus reducing her judgment to $90,000 under comparative negligence rules. The jury also finds that A was chargeable with 60% of the fault and B with 30%. Under a joint and several liability system, if the plaintiff enforced her judgment entirely against A, A would pay $90,000 but would be entitled to $30,000 in contribution from B. As always with the traditional joint and several liability system, A may get a judgment for contribution from B but may not be able to collect it. If the plaintiff was wholly without legal fault, this result would be sound, for it would require the negligent tortfeasor rather than the innocent plaintiff to bear the risks of another tortfeasor's insolvency. However, when the plaintiff herself is also at fault, it seems more logical to require that the plaintiff and tortfeasor A share the risk of B's insolvency in proportion to their respective fault shares.[150] In a jurisdiction with reapportionment for an uncollectible share, since A's negligence was 60% of the total and the plaintiff's 10%, they would presumably absorb B's share of liability between them in the same proportion, six to one. The same figure results if you use that ratio for the $100,000 damages figure, ignoring B altogether. A's liability would then by 6/7 of the $100,000 and the plaintiff would absorb 1/7 of that sum.

The argument in favor of reallocation. This outcome is attractive because neither the plaintiff nor defendant A will bear the entire insolvency, nor will the plaintiff's recovery be in proportion to one defendant's responsibility relative to another's. Instead the plaintiff's recovery for the uncollectible share is in proportion to the defendant's responsibility relative to the plaintiff's. With its greater claim of fairness to both plaintiffs and defendants, scholars from other countries have found the doctrine appealing.[151] The approach is quite new and is typically adopted by statute.[152] It may become increasingly popular given the theoretical appeal of the framework and the

---

[150] See Martignetti v. Haigh-Farr Inc., 425 Mass. 294, 680 N.E.2d 1131 (1997) (where plaintiff and defendants are all responsible for release of hazardous materials, plaintiff who bore the cost of cleanup can get contribution from others, but orphan shares of responsibility due to insolvency of any defendant must be borne equitably among all parties).

[151] Zhu Wang, Research on Apportionment of Tort Liability—A General Theory of Apportionment of Tort Liability Among Multiple Parties (2010) (discussing the idea as a model for Chinese tort law).

[152] Conn. Gen. Stat. Ann. § 52–572h(g) & (h); Mich. Comp. L. Ann. § 600.6304(6)(b). Distinguish reallocation statutes that merely provide for reallocation among defendants in contribution actions. See Rodgers v. Colby's Ol' Place, Inc., 802 A.2d 1159 (N.H. 2002).

influence of significant groups who support it including the National Commissioners on Uniform State Laws.

§ 35.12   Hybrid Systems: Joint and Several Liability Based on Threshold Percentages or Type of Damages

Types of hybrid systems. In truth, most jurisdictions' systems could be defined as hybrid systems—state statutes and common law typically provide for some blend of several and joint and several liability rules.[153] However, the Restatement of Apportionment highlights two particular forms of hybrid systems. In one, joint and several liability is retained for tortfeasors whose comparative responsibility share is above a set percentage, but denied if the tortfeasor's comparative responsibility share is below that percentage.[154] In the other, the availability of joint and several liability hinges on the type of damages sought. Typically, joint and several liability applies to plaintiff's economic damages, but several liability applies to the defendant's share of noneconomic damages.[155]

Threshold percentages. In jurisdictions that adopt a threshold percentage for joint and several liability, the purpose is generally to retain the joint and several liability of more significant actors, but deny it in the case of minimally responsible defendants. To be sure, there are problems with this approach and to some extent the actual legal threshold selected is arbitrary.[156] But a number of jurisdictions have embraced this sort of compromise, adopting threshold percentages ranging from 10% to 60%, with 50% as a typical threshold.[157] In some states the threshold is whether the defendant's share of the responsibility is greater than the plaintiff's.[158]

Types of damage. In jurisdictions that determine joint and several liability based on the type of damages for which liability is sought, an underlying idea is that replacement for economic damages is more important than replacement for intangible losses such as pain and suffering, emotional distress, disfigurement, loss of consortium and the like.[159] The split may also reflect a sense that noneconomic losses are more difficult to value and thus more likely to represent a windfall to the plaintiff rather than an appropriate level of compensation.[160] Criticism has centered on the way in which these systems 1) devalue losses that are substantial yet noneconomic, such as with the loss of a plaintiff's reproductive capacity or the loss of plaintiff's child,[161] 2) impact women[162] and

---

[153]   Restatement (Third) of Torts: Apportionment of Liability § D18 cmt. b (2000).

[154]   Id. §§ D18–19.

[155]   Id. §§ E18–21.

[156]   Id. § D18 cmt. c and g.

[157]   Id. § D18 rptrs. notes cmt. g. E.g., N.Y. C.P.L.R. § 1601 (50%). About 10 states use a threshold at some level, sometimes in combination with a distinction between economic loss and noneconomic loss. Ohio's law abolishing joint and several liability for tortfeasors chargeable with less than 50% of the overall responsibility was held unconstitutional in Ohio Acad. of Trial Lawyers v. Steward, 715 N.E.2d 1062 (Ohio 1999).

[158]   See Fla. Stat. Ann. § 768.81; Haw. Rev. Stat. § 663–31.

[159]   Restatement (Third) of Torts: Apportionment of Liability § E18 cmt. c and d (2000).

[160]   See David Baldus, John C. McQueen, & George Woodworth, Improving Judicial Oversight of Jury Damages Assessments: A Proposal for the Comparative Additur/Remittitur Review of Awards for Nonpecuniary Harms and Punitive Damages, 80 Iowa L. Rev. 1109 (1995).

[161]   Lucinda Finley, The Hidden Victims of Tort Reform: Women, Children and the Elderly, 53 Emory L.J. 1263 (2004).

[162]   Id.

3) undermine deterrence.[163] One such law has been held unconstitutional.[164] Nevertheless, a number of other jurisdictions apply this approach by statute.[165] A variation applies joint and several liability only to a specified percentage of the damages award instead of to economic damages.[166]

Type of damage and type of tort. New York's statute abolishes joint and several liability for noneconomic damages as to relatively low-fault defendants. This has been held to permit a 50–50 apportionment between a negligent landlord and the tenant's attacker.[167] However, the statute goes on to provide, in effect, that the negligent tortfeasor loses this protection when he is liable for any tort requiring proof of intent or for recklessness.[168] This is a recognition that some negligent torts are quite seriously wrongful even if, on a comparative basis, only a small percentage of fault can be attributed to those negligent wrongdoers. In *Lubecki v. City of New York*,[169] a bank robber took innocent bystander hostage. He was quickly surrounded by as many as thirty police officers. He held the hostage in front of him. Allegedly in violation of rules, one officer fired, then others followed suit. The hostage was killed. The court held that the plaintiff could amend the pleadings to assert the recklessness exception to the several liability statute.

---

[163] Kwansy v. United States, 823 F.2d 194 (7th Cir. 1987).

[164] Ohio's law abolishing joint and several liability for tortfeasors chargeable with less than 50% of the overall responsibility was held unconstitutional in Ohio Academy of Trial Lawyers v. Steward, 715 N.E.2d 1062 (Ohio 1999).

[165] See, e.g., Cal. Civ. Code § 143; Neb. Rev. Stat. § 25–21,185. Cal. Civ. Code § 1431.2; Neb. Rev. Stat. § 25–21,185.10. California's provision was held inapplicable to strict products liability actions in Bostick v. Flex Equip. Co., 147 Cal. App. 4th 80, 54 Cal. Rptr. 3d 28 (2007). See also Restatement (Third) of Torts: Apportionment of Liability § E18 rptrs note cmt. b (2000).

[166] See Narkeeta Timber Co., Inc. v. Jenkins, 777 So. 2d 39 (Miss. 2001) (construing the Mississippi statute).

[167] Chianese v. Meier, 98 N.Y.2d 270, 746 N.Y.S.2d 657, 774 N.E.2d 722 (2002).

[168] N.Y. C.P.L.R. § 1602.

[169] Lubecki v. City of New York, 304 A.D.2d 224, 758 N.Y.S.2d 610 (2003).

Chapter 36

ALTERNATIVE SYSTEMS FOR COMPENSATING INJURY

Analysis

A. CRITICISM OF TORT
§ 36.1   Criticisms of the Tort System

B. WORKERS' COMPENSATION
§ 36.2   The Workers' Compensation System
§ 36.3   Workers' Compensation: Injury Arising Out of and In the Course of Employment
§ 36.4   Workers' Compensation: Accident vs. Disease
§ 36.5   Workers' Compensation: Exclusive Remedy and Third Parties

C. OTHER INJURY SYSTEMS
§ 36.6   Social Security Disability
§ 36.7   The Private Insurance Alternative
§ 36.8   Government Compensation Funds
§ 36.9   Taxing Industry to Create Compensation Funds

A. CRITICISM OF TORT

§ 36.1 Criticisms of the Tort System

The traditional view. Critics of the tort system have appeared on all sides. The traditional view is that tort law should both compensate victims of wrongful behavior and deter that behavior. Ideally, defendants required to make full compensation would make their behavior safer. In the case of intentional or malicious torts, punitive damages might be invoked to do the job.

Main criticisms. One wave of criticism variously asserted that the tort system (1) does not adequately compensate because many injuries are uncompensated or under compensated, (2) does not deter or does not deter adequately, either because deterrence simply is not accomplished by legal rules and liabilities or because actual liability systematically tends to be less than theoretically required, and (3) is inefficient in its use of resources and in its use of costly liability insurance. Related criticisms pointed to delays that prevented recovery when it was needed and to the limited resources provided by the pool of liability insurance that was sometimes exhausted by recoveries for pain, leaving nothing for what was regarded as more essential—basic economic harms such as wage loss.

Studies on under- and overcompensation. Quite a few studies amply support most of the criticisms about undercompensation, administrative cost and delay except that the deterrence effects remain controversial.[1] One of the earliest empirical studies showed that of 86,000 persons who suffered economic loss, some 20,000 received no compensation, and most of those who were compensated did not draw their compensation from the tort system.[2] There is some argument that undercompensation may be one of tort law's most significant problems.[3] While undercompensation has been common for many serious harms, overcompensation may occur for small losses. This overcompensation is dreadfully costly because so many small losses occur.

Inefficiency. On top of this, liability insurance, which fuels most of the tort system, is said to be relatively inefficient because expenses attributable to litigation consume a significant share of premium dollars[4] (though the significance of these amounts may be fueled by some insurance company practices).[5]

The tort lottery and proposed changes. The uncertainties of tort litigation contribute to the feeling that it is largely a lottery rather than a system for redressing wrongs or assuring compensation.[6] These and many related concerns have led some observers to suggest that many tort problems should be allocated to some other kind of system to be resolved by regulation, by social welfare programs or social insurance, or administrative agencies,[7] although those proposed solutions are not without critics either.[8]

Excessive liability criticisms. A second wave of criticism, associated with "tort reform" mainly of the 1980s, has asserted that the tort system is out of control and that Americans have become lawsuit prone and greedy, suing over every little injury, and driving up the cost of doing business. Critics in this wave argue that insurance has

---

[1]   Compare A. Mitchell Polinsky & Steven Shavell, The Uneasy Market for Products Liability, 123 Harv. L. Rev. 1437 (2000) (suggesting that market forces and regulation can reduce the need for product liability law to encourage safety), and Stephen D. Sugarman, Doing Away with Tort Law, 73 Cal. L. Rev. 556 (1985), with William M. Landes & Richard A. Posner, The Economic Structure of Tort Law (1987), Guido Calabresi, The Cost of Accidents: A Legal and Economic Analysis (1970), and Gary T. Schwartz, Reality in the Economic Analysis of Tort Law: Does the Tort Law Really Deter?, 42 UCLA L. Rev. 377 (1994).

[2]   Alfred F. Conard et al., Automobile Accidents Costs and Payments (1964). However more recent data reflecting widespread automobile insurance coverage show that in the case of automobile accidents, two-thirds of those injured receive at least some compensation. Gary T. Schwartz, Auto No-Fault and First-Party Insurance: Advantages and Problems, 73 S. Cal. L. Rev. 611, 624 (2000).

[3]   See Deborah L. Rhode, Frivolous Litigation and Civil Justice Reform: Miscasting the Problem, Recasting the Solution, 54 Duke L.J. 447, 460 (2004) (contending that "although excessive litigation is the pathology dominating public discussion and policy agendas, systemic research reveals that more serious problems are undercompensation of victims"). See also Joni Hersch & W. Kip Viscusi, Saving Lives Through Punitive Damages, 83 S. Cal. L. Rev. 229 (2010) (proposing increase in wrongful death damages through punitive rather than hedonic damages); Eric A. Posner & Cass R. Sunstein, Dollars and Death, 72 U. Chi. L. Rev. 537 (2005) (supporting higher damage awards in wrongful death claims to promote optimal deterrence).

[4]   See A. Mitchell Polinsky & Steven Shavell, The Uneasy Market for Products Liability, 123 Harv. L. Rev. 1437, 1469–70 (2010) (citing data suggesting injury victims receive 40 to 60 cents of every dollar paid for liability insurance); Joni Hersch & W. Kip Viscusi, Tort Liability Litigation Costs for Commercial Claims, 9 Am. L. & Econ. Rev. 330 (2007) (costs of defending claims were 18% of insurers' total expenditures); Jeffery O'Connell, Why Economists and Philosophers Flunk Torts: With a Guide to Getting a Good Grade, 53 Emory L.J. 1349 (2004); Deborah H. Hensler et al., "Trends in Tort Litigation: The Story Behind the Statistics" in RAND Institute for Civil Justice, R-3583-ICJ (1987).

[5]   Jay M. Feinman, Delay, Deny, Defend (2010).

[6]   See Marc A. Franklin, Replacing the Negligence Lottery: Compensation and Selective Reimbursement, 53 Va. L. Rev. 774 (1967).

[7]   E.g., Stephen Sugarman, Doing Away with Personal Injury Law (1989); W. Kip Viscusi, Toward a Diminished Role for Tort Liability: Social Insurance, Government Regulation, and Contemporary Risks to Health and Safety, 6 Yale J. Reg. 65 (1989); Richard B. Stewart, Crisis in Tort Law? The Institutional Perspective, 54 U. Chi. L. Rev. 184 (1987).

[8]   See Jerry Mashaw & David Harfst, The Struggle for Auto Safety (1990); Michael J. Trebilcock, Requiem for Regulators: The Passing of a Counter-Culture, 8 Yale J. Reg. 497 (1991).

become too costly as a result of overcompensating the injured, and that in some cases insurance has become unavailable. They also say that some valuable products like prescription drugs and vaccines may be driven from the market because of the tort liabilities they produce. These criticisms have already affected tort law in most jurisdictions. Many states have imposed caps on compensatory and punitive damages, reintroduced, expanded or created new immunities, barred some claims before they have accrued, or abolished joint and several liability.[9] Overall, the reforms make the individual and the individual case less important by making the facts about liability and damages less significant and categorical rules more significant.[10]

Data on excessive liability criticism. Much of the support for the tort reform criticisms is anecdotal and impressionistic.[11] There is not much good evidence that litigation has increased overall when population increases are taken into account,[12] even in states said to be experiencing a litigation crisis.[13] In fact, the percentage of tort cases today may actually be smaller than it was in earlier years.[14] Similarly, there is not much reason to think that juries are "running amok."[15] According to a Bureau of Justice Statistics sample, juries found for plaintiffs in 52% of the cases and judges found for the plaintiff a little more often.[16] Moreover, data indicates that when judges act as triers of fact they make similar awards to those made by juries, even with respect to punitive damages.[17] Neither is there reason to believe that damages awards have generally increased. An intensive, 12-year study in a major metropolitan area concluded that before tort reform, neither the number of products and medical claims nor the amounts awarded had increased. Similarly, win rates for plaintiffs in those cases are especially low.[18] Recent data puts the median total award in a sample of tort cases at $24,000.[19] This figure is less than the average economic cost of injury in at least some types of cases.[20] In 2006, the prestigious *New England Journal of Medicine* published a study of over 1,400 medical malpractice claims. The study, carried out by medical doctors, lawyers, nurses, and public health experts, found that about 60% of the claims did in

---

[9]   See Michael L. Rustad & Thomas H. Koening, Taming the Tort Monster: The American Civil Justice System as a Battleground of Social Theory, 68 Brook. L. Rev. 1, 66–72 (2002); Joseph Sanders & Craig Joyce, "Off to the Races": The 1980s Tort Crisis and the Law Reform Process, 27 Hous. L. Rev. 207 (1990).

[10]   See Kenneth S. Abraham, What Is a Tort Claim? An Interpretation of Contemporary Tort Reform, 51 Md. L. Rev. 172 (1992) (noting also that some changes favorable to plaintiffs do the same).

[11]   See Marc Galanter, Real World Torts: An Antidote to Anecdote, 55 Md. L. Rev. 1093 (1996). Some of the anecdotes reporting absurd awards were not true. See Joseph A. Page, Deforming Tort Reform, 78 Geo. L.J. 649 (1990) (book review of Peter W. Huber, Liability: The Legal Revolution and Its Consequences (1988)).

[12]   Brian Ostrom et al., Examining the Work of State Courts 2002, at 24 (National Center for State Courts, 2003); David J. Nye & Donald G. Gifford, The Myth of Liability Insurance Claims Explosion: An Empirical Rebuttal, 41 Vand. L. Rev. 909 (1988).

[13]   See Bernard Black et al., Stability, Not Crisis: Medical Malpractice Claims Outcomes in Texas, 1998–2002, 2 J. Empirical Legal Stud. 207, 210 (2005).

[14]   See Michael J. Saks, Do We Really Know Anything About the Behavior of the Tort Litigation System—And Why Not?, 140 U. Pa. L. Rev. 1147 (1992).

[15]   Much tort reform criticism is based upon a distrust of juries, who are collectively perceived as "running amok." E.g., 135 Cong. Rec. S5989–02 (June 1, 1989).

[16]   Bureau of Justice Statistics, Civil Bench and Jury Trials in State Courts, 2005 (2008).

[17]   See Theodore Eisenberg et al., Juries, Judges, and Punitive Damages: an Empirical Study, 87 Cornell L. Rev. 743 (2002).

[18]   Deborah Jones Merritt & Kathryn Ann Barry, Is the Tort System in Crisis? New Empirical Evidence, 60 Ohio St. L.J. 315, 334, 350, 352 (1999).

[19]   Bureau of Justice Statistics, Civil Bench and Jury Trials in State Courts, 2005 (2008).

[20]   National Safety Council, Injury Facts 91 (2003) (putting the average economic cost of injury in automobile cases at $52,000 without factoring in human costs).

fact involve medical errors, and in addition that where no medical error was demonstrated, the claims were mostly denied compensation.[21] Reviewing a large number of studies in the medical field, one set of commentators evaluated the data this way: "Plaintiffs who received substandard care generally obtained compensation; plaintiffs who received proper care generally did not; and plaintiffs whose care quality was uncertain wound up in between."[22]

Increase in litigation: economic tort claims. Economic tort litigation appears to have grown, but that is largely litigation by business enterprises among themselves, not personal injury claims by individuals.[23]

Insurance costs. As to insurance costs, it is assuredly true that in some periods premiums have risen, and this was especially painful to health care providers. However, increased premium costs is a complex matter. Premiums are raised at least in part when insurance investment income is reduced in a slow economy, not necessarily because of tort claims. The data available are always limited and can never be fully current, but overall they suggest that in fact, many people with very good claims do not sue or even assert a claim,[24] and that restricting tort law does not solve all health care worries.[25]

Interest groups affecting perceptions. The question whether the tort system has serious problems and how to resolve them has been highly politicized by interest groups.[26] Neutral and objective reporting of the facts and assessment of the arguments is very difficult to obtain.[27] However, serious study has been undertaken.[28]

---

[21]   David M. Studdert et al., Claims, Errors, and Compensation Payments in Medical Malpractice Litigation, 354 New Eng. J. Med. 2024 (2006).

[22]   David A. Hyman & Charles Silver, Medical Malpractice Litigation and Tort Reform: It's the Incentive Stupid, 59 Vand. L. Rev. 1085, 1097 (2006).

[23]   See John T. Nockleby & Shannon Curreri, 100 Years of Conflict: The Past and Future of Tort Retrenchment, 38 Loy. L.A. L. Rev. 1021, 1080–85 (2005) (discussing dramatic increases in business litigation despite overall decreases in tort filings).

[24]   See A. Russell Localio et al., Relation Between Malpractice Claims and Adverse Events Due to Negligence, 325 New Eng. J. Med. 245 (July 25, 1991) (study by health care providers of negligence in health care).

[25]   See Charles R. Ellington et. al., State Tort Reforms and Hospital Malpractice Costs, 38 J. of L. Med. & Ethics 127 (2010) (finding that some caps on noneconomic damages reduced malpractice costs and some did not, but that no tort reform measures were associated with improved financial solvency of hospitals).

[26]   See Elizabeth G. Thornburg, Judicial Hellholes, Lawsuit Climates and Bad Social Science: Lessons from West Virginia, 100 W.Va. L. Rev. 1097 (2008) (discussing campaigns to shape public opinion in a misleading way); Stephen Daniels & Joanne Martin, The Strange Success of Tort Reform, 53 Emory L.J. 1225 (2004) (discussing the impact of public tort reform campaigns on public suspicion of the tort law); Joseph Sanders & Craig Joyce, "Off to the Races": The 1980s Tort Crisis and the Law Reform Process, 27 Hous. L. Rev. 207 (1990) (describing one legislative process).

[27]   With respect to those difficulties, see Marc Galanter, Shadow Play: The Fabled Menace of Punitive Damages, 1998 Wis. L. Rev. 1, 13–14 (reporting that one group tried to get the American Bar Association to repudiate a conference discussing pros and cons of tort reform and then boycotted it); Jerome B. Meites et al., Justice James D. Heiple: Impeachment and the Assault on Judicial Independence, 29 Loy. U. Chi. L.J. 741 (1998) (reporting impeachment investigation after the Supreme Court of Illinois held a tort reform statute unconstitutional and an attack on the court by the Illinois Manufacturers' Association).

[28]   See John T. Nockleby, How to Manufacture a Crisis: Empirical Claims Behind "Tort Reform," 86 Or. L. Rev. 533 (2007) (reviewing empirical studies on the tort reform issue); Bernard Black et al., Stability, Not Crisis: Medical Malpractice Claims Outcomes in Texas, 1998–2002, 2 J. Empirical Legal Stud. 207, 210 (2005) (studying closed medical malpractice claims in Texas); Gary R. Smith, The Future of Tort Reform: Reframing the Remedy, Re-balancing the Scales, 53 Emory L.J. 1219 (2004) (introducing a thoughtful academic symposium on tort reform efforts).

Mass torts and class actions advantages. The development of mass tort litigation in the 1980s—hundreds of thousands of asbestos claims, for example[29]—has generated a third set of critic-observers and a large body of literature.[30] Mass torts claims have clogged courts. Critics say the system has been inefficient, expensive, and unfair.[31] Tort law grew out of judicial efforts to resolve cases one by one. That setting enhanced the courts' commitment to the rights of both parties based on the unique facts of each claim and defense. With the development of mass tort litigation, lawyers may carry large "inventories" of claims against a product manufacturer or others—perhaps as many as 10,000 claims aggregated and settled in a batch. Some of the dangers, including collusive settlements that benefit primarily lawyers and defendants but not plaintiffs,[32] may be obvious, but even in the absence of venal behavior, individuals are likely to be submerged in the mass claim. There are some protections for class members.[33] Moreover, class actions present certain advantages. Some individuals' only hope of success may be through the enhanced investment and services they obtain as part of the lawyer's inventory of cases. Moreover, some claims are so small that one-by-one litigation would essentially give the plaintiff the only option of no vindication of rights.[34] Some critics have suggested that injured individuals should be permitted to sell their claims to brokers who would amass claims in a group for more efficient handling.[35] Others suggests that mass torts be removed from the tort system for some kind of alternative resolution, either one more individually oriented[36] or one less so.[37] A variation is to preserve the tort system until the mass claim is mature, then invoke some kind of administrative or "claims center" approach for remaining issues.[38] One possibility is to combine bellwether trials with non-class but aggregate settlements facilitated through multidistrict litigation.[39] However these systems pose a number of ethical risks. For

---

[29]   See Stephen J. Carroll et al., Asbestos Litigation 104 (2005); Deborah R. Hensler & Mark A. Peterson, Understanding Mass Personal Injury Litigation: A Socio-legal Analysis, 59 Brook. L. Rev. 961 (1993) (defining mass torts partly with reference to commonality of issues and interdependence that distinguishes the half million automobile accident cases disposed of each year).

[30]   Richard A. Nagareda, Mass Torts in a World of Settlement (2007); John C. Coffee, Jr., Class Wars: The Dilemma of the Mass Tort Class Action, 95 Colum. L. Rev. 1343 (1995) (an excellent summary of facts, issues, and viewpoints).

[31]   For factual histories of a number of mass tort litigations, see Deborah R. Hensler & Mark A. Peterson, Understanding Mass Personal Injury Litigation: A Socio-legal Analysis, 59 Brook. L. Rev. 961 (1993); Francis E. McGovern, Resolving Mature Mass Tort Litigation, 69 B.U. L. Rev. 659 (1989).

[32]   See John C. Coffee, Jr., Class Wars: The Dilemma of The Mass Tort Class Action, 95 Colum. L. Rev. 1343, 1367–84 (1995) (summarizing various forms of "collusion" between plaintiffs' lawyers and defendants in mass tort settlements).

[33]   Amchem Prods., Inc. v. Windsor, 521 U.S. 591 (1997).

[34]   Carnegie v. Household Int'l, Inc., 376 F.3d 656 (7th Cir. 2004).

[35]   The original idea, see Robert Cooter & Stephen D. Sugarman, A Regulated Market in Unmatured Tort Claims: Tort Reform by Contract, in New Directions in Liability Law 174 (Walter Olson ed.1988), was not about mass torts, but can be adapted to deal with the mass tort problem. See Peter H. Schuck, Mass Torts: an Institutional Evolutionist Perspective, 80 Cornell L. Rev. 941 (1995).

[36]   Richard A. Nagareda, Mass Torts in a World of Settlement (2007). Cf. Carrie Menkel-Meadow, Taking the Mass Out of Mass Torts: Reflections of a Dalkon Shield Arbitrator on Alternative Dispute Resolution, Judging, Neutrality, Gender, and Process, 31 Loy. L.A. L. Rev. 513 (1998) (discussing ADR with mediation and story-telling as part of a mass tort resolution).

[37]   Cf. Robert L. Rabin, Some Thoughts on the Efficacy of a Mass Toxics Administrative Compensation Scheme, 52 Md. L. Rev. 951, 981 (1993) (expressing cautious attitude about substituting administrative compensation systems for mass tort litigation, but also suggesting that if another major wave of mass tort litigation is to be foreseen, the case for a no-fault administrative compensation system would be very strong).

[38]   Francis E. McGovern, Resolving Mature Mass Tort Litigation, 69 B.U. L. Rev. 659 (1989).

[39]   Thomas E. Willging & Emery G. Lee III, From Class Actions to Multidistrict Consolidations: Aggregating Mass-Tort Litigation After Ortiz, 58 U. Kan. L. Rev. 775 (2010).

example, plaintiffs' lawyers may be at risk for losing their attorney fees unless they pressure clients to sign-off on settlements.[40] Another possibility, although it seems adapted to a narrow range of cases, is to create a state or federal compensation fund that operates independently of tort law, as Congress did in the case of victims of the September 11 terrorist attack on the Pentagon and World Trade Center.[41] A company or industry paid fund is another approach.[42]

Alternatives

Different systems. Deep-seated criticisms assert that the tort way of resolving disputes, providing compensation, and seeking deterrence is so inadequate that alternative systems should be sought out. A number of different systems are actually now in place. They do not displace the tort system over a wide spectrum. Instead, they supplement it in providing some degree of relief for injury when tort law provides none or an inadequate amount, or providing a more efficient (and less individualized) system for administering compensation. In fact, these compensation systems are so vast that tort law might be seen as a supplement to some of them.[43] The alternatives in place generally provide caps or limits on compensation. Some alternatives are limited welfare systems, providing for emergency medical care[44] or funds for rehabilitation.[45] In mass tort cases, the bankruptcy court has also become a kind of alternative for administering relief.[46] Alternative dispute resolution (ADR), emphasizing party control of the dispute, mediation, and negotiation, and, quite distinctly, arbitration,[47] also represent possible approaches to claims now allocated to the tort system.

Five important alternatives. Five alternative systems are especially important because they represent some of the divergent approaches that may suggest the pitfalls and advantages of different alternative systems. At the same time, these five systems are not only in place but are sometimes critical in determining tort rights and liabilities and consequently deserve notice of tort lawyers. These five systems are (1) workers' compensation, (2) social security disability or welfare rights, (3) private insurance such

---

[40]   See L. Elizabeth Chamblee, Unsettling Efficiency: When Non-Class Aggregation of Mass Torts Creates Second-Class Settlements, 65 La. L. Rev. 157 (2004) (discussing ethical issues in settlements of aggregated but uncertified claims); Heather Won Tesoriero & Nathan Koppel, Vioxx Settlement Plan Heads For Key Deadlines, Wall St. J., Jan. 10, 2008, at B1 (outlining agreement requiring participating lawyers to recommend settlement to all of their clients and withdraw from cases in which clients did not accept settlement).

[41]   Air Transportation Safety and System Stabilization Act of 2001, Pub.L. No. 107–42, 115 Stat 230. The Victims' Compensation portion is Title IV. The statute excludes tort claims for those who assert a claim to the fund and caps tort claims for those who do not. See 3 Dobbs, Hayden & Bublick, The Law of Torts § 510 (2d ed. 2011 & Supp.).

[42]   The BP Oil Spill Victim Compensation Fund is one example. See Jackie Calmes & Helene Cooper, BP Chief to Express Contrition in Remarks to Panel, N.Y. Times at A1, June 16, 2010.

[43]   See Kenneth S. Abraham, The Liability Century 2–3 (2008) (estimating that tort law accounts for approximately $200 billion dollars of $1.5 trillion in total compensation for injury, illness and death in this country). See alsoJulie Davies, Reforming the Tort Reform Agenda, 25 Wash. U. J.L. & Pol'y 11 (2007) (discussing the way in which tort law and health care are connected and the way in which "uninsured Americans are forced by need to seek de facto health coverage through the tort system when they are injured").

[44]   See 2 Dobbs, Hayden & Bublick, The Law of Torts § 317 (2d ed. 2011 & Supp.).

[45]   See 29 U.S.C.A. §§ 701 et seq. (structuring a vocational rehabilitation program).

[46]   John C. Coffee, Jr., Class Wars: The Dilemma of the Mass Tort Class Action, 95 Colum. L. Rev. 1343, 1387 (1995).

[47]   See Harold Brown, Alternative Dispute Resolution, 30 Suffolk U. L. Rev. 743 (1997) (expressing concerns in the area of commercial ADR); William P. Zdancewicz, Alternative Dispute Resolution in the Personal Injury Forum, 26 U. Mem. L. Rev. 1169 (1996) (supporting mediation or arbitration in personal injury context).

as that found in no-fault plans, (4) government compensation funds and (5) a system for taxing dangerous activities and using the funds created by the tax to pay for harms. Each of these alternatives could be adopted as a way of dealing with some personal injuries. In fact, four of the five have actually been substituted for the tort system somewhere. Each has advantages and disadvantages in the kind of deterrence that might be generated, the extent and appropriateness of compensation, and the kind of process used. Whether they are deemed better than the tort system or worse, they all throw a strong sidelight on it.

B. WORKERS' COMPENSATION

§ 36.2   The Workers' Compensation System

Common Law and the Adoption of Workers' Compensation

Common law liabilities of employers. Nineteenth century employers owed a duty of care to employees, usually described in specific terms as a duty to provide employees with a reasonably safe place in which to work, reasonably safe tools and appliances, warnings of dangers likely to be unknown to employees, a sufficient number of suitable fellow servants, and rules that would make work safe.[48] However, the ordinary rules of vicarious liability did not apply; under the fellow servant rule, the employer was not liable for injuries to an employee caused by the negligence of another employee.[49] In addition, injured employees were barred from recovery by contributory negligence and a broad application of assumed risk. Beyond this, much of the work around machinery was unavoidably dangerous, so that injuries occurred often enough even without provable fault. All these things plus the delay and uncertainty of compensation made life for the injured worker almost intolerably difficult, especially in a day when no welfare backup of any kind was available.

Early compensation systems. There were niches of liability. Admiralty law recognized a kind of judge-made no-fault compensation system for seamen, who would be entitled to maintenance and care during a recuperative period, that is, basic support and medical attention.[50] In addition, a few statutes were passed to require safer working places, but these were construed narrowly to avoid liability in many instances.[51] Congress provided for automatic couplings and other safety devices on railroad trains.[52] The Federal Employers' Liability Act established a rule of comparative negligence and eliminated the bar of contributory fault and assumed risk for employees of interstate railroads,[53] but at best these statutes applied only to railroad workers.

Development of workers' compensation. Given the limited hopes a worker might have under the common law rules, workers' compensation statutes represented

---

[48] See Glass v. Hazen Confectionery Co., 211 Mass. 99, 97 N.E. 627 (1912) (instructions, suitable appliances); Carriere v. Merrick Lumber Co., 203 Mass. 322, 89 N.E. 544 (1909) (safe place); Thomas M. Cooley, Law of Torts 647–62 (2d ed. 1888).

[49] Farwell v. Boston & Worcester R.R., 45 Mass. 49 (1842); Priestly v. Fowler, 3 M. & W. 1, 150 Eng. Rep. 1030 (Exch. 1837).

[50] Thomas Schoenbaum, Admiralty and Maritime Law §§ 5–1 through 5–23 (2004).

[51] E.g., Jaeger v. Evangelical Lutheran Holy Ghost Congregation, 219 Wis. 209, 262 N.W. 585, 101 A.L.R. 405 (1935) (safe place requirement did not apply to transient conditions like a dangerous stack of chairs that might fall upon the plaintiff).

[52] 27 Stat. 531 (1893); the coupling requirement now appears as 49 U.S.C.A. § 20302.

[53] 45 U.S.C.A. § 53. The Jones Act did the same for seamen. 46 U.S.C.A. § 688.

progressive reform.[54] However, it originated in Germany, as Bismarck's defense against Marxism[55] and workers' compensation ever since has shown a side favorable to workers and another side quite favorable to employers. In 1910 New York became the first state to enact a workers' compensation statute. This was held unconstitutional as a taking of property without due process because it imposed liability without fault,[56] but with an amendment of its constitution New York got a statute that held up. Other states followed, most of them quickly. All states now have workers' compensation statutes. A federal compensation plan provides for federal workers[57] and another for longshoremen.[58] Workers' compensation plans reflect the clearest expression of the enterprise liability ideas—that enterprise should bear the costs it systematically produces, including the costs of injury. But they also show a strong intent to limit significantly the employers' liabilities.

The Architecture of Workers' Compensation

Basic information. Workers' compensation requires employers to pay benefits for disability caused by accidental injuries arising out of and in the course of employment and for injuries resulting from an occupational disease incurred in employment, subject to some careful exclusions. Some employments and some types of employees are excluded[59] or included[60] by statute and some statutes still permit workers or employers to opt out of a workers' compensation system. The incentives favor staying within the system and few elect to return to the common law system. Otherwise, workers' compensation is generally mandatory. It may even impose responsibility upon "statutory employers" whose "employees" are actually independent contractors.[61] The structure of workers' compensation statutes in most states is described below.

Compensation rules. The employer (1) is strictly liable for injury incurred in the course and scope of employment and (2) is required to purchase private insurance or participate in a state-managed insurance fund to guarantee payments of benefits as required by the statute; (3) cannot limit liability by reason of the workers' contributory negligence or assumed risk, or under the fellow servant rule, although he is not liable for an employee's self-inflicted intentional injury; (4) benefits from limited liability (for example, in the case of an employee's total disablement, the employee's recovery may be two-thirds of her average wage for a limited period of years plus medical expenses, but

---

[54]   United States v. City of New York, 359 F.3d 83 (2d Cir. 2004) (classifying eligibility for workers' compensation as a benefit of city program); Darryll M. Halcomb Lewis, An Analysis of Brown v. National Football League, 9 Vill. Sports & Ent. L.J. 263 (2002) (arguing that workers compensation may provide remedies superior to tort law for some injured football players).

[55]   See Arthur Larson & Lex K. Larson, Workers' Compensation § 5.10.

[56]   Ives v. South Buffalo Ry. Co., 201 N.Y. 271, 94 N.E. 431 (1911).

[57]   5 U.S.C.A. §§ 8101 et seq.

[58]   33 U.S.C.A. §§ 901 et seq.

[59]   Employers of agricultural workers, casual and domestic workers, and a few employees may be exempted from workers' compensation coverage. Many statutes cover undocumented workers. See, e.g., Moyera v. Quality Pork Int'l, 825 N.W.2d 409 (Neb. 2013).

[60]   Md. Code Ann. Lab. & Empl. § 9–231.1 (2008) (volunteers for state government are covered for medical benefits under workers' compensation); Va. Code Ann. § 65.2–102(B) (2008) (off-duty police who undertake law enforcement or rescue activities are entitled to workers compensation). Statutes may also specify who must pay workers' compensation benefits where an employee has been loaned by one employer to another. See, e.g., Cattlemen's Steakhouse, Inc. v. Waldenville, 318 P.3d 1105 (Okla. 2013).

[61]   E.g., Pinter Constr. Co. v. Frisby, 678 P.2d 305 (Utah 1984).

notably not for pain and suffering); (5) pays benefits (through the insurer or state fund) periodically and immediately, with payment processed automatically.

Administrative enforcement. Enforcement is ordinarily in the hands of an administrative agency, so there is no jury trial in most states. The role of courts in reviewing the administrative decision is to determine issues of law and the sufficiency of evidence to meet the legal requirements.[62] The workers' compensation remedy is exclusive; the worker cannot recover from the employer in tort, even if the employer is negligent. Moreover, the employee cannot recover unless she suffers medically treatable harm or a disability. Some states do permit a tort recovery against the employer for his intentional torts, however. Occupational disease and disability without external injury may be treated much more cautiously.

Workers' Compensation as a Model for Changing Tort Law?

Standardization. In comparison to the individualized approach of the tort system, workers' compensation is highly standardized. In workers' compensation, the fact of injury is a matter to be determined individually, case by case, but the amount of compensation and its cap is standardized. The issue of negligence simply does not arise. Standardization and severely limited benefits yield efficiency in the sense that a relatively high percentage of dollars invested in insurance are returned as benefits. Yet the original hope that lawyers would be unnecessary has proved to be too optimistic. A high percentage of claims are disposed of without serious dispute or administrative resolution, but in disputed claims, lawyers are quite often needed. The original hope that payments would be prompt has sometimes been disappointed, too, although the system performs far better in that regard than the tort system.

Concerns. Some critics object that benefits are too low and too limited; others object that the system, efficient as it is, costs too much. Recent statutes in some states reflect some doubts; they have made it permissible for the first time for unions and employers to provide themselves with an alternative dispute resolution (ADR) system in certain employments.[63]

Exclusive remedy. The workers' compensation system also poses problems in the way that it relates to the tort system. The exclusive remedy provision bars claims even against the egregiously negligent employer and it also protects the employer against liability for contribution when third persons are held liable.[64] Employer-oriented criticisms, however, suggest that the exclusive remedy is not exclusive enough because employees can "circumvent" workers' compensation and sue in tort when the employer is guilty of an intentional tort, when other statutes provide a remedy, and several other instances.[65] Yet when workers are guilty of intentional[66] or reckless misconduct, employers may well want out of the workers compensation system themselves.[67]

---

[62]   Straub v. City of Scottsbluff, 280 Neb. 163, 784 N.W.2d 886 (2010).

[63]   See Ellyn Moscowitz & Victor J. Van Bourg, Carve-outs and the Privatization of Workers' Compensation in Collective Bargaining Agreements, 46 Syracuse L. Rev. 1 (1995).

[64]   See 3 Dobbs, Hayden & Bublick, The Law of Torts § 506 (2d ed. 2011 & Supp.).

[65]   Joan T.A. Gabel et al., The New Relationship Between Injured Worker and Employer: An Opportunity for Restructuring the System, 35 Am. Bus. L.J. 403 (1998).

[66]   See Brackett v. Focus Hope, Inc., 753 N.W.2d 201 (Mich. 2008) (state statute bars compensation where employee has engaged in "intentional and willful misconduct").

[67]   See Arreola v. Administrative Concepts, 17 So.3d 792, 794 (Fla. Dist. Ct. App. 2009) (illegal status of employee was not a bar to receiving workers compensation benefits but providing a false social security

§ 36.3   Workers' Compensation: Injury Arising Out of and In the Course of Employment

Course of employment. The statutes provide for benefits only for accidental injury occurring in the course of and arising out of employment. Course of employment refers mainly to time and place; injuries that occur going from or coming to work are not covered[68] unless the employee is on a special errand or holds a traveling job for the employer, in which case injury during the travel falls within the course of employment.[69] There are many borderline cases requiring adjudication, as where the employee is injured in the company parking lot on the way to work,[70] injured during a break[71] or company event,[72] or telecommuting from home.[73]

Arising out of employment. An injury is not necessarily compensable because it occurs in the course of employment; it must also arise out of employment. That is, the injury must be associated with risks of employment. Broadly speaking, the issue is like the scope-of-risk issue in proximate or legal cause cases, except that, because liability for workers' compensation is strict, the risk need not be negligently created or even foreseeable.[74] It is enough if it is a risk associated with employment, even if the risk itself is small or unexpected. In the main, the arising out of employment rule excludes personal risks. If an employee acting in the course of employment is attacked by a stranger, or by a fellow employee in a job-related dispute, the injury arises out of employment.[75] But if

number with the purpose of obtaining those benefits was fraud which was a bar); Travis M. Wheeler, Grammatico v. Industrial Commission: Invalidating Statutes Making Alcohol or Drug Use a Bar to Workers' Compensation Claims in Arizona, 48 Ariz. L. Rev. 211 (2006).

[68]   E.g., Haslam's Case, 451 Mass. 101, 883 N.E.2d 949 (2008); Harris v. Westin Mgmt. Co. East, 230 S.W.3d 1 (Mo. 2007); Heath v. Montana Mun. Ins. Auth., 959 P.2d 480 (Mont. 1998).

[69]   E.g., Khan v. Parsons Global Servs., Ltd., 428 F.3d 1079 (D.C. Cir. 2005) (kidnapped employee was "traveling employee"); Mulready v. University Research Corp., 360 Md. 51, 756 A.2d 575 (2000) (fall in bathtub while preparing to give presentation away from home compensable); Bob Allyn Masonry v. Murphy, 183 P.3d 126 (Nev. 2008) (special errand); Leordeanu v. American Protection Ins. Co., 330 S.W.3d 239 (Tex. 2010) (claimant was on her way home from an employer-sponsored dinner and had the intention to stop first an employer-provided storage facility to empty her company car of business supplies); Ball-Foster Glass Container Co. v. Giovanelli, 163 Wash.2d 133, 177 P.3d 692 (2008) (traveling employee injured while walking to a park; injury compensable).

[70]   E.g., Hersh v. County of Morris, 86 A.3d 140 (N.J. 2014) (injuries from parking garage not owned by employer to place of employment); Cf. Jaeger Baking Co. v. Kretschmann, 96 Wis.2d 590, 292 N.W.2d 622 (1980) (statute making travel between parking lot and work site compensable did not apply to worker who arrived by bus and was on the parking lot-to-work route but never in the parking lot).

[71]   Ray Bell Constr. Co. v. King, 281 Ga. 853, 642 S.E.2d 841 (2007); K-Mart Corp. v. Herring, 188 P.3d 140 (Okla. 2008) (night watchman who was shot during a trip to a fast-food restaurant during a 7-hour shift with no scheduled breaks was still acting in the course of employment); City of Eugene v. McDermed, 250 Or. App. 572, 282 P.3d 947 (2012) (police officer hit by a car while crossing the street on a break to get a cup of coffee); Gooden v. Coors Technical Ceramic Co., 236 S.W.3d 151 (Tenn. 2007) (employee's heart attack while playing basketball on company premises during work break was in the course of employment).

[72]   Frost v. Salter Path Fire & Rescue, 639 S.E.2d 429 (N.C. 2007).

[73]   Wait v. Travelers Indem. Co., 240 S.W.3d 220 (Tenn. 2007) (injury that occurred at plaintiff's home during her lunch hour took place "in the course of employment").

[74]   Courts may conflate "proximate cause" with "arising out of employment," however, when denying compensation. See, e.g., Sapko v. State, 305 Conn. 360, 44 A.3d 827 (2012) (employee's ingestion of excess quantity of prescribed medications, for reasons that had no relation to his employment, "constituted an intervening event that broke the chain of causation").

[75]   Hartford Accident & Indem. Co. v. Cardillo, 112 F.2d 11 (D.C. 1940); but see Horodyskyj v. Karanian, 32 P.3d 470 (Colo. 2001) (discussing standards for and limits of the rules).

the employee is attacked in an injury that arises from the employee's personal life, there is no recovery.[76]

Neutral risk cases. When the risk that eventuates in injury is "neutral," neither especially personal nor especially job-related, courts sometimes have difficulty in determining whether the injury arose out of employment. If the employment increased the risk,[77] or in some states, if the employment was merely a but-for cause of the harm, the employer will owe compensation in neutral risk cases, as where the employee merely slips and falls.[78] Many variations on the theme arise, almost always turning on factual details that help associate or disassociate the injury from employment risks.[79]

§ 36.4   Workers' Compensation: Accident vs. Disease

Accidental Injury

Intent. Occupational disease aside, compensation statutes also require "accidental injury," or as sometimes phrased, "injury by accident."[80] The requirement of an accident certainly implies that an injury intentionally self-inflicted would not qualify for compensation. However, when a third person attacks the employee on the job, the injury remains an accident from the point of view of both the employee and the employer, so compensation is awarded in such cases if the attack arose out of employment,[81] and the same kind of reasoning has led courts to treat co-employee attacks as compensable accidental injuries so far as the employer is concerned.[82]

---

[76]   Guillory v. Interstate Gas Station, 653 So.2d 1152 (La. 1995); Brookhaven Steam Laundry v. Watts, 214 Miss. 569, 59 So. 2d 294 (1952) (lover's spouse shot employee). Factual details are determinative and there are many factual variations. See, e.g., Lane v. Industrial Comm'n of Ariz., 218 Ariz. 44, 178 P.3d 516 (Ct. App. 2008) (off-duty police officer's shooting did not have the necessary quantum of connection to the employment to be compensable).

[77]   E.g., Jivan v. Economy Inn & Suites, 370 Ark. 414, 260 S.W.3d 281 (2007) (claimant's duties as assistant hotel manager required her to reside at the hotel, which put her at more risk than someone who did not live on premises); Brady v. Louis Ruffolo & Sons Constr. Co., 143 Ill.2d 542, 578 N.E.2d 921, 161 Ill.Dec. 275 (1991) (if risk is not related to employment it must be peculiar or increased by employment); Mitchell v. Clark County Sch. Dist., 111 P.3d 1104 (Nev. 2005) (liability rejected for fall for no identified reason; rejecting positional risk test that but-for cause is sufficient when risk is neutral).

[78]   Circle K Store No. 1131 v. Industrial Comm'n of Ariz., 165 Ariz. 91, 796 P.2d 893 (1990); Logsdon v. Isco Co., 260 Neb. 624, 618 N.W.2d 667 (2000) (unexplained fall in the course of employment is compensable as a neutral risk to which the positional risk test applies); cf. Wilson v. State Farm Ins., 326 Or. 413, 952 P.2d 528 (1998) (tendon injured when employee carrying out normal tasks "skip stepped"). But see Johme v. St. John's Mercy Healthcare, 366 S.W.3d 504 (Mo. 2012) (claimant who twisted her ankle and fell after making coffee at work; because this was a risk to which the claimant would have been exposed in her non-employment life, injury not compensable); Dykhoff v. Xcel Energy, 840 N.W.2d 821 (Minn. 2013) (slip and fall where floor was not hazardous and employment did not create special hazard).

[79]   E.g., Wait v. Travelers Indem. Co., 240 S.W.3d 220 (Tenn. 2007) (criminal attack on telecommuter was in the course of employment, but did not arise out of employment since "there is nothing to indicate that she was targeted because of her association with her employer or that she was charged with safeguarding her employer's property"); see also Feiereisen v. Newpage Corp., 5 A.3d 669 (Me. 2010) (injury did not arise out of and in the course of claimant's employment where he was injured while traveling to a workers' compensation mediation for a previous injury).

[80]   Workers' compensation statutes themselves may define particular types of compensable injuries. Where that is the case, a claimant who fails to prove that he has an "injury" under the statute will be entitled to no compensation. See, e.g., State ex rel. Baker v. Coast to Coast Manpower, LLC, 129 Ohio St.3d 138, 950 N.E.2d 924 (2011).

[81]   E.g., Mullins v. Tanksleary, 376 P.2d 590 (Okla. 1962); Barkley v. Corrections Div., 111 Or.App. 48, 825 P.2d 291 (1992).

[82]   PF Chang's v. Industrial Comm'n of Ariz., 166 P.3d 135 (Ariz. Ct. App. 2007); Wal-Mart Stores, Inc. v. Reinholtz, 955 P.2d 223 (Okla. 1998) (supervisor raped plaintiff, employer responsible to make compensation for resulting psychological harm).

Definite occasion. The requirement of accidental injury or injury by accident may imply not only an unintended injury but (1) a definite occasion or time when injury occurred and (2) an external event. Injuries that occur through repetitive stress over a long period do not fit the definite occasion rule, and some courts have excluded compensation for such injuries.[83] However, in many cases courts ignore or depart from the definite occasion rule and permit compensation for repetitive stress injuries or allergies that develop from exposure over time.[84] Others may address such problems under the rubric of occupational disease.

External event. The employer takes the employee with all her preexisting conditions. A compensable injury may therefore result if an accident aggravates or triggers a preexisting condition.[85] On the other hand, courts may narrow the road to compensation for heart attacks, hernias, or strokes on the job by saying that an internal bodily breakdown is not an external event and thus not an accident unless the heart attack or the like is triggered by some unusual activity such as heavy lifting.[86] A more liberal view permits compensation if the job exertion contributes in part to the attack or stroke, whether or not the exertion is unusual.[87]

Emotional or "mental" injury. The strongest case for emotional distress compensation arises when the employee is physically injured on the job and suffers disabling emotional distress as a result of that injury. In that case, compensation is appropriately granted.[88] The obverse, the case of mental stimulus producing physical injury, also seems to touch the core purpose of workers' compensation.[89] When mental or emotional injury arises from a purely mental stimulus—the so-called mental/mental case—courts usually become more cautious. Some courts have rejected the mental/mental claim altogether, limiting recovery for mental or emotional injury to cases

[83] Nelson v. Ponsness-Warren Idgas Enters., 126 Idaho 129, 879 P.2d 592 (1994) (carpal tunnel syndrome not "accident," not compensable); Young v. Melrose Granite Co., 152 Minn. 512, 189 N.W. 426 (1922) (atrophy of muscles through years of vibration working at a machine not compensable).

[84] Schlup v. Auburn Needleworks, Inc., 239 Neb. 854, 479 N.W.2d 440, 14 A.L.R.5th 963 (1992) (carpel tunnel syndrome compensable when it developed over a few months); Johannesen v. New York City Dep't of Hous. Pres. & Dev., 84 N.Y.2d 129, 638 N.E.2d 981, 615 N.Y.S.2d 336 (1994) (asthma from office smoke could be an accident); cf. Noble v. Lamoni Prods., 512 N.W.2d 290 (Iowa 1994) (carpel tunnel syndrome compensable where "accident" was not a statutory requirement).

[85] See Martinez v. Indus. Comm'n of Ariz., 192 Ariz. 176, 962 P.2d 903 (1998); Gartrell v. Department of Corr., 259 Conn. 29, 787 A.2d 541 (2002); McCamey v. District of Columbia Dep't of Employment Servs., 947 A.3d 1191 (D.C. 2008); Rakestraw v. General Dynamics Land Sys., Inc., 666 N.W.2d 199 (Mich. 2003).

[86] Virginia Elec. & Power Co. v. Cogbill, 223 Va. 354, 288 S.E.2d 485 (1982) (sitting in a bent position all day too similar to employee's ordinary work, not compensable); Wyoming Workers' Comp. Div. v. Harris, 931 P.2d 255 (Wyo. 1997) (changing tire on a large trailer sufficient).

[87] Bush v. Industrial Comm'n, 136 Ariz. 522, 667 P.2d 222 (1983); Baggett v. Industrial Comm'n, 201 Ill.2d 187, 775 N.E.2d 908, 266 Ill.Dec. 836 (2002) (heart attack supposedly resulting from job stress; the stress must be more than public generally subjected to, but need not be unusual in the job or more than other employees subjected to; special susceptibility of employee no defense).

[88] T.W.M. Custom Framing v. Industrial Comm'n, 198 Ariz. 41, 6 P.3d 745 (Ct. App. 2000) (injury caused depression which caused suicide, compensable); McCamey v. District of Columbia Dep't of Employment Servs., 947 A.3d 1191 (D.C. 2008); Simmons v. Comfort Suites Hotel, 968 A.2d 1123 (Md. Ct. Spec. App. 2009) (home security system compensable for employee who had been attacked with a bat during a robbery and left for dead); Vredenburg v. Sedgwick CMS, 188 P.3d 1084 (Nev. 2008); Anderson v. Baptist Med. Ctr., 343 S.C. 487, 541 S.E.2d 526 (2001) (physical injury aggravating preexisting depression, aggravation compensable).

[89] In Baggett v. Industrial Comm'n, 201 Ill.2d 187, 775 N.E.2d 908, 266 Ill.Dec. 836 (2002), the court refused to import special proof requirements frequently applied in the mental/mental cases. Some other authority, however, requires a sudden event or unusual or abnormal stress in the case of stress induced heart attacks. See Anderson v. Baptist Med. Ctr., 343 S.C. 487, 541 S.E.2d 526 (2001).

of physical trauma.[90] More commonly, however, courts entertain the claim but impose special proof requirements, for example, holding that the initial stimulus must have been abnormal or unusual and not an ordinary part of the job,[91] or that the mental stimulus must have been sudden and unexpected, a rule that resembles the definite occasion requirement.[92] However, if the stress is greater than usual or normal, then compensation may be due even though the stress did not arise from a single, sudden, and definite occasion.[93] Compensation will be denied if the emotional harm is not disabling and requires no medical attention, since no award is made for pain or suffering.[94] Compensation will also be denied if the mental distress is not reasonable.[95]

Occupational Disease

Diseases. Although a work-related disease can sometimes count as an injury by accident,[96] the definite occasion and external event rules often exclude compensation for diseases. Earlier workers' compensation statutes had no provisions for occupational disease, as distinct from injury, or at best recognized only a limited number of diseases. Modern statutes allow compensation for disability resulting from occupational diseases, but compensation is usually permitted only if the disease is distinctively related to the employee's occupation or the employee was subjected to some unusual exposure.[97] For example, in a New York case, the court refused to entertain a social worker's claim of occupational disease for an eye disorder brought about by exposure to cigarette smoke in a poorly ventilated room on the ground that the disease must derive "from the very nature of the employment, not a specific condition peculiar to the employee's place of work."[98] However, a police officer who saw his partner bleed to death was allowed to

---

[90]   See Boutwell v. Domino's Pizza, 25 Kan.App. 2d 110, 959 P.2d 469 (1998); Kerans v. Porter Paint Co., 61 Ohio St.3d 486, 575 N.E.2d 428 (1991) (mental injury from non-physical sexual harassment not compensable and outside the compensation system, hence employee has potential tort claim against employer); Emmanuel S. Tipon, Annotation, Right to Workers' Compensation for Emotional Distress or Like Injury Suffered by Claimant as Result of Sudden Stimuli Involving Nonpersonnel Action—Compensability under Particular Circumstances, 84 A.L.R.5th 249 (2000).

[91]   Spencer v. Time Warner Cable, 717 N.Y.S.2d 711 (App. Div. 2000) (office worker taking large number of customer calls, compensation denied); Anderson v. Baptist Med. Ctr., 343 S.C. 487, 541 S.E.2d 526 (2001). Statutes may impose the requirement of unusual stress. See Williams v. State Dep't of Revenue, 938 P.2d 1065 (Alaska 1997) (applying such a statute).

[92]   Brown v. Quik Trip Corp., 641 N.W.2d 725 (Iowa 2002) (two frightening robberies; employee's stress need not be greater than other similarly situated where emotional harm resulted from sudden traumatic event); Partin v. Merchants & Farmers Bank, 810 So.2d 1118 (La. 2002) (statute so providing); McGrath v. State Dep't of Pub. Safety, 159 P.3d 239 (Nev. 2007) (status as a patrol woman not enough by itself).

[93] See City of Fort Smith v. Brooks, 40 Ark.App. 120, 842 S.W.2d 463 (1992) (police officer forced to kill a man in the line of duty suffered disability when later abnormal job stresses added to the strain).

[94]   Scheduled injuries, under which a fixed sum is paid for, say, loss of a thumb, may be regarded as a partial exception. Some statutes also allow a relatively small payment for bodily disfigurement to take care of cases in which, for example, a worker is castrated but is not disabled from working. For a discussion of bodily disfigurement, see Rison v. Air Filter Sys., Inc., 707 A.2d 675 (R.I. 1998).

[95]   Guess v. Sharp Mfg. Co. of Am., 114 S.W.3d 480 (Tenn. 2003) (denying recovery for employee's fear of AIDS from tactile contact with fellow worker's blood when there was no proof that blood was HIV positive).

[96]   Johannesen v. New York City Dep't of Hous. Pres. & Dev., 84 N.Y.2d 129, 638 N.E.2d 981, 615 N.Y.S.2d 336 (1994) (exposure to secondhand tobacco smoke aggravating previous condition compensable as accident under rule that gradual development over a reasonably definite time period is sufficient).

[97]   See, e.g., Potter v. Department of Labor & Indus., 289 P.3d 727 (Wash. Ct. App. 2012) (denying compensation for an alleged occupational disease, multiple chemical sensitivity disorder, in claim brought by lawyer claiming her disorder arose from her employment in her former law firm; claimant failed to show that her disease arose from conditions of her particular occupation, as opposed to condition coincidentally occurring in her workplace).

[98]   Mack v. County of Rockland, 71 N.Y.2d 1008, 1009, 525 N.E.2d 744, 530 N.Y.S.2d 98, 99 (1988).

pursue a claim for workers compensation benefits on the theory that PTSD is a natural hazard of police work.[99] At times, state statutes create a presumption that a particular disease is related to employment.[100] Where a disease has been caused in part by an employee's personal habits and in part by employment-related factors, most states allow recovery of workers' compensation benefits upon a showing that the work-related exposures or conditions were a substantial contributing factor to the employee's disability.[101] Where a disease is caused in part by work-related exposure and in part by a concurrently-developing non-occupational disease (such as cigarette smoking-related emphysema), some courts allow the employer to apportion partial workers' compensation disability benefits.[102]

Multiple Employers and the Alternative to Joint Liability

Allocating liability. When injury or disability results from a compensable disease to which the employee was exposed in two or more employments, the compensation statutes use a remarkable rule for allocating liability among the employers that is quite different from any of the common law apportionment rules. They simply allocate all liability to the last employment in which the employee suffered injurious exposure.[103] In line with other features of workers' compensation that standardize benefits and liabilities, this one economizes by eliminating the need for individualized and complex factual evidence. In the long run, the rule may work out to approximately the right set of ultimate costs for the employer because so long as the employment characteristically exposes workers to a disease, as asbestos-related employments did, an employer liable in one case for all compensation will escape liability entirely in another case.

§ 36.5 Workers' Compensation: Exclusive Remedy and Third Parties

Barring the tort claim. One of the most difficult problems in meshing workers' compensation with tort law arises from the common provisions that the employee's compensation remedy is her exclusive remedy against the employer. The effect is that one who employs the worker at the time of injury[104] is immune from liability for its negligence.[105] The immunity not only bars tort actions by injured employees but also

---

[99]   Brunell v. Wildwood Crest Police Dep't, 822 A.2d 576 (N.J. 2003).

[100]   Alaska Stat. § 23.30.121 (2008) (presumption of coverage for firefighters with disability claims related to certain illnesses such as respiratory diseases, certain cancers, and cardiovascular problems that occur within 72 hours after exposure to a fire).

[101]   Lindquist v. City of Jersey City Fire Dept., 175 N.J. 244, 814 A.2d 1069 (2003); Manske v. Workforce Safety & Ins., 748 N.W.2d 394 (N.D. 2008) (citing cases and statutes from other jurisdictions).

[102]   Deschenes v. Transco, Inc., 288 Conn. 303, 953 A.2d 13 (2008) (placing burden on employer to prove that the disability resulted in part from non-occupationally-related disease, and that the claimant's occupation had no influence on the development of the non-occupational disease).

[103]   Union Carbide Corp. v. Industrial Comm'n, 196 Colo. 56, 581 P.2d 734 (1978); cf. Bouse v. Fireman's Fund Ins. Co., 932 P.2d 222 (Alaska 1997) (last employer responsible if second injury was a substantial factor in causing disability).

[104]   Ex Parte Weaver, 871 So. 2d 820 (Ala. 2003) (former employer, whose negligence during employment resulted in injury after employment was terminated was not immune, discussing cases, including one to the contrary).

[105]   This immunity may also extend to protect employers against tort suits by employees of independent contractors. Tatera v. FMC Corp., 328 Wis. 2d 320, 786 N.W.2d 810 (2010).

derivative claims for loss of consortium[106] and wrongful death.[107] The rule does not, however, bar independent claims such as those of a fetus injured by the employee-mother's exposure to toxic substances on the job.[108] The employer's immunity is usually shared by co-employees who negligently cause on-the-job injury[109] so long as the co-employee has not departed from the scope of his employment by committing an intentional tort unrelated to his employment.[110] Although the immunity does not logically extend to a parent corporation of the employer,[111] or indeed to any shareholder,[112] it may extend to the parent or any other corporation which is in fact an alter ego of the employer, as where, through common ownership or management, two companies operate as a single employer.[113] The immunity usually extends as well to limited partners of the employer,[114] to insurers,[115] and executives[116] of the employer.

Tortfeasor's contribution claim against employer. The exclusive remedy provision does not bar the injured employee's tort claim against third parties like manufacturers of defective products that contributed to the workplace harm. However, when a suit can be maintained against a third party, issues arise about the fair allocation of responsibility among third parties and the employer. In one situation, the tortfeasor, liable to the employee for an injury also covered by workers' compensation, seeks contribution from the employer. A few courts require the employer to make contribution to the tortfeasor but never in excess of the employer's workers' compensation liability.[117] This preserves the employer's tort immunity. Most courts, however, reject contribution

---

[106] See, e.g., LeFiell Mfg. Co. v. Superior Court, 55 Cal.4th 275, 145 Cal.Rptr.3d 543, 282 P.3d 1242 (2012); see also Pittman v. Western Eng'g Co., Inc., 283 Neb. 913, 813 N.W.2d 487 (2012) (spouse of employee killed on the job was barred by exclusivity provision from suing employer for negligent infliction of emotional distress).

[107] Estate of Moulton v. Puopolo, 5 N.E.3d 908 (Mass. 2014); Saab v. Massachusetts CVS Pharmacy, LLC, 452 Mass. 564, 896 N.E.2d 615 (2008). But see Lewis v. Gilmore, 366 S.W.3d 522 (Mo. 2012).

[108] Snyder v. Michael's Stores, Inc., 16 Cal.4th 991, 945 P.2d 781, 68 Cal.Rptr.2d 476 (1997); Meyer v. Burger King Corp., 26 P.3d 925 (Wash. 2001).

[109] Mitchell v. Sanborn, 536 N.W.2d 678 (N.D. 1995); Progressive Halcyon Ins. Co. v. Philippi, 754 N.W.2d 646 (S.D. 2008).

[110] O'Connell v. Chasdi, 400 Mass. 686, 511 N.E.2d 349 (1987) (co-employee liable for assault, battery, intentional infliction of emotional distress); Stringer v. Minnesota Vikings Football Club, LLC, 705 N.W.2d 746 (Minn. 2005) (holding that team medical services coordinator was not guilty of an intentional tort). State statutes may contain specific provisions on this topic. See, e.g., Burns v. Smith, 214 S.W.3d 335 (Mo. 2007).

[111] E.g., McQuade v. Draw Tite, Inc., 659 N.E.2d 1016 (Ind. 1995); see Annotation, Workers' Compensation Immunity as Extending to One Owning Controlling Interest in Employer Corporation, 30 A.L.R.4th 948 (1984).

[112] Lyon v. Barrett, 89 N.J. 294, 445 A.2d 1153 (1982) (plaintiff employed by professional law corporation wholly owned by individual attorney could recover compensation from corporation and sue the individual attorney for negligence as landlord).

[113] See Ioerger v. Halverson Constr. Co., 232 Ill.2d 196, 327 Ill.Dec. 524, 902 N.E.2d 645 (2008) (joint venturers); Thompson v. Bernard G. Janowitz Constr. Corp., 301 A.D.2d 588 754 N.Y.S.2d 50 (2003).

[114] Currier v. Amerigas Propane, L.P., 144 N.H. 122, 737 A.2d 1118 (1999).

[115] See, reflecting the usual immunity of insurers and some cases to the contrary, Frank J. Wozniak, Annotation, Breach of Assumed Duty to Inspect Property as Ground for Liability to Third Party, 13 A.L.R.5th 289 (1993). The immunity does not apply to the intentional misconduct of the insurer. Aquilera v. Inservices, Inc., 905 So.2d 84 (Fla. 2005).

[116] Gunderson v. Harrington, 632 N.W.2d 695 (Minn. 2001) (sole shareholder-manager of corporate employer); Ingalls v. Standard Gypsum, LLC, 70 S.W.3d 252 (Tex. App. 2001).

[117] Kotecki v. Cyclops Welding Corp., 146 Ill.2d 155, 166 Ill.Dec. 1, 585 N.E.2d 1023 (1991); Lambertson v. Cincinnati Corp., 312 Minn. 114, 257 N.W.2d 679, 100 A.L.R. 3d 335 (1977).

claims against the immune employer altogether.[118] The result is that the negligent employer pays the limited amount required as workers' compensation while the third party in a joint and several liability system pays full tort liability. Where joint and several liability has been completely abolished, the tortfeasor will pay only his own comparative fault share.[119] But that means that the employee must bear the loss to the extent that it is caused by the employer's fault and is not fully compensated by workers' compensation. Thus if an employer and tortfeasor are each chargeable with 50% of the fault and the damages are $100,000, the workers' compensation payments might be, say, $10,000 only. That leaves the employee recovering $50,000 from the tortfeasor and $10,000 in compensation payments; she must bear the remaining $40,000 loss herself unless the court reinstates joint and several liability for this situation.[120]

Employer's claim against tortfeasor for reimbursement. Workers' compensation statutes provide that the employer or its insurance carrier will be reimbursed from the recovery available from the tortfeasor to the extent it has or will pay compensation. They create a lien against the tort recovery to protect this right of reimbursement. Some cases have allowed reimbursement from the tort recovery even when the damages recovered are only for pain and suffering for which no compensation at all was paid.[121] Where joint and several liability has been abolished, this system, too, raises problems because the employee would recover from the tortfeasor only a percentage of her damages reflecting the tortfeasor's proportionate share. Her recovery, then, is reduced by the employer's negligence. If she must then fully reimburse the negligent employer for compensation paid, the employer bears no share at all of the injury, and the employee bears the burden of paying for the employer's share. Some courts feel that the problem must be resolved by statutes, but others have concluded that the employer's reimbursement right should be limited to exclude its proportionate share of fault.[122] If the jury may have deducted the workers' compensation payments from the judgment against the third party, the employer cannot take reimbursement from that award.[123]

Permitting tort suit against employer. When no third party tortfeasor is in the picture, workers' compensation systems provide a great deal of assurance that injured employees will receive financial assistance in the event of physical injury causing work loss or medical expenses. On the other hand, the employee has no tort claim even if the employer was negligent and if the injury is serious. Consequently, employees have sought exceptions to the exclusive remedy rule. They have found several, though they are not adopted everywhere. At least some states have recognized an employee's right to sue the employer in tort, even though injury was inflicted arising out of employment, in these cases:

    (1) Fraudulent concealment, bad faith. When the employee's on-the-job injury is aggravated because the employer fraudulently conceals it and thus

---

[118] Joel E. Smith, Annotation, Modern Status of Effect of State Workmen's Compensation Act on Right of Third-Person Tortfeasor to Contribution or Indemnity from Employer of Injured or Killed Workman, 100 A.L.R.3d 350 (1980).

[119] Allied-Signal, Inc. v. Fox, 623 So.2d 1180 (Fla. 1993); DaFonte v. Up-Right, Inc., 2 Cal.4th 593, 7 Cal.Rptr.2d 238, 828 P.2d 140 (1992).

[120] See Ridings v. Ralph M. Parsons Co., 914 S.W.2d 79 (Tenn. 1996) (holding third-person tortfeasor fully liable).

[121] United States v. Lorenzetti, 467 U.S. 167 (1984).

[122] Aitken v. Industrial Comm'n, 183 Ariz. 387, 904 P.2d 456 (1995).

[123] Travelers Indem. Co. of Am. v. Jarrells, 927 N.E.2d 374 (Ind. 2010).

delays treatment.[124] Similarly, the employer's bad faith in delaying benefits due is actionable in some states.[125]

(2) Dual capacity. When the employer causes harm while acting in some capacity other than an employer. For example, if the employer is a manufacturer and the employee is injured by the employer's defective product, courts can think of the employer as having two roles or capacities, one as manufacturer of a product and one as employer. In this view, the employee can sue the employer in tort in its capacity as a product manufacturer.[126] Similarly, if the employer is a health care provider and negligently causes injury while it is acting in that capacity, a common law suit may be permitted.[127] But since an employer's negligent treatment of an on-the-job injury is itself covered by workers' compensation, tort liability in such cases is generally rejected.[128] Some courts say they reject the dual capacity doctrine altogether.[129] But even these courts may nevertheless permit liability in "dual transaction" cases where the employer's tort is in no way related to employment injury, as where the employer leases an apartment to an employee, who is injured when the apartment ceiling collapses.[130]

(3) Intentional physical harms. A number of statutes provide, that the exclusive remedy provision does not bar a tort claim against an employer guilty of an intentional tort.[131] Some of the decisions recognize the traditional alternative definitions of intent,[132] so that the employer will be liable in tort if he has either purpose to harm or a substantial certainty that harm will follow.[133] Mere risk, however great, is not enough to show intent under the traditional concept of substantial certainty.[134] Some jurisdictions, perhaps

---

[124] Martin v. Lancaster Battery Co., Inc., 530 Pa. 11, 606 A.2d 444 (1992).

[125] Falline v. GNLV Corp., 107 Nev. 1004, 823 P.2d 888 (1991) (action for negligent or fraudulent delay in payment permitted).

[126] Bell v. Industrial Vangas, Inc., 30 Cal.3d 268, 637 P.2d 266, 179 Cal.Rptr. 30 (1981). Cal. Lab. Code § 3602(b)(3) now limits this to cases in which the product was sold by the employer-manufacturer to third persons. See also Price v. Howard, 236 P.3d 82 (Okla. 2010).

[127] Duprey v. Shane, 39 Cal. 2d 781, 249 P.2d 8 (1952). Where the employer is a health care provider that furnishes medical care causing injury, see Hollingshed v. Levine, 307 A.D.2d 850, 763 N.Y.S.2d 595 (2003) (patient went to hospital emergency room not as employee but as private patient). A California statute has trimmed the use of the dual capacity doctrine in that state. See Cal. Lab. Code § 3602.

[128] See Suburban Hosp., Inc. v. Kirson, 362 Md. 140, 763 A.2d 185 (2000); Payne v. Galen Hosp. Corp., 28 S.W.3d 15 (Tex. 2000).

[129] E.g., Johnson v. Rental Unif. Serv. of Greenville, S.C., Inc., 316 S.C. 70, 447 S.E.2d 184 (1994).

[130] See Suburban Hosp., Inc. v. Kirson, 362 Md. 140, 763 A.2d 185 (2000) (rejecting dual capacity, so hospital that negligently treated injured employee was liable for compensation, not for tort damages; but perhaps recognizing potential for "dual transaction" liability of employer leasing negligently maintained apartment).

[131] E.g., N.J. Stat. Ann. § 34:15–8.

[132] See 1 Dobbs, Hayden & Bublick, The Law of Torts § 29 (2d ed. 2011 & Supp.).

[133] See Bakerman v. The Bombay Co., 961 So.2d 259 (Fla. 2007) (liability found where employer engaged in conduct that was substantially certain to result in injury to the employee); Alexander v. Bozeman Motors, Inc., 356 Mont. 439, 234 P.3d 880 (2010) (fact question regarding certainty); Kaminski v. Metal & Wire Prods. Co., 125 Ohio St.3d 250, 927 N.E.2d 1066 (2010); Jordan v. Western Farmers Elec. Co-op., 290 P.3d 9, 34 I.E.R. Cas. (BNA) 1128 (Okla. 2012) (pleading sufficiently alleged that employer acted with knowledge that the employee's injury was substantially certain to result from the employer's conduct; thus action was not barred by exclusivity provision). Mere risk, however great, is not enough to show intent under the traditional concept of substantial certainty.

[134] See Miller v. Ensco, Inc., 286 Ark. 458, 692 S.W.2d 615 (1985); Danos v. Boh Bros. Constr. Co., LLC, 132 So.3d 958 (La. 2014); Tomeo v. Thomas Whitesell Constr. Co., 176 N.J. 366, 823 A.2d 769 (2003) (deliberate

reacting to the danger that high risk could easily be treated like substantial certainty, have rejected the substantial certainty rule altogether and have held the employer liable in tort only when he had a purpose to harm.[135] Other jurisdictions have defined terms like "deliberate harm" in a way that seems to encompass more than ordinary intentional tort terminology might.[136]

Non-injury torts. Many torts can involve an element of intent without producing a disabling injury. For instance, an employer might falsely imprison an employee. If the employee is not disabled and has no medical expense, there would normally be no workers' compensation benefits payable. In these circumstances, the California court has held that the exclusive remedy clause did not bar a tort recovery because such cases were outside the workers' compensation "bargain" or basic plan.[137] The same kind of argument can be applied to permit a tort suit for fraud by the employer that imposes economic costs but not physical injury,[138] or a libel that harms reputation without causing disablement.[139] Some sexual harassment or assault may present a special case of this kind of tort.

C. OTHER INJURY SYSTEMS

§ 36.6   Social Security Disability

Background. The Social Security program signed into law in 1935 under President Franklin D. Roosevelt was designed to pay benefits to workers over 65 years old. Amendments signed under President Eisenhower in 1956 and additional amendments enacted over the next decade extended the program to cover disabled workers, disabled children and some family members of those individuals.[140] In December 2009, the

---

risk falls short of intent to harm with substantial certainty). Nor is certainty in the statistical sense that the defendant's activity is "certain" to cause harm sooner or later if it is carried on for a longer period of time. See Restatement (Third) of Torts: Liability for Physical Harm § 1 cmt. e (2010).

[135]   Rudisill v. Ford Motor Co., 709 F.3d 595 (6th Cir. 2013) (Ohio law; deliberate intent to cause injury); Harris v. State, Dep't of Corr., 294 P.3d 382 (Mont. 2013) (employer specifically intended to cause injury); Bowden v. Young, 120 So.3d 971 (Miss. 2013). The court in Blankenship v. Cincinnati Milacron Chems., Inc., 69 Ohio St.2d 608, 433 N.E.2d 572 (1982), thought that substantial certainty intent could be shown if the employer knew certain diseases were being contracted in plant with noxious fumes. The Ohio legislature apparently took a different view in enacting Ohio Rev. Code Ann. § 2745.01, but that statute was then held unconstitutional in Johnson v. BP Chems., Inc., 85 Ohio St.3d 298, 707 N.E.2d 1107 (1999). A subsequent statute which limited suits against employers to cases in which there was an intent to injure or belief that injury was substantially certain was upheld. See Kaminski v. Metal & Wire Prods. Co., 927 N.E.2d 1066 (Ohio 2010).

[136]   Pixley v. Pro-Pak Indus., Inc., 28 N.E.3d 1249 (Ohio 2014) ("deliberate intent to cause injury to an employee"); Walston v. Boeing Co., 334 P.3d 519 (Wash. 2014) ("actual knowledge of certain injury"); Coleman Estate ex rel. Coleman v. R.M. Logging, Inc., 696 S.E.2d 28 (W.Va. 2010) (test is whether employer actually possessed knowledge of specific unsafe working condition and of the strong probability of serious injury or death presented by that condition). These decisions might be viewed as efforts to preserve tort liability, not for intentional torts as such, but for atrocious misconduct by the employer.

[137]   Fermino v. Fedco, 7 Cal.4th 701, 30 Cal.Rptr.2d 18, 872 P.2d 559 (1994). If the false imprisonment or other intentional tort actually causes physical harm to the worker, his claim is logically limited to the workers' compensation award. Nelson v. Winnebago Indus., Inc., 619 N.W.2d 385 (Iowa 2000).

[138]   See Nassa v. Hook-SupeRx, Inc., 790 A.2d 368 (R.I. 2002); Aslakson v. Gallagher Bassett Servs., Inc., 300 Wis.2d 92, 729 N.W.2d 712 (2007).

[139]   Howland v. Balma, 143 Cal.App.3d 899, 192 Cal.Rptr. 286 (1983); Foley v. Polaroid Corp., 381 Mass. 545, 413 N.E.2d 711 (1980); Nassa v. Hook-SupeRx, Inc., 790 A.2d 368 (R.I. 2002). When an emotional injury is compensable under the workers' compensation act, claims for it are barred by the exclusivity provisions. See Tennaro v. Ryder Sys., Inc., 832 F.Supp. 494 (D. Mass. 1993).

[140]   Social Security Administration, Annual Statistical Report of the Social Security Disability Insurance Program 2009, at 2 (2010).

program provided disability benefits to approximately 8.9 million people, 7.8 million of whom were disabled workers.[141] Average monthly benefits received by disabled workers under the system are about $1,000 per month.[142] In December 2009, payments to disabled workers by the government totaled $8.2 billion per month.[143]

The Social Security disability system. Social Security disability benefits resemble workers' compensation in several respects. Like workers' compensation, it is a no-fault system and it is enforced ultimately in administrative hearings (before federal administrative law judges by a limited review of their decisions, in the case of social security).[144] As in workers' compensation systems, the fact of disability that prevents work is the critical fact to be determined in Social Security claims.

A universal tax-funded program. Likewise, Social Security determinations are highly standardized, leaving no room to individuate benefits and little room to individuate findings of disability. In contrast to workers' compensation systems, Social Security is universal; it is not limited to injury cases at all, much less to on-the-job injuries. One of the most notable differences is that although workers' compensation is a no-fault system, the enterprise that causes the workers' harm is also the one that pays the costs. With social security disability benefits, payments, like Social Security retirement payments, are ultimately derived from tax funds.[145] (Individual contributions to the system, in the form of Social Security taxes, are insufficient to pay the retirement or disability benefits.)

Disability and impairment. Social Security disability payments are viewed as early retirement payments. Disability is not partial or momentary; only persons whose impairment prevents "any substantial gainful activity" are entitled to benefits, and then only if the disability has lasted or will last at least a year or can be expected to result in death.[146] Medical impairment is only half of the story. An impairment that might not prevent a trained lawyer from practicing might completely eliminate an uneducated worker from the job market. The statute specifically recognizes that disability is determined partly by medical impairment and partly by education, training and the like. However, the statute also provides that if the claimant can perform any type of work that exists in the national economy, she is not disabled, even if that work is not available locally and even if no actual job vacancy exists.[147] By definition, disability need not result from injury. Frequently the impairment that leads to disability is disease like multiple

---

[141] Id. at 11.

[142] Id. at 18.

[143] Id. at 21.

[144] See Harvey McCormick, Social Security Claims and Procedures (6th ed. 2009).

[145] Under the portion called OASI, individuals have paid Social Security taxes, but these taxes are not sufficient to pay the retirement or disability benefits. Under the portion called SSI, the system is a form of welfare for persons of inadequate means.

[146] 42 U.S.C.A. § 423(d). Blind persons over 55 years of age are defined as disabled if blindness prevents substantial gainful employment using the skills they previously used. See also Castile v. Astrue, 617 F.3d 923 (7th Cir. 2010) (claimant could perform sedentary work and therefore did not meet the definition of disability in the statute).

[147] 42 U.S.C.A. § 423(d)(2)(A). The type of work for which the claimant is qualified must, however, exist either in the "region" where she lives or in several regions of the country.

sclerosis, mental limits or breakdown.[148] Pain resulting from a medically determinable condition may lead to a disability.[149]

Standardizing: listings. Because disability requires both an impairment and an inability to work, hearings on disputed claims at one time routinely involved a good deal of vocational testimony as to jobs available and how they matched the claimant's physical or mental abilities. Much of this was repetitious and wasteful and the governing administrative regulations now contain "listings" of impairments that automatically qualify as a disability.[150] The listings work in favor of the claimant but cannot be used to automatically exclude a disability finding.[151]

Standardizing: the grids. A quite different form of standardizing utilizes the medical-vocational guidelines or "the grids." When the listings do not show an automatic disability finding, the grids are invoked in cases involving exertional limits[152] to provide a disability profile of the claimant by applying a table of several factors. The administrative law judge (ALJ) is required to make a rough finding about the degree of "residual functional capacity" considering impairment. For example, the claimant might be limited to light work or medium work. The ALJ also makes findings about other categories in the table—age, previous work experience, and education. When those findings are plugged in, the table provides the ultimate conclusion—disability or not. The table or grid provides an automatic finding of disability in some cases, as where the claimant is approaching advanced age, has no skilled work experience. But the grids may also automatically determine that the claimant is not disabled, as where a 45-year-old has the same impairment and education.[153] The Supreme Court has upheld the grids, noting that the claimant still gets individualized adjudication on the specific components such as impairment, age, and education.[154] Indeed, individual determinations of disability consume most of the resources of the social security administration.[155]

Social Security as a model for tort law change? Some torts scholars doubt the capacity of tort law either to deter wrongdoing or to provide appropriate compensation

---

[148] E.g., Hardt v. Reliance Standard Life Ins. Co., 560 U.S 242, 130 S.Ct. 2149 (2010) (neuropathy); McLain v. Schweiker, 715 F.2d 866 (4th Cir. 1983) (nervous disorders, inadequate personality); Foreman v. Callahan, 122 F.3d 24 (8th Cir. 1997) (limited intellectual ability). See also Social Security Administration, Annual Statistical Report of the Social Security Disability Insurance Program 2009, at 16 (2010) (listing musculoskeletal and mental issues as the cause of over 50% of all worker disability claims).

[149] See 42 U.S.C.A. § 423(d)(5)(A); Lingenfelter v. Astrue, 504 F.3d 1028 (8th Cir. 2007); Kelley v. Callahan, 133 F.3d 583 (8th Cir. 1998). Professor Pryor believes that too little scope is given for findings of disability based upon pain. She argues that pain professionals can detect malingering and that no special rules are needed to fence-out that possibility. See Ellen Smith Pryor, Compensation and the Ineradicable Problems of Pain, 59 Geo. Wash. L. Rev. 239 (1991).

[150] 20 C.F.R. part 404, Subpart P, Appendix I.

[151] See Sullivan v. Zebley, 493 U.S. 521 (1990); Vossen v. Astrue, 612 F.3d 1011 (8th Cir. 2010) (claimant did not prove listed impairment, consequently administrative law judge had to consider issues related to claimant's residual functional capacity); Colon v. Apfel, 133 F.Supp.2d 330 (S.D.N.Y. 2001) (discussing qualification standards for children).

[152] Jordan v. Commissioner of Soc. Sec., 548 F.3d 417(6th Cir. 2008).

[153] Lockwood v. Commissioner Soc. Sec. Admin., 616 F.3d 1068 (9th Cir. 2010) (ALJ could consider a person one month away from her 55th birthday as a person "approaching advanced age" rather than a person of "advanced age").

[154] Heckler v. Campbell, 461 U.S. 458 (1983).

[155] See Frank S. Boch, Medical Proof, Social Policy, and Social Security's Medically Centered Definition of Disability, 92 Cornell L. Rev. 189 (2007) (although disability benefits claimants are less than 20% of the total number of Social Security claims, "determining whether disability benefit claimants are disabled consumes the bulk of the administrative resources of the Social Security Administration" as 4.5 million new disability claims were filed in 2004 alone).

to victims. Consequently, they argue for an out and out welfare program for injured or disabled persons.[156] Those who hope or believe that tort law is part of the culture that helps deter wrongdoing, indirectly if not directly, on the other hand, would prefer that benefits be provided by someone in a position to reduce injury. In that respect, Social Security seems to offer limited lessons for improving tort law. Its use of standardizing techniques and their acceptance in the courts point to ways in which efficiencies may be gained for some aspects of tort law, or alternatively, may provide cautionary examples against too much streamlining.[157]

§ 36.7 The Private Insurance Alternative

Liability insurance. So far as personal injury results from automobile accidents— and a very large amount does—the tort system is largely fueled by liability insurance.[158] If the defendant has liability insurance, it will pay his legal liability for harm he causes (and will also investigate and defend the suit against him). Liability insurance is costly, not only in relation to the earnings of many people, but also in the sense that most of the premium dollar is used up in cost of administration, investigation, and trial.[159] Liability insurance as the financial backbone of tort law has some other limitations. No matter how much liability insurance you buy, it will not help you when you yourself are injured. And you have no control over whether the person who injures you has purchased any insurance at all or what amount. A number of states now make liability insurance compulsory, but enforcement is difficult and the limits of the insurance purchased severely limit the damages recoverable. Persons who want protection from others' negligence are forced to purchase uninsured motorist insurance, or accident insurance in addition to their own liability insurance.[160]

The Keeton-O'Connell Plan. These problems, coupled with the problems of delay and uncertainty and injustice in tort litigation, led then Professor (later Judge) Robert Keeton and Professor Jeffrey O'Connell to work up a detailed plan that would guarantee everyone injured from use of an automobile some minimal protection against wage loss and medical expense.[161]

No-fault insurance. The Keeton-O'Connell Plan, also called no-fault auto insurance, set up a system under which no one had to rely exclusively upon others to purchase insurance. Instead, each auto owner would be required to purchase insurance that would provide two tiers of benefits. In the first tier, the insurance would pay the owner, his passengers, and pedestrians injured by his automobile, for wage loss and medical expenses, but not pain and suffering. The amounts to be paid were limited. As long as the limit was not exhausted, no tort suit was permitted.

Operation of no-fault. If damages were greater than the coverage, the injured person could go to the tort tier. There he would recover for damage greater than those paid for

[156] Stephen D. Sugarman, Doing Away with Personal Injury Law (1989).

[157] Frank S. Bloch, et al., Developing Full and Fair Evidentiary Record in a Nonadversary Setting: Two Proposals for Improving Social Security Disability Adjudications, 25 Cardozo L. Rev. 1 (2003).

[158] See Kenneth S. Abraham, The Liability Century 69 (2008) (putting the amount of insurance against liability for auto accidents in the United States at 110 billion dollars per year).

[159] See Polinsky & Shavell, supra n.4.

[160] Kenneth S. Abraham, The Liability Century 69 (2008) (noting that in addition to the 110 billion dollars a year of liability insurance, people in the U.S. spend an additional 70 billion dollars on first-party insurance against damage caused by collision or other vehicle-related property damage).

[161] Robert E. Keeton & Jeffrey O'Connell, Basic Protection for the Traffic Victim (1965).

by his insurance in the first tier. In a two-car collision, if each driver were injured, each would recover the benefits he had paid for from his own insurer. If one or both drivers were negligent, and their damages high enough, they might also litigate tort claims against each other for the excess.

Since the great bulk of claims are small claims that could fall exclusively within the first tier, litigation might be reduced if the first tier was big enough. Basic losses would be paid in all cases, but pain and suffering would be paid only if basic losses were high and tort rules would permit recovery.

Adoption. The Keeton-O'Connell plan provided a detailed model and a number of states adopted some form of it.[162] To make the plan work well, however, it is necessary to exclude tort claims in the first tier and to make the first tier large enough to cover a very large number of cases. That is, the threshold for entrance to the second or torts tier must be high enough to make sure that most relatively small injuries would be resolved in the no-fault tier. If legislation established a $1,000 top damage in the first tier, the plan would fail to insure against substantial losses in the first tier and would fail to reduce tort litigation by any significant amount. If legislation merely permitted you to buy accident insurance without eliminating the tort suit in the first tier, it would have no beneficial effects at all, since you could already buy accident insurance. A number of states that adopted no-fault plans either used an inadequate first tier or merely provided for add-on insurance, with the result in either case that the plan failed to work. A very few states adopted no-fault plans with substantial first-tiers. For instance, New York uses $50,000 as the cap on economic damages recoverable in the first or no-fault tier. If economic damages exceed that sum or injury is otherwise "serious" as defined in the statute, the injured person can then sue in tort.[163]

A two-tier system. The Keeton-O'Connell no-fault plan differed more from the workers' compensation and Social Security systems than it did from the tort system. In one respect it was like neither. It envisioned that most claims in the no-fault tier would not require litigation. The claimant would be claiming against his own insurer, just as she would with a fire insurance or collision policy. The terms of the plan left little to dispute and provided a penalty if the insurer did not properly pay claims. So the bureaucratic or administrative hearings contemplated by workers' compensation and Social Security had no place in the no-fault plan. The plan was perhaps best adapted to the automobile injury problem.[164] But the two-tier structure of the no-fault plan might prove to be quite useful in managing tort claims. For instance, the strategy of standardizing of damages and disability seen in workers' compensation and Social Security systems may be more acceptable for tort cases if it were limited to the lower tier of claims. Compared to caps that harm the most seriously injured, a two-tier system of torts that standardized and limited damages in the first tier might prove much more desirable.

---

[162] See Gary T. Schwartz, Auto No-Fault and First-Party Insurance: Advantages and Problems, 73 S. Cal. L. Rev. 611 (2000); Roger C. Henderson, No-Fault Insurance for Automobile Accidents: Status and Effect in the United States, 56 Or. L. Rev. 287 (1977).

[163] See N.Y. Ins. Law §§ 5104, 5102(d) (defining serious injury); Toure v. Avis Rent A Car Sys., Inc., 98 N.Y.2d 345, 774 N.E.2d 1197 (2002) (holding that there must be "objective proof" by an expert—usually a medical expert—to prove serious injury).

[164] Gary T. Schwartz, Auto No-Fault and First-Party Insurance: Advantages and Problems, 73 S. Cal. L. Rev. 611 (2000).

Criticisms. However, ample criticisms have been raised about no-fault plans too. The most frequent and notable of these criticisms concerns the loss of deterrence in no-fault systems,[165] though insurance features like experience rating may improve deterrence.[166] In addition, significant concerns have been voiced about fraud in no-fault systems.[167]

§ 36.8 Government Compensation Funds

Compensation funds. Congress has sometimes provided cash benefits directly or indirectly from public money for specific groups of victims, either to provide compensation to victims or to limit the tort liability of potential defendants. The scope and methods in doing so can be quite different.

The 9/11 fund. The terrorist attacks of September 11, 2001, prompted a federal statute[168] intended primarily to protect airlines from potential economic losses, providing billions to make up for losses they suffered when planes were grounded and otherwise. The statute then added a compensation program for the thousands injured and killed, partly to provide benefits and partly to make suits against airlines less likely. The statute left victims with tort options against the airlines and others, but capped airline liability at the limit of their insurance and required victims to sue in a federal court in New York.[169]

Operation of the fund. The compensation option, pursued by claims presented to a Special Master, allowed substantial compensation for economic loss, but less than traditional tort law would allow in at least five respects. (1) The victim's personal needs and her other financial resources are to be considered in determining the award.[170] (2) The regulations promulgated by the Special Master use a series of presumed damages awards for various circumstances, reducing the likelihood of individualized measurement of damages and flattening out the top awards.[171] (3) Future losses, such as those likely to arise from exposure to toxic materials during rescue operations, are

---

[165] J. David Cummins, et al., The Incentive Effects of No-Fault Automobile Insurance, 44 J.L. & Econ. 427 (2001) (studying empirically no-fault and tort compensation systems and finding support for the hypothesis that no-fault is significantly associated with higher fatal accident rates than tort law).

[166] Gary Schwartz, Auto No-Fault and First-Party Insurance: Advantages and Problems, 73 S. Cal. L. Rev. 611 (2000) (arguing that the no-fault plan should have about the same deterrent effect as tort law if premiums are experience rated).

[167] Fair Price Med. Supply Corp. v. Travelers Indem. Co., 10 N.Y.3d 556, 567, 890 N.E.2d 233, 860 N.Y.S.2d 471 (2008) (Smith, J., dissenting) ("The impact of fraud on this State's no-fault system is notorious.").

[168] Air Transportation Safety and System Stabilization Act (ATSSSA), Pub.L. No. 107–42, 115 Stat. 230 (2001). Uncodified sections are available in the United States Code Annotated notes following 49 U.S.C.A. § 40401. They are cited here by the section numbers appearing in the original enactment, e.g., ATSSSA § 405.

[169] ATSSSA, supra note 168, § 408 (b). A comprehensive report detailing the fund's structure, process and payouts is Kenneth R. Feinberg, et al., Final Report of the Special Master for the September 11th Victim Compensation Fund of 2001 (2004) (available at http://www.justice.gov/final_report.pdf).

[170] See 28 C.F.R. § 104.41 ("the Special Master shall take into consideration the harm to the claimant, the facts of the claim, and the individual circumstances of the claimant. The individual circumstances of the claimant may include the financial needs or financial resources of the claimant or the victim's dependents and beneficiaries").

[171] The United States Department of Justice published tables on the internet. Users could identify the wage loss and age of the deceased victim, then read out the presumed damages. Formal regulations on presumed losses are contained in 28 C.F.R. §§ 104.41 to 104.45.

excluded.[172] (4) The victims' award is reduced by collateral sources;[173] (5) pain and suffering damages are effectively capped at $250,000 for most victims.[174]

Participation and awards. Ninety-seven percent of the families of victims who died on September 11th elected to receive compensation through the compensation fund rather than pursue a lawsuit.[175] For claims based on the death of a victim, awards ranged from $250,000 to $7.1 million. The average award was $2.08 million and the median award was $1.68 million.[176] In total, the Fund distributed more than $7 billion to the families of 2,880 people killed in the September 11th attacks and the 2,680 people who were injured in the attacks or later rescue efforts.[177] The average award for injury victims was nearly $400,000.

Only 96 families chose to file lawsuits. The trial judge issued a number of rulings that would have allowed the suits to go to trial.[178] Nearly all of the lawsuits settled in light of these favorable rulings.

Criticisms. When the government is not legally responsible for the victims' injuries—probably the case here, given the discretionary immunity and arguably the absence of negligence—substantial and direct cash benefits for highly selective groups seem to be unique. Critics have argued that such substantial benefits, not precisely capped on the model of workers' compensation, are difficult to justify for a particular set of victims[179] and are inappropriate where the government is not a tortfeasor and where others similarly situated—victims of the Oklahoma City bombing, for example—are not given similar benefits.[180] Other critics have suggested constitutional concerns and undue federal intervention into state tort law.[181] It is quite possible, however, that the victim's compensation fund can and will serve as a model in other situations and to tort law as a whole.[182]

---

[172] ATSSSA, supra note 168, § 405(a)(3). The exclusion results because all claims must be filed within two years from the time regulations were promulgated. Latent injuries to rescue workers and pregnant women exposed to the "toxic brew" of chemicals released from the ruins of the WTC were thus excluded. Robert L. Rabin, Indeterminate Future Harm in the Context of September 11, 81 Va. L. Rev. 1831 (2002).

[173] ATSSSA, supra note 168, § 405(b)(6). Collateral sources are defined to include life insurance benefits. ATSSSA § 402 (6).

[174] 28 C.F.R. § 104.44 ("The presumed non-economic losses for decedents shall be $250,000 plus an additional $100,000 for the spouse and each dependent of the deceased victim. Such presumed losses include a noneconomic component of replacement services loss").

[175] See Final Report of the Special Master, supra note 169.

[176] Id. at 110.

[177] Id. at 1.

[178] See, e.g., In re September 11 Litig., 280 F.Supp.2d 279 (S.D.N.Y. 2003) (holding that the airlines owed a duty of reasonable care to those on the ground but not deciding breach and causation issues).

[179] See Robert L. Rabin, The Renaissance of Accident Law Plans Revisited, 64 Md. L. Rev. 699 (2005).

[180] John G. Cullhane, Tort, Compensation, and Two Kinds of Justice, 55 Rutgers L. Rev. 1027 (2003) (arguing that the benefits are tort-like but not justified by considerations of corrective justice, since the government is not the wrongdoer, and that the distributive justice aspects of the benefits are unjustified because similar benefits are not provided to other victims of terrorism or disaster).

[181] See Erin G. Holt, The September 11 Victim Compensation Fund: Legislative Justice Sui Generis, 59 N.Y.U. Ann. Surv. Am. L. 513 (2004).

[182] See Linda S. Mullinex, The Future of Tort Reform: Possible Lessons From the World Trade Center Victim Compensation Fund, 53 Emory L.J. 1315 (2004).

Private settlement "funds." Private companies that cause widespread damage may find it in their interests to create a fund option.[183] In the setting in which the company administers the process and distributions, however, a fund is really just a means of providing structured and consistent settlement offers.

§ 36.9   Taxing Industry to Create Compensation Funds

Funds from taxes on industry. In contrast to the direct award of public money to victims, some other programs have taxed industries that cause specified harms, then use the fund so created to pay benefits. Congress did this with one of the stages provided for in the Black Lung Act.[184]

National Childhood Vaccine Injury Act. The substance tax is also the approach taken more recently in the National Childhood Vaccine Injury Act.[185] That statute confronts the fact that vaccines mandated by statute and by public health policy do regularly cause devastating injury to vaccinated children and adults. The injury occurs, not because the vaccines are defective, but because some adverse reactions are unavoidable.[186] Taxing vaccines is likely to raise their costs to public health agencies that provide them and to private users. This increased cost can be limited if the benefits provided are limited and the liabilities standardized. The vaccine act does both of those things. The compensation for pain is limited to $250,000 and the compensation for death the same. Other types of compensation include medical expense and loss of earnings.[187] The claim must be pursued in the Vaccine Court before a tort suit is possible. If the award under the statute is unacceptable to the claimant, she can seek a tort recovery, but cannot recover for unavoidable side effects.[188]

Operation of the vaccine-injury program. The act's standardizing techniques as well as its financing are especially interesting. The plaintiff is permitted to establish that the vaccine actually caused her injury by the usual method of medical evidence if she can, which may be a difficult task.[189] However, as with the listings in Social Security disability claims, the plaintiff can rely instead upon a table with a predetermined list of injuries or symptoms correlated with each type of vaccine. For example, if the vaccine is the basic DPT vaccine and anaphylaxis or anaphylactic shock occurs within 24 hours, the table establishes that the vaccine is a cause. For the same vaccine, however, if the

---

[183] See Ian Urbina, BP Settlements Likely to Shield Top Defendants, N.Y. Times, August 20, 2010, at A1.

[184] 30 U.S.C.A. §§ 901 et seq., later repealed as noted in West Virginia CWP Fund v. Stacy, 671 F.3d 378 (4th Cir. 2011).

[185] 42 U.S.C.A. §§ 300aa–1 et seq.

[186] See Joanna B. Apolinsky & Jeffrey A. Van Detta, Rethinking Liability for Vaccine Injury, 19 Cornell J.L. & Pub. Pol'y 537 (2010) (identifying six different classes of risk).

[187] See Zatuchni v. Secretary of Health & Human Servs., 516 F.3d 1312 (Fed. Cir. 2008) (allowing recovery for both death benefit and for lifetime economic losses).

[188] Judge (now Justice) Breyer summarized the act succinctly in Schafer v. American Cyanamid Co., 20 F.3d 1 (1st Cir. 1994). The Court held that the NCVIA preempts all design defect claims against vaccine manufacturers by plaintiffs who seek compensation for injuries caused by the side-effects of vaccines, in Bruesewitz v. Wyeth LLC, 562 U.S. 223, 131 S.Ct. 1068, 179 L.Ed.2d 1, Prod. Liab. Rep. (CCH) P 18580 (2011).

[189] See Katherine E. Strong, Note, Proving Causation Under the Vaccine Injury Act: A New Approach for a New Day, 75 Geo. Wash. L. Rev. 426 (2007). Before establishing causation, the claimant must prove that she actually has the condition she alleges. See, e.g., Hibbard v. Secretary of Health & Human Servs., 698 F.3d 1355 (Fed. Cir. 2012) (Special Master did not err in focusing on that question, and did not act arbitrarily in finding that the claimant did not prove by a preponderance of the evidence that she actually had autonomic neuropathy).

harm is encephalopathy or encephalitis, causation is established if the problem is first manifest anytime up to three days after vaccination.[190] The table does not resolve all problems[191] and assuredly leaves it open to the plaintiff to prove causation, the only issue, in other ways. Whether vaccines cause certain types of injury has been hugely controversial.[192]

Criticisms and suggestions. Tax-created injury funds may not be suitable for the great mass of tort cases. The vaccine plan has been criticized as slow,[193] limiting,[194] and inconsistent.[195] Its best use may be for those cases in which liability is doubtful or would likely be financially destructive. The idea has been raised, however, as a possible solution for alcohol related injuries.[196] The injured victims of a drunk driver can seldom enforce a substantial judgment against the drinker and often cannot do so against the alcohol provider. In those circumstances, an injury fund created by taxes on the substance may prove a useful solution, especially if, as in the Vaccine Injury Act, the victim still has an option to seeking redress in the tort system.

---

[190] The table is enacted and codified at 42 U.S.C.A. § 300aa–14.

[191] See Shalala v. Whitecotton, 514 U.S. 268 (1995) (holding against the claimant where evidence indicated that the condition in question existed before the vaccination). See also Russell G. Donaldson, Annotation, Construction and Application of National Childhood Vaccine Injury Act (42 U.S.C.A. §§ 300aa et seq.), 129 A.L.R. Fed. 1 (1996).

[192] See Michael J. Donovan, The Impact of "Hurricane" Hannah: The Government's Decision to Compensate One Girl's Vaccine Injury Case Could Drastically Alter the Face of Public Health, 50 Jurimetrics J. 229 (2010).

[193] Data from the Department of Health and Human Services show that between 1988 and 2010 over 13000 claims had been filed, but only 7000 adjudicated. The average time to adjudication was 2–3 years. Of the adjudicated claims approximately 2500 were granted and 4500 denied. The vast majority of unadjudicated claims were autism claims. See U.S. Department of Health and Human Services, National Vaccine Injury Compensation Program, Statistics Report, July 14 2010 (available at http://www.hrsa.gov/vaccine compensation/statistics_report.htm).

[194] Elizabeth A. Breen, A One Shot Deal: The National Childhood Vaccine Injury Act, 41 Wm. & Mary L. Rev. 309 (1999).

[195] Claimants have a markedly better chance with some special masters than with others. See Derry Ridgway, No-Fault Vaccine Insurance: Lessons from the National Vaccine Injury Compensation Program, 24 J. Health Pol'y & L. 59 (1999).

[196] Paul LeBel, John Barleycorn Must Pay: Compensating the Victims of Drinking Drivers 135–48 (1992).

Part VIII

DIGNITARY AND ECONOMIC TORTS

Distinguishing physical harm torts. Beginning with this chapter, the subject-matter focus turns to stand-alone dignitary and economic harms. Stand-alone or "pure" dignitary or economic harms occur without the direct invasion of the plaintiff's legal interest in physical security of her person or property. In contrast, the preceding chapters were devoted to cases in which the core harm was to the plaintiff's interest in physical security of persons or things. The stand-alone dignitary or economic harm discussed in the chapters that follow are often communicative torts—they result from the defendant's use of words or other means of communication. To defame, to persuade someone to cease doing business with the plaintiff, to give the plaintiff misinformation in a business deal are examples of words that may be actionable without causing physical harm. Many dignitary and economic torts are also relational torts; they damage the plaintiff's relationship, personal or economic, with other persons, but again they cause no direct physical harm.

Different rules and approaches. The distinction between stand-alone dignitary or economic harm and physical harm to persons and property is not merely an idle classification. Both the explicit rules and the guiding policies of dignitary and economic torts usually differ radically from the rules of negligence and the rules of trespassory torts like battery. The mode of legal analysis also differs in most cases. For example, negligence is seldom the basis for liability in dignitary and economic torts.[1] In terms of guiding policy, free speech considerations, which are not an issue in ordinary physical harm torts, will often be significant or even determinative in the case of dignitary torts based on non-commercial communications by the defendant.[2] And in economic tort claims, courts are increasingly concerned to preserve a large, sometimes a very large role for contracts, to the exclusion of tort claims.[3] Similar issues have not traditionally been significant in physical harm cases.

Characteristic overlap in dignitary and economic tort claims. The dignitary and economic torts are often conceived so loosely that they overlap with one another, even though different rules apply to each tort. For example, a defendant's published statement might be either defamation, or invasion of privacy, or interference with contract, or even intentional infliction of emotional distress—or all of the above. Possibly it could also be an injurious falsehood such as commercial disparagement, an invasion of the "right of publicity," or even a trademark infringement. Another example is the case of identity theft, which might support invasion of privacy claims, conversion of

---

[1] An important but partial exception is that, although defamation was traditionally a kind of strict liability tort, free speech considerations have led courts to require intentional or negligent falsehood in many cases. See § 519.

[2] See § 554 (constitutional limitations on defamation claims). Commercial speech is sometimes given substantial constitutional protection, see e.g., § 632 (persuasion to breach a contract), but not always, see § 579 (use of plaintiff's "personality" characteristics for commercial purposes).

[3] See §§ 515 & 686 and Chapter 41 generally.

intangibles, or interference with contract, among others.[4] The conceptual imprecision that makes these overlapping theories possible creates several problems.

Practical problems. The plaintiff's lawyer may be required to make numerous separate claims to avoid the risk of a malpractice claim if the case is lost. This will add work for the plaintiff's lawyer and additional work for the defense firm. Defendants, typically earning hourly fees, are likely to respond aggressively on each separate overlapping claim, generating not only work for themselves but also additional work for the plaintiff's lawyer and the courts. Among other problems created by overlapping dignitary and economic claims is the problem of avoiding duplicative damages.[5] Another is to determine whether the policy reasons that bar a cause of action for one of the overlapping torts should defeat an action under other theories of recovery upon the same essential facts. For instance, if the tort consists of a communication but is defeated by defamation rules, can the plaintiff sidestep the rules of defamation by recasting the tort as one for emotional distress, privacy invasion, or interference with contract? The problem represented by this question arises partly because courts and lawyers have not always recognized that conflicting tort rules require attention.

Dignitary torts. Dignitary torts involve legally cognizable invasions of rights that stand independent of both physical and economic harms, that is, invasions of human dignity in the sense of human worth. Battery may entail physical harm, but in some cases the harm from a battery is interference with the plaintiff's autonomy, her right to prevent unconsented-to touchings. The dignitary torts in the chapters that follow, however, involve no physical invasion and no direct threat of it. The best examples of stand-alone dignitary torts are defamation[6] and invasion of privacy,[7] although various misuses of the judicial process can be classified in the same way.[8] Intentional interference with important family relationships is a further example of a dignitary tort.[9] Discrimination, where it is a tort, statutory or otherwise, can also be a dignitary tort, although coverage of that topic has been left largely to more specialized materials.

Emotional harm claims. Claims for stand-alone emotional harm also fit the idea of dignitary harm, and it is true that special rules, not ordinary negligence or intentional tort rules apply in most cases. Nevertheless, this book groups emotional harm claims with physical torts because, for the most part, emotional harm claims are contextually rooted in physical harm or threats of it even when the particular plaintiff suffers no physical harm.[10]

Nuisance. The tort of nuisance, where the plaintiff loses "enjoyment" of land but does not necessarily suffer physical harm to it, is also hard to classify, but it can certainly be said that it is a tort with rules of its own and that simple negligence analysis alone will not suffice.[11]

---

[4] See §§ 580 (privacy invasion generally); 710 (conversion of intangibles); 650 (identity theft and reputational loss) & 659 (injurious falsehood).

[5] See § 617.

[6] Chapter 37.

[7] Chapter 38.

[8] Chapter 39.

[9] Chapter 40.

[10] See Chapter 29.

[11] Chapter 30.

The meaning of pure economic torts. With pure or "stand alone" economic torts, economic harm is the gist of the action. More than that, however, the economic harm stands alone in that does not result from some other actionable tort. For instance, in a pure economic tort, the plaintiff's economic harm does not result from actionable personal injury, property damage or emotional harm. If economic harm is a consequence of some actionable tort, it is merely an item of recoverable damages in a suit for that tort, and no special tort rules are invoked.

Examples of pure economic torts. The law is host to many pure economic torts. A huge category is interference with contract and the related tort of interference with economic opportunity. Where such interference is accomplished by tortious means, say by physically beating the plaintiff, the plaintiff can recover proven economic losses as consequential damages resulting from the tortious battery. In contrast, the pure economic tort of interference with contract arises only if the plaintiff suffers such interference in the absence of any physical tort. For example, the defendant may interfere with the plaintiff's contract by offering a better deal to the plaintiff's promisor or by using its economic power to make the plaintiff's deal costly.[12] In some jurisdictions these interference torts are so broadly conceived that they cover much the same ground as many other torts with more specific rules. Examples of other economic torts include cases of pure economic harm caused by breach of fiduciary duty,[13] by fraud or misrepresentation,[14] conversion of intangibles, injurious falsehoods that do not affect personal reputation but that cause financial harm,[15] and malpractice of lawyers,[16] auditors, and architects whose fault causes no physical harm but does result in economic loss to those who rely.

Negligence in economic torts. Negligence is often an insufficient basis for liability when it comes to pure economic torts. Negligent interference with contract, for example, is not ordinarily actionable. However, in some cases the defendant owes the plaintiff a duty of care because of his undertaking or special relationship with the plaintiff, in which case, a negligence action is permitted for pure economic harm. Legal malpractice claims are examples.

The special role of contract—an "economic loss rule." The potential role of contract in economic harm claims is a major concern. Where the plaintiff and defendant have contracted with respect to a given matter, many courts have insisted that the plaintiff's claim with respect to that must be in contract. If the contract between the parties gives the plaintiff ground for relief, she may pursue the contract claim but not a tort claim. If the contract does not afford the plaintiff relief, then it is frequently held that she cannot have relief under tort law either. The rule that often limits the plaintiff to her contract claim (if she has one at all) is one of the several rules often referred to as the economic loss rule or doctrine.[17] Some courts have gone much, much further, refusing to entertain tort claims when the plaintiff could have but did not actually contract about a matter. The exact scope and application of the economic loss rule has probably not been fully delineated, although it figures in a multitude of cases.

---

[12] See generally Chapter 42.
[13] Chapter 43.
[14] Chapter 43.
[15] Chapter 43.
[16] Chapter 45.
[17] Chapter 41.

Scope of Coverage. Several kinds of economic interference have been excluded from coverage in this treatise, partly because they are now well-developed specialties. Antitrust law is thus omitted. Although intellectual property and unfair competition torts are summarized in this book,[18] specialized works deal with those subjects in more detail.

---

[18] Chapter 46.

Subpart A

DIGNITARY TORTS

Chapter 37

DEFAMATION

Analysis

A. INTRODUCING DEFAMATION

§ 37.1   Defamation: Scope
§ 37.2   Historical Development of Defamation Law

B. COMMON LAW REQUIREMENTS

§ 37.3   Elements of Defamation—Common Law and Constitution
§ 37.4   Requirement of Publication Generally
§ 37.5   The Requirement of Defamatory Content and Its Test
§ 37.6   Interpreting Meaning and Effect
§ 37.7   Defamation of and Concerning the Plaintiff
§ 37.8   The Requirement of Falsity vs. "The Truth Defense"
§ 37.9   Special Slander Rules
§ 37.10   Libel Per Quod

C. DEFENSES

§ 37.11   Absolute Privileges & Common Law Qualified Privileges
§ 37.12   Abuse or Loss of Privilege
§ 37.13   Revising Privileges After the Constitutional Cases
§ 37.14   The Anti-SLAPP Statutes

D. CONSTITUTIONAL LIMITATIONS ON RECOVERY

§ 37.15   Constitutional Limitations on Recovery
§ 37.16   Who Are Public Officials
§ 37.17   Who Are Public Figures
§ 37.18   Proving Constitutional Levels of Fault
§ 37.19   Opinion Statements—Constitutional Protections

E. REMEDIES

§ 37.20   Remedies—Damages
§ 37.21   Non-Damages Remedies Including Money Disgorgement

A. INTRODUCING DEFAMATION

§ 37.1 Defamation: Scope

Reputation and free speech interests. Defamation law, executed through the rules of libel and slander, aims at protecting reputation and good name against false and derogatory communications.[1] Reputation is much prized in the law.[2] So is free speech. These two interests are often in conflict. Accordingly much contemporary defamation law is engaged in seeking an appropriate range of protection for the plaintiff's reputation without sacrificing the defendant's speech rights.

Exclusive means of protecting reputation interests. Reputational harm is protected almost exclusively by the rules of defamation, malicious prosecution type torts,[3] privacy,[4] and injurious falsehood.[5] Although occasionally a plaintiff will claim emotional distress or some other tort based on defamation-type facts, the defamation rules will ordinarily control.[6] Under traditional rules, then, the plaintiff cannot ordinarily avoid the defamation rules by pleading simple negligence. Instead, she must prove the elements of defamation, and she is subject to its limits.[7] Only a few cases have allowed the plaintiff to proceed on a negligence claim, and those have involved unusual and indirect conduct.[8]

Protection of reputation only. Because defamation law aims to redress harms to reputation, it is not used to recover for other types of harm that do not result from reputational harm. For instance, the plaintiff can recover for emotional harm resulting from harm to her reputation, but if the defendant's publication did not harm her reputation, a defamation claim will not lie for emotional harm resulting from the publication.[9]

§ 37.2 Historical Development of Defamation Law

History. Reputational harm may not always have been the focus of defamation law. Primitive law may have been concerned more with insult or dishonor that could lead to blood feud.[10] Legal redress for harsh words or name-calling formalized the victim's vengeance and made the violence of revenge unnecessary. In the medieval English law, oral statements demeaning to others were punished as sin in the Church courts, which

---

[1]   E.g., Little Rock Newspapers, Inc. v. Dodrill, 281 Ark. 25, 660 S.W.2d 933 (1983). For various kinds of reputation and injury to it, see David A. Anderson, Reputation, Compensation, and Proof, 25 Wm. & Mary L. Rev. 747 (1984).

[2]   Reputation is not, however, protected under the United States Constitution. Paul v. Davis, 424 U.S. 693, 96 S.Ct. 1155, 47 L.Ed.2d 405 (1976) (no action may be brought under § 1983 for defamation carried out under color of state law).

[3]   Chapter 39.

[4]   Chapter 38.

[5]   Chapter 43.

[6]   See, e.g., Hustler Magazine v. Falwell, 485 U.S. 46, 108 S.Ct. 876, 99 L.Ed.2d 41 (1988); Hatfill v. New York Times Co., 532 F.3d 312 (4th Cir. 2008).

[7]   See Texas Beef Group v. Winfrey, 11 F.Supp.2d 858, 864 (N.D. Tex. 1998); Hall v. United Parcel Serv. of Am., Inc., 76 N.Y.2d 27, 555 N.E.2d 273 (1990).

[8]   See 3 Dobbs, Hayden & Bublick, The Law of Torts § 649 (2d. ed. 2011 & Supp.).

[9]   See Kenney v. Wal-Mart Stores, Inc., 100 S.W.3d 809 (Mo. 2003).

[10]   The capacity of libel to incite a breach of the peace was given as one reason for imposing criminal liability in Coke's De Libelis Famosis, 50 Co.Rep. 125a, 77 Eng. Rep. 250 (Star Chamber 1605).

is to say that the priest demanded a penance. Eventually, however, common law torts in the 1500s took over these slander actions and converted them into actions for damages.[11]

The history of libel based on printed or tangible communications, such as those found in pamphlets is quite different. By 1600 or before, the printed word was considered a threat to political stability. Printers in England had to be licensed and to give a bond. At that time a libel included any criticism of the English government or even of "great men."[12] Truth was no defense;[13] even to laugh at a libel was a crime.[14] This ruthless program of suppression was carried out by the Court of the Star Chamber, called by Andrew Hamilton "the most dangerous Court to the Liberties of the People of England, that ever was known in that Kingdom. . . ."[15]

Libel was historically used to silence political opposition in England and the United States. New York's British-appointed Governor Cosby used libel law to prosecute John Peter Zenger, the editor of a politically independent paper, *The New York Weekly Journal,* for reporting the Governor's misdemeanors. Zenger was forced to spend nine months in prison awaiting trial because his bail was set so high. (Anna Catherine Zenger published the paper while her husband was incarcerated.) Ultimately, Andrew Hamilton came to Zenger's defense, securing a jury acquittal in 1735.

Zenger's acquittal did not establish a free press in the Colonies, but it has ever since been a rallying point against the scheme of criminal punishment for truthful words. Since the 19th and 20th centuries, defamation law has been largely private and civil. The states received a good deal of English law on the subject of defamation. In particular, the American courts thought from the beginning that written defamation is to be treated differently from oral defamation; the categories that limit liability for slander do not apply when the defamation is in writing.[16] American courts also adopted some obscure and even bizarre doctrines best left for later discussion.[17] Although the private or tort law of defamation aims to protect reputation and good name, some of its particular rules seem derived from the roots of defamation in sin, sedition, dishonor, and punishment.

The history of libel and slander forecasts the concern of contemporary law to balance reputational interests against the interest of the individual defendant and of society at large in free speech. Since 1964, the Supreme Court of the United States has attempted to affect an appropriate balance of those interests under the First Amendment's free speech guarantee,[18] which has required changes in some of the common law rules for many cases.

The history of libel and slander also makes a narrower point. Defamation law long antedated the development of general negligence law. Liability for defamation under the

---

[11]   On all this early development, see R.H. Helmholz, Introduction, Select Cases on Defamation to 1600 xiv–xv (Selden Society 1985).

[12]   Punishment for defamation of important persons goes back to a statute of 1275. Unimportant persons were not so protected for centuries.

[13]   De Libelis Famosis, 50 Co.Rep. 125a, 77 Eng. Rep. 250 (Star Chamber 1605).

[14]   S.F.C. Milsom, Historical Foundations of the Common Law 389 (2d ed.1981).

[15]   See Vincent Buranelli, The Trial of Peter Zenger 103 (1957); Leonard Levy, Freedom of the Press from Zenger to Jefferson 45 (1966).

[16]   Clark v. Binney, 19 Mass. 113 (1824).

[17]   Notably the doctrines of libel per quod and innocent construction. See § 37.10.

[18]   New York Times v. Sullivan, 376 U.S. 254, 84 S.Ct. 710, 11 L.Ed.2d 686, 95 A.L.R.2d 1412 (1964). See § 37.15.

common law rules thus did not depend upon proof of negligence. Equally, an ordinary negligence action ordinarily cannot be maintained for loss of reputation.[19] Defamation law is also wholly unrelated to those intentional torts like battery and assault that are derived from the writ of trespass and that entail direct application of force. The law of defamation, true to its unhappy history, developed its own complex rules unrelated to the law of negligence and intent.

B. COMMON LAW REQUIREMENTS

§ 37.3   Elements of Defamation—Common Law and Constitution

Traditional common law elements—libel. Defamation by writing and by contemporary means analogous to writing is libel. Defamation communicated orally is slander. Communication in any form can be defamatory, but defamation is most commonly communicated in words, pictorial elements, acts or some combination of these methods. This chapter often uses the term defamation to include any form of communication. In claims for libel, once the plaintiff showed a publication of defamatory material about the plaintiff, the traditional rule permitted courts to presume that the publication was made with malice,[20] that the words were false,[21] and that the plaintiff suffered damages.[22] The upshot was that the plaintiff could recover substantial damages for libel upon proof of three elements: (1) defendant's publication of defamatory material (2) of and concerning the plaintiff (3) to a third person. These rules created a regime of prima facie strict liability, because no proof of the defendant's fault was required. As usual with such extremes, courts then created a limited number of affirmative defenses with the burden on the defendant.[23]

Additional elements required in contemporary law. Many contemporary cases have announced that three non-traditional requirements are now necessary to sustain a libel claim. These cases tend to say the plaintiff must prove, besides the elements listed above, that (4) the defendant was guilty of fault equivalent to negligence or something greater in all cases,[24] (5) the publication was false,[25] and (6) the plaintiff suffered actual

---

[19]   Lawrence v. Grinde, 534 N.W.2d 414 (Iowa 1995).

[20]   See, e.g., Senna v. Florimont, 196 N.J. 469, 958 A.2d 427 (2008) (but holding that fault is now required when the publication touches on an issue of public concern); Doss v. Jones, 5 Howard 158 (Miss. 1840) ("the law imputes malice or an evil intention in all cases, when words actionable in themselves are spoken").

[21]   See Hepps v. Philadelphia Newspapers, Inc., 506 Pa. 304, 485 A.2d 374, 379 (1984) ("falsity of the defamatory words is presumed," truth is an affirmative defense), rev'd, Philadelphia Newspapers, Inc. v. Hepps, 475 U.S. 767, 106 S.Ct. 1558, 89 L.Ed.2d 783 (1986) (constitutional rules require the plaintiff to prove falsity, at least in certain cases).

[22]   See Greenmoss Builders, Inc. v. Dun & Bradstreet, Inc., 143 Vt. 66, 76, 461 A.2d 414, 419 (1983), aff'd, Dun & Bradstreet, Inc. v. Greenmoss Builders, Inc., 472 U.S. 749, 105 S. Ct. 2939, 86 L. Ed. 2d 593 (1985); In re Storms v. Action Wis., Inc., 309 Wis.2d 704, 748, 750 N.W.2d 739, 761 (2008) ("Damages are presumed from proof of the defamation by libel"; but holding that constitutional fault levels were required when a public figure sues).

[23]   See generally § 37.11.

[24]   See Seaton v. TripAdvisor, LLC, 728 F.3d 592 (6th Cir, 2013) (applying Tennesssee law); Blodgett v. University Club, 930 A.2d 210 (D.C. 2007); Morgan v. Kooistra, 941 A.2d 447 (Me. 2008); Higginbotham v. Public Serv. Comm'n of Md., 412 Md. 112, 985 A.2d 1183 (2009); Smith v. Anonymous Joint Enter., 487 Mich. 102, 793 N.W.2d 533 (2010); Sullivan v. Baptist Mem'l Hosp., 995 S.W.2d 569 (Tenn. 1999); Belcher v. Wal-Mart Stores, Inc., 211 W.Va. 712, 568 S.E.2d 19 (2002).

[25]   Eckman v. Cooper Tire & Rubber Co., 893 So.2d 1049 (Miss. 2005); Mark v. Seattle Times, 96 Wash.2d 473, 635 P.2d 1081 (1981).

damages.[26] Others list only some of these added elements.[27] These added elements came about as courts attempted to integrate federal constitutional rules of free-speech into the common law of libel. When the Restatement Second introduced these additional requirements in 1977,[28] they appeared to reflect the constitutional requirements. A later Supreme Court decision, however, suggests that the Constitution does not require these added elements where the defendant defames a purely private person on an issue that is not of public concern.[29] Nevertheless, states apparently continue to state these added elements of proof for all cases, not merely those involving public figures or issues of public concern.[30]

Slander, special requirements. In the case of slander, the plaintiff must also prove either (a) special (pecuniary) harm *or* (b) a publication asserting that the plaintiff has committed a serious crime, or that the plaintiff has a character trait or a practice incompatible with her trade, business, or profession, or that the plaintiff suffers an incurable and communicable disease.[31] The requirement of pecuniary harm is significantly more demanding than the requirement of actual harm or damages.[32]

Constitutional Limitations. Since 1964, the structure of the common law defamation case has been radically altered by constitutional rulings based upon defendants' rights to free speech. All three of the common law presumptions—fault, falsity, and damages—have been reversed by constitutional decisions governing a substantial number of cases.[33]

Although some issues remain undecided, the constitutional rules probably cover the following territory. [34] (1) If the plaintiff is a public official or a public figure, she must now prove that the defendant published a knowing or reckless falsehood, but states are free to permit recovery of presumed damages if they choose to do so. (2) If the plaintiff is a private person but the issue involved in the publication is one of public concern, the plaintiff is required to prove falsity of the publication, some fault on the part of the defendant (usually negligence), plus actual injury or damages. Upon such proof, she cannot recover punitive damages, and without such proof she cannot recover anything. (3) If the plaintiff is a private person and the alleged defamation is of no public concern,

---

[26]   Nazeri v. Missouri Valley Coll., 860 S.W.2d 303 (Mo. 1993). Traditionally, slander claims required proof of *pecuniary* damages while libel cases presumed damages. Under a rule developed in some 19th century American cases, pecuniary damages must be proved in certain libel cases, but not all. See § 535.

[27]   E.g., Hopkins v. O'Connor, 282 Conn. 821, 925 A.2d 1030 (2007) (adding to the traditional common law elements only that the plaintiff must show reputational injury resulting from the defendant's publication).

[28]   Restatement (Second) of Torts § 558 (1977); see § 37.15.

[29]   Id.

[30]   In some instances it is difficult to be sure of the weight to be given to the state-court cases requiring proof of additional elements. Compare Mathis v. Cannon, 276 Ga. 16, 573 S.E.2d 376 (2002) (stating that fault amounting at least to negligence would be required to impose liability for publications *on matters of public concern*), with Smith v. Stewart, 291 Ga. App. 86, 660 S.E.2d 822 (2008) (stating without limitation that fault amount at least to negligence must be shown in all cases, but citing Mathis as authority). Some of the statements turn out to be inherently ambiguous, as where a court says damages are required but later in the opinion that damages may be presumed in certain cases. See, e.g., Dugan v. Mittal Steel USA Inc., 929 N.E.2d 184 (Ind. 2010).

[31]   Unchastity is a fourth category once recognized, but perhaps no longer. See § 37.9.

[32]   See id. (pecuniary harm required in certain slander cases).

[33]   § 37.15.

[34]   Id.

the states are free to permit recovery of presumed damages; probably the states are free to invoke common law strict liability rules as well.

Where falsity is required, the effect is to protect opinion statements that cannot be said to be either true or false.[35] Even where the constitutional limitations may not apply, some states have now adopted some of these constitutional limitations as a part of their common law.[36]

§ 37.4 Requirement of Publication Generally

The meaning of publication. The concept of publication is used in defamation law not only in stating the elements of a claim but also in determining what law applies, whether the statute of limitations has run, and other procedural matters.[37] *Publication* is a word of art. It includes any communication, by any method,[38] to one or more persons who can understand the meaning.[39] The threat or danger of a future communication is not a publication in any sense.[40] By inference or by direct evidence,[41] the plaintiff claiming libel or slander must prove that the defendant published defamatory material about the plaintiff to a third person; publication only to the plaintiff herself is insufficient to establish defamation, though it may amount to some other tort.[42] No rule requires a mass audience, but if the publication reaches only a few persons, damages may be limited. Anyone who participates in publication can be a publisher subject to liability for defamation.[43] Courts sometimes treat issues of privilege to publish as issues about publication itself.[44] It has been held that publication to an agent of the plaintiff who is acting for her in matters touched by the defamation may be considered to be no more than publication to the plaintiff herself,[45] but this seems doubtful, since the plaintiff is entitled to her reputation with her agents as well as with others.

Forms of publication. Books and newspapers are publications if distributed to at least one person besides the plaintiff, as many cases imposing liability show. At the other

---

[35] § 37.19.

[36] See, e.g., United Ins. Co. of Am. v. Murphy, 331 Ark. 364, 961 S.W.2d 752 (1998) (prospectively abolishing presumed damages); Thomas v. Jacksonville Television, Inc., 699 So.2d 800 (Fla. Dist. Ct. App. 1997) (fault is element of defamation); Simpson v. Mars Inc., 929 P.2d 966 (Nev. 1997) (same); Hupp v. Sasser, 200 W.Va. 791, 490 S.E.2d 880 (1997) (listing falsity as element).

[37] See § 573.

[38] See Restatement (Second) of Torts § 577 cmt. a (1977).

[39] Simpson Strong-Tie Co., Inc. v. Stewart, Estes & Donnell, 232 S.W.3d 18 (Tenn. 2007). Words spoken in a foreign language to a person who does not understand that language is not a publication. See Economopoulos v. A.G. Pollard Co., 218 Mass. 294, 105 N.E. 896 (1914). Distinguish understanding of the words' meaning from belief in the truth of the words. The fact that the only recipient of the words does not believe them goes only to the issue of damages and does not show non-publication. Marble v. Chapin, 132 Mass. 225 (Mass. 1882). But cf. Silverman v. Progressive Broad., Inc., 964 P.2d 61 (N.M. 1998) (there is no publication if the recipient knows the statement is false, perhaps treating recipient's lack of belief in the statement in the same way).

[40] Dible v. Haight Ashbury Free Clinics, 170 Cal.App.4th 843, 88 Cal.Rptr.3d 464, 471 (2009).

[41] With mass media publications publication is easily inferred, but it might be rebuttably inferred from circumstantial evidence in other cases as well, as where an institution exhibits defamatory matter in a public display. LaMon v. City of Westport, 44 Wash.App. 664, 723 P.2d 470 (1986).

[42] See Kamelgard v. Macura, 585 F.3d 334, 342 (7th Cir. 2009); Brauer v. Globe Newspaper Co., 351 Mass. 53, 217 N.E.2d 736 (1966); Restatement (Second) of Torts § 577 cmt. b (1977); but see the paragraph, "Traditional Self-Publication," below.

[43] Missner v. Clifford, 393 Ill.App.3d 751, 914 N.E.2d 540 (2009).

[44] See 3 Dobbs, Hayden & Bublick, The Law of Torts § 523 (2d. ed. 2011 & Supp.).

[45] Delval v. PPG Indus., Inc., 590 N.E.2d 1078, 1081 (Ind. Ct. App. 1992).

end of the spectrum, oral personal remarks made to a neighbor over the back fence equally count as publication.[46] Suggestive questions as well as declaratory statements can communicate defamatory meaning.[47] Photos,[48] motion pictures,[49] and computer communications[50] can all count as publications. Even some signs or writing on the restroom wall[51] or conduct without words can communicate a defamatory falsehood. The defendant's conduct may be innocent in itself but may become defamatory when combined with his words and with his implied adoption of another's words.[52] A publisher who gives a false and defamatory impression by truthfully reporting some facts but omitting exculpatory facts or facts that put the matter in an innocent light is subject to liability because the gist of the publication as a whole in that case is false and defamatory.[53] But bare silence, not coupled with revelation of other material, may not easily fit into the concept of publication, even when silence implies something derogatory.[54]

Intent and negligence. To be responsible for defamatory material, the defendant need not be the author, but he must be a publisher of it. That means that he is not liable unless he communicates the material intentionally or negligently.[55] If he is under a duty to remove or prevent a publication, a negligent or intentional failure to do so counts as a publication.[56] Negligent publication is relatively rare, but possible. If I write in my diary that you robbed the bank there is no publication at all, but if I leave the diary open on the coffee table where guests might read it, I am a negligent publisher if one of them does so.[57]

---

[46]   See McCune v. Neitzel, 235 Neb. 754, 457 N.W.2d 803 (1990) (affirming a judgment for the plaintiff, victim of neighbor talk that he had AIDS).

[47]   E.g., Keohane v. Stewart, 882 P.2d 1293 (Colo. 1994) (was he paid off in cash or cocaine?); Lara v. Thomas, 512 N.W.2d 777 (Iowa 1994) (does she have a drug problem?).

[48]   Kiesau v. Bantz, 686 N.W.2d 164 (Iowa 2004) (photo of plaintiff, a sheriff's officer, altered to make it appear that she was exposing her breasts, was actionable).

[49]   E.g., Muzikowski v. Paramount Pictures Corp., 322 F.3d 918 (7th Cir. 2003) (error to dismiss claim).

[50]   Lott v. Levitt, 469 F.Supp. 2d 575 (N.D. Ill. 2007) (email to third person actionable).

[51]   Hellar v. Bianco, 111 Cal.App.2d 424, 244 P.2d 757, 28 A.L.R.2d 1451 (1952) (actionable if owner maintained the writing, though he did not originate it).

[52]   Clampitt v. American Univ., 957 A.2d 23, 39 (D.C. 2008).

[53]   Karage v. First Advantage Corp., 2010 WL 1062601 (N.D.Tex. 2010) (unreported) ("A publication as a whole may be defamatory if it creates a false impression by omitting material facts"); Mohr v. Grant, 153 Wash.2d 812, 108 P.3d 768, 776 (2005) ("In a defamation by omission case, the plaintiff must show with respect to the element of falsity that the communication left a false impression that would be contradicted by the inclusion of omitted facts").

[54]   See Mbarika v. Board of Supervisors of La. State Univ., 992 So.2d 551, 563 (La. Ct. App. 2008) ("allegations that Dr. Schneider defamed Dr. Mbarika by failing to make a statement about some of his accomplishments cannot support a claim of defamation"). Cf. Trail v. Boys & Girls Clubs of Nw. Ind., 845 N.E.2d 130 (Ind. 2006).

[55]   Haley v. Casa Del Rey Homeowners Ass'n, 153 Cal. App. 4th 863, 63 Cal. Rptr. 3d 514 (2007) (defendant made defamatory accusations at the plaintiff's front door, but did not know or have reason to believe that anyone else was in the house who could hear them; this was neither intentional nor negligent publication); Restatement (Second) of Torts § 577(1) (1977).

[56]   Hellar v. Bianco, 111 Cal.App.2d 424, 244 P.2d 757, 28 A.L.R.2d 1451 (1952) (remarks about the plaintiff's sexual activity, along with her home phone number, written on the restroom wall of a bar; liability for failure to remove promptly after learning the content); Restatement (Second) of Torts § 577(2) (1979); cf. Tacket v. General Motors Corp., 836 F.2d 1042 (7th Cir. 1987) (liability based on theory that defendant implicitly adopted the defamatory statement; adoption could not be found without a significant time in which to remove the defamatory material).

[57]   See Restatement (Second) of Torts § 577 cmt. k and Illus. 4 to 6 (1977); see also id. cmt. l (mistaken identity of recipient).

Intent to publish versus intent to defame. The traditional requirement of intent or negligence has sometimes been misunderstood as a requirement of fault. The only intent required is an intent to publish (that is, to communicate), not an intent to harm or even an intent to relay a falsehood. Although fault in some more substantive sense is required in some cases under the Constitution, the role of fault in determining whether the defendant published material does not touch issues of truth, justification, or reasonableness of the publication. The issue of publication is about communication.

Original publisher as publisher of repeater's republication. A publisher is responsible for reputational harms proximately caused by publication of defamatory material, including harms resulting from a repeater's foreseeable publication[58] to at least one person other than the plaintiff herself.[59] The publisher is liable only if the repeater is in fact repeating the substance of the original publication and not the same defamation derived from some other source,[60] and if all the other requirements of a defamation action are met.[61]

Transmitters, distributors, or disseminators of information. Some primary publishers like newspapers are responsible as publishers even for materials prepared by others, as in the case of advertisements.[62] On the other hand, many other publishers such as telephone companies, libraries, news vendors, radio stations, and internet services are called transmitters, distributors, or secondary publishers rather than primary publishers. The disseminator is essentially a conduit, not an originator or promoter of content.

Protections for secondary publishers. Protection for distributors or secondary publishers who merely carry the publications of others, or furnish a forum in which others may be heard, seems increasingly accepted in the United States.[63] In the case of radio and similar broadcasts, statutes today frequently immunize the broadcaster who merely provides a forum for the speech of others by leasing air time.[64] A federal statute, the Communications Decency Act (CDA), immunizes internet service providers and users so that they are not to be treated as "publishers" and are not legally responsible

---

[58]   Barnette v. Wilson, 706 So.2d 1164 (Ala. 1997); Wright v. Bachmurski, 29 Kan. App. 2d 595, 29 P.3d 979 (2001); Trentecosta v. Beck, 703 So.2d 552 (La. 1997); Murphy v. Boston Herald, Inc., 449 Mass. 42, 865 N.E.2d 746 (2007); Restatement (Second) of Torts § 576 (1977) (also recognizing liability where repeater was privileged to repeat).

[59]   If the repeater's communication of the defamatory material is made only to the plaintiff herself, that is not a publication and does not start the statute of limitations running anew. Oparaugo v. Watts, 884 A.2d 63 (D.C. 2005).

[60]   Longbehn v. Schoenrock, 727 N.W.2d 153 (Minn. Ct. App. 2007).

[61]   The topic is developed at greater length in 3 Dobbs, Hayden & Bublick, The Law of Torts § 521 (2d. ed. 2011 & Supp.).

[62]   Triangle Publ'ns, Inc. v. Chumley, 253 Ga. 179, 317 S.E.2d 534 (1984); Pettengill v. Booth Newspapers, Inc., 88 Mich. App. 587, 278 N.W.2d 682 (1979).

[63]   The question remains whether the neutral distributor such as a library is liable if the distributor knows of the defamation. An English case decided in 1900 held that such liability was appropriate. Vizetelly v. Mudie's Select Library, Ltd., [1900] 2 Q.B. 170, 69 L.J.Q.B. 645 (C.A.). Contemporary American ideas about liability for speech seem to be quite different. See 3 Dobbs, Hayden & Bublick, The Law of Torts § 522 (2d. ed. 2011 & Supp.).

[64]   E.g., Cal. Civ. Code § 48.5; N.Y. Civ. Rights Law § 75. Before the statutes, common law decisions were divided on the point.

for defamatory material created by others.[65] The immunity does not extend to website operators who are in part responsible for the creation or development of content.[66]

Traditional self-publication. One peculiar kind of case is strangely labeled as self-publication. In this kind of case, the defendant directly communicates defamatory material about the plaintiff only to the plaintiff herself. That is ordinarily not publication in the law of defamation. However, in some cases, the defendant can foresee that the plaintiff will feel compelled to communicate the defamatory materials to others, and the defendant thus is himself a publisher. For instance, if the defendant hands a written defamation to an unsighted person, the defendant can expect that the recipient will have others read it.[67] The Restatement Second adds that the defendant is only a publisher in these cases because the plaintiff was unaware of the defamatory character of the communication she transmitted to third persons.[68] However, in some cases the self-publication doctrine has been expanded. A few cases have held that when the defendant can foresee publication by the plaintiff under compelling circumstances, as with a discharged employee seeking employment elsewhere, the defendant is subject to liability for defamation.[69] Other cases, said to be the large majority, however, have expressly rejected the whole idea, at least as applied in employment cases and where the plaintiff is aware of the defamatory content. These decisions theorize that the defaming employer is simply not a publisher at all.[70] The policy bases for excluding liability is that open and honest communication is important in the conduct of business, that a culture of silence in the workplace would be harmful to both employer and employee, and that liability would undermine the plaintiff's duty to mitigate damages.[71] These policies do not support the no-publication conclusion, but rather support a privilege.[72]

§ 37.5 The Requirement of Defamatory Content and Its Test

Defamatory content required. No action for libel or slander is stated unless the plaintiff can prove that the defendant has published something of a defamatory nature about her. Publications that are expected to harm and do in fact harm the plaintiff may count as some other tort but they cannot count as libel or slander unless they have defamatory quality.[73]

---

[65]   See § 37.11. "No provider or user of an interactive computer service shall be treated as the publisher or speaker of any information provided by another information content provider." 47 U.S.C.A. § 230(c)(1).

[66] See Jones v. Dirty World Entm't Recordings, LLC, 755 F.3d 398 (6th Cir. 2014); Klayman v. Zuckerberg, 753 F.3d 1354 (D.C. Cir.), cert. denied, 135 S.Ct. 680, 190 L.Ed.2d 391 (2014).

[67]   Lane v. Schilling, 130 Or. 119, 279 P. 267 (1929).

[68]   Restatement (Second) of Torts § 577 cmt. m (1977). Accord: Austin v. Inet Techs., Inc., 118 S.W.3d 491 (Tex. App. 2003).

[69]   Lewis v. Equitable Life Assurance Soc'y of the U.S., 389 N.W.2d 876, 62 A.L.R.4th 581 (Minn. 1986) (a leading case); David P. Chapus, Annotation, Publication of Allegedly Defamatory Matter by Plaintiff ("Self-publication") as Sufficient to Support Defamation Action, 62 A.L.R.4th 616 (1989). The Lewis case, mentioned in this note, has been largely superseded by Minn. Stat. Ann. § 181.933.

[70]   Gonsalves v. Nissan Motor Corp. in Haw., Ltd., 100 Haw. 149, 58 P.3d 1196 (2002); White v. Blue Cross & Blue Shield of Mass., Inc., 442 Mass. 64, 809 N.E.2d 1034 (2004); Sullivan v. Baptist Mem'l Hosp., 995 S.W.2d 569 (Tenn. 1999); Bettinger v. Field Container Co., 221 Wis.2d 221, 584 N.W.2d 233 (Ct. App. 1998).

[71]   All these grounds are reviewed and accepted in Cweklinsky v. Mobile Chemical Co., 267 Conn. 2109, 837 A.2d 759 (2004).

[72]   For greater detail, see 3 Dobbs, Hayden & Bublick, The Law of Torts § 523 (2d. ed. 2011 & Supp.).

[73]   Frinzi v. Hanson, 30 Wis.2d 271, 140 N.W.2d 259 (1966); see Kirch v. Liberty Media Corp., 449 F.3d 388, 398 (2d Cir. 2006) (noting that injury without defamation of the plaintiff would not be actionable as defamation).

Definitions of "defamatory." Under the classic English definition, words had a defamatory quality if they exposed the plaintiff to hatred, ridicule, or contempt.[74] American decisions added that defamation included anything that subjected the plaintiff to obloquy, odium, shame, disgrace, or other forms of discredit or harm to reputation.[75] They also recognized that a publication would be defamatory if it caused the plaintiff to be shunned or avoided by others, even if she were not discredited or subjected to disgrace.[76] Courts have generally come to adopt the Restatement's more accurate statement[77] that a communication is defamatory if it tends to harm the plaintiff's reputation, lowering her in the esteem of a substantial and respectable minority in the community or deterring people from associating or dealing with her.[78] Tendency to harm, however, is an estimate of the judges and jurors from their experience in life; it is almost never a matter of evidence or poll-taking.[79] When reasonable people could differ as to whether a communication is defamatory, the question is left to the jury.[80] A statement raising suspicion that the plaintiff had poisoned people with anthrax might fit these broad definitions even if the statement could not be construed to mean that the plaintiff was in fact guilty of the poisoning.[81]

Right-thinking people test. Even the Restatement's definition does not adequately explain why recovery is excluded in some cases. In a diverse society, almost any statement about the plaintiff would tend to lower the plaintiff in the esteem of someone. Statements that the plaintiff cooperated with police or voted for one party or another in an election are not accepted as defamatory,[82] but some people will feel that such conduct is disgraceful and contemptible. Courts, especially in New York, once attempted to deal with this problem by saying that to be defamatory the statement must lower the plaintiff in the esteem of "right-thinking people,"[83] but as there is no standard for determining what right-thinking people would think, and since a democratic and individualistic society recognizes all people's right to hold their own opinions, the right-thinking test is

---

[74]   Parmiter v. Coupland, 151 Eng. Rep. 340 (Exch. Pleas 1840).

[75]   E.g., Thomas v. Jacksonville Television, Inc., 699 So.2d 800 (Fla. Dist. Ct. App. 1997) (distrust); Brock v. Thompson, 948 P.2d 279 (Okla. 1997) (obloquy). All the terms refer to the same general idea. The plaintiff must prove actual injury to reputation before being awarded damages. Smith v. Durden, 276 P.3d 943 (N.M. 2012).

[76]   Katapodis v. Brooklyn Spectator, 287 N.Y. 17, 38 N.E.2d 112 (1941).

[77]   Restatement (Second) of Torts § 559 & cmt. e (1977), based on Peck v. Tribune Co., 214 U.S. 185, 29 S.Ct. 554, 53 L.Ed. 960 (1909).

[78]   See, e.g., Jews For Jesus, Inc. v. Rapp, 997 So.2d 1098 (Fla. 2008); Tuite v. Corbitt, 224 Ill. 2d 490, 866 N.E.2d 114, 310 Ill. Dec. 303 (2006); Brown v. Gatti, 341 Or. 452, 145 P.3d 130 (2006). Courts may use the Restatement's test alone or use it as the primary definition followed by references to the older language. E.g., Hupp v. Sasser, 200 W.Va. 791, 490 S.E.2d 880 (1997).

[79]   See Lyrissa Barnett Lidsky, Defamation, Reputation, and the Myth of Community, 71 Wash. L. Rev. 1, 18 (1996); 3 Dobbs, Hayden & Bublick, The Law of Torts § 574 (2d. ed. 2011 & Supp.)(admissibility of evidence that people believed or reacted negatively establishes harm).

[80]   E.g., Frinzi v. Hanson, 30 Wis.2d 271, 140 N.W.2d 259 (1966).

[81]   In Hatfill v. New York Times Co., 416 F.3d 320 (4th Cir. 2005), the defendant published statements suggesting that the FBI should investigate Hatfill more vigorously in connection with anthrax mailed to various people. In a lengthy analysis, the court concluded that reasonable people could conclude from alleged misstatements of fact that Hatfill "was responsible for the anthrax mailings in 2001." The plaintiff in Hatfill, however, ultimately lost on a different ground, for failure to prove knowing or reckless falsehood. Hatfill v. New York Times Co., 532 F.3d 312 (4th Cir. 2008).

[82]   See Saunders v. Bd. of Dirs., WHYY-TV, 382 A.2d 257 (Del. Super. 1978) (to identify plaintiff as an FBI informer is not defamatory even though the plaintiff was a prison inmate at the time).

[83]   See Foster v. Churchill, 87 N.Y.2d 744, 665 N.E.2d 153, 642 N.Y.S.2d 583 (1996).

unhelpful, if not downright sinister. The test has sometimes been expressly rejected[84] and in the last generation, hardly been mentioned except in the application of New York and Kentucky law.

Substantial number test. The best courts have been able to do with the problem is to say that the publication is not defamatory unless it would cause a substantial number in the community to reduce dealings with the plaintiff or to hold her in lower esteem.[85] This does not mean, however, that the plaintiff must show that anyone actually *believed* the defamatory statement.[86] Under the presumed damages rule, it is enough that the publication is of a defamatory nature, even if no actual harm is demonstrable. The inquiry, in other words, is about the defamatory nature of the statement, not about the extent of harm it wreaked.

Common categories of defamation. The tests of defamation permit courts to judge each case on its facts without limiting recovery to any artificial categories. However, as a matter of description, most defamation cases involve publications that expressly or impliedly impute to the plaintiff (1) a serious crime involving moral turpitude or a felony; (2) a character trait that makes her unfit for, or conduct incompatible with, her business, trade, or profession; (3) acts or views opposing some deeply held moral standard of the community, even when no crime has been asserted; or (4) physical or other traits that show no violation at all of community standards but would nevertheless induce others to shun the plaintiff or avoid dealing with her. The first two categories are used in the law of slander for somewhat different purposes, but they also describe the patterns in a great many libel actions.[87]

Crime. Examples of the first two categories are easy to imagine. Publications asserting that the plaintiff committed murder or any other serious crime are certainly defamatory, whether the claim is for libel or slander. And the accusation may lie in the recitation of evidence against the plaintiff as well as in direct or conclusory accusations.[88]

Incompetence, bad credit. Publications asserting or implying that a physician is not trained in his work, is incompetent to do it,[89] or that he does medically unnecessary surgeries[90] are examples of the second category. Even a garbled letter, sent out over the plaintiff's name to prospective employers looking for editorial employees, could imply

---

[84]   Herrmann v. Newark Morning Ledger Co., 49 N.J.Super. 551, 140 A.2d 529 (1958).

[85]   Burns v. McGraw Hill Broad. Co., Inc., 659 P.2d 1351 (Colo. 1983); Brauer v. Globe Newspaper Co., 351 Mass. 53, 217 N.E.2d 736 (1966). Shay v. Walters, 702 F.3d 76 (1st Cir. 2012), affirmed dismissal of plaintiff's complaint based on the conclusion that only a "tiny group of people might recognize the plaintiff" as the person referenced in the book under a different name. The plaintiff argued that a "more expansive segment of the population" know her identity following the filing of her lawsuit, but the court noted, "there is a rub: the filing of the suit was the plaintiff's doing, and, in all events, the republished statements were not made by the defendant."

[86]   See Plumley v. Landmark Chevrolet, Inc., 122 F.3d 308 (5th Cir. 1997); In re Peck, 295 B.R. 353 (B.A.P. 9th Cir. 2003); Marble v. Chapin, 132 Mass. 225 (1882); cf. Bell v. National Republican Cong. Comm., 187 F.Supp.2d 605 (S.D. W. Va. 2002) (presuming harm even if no recipient shares plaintiff's interpretation of defendant's statement); but cf. Silverman v. Progressive Broad., Inc., 964 P.2d 61 (N.M. 1998) (publication to one who knows statement is untrue is no publication at all, perhaps treating recipient's belief in truth as the same thing).

[87]   On the slander categories, see § 37.9.

[88]   E.g., Hatfill v. New York Times Co., 416 F.3d 320 (4th Cir. 2005) (newspaper column allegedly erroneously reciting evidence pointing to plaintiff as a primary suspect in sending deadly anthrax by mail).

[89]   Saunders v. VanPelt, 497 A.2d 1121 (Me. 1985) (that psychologist not competent to work with children is defamatory).

[90]   Slaughter v. Friedman, 32 Cal.3d 149, 649 P.2d 886, 185 Cal.Rptr. 244 (1982).

that the plaintiff is a sloppy writer or fails to proof her letters and is incompetent for an editorial position.[91] Courts have also extended this category to include assertions that may damage the plaintiff's credit because they bear upon the plaintiff's ability or willingness to pay her debts.[92]

Views or acts offending prevailing cultural or moral views. Examples of the third group include a few cases finding defamatory quality in assertions that the plaintiff is a liar,[93] or that the plaintiff engages in or supports sexual activity that members of the community regard as fundamentally wrong, even when that activity is not a crime at all.[94] Similarly, the implication that an African-American politician makes deals that reduce the power of blacks in the community has been considered defamatory.[95] Even statements that make the plaintiff seem "insincere, excessively litigious, avaricious, and perhaps unstable" have been held to count as defamatory.[96] False attribution of offensive views to the plaintiff may be actionable,[97] as where the defendant misquoted the plaintiff in a way that made the plaintiff seem particularly insensitive to rape victims.[98] At least in one era, imputations of communist sympathy, though again not illegal, were held to be defamatory.[99] Sometimes publications asserting that the plaintiff is a racist, homophobic or otherwise hostile to particular groups are dismissed because they are, on the facts, mere name-calling or opinion,[100] or because some other element of the

---

[91] Uebelacker v. Paula Allen Holdings, Inc., 464 F.Supp. 2d 791 (W.D. Wis. 2006).

[92] E.g., Alaska State Bank v. Fairco., 674 P.2d 288 (Alaska 1983); Student Loan Fund of Idaho, Inc. v. Duerner, 951 P.2d 1272 (Idaho 1998). The Fair Credit Reporting Act imposes some special duties on credit reporting agencies and also preempts some defamation claims. See 15 U.S.C.A. §§ 1681h & 1681t. Cushman v. Trans Union Corp., 920 F.Supp. 80 (E.D. Pa. 1996); 3 Dobbs, Hayden & Bublick, The Law of Torts § 536 (2d. ed. 2011 & Supp.).

[93] E.g., Paxton v. Woodward, 31 Mont. 195, 78 P. 215 (1904). Most "liar" accusations may imply crime or unfitness for a vocation and hence may be actionable on one of those grounds, depending on the facts. See Cook v. Winfrey, 141 F.3d 322 (7th Cir. 1998); Edwards v. National Audubon Soc'y, Inc., 556 F.2d 113 (2d Cir. 1977).

[94] See Ogle v. Hocker, 279 Fed. Appx. 391(6th Cir. 2008) (homosexual desires attributed to a minister of the Church of God); Nazeri v. Missouri Valley Coll., 860 S.W.2d 303, 312 (Mo. 1993) ("[H]omosexuality is still viewed with disfavor, if not outright contempt, by a sizeable proportion of our population. . . . [A] false allegation of homosexuality is defamatory in Missouri"); Rejent v. Liberation Publ'ns, Inc., 197 A.D.2d 240, 611 N.Y.S.2d 866 (1994). Contra, as to imputations of homosexuality, Albright v. Morton, 321 F.Supp.2d 130 (D. Mass. 2004); Hayes v. Smith, 832 P.2d 1022, 1025 (Colo. Ct. App. 1992) ("A court should not classify homosexuals with those miscreants who have engaged in actions that deserve the reprobation and scorn"); Yonaty v. Mincolla, 97 A.D.3d 141, 945 N.Y.S.2d 774, 40 Media L. Rep. (BNA) 2014 (2012), leave to appeal denied, 20 N.Y.3d 855, 959 N.Y.S.2d 126, 982 N.E.2d 1260 (2013) (statements that plaintiff was gay or bisexual were not slanderous per se, "in light of the tremendous evolution in social attitudes regarding homosexuality").

[95] Wilder v. Johnson Publ'g Co., Inc., 551 F.Supp. 622 (E.D. Va. 1982); cf. State Press Co. v. Willett, 219 Ark. 850, 245 S.W.2d 403 (1952) (implication that African American minister vilified African Americans to please whites); but cf. Moore v. P.W. Publ'g Co., 3 Ohio St.2d 183, 209 N.E.2d 412 (1965) (statement that plaintiff, a an African American, was an "Uncle Tom" was not defamatory per se).

[96] Tucker v. Fischbein, 237 F.3d 275 (3d Cir. 2001); Tucker v. Philadelphia Daily News, 577 Pa. 598, 848 A.2d 113 (2004).

[97] See MacElree v. Philadelphia Newspapers, Inc., 544 Pa. 117, 674 A.2d 1050 (1996) ("the David Duke of Chester County"); Gregory G. Sarno, Imputation of Allegedly Objectionable Political or Social Beliefs or Principles as Defamation, 62 A.L.R.4th 314 (1989).

[98] Murphy v. Boston Herald, Inc., 449 Mass. 42, 865 N.E.2d 746 (2007) (judge reported to have said of rape victim words to the effect that she was 14, she got raped, tell her to get over it; report was defamatory).

[99] Grant v. Reader's Digest Ass'n, Inc., 151 F.2d 733 (2d Cir. 1945) (asserting that plaintiff was a lobbyist for the communist party); see Gregory G. Sarno, Imputation of Allegedly Objectionable Political or Social Beliefs or Principles as Defamation, 62 A.L.R.4th 314 (1989).

[100] E.g., Stevens v. Tillman, 855 F.2d 394, 402 (7th Cir. 1988) ("In daily life 'racist'; is hurled about so indiscriminately that it is no more than a verbal slap in the face. . . . It is not actionable unless it implies the existence of undisclosed, defamatory facts. . . .").

defamation claim has not been proved.[101] However, false factual assertions that impute racism to the plaintiff are defamatory,[102] although what counts as defamatory in this context will vary with the exact words, the time and place and the experience and sensibilities of judges.[103] This third group can also sometimes be subsumed within the second, since any character trait that deeply offends the prevailing views may also be regarded as affecting the plaintiff's fitness for her calling.

Conditions causing people to shun the plaintiff. In the fourth group are cases in which the plaintiff is not said to have done or even thought anything discreditable by anyone's standards, but is held to be defamed nonetheless. For example, it may be defamatory to assert that the plaintiff is insane[104] or mentally impaired,[105] that she has a contagious disease through no fault of her own,[106] that she is an African American,[107] or even that she has been a victim of rape.[108] Such decisions can be troubling because they may seem to institutionalize various forms of bigotry and ignorance. On the other hand, the plaintiff's harm in a world where ignorance and bigotry exist can be very real. The defendant whose negligent or intentional falsehood causes such harm is not necessarily entitled to benefit from a judicial condemnation of the prejudice that he himself has invoked. Perhaps the plaintiff is entitled to maintain her reputation and good relationship even with people who hold wrong-thinking opinions on particular subjects.

Examples of nondefamatory content. On the other hand, a good many publications may cause actual harm without being defamatory, especially if they do not assert a moral flaw. Ridicule was once considered to carry a defamatory quality, although it might be privileged on occasions. Constitutional decisions, however, have protected ridicule and other communications that do not falsely assert facts.[109] The common law also rejected suits based upon name-calling,[110] although it must be apparent that in many groups

---

[101] E.g., Smith v. Huntsville Times Co., Inc., 888 So.2d 492 (Ala. 2004) (knowing or reckless falsehood required, not shown).

[102] Puchalski v. Sch. Dist. Of Springfield, 161 F.Supp.2d 395, 408 (E.D. Pa. 2001) ("Mr. McGovern may have articulated the specific offensive statement attributed to Mr. Puchalski, taking it beyond the realm of mere opinion or general characterization"); Tech Plus, Inc. v. Ansel, 59 Mass. App. Ct. 12, 793 N.E.2d 1256 (2003) (defendant allegedly told third persons that plaintiff persecuted him because of his Jewish heritage, alleges defamatory publication); Schermerhorn v. Rosenberg, 73 A.D.2d 276, 426 N.Y.S.2d 274 (1980) (newspaper headline that plaintiff said public board could do without blacks as directors was defamatory).

[103] See Schermerhorn v. Rosenberg, 73 A.D.2d 276, 284, 426 N.Y.S.2d 274, 282 (1980).

[104] E.g., Powers v. Gastineau, 568 N.E.2d 1020 (Ind. Ct. App. 1991); Annotation, Libel and Slander: Actionability of Imputing to Private Person Mental Disorder or Incapacity, or Impairment of Mental Faculties, 23 A.L.R.3d 652 (1969).

[105] Brauer v. Globe Newspaper Co., 351 Mass. 53, 217 N.E.2d 736 (1966) (defendant's concession).

[106] See McCune v. Neitzel, 235 Neb. 754, 457 N.W.2d 803 (1990) (assertion that plaintiff had AIDS).

[107] Bowen v. Independent Publ'g Co., 230 S.C. 509, 96 S.E.2d 564 (1957). But see Lyrissa Barnett Lidsky, Defamation, Reputation, and the Myth of Community, 71 Wash. L. Rev. 1, 30–31 (1996) (asserting that after 1950 such claims began to disappear but also that modern cases tend to assume that the allegation is not defamatory; apparently finding no actual decisions to that effect).

[108] Youssoupoff v. Metro-Goldwyn-Mayer Pictures, Ltd., 50 T.L.R. 581, 99 A.L.R. 864 (C.A. 1934).

[109] See Hustler Magazine v. Falwell, 485 U.S. 46, 108 S.Ct. 876, 99 L.Ed.2d 41 (1988); but cf. Doe v. TCI Cablevision, 110 S.W.3d 363 (Mo. 2003) (fictional comic book character deliberately given plaintiff-celebrity's name; this was a ploy to sell comic books and violated the celebrity's right of publicity).

[110] Finck v. City of Tea, 443 N.W.2d 632 (S.D. 1989) (statement that police chief was a dumb son of a bitch not actionable); see 3 Dobbs, Hayden & Bublick, The Law of Torts § 572 (2d. ed. 2011 & Supp.).

name-calling can be quite destructive of the plaintiff's reputation.[111] Beyond ridicule and name-calling, many assertions can cause harm to the plaintiff's reputation but are not defamatory. It is not actionable to assert that the plaintiff is a Republican or supports Senator Hatch when she does not,[112] that a Democratic candidate is not really a Democrat,[113] or that another candidate voted to raise taxes.[114] New York seems to have held that it is not defamatory to imply that a competing retailer of Korean origin does not speak English.[115] In some cases, the plaintiff is falsely accused of doing something socially useful but inimical to the interests of the plaintiff's own group. In a well-known case,[116] a truck-stop owner was accused of reporting truckers' violations to the Interstate Commerce Commission, and naturally enough lost the truckers' business as a result. Since supporting the interests of the larger community was not reprehensible, the court found the communication not defamatory. This result seems to contradict the premise suggested for the third group, that the plaintiff is entitled to good relationships even with people whose own attitudes are antisocial.

§ 37.6 Interpreting Meaning and Effect

The meaning of words. Logically speaking, courts can determine the defamatory content[117] of a publication only after they have first determined its meaning. The meaning of words, pictures, or other communicative elements is critical not only on the issue of defamatory quality but also on the issue of truth or falsity, even though those issues are distinct from one another.

Judge and jury. The first question is whether the words used are capable of bearing a defamatory meaning. This question is for the judge to decide.[118] If the answer is no, judgment must go for the defendant. If the answer is that reasonable people could find a defamatory meaning, the jury must decide what meaning the words conveyed and whether that meaning was defamatory.[119] Those questions are ordinarily decided on the basis of the jurors' own experience and understanding rather than on the basis of expert testimony.[120] No rule requires that all people would understand the words in a

---

[111] "Racist" of a white professor, "sexist" of an employer, "Uncle Tom" of an African American are among the possibilities for serious harm, but unless the accusation is made specific, it is likely to be dismissed as name-calling. See Stevens v. Tillman, 855 F.2d 394, 402 (7th Cir. 1988).

[112] Cox v. Hatch, 761 P.2d 556 (Utah 1988).

[113] See Frinzi v. Hanson, 30 Wis.2d 271, 140 N.W.2d 259 (1966).

[114] Tatur v. Solsrud, 167 Wis.2d 266, 481 N.W.2d 657 (1992). But cf. Wilder v. Johnson Publ'g Co., Inc., 551 F.Supp. 622 (E.D. Va. 1982) (defamatory to assert that African-American had swung vote against black leader).

[115] Lenz Hardware, Inc. v. Wilson, 94 N.Y.2d 913, 729 N.E.2d 338, 707 N.Y.S.2d 619 (2000) (the defendant's advertisement directly compared defendant's prices with plaintiff's, and ended with the statement that "We Speak English, Plumbing, Farming and Dabble in Pig Latin"; the court concluded that the phrase is not reasonably susceptible of a defamatory connotation).

[116] Connelly v. McKay, 176 Misc. 685, 28 N.Y.S.2d 327 (1941).

[117] Discussed in § 37.5.

[118] E.g., Clampitt v. American Univ., 957 A.2d 23, 39 (D.C. 2008); McKee v. Laurion, 825 N.W.2d 725 (Minn. 2013); Restatement (Second) of Torts § 614 (1965).

[119] Stevens v. Iowa Newspapers, Inc., 728 N.W.2d 823 (Iowa 2007).

[120] See Seropian v. Forman, 652 So.2d 490, 498 (Fla. Dist. Ct. App. 1995) ("If influence peddling conveyed the obloquy that plaintiff suggests, that fact should be readily understood by the ordinary jury without a political scientist swearing that it does"); contra, Weller v. American Broad. Cos., Inc., 232 Cal. App. 3d 991, 283 Cal.Rptr. 644 (1991) (permitting expert testimony).

defamatory sense. The logic is that if only some people would understand the words in a defamatory sense, the damages award should be smaller than otherwise.

Meaning vs. defamatory quality. The *meaning* of words raises a question distinct from their defamatory quality. A statement that a police officer tested positively for drugs but that his friends in the department falsified the test to show a negative would clearly be a statement having the quality of defamation. But a statement that the police department did not follow required procedures in testing the same police officer may not mean the same thing at all because the department's failure to follow procedures may or may not imply falsification. The second statement raises a problem about the meaning of the words used; once that is resolved, the question whether the words were defamatory may become quite simple.

The meaning of meaning. Under the Restatement, the meaning (as distinct from the defamatory quality) of a publication is either (1) that which the publisher intended or (2) that which the recipient of the publication reasonably understood to have been intended.[121] Under the first part of this definition, the meaning is that intended by the defendant even if that meaning differs from that conveyed by the words themselves.[122] Under the second part of the definition, the recipients' own reasonable understanding of the words controls. Courts consider not only the meaning recipients would attach to individual words,[123] but the recipients' "habits of deduction,"[124] subject, however, to judicial limits on irrational interpretations.

Factors in assessing meaning. Courts tend to consider questions of meaning by taking into account (1) the words themselves, especially where the meaning is precise and standardized, together with reasonable implications; (2) the literary context, that is, the entire message; (3) the social context, that is, events, disputes, purposes of the communication and other factors outside the publication itself; and (4) the group feelings or culture of the recipients.

Literal words and implications. Sometimes words mean what they say, no more, no less, but ambiguities and shifts in word usage over time[125] complicate interpretations. When words are ambiguous, with one possible meaning defamatory and one not, most courts permit the jury to resolve the issue.[126] Both judges and juries are to go by the plain and natural meaning as persons of ordinary intelligence would understand it.[127] Much of the difficulty comes when the defamation, if there is any, arises from an implied meaning carried by the literal words. A literal statement that is false but not literally

---

[121] Restatement (Second) of Torts § 563 (1977).

[122] See White v. Fraternal Order of Police, 909 F.2d 512, 521 (D.C. Cir. 1990) (one of the publications "provided a clear signal from which a reader could conclude, rightly or wrongly, that the defamatory inference was intended or endorsed").

[123] See Wildstein v. New York Post Corp., 40 Misc.2d 586, 243 N.Y.S.2d 386 (1963) (to say the police questioned plaintiff as one of the women "associated" with a murdered man may imply meretricious relationship because the word associated was placed in quotation marks).

[124] Herrmann v. Newark Morning Ledger Co., 48 N.J.Super. 420, 440, 138 A.2d 61, 72 (1958).

[125] See Bryson v. News Am. Publ'ns, Inc., 174 Ill.2d 77, 96, 672 N.E.2d 1207, 1218, 220 Ill.Dec. 195, 206 (1996) (discussing shifted meanings of slut and fag).

[126] See, e.g., New Times, Inc. v. Isaacks, 146 S.W.3d 144, 155 (Tex. 2004).

[127] Ramunno v. Cawley, 705 A.2d 1029 (Del. 1998); Cox Enters., Inc. v. Nix, 274 Ga. 801, 560 S.E.2d 650 (2002). Illinois law is a partial exception, requiring courts to place an innocent construction of the publication if possible, unless the plaintiff proves pecuniary loss. See Bryson v. News Am. Publ'ns, Inc., 174 Ill.2d 77, 672 N.E.2d 1207, 220 Ill.Dec. 195 (1996).

defamatory[128] may imply a further false statement that is entirely defamatory.[129] Some implications are analytically inescapable. If the plaintiff says he saw the defendant strike a woman and that he could not be mistaken, the defendant's denial is equivalent to saying that the plaintiff was lying. If a company has a rule against extending credit, then to say that the plaintiff-employee extended the company's credit to a customer inescapably says that the plaintiff violated company rules.[130]

Implication from words or context. Many other implications cannot be derived analytically from the published language. The defendant's statement that a former employee is no longer available to serve clients might be understood by someone to mean that the employee was discharged for wrongdoing, but the statement neither says nor, standing alone, does it imply anything of the kind.[131] When the plaintiff cannot show defamatory implication from the words themselves, however, she may be able to do so by pointing to materials outside the words, that is, to literary or social context, which are in part, the same materials considered in determining whether a statement is one of fact or one of opinion.

Literary or internal context. Courts frequently recognize the importance of literary context in determining whether a publication is defamatory. For example, a single word or phrase in a news story might seem defamatory if read alone, but not if read with the entire story.[132] Equally, individual items in a news report may be nondefamatory when taken alone, but the report as a whole may be defamatory because of its omissions or its juxtaposition of facts or otherwise.[133] Thus literary context (as distinct from social context) is often critical in interpreting both defamatory and nondefamatory publications. Trying to focus on the defamatory words alone would be like trying to appreciate a pointillist painting by Seurat with a magnifying glass—the telling pattern would be lost in a maze of dots.[134] Beyond that, courts have recognized that context (including tone and type of publication) may show that language is asserting no defamatory fact because context can show that the words should not be understood as literal statements but as whimsy, irony, hyperbole, or meaningless invective.[135] One context issue arises with headlines which, read alone, look defamatory. Courts have usually said that the headline must be interpreted by reading it with the accompanying story, which may negate its defamatory meaning.[136] The point of examining context, however, is to assist in determining meaning, not to make a rule. In some cases a sensational headline (or television teaser) will overwhelm the more detailed text, while

[128] As to *true* statements carrying defamatory implications, see § 37.8.

[129] See, e.g., Jews For Jesus, Inc. v. Rapp, 997 So.2d 1098 (Fla. 2008).

[130] Quartana v. Utterback, 789 F.2d 1297 (8th Cir. 1986).

[131] McCullough v. Visiting Nurse Serv. of S. Me., Inc., 691 A.2d 1201 (Me. 1997).

[132] Karage v. First Advantage Corp., 2010 WL 1062601 (N.D.Tex. 2010) (unreported) ("A publication as a whole may be defamatory if it creates a false impression by omitting material facts"); Clawson v. St. Louis Post-Dispatch, LLC, 906 A.2d 308 (D.C. 2006) ("informer" and "FBI informer" not defamatory read in light of entire story).

[133] Turner v. KTRK Television, Inc., 38 S.W.3d 103, 114 (2000) ("a publication can convey a false and defamatory meaning by omitting or juxtaposing facts, even though all the story's individual statements considered in isolation were literally true or non-defamatory").

[134] Chapin v. Knight-Ridder, Inc., 993 F.2d 1087 (4th Cir. 1993).

[135] E.g., Morse v. Ripken, 707 So.2d 921(Fla. App. 1998); see § 572.

[136] E.g., Blomberg v. Cox Enters., Inc., 228 Ga.App. 178, 491 S.E.2d 430 (1997); but cf. Burgess v. Reformer Publ'g Corp., 146 Vt. 612, 618, 508 A.2d 1359, 1362 (1986) ("If the headline is a fair index of an accurate article, it is not actionable. If it is not a fair index then the headline must be examined independently to determine whether it is actionable under general principles of libel.").

in others, the nature of the headline and story are such that many readers will not read or absorb the supposedly redemptive text. Similarly, if a photograph of the plaintiff is erroneously identified as the perpetrator of a crime, the visual impact may overwhelm the more accurate identification contained in the accompanying news story. Not surprisingly, then, in some cases defamatory headlines and photographs have been sufficient for liability in spite of qualifications that might be found in accompanying text.[137]

Social or external context. Social context of a publication includes a wide variety of facts extrinsic to the publication itself. A statement that a butcher shop sells bacon or that a woman is engaged to marry Mr. Arbuckle carries no defamatory implications on its face. But when facts extrinsic to the publication are added, serious implications may arise. If the butcher is an Orthodox Jew or the woman is already married, the first publication implies a violation of religious tenets or practices,[138] and the second implies a violation of sexual standards strongly held in many communities.[139] A number of publications that do not obviously mean anything defamatory may be understood to convey additional and defamatory meanings when the full dispute and background issues that led to publication are shown.[140] Some courts require proof of special damages when extrinsic facts are necessary to show the defamatory quality of the communication,[141] but whether that added requirement is imposed or not, the prior issue of meaning itself must often be gleaned from the social context of the publication.

Recipient's culture or outlook. The recipient's culture, outlook, and knowledge clearly shape his reaction to the published message, but they may also shape his interpretation of the words used. This is most obviously true with the recipients' knowledge, which may vary from time to time and place to place. To say that the plaintiff is the David Duke of Chester County harbors no meaning except to those who know or think they know something about David Duke.[142] Different cultures may also attribute different meanings to words or styles of communication. Interpretation of publications in light of the understandings and assumptions of the culture to which they were addressed is therefore appropriate.

§ 37.7 Defamation of and Concerning the Plaintiff

Publication must refer to plaintiff. A defamatory publication is actionable only if it is "of and concerning" the plaintiff. In the language of the Restatement,[143] quoted or paraphrased by a number of courts,[144] the trier must find that recipients of the

---

[137] Kaelin v. Globe Commc'ns Corp., 162 F.3d 1036 (9th Cir. 1998) (jury could find that headline, 17 pages removed from text of the story and implying plaintiff was suspected of murdering Nicole Brown Simpson, was libelous because text so far removed would not clean up the headline); Little Rock Newspapers, Inc. v. Fitzhugh, 330 Ark. 561, 954 S.W.2d 914 (1997) (wrong photo); Schermerhorn v. Rosenberg, 73 A.D.2d 276, 426 N.Y.S.2d 274 (1980) (headline); Sprouse v. Clay Commc'ns, Inc., 211 S.E.2d 674 (W.Va. 1975) (where the publisher systematically, repeatedly, and intentionally printed misleading political headlines).

[138] See Braun v. Armour & Co., 254 N.Y. 514, 173 N.E. 845 (1930) (cause of action stated).

[139] Sydney v. MacFadden Newspaper Publ'g Corp., 242 N.Y. 208, 151 N.E. 209 (1926).

[140] E.g., Ramunno v. Cawley, 705 A.2d 1029 (Del. 1998) (long-lasting community dispute).

[141] See § 37.10.

[142] See MacElree v. Philadelphia Newspapers, Inc. 544 Pa. 117, 126, 674 A.2d 1050, 1055 (1996) ("the statement could be construed to mean that appellant was acting in a racist manner").

[143] Restatement (Second) of Torts § 564 (1977).

[144] MacDonald v. Riggs, 166 P.3d 12, 15 (Alaska 2007) ("the recipient of the defamatory communication [must] understand it as intended to refer to the plaintiff"); Keohane v. Stewart, 882 P.2d 1293, 1300 (Colo.

publication would reasonably or correctly believe that it was intended to refer to the plaintiff. Although courts often state the rule in abbreviated form,[145] the rule actually requires several things. The court must first determine that reasonable people could believe that the published statement referred to the plaintiff.[146] If evidence is sufficient to make a question for the trier, the trier must then find that at least one person actually did believe the statement referred to the plaintiff.[147] And finally, under the Restatement's test, the hypothetical reasonable person and the actual recipient must rationally believe that the defendant intended a reference to the plaintiff. Issues concerning the defendant's state of mind, as well as evidence and inference to identify the plaintiff is developed at greater length elsewhere.[148] Works of fiction thought to be understood as referring to a living plaintiff, present special issues as well.[149]

Defaming plaintiff by defaming others. In general, plaintiff has no defamation claim resulting solely from defamation of another.[150] For example, the commissioner of police is not defamed by defamatory criticisms of police under the commissioner's command,[151] nor is one police officer necessarily defamed when another one is.[152] There are of course cases in which defamation of one person defames another as well, but only if a reasonable recipient of the publication can and does interpret the defamation "as being, in substance, actually *about* him or her."[153] For example, defamation of a corporation is not routinely defamation of shareholders or officers,[154] but conceivably defamatory statements that the corporation engaged in certain illegal financial activities defames the CEO if the CEO makes all the financial decisions.[155]

Defaming plaintiff by defaming a group. Recent years have seen repeated efforts to condemn group defamation, but so far without an impact on domestic tort law.[156] An

---

1994); Gonzalez v. Sessom, 137 P.3d 1245, 1248 (Okla. Civ. App. 2006); Gazette, Inc. v. Harris, 229 Va. 1, 37, 325 S.E.2d 713, 738 (1985).

[145] Thus a court may simply say that the test is whether a character in fiction "could reasonably understood as a portrayal of plaintiff." Middlebrooks v. Curtis Publ'g Co., 413 F.2d 141, 142 (4th Cir. 1969). This brief statement does not address the need to find additionally that a recipient would correctly or reasonably believe that the author intended such an understanding, but does not rule out such a requirement.

[146] See, e.g., Houseman v. Publicaciones Paso del Norte, S.A. DE C.V., 242 S.W.3d 518 (Tex. App. 2007).

[147] SDV/ACCI, Inc. v. AT & T Corp., 522 F.3d 955, 960 (9th Cir. 2008).

[148] 3 Dobbs, Hayden & Bublick, The Law of Torts § 527 (2d. ed. 2011 & Supp.).

[149] Id. § 529.

[150] See Kirch v. Liberty Media Corp., 449 F.3d 388, 398 (2d Cir. 2006) ("A false disparaging statement about IBM, for example, would not, we think, ordinarily be a defamatory statement 'of and concerning' all of IBM's suppliers, employees and dealers, however much they may be injured as a result"); Johnson v. Southwestern Newspapers Corp., 855 S.W.2d 182 (Tex. App. 1993). The rule that defamation of the dead does not ordinarily defame the living, 3 Dobbs, Hayden & Bublick, The Law of Torts § 532 (2d. ed. 2011 & Supp.), is a specific instance of the same principle.

[151] New York Times v. Sullivan, 376 U. S. 254, 84 S.Ct. 710, 11 L.Ed.2d 686 (1964).

[152] Arcand v. Evening Call Publ'g Co., 567 F.2d 1163 (1st Cir. 1977).

[153] Kirch v. Liberty Media Corp., 449 F.3d 388, 399 (2d Cir. 2006). A few cases may have skirted this rule. In Williams v. Gannett Satellite Information Network, Inc., 162 Ohio App. 3d 596, 834 N.E.2d 397 (2005), media published a story that X was arrested for a crime, had been previously convicted of selling drugs, and was the son of the plaintiff, a police officer. This was held sufficient to show defamation of the officer plaintiff because it would tend to injured him in his occupation, but perhaps the "of and concerning" issue was not clearly presented.

[154] SDV/ACCI, Inc. v. AT & T Corp., 522 F.3d 955, 960 (9th Cir. 2008) (reviewing cases).

[155] See Caudle v. Thomason, 942 F.Supp. 635, 638 (D.D.C. 1996). Judge Sack reviewed a number of cases in Kirch v. Liberty Media Corp., 449 F.3d 388 (2d Cir. 2006).

[156] See Lorenz Langer, The Rise (And Fall?) of Defamation of Religions, 35 Yale J. Int'l L. 257 (2010).

Illinois criminal statute against group defamation was once upheld,[157] and "veggie libel laws" create claims for all producers of a general food that is falsely said to be unsafe.[158] Otherwise, however, defamation of large groups, for example by claims that lawyers are shysters,[159] is almost never actionable by the group itself.[160] Rationales and permutations can be complex.[161]

Corporations; injurious falsehood or disparagement. Corporations and other businesses can and do recover for libel or slander when they have been defamed by charges that import wrongdoing such as charges of crime, fraud, or incompetence in business operations.[162] But when the publication asserts that the corporate product is defective, inadequate, or harmful without asserting "personal" defamation, the traditional view regards the claim as essentially different from the claim for defamation.[163] Such claims, along with other false and harmful statements affecting business are called injurious falsehood, commercial disparagement, or slander of title claims. Statutes may also create causes of action for some injurious falsehoods. Such claims, which do not follow the early common law rules of libel, really involve economic, not personal torts, and are accordingly considered elsewhere.[164] However, many claims by corporations or other businesses are asserted and analyzed in the terminology of libel or defamation, even though the rules of injurious falsehood, disparagement or slander of title would be more appropriate.[165]

Government entities as plaintiffs. Few cases have been brought by government entities against private individuals. The Supreme Court affirmed that the Sedition Act was unconstitutional in prohibiting criticism of government, and said that a civil libel claim was equally prohibited.[166] It may be arguable that a false publication of fact harmful financially to a governmental entity should be actionable, if not as defamation then as injurious falsehood. However, the Illinois Supreme Court rejected such a claim, saying that the action "is out of tune with the American spirit, and has no place in

---

[157] Beauharnais v. Illinois, 343 U.S. 250, 72 S.Ct. 725, 96 L.Ed. 919 (1952). The case was decided at a time when it was thought that defamation was not entitled to First Amendment protection, so the case may be outdated.

[158] E.g., N.D. Cent. Code § 32–44–03. These statutes may be vulnerable to constitutional attack.

[159] Cf. Brock v. Thompson, 948 P.2d 279 (Okla. 1997) (reflecting on trial lawyers).

[160] See AIDA v. Time Warner Entm't Co., L.P., 332 Ill. App. 3d 154, 772 N.E.2d 953 (2002) (non-profit organization interested in fair presentation of Italian-Americans had no standing to sue and no cause of action against those responsible for a TV series depicting Italian-Americans negatively); Lega Siciliana Social Club, Inc. v. St. Germaine, 77 Conn. App. 846, 825 A.2d 827 (2003).

[161] See Dobbs, Hayden & Bublick, The Law of Torts § 531 (2d ed. 2011 & Supp.).

[162] Ampex Corp. v. Cargle, 128 Cal. App. 4th 1569, 27 Cal. Rptr. 3d 863 (2005) (internet postings claiming specific examples of business incompetence); Joseph v. Scranton Times L.P., 959 A.2d 322 (Pa. Super. 2008) (charges associating corporation with money laundering, drugs and prostitution); Harwood Pharmacal Co. v. National Broad. Co., 9 N.Y.2d 460, 174 N.E.2d 602, 214 N.Y.S.2d 725 (1961); Waste Mgmt. of Tex., Inc. v. Texas Disposal Sys. Landfill, Inc., 434 S.W.3d 142 (Tex. 2014).

[163] See National Ref. Co. v. Benzo Gas Motor Fuel Co., 20 F.2d 763 (8th Cir. 1927).

[164] Chapter 43.

[165] 3 Dobbs, Hayden & Bublick, The Law of Torts § 661 (2d. ed. 2011 & Supp.).

[166] New York Times v. Sullivan, 376 U.S. 254, 84 S.Ct. 710, 11 L.Ed.2d 686 (1964); accord: Nampa Charter Sch., Inc. v. DeLaPaz, 140 Idaho 23, 89 P.3d 863 (2004) (charter school was public entity and as such "cannot maintain an action for libel and slander against an individual when that individual is speaking out on an issue of public concern").

American jurisprudence."[167] Somewhat analogously a California court held that a city could not sue for malicious prosecution.[168]

Defamation of the dead. No civil action lies for defamation of the dead.[169] This means that neither the estate of the deceased person nor her relatives can recover for statements made after her death.[170]

Survival of defamation actions. As to defamation published before death, whether suit is permitted depends upon the state's survival statute.[171] The common law rule terminated tort actions at the death of either party. Survival statutes changed that rule with respect to claims arising from personal injury and some have done so with respect to defamation claims as well, thus permitting the estate to sue for a defamatory publication made during the deceased's lifetime.[172] Other survival statutes, however, have continued the common law rule with respect to claims for libel and slander. Where that is the case, the claim of a person defamed during her lifetime is terminated at her death,[173] unless, as a little authority has said, the survival statute is unconstitutional insofar as it prescribes a special rule for defamation.[174]

§ 37.8 The Requirement of Falsity vs. "The Truth Defense"

Traditional burden of proof. Under the traditional common law view of defamation, a publication was presumed false once it was shown to be defamatory.[175] Under the original English practice of using criminal libel suits to punish political dissent, it was said that the greater the truth, the greater the libel, and even in some American states it was said that truth was no defense if libel was published maliciously. These approaches suggested another rule—that even the assertion of truth as a defense in court might be reviewed as a repetition of the libel that justifies inflicting punitive damages on the defendant.[176] Such rules are obviously at odds with the American notion

---

[167] Chicago v. Tribune Co., 307 Ill. 595, 610, 139 N.E. 86, 91, 28 A.L.R. 1368 (1923); see J. A. Bryant, Jr., Right of Governmental Entity to Maintain Action for Defamation, 45 A.L.R.3d 1315 (1972) (reflecting general accord that no such action will be entertained).

[168] City of Long Beach v. Bozek, 31 Cal.3d 527, 645 P.2d 137, 183 Cal.Rptr. 86 (1982), reiterated after vacation, 33 Cal.3d 727, 661 P.2d 1072, 190 Cal.Rptr. 918 (1983).

[169] Gillikin v. Bell, 254 N.C. 244, 118 S.E.2d 609 (1961).

[170] Johnson v. KTBS, Inc., 889 So.2d 329 (La. Ct. App. 2004) (no action for defaming the dead, and children of deceased have no action for defamation of their parents); Drake v. Park Newspapers of Ne. Okla., Inc., 683 P.2d 1347 (Okla. 1984); Restatement (Second) of Torts § 560 (1977).

[171] See generally 2 Dobbs, Hayden & Bublick, The Law of Torts § 373 (2d. ed. 2011 & Supp.).

[172] See, e.g., Plumley v. Landmark Chevrolet, Inc., 122 F.3d 308 (5th Cir. 1997). The results are mixed when the statute does not specify defamation actions either way. See Francis M. Dougherty, Annotation, Defamation Action as Surviving Plaintiff's Death, Under Statute Not Specifically Covering Action, 42 A.L.R.4th 272 (1986).

[173] Innes v. Howell Corp., 76 F.3d 702 (6th Cir. 1995) (upholding constitutionality of Kentucky statute); Drake v. Park Newspapers of Ne. Okla., Inc., 683 P.2d 1347 (Okla. 1984).

[174] Moyer v. Phillips, 462 Pa. 395, 341 A.2d 441 (1975); cf. Thompson v. Estate of Petroff, 319 N.W.2d 400 (Minn. 1982) (survival statute was irrational in not permitting survival for intentional torts).

[175] E.g., Post Publ'g Co. v. Moloney, 50 Ohio St. 71, 33 N.E. 921 (1893); Bird v. Hudson, 113 N.C. 203, 18 S.E. 209 (1893).

[176] Marley v. Providence Journal Co., 86 R.I. 229, 134 A.2d 180 (1957) ("in an action of libel or slander the plea of 'truth' of itself constitutes a reaffirmation of the libel or slander which, when not substantiated to the satisfaction of the jury, may be regarded by them as an aggravation of the wrong showing actual malice and warranting an award of punitive damages"); Bentley v. Bunton, 94 S.W.3d 561 (Tex. 2002) ("Bunton's consistent position at trial that his accusations of corruption were true is a compelling indication that he himself regarded his statements as factual and not mere opinion, right up until the jury returned its verdict"); cf. Dodson v. Allstate Ins. Co., 345 Ark. 430, 47 S.W.3d 866 (2001) (withdrawn counterclaim that had re-

of free speech, the value of truth, and access to courts. They may now be unconstitutional,[177] although their ragged threads can occasionally be found.[178]

Constitutional reallocation of burden to plaintiff to prove falsity. Constitutional decisions have now allocated the burden of proof to the plaintiff on the issue of truth or falsity in cases where the plaintiff is a public official or public figure and also where the defamation touches an issue of public concern. The Supreme Court has not excluded the possibility that the burden will fall upon the plaintiff in all cases.[179] Some states have also independently said that falsity of the publication is an element of defamation and hence to be proved by the plaintiff.[180] Casual statements sometimes ventured by courts to the effect that truth is a "defense" in defamation cases generally[181] are not to be taken literally. Burden of proof aside, underlying issues about truth remain.

Substantial truth. The publication need not be literally true to receive protection. It is enough if the publication is substantially true. That means the gist or sting of the defamation must be true even if details are not.[182] Read literally, some judicial statements seem to say that a publication is true if it generates no more opprobrium or distaste in the readers' minds than the truth.[183] That may make good sense only when the published statement and the truth are factually similar. Benedict Arnold's treason was more shameful than shoplifting, but it is not true that he was a shoplifter merely because he was guilty of more serious misbehavior.[184] Arnold's treason is too factually different from shoplifting to show the truth of the shoplifting charge. But there is another possibility. If the publication consists of more than one defamatory item, the substantial truth of each item is judged separately, although each item is to be understood in the

---

asserted the allegedly defamatory statements could be admitted to "impeach" defendant's trial court position that it had never made such statements).

[177] Shaari v. Harvard Student Agencies, Inc., 427 Mass. 129, 691 N.E.2d 925 (1998) (statute allowing truth defense only for nonmalicious statements unconstitutional where issue in defamation was a matter of public interest).

[178] See Noonan v. Staples, Inc., 556 F.3d 20 (1st Cir. 2009) (where constitutional issue was not timely raised, federal court applied Massachusetts statutes that deprived the publisher of the "truth defense" where the publisher acted with malice in the sense of ill will), discussed in Recent Case, Noonan v. Staples, Inc., 123 Harv. L. Rev. 784 (2010); Young v. First United Bank of Bellevue, 246 Neb. 43, 516 N.W.2d 256 (1994).

[179] See Philadelphia Newspapers, Inc. v. Hepps, 475 U.S. 767, 106 S.Ct. 1558, 89 L.Ed.2d 783 (1986); § 568.

[180] E.g., Cox Enters., Inc. v. Nix, 274 Ga. 801, 560 S.E.2d 650 (2002); Voyles v. Sandia Mortgage Corp., 196 Ill.2d 288, 751 N.E.2d 1126, 256 Ill. Dec. 289 (2001); Armistead v. Minor, 815 So.2d 1189 (Miss. 2002); Simpson v. Mars Inc., 929 P.2d 966 (Nev. 1997) (listing falsity as an element of the claim); Belcher v. Wal-Mart Stores, Inc., 211 W.Va. 712, 568 S.E.2d 19 (2002) (same). A persistent tendency to speak of the "truth defense," as if the burden of proving truth fell upon the defendant, e.g., Choksi v. Shah, 8 So.3d 288 (Ala. 2008), probably does not reflect a rejection of constitutional mandates but only the use of language in its accustomed form.

[181] E.g., G.D. v. Kenny, 205 N.J. 275, 15 A.3d 300, 39 Media L. Rep. (BNA) 1699 (2011) (saying several times that "truth is a defense," yet recognizing that speech involving matters of public interest and concern, such as the speech involved in the case, requires that the plaintiff prove that the defamatory statement was published "with knowledge that it was false or with reckless disregard of its truth or falsity"). Courts sometimes cite the Restatement for the proposition that truth is a defense, but that is not what the Restatement says. See Restatement (Second) of Torts § 581A & cmt. b (1977).

[182] Hogan v. Winder, 762 F.3d 1096 (10th Cir. 2014); Armstrong v. Thompson, 80 A.3d 177 (D.C. 2013); Thomas v. Telegraph Publ'g Co., 155 N.H. 314, 929 A.2d 993 (2007); Neely v. Wilson, 418 S.W.3d 52 (Tex. 2013).

[183] See, e.g., Air Wisconsin Airlines Corp. v. Hoeper, 134 S.Ct. 852, 861, 187 L.Ed.2d 744 (2014).

[184] See Liberty Lobby, Inc. v. Anderson, 746 F.2d 1563, 1568 (D.C. Cir. 1984), *vacated, as to applicable standard on summary judgment*, 477 U.S. 242, 106 S.Ct. 2505, 91 L.Ed.2d 202 (1986) (Scalia, J.).

context of the whole article.[185] Even if the defendant intentionally misquotes the plaintiff, that does not necessarily show a deviation from substantial truth.[186]

Examples of substantial truth. To say that the plaintiff evicted a wounded Marine is substantially true if the plaintiff actually evicted the Marine's family with whom the Marine resided.[187] Statements about crimes are often technically incorrect but substantially true. To laypersons, "theft" may mean any wrongful taking, including such distinct crimes as embezzlement, and might even include a simple conversion of property.[188] A statement that the plaintiff has been disbarred is substantially true even if a motion for rehearing is pending and the judgment is not final.[189] A statement that the plaintiff, booked for a crime, had been identified by his own children is substantially true if he was identified by his former wife's children.[190]

Evidence of truth. Some defamation charges the plaintiff with specific conduct like perjury in a trial (or with having a specific condition such as a disease). Other defamation attributes to the plaintiff a general character trait, as where the plaintiff is said to be a liar or incompetent at her profession. If the defamation charges specific conduct, the only admissible evidence of truth is specific evidence of that conduct or conduct substantially similar and carrying the equivalent sting. Evidence of general bad reputation does not tend to prove specific charges. The plaintiff may have a bad reputation as an alcoholic but that does not prove she passed out in an alcoholic stupor last Saturday at the tavern.[191] When the defamation attributes an ongoing course of behavior to the plaintiff, however, evidence of such behavior on particular occasions will tend to show truth and is admissible.[192] Likewise, if the defamation attributes a character trait to the plaintiff, evidence of either specific misconduct that manifests the trait charged or opinion or reputation evidence concerning the trait in question will be admissible.[193]

Truth vs. limited damages. Even when the defendant cannot show the truth of the charge, he may be able to show that actual harm to reputation was small because the plaintiff's reputation in the community was already bad. This argument does not bar the claim; it only permits the trier to consider evidence on the damages issue.[194] For this

---

[185] Thomas v. Telegraph Publ'g Co., 155 N.H. 314, 929 A.2d 993 (2007).

[186] See Masson v. New Yorker Magazine, Inc., 501 U.S. 496, 111 S.Ct. 2419, 115 L.Ed.2d 447 (1991).

[187] Harnish v. Herald-Mail Co., 264 Md. 326, 286 A.2d 146, 49 A.L.R.3d 1056 (1972).

[188] Russin v. Wesson, 183 Vt. 301, 949 A.2d 1019 (2008).

[189] Hamilton v. Lake Charles Am. Press, Inc., 372 So. 2d 239 (La. Ct. App. 1979).

[190] Rouch v. Enquirer & News of Battle Creek, Mich., 440 Mich. 238, 487 N.W.2d 205 (1992).

[191] See Fed. R. Evid. 405(a) (subject to exceptions, "Evidence of a person's character or a trait of character is not admissible for the purpose of proving action in conformity therewith on a particular occasion").

[192] Guccione v. Hustler Magazine, Inc., 800 F.2d 298, 300 (2d Cir. 1986) (if the statement published could be read as asserting adultery in 1983, proof of adultery at some other time would not show truth, but statement here was more general, asserting ongoing marriage and ongoing adultery, so proof of adultery at one time was sufficient to show the truth).

[193] See Fed. R. Evid. 405(a) & (b) ("proof may be made by testimony as to reputation or by testimony in the form of an opinion. . . . In cases in which character or a trait of character of a person is an essential element of a charge, claim, or defense, proof may also be made of specific instances of that person's conduct").

[194] See Marcone v. Penthouse Int'l Magazine for Men, 754 F.2d 1072, 1079 (3d Cir. 1985) (widespread negative publicity before defamation was published); McBride v. New Braunfels Herald-Zeitung, 894 S.W.2d 6 (Tex. App. 1994) (if plaintiff's earlier convictions of theft and burglary were well known, that would affect damages but would not justify a summary judgment for the defendant).

purpose, courts might reject evidence of the plaintiff's conduct on specific occasions,[195] but such evidence has sometimes been admitted,[196] and evidence of the plaintiff's general reputation would be admissible,[197] at least aspects of her reputation affected by the defamation.[198] Indeed, under the libel-proof plaintiff doctrine, it is sometimes argued that the reputation of some plaintiffs is so bad that no award at all could be justified, even when the publication is defamatory and untrue.[199]

False and defamatory implications embedded in a literally true statement. Several kinds of statements may be literally or formally true, yet contain an explicitly false and defamatory statement. Examples of embedded defamation are: (1) "John told me that Pat robbed the bank on Friday," where it is true that John made the statement but false that Pat robbed the bank; (2) "In my opinion, Linda is an embezzler," where it is true that the speaker holds the opinion but false that Linda is an embezzler; and (3) "Either I added incorrectly or the cashier stole $10," where it is true that one of the two conditions must exist but false that the cashier stole the money. In such cases, the defamatory statement may do its dirty work even though the non-defamatory portion of the statement is true. In the first example, if truth were a defense, it would negate the rule of repeaters' liability. If truth is to be a defense in such cases, it must be truth as to the defamatory sting. So if Pat did not rob the bank and Linda is not an embezzler, the defendant cannot avoid liability under the truth defense merely because he accurately quoted someone's accusation.[200] The same idea applies to other cases of embedded defamation. If the defendant asks the question "Did Phil attempt to bribe the juror?" he conveys the thought that he believes Phil may have attempted bribery. To assert truth, the defendant would be required to show that Phil did indeed attempt bribery.[201] The truth issue is sometimes confused with the issue of privilege. The fact that the publisher truthfully attributes defamatory statements to others does not raise the truth defense, but in some circumstances he may be privileged to convey information gleaned from others.[202]

---

[195] See Fraser v. Park Newspapers of St. Lawrence Inc., 257 A.D.2d 961, 684 N.Y.S.2d 332 (1999); Shirley v. Freunscht, 303 Or. 234, 735 P.2d 600 (1987); Towle v. St. Albans Publ'g Co., Inc., 122 Vt. 134, 165 A.2d 363 (1960).

[196] Schafer v. Time, Inc., 142 F.3d 1361(11th Cir. 1998) (alleged libel that the plaintiff was a traitor and helped those who caused the bombing of Pan Am Flight 103; defendant could question plaintiff about "a felony conviction, a possible violation of his subsequent parole, convictions for driving under the influence, an arrest for writing a bad check, failure to file tax returns, failure to pay alimony and child support, and evidence concerning Schafer's efforts to change his name and social security number").

[197] E.g., Dunagan v. Upham, 214 Ark. 66, 214 S.W.2d 786 (1948); Martin v. Roy, 54 Mass. App. 642, 767 N.E.2d 603 (2002) (evidence of plaintiff's alleged anti-Semitism admissible).

[198] Gosden v. Louis, 116 Ohio App.3d 195, 687 N.E.2d 481 (1996).

[199] See 3 Dobbs, Hayden & Bublick, The Law of Torts § 575 (2d. ed. 2011 & Supp.).

[200] See e.g., Erickson v. Jones St. Publishers, LLC, 368 S.C. 444, 459, n. 2, 629 S.E.2d 653, 661, n. 2 (2006) ('A defendant or publisher asserting truth as a defense must prove that the statement or purported fact is true, not that the person quoted actually made the statement"); Restatement (Second) of Torts § 581A cmt. e (1977). Put the other way around, the repeater is liable for the defamatory statement and does not escape this liability merely because he has repeated the statement with precision. E.g., Taj Mahal Travel, Inc. v. Delta Airlines, Inc., 164 F.3d 186 (3d Cir. 1998).

[201] See Lutz v. Watson, 136 A.D.2d 888, 525 N.Y.S.2d 80 (1988); Meaney v. Loew's Hotels, Inc., 29 A.D.2d 850, 288 N.Y.S.2d 217 (1968). Not all questions, even about wrongdoing, carry defamatory implications. See Schupmann v. Empire Fire & Marine Ins. Co., 689 S.W.2d 101, 53 A.L.R.4th 445 (Mo. Ct. App. 1985) (question whether plaintiff was pregnant was not implication of unchastity).

[202] See, e.g., Magnusson v. New York Times Co., 98 P.3d 1070 (Okla.2004) (in determining fair comment privilege, court noted that the defendant truthfully reported what witnesses had said); 3 Dobbs, Hayden & Bublick, The Law of Torts § 549 (2d. ed. 2011 & Supp.).

Similarly, the publisher may characterize facts that are literally true in a way that makes the publication as a whole defamatory. Truth might be a justification if the defendant correctly asserts that the plaintiff used county building materials in constructing the plaintiff's own driveway, even if in fact the plaintiff was properly authorized to do so. But if the defendant goes further and characterizes the plaintiff as the perpetrator of a crime, the only truth that will aid the defendant is truth of the assertion that the plaintiff committed a crime.[203] The problem of implied defamation is discussed elsewhere.[204]

§ 37.9 Special Slander Rules

The damages difference. The traditional common law made much of the distinction between libel and slander. All libel was originally actionable without proof of special damages.[205] Put differently, damages were presumed in the case of libel. General slander, sometimes called slander per quod, however, was not actionable at all unless it caused the plaintiff pecuniary loss, often called special harm or special damages.[206] The effect of the rule was that harm to reputation that did not show itself in pecuniary loss was insufficient to permit recovery in the case of slander per quod. At the same time, several categories of slander were treated like libel so that damages were in effect presumed. This kind of categorical slander is called slander per se, a term that means the plaintiff need not prove pecuniary loss and that contrasts it with slander per quod.

Distinguishing slander from libel. The traditional distinction between slander and libel had it that slander was oral, libel was written. That difference is not wholly adequate to distinguish the two forms of defamation today. Courts now may consider several factors: whether the publication is in tangible form, whether it has the potential harmful qualities characteristic of written words, whether it is widely disseminated, and whether it was premeditated.[207] A "yes" answer in each case tends to indicate that the publication is libel rather than slander. Perhaps the ultimate question on which these factors bear is whether the publication and the harm expected from it is merely transitory and thus to be classified as slander.[208]

Examples of publications that count as libel. Today, libel includes not only writing but all forms of communication embodied in some physical form such as movie film or video tapes, and mass communications through radio broadcasts even if they are not produced from a written script.[209] Most communications by computer are no doubt in the

---

[203] Ratcliff v. Barnes, 750 N.E.2d 433 (Ind. Ct. App. 2001).

[204] 3 Dobbs, Hayden & Bublick, The Law of Torts § 566 (2d. ed. 2011 & Supp.).

[205] Restatement (Second) of Torts § 569 (1977).

[206] See, e.g., Marcil v. Kells, 936 A.2d 208, 212 (R.I. 2007).

[207] Too Much Media, LLC v. Hale, 413 N.J.Super. 135, 993 A.2d 845, 865 (App. Div. 2010) ("Defendant's [internet] postings are written words published through a 'mechanical device' (the computer) akin to the typewriter. As a general proposition, it may take more aforethought to type an internet posting than it does to blurt out spoken words. Also, unlike spoken words that evaporate, Internet postings have permanence, as the posts can remain on that particular site for an indefinite period and can easily be copied and forwarded. The name 'the world wide web' is an indication that unlike spoken words, Internet postings have the widest distribution possible-globally"); Restatement (Second) of Torts § 568 (1977).

[208] See Weitz v. Green, 148 Idaho 851, 230 P.3d 743, 754 (2010) ("Slander is '[a] defamatory assertion expressed in a transitory form' "); Spence v. Funk, 396 A.2d 967 (Del. 1978) ("the written word leaves a more permanent blot on one's reputation," also noting capacity of writings for widespread circulation).

[209] Restatement (Second) of Torts § 568A (1977). Statutes, however, may limit the liability of broadcasters to special or actual damages. E.g., N.Y. Civ. Rights Law § 75.

category of libel.[210] Reading aloud from written text may constitute libel.[211] An oral defamatory statement may also result in a libel if the speaker knows, intends, or foresees that it will be reduced to writing or other permanent form, and it is in fact published in such a form. For example, a speaker at a meeting who knows his words are being transcribed and will be printed in the newspaper may be subjected to a libel suit rather than one for slander only.[212] Slander, in contrast, includes ordinary, unamplified oral communications and transitory defamatory gestures.[213] The slander-libel distinction prompts endless analysis of close cases such as the loudspeaker in the stadium filled with 50,000 people, but the whole classification process is usually unsatisfactory because, traditionally at least, it leads to extreme damages rules no matter what classification is adopted.

Slander per se. If the publication is classified as slander rather than libel, a subsidiary classification is required. If the slander is the kind called "per se," then after all it is treated more like libel—in particular, the plaintiff will not be required to prove pecuniary damages and can recover for harm to reputation[214] and emotional harm[215] even when the plaintiff suffers no monetary harm. In fact, as in traditional libel cases, the plaintiff will be permitted to recover damages without proof of any harm to reputation at all[216] except when constitutional rules dictate otherwise.[217] Slander per se is that which charges a (1) serious criminal offense or one of moral turpitude,[218] (2) a "loathsome" and communicable disease,[219] (3) any matter incompatible with business, trade, profession, or office,[220] and, sometimes, (4) serious sexual misconduct.[221]

Serious crime. Each of these per se categories can prompt its own litigation without getting any closer to the real merits of the claim or defense. Lawyers may find themselves

---

[210] See Too Much Media, LLC v. Hale, 413 N.J.Super. 135, 993 A.2d 845 (App. Div. 2010); David J. Loundy, E-law 4: Computer Information Systems Law and System Operator Liability, 21 Seattle U. L. Rev. 1075 (1998). Operators of interactive systems are protected against liability for defamation posted by others. 47 U.S.C.A. § 230(c)(1); § 37.11.

[211] See Christy v. Stauffer Publ'ns, Inc., 437 S.W.2d 814 (Tex. 1969).

[212] See Cohen v. Bowdoin, 288 A.2d 106 (Me. 1972) (oral statements reduced to minutes of meeting then passed to newspaper); Bell v. Simmons, 247 N.C. 488, 101 S.E.2d 383 (1958), citing Restatement of Torts § 577 cmt. f.

[213] Restatement (Second) of Torts § 568(2) (1977).

[214] MacDonald v. Riggs, 166 P.3d 12, 18 (Alaska 2007); Riddle v. Golden Isles Broad., LLC, 292 Ga.App. 888, 891, 666 S.E.2d 75, 78 (2008) (when the words uttered are slander per se, "the law infers an injury to the reputation without proof of special damages. Such an injury falls within the category of general damages, 'those which the law presumes to flow from any tortious act; they may be recovered without proof of any amount' ").

[215] Tranum v. Broadway, 283 S.W.3d 403, 422 (Tex. App. 2008) ("Because Tranum's statements were slanderous per se, Broadway was not required to present independent proof of mental anguish, as the slander itself gives rise to a presumption of these damages").

[216] See Biondi v. Nassimos, 300 N.J.Super. 148, 153, 692 A.2d 103, 106 (1997).

[217] In some settings, constitutional decisions require the plaintiff to show "actual" (not necessarily pecuniary) harm. See § 3 Dobbs, Hayden & Bublick, The Law of Torts § 556 (2d. ed. 2011 & Supp.).

[218] E.g., Pensacola Motor Sales, Inc. v. Daphne Auto., LLC, 155 So.3d 930 (Ala. 2013); Donovan v. Fiumara, 114 N.C.App. 524, 442 S.E.2d 572 (1994); Restatement (Second) of Torts § 571 (1977). States embrace slightly different verbal formulas. See Cottrell v. National Collegiate Athletic Ass'n, 975 So.2d 306, 345 (Ala. 2007) ("indictable offense involving infamy or moral turpitude"); MacDonald v. Riggs, 166 P.3d 12, 18 (Alaska 2007) ("serious crime").

[219] McCune v. Neitzel, 235 Neb. 754, 457 N.W.2d 803 (1990) (AIDS); Restatement (Second) of Torts § 572 (1977).

[220] E.g., Restatement (Second) of Torts § 573 (1977).

[221] See, e.g., French v. Jadon, Inc., 911 P.2d 20 (Alaska 1996); City of Fairbanks v. Rice, 20 P.3d 1097 (Alaska 2000) (allegations of marital infidelity).

debating whether an accusation that the plaintiff is an adulterer charges a "serious crime,"[222] whether a charge that the plaintiff is a voyeur charges a crime of moral turpitude[223] and whether an accusation that the plaintiff is a "thief and a liar" charges a serious crime when the only "theft" referred to was a few pieces of paper.[224] Sometimes the result of working in these categories is surprising. For example, it has been held that to state that the plaintiff has mob connections and might order a hit upon an adversary does not count as an accusation of crime because it does not assert that a crime has in fact been committed.[225]

Business, trade or profession. The third category deals with matters incompatible with the plaintiff's trade, business, or profession. The category is especially indeterminate and must be defined largely as cases arise. It is probably fair to say that it includes any charges of seriously unprofessional conduct or serious departure from professional ethics.[226] Even a statement that the plaintiff, a physician, is terminally ill has been held sufficient;[227] although such a statement implies no personal fault, it does imply an inability to carry out a long-term physician-patient relationship. On the other hand, a mere conclusion or opinion that the plaintiff is incompetent in her job, without any express or implied assertion of facts, will probably not be accepted as a sufficient basis for a defamation claim.[228]

Reflection on plaintiff's business. It has been suggested that either the words or the circumstances must connect the defamatory assertion with the plaintiff's vocation,[229] but if that is too strong, it is at least true that the statements must reflect upon the proper conduct of, or reputation in[230] the plaintiff's business, trade, or profession and not merely upon the plaintiff's general characteristics.[231] For example, the accusation that the

---

[222] Gallo v. Alitalia-Linee Aeree Italiane-Societa per Azioni, 585 F.Supp.2d 520 (S.D.N.Y. 2008) ("Adultery is not a serious crime, and therefore is not included in that slander per se category. Adultery is a class B misdemeanor").

[223] See Gosden v. Louis, 116 Ohio App. 3d 195, 687 N.E.2d 481 (1996) (voyeurism might not be crime of moral turpitude but if in writing the charge of any crime would be libel and actionable).

[224] Speed v. Scott, 787 So.2d 626 (Miss. 2001) ("thief and liar" not slander per se under the circumstances; dissenters argued that listeners might not know the reference was so limited).

[225] Biondi v. Nassimos, 300 N.J.Super. 148, 692 A.2d 103 (1997); cf. Restatement (Second) of Torts § 571 cmt. c (1977).

[226] See Greene v. Tinker, 332 P.3d 21 (Alaska 2014) (breach of medical confidentiality); White v. Wilkerson, 328 S.C. 179, 493 S.E.2d 345 (1997) (attorney said to have taken over 90% of a settlement). Statements suggesting that the plaintiff was disloyal to his employer by taking kickbacks from those dealing with the employer are easily slander per se. See Nassa v. Hook-SupeRx, Inc., 790 A.2d 368 (R.I. 2002).

[227] Ravnikar v. Bogojavlensky, 438 Mass. 627, 782 N.E.2d 508 (2003).

[228] Finck v. City of Tea, 443 N.W.2d 632 (S.D. 1989) (statement that police chief was a dumb son of a bitch and incompetent was opinion only and not actionable). An opinion offered by an expert or one who seems to have special knowledge of the facts, however, may imply unstated facts and may be accepted as slander per se. See Lawnwood Med. Ctr., Inc. v. Sadow, 43 So.3d 710 (Fla. Dist. Ct. App. 2010) (hospital senior executive told new doctor that the plaintiff doctor was not competent to operate on a dog).

[229] Gunsberg v. Roseland Corp., 34 Misc.2d 220, 225 N.Y.S.2d 1020 (Sup. Ct. 1962).

[230] Smith v. IMG Worldwide, Inc., 437 F.Supp.2d 297 (E.D. Pa. 2006) (alleged statements to potential recruit by sports agent that the plaintiff, a competing sports agent, "played the race card" in negotiating with the NFL on behalf of players are slander per se because they "are peculiarly harmful to plaintiff because his ability to represent professional football players is directly tied to his relationships with the general managers of NFL clubs").

[231] See Pippen v. NBCUniversal Media, LLC, 734 F.3d 610 (7th Cir. 2013) (assertion of personal bankruptcy did not imply former basketball star's lack of competence or integrity to serve as goodwill ambassador for professional team, basketball analyst, or celebrity product endorser); Hancock v. Variyam, 400 S.W.3d 59 (Tex. 2013) (assertion that physician was "lacking veracity" did not affect fitness for proper conduct as physician).

plaintiff, a landlord, had threatened the defendant's life and tried to bribe a police officer does not reflect upon the plaintiff's status as a landlord and hence is not actionable without proof of pecuniary damages.[232]

Slander per quod and the requirement for special damages or pecuniary harm. Unless the slander falls in one of the four categories, the slander is called *per quod* and the plaintiff must plead and prove "special harm." Special harm in this instance means specifically identified pecuniary harm resulting from the slander.[233] Special harm in this sense is not the same as actual harm, which includes any actual loss to reputation, whether pecuniary harm results or not.[234] As a result of the special or pecuniary harm rule for slander per quod, the plaintiff who suffers no loss of anything of pecuniary value but suffers a proven loss of reputation and resulting emotional harm has no slander claim at all.[235] The rule equally implies, however, that if the plaintiff can prove some slight pecuniary loss, she recovers all her damages, including loss of reputation and emotional harm.[236] Pecuniary loss is easy to find in the loss of a job[237] and in the loss of customers or business income[238] but it can take the form of "any material loss capable of being measured in money," such as the loss of a free cruise.[239] It has been said that anticipated loss that has not actually occurred at the time of trial, however, is insufficient to permit the slander per quod action.[240] However, if such loss is proven with the degree of certainty required to establish other future damages, it is not easy to see why that item of damage should be ruled out here.

Reform. Both the damages rules for libel and those for slander are extreme in different ways. The libel rules might be reformed by eliminating the presumption of harm and requiring some evidence that actual harm occurred.[241] The slander rules might be reformed in the other direction, by permitting the plaintiff to prove a real loss of reputation even if it did not result in pecuniary harm, at least where the plaintiff must also prove that the defendant was guilty of publishing a knowing, reckless, or negligent

---

[232] Liberman v. Gelstein, 80 N.Y.2d 429, 605 N.E.2d 344, 590 N.Y.S.2d 857 (1992).

[233] A general allegation of economic loss is usually insufficient. See Becker v. Zellner, 292 Ill.App.3d 116, 684 N.E.2d 1378, 226 Ill.Dec. 175 (1997); contra, Johnson v. Bollinger, 86 N.C.App. 1, 356 S.E.2d 378 (1987). Authorities on special harm in analogous libel per quod and injurious falsehood cases have sometimes insisted that the plaintiff must prove such items as the loss of named customers.

[234] Actual harm is required by the constitutional decisions to establish certain defamation claims. See § 37.15.

[235] Terwilliger v. Wands, 17 N.Y. 54 (1858); Scott v. Harrison, 215 N.C. 427, 2 S.E.2d 1 (1939); Restatement (Second) of Torts § 575 cmt. b (1977).

[236] Restatement (Second) of Torts § 623 (1977).

[237] Leonardo v. Sley Sys. Garages, Inc., 166 Pa.Super. 633, 74 A.2d 712 (1950).

[238] Claims for lost profits and the like arise equally in slander per se, libel and injurious falsehood cases, which provide many of the authorities on evidence required. See, e.g., Erick Bowman Remedy Co. v. Jensen Salsbery Labs., Inc., 17 F.2d 255 (8th Cir. 1926) (injurious falsehood, with emphasis on the need to show loss of specific customers in some cases); Schoen v. Washington Post, 246 F.2d 670 (D.C. Cir. 1957) (libel with claims of lost customers; plaintiff would be required to segregate losses due to true portion of the publication); Van Gundy v. Wilson, 84 Ga.App. 429, 66 S.E.2d 93 (1951) (slander per se as to eating establishment but not as to other businesses operated in the same place).

[239] Restatement (Second) of Torts § 575 & ill. 4 (1977).

[240] Scott v. Harrison, 215 N.C. 427, 2 S.E.2d 1 (1939).

[241] See Rocci v. Ecole Secondaire Macdonald-Cartier, 165 N.J. 149, 755 A.2d 583 (2000) (requiring either proof of actual harm or "actual malice" when speech is of public concern, even if the plaintiff is not a public figure; also leaving open the issue of whether the presumption of damages should be abolished).

falsehood. Major commentators have suggested one or more of these reforms[242] and several courts have said that proof of actual damages is now required in all defamation cases.[243]

§ 37.10　Libel Per Quod

Rule that all libel is libel per se. The common law rule was that all libel was actionable without proof of harm; harm to reputation was conclusively presumed once defamatory content was published. In addition, the plaintiff could of course recover for any actual damages proved, including actual loss of reputation and distress, whether or not the plaintiff suffered pecuniary loss. The rule can be expressed by saying that all libel is libel per se (or "actionable per se").[244] That remains the rule followed in many courts[245] and by the Restatement[246] where the constitutional decisions do not compel a different result.[247] The rule authorizes the jury to award substantial damages even if no loss of reputation has been proved,[248] although the defendant may present evidence tending to show that damages were limited.[249]

The contrary rule of libel per quod. However, in the 19th century, a number of courts began to say that some libel was "per quod," meaning that after all the plaintiff would be required in libel as well as in slander cases to prove pecuniary loss in order to recover. But these courts did not provide a parallel set of rules for libel and slander. Slander per quod was any slander not falling into one of the special categories, while libel per quod was any libel that was not defamatory "on its face."[250] Perhaps most courts adopt some form of the libel per quod rule requiring proof of pecuniary (not merely actual) damages, but it has been argued that many of the earlier cases identified with the per quod rule were actually cases of injurious falsehood where pecuniary harm is regularly required in any event.[251] Whether few or many, the cases have managed to add technicalities and complications to a body of law already known as a lawyer's labyrinth.

---

[242] David A. Anderson, Reputation, Compensation, and Proof, 25 Wm. & Mary L. Rev. 747 (1984) (requiring actual harm which could sometimes be inferred from other facts); See also Rodney A. Smolla, Law of Defamation § 7.33 (updated, available on Westlaw).

[243] Arthaud v. Mutual of Omaha Ins. Co., 170 F.3d 860 (8th Cir. 1999); Synygy, Inc. v. Scott-Levin, Inc., 51 F.Supp.2d 570 (E.D.Pa. 1999); United Ins. Co. of Am. v. Murphy, 331 Ark. 364, 961 S.W.2d 752 (1998); Schlegel v. Ottumwa Courier, 585 N.W.2d 217 (Iowa 1998); Zoeller v. American Fam. Mut. Ins. Co., 17 Kan. App.2d 223, 834 P.2d 391 (1992); Nazeri v. Missouri Valley Coll., 860 S.W.2d 303 (Mo. 1993); Walker v. Grand Cent. Sanitation, Inc., 430 Pa. Super. 236, 634 A.2d 237 (1993).

[244] Holtzscheiter v. Tomson Newspapers, Inc., 332 S.C. 502, 506 S.E.2d 497 (1998), concluded that all libel is *actionable per se,* that is without proof of special damages. It reserved the term libel per quod, usually contrasted with libel per se, to mean only that extrinsic circumstances could be introduced to show defamatory meaning.

[245] Vanover v. Kansas City Life Ins. Co., 553 N.W.2d 192 (N.D. 1996) (repudiating earlier authority supporting the per quod rule); Maison de France v. Mais Oui!, Inc., 126 Wash. App. 34, 108 P.3d 787 (2005); In re Storms v. Action Wis. Inc., 309 Wis.2d 704, 748, 750 N.W.2d 739, 761 (2008) ("We adhere to and adopt the common-law rule of libel . . . that all libels are actionable without alleging or proving special damages").

[246] Restatement (Second) of Torts § 569 (1977).

[247] See § 37.15 (where a private person sues and the issue involved in the alleged defamation is one of public concern, the plaintiff must prove some actual harm or else knowing or reckless falsehood).

[248] See Wilhoit v. WCSC, Inc., 293 S.C. 34, 358 S.E.2d 397 (1987); Poulston v. Rock, 251 Va. 254, 467 S.E.2d 479 (1996) (trial judge erred in reducing award merely because no harm had been shown).

[249] Williams v. District Court, 866 P.2d 908 (Colo. 1993)

[250] See Baker v. Tremco Inc., 890 N.E.2d 73 (Ind. Ct. App. 2008), vacated by Baker v. Tremco Inc., 917 N.E.2d 650 (Ind. 2009).

[251] See Laurence H. Eldredge, The Law of Defamation § 24 (1978). Prosser and Eldredge heavily debated the question of "how many" authorities support the rule. See William L. Prosser, Libel Per Quod, 46 Va. L.

Example of statement not defamatory on its face. If the defendant published a statement that the plaintiff was the only person present at T's home during the entire day yesterday, the statement on its face seems innocuous. However, if the recipient of the statement knows that T was murdered at his home during the day yesterday, the statement can be understood to accuse the plaintiff of murder. Unless some qualification applies,[252] the traditional libel per quod rule would require the plaintiff to prove pecuniary harm even though the plaintiff could prove by extrinsic evidence that the statement was reasonably understood to accuse the plaintiff of a felony.[253]

Relevance of slander categories in libel per se/per quod cases. Confusion is the norm for defamation cases. Although "not defamatory on its face" is the test of libel per quod, some courts define libel per se in terms of the slander per se categories even when they also define libel per se as defamation that does not require extrinsic evidence.[254] A court may state both the extrinsic evidence test and the test based on slander per se categories without explaining how they can both be tests of libel per se.[255] Or a court may insist that libel is per quod unless the plaintiff meets both tests, in which case, the plaintiff must prove pecuniary harm unless the defamatory quality of the publication is apparent on its face without resort to extrinsic facts *and* the publication accuses the plaintiff of conduct that falls within one of the slander per se categories.[256] Sometimes other consequences of the per se/per quod classification have been attached, too, so that if the libel is not per se, the plaintiff may be required to prove falsity and fault not required in the traditional common law libel cases.[257]

Rationales for per quod rule. Rationales for a per quod rule are also poorly developed. One possibility, suggested above, is that in one type of libel per quod—when extrinsic facts are required to show any defamatory meaning at all—the publisher is not likely to be at fault and perhaps should not be held strictly liable unless the plaintiff suffers some special damages. Another is that when libel is not apparent on the face of the publication, the plaintiff is likely to suffer little harm; in that case, so the reasoning might go, it is reasonable to require proof of special damages.

Rev. 839 (1960); Laurence H. Eldredge, The Spruious Rule of Libel Per Quod, 79 Harv. L. Rev. 733 (1966); William L. Prosser, More Libel Per Quod, 79 Harv. L. Rev. 1629 (1966).

[252] See the paragraph, *Relevance of the slander categories in libel per se/per quod cases,* below.

[253] See Ilitzky v. Goodman, 57 Ariz. 216, 112 P.2d 860 (1941); Bryson v. News Am. Publ'ns, Inc., 174 Ill.2d 77, 103, 672 N.E.2d 1207, 1121, 220 Ill.Dec. 195, 209 (1996) ("a per quod claim is appropriate where the defamatory character of the statement is not apparent on its face, and resort to extrinsic circumstances is necessary to demonstrate its injurious meaning").

[254] E.g., Bryson v. News Am. Publ'ns, Inc., 174 Ill. 2d 77, 672 N.E.2d 1207, 220 Ill. Dec. 195 (1996); DaimlerChrysler Corp. v. Kirkhart, 148 N.C.App. 572, 561 S.E.2d 276 (2002); Robert D. Sack, Sack on Defamation: Libel, Slander and Related Problems § 2.8 (2008) (available on Westlaw).

[255] See Smith v. Stewart, 291 Ga.App. 86, 96, 660 S.E.2d 822, 831 (2008) ("Libel per se consists of a charge that one is guilty of a crime, dishonesty[,] or immorality. . . . Defamatory words which are actionable per se are those which are recognized as injurious on their face-without the aid of extrinsic proof. . . . [I]f the defamatory character of the words does not appear on their face but only become defamatory by the aid of extrinsic facts, they are not defamatory per se. . . ." (quoting)). On the surface, the two tests are antithetical, but a court could require that the plaintiff meet both tests in order to show libel per se, or it could hold that meeting either would suffice.

[256] See Mercer v. Cosley, 110 Conn.App. 283, 294, 955 A.2d 550, 559 (2008) ("To recover on a claim that the libel was actionable per se, a plaintiff must show that the libel, on its face, either charged some impropriety in the plaintiff's business or profession or that it charged a crime of moral turpitude"); Kennedy v. Sheriff of E. Baton Rouge, 920 So.2d 217 (La. 2006). See also Holleman v. Aiken, 668 S.E.2d 579 (N.C. Ct. App. 2008).

[257] See Kennedy v. Sheriff of E. Baton Rouge, 920 So.2d 217 (La. 2006).

Inadequacy of rationales. Both rationales are now deficient. First, the requirement of pecuniary loss rather than actual harm to reputation is as artificial here as it is with slander. Second, fault is now often required by constitutional and even common law decisions; when it is required, the artificial technicalities of libel per quod cannot be justified as an indirect and complicated way of preventing strict liability. If fault is the hidden issue in libel per quod cases, the court can simply require proof of fault in all cases or at least when extrinsic facts are required to show defamatory meaning.[258] Third, the extrinsic facts that show defamatory quality may be well known to both the publisher and the readers. The "common-sense idea [is] that a fact not expressed in the newspaper but presumably known to its readers is part of the libel"[259] so in all such cases the requirement of special damages in the sense of pecuniary loss rather than actual harm is out of place.

The complex case of "defamatory" credit reports. Identity theft and similar cases aside,[260] aspersions on the plaintiff's creditworthiness have been treated as defamation.[261] Courts recognizing the claim for aspersions on creditworthiness have sometimes invoked two rules that bring the claim close to the injurious falsehood rules. First, in some jurisdictions, courts may invoke the per quod rule, saying that the plaintiff would be required to show pecuniary loss.[262] Second, courts traditionally interposed a privilege in favor of the defendant who provided credit information to actual or potential creditors or other persons with a legitimate interest.[263] The privilege in most courts was lost only if the credit reporter acted in bad faith or with malice, or engaged in excessive publication.[264] The end result of those rules turned the claim, nominally one for defamation, into something close to the more restricted injurious falsehood claim.[265] However, Congress passed the Fair Credit Reporting Act[266] in 1970 and has since amended it. That statute may provide a better set of rules than the common law libel claims.[267]

---

[258] As in Reed v. Melnick, 81 N.M. 608, 471 P.2d 178, 49 A.L.R.3d 156 (1970), overruled on other grounds, Marchiondo v. Brown, 98 N.M. 394, 649 P.2d 462 (1982). A fault requirement may be the point in cases like DaimlerChrysler Corp. v. Kirkhart, 148 N.C. App. 572, 561 S.E.2d 276 (2002) (requiring publisher in a per quod case to intend "to defame" or recipient understand the communication "to be defamatory").

[259] Hinsdale v. Orange County Publ'ns, Inc., 17 N.Y.2d 284, 290, 217 N.E.2d 650, 653, 270 N.Y.S.2d 592 (1966).

[260] See 3 Dobbs, Hayden & Bublick, The Law of Torts § 650 (2d. ed. 2011 & Supp.).

[261] E.g., Beuster v. Equifax Info. Servs., 435 F.Supp. 2d 471 (D. Md. 2006) (holding libel action not preempted by federal Fair Credit Reporting Act); Student Loan Fund of Idaho, Inc. v. Duerner, 951 P.2d 1272 (Idaho 1998); Ruder & Finn, Inc. v. Seaboard Surety Co., 52 N.Y.2d 663, 422 N.E.2d 518 (1981) ("Where a statement impugns the basic integrity or creditworthiness of a business, an action for defamation lies and injury is conclusively presumed").

[262] See § 37.10.

[263] Fischer v. Unipac Serv. Corp., 519 N.W.2d 793 (Iowa 1994).

[264] Sunderlin v. Bradstreet, 1 Sickels 188, 46 N.Y. 188 (1871); Weir v. Citicorp Nat'l Servs., Inc., 312 S.C. 511, 435 S.E.2d 864 (1993); Calhoun v. Chase Manhattan Bank, 911 S.W.2d 403 (Tex. App. 1995).

[265] The main difference was that the defendant would have the burden of showing a privileged occasion, but that would ordinarily be easy enough, and once the privilege was invoked, the burden of showing malice would fall upon the plaintiff, just as it does in injurious falsehood claims.

[266] Currently codified as 15 U.S.C.A. §§ 1681 et seq.

[267] The topic of defamatory credit reports is developed more fully in Dobbs, Hayden & Bublick, The Law of Torts § 536 (2d ed. 2011 & Supp.).

C. DEFENSES

§ 37.11 Absolute Privileges and Common Law Qualified Privileges

Absolute Privileges or Immunities

Absolute privileges. Although the common law defamation plaintiff could make out a case without proof of fault, the defendant might defeat the claim by presenting the affirmative defense of privilege. Privileges are either absolute or qualified. A privilege is described as "absolute" when it prevails despite the defendant's malice, which, under common law notions, involved ill will, spite, improper purpose, or the like. The privilege is in effect a complete immunity.[268] Although it protected malicious statements as well as others, it must be remembered that even the defendant who spoke with ill will might nevertheless have reasonably believed in the truth of what he said.

Recognized categories of absolute privilege. Subject to certain limitations, the absolute privilege applies principally to the following categories, discussed further below: (1) judicial proceedings and certain preparations therefore; (2) legislative proceedings; (3) to a limited number of executive publications; (4) publications consented to, (5) publications between spouses;[269] (6) publications required by law,[270] and (7) any absolute privilege accorded by statute, including the immunity of internet service providers for defamatory material posted by others.[271]

Speech protections. In addition, some states, proceeding from the constitutional right to petition government under the so-called anti-SLAPP statutes, give special protections to communications made in the course of participation in public affairs.[272] Although legal professionals sometimes use the term "constitutional privilege" to describe one or more of the constitutional speech protections, those rules are not technical privileges. They do not shield defendants by offering them affirmative defenses but rather require the plaintiff to establish certain facts or characteristics in the first place.

Judicial and Quasi-Judicial Proceedings and Complaints to Police

Judicial and quasi-judicial proceedings. The absolute privilege in judicial and quasi-judicial proceedings protects judges and other judicial officers with respect to statements made in the performance of judicial functions and having some relationship to those functions.[273] The privilege also protects defamatory matter in pleadings,[274] and statements made by attorneys, parties, witnesses, and jurors so far as they are involved

---

[268] See Simpson Strong-Tie Co., Inc. v. Stewart, Estes & Donnell, 232 S.W.3d 18, 22 (Tenn. 2007).

[269] Restatement (Second) of Torts § 592 (1977).

[270] Stecks v. Young, 38 Cal. App. 4th 365, 45 Cal. Rptr. 2d 475 (1995) (mandatory child abuse reports); Anderson v. Beach, 897 N.E.2d 361, 325 Ill. Dec. 113 (Ct. App. 2008) (duty to report police officers' rule infractions to superior officer absolutely privileged); Restatement (Second) of Torts § 592A (1977); see Farmers Educ. & Coop. Union of Am. v. WDAY, Inc., 360 U.S. 525, 79 S.Ct. 1302, 3 L.Ed.2d 1407 (1959).

[271] See Cucinotta v. Deloitte & Touche, LLP, 302 P.3d 1099 (Nev. 2013) (absolute privilege for accounting firm's communications with corporations audit committee, pursuant to SEC Act); § 37.11 (internet providers).

[272] "SLAPP" stands for "strategic lawsuit against public participation." See § 37.14.

[273] Restatement (Second) of Torts § 585 (1977).

[274] Prokop v. Cannon, 7 Neb. App. 334, 583 N.W.2d 51 (1998); Titan Am., LLC v. Riverton Inv. Corp., 264 Va. 292, 569 S.E.2d 57 (2002) (absolute privilege though case had been settled and some of the allegations had not been "tested" by judicial action).

in and related to judicial proceedings.[275] As this privilege perhaps implies, there is no separate tort of perjury.[276] Attorneys, parties, and their representatives, as well as witnesses, may also be absolutely protected from liability for communications made in preparation for trial[277] or in connection with post-trial determinations.[278] Even statements made in soliciting a purely potential client for a merely possible lawsuit have been granted absolute protection.[279] So have letters written as provided by a settlement agreement, even when those letters are not part of public records.[280] The privilege has been extended to administrative proceedings that are adversary and quasi-judicial, that is, when they apply law to facts and are subject to judicial review.[281] Several courts have held that even an individual's out-of-court charge or a report to police is absolutely privileged and that the privilege will defeat all claims except a valid claim for malicious prosecution and perhaps a civil rights claim.[282]

Occasion and content must be privileged. The publication is not protected by the absolute privilege unless both the occasion for publication and the content of the publication have some relation or "pertinence" to the proceeding. An attorney who makes defamatory remarks at a press conference or other media presentation would not ordinarily enjoy the absolute privilege.[283] Outside repetition or republication of defamatory statements made in judicial proceedings may be sometimes denied automatic or absolute protection,[284] and even that providing a copy of a filed complaint to the media forfeits the privilege, although the complaint is a public record and available to the press in any event.[285] In such cases, however, the qualified privilege to make a fair

---

[275] The absolute privilege does not bar an action for malicious prosecution. See, e.g., McKinney v. Okoye, 282 Neb. 880, 806 N.W.2d 571 (2011); see Chapter 39.

[276] Witzke v. City of Bismarck, 718 N.W.2d 586 (N.D. 2006); see Cooper v. Parker-Hughey, 894 P.2d 1096 (Okla. 1995) (citing cases from many states).

[277] Kelley v. Bonney, 221 Conn. 549, 606 A.2d 693, 708 (1992); Helena Chem. Co. v. Uribe, 281 P.3d 237 (N.M. 2012); Francis v. Gallo, 59 A.3d 69 (R.I. 2013).

[278] Van Eaton v. Fink, 697 N.E.2d 490 (Ind. Ct. App. 1998). Prokop v. Cannon, 7 Neb. App. 334, 583 N.W.2d 51 (1998), goes much further in protecting a comment made by an attorney after the cases had been dropped.

[279] Rubin v. Green, 4 Cal.4th 1187, 847 P.2d 1044, 17 Cal. Rptr. 2d 828 (1993) (interference with contract claim based upon statements to potential clients); Simpson Strong-Tie Co., Inc. v. Stewart, Estes & Donnell, 232 S.W.3d 18, 22 (Tenn. 2007) (requiring that the statements be relevant to a potential lawsuit seriously contemplated in good faith; the privilege extends to publically published solicitation where more closely targeted communication is not feasible).

[280] Sodergren v. Johns Hopkins Univ. Applied Physics Lab., 138 Md.App. 686, 773 A.2d 592 (2001).

[281] E.g., Morgan & Pottinger, Attorneys, P.S.C. v. Botts, 348 S.W.3d 599 (Ky. 2011) (attorney disciplinary proceeding); Reichardt v. Flynn, 374 Md. 361, 823 A.2d 566 (2003) (teacher disciplinary action); Cottrell v. Zagami, LLC, 94 A.3d 878 (N.J. 2014) (municipal liquor license hearing). For greater discussion of the issue see Dobbs, Hayden & Bublick, The Law of Torts § 539 (2d ed. 2011 & Supp.).

[282] Ledvina v. Cerasani, 146 P.3d 70 (Ariz. Ct. App. 2006); Hagberg v. California Fed. Bank FSB, 32 Cal. 4th 350, 81 P.3d 244, 7 Cal. Rptr. 3d 803 (2004).

[283] Medical Informatics Eng'g, Inc. v. Orthopaedics Ne., P.C., 458 F.Supp. 2d 716 (N.D. Ind. 2006) (citing many cases); Green Acres Trust v. London, 141 Ariz. 609, 688 P.2d 617 (1984). But see Norman v. Borison, 418 Md. 630, 17 A.3d 697, 39 Media L. Rep. (BNA) 1673 (2011) (extending absolute privilege to statements made by lawyers to newspaper reporter after the filing of a complaint, holding that the allegedly defamatory statements made to the newspaper were relevant to the judicial proceedings).

[284] Wagner v. Miskin, 660 N.W.2d 593 (N.D. 2003) ("A privileged statement, such as one made in a judicial proceeding, is not privileged for all subsequent publications by virtue of initially being spoken in a privileged proceeding").

[285] Williams v. Kenney, 379 N.J.Super. 118, 877 A.2d 277, 287 (2005) (transcript of telephone conversation attached to complaint sent to newspaper; "extra-judicial distribution of papers filed in court" is not ordinarily deemed privileged because "[s]uch publications are made beyond the controls and inhibitions inherent in the judicial process"); Bochetto v. Gibson, 580 Pa. 245, 860 A.2d 67 (2004); Pratt v. Nelson, 164

report of public proceedings may protect the defendant, though the judicial privilege does not.[286] The judge who makes a defamatory remark at lunch or in the course of hiring or firing an employee is not absolutely privileged.[287] Nor is any participant in a contract suit who simply takes the occasion to let the world know what he thinks of a business rival who is in no way involved.[288] However, statements that have some bearing on the matter at issue and are made in connection with the proceeding are protected, even if they would not be admissible in evidence or would be counted as improper argument.[289]

Purpose and scope of judicial proceedings privilege. The purpose of absolute privilege in this context is to immunize participants in the judicial process so as to assure all concerned that they can speak truly (or in their client's interest in the case of a lawyer) without fear of personal liability or an expensive lawsuit.[290] The immunity may sometimes protect scoundrels and liars, but it has always been thought necessary, because if each case is judged on its own merits, honest witnesses and other participants in the trial cannot be assured of protection from suit. The privilege does not reflect a rule peculiar to defamation claims but a rule protecting litigation itself. Consequently, the privilege protects the communications in litigation whether the plaintiff labels her claim as one for defamation, or false light, or interference with business prospects.[291] The privilege has even been applied to protect a party to litigation who induces a settlement

---

P.3d 366, 377 (Utah 2007) ("the Nelsons' statements made during the press conference, including the Kingston Complaint, the Prepared Statement, and other oral statements, lost through excessive publication any privileged status they may have otherwise enjoyed"). But see Norman v. Borison, 418 Md. 630, 17 A.3d 697, 39 Media L. Rep. (BNA) 1673 (2011) (extending absolute privilege to protect lawyers who spoke to newspaper reporter and gave reporter a copy of a complaint filed in a case, holding that the allegedly defamatory statements made to the newspaper were relevant to the judicial proceedings).

[286] See Rosenberg v. Helinski, 328 Md. 664, 616 A.2d 866 (1992).

[287] Cf. Forrester v. White, 484 U.S. 219, 108 S.Ct. 538, 98 L.Ed.2d 555 (1988) (distinguish judicial from administrative capacity of judge; judge who violates constitutional rights in the course of discharging an employee does not enjoy absolute, only qualified, protection).

[288] Cf. Post v. Mendel, 510 Pa. 213, 507 A.2d 351 (1986) (lawyer's letter attacking opposing counsel; copy to the judge, written and received during trial was not absolutely privileged as part of the proceeding).

[289] See Kocontes v. McQuaid, 279 Neb. 335, 340, 778 N.W.2d 410, 416 (2010) (required relevancy "of the defamatory matter is not a technical legal relevancy but instead a general frame of reference and relationship to the subject matter of the action"); Irwin v. Ashurst, 158 Or. 61, 74 P.2d 1127 (1938) (attorney's closing argument to the jury: plaintiff was not truthful and "was lower than a rattlesnake because a rattlesnake gives warning before it strikes"; absolutely privileged if pertinent and jury found it was).

[290] See Rosenberg v. Helinski, 328 Md. 664, 616 A.2d 866 (1992); Paul T. Hayden, Reconsidering the Litigator's Absolute Privilege to Defame, 54 Ohio St. L.J. 985 (1993) (detailed examination of rationales). The rationales behind and purposes of the privilege do not support its application to a legal malpractice suit by the client against the lawyer based on statements the lawyer made in connection with a judicial proceeding. See Buchanan v. Leonard, 428 N.J. Super. 277, 52 A.3d 1064 (App. Div. 2012).

[291] The principle seems actually broader: restrictions on liability imposed in defamation cases, whether through privileges or free speech rules, are not to be subverted by allowing a recovery for derogatory words on the theory that some other tort has been committed. See Sullivan v. Conway, 157 F.3d 1092 (7th Cir. 1998) ("the same privileges are applicable to the false-light tort as to the defamation tort. Otherwise privilege could be defeated by relabeling;" not addressing litigation privilege, however); Levin, Middlebrooks, Mabie, Thomas, Mayes & Mitchell, P. A. v. United States Fire Ins. Co., 639 So.2d 606 (Fla. 1994) (absolute privilege for communications in litigation applied to interference claim); Crain v. The Unauthorized Practice of Law Comm. of the Supreme Court of Tex., 11 S.W.3d 328 (Tex. App. 1999) ("the judicial privilege is not limited to claims of libel or slander, and it should be applied to claims arising out of communications made in the course of judicial proceedings, regardless of the label placed on the claim," mentioning tortious interference claims specifically); Moss v. Parr Waddoups Brown Gee & Loveless, 285 P.3d 1157 (Utah 2012) (litigation privilege protected lawyers from claims of breach of settlement agreement, abuse of process and invasion of privacy, where alleged wrong was in drafting and serving civil discovery orders authorizing entry into the plaintiffs' homes); contra, Trau-Med of Am., Inc. v. Allstate Ins. Co., 71 S.W.3d 691(Tenn. 2002).

by fraud in the litigation.[292] At least one scholar has argued that the privilege does not in fact work to support justice and that a qualified privilege would suffice.[293]

Legislative Business

Legislators and aides. Similar policies apply to legislative proceedings. The United States Constitution provides that "for any Speech or Debate in either House," members of Congress "shall not be questioned in any other Place."[294] State constitutional provisions, statutes, or common law provides essentially the same immunity for state legislators[295] and sometimes to local council members.[296] The legislative privilege extends to aides engaged in assisting legislators.[297] Legislative functions covered by the privilege include not only speeches on the floor but committee and other work related to the business of the legislature.[298] They do not, however, include electioneering or the communication of defamatory material to constituents outside the business of the legislature.[299]

Witnesses and citizen participants. In the view of the Restatement and a number of courts, the privilege also covers witnesses or citizen participants at legislative hearings,[300] in order to secure citizen participation in the political process that will more fully inform legislators.[301] This view is most easily supported when the proceeding has a formal character and procedural safeguards and when the witness is subpoenaed or gives testimony under oath.[302] When the proceeding merely asks members of the public to offer their opinions, some courts have rejected the absolute privilege for witnesses, limiting their protection to the qualified privilege,[303] but others afford the citizen-witness absolute protection even when he volunteers testimony and even when it is not given under oath.[304]

Executive Branch Business

Generally not privileged. The executive branch, including police, administrators at all levels, and most other governmental employees,[305] is quite different from the judicial

---

[292] Florida Evergreen Foliage v. E.I. DuPont De Nemours & Co., 470 F.3d 1036 (11th Cir. 2006); Simms v. Seaman, 308 Conn. 523, 69 A.3d 880 (2013).

[293] Paul T. Hayden, Reconsidering the Litigator's Absolute Privilege to Defame, 54 Ohio St. L.J. 985 (1993) (arguing that the privilege as applied to lawyers gets in the way of justice and casts doubt on the integrity of the legal profession, and that a qualified privilege would suffice).

[294] U.S. Const. art I, § 6, cl. 1.

[295] E.g., Colo. Rev. Stat. Ann. § 2–2–304; Conn. Const. art. 3, § 15; Ind. Const. art. 4, § 8; Restatement (Second) of Torts § 590 (1977).

[296] Sanchez v. Coxon, 854 P.2d 126 (Ariz. 1993). Iowa applies only a qualified, rather than absolute, privilege to local council members. On the other hand, it has been held that the privilege is not destroyed by bad motive, only by knowing or reckless falsehood. Barreca v. Nickolas, 683 N.W.2d 111 (Iowa 2004).

[297] Gravel v. United States, 408 U.S. 606, 92 S.Ct. 2614, 33 L.Ed.2d 583 (1972).

[298] Id.

[299] Hutchinson v. Proxmire, 443 U.S. 111, 99 S.Ct. 2675, 61 L.Ed.2d 411 (1979).

[300] DeSantis v. Employees Passaic County Welfare Ass'n, 237 N.J.Super. 550, 568 A.2d 565 (1990) (allegedly defaming public official); Restatement (Second) of Torts § 590A (1977).

[301] See Krueger v. Lewis, 359 Ill. App. 3d 515, 522, 834 N.E.2d 457, 464, 295 Ill. Dec. 876, 883 (2005).

[302] As in Kelly v. Daro, 47 Cal.App.2d 418, 118 P.2d 37 (1941).

[303] Vultaggio v. Yasko, 215 Wis.2d 326, 572 N.W.2d 450 (1998).

[304] Krueger v. Lewis, 359 Ill. App. 3d 515, 834 N.E.2d 457, 295 Ill. Dec. 876 (2005); Riddle v. Perry, 40 P.3d 1128 (Utah 2002).

[305] "Employee" is used inclusively here to mean any person employee by the public entity in question, including those who may be classed as "officers," and those who are elected.

and legislative branch. Except in quasi-judicial proceedings where the absolute judicial privilege would apply, employees in the executive branch do not regularly operate in structured forums like the Congress or the judiciary; they are not often subject to institutional, professional, or even regular political constraints; they seldom if ever have need of privileges not enjoyed by the citizens they are obliged to serve. To the extent that they defame other officials, they are protected by the rules developed under the First Amendment. To the extent that they defame non-governmental citizens, immunity is questionable at best. Apart from statute, executive branch employees were not traditionally afforded the same broad and absolute immunity granted to employees in the judicial and legislative branches.

Federal executive branch immunities. At the federal level, however, Congress has immunized all federal employees for all torts within the scope of their employment.[306] In doing so, it substituted the government itself as a potential defendant, but only under the terms of the Federal Tort Claims Act, which leaves the government itself immune in many instances and specifically immune in suits for libel or slander.[307] Congress did not abrogate the constitutional constraints upon federal officials,[308] so the defamed plaintiff may have a direct constitutional claim against the official.[309] However, the Supreme Court has held that defamation alone does not violate any constitutional right.[310] The effect is that the federal official is absolutely free to defame citizens and that neither he nor the government is liable in a common law or constitutional action for defamation alone.[311]

State executive branch immunities. The states have come up with at least four views on immunity for their executive branch employees. (1) Officers or employees have an absolute immunity for acts, including defamation, that fall within the scope of their employment and are considered discretionary, though not for acts that are considered to be merely non-discretionary or ministerial.[312] (2) High-level officers in the state government are entitled to the absolute privilege; lower-level officers are not.[313] (3) A substantial number of state executive branch employees are protected, including those below cabinet rank.[314] (4) No state officers have an absolute common law privilege to defame; their privilege is qualified and destroyed by malice or knowing falsehood.[315]

---

[306] 28 U.S.C.A. § 2679. See § 351.

[307] 28 U.S.C.A. § 2680(h).

[308] See 28 U.S.C.A. § 2679(b)(2) (the statutory immunity "does not extend or apply to a civil action against an employee of the Government—(A) which is brought for a violation of the Constitution of the United States, or (B) which is brought for a violation of a statute of the United States under which such action against an individual is otherwise authorized").

[309] Under the rule in Bivens v. Six Unknown Named Agents of Federal Bureau of Narcotics, 403 U.S. 388, 91 S. Ct. 1999, 29 L.Ed.2d 619 (1971).

[310] Paul v. Davis, 424 U.S. 693, 96 S.Ct. 1155, 47 L.Ed.2d 405 (1976).

[311] Aversa v. United States, 99 F.3d 1200 (1st Cir. 1996).

[312] District of Columbia v. Jones, 919 A.2d 604 (D.C. 2007).

[313] Bauer v. State, 511 N.W.2d 447 (Minn. 1994); Stukuls v. State, 42 N.Y.2d 272, 397 N.Y.S.2d 740, 366 N.E.2d 829 (1977); Jones v. State, 426 S.W.3d 50 (Tenn. 2013).

[314] Cf. Liberty Bank of Seattle, Inc. v. Henderson, 75 Wash. App. 546, 878 P.2d 1259 (1994) (refusing to state a rule, but indicating that officers below the "cabinet rank" are protected).

[315] Gibson v. Abbott, 529 So.2d 939 (Ala. 1988); Chamberlain v. Mathis, 729 P.2d 905 (Ariz. 1986); cf. Aspen Exploration Corp. v. Sheffield, 739 P.2d 150 (Alaska 1987) (governor had only qualified privilege as to defamation; choice between absolute and qualified privilege depends upon the facts).

States may[316] or may not[317] immunize governmental entities themselves from responsibility for libeling citizens, usually depending on construction of the state's statutes on sovereign immunity.

Consent

Consent as bar. The plaintiff's consent or apparent consent to publication of defamatory materials is a complete bar to the plaintiff's recovery for defamation.[318] The reasons for this rule are in no way related to the reasons given for the immunities of those engaged in legislative and judicial functions. Consent is a bar, not only for reasons of policy, but also for reasons of justice. The ordinary rules for consent and apparent consent apply,[319] so that, for example, if consent is obtained by fraud, that "consent" is no bar to the defamation claim.

Applications. One application of the consent rule occurs when the plaintiff authorizes evaluations of her past work to be communicated to a prospective employer.[320] There are elements of economic compulsion in some such cases, so it may be that consent to publish should not be interpreted to permit publication of a knowing or reckless falsehood. In addition, a rule of fair play that warns the plaintiff about the nature of the evaluation before consent is given might also represent good policy.[321] Consent is implied when the plaintiff accepts or applies for membership in an organization contemplating an investigation of the plaintiff and report to membership or governing boards[322] or other publications about the plaintiff.[323] For example, a priest accedes to the canons and by implication to communication of complaints by parishioners to his superiors.[324]

Internet Communications

General statutory rule. Under the federal Communications Decency Act (CDA),[325] internet service providers who facilitate the communication of internet messages by others are immune from liability for the content of those messages. Those who actually create defamatory content, however, are theoretically subject to liability for the defamation.

---

[316] See Brown v. Blaine, 833 A.2d 1166 (Pa. Commw. Ct. 2003) (state and its agencies are immune except as legislature has specifically waived immunity; it has not waived immunity for libel); Texas Dep't of Health v. Rocha, 102 S.W.3d 348 (Tex. App. 2003) (similar).

[317] Rudloe v. Karl, 899 So.2d 1161 (Fla. Dist. Ct. App. 2005) (state university was not immune from liability for negligently publishing defamatory material; there was no governmental policy-making).

[318] Restatement (Second) of Torts § 583 & cmt. c (1977).

[319] Chapter 8.

[320] Smith v. Holley, 827 S.W.2d 433 (Tex. App. 1992); Woodfield v. Providence Hosp., 779 A.2d 933 (D.C. 2001) (assuming arguendo that consent would only be a qualified privilege; but consent protected former employer even if it gave out information it was contractually obliged to keep confidential); but cf. McQuirk v. Donnelley, 189 F.3d 793 (9th Cir. 1999) (California statute invalidating releases in advance for intentional torts held to include defamation, no discussion whether any wrongful intent was involved). When the plaintiff has not consented to a reference, former employers are often protected by a conditional or qualified privilege, destructible if abused by malice or the like. Statutes sometimes offer specific protection. E.g., Ga. Code § 34–1–4.

[321] See Horkan, Note, Contracting around the Law of Defamation and Employment References, 79 Va. L. Rev. 517 (1993).

[322] Rosenberg v. American Bowling Cong., 589 F.Supp. 547 (M.D. Fla. 1984).

[323] O'Connor v. Diocese of Honolulu, 77 Haw. 383, 885 P.2d 361 (1994).

[324] Hiles v. Episcopal Diocese of Mass., 437 Mass. 505, 773 N.E.2d 929 (2002).

[325] 47 U.S.C.A. § 230(c)(1).

Scope. The CDA expresses the immunity of internet service providers by stating that internet service providers and users are not to be treated as "publishers." The immunity protects the service provider, even though the provider permits posting on the provider's web site or its servers carry defamatory email.[326] In addition, the provider has no duty to remove such postings or emails even when notified of their defamatory content. This result follows from the courts' interpretation of immunity for "publishers" to include immunity for distributors, who constitute a subset of publishers. Thus the immunity protects the provider whether he is considered a "publisher" or "distributor."[327] Although the motivation behind the statute was to promote "decency" on the internet, the statutory immunity also promotes free speech, since if a provider were under a duty to remove offensive speech, it would tend to remove nondefamatory as well as defamatory speech.[328]

Content providers and users under CDA. The statute does not protect those who originate and secure publication of defamatory content. So, in theory, one who posts a defamatory message on an internet site or sends a defamatory email is not immunized.[329] However, such originators may enjoy the near-immunities created by anti-SLAPP statutes,[330] and as a practical matter, anonymous internet posters can most often stand completely protected by the shield of anonymity unless courts force providers to reveal their identity.

Judicial protection of anonymity. Free speech protections include some degree of protection for anonymity,[331] and courts have rightly exercised caution in forcing internet providers or other third persons to reveal the identity of those who anonymously post internet messages, whether the underlying claim is one for defamation or for something else.[332] Although courts have not agreed on every detail, the more recent decisions have coalesced around broadly similar rules for the protection of internet anonymity.[333]

Indirect content providers-repeaters. More significantly, perhaps, some courts have created rules that will immunize providers and users from all responsibility even though

---

[326] "No provider or user of an interactive computer service shall be treated as the publisher or speaker of any information provided by another information content provider." 47 U.S.C.A. § 230(c)(1). Before the statute, Cubby, Inc. v. Compuserve, Inc., 776 F.Supp. 135 (S.D. N.Y. 1991) got the same result. On email, see Lunney v. Prodigy Servs. Co., 701 N.Y.S.2d 684, 723 N.E.2d 539 (1999).

[327] Zeran v. America Online, Inc., 129 F.3d 327, 333 (4th Cir. 1997); Barrett v. Rosenthal, 40 Cal. 4th 33, 146 P.3d 510, 51 Cal. Rptr. 3d 55 (2006).

[328] See Zeran v. America Online, Inc., 129 F.3d 327, 333 (4th Cir. 1997).

[329] Cf. Too Much Media, LLC v. Hale, 206 N.J. 209, 20 A.3d 364, 30 Media L. Rep. (BNA) 1849 (2011) (without citing the CDA, holding that the state Shield Law which creates a newsperson's privilege does not protect people who post defamatory comments on Internet message boards).

[330] See Barrett v. Rosenthal, 40 Cal. 4th 33, 146 P.3d 510, 51 Cal. Rptr. 3d 55 (2006) (internet web site available to public is a public forum protected under anti-SLAPP statute). As to those statutes, see § 553.

[331] It has been argued that freedom to defame behind a cloak of anonymity has great social value because it encourages good as well as libelous speech. Lyrissa Barnett Lidsky, Silencing John Doe: Defamation & Discourse in Cyberspace, 49 Duke L.J. 855 (2000).

[332] Similar issues can occur in invasion of privacy claims, anonymous emailers, see Mobilisa, Inc. v. Doe, 217 Ariz. 103, 170 P.3d 712 (2007), and even in trademark claims, see Salehoo Group, Ltd. v. ABC Co., 722 F.Supp.2d 1210 (W.D. Wash. 2010).

[333] See Mobilisa, Inc. v. Doe, 217 Ariz. 103, 170 P.3d 712 (2007); Krinsky v. Doe 6, 159 Cal.App.4th 1154, 72 Cal.Rptr.3d 231, 245–246 (2008); Doe v. Cahill, 884 A.2d 451(Del. 2005); Solers, Inc. v. Doe, 977 A.2d 941 (D.C. 2009); Independent Newspapers, Inc. v. Brodie, 407 Md. 415, 966 A. 2d 432 (2009); Mortgage Specialists, Inc. v. Implode-Explode Heavy Indus., Inc., 160 N.H. 227, 999 A.2d 184 (2010); Dendrite Int'l, Inc. v. Doe, 342 N.J. Super. 134, 775 A.2d 756 (2001). For greater explication of the rules, see 3 Dobbs, Hayden & Bublick, The Law of Torts § 543 (2d. ed. 2011 & Supp.).

the provider or user selected and posted allegedly defamatory material written by another,[334] or even paid a writer to provide it. The theory is that even though the defendant was instrumental in creating the libel, it was nevertheless defamation "provided by another content provider."[335] Complete protection for those who provide fora and serve as a conduit for information and ideas seems entirely justified, but a rule that protects users or providers who set out to defame by quoting the words of others "has disturbing implications."[336]

Common Law Qualified Privileges

Qualified privilege as affirmative defense. Except for the immunities of internet providers, the absolute privileges discussed above are relatively circumscribed. The qualified or conditional privileges, however, cover much ground. The common law imposed something like a prima facie strict liability in libel cases. If the plaintiff established that the defendant published defamatory material about the plaintiff, liability would follow without proof of any fault. That liability could be avoided only if the defendant was able to meet the burden of establishing an affirmative defense—truth or one of the privileges.[337] If a qualified privilege was established, the plaintiff might still prevail by proving that the defendant had abused the privilege.[338]

Where plaintiff must prove fault in the first instance. Today, the plaintiff is often required to prove in the first instance elements such as reckless falsehood that formerly were relevant on the affirmative defense of privilege.[339] Where such fault has become part of the plaintiff's prima facie case, the privilege analysis might therefore be regarded as superfluous. At the very least, the role of privilege could be reduced without substantially changing the defendant's ultimate liability.

Main qualified privileges. Courts have recognized four basic qualified privileges: (1) the public interest privilege, to publish materials to public officials on matters within their public responsibility; (2) the privilege to publish to someone who shares a common interest, or, relatedly, to publish in defense of oneself or in the interest of others; (3) the

---

[334] See Barrett v. Rosenthal, 40 Cal. 4th 33, 146 P.3d 510, 51 Cal. Rptr. 3d 55 (2006) (apparently conceiving its rule protecting "users" to include users who actively select defamatory material for internet posting).

[335] In Blumenthal v. Drudge, 992 F.Supp. 44 (D. D.C. 1998), AOL hired Drudge to write gossip and made it available through its online service. AOL was held immune from liability for its defamatory content because AOL had not developed the material "itself." When the service provider has some input into content based on the computer user's interactive input, it may still be protected. See Carafano v. Metrosplash.com., Inc., 339 F.3d 1119, 1124 (9th Cir. 2003). In Donato v. Moldow, 374 N.J.Super. 475, 865 A.2d 711 (2005), the interactive computer service selectively deleted messages and thus affected the overall content, but again the immunity remained. HY Cite Corp. v. Badbusinessbureau.Com, LLC, 418 F.Supp. 2d 1142 (D. Ariz. 2005), rejected a motion to dismiss a claim against a website operator, seemingly in part because the plaintiff alleged that the operator solicited negative reports about the plaintiff's products and business and might thus be shown to be responsible for the development of the defamatory information. And in Murphy v. Boston Herald, Inc., 449 Mass. 42, 865 N.E.2d 746 (2007), the defendant newspaper ran a blog or chat room and was held liable for libel in comments posted by readers there on the ground that the defendant had published the original libel in print and would be responsible for repetition of others under the common law repeaters' rule.

[336] Barrett v. Rosenthal, 40 Cal. 4th 33, 63,146 P.3d 510, 528, 51 Cal. Rptr. 3d 55, 77 (2006).

[337] Smith v. Des Moines Pub. Sch., 259 F.3d 942 (8th Cir. 2001); Cortez v. Jo-Ann Stores, Inc., 827 N.E.2d 1223 (Ind. Ct. App. 2005); Boone v. Sunbelt Newspapers, Inc., 347 S.C. 571, 556 S.E.2d 732 (2001). West Virginia says that one element of the plaintiff's case is to prove the absence of a privilege. Belcher v. Wal-Mart Stores, Inc., 211 W.Va. 712, 568 S.E.2d 19 (2002). The logic of that proposition is to put the burden on the plaintiff to negate the privilege rather than upon the defendant to establish it.

[338] § 37.12.

[339] See § 37.15 (constitutional limitations on certain libel actions).

fair comment privilege; and (4) the privilege to make a fair and accurate report of public proceedings. Some courts apply a qualified rather than the absolute privilege when it comes to publications by certain local officers.[340]

Interest Privileges

"Legal, moral, or social duty." The qualified privilege to publish to protect one's own interest, the interest of a recipient or the public, or in a common interest is often introduced in the cases with antique language: "A communication, made in good faith, on a subject matter in which the person communicating has an interest, or owes a duty, legal, moral, or social, is qualifiedly privileged if made to a person having a corresponding interest or duty."[341] The language of moral or social duty is little more than a chant; it seems almost impervious to analysis and at best begs the question what moral and social duties one might have.[342] It seems particularly strange to say that one might have a "a legal or moral duty . . . to protect his own interests" by speaking out.[343] A better approach is to identify particular interests to be served by a publication that turns out to be defamatory and to weigh those interests against the risk of reputational loss.

Public Interest Privilege

Charges made to public officials. Citizen complaints about the supposed crimes of an identifiable person are necessarily defamatory, but so long as the complaint is made to appropriate officials who have authority to deal with the case, the publication is at least qualifiedly privileged.[344] A number of the qualified privilege cases of this sort involve simple reports to the police.[345] However, it has been argued that the privilege goes further in two ways. The first way would afford the privilege to the defendant who makes defamatory reports to a private person who in turn would be authorized or privileged to deal with the matter if the defamatory report were true.[346] The second way would afford the privilege to a defendant who cooperates with a police investigation by making defamatory statements to third persons when authorized by police in the course of an investigation.[347] While the first extension of the privilege is logical, the second runs a risk because it may in effect give police or other officials the privilege of fostering defamation through the cooperation of a citizen, and may delegate to the police the power

---

[340] Barreca v. Nickolas, 683 N.W.2d 111(Iowa 2004).

[341] E.g., Great Coastal Express, Inc. v. Ellington, 230 Va. 142, 153, 334 S.E.2d 846, 853 (1985), overruled by Cashion v. Smith, 749 S.E.2d 526 (Va. 2013). This form of expression originated in Toogood v. Spyring, 1 C.M. & R. 181 (1834). See Patrick Milmo & W.V.H. Rogers, Gatley in Libel and Slander § 14.5 (9th ed. 1998).

[342] A *legal* duty to publish, of course provides a privilege and in fact an absolute one. See Restatement (Second) of Torts § 592A (1977).

[343] Powers v. Carvalho., 117 R.I. 519, 531, 368 A.2d 1242, 1249 (1977).

[344] Skaskiw v. Vermont Agency of Agric., 112 A.3d 1277 (Vt. 2014); Restatement (Second) of Torts § 598 (1977). The privilege may be codified in some cases, as with child abuse reports. See F.A. v. W.J. F., 280 N.J.Super. 570, 656 A.2d 43 (1995).

[345] E.g., Tidwell v. Winn-Dixie, Inc., 502 So.2d 747 (Ala. 1987) (report to police); Flanagan v. McLane, 87 Conn. 220, 87 A. 727 (1913); Kennedy v. Sheriff of East Baton Rouge, 920 So.2d 217 (La. 2006) (report to police that plaintiff tried to pass a counterfeit bill, which later proved to be genuine); Pope v. Motel 6, 114 P.3d 277 (Nev. 2005); Levy v. Gandone, 14 A.D.3d 660, 789 N.Y.S.2d 291 (2005); Shillington v. K-Mart Corp., 102 N.C. App. 187, 402 S.E.2d 155 (1991) (accusation communicated to fellow security guard and to police officer); DeLong v. Yu Enters., Inc., 334 Or. 166, 47 P.3d 8 (2002); see Matter of Disciplinary Action Against Mertz, 712 N.W.2d 849 (N.D. 2006) (dictum, privilege is only a qualified, not absolute one).

[346] Restatement (Second) of Torts § 598 cmt. f (1977).

[347] Kelley v. Tanoos, 865 N.E.2d 593 (2007).

to determine occasions for privilege and to furnish a privilege to a citizen who is all too willing to take the occasion to defame another.

Absolute privilege and analogy to judicial proceedings. A few courts have said the privilege to report a supposed crime to the police is not merely qualified but is absolute,[348] a view that treats a complaint to the police like statements made in, or in preparation for judicial proceedings.[349] Certainly it is true that when the same defamatory statement is made as part of a judicial process, the absolute judicial privilege applies instead.[350] Some cases of reports of authorities do not plainly resemble judicial proceedings. Courts can regard a communication to a prosecuting attorney in an ongoing investigation, for example, as similar to statements before a grand jury and thus in the nature of a judicial proceeding to which absolute privilege should attach. Or, especially when no subpoena has been issued and no oath administered, they can regard communications to the prosecutor as reports to a law enforcement officer. Accordingly they may provide an absolute privilege[351] or only a qualified one.[352] In a Maryland case, public school students who complained to authorities about their teacher got an absolute immunity because the teacher was entitled to a number of procedural safeguards and right to appeal any decision the authorities made.[353]

Malicious prosecution claims not barred. The qualified or absolute privilege to report crime may cut off liability for defamation but it may leave the victim of a false accusation the possibility of a malicious prosecution suit if the defamatory charge actually results in a prosecution without probable cause and other elements of that tort are shown.[354]

Publication in Self-Interest, Interest of Others, and Common Interest

Self-interest. Anyone who has or reasonably believes he has an important interest at stake is conditionally privileged to protect that interest by relevant communications to appropriate recipients.[355] For example, one who is defamed by another may respond to the defamation in any way that appears reasonable so long as the privilege is not

---

[348] Ledvina v. Cerasani, 146 P.3d 70 (Ariz. Ct. App. 2006); Hagberg v. California Fed. Bank FSB, 32 Cal. 4th 350, 81 P.3d 244, 7 Cal. Rptr. 3d 803 (2004).

[349] See Ledvina v. Cerasani, 146 P.3d 70 (Ariz. Ct. App. 2006) (relying in part on Victims' Bill of Rights and in part on cases of reports to prosecutors or grand juries, rather than to police, or else on cases involving the privilege involved in preparing for civil litigation); Rodney A. Smolla, Law of Defamation § 8:58 (available on Westlaw).

[350] See § 37.11 (absolute privilege in judicial process). Thus Cutts v. American United Life Ins. Co., 505 So.2d 1211 (Ala. 1987), applied an absolute privilege for a defamatory answer to a prosecuting attorney's investigative question, but in the same year the same court in Tidwell v. Winn-Dixie, Inc., 502 So.2d 747 (Ala. 1987), applied a qualified privilege for a report to the police. Statements made in preparing for litigation are also distinguishable from mere reports to public officials, and these too may generate an absolute privilege, as in General Elec. Co. v. Sargent & Lundy, 916 F.2d 1119 (6th Cir. 1990), which has sometimes been cited as if it were a report to police.

[351] Bergman v. Hupy, 64 Wis.2d 747, 221 N.W.2d 898 (1974).

[352] Toker v. Pollak, 44 N.Y.2d 211, 376 N.E.2d 163, 405 N.Y.S.2d 1 (1978).

[353] Reichardt v. Flynn, 374 Md. 361, 23 A.2d 566 (2003).

[354] See Chapter 39.

[355] Washburn v. Lavoie, 437 F.3d 84 (D.C. Cir. 2006) (student neighbors of the plaintiff could respond to plaintiff's report to university and landlord of excessive noise by responding to the same recipients that plaintiff's tape recording of the alleged noise was illegal); Restatement (Second) of Torts § 594 (1977); cf. Gregory's Inc. v. Haan, 545 N.W.2d 488 (S.D. 1996) (conditional privilege to file lien of record, although this is not considered a judicial proceeding).

abused.[356] What is reasonable depends in part on the importance of the interest at stake, in part on the need for publication.[357] Possibly some courts would limit the privilege to cases in which the defendant publishes to a well-defined group of people.[358] The privilege to make a response of this kind is a species of the self-defense privilege, and like its physical counterpart, it authorizes the defendant to meet the attack, not to launch a new one of his own on the same or a different subject.[359]

Interest of recipient or third person. The same kind of principle applies to publications made to protect the interest of the recipient.[360] The recipient's interest, however, must be important enough to justify the defamatory communication and sometimes that turns on the relationship between the defendant and the recipient.[361] A stranger might enjoy a privilege to warn the recipient that the plaintiff was planning to kill him,[362] but might not enjoy a privilege to tell him that his wife was flirting with men at the tavern.[363] The interest of a prospective employer of the plaintiff is sufficient to justify a former employer in providing negative evaluations.[364]

Common interest. Many publications are privileged because they are made in the common interest of the publisher and recipient. Common interests are usually found among members of identifiable groups in which members share similar goals or values or cooperate in a single endeavor. The idea is to promote free exchange of relevant information among those engaged in a common enterprise or activity and to permit them to make appropriate internal communications and share consultations without fear of suit.

Examples of common interest privilege. Employers and employees share many interests in the employment, so an employee may be privileged to communicate information about third persons involved with the business[365] and certainly to

---

[356] E.g., Dickins v. Int'l Bhd. of Teamsters., 171 F.2d 21 (D.C. Cir. 1948); State v. Eighth Judicial Dist. Court ex rel. County of Clark, 42 P.3d 233 (Nev. 2002) (state official's letter to newspaper responding to charges allegedly made by the plaintiff); Gattis v. Kilgo, 128 N.C. 402, 38 S.E. 931 (1901); see J. A. Bryant, Annotation, Libel and Slander: Qualified Privilege of Reply to Defamatory Publication, 41 A.L.R.3d 1083 (1972).

[357] Cf. Foretich v. Capital Cities/ABC, Inc., 37 F.3d 1541 (4th Cir. 1994) (plaintiffs, previously accused of child abuse in highly publicized case, had privilege to respond with attacks on accuser and did not become public figures under constitutional rules by so responding).

[358] See Konikoff v. Prudential Ins. Co. of Am., 234 F.3d 92 (2d Cir. 2000) (noting that New York law had so far not accorded the privilege to publications made in the public media). But where public charges are made, public self-defense seems appropriate if it does not otherwise exceed the privilege. See State v. Eighth Judicial Dist. Court ex rel. County of Clark, 42 P.3d 233 (Nev. 2002).

[359] See Reynolds v. Pegler, 223 F.2d 429 (2d Cir. 1955) (choice example of Pegler's wide-ranging attack); State v. Eighth Judicial Dist. Court ex rel. County of Clark, 42 P.3d 233 (Nev. 2002) ("The privilege may be lost, however, if the reply: (1) includes substantial defamatory matter that is irrelevant or non-responsive to the initial statement; (2) includes substantial defamatory material that is disproportionate to the initial statement; (3) is excessively publicized; or (4) is made with malice in the sense of actual spite or ill will").

[360] Restatement (Second) of Torts § 595 (1977).

[361] Id. §§ 595 & 597.

[362] See id. § 595 cmt. g.

[363] Cf. Watt v. Longsdon, [1930] 1 K.B. 130 (1929) (no privilege to communicate all the gossip one hears at "men's clubs or women's bridge parties" to the spouses affected).

[364] See Sigal Constr. Corp. v. Stanbury, 586 A.2d 1204 (D.C. 1991); cf. Hassan v. Mercy Am. River Hosp., 31 Cal. 4th 709, 74 P.3d 726, 3 Cal. Rptr. 3d 623 (2003) (hospital where plaintiff had worked giving material to another hospital where plaintiff had applied for staff privileges; statute provided qualified privilege); Gohari v. Darvish, 363 Md. 42, 767 A.2d 321 (2001) (interest of others' privilege protected franchisee's statements to franchisor about a former employee who was now a prospective competitor). This is sometimes treated as a common interest privilege, but the main interest seems to be that of the recipient.

[365] Van Eaton v. Fink, 697 N.E.2d 490 (Ind. Ct. App. 1998) (paralegal).

communicate information about fellow employees.[366] Equally, the shared interest warrants the employer's privilege to explain to its employees why some of them were discharged.[367] The common interest privilege has protected a franchisee's discussions with his franchisor about prospective competitors,[368] an insured's communications to his insurer about a person alleged to have caused a loss,[369] church members' communications to each other about the supposed proclivities of their ministers,[370] a speaker's professional address to a conference on the subject matter of the conference,[371] and even neighbors' discussions with each other about neighborhood concerns.[372] Credit reporting agencies and others similarly situated likewise have been traditionally privileged to furnish actual and potential creditors with reports on the plaintiff's finances.[373] The common interest privilege may protect a lawyer's communications with his clients, where the lawyer has an ethical duty to say some unpleasant things in the fulfillment of such a duty.[374]

Limiting common interest privilege. Possibly the privilege permits publication to a limited segment of the public where the common interest is a strong one,[375] but it has not been broad enough to justify a defamatory report to the general public merely because material is newsworthy.[376] Some cases have characterized common interest quite narrowly. One decision insisted that although both the publisher and recipient had an interest in the matters communicated, the privilege would not apply unless their interests were based on precisely the same concerns or the same reasons.[377]

Dueling privileges—employment discrimination. Employees are of course privileged to communicate to their employer as well as to officials that they have been sexually harassed or otherwise unlawfully discriminated against in violation of statute. Under the ordinary self-interest privileges, the employer or supervisor would be qualifiedly privileged to answer the charges in self-defense and that might include an attack on the truthfulness and motives of the employee who made the charge. Since a charge of discrimination is a serious one in most employment environments, the supervisor or

---

[366] Ikani v. Bennett, 284 Ark. 409, 682 S.W.2d 747 (1985); Toler v. Sud-Chemie, Inc., 458 S.W.3d 276 (Ky. 2015); Gautschi v. Maisel, 565 A.2d 1009 (Me. 1989).

[367] Schrader v. Eli Lilly & Co., 639 N.E.2d 258 (Ind. 1994); Olson v. 3M Company, 523 N.W.2d 578 (Wis.App. 1994).

[368] Gohari v. Darvish, 363 Md. 42, 767 A.2d 321 (2001).

[369] Delta Health Group, Inc. v. Stafford, 887 So.2d 887 (Ala. 2004); Turner v. Welliver, 226 Neb. 275, 411 N.W.2d 298 (1987).

[370] Rasmussen v. Bennett, 741 P.2d 755 (Mont. 1987); Berger v. Temple Beth-El of Great Neck, 41 A.D.3d 626, 839 N.Y.S.2d 504 (2007).

[371] Taus v. Loftus, 40 Cal. 4th 683, 721, 151 P.3d 1185, 1210,54 Cal. Rptr. 3d 775 (2007).

[372] Christenson v. Gutman, 671 N.Y.S.2d 835 (App. Div. 1998).

[373] See See 3 Dobbs, Hayden & Bublick, The Law of Torts § 536 (2d. ed. 2011 & Supp.).

[374] Gagan v. Yast, 966 N.E.2d 177 (Ind. Ct. App. 2012).

[375] Cf. Richmond v. Southwire Co., 980 F.2d 518 (8th Cir. 1992); Olson v. 3M Company, 523 N.W.2d 578 (Wis. Ct. App. 1994).

[376] Draghetti v. Chmielwski, 416 Mass. 808, 626 N.E.2d 862 (1994). In Konikoff v. Prudential Ins. Co. of America, 234 F.3d 92 (2d Cir. 2000), the court refused to determine whether the interest privileges could be applied to a publication made to the general public in the media, saying that under governing New York law, the privilege had so far been confined to publications made to limited, clearly defined groups with a definite relationship to the publisher.

[377] Kelley v. Tanoos, 865 N.E.2d 593 (2007) (defendant discussed with plaintiff's employer, a school, the idea that the plaintiff might be guilty of firing a weapon at the defendant, but defendant's interest in establishing guilt was not same as the school's interest in repairing strained relations that arose out of the shooting, hence no common interest privilege applied).

employer who is so charged might also bring a defamation suit against the employee. The policy problem is that if the employee who makes a charge of discrimination will be subject to either a defamation suit or a privileged attack on her motives, employees may be forced to forgo their rights against discrimination lest they lose all in defending a lawsuit.

Fair Report Privilege: Reports of Public Documents and Proceedings

Privilege, scope, and loss. The common law did not traditionally recognize a privilege to report newsworthy events. The common law does, however, recognize a qualified privilege to provide a fair and accurate report of public proceedings and documents and even to report meetings open to the public and dealing with matters of public concern.[378] The privilege is lost if the report is inaccurate or unfair, although even in that case constitutional rules may protect the defendant.[379] "Accuracy means 'substantially correct,' while fair means balanced."[380] Fairness requires that the report must substantially represent the matter contained in the public records or proceedings[381] and provide appropriate context for statements reported so that the inevitable summary and omissions do not distort the overall picture.[382] Some authority adds that the privilege does not arise unless the public proceeding or document is referred to in the report and the reporter actually knows about and relies upon the document or proceeding.[383] Even if the reporter knows the underlying facts are false, as where he reports a false statement in a legislative document, he does not lose the privilege, since he is a conduit for information that citizens have a right to see for themselves.[384]

Application. The privilege to report public proceedings protects fair and accurate reports of judicial,[385] legislative,[386] and official executive proceedings or reports[387] arrests,[388] official hearings or meetings of public bodies,[389] and in a few instances private

---

[378] Restatement (Second) of Torts § 611 (1977). Even statements of public officials might qualify, see Maples Lanes, Inc. v. New Media Corp., 322 Ill. App. 3d 842, 256 Ill. Dec. 124, 751 N.E.2d 177 (2001); but cf. Greenbelt Coop. Publ'g Ass'n v. Bresler, 253 Md. 324, 252 A.2d 755 (1969), rev'd on other grounds, 398 U.S. 6, 90 S.Ct. 1537, 26 L.Ed.2d 6 (1970) (suggesting the privilege might not apply to report of an open city council meeting as contrasted an official report by the same council).

[379] If the plaintiff is a public figure, she will be required to show knowing or reckless falsehood. If she is a private person and the issue is one of public concern, she will be required to show at least negligence. See § 556.

[380] Green Acres Trust v. London, 141 Ariz. 609, 618, 688 P.2d 617, 626 (1984).

[381] Northland Wheels Roller Skating Center, Inc. v. Detroit Free Press, Inc., 213 Mich.App. 317, 539 N.W.2d 774 (1995). But a report of a witness' testimony need not include a comprehensive report of the entire trial. Rosenberg v. Helinski, 328 Md. 664, 616 A.2d 866 (1992).

[382] See Costello v. Ocean County Observer, 136 N.J. 594, 643 A.2d 1012 (1994).

[383] See Dameron v. Washington Magazine, 779 F.2d 736 (D.C. Cir. 1985); Bufalino v. Associated Press, 692 F.2d 266 (2d Cir. 1982).

[384] See § 37.12 (abuse of privilege).

[385] E.g., Rushford v. New Yorker Magazine, Inc., 846 F.2d 249 (4th Cir. 1988); Piscatelli v. Van Smith, 424 Md. 294, 35 A.3d 1140, 40 Media L. Rep. (BNA) 1262 (2012) (fair reporting privilege protected newspaper and reporter from defamation claims when challenged statements about plaintiff were taken from plaintiff's own testimony during criminal trial and documents admitted at that trial).

[386] E.g., Cresson v. Louisville Courier-Journal, 299 F. 487 (6th Cir. 1924).

[387] E.g., Brandon v. Gazette Publ'g Co., 234 Ark. 332, 352 S.W.2d 92 (1961).

[388] Trentecosta v. Beck, 703 So.2d 552 (La. 1997) (the fact of the arrest and investigation but not evidence that is no part of a public record).

[389] Bray v. Providence Journal Co., 101 R.I. 111, 220 A.2d 531 (1966) (school committee meeting).

meetings open to the public where issues of public concern are discussed.[390] The privilege also applies to reports of documents open to public inspection, including recall petitions,[391] police reports,[392] pleadings,[393] and others.[394] Some cases have extended the privilege or something analogous to it to protect reports of oral statements to the press made by police officers and others similarly placed,[395] but this extension may be limited to remarks of police officers that are part of their official duties, as distinct from police remarks about the facts of an investigation or the facts of the police case against the plaintiff.[396] The privilege has even been applied to protect "self-reports"—publication by a witness or pleader of his own testimony or pleadings—so long as they are not corruptly designed to foster defamation and protect the defamer.[397] The Restatement Second took the opposite view, providing that one quoting his own pleading, for example, does not enjoy the privilege.[398] The Restatement now has some support.[399] The privilege is not limited to media publications but protects even a letter by a private citizen as long as it fairly and accurately reports a public proceeding.[400]

Rationales. The privilege is based in part on the principle that government activities must always be conducted in the daylight of public scrutiny and in part on the right of members of the public to read public materials for themselves—the reporter being a kind of agent for the readers who as a practical matter cannot always exercise their rights to be present or to read public documents on file.[401]

Judicial action rule for pleadings. The Restatement and a number of courts implicitly reject the second ground by insisting that pleadings cannot be reported, even accurately and fairly, until they have been subjected to some kind of judicial action.[402] The fear behind the Restatement's version is that intentional defamers will file defamatory pleadings protected by the absolute judicial immunity, and then spread the defamation by reporting those pleadings under the protection of the qualified privilege

---

[390] Phoenix Newspapers, Inc. v. Choisser, 82 Ariz. 271, 312 P.2d 150 (1957) (Junior Chamber of Commerce open forum for candidates); Restatement (Second) of Torts § 611 cmt. i (1977).

[391] Herron v. Tribune Publ'g Co., Inc., 108 Wash.2d 162, 736 P.2d 249 (1987).

[392] Dinkel v. Lincoln Publ'g (Ohio), Inc., 93 Ohio App.3d 344, 638 N.E.2d 611 (1994) (under statutory version of the privilege); cf. Gist v. Macon County Sheriff's Dept., 284 Ill.App.3d 367, 671 N.E.2d 1154, 219 Ill.Dec. 701 (1996) (newspaper published sheriff's "most wanted" flyer accurately stating warrant existed for plaintiff); Wright v. Grove Sun Newspaper Co., Inc., 873 P.2d 983 (Okla. 1994) (district attorney's press conference about drug investigation by his office).

[393] E.g., Newell v. Field Enters., Inc., 91 Ill.App.3d 735, 415 N.E.2d 434, 47 Ill.Dec. 429, 20 A.L.R.4th 551 (1980).

[394] E.g., the contents of search warrants. Pearce v. Courier-Journal, 683 S.W.2d 633 (Ky. 1985).

[395] Yohe v. Nugent, 321 F.3d 35 (1st Cir. 2003) (police chief's statement which itself was a summary of an oral report made to the police department); Molnar v. Star-Ledger, 193 N.J. Super. 12, 471 A.2d 1209 (1984) (asserting a common interest type privilege and also report of *official* conduct as analogy to fair report privilege).

[396] Thomas v. Telegraph Publ'g Co., 155 N.H. 314, 929 A.2d 993 (2007); cf. Phillips v. Evening Star Newspapers Co., 424 A.2d 78 (D.C. 1980) (oral statement of official (recorded on a hot line for newspapers) not weighty enough to be entitled to the privilege).

[397] Rosenberg v. Helinski, 328 Md. 664, 616 A.2d 866 (1992) (relying in part on Harper, James & Gray).

[398] Restatement (Second) of Torts § 611 cmt. c (1977) ("A person cannot confer this privilege upon himself").

[399] Republic Tobacco Co. v. North Atl. Trading Co., Inc., 381 F.3d 717 (7th Cir. 2004).

[400] Sahara Gaming Corp. v. Culinary Workers Union Local 226, 115 Nev. 212, 984 P.2d 164 (1999).

[401] See Cox Broad. Corp. v. Cohn, 420 U.S. 469, 491–92, 95 S.Ct. 1029, 1044–45, 43 L.Ed.2d 328 (1975).

[402] Restatement (Second) of Torts § 611 cmt. e (1977). For an evaluation of the Restatement position, see 3 Dobbs, Hayden & Bublick, The Law of Torts § 548 (2d. ed. 2011 & Supp.).

to report public documents. There is case support for the Restatement's narrow view of the privilege,[403] but a number of more recent decisions hold that the privilege applies as soon as the action is commenced.[404]

Reports of News—Neutral Reportage

History. Traditionally, the common law recognized no privilege to report defamatory matter simply because it was newsworthy. The absence of a privilege, combined with the rule that repeaters are liable for defamation, meant that a newspaper could be held liable for reporting a newsworthy event or accusation if it was also defamatory. The fact that events or accusations took place in public would not itself provide a privilege.

Development of rule. However, in *Edwards v. National Audubon Society*,[405] the court held that at least under some circumstances, the press would be privileged to report serious and defamatory charges made against a public figure by responsible organizations as part of a controversial public issue. The court appeared to have in mind an analogy to the fair reporting privilege for public proceedings and documents; the reporter's doubts about the truth of the statements would be irrelevant. "What is newsworthy about such accusations is that they were made. We do not believe that the press may be required under the First Amendment to suppress newsworthy statements merely because it has serious doubts regarding their truth."[406] The *Edwards* court called its rule a privilege of "neutral reportage" based upon the First Amendment.

A number of courts have rejected the neutral reportage privilege.[407] And of course courts may accept the principle but hold that it is inapplicable on the facts, as where the reporter's stance is not neutral at all but actually seconds the defamation.[408] The Supreme Court has not passed on it. A few courts have adopted the privilege in some form;[409] some have avoided passing on it.[410]

State development. Courts would be free to accept the privilege as a matter of state law even if the Constitution does not dictate such a privilege. Many cases, however, have used both ordinary and arcane doctrine to relieve defendants of liability. Some decisions more directly seek protection by expanding the fair report privilege to include reports of things like a witness' repetition for television cameras of testimony he gave in court,[411] a governor's press conference,[412] a private meeting,[413] and even unofficial remarks of a

---

[403] See John E. Theuman, Annotation, Libel and Slander: Reports of Pleadings as Within Privilege for Reports of Judicial Proceedings, 20 A.L.R.4th 576 (1981).

[404] See Solaia Tech., LLC. v. Specialty Publ'g Co., 221 Ill. 2d 558, 852 N.E.2d 825, 304 Ill. Dec. 369 (2006); Mark v. King Broad. Co., 27 Wash. App. 344, 618 P.2d 512 (1980); Rodney A. Smolla, Law of Defamation 8.70 (updated, available on Westlaw).

[405] 556 F.2d 113 (2d Cir. 1977).

[406] Id. at 120.

[407] E.g., Dickey v. CBS, Inc., 583 F.2d 1221 (3d Cir. 1978); Young v. The Morning Journal, 76 Ohio St.3d 627, 669 N.E.2d 1136 (1996); Norton v. Glenn, 860 A.2d 48 (Pa. 2004).

[408] See Condit v. Dunne, 317 F.Supp.2d 344 (S.D. N.Y. 2004) ("Defendant's comments in each medium were not neutral. Defendant concurred in the allegations he reported, making clear in each publication that he believed that plaintiff was criminally involved in Ms. Levy's disappearance").

[409] Krauss v. Champaign News Gazette, Inc., 59 Ill. App. 3d 745, 375 N.E.2d 1362, 17 Ill. Dec. 78 (1978).

[410] Khawar v. Globe Int'l, Inc., 19 Cal. 4th 254, 19 Cal. 4th 1073A, 965 P.2d 696, 79 Cal. Rptr. 2d 178 (1998) (rejecting the privilege when purely private persons are defamed, not passing on the privilege as to public figures).

[411] Rosenberg v. Helinski, 328 Md. 664, 616 A.2d 866 (1992).

[412] Brandon v. Gazette Pub. Co., 234 Ark. 332, 352 S.W.2d 92 (1961).

[413] Phoenix Newspapers, Inc. v. Choisser, 82 Ariz. 271, 312 P.2d 150 (1957).

member of Congress.[414] Other lines of decision have reached results similar to those under the neutral reportage rule, not by creating a privilege, but by administering rules of truth or fault to protect news reports. Some of these simply change the ordinary truth rules[415] when a defendant reports newsworthy but false accusations, so that defendant is regarded as publishing the truth if he accurately reports the false accusation itself, even though its sting is false.[416] Another line of decisions holds that the defendant who publishes defamatory material is not at fault and not liable if he relied on previous publications of the same defamation by others.[417] Taken as a whole, the decisions come increasingly close to a newsworthiness privilege, so frank adoption of the privilege seems quite possible. If the neutral reportage privilege is to be adopted, its contours almost certainly require further thought.[418]

§ 37.12   Abuse or Loss of Privilege

Exceeding scope of privilege. In some instances the claimed privilege never arises because defendant's publication went beyond the scope of the privilege.[419] For instance, an insurer canceling a policy may be privileged to state concerns about the insured, but not irrelevant concerns about her husband.[420]

Fault. If the defendant shows that the publication was privileged, however, he is not subject to liability unless the plaintiff then sustains the burden of proving that the defendant abused the privilege.[421] Abuse is usually shown by proving some species of fault; in most instances proof that the defendant was negligent did not traditionally suffice to show abuse of the privilege.[422] Depending upon the privilege asserted, abuse can take several forms.

Excessive publication. When the facts or the nature of the privilege calls for publication only to a limited group, the privilege is lost by excessive publication.[423] For

---

[414] Chapin v. Knight-Ridder, Inc., 993 F.2d 1087 (4th Cir. 1992); Coleman v. Newark Morning Ledger Co., 29 N.J. 357, 149 A.2d 193 (1959) (report of a press conferences held by Senator Joseph McCarthy about a secret congressional committee meeting).

[415] The normal truth rules hold that the defendant cannot rely on the fact that he accurately reported defamatory statements of others; he must instead prove the truth of the underlying assertions, not merely the truth of the fact that the accusation was made. See § 533.

[416] See Shepard v. Schurz Commc'ns, Inc., 847 N.E.2d 219 (Ind. 2006) (defendant "accurately reported a quotation upon a matter of public concern. . . . Litz's statements were quoted, but not adopted or endorsed by the Times"; summary judgment for publisher affirmed). See also Green v. CBS Inc., 286 F.3d 281 (5th Cir. 2002); Howard v. Antilla, 294 F.3d 244 (1st Cir. 2002); KTRK Television v. Felder, 950 S.W.2d 100, 106 (Tex. Ct. App. 1997).

[417] Cole v. Star Tribune, 581 N.W.2d 364 (Minn. App. Ct. 1998) (publisher's reliance on wire services report); Karaduman v. Newsday, Inc., 51 N.Y.2d 531, 549, 416 N.E.2d 557, 566, 435 N.Y.S.2d 556, 566 (1980) ("a company or concern which simply republishes a work is entitled to place its reliance upon the research of the original publisher, absent a showing that the republisher had, or should have had, substantial reasons to question the accuracy").

[418] For further assessment, see 3 Dobbs, Hayden & Bublick, The Law of Torts § 549 (2d. ed. 2011 & Supp.)

[419] See SDV/ACCI, Inc. v. AT & T Corp., 522 F.3d 955 (9th Cir. 2008).

[420] Emo v. Milbank Mut. Ins. Co., 183 N.W.2d 508 (N.D. 1971).

[421] E.g., Ikani v. Bennett, 284 Ark. 409, 682 S.W.2d 747 (1985); Gattis v. Kilgo, 128 N.C. 402, 38 S.E. 931 (1901).

[422] Williams v. Tharp, 889 N.E.2d 870, 877 (Ind. Ct. App. 2008); Dragonas v. School Comm. of Melrose, 64 Mass. App. Ct. 429, 439, 833 N.E.2d 679, 688 (2005) ("Simple negligence, want of sound judgment, or hasty action will not cause loss of the privilege" (quoting)).

[423] Elliott v. Roach, 409 N.E.2d 661 (Ind. Ct. App. 1980); Pratt v. Nelson, 164 P.3d 366, 377 (Utah 2007); Restatement (Second) of Torts § 604 (1977). Sometimes courts view excessive publication as merely one way of

example, if the defendant has a common interest privilege to discuss church affairs with fellow church members, the privilege would be lost if he published defamatory material about church affairs on a radio talk show.[424] What is excessive is determined in part by the nature of the privilege, in part by practicality. A defendant is entitled to use a method of publication that involves an incidental communication to persons not within the scope of the privilege. If an employer is privileged to communicate materials to its employees in a company newsletter, the fact that the employees will sometimes circulate the letter in the community at large does not necessarily reflect excessive publication.[425] In contrast, a doctor, writing letters to individual patients to explain the departure of another doctor from the clinic, may be publishing excessively if he sends copies of the letter to physicians in other states.[426]

Inaccuracy in reporting public documents and proceedings. The privilege to make a fair report of public documents and proceedings is lost by substantial inaccuracy or unfair or slanted reporting, regardless of the publisher's intent. "If the gist or sting of the defamation in the official report is the same as the gist or sting in the news account, then the news item is a fair abridgement of the proceedings. The accuracy of the summary, not the truth or falsity of the information being summarized, is the 'benchmark of the privilege.' "[427] Neither the publisher's knowing falsehood nor his ill will is logically irrelevant, since publication of public documents and official proceedings is in the public interest. Either the publisher is the "agent" of the public which is entitled to read the original document, or the publisher is serving the public good by providing the basis for public monitoring of government. Consequently, the privilege is not lost when the publisher harbors "malice or knows that the public document contains defamatory falsehood."[428] Some authority, however, states that the privilege is lost if the public information is published with common law malice.[429]

Common law malice. The common law traditionally held that a privilege is abused or lost if the plaintiff showed that the defendant acted out of common law malice, meaning spite, ill will, or any purpose other than the one for which the privilege was intended to serve.[430] Some courts continue to repeat the old rule that the defendant's

---

showing common law malice or ill will. See Wayment v. Clear Channel Broad., Inc., 116 P.3d 271, 288 (Utah 2005) ("Evidence of malice in this context may include indications that the [statements] were excessively published").

[424] Cf. Kliebenstein v. Iowa Conference of the United Methodist Church, 663 N.W.2d 404 (Iowa 2003) (letter about member of congregation sent both to congregation and to others in the larger community would not be protected).

[425] Zinda v. Louisiana Pac. Corp., 149 Wis.2d 913, 440 N.W.2d 548 (1988).

[426] See Setliff v. Akins, 616 N.W.2d 878 (S.D. 2000).

[427] Maple Lanes, Inc. v. New Media Corp., 256 Ill. Dec. 124, 126, 751 N.E.2d 177, 179 (2001); see also Weber v. Lancaster Newspapers, Inc., 878 A.2d 63 (Pa. Super. 2005).

[428] Green Acres Trust v. London, 141 Ariz. 609, 618, 688 P.2d 617, 626 (1984); Wilson v. Meyer, 126 P.3d 276 (Colo. Ct. App. 2005); Solaia Tech., LLC. v. Specialty Publ'g Co., 221 Ill.2d 558, 304 Ill. Dec. 369, 852 N.E.2d 825 (2006); Wright v. Grove Sun Newspaper Co., 873 P.2d 983 (Okla. 1994); Restatement (Second) of Torts § 611 cmt. a (1977).

[429] Thomas v. Telegraph Publ'g Co., 155 N.H. 314, 929 A.2d 993 (2007).

[430] E.g., Smith v. Des Moines Pub. Sch., 259 F.3d 942 (8th Cir. 2001) (Iowa law); Delta Health Group, Inc. v. Stafford, 887 So.2d 887, 897 (Ala. 2004); Coleman v. Newark Morning Ledger Co., 29 N.J. 357, 375, 149 A.2d 193, 202 (1959) ("the privilege is lost if the publication is not made primarily for the purpose of furthering the interest which is entitled to protection" (quoting Prosser)); Brehany v. Nordstrom, Inc., 812 P.2d 49 (Utah 1991). Sometimes it is said that it is not malice itself that destroys the privilege but the fact that the defendant has gone beyond the purpose for which the privilege exists. Kelley v. Tanoos, 865 N.E.2d 593 (Ind. 2007). A purpose to undermine or prevent potential criticism of job performance might suffice. See Albert v. Loksen, 239 F.3d 256 (2d Cir. 2001). It may be that either common law malice in the sense of ill will or constitutional

spite or ill will suffices to destroy the privilege,[431] but the emphasis appears to be shifting to require proof, not merely that the defendant had unpleasant subjective motives, but rather that he was objectively at fault because he knowingly published a falsehood, or else was reckless, or at least negligent, with respect to the truth.[432] Malice in this sense could be shown by evidence that the defendant's chief motivation in publishing the defamation was based upon "ill will, hostility, threats, rivalry,"[433] a direct intent to injure, or a reckless disregard of the reputational consequences.[434] Occasionally courts say they permit an inference of common law malice from the intemperate or abusive language of the publication itself.[435] When a privilege exists, the common law presumption of malice from the mere publication of defamation disappears.

Malice that does not motivate publication. However, evidence of ill will is not by itself enough; the trier must have a basis for believing that the ill will motivated the publication. "If the defendant's statements were made to further the interest protected by the privilege, it matters not that defendant also despised plaintiff."[436] Even if one of the motives for publication was improper, the privilege is not lost unless the improper motive is the predominant one.[437]

§ 37.13 Revising Privileges After the Constitutional Cases

Two differences in constitutional fault. In a series of decisions beginning in 1964, the Supreme Court held that the First Amendment's free speech guarantee requires the libel suit plaintiff to prove fault in a wide band of cases described in later sections. For constitutional purposes, the treatment of fault differs in two distinct ways. First, the common law privileges introduced fault defensively, but under the constitutional decisions governing certain claims, the plaintiff must prove the defendant's fault as part of the plaintiff's prima facie case. If the plaintiff's proof of fault in her prima facie case would also suffice to defeat any privilege, the privilege issue becomes superfluous. Second, the fault sufficient to defeat the common law privilege was often a matter of motive or a bad state of mind, not desire to utter a falsehood; but under the constitutional decisions, the fault to be proven is the defendant's fault with respect to accuracy, such

---

malice in the sense of reckless disregard of the truth will suffice to destroy the privilege. See Hailstone v. Martinez, 169 Cal. App. 4th 728, 87 Cal. Rptr. 3d 347 (2008). One group of cases applies the same rule even to the public interest privilege, with the result that it will be dangerous for a citizen to report evidence to the police if the citizen also dislikes the supposed criminal. See Otten v. Schutt, 15 Wis. 2d 497, 113 N.W.2d 152 (1962); Kroh v. Kroh, 152 N.C. App. 347, 567 S.E.2d 760 (2002) (report to child protection agency that husband had abused defendant's children was unfounded and malicious, no privilege). Liability for honest report of evidence to officials merely because the reporter doubts the evidence was criticized in Dan B. Dobbs, Belief and Doubt in Malicious Prosecution and Libel, 21 Ariz. L. Rev. 607 (1979), arguing that the citizen-accuser should be free to rely upon officers to make the appropriate decision.

[431] Taus v. Loftus, 40 Cal. 4th 683, 721, 151 P.3d 1185, 1210,54 Cal. Rptr. 3d 775, 805 (2007); Dragonas v. School Comm. of Melrose, 64 Mass. App. Ct. 429, 833 N.E.2d 679 (2005); Richmond v. Nodland, 552 N.W.2d 586 (N.D. 1996).

[432] See Barreca v. Nickolas, 683 N.W.2d 111(Iowa 2004); Costello v. Hardy, 864 So.2d 129, 148 n.18 (La. 2004); Jackson v. Columbus, 117 Ohio St.3d 328, 331, 883 N.E.2d 1060, 1064 (2008).

[433] Clark v. America's First Credit Union, 585 So.2d 1367, 1371 (Ala. 1991).

[434] Kuwik v. Starmark Star Mktg. & Admin., Inc., 156 Ill.2d 16, 30, 619 N.E.2d 129, 135, 188 Ill.Dec. 765, 771 (1993).

[435] E.g., Blodgett v. University Club, 930 A.2d 210 (D.C. 2007) (language "so excessive, intemperate, unreasonable, and abusive as to forbid any other reasonable conclusion than that the defendant[s] [were] actuated by express malice"); Bauer v. State, 511 N.W.2d 447 (Minn. 1994).

[436] Liberman v. Gelstein, 80 N.Y.2d 429, 439, 605 N.E.2d 344, 350, 590 N.Y.S.2d 857, 863 (1992).

[437] Caudle v. Thomason, 992 F.Supp. 1 (D.D.C. 1997); DeNardo v. Bax, 147 P.3d 672 (Alaska 2006).

as intent to publish a falsehood. In particular, the plaintiff must prove either knowing or reckless falsehood or something like negligence with respect to the truth, but in neither case is the fault determined by motive. This difference is important because under the constitutional decisions a defendant's subjective motives are of no interest as long as he believed (or sometimes reasonably believed) he was publishing the truth.

Potential common law responses. To avoid needless complexity, the common law could respond to these constitutional changes by (1) putting the burden upon the plaintiff to prove some kind of fault in the first instance and dropping the whole privilege-defense approach applied in the "interest" privileges; and (2) using the fault concepts and terminology applied in the constitutional cases and dropping the malice and motive approaches to fault on the ground that one set of fault principles is quite sufficient and that using two confuses and complicates needlessly. Specifically, the plaintiff would be required to prove knowing, reckless, or at least negligent falsehood in all cases. The degree of fault required could vary according circumstances, just as it does in the constitutional cases. Such a common law response would help simplify and modernize libel law. Under this approach, if the plaintiff proves the requisite fault as part of her case, there is no need to reconsider fault again in a defense. If she does not prove fault, her prima facie case fails, and the issue of privilege is again unnecessary.

Restatement. The Second Restatement takes a view something like this in providing that where common law malice formerly destroyed a privilege, the privilege would now be destroyed only by proof that the defendant knowingly or recklessly published a falsehood.[438] Thus proof of knowing or reckless falsehood as part of the plaintiff's prima facie case would destroy any of the interest privileges.[439] None of this applies, however, to the privilege of fair reporting of public materials, which turns on accuracy and fairness.

Authorities. The implications of the constitutional changes have not been universally recognized and the jurisprudence of privilege has not fully developed these ideas. Some courts have not altered their approach to the common law privilege in light of the constitutional decisions. Among those courts that have modified their abuse of privileges rules, some, with the Restatement, drop common law malice out of the picture and hold that the interest privileges are destroyed only by knowing or reckless falsehood.[440] Alternatively, courts may require the plaintiff to prove knowing or reckless falsehood as part of her prima facie case, so that the issue of privilege is implicitly decided before it is reached even when constitutional rules do not require such a

---

[438] Restatement (Second) of Torts § 600 (1977).

[439] See Haworth v. Feigon, 623 A.2d 150 (Me. 1993) (trial judge charged jury that the plaintiff had to prove knowing or reckless falsehood, consequently it was not reversible error that trial judge failed to charge on privilege).

[440] De Leon v. Saint Joseph Hosp., Inc., 871 F.2d 1229 (4th Cir. 1989); Barreca v. Nickolas, 683 N.W.2d 111 (Iowa 2004) (dropping motive or malice test in favor of a knowing or reckless falsehood test when local councilman invokes a qualified privilege); Kennedy v. Sheriff of E. Baton Rouge, 920 So.2d 217 (La. 2006) (knowing or reckless falsehood required to show abuse of the public interest privilege to report suspected crime to police); Eckman v. Cooper Tire & Rubber Co., 893 So.2d 1049, 1053 (Miss. 2005); Pope v. Motel 6, 114 P.3d 277 (Nev. 2005) (report to police given a qualified privilege; "the plaintiff must prove by a preponderance of the evidence that the defendant abused the privilege by publishing the defamatory communication . . . demonstrating that a statement is published with knowledge that it was false or with reckless disregard for its veracity"); Hagler v. Proctor & Gamble Mfg. Co., 884 S.W.2d 771 (Tex. 1994).

result.[441] A third reaction to the constitutional decisions treats either knowing or reckless falsehood or common law malice as sufficient to destroy the privilege.[442]

§ 37.14 The Anti-SLAPP Statutes

Petition and association. The First Amendment guarantees the right to petition government. Petitioning activity is understood in a broad sense to include all kinds of public participation in issues facing governmental bodies and even issues that may face them in the future. Such petitioning activity is not protected by absolute immunity,[443] but is constitutionally protected in the same way as other forms of speech and protected by antitrust law.[444]

Statutory protections. Following a series of articles and speeches claiming that individuals who speak out on public issues are subject to retaliatory lawsuits on a vast scale,[445] a number of states enacted statutes providing special absolute immunities[446] or qualified immunities[447] to citizens who exercise their right to petition by speaking on

---

[441] Turf Lawnmower Repair, Inc. v. Bergen Record Corp., 139 N.J. 392, 655 A.2d 417 (1994) (recognizing knowing or reckless falsehood standard for some cases, negligence for others). In Kennedy v. Sheriff of East Baton Rouge, 920 So.2d 217 (La. 2006), the court required proof of negligence or greater fault on the plaintiff's prima facie case, but held that once the defendant established grounds for a privileged report to the police, the plaintiff would have the burden of showing the defendant was guilty of even greater fault, knowing or reckless falsehood in making the report. Since a report to the police would always establish the privilege, with only the abuse issue remaining, this seems to work out to be substantively the same as saying that the plaintiff must prove knowing or reckless falsehood in this category of cases.

[442] Schrader v. Eli Lilly & Co., 639 N.E.2d 258 (Ind. 1994); Haworth v. Feigon, 623 A.2d 150 (Me. 1993); Liberman v. Gelstein, 80 N.Y.2d 429, 605 N.E.2d 344, 590 N.Y.S.2d 857 (1992).

[443] McDonald v. Smith, 472 U.S. 479, 105 S.Ct. 2787, 86 L.Ed.2d 384 (1985).

[444] A line of Supreme Court decisions established that federal antitrust laws did not apply to petitioning activity unless the petitioning was a sham to carry forward anti-competitive conduct. To show sham litigation and thus to circumvent the right to petition defense, the plaintiff had to show that the litigation was objectively baseless and also, subjectively, brought for some improper purpose, to gain collateral advantage, not to win. See Professional Real Estate Investors, Inc. v. Columbia Pictures Indus., Inc., 508 U.S. 49, 113 S.Ct. 1920, 123 L.Ed.2d 611 (1993). The Court perhaps implied that the First Amendment right of petition would dictate such a rule aside from statutory construction, and some other courts have explicitly so held. See Titan Am., LLC v. Riverton Inv. Corp., 264 Va. 292, 569 S.E.2d 57 (2002).

[445] See George W. Pring & Penelope Canan, SLAPPs: Getting Sued for Speaking Out (1996); Penelope Canan & George W. Pring, Studying Strategic Lawsuits Against Public Participating: Mixing Quantitative and Qualitative Approaches, 22 L. & Soc'y Rev. 385 (1988); George W. Pring, SLAPPS: Strategic Lawsuits Against Public Participation, 7 Pace Envt'l L. Rev. 3 (1989); George W. Pring & Penelope Canan, "Strategic Lawsuits Against Public Participation" ("Slapps"): An Introduction for Bench, Bar and Bystanders, 12 Bridgeport L. Rev. 937 (1992).

[446] Some statutes appear to afford an absolute immunity by protecting all petitioning activity unless it is a sham in the sense that it is not really aimed at procuring favorable government action. R.I. Gen. L. § 9–33–2 (labeling the immunity conditional, however). The Massachusetts practice is structured. The defendant raising the anti-SLAPP statute must first make a threshold showing that the suit against him was based on petitioning activities and only on such activities. Once that is shown, the plaintiff must suffer dismissal unless she can show that "the defendants' [petitioning] activities were devoid of any reasonable factual support or any arguable basis in law." The defendant must make this showing by a preponderance of the evidence. Baker v. Parsons, 434 Mass. 543, 750 N.E.2d 953 (2001). California's statute halts discovery, Cal. Code Civ. Proc. § 425.16 (g), and grants a motion to strike the claim unless the plaintiff can show she will probably prevail. Id. § 425.16 (b). This has worked out to be an absolute immunity or something close to it in some instances. See Dixon v. Superior Court Scientific Res. Surveys, Inc., 30 Cal. App. 4th 733, 36 Cal. Rptr. 2d 687 (1994).

[447] Some statutes offer a qualified immunity only, defeasible if the defendant publishes in bad faith. Nev. Rev. Stat. § 41.650; Rev. Code. Wash. Ann. § 4.24.510. The Delaware and New York statutes do not grant an absolute immunity but merely invoke, on behalf of public participants, the constitutional rules requiring proof of knowing or reckless falsehood. 10 Del. Code Ann. § 8136; N.Y. Civ. Rts. L. § 76–a. Georgia merely requires the plaintiff to verify the complaint if it is directed at speech or petitioning activity. See Denton v. Browns Mill Dev. Co., Inc., 275 Ga. 2, 561 S.E.2d 431 (2002).

public issues[448] or by addressing public officers or agencies, including courts,[449] to express their claims or grievances.[450] The statutes provide protection by authorizing a special motion to strike or dismiss when it appears that the suit against the defendant, whether for defamation or otherwise,[451] complains of the defendant's petitioning activity on a matter of public interest.[452] The motion must be granted unless the plaintiff can convince the court that she will probably prevail on the merits.[453] If speech counts as petitioning activity, the motive for the speech would seem to be irrelevant to the statutory immunity.[454] Similarly, statutes apply to protect the defendant's petitioning activity even if the plaintiff has no intent to chill the defendant's exercise of this constitutional right and even if the plaintiff's suit has no actual chilling effect.[455]

Varied standards. Case results are somewhat dependent upon statutory terms. Some authority protects even those defendants who indulge in knowing or reckless falsehood,[456] but other authority holds that the plaintiff may prevail by proving that the defendant's petitioning activity or speech is without factual or legal basis,[457] a test that sounds similar to the knowing or reckless falsehood test used in First Amendment libel cases.[458] Similarly, it has been held that the defendant cannot successfully invoke the

---

[448] In Massachusetts, the statute applies even when the defendant is addressing a private interest. See Duracraft Corp. v. Holmes Prods. Corp., 427 Mass. 156, 691 N.E.2d 935 (1998). But other statutes may apply more restrictively, sometimes only when the plaintiff has applied for a public permit or licenses or the like, e.g., N.Y. Civ. Rts. L. § 76–a, or where the defendant speaks in a public forum or on a public issue, leaving issues about what counts as public forum for petitioning activity and what counts as a public issue. A single statute may be interpreted quite narrowly or quite broadly in determining public interest and public fora. Compare Condit v. Nat'l Enquirer, Inc., 248 F.Supp. 2d 945 (E.D. Cal. 2002) (seemingly, a tabloid publication which published a statement that the plaintiff "verbally attacked" Chandra Levy just days before Levy's disappearance was not addressing an issue of public interest; the case was "not the type of meritless case brought to obtain a financial or political advantage over or to silence opposition from a defendant, which California's anti-SLAPP statute is designed to discourage"), with Nygard, Inc. v. Uusi-Keerttula, 159 Cal. App. 4th 1027, 72 Cal. Rptr. 3d 210 (2008) (defendant's interview in a magazine discussing work conditions when he was employed by plaintiff was an issue of public significance because public was interested and publication in a magazine is publication in a public forum).

[449] Navellier v. Sletten, 29 Cal. 4th 82, 52 P.3d 703, 124 Cal. Rptr. 2d 530 (2002) (by statutory definition).

[450] In Kobrin v. Gastfriend, 443 Mass. 327, 821 N.E.2d 60 (2005), the court concluded that a paid witness was not entitled to the protection of the anti-SLAPP statute because he was not seeking redress or petitioning on his own behalf.

[451] E.g., Kibler v. Northern Inyo County Local Hosp. Dist., 39 Cal.4th 192, 138 P.3d 193 (2006) (defamation, abuse of process, and interference with plaintiff's practice of medicine); Huntingdon Life Scis., Inc. v. Stop Huntingdon Animal Cruelty USA, Inc., 129 Cal. App. 4th 1228, 29 Cal. Rptr. 3d 521 (2005) (suit for harassment and emotional distress by protestors at the plaintiff's home; statute applied but the plaintiff met her burden of showing probability of success); Adams v. Whitman, 62 Mass. App. Ct. 850, 822 N.E.2d 727 (2005) (abuse of process claim dismissed under the anti-SLAPP statute; it was devoid of legal and factual support because essential allegations were both unverified and conclusory).

[452] Some statutes are tailored much more narrowly, to protect only petitioning activity addressed to government or quasi-governmental bodies.

[453] See Cal. Civ. Proc. Code § 425.16(b)(1). Thus the statute "subjects to potential dismissal only those actions in which the plaintiff cannot state and substantiate a legally sufficient claim." Navellier v. Sletten, 29 Cal. 4th 82, 52 P.3d 703 (2002).

[454] See Equilon Enters., LLC v. Consumer Cause, Inc., 29 Cal.4th 53, 52 P.3d 685, 124 Cal.Rptr.2d 507 (2002); Office One, Inc. v. Lopez, 437 Mass. 113, 769 N.E.2d 749 (2002).

[455] City of Cotati v. Cashman, 29 Cal.4th 69, 52 P.3d 695, 124 Cal.Rptr.2d 519 (2002).

[456] See Dixon v. Superior Court Scientific Res. Surveys, Inc., 30 Cal. App. 4th 733, 36 Cal. Rptr. 2d 687 (1994).

[457] Office One, Inc. v. Lopez, 437 Mass. 113, 769 N.E.2d 749 (2002).

[458] See § 37.15.

anti-SLAPP statutes to protect speech or petitioning activity that was illegal as a matter of law.[459]

Attorney fees, discovery and unequal protections? The statutes also provide for attorney fee awards to the defendant who prevails on the special motion to dismiss[460] as well as a halt to discovery.[461] These statutory provisions raise the question whether the statutes adequately protect the plaintiff's own right to petition for redress of grievances by way of a lawsuit.[462] As the Massachusetts court said, "By protecting one party's exercise of its right of petition, unless it can be shown to be sham petitioning, the statute impinges on the adverse party's exercise of its right to petition, even when it is not engaged in sham petitioning."[463] New Hampshire has held that such a statute would be unconstitutional as a deprivation of jury trial rights.[464]

D. CONSTITUTIONAL LIMITATIONS ON RECOVERY

§ 37.15   Constitutional Limitations on Recovery

First Amendment. The First Amendment to the United States Constitution applies through the Fourteenth Amendment[465] to restrict some liabilities for defamation. The Constitution may similarly restrict other torts growing out of communication or otherwise,[466] but this chapter concerns only the impact on defamation claims. In some cases, the First Amendment completely immunizes publishers of allegedly defamatory material; in others, it adds new elements to be proved by the plaintiff and a qualitatively heavier burden of proving them by convincing evidence.

Constitutionally overriding common law rules. Beginning in 1964, the Supreme Court recognized that the First Amendment's free speech provisions imposed limits on common law strict liability for defamation. The common law rules did not require a defamation plaintiff to prove fault, falsity, or actual damages. Each of these elements, sometimes all of them, is now constitutionally required in some cases. These elements are only minimum constitutional protections for speech; the states are free to restrict tort liability further. The exact constitutional requirements vary, however, depending largely upon the status of the plaintiff, so the rules for public officials and public figures are different from those applied to private persons.

---

[459]   Flatley v. Mauro, 39 Cal. 4th 299, 139 P.3d 2, 46 Cal. Rptr. 3d 606 (2006) (plaintiff asserted several claims, including "extortion" and defamation based on defendant's threats to expose the plaintiff's alleged misdeeds; defendant's threats as a matter of law were extortionate under a criminal statute and that prevented his reliance upon the anti-SLAPP statute).

[460]   See Equilon Enters., LLC, 29 Cal.4th 53, 52 P.3d 685, 124 Cal.Rptr.2d 507 (2002).

[461]   E.g., Cal. Civ. Proc. Code § 425.16 (g).

[462]   See Joseph W. Beatty, The Legal Literature on SLAPPs: A Look Behind the Smoke Nine Years after Professor Pring and Canan First Yelled "Fire!", 9 U. Fla. J.L. & Pub. Pol'y 85 (1997).

[463]   Duracraft Corp. v. Holmes Prods. Corp., 427 Mass. 156, 691 N.E.2d 935 (1998).

[464]   Opinion of the Justices (SLAPP Suit Procedure), 138 N.H. 445, 641 A.2d 1012 (1994).

[465]   Many cases have so held, including the best-known libel case, New York Times Co. v. Sullivan, 376 U.S. 254, 84 S.Ct. 710, 11 L.Ed.2d 686 (1964).

[466]   E.g., Westbrook v. Penley, 231 S.W.3d 389 (Tex. 2007) (plaintiff's clergyman was also her professional counselor, but he revealed confidential communications to the church, condemning the plaintiff; the defamation claim dismissed below and the remaining professional negligence claim was dismissed on Constitutional grounds by the Texas Supreme Court). The case is criticized in Recent Cases, 121 Harv. L. Rev. 676 (2007).

Some basic constitutional modifications. Much contemporary litigation in defamation actions is concerned with the First Amendment's guarantee of free speech and press. Whether freedom of speech and freedom of the press are merely two instances of the same underlying freedom or not, together or separately they have come to modify common law rules of defamation liability:

(1) *Issues of public concern and public official or figure.* If the plaintiff is a public official or public figure, she is required to prove (a) falsity of the defendant's publication, and (b) that the defendant knowingly or recklessly published the falsehood.

(2) *Issues of public concern, private plaintiff.* If the plaintiff is not a public official or public figure but the issue is one of public concern, the plaintiff is required to prove (a) falsity, (b) "some fault" and (c) actual damages.

(3) *Opinion.* In addition, statements that do not assert matters that are provably false—often called opinion statements—are protected, at least where issues of public concern are involved.[467]

(4) *Private issues, private plaintiffs.* Purely private persons are not necessarily governed by these rules where the defamation involves no issue of public concern.

Rationales for protecting criticism of public officials. The constitutional basis for rules requiring fault and falsity lies in the First Amendment to the United States Constitution, which broadly protects free speech against legal constraints. Because libel judgments, or even the possibility of a libel suit, can promote self-censorship that chills criticism of government and other public discussion, defamation actions potentially infringe rights of speech, rights of association and rights to petition government. This is most especially true when the plaintiff is a public official suing for a publication that may throw light on governmental operations. Criticism of government is at the very heart of the free speech right and such criticism is focused most often and most effectively on a particular official. For these reasons, and because some factual error is inevitable in robust debate, the strict liability imposed at common law is problematic in a democratic society.[468] In a sense, it is the public, not the courts, that must always judge public officials. Ideas like these were developed at length in the landmark 1964 decision, *New York Times Co. v. Sullivan.*[469]

---

[467] § 37.19.

[468] A circumscribed form of strict liability, analogous to the strict liability of product manufacturers, might have been more justified as applied to defendants whose product is culture- and value-shaping communication, especially in light of the enormous power mass publishers wield. That was not the common law system, however, and the argument for such a system now is undercut to some degree by the capacity of individuals to reach wide audiences on the internet.

[469] New York Times Co. v. Sullivan, 376 U.S. 254, 84 S.Ct. 710, 11L.Ed.2d 686 (1964), arose out of the controversies and feelings of the civil rights struggle in the 1960s. A group of responsible persons published an advertisement in the New York Times soliciting donations, in part to defend Dr. Martin Luther King, who stood charged with perjury in Alabama. The advertisement asserted that those upholding civil rights were being subjected to a "wave of terror," and that "Southern violators" had bombed King's home and that "They have arrested him seven times. . . ." The police commissioner of Montgomery, Sullivan, sued the New York Times claiming defamation. He argued that the advertisement implicitly identified those who arrested King as Southern violators who also bombed his home. Since the police commissioner was supervisor of the police, he claimed the advertisement libeled him even though he was not named. The Alabama Supreme Court affirmed a judgment against the New York Times for $500,000. It was this judgment that was reversed by the Supreme Court's requirement of a knowing or reckless falsehood.

Rationales for the Modifications

Rationales for protecting criticism of public figures. Three years after the *Times-Sullivan* decision, the Supreme Court extended its knowing or reckless falsehood rules to cover publications about public figures who were not public officials.[470] The reason given in Chief Justice Warren's opinion was that public figures can exercise informal power and influence over government and social decisions that may be as important as the power exercised by officials. However, the Court also seemed to say that public figures had ready access to media so that they could counter criticism, and later the Court seemed to put a great deal of emphasis on the fact that public figures are ordinarily in the public eye because they choose to be.[471]

Rationales for protections for private persons, issues of public concern. Observers think that public officials and public figures in the constitutional rules were really stand-ins for efforts to foster freedom of speech about public issues. In fact, in 1971, the governing plurality in *Rosenbloom v. Metromedia*[472] adopted the view that publications about matters of public concern fell under the *Times-Sullivan* protections. However, three years later, in *Gertz*,[473] a divided Court rejected the *Rosenbloom* decision. The *Gertz* argument for the proposition that "some" fault was enough in private plaintiff cases turned on its view that First Amendment values had to be accommodated to the states' interests in redressing defamation. The *Gertz* Court thought the state's interest in redressing defamation of private persons was much stronger than its interest in redressing defamation of public figures, who, after all, would ordinarily have often chosen the limelight and its risks of defamation. Given the Court's balancing of the states' general interest and the First Amendment concerns, the Court hit on the requirement of "some fault" plus actual damages as the appropriate compromise or "accommodation" of those interests.[474]

Rationales for no constitutional protections: private persons, issues not of public concern. In the case of private plaintiffs suing for defamation that does not involve issues of public concern, the same balancing of state interests against the First Amendment led the Court to hold in *Dun & Bradstreet* that the states were free to revert to the common law of presumed damages.[475]

An extra layer of constitutional analysis. The constitutional rules requiring fault, falsity, and damages hold a potential for rationalizing and simplifying the law of defamation. In fact, however, because the rules vary in each category, much of the dispute in libel cases now turns on how to categorize the plaintiff and the alleged defamation. The result is that new layers have been added to the law of defamation and that it has become more, not less, complex.

Special Rules for Public Issues and Public Official or Figure Plaintiffs

Fault required in suits by public official and public figures. Under the rule developed in and after *New York Times Co. v. Sullivan*, when the plaintiff is a public

---

[470]   Curtis Publ'g Co. v. Butts, 388 U.S. 130, 87 S.Ct. 1975, 18 L.Ed.2d 1094 (1967).

[471]   Gertz v. Robert Welch, Inc., 418 U.S. 323, 94 S.Ct. 2997, 41 L.Ed.2d 789 (1974).

[472]   403 U.S. 29, 91 S.Ct. 1811, 29 L.Ed.2d 296 (1971).

[473]   Gertz v. Robert Welch, Inc., 418 U.S. 323, 94 S.Ct. 2997, 41 L.Ed.2d 789 (1974).

[474]   States may thus adopt a negligence standard or any more demanding standard of fault. See § 565.

[475]   Dun & Bradstreet, Inc. v. Greenmoss Builders, Inc., 472 U.S. 749, 105 S.Ct. 2939, 86 L.Ed.2d 593 (1985).

official, a candidate for public office, or a public figure suing for defamation, the plaintiff's claim must be established by proving whatever is required under state tort law *and,* as a constitutional requirement, that the defendant published (a) a falsehood, (b) knowing it to be false or acting in reckless disregard whether it was true or false. [476] If the defendant originally published knowing of the falsehood or acting recklessly because he entertained serious doubts about the truth of his publication,[477] he would be liable for repetition by others under the common law rule, even if the repeaters themselves did not publish knowingly or recklessly.[478]

"Actual malice" vs. knowing or reckless falsehood. The Supreme Court characterized its requirement of a knowing or reckless falsehood as "actual malice." The term has caused confusion, because constitutional "actual malice" does not mean common law malice in the sense of spite or ill will. Instead the actual malice terminology in the constitutional decisions is only a label applied to the requirement of knowing or reckless falsehood. Thus, while the defendant's knowing falsehood about the plaintiff might be evidence of ill will or spite, spite without a knowing or reckless falsehood will not be sufficient where public officials or public figures are plaintiffs in the defamation action.[479] As courts have said, the constitutional focus on is the defendant's attitude toward the truth, not his attitude toward the plaintiff.[480] Consequently, it may facilitate analysis to avoid the actual malice terminology and specify knowing or reckless falsehood instead.

Quantum of proof and damages. The constitutionally required elements must be proved with "convincing clarity."[481] This rule for public official and public figure plaintiffs does not require proof of actual harm to reputation.[482] Thus if the plaintiff makes the required showing of knowing or reckless falsehood, she will be constitutionally permitted to recover presumed damages and punitive damages where state law itself permits such recoveries.[483]

Fair comment distinguished. The constitutional public official/public figure rule is not a constitutional version of the fair comment privilege. The fair comment privilege protects only "comment" and not errors of facts. In addition, it leaves the burden upon the defendant to justify the publication. Because the burden under the *Times-Sullivan* rule is upon the plaintiff, it is not even helpful to think of the constitutional rule as a

---

[476] New York Times Co. v. Sullivan, 376 U.S. 254, 84 S.Ct. 710, 11 L.Ed.2d 686 (1964) (public officials); Curtis Publ'g Co. v. Butts, 388 U.S. 130, 87 S.Ct. 1975, 18 L.Ed.2d 1094 (1967) (public figures).

[477] On the recklessness standard, see See 3 Dobbs, Hayden & Bublick, The Law of Torts § 564 (2d. ed. 2011 & Supp.).

[478] Murphy v. Boston Herald, Inc., 449 Mass. 42, 865 N.E.2d 746 (2007).

[479] See, e.g., Greenbelt Coop. Publ'g Ass'n v. Bresler, 253 Md. 324, 252 A.2d 755 (1969) (reversed partly because trial judge instructed on ill will or spite as malice).

[480] Thomas v. Telegraph Publ'g Co., 155 N.H. 314, 328, 929 A.2d 993, 1007 (2007); Jackson v. Columbus, 117 Ohio St.3d 328, 334, 883 N.E.2d 1060, 1067 (2008).

[481] Some courts do not apply that standard to the issue of falsity as distinct from issues of fault. See § 37.18.

[482] New York Times Co. v. Sullivan, 376 U.S. 254, 84 S.Ct. 710, 11 L.Ed.2d 686 (1964). See Walker v. Kiousis, 93 Cal. App. 4th 1432, 114 Cal. Rptr. 2d 69 (2001).

[483] E.g., Lyons v. Nichols, 63 Conn. App. 761, 778 A.2d 246 (2001) (presumed damages permitted to a public figure upon showing of knowing or reckless falsehood, and where no harm was proven, the court would be free to award "nominal" damages of $100 plus punitive damages); Hanlon v. Davis, 76 Md. App. 339, 545 A.2d 72 (1988) (even private person could recover presumed damages if he proves knowing or reckless falsehood); Mitchell v. Griffin Television, LLC, 60 P.3d 1058 (Okla. Civ. App. 2002) (similar); Bentley v. Bunton, 94 S.W.3d 561 (Tex. 2002).

"privilege." A privilege is sustained only if the defendant carries the burden of proof and persuasion.

Special Rules for Public Issues and Private Plaintiffs

On issues of public concern—constitutional rules. Constitutional rules applied to private persons suing for defamation differ considerably from those applied to public official/public figure plaintiffs. A private person plaintiff who sues for defamation arising from publication of matters of public concern must prove whatever is required under state tort law *and* that the defendant (a) published a falsehood; (b) that he was negligent or otherwise at fault in failing to ascertain or state the truth; and (c) that the plaintiff suffered actual harm to reputation as a result.

Not only must the plaintiff prove actual harm, but she is limited to a recovery of "actual damages." This rule operates to exclude recoveries of the old common law presumed damages and likewise to exclude punitive damages unless the plaintiff proves a knowing or reckless falsehood.[484] However, the requirement of actual injury or actual harm is not a requirement of pecuniary loss; genuine loss of reputation or emotional harm will qualify as actual injury.[485] A few doubts remain about the exact scope of the rules, for example, whether they apply only to media publications.[486]

Added state requirements. States are free to impose more demanding requirements than those imposed by the Constitution. Many states impose a negligence standard for private person plaintiffs where the issue involves public concern, but some require such plaintiffs to make proof under the more demanding knowing or reckless falsehood standard.[487] The anti-SLAPP statutes may also, in effect, impose special burdens on private plaintiffs.[488]

No Special Protections for Private Issues and Private Plaintiffs

On issues of no public concern. The United States Supreme Court, in *Dun & Bradstreet, Inc. v. Greenmoss Builders, Inc.,*[489] held that when a private person who is neither a public official nor a public figure sues for defamation arising from publication of matters that are *not* of public concern, she need not prove actual damages as required in the private person, public concern cases. Thus the common law rule of presumed damages can be applied by the states to cases in this category if the states are so minded.[490]

Several decisions have said or assumed that the *Dun & Bradstreet* case means that *all* of the common law rules remain intact, not merely the damages rule.[491] That would

---

[484] Gertz v. Robert Welch, Inc., 418 U.S. 323, 94 S.Ct. 2997 (1974).

[485] Id. at 350 n.1, 94 S.Ct. at 3012 n.1 ("actual injury is not limited to out-of-pocket loss" but includes "impairment of reputation and standing in the community, personal humiliation, and mental anguish and suffering" and "there need be no evidence which assigns an actual dollar value to the injury").

[486] Francis M. Dougherty, Annotation, Defamation: Application of New York Times And Related Standards to Nonmedia Defendants, 38 A.L.R.4th 1114 (1981).

[487] See 3 Dobbs, Hayden & Bublick, The Law of Torts § 565 (2d. ed. 2011 & Supp.).

[488] See § 37.14.

[489] 472 U.S. 749, 105 S.Ct. 2939, 86 L.Ed.2d 593 (1985).

[490] See, e.g., W.J.A. v. D.A., 210 N.J. 229, 43 A.3d 1148, 40 Media L. Rep. (BNA) 1830 (2012) (false accusations of child molestation; where statements involved only matters of private concern and the plaintiff is a private person, doctrine of presumed damages would be retained).

[491] See Dombey v. Phoenix Newspapers, Inc., 150 Ariz. 476, 724 P.2d 562 (1986); Cox v. Hatch, 761 P.2d 556 (Utah 1988).

mean that in the private person case where the issue is not of public concern, the states would also be free to presume falsehood as well as damages, and possibly even to presume that the defendant was at fault; courts could go back to the old common law of prima facie strict liability in this class of cases. If the rules develop along these lines, courts in private person cases will be required to determine what counts as an issue of public concern.[492]

§ 37.16   Who Are Public Officials

Status a question of law. Public officials and public figures come under the same substantive rule: both must prove knowing or reckless falsehood. The determination of public official[493] and public figure[494] status on any given set of facts is for the judge, not the jury.

Definitions and limitations. States sometimes have their own definitions of "official" for various purposes, but those definitions do not control the constitutional rule. Under the Supreme Court's decision in *Rosenblatt v. Baer*, public officials include, "at the very least," all government employees who have substantial responsibility in government affairs.[495]

Other factors and limitations. Some courts have added other significant factors. For example, a public employee whose work could have an impact on everyday life of citizens or could wreak social harm might well be considered to be a public official for purposes of the *Times-Sullivan* rule.[496] These definitions do not limit the public official category to government employees who issue orders or those who are at upper levels of the political hierarchy. There is, however, a limit. The plaintiff is not a public official under the *Times-Sullivan* rule unless she holds a position that "would invite public scrutiny and discussion of the person holding it, entirely apart from the scrutiny and discussion occasioned by the particular charges in controversy."[497] In what seems to be a departure from the text of the *Rosenblatt* test, some courts seem to be conflating the public official test with the public figure test.[498]

Former public officials and candidates for public position. Departure or retirement from public office does not make the activities of public officials of any less public

---

[492]   Robert D. Sack, Sack on Defamation: Libel, Slander, and Related Problems § 6.6 (available, updated, on Westlaw).

[493]   See Dixon v. International Bhd. of Police Officers, 504 F.3d 73, 87 (1st Cir. 2007).

[494]   Costello v. Ocean County Observer, 136 N.J. 594, 643 A.2d 1012, 44 A.L.R.5th 799 (1994); Krueger v. Austad, 545 N.W.2d 205 (S.D. 1996).

[495]   Rosenblatt v. Baer, 383 U.S. 75, 85, 86 S. Ct. 669, 676 (1966). But in Mandel v. The Boston Phoenix, Inc., 322 F.Supp.2d 39, 42 (D. Mass. 2004), vacated on other grounds, 456 F.3d 198 (1st Cir. 2006), "at the very least" became "only"—"only those employees with 'substantial responsibility for or control over the conduct of government affairs' are deemed public officials." Mandel did not invent this twist, but got it from Kassel v. Gannett Co., Inc., 875 F.2d 935 (1st Cir. 1989), where the court also imported tests of "public figure" to determine "public official" status.

[496]   Lane v. MPG Newspapers, 438 Mass. 476, 781 N.E.2d 800 (2003).

[497]   Rosenblatt v. Baer, 383 U.S. 75, 86, 86 S. Ct. 669, 676 n.13 (1966).

[498]   In Mandel v. Boston Phoenix, Inc., 456 F.3d 198 (1st Cir. 2006), the court seemed to say that public official status is determined by "taking into account: (i) the extent to which the inherent attributes of a position define it as one of influence over issues of public importance; (ii) the position's special access to the media as a means of self-help; and (iii) the risk of diminished privacy assumed upon taking the position." The latter two points seem to be taken directly from the public figure test. In fact, the First Circuit, in its earlier decision in Kassel v. Gannet Co., Inc., 875 F.2d 935 (1st Cir. 1989), expressly took them from Gertz' definition of public *figures*. As to public figure tests, see § 560.

concern. Consequently, discussion of former public officials, at least in connection with their activities while holding public office, are protected under the rule for public officials.[499] The same applies to candidates for governmental positions.[500]

Examples of public officials. A number of persons in governmental positions easily qualify as public officials because of their substantial responsibility in the conduct of government affairs. Federal, state, and local elected officials would almost always count as public officials.[501] So would a good many others who act in positions of authority, management, or independence in their sphere of operation.[502] Police officers, with their potential for substantial effects on lives of citizens, are usually held to be public officials.[503] But the same reasoning is not always applied; a few cases have held that public school teachers and even school principals, whose effect on the lives of citizens for good or bad is profound, are not public officials.[504] Other courts insist that as public education is a vital matter to society, public school principals and teachers are public officials whose capacities can be discussed under the *Times-Sullivan* rule.[505] Numerous other government employees have litigated these issues with similar differences in results.[506]

§ 37.17 Who Are Public Figures

Public figures. Because public figures as well as public officials come under the *Times-Sullivan* rules requiring the plaintiff to prove knowing or reckless falsehood by clear and convincing evidence,[507] courts are called upon to determine which plaintiffs are public figures. The Supreme Court has recognized two categories of public figure, with

---

[499] Rosenblatt v. Baer, 383 U.S. 75, 87, 86 S.Ct. 669, 676, 15 L.Ed.2d 597 (1966); Revell v. Hoffman, 309 F.3d 1228 (10th Cir. 2002).

[500] Monitor Patriot Co. v. Roy, 401 U.S. 265, 91 S.Ct. 621, 28 L.Ed.2d 35 (1971) (candidates could be considered either public officials or public figures).

[501] See Ocala Star-Banner Co. v. Damron, 401 U.S. 295, 91 S.Ct. 628, 28 L.Ed.2d 57 (1971) (mayor); Lane v. MPG Newspapers, 438 Mass. 476, 781 N.E.2d 800 (2003); Krueger v. Austad, 545 N.W.2d 205 (S.D. 1996) (state senator).

[502] Barnett v. Mobile County Personnel Bd., 536 So.2d 46 (Ala. 1988) (town clerk in charge of payroll); Demby v. English, 667 So.2d 350 (Fla. Dist. Ct. App. 1995) (director of animal control).

[503] Moriarty v. Lippe, 162 Conn. 371, 378, 294 A.2d 326, 330–331 (1972) (although low-ranking, "a patrolman's office, if abused, has great potential for social harm and thus invites independent interest in the qualifications and performance of the person who holds the position"); Rotkiewicz v. Sadowsky, 431 Mass. 748, 730 N.E.2d 282 (2000); Costello v. Ocean County Observer, 136 N.J. 594, 643 A.2d 1012, 44 A.L.R.5th 799 (1994); Hall v. Rogers, 490 A.2d 502 (R.I. 1985) (police officers are public officials, semble, as a matter of law). But cf. Nash v. Keene Publ'g Corp., 498 A.2d 348 (N. H. 1985) (jury question whether officer was public official).

[504] McCurcheon v. Moran, 99 Ill. App.3d 421, 424, 425 N.E.2d 1130, 1133, 54 Ill. Dec. 913, 916 (1981).

[505] Johnson v. Robbinsdale Indep. Sch. Dist. No. 281, 827 F.Supp. 1439, 1443 (D. Minn. 1993) ("Education of children is of vital importance to our society. . . . A contrary holding would stifle public debate about important local issues"); Sewell v. Brookbank, 119 Ariz. 422, 581 P.2d 267 (Ct. App. 1978); Kelley v. Bonney, 221 Conn. 549, 606 A.2d 693, 709 (1992).

[506] E.g., Fiacco v. Sigma Alpha Epsilon Fraternity, 528 F.3d 94 (1st Cir. 2008) (a university administrator a public official, but conflating the public official test with public figure tests); Ortego v. Hickerson, 989 So.2d 777 (La. Ct. App. 2008) (executive director of housing authority a public official); Porcari v. Gannett Satellite Info. Network, Inc., 50 A.D.3d 993, 856 N.Y.S.2d 217 (2008) (lawyer employed in city attorney's office was *not* a public official); Scaccia v. Dayton Newspapers, Inc., 170 Ohio App.3d 471, 867 N.E.2d 874 (2007); ("chief of the criminal section of the City of Dayton Law Department meets the public official test"); Cloud v. McKinney, 228 S.W.3d 326 (Tex. App. 2007) (executive director of lottery commission a public figure); O'Connor v. Burningham, 165 P.3d 1214 (Utah 2007) (high school basketball coach *not* a public official); see Danny R. Veilleux, Annotation, Who Is "Public Official" For Purposes of Defamation Action, 44 A.L.R.5th 193 (1996).

[507] Curtis Publ'g Co. v. Butts, 388 U.S. 130, 87 S.Ct. 1975, 18 L.Ed.2d 1094 (1967).

different rules governing their status—1) all purpose public figures and 2) limited purpose public figures.[508] These two categories and the rules that go with each have dominated most of the judicial effort to determine who counts as a public figure.

All purpose public figures. To prove that the plaintiff is this kind of public figure, the defendant would rely upon proof that the plaintiff enjoyed "pervasive power and influence" or "pervasive fame and notoriety" in public affairs.[509] Famous sports figures may be classed as public figures.[510] The decisions as a whole do not present a uniform picture. Thus while the football player may be a public figure because of fame, a famous medical doctor[511] or a television reporter who appears daily[512] may be placed outside that category on the ground that they lack pervasive power and influence in society. Perhaps the slipperiness of the all-purpose concept is due to the fact that its principle and purpose is not clear or because rules for all-purpose public figures are less commonly used than those for limited purpose figures.[513]

Entities. A public figure is often an individual, but various organizations including businesses,[514] public interest groups,[515] charities,[516] and religious organizations[517] may also count as public figures who are required to prove knowing or reckless falsehood in defamation suits.

Limited purpose public figures. To prove the plaintiff is a limited purpose public figure, the defendant must ordinarily show not only a controversy, but that the plaintiff voluntarily thrust herself into the controversy,[518] or at least is drawn into it[519] and attempted to influence its outcome. The Supreme Court in *Gertz* thought the plaintiff would be a public figure in these cases because (a) she assumed the risk of public scrutiny by her voluntary involvement in an issue or controversy, and (b) she would have access to media and hence to self-defense against defamatory publications. In such a case, public figure status is limited to that controversy.[520] Some courts have elaborated the two *Gertz* points into a series of three to five "factors" to be considered in determining limited-purpose public-figure status.[521] In some opinions, the "factors" become hard and

---

[508] Gertz v. Robert Welch, Inc., 418 U.S. 323, 94 S.Ct. 2997, 41 L.Ed.2d 789 (1974).

[509] Gertz, 418 U. S. at 345, 351, 94 S. Ct. at 3009, 3013.

[510] See Curtis Publ'g Co. v. Butts, 388 U.S. 130, 155, 87 S.Ct. 1975, 1991, 18 L.Ed.2d 1094 (1967) (Harlan, J.); Chuy v. Philadelphia Eagles Football Club, 595 F.2d 1265, 1280 (3d Cir. 1977).

[511] Bongiovi v. Sullivan, 138 P.3d 433 (Nev. 2006).

[512] Wayment v. Clear Channel Broad., Inc., 116 P.3d 271 (Utah 2005).

[513] National Found. for Cancer Research, Inc. v. Council of Better Bus. Bureaus, Inc., 705 F.2d 98 (4th Cir. 1983).

[514] E.g., Steaks Unlimited, Inc. v. Deaner, 623 F.2d 264 (3d Cir. 1980).

[515] E.g., Friends of Animals, Inc. v. Associated Fur Mfrs., Inc., 46 N.Y.2d 1065, 390 N.E.2d 298, 416 N.Y.S.2d 790 (1979).

[516] National Found. for Cancer Research, Inc. v. Council of Better Bus. Bureraus, Inc., 705 F.2d 98 (4th Cir. 1983).

[517] E.g., Reader's Digest Ass'n v. Superior Court, 37 Cal.3d 244, 690 P.2d 610, 208 Cal.Rptr. 137 (1984) (church).

[518] Id. at 345, 94 S.Ct. at 3009.

[519] Id. at 351, 94 S.Ct. at 3013 ("an individual voluntarily injects himself or is drawn into a particular public controversy and thereby becomes a public figure for a limited range of issues").

[520] See 3 Dobbs, Hayden & Bublick, The Law of Torts § 561 (2d. ed. 2011 & Supp.).

[521] Hatfill v. New York Times Co., 532 F.3d 312, 319 (4th Cir. 2008) (five factors, asking "whether (1) the plaintiff has access to channels of effective communication, (2) the plaintiff voluntarily assumed a role of special prominence in the controversy, (3) the plaintiff sought to influence the resolution of the controversy,

fast elements that the defendant must prove to show that the plaintiff is a public figure.[522]

Relevance of defamatory statements to the plaintiff's status. Statements about limited purpose public figures must be germane to their public figure status,[523] but when it comes to public officials, almost anything is relevant to the public official's qualifications, including misbehavior that is remote in time or considered to be minor or purely personal by many people.[524]

§ 37.18   Proving Constitutional Levels of Fault

Clear and convincing evidence. Under *New York Times Co. v. Sullivan*, public officials and public figures suing for defamation are required to prove with convincing clarity[525] that the defendant was guilty of publishing a knowing or reckless falsehood. It has been said that the convincing clarity or "clear and convincing evidence" standard requires evidence that must support a firm conviction that the fact asserted is true.[526] The Supreme Court has said that it will independently review issues of constitutional fact, which has been interpreted to mean that the appellate judges must themselves believe the defendant was guilty of a knowing or reckless falsehood.[527]

Scope and exceptions. Most courts say the convincing-clarity standard of proof applies to the issue of falsity as well as to the question of knowledge of falsity or recklessness,[528] but some have embraced a preponderance of the evidence standard for the issue of falsity.[529] And some courts believe the convincing-clarity standard is limited

---

(4) the controversy existed prior to the publication of the defamatory statements, and (5) the plaintiff retained public figure status at the time of the alleged defamation").

[522]   Contemporary Mission, Inc. v. New York Times Co., 842 F.2d 612, 6127 (2d Cir. 1988) (four elements of proof required: "A defendant *must show* the plaintiff has: (1) successfully invited public attention to his views in an effort to influence others prior to the incident that is the subject of litigation; (2) voluntarily injected himself into a public controversy related to the subject of the litigation; (3) assumed a position of prominence in the public controversy; and (4) maintained regular and continuing access to the media") (emphasis added); see also Neely v. Wilson, 418 S.W.3d 52 (Tex. 2013) (three elements).

[523]   E.g., Mathis v. Daly, 695 S.E.2d 807 (N.C. Ct. App. 2010); Klentzman v. Brady, 312 S.W.3d 886, 905 (Tex. App. 2009).

[524]   Monitor Patriot Co. v. Roy, 401 U.S. 265, 91 S.Ct. 621, 28 L.Ed.2d 35 (1971) (charge that plaintiff candidate was former small-time bootlegger; charge of criminal conduct, no matter how remote, is protected by the rule); Dixon v. International Bhd. of Police Officers, 504 F.3d 73, 87 (1st Cir. 2007) (noting that almost any statement regarding a public official will be relevant and holding that defamation relating to the plaintiff's alleged sexual conduct was mixed with other defamation clearly germane to her fitness for office).

[525]   New York Times Co. v. Sullivan, 376 U.S. 254, 286, 84 S.Ct. 710, 729, 11 L.Ed.2d 686 (1964). Presumably convincing clarity can be equated with the familiar clear and convincing evidence standard.

[526]   See Bentley v. Bunton, 94 S.W.3d 561 (Tex. 2002).

[527]   See Eastwood v. National Enquirer, Inc., 123 F.3d 1249, 1252 (9th Cir. 1997) (recognizing the more or less impossible task of de novo review while giving deference to jury decisions on credibility).

[528]   Dibella v. Hopkins, 403 F.3d 102 (2d Cir. 2005); Deutcsh v. Birmingham Post Co., 603 So.2d 910 (Ala. 1992). Dibella listed and discussed a number of cases, concluding that most courts to consider the issue have held that this standard applies to the issue of falsity as well as to the issue of fault or "actual malice." The court went on to predict that New York would follow this standard even if it is not a constitutional requirement.

[529]   Some judges have suggested that the convincing-clarity requirement applied only to the knowing or reckless elements and that falsity could be proved by a preponderance of the evidence. See Ayala v. Washington, 679 A.2d 1057 (D.C. 1996); Yeakey v. Hearst Commc'ns, Inc., 234 P.3d 332 (Wash. Ct. App. 2010).

to suits against media defendants,[530] while others reject any such special disability for individual speakers.[531] The Supreme Court has never resolved that issue.

Types of evidence. What constitutes adequate evidence is a crucial issue only touched on here.[532] Since the *Times-Sullivan* rule clearly requires that the plaintiff must prove more than common law malice, she must prove fault with respect to the substantial truth of the defamatory statement, that is, knowing or reckless falsehood.[533] For example, the publisher's motive to increase its profits is not evidence of a knowing or reckless falsehood.[534] Nor does the publisher's ill will or spite prove knowing or reckless falsehood.[535] Similarly, the defendant who is merely negligent in failing to investigate or otherwise ascertain the truth of a defamatory statement is not liable to a public official or public figure plaintiff; by itself, failure to investigate is not reckless.[536]

State law under the "some fault" rule. Under the *Gertz* rule, even a private person suing for defamation—or perhaps media defamation—is constitutionally required to prove "some fault" when the defamation touches an issue that is not of purely private concern.[537] *Gertz* leaves the states free to set the level of fault required, but presumably it must be fault in publishing a falsehood, not "fault" in the sense of common law malice such as hatred or ill will.[538] The states have overwhelmingly adopted negligence as the standard of fault to be required when a private person sues.[539] Several states have adopted the stronger standard based upon knowing or reckless falsehood when speech touches public concerns, even if the plaintiff is a private person and not a public figure

---

[530] Denny v. Mertz, 106 Wis.2d 636, 318 N.W.2d 141 (1982) (holding, over a dissent by Justice Abrahamson, that a magazine publishing a quotation from an individual was protected by the Gertz rule but that the individual who supplied the quotation was not).

[531] Kennedy v. Sheriff of E. Baton Rouge, 920 So.2d 217 (La. 2006); Jacron Sales Co., Inc. v. Sindorf, 276 Md. 580, 592, 350 A.2d 688, 695 (1976) (as a matter of tort law, it would be bizarre to impose strict liability upon individuals while relieving an enterprise); Wampler v. Higgins, 93 Ohio St.3d 111, 752 N.E.2d 962 (2001) (state constitution's protection for opinion statements extends to non-media defendants, criticizing cases limiting speech protection to media defendants).

[532] For a fuller discussion see 3 Dobbs, Hayden & Bublick, The Law of Torts §§ 564–565 (2d ed. 2011 & Supp.).

[533] Literal falsity is not enough to meet the constitutional demand. If the publisher knows the statement he is publishing is literally false, as in the case of a known misquotation, the defendant is still not liable if the statement is substantially true in the sense that it caused no more injury to the plaintiff's reputation than a similar and true statement. See Masson v. New Yorker Magazine, Inc., 501 U.S. 496, 111 S.Ct. 2419, 115 L.Ed.2d 447 (1991).

[534] Cobb v. Time, Inc., 278 F.3d 629 (6th Cir. 2002) (also holding that the fact that a witness is paid for his sensational story is not enough to show knowing or reckless falsehood).

[535] DeAngelis v. Hill, 180 N.J. 1, 847 A.2d 1261 (2004); New Times, Inc. v. Isaacks, 146 S.W.3d 144, 157 (Tex. 2004) (actual malice concerns the defendant's attitude toward the truth, not toward the plaintiff).

[536] Cobb v. Time, Inc., 278 F.3d 629 (6th Cir. 2002) (failure to interview all witnesses); New York Times Co. v. Connor, 365 F.2d 567 (5th Cir. 1966); Bertrand v. Mullin, 846 N.W.2d 884 (Iowa), cert. denied, 135 S.Ct. 373 (2014); Hearst Corp. v. Skeen, 159 S.W.3d 633 (Tex. 2005) (critic suggesting criminal justice system in county was tainted and based on "win at all costs" approach only studied ten cases out of thousands; this is no evidence of known falsehood); but cf. Curtis Publ'g Co. v. Butts, 388 U.S. 130, 87 S.Ct. 1975, 18 L.Ed.2d 1094 (1967) (some Justices found reckless disregard of the truth largely because of slipshod investigation of serious allegation and a source regarded as untrustworthy).

[537] Dun & Bradstreet, Inc. v. Greenmoss Builders, Inc.,472 U.S. 749, 105 S.Ct. 2939, 86 L.Ed.2d 593 (1985).

[538] See Hustler Magazine v. Falwell, 485 U.S. 46, 108 S.Ct. 876, 99 L.Ed.2d 41 (1988) (expressing the view that fault must relate to falsehood in a privacy claim); Kennedy v. Sheriff of E. Baton Rouge, 920 So.2d 217 (La. 2006).

[539] E.g., Peagler v. Phoenix Newspapers, Inc., 114 Ariz. 309, 560 P.2d 1216 (1977); Kennedy v. Sheriff of E. Baton Rouge, 920 So.2d 217 (La. 2006); Memphis Publ'g Co. v. Nichols, 569 S.W.2d 412 (Tenn. 1978); Restatement (Second) of Torts § 580B (1977).

or official.[540] A media publisher's negligence is perhaps most easily imaginable when the publisher fails to investigate facts and when such a failure can be evaluated under the professional standards of journalists.[541]

§ 37.19 Opinion Statements—Constitutional Protections

Earlier common law offered no general doctrine protecting non-factual statements such as statements of opinion[542] or statements ridiculing the plaintiff without the use of any false factual statement.[543]

Constitutional requirement; the publication must be provably false. Beginning in 1964, constitutional rules required the public official or public figure plaintiff to prove a knowing or at least reckless falsehood.[544] This seems to imply that the plaintiff must prove falsity of the publication. In *Philadelphia Newspapers, Inc. v. Hepps*,[545] the Court went further, holding that, at least in some situations, the plaintiff has the burden of proving falsity of the putative defamation even when the plaintiff was a purely private person.

Scope of Hepps. Some uncertainties remain about the scope of *Hepps*. In most cases, the plaintiff must bear the burden of proving falsity of the defamatory sting, but the *Hepps* Court did not decide whether the same rule applies (1) when the issue involved in the defamation is of no public concern; or (2) when the defendant is a non-media defendant.

Media and non-media defendants. On the latter point, Judge Sack's authoritative treatise concludes that lower courts routinely apply the *Hepps* rule to non-media defendants and indeed suggests that in the age of the internet it is hard to tell the difference between media and non-media.[546] In the words of one court, "a distinction drawn according to whether the defendant is a member of the media or not is untenable."[547]

---

[540] Mount Juneau Enters., Inc. v. Juneau Empire, 891 P.2d 829 (Alaska 1995); Diversified Mgmt., Inc. v. Denver Post, Inc., 653 P.2d 1103, 33 A.L.R.4th 193 (Colo. 1982) (but rejecting the subjective test of reckless disregard); Shepard v. Schurz Commc'ns, Inc., 847 N.E.2d 219 (Ind. 2006).

[541] Gobin v. Globe Pub. Co., 216 Kan. 223, 531 P.2d 76, 84 (1975); Seegmiller v. KSL, Inc., 626 P.2d 968 (Utah 1981).

[542] Restatement (First) of Torts § 566 (1938); see George C. Christie, Defamatory Opinions and the Restatement (Second) of Torts, 75 Mich. L. Rev. 1621 (1977). The First Restatement's illustration has it that one making a political speech and truthfully describing the plaintiff's actions with particularity is guilty of defamation if he characterizes the plaintiff's acts as like those of a murderer. It leaves open the possibility of a privilege. The Second Restatement, however, restated the rule of § 566 to say that an opinion statement would be actionable only if it implied the allegation of undisclosed defamatory facts.

[543] Burton v. Crowell Publ'g Co., 82 F.2d 154 (2d Cir. 1936) (by accident of lighting and composition photo made it appear that a piece of the plaintiff's saddle was a part of the plaintiff's person and that he was exposing himself; although any viewer would recognize that this was not in fact the case, viewer might still laugh and the plaintiff would suffer from the ridiculous association); see also Spence v. Flynt, 816 P.2d 771 (Wyo. 1991) (labeling plaintiff as "asshole of the month" and offering other epithets was actionable). Courts also held that a privilege to publish would be destroyed if the defendant's purpose was to ridicule the plaintiff. Hogan v. New York Times Co., 313 F.2d 354 (2d Cir. 1963) (misstatements of fact; reference to police as "Keystone Cops" showed abuse of privilege because of intent to ridicule and thus abuse of privilege).

[544] § 37.15.

[545] 475 U.S. 767, 106 S.Ct. 1558, 89 L.Ed.2d 783 (1986). Hepps, like most other important decisions, involved a media publication.

[546] Robert D. Sack on Defamation: Libel, Slander & Related Problems. § 3:3.2 (updated on Westlaw).

[547] Flamm v. American Ass'n of Univ. Women, 201 F.3d 144, 149 (2d Cir. 2000).

Constitutional "opinion" principle. The constitutional protection for truthful speech has led to a constitutional principle, expressed by the Supreme Court in the *Milkovich* case, that liability may be imposed for speech on matters of public concern only if the defendant's publication contains statements that are "provably false."[548] Presumably statements would be factual in nature and therefore provably false if they could be verified or falsified by use of the senses (had witnesses been present), even if reasonable inferences were also needed. The same could be said if the defendant's statements could be verified or falsified by the application of accepted scientific or mathematical methods. If not capable of that kind of verification, the statements would be protected and could form no basis for liability in a defamation claim.

The opinion word. Although the Supreme Court rejected any separate protection for "opinion," a statement of opinion that implied no facts at all would not be provably false and hence would be constitutionally protected. Perhaps for this reason, courts often continue use the term "opinion" to cover statements that are not provably false.[549] The constitutional rule is thus largely congruent with the Restatement's rule protecting opinion statements[550] even though the constitutional rule is expressed differently. The provably false/opinion rule also correlates to a large extent with the independent rule that courts will not adjudicate religious matters.[551]

The unknown scope of protection for opinion statements. Judge Sack has suggested that since *Milkovich* grounded constitutional protection of opinion-type statements in the provably false rule of *Hepps*,[552] the scope of *Hepps* might determine the scope of opinion protection. In particular, unless *Hepps* is extended to require provable falsity of statements involving no public issue, then opinion statements not involving public issues (or mere invective or hyperbole) might be left without constitutional protection,[553] though common law protection might remain. Evaluative opinions that imply facts may also enjoy lesser protections.[554] Of course, this makes the means of distinguishing opinion from fact an important question.[555] And state courts are free to adopt more protective rules for "opinion" statements.[556] Name-calling, rhetorical hyperbole, satire

---

[548] Milkovich v. Lorain Journal, 497 U.S. 1, 110 S.Ct. 2695, 111 L.Ed.2d 1 (1990). The provably false standard does not ask whether there is sufficient evidence in the particular case to prove the statement false, but whether the nature of the statement is such that one could falsify or verify it by examining facts.

[549] E.g., Madison v. Frazier, 539 F.3d 646, 653 (7th Cir. 2008); McKee v. Laurion, 825 N.W.2d 725 (Minn. 2013).

[550] Restatement (Second) of Torts § 566 (1977) (providing that opinion statements are not actionable unless they imply defamatory factual statements).

[551] For example, in Harvest House Publishers v. Local Church, 190 S.W.3d 204 (Tex. App. 2006), the publication may have indirectly asserted that the plaintiff church held doctrines incompatible with Christianity. The court rejected liability. "The issue of whether a group's doctrines are compatible with Christianity depends upon the religious convictions of the speaker." On a related claim, the court observed: "Because the statement concerns the speaker's religious beliefs, which cannot be proved true or false, an allegation that one is an idolator and accepts occult powers is not actionable."

[552] Robert D. Sack on Defamation: Libel, Slander & Related Problems. § 3:3.2 (updated on Westlaw).

[553] Robert D. Sack, Protection of Opinion under the First Amendment: Reflections on Alfred Hill, "Defamation and Privacy under the First Amendment," 100 Colum. L. Rev. 294, 326–27 (2000).

[554] See 3 Dobbs, Hayden & Bublick, The Law of Torts § 569 (2d. ed. 2011 & Supp.).

[555] Id. § 570.

[556] Id. § 571. In Shepard v. Schurz Communications, Inc., 847 N.E.2d 219 (Ind. 2006), the publication was: "Cliff Shepard is a liar. His statement is false." Although "liar" was the very charge the Milkovich Court held to be provably false, the Shepard court exculpated the publisher in this language: "The Times made a prima facie showing that it acted without malice and merely reported statements that were essentially rhetorical hyperbole by an opposing attorney, statements incapable of being proved true or false by the Times." Although the Shepard court described the "liar" language as rhetorical hyperbole—a species of non-factual

and the like may carry meanings that are not literal. When their non-literal meaning is perceived, it is often easy to see that theses communications have no factual content and are therefore not actionable.[557]

E. REMEDIES

§ 37.20 Remedies—Damages

Defamation cases involve a number of special procedural rules.[558] Once those procedures are satisfied, and a jury finds for the plaintiff, the usual remedy is money damages.

Defamation law purports to redress claims for harm to reputation. The specific harms resulting from reputational injury may vary considerably, and might include presumed damages, actual but unquantifiable harm to reputation, pecuniary loss, and emotional distress as well as other consequential damages.

Presumed damages under common law. The common law rule, which can still govern some cases, allows juries to presume that a defamatory publication has caused harm to reputation and then to award substantial sums of money even in the absence of evidence as to any particular amount of damages.[559] However, an award of presumed damages may be deemed excessive if the defamation is not serious or widespread, and if it appears to cause neither serious reputational nor emotional harm.[560] The presumed damages rule may be headed for extinction.[561] Commentators have attacked it, and some states have abandoned it even when the Constitution does not require them to do so.[562]

Constitutional limits on presumed and punitive damages. Under *Gertz v. Robert Welch, Inc.*,[563] the First Amendment is held to bar recovery of presumed damages when the plaintiff is a private person defamed on a topic of public concern and evidence of fault falls short of showing knowing or reckless falsehood.[564] In such a case, the plaintiff can

---

statement—its central concern may have rested elsewhere, with the idea that a newspaper should be permitted to quote newsworthy statements. On this, see § 37.11.

[557] See 3 Dobbs, Hayden & Bublick, The Law of Torts § 572 (2d. ed. 2011 & Supp.).

[558] See id. § 573.

[559] See Dugan v. Mittal Steel USA Inc., 929 N.E.2d 184, 186 (Ind. 2010) (damages presumed in cases of defamation per se); Kiesau v. Bantz, 686 N.W.2d 164 (Iowa 2004).

[560] In Republic Tobacco Co. v. North Atlantic Trading Co., Inc., 381 F.3d 717 (7th Cir. 2004), the jury awarded $8.4 million in presumed damages based on a competitor's defamatory letters to dealers. On appeal, this was reduced to $1 million (along with punitive damages) on the ground that no more could be fairly "presumed" in the absence of general publication or evidence of some economic loss. In Bongiovi v. Sullivan, 138 P.3d 433 (Nev. 2006), one plastic surgeon sued another for slander per se for falsely stating that the plaintiff had negligently caused the death of a patient. The jury's award of $250,000 compensatory damages was affirmed as a reasonable range for presumed damages given the emotional harm to the plaintiff and perhaps because of the seriousness of the defamation.

[561] It is not dead yet, however. See W.J.A. v. D.A., 210 N.J. 229, 43 A.3d 1148, 40 Media L. Rep. (BNA) 1830 (2012) (false accusations of child molestation; where statements involve only matters of private concern and the plaintiff is a private person, doctrine of presumed damages is retained, allowing recovery of nominal damages "thus vindicating his good name").

[562] Arthaud v. Mutual of Omaha Ins. Co., 170 F.3d 860 (8th Cir. 1999); Synygy, Inc. v. Scott-Levin, Inc., 51 F.Supp.2d 570 (E.D.Pa. 1999), aff'd, 229 F.3d 1139 (3d Cir. 2000) (table); United Ins. Co. of Am. v. Murphy, 331 Ark. 364, 961 S.W.2d 752 (1998); Walker v. Grand Cent. Sanitation, Inc., 430 Pa. Super. 236, 634 A.2d 237 (1993); see David Anderson, Reputation, Compensation, and Proof, 25 Wm. & Mary L. Rev. 747, 758 (1984).

[563] 418 U.S. 323, 339, 94 S.Ct. 2997, 3007, 41 L.Ed.2d 789 (1974).

[564] Independent of these rules, the Constitution bars the claim altogether if it is brought by a public official or public figure without proof of knowing or reckless falsehood. This rule does not depend upon damages proof. See § 37.15.

recover only her "actual" damages. The rule excludes both the common law presumed damages and punitive damages. On the other hand, "actual" damages permitted in such cases are not limited to special or pecuniary damages required by the common law rules in slander cases. For example, actual damages may include any proven harm to reputation and also emotional harm without proof of pecuniary loss.[565] In addition, if the plaintiff can go beyond the minimal showing required in *Gertz* and prove that the defendant was guilty of a knowing or reckless falsehood, damages can be constitutionally presumed if state law continues to permit presumed damages.[566]

Elements of damages. In addition to damages for estimated loss of reputation, the award may include damages for pecuniary losses, so long as they are proximately caused by the defamatory publication.[567] For example, the plaintiff may recover for loss of employment or harm to her career resulting from the defamation.[568] The plaintiff may also recover for emotional distress[569] and resulting bodily harm,[570] and for costs of corrective advertising by the plaintiff[571] and other expenses incurred in defending her reputation.[572] Courts have even allowed loss of consortium recovery by the spouse of a defamed person.[573] So far as the plaintiff claims actual damages, she must of course prove them. If the publication has caused loss of business, she may be required to show how much of the business loss was due to true portions of the defamation and how much due to the untrue and defamatory portion.[574] And on the ground that excessive damages may chill free speech, expressing disapproval of the defendant rather than real

---

[565] Gertz v. Robert Welch, Inc., 418 U.S. 323, 350, 94 S.Ct. 2997, 3012 41 L.Ed.2d 789 (1974).

[566] Gertz, id., implied so in saying "we hold that the States may not permit recovery of presumed or punitive damages, at least when liability is not based on a showing of knowledge of falsity or reckless disregard for the truth." It is generally assumed that recovery of presumed damages, which would be permitted to a public figure upon proof of knowing or reckless falsehood, would a fortiori be permitted to a private person in the Gertz category. Some cases have expressly said so. Mitchell v. Griffin Television, L.L. C., 60 P.3d 1058 (Okla. Civ. App. 2002) ("Upon a showing of actual malice, the plaintiff may recover punitive damages, and, where otherwise allowed, presumed damages"). The rule that punitive damages, forbidden by Gertz when only negligence is proved by a private person, is exactly analogous, and in that case, proof of knowing or reckless falsehood is constitutionally sufficient to permit punitive damages if state law would also permit such damages. E.g., Cochran v. Piedmont Publ'g Co. Inc., 62 N.C. App. 548, 302 S.E.2d 903 (1983).

[567] Lara v. Thomas, 512 N.W.2d 777 (Iowa 1994) ("natural and probable consequences"). In Longbehn v. Schoenrock, 727 N.W.2d 153 (Minn. Ct. App. 2007), the court recognized the general rule permitting proximately caused pecuniary damages, but held that the plaintiff's pecuniary damages were not caused by the defendant's publication; many people in the community communicated the defamation and they did not derive it from the defendant. In addition, the defamation was not a substantial factor in causing the plaintiff's pecuniary harm from loss of employment.

[568] E.g., Sigal Const. Corp. v. Stanbury, 586 A.2d 1204 (D.C. 1991); Ayash v. Dana-Farber Cancer Inst., 822 N.E.2d 667 (Mass. 2005) (successful research physician with a "bright future" was forced to accept purely clinical employment in another state after the libel).

[569] Prozeralik v. Capital Cities Commc'ns, 188 A.D.2d 178, 593 N.Y.S.2d 662 (1992), rev'd on other grounds, 82 N.Y.2d 466, 626 N.E.2d 34, 605 N.Y.S.2d 218 (1993); Southern Baptist Hosp. of Fla., Inc. v. Welker, 908 So. 2d 317 (Fla. 2005) (holding that rules limiting right to recovery for stand-alone emotional distress had no application to limit distress damages resulting from an established tort such as libel).

[570] Vinson v. Linn-Mar Cmty. Sch. Dist., 360 N.W.2d 108 (Iowa 1984).

[571] Den Norske Ameriekalinje Actiesselskabet v. Sun Printing & Publ'g Ass'n, 226 N.Y. 1, 122 N.E. 463 (1919).

[572] Bolduc v. Bailey, 586 F.Supp. 896 (D. Colo. 1984).

[573] Hudnall v. Selner, 800 F.2d 377 (4th Cir. 1988); Garrison v. Sun Printing & Publ'g Ass'n, 207 N.Y. 1, 100 N.E. 430 (1912).

[574] See Schoen v. Washington Post, 246 F.2d 670 (D.C. Cir. 1957).

compensation for the plaintiff, a court may scrutinize damages awards for libel with special care.[575]

Harm to reputation. Harm to reputation itself, though often not quantifiable, is the chief item for which recovery is permitted. The traditional common law rule did not require the plaintiff to prove that any person believed the defamatory publication,[576] but evidence that people did in fact believe the defamation and that they held the plaintiff in lower esteem as a result is relevant to show harm to reputation.[577] Equally, evidence that no one believed it tends to show that little harm was inflicted.[578] Other factors bear on the assessment of reputational loss: Was the accusation specific or vague, did it touch highly emotional issues or charge serious departures from well-established and important community standards, would it tend to be permanent and have repeated effects, did it reach a large audience or one especially relevant to the reputational issue? Perhaps the source of the defamation itself is an important factor. Defamation contained in a magazine with a poor reputation will perhaps have less effect than defamation contained in a respected news magazine.[579] The plaintiff's own existing reputation is of course central to the estimate of damages. That point requires further attention.

Emotional harm damages without reputational loss. The plaintiff's claim for emotional harm is usually that she suffered anxiety, depression, or other emotional harm because her reputation was damaged. The question is whether the plaintiff can sever her claim for emotional distress and avoid constitutional requirements and defenses. The Supreme Court has held that an emotional harm claim cannot be asserted for brutal satire that does not include false statements of fact.[580]

However, in the *Firestone* case, the Court permitted the plaintiff to drop the defamation claim and proceed on an emotional distress claim standing alone.[581] In that case, Time Magazine said the plaintiff's husband had divorced her for adultery. This was not true, although the trial judge had mentioned evidence of extramarital escapades. In a defamation case, a private person like the plaintiff cannot recover presumed damages

---

[575] Bentley v. Bunton, 94 S.W.3d 561 (Tex. 2002) ("the First Amendment requires appellate review of amounts awarded for non-economic damages in defamation cases to ensure that any recovery only compensates the plaintiff for actual injuries and is not a disguised disapproval of the defendant"). See also, rejecting multi-million dollar damage verdicts, Burbage v. Burbage, 47 S.W.3d 249 (Tex. 2014); Waste Mgmt. of Tex., Inc. v. Texas Disposal Sys. Landfill, Inc., 434 S.W.3d 142 (Tex. 2014).

[576] E.g., See Plumley v. Landmark Chevrolet, Inc., 122 F.3d 308 (5th Cir. 1997); In re Peck, 295 B.R. 353 (B.A.P. 9th Cir. 2003).

[577] Ellis v. Price, 337 Ark. 542, 990 S.W.2d 543 (1999) (in state requiring actual damages, testimony that after wife had been defamed, husband was angry with her, slept in a different room, and would not touch wife sufficed to show reputational loss); Murphy v. Boston Herald, Inc., 449 Mass. 42, 865 N.E.2d 746 (2007) (no error to admit evidence of hate mail received by plaintiff and reactions to the plaintiff posted in an internet chat room after defamation was published); Poleski v. Polish Am. Publ'g Co., 254 Mich. 15, 235 N.W. 841 (1931) (testimony showing how the plaintiff's Polish-ancestry constituency reacted to defamation associating plaintiff with the Klan). However, in Macy v. New York World-Telegram Corp., 2 N.Y.S.2d 416, 141 N.E.2d 566, 161 N.Y.S.2d 55 (1957), the court disapproved of some testimony about reactions of third persons to the defendant following publication of the defamation, saying that the "better practice would be to call as witnesses for plaintiff subject to cross-examination, the persons who were supposed to have spoken or acted adversely to plaintiff and to demonstrate, if such demonstration be possible, a connection to the libel," and in a holding uncertain scope said that some of the testimony in the case was inadmissible.

[578] E.g., Gazette, Inc. v. Harris, 229 Va. 1, 325 S.E.2d 713, 745, 54 A.L.R. 4th 685 (1985). Some courts have refused to admit such evidence. E.g., Clay v. Lagiss, 143 Cal. App. 2d 441, 448, 299 P.2d 1025, 1030 (1956).

[579] See 2 Dan Dobbs, Law of Remedies § 7.2(7) (2d ed. 1993).

[580] Hustler Magazine v. Falwell, 485 U.S. 46, 108 S.Ct. 876, 99 L.Ed.2d 41 (1988).

[581] Time, Inc. v. Firestone, 424 U.S. 448, 96 S.Ct. 958, 47 L.Ed.2d 154 (1976).

without proof of knowing or reckless falsehood. One risk of the stand-alone emotional harm claim based upon publication is that presumed damages may be allowed under the name of emotional harm.[582] Another possibility is that if a plaintiff is permitted to drop the defamation claim but recover for stand-alone emotional harm, evidence of the plaintiff's reputation would be excluded on the ground that it would be highly relevant to the defamation claim but quite irrelevant to emotional harm.[583] The result would be that some plaintiffs might recover damages based upon a loss of reputation they did not enjoy in the first place. A number of state courts have avoided these results.[584]

Punitive damages. When the plaintiff proves a knowing or reckless falsehood, punitive damages are constitutionally permissible. This is the level of fault required under the *Times-Sullivan* rule for public officials and public figures to recover even compensatory damages,[585] so, as far as the First Amendment is concerned, no additional fault is required when such plaintiffs claim punitive damages.

Proof required. When the plaintiff is a private person defamed in connection with a matter of public concern, she may recover proven compensatory damages under *Gertz* upon proof of some fault such as negligence. But she cannot recover punitive damages on such proof.[586] Only if she goes further and proves knowing or reckless falsehood can she recover punitive damages.[587]

Common law damages. When the plaintiff is a private person defamed on a matter that is of no public concern, *Dun & Bradstreet* permits the plaintiff to recover both common law presumed damages and punitive damages without restrictions imposed by the First Amendment.[588]

Damages within limits. So long as constitutional limits are observed, state rules of punitive damages may determine the grant or denial of relief. Thus courts often hold that no punitive award may be made unless compensatory damages are also awarded or at least proved.[589] And in defamation cases specifically, New York has held that something more than knowing or reckless falsehood is required to establish a claim for punitive damages; a malicious motive for publishing the falsehood is also required.[590] In

[582] David Anderson, Reputation, Compensation, and Proof, 25 Wm. & Mary L. Rev. 747, 758 (1984); see also 2 Dan Dobbs, Law of Remedies § 7.2(6) (2d ed. 1993).

[583] See 2 Dan Dobbs, Law of Remedies § 7.2(6) (2d ed. 1993).

[584] See Little Rock Newspapers, Inc. v. Dodrill, 281 Ark. 25, 660 S.W.2d 933 (1983); Schlegel v. Ottumwa Courier, 585 N.W.2d 217 (Iowa 1998); Gobin v. Globe Publ'g Co., 232 Kan. 1, 649 P.2d 1239 (1982); Kenney v. Wal-Mart Stores, Inc., 100 S.W.3d 809 (Mo. 2003) (error to permit jury to award damages in libel cases on proof of emotional harm without proof of reputational harm). However, claims of emotional harm arising from publication but not from reputational harm have been permitted. See State v. Carpenter, 171 P.3d 41 (Alaska 2007).

[585] See § 37.15.

[586] Gertz v. Robert Welch, Inc., 418 U.S. 323, 94 S.Ct. 2997, 41 L.Ed.2d 789 (1974).

[587] See Milkovich v. Lorain Journal Co., 497 U.S. 1, 16, 110 S.Ct. 2695, 2704 (1990) (states cannot "permit recovery of presumed or punitive damages on less than a showing of New York Times malice"); Cochran v. Piedmont Publ'g Co. Inc., 62 N.C. App. 548, 302 S.E.2d 903 (1983); Mitchell v. Griffin Television, L.L. C., 60 P.3d 1058, 1061 (Okla. Civ. App. 2002) ("Upon a showing of actual malice, the plaintiff may recover punitive damages, and, where otherwise allowed, presumed damages").

[588] Dun & Bradstreet, Inc. v. Greenmoss Builders, Inc., 472 U.S. 749, 105 S.Ct. 2939, 86 L.Ed.2d 593 (1985).

[589] See 3 Dobbs, Hayden & Bublick, The Law of Torts § 483 (2d. ed. 2011 & Supp.). Lawnwood Med. Ctr., Inc. v. Sadow, 43 So.3d 710 (Fla. Dist. Ct. App. 2010), holds that in defamation cases where compensatory damages can be presumed, that is enough basis for punitive damages.

[590] Prozeralik v. Capital Cities Commc'ns, Inc., 82 N.Y.2d 466, 626 N.E.2d 34, 605 N.Y.S.2d 218 (1993).

addition, the Supreme Court has held that due process requires judicial scrutiny of all punitive awards, and that some punitive awards may be stricken as constitutionally excessive.[591]

Libel-proof plaintiffs. If the defamation plaintiff already has a bad reputation on the topic involved in the defamation, her damages are at least arguably less than if she enjoyed a good reputation or no reputation at all. Consequently, evidence of the plaintiff's reputation prior to publication of defamatory material is highly relevant in most cases to show that damages should be limited.[592] However, the libel-proof plaintiff doctrines, where applied, go further by permitting summary judgment for the defendant on the ground that the plaintiff's reputation could not be further harmed by the defendant's publication.[593]

§ 37.21 Non-Damages Remedies Including Money Disgorgement

Restitution

Many people have been confused by the word restitution and some of them appear to believe that the measure of restitution is the same as the measure of damages. This may be true in the criminal cases where the offender can be required to "make restitution" to his victim. More generally, however, restitution refers to the defendant's liability to disgorge gains he has made from wrongdoing. In that case, his liability is measured by his gain, not, as with damages, by the plaintiff's loss. That makes restitution an attractive measure of liability when the defendant's tort provides him extraordinary gain in excess of the plaintiff's loss. The publisher of a book, for example, might make great profits from it, and if the book's premise and theme defames the plaintiff, the plaintiff might conceivably prefer to recover the book's profits rather than ordinary damages. The limited authority on such publisher's liability, however, excludes restitutionary recovery[594] and that is indeed in accord with free speech concerns, at least in the absence of knowing or reckless falsehood.

Injunctions

Quite apart from constitutional constraints, a long tradition has it that equity will not enjoin defamation.[595] To a large extent the precedents against injunctions are the

---

[591] § 485.

[592] Longbehn v. Schoenrock, 2010 WL 3000283 (Minn. Ct. App. 2010) (unreported) (aptly adducing authority that makes the same point by saying that the plaintiff's "bad character" "may be shown in mitigation of damages by presenting evidence of the plaintiff's general reputation in that respect").

[593] Forms and use of the libel-proof doctrine are developed in 3 Dobbs, Bublick & Hayden, The Law of Torts § 575 (2d. ed. 2011 & Supp.).

[594] Hart v. E.P. Dutton & Co., 197 Misc. 274, 93 N.Y.S.2d 871 (1949), *aff'd*, 277 A.D. 935, 98 N.Y.S.2d 773 (1949); cf. Simon & Schuster, Inc. v. Members of the N.Y. State Crime Victims Bd., 502 U.S. 105, 112 S.Ct. 501, 116 L.Ed.2d 476 (1991) (statutes allocating profits criminal makes from writing about his crime toward payment of victims unconstitutional). In Snepp v. United States, 444 U.S. 507, 100 S.Ct. 763 (1980), however, a former CIA agent, Snepp, wrote a book about his experiences and it was published without prior permission by the CIA. Although it revealed no classified information, the government was allowed to take all of the royalties earned—restitution for fiduciary breach.

[595] E.g., Kramer v. Thompson, 947 F.2d 666 (3d Cir. 1991) (even though jury has first found statements libelous and awarded damages, no injunction and no compulsory retraction); High Country Fashions, Inc. v. Marlenna Fashions, Inc., 257 Ga. 267, 357 S.E.2d 576, 577 (1987). See generally 2 Dan B. Dobbs, Law of Remedies § 7.2(14) (2d ed. 1993).

products of state law based upon judicial reluctance to censor speech and sometimes upon state constitutions.[596]

However, courts have sometimes in effect engaged in censorship, in effect issuing injunctions against publishing public records by ordering them to be sealed or even expunged.[597] In addition, although "prior restraint" on speech is a violation of the United States Constitution,[598] cases have held that the Constitution does not forbid an injunction against repetition of defamatory statements that have been made in the past and have been adjudicated to be defamation.[599] The question remains whether even such a constitutionally permissible injunction is appropriate under state law, especially where damages may be an adequate remedy or where discretion counsels caution. The scope and detail of injunctions against speech is of special concern, and even where an injunction against libel is constitutionally permissible, it must be tailored narrowly. For example, an injunction that forbids all repetition of speech adjudicated to be defamatory would be too broad, because such an injunction must not exclude the right of the defendant to repeat her claims to public officials in seeking redress of grievances.[600]

Retraction and Reply

The damages action for defamation is expensive to defendants, risks a chill on free speech, and is so clogged with distinctions and decision points it cannot be counted upon to clear the plaintiff's name, to provide measured redress of her rights, or fully protect the rights of speakers and society. Critics have often proposed reforms, but most of these proposals have their deficits, too.

Retraction. The common law recognized that the defendant's full and fair retraction of the defamatory statement would be admissible in evidence as tending to show that harm to reputation may have been minimized[601] and as tending to negate grounds for punitive damages.[602] Most states have enacted statutes governing retraction by media publishers.[603] If no statutory demand is made for retraction or if a statutory retraction is published, then damages may be limited, for example, by eliminating presumed damages. The statutes do not require retraction and almost certainly could not

---

[596] See Willing v. Mazzocone, 482 Pa. 377, 393 A.2d 1155 (1978); Robert A. Leflar, Legal Remedies for Defamation, 6 Ark. L. Rev. 423 (1952).

[597] See In re Smith, 63 Misc. 2d 198, 310 N.Y.S.2d 617 (1970) (physical obliteration of the names from all records to prevent employer's knowledge that juveniles had been arrested); See 3 Dobbs, Hayden & Bublick, The Law of Torts § 583 (2d. ed. 2011 & Supp.).

[598] See Near v. State of Minn., 283 U.S. 697, 51 S.Ct. 625, 75 L.Ed. 1357 (1931). The exact scope of the rule against prior restraints is debated.

[599] Balboa Island Vill. Inn, Inc. v. Lemen, 40 Cal. 4th 1141, 156 P.3d 339, 57 Cal. Rptr. 3d 320 (2007) (noting that if the enjoined statements became justified later on, the plaintiff could seek modification of the injunction).

[600] Id.; see also Kinney v. Barnes, 443 S.W.3d 87 (Tex. 2014), cert. denied, 135 S.Ct. 1164 (2015).

[601] Webb v. Call Publ'g Co., 173 Wis. 45, 180 N.W. 263 (1920). In Whitcomb v. Hearst Corp., 329 Mass. 193, 107 N.E.2d 295 (1952), the court approved an instruction that told the jury it could find the retraction reduced damages to a nominal level, did not reduce them at all, or reduced them to some extent in between.

[602] Kehoe v. New York Tribune, 229 A.D. 220, 241 N.Y.S. 676 (1930) (admissible to reduce punitive but not compensatory damages). The defendant's refusal to retract after being fully informed of the facts is evidence of common law malice, e.g., Myers v. Pickering Firm, Inc., 959 S.W.2d 152 (Tenn. Ct. App. 1997), but not necessarily evidence of knowing or reckless falsehood. New York Times Co. v. Sullivan, 376 U.S. 254, 84 S.Ct. 710, 11 L.Ed.2d 686 (1964). A statute that merely required a request for retraction before punitive damages could be claimed was held to apply to internet publications in Mathis v. Cannon, 573 S.E.2d 376 (Ga. 2002).

[603] See Robert D. Sack & Sandra S. Baron, Libel, Slander and Related Problems, Appendix 2 (2d ed. 1994) (setting out all of the retraction statutes).

constitutionally do so, partly for reasons that appear in the next paragraph and because an official, governmentally prescribed "truth" would raise even more fundamental questions. The retraction-statute cases litigate various collateral issues such as the sufficiency of the demand for retraction, or the retraction itself, its timing, and other statutory terms.[604]

Right of reply. Conceivably a statute might structure some kind of intelligible right of reply to media defamation in lieu of a damages recovery. Florida once had a rather inadequate version of such a statute, triggering a right of reply whenever the plaintiff was "assailed" in a newspaper, which was then required to devote equal space to the plaintiff's reply. The Supreme Court held this to be an unconstitutional intrusion upon the editorial decisions of the press, a kind of compelled speech.[605]

---

[604] See id. § 9.2. Arizona held its statute unconstitutional in Boswell v. Phoenix Newspapers, Inc., 152 Ariz. 9, 730 P.2d 186 (1986).

[605] Miami Herald Pub. Co. v. Tornillo, 418 U.S. 241, 94 S.Ct. 2831, 41 L.Ed.2d 730 (1974). But cf. Pruneyard Shopping Ctr. v. Robins, 447 U.S. 74, 100 S.Ct. 2035, 64 L.Ed.2d 741 (1980) (state could compel privately owned shopping center to permit people to distribute leaflets on its property).

Chapter 38

PRIVACY

Analysis

§ 38.1   Privacy Torts: An Introduction
§ 38.2   Appropriation of the Plaintiff's Personality
§ 38.3   Intrusion: Private Life and Information
§ 38.4   Publicizing Private Life
§ 38.5   False Light

§ 38.1 Privacy Torts: An Introduction

Categories of privacy claims. Sometimes it is said that the right of privacy is the right to be let alone, but the phrase does not reflect the varieties of privacy invasion.[1] Scholars eventually posited four forms of privacy invasion (or four different torts). Dean Prosser and the Restatement posited that privacy is invaded by (a) an unreasonable intrusion upon the plaintiff's seclusion, (b) the appropriation of the plaintiff's name or likeness, (c) unreasonably giving publicity to the plaintiff's private life, and (d) publicizing the plaintiff in a false light.[2] This set of four categories, with its frequent overlaps,[3] is the one that prevails in the common law today, for better or for worse.[4]

Concerns. Within the current common law framework, the right of privacy leaves a good many problems in its wake. So far as privacy is said to be violated by publication or communication, the free speech considerations that limit liability for defamation may have similar application when the plaintiff switches to the privacy theory.[5] In addition, the anti-SLAPP statutes, ostensibly protecting the right to petition government, may be invoked in privacy claims.[6]

§ 38.2 Appropriation of the Plaintiff's Personality

Gist of the tort. The early cases establishing privacy as a separate tort were based upon the defendant's use of the plaintiff's name or likeness in commercial advertising.[7] It later became apparent that appropriation of the plaintiff's identity for other purposes

---

[1]   See Daniel Solove, A Taxonomy of Privacy, 154 U. Pa. L. Rev. 477 (2006) (grouping the potentially harmful activities to privacy into four categories: information collection, information processing, information dissemination, and invasion into private spaces and decisions).

[2]   Restatement (Second) of Torts §§ 652A–652E (1976).

[3]   Id. § 652A cmt. d.

[4]   See Lior Jacob Strahilevitz, Reunifying Privacy Law, 98 Cal. L. Rev. 2007 (2010) (arguing that courts should renounce the divisions Prosser introduced into common law cases dealing with informational privacy and instead combine the torts of intrusion on seclusion and public disclosure of social facts by asking if the defendant intruded on private information in a way that was highly offensive to a reasonable person).

[5]   See 3 Dobbs, Hayden & Bublick, The Law of Torts § 581 (2d ed. 2011 & Supp.).

[6]   Gates v. Discovery Commc'ns, Inc., 34 Cal.4th 679, 101 P.3d 552 (2004); Stern v. Doe, 806 So.2d 98 (La. Ct. App. 2001).

[7]   Pavesich v. New England Life Ins. Co., 122 Ga. 190, 50 S.E. 68 (1905); Kunz v. Allen, 102 Kan. 883, 172 P. 532 (1918); Flake v. Greensboro News Co., 212 N.C. 780, 195 S.E. 55 (1938).

could be actionable,[8] subject to free speech constraints. Since the gist of the tort is the unconsented to[9] appropriation of the plaintiff's identity or reputation, or some substantial aspect of it,[10] for the defendant's own use or benefit, no element of falsity is required.

Dignitary tort vs. property right. The earliest plaintiffs were mostly private individuals, not public figures. The emphasis was personal and dignitary. The individual had liberty interests at stake; she could associate with others or not according to her personality and preferences; she might be humiliated if people thought she sold her picture for advertising. Later cases adapted this form of privacy invasion to the case of public figures who do not seek privacy but on the contrary seek out opportunities for public exposure and who wish to use their name, likeness, voice or other aspects of "identity" as a property to be sold.[11] In this form, the claim is sometimes strangely called a right of publicity.[12] The recent appropriation cases of note have been of this kind and are closer to the fields of intellectual property, unfair competition, and trademarks than to the purely dignitary torts.[13] The characterization of the tort interest as intellectual property may avoid limitations on recovery imposed on some of the other privacy torts.[14]

Plaintiffs with and without commercially valuable identities. Consistent with the property characterization, some courts have apparently rejected the earlier emphasis upon the plaintiff's personal rights and liberties that gave rise to this cause of action. These courts refuse to allow recovery for appropriation of the plaintiff's name or likeness unless the plaintiff was a famous person who could sell her identity for endorsements or the like.[15] However, other courts have taken care to recognize that while some cases of appropriation might involve rights of public figures, others would be harmful even to

---

[8] AFL Philadelphia LLC v. Krause, 639 F.Supp.2d 512 (E.D. Pa. 2009) (signing plaintiff's name to a widely distributed letter); Faegre & Benson LLP v. Purdy, 367 F.Supp.2d 1238, 1247–48 (D. Minn. 2005) (posting statements falsely attributed to attorney); Bosley v. Wildwett.com, 310 F.Supp.2d 914, 920 (N.D. Ohio 2004) (economic gain other than advertising); Hinish v. Meier & Frank Co., Inc., 166 Or. 482, 113 P.2d 438 (1941) (signing plaintiff's name to a communication to the governor).

[9] Gignilliat v. Gignilliat, Savitz & Bettis, LLP, 385 S.C. 452, 684 S.E.2d 756 (2009) (law partner consented to law firm's continued use of his name).

[10] Trevino v. MacSports, Inc., 2010 WL 890992 (E.D. La. 2010) (use of artist's signature).

[11] Lemon v. Harlem Globetrotters Int'l, Inc., 437 F.Supp.2d 1089, 1100 (D. Ariz. 2006). The Restatement treats all appropriation cases as "property" cases, although it recognizes that personal feelings and emotional distress of the plaintiff were part of the reason for recognizing the right in the first place. See Restatement (Second) of Torts § 652C cmt. a (1976).

[12] See J. Thomas McCarthy, The Rights of Publicity and Privacy (1998) (expansive definitions of right of publicity).

[13] E.g., ETW Corp. v. Jireh Publ'g, Inc., 332 F.3d 915, 930 (6th Cir. 2003); Midler v. Ford Motor Co., 849 F.2d 460 (9th Cir. 1988) (voice imitation); Carson v. Here's Johnny Portable Toilets, Inc., 698 F.2d 831 (6th Cir. 1983) (phrase used to introduce famous television person); Armstrong v. Eagle Rock Entm't, Inc., 655 F.Supp.2d 779 (E.D. Mich. 2009). See Chapter 46.

[14] Doe v. Friendfinder Network, Inc., 540 F.Supp.2d 288, 303 (D.N.H. 2008) (claim against web operators related to false personal advertisements about the plaintiff was not barred by Communications Decency Act because right of publicity sounded in intellectual property law).

[15] Cox v. Hatch, 761 P.2d 556 (Utah 1988) (Senator Hatch posed for photos with federal postal workers, then used pictures in his political campaign; workers had no claim as their likeness had no intrinsic value). See also Barnhart v. Paisano Publ'ns, LLC, 457 F.Supp.2d 590, 595–96 (D. Md. 2006). At times the fact that the plaintiff had a high profile status is enough to warrant the claim. See Tripp v. United States, 257 F.Supp.2d 37, 40–42 (D.D.C. 2003).

utterly private persons. The latter, the court said, could have a damages claim for distress even if their name or identity had no commercial value.[16]

Intent and appropriation. The Restatement Second is not specific about the intent required to support the appropriation tort. It requires "appropriation," which perhaps implies that intent to utilize the plaintiff's identity is required.[17] But the Restatement also characterizes the plaintiff's right as one of property, perhaps as if to say that even an innocent taking of that property right in identity is actionable. Some authority might be read to support liability even if the defendant does not intend to appropriate the plaintiff's identity or reap the benefits of her fame.[18] However, the defendant does not appropriate the plaintiff's identity by incidental mention.[19] A public figure may be mentioned in a work of fiction if her identity is not used to tout a product or imply her sponsorship and if the work is clearly not a factual report about the public figure. So fictional work involving Notre Dame and its mention of its president does not offend the rights of either the school or the individual, and even more clearly so if the work is one of criticism or satire.[20]

Newsworthiness. In any event, reporting of matters that are newsworthy or of public concern is not an appropriation for which liability is imposed, even though the reported matter increases circulation or profits of the publisher.[21] In privacy law, newsworthiness is a broad concept that includes much more than hot news,[22] so a magazine article discussing a public figure or a newsworthy or educational topic is free to use names and photographs as much as a newspaper.[23] In the same way, nothing limits the right to publish a biography of a public figure so long as it is not false.[24] However, not every matter that might interest readers qualifies as a newsworthy item subject to protection from suit.[25]

---

[16]   Joe Dickerson & Assocs., LLC v. Dittmar, 34 P.3d 995 (Colo. 2001) (plaintiff identified by name and picture in a newsletter).

[17]   Restatement (Second) of Torts § 652C (1976). See Yeager v. Cingular Wireless LLC, 673 F.Supp.2d 1089 (E.D. Cal. 2009) (examining whether plaintiff's likeness is used to take advantage of his reputation or prestige); Tropeano v. Atlantic Monthly Co., 379 Mass. 745, 400 N.E.2d 847 (1980) (contrasting incidental use, which is not actionable, with an effort "deliberately to exploit" the plaintiff's likeness for advertising).

[18]   See Kerby v. Hal Roach Studios, Inc., 53 Cal.App.2d 207, 127 P.2d 577 (1942) (plaintiff's name was same as fictional movie character; the name was "signed" to printed and suggestive letters advertising the movie; no intent was required, but the case might be a false light case if that matters).

[19]   Comins v. Discovery Commc'ns, Inc., 200 F.Supp.2d 512, 523 (D. Md. 2002); Tropeano v. Atlantic Monthly Co., 379 Mass. 745, 400 N.E.2d 847 (1980) (photo of several unidentified people to illustrate "sociological commentary" on the sexual revolution was not effort to sell goods but only an incidental use of the plaintiff's likeness).

[20]   University of Notre Dame Du Lac v. Twentieth Century-Fox Film Corp., 22 A.D.2d 452, 256 N.Y.S.2d 301, aff'd, 15 N.Y.2d 940, 207 N.E.2d 508, 259 N.Y.S.2d 832 (1965).

[21]   Whitehurst v. Showtime Networks, Inc., 2009 WL 3052663 (E.D. Tex. 2009); Chapman v. Journal Concepts, Inc., 528 F.Supp. 2d 1081 (D. Haw. 2007); Battaglieri v. Mackinac Ctr. for Pub. Policy, 680 N.W.2d 915 (Mich. Ct. App. 2004); Freihofer v. Hearst Corp., 65 N.Y.2d 135, 480 N.E.2d 349, 490 N.Y.S.2d 735 (1985).

[22]   See Shulman v. Group W Prods., Inc., 18 Cal.4th 200, 955 P.2d 469, 74 Cal.Rptr.2d 843 (1998).

[23]   E.g., Rozhon v. Triangle Publ'ns., 230 F.2d 359 (7th Cir. 1956); Raymen v. United Senior Ass'n, Inc., 409 F.Supp.2d 15 (D.D.C. 2006).

[24]   See Spahn v. Julian Messner, Inc., 18 N.Y.2d 324, 221 N.E.2d 543, 274 N.Y.S.2d 877 (1966), on reargument after review in the Supreme Court, 21 N.Y.2d 124, 233 N.E.2d 840, 286 N.Y.S.2d 832, 30A.L.R.3d 196 (1967) (biography protected but fictionalized biography of famous baseball pitcher actionable as use of personality for trade or business).

[25]   Toffoloni v. LFP Publ'g Group, LLC, 572 F.3d 1201 (11th Cir. 2009) (nude photos of murdered female wrestler that were taken 20 years earlier did not satisfy newsworthiness standard).

First Amendment. Although the First Amendment's protection of free speech requires proof of falsity as a prerequisite to recovery in defamation cases and in some other kinds of privacy cases,[26] no such requirement has been imposed in the commercial appropriation cases. Perhaps that is partly because commercial speech is sometimes given less First Amendment protection and partly because the plaintiff's right in her own identity is treated as a species of property.[27] It is especially easy to think of the plaintiff's right as one analogous to intellectual property when the plaintiff has created a public personality, style, or characteristic performance. In that kind of case, at least, the Supreme Court has held that states may impose liability when the defendant appropriates the plaintiff's entire public performance.[28] Although falsity is probably never required to establish a claim, it appears unlikely that an accurate report on a newsworthy matter or one of public concern could be actionable without a very substantial appropriation indeed. Presumably, noncommercial speech would receive full protection from privacy law and the Constitution, so that, for example, truthful publications of public concern could not by themselves count as an invasion of privacy.[29] Whether speech is primarily commercial can be a difficult line to draw.[30]

§ 38.3 Intrusion: Private Life and Information

The outlines of the tort. Intrusive invasion of privacy is a rule desert; such rules as there are turn out to be shimmering mirages. The Restatement's rule is that an intentional intrusion upon the solitude or seclusion of another or upon her private affairs is subject to liability if the intrusion would be highly offensive to a reasonable person.[31] However, the Restatement provides little guidance as to what counts as protected seclusion or private affairs or what conduct that is not already some other tort would offend a reasonable person. Many times the emphasis in the intrusion tort is on an intrusive act. The cases clearly allow recovery where the defendant commits a virtual trespass, entering the plaintiff's possession or domain by electronic means such as tapping telephones or using other listening devices,[32] or by hacking into the plaintiff's email account,[33] or by secretly videotaping a person changing clothes in a dressing room,[34] or even by peeping into the plaintiff's home through cracks in the blinds.[35] At

---

[26]   See § 37.15.

[27]   Doe v. TCI Cablevision, 110 S.W.3d 363 (Mo. 2003).

[28]   See Zacchini v. Scripps-Howard Broad. Co., 433 U.S. 562, 97 S.Ct. 2849, 53 L.Ed.2d 965 (1977) (defendant broadcast video of the plaintiff's entire act as a human cannonball, state may impose liability).

[29]   See Raymen v. United Senior Ass'n, Inc., 409 F.Supp.2d 15 (D.D.C. 2006) (photograph of two men, about to be married under Oregon's same sex marriage law, kissing; defendant used the photograph in ad attacking AARP, claiming AARP supported such marriages; individuals depicted had no privacy rights because issue was of public concern); Joe Dickerson & Assocs., LLC v. Dittmar, 34 P.3d 995 (Colo. 2001).

[30]   For example, in Hart v. Electronic Arts, Inc., 740 F.Supp.2d 658 (D.N.J. 2010), the defendant's football video games may have used the plaintiff's likeness, replicating actual games in which he played. The court thought such a use would not be commercial unless the likeness was used to increase sales of the games and also that a celebrity's identity might serve dual purposes as newsworthy speech and also as speech designed to sell products, substantially complicating the newsworthy-commercial distinction.

[31]   Restatement (Second) of Torts § 652B (1976).

[32]   E.g., Hamberger v. Eastman, 106 N.H. 107, 206 A.2d 239 (1964); Roach v. Harper, 143 W.Va. 869, 105 S.E.2d 564 (1958). Statutes provide an independent ground for relief in the case of wiretapping. See 3 Dobbs, Hayden & Bublick, The Law of Torts § 584 (2d ed. 2011 & Supp.).

[33]   Garback v. Lossing, 2010 WL 3733971 (E.D. Mich. 2010) (need to show that private information from e-mail was obtained in an objectionable manner).

[34]   See American Guarantee & Liab. Ins. Co. v. 1906 Co., 273 F.3d 605 (5th Cir. 2001).

[35]   Alderson v. Bonner, 142 Idaho 733, 132 P.3d 1261 (Ct. App. 2006).

other times, the emphasis is on the plaintiff's interest in controlling information about herself, whether the defendant's act in obtaining or perpetuating data about the plaintiff is intrusive by itself or not. For instance, controlling use of credit card or social security numbers would fall into this category.[36]

Reasonable expectation of privacy. It is clear that no action for intrusive invasion of privacy will lie unless the plaintiff has a reasonable[37] and actual[38] expectation of privacy in the place, the materials involved, or the subject matter. Except as her conduct or consent might show otherwise, the plaintiff has expectations of privacy in her home[39] and even in public places that provide privacy protection like dressing rooms or restroom stalls.[40] An employee might even have some limited expectation of privacy in the workplace,[41] but here perhaps only with respect to personal as opposed to business information.[42] On the public street, the plaintiff might have an expectation of privacy as to a whispered conversation with a companion, but has no reasonable expectation of privacy as to her presence.[43]

Data privacy. Privacy expectations may also arise with respect to certain data, such as the plaintiff's social security number,[44] although an investigation of public records or information already known to individuals and not held in confidence may not in itself be an intrusive invasion.[45] Nor is it an invasion of privacy to read the plaintiff's private computer files if the plaintiff has no expectation of privacy in those files, as might be the case if, by custom in the business or by his own consent, he expects the employer defendant to monitor his computer.[46] However, even if individual records in a data base or file system are separately available on a one-at-a-time basis, privacy rights in aggregated data about the plaintiff might be legally protected.[47] Statutes provide an

---

[36]   Remsburg v. Docusearch, Inc., 816 A.2d 1001 (N.H. 2003).

[37]   E.g., Cheatham v. Paisano Publ'ns., Inc., 891 F.Supp. 381 (W.D. Ky. 1995) (at a large public bikers' event, plaintiff wore clothing that partly revealed her "bottom"; a photograph made at the event was not an intrusive invasion of privacy).

[38]   It is said that the plaintiff must have an actual, subjective expectation of privacy as well, but this is shown by objective facts. See Medical Lab. Mgmt. Consultants v. American Broad. Cos., Inc., 306 F.3d 806 (9th Cir. 2002).

[39]   Clearly homes are private places as far as outsiders go. As between husband and wife or domestic partners living in the home, expectations of privacy may be altered by the marital relationship. "Privilege" may be an alternate way of expressing the same essential idea. See Hennig v. Alltel Commc'ns, Inc., 903 So. 2d 1137 (La. Ct. App. 2005).

[40]   Thus when surveillance of a public restroom stall is planned or intentional, liability is appropriate. See Houghum v. Valley Mem'l Homes, 574 N.W.2d 812 (N.D. 1998). Georgia agrees, but says that if a public restroom is used for sexual activity, the user has no expectation of privacy. Johnson v. Allen, 272 Ga.App. 861, 613 S.E.2d 657 (2005).

[41]   Hernandez v. Hillsides, Inc., 47 Cal.4th 272, 211 P.3d 1063 (2009) (undisclosed video surveillance).

[42]   See Medical Lab. Mgmt. Consultants v. American Broad. Cos., Inc., 306 F.3d 806 (9th Cir. 2002).

[43]   E.g., Johnson v. Stewart, 854 So.2d 544 (Ala. 2002) (surveillance of plaintiff in public places not actionable); Stern v. Doe, 806 So.2d 98 (La. Ct. App. 2001) (young man arrested for truancy, pockets emptied while television camera rolled, no expectation of privacy).

[44]   See Remsburg v. Docusearch, Inc., 816 A.2d 1001 (N.H. 2003) (firm doing computer information searches found social security number for person as requested by client, there is expectation of privacy in light of legal and contractual constraints on releasing the SSN even if that data is often illicitly obtained).

[45]   Myrick v. Barron, 820 So. 2d 81 (Ala. 2001).

[46]   TBG Ins. Servs. Corp. v. Superior Court, 96 Cal.App.4th 443, 117 Cal.Rptr.2d 155 (2002).

[47]   United States Dep't of Justice v. Reporters Comm. for Freedom of the Press, 489 U.S. 749, 109 S.Ct. 1468, 103 L.Ed.2d 774 (1989) (under Freedom of Information Act, disclosure of FBI rap sheet that could contain information about many individual state investigations or records could compromise privacy interests); Best v. Malec, 2010 WL 3721475 (N.D. Ill. 2010) (broadcasting a police computer screen of data about plaintiff). Distinguish aggregated data that contains no personally identifiable information.

independent ground for relief for interception of electronic submissions and disclosure of personal information in several instances.[48]

Limited expectations of privacy. Plaintiff's reasonable expectation need not be an expectation of complete privacy. Something less may be sufficient for the tort, so long as the limited privacy expected excludes the kind of intrusion launched by the defendant. Surreptitious videotaping at work[49] or home[50] is a prime example. Consequently, even if the plaintiff shares a marital bedroom with a spouse so that complete privacy is not expected, when the plaintiff is alone in the bedroom there is still a reasonable expectation that activities in the room will not be recorded by a hidden camera.[51] Similarly, the California Supreme Court has held that if A covertly records his own conversation with B that is also heard by others, the recording itself can violate B's limited expectation of privacy and may be actionable. The theory is that although B can have no expectation of confidentiality, she has an expectation that it will not be recorded.[52] However, courts have reached different conclusions.[53]

Intentional and highly offensive intrusion. Given a reasonable expectation of privacy, the intentional and highly offensive intrusion that defeats the expectation is itself tortious. If that intrusion is carried out under color of law, it may violate the standards of the Fourth Amendment or Due Process clause and be actionable as a civil rights tort under § 1983.[54] Intrusions that would not be highly offensive to a reasonable person are not actionable under the tort.[55] One factor that may be relevant to evaluating offensiveness to a reasonable person is the value of the social interest in disclosure that rivals the privacy interest.[56] In addition to a highly offensive intrusion, the Restatement's version of this tort requires intent, presumably intent to commit the act

---

[48]   See 3 Dobbs, Hayden & Bublick, The Law of Torts § 584 (2d ed. 2011 & Supp.).

[49]   Sanders v. American Broad. Cos., Inc., 20 Cal.4th 907, 85 Cal.Rptr.2d 909, 978 P.2d 67 (1999).

[50]   In Miller v. Brooks, 123 N.C. App. 20, 472 S.E.2d 350 (1996), the husband and wife were separated and the wife's use of surveillance cameras in the husband's home was considered intrusive.

[51]   In re Marriage of Tigges, 758 N.W.2d 824 (Iowa 2008) (husband had no right to videotaped wife in the bedroom without her knowledge and consent); Clayton v. Richards, 47 S.W.3d 149 (Tex. App. 2001) (privacy cause of action when wife installed video camera to tape husband in the bedroom while she was out of town).

[52]   Flanagan v. Flanagan, 27 Cal.4th 766, 41 P.3d 575, 117 Cal.Rptr.2d 574 (2002) (expectation of privacy or confidentiality arises without proof that victim also reasonably expected that contents of call would not be later divulged); Sanders v. American Broad. Cos., Inc., 20 Cal.4th 907, 85 Cal.Rptr.2d 909, 978 P.2d 67 (1999).

[53]   Compare Caro v. Weintraub, 618 F.3d 94 (2d Cir. 2010) (setting up iPhone and hitting record in conversation to which defendant was a party could be intrusion tort), with Bradley v. Atlantic City Bd. of Educ., 736 F.Supp.2d 891 (D.N.J. 2010) (secretly recording telephone call concerning harassment did not warrant intrusion claim). Individual state laws about the legality of such recordings may affect the conclusion.

[54]   Wilson v. Layne, 526 U.S. 603, 119 S.Ct. 1692 (1999) (establishing the principle that officers violate the Fourth Amendment by inviting media representatives to enter the plaintiff's home while officers executed a warrant); see also Hill v. McKinley, 311 F.3d 899 (8th Cir. 2002) (prisoner strapped down to a restraining board naked for three hours); James v. City of Douglas, Ga., 941 F.2d 1539 (11th Cir. 1991) (video tape of sexual conduct of the plaintiff seized by police from another person was not logged in as evidence but kept in a drawer and viewed by various persons); York v. Story, 324 F.2d 450 (9th Cir. 1963) (police required nude photos of assault victim).

[55]   Hernandez v. Hillsides, Inc., 47 Cal.4th 272, 211 P.3d 1063 (Cal. 2009) (covert videotaping of the plaintiff's office after her shift ended to see who was using her computer to display pornography in a residential facility for abused and neglected children was not highly offensive).

[56]   See Wolfe v. Schaefer, 619 F.3d 782 (7th Cir. 2010) ("If Congress required airline passengers to fly nude in order to reduce the risk of a terrorist incident, one imagines that the law might well be held to infringe a constitutional right to privacy even though there is a substantial social interest in airline safety"); Muick v. Glenayre Elecs., 280 F.3d 741 (7th Cir. 2002) (employer's valid interest in investigation relevant to intrusion claim).

that the court considers an intrusion. A knowing and reckless falsehood known to lead to the intrusion may be adequate.[57] Some courts, however, may treat negligent intrusion as actionable.[58]

Overlap with other torts: trespass and battery. Courts say that intrusive invasion of privacy is independent of any other tort such as trespass, but in fact a number of privacy cases could be resolved under better-defined rules of trespass, battery, Fourth Amendment violation, or the like. No doubt a defendant who enters the plaintiff's home on the basis of a "consent" procured by deceit should be liable on a close analogy to trespass.[59] In 1881, the Michigan court held that a doctor was liable for bringing an untrained man into the room where the plaintiff was delivering a child.[60] The plaintiff's "consent" was not valid because she had been under the mistaken belief that the man was a doctor or medical student, so recovery could have been justified on a trespass theory as well as any other. A well-known Missouri case is only a little different because the plaintiff was in a hospital room rather than her home; journalists invaded the room over her express objection, photographed her in bed against her will, and published the photograph with a story about her disease. This was said to be an invasion of privacy, but its substantial core is only a technical variation on trespass in which the plaintiff lacked a present possessory interest in the hospital room.[61] Courts have also said that the right to reject medical treatment or the like is grounded in a privacy right when they could as well have said that forced medical treatment is a battery.[62]

Overlap with intentional infliction of emotional distress. Some forms of the intrusive privacy action appear to be especially like the claim for intentional infliction of emotional distress. In a Washington case,[63] individual county employees retained for their personal use autopsy photos of deceased persons. Relatives of the deceased were allowed to pursue an invasion of privacy claim although their claim for intentional infliction of emotional distress failed because they were not present when the defendants took or used the photos.[64] Likewise, harassment—repeated and unwanted attentions—may be characterized as an intrusive invasion of privacy rather than as an intentional infliction of emotional distress. A bill collector hounds a debtor,[65] an employer repeatedly broaches

---

[57]   Leang v. Jersey City Bd. of Educ., 969 A.2d 1097 (N.J. 2009).

[58]   Prince v. St. Francis-St. George Hosp., Inc., 20 Ohio App.3d 4, 484 N.E.2d 265 (1985) (bill with medical diagnosis of alcoholism sent to patient's employer, a privacy claim would be actionable regardless whether the defendant acted intentionally or negligently).

[59]   E.g., Dietemann v. Time, Inc., 449 F.2d 245 (9th Cir. 1971); but cf. Desnick v. American Broad. Cos., Inc., 44 F.3d 1345 (7th Cir. 1994) (journalists fraudulently presenting themselves as patients in order to obtain incriminating evidence about an eye clinic were not liable as trespassers or for invasion of privacy).

[60]   Dalley v. Dykema Gossett, P.LLC, 788 N.W.2d 679, 287 Mich.App. 296 (2010) (defendants "gained admission to plaintiff's premises by deceit"); De May v. Roberts, 46 Mich. 160, 9 N.W. 146 (1881).

[61]   Barber v. Time, Inc., 348 Mo. 1199, 159 S.W.2d 291 (1942); cf. Sanchez-Scott v. Alza Pharm., 86 Cal.App.4th 365, 103 Cal.Rptr.2d 410 (2001) (drug salesman with physician during plaintiff's breast examination without revealing his identity as a salesman, trial court erred in dismissing complaint); Froelich v. Adair, 213 Kan. 357, 516 P.2d 993 (1973) (defendant paid hospital orderly to obtain plaintiff's body tissue from a discarded bandage).

[62]   In re Schuoler, 106 Wash.2d 500, 723 P.2d 1103 (1986).

[63]   Reid v. Pierce County, 136 Wash.2d 195, 961 P.2d 333 (1998).

[64]   Id. The claim was not based on survival of the deceased persons' causes of action but on the relatives' claims analogous to claims for intentional interference with a dead body. See also Catsouras v. Dep't of Cal. Highway Patrol, 181 Cal.App.4th 856 (2010).

[65]   A federal statute now heavily regulates debt collection. 15 U.S.C.A. § 1692.

sexual questions to an employee,[66] a stalker repeatedly follows or threatens the object of his obsession,[67] or telemarketers repeatedly call the homes of victims[68] or send unwanted faxes;[69] all are subject to liability for invasion of privacy.

Employee privacy rights. Employee rights of privacy vis-a-vis employers has developed into something of a specialty itself.[70] A federal statute now prohibits employers from administering, demanding, or even suggesting a polygraph test to employees, and creates a federal cause of action against employers who violate the statute.[71] Drug testing by employers as a condition of employment or by schools and private associations as a condition to participation in sports or other activities,[72] is a different matter. So far as the employer is a governmental entity, the Fourth Amendment forbids unreasonable searches (including drug testing). A search is reasonable when there is reasonable ground for suspicion of wrongdoing and when compelling governmental interests and special needs outweigh privacy concerns. Compelling interests and special needs have been found in a number of cases,[73] but not all.[74] Private employers are generally constitutionally free to enforce rules requiring employee searches and to discharge employees who do not comply. Even so, states are free to hold that privacy rights trump the employer's right to discharge an employee. Some states have thus held that private employers may not discharge an employee for refusing to accept a suspicionless drug test unless safety issues made such testing reasonable.[75] Other courts and statutes, however, have left little or no room for claims based upon private employer drug testing.[76]

Intrusion and speech. Because the basic nature of the tort is intrusion, liability does not turn upon publication of any kind.[77] For that reason, liability for intrusion alone would not ordinarily raise free speech considerations that may concern other forms of privacy invasion. In particular, an intrusion upon privacy is not justified by newsworthiness of material that may be gained.[78]

---

[66] Phillips v. Smalley Maint. Servs., Inc., 435 So. 2d 705 (Ala. 1983); cf. McSurely v. McClellan, 753 F.2d 88 (D.C. Cir. 1985) (wife's pre-marriage relations with others revealed to husband).

[67] Rumbauskas v. Cantor, 138 N.J. 173, 649 A.2d 853 (1994).

[68] Irvine v. Akron Beacon Journal, 147 Ohio App.3d 428, 770 N.E.2d 1105 (2002); Charvat v. Dispatch Consumer Servs., Inc., 95 Ohio St.3d 505, 769 N.E.2d 829 (2002) (under federal statute, consumer placing name on do-not-call list terminates caller's former privilege derived from established business relationship).

[69] Resource Bankshares Corp. v. St. Paul Mercury Ins. Co., 407 F.3d 631 (4th Cir. 2005).

[70] See Matthew W. Finkin, Privacy in Employment Law (1995 & 1997 Supp.); Pauline T. Kim, Privacy Rights, Public Policy, and the Employment Relationship, 57 Ohio St. L.J. 671 (1996).

[71] The Employee Polygraph Protection Act of 1988, 29 U.S.C.A. §§ 2001–09 (1994).

[72] As to testing as a condition of sports, see Hill v. National Collegiate Athletic Ass'n, 7 Cal.4th 1, 865 P.2d 633, 26 Cal.Rptr.2d 834 (1994) (testing college athletes permissible).

[73] Skinner v. Railway Labor Executives' Ass'n, 489 U.S. 602, 109 S.Ct. 1402, 103 L.Ed.2d 639 (1989).

[74] Chandler v. Miller, 520 U.S. 305, 117 S.Ct. 1295, 137 L.Ed.2d 513 (1997).

[75] Twigg v. Hercules Corp., 185 W.Va. 155, 406 S.E.2d 52 (1990); see Hennessey v. Coastal Eagle Point Oil Co., 129 N.J. 81, 609 A.2d 11 (1992); Edward L. Raymond, Jr., Annotation, Liability for Discharge of At-will Employee for Refusal to Submit to Drug Testing, 79 A.L.R.4th 105 (1991).

[76] See Ariz. Rev. Stat. § 23–493.04; Roe v. Quality Transp. Servs., 67 Wash.App. 604, 838 P.2d 128 (1992).

[77] Alexander v. Federal Bureau of Investigation, 971 F.Supp. 603 (D.D.C. 1997); Dalley v. Dykema Gossett, P.LLC, 287 Mich.App. 296, 788 N.W.2d 679 (2010); Clayton v. Richards, 47 S.W.3d 149 (Tex. App. 2001) (estranged wife hired private investigator to install and monitor hidden video camera in couple's bedroom).

[78] See Shulman v. Group W Prods., Inc., 18 Cal.4th 200, 955 P.2d 469, 74 Cal.Rptr.2d 843 (1998).

§ 38.4 Publicizing Private Life

Actions based on truthful speech. Although truth was a complete defense in latter-day libel actions and under the constitutional decisions the plaintiff is often required to prove falsehood of defamatory statements, these restrictions may be ignored under the Restatement's private facts privacy claim. In part, this is due to the fact that the Restatement confines liability to private matters that are not the subject of legitimate public concern.[79]

Elements. As the Restatement states the rule, the "private facts" category of privacy invasion occurs when the defendant gives publicity to a private fact about the plaintiff when disclosure would be highly offensive to a reasonable person and is not of legitimate public concern.[80] The tort "is illustrated by the unauthorized publicizing of a person's medical condition, personal finances, or sexual proclivities or activities."[81] Which disclosures would be highly offensive to a reasonable person is a matter at times left to a jury[82] and at times resolved as a matter of law.[83]

Publicity to private matters. The facts published about the plaintiff must be "private," which means that they must not be a matter of public record[84] or generally known.[85] When proper or privileged disclosure about A entails publication of private facts about B, courts are reluctant to entertain the claims.[86] At times, however, family members have protected privacy interests.[87] The defendant must give "publicity" to the private facts, which means that publication must be to the public at large or to a

---

[79] Restatement (Second) of Torts § 652D (1976). In some cases, the truth of the disclosure will establish a legitimate public concern. For example, if the plaintiff has tested positive for drug use, it is not a privacy tort for the employer to receive the results and pursue disciplinary action. Garofolo v. Fairview Park, 2009 WL 4694877 (Ohio Ct. App. 2009).

[80] Restatement (Second) of Torts § 652D (1976).

[81] Wolfe v. Schaefer, 619 F.3d 782 (7th Cir. 2010) (citing cases).

[82] Catsouras v. Department of Cal. Highway Patrol, 181 Cal.App.4th 856, 104 Cal.Rptr.3d 352 (2010) (highway patrol officers' e-mail of gruesome photos of 18-year-old's decapitated corpse to friends and family members for Halloween could support privacy claim); Johnson v. K-Mart Corp., 311 Ill.App.3d 573, 723 N.E.2d 1192, 243 Ill.Dec. 591 (2000) (employer placed private detectives in work force to pose as plaintiffs' co-workers and to obtain private information about workers' sex lives and other matters; such information was then published to employer; facts made a jury question whether the material was highly offensive to a reasonable person). Perhaps "deeply shocking" rather than "highly offensive" would better express the requirement. See Haynes v. Alfred A. Knopf, Inc., 8 F.3d 1222 (7th Cir. 1993).

[83] Scroggins v. Bill Furst Florist & Greenhouse, Inc., 2004 WL 41716 (Ohio Ct. App. 2004) (photo of female plaintiff in "teddy," in no way vulgar or revealing, as a matter of law was not highly offensive).

[84] Hatch v. Town of Middletown, 311 F.3d 83, 91 (1st Cir. 2002); Green v. CBS Inc., 286 F.3d 281 (5th Cir. 2002) ("once information is part of a public record, there can be no liability for publicizing it"); Washington v. City of Georgetown, 2009 WL 530782 (E.D. Ky. 2009).

[85] Moreno v. Hanford Sentinel, Inc., 172 Cal.App.4th 1125, 91 Cal.Rptr.3d 858 (2009) (essay posted on Myspace for less than a week was "open to the public at large" so information was already public). See Rodney A. Smolla, Law of Defamation § 10.04.

[86] See Bonome v. Kaysen, 2004 WL 1194731 (Mass. Super. Ct. 2004) (author of Girl, Interrupted is protected in discussing her sexual relationship which tells her own personal story which inextricably involves her boyfriend). See also Olson v. Red Cedar Clinic, 681 N.W.2d 306 (Wis. Ct. App. 2004); Livsey v. Salt Lake County, 275 F.3d 952 (10th Cir. 2001).

[87] National Archives & Records Admin. v. Favish, 541 U.S. 157, 124 S.Ct. 1570, 158 L.Ed.2d 319 (2003) (recognizing relatives' privacy interest in photos of deceased who died of gunshot wounds); Catsouras v. Department of Cal. Highway Patrol, 181 Cal.App.4th 856, 104 Cal.Rptr.3d 352 (2010) (family members have a common law right of privacy in the images of their deceased daughter); Reid v. Pierce County, 136 Wash.2d 195, 961 P.2d 333 (1998) (family have a privacy interest in autopsy photos).

substantial group of people,[88] though occasionally courts use a different standard for web pages[89] and could do so for other disclosures.[90] The publicity rule requires some qualification. First, a defendant who owes a duty of confidentiality is liable for breach of that duty by publishing to a small group or even to one person, as in the case of a physician who reveals his patient's medical history.[91] However, the defendant must intend to reveal that information,[92] and the defendant may be privileged to reveal confidential information to a person who has an interest of his own to protect.[93] Second, some authority allows recovery for communication to a small group, "if those people have a special relationship with the plaintiff that makes the disclosure as devastating as disclosure to the public at large."[94]

Free speech and legitimate public concern. Because this cause of action always entails communication to others, it runs squarely into the issue of free speech and the First Amendment. The Restatement's version of the rule attempts to stay within the limits of the First Amendment by restricting liability to publications that are not newsworthy or of legitimate public concern, since truthful communications on matters of public concern, and matters involving public figures appear to be constitutionally protected.[95] One thinker has gone so far as to say that the "shocking character of the disclosure" is a sufficiently good basis for liability, even in the light of First Amendment

---

[88] Willan v. Columbia County, 280 F.3d 1160 (1st Cir. 2002); Quinn v. Thomas, 2010 WL 3021795 (D. Nev. 2010); Randolph v. ING Life Ins. & Ann. Co., 973 A.2d 702 (D.C. 2009) (data concerning employee participants in a deferred compensation plan was stolen from the laptop computer of the plan administrator but never used or distributed after the theft; publicity rule had not been met); Restatement (Second) of Torts § 652D cmt. a (1976); David A. Elder, Privacy Torts § 3:3 (2002) (criticizing cases following this rule in "knee-jerk" fashion).

[89] Yath v. Fairview Clinics, N.P., 767 N.W.2d 34 (Minn. Ct. App. 2009) ("a publicly accessible webpage can present the story of someone's private life . . . to more than one billion Internet surfers worldwide. This extraordinary advancement in communication argues for, not against, a holding that the Myspace posting constitutes publicity" even though few people had accessed it). See also Steinbuch v. Cutler, 463 F.Supp.2d 1 (D.D.C. 2006) (claim of invasion of privacy on A's website, a claim against B whose own website allegedly carried a link to A's, was allowed to proceed, but seemingly not because the link itself was sufficient but only because the plaintiff alleged the two "worked together" to give publicity to the material).

[90] In some cases a court could drop the requirement of publicity and substitute a privilege or reasonableness analysis instead. For instance, in Bodah v. Lakeville Motor Express, Inc., 663 N.W.2d 550 (Minn. 2003), the employee-plaintiffs' social security numbers were distributed to over two hundred people in the business. The court concluded that was not enough "publicity." Under a privilege analysis, the court would ask instead whether the distribution was unreasonable or unprivileged. Distribution to managers in the business might be reasonable and even expected, but if not, the seriousness of identity theft would suggest that the distribution should be actionable.

[91] Horne v. Patton, 291 Ala. 701, 287 So.2d 824 (1974) (doctor gave information on patient to patient's employer; tort of privacy invasion); Yath v. Fairview Clinics, N.P., 767 N.W.2d 34 (Minn. Ct. App. 2009) (clinic employee disclosed acquaintance's medical file concerning sexually transmitted disease and sexual partners to another employee, who disclosed it to others who posted it on a Myspace account viewed by a small number of people—valid privacy claim and claim under state statute). See Andrew J. McClurg, Kiss and Tell: Protecting Intimate Relationship Privacy Through Implied Contracts of Confidentiality, 74 U. Cin. L. Rev. 887 (2006).

[92] Randolph v. ING Life Ins. & Ann. Co., 973 A.2d 702 (D.C. 2009).

[93] See Hennig v. Alltel Commc'ns, Inc., 903 So.2d 1137 (La. Ct. App. 2005) (cell phone company revealed wife's phone records to husband, not actionable because husband had a legal right to inspect records concerning debt of the marital community).

[94] See Karraker v. Rent-A-Center, Inc., 411 F.3d 831 (7th Cir. 2005); Olson v. Red Cedar Clinic, 681 N.W.2d 306 (Wis. Ct. App. 2004); contra Bodah v. Lakeville Motor Express, Inc., 663 N.W.2d 550 (Minn. 2003) (rejecting the special relationship or "particular public" approach).

[95] Wilson v. Freitas, 121 Haw. 120, 214 P.3d 1110 (Ct. App. 2009) (identifying suspect in serial murder investigation was legitimate public concern).

considerations.[96] Disclosure of private names and addresses in a way that constitutes a threat to life, as with abortion providers, may pass constitutional muster on the ground that threats are not protected speech.[97]

Wrongfully obtained information. Some cases that may be thought to support the Restatement's broad liability are actually much narrower. Those cases impose liability for revelation of private facts when the defendant obtained the private information by wrongful means such as trespass, deceit, betrayal, or breach of confidence.[98] Such cases do not seem to raise First Amendment or common law free speech issues because the information itself is obtained by wrongdoing.[99] A number of cases imposing liability can be justified on the ground that the published information was wrongfully obtained. In *Dietemann v. Time, Inc.*,[100] journalists got into the plaintiff's den by deceit and secretly photographed and recorded events, then published. The tort was the deceitful intrusion, but the proximate damages included harm resulting from publication. In *Barber v. Time, Inc.*,[101] journalists forced their way into the plaintiff's hospital room over her protests and then by trickery photographed her and published the photograph. In the famous *Sidis* case,[102] a former child prodigy turned into an obsessive recluse who valued privacy above all was the subject of a New Yorker profile that subjected him to merciless treatment. The court went off on a newsworthiness issue, but if the interviewer had gained entry into Sidis' room and mind by deceit and breach of confidence, liability of the interviewer would have been entirely appropriate. Such cases need not turn on such subjective criteria as the shocking nature of the disclosure or the private quality of the facts. Liability would be appropriate because the information was gained by a wrong to the plaintiff. However, when the information is obtained illegally by a third person, then published by the defendant who knows of the illegal act but who is in no way responsible for it, the defendant is constitutionally protected from liability, provided the information is of public concern.[103]

Newsworthiness: reporting on issues of public concern. Courts recognize that newsworthy events are matters of public concern and that the defendant may publicize those events even when they relate to private persons who are involuntarily involved in them.[104] For example, a television broadcaster may provide a videotaped report of an

---

[96] Alfred Hill, Defamation and Privacy Under the First Amendment, 76 Colum. L. Rev. 1205, 1258 (1976).

[97] Planned Parenthood of the Columbia/Willamette, Inc. v. American Coal. of Life Activists, 290 F.3d 1058 (9th Cir. 2002) (statutory action).

[98] Horne v. Patton, 291 Ala. 701, 287 So.2d 824 (1973) (medical information in breach of confidence); MacDonald v. Clinger, 84 A.D.2d 482, 446 N.Y.S.2d 801 (1982) (similar); Doe v. Roe, 400 N.Y.S.2d 668 (Sup. Ct. 1977) (therapist's book made her patient recognizable); Humphers v. First Interstate Bank of Or., 298 Or. 706, 696 P.2d 527 (1985) (doctor's breach of confidence in disclosing child's identity was actionable as breach of confidence, not as privacy invasion).

[99] However, the fact that information was wrongfully obtained does not automatically lead to liability where the defendant's wrongdoing is deemed collateral. Desnick v. American Broad. Cos., Inc., 44 F.3d 1345 (7th Cir. 1994). As to liability for publishing information wrongfully obtained by another where the information is of public concern, see Bartnicki v. Vopper, 532 U.S. 514, 121 S.Ct. 1753, 149 L.Ed.2d 787 (2001).

[100] Dietemann v. Time, Inc., 449 F.2d 245 (9th Cir. 1971).

[101] Barber v. Time, Inc., 348 Mo. 1199, 159 S.W.2d 291 (1942).

[102] Sidis v. F-R Publ'g Corp., 113 F.2d 806 (2d Cir. 1940).

[103] Bartnicki v. Vopper, 532 U.S. 514, 121 S.Ct. 1753, 149 L.Ed.2d 787 (2001). See Pearson v. Dodd, 410 F.2d 701 (D.C. Cir. 1969) (publishers, who did not obtain information by trespass or betrayal and did not authorize such conduct, nevertheless published the information; publishers not liable).

[104] California courts have held that lack of newsworthiness is an element of the prima facie case, making newsworthiness a "complete bar" to liability for public disclosure of private facts. See Taus v. Loftus, 40 Cal.4th

auto accident showing the victims[105] or even a frantic woman covered only with a dishtowel escaping from her husband's attack.[106] The freedom to report truthfully on newsworthy events or matters of public concern does not depend upon the plaintiff's preexisting public figure status, and in that respect it differs from the false defamatory report. Newsworthiness, moreover, is a shorthand expression rather than a precise description; the term is defined broadly to include many matters of public interest that are by no means news, including educational and entertaining materials, and the quotidian details of life involving births, deaths, personal heroism and tragedy.[107]

An example. The newsworthiness protection does not necessarily provide clear rights for speakers and publishers or clear protections for privacy. Perhaps it is not even capable of definition.[108] For example, Oliver Sipple, otherwise a private citizen, obstructed an effort to shoot former President Gerald Ford and became famous for it. Two days later, a columnist publicly revealed that Sipple was homosexual. Sipple suffered various humiliations, some at the hands of his own family, but his privacy claim was rejected, in part because his sexual preference was regarded as newsworthy. "Newsworthy" turned out to be a matter of the publisher's subjective motive. The court thought that the publisher's purpose to dispel false ideas about gays by using Sipple's life as an example showed that the publisher had no motive based upon sensational prying, and that, for the court, seemed to make the story newsworthy as a matter of law.[109]

What is newsworthy. However, newsworthiness has not been read to be all-encompassing. When information is not of public concern, the fact that it was lawfully obtained does not necessarily shield the defendant from liability. A publication that associates photographs of unnamed little league members with victims of a coach's molestation, may be actionable under California law as a wrongful revelation of a private fact.[110] Revelation that a student body president involved in a dispute with a college was transsexual was thought not to be newsworthy as a matter of law,[111] and some argue that private sexual matters are seldom or never newsworthy.[112] A California court also held that dissemination of photos showing a decapitated 18-year-old was not a matter of

---

683, 54 Cal.Rptr.3d 775, 151 P.3d 1185 (2007) (prominent psychology professor and author who disclosed various aspects of plaintiff's family background and personal life in connection with her scholarly studies of repressed memory in childhood sexual abuse cases).

[105]   Shulman v. Group W Prods., Inc., 18 Cal.4th 200, 955 P.2d 469, 74 Cal.Rptr.2d 843 (1998).

[106]   Cape Publ'ns, Inc. v. Bridges, 423 So.2d 426 (Fla. Dist. Ct. App. 1982). See also Anderson v. Suiters, 499 F.3d 1228, 1235–37 (10th Cir. 2007) (videotape of assault of rape victim).

[107]   See Alvarado v. KOB-TV, LLC, 493 F.3d 1210, 1218–20 (10th Cir. 2007) (allegations of misconduct by undercover police officers); Rodney A. Smolla, Law of Defamation § 10.04[2][b]; cf. Riley v. Harr, 292 F.3d 282 (1st Cir. 2002) (private fact that was seemingly not in itself newsworthy was nonetheless protected because it was substantially relevant to the matters of public concern reported).

[108]   The term itself is not treated as a mere description of what the public wants to know, but a normative term standing for the court's willingness to protect the publication. See Shulman v. Group W Prods., Inc., 18 Cal.4th 200, 955 P.2d 469, 74 Cal.Rptr.2d 843 (1998).

[109]   Sipple v. Chronicle Publ'g Co., 154 Cal.App.3d 1040, 1049, 201 Cal.Rptr. 665, 670 (1984).

[110]   M.G. v. Time Warner, Inc., 89 Cal.App.4th 623, 107 Cal.Rptr.2d 504 (2001).

[111]   Diaz v. Oakland Tribune, Inc., 139 Cal.App.3d 118, 188 Cal.Rptr. 762 (1983).

[112]   See John P. Elwood, Note, Outing, Privacy, and the First Amendment, 102 Yale L.J. 747 (1992).

public interest where "a reasonable member of the public, with decent standards, would say that he has no concern" beyond a morbid or sensational interest.[113]

Balancing privacy and speech. Both speech and privacy represent fundamental values sometimes given constitutional protection. Whether newsworthiness or public concern is a concept capable of sufficient development to balance the two remains to be seen.

Public information. Other cases, no longer valid, went far, far beyond liability for publishing wrongfully obtained information or information not of legitimate public interest. The most notable and extreme cases once held the defendant liable for publishing truthful information gleaned from records open to the public. In *Melvin v. Reid*,[114] the defendants made a movie in which true incidents of the plaintiff's life and her involvement in a murder trial were shown and her real name was used so that she could be identified. Although the court conceded that the defendants could use the incidents from the public record, it thought it was "unnecessary" and uncharitable to give the plaintiff's name. On this ground it held that the plaintiff stated a cause of action. Cases like this raise serious constitutional questions first because they decide what the public has a right to know—in this particular case, about crimes and criminals—and second because they penalize publication of the truth. California has now held that at least when the published information is rightfully obtained from public records, federal constitutional rules prohibit recovery.[115]

Constitutional rules about reports on public information. The Supreme Court of the United States has considered the First Amendment's impact in a series of cases in which the media lawfully obtained information about the plaintiff from public records and then publicized it. In each of the cases so far, the media's right to publish the information was upheld. Some of the claims for the plaintiff are especially sympathetic. In two, the plaintiffs were rape victims. Revealing names of rape victims will often compound the grievous injury; and it may at times also endanger the victims further. In the first case, *Cox Broadcasting Corp. v. Cohn*,[116] the Court held that the state could not prohibit publication of a rape victim's name when the name was obtained by the media from an indictment available for inspection. Part of the reason was that the press served as a kind of agent for individual members of the public who would have a right to inspect public records for themselves. Public scrutiny was particularly important as a means of helping to guarantee fair trials.

The Court later went beyond trial records. It has said that media may publish the names of juveniles charged with a crime when the names are obtained by listening to police band radio and may publish rape victims' names obtained from police reports (as distinguished from trial records). When "a newspaper lawfully obtains truthful information about a matter of public significance then state officials may not

---

[113] Catsouras v. Department of Cal. Highway Patrol, 181 Cal.App.4th 856, 874, 104 Cal.Rptr.3d 352, 366 (2010). Other language, however, suggested that the defendant's morbid or sensational motive would be enough to rule out public interest in the published content.

[114] Melvin v. Reid, 112 Cal.App. 285, 297 P. 91 (1931).

[115] Gates v. Discovery Commc'ns, Inc., 34 Cal.4th 679, 101 P.3d 552, 21 Cal.Rptr.3d 663 (2004).

[116] Cox Broad. Corp. v. Cohn, 420 U.S. 469, 95 S.Ct. 1029, 43 L.Ed.2d 328 (1975). Cox was applied in Uranga v. Federated Publ'ns. Inc., 138 Idaho 550, 67 P.3d 29 (2003), to protect publication of a statement that had been inserted in a court file by an unknown person forty years earlier.

constitutionally punish publication of the information, absent a need to further a state interest of the highest order."[117]

Restricting access to public information. These Supreme Court decisions recognize two potential conditions in which a truthful report of public records might be actionable. First, if there is a state need of the highest order, the state might forbid publication of records that are otherwise open to public access. Second, the state might restrict public access to records.[118] The first instance is hard to imagine in the light of the second,[119] and the second raises a new realm of concern. If government can be carried out secretly by invoking privacy rights of individuals, government will not be open or democratic. Public records are addressed to a greater extent in § 428A.

Scope of the tort. All in all, the privacy invasion tort most closely related to the Brandeis and Warren proposal has presented serious problems. Neither adjudications nor statutory solutions have proved entirely satisfactory. Not surprisingly, commentators have argued against this form of the privacy right.[120] New York, with a statutory right of privacy limited to appropriation cases, rejects the private facts version of privacy invasion.[121] Oregon has held that publication about the plaintiff is not actionable "unless the manner or purpose of defendant's conduct is wrongful in some respect apart from causing the plaintiff's hurt feelings."[122] A plurality decision in Indiana agreed, noting that emotional injuries from disclosure were not worse than other emotional injuries, so that the plaintiff should recover, if at all, for intentional infliction of emotional distress,[123] although later Indiana cases suggest that the state may yet recognize the tort.[124] North Carolina flatly rejected the private facts tort with the observation that at best it was constitutionally suspect.[125] Such decisions leave potential for liability when the defendant is a wrongdoer in some respect other than in publishing the truth, as where he breaches confidence or obtains information wrongfully, and where he intentionally inflicts severe emotional distress. Otherwise, the intrusion tort rather than the publicity tort may come closer to the core privacy value.

---

[117] Florida Star v. B.J.F., 491 U.S. 524, 109 S.Ct. 2603, 105 L.Ed.2d 443 (1989) (police report) (quoting Smith v. Daily Mail Publ'g Co., 443 U.S. 97, 99 S.Ct. 2667, 61 L.Ed.2d 399 (1979) (police radio)). See also Uranga v. Federated Publ'ns. Inc., 138 Idaho 550, 67 P.3d 29 (2003) (40-year-old unsworn statement inserted in court file by unknown person and not part of any pleading was protected).

[118] See National Archives & Records Admin. v. Favish, 541 U.S. 157, 124 S.Ct. 1570, 158 L.Ed.2d 319 (2003); Los Angeles Police Dep't v. United Reporting Publ'g Co., 528 U.S. 32, 120 S.Ct. 483, 145 L.Ed.2d 451 (1999); Florida Star v. B.J.F., 491 U.S. 524, 109 S.Ct. 2603, 105 L.Ed.2d 443 (1989).

[119] Ostergren v. Cuccinelli, 615 F.3d 263 (4th Cir. 2010) (state could not prevent private party from posting social security numbers from land records when it had not yet redacted social security numbers from records it put online).

[120] Diane L. Zimmerman, Requiem for a Heavyweight: a Farewell to Warren and Brandeis's Privacy Tort, 68 Cornell L. Rev. 291 (1983).

[121] Freihofer v. Hearst Corp., 65 N.Y.2d 135, 480 N.E.2d 349, 490 N.Y.S.2d 735 (1985). But the state consumer protection statute may prevent certain disclosures of private information. See Meyerson v. Prime Realty Svcs., LLC, 796 N.Y.S.2d 848, 853 (N.Y. Sup. Ct. 2005).

[122] Anderson v. Fisher Broad. Cos., Inc. 300 Or. 452, 469, 712 P.2d 803, 814 (1986).

[123] Doe v. Methodist Hosp., 690 N.E.2d 681 (Ind. 1997).

[124] Dietz v. Finlay Fine Jewelry Corp., 754 N.E.2d 958 (Ind. Ct. App. 2001).

[125] Hall v. Post, 323 N.C. 259, 372 S.E.2d 711 (1988). However, the court allowed an intentional infliction of emotional distress claim in a related setting. See Burgess v. Busby, 142 N.C.App. 393, 544 S.E.2d 4 (2001) (doctor sent letter to other doctors in the county naming jurors as people who found a doctor guilty of malpractice).

§ 38.5 False Light

Elements. The fourth privacy tort recognized by the Restatement and conventional wisdom is the false light tort. The tort is established only if the plaintiff proves that (a) the defendant publicized a matter about the plaintiff to a substantial group of persons or to the public; (b) the matter put the plaintiff in a false light; (c) the false light would be highly offensive to a reasonable person; and (d) the defendant knew of the falsity or acted in reckless disregard of whether the matter was false or not.[126] The Restatement contemplates "publicity," rather than publication of a lesser scope, such as communication to a few people.[127] The cases mostly agree.[128] The false light claim, like the claim for defamation, commonly does not survive the death of the victim.[129]

False light and defamation. The tort theoretically goes beyond defamation because the objectionable false light is not necessarily a defamatory one, only false and offensive. For example, a false light claim was established when a newspaper feature article made false statements about the plaintiff's poverty and her stoic attitude following the death of her husband in a disaster.[130] Likewise, a false light claim was made out when a television program, by splicing shots, falsely depicted the plaintiff as a hunter who shot wild geese on the ground rather than in flight.[131] A claim was also stated when a magazine cover falsely implied that the plaintiff had posed nude for the magazine.[132] Publication of a photo of a little league baseball team, whose coach had molested some members of the team, was enough to count as false light in a suit by the players and coaches depicted.[133] Possibly, but not certainly, these are cases in which defamation could not be established.[134]

Overlap with other torts. On the other hand, many of the false light cases appear to be cases of defamation or infliction of emotional distress under another name. Where the

---

[126] Restatement (Second) of Torts § 652E (1976).

[127] Bean v. Gutierrez, 980 A.2d 1090 (D.C. 2009) (communication from one individual to another without knowledge or intent that the second person would publish it in a newsletter is not sufficient to satisfy the "publicity" requirement); Restatement (Second) of Torts § 652E cmt. a (1976) (incorporating the publicity requirement of § 652D cmt. a).

[128] Steinbuch v. Cutler, 463 F.Supp.2d 1 (D.D.C. 2006) (claim of invasion of privacy on A's website; an additional claim against B, whose own website allegedly carried a link to A's, was allowed to proceed, seemingly not because the link itself was sufficient but only because the plaintiff alleged the two "worked together" to give publicity to the material); Cole v. Chandler, 752 A.2d 1189 (Me. 2000) (communicating to public at large or to so many that eventual public knowledge is substantially certain). But see Wal-Mart Stores, Inc. v. Lee, 348 Ark. 707, 74 S.W.3d 634 (2002) (requiring publicity but publication "to police, Wal-Mart supervisory personnel, and the prosecuting attorney" was treated as sufficient publicity). Solano v. Playgirl, Inc., 292 F.3d 1078 (9th Cir. 2002), said the requirement was disclosure "to one or more persons," but that seems to be a mistake about California law, which appeared to govern. See generally David A. Elder, Privacy Torts § 4:3 (2002); Russell G. Donaldson, Annotation, False Light Invasion of Privacy—Cognizability and Elements, 57 A.L.R.4th 22 (1987).

[129] West v. Media Gen. Convergence, Inc., 53 S.W.3d 640 (Tenn. 2001).

[130] See Cantrell v. Forest City Pub. Co., 419 U.S. 245, 95 S.Ct. 465, 42 L.Ed.2d 419 (1974) (in effect reinstating a jury verdict).

[131] Uhl v. Columbia Broad. Sys., Inc., 476 F.Supp. 1134 (W.D. Pa. 1979).

[132] Solano v. Playgirl, Inc., 292 F.3d 1078 (9th Cir. 2002) (given nature of magazine, it was a jury question whether photo and text on cover implied falsely that plaintiff had posed nude for magazine, which plaintiff claimed in turn implied that "he was willing to degrade himself and endorse such a magazine").

[133] M.G. v. Time Warner, Inc., 89 Cal.App.4th 623, 107 Cal.Rptr.2d 504 (2001).

[134] See also Flowers v. Carville, 310 F.3d 1118, 1132 (9th Cir. 2002) (false light claim by plaintiff who allegedly had affair with former President of the United States could go forward; in false light, unlike defamation, plaintiff did not need to allege injury to her reputation).

defamation claim requires derogatory content that would lower the plaintiff in the esteem of others, the false light privacy claim requires that the content would be highly offensive to a reasonable person. If a reasonable person would find the publication highly offensive, it is quite likely that the content is also defamatory under contemporary definitions.[135] Not surprisingly then, the Supreme Court, after holding that defamation under color of state law violated no constitutional rights, held that false light publicity violated none either.[136]

False light as element of damage resulting from other torts. Sometimes conduct that in fact puts the plaintiff in a false light is actionable for entirely different reasons, so that the false light is merely one element of damages resulting from some other tort. In a Minnesota case,[137] the plaintiff alleged that a photo developer retained a copy of a photo showing the plaintiff and another person in a shower together, then circulated the photo to others. The plaintiff alleged that as a result, some people questioned her sexual orientation. The court concluded that no false light claim would be permitted but remanded for trial to determine the plaintiff's intrusion and appropriation claims. In an Oregon case, the defendant signed the plaintiff's name to a petition sent to the governor. The court held the claim actionable, but as fraud and an appropriation of the plaintiff's name, not as a false light tort.[138]

Perhaps most of the cases of false light are cases of defamatory communications, appropriation of name or likeness, intrusive invasion of privacy followed by publication of matters wrongfully gained in the intrusion, or some other tortious activity. In all of these cases the plaintiff would be entitled to recover for the harms done by placing her in a false light, even if there were no separate false light tort. Consequently, a serious question is raised whether the false light tort is a helpful addition to the armory or merely another piece of baggage that gets in the way.[139] In addition, the false light claim always involves publication or publicity and hence is either entitled to some kind of constitutional and common law free speech protection[140] or else is merely an evasion of those constitutional protections.

Rejecting the false light tort. With these considerations in mind, the highest courts of some states have flatly rejected any false light tort.[141] Others doubted that the tort

---

[135] Jews For Jesus, Inc. v. Rapp, 997 So.2d 1098 (Fla. 2008) ("conduct that defames will often be highly offensive to a reasonable person, just as conduct that is highly offensive will often result in injury to one's reputation"); compare Solano v. Playgirl, Inc., 292 F.3d 1078 (9th Cir. 2002) (false light claim based on magazine's implication that plaintiff would "endorse" the magazine by posing for it), with Eastwood v. National Enquirer, Inc., 123 F.3d 1249 (9th Cir. 1997) (defamation claim based on publication's implication that plaintiff gave it an interview, perhaps implying that actor was washed up, else he would not interview with such a publication).

[136] Paul v. Davis, 424 U.S. 693, 96 S.Ct. 1155, 47 L.Ed.2d 405 (1976).

[137] Lake v. Wal-Mart Stores, Inc., 582 N.W.2d 231 (Minn. 1998).

[138] Hinish v. Meier & Frank Co., Inc., 166 Or. 482, 113 P.2d 438 (1941).

[139] Wilson v. Freitas, 121 Haw. 120, 214 P.3d 1110 (Ct. App. 2009) (false light claim is derivative of defamation claim: if latter is dismissed, former will be as well).

[140] Roux v. Pflueger, 16 So. 3d 590 (La. Ct. App. 2009) (speech on an issue of public concern—vicar giving away valuable church property—as a matter of law was not false light tort).

[141] Denver Publ'g Co. v. Bueno, 54 P.3d 893 (Colo. 2002) (emphasizing overlap with libel, availability of other privacy and emotional distress claims, and constitutional free speech concerns, three judges dissenting); Jews For Jesus, Inc. v. Rapp, 997 So.2d 1098 (Fla. 2008); Cain v. Hearst Corp., 878 S.W.2d 577, 579 (Tex. 1994).

should be recognized and so far have refused to do so[142] or suggested special impediments to it.[143] In addition, legislation in some states codifying a limited right of privacy has been deemed to exclude all forms of privacy actions not established by statute, including false light claims.[144] The Supreme Court of Arizona, on the other hand, has insisted that even when the plaintiffs allege that the publication accused them of incompetence in office, illegal activities, misuse of public funds, and police brutality, all clearly defamatory, the plaintiff could assert the false light tort and would not be limited to a defamation action.[145] One potential advantage in retaining the false light claim is that it can be and has been used to avoid some of the more arcane and complex rules of defamation.[146] However, that hardly seems to be a justification for the false light claim. It would be more clear, and more just, to simply abolish undesirable defamation rules. If, instead, the rules in defamation cases are sound, the false light claim may be an undesirable evasion of the rules, unless courts go on to apply those rules to the false light claim as well.[147]

Constitutional constraints. In any event, where the false light tort is recognized, the Constitution imposes limits in the interest of free speech, just as it does in libel cases. Under the rule for defamation cases, the plaintiff who is a public official or public figure must prove knowing or reckless falsehood[148] and do so by clear and convincing evidence.[149] A more lenient rule applies to libel cases brought by private figures; in that case, the plaintiff is required to show "some fault" such as negligence and can recover only actual damages.[150] The Supreme Court handed down its initial false light privacy decision before the more lenient rule for private plaintiffs had been announced and consequently required a knowing or reckless falsehood without regard to the plaintiff's status as a private figure.[151] Because of the parallel to libel cases, it may well be that a

---

[142] Lake v. Wal-Mart Stores, Inc., 582 N.W.2d 231 (Minn. 1998); cf. Sullivan v. Pulitzer Broad. Co., 709 S.W.2d 475 (Mo. 1986) (plaintiff could not evade defamation statute of limitation by casting claim as one for false light privacy). See Russell G. Donaldson, Annotation, False Light Invasion of Privacy—Cognizability and Elements, 57 A.L.R.4th 22 (1988).

[143] See Colbert v. World Publ'g Co., 747 P.2d 286, 292 (Okla. 1987) (linking the tort to intentional infliction of emotional distress and requiring a knowing or reckless falsehood).

[144] Costanza v. Seinfeld, 279 A.D.2d 255, 719 N.Y.S.2d 29 (2001); WJLA-TV v. Levin, 264 Va. 140, 564 S.E.2d 383 (2002).

[145] Godbehere v. Phoenix Newspapers, Inc., 162 Ariz. 335, 783 P.2d 781 (1989); cf. West v. Media Gen. Convergence, Inc., 53 S.W.3d 640 (Tenn. 2001) (upholding the false light tort in a case where plaintiffs alleged a publication implying a sexual or "cozy" relationship with a judge who referred business to the plaintiff).

[146] See, e.g., Zechman v. Merrill Lynch, Pierce, Fenner & Smith, Inc., 742 F.Supp. 1359, 1373 (N.D. Ill. 1990) (Illinois' innocent construction rule and distinction between per se and per quod defamation avoided by false light privacy claim). But other courts have carried over the per quod rules of defamation to privacy claims as well. Fellows v. National Enquirer, Inc., 42 Cal.3d 234, 721 P.2d 97, 228 Cal.Rptr. 215, 57 A.L.R.4th 223 (1986).

[147] Yeung v. Maric, 224 Ariz. 499, 232 P.3d 1281 (Ct. App. 2010) (absolute judicial proceedings privilege applies to false light as it would to defamation claims); Swan v. Boardwalk Regency Corp., 969 A.2d 1145 (N.J. 2009) (to avoid end run around defamation requirements, one year statute of limitations for defamation actions applies to false light privacy claims).

[148] Falsity itself is a hurdle in a number of cases. See S.B. v. Saint James Sch., 959 So. 2d 72 (Ala. 2006) (schoolgirls who took nude pictures of themselves that were circulated among classmates could not show that expulsion put them in false light); Mann v. Cincinnati Enquirer, 2010 WL 3328631 (Ohio Ct. App. 2010) ("privacy is not invaded when unimportant false statements are made").

[149] § 37.18.

[150] Id.

[151] Time, Inc. v. Hill, 385 U.S. 374, 87 S.Ct. 534, 17 L.Ed.2d 456 (1967).

negligent falsehood would suffice in a false light claim by a private person,[152] provided that such a plaintiff could only recover actual damages.[153] The Supreme Court has implied that the question is open for consideration.[154] However, states may require the plaintiff to prove not merely negligence, but a knowing or reckless falsehood even when a private person sues, and some, in line with the Restatement's rule, have done so.[155]

---

[152] Such a rule has been applied or stated. See Wood v. Hustler Magazine, Inc., 736 F.2d 1084 (5th Cir. 1984) (Texas law before Texas rejected false light claims altogether); West v. Media Gen. Convergence, Inc., 53 S.W.3d 640 (Tenn. 2001). To complete the parallel, the plaintiff would be limited to a recovery of actual damages in such a case.

[153] Haynes v. Alfred A. Knopf, Inc., 8 F.3d 1222 (7th Cir. 1993); West v. Media Gen. Convergence, Inc., 53 S.W.3d 640 (Tenn. 2001).

[154] Cantrell v. Forest City Publ'g Co., 419 U.S. 245, 95 S.Ct. 465, 42 L.Ed.2d 419 (1974).

[155] See Pfannenstiel v. Osborne Publ'g Co., 939 F.Supp. 1497 (D. Kan. 1996) (predicting Kansas law to this effect and citing a number of cases); Colbert v. World Publ'g. Co., 747 P.2d 286 (Okla. 1987); Robert D. Sack & Sandra S. Baron, Libel, Slander and Related Problems § 10.3.6.2 (3d ed. 2008) (reviewing cases on all positions). Cf. Corey v. Pierce County, 154 Wash. App. 752, 225 P.3d 367 (2010) (knowing or reckless falsehood required with defamation and false light in case involving prosecutor).

Chapter 39

MISUSING JUDICIAL PROCESS

Analysis

A. INTRODUCTION: TORTIOUS USE OF THE LEGAL PROCESS

§ 39.1   Scope, Policies and Immunities

B. MALICIOUS PROSECUTION

§ 39.2   Elements
§ 39.3   Instigating or Continuing the Criminal Proceeding
§ 39.4   Absence of Probable Cause
§ 39.5   Improper Purpose or "Malice"
§ 39.6   Favorable Termination of the Prosecution
§ 39.7   Special Defenses

C. WRONGFUL CIVIL LITIGATION

§ 39.8   Elements
§ 39.9   Probable Cause in Wrongful Civil Litigation
§ 39.10   Malice or Improper Purpose
§ 39.11   Favorable Termination of Former Civil Suit
§ 39.12   Special-Injury or Special-Grievance Requirement

D. ABUSE OF PROCESS

§ 39.13   Elements
§ 39.14   The Meaning of "Process" and Examples of Abuse
§ 39.15   Collateral Advantage and the "Act After" Requirement

E. REFORMS AND NEW DIRECTIONS

§ 39.16   SLAPP Suits, Sanctions, and Counterclaims

A. INTRODUCTION: TORTIOUS USE OF THE LEGAL PROCESS

§ 39.1 Scope, Policies and Immunities

The integrity of the legal system can be undermined by the innocent, negligent, or intentional conduct of many people, including lawyers, litigants, witnesses, judges, and juries. A judge who makes a palpably erroneous ruling, a witness who commits perjury, and a litigant who brings wholly unjustified suits all inflict harm on the legal system and the public interest. They may also inflict private harm upon others in the process. This chapter addresses the torts of malicious prosecution, wrongful civil litigation, and abuse of process that may allow recovery when such private harm occurs.[1]

---

[1]   An aggrieved plaintiff may be able to bring a federal constitutional or civil rights claim under narrow circumstances. See 3 Dobbs, Hayden & Bublick, The Law of Torts § 597 to 600 (2d ed. 2011 & Supp.).

In the most common kind of case, the plaintiff is complaining because the defendant unjustifiedly instigated an earlier suit or criminal prosecution against the plaintiff, causing the plaintiff expense and perhaps loss of reputation. The injustice felt by one who has been wrongly prosecuted is clear enough. The chief policy against redress for such a victim is that prosecutions of the arguably guilty should not be discouraged by the threat that the complaining witness will be held liable in damages. Moreover, if a second court could impose liability for what was done in the first, then a third court could question the second, and a fourth could question the third. Much more substantially, litigation in the first court's resolution of the issues represents the appropriate solution to the dispute. These policies translate into great caution about imposing liability upon those who instigate criminal or civil litigation or utilize the process of the courts.[2]

The policy of limiting liability of those involved in legal processes is expressed in two major ways. First, courts protect many actors in the legal process by recognizing privileges or immunities. Second, courts require the plaintiff who asserts harm resulting from litigation to prove a series of difficult elements to make out a prima facie case.

Litigation privilege or immunity. Almost everyone directly involved in litigation enjoys an absolute immunity from liability for communications made in the litigation or even in preparation for it[3] lest the voices of the honest be stilled by fear of liability.[4] Beyond that, judges are immune from suit based upon their rulings in a case over which they have jurisdiction, even if the ruling is erroneous or malicious.[5] Although in some states a witness retained as an expert is subject to liability for expert malpractice,[6] this liability runs only to the party who retained him. Otherwise, witnesses are immune; even those who testify to a knowing falsehood avoid liability to those harmed by his testimony, either on the ground that perjury is not a tort or that the witness is absolutely immune.[7] And no civil rights action lies even though the lying witness is a government

[2] See Sheldon Appel Co. v. Albert & Oliker, 47 Cal.3d 863, 872, 765 P.2d 498, 501, 254 Cal.Rptr. 336, 340 (1989) (claim is "disfavored" because of its chilling effect); Richey v. Brookshire Grocery Co., 952 S.W.2d 515, 517 (Tex. 1997) ("Malicious prosecution actions involve a delicate balance between society's interest in the efficient enforcement of the criminal law and the individual's interest in freedom from unjustifiable and oppressive criminal prosecution.").

[3] See § 37.11.

[4] See Briscoe v. LaHue, 460 U.S. 325, 333, 103 S.Ct. 1108, 1114, 75 L.Ed.2d 96 (1983) ("A witness's apprehension of subsequent damages liability might induce two forms of self-censorship. First, witnesses might be reluctant to come forward to testify. And once a witness is on the stand, his testimony might be distorted by the fear of subsequent liability.").

[5] See, e.g., K.D. v. Bozarth, 313 N.J.Super. 561, 713 A.2d 546 (App. Div. 1998).

[6] Marrogi v. Howard, 805 So.2d 1118 (La. 2002) (math errors, no immunity); LLMD of Mich., Inc. v. Jackson-Cross Co., 559 Pa. 297, 740 A.2d 186 (1999) (same); contra, Bruce v. Byrne-Stevens & Associates Engineers, Inc. 113 Wash.2d 123, 776 P.2d 666 (1989) (engineer retained to show cost of repairs grossly understated costs, resulting in inadequate jury verdict, retained witness is immune like others).

[7] E.g., Witzke v. City of Bismarck, 718 N.W.2d 586 (N.D. 2006); Cooper v. Parker-Hughey, 894 P.2d 1096 (Okla. 1995); Wilson v. Bernet, 218 W.Va. 628, 625 S.E.2d 706 (2005) (adverse witness in child-custody proceeding immune).

official.[8] Official prosecutors,[9] grand juries,[10] and those in similar roles[11] are absolutely immune for their decision to prosecute as well as for their in-trial conduct.

Litigation privilege or immunity inapplicable to wrongfully brought actions. Private persons and police officers who wrongfully institute legal actions are not protected by the litigation privilege against a malicious prosecution claim.[12] This result reflects the tendency of many courts to limit liability for conduct occurring after suit is brought[13] but to permit liability for wrongfully bringing suit in the first place. For instance, although perjury is not ordinarily actionable, pre-litigation spoliation of evidence sometimes is.[14] More central in this chapter, citizens and officers who procure the institution of a prosecution, civil suit, or even misuse a process within the suit may be held liable if they have done so wrongfully.[15] Attorneys fall under the same rule. They are not liable vicariously for the acts of their clients, but for their own decisions to sue when the known facts show that there is no probable cause to do so, and for their own abuse of process, they enjoy no more immunity than others[16] and are subject to liability.[17]

Damages. Damages awardable for malicious prosecution, wrongful civil litigation and abuse of process are dependent upon the facts and upon proof of losses, but when evidence shows the harm claimed, the principles of damages are essentially the same with all three torts. As with all torts, recovery is limited to those harms fairly attributable to the defendant's wrongful acts. Compensatory damages for tangible losses or harm normally include reasonable attorney's fees and other expenses incurred in defending the wrongful criminal or civil litigation[18] or avoiding or quashing abusive process,[19] other consequent losses such as lost earnings,[20] damages for dispossession of

---

[8]   Briscoe v. LaHue, 460 U.S. 325, 103 S.Ct. 1108, 75 L.Ed.2d 96 (1983).

[9]   Van de Kamp v. Goldstein, 555 U.S. 335, 129 S.Ct. 855, 172 L.Ed.2d 706 (2009); Imbler v. Pachtman, 424 U.S. 409, 96 S.Ct. 984, 47 L.Ed.2d 128 (1976) (immunity of prosecutor extends to § 1983 actions).

[10]   Crawford v. Busbee, 164 Ga.App. 559, 298 S.E.2d 278 (1982).

[11]   The immunity follows the prosecutor's function rather than his status. Van de Kamp v. Goldstein, 555 U.S. 335, 129 S.Ct. 855, 172 L.Ed.2d 706 (2009). When the prosecutor becomes a complaining witness, the immunity becomes qualified. Kalina v. Fletcher, 522 U.S. 118, 118 S.Ct. 502, 139 L.Ed.2d 471 (1997).

[12]   Silberg v. Anderson, 50 Cal.3d 205, 786 P.2d 365, 266 Cal.Rptr. 638 (1990); McKinney v. Okoye, 282 Neb. 880, 806 N.W.2d 571 (2011); Rainier's Dairies v. Raritan Valley Farms, 19 N.J. 552, 117 A.2d 889 (1955).

[13]   Thus some courts invoke the litigation privilege in abuse of process claims, at least in the form that depends upon conduct occurring after suit is commenced. See § 37.11. Where a lawyer is sued for abuse of process, and the pleadings allege no act independent of the legal process itself and no act "beyond the scope of her representation of the client or in her own interests," the judicial privilege may protect the lawyer from liability even where the conduct occurred before a judicial proceeding has commenced. See Moss v. Parr Waddoups Brown Gee & Loveless, 285 P.3d 1157 (Utah 2012) (lawyers obtained civil discovery orders authorizing search).

[14]   E.g., Henry v. Deen, 310 N.C. 75, 310 S.E.2d 326 (1984); see §§ 44.4 to 44.7.

[15]   However, some states may provide a non-traditional immunity for officers guilty of malicious prosecution. See Cal. Gov. Code § 821.6.

[16]   Mozzochi v. Beck, 204 Conn. 490, 529 A.2d 171 (1987); Baglini v. Lauletta, 315 N.J.Super. 225, 717 A.2d 449 (1998).

[17]   See Sheldon Appel Co. v. Albert & Oliker, 47 Cal.3d 863, 765 P.2d 498, 254 Cal.Rptr. 336 (1989) (recognizing potential liability); Manuel v. Wilka, 610 N.W.2d 458 (S.D. 2000) (summary judgment for attorney held improper); Vazquez v. Reeves, 138 Or.App. 153, 907 P.2d 254 (1995).

[18]   Tri-State Hospital Supply Corp. v. United States, 341 F.3d 571 (D.C. Cir. 2003); Ziobron v. Crawford, 667 N.E.2d 202 (Ind. Ct. App. 1996).

[19]   Hewes v. Wolfe, 74 N.C.App. 610, 330 S.E.2d 16 (1985).

[20]   Thrift v. Hubbard, 974 S.W.2d 70 (Tex.Ct.App. 1998) (almost $10,000 in lost earnings during court appearances).

or cloud on the title of property[21] and for physical illness or pain resulting from the tort,[22] subject to the usual limitations that they must result proximately from the wrong and that damages will not be awarded for speculative or conjectural items of loss.[23] Intangible damages recoverable include damages for harm to reputation[24] and damages for emotional harm.[25] Punitive damages can be awarded against the tortfeasor,[26] subject to all the rules governing such awards in the particular jurisdiction.[27]

B. MALICIOUS PROSECUTION

§ 39.2 Elements

A malicious prosecution suit asserts that the plaintiff was formerly prosecuted and that the prosecution was wrongfully instigated by the now defendant. It differs from false arrest in that the prosecution does not necessarily involve any detention of the plaintiff at all and in that any detention that does occur is the result of legal process that would defeat a false imprisonment claim. Malicious prosecution focuses upon the elements necessary to show that the process is wrongful; detention or confinement is not part of the issue, although the plaintiff who has a malicious prosecution suit may also have a false arrest action. Malicious prosecution always involves defamation, since it entails charging the now-plaintiff with a crime, but a defamation action as such would be defeated by the privilege to report suspected crimes to appropriate authorities. In the usual view, malicious prosecution also differs from abuse of process, which requires misuse of legal process after it has been rightly issued.

One common illustration of the malicious prosecution case is this: a store manager believes the plaintiff has secreted merchandise on her person and has left the premises without paying. The manager swears out a warrant charging the plaintiff with shoplifting or some similar crime. The jury returns a not guilty judgment. The plaintiff then sues the store for malicious prosecution. Indeed, any charge of crime can produce a tort claim that the accused was maliciously prosecuted—a retailer's bad-check charge, a lender's charge of criminal fraud, or an employer's charge of embezzlement, for example.

The plaintiff who is unjustifiably prosecuted suffers a number of harms that are worthy of redress, but redress does not come easily. The malicious prosecution claim must assert that the plaintiff's wrongful prosecution was (1) directly or indirectly instigated or continued by the defendant,[28] (2) without probable cause, (3) with improper

---

[21]   Kleinschmidt v. Morrow, 642 A.2d 161 (Me. 1994) (lost rental value resulting because of excessive lien claim); Ruiz v. Varan, 110 N.M. 478, 797 P.2d 267 (1990) ("nominal" damages of $5,000 when wrongful lis pendens clouded title but did not result in any loss of use).

[22]   Avildsen v. Prystay, 204 A.D.2d 154, 611 N.Y.S.2d 188 (1994).

[23]   E.g., MTW Inv. Co. v. Alcovy Properties, Inc., 228 Ga.App. 206, 491 S.E.2d 460 (1997) (land tied up by lis pendens, but owner's claims that he would have subdivided land and made profit was too speculative).

[24]   Papa v. City of New York, 194 A.D.2d 527, 598 N.Y.S.2d 558 (1993); Junior Food Stores, Inc. v. Rice, 671 So.2d 67 (Miss. 1996).

[25]   E.g., Martinez v. The Port Authority of New York and New Jersey, 445 F.3d 158 (2d Cir. 2002); K-Mart Corp. v. Kyles, 723 So.2d 572 (Ala. 1998); Ford Motor Credit Co. v. Hickey Ford Sales, Inc., 62 N.Y.2d 291, 465 N.E.2d 330, 476 N.Y.S.2d 791 (1984).

[26]   E.g., Harold McLaughlin Reliable Truck Brokers, Inc. v. Cox, 324 Ark. 361, 922 S.W.2d 327 (1996); Alamo Rent-A-Car, Inc. v. Mancusi, 632 So.2d 1352 (Fla. 1994).

[27]   See §§ 34.4 to 34.6.

[28]   This can be broken into two elements: (a) a prosecution must be commenced, for example, a mere charge to authorities is not a commencement; and (b) the accuser must be legally responsible for it. See, e.g.,

purpose ("malice"), and (4) terminated favorably to the plaintiff.[29] The plaintiff is also required to prove damages, but that is seldom a problem. Since all of these elements are required to establish the claim, there is no such thing as a valid claim for negligent prosecution.[30] It is difficult to prove all four of the required elements and it is meant to be, since those who report a perception of crime should not be led by fear of liability to withhold information from police and prosecutors.

§ 39.3   Instigating or Continuing the Criminal Proceeding

Criminal proceeding required. Malicious prosecution can be established only if the defendant has instigated or continued to pursue a criminal proceeding.[31] The Restatement Second of Torts rightly points out that a criminal proceeding must be formally begun by issuance of criminal process, by an indictment, or at least by an official arrest on a criminal charge.[32] Almost any kind of criminal proceeding will qualify, and most courts say that a proceeding has been instituted even if the court lacks jurisdiction.[33] On the other hand a mere complaint to authorities that never results in arrest, indictment or information does not initiate a criminal proceeding.[34]

Reporting facts to prosecutor or officer. To be an instigator, the defendant must necessarily make a complaint, induce another to do so,[35] or otherwise communicate directly or indirectly with the prosecutor; and prosecution must in fact follow. But while that is necessary, it is not sufficient. If the officer or prosecutor makes his own decision to prosecute, it is he, not the complaining witness, who is regarded as instituting the action.[36] The defendant is free to report the facts to the prosecutor. The defendant's provision of facts leaves the decision to the prosecutor, and the defendant is not responsible for his decisions to prosecute.[37]

Falsity, inaccuracy, or undue influence required. As these limitations imply, the defendant can be regarded as an instigator of the proceeding only if (a) he communicates material information falsely or inaccurately and the prosecutor relies upon his statement,[38] or (b) the defendant uses his power or position to influence the prosecutor

---

McKinney v. Okoye, 287 Neb. 261, 842 N.W.2d 581 (2014). The latter element reflects a requirement of both factual and proximate causation.

[29] See Restatement Second of Torts § 653 (1977).

[30] See Lawson v. Kroger Co., 997 F.2d 214 (6th Cir. 1993).

[31] See LaMantia v. Redisi, 118 Nev. 27, 38 P.3d 877 (2002).

[32] Restatement Second of Torts § 654 (1977).

[33] See, e.g., Calhoun v. Bell, 136 La. 149, 66 So. 761 (1914).

[34] Restatement Second of Torts § 654 (1977).

[35] Id. § 653, cmt. d (1977).

[36] See State Farm Bureau v. Cully's Motorcross Park, 366 N.C. 505, 742 S.E.2d 781 (2013) (police officer independently exercised his discretion to prosecute an insured with information provided by insurer; insurer did not instigate); see also Limone v. United States, 579 F.3d 79 (1st Cir. 2009) (merely providing false information to law enforcement in response to official queries during an investigation is insufficient to constitute instigating criminal proceedings).

[37] Bankston v. Pass Road Tire Ctr., Inc., 611 So.2d 998 (Miss. 1992); Lester v. Buchanen, 112 Nev. 1426, 929 P.2d 910 (1996); Restatement Second of Torts § 653, cmt. g; see Dan B. Dobbs, Belief and Doubt in Malicious Prosecution and Libel, 21 Ariz. L. Rev. 607 (1979) (arguing that the citizen-accuser should be free to rely on officers to make the appropriate decision).

[38] Bank of Eureka Springs v. Evans, 353 Ark. 438, 109 S.W.3d 672 (2003); Matthews v. Blue Cross and Blue Shield of Michigan, 456 Mich. 365, 572 N.W.2d 603 (1998).

in favor of prosecution.[39] An inaccurate statement of facts can be found when the defendant omits material information such as exculpatory evidence that might induce a prosecutor not to proceed.[40]

An important question arises when the defendant believes that he has reported the information accurately to the prosecutor but it is in fact false, so that by honest error the prosecutor is misled. The Restatement Second of Torts and most cases protect the defendant who honestly believes the information he has furnished the prosecutor, even if it turns out to be false.[41] For example, if the defendant honestly identifies the plaintiff as the person who committed a crime, the plaintiff is not an instigator of the prosecution and not liable even though the identification is in fact false.[42] In effect, this requires a knowing or reckless falsehood. The danger of penalizing one who cooperates with law enforcement is so great that it is appropriate to require more than negligence.

§ 39.4 Absence of Probable Cause

The plaintiff must prove that the defendant instigated criminal proceedings without probable cause.[43] Probable cause turns on the reasonableness of the accusation made against the plaintiff,[44] rather than on the accuser's improper purpose or malice. If the defendant had probable cause to procure the prosecution, the fact that he harbored malice or improper purpose will not help the plaintiff. The accuser's malice, as the saying goes, does not permit an inference that probable cause was lacking.[45]

Definitions. Many courts have defined probable cause in similar language. One version of the definition says that probable cause is a state of facts known to the accuser that would permit a person of ordinary prudence to believe that the accused committed the *offense* charged,[46] although the facts need not show guilt beyond a reasonable doubt.[47] A second version, perhaps more accurately, says that the facts must permit a reasonable person to believe that the accused committed the *act* of which the accuser complains.[48] The first version suggests that a citizen-accuser is responsible for failing to

---

[39]   Police officers, like others, are subject to liability for malicious prosecution, unless they are performing purely prosecutorial duties. If they initiate a criminal proceeding by presentation of false statements, or by withholding exculpatory information from the prosecutor, for example, they are clearly instigators. E.g., Martin v. City of Albany, 42 N.Y.2d 13, 364 N.E.2d 1304, 369 N.Y.S.2d 612 (1977).

[40]   E.g., Jones v. City of Chicago, 856 F.2d 985 (7th Cir. 1988).

[41]   Papa John's Intern., Inc. v. McCoy, 244 S.W.3d 44 (Ky. 2006) (false statement must be made intentionally or there is no tort of malicious prosecution); Lester v. Buchanen, 112 Nev. 1426, 1429, 929 P.2d 910, 913 (1996) (defendant "cannot be held liable for commencing the criminal action because they merely reported information they believed to be true"); Restatement Second of Torts § 653, cmt. g (1977) (information must be "known to be false").

[42]   E.g., Cedars-Sinai Med. Ctr. v. Superior Court, 206 Cal.App.3d 414, 253 Cal.Rptr. 561 (1988).

[43]   See Brunson v. Affinity Federal Credit Union, 199 N.J. 381, 972 A.2d 1112 (2009) (lack of probable cause is the "essence" of the malicious prosecution claim, and plaintiff must establish it).

[44]   The issue is whether the probable cause existed for the prior proceeding as a whole, as opposed to each specific claim in that proceeding. See, e.g., Brunson v. Affinity Fed. Credit Union, 199 N.J. 381, 972 A.2d 1112 (2009); Fleetwood Retail Corp. of New Mexico v. LeDoux, 142 N.M. 150, 164 P.3d 31 (2007).

[45]   E.g., Cordes v. Outdoor Living Ctr., Inc., 301 Ark. 26, 781 S.W.2d 31 (1989); Restatement Second of Torts § 669A (1977). Similarly, evidence that the accuser misstated or withheld facts in making a report to the police may establish malice, but it does not establish a want of probable cause. First Valley Bank of Los Fresnos v. Martin, 144 S.W.3d 466 (Tex. 2004).

[46]   E.g., Adams v. Sussman & Hertzberg, Ltd., 292 Ill.App.3d 30, 684 N.E.2d 935, 225 Ill.Dec. 944 (1997); Bacon v. Towne, 4 Cush. (58 Mass.) 217 (1849).

[47]   E.g., Strickland v. University of Scranton, 700 A.2d 979 (Pa.Super. 1997).

[48]   See Lawson v. Kroger Co., 997 F.2d 214 (6th Cir. 1993) ("without probable cause to believe the facts upon which the claim was based") (Tennessee law); Pallares v. Seinar, 407 S.C. 359, 756 S.E.2d 128 (2014)

name the crime correctly,[49] except that in very unusual cases he can avoid liability because of an honest mistake of law.[50] The second suggests that he need only state the facts accurately.

Which definition? The first version may be more appropriate when the accuser is an officer who should know or find out the appropriate charge. The second version is more appropriate when the accuser is a private person whose responsibility should be limited to accurate reporting of the facts. Sometimes, however, the accusation of a crime implies the assertion of some specific facts. If a reasonable person would not believe the implied assertions of fact, then probable cause is lacking even under the second version. For instance, a storekeeper might accuse someone of larceny when the crime actually shown by the facts is only a crime called shoplifting. The second version of the probable cause definition does not require the storekeeper to take the risk that his legal language is inappropriate but it does require reasonable grounds for believing facts. But the charge of larceny, like the more accurate charge of shoplifting, implies grounds for believing that the accused took something. If the facts do not warrant such a belief by a reasonable person, probable cause is lacking under either version of the definition.

Factual analysis. Under any definition, the determination of probable cause or its absence usually requires detailed factual analysis. A shopper's concealment of merchandise coupled with prompt departure may warrant an inference of theft, but a customer's departure with openly carried merchandise may not.[51] There are, of course, easy cases in which courts can simply say that the defendant was irrational in drawing an inference of guilt. The officer who overhears Person A say he smoked marijuana in Person B's presence can hardly rationally conclude that Person B possessed marijuana.[52] The officer who relies on a child's contradictory statements, when that child has been beaten so badly he cannot coherently identify the plaintiff as a criminal when all other evidence exculpates him, obviously has no probable cause for accusing the plaintiff.[53]

Reasonable appearance of facts at the time. Probable cause—the reasonableness of inferences of guilt—is to be judged by facts as they appeared at the time, not by later-discovered facts.[54] When liability is based upon continuance rather than initiation of the prosecution, probable cause must be judged on appearances at the time the accuser acts to continue the prosecution, as where he refuses to withdraw his complaint even after he has learned of the accused's innocence.[55] Non-lawyers may judge appearances by relying in good faith upon advice of fully informed counsel who is admitted to the bar in the state or otherwise appears to be reasonably competent.[56]

("[P]robable cause exists if the facts and circumstances would lead a person of ordinary intelligence to believe that the plaintiff committed one or more of the acts alleged in the opponent's complaint.").

[49] See Restatement Second of Torts § 662, Ill. 1 (1977) (based on Parli v. Reed, 30 Kan. 534, 2 P. 635 (1883)).

[50] See id. § 662, cmt. i (limiting the mistake of law defense to such cases as those in which a statute that is facially valid is later held unconstitutional).

[51] Gustafson v. Payless Drug Stores Northwest, Inc., 269 Or. 354, 525 P.2d 118 (1974).

[52] Cf. Malley v. Briggs, 475 U.S. 335, 106 S.Ct. 1092, 89 L.Ed.2d 271 (1986) (on similar facts).

[53] Jones v. City of Chicago, 856 F.2d 985 (7th Cir. 1988).

[54] Brunson v. Affinity Fed. Credit Union, 199 N.J. 381, 972 A.2d 1112 (2009).

[55] Branson v. Donaldson, 206 Ga.App. 723, 426 S.E.2d 218 (1992).

[56] Strickland v. University of Scranton, 700 A.2d 979 (Pa.Super. 1997); Restatement Second of Torts § 666 (1977). Most courts regard this as a defense, on which the defendant bears the burden of proof. See § 39.8.

Further investigation required. When appearances leave heavy doubts, or create serious ambiguities, and when they indicate that other information is available that will confirm or dispel suspicions, an accusation made without further investigation may be premature and lacking in probable cause. For example, when a store customer walks out with an unpaid-for item of merchandise, courts often say that the inference of theft is reasonable, so the store manager has probable cause to prosecute,[57] but when the evidence is ambiguous or doubtful, the accuser's failure to investigate, or at least to utilize all the evidence at hand, may be enough to indicate a want of probable cause. An officer who has only an unsupported accusation of the plaintiff from a felon with a motive for revenge should not lodge a serious charge of armed robbery when further leads remain to be investigated.[58] On the other hand, where a reasonable person would not investigate the facts further before instituting criminal proceedings, the lack of such an investigation will not show lack of probable cause.[59] Similarly, the mere fact that some evidence can be found that tends to exculpate the accused does not eliminate probable cause to believe in guilt.[60]

Objective vs. subjective judgments of reasonableness. The reasonableness standard of probable cause is an objective standard.[61] If the citizen-accuser only states facts to an officer or prosecutor, and he honestly believes those facts, the whole matter is left to the prosecutor, and the accuser is not an instigator of the prosecution at all.[62] However, when it comes to the issue of probable cause, the accuser's own honest belief in guilt is not sufficient; the facts must warrant a reasonable person's belief in guilt.[63] However, a formula recited by a number of courts implies or states that while the accuser's subjective belief in guilt is not enough to show probable cause, his subjective belief in the accused's innocence is enough to show the lack of it.[64] If the facts warrant prosecution, however, the citizen's belief in innocence seems irrelevant. A completely objective test would be more appropriate,[65] and some recent decisions have explicitly rejected subjective elements.[66] Perhaps in most cases the citizen-accuser would be protected because he is not an instigator at all.

Presuming want of probable cause from judicial actions. Since the criminal trial itself does not deal with the issue of probable cause but with the issue of ultimate guilt

---

[57] E.g., Richey v. Brookshire Grocery Co., 952 S.W.2d 515 (Tex. 1997).

[58] Miller v. East Baton Rouge Parish Sheriff's Dept., 511 So.2d 446 (La. 1987). On the other hand, if an officer learns about a crime from a co-perpetrator in connection with that person's confession, courts may view this information as "highly credible" and "more reliable" than other types of statements, because it is a statement against penal interest. See Gibson v. State, 758 So.2d 782 (La. 2000).

[59] Van v. Grand Casinos of Mississippi, Inc., 767 So.2d 1014 (Miss. 2000).

[60] E.g., Gray v. State, 624 A.2d 479 (Me. 1993) (evidence of mother's child abuse justified reasonable belief in her guilt, although some therapists could pose alternative explanations for the evidence).

[61] Matthews v. Blue Cross and Blue Shield of Michigan, 456 Mich. 365, 572 N.W.2d 603 (1998); Jordan v. Bailey, 113 Nev. 1038, 944 P.2d 828 (1997).

[62] See § 39.3.

[63] Bacon v. Towne, 4 Cush. (58 Mass.) 217, 238 (1849) ("Probable cause is such a state of facts in the mind of the prosecutor as would lead a man of ordinary caution and prudence to believe, or entertain an honest and strong suspicion, that the person arrested is guilty.").

[64] Torian v. Ashford, 216 Ala. 85, 112 So. 418 (1927); see Hitson v. Simms, 69 Ark. 439, 64 S.W. 219 (1901).

[65] See Dan B. Dobbs, Belief and Doubt in Malicious Prosecution and Libel, 21 Ariz. L. Rev. 607 (1980).

[66] Sheldon Appel Co. v. Albert & Oliker, 47 Cal.3d 863, 765 P.2d 498, 254 Cal.Rptr. 336 (1989); Matthews v. Blue Cross and Blue Shield of Michigan, 456 Mich. 365, 572 N.W.2d 603 (1998); Roberts v. Federal Express Corp., 842 S.W.2d 246 (Tenn. 1992).

beyond a reasonable doubt, an acquittal of the accused at trial does not tend to prove that the accuser lacked probable cause.[67] Some courts, however, have said that when the examining magistrate finds no probable cause, or the grand jury rejects an indictment, a rebuttable presumption or an inference arises that the accuser lacked probable cause.[68] Some have even said so when the public prosecutor enters a *nolle prosqui* or abandons the prosecution.[69] Other courts have rejected such presumptions.[70]

The presumption or inference is usually a diversion. At best, it puts the burden upon the defendant to show he had probable cause and hence places upon him the risk of uncertainty. It may promote a substantial diversion from the merits because the presumption may be attacked on the ground that the magistrate's discharge was not upon the merits, or was a mistaken adjudication of the ultimate guilt rather than probable cause, or was based upon misconduct.[71] If the evidence bearing upon probable cause is before the court, the presumption satisfies no need, especially under the usual rule that the probable cause issue is for the judge, not the jury.[72] In addition, if the court indulges a presumption that the defendant lacked probable cause because a magistrate so determined at a preliminary criminal hearing, the court is binding the present defendant by the results of a proceeding in which the defendant was not a party. If that is not actually unconstitutional, it is at least unfair,[73] and since it is also unneeded, such presumptions could be dropped without loss.

Presuming probable cause. The converse case is one in which the accused is bound over by the magistrate, or indicted by the grand jury. Courts in these cases have held that such determinations make a prima facie showing that the accuser had probable cause,[74] rebuttable by proof that the magistrate in fact made the determination on some other ground.[75] The requirement of favorable termination of the criminal proceeding bars the accused who is found guilty at trial and does not succeed in reversing the conviction; but even if the conviction is reversed on appeal, the now-reversed guilty finding has been treated as establishing prima facie evidence of probable cause.[76]

---

[67] E.g., Banks v. Montogomery Ward & Co., Inc., 212 Md. 31, 128 A.2d 600 (1957); Shoemaker v. Selnes, 220 Or. 573, 349 P.2d 473 (1960). See also H.D. Warren, Annotation, Acquittal, discharge, or discontinuance of criminal charge as evidence of want of probable cause in malicious prosecution action, 59 A.L.R.2d 1413 (1958).

[68] Schnathorst v. Williams, 240 Iowa 561, 36 N.W.2d 739 (1949); Tritchler v. West Virginia Newspaper Pub. Co., 156 W.Va. 335, 193 S.E.2d 146 (1972).

[69] Thompson v. Harris, 603 So.2d 1086 (Ala. Civ. App. 1992).

[70] Sundeen v. Kroger, 355 Ark. 138, 133 S.W.3d 393 (2003) (entry of nolle prosqui, standing alone, is not evidence that probable cause was lacking); Miessner v. All Dakota Ins. Assocs., Inc., 515 N.W.2d 198 (S.D. 1993) (nolle prosqui or abandonment creates no presumption); Roberts v. Federal Express Corp., 842 S.W.2d 246 (Tenn. 1992) (grand's jury's refusal to indict creates no presumption).

[71] See Restatement Second of Torts § 663 (1977).

[72] See Palmer Ford, Inc. v. Wood, 298 Md. 484, 471 A.2d 297 (1984).

[73] See Davis v. McMillan, 142 Mich. 391, 105 N.W. 862 (1905) (rejecting the presumption on the ground that an act that is not the defendant's cannot bind him).

[74] E.g., Rothstein v. Carriere, 373 F.3d 275 (2d Cir. 2004); Miessner v. All Dakota Ins. Assocs., Inc., 515 N.W.2d 198 (S.D. 1994).

[75] E.g., Rodgers v. W.T. Grant Co., 341 So.2d 511 (Fla. 1976) (magistrate bound the accused over because she would not release her potential civil action; this was not a determination of probable cause).

[76] E.g., Ex parte City of Gadsden, 718 So.2d 716 (Ala. 1998). Some courts give it even greater weight. See Sundeen v. Kroger, 355 Ark. 138, 133 S.W.3d 393 (2003) (conviction is "conclusive evidence of probable cause, even where the judgment is later reversed").

Judge and jury. Under the traditional view, the jury determines any disputed facts bearing on probable cause, but the question whether the facts so determined count as probable cause is a question of law for the judge.[77] Some courts reject this view and leave both the facts and the ultimate issue of probable cause to the jury;[78] others sometimes use an ambiguous formulation that leaves the roles of judge and jury in doubt.[79]

§ 39.5 Improper Purpose or "Malice"

The malicious prosecution plaintiff must prove, in addition to the other elements, that the now-defendant instigated the earlier prosecution for an improper purpose—for a purpose other than to bring the accused to justice.[80] This is the element traditionally referred to as "malice," and is for the jury to decide.[81]

Mixed motives. All tests that turn on the defendant's supposed motive or purpose raise difficult problems, first because motives can only be guessed at from actions, and second because motives are usually quite mixed. The Restatement Second of Torts resolves the mixed-motive problem by providing that the accuser must act "primarily" for a purpose other than to bring the supposed offender to justice.[82] For example, there is a good deal of abuse of the criminal process by merchants who use it as a means of collecting bad checks, but the fact that a merchant prosecutes those who bounce checks partly because the merchant hopes to collect the check is not enough to show malice.[83] The primary-purpose test may be less suited than a but-for test used in some other circumstances. Under a but-for test, the prosecutor's supposed improper purpose would not count against him if he would have instituted the prosecution even without the improper purpose.[84]

Improper purposes. The mixed-motive problem aside, the Restatement Second of Torts takes the view that any purpose other than to bring the offender to justice is improper and establishes the "malice" element of malicious prosecution. Use of the criminal process solely to enforce a supposed debt or to extort money from the accused shows improper purpose,[85] and so does personal hostility or ill-will,[86] or impersonal

---

[77] Palmer Ford, Inc. v. Wood, 298 Md. 484, 471 A.2d 297 (1984); Matthews v. Blue Cross and Blue Shield of Michigan, 456 Mich. 365, 381, 572 N.W.2d 603, 611 (1998); Van v. Grand Casinos of Mississippi, Inc., 767 So.2d 1014 (Miss. 2000); Restatement Second of Torts § 673(1) (1977).

[78] Schnathorst v. Williams, 240 Iowa 561, 36 N.W.2d 739 (1949).

[79] Courts often state that probable cause is for the judge unless facts are not in dispute, but that if facts are disputed, the issue becomes one of mixed law and fact, to be resolved by the jury. Thrifty Rent-A-Car v. Jeffrey, 257 Ark. 904, 520 S.W.2d 304 (1975); Richey v. Brookshire Grocery Co., 952 S.W.2d 515 (Tex. 1997). Conceivably such a statement means only that the hard facts are to be resolved by the jury, after which the judge decides probable cause on the basis of the jury's factual determination.

[80] Restatement Second of Torts § 668 (1977).

[81] E.g., Mitchell v. Folmar & Assoc., LLP, 854 So.2d 1115 (Ala. 2003); Nassar v. Concordia Rod and Gun Club, Inc., 682 So.2d 1035 (Miss. 1996); Lambert v. Sears, Roebuck & Co., 280 Or. 123, 570 P.2d 357 (1977).

[82] See Restatement Second of Torts § 668, cmt. c (1977).

[83] Lawson v. Kroger Co., 997 F.2d 214 (6th Cir. 1993).

[84] Mt. Healthy City Sch. Dist. Bd. of Educ. v. Doyle, 429 U.S. 274, 97 S.Ct. 568, 50 L.Ed.2d 471 (1977) (discharge for both unconstitutional and constitutional reasons); Greenwich Citizens Comm., Inc. v. Counties of Warren and Washington Indus. Dev. Agency, 77 F.3d 26 (2d Cir. 1996).

[85] Hodges v. Gibson Prods. Co., 811 P.2d 151 (Utah 1991); Restatement Second of Torts § 668, cmt. g (1977).

[86] Restatement Second of Torts § 668, cmt. f (1977); Kingstown Mobile Home Park v. Strashnick, 774 A.2d 847 (R.I. 2001). Cf. McClinton v. Delta Pride Catfish, Inc., 792 So.2d 968 (Miss. 2001) (malice means improper objective, not improper attitude).

hostility based upon race or other group characteristics.[87] In some of the cases malice seems more like oppressive behavior or abuse of power or authority than anything else.[88] Courts can easily infer malice if the accuser knowingly asserts falsehoods. On the other hand, it is difficult to see how he can be malicious if he honestly reports facts pointing toward guilt, even if he does not believe the inference of guilt. The Restatement flatly states, however, that the accuser who does not believe in guilt is necessarily malicious.[89] This seems wrong because an honest citizen can believe it is his duty to report facts even if he does not believe their negative implications.[90]

Relation to probable cause. Courts sometimes appear to confuse or conflate probable-cause and malice issues. The most serious problem arises in applying the old saw that while malice is not evidence of a lack of probable cause, a lack of probable cause is evidence of malice.[91] The inference of malice from a want of probable cause has been permitted even when the want of probable cause itself is merely "presumed" from a grand jury's refusal to indict.[92] But if malice or improper purpose can be inferred any time probable cause is lacking, then malice does not look like an independent element of the plaintiff's case at all. The Restatement has accordingly attempted to limit the inference to cases in which the lack of probable cause shows the accuser did not believe the charges he brought.[93] Perhaps, as Judge Linde argued, it would be more accurate to say that the same evidence that shows a want of probable cause might sometimes show malice as well.[94] For example, when an accuser reports incriminating evidence he knows to be false, the facts might permit a reasonable inference of instigation, malice, and a want of probable cause. But not necessarily. If probable cause has been shown to exist by other evidence, the accuser's knowing falsehoods may permit an inference of his malice, but they prove nothing about probable cause.[95]

§ 39.6 Favorable Termination of the Prosecution

The malicious-prosecution plaintiff must show not only that the criminal prosecution of which he complains has been terminated, but also that it has been terminated in his favor.[96] The requirement of termination serves to minimize a threat of civil liability that might chill testimony in the criminal action and to avoid litigation that may become needless if a conviction is obtained and upheld. The additional requirement that termination must be in the accused's favor of the accused serves a different purpose. If the accused was convicted, a malicious prosecution action should be impermissible because courts should not be permitted to collaterally attack the conviction.[97]

---

[87]   Lippay v. Christos, 996 F.2d 1490 (3d Cir. 1993).

[88]   See Lippay v. Christos, 996 F.2d 1490 (3d Cir. 1993); Martin v. City of Albany, 42 N.Y.2d 13, 396 N.Y.S.2d 612, 364 N.E.2d 1304 (1977) (civil rights claim adopting state law; oppressive behavior may warrant finding of malice); Lambert v. Sears, Robebuck & Co., 280 Or. 123, 570 P.2d 357 (1977).

[89]   Restatement Second of Torts § 668, cmt. e (1977).

[90]   Dan B. Dobbs, Belief and Doubt in Malicious Prosecution and Libel, 21 Ariz. L. Rev. 607 (1979).

[91]   See, e.g., Montgomery Ward v. Wilson, 339 Md. 701, 664 A.2d 916 (1995); Moore v. Evans, 124 N.C.App. 35, 476 S.E.2d 415 (1996); Pallares v. Seinar, 407 S.C. 359, 756 S.E.2d 128 (2014).

[92]   Schnathorst v. Williams, 240 Iowa 561, 36 N.W.2d 739 (1949).

[93]   Restatement Second of Torts § 669 (1977).

[94]   Lambert v. Sears, Roebuck & Co., 280 Or. 123, 570 P.2d 357 (1977) (Linde, J., concurring).

[95]   First Valley Bank of Los Fresnos v. Martin, 144 S.W.3d 466 (Tex. 2004).

[96]   Restatement Second of Torts § 658 (1977); see Yacubian v. United States, 750 F.3d 100 (1st Cir. 2014); Kossler v. Crisanti, 564 F.3d 181 (3d Cir. 2009) (en banc).

[97]   See Heck v. Humphrey, 512 U.S. 477, 114 S.Ct. 2364, 129 L.Ed.2d 383 (1994).

An acquittal of the accused after a trial or on a dispositive motion is of course a termination favorable to the accused.[98] Short of that, courts have looked for dispositions that tend to show the accused's innocence or at least a determination that a criminal case could not be proved,[99] saying that a mere procedural victory would not suffice.[100] Maybe it would be more accurate to say that a disposition of the criminal proceedings that probably entailed some judgment about the merits will count as a favorable termination, or at least that the dismissal of the criminal prosecution was not inconsistent with innocence.[101] Under such a rule, a favorable termination may sometimes occur even though the termination is not "final" because the prosecution can be revived or reinstituted. For example, if a magistrate determines that no probable cause has been shown and discharges the accused, jeopardy has not attached and the same charge may be laid again.[102] Nevertheless, a magistrate's discharge and a grand jury's refusal to indict can count as sufficient terminations.[103]

When the criminal prosecution is terminated because of a mere lapse of time or because the accused has left the jurisdiction,[104] because of a compromise settlement,[105] or for other reasons that do not bear even remotely upon the merits,[106] courts have held that the termination is not favorable to the accused, with the result that he cannot bring a malicious prosecution action based upon the criminal proceeding. Sometimes a *nol pros* reflects a compromise or mercy or some other reason for abandoning the prosecution that does not touch the merits and hence leaves the accused without a favorable termination.[107] Some courts have assumed that the unexplained *nol pros* is a compromise;[108] others have permitted or required evidence to show the reasons for the *nol pros*.[109] Still others have tacitly or expressly treated a *nol pros* as a termination.

---

[98]   Restatement Second of Torts § 659 (1977).

[99]   Jaffee v. Stone, 18 Cal.2d 146, 114 P.2d 335 (1941); MacFawn v. Kresler, 88 N.Y.2d 859, 666 N.E.2d 1359, 644 N.Y.S.2d 486 (1996); Ash v. Ash, 72 Ohio St.3d 520, 651 N.E.2d 945 (1995).

[100]   E.g., Foshee v. Southern Finance & Thrift Corp., 967 S.W.2d 817 (Tenn.Ct. App. 1997) (dismissal of the first action on double jeopardy grounds was not a favorable termination).

[101]   Cantalino v. Danner, 96 N.Y.2d 391, 754 N.E.2d 164, 729 N.Y.S.2d 405 (2001) (dismissal in the interests of justice was favorable termination on the facts of the particular case but would not be favorable termination if dismissal was a matter of mercy); Smith-Hunter v. Harvey, 95 N.Y.2d 191, 734 N.E.2d 750, 712 N.Y.S.2d 438 (2000) (dismissal on speedy trial grounds—failure to prosecute—was a favorable termination and "not inconsistent with plaintiff's innocence").

[102]   U.S. ex rel. Rutz v. Levy, 268 U.S. 390, 45 S.Ct. 516, 69 L.Ed. 1010 (1925); Richmond v. State, 554 P.2d 1217 (Wyo. 1976).

[103]   Jaffee v. Stone, 18 Cal.2d 146, 114 P.2d 335 (1941); but cf. MacFawn v. Kresler, 88 N.Y.2d 859, 666 N.E.2d 1359, 644 N.Y.S.2d 486 (1996) (dismissal of criminal charge on the ground that facts as stated were not sufficient to show a crime was not a sufficient termination).

[104]   Halberstadt v. New York Life Ins. Co., 194 N.Y. 1, 86 N.E. 801 (1909).

[105]   Martinez v. City of Schenectady, 97 N.Y.2d 78, 735 N.Y.S.2d 868, 761 N.E.2d 560 (2001); Cimino v. Rosen, 193 Neb. 162, 225 N.W.2d 567 (1975).

[106]   Restatement Second of Torts § 660 (1977) (listing compromise; accused's misconduct that prevents a proper trial; mercy; and institution of a new proceeding for the same offense).

[107]   See id. §§ 660 & 661; cf. O'Brien v. Alexander, 101 F.3d 1479 (2d Cir. 1996) (voluntary dismissal).

[108]   Tucker v. Duncan, 499 F.2d 963 (4th Cir. 1974).

[109]   Alamo Rent-A-Car, Inc. v. Mancusi, 632 So.2d 1352, 1356 (Fla. 1994).

§ 39.7 Special Defenses

Aside from immunities[110] and ordinary defenses such as the statute of limitations,[111] three special defenses may be raised: guilt in fact, release, and advice of counsel.

Guilt in fact. If the defendant instigated a prosecution of the plaintiff without probable cause but with malice, and the plaintiff was fully vindicated by a favorable termination, it is still possible that the plaintiff was in fact guilty of the crime for which she was prosecuted or one quite similar. Authorities agree that in such a case, the plaintiff cannot recover for malicious prosecution.[112] The rule is essentially similar to the rules applied in defamation and false arrest cases, relieving the defendant of all liability when the defamation turns out to be true[113] or the arrest justified because the arrested person is guilty in fact.[114] A different rule applies to the case of a discriminatory discharge from employment, which is not justified by the later discovery of non-discriminatory grounds for discharge; but even here, the employer-accuser is liable only for a limited remedy.[115] The guilt-in-fact rule does not exactly permit a collateral attack, since the earlier criminal action only determines that guilt has not been proven beyond a reasonable doubt, while the later malicious prosecution suit determines that guilt is established by a preponderance of the evidence.

Release. Public prosecutors not uncommonly agree to drop criminal charges in exchange for the accused's release of all claims against the prosecutor and others who have participated in the prosecution. If the release is valid, it forecloses legitimate complaints as well as frivolous complaints of malicious prosecution or analogous civil rights violations. States have split as to whether such releases are invalid per se.[116] The Supreme Court of the United States, in a decision governing federal civil rights claims for malicious prosecution, took the position that such releases were not necessarily invalid, but might be held so in particular cases, as where there is prosecutorial misconduct.[117] Following that lead, federal courts have developed a small jurisprudence of release law.[118] They have held that the prosecutor would be required to show a public interest favoring the release in the particular case so that a blanket policy of obtaining releases in all cases of abandoned prosecution would not be valid.[119] They have also

---

[110] E.g., McEachern v. Black, 329 S.C. 642, 496 S.E.2d 659 (1998) (judge); Andrews v. Ring, 266 Va. 311, 585 S.E.2d 780 (2003) (county attorney).

[111] The malicious prosecution action normally accrues upon termination of the criminal prosecution and the statute begins to run at that point. Lopes v. Farmer, 286 Conn. 384, 944 A.2d 921 (2008); Ferguson v. City of Chicago, 213 Ill.2d 94, 289 Ill.Dec. 679, 820 N.E.2d 455 (2004).

[112] Wal-Mart Stores, Inc. v. Blackford, 264 Ga. 612, 449 S.E.2d 293 (1994) (theorizing that guilt in fact eliminates damages and describing it as a "defense"); Rogers v. Hill, 281 Or. 491, 576 P.2d 328 (1978).

[113] See § 37.8. For further comparison of defamation and malicious prosecution, see § 39.2.

[114] Restatement Second of Torts § 119(a) (1965). Similarly, if a client is convicted because of a lawyer's malpractice but the client is in fact guilty of the crime, the lawyer will usually escape liability. See § 45.13.

[115] McKennon v. Nashville Banner Pub. Co., 513 U.S. 352, 115 S.Ct. 879, 130 L.Ed.2d 852 (1995).

[116] *Compare* Cowles v. Brownell, 73 N.Y.2d 382, 538 N.E.2d 325, 540 N.Y.S.2d 973 (1989) (per se invalid), *with* Hoines v. Barney's Club, Inc., 28 Cal.3d 603, 620 P.2d 628, 170 Cal.Rptr. 42 (1980) (not per se invalid).

[117] Town of Newton v. Rumery, 480 U.S. 386, 107 S.Ct. 1187, 94 L.Ed.2d 405 (1987); see, applying the *Rumery* factors to uphold a release, MacBoyle v. City of Parma, 383 F.3d 456 (6th Cir. 2004).

[118] See David B. Sweet, Annotation, Validity, as Against Claim under 42 U.S.C.A. § 1983, of Accused's Release Etc., 139 A.L.R. Fed. 1 (1997).

[119] Cain v. Darby Borough, 7 F.3d 377, 139 A.L.R. Fed. 677 (3d Cir. 1993).

considered whether particular releases were given voluntarily, taking into account a variety of factors. The release is less likely to be voluntary if the accused signs it while in custody, is not represented by counsel, is unsophisticated or is not fully informed about its effects.[120] Several courts have said that the burden of proof to show the validity of the release is upon the prosecutor.[121] Where police misconduct is part of the underlying civil rights claim, the release may deserve special scrutiny, since police might file charges as bargaining chips when their own misconduct is called into question.[122]

Advice of counsel. The defendant in a malicious prosecution action can also escape all liability by pleading and proving as an affirmative defense that the action was commenced or continued on the advice of counsel.[123] In order for the defense to be established, however, the defendant must show that he gave counsel all of the relevant information with respect to the claim.[124] The dominant rationale is that acting in good faith on the advice of counsel after giving the lawyer such information establishes that the defendant acted with probable cause.[125] Acting on the advice of counsel is a complete defense even where counsel's advice turned out to be entirely wrong.[126]

C. WRONGFUL CIVIL LITIGATION

§ 39.8 Elements

Wrongful institution of a civil action is actionable under rules similar to those for malicious prosecution of a criminal proceeding. The policy of protecting the right to resort to court, analogous to, if not grounded in, the First Amendment's right to petition government, applies to protect a certain amount of wrongful civil litigation, a point recognized under federal law as well as under the common law.[127] On the other hand, wrongful civil suits can destroy a livelihood, devastate a business, or chill debate on public issues.[128] Balance between these competing and core concerns is critical, and the rules aim with varying success at striking that balance.

The analogy to malicious prosecution led lawyers and courts to focus on wrongful initiation or continuation of civil proceedings or wrongful assertion of a counterclaim,[129] rather than wrongful or unjustified defensive tactics.[130] Under the traditional view, then,

---

[120] Livingstone v. North Belle Vernon Borough, 12 F.3d 1205 (3d Cir. 1993).

[121] E.g., Lynch v. City of Alhambra, 880 F.2d 1122 (9th Cir. 1989).

[122] Coughlen v. Coots, 5 F.3d 970 (6th Cir. 1993).

[123] This defense applies in cases of both criminal malicious prosecution and wrongful civil litigation.

[124] South Arkansas Petroleum Co. v. Schiesser, 343 Ark. 492, 36 S.W.3d 317 (2001); Verspyck v. Franco, 274 Conn. 105, 874 A.2d 249 (2005); Schnathorst v. Williams, 240 Iowa 561, 36 N.W.2d 739 (1949); Garcia v. Whitaker, 400 S.W.3d 270 (Ky. 2013).

[125] See, e.g., Pannell v. Reynolds, 655 So.2d 935 (Ala. 1994).

[126] See Vandersluis v. Weil, 176 Conn. 353, 407 A.2d 982 (1978); Andrews v. Ring, 266 Va. 311, 585 S.E.2d 780 (2003) (citing Noell v. Angle, 217 Va. 656, 231 S.E.2d 330 (1977)).

[127] Professional Real Estate Investors, Inc. v. Columbia Pictures Indus., Inc., 508 U.S. 49, 113 S.Ct. 1920, 123 L.Ed.2d 611 (1993) (all but "sham" litigation [essentially that brought without probable cause and with malice] is protected from claims that litigation is used to violate antitrust laws); Titan Am., LLC v. Riverton Investment Corp., 264 Va. 292, 569 S.E.2d 57 (2002) (applying the protection to state tort suits).

[128] On special anti-SLAPP statutes, see § 39.16.

[129] E.g., Harrison v. Springdale Water & Sewer Com'n, 780 F.2d 1422 (8th Cir. 1986) (public entity's counterclaim, § 1983 civil rights action was viable); Bertero v. National General Corp., 13 Cal.3d 43, 118 Cal.Rptr. 184, 529 P.2d 608 (1974) (cross-complaint seeking affirmative relief may be subject to a malicious prosecution claim).

[130] For changes in this view, see § 39.16.

the elements of the plaintiff's claim for wrongful civil proceedings were variations on those in malicious prosecution.[131] The plaintiff can recover if the defendant had participated in instigating or continuing[132] a civil proceeding, including a declaratory judgment action[133] or even a quasi-judicial administrative proceeding,[134] without probable cause and for an improper purpose, provided that the proceeding had been terminated favorably to the now-plaintiff. As a matter of *pleading*, conclusory allegations may be insufficient so that the plaintiff may be required to state facts from which a want of probable cause and malice could be inferred.[135] A substantial number of states add a requirement not found in malicious criminal prosecution cases: the plaintiff cannot recover unless she suffers special injury, usually meaning that her person or property was seized in the former action.[136]

Circumventing rules by pleading other torts. As with the malicious prosecution of a criminal charge,[137] the plaintiff cannot avoid the burden of proving these elements by claiming on a theory of negligence.[138] The protections for court access erected by the rules for wrongful litigation claims presumably cannot be avoided by framing the claim on a theory of defamation, privacy invasion, outrage, interference with contract, or professional negligence of lawyers, either. In fact, courts have rejected such claims under the rules for those particular torts.[139] But some courts have allowed plaintiffs to circumvent the rules protecting access to courts. If the plaintiff alleges that a lawsuit caused emotional harm[140] or interference with prospective economic relations,[141] a few cases have allowed the claim to proceed without evidence that the lawsuit was brought without probable cause. For this reason, it is important to recognize straightforwardly that no alternative theory can be permitted to subvert the rules by permitting liability for maintaining a suit when the conduct involved would not show wrongful civil litigation.[142] The original suitor's lawyer owes a duty of care only to his client, so although he may be liable for malicious prosecution or abuse of process, he is not liable to his client's adversary for negligence.[143] Taken together, these rules are a formidable barrier to recovery in many cases. For example, almost all of the physicians' countersuits

---

[131] Courts sometimes also invoke "presumptions" based on judicial determinations in the prior litigation. See Hornstein v. Wolf, 67 N.Y.2d 721, 490 N.E.2d 857, 499 N.Y.S.2d 938 (1986).

[132] E.g., Zamos v. Stroud, 32 Cal.4th 958, 12 Cal.Rptr.3d 54, 87 P.3d 802 (2004).

[133] George F. Hillenbrand, Inc. v. Ins. Co. of North America, 104 Cal.App.4th 784, 128 Cal.Rptr.2d 586 (2003).

[134] Hardy v. Vial, 48 Cal.2d 577, 311 P.2d 494, 66 A.L.R.2d 739 (1957); Label Systems Corp. v. Aghamohammadi, 270 Conn. 291, 852 A.2d 703 (2004); Restatement Second of Torts § 680 (1977).

[135] Prokop v. Hoch, 258 Neb. 1009, 607 N.W.2d 535 (2000).

[136] See § 39.12.

[137] See Brunson v. Affinity Fed. Credit Union, 199 N.J. 381, 972 A.2d 1112 (2009) (rejecting a claim of negligent investigation of purported fraud as a "surrogate" for a malicious prosecution claim).

[138] O'Toole v. Franklin, 279 Or. 513, 569 P.2d 561 (1977).

[139] See, e.g., Tappen v. Ager, 599 F.2d 376 (10th Cir. 1979) (physician who won malpractice action had no claim based upon libel, privacy invasion, and intentional infliction of emotional distress); Bidna v. Rosen, 19 Cal.App.4th 27, 23 Cal.Rptr.2d 251 (1993) (intentional infliction of emotional distress claim would require acts other than those supporting malicious prosecution).

[140] Green Bay Packaging, Inc. v. Preferred Packaging, Inc., 932 P.2d 1091 (Okla. 1996).

[141] See Nesler v. Fisher & Co., 452 N.W.2d 191 (Iowa 1990).

[142] See Palazzo v. Alves, 944 A.2d 144 (R.I. 2008) (failure of malicious prosecution claim necessarily means that separate claim under anti-SLAPP statute must also fail).

[143] Friedman v. Dozorc, 412 Mich. 1, 312 N.W.2d 585 (1981); see also Buscher v. Boning, 114 Hawai'i 202, 159 P.3d 814 (2007); Clark v. Druckman, 218 W.Va. 427, 624 S.E.2d 864 (2005).

against lawyers and former patients for bringing unjustified medical malpractice actions have been defeated by at least one of these rules.[144]

§ 39.9 Probable Cause in Wrongful Civil Litigation

The special-injury rule aside, one of the chief differences between the claim for malicious prosecution and the claim for wrongful civil litigation is that "probable cause" in the civil context means only that the original suitor must believe in the facts he asserts and that a civil claim is plausible, or he has a good chance at establishing the case to the satisfaction of judge and jury,[145] or that he "may" have a claim.[146] In this respect, he may rely upon advice of apparently competent and unbiased counsel after full disclosure of all relevant facts.[147] When the lawyer himself is sued for his part in instigating the former civil action, the lawyer is held to a kind of objective professional standard[148] and is liable only if the claim he fosters is not legally tenable.[149] This lenient approach to probable cause reflects the fact that in American litigation courts are constantly drawing distinctions, modifying formulations of rules, and recognizing new claims and defenses, so that even arguments that have been previously rejected are not necessarily untenable, and the further fact that much of the evidence in complex cases must be developed by discovery rather than before suit is commenced.

Effect of rulings in the underlying suit. As in criminal cases,[150] rulings in the underlying first suit may tend to establish or disestablish the existence of probable cause to bring that suit, and thus directly affect the malicious prosecution claim. Subject to limited exceptions,[151] courts say that when the first-suit plaintiff *won* on the merits of that suit, his win conclusively establishes that he had probable cause to pursue that suit, even if the plaintiff's judgment is later reversed on appeal.[152] When the first-suit plaintiff survives a motion for summary judgment but ultimately loses the case, authorities differ a little. A California case has said that survival of a defendant's summary judgment

---

[144] See Linda A. Sharp, Annotation, Medical Malpractice Countersuits, 61 A.L.R.5th 307 (1998).

[145] Bradshaw v. State Farm Mut. Auto. Ins., 157 Ariz. 411, 758 P.2d 1313 (1988).

[146] Restatement Second of Torts § 675 (1977).

[147] E.g., Bisno v. Douglas Emmett Realty Fund 1988, 174 Cal.App.4th 1534, 95 Cal.Rptr.3d 492 (2009); Neumann v. Indus. Sound Eng'g, Inc., 31 Wis.2d 471, 143 N.W.2d 543 (1966); see § 39.8.

[148] Sheldon Appel Co. v. Albert & Oliker, 47 Cal.3d 863, 765 P.2d 498, 254 Cal.Rptr. 336 (1989); Paulus v. Bob Lynch Ford, Inc., 139 Cal.App.4th 659, 43 Cal.Rptr.3d 148 (2006) (resolution of probable cause issue in suit against attorney "calls for the application of an objective standard").

[149] See Shannahan v. Gigray, 131 Idaho 664, 962 P.2d 1048 (1998) (in civil case, probable cause exists "if the attorney has a reasonable and honest belief that the client has a tenable claim"); Nagy v. McBurney, 120 R.I. 925, 392 A.2d 365 (1978) (lawyer who brings civil action has probable cause to do so "if he reasonably believes he has a good chance of establishing it to the satisfaction of the court or the jury").

[150] See § 39.5.

[151] (1) Probable cause is not conclusively shown if the first-suit plaintiff procured a favorable result by fraud or similar misconduct, or if the first court lacked jurisdiction. E.g., Cowles v. Carter, 115 Cal. App.3d 350, 357, 171 Cal. Rptr. 269, 272 (1981); Nagy v. McBurney, 120 R.I. 925, 392 A.2d 365 (1978). (2) Probable cause is not conclusively shown where the first-suit plaintiff wins only an ex parte injunctive order, but even that is said to be prima facie evidence that he had probable cause. Bokum v. Elkins, 67 N.M. 324, 331, 355 P.2d 137, 141 (1960); see also Paul v. Sherburne, 53 N.H. 747, 903 A.2d 1011 (2006) (applying same rule to ex parte protective order).

[152] Dacey v. New York County Lawyers' Ass'n, 423 F.2d 188 (2d Cir. 1969) (order granting injunction shows probable cause even where it is later reversed); Goldstein v. Sabella, 88 So.2d 910 (Fla. 1956); Condon v. Vickery, 270 Ga. App. 322, 606 S.E.2d 336 (2004); see L.C. Warden, Annotation, Judgment in Prior Civil Proceedings Adverse to Instant Plaintiff in Malicious Prosecution as Evidence of Probable Cause, 58 A.L.R.2d 1422 (1958).

motion in the first case is "persuasive evidence" that the plaintiff had probable cause;[153] an Arizona case held that the first-suit plaintiff's survival of a summary judgment motion is evidence, but not conclusive evidence, bearing on probable cause.[154]

The first-suit plaintiff's *loss* on the merits does not show a want of probable cause to bring the suit.[155] Similarly, when the first-suit plaintiff loses on summary judgment rather than on a jury verdict, his loss does not ordinarily establish as a matter of law that he lacked probable cause to sue.[156] This is obviously correct where the summary judgment was granted on procedural grounds, such as the statute of limitations or lack of standing, since that is not a "favorable termination on the merits" at all.[157] Sometimes, however, the trial court's ruling on a dispositive motion may furnish some degree of evidence on the issue,[158] and some other kinds of determinations made by judge or jury in the first suit may imply that the first-suit plaintiff lacked probable cause.[159]

§ 39.10 Malice or Improper Purpose

The requirement of improper purpose (or "malice") in wrongful civil litigation actions is again similar to its analog in malicious prosecution cases. The suitor is not liable for his failed suit unless he brought it for an improper purpose—that is, "primarily" for any purpose other than securing proper adjudication of the claim.[160] Spite itself is not enough; few tort suits are brought without a degree of rancor.[161] A motive that includes a spiteful desire to harass or a calculated desire to extort a settlement by a suitor who knows that the facts do not support his claim will suffice, however.[162] A complaint based upon knowing or reckless falsehoods shows improper purpose, but mere negligence of a lawyer in failing to discover that he has no case does not.[163] At the same time, purposeful avoidance of the evidence might show a knowing or reckless falsehood in libel cases;[164] a lawyer's complete lack of evidence in support of a claim might be understood to show that his motive for suit was primarily extortionate, not colorably legitimate. It should go without saying that a lawyer's contingent fee arrangement assuredly does not show malice in bringing the suit.[165] As in the malicious prosecution

---

[153] Roberts v. Sentry Life Ins., 76 Cal. App.4th 375, 90 Cal. Rptr.2d 408 (1999).

[154] Wolfinger v. Cheche, 206 Ariz. 504, 80 P.3d 783 (Ct. App. 2003).

[155] Royce v. Hoening, 423 N.W.2d 198 (Iowa 1988) (counterclaim dismissed after trial; no inference that counterclaimant lacked probable cause to pursue the counterclaim); Hill v. Carlstrom, 216 Or. 300, 338 P.2d 645 (1959).

[156] Jarrow Formulas, Inc. v. LaMarche, 31 Cal. 4th 728, 74 P.3d 737, 3 Cal. Rptr.3d 636 (2003).

[157] Parrish v. Marquis, 172 S.W.3d 526 (Tenn. 2005).

[158] See Neumann v. Industrial Sound Eng'g, Inc., 31 Wis.2d 471, 143 N.W.2d 543 (1966) (trial judge's dismissal of involuntary bankruptcy petition in the first suit is prima facie evidence of lack of probable cause, drawing analogy to criminal cases).

[159] See Slaney v. Ranger Ins. Co., 115 Cal. App.4th 306, 8 Cal. Rptr.3d 915 (2004).

[160] Restatement Second of Torts § 676 (1977).

[161] See DeVaney v. Thriftway Mktg. Corp., 124 N.M. 512, 953 P.2d 277 (1997), *overruled on other grounds*, Durham v. Guest, 145 N.M. 694, 204 P.3d 19 (2009).

[162] E.g., Bradshaw v. State Farm Mut. Auto. Ins., 157 Ariz. 411, 758 P.2d 1313 (1988) (insurer induced insured to file a suit as part of strategy to defend against a valid claim; this shows "malice").

[163] Spencer v. Burglass, 337 So.2d 596 (La.Ct.App. 1976).

[164] See Harte-Hanks Communications, Inc. v. Connaughton, 491 U.S. 657, 109 S.Ct. 2678, 105 L.Ed.2d 562 (1989); § 37.18.

[165] Miskew v. Hess, 21 Kan.App.2d 927, 910 P.2d 223 (1996).

cases, courts say that malice may be inferred from a want of probable cause.[166] The same objections can be raised as in malicious prosecution cases.

§ 39.11   Favorable Termination of Former Civil Suit

Termination of the former civil suit is important in two ways. First, the wrongful litigation claim accrues at termination of the former suit, so that the statute of limitations begins running at that time.[167] Second, favorable termination of the former suit is a substantive element of the plaintiff's claim for wrongful litigation.[168] The termination requirement leads courts to say that wrongful civil litigation cannot be challenged by a counterclaim in the same action, since that litigation could not have terminated when the counterclaim is filed.[169]

Favorable termination is not necessarily a termination on the merits, but it is usually a termination that tends to reflect on the probable merits. A disposition of the former suit that is on appeal is not regarded as a sufficient termination until the appeal is decided.[170] Otherwise, however, a determination on the merits that the defendant in the prior suit is not liable will be sufficient to show favorable termination, whether the termination is based upon trial or upon summary judgment or other motion.[171] But courts have said that a dismissal of the prior suit because the statute of limitations has run does not reflect the innocence of the defendant in the former suit and hence does not show favorable termination.[172] The Restatement view is that a dismissal for failure to prosecute the former suit is a sufficiently favorable termination, and that a withdrawal or voluntary dismissal by the plaintiff in that suit is likewise.[173] Some courts have taken a contrary view on the latter issue, holding that a voluntarily dismissal without prejudice is not a favorable termination, because it is "not an adjudication on the merits of the case but is merely a procedural option available to plaintiffs as a matter of right."[174]

[166]   One Thousand Fleet Ltd. Partnership v. Guerriero, 346 Md. 29, 694 A.2d 952 (1997).

[167]   Christian v. Lapidus, 833 S.W.2d 71 (Tenn. 1992) (abandonment of claim by filing a complaint not naming the present plaintiffs terminated the action and started the statute of limitations running).

[168]   New Mexico, which first consolidated the wrongful litigation and abuse of process torts into a single tort called "malicious abuse of process" in DeVaney v. Thriftway Mktg. Corp., 124 N.M. 512, 521, 953 P.2d 277, 286 (1997), *abrogated on other grounds*, Fleetwood Retail Corp. of New Mexico v. LeDoux, 142 N.M. 150, 164 P.3d 31 (2007), treats favorable termination as evidence bearing on probable cause but not as a separate element. See Durham v. Guest, 145 N.M. 694, 204 P.3d 19 (2009) (one way of proving "an improper use of process," an element of the new tort, is to show that the defendant filed a complaint without probable cause).

[169]   E.g., Bismarck Hotel Co. v. Sutherland, 175 Ill. App.3d 739, 529 N.E.2d 1091, 125 Ill.Dec. 15 (1988); Flugge v. Flugge, 681 N.W.2d 837 (S.D. 2004); Anello v. Vinci, 142 Vt. 583, 458 A.2d 1117 (1983); see Vitauts M. Gulbis, Annotation, Nature of termination of civil action required to satisfy element of favorable termination to support action for malicious prosecution, 30 A.L.R.4th 572, § 4[a] (1984).

[170]   One Thousand Fleet Ltd. Partnership v. Guerriero, 346 Md. 29, 694 A.2d 952 (1997).

[171]   Restatement Second of Torts § 674, cmt. j (1977).

[172]   Lackner v. LaCroix, 25 Cal.3d 747, 602 P.2d 393, 159 Cal.Rptr. 693 (1979); Miskew v. Hess, 21 Kan.App.2d 927, 910 P.2d 223 (1996); Palmer Dev. Corp. v. Gordon, 723 A.2d 881 (Me. 1999).

[173]   Restatement Second of Torts § 674, cmt. j (1977); accord, Siebel v. Mittlesteadt, 41 Cal.4th 735, 62 Cal.Rptr.3d 155, 161 P.3d 527 (2007); Cult Awareness Network v. Church of Scientology Intern., 177 Ill.2d 267, 685 N.E.2d 1347, 226 Ill.Dec. 604 (1997).

[174]   Himmelfarb v. Allain, 380 S.W.3d 35 (Tenn. 2012).

§ 39.12   Special-Injury or Special-Grievance Requirement

While most courts do not require the plaintiff in a wrongful civil litigation claim to show any "special injury" caused by the litigation to recover,[175] a substantial number have imposed such a requirement.[176] And many cases that purport to ignore special-injury requirements are actually decided on facts consistent with such requirements.[177] Special injury must be something more than the expense, distress, and reputational loss that is ordinarily suffered as a result of wrongful litigation.[178] Rather, the interference must result directly from the suit itself or the court's pre-judgment orders.[179] The wrongful litigation claim is allowed when the defendant has repeatedly brought unjustified suits.[180]

It is also allowed when a single suit directly results in pre-judgment impairment or suspension of the plaintiff's rights in property, income, or credit, or detention of the plaintiff's person.[181] Unjustified insanity proceedings are actionable, at least when they constrain the plaintiff's person for examination or otherwise,[182] while unjustified bankruptcy proceedings are actionable because they put the plaintiff's property under the control of the bankruptcy court.[183] Maliciously obtained provisional remedies such as injunctions, replevin, garnishment, attachment and receivership may give rise to liability.[184] Similar considerations might control when the original suitor files an

---

[175] Greenberg v. Wolfberg, 890 P.2d 895 (Okla. 1994). Statutes may so provide. See Or. Rev. Stats. § 31.230.

[176] Foley v. Argosy Gaming Co., 688 N.W.2d 244 (Iowa 2004); Robb v. Chagrin Lagoons Yacht Club, Inc., 75 Ohio St.3d 264, 662 N.E.2d 9 (1996) (prejudgment seizure of property required); Friedman v. Dozorc, 412 Mich. 1, 312 N.W.2d 585 (1981); Engel v. CBS, Inc., 93 N.Y.2d 195, 689 N.Y.S.2d 411, 711 N.E.2d 626 (1999); Kingstown Mobile Home Park v. Strashnick, 774 A.2d 847 (R.I. 2001); Texas Beef Cattle Co. v. Green, 921 S.W.2d 203 (Tex. 1996).

[177] E.g., Ackerman v. Kaufman, 41 Ariz. 110, 15 P.2d 966 (1932) (rejecting the special injury requirement where facts actually showed many harassing prior suits that would count as special injury); Greenberg v. Wolfberg, 890 P.2d 895 (Okla. 1995) (similar).

[178] E.g., Whalen v. Connelly, 621 N.W.2d 681 (Iowa 2000) (expense of litigation—allegedly $1 million— is not special injury).

[179] Thus the fact that the victim of wrongful litigation takes voluntary bankruptcy does not show special grievance, since it results only indirectly from the wrongful litigation. Venuto v. Carella, Byrne, Bain, Gilfillan, Cecchi & Stewart, P.C., 11 F.3d 385 (3d Cir. 1993).

[180] Cult Awareness Network v. Church of Scientology Int'l, 177 Ill.2d 267, 685 N.E.2d 1347, 226 Ill.Dec. 604 (1997) (21 allegedly meritless suits in 17 months in various jurisdictions sufficient showing of special injury); Restatement Second of Torts § 679 (1977).

[181] Royce v. Hoenig, 423 N.W.2d 198 (Iowa 1988) (requiring "proof of arrest, seizure of property, or other 'special injury' . . . which would not necessarily result in all suits prosecuted to recover for like causes of action"); Palazzo v. Alves, 944 A.2d 144 (R.I. 2008) (requiring "in the absence of a person's arrest or seizure of his or her property, a showing of 'special injury' beyond the trouble, cost, and other consequences normally associated with defending oneself against an unfounded legal charge"); but see Foley v. Argosy Gaming Co., 688 N.W.2d 244 (Iowa 2004) (consequential impairment of credit and loss of insurance coverage resulting indirectly from the prior suit is not a special injury).

[182] Pellegrini v. Winter, 476 So.2d 1363 (Fla.Dist.Ct.App. 1985); Fowle v. Fowle, 263 N.C. 724, 140 S.E.2d 398 (1965).

[183] Norin v. Sheldt Mfg. Co., 297 Ill. 521, 130 N.E. 791 (1921); Hubbard v. Beatty & Hyde, Inc., 343 Mass. 258, 178 N.E.2d 485 (1961); Specialty Mills, Inc. v. Citizens State Bank, 558 N.W.2d 617 (S.D. 1997). Some courts, however, require an actual seizure of the property. See Peter G. Guthrie, Annotation, Action For Malicious Prosecution Based on Institution of Involuntary Bankruptcy, Insolvency, or Receivership Proceedings, 40 A.L.R.3d 296 (1971).

[184] See O'Brien v. Alexander, 101 F.3d 1479 (2d Cir. 1996) (listing remedies and many cases); Blankenship v. Staton, 348 S.W.2d 925 (Ky. 1961) (attachment); Mayflower Indus. v. Thor Corp., 15 N.J.Super. 139, 83 A.2d 246 (1951) (injunction); Shute v. Shute, 180 N.C. 386, 104 S.E. 764 (1920) (injunction; bond is not exclusive remedy); Novick v. Becker, 4 Wis.2d 432, 90 N.W.2d 620 (1958) (garnishment).

unjustified *lis pendens*,[185] which clouds or encumbers the plaintiff's title to property and impairs its marketability. Consequently, some courts have permitted the victim to recover[186] on a wrongful litigation or some other theory[187] when a lis pendens is filed improperly or without probable cause. In the case of *lis pendens*, however, some other courts have rejected the action on the ground that the special-injury rule requires physical seizure[188] or on the ground that the filing of a *lis pendens* is absolutely privileged as a judicial act, at least where it is based upon underlying litigation that claims title to the disputed land.[189]

D. ABUSE OF PROCESS

§ 39.13   Elements

The gist of the abuse of process tort is the misuse of legal process primarily to accomplish a purpose for which it was not designed,[190] usually to compel the victim to yield on some matter not involved in the suit, or to harass litigation opponents by clearly wrongful conduct.[191] The victim might even be a person who is not sued at all but who is directly affected by the process, as where an injunction forbids the conduct of nonparties[192] or a lis pendens ties up the property of a person against whom no suit has been filed.[193]

The abuse of process tort could readily be integrated with the malicious prosecution and wrongful litigation torts,[194] but the traditional view treats them as separate torts with distinct elements. If the plaintiff can show instigation of a suit for an improper purpose without probable cause and with a termination favorable to the now-plaintiff, she has a malicious prosecution or a wrongful litigation claim, not a claim for abuse of process. Conversely, if the plaintiff cannot show those elements, she may still have a good abuse of process claim.[195] Specifically, the abuse of process claim permits the plaintiff to recover without showing the traditional absence of probable cause for the original suit and without showing favorable termination of that suit. The abuse of

---

[185] *Lis pendens* is an official record notifying prospective purchasers of real property that a suit is pending asserting a legal interest in the property. It is not authorized merely because the suitor has a claim for money damages that might ultimately be enforced against the property. See National City Bank, Indiana v. Shortridge, 689 N.E.2d 1248 (Ind. 1997).

[186] Wyatt v. Wehmueller, 163 Ariz. 12, 785 P.2d 581 (Ct. App. 1989) (filing *lis pendens* when statutory criteria were clearly not met, statutory penalty), *rev'd on other grounds*, 167 Ariz. 281, 806 P.2d 870 (1991); Cok v. Cok, 558 A.2d 205 (R.I. 1989) (both wrongful litigation and abuse of process theories); Kensington Dev. Corp. v. Israel, 142 Wis.2d 894, 419 N.W.2d 241 (1988).

[187] See Hewitt v. Rice, 154 P.3d 408 (Colo. 2007) (wrongful *lis pendens* filing may be remedied by an action for malicious prosecution, abuse of process, slander of title, and intentional interference with contractual relationship). Other courts have analyzed unjustified filing of *lis pendens* under theories of interference with contract, see National City Bank, Indiana v. Shortridge, 689 N.E.2d 1248 (Ind. 1997), slander of title, see Montecalvo v. Mandarelli, 682 A.2d 918 (R.I. 1996), abuse of process, and wrongful civil litigation, see Cok v. Cok, 558 A.2d 205 (R.I. 1989) (both abuse of process and malicious use of process).

[188] Sharif-Munir-Davidson Dev. Corp. v. Bell, 788 S.W.2d 427 (Tex. Ct. App. 1990).

[189] Ringier America, Inc. v. Enviro-Technics, Ltd., 284 Ill. App. 3d 1102, 673 N.E.2d 444, 220 Ill. Dec. 532 (1996).

[190] See Restatement Second of Torts § 682 (1977).

[191] See General Refractories Co. v. Fireman's Fund Ins. Co., 337 F.3d 297 (3d Cir. 2003).

[192] See Sands v. Living Word Fellowship, 34 P.3d 955 (Alaska 2001).

[193] See § 39.12.

[194] See Durham v. Guest, 145 N.M. 694, 204 P.3d 19 (2009) (stating revised elements for the new tort of "malicious abuse of process"), discussed in § 39.16.

[195] See Hewitt v. Rice, 154 P.3d 408 (Colo. 2007).

process claim may also permit the plaintiff to avoid the special-injury requirement applied in some wrongful litigation cases.

The elements of the abuse of process claim can be stated in slightly different ways, but, however stated, they are both vague and simple: first, the original suitor must have a primary purpose to use the criminal or civil process for an end for which it was not designed; and second, he must use that process in a way not proper in the regular course of the proceeding,[196] or in other words, bad motive plus some use of the court's process. More simply, "a court should ask whether there has been a 'perversion' of the process, or, whether a legal process has been used 'as a tactical weapon to coerce a desired result that is not the legitimate object of the process.' "[197] The First Restatement limited the tort to cases of pecuniary harm,[198] but that requirement was dropped in the Second Restatement.[199] Some courts add that actual seizure of person or property is also required,[200] but in most cases motive or purpose is the centerpiece of the tort.[201] In one of its common versions, the suitor attempts to use the suit itself or some process issued after suit has commenced as a form of extortion.[202] For example, a suitor may attach all the plaintiff's property so that the plaintiff cannot operate her business; the suitor then explicitly or implicitly offers to drop the attachment if the plaintiff will pay the suitor money she does not owe.[203]

§ 39.14   The Meaning of "Process" and Examples of Abuse

In its narrowest sense, "process" refers to enforceable court orders, although many of these are in fact issued routinely by the clerk of court. These include the summons, subpoenas, attachments, garnishments, replevin or claim and delivery writs, arrest under a warrant, injunctive orders, and other orders directly affecting obligations of persons or rights in property. Abuse of any of these processes is actionable upon appropriate proof.[204] But in this context, "process" can refer to judicial procedures of

---

[196] E.g., Simpson v. Laytart, 962 S.W.2d 392 (Ky. 1998); Yaklevich v. Kemp, Schaeffer & Rowe Co., L.P.A., 68 Ohio St.3d 294, 626 N.E.2d 115 (1994).

[197] General Refractories Co. v. Fireman's Fund Ins. Co., 337 F.3d 297 (3d Cir. 2003).

[198] Restatement of Torts § 682 (1938).

[199] Restatement Second of Torts § 682 (1977).

[200] See Parks v. Neuf, 218 Ill.App.3d 427, 578 N.E.2d 282, 161 Ill.Dec. 155 (1991); Lee v. Mitchell, 152 Or.App. 159, 953 P.2d 414 (1998).

[201] See Hatch v. Davis, 147 P.3d 383 (Utah 2006) (saying "the 'essence' of the tort of abuse of process [is] 'a perversion of the process to accomplish some improper purpose,' " finding that the defendant was engaged in "a campaign of hate and terror" and an "ill-intentioned crusade to intimidate" the plaintiff and others).

[202] See, e.g., Fuller v. Local Union No. 106, United Brotherhood of Carpenters and Joiners of America, 567 N.W.2d 419, 421 (Iowa 1997).

[203] Cf. Grainger v. Hill, 4 Bing. N.C. 212, 132 Eng.Rep. 769 (1838) (the classic case; the original suitor had the plaintiff arrested under civil process available at that time in order to induce the plaintiff to yield control of the vessel by which the plaintiff earned his livelihood); South Arkansas Petroleum Co. v. Schiesser, 343 Ark. 492, 36 S.W.3d 317 (2001) ("the test of abuse of process is whether a judicial process is used to extort or coerce"; demand for money not owed followed by instigation of prosecution, followed by testimony that did not reveal facts exculpating the plaintiff).

[204] E.g., Sands v. Living Word Fellowship, 34 P.3d 955 (Alaska 2001) (person not sued but who was enjoined as a result of the suit had standing to sue); White Lighting Co. v. Wolfson, 68 Cal.2d 336, 66 Cal.Rptr. 697, 438 P.2d 345 (1968) (attachment); Czap v. Credit Bureau of Santa Clara Valley, 7 Cal.App.3d 1, 86 Cal.Rptr. 417 (1970) (garnishment); Board of Educ. of Farmingdale Union Free Sch. Dist. v. Farmingdale Classroom Teachers Ass'n, Inc., Local 1899, 38 N.Y.2d 397, 403, 343 N.E.2d 278, 283, 380 N.Y.S.2d 635, 642 (1975) (subpoena).

various kinds that do not actually entail a court order or a writ.[205] Some courts have in mind the narrowest conception of process and hold that filing a wrongful *lis pendens* is not a tort because lis pendens is not a process.[206] Other courts, taking process more broadly to include all the procedures in the litigation process, include *lis pendens* as process, so that abuse is actionable.[207] Such a view holds that repeated filings in the wrong venue,[208] and even abusive discovery techniques or oppressive litigation tactics, can be an abuse of process.[209]

Abuse by coercive process plus offer to abandon it for illegitimate objective. Abuse appears in several forms. In the most commonly mentioned case, the original suitor offers to release or withdraw a justly procured process such as attachment or arrest in exchange for some collateral advantage unrelated to the lawsuit or which the court itself would be powerless to order.[210] For example, the original suitor may procure an arrest of the plaintiff pursuant to a warrant and then offer to have the prosecution dismissed if the plaintiff will work in the suitor's fertilizer factory. Since the only purpose of a criminal prosecution is punishment of crime, the use of the prosecution as a means of extorting payment of a debt is an abuse for which the action lies, even if the prosecution itself was proper.[211] Even if the offer for an illicit exchange is not explicit, the improper purpose to release the process in exchange for improper benefit may be inferred from what is said or done.[212] The gist of this form of abuse of process is that the original suitor attempts to use the court's process to gain an advantage to which he is not entitled. If he uses the court's process to obtain the very thing to which he is entitled, his motive for doing so and his plans for using his lawful entitlement are irrelevant.[213]

Other forms of abuse of process. In a number of cases, abuse of process can be found even though the original suitor makes no express extortionate demand at all. At least three patterns or explanations can be found for these cases. (1) Excessive attachments[214] and wrongful *lis pendens*[215] often amount to an abuse of process regardless of any

---

[205] Nienstedt v. Wetzel, 133 Ariz. 348, 352, 651 P.2d 876, 880, 33 A.L.R.4th 635 (Ct. App. 1982) (process "encompasses the entire range of procedures incident to the litigation process").

[206] Podolsky v. Alma Energy Corp., 143 F.3d 364 (7th Cir. 1998); Stahl v. St. Elizabeth Med. Ctr., 948 S.W.2d 419 (Ky.Ct.App. 1997).

[207] National City Bank, Indiana v. Shortridge, 689 N.E.2d 1248 (Ind. 1997); Cok v. Cok, 558 A.2d 205 (R.I. 1989); Broadmoor Apartments of Charleston v. Horwitz, 306 S.C. 482, 413 S.E.2d 9 (1991).

[208] Barquis v. Merchants Collection Ass'n of Oakland, 7 Cal.3d 94, 496 P.2d 817, 101 Cal.Rptr. 745 (1972).

[209] See, e.g., Simon v. Navon, 71 F.3d 9 (1st Cir. 1995); General Refractories Co. v. Fireman's Fund Ins. Co., 337 F.3d 297 (3d Cir. 2003).

[210] See Robb v. Chagrin Lagoons Yacht Club, Inc., 75 Ohio St.3d 264, 271, 662 N.E.2d 9, 14 (1996).

[211] Palmer Ford, Inc. v. Wood, 298 Md. 484, 471 A.2d 297 (1984); Ellis v. Wellons, 224 N.C. 269, 29 S.E.2d 884 (1944).

[212] See, e.g., Tranchina v. Arcinas, 78 Cal.App.2d 522, 178 P.2d 65 (1947); Robb v. Chagrin Lagoons Yacht Club, Inc., 75 Ohio St.3d 264, 662 N.E.2d 9 (1996).

[213] See Palazzo v. Alves, 944 A.2d 144 (R.I. 2008) (state senator sued public meeting participants for defamation; affirming trial court's dismissal of the abuse of process claim by the participants, noting "even a pure spite motive is not sufficient where process is used only to accomplish the result for which it was created"); Schmit v. Klumpyan, 663 N.W.2d 331 (Wis. App. 2003) (A and B were co-owners of a parcel of land; A wished to sell but B did not; A brought a partition action to force a sale; as this was the very purpose of a partition action, the fact that A's motive was to coerce B was essentially irrelevant).

[214] White Lighting Co. v. Wolfson, 68 Cal.2d 336, 66 Cal.Rptr. 697, 438 P.2d 345 (1968); see also Thomas J. Goger, Annotation, Liability of Creditor for Excessive Attachment or Garnishment, 56 A.L.R.3d 493 (1974).

[215] E.g., Cok v. Cok, 558 A.2d 205 (R.I. 1989); see also § 39.12.

extortionate demand.[216] Many or all of these can be explained on the ground that the suitor's act is, in the circumstances, an implicit proposal to abandon the process in exchange for an obvious quid pro quo. (2) In other cases, the process itself seems to be inherently or definitionally wrongful and that seems to be sufficient, even if the suitor commits no further act. Wrongful *lis pendens* and excessive-attachment cases may fall in this category as well as in the category of implicit threats. The abuse in such cases lies in the "illegitimate use of the attachment process to tie up more property than is reasonably necessary to secure the attaching creditor's claim," and no improper threat or bargaining is required.[217] Even a process server's falsification of an affidavit of service without more has been held to be an abuse of process.[218] (3) In some cases intended detriment to the adversary without any necessary benefit to the suitor may suffice,[219] as where the suitor repeatedly garnishes the plaintiff's wages solely to induce the harassed employer to fire the plaintiff,[220] or the suitor subpoenas all the teachers in a school system to impose financial hardship on the school,[221] sues debtors in the wrong venue in hopes of obtaining more default judgments,[222] or, in the case of a defendant in the original suit, repeatedly and illegitimately delays for unfair advantage.[223] In the category of illegitimate and harassing litigation tactics, even the opposing attorney may be liable to the plaintiff for the abuse of process.[224]

§ 39.15 Collateral Advantage and the "Act After" Requirement

Collateral advantage. When the claim for abuse of process rests upon the suitor's attempt to use the court's process to extort some special advantage, courts usually say that the advantage sought must be *collateral*, meaning that it is not a benefit to the suitor that the process was designed to secure. However, emphasis on the collateral character of the advantage sought can be misleading. First, the advantage need not always be collateral in the sense that it would be outside the court's power to grant. An attempt to gain a nuisance-value settlement for a bad medical malpractice suit was regarded as sufficient in one case,[225] although a money judgment for the same small amount would easily be within the court's jurisdiction. And there is nothing collateral about harassing the adversary in litigation, but serious misbehavior in doing so may nonetheless count as an abuse of process.[226] On the other side of the coin, even when the

---

[216]   E.g., Broadmoor Apartments of Charleston v. Horwitz, 306 S.C. 482, 413 S.E.2d 9 (1991).

[217]   White Lighting Co. v. Wolfson, 68 Cal.2d 336, 66 Cal.Rptr. 697, 438 P.2d 345 (1968).

[218]   Parks v. Neuf, 218 Ill.App.3d 427, 578 N.E.2d 282, 161 Ill.Dec. 155 (1991).

[219]   Bd. of Educ. of Farmingdale Union Free Sch. Dist. v. Farmingdale Classroom Teachers Ass'n, Inc., Local 1899, 38 N.Y.2d 397, 403, 343 N.E.2d 278, 283, 380 N.Y.S.2d 635, 642 (1975) (defendant must seek collateral advantage or a "corresponding detriment to the plaintiff which is outside the legitimate ends of the process").

[220]   Peterson v. Worthen Bank & Trust Co., 296 Ark. 201, 753 S.W.2d 278 (1988) (repeated wage garnishments pursued to induce employer to fire the employee).

[221]   Cf. Bd. of Educ. of Farmingdale Union Free Sch. Dist. v. Farmingdale Classroom Teachers Ass'n, Inc., Local 1899, 38 N.Y.2d 397, 343 N.E.2d 278, 380 N.Y.S.2d 635 (1975) (subpoena of 87 teachers to appear at the same time, forcing school to hire substitutes, although not all could appear on any one day).

[222]   Barquis v. Merchants Collection Ass'n of Oakland, Inc., 7 Cal.3d 94, 496 P.2d 817, 101 Cal.Rptr. 745 (1972) (debt collection agency's pattern of filing claims in wrong venue to impose hardship and make default judgment more likely).

[223]   General Refractories Co. v. Fireman's Fund Ins. Co., 337 F.3d 297 (3d Cir. 2003).

[224]   Giles v. Hill Lewis Marce, 195 Ariz. 358, 988 P.2d 143 (Ct. App. 1999).

[225]   Bull v. McCuskey, 96 Nev. 706, 615 P.2d 957 (1980), *overruled on other grounds*, Ace Truck v. Kahn, 103 Nev. 503, 746 P.2d 132 (1987).

[226]   General Refractories Co. v. Fireman's Fund Ins. Co., 337 F.3d 297 (3d Cir. 2003).

demand is for collateral advantage, it is not necessarily a wrong. A collateral demand may reflect nothing more than an insistence upon a comprehensive settlement of all disputes among the parties. In a California case,[227] a husband had the wife's property seized under claim-and-delivery or replevin proceedings. He then offered to drop the proceedings if the wife would drop her suit to establish the validity of their marriage. That was held an abuse of process. The husband's offer clearly sought an advantage that was collateral to his claim-and-delivery suit, and perhaps the detailed facts warranted liability. But the case can hardly reflect a rule of law that makes it tortious to work out a comprehensive settlement of all disputes between the parties.[228]

Act after process has issued. A number of courts have said that abuse of process is shown by showing the original suitor's ulterior purpose and his willful use of the process in a way not proper in the regular conduct of the proceeding or words to that effect.[229] As such formulations imply, the very issuance of the process may be abusive in some cases without additional acts.[230] But courts have repeatedly quoted or paraphrased[231] Prosser's comment[232] that the defendant is not liable if he has done nothing more than to carry a process to its authorized conclusion, even if he acted with bad intentions. Or similarly courts have said that abuse after issuance, not merely issuance itself, is required to establish the claim.[233] That observation is similar to the added requirement adopted in some courts that the suitor must commit some further act after the process has issued.[234] As shown by those cases allowing a recovery for excessive attachment or wrongful lis pendens, however, the requirement of a post-process act has no place when the process is itself wrongful.

E. REFORMS AND NEW DIRECTIONS

§ 39.16 SLAPP Suits, Sanctions, and Counterclaims

Many abuse of process cases reflect the fact that in our legal system, individuals not only have the power to invoke legal processes but to do so without supervision by responsible judges or notice to the opposing party. In 1991, the Supreme Court held that a statute permitting ex parte attachment before judgment was unconstitutional for want

---

[227] Spellens v. Spellens, 49 Cal.2d 210, 317 P.2d 613 (1957).

[228] See Baglini v. Lauletta, 338 N.J. Super. 282, 768 A.2d 825 (2001) (defendant's offer to drop suit against plaintiff if plaintiffs would drop their suit against defendant was not an abuse of process).

[229] E.g., Yaklevich v. Kemp, Schaeffer & Rowe Co., L.P.A., 68 OhioSt.3d 294, 626 N.E.2d 115 (1994) (a legal proceeding has been set in motion with probable cause but the proceeding has been perverted to accomplish an ulterior purpose); Hatch v. Davis, 147 P.3d 383 (Utah 2006) ("To satisfy the 'willful act' requirement, a party must point to conduct independent of the legal process itself that corroborates the alleged improper purpose. . . . [A] corroborating act of a nature other than legal process is also necessary.").

[230] Mills County State Bank v. Roure, 291 N.W.2d 1, 5 (Iowa 1980) (refusing to protect the tortfeasor "where the issuance of the process alone is sufficient to accomplish the collateral purpose"); see also Givens v. Mullikin, 75 S.W.3d 383 (Tenn. 2002) (the "process" referred to in the "act after" rule is the original process, such as complaint, summons, and responsive pleading, so that any abusive and improper act thereafter may suffice to meet the act after rule).

[231] E.g., Cabletron Sys., Inc. v. Miller, 140 N.H. 55, 662 A.2d 304 (1995).

[232] Prosser & Keeton on Torts § 121, at 898 (5th ed. 1984).

[233] Willis v. Parker, 814 So.2d 857 (Ala. 2001); Snyder v. Icard, Merrill, Cullis, Timm, Furen and Ginsburg, P.A., 986 S.W.2d 550 (Tenn. 1999).

[234] See Gibson v. Regions Financial Corp., 557 F.3d 842 (8th Cir. 2009) (Arkansas law) (quoting: "The key to an abuse of process claim is improper use of process *after* issuance, even when issuance has been properly obtained.") (emphasis in original); Sands v. Living Word Fellowship, 34 P.3d 955 (Alaska 2001).

of notice to and opportunity to be heard by the owner.[235] Notice to the owner is the first step in early termination of an abusive suit. A much more aggressive solution calls for early dismissal in certain cases and some states have so provided in the case of the so-called SLAPP[236] suits. These are suits brought against individuals whose exercise of speech or petitioning rights[237] allegedly causes tortious harm to the plaintiff.[238] Some states put these suits on a fast track, terminating discovery early and making dismissal especially easy.[239] California has said that there is no exemption for malicious prosecution suits under its anti-SLAPP statute, so the malicious-prosecution plaintiff must show a probability of winning, else suffer dismissal.[240] Some of the statutes are themselves subject to abuse, but, right or wrong, they point to the possibility that abusive litigation can be dealt with at the point of abuse, not later in a tort suit.

Sanctions during trial. A closely related means of dealing with abusive litigation tactics is to permit sanctions for abuse during the trial itself. Sanctions can include awarding attorney's fees to the victim for the costs of dealing with abusive process such as excessive attachment or even harassing delay, for example.[241] To the extent that sanctions are imposed, separate suits for abusive litigation may be unnecessary and courts might even bar such suits where sanctions have proved adequate.[242]

Counterclaims. If dealing with abuse when it occurs rather than later is a good idea when it comes to sanctions or dismissal, it is also a good idea to permit counterclaims in civil cases for wrongful litigation.[243] Under the present rule, a counterclaim can be asserted for abuse of process but not for wrongful litigation. That prohibition in turn results from the requirement that the unjustified original action must have terminated favorably to the now-plaintiff. The favorable termination rule makes good sense when the plaintiff complains of an unjustified criminal prosecution, but it serves no useful purpose when the plaintiff complains of a former civil suit. On the contrary, the original suit is by far the best place to resolve the issues, although bifurcation of trial might be required when a particular counterclaim raises serious dangers of prejudice.

---

[235] Connecticut v. Doehr, 501 U.S. 1, 111 S.Ct. 2105, 115 L.Ed.2d 1 (1991).

[236] The acronym stands for "strategic lawsuit against public participation." See, e.g., Palazzo v. Alves, 944 A.2d 144 (R.I. 2008) (explaining the purposes of Rhode Island's anti-SLAPP statute).

[237] See Leiendecker v. Asian Women United of Minnesota, 848 N.W.2d 224 (Minn. 2014) ("Typically, anti-SLAPP statutes protect the exercise of two types of public-participation rights: the right to free speech and the right to petition the government."). The *Noerr-Pennington* doctrine provides for an immunity from statutory liability for those who petition government for redress and are sued for that conduct. See BE&K Const. Co. v. NLRB, 536 U.S. 516, 122 S.Ct. 2390, 153 L.Ed.2d 449 (2001).

[238] See, e.g., Morse Bros., Inc. v. Webster, 772 A.2d 842 (Me. 2001).

[239] See Leiendecker v. Asian Women United of Minnesota, 848 N.W.2d 224 (Minn. 2014) (applying state statute that requires the trial court "to suspend discovery once an anti-SLAPP motion is filed unless the responding party can show 'good cause' for 'specified and limited discovery' "; the responding party must then produce "clear and convincing evidence that the moving party is not entitled to immunity").

[240] Jarrow Formulas, Inc. v. LaMarche, 31 Cal. 4th 728, 74 P.3d 737, 3 Cal. Rptr.3d 636 (2003).

[241] Linscott v. Foy, 716 A.2d 1017 (Me. 1998).

[242] Bidna v. Rosen, 19 Cal.App.4th 27, 23 Cal.Rptr.2d 251 (1993), barred wrongful litigation suits in family court matters in favor of a complete sanctions approach.

[243] See DeVaney v. Thriftway Mktg. Corp., 124 N.M. 512, 953 P.2d 277 (1997) (eliminating the termination requirement and permitting counterclaims for wrongful civil litigation, as well as restructuring the wrongful litigation and abuse of process torts as a single tort called "malicious abuse of process"); see also Fleetwood Retail Corp. of New Mexico v. LeDoux, 142 N.M. 150, 164 P.3d 31 (2007) (modifying one aspect of *DeVaney*, but retaining its essential reforms); Durham v. Guest, 145 N.M. 694, 204 P.3d 19 (2009) (tort does not require the plaintiff to prove that the defendant initiated judicial proceedings against the plaintiff, overruling *DeVaney* on that point; plaintiff need only show some improper use of process in a proceeding).

Alternatives to the counterclaim are possible. For instance, courts could award attorney's fees for wrongful litigation on motion, as part of an award of costs or otherwise, and could provide that if such fees are claimed and awarded, no separate tort action could be brought for the wrongful litigation or abuse of process.

Chapter 40

INTERFERENCE WITH FAMILY RELATIONSHIPS

Analysis

§ 40.1   Alienation of Affections and Criminal Conversation
§ 40.2   Interference with Parental Custody and Other Rights in Children
§ 40.3   Alienation of a Parent's or Child's Affections

§ 40.1 Alienation of Affections and Criminal Conversation

Tort law and the family: background. Families and family relationships have been important in tort law in a number of ways. The present chapter focuses only upon the potential liability of those who interfere with family relationships where physical harm to the claimant is no part of the claim. "Relational injury" or injury to the family relationship itself with the concomitant emotional harm and loss of well-being is the essential concern here. The most notable historical example is the claim by a spouse that the defendant has alienated the affections of the other spouse, but contemporary custody battles and the seduction of children by religious groups has raised issues about "interference" and alienation in new contexts.

Common law view of relationships. At one time the common law treated a husband and father as the master of his wife and children. If the defendant injured a servant or enticed him away from service, the master would have a cause of action for the loss.[1] Similar rules applied if the master's wife was injured or enticed away.[2] By the latter part of the 19th century courts developed two or three semi-distinct torts from this beginning. Together they protected the husband's interest in his wife's services, society, affection, and honor against interference by others. Later, courts became more even-handed and provided wives with the same rights. These interference torts are now abolished in most states,[3] but lawyers sometimes attempt to resurrect them under another label.

Criminal conversation. Criminal conversation merely meant adultery or sexual relations. The defendant who engaged in adultery with the plaintiff's spouse would be liable to the plaintiff. The authorities state the elements of the tort with almost alarming simplicity: the tort consists of having sexual relations with one spouse.[4] "The fact that the wife consented, that she was the aggressor, that she represented herself as single, that she was mistreated or neglected by her husband, that she and her husband were separated through no fault of her own, or that her husband was impotent, were not valid

---

[1]   See §§ 36.2 to 36.5.

[2]   See William Blackstone, 3 Commentaries *139.

[3]   See *Abolishing the Torts* below.

[4]   See Brown v. Hurley, 124 N.C.App. 377, 477 S.E.2d 234 (1996) (actual existing marriage plus sexual intercourse); Russo v. Sutton, 310 S.C. 200, 422 S.E.2d 750 (1992) (same); Restatement (Second) of Torts § 685 (1977).

defenses."[5] The only defense was the nonparticipating spouse's own consent.[6] In other words, the defendant was liable to the husband although he had committed no tort to the wife and was guilty of no fraud, force, or deception.

Alienation of affections. If the defendant deprived one spouse of the other's affections but did not engage in sexual relations, that too became a tort by the latter half of the 19th century.[7] The defendant here must ordinarily have known of the marital relationship and acted for the purpose of affecting it adversely,[8] but neither sexual nor romantic involvement was required. Indeed, the defendant could be held liable though he was only a minister or a family member who, without a privilege,[9] urged one spouse to leave the other.[10] The defendant was not subject to liability unless his conduct was a substantial factor, along with other causes, for the alienation,[11] and of course there was no alienation if no affection remained in the marriage at the time of the defendant's conduct.[12] However, causation and wrongful intent were both elements that might be proved by circumstances.[13] As with criminal conversation, the defendant would be liable without a tort to the person whose affections were alienated and without any kind of falsehood.

Enticement. A defendant who abducted the plaintiff's spouse might be liable to the abducted spouse for false imprisonment, and the other spouse might plausibly claim loss of consortium as in the case of other physical harms. Historically, courts took a shortcut across such reasoning by holding simply that one who abducted a spouse would be liable to the other spouse, and by extension of this, that one who enticed one spouse to separate from the other would also be liable. In line with this history the Restatement recognized enticement as a separate tort.[14] It is apparent, however, that enticement is merely one form of, or at most an extension of, alienation of affections and like alienation, turns on an intent to disrupt the marriage.[15]

Abolishing the torts. Criminal conversation[16] and alienation of affections[17] have now been abolished in the great majority of states, either by explicit legislation or by judicial

---

[5]   Kline v. Ansell, 287 Md. 585, 587, 414 A.2d 929, 930 (1980).

[6]   Restatement (Second) of Torts § 687 (1977).

[7]   See, e.g., Foot v. Card, 58 Conn. 1, 18 A. 1027 (1889) (also recognizing that the right to sue for alienation extended to the wife).

[8]   Restatement (Second) of Torts § 683 (1977).

[9]   Under Restatement (Second) of Torts § 686 (1977), a parent or near relative had a privilege to give advice in good faith and reasonably to advance the interest of the alienated spouse, but not for the purpose of "appropriating the affections" of that spouse. But cf. Poulos v. Poulos, 351 Mass. 603, 222 N.E.2d 887 (1967). (mother who aggressively tries to persuade her son to leave his wife and tells him nine times that the marriage is a disgrace may be liable for abusing her privilege by going further than is "reasonable").

[10]   Boland v. Stanley, 88 Ark. 562, 115 S.W. 163 (1909) (parents of alienated spouse); Carrieri v. Bush, 69 Wash.2d 536, 419 P.2d 132 (1966) (minister who taught that God had come to separate husband from wife).

[11]   Norton v. MacFarlane, 818 P.2d 8 (Utah 1991) (controlling or primary cause as opposed to incidental cause).

[12]   See McCutchen v. McCutchen, 624 S.E.2d 620 (N.C. 2006); Pickering v. Pickering, 434 N.W.2d 758, 763 (S.D. 1989).

[13]   See Kirk v. Koch, 607 So.2d 1220 (Miss. 1992).

[14]   Restatement (Second) of Torts § 684 (1977).

[15]   Id. § 684(2) & cmt. f (1977).

[16]   By statute in most states, e.g., Or. Rev. Stat. § 30.850; Va. Code § 8.01–220. Among decisions abolishing criminal conversation, see Bearbower v. Merry, 266 N.W.2d 128 (Iowa 1978); Thomas v. Siddiqui, 869 S.W.2d 740 (Mo. 1994); Feldman v. Feldman, 125 N.H. 102, 480 A.2d 34 (1984).

[17]   Statutes abolishing the tort have been enacted in most states. E.g., N.Y. Civ. Rights Law § 80–a; Tex. Fam. Code § 1.107. Among judicial decisions abolishing the tort, see O'Neil v. Schuckardt, 112 Idaho 472, 733

decision. Indeed, an attorney who files a complaint for this defunct cause of action may be subject to sanctions.[18] Only a handful of states have continued the alienation of affections action and some of those have abolished the criminal conversation claim.[19] A few other states seem not to have passed on the issue.[20] The reasons to abolish the torts are numerous and they run deep.[21]

Rationales. Courts and legislatures have been moved in part by the conclusion that these torts lent themselves to blackmail and to vindictiveness pursued by a spouse whose marriage is over and who seeks merely to inflict harm. With the advent of no fault divorce everywhere and the decriminalization of adultery in many states, these torts also came to seem illogical and inimical to the reforms enacted in divorce and criminal laws.[22] Beyond this, the torts have become offensive because they have, sometimes quite explicitly, treated a spouse as the property of the other spouse and because they are thoroughly inimical to the freedom of all human beings to choose their associations and to choose to depart dangerous, stultifying, or deeply unhappy homes. These torts could also operate unjustly by punishing the defendant for conduct to which both participants consent. Finally, some of the cases turned on nothing more than words that were by no means false and thus punished speech. The grounds for abolishing the torts are thus ample, although one commentator has argued to the contrary and thinks more limited versions of the torts would save families and prevent adultery.[23] Where the torts are abolished, the question now arises whether their abolition also prevents recovery on other theories.

Alternative theories after abolition. After the abolition of the interference torts, lawyers began to assert claims on the same facts but under other theories. For instance, a spouse might assert that the defendant's adultery with the other spouse was an intentional or negligent infliction of distress or an interference with contract. Alert to such "artful pleading," courts have rejected the emotional harm,[24] interference with

---

P.2d 693 (1986); Hoye v. Hoye, 824 S.W.2d 422 (Ky. 1992); Russo v. Sutton, 310 S.C. 200, 422 S.E.2d 750 (1992). A recent decision abolishing the tort is Helsel v. Noellesch, 107 S.W.3d 231 (Mo. 2003). For an intriguing post mortem on the tort, see Kyle Graham, Why Torts Die, 35 Fla. St. U. L. Rev. 359 (2008).

[18]   Attorney Grievance Comm'n of Md. v. James, 870 A.2d 229 (Md. 2005).

[19]   Brown v. Ellis, 678 S.E.2d 222 (N.C. 2009); Fitch v. Valentine, 959 So.2d 1012 (Miss. 2007); Dowling v. Bullen, 94 P.3d 915 (Utah 2004); Veeder v. Kennedy, 589 N.W.2d 610 (S.D. 1999). A limited recovery is possible in Illinois, but suits are discouraged as a practical matter by statutes limiting recovery to "actual damages," 740 Ill. Comp. Stat. § 5/2, and forbidding recovery of the normal damage elements such as injury to the plaintiff's feelings, shame, or the like. 740 Ill. Comp. Stat. § 5/4. North Carolina has the largest number and widest breadth of recent actions. See Misenheimer v. Burris, 637 S.E.2d 173 (N.C. 2006) (tolling criminal conversation action under the discovery rule); Oddo v. Presser, 592 S.E.2d 195 (N.C. 2004) (affirming large compensatory and punitive damages verdict).

[20]   Even when an action may be possible in theory, the absence of decisions in the area for decades suggests the decline of the tort if not its demise. See Hunt v. Chang, 594 P.2d 118 (Haw. 1979).

[21]   See Kay Kavanagh, Note, Alienation of Affections and Criminal Conversation: Unholy Marriage in Need of Annulment, 23 Ariz. L. Rev. 323 (1981); Jamie Heard, Comment, The National Trend of Abolishing Actions for the Alienation of a Spouse's Affection and Mississippi's Refusal to Follow Suit, 28 Miss. L. Rev. 313 (2009). See also, Helsel v. Noellsch, 107 S.W.3d 231 (Mo. 2003).

[22]   On the relation of these and other tort claims to divorce, see Ira Mark Ellman & Stephen D. Sugarman, Spousal Emotional Abuse as a Tort?, 55 Md. L. Rev. 1268 (1996).

[23]   William R. Corbett, A Somewhat Modest Proposal to Prevent Adultery and Save Families: Two Old Torts Looking for a New Career, 33 Ariz. St. L.J. 985 (2001). See also Jill Jones, Comment, Fanning an Old Flame: Alienation of Affections and Criminal Conversation Revisited, 26 Pepp. L. Rev. 61 (1999).

[24]   McDermott v. Reynolds, 530 S.E.2d 902 (Va. 2000); Padwa v. Hadley, 981 P.2d 1234 (N.M. Ct. App. 1999); R.E.R. v. J.G., 552 N.W.2d 27 (Minn. Ct. App. 1996); Lotring v. Philbrook, 701 A.2d 1034 (R.I. 1997).

contract,[25] and other claims[26] as mere disguises for the alienation and criminal conversation claims. Negligent interference was never enough to show alienation of affections and is of course not enough once the tort has been abolished.[27] Moreover, the claim cannot be pursued by chidren of the marriage.[28] Even if the claim adds aggravating facts not necessary to the alienation or criminal conversation theory, it may still be denied when the underlying facts are in the patterns of those torts.[29]

Duty to one or both spouses. In the counseling setting, when a therapist or counselor has sexual relations with the spouse who is his patient, the patient herself may well have a claim for malpractice.[30] But the spouse who is not a patient has no malpractice claim of his own for the very reason that professional duties are ordinarily owed only to patients or clients.[31] With the claim for criminal conversation abolished, that leaves the non-patient spouse with no claim at all. The same analysis is made when a clergyman has an affair with a parishioner to the dismay of the parishioner's spouse.[32] However, the story may be different if the therapist owes an independent duty to both spouses or to the complaining spouse.[33] For instance, when a counselor undertakes to professionally treat the marital problems of both spouses, he may be liable for professional negligence if sexual relations or romantic affairs with one of them violates the duty owed to both.[34]

Independent torts. Similarly, an independent tort like libel or slander is presumably actionable, even though its effect is to reduce spousal affection.[35] Moreover, a tort action for sexual assault brought by both husband and wife for an assault against one of the two is not barred by the abolition of the alienation of affections tort. The non-consensual contact distinguishes the case from the abolished torts.[36]

---

[25]   E.g., Speer v. Dealy, 242 Neb. 542, 495 N.W.2d 911 (1993).

[26]   State ex rel. Golden v. Kaufman, 760 S.E.2d 883 (W. Va. 2014) (breach of fiduciary duty rejected).

[27]   Helena Labs. Corp. v. Snyder, 886 S.W.2d 767 (Tex. 1994).

[28]   Brent v. Mathias, 154 So.2d 842 (Miss. 201).

[29]   Doe v. Doe, 747 A.2d 617 (Md. 2000) (wife's misrepresentation of the paternity of the children born during the marriage; barred); Koestler v. Pollard, 162 Wis.2d 797, 471 N.W.2d 7 (1991) (defendant's sexual intercourse with the plaintiff's wife resulted in conception and birth of a child, which plaintiff discovered after a period of the defendant's concealment; added facts not sufficient for a claim); contra, Bailey v. Searles-Bailey, 140 Ohio App.3d 174, 746 N.E.2d 1159 (2001) (claim against paramour who failed to reveal that he had fathered the child husband believed was his own; not barred but not sufficiently outrageous for liability on intentional infliction of emotional distress theory). For an argument that courts should allow a tort cause of action between spouses in light of intentional lies that interfere with the establishment and continuation of parent-child relationships, see Linda Berger, Lies Between Mommy and Daddy: The Case for Recognizing Spousal Emotional Distress Claims Base on Domestic Deceit that Interferes with Parent-Child Relationships, 33 Loy. L.A. L. Rev. 449 (2000).

[30]   See 2 Dobbs, Hayden & Bublick, The Law of Torts §§ 329 & 332 (2d ed. 2011 & Supp.).

[31]   Smith v. Pust, 19 Cal.App.4th 263, 23 Cal.Rptr.2d 364 (1993).

[32]   Cherepski v. Walker, 323 Ark. 43, 913 S.W.2d 761 (1996). See 2 Dobbs, Hayden & Bublick, The Law of Torts §§ 329 to 332 (2d ed. 2011 & Supp.), on clergy malpractice, including claims based on sexual relations in therapy.

[33]   Doe v. Zwelling, 620 S.E.2d 750 (Va. 2005).

[34]   Odenthal v. Minn. Conference of Seventh Day Adventists, 649 N.W.2d 426 (Minn. 2002); Figueiredo-Torres v. Nickel, 321 Md. 642, 584 A.2d 69 (1991); Rowe v. Bennett, 514 A.2d 802 (Me. 1986). Courts are not of a single mind on this proposition however. See Bailey v. Faulkner, 940 So.2d 247 (Ala. 2006).

[35]   See Ellis v. Price, 337 Ark. 542, 990 S.W.2d 543 (1999) (wife's recovery for defamation that reduced husband's trust and good feelings for her).

[36]   See Choski v. Shah, 8 So.3d 288 (Ala. 2008).

§ 40.2 Interference with Parental Custody and Other Rights in Children

From common law to today. Early common law recognized a right in the father of a child to have the child's services and hence a right to recover for loss of those services when the defendant abducted or injured the child. This approach is largely obsolete, first because rights in the parent-child relationship are no longer those of the father alone but belong to the mother or other custodian as well, and second because loss of services is no longer the essence of the loss.[37] In most cases a full range of damages for the loss of society and affection and other values in the relationship is now permitted. So far as the parent-child relationship is damaged by negligent physical injury to the child, only a few courts have accepted the parent's claim for loss of the child's society and affection.[38] This section addresses the remaining issues—interference with relationships in the family by abduction, alienation of affections of a child or parent and the like.

Interference with custody rights: enticing, abducting or harboring. When the minor child is enticed, or abducted, or "harbored," the custodians of the child are entitled by common law or statute to recover.[39] The claim is not for alienation of affections, but for deprivation of physical custody.[40] On the other hand, damages are no longer limited to an award for loss of the child's services, but may include awards for the parents' distress, their loss of the child's society, and the expenses incurred in recovering custody as well as punitive damages in an appropriate case.[41] The action can be characterized as an intentional and unjustified interference with the parental right of custody of a minor.[42] As this implies, the defendant must have notice of the plaintiff's custodial rights. The consent of the child is no defense to the custodians' action.[43]

Abduction versus privileged shelter. The claim by its terms covers out-and-out abduction with criminal intent to harm or ransom, as well as cases of sexual enticement,[44] but most of the contemporary cases are more complex. When an outsider provides a haven for the child in the reasonable suspicion that the child is abused at home,[45] or merely exercises his freedom of religion when speaking to the minor,[46] he may

---

[37] Khalifa v. Shannon, 945 A.2d 1244 (Md. 2008); Pickle v. Page, 252 N.Y. 474, 169 N.E. 650 (1930).

[38] See § 29.11.

[39] Magnuson v. O'Dea, 75 Wash. 574, 135 P. 640 (1913); Restatement (Second) of Torts § 700 (1977).

[40] See Murphy v. I.S.K. Con. of New England, Inc., 409 Mass. 842, 860, 571 N.E.2d 340, 351 (1991); Khalifa v. Shannon, 404 Md. 107, 945 A.2d 1244 (2008) (mother and maternal grandmother fled to Egypt with plaintiff's two children).

[41] Khalifa v. Shannon, 404 Md. 107, 945 A.2d 1244 (2008) (upholding punitive damages award of $2 million in case where mother and grandmother fled to Egypt with plaintiff's children); Murphy v. I.S.K.Con. of New England, Inc., 409 Mass. 842, 571 N.E.2d 340 (1991); Howell v. Howell, 162 N.C. 283, 78 S.E. 222 (1913); Kessel v. Leavitt, 511 S.E.2d 720 (W.Va. 1998).

[42] See Anonymous v. Anonymous, 672 So.2d 787 (Ala. 1995). The Iowa Supreme Court recently outlined elements of the tort which include the parent's right to a custodial relationship, the defendant's knowledge of that right and the defendant's willful effort to abduct, compel or induce the child to leave in spite of that knowledge. Wolf v. Wolf, 690 N.W.2d 887 (Iowa 2005).

[43] Surina v. Lucey, 168 Cal.App.3d 539, 214 Cal.Rptr. 509 (1985).

[44] Id. (allegations that uncle took minor child and engaged in sexual relations with her).

[45] Robbins v. Hamburger Home for Girls, 32 Cal.App.4th 671, 38 Cal.Rptr.2d 534 (1995); Restatement (Second) of Torts § 700 cmt. e (1977).

[46] Cf. Murphy v. I.S.K.Con. of New England, Inc., 409 Mass. 842, 571 N.E.2d 340 (1991) (emotionally disturbing religious arguments not actionable as intentional infliction of distress).

be guilty of no wrongdoing at all or may be protected by a privilege or a constitutional right.

Suits between parents and kidnappers and abetters. One important group of cases arises when a parent or other family member kidnaps a child following a divorce and a lost custody battle. Most courts dealing with the issue have recognized the action brought by the custodial parent against the non-custodial parent or family members who aid and abet the kidnaping.[47] It has been said that tort claims better serve "both to prevent child-snatching and to pick up the pieces if it does occur" than any of the alternative sanctions such as those provided by the Uniform Child Custody Jurisdiction Act, or by kidnaping or contempt prosecutions.[48] The view, however is not unanimous. A Minnesota case is the principal authority rejecting the action against a parental kidnaper.[49] The Minnesota court did so on the theory that it would not be best for the child to undergo such litigation. Supporters of this view have suggested that statutes enhancing power over the kidnaper who flees the jurisdiction,[50] coupled with other litigation against the kidnaper, may ameliorate the problem. But these other types of litigation—criminal felony prosecutions, contempt of court, and tort claims for infliction of emotional distress[51]—seem no less harmful to the child than the interference with custody claim. To some extent the conflict about whether to recognize a tort cause of action for interference with custody by a parental kidnapper may represent a conflict of two legal cultures, one associated with tort practice and emphasizing rights and responsibilities, the other associated with family law practice and emphasizing a kind of social work role for judges and court staff.

Custody required; joint custody. The right protected in interference with custody cases is the right to custody of the child. If the plaintiff does not have custody rights, she has no claim.[52] The Restatement (Second) of Torts, in a passage accepted by a number of courts, takes the position that when parents have joint custody of a child, neither may recover from the other for denying access to the child.[53] The rule makes sense if it only means that joint custody does not give either parent an absolute right to sole custody of the child for a percentage of the time. A third person who assists the joint-custody father in permanently hiding the children from the mother cannot logically be aiding and

[47] Matsumoto v. Matsumoto, 792 A.2d 1222 (N.J. 2002); Lozano v. Lozano, 52 S.W.3d 141 (Tex. 2001); Stone v. Wall, 734 So.2d 1038 (Fla. 1999); Wood v. Wood, 338 N.W.2d 123 (Iowa 1983); Weirich v. Weirich, 833 S.W.2d 942 (Tex. 1992); William B. Johnson, Annotation, Liability of Legal or Natural Parent, or One Who Aids and Abets, for Damages Resulting from Abduction of Own Child, 49 A.L.R.4th 7 (1987); see Kessel v. Leavitt, 511 S.E.2d 720 (W.Va. 1998) (recognizing claim where plaintiff has sole custody right and applying it to mother's adoption placement of child out of the country).

[48] Wolf v. Wolf, 690 N.W.2d 887 (Iowa 2005).

[49] Larson v. Dunn, 460 N.W.2d 39 (Minn. 1990); Mantooth v. Richards, 557 So.2d 646 (Fla. Dist. Ct. App. 1990); Friedman v. Friedman, 79 Misc.2d 646, 361 N.Y.S.2d 108 (Sup. Ct. 1974). Politte v. Politte, 727 S.W.2d 198 (Mo. Ct. App. 1987), expressed doubts about the action but apparently went off on the fact that the plaintiff had no custodial rights. Mantooth, supra, was effectively set aside by the decision in Stone v. Wall, 734 So.2d 1038 (Fla. 1999), which allowed a common law action.

[50] Parental Kidnapping Prevention Act (PKPA), 28 U.S.C.A. § 1738A; Unif. Child Custody Jurisdiction & Enforcement Act. Support of an international convention is reflected in 42 U.S.C.A. § 11601. Expenses and attorney fees can be recovered under § 312 of the Uniform Act where that act applies.

[51] See Larson v. Dunn, 460 N.W.2d 39, 46, 47 (Minn. 1990) (emotional distress claim might be entertained); Joseph R. Hillebrand, Parental Kidnapping and the Tort of Custodial Interference: Not in a Child's Best Interests, 25 Ind. L. Rev. 893, 915 (1991) (proposing tougher enforcement of criminal laws against kidnaping).

[52] Stevens v. Redwing, 146 F.3d 538 (8th Cir. 1998).

[53] Restatement (Second) of Torts § 700 cmt. c (1977).

abetting a tort if it would be no tort for the father to do the same things by himself. While some authority supported this analysis,[54] in more recent cases, courts generally have supported claims against those who aid a joint-custody parent in abducting the child.[55] If joint custody means anything, it must mean that one parent cannot be the sole custodian. When a father carries children abroad and hides them, it seems absurd to say that he is respecting the mother's right of joint custody. Indeed, recent cases hold that a claim of interference with custody can be brought against a parent who has shared custody.[56]

Cases against third parties. On occasion, courts permit recovery for custodial interference by parties other than the absconding parent and conspiratorial relatives. For example, a $27 million jury award was upheld against an air charter operator who negligently facilitated a father's abduction of his children by plane to Egypt.[57] In another negligence case, a malpractice claim for damages from loss of custody could be maintained when an attorney's faulty legal advice caused the biological parents to lose partial custody of their child.[58] Where independent duties to the parents or children do not exist, the plaintiff must prove intentional interference.[59] Moreover, immunities protect persons who intentionally attempt to influence child custody in legal proceedings. In accord with testimonial immunities generally, a cause of action is not available simply because a party testified in a way that caused a court to grant custody in favor of one spouse rather than another. Courts are justifiably wary of such suits because of the chilling effect on the truth seeking process in child custody cases.[60] In addition to common law protections, state statutes may afford a privilege to report concerns about child welfare even when those reports will logically lead to custody deprivation or modification.[61]

Visitation rights. Where one parent interferes with the other's rights of visitation rather than rights of custody, some courts have refused to permit a tort recovery,[62] at least for what they considered to be minor infringements of visitation rights remediable

---

[54]   Marshak v. Marshak, 226 Conn. 652, 628 A.2d 964 (1993), overruled by State v. Vakilzaden, 628 A.2d 964 (Conn. 1993) (holding that a joint custodian may be subject to criminal interference statutes).

[55]   Rosefield v. Rosefield, 221 Cal.App.2d 431, 34 Cal.Rptr. 479 (1963); cf. Kessel v. Leavitt, 511 S.E.2d 720 (W.Va. 1998) (unwed father has no custody rights but prevailed against child's grandparents who helped place the child for adoption outside the country as soon as he was born).

[56]   See Wolf v. Wolf, 690 N.W.2d 887 (Iowa 2005). The Connecticut Supreme Court has now held, in a criminal prosecution, that "a joint custodian is not inherently immune . . . based solely on his or her status as joint custodian" where all the elements of custodial interference are proved, including both knowledge and intent. State v. Valkilzaden, 251 Conn. 656, 742 A.2d 767 (1999).

[57]   Streeter v. Executive Jet Mgmt., Inc., 2005 WL 4357633 (Conn. Super. Ct. 2005) (unpublished opinion).

[58]   Collins v. Mo. Bar Plan, 157 S.W.3d 726 (Mo. Ct. App. 2005).

[59]   In Wyatt v. McDermott, 283 Va. 685, 725 S.E.2d 555 (2012), the court, answering a certified question, held that Virginia recognizes a common law action for tortious interference with parental rights. The elements of the cause of action are: (1) the complaining parent has a right to custody; (2) a party outside the relationship between the complaining parent and the child intentionally interfered with that relationship; (3) and caused harm to the custodial or parental relationship; (4) causing damages. The court traced the cause of action back to at least 1607.

[60]   Wilson v. Bernet, 218 W.Va. 628, 625 S.E.2d 706 (2005) (expert witness in a child custody hearing, testified in support of the wife's custody; wife prevailed; complete immunity of adverse witnesses; testimony was not like removing the child or detaining him and not the kind of conduct that would be actionable).

[61]   Myers v. Lashley, 44 P.3d 553 (Okla. 2002).

[62]   Politte v. Politte, 727 S.W.2d 198 (Mo. Ct. App. 1987).

by injunction or contempt proceedings.[63] When the custodial parent totally removes the child from the jurisdiction and hides him, the other parent's right of visitation is completely destroyed for which an action has been approved in some cases,[64] but not in others.[65] The difficulty of justly monitoring the seething relations between former spouses and their various allies may warrant a refusal to entertain actions for the kind of minor guerrilla warfare that regularly occurs, but when the defendant's action is a substantial and long-term interference, courts should not lightly put aside their own fundamental purposes to do justice nor too readily assume that a tort action will be against the child's long-term best interest.

Seduction of a minor child. When a minor female child was seduced, old common law recognized a claim by the father both for medical expenses and for loss of his daughter's services resulting from the seduction.[66] The seduction claim belonged to the father, not the child.[67] The loss of services here became the fictional basis of the action which in reality was a reflection of judicial outrage coupled with the belief that the father had legal rights in his female children. Social change brought more independence to women and procedural reforms required suit to be brought by the real party in interest.[68] After these changes and sometimes as a result of explicit statutes, courts began to permit the seduced woman to bring her own suit.[69] The effect was to convert the relational injury claim into a kind of battery claim, or perhaps one for fraud,[70] but either way to be pursued by the immediate victim. But in any event, the parental claim for anything more than obligatory medical expenses may be abolished along with the alienation and criminal conversation claims.[71]

§ 40.3 Alienation of a Parent's or Child's Affections

Basic rules. The usual rule is that there is no independent action for the defendant's acts alienating the affections of either a parent[72] or a child.[73] The child's claim, asserted

---

[63] Hixon v. Buchberger, 306 Md. 72, 507 A.2d 607 (1986).

[64] Khalifa v. Shannon, 945 A.2d 1244 (Md. 2008); Brown v. Denny, 72 Ohio App.3d 417, 594 N.E.2d 1008 (1991) (under statute); Hershey v. Hershey, 467 N.W.2d 484 (S.D. 1991). Even if a court does not allow an interference with custody claim when one parent removes the child so that visitation rights are thwarted, it may allow a similar claim under another name. See Stewart v. Walker, 5 So.3d 746 (Fl. Ct. App. 2009) (father did not have standing to claim tortious interference in parent-child relationship, but did have standing to claim intentional infliction of emotional distress when mother took the child out of state without father's consent).

[65] Cosner v. Ridinger, 882 P.2d 1243 (Wyo. 1994).

[66] Restatement (Second) of Torts § 701 (1977).

[67] On the wrongs of this system, see Lea Vandervelde, The Legal Ways of Seduction, 48 Stan. L. Rev. 817 (1996).

[68] See Franklin v. Hill, 264 Ga. 302, 444 S.E.2d 778 (1994) (statute applying only to men unconstitutional).

[69] See Piggott v. Miller, 557 S.W.2d 692 (Mo. Ct. App. 1977); Lea Vandervelde, The Legal Ways of Seduction, 48 Stan. L. Rev. 817 (1996).

[70] Many discussions treat the claim as one of "fraud," focusing on the misrepresentation required to invalidate the plaintiff's consent. See Jane E. Larson, "Women Understand So Little, They Call My Good Nature 'Deceit' ": A Feminist Rethinking of Seduction, 93 Colum. L. Rev. 374 (1993) (proposing a tort of sexual fraud). With consent invalidated, however, the sexual touching perfectly fits the definition of battery as well.

[71] N.Y. Civ. Rights Law § 80–a; Okla. Stat. tit. 76, § 8.1 (as to persons of legal age and sound mind).

[72] Taylor v. Keefe, 134 Conn. 156, 56 A.2d 768 (1947); Whitcomb v. Huffington, 180 Kan. 340, 304 P.2d 465 (1956). See Jeffery F. Ghent, Annotation, Right of Child or Parent to Recover for Alienation of Other's Affections, 60 A.L.R.3d 931 (1975). Contra Johnson v. Luhman, 330 Ill.App. 598, 71 N.E.2d 810 (1947); Miller v. Monsen, 228 Minn. 400, 37 N.W.2d 543 (1949).

[73] Stevens v. Redwing, 146 F.3d 538 (8th Cir. 1998) (holding also that this rule is not to be circumvented by allowing an emotional distress claim); Restatement Second of Torts § 699 (1977). Cf. Mackintosh v. Carter,

against a parent's new spouse or lover, seems inconsistent with the general abolition of alienation claims and also with the right of the parent to obtain a divorce. If the rule against a recovery for alienation of a parent's affections is to be effective, courts must also deny the claim when it is asserted on the same essential facts under the theory of privacy invasion, or interference with contract, or intentional infliction of emotional distress.[74]

Alienation of a child's affections: difficulties of claims between parents. The parents' claim for alienation of a child's affection might stand on substantially higher ground and at least one notable case supports it.[75] So far as the claim is asserted against the child's other parent or against the child's custodian, however, the problem of monitoring the persistent destructive behavior of divorced parents may make it difficult to be confident that adjudications would produce just results with appropriate consistency. On the other hand, when the issue is not tort recovery but custody of the child, courts have been perfectly willing to consider whether one parent has been guilty of alienating the child's affections for the other.[76]

Liability of therapists for alienating a child's affections. When therapists induce an adult to believe falsely that a parent sexually abused her as a child, standard doctrine holds that the therapist is not liable to the parent for mere negligence in diagnosis because a professional's duty of care ordinarily runs to the patient or client, not to others, and because so far as the therapist reports suspected child abuse, he may be privileged as well.[77] Expressed in policy terms, a professional's duty of care should not run to his client's or patient's adversary lest his professional conduct be shaped by fear of liability rather than by duty to his patient or client.[78]

---

451 N.W.2d 285 (S.D. 1990) (defendants providing shelter to child when they reasonably thought she was in danger).

[74]   See Kane v. Quigley, 1 Ohio St.2d 1, 203 N.E.2d 338 (1964). Defamation of a family member, however, is distinguishable because, unlike the claim for interference and emotional harm, it now requires at least a publication of a falsehood. See Tuman v. Genesis Assocs., 894 F.Supp. 183 (E.D. Pa. 1995).

[75]   Strode v. Gleason, 9 Wash.App. 13, 510 P.2d 250 (1973). Hershey v. Hershey, 467 N.W.2d 484 (S.D. 1991), allowed recovery where the child was taken from the jurisdiction and hidden until he reached adulthood, calling the claim one for alienation of affections.

[76]   E.g., Stevens v. Stevens, 977 S.W.2d 305 (Mo. Ct. App. 1998).

[77]   J.A.H. v. Wadle & Assocs., 589 N.W.2d 256 (Iowa 1999) (public policy: confidentiality and divided loyalties of therapist would ensue if liability is imposed; in any event, no negligent treatment was proven); Bird v. W.C.W., 868 S.W.2d 767 (Tex. 1994). Contra Montoya v. Bebensee, 761 P.2d 285 (Colo. Ct. App. 1988).

[78]   See Zamstein v. Marvasti, 240 Conn. 549, 561, 692 A.2d 781, 787 (1997); Doe v. McKay, 183 Ill.2d 272, 700 N.E.2d 1018, 233 Ill.Dec. 310 (1998); cf. Ryder v. Mitchell, 54 P.3d 885 (Colo. 2002) (mother's suit against her children's therapist for communicating to their father a diagnosis unfavorable to mother was not actionable; the therapist had duty only to her patients, since a threat of liability could present a barrier to appropriate treatment of the patient). Similarly, so far as the claim is based on reporting suspected child abuse, statutory privileges will usually protect the therapist. See Myers v. Lashley, 44 P.3d 553 (Okla. 2002).

Subpart B

ECONOMIC TORTS

Chapter 41

ECONOMIC TORTS AND ECONOMIC LOSS RULES

Analysis

A. ECONOMIC LOSS: AN INTRODUCTION

§ 41.1   Economic Loss
§ 41.2   Specific Economic Torts vs. General Negligence Claims for Economic Loss
§ 41.3   The Core Economic Loss Rules: Contracting Parties and Strangers
§ 41.4   Categories of Economic Torts

B. NEGLIGENT ECONOMIC LOSS IN THE STRANGER CONTEXT

§ 41.5   Strangers: Negligence Toward a Third Person Causing Economic Loss to the Plaintiff
§ 41.6   Strangers: General Nonliability for Negligently Caused Stand-Alone Economic Harm
§ 41.7   Strangers: Policies or Rationales for Limiting Liability
§ 41.8   Strangers: Exceptions

C. NEGLIGENT ECONOMIC LOSS AND CONTRACTING PARTIES

§ 41.9   Contracting Parties: The Economic Loss Rule Generally
§ 41.10   Contracting Parties: Rationales and Policies for the Economic Loss Rule

D. SCOPE AND EXCEPTIONS

§ 41.11   Scope of and Exceptions to the No-Duty Economic Loss Rule

A. ECONOMIC LOSS: AN INTRODUCTION

§ 41.1 Economic Loss

Scope of the chapter. This chapter summarizes the general economic loss rules in ordinary negligence cases and their two basic forms, along with general exceptions and rationales. Many particular economic torts are discussed in the following chapters. The economic torts now constitute a major portion of tort law, and have increasingly drawn the attention of commentators in this country.[1] However, at present, the most detailed

---

[1]   See Ellen M. Bublick, Economic Torts: Gain in Understanding Losses, 48 Ariz. L. Rev. 693 (2006) (introducing and highlighting many articles in Symposium, Economic Tort Law, 48 Ariz. L. Rev. 693–1127 (2006)); Vincent Johnson, The Boundary-Line Function of the Economic Loss Rule, 66 Wash. & Lee L. Rev. 533 (2009).

studies in this area have come from Australian, Canadian, European and English scholars and lawyers.[2]

Pure economic loss. Economic harms or losses are financial costs to the plaintiff that do not arise from personal injury to the plaintiff or damage to tangible property in which the plaintiff has a legally recognized possessory or ownership interest.[3] To take a single example of such pure economic loss, the defendant might negligently block access to the plaintiff's retail store, without trespassing or harming the property itself. In such a case, the plaintiff's only claim is for pure economic loss that results because customers could not reach the store. Such a claim for pure economic loss will often be rejected under one of the economic loss rules.[4]

Economic loss as an item of damages versus economic torts. Any kind of tort can cause financial harm. A personal injury tort may result in medical bills and wage loss. Physical harm to property can reduce the value of the property or result in repair costs. Even emotional harms without physical injury may result in medical costs and lost wages. In all such cases, however, the economic loss is not itself the tort; it is only an item of damages resulting from a personal or a property tort. In contrast, economic torts inflict pecuniary or financial costs upon the plaintiff that do not result from injury to person or property or even from stand-alone emotional distress.[5] The first category— torts to person and tangible property accompanied by economic loss—are not economic torts and come under none of the strictures applied to economic tort claims. Special rules are for pure economic loss claims.

§ 41.2　Specific Economic Torts vs. General Negligence Claims for Economic Loss

Overview. With parties who have no contract-like relationship, pure economic loss is addressed in tort law in two different ways that are treated completely differently. The first is through recognized tort causes of action. The second is through ordinary negligence claims seeking recovery for pure economic loss.

Addressing economic harm in specific or named economic torts. In the first approach, tortious acts causing pure economic harm are traditionally dealt with under the rules of specific or named economic torts developed to address particular kinds of economic harm cases. For example, the action of "deceit" provides redress for economic harm caused by fraud that induced the plaintiff to enter a contract; the action of injurious falsehood or commercial disparagement provides redress for economic harm caused by false statements about the plaintiff's products. These and other torts aimed at specific kinds

---

[2]　Bruce Feldthusen, Economic Negligence—The Recovery of Pure Economic Loss (5th ed. 2008) (discussing a wide variety of cases from Canada, the United States, England and Australia); Helmut Koziol, Recovery for Economic Loss in the European Union, 48 Ariz. L. Rev. 871 (2006) (working through important factors in liability); Jane Stapleton, Comparative Economic Loss: Lessons from Case-Law-Focused "Middle Theory," 50 UCLA L. Rev. 531 (2002); Willem H. van Boom, Pure Economic Loss—A Comparative Perspective, in Pure Economic Loss 1, 2 (Willem H. van Boom, Helmut Koziol & Christian A. Witting eds., 2004).

[3]　Restatement (Third) of Torts: Liability for Economic Harms § 2 (2012) ("For purposes of this Restatement., "economic loss" is pecuniary damage not arising from injury to the plaintiff's person or from physical harm to the plaintiff's property."); Davencourt at Pilgrims Landing Homeowners Ass'n v. Davencourt at Pilgrims Landing, LC, 221 P.3d 234 (Utah 2009).

[4]　See Restatement (Third) of Torts: Liability for Economic Harms § 1 (2012).

[5]　See, e.g., Bayer CropScience LP v. Schafer, 385 S.W.3d 822 (Ark. 2011) (economic loss rule had no application where plaintiff rice farmers showed that defendant caused physical harm to their lands, crops and equipment).

of acts are supplemented by a catch-all pair of torts—interference with contract and interference with economic opportunity. Although all of these torts have their own rules and are considered in the chapters that follow, the significant thing about them in the present chapter is that with the most limited exceptions,[6] they reject liability based upon negligence, requiring instead intent or "malice" unless the parties are in a special relationship, such as, for example, the special relationship of lawyer and client.

Addressing economic harm in ordinary negligence claims. A radically different way of addressing claims for pure economic harm is to assert a claim for ordinary negligence, or possibly strict liability.[7] But if courts were to permit recovery for general negligence in a case addressed by one of the named economic torts, they would be negating the rules against negligence liability that are established in the named torts. Logically, then, if a named or more specific economic tort addresses the kind of facts the plaintiff presents, the plaintiff's claim should stand or fall under the rules for that tort, not under a general negligence theory, much less under a theory of strict liability.[8]

Effects of economic loss rules on the ordinary negligence claims. Economic loss rules are applied in claims asserting ordinary negligence for economic harm. Economic loss rules tend to exclude liability for mere negligence, although there are exceptions. For example, the Restatment Third of Torts, in its very first rule, establishes that "An actor has no general duty to avoid the unintentional infliction of economic loss on another," and then recognizes exceptions for some forms of professional negligence, negligent misrepresentation and negligent performance of services.[9] That brings the specific-tort approach and the negligence approach into a degree of harmony where the facts in issue are addressed by some specific tort. At the very least, coherence and consistency demand that in considering the negligence claims for pure economic loss, the named economic torts must be considered wherever they address the issues before the court. However, the economic loss rules in negligence cases may go further; economic loss rules might deny economic harm claims that are not addressed at all by the specific economic torts.

§ 41.3 The Core Economic Loss Rules: Contracting Parties and Strangers

Economic loss rules in context. In reality, courts very often reject liability for pure economic loss caused by negligence. In doing so, they often refer to "the" economic loss rule, mainly meaning that defendants are not liable for mere negligence that causes pure economic harm, much less are they strictly liable.[10] But because negligent infliction of stand-alone economic harm sometimes suffices for liability and sometimes not, commentators have doubted whether any single normative principle lies behind the

---

[6] Wrongful death actions, see Chapter 28, fit the formal paradigm of economic torts because the surviving plaintiffs were not themselves injured and they are seeking compensation for harm to another. Viewed in that way, wrongful death actions are statutory exceptions to economic loss rules that might otherwise exclude liability based on negligence or strict liability.

[7] Economic loss rules barring negligence claims would almost always bar strict liability claims as well. These usually occur in product-defect cases. In a few instances, intentional tort claims for pure economic loss have been barred by the rules. See 3 Dobbs, Hayden & Bublick, The Law of Torts § 686 (2d ed. 2011 & Supp.).

[8] See id. § 617 (discussing the overlap problem and giving other examples).

[9] Restatement (Third) of Torts: Liability for Economic Harms §§ 1, 4–6 (2012).

[10] E.g., Aguilar v. RP MRP Washington Harbour, LLC, 98 A. 3d 979 (D.C. 2014) (negligence action seeking to recover lost wages caused by flooding; claim barred by economic loss rule); LAN/STV v. Martin K. Eby Constr. Co., 435 S.W.3d 234 (Tex. 2014) (economic loss rule precluded general contractor from recovering damages in tort action from project architect for delay in project).

economic loss rule's rejection of many potential claims. They have correspondingly suggested that details and factual contexts are likely to be more compelling than a sweeping rule.[11] It is also possible that in some instances liability for pure economic harm is rejected under the tort no-duty rules of particular torts rather than because of the economic loss rule.[12] Economic losses arise in several distinctive situations, supported by different rationales and requiring different analyses.[13] Any reference to "the" economic loss rule in this treatise is therefore a reference to the particular economic loss rule relevant in the specific discussion and is not intended to suggest that there is a single over-arching rule.

Contracting parties. When the plaintiff and defendant have a contract that can be treated as allocating the relevant economic risks, tort liability for those risks would undermine the parties' contractual ordering of responsibilities. Accordingly, as to pure economic harm, such contracts usually replace the tort duty of reasonable care and sometimes other tort duties as well, leaving the plaintiff to any contract action she might have.[14] The contract action may also be barred, for example by disclaimers, statutes of limitation or damages limitations. In that case, the plaintiff will have neither a contract nor a tort action against a negligent defendant. The Restatement Third[15] and some courts[16] have adopted the term "economic loss rule" to apply only in the context of contracting parties.

Non-contracting strangers. The plaintiff's economic harm claim may also be barred when the parties are strangers, which is to say when they are *not* in a contractual relationship. Some courts have considered this too as one of the economic loss rules.[17] However, other courts reject liability for negligence causing pure economic harm on a different ground—the relevant tort does not recognize negligence as a basis for a tort action, as in the case of interference with contract or business opportunity.[18] In an ordinary negligence action, the plaintiff also may be denied all recovery for pure

---

[11]   See Vincent Johnson, The Boundary-Line Function of the Economic Loss Rule, 66 Wash. & Lee L. Rev. 533 (2009); Robert L. Rabin, Boundaries and the Economic Loss Rule in Tort, Respecting Boundaries and the Economic Loss Rule in, 48 Ariz. L. Rev. 857 (2006) (distinguishing cases of disappointed contractual expectation, economic harm to the plaintiff resulting from physical harms to others, and negligent performance of obligations to one person resulting in stand-alone economic loss to the plaintiff); Jay M. Feinman, The Economic Loss Rule and Private Ordering, 48 Ariz. L. Rev. 813 (2006) (noting the diversity of economic loss cases and discussing the importance of context-sensitive adjudication as distinct from abstract or formal rules); Helmut Koziol, Recovery for Economic Loss in the European Union, 48 Ariz. L. Rev. 871 (2006) (balancing various factors to determine liability for economic loss in particular cases, including indeterminate liabilities, and the nature and value of the interests at stake); cf. Anita Bernstein, Keep It Simple: An Explanation of the Rule of No Recovery for Pure Economic Loss, 48 Ariz. L. Rev. 773 (2006) (proposing an overall rule for economic loss but distinguishing many disparate situations such as product cases, transferred loss cases, flawed services and other).

[12]   See Flagstaff Affordable Housing Ltd. P'ship v. Design Alliance, Inc., 223 Ariz. 320, 223 P.3d 664 (2010).

[13]   E.g., Tiara Condo. Ass'n, Inc. v. Marsh & McLennan Cos., Inc., 110 So.3d 399 (Fla. 2013) (economic loss rule applies only in product liability context in Florida).

[14]   See generally § 41.9.

[15]   Restatement (Third) of Torts: Liability for Economic Harms § 3 (2012).

[16]   Sullivan v. Pulte Home Corp., 306 P.3d 1 (Ariz. 2013).

[17]   Thus Excavation Technologies, Inc. v. Columbia Gas Co. of Pa., 985 A.2d 840 (Pa. 2009), defined economic loss rule to include non-contracting parties by saying "no cause of action exists for negligence that results solely in economic damages unaccompanied by physical injury or property damage." It also treated the leading non-contracting case, Robins Dry Dock & Repair Co. v. Flint, 275 U.S. 303, 48 S.Ct. 134, 72 L.Ed. 290 (1927), as representing the economic loss rule.

[18]   See Chapters 41–42.

economic loss on the ground that there is generally no liability for negligently inflicted economic harm, as where the defendant negligently injures the plaintiff's key employee, with resulting business losses to the plaintiff.[19] The general approach of denying liability for negligently inflicted economic harm is the approach taken by the Restatement Third of Torts.[20] However, it must always be borne in mind that there are exceptions to this economic loss rule.[21]

Contracting parties and strangers: a continuum of relationships. The reasons for denying tort liability in the two kinds of cases are different. The case of non-contracting parties may involve concerns about unpredictable and limitless liabilities, but the case of contracting parties involves the policy of honoring the contract. For this reason— because the scope of the rules is different—it is important to distinguish the two patterns. At the same time it may be important to recognize that relationships of the parties may be neither clear-cut, direct-contract relationships nor total stranger relationships. Many two-party contracts may also be part of a single project involving other parties. For example, architects or engineers may contract only with a landowner, but they know that building contractors and subcontractors will rely on their plans in bidding. Banks and financial institutions involved in the huge, many-layered credit card industry may construct multiple bilateral contracts, creating a web of relationships which affect, say, victims of identity theft who may have no contract at all. In such cases, it may be worthwhile to recognize a continuum of relationships, some of which might create tort duties.

§ 41.4 Categories of Economic Torts

Factual categories of economic torts. Economic torts can be categorized in many different ways. The following five categories suggest the general factual settings for economic torts. They cover most of the common economic tort cases:

(1) The defendant's improper communications to third persons cause the plaintiff financial harm.

(2) The defendant's false statements to the plaintiff herself induce the plaintiff to enter into an economically damaging transaction.

(3) The defendant appropriates some intangible value belonging to the plaintiff, a trade secret, for example.

(4) The defendant provides a defective tangible product or services, causing pure economic harm such as losses in production or added costs without physical harm to other property.

(5) The defendant causes physical harm to person or property of another person which in turn causes pure economic harm to the plaintiff.

It must be remembered that in all these categories, the putative tort is an economic tort and invokes the economic tort rules only if the plaintiff's economic harm does not result

---

[19] E.g., Local Joint Exec. Bd. of Las Vegas, Culinary Workers Union, Local No. 226 v. Stern, 98 Nev. 409, 651 P.2d 637 (1982).

[20] Restatement (Third) of Torts: Liability for Economic Harms § 1 (2012).

[21] § 41.11.

from physical harm to the plaintiff's person or property[22] or from a personal tort such as defamation.

Communications to others causing stand-alone economic harm. One type of economic harm occurs when the defendant communicates, not to the plaintiff, but to third persons. For example, the defendant tells the plaintiff's customers that the plaintiff is selling goods with hidden defects. If some customers cease buying from the plaintiff as a result, the plaintiff has a potential claim for intentional interference with business relations or contract[23] and perhaps also a claim for product disparagement.[24] But negligence alone seldom suffices in this category. Courts have even held that banks are free to act negligently in providing credit cards in the plaintiff's name to imposters whose identity theft then results in financial harm to the plaintiff.[25]

Communications to the plaintiff causing stand-alone economic harm. The category of economic torts based on communications to the plaintiff consists almost entirely of claims for fraud, deceit, or misrepresentation. These claims arise mainly in bargaining transactions between the plaintiff and defendant. For example, the defendant falsely represents that an oil painting is a Titian when in fact it is a modern copy and worth little. The plaintiff who buys in reliance may have an economic tort claim to recover for his loss or perhaps for the loss of his expected gain in the transaction. In the category of economic harm resulting from communications to the plaintiff, litigation may raise a number of issues—whether the plaintiff relied on the statement, whether the plaintiff was justified in relying, whether the statement was merely a promise about the future that can be redressed only through a contract claim, whether the statement was an intentional falsehood and if not whether negligence or strict liability could be a sufficient ground for relief.[26] A number of courts have now applied the economic loss rule not only to bar negligence claims but also to bar claims for intentional fraud where that fraud is related to the subject matter of the contract.[27]

Misappropriation of intangible values. Much of the economic value in the world today lies outside the realm of tangible property. Stocks and bonds, promissory notes, trade secrets, performance rights, trademarks, copyright, and patents are examples. In contrast to the single set of rules involved in misrepresentations to the plaintiff, the rules in misappropriation cases vary with the particular kind of tort claimed or interest asserted. For example, the rules of copyright (based on statute)[28] are not like the rules of patent or trademark.[29] Trade secrets could be protected by an expansive notion of the

---

[22] See, e.g., Bayer CropScience LP v. Schafer, 385 S.W.3d 822 (Ark. 2011) (economic loss rule had no application where plaintiff rice farmers showed that defendant caused physical harm to their lands, crops and equipment; "the rule does not apply if the plaintiff's economic harm results from physical harm to the plaintiff's person or other property") (citing Dobbs, Hayden & Bublick, The Law of Torts (2d ed. 2011).

[23] Chapter 43.

[24] See § 43.1. A defamation claim may be possible, but defamation is a personal, not a purely economic tort.

[25] See 3 Dobbs, Hayden & Bublick, The Law of Torts §§ 650 (banks' liability or not) & 712 (same in context of computer hacking) (2d ed. 2011 & Supp.). Both the card issuer and the identity thief, of course, are, directly or indirectly, making representations to third persons about the identity of the thief and about the plaintiff's credit.

[26] See Chapter 43.

[27] See 3 Dobbs, Hayden & Bublick, The Law of Torts § 686 (2d ed. 2011 & Supp.).

[28] Id. § 741.

[29] Id. §§ 735–38.

ancient tort of conversion,[30] but trade secret law may represent the exclusive approach in that particular instance, leaving claims for conversion of intangibles for other interests.[31] Here again there are possible overlaps and preemption issues. The right of publicity—rights in certain commercially valuable personae[32]—may overlap and tread upon the rules of copyright, for example.

Supplying defective chattels, services, or real property. Defective products may cause economic loss if they do not work well; but so long as they do not cause physical harm to person or property other than the product itself,[33] most courts invoke the economic loss rule to reject tort liability. In products cases, for example, courts limit the manufacturer's liability to contract or warranty claims[34] unless the defendant commits a tort that is somehow "independent" of the contract and unrelated to the protection the contract afforded.[35] The same rule has been applied to cases of defective real property[36] and, somewhat unevenly, to services.[37] The Restatement Third of Torts recognizes liability in this situation in limited situations.[38]

Harm to another's interest with indirect economic harm to the plaintiff. Almost everyone is dependent to some degree upon other people. For example, a product manufacturer is dependent upon power supplies from the electric company, but does not own the electrical equipment that generates electricity. A defendant who negligently destroys the generating plant may cause the manufacturer to lose production and thus to lose sales. In such a case, however, the manufacturing company that suffers no physical harm to its own property is likely to find that the economic loss rule bars any claim for lost production and lost profits.[39]

B. NEGLIGENT ECONOMIC LOSS IN THE STRANGER CONTEXT

§ 41.5 Strangers: Negligence Toward a Third Person Causing Economic Loss to the Plaintiff

Physical harm to A's property resulting in stand-alone economic harm to B. A stranger who negligently, but not intentionally, causes physical harm to one person or his property, with resulting economic harm to another person, is not liable for that

---

[30] §§ 44.1–44.3.

[31] § 46.5.

[32] § 46.6.

[33] As to what counts as "other property," see 2 Dobbs, Hayden & Bublick, The Law of Torts § 449 (2d ed. 2011 & Supp.).

[34] E.g., East River S.S. Corp. v. Transamerica Delaval, Inc., 476 U.S. 858, 106 S.Ct. 2295, 90 L.Ed.2d 865 (1986); Moorman Mfg. Co. v. National Tank Co., 91 Ill. 2d 69, 61 Ill. Dec. 746, 435 N.E.2d 443 (1982). Some authority goes further, imposing only contract liability even when a defective product causes harm to other property in some instances. Fleetwood Enters., Inc. v. Progressive N. Ins. Co., 749 N.E.2d 492 (Ind. 2001) (harm to product itself treated as stand-alone economic harm for which recovery is denied, even if the plaintiff also suffers damages to person or other property); Neibarger v. Universal Coops., Inc., 439 Mich. 512, 486 N.W.2d 612 (1992).

[35] See 3 Dobbs, Hayden & Bublick, The Law of Torts § 615 (2d ed. 2011 & Supp.).

[36] Blahd v. Richard B. Smith, Inc., 141 Idaho 296, 108 P.3d 996 (2005).

[37] See Insurance Co. of N. Am. v. Cease Elec. Inc., 276 Wis.2d 361, 688 N.W.2d 462 (2004) (refused to apply the economic loss rule to services).

[38] Restatement (Third) of Torts: Liability for Economic Harms § 6 (2012).

[39] See 3 Dobbs, Hayden & Bublick, The Law of Torts § 647 (2d ed. 2011 & Supp.) (viewing such cases as claims for negligent interference with contract).

economic harm. The leading case, *Robins Dry Dock & Repair Co. v. Flint*,[40] long ago established that a defendant owed no duty of care to protect the plaintiff from pure economic loss merely because it harmed property of a third person in which the plaintiff had no possessory or ownership interests. This was the rule, even though the defendant's negligence caused physical damage to the third person or his property and that damage resulted in economic loss to the plaintiff. The Third Restatement is in accord with the traditional rule.[41] Of course, wrongful death statutes provide an exception to the general rule.

The Robins case. The defendant in *Robins*, carrying out a contract with A to do maintenance work on A's sea-going vessel, actually caused damage to the vessel. That damage required further repairs. During the added repair period, the plaintiff was unable to exercise his right to transport goods on the ship and suffered economic loss as a result. But the plaintiff had no possessory or property interest in the ship itself, and the Supreme Court, in an opinion by Justice Holmes, held that the plaintiff had no cause of action based on the defendant's negligent physical harm to the vessel owned by another. Two easily acceptable corollaries apply the same rule to deny liability to the plaintiff when the defendant negligently causes either physical[42] or pure economic harm to A with resulting economic loss to the plaintiff.[43] A number of illustrative cases are given in the discussion of negligent interference with contract or economic opportunity.[44]

Foreseeability. Under the *Robins* rule, liability for the plaintiff's pure economic loss is rejected even if the defendant could foresee economic harm to the plaintiff, which is to

---

[40]   Robins Dry Dock & Repair Co. v. Flint, 275 U.S. 303, 48 S.Ct. 134, 72 L.Ed. 290 (1927).

[41]   Restatement (Third) of Torts: Liability for Economic Harms § 7 (2014) (unless recognized in a specific tort, there is no liability for economic loss caused by unintentional injury to another person or property in which the claimant has no proprietary interest).

[42]   See Fifield Manor v. Finston, 54 Cal.2d 632, 7 Cal.Rptr. 377, 354 P.2d 1073 (1960). The same result may be obtained, at least in some claims, by saying that the plaintiff suffered only indirect harm and has no standing to sue. See Ganim v. Smith & Wesson Corp., 258 Conn. 313, 780 A.2d 98 (2001) (city had no standing to sue for losses incurred, inter alia, in public health and police costs caused by sale of certain handguns). Likewise, statutes may impose duties to provide care for the plaintiff's personal well-being, but not for the plaintiff's economic interests. See Sabeta v. Baptist Hosp. of Miami, Inc., 410 F.Supp. 2d 1224 (S.D. Fla. 2005) (emergency medical care required by federal statute did not protect against economic loss). On economic loss claims based on nuisance, including gun-marketing cases, and the 2005 statute affecting the gun cases, see 2 Dobbs, Hayden & Bublick, The Law of Torts § 403 (2d ed. 2011 & Supp.). See also id. § 452 (products liability analysis in the gun marketing cases).

[43]   In Banknorth, N.A. v. BJ's Wholesale Club, Inc., 442 F.Supp.2d 206 (M.D. Pa. 2006), a merchant failed to properly secure customers' credit card data. Hackers used data to run up charges on credit cards. The plaintiff, a bank that guaranteed customers against liability for fraudulent use of their cards, had no negligence claim against merchant. Instead of conceptualizing the case in terms of the stranger rule, the court crammed it into the contract category, saying that although there was no contract between the parties, the bank "could have" bargained with Visa for protection and failed to do so.

[44]   § 42.11.

say the rule is a bright-line, no-duty rule.[45] The rule is thus not merely an application of the *Palsgraf* foreseeability rule.[46]

Interruptions of power or supplies. Another version of the basic idea in *Robins* occurs when the defendant causes harm to the property of a supplier who provides the plaintiff with goods or power necessary to operate the plaintiff's business, with the result that the business is interrupted without physical harm to any property of the plaintiff. In such cases, courts have applied the rule to exclude the liability of the negligent defendant.[47]

Negligently blocking walks or highways, reducing traffic to the plaintiff's business. Similarly, a business may lose customers because traffic is reduced after the defendant's negligence requires closure of a bridge, but no claim for economic loss lies against the negligent defendant[48] unless the business owner's property right is invaded by denial of access to her land.[49]

An illustration. The principle was dramatically illustrated when two buildings collapsed in Manhattan in 1997 and 1998. Streets were closed and businesses served by those streets suffered economic losses without physical harms. The New York Court of Appeals rejected recovery, holding that although a building owner owes duties to those with whom it has a special relationship, the vast number of claims that could arise in an urban disaster required the court to hold that stand-alone economic loss was beyond the scope of the defendant's duty.[50] Under the same general principle, a contractor whose work is delayed because of pollution is denied recovery for his purely economic loss.[51]

Limitations: independent duty to the plaintiff. The economic loss rules mean that a duty owed by the defendant to a third person does not, by itself, show that the defendant owed a duty to protect the plaintiff against economic harm. Although the plaintiff can

---

[45]   See Consolidated Aluminum Corp. v. C.F. Bean Corp., 772 F.2d 1217, 1222 (5th Cir. 1985) (the determinative issue is not "whether a plaintiff's harm is 'foreseeable' or 'remote' in a factual sense but instead on 'the character of the interest harmed' for which a plaintiff seeks relief"); State of La. ex rel. Guste v. M/V Testbank, 752 F.2d 1019, 1023 (5th Cir. 1985) (rejecting foreseeability and remoteness tests in favor of a bright-line no-duty rule). Sometimes, however, similar results in similar economic harm cases are explained on the ground that the link between the defendant's fault and the economic damage suffered is too tenuous or remote—the language of "legal" or proximate cause that antedated scope-of-risk analysis. See Petitions of Kinsman Transit Co., 388 F.2d 821 (2d Cir. 1968) (defendant's damage to a draw-bridge temporarily prevented shipping from proceeding to deliver goods up river, to the economic loss of owners of undamaged goods down river that could not be delivered).

[46]   Palsgraf v. Long Island R.R., 248 N.Y. 339, 162 N.E. 99 (1928) (limiting liability to persons within the scope of foreseeable harm), discussed in § 15.7. Dissenters from the Robins rule have suggested that some kind of foreseeability or "proximate cause" rule could be used to permit recover for some but not all economic loss. See Petitions of Kinsman Transit Co., 388 F.2d 821 (2d Cir. 1968). This position has not received general approbation.

[47]   Kaiser Aluminum & Chem. Corp. v. Marshland Dredging Co., 455 F.2d 957 (5th Cir. 1972); Byrd v. English, 117 Ga. 191, 43 S.E. 419 (1903). Consolidated Aluminum Corp. v. C.F. Bean Corp., 772 F.2d 1217 (5th Cir. 1985); Newlin v. New England Tel. & Tel. Co., 316 Mass. 234, 54 N.E.2d 929 (1944). Distinguish interruptions caused by the supplier himself, who is in privity with the plaintiff. See § 41.9. In that case the result may be the same, but the rationales, scope and exceptions may differ. E.g., Bamberger & Feibleman v. Indianapolis Power & Light Co., 665 N.E.2d 933 (Ind. Ct. App. 1996).

[48]   Nebraska Innkeepers, Inc. v. Pittsburgh-Des Moines Corp., 345 N.W.2d 124 (Iowa 1984).

[49]   Denial of access to property invades a property right, see Restatement (Second) of Torts § 821C cmt. f (1979). Consequently liability for denial of access to an abutting owner is appropriate. Stop & Shop Cos., Inc. v. Fisher, 387 Mass. 889, 444 N.E.2d 368 (1983).

[50]   532 Madison Ave. Gourmet Foods, Inc. v. Finlandia Ctr., Inc., 96 N.Y.2d 280, 750 N.E.2d 1097, 727 N.Y.S.2d 49 (2001). The court also rejected the plaintiffs' claim for public nuisance with private harm.

[51]   Garweth Corp. v. Boston Edison Co., 415 Mass. 303, 613 N.E.2d 92 (1993).

get no advantage from a breach of defendant's duty to a third person, the defendant might owe a second, independent duty to the plaintiff's economic interests, as through a special relationship with the plaintiff.[52] Statutes can also create a duty to protect the plaintiff's economic interests; wrongful death statutes allow certain family members to recover for economic losses that arise from negligent physical harm to others.

Limitations: Third party beneficiary under contract law. The Robins rule bars the tort claim for negligence but does not bar a contract claim. If the Robins plaintiff had been a third party beneficiary of the contract and the defendant's acts constituted a breach, the plaintiff could have been permitted to recover under the contract, though not in tort.

Limitations: economic loss accompanying physical injury to person or property. Unless barred by some other rules, a plaintiff whose own person or property is injured can recover in tort for accompanying economic harm.[53] In Robins, the plaintiff's problem as the Court saw it was that he did not have a property interest in the vessel; he had only a contract right under which A would carry the goods, not a leasehold interest or "demise." If the third party had a property interest in the vessel, the case might well have come out differently. In a number of cases the defendant negligently pollutes waters and commercial fishers have been allowed recovery for their purely economic losses.[54] Such cases are sometimes viewed as public nuisance cases with special private harm,[55] or as a limited property interest in the waters, not extended to others.[56]

§ 41.6   Strangers: General Nonliability for Negligently Caused Stand-Alone Economic Harm

Negligence generally an insufficient basis for liability. In the absence of an exception or a particular tort duty, liability is generally not imposed upon strangers—those not in privity or near-privity—for negligent infliction of pure economic harm.[57] Put differently, when strangers negligently cause economic harm to the plaintiff without causing physical harm to the person or property of others, the general rule typically bars the

---

[52] For example, an auditor's breach of duty to use care in the audit of a business may sometimes also be a breach of duty to lenders who rely on the audit, provided the auditor has certain relationships with the lenders. See 3 Dobbs, Hayden & Bublick, The Law of Torts § 681 (2d ed. 2011 & Supp.).

[53] E.g., Souci v. William C. Smith & Co., 763 A.2d 96 (D.C. 2000) (tenant can recover against third person for negligent repairs contracted for by landlord); McClosky v. Martin, 56 So.2d 916 (Fla. 1951) (tenant could recover against "adjoining landowner" for nuisance that caused only economic harm in reduced restaurant business); Nichols v. Mid-Continent Pipe Line Co., 933 P.2d 272 (Okla. 1996) (tenant in possession could recover against third person for physical harms resulting from nuisance, even if lessor could have repudiated the tenancy).

[54] Union Oil Co. v. Oppen, 501 F.2d 558 (9th Cir. 1974); Carson v. Hercules Powder Co., 240 Ark. 887, 402 S.W.2d 640 (1966) ("public nuisance" on a non-navigable stream or bayou, plaintiff had permission of riparian owners to fish there and earned his living doing so; polluter was subject to liability); Hampton v. North Carolina Pulp Co., 223 N.C. 535, 27 S.E.2d 538 (1943).

[55] Restatement (Third) of Torts: Liability for Economic Harms § 8 (2014).

[56] Louisiana ex rel. v. Guste v. M/V Testbank, 752 F.2d 1019, 88 A.L.R.Fed. 239 (5th Cir. 1985).

[57] Plourde Sand & Gravel v. JGI E., Inc., 154 N.H. 791, 917 A.2d 1250, 1254 (2007); Loosli v. City of Salem, 345 Or. 303, 194 P.3d 623 (2008) (city had no duty to use care in certifying that citizen's proposed business location was permissible under zoning law and was not liable for cost of a move it later required); Excavation Techs., Inc. v. Columbia Gas Co. of Pa., 985 A.2d 840 (Pa. 2009) (defendant was not liable for negligently marking underground gas lines, resulting in economic loss to the plaintiff excavator who struck the lines as a result of the markings); Hamill v. Pawtucket Mut. Ins. Co., 179 Vt. 250, 892 A.2d 226 (2005). The rule is broad enough to cover cases of contracting parties as well as strangers and has been asserted in such contracting cases. E.g., Nelson v. Anderson Lumber Co., 140 Idaho 702, 99 P.3d 1092 (Ct. App. 2004). The Robins case, discussed in the preceding section, may be viewed as supporting this general rule.

claim for negligence.[58] In some jurisdictions, this is considered one form of the economic loss rule.[59] In others, the economic loss rule only involves claims by a plaintiff who has a contractual, or at least near-privity relationship with the defendant.[60] The Restatement Third has sided with this latter group and used the term "economic loss rule" solely in conjunction with contracting parties,[61] although the Restatement also would generally deny liability in the stranger context, just under the general rule that "An actor has no general duty to avoid the unintentional infliction of economic loss on another."[62] Whatever the terminology, the rule in effect says there is no general tort duty to use reasonable care to protect strangers from pure economic harm and it has been held to bar consumers as well as sophisticated or entrepreneurial plaintiffs.

Overstatements of the stranger rule. Courts have at times stated the stranger rule too broadly, for example, by stating it as a flat rule rather than as a rule to be applied generally, but subject to exceptions.[63] Courts have also sometimes said that the rule bars *tort* actions instead of negligence and strict liability actions, implying, perhaps unintentionally, that the rule also bars actions for intentional torts.[64] It is true that where the parties, plaintiff, and defendant are in contractual relationship, even claims for intentional torts may be barred under some circumstances,[65] but that is not the case with the rule applied in stranger cases. For instance, the tort of intentional interference with contract is well established.

Economic loss rule: basis in rules of specific or named economic torts. The economic loss rule in stranger cases is less a matter of capturing the verbal expressions of courts than a matter of capturing their usual actions. As already stated, the economic loss rule in stranger cases reflects the common rules of specific economic torts, which, with the limited exception of negligent misrepresentation,[66] generally require more than negligence to support liability.[67] Thus many cases of economic loss fit within the concept of interference with contract or interference with economic relations, and the firm rule for those interference cases is that no action will lie for mere negligence.[68] This rule against negligence liability can be seen as a specific instance of the more broadly stated

---

[58] E.g., Western Mass. Blasting Corp. v. Metropolitan & Cas. Ins. Co., 783 A.2d 398 (R.I. 2001) (plaintiff claimed that defendant's negligent investigation of damage to property of defendant's insured led defendant to assert a claim for damages, which, if paid, would damage the plaintiff's business reputation; held, negligence is insufficient basis for liability).

[59] See Excavation Techs., Inc. v. Columbia Gas Co. of Pa., 985 A.2d 840 (Pa. 2009).

[60] E.g., Flagstaff Affordable Housing Ltd. P'ship v. Design Alliance, Inc., 223 Ariz. 320, 223 P.3d 664 (2010); Sullivan v. Pulte Home Corp., 306 P.3d 1 (Ariz. 2013); Sunridge Dev. Corp. v. RB&G Eng'g, Inc., 230 P.3d 1000 (Utah 2010); § 41.9 (the contracting version of the economic loss rules).

[61] Restatement (Third) of Torts: Liability for Economic Harms § 3 (2012).

[62] Id. § 1.

[63] E.g., Franklin Grove Corp. v. Drexel, 936 A.2d 1272, 1275 (R.I. 2007) (a plaintiff is precluded from recovering purely economic losses in a negligence cause of action, but later noting an exception for consumer-plaintiffs).

[64] E.g., In re Ill. Bell Switching Station Litig., 161 Ill.2d 233, 641 N.E.2d 440, 204 Ill.Dec. 216 (1994).

[65] § 41.11.

[66] § 43.5. Even liability for negligent misrepresentation can be seen as less a special exception than a product of the rule that special relationships create a duty of care, even in economic tort cases.

[67] See, e.g., Offshore Rental Co. v. Continental Oil Co., 22 Cal.3d 157, 168, 583 P.2d 721, 728, 148 Cal.Rptr. 867, 874 (1978); Alvord & Swift v. Stewart M. Muller Constr. Co., Inc. 46 N.Y.2d 276, 281, 385 N.E.2d 1238, 1241–42, 413 N.Y.S.2d 309, 312 (1978). Examples include: (1) interference with contract, (2) interference with economic expectancies, (3) disparagement and injurious falsehood, (4) malicious prosecution, and, usually, (5) conversion of intangibles and trade secret appropriation, and (6) infringement of the right of publicity.

[68] § 42.11.

economic loss rule as applied among strangers.[69] In other words, the stranger economic loss rule is a generalization of the near-uniform rules of specific economic torts. In cases of this kind, the economic loss rule for strangers is merely a recognition that the rule of torts designed to deal with the specific situation should not be subverted simply by calling the claim one for negligence rather than, say, interference with contract or some other specific economic tort.[70] For these reasons, even if an economic loss rule is not invoked by name, negligent infliction of stand-alone economic harm is still not ordinarily sufficient for liability.[71] A number of examples are discussed elsewhere.[72]

Clarifying the role of the economic loss rule in stranger cases. From what has just been said, it seems apparent that the economic loss, no-duty rule in stranger cases is partly a way of saying that the rules of specific economic torts with usual rejection of the negligence basis of liability are not to be subverted simply by treating the claim as a negligence action instead of one for intentional interference with contract.[73]

Privity. Courts long ago eliminated the need to show privity in most tort cases,[74] retaining the requirement for only contract claims. Privity can be relevant in economic loss claims, however, because the reasons for barring such claims and hence the scope of the rules differ according to whether the parties are in a contractual or semi-contractual relationship or whether they are strangers.[75] Defendants who have tried to make economic loss arguments in terms of privity rather in terms of the principles may have confused the issue and perhaps have made it easy for courts to reject their arguments.[76]

---

[69]   See Lips v. Scottsdale Healthcare Corp., 224 Ariz. 266, 229 P.3d 1008 (2010) (stating that courts generally recognize no duty to exercise reasonable care for purely economic well-being and giving the rule against negligence-based liability for interference with contract as one example).

[70]   Thus, the Arizona Court initially avoided deciding a claim on the basis of the economic tort rule and instead favored focusing on the rules of the particular tort applicable to the facts. Flagstaff Affordable Housing Ltd. P'ship v. Design Alliance, Inc., 223 Ariz. 320, 223 P.3d 664 (2010). The same court later acknowledged that "[c]ourts have not recognized a general duty to exercise reasonable care for the purely economic well-being of others," and gave the rule against negligence-based liability for interference with contract or prospects as an example. Lips v. Scottsdale Healthcare Corp., 224 Ariz. 266, 229 P.3d 1008 (2010).

[71]   E.g., Reserve Mooring, Inc. v. American Commercial Barge Line, LLC, 251 F.3d 1069 (5th Cir. 2001) (vessel sunk near the claimant's commercial mooring site, blocking customers; no liability for economic harm without damage to the plaintiff's property); Nelson v. Anderson Lumber Co., 99 P.3d 1092 (Idaho Ct. App. 2004) (absent special relationship, no tort duty to prevent economic losses to another); 532 Madison Ave. Gourmet Foods, Inc. v. Finlandia Ctr., Inc., 96 N.Y.2d 280, 750 N.E.2d 1097, 727 N.Y.S.2d 49 (2001); Adams v. Copper Beach Townhome Communities, L.P., 816 A.2d 301 (Pa. Super. Ct. 2003) (employees thrown out of work by defendants' negligent damage to factory where they worked had no cause of action); Aikens v. Debow, 541 S.E.2d 576 (W.Va. 2000) (motel lost business when defendant negligently damaged an access bridge; no duty absent contract or special relationship).

[72]   See 3 Dobbs, Hayden & Bublick, The Law of Torts §§ 645–51 (2d ed. 2011 & Supp.).

[73]   See § 41.2.

[74]   See Greenman v. Yuba Power Prods., Inc., 59 Cal. 2d 57, 27 Cal. Rptr. 697, 377 P.2d 897 (1963) (strict liability in products cases); Peters v. Forster, 804 N.E.2d 736, 742 (Ind. 2004) (privity not required between building contractor and one injured by his negligent work); MacPherson v. Buick Motor Co., 217 N.Y. 382, 390, 111 N.E. 1050 (1916) (negligence in products cases, foreseeability, not privity is the test).

[75]   See §§ 41.7 (rationales for the stranger rule) & 41.10 (rationales for the contracting-party rules).

[76]   See Jim's Excavating Serv., Inc. v. HKM Assocs., 265 Mont. 494, 502, 878 P.2d 248, 253 (1994); cf. Aikens v. DeBow, 208 W.Va. 486, 541 S.E.2d 576 (2000) (a special relationship is required to establish duty to protect against stand-alone economic loss; privity or close relationship might be one way of showing special relation).

As courts have sometimes said, in many of the stranger or non-privity cases, the concern is not privity as such but the risk of indeterminate liability.[77]

§ 41.7 Strangers: Policies or Rationales for Limiting Liability

General policies for excluding liability based on negligence alone: economic freedom. Several reasons support the rule requiring intent—or sometimes "malice"—for most economic torts, although those reasons may vary with the factual context.[78] In general, freedom to act in the economic sphere for self-interest and competition is a generally accepted policy. Liability for mere negligence could undermine competition and economic freedom, at least in many circumstances, especially where the parties have adverse economic interests.

Suggesting limits to economic freedom rationale. Limits to this rationale have not been much explored in the cases and probably should be. The economic freedom rationale seems inapplicable, for instance, where both the plaintiff and the defendant have unconditional economic interests that would be served by the defendant's reasonable care. Suppose a gas company negligently marks the location of its underground gas lines for an excavator, thus leading the excavator to operate in the wrong area, with damage to the pipes. Necessary repair of the pipes delays the excavator's work, to the excavator's resulting economic loss. In such a case, the economic loss rule seems to serves none of the defendant's interests in economic freedom to negligently mark the pipes' location. On the contrary, the defendant's interest is to use reasonable care, since damaged or exploding gas lines can cause it significant damage. Nor would the defendant's cost of making reasonably accurate markings be a factor in favor of eliminating the duty of care, since, again, reasonably careful marking is to the company's own interest.[79] When the parties' interests are not adversarial on the issue involved, or not entrepreneurial, it may be that courts should weigh the value of no-duty rule solely in light of the other rationales.

Indeterminate liability and the domino effect. An unmitigated statement of the no-duty or economic loss rule in stranger cases is a very broad and general response to a narrow and particular problem. In some cases, A's economic loss is likely to cause a new economic loss to B, and B's loss likely to cause one to C, with no predictable end in sight. This domino effect is one that cannot be calculated by the defendant and probably not efficiently insured for.[80] Something similar can be said when the defendant's negligence toward A could result in unlimited liabilities to parties whose number and economic losses cannot be guessed in advance, as where the defendant accountant erroneously certifies that A has a large net worth, with the result that many lenders separately lose money investing in A's failing enterprise.[81] Liability "in an indeterminate amount for an

[77] See Rozny v. Marnul, 43 Ill.2d 54, 65, 250 N.E.2d 656, 662 (1969); Klecan v. Countrywide Home Loans, Inc., 351 Ill. Dec. 548, 951 N.E.2d 1212 (App. Ct. 2011); Plourde Sand & Gravel v. JGI E., Inc., 154 N.H. 791, 917 A.2d 1250, 1254 (2007) (citing 4 Harper, James & Gray, The Law of Torts § 25.18A (2d ed.1986)).

[78] See Robert L. Rabin, Respecting Boundaries and the Economic Loss Rule in Tort, 48 Ariz. L. Rev. 857 (2006).

[79] The example is based on the facts in Excavation Technologies, Inc. v. Columbia Gas Co. of Pennsylvania, 985 A.2d 840 (Pa. 2009), where the court invoked the economic loss rule to protect the gas company from liability. Neither of the points mentioned in the text was raised.

[80] See Louisiana ex rel. Guste V. M/v Testbank, 752 F.2d 1019 (5th Cir. 1985).

[81] See 3 Dobbs, Hayden & Bublick, The Law of Torts § 679 (2d ed. 2011 & Supp.).

indeterminate time to an indeterminate class"[82] is likely to impact both fairness and the policy of free economic activities.

Examples. The domino effect is a real risk when a third party's goods or property used in commerce are damaged or access to them is delayed. If the defendant negligently damages A's ship, shippers who would have used the vessel for shipping food to foreign buyers will lose profits. The foreign buyers will then have economic losses because they will not have the goods for resale to foreign manufactures of food products. Similarly, closure of a river due to the defendant's oil spill or toxic contamination may bring river transport to a halt with the same domino effect and collateral economic effects as well.

Drawing boundaries on the negligence tort. Somewhat differently, it may be difficult in many cases to draw appropriate boundaries on liability for negligence. An employee who sleeps late one Monday morning might reduce his employer's production, which in turn may have further effects on others in the economic world. But negligent sleeping sounds like a tort no one would want to recognize as a ground for recovery of economic loss.

The traffic cop function—economic loss rule directs the claim to the most appropriate rules. A rule imposing liability for negligence alone in all economic harm cases would sabotage the rules crafted for many particular torts. Economic harm from commercial disparagement or conversion of intangibles or interference with contract would become actionable upon proof of negligence alone, contrary to many of the rules applied in those and other particular torts. Consequently, it has been argued that the general rule against negligence liability for economic harms is a kind of intellectual traffic cop, channeling claims to the tort rules that most specifically apply.[83] The rule functions in part to preserve the integrity of other tort rules. An illustration of the argument is in cases of harm to reputation causing economic loss. Often, though not always, negligence cases asserting these harms are displaced by the laws of specific torts.[84]

The rule or practice is usually normatively right. In the absence of more specific rules addressed to particular conduct, it may be argued that strangers should not usually be required to exercise reasonable care for the protection of others' economic well-being. Perhaps a worker can foresee that if he negligently delays repairs on my truck, others who count on me to haul their goods will lose their profits. But maybe the worker should not be required to consider the potential loss to non-owners unless they are third party beneficiaries.

Economic losses are not social losses. Some economic thinkers, like Judge Posner, hold that economic losses are not social losses and that only social losses should be compensated.[85] Judge Posner has pointed out that economic harm to one person often means economic gain to another. He suggested that "since the tortfeasor is not entitled to sue for the benefits, neither should he have to pay for the losses."[86] Perhaps, however,

---

[82]   Ultramares Corp. v. Touche, 255 N.Y. 170, 174 N.E. 441 (1931) (Cardozo, J., on negligent misrepresentation claims against an auditor).

[83]   Dan B. Dobbs, An Introduction to Non-Statutory Economic Loss Claims, 48 Ariz. L. Rev. 713, 715 (2006).

[84]   See 3 Dobbs, Hayden & Bublick, The Law of Torts § 649 (2d ed. 2011 & Supp.).

[85]   Richard A. Posner, Common-Law Economic Torts: An Economic and Legal Analysis, 48 Ariz. L. Rev. 735, 736–37 (2006).

[86]   See All-Tech Telecom, Inc. v. Amway Corp., 174 F.3d 862, 865 (7th Cir. 1999). It is possible to argue that there is no need to limit compensation to cases where social loss has been inflicted and that in any event

many would argue that a particular individual's right to economic security should not turn on whether there is a net social loss but instead on considerations of fairness and justice, at least in part.

Policies opposed to economic loss limitations. Although some of the reasons just discussed do indeed support a limited application of the stranger economic loss rules, there are also reasons to impose measured liability for some economic harms caused by negligence, certainly reasons not to overstate the rules against liability, and these reasons come from the heart of tort law. Prima facie, essential fairness requires that when one person's fault causes harm to another, the person at fault should recompense the victim for the harms done to the victim. That is a settled policy—or sense of justice— in tort law, although pragmatic concerns, such as the concern about indeterminate liability, may override that policy in some instances. A distinct reason is deterrence; if negligent activity carries risks to others but the tortfeasor is not held accountable for the harm done, he will have little or no motive to take appropriate precautions. Here again, pragmatic concerns may call for a different answer in particular cases, but a general absolution that forgives all economic torts in advance is unwarranted. For these reasons, a measured and careful delineation of the stranger rules and careful attention to the exceptions and other limitations is especially desirable.

§ 41.8 Strangers: Exceptions

Exceptions—when negligence is a sufficient basis for liability. The general rule in stranger cases does not bar negligence claims against a defendant who is under a specific duty to use reasonable care for plaintiff's economic interests, or when special reasons of principle and policy warrant a different rule.

Special Relationship

Special relationship rule. The economic loss rule does not bar claims against defendants who have undertaken tort duties to protect economic interests[87] or against those who are in a special relationship which creates such a duty[88] independent of the contract duty. Special relationship is a capacious and open-ended term, and it is meant to be. It includes any relationship of the parties that courts believe calls for a duty of reasonable care with respect to pure economic loss, all things considered.[89]

Examples of special relationship. Among those who are subject to liability for negligent infliction of economic harm because of undertakings or special relationships

---

at least some of the economic-loss cases entail social loss. See Anita Bernstein, Keep It Simple: An Explanation of the Rule of No Recovery for Pure Economic Loss, 48 Ariz. L. Rev. 773, 775, 781, 799–802 (2006).

[87] For example, a defendant who undertakes to protect tangible evidence needed by the plaintiff to pursue or defend a lawsuit may be under a duty to exercise the care he undertook. The issue of spoliation of evidence is complex, however. See §§ 44.4–44.7.

[88] See 532 Madison Ave. Gourmet Foods, Inc. v. Finlandia Ctr., Inc., 96 N.Y.2d 280, 289, 750 N.E.2d 1097, 1101, 727 N.Y.S.2d 49, 51 (2001) (recognizing that a duty may arise from a special relationship); Tommy L. Griffin Plumbing & Heating Co. v. Jordan, Jones & Goulding, Inc., 320 S.C. 49, 463 S.E.2d 85 (1995); EBWS, LLC v. Britly Corp., 181 Vt. 513, 928 A.2d 497 (2007) (suggesting that recovery against professionals for economic loss is an example of a special relationship duty); Eastern Steel Constructors, Inc. v. City of Salem, 209 W.Va. 392, 549 S.E. 2d 266 (2001).

[89] See Blahd v. Richard B. Smith, Inc., 141 Idaho 296, 301, 108 P.3d 996, 1001 (2005) (special relationship exists "where the relationship between the parties is such that it would be equitable to impose such a duty"); Bell v. Michigan Council 25 of Am. Fed'n of State, County, & Mun. Employees, AFL-CIO, Local 1023, 2005 WL 356306 (Mich. Ct. App. 2005) (considering numerous factors, including plaintiff's entrustment of his interests to the control by the defendant; "The scope and extent of the duty to protect against third parties is essentially a question of public policy").

are engineers,[90] fiduciaries,[91] attorneys,[92] accountants,[93] expert witnesses retained to testify in litigation or provide support services in litigation,[94] insurance brokers,[95] notaries,[96] and sometimes even title insurers who perform a negligent title search.[97]

Transferred Loss

The indeterminate liability problem and transferred or single loss. Another case in which courts may decide to recognize a duty is when principle or policy warrants an exception. One of the foundation policies for the economic loss rule in litigation between persons who are not in contractual privity with one another is to avoid the risk of indeterminate liability for an indeterminate time and to an indeterminate class—that is, to avoid the domino effect that occurs when each economic loss begets another.[98] That policy has no application, however, when the defendant's negligence causes a harm that falls upon a single person without the risk of creating new economic losses for others.

Transferred loss terminology. The term "transferred loss" refers to a particular type of case in which the defendant's negligence causes economic harm to A, but in which the loss is transferred, by contract or otherwise, to another person, and in which liability is determinate, without the risk of harms and liabilities to others downstream. The term

---

[90]   Hydro Investors, Inc. v. Trafalgar Power Inc., 227 F.3d 8 (2d Cir. 2000); contra BRW, Inc. v. Dufficy & Sons, Inc., 99 P.3d 66 (Colo. 2004).

[91]   § 43.10.

[92]   E.g., Collins v. Reynard, 154 Ill.2d 48, 607 N.E.2d 1185 (1992); Clark v. Rowe, 428 Mass. 339, 701 N.E.2d 624 (1998); contra BRW, Inc. v. Dufficy & Sons, Inc., 99 P.3d 66, 74 (Colo. 2004).

[93]   Congregation of the Passion, Holy Cross Province v. Touche Ross & Co., 159 Ill.2d 137, 161, 636 N.E.2d 503, 514, 201 Ill.Dec. 71, 82 (1994).

[94]   Several cases have held that the absolute privilege of witnesses does not protect the expert witness from suit by his client based on breach of the standard of care. See Mattco Forge, Inc. v. Arthur Young & Co., 5 Cal.App.4th 392, 6 Cal. Rptr. 2d 781 (1992); Marrogi v. Howard, 805 So.2d 1118 (La. 2002); LLMD of Mich., Inc. v. Jackson-Cross Co., 559 Pa. 297, 740 A.2d 186 (1999).

[95]   See Filip v. Block, 879 N.E.2d 1076 (Ind. 2008) (recognizing a general duty of care owed by agent to procure the insurance but not a duty to advise of further insurance available); Graff v. Robert M. Swendra Agency, Inc., 800 N.W.2d 112 (Minn. 2011) (affirming jury verdict for insured against insurance agent who negligently failed to procure additional underinsured motorist coverage in an umbrella policy); Broad ex rel. Estate of Schekall v. Randy Bauer Ins. Agency, Inc., 275 Neb. 788, 749 N.W.2d 478 (2008) (distinguishing between agent of a disclosed principal (the insurer) and broker who acts for the buyer as to the agent's individual liability in contract); American Bldg. Supply Corp. v. Petrocelli Group, Inc., 19 N.Y.3d 730, 955 N.Y.S.2d 854, 979 N.E.2d 1181 (2012) (reversing summary judgment for insurance broker on negligence and breach of contract claims brought by insured; broker could have negligence liability for failing to procure adequate general liability coverage after insured had requested it, and insured's failure to read the policy was not an absolute bar to recovery on such facts); Eric Mills Holmes, Holmes' Appleman on Insurance § 83.4 (2d. ed. & Supp.).

[96]   City Consumer Servs., Inc. v. Metcalf, 161 Ariz. 1, 775 P.2d 1065 (1989); Guaranty Residential Lending, Inc. v. International Mortgage Ctr., Inc., 305 F.Supp.2d 846 (N.D. Ill. 2004).

[97]   See Cottonwood Enters. v. McAlpin, 111 N.M. 793, 810 P.2d 812 (1991) (relying on statutory duty of insurer to search title). Other courts hold that the title insurer only agrees to insure, not to search, and thus is not liable in tort for a negligent search. First Midwest Bank v. Stewart Title Guaranty Co., 218 Ill. 2d 326, 300 Ill. Dec. 69 (2006) (invoking the economic loss rule and holding that the plaintiff could not proceed on a theory of negligent misrepresentation because title insurers are not in the business of supplying information); Walker Rogge, Inc. v. Chelsea Title & Guaranty Co., 116 N.J. 517, 562 A.2d 208 (1989) (excellent summary of case law); Hulse v. First Am. Title Co. of Crook County, 33 P.3d 122 (Wyo. 2001). Some cases imposing liability involve, not a negligent title search, but an affirmative misrepresentation about some other matter, as in Bank of Cal., N.A. v. First Am. Title Ins. Co., 826 P.2d 1126 (Alaska 1992), or alternatively, an undertaking to do a title search and a negligent report, Heyd v. Chicago Title Ins. Co., 218 Neb. 296, 354 N.W.2d 154 (1984). Such cases of course do not speak against the rule of non-liability where the insurer does not undertake to make a search and where he misrepresents nothing. On the whole topic, see Jay M. Zitter, Annotation, Title Insurer's Negligent Failure to Discover and Disclose Defect as Basis for Liability in Tort, 19 A.L.R.5th 786 (1993).

[98]   See § 41.7.

"single loss" includes the case of transferred loss and also the case where only one loss can be suffered, regardless of transfer.[99] Where the plaintiff establishes a transferred or single loss, the claim cannot logically be rejected on grounds associated with the problem of indeterminate liability.

State of conceptual development. The concept is widely recognized in discussions of Canadian and European law[100] under the name of transferred loss. American courts have not yet developed a jurisprudence on this topic by name. However, the pattern of the cases mentioned below, and sometimes explicit recognition of the policy,[101] show that the single loss concept has power.

The surveyor example of transferred loss. In a number of cases, a surveyor negligently surveys land on behalf of A, erroneously marking the boundaries. As a result, A buys the land at a price that proves excessive for the actual size of the parcel, or A builds structures that are not entirely on the land. Before the error is discovered, A sells the property to B, who ultimately suffers economic loss when he must move or destroy the structures or when the parcel proves to be smaller than shown on the survey.

Significant characteristics of the transferred loss case. The special characteristic of cases of this type is that no matter how many times the property is sold to a new owner, only one of the sales will ultimately produce an economic loss. If A discovered the error and sued, the surveyor would have been liable to him. If ownership is transferred to B and B is the one who discovers the error, then the surveyor will be liable to him, but not to A.[102] The loss for which the surveyor is liable is not increased because it is B who sues; it is the same loss for which the surveyor would be liable had it been discovered by A at the same time. It is therefore no surprise that courts find some ground on which impose liability in surveyor cases like this.[103] The same is true with notaries who negligently misidentify a party to a deed or other document, leaving someone to bear the loss of ownership, although it cannot be known in advance which party that will be.[104] In many of these cases, the analogy is to subrogation or assignment of A's claim. Since the defendant breached a duty to A, he is not prejudiced by the law's recognition that B was

---

[99] The term transferred loss is a term also used in tax law. The term "single loss" may be more useful as covering both transferred loss and other determinate liability cases and as avoiding use of a technical tax term.

[100] Bruce Feldthusen, Economic Negligence—The Recovery of Pure Economic Loss 257–64 (5th ed. 2008); Willem H. van Boom, Pure Economic Loss—A Comparative Perspective, in Pure Economic Loss 1, 38–40 (Willem H. van Boom, Helmut Koziol & Christian A. Witting eds., 2004).

[101] Harris v. Suniga, 344 Or. 301, 180 P.3d 12 (2008) (builder who sold defective structure to A, who sold it to the plaintiff, is subject to liability for negligent construction which led to leaks in the building; there is no risk of indeterminate liability because "[o]nce a party has paid damages related to the physical injury to property caused by its negligence, its liability is at an end").

[102] If A discovers the loss before selling, reveals it to B and in consequence must concede a reduction in purchase price, A can use the documents of sale to protect his right to sue the negligent surveyor.

[103] Rozny v. Marnul, 43 Ill.2d 54, 250 N.E.2d 656 (1969) (using a negligent misrepresentation theory); Hanneman v. Downer, 110 Nev. 167, 871 P.2d 279 (1994) (using an ordinary negligence theory).

[104] Guaranty Residential Lending, Inc. v. International Mortgage Ctr., Inc., 305 F.Supp.2d 846 (N.D. Ill. 2004); see Restatement (Second) of Torts § 552 illus. 16 (1977). Distinguish the claim against a notary who fails to verify the identity of the person subscribing to a deed. If the signature was not genuine, any claim the person whose signature was forged has against the notary cannot be for misrepresentation, since a non-party could not have relied. See City Consumer Servs., Inc. v. Metcalf, 161 Ariz. 1, 775 P.2d 1065 (1989) (permitting recovery for "negligence" without reference to misrepresentation rules or to the possibility of recovery on an injurious falsehood theory).

the party who suffered the loss any more than he would be prejudiced by A's assignment of the claim to B.

Another example. Termite inspectors, whose negligent reports permit sellers to obtain full price for a building that is in fact riddled with termites, have likewise been held liable to the subsequent buyers who suffer the loss.[105] Once again, it must be said that many of these cases rely on the ideas and precedents associated with negligent misrepresentation.[106]

Statutes

Statutes. If courts do not create common law liability for negligently caused economic harms, legislatures are, of course, free to create statutory causes of action. State consumer fraud acts often permit such recoveries. Similarly, one federal statute imposes liability for economic harm in the case of oil spills in navigable waters.[107] Another, the Medical Care Recovery Act, allows the federal government to recover its economic costs in treating a member of the armed forces who is injured by a tortfeasor.[108] This is not necessarily a rejection of the common law rule but a compliment to it. Legislatures can supplement and define recoveries for negligently caused economic loss.

Cases Rejecting the General Rule

Cases that seemed to reject the usual rule. Some common law cases may once have seemed to discard the stranger economic loss rule more generally. One leading case in this regard was *People Express Airlines, Inc. v. Consolidated Rail Corp.*,[109] where the defendant allegedly handled dangerous chemicals negligently with the result that the plaintiff's airline office had to be evacuated. No physical harm was done, but the plaintiff lost profits when business operations were shut down. Possibly the plaintiff could have claimed a right to recover on the authority of public nuisance/private harm cases, because the defendant in effect blocked access to the plaintiff's business, but that argument was not directly in issue.[110] Instead, the court concluded that the general rule against liability was wrong. It held that the defendant would owe a duty of reasonable care to protect against economic harm when "particular plaintiffs or plaintiffs comprising an identifiable class" suffered stand-alone economic harm, provided the defendant knew or had reason to know that such harm was likely. Other cases that tend to support a broad recovery for negligent interference with economc interests are *Mattingly v. Sheldon Jackson College,*[111] and *J'Aire Corp v. Gregory.*[112] More than 30 or

---

[105] Barrie v. V.P. Exterminators, Inc., 625 So.2d 1007 (La. 1993) (long opinion struggling with negligent misrepresentation theory, consistent with the single liability point but not discussing it).

[106] See § 43.8.

[107] 33 U.S.C.A. § 2702(b)(2)(E). See South Port Marine, LLC v. Gulf Oil Ltd. P'ship, 234 F.3d 58 (1st Cir. 2000) (approving a recovery of a marina's lost future profits where a gasoline spill not only damaged the marina's property but also required the marina to reallocate capital and staff work, resulting in delay of planned expansion; also approving jury trial). The statute also imposes liability limitations. State statutes may impose similar liabilities for stand-alone economic harm. See Ballard Shipping Co. v. Beach Shellfish, 32 F.2d 623 (1st Cir. 1994); Kodiak Island Borough v. Exxon Corp., 991 P.2d 757 (Alaska 1999).

[108] 42 U.S.C.A. § 2651.

[109] People Express Airlines, Inc. v. Consolidated Rail Corp., 100 N.J. 246, 495 A.2d 107 (1985).

[110] The court only referred to the nuisance cases to advance its idea that some kind of foreseeability would be sufficient basis for liability.

[111] 743 P.2d 356 (Alaska 1987) (confusingly holding that the plaintiff employer cannot recover for negligent injury to the employee that causes loss of services or loss of profits but that he can recover for negligently caused economic loss, which is evidenced by the same injury to the same employee).

[112] J'Aire Corp v. Gregory, 24 Cal.3d 799, 598 P.2d 60, 157 Cal.Rptr. 407 (1979).

40 years old at this writing, those cases have sometime generated anomalies[113] but have garnered almost no lasting support outside their home states.

C. NEGLIGENT ECONOMIC LOSS AND CONTRACTING PARTIES

§ 41.9 Contracting Parties: The Economic Loss Rule Generally

Contract between the parties explicitly or implicitly excluding tort liability. The core principle behind the economic loss rule excludes tort liability for negligence and perhaps some other torts[114] when a contract between the parties expressly or impliedly covers all their responsibilities attendant to performance of the contract.[115] In essence, application of the principle honors the parties' own allocations of risks and responsibilities by limiting the plaintiff to whatever recovery may be permitted under the contract, which may be no remedy at all where the contract disclaims liability.[116] There may be exceptions even to this core version of the rule, as where an at-will employee is permitted to sue in tort for wrongful discharge carried out in violation of public policy.[117]

Where contract does not exclude tort liability. Conversely, under this core view, when the contract does *not* address the conduct or the risk that forms the tort claim and does not reflect an intent to make the contractual remedy exclusive, the logic of the rule permits the tort claim to proceed if it is otherwise viable.[118] This conception of the relevant economic loss rule also leaves room for tort liability when the defendant is under a duty in tort wholly independent of the contract and the contract has not released the defendant from that duty.[119]

Expanded versions of the contractual economic loss rule. The principle that respects the parties' private ordering is to some extent undermined when courts assume, without

---

[113] In California, the odd opinion in J'Aire, id., may have resulted in a rule that permits negligence-based recovery for interference with non-contractual economic prospects but that insists that intent is required before liability can be imposed for interference with an actual contract. See Davis v. Nadrich, 174 Cal.App.4th 1, 94 Cal.Rptr.3d 414 (2009). This result is out of line with the settled principle that greater protection, not lesser, is to be afforded to contracts than to uncontracted-for opportunities.

[114] Even some intentional torts may be protected by the economic loss rule in some instances. See 3 Dobbs, Hayden & Bublick, The Law of Torts § 615 (the paragraph *Intentional torts*) (2d ed. 2011 & Supp.).

[115] See, e.g., Sunridge Dev. Corp. v. RB&G Eng'g, Inc., 230 P.3d 1000 (Utah. 2010) ("the economic loss rule prevents parties who have contracted with each other from recovering beyond the bargained-for risks"). But some courts treat the mere existence of a contract as sufficient to exclude tort liability, regardless whether the contract itself implied such a purpose. See the paragraph, *Expanded versions of the contractual economic loss rule*, below.

[116] See Seely v. White Motor Co., 63 Cal.2d 9, 403 P.2d 145, 45 Cal.Rptr. 17 (1965).

[117] § 43.10. On the other hand, when no public policy supports the at-will employee, the rule rejects a tort action and to that extent can be viewed as a collateral support for the contractual economic loss rule.

[118] In re Gosnell Dev. Corp. of Ariz., 331 Fed.Appx. 440 (9th Cir. 2009) (reversing district court's elimination of fiduciary duty where contract duties arose from same facts; the economic loss rule applies only where "an underlying contract shows the parties already bargained for and allocated their risk of loss"). But some established views of contract interpretation may treat the contract's silence on a topic as negating any rights on that subject. Thus contracts for employment are presumptively at-will unless the contract states or implies otherwise. § 43.10.

[119] See Robinson Helicopter Co., Inc. v. Dana Corp., 34 Cal.4th 979, 102 P.3d 268, 22 Cal.Rptr. 3d 352 (2004); Indemnity Ins. Co. of N. Am. v. American Aviation, Inc., 891 So.2d 532 (Fla. 2004). Phrased differently, the tort duty, to be actionable, must not be interwoven with the contract. Huron Tool & Eng'g Co. v. Precision Consulting Servs., Inc., 209 Mich. App. 365, 532 N.W.2d 541 (1995).

analyzing the contract, that the contract has allocated risks on the matter in dispute.[120] In addition, some courts have applied the contract version of the economic loss rules much more broadly than the core idea suggests. For example, courts may exclude the tort claim because the contract imposes a duty that is the same as or similar to the duty imposed by an independent tort rule.[121] Courts may also exclude the tort claim that arises from an independent tort duty if the tort claim deals with the same "subject matter" covered by the contract, or is "interwoven" with the contract,[122] or even when the tort claim merely arises from the same set of facts as the contract claim.[123] Professor Johnson has carefully criticized these broad approximations.[124] It is possible that fine-tuning overbroad statements will come as case law develops with more attention to effectuating the parties' intent in contracting.[125] In the most extreme cases, though, courts have expressly departed from any effort to honor the contract the parties made, holding that if they *could* have bargained about a foreseeable issue but did not do so, they may not pursue traditional tort claims.[126]

Applying the rules without the economic loss label. Like its cousin, the stranger rule, the contracts version of the economic loss rule is a no-duty rule, eliminating the tort duty to use care but leaving the defendant subject to liability in contract if actionable breach can be shown. Where it applies without expansion,[127] the rule gives primacy to the

---

[120] This assumption is played out in many cases where the terms of the contract are not considered and in cases that make existence of the contract, not its content, the determinative condition. E.g., Jorgensen v. Colorado Rural Props., LLC, 226 P.3d 1255 (Colo. Ct. App. 2010) ("a party suffering only economic loss from the breach of an express or implied contractual duty may not assert a tort claim for such breach absent an independent duty of care"). See Jay M. Feinman, The Economic Loss Rule and Private Ordering, 48 Ariz. L. Rev. 814 (2006) (noting that courts have become more formal and less attentive to context, and that they have applied the economic loss rule to bar tort claims even when the contract has not in fact allocated the risks bearing on the negligence claim). In addition, some courts may simply believe that the actual contract terms are irrelevant because they believe it is enough that the parties *could* have contracted to deal with the tort issue, even if they did not in fact attempt to exclude tort liability. See § 41.10.

[121] Dubinsky v. Meermart, 595 F.3d 812 (8th Cir. 2010) ("The economic loss doctrine bars 'recovery of purely pecuniary losses in tort where the injury results from a breach of a contractual duty'"); Gulfstream Aerospace Servs. Corp. v. United States Aviation Underwriters, Inc., 280 Ga.App. 747, 635 S.E.2d 38 (2006) (if the contract sets a duty relevant to the claim, the contract will control even if there would also be a tort duty independent of the claim; reviewing Utah and Colorado cases); Plourde Sand & Gravel v. JGI E., Inc., 154 N.H. 791, 917 A.2d 1250 (2007) (quoting a broad statement that the economic loss rule precludes "contracting parties from pursuing tort recovery for purely economic or commercial losses *associated with the contract relationship*" (emphasis added)); cf. Grynberg v. Questar Pipeline Co., 70 P.3d 1, 43 (Utah 2003) (if duty arises from contract, not tort action, even for physical harm). The unavoidable implications of these statements in excluding liability for established tort duties may be broader than the courts had in mind.

[122] E.g., Rubesa v. Bull Run Jumpers, LLC, 2010 WL 376320 (S.D. Fla. 2010); Huron Tool & Eng'g Co. v. Precision Consulting Servs., Inc., 209 Mich.App. 365, 532 N.W.2d 541 (1995).

[123] See General Motors Corp. v. Alumi-Bunk, Inc., 482 Mich. 1080, 757 N.W.2d 859 (2008) (a single "promise" made in negotiations was the sole basis for breach of contract and tort claim, therefore tort claim was properly dismissed to prevent contract from drowning in a sea of tort) (Young, J., concurring); cf. Grynberg v. Questar Pipeline Co., 70 P.3d 1, 14 (Utah 2003) (interpreting Wyoming law, once the contract prescribes duties identical to tort duties, the tort duty is wiped out, at least where same conduct is described in both tort and contract claims).

[124] Vincent Johnson, The Boundary-Line Function of the Economic Loss Rule, 66 Wash. & Lee L. Rev. 533, 575–81 (2009).

[125] The point is to honor the contract, or as Professor Johnson says, to "ensure that the adjudication of tort remedies defers to private ordering." Id. at 580.

[126] See § 41.10.

[127] On exceptions, see § 41.11. See also Jane Stapleton, Comparative Economic Loss: Lessons from Case-Law-Focused "Middle Theory," 50 UCLA L. Rev. 531, 551–54, 561–63 (2002) (arguing for limitations on the rule, especially that it should not apply unless the plaintiff has realistic opportunities to bargain for protection from the defendant's conduct).

contract. The term "economic loss rule" or "economic loss doctrine" came into use only after the decision in *Seely v. White Motor Co.*[128] in 1965, but courts used other language to obtain similar results much earlier,[129] seemingly with the same goals in mind. Even today the rule or its principles may be applied without referring to the economic loss rules by name,[130] or even by identifying some versions by other names entirely[131] or by deciding that the "gist" of the action is contract, not tort.[132] And, as already noted, the rules of particular economic torts are in accord in requiring something more than negligence to establish the tort.[133] The bases for believing that the contracting economic loss rules have widespread application is thus found in many cases that do not use the terminology. On the other hand, it must be noted that when the arguments for this principle are not addressed, the principle may be ignored and the tort action permitted.[134]

Examples of the contracting no-duty rule. For example, a defendant who has contracted to provide the plaintiff with wheat on October 1 may negligently fail to acquire the wheat, with the result that he cannot supply it to the plaintiff as promised. The plaintiff in such a case has a breach of contract claim, but not a negligence claim.[135] Negligent breach of contract is still breach of contract and the contract controls. Another prominent application of the rule occurs in defective product cases, where the defendant's product is reduced in economic value or causes economic harm because of its defect, but where no physical harm is done to person or to property other than the product. In such cases, the economic loss rule bars tort claims against the manufacturer.[136]

---

[128] 63 Cal.2d 9, 403 P.2d 145, 45 Cal. Rptr. 17 (1965) (stating one phase of the doctrine). The full terms, "economic loss rule" or "economic loss doctrine" to refer to the underlying ideas, came into common use in the courts only in the late 1980s, after which time the rule was more frequently presented to courts in arguments and became better understood. As a result, earlier cases may not control contemporary decisions. See Berschauer/Phillips Constr. Co. v. Seattle Sch. Dist. No. 1, 124 Wash.2d 816, 824, 881 P.2d 986, 991 (1994).

[129] E.g., Russell v. Western Union Tel. Co., 19 N.W. 408 (Dakota Terr. 1884) (gist of action for defendant's negligent failure to transmit telegram was contract, not tort).

[130] E.g., Robin Bay Assocs., LLC v. Merrill Lynch & Co., 2008 WL 2275902 (S.D.N.Y. 2008) (under New York law, a claim for breach of fiduciary duty that duplicates a breach of contract claim cannot stand); Carvel Corp. v. Noonan, 3 N.Y.3d 182, 818 N.E.2d 1100, 785 N.Y.S.2d 359 (2004) (rejecting claim that defendant franchisor had interfered with plaintiff-franchisee's business relations with its customers on the ground that the franchise contract governed, not tort); Gus' Catering, Inc. v. Menusoft Sys., 171 Vt. 556, 762 A.2d 804 (2000). The rule that a contracting party cannot be liable for tortiously interfering with his own contract, is still another reflection of the economic loss rule or the principle behind it. See 3 Dobbs, Hayden & Bublick, The Law of Torts § 635 (2d ed. 2011 & Supp.).

[131] See Russo v. NCS Pearson, Inc., 462 F.Supp.2d 981 (D. Minn. 2006) (identifying one version of the rule as "the independent duty rule").

[132] As applied in economic loss cases, the court's declaration that the "gist" of the action is contract operates like the no-duty or economic loss rule, excluding the tort claim and sometimes for the same basic reasons. See eToll, Inc. v. Elias/Savion Adver., Inc., 811 A.2d 10 (Pa. Super. Ct. 2002). Similarly, the same policies are reached in some cases that simply say the action "sounds in" contract. See Heath v. Palmer, 181 Vt. 545, 915 A.2d 1290 (2006).

[133] §§ 41.2 & 41.7 (pointing out respectively that the rules of specific economic torts requiring intent, not merely negligence, would be subverted if the plaintiff could ignore the tort designed to deal with the particular facts and simply claim "negligence" and that the economic loss rule serves as a traffic cop function, directing analysis to the appropriate specific torts).

[134] E.g., Hawaii Med. Ass'n v. Hawaii Med. Serv. Ass'n, Inc., 113 Haw. 77, 116, 148 P.3d 1179, 1218 (2006) (health insurer, a contracting party, by non-payment or slow payment to physicians, allegedly tortiously interfered with plaintiffs' prospective economic relations with patients; the claim survived a motion to dismiss).

[135] See Springfield Hydroelectric Co. v. Copp, 779 A.2d 67 (Vt. 2001); Cf. Smith Mar., Inc. v. L/B Kaitlyn Eymard, 710 F.3d 560 (5th Cir. 2013) (plaintiff ship buyer culd not sue in tort; limited to contract remedies).

[136] § 33.3.

Multiple effects of the rule. In the contract setting, one effect of the economic loss no-duty rule is that the plaintiff cannot recover tort damages but is limited to damages available in contract actions. That normally excludes punitive damages.[137] And since the only claim is on the contract, any valid limitations on liability contained in the contract apply, as where a sales contract effectively disclaims any warranty.[138] The contract statute of limitations may apply to bar the contract action.[139] With tort action barred by the economic loss no-duty rule and the contract action barred by contract rules, the plaintiff in such cases is without a common law remedy.

A separate rule: contract duties are enforced only in contract claims. A rule related to the economic loss rules, but distinct from them, is that if the defendant's duty arises *solely* from a contract, then by definition he has no duty in tort; his claim, if he has one, must be brought as a contract claim with all the limitations that implies.[140] This rule is potentially broader than the economic loss rules because it is not limited to pure economic loss; it might bar tort claims for damage to tangible property where the only duty is the contract duty. The rule is also narrower than the economic loss rules, however, because in many cases tort duties can coexist with contract duties. In fact, some tort duties arise out the contract itself. For example, a client who has a contract with her attorney for a representation nevertheless has a tort action against the attorney for negligence or breach of fiduciary duty.[141] The bailor of tangible goods, though in a contractual relationship with the bailee, traditionally has a choice of suing either in contract or tort when the bailee negligently damages the goods.[142] The separate rule must be formulated accordingly, to recognize that the existence of a contract duty does not preclude construction of a tort duty where considerations of justice and policy warrant liability. That is true even in pure economic loss cases, as the attorney example shows.

§ 41.10   Contracting Parties: Rationales and Policies for the Economic Loss Rule

Honoring the contract. Courts have stated several purported rationales for the economic loss rule as illustrated above, although commentators have sometimes criticized some or all of them.[143] Perhaps the strongest is to honor the contract by enforcing its express or implied allocations of responsibility. As courts have said, the

---

[137] See Richard Swaebe, Inc. v. Sears World Trade, Inc., 639 So. 2d 1120 (Fla. Dist. Ct. App. 1994) (barring punitive damages under the economic loss rule); Tietsworth v. Harley-Davidson, Inc., 677 N.W.2d 233 (Wis. 2004) (recognizing that punitive damages unrecoverable where economic loss rule eliminated the tort claim).

[138] E.g., N.Y. State Elec. & Gas Corp. v. Westinghouse Elec. Corp., 564 A.2d 919 (Pa. Super. 1989); see the leading early discussion in Seely v. White Motor Co., 63 Cal. 2d 9, 403 P.2d 145, 45 Cal. Rptr. 17 (1965) ("Had defendant not warranted the truck, but sold it 'as is,' it should not be liable for the failure of the truck to serve plaintiff's business needs").

[139] See Marvin Lumber & Cedar Co. v. PPG Indus., Inc., 223 F.3d 873 (8th Cir. 2000); Grynberg v. Questar Pipeline Co., 70 P.3d 1 (Utah 2003).

[140] See, e.g., Southwestern Bell Tel. Co. v. Delanney, 809 S.W.2d 493 (Tex. 1991).

[141] Chapter 45.

[142] § 6.11.

[143] See Jay M. Feinman, The Economic Loss Rule and Private Ordering, 48 Ariz. L. Rev. 814 (2006) (arguing that the rationales giving primacy to contractual or private ordering solutions are inadequate because parties do not in fact specify performance terms and allocate risks during the contracting process and noting that contract rules and interpretation have become more abstract and formal and less context oriented); Anita Bernstein, Keep It Simple: An Explanation of the Rule of No Recovery for Pure Economic Loss, 48 Ariz. L. Rev. 773 (2006) (criticizing all rationales, suggesting they are fatuous).

economic loss doctrine "protects the parties' freedom to allocate economic risk by contract,"[144] a freedom that would be lost if tort law were allowed to envelop the responsibilities allocated by contract.[145] Put more strongly, if the contract limits liability, the rule eliminating tort claims prevents the plaintiff from circumventing the contract's allocation of loss.[146]

The distinction rationale. Courts have phrased this essential point as a separate rationale by saying that the purpose of the contractual economic loss rule is to preserve the distinction between torts and contracts.[147] That change in expression, however, seems only to be a truncated statement of the perception that, where the contract deals with the subject matter, its allocations of risks and responsibilities should not be undermined by a tort claim that ignores the contract limitations. That observation in turn makes the "distinction" rationale largely the equivalent to the rationale that seeks to honor the parties' reasonable expectations under the contract.

Encouraging contract or insurance. Another rationale, the encouragement rationale, is almost the opposite of the practice of honoring the parties' contract and some courts may reject it.[148] The encouragement rationale supports the economic loss rule as a rule of imposed by law, not by the contract. It theorizes that courts should impose this rule to force future plaintiffs either to provide contractually for all contingencies or to buy insurance, or else suffer the economic loss that results from the defendant's negligence.[149] This theory has sometimes led courts to bar recovery even when the plaintiff was in no contractual relationship with the defendant at all—on the ground that the plaintiff *could* have tried to contract with the defendant, and also where the plaintiff did in fact bargain with some *other* person for a degree of protection.[150]

---

[144] Wausau Tile, Inc. v. County Concrete Corp., 226 Wis. 2d 235, 593 N.W.2d 445 (1999).

[145] Fireman's Fund Ins. Co. v. SEC Donohue, Inc., 176 Ill.2d 160, 164, 679 N.E.2d 1197, 1199, 223 Ill.Dec. 424, 426 (1997) (quoting, "tort law would, if allowed to develop unchecked, eventually envelop contract law").

[146] Indemnity Ins. Co. of N. Am. v. American Aviation, Inc., 891 So.2d 532 (Fla. 2004) ("The prohibition against tort actions to recover solely economic damages for those in contractual privity is designed to prevent parties to a contract from circumventing the allocation of losses set forth in the contract by bringing an action for economic loss in tort"); Carvel Corp. v. Noonan, 3 N.Y.3d 182, 818 N.E.2d 1100, 785 N.Y.S.2d 359 (2004) (emphasizing that contractual allocation of losses between the parties should control).

[147] E.g., Wausau Tile, Inc. v. County Concrete Corp., 226 Wis.2d 235, 593 N.W.2d 445 (1999).

[148] Presumably courts would not accept an encouragement rationale if they require a contract or privity between the parties as a condition of imposing the "contract" type of economic loss rule. So requiring, see, Indemnity Ins. Co. of N. Am. v. American Aviation, Inc., 891 So.2d 532, 534, 542 (Fla. 2004) ("We conclude that the 'economic loss doctrine' or 'economic loss rule' bars a negligence action to recover solely economic damages only in circumstances where the parties are either in contractual privity or the defendant is a manufacturer or distributor of a product, and no established exception to the application of the rule applies;" and the rule applies only "when the parties have negotiated remedies for nonperformance pursuant to a contract," in which case, "one party may not seek to obtain a better bargain than it made by turning a breach of contract into a tort for economic loss"); Camp St. Mary's Ass'n of the W. Ohio Conference of United Methodist Church, Inc. v. Otterbein Homes, 176 Ohio App.3d 54, 889 N.E.2d 1066 (2008).

[149] Palmetto Linen Serv., Inc. v. U.N.X., Inc., 205 F.3d 126 (4th Cir. 2000); BRW, Inc. v. Dufficy & Sons, Inc., 99 P.3d 66 (Colo. 2004) (by forbidding tort damages, the rule encourages the plaintiff "to build the cost considerations into the contract because they will not be able to recover economic damages in tort").

[150] E.g., Rissler & McMurry Co. v. Sheridan Area Water Supply Joint Powers Bd., 929 P.2d 1228 (Wyo. 1996) (construction contractor had contract only with the public entity initiating construction, but this contract barred his recovery against negligent architect, even though he could not recover under the contract with the public entity). Similarly, when the parties are in a contractual relationship but the defendant negligently harms property that was not part of the transaction, it has been held that the economic loss rule barred recovery for negligence on the ground that harm to other property *could* have been provided for in the contract. Palmetto Linen Serv., Inc. v. U.N.X., Inc., 205 F.3d 126 (4th Cir. 2000). In Banknorth, N.A. v. BJ's Wholesale

The plaintiff is "best suited" to allocate risks. Where the contract does not even impliedly allocate the risk of the defendant's negligence, some courts have said that the plaintiff ought still be denied a claim for negligence on the ground that the plaintiff knows better than the defendant what losses he might suffer and consequently should either purchase insurance or contract with the potential tortfeasor for protection. If the plaintiff does not affirmatively protect himself by premium payments for insurance or contractual arrangement with the defendant, this theory holds that he must suffer the loss resulting from the defendant's negligence, or, sometimes, even from the defendant's intentional fraud.[151]

Is the plaintiff best suited to allocate risks? The assertion that the purchaser or plaintiff is the party "best suited" to protect himself seems to be an article of faith rather than a matter on which evidence is required. While it may be more or less evidently true in some cases,[152] it is surely not so in all cases.[153] The architect or engineer who negligently tells the building contractor to dig a tunnel 100 yards south of the correct location is very likely to know far better than the contractor what risks he creates if his instructions are negligent. He is also likely to be the only one in position to avoid the waste that will be incurred if the contractor, following plans, tunnels into a lake instead of the appropriate land. At least some sellers of goods and services, perhaps all of them, can also avoid injury at a cost less than the cost of harms inflicted.[154] A position more moderate than the encouragement rationale and the claim that the plaintiff is best suited to protect himself has been worked out by theorists and some Commonwealth

---

Club, Inc., 442 F.Supp.2d 206 (M.D. Pa. 2006), the court held that a bank that had guaranteed its customers would not be held liable for fraudulent charges on VISA credit cards it issued could not recover from a merchant for losses it sustained when the merchant failed to properly guard customer's credit card information and hackers fraudulently ran up charges against the cards, ultimately paid by the bank. The court reasoned that the bank should not recover for the merchant's negligence because, although the bank had no contractual relationship with the merchant, it "could have" bargained with VISA for protection. This reasoning is criticized in Vincent Johnson, The Boundary-Line Function of the Economic Loss Rule, 66 Wash. & Lee L. Rev. 533, 562–64 (2009). The encouragement rationale may at times be superfluous, under the oft-applied rule for strangers that negligence is insufficient in any event. However, in the architect-engineer-landowner-contractor setting, the relationships of the parties may be a "special relationship" that would displace the stranger rule and permit recovery. See, permitting the tort recovery, Eastern Steel Constructors, Inc. v. City of Salem, 209 W.Va. 392, 549 S.E.2d 266 (2001).

[151] Below v. Norton, 751 N.W.2d 351 (Wis. 2008) (the economic loss doctrine is "meant to encourage the purchaser, who is the party best situated to assess the risk of his or her economic loss, to assume, allocate, or insure against that risk"). A Wisconsin statute subsequently allowed some but not all purchasers of real estate to recover in for intentional fraud by the seller. Wis. Stat. Ann. § 895.10.

[152] Cf. State of La. ex rel. Guste v. M/V Testbank, 752 F.2d 1019, 1029 (5th Cir. 1985) (businesses suffered losses when defendant negligently spilled chemicals, causing the river to be closed for cleanup; "[F]irst party insurance is feasible for many of the economic losses claimed here. Each businessman who might be affected by a disruption of river traffic or by a halt in fishing activities can protect against that eventuality at a relatively low cost since his own potential losses are finite and readily discernible.").

[153] A number of decisions have now supported use of a no-duty economic loss rule to protect a fraudulent defendant who induces a contract by intentional misrepresentation, see Below v. Norton, 751 N.W.2d 351 (Wis. 2008). However, these do not seem supportable on the ground that the deceived buyer is in better position to protect himself than is the lying seller. "When a seller is lying about the subject matter of the contract, the party best situated to assess and allocate the risk of economic loss is the seller, not the buyer . . . a party to a contract cannot rationally calculate the possibility that the other party will deliberately lie. . . . When a seller is lying about the subject matter of a contract, the party best suited to assess the risk of economic loss switches from being the purchaser, who cannot possibly know which of several statements may be a lie, to the seller, who clearly knows." Budgetel Inns, Inc. v. Micros Sys., Inc., 34 F.Supp. 2d 720, 723, 725 (E.D. Wis. 1999). Some cases have expressly rejected the relevance of realistic ability to bargain for self-protection. See Foremost Farms USA Co-op. v. Performance Process, Inc., 297 Wis.2d 724, 742, 726 N.W.2d 289, 297 (Ct. App. 2006).

[154] This is so because the defendant is not negligent and not liable at all unless the cost of avoiding harm is less than the cost of injury with probability factored in. See §§ 12.3–12.4.

courts. This position is similar in excluding recovery when the plaintiff could have protected herself, but different in adding that self-protection must be realistically possible, not merely a theoretical ability to contract.[155] Some American authority appears to be in line with this notion as well.[156]

Rule of law, not analysis of parties' contractual expectations. The encouragement rationale, at least as baldly stated in the cases, appears to be inconsistent with the rationale emphasizing freedom of contract and the importance of honoring the contract; it does not seek to enforce the expectations of the parties but instead penalizes the plaintiff for failure to contractually allocate losses. Another indicator that the parties' expectations and the freedom of contract premise are not fully followed lies in the way this form of an economic loss rule is applied. For example, when the manufacturer issues a limited warranty to the buyer, the existence of a warranty may not necessarily mean that the parties meant to absolve the manufacturer of all liability for negligence. Nevertheless, the rule treats the existence of the contract as foreclosing tort liability, without inquiry into the parties' objectively expressed intent or reasonable expectations.[157]

D. SCOPE AND EXCEPTIONS

§ 41.11 Scope of and Exceptions to the No-Duty Economic Loss Rule

Scope: consumers, unsophisticated parties. A little authority has flatly held that the contractual version of the economic loss rule bars the tort claim for pure economic loss when the aggrieved plaintiff is a business entity engaged in a "commercial" deal, but not when the plaintiff is a "consumer."[158] Consumer protection statutes may likewise provide relief for "consumers" that would be barred under the no-duty economic loss rule for contracting parties.[159] Some courts, seemingly with a similar view, have defined the economic loss rule as a bar to the tort action when "the parties to a transaction are sophisticated business entities,"[160] although such statements do not specifically address the position of consumers. Some have similarly indicated that the plaintiff with relative lack of bargaining power might not be limited to the contract claim, if any, but could proceed on a negligence claim.[161] Finally, a court may buttress its decision to bar the tort claim by pointing out that the plaintiff in the case before the court was a sophisticated

---

[155] See Jane Stapleton, Comparative Economic Loss: Lessons from Case-Law-Focused "Middle Theory," 50 UCLA L. Rev. 531, 551–54, 561–63 (2002).

[156] See Apollo Group, Inc. v. Avnet, Inc., 58 F.3d 477 (9th Cir. 1995) (explaining that recovery was properly allowed in certain cases where the parties were not in privity, which "limited the contractual remedies available to plaintiffs, rendering commercial law an inadequate framework in which to resolve plaintiffs' claims" in those cases); Sports Imaging of Ariz., LLC v. 1993 CKC Trust, 2008 WL 4448063 (Ariz. Ct. App. 2008) (unreported, available on Westlaw) (defendant's contract with the plaintiff "was limited to that of a passive member-investor" so that the parties "were never in a position to negotiate the economic risks themselves;" economic loss rule was no bar).

[157] Seely v. White Motor Co., 63 Cal.2d 9, 403 P.2d 145, 45 Cal.Rptr. 17 (1965), is the leading case.

[158] Franklin Grove Corp. v. Drexel, 936 A.2d 1272 (R.I. 2007); Rousseau v. K.N. Constr., Inc., 727 A.2d 190, 193 (R.I. 1999).

[159] E.g., Washington State Physicians Ins. Exch. & Ass'n v. Fisons Corp., 122 Wash.2d 299, 858 P.2d 1054 (1993).

[160] PTI Assocs., LLC v. Carolina Int'l Sales Co., Inc., 2010 WL 363330 (D. Conn. 2010); 425 Beecher, LLC v. Unizan Bank, Nat'l Ass'n, 186 Ohio App.3d 214, 927 N.E.2d 46 (2010).

[161] Alloway v. General Marine Indus., L.P., 149 N.J. 620, 628, 695 A.2d 264, 268 (1997).

party[162] or suggest that the rule applies more broadly or with exceptional rigor if the plaintiff is a sophisticated entrepreneur.[163]

Commercial versus consumer contracts. However, most courts that have addressed or made assumptions about the issue appear to apply the contracting parties' economic loss rule across the board, with no distinction between "commercial" and "consumer" contracts or between sophisticated and unsophisticated buyers.[164] The leading decisions adopting the contractual version of the economic loss rule in the case of defective products that cause no physical harm to persons or other property drew no distinction between "commercial" and "consumer" contracts or between sophisticated and unsophisticated buyers.[165] Other courts have specifically rejected the distinction, applying the rule to bar a tort claim in both cases.[166] Even so, some particular consumers may be permitted to sue in tort on the basis of some other exception to the economic loss rule.[167]

Independent duty in tort. The economic loss rule does not apply to bar the tort claim for economic harms if the defendant breached a duty of care that was independent of the contract.[168] This may occur because the duty did not arise out of the contract and is not intertwined with the contract duty of performance.[169] Phrased differently, the tort duty, to be actionable, must not be "interwoven" with the contract.[170] Where a contract creates

---

[162] Desert Healthcare Dist. v. PacifiCare FHP, Inc., 94 Cal.App. 4th 781, 793, 114 Cal.Rptr. 2d 623, 632 (2001) (noting that plaintiff "is a large corporate entity well versed in the intricacies of the health care financing system," and "more than capable of protecting itself through diligence and prudence, and by exercising its own considerable contracting power," but possibly limiting the rule to such cases); Rissler & McMurry Co. v. Sheridan Area Water Supply Joint Powers Bd., 929 P.2d 1228, 1235 (Wyo. 1996) (agreeing with other authority that, given "the abilities of sophisticated businessmen to provide contractual remedies in their business dealings . . . the contractor's claims against the architect must fail under the economic loss doctrine").

[163] Palmetto Linen Servs., Inc. v. U.N.X., Inc., 205 F.3d 126, 129–30 (4th Cir. 2000); Grynberg v. Questar Pipeline Co., 70 P.3d 1 (Utah 2003).

[164] E.g., Alejandre v. Bull, 159 Wash.2d 674, 684–85, 153 P.3d 864, 869 (2007) ("the economic loss rule applies to tort claims brought by home buyers").

[165] East River S.S. Corp. v. Transamerica Delaval, Inc. 476 U.S. 858, 106 S.Ct. 2295, 90 L.Ed.2d 865 (1986) (ship's engines); Seely v. White Motor Co., 63 Cal. 2d 9, 45 Cal. Rptr. 17, 403 P.2d 145 (1965). Commercial and consumer are unfortunately ambiguous terms. All sales transactions are in a sense commercial and all buyers who use the product instead of reselling are in a sense consumers.

[166] E.g., Federal Ins. Co. v. Lazzara Yachts of N. Am., Inc., 2010 WL 1223126 (M.D. Fla. 2010) (weight of authority holds the economic loss rule as applied in defective product cases "applies in the consumer context"); Ace Am. Ins. Co. v. Grand Banks Yachts, Ltd., 587 F.Supp.2d 697 (D. Md. 2008).

[167] See Sapp v. Ford Motor Co., 386 S.C. 143, 687 S.E.2d 47 (2009) (recognizing a special exception that would permit *home buyers* to sue for negligence, but refusing to extend that exception to the plaintiffs who seemed to be ordinary consumers who had purchased defective automobiles causing only pure economic loss).

[168] This "independent duty rule" appears to be gaining some momentum. See, e.g., David v. Hett, 293 Kan. 679, 270 P.3d 1102 (2011) (remanding for a determination of whether the plaintiffs could assert an independent tort duty, but holding that the economic loss doctrine does not bar claims by homeowners seeking to recover economic damages resulting from negligently performed residential construction services, reviewing the history of and policies behind the economic loss rules); see also Town of Alma v. Azco Constr., Inc., 10 P.3d 1256 (Colo. 2000) (saying that a "more accurate designation of what is commonly termed 'the economic loss rule' would be an 'independent duty rule,'" holding that "a party suffering only economic loss from the breach of an express or implied contractual duty may not assert a tort claim for such breach absent an independent duty of care under tort law"); Eastwood v. Horse Harbor Found., Inc., 170 Wash. 2d 380, 241 P.3d 1256 (2010) (a plaintiff's injury is remediable in tort where the injury can be traced back to a tort duty arising independently from the contract); Affiliated FM Ins. Co. v. LTK Consulting Servs., Inc., 170 Wash.2d 442, 243 P.3d 521 (2010) (same).

[169] See Robinson Helicopter Co., Inc. v. Dana Corp., 34 Cal.4th 979, 102 P.3d 268, 22 Cal.Rptr. 3d 352 (2004); Indemnity Ins. Co. of N. Am. v. American Aviation, Inc., 891 So.2d 532 (Fla. 2004).

[170] Huron Tool & Eng'g Co. v. Precision Consulting Servs., Inc., 209 Mich.App. 365, 532 N.W.2d 541 (1995).

a special relationship between the parties, such as a status like lawyer and client, the duties arising from the relationship may often be enforced in tort, not merely in contract.[171] However, according to some authority, if the contract sets a duty relevant to the claim, the contract will control even if there would also be a tort duty independent of the claim.[172]

Tangible, "other property." If the defendant manufactures a product that is flawed and worthless but causes no physical harm to persons or to other property, the purchaser suffers only pure economic harm in the form of deficient economic value of the product. Under the economic loss rule, the purchaser therefore has no tort claim.[173] Courts usually hold the same if the product flaw results in physical harm only to the product itself.[174] If the defendant's product causes physical harm to "other property," *not* associated with the contract, however, he is subject to liability as with any other property damage. For example, if, because of a manufacturing flaw, the product explodes and damages the purchaser's nearby home, the plaintiff has an ordinary property damage claim for the physical harm to the home.[175] Such a case is not one of pure economic harm; instead, it is a case of economic harm arising from physical harm to property. Some courts have expanded the rule against liability for pure economic losses to exclude liability in tort for physical destruction of entirely different goods where the product was expected to interact with such goods, with the result that the plaintiff's tort claim is barred altogether even though it is not one for pure economic harm but for property damage.[176]

Sudden calamitous event or risks thereof and the other property rule. Some older cases accepted the rule that physical harm to a product from its own defect is still an economic loss governed by contract, but if the self-damage occurred in a sudden and dangerous event, the plaintiff could sue in tort.[177] Later, however, the Supreme Court of the United States, in an admiralty products liability case, rejected the relevance of sudden and dangerous events, holding that the product's damage to itself was simply economic loss—no different from the product's failure to function.[178] Consequently, some

---

[171] See the paragraph *Actions for certain negligent services permitted; attorneys and others*, below, this section. For analysis of the duties owed by lawyer to clients, see Chapter 45.

[172] See Gulfstream Aerospace Servs. Corp. v. United States Aviation Underwriters, Inc., 280 Ga. App. 747, 635 S.E.2d 38 (2006) (reviewing Utah and Colorado cases); Robin Bay Assocs., LLC v. Merrill Lynch & Co., 2008 WL 2275902 (S.D.N.Y. 2008) (under New York law, a claim for breach of fiduciary duty that duplicates a breach of contract claim cannot stand).

[173] See § 33.3.

[174] East River S.S. Corp. v. Transamerica Delaval, Inc. 476 U.S. 858, 106 S.Ct. 2295, 90 L.Ed.2d 865 (1986) (ship's engines); Seely v. White Motor Co., 63 Cal. 2d 9, 45 Cal. Rptr. 17, 403 P.2d 145 (1965); contra, as to real property, Harris v. Suniga, 344 Or. 301, 180 P.3d 12 (2008).

[175] E.g., Sarasota Fishing Co. v. J.M. Martinac & Co., 520 U.S. 875, 117 S.Ct. 1783, 138 L.Ed.2d 76 (1997) (equipment added to vessel after manufacturer sold it is other property); A.J. Decoster Co. v. Westinghouse Elec. Corp., 333 Md. 245, 634 A.2d 1330 (1994) (backup power system manufactured by defendant allegedly did not work, resulting in loss of 140,000 chickens in a power failure; upon proof, the plaintiff can recover its losses). What counts as other property and what does not may be surprising.

[176] See Palmetto Linen Serv., Inc. v. U.N.X., Inc., 205 F.3d 126 (4th Cir. 2000).

[177] Pennsylvania Glass Sand Corp. v. Caterpillar Tractor Co., 652 F.2d 1165, 1174–75 (3d Cir. 1981) ("Here, the damage to the front-end loader was the result of a fire a sudden and highly dangerous occurrence. . . . Thus, the complaint brought by PGS appears to fall within the policy of tort law that the manufacturer should bear the risk of hazardous products."), receded from by Aloe Coal Co. v. Clark Equip. Co., 816 F.2d 110 (3d Cir. 1987).

[178] East River S.S. Corp. v. Transamerica Delaval, Inc., 476 U.S. 858, 106 S.Ct. 2295, 90 L.Ed.2d 865 (1986).

courts that once permitted tort suits for calamitous self-damaging product defects have receded from that position.[179] The Restatement of Products Liability ignores the sudden and dangerous test entirely in its statement of the blackletter rule.[180] In some states, however, the older rule that allows a tort action when a product's defect results in a sudden self-damaging event such as an explosion that damages the product, but nothing else, is still on the books.[181] In some courts that recognize an exception for sudden dangerous events, that exception may have been unmoored from the "other property" issue, becoming a general "factor" courts can use to discard the economic loss rule.[182] In the most extreme version, the court may treat a product's mere *risk* of sudden accidental physical harm as grounds for discarding the economic loss rule, even though no physical harm has in fact occurred.[183] At the other end of the spectrum, loose statements may create doubts about the role of sudden danger. Some judicial statements about the effect of sudden and dangerous harm might be read too broadly to imply that even if a defective product caused physical injury to a person, the economic loss rule would bar the claim unless the injury results from a sudden, dangerous event.[184] If such a rule were intended, it would clearly depart from the economic loss rule and the policies behind it, and it seems unlikely that such a statement would be applied literally.

Goods vs. services. Early and prominent cases stated the economic loss rule in the context of products liability, holding that a purchaser of a defective product that caused no physical harms could not sue in tort but was forced to rely on the warranty or other

---

[179] Aloe Coal Co. v. Clark Equip. Co., 816 F.2d 110 (3d Cir. 1987).

[180] Restatement (Third) of Torts: Products Liability § 21 (1998) ("harm to persons or property includes economic loss if caused by harm to: (a) the plaintiff's person; or (b) the person of another when harm to the other interferes with an interest of the plaintiff protected by tort law; or (c) the plaintiff's property other than the defective product itself").

[181] Salt River Project Agric. Improvement & Power Dist. v. Westinghouse Elec. Corp., 143 Ariz. 368, 379, 694 P.2d 198, 209 (1984), overruled as to construction contracts, Flagstaff Affordable Housing Ltd. P'ship v. Design Alliance, Inc., 223 Ariz. 320, 223 P.3d 664 (2010) (under a test that weighs several factors, "It is in the realm of this direct property damage that we believe the unreasonably dangerous nature of the product defect and the occurrence of the loss in a sudden, accidental manner would tip the balance in favor of strict tort liability even though the damage fortuitously was confined to the product itself.").

[182] Thus a court may simply declare generally that the plaintiff can recover in tort if a sudden and dangerous event causes damage, without connecting this rule to the problem of suing for damage to the product itself. See Nobl Park, LLC of Vancouver v. Shell Oil Co., 122 Wash.App. 838, 848, 95 P.3d 1265, 1721 (2004). Although mainly emphasizing sudden events as significant in cases where a product damages itself, not other property, the court in Salt River Project Agric. Improvement & Power Dist. v. Westinghouse Elec. Corp., 143 Ariz. 368, 379, 380, 694 P.2d 198, 209, 210 (1984), a products liability case, also appeared to say that harm by way of a sudden event was a factor that could be considered in any kind of case: "Each case must be examined to determine whether the facts preponderate in favor of the application of tort law or commercial law exclusively or a combination of the two. In weighing the evidence to make this determination, the trial court should examine the three factors—1) the nature of the product defect, 2) the manner in which the loss occurred, and 3) the type(s) of loss or damage that resulted." Without overruling Salt River in the products liability context, the Arizona Supreme Court has now held that the economic loss rule applies to bar tort claims in the context of construction contracts. Flagstaff Affordable Housing Ltd. P'ship v. Design Alliance, Inc., 223 Ariz. 320, 223 P.3d 664 (2010).

[183] E.g., Lloyd v. General Motors Corp., 397 Md. 108, 916 A.2d 257 (2007).

[184] See First Midwest Bank, N.A. v. Stewart Title Guar. Co., 218 Ill.2d 326, 843 N.E.2d 327, 300 Ill.Dec. 69 (2006) ("We recognized three exceptions to [the economic loss rule]: (1) where the plaintiff sustained damage, *i.e.,* personal injury or property damage, resulting from a sudden or dangerous occurrence"). The quoted language suggests that a manufacturer of a product that is defective because it emits unsafe levels of radiation causing cancer over a period of time would be immune from liability because there was no sudden and dangerous event. That would not only be out of line with products liability law generally but would be out of line with any conceivable policy behind the economic loss rule. Presumably the quoted language should be regarded as an incomplete statement that states a sufficient but not necessary basis for physical harm recovery based on negligence or strict liability. On the rule in products cases generally, see § 33.3.

contractual terms. Some authority has limited the economic loss rule to such products cases, or has at least exempted services from its reach.[185] Since it would be as important to honor the provisions of a service contract as well as a property contract,[186] other courts have applied the economic loss rule to bar claims against a defendant who contracted to provide services[187] or other value,[188] as well as against product sellers.

Actions for certain negligent services permitted; attorneys and "professionals." Application of the economic loss rule to services seems consistent with the policy behind the rule, but it opens up a new problem. Courts continue to permit negligence actions by clients against such service providers as attorneys, accountants, insurance brokers, notaries and sometimes even title insurers who perform a negligent title search.[189] On the other hand, the economic loss rule often protects other providers of services, such as building contractors, against liability for their negligence.[190] Some courts have sought to explain the uneven treatment of service providers by saying that the economic loss rules does not apply to bar negligence actions against defendants who are professionals,[191] or defendants who are in a special relationship with the plaintiff,[192] or those whose contract obligation does not include production or delivery of a tangible object.[193] It may be that all of these efforts to describe the exception are heuristics—pragmatic short-cuts that might usually but not always coincide with a principled exception. Perhaps the overriding principle is that defendants who, like attorneys, are in a special relationship with the plaintiff, or who contract to foster the plaintiff's interests and who are not

---

[185] Cargill, Inc. v. Boag Cold Storage Warehouse, Inc., 71 F.3d 545 (6th Cir. 1995); Insurance Co. of N. Am. v. Cease Elec. Inc., 276 Wis.2d 361, 688 N.W.2d 462 (2004).

[186] See Congregation of the Passion, Holy Cross Province v. Touche Ross & Co., 159 Ill.2d 137, 161, 636 N.E.2d 503, 514, 201 Ill.Dec. 71, 82 (1994) ("A provider of services and his client have an important interest in being able to establish the terms of their relationship prior to entering into a final agreement. The policy interest . . . parallels the policy interest [in the case of] the sale of goods.").

[187] BRW, Inc. v. Dufficy & Sons, Inc., 99 P.3d 66 (Colo. 2004); Blahd v. Richard B. Smith, Inc., 141 Idaho 296, 108 P.3d 996 (2005); Corporex Dev. & Constr. Mgmt., Inc. v. Shook, Inc., 106 Ohio St.3d 412, 835 N.E.2d 701 (2005) (under the economic loss rule, landowner could not recover against subcontractor for defective performance); Trans-Gulf Corp. v. Performance Aircraft Servs, Inc., 82 S.W.3d 691 (Tex. App. 2002). Some cases so stating, however, may be applying the stranger rather than the contractual version of the rule. Heath v. Palmer, 181 Vt. 545, 915 A.2d 1290 (2006) (contractor's negligence resulted in home of inadequate value, contract claim only).

[188] Hamill v. Pawtucket Mut. Ins. Co., 179 Vt. 250, 892 A.2d 226 (2005) (insurance; negligent investigation by adjuster caused economic loss related to the plaintiff expectations of insurance coverage, contract action only).

[189] For all these, see 3 Dobbs, Hayden & Bublick, The Law of Torts § 653 (2d ed. 2011 & Supp.).

[190] See id.

[191] Restatement (Third) of Torts: Liability for Economic Harms § 4 (2012) ("professionals" are subject to liability for economic loss caused by negligent performance of an undertaking to serve a client). SMI Owen Steel Co., Inc. v. Marsh USA, Inc., 520 F.3d 432 (5th Cir. 2008) (negligence action would lie against insurance broker for negligent failure to procure insurance as contracted; duties of professionals are prescribed by law and hence are independent of the contract; predicting Nevada law); Plourde Sand & Gravel v. JGI E., Inc., 154 N.H. 791, 917 A.2d 1250 (2007) (economic loss rule does not bar claim against design professional, but ordinary construction contractors and others rendering service in that connection are barred by the rule); see Blahd v. Richard B. Smith, Inc., 141 Idaho 296, 301,108 P.3d 996, 1001 (2005).

[192] Duffin v. Idaho Crop Improvement Ass'n, 126 Idaho 1002, 895 P.2d 1195 (1995) (noting that this formulation is not equivalent to an exception based on professional status); EBWS, LLC v. Britly Corp., 181 Vt. 513, 928 A.2d 497, 507–08 (2007) ("Purely economic losses may be recoverable in professional services cases because the parties have a special relationship, which creates a duty of care independent of contract obligations. . . . [T]he determining factor is the type of relationship created between the parties. . . . Although a license may be indicative of this relationship, it is not determinative;" but holding that a contractor was not a professional).

[193] Congregation of the Passion, Holy Cross Province v. Touche Ross & Co., 159 Ill.2d 137, 161, 636 N.E.2d 503, 514, 201 Ill.Dec. 71, 82 (1994).

contracting as adversarial bargainers or competitors, should be subject to the duties of care imposed by negligence law. That would explain the cases and offer a realistic basis for judicial decision-making.

Intentional torts. Both the stranger rule and the contract rule originally only operated to forbid negligence and strict liability actions for pure economic loss. The rule was soon adapted by some courts to bar claims for certain intentional torts, particularly fraud and deceit, between parties in a contractual or semi-contractual relationship. Other courts, however, have followed the historical rule that fraud inducing the plaintiff to enter into a contract is a basis for the plaintiff's action to rescind or to recover damages or the defendant's unjust enrichment. Courts that apply the economic loss rule bar the claim for intentional fraud unless the fraud is independent of or unrelated to the contract obligations.[194] Such a rule, applied literally, would obliterate most claims for intentional deceit. However, this expansion of the economic loss rule is largely congruent with the view taken by some courts that the deceitful defendant may effectively disclaim liability for intentional fraud in the contract itself.[195]

Other expansions. Although the economic loss rules by definition cover only stand-alone economic loss, not property damage, some courts have insisted that even when the defendant damages the plaintiff's tangible property, the plaintiff who has some kind of contractual relationship with the defendant has no negligence claim. This expansion has occurred when the defendant has damaged or refused to return the plaintiff's bailed property.[196] In addition, one broad pronouncement states that the relevant concern is not the type of harm—pure economic loss—but the source of the duty in contract.[197] It is certainly true that if the *only* duty is one created by contract, the plaintiff has only a contract action. However, the bare existence of a contract has not traditionally negated all tort duties with respect to tangible property.[198] Indeed, it does not do so with respect to all economic harm, as the case of attorney liability shows.[199]

---

[194] See 3 Dobbs, Hayden & Bublick, The Law of Torts § 686 (2d ed. 2011 & Supp.).

[195] Id. § 684.

[196] See § 6.11.

[197] See Grynberg v. Questar Pipeline Co., 70 P.3d 1, 43 (Utah 2003) ("the modern focus is not on the harm that occurs but instead is on the source of the duty that was breached. . . . All contract duties, and all breaches of those duties—no matter how intentional—must be enforced pursuant to contract law").

[198] See, e.g., Abraham v. T. Henry Constr., Inc., 350 Or. 29, 249 P.3d 534 (2011) (homeowners allowed to sue contractor in tort despite the existence of contract between them where contract did not create or define any duty that the contractors did not already have; the negligence claim that the plaintiff would have in the absence of a contract was not limited or defined in any way in the contract).

[199] See the paragraph, *Actions for certain negligent services permitted; attorneys and others,* supra, this section. For analysis of attorneys' liability to clients generally, see Chapter 45.

Chapter 42

INTERFERENCE WITH CONTRACT AND ECONOMIC INTERESTS

Analysis

A. THE CORE RULES OF INTENTIONAL INTERFERENCE WITH CONTRACT

§ 42.1   The Intentional Interference Tort
§ 42.2   Interference with Economic Relations by Committing Other Torts
§ 42.3   General Rules of Intentional Interference Claims
§ 42.4   Elements of the Interference Claims

B. IMPROPER INTERFERENCE

§ 42.5   The Improper Interference Requirement
§ 42.6   Improper Motive or Purpose as a Basis for Liability
§ 42.7   Improper Means or Effects—Independently Tortious Acts, Crimes or Violation of Statutes
§ 42.8   Specific Rules or Principles Protecting Interference, Including Right of Competition, Advice, and Truth

C. INTENTIONAL INTERFERENCE WITH ECONOMIC OPPORTUNITY

§ 42.9   Intentional Interference with Economic Opportunity: General Rules

D. THE PRIMA FACIE TORT

§ 42.10   The Prima Facie Tort

E. NEGLIGENT INTERFERENCE WITH CONTRACT AND OPPORTUNITY

§ 42.11   General Rule Inhibition Against Recovery for Negligently Caused Economic Harm

A. THE CORE RULES OF INTENTIONAL INTERFERENCE WITH CONTRACT

§ 42.1 The Intentional Interference Tort

Harms covered. This section considers torts that redress stand-alone economic harm[1] resulting from the defendant's intentional disruption of the plaintiff's contracts with other persons or disruption of the plaintiff's economic opportunities that are not represented by actual contracts. In interference with contract cases, the defendant's interference commonly causes a third person to breach his contract with the plaintiff, but breach is not necessarily required to establish harm from the interference. In the case of intentional interference with economic opportunities that are not represented by

---

[1]   Economic harm that results from physical or dignitary harm is distinguished from economic harm that stands alone, not the result of tortious physical or dignitary injury. See 3 Dobbs, Hayden & Bublick, The Law of Torts § 605 (2d ed. 2011 & Supp.).

contract, the harm is the plaintiff's lost prospect of a reasonably likely profit or benefit, usually from an established and gainful business relationship.

Means of interference. The disruption of the plaintiff's contracts with others or of the plaintiff's economic opportunities elsewhere does not result from physical harms to the plaintiff, so torts like trespass or battery are not available to the plaintiff to redress the claimed grievance. When the defendant interferes with an actual contract between the plaintiff and a third person, he often does so by simple persuasion—offering more money for the performance that is due to the plaintiff under the contract. The defendant can interfere in many ways, but most interference falls into one of four categories: (1) persuasion (in the case of interference with existing contracts), (2) economic or other coercion of pressure, (3) misappropriation of commercial values, or (4) falsehoods.

The torts. The main torts invoked to deal with these situations, sometimes traveling under slightly different names, are:

(1) Interference with contract;

(2) Interference with economic opportunities, business relationships, prospects, prospective advantage, or prospective contractual relations, none of which are represented by an enforceable contract; all these names refer to essentially the same tort;[2] and

(3) The "prima facie tort."[3]

These three torts are similar in that they all involve interference with economic expectancies, and some courts use a single general rule to cover both the interference with contract and the interference with economic prospects claim,[4] although in practice courts recognize critical differences between the two torts.[5] Courts give the broadest protection to the plaintiff's interest in an existing contract, providing much less protection to mere business relationships or prospects. Accordingly, the rules for interference with opportunities of this kind are usually more stringent.[6] The prima facie tort is frankly reserved for cases that are perceived as falling outside the purview of any other tort and yet deserving redress.

Peculiarities of the torts. The three torts are peculiar to the point of being unique. They have developed without elements that describe the wrongful conduct required to impose liability.[7] Instead, the names of the interference torts describe the type of harm inflicted—interference with contract or other economic opportunity. Intended interference with contracts or business relations describes a wide range of conduct that is entirely legitimate, for example, competition for business or opposition to discrimination. By omitting to prescribe elements of the interference claims, the original rules turned perfectly legitimate and even desirable conduct into a tort. In the more

---

[2]   § 42.9.

[3]   See § 42.10.

[4]   E.g., Pacific Nw. Shooting Park Ass'n v. City of Sequim, 158 Wash.2d 342, 144 P.3d 276 (2006).

[5]   For example, a competitor may ordinarily interfere with a business relationship but not with a contract. See § 42.8. Occasionally courts create confusion by treating a claim for interference with prospective contracts differently from interference with economic opportunities. See, expressing perplexity at this, Bodell Constr. Co. v. Ohio Pac. Tech, Inc., 458 F.Supp.2d 1153, 1163 n.17 (D. Haw. 2006).

[6]   § 42.9.

[7]   Courts often list the elements of the torts, but those elements do not escribe the forbidden acts other than the intended interference itself. See §§ 42.3–42.4.

contemporary versions of the torts, some impropriety is required, but the rules still do not define the specific elements required.

§ 42.2 Interference with Economic Relations by Committing Other Torts

Overlapping or duplicative torts. Sometimes the claimed interference with contract is really nothing more than a breach of contract claim.[8] Beyond that, claims for interference overlap considerably with many named or nominate torts which are defined by their specific elements. For example, the defendant might interfere with the plaintiff's contracts with others by defaming the plaintiff or by publishing injurious falsehoods about the plaintiff's product. In a large percentage of cases, plaintiffs plead specific torts in addition to their claims for interference with contract or prospects. These specific torts may be based on the same core facts involved in the interference claim. A representative but not an exhaustive list includes abuse of process,[9] antitrust violations and common law restraint of trade,[10] bribery,[11] conversion,[12] copyright infringement,[13] defamation,[14] disparagement or slander of title,[15] breach of fiduciary duty,[16] injurious falsehood, intentional infliction of emotional distress,[17] malicious prosecution,[18] misrepresentation,[19] prima facie tort,[20] and trade secret misappropriation and unfair competition.[21] Just as a plaintiff might claim interference to avoid limitations imposed by the most appropriate specific tort, the plaintiff may claim interference to avoid pursuing a will contest in a probate court.[22] In some instances, the specific torts sued upon do not fully overlap because they are based on conduct and harms somewhat distinct from the interference. When the overlap exists, several questions arise.

Claims normally governed by a more specific tort. Perhaps the most significant practical issue arises when the claim is one normally governed by rules of a specific tort. For example, if the defendant communicates negative information about the plaintiff to the plaintiff's promisor, the promisor may breach his contract with the plaintiff. Such a case looks like one for defamation or disparagement because it is based on an arguably

---

[8]   See § 46.2.

[9]   E.g., Pinewood Homes, Inc. v. Harris, 646 S.E.2d 826 (N.C. Ct. App. 2007).

[10]   E.g., Omega Envtl., Inc. v. Gilbarco, Inc., 127 F.3d 1157 (9th Cir. 1997).

[11]   Ballard Group, Inc. v. BP Lubricants USA, Inc., 436 S.W.3d 445 (Ark. 2014); Korea Supply Co. v. Lockheed Martin Corp., 29 Cal.4th 1134, 63 P.3d 937, 131 Cal.Rptr. 2d 29 (2003) (where bribery violates a statute). Bribery may also be the *means* of committing a tort. See § 43.10.

[12]   E.g., Van Sickle v. Hallmark & Assocs., Inc., 744 N.W.2d 532 (N.D. 2008).

[13]   E.g., Altera Corp. v. Clear Logic, Inc., 424 F.3d 1079 (9th Cir. 2005) (holding that copyright law did not preempt interference with contract claims because, although the core facts were the same, the interference claim turned on an extra element, the violation of contract rights).

[14]   E.g., Hartman v. Keri, 883 N.E.2d 774 (Ind. 2008).

[15]   E.g., Dominant Semiconductors SDN. BHD. v. Osram GMBH, 524 F.3d 1254 (Fed. Cir. 2008).

[16]   E.g., McConnell v. Hunt Sports Enters., 132 Ohio App.3d 657, 725 N.E.2d 1193 (1999).

[17]   E.g., Gilbert v. Sykes, 147 Cal.App.4th 13, 53 Cal.Rptr. 3d 752 (2007).

[18]   E.g., Nocula v. UGS Corp., 520 F.3d 719 (7th Cir. 2008).

[19]   E.g., BMK Corp. v. Clayton Corp., 226 S.W.3d 179 (Mo. Ct. App. 2007).

[20]   E.g., Deflon v. Sawyers, 139 N.M. 637, 137 P.3d 577 (2006).

[21]   Central Trust & Inv. Co. v. Signalpoint Asset Mgmt., LLC, 422 S.W.3d 312 (Mo. 2014) (en banc) (misappropriation of trade secrets); Alpha Funding Group v. Continental Funding, LLC, 17 Misc.3d 959, 848 N.Y.S.2d 825 (Sup. Ct. 2007).

[22]   Storm v. Storm, 328 F.3d 941, 945 (7th Cir. 2003) (finding the claim was a will contest in disguise and accordingly belonged in a state court).

defamatory communication; but it also looks like an interference with contract case because interference is the harm that resulted.

Specific tort foreclosing recovery. Suppose that defamation law requires evidence that the plaintiff is unable to produce, say, evidence of knowing or reckless falsehood.[23] Should the plaintiff be permitted to claim interference with contract where such a claim would subvert the defamation rules that are intended to protect the defendant's speech? The principle seems to be that if the defendant's conduct is within the general realm governed by a specific tort, the plaintiff cannot subvert the rules of that realm by claiming interference with contract or prospects. Put differently, the *fact* of interference with contract is best understood as representing an element of damages for the specific or named tort, not as a separate cause of action for interference.[24] In the example given, the rules that foreclosed the defamation claim would also foreclose the interference claim.[25] Similarly, if the interference occurs because the defendant filed a lawsuit against the plaintiff, the restrictive rules of malicious prosecution should control.[26] Possibly constitutional rights to petition government would also preclude liability for interference.[27]

Duplication of damages. In the reverse situation, the plaintiff is not barred by rules of a specific tort, but instead can prove her case under the substantive rules of some specific tort and also under the rules for interference with contract or prospects. There is no prohibition against suing on both theories or indeed on recovering on both theories. However, doing so adds work for all the lawyers involved and for the courts. The implication is not that lawyers should drop potentially valid claims, but that it would be desirable to streamline the economic torts to avoid overlaps. Multiple claims raise a second point. The compensation principle of damages law forbids duplicated recoveries.[28] If the harm claimed results from interference with contract, the plaintiff should not

---

[23] Knowing or reckless falsehood is constitutionally required in certain cases when public officials or public figures sue for defamation. See §§ 37.15–37.16. Perhaps the same or a similar requirement is imposed by common law rules when the communication is an injurious falsehood such as commercial disparagement. See Chapter 43.

[24] See § 42.10. Green Bay Packaging, Inc. v. Preferred Packaging, Inc., 932 P.2d 1091 (Okla. 1996), did it the other way around, upholding a jury award in the interference with contract claim, but holding that damages could not be awarded on the defamation claim arising from identical facts and harms.

[25] Medical Lab. Mgmt. Consultants v. American Broad. Cos., Inc., 306 F.3d 806 (9th Cir. 2002) (where interference accomplished through publication on a matter of public concern, plaintiff must prove both fault and falsity); Serio-US Indus., Inc. v. Plastic Recovery Techs. Corp., 459 F.3d 1311 (Fed. Cir. 2006) (interference by asserting that claimant infringed patent preempted or subject to patent law rule that such a claim could be actionable only if asserted in bad faith); Aequitron Med., Inc. v. CBS, Inc., 964 F.Supp. 704 (S.D.N.Y. 1997) (good discussion, citing cases); Blatty v. New York Times Co., 42 Cal.3d 1033, 728 P.2d 1177, 232 Cal.Rptr. 542 (1987).

[26] Kollar v. Martin, 167 Vt. 592, 706 A.2d 945 (1997) (also extending the rule to insulate threats of suit from liability under the interference with contract rules); but cf. Voorhees v. Guyan Mach. Co., 191 W.Va. 450, 446 S.E.2d 672 (1994) (defendant's threat to enforce a non-competition covenant led defendant's competitor to discharge the plaintiff).

[27] Structure Bldg. Corp. v. Abella, 377 N.J. Super. 467, 873 A.2d 601 (2005) (applying the federal antitrust law rule as a matter of state common law); Titan Am., LLC v. Riverton Inv. Corp., 569 S.E.2d 57 (Va. 2002) (interference with prospects claim based on a series of civil litigations was subject to First Amendment rules on right to petition government under Noerr-Pennington doctrine). The rule limiting liability for bringing civil actions has been developed by the Supreme Court in antitrust cases, but it appears to have a constitutional basis. See Professional Real Estate Investors, Inc. v. Columbia Pictures Indus., Inc., 508 U.S. 49, 113 S.Ct. 1920, 123 L.Ed.2d 611 (1993) (under Noerr-Pennington lines of antitrust cases, the institution of a lawsuit can furnish a basis for liability only if it is brought without objective basis and with subjective bad faith).

[28] See generally 1 Dan B. Dobbs, Law of Remedies § 3.3(7) (2d ed. 1993).

recover for that once under the defamation count and then again under the interference with contract count.[29] The point seems obvious, but it is sometimes overlooked.

Suing for interference only. When the plaintiff has a potentially good claim for a specific tort but asserts only the claim for interference with contract, the case can become more complex than need be. That is because, with limited exceptions,[30] specific torts can provide specific rules and guidance for analysis that is largely missing in the interference torts. If the plaintiff loses contract benefits because the defendant battered her, the court can simply apply the battery rules and permit or deny recovery as they dictate. Foreseeable damages from the battery, including those resulting from an intended interference, would easily be recoverable. If the defendant interferes with a contract by bringing a lawsuit, the rules of wrongful litigation offer the historical guidance needed to preserve access to courts. Even if the plaintiff has not sued on the specific tort, courts can consider the rules of the specific tort in determining whether the interference is improper, or indeed, whether the rules of the specific tort trump the interference claim.

Implications? Critics have suggested that at least in large part the interference torts should be abolished in favor of torts like fraud, defamation, or restraint of trade that focus on identifiable wrongful acts,[31] or that the torts should at least be limited so as not to interfere with appropriate competition.[32] Others critics, however, have offered a degree of support for the interference torts.[33]

§ 42.3 General Rules of Intentional Interference Claims

Historical prima facie liability. Courts originally treated a defendant's intended interference with contract as prima facie tortious if it induced breach and caused harm to the plaintiff as a contracting party, his assignee, or to third party beneficiaries.[34] This

---

[29] Green Bay Packaging, Inc. v. Preferred Packaging, Inc., 932 P.2d 1091 (Okla. 1996) (striking the damages award based on a defamation theory, leaving standing the award based on interference with contract). The fact that the elements of the defamation claim and the interference claim are different does not affect this point. If the plaintiff suffers only one harm, her recovery must not be doubled merely because she advances two theories. See Graff v. Motta, 695 A.2d 486 (R.I. 1997) (harm suffered was a total of $1,000; jury awards of $1,000 on each of separate counts for false imprisonment, malicious prosecution and abuse of process reversed; the plaintiff cannot recover three times for the same loss). If the harm from defamation includes harms not awarded in the claim for interference with contract, damages for those distinct harms would be recoverable.

[30] Two specific torts, however, bear a little resemblance to interference with contract/prospects torts in offering only highly abstract elements. Abuse of process turns on "improper purpose," much like the interference torts. Intentional infliction of emotional distress turns on extreme and outrageous conduct inflicting distress.

[31] Dan B. Dobbs, Tortious Interference with Contractual Relationships, 34 Ark. L. Rev. 335 (1980); Harvey S. Perlman, Interference with Contract and Other Economic Expectancies: A Clash of Tort and Contract Doctrine, 49 U. Chi. L. Rev. 61 (1982). Mark P. Gergen, Tortious Interference: How It Is Engulfing Commercial Law, Why This Is Not Entirely Bad, and a Prudential Response, 38 Ariz. L. Rev. 1175 (1996), argues that the present interference claims should be limited to misappropriation of the plaintiff's contract relations rather than mere interference with them.

[32] Gary Myers, The Differing Treatment of Efficiency and Competition in Antitrust and Tortious Interference Law, 77 Minn. L. Rev. 1097 (1993).

[33] Marina Lao, Tortious Interference and the Federal Antitrust Law of Vertical Restraints, 83 Iowa L. Rev. 35 (1997) (arguing against certain limits in federal antitrust law and suggesting that the common law interference torts can to some extent supply the claimed deficiency in antitrust law). Lillian R. BeVier, Reconsidering Inducement, 76 Va. L. Rev. 877 (1990), supports the liability for one range of cases, but thinks it is not justified for another.

[34] See CSY Liquidating Corp. v. Harris Trust & Sav. Bank, 162 F.3d 929 (7th Cir. 1998); Debary v. Harrah's Operating Co., Inc., 465 F.Supp.2d 250 (S.D.N.Y. 2006); Tamposi Assocs., Inc. v. Star Mkt. Co., Inc., 119 N.H. 630, 406 A.2d 132 (1979). As to the liability of a third party beneficiary for interfering, see 3 Dobbs, Hayden & Bublick, The Law of Torts § 636 (2d ed. 2011 & Supp.).

meant that the mere fact of intended interference was enough to make out a prima facie case for the plaintiff.[35] Motives were deemed to be malicious if the interference was intended; that was enough, prima facie, for liability.[36] In effect, the contract between A and B was treated as a property right good against interference by third persons. The same idea was carried over and applied to the case of intentional interference with non-contractual opportunities.[37]

Privilege or justification. Under this early regime, the defendant might be able to avoid liability, but only if he shouldered the burden of proof by affirmatively establishing a justification or a privilege. However, no rule defined the privileges available; judges would decide that by applying "good sense."[38] If good sense did not tell the judges that the defendant was privileged, the defendant would automatically be liable. In general, however, the judges' "good sense" permitted a wider range of interference with mere business opportunities than with actual contracts.[39]

Requiring improper means or motive. Some contemporary courts have said, in line with the older rule describe above, that intentional interference with contract is by itself a wrong,[40] but most courts today require more—something wrongful beyond the act of interference itself.[41] They hold that the defendant who acts with an acceptable motive and by proper means is not liable for interference with contract and even more clearly not liable for interference with non-contractual economic relations.[42] In some instances, courts have gone on to hold that malice or improper motive is not enough because improper means must be proved.[43] Because of these and other shifts in the rules and

---

[35] Lumley v. Gye, 2 El. & Bl. 216, 118 Eng. Rep. 749 (Q.B. 1853), discussed in 3 Dobbs, Hayden & Bublick, The Law of Torts § 632 (2d ed. 2011 & Supp.).

[36] Restatement (First) of Torts § 766 (1939) (requiring neither improper motive nor improper means; upon proof of intentional interference, the plaintiff made a prima facie case).

[37] Thus inducing an at-will employee to strike for better pay or working conditions was tortious because it interfered with the employer's prospects of manufacturing or selling goods. See O'Brien v. People ex rel. Kellogg Switchboard & Supply Co., 216 Ill. 354, 75 N.E. 108 (1905); Walker v. Cronin, 107 Mass. 555 (1871). African-Americans were likewise tortfeasors who could be enjoined when they peaceably picketed a Harlem shoe store that refused to hire African-American employees. A.S. Beck Shoe Corp. v. Johnson, 153 Misc. 363, 274 N.Y.S. 946 (1934). Federal statutes on labor relations have made the first holdings obsolete and contemporary rules concerning freedom of speech and association uphold the right to speak on social and political issues.

[38] Brimelow v. Casson, [1924] 1 Ch. 302 (good sense showed that a labor association was justified in inducing theater owners to breach contracts with a touring group known as the King Wu Tut Tut Revue because the manager paid such small wages to women that they were induced to enter prostitution; interference with contract was the only means available to induce the manager to pay sufficient wages).

[39] See § 42.8.

[40] Korea Supply Co. v. Lockheed Martin Corp., 29 Cal.4th 1134, 1158, 63 P.3d 937, 953, 131 Cal.Rptr.2d 29, 49 (2003) ("Intentionally inducing or causing a breach of an existing contract is . . . a wrong in and of itself").

[41] Della Penna v. Toyota Motor Sales, U.S.A., Inc.11 Cal.4th 376, 45 Cal.Rptr.2d 436, 902 P.2d 740 (1995) (interference with prospective business relations; defendant's conduct must be wrongful "by some measure beyond the fact of the interference itself"); Larsen Chelsey Realty Co. v. Larsen, 232 Conn. 480, 503, 656 A.2d 1009, 1022 n.24 (1995) (interference with contract claim; defendant's conduct must be "wrongful by some measure beyond the fact of the interference itself"); KACT, Inc. v. Rubin, 62 Mass.App.Ct. 689, 819 N.E.2d 610 (2004) (same).

[42] § 42.4. The Restatement summarizes the rule by saying one is subject to liability if he "intentionally and improperly interferes." See Restatement (Second) of Torts §§ 766, 766A, 766B (1979). What is improper is determined by considering means or method of interference and purpose, motive or ill will. E.g., id. § 766 cmts. c & r.

[43] Kirkland v. Tamplin, 285 Ga.App. 241, 645 S.E.2d 653 (2007) (improper means such as fraud or defamation are required to support an action for interference with contract; merely persuading one to breach is not enough). On this requirement in interference with prospects cases, see § 42.7. On the requirement in prospective advantage cases, see 3 Dobbs, Hayden & Bublick, The Law of Torts § 638 (2d ed. 2011 & Supp.).

attitudes, more recent decisions that involve no independent basis for tort liability, such as defamation, have often tended to conclude that the facts did not support the interference claim.[44] In courts that accept conclusory allegations of improper interference, though, the plaintiff may get past motions to dismiss or for summary judgment.[45] Likewise, courts that do not require that the interference be wrongful may readily find for the plaintiff.[46]

Privilege and burden of proof. The burden of proof, under the older rule, clearly fell upon the defendant to justify an interference. Most courts now appear to put the burden on the plaintiff to show improper purpose or improper means of interference in order to establish a prima facie case. Some, however, may adhere to the older prima facie rule that required the defendant to prove his innocence before any bad purpose or means was ever demonstrated.[47] Some courts appear to put the burden on the plaintiff when the claim is only for interference with economic relations, but on the defendant when the claim is for interference with an actual existing contract.[48]

Defining improper means or purpose. Most courts still decide what is an improper means or improper purpose in the way English courts did in the 19th century—by simply applying what the judge thinks is "good sense."[49] Courts usually apply this "good sense" rule by adverting to a number of abstract "factors."[50] The absence of any firm concept of the tortious misconduct required continues to plague these decisions. Courts take similar approaches in cases of interference with business relations, but liability is more restricted in such cases, and they must be discussed separately on this point.[51]

§ 42.4 Elements of the Interference Claims

Elements of the interference claims generally. As already pointed out, the traditional view held that intentional interference with an existing and enforceable contract was itself a wrong if damages flowed from that interference. The plaintiff was not required

---

[44] E.g., Marin Tug & Barge, Inc. v. Westport Petroleum, Inc., 271 F.3d 825 (9th Cir. 2001) (interference with economic prospects); Green v. Racing Ass'n of Cent. Iowa, 713 N.W.2d 234 (Iowa 2006) (interference with contract); Blackstone v. Cashman, 448 Mass. 255, 860 N.E.2d 7 (2007) (interference with prospects); Avilla v. Newport Grand Jai Alai LLC, 935 A.2d 91 (R.I. 2007) (interference with prospects); Eldeco, Inc. v. Charleston Cnty. Sch. Dist., 372 S.C. 470, 642 S.E.2d 726 (2007) (interference with prospects); Briesemeister v. Lehner, 295 Wis.2d 429, 720 N.W.2d 531 (Ct. App. 2006) (interference with contract).

[45] As in, apparently, Landskroner v. Landskroner, 154 Ohio App.3d 471, 797 N.E.2d 1002 (2003).

[46] See Harris v. Bornhorst, 513 F.3d 503 (6th Cir. 2008) (improper interference not listed in elements). The Harris opinion relied on a list of elements that may have been obsolete after the decision in Fred Siegel Co., L.P.A. v. Arter & Hadden, 85 Ohio St. 3d 171, 707 N.E.2d 853 (1999), which specifically required improper interference.

[47] § 42.4.

[48] As in Commercial Ventures, Inc. v. Rex M. & Lynn Lea Family Trust, 145 Idaho 208, 177 P.3d 955 (2008) (elements of interference with business relationships require showing improper interference, but elements of interference with contract do not).

[49] The Mogul S.S. Co., Ltd. v. McGregor, Gow, & Co., (1889) L.R. 23 Q.B.D. 598, 618–619, aff'd, [1892] A.C. 25, [1891–94] All E.R. Rep. 263 (H.L.) (Bowen, L.J.: the defendant's purpose would be judged by "[t]he good sense of the tribunal"); Brimelow v. Casson, [1924] 1 Ch. 302.

[50] The idea of listing a series of abstract considerations appeared in Glamorgan Coal Company, Limited, and Others v. South Wales Miners' Federation and Others, [1903] 2 K.B. 545, 574, where the judge thought that "regard might be had to the nature of the contract broken; the position of the parties to the contract; the grounds for the breach; the means employed to procure the breach; the relation of the person procuring the breach to the person who breaks the contract; and I think also to the object of the person in procuring the breach." The Restatement's somewhat similar factors are discussed in § 42.5.

[51] § 42.9.

to prove improper means or even improper purpose or ill-will.[52] Today, courts more commonly require the plaintiff to prove something showing the interference with contract or economic opportunity was carried out by improper means or with improper motive or both.[53] Perhaps because of this shift, courts now often list elements of the interference with contract claim. In various expressions most courts say in essence that the plaintiff must prove:

(1) the existence of an enforceable contract between the plaintiff and another,

(2) the defendant's knowledge of the contract's existence,[54]

(3) the defendant's intentional interference with the contract[55] of specific persons[56]

(4) with improper motive or by improper means,[57]

(5) which causes breach of the contract[58] and

(6) resulting damage to the plaintiff,[59] unjust enrichment to the defendant,[60] the prospect of injury that warrants an injunction against interference, or, possibly, the threat of public harm because the interference is anti-competitive or in restraint of trade.

Some courts, seemingly following the older practice, omit the fourth element, thus ostensibly permitting recovery without requiring evidence that the interference was

---

[52] § 42.3.

[53] See, e.g., Harrison v. NetCentric Corp., 433 Mass. 465, 744 N.E.2d 622 (2001); Fikes v. Furst, 134 N.M. 602, 609, 81 P.3d 545, 552 (2003); Greensleeves, Inc. v. Smiley, 68 A.3d 425 (R.I. 2013); Anderson Dev. Co., L.C. v. Tobias, 116 P.3d 323 (Utah 2005); see Restatement (Second) of Torts §§ 766 to 766B (1979). Even if the ultimate burden of proof is cast upon the defendant to justify his interference, improper interference is still the ultimate issue. See, e.g., Kollar v. Martin, 167 Vt. 592, 706 A.2d 945 (1997) (not deciding burden of proof issue but requiring improper interference). Some cases that appear to require both improper means *and* improper motive may in fact blend the two so that proof of one tends to be regarded as proving the other. Australian Gold, Inc. v. Hatfield, 436 F.3d 1228 (10th Cir. 2006), may be an example.

[54] See § 42.4.

[55] Id.

[56] Restatement (Second) of Torts § 766 cmt. p (1979). The Restatement instances the case of a speaker who extols economic opportunities in the west, knowing that he will thereby induce many people to breach contracts in the east to seek better opportunities elsewhere. He is not liable for interference because he lacks the intent to interfere with a specific person's contract.

[57] E.g., Fred Siegel Co., L.P.A. v. Arter & Hadden, 85 Ohio St.3d 171, 707 N.E.2d 853 (1999); Selle v. Tozser, 786 N.W.2d 748 (S.D. 2010) (also holding that defendant's consultation with counsel did not preclude a finding of improper motive); Nostrame v. Santiago, 61 A.3d 893 (N.J. 2013).

[58] The Restatement supports liability for tortious interference with contract if the defendant causes a person "not to perform" the contract with the plaintiff. Restatement (Second) of Torts § 766 (1979). In some cases, liability is imposed for interference with contract only if the defendant causes an actual *breach*. Kirch v. Liberty Media Corp., 449 F.3d 388 (2d Cir. 2005); Health Call of Detroit v. Atrium Home & Health Care Servs., Inc., 268 Mich.App. 83, 706 N.W.2d 843 (2005) (but permitting the claim for interference with economic prospects, where no breach is required). Actual breach of the contract with the plaintiff is not required where the court recognizes a claim for (a) interference that makes the plaintiff's own performance more costly, see 3 Dobbs, Hayden & Bublick, The Law of Torts § 634 (2d ed. 2011 & Supp.), or (b) interference with business relations, see id. § 638.

[59] Quelimane Co., Inc. v. Stewart Title Guar. Co., 19 Cal. 4th 26, 960 P.2d 513, 77 Cal. Rptr. 2d 709 (1998); Foster v. Churchill, 87 N.Y.2d 744, 665 N.E.2d 153, 642 N.Y.S.2d 583 (1996); Mills v. C.H.I.L.D., Inc., 837 A.2d 714 (R.I. 2003); see 3 Dobbs, Hayden & Bublick, The Law of Torts § 644 (2d ed. 2011 & Supp.).

[60] APG, Inc. v. MCI Telecomms. Corp., 436 F.3d 294 (1st Cir. 2006) (although the plaintiff could not prove it would have realized the business opportunity had there been no interference, it might still recover by showing that the defendant was unjustly enriched as a result of the interference).

improper.[61] However, omission of the "improper" requirement sometimes appears to result from oversight or error,[62] so it is sometimes difficult to pinpoint a state's interference rules without comprehensive review of its cases.

Elements—unitary or separate formula for prospects claims. Some courts write a separate set of elements of the interference with economic prospects claim,[63] while others attempt to write a unitary formula covering both claims.[64] In either case, the interference with business opportunity case today generally requires the elements listed above, verbally adapted to reflect the business opportunity in issue.

Elements without identified misconduct conduct. However stated, the elements listed fail to describe specific wrongful conduct that makes interference "improper"; they may function as general guidelines for analysis, but not as actual rules of conduct or decision.

Traditional burden of proof. Courts traditionally held that proof of intentional interference was by itself prima facie proof of the tort. In effect, they presumed that the defendant had acted with wrongful motive or improper purpose when he intentionally interfered with the plaintiff's contract or economic opportunity. Under that rule, the defendant could escape liability only by showing a privilege and shouldering the burden of justifying the interference.[65] Even if the defendant showed a privilege, the privilege could be defeated if the plaintiff proved that the defendant's conduct was unjustified.[66]

Placing the burden on the plaintiff to prove wrongfulness. Most contemporary cases put the burden of proof where it normally is—on the plaintiff. This burden of proving some species of fault has been adopted both in cases of interference with an existing contract[67] and in cases of interference with economic opportunities or business

---

[61]   E.g., Parker v. Learn Skills Corp., 530 F.Supp. 2d 661 (D. Del. 2008); Bowl-Mor Co., Inc. v. Brunswick Corp., 297 A.2d 61 (Del. Ch. 1972) (relying on the First Restatement of Torts, which used the older approach); Serra Chevrolet, Inc. v. Edwards Chevrolet, Inc., 850 So.2d 259 (Ala. 2002).

[62]   Thus Harris v. Bornhorst, 513 F.3d 503 (6th Cir. 2008), did not include improper means or motive in its list of elements required by Ohio law, apparently overlooking Fred Siegel Co., L.P.A. v. Arter & Hadden, 85 Ohio St.3d 171, 707 N.E.2d 853 (1999), which specifically required improper interference in interference with contract cases and which adopted the Restatement's rule requiring the same kind of wrongfulness for interference with economic opportunities. In Windsong Enterprises, Inc. v. Upton, 366 Ark. 23, 233 S.W.3d 145 (2006), the court similarly listed the elements of the tort without requiring improper means or motive, although the same court had previously explained several times that the interference must be improper. See Baptist Health v. Murphy, 365 Ark. 115, 226 S.W.3d 800 (2006); Stewart Title Guar. Co. v. American Abstract & Title Co., 363 Ark. 530, 540, 215 S.W.3d 596, 601 (2005).

[63]   Commercial Ventures, Inc. v. Rex M. & Lynn Lea Family Trust, 145 Idaho 208, 177 P.3d 955 (2008).

[64]   Pacific Nw. Shooting Park Ass'n v. City of Sequim, 158 Wash.2d 342, 144 P.3d 276 (2006).

[65]   The older English cases spoke of justification, which is an affirmative defense with the burden upon the defendant to raise the issue and to persuade judge or jury. See, e.g., Ross v. Wright, 286 Mass. 269, 271, 190 N.E. 514, 515 (1934). In some cases, placing the burden upon the defendant has dramatic effect. Alyeska Pipeline Serv. Co. v. Aurora Air Serv., Inc., 604 P.2d 1090 (Alaska 1979).

[66]   See HPI Health Care Servs., Inc. v. Mt. Vernon Hosp., Inc., 131 Ill.2d 145, 545 N.E.2d 672, 137 Ill.Dec. 19 (1989).

[67]   See Palmer v. Arkansas Council on Econ. Educ., RPL, 344 Ark. 461, 40 S.W.3d 784 (2001) ("plaintiff must establish . . . intentional and improper interference . . ."); Robert S. Weiss & Assocs., Inc. v. Wiederlight, 208 Conn. 525, 535–36, 546 A.2d 216 222–23 (1988) ("not every act that disturbs a contract or business expectancy is actionable. [F]or a plaintiff successfully to prosecute such an action it must prove that the defendant's conduct was in fact tortious. This element may be satisfied by proof that the defendant was guilty of fraud, misrepresentation, intimidation or molestation . . . or that the defendant acted maliciously."); Morsani v. Major League Baseball, 663 So.2d 653, 656 (Fla. Dist. Ct. App. 1995) ("plaintiff must allege and prove . . . an intentional and unjustified interference with that relationship by the defendant," noting that the requirement was the same for interference with contract and interference business relationships); Green v. Racing Ass'n of Cent. Iowa, 713 N.W.2d 234 (Iowa 2006); Buster v. George W. Moore, Inc., 438 Mass. 635, 783

relationships.[68] The effect is that issues previously tried as questions of justification or privilege will now ordinarily go to the question of improper interference with the burden on the plaintiff. Thus, the affirmative defense of privilege or justification becomes relevant, if ever, only after the plaintiff first proves wrongful interference.[69]

B. IMPROPER INTERFERENCE

§ 42.5   The Improper Interference Requirement

Improper motive or means approached through the Restatement's factors. Interference that is improper and therefore potentially actionable falls into two broad categories. First, the defendant may interfere with a bad purpose or motive or with ill will toward the plaintiff. Second, the defendant may interfere by improper means. To determine what is improper motive or means, the Restatement Second's main approach is to keep analysis as vague as possible by stating abstract factors, ostensibly to guide analysis.

The Restatement factors and others. According to the Restatement Second,[70] judges are to consider no less than seven non-exclusive factors in determining the whether the defendant's conduct was improper or wrongful:

N.E.2d 399 (2003) (claims for interference with contract requires a showing that defendant interfered "for an improper purpose or by improper means"); Stokes v. State ex rel. Mont. Dep't of Transp., 338 Mont. 165, 162 P.3d 865 (2007) (treating easement right as a "contract," but finding that plaintiff had not shown interference to be improper); Scruggs, Millette, Bozeman & Dent, P.A. v. Merkel & Cocke, P.A., 910 So.2d 1093, 1099 (Miss. 2005) ("plaintiff must show that the defendant knew of the existence of a contract and did a wrongful act without legal or social justification"); National Emp't Serv. Corp. v. Olsten Staffing Serv., Inc., 145 N.H. 158, 761 A.2d 401 (2000) ("to prove tortious interference with contractual relations, the plaintiff must prove . . . that the defendant wrongfully induced the employees to breach that contract. 'Only improper interference is deemed tortious in New Hampshire' "); Fikes v. Furst, 134 N.M. 602, 81 P.3d 545 (2003) (repeatedly asserting that plaintiff must prove improper motive or means, although some language presents issues in terms of privilege); White Plains Coat & Apron Co., Inc. v. Cintas Corp., 8 N.Y.3d 422, 426, 867 N.E.2d 381, 383, 835 N.Y.S.2d 530, 532 (2007) (plaintiff "must show" improper procurement of breach); Van Sickle v. Hallmark & Assocs., Inc., 744 N.W.2d 532, 540 (N.D. 2008) (to establish a prima facie case, plaintiff must prove, among other things, that "defendant instigated the breach without justification;" interference must be "wrongful"); Greensleeves, Inc. v. Smiley, 942 A.2d 284 (R.I. 2007) (plaintiff "must also show that the alleged wrongdoer . . . intended to do harm to the contractual relationship without any legally recognized privilege or justification"); Anderson Dev. Co. v. Tobias, 116 P.3d 323 (Utah 2005) (plaintiff must prove improper purpose or improper means whether the claim is for interference with existing contract or with business relationships); First Wyo. Bank, Casper v. Mudge, 748 P.2d 713 (Wyo. 1988) (approving instruction placing the burden on plaintiff to prove improper interference). Courts making forceful statements requiring the plaintiff to prove wrongful or improper conduct sometimes lapse into casual references to privilege.

[68]   See Advance Sign Group, LLC v. Optec Displays, Inc., 722 F.3d 778 (6th Cir. 2013); Bodell Constr. Co. v. Ohio Pac. Tech, Inc., 458 F.Supp. 2d 1153 (D. Haw. 2006); Sisters of Providence in Wash. v. A.A. Pain Clinic, Inc., 81 P.3d 989 (Alaska 2003); Della Penna v. Toyota Motor Sales, U.S.A., Inc., 11 Cal.4th 376, 902 P.2d 740, 45 Cal.Rptr.2d 436 (1995); Carvel Corp. v. Noonan, 3 N.Y.3d 182, 818 N.E.2d 1100, 785 N.Y.S.2d 359 (2004); Straube v. Larson, 287 Or. 357, 600 P.2d 371 (1979); Wal-Mart Stores, Inc. v. Sturges, III, 52 S.W.3d 711 (Tex. 2001); see Restatement (Third) of Unfair Competition § 1 cmt. a (1995). Alaska now appears to put the burden on the plaintiff to show unjustified interference, see Sisters of Providence in Wash., supra, but does not seem to have formally overruled Alyeska Pipeline Serv. Co. v. Aurora Air Serv., Inc., 604 P.2d 1090 (Alaska 1979), involving an at-will contract analytically equivalent to an interference with prospects claim.

[69]   See, e.g., Pleas v. City of Seattle, 112 Wash.2d 794, 804, 774 P.2d 1158, 1163 (1989). A few issues that are truly affirmative defenses with the burden on the defendant may remain, but not those going to the question of the defendant's culpability. For example, the absolute judicial privilege may be an affirmative defense available even when the plaintiff has proved wrongdoing, say by a witness' false testimony that leads others to breach contracts with the plaintiff.

[70]   Restatement (Second) of Torts § 767 (1979).

(1) "the nature of the defendant's conduct;"

(2) his motive;

(3) the plaintiff's interests;

(4) the interests the defendant seeks to protect;

(5) a weighing of the defendant's freedom of action compared to the plaintiff's interests in his contracts with others;

(6) the "proximity or remoteness" of the defendant's conduct; and

(7) the relationship between the plaintiff and defendant.

Other considerations may include relevant business ethics and customs, or rules of a business or trade association that are binding on the parties.[71]

Courts' acceptance of the factors and criticism. Courts undoubtedly find the Restatement factors useful in structuring discussion, and many of them have used the factors to determine whether the defendant's interference was sufficiently culpable to warrant liability.[72] However, different judges can emphasize different factors or weigh them differently. They can also characterize the facts to fit the factors or fall outside them. The factors are almost always capable of leading courts where their predisposition takes them. The problem with such factors is not merely that they fail to guide those engaged in economic activity. The problem is that a process of decision-making that cannot describe the wrongful acts it condemns runs the risk of being neither judicial nor fair.[73]

§ 42.6 Improper Motive or Purpose as a Basis for Liability

If the defendant uses no improper means, is his "malice" or improper motive by itself a sufficient basis for liability for interference with contract or economic opportunities?

The first stage. Decisions have gone through several more or less distinct stages. Earlier cases treated the defendant's bare intent to interfere with the plaintiff's contracts as "malicious" in itself.[74] Under this older approach, the defendant was, prima facie, liable even though he had no improper purpose and had used no improper means. In some interference with contract cases, some authority still appears to follow this older approach.[75]

---

[71] See § 42.7.

[72] E.g., Wells Fargo Bank v. Arizona Laborers, Teamsters & Cement Masons Local No. 395 Pension Trust Fund, 201 Ariz. 474, 38 P.3d 12 (2002); Seminole Tribe of Fla. v. Times Publ'g Co., Inc., 780 So.2d 310 (Fla. Dist. Ct. App. 2001); Bridge v. Park Nat'l Bank, 179 Ohio App.3d 761, 903 N.E.2d 702 (2008).

[73] See Dan B. Dobbs, Tortious Interference with Contractual Relationships, 34 Ark. L. Rev. 335, 346 (1980).

[74] See e.g., Carroll Anesthesia Assocs., P.C. v. Anesthecare, Inc., 234 Ga.App. 646, 507 S.E.2d 829 (1998); Nesler v. Fisher & Co., Inc., 452 N.W.2d 191 (Iowa 1990). Thus the First Restatement required neither malice, ill will, nor any other improper motive or purpose. Restatement (First) of Torts § 766 (1939). The judges in Lumley v. Gye, 2 El. & Bl. 216, 118 Eng. Rep. 749 (Q.B. 1853), used the "malice" and derivative terms dozens of times. There are peculiar formulations consistent with this, for example, a formulation that says the interference is in itself wrongful and that its wrongfulness supports the inference of malicious motive, as if the motive, not the wrongfulness of interference were the critical point. See Allison v. Union Hosp., Inc., 883 N.E.2d 113 (Ind. Ct. App. 2008) (quoting).

[75] Reeves v. Hanlon, 33 Cal.4th 1140, 95 P.3d 513, 17 Cal.Rptr.3d 289 (2004).

The second stage. As the law developed, however, courts realized that not all intended interference was culpable; some was entirely justified. The Restatement and most courts came to require some kind of improper interference—improper either because the defendant had an improper purpose or motive for interfering, or because he used tortious or improper means to interfere.[76] The defendant's supposed motive or purpose can thus become central to the interference claim.

Forming a third stage. A third stage may be forming. Courts and critics have increasingly thought that liability for interference should not be based upon the defendant's supposed bad motive or purpose but only upon his use of tortious or otherwise improper means of interference, especially where the defendant has legitimate interests of his own to protect[77] and where the defendant interferes only with economic prospects, not with valid existing contracts.[78] Some authority goes further, requiring improper means not only to establish interference with economic prospects but also to establish an interference with contract claim.[79]

Malice or the like sufficient to show improper motive. Where improper purpose remains a ground for liability, the defendant's spite, a desire to do harm for harm's sake, or malice can be sufficient to show such a purpose, even when no improper means are used.[80] However, proof of such malice is not necessary to a finding of improper motive.[81]

Bases for judging improper motive. Courts have been cautious or even obscure about what would count as an improper motive other than personal ill-will or the like. They may insist that motive be judged case-by-case by the judge's "good sense" rather than by

---

[76]   Fikes v. Furst, 134 N.M. 602, 609, 81 P.3d 545, 552 (2003); Eldeco, Inc. v. Charleston Cnty. Sch. Dist., 372 S.C. 470, 642 S.E.2d 726 (2007) (improper purpose, not necessarily "malice"); Anderson Dev. Co., L.C. v. Tobias, 116 P.3d 323 (Utah 2005).

[77]   See, e.g., Marin Tug & Barge, Inc. v. Westport Petroleum, Inc., 271 F.3d 825 (9th Cir. 2001) (interpreting California law to hold either that in interference with prospects claims motive alone will normally be insufficient basis for liability, or else that the motive must be independently wrongful, as where discrimination is forbidden by statute); Wal-Mart Stores, Inc. v. Sturges, III, 52 S.W.3d 711 (Tex. 2001); see 3 Dobbs, Hayden & Bublick, The Law of Torts § 639 (2d ed. 2011 & Supp.).

[78]   See § 42.9.

[79]   Kirkland v. Tamplin, 285 Ga.App. 241, 645 S.E.2d 653 (2007) (persuading one to breach a contract with the plaintiff is insufficient basis for liability because "the plaintiff must adduce evidence of improper action or wrongful conduct," generally meaning "predatory tactics such as physical violence, fraud or misrepresentation, defamation, use of confidential information, abusive civil suits, and unwarranted criminal prosecutions"). See Pratt v. Prodata, Inc., 885 P.2d 786, 789 (Utah 1994) ("The author of this opinion has grave doubts about the future vitality of [the] improper-purpose prong, especially in the context of commercial dealings. [Precedent] provides no standards by which a court or jury can determine when to apply the improper-purpose test to commercial conduct. Absent such standards, [the] improper-purpose test creates a trap for the wary and unwary alike: business practices that are found to be 'proper means' by a finder of fact and may otherwise be regarded as wholly legitimate under our capitalistic economic system may be recast through a jury's unguided exercise of its moral judgment into examples of spite or malice. For example, the enforcement of a binding, valid contractual noncompete provision can result in liability under [precedent] merely upon a jury finding of some ill-defined 'improper purpose' "), overruled by Eldridge v. Johndrow, 345 P.3d 553 (Utah 2015).

[80]   See Hawaii Med. Ass'n v. Hawaii Med. Serv. Ass'n, Inc., 113 Haw. 77, 116, 148 P.3d 1179, 1218 (2006) (in interference with economic opportunity case, "[t]he plaintiff must prove that the defendant either pursued an improper objective of harming the plaintiff or used wrongful means that caused injury in fact."); Kern v. Palmer Coll. of Chiropractic, 757 N.W.2d 651 (Iowa 2008) (spite or ill will).

[81]   See Eldeco, Inc. v. Charleston Cnty. Sch. Dist., 372 S.C. 470, 642 S.E.2d 726 (2007). Some cases still speak as if malice or ill will were actually required, not merely sufficient. E.g., Akins v. ICI Americas Inc., 1993 WL 832408 (M.D. Tenn. 1993), aff'd, 62 F.3d 1417 (6th Cir. 1995) (unpublished). "Actual malice" is sometimes required in suits against a supervisor for interfering with the plaintiff-employee's employment contract. See Sklar v. Beth Israel Deaconess Med. Ctr., 797 N.E.2d 381 (Mass. App. Ct. 2003).

any rules than can be identified,[82] and may invoke the Restatement's numerous abstract factors[83] to judge motive, although motive itself is one of those factors.[84] Some cases do not make it clear what conduct or purpose was improper or why.

Sole and mixed motives. When courts focus on improper motive in claims for interference with economic prospects, they sometimes insist that the improper motive must be the sole motive.[85] The sole motive rule may also be invoked when the court finds other special reason to protect the defendant.[86] Pragmatically, the rule serves to filter out many undesirable claims. For this reason, it may be a step toward eventually discarding motive as a basis for liability in these cases. In many cases it is difficult to fairly assign motives at all and even more difficult to determine whether a motive is the sole one, if indeed it is even possible to have a single motive.[87] In mixed motive cases, to count against the defendant in the interference claim, some say the improper motive must be the predominant or primary one.[88]

Alternative approaches. Given the difficulty of knowing motives and the much greater difficulty of weighing motives against each other, the kind of approach taken by the Supreme Court with analogous motive issues seems better.[89] This approach would ask whether the interference would have taken place even without the bad motive; that is, whether the acceptable motive would have produced the same interference. If so, the bad motives are to be ignored because they were not but-for causes of the interference.

Criticism of motive-based liability. In the interference, motive is irrelevant to the policy objectives—the desirability of the defendant's interference seldom correlates with the defendant's motives. Instead, the social concern is with his conduct and its effects.[90] And since motive is seldom an observable fact but must be inferred, to make motive a key issue is to invite decision-makers to exercise their biases, conscious or unconscious.[91] When courts decide not only the existence of motive but also its weight and quality, as

---

[82]   The Mogul S.S. Co., Ltd. v. McGregor, Gow, & Co., (1889) L.R. 23 Q.B.D. 598, 618–619, aff'd, [1892] A.C. 25, [1891–94] All E.R. Rep. 263 (H.L.) ("[t]he good sense of the tribunal").

[83]   § 42.6.

[84]   Presumably a relevant factor in motive would be "the interests the defendant seeks to protect."

[85]   Carvel Corp. v. Noonan, 3 N.Y.3d 182, 818 N.E.2d 1100, 785 N.Y.S.2d 359 (2004) (interference with economic opportunity rather than contract case, if motive is basis for liability, motive to inflict harm must be sole motive).

[86]   See Los Angeles Airways, Inc. v. Davis, 687 F. 2d 321 (9th Cir. 1982) (agent advising principal to breach contract not liable in part if motive was to serve principal).

[87]   Even a defendant motivated by malice toward the plaintiff is likely to be motivated as well by a desire to gain advantage. See Havana Cent. NY2 LLC v. Lunney's Pub, Inc., 49 A.D.3d 70, 852 N.Y.S.2d 32 (2007) (defendant did not have the required sole motive to harm the plaintiff because defendant was motivated to gain profits).

[88]   Alyeska Pipeline Serv. Co. v. Aurora Air Serv., Inc., 604 P.2d 1090 (Alaska 1979) ("predominant" motive); Fikes v. Furst, 134 N.M. 602, 81 P.3d 545 (2003) (if motive was "primarily improper" the defendant is not justified).

[89]   See Mt. Healthy City Sch. Dist. Bd. of Educ. v. Doyle, 429 U.S. 274, 97 S.Ct. 568, 50 L.Ed.2d 471 (1977) (discharge of public employee partly for the illegitimate reason that he exercised First Amendment rights and partly for legitimate reasons, no civil rights action by employee if the legitimate reasons were sufficient to cause the discharge); cf. McKennon v. Nashville Banner Pub. Co., 513 U.S. 352, 115 S.Ct. 879, 130 L.Ed.2d 852 (1995) (wrongful motive, but after-acquired evidence would have provided acceptable motive, remedy limited). In the case of employment sex discrimination, however, 42 U.S.C.A. § 2000e–2(m) now provides that if discriminatory motives are established for any employment practice, that practice is unlawful even if other factors also motivated it.

[90]   See Restatement (Third) of Unfair Competition § 1 cmt. c (1995).

[91]   See Pratt v. Prodata, Inc., 885 P.2d 786, 789 (Utah 1994), overruled by Eldridge v. Johndrow, 345 P.3d 553 (Utah 2015).

where liability turns on the defendant's predominant motive, we invest both judicial and private resources in litigating an issue that seldom matters and cannot be accurately determined in any event. If these criticisms are accurate, if the defendant interferes by competition, competition should not be stifled because the defendant has bad thoughts. Instead, courts could concentrate on whether the defendant's acts were in fact anticompetitive or otherwise wrongful by some independent standard.

§ 42.7   Improper Means or Effects—Independently Tortious Acts, Crimes or Violation of Statutes

Improper means in the scheme of liability. Even where it is possible to recover for intentional interference with contract on the basis of improper motive, proof of improper means presents a stronger case.[92] Plaintiffs often assert that the defendant interfered with a contract or business relationship by committing some specific tort.[93] Interference by committing a crime is also easily improper and facially actionable as an interference with contract or prospects, as are some violations of statute or regulation, although not every violation of statute conclusively shows improper means.[94] Some authority holds that violation of established standards or ethical rules of a trade or profession can count as improper so as to permit the interference action,[95] at least if the violation subjects the defendant to liability or some kind of sanction.[96] However, this idea has been criticized.[97]

Scope and examples. Examples of specific torts that can improperly interfere with a contract or business relationship include the case of defamation that induces the promisor to breach his contract with the plaintiff[98] and a physical tort such battery, trespass or nuisance that blocks performance of a contract.[99] In more general terms, it

---

[92]   Stehno v. Sprint Spectrum, L.P., 186 S.W.3d 247, 252 (Mo. 2006) ("Even if there is an economic justification for interfering with a business expectancy, the interfering party must not employ improper means").

[93]   § 42.2.

[94]   KACT, Inc. v. Rubin, 819 N.E.2d 610 (Mass. App. Ct. 2004) (where statute is intended to protect only rights of individual, not the public, the individual can waive the statutory protection).

[95]   Saglioccolo v. Eagle Ins. Co., 112 F.3d 226 (6th Cir. 1997); Duggin v. Adams, 234 Va. 221, 228, 360 S.E.2d 832, 837 (1987) ("Methods also may be improper because they violate an established standard of a trade or profession or involve unethical conduct. Sharp dealing, overreaching, or unfair competition may also constitute improper methods").

[96]   See Stevenson Real Estate Servs., Inc. v. CB Richard Ellis Real Estate Servs., Inc., 138 Cal.App.4th 1215, 42 Cal.Rptr.3d 235 (2006) (but holding that the association's own internal remedies, such as arbitration, would suffice under this rule).

[97]   Speakers of Sport, Inc. v. ProServ, Inc., 178 F.3d 862, 867 (7th Cir. 1999); cf. Wal-Mart Stores, Inc. v. Sturges, III, 52 S.W.3d 711 (Tex. 2001) ("Conduct that is merely 'sharp' or unfair is not actionable and cannot be the basis for an action for tortious interference with prospective relations").

[98]   E.g., Fabricor, Inc. v. E.I. DuPont de Nemours & Co., 24 S.W.3d 82 (Mo. Ct. App. 2000) (false statements about plaintiff's ability to carry out a contract counted as improper interference); Kraemer v. Harding, 159 Or.App. 90, 976 P.2d 1160 (1999) (defamatory statement counted as improper means of interfering with the plaintiff's employment as a school bus driver); cf. Vito v. Inman, 286 Ga.App. 646, 649 S.E.2d 753 (2007) (claim that defendant left messages for podiatrist's patient causing patient to sever relationship with podiatrist, but since the messages were not actionable as defamation they were not improper for purposes of interference claim either).

[99]   See Sunshine Custom Paints & Body, Inc. v. South Douglas Highway Water & Sewer Dist., 173 P.3d 398 (Wyo. 2007) (defendant physically blocked plaintiff's road, thus interfering with contracts or prospects, held actionable on the ground that the blockage was vigilante activity). In general, if the defendant physically blocks use of the plaintiff's property, delaying completion of a contract, a trespass or nuisance action would ordinarily be available and damages could easily include all proximate harms, including the costs resulting from interference with a known contract or economic opportunity. See Little v. Chesser, 256 Ga.App. 228, 568 S.E.2d 54 (2002) (damages for interference with road easement could include plaintiff's cost in paying workers

has been said that "violence, threats or intimidation, bribery, unfounded litigation, fraud, misrepresentation or deceit, defamation, duress, undue influence, misuse of insider or confidential information, or breach of a fiduciary relationship" count as improper acts causing interference.[100] Restraint of trade is in the same category,[101] as are other torts such as injurious falsehood.

Tortious conduct that is not actionable under the rules of a specific tort. Some courts have held that the tortious conduct counts as interference with contract by improper means, even if that conduct is not actionable by the plaintiff on the particular facts. For example, if the statute of limitations has run on the specific tort but not on the interference claim, improper means can be shown by showing the specific tort.[102]

Non-tortious conduct not subject to legal sanction. Conceivably, even conduct that is not subject to legal sanction may count as improper in the context of interference with contract or prospects claims. Intentionally false statements of fact might be considered improper even if those statements do not amount to a tort.[103] Interference with prospects resulting from a public official's discriminatory administration of the law might well be deemed to show wrongful conduct as well as wrongful motive.[104] Such examples suggest that near-torts might qualify.

§ 42.8 Specific Rules or Principles Protecting Interference, Including Right of Competition, Advice, and Truth

The Restatement, with a basis in the cases, offers several specific rules and principles that protect the defendant from liability for interference.

Marriage contracts. Most clearly and most narrowly, in the absence of a specific tort, it is not wrongful to induce another to breach a marriage contract (or to interfere with prospects of marriage).[105] And of course it is not actionable to interfere with a putative contract that is illegal.[106]

Competition. Economic competition does not justify improper interference with a valid existing contract.[107] At the same time, it is privileged, or not improper, to compete

---

whose work was disrupted); Berliner v. Clukay, 150 N.H. 80, 834 A.2d 297 (2003) (one with right to use public road properly recovered damages against trespasser who damaged it, including the cost of repairing the road).

[100] Commerce Funding Corp. v. Worldwide Sec. Servs. Corp., 249 F.3d 204 (4th Cir. 2001), relying on Duggin v. Adams, 234 Va. 221, 360 S.E.2d 832 (1987).

[101] See Jackson v. Stanfield, 137 Ind. 592, 36 N.E. 345 (1894).

[102] Kraemer v. Harding, 159 Or.App. 90, 976 P.2d 1160 (1999).

[103] See Manufacturing Research Corp. v. Greenlee Tool Co., 693 F.2d 1037 (11th Cir. 1982) (identifying false statements "calculated to diminish the market" for the plaintiff's product as improper means without asserting that the false statements qualified as disparagement/injurious falsehood, defamation or misrepresentation). *Caveat:* If the false statement is protected by a rule of the specific tort, many cases have held that the statement cannot form a basis for liability under an interference with contract or prospects theory. See § 42.2.

[104] Pleas v. City of Seattle, 112 Wash.2d 794, 805, 774 P.2d 1158, 1163 (1989) (regarding something similar as involving both improper motive and improper means).

[105] Restatement (Second) of Torts §§ 766, 766A & 766B (1979).

[106] Access Telecom, Inc. v. MCI Telecomms. Corp., 197 F.3d 694 (5th Cir. 1999); Jackson v. Bi-Lo Stores, Inc., 313 S.C. 272, 277–78, 437 S.E.2d 168, 171 (1993) ("A contract which contravenes public policy is void, and an action cannot be maintained for either its breach or for inducing its breach").

[107] White Plains Coat & Apron Co., Inc. v. Cintas Corp., 8 N.Y.3d 422, 867 N.E.2d 381, 835 N.Y.S.2d 530 (2007); Wal-Mart Stores, Inc. v. Sturges, 52 S.W.3d 711, 716–17 (Tex. 2001) (competition is limited "by promises already made," but absent such promises, competitors are free to use lawful means to obtain advantage).

by lawful means for economic prospects not represented by such a contract, for example, to compete for customers who are not bound to the plaintiff by contract.[108] The defendant can properly induce the plaintiff's non-contracting customers to buy from the defendant instead, but can also interfere in other ways as well,[109] say, by bringing or threatening a bona fide suit to protect his own interests,[110] at least in the absence of other factors that warrant liability.[111] A more or less separate rule is that advertising is not improper interference, even if it is intended to and does interfere, not only with the plaintiff's business prospects but also with the plaintiff's actual existing contracts.[112]

Defendant protecting his own interests. The defendant is also free to protect his own preexisting financial interests by interfering with the plaintiff's contracts with others, so long as the interference is carried out by lawful means such as persuasion.[113] The principle is broader than a right to compete for economic prospects. The Restatement and the cases recognize that the defendant who has a legitimate interest of his own is free to protect his interests even by interfering with an existing contract[114] and even if the plaintiff and defendant are not competitors.[115] If the defendant's subjective purpose

---

[108] E.g., International Sales & Serv., Inc. v. Austral Insulated Prods., Inc., 262 F.3d 1152 (11th Cir. 2001); Networkip, LLC v. Spread Enters., Inc., 922 So.2d 355 (Fla. Dist. Ct. App., 2006); Miller v. Lockport Realty Group, Inc., 377 Ill.App.3d 369, 878 N.E. 2d 171, 315 Ill.Dec. 945 (2007); Restatement (Second) of Torts § 768 (1979). In courts that continue to put the initial burden of proof upon the defendant to justify interference, see § 42.4, the opinions may say the defendant is privileged to compete rather than saying that competition is not wrongful in the first place. Some courts that have placed the burden of proof on the plaintiff may continue to use the older terminology by speaking of the "privilege" of competition. See Fred Siegel Co., L.P.A. v. Arter & Hadden, 85 Ohio St.3d 171, 707 N.E.2d 853 (1999). Either way, however, competition is protected.

[109] Green v. Racing Ass'n of Cent. Iowa, 713 N.W.2d 234 (Iowa 2006) (racing association did not act improperly in barring plaintiff-jockeys from access to track while allegations of racial harassment against jockeys were investigated).

[110] Westfield Dev. Co. v. Rifle Inv. Assocs., 786 P.2d 1112 (Colo. 1990) (asserting claim by filing lis pendens); Wilkin Elevator v. Bennett State Bank, 522 N.W.2d 57 (Iowa 1994) (bank took ownership of security for loan, this was legitimate self-interest and reflected a legal right); contra Voorhees v. Guyan Mach. Co., 191 W.Va. 450, 446 S.E.2d 672 (1994) (not citing the Restatement); Restatement (Second) of Torts § 773 (1979).

[111] Some courts may hold that a bad motive overrides the financial interest protection. See Kinzel v. Discovery Drilling, Inc., 93 P.3d 427, 444 (Alaska 2004).

[112] White Plains Coat & Apron Co., Inc. v. Cintas Corp., 8 N.Y.3d 422, 427, 867 N.E.2d 381, 384, 835 N.Y.S.2d 530, 533 (2007) ("Sending regular advertising and soliciting business in the normal course does not constitute inducement of breach of contract"); Restatement (Second) of Torts § 766 cmts. m & p (1979).

[113] Hassan v. Deutsche Bank A.G., 515 F.Supp.2d 426 (2007); Green v. Racing Ass'n of Cent. Iowa, 713 N.W.2d 234 (Iowa 2006) (one "does not improperly interfere with another's contract by exercising its own legal rights in protection of its own financial interests"); Fikes v. Furst, 134 N.M. 602, 81 P.3d 545 (2003) (interfering to protect reputational interest); Eldeco, Inc. v. Charleston Cnty. Sch. Dist., 372 S.C. 470, 642 S.E.2d 726 (2007) (not improper to interfere to protect own contractual rights).

[114] Bendix Corp. v. Adams, 610 P.2d 24 (Alaska 1980); Felsen v. Sol Cafe Mfg. Corp., 24 N.Y.2d 682, 249 N.E.2d 459 (1969). See APG, Inc. v. MCI Telecomms. Corp., 436 F.3d 294, 304 n.12 (1st Cir. 2006) ("[c]onduct in furtherance of business competition is generally held to justify interference with others' contracts, so long as the conduct involves neither 'wrongful means' nor 'unlawful restraint of trade,'" citing authority that applied only to interference with prospects); Australian Gold, Inc. v. Hatfield, 436 F.3d 1228, 1236 (10th Cir. 2006) (seemingly suggesting that the rule of no liability where means and motive are proper is a special dispensation for bettering "one's own business"). Where the court limits liability to cases of improper means, a motive to compete by lawful competition is necessarily inadequate. See, e.g., Kirkland v. Tamplin, 285 Ga.App. 241, 645 S.E.2d 653 (2007).

[115] Langer v. Becker, 176 Ill.App.3d 745, 531 N.E.2d 830, 126 Ill.Dec. 203 (1988) (defendant can interfere to protect his own equal or greater economic interest); St. Benedict's Dev. Co. v. St. Benedict's Hosp., 811 P.2d 194 (Utah 1991) (but indicating that liability might be imposed if desire to harm was predominant purpose); Carvel Corp. v. Noonan, 3 N.Y.3d 182, 191, 818 N.E.2d 1100, 1104, 785 N.Y.S.2d 359, 363 (2004) (the issue "does not ... depend on the parties' status as competitors. ... [A]s long as the defendant is motivated by legitimate economic self-interest, it should not matter if the parties are or are not competitors in the same marketplace").

is to further his own legitimate ends, some courts express the idea that his interference is justified by saying that interference is only "incidental" and is protected for that reason[116] or even by saying that the defendant did not "intend" to interfere.[117] The defendant's general right to protect his own interests by interfering, however, has not traditionally provided him with protection when he interferes without a preexisting contract or property right of his own.[118]

Where the defendant does not obtain the very performance due the plaintiff. In the core case of liability for interference with contract, the defendant's interference allows him to obtain the very goods or services promised to the plaintiff. When the interfering defendant acts in his own interests and does not in fact gain the performance due the plaintiff under the contract, courts have tended to reject liability, sometimes on the ground that the defendant's self-protective or self-aggrandizing motives are not wrongful. For example, if a racing association excludes jockeys for alleged misconduct, it interferes with the contracts between the jockeys and horse owners. But the racing association's interference does not give the association the jockeys' contract rights to ride the horses. Consequently, its motive to protect its own interests does not count as an improper purpose.[119]

Advice in another's interests; truth; free speech. The defendant is also free to advise breach when the defendant has taken responsibility for the third person's welfare,[120] as where the defendant advises a friend to breach a contract that is dangerous to his health,[121] a director of a corporation advises other directors to terminate the plaintiff's employment by the corporation,[122] or an agent or attorney acting within the scope of his employment advises his principal[123] or client[124] to breach. Somewhat strangely in the light of liability for honest persuasion to breach, the Restatement also recognizes that the defendant is free to provide truthful information and honest advice within the scope of a request.[125] Under the free speech rules, the defendant can also take a position on social and political issues, even though the position will induce others to cease all dealings with the plaintiff and even if that is the purpose of his advocacy.[126]

---

[116] See K & K Mgmt., Inc. v. Lee, 316 Md. 137, 557 A.2d 965 (1989) (reviewing cases).

[117] Kreuzer v. George Washington Univ., 896 A.2d 238 (D.C. 2006). In Kreuzer, the defendant knew its activity interfered with the plaintiff's economic prospects, but the court held that it did not intend to interfere, seemingly meaning either that its purpose was not interference or that its purpose was justified. On the meaning of intent, see § 42.4.

[118] See BMK Corp. v. Clayton Corp., 226 S.W.3d 179 (Mo. Ct. App. 2007) (ownership interest or prior contract interest); White Plains Coat & Apron Co., Inc. v. Cintas Corp., 8 N.Y.3d 422, 867 N.E.2d 381, 835 N.Y.S.2d 530 (2007) (giving examples, including interest of stockholders in the breaching party's business, parent and subsidiary corporations, and creditor of breaching party); Restatement (Second) of Torts § 769 cmt. c (1979) (dealing only with interference with prospects).

[119] Green v. Racing Ass'n of Cent. Iowa, 713 N.W.2d 234 (Iowa 2006).

[120] Langer v. Becker, 176 Ill.App.3d 745, 531 N.E.2d 830, 126 Ill.Dec. 203 (1988); Restatement (Second) of Torts § 769 (1979).

[121] Restatement (Second) of Contracts § 770 & illus. 4 (1979).

[122] Foster v. Churchill, 87 N.Y.2d 744, 665 N.E.2d 153, 642 N.Y.S.2d 583 (1996).

[123] E.g., Lachenmaier v. First Bank Sys., Inc., 246 Mont. 26, 803 P.2d 614 (1990). When the agent acts exclusively in his own interests and outside the scope of his employment, however, this justification does not apply. E.g., Ives v. Guilford Mills, Inc., 3 F.Supp.2d 191 (N.D.N.Y. 1998).

[124] Los Angeles Airways, Inc. v. Davis, 687 F. 2d 321 (9th Cir. 1982).

[125] Restatement (Second) of Torts § 772 (1979). See Allen v. Safeway Stores, Inc., 699 P.2d 277 (Wyo. 1985) (truthful information given by customer or business contact about treatment by business employee is fully protected whether requested or not).

[126] NAACP v. Claiborne Hardware Co., 458 U.S. 886, 102 S.Ct. 3409, 73 L.Ed.2d 1215 (1982).

Consent. In the absence of public policy reasons to the contrary, consent to the defendant's conduct usually negates the tortious elements or provides a "defense." Some authority has held in essence that the plaintiff's consent to acts that interfere with contract is a bar to the interference claim as well.[127]

Types of interference: situational analysis. There are many specific types of interference cases. These include intentional interference with the performance of the plaintiff's promisor, interference by persuasion of offers to the plaintiff's promisor, interference by coercive conduct or threats, and intentional interference with the plaintiff's contractual performance. Moreover, interference can be effected by a contracting party or a person identified with a contracting party such as an agent, and may be achieved by the contracting party's independent tort. Although not developed here, each of these categories merits special discussion.[128]

C. INTENTIONAL INTERFERENCE WITH ECONOMIC OPPORTUNITY

§ 42.9 Intentional Interference with Economic Opportunity: General Rules

Characteristics and elements. The tort variously called interference with business relations, interference with economic opportunities, interference with prospective advantage or the like is an economic tort accomplished without physical harm to person or property.[129] The tort is generally recognized in American courts.[130] The basic elements of the tort are not identical to those for the tort of interference with contract, but they are similar—the plaintiff must show (1) that the defendant knew of and intended to interfere with the plaintiff's economic opportunity, (2) that the opportunity was reasonably likely of fruition, (3) that the defendant did in fact interfere by improper means, or in some cases, by improper motive, and (4) that the interference caused reasonably provable harms.[131] On analogy to interference with contract, courts may also require the plaintiff to prove that the interfering defendant was a stranger to the economic opportunity involved.[132]

---

[127] See Harrison v. Netcentric Corp., 433 Mass. 465, 744 N.E.2d 622 (2001) ("By signing this agreement, the plaintiff accepted that NetCentric had an interest in his unvested shares and that the vesting of those shares was connected to his continued employment relationship with NetCentric. Thus, the plaintiff implicitly agreed that his at-will contract could be interfered with in this manner: he was subject to discharge without cause, and NetCentric could exercise its right to repurchase the plaintiff's unvested shares").

[128] 3 Dobbs, Hayden & Bublick, The Law of Torts §§ 631–37 (2d ed. 2011 & Supp.).

[129] On economic torts generally, see Chapter 41.

[130] See, e.g., Hawaii Med. Ass'n v. Hawaii Med. Servs. Ass'n, Inc., 113 Haw. 77, 148 P.3d 1179 (2006); Mortgage Specialists, Inc. v. Davey, 904 A.2d 652 (N.H. 2006); Caprer v. Nussbaum, 36 A.D.3d 176, 825 N.Y.S.2d 55 (2006); Burbank Grease Servs., LLC v. Sokolowski, 717 N.W.2d 781 (Wis. 2006); James O. Pearson, Liability For Interference With At Will Business Relationship, 5 A.L.R.4th 9 (1981).

[131] See, e.g., listing elements in slightly varied formulations, Korea Supply Co. v. Lockheed Martin Corp., 29 Cal.4th 1134, 63 P.3d 937 (2003); McGanty v. Staudenraus, 321 Or. 532, 901 P.2d 841 (1995).

[132] ASC Constr. Equip. USA, Inc. v. City Commercial Real Estate, Inc., 303 Ga.App. 309, 693 S.E.2d 559 (2010) (relating third party rule to rule that defendant could be protected by privilege to interfere); cf. McGanty v. Staudenraus, 321 Or. 532, 901 P.2d 841 (1995) (applying third party rule to interference with economic relations but perhaps meaning interference with contract). In case of interference with actual contracts, the third party rule is merely an indirect way of stating an economic loss rule, saying that, between parties and privies, the contract itself ordinarily controls, not tort law. See Chapter 41. In the case of interference with economic opportunity, however, a "third party" requirement seems at least in part to indirectly address a

Differences between the two interference torts. The interference with economic opportunity tort differs from interference with contract in two broad respects. First, it redresses interferences with mere economic opportunities that are not represented by existing, enforceable contracts. Second, the economic opportunities tort may require significantly more proof of wrongdoing than is required in the most traditional interference with contract claim.[133] Phrased in the older language of privilege, the same point can be made by saying that the defendant is privileged to interfere with certain opportunities even though he would not be privileged to interfere in the case of an existing and enforceable contract.

Burden of proof. Traditional thought held that the defendant had the burden of justifying interference. This has substantially changed in most states,[134] but most emphatically in interference with opportunity cases.[135] Even in those states that still put the burden on the defendant to justify an interference with an existing contract, the burden may be placed upon the plaintiff to show affirmative wrongdoing when the interference is merely with an economic opportunity.[136]

Examples of interference with opportunity tort. A variety of economic relationships not sealed by contract may be protected. The opportunity to buy or sell goods or land, to employ others, or to be employed at will are examples,[137] but protection is not limited to merchants or employment. Suppose the defendant persuades a hospital to reverse its long-standing policy of renewing a physician's staff privileges. Staff privilege is essential to the physician's business, but her contract with the hospital does not guarantee a renewal of her privilege to work in the hospital. If the facts warrant a finding that the defendant acted improperly and that the existing relationship between physician and hospital was significant enough to deserve protection, the defendant may be subject to liability in tort for interfering with a prospective business relationship.[138]

Reasonable probability of reaping the economic benefit. The plaintiff's prospect or economic opportunity must be one that the plaintiff would likely have captured but for the defendant's interference.[139] Although some courts have defined the necessary

---

slightly different question—whether the defendant was a wrongdoer (or privileged), or whether the defendant merely withdrew from an economic relationship he was not obliged to accept in the first place.

[133] See Korea Supply Co. v. Lockheed Martin Corp., 29 Cal.4th 1134, 63 P.3d 937 (2003) ("while intentionally interfering with an existing contract is "a wrong in and of itself," intentionally interfering with a plaintiff's prospective economic advantage is not. To establish a claim for interference with prospective economic advantage . . . a plaintiff must plead that the defendant engaged in an independently wrongful act. An act is not independently wrongful merely because defendant acted with an improper motive.").

[134] § 42.4.

[135] See Clinch v. Heartland Health, 187 S.W.3d 10 (Mo. Ct. App. 2006).

[136] Compare Penna v. Toyota Motor Sales, U.S.A., Inc., 11 Cal.4th 376, 902 P.2d 740, 45 Cal.Rptr.2d 436 (1995), with Quelimane Co., Inc. v. Stewart Title Guar. Co., 19 Cal.4th 26, 960 P.2d 513, 77 Cal.Rptr.2d 709 (1998).

[137] Restatement (Second) of Torts § 766B cmt. c (1979).

[138] E.g., Straube v. Larson, 287 Or. 357, 600 P.2d 371 (1979). As pointed out at length elsewhere, there are often other possible claims, based on specific torts. Depending on the facts, these may include defamation and violation of antitrust statutes. See § 42.2.

[139] Santana Prods. Inc. v. Bobrick Washroom Equip. Inc., 401 F.3d 123 (3d Cir. 2005) (plaintiff was excluded from making a bid, but there were several other bidders and no showing that the plaintiff was likely to have won the contract); Stehno v. Spring Spectrum, 186 S.W.3d 247, 250 (Mo. 2006) ("The valid business expectancy requirement involves more than a mere subjective expectancy—it must be a *reasonable* expectancy of continued employment. The plaintiff must have more than a 'mere hope' of continued employment.").

economic opportunity or relationship to require a specific, identifiable opportunity[140] the plaintiff need not have a prospect of obtaining a contract as such. It is enough if she has a probable prospect of economic gain and provable losses resulting from the interference,[141] provided the economic opportunity is sufficiently definite to warrant protection.

Historical liability for improper motive or purpose. At one time judges stood ready to impose tort liability for ordinary business decisions—seeking tenants for a mall,[142] choosing a means of company transport,[143] discharging managerial employees believed to be working against the company's interests[144]—if a bad motive was perceived. And judges were sometimes equally ready to perceive a bad motive.[145] Occasionally, liability for loss of economic opportunity has been imposed without any objective indication of wrongdoing at all.[146]

Contemporary rejection or limitation of motive-based liability. In interference with prospects case, contemporary courts have increasingly expressed skepticism about liability based upon motive or purpose, as distinct from wrongful means. Some have said that motive ordinarily is not sufficient.[147] Others have gone further and rejected motive-based liability altogether. Such courts require improper means of interference, or even proof of specific, named torts,[148] violation of statute, constitution, regulation or

---

[140] See Table Steaks v. First Premier Banks, 650 N.W.2d 829 (S.D. 2002) (relationship with identifiable third person required); DaimlerChrysler Corp. v. Kirkhart, 148 N.C.App. 572, 561 S.E.2d 276 (2002) (communications to large number of people suggesting they had potential lawsuits against vehicle manufacturer was not an interference with prospects of a contract and not actionable).

[141] Hannex Corp. v. GMI, Inc., 140 F.3d 194 (2d Cir. 1998); Restatement (Second) of Torts § 766B cmt. c (1979).

[142] In Deauville Corp. v. Federated Dep't Stores, Inc., 756 F.2d 1183 (5th Cir. 1985), Federated was developing a large shopping mall and had some anchor tenants. It induced Ward, a retailer, to sign on as a tenant, knowing that Ward had earlier signed on with the plaintiff's competing mall. However, Federated also knew also that Ward had the right to withdraw from its contract with the plaintiff. Ward did withdraw and the plaintiff sued Federated for interfering with its contract with Ward. The court concluded that Federated and Deauville were competitors for Ward's tenancy and that Ward was not contractually committed to remain with Deauville. Nevertheless, the court held that a jury could find that Federated's motive was "only to harm Deauville" and that if the jury so found, Federated would be liable.

[143] Alyeska Pipeline Serv. Co. v. Aurora Air Serv., Inc., 604 P.2d 1090 (Alaska 1979), summarized in part in § 42.6.

[144] In Smith v. Ford Motor Co., 289 N.C. 71, 221 S.E.2d 282, 79 A.L.R.3d 651 (1976), plaintiff was a manager for a Ford dealership, which had the contractual right to terminate the plaintiff's employment. Ford Motor Company, believing that the plaintiff's membership in a dealer alliance was inimical for Ford's interest, induced the dealership to exercise its rights by terminating the plaintiff's employment. Ford's motive was to protect its own interests as it saw them, but the court made its own determination that Ford's action did not in fact protect its business interests and that its motive was therefore improper. On this basis, Ford would be liable for interference with the plaintiff's contract, even though the dealer acted within its rights in terminating.

[145] See, on inferring bad motives, § 42.6.

[146] Fossett v. Davis, 531 So.2d 849 (Ala. 1988) (defendant who merely explained to a landlord that she had a right to evict a tenant and procured a lawyer to initiate an eviction was held liable, although he apparently only assisted the landlord in exercising her rights and the tenant lost nothing she had a right to keep; the tenant moved out upon second eviction notice, no indication that landlord lacked right to evict).

[147] Tom's Foods, Inc. v. Carn, 896 So.2d 443, 458 (Ala. 2004); Avilla v. Newport Grand Jai Alai LLC, 935 A.2d 91 (R.I. 2007); see also Saab Auto. AB v. General Motors Co., 770 F.3d 436 (6th Cir. 2014).

[148] Speakers of Sport, Inc. v. ProServ, Inc., 178 F.3d 862 (7th Cir. 1999) (Illinois law; "We agree with Professor Perlman that the tort of interference with business relationships should be confined to cases in which the defendant employed unlawful means to stiff a competitor, Harvey S. Perlman, "Interference With Contract and Other Economic Expectancies: A Clash of Tort and Contract Doctrine," 49 U. Chi. L.Rev. 61 (1982), and we are reassured by the conclusion of his careful analysis that the case law is generally consistent with this position as a matter of outcomes as distinct from articulation."); Great Escape, Inc. v. Union City Body Co.,

independent common law rule.[149] Short of formally eliminating considerations of motive in determining liability, some courts have imposed a strong practical constraint on motive-based liability by insisting that when the defendant's bad motive is a basis for liability, the bad motive must be the defendant's sole motive.[150] This rule is hard to meet and restricts liability far more than the traditional rule, which held the defendant could be liable if any or a predominant part of his motive was improper. Altogether, the cases seem to be part of a definite movement toward limiting or even eliminating motive-based liability for interference with prospects. This is to the good. In addition to risks of liability, litigation costs in defending claims that often appear to be unjustified can be substantial for the judicial system as well as the defendant.

Rules protecting interference. As with interference with contract, in an interests case, the defendant is also privileged to compete, to act in self-interest, and to exercise other privileges. Competition is merely a particular example of the principle that the defendant is free to pursue his self-interest as long as the means are not wrongful. Thus the defendant may be free to interfere with the plaintiff's prospects even if the two are not competitors. Interference is not wrongful, then, when it is carried out by proper means and the motive is to protect the defendant's interests.

What counts as a protected economic opportunity; specific business relationships. The Restatement,[151] with explicit agreement of some courts,[152] protects any kind of reasonable economic expectancy against intentional and improper interference, so long as the plaintiff can prove a reasonable probability that the opportunity would have been

---

Inc., 791 F.2d 532 (7th Cir. 1986) (Indiana law; motive alone is insufficient; there must be something "illegal"); Reeves v. Hanlon, 33 Cal. 4th 1140, 95 P.3d 513, 17 Cal. Rptr.3d 289 (2004); Rutland v. Mullen, 798 A.2d 1104 (Me. 2002) (fraud or unlawful coercion); Nazeri v. Missouri Valley Coll., 860 S.W.2d 303 (Mo. 1993) ("If the defendant has a legitimate interest, economic or otherwise, in the contract or expectancy sought to be protected, then the plaintiff must show that the defendant employed improper means in seeking to further only his own interests. . . . [I]mproper means are those that are independently wrongful, such as threats, violence, trespass, defamation, misrepresentation of fact, restraint of trade, or any other wrongful act recognized by statute or the common law"); Wal-Mart Stores, Inc. v. Sturges, 52 S.W.3d 711 (Tex. 2001); Peace v. Conway, 246 Va. 278, 435 S.E.2d 133 (1993). A little authority has applied this restriction even in interference with contract cases. Kirkland v. Tamplin, 285 Ga.App. 241, 645 S.E.2d 653 (2007) (improper means such as fraud or defamation are required to support an action for interference with contract; merely persuading one to breach is not enough for liability). Presumably the same authority would adopt the rule for interference with prospects claims where liability is generally more limited.

[149] Reeves v. Hanlon, 33 Cal.4th 1140, 95 P.3d 513, 17 Cal.Rptr.3d 289 (2004).

[150] Scutti Enters., LLC. v. Park Place Entm't Corp., 322 F.3d 211, 215 (2d Cir. 2003); Fikes v. Furst, 134 N.M. 602, 609, 81 P.3d 545, 552 (2003); Carvel Corp. v. Noonan, 3 N.Y.3d 182, 818 N.E.2d 1100, 785 N.Y.S.2d 359 (2004); cf. Lake Panorama Servicing Corp. v. Central Iowa Energy Coop., 636 N.W.2d 747 (Iowa 2001) ("A defendant's conduct is improper only if it is undertaken with '*the sole or predominant purpose* to injure or financially destroy' another. If the interference is a necessary consequence of actions taken for a different purpose, the acts may be deemed intentional, but are not improper."). Another view rejects liability if the justifiable motive would have produced the same conduct by the defendant. See Mt. Healthy City Sch. Dist. Bd. of Ed. v. Doyle, 429 U.S. 274, 97 S.Ct. 568, 50 L.Ed.2d 471 (1977); § 42.6.

[151] The Restatement (Second) of Torts § 766B (1979) was given a misleading title which speaks of interference with prospective contractual relations, but in comments it is clear that it equally protects ordinary sales, for example, in a retail business, where no contracts at all are involved. See id. cmt. c.

[152] See Abbott Labs. v. TEVA Pharms. USA, Inc., 432 F.Supp.2d 408 (D. Del. 2006) (claimed interference with prospective sales of pharmaceuticals, no need to "identify specific relationships that have been disrupted"); Hawaii Med. Ass'n v. Hawaii Med. Servs. Ass'n, Inc., 148 P.3d 1179, 1220 (Haw. 2006) (emphasizing that plaintiffs "are not required to allege the existence of a potential or actual contract, nor are they required to specifically name the third party with whom they have a business expectancy, provided that they have alleged a relationship or potential relationship that 'would have inured to [their] economic benefit' "). For a fuller discussion, see 3 Dobbs, Hayden & Bublick, The Law of Torts § 642 (2d ed. 2011 & Supp.).

realized but for the defendant's intentional interference and that there is a reasonable basis for estimating damages.

Intentional interference with noncommercial opportunities. Courts have extended liability for interference with economic opportunity to some but not all noncommercial opportunities. Liability is sometimes imposed for interference with a reasonably expected gift or inheritance and for interference with a good opportunity to recover in a lawsuit. Even so, in the few decisions on point, courts have been loath to permit recovery for interference with elections and sporting events that do not involve some specific tort. They have also tended to reject liability for spoliation of evidence which affects the plaintiff's opportunity to prevail in a lawsuit against someone else.[153]

D. THE PRIMA FACIE TORT

§ 42.10 The Prima Facie Tort

Nature of the prima facie tort. Several states have recognized some version of an economic tort separate from all others, calling it the prima facie tort.[154] The tort stems from Justice Holmes' argument that intended infliction of harm is prima facie tortious, even if the defendant's conduct did not amount to a specific or named tort.[155] Given intentional infliction of economic loss, then, the defendant would be liable unless he proved affirmatively some justification.

Relation to interference with contract or economic opportunity. The prima facie tort idea, which makes everything tortious *prima facie* and puts the burden on the defendant to justify his actions, actually describes the older rule for interference with contract[156]— that is, given intended interference, the defendant was liable unless he convinced judge and jury that he was somehow justified in doing so.[157] Many intended *harms* are entirely rightful, as in the case of a business that successfully competes for customers, thus harming its rivals, or the lawyer who successfully wins a case, thus harming opposing parties and perhaps their lawyers as well. For this reason, the prima facie tort rule, as it worked out in interference with contract cases, proved to be more like a bludgeon than a scalpel. Consequently, the prima facie tort approach in interference cases has largely given way to a rule requiring the plaintiff at least to prove some improper means or motive, not merely an intent to harm.[158]

Limited adoption in the courts. Incongruously, while many courts have moved away from the prima facie tort idea in interference cases, both by putting the burden of proof on the plaintiff and by requiring some kind of wrongful conduct as a condition of liability, several courts have adopted the "prima facie tort" as a separate tort. The only significant

---

[153] Spoliation is discussed separately from other interferences. §§ 44.4–44.7.

[154] Distinguish the prima facie tort from the principle that intended physical harm is prima facie actionable. See Restatement (Third) of Torts: Liability for Physical and Emotional Harm § 5 (2010). Prima facie actionability of intended physical harm summarizes one effect of the specific rules of battery, assault, false imprisonment, and trespass.

[155] Aikens v. Wisconsin, 195 U.S. 194, 204, 25 S.Ct. 3, 5, 49 L.Ed. 154, 158 (1904).

[156] See Mark P. Gergen, Tortious Interference: How It Is Engulfing Commercial Law, Why This Is Not Entirely Bad, and a Prudential Response, 38 Ariz. L. Rev. 1175 (1996) (prima facie tort was really the source of intentional interference law).

[157] § 42.3.

[158] § 42.4 (improper purpose or motive & burden of proof).

jurisprudence on the prima facie tort is found in the courts of Missouri,[159] New Mexico[160] and New York[161] and in the Restatement Second of Torts.[162] Even among these jurisdictions, however, the court may require the plaintiff to prove a lack of justification in the first place, which takes the case out of the prima facie tort category altogether by putting a burden on the plaintiff to prove improper acts.[163] Consequently, the doctrine is more important in theory than it is in practice.

Limitations on the tort—relation to named torts. The prima facie tort could engulf all intentional torts. For instance, if the prima facie tort theory is adopted without restriction, a plaintiff could recover for emotional distress or defamation even though the plaintiff could not prove the elements required to establish those torts. This kind of subversion of the tort rules has been rejected in the cases, which insist that "prima facie tort may not be used to evade the essential elements of traditional tort."[164] Yet the plaintiff is also barred if the defendant's act is unlawful;[165] and, at least under New York's rule, if the plaintiff can state a claim under a specific named tort, the prima facie theory must be discarded.[166] At least some aspects of the economic loss rules may also bar the prima facie tort claims.[167]

Other limitations. Courts have also required the plaintiff to show special damages in order to recover under the prima facie tort theory. Although the term special damages is not always clearly defined,[168] the term often means pecuniary loss, as opposed to intangible harms[169] or unrealized or bookkeeping losses.[170] That seems to be what the New York Court of Appeals had in mind in requiring evidence that plaintiff "suffered specific and measurable loss."[171] New York cases often say as well that damages must be pleaded with specificity, and the complaint is dismissed when the plaintiff does not

---

[159] Porter v. Crawford & Co., 611 S.W.2d 265 (Mo. Ct. App. 1980).

[160] Schmitz v. Smentowski, 109 N.M. 386, 785 P.2d 726 (1990).

[161] Advance Music Corp. v. American Tobacco Co., 296 N.Y. 79, 70 N.E.2d 401 (1946).

[162] Restatement (Second) of Torts § 870 (1979) (providing no illustrations of the prima facie tort in the context of economic harms).

[163] LPP Mortg., Ltd. v. Marcin, Inc., 224 S.W.3d 50, 55 (Mo. Ct. App. 2007) ("In order to make a submissible claim, claimants in prima facie tort must 'demonstrate that they have substantial evidence on each of the four elements,'" the fourth of which is the defendant's lack of justification).

[164] Fromson v. State, 176 Vt. 395, 848 A.2d 344 (2004); see also Engel v. CBS, Inc., 93 N.Y.2d 195, 689 N.Y.S.2d 411, 711 N.E.2d 626 (1999) (if the jurisdiction follows the special grievance rule of malicious prosecution/wrongful civil litigation, that rule cannot be avoided by claiming prima facie tort instead).

[165] Kelly v. Golden, 352 F.3d 344 (8th Cir. 2003) (Missouri law, lawfulness of the defendant's act is an element of the claim for prima facie tort); Druyan v. Jagger, 508 F.Supp. 2d 228 (S.D.N.Y. 2007) (same); Portales Nat'l Bank v. Ribble, 134 N.M. 238, 75 P.3d 838 (Ct. App. 2003) (same).

[166] Freihofer v. Hearst Corp., 65 N.Y.2d 135, 143, 480 N.E.2d 349, 355, 490 N.Y.S.2d 735, 741 (1985) ("Where relief may be afforded under traditional tort concepts, prima facie tort may not be invoked as a basis to sustain a pleading which otherwise fails to state a cause of action in conventional tort."); Curiano v. Suozzi, 63 N.Y.2d 113, 117, 469 N.E.2d 1324, 1327, 480 N.Y.S.2d 466, 469 (1984) ("once a traditional tort is established the cause of action for prima facie tort disappears").

[167] See Druyan v. Jagger, 508 F.Supp. 2d 228 (S.D.N.Y. 2007) (a concert ticket was a contract which limited the plaintiff's recovery in case the performance was not given; this prevented the plaintiff's recovery for fraud and, given that limitation, the prima facie tort claim was also barred).

[168] See D'Angelo-Fenton v. Town of Carmel, 470 F.Supp. 2d 387 (S.D. N.Y. 2007).

[169] As in claims for slander. See § 534. The term is widely used to contrast intangible or nonpecuniary harms. See Washington Metro. Area Transit Auth. v. Jeanty, 718 A.2d 172 (D.C. 1998); Strahin v. Cleavenger, 216 W.Va. 175, 603 S.E.2d 197 (2004); Dan B. Dobbs, Law of Remedies § 12.2(3) (2d ed. 1993).

[170] See Dan B. Dobbs, Law of Remedies § 3.4 (2d ed. 1993).

[171] Freihofer v. Hearst Corp., 65 N.Y.2d 135, 143, 480 N.E.2d 349, 355 (1985).

do so.[172] Courts have also circumscribed the prima facie tort by demanding especially clear evidence of a specific intent to harm the plaintiff.[173]

E. NEGLIGENT INTERFERENCE WITH CONTRACT AND OPPORTUNITY

§ 42.11 General Rule Inhibition Against Recovery for Negligently Caused Economic Harm

General rule that negligent interference with contract or prospects is an insufficient basis for liability. Intentional interference is required to establish a claim for interference with contract or for interference with economic prospects.[174] Correspondingly, negligent interference is no ground for recovery, either in the case of interference with actual contracts or in the case of interference with economic opportunities.[175] Less than a handful of courts hold otherwise.[176]

Interference claims and the economic loss rules. Although economic loss rules have been discussed in an earlier chapter,[177] it is important here to recognize that so far as the economic loss rule forbids recovery for negligently caused pure economic loss it is substantially identical to the rules for interference with contract or economic opportunities. Indeed, the economic loss rules in cases among strangers—those who are not in a contract-like relationship—are largely built on the interference rules; the great mass of economic torts among strangers could easily be conceived as claims for interference with contract or interference with economic opportunity. Likewise, the interference torts in turn can be viewed as specific instances of the more general economic loss rule that defendants owe no duty to use care to protect strangers against stand-alone economic harm.[178]

---

[172] Lynch v. McQueen, 309 A.D.2d 790, 765 N.Y.S.2d 645 (2003).

[173] See Tamko Roofing Prods., Inc. v. Smith Eng'g Co., 450 F.3d 822 (8th Cir. 2006).

[174] § 42.4.

[175] Misany v. United States, 873 F.2d 160 (7th Cir. 1989) (Wisconsin law, intent required for interference with contract or prospects); Williams v. University Med. Ctr. of S. Nev., 688 F.Supp.2d 1134 (D. Nev. 2010) (Nevada does not recognize claim for negligence interference with economic expectancies); Great Sw. Fire Ins. Co. v. CNA Ins. Cos., 557 So.2d 966 (La. 1990); King's Daughters & Sons Circle No. Two of Greenville v. Delta Reg'l Med. Ctr., 856 So.2d 600, 606 (Miss. Ct. App. 2003) ("mere negligent interference is no cause of action at all"); Hatfield v. Health Mgmt. Assocs. of W. Va., 223 W.Va. 259, 672 S.E.2d 395 (2008) (negligence insufficient basis for liability either for interference with contract or with economic expectancy).

[176] §§ 42.11, 41.11.

[177] Chapter 41.

[178] See 2 Harper, James & Gray, The Law of Torts § 6.10 (3d ed. 2006 (with Supps.)); but cf. Flagstaff Affordable Housing Ltd. P'ship v. Design Alliance, Inc., 223 P.3d 664 (Ariz. 2010) (seemingly doubting the generality of the stranger version of the economic loss rule and suggesting that the cases against liability are best explained as products of rules internal to particular torts).

Chapter 43

MISREPRESENTATION AND FALSEHOODS

Analysis

A. INJURIOUS FALSEHOOD
§ 43.1   Falsehoods Published to Others Causing Plaintiff's Economic Harm

B. FRAUDULENT MISREPRESENTATIONS
§ 43.2   Misrepresentation Torts: An Overview
§ 43.3   Misrepresentation as a Fact vs. a Tort
§ 43.4   Fraudulent Misrepresentation

C. NEGLIGENT MISREPRESENTATION
§ 43.5   Negligent Misrepresentation

D. INNOCENT MISREPRESENTATION
§ 43.6   Innocent Misrepresentation

E. MAJOR ISSUES
§ 43.7   Reliance
§ 43.8   Factual Representations: Opinion, Law and Prediction
§ 43.9   Defenses and Remedies

F. ECONOMIC HARMS IN SPECIAL RELATIONSHIPS
§ 43.10 Breach of Fiduciary Duty, Bad Faith, Wrongful Discharge and Economic Duress

---

A. INJURIOUS FALSEHOOD

§ 43.1 Falsehoods Published to Others Causing Plaintiff's Economic Harm

Interests protected in injurious falsehood. The law of injurious falsehood applies to derogatory publications about the plaintiff's economic or commercial interests that diminish those interests or their value. For example, a false statement communicated to others asserting that the plaintiff's product is inferior may cause loss of sales.[1] Injurious falsehood law does not redress dignitary harms.[2] Courts and lawyers often call injurious falsehood by more specific names like commercial disparagement or trade libel when the defendant disparages a product,[3] or slander of title when the defendant casts doubt on the plaintiff's interest in property.[4] The principle behind the injurious falsehood tort is not limited to those particular forms of the tort. False statements about the plaintiff's

---

[1]   Martin v. Reynolds Metals Co., 224 F.Supp. 978 (D. Or. 1963) (enjoining such a "libel" on business interests). See also Black & Yates v. Mahogany Ass'n, 129 F.2d 227 (3d Cir. 1941).

[2]   The distinction has been long recognized even though it is imperfectly expressed. See Black & Yates v. Mahogany Ass'n, 129 F.2d 227 (3d Cir. 1941) (a leading case; defamation "is concerned with interests of personality" while injurious falsehood is concerned "with interests in property").

[3]   E.g., Auvil v. CBS 60 Minutes, 67 F.3d 816 (9th Cir. 1995).

[4]   E.g., Rorvig v. Douglas, 123 Wash.2d 854, 873 P.2d 492 (1994).

pecuniary interests may qualify even if they are not about the property, product or services offered by the plaintiff.[5]

Examples of injurious falsehood. In the slander of title form of injurious falsehood, the defendant casts doubt on the plaintiff's title to a legally recognized interest. It is enough that the defendant claims the plaintiff's title is subject to an encumbrance that would affect marketability or value. This is often done by filing or recording an unjustified lien, lis pendens, or option contract.[6] Intangible as well as tangible property is protected against attacks on the plaintiff's title. For instance, intellectual property rights may be subject to a slander of title claim when federal law does not preempt the claim under patent or other federal laws.[7]

A false statement that the ratings of the plaintiff's radio show are too low to justify continuing the show can be an actionable disparagement.[8] Even a publication falsely stating the price the plaintiff charges for his goods has been held actionable.[9] Likewise actionable are statements that the plaintiff has insufficient funds to continue in business.[10]

Carrying over defamation rules and concepts. Many legal conceptions important in defamation cases carry over and apply in injurious falsehood cases as well.[11] Similarly, constitutional protections for the defendant that apply when the facts are adjudicated as a claim for defamation may equally apply when the same facts are adjudicated as a claim for injurious falsehood[12] unless the court excludes constitutional protection because the falsehood is unprotected commercial speech.[13] However, the common law injurious

---

[5] Restatement (Second) of Torts § 623A & cmt. a (1977) (false statements are actionable if they are harmful to the pecuniary interests of another and the other elements of the tort are proved; for example, imputations of bad credit that do not also imply a want of integrity).

[6] E.g., Peckham v. Hirshfeld, 570 A.2d 663 (R.I. 1990) (option to purchase recorded); Gregory's, Inc. v. Haan, 545 N.W.2d 488 (S.D. 1996) (materialman's lien filed, jury question on whether requisite fault was established). Recording a lien or lis pendens is privileged in some states. See 3 Dobbs, Hayden & Bublick, The Law of Torts § 661 (2d ed. 2011 & Supp.).

[7] See Chamilia, LLC v. Pandora Jewelry, LLC, 2007 WL 2781246 (S.D.N.Y. 2007) (recognizing that a slander of title to patent would be actionable); Macia v. Microsoft Corp., 152 F.Supp.2d 535 (D. Vt. 2001) (slander of title to trademark adequately pleaded and not preempted).

[8] Menefee v. Columbia Broad. Sys., Inc., 458 Pa. 46, 329 A.2d 216 (1974); see also Neurotron Inc. v. Medical Serv. Ass'n of Pa., Inc., 254 F.3d 444 (3d Cir. 2001) (opining that on the Menefee facts today, the Pennsylvania Court would require knowing or reckless falsehood). In Advance Music Corp. v. American Tobacco Co., 296 N.Y. 79, 70 N.E.2d 401 (1946), the defendant purported to list the top selling songs, but omitted plaintiff's songs from list, thereby implying that the plaintiff's songs did not sell that well. This disparagement was held actionable but the theory advanced for liability was not disparagement but prima facie tort.

[9] Kings Creations Ltd. v. Conde Nast Publ'ns Inc., 34 A.D.2d 935, 311 N.Y.S.2d 757 (1970).

[10] Primiani v. Federal Ins. Co., 203 Fed.Appx. 902 (9th Cir. 2006).

[11] E.g., Western Techs., Inc. v. Sverdrup & Parcel, Inc., 739 P.2d 1318 (Ariz. Ct. App. 1986) (judicial proceedings privilege).

[12] TMJ Implants, Inc. v. Aetna, Inc., 498 F.3d 1175 (10th Cir. 2007) ("opinion" statements protected both in defamation and injurious falsehood); Suzuki Motor Corp. v. Consumers Union of U.S., Inc., 330 F.3d 1110 (9th Cir. 2003) (public figure plaintiff suing for disparagement must constitutionally prove that defendant's statement was a knowing or reckless falsehood); Reliance Ins. Co. v. Shenandoah S., Inc., 81 F.3d 789 (8th Cir. 1996) ("Under Missouri law, defamation or disparagement actions brought by public figures require a showing of the following elements: . . . that the defendant published the statement either with knowledge of its falsity or with reckless disregard for whether it was true or false. . . ."); Abernathy & Closther v. Buffalo Broad. Co., Inc., 176 A.D.2d 300, 574 N.Y.S.2d 568 (1991) (constitutional "clear and convincing evidence" standard applies to public figure's product disparagement claim).

[13] U.S. Healthcare, Inc. v. Blue Cross of Greater Philadelphia, 898 F.2d 914 (3d Cir. 1990).

falsehood rules will frequently require the same proof as required by the Constitution, so constitutional questions may be superfluous.

Rejecting defamation rules. Injurious falsehood claims are also different from defamation claims in a number of ways. Damages are of course different because the nature of the harm, which is purely pecuniary, differs from the reputational harm in defamation cases. More importantly, the plaintiff in injurious falsehood must prove three major elements that a plaintiff suing for libel was *not* required to prove in traditional common law defamation suits—falsity of the statement, fault on the part of the defendant, and pecuniary harm.[14]

Elements of injurious falsehood claims. To sustain a claim for injurious falsehood (in any of its forms), the plaintiff must prove that the defendant

　　(1)　published a provably false communication;[15]

　　(2)　of and concerning the plaintiff or the plaintiff's pecuniary interests;[16]

　　(3)　with knowledge of the statement's falsity or with recklessness as to its falsity, or, in some states, with malice in the sense of ill will;

　　(4)　when pecuniary harm to the defendant was either intended or foreseeable;[17] and

　　(5)　resulting pecuniary harm to the plaintiff.

Some courts agree in essence with these requirements but continue the older habit of invoking them in determining the defendant's privilege rather than as elements of the plaintiff's case.[18] In addition, some courts invoke the knowing or reckless falsehood rule as a matter of constitutional law applicable to cases in which the plaintiff is a public figure,[19] rather than as a matter of state law applicable to all cases.

The fault required by the tort, its relationship to truth or falsity, the pecuniary harm requirement, and the tort's interrelationship with other torts are all important issues developed more fully in other publications.[20]

B.　FRAUDULENT MISREPRESENTATIONS

§ 43.2　Misrepresentation Torts: An Overview

Misrepresentation inducing an economic transaction. Both the torts of intentional misrepresentation and negligent misrepresentation are derived from the old tort of *Deceit*, which covered pure economic harm caused by misrepresentations of fact made directly or indirectly to, and justifiably relied upon by the plaintiff. The

---

[14]　In libel cases, earlier common law and to some extent contemporary law as well, held that, with limited exceptions, "falsity, malice, and injury are presumed and proof of these elements is not necessary." Kiesau v. Bantz, 686 N.W.2d 164 (Iowa 2004).

[15]　See Auvil v. CBS 60 Minutes, 67 F.3d 816 (9th Cir. 1995).

[16]　Blatty v. New York Times Co., 42 Cal.3d 1033, 728 P.2d 1177, 232 Cal.Rptr. 542 (1987); Sanderson v. Indiana Soft Water Servs., Inc., 2004 WL 1784755 (S.D. Ind. 2004) ("But as under the law of defamation, a statement is not actionable unless it is clear from its content and context that it refers specifically to the plaintiff's products.").

[17]　Restatement (Second) of Torts § 623A(a) (1977).

[18]　E.g., Gregory's, Inc. v. Haan, 545 N.W.2d 488 (S.D. 1996).

[19]　E.g., Suzuki Motor Corp. v. Consumers Union of U.S., Inc., 330 F.3d 1110 (9th Cir. 2003).

[20]　See 3 Dobbs, Hayden & Bublick, The Law of Torts ch. 43 (2d ed. 2011 & Supp.).

misrepresentation normally must induce the plaintiff to enter into a transaction, or sometimes to avoid a transaction, as where it induces the plaintiff to retain shares of stock rather than sell them. The traditional tort of deceit required an intentional misrepresentation as well as certain other elements. False communications, including misleading nondisclosures, are often referred to as fraud or deceit when the falsity is intentional.

Statutes. Statutes are often important in contemporary misrepresentation cases and often must be consulted. Statutes covering particular situations like the civil RICO statute,[21] securities statutes,[22] and consumer protection statutes,[23] have helped create specialized and sometimes intricate fields that may or may not offer more protection against fraud than the common law. The federal Qui Tam statute permits private persons to sue contractors who make false claims against the government, in effect permitting the private plaintiff to share part of the recovery.[24]

Examples. Examples of tortious misrepresentation include the homeowner who induces a sale by falsely representing that the basement does not flood;[25] the employer who recruits desirable employees by falsely representing that it had no plans to move or close[26] or who induces older employees to quit by falsely representing retirement options;[27] the adjuster who falsely says that a release to be signed by an injured person is merely a receipt;[28] and even the HMO that induces members to join by falsely representing that it will expeditiously arbitrate disputes when in fact it stonewalls even the dying patient.[29] If such representations are culpably false, the plaintiff who justifiably relies upon them may have a claim for damages[30] or, in some cases, for equitable relief such as rescission of the transaction.

---

[21]   See 18 U.S.C.A. §§ 1961–64. Although the statute requires proof that the defendant engaged in a pattern of racketeering activity, that term is defined broadly. A number of common if shady and dishonest business dealings may be included if a "pattern" of illegal activity can be found. See, e.g., Corley v. Rosewood Care Ctr., Inc. of Peoria, 142 F.3d 1041 (7th Cir. 1998) (use of mails in furtherance of scheme to defraud in a kind of bait and switch operation).

[22]   Of many statutes, 15 U.S.C.A. § 78j is perhaps the most used and best known. See generally 7 & 8 Louis Loss & Joel Seligman, Securities Regulation, Chs. 9 & 10 (fraud and manipulation) (3d ed. 1991 & Supps.). One federal statute, the Securities Litigation Uniform Standards Act of 1998 (SLUSA), 15 U.S.C.A. § 78bb (f), preempted many class actions brought as *state-law* securities fraud claims, forcing them into federal court and then requiring their dismissal. See 1 Thomas Lee Hazen, Treatise on The Law of Securities Regulation § 7.17 (4th ed. 2002).

[23]   Some consumer protection law is public law, but most state statutes recognize a private right of action for misleading or deceptive practices. See Restatement of Unfair Competition § 1, Reporter's Note (listing all state statutes).

[24]   Anyone who knowingly presents a false claim against the United States is criminally liable and also liable for a civil fine and treble damages. 18 U.S.C.A. § 287 & 31 U.S.C.A. § 729.

[25]   Cf. Wasson v. Schubert, 964 S.W.2d 520 (Mo. Ct. App. 1998) (similar).

[26]   Cf. Meade v. Cedarapids, Inc., 164 F.3d 1218 (9th Cir. 1999) (similar); see Richard P. Perna, Deceitful Employers: Intentional Misrepresentation in Hiring and the Employment-at-Will Doctrine, 54 U. Kan. L. Rev. 587 (2006) (discussing both employer and employee fraud).

[27]   Cf. Voilas v. General Motors Corp., 170 F.3d 367 (3d Cir. 1999) (similar claim not preempted by labor laws).

[28]   Cf. Lubin v. Johnson, 169 Ariz. 464, 820 P.2d 328 (1991) (similar).

[29]   Cf. Engalla v. Permanente Med. Group, Inc., 15 Cal.4th 951, 938 P.2d 903, 64 Cal.Rptr.2d 843 (1997) (similar).

[30]   Dier v. Peters, 815 N.W.2d 1 (Iowa 2012) (mother of a child intentionally misrepresented that the plaintiff was the child's father, inducing him to pay money to them in reliance on her misrepresentations; court found that the public policy of "providing a remedy for fraud" outweighed any policy concerns to the contrary); Hodge v. Craig, 382 S.W.3d 325 (Tenn. 2012) (allowing ex-husband to recover damages in the form of child

Damages vs. rescission and other equitable remedies; constructive fraud. The plaintiff who suffers financial harm from reliance upon a misrepresentation can frequently seek rescission of any agreement that resulted from that reliance or can raise the misrepresentation as a defense when she is sued for breach of the agreement. Sometimes she can capture whatever gains the defendant made from his fraud. The old equity courts applied the term constructive fraud to any conduct that would warrant equitable relief such as rescission or reformation[31] and to any ground for equitable relief against fiduciaries.[32] Constructive fraud in this sense is not actual fraud at all; it includes even innocent misrepresentations that will warrant rescission or reformation.[33] Thus rescission or avoidance of the transaction is permitted for innocent material misrepresentations, subject to timeliness rules and other equities. The term constructive fraud is perhaps best avoided because it invites lawyers to confuse the rules for equitable relief and fiducial obligation with the rules for damages that traditionally require a knowing falsehood.[34] The rules stated in this chapter are those governing the tort claim for damages except when specifically noted otherwise.

§ 43.3 Misrepresentation as a Fact vs. a Tort

"Misrepresentation" as description of a fact in claims for physical or emotional harm or as a tort. The terms fraud, deceit, and misrepresentation are used as the name of the economic tort. However, these terms can also be used, not as a name for a cause of action but as a description of facts such as an actual event or the communication unrelated to economic transactions.

Misrepresentation as a way of establishing negligent physical harm. In that descriptive sense, many misrepresentations are important in establishing legal liability for some tort other than misrepresentation or fraud. For example, a former employer might subject others to danger by recommending a sexual predator for a job with children.[35] A physician might cause emotional distress by representing to a patient that she has a disease when she does not.[36] A potential sexual partner might obtain consent to sexual relations by representing that he is not infected with disease or that he cannot

---

support, medical expenses, and insurance payments he had made after his ex-wife's intentional misrepresentations that he was the child's biological father).

[31]   E.g., Wells v. Schuster-Hax Nat'l Bank, 23 Colo. 534, 48 P. 809 (1897) (conveyance without consideration that could defeat creditors' rights would be fraud in law though there was no specific misrepresentation or even intent); Gibson v. Gibson, 102 Wis. 501, 78 N.W. 917 (1899) (equitable suit to alter record title).

[32]   See Barger v. McCoy Hillard & Parks, 346 N.C. 650, 488 S.E.2d 215 (1997) (defining constructive fraud); Stanley v. Luse, 36 Or. 25, 58 P. 75 (1899) (self-dealing by fiduciary as constructive fraud).

[33]   In the lore of constructive fraud in some jurisdictions, the term may even be applied to cases of actual fraud, as where the defendant misleads by active concealment of material facts or by stating misleading half-truths. See Specialty Beverages, LLC v. Pabst Brewing Co., 537 F.3d 1165 (10th Cir. 2008) (Oklahoma law).

[34]   See, e.g., Pugh's IGA, Inc. v. Super Food Servs., Inc., 531 N.E.2d 1194 (Ind. Ct. App. 1988) (discussing but not applying constructive fraud rules in an ordinary damages claim).

[35]   Cf. Randi W. v. Muroc Joint Unified Sch. Dist., 14 Cal.4th 1066, 929 P.2d 582, 60 Cal.Rptr.2d 263 (1997) (claim that school failed to qualify its positive recommendation for teacher who allegedly had been subject of previous complaints of sexual impropriety with students; in his new job, teacher allegedly molested a middle school student); cf. Estate of Shinaul v. State Dep't of Soc. & Health Servs., 980 P.2d 800 (Wash. Ct. App. 1999) (social worker allegedly gave misleading information leading guardians to place child in allegedly unsafe institution where he met his death).

[36]   See Molien v. Kaiser Found. Hosps., 27 Cal.3d 916, 167 Cal.Rptr. 831, 616 P.2d 813, 16 A.L.R. 4th 518 (1980), modified, Burgess v. Superior Court, 2 Cal.4th 1064, 831 P.2d 1197, 9 Cal.Rptr.2d 615 (1992).

have children.[37] A driver might cause a collision by giving signals representing that it is safe to pass when it is not.[38] In these examples, the misrepresentation is merely a way in which personal injury or direct emotional harm is inflicted and need not be viewed as a distinct tort called misrepresentation or fraud. Although some courts do treat the plaintiff's claims in such cases as involving the tort of misrepresentation,[39] liability for personal injury, property damage or emotional harm in such those cases is actually supported by the rules of negligence or those of intentional torts such as battery.[40] Thus for coherence and convenience, it may be best to recognize that personal injury actions based on risks created by misrepresentation are negligence actions or possibly in rare cases they are battery actions.[41]

False statements to the plaintiff. The false statements or misrepresentations at the core of this chapter differ fundamentally from those involved in defamation[42] or injurious falsehood,[43] where the defendant makes a false statement to third persons that damages the personal reputation of the plaintiff or the reputation of the plaintiff's property or product. The misrepresentations in this chapter, in contrast, are made to the plaintiff in connection with explicit or implicit effort to induce the plaintiff's reliance.

§ 43.4   Fraudulent Misrepresentation

Overview

Intentional misrepresentation: fraud. Intentional misrepresentation is often called fraud or fraudulent misrepresentation. Scienter or knowing fraud means the same. The Restatement Third of Torts new blackletter rule for fraud provides that "One who fraudulently makes a material misrepresentation of fact, opinion, intention, or law, for the purpose of inducing another to act or refrain from acting, is subject to liability for economic loss caused by the other's justifiable reliance on the misrepresentation."[44]

Elements: Courts list anywhere from four to nine elements of the common law claim for such misrepresentations.[45] However the elements are formulated, courts agree in substance that the plaintiff must prove the following elements:

---

[37]   See Stephen K. v. Roni L., 105 Cal.App. 3d 640, 164 Cal.Rptr. 618 (1980) (liability denied); Pamela P. v. Frank S., 110 Misc.2d 978, 443 N.Y.S.2d 343 (1981) (indirectly recognized); Conley v. Romeri, 60 Mass. App. Ct. 799, 806 N.E.2d 933 (2004) (claim denied).

[38]   See Restatement (Second) of Torts § 311 (1965).

[39]   E.g., Behr v. Richmond, 193 Cal.App.4th 517, 123 Cal.Rptr.3d 97 (4th Dist. 2011) (infected boyfriend who negligently and fraudulently concealed from plaintiff-girlfriend the risk of her contracting herpes; court found evidence sufficient to support finding that plaintiff's reliance on his representations was reasonable).

[40]   Courts may use the term misrepresentation in describing liability for personal injury but at the same time use the language of ordinary negligence law in describing the basis for liability. See Roe v. Catholic Charities of the Diocese of Springfield, 225 Ill.App.3d 519, 588 N.E.2d 354, 167 Ill.Dec. 713 (1992) (recognizing negligence action against adoption agency that did not disclose child's health problems); R.A.P. v. B.J.P., 428 N.W.2d 103, 109 (Minn. Ct. App.1988) ("people who know that they have genital herpes have a legal duty to take reasonable care to prevent the disease from spreading").

[41]   See Doe v. Dilling, 228 Ill.2d 324, 888 N.E.2d 24, 320 Ill.Dec. 807 (2008) (defendants, parents of the plaintiff's lover, knew but failed to disclose that her lover had HIV and then AIDS; the court did not reject claims based on negligence or battery).

[42]   See Chapter 37.

[43]   See Chapter 43.

[44]   Restatement (Third) of Torts: Liability for Economic Harm § 9 (2014).

[45]   Restatement (Second) of Torts § 525 (1977) requires a (1) fraudulent misrepresentation (2) of fact, opinion, intention, or law, (3) for the purpose of inducing reliance, and (4) justifiable reliance. Similar formulations are found in some cases. E.g., Walker v. Percy, 142 N.H. 345, 702 A.2d 313 (1997). Courts often

(1) an intentional misrepresentation

(2) of fact (or something similar to fact)

(3) that proximately causes pecuniary harm[46] and

(4) is material,

(5) intended to induce reliance and

(6) does induce reliance by the plaintiff,

(7) which is reasonable or "justifiable."

Procedural requirements. Procedurally, the plaintiff is usually required to plead fraud with particularity.[47] Many courts add that fraud must be proved by clear and convincing evidence,[48] although a number say a preponderance of the evidence is sufficient, at least under some conditions[49] and in negligent misrepresentation claims.[50]

---

add that the misrepresentation must be material, e.g., D'Ambrosio v. Colonnade Council of Unit Owners, 717 A.2d 356 (1998), but justifiable reliance may be regarded as encompassing materiality. The legal requirements imposed by this list of elements are not changed if the elements are broken down into more detailed parts. For example, the single element of fraudulent representation can be expressed as three elements—(i) a representation, (ii) which is false in fact, and (iii) known to be false. By a process like this, Arizona comes up with nine elements, see e.g., Nielson v. Flashberg, 101 Ariz. 335, 419 P.2d 514 (1966), but they appear to demand essentially the same proof as required by the Restatement's more economical four elements.

[46]   The harm typically must be pecuniary in nature. E.g., Ironworkers Local Union 68 v. AstraZeneca Pharm., LP, 634 F.3d 1352, R.I.C.O. Bus. Disp. Guide (CCH) P 12026 (11th Cir. 2011) (under applicable laws of the three states involved, "without allegations of injury, a claim is not remediable when based either on common law fraud, or negligent misrepresentation"; here, the plaintiffs failed to allege any economic injury arising from pharmaceutical manufacturer's alleged misrepresentations about the safety and effectiveness of their drugs); Bicknese v. Sutula, 260 Wis. 2d 713, 660 N.W.2d 289 (2004). Illinois courts have limited the tort of fraudulent misrepresentation to commercial or business settings. See Bonhomme v. St. James, 361 Ill.Dec. 1, 970 N.E.2d 1 (2012) (plaintiff's purely personal relationships "is simply not something the state regulates or in which the state possesses any kind of valid public policy interest").

[47]   Fed. R. Civ. Proc. 9(b); Ashworth v. Albers Med., Inc., 410 F.Supp.2d 471 (S.D. W.Va. 2005) (plaintiff must plead time, place, and contents of the false representation, the identity of the person making the misrepresentation, and what defendant obtained by the fraud); Hobson v. American Cast Iron Pipe Co., 690 So.2d 341 (Ala. 1997); Hames v. Cravens, 332 Ark. 437, 966 S.W.2d 244 (1998).

[48]   In re Marriage of Cutler, 588 N.W.2d 425 (Iowa 1999); Richmond Metro. Auth. v. McDevitt Street Bovis, Inc., 256 Va. 553, 507 S.E.2d 344 (1998). Where heightened standard is imposed, courts usually say the standard applies to all elements of the fraud claim, but some courts have reasonably said that it does not apply to proof of damages. See Kilduff v. Adams, Inc., 219 Conn. 314, 593 A.2d 478 (1991). In class actions for securities laws violations, federal law now displaces state law in some instances, forcing it into federal court, where it may be dismissed or face stern proof demands requiring the plaintiffs to plead facts that warrant a "strong" inference of scienter fault. 15 U.S.C.A. § 78u–4 (b)(2). Some authority treats this requirement as more demanding than the clear and convincing evidence standard and as displacing the jury's role in deciding inferences as well. See Gompper v. Visz, Inc., 298 F.3d 893 (9th Cir. 2002). But see Pirraglia v. Novell, Inc., 339 F.3d 1182 (10th Cir. 2003).

[49]   See Huffman v. Poore, 6 Neb.App. 43, 569 N.W.2d 549 (1997) (preponderance sufficient in actions at law for damages, though not for suits in equity); Clay v. Brand, 236 Ark. 236, 365 S.W.2d 256 (1963) (preponderance sufficient unless the misrepresentation claimed would contradict a solemn writing); In re Estate of Kindsfather, 326 Mont. 192, 108 P.3d 487 (2005).

[50]   McLaughlin v. Williams, 379 S.C. 451, 665 S.E.2d 667 (Ct. App. 2008); Dewey v. Wentland, 38 P.3d 402 (Wyo. 2002).

Intent Required

Traditional rule—scienter—a false representation made knowingly. In the leading 19th century case, *Derry v. Peek*,[51] Lord Herschell laid down a rule that has been widely accepted in American decisions.[52] Lord Herschell said:

> Fraud is proved when it is shown that a false representation has been made (1) knowingly [*scienter*], or (2) without belief in its truth, or (3) recklessly, careless whether it be true or false.

The second category really includes both the first and the third. If the defendant represents a fact knowing it to be false he is making a representation without belief in the truth of his statement. Likewise, if he falsely asserts a fact without caring whether it is true or not he probably, if not certainly, lacks a belief in its truth and it is entirely fair to treat the case as an intentional fraud.

Knowing falsehood. The common case falls in the first category—a knowing falsehood. The seller who assures the buyer that the basement has never been flooded when she knows that it has is guilty of a knowing falsehood.[53] But the key principle is expressed in the second category—a statement made without belief in its truth. The language of recklessness in the third category may be misleading to contemporary Americans who might be led to think of highly irresponsible driving. The context makes it clear, however, that the test was not about some extreme form of negligence, but about a lack of belief in the truth of the representation.[54]

Types of intentional misstatements. Under the rules in *Derry v. Peek*, the defendant may be liable not only for unadorned lies but also for half-truths uttered *scienter*,[55] for intentionally misleading ambiguities,[56] and even for misrepresentations of his own present intention to provide benefits in the future. The defendant may also fall under a duty to correct a representation that was true when made but has since become untrue.[57] The defendant's argument that he misrepresented a fact only because the truth would have been misleading and that his ultimate aim was to communicate the real truth by lying about details has deservedly been rejected.[58]

Scienter in the Restatement Third of Torts: The Restatment Third of Torts says that a misrepresentation is fraudulent in three circumstances: if the maker of the misrepresentation "(a) knows or believes that the matter is not as he represents it to be, (b) knows that he does not have the confidence in the accuracy of his representation that

---

[51]   Derry v. Peek, 14 App.Cas. 337 (H.L. 1889) (judgment of Lord Herschell).

[52]   E.g., Kimber v. Young, 137 F. 744 (8th Cir. 1905). Many opinions reflect Derry v. Peek in stating the elements of fraud even when the case is not cited.

[53]   Nielsen v. Adams, 223 Neb. 262, 388 N.W.2d 840 (1986).

[54]   Modern courts recognize this point. See, e.g., Davis v. McGuigan, 325 S.W.3d 149 (Tenn. 2010) (equating "recklessness" with knowledge that a representation was false or without a belief that the representation was true, finding genuine issue of material fact on the issue).

[55]   E.g., Junius Constr. Co. v. Cohen, 257 N.Y. 393, 178 N.E. 672 (1931).

[56]   Restatement (Second) of Torts § 527 (1977).

[57]   See id. § 535.

[58]   Bangert Bros. Constr. Co. v. Kiewit W. Co., 310 F.3d 1278 (10th Cir. 2002) (rejecting the truth-through-lies argument on the ground that the fact misrepresented, not the ultimate conclusion to which it led, was the material fact); Nielsen v. Adams, 223 Neb. 262, 388 N.W.2d 840 (1986) (rejecting the argument on the ground that knowing falsehood and intent to induce reliance are required, but not intent to deceive).

he states or implies, or (c) knows that he does not have the basis for the representation that he states or implies."[59]

Circumstantial evidence and the relevance of negligence. Under the *scienter* test, ordinary negligence, such as the defendant's failure to ascertain facts with reasonable care or his failure to formulate misrepresentations more accurately, is not enough for liability in a claim for intentional misrepresentation.[60] On the other hand, short of the defendant's own admission, the plaintiff can often prove knowing falsehood only by circumstantial evidence. Such evidence must not be merely speculative,[61] but if it is strong enough, it is not only admissible[62] but may meet the clear and convincing standard.[63] If the defendant makes a representation that, given his other knowledge, a reasonable person *should* know to be false, the trier of fact may at times be permitted to infer that he *did* know it to be false and hence that he had made a knowingly false statement.[64]

Conscious ignorance. In line with the rules in *Derry v. Peek*, the defendant who is consciously aware that he does not know the truth of his representation is held responsible for the falsehood.[65] A similar idea is that the defendant is subject to liability if he asserts something of his own knowledge when he does not know the truth or falsity of the proposition,[66] knows he lacks information necessary to support such a statement,[67] or should expect that he will be understood as implicitly asserting knowledge he does not have.[68] If a fact is the kind that the defendant would be expected to know, his unqualified assertion of the fact implies that he does know it, so if the defendant does not have knowledge of the asserted fact, he can be found to have fraudulent intent. For example, a seller who assures the buyer that the slip covers are washable may imply that he has at least some basis for knowing that their colors will not run and may be liable when they do.[69]

---

[59]   Restatement (Third) of Torts: Liability for Economic Harm § 10 (2014).

[60]   Johnson v. Wysocki, 990 N.E.2d 456 (Ind. 2013) ("should have known" standard is insufficient for fraud); VF Corp. v. Wrexham Aviation Corp.,350 Md. 693, 704, 715 A.2d 188, 193 (1998) ("Negligence or misjudgment, however gross, does not satisfy the knowledge element").

[61]   Four R Cattle Co. v. Mullins, 253 Neb. 133, 570 N.W.2d 813 (1997).

[62]   See Edwards v. Travelers Ins. of Hartford, Conn., 563 F.2d 105 (6th Cir. 1977).

[63]   Clark v. Iowa Dep't of Revenue & Fin., 644 N.W.2d 310 (Iowa 2002); Kuo Feng Corp. v. Ma, 248 A.D.2d 168, 669 N.Y.S.2d 575 (1998).

[64]   See Stromberger v. 3M Co., 990 F.2d 974, 978 (7th Cir. 1993) ("No doubt some statements are so outlandish that no one in his right mind could think them true when he said them, and then intent to defraud could be inferred from the statement itself"); Ultramares Corp. v. Touche, 255 N.Y. 170, 191, 174 N.E. 441, 449 (1931) ("negligence or blindness, even when not equivalent to fraud, is nonetheless evidence to sustain an inference of fraud"); Restatement (Second) of Torts § 526 cmt. d (1977).

[65]   Receivables Purchasing Co., Inc. v. Engineering & Prof'l Servs., Inc., 510 F.3d 840, 843 (8th Cir. 2008) ("knowingly ignorant misrepresentations"); Borcherding v. Anderson Remodeling Co., Inc., 253 Ill. App. 3d 655, 660, 705, 624 N.E.2d 887, 893 (1993) (statement made "in culpable ignorance of its truth or falsity"); Gross v. Sussex Inc., 332 Md. 247, 630 A.2d 1156 (1993) (knowingly or in conscious disregard of its truth).

[66]   Florenzano v. Olson, 387 N.W.2d 168 (Minn. 1986).

[67]   Anchorage Chrysler Ctr., Inc. v. DaimlerChrysler Corp., 129 P.3d 905, 914 n.21 (Alaska 2006) (scienter requirement is met when the defendant "knows that he does not have the basis for his representation that he states or implies"); see Page Keeton, Fraud: The Necessity for an Intent to Deceive, 5 UCLA L. Rev. 583, 592 (1958) (defendant who makes an unqualified representation of fact realizing information was inadequate to justify a feeling of certainty about it).

[68]   See Schlossman's, Inc. v. Niewinski, 12 N.J. Super. 500, 507–08, 79 A.2d 870, 874 (1951).

[69]   Id. (rescission of the contract).

Defendant knows he does not know. Even if a defendant believes what he has asserted, he knows he lacks knowledge about the facts represented. Such a defendant has dishonestly represented at least one thing, namely the extent of his knowledge. He can readily avoid liability if he avoids making a statement as one of known fact, for example, by stating his belief or by indicating the limits of his knowledge. Liability in such cases is not only recognized, it is appropriate.

Slipping into negligence or strict liability. The term *knowledge* is highly uncertain. Suppose the defendant is in possession of a surveyor's map of his property showing ownership of 180 acres and relies upon it in representing to a potential buyer that the tract contains such acreage. He has not personally surveyed the area. Does he "know" the acreage? Or suppose he once knew a fact that put the acreage in doubt, such as the surveyor's assumption that a certain marker was the southwest corner, but that he forgot the assumption and relied quite honestly upon the map. A well-known older case imposed liability on similar facts,[70] although it would be hard to say that anything more than negligence was involved.

Intent to deceive. A number of opinions have said that the defendant must have an intent to deceive. Some statements of the rule appear to use the term interchangeably with or as a substitute for the *scienter* requirement.[71] Following this view, the Nebraska Court concluded that a separate instruction on intent to deceive was undesirable where an instruction on *scienter* falsehood was also given.[72] Others appear to state intent to deceive as a separate element of the claim, to be proved in addition to the elements listed in *Derry v. Peek*.[73] If intent to deceive is a separate element of the claim, then it may be difficult or impossible to impose liability merely on the ground that the defendant knows he does not know the truth, because a person who knows he does not know may nevertheless hold a strong belief in his statement and may wholly lack any intent to deceive. A court that wishes to enforce the liabilities envisioned in *Derry v. Peek* could avoid language on intent to deceive and say instead that the defendant must state a fact lacking belief in its truth and have an intent to induce reliance on that statement. Intent to induce reliance is in fact the language of the Restatement[74] and of some opinions.[75]

---

[70]   Chatham Furnace Co. v. Moffatt, 147 Mass. 403, 18 N.E. 168 (1888).

[71]   Johnson v. University Health Servs., Inc., 161 F.3d 1334 (11th Cir. 1998); Kimber v. Young, 137 F. 744 (8th Cir. 1905); Marten's Chevrolet, Inc. v. Seney, 292 Md. 328, 439 A.2d 534 (1982). The structure of the rule as envisioned in Prosser and Keeton § 107 is that the rule requires intent to deceive, which is then proved by proving a knowing falsehood, or a lack of belief in the statement, or a statement made in conscious ignorance.

[72]   Nielsen v. Adams, 223 Neb. 262, 388 N.W.2d 840 (1986).

[73]   Myers & Chapman, Inc. v. Thomas G. Evans, Inc., 323 N.C. 559, 374 S.E.2d 385 (1988). A single jurisdiction may sometimes state that, besides scienter, intent to deceive is required, while at other times may state that intent to induce reliance is the test. Compare In re Estate of McKenney, 953 A.2d 336 (D.C. 2008) (intent to deceive), with Media Gen., Inc. v. Tomlin, 532 F.3d 854 (D.C. Cir. 2008) (District of Columbia law, intent to induce reliance).

[74]   Restatement (Second) of Torts § 525 (1977) (requiring a "purpose" of inducing reliance); cf. id. § 531 ("reason to expect" reliance).

[75]   Seybert v. Cominco Alaska Exploration, 182 P.3d 1079, 1094 (Alaska 2008) (elements include scienter and intent to induce reliance); Foreman v. AS Mid-America, Inc., 255 Neb. 323, 586 N.W.2d 290 (1998); Marchant v. Cook, 967 P.2d 551 (Wyo. 1998).

C. NEGLIGENT MISREPRESENTATION

§ 43.5   Negligent Misrepresentation

Overview

Liability for negligent misrepresentation. Courts fully accept liability for *personal injury or property damage* resulting from negligent misrepresentations. However, negligence is frequently held to be an insufficient basis for liability in the case of pure or stand-alone *economic* harm.[76] Most courts hold only when defendants are under a duty, typically based on a special relationship or affirmative undertaking, can they be liable for negligent misrepresentation.[77] Where the negligent misrepresentation action is entertained because a duty of reasonable care is recognized, that duty supports a less favorable damages award.[78]

Key questions. Negligent misrepresentation claims raise two special problems. First, under what conditions is a duty of care owed to make one's representations accurate?[79] Second, given that a duty of care is owed to someone, does that duty run in favor of some third person who relies on the representation?[80]

Duty of Care

No duty. No precise formula for determining the existence of a duty of care has yet been authoritatively stated. Aside from fiduciaries and those in special relations of confidence, persons who are neither in the business of supplying information nor have a pecuniary interest in dealing with the plaintiff ordinarily have no duty of care and are thus liable only for knowingly false misrepresentations.[81] More broadly, the ordinary commercial adversary bargainer ordinarily has no duty to use care in supplying information to those with whom he bargains.[82] Likewise, one giving an ordinary business reference may be under no duty of care to verify the good qualities he to attributes a job seeker.[83] Where the plaintiff and defendant are in a contractual relationship, the

---

[76]   See Chapters 41 & 42.

[77]   See e.g., St. Joseph's Hosp. & Med. Ctr. v. Reserve Life Ins. Co., 154 Ariz. 307, 742 P.2d 808 (1987); Small v. Fritz Cos., Inc., 30 Cal.4th 167, 65 P.3d 1255 (2003); Barton v. City of Bristol, 291 Conn. 84, 967 A.2d 482 (2009); Holmes v. Grubman, 286 Ga. 636, 691 S.E.2d 196; Rinehart v. Morton Bldgs., Inc., 305 P.3d 622 (2013); D.R. Strong Consulting Eng'rs, Inc., 312 P.3d 620 (2013); Sturm v. Peoples Trust & Sav. Bank, 713 N.W.2d 1 (Iowa 2006) (limited to representations inducing dealings with third parties); Gossels v. Fleet Nat'l Bank, 453 Mass. 366, 902 N.E.2d 370 (2009); Valspar Refinish, Inc. v. Gaylord's, Inc., 764 N.W.2d 359 (Minn. 2009); Avanta Fed. Credit Union v. Shupak, 354 Mont. 372, 223 P.3d 863 (2009); Heard v. City of New York, 82 N.Y.2d 66, 623 N.E.2d 541 (1993); Restatement (Second) of Torts § 552 (1977).

[78]   Restatement (Second) of Torts § 552B (1977) (excluding benefit of the bargain damages). It is also possible that the plaintiff's comparative fault will reduce the award in negligent misrepresentation cases when it would not do so in intentional fraud cases. See 3 Dobbs, Hayden & Bublick, The Law of Torts § 672 (2d ed. 2011 & Supp.).

[79]   See 3 Dobbs, Hayden & Bublick, The Law of Torts § 667 (2d ed. 2011 & Supp.).

[80]   Id. § 681.

[81]   Restatement (Second) of Torts § 552(1) (1979) (providing for a duty of care if defendant has pecuniary interest in transaction, not requiring defendant be in the business of supplying the information).

[82]   Badger Pharmacal, Inc. v. Colgate-Palmolive Co., 1 F.3d 621 (7th Cir. 1993) (the plaintiff has "not persuaded us that, in the context of business dealings between sophisticated parties, Wisconsin law would impose a duty on each not to utter words negligently"); Sain v. Cedar Rapids Cmty. Sch. Dist., 626 N.W.2d 115 (Iowa 2001) (duty arises only when defendant is in the business of supplying information); Onita Pac. Corp. v. Trustees of Bronson, 315 Or. 149, 843 P.2d 890 (1992); see Alfred Hill, Damages for Innocent Misrepresentation, 73 Colum. L. Rev. 679, 685–88 (1973).

[83]   Hale v. George A. Hormel & Co., 48 Cal.App.3d 73, 121 Cal.Rptr. 144 (1975) (recommending a seller of goods); Richland Sch. Dist. v. Mabton Sch. Dist., 111 Wash. App. 377, 45 P.3d 580 (2002) (school district

economic loss rule will force the same result in some cases, leaving the plaintiff to rely on her contract rights, if any.[84]

Special duties. A duty of care not to be negligent in supplying information is the exception, not the rule. The duty of care arises only when the defendant undertakes such a duty, [85] or when, based on a special relationship, the plaintiff is led reasonably to expect reasonable care for her interests.

Defendants retained to exercise reasonable care in providing information. The clear cases for a duty of care and concomitant liability for negligent misrepresentations are those in which the defendant has expressly or implicitly undertaken to exercise care for the benefit of the plaintiff. That is ordinarily the case when the defendant is retained for the very purpose of providing accurate information. In such a case, the relationship of the parties suggests that the defendant has implicitly undertaken to use reasonable or professional care. Consequently, their clients can recover for economic damages inflicted by the negligent misstatements of lawyers,[86] accountants,[87] abstractors,[88] notaries,[89] and others retained or consulted to determine or certify a given state of facts[90] or who assume such duties.[91]

Statutes. Sometimes statutes prescribe particular duties and the liability that follows from breach.[92] Where a professional is under a duty of reasonable investigation, his negligence in failing to discover facts the client is entitled to know is actionable on

---

gave laudatory recommendations for an employee, omitting to mention that he had been charged with child molesting).

   [84]   See Alejandre v. Bull, 159 Wash.2d 674, 153 P.3d 864 (2007).

   [85]   See Krahmer v. Christie's Inc., 903 A.2d 773 (Del. Ch. 2006) ("A plaintiff may only recover for negligent misrepresentation where there is a fiduciary or special relationship between the parties"; there was no special relation between buyer of painting and auction house); Cooper v. Berkshire Life Ins. Co., 148 Md.App. 41, 810 A.2d 1045 (2002) ("the duty to furnish the correct information arises when the relationship is of the nature that one party has the right to rely upon the other for information. The precise degree of the relationship that must exist before recovery will be allowed is a question that defies generalization"); Loosli v. City of Salem, 345 Or. 303, 194 P.3d 623 (2008) (statute imposed duty on city only for benefit of public, not for guidance of citizen who suffered economic loss when the city negligently approved business location forbidden by city's zoning rules, forcing the citizen to move afterward); Stillwater Condo. Ass'n v. Town of Salem, 140 N.H. 505, 668 A.2d 38 (1995) (no special relationship existed and defendant did not undertake a duty).

   [86]   When the claim is asserted by the client, it may be conceptualized as one for "malpractice" rather than "misrepresentation," even though based upon a misstatement of fact. Mecca v. Shang, 685 N.Y.S.2d 458 (App. Div. 1999) (negligent misrepresentation claim should have been dismissed as it was but one form of the lawyer malpractice claim and duplicative); Safeway Managing Gen. Agency, Inc. v. Clark & Gamble, 985 S.W.2d 166 (Tex. App. 1998) (since insurer who retained attorneys to defend insured was not "client," the claim was not one for malpractice but for negligent misrepresentation). Lawyers may be liable to non-clients for negligent "misrepresentation."

   [87]   E.g., Cordial v. Ernst & Young, 199 W.Va. 119, 483 S.E.2d 248 (1996).

   [88]   Williams v. Polgar, 391 Mich. 6, 215 N.W.2d 149 (1974).

   [89]   Keck v. Keck, 54 OhioApp.2d 128, 375 N.E.2d 1256 (1977).

   [90]   Barrie v. V.P. Exterminators, Inc., 625 So.2d 1007 (La. 1993) (termite inspector's certificate); Glanzer v. Shepard, 233 N.Y. 236, 135 N.E. 275 (1922) (public weighmaster certificate of weight in commercial transaction); Aesoph v. Kusser, 498 N.W.2d 654 (S.D. 1993) (insurance agent representing that coverage was not available).

   [91]   Culp Constr. Co. v. Buildmart Mall, 795 P.2d 650 (Utah 1990) (title company may have assumed duty of abstractor).

   [92]   E.g., Cal. Gov't. Code § 8214 (liability of notary).

the same basis.[93] By statute, a real estate agent for the seller may owe a duty to the buyer to independently substantiate the information in the listing.[94]

Fiduciaries. Courts have recognized that a fiduciary, confidential, or other special relationship between the parties implies such an undertaking or expectation that the defendant would exercise reasonable care. Fiduciaries and those in similar confidential relationships are accordingly liable for negligent misrepresentation.[95] When the facts are peculiarly within the knowledge of the defendant and inaccessible to the plaintiff, commercial dealings between the parties must come to a halt unless the plaintiff can put confidence in reasonable accuracy of the defendant's statements. So courts sometimes impose a duty of care when the defendant had peculiar knowledge or expertise.[96] Perhaps in some of these cases, the plaintiff has reposed confidence in the defendant's special knowledge and the defendant has accepted that confidence as a basis for their dealings.[97] Similarly, the particular facts or the words or deeds of the defendant may warrant the belief that he has undertaken to exercise care in the plaintiff's behalf.[98] That may be the case even though on some issues in the transaction the plaintiff and the defendant are bargaining adversely to each other.[99]

Duty of care under the Restatement. The Restatement provides that anyone who has a pecuniary interest in a transaction is subject to liability for negligently supplying information intended for the guidance of others.[100] As phrased, the Restatement does not require the defendant to be in the business of supplying information, only that he supply it either (a) in the *course* of his business (whatever that business may be) or (b) in connection with a transaction in which he is financially interested. The formulation is

---

[93]   Glanzer v. Shepard, 233 N.Y. 236, 135 N.E. 275 (1922); see Lumbermens Mut. Cas. Co. v. Thornton, 92 S.W.3d 259 (Mo. Ct. App. 2002) (auditor's failure to discover lack of appropriate internal controls that would have prevented embezzlement losses).

[94]   See Fisher v. Kahler, 641 N.W.2d 122 (S.D. 2002).

[95]   See McAuley v. Int'l Bus. Mach. Corp., 165 F.3d 1038 (6th Cir. 1999) (ERISA fiduciary's duties); Kimmell v. Schaefer, 89 N.Y.2d 257, 675 N.E.2d 450, 652 N.Y.S.2d 715 (1996) (even though defendant was to gain a commission if the plaintiff invested in project, defendant's expertise and special relation sufficed to require reasonable care).

[96]   See, e.g., Fine Host Corp. Sec. Litig., 25 F.Supp.2d 61 (D. Conn. 1998) (emphasizing unique knowledge or specialized expertise); Colonial Imports, Inc. v. Carlton Nw., Inc., 121 Wash.2d 726, 853 P.2d 913 (1993); cf. Westby v. Gorsuch, 112 Wash.App. 558, 50 P.3d 284 (2002) (trial court not in error in submitting negligent misrepresentation claim as well as fraud claim against knowledgeable buyer-dealer who told seller the item in question wasn't worth even $500 when in fact it later sold for over $100,000; no actual discussion of duty).

[97]   Confidence reposed and accepted establishes a confidential relationship and a duty of care. See City of Atascadero v. Merrill Lynch, Pierce, Fenner & Smith, Inc., 68 Cal.App.4th 445, 80 Cal.Rptr.2d 329 (1999).

[98]   Cf. Lacher v. Superior Court, 230 Cal.App.3d 1038, 281 Cal.Rptr. 640 (1991) (developer, to obtain neighbor's support for development, assured neighbors that buildings would be one story and not block views, public policy imposed duty of care in making representations).

[99]   See Jackson v. State, 287 Mont. 473, 956 P.2d 35 (1998) (state revealing some information about prospective adoptee in state's custody was undertaking duty to prospective adopting family to exercise care in its representations). Along these lines, cases have held or assumed that a prospective employer, inducing a recruit to accept a job, is under a duty of care and hence liable for negligent misrepresentations. E.g., Van Buren v. Pima Cmty. Coll. Dist., 113 Ariz. 85, 546 P.2d 821 (1976); Pollmann v. Belle Plaine Livestock Auction, Inc., 567 N.W.2d 405 (Iowa 1997); Griesi v. Atlantic Gen. Hosp. Corp., 360 Md. 1, 756 A.2d 548 (2000); cf. Craine v. Trinity Coll., 259 Conn. 625, 791 A.2d 518 (2002) (college advising tenure-track professor to continue along lines she was following could be found to be a negligent representation that if she did so, tenure would follow); but cf. Conway v. Pacific Univ., 324 Or. 231, 924 P.2d 818 (1996) (university owed no duty of care in its representations about tenure in the absence of some relationship beyond employment).

[100]   Restatement (Second) of Torts § 552 (1977).

thus more favorable to plaintiffs than the narrowest rules stated in some cases.[101] Unfortunately, the formulation could also be read to include adversary bargainers who do not undertake to exercise reasonable care for the other's informational interests. The Restatement Third follows the Restatement Second "with small changes" requiring invited reliance.[102]

Negligent misrepresentation to a contracting party and the economic loss rule. Although most courts appear to recognize negligent misrepresentation as an exception to the economic loss rule, thus permitting a claim for pure economic loss based on negligent representations that induce a contract,[103] some courts have said that the economic loss rules bar the plaintiff, or at least a sophisticated plaintiff's negligent misrepresentation claim for commercial harm against a defendant with whom he has a contractual relationship.[104] In that view, if the claim cannot be asserted on grounds of intentional misrepresentation, it must be asserted as a contract claim or not at all. The idea is that, between contracting parties, the contract's provisions should control. There is also the idea that if a point covered by a misrepresentation was important to the plaintiff, that point would have been expressed in the contract, and if it was not, then the plaintiff should suffer the risk that the trier of fact will believe the point was not so important as the plaintiff now claims.[105] However, not all agreements between sophisticated bargainers call for the same result. A lawyer's contract with his client, for example, should not preclude recovery by the client for a negligent misrepresentation upon which the client relied to her detriment.[106] Statutes may impose duties of care upon adversary bargainers, thus permitting a tort claim,[107] and the defendant's undertakings

---

[101] Excavation Technologies, Inc. v. Columbia Gas Co. of Pa., 985 A.2d 840 (Pa. 2009) (gas company was under a statutory duty to mark location of its underground lines and mis-marked some; when contractor struck lines, causing him expensive delay, court held gas company was not in the business of providing information and denied liability, also saying that the economic loss rule applied to bar the claim in such a case).

[102] Restatement (Third) of Torts: Liability for Economic Harms § 5 (2012).

[103] See, e.g., Level 3 Commc'ns, LLC v. Liebert Corp., 535 F.3d 1146 (10th Cir 2008) (distinguishing BRW, Inc. v. Dufficy & Sons, Inc., 99 P.3d 66 (Colo.2004), where the contract created the specific duty to communicate certain information so that it was appropriate to limit the plaintiff to its contract remedy); In re TJX Cos. Retail Sec. Breach Litig., 564 F.3d 489 (1st Cir. 2009) (upholding negligent misrepresentation claim against a motion to dismiss, while dismissing plain negligence claim on the same facts under the economic loss rule); Van Sickle Constr. Co. v. Wachovia Commercial Mortg., Inc., 783 N.W.2d 684 (Iowa 2010) ("Application of the economic loss doctrine in negligent misrepresentation cases would essentially eliminate the tort."); Terracon Consultants W., Inc. v. Mandalay Resort Group, 206 P.3d 81, 88 (Nev. 2009) ("negligent misrepresentation is a special financial harm claim for which tort recovery is permitted because without such liability the law would not exert significant financial pressures to avoid such negligence"); Plourde Sand & Gravel v. JGI E., Inc., 154 N.H. 791, 917 A.2d 1250, 1254 (2007) ("we recognize that a cause of action in tort for economic damages may be maintained under the 'special relationship' or negligent misrepresentation exceptions"). On the economic loss rules, see Chapters 41 & 42 and 3 Dobbs, Hayden & Bublick, The Law of Torts § 686 (2d ed. 2011 & Supp.).

[104] E.g., Apollo Group, Inc. v. Avnet, Inc., 58 F.3d 477 (9th Cir. 1995) (forecasting Arizona law); Borish v. Russell, 230 P.3d 646 (Wash. Ct. App. 2010) (negligent misrepresentation claim against contracting party barred by economic loss rule); Excel Constr., Inc. v. HKM Eng'g, Inc., 228 P.3d 40 (Wyo. 2010) ("While a party may be entitled to maintain a claim for intentional misrepresentation or fraud . . . notwithstanding the economic loss rule . . . Excel did not present such a claim . . . and Excel's claim for negligent misrepresentation is barred.").

[105] Cf. All-Tech Telecom, Inc. v. Amway Corp., 174 F.3d 862 (7th Cir. 1999) (discussing the concerns).

[106] Collins v. Reynard, 154 Ill.2d 48, 607 N.E.2d 1185 (1992).

[107] See Beaux v. Jacob, 30 P.3d 90 (Alaska 2001) (liability for negligent failure to communicate in responding to required real estate transfer disclosure form).

or special relationships with the plaintiff may counsel liability for negligent misrepresentations.[108]

D. INNOCENT MISREPRESENTATION

§ 43.6 Innocent Misrepresentation

General rule. Most cases impose strict liability for misrepresentations only in one of two special and limited cases—when the representation is construed to be a warranty, and when the plaintiff's suit is for rescission or rescission-equivalent damages. These forms of strict liability would ordinarily apply only to the contracting parties.[109] Innocent misrepresentation may also operate to toll the statute of limitations[110] or furnish a defense to a breach of contract against one who relied on the representation.[111]

Liability for innocent misrepresentations under warranty theory. The defendant may be subjected to liability for innocent misrepresentation causing stand-alone economic harm when the defendant undertakes to guarantee the truth of the matter represented; that is, when his representation is a warranty. Where a warranty is breached, the plaintiff may recover the contract or loss of bargain measure of damages.[112] The most familiar warranties are the UCC warranties by sellers of goods. The UCC treats any affirmation of fact relating to the goods sold as a warranty. Samples, models, and descriptions may have the same effect.[113] In addition, the UCC imposes an implied warranty of merchantability which requires that the goods must be at least able to pass without objection in the trade and that they are fit for the ordinary purposes for which such goods are used.[114] If the seller breaches these warranties, he is liable for the economic harm suffered as a result, without proof of fraud or even negligence.

Express warranties. The implied warranty described by the UCC is ordinarily limited to sales of tangible chattels. But an express warranty is still possible in any kind of transaction. For instance, the seller of a business may warrant in writing that the financial records attached to the closing documents are accurate and may be liable without fault of any kind for breach of such a warranty.[115] And some representations, especially by sellers, may be construed as warranties under the particular circumstances of the case.[116]

---

[108] See Chapters 41 & 42.

[109] See Restatement (Second) of Torts § 552C (1977).

[110] See University of Pittsburgh v. Townsend, 542 F.3d 513 (6th Cir. 2008) (Pennsylvania law, calling it "fraud and concealment," but nevertheless recognizing that unintended "concealment" can stop the defendant from pleading the statute of limitations).

[111] E.g., Jocelyn Canyon, Inc. v. Lentjes, 292 Ga. App. 608, 664 S.E.2d 908 (2008).

[112] Johnson v. Healy, 176 Conn. 97, 405 A.2d 54 (1978); as to damages measures, see 3 Dobbs, Hayden & Bublick, The Law of Torts §§ 687–92 (2d ed. 2011 & Supp.).

[113] UCC § 2–313. An affirmation that is mere puffery, however, is not a warranty, though some "opinion" type statements may fall into the warranty rather than the puffery category. See David A. Hoffman, The Best Puffery Article Ever, 91 Iowa L. Rev. 1395, 1411–15 (2006).

[114] UCC § 2–314.

[115] VF Corp. v. Wrexham Aviation Corp., 350 Md. 693, 715 A.2d 188 (1998).

[116] Johnson v. Healy, 176 Conn. 97, 405 A.2d 54 (1978) (homebuilder assertions); Richard v. A. Waldman & Sons, Inc., 155 Conn. 343, 232 A.2d 307 (1967) (real estate developer sold a house and lot with a plot plan showing a 20-foot side yard that complied with zoning regulations; the parties later discovered that the house was so close to the next lot that to enter the house required a trespass; the representation was construed as a warranty). At one time, Alaska imposed strict liability for innocent misrepresentations by real estate sellers, but that has been changed by statute. See Amyot v. Luchini, 932 P.2d 244 (Alaska 1997).

Limits on warranty; oral representation. Apart from the implied warranties in chattel sales, an oral representation is not ordinarily construed to be a warranty unless the contract specifies it as such. Even if an oral representation is construed as a contractual warranty or promise, the parol evidence rule[117] and any valid disclaimer clause[118] will likely bar the warranty claim if the transaction is later reduced to a complete writing. If the oral representation is conceived as a warranty that amounts to a tort rather than a contract obligation, the economic loss rule, which requires courts to focus upon the contractual rights, will probably bar the claim.[119]

Liability for innocent misrepresentation in rescission or for rescission-equivalent damages. Rescission is distinct from the tort action for damages. Rescission voids the transaction and requires each party to restore what he received in it. Since the defendant's misrepresentation is innocent, neither intentional nor negligent, it is essentially like a mistake. Given that the defendant and the plaintiff share that mistake, rescission on the same basis as mutual mistake is appropriate even though the defendant is not at fault. Courts traditionally avoid or rescind transactions for innocent misrepresentations, even though the same court would reject a tort damages claim for such a misrepresentation. That is to say, scienter is not required to permit rescission.[120] Rescission may thus be the more advantageous claim for the plaintiff whose evidence of intent or negligence is weak. In addition, courts may use the preponderance of evidence standard of proof rather than the clear and convincing standard.[121] For rescission, however, the plaintiff must act promptly,[122] perhaps long before the statute of limitations has run on the damages claim.

Fact represented must be basic or material. Rescission for mutual mistake was traditionally limited to mistakes that went to the very basis of the transaction; a mistake about a material matter that was not basic or of the essence was insufficient.[123] To the extent that innocent misrepresentation is a special case of mutual mistake, the same requirement should apply. However, courts and authorities insist that in spite of the defendant's innocence, a misrepresentation that is merely material and not basic at all will suffice to permit rescission.[124] This rule would, at least in theory, permit the plaintiff

---

[117] Betaco, Inc. v. Cessna Aircraft Co., 103 F.3d 1281 (7th Cir. 1996) (if writing fully integrates agreement, parol evidence of other terms is not admissible; disclaimer of warranty and merger clause are among factors indicating integration); Martin & Martin, Inc. v. Bradley Enters., Inc., 256 Va. 288, 504 S.E.2d 849 (1998) (enforcing merger clause).

[118] Gibson v. Capano, 241 Conn. 725, 699 A.2d 68 (1997).

[119] Apollo Group, Inc. v. Avnet, Inc., 58 F.3d 477 (9th Cir. 1995).

[120] E.g., In re Estate of McKenney, 953 A.2d 336, 342 (D.C. 2008) (a "party to a contract can seek rescission relying on a material misrepresentation without establishing fraud. . . . Fraud need not be proven to rescind a contract; instead, a party must only show that the misrepresentation 'would have been likely to have induced a reasonable recipient to make the contract.' "); Bortz v. Noon, 729 A.2d 555 (Pa. 1999) (recognizing rescission for innocent misrepresentations but rejecting liability in damages).

[121] See Estate of McKenney, 953 A.2d 336, 342 (D.C. 2008).

[122] Knudsen v. Jensen, 521 N.W.2d 415 (S.D. 1994).

[123] See 2 Dan B. Dobbs, Law of Remedies § 11.3 (2d ed. 1993); Restatement (Second) of Contracts § 152 (1981).

[124] Hyler v. Garner, 548 N.W.2d 864 (Iowa 1996); French Energy, Inc. v. Alexander, 818 P.2d 1234, 1238 (Okla. 1991) ("Where innocent misrepresentation or non-disclosure is the sole ground for restitution, restitution is granted only if the misrepresentation or non-disclosure was material. Where mutual mistake is the sole ground for restitution, restitution is granted only if the mistake was basic"); Halpert v. Rosenthal, 107 R.I. 406, 267 A.2d 730 (1970); Restatement (Second) of Contracts § 164(a) (1981) (permitting the plaintiff to avoid a contract if it was induced either by a fraudulent or a material, non-fraudulent misrepresentation); id.

to overthrow a whole deal by rescission merely because of an erroneous statement about price or costs that could be remedied fully by a small damages award.[125]

Contract limitations on liability for innocent representation; disclaimers. If, by disclaimers or otherwise, the contract indicates that the defendant will not be liable for mistakes, and the defendant delivers the performance promised by the contract, rescission must be denied if the contract is to be honored.[126] At least in the case of formal non-consumer contracts, it would seem that the plaintiff cannot justifiably rely upon representations plainly inconsistent with the contract's own provisions or disclaimers,[127] a result also obtained by excluding evidence of prior misrepresentations under the parol evidence rule.[128] As in the case of a claimed warranty, a written and fully integrated contract will determine the rights of the parties.

Limited damages in innocent misrepresentation cases. The plaintiff deceived by an innocent misrepresentation is one of two innocent and mistaken parties and at most should recover out of pocket damages. Such a measure would ordinarily be the financial equivalent of rescission.[129] And since the plaintiff could not rescind against a third person who is not a party to the contract, she should not recover damages for innocent misrepresentation against a third person, either.[130] Besides these limitations, some forms of rescission or rescission-equivalent damages recoveries can have unjust and undesirable effects that are discussed below in connection with the topic of remedies.

E. MAJOR ISSUES

§ 43.7 Reliance

Reliance in Fact

Requirement of reliance. A representation is not actionable unless the plaintiff in fact relies upon it.[131] To rely, the plaintiff must enter a transaction in whole or part because of the representation.[132] For example, the plaintiff who enters into a transaction

---

§ 476 (same rule as to acts in performance induced by innocent misrepresentations). Statutes may eliminate this liability. See Amyot v. Luchini, 932 P.2d 244 (Alaska 1997).

[125] "Sometimes avoidance of a contract or rescission is a benign and moderate remedy as compared to damages. At other times rescission is a disruptive remedy." 2 Dan B. Dobbs, The Law of Remedies § 11.3 (2d ed. 1993).

[126] As in, e.g., Knieper v. United States, 38 Fed.Cl. 128 (1997).

[127] See Morris v. United States, 33 Fed.Cl. 733, 746 (1995); but cf. Halpert v. Rosenthal, 107 R.I. 406, 267 A.2d 730 (1970) (general merger clause did not prevent rescission for innocent misrepresentation).

[128] See Calomiris v. Woods, 353 Md. 425, 727 A.2d 358 (1999) (parol evidence rule bars admission of evidence of prior representations when the plaintiff claims only innocent misrepresentations).

[129] Restatement (Second) of Torts § 552C (1977) (limited to sale, rental, or exchanges but purporting to permit out of pocket damages in all such cases of innocent misrepresentation); Anzalone v. Strand, 14 Mass. App. Ct. 45, 436 N.E.2d 960 (1982) (innocent misrepresentation). Some opinions seem to have been unaware of the distinction, but possibly because the liability was imposed on the ground of contractually implicit warranty rather than on the basis of the mistake-rescission analysis. See Richard v. A. Waldman & Sons, Inc., 155 Conn. 343, 232 A.2d 307 (1967).

[130] Norman v. Brown, Todd & Heyburn, 693 F.Supp. 1259 (D. Mass. 1988); see M & D, Inc. v. McConkey,231 Mich.App. 22, 585 N.W.2d 33 (1998) (privity required).

[131] Restatement (Third) of Torts: Liability for Economic Harms § 11 (2014) (fraud). Restatement (Second) of Torts §§ 537(a) (fraudulent representations), 552(1) (negligent representations), 552C (innocent representation) (1977).

[132] Small v. Fritz Cos., Inc., 30 Cal.4th 167, 132 Cal.Rptr.2d 490, 65 P.3d 1255 (2003) (owner who refrains from selling his securities because of a misrepresentation has relied); St. Paul Fire & Marine Ins. Co. v. Russo Bros., Inc., 641 A.2d 1297 (R.I. 1994); Restatement (Second) of Torts § 537(a) (1977). Thus the bare

with the defendant does not rely upon the defendant's misrepresentation if she enters into the transaction without a belief in its truth, or doesn't learn of the misrepresentation until after the transaction has closed,[133] or would have entered the transaction whether or not the misrepresentation had been made.[134] The plaintiff may rely on several things, but the defendant's representation must be one of them.[135]

Reliance and causation. The requirement of reliance is one of the requirements of causation in misrepresentation cases—if the plaintiff has not relied, the misrepresentation has caused no harm. The requirement of pecuniary harm is the other causal requirement—if there is no pecuniary harm, the defendant's misrepresentation has not caused cognizable damages. Reliance is thus necessary to show causation, but not sufficient to do so. It may be that reliance serves other principles of fraud law, too,[136] but liability will be imposed only if the defendant's misrepresentation causes cognizable harm, tested in part by the reliance requirement.

Justified Reliance and Comparative Fault

Requirement of justified reliance. According to most courts, bare reliance is not enough.[137] The plaintiff must go on to show that she justifiably relied.[138] This is also the position of the Restatement Third of Torts.[139] Reliance upon the defendant's material representations is ordinarily justified unless the plaintiff is on notice that the statement

claim that the defendant is guilty of "fraud" for intentionally overcharging or underpaying the plaintiff sums due will fail because the plaintiff has relied upon nothing. Such a claim looks like a plain contract claim. See Pioneer Res. Corp. v. Nami Res. Co., LLC, 2006 WL 1778318 (E.D. Ky. 2006) (unreported).

[133] Lovejoy v. AT&T Corp., 92 Cal.App.4th 85, 111 Cal.Rptr.2d 711 (2001) (allegation of AT&T's slamming, falsely representing to plaintiff's carrier for an 800 number that plaintiff wished to switch to AT&T; plaintiff knew nothing of the switch until AT&T then cut off his 800 service; no reliance on the alleged misrepresentation; however, plaintiff had a good claim for fraudulent *concealment*).

[134] Schaaf v. Highfield, 127 Wash.2d 17, 896 P.2d 665 (1995) (plaintiff-buyer did not rely upon negligent representation about roof because he intended to construct a new roof anyway, and further because he received the representation after purchase, not before).

[135] Engalla v. Permanente Med. Group, Inc., 15 Cal.4th 951, 976–77, 938 P.2d 903, 64 Cal.Rptr.2d 843 (1997) ("It is not . . . necessary that [a plaintiff's] reliance upon the truth of the fraudulent misrepresentation be the sole or even the predominant or decisive factor in influencing his conduct. . . . It is enough that the representation has played a substantial part, and so has been a substantial factor, in influencing his decision.") (quoting Restatement (Second) of Torts § 546 cmt. b); Horton v. Tyree, 104 W.Va. 238, 139 S.E. 737 (1927).

[136] John C.P. Goldberg, Anthony J. Sebok, & Benjamin C. Zipursky, The Place of Reliance in Fraud, 48 Ariz. L. Rev. 1001 (2006). The authors argue that the tort of fraud protects the plaintiff's interest in freedom to make economic decisions undistorted by misinformation generated by others, and this interest is not invaded unless the plaintiff relies in fact on that misinformation. In that view, the plaintiff's interest in avoiding harm from fraud is not so much the point as protecting the plaintiff's freedom to make decisions undistorted by false information.

[137] Some consumer fraud statutes eliminate the justified reliance requirement in cases brought under those statutes. See, e.g., Gennari v. Weichert Co. Realtors, 148 N.J. 582, 691 A.2d 350 (1997); see also White v. Wyeth, 227 W.Va. 131, 705 S.E.2d 828 (2010) (surveying virtually all states' unfair competition statutes on whether they require reliance of any kind, holding that such West Virginia's Consumer Credit and Protection Act does require reliance in a private consumer fraud action).

[138] E.g., Stewart Title Guar. Co. v. Dude, 708 F.3d 1191 (10th Cir. 2013); Hyler v. Garner, 548 N.W.2d 864 (Iowa 1996). Justified reliance is a jury issue if reasonable people can differ. See Jeffrey v. Methodist Hosps., 956 N.E.2d 151 (Ind. Ct. App. 2011); Marcus Bros. Textiles, Inc. v. Price Waterhouse, LLP, 350 N.C. 214, 513 S.E.2d 320 (1999); Doyle v. Fairfield Mach. Co., Inc., 120 Ohio App.3d 192, 697 N.E.2d 667 (1997). Where representations are immaterial, or may count as opinion, statements of law, future predictions, or puffing, however, the plaintiff's reliance may be found to be unjustified as a matter of law. See 3 Dobbs, Hayden & Bublick, The Law of Torts §§ 675–78 (2d ed. 2011 & Supp.). Reliance on ambiguous remarks may also be found to be unreasonable as a matter of law. See Greenberg, Trager & Herbst, LLP v. HSBC Bank USA, 17 N.Y.3d 565, 934 N.Y.S.2d 43, 958 N.E.2d 77, 75 U.C.C. Rep. Serv. 2d 775 (2011) (alleged oral statement by bank representative that check had "cleared").

[139] Restatement (Third) of Torts: Liability for Economic Harm § 11 (2014).

is not to be trusted or knows the statement to be false. Reliance is ordinarily not justifiable if the misrepresentation (a) is not material; (b) is mere puffing, or states an opinion or judgment of one without specialized knowledge and that does not imply assertions of fact; (c) predicts some future course of events over which the defendant has little or no control; (d) states a legal conclusion by one without specialized knowledge and who does not imply assertions of fact. The rule is not a causal rule; reliance of any kind, justifiable or not, establishes bare causation. Instead, the justifiable reliance requirement is a limitation on the defendant's duty.

Distinguishing justifiable reliance from comparative fault. Some courts still use the term "reasonable reliance" rather than "justifiable reliance," and tend to equate it with contributory negligence of the plaintiff.[140] Although some opinions use the language loosely, most courts use the term justifiable reliance and treat that term as something quite different from contributory negligence or comparative fault.[141]

Comparative fault as a separate and additional issue in misrepresentation cases. Courts have applied comparative fault rules under the objective reasonable person standard to bar or reduce damages when the defendant's misrepresentation is merely negligent.[142] Comparative fault rules have generally not been applied in cases of intentional, fraudulent misrepresentations[143] or to cases of breach of fiduciary duty.[144] However, a little authority suggests that comparative fault of the plaintiff could reduce damages or even in extreme cases bar recovery against a fraudulent tortfeasor,[145] and a little goes to the other end of the spectrum by rejecting comparative fault apportionment even in negligent misrepresentation cases.[146] Courts have also limited the use of the comparative fault defense by professionals like accountants or auditors to cases in which

---

[140] See Foremost Ins. Co. v. Parham, 693 So.2d 409 (Ala. 1997) (returning to "reasonable reliance" standard when plaintiff fails to read a document she signed).

[141] See Field v. Mans, 516 U.S. 59, 116 S.Ct. 437, 133 L.Ed.2d 351 (1995) (discussing and reviewing many authorities); Cocchiara v. Lithia Motors, Inc., 297 P.3d 1277 (Or. 2013).

[142] E.g., Williams Ford, Inc. v. Hartford Courant Co., 232 Conn. 559, 657 A.2d 212 (1995) (although comparative fault statute covered only personal injury and property damages, court would use comparative fault approach to the plaintiff's contributory fault in negligent misrepresentation case); ESCA Corp. v. KPMG Peat Marwick, 135 Wash.2d 820, 959 P.2d 651 (1998) (similar). Sonja Larsen, Annotation, Applicability of Comparative Negligence Doctrine to Actions Based on Negligent Misrepresentation, 22 A.L.R.5th 464 (1995). Traditionally, contributory negligence had no role in strict liability claims, but that has changed in products liability suits for injury and property damage. See 2 Dobbs, Hayden & Bublick, The Law of Torts § 470 (2d ed. 2011 & Supp.). Unless the rule of strict liability for misrepresentations is intended to protect the negligent plaintiff from her own fault, comparative negligence seems as appropriate in innocent as in negligent misrepresentation cases. Comparative fault principles were invoked in Gennari v. Weichert Co. Realtors, 148 N.J. 582, 691 A.2d 350 (1997), as between defendants. Contra, for reasons that may be hard to generalize, Reda v. Sincaban, 145 Wis.2d 266, 426 N.W.2d 100 (Ct. App. 1988).

[143] See Edwards v. Travelers Ins. of Hartford, Conn., 563 F.2d 105 (6th Cir. 1977); Greycas, Inc. v. Proud, 826 F.2d 1560, 23 Fed. R. Evid. Serv. 888 (7th Cir. 1987).

[144] Neff v. Bud Lewis, Co., 89 N.M. 145, 548 P.2d 107 (1976).

[145] Bangert Bros. Constr. Co. v. Kiewit W. Co., 310 F.3d 1278 (10th Cir. 2002); see Andrew R. Klein, Comparative Fault and Fraud, 48 Ariz. L. Rev. 983, 992–93 (2006). In Bangert, supra, the Tenth Circuit relied on a decision of the Colorado Supreme Court holding that comparative fault apportionment was required in a personal injury case when one actor was guilty of intentional wrong and another chargeable only with negligence. However, the Colorado statute requiring comparative fault apportionment by its own terms applied only in suits brought for "death or an injury to person or property." Colo. Rev. Stat. Ann. § 13–21–111.5. The claim in Bangert Bros. was for stand-alone economic harm, that is, money losses without damage to the claimant's property or person, so the statute seems facially inapt. The Bangert Bros. approach could be upheld by saying that "property" in the statute includes stand-alone economic loss but until such an unusual and expansive interpretation is advanced by the Colorado Court, Bangert Bros. might be regarded as fragile authority for apportionment that favors an intentionally fraudulent actor.

[146] Estate of Braswell v. People's Credit Union, 602 A.2d 510 (R.I. 1992).

the fault of the plaintiff-client contributes to the accountants' failure to perform their work.[147] Professor Klein has argued in favor of applying comparative fault rules in intentional fraud cases, not in addition to the justifiable reliance rules, but instead of them.[148]

Plaintiff's failure to investigate—general rule. When the defendant is guilty of actual *scienter* fraud and not merely negligent misrepresentation, the plaintiff is ordinarily justified in relying upon the defendant's material representations without any investigation at all,[149] even though those representations come from an adverse bargainer[150] and could be checked by examining courthouse records.[151] Commerce thrives when parties can conclude transactions without extensive investigation of representations, which can add significant transaction costs as well as delay. As Judge Easterbrook said, "Telling the truth is cheap, while nosing out deceit is expensive. Requiring all lenders, investors, and so on to investigate every representation made to them would be extravagantly wasteful. . . ."[152] The rule permitting reliance unless the plaintiff is on notice that would excite suspicions in a reasonable person thus serves good commercial policy as well as ordinary considerations of fairness.

§ 43.8 Factual Representations: Opinion, Law and Prediction

General rules. Courts have said repeatedly that a claim for misrepresentation lies only for misrepresentation of a fact, or as they say for emphasis, a past or existing fact.[153] Statements that are merely opinion and statements that are merely promises or predictions of the future,[154] do not qualify as representations of fact. Puffery, exaggerated and vague statements such as those praising a product as "first class" or

---

[147] Steiner Corp. v. Johnson & Higgins of Cal., 135 F.3d 684, 688 (10th Cir. 1998); ("a professional holding himself out to serve clients or patients is liable for his negligent performance of duties undertaken and may not be relieved of such liability by his clients' or patients' actions in causing or getting involved in the very conditions which the professional was employed and undertook to treat or remedy"); Board of Trs. of Cmty. Coll. Dist. No. 508, County of Cook v. Coopers & Lybrand, 208 Ill.2d 259, 281 Ill.Dec. 56 (2003); Stroud v. Arthur Andersen & Co., 37 P.3d 783 (Okla. 2001).

[148] Andrew R. Klein, Comparative Fault and Fraud, 48 Ariz. L. Rev. 983 (2006).

[149] Gross v. Sussex, Inc., 332 Md. 247, 630 A.2d 1156 (1993) (excellent discussion of various statements of the rule); Townsend v. Felthousen, 156 N.Y. 618, 51 N.E. 279 (1898); Horton v. Tyree, 104 W.Va. 238, 139 S.E. 737 (1927); Halpert v. Rosenthal, 107 R.I. 406, 267 A.2d 730 (1970) (nothing absurd in statement that house had no termites that would put buyer on notice to investigate). Some early cases took the view that bargainers should distrust and hence investigate everything said. The change in this attitude has been attributed to changed standards of business ethics. See 2 Harper, James & Gray, The Law of Torts § 7.12 (3d ed. 2006); Prosser & Keeton § 108, at 751. The change may also be due to better perception that, subject to the economic loss rule and any effective exculpatory clauses, commercial transactions would be unduly costly and even at times impossible if the plaintiff were required to investigate every fact asserted by the defendant.

[150] Hoyt Props., Inc. v. Productions Res. Group, LLC, 716 N.W.2d 366 (Minn. Ct. App. 2006) ("A party's reliance is reasonable unless the party is on notice that the representation is not to be trusted or knows or has reason to know that the representation is false" even if representation is made by adverse bargainer).

[151] Cf. Field v. Mans, 516 U.S. 59, 116 S.Ct. 437 (1995) (creditor who justifiably relied upon debtor's representations is not barred by debtor's bankruptcy, even if he could readily have learned the truth by checking deed records); see Restatement (Second) of Torts § 545A cmt. b (1977).

[152] U.S. v. Rosby, 454 F.3d 670, 677 (7th Cir. 2006). Judge Easterbrook continued: "Thus investors' gullibility and carelessness do not excuse willfully false statements or reduce the damages available to the victims."

[153] E.g., Ruff v. Charter Behavior Health Sys. of Nw. Ind., Inc., 699 N.E. 2d 1171 (Ind. Ct. App. 1998); Sales v. Kecoughtan Housing Co., Ltd., 279 Va. 475, 690 S.E.2d 91 (2010); Adams v. King Cnty., 164 Wash.2d 640, 192 P.3d 891 (2008).

[154] Radioshack Corp. v. ComSmart, Inc., 222 S.W.3d 256 (Ky. Ct. App. 2007); Adams v. King County, 164 Wash.2d 640, 192 P.3d 891 (2008) (a "false" promise does not constitute an existing fact).

asserting that a given product will last a lifetime, is one particular form of the opinion or prediction statement. The rules against recovery for opinion, puffery, or predictions turn on the courts' characterization of the representation and may apply whether or not the defendant himself purports to be offering opinion.[155]

Exceptions. The rule that requires factual representation and denies liability for opinions and predictions is often broadly stated, but in fact courts recognize a number of undermining exceptions. Courts have expressly said that liability may be imposed for false and material misrepresentations of opinion when the defendant is a fiduciary,[156] when he is a disinterested person or an expert upon whom the plaintiff can justifiably rely or when he has special knowledge,[157] and when the opinion implies material facts.[158] This is the position of the Restatement Third of Torts.[159]

Examples. For example, the dealer who says that his goods are "first class" is puffing his wares but asserting no fact at all.[160] The securities dealer who tells a client that a stock is bound to rise in the next year is not asserting a fact but predicting the future.[161] The auction house that says a painting is beautiful is merely expressing an opinion. Since none of these assertions explicitly states a fact and none seem to imply any particular fact, none is actionable.

Reasons for the rule. The reason most prominently addressed is that the plaintiff does not rely upon such statements, or if she relies, she is not justified in doing so. As already suggested, justified-reliance analysis may be merely one way of considering whether the defendant is culpable.[162] But if it is a separate ground, the justifications for reliance vary from case to case and do not support an invariant rule against recovery. For instance, the relationship of the parties and their relative knowledge may indicate that reliance is justified. If a court concludes that the plaintiff's reliance is justified, it may declare that the defendant's statement is one of fact, not opinion.[163]

The second reason supporting the opinion rule is what courts sometimes have in mind when they classify a statement as one of opinion is that the defendant has not exceeded the rules of the particular kind of bargaining game and hence is not culpable at all. The buyer's assertion that $250 is his top-dollar price is to be understood as a step in the process to getting to $300 or some other figure, not as a literal factual statement.

---

[155] The meaning, not the form of the statement, determines whether it will be counted as non-actionable opinion. See Restatement (Second) of Torts § 538A cmt. d (1977). When reasonable minds can differ about whether a statement of is opinion or fact, it is a jury question. Restatement (Third) of Torts: Liability for Economic Harms § 14 cmt.a (2012). See the detailed analysis in W. Page Keeton, Fraud: Misrepresentations of Opinion, 21 Minn. L. Rev. 643 (1937). See also United Concrete & Constr., Inc. v. Red-D-Mix Concrete, Inc., 836 N.W.2d 807 (Wis. 2013).

[156] Papatheofanis v. Allen, 242 P.3d 358 (N.M. Ct. App. 2010) (if statement was opinion, defendant as fiduciary was nevertheless subject to liability if other elements of the tort were shown).

[157] 625 3rd St. Assocs., L.P. v. Alliant Credit Union, 633 F.Supp.2d 1040, 1052 (N.D. Cal. 2009) ("opinions expressed by persons deemed to have superior knowledge over or special information regarding transactions can form the basis of a misrepresentation claim").

[158] See Cummings v. HPG Int'l, Inc., 244 F.3d 16 (1st Cir. 2001) (statement indicated that defendant knew facts to justify its "opinion"); Restatement (Second) of Torts § 542 (1977).

[159] Restatement (Third) of Torts: Liability for Economic Harm § 14 (2014).

[160] Ed Miller & Sons, Inc. v. Earl, 243 Neb. 708, 502 N.W.2d 444 (1993).

[161] Kennedy v. Flo-Tronics, Inc., 274 Minn. 327, 143 N.W.2d 827 (1966).

[162] 3 Dobbs, Hayden & Bublick, The Law of Torts § 672 (2d ed. 2011 & Supp.).

[163] See Transport Ins. Co. v. Faircloth, 898 S.W.2d 269 (Tex. 1995).

The third reason is that many opinion or puffing statements are not provably false, or rather that they are provably false only in extreme cases. Here again, the defendant may not be culpable because he has attempted to persuade but not to deceive about facts. This, too, varies with the evidence, for as shown below, some statements are false even when they are taken as approximations.

As these observations suggest, the putative rules about statements of opinion, prediction and law are really guidelines for analysis of larger questions—whether the plaintiff could have justifiably relied, whether the defendant was culpable, and whether the defendant's statements could be false in any meaningful sense. The guidelines are important, but in light of the "exceptions," it is probably best not to treat them as bright-line rules except in extreme cases.

Special types of representation. Special rules have grown up around a number of types of representations, particularly statements of value, predictions about the future, misrepresentation about the defendant's present intent to perform (promissory fraud), and implied representations of exisiting fact. All of these subjects are discussed at greater length elsewhere.[164]

Scope of third persons entitled to rely on representations: fraud. In addition, the scope of the defendant's duty for representations that influence persons the defendant did not intend to influence is another significant question. For example, suppose the defendant misrepresents the condition of his house to A, who passes the information on to B, who buys the defendant's house in reliance. Under the Restatement Second, the maker of a fraudulent representation was liable not only to those persons he directly addressed or intended to influence, but also to the entire class of persons he intends or has reason to expect will rely upon the representations.[165] The Restatement Third, in a slight variation, says an actor is subject to liability for harm "only if the risk of the harm was foreseeably increased by the fraud."[166] The Restatement Third notes that defendant's liability extend to damages suffered by "those whose reliance defendant intended to induce" as well as those "who the defendant had reason to expect" would "receive the statement and rely on it."[167]

Scope of third persons entitled to rely: negligent misrepresentation. In negligent misrepresentation, the Second Restatement provided that the defendant is subject to liability if he intends to supply the information to a small group of which the plaintiff is a member. He is also liable if he knows the recipient of the information he provides will pass it on to others in the limited group of people he expects would be influenced.[168] A similar rule is echoed in the Restatement Third.[169] Most courts adopt the Restatement's

---

[164] See 3 Dobbs, Hayden & Bublick, The Law of Torts §§ 676–79 (2d ed. 2011 & Supp.).

[165] See, supporting liability for fraudulent representations to those whose reliance is reasonably foreseeable or expected, Bily v. Arthur Young & Co., 3 Cal.4th 370, 11 Cal.Rptr.2d 51, 834 P.2d 745 (1992) (accountant performing audit); Geernaert v. Mitchell, 31 Cal.App.4th 601, 37 Cal.Rptr.2d 483 (1995) (homeowner-seller expecting repetition of falsehood in subsequent sales); Clark v. McDaniel, 546 N.W.2d 590 (Iowa 1996); Rhee v. Highland Dev. Corp., 182 Md.App. 516, 958 A.2d 385 (2008); cf. Ernst & Young, LLP v. Pacific Mut. Life Ins. Co., 51 S.W.3d 573 (Tex. 2001) (approving the Restatement's "reason to expect" language but insisting that this requires more than mere foreseeability).

[166] Restatement (Third) of Torts: Liability for Economic Harm § 12 (2014).

[167] Id. § 12 cmt. b (2014).

[168] Restatement (Second) of Torts § 552(2) (1977).

[169] Restatement (Third) of Torts: Liability for Economic Harm § 6 (2014).

position or something close to it.[170] However, many methods of resolving the issue are possible and discussed elsewhere in greater depth.[171]

Nondisclosure. When nondisclosure without active concealment is actionable is also a highly contested issue. Traditionally, affirmative duties of disclosure are imposed only when (1) statutes so provide; (2) the defendant is in a confidential relationship or under a fiduciary duty to the plaintiff;[172] (3) the defendant has made a representation that is true at the time it was made but that becomes untrue or misleading before the bargain is consummated;[173] (4) the statement was untrue at the time it was made and the defendant later realizes that it has become material or that the plaintiff is relying upon it;[174] or (5) the defendant has communicated a half-truth, that is, a partial or ambiguous statement that is misleading unless additional facts are disclosed,[175] as where the seller of a lot discloses that the city has the right to widen a street bounding the lot but saying nothing about the fact that the city also has the right to open a street that will divide the lot in half.[176] Some contemporary cases add an obligation (6) to disclose a material fact when the defendant knows that the plaintiff is acting under a mistake that is not merely material to the transaction but "basic" to it and disclosure would reasonably be expected.[177] The Restatement Third suggests a duty to disclose might arise in any of these situations.[178] The critical questions in nondisclosure cases are whether there is a

---

[170]   See Bily v. Arthur Young & Co., 3 Cal.4th 370, 11 Cal.Rptr. 51, 834 P.2d 745 (1992); First Fla. Bank, N.A. v. Max Mitchell & Co., 558 So.2d 9 (Fla. 1990); Rozny v. Marnul, 43 Ill.2d 54, 250 N.E.2d 656 (1969); Van Sickle Constr. Co. v. Wachovia Commercial Mortg., Inc., 783 N.W.2d 684 (Iowa 2010) (approving Restatement formulation generally); NYCAL Corp. v. KPMG Peat Marwick LLP., 426 Mass. 491, 688 N.E.2d 1368 (1998); Lucky 7, LLC v. THT Realty, LLC, 278 Neb. 997, 775 N.W.2d 671 (2009) (reiterating court's adoption of Restatement rules); Raritan River Steel Co. v. Cherry, Bekaert & Holland, 322 N.C. 200, 367 S.E.2d 609 (1988); Bethlehem Steel Corp. v. Ernst & Whinney, 822 S.W.2d 592 (Tenn. 1991).

[171]   See 3 Dobbs, Hayden & Bublick, The Law of Torts §§ 679–80 (2d ed. 2011 & Supp.).

[172]   See Old Harbor Native Corp. v. Afognak Joint Venture, 30 P.3d 101 (Alaska 2001) (fiduciary duty of joint venturer to disclose continues after notice of withdrawal from venture until complete winding up of the venture's affairs); Burkons v. Ticor Title Ins. Co. of Cal., 168 Ariz. 345, 813 P.2d 710 (1991) (escrow agent's duty to reveal evidence of fraud by one of the parties upon the other); Pacelli Bros. Transp., Inc. v. Pacelli, 189 Conn. 401, 456 A.2d 325 (1983) (obligation may continue after relationship terminated); Martin v. Heinold Commodities, Inc., 163 Ill.2d 33, 643 N.E.2d 734 (1994) (precontract negotiations to create fiducial relationship required disclosure of special commissions). With appropriate adjustments, a fiduciary's concealment or nondisclosure of information needed for the *physical* safety of a beneficiary can also be actionable. See Doe 67C v. Archdiocese of Milwaukee, 700 N.W.2d 180 (Wis. 2005) (recognizing principle).

[173]   Refrigeration Indus., Inc. v. Nemmers, 880 S.W.2d 912 (Mo. Ct. App. 1994); Shafmaster v. Shafmaster, 138 N.H. 460, 642 A.2d 1361 (1994); Restatement (Second) of Torts § 551(2)(c) (1977).

[174]   Restatement (Second) of Torts § 551(d) (1977).

[175]   Meade v. Cedarapids, Inc., 164 F.3d 1218 (9th Cir. 1999); OCM Principal Opportunities Fund v. CIBC World Mkts. Corp., 157 Cal.App.4th 835, 68 Cal.Rptr.3d 828 (2007); St. Joseph Hosp. v. Corbetta Constr. Co., Inc., 21 Ill.App.3d 925, 316 N.E.2d 51 (1974); Restatement (Second) of Torts § 551(2)(b) (1977). In Sarvis v. Vermont State Colleges, 772 A.2d 494 (Vt. 2001), a man convicted of bank fraud was imprisoned for several years and legally obliged to repay $12 million. Quickly out of prison, he applied for a teaching job, presenting a resume that did not reveal that he had been in prison. When discovered and discharged, he sued the college. The college relied on his fraud as justification for termination. He argued that he had no duty to reveal his conviction or imprisonment, but the court answered that under the half-truth rule and also because of affirmative misrepresentations, he was chargeable with fraud and his termination was just.

[176]   Junius Constr. Co. v. Cohen, 257 N.Y. 393, 178 N.E. 672 (1931) (the ennumeration of "a risk like in kind but vastly greater in degree" tacitly implied there were no others).

[177]   Restatement (Second) of Torts § 551(e) (1977); cf. Alejandre v. Bull, 159 Wash.2d 674, 689 153 P.3d 864, 872 (2007) (duty to disclose defects in property that present a danger to property itself, health, or life of the purchaser). Maybee v. Jacobs Motor Co., Inc., 519 N.W.2d 341 (S.D. 1994).

[178]   Restatement (Third) of Torts: Liability for Economic Harm § 13 (2014).

duty to disclose and whether the defendant's silence in the particular context implied a representation.[179]

§ 43.9 Defenses and Remedies

Contract Defenses

Negligent misrepresentation cases. Defendants charged with misrepresentation often assert that the claim is barred, either by legal rules such as the parol evidence rule, or by contract provisions. When the misrepresentation is merely negligent, contract clauses that exculpate the defendant are usually enforced and the plaintiff's misrepresentation claim rejected.[180]

Scienter fraud. When the plaintiff's claim is one of scienter fraud, the traditional approach more or less flatly rejects exculpatory mechanisms, often in very broad and absolute terms, frequently saying that fraud vitiates everything it touches,[181] or that enforcing contract clauses that would protect fraud is against public policy.[182] Under these broad traditional principles, the parol evidence rule cannot be invoked to bar a claim of scienter fraud.[183] The result is that the plaintiff can introduce evidence of the defendant's alleged representations that are contradicted by the contract provisions. Likewise, a court may reject a statute of frauds defense when the defendant is charged with intentional misrepresentation.[184] A merger or integration clause in the contract merely stipulates that the conditions for invoking the parol evidence rule are met, that is, that the contract is the complete agreement of the parties. Since the parol evidence rule itself does not apply to bar the fraud claim under the traditional view, the merger clause adds nothing to prevent the fraud claim from proceeding.[185] Consequently, the plaintiff is permitted to proceed with a scienter fraud claim in spite of a contract clause that purports to exculpate the defendant.[186]

---

[179] MacDonald v. Thomas M. Cooley Law Sch., 724 F.3d 654 (6th Cir. 2013); Littau v. Midwest Commodities, Inc., 316 N.W.2d 639 (S.D. 1982).

[180] See RepublicBank Dallas, N.A. v. First Wis. Nat'l Bank of Milwaukee, 636 F.Supp. 1470 (E.D. Wis. 1986) (clauses would be effective to bar claims for misrepresentation grounded in negligence or strict liability); Van Der Stok v. Van Voorhees, 151 N.H. 679, 866 A.2d 972 (2005) (by implication, exculpatory clauses would bar negligent misrepresentation claims); Snyder v. Lovercheck, 992 P.2d 1079, 1086 (Wyo. 1999). *Contra:* Formento v. Encanto Bus. Park, 154 Ariz. 495, 744 P.2d 22 (Ct. App. 1987).

[181] Stegman v. Professional & Bus. Men's Life Ins. Co., 173 Kan. 744, 750, 252 P.2d 1074, 1080 (1953) ("An invariable qualification of the rule which makes parol evidence inadmissible to vary the terms of a written instrument is the one which permits such testimony where a contract is induced or procured by fraud. . . . Fraud vitiates whatever it touches including final judgments and final orders as well as contracts.").

[182] Bates v. Southgate, 308 Mass. 170, 31 N.E.2d 551 (1941) ("contracts or clauses attempting to protect a party against the consequences of his own fraud are against public policy and void where fraud inducing the contract is shown").

[183] McClain v. Octagon Plaza, LLC, 159 Cal.App.4th 784, 71 Cal.Rptr.3d 885 (2008); Aspiazu v. Mortimer, 139 Idaho 548, 82 P.3d 830 (2003); Meland v. Youngberg, 124 Minn. 446, 145 N.W. 167 (1914); Slack v. James, 364 S.C. 609, 614 S.E.2d 636 (2005) (parol evidence rule does not bar proof of either scienter fraud or negligent misrepresentation); see Still v. Cunningham, 94 P.3d 1104 (Alaska 2004).

[184] Tenzer v. Superscope, Inc., 39 Cal.3d 18, 702 P.2d 212, 216 Cal.Rptr. 130 (1985); Burgdorfer v. Thielemann, 153 Or. 354, 55 P.2d 1122 (1936); Restatement (Second) of Torts § 530 cmt. c (1977).

[185] See, permitting the fraud claim in spite of a merger clause, Blanchard v. Blanchard, 108 Nev. 908, 919, 839 P.2d 1320, 1322–23 (1992) (clause providing that one party did not rely on values in financial statement did not bar fraud claim; "integration clauses do not bar claims for misrepresentation" and neither do waiver clauses); Travers v. Spidell, 682 A.2d 471 (R.I. 1996).

[186] Pearson & Son, Ltd. v. Lord Mayor of Dublin, [1907] A.C. 351, 353–354 (H.L. 1907) ("no one can escape liability for his own fraudulent statements by inserting in a contract a clause that the other party shall not rely upon them;" per Lord Loreburn, L.C.); Cummings v. HPG Int'l, Inc., 244 F.3d 16 (1st Cir. 2001)

Rejecting traditional view. Some courts have created a rule couched in terms just as absolute as the traditional rule, but providing for the opposite result. Subject perhaps to a limited exception,[187] this rule appears to say flatly that the defendant can invoke both the parol evidence rule[188] and contract clauses like those in which the plaintiff acknowledges she had not relied on certain representations[189] to defeat the plaintiff's claim of fraud in the inducement. Similarly, the plaintiff might be deemed to waive the fraud claim by executing a new contract on the same subject matter after learning of the alleged misrepresentation.[190]

Remedies

The main remedies. To some extent the remedies available for misrepresentation depend upon the facts. In general, the remedies are:

> *(1) Reformation.* When the written document does not correctly express the parties' actual agreement because of fraud or mistake, the plaintiff is entitled to reformation of the document to make it reflect the real agreement.[191]

(Massachusetts law, contract cannot protect defendant against his own fraud, but in some cases may bar negligent misrepresentation action); Bates v. Southgate, 308 Mass. 170, 31 N.E.2d 551 (1941); Hess v. Chase Manhattan Bank, USA, N.A., 220 S.W.3d 758 (Mo. 2007) ("a party may not, by disclaimer or otherwise, contractually exclude liability for fraud in inducing that contract"); Bowman v. Presley, 212 P.3d 1210, 1220 (Okla. 2009) (terms of contract did not prevent buyers' claim of fraud; "A whisper of fraud can topple the pillars of even the most impregnable contract, for to base a contract upon fraud is to build it upon sand. . . . Fraud vitiates everything it touches, and a contract obtained thereby is voidable"). In most of these cases and a number of others that allow the fraud claim to proceed, the person claiming fraud is a consumer or small investor while the fraud is alleged against a relatively sophisticated repeat player who is engaged in a business operation. However, in ABRY Partners V, L.P. v. F & W Acquisition LLC, 891 A.2d 1032 (Del. Ch. 2006), the court allowed a scienter fraud claim by a sophisticated buyer to proceed in spite of non-reliance clauses, where the seller's misrepresentation was contained in the written contract documents themselves.

[187] The defendant's fraud in procuring the exculpatory clause itself will not bar the plaintiff's fraud claim, though fraud in inducing the contract as a whole will. See UAW-GM Human Res. Ctr. v. KSL Recreation Corp., 228 Mich.App. 486, 503, 579 N.W.2d 411, 419 (1998). A similar rule is applied when the contract contains an arbitration clause. One claiming the contract was procured by fraud does not avoid the clause that submits disputes to arbitration unless she can also show that the clause itself was induced by fraud, Prima Paint v. Flood & Conklin, 388 U.S. 395, 87 S.Ct. 1801 (1967); Buckeye Check Cashing, Inc. v. Cardegna, 546 U.S. 440, 126 S.Ct. 1204 (2006); Ericksen, Arbuthnot, McCarthy, Kearney & Walsh, Inc. v. 100 Oak St., 35 Cal.3d 312, 197 Cal.Rptr. 581, 673 P.2d 251 (1983), or that the entire contract was procured by fraud *in the execution*, see Rosenthal v. Great Western Fin. Sec. Corp., 14 Cal.4th 394, 926 P.2d 1061, 58 Cal.Rptr.2d 875 (1996).

[188] See Northrop v. Piper, 199 Minn. 244, 271 N.W. 487 (1937) (contract provision contradicted alleged prior representation; "That ends the case. . . . [T]he inescapable answer is that, whatever negotiations, or even contracts, had preceded in respect to his actual or hoped for status in the new business, he agreed contractually that from August 27, 1928, on he was to be a salesman only," notwithstanding the plaintiff's claim of fraud); Yocca v. Pittsburgh Steelers Sports, Inc., 578 Pa. 479, 854 A.2d 425, 437 n.26 (2004) ("parol evidence may not be admitted based on a claim that there was fraud in the inducement of the contract, i.e., that an opposing party made false representations that induced the complaining party to agree to the contract").

[189] See U.S. v. Rosby, 454 F.3d 670 (7th Cir. 2006) ("an investor's disclaimer of reliance on certain representations, as part of a declaration that the investor has done and is relying on his own investigation, defeats a private damages action for securities fraud"); Head v. Head, 59 Md.App. 570, 477 A.2d 282 (1984) (ordinary integration clause would not bar fraud claim, but provision that plaintiff who accepted $1.5 million knew she did not know defendant's total assets and realized they might be disproportionately greater would be a bar).

[190] Oakland Raiders v. Oakland-Alameda County Coliseum, Inc., 144 Cal.App.4th 1175, 51 Cal.Rptr.3d 144 (2006) (a negligent misrepresentation claim; "if, after discovery of the alleged fraud, he enters into a new contract with the defendant regarding the same subject matter that supersedes the former agreement and confers upon him significant benefits the plaintiff has waived the misrepresentation;" also suggesting that estoppel underlies the rule).

[191] See 2 Dan B. Dobbs, Law of Remedies § 9.5 (2d ed. 1993).

(2) Rescission. When the transaction was induced by fraud or even by innocent misrepresentation of a basic fact, the plaintiff may be entitled to rescission, provided circumstances have not so changed as to make rescission inequitable.[192]

(3) Damages. In all cases in which the misrepresentation is actionable in tort, the plaintiff is entitled to recover damages instead of rescission, but the measure of damages may be less favorable to the plaintiff if the basis for liability is an innocent or negligent representation.[193] Apart from interest, costs, attorney fees, set-offs and other adjustments, damages may be calculated by looking to the market value of what the plaintiff received and was promised,[194] or by assessing consequential damages.[195]

(4) Disgorgement of defendant's gains—restitution. When the defendant has gained from a transaction induced by scienter fraud or breach of fiduciary relationship, the plaintiff may be entitled to recover, on a theory of constructive trust or otherwise, the defendant's gains from the transaction, even if those gains exceed the plaintiff's losses.[196]

Market-based damages measures. Courts have recognized three potential measures of damages calculated on the basis of market or capital values (as distinct from consequential damages).

(1) Benefit of bargain measure. The loss of bargain measure gives the plaintiff the difference between what she received in value and the value she would have received had matters been as represented. If the misrepresentation induces the plaintiff to pay $5,000 for a car that is worth $5,000 but would have been worth $10,000 had it been as represented, the plaintiff recovers $5,000 under the loss of bargain rule, giving her a total value of $10,000 (the car plus the damages)—the benefit of the bargain.[197]

(2) Out of pocket measure. The out of pocket measure allows the plaintiff to recover the loss she sustained in the transaction but not her expected gain. Consequential damages aside, that loss is the difference between what the plaintiff paid in the transaction and what she received at the time the transaction was completed. If the misrepresentation induces the plaintiff to pay $5,000 for a chattel worth only $4,000, the plaintiff recovers $1,000. In effect, the exchange is equalized.[198]

(3) "Rescissory damages." The third potential measure has been used almost not at all. It calculates the out of pocket measure at a later date, giving the plaintiff a recovery that resembles the financial effect of a rescission. It is sometimes called rescissory damages. If the plaintiff is induced to buy shares of stock for $100,000 at a

---

[192] Id. §§ 9.3(1) & 9.6.

[193] See 3 Dobbs, Hayden & Bublick, The Law of Torts § 692 (2d ed. 2011 & Supp.).

[194] Id. § 688.

[195] Id. § 689.

[196] 2 Dan B., Dobbs, Law of Remedies § 9.3(4) (2d ed. 1993).

[197] See, e.g., Finderne Mgmt. Co., Inc. v. Barrett, 402 N.J.Super. 546, 955 A.2d 940 (2008) (but holding that tax benefits represented were not established with sufficient certainty); Schnellmann v. Roettger, 373 S.C. 379, 645 S.E.2d 239 (2007) (but finding reliance unjustified).

[198] When the misrepresentation induces the plaintiff either to forgo or enter into a transaction with some person other than the defendant, none of these market value rules seem to portray the problem. See Trytko v. Hubbell, Inc., 28 F.3d 715 (7th Cir. 1994), discussing some such cases. In those instances, the claim can appropriately be viewed as a consequential damages claim involving none of the market measures.

time when their market value is $80,000 and does not get a judgment until a year later when the market has dropped and the shares are worth only $50,000, rescissory damages would permit the plaintiff to recover $50,000, not merely the $20,000 authorized by the traditional out of pocket measure. That is, the damage award would put the plaintiff in the same financial position as rescission on the date of the court's decree. Rescission itself would give the plaintiff back the $100,000 purchase price and she would return stock now worth only $50,000. The damage award would give the plaintiff $50,000 and let her keep the $50,000 worth of stock.

Consequential damages. When misrepresentation is actionable in tort, the plaintiff may recover consequential damages instead of or, in proper cases,[199] in addition to damages based on market value like the benefit of the bargain measure. Consequential damages are measured, not by the value of the items promised and received, but by losses incurred in *consequence* of the fact that the plaintiff did not receive what was represented. In a jurisdiction that permits loss of bargain damages, consequential damages can include compensation for reliance expenses, even if the transaction is not completed.[200] Thus consequential damages include expenses incurred or profits lost as a proximate result of the misrepresentation,[201] provided such damages are proved with reasonable certainty and do not duplicate an out of pocket or loss of bargain award.[202] While market losses may be paper losses that are never actually realized, consequential damages must either be realized or more likely than not to be realized in the future.[203]

Emotional harm damages. Emotional harm damages are not ordinarily recoverable in a misrepresentation action based on commercial dealings such as ordinary purchases of property,[204] although they might be recovered when misrepresentation is an operative fact in some other cause of action[205] and in cases where the fraud invades personal rights such as those recognized in insurance bad faith claims.[206] Emotional harm damages might also be recoverable if the defendant's misrepresentation also amounted to the independent tort of intentional infliction of emotional distress. And where punitive

---

[199] When the market-based damage measure duplicates the consequential damages, both should not be awarded. Damages under the two measures may be duplicative even if they do not produce the same final figure. Duplication arises from the fact that market value may be based on prospects of producing profits, so lost profits and inadequate market value may be only two ways of estimating the same single loss. See, with an example, 2 Dan B. Dobbs, Law of Remedies § 9.2(3) (2d ed. 1991).

[200] Zanakis-Pico v. Cutter Dodge, Inc., 98 Haw. 309, 47 P.3d 1222 (Haw. 2002).

[201] E.g., Lazar v. Superior Court, 12 Cal.4th 631, 909 P.2d 981, 49 Cal.Rptr.2d 377 (1996) (items like moving expenses in addition to loss of bargain damages for employee fraudulently induced to move to new job). See generally 2 Dan B. Dobbs, Law of Remedies § 9.2(3) (2d ed. 1993). New York, with a strong policy of limiting damages to out of pocket losses, has rejected some consequential damages on the ground that allowance will tend to match a loss of bargain rule. See Alpert v. Shea Gould Climenko & Casey, 160 A.D.2d 67, 559 N.Y.S.2d 312 (1990).

[202] Loss of expected profits and loss of bargain may turn out on some facts to be two ways of measuring the same thing. See 2 Dan B. Dobbs, Law of Remedies § 9.2(4), p. 558 (2d ed. 1993).

[203] See id. §§ 3.3 (3) & 3.4 (2d ed. 1991); for more detail, see 3 Dobbs, Hayden & Bublick, The Law of Torts § 694 (2d ed. 2011 & Supp.).

[204] E.g., Brogan v. Mitchell Int'l, Inc., 181 Ill.2d 178, 692 N.E.2d 276, 229 Ill.Dec. 503 (1998); Cornell v. Wunschel, 408 N.W.2d 369 (Iowa 1987) (denying mental distress damages in the tort of deceit; "deceit is an economic, not a dignitary tort"); Jourdain v. Dineen, 527 A.2d 1304 (Me. 1987); 2 Dan B. Dobbs, Law of Remedies § 9.2(4) (2d ed. 1993); cf. McConkey v. Aon Corp., 354 N.J. Super. 25, 804 A.2d 572 (2002) (fraud inducing an employment contract, emotional damages not recoverable).

[205] 3 Dobbs, Hayden & Bublick, The Law of Torts § 663 (2d ed. 2011 & Supp.).

[206] Cf. Campbell v. State Farm Mut. Auto. Ins. Co., 98 P.3d 409 (Utah 2004) (fraud claim embedded in bad faith claim against insurer; on remand from the Supreme Court on issue of punitive damages, original award of $145 million reduced to less than $10 million).

damages awards are made, they may represent in part unacknowledged damages for emotional distress.

Punitive damages. Punitive damages are recoverable if the defendant's intentional fraud qualifies as sufficiently malicious or oppressive.[207] Statutes, such as consumer protection statutes may also authorize punitive damages, double or treble damages and other enhancements of the traditional damage award.[208]

Damages for intentional misrepresentation. When the defendant's fraud is intentional, most courts, including some that formerly supported the out of pocket measure, now permit the plaintiff to recover the loss of bargain,[209] or say with the Restatement that the plaintiff can recover under either loss of bargain or out of pocket, at her option.[210] Sometimes courts choose the measure they deem best to fit the facts.[211]

Damages for negligent misrepresentation. When the defendant's misrepresentation is merely negligent, the Restatement provides that liability is limited to the out of pocket measure and/or consequential damages that are not the equivalent of benefit of the bargain damages.[212] Earlier cases of negligence did not discuss the damages issue or failed to realize that negligence might call for a milder measure. More recent cases alluding to the issue have followed or acknowledged the Restatement limitations on damages.[213]

Damages for innocent misrepresentations—Rescission-equivalent damages. The Restatement also provides that the out of pocket measure is to be applied in the case of innocent misrepresentations.[214] There are, however, two logically distinct grounds for

[207] E.g., Casciola v. F.S. Air Serv., Inc., 120 P.3d 1059 (Alaska 2005) ($30,000 actual damages, $300,000 punitive damages upheld for reprehensible fraud); Medasys Acquisition Corp. v. SDMS, P.C., 203 Ariz. 420, 55 P.3d 763 (2002) (punitive damages recoverable even where the plaintiff seeks and obtains rescission for fraud; the requirement of actual damages to support punitive awards is met here); Midwest Home Distributor, Inc. v. Domco Indus. Ltd., 585 N.W.2d 735 (Iowa 1998); McConkey v. Aon Corp., 354 N.J.Super. 25, 804 A.2d 572 (2002); Campbell v. State Farm Mut. Auto. Ins. Co., 98 P.3d 409 (Utah 2004).

[208] E.g., Ga. Code Ann., § 31–38–10 (punitive damages authorized for intentional violations of statute); N. M. Stat. § 57–27–5 (treble damages or $300, whichever is greater). These statutes may provide for recovery of some minimum sum, such as $1,000, even if actual damages are less. E.g., Idaho Code § 48–608(1).

[209] E.g., American Family Serv. Corp. v. Michelfelder, 968 F.2d 667 (8th Cir. 1992); Bechtel v. Liberty Nat'l Bank, 534 F.2d 1335 (9th Cir. 1976); Turnbull v. LaRose, 702 P.2d 1331 (Alaska 1985). A number of cases have stated the formula as "the difference between the value of the goods received and the value of the goods as represented." E.g., Lancaster v. Schilling Motors, Inc., 299 Ark. 365, 369, 772 S.W.2d 349, 351 (1989); Gerill Corp. v. Jack L. Hargrove Builders, Inc., 128 Ill.2d 179, 131 Ill.Dec. 155, 538 N.E.2d 530 (1989); LeFlore v. Reflections of Tulsa, Inc., 708 P.2d 1068 (Okla. 1985); Danca v. Taunton Sav. Bank, 385 Mass. 1, 429 N.E.2d 1129 (1982); Terry v. Panek, 631 P.2d 896 (Utah 1981); Kramer v. Chabot, 564 A.2d 292 (Vt. 1989).

[210] Hall v. Lovell Regency Homes Ltd. P'ship, 121 Md.App. 1, 708 A.2d 344 (1998); Aquaplex, Inc. v. Rancho La Valencia, Inc., 297 S.W.3d 768, 776 (Tex. 2009); see Restatement (Second) of Torts § 549 (1977); cf. O'Neal Ford, Inc. v. Davie, 299 Ark. 45, 770 S.W.2d 656 (1989) (a preference for loss of bargain but approving a recovery based upon out of pocket).

[211] Walston v. Monumental Life Ins. Co., 129 Idaho 211, 923 P.2d 456 (1996).

[212] Restatement (Second) of Torts § 552B (1977). In any event, recovery of money damages on a negligent misrepresentation claim requires proof of injury. See, e.g., Ironworkers Local Union 68 v. AstraZeneca Pharm., LP, 634 F.3d 1352, R.I.C.O. Bus. Disp. Guide (CCH) P 12026 (11th Cir. 2011) (under applicable laws of the three states involved, "without allegations of injury, a claim is not remediable when based either on common law fraud, or negligent misrepresentation"; here, the plaintiffs failed to allege any economic injury arising from pharmaceutical manufacturer's alleged misrepresentations about the safety and effectiveness of their drugs and were therefore not entitled to any recovery).

[213] E.g., Trytko v. Hubbell, Inc., 28 F.3d 715 (7th Cir. 1994); BDO Seidman, LLP v. Mindis Acquisition Corp., 276 Ga. 311, 578 S.E.2d 400 (2003); First Interstate Bank of Gallup v. Foutz, 107 N.M. 749, 764 P.2d 1307 (1988); Washington Mut. Bank v. Houston Windcrest West Rd. I, L.P., 262 S.W.3d 856 (Tex. App. 2008).

[214] Restatement (Second) of Torts § 552C (1977).

imposing liability in innocent misrepresentation cases, and they do not necessarily suggest the same damages measure. The first is that the innocent misrepresentation is a true contractual warranty, that is, an implicit or explicit contractual guarantee. Some warranties are redressed by a benefit of the bargain measure of damages, as provided in the UCC.[215] Other warranties are not likely to imply a benefit of the bargain measure of damages, but where they do, they should be honored as part of the parties' agreement. Where liability for innocent misrepresentation is essentially based on breach of a warranty, then, damages may properly be based on benefit of the bargain in some cases and not in others.

Innocent misrepresentation as mistake justifying rescission-equivalent damages. The other ground for recognizing innocent misrepresentations as actionable is rooted in equitable notions and in the remedy of rescission. Rescission was granted for honest mutual mistakes about truly basic—not merely material—incidents of an agreement. It seemed, therefore, that rescission should equally be granted when the defendant honestly but mistakenly asserted a fact and the plaintiff honestly and mistakenly relied upon it.

Once a court goes that far, it is easy to say that if rescission can be granted for an honest misrepresentation of basic fact, then the court could also grant damages that have a substantially similar impact. Out of pocket damages do have an impact similar to rescission in many cases. You give me $100 for a dog that I honestly and reasonably represent to be pedigreed, but it turns out that I am wrong and the dog is worth only $50. You can rescind the dog deal and get your $100 back. If you recover out of pocket damages, you keep the $50 dog and get damages of $50, ending up with $100 in assets.

Economic entitlement or market-measured damages. Damages rules in misrepresentation cases can be called economic entitlement rules. Loss of bargain rules aim to award the plaintiff damages in a sum that will give her the value she was entitled to have under the representation or warranty. Specifically, they attempt to place the plaintiff in the economic position she would have enjoyed if the representation had been correct. Under the narrower out of pocket rule, the rules attempt to place the plaintiff in the position she would have enjoyed if the items she received had been worth what she paid.[216]

These rules require the plaintiff to prove a loss, but they do not require the plaintiff to *realize* a loss. That is, they do not require the plaintiff to re-sell the purchased goods at a loss, to pay for repair or upgrading of the goods, or to suffer any kind of physical injury as a result of the item's poor qualities. There is nothing unusual in the law of damages about using this kind of entitlement or bookkeeping measure of damages.[217] In

---

[215] UCC § 2–714 (2) ("The measure of damages for breach of warranty is the difference at the time and place of acceptance between the value of the goods accepted and the value they would have had if they had been as warranted, unless special circumstances show proximate damages of a different amount").

[216] See 3 Dobbs, Hayden & Bublick, The Law of Torts §§ 687–88 (2d ed. 2011 & Supp.) (reflecting these alternative aims in the benefit of bargain and out of pocket measures of damages). Misrepresentation may also be a relevant fact in other torts, in which case physical harm and other damages may be appropriate. Id. § 663.

[217] Variations on the entitlement rules can be found in ordinary trespass cases, conversion cases, contract cases, nuisance cases, and in breach of warranty cases, including breach of the warranty of habitability in a lease. See Williard v. Parsons Hill P'ship, 178 Vt. 300, 882 A.2d 1213 (2005). Except to provide some special rules to deal with market fluctuation, in none of these cases do courts ordinarily inquire whether the present economic loss might be nullified by subsequent events that would nullify the plaintiff's apparent loss. Risks that an apparent loss is only a "blip" on the screen, to be erased when the market rises a few days later, may be addressed by treating a three-month market average as the appropriate market value, see 15

fact, the damages measure is like the buyer's measure of damages for breach of warranty which is codified in the UCC.[218]

Example. For example, suppose the seller fraudulently represents that a house has a new roof in excellent condition when in fact the roof is rotting and ready to leak at the first rain. With a roof like that represented, the house would be worth $300,000, but with the bad roof it is worth only $290,000. The misrepresentation puts the plaintiff purchaser at risk for rain damage in the future, but that future risk also creates a present loss in value.[219] The plaintiff's claim in such a case is a market-based loss for her economic entitlement. Under the loss of bargain measure of damages, the plaintiff is entitled to recover $10,000, even though she has not actually sold at a loss, incurred expenses of repair, or suffered damage from leaks.[220]

Consequential damages—when harm must be realized or likely to be realized. The rule is different when the plaintiff seeks to recover consequential damages. Consequential damages are not based on the market value of the very thing to which the plaintiff is entitled but upon collateral costs incurred or lost profits suffered. For example, the defendant who misrepresents the condition of the roof to the home buyer is liable to make the plaintiff's economic entitlement good by paying damages based on the difference between the value of the house with the roof as represented and the value the plaintiff received. In contrast, though, if the plaintiff claims that the rains came and the roof leaked, causing rain damage to the plaintiff's antique furniture, the claim is for consequential damages and the plaintiff will be required to prove that the damages were in fact realized or will more likely than not be realized in the future.[221] Consequential damages claims are also limited by a series of other rules, requiring rather clear proof as to causation and damage[222] and also requiring the plaintiff to minimize damages.[223]

The upshot is that in the ordinary misrepresentation claim (and in the claim of economic damages for breach of warranty as well), the buyer-plaintiff can claim economic damages if the property is worth less than the value she was entitled to; but if she claims consequential damages, she must prove that the loss has been realized or will probably be realized in the future by way of physical harm, repair costs, or sale at a loss.

U.S.C.A. § 78u–4(e), or by some similar adjustment, see 15 U.S.C.A. § 73 (similar adjustments to deal with fluctuating markets in converted goods).

[218] UCC § 2–714 (2) ("The measure of damages for breach of warranty is the difference at the time and place of acceptance between the value of the goods accepted and the value they would have had if they had been as warranted, unless special circumstances show proximate damages of a different amount").

[219] That is only to recognize that value of property reflects what buyers would pay and that buyers would take into account risks of future harm as well as opportunities for future gain. See Almota Farmers Elevator & Warehouse Co. v. United States, 409 U.S. 470, 93 S.Ct. 791, 35 L.Ed.2d 1 (1973); City of Harlingen v. Estate of Sharboneau, 48 S.W.3d 177 (Tex. 2001).

[220] For example, in Artilla Cove Resort, Inc. v. Hartley, 72 S.W.3d 291 (Mo. Ct. App. 2002), the building sold to the plaintiffs did not have the structural strength represented (by concealment or nondisclosure); extensive repairs would be needed, but the plaintiffs had neither taken a loss through selling the building at a lower price or by paying for the repairs. They were entitled to recover the difference between a building as represented and the unsound building they received. Although not involving fraud, the damages principle in Williard v. Parsons Hill Partnership, 178 Vt. 300, 313, 882 A.2d 1213, 1222 (2005), was the same. The court there held that landlords who provided a toxin-contaminated water supply were subject to liability under a warranty of habitability for the difference between the value of the lease with and without drinkable water, regardless whether personal injuries had been proven. On unrealized losses generally see 1 Dan B. Dobbs, Law of Remedies §§ 3.2 & 3.3(3) (2d ed. 1993).

[221] See 1 Dan B. Dobbs, Law of Remedies §§ 3.3(4) & 3.4 (2d ed. 1993).

[222] See id.

[223] Id. §§ 3.4 & 3.9.

F. ECONOMIC HARMS IN SPECIAL RELATIONSHIPS

§ 43.10   Breach of Fiduciary Duty, Bad Faith, Wrongful Discharge and Economic Duress

Special relationship and fiduciary duties. While some tort duties are imposed independent of the parties' relationship, others are imposed *because* of the parties' relationship. For example, a defendant may owe a special tort duty to a plaintiff because the defendant is perceived by the courts to be a fiduciary. All the torts covered in this part of the chapter—bad faith, economic duress, and wrongful discharge—can involve fragments of the fiduciary duty. This chapter outlines the gist of the torts, leaving more exhaustive coverage to other works.[224]

Who is a fiduciary? Fiduciary issues arise in a wide variety of factual settings, leading courts to advance inconsistent definitions of fiduciaries. Broadly speaking, however, fiduciaries are individuals or corporations who appear to accept, expressly or impliedly, an obligation to act in a position of trust or confidence for the benefit of another or who have accepted a status or relationship understood to entail such an obligation, generating the beneficiary's justifiable expectations of loyalty.[225] Examples of fiduciary relationships include formal trustee-beneficiary relationships, agent-principal relationships, partnerships, and lawyer-client relationships.

Informal confidential relationships. Fiduciary duties may also arise in less formal settings when a defendant stands in a relationship of special trust or confidence to a beneficiary.[226] In determining whether a fiduciary relation exists, courts will consider evidence bearing on the plaintiff's reasonable expectations based on the defendant's apparent acceptance of the plaintiff's confidence and his own fiduciary responsibility.[227] Broadly stated, factors a court would consider include the course of the parties' prior

---

[224] 3 Dobbs, Hayden & Bublick, The Law of Torts §§ 695–707 (2d ed. 2011 & Supp.).

[225] "A fiduciary relation exists between two persons when one of them is under a duty to act for or to give advice for the benefit of another upon matters within the scope of the relation." Restatement (Second) of Torts § 874 cmt. a (1977); accord, Hoopes v. Hammargren, 102 Nev. 425, 431, 725 P.2d 238, 242 (1986) ("A fiduciary relationship is deemed to exist when one party is bound to act for the benefit of the other party."). This test defines the existence of a fiduciary duty by referring to its legal effect, not by reference to a state of facts. Consequently, if you want to know whether a fiduciary relation exists, you in effect ask whether there is a fiduciary duty. To find out, you would ask whether there was a fiduciary relation, leaving an endless circle. A different criticism of this definition is given in Deborah A. DeMott, Breach of Fiduciary Duty: On Justifiable Expectations of Loyalty and Their Consequences, 48 Ariz. L. Rev. 925, 933–34 (2006).

[226] Ware v. Ware, 161 P.3d 1188 (Alaska 2007) ("when one imposes a special confidence in another, so that the latter, in equity and good conscience, is bound to act in good faith and with due regard to the interests of the one imposing the confidence"); Scheffler v. Adams & Reese, LLP, 950 So.2d 641, 647 (La. 2007) ("when confidence is reposed on one side and there is resulting superiority and influence on the other"). Restatement (Third) of Trusts § 2 cmt. b (2003), prefers to say that confidential relationships are not fiduciary relationships, and, to distinguish the formal or categorical fiduciary cases, courts sometimes refer to these cases as confidential relationship cases. However, the terminology does not eliminate the fiduciary type duty.

[227] Kent v. United of Omaha Life Ins. Co., 484 F.3d 988 (8th Cir. 2007) ("when one party places 'peculiar confidence' and trust in another and the trusted party 'undertakes to act primarily for another's benefit'); Gracey v. Eaker, 837 So.2d 348 (Fla. 2002) ("where confidence is reposed by one party and a trust accepted by the other, or where confidence has been acquired and abused"); Mabus v. St. James Episcopal Church, 884 So.2d 747 (Miss. 2004) ("must be evidence that both parties understood that a special trust and confidence was being reposed"); Groob v. KeyBank, 108 Ohio St.3d 348, 351, 843 N.E.2d 1170, 1173 (2006) (a fiduciary's duty is "created by his undertaking, to act primarily for the benefit of another in matters connected with his undertaking"); Johnson v. Reiger, 93 P.3d 992 (Wyo. 2004) (fiduciary relations "not created by the unilateral decision to repose trust and reliance, but derive from the conduct or undertaking of the purported beneficiary").

relationship over time, the defendant's evident allegiances, the inability of the putative beneficiary to protect herself and analogies to the recognized categories of fiduciaries.[228]

Arm's length transactions. Ordinary commercial transactions are conducted at arm's length between parties, each of whom expects the other to serve his own interests. Consequently, commercial transactions usually involve no formal fiduciary relationship unless the defendant has special powers of control over the plaintiff's rights or if the plaintiff reposes special confidence in the defendant.[229]

Limitations on fiduciary duties: contracts and statutes. Some fiduciary duties can be limited by contract and some cannot. This accords with the rules for ordinary contracts—some provisions are unconscionable or against public policy and won't be enforced. It also accords with the rules for exculpatory provisions purporting to limit liability for tort—sometimes they work and sometimes they do not. In addition, statutes may eliminate some fiduciary duties or immunize some fiduciaries.[230]

Fiduciaries: duties owed. Fiduciaries owe to their beneficiaries a duty of the "utmost" good faith and loyalty.[231] Given the duty of good faith and loyalty, fiduciaries must, with reasonable care, subordinate their own interests to those of their beneficiaries, keep their beneficiaries' information confidential, and disclose all relevant information they acquire to their beneficiaries.[232] Fiduciaries must also avoid conflicts of interest, or at least obtain the beneficiaries' knowing consent to the conflict.[233]

Fiduciaries: breach of duty. The fault required to show breach of a fiduciary duty depends on the specific duty in issue. Sometimes the fiduciary duty in issue is essentially a duty of reasonable care, in which case the fiduciary is liable for inadvertence or

---

[228] Deborah A. DeMott, Breach of Fiduciary Duty: On Justifiable Expectations of Loyalty and Their Consequences, 48 Ariz. L. Rev. 925, 941–49 (2006).

[229] In re Express Scripts, Inc., PBM Litig., 522 F.Supp.2d 1132 (E.D. Mo. 2007) (business contracts "do not generally give rise to a fiduciary relationship, absent extraordinary circumstances"; the "parties deal with each other at arm's length").

[230] 3 Dobbs, Hayden & Bublick, The Law of Torts § 698 (2d ed. 2011 & Supp.).

[231] "Not honesty alone, but the punctilio of an honor the most sensitive, is then the standard of behavior." Meinhard v. Salmon, 249 N.Y. 458, 464, 164 N.E. 545, 546 (1928) (Cardozo, C.J.). Cardozo's language has been quoted or paraphrased in hundreds of cases. See also Blair v. McDonagh, 177 Ohio App.3d 262, 894 N.E.2d 377 (2008) (the fiduciary "relationship imposes on the members a duty to exercise the utmost good faith and honesty in all dealings and transactions"); Today Homes, Inc. v. Williams, 272 Va. 462, 634 S.E.2d 737 (2006); see generally Deborah A. DeMott, Breach of Fiduciary Duty: On Justifiable Expectations of Loyalty and Their Consequences, 48 Ariz. L. Rev. 925 (2006).

[232] See Doe v. Liberatore, 478 F.Supp. 2d 742, 766 (M.D. Pa. 2007) ("One in a fiduciary relationship with another is under a duty to act solely in the interest of that person"); In re Estate of Green, 912 A.2d 1198 (D.C. 2006) ("An important aspect of a personal representative's fiduciary duty is that he must place the best interests of the heirs ahead of his own interests"); Zastrow v. Journal Commc'ns, Inc., 291 Wis.2d 426, 718 N.W.2d 51 (2006) (similar).

[233] See EBC I, Inc. v. Goldman Sachs & Co., 5 N.Y.3d 11, 832 N.E.2d 26 (2005) (underwriter had fiduciary obligation to disclose alleged secret deals that would give it incentive to underprice initial public offering price of plaintiff's stock).

negligence.[234] Other cases may call for evidence of bad acts[235] or conversely, for strict liability.[236]

Fiduciary breach as a tort with remedies. A breach of fiduciary duty, including the kind of fiduciary duty called a confidential relationship, is a tort.[237] In some cases, the facts may also support a breach of contract theory,[238] while in others the claim is viewed as one in tort only.[239] As with other torts, those who aid and abet violation of fiduciary duties are generally subject to liability for the breach.[240] Thus one who bribes the fiduciary is liable along with the fiduciary himself.[241]

Variable remedies. Remedies available for fiduciary breach vary with the facts.[242] Remedies may include relief at law in the form of compensatory[243] and punitive damages[244] in appropriate cases.[245] Depending on the facts and the claims asserted, available remedies may also include equitable relief such as injunctions and similar orders,[246] rescission, restitution of payments made to the fiduciary or disgorgement of

---

[234] Deborah A. DeMott, Breach of Fiduciary Duty: On Justifiable Expectations of Loyalty and Their Consequences, 48 Ariz. L. Rev. 925, 931 (2006).

[235] See Brehm v. Eisner, 746 A.2d 244, 264 n.66 (Del. 2000) ("directors' decisions will be respected by courts unless the directors are interested or lack independence relative to the decision, do not act in good faith, act in a manner that cannot be attributed to a rational business purpose or reach their decision by a grossly negligent process that includes the failure to consider all material facts reasonably available").

[236] Meinhard v. Salmon, 249 N.Y. 458, 467–68, 164 N.E. 545, 548 (1928). Judge Cardozo for the majority said: "We have no thought to hold that Salmon was guilty of a conscious purpose to defraud. Very likely he assumed in all good faith that with the approaching end of the venture he might ignore his coadventurer and take the extension for himself." Even so, the majority held him responsible. Judge Andrews, dissenting, thought liability should be judged by assessing fairness, not merely by the fact that the innocent co-adventurer took an opportunity he thought was his to take.

[237] E.g., Diamond v. Pappathanasi, 78 Mass.App.Ct. 77, 935 N.E.2d 340 (2010); IDT Corp. v. Morgan Stanley Dean Witter & Co., 12 N.Y.3d 132, 907 N.E.2d 268 (2009); Restatement (Second) of Torts § 874 (1979); Deborah A. DeMott, Breach of Fiduciary Duty: On Justifiable Expectations of Loyalty and Their Consequences, 48 Ariz. L. Rev. 925, 927–34 (2006).

[238] Collins v. Reynard, 154 Ill.2d 48, 607 N.E.2d 1185 (1992) (client can proceed against his attorney either in tort or contract); Burbank Grease Servs., LLC v. Sokolowski, 717 N.W.2d 781 (Wis. 2006) (agent's duty of loyalty redressable either in tort or contract).

[239] Ash v. Continental Ins. Co., 932 A.2d 877 (Pa. 2007).

[240] See In re Adelphia Commc'ns Corp., 365 B.R. 24 (S.D.N.Y. 2007) (also recognizing some contrary authority and special circumstances warranting an exception); Arcidi v. Nat'l Ass'n of Gov't Employees, Inc., 447 Mass. 616, 856 N.E.2d 167 (2006) (dictum; the aider is not liable unless he actively participates or substantially assists in or encourages the breach "to the degree that he or she could not reasonably be held to have acted in good faith"); Burbank Grease Servs., LLC v. Sokolowski, 717 N.W.2d 781 (Wis. 2006); Restatement of Restitution § 138 (1937).

[241] Williams Elec. Games, Inc. v. Garrity, 366 F.3d 569 (7th Cir. 2004).

[242] "[I]dentifying a breach of fiduciary duty [is] the beginning of the analysis, and not its conclusion. Counsel are required to identify the particular fiduciary relationship involved, identify how it was breached, consider the remedies available, and select those remedies appropriate to the client's problem. Whether the cause or causes of action selected carry the right to a jury trial will have to be determined by an historical analysis." Kann v. Kann, 344 Md. 689, 713, 690 A.2d 509, 521 (1997).

[243] Rhue v. Dawson, 173 Ariz. 220, 841 P.2d 215 (Ct. App. 1992).; In re Guardianship of Dorson, 156 N.H. 382, 934 A.2d 545 (2007) (fiduciary took non-cash assets, which had appreciated in value at the time of trial; held, the fiduciary and its surety would be liable for the appreciated value).

[244] E.g., Bardis v. Oates, 119 Cal.App.4th 1, 14 Cal.Rptr.3d 89 (2004); Jordan v. Holt, 362 S.C. 201, 608 S.E.2d 129 (2005); Cooper v. Cooper, 173 Vt. 1, 783 A.2d 430 (2001).

[245] Statutes like ERISA, prescribing only equitable enforcement, may prohibit the award of damages against the statutory fiduciary. See Callery v. U.S. Life Ins. Co. in the City of New York, 392 F.3d 401 (10th Cir. 2004).

[246] Biosynexus, Inc. v. Glaxo Group Ltd., 40 A.D.3d 384, 836 N.Y.S.2d 126 (2007) (preliminary injunction in connection with defendant's assignment of rights, allegedly in violation of fiduciary duty); Sharma v. Vinmar Int'l, Ltd., 231 S.W.3d 405, 429 (Tex. App. 2007) ("injunctive relief must, of necessity, be full and complete so

his profits and gains in the breaching transaction[247] and any other equitable remedy the court deems appropriate.[248] Disgorgement, meaning recovery of the breachor's profits or other gains, may be especially significant when the plaintiff has little or no loss but the fiduciary has reaped a gain through fiduciary breach.

Bad faith breach of contract. For a brief period, several cases supported tort liability for bad faith breach of ordinary commercial contracts,[249] but the tort approach to bad faith breach in those contracts has now been forsaken in the states that adopted it.[250] The general rule today is that the defendant who is guilty of a bad faith breach of contract—that is, guilty of breaching the implied covenant of good faith and fair dealing—is generally liable only in contract, not in tort,[251] unless the breach creates some unreasonable risk of physical harm.[252] Tort liability for bad faith breach is still possible, however, in certain insurance bad faith cases discussed below.

Third-party insurance cases. Third-party insurance cases are best illustrated by the ordinary liability insurance claim. The insurer insures the insured against liability to others, who are third parties. The insurer then owes the insured a duty to defend if the insured is sued by someone claiming a tort covered by the policy. It also owes the insured the duty to pay any legal liability up to the policy limits. The third-party insurance cases recognize that an insurer's breach of contract obligation to its insured will be a tort under certain circumstances. The tort is usually characterized as a "bad faith" breach of the insurer's duty to fairly secure the benefits of the policy to its insured. The liability insurer

---

that those who have acted wrongfully and have breached their fiduciary relationship, as well as those who willfully and knowingly have aided them in doing so, will be effectively denied the benefits and profits flowing from the wrongdoing;" approving injunction against use of trade secrets by former employees).

[247] E.g., Williams Elec. Games, Inc. v. Garrity, 366 F.3d 569 (7th Cir. 2004); United States v. Kearns, 595 F.2d 729 (D.C. Cir. 1978); Lingo v. Lingo, 3 A.3d 241 (Del. 2010); In re Paxson Trust I, 893 A.2d 99 (Pa. Super. 2006) (trustee who used trust property as collateral for a personal loan is subject to liability for the "profit" thus obtained); ERI Consulting Eng'rs, Inc. v. Swinnea, 318 S.W.3d 867 (Tex. 2010); 1 Dan B. Dobbs, Law of Remedies §§ 4.3(5), 4.5(3), 10.6 (2d ed. 1993) (among many discussions on recovery of the breacher's profits, both against fiduciaries and others).

[248] See In re Guardianship of Dorson, 156 N.H. 382, 934 A.2d 545 (2007) ("when crafting a remedy for a trustee's breach of trust and breach of loyalty, '[t]he court is not confined to a limited list of remedies but rather will mold the relief to protect the rights of the beneficiary according to the situation involved,' " quoting G.G. Bogert & G.T. Bogert, The Law of Trusts and Trustees § 861, at 4 (2d ed. rev.1995)).

[249] Seaman's Direct Buying Serv. Inc. v. Standard Oil Co. of Cal., 36 Cal.3d 752, 206 Cal.Rptr. 354, 686 P.2d 1158 (1984) (creating a tort based upon the defendant's bad faith denial that it had a valid contract to supply oil to the plaintiff); Nicholson v. United Pac. Ins. Co., 219 Mont. 32, 710 P.2d 1342 (1985).

[250] See Freeman & Mills, Inc. v. Belcher Oil Co., 11 Cal.4th 85, 900 P.2d 669, 44 Cal.Rptr.2d 420 (1995) (limiting the bad faith claim in tort to insurance cases and those where an independent tort is committed); Stephen S. Ashley, Bad Faith Actions: Liability and Damages § 11.01 (2d ed., current on Westlaw).

[251] E.g., JP Morgan Trust Co. Nat'l Ass'n v. Mid-America Pipeline Co., 413 F.Supp.2d 1244 (D. Kan. 2006); LaSalle Nat'l Leasing Corp. v. Lyndecon, LLC, 409 F.Supp.2d 843 (E.D. Mich. 2005) (Michigan law); Laeroc Waikiki Parkside, LLC v. K.S.K. (Oahu) Ltd. P'ship, 115 Haw. 201, 229, 166 P.3d 961, 989 (2007) ("there is no tort of bad faith outside the context of insurance claims"); Gorski v. Smith, 812 A.2d 683, 710 (Pa. Super. 2002) ("Where a duty of good faith arises, it arises under the law of contracts, not under the law of torts"); see Stephen S. Ashley, Bad Faith Actions Liability & Damages § 11.2 (available on Westlaw with updates) ("the courts have . . . uniformly declined to extend the cause of action for bad faith beyond the insurance context").

[252] E.g., Mobil Oil Corp. v. Thorn, 401 Mich. 36, 258 N.W.2d 30 (1977) (landlord's contract to repair premises); cf. DCR Inc. v. Peak Alarm Co., 663 P.2d 433, 37 A.L.R.4th 35 (Utah 1983) (negligent performance of burglar alarm contract permitted burglary). The point is often raised in nonfeasance cases, where the rule creates a tort duty if the defendant undertakes to act for the plaintiff's safety and certain other conditions are met.

should accept a reasonable opportunity to settle within its policy limits, or at least act in good faith in deciding whether to settle.[253]

First-party insurance cases. First-party insurance cases are illustrated by fire insurance. The insured pays the insurer premiums to assure payment in case of fire damage to the insured's property. When one or more of the insured persons makes a claim against the insurer for payment, the case is a first-party insurance case. The leading case, *Gruenberg v. Aetna Insurance Co.*, for example, held that a fire insurer who unreasonably and in bad faith withheld payment of a claim covered by its policy would be liable, not merely on contractual provisions of the policy, but in both contract and tort.[254]

Elements of the first-party bad faith claim. A little authority requires only proof of negligence as ground for the insurer's tort liability.[255] But the mainstream core test for judging tortious bad faith requires the plaintiff to prove that (1) the insurer lacked a reasonable basis for denying policy benefits to the insured and (2) that the insurer acted with knowing or reckless disregard of the inadequate ground for denying the benefits.[256]

Conduct indirectly affecting payment. Liability in first-party insurance cases has also been extended to cover conduct that may indirectly affect nonpayment or delay. For example, the insurer's failure to properly and promptly investigate may count as bad faith or at least evidence of it.[257] Other collateral conduct, perhaps some that does not affect payment, may also reflect bad faith.[258]

Wrongful discharge: breach of contract. In the absence of statute, the traditional view holds that employees are employed at will unless their contract specifies otherwise.[259] Thus employers are free to discharge employees for any reason or no reason. The discharged employee has a breach of contract action if employment was for a particular duration or if the contract of employment permitted discharge only for just cause. At one time it appeared that courts would treat discharge of an at-will employee as a tort based on the employer's breach of an implied covenant of good faith and fair dealing.[260] This is no longer part of the picture. Instead the claim of tortious wrongful discharge is now commonly predicated upon a specific and identifiable public policy that

---

[253] See 3 Dobbs, Hayden & Bublick, The Law of Torts § 701 (2d ed. 2011 & Supp.).

[254] Gruenberg v. Aetna Ins. Co., 9 Cal.3d 566, 510 P.2d 1032, 108 Cal.Rptr. 480 (1973).

[255] Zoppo v. Homestead Ins. Co., 71 Ohio St.3d 552, 644 N.E.2d 397 (1994).

[256] See Dale v. Guaranty Nat'l Ins. Co., 948 P.2d 545, 551 (Colo. 1997) (the plaintiff must prove that "the insurer acted: (1) unreasonably and (2) with knowledge of or reckless disregard of its unreasonableness"); Bellville v. Farm Bureau Mut. Ins. Co., 702 N.W.2d 468 (Iowa 2005); Hein v. Acuity, 731 N.W.2d 231 (S.D. 2007); Anderson v. Continental Ins. Co., 85 Wis.2d 675, 691, 271 N.W.2d 368, 376 (1978). Douglas G. Houser, Ronald J. Clark & Linda M. Bolduan, Good Faith as a Matter of Law-an Update on the Insurance Company's "Right to Be Wrong," 39 Tort Trial & Ins. Prac. L.J. 1045 (2004).

[257] E.g., Brown v. Patel, 157 P.3d 117, 122 (Okla. 2007) ("a duty to *timely* and *properly* investigate an insurance claim is intrinsic to an insurer's contractual duty to *timely* pay a valid claim").

[258] See Roger C. Henderson, The Tort of Bad Faith in First-Party Insurance Transactions after Two Decades, 37 Ariz. L. Rev. 1153 (1995) (noting among other examples, potential liability for falsely accusing the insured of wrongdoing). In Hollock v. Erie Ins. Exchange, 842 A.2d 409 (Pa. Super. 2004), an uninsured motorist claim, which bears more resemblance to first-party claims than not, the court emphasized collateral conduct of the insurer in misleading the plaintiff's counsel about amounts of coverage and in putting the insured-claimant under surveillance.

[259] For a summary of some of the arguments over at-will employment and support for contract-based good faith obligations, see Stewart J. Schwab, Life-Cycle Justice: Accommodating Just Cause and Employment at Will, 92 Mich. L. Rev. 8 (1993).

[260] Monge v. Beebe Rubber Co., 114 N.H. 130, 316 A.2d 549, 62 A.L.R.3d 264 (1974).

would be undermined if the employer were free to take adverse action against the employee who acts in accord with that policy.[261]

Elements of the wrongful discharge claim. The elements of the public policy claim are essentially adaptations of the elements in tort claims generally, requiring both causation of harm and fault on the part of the employer that would tend to undermine public policy. The precise expressions of these elements have varied. One type of formula requires the plaintiff to prove that: (1) a clear and perhaps substantial public policy existed; (2) the policy would be jeopardized if employees could be freely punished by the employer for the employee's actions in accord with that policy; (3) the employee's conduct in accord with the public policy caused the employer to discharge the employee or to take other adverse employment action, and (4) no overriding justification for the employer's action existed.[262]

What counts as public policy in wrongful discharge claims. Generally, the public policy must be a "clear mandate" and a specific one. It must be well-defined and substantial, and it must be widely perceived so that both employees and employers will recognize it. Most courts also insist that any public policy must derive from constitutions or statutes or from administrative regulations, or sometimes from applicable rules of professional ethics. The defendant's liability does not depend upon proof that he violated the statute. It depends rather upon proof that his actions in discharging the plaintiff undermined the policy reflected in the statute.[263]

Examples. Examples of public policy claims include cases in which the employer fires the at-will employee for refusing to engage in illegal conduct, for performing a public duty, for blowing the whistle on the employer's illegal conduct, or for asserting her rights, as where she claims workers' compensation benefits for an employment injury or for merely exercising her free speech rights.[264]

Economic duress. Threats of physical harm that are made to extract a contract, gift, conveyance or other disposition of property rights are usually tortious if the plaintiff, having no reasonable alternative, accedes to the threats. In such cases, the plaintiff is, at a minimum, entitled to avoid the transaction and to recover either what she has transferred under threat or appropriate compensatory damages.[265]

Elements of a claim. Courts state the elements of economic duress in various ways.[266] In substance they require that (1) the victim entered into a transaction that was disproportionate or unfair (2) as a result of a threat that the courts consider to be legally

---

[261] Howard v. Dorr Woolen Co., 120 N.H. 295, 414 A.2d 1273 (1980) (limiting the bad faith approach of Monge v. Beebe Rubber Co., to discharge in violation of public policy). See Mont. Code Ann. § 39–2–904. Courts sometimes say that the claim lies for breach of "implied covenants of good faith and fair dealing" but then add that the discharge must violate an important public policy. See Lewis v. Cowen, 165 F.3d 154 (2d Cir. 1999).

[262] Jaynes v. Centura Health Corp., 148 P.3d 241 (Colo. Ct. App. 2006); Ballalatak v. All Iowa Agric. Ass'n, 781 N.W.2d 272, 275 (Iowa 2010) ("the employee must show: (1) existence of a clearly defined public policy that protects employee activity; (2) the public policy would be jeopardized by the discharge from employment; (3) the employee engaged in the protected activity, and this conduct was the reason for the employee's discharge; and (4) there was no overriding business justification for the termination").

[263] See 3 Dobbs, Hayden & Bublick, The Law of Torts § 704 (2d ed. 2011 & Supp.) for citations and a fuller discussion.

[264] Id. §§ 704–706.

[265] Restatement (Second) of Torts § 871 cmt. f (1979) (proposing general liability for threats of unlawful conduct that result in interference with a legally protected property interest).

[266] E.g., International Paper Co. v. Whilden, 469 So.2d 560 (Ala. 1985); Kelso v. McGowan, 604 So.2d 726, 732 (Miss. 1992); Troutman v. Facetglas, Inc., 281 S.C. 598, 316 S.E.2d 424 (Ct. App. 1984).

unacceptable on the facts of the particular case and (3) the victim had no reasonable alternative but to yield to the threat, or, commonly, that the victim's free will to choose was overborne by the threat.[267] Some courts have added an ambiguous requirement that (4) the circumstances eliminating the victim's reasonable choices were created by the defendant.[268]

Remedies. A restitutionary recovery may be available as a claim independent of tort or as one kind of remedy given in tort cases where appropriate. Other tort remedies are seldom recoverable for economic duress. However, a few economic threats may warrant the full range of tort relief, including any damages that exceed the defendant's wrongful gains and that thus exceed restitution. While only restitutionary remedies would be awarded in most cases, characterizing economic duress as a tort thus leaves the courts free to award compensatory consequential damages or even punitive damages in a proper case.[269]

---

[267] Superior bargaining power on one side and relative weakness on the other is often mentioned. E.g., U.S. v. Bethlehem Steel Corp., 315 U.S. 289, 300, 62 S.Ct. 581, 587 (1942). For types of threats that are actionable, see 3 Dobbs, Hayden & Bublick, The Law of Torts § 708 (2d ed. 2011 & Supp.).

[268] W. R. Grimshaw Co. v. Nevil C. Withrow Co., 248 F.2d 896, 904 (8th Cir. 1957).

[269] See 3 Dobbs, Hayden & Bublick, The Law of Torts § 707 (2d ed. 2011 & Supp.).

Chapter 44

ECONOMIC HARM TO INTANGIBLE
INTERESTS BY CONVERSION
OR SPOLIATION

Analysis

A. CONVERSION OF INTANGIBLE ECONOMIC INTERESTS
§ 44.1   Expanding the Traditional Conversion Action
§ 44.2   Conversion of Money and Accounts
§ 44.3   Conversion and Contract

B. SPOLIATION OF EVIDENCE
§ 44.4   Intentional Spoliation by a Party to Litigation
§ 44.5   Intentional Spoliation by a Non-Party
§ 44.6   Negligent Spoliation of Evidence
§ 44.7   Factual Causation in Spoliation Cases

A. CONVERSION OF INTANGIBLE ECONOMIC INTERESTS

§ 44.1 Expanding the Traditional Conversion Action

Traditional rules. Under the traditional common law rules, the action for conversion would lie only for interference with rights in tangible personal property.[1] Thus traditionally no conversion action lies for interference with intangible rights, such as choses in action,[2] or for the use of the plaintiff's ideas.[3] In the same way, infringement of a copyright or trademark, interference with business opportunities,[4] the "taking" of one's personality or performance for commercial purposes,[5] the misappropriation of trade secrets, and the misappropriation of ideas[6] may all be torts, but under the traditional rule such actions could not constitute conversion. The rule limiting the conversion action is thus not necessarily a claim-destroying rule. Instead it is often merely a channeling rule, guiding claims for stand-alone economic harm to the most appropriate tort analysis.[7]

---

[1]   § 6.5.

[2]   Shebester v. Triple Crown Insurers, 826 P.2d 603 (Okla. 1992).

[3]   Matzan v. Eastman Kodak Co., 134 A.D.2d 863, 521 N.Y.S.2d 917 (1987).

[4]   H.J., Inc. v. International Telephone & Telegraph Corp., 867 F.2d 1531 (8th Cir. 1989) (manufacturer who terminated distributor and sold directly to dealers was not liable for "conversion" of the dealer network).

[5]   Ippolito v. Lennon, 150 A.D.2d 300, 542 N.Y.S.2d 3 (1989) (rights in a performance, no conversion action unless right is merged in and identified with a document).

[6]   Bloom v. Hennepin County, 783 F. Supp. 418, 440 (D.Minn. 1992) (medical procedure or "protocol" allegedly misappropriated by defendants, intellectual property law, not conversion law, should govern).

[7]   See Dan B. Dobbs, An Introduction to Non-Statutory Economic Loss Claims, 48 Ariz. L. Rev. 713, 722 (2006).

Expansion of conversion: overview. Courts have expanded the conversion action to permit recovery for economic torts in certain cases. Some of the cases that have done so have merely made awards equivalent to restitution of the defendant's gains rather than awards of consequential or punitive damages.[8] Most of the other expansive cases protect the plaintiff's economic interest by a conversion action when that interest can be conceived of as one that is functionally equivalent to an interest in tangible property. A tangible property interest in this sense includes an equitable interest in tangible property offering protection by specific performance or constructive trust; legal rights fully controlled by a tangible document (like a bearer bond); interests that are themselves bought, sold or otherwise exchanged in a market; and information such as computer data and programs that function in the business world like a tangible document. Otherwise, the claim that a pure economic interest has been converted is likely to be rejected, either because the tort is limited to redress only property-like interests, or because some version of the economic loss rule prevents recovery. Thus spoliation of evidence, even when it is a tort, is not conceived as conversion.[9]

Documents embodying rights; negotiable instruments. One of the more clearly justified departures from the traditional rules comes when the defendant takes or wrongly retains a negotiable instrument that is not merely evidence of a right but that can itself be bought and sold as an embodiment of the right to collect. A promissory note payable to the plaintiff, for example, represents the plaintiff's rights to recover money from the maker of the note and courts have generally recognized that conversion of such a note is conversion of the right it embodies, that is, conversion of the value of the note, not merely the value of the paper it is written on.[10] A deed to land, once recorded, has a similar quality and its recording may count as a conversion.[11] Checks, bonds, stock certificates and other similar instruments have been treated the same way,[12] and the plaintiff can recover for their conversion, provided she was entitled to possession of the instrument.[13] The measurement of damages in such cases, however, frequently presents a problem; a promissory note for $100 is not necessarily worth that sum, and certainly is not if the maker is insolvent or has a good defense.[14] In some instances, too, the plaintiff's claim will be for negligence rather than conversion, as where the plaintiff suffers a loss when the defendant bank allows deposit of a check to the account of a person other than the payee.[15]

---

[8] See 3 Dobbs, Hayden & Bublick, The Law of Torts § 709 (2d ed. 2011 & Supp.).

[9] See §§ 44.4 to 44.7.

[10] Teper v. Weiss, 115 Ga. App. 621, 155 S.E.2d 730 (1967); Lappe and Associates, Inc. v. Palmen, 811 S.W.2d 468 (Mo. App. 1991); Save Charleston Foundation v. Murray, 286 S.C. 170, 333 S.E.2d 60 (Ct. App. 1985); United Leasing Corp. v. Thrift Ins. Corp., 247 Va. 299, 440 S.E.2d 902 (1994).

[11] Montano v. Land Title Guarantee Co., 778 P.2d 328 (Colo. App. 1989) (deed from A to C held by bailee in three-party transaction; bailee recorded it without authority, whereupon C borrowed money on it; B, who was to pay A left for parts unknown; held, the bailee is a converter).

[12] Carmichael v. Halstead Nursing Center, Ltd., 237 Kan. 495, 701 P.2d 934 (1985) (corporate defendant, with name similar to payee's, deposited check in its own bank account; this was a conversion); Dayton Construction, Inc. v. Meinhardt, 882 S.W.2d 206 (Mo. App. 1994) (specific checks); see UCC § 3–420 (with certain exceptions, "[t]he law applicable to conversion of personal property applies to instruments").

[13] Great Lakes Higher Education Corp. v. Austin Bank of Chicago, 837 F.Supp. 892 (N.D.Ill. 1993).

[14] See Annotation, Measure of damages for conversion or loss of commercial paper, 85 A.L.R.2d 1349 (1962).

[15] Chicago Title Ins. Co. v. Allfirst Bank, 394 Md. 270, 905 A.2d 366 (2006).

§ 44.2   Conversion of Money and Accounts

Money. Specific coins or bills are subject to conversion if they are identifiable as the particular coins or bills taken from the plaintiff.[16] The old idea that money could be converted only if it was in a "bag"[17] now seems obsolete. Today, it might be plausible to say that when the defendant commits an affirmative act and physically takes control of particular paper monies he is guilty of conversion, even if the particular bills or coins cannot be identified,[18] although perhaps not to gain priority over other creditors with respect to the unidentified monies. Certainly the plaintiff is entitled to recover on restitutionary grounds to prevent the defendant's unjust enrichment, even if not on the basis of conversion.[19]

Accounts or funds. Interference with accounts or "funds" can be conceptualized in various ways. Where the defendant wrongfully attached a bank account, the Colorado court treated the claim as one for "wrongful attachment," which it considered to be a specific kind of interference with contract, not conversion.[20] But it is also plausible to treat some accounts or "funds" as subject to conversion even where the defendant does not physically withhold a negotiable instrument from its owner. If the defendant, without authority, transfers funds from the plaintiff's account to his own or another account, he is a converter[21] even though the transfer is purely a bookkeeping entry, not a physical movement of cash.[22] Some courts have said that a fund or account may be subject to conversion if the defendant is under an obligation to treat specific funds in a particular manner,[23] although stated this broadly the proposition may conflict with the usual rule that breach of a contract or non-payment of a debt does not qualify.[24]

---

[16] In Moody v. Smith, 899 F.2d 383 (5th Cir. 1990), the defendant was held to have converted a pedigreed 1879 gold four-dollar coin worth between $75,000 and $88,000. In Little v. Gibbs, 4 N.J.L. 211 (1818), the court thought identification by numbers on bills would suffice: "If money or cash be lost or stolen the loser cannot maintain trover to recover it, because it cannot be distinguished. But notes and bank bills may be recovered in such an action, because the interest of the owner in them is sufficient, and they may be distinguished by names, marks and numbers on them."

[17] See Kinaston v. Moor, Cro. Car. 89, 79 Eng.Rep. 678 (1627) (perhaps suggesting that the bag was only important as one piece of evidence showing that it was the plaintiff's money held by the defendant, but an unnecessary piece of evidence if the evidence showed that the defendant took the money directly from the plaintiff); Campbell v. Naman's Catering, Inc., 842 So.2d 654 (Ala. 2002) ("earmarked money or specific money capable of identification, e.g., money in a bag or coins or notes which have been entrusted to defendants' care," but recognizing that monies in a special account could be subject to conversion).

[18] Cf. Lappe and Associates, Inc. v. Palmen, 811 S.W.2d 468 (Mo.App. 1991) (check payable to defendant for one purpose, fund diverted to another purpose, held, conversion).

[19] Assumpsit, to use the name of an old form of action, would lie for money received by the defendant that belongs to the plaintiff. See 1 Dan B. Dobbs, Law of Remedies § 6.1(1) (2d ed. 1993).

[20] Vanderbeek v. Vernon Corp., 50 P.3d 866 (Colo. 2002).

[21] Kenet v. Bailey, 679 So.2d 348 (Fla. Dist. Ct. App. 1996) (attorney transferred client's funds from trust-escrow account to himself, he is a converter and punitive damages may be recoverable); Evans v. Dean Witter Reynolds, Inc., 116 Nev. 598, 5 P.3d 1043 (2000) (approving multi-million punitive damages award and holding that brokerage firm guilty of aiding and abetting or "conspiring" to convert assets was liable without offsets for amounts repaid to owners of assets by other tortfeasors); Methodist Manor of Waukesha, Inc. v. Martin, 255 Wis. 2d 707, 647 N.W.2d 409 (Ct. App. 2002) (allegation that defendant diverted monies from his mother's bank account, which monies were required by law to be paid to nursing home supporting mother, is an allegation of conversion).

[22] Brown v. Oklahoma State Bank & Trust Co. of Vinita, 860 P.2d 230 (1993); see also UCC § 3–420 (with certain exceptions, "[t]he law applicable to conversion of personal property applies to instruments" covered by the UCC).

[23] Hoffman v. Unterberg, 9 A.D.3d 386, 780 N.Y.S.2d 617 (2004), *abrogated on other grounds*, Tzolis v. Wolff, 10 N.Y.3d 100, 855 N.Y.S.2d 6 (2008).

[24] § 44.3.

Mispayment of a negotiable instrument like a check by paying the wrong person on a forged indorsement or by other mispayments is an example.[25] Likewise, if an identified fund of money represented by a check belongs to the plaintiff, deposit of the check to the defendant's account,[26] or the defendant's refusal release money represented by account,[27] is a conversion.

Relationships of the parties sometimes matters. One who deposits funds in a bank is a creditor, not a bailor of the funds,[28] and is thus likely to be limited to a recovery in contract or under restitutionary principles.[29] Liability based on transfer of a fund by bookkeeping (or computer) entry is consonant with commercial practice that treats such entries as an effective transfer, and consonant as well with the protection given to account transfers and the like under constructive trust and other equitable rules.[30]

The plaintiff has no claim for conversion merely because the defendant has a bank account and owes the plaintiff money. To support a conversion action, the plaintiff must show that the defendant in some way transferred the plaintiff's funds to the defendant's accounts,[31] or that the defendant retained in his account funds specifically belonging to the plaintiff.[32]

Negotiable instruments. So far as the putative conversion of an account is accomplished through negotiation, endorsement, transfer or payment of a negotiable instrument, the intricacies of banking practice complicate the picture both on the question of liability and on its basis. UCC provisions are likely to determine which parties are entitled to recover and whether and on what conditions recovery is to be

---

[25] UCC § 3–420; Stromberg v. Moore, 170 S.W.3d 26 (Mo. App. 2005); Restatement Second of Torts § 241A (1965); cf. Decatur Auto Ctr. v. Wachovia Bank, 276 Ga. 817, 583 S.E.2d 6 (2003) (customer paid bank to stop payment on customer's check, but bank knowingly paid the check anyway, conversion); Stebbins v. North Adams Trust Co., 243 Mass. 69, 136 N.E. 880 (1922) (under a system in which the passbook was required to make a withdrawal and in which its assignment operated to assign the account and not merely the book itself, defendant was liable for the amount in the account).

[26] Commonwealth v. Caparella, 70 Mass. App. Ct. 506, 874 N.E.2d 682 (2007) (defendant deposited checks payable to employer in a secret account defendant created in employer's name with defendant in control of the account; this was criminal embezzlement which is conversion by one in a position of trust); In re Baez, 42 A.D.3d 157, 836 N.Y.S.2d 591 (2007) (attorney deposited escrow check into his personal account; he was a converter and suspended from practice).

[27] Giles v. General Motors Acceptance Corp., 494 F.3d 865 (9th Cir. 2007) (defendant held money due to the plaintiff in a separate account, then withheld the money, held, a conversion).

[28] See Leather Manufacturers' Nat'l Bank v. Merchants' Nat'l Bank, 128 U.S. 26, 34, 9 S.Ct. 3, 4, 32 L.Ed. 342 (1888) (because bank does not owe depositor a refund of specific funds, only a money equivalent).

[29] See Gossels v. Fleet Nat'l Bank, 453 Mass. 366, 372, 902 N.E.2d 370, 378 (2009) (emphasizing that bank is a debtor to its depositor, not a bailee, and that the customer has no right to specific funds transferred by the bank; hence the bank transferring funds is not a converter).

[30] For example, a constructive trust may be imposed on a bank account, although the account is not a separate accumulation of money but only a bookkeeping credit to the owner. See Dan B. Dobbs, Law of Remedies § 6.1(4) (2d ed. 1993).

[31] See Citadel Management, Inc. v. Telesis Trust, Inc., 123 F.Supp.2d 133 (S.D.N.Y. 2000).

[32] See Giles v. General Motors Acceptance Corp., 494 F.3d 865 (9th Cir. 2007).

permitted at all.[33] And, once again, restitution may prove to be a quite satisfactory alternative.[34]

§ 44.3 Conversion and Contract

Contracts between the parties potentially affect liability for conversion of economic interests in two major ways, one of which favors defendants and one of which favors plaintiffs.

Defendant-favorable provisions. First, the defendant does not convert either a tangible or intangible interest of the plaintiff's if the defendant is acting rightfully. A contract provision favorable to the defendant may show that the defendant's action with respect to the plaintiff's economic interest is rightful, not wrongful. A pledge of a tangible chattel as security for a debt is an easy example. The defendant is not acting wrongfully in retaining the pledged goods until the debt is paid; that is the very thing the pledge contract contemplates.[35] The same is true with economic rights. If the defendant retains a down payment when the plaintiff breaches a contract to purchase, that is no conversion if the contract lawfully permits the retention.[36]

The defendant-favorable contract effect is circumscribed by the statutory or common law public policy against the use of force to recover property, so the defendant who might retain the down payment of the contract breacher would have no privilege to take an equivalent sum by hacking into the breacher's bank account.[37] It may be circumscribed as well by the sometime rule for bailments that a bailee cannot avoid liability for conversion or damage to bailed property by writing an exculpatory clause into the bailment contract.[38]

Plaintiff-favorable provisions. Second, a plaintiff-favorable contract provision may obligate the defendant to provide the plaintiff with some kind of economic advantage. If the contract requires the defendant to return tangible property, title to which is in the plaintiff, the plaintiff may have an option to sue in tort for conversion or on the contract.[39] However, if the contract requires the defendant to provide some purely economic benefit, as distinct from a return of the plaintiff's property, the conversion action may not be an option. For one thing, the contract right may not count as a "property" interest, which is required for conversion.[40] For another, a recovery in conversion may fail to honor the contract provisions between the parties.

---

[33]   E.g., UCC § 3–420 (setting forth who may sue for conversion of an instrument); setting § 4–401 & 4–402 (wrongful dishonor of a check; limitations on damages). Uniform statutes have addressed negotiable instrument rules for well over a century in versions that have been revised at various times. Lawyers may need to construe case law in light of the version in force when cases were decided. See Philip E. Cleary, Statutory Overkill: Why Section 3–420(a) of the Uniform Commercial Code May Not *Really* Mean What It Says About the Issuer's Cause of Action for Conversion of a Negotiable Instrument, 39 UCC L.J. 399 (2007).

[34]   See, e.g., B.D.G.S., Inc. v. Balio, 8 N.Y.3d 106, 861 N.E.2d 813, 829 N.Y.S.2d 449 (2006).

[35]   See §§ 6.9 & 6.11.

[36]   E.g., Bradley v. Sanchez, 943 So.2d 218 (Fla. Dist. Ct. App. 2006).

[37]   See § 7.14 (forceful repossession of chattels).

[38]   § 6.10.

[39]   See § 44.1. The plaintiff in a tangible chattel case may have the option to sue for negligence. § 6.11.

[40]   See § 6.5.

Courts commonly say that the defendant who fails to pay a debt is not a converter of the money withheld; he is simply liable or not according to the contract's terms,[41] unless he commits some independently tortious act. Thus a buyer of natural gas who underpays the seller because the buyer wrongly attributes poor quality to the gas may be in breach of contract but cannot be held for conversion of the sums due to the seller.[42] This rule can be viewed as an insistence that conversion rules, if applied to pure economic interests at all, should be limited to interests that bear more similarity to property interests than to contract rights.

Economic loss rule. The rule can also be viewed belonging to the cluster of economic loss rules, which generally reject tort liability for non-physical economic harms on issues within the scope of a contract between the parties.[43] A few decisions reject the economic loss rule in cases of intentional torts such as conversion.[44] Others have effectuated the economic loss rule by limiting the plaintiff to a contract rather than a conversion claim,[45] allowing the conversion action only if the defendant has breached a duty that is independent of or extraneous to the contract.[46] The same policy also makes an appearance in restitution doctrine.[47] However, it is important to observe that at least some contract provisions can be given due respect even if the action is one in conversion, because even in a conversion action, the defendant who acts in accord with the contract is not a converter.

Practical effect of the limit to contract. The practical effect of limiting the plaintiff to a contract claim may include the following: (1) the statute of limitations has run on contract claims, though not on tort claims;[48] (2) contract damages are more limited, notably in their basic measure, in their disallowance of punitive and emotional distress damages, and in their substitution of liquidated damages for actual damages;[49] (3) other contract provisions may eliminate the possibility of practical recovery under the

---

[41]   In re McDaniel, 368 B.R. 515 (M.D. La. 2007); Morris v. National Western Life Ins. Co., 208 Ga. App. 443, 430 S.E.2d 813, 815 (1993); cf. Shebester v. Triple Crown Insurers, 826 P.2d 603 (Okla. 1992) (insurer allegedly paid wrong person, held not a conversion).

[42]   Grynberg v. Questar Pipeline Co., 70 P.3d 1 (Utah 2003).

[43]   See Ch. 41.

[44]   Indemnity Ins. Co. of N. Am. v. American Aviation, Inc., 891 So.2d 532 (Fla. 2004) ("Intentional tort claims such as fraud, conversion, intentional interference, civil theft, abuse of process, and other torts requiring proof of intent generally remain viable either in the products liability context or if the parties are in privity of contract."), *receded from on other grounds*, Tiara Condominium Ass'n v. Marsh & McLennan Companies, Inc., 110 So.3d 399 (Fla. 2013) (economic loss rule applies only in products context).

[45]   See Pittsburgh Construction Co. v. Griffith, 834 A.2d 572 (Pa. Super. 2003) (homeowner withheld escrowed funds due builder under contract, but builder's claim was only for breach of contract, not conversion); see also Pioneer Commercial Funding Corp. v. American Financial Mortgage Corp., 855 A.2d 818, 827 (Pa. 2004) (although the plaintiff's claim was styled as one of conversion, commercial law rules trumped conversion rules by providing a justification for the defendant's dominion of the disputed property).

[46]   See, e.g., Giles v. General Motors Acceptance Corp., 494 F.3d 865 (9th Cir. 2007) (at least where a duty is imposed by law independent of the contract duty, an economic loss claim can proceed in tort, permitting a claim for conversion of funds).

[47]   Independently of tort rules, restitution doctrine refuses to permit restitution for breach of contract where the defendant's only remaining obligation is to pay the plaintiff money. See, e.g., 3 Dan B. Dobbs, Law of Remedies § 12.7(5) (2d ed. 1993). The effect of this rule is to limit the plaintiff to the contract price and to prevent recovery of whatever gains the defendant made by reason of his breach.

[48]   E.g., Grynberg v. Questar Pipeline Co., 70 P.3d 1 (Utah 2003).

[49]   Cf. Bradley v. Sanchez, 943 So.2d 218 (Fla. Dist. Ct. App. 2006) (forfeiture of down payment under contract provision permitted, hence no conversion for seller to keep the down payment).

contract, as where a contract provision would require the plaintiff to indemnify the defendant for any losses the defendant incurs in contract liability.[50]

B. SPOLIATION OF EVIDENCE

§ 44.4 Intentional Spoliation by a Party to Litigation

Rejecting the tort claim. When a party to pending or probable litigation intentionally destroys or otherwise spoliates evidence that substantially impairs the opposing party's ability to prove her claim, the victim of intentional spoliation sometimes asserts a tort claim against the spoliator. This claim seems not to have been thought of as a claim for conversion of intangible rights or as an interference with the judicial process. It is sometimes thought of as a new tort and a cause of action for spoliation, although all such claims appear to be particular instances of an older tort—intentional interference with economic prospects. A number of courts reject this independent tort claim for spoliation of evidence by a party or prospective party to litigation.[51]

Reasons for rejecting the tort; alternative remedies. Several reasons are given for this outcome.[52] One major argument against tort liability for spoliation is that other sanctions and remedies are available against parties who destroy evidence. In particular, the trial judge in the underlying litigation in which the lost evidence is relevant may provide a remedy. The judge may allow the victim to introduce evidence that the defendant destroyed or otherwise spoliated evidence, then give a jury instruction that, if intentional spoliation is established, the jury may presume or infer that the spoliated evidence was favorable to the victim and unfavorable to the spoliator.[53]

Cases may apply this approach not only cases of destroyed or secreted physical evidence but also to "missing witness" cases in which one party fails to produce a witness who apparently knows all the relevant facts. In fact, concerns about spoliation lie behind several kinds of res ipsa loquitur cases.[54] In a case of plaintiff-spoliation,[55] the plaintiff's investigators, examining a vehicle before the manufacturer defendant was notified of its involvement in the plaintiff's injury, removed a part for scrutiny, making it impossible to determine whether it had been misaligned. When misalignment later became a critical issue, the court held that the plaintiff could not use res ipsa loquitur, partly because of

---

[50]   See Giles v. General Motors Acceptance Corp., 494 F.3d 865 (9th Cir. 2007).

[51]   Gribben v. Wal-Mart Stores, Inc., 824 N.E.2d 349 (Ind. 2005); Fletcher v. Dorchester Mutual Ins. Co., 437 Mass. 544, 773 N.E.2d 420 (2002); Dowdle Butane Gas Co. v. Moore, 831 So.2d 1124 (Miss. 2002); Trevino v. Ortega, 969 S.W.2d 950 (Tex. 1998). See generally Thomas G. Fischer, Intentional Spoliation of Evidence, Interfering With Prospective Civil Action as Actionable, 70 A.L.R.4th 984 (1990).

[52]   Among them: (1) It would be difficult to be certain that, even armed with the lost evidence, the victim would have prevailed in the initial dispute. See § 44.7. (2) It has also been argued that, in some cases, the spoliator is merely disposing of his own property and should have a right to do that. But the spoliator's property interest—when he has one—does not prevent sanctions and inferences adverse to the spoliator, e.g., Gath v. M/A-Com, Inc., 440 Mass. 482, 802 N.E.2d 521 (2003), so it seems unclear why it should bar a separate tort claim. (3) Not every piece of evidence is important enough to warrant a tort suit over its destruction, but it will be hard to know whether evidence that has been destroyed is important or not and hard to draw the line between important and unimportant in any event.

[53]   E.g., Banks v. Sunrise Hosp., 102 P.3d 52 (Nev. 2004); Murray v. Developmental Servs. of Sullivan County, Inc., 149 N.H. 264, 818 A.2d 302 (2003); Jerista v. Murray, 185 N.J. 175, 883 A.2d 350 (2005). The foundation for the adverse inference is that the spoliator knew or should have known that the evidence was important in actual or potential litigation and then intentionally destroyed it. See Wal-Mart Stores, Inc. v. Johnson, 106 S.W.3d 718 (Tex. 2003).

[54]   See generally §§ 13.3 to 13.6.

[55]   Lawson v. Mitsubishi Motor Sales of America, Inc., 938 So.2d 35 (La. 2006).

her investigator's interference with the evidence, a result that may or may not be comparable to the spoliation inference against a defendant spoliator.

Other in-trial sanctions without a separate tort suit are possible, too. In Massachusetts, a trial judge remedied the spoliation by imposing a sanction that prevented the spoliator from offering his own evidence and argument on certain related issues, then permitting the adverse inference as well.[56] If the plaintiff destroys evidence, such as a product manufactured by the defendant and claimed to be defective, the court might conceivably even dismiss the plaintiff's claim altogether.[57] For the courts rejecting the tort claim for spoliation, such potential sanctions and remedies are sufficient.

Recognizing the tort claim. Some courts, however, have held that where vital or critical evidence is impaired, concealed, or destroyed, such intentional spoliation by a party or prospective party to probable litigation is actionable under existing tort principles[58] or as a separate tort for spoliation.[59] One argument for this position is that intentional spoliation of vital evidence "is misconduct of such a serious nature, the existing remedies are not a sufficient response," so that an independent tort action, with its potential for punitive damages, is permissible or even desirable in the interests of justice.[60] And spoliation can "destroy fairness and justice" and increase the costs of litigation as parties attempt to reconstruct evidence.[61]

The duty not to spoliate evidence, however, is discharged if the alleged spoliator has given the other party a full and fair opportunity to examine the evidence.[62] (The same result could be reached in jurisdictions that predicate the spoliation action on an intent to defeat the opposing party's action, since destruction of evidence after the opposing party has a full and fair chance to inspect the evidence would not normally evince such intent.) On a more controversial note, some authority has played with the idea that the spoliation claim must be dismissed unless the plaintiff has actually pursued the underlying claim and lost for lack of the evidence destroyed by the defendant.[63] Other

---

[56]   Gath v. M/A-Com, Inc., 440 Mass. 482, 802 N.E.2d 521 (2003) (affirming the trial judge's decision, nothing that the adverse inference piled on the prohibition of evidence could be justified because the defendant may have evaded the prohibition).

[57]   Verchot v. General Motors Corp., 812 So.2d 296 (Ala. 2001) (after brakes failed, plaintiff's insurer disposed of the car manufactured by defendant; court appears to treat this as if the plaintiff herself had disposed of the car; dismissal upheld).

[58]   E.g., Allstate Ins. Co. v. Dooley, 243 P.3d 197 (Alaska 2010) (where evidence is intentionally concealed until after the entry of judgment and the expiration of the time to seek relief from that judgment, the proper cause of action is fraudulent concealment of evidence, not spoliation; if evidence is completely destroyed, then an action for spoliation might lie); Rosenblit v. Zimmerman, 166 N.J. 391, 766 A.2d 749 (2001) ("fraudulent concealment").

[59]   E.g., Williams v. BASF Catalysts LLC, 765 F.3d 306 (3d Cir. 2014) (N.J. law); Rizzuto v. Davidson Ladders, Inc., 280 Conn. 225, 905 A.2d 1165 (2006); Davis v. Wal-Mart Stores, Inc., 93 Ohio St. 3d 488, 756 N.E.2d 657 (2001). Some courts say the plaintiff must prove the "underlying claim was significantly impaired due to the spoliation of evidence," Holmes v. Amerex Rent-A-Car, 710 A.2d 846 (D.C. 1998), the same essential idea as the requirement in other formulations that the spoliated evidence must be "vital" in establishing the underlying claim.

[60]   State v. Carpenter, 171 P.3d 41 (Alaska 2007); Hannah v. Heeter, 213 W.Va. 704, 584 S.E.2d 560 (2003).

[61]   Rizzuto v. Davidson Ladders, Inc., 280 Conn. 225, 905 A.2d 1165 (2006).

[62]   American Family Mut. Ins. Co. v. Golke, 319 Wis.2d 397, 768 N.W.2d 729 (2009).

[63]   Mayfield v. Acme Barrel Co., 258 Ill. App.3d 32, 629 N.E.2d 690 (1994) (reflecting Illinois decisions that a spoliation claim is premature until the plaintiff has tried and lost the underlying tort claim).

authority has declined "to require a spoliation plaintiff to pursue a futile lawsuit" as a prerequisite to the spoliation claim.[64]

§ 44.5 Intentional Spoliation by a Non-Party

Inadequacy of alternative sanctions against a party. When it comes to destruction by non-parties, the problem is surprisingly complex. An unrelated third person's destruction of evidence clearly does not warrant a presumption against the defendant in the initial action who had nothing to do with the destruction.[65] In that case, a tort action against the spoliator may be the plaintiff's only hope of compensation.

Ownership of destroyed evidence. One factor that may be important is ownership of the destroyed evidence. If the physical evidence is property rightfully owned or possessed by the plaintiff, T's intentional destruction will ordinarily be actionable as a conversion or trespass, but proximate cause and reasonable certainty rules of damages may tend to limit liability to the value of the property as a tangible good unless T knew of its importance in existing or probable litigation and a separate spoliation action is permitted.

Split in authority. Some authority has permitted an action for intentional spoliation against a third person who has actual knowledge that the destroyed evidence is important in the plaintiff's litigation.[66] But other courts have rejected the intentional spoliation action against a non-party.[67] Even where the claim of spoliation is recognized against a non-party, the claim may fail in particular cases because the defendant was, in effect, privileged to dispose of the evidence on the facts of the case, because the plaintiff herself failed to take reasonable steps to preserve or inspect the evidence,[68] because a party who could be sanctioned was partly responsible for the destruction along with the non-party,[69] or because of other particular circumstances.[70]

---

[64] Rizzuto v. Davidson Ladders, Inc., 280 Conn. 225, 233, 905 A.2d 1165, 1172 (2006); Holmes v. Amerex Rent-A-Car, 710 A.2d 846 (D.C. 1998).

[65] Cf. Boyd v. Travelers Ins. Co., 166 Ill.2d 188, 652 N.E.2d 267, 209 Ill.Dec. 727 (1995) (refusing also to apply a presumption against the third person that the loss of evidence caused loss of the suit).

[66] Hannah v. Heeter, 213 W.Va. 704, 584 S.E.2d 560 (2003) (negligent spoliation is a stand-alone tort if third person had a duty to use care to preserve evidence, as where the duty is assumed by undertaking; intentional spoliation by a third person is also actionable); cf. Lips v. Scottsdale Healthcare Corp., 224 Ariz. 266, 229 P.3d 1008 (2010) (holding that no "specific intent . . . to disrupt or injure the plaintiff's lawsuit" had been shown, and stating that such an intent would be required if the tort were to be recognized).

[67] Temple Community Hospital v. Superior Court, 20 Cal.4th 464, 84 Cal.Rptr.2d 852, 976 P.2d 223 (1999); Fletcher v. Dorchester Mutual Insurance Company, 437 Mass. 544, 773 N.E.2d 420 (2002); Dowdle Butane Gas Co., Inc. v. Moore, 831 So.2d 1124 (Miss. 2002); Thomas G. Fischer, Intentional Spoliation of Evidence, Interfering with Prospective Civil Action, as Actionable, 70 A.L.R.4th 984 (1990).

[68] Dardeen v. Kuehling, 213 Ill.2d 329, 821 N.E.2d 227, 290 Ill.Dec. 176 (2004); Hennessey v. Restaurant Assocs., Inc., 25 A.D.3d 340, 807 N.Y.S.2d 349 (2006).

[69] Cf. Ortega v. City of New York, 9 N.Y.3d 69, 876 N.E.2d 1189, 845 N.Y.S.2d 773 (suggesting this possibility).

[70] In Glotzbach v. Froman, 854 N.E.2d 337 (Ind. 2006), the spoliator was the employer of the deceased whose death arose out of employment and was subject to workers' compensation. By destroying the evidence, the employer eliminated any hope of a claim by the estate against the manufacturer of equipment that may have caused the employee's death. The court found workers' compensation doubly important. First, it would be in the employer's interest to preserve the evidence against a manufacturer whose liability might reduce the employer's ultimate workers' compensation payout. Second, the workers' compensation act was intended to eliminate "satellite litigation against the employer," and to allow the spoliation claim would tend to undermine that purpose.

§ 44.6 Negligent Spoliation of Evidence

Liability for negligent interference with the plaintiff's lawsuit prospects is perhaps even more problematical than liability for intentional interference. As with intentional interference, courts are likely to label damages speculative because of uncertainty whether the lost evidence would in fact have produced a winning case for the plaintiff or even whether it would have helped the plaintiff at all.[71]

In addition, in the absence of a special exception, tort law seldom imposes a duty of care to protect strangers from stand-alone economic harm.[72] Likewise under the nonfeasance rules, people in general have no duty to act positively to aid others.[73] If the spoliator is a party or prospective party to the initial suit, a duty to use reasonable care might conceivably be based on his special control of evidence in a suit to which he is a party, or on the fact that destruction of evidence not only harms the other party but affirmatively aids the spoliator. But the argument that trial sanctions against a party to the suit will be sufficient protection for the plaintiff may bar the claim for negligence spoliation as well as for the intentional variety.

If the negligent spoliator is neither a party nor aligned in interest with a party, he can argue the nonfeasance and economic loss rules against any duty to use care to protect a stranger, even if he is under a duty not to intentionally destroy evidence. Courts would ordinarily impose a duty of care only if the non-party defendant undertook to preserve the evidence,[74] if he stood in a fiduciary[75] or other special relationship to the plaintiff,[76] if he had a statutory duty to preserve it[77] or if he had been subjected to a court order

---

[71] E.g., Ortega v. City of New York, 9 N.Y.3d 69, 845 N.Y.S.2d 773 (2007); see § 44.7.

[72] See Chapter 41.

[73] See §§ 25.1 to 25.7.

[74] Holmes v. Amerex Rent-A-Car, 710 A.2d 846 (D.C. 1998); Boyd v. Travelers Ins. Co., 166 Ill.2d 188, 652 N.E.2d 267, 209 Ill.Dec. 727 (1995) (saying that this is not a separate tort, but ordinary negligence, based on an assumed duty of care); Callahan v. Stanley Works, 306 N.J.Super. 488, 703 A.2d 1014 (1997) (voluntary assumption of a duty to preserve would be a jury question where defendant placed evidence tag on harmful instrumentality then lost it); cf. Dardeen v. Kuehling, 213 Ill. 2d 329, 821 N.E.2d 227, 290 Ill. Dec. 176 (2004) (in a negligent spoliation claim, the plaintiff must show a duty to preserve evidence arising by contract, agreement, assumption of duty by voluntary undertaking or otherwise; homeowner's liability insurer had no duty to instruct homeowner to preserve evidence of condition that caused harm to plaintiff). In New York, even an oral undertaking by itself is not sufficient to create a duty. See Metlife Auto & Home v. Joe Basic Chevrolet, Inc., 1 N.Y.3d 478, 807 N.E.2d 865, 775 N.Y.S.2d 754 (2004).

[75] Fuller Family Holdings, LLC v. Northern Trust Co., 371 Ill. App. 3d 605, 624, 863 N.E.2d 743, 761, 309 Ill. Dec. 111, 129 (2007) (trustee lost written guarantee of an obligation to the beneficiaries; trustee had "a duty to preserve the guarantee based on the fiduciary relationship between the trustee and the trust beneficiaries and upon the trustee's obligation to maintain all records that relate to the assets and interests of the trust").

[76] Hannah v. Heeter, 213 W.Va. 704, 584 S.E.2d 560 (2003) (no general duty to preserve evidence; defendant will be liable only if he is under a special duty by virtue of a contract, assumed duty, or special relationship or otherwise).

[77] As in Bondu v. Gurvich, 473 So.2d 1307 (Fla. Dist. Ct. App. 1984) (allowing independent spoliation claim where hospital, which was a defendant in the underlying negligence action, had a duty to preserve medical records). The Florida Supreme Court later disapproved of first-party spoliation claims, holding that adverse inferences or presumptions against the spoliator could be used instead. Martino v. Wal-Mart Stores, Inc., 908 So.2d 342 (Fla. 2005).

requiring him to do so.[78] Consequently, liability of a third person for negligent interference with evidence is frequently rejected.[79]

§ 44.7 Factual Causation in Spoliation Cases

Causation and damages raise difficult issues in all spoliation cases. The plaintiff must contend that the spoliator has destroyed evidence that would have allowed the plaintiff to recover in the underlying suit and that she cannot recover because the evidence is missing. But if the plaintiff cannot prove what the evidence would show, she cannot possibly prove that it would have saved her suit or defense. If she can prove indirectly what the evidence would have shown, she could presumably have proved the same thing in the underlying suit. Courts that reject the spoliation claim completely usually point to this problem of proving factual causation.[80]

Relaxing the but-for causation rule—value-of-the-chance recovery. Perhaps some of the courts that recognize the tort claim assume that the normal burden of proof is to be relaxed. The District of Columbia Court has specifically said that the plaintiff need only prove "that the underlying lawsuit was significantly *impaired*, that the spoliated evidence was *material* to that impairment, and that the plaintiff enjoyed a *significant possibility of success* in the underlying claim."[81] Recovery under the District of Columbia rule would then be limited to the value of the chance of recovery.[82]

Relaxing the but-for causation rule—presumption of causation. Other courts have allowed the plaintiff to recover all her damages. West Virginia has held that the spoliated evidence must be found to have been "vital to a party's ability to prevail in a pending or potential civil action," but that once this and other elements of the claim have been proved, "there arises a rebuttable presumption that but for the fact of the spoliation of evidence, the party injured by the spoliation would have prevailed in the pending or potential litigation."[83] The Connecticut Court thought that while the plaintiff may get a windfall by prevailing in the spoliation claim when—possibly—she could not have prevailed in the underlying claim, requiring the plaintiff to prove intentional and bad faith destruction of the evidence minimized that danger. Even if some risk of windfall remained, the court said, "the defendant should bear this risk in light of its egregious litigation misconduct."[84] It may be added that when the defendant creates a definite risk of loss by misconduct that also renders proof of causation difficult, tort cases in other areas have also been willing to permit findings of causation if the evidence is otherwise satisfactory.

---

[78] Ortega v. City of New York, 9 N.Y.3d 69, 845 N.Y.S.2d 773 (2007) (recognizing a duty of care, but holding nevertheless that no cause of action exists against non-party for negligent spoliation).

[79] Lips v. Scottsdale Healthcare Corp., 224 Ariz. 266, 229 P.3d 1008 (2010); Martin v. Keeley & Sons, Inc., 2012 IL 113270, 365 Ill. Dec. 656, 979 N.E.2d 22 (2012); Richardson v. Sara Lee Corp., 847 So.2d 821 (Miss. 2003).

[80] Temple Community Hospital v. Superior Court, 20 Cal.4th 464, 84 Cal.Rptr.2d 852, 976 P.2d 223, 229 (1999); Ortega v. City of New York, 9 N.Y.3d 69, 845 N.Y.S.2d 773 (2007).

[81] Holmes v. Amerex Rent-A-Car, 710 A.2d 846 (D.C. 1998) (emphasis added).

[82] Id. (if plaintiff would have had 60% chance of recovering $100,000 given the missing evidence, plaintiff's recovery for its destruction would be $60,000).

[83] Hannah v. Heeter, 213 W.Va. 704, 584 S.E.2d 560 (2003). Although the presumption seems to establish that a loss occurred, it appears that the plaintiff would still be required to prove the damages that would have been recovered or recoverable. In that respect, the spoliation claim would resemble the case-within-the-case proof in legal malpractice cases. See §§ 45.6 & 45.12.

[84] Rizzuto v. Davidson Ladders, Inc., 280 Conn. 225, 905 A.2d 1165 (2006).

Chapter 45

LEGAL MALPRACTICE

Analysis

A. MALPRACTICE IN CIVIL MATTERS: PRIMA FACIE CASE

§ 45.1   Scope, Duties, and Elements
§ 45.2   Duty: Establishing a Client-Lawyer Relationship
§ 45.3   The Professional Standard of Care
§ 45.4   Breach of Duty
§ 45.5   Causation of Harm: General Rules
§ 45.6   Causation: The Case Within a Case
§ 45.7   Liability to Non-clients

B. MALPRACTICE IN CIVIL MATTERS: DEFENSES

§ 45.8   Contributory Negligence/Comparative Fault
§ 45.9   *In Pari Delicto* and Quasi-Judicial Immunity
§ 45.10 Statute of Limitations

C. MALPRACTICE IN CIVIL MATTERS: DAMAGES

§ 45.11 Compensatory Damages Generally
§ 45.12 Compensatory Damages in the Case-Within-a-Case Suit

D. MALPRACTICE IN CRIMINAL CASES

§ 45.13 Criminal Malpractice: Prima Facie Case
§ 45.14 Criminal Malpractice: Defenses and Immunities

A. MALPRACTICE IN CIVIL MATTERS: PRIMA FACIE CASE

§ 45.1 Scope, Duties, and Elements

Scope of malpractice. Legal malpractice is ordinarily an economic tort, causing financial harm without personal injury or property damage.[1] The topic deals only with violation of a lawyer's duty arising out of the lawyer's representation of a client.[2] Legal malpractice, in other words, entails breach of a duty created by the contract[3] or by the

---

[1]   See Meyers v. Livingston, Adler, Pulda, Meiklejohn and Kelly, P.C., 311 Conn. 282, 87 A.3d 534 (2014); Tri-G, Inc. v. Burke, Bosselman & Weaver, 222 Ill.2d 218, 226, 856 N.E.2d 389, 394–95, 305 Ill.Dec. 584, 589–90 (2006). Malpractice in a criminal representation is a different matter; the harm alleged in that case is usually to a liberty interest, not to a purely economic one. See §§ 45.13 to 45.14.

[2]   Representation of the client may, however, create duties to non-clients. See § 45.7.

[3]   See Credit Union Central Falls v. Groff, 966 A.2d 1262, 1271 (R.I. 2009) ("The attorney-client relationship is contractual in nature and the gravamen of an action for attorney malpractice is the negligent breach of a contractual duty."); see also Horn v. Wooster, 165 P.3d 69 (Wyo. 2007) ("Although the standard of care element reflects the law of torts, we have consistently held the legal relationship between an attorney and his client is contractual in nature.").

relationship with the client. Indeed, in some cases the claim may be brought as a contract claim as well as a negligence claim,[4] although where the breach of contract claim is based on the same facts as a tort claim for legal malpractice, the former may be stricken as redundant.[5] In any event, the contract between client and lawyer itself may not only create professional duties but limit them.[6] Because a lawyer is in a fiduciary relationship with a client, the client may also be able to bring a separate claim for breach of fiduciary duty against a lawyer, especially where the lawyer has violated duties of loyalty or confidentiality; otherwise a separate claim for breach of fiduciary duty may also be considered redundant.[7]

Core duties. A lawyer's core duties, often implicated in legal malpractice cases, include the duties of professional care and competence, but also includes the special duties of fiduciaries[8] and the duty to provide certain information to the client, somewhat analogous to the obligation of medical practitioners to provide patients with information as part of getting their "informed consent" to treatment.[9]

Agency law and the malpractice claim. The legal malpractice claim is often the only avenue of compensatory financial relief[10] for an aggrieved client, because of the rule that the client (as principal) is bound by the negligent acts of her lawyer (as agent).[11] That is, "a client is ordinarily chargeable with his counsel's negligent acts,"[12] and "the sins of the

---

[4]   See e.g., Collins v. Reynard, 154 Ill.2d 48, 607 N.E.2d 1185 (1992) (allowing pleading in the alternative); Pancake House, Inc. v. Redmond, 239 Kan. 83, 716 P.2d 575 (1986) ("Where the essential claim of the action is a breach of a duty imposed by law upon the relationship of attorney/client and not of the contract itself, the action is in tort"); Christensen & Jensen, P.C. v. Barrett & Daines, 194 P.3d 931 (Utah 2008) (clients wronged by their lawyers may sue based on negligence, breach of contract, or breach of fiduciary duty); see also Ray Ryden Anderson & Walter W. Steele, Jr., Fiduciary Duty, Tort and Contract: A Primer on the Legal Malpractice Puzzle, 47 SMU L. Rev. 235 (1994).

[5]   See, e.g., Nettleton v. Stogsdill, 387 Ill.App.3d 743, 899 N.E.2d 1252, 326 Ill.Dec. 601 (2008); Beck v. Law Offices of Edwin J. (Ted) Terry, Jr., P.C., 284 S.W.3d 416 (Tex. App. 2009) (discussing Texas rule against "fracturing" professional negligence claims against lawyers).

[6]   See, eg, AmBase Corp. v. Davis Polk & Wardwell, 8 N.Y.3d 428, 866 N.E.2d 1033 (2007) (limiting duty); see also ABA Model Rules of Professional Conduct 1.2(e) (allowing lawyer to limit scope of representation to particular stages of a case or to certain aspects of a legal problem, as long as the limitation is reasonable and the client gives informed consent). While the scope of a lawyer's duty may be limited by agreement, ethics rules prohibit a lawyer from making an agreement prospectively limiting malpractice liability to a client. See ABA Model Rules of Professional Conduct 1.8(h) (prohibited unless the client is independently represented in making such an agreement); see also Restatement Third of the Law Governing Lawyers § 54(1) (2000) (such agreements are unenforceable).

[7]   See 4 Dobbs, Hayden & Bublick, The Law of Torts § 724 (2d ed. 2011 & Supp.) (breach of fiduciary duty by lawyers); 2 Ronald E. Mallen & Jeffrey M. Smith, Legal Malpractice § 15:2 (2009 ed.) (hereinafter Mallen & Smith, Legal Malpractice).

[8]   See 4 Dobbs, Hayden & Bublick, The Law of Torts § 724 (2d ed. 2011 & Supp.).

[9]   See §§ 21.9 to 21.12.

[10]   Lawyers are subject to disciplinary actions by state authorities, but clients are generally not entitled to obtain any compensatory damages in connection with such proceedings. See ABA Standards for Imposing Lawyer Sanctions (1986) (followed substantially by most states). Further, mere lawyer negligence seldom gives rise to discipline. See, e.g., In re Disciplinary Action Against McKechnie, 656 N.W.2d 661 (N.D. 2003). All states now have client protection or client security funds that may provide some financial reimbursement to clients who are aggrieved by their lawyer's misdeeds. However, such funds are typically limited in scope and do not serve as a substitute for the legal malpractice case where the plaintiff seeks compensatory damages for a lawyer's negligence. See 1 Mallen & Smith, Legal Malpractice § 2:51 (2009 ed.).

[11]   See Link v. Wabash Co., 370 U.S. 626, 82 S.Ct. 1386, 8 L.Ed.2d 734 (1962); Panzino v. City of Phoenix, 196 Ariz. 442, 999 P.2d 198 (2000) ("Under general rules of agency, which apply to the attorney-client relationship, the neglect of the attorney is equivalent to the neglect of the client himself when the attorney is acting within the scope of his authority.").

[12]   Community Dental Services v. Tani, 282 F.3d 1164 (9th Cir. 2002).

lawyer as agent are visited upon the client as principal."[13] With narrow exceptions,[14] whatever error the lawyer's malpractice caused in the underlying case or transaction cannot usually be undone in that underlying matter; the harm is done, and the client is left with a decidedly second-best remedy—a civil suit for damages against the lawyer.

Elements. To prove a legal malpractice claim, the plaintiff must first prove the existence of a client-lawyer relationship that establishes a duty on the lawyer's part.[15] The contract or relationship between lawyer and client establishes the general duty to provide professional care.[16] Given the relationship, the economic loss rule[17] does not apply to eliminate liability for negligence.[18] A lawyer may also owe non-clients a duty of professional care under narrow circumstances.[19] The remaining elements of the legal malpractice claim are those of other negligence cases: The plaintiff must prove a breach of the duty, factual and proximate cause,[20] and damages.[21] Additional elements may be required in the case of criminal-case malpractice.[22] Expert testimony is usually required to determine both the standard of care[23] and its breach,[24] and may be required to establish that the breach caused the plaintiff's harm.[25]

§ 45.2 Duty: Establishing a Client-Lawyer Relationship

Where the plaintiff has signed a retainer agreement with the lawyer, the lawyer clearly owes the client a duty of care with respect to legal work done pursuant to that agreement. While most client-lawyer relationships are formed by express agreement,[26] such a relationship may also arise by implication. In those situations and some others,

---

[13] Bailey v. Algonquin Gas Transmission Co., 788 A.2d 478 (R.I. 2002).

[14] State and federal procedural rules provide for relief from a final judgment on a showing of "excusable neglect." FRCP 60(b). But almost all jurisdictions have held that there must be some significant extenuating circumstances to excuse a lawyer's neglect. See Pioneer Investment Services Co. v. Brunswick Assocs. Ltd. Partnership, 507 U.S. 380, 113 S.Ct. 1489, 123 L.Ed.2d 74 (1993) (holding that "inadvertence, ignorance of the rules, or mistakes construing the rules do not usually constitute 'excusable' neglect" under the federal rule); Bailey v. Algonquin Gas Transmission Co., 788 A.2d 478 (R.I. 2002) (adopting a similarly strict reading of Rhode Island's rule). Some states do not bind a client to a lawyer's errors where the lawyer has completely abandoned the client. See Amco Builders & Developers, Inc. v. Team Act Joint Venture, 469 Mich. 90, 666 N.W.2d 623 (2003); Cal. Code Civ. Proc. § 473.1. An even smaller number of courts do not bind the client where the lawyer was guilty of "gross negligence." See, e.g., Resolution Trust Corp. v. Ferri, 120 N.M. 320, 901 P.2d 738 (1995).

[15] See § 45.2. Prospective clients—those who have discussed with a lawyer the possibility of forming a relationship—are owed a duty of reasonable care to the extent the lawyer provides legal services during the preliminary discussion. Restatement of the Law Governing Lawyers § 15(1) (2000).

[16] McColm-Traska v. Baker, 139 Idaho 948, 88 P.3d 767 (2004).

[17] See Chapter 41.

[18] Collins v. Reynard, 154 Ill.2d 48, 607 N.E.2d 1185 (1992); Clark v. Rowe, 428 Mass. 339, 701 N.E.2d 624 (1998).

[19] See § 45.7.

[20] See §§ 45.5 to 45.6.

[21] See §§ 45.11 to 45.12.

[22] See §§ 45.13 to 45.14.

[23] See § 45.3.

[24] See § 45.4.

[25] See § 45.5.

[26] Where this is the case, the agreement itself usually specifies the basic duties owed by the lawyer, and the scope of the lawyer's undertaking. 1 Mallen & Smith, Legal Malpractice § 8:2 (2009 ed.).

the existence of a duty is indeed a live issue:[27] without a client-lawyer relationship, there is rarely a duty, and without a duty, there can be no malpractice liability.[28]

Proving a relationship by implication. A client-lawyer relationship may be implied by circumstances when a person manifests to the lawyer his authorization for the lawyer to act on his behalf, and the lawyer manifests his acceptance of that authorization.[29] The lawyer may manifest this acceptance explicitly, or simply by failing to manifest such consent where she knows or reasonably should know that the would-be client is relying reasonably on the lawyer to provide legal services.[30] In essence, then, courts are looking for an implied contract between client and lawyer for the lawyer to perform legal work.[31] Many courts have said that neither a unilateral nor an unreasonable belief on the putative client's part that the lawyer is representing her will suffice to create a relationship.[32] Indeed, many require that there is first some "concrete communication by the plaintiff requesting that the attorney represent him."[33] Courts agree also that neither the payment of fees nor the signing of a retainer agreement is necessary,[34] although such facts are not irrelevant to the inquiry as to whether a client-lawyer relationship has been formed.[35] While the existence of a duty is a question of law for the court, a number of courts leave it to the jury to resolve any contested issues of fact on this issue.[36] Thus, in many of the cases in which the existence of an implied client-lawyer relationship is in question, the lawyer will be unable to escape on summary judgment.[37]

---

[27] See Restatement of the Law Governing Lawyers § 14, Introductory Note (2000) ("A fundamental distinction is involved between clients, to whom lawyers owe many duties, and nonclients, to whom lawyers owe few duties.").

[28] See, e.g., Great American E & S Ins. Co. v. Quintairos, Prieto, Wood & Boyer, P.A., 100 So.3d 420 (Miss. 2012) (excess insurer could not maintain a direct claim of legal malpractice against the lawyers that represented the insured).

[29] See Kehoe v. Saltarelli, 337 Ill.App.3d 669, 786 N.E.2d 605, 272 Ill.Dec. 66 (2003); Miller v. Mooney, 431 Mass. 57, 725 N.E.2d 545 (2000); Baker Donelson Bearman Caldwell & Berkowitz, P.C. v. Seay, 42 So.3d 474 (Miss. 2010); Restatement of the Law Governing Lawyers § 14(1) (2000).

[30] See Miller v. Mooney, 431 Mass. 57, 725 N.E.2d 545 (2000) (plaintiff may establish lawyer's implied consent to form the relationship "by proof of detrimental reliance, when the person seeking legal services reasonably relies on the attorney to provide them and the attorney, aware of such reliance, does nothing to negate it"); In re Disciplinary Action Against McKechnie, 656 N.W.2d 661 (N.D. 2003); Restatement of the Law Governing Lawyers § 14(1)(b) (2000).

[31] See Zenith Ins. Co. v. Cozen O'Connor, 148 Cal.App.4th 998, 55 Cal.Rptr.3d 911 (2007); Edmonds v. Williamson, 13 So.3d 1283 (Miss. 2009).

[32] See, e.g., Mansur v. Podhurst Orseck, P.A., 994 So.2d 435 (Fla. Dist. Ct. App. 2008); Cleveland Campers, Inc. v. McCormack, 280 Ga.App. 900, 635 S.E.2d 274 (2006); Bloom v. Hensel, 59 A.D.3d 1026, 872 N.Y.S.2d 776 (2009); Meyer v. Mulligan, 889 P.2d 509 (Wyo. 1995).

[33] International Strategies Group, Ltd. v. Greenberg Traurig, LLP, 482 F.3d 1 (1st Cir. 2007).

[34] See Warren v. Williams, 313 Ill.App.3d 450, 730 N.E.2d 512, 246 Ill.Dec. 487 (2000) (city attorney who entered an appearance for a police officer who knew nothing of the suit created an attorney-client relationship with the officer); Togstad v. Vesely, Otto, Miller & Keefe, 291 N.W.2d 686 (Minn. 1980) (consultation about a potential medical malpractice claim; seeking and receiving advice when reasonable person would rely upon it is enough); Edmonds v. Williamson, 13 So.3d 1283 (Miss. 2009) (husband of injured party in products liability case neither signed a retainer nor paid a fee, but accepted lawyer's services, forming client-lawyer relationship).

[35] See Cleveland Campers, Inc. v. McCormack, 280 Ga.App. 900, 635 S.E.2d 174 (2006).

[36] E.g., Credit Union Central Falls v. Groff, 966 A.2d 1262 (R.I. 2009); Bangs v. Schroth, 201 P.3d 442 (Wyo. 2009). See also 4 Mallen & Smith, Legal Malpractice § 35:21 (2009 ed.) ("There is diversity whether the existence of the relationship is an issue of fact or law.").

[37] See, e.g., Dixon Ticonderoga Co. v. Estate of O'Connor, 248 F.3d 151 (3d Cir. 2001) (on the evidence before the court, it was a question of fact whether lawyer agreed to pursue claim against another lawyer or knew or should have known that client thought he was agreeing); Mansur v. Podhurst Orseck, P.A., 994 So.2d 435 (Fla. Dist. Ct. App. 2008) (reversing summary judgment for lawyers, finding triable issue of fact on whether

Representing entities. Issues of client identity sometimes arise when a lawyer has been retained to represent a legal entity, such as a corporation. Although the lawyer in such a situation is giving legal advice to the entity through the entity's constituents who are acting within that capacity, the lawyer's client is the entity itself, not those individuals.[38] Thus a lawyer representing an entity could be sued for legal malpractice by the entity itself, but not by its CEO or its General Counsel, let alone a lower-level employee or shareholders.[39] A lawyer may also represent constituents within the organization, however, either by express agreement or by implication.[40] In that case both the entity and those constituents would be owed a duty enforceable in a malpractice case.

Third-party fee payors. The rule that the payment of a lawyer's fee is not necessary to create a client-lawyer relationship has a flip side, also: The mere payment of a fee does not create such a relationship. Thus where a lawyer is retained to represent a person, but another person or entity is paying the fee, the fee payor is not a client based on that payment alone,[41] and thus would not be owed a duty enforceable in a legal malpractice action absent an express agreement to the contrary, or other facts that would create an implied relationship.[42]

Representing insured persons. Traditionally, a lawyer retained and paid by an insurance company to provide representation to an insured person was thereby thrust into a "tripartite relationship" in which both the insurer and the insured were dual clients.[43] But beginning with a 1991 Michigan decision,[44] a growing number of jurisdictions have held that the insured is the *only* client.[45] Under either approach, the insured person would have standing to sue the lawyer for malpractice, even where the insurer was paying the bills. Under the dual-client approach the insurer would be similarly situated. Even under the insured-as-sole-client view, however, the insurer may be able to sue the lawyer for legal malpractice if the retainer agreement makes the

---

plaintiffs were clients of the defendant lawyers); Bloom v. Hensel, 59 A.D.3d 1026, 872 N.Y.S.2d 776 (2009) (same).

[38] ABA Model Rule of Professional Conduct 1.13(a) ("A lawyer employed or retained by an organization represents the organization acting through its duly authorized constituents.").

[39] E.g., In re Banks, 283 Or. 459, 583 P.2d 284 (1978); Bovee v. Gravel, 174 Vt. 486, 811 A.2d 137 (2002).

[40] ABA Model Rule of Professional Conduct 1.13(g) (but cautioning lawyers that such dual representation requires compliance with rules on conflicts of interest). A lawyer who represents a constituent of an organization does not, by virtue of that relationship alone, also represent the organization itself. See New Destiny Treatment Ctr., Inc. v. Wheeler, 129 Ohio St.3d 39, 950 N.E.2d 157 (2011).

[41] See, e.g., Helms v. Helms, 317 Ark. 143, 875 S.W.2d 849 (1994) (payor of wife's fees in divorce action); Fox v. White, 215 S.W.3d 257 (Mo.App. 2007) (stepfather who paid legal fees on behalf of stepson); Krug v. Krug, 179 A.D.2d 1041, 580 N.Y.S.2d 599 (1992) (man who paid fees for the representation of the woman he later married, in her divorce proceeding); Restatement of the Law Governing Lawyers § 134 (2000).

[42] See Fox v. White, 215 S.W.3d 257 (Mo. App. 2007) (affirming dismissal of malpractice suit by third-party fee payor).

[43] See Charles Silver & Kent Syverud, The Professional Responsibilities of Insurance Defense Lawyers, 45 Duke L.J. 255, 273–75 (1995); 4 Mallen & Smith, Legal Malpractice § 30:6 (2009 ed.) (strongly endorsing this as the best view). Many courts adhere to this position. See, e.g., Nevada Yellow Cab Corp. v. Eighth Judicial Dist. Court ex rel. County of Clark, 123 Nev. 44, 152 P.3d 737 (2007); Spratley v. State Farm Mut. Auto. Ins. Co., 78 P.3d 603 (Utah 2003).

[44] Atlanta Int'l Ins. Co. v. Bell, 438 Mich. 512, 475 N.W.2d 294 (1991).

[45] See, e.g., Paradigm Ins. Co. v. Langerman Law Offices, P.A., 200 Ariz. 146, 24 P.3d 593 (2001); Higgins v. Karp, 239 Conn. 802, 687 A.2d 539 (1997); Pine Island Farmers Coop v. Erstad & Reimer, P.A., 649 N.W.2d 444 (Minn. 2002); Lieberman v. Employers Ins. of Wausau, 84 N.J. 325, 419 A.2d 417 (1980); State Farm Mutual Auto Ins. Co. v. Traver, 980 S.W.2d 625 (Tex. 1998); see also Restatement of the Law Governing Lawyers § 134, cmt. f (2000) (insured person is a client; insurer is not a client "simply by the fact that it designates the lawyer").

insurer a client, or if a relationship arises by implication, as where the lawyer has given legal advice directly to the insurer.[46]

§ 45.3   The Professional Standard of Care

Subject to slight variations in expression, attorneys owe clients the skill, care, knowledge, and diligence exercised by reasonable and prudent lawyers in similar circumstances.[47] The general standard of care is an issue of law, but is usually intertwined with the fact issue of "what an attorney's specific conduct should be in a particular case."[48]

Geographical limits and specialists. The usual geographic scope of a lawyer's standard of care is the state in which the lawyer practices.[49] This makes perfect sense, because each state regulates the practice of law within its own borders in terms of bar admissions requirements and lawyer discipline. The locality rule seems never to have had the major place in legal malpractice cases that it once had in the medical cases. This is not to say that local practices are irrelevant in a legal malpractice action; however, local practices are most properly seen as determining the propriety of the lawyer's conduct rather than changing the standard of care.[50] In many specialized areas of practice, a national standard seems entirely appropriate.[51]

Role of ethics rules. Lawyer codes of conduct or ethics, adopted by the states for disciplinary purposes,[52] may be relevant to a court determining the civil obligations of lawyers,[53] but they do not normally set the standard of care[54] or create a cause of action against lawyers.[55] While experts may usually offer testimony about ethics rules, they

---

[46]   See, e.g., Paradigm Ins. Co. v. Langerman, 200 Ariz. 146, 24 P.3d 593 (2001); Pine Island Farmers Coop v. Erstad & Reimer, P.A., 649 N.W.2d 444 (Minn. 2002) (also holding that a lawyer owes a duty to the insurer, even if the insurer is nonclient, because the lawyer's services are ordinarily intended to benefit both the insured and the insurer). On suits against lawyers by non-clients, see § 45.7.

[47]   See Radiology Services, P.C. v. Hall, 279 Neb. 553, 780 N.W.2d 17 (2010); Leder v. Spiegel, 9 N.Y.3d 836, 872 N.E.2d 1194, 840 N.Y.S.2d 888 (2007); Olson v. Fraase, 421 N.W.2d 820 (N.D. 1988); Restatement of the Law Governing Lawyers § 52(1) (2000).

[48]   Wolski v. Wandel, 275 Neb. 266, 746 N.W.2d 143 (2008).

[49]   E.g., Kellos v. Sawilowsky, 325 S.E.2d 757 (Ga. 1985); Smith v. Haynesworth, Marion, McKay & Geurard, 472 S.E.2d 612 (S.C. 1996); Chapman v. Bearfield, 207 S.W.3d 736 (Tenn. 2006); Russo v. Griffin, 147 Vt. 20, 510 A.2d 436 (1986).

[50]   See 2 Mallen & Smith, Legal Malpractice § 20:5 (2009 ed.). This would impact on the admissibility of expert testimony; where the court rejects a local standard of care, it would be improper for the trial judge to discount non-local expert testimony on the standard of care. See Russo v. Griffin, 147 Vt. 20, 510 A.2d 436 (1986).

[51]   See Restatement of the Law Governing Lawyers § 52, cmt. b (2000) (referencing various types of federal-law oriented practice).

[52]   Virtually all have patterned their rules on models drafted by the American Bar Association, the current version of which is found in the ABA Model Rules of Professional Conduct.

[53]   Restatement of the Law Governing Lawyers § 52(2)(c) (2000).

[54]   E.g., Byers v. Cummings, 320 Mont. 339, 87 P.3d 465 (2004) ("Rules of Professional Conduct do not establish substantive legal duties."); Lazy Seven Coal Sales, Inc. v. Stone & Hinds, P.C., 813 S.W.2d 400 (Tenn. 1991) (Code of Professional Responsibility does not set the standard of care, so a law professor's proffered testimony based solely on the Code was inadequate to establish the standard); see ABA Model Rules of Professional Conduct, Preamble ("nothing in the Rules should be deemed to augment any substantive legal duty of lawyers or the extra-disciplinary consequences of violating such a duty").

[55]   E.g., Allen v. Allison, 356 Ark. 403, 155 S.W.3d 682 (2004) (rejecting plaintiff's attempt to use the ethics rules to establish an element of a civil conspiracy claim); Liggett v. Young, 877 N.E.2d 178 (Ind. 2007) (Professional Conduct Rule on business transactions with client did not create a cause of action); Shamberg, Johnson & Bergman, Chtd. v. Oliver, 289 Kan. 891, 220 P.3d 333 (2009) (lawyer's violation of ethical rule

must do so with reference to the rules' relationship to the common law standard of care.[56] In any event, the rules of conduct for lawyers are perhaps less relevant to ordinary negligence actions than to breaches of fiduciary and other special duties.[57]

Expert testimony required. At one time, courts weren't so sure they would even admit expert testimony to establish the standard of care or its breach.[58] That has all passed, and courts now not only admit but generally require expert testimony to establish the standard of care[59] unless it is a matter of common knowledge.[60]

Expert testimony as to specialists. If the defendant lawyer is a specialist, a witness who knows the specialist's standards is required, or at least appropriate.[61] A dictum in a California case has it that *only* a specialist can provide evidence of the standard of care for specialists.[62] That is probably right for many cases; a personal injury lawyer could hardly help the trier understand whether a tax lawyer's estate plan met standards or not. However, the usual view is that the standard for specialists is more exacting than the standard for non-specialists, so in some cases, proof that the specialist breached the less exacting standard for non-specialists would also show that he breached the more exacting standard for specialists.

§ 45.4 Breach of Duty

The second element of the legal malpractice claim is breach of duty. The plaintiff must prove that the lawyer's conduct fell below the professional standard of care—that is, that the lawyer failed to use such skill, prudence and diligence as lawyers of ordinary skill and capacity usually possess and exercise in the performance of the kinds of tasks the lawyer undertook. This is a "foresight" test; the focus is on what a reasonable lawyer "would have done at the time, excluding the benefit of hindsight."[63] Good faith is no defense if the lawyer violates the standard.[64] However, the lawyer need not be perfect to

---

neither creates a cause of action nor necessarily warrants any other non-disciplinary remedy); Olson v. Fraase, 421 N.W.2d 820 (N.D. 1988) (violation of ethics code provision is not a tort).

[56] See Fishman v. Brooks, 396 Mass. 643, 487 N.E.2d 1377 (1986) (allowing testimony about ethics rules on the ground that violation of rules could be "some evidence" of negligence); see also Hizey v. Carpenter, 119 Wash.2d 251, 830 P.2d 646 (1992) (approving expert testimony on the content of ethics rules, but only if the expert did not actually refer to the rules as such).

[57] Griva v. Davison, 637 A.2d 830 (D.C. 1994) (violation of ethic rule can constitute a breach of fiduciary duty to the client); see also Ronald D. Rotunda & John S. Dzienkowski, Legal Ethics—The Lawyer's Deskbook on Professional Responsibility § 1–9(c)(3) (2010–11 ed.) (discussing many complexities about the uses of ethics rules in civil cases); 4 Dobbs, Hayden & Bublick, The Law of Torts § 724 (2d ed. 2011 & Supp.).

[58] Developments in the Law—Lawyers' Responsibilities and Lawyers' Responses, II. Lawyers' Responsibilities to the Client: Legal Malpractice and Tort Reform, 107 Harv. L. Rev. 1557 (1994).

[59] E.g., Crookham v. Riley, 584 N.W.2d 258 (Iowa 1998); Bergstrom v. Noah, 266 Kan. 847, 974 P.2d 531 (1999); Boyle v. Welsh, 256 Neb. 118, 589 N.W.2d 118 (1999); Roberts v. Chimileski, 175 Vt. 480, 820 A.2d 995 (2003); Rino v. Mead, 55 P.3d 13 (Wyo. 2002). See also Michael A. DiSabatino, Annotation, Admissibility and necessity of expert evidence as to standards of practice and negligence in malpractice action against attorney, 14 A.L.R.4th 170 (1982).

[60] See, e.g., Pierce v. Cook, 992 So.2d 612 (Miss. 2008) (lawyer had adulterous affair with client's wife, no expert required); Vandermay v. Clayton, 328 Or. 646, 984 P.2d 272 (1999) (error in drafting agreement pursuant to explicit instructions by client).

[61] Lentino v. Fringe Emp. Plans, Inc., 611 F.2d 474 (3d Cir. 1979); Conley v. Lieber, 97 Cal.App.3d 646, 158 Cal.Rptr. 770 (1979).

[62] Wright v. Williams, 47 Cal.App.3d 802, 121 Cal.Rptr. 194 (1975).

[63] Hopp & Flesch, LLC v. Backstreet, 123 P.3d 1176 (Colo. 2005); Accord, e.g., Darby & Darby, P.C. v. VSI Intern., Inc., 95 N.Y.2d 308, 739 N.E.2d 744, 716 N.Y.S.2d 378 (2000).

[64] See Meyer v. Wagner, 429 Mass. 410, 709 N.E.2d 784 (1999); Nesvig v. Nesvig, 676 N.W.2d 73 (Nev. 2004).

satisfy the duty of care, and "a failure to be brilliant" is certainly not legal malpractice.[65] Breach of duty is an issue of fact for the jury, as in any other negligence case.[66]

Types of negligent conduct. A lawyer may breach the professional duty of care in any number of ways. For example, fiduciary breach aside, lawyers may fail to recognize a cause of action or may fail to file a claim or defense within required time limits,[67] may inadequately prepare for trial,[68] or use substandard strategies or techniques in trial itself.[69] Lawyers must keep clients informed about developments relating to the representation,[70] and may be negligent in negotiating a settlement[71] or advising its acceptance.[72] Of course, malpractice claims are not confined to litigation malpractice; they can arise in any kind of representation. Lawyers may be negligent in drafting[73] or recording[74] documents, in searching records,[75] in giving advice,[76] and possibly even in accepting a case beyond their experience and competence.[77] Each area of practice tends to have its own unique problems. Joint representation of clients—both spouses in preparing wills, for example—may run risks that the lawyer will have conflicts of interest or will face confidentiality issues unlike those routinely faced by, say, a personal-injury lawyer.[78]

The "error of judgment" rule. Not every professional mistake is negligence.[79] In fact, courts often say that lawyers are not liable for good faith errors in judgment,[80] but taken

---

[65] McKnight v. Dean, 270 F.3d 513 (7th Cir. 2001) (Posner, J.).

[66] See, e.g., Blanks v. Seyfarth Shaw, 171 Cal.App.4th 336, 89 Cal.Rptr.3d 710 (2009) (reversing trial judge's ruling that law firm breached its duty to client as a matter of law); Jerry's Enterprises, Inc. v. Larkin, Hoffman, Daly & Lindgren, Ltd., 711 N.W.2d 811 (Minn. 2006); McIntire v. Lee, 149 N.H. 160, 816 A.2d 993 (2003).

[67] E.g., Phillips v. Clancy, 152 Ariz. 415, 733 P.2d 300 (Ct. App. 1986); Bebo Const. Co. v. Mattox & O'Brien, P.C., 990 P.2d 78 (Colo. 1999).

[68] Waldman v. Levine, 544 A.2d 683, 78 A.L.R.4th 703 (D.C. 1988); McIntire v. Lee, 149 N.H. 160, 816 A.2d 993 (2003) (failure to conduct adequate discovery or prepare the plaintiff for trial).

[69] Wartnick v. Moss & Barnett, 490 N.W.2d 108 (Minn. 1992) (lawyer's admission in opening statement); McIntire v. Lee, 149 N.H. 160, 816 A.2d 993 (2003) (failure to present relevant evidence).

[70] The duty to provide information to the client clearly extends to relating settlement offers and giving the client enough facts to assess them. See Moores v. Greenberg, 834 F.2d 1105 (1st Cir. 1987); Wood v. McGrath, North, Ullin & Kratz, P.C., 256 Neb. 109, 589 N.W.2d 103 (1999).

[71] E.g., Meyer v. Wagner, 429 Mass. 410, 709 N.E.2d 784 (1999) (following the usual rule that judicial approval of a settlement does not foreclose the malpractice action based upon the attorney's negligence).

[72] Thomas v. Bethea, 351 Md. 513, 718 A.2d 1187 (1998) (analyzing a number of settlement cases).

[73] E.g., Lucas v. Hamm, 56 Cal.2d 583, 364 P.2d 685, 15 Cal.Rptr. 821 (1961).

[74] See Pizel v. Zuspann, 247 Kan. 54, 795 P.2d 42, 10 A.L.R. 5th 1098 (1990).

[75] Cf. Greycas, Inc. v. Proud, 826 F.2d 1560 (7th Cir. 1987) (failure to search for UCC filings followed by a misrepresentation that no liens existed).

[76] Conklin v. Hannoch Weisman, 145 N.J. 395, 678 A.2d 1060 (1996) (plaintiff claimed lawyer gave inadequate explanation of subordination agreement).

[77] See Battle v. Thornton, 646 A.2d 315 (D.C. 1994). However, mere acceptance of a case would not necessarily cause harm unless the attorney fell below the standard of care in some particular act. The Model Rules provide that a lawyer who takes on a case in an unfamiliar or "wholly novel" field is not acting incompetently if the lawyer engages in "necessary study," "reasonable preparation," or associates with a lawyer who has "established competence in the field in question." ABA Model Rules of Professional Conduct 1.1, Comment ¶¶ 2 & 4.

[78] See A. v. B., 158 N.J. 51, 726 A.2d 924 (1999); Spencer v. Barber, 299 P.3d 388 (N.M. 2013).

[79] Lucas v. Hamm, 56 Cal.2d 583, 364 P.2d 685, 15 Cal.Rptr. 821 (1961) (not negligent to misapply the rule against perpetuities).

[80] E.g., Woodruff v. Tomlin, 616 F.2d 924 (6th Cir. 1980); Nash v. Hendricks, 369 Ark. 60, 250 S.W.3d 541 (2007); Biomet v. Finnegan Henderson LLP, 967 A.2d 662 (D.C. 2009); Sun Valley v. Rosholt, Robertson & Tucker, 133 Idaho 1, 981 P.2d 236 (1999). Pattern jury instructions often contain similar statements. See, e.g., Cal. Jury Instr.—Civ. 6–37–2; Ind. Pattern Jury Instr.—Civ. No. 23.35. The rule originates in an

literally this would virtually eliminate all lawyer liability. The error-of-judgment rule is therefore confined by most courts to situations where reasonable professional judgments could differ, in which case the lawyer simply has not violated the professional standard.[81] More specifically, many cases limit their use of the error-of-judgment rule to cases in which the lawyer has been faced with an "unsettled" area of law.[82] Even where an area of law is unsettled, however, a lawyer may fall below the standard of care,[83] as by conducting inadequate research,[84] especially where research would reveal alternative courses of conduct that would avoid placing the client in a "murky" area of law rife with uncertainties.[85] At bottom, neither "good faith" nor the uncertainty of the legal terrain should protect the lawyer who acts unreasonably when compared to prudent lawyers faced with a similar situation.[86]

Expert testimony. Expert testimony is almost always required to prove that the lawyer's conduct constituted a breach of the duty of care.[87] As with medical expert testimony, it is not enough for the legal expert to testify that he would have acted differently than the defendant did; instead the expert must testify that the lawyer's conduct fell below the professional standard of care of lawyers under similar circumstances.[88] Courts recognize a "common knowledge" exception to the expert testimony requirement where the ordinary layperson can assess the professional's breach without any expert assistance.[89] A typical example of such an exceptional situation is where an attorney takes no action at all to protect a client's interests,[90] or fails to file what would have been a meritorious lawsuit within the statute of

---

eighteenth century malpractice case announced by Lord Mansfield in the House of Lords, Pitt v. Yalden, 98 Eng. Rep. 74 (K.B. 1767), discussed in 2 Mallen & Smith, Legal Malpractice § 19:2 (2009 ed.).

[81]   See Bergstrom v. Noah, 266 Kan. 847, 974 P.2d 531 (1999).

[82]   E.g., Jerry's Enterprises, Inc. v. Larkin, Hoffman, Daly & Lindgren, Ltd., 711 N.W.2d 811 (Minn. 2006); Baker v. Fabian, Thielen & Thielen, 254 Neb. 697, 578 N.W.2d 446 (1998); Roberts v. Chimileski, 175 Vt. 480, 820 A.2d 995 (2003).

[83]   See L.D.G., Inc. v. Robinson, 290 P.3d 215 (Alaska 2012) (in dram shop action, failing to join an intoxicated consumer as an additional defendant could breach duty of care despite unsettled nature of the law on who could be liable in such a case); Collins v. Miller & Miller, Ltd., 189 Ariz. 387, 943 P.2d 747 (Ct. App. 1996) (fact issue whether lawyer breached duty of care despite unsettled statute of limitations issue, where lawyer could have filed claim in a timely manner nonetheless).

[84]   Biomet Inc. v. Finnegan Henderson LLP, 967 A.2d 662 (D.C. 2009); Jerry's Enterprises, Inc. v. Larkin, Hoffman, Daly & Lindgren, Ltd., 711 N.W.2d 811 (Minn. 2006); Kempf v. Magida, 37 A.D.3d 763, 832 N.Y.S.2d 47 (2007).

[85]   Blanks v. Seyfarth Shaw, 171 Cal.App.4th 336, 89 Cal.Rptr.3d 710 (2009).

[86]   See, e.g., Biomet Inc. v. Finnegan Henderson LLP, 967 A.2d 662 (D.C. 2009); Equitania Ins. Co. v. Slone & Garrett, P.S.C., 191 S.W.3d 552 (Ky. 2006).

[87]   E.g., Ball v. Birch, Horton, Bittner and Cherot, 58 P.3d 481 (Alaska 2002); Jerry's Enterprises, Inc. v. Larkin, Hoffman, Daly & Lindgren, Ltd., 711 N.W.2d 811 (Minn. 2006); Davis v. Enget, 779 N.W.2d 126 (N.D. 2010); but see Dubreil v. Witt, 271 Conn. 782, 860 A.2d 698 (2004) (trial judge properly excluded expert testimony on standard of care and breach in bench trial, where judge himself was fully aware of both the standard and the kind of conduct that would breach it).

[88]   See Wolski v. Wandel, 275 Neb. 266, 746 N.W.2d 143 (2008) (difference of opinion between lawyers does not prove that one of them was negligent).

[89]   E.g., In re R & R Associates of Hampton, 402 F.3d 257 (1st Cir. 2005) (N.H. law); Flax v. Schertler, 935 A.2d 1091 (D.C. 2007); Samuel v. Hepworth, Nungester & Lezamiz, Inc., 134 Idaho 85, 996 P.2d 303 (2000); Wolski v. Wandel, 275 Neb. 266, 746 N.W.2d 143 (2008); Davis v. Enget, 779 N.W.2d 126 (N.D. 2010).

[90]   See, e.g., Zok v. Collins, 18 P.3d 39 (Alaska 2001) (lawyer failed to file papers or oppose motions); Paul v. Gordon, 58 Conn.App. 724, 754 A.2d 851 (2000) (lawyer had done "absolutely nothing" in response to a complaint filed against his client, resulting in a default judgment).

limitations.[91] Even there, however, if the statute of limitations is missed because of a legal judgment by the lawyer, expert testimony is required to show that the judgment fell below professional standards.[92]

§ 45.5   Causation of Harm: General Rules

Proximate cause: scope of risk. Whether the harm was within the scope of risks created by the lawyer's malpractice is not often raised in the cases, simply because where the plaintiff was a client and the harm caused is economic, the usual foreseeability tests[93] are clearly met. For example, if the lawyer does not file a lien that could have secured the plaintiff's right to payment from a debtor, and that debtor then sells the property and absconds, the lawyer's malpractice clearly created the very risk that came to fruition.[94] Where scope of risk is a live issue, it is usually due to the type of harm being unusual or unforeseeable.[95]

Factual cause. As in other negligence cases, the malpractice plaintiff must show that her harm was factually caused by the defendant's negligence. Under the but-for test of factual cause,[96] liability is rejected when the plaintiff's loss would have occurred even had the lawyer not committed malpractice,[97] or when the breach of duty did not cause any harm at all.[98] If the lawyer fails to file a viable claim, but the claim can still be pursued without prejudice, the lawyer's negligence caused no harm and he is not liable for his failure.[99] If the claim was not viable because the statute of limitations had already expired, the lawyer failure to file it is not a factual cause of any harm.[100] If a lawyer fails to file an answer to a complaint, but the client had no defense to the claims, that failure has not caused harm and is not actionable.[101] A lawyer who negligently fails to search for attachable assets of a judgment debtor is not liable for malpractice where the

---

[91]   E.g., Giron v. Koktavy, 124 P.3d 821 (Colo.App. 2005) (collecting cases); Byrd v. Bowie, 933 So.2d 899 (Miss. 2006); Allyn v. McDonald, 112 Nev. 68, 910 P.2d 263 (1996).

[92]   See Boyle v. Welsh, 256 Neb. 118, 589 N.W.2d 118 (1999).

[93]   See §§ 15.1 & 15.10.

[94]   Cf. Rhine v. Haley, 238 Ark. 72, 378 S.W.2d 655 (1964) (divorce settlement, attorney failed to require a lien on property of husband, who saw his opportunity and "absconded to Louisiana with his new wife").

[95]   E.g., TIG Ins. Co. v. Giffin Winning Cohen & Bodewes, P.C., 444 F.3d 587 (7th Cir. 2006) (law firm's negligence in producing documents pursuant to a discovery request did not, as a matter of law, proximately cause a tangled legal battle that ultimately cost the client over a million dollars in attorney's fees; such an injury "was not reasonably foreseeable"); Hansen v. Anderson, Wilmarth & Van Der Maaten, 657 N.W.2d 711 (Iowa 2003) (the hazard posed by law firm's negligence "was not the hazard that produced the judgment against [the plaintiffs]" in the underlying action); Worsham v. Nix, 83 P.3d 879 (Okla. App. 2003) (legal malpractice did not proximately cause client's suicide); Roberts v. Healy, 991 S.W.2d 873 (Tex. App. 1999) (lawyer's failure to secure a protective order against client's estranged husband not a proximate cause of the husband's murdering the children).

[96]   See §§ 14.4 & 14.5.

[97]   McColm-Traska v. Baker, 139 Idaho 948, 88 P.3d 767 (2004); Gregory v. Hawkins, 251 Va. 471, 468 S.E.2d 891 (1996).

[98]   See, e.g., Vallinoto v. DiSandro, 688 A.2d 830 (R.I. 1997) (client's divorce lawyer engaged in numerous sex acts with her, but malpractice claim failed because she failed to prove that her legal position was damaged by the relationship); see also Hand v. Howell, Sarto & Howell, 131 So.3d 599 (Ala. 2013) (failure to name particular defendant would not have made any difference); Pietrangelo v. Wilmer Cutler Pickering Hale & Dorr, LLP, 68 A.3d 697 (D.C. 2013) (failure to file writ of certiorari; "pure speculation" that writ would have made any difference to client).

[99]   Moscatello v. Univ. of Medicine and Dentistry of New Jersey, 342 N.J.Super. 351, 776 A.2d 874 (2001).

[100]   Minn-Kota Ag Products, Inc. v. Carlson, 684 N.W.2d 60 (N.D. 2004).

[101]   Brodeur v. Hayes, 18 A.D.3d 754, 760 N.Y.S.2d 761 (2005).

judgment debtor had no assets of value anyway.[102] Even a failure to inform a client of a settlement offer—a clear breach of duty—is not actionable as malpractice without proof that such failure cost the client some money.[103]

The same point applies to bad legal advice and to transactional malpractice.[104] In many cases courts say that the plaintiff must prove that had the lawyer acted properly, the plaintiff would have obtained a more favorable result in the underlying transaction.[105] Thus a lawyer who fails to reasonably describe the risks involved in a development scheme is not liable to clients who would have gone ahead with the scheme even if they had been aware of the risks.[106] A lawyer who drafts faulty contracts likewise escapes liability unless the plaintiff can prove the faulty documents were a but-for cause of some financial harm to her.[107] Incomplete tax advice is not actionable where the plaintiff alleges it caused a loss of business opportunities, but fails to produce evidence that those opportunities would not have been lost in any event.[108] If a lawyer fails to file timely patent applications on a client's inventions, but the plaintiff cannot prove that the inventions were patentable, the malpractice case dies for want of factual cause.[109]

§ 45.6 Causation: The Case Within a Case

In litigation malpractice, the plaintiff must frequently prove causation of loss by specifically proving that, had the lawyer properly fulfilled his duties, the client would have achieved a better result in that underlying case.[110] To do that, the client-plaintiff must often prove her original claim or defense and the amount of damages she would have recovered or avoided.[111] This is known as the "case within a case" or "trial within a trial" requirement. The plaintiff must "prove two claims: first, the one that was lost, and second, the claim that his attorney's negligence caused that loss."[112] For example, if the lawyer negligently lost a procedural entitlement such as jury trial, leaving his client to a bench trial that was conducted without error, the fact that the client loses the case does not by itself show damages, for the client might have lost the case even if it had been tried to a jury.[113] A lawyer who negligently lost a military client's medical malpractice case against a government doctor will prevail in the subsequent legal malpractice case where the evidence shows that the claim was barred by the *Feres* doctrine[114] and thus would have been lost even by a non-negligent lawyer.[115] On the

---

[102] Brown v. Kelly, 140 Vt. 336, 437 A.2d 1103 (1981).

[103] Coastal Orthopaedic Institute, P.C. v. Bongiorno, 61 Mass.App.Ct. 55, 807 N.E.2d 187 (2004).

[104] See, e.g., Radiology Services, P.C. v. Hall, 279 Neb. 553, 780 N.W.2d 17 (2010) (lawyer's alleged negligence in sending letters to client's customers did not cause customers to stop doing business with client).

[105] See, e.g., Jerry's Enterprises, Inc. v. Larkin, Hoffman, Daly & Lindgren, Ltd., 711 N.W.2d 811 (Minn. 2006).

[106] Roberts v. Chimileski, 175 Vt. 480, 820 A.2d 995 (2003).

[107] Viner v. Sweet, 30 Cal. 4th 1232, 70 P.3d 1046, 135 Cal. Rptr. 2d 629 (2003).

[108] AmBase Corp. v. Davis Polk & Wardwell, 8 N.Y.3d 428, 866 N.E.2d 1033, 834 N.Y.S.2d 705 (2007).

[109] Davis v. Brouse McDowell, L.P.A., 586 F.3d 1355 (Fed. Cir. 2010).

[110] See Osborne v. Keeney, 339 S.W.3d 1 (Ky. 2012).

[111] E.g., Thomas v. Bethea, 351 Md. 513, 718 A.2d 1187 (1998); Restatement of the Law Governing Lawyers § 53, cmt. b (2000).

[112] Dan Nelson Const., Inc. v. Nodland & Dickson, 608 N.W.2d 267 (N.D. 2000); Encinias v. Whitener Law Firm, P.A., 310 P.3d 611 (N.M. 2013); Schmidt v. Coogan, 162 Wash.2d 488, 173 P.3d 273 (2007).

[113] Cf. Jones Motor Co., Inc. v. Holtkamp, Liese, Beckemeier & Childress, P.C., 197 F.3d 1190 (7th Cir. 1999) (suggesting that proof of damages in such a case would be difficult if not impossible).

[114] See § 22.4.

[115] Nash v. Hendricks, 369 Ark. 60, 250 S.W.3d 541 (2007).

other hand, where the plaintiff shows that the negligence of trial counsel in failing to argue a key issue to court resulted in a lower verdict than would have been obtained had the issue been argued competently, the plaintiff will recover the difference between what should have been obtained absent the negligence and the amount of the actual (tainted) verdict.[116]

In many instances, the malpractice plaintiff will be compelled to actually stage the original trial by putting on testimony that should have been put on but for the lawyer's alleged malpractice.[117] As one court has described it, "the litigants reconstruct the underlying action, absent the supposed breach of duty. The tribunal must not only determine how the parties would have proceeded had there been no breach, but must also assume the role of the earlier adjudicator in order to ascertain the probable outcome of the case."[118] If the plaintiff's original suit was a malpractice suit against a surgeon, for example, she would put on evidence of the surgery, the injury following, the doctor's negligence, and medical causation.[119] For this purpose she will ordinarily require one or more medical experts.[120] And to show that her former lawyer was negligent, she will also need a legal expert unless the lawyer's negligence is obvious.[121]

Settlements. In most states a malpractice suit may be maintained even after the client has either accepted or paid a settlement.[122] The plaintiff may claim that the settlement paid out is too high, or more commonly that the settlement accepted was too low, due to her lawyer's negligence.[123] Or the client might claim that the lawyer failed to recommend a settlement, or failed to memorialize or execute a settlement, that resulted in a continuation of proceedings that caused greater damages to the client.[124] The protection of the "error of judgment" rule,[125] however, is particularly strong in this context, protecting lawyers from liability where they have recommended or recommended against a settlement based on the exercise of reasonable professional judgment.[126] Further, a plaintiff's argument that a non-negligent lawyer would have obtained a greater settlement, or would have taken the claim to trial and obtained a

---

[116] Clary v. Lite Machines Corp., 850 N.E.2d 423 (Ind. App. 2006) (malpractice plaintiff won jury award of $3.6 million, where trial judge had awarded plaintiff $260,000 in underlying action).

[117] See, e.g., Deramus v. Donovan, Leisure, Newton & Irvine, 905 A.2d 164 (D.C. 2006); Tri-G, Inc. v. Burke, Bosselman & Weaver, 222 Ill.2d 218, 856 N.E.2d 389, 305 Ill.Dec. 584 (2006); Osborne v. Keeney, 339 S.W.3d 1 (Ky. 2012).

[118] Suder v. Whiteford, Taylor & Preston, LLP, 413 Md. 230, 922 A.2d 413 (2010).

[119] See, e.g., Stanski v. Ezersky, 228 A.D.2d 311, 644 N.Y.S.2d 220 (1996).

[120] See § 21.8.

[121] Alexander v. Turtur & Assocs., Inc., 146 S.W.3d 113 (Tex. 2004); see §§ 45.3 & 45.4.

[122] See 4 Mallen & Smith, Legal Malpractice § 31.43 (2009 ed.). The decision to accept or reject a settlement is the client's alone. See ABA Model Rules of Professional Conduct 1.2(a). As recognized in McWhirt v. Heavey, 250 Neb. 536, 550 N.W.2d 327 (1996), however, "litigants rely heavily on the professional advice of counsel when they decide whether to accept or reject offers of settlement."

[123] E.g., McKnight v. Dean, 270 F.3d 513 (7th Cir. 2001); Garcia v. Kozlov, Seaton, Romanini & Brooks, P.C., 179 N.J. 343, 845 A.2d 602 (2004); Environmental Network Corp. v. Goodman Weiss Miller, LLP, 119 Ohio St.3d 209, 893 N.E.2d 173 (2008).

[124] E.g., McColm-Traska v. Baker, 139 Idaho 948, 88 P.3d 767 (2004) (but finding that client was not damaged by the lawyer's failure to memorialize an oral settlement agreement); Bellino v. McGrath North Mullin & Kratz, PC LLO, 274 Neb. 130, 738 N.W.2d 434 (2007) (adversary offered to settle for $1.5 million, but lawyers advised plaintiff he could "do much better," resulting in ultimate losses to plaintiff of $3.1 million; jury verdict for plaintiff reinstated).

[125] See § 45.4.

[126] See, e.g., Schweizer v. Mulvehill, 93 F.Supp.2d 376 (S.D.N.Y. 2000); Cook v. Connolly, 366 N.W.2d 287 (Minn. 1985); Wolski v. Wandel, 275 Neb. 266, 746 N.W.2d 143 (2008).

larger amount, may be seen as too speculative to allow any recovery.[127] In any event, the case-within-a-case approach applies to this setting, and a plaintiff can prevail only by showing that a more favorable outcome would have likely been obtained[128]—"the same burden the plaintiff would have had to satisfy if the underlying case had gone to trial."[129]

§ 45.7　Liability to Non-Clients

At one time courts said that lawyers owed no duty to non-clients. They often invoked a privity requirement to bar a non-client's claim to reap the benefits of the lawyer-client contract. The convenient model for discussion is the case of the lawyer who negligently drafts his client's will so that it is invalid or fails to pass the client's estate in accord with the client's wishes. The intended beneficiary in such a case is the non-client plaintiff suing the lawyer-draftsman. While a number of courts still retain the privity rule or some slightly liberalized version of it,[130] most now reject it.[131]

Limiting the class of non-clients who can sue for malpractice. Even with the blanket rule abolished, however, the lawyer's professional duty does not extend to all non-clients; but it extends to those the lawyer was retained to benefit, such as the beneficiary of the will, and also to those who are involved in a transaction with the client and who rely upon the lawyer's work after the lawyer has invited them to do so.[132] This certainly excludes most non-clients. For example, lawyers do not owe a duty of care to co-counsel to protect co-counsel's prospective fee recovery, because imposing such a duty would create impermissible conflicts of interest.[133]

Intended beneficiaries. When a lawyer knows that his client intends a third person to be a primary beneficiary of the lawyer's work, and imposing such a duty would not interfere with the duty the lawyer owes the client, then that third person is owed a duty of care and may sue for breach if harm results.[134] It is not enough, however, for a plaintiff

---

[127] E.g., McKnight v. Dean, 270 F.3d 513 (7th Cir. 2001) (noting that lawyer did the client "a favor in 'coercing' a $765,000 settlement, if that is what really happened"); Slovensky v. Friedman, 142 Cal.App.4th 1518, 49 Cal.Rptr.3d 60 (2006).

[128] See Moores v. Greenberg, 834 F.2d 1105 (1st Cir. 1987) (affirming jury verdict for client in malpractice case, measuring damages by the amount of a settlement offer that lawyer did not relay to client, less the monies the client received subsequently from a workers' compensation carrier, plus attorney's fees).

[129] Environmental Network Corp. v. Goodman Weiss Miller, LLP, 119 Ohio St.3d 209, 893 N.E.2d 173 (2008) (citing many other cases and Restatement of the Law Governing Lawyers § 53, cmt. b (2000)).

[130] See, e.g., Robinson v. Benton, 842 So.2d 631 (Ala. 2002); First Arkansas Bank & Trust, Trustee v. Gill Elrod Ragon Owen & Sherman, P.A., 2013 Ark. 159, 427 S.W.3d 47 (2013); LeRoy v. Allen, Yurasek & Merklin, 114 Ohio St. 3d 323, 872 N.E.2d 254 (2007); Belt v. Oppenheimer, Blend, Harrison & Tate, Inc., 192 S.W.3d 780 (Tex. 2006).

[131] E.g., Lucas v. Hamm, 56 Cal.2d 583, 364 P.2d 685, 15 Cal.Rptr. 821 (1961) (but finding no negligence on the facts); Stowe v. Smith, 184 Conn. 194, 441 A.2d 81 (1981); Harrigfeld v. Hancock, 140 Idaho 134, 90 P.3d 884 (2004); Hale v. Groce, 304 Or. 281, 744 P.2d 1289 (1987); Friske v. Hogan, 698 N.W.2d 526 (S.D. 2005). See Joan Teshima, Annotation, Attorney's liability, to one other than the immediate client, for negligence in connection with legal duties, 61 A.L.R.4th 615 (1988).

[132] See Restatement of the Law Governing Lawyers § 51 (2000). See also, applying the general rule that in the absence of such facts no duty is owed to a non-client because it would create conflicts of interest with the duties owed to the client, Leonard v. Dorsey & Whitney, LLP, 553 F.3d 609 (8th Cir. 2009).

[133] See Beck v. Wecht, 28 Cal. 4th 289, 48 P.3d 417, 121 Cal. Rptr.2d 384 (2002); Scheffler v. Adams & Reese, LLP, 950 So. 2d 641 (La. 2007); Mazon v. Krafchick, 158 Wash.2d 440, 144 P.3d 1168 (2006); Horn v. Wooster, 165 P.3d 69 (Wyo. 2007).

[134] E.g., Paradigm Ins. Co. v. Langerman Law Offices, P.A., 200 Ariz. 146, 24 P.3d 593 (2001) (lawyer can owe a duty of care to an insurer, even where insurer is not a client, where lawyer knows that client intends as one of the primary objectives of the representation that the lawyer's services benefit the insurer); see Restatement of the Law Governing Lawyers § 51(3) (2000).

to prove that she would get some incidental benefit from the lawyer's work for his client, even where the lawyer knows that fact.[135] Rather, the non-client must be a "direct and intended beneficiary" for a duty to arise.[136] As noted above, the classic example is an intended beneficiary of a client's will; most courts have now recognized that such persons are owed a duty of professional care and can sue the lawyer directly for malpractice if his breach causes them harm.[137] Some states, however, have drawn the line at named beneficiaries, holding that no duty is owed to intended but *unnamed* beneficiaries.[138]

Those invited to rely. If a lawyer, or the client with the lawyer's consent, invites a third party to rely on the lawyer's work, and the third party reasonably relies on that work, then that third party is also owed a duty of care enforceable in a malpractice action.[139] The lawyer must either know or should know that the non-client is relying on his services, and the imposition of a duty must not conflict with the duty owed to the client.[140] Perhaps the most common example of this situation is where the client retains the lawyer to draft an opinion letter to send to a bank so that the client can get a loan.[141]

Duty to adversaries and those with conflicting interests. The privity rule might have been an overstatement of an enduring policy. The lawyer owes no duty of professional care to his client's adversary.[142] That much is essential to the adversary system and required to prevent conflicts of interest.[143] Likewise, the lawyer must owe no duty of care even to friendly third persons where efforts to comply with such a duty would impair the lawyer's obligation to his client.[144] A lawyer is not immune from liability for malicious prosecution or abuse of process, however.[145] And a non-client may sue a lawyer for negligent misrepresentation if the elements of that tort are proved.[146] Finally a lawyer may owe fiduciary duties to non-clients, with resulting liability for breach.[147]

---

[135]   Zenith Ins. Co. v. Cozen O'Connor, 148 Cal.App.4th 998, 55 Cal.Rptr.3d 911 (2007).

[136]   Leonard v. Dorsey & Whitney LLP, 553 F.3d 609 (8th Cir. 2009).

[137]   See Joan Teshima, Annotation, Attorney's liability, to one other than the immediate client, for negligence in connection with legal duties, 61 A.L.R.4th 615 (1988).

[138]   See, e.g., St. Malachy Roman Catholic Congretation of Geneseo v. Ingram, 841 N.W.2d 338 (Iowa 2013); Miller v. Mooney, 431 Mass. 57, 725 N.E.2d 545 (2000); Rydde v. Morris, 381 S.C. 643, 675 S.E.2d 431 (2009).

[139]   See Taylor v. Riley, 157 Idaho 323, 336 P.3d 256 (2014) (corporate counsel owed duty to non-client shareholder where counsel drafted opinion letter addressed to shareholder stating that the shareholder could rely on the opinions given in the letter); Restatement of the Law Governing Lawyers § 51(2) (2000).

[140]   See International Strategies Group, Ltd. v. Greenberg Traurig, LLP, 482 F.3d 1 (1st Cir. 2007).

[141]   E.g., Greycas, Inc. v. Proud, 826 F.2d 1560 (7th Cir. 1987) (lawyer told lender that collateral for a loan to client was not subject to other liens, but did not check records that would have shown otherwise); see also Petrillo v. Bachenberg, 139 N.J. 472, 655 A.2d 1354 (1995) (lawyer for real estate seller assumed a duty to the purchaser by submitting an incomplete percolation-test report, knowing purchaser was relying on its accuracy).

[142]   E.g., Lamare v. Basbanes, 636 N.E.2d 218 (Mass. 1994); Friedman v. Dozorc, 312 N.W.2d 585 (Mich. 1981); Brooks v. Zebre, 792 P.2d 196 (Wyo. 1990); see also Restatement of the Law Governing Lawyers § 51, cmt. c (2000).

[143]   See Chu v. Hong, 249 S.W.3d 441 (Tex. 2008).

[144]   See Restatement of the Law Governing Lawyers § 51 (2000).

[145]   E.g., Zamos v. Stroud, 87 P.3d 802 (Cal. 2004); see Debra E. Was, Annotation, Liability of Attorney, Acting for Client, for Malicious Prosecution, 46 A.L.R.4th 249 (1987). In malicious prosecution claims, the action must first terminate favorably to the original defendant who is now suing. See § 39.6.

[146]   E.g., Allen v. Steele, 252 P.3d 476 (Colo. 2011).

[147]   E.g., Graubard Mollen Dannett & Horowitz v. Moskovitz, 86 N.Y.2d 112, 653 N.E.2d 1179, 629 N.Y.S.2d 1009 (1995) (departing partner in law firm breached fiduciary duty owed to firm); see §§ 696 & 697.

B. MALPRACTICE IN CIVIL MATTERS: DEFENSES

§ 45.8　Contributory Negligence/Comparative Fault

Comparative fault as a valid defense. When the malpractice claim is based upon negligence, courts have been quite ready to adopt the defense or partial defense of contributory negligence or comparative fault,[148] although some comparative fault statutes are addressed only to personal injury cases and the like.[149] Relatedly but quite distinctly, courts may sometimes conclude that the plaintiff's conduct is the sole proximate cause of her own harm, in which case recovery is altogether barred.[150] Perhaps the best candidates for a comparative negligence reduction are the clients who fail to provide requested information or to follow the lawyer's instructions or advice.[151] In many of these cases, the plaintiff's contributory negligence may be an awkward way of recognizing that the lawyer was not negligent in the first place.[152] If the client fails to follow the lawyer's good instructions, the lawyer seems not to be at fault;[153] if the lawyer's instructions were bad, the client is not likely to be at fault for failure to follow them.[154] Ultimately, however, whether a client's fault should be given legal effect must be appraised in light of a lawyer's duties to the client, which vary from case to case.[155]

Failure to read or understand legal documents before signing. These general principles have been applied numerous times to a common situation, in which a client signs a legal document prepared by the lawyer, without reading it or understanding it, then sues the lawyer for malpractice in connection with the document. Whether the lawyer is negligent on these facts, and if so, whether the client is contributorily negligent, will often produce a jury question.[156] Courts recognize that in some of these cases the client is at fault (and perhaps the lawyer is not at all), whereas in others the client is entitled to rely on the lawyer's skill and advice in drafting the document. The client's sophistication (or more properly her degree of knowledge about the matter covered by the document) may be a factor in the analysis. A knowledgeable and sophisticated client

---

[148] E.g., Kirsch v. Duryea, 21 Cal.3d 303, 146 Cal.Rptr. 218, 578 P.2d 935, 6 A.L.R.4th 334 (1978); Pizel v. Zuspann, 247 Kan. 54, 795 P.2d 42, 10 A.L.R.5th 1098 (1990); Wheeler v. White, 714 A.2d 125 (Me. 1998); Clark v. Rowe, 428 Mass. 339, 701 N.E.2d 624 (1998); see 3 Mallen & Smith, Legal Malpractice § 22:2 (2009 ed.) (citing cases from virtually every jurisdiction).

[149] E.g., Ind. Code § 34–6–2–45; see Clark v. Rowe, 428 Mass. 339, 701 N.E.2d 624 (1998) (comparative negligence statute does not apply to economic harms caused by legal malpractice, but modified comparative fault defense adopted as a common law rule based on the "public policy considerations underlying" the statute).

[150] These are cases, then, not of a contributory negligence defense at all, but rather a failure of an element of the plaintiff's prima facie case. E.g., Hansen v. Anderson, Wilmarth & Van Der Maaten, 657 N.W.2d 711 (Iowa 2003); Blackstock v. Kohn, 994 S.W.2d 947 (Mo. 1999).

[151] E.g., Ott v. Smith, 413 So.2d 1129 (Ala. 1982); Western Fiberglass, Inc. v. Kirton, McConkie and Bushnell, 789 P.2d 34 (Utah Ct App. 1990) (client 50% at fault for failing to keep lawyers informed, and failing to follow lawyers' instructions).

[152] E.g., Conklin v. Hannoch Weisman, 145 N.J. 395, 678 A.2d 1060 (1996) (recognizing that where a client violates the professional's instructions or advice, "the analysis is that of causation, not contributory negligence"). The phenomenon is not limited to malpractice cases. See § 16.5.

[153] E.g., Sierra Fria Corp. v. Donald J. Evans, P.C., 127 F.3d 175 (1st Cir. 1997) (Mass. law) (lawyer did not breach duty to client where client did not heed lawyer's warnings).

[154] E.g., Michael E. Greene, P.A. v. Leasing Associates, Inc., 935 So.2d 21 (Fla. Dist. Ct. App. 2006) (client cannot be found comparatively negligent for relying on a lawyer's erroneous advice or for failing to correct a lawyer's errors).

[155] See Restatement of the Law Governing Lawyers § 54, cmt. d (2000).

[156] See, e.g., Paul v. Smith, Gambrell & Russell, 283 Ga.App. 584, 642 S.E.2d 217 (2007); Mandel, Resnik & Kaiser, P.C. v. E.I. Electronics, Inc., 41 A.D.3d 386, 839 N.Y.S.2d 68 (2007).

may be contributorily negligent for signing a legal document without reading and understanding it,[157] but an unsophisticated client may not be negligent for assuming that the lawyer has fulfilled his duty to draft a proper document and explain its effects before the client signs.[158] The nature of the document is also a factor; where it is not ambiguous or "laced with legal jargon," then the client owes a duty to herself to read it before signing.[159] New York courts have developed a rule that a party who signs a document is conclusively bound by its terms, absent a valid excuse for having failed to read it, and found such an excuse where the lawyers made affirmative representations to their clients about the contents of the document, in essence telling them that they did not need to read it.[160]

§ 45.9 *In Pari Delicto* and Quasi-Judicial Immunity

Two other defenses will provide a complete bar to a plaintiff's malpractice recovery if established. The first, *in pari delicto,* relates to the contributory negligence defense in that it involves proof of the client's wrongdoing. The second defense arises when the attorney being sued was appointed by the court to represent the interests of a minor, often in a custody or dissolution proceeding; in many states the lawyer (usually denominated a guardian ad litem) is granted either a qualified or absolute immunity from civil liability for actions taken within the scope of the lawyer's duties.

In pari delicto. The *in pari delicto*[161] (sometimes called unclean hands) defense applies when the client is guilty of highly culpable and illegal conduct and his claim or injury arises in part from that conduct as well as from the lawyer's fault.[162] A lawyer who advises his client to perjure herself is guilty of malpractice; but a client to follows the advice is barred by the *in pari delicto* defense.[163] The client's conduct in these cases is usually intentional, not merely negligent.[164] In some jurisdictions, the culpability of the client must either exceed or equal that of the lawyer.[165] Courts often cite the policy of not allowing a client to benefit from her own intentional wrongdoing and to seek what amounts to an indemnity from her lawyer to escape full responsibility.[166] The defense is

---

[157] E.g., Pontiac School Dist. v. Miller, Canfield, Paddock & Stone, 221 Mich. App. 602, 563 N.W.2d 693 (1997); Cicorelli v. Capobianco, 89 A.D.2d 842, 453 N.Y.S.2d 21 (1982).

[158] E.g., TCW/Camil Holding LLC v. Fox Horan & Camerini, LLP, 330 B.R. 117 (D. Del. 2005) (client was not contributorily negligent for signing documents where law firm failed to advise him of their legal effect); Tarleton v. Arnstein & Lehr, 719 So.2d 325 (Fla. Dist. Ct. App. 1998); Gorski v. Smith, 812 A.2d 683 (Pa. Super. 2002).

[159] Berman v. Rubin, 138 Ga.App. 849, 227 S.E.2d 802 (1976) (lawyer not liable for malpractice where the document was signed on every page by the client, who was well-educated).

[160] Arnav Industries, Inc. Retirement Trust v. Brown, Raysman, Millstein, Felder & Steiner, LLP, 96 N.Y.2d 300, 727 N.Y.S.2d 688, 751 N.E.2d 936 (2001), *overruled on other grounds*, Oakes v. Patel, 20 N.Y.3d 633, 988 N.E.2d 488, 965 N.Y.S.2d 752 (2013).

[161] *In pari delicto* literally means "in equal fault."

[162] See, e.g., Whiteheart v. Waller, 681 S.E.2d 419 (N.C.App. 2009) (client "continued to assert his non-existent interests" in court papers, giving rise to a claim against him and his lawyers for malicious prosecution, among other things; he was thus barred from suing his own lawyers for malpractice in connection with the cases, despite his lawyers' many violations of ethics rules).

[163] E.g., Blain v. Doctor's Company, 222 Cal.App.3d 1048, 272 Cal.Rptr. 250 (1990); Turner v. Anderson, 704 So.2d 748 (Fla. Dist. Ct. App. 1998); Quick v. Samp, 697 N.W.2d 741 (S.D. 2005).

[164] See 3 Mallen & Smith, Legal Malpractice § 22:4 (2009 ed.).

[165] See State v. Therrien, 175 Vt. 342, 830 A.2d 28 (2003) (client barred where she and her late husband committed fraud; lawyers were sued for negligently allowing them to execute deeds and complete land transfers that constituted the fraud).

[166] Heyman v. Gable, Gotwals, Mock, Schwabe, Kihle, Gabarino, 994 P.2d 902 (Okla. Civ. App. 1999).

based on the impropriety of the client's act, not the lawyer's lack of fault or blame.[167] It has been used numerous times in connection with bankruptcy proceedings, but its contours remain uncertain.[168] Courts have allowed the defense even where the lawyer did not participate in the client's misconduct at all.[169]

Quasi-judicial immunity. Lawyers appointed by the court as a guardian ad litem to represent a person's interests in litigation are granted an immunity from suits, including malpractice suits, in a number of states.[170] Some grant an immunity by statute to court-appointed guardians at litem,[171] while a few others have adopted an immunity as a matter of common law.[172] Often the immunity is absolute[173] and sometimes it is qualified. When the immunity is qualified, it is lost if the lawyer acts with malice, wantonness or an intent to injure.[174] In all states that allow an immunity, the lawyer must be acting within the scope of his duties or the privilege is lost.[175]

Courts that have applied the immunity have stressed the policy rationale that lawyers in this role must be allowed to take positions in the ward's best interests, even where those positions are at odds with the wishes of the ward herself, or in the case of a minor ward, adverse to the interests of the child's parents.[176] Another factor of key importance to many courts is that the lawyer's role in such cases is a hybrid of advocate and guardian, with duties to the court as well as to the client.[177] In some of those states, the existence of the immunity turns on whether the lawyer is acting principally as an advocate rather than as an arm of the court; if the former, then there is no immunity at all against a malpractice action.[178]

§ 45.10   Statute of Limitations

Contract and tort: occurrence rule. Decisions on the statute of limitations in lawyer malpractice claims are quite diverse if not actually chaotic.[179] Since malpractice arises out of a consensual relationship, the claim has some connection to contract and that connection may affect the statute of limitations defense in two ways. First, if the plaintiff

---

[167]   See Mettes v. Quinn, 89 Ill.App.3d 77, 411 N.E.2d 549, 44 Ill.Dec. 427 (1980).

[168]   E.g., Choquette v. Isacoff, 65 Mass.App.Ct. 1, 836 N.E.2d 329 (2005) (client knew his bankruptcy petition contained false statements about his income and assets).

[169]   Goldstein v. Lustig, 154 Ill.App.3d 595, 507 N.E.2d 164, 107 Ill.Dec. 500 (1987).

[170]   Perhaps the most common example is the lawyer appointed to represent the interests of a child in a divorce case between the child's parents, see, e.g., Sarkissian v. Benjamin, 62 Mass.App.Ct. 741, 820 N.E.2d 263 (2005). Lawyers have also been appointed as guardians ad litem to represent the interests of adults in conservatorship proceedings, see, e.g., Estate of Leonard v. Swift, 656 N.W.2d 132 (Iowa 2003).

[171]   See, e.g., Ariz. Rev. Stat. § 8–522 (H).

[172]   E.g., Paige K.B. v. Molepske, 219 Wis.2d 418, 580 N.W.2d 289 (1998).

[173]   E.g., Billups v. Scott, 253 Neb. 287, 571 N.W.2d 603 (1997).

[174]   Carrubba v. Moskowitz, 81 Conn.App. 382, 840 A.2d 557 (2004).

[175]   See Sarkisian v. Benjamin, 62 Mass.App.Ct. 741, 820 N.E.2d 263 (2005); Kimbrell v. Kimbrell, 331 P.3d 915 (N.M. 2014); Falk v. Sadler, 341 S.C. 281, 533 S.E.2d 350 (Ct. App. 2000).

[176]   See Short by Oosterhous v. Short, 730 F.Supp. 1037 (D. Colo. 1990); Carrubba v. Moskowitz, 81 Conn.App. 382, 840 A.2d 557 (2004).

[177]   See, e.g., Bradt v. White, 190 Misc.2d 526, 740 N.Y.S.2d 777 (2002).

[178]   See Fox v. Wills, 390 Md. 620, 890 A.2d 726 (2006); Hunnicutt v. Sewell, 147 N.M. 272, 219 P.3d 529 (Ct. App. 2009); see also 3 Mallen & Smith, Legal Malpractice § 22:7 (2009 ed.).

[179]   See Francis M. Dougherty, Annotation, When Statute of Limitations Begins to Run upon Action Against Attorney for Malpractice, 32 A.L.R.4th 260 (1981); George L. Blum, Annotation, When Statute of Limitations Begins to Run upon Action Against Attorney for Legal Malpractice—Deliberate Wrongful Acts or Omissions, 67 A.L.R.5th 587 (1999); George L. Blum, Annotation, Attorney Malpractice—Tolling or Other Exceptions to Running of Statute of Limitations, 87 A.L.R.5th 473 (2001).

is permitted to sue on a contract rather than negligence theory, the contract statute of limitations may apply as it does in other contract cases.[180] Even when the claim is asserted in tort for negligence, the old connection with contract nevertheless led courts to say that the plaintiff could recover nominal damages when the contract was breached by the lawyer's negligent act. That in turn meant that the cause of action would accrue upon breach, not later when damages were inflicted.[181] The occurrence rule can foreclose the plaintiff's claim before harm is done or discovered. In spite of its problems, a very small number of state statutes continue to provide that the limitation period begins on the date that the malpractice occurs.[182] Some other state statutes reference an occurrence rule but expressly provide for tolling of the limitations period if the malpractice is not and could not reasonably have been discovered.[183] Accrual at the time of breach does not invariably cause difficulties for the plaintiff, of course. Depending on the defendant's duty, breach may not occur until quite late in a series of transactions.[184] The unadorned occurrence rule, however, has largely been abandoned in legal malpractice actions.

Time-of-harm rule. The conventional negligence case would start the statute at the moment when the defendant's negligence has actually caused damages, whether or not the plaintiff was aware of the harm at the time. Some courts apply this rule in legal malpractice cases—essentially rejecting the discovery rule[185]—especially but not only in cases of drafting errors in the preparation of a will that can cause injury only after the putative testator dies.[186] "Harm" may be a flexible term in some cases. A lawyer's error in failing to secure a judgment for definite benefits that would be payable in the future may be deemed to create actual harm on the date of the judgment if future loss could be calculated at that time.[187] Even when the time of harm is not itself the ultimate governing rule, the time of harm may be a significant component in some other rule.

Discovery rule. Most states have now adopted some form of the discovery rule for legal malpractice cases; many have done so by statute.[188] The rule usually postpones accrual of a claim until the plaintiff-client discovered or could reasonably have

---

[180] Van Dam v. Gay, 280 Va. 457, 699 S.E.2d 480 (2010).

[181] See 3 Mallen & Smith, Legal Malpractice § 23:10 (2009 ed.) (tracing the genesis of the rule's application in legal malpractice cases to Wilcox v. Plummer's Executors, 29 U.S. 172, 7 L.Ed. 821 (1830)).

[182] See 14 Me. Rev. Stat. Ann. § 753A (six-year statute of limitations begins to run "from the date of the act or omission giving rise to the injury" with a few narrow exceptions); S.D. Codified Laws § 15–2–14.2 (with a few exceptions, action must be brought "within three years after the alleged malpractice, error, mistake or omission shall have occurred").

[183] E.g., 735 Ill. Comp. Stat. 5/13–214.3(c); Neb. Rev. Stat. § 25–222.

[184] See, e.g., Barnes v. Turner, 278 Ga. 788, 606 S.E.2d 849 (2004) (failure to file UCC financing statement).

[185] Tingley v. Harrison, 125 Idaho 86, 867 P.2d 960 (1994); Michels v. Sklavos, 869 S.W.2d 728 (Ky. 1994) (in the litigation malpractice, case-within-a-case setting, the plaintiff-client's claim accrues when the first case is terminated, not when the lawyer commits the earlier act of negligence); Uhler v. Doak, 268 Mont. 191, 885 P.2d 1297 (1994); McCoy v. Feinman, 99 N.Y.2d 295, 755 N.Y.S.2d 693, 785 N.E.2d 714 (2002).

[186] Cf. Pizel v. Zuspann, 247 Kan. 54, 795 P.2d 42, 10 A.L.R.5th 1098 (1990) (trust instrument).

[187] See McCoy v. Feinman, 99 N.Y.2d 295, 755 N.Y.S.2d 693, 785 N.E.2d 714 (2002).

[188] See 3 Mallen & Smith, Legal Malpractice §§ 23:15 & 23:16 (2009 ed.). Only a few states have rejected the rule; many of those have said that only the legislature can adopt a discovery rule. E.g., Moix-McNutt v. Brown, 348 Ark. 518, 74 S.W.3d 612, 11 A.L.R.6th 795 (2002); Martin v. Clements, 98 Idaho 906, 575 P.2d 885 (1978); Madlem v. Arko, 592 N.E.2d 686 (Ind. 1992); McCoy v. Feinman, 99 N.Y.2d 295, 785 N.E.2d 714, 755 N.Y.S.2d 693 (2002).

discovered both the lawyer's negligent conduct and the plaintiff's injury.[189] One reason
for the rule lies in the lawyer's fiduciary obligation to disclose his own malpractice.[190] A
client need not know the full extent of the injuries caused by the lawyer's negligence in
order for the discovery rule to trigger accrual of the claim.[191] The focus is on the plaintiff's
knowledge of *facts,* not law; the key is whether the plaintiff knew or should have known
facts that would give rise to a legal claim.[192]

Continuous-representation rule. An increasing number of decisions recognize
termination of the relationship or representation as an appropriate time for starting the
statute.[193] The representation qualifies as continuing only if it concerns the same or a
related subject matter.[194] Thus where a lawyer commits malpractice in one matter, but
continues to represent the client in one or more unrelated matters, the continuous-
representation rule does not assist the plaintiff.[195] Nor does the continuous-
representation rule apply to interrupted or sporadic representations; as the name
indicates, the representation must in fact be "continuous," as opposed to "sporadic."[196]

Supporting rationales for the continuous-representation doctrine. Termination of the
relationship on the particular legal matter may represent an important starting time for
the statute of limitations in litigation-malpractice cases for several different reasons, not
at all alike. One reason is that the termination may be a good index to the client's
discovery or probable discovery of the elements of a claim against her lawyer. Another is
that the lawyer's negligence may be remediable or at least that the damages he inflicts
can be minimized if he takes steps to reduce the harm after his initial act of negligence.[197]
A third reason recognizes that the client cannot very well be expected to sue her attorney
while representation continues;[198] in that sense the rule also prevents the disruption of
the client-lawyer relationship.[199] Even the attorney who does nothing to carry out his
representation may be continuously representing the client if the client reasonably

---

[189] See, e.g., Bleck v. Power, 955 A.2d 712 (D.C. 2008); Bank of New York v. Sheff, 382 Md. 235, 854 A.2d 1269 (2004); Channel v. Loyacono, 954 So.2d 415 (Miss. 2007); Guest v. McLaverty, 332 Mont. 421, 138 P.3d 812 (2006); Vastano v. Algeier, 178 N.J. 230, 837 A.2d 1081 (2003).

[190] Where the lawyer has actually concealed his malpractice, the rule in virtually all jurisdictions is that the statute of limitations is tolled until the client discovers or should reasonably have discovered the facts. See 3 Mallen & Smith, Legal Malpractice § 23:14 (2009 ed.); e.g., Bennett v. Hill-Boren, P.C., 52 So. 3d 364 (Miss. 2011).

[191] E.g., Larson & Larson, P.A. v. TSE Indus., Inc., 22 So.3d 36 (Fla. 2009); Channel v. Loyacono, 954 So.2d 415 (Miss. 2007).

[192] See, e.g., Jeanes v. Bank of America, N.A., 296 Kan. 870, 295 P.3d 1045 (2013); Guinn v. Murray, 286 Neb. 584, 837 N.W.2d 805 (2013); Vastano v. Algeier, 178 N.J. 230, 837 A.2d 1081 (2003); Sharkey v. Prescott, 19 A.3d 62 (R.I. 2011).

[193] O'Neill v. Tichy, 19 Cal.App.4th 114, 25 Cal.Rptr.2d 162 (1994); Murphy v. Smith, 411 Mass. 133, 579 N.E.2d 165 (1991); Bjorgen v. Kinsey, 466 N.W.2d 553 (N.D. 1991).

[194] See Lockton v. O'Rourke, 184 Cal.App.4th 1051 (2010); Bleck v. Power, 955 A.2d 712 (D.C. 2008); Shumsky v. Eisenstein, 96 N.Y.2d 164, 750 N.E.2d 67, 726 N.Y.S.2d 365 (2001).

[195] See, e.g., Duane Morris LLP v. Astor Holdings Inc., 61 A.D.3d 418, 877 N.Y.S.2d 250 (2009) (lawyers' alleged malpractice was in a litigation that ended in 2002; claim accrued at that point, and was not tolled until 2004 although the lawyers represented the plaintiffs in another litigation until then).

[196] See, e.g., Byron Chemical Co. v. Groman, 61 A.D.3d 909, 877 N.Y.S.2d 457 (2009); Williams v. Maulis, 672 N.W.2d 702 (S.D. 2003).

[197] Beal Bank, SSB v. Arter & Haddon, LLP, 42 Cal.4th 503, 167 P.3d 666, 66 Cal.Rptr.3d 52 (2007).

[198] Shumsky v. Eisenstein, 96 N.Y.2d 164, 750 N.E.2d 67, 726 N.Y.S.2d 365 (2001).

[199] See 3 Mallen & Smith, Legal Malpractice § 23:13 (2009 ed.).

expects or understands that representation is continuing.[200] Some authority regards the continuous-representation doctrine as an equitable one and determines on a case-by-case basis whether to apply it.[201] A few modern courts have rejected the continuous-representation doctrine,[202] sometimes on the ground that only the legislature can adopt the rule,[203] but it has become quite well-established.

C. MALPRACTICE IN CIVIL MATTERS: DAMAGES

§ 45.11 Compensatory Damages Generally

Punitive damages aside,[204] the general principle of damages measurement is to provide compensation; thus the client-plaintiff is entitled to recover a sum that will put her in the financial position she would have been in but for the malpractice. The plaintiff can potentially claim three layers of damages: (1) The loss incurred (or gain prevented) as a result of the defendant's malpractice; (2) consequential damages, meaning collateral losses that would not have been recovered in any underlying litigation, potentially including items such as loss of credit; and (3) damages based on costs in the malpractice suit itself, such as the fees incurred in pursuing the malpractice claim.

First-layer damages. In the first category, many examples are straightforward in principle even if proof is sometimes difficult. The attorney negligently causes the client to lose his property; the client is entitled to recover the value of the property lost.[205] The attorney negligently causes a trust in favor of the beneficiary to fail; the beneficiary recovers what she would have taken if the trust had been properly handled.[206] The attorney negligently recommends that the client accept an inadequate settlement on dissolution of her marriage; he is liable to the client for the settlement or recovery that she could have recovered had the advice been appropriate.[207] Courts have disagreed over whether any such recovery should be reduced by the amount of fees that the client would have paid for competent lawyering; most hold that there should be no such reduction.[208]

Second-layer or consequential damages. One example of recoverable consequential damages occurs when the malpractice requires the plaintiff to carry on litigation with others. If the attorney's bad advice or negligent drafting results in a criminal prosecution

---

[200] McCoy v. Feinman, 99 N.Y.2d 295, 785 N.E.2d 714, 755 N.Y.S.2d 693 (2002) ("The continuous representation doctrine tolls the statute of limitations only where there is a mutual understanding of the need for further representation on the specific subject matter underlying the malpractice claim.").

[201] Hendrick v. ABC Ins. Co., 787 So.2d 283 (La. 2001).

[202] See, e.g., Channel v. Loyacono, 954 So.2d 415 (Miss. 2007) (implying that the rule was not needed where the discovery rule applied).

[203] See, e.g., Larson & Larson, P.A. v. TSE Industries, Inc., 22 So.3d 36 (Fla. 2009) (finding that the doctrine is a species of tolling and that the tolling statute does not mention lawyers or legal malpractice cases).

[204] Most states allow recovery of punitive damages against lawyers in legal malpractice cases, but only where the lawyer engages in particularly egregious misconduct. See 4 Dobbs, Hayden & Bublick, The Law of Torts § 731 (2d ed. 2011 & Supp.). For a discussion of punitive damages generally, see id. § 483. Liability for punitive damages that were lost because of the lawyer's negligence in the underlying case is discussed in § 45.12.

[205] Rafferty v. Scurry, 117 Ohio App.3d 240, 690 N.E.2d 104 (1997).

[206] As in Pizel v. Zuspann, 247 Kan. 54, 795 P.2d 42, 10 A.L.R.5th 1098 (1990) (subject to comparative fault reduction).

[207] E.g., Grayson v. Wofsey, Rosen, Kweskin and Kuriansky, 231 Conn. 168, 646 A.2d 195 (1994) ($1,500,000 recovery).

[208] See, e.g., Hook v. Trevino, 839 N.W.2d 434 (Iowa 2013); Shoemake v. Ferrer, 143 Wash.App. 819, 182 P.3d 992 (2008); see Restatement of the Law Governing Lawyers § 53, cmt. c (2000).

or civil suit against his client, the client's costs of that collateral litigation are recoverable items of consequential damage.[209] All the reasonable costs of such litigation, including attorneys fees incurred there, are recoverable against the malpracticing defendant.[210]

Emotional harm. A few courts have stated without qualification that emotional distress recovery is allowed in legal malpractice cases, at least where the distress is severe.[211] But in keeping with the general attitude toward economic torts, most courts have subjected emotional harm damages to special limitations or have rejected them outright,[212] except under the case-within-a-case rules.[213] For instance, Minnesota has said that emotional harm damages could be recovered in a legal malpractice case only if the lawyer directly caused the harm by willful, wanton, or malicious conduct[214] and a number of other courts have placed similar restrictions on the recovery.[215] A number of courts have concluded that emotional distress damages may not be recovered where the emotional distress results from other damages caused by the lawyer's negligence, because of a lack of general foreseeability.[216] If lawyers are not liable for negligently causing their clients emotional distress, they are presumably not liable for the suicide that results from such distress.[217] This result is perhaps more understandable when the malpractice implicates no dignitary interests of the client.[218] But emotional harm damages seem appropriate without any proof of physical harm if the defendant's malpractice is the kind that runs the risk of substantial emotional distress, and courts have allowed emotional harm damages in some such cases.[219] The lawyer who negligently allows an entirely sane client to be dispatched to a mental hospital would be an obvious example.[220] If malpractice runs the risk of stigmatizing the client or destroying her reputation, emotional distress damages seem entirely appropriate.[221] An

---

[209] Dessel v. Donohue, 431 N.W.2d 359 (Iowa 1988); Rudolph v. Shayne, Dachs, Stanisci, Corker & Sauer, 8 N.Y.3d 438, 867 N.E.2d 385, 835 N.Y.S.2d 534 (2007).

[210] See Restatement Second of Torts § 914(2) (1979).

[211] See Sherwin-Williams Co. v. First Louisiana Const., Inc., 915 So.2d 841 (La. App. 2005) (negligently-handled real estate transaction); Gore v. Rains & Block, 189 Mich.App. 729, 473 N.W.2d 813 (1991) (failure to file a timely medical malpractice claim).

[212] For example, some states disallow emotional distress damages cases absent physical injury, and carry that restriction over to legal malpractice cases. See, e.g., Leonard v. Walthall, 143 F.3d 466 (8th Cir. 1998) (Arkansas law). Other courts apply the basic rule that emotional distress damages are unavailable in economic-loss cases. See, e.g., Douglas v. Delp, 987 S.W.2d 879 (Tex. 1999).

[213] See § 45.12.

[214] Lickteig v. Alderson, Ondov, Leonard & Sween, 556 N.W.2d 557 (Minn. 1996).

[215] See, e.g., Boros v. Baxley, 621 So.2d 240 (Ala. 1993); Garland v. Roy, 976 A.2d 940 (Me. 2009) (only where the distress is severe and the lawyer's actions were "egregious"); Akutagawa v. Laflin, Pick & Heer, P.A., 138 N.M. 774, 126 P.3d 1138 (2005) (only where lawyer acted intentionally, or in breach of contract cases where protecting client from emotional harm was contemplated).

[216] E.g., Reed v. Mitchell & Timbanard, P.C., 183 Ariz. 313, 903 P.2d 621 (Ct. App. 1995); Kahn v. Morse & Mobray, 121 Nev. 464, 117 P.3d 227 (2005) (asserting that several other jurisdictions follow the rule).

[217] See Cleveland v. Rotman, 297 F.3d 569 (7th Cir. 2002).

[218] E.g., Cornell v. Wunschel, 408 N.W.2d 369 (Iowa 1987).

[219] E.g., Miranda v. Said, 836 N.W.2d 8 (Iowa 2013) (immigration case); Kohn v. Schiappa, 281 N.J. Super. 235, 656 A.2d 1322 (1995) (lawyer retained to help adopt a child).

[220] Wagenmann v. Adams, 829 F.2d 196 (1st Cir. 1987) (a long but fascinating tale of human error, panic, grief, and pain). Recovery of emotional distress damages against a criminal defense lawyer whose negligence resulted in the client's incarceration would often appear justified, because the harm caused in such a case is not purely economic and is also a reasonably foreseeable result of the negligence. See § 45.13.

[221] See Salley v. Childs, 541 A.2d 1297 (Me. 1988) (lawyer failed to discover evidence that would exculpate horse trainer whose license was revoked because a horse was drugged).

attorney may also be liable for intentional infliction of emotional distress where the elements of that tort are met.[222]

Third-layer damages: costs of malpractice litigation. Under the basic American rule, neither party to a litigation is liable to the other for attorney's fees incurred in that litigation,[223] although as noted above, costs of collateral litigation is another matter. This rule governs malpractice litigation, except for the potential peculiarity resulting from case-within-the-case proof.

§ 45.12 Compensatory Damages in the Case-Within-a-Case Suit

Elements recoverable. When the lawyer's malpractice allegedly deprived the plaintiff of an appropriate litigation outcome, as where the lawyer fails to file a claim within the statute of limitations period, or negotiates or counsels an inadequate settlement, the malpractice plaintiff must normally prove what she would have recovered had the case been tried and tried properly, or if she was a defendant in the underlying case, what losses she would have avoided by proper representation.[224] This rule impacts damages. For example, if the client would have recovered a fund of money or a share in property, he is entitled to recover its value against the attorney.[225] If the plaintiff would have recovered lost wages[226] and medical expenses,[227] pain and suffering, or emotional distress[228] or lost consortium[229] damages, those items of damage are recoverable against the malpracticing lawyer. If prejudgment interest or attorney fees would have been available in the first suit, those items are also recoverable against the lawyer whose fault caused the loss of the original recovery.[230]

Punitive damages as compensatory damages in case-within-a-case suit. Perhaps the same principle recited above applies to punitive damages,[231] so that if such items were recoverable in the first action they would also be recoverable against the attorney, though the attorney did not engage in the kind of malicious behavior that would

---

[222] See Pierce v. Cook, 992 So.2d 612 (Miss. 2008) (affirming jury verdict of $1 million for intentional infliction of emotional distress against lawyer who had an affair with his client's wife); Vallinoto v. DiSandro, 688 A.2d 830 (R.I. 1997) (but determining that plaintiff failed to prove that severe emotional distress was caused by her lawyer's sexual abuse during his representation of her in her divorce).

[223] See 1 Dan B. Dobbs, Law of Remedies § 3.10(1) (2d ed. 1993); 3 Mallen & Smith, Legal Malpractice § 21:14 (2009 ed.).

[224] See §§ 45.5 & 45.6.

[225] Martin v. Northwest Washington Legal Services, 43 Wash. App. 405, 717 P.2d 779 (1986) (divorce, value of husband's pension rights which lawyer failed to claim).

[226] E.g., Williams v. Bashman, 457 F. Supp. 322 (E.D. Pa. 1978) (loss of wages would have been recovered, but only for part-time work in light of plaintiff's physical ailments).

[227] Harris v. Kissling, 80 Or. App. 5, 721 P.2d 838 (1986) (future medical expenses included).

[228] Harris v. Kissling, 80 Or. App. 5, 721 P.2d 838 (1986) (lawyer failed to file suit against hospital which had failed to make routine blood tests for Rh factors, resulting in serious complications for the plaintiff's subsequent pregnancies, emotional distress damages could have been recovered against hospital, therefore recoverable against lawyer).

[229] Togstad v. Vesely, Otto, Miller & Keefe, 291 N.W.2d 686 (Minn. 1980).

[230] See Glamann v. St. Paul Fire & Marine Ins. Co., 144 Wis.2d 865, 424 N.W.2d 924 (1988).

[231] See Marjorie A. Shields, Allowance of Punitive Damages in Action Against Attorney for Malpractice, 9 A.L.R.6th 285 (2005) (§§ 15 & 16, collecting cases going both ways).

otherwise warrant a punitive award against him.[232] However, many courts do not allow recovery of punitive awards that would have been recovered in the underlying action.[233]

Collectibility. The plaintiff should recover in compensatory damages what she lost, but no more. This general principle has led most courts to conclude that the plaintiff who claims she would have recovered a judgment (or a higher judgment) must ordinarily also establish that it would have been collectible against the adversary in the underlying case.[234] If she cannot establish that, she cannot establish that she has a loss. A number of other courts, however, have taken the view that the defendant lawyer must shoulder the burden of proving that a judgment in the underlying case would *not* have been collectible, typically on the rationale that the lawyer's malpractice created the problem of uncollectibility in the first place.[235]

Settlement. In the world of what might have happened if the lawyer had not been negligent, there is one more important variation: the plaintiff might have settled the case (since the vast majority of cases settle) or she might have gone to trial. Settlement values vary over the course of a long preparation and negotiation period and verdicts are hard to predict, but if the plaintiff can mount sufficient evidence to provide a basis for estimation, the question is whether the jury should be estimating settlement value or the probable verdict. If the plaintiff can prove that she would have gone to trial and received a verdict, then that is the basis for calculating her damages. If, on the other hand, she can show that a settlement was likely in a given amount (or in a given range), then that would be the basis for determining damages.[236]

Attorney's fees. If, but for the defendant's malpractice, the plaintiff would have won a collectible verdict and judgment, she would normally have been required to pay her lawyer a fee. If she recovers from the lawyer the amount she would have recovered had the lawyer properly tried the case, she will be more than compensated unless a fee for the lawyer is deducted. For this reason, some courts have deducted a reasonable fee from the malpractice judgment.[237] On the other hand, the lawyer did not earn any fee;[238] far from it, he was guilty of malpractice. In addition, the plaintiff may have incurred fees to pursue the malpractice claim, so that deduction of the negligent lawyer's fee would in

---

[232] Elliott v. Videan, 164 Ariz. 113, 791 P.2d 639 (1989); Haberer v. Rice, 511 N.W.2d 279 (S.D. 1994).

[233] See Ferguson v. Lieff, Cabraser, Heimann & Bernstein, LLP, 30 Cal.4th 1037, 69 P.3d 965, 135 Cal.Rptr.2d 46 (2003); Tri-G, Inc. v. Burke, Bosselman & Weaver, 222 Ill.2d 218, 856 N.E.2d 389, 305 Ill.Dec. 584 (2006); Osborne v. Keeney, 339 S.W.3d 1 (Ky. 2012); see also Restatement of the Law Governing Lawyers § 53, cmt. h (2000) ("Collecting punitive damages from the lawyer will neither punish nor deter the original tortfeasor and calls for a speculative reconstruction of a hypothetical jury's reaction.").

[234] See, e.g., Klump v. Duffus, 71 F.3d 1368 (7th Cir. 1995); Paterek v. Petersen & Ibold, 118 Ohio St.3d 503, 890 N.E.2d 316 (2008); Thomas v. Bethea, 351 Md. 513, 718 A.2d 1187 (1998); Akin, Gump, Strauss, Hauer & Feld, LLP v. National Development and Research Corp., 299 S.W.3d 106 (Tex. 2009).

[235] E.g., Carbone v. Tierney, 151 N.H. 521, 864 A.2d 308 (2004); Kituskie v. Corbman, 714 A.2d 1027 (Pa. 1998); Schmidt v. Coogan, 335 P.3d 424 (Wash. 2014).

[236] See, e.g., Blanks v. Seyfarth Shaw, 171 Cal.App.4th 336, 89 Cal.Rptr.3d 710 (2009); Pike v. Mullikin, 158 N.H. 267, 965 A.2d 987 (2009); Thomas v. Bethea, 351 Md. 513, 718 A.2d 1187 (1998).

[237] Moores v. Greenberg, 834 F.2d 1105 (1st Cir. 1987).

[238] Kane, Kane & Kritzer, Inc. v. Altagen, 107 Cal.App. 3d 36, 165 Cal.Rptr. 534, 538 (1980) (lawyer "failed to earn" fee and crediting him "rewards his wrongdoing"); Campagnola v. Mulholland, Minion & Roe, 76 N.Y.2d 38, 556 N.Y.S.2d 239, 555 N.E.2d 611 (1990) ("defendant attorneys performed absolutely no services in connection with the disputed claim, and thus, even if discharged by plaintiff without cause, would not have been entitled to any quantum merit compensation").

effect require the plaintiff to pay fees twice.[239] With such arguments in mind, a number of cases have rejected any reduction.[240]

D. MALPRACTICE IN CRIMINAL CASES

§ 45.13   Criminal Malpractice: Prima Facie Case

Where a lawyer is sued for legal malpractice by a client he has previously represented in a criminal case—commonly called "criminal malpractice"[241]—most of the general principles of legal malpractice continue to apply. These general rules will often resolve the case without any resort to special rules. Some significant differences exist between suits for malpractice in a civil matter and those arising from lawyer negligence in a criminal case, however, meaning that the usual civil-setting rules do not always resolve the case. Most fundamentally, the interest harmed by a criminal defense lawyer's malpractice is not purely economic; rather, it is a liberty interest.[242] That key distinction may mean, for example, that some of the limitations on remedies that are entirely appropriate for an economic tort should not stand in the criminal-malpractice context. Second, the criminal defendant who claims to have been convicted because of the lawyer's negligent representation has other avenues of relief that actually protect the liberty interest more directly, most notably a claim of ineffective assistance of counsel.[243] Third, the plaintiffs in criminal malpractice actions were convicted of or pleaded guilty to criminal offenses in the underlying criminal case in which the malpractice allegedly occurred, leaving many courts reluctant or unwilling to allow recovery as a policy matter.[244] Finally, many plaintiffs in criminal malpractice cases were represented in their underlying criminal case by public defenders; this leads some courts to conclude that special protections are needed for the lawyers who take on these difficult cases,[245]

---

[239]   See Togstad v. Vesely, Otto, Miller & Keefe, 291 N.W.2d 686 (Minn. 1980) ("a reduction for attorney fees is unwarranted because of the expense incurred by the plaintiff in bringing an action against the attorney").

[240]   See, e.g., Hook v. Trevino, 839 N.W.2d 434 (Iowa 2013).

[241]   The term was apparently coined in Otto M. Kaus & Ronald E. Mallen, The Misguiding Hand of Counsel—Reflections on "Criminal Malpractice," 21 U.C.L.A. L. Rev. 1191 (1974).

[242]   See Wagenmann v. Adams, 829 F.2d 196 (1st Cir. 1987); Ovando v. County of Los Angeles, 159 Cal.App.4th 42, 71 Cal.Rptr.3d 415 (2008); see also 3 Mallen & Smith, Legal Malpractice § 27:1 (2009 ed.).

[243]   See, e.g., Stevens v. Bispham, 316 Or. 221, 851 P.2d 556 (1993). A claim of ineffective assistance of counsel is a type of post-conviction relief based on the Sixth Amendment's right to counsel in criminal cases. To succeed on the claim, the petitioner must prove both deficient attorney performance and resulting prejudice. See Strickland v. Washington, 466 U.S. 668, 104 S.Ct. 2052, 80 L.Ed.2d 674 (1984). The lawyer's deficient performance may involve some affirmative act, or an omission such as the failure to advise a client about the risk of deportation created by a guilty plea to a criminal offense. Padilla v. Kentucky, 130 S.Ct. 1473, 176 L.Ed.2d 284 (2010). The remedy is either a reversal of the conviction or, less commonly, a reduction in sentence. It is not a tort claim; no damages of any kind are awarded. Thus the successful ineffective assistance claim prevents a further deprivation of liberty but does not at all address the damages caused by that deprivation.

[244]   See, e.g., Wiley v. County of San Diego, 19 Cal.4th 532, 79 Cal.Rptr.2d 672, 966 P.2d 983 (1998); Canaan v. Bartee, 276 Kan. 116, 72 P.3d 911 (2003); Peeler v. Hughes & Luce, 909 S.W.2d 494 (Tex. 1995). This rationale is criticized as resting on "specious" grounds, in Joseph H. King, Jr., Outlaws and Outlier Doctrines: The Serious Misconduct Bar in Tort Law, 43 Wm. & Mary L. Rev. 1011 (2002).

[245]   E.g., Glenn v. Aiken, 409 Mass 699, 569 N.E.2d 783 (1991); Belk v. Cheshire, 159 N.C.App. 325, 583 S.E.2d 700 (2003).

and also makes applicable some governmental-liability requirements[246] and possible immunities.[247]

Special rules. These and perhaps other distinctions between civil and criminal malpractice have led a growing number of courts to add additional elements to the plaintiff's prima facie case, or to modify the civil-malpractice elements. Pennsylvania, for example, requires the plaintiff to make a heightened showing of lawyer fault.[248] The most common additions, however, have made the plaintiff's burden in this setting even more difficult: proof that the former criminal defendant has obtained post-conviction relief, or that the client was actually innocent of the criminal charges, or both. Some courts see this simply as a logical causation requirement in this setting, reasoning that a plaintiff who cannot prove that he would not have been convicted but for the lawyer's negligence cannot prevail under ordinary factual causation rules.[249] Others characterize one or both of these requirements as "proximate cause" limitations, often stressing public policy grounds for limiting defense-lawyer liability.[250] These special requirements have been criticized as making a criminal malpractice plaintiff's burden virtually impossible to meet, and the reported cases would seem to indicate that plaintiffs rarely succeed where they are imposed.[251] The plaintiffs' success rate is not improved by the fact that a very high percentage of criminal malpractice cases are pursued by the plaintiffs acting pro se.[252]

Exoneration or post-conviction relief requirement. A number of courts have added the requirement that in order to succeed in a case claiming malpractice by a criminal defense lawyer, the convicted client must show that he has been exonerated in a post-conviction proceeding.[253] Post-conviction relief typically takes the form of a direct appeal, a collateral attack on the conviction, or a habeas claim alleging ineffective assistance of counsel. Not surprisingly, it has been held that when the client gets a second trial and pleads *nolo contendere,* the client's plea bars his malpractice claim.[254]

---

[246] A defense lawyer acting as an advocate is not a "state actor" and thus does not act under color of law within the meaning of 42 U.S.C. § 1983. Polk County v. Dodson, 454 U.S. 312, 102 S.Ct. 445, 70 L.Ed.2d 509 (1981). This is true even where the lawyer has been appointed by a state court to represent the accused. See, e.g., Laurence v. Sollitto, 788 A.2d 455 (R.I. 2002). However, a government-employed lawyer may be liable on other grounds.

[247] See § 22.12.

[248] See Bailey v. Tucker, 533 Pa. 237, 621 A.2d 108 (1993) (reckless or wanton conduct).

[249] See, e.g., Brewer v. Hagemann, 771 A.2d 1030 (Me. 2001).

[250] See, e.g., Canaan v. Bartee, 276 Kan. 116, 72 P.3d 911 (2003); Butler v. Mooers, 771 A.2d 1034 (Me. 2001); Peeler v. Hughes & Luce, 909 S.W.2d 494 (Tex. 1995).

[251] See Meredith J. Duncan, Criminal Malpractice: A Lawyer's Holiday, 37 Ga. L. Rev. 1251 (2003); Meredith J. Duncan, The (So-Called) Liability of Criminal Defense Attorneys: A System in Need of Reform, 2002 B.Y.U. L. Rev. 1 (2002); 3 Mallen & Smith, Legal Malpractice § 27:1 (2009 ed.) ("Civil legal malpractice suits brought against criminal attorneys have increased, but rarely has an appellate court affirmed a judgment against an attorney.").

[252] This phenomenon is observable in the reported cases simply by looking at the listing of counsel. It may be explainable by the fact that criminal malpractice cases are extraordinarily difficult to win and may result in "little or no damages," leading private counsel to decline such cases. Jenny Roberts, Ignorance Is Effectively Bliss: Collateral Consequences, Silence, and Misinformation in the Guilty-Plea Process, 95 Iowa L. Rev. 119, 166 n.193 (2009).

[253] See, e.g., Glaze v. Larsen, 207 Ariz. 26, 83 P.3d 26 (2004); Coscia v. McKenna & Cuneo, 25 Cal.4th 1194, 108 Cal.Rptr.2d 471, 25 P.3d 670 (2001); Trobaugh v. Sondag, 668 N.W.2d 577 (Iowa 2003); McKnight v. Office of Public Defender, 197 N.J. 180, 962 A.2d 482 (2008). See also Heck v. Humphrey, 512 U.S. 477, 114 S.Ct. 2364, 129 L.Ed.2d 383 (1994) (requiring post-conviction relief as a predicate to a § 1983 action).

[254] Brown v. Theos, 345 S.C. 626, 550 S.E.2d 304 (2001).

Actual innocence requirement. A growing number of courts have held that when a convicted client sues for malpractice, he must prove by a preponderance of the evidence that he was actually innocent of the crime.[255] This is a more difficult burden than proving exoneration, since most forms of post-conviction relief do not require proof of actual innocence, and exoneration may be obtained on grounds other than actual innocence.[256] Courts adopting the actual innocence requirement often contemplate that the client's innocence will be proved in a post-conviction proceeding, making the actual innocence requirement sometimes an addition, rather than an alternative, to the exoneration requirement.[257] The actual innocence requirement means quite simply that any client who is actually guilty cannot sue his former defense lawyer for malpractice at all.[258] Nor can an actually innocent client sue, if he cannot affirmatively prove his innocence by a preponderance of the evidence. Some judges have been sharply critical of the actual innocence rule,[259] but it has obvious momentum.

Exceptions to and rejections of special rules. A minority of states that have considered the issue have rejected both of the special rules described above.[260] Additionally, even in those states that have adopted one or both, some exceptions have emerged. For example, some states have recognized that the actual innocence requirement does not apply where the client's malpractice claims are unrelated to underlying guilt or innocence, such as when the client who pleaded guilty complains that the lawyer's negligence caused him to be given an unlawful sentence.[261] Washington has crafted a "very limited exception" to its innocence rule on similar facts, where the lawyer's negligence caused the criminal defendant to be sentenced to a term longer than the maximum allowed by statute, and the criminal defendant actually served prison time

---

[255] See, e.g., Winniczek v. Nagelberg, 394 F.3d 505 (7th Cir. 2005) (Illinois law); Wiley v. County of San Diego, 19 Cal.4th 532,79 Cal. Rptr.2d 672, 966 P.2d 983 (1998); Schreiber v. Rowe, 814 So.2d 396 (Fla. 2002); Gaylor v. Jeffco, 999 A.2d 290 (N.H. 2010); Carmel v. Lundy, 70 N.Y.2d 169, 518 N.Y.S.2d 605, 511 N.E.2d 1126 (1987); Humphries v. Detch, 227 W. Va. 627, 712 S.E.2d 795 (2011).

[256] In this context, courts distinguish between "actual innocence" and "legal innocence." Post-conviction relief may establish the latter, but not the former. See, e.g., Correia v. Fagan, 452 Mass. 120, 891 N.E.2d 227 (2008); Ang v. Martin, 154 Wash.2d 477, 114 P.3d 637 (2005).

[257] See Kevin Bennardo, Note, A Defense Bar: The "Proof of Innocence" Requirement in Criminal Malpractice Claims, 5 Ohio St. J. Crim. L. 341, 344 (2007).

[258] See, e.g., Lamb v. Manweiler, 129 Idaho 269, 923 P.2d 976 (1996); Bailey v. Tucker, 533 Pa. 237, 621 A.2d 108 (1993); Brown v. Theos, 345 S.C. 626, 550 S.E.2d 304 (2001) It is perhaps accurate to conclude that the requirement "creates an almost impossible burden and provides almost absolute immunity to criminal defense lawyers." Ang v. Martin, 154 Wash.2d 477, 114 P.3d 637 (2005) (Chambers, J., dissenting). More benignly, however, the rule has close affinity with the rule in malicious prosecution that the prosecuted plaintiff who is guilty in fact cannot recover even if prosecuted without probable cause. See § 591.

[259] See, e.g., Peeler v. Hughes & Luce, 909 S.W.2d 494 (Tex. 1995) (Phillips, C.J., dissenting) (adoption of the actual innocence rule on the ground that criminals should not profit from their crimes means "[t]he public morality is thus protected at the expense of shielding all criminal defense attorney malpractice, no matter how egregious, from any redress in the civil justice system"); Ang v. Martin, 154 Wash.2d 477, 114 P.3d 637 (2005) (Sanders, J., dissenting) ("Forcing criminal defendants to prove actual innocence does not serve any purpose except to frustrate the client's right to competent representation. . . . The majority's rule simply invites malpractice since the defense attorney knows he is held to a lower standard. Proving innocence is impossible since a negative cannot be proved.").

[260] See, e.g., Mylar v. Wilkinson, 435 So.2d 1237 (Ala. 1983); Rantz v. Kaufman, 109 P.3d 132 (Colo. 2005); Gebhardt v. O'Rourke, 444 Mich. 535, 510 N.W.2d 900 (1994); Vahila v. Hall, 77 Ohio St.3d 421, 674 N.E.2d 1164 (1997) see also Restatement of the Law Governing Lawyers § 53, cmt. d (2000) (expressly disapproving the actual innocence requirement).

[261] Hilario v. Reardon, 158 N.H. 56, 960 A.2d 337 (2008); Johnson v. Babcock, 206 Or.App. 217, 136 P.3d 77 (2006).

in excess of the legal maximum before filing suit.[262] Others have found lack of proof of actual innocence irrelevant where the plaintiff's suit sought a refund of fees, and was not attacking the actual conviction at all.[263] One court has held that the actual innocence rule is inapplicable to a claim against a criminal defense lawyer for breach of fiduciary duty;[264] another has recognized an exception where the client alleged that he was actually innocent because the crime for which he was convicted did not constitute a crime at the time he was charged, and that he could not establish his actual innocence in a post-conviction proceeding because of his lawyer's negligence.[265]

Emotional distress recovery. In civil malpractice, recovery of emotional distress damages is both difficult and rare.[266] In the criminal-malpractice setting, however, if the plaintiff succeeds on the malpractice claim it may be even easier to recover damages for emotional harm.[267] Certainly emotional distress is a foreseeable consequence of an unjustified loss of liberty caused by a defense lawyer's negligence.[268] As a California court put it, "the recovery of damages for emotional distress in a legal malpractice case— if it is to be limited at all—should turn on the nature of plaintiff's interest which is harmed and not merely on the reprehensibility of the defendant's conduct."[269] Where a liberty interest rather than an economic one has been invaded, substantial emotional distress damages may be awarded upon proper proof.[270] In a case from the First Circuit, the court affirmed an award of $50,000 for emotional distress when a lawyer's negligence resulted in his client's wrongful incarceration in a state mental hospital for a single night, where the plaintiff proved lasting emotional effects from the event.[271] Of course, at a minimum, a plaintiff must prove that the emotional distress was caused by the defense lawyer's negligence and not simply from the usual stresses of an encounter with the criminal justice system.[272]

---

[262] Powell v. Associated Counsel for the Accused, 125 Wash. App. 773, 106 P.3d 271 (2005) (finding on those facts that the case "is more akin to that of an innocent person wrongfully convicted than of a guilty person attempting to take advantage of his own wrongdoing," despite the fact that the criminal defendant had pleaded guilty).

[263] E.g., Bird, Marella, Boxer & Wolpert v. Superior Court, 106 Cal.App.4th 419, 130 Cal.Rptr.2d 782 (2003); Labovitz v. Feinberg, 47 Mass. App. Ct. 306, 713 N.E.2d 379 (1999); Van Polen v. Wisch, 23 S.W.3d 510 (Tex. App. 2000).

[264] Morris v. Margulis, 307 Ill.App.3d 1024, 718 N.E.2d 709, 241 Ill.Dec. 138 (1999), *rev'd on other grounds,* 197 Ill.2d 28, 754 N.E.2d 314, 257 Ill.Dec. 656 (2001).

[265] Taylor v. Davis, 265 Va. 187, 576 S.E.2d 445 (2003).

[266] See § 45.11.

[267] See Rowell v. Holt, 850 So.2d 474 (Fla. 2003) (lawyer had document that would have procured client's immediate release from pre-trial detention but failed to produce it).

[268] See Ovando v. County of Los Angeles, 159 Cal.App.4th 42, 71 Cal.Rptr.3d 415 (2008) ("An emotional injury resulting from the incarceration of an innocent defendant is plainly foreseeable."); see also Snyder v. Baumecker, 708 F.Supp. 1451 (D. N.J. 1989) (incarcerated client became depressed and committed suicide; no liability for the suicide, but liability for emotional distress); Restatement of the Law Governing Lawyers § 53, cmt. g, Reporter's Note (2000) (citing cases allowing emotional-distress damages in criminal malpractice cases, opining that the likely explanation is that when malpractice results in imprisonment, "distress is likely and financial damages difficult to prove").

[269] Holliday v. Jones, 215 Cal.App.3d 102, 264 Cal.Rptr. 448 (1989).

[270] Id. (affirming jury award of $400,000 to former client for emotional distress, where lawyer's negligence resulted in the plaintiff's wrongful conviction and imprisonment under horrible conditions); see also Bowman v. Doherty, 235 Kan. 870, 686 P.2d 112 (1984) ("One being negligently deprived of his freedom suffers an injury which could cause mental distress.").

[271] Wagenmann v. Adams, 829 F.2d 196 (1st Cir. 1987).

[272] See Lancaster v. Stevens, 961 So.2d 768 (Miss. 2007).

§ 45.14   Criminal Malpractice: Defenses and Immunities

Statute of limitations. States do not have special statutes of limitation for criminal malpractice, so the general rules applicable to civil malpractice suits still obtain.[273] Criminal malpractice cases present some unique situations, however, making some additional rules relevant. For example, the statute of limitations may be tolled in some states during the malpractice plaintiff's incarceration; this may be by statute or by equitable tolling principles.[274] Other states reject tolling for incarceration.[275] Further, the availability of post-conviction relief raises an accrual issue that courts must resolve in many criminal-malpractice cases. In a state that requires exoneration, the question is whether the claim for malpractice accrues at the time post-conviction relief is granted, or at some earlier time. Some courts have held that the statute of limitations begins to run only after post-conviction relief has been obtained.[276] Others have rejected that date and hold that the claim accrues before then.[277] Many of those latter courts—those that start the clock before termination of post-conviction proceedings—have adopted a "two-track" approach in which the criminal-malpractice plaintiff must file his claim within the usual statutory period, but can obtain a stay of the malpractice case until those post-conviction proceedings have terminated.[278]

Collateral estoppel. Collateral estoppel, or issue preclusion, is a defense in legal claims generally, prohibiting a party from relitigating an issue that was actually and necessarily litigated and determined in a prior action.[279] In the context of criminal malpractice, this defense has special force, one that connects to the element of causation and to the oft-imposed special requirements of post-conviction relief and proof of actual innocence. The lawyer's use of defensive collateral estoppel is particularly common, and often successful, when the client has previously pleaded guilty. There, the doctrine may bar the client from arguing that he was actually innocent, or that the lawyer's negligence

---

[273] See § 45.10.

[274] E.g., Swan v. Matthews, 555 F.Supp. 495 (D. Mont. 1982) (maximum of five years tolling for imprisonment under Montana law); Shaw v. State, Dep't of Admin., 816 P.2d 1358 (Alaska 1991); Herzog v. Yuill, 399 N.W.2d 287 (N.D. 1987) (statute tolled for one year after termination of imprisonment); Cal. Code Civ. Proc. § 352.1 (tolling for imprisonment not to exceed two years); S.C. Code § 15–3–40 (tolling for imprisonment, except for life sentence).

[275] E.g., Tenamee v. Schmukler, 438 F.Supp.2d 438 (S.D.N.Y. 2006) (incarceration not a "rare and exceptional circumstance" so as suspend the statute of limitations under equitable tolling principles); Johnson v. Marks, 224 Mich.App. 356, 568 N.W.2d 689 (1997) (legislature removed incarceration as a basis for tolling); Seevers v. Potter, 537 N.W.2d 505 (Neb. 1995) (statute provides that claim accrues upon occurrence of the negligent act; no tolling for incarceration); Ballinger v. Thompson, 118 P.3d 429 (Wyo. 2005) (civil malpractice case; statute interpreted not to authorize tolling for incarceration).

[276] E.g., Glaze v. Larsen, 207 Ariz. 26, 83 P.3d 26 (2004); Trobaugh v. Sondag, 668 N.W.2d 577 (Iowa 2003); Canaan v. Bartee, 276 Kan. 116, 72 P.3d 911 (2003); Therrien v. Sullivan, 153 N.H. 211, 891 A.2d 560 (2006); McKnight v. Office of Public Defender, 197 N.J. 180, 962 A.2d 482 (2008).

[277] E.g., Morrison v. Goff, 91 P.3d 1050 (Colo. 2004) (applying discovery rule; underlying appeal or motion for post-conviction relief does not affect accrual of the claim); Bailey v. Tucker, 533 Pa. 237, 621 A.2d 108 (1993) (statute begins to run no later than date plaintiff files petition for post-conviction relief, with new counsel).

[278] E.g., McCord v. Bailey, 636 F.2d 606 (D.C. Cir. 1980); Gebhardt v. O'Rourke, 444 Mich. 535, 510 N.W.2d 900 (1994); Ereth v. Cascade County, 318 Mont. 355, 81 P.3d 463 (2003); Seevers v. Potter, 248 Neb. 621, 537 N.W.2d 505 (1995).

[279] Rantz v. Kaufman, 109 P.3d 132 (Colo. 2005); Krahn v. Kinney, 43 Ohio St.3d 103, 538 N.E.2d 1058 (1989); see also Meredith J. Duncan, The (So-Called) Liability of Criminal Defense Attorneys: A System In Need of Reform, 2002 B.Y.U. L.Rev. 1, 32–37 (2002) (describing requirements of collateral estoppel and analyzing how the defense has been applied in criminal malpractice cases).

caused his incarceration.[280] Lawyers have also been successful in arguing that the plaintiff-client is collaterally estopped from relitigating issues that were decided against the plaintiff in post-conviction proceedings.[281]

Immunity of public defenders and court-appointed attorneys. Criminal defendants are often represented by public defenders, who are employed by the government, or court-appointed lawyers, who are paid by the government. Although these lawyers may be paid by a public entity, their client is the individual accused. Indeed, the lawyer owes undivided loyalty to the accused and must act independently of the government. On reasoning of this sort, the Supreme Court held that as a matter of federal law, no absolute immunity attaches to lawyers appointed by federal courts to defend those accused of crime.[282] The Court has also held that a court-appointed lawyer lacks immunity when sued for civil rights violations under § 1983.[283]

When the issue is one of state law, however, some authority supports an immunity on the ground that public defenders or appointed counsel[284] are not so much like private practitioners because they cannot reject clients and because, at least with respect to public defenders, they are typically overworked and undersupported.[285] Other state courts have lined up against an absolute immunity.[286] However, in some states the public defender may be regarded as a state employee, and may benefit from whatever immunity or procedural advantage is accorded to state employees by local law.[287]

---

[280] See, e.g., Coscia v. McKenna & Cuneo, 25 Cal.4th 1194, 108 Cal.Rptr.2d 471, 25 P.3d 670 (2001); Allen v. Martin, 203 P.3d 546 (Colo. App. 2008); Krahn v. Kinney, 43 Ohio St.3d 103, 538 N.E.2d 1058 (1989); contra, Mrozek v. Intra Financial Corp., 281 Wis.2d 448, 699 N.W.2d 54 (2005).

[281] E.g., Brewer v. Hagemann, 771 A.2d 1030 (Me. 2001); Gibson v. Trant, 58 S.W.3d 103 (Tenn. 2001). For collateral estoppel to apply, the issue in the malpractice case must have been actually decided in the former proceeding. See Stanton v. Schultz, 222 P.3d 303 (Colo. 2010).

[282] Ferri v. Ackerman, 444 U.S. 193, 100 S.Ct. 402, 62 L.Ed.2d 355 (1979).

[283] Tower v. Glover, 467 U.S. 914, 104 S.Ct. 2820, 81 L.Ed.2d 758 (1984).

[284] E.g., Morgano v. Smith, 110 Nev. 1025, 879 P.2d 735 (1994) (extending statutory immunity to court-appointed counsel); Mooney v. Frazier, 225 W.Va. 358, 693 S.E.2d 333 (2010) (same).

[285] Dziubak v. Mott, 503 N.W.2d 771 (Minn. 1993). Some public defender or indigent defense statutes support this view. E.g., Tenn. Code Ann. § 8–14–209. See Coyazo v. State, 120 N.M. 47, 897 P.2d 234 (Ct. App. 1995).

[286] E.g., Johnson v. Halloran, 194 Ill.2d 493, 742 N.E.2d 741, 252 Ill.Dec. 203 (2000); Donigan v. Finn, 95 Mich.App. 28, 290 N.W.2d 80 (1980); Reese v. Danforth, 486 Pa. 479, 406 A.2d 735, 6 A.L.R.4th 758 (1979); Adkins v. Dixon, 253 Va. 275, 482 S.E.2d 797 (1997).

[287] E.g., Bradshaw v. Joseph, 666 A.2d 1175 (Vt. 1995) (complete immunity); Conn. Gen. Stat. § 4–165 (qualified immunity for state officers, listing public defenders as "officers").

Chapter 46

UNFAIR COMPETITION: TRADEMARKS, TRADE SECRETS AND PUBLICITY RIGHTS

Analysis

§ 46.1   Unfair Competition and Trademark Infringement
§ 46.2   Sponsorship Confusion and Dilution in Trademark Law
§ 46.3   False Advertising and § 43(a) of the Lanham Act
§ 46.4   Product Design, Trade Dress, and Functional Features
§ 46.5   Ideas and Trade Secrets
§ 46.6   Rights in Personality and Publicity

---

§ 46.1 Unfair Competition and Trademark Infringement

Terms and scope. Unfair competition is a general term that includes deceptive trade practices, acts such as trademark infringement, and appropriation of trade values or rights in publicity.[1] All of these are torts under common law rules. Some are enhanced or limited by statutory provisions. Both state and federal law recognize claims against defendants for (1) using marks or identifiers for goods or services that are confusingly similar to identifiers the plaintiff has the right to use;[2] (2) dilution of the plaintiff's trademark, for example, by associating it with something undesirable;[3] and (3) the publication of false advertising[4] (and sometimes false statements outside of advertising). Three other kinds of claims are quite distinct. These are intellectual property claims that emphasize content of the plaintiff's rights in confidential information, inventions, and works of authorship, protected respectively by the states' laws of trade secrets,[5] by federal patent law,[6] and by federal copyright law.[7]

Passing off. The core unfair competition case and the core trademark infringement case are similar, and both have roots in the passing-off cases. In these, the defendant is likely to mislead purchasers by misrepresenting that his goods are produced or sponsored by the plaintiff, or by representing himself as an agent or affiliate of the plaintiff.[8] For example, if a customer orders "Coca-Cola" but the restaurant provides

---

[1]   Restatement of Unfair Competition § 1 (1995). Among the multi-volume treatises discussing this topic are J. Thomas McCarthy, Trademarks and Unfair Competition (4th ed., updated on Westlaw in MCCARTHY database) (hereinafter McCarthy on Trademarks); and Louis Altman & Malla Pollack, Callman on Unfair Competition, Trademarks & Monopolies (4th ed., updated on Westlaw in CALLMAN database) (hereinafter Callman on Unfair Competition).

[2]   See § 46.4.

[3]   See § 46.2.

[4]   See § 46.3.

[5]   See § 46.5.

[6]   See Bonito Boats, Inc. v. Thunder Craft Boats, Inc., 489 U.S. 141, 109 S.Ct. 971, 103 L.Ed.2d 118 (1989).

[7]   See 4 Dobbs, Hayden & Bublick, The Law of Torts § 741 (2d ed. 2011 & Supp.).

[8]   Restatement of Unfair Competition § 4 (1995).

Pepsi-Cola without warning of the substitution, the restaurant is passing off Pepsi for Coca-Cola.[9] Reverse passing off is similar—the vendor sells a herbal supplement as one composed of his own secret formula when in fact the product is one made by the plaintiff.[10] In effect, the defendant is making a misrepresentation about both his product and his competitor's. The customer who is misled might have an action for deceit, but it is the competitor who can recover for unfair competition accomplished by passing off or reverse passing off. It is but a short step from these cases to provide that cans of one soft drink must not be labeled so they are likely to be taken for cans of another. That is a central notion of both common law unfair competition rules and federal statutory trademark rules under the Lanham Act.[11]

Trademark. Any words, symbols, or designs can qualify as a protected trademark if they sufficiently distinguish one person's goods or services from another's.[12] Labels, packaging, even the design or color[13] of the product itself, can count as trademarks if they are distinctive and non-functional.[14] Trade names—the name by which an enterprise is known—receive similar protection.[15] Some trademarks may be protected more broadly than others. Marks fall on a spectrum between generic, descriptive, and suggestive, to arbitrary and fanciful; the strength of the mark, and of its protection, increases as you move towards the "fanciful" end of that spectrum.[16]

For brevity, the term *trademark* will be used here to stand for all identifiers of goods, including trade names. In the original passing-off or unfair-competition cases, courts tended to make liability turn on the defendant's wrongful conduct such as intentional deceit.[17] In contrast, contemporary law holds that any valid mark is infringed by similar marks if they in fact are likely to cause customer confusion about the source of the marked goods.[18] Non-trademark uses, as where the plaintiff's product is named by reference to its trademark in comparative advertising or otherwise, is not ordinarily an infringement.[19]

Acquisition of rights. Rights in trademarks are usually acquired only by using the mark to identify goods with the plaintiff as their source.[20] Once used, the mark may be

---

[9]   E.g., Coca-Cola Co. v. Overland, Inc., 692 F.2d 1250 (9th Cir. 1982).

[10]   See Dastar Corp. v. Twentieth Century Fox Film Corp., 539 U.S. 23, 123 S.Ct. 2041, 156 L.Ed.2d 18 (2003).

[11]   See 15 U.S.C.A. § 1114 (1) (any person who uses in commerce a reproduction, counterfeit, copy or imitation of a registered mark in connection with a sale or advertising of any goods or services is liable in a civil action brought by the registrant).

[12]   See Board of Supervisors for Louisiana State University Agricultural and Mechanical College v. Smack Apparel Co., 550 F.3d 465 (5th Cir. 2008) (clothing manufacturer who used universities' color schemes and other indentifying indicia, which created a likelihood of confusion); Restatement of Unfair Competition § 9 (1995).

[13]   See Qualitex Co. v. Jacobson Products Co., 514 U.S. 159, 115 S.Ct. 1300, 131 L.Ed.2d 248 (1995).

[14]   Restatement of Unfair Competition § 16 (1995); see § 46.4.

[15]   Restatement of Unfair Competition § 12 (1995).

[16]   See American Rice, Inc. v. Producers Rice Mill, Inc., 518 F.2d 321 (5th Cir. 2008).

[17]   See McCarthy on Trademarks § 5:2.

[18]   Evidence of the defendant's intent to confuse is relevant, but not determinative of the issue of likelihood of confusion. American Rice, Inc. v. Producers Rice Mill, Inc., 518 F.2d 321 (5th Cir. 2008). With trade names, collective and certifying marks, the relevant confusion is about the business, collective, or certifying organization. See Restatement of Unfair Competition § 20 (1995).

[19]   Tiffany (NJ) Inc. v. eBay, Inc., 600 F.3d 93 (2d Cir. 2010); August Storck K.G. v. Nabisco, Inc., 59 F.3d 616 (7th Cir. 1995); Playboy Enterprises, Inc. v. Welles, 279 F.3d 796 (9th Cir. 2002).

[20]   McCarthy on Trademarks §§ 16:1 & 16:4.

registered under federal and state statutes. Registration gives the mark's owner some evidentiary and procedural advantages in litigation and may help forestall imitation by others. Once the mark is established, it may be sold or licensed with the product.

Arbitrary, fanciful, or inherently distinctive marks. A mark is valid and protectable only if it is distinctive, that is, capable of unambiguously identifying goods as those of the mark's owner in the minds of a large number of consumers. The mark is distinctive either because it is fanciful or arbitrary or because from public usage it has come to identify the owner's goods in the public mind.[21] For example, Kodak is a fanciful word coined as a trademark; when coined, it had no meaning except as a trademark. By itself, it describes nothing about the product. It is thus inherently distinctive as an identifier and protectable without proof that the public associates it with a particular producer of goods.[22] Marks that are not arbitrary or fanciful but are suggestive without being descriptive may also be distinctive and protected.[23]

Descriptive marks, secondary meaning. Other words or symbols are not naturally distinctive because they have existing meaning that tends to describe characteristics of other things as well as characteristics of the plaintiff's product. The Restatement illustration is helpful: TRAQ as a trademark for steel girders is fanciful or arbitrary and distinctive without further proof. On the other hand RIGID may be taken to describe some characteristic of the girders and is not by itself distinctive.[24] Similarly, the personal name of the producer and geographical terms describing origin are usually descriptive and have no arbitrary meaning that makes them distinctive.[25] Such descriptive marks, however, can become distinctive if consumers come to identify the mark with the owner's products. In such a case, the mark is said to acquire distinctiveness through secondary meaning. Once it is found to be distinctive, it can be protected against infringement.[26]

Generic terms and loss of distinctiveness. There is a limit to acquired distinctiveness: no one can acquire rights in words understood to be generic descriptions of a category of goods rather than merely descriptive.[27] "Bank" and "camera" are examples.[28] More than this, a once-distinctive mark may cease to be distinctive if the public comes to use the trademark as a description. "Aspirin" is a traditional example. Once a fanciful term, it is now used as a descriptive name for a type of pain reliever, regardless of the manufacturer. The term is no longer distinctive of a particular manufacturer and is thus no longer a trademark.

Infringement: likelihood of confusion. A defendant infringes a mark by using the same mark or one that is sufficiently similar to make it likely that consumers will be

---

[21] See, e.g., American Rice, Inc. v. Producers Rice Mill, Inc., 518 F.3d 321 (5th Cir. 2008) (girl design used on rice bags).

[22] Wal-Mart Stores, Inc. v. Samara Bros., 529 U.S. 205, 120 S.Ct. 1339, 146 L.Ed.2d 182 (2000).

[23] See Douglas Labs. Corp. v. Copper Tan, 210 F.2d 453 (2d Cir. 1952) ("Coppertone" designation for sun tan lotion is fanciful, not descriptive).

[24] Restatement of Unfair Competition § 13, Ills. 1 & 4 (1995).

[25] Id. § 14.

[26] Even a famous person's name may be protectable on this ground. See Parks v. LaFace Records, 329 F.3d 437 (6th Cir. 2003) (civil rights icon Rosa Parks stated a Lanham Act claim against defendants who used her name as a song title without her permission).

[27] See, e.g., Ward One Democrats, Inc. v. Woodland, 898 A.2d 356 (D.C. 2006) (political organization's name, "Ward One Democrats," was generic and thus not entitled to trademark protection).

[28] Restatement of Unfair Competition § 15 & cmt. a (1995).

confused about the source or sponsorship of the marked goods.[29] The party claiming infringement bears the burden of proving a likelihood of confusion.[30] Judgments about the likelihood of confusion draw upon sophisticated analysis.[31] Similarity itself may take several forms; even if a spelling is different, the phonetic similarity may indicate a danger of confusion. The nature of the market for the goods matters, too; if two disparate groups of consumers purchase the plaintiff's and defendant's goods respectively, confusion may not be likely in spite of similarities in two marks.[32] Conversely, where the defendant markets a similarly named product that is sold within the plaintiff's "natural zone of expansion," a likelihood of confusion might be found.[33] Free speech rights are intimately related to the likelihood-of-confusion rule.[34] Use of a trademark in a satire of the product, or even merely as a means of referring to a set of values, ideas, or cultural exemplars, is not likely to confuse the plaintiff's goods with the defendant's. The defendant is thus free to produce songs about the plastic world of Barbie and Ken, even though Barbie and Ken are trademarks as well as the names of dolls.[35] A defendant may even be free to market a non-competing product that parodies the plaintiff's trade name, such as "Tommy Holedigger" dog perfume[36] or "Chewy Vuiton" pet chew-toys.[37]

§ 46.2 Sponsorship Confusion and Dilution in Trademark Law

Sponsorship confusion. Trademark protection originally aimed to redress or prevent a diversion of trade that would occur if customers intended to purchase the plaintiff's product but mistakenly chose the defendant's product with a confusingly similar mark. This was called source confusion because the purchaser might believe that the plaintiff was the source of the defendant's product. That would mean that if A sold a magazine called Seventeen and B sold girdles called Seventeen, the likelihood of confusion was

---

[29] See, e.g., One Industries, LLC v. Jim O'Neal Distributing, Inc., 578 F.3d 1154 (9th Cir. 2009) (no likelihood of confusion between marks used by two competitors for motocross clothing); Water Pik, Inc. v. Med-Systems, Inc., 725 F.3d 1136 (10th Cir. 2013) (isolated instances of actual confusion between SinuSense mark and SinuCleanse mark of competitor were insufficient to prove a likelihood of confusion; "Sinu" is essentially generic, making the SinuCleanse mark "conceptually weak"); North Am. Medical Corp. v. Axiom Worldwide, Inc., 522 F.3d 1211 (11th Cir. 2008) (defendant's use on its website of "metatags" of plaintiff's trademarks resulted in a likelihood of confusion).

[30] KP Permanent Make-Up, Inc. v. Lasting Impressions I, Inc., 543 U.S. 111, 125 S.Ct. 542, 160 L.Ed.2d 440 (2004) (availability of a "fair use" defense does not alter the burden of proof on the likelihood of confusion issue); Network Automation, Inc. v. Advanced Systems Concepts, Inc., 638 F.3d 1137 (9th Cir. 2011) (plaintiff's showing of likelihood of consumer confusion insufficient to support injunctive relief; in internet context, emerging technologies require a "flexible approach" to the issue).

[31] See, e.g., Elvis Presley Enterprises, Inc. v. Capece, 141 F.3d 188 (5th Cir. 1998) (discussing complex factors that trial court should have weighed to determine likelihood of confusion); see also, e.g., Hormel Foods Corp. v. Jim Henson Productions, 73 F.3d 497 (2d Cir. 1996); Fortress Grand Corp. v. Warner Bros. Entertainment Inc., 763 F.3d 696 (7th Cir. 2014).

[32] See Restatement of Unfair Competition § 21 (1995) (listing evidentiary considerations).

[33] Westchester Media v. PRL USA Holdings, Inc., 214 F.3d 658 (5th Cir. 2000) (magazine publisher using the name "Polo" infringed the trademark of the designer Ralph Lauren, where the public could think the designer would publish a magazine with that name even though he did not).

[34] See, e.g., E.S.S. Entertainment 2000, Inc. v. Rock Star Videos, Inc., 547 F.3d 1095 (9th Cir. 2008) (video-game creator's depiction of a club called "Pig Pen" was protected by First Amendment in infringement suit brought by owner of a strip club called "Play Pen Gentlemen's Club"; no likelihood of confusion).

[35] See Mattel, Inc. v. MCA Records, Inc., 296 F.3d 894 (9th Cir. 2002); but see Parks v. LaFace Records, 329 F.3d 437 (6th Cir. 2003).

[36] Tommy Hilfiger Licensing, Inc. v. Nature Labs, LLC, 221 F.Supp.2d 410 (S.D.N.Y. 2002) (granting summary judgment for defendant).

[37] Louis Vuitton Malletier S.A. v. Haute Diggity Dog, LLC, 464 F.Supp.2d 495 (E.D. Va. 2006) (granting summary judgment for defendant, who used the name for its low-priced pet chew-toys, in suit by "Louis Vuitton" trademark holder, a manufacturer of high-end consumer products).

practically nil, since hardly anyone would think a magazine was a girdle or vice versa. Nevertheless, courts came to say that confusion about sponsorship of a product would suffice to show infringement. So if a prospective girdle purchaser might think that Seventeen Girdles were somehow sponsored or approved by Seventeen Magazine, the girdle manufacturer's use of the term Seventeen would infringe the magazine's trademark.[38] Sometimes this idea is taken to the edge or perhaps invoked as a conscious fiction for something else. In one case,[39] a pornographic movie depicted young women who wished to become "Texas Cowgirl" cheerleaders and who wore a uniform similar to that worn by cheerleaders for the Dallas Cowboys football team. The court granted a preliminary injunction against showing the movie on the likelihood that the uniform was a trademark and that the movie infringed it because the viewers of pornographic movies might believe that the Dallas Cowboys Cheerleaders, Inc., had authorized use of the similar uniforms.

Dilution. As the sponsorship-confusion cases show, trademark protection underwent a mutation. What began as a protection against customer confusion and diversion of trade became an effort to enhance or maintain the selling power of trade symbols. Since around 1950, state[40] and federal[41] anti-dilution statutes have explicitly embraced this selling-power ideal[42] by protecting trademarks against "dilution" of a mark even when no confusion of any kind is to be found.[43] For instance, "the proliferation of various noncompetitive businesses utilizing the name Tiffany's" dilute "the public's association of the name Tiffany's solely with fine jewelry."[44] This type of dilution is known as the "blurring" or "whittling down" kind. The claim for dilution is appropriate, however, only when the plaintiff's mark is highly distinctive[45] or, in the terms of the federal statute, "famous."[46] A mark containing the phrase "Blue Ribbon" or "Allied" is not distinctive and cannot be diluted.[47]

Tarnishment. Another form of dilution is tarnishment, which occurs when the plaintiff's trademark or a similar mark is used for products that are inconsistent with the image the plaintiff's goods or their mark seeks to project. If the use of a bank's

---

[38] Triangle Publ'ns, Inc. v. Rohrlich, 167 F. 2d 969 (2d Cir. 1948), *overruled on other grounds*, Monsanto Chem. Co. v. Perfect Fit Products Mfg. Co., 349 F.2d 389 (2d Cir. 1965).

[39] Dallas Cowboys Cheerleaders, Inc. v. Pussycat Cinema, Ltd., 604 F. 2d 200 (2d Cir. 1979).

[40] E.g., Mass. Gen. L. Ann. 110B § 12; Tex. Stat. & Code Ann. § 16.29.

[41] 15 U.S.C.A. § 1125 (c).

[42] See Allied Maintenance Corp. v. Allied Mechanical Trades, Inc., 42 N.Y.2d 538, 369 N.E.2d 1162, 399 N.Y.S.2d 628 (1977) (reflecting legislative purpose to stop "the whittling away of an established trademark's selling power and value through its unauthorized use by others upon dissimilar products").

[43] See Moseley v. V Secret Catalogue, Inc., 537 U.S. 418, 123 S.Ct. 1115, 155 L.Ed.2d 1 (2003) (no likelihood of confusion needed, but proof of actual dilution required to prove a federal dilution claim); Restatement of Unfair Competition § 25(1) (1995).

[44] Allied Maintenance Corp. v. Allied Mechanical Trades, Inc., 42 N.Y.2d 538, 545, 369 N.E.2d 1162, 1166, 399 N.Y.S.2d 628 (1977).

[45] Restatement of Unfair Competition § 25 (1995); see New York Stock Exchange, Inc. v. New York, New York Hotel, LLC, 293 F.3d 550 (2d Cir. 2002) (under federal anti-dilution law, the mark must be inherently distinctive; acquired distinctiveness is not enough).

[46] A mark may be "famous" in a niche market and still be entitled to protection, where the parties are both operating in that niche market. See Times Mirror Magazines v. Las Vegas Sports News, 212 F.3d 157 (3d Cir. 2000) (affirming injunction against publisher of the "Las Vegas Sporting News" by the publisher of "The Sporting News," a national publication); Syndicate Sales, Inc. v. Hampshire Paper Corp., 192 F.3d 633 (7th Cir. 1999) ("famous" trade dress in niche floral market).

[47] Allied Maintenance Corp. v. Allied Mechanical Trades, Inc., 42 N.Y.2d 538, 369 N.E.2d 1162, 399 N.Y.S.2d 628 (1977).

trademark for a place of adult entertainment[48] or a beer's trademark for an insecticide[49] tarnishes the original trademark, such use is enjoinable.[50] However, where the defendant's use of the plaintiff's trademark does not replace positive associations with negative ones, the mark has not been tarnished at all.[51] Nor is it actionable tarnishment for the defendant to use the plaintiff's trademark to correctly identify the second-hand trademarked goods sold by the defendant, as in "used Beanie Babies sold here."[52] Where the plaintiff's trademark is used not to identify goods or services but as commentary, satire, or parody, protection is inappropriate. Similarly, discussion or comparative advertising that uses an unaltered mark must be permitted.[53] Consequently, the Restatement of Unfair Competition provides that if the defendant uses the mark to disparage it without using it to identify goods, liability may be appropriate only under the rules of defamation or injurious falsehood, not under trademark law.[54] And since the rules for defamation, injurious falsehood, and privacy invasion take account of free speech interests, satiric or parodic use of the plaintiff's mark may not be actionable.[55] Speech rights may be undermined in tarnishment cases, however, if the court declares that confusion is likely and brings the case within the framework of traditional trademark infringement.[56] The internet has brought dilution problems as well as many others.[57]

§ 46.3   False Advertising and § 43(a) of the Lanham Act

Lanham Act § 43(a): Protection for unregistered marks under trademark rules. The federal Lanham Trademark Act, as expanded by amendments, has an enormous impact, creating a federal law of unfair competition independent of any protection for registered trademarks.[58] First, under the A-clause, one who is damaged when a defendant makes

---

[48]   E.g., Community Fed. Sav. & Loan Ass'n v. Orondorff, 678 F.2d 1034 (11th Cir. 1982) (bank's "cookie jar" mark for ATM diluted by use of "Cookie Jar" for place of adult entertainment); cf. Dallas Cowboys Cheerleaders, Inc. v. Pussycat Cinema, Ltd., 604 F. 2d 200 (2d Cir. 1979).

[49]   Chemical Corp. of America v. Anheauser-Busch, Inc., 306 F.2d 433, 2 A.L.R.3d 739 (1962).

[50]   See Moseley v. V Secret Catalogue, Inc., 537 U.S. 418, 123 S.Ct. 1115, 155 L.Ed.2d 1 (2003) (while many state statutes require only a likelihood of dilution, the federal statute requires proof of *actual* dilution).

[51]   See Id. (no tarnishment where there was no evidence that anyone "formed a different impression" of Victoria's Secret as a result of defendant's use of the name "Victor's Little Secret" for its store).

[52]   Ty Inc. v. Perryman, 306 F.3d 509 (7th Cir. 2002).

[53]   See Deere & Co. v. MTD Products, Inc., 41 F.3d 39 (2d Cir. 1994).

[54]   Restatement of Unfair Competition § 25(2) (1995).

[55]   L.L. Bean, Inc. v. Drake Publishers, Inc., 811 F.2d 26 (1st Cir. 1987); Charles Atlas, Ltd. v. DC Comics, Inc., 112 F.Supp.2d 330 (S.D.N.Y. 2000) (use of plaintiff's character in a comic-book story that parodied him); see also Mattel, Inc. v. MCA Records, Inc., 296 F.3d 894 (9th Cir. 2002) (song lampooning Barbie doll and values attributed to the doll was not purely commercial and was thus exempted from the interdictions of the federal antidilution statute). The U.S. Olympic Committee enjoys special statutory protection so that its trademark will not be diluted or tarnished. See San Francisco Arts & Athletics, Inc. v. United States Olympic Committee, 483 U.S. 522, 107 S.Ct. 2971, 97 L.Ed.2d 427 (1987) (prohibiting the use of the word "Olympic" for "Gay Olympic Games").

[56]   See Mutual of Omaha Ins. Co. v. Novak, 775 F.2d 247 (8th Cir. 1985) (affirming injunction; "Mutant of Omaha" name used on clothing by opponent of nuclear war would confuse purchasers).

[57]   See Dan L. Burk, Cybermarks, 94 Minn. L. Rev. 1375 (2010). Federal statutes increasingly address some of these issues. The Anticybersquatting Consumer Protection Act (ACPA), 15 U.S.C.A. § 1125 (d), (section 43(d) of the Lanham Act), provides a remedy to trademark holders against those who register distinctive marks as Internet domain names with the intent to profit from their goodwill. See Coca-Cola Co. v. Purdy, 382 F.3d 774 (8th Cir. 2004) (upholding injunction against defendant who registered such domain names as "drinkcoke.org," "mycocacola.com," and "mypepsi.org," and linked those names to the website "abortionismurder.com," which contained anti-abortion messages and graphic photos of aborted fetuses).

[58]   See McCarthy on Trademarks § 27:7.

confusion likely as to the origin or sponsorship of his goods has a cause of action under § 43(a).[59] That section covers not only the case in which the defendant passes off his goods as those of the plaintiff, but also reverse passing off, in which the defendant passes off the plaintiff's goods as the defendant's own.[60] In fact, § 43(a) gives unregistered marks substantially the same protection accorded to registered trademarks and on the same conditions.[61] Protection can extend to trade-dress[62]—containers of goods or the like—where the container or other appearance elements distinguish the plaintiff's goods. A likelihood of confusion exits for purposes of trade dress infringement "when consumers viewing the defendant's trade dress probably would assume that the product it represents is associated with the source of a different product identified by the plaintiff's similar trade dress."[63] The protection may also extend to product designs as such if the plaintiff proves[64] that those designs are non-functional and that they distinguish the plaintiff's goods in the eyes of consumers.[65]

False advertising: common law. The defendant who falsely disparages the products of a competitor may be liable for injurious falsehood under state common law rules.[66] If, instead of disparaging his competitor's products, he advertises or otherwise misrepresents material qualities of his own goods, he might also be liable to the purchaser who is deceived. But in that case, earlier common law tended to deny competitors any recovery on the ground that they could not show any direct losses.[67]

Lanham Act § 43(a): protection against false advertising and disparagement. The B-clause of § 43(a),[68] however, creates a cause of action against defendants who are responsible for false advertising that "misrepresents the nature, characteristics, qualities, or geographic origin of his or her or another person's goods, services or commercial activities."[69] State statutes may now do the same.[70] The B-clause creates a

---

[59]   "(1) Any person who, on or in connection with any goods or services, or any container for goods, uses in commerce any word, term, name, symbol, or device, or any combination thereof, or any false designation of origin, false or misleading description of fact, or false or misleading representation of fact, which—

(A) is likely to cause confusion, or to cause mistake, or to deceive as to the affiliation, connection, or association of such person with another person, or as to the origin, sponsorship, or approval of his or her goods, services, or commercial activities by another person. . . ."
§ 43(a)(1)(A), 15 U.S.C. § 1125(a)(1)(A).

[60]   "Section 43(a) of the Lanham Act prohibits actions like trademark infringement that deceive consumers and impair a producer's goodwill. It forbids, for example, the Coca-Cola Company's passing off its product as Pepsi-Cola or reverse passing off Pepsi-Cola as its product." Dastar Corp. v. Twentieth Century Fox Film Corp., 539 U.S. 23, 123 S.Ct. 2041, 156 L.Ed.2d 18 (2003).

[61]   Two Pesos, Inc. v. Taco Cabana, Inc., 505 U.S. 763, 112 S.Ct. 2753, 120 L.Ed.2d 615 (1992); Courtenay Communications Corp. v. Hall, 334 F.3d 210 (2d Cir. 2003).

[62]   See § 46.4.

[63]   McNeil Nutritionals, LLC v. Heartland Sweeteners, LLC, 511 F.3d 350 (3d Cir. 2007).

[64]   § 43(a)(3), 15 U.S.C.A. § 1125(a)(3).

[65]   Wal-Mart Stores, Inc. v. Samara Bros., 529 U.S. 205, 120 S.Ct. 1339, 146 L.Ed.2d 182 (2000).

[66]   E.g., Vascular Solutions, Inc. v. Marine Polymer Technologies, Inc., 590 F.3d 56 (1st Cir. 2009); see § 43.1.

[67]   E.g. American Washboard Co. v. Saginaw Mfg. Co., 103 F. 281 (6th Cir. 1900). For history and exceptions, see Restatement of Unfair Competition § 2, cmt. b (1995).

[68]   § 43(a)(1)(B), 15 U.S.C.A. § 1125(a)(1)(B).

[69]   15 U.S.C.A. § 1125(a)(2). The Supreme Court has held that one competitor may sue another for false advertising under the Lanham Act over FDCA-compliant food labels. POM Wonderful LLC v. Coca-Cola Co., 134 S.Ct. 2228 (2014) (claim that Minute Maid's "Pomegranate Blueberry" juice label misled consumers into believing it was primarily made up of those two juices, when it is less than one percent of either, resulting in a loss of sales for POM's Pomegranite Blueberry juice, which is 100 percent those two juices).

[70]   See Uniform Deceptive Trade Practices Act § 2.

cause of action for two different kinds of false statements in promotions of goods and services—first, the defendant's false (and favorable) statements about his *own* goods; and second, the defendant's false (and *un*favorable) statements about the *plaintiff's* goods. The second kind of representation is redressed as a federal disparagement or injurious falsehood claim,[71] subject to certain limitations. However, the statute does not expressly require intentional falsehood as a basis for liability. Unless such a requirement can be derived from construction,[72] the § 43(a) false advertising and disparagement claims differ considerably from the common law disparagement or injurious falsehood claims, at least at they are described in the Restatement, which imposes liability only if the defendant intends a falsehood or is at least reckless with respect to falsity.[73]

Limitations on the false advertising claim under § 43(a). Although liability under the B-clause may not require intentional falsehood, there are statutory limitations on the claim. The falsity or misrepresentation must be in advertising or promotion, presumably excluding liability for political or social observations. The commercial requirement also excludes liability for, say, disparagement in conversation or in magazine articles.[74] A plaintiff suing for false advertising under the Lanham Act ordinarily must show economic or reputational injury flowing directly from the deception wrought by the defendant's false advertising; a plaintiff's complaint must sufficiently allege harm proximately caused by the defendant's actions, or it will be subject to dismissal.[75] The statement must also be "false" or misleading,[76] a requirement that leaves the advertiser free to engage in puffing and opinion statements that imply no false statement of fact.[77] Although the statute does not use the term, courts have also said that the representation used in promotion or advertising will not be actionable unless it is "material."[78] These last two requirements are in line with similar rules in common law fraud cases.[79]

Remedies. For a private party such as a competitor to prevail on a false advertising claim under § 43(a), it must show injury, either in the form of past financial loss, or

---

[71]   For the common law claims of disparagement or injurious falsehood, see § 43.1.

[72]   McCarthy favors importing the common law rules into the statutory action. See McCarthy on Trademarks § 27:91.

[73]   See § 43.1.

[74]   Gmurzynska v. Hutton, 355 F.3d 206 (2d Cir. 2004); cf. NXIVM Corp. v. Ross Institute, 364 F.3d 471 (2d Cir. 2004) (cult de-programmer's critique of executive success seminar was not "commercial advertising or promotion" under § 43(a) because the contested representations were not "part of an organized campaign to penetrate the relevant market").

[75]   See Lexmark Intern., Inc. v. Static Control Components, Inc., 134 S.Ct. 1377, 188 L.Ed.2d 392 (2014). State consumer protection statutes may allow a broader class of plaintiffs to sue for false advertising and other deceptive trade practices. See, e.g., N.Y. Gen Bus. Law § 349 (h); Pa. Stat. § 201–9.2.

[76]   "Under section 43(a), two categories of actionable statements exist: (1) literally false factual commercial claims; and (2) literally true or ambiguous factual claims which implicitly convey a false impression, are misleading in context, or [are] likely to deceive consumers." American Italian Pasta Co. v. New World Pasta Co., 371 F.3d 387 (8th Cir. 2004) (quoting). If a statement in an ad is literally false, it may be actionable without any reference to the ad's impact on the buying public; where it is not literally false, the evidentiary burden is higher. See Hall v. Bed Bath & Beyond, Inc., 705 F.3d 1357 (Fed. Cir. 2013).

[77]   American Italian Pasta Co. v. New World Pasta Co., 371 F.3d 387 (8th Cir. 2004) ("Puffery exists in two general forms: (1) exaggerated statements of bluster or boast upon which no reasonable consumer would rely; and (2) vague or highly subjective claims of product superiority, including bald assertions of superiority."); Pizza Hut, Inc. v. Papa John's Intern., Inc., 227 F.3d 489 (5th Cir. 2000) ("Bald assertions of superiority or general statements of opinion cannot form the basis of Lanham Act liability.").

[78]   Pizza Hut, Inc. v. Papa John's Intern., Inc., 227 F.3d 489 (5th Cir. 2000); McCarthy on Trademarks § 27:35.

[79]   See §§ 43.4 & 43.8.

likelihood of future business losses.[80] A recovery of damages,[81] or an accounting for profits,[82] or both, is appropriate if the plaintiff's loss or the defendant's gain from the false advertising is proved with sufficient certainty.[83] Further, section 43(a) permits trebling of the recovery "as compensation."[84] If monetary damages cannot be proved, the aggrieved competitor can at least enjoin the false representations.[85]

§ 46.4   Product Design, Trade Dress, and Functional Features

Trade dress. In contemporary law, a distinctive overall appearance of a container, label, or means of packaging a product can be protected as a mark under § 43(a) independent of any specific trademark accompanying such packaging.[86] This kind of overall appearance is often called trade dress. The fundamental rules of trademark apply. Trade dress is protected as a trademark only when it is inherently distinctive or acquires distinctiveness through secondary meaning and identifies the product's source or sponsorship.[87] A wide range of attributes, including restaurant decor,[88] the special color of pads for dry cleaners,[89] the shape and texture of a bottle in which a product is marketed,[90] and many others can count as protectable trade dress, as long as the total look distinguishes the plaintiff's goods or services from others.[91]

Product design. A product's design itself can also function as a distinctive mark and is also sometimes called trade dress. Special limits apply when trade dress, and especially product design, is claimed as a trademark, first because functional features cannot be protected (except under patent law), and second because designs cannot be inherently distinctive but must instead have acquired "secondary meaning."

Functional features. Functional features cannot be protected as trademarks.[92] This means that competitors can copy any feature of a product's design that is functional and not protected by patent.[93] Although functionality can be defined in varied formulas,[94] the

---

[80]   See B. Sanfield, Inc. v. Finlay Fine Jewelry Corp., 258 F.3d 578 (7th Cir. 2001) (citing cases from many jurisdictions).

[81]   See Restatement of Unfair Competition § 36 & cmt. a (1995) ("The general rules relating to recovery of compensatory damages in tort actions apply in actions for unfair competition.").

[82]   See Id. § 37. Accounting for profits permits a recovery of the gains obtained by the defendant as a result of the tort and presents special problems of measurement. See 2 Dan B. Dobbs, Law of Remedies § 6.4(4) (2d ed. 1993).

[83]   Tim Torres Enterprises, Inc. v. Linscott, 142 Wis.2d 56, 416 N.W.2d 670 (1987).

[84]   See 2 Dan B. Dobbs, Law of Remedies § 6.4(3) (2d ed. 1993).

[85]   See Id., § 6.4(5); North American Medical Corp. v. Axiom Worldwide, Inc., 522 F.3d 1211 (11th Cir. 2008) (discussing requirements for an injunction in a Lanham Act case).

[86]   Two Pesos, Inc. v. Taco Cabana, Inc., 505 U.S. 763, 112 S.Ct. 2753, 120 L.Ed.2d 615 (1992); see also Restatement of Unfair Competition § 16 (1995).

[87]   Wal-Mart Stores, Inc. v. Samara Bros., Inc., 529 U.S. 205, 120 S.Ct. 1339 (2000); See McCarthy on Trademarks § 8:1.

[88]   See Two Pesos, Inc. v. Taco Cabana, Inc., 505 U.S. 763, 112 S.Ct. 2753, 120 L.Ed.2d 615 (1992).

[89]   Qualitex Co. v. Jacobson Products Co., Inc., 514 U.S. 159, 115 S.Ct. 1300 (1995).

[90]   E.g., Nora Beverages, Inc. v. Perrier Group of America, Inc., 164 F.3d 736 (2d Cir. 1998).

[91]   Amazing Spaces, Inc. v. Metro Mini Storage, 608 F.3d 225 (5th Cir. 2010).

[92]   E.g., American Greetings Corporation v. Dan-Dee Imports, Inc., 807 F.2d 1136 (3d Cir. 1986); Groenevelt Transport Efficiency, Inc. v. Lubecore Intern., Inc., 730 F.3d 494 (6th Cir. 2013); Restatement of Unfair Competition § 16 (1995).

[93]   Eppendorf-Netheler-Hinz GMBH v. Ritter GMBH, 289 F.3d 351 (5th Cir. 2002).

[94]   Qualitex Co. v. Jacobson Products Co., Inc., 514 U.S. 159, 165, 115 S.Ct. 1300, 1304, 131 L.Ed.2d 248 (1995) ("if it is essential to the use or purpose of the article or if it affects the cost or quality of the article"); Restatement of Unfair Competition § 17 (1995) (a feature is functional if it affords benefits in marketing

general idea is that a feature is functional if it makes the product more workable, useful, or efficient than reasonable alternatives, or if it affects the quality or cost of the product. For example, the first automobile might have had a distinctive appearance, "but if its distinctiveness was due to the fact that it had an engine in front instead of horses, and a crank, radiator grill, and steering wheel, the producer would not be able to claim that this combination of functional features constituted trade dress; for that would give him a monopoly of the production of automobiles, and trademark law is not intended to confer product monopolies."[95] The fact that the product's feature was once patented is strong evidence that, although the patent has expired, the feature remains functional.[96] A product might even have aesthetically functional features, features that command a premium in the market because they appeal to tastes so strongly that they are essential characteristics for marketing the particular product.[97]

Policy and effect of the functionality rule. The functionality rule is a part of the balance between free competition and protection of identifying marks. Copying of useful ideas and designs not protected by patent laws is entirely desirable and permissible. It is in fact a part of the balance dictated by the patent laws. Under the Constitution, federal patent laws are the exclusive source for rights in inventions.[98] They grant inventors of useful items a monopoly or patent for a period of years, after which anyone may copy the invention and go into competition with the inventor. The laws restrict patents to specific devices; general ideas are not patentable.[99] In addition, the device must be inventive and novel and not merely an extension of earlier ideas.[100] Trademark protection for functional features of a product that is not protected by a patent would subvert the balance of competition and property rights struck by the patent laws. That is because trademark of functional items would provide protection for devices that patent laws might refuse to protect altogether, and would provide protection in perpetuity where patent laws would at most protect for 20 years.[101]

Preemption of state patent-like laws. With these ideas in mind, the Supreme Court has held that federal patent laws preempt state laws that attempt to create patent-like rules to forbid copying of products that are not protected by federal patent law. In one of the leading cases, the defendant made a mold of the plaintiff's boat design, then cast copies and competed with the plaintiff. Since the boat design was not patented, copying was not only permitted but, under the patent scheme, desirable as a means of promoting

---

independent of the feature's value as indicating the source of the goods and if those benefits are important in effective competition and if they cannot be captured in other ways); McCarthy on Trademarks, supra n.2, at § 7:69.

[95] Publications Intern., Ltd. v. Landoll, Inc., 164 F.3d 337, 340 (7th Cir. 1998).

[96] Traffix Devices, Inc. v. Marketing Displays, Inc., 532 U.S. 23, 149 L.Ed.2d 164, 121 S.Ct. 1255 (2001).

[97] Restatement of Unfair Competition § 17 (1995). See Dippin' Dots, Inc. v. Frosty Bites Distribution, LLC, 369 F.3d 1197, 1203 (11th Cir. 2004) (size, shape, and color of small spheres of flash frozen ice cream were aesthetically functional under "the competitive necessity test . . . generally applied in cases of aesthetic functionality," namely, that a product's feature is functional if its exclusive use by one competitor would put other competitors at "a significant non-reputation-related disadvantage"). Judge Posner gave this example of aesthetic functionality: "Mink coats are normally sold dyed. The dye does not make the coat any warmer, but it makes it more beautiful, and, once again, it could not be claimed as trade dress by the first furrier to have hit on the idea." Publications Intern., Ltd. v. Landoll, Inc., 164 F.3d 337 (7th Cir. 1998).

[98] U.S. Const., Art. I, § Cl. 8; Bonito Boats, Inc. v. Thunder Craft Boats, Inc., 489 U.S. 141, 109 S.Ct. 971, 103 L.Ed.2d 118 (1989) (preemption of patent-like laws).

[99] Gottschalk v. Benson, 409 U.S. 63, 93 S.Ct. 253, 34 L.Ed.2d 273 (1972).

[100] See 35 U.S.C.A. §§ 102 & 103.

[101] 35 U.S.C.A. § 154 (with some variation in the term depending upon circumstances and patent type).

competition. A state statute that attempted to prohibit such copying was thus invalid.[102] Earlier cases had taken a similar view about copying of lamp designs.[103]

Federal claims and functionality. The preemption analysis does not apply to claims for trademark infringement under the federal trademark laws, which permit a claim for infringement of trademarks in trade dress and product design.[104] But the policy behind the patent preemption decisions applies to federal claims by way of the functionality rules: a functional feature cannot count as a trademark, even if it also identifies the plaintiff as producer of the goods.[105] The plaintiff must protect functional features under the law of trade secrets or patents or not at all.

Designs without distinctiveness. Product designs—as opposed to trade dress like a container for the goods—are not so likely to be capable of exclusively identifying the plaintiff's goods. In fact, the Supreme Court has held that product *designs* cannot be inherently distinctive. At the same time, however, product designs can be distinctive if, but only if, they have acquired a secondary meaning.[106]

§ 46.5 Ideas and Trade Secrets

General ideas not protected. Ideas as such are not protected, either by statutes or by the common law. Newton did not own gravity. If the idea is sufficiently inventive and novel and also reduced to a specific useful design, it may be patented for a limited period of years, otherwise not.[107] A person with an idea may exploit it by going into business using the idea, but she cannot prevent others from using it as well once she reveals it. In such a case, her rewards for developing a good idea must come from the fact that she is the first to exploit it and from her efficient use of it, not from static ownership.

Protection from breach of confidence or contract. However, ideas and information can be protected to some extent by divulging them only to fiduciaries, or in confidence, or pursuant to a contract. A stranger or an employee may suggest improvements to a business, which may be liable if it contracts to pay for ideas and perhaps on an implied contract if it uses the idea,[108] but otherwise liability must be founded upon the trade-secret rules[109] or not at all.[110]

---

[102] Bonito Boats, Inc. v. Thunder Craft Boats, Inc., 489 U.S. 141, 109 S.Ct. 971, 103 L.Ed.2d 118 (1989). As to boat hulls specifically, Congress itself has now provided protection against copying in 1998. 17 U.S.C.A. § 1301.

[103] Sears, Roebuck & Co. v. Stiffel Co., 376 U.S. 225, 84 S.Ct. 784, 11 L.Ed.2d 661 (1964); Compco Corp. v. Day-Brite Lighting, Inc., 376 U.S. 234, 84 S.Ct. 779, 11 L.Ed.2d 669 (1964).

[104] See McCarthy on Trademarks § 7:58.

[105] Two Pesos, Inc. v. Taco Cabana, Inc., 505 U.S. 763, 112 S.Ct. 2753, 120 L.Ed.2d 615 (1992); Publications Intern., Ltd. v. Landoll, Inc., 164 F.3d 337 (7th Cir. 1998).

[106] Wal-Mart Stores, Inc. v. Samara Bros., 529 U.S. 205, 120 S.Ct. 1339, 146 L.Ed.2d 182 (2000). This decision will require courts to draw a distinction between trade dress, which may be inherently distinctive, and product design, which the Court holds cannot be.

[107] Gottschalk v. Benson, 409 U.S. 63, 93 S.Ct. 253, 34 L.Ed.2d 273 (1972).

[108] See Phillips v. Frey, 20 F.3d 623 (5th Cir. 1994) (prospective seller enthusiastically revealed too much; buyers implicitly accepted the information in confidence).

[109] See Restatement of Unfair Competition § 39, cmt. h (1995).

[110] Joyce v. General Motors Corp., 49 Ohio St.3d 93, 551 N.E.2d 172 (1990) (employee not entitled to compensation under the terms of employee suggestion program); Martin v. Little, Brown and Co., 304 Pa. Super. 424, 450 A.2d 984 (1981) (stranger not entitled to compensation for notifying publisher that its copyright had been infringed by others).

Protected information. A trade secret[111] is any kind of secret information used in an enterprise for actual or potential economic advantage,[112] at least if it has independent value because it is secret.[113] It must not be readily ascertainable[114] or widely known.[115] Many courts insist that for information to be deemed a trade secret, the plaintiff must have taken reasonable measures to maintain its secrecy.[116] A trade secret is often a formula or a compilation of information used in business. Sometimes it is a process or a combination of elements, each of which is publicly known, although the combination is not.[117] The trade secret is protected even though it is not novel enough to justify a patent,[118] and though it is not actually used by the plaintiff.[119] One great advantage for the owner of a trade secret is that, unlike a patent, it does not expire at the end of a fixed term. A company that developed a formula or process in 1900 and never divulged it may still be exploiting that process to its competitive advantage today.

Grounds for liability. Liability turns on a finding that the defendant misappropriated the information by tortious or improper means such as fraud, theft, or the like,[120] or the finding that he was guilty of, or took advantage of, a breach of confidence.[121] For example, if the owner of a trade secret discloses it in confidence to the defendant as a prospective buyer of the business, the defendant's use of the trade secret without making the purchase is a breach of confidence and a wrongful use of the trade secret.[122] The same is true when the plaintiff discloses the trade secret to employees who must use it in their work. Because the focus is on wrongdoing and breach of confidence,

---

[111] See Roger M. Milgrim, Trade Secrets (4 vols. with supps. 2010).

[112] Restatement of Unfair Competition § 39 (1995).

[113] E.g., Faiveley Transport Malmo AB v. Wabtec Corp., 559 F.3d 110 (2d Cir. 2009); In re Bass, 113 S.W.3d 735 (Tex. 2003). Information is not "secret" if it has been actually disclosed earlier to a person with no duty to keep it confidential. See, e.g., Ruckelshaus v. Monsanto Co., 467 U.S. 986, 104 S.Ct. 2862, 81 L.Ed.2d 815 (1984); BondPro Corp. v. Siemens Power Generation, Inc., 463 F.3d 702 (7th Cir. 2006).

[114] See Western Forms, Inc., 308 F.3d 930 (8th Cir. 2002) (customer lists, pricing information and "bidding structure" not protectable trade secrets because they were readily ascertainable); Buffets, Inc. v. Klinke, 73 F.3d 965 (9th Cir. 1996) (recipes and employee manuals could easily be discovered by others; plaintiff failed to make reasonable efforts to maintain their secrecy); Aetna Building Maintenance Co., Inc. v. West, 39 Cal.2d 198, 246 P.2d 11 (1952) (prospective customers readily discoverable); Cemen Tech, Inc. v. Three D Industries, LLC, 753 N.W.2d 1 (Iowa 2008) (issue of fact whether information used by plaintiff's former employee to develop a competing cement mixer was "readily ascertainable"); Uniform Trade Secrets Act § 1 (4).

[115] E.g., MP TotalCare Services, Inc. v. Mattimoe, 648 F.Supp.2d 956 (N.D. Ohio 2009).

[116] See, e.g., Hertz v. Luzenac Group, 576 F.3d 1003 (10th Cir. 2009); Incase Inc. v. Timex Corp., 488 F.3d 46 (1st Cir. 2007); Air Turbo Systems AG v. Turbousa, Inc., 774 F.3d 979 (Fed. Cir. 2014); Tyson Foods v. Con Agra, Inc., 349 Ark. 469, 79 S.W.3d 326 (2002); Callman on Unfair Competition § 14:26.

[117] Integrated Cash Management Services, Inc. v. Digital Transactions, Inc., 920 F.2d 171 (2d Cir. 1990); Pinchera v. Allstate Ins. Co., 144 N.M. 601, 190 P.3d 322 (2008).

[118] Learning Curve Toys, Inc. v. Playwood Toys, Inc., 342 F.3d 714 (7th Cir. 2003); Softel, Inc. v. Dragon Medical and Scientific Communications, Inc., 118 F.3d 955 (2d Cir. 1997); Dionne v. Southeast Foam Converting & Packaging, Inc., 240 Va. 297, 397 S.E.2d 110 (1990).

[119] Restatement of Unfair Competition § 39, cmt. e (1995).

[120] E.I. du Pont de Nemours & Co. v. Christopher, 431 F.2d 1012 (5th Cir. 1970) (overflights with photography to reveal plant structure which in turn would reveal nature of secret process). The set of special trade secret rules displaces an ordinary conversion analysis. See 4 Dobbs, Hayden & Bublick, The Law of Torts § 712 (2d ed. 2011 & Supp.).

[121] See generally Restatement of Unfair Competition § 40 (1995).

[122] E.g., Roton Barrier, Inc. v. Stanley Works, 79 F.3d 1112 (Fed. Cir. 1996).

a person who acquires the trade secret from a wrongdoer without reason to know of the wrong is not subject to liability.[123]

Remedies. If a trade secret is misappropriated or revealed in breach of confidence, the owner may have relief measured by her own damages or by the defendant's unjust enrichment; where future revelation is threatened, the owner may frequently obtain an injunction.[124] Damages may include lost profits resulting because use of the trade secret permitted the defendant to sell goods in competition with the plaintiff[125] and also erosion of prices made necessary by the competition founded on misappropriation of the trade secret.[126] Punitive damages may be available where the misappropriation was willful and malicious.[127] The Uniform Trade Secrets Act embodies the common law rules protecting trade secrets and a federal statute makes misappropriation of trade secrets a crime.[128]

Preemption or displacement of other claims. The Uniform Trade Secrets Act preempts or displaces all other claims for misappropriation of trade secrets, such as claims for "conversion" of secrets or interference with contract by use of trade secrets.[129] Some courts hold that all other claims are displaced even if the information taken does not count as a trade secret at all.[130] Others take the view that the displacement clause applies only if the information misappropriated counts as a trade secret.[131] Even the broader view of displacement allows claims that are distinct from the misappropriation of information.[132]

Losing rights in trade secrets. Trade secret protection is lost when the secret becomes publicly or widely known, either because of the plaintiff's divulgence[133] or in spite of the plaintiff's best efforts to keep it secret.[134] Furthermore, the defendant is free to develop the same information covered by a trade secret, so long as he does not take

---

[123] See Forest Laboratories, Inc. v. Pillsbury Co., 452 F.2d 621 (7th Cir. 1971); Restatement of Unfair Competition § 40(b) & cmt. d (1995).

[124] E.g., Henry Hope X-Ray Products, Inc. v. Marron Carrel, Inc., 674 F.2d 1336 (9th Cir. 1982). For all these remedies, see 2 Dan B. Dobbs, Law of Remedies § 10.5(3) (2d ed. 1993).

[125] See, e.g., Pioneer Hi-Bred Intern. v. Holden Foundation Seeds, Inc., 35 F.3d 1226 (8th Cir. 1994).

[126] Roton Barrier, Inc. v. Stanley Works, 79 F.3d 1112 (Fed. Cir. 1996); see also World Wide Prosthetic Supply, Inc. v. Mikulsky, 251 Wis.2d 45, 640 N.W.2d 764 (2002) (approving broader damages, including the plaintiff's loss of profits resulting because the defendant used the trade secret in its production of defective products for which the plaintiff might be blamed by customers).

[127] Learning Curve Toys, Inc. v. Playwood Toys, Inc., 342 F.3d 714 (7th Cir. 2003) (applying Illinois law). The Uniform Trade Secrets Act § 3(b) limits punitive damages to double the compensatory damages.

[128] 18 U.S.C.A. §§ 1831 to 1839.

[129] See 4 Dobbs, Hayden & Bublick, The Law of Torts § 712 (2d ed. 2011 & Supp.).

[130] Mortgage Specialists, Inc. v. Davey, 153 N.H. 764, 904 A.2d 652 (2006).

[131] See Orca Communications Unlimited, LLC v. Noder, 337 P.3d 545 (Ariz. 2014) (state Trade Secrets Act does not displace common law claims based on alleged misappropriation of confidential information that does not constitute trade secrets); Burbank Grease Services, LLC v. Sokolowski, 294 Wis.2d 274, 717 N.W.2d 781 (2006) (interference with contract or prospects claim for taking employer's information not preempted or displaced by trade secret statute).

[132] Mortgage Specialists, Inc. v. Davey, 153 N.H. 764, 904 A.2d 652 (2006) ("a claim is not preempted where the elements of the claim require some allegation or factual showing in addition to that which forms the basis for a claim of misappropriation of a trade secret;" statements made by defendant to plaintiff's customers were not part of the misappropriation and permitted a claim for interference with economic opportunity).

[133] E.g., BondPro Corp. v. Siemens Power Generation, Inc., 463 F.3d 702 (7th Cir. 2006).

[134] Religious Technology Center v. F.A.C.T.NET, Inc., 901 F.Supp. 1519 (D. Colo. 1995) (secret works of Scientology's founder had escaped into the public domain, although the Church had worked hard to keep the works secret).

advantage of a breach of confidence or commit an independent tort to do so. In particular, he is free to analyze or reverse-engineer the plaintiff's products and to acquire the secret in that manner if he can.[135] These rules reflect disadvantages of trade secret ownership compared to patents. They also reflect the fact that trade secrets are property protected by tort law mainly in the limited sense that tort law will impose liability for breach of confidence or some independent tort.[136]

Employees joining a competitor. The breach of confidence issue often arises when employees who are knowledgeable about the employer's trade secrets set up a competing business or go to work for an existing competitor. The employee owes a fiduciary duty to his employer,[137] so it is clear that he cannot take the employer's secret information or use it for his own unauthorized purposes.[138] On the other hand, in the absence of a valid agreement to the contrary, the employee is entitled to take her own skills and general knowledge with her to another employment. If a customer list is a trade secret— sometimes they are, sometimes not[139]—the employee may still be entitled to use his memory of faces and names in his new job.[140] The conflict between the employee's right to work with her own skills and the employer's right to protect trade secrets leads to difficult decisions. In extreme cases, the developing inevitable-disclosure doctrine permits the court to enjoin the former employee from working for a competitor for a period of time on the theory that he would inevitably reveal trade secrets.[141]

§ 46.6   Rights in Personality and Publicity

The earliest right of privacy claims sought relief because the defendant, without permission, had used the plaintiff's name or picture in commercial advertising.[142] Privacy invasion claims with their dignitary emphasis remain valid to redress dignitary harms such as personal distress. When the claim is that the defendant has appropriated

---

[135] Roboserve, Ltd. v. Tom's Foods, Inc., 940 F.2d 1441 (11th Cir. 1991); see Restatement of Unfair Competition § 43 (1995).

[136] As Holmes put it, "The word 'property' as applied to trademarks and trade secrets is an unanalyzed expression of certain secondary consequences of the primary fact that the law makes some rudimentary requirements of good faith. Whether the plaintiffs have any valuable secret or not the defendant knows the facts, whatever they are, through a special confidence that he accepted. The property may be denied, but the confidence cannot be. Therefore the starting point for the present matter is not property or due process of law, but that the defendant stood in confidential relations with the plaintiffs. . . ." E.I. du Pont de Nemours Powder Co. v. Masland, 244 U.S. 100, 37 S.Ct. 575, 61 L.Ed. 1016 (1917). There are indisputably some property aspects; for example, trade secrets may also be "taken" by the government, and if so, due process requires compensation. See Ruckelshaus v. Monsanto Co., 467 U.S. 986, 104 S.Ct. 2862, 81 L.Ed.2d 815 (1984).

[137] Restatement Third of Agency § 8.01, cmt. c (2006); Restatement Second of Agency §§ 395 & 396 (1959).

[138] Restatement Third of Agency § 8.05(2) (2006).

[139] E.g., Leo Publications, Inc. v. Reid, 265 Ga. 561, 458 S.E.2d 651 (1995) (list of employer's customers not a trade secret, but employee must return the original list, made in the course of employment, to the employer after the employee has left the company); Home Pride Foods, Inc. v. Johnson, 262 Neb. 701, 634 N.W.2d 774 (2001) (customer list a trade secret where list had independent economic value, was kept secret, and competitor paid $800 for a stolen copy); see K. H. Larsen, Annotation, Former Employee's Duty, in Absence of Express Contract, Not to Solicit Former Employer's Customers or Otherwise Use His Knowledge of Customer Lists Acquired in Earlier Employment, 28 A.L.R.3d 7 (1970).

[140] Carl A. Colteryahn Dairy, Inc. v. Schneider Dairy, 415 Pa. 276, 203 A.2d 469 (1964).

[141] PepsiCo, Inc. v. Redmond, 54 F.3d 1262 (7th Cir. 1995) (marketing strategies, six month injunction against work for direct competitor).

[142] See § 38.2.

the plaintiff's "identity" for trade or commercial purposes,[143] the harm is different; it is economic harm to the plaintiff (or unjust economic gain to the defendant). In that case, the tort can be viewed as an invasion of privacy in which damages happen to be economic, or as a separate tort for the commercial appropriation of identity or personality or as a vindication of the "right of publicity."[144] A fair number of states so provide by statute, the terms of which are sometimes exclusive.[145]

If the defendant's use of the plaintiff's identity is not for trade or commerce, the right of publicity is not infringed,[146] or if it is, the plaintiff's claim is subject to First Amendment free speech defenses.[147] Thus a biography, fictionalized or not, does not violate the right of publicity, and the plaintiff loses unless she can prove some other tort such as defamation.[148] In addition, First Amendment free speech rights may protect a defendant who appropriates the plaintiff's identity as part of his own creative, transformative work such as a song,[149] a portrait that is creative rather than a literal depiction,[150] fantasy-baseball games,[151] or bizarre comic-book fiction utilizing the plaintiffs' well-known names for a character that is half-worm.[152] This First Amendment protection does not require literary or creative quality, but perhaps the new, creative,

---

[143] The leading treatise on this topic is J. Thomas McCarthy, Publicity and Privacy (2d ed., updated on Westlaw in RTPUBPRIV database) (hereinafter McCarthy on Publicity and Privacy).

[144] See Restatement of Unfair Competition §§ 46 to 49 (1995); 1 McCarthy on Publicity and Privacy § 5:63. If the plaintiff's identity has become associated with goods or services he produces, he may have a trademark interest in it as well.

[145] See Stephano v. News Group Publications, Inc., 64 N.Y.2d 174, 474 N.E.2d 580, 485 N.Y.S.2d 220 (1984).

[146] See Restatement of Unfair Competition § 47 (1995) (defining "for purposes of trade"). In Tyne v. Time Warner Entertainment Co., L.P., 901 So.2d 802 (Fla. 2005), a movie, *The Perfect Storm*, was a fictionalized version of a real event in which several men died. Their survivors sued, complaining of the fictional depiction of the men and of themselves. The court held that a movie that does not promote the sale of a product is not a commercial or advertising purpose and hence not actionable under the state's commercial appropriation statute.

[147] Hoffman v. Capital Cities/ABC, Inc., 255 F.3d 1180 (9th Cir. 2001) (use of an image of Dustin Hoffman's face with a digitally grafted body in a feature story was not commercial and would not be actionable absent knowing or reckless falsehood required for protection of noncommercial speech); Montgomery v. Montgomery, 60 S.W.3d 524 (Ky. 2001) (music video). See also Jordan v. Jewel Food Stores, Inc., 743 F.3d 509 (7th Cir. 2014) (advertisement for defendant's store that used Michael Jordan's name and a photo of his basketball shoes, and purported to congratulate him on his induction into the NBA Hall of Fame, was commercial speech for First Amendment purposes).

[148] Ruffin-Steinback v. dePasse, 267 F.3d 457 (6th Cir. 2001) (fictionalized biographical treatment of musical group The Temptations in a television miniseries not actionable as invasion of right of publicity); Seale v. Gramercy Pictures, 949 F.Supp. 331 (E.D. Pa. 1996) (former Black Panther and civil rights activist Bobby Seale did not state a claim for violation of the right of publicity where defendant used his name and likeness in film, book, and home video, but fact questions remained on whether film portrayed him in a false light).

[149] See Parks v. LaFace Records, 329 F.3d 437 (6th Cir. 2003) (civil rights pioneer Rosa Parks established a state-law right of publicity claim against defendant who used her name as the title of a song, but fact issues remained on whether defendants were protected by the First Amendment).

[150] Cardtoons, L.C. v. Major League Baseball Players Ass'n, 95 F.3d 959 (10th Cir. 1996); see also Comedy III Productions, Inc. v. Gary Saderup, Inc., 25 Cal.4th 387, 21 P.3d 797, 106 Cal.Rptr.2d 126 (2001) (strong statements recognizing protection for transformative uses). In both these cases, the alleged appropriation was embodied in a product—parodic baseball cards and tee-shirts respectively—so the defendants' purposes were for trade even though there was no advertisement.

[151] C.B.C. Distribution and Marketing, Inc. v. Major League Baseball Advanced Media, L.P., 505 F.3d 818 (8th Cir. 2007).

[152] Hart v. Electronic Arts, Inc., 717 F.3d 141 (3d Cir. 2013) (manner in which former college football player's identity was incorporated into football-related video games did not satisfy transformative use test); Winter v. DC Comics, 30 Cal.4th 881, 69 P.3d 473, 134 Cal.Rptr.2d 634 (2003) (defendants' fictional work that used "Autumn Brothers" to refer to plaintiffs, rock and blues musicians and siblings Edgar and Johnny Winter, and gave the fictional Autumns displeasing characteristics, was transformative and thus protected).

and transformative elements must be substantial, and perhaps must predominate in the work.[153]

The broad term "identity" here means the plaintiff's name, likeness, or other singular or notable characteristics associated peculiarly with the plaintiff. The forbidden commercial use includes use of the plaintiff's identity in an advertisement, as where the plaintiff's name,[154] voice[155] or likeness[156] is used or imitated in an advertisement and where the plaintiff's identity is used as part of the defendant's trademark,[157] or sold directly as a poster, tee-shirt, statuette or the like.[158] The emphasis is on the fact that the plaintiff's identity has commercial value, so plaintiffs in such cases are usually celebrities. But even a little-known recluse may have a reasonable claim if her identity has commercial value,[159] and in any event such a person may have a claim for emotional or other dignitary harm on right of privacy grounds.[160]

Extending identity or style. One kind of problem case involves the plaintiff's claim to protection for her public style or distinctive performing persona rather than her name or likeness–that is, protection for a combination of demeanor, dress, and intangible aspects of personality.[161] Courts have held that an Elvis Presley imitation infringed rights of publicity,[162] and that a TV news publication depiction of the late Zacchini's entire cannon-ball act would be an infringement, even though the tape was legitimately made.[163] The Ninth Circuit held that a parodic ad showing a robot, dressed in clothes and jewelry similar to those worn by television personality Vanna White, and sporting her hair style, was an infringement of her right of publicity.[164] The reference to Vanna White was unmistakable to those who watch TV game shows. Although White did not own the exclusive right to dress and bejewel herself in that particular way, the court

---

[153] Winter v. DC Comics, 30 Cal.4th 881, 889, 69 P.3d 473, 478, 134 Cal.Rptr.2d 634, 640 (2003); Doe v. TCI Cablevision, 110 S.W.3d 363 (Mo. 2003) ("[T]he metaphorical reference to Twist, though a literary device, has very little literary value compared to its commercial value. On the record here, the use and identity of Twist's name has become predominantly a ploy to sell comic books and related products rather than an artistic or literary expression, and under these circumstances, free speech must give way to the right of publicity.").

[154] See Henley v. Dillard Department Stores, 46 F.Supp.2d 587 (N.D. Tex. 1999) (department store advertisement for shirt, labeling it "Don's henley," wrongfully appropriated famous rock musician's name for the value associated with it); Hirsch v. S.C. Johnson & Son, Inc., 90 Wis.2d 379, 280 N.W.2d 129 (1979) (use of famous athlete plaintiff's nickname "Crazylegs").

[155] Waits v. Frito-Lay, Inc., 978 F.2d 1093 (9th Cir. 1992) (wrongful use of Tom Waits "sound-alike" in radio commercial), *abrogated on other grounds*, Lexmark Intern., Inc. v. Static Control Components, Inc., 134 S.Ct. 1377, 188 L.Ed.2d 392 (2014); Midler v. Ford Motor Co., 849 F.2d 460 (9th Cir. 1988) (wrongful use of Bette Midler "sound-alike" in television commercial).

[156] Ali v. Playgirl, Inc., 447 F.Supp. 723 (S.D.N.Y. 1978) (seemingly realistic drawing or cartoon depicting Muhammad Ali nude). So far as an advertisement implies the plaintiff's endorsement by using a look-alike actor, the advertiser may also be guilty of false advertising or passing off. Allen v. National Video, Inc., 610 F.Supp. 612 (S.D.N.Y. 1985) (Woody Allen look-alike in ad).

[157] Carson v. Here's Johnny Portable Toilets, Inc., 698 F.2d 831 (6th Cir. 1983).

[158] E.g., Comedy III Productions, Inc. v. Gary Saderup, Inc., 25 Cal.4th 387, 21 P.3d 797, 106 Cal.Rptr.2d 126 (2001); Martin Luther King, Jr., Center for Social Change, Inc. v. American Heritage Products, Inc., 250 Ga. 135, 296 S.E.2d 697 (1982) (bust of Dr. Martin Luther King infringed right of publicity). Once the plaintiff has licensed the use of her identity on items like tee-shirts, the purchaser of the tee-shirt is entitled to use it and even to resell it. See Allison v. Vintage Sports Plaques, 136 F.3d 1443 (11th Cir. 1998).

[159] See Landham v. Lewis Galoob Toys, Inc., 227 F.3d 619 (6th Cir. 2000); Hauf v. Life Extension Foundation, 547 F.Supp.2d 771 (W.D. Mich. 2008).

[160] See Restatement of Unfair Competition § 49, cmt. b (1995).

[161] See Landham v. Lewis Galoob Toys, Inc., 227 F.3d 619 (6th Cir. 2000) (discussing several cases).

[162] Presley's Estate v. Russen, 513 F.Supp. 1339 (D.N.J. 1981).

[163] Zacchini v. Scripps Howard Broadcasting Co., 433 U. S. 562, 97 S.Ct. 2849 53 L.Ed.2d 965 (1977).

[164] White v. Samsung Electronics America, Inc., 971 F.2d 1395 (9th Cir. 1992).

thought the advertiser could be liable for using her "identity" for commercial purposes.[165] Proof that defendant published a TV commercial in which a bandleader is shown playing Auld Lang Syne on New Year's Eve with the tempo and gestures of Guy Lombardo, was sufficient to create a factual question whether the defendant was guilty of a commercial appropriation of Lombardo's identity.[166] Other cases have given actors rights in their portrayal of fictional characters, even though the actors do not own the copyright on the script and did not create the set in which they acted.[167] Such cases raise questions whether the defendant has appropriated something of the plaintiff's personality or has merely appropriated the role he was playing, which, in the medieval metaphysics of intellectual property, is owned by someone else altogether.

Descendability. Some courts and legislatures have expanded[168] the right of publicity in another direction by holding that the right of publicity survives the death of the person whose identity is used, permitting the estate of performers like Elvis Presley or their licensees to control the uses of the image and even the general style of the performer long after the performer's death.[169] Some other states, by statute or otherwise, have limited the right of publicity to the protection of living persons,[170] and England does not recognize the claim at all with the result that, where English law governs, American entrepreneurs can sell dolls and plates commemorating Princess Diana without approval from her estate.[171] But about half of the states, by statute or court decision, have permitted descent of the right to heirs or devisees.[172]

Criticisms and alternatives. The leading treatise author on the subject strongly favors the right of publicity,[173] but some thinkers have suggested that protection ought to extend mainly to the use of name or likeness. One potential limitation upon the more expansive forms of the publicity right is that the federal copyright statute could be interpreted to preempt some publicity rights, as the Seventh Circuit actually held.[174] More recently, it has become possible to see that protection of intangible rights in a performer's persona apart from name and likeness is really not protection of identity but protection for creative efforts. Protection for creative efforts, it can be argued, should be

---

[165] Some courts have rejected the notion that a "character" created by a person is the same as that person's "identity." See Donchez v. Coors Brewing Co., 392 F.3d 1211 (10th Cir. 2004) (brewery's use of term "beerman" in advertising did not violate the right of publicity of plaintiff beer vendor who had developed the character "Bob the Beerman" at athletic events; while the "character might have been a celebrity, the vendor was not," and the brewery did not use the vendor's actual likeness in its ads).

[166] Lombardo v. Doyle, Dane & Bernbach, Inc., 58 A.D.2d 620, 396 N.Y.S.2d 661 (1977).

[167] Wendt v. Host Intern., Inc., 125 F.3d 806 (9th Cir. 1997) ("Norm" and "Cliff" of the television program *Cheers*).

[168] Rights of privacy and reputation traditionally die with the person, so that, for example, there is no liability for "defaming" the dead.

[169] Cal. Civ. Code § 990 (only specifying name, voice, signature, photograph or likeness); Presley's Estate v. Russen, 513 F.Supp. 1339 (D.N.J. 1981) (performance style and pose); Martin Luther King, Jr., Center for Social Change, Inc. v. American Heritage Products, Inc., 250 Ga. 135, 296 S.E.2d 697 (1982).

[170] New York's statute refers specifically to living persons, and has been held to be the exclusive source of rights in New York. Stephano v. News Group Publications, Inc., 64 N.Y.2d 174, 474 N.E.2d 580, 485 N.Y.S.2d 220 (1984).

[171] Cairns v. Franklin Mint Co., 292 F.3d 1139 (9th Cir. 2002) (holding that California statutory rights did not govern and that the estate its assignees had no right under English law).

[172] See 2 McCarthy on Publicity and Privacy § 9.18 (listing states). E.g., Toffoloni v. LFP Publ'g Group, LLC, 572 F.3d 1201 (11th Cir. 2009) (estate of professional female wrestler stated claim for violation of right of publicity against publisher of nude photographs taken 20 years prior to her death).

[173] See 1 McCarthy on Publicity and Privacy § 5:67.

[174] Baltimore Orioles, Inc. v. Major League Baseball Players Ass'n, 805 F.2d 663 (7th Cir. 1986).

left to copyright laws when the creation is fixed in a tangible medium, and otherwise left to confidentiality agreements or to the public domain.[175] Behind the desire to restrict liability for less-tangible aspects of persona are concerns for free speech and free competition. In addition, as has been noted in connection with copyright issues, art historically builds on art, even if it uses ideas or forms peculiarly associated with others artists. Too much restriction on the ability of one artist such as an Elvis impersonator may not only reward fame; it may defeat creativity as well.

---

[175] See David W. Melville & Harvey S. Perlman, Protection for Works of Authorship Through the Law of Unfair Competition: Right of Publicity and Common Law Copyright Reconsidered, 42 St. Louis U. L.J. 363 (1998).

Table of Cases

509 Sixth Avenue Corp. v. New York City Transit Authority.................................. 95

532 Madison Avenue Gourmet Foods, Inc. v. Finlandia Center, Inc. 745

625 3rd St. Assocs., L.P. v. Alliant Credit Union.. 1133

A. v. B.. 1170

A.B., Matter of....................................... 173

A.C., In re.. 514

A.H. v. Rockingham Publ'g Co., Inc......... 266

A.J. Decoster Co. v. Westinghouse Elec. Corp.. 804, 1085

A.O. Smith Corp. v. United States 556

A.R.B. v. Elkin.. 83

A.R.H. v. W.H.S. 621

A.S. Beck Shoe Corp. v. Johnson 1094

A.W. v. Lancaster Cnty. Sch. Dist. 0001 ....205, 212, 647, 713

Abbott Labs. v. TEVA Pharms. USA, Inc. 1109

Abebe v. Benitez 292

Abernathy & Closther v. Buffalo Broad. Co., Inc. 1114

Ablin v. Richard O'Brien Plastering Co. 694

ABN AMRO Verzekeringen BV v. Geologistics Americas, Inc.................... 120

Abraham v. T. Henry Constr., Inc. 1088

Abrams v. City of Mattoon 855

Abramson v. Reiss 597

ABRY Partners V, L.P. v. F & W Acquisition LLC 1137

Absolon v. Dollahite 249

Access Telecom, Inc. v. MCI Telecomms. Corp. 1103

Acculog, Inc. v. Peterson 408

Ace Am. Ins. Co. v. Grand Banks Yachts, Ltd. 1084

Ackerman v. Kaufman 1041

Ackerman v. Lerwick 514

Acuna v. Turkish 517, 520, 671

Adames v. Sheahan 361, 757

Adams Bros. v. Clark 778

Adams v. Cleveland-Cliffs Iron Co. 736

Adams v. Copper Beach Townhome Communities, L.P. 1070

Adams v. Department of Motor Vehicles 150

Adams v. King Cnty. 704, 729, 1132

Adams v. Mills.. 243

Adams v. Murakami.................................. 865

Adams v. N. Ill. Gas Co. 218

Adams v. N.Y.C. Transit Auth................. 703

Adams v. National Bank of Detroit 42

Adams v. Star Enterprise 744

Adams v. State... 574

Adams v. Sussman & Hertzberg, Ltd... 1028

Adams v. United States 692

Adams v. Via Christi Reg'l Med. Ctr...... 497, 498, 874

Adams v. Wal-Mart Stores, Inc. 73

Adams v. Whitman 985

Adamsky v. Buckeye Local Sch. Dist. 438

Addy v. Jenkins....................................... 342

Adel v. Parkhurst.................................... 865

Adelphia Commc'ns Corp., In re............ 1145

Adickes v. Kress & Co............................. 582

Adkins v. Chevron, USA, Inc.................. 468

Adkins v. GAF Corp................................ 806

Adkins v. Thomas Solvent Co.................. 743

Admiral Ins. Co. v. Price-Williams............ 48

Advance Music Corp. v. American Tobacco Co. 1111, 1114

Advance Sign Group, LLC v. Optec Displays, Inc. 1098

Advincula v. United Blood Servs............ 496, 507, 529

Advocat, Inc. v. Sauer 538, 541, 544

Aebischer v. Stryker Corp. 430

Aegis Ins. Servs., Inc. v. 7 World Trade Co., L.P. 327

Aequitron Med., Inc. v. CBS, Inc........... 1092

Aesoph v. Kusser..................................... 1124

Aetna Building Maintenance Co., Inc. v. West 1204

Aetna Health Inc. v. Davila..................... 536

Afarian v. Massachusetts Elec. Co.......... 390

Affiliated FM Ins. Co. v. LTK Consulting Servs., Inc. 496, 1084

AFL Philadelphia LLC v. Krause.......... 1006

Afoa v. Port of Seattle 466

AG Capital Funding Partners, L.P. v. State St. Bank & Trust Co..................... 285, 288

Agar v. Orda 111

Agricultural Ins. v. Constantine 120

Aguallo v. City of Scottsbluff.................. 387

Aguilar v. Atl. Richfield Co...................... 240

Aguilar v. RP MRP Washington Harbour, LLC 1061

Ahles v. Aztec Enterprises, Inc. 126

Ahlstrom v. Salt Lake City Corp............. 759

Ahmed v. Pickwick Place Owners' Ass'n.. 474

AIDA v. Time Warner Entm't Co., L.P... 953

Aikens v. Debow............................373, 1070

Aikens v. Wisconsin 1110

Air Crash at Belle Harbor, N.Y. on Nov. 12, In re 692, 714

Air Wisconsin Airlines Corp. v. Hoeper... 955

1211

Aitken v. Industrial Comm'n 920
Aka v. Jefferson Hosp. Ass'n, Inc............ 670
Ake v. General Motors Corp............ 289, 818
Akin, Gump, Strauss, Hauer & Feld, LLP v.
    National Dev. & Research Corp. 317,
    1185
Akins v. Glens Falls City Sch. Dist. 422
Akins v. ICI Americas Inc. 1100
Akutagawa v. Laflin, Pick & Heer,
    P.A. 1183
Alabama Baptist Hosp. Bd. v. Carter..... 598
Alabama Power Co. v. Moore................. 391
Alaface v. Nat'l Investment Co. 244, 432
Alami v. Volkswagen of America, Inc..... 840
Alamo Rent-A-Car, Inc. v. Hamilton 362
Alamo Rent-A-Car, Inc. v. Mancusi..... 1026,
    1034
Alarid v. Vanier....................................... 259
Alaska State Bank v. Fairco. 946
Albala v. City of New York..................... 676
Alberino v. Balch 741
Albert v. Loksen 981
Alberts v. Schultz 333
Albrecht v. Zwaanshoek Holding en
    Financiering, B.V................................ 117
Albright v. Morton.................................. 946
Albritton v. Neighborhood Ctrs. Ass'n for
    Child Dev. 598
Alcala v. City of Corcoran 575
Alcorn v. Union Pacific R.R. Co. 356
Aldana v. School City of E. Chicago 305,
    307
Alder v. Bayer Corp., AGFA Div.... 314, 326,
    356, 629
Alderman's Inc. v. Shanks 244
Alderson v. Bonner........................... 705, 706
Alejandre v. Bull..................803, 1084, 1124
Alessio v. Fire & Ice, Inc. 611
Alexander v. Bozeman Motors, Inc........ 707,
    921
Alexander v. DeAngelo........................... 175
Alexander v. Federal Bureau of
    Investigation 1012
Alexander v. Medical Assocs. Clinic 460
Alexander v. Scheid................ 332, 333, 334
Alexander v. Turtur & Assocs., Inc. 1174
Ali v. City of Boston............................... 481
Ali v. Fisher 754, 896
Ali v. Playgirl, Inc.................................. 1208
Aliotta v. Nat'l R.R. Passenger Corp. 448,
    450, 451
Allaire v. St. Luke's Hosp....................... 669
Alldedge v. Good Samaritan Home,
    Inc.. 697
Allen, In re Estate of 182
Allen v. Allison 1168
Allen v. Bos. & M. R.R............................ 225
Allen v. Cox 780
Allen v. Dover Co-Recreational Softball
    League...................................... 421, 426
Allen v. Martin 1191
Allen v. Muskogee, Oklahoma 587

Allen v. National Video, Inc...................1208
Allen v. Safeway Stores, Inc. 1105
Allen v. Steele 1176
Allen v. Sully-Miller Contracting Co.......873
Allen v. Uni-First Corp. 743
Allen v. Walker 71
Alley v. Siepman 233, 258, 284
Allied Maintenance Corp. v. Allied
    Mechanical Trades, Inc. 1197
Allied-Signal, Inc. v. Fox 920
Allison v. Cnty. of Ventura 156
Allison v. Fiscus 142, 143, 145
Allison v. Ideal Laundry & Cleaners.......788
Allison v. Manetta...................................297
Allison v. Snelling & Snelling, Inc. 696
Allison v. Union Hosp., Inc. 1099
Allison v. Vintage Sports Plaques.........1208
Alloway v. General Marine Indus.,
    L.P...1083
Allred v. Harris 90
Allright Phoenix Parking, Inc. v.
    Shabala 120
Allstate Ins. Co. v. Dooley......................1158
Allstate Ins. Co. v. Hamilton Beach/Proctor
    Silex, Inc. 811
Allstate Ins. v. Campbell 57
All-Tech Telecom, Inc. v. Amway
    Corp..................................... 1072, 1126
Allyn v. McDonald..................................1172
Alma, Town of v. Azco Constr., Inc. 1084
Almota Farmers Elevator & Warehouse Co.
    v. United States.................................1142
Almy v. Grisham 707
Aloe Coal Co. v. Clark Equip. Co..........1085,
    1086
Alpert v. Shea Gould Climenko &
    Casey...1139
Alpha Funding Group v. Continental
    Funding, LLC 1091
Alphin v. Huguley Nursing Center 539
Alphonso v. Charity Hosp. of La. at New
    Orleans 854
Alsenz v. Clark County Sch. Dist. 693
Alston v. Advanced Brands and Importing
    Co...361
Alston v. City of Camden.........................575
Alston v. Hormel Foods Corp...................436
Alteiri v. Colasso......................................80
Altera Corp. v. Clear Logic, Inc. 1091
Alterra Healthcare Corp. v. Bryant 547
Altria Group, Inc. v. Good........................845
Aluminum Company of American v.
    Guthrie 460
Alvarado v. KOB-TV, LLC.....................1016
Alyeska Pipeline Serv. Co. v. Aurora Air
    Serv., Inc.............. 1097, 1098, 1101, 1108
Amann v. Faidy.......................................669
Amarillo, City of v. Martin 575
Amatulli v. Delhi Const. Corp. 838
Amaya v. Home Ice, Fuel & Supply
    Co. 209, 714

Amazing Spaces, Inc. v. Metro Mini
Storage 1201
AmBase Corp. v. Davis Polk &
Wardwell.................................... 1164, 1173
Ambling Management Co. v. Miller 759
Amchem Prods., Inc. v. Windsor............. 909
Amco Builders & Developers, Inc. v. Team
Act Joint Venture 1165
Amend v. Bell 408
America v. Sunspray Condo. Ass'n 312
American Bldg. Supply Corp. v. Petrocelli
Group, Inc. 1074
American Family Mut. Ins. Co. v.
Golke 1158
American Family Serv. Corp. v.
Michelfelder 1140
American Greetings Corporation v. Dan-
Dee Imports, Inc. 1201
American Guarantee & Liab. Ins. Co. v.
1906 Co...................................... 199, 1008
American Home Assurance Co. v. National
R.R. Passenger Corp. 767
American Italian Pasta Co. v. New World
Pasta Co. 1200
American Motorcycle Ass'n v. Superior
Court 882
American Multi-Cinema, Inc. v.
Brown 469
American Nat'l Fire Ins. Co. v. Schuss..... 58
American Nat'l Watermattress Corp. v.
Manville 853
American Powerlifting Ass'n v. Cotillo... 426
American Print Works v. Lawrence 159
American Rice, Inc. v. Producers Rice Mill,
Inc.. 1194, 1195
American States Ins. Co. v.
Guillermin 782, 783
American Tobacco Co., Inc. v.
Grinnell 809, 813
American Transmission, Inc. v. Channel 7
of Detroit, Inc..................................... 177
American Washboard Co. v. Saginaw Mfg.
Co... 1199
Amish v. Walnut Creek Development,
Inc.. 789
Ammondson v. Northwestern Corp. 700
Amos, Estate of v. Vanderbilt Univ. 500,
502, 660, 676
Ampex Corp. v. Cargle 953
Amphitheaters, Inc. v. Portland
Meadows... 735
AmSouth Bank, N.A. v. City of Mobile..... 91
Amyot v. Luchini 1127, 1129
Ananda Church of Self Realization v.
Massachusetts Bay Ins. Co. 111
Anaya v. Superior Court 369
Anchorage Chrysler Ctr., Inc. v.
DaimlerChrysler Corp..................... 1121
Andersen v. Edwards 857
Andersen v. Two Dot Ranch, Inc. ... 214, 779
Andersen v. Whitley.............................. 61, 62

Anderson Dev. Co., L.C. v. Tobias........1096,
1098, 1100
Anderson v. Am. Family Mut. Ins...........232
Anderson v. Baptist Med. Ctr..........916, 917
Anderson v. Beach 965
Anderson v. Cahill 477
Anderson v. Ceccardi 419
Anderson v. Chrysler Corp. 810
Anderson v. City of Springfield 483
Anderson v. Claiborne County Recreation
Club, Inc. 475
Anderson v. Continental Ins. Co. 1147
Anderson v. Creighton 586
Anderson v. Fisher Broad. Cos., Inc......1018
Anderson v. Fox Hill Village Homeowners
Corp..483, 630
Anderson v. Hollingsworth 520
Anderson v. Low Rent Housing Com'n of
Muscatine 163
Anderson v. Massillon..........................59, 60
Anderson v. Minneapolis, St. Paul & Sault
Ste. Marie Ry.......................................322
Anderson v. Morgan................................232
Anderson v. Nashua Corp........................217
Anderson v. Nebraska Dep't of Social
Services..342, 576
Anderson v. Owens-Corning Fiberglas
Corp..825
Anderson v. PPCT Management Systems,
Inc. 635
Anderson v. Serv. Merchandise Co.,
Inc. 304, 307, 308
Anderson v. St. Francis-St. George
Hosp. 62
Anderson v. State....................................569
Anderson v. Stream 594
Anderson v. Suiters 1016
Anderson v. W.R. Grace & Co..................746
Anderson v. Watson 407
Andres v. Alpha Kappa Lambda
Fraternity 665
Andrews v. Burke 302
Andrews v. Piedmont Airlines..................78
Andrews v. Ring........................... 1035, 1036
Andrews v. United States........................554
Anello v. Vinci 1040
Angelini v. OMD Corp. 669
Anglado v. Leaf River Forest Products,
Inc..743
Angland v. Mountain Creek Resort, Inc. 240
Angle v. Koppers, Inc...............................431
Anglin v. Kleeman 294
Anicet v. Gant 420, 612
Ann M. v. Pacific Plaza Shopping
Ctr...212, 640
Anonymous v. Anonymous 1053
Anselmo v. Tuck....................................341, 346
Anthony v. Abbott Labs...........................431
Antisdel v. Ashby 694
Antoniewicz v. Reszcynski......................460
Antwaun A. v. Heritage Mut. Ins. Co. ...491,
492

Anzalone v. Strand 1129
APG, Inc. v. MCI Telecomms. Corp. 1096, 1104
Apollo Group, Inc. v. Avnet, Inc. 1083, 1126
Appelgren v. Walsh 140
Applebaum v. Nemon 621
Aquilera v. Inservices, Inc. 919
Arato v. Avedon 519, 520
Arbino v. Johnson & Johnson 874
Arbogast v. Mid-Ohio Valley Med. Corp. 509
Arcand v. Evening Call Publ'g Co. 952
Archambault v. Soneco/Northeastern, Inc. 376
Arche v. United States 678, 681
Archer v. Sisters of Mercy Health Sys., St. Louis, Inc. 598, 599
Arcidi v. Nat'l Ass'n of Gov't Employees, Inc. 1145
Ardinger v. Hummell 236, 402
Arena v. Gingrich 522
Argoe v. Three Rivers Behavioral Ctr. & Psychiatric Solutions 713
Argus v. Scheppegrell 394, 528
Arkansas Release Guidance Foundation v. Needler 743
Arlowski v. Foglio 152
Armantrout v. Carlson 689
Armijo v. Miles 695
Armistead v. Minor 955
Armitage v. Decker 86, 97
Armoneit v. Elliott Crane Service, Inc. 774
Armory Park Neighborhood Ass'n v. Episcopal Community Services in Arizona 738, 741, 744, 745
Arms v. Halsey 260
Armstrong v. Best Buy Co. 470
Armstrong v. Eagle Rock Entm't, Inc. 1006
Armstrong v. Paoli Mem'l Hosp. 722
Armstrong v. United States 160
Arnold v. City of Cedar Rapids, Iowa 418, 422
Arnold v. Laird 781
Arnold v. Turek 694
Aronberg v. Tolbert 403
Aronson v. Harriman 515
Arpin v. United States 721, 855
Arreola v. Administrative Concepts 913
Arthaud v. Mutual of Omaha Ins. Co. 962, 998
Artilla Cove Resort, Inc. v. Hartley 1142
Artis v. Corona Corp. of Japan 821, 822
ASC Constr. Equip. USA, Inc. v. City Commercial Real Estate, Inc. 1106
Asgari v. City of Los Angeles 73, 78
Ash v. Ash 1034
Ash v. Continental Ins. Co. 1145
Ashcraft v. King 170
Ashcroft v. al-Kidd 585

Ashe v. Radiation Oncology Assocs. 515, 516, 521
Ashland Dry Goods Co. v. Wages 75
Ashley County, Arkansas v. Pfizer, Inc. 745
Ashworth v. Albers Med., Inc. 1119
Aslakson v. Gallagher Bassett Servs., Inc. 922
Aspen Exploration Corp. v. Sheffield 969
Aspiazu v. Mortimer 1136
Atascadero v. Merrill Lynch, Pierce, Fenner & Smith, Inc., City of 1125
Atchison v. District of Columbia 588
Atchison, T. & S. F. R. Co. v. Stanford 356
Atherton v. Devine 369
Atienza v. Taub 180
Atkins v. Swimwest Family Fitness Ctr. 411
Atkinson v. Bernard, Inc. 94, 734
Atlanta Coca-Cola Bottling Co. v. Ergle 305
Atlanta Enters. v. James 286
Atlanta Int'l Ins. Co. v. Bell 1167
Atlanta Transit Sys., Inc. v. Nowell 853
Atlanta, City of v. Chambers 566
Atlanta, City of v. Kleber 737
Atlantic Coast Airlines v. Cook 722
Atlantic Mut. Ins. Co. v. Kenney 367
Atlas Chemical Industries, Inc. v. Anderson 789
Attorney Grievance Comm'n of Md. v. James 1051
Auckenthaler v. Grundmeyer 426
Auer v. Paliath 757
Augsburger v. Homestead Mut. Ins. Co. 781
August Storck K.G. v. Nabisco, Inc. 1194
Ault v. International Harvester Co. 823
Auman v. School Dist. of Stanley-Boyd 481, 483
Austermiller v. Dosick 365
Austin v. City of Buffalo 613
Austin v. Inet Techs., Inc. 943
Austin v. Kaness 757
Austin v. Litvak 430
Australian Gold, Inc. v. Hatfield 1096, 1104
Auvil v. CBS 60 Minutes 1113, 1115
Avanta Fed. Credit Union v. Shupak 1123
Aversa v. United States 969
Averyt v. Wal-Mart Stores, Inc. 36, 856
Aviation Cadet Museum v. Hammer 734, 741, 747
Avila v. Citrus Cmty. Coll. Dist. 166, 423, 424
Avildsen v. Prystay 1026
Avilla v. Newport Grand Jai Alai LLC 1095, 1108
Ayala v. B & B Realty Co. 489
Ayala v. Washington 994
Ayash v. Dana-Farber Cancer Inst. 999
Aycock v. Wilmington & W. R. Co. 217

Ayers v. Jackson Twp. 441, 854
Ayres v. French 111
Ayuluk v. Red Oaks Assisted Living,
    Inc. 172, 539
Azzolino v. Dingfelder 679
B. Sanfield, Inc. v. Finlay Fine Jewelry
    Corp. 1201
B.D.G.S., Inc. v. Balio 1155
B.D.H. ex rel. S.K.L. v. Mickelson 677
Babb v. Lee Cnty. Landfill SC, LLC ... 89, 92
Babcock v. Mason County Fire Dist.
    No. 6 571
Babes Showclub, Jaba, Inc. v. Lair 607
Baby Boy Doe, Interest of v. Doe 62
Bachtel v. Miller County Nursing Home
    Dist. 546
Backiel v. Citibank, N.A. 468
Backlund v. Univ. of Washington 513
Badahman v. Catering St. Louis 356
Bader v. Johnson 677
Badger Pharmacal, Inc. v. Colgate-
    Palmolive Co. 1123
Bae v. Dragoo & Assoc., Inc. 474
Baer v. Slater 117
Baez, In re 1154
Bagent v. Blessing Care Corp. 758
Baggett v. Industrial Comm'n 916
Bagley v. Mazda Motor Corp. 821, 822
Bagley v. Mt. Bachelor, Inc. 413
Baglini v. Lauletta 1025, 1046
Bagnana v. Wolfinger 465
Bahr v. Harper-Grace Hosps. 509
Bahrle v. Exxon Corp. 767
Bailey v. Algonquin Gas Transmission
    Co. 1165
Bailey v. Bayer Cropscience 731
Bailey v. C.S. 58
Bailey v. Edward Hines Lumber Co. 631
Bailey v. Faulkner 1052
Bailey v. Lewis Farm, Inc. 353
Bailey v. Rose Care Ctr. Div. of C.A.R.E.,
    Inc. 538, 541
Bailey v. Searles-Bailey 728, 1052
Bajwa v. Metropolitan Life Ins. Co. 637
Baker Donelson Bearman Caldwell &
    Berkowitz, P.C. v. Seay 1166
Baker v. Burbank-Glendale-Pasadena
    Airport Authority 99
Baker v. Fabian, Thielen & Thielen 1171
Baker v. Howard County Hunt 778
Baker v. Joyal 224
Baker v. McCollan 156, 583
Baker v. Morrison 405
Baker v. Parsons 984
Baker v. Saint Francis Hosp. 757,
    758, 762
Baker v. Superior Court (Leach) 611
Baker v. Tremco Inc. 962
Baker, State ex rel. v. Coast to Coast
    Manpower, LLC 915
Bakerman v. The Bombay Co. 921

Balas v. Huntington Ingalls Industries,
    Inc. 63, 67
Balboa Island Vill. Inn, Inc. v.
    Lemen 1003
Baldonado v. El Paso Natural Gas Co. ... 610
Baldwin v. Mosley 478
Baliva v. State Farm Mut. Auto. Ins.
    Co. 706
Ball v. Birch, Horton, Bittner and
    Cherot 1171
Ball v. Nye 785
Ballalatak v. All Iowa Agric. Ass'n 1148
Ballard Group, Inc. v. BP Lubricants USA,
    Inc. 1091
Ballard Shipping Co. v. Beach
    Shellfish 1076
Ballard v. Uribe 267
Ballard v. Ypsilanti Tp. 483
Ball-Foster Glass Container Co. v.
    Giovanelli 914
Ballinger v. Thompson 1190
Ballou v. Sigma Nu Gen. Fraternity 232
Baltimore & O.R. Co. v. Goodman 10
Baltimore Gas & Elec. Co. v. Flippo 459
Baltimore Gas & Elec. Co. v. Lane 368
Baltimore Orioles, Inc. v. Major League
    Baseball Players Ass'n 1209
Bamberger & Feibleman v. Indianapolis
    Power & Light Co. 1067
Bamford v. Turnley 277
Bammerlin v. Navistar Intern. Transp.
    Corp. 844
Banaghan v. Bay State Elevator Co. 629
Bangert Bros. Constr. Co. v. Kiewit W.
    Co. 1120, 1131
Bangert v. Shaffner 425
Bangs v. Schroth 1166
Bank of California, N.A. v. First American
    Title Ins. Co. 1074
Bank of Eureka Springs v. Evans 1027
Bank of New York v. Sheff 1181
Banker v. McLaughlin 476, 477
Bankhead v. ArvinMeritor, Inc. 866, 869
Banknorth, N.A. v. BJ's Wholesale Club,
    Inc. 1066, 1081
Banks v. Beckwith 292, 297, 300, 307
Banks v. Fritsch 706
Banks v. ICI Americas, Inc. 821
Banks v. Montogomery Ward & Co.,
    Inc. 1031
Banks v. Sunrise Hosp. 856, 1157
Banks, In re 1167
Bankston v. Pass Road Tire Ctr.,
    Inc. 1027
Baptist Health v. Murphy 1097
Baptist Memorial Hosp. System v.
    Sampson 771
Barber v. LaFromboise 40
Barber v. Time, Inc. 1011, 1015
Barbera v. Brod-Dugan Co. 769
Barbie v. Minko Constr., Inc. 294
Barbina v. Curry 571

Barcai v. Betwee 517
Barclay v. Briscoe 758
Bardis v. Oates 1145
Barger v. McCoy Hillard & Parks 1117
Barillari v. City of Milwaukee 574
Barker v. Kallash 402
Barker v. Lull Engineering Co 815, 822, 824
Barkley v. Corrections Div 915
Barnaby v. A. & C. Properties 244
Barnes v. Koppers 430
Barnes v. Martin 150, 151
Barnes v. Paulin 407
Barnes v. Turner 1180
Barnes v. United States 267
Barnett v. Clark 757, 761, 762
Barnett v. Mobile County Personnel
   Bd. 992
Barnette v. Wilson 942
Barnhart v. Paisano Publ'ns, LLC 1006
Barnish v. KWI Building Co. 810, 811
Barquis v. Merchants Collection Ass'n of
   Oakland 1044, 1045
Barreca v. Nickolas 968, 973, 982, 983
Barret, Doering ex rel. v. Copper Mountain,
   Inc. 596
Barrett v. Danbury Hosp. 726
Barrett v. Lucky Seven Saloon, Inc. 251
Barrett v. Montesano 430
Barrett v. Mt. Brighton, Inc. 423
Barrett v. Rosenthal 971, 972
Barrie v. V.P. Exterminators, Inc. 1076, 1124
Barrio v. San Manuel Div. Hosp. For
   Magma Copper Co. 437
Barris v. County of Los Angeles 532
Barry v. Quality Steel Products, Inc. 376, 377
Bartell v. State 176
Barth v. Coleman 896
Bartnicki v. Vopper 1015
Barton v. Adams Rental, Inc. 815
Barton v. City of Bristol 1123
BASF Corp. v. Symington 432
Basham v. Hunt 381
Baska v. Scherzer 59, 65, 79, 81
Bass v. Stryker Corp. 847
Bass, In re 1204
Basso v. Miller 478
Bateman v. Mello 477
Bates v. Southgate 1136, 1137
Battaglieri v. Mackinac Ctr. for Pub.
   Policy 1007
Battalla v. State 721, 722
Battle v. Thornton 1170
Baudanza v. Comcast of Mass. I, Inc. 386
Bauer v. State 579, 969
Baugh v. CBS, Inc. 87
Bauldock v. Davco Food, Inc. 759
Baum v. Burrington 671
Baum v. United States 557

Bauman ex rel. Chapman v.
   Crawford 233, 258
Baumeister v. Plunkett 761
Baxter v. Noce 394
Bayer CropScience LP v. Schafer 875, 1060
Bayer v. Crested Butte Mountain Resort,
   Inc. 450
BDO Seidman, LLP v. Mindis Acquisition
   Corp 1140
BE&K Const. Co. v. NLRB 1047
Beach v. Lipham 505
Beach v. University of Utah 648
Beacon Residential Cmty. Ass'n v.
   Skidmore, Owings & Merrill LLP 204
Beal Bank, SSB v. Arter & Haddon,
   LLP 1181
Beal v. City of Seattle 626
Bean v. Gutierrez 1019
Bearbower v. Merry 1050
Beard v. Flying J, Inc. 83
Beard v. Johnson and Johnson, Inc. 817
Beardsley v. Wierdsma 682
Beatty v. Central Iowa Ry. Co. 269
Beaudrie v. Henderson 572
Beauharnais v. Illinois 953
Beaulieu v. Elliott 859
Beaux v. Jacob 1126
Beaver v. Grand Prix Karting Ass'n,
   Inc. 720
Beaver v. Howard Miller Clock Co. 818
Beavers v. West Penn Power Co 101
Bebo Const. Co. v. Mattox & O'Brien,
   P.C. 1170
Bechtel v. Liberty Nat'l Bank 1140
Beck v. Dobrowski 200
Beck v. Law Offices of Edwin J. (Ted) Terry,
   Jr., P.C. 1164
Beck v. State 716
Beck v. Wecht 1175
Beck v. Woodward Affiliates 767
Beckles v. Madden 512
Beddingfield v. Linam 787
Bedor v. Johnson 220
Beecher v. Dull 748
Beecher, LLC v. Unizan Bank, Nat'l
   Ass'n 1083
Beggs v. State, Dep't of Soc. & Health
   Servs. 247
Behr v. Richmond 1118
Behrendt v. Gulf Underwriters Ins. 212, 265
Behrens v. Raleigh Hills Hosp., Inc. 694
Belcher v. Wal-Mart Stores, Inc. 938, 955, 972
Belhumeur v. Zilm 624, 629, 734
Belk v. Cheshire 1186
Bell v. Chisom 568
Bell v. Hutsell 665
Bell v. Industrial Vangas, Inc. 921

Bell v. Michigan Council 25 of Am. Fed'n of State, County & Mun. Employees, AFL-CIO, Local 1023 1073

Bell v. National Republican Cong. Comm. 945

Bell v. Simmons 959

Bell, Bell ex rel. v. Dawson 621

Bella v. Aurora Air, Inc. 785

Bellah v. Greenson 501

Bellino v. McGrath North Mullin & Kratz, PC LLO 1174

Bellville v. Farm Bureau Mut. Ins. Co. 1147

Below v. Norton 1082

Bemis v. Estate of Bemis 128

Bendix Corp. v. Adams 1104

Bendix Corp. v. Stagg 847

Benefield v. Pep Boys-Manny, Moe & Jack, Inc. 604

Benesh v. New Era, Inc. 768

Benham v. King 305, 468

Benik v. Hatcher 492

Beninati v. Black Rock City, LLC 416

Benjamin v. Wal-Mart Stores, Inc. 829

Bennett v. Butlin 511

Bennett v. Dunn 136

Bennett v. Gordon 688

Bennett v. Hill-Boren, P.C. 1181

Bennett v. Ohio Dep't of Rehab. & Correction 77, 163

Bennett v. Stanley 475

Bennett v. State 225

Bennett v. Trevecca Nazarene Univ. 603, 604

Bennett v. United States 563

Bennett, In re Estate of 694

Benson v. Kutsch 570, 571

Bentley v. Bunton 954

Berberian v. Lynn 226, 420

Berdyck v. Shinde 496

Berenger v. Frink 688

Berg v. Reaction Motors Division 787

Berg v. Wiley 148, 152

Berger v. Temple Beth-El of Great Neck 976

Bergman v. Hupy 974

Bergstreser v. Mitchell 676

Bergstrom v. Noah 1169, 1171

Berkovitz by Berkovitz v. United States 554, 555

Berlangieri v. Running Elk Corp. 413

Berliner v. Clukay 1103

Berman v. Rubin 1178

Bernard v. Char 521

Bernethy v. Walt Failor's Inc. 653

Bernier v. Boston Edison Co. 272

Berrios v. United Parcel Serv. 413

Berry v. Sugar Notch Borough 354

Berry v. Watchtower Bible and Tract Soc'y of New York 455, 456

Berschauer/Phillips Constr. Co. v. Seattle Sch. Dist. No. 1 1079

Berte v. Bode 316, 317, 338

Bertelmann v. Taas Associates 663

Berten v. Pierce 314

Bertero v. National General Corp. 1036

Bertrand v. Mullin 995

Besette v. Enderlin Sch. Dist. No. 22 283

Beshears v. United Sch. Dist. No. 305 647

Best v. Malec 1009

Best v. Taylor Mach. Works 433, 875

Betaco, Inc. v. Cessna Aircraft Co. 1128

Bethlehem Steel Corp. v. Ernst & Whinney 1135

Bethlehem Steel Corp., United States v. 1149

Betsinger v. D.R. Horton, Inc. 700

Bettel v. Yim 79

Betterton v. Leichtling 515, 517

Bettinger v. Field Container Co. 943

Beupre v. Pierce County 608

Beuster v. Equifax Info. Servs. 964

Bevan v. Fix 709, 712

Bexiga v. Havir Mfg. Corp. 375, 393, 837

Bey v. Sacks 523

Beyer v. Todd 220

Bhatia v. Mehak, Inc. 600

Bhinder v. Sun Co. 896

Biakanja v. Irving 209

Bible Baptist Church v. City of Cleburne 734

BIC Pen Corp. v. Carter 805, 846

Bicknese v. Sutula 1119

Biddle v. Sartori Memorial Hospital 530

Bidiman v. Gehrts 467

Bidna v. Rosen 1037, 1047

Biercyznski v. Rogers 881

Bigbee v. Pac. Tel. & Tel. Co. 265, 367

Billups v. Scott 1179

Bily v. Arthur Young & Co. 1134, 1135

Binder v. General Motors Acceptance Corp. 151

Bing v. Thunig 529

Biomet v. Finnegan Henderson LLP 1170, 1171

Biondi v. Nassimos 959, 960

Biosera, Inc. v. Forma Scientific, Inc. 812

Biosynexus, Inc. v. Glaxo Group Ltd. 1145

Bird v. Holbrook 144

Bird v. Hudson 954

Bird v. Saenz 718

Bird v. W.C.W. 1057

Bird, Marella, Boxer & Wolpert v. Superior Court 1189

Birkner v. Salt Lake Cty. 226

Birmingham Coal & Coke Co. v. Johnson 787

Birnbaum v. United States 562

Bishop Processing Co. v. Davis 747

Bishop v. Poore 853

Bishop v. TES Realty Trust 489

Bismarck Hotel Co. v. Sutherland 1040

Bisno v. Douglas Emmett Realty Fund 1988 1038

Bissell v. Town of Amherst 855
Bisso v. Inland Waterways Corp. 120
Bitar v. Rahman 504
Bivens v. Six Unknown Named Agents of
    Fed. Bur. of Narcotics 248, 582, 969
BJ's Wholesale Club, Inc. v. Rosen 414
Bjerke v. Johnson 172
Bjorgen v. Kinsey 437, 1181
Bjorndal v. Weitman 221
Black & Yates v. Mahogany Ass'n 1113
Black v. Comer 854
Black v. Kroger Co................................... 76
Black v. Power 437
Blackford v. Prairie Meadows Racetrack
    and Casino, Inc. 111
Blackstock v. Kohn.............................. 1177
Blackstone v. Cashman........................ 1095
Blackwell v. Wyeth................................. 674
Bladen v. First Presbyterian Church of
    Sallisaw... 180
Blahd v. Richard B. Smith, Inc. 1065,
    1087
Blain v. Doctor's Company 1178
Blair v. Campbell........................... 214, 604
Blair v. McDonagh............................... 1144
Blair v. Ohio Dep't of Rehab. & Corr..... 465,
    466
Blair v. West Town Mall 469
Blakeley v. Shortal's Estate............ 688, 711
Blakely v. Austin-Weston Ctr. for Cosmetic
    Surgery LLC 59
Blakes v. Blakes 229
Blanchard v. Kellum 515
Blankenship v. Cincinnati Milacron
    Chems., Inc. 922
Blankenship v. Staton........................... 1041
Blanks v. Seyfarth Shaw....1170, 1171, 1185
Blatty v. New York Times Co. 1092, 1115
Blazevska v. Raytheon Aircraft Co......... 434
Bleck v. Power 1181
Block v. Neal... 562
Blodgett v. University Club 938, 982
Blomberg v. Cox Enters., Inc. 950
Blonski v. Metropolitan Dist. Com'n 483
Bloom v. Hennepin County 1151
Bloom v. Hensel 1166, 1167
Bloskas v. Murray 514
Blount v. Bordens, Inc........................... 296
Bloxom v. Bloxom 829
Blue Fox Bar, Inc. v. City of Yankton..... 566
Blue v. Environmental Engineering,
    Inc... 820
Blueflame Gas, Inc. v. Van Hoose........... 217
Blum v. Airport Terminal Servs., Inc..... 856
Blumenthal v. Drudge............................ 972
Blunt v. Medtronic, Inc. 719, 720
Bly v. Tri-Continental Indus., Inc. 330
BMK Corp. v. Clayton Corp. 1091, 1105
BMW of N. Am. v. Gore.................. 868, 871
Board of Comm'rs v. Nevitt.................... 721
Board of County Com'rs of Cecil County v.
    Dorman 487

Board of Educ. of Farmingdale Union Free
    Sch. Dist. v. Farmingdale Classroom
    Teachers Ass'n, Inc., Local 1899.......1043,
    1045
Board of Regents of the University System
    of Georgia v. Riddle...............................576
Board of Supervisors for Louisiana State
    University Agricultural and Mechanical
    College v. Smack Apparel Co.............1194
Board of Trs. of Cmty. Coll. Dist. No. 508,
    County of Cook v. Coopers &
    Lybrand 1132
Bob Allyn Masonry v. Murphy 914
Bobb v. Bosworth 150
Bochetto v. Gibson 966
Bodah v. Lakeville Motor Express,
    Inc. 1014
Bode v. Clark Equipment Co. 889, 890
Bodell Constr. Co. v. Ohio Pac. Tech,
    Inc. 1090, 1098
Bodenheimer v. Confederate Mem'l
    Ass'n...597
Bodiford v. Lubitz 511
Boeken v. Philip Morris USA, Inc. 720
Boerner v. Brown & Williamson Tobacco
    Corp..821
Bogan v. Scott-Harris 578, 585
Bohrer v. DeHart 899
Boies v. Cole 693
Boisdore v. International City Bank &
    Trust Co. 116
Boiter v. South Carolina Dep't of
    Transp..873
Bokum v. Elkins....................................1038
Boland v. Stanley...................................1050
Bolduc v. Bailey.......................................999
Boles v. Sun Ergoline, Inc......................801
Bolick v. Sunbird Airlines.......................219
Bolin v. Wingert.....................................670
Bollin v. Elevator Const. & Repair Co. ...629
Boltax v. Joy Day Camp 373
Bonbrest v. Kotz......................................669
Bond v. Lincoln Elec. Co. 828
BondPro Corp. v. Siemens Power
    Generation, Inc. 1204, 1205
Bondu v. Gurvich 1160
Bondy v. Allen 450
Bonhomme v. St. James 1119
Bonilla v. University of Mont. 307
Bonin v. Vannaman 594
Bonito Boats, Inc. v. Thunder Craft Boats,
    Inc. 1193, 1202, 1203
Bonome v. Kaysen..................................1013
Bonpua v. Fagan 400
Bonte v. Bonte 675
Booker, Inc. v. Morrill..............................59
Boomer v. Atlantic Cement Co. 735, 747
Boomer v. Frank 383
Boone v. Boone 592
Boone v. William W. Backus Hosp. 333
Boorman v. Nev. Mem'l Cremation
    Soc'y 112, 704, 729

Booth v. Quality Carriers, Inc. 447
Booth v. Santa Barbara Biplanes,
  LLC.. 411
Borcherding v. Anderson Remodeling Co.,
  Inc.. 1121
Boren v. Weeks....................................... 770
Boren v. Worthen Nat'l Bank of
  Arkansas 466, 640
Borish v. Russell................................... 1126
Borland v. Sanders Lead Co. 92, 736
Borley Storage & Transfer Co. v.
  Whitted...................................... 403, 404
Boros v. Baxley 1183
Boroughs v. Joiner.................................. 767
Borrelli, People v. 73
Bortz v. Noon 1128
Boryla v. Pash... 856
Bosley v. Wildwett.com 1006
Bostick v. Flex Equip. Co. 903
Boswell v. Phoenix Newspapers, Inc. ... 1004
Botelho v. Caster's, Inc........... 292, 293, 382
Boulter v. Eli & Bessie Cohen Found. 609
Bourgonje v. Machev 625, 627
Bourne v. Mary Gilman, Inc. 820
Bouse v. Fireman's Fund Ins. Co............ 918
Boutwell v. Domino's Pizza 917
Bovee v. Gravel.................................... 1167
Bovsun v. Sanperi........................... 714, 715
Bowan, Bowan ex rel. v. Express Med.
  Transporters, Inc. 286
Bowden v. Caldor 866
Bowden v. Young..................................... 922
Bowen v. City of New York 438
Bowen v. Independent Publ'g Co. 947
Bowen v. Lumbermens Mut. Cas. Co. ... 716,
  718, 723
Bower v. Harrah's Laughlin, Inc. 363
Bower v. Westinghouse Elec. Corp. 854
Bowers v. Westvaco Corp. 734
Bowie v. Murphy 70
Bowler v. Joyner.................................... 114
Bowling v. City of Oxford 789
Bowling v. Foster.................................... 514
Bowling v. Heil Co................................... 836
Bowl-Mor Co., Inc. v. Brunswick
  Corp.. 1097
Bowman v. Doherty............................... 1189
Bowman v. Presley................................ 1137
Bowman v. United States 569
Bowyer v. Loftus...................................... 758
Boyanton v. Reif...................................... 505
Boycher v. Livingston Parish School
  Board 478
Boyd v. Albert Einstein Medical
  Center... 534
Boyd v. Goffoli 870
Boyd v. Moore 216
Boyd v. Nat'l R.R. Passenger Corp. 242
Boyd v. Racine Currency Exchange,
  Inc.. 643
Boyd v. Travelers Ins. Co. 1159, 1160
Boyer v. Anchor Disposal 612

Boyer v. Iowa High Sch. Athletic
  Ass'n..422
Boyer v. Johnson.....................................234
Boyer v. Waples...............................132, 135
Boyle v. Revici................................410, 420
Boyle v. United Technologies Corp. 580
Boyle v. Welsh.............................1169, 1172
Boyrie v. E & G Property Services 460
Brabant v. Republic Servs., Inc.......593, 594
Brabazon v. Joannes Bros. 101
Brackett v. Focus Hope, Inc....................913
Brackett v. Peters 732
Braden v. Workman..................................286
Bradford v. Feeback.................................474
Bradford v. Universal Const. Co. 365, 485
Bradley v. American Smelting & Refining
  Co...56, 736
Bradley v. Armstrong Rubber Co. 742
Bradley v. Atlantic City Bd. of Educ. 1010
Bradley v. Hunter 135
Bradley v. Sanchez....................1155, 1156
Bradley v. United States 560
Bradley v. Welch 475
Bradshaw v. Daniel.........................366, 501
Bradshaw v. Joseph 578, 1191
Bradshaw v. State Farm Mut. Auto.
  Ins. 1038, 1039
Bradt v. White.......................................1179
Bradway v. American Nat'l Red Cross....434
Brady v. Louis Ruffolo & Sons Constr.
  Co...915
Brady v. Maryland...................................583
Brady, People v. 352, 354
Bragg v. Genesee County Agr. Soc. 482
Bramble v. Thompson.............................147
Bramlette v. Charter-Medical-
  Columbia..................................227, 394
Brammer v. Dotson..................................727
Branch v. Western Petroleum, Inc..........789
Brandenburg v. Briarwood Forestry
  Services 767
Brandert v. Scottsbluff Nat'l Bank & Trust
  Co. 470
Brandon v. Cnty. of Richardson 382, 390,
  692, 708, 892
Brandon v. Gazette Pub. Co. 977, 979
Brandt v. Cnty. of Pennington 98
Branham v. Ford Motor Co.....................295
Branham v. Loews Orpheum Cinemas,
  Inc..295
Branks v. Kern.......................................466
Branson v. Donaldson............................1029
Braswell v. Braswell 571
Braswell v. Cincinnati Inc.....................820
Braswell, Estate of v. People's Credit
  Union 1131
Bratton v. Bond......................................506
Bratton v. McDonough............................709
Brauer v. Globe Newspaper Co. 940, 945,
  947
Braun v. Armour & Co.............................951
Bravman v. Baxter Healthcare Corp. 816

Bravo v. United States 855

Brawner v. Richardson............................ 383

Bray v. Providence Journal Co. 977

Bray v. St. John Health System, Inc. 639

Breger v. City of New York 486

Brehany v. Nordstrom, Inc. 981

Brehm v. Eisner..................................... 1145

Breiggar Properties, L.C. v. H.E. Davis &
  Sons, Inc. 98

Brent v. Mathias.................................... 1052

Brett v. Great Am. Recreations, Inc. 423

Breunig v. American Family Ins. 225

Brewer v. Furtwangler 147

Brewer v. Hagemann 1187, 1191

Brewer v. J.B. Hunt Transp. Inc. 895

Brewer v. State............................. 158, 160

Brewster v. Colgate-Palmolive Co. 603,
  605

Brewster v. Rush-Presbyterian-St. Luke's
  Medical Center.................................... 635

Brewster v. United States....... 293, 297, 309

Brewster, United States v...................... 581

Briarcliff Nursing Home, Inc. v.
  Turcotte.. 694

Bridge v. Park Nat'l Bank...................... 1099

Bridges v. Park Place Entertainment 663

Bridgestone/Firestone North America Tire,
  LLC v. Naranjo 881

Bridgestone/Firestone, Inc. v.
  Glyn-Jones 408

Bridport, Town of v. Sterling Clark Lurton
  Corp. 828, 829, 833

Briesemeister v. Lehner........................ 1095

Brigance v. Velvet Dove Rest., Inc......... 280,
  662

Briggs v. Morgan 287

Bright v. Cargill, Inc. 774

Brimelow v. Casson................... 1094, 1095

Brisbon v. Mount Sinai Hosp................ 308

Briscoe v. LaHue 1024, 1025

Bristol, City of v. Tilcon Minerals, Inc. ... 88,
  91, 99

Bristow v. Flurry................................... 293

Britt Builders, Inc. v. Brister.................. 97

Britton v. Soltes.................................... 502

Britton v. Wooten 363, 364

Broadbent v. Broadbent 594, 595

Broadley v. State 70

Broadmoor Apartments of Charleston v.
  Horwitz....................................... 1044, 1045

Broadnax v. Gonzalez............................ 730

Broadwell v. Holmes 594

Brochu v. Ortho Pharmaceutical
  Corp... 806, 828

Brock v. Peabody Coop. Equity Exch..... 382,
  383

Brock v. Thompson.......................... 944, 953

Brock v. United States 563

Brock v. Watts Realty Co., Inc........ 244, 644

Brodeur v. Hayes.................................. 1172

Brodie v. Summit County Children Services
  Board.. 570

Brogan v. Mitchell Int'l, Inc................... 1139

Brogdon v. National Healthcare Corp.....546

Brokaw v. Winfield-Mt. Union Cmty. Sch.
  Dist.......................................216, 267, 862

Bronsen v. Dawes County................479, 483

Brookhaven Steam Laundry v. Watts.....915

Brooks v. Beech Aircraft Corp.................801

Brooks v. Lewin Realty III, Inc. 36

Brooks v. United States....................559, 560

Brooks v. Zebre.....................................1176

Brotherton v. Day & Night Fuel Co. 259

Brown Eyes v. South Dakota Dep't of Social
  Services...580

Brown Transport Corp. v. James 438

Brown v. Blaine.....................................970

Brown v. Brown.....................................592

Brown v. Buffalo & State Line R.R. 250

Brown v. Campbell..................................125

Brown v. Collins.....................................785

Brown v. Commonwealth of Pennsylvania,
  Dep't of Health Emergency Medical
  Services Training Institute..................649

Brown v. Crown Equipment Corp. 821

Brown v. Dellinger 85, 87, 101

Brown v. Denny......................................1056

Brown v. Dibbell............................393, 523

Brown v. Dillard's, Inc. 759

Brown v. Diversified Hospitality Group,
  Inc..56

Brown v. Ellis..1051

Brown v. Florida Chautauqua Ass'n 745

Brown v. Gatti.......................................944

Brown v. Glaxo, Inc.................................828

Brown v. Hurley......................................1049

Brown v. Kelly..1173

Brown v. Kendall 29, 194, 777

Brown v. Martinez 80

Brown v. Mayor......................................762

Brown v. Merlo........................47, 241

Brown v. North Carolina Wesleyan
  College 648

Brown v. Oklahoma State Bank & Trust Co.
  of Vinita 1153

Brown v. Patel..1147

Brown v. Patterson 183

Brown v. Pine Bluff Nursing Home 697

Brown v. Poway Unified Sch. Dist. 300,
  308

Brown v. Quik Trip Corp. 917

Brown v. Racquet Club of Bricktown 308

Brown v. Robishaw 59

Brown v. Shyne.............................253, 494

Brown v. Soh 414

Brown v. Spokane Cty. Fire Prot. Dist.
  No. 1...220

Brown v. Superior Court.................330, 823

Brown v. Theos............................1187, 1188

Brown v. United States...........................560

Brown v. United States Stove Co. 839

Brown, United States v....................559, 560

Brownelli v. McCaughtry.........................621

Browning-Ferris Indus. of Vt., Inc. v. Kelco Disposal, Inc. 867

Bruce v. Byrne-Stevens & Associates Engineers, Inc. 113 Wash.2d 123 1024

Brucker v. Mercola 674

Bruesewitz v. Wyeth LLC 845, 929

Brugh v. Peterson 296

Brune v. Belinkoff 508, 509

Brunell v. Wildwood Crest Police Dep't 918

Bruns v. City of Centralia 471

Brunson v. Affinity Federal Credit Union 1028, 1029, 1037

Brunswick, Town of v. Hyatt 566, 567

BRW, Inc. v. Dufficy & Sons, Inc. 1074, 1081, 1126

Bryan v. Burt 506

Bryan v. Sherick 505

Bryant County, Board of County Comn'rs of v. Brown 586, 587, 588

Bryant v. Calantone 403

Bryant v. HCA Health Servs. of No. Tennessee, Inc. 514

Bryant v. Hoffmann-La Roche, Inc. 815

Bryant, Madison ex rel. v. Babcock Center, Inc. 384, 570, 633, 770

Bryson v. News Am. Publ'ns, Inc. 949, 963

Bubb v. Brusky 518

Buchanan v. Doe 3

Buchanan v. Leonard 967

Buckeye Check Cashing, Inc. v. Cardegna 1137

Buckley v. Bell 374

Buckman Co. v. Plaintiffs' Legal Committee 442, 845

Buczkowski v. McKay 284, 287

Budgetel Inns, Inc. v. Micros Sys., Inc. 1082

Buel v. ASSE Int'l, Inc. 396

Bufalino v. Associated Press 977

Buffets, Inc. v. Klinke 1204

Bufkin v. Felipe's Louisiana, LLC 473

Bullard v. Barnes 690

Buono v. Scalia 595

Burbage v. Burbage.............................. 1000

Burbank Grease Servs., LLC v. Sokolowski 1106, 1145, 1205

Burch v. Nedpower Mount Storm, LLC 739

Buren v. Midwest Indus., Inc. 606

Burgbacher v. Lazar 258

Burgdorfer v. Thielemann...................... 1136

Burgess v. Busby 1018

Burgess v. Clements................................ 191

Burgess v. Reformer Publ'g Corp. 950

Burgess v. Shampooch Pet Indus., Inc. 857

Burke v. Rivo 682

Burkons v. Ticor Title Ins. Co. of Cal. 1135

Burless v. West Virginia University Hospitals, Inc. 770

Burley v. Kytec Innovative Sports Equipment, Inc. 810, 817

Burlington N. & Santa Fe Ry. Co. v. United States...............................878, 885

Burnett v. Al Baraka Inv. & Dev. Corp. 712

Burnett v. Columbus McKinnon Corp. ...890

Burns v. Hanson 678, 680

Burns v. McGraw Hill Broad. Co., Inc. ...945

Burns v. Metz 505

Burns v. Reed 578

Burns v. Smith 919

Burr v. Board of Cnty. Comm'rs of Stark Cnty. 678, 728

Burrow v. K-Mart Corp............................75

Burton v. Crowell Publ'g Co. 996

Burton v. Des Moines Metro. Transit Auth. 448

Burton v. R.J. Reynolds Tobacco Co..........40

Busby v. Quail Creek Golf & Country Club 254, 258, 663

Buscaglia v. United States 556

Buscher v. Boning..................................1037

Bush v. Industrial Comm'n 916

Bushong v. Garman Co............................833

Business Men's Assurance Co. of Am. v. Graham.................................405, 406

Busta v. Columbus Hosp. Corp. 350, 351

Buster v. George W. Moore, Inc.............1097

Busy Fee Buffet v. Ferrell 466

Butcher v. Gay 214

Butigan v. Yellow Cab Co. of Cal. 221

Butler v. Acme Markets, Inc. 639

Butler v. Flint Goodrich Hosp. 873, 875

Butler v. Mooers....................................1187

Butler v. Town of Argo............................578

Butler-Tulio v. Scroggins........................303

Butz v. Economou 581, 585

Byers v. Cummings................................1168

Bylsma v. Burger King Corp. 805

Byrd Theatre Found. v. Barnett.............598

Byrd v. Bowie..1172

Byrd v. English 1067

Byrd v. Faber 763

Byrne v. Schneider's Iron & Metal, Inc. 696

Byrns v. Riddell, Inc. 814

Byron Chemical Co. v. Groman.............1181

C.A. v. William S. Hart Union High School Dist.................................647, 658

C.A.R. Transp. Brokerage Co., Inc. v. Seay...125

C.B.C. Distribution and Marketing, Inc. v. Major League Baseball Advanced Media, L.P...1207

C.H. v. Los Lunas Schools Bd. of Educ. 267

C.R. v. Tenet Healthcare Corp. 754

C.R.S. v. United States 557

C.T.W. v. B.C.G. & D.T.G. 226, 228

C.W. v. Cooper Health System 660

Cabaness v. Thomas 708, 709

Cabe v. Lunich.. 863

Cabletron Sys., Inc. v. Miller 1046

Caboni v. General Motors Corp. 807

Cabral v. Ralphs Grocery Co.......... 319, 386

Caddo Valley, City of v. George 575

Cadena v. Chicago Fireworks Mfg.
Co... 787

Caiazzo v. Volkswagenwerk.................... 406

Cain v. Darby Borough........................... 1035

Cain v. Hearst Corp................................ 1020

Cain v. McKinnon..................................... 61

Cairl v. City of St. Paul 161

Cairns v. Franklin Mint Co.................... 1209

Calabretta v. Nat'l Airlines, Inc. 303

Caldwell v. CVS Corp................................ 66

Calhoun v. Bell 1027

Calhoun v. Chase Manhattan Bank 964

Caliri v. State Dep't of Transp................ 215

Callahan v. Stanley Works 1160

Callery v. U.S. Life Ins. Co. in the City of
New York 1145

Calles v. Scripto-Tokai Corp. 813, 814,
815

Calloway v. City of New Orleans.... 287, 530

Calloway v. Kinkelaar............................. 241

Calomiris v. Woods 1129

Caltex, Inc., United States v. 159

Calvillo-Silva v. Home Grocery.............. 402

Calvin Klein Ltd. v. Trylon Trucking
Corp.. 120

Calwell v. Hassan............................ 501, 502

Camacho v. Honda Motor Co. 814

Camden Oil Co., LLC v. Jackson 244

Camerlinck v. Thomas 234

Cameron v. Abatiell................................ 606

Camicia v. Howard S. Wright Construction
Co... 481

Camp St. Mary's Ass'n of the W. Ohio
Conference of United Methodist Church,
Inc. v. Otterbein Homes 1081

Campagnola v. Mulholland, Minion &
Roe... 1185

Campbell v. City of Elmira 241

Campbell v. Delbridge............................ 731

Campbell v. General Motors Corp. 825

Campbell v. Naman's Catering, Inc...... 1153

Campbell v. Ohio State Univ. Medical
Center 659

Campbell v. State Farm Mut. Auto. Ins.
Co. 710, 1139

Campbell v. Van Roekel 863

Campen v. Stone..................................... 865

Camper v. Minor................... 714, 723, 724

Campos v. Firestone Tire & Rubber
Co... 829

Canaan v. Bartee.............. 1186, 1187, 1190

Canal Barge Co., Inc. v. Torco Oil Co. 283

Canape v. Petersen................................. 249

Canavan v. Galuski 329

Candy H. v. Redemption Ranch, Inc. 77

Canesi v. Wilson 679

Caneyville Volunteer Fire Department v.
Green's Motorcycle Salvage, Inc. 566

Canipe v. National Loss Control Serv.
Corp..629, 630

Cannon v. Dunn 95

Cannons Eng'g Corp., United States v......17

Cantalino v. Danner.............................1034

Canterbury v. Spence.......................182, 516

Canton v. Graniteville Fire Dist. No. 4....89,
93

Canton, City of v. Harris 584, 587, 588

Cantrell v. Forest City Pub. Co. 1019,
1022

Caparella, Commonwealth v. 1154

Cape Publ'ns, Inc. v. Bridges.................1016

Capital Transit Co. v. Jackson 448

Caporale v. C.W. Blakeslee and Sons,
Inc. 787

Caprara v. Chrysler Corp. 816, 823

Caprer v. Nussbaum 1106

Caputzal v. Lindsay Co...........................340

Car Transportation v. Garden Spot
Distributors 108, 110, 118

Carafano v. Metrosplash.com., Inc..........972

Caravaggio v. D'Agostini 431

Carbone v. Tierney.................................1185

Cardenas v. Muangman..........................719

Cardina v. Kash N' Karry Food Stores,
Inc. 304

Cardtoons, L.C. v. Major League Baseball
Players Ass'n 1207

Carey v. Berkshire R.R. 685

Carey v. Lovett.......................................730

Carey v. Piphus 150

Cargill, Inc. v. Boag Cold Storage
Warehouse, Inc....................................1087

Carignan v. New Hampshire Int'l
Speedway, Inc......................................624

Carignan v. Wheeler...............................295

Caristo v. Sanzone 219, 220

Carl A. Colteryahn Dairy, Inc. v. Schneider
Dairy 1206

Carlin v. Superior Court.........................826

Carlsen v. Koivumaki 65

Carmago v. Tjaarda Dairy 657

Carmel v. Lundy 1188

Carmichael v. Halstead Nursing Center,
Ltd..1152

Carnegie v. Household Int'l, Inc..............909

Carnes v. Thompson 79

Caro v. Weintraub.................................1010

Carona de Camargo v. Schon 687

Carpenter, State v.......................1001, 1158

Carpenter v. Doubler Cattle Co., Inc. 742

Carpenter v. O'Day 611

Carpentier v. Tuthill................................83

Carr v. Mobile Video Tapes, Inc. 165

Carr v. Strode................................293, 517

Carr v. Turner 661

Carr v. Wm. C. Crowell Co. 761

Carrano v. Yale-New Haven Hosp. 691

Carranza v. United States...............671, 686

Carraway v. Kurtts 539
Carrel v. Allied Prods. Corp. 835
Carrera v. Maurice J. Sopp & Son 655
Carrier v. City of Amite 827
Carrier v. Lake Pend Oreille School
    Dist. 646
Carriere v. Merrick Lumber Co. 911
Carrieri v. Bush 1050
Carrillo v. Boise Tire Co., Inc. 60, 860
Carroll Air Sys., Inc. v. Greenbaum 758
Carroll Anesthesia Assocs., P.C. v.
    Anesthecare, Inc. 1099
Carroll Towing Co., United States v. 271
Carroll v. Owens-Corning Fiberglas
    Corp. 441
Carroll v. Sisters of Saint Francis Health
    Servs., Inc. 726
Carroll v. United States 551
Carroll v. W.R. Grace & Co. 697
Carrow Co. v. Lusby 779
Carrubba v. Moskowitz 1179
Carson v. Headrick 606
Carson v. Hercules Powder Co. 1068
Carson v. Here's Johnny Portable Toilets,
    Inc. 1006, 1208
Carson v. Maurer 526
Carter v. Kinney 462, 463
Carter v. Kurn 449
Carter v. Reynolds 756, 759
Carter v. SSC Odin Operating Co.,
    LLC 538
Cartier v. Northwestern Elec., Inc. 404
Cartwright v. Equitable Life Assurance
    Soc'y 399, 400
Carvel Corp. v. Noonan 1079, 1081, 1098
Carver v. Salt River Valley Water Users'
    Ass'n 484
Casciola v. F.S. Air Serv., Inc. 1140
Casebolt v. Cowan 208
Casey v. Estes 490
Casey v. Merck & Co., Inc. 438
Casey v. Toyota Motor Engineering & Mfg.
    North America, Inc. 810, 822
Cash v. Otis Elevator Co. 450
Cassady v. Goering 585
Cassady v. Tackett 75
Cassinos v. Union Oil Co. of California ... 93,
    95
Castenada v. Olsher 643
Castile v. Astrue 923
Castillo v. E.I. Du Pont de Nemours & Co.,
    Inc. 188
Castillo, A.Q.C. ex rel. v. United
    States 551
Castle Rock, Town of v. Gonzales 588
Castro v. Hernandez-Davila ... 256, 267, 357
Castronovo v. Murawsky 183
Caterpillar Tractor Co. v. Beck 821, 824
Caterpillar, Inc. v. Shears 827
Cates v. Cates 594
Cates v. Taylor 83
Cates v. Wilson 860

Catron v. Lewis 715, 717
Catsouras v. Dep't of Cal. Highway
    Patrol 1011
Cattlemen's Steakhouse, Inc. v.
    Waldenville 912
Caudle v. Betts 65, 82
Caudle v. Thomason 952, 982
Caulfield v. Kitsap County 621
Cauman v. George Washington Univ. 727,
    730
Cavanaugh, Estate of v. Andrade 575
Cavazos v. Franklin 670
Cavens v. Zaberdac 395, 527
Cavillo-Silva v. Home Grocery 240
Cedar Falls, City of v. Cedar Falls
    Community School Dist. 368
Cedars-Sinai Med. Ctr. v. Superior
    Court 1028
Celanese Corp. of America v. Mayor and
    Council of Wilmington 121
Cemen Tech, Inc. v. Three D Industries,
    LLC 1204
Centocor, Inc. v. Hamilton 830, 831
Central GMC, Inc. v. Helms 116
Central Pathology Serv. Med. Clinic, Inc. v.
    Superior Court 58
Central Trust & Inv. Co. v. Signalpoint
    Asset Mgmt., LLC 1091
Cerny v. Cedar Bluffs Junior/Senior Pub.
    Sch. 214, 215, 231, 496
Certification of a Question of Law from the
    United States District Court, In re 524,
    623
Certified Question from the Fourteenth
    District Court of Appeals of Texas,
    In re 485
Cervantez v. J.C. Penney Co. 154
Cervelli v. Graves 231
Chadbourne, III v. Kappaz 252
Chaffee v. Seslar 680, 681
Chairez v. James Hamiliton Const.
    Co. 841
Chakalis v. Elevator Solutions, Inc. 512
Chamberlain v. Chandler 703
Chamberlain v. Mathis 969
Chamberland v. Roswell Osteopathic Clinic,
    Inc. 352
Chambers v. St. Mary's School 468
Chambers v. Village of Moreauville 268
Chamilia, LLC v. Pandora Jewelry,
    LLC 1114
Chance v. BP Chemicals 96, 743
Chance v. Dallas County, Ala. 603, 604
Chandler v. Miller 1012
Chang v. Michiana Telecasting Corp. 47
Chang v. State Farm Mut. Auto. Ins.
    Co. 694
Channel v. Loyacono 1181, 1182
Chaparro v. Carnival Corp. 715
Chapel v. Allison 509
Chapin v. Knight-Ridder, Inc. 950, 980
Chapman v. Bearfield 1168

Chapman v. Cardiac Pacemakers, Inc............ 697
Chapman v. Chapman 462, 463
Chapman v. Harner........................ 300
Chapman v. Journal Concepts, Inc....... 1007
Chapman v. Maytag Corp.............. 838, 842
Chapman v. Willey...................... 468
Chappell v. Wallace..................... 559
Charbonneau v. MacRury.................. 235
Charette v. Santspree 489, 490, 492
Charles Atlas, Ltd. v. DC Comics, Inc............ 1198
Charleston Joint Venture v. McPherson 96
Charvat v. Dispatch Consumer Servs., Inc............ 1012
Chase v. Independent Practice Ass'n, Inc............ 534
Chase v. Sabin 431
Chatelain v. Kelley...................... 670
Chatham Furnace Co. v. Moffatt......... 1122
Chavez v. Cedar Fair, LP............... 217, 448
Cheape v. Town of Chapel Hill 94
Cheatham v. Paisano Publ'ns, Inc. 1009
Cheatham v. Pohle 876
Cheeks v. Dorsey........................ 500
Chemical Corp. of America v. Anheauser-Busch, Inc............ 1198
Chemical Express Carriers, Inc. v. French 858
Chenault v. Huie 675
Cherepski v. Walker.................... 1052
Chesapeake & Ohio Ry. v. Kelly............ 859
Chesher v. Neyer 729
Chevron Chemical Co., Ex parte 801, 827
Chianese v. Meier...................... 889, 903
Chicago & N.W. Ry. v. Tyler 789
Chicago City Ry. Co. v. Saxby.............. 355
Chicago Flood Litigation, In re 744, 787
Chicago Title Ins. Co. v. Allfirst Bank... 271, 1152
Chicago v. Tribune Co. 954
Chicago, B & Q Ry. Co. v. Krayenbuhl... 269
Chicago, B & Q Ry. Co. v. Chicago 564
Chicago, City of v. Berretta U.S.A. Corp........................... 342
Child v. Central Maine Med. Ctr. 599
Childress v. Bowser...................... 489
Childs v. Purll.......................... 250, 492
Chiu v. City of Portland 488, 491, 542
Chizmar v. Mackie 723, 725, 727
Chlopek v. Schmall...................... 857
Choate v. Ind. Harbor Belt R.R. 233
Chodorov v. Eley........................ 220
Choi v. Anvil 314, 855
Choksi v. Shah.......................... 955
CHoPP Computer Corporation, Inc. v. United States 562
Choquette v. Isacoff.................... 1179
Choski v. Shah.......................... 1052
Chouinard v. Health Ventures............ 722
Chrismon v. Brown....................... 425

Christensen & Jensen, P.C. v. Barrett & Daines 1164
Christensen v. Munsen.................. 506
Christensen v. Murphy.................. 608
Christensen v. Royal Sch. Dist. No. 160............ 391, 393, 396, 399
Christensen v. Superior Court (Pasadena Crematorium of Altadena).......... 729
Christenson v. Bergeson................ 40
Christenson v. Gutman................... 976
Christian v. Lapidus.................... 1040
Christiansen v. Providence Health Sys. of Or. Corp............ 437
Christman v. Davis................. 169, 515
Christy v. Stauffer Publ'ns, Inc.......... 959
Chu v. Bowers.......................... 392
Chu v. Hong............................ 1176
Church of Christ in Hollywood v. Superior Court 96
Chuy v. Philadelphia Eagles Football Club 993
Cicorelli v. Capobianco 1178
Ciervo v. City of New York 610
Cilley v. Lane 615, 621
Cimino v. Rosen 1034
Cipollone v. Liggett Group, Inc. 45, 405, 441, 830
Circle K Store No. 1131 v. Industrial Comm'n of Ariz. 915
Cislaw v. Southland Corp. 766
Citadel Management, Inc. v. Telesis Trust, Inc. 1154
Cities Service Co. v. State.......... 789
Citizen Publ'g Co. v. Miller.......... 710
City Consumer Servs., Inc. v. Metcalf 1074, 1075
Ciup v. Chevron U.S.A., Inc. 766
Clampitt v. American Univ. 941, 948
Clark v. America's First Credit Union.... 982
Clark v. Binney......................... 937
Clark v. Children's Mem'l Hosp. 677, 681
Clark v. District of Columbia 510
Clark v. Druckman 1037
Clark v. Iowa Dep't of Revenue & Fin............ 1121
Clark v. McDaniel................... 1134
Clark v. Rowe 1074, 1165
Clark v. Southview Hosp. & Family Health Ctr............ 530, 772, 773
Clark v. St. Dominic-Jackson Mem'l Hosp............ 267, 530
Clarke v. Martucci................... 314
Clarke v. Oregon Health Sciences Univ............ 873
Clary v. Lite Machines Corp.......... 1174
Clawson v. St. Louis Post-Dispatch, LLC............ 950
Clay City Consol. Sch. Corp.v. Tiberman 385
Clay Elec. Coop., Inc. v. Johnson........... 629
Clay v. Brand 1119
Clay v. Lagiss.......................... 1000

Clayton v. Richards 1010, 1012
Claytor v. Owens-Corning Fiberglas
  Corp. 315
Cleary v. Manning................................ 302
Cleland v. Bronson Health Care Group,
  Inc.. 532
Clem v. Lomeli.................................... 585
Clemensen v. Providence Alaska Med.
  Ctr. 732
Cleveland Campers, Inc. v.
  McCormack 1166
Cleveland Park Club v. Perry 87
Cleveland v. Mann................................ 694
Cleveland v. Rotman 209, 1183
Clift v. Narragansett Television L.P. 372
Clinch v. Heartland Health 1107
Clinic & Hospital v. McConnell 738, 739
Clinkscales v. Carver 251
Clinkscales v. Nelson Secs., Inc. 298, 304,
  349, 472
Clinton v. Jones 581
Clites v. State 540, 542
Clo v. McDermott 781
Clohessy v. Bachelor 718
Clohesy v. Food Circus Supermarkets,
  Inc. 213, 466, 639
Cloud v. McKinney 992
Clymer v. Webster 694
Coachmen Indus. v. Crown Steel Co. 239
Coan v. New Hampshire Dep't of
  Environmental Services 482
Coastal Orthopaedic Institute, P.C. v.
  Bongiorno 1173
Coates v. Southern Maryland Co-op.,
  Inc.. 487
Coates v. United States........................... 553
Cobb v. Time, Inc.................................... 995
Cobbs v. Grant............................... 63, 515
Coburn v. City of Tucson......... 207, 216, 485
Coca-Cola Bottling Co. v. Hagan 726
Coca-Cola Co. v. Overland, Inc. 1194
Coca-Cola Co. v. Purdy........................ 1198
Cocchiara v. Lithia Motors, Inc. 1131
Cochran v. Burger King Corp. 462
Cochran v. Piedmont Publ'g Co. Inc. 999,
  1001
Cockrum v. Baumgartner 681
Coffee v. McDonnell-Douglas Corp......... 651
Coffman v. Keene Corp. 327, 833
Coggs v. Bernard 238
Cohen v. Alliant Enterprises, Inc. 756
Cohen v. Bowdoin................................ 959
Cohen v. Cabrini Med. Ctr. 209
Cohen v. Five Brooks Stable 410, 411,
  423
Cohen v. Smith 63
Coho Res., Inc. v. Chapman 603
Cok v. Cok..................................... 1042, 1044
Coker v. Wal-Mart Stores, Inc. 244
Colavito v. New York Organ Donor
  Network, Inc. 112
Colbert v. Mooba Sports, Inc.................. 716

Colbert v. World Publ'g Co. 1021, 1022
Colboch v. Uniroyal Tire Co. 810
Colby v. Carney Hosp. 597
Cole v. Atlanta & W.P.R. Co.................... 703
Cole v. Chandler................................... 1019
Cole v. Fairchild................................... 465
Cole v. Hubanks............................ 605, 608
Cole v. South Carolina Elec. and Gas,
  Inc.. 479
Cole v. Star Tribune.............................. 980
Cole v. Taylor 402
Coleman Estate ex rel. Coleman v. R.M.
  Logging, Inc....................................... 922
Coleman v. Newark Morning Ledger
  Co. 980, 981
Coleman v. Oregon Parks and Recreation
  Dept.. 479
Coleman v. Soccer Ass'n of Columbia 384
Coleman v. Steinberg............................ 491
Coleson v. City of New York 715
Collazo v. United States 557
College of Charleston Foundation v.
  Ham 96
Collette v. Tolleson Unified School Dist. No.
  214..658
Collins v. City of Harker Heights,
  Texas..583, 587
Collins v. Eli Lilly Co............................. 329
Collins v. King...................................... 860
Collins v. Mo. Bar Plan........................ 1055
Collins v. Navistar, Inc.................... 840, 841
Collins v. Otto 783
Collins v. Reynard............. 1074, 1126, 1164
Collins v. Scenic Homes, Inc................... 433
Collins v. Straight, Inc............ 74, 75, 76, 77
Collins v. Superior Air-Ground Ambulance
  Serv., Inc...................................308, 309
Collins v. Thomas................................. 622
Collins v. United States..................556, 557
Collyer v. S.H. Kress Co. 153, 154
Colon v. Apfel...................................... 924
Colonial Imports, Inc. v. Carlton Nw.,
  Inc. 1125
Colosimo v. Roman Catholic Bishop of Salt
  Lake City 430, 439
Colt v. M'Mechen 193
Colton v. Onderdonk 791
Columbia Med. Ctr. of Las Colinas,
  In re..695
Columbia Med. Ctr. of Las Colinas, Inc. v.
  Hogue..317
Columbia Rio Grande Healthcare, L.P. v.
  Hawley...331, 369
Columbia, District of v. Harris............... 297
Colwell v. Holy Family Hosp. 512
Comeau v. Lucas 399
Comedy III Productions, Inc. v. Gary
  Saderup, Inc. 1207, 1208
Comer v. Texaco, Inc.............................. 603
Comins v. Discovery Commc'ns, Inc...... 1007
Command Cinema Corp. v. VCA Labs,
  Inc. 121

Commerce Bank v. Augsburger 594
Commerce Funding Corp. v. Worldwide Sec.
     Servs. Corp. 1103
Commerce Ins. Co. v. Ultimate Livery Serv.,
     Inc. 204
Commercial Carrier Corp. v. Indian River
     County 572
Commercial Ventures, Inc. v. Rex M. &
     Lynn Lea Family Trust 1095, 1097
Comminge v. Stevenson 743
Commonwealth, Transp. Cabinet, Dep't of
     Highways v. Sexton 484, 569
Community Dental Services v. Tani..... 1164
Community Fed. Sav. & Loan Ass'n v.
     Orondorff 1198
Community Resources for Justice, Inc. v.
     City of Manchester 526
Compco Corp. v. Day-Brite Lighting,
     Inc. 1203
Concerned Parents of Pueblo v.
     Gilmore 600
Concord Florida, Inc. v. Lewin 364
Condit v. Dunne 979
Condit v. Nat'l Enquirer, Inc. 985
Condon v. Vickery 1038
Condra v. Atlanta Orthopaedic Group,
     P.C. 510
Coney v. J.L.G. Indus., Inc...... 836, 838, 842
Congregation of the Passion, Holy Cross
     Province v. Touche Ross & Co. 1074,
     1087
Conklin v. Hannoch Weisman 1170, 1177
Conley v. Boyle Drug Co. 330
Conley v. Lieber 1169
Conley v. Life Care Centers of America,
     Inc. 546
Conley v. Romeri 1118
Connecticut v. Doehr 1047
Connell v. Call-A-Cab, Inc. 763
Connell, Fandrey ex rel. v. American
     Family Mut. Ins. Co. 340
Connelly v. City of Omaha 566
Connelly v. McKay 948
Conner v. Farmers and Merchs.
     Bank 229
Conner v. Menard, Inc. 304
Connick v. Thompson 586, 587
Connolley v. Omaha Pub. Power
     District 101
Connolly v. Holt 594
Connor v. Hodges 721
Conservatorship of Gregory 252, 545
Considine v. City of Waterbury 250,
     292, 566
Consolidated Aluminum Corp. v. C.F. Bean
     Corp. 1067
Consolidated Rail Corp. v. Gottshall 715
Conte v. Girard Orthopaedic Surgeons Med.
     Group 62, 169
Contemporary Mission, Inc. v. New York
     Times Co. 994
Conti v. Ford Motor Co. 834

Contreras v. Crown Zellerbach Corp. 709
Contreras v. Vannoy Heating & Air
     Conditioning, Inc. 307
Control Techniques, Inc. v. Johnson 376,
     377, 390
Convit v. Wilson 369
Conway v. Pacific Univ. 1125
Cook ex rel. Uithoven v. Spinnaker's of
     Rivergate, Inc. 232
Cook v. Connolly 1174
Cook v. DeSoto Fuels, Inc. 89, 98
Cook v. Shoshone Nat'l Bank 372
Cook v. Winfrey 946
Coombes v. Florio 500, 501
Coombs v. Curnow 314
Coomer v. Kansas City Royals Baseball
     Corp. 422
Cooper Clinic, P.A. v. Barnes 757
Cooper Indus., Inc. v. Leatherman Tool
     Group, Inc. 868
Cooper v. Berkshire Life Ins. Co. 1124
Cooper v. Cooper 1145
Cooper v. Corporate Property
     Investors 463, 464
Cooper v. Horn 93
Cooper v. Parker-Hughey 966, 1024
Copart Indus., Inc. v. Consolidated Edison
     Co. of New York, Inc. 734, 737, 738
Cope v. Scott 556, 557
Copeland v. Baltimore & Ohio R. Co. 460
Copeland v. Compton 199
Copier v. Smith & Wesson Corp. 788
Copple v. Warner 370
Corales v. Bennett 732
Corcoran v. United Healthcare, Inc. 536
Cordes v. Outdoor Living Ctr., Inc. 1028
Cordial v. Ernst & Young 1124
Corey v. Pierce County 1022
Corgan v. Muehling 253, 723, 746
Corinaldi v. Columbia Courtyard,
     Inc. 453
Corley v. Rosewood Care Ctr., Inc. of
     Peoria 1116
Cornell v. Wunschel 728, 1139, 1183
Cornett v. Johnson & Johnson 847
Corporex Dev. & Constr. Mgmt., Inc. v.
     Shook, Inc. 1087
Correa v. Hospital San Francisco 533
Correia v. Fagan 1188
Cortez v. Jo-Ann Stores, Inc. 972
Coscia v. McKenna & Cuneo 1187, 1191
Cosgrove v. Commonwealth Edison
     Co. 305
Cosner v. Ridinger 1056
Costa v. Cmty. Emergency Med. Servs.,
     Inc. 240
Costanza v. Seinfeld 1021
Costello v. Ocean County Observer 977,
     991, 992
Coster v. Crookham 863
Costo v. United States 561
Costos v. Coconut Island Corp. 543, 758

Cotati, City of v. Cashman 985
Cottam v. CVS Pharmacy 627
Cotton v. Buckeye Gas Products Co. 827
Cottonwood Enters. v. McAlpin 1074
Cottrell v. Kaysville City, Utah 583
Cottrell v. National Collegiate Athletic
  Ass'n 959
Cottrell v. Zagami, LLC 966
Couch v. Red Roof Inns, Inc. 880, 889
Coughlen v. Coots 1036
Coulombe v. Salvation Army 599
Coulter v. Michelin Tire Corp. 303
Countrywide Home Loans, Inc. v.
  Thitchener 862
Coursey v. Westvaco Corp. 480, 481
Court v. Grzelinski 606
Courtenay Communications Corp. v.
  Hall 1199
Cousins v. Lockyer 585
Coveleski v. Bubnis 671
Covell v. McCarthy 75
Covenant Health & Rehab. of Picayune, LP
  v. Estate of Moulds 413, 694
Cover v. Cohen 282
Cover v. Phillips Pipe Line Co. 88
Coville v. Liberty Mut. Ins. Co. 622
Cowan v. Doering 227, 372, 394
Cowan v. Hospice Support Care,
  Inc. 240, 598
Cowart v. Widener 314
Cowe v. Forum Group, Inc. 677
Cowell v. Thompson 259
Cowles v. Brownell 1035
Cowles v. Carter 1038
Cox Broad. Corp. v. Cohn 978, 1017
Cox Enters., Inc. v. Nix 949, 955
Cox v. City of Dallas 885
Cox v. Crown Coco, Inc. 859
Cox v. Hatch 948, 990, 1006
Cox v. M.A. Primary and Urgent Care
  Clinic 496, 530
Cox v. May Dep't Store Co. 309
Cox v. Paul 505
Coyazo v. State 1191
Coyle v. Englander's 625
Coyle v. Richardson-Merrell, Inc. ... 830, 831
Coyne's & Co., Inc. v. Enesco, LLC 111
Crabtree v. Dawson 135
Craft v. Peebles 831
Craig & Bishop, Inc. v. Piles 126
Craig v. Driscoll 248, 356
Craig Wrecking Co. v. S.G. Loewendick &
  Sons, Inc. 150
Crain v. The Unauthorized Practice of Law
  Comm. of the Supreme Court of
  Tex. 967
Craine v. Trinity Coll. 1125
Cramer v. Hous. Opportunities Comm'n of
  Montgomery Cty. 230
Cramer v. Slater 341, 342, 369, 372, 696,
  732
Crane v. Neal 390

Cranshaw v. Cumberland Farms, Inc. 483
Crawford v. Busbee 1025
Crawford v. French 85, 87
Crawford v. Mintz 384
Crawford v. Sears Roebuck & Co. 811
Crawford v. Tilley 482
Crawn v. Campo 8, 425
Creasey v. Hogan 494, 511
Creasy v. Rusk 226, 420, 613
Credit Union Central Falls v. Groff 1163,
  1166
Creech v. South Carolina Wildlife and
  Marine Resources Dept. 569
Creel v. L & L, Inc. 422
Cresson v. Louisville Courier-
  Journal 977
Crews v. Hollenbach 415
Crinkley v. Holiday Inns, Inc. 773
Criscuola v. Andrews 691
Croaker v. Mackenhausen 476
Crocker v. Morales-Santana 764
Crocker v. Pleasant 704
Crookham v. Riley 1169
Crosby v. Glasscock Trucking Co.,
  Inc. 671
Crosby v. Hummell 236
Cross v. Trapp 518
Crosslin v. Health Care Auth. of City of
  Huntsville 429
Crotteau v. Karlgaard 136
Crouch v. Cameron 73
Crowell v. Crowell 176
Crowley v. N. Am. Telecomms. Ass'n 708
Crowne Investments, Inc. v. Reid 541
Cruz v. City of New York 367
Cruz v. DaimlerChrysler Motors
  Corp. 307
Cruz v. Middlekauff Lincoln-Mercury,
  Inc. 363
Cruz-Vazquez v. Mennonite General
  Hospital, Inc. 533
CSX Transp., Inc. v. Begley 384
CSX Transp., Inc. v. Continental Ins.
  Co. 346
CSX Transp., Inc. v. Easterwood 45, 441,
  442
CSX Transp., Inc. v. Hensley 725
CSX Transp., Inc. v. McBride 247
CSX Transp., Inc. v. Miller 331, 401, 890
CSY Liquidating Corp. v. Harris Trust &
  Sav. Bank 1093
CTL Distrib., Inc., State v. 329
Cucinotta v. Deloitte & Touche, LLP 965
Culbert v. Sampson's Supermarkets,
  Inc. 723, 731
Cullip v. Domann 243
Cullison v. Medley 71, 97
Cullum v. McCool 638
Culp Constr. Co. v. Buildmart Mall 1124
Culpepper v. Pearl St. Bldg., Inc. 112, 704
Cult Awareness Network v. Church of
  Scientology Intern. 1040, 1041

Cumberland Torpedo Co. v. Gaines 743
Cummings v. HPG Int'l, Inc. 1133, 1136
Cummins v. Lewis County 625
Cunningham v. Yankton Clinic 182
Cunnington v. Gaub 767
Cuonzo v. Shore 329
Curiano v. Suozzi 1111
Curran v. Bosze 174
Curran v. Buser 521
Currie v. Silvernale 157, 158
Currier v. Amerigas Propane, L.P. 919
Curtis Publ'g Co. v. Butts 989, 992, 993, 995
Curtis v. Carey 116
Curtis v. Firth 711
Curtis v. MRI Imaging Servs., II 731, 732
Curtis v. Porter 56
Curtis v. Traders Nat'l Bank 415
Cushing v. Time Saver Stores, Inc. 672
Cushman v. Trans Union Corp. 946
Custodi v. Town of Amherst 425
Customer Co. v. City of Sacramento 161
Cutshall v. United States 561
Cutts v. American United Life Ins. Co. 974
Cuyler v. United States 246
Cweklinsky v. Mobile Chemical Co. 943
Cygan v. Kaleida Health 532
Cyr v. State 157
Czap v. Credit Bureau of Santa Clara Valley 1043
D.L. v. Huebner 282
D.R. Strong Consulting Eng'rs, Inc. 1123
D'Ambrosio v. Colonnade Council of Unit Owners 1119
D'Ambrosio v. Philadelphia 258
D'Amico v. Christie 664, 665
D'Angelo-Fenton v. Town of Carmel 1111
D'Ascanio v. Toyota Industries Corp. 809, 812
d'Hedouville v. Pioneer Hotel Co. 364
Dacey v. New York County Lawyers' Ass'n 1038
DaFonte v. Up-Right, Inc. 890, 920
Dagley v. Thompson 232
Dahlin v. Evangelical Child & Family Agency 728
Dahna v. Clay County Fair Ass'n 451
Dailey v. Methodist Med. Ctr. 312
Daily v. New Britain Mach. Co. 848
DaimlerChrysler Corp. v. Kirkhart 963, 964, 1108
Dakter v. Cavallino 231
Dale v. Guaranty Nat'l Ins. Co. 1147
Dalehite v. United States 551, 553, 554
Daley v. A.W. Chesterton, Inc. 441
Daley v. United States 556
Dallas Cowboys Cheerleaders, Inc. v. Pussycat Cinema, Ltd. 1197, 1198
Dallas, City of v. Heard 782
Dalley v. Dykema Gossett, P.LLC 1011, 1012

Dalley v. Utah Valley Reg'l Med. Ctr. 307, 309
Dalton v. Favour 192
Daluiso v. Boone 148, 149
Dalury v. S-K-I, Ltd. 413
Daly v. General Motors Corp. 835, 837, 838, 842
Daly v. McFarland 220
Dameron v. Washington Magazine 977
Dan Nelson Const., Inc. v. Nodland & Dickson 1173
Danca v. Taunton Sav. Bank 1140
Daniel v. Ben E. Keith Co. 833
Daniel v. City of Colorado Springs 482
Danielle A. v. Christopher P. 654
Daniels v. Gamma West Brachytherapy, LLC 516
Daniels v. Twin Oaks Nursing Home 542
Daniels v. Williams 583, 587
Danos v. Boh Bros. Constr. Co., LLC 921
Darby & Darby, P.C. v. VSI Intern., Inc. 1169
Darcars Motors of Silver Springs, Inc. v. Borzym 110, 112, 114, 126
Dardeen v. Kuehling 1159, 1160
Dare v. Sobule 408
Darling v. Charleston Cmty. Mem. Hosp. 282, 530, 657
Darling v. J.B. Expedited Servs., Inc. 291
Darnell v. Eastman 314
Darrough v. Glendale Heights Cmty. Hosp. 309
Dart v. Wiebe Mfg., Inc. 821
Dastar Corp. v. Twentieth Century Fox Film Corp. 1194, 1199
Daubert v. Merrell Dow Pharms., Inc. 293, 673
Daugherty v. Allee's Sports Bar & Grill 762
Daughten v. Fox 857
Dausch v. Rykse 457
Dauzat v. Curnest Guillot Logging Inc. 268
Davencourt at Pilgrims Landing Homeowners Ass'n v. Davencourt at Pilgrims Landing, LC 1060
Davey Compressor Co. v. City of Delray Beach 97
David v. DeLeon 355
David v. Hett 1084
David v. McLeod Regional Med. Ctr. 506
Davidson v. Lindsey 264
Davies v. Butler 231, 232, 400
Davis v. Berwind Corp. 829, 836, 841
Davis v. Brouse McDowell, L.P.A. 1173
Davis v. Caldwell 516
Davis v. Devereux Foundation 761
Davis v. Enget 1171
Davis v. Graviss 725
Davis v. Landis Outboard Motor Co. 239, 240
Davis v. Marathon Oil Co. 245

Davis v. McGuigan 1120
Davis v. McMillan 1031
Davis v. Monahan.................................. 128
Davis v. Nadrich 1077
Davis v. Pickell 708
Davis v. Provo City Corp........................ 428
Davis v. Rodman.................................. 660
Davis v. South Side Elevated R.R.......... 451
Davis v. Sun Valley Ski Educ. Found.,
    Inc.. 410
Davis v. Toshiba Machine Co.,
    America 848
Davis v. Van Camp Packing Co. 800
Davis v. Venture One Const., Inc. 623
Davis v. Wal-Mart Stores, Inc............... 1158
Davis v. Westwood Group 484, 627
Davis v. White 79, 81
Dawe v. Dr. Reuven Bar-Levav &
    Associates, P.C................................. 659
Dawson v. Bunker Hill Plaza
    Associates... 466
Dawson v. Payless for Drugs 472
Day v. Providence Hosp. 73
Day, Estate of v. Willis........................... 575
Dayton Construction, Inc. v.
    Meinhardt 1152
Daytona Beach, City of v. Palmer........... 574
DCR Inc. v. Peak Alarm Co.................... 1146
De Laveaga, Estate of 96
De Leon Lopez v. Corporacion Insular de
    Seguros.. 300
De Leon v. Saint Joseph Hosp., Inc........ 983
De Long v. County of Erie.............. 572, 574
De May v. Roberts 1011
Deadman v. Valley Nat'l Bank of Ariz. 73
Deal v. Bowman 292
DeAmiches v. Popczun 416
DeAngelis v. Hill 995
DeAngelis v. Jamesway Dep't Store 76
Deasy v. United States............................ 557
Deauville Corp. v. Federated Dep't Stores,
    Inc.. 1108
Debary v. Harrah's Operating Co.,
    Inc.. 1093
DeBusscher v. Sam's East, Inc. 471
DeCarlo v. Eden Park Health Servs.,
    Inc.. 306
Decatur Auto Ctr. v. Wachovia
    Bank 1154
Deere & Co. v. MTD Products, Inc. 1198
Deerings West Nursing Center v.
    Scott.. 543
Deflon v. Sawyers 1091
Defoor v. Evesque............................ 568, 569
Degennaro v. Tandon 513
DeGrella v. Elston 174
Dehn v. Edgecombe 527
Dehn v. S. Brand Coal & Oil Co. 475
DeJesus v. United States Dep't of Veterans
    Affairs.. 656, 659
Del E. Webb Corp. v. Super. Ct. 232, 401
Del Lago Partners, Inc. v. Smith 392, 397

Del Rio v. United States 561
Delahoussaye v. Mary Mahoney's,
    Inc...662
DeLaire v. Kaskel 608
DeLaney v. Baker 541, 548
DeLaney v. Deere and Co. 809, 821
Delaney v. Reynolds...............................372
Delaware, Lackawanna and Western R. Co.
    v. Salmon 360
Delbrel v. Doenges Bros. Ford, Inc.........342
Delfino v. Griffo....................................241
Delgado v. Interinsurance Exch. of Auto.
    Club of S. Cal....................................321
Delgado v. Trax Bar & Grill 620, 640
Deliso v. Cangialosi......................233, 234
Della Penna v. Toyota Motor Sales, U.S.A.,
    Inc...1098
Dellwo v. Pearson...........................236, 237
Delmarva Power & Light v. Stout...........292
DeLong v. Yu Enters., Inc. 973
Delta Farms Reclamation Dist. v. Super.
    Ct...483
DeLuna v. Burciaga 438
Delval v. PPG Indus., Inc. 940
Delvaux v. Ford Motor Co.......................813
Demag v. Better Power Equip., Inc........478,
    606
Demby v. English....................................992
DeMendoza v. Huffman 876
DeMoss v. Hamilton...............................395
Den Norske Ameriekalinje Actiesselskabet
    v. Sun Printing & Publ'g Ass'n 999
DeNardo v. Bax 982
DeNardo v. Corneloup 787
Dendrite Int'l, Inc. v. Doe 971
Denison Parking, Inc. v. Davis................483
Denny v. Ford Motor Co. 809
Denny v. Mertz......................................995
Dentists' Supply Co. of New York v.
    Cornelius..128
Denton v. Browns Mill Dev. Co., Inc.......984
Denver Publ'g Co. v. Bueno 1020
Department of Health & Soc. Servs., State
    v. Mullins..894
DePerno v. Hans 236
Depue v. Flatau 141, 157
Deramus v. Donovan, Leisure, Newton &
    Irvine 1174
DeRobertis ex rel. DeRobertis v.
    Randazzo..217
Derricotte v. United Skates of Am. 423
Desai v. SSM Health Care........................73
DeSantis v. Employees Passaic County
    Welfare Ass'n.....................................968
Deschenes v. Transco, Inc. 918
Desert Healthcare Dist. v. PacifiCare FHP,
    Inc...1084
DeShaney v. Winnebago County Dep't of
    Social Services 588, 649
Desnick v. American Broad. Cos.,
    Inc. 177, 1011
Dessel v. Donohue.................................1183

Destefano v. Grabrian 181, 456, 713, 763
Dethloff v. Zeigler Coal Co. 90
Detwiler v. Bristol-Myers Squibb Co...... 438
Deuel v. Surgical Clinic, PLLC 300
Deuley v. DynCorp Int'l, Inc. 410
Deutcsh v. Birmingham Post Co............ 994
DeVane, United States v........................ 623
DeVaney v. Thriftway Mktg. Corp. 1039,
    1040, 1047
Dew v. Crown Derrick Erectors, Inc....... 367
Dewey v. Wentland............................... 1119
DeWolf v. Ford...................................... 703
DeYoung v. Providence Med. Ctr............ 435
Di Ponzio v. Riordan........................ 346, 349
Diamond v. E.R. Squibb and Sons,
    Inc... 848
Diamond v. Pappathanasi.................... 1145
Dias v. Brigham Med. Assocs., Inc. 529,
    764
Diaz v. Carcamo 657, 754
Diaz v. Oakland Tribune, Inc............... 1016
Diaz v. Phoenix Lubrication Serv.,
    Inc... 283
Dibella v. Hopkins................................ 994
Dible v. Haight Ashbury Free Clinics 940
DiCaprio v. New York Cent. R.R. 257
Dickens v. Puryear..................... 71, 84, 706
Dickens v. Sahley Realty Co., Inc. 297
Dickey v. CBS, Inc................................. 979
Dickhoff v. Green.................................. 333
Dickins v. Int'l Bhd. of Teamsters. 975
Dickinson v. Clark................................ 480
Didato v. Strehler 497, 679
Didier v. Ash Grove Cement Co............. 650
Dier v. Peters....................................... 1116
Dietemann v. Time, Inc.............. 1011, 1015
Dietrich v. Northhampton...................... 669
Dietz v. Finlay Fine Jewelry Corp. 1018
Dietz v. General Elec. Co. 890
DiFranco v. Klein 509
Digicorp, Inc. v. Ameritech Corp. 803
Dillard Dep't Stores, Inc. v. Silva 154
Dillon v. Callaway 180
Dillon v. Evanston Hosp................. 334, 440
Dillon v. Frazer..................................... 293
Dillon v. Legg 209, 715
Dillon v. Nissan Motor Co....................... 844
Dillworth v. Gambardella 308
DiMarco v. Lynch Homes-Chester County,
    Inc.................189, 366, 500, 660
Dimond v. Kling...................................... 234
Dincher v. Marlin Firearms Co.............. 435
Dini v. Naiditch 606
Dinkel v. Lincoln Publ'g (Ohio), Inc........ 978
Dionne v. Southeast Foam Converting &
    Packaging, Inc. 1204
DiPino v. Davis...................................... 579
Dippin' Dots, Inc. v. Frosty Bites
    Distribution, LLC 1202
Disciplinary Action Against McKechnie, In
    re... 1164, 1166

Disciplinary Action Against Mertz, Matter
    of..973
Distefano v. Forester............................424
Distinctive Printing & Packaging Co. v.
    Cox..861
District of Columbia v. Chinn............58, 133
District of Columbia v. Hampton 496, 765
District of Columbia v. Howell 767
District of Columbia v. Jones 969
District of Columbia v. Tulin.................708
Diversicare General Partner, Inc. v.
    Rubio..540
Diversified Mgmt., Inc. v. Denver Post,
    Inc. 996
Dixon Ticonderoga Co. v. Estate of
    O'Connor 1166
Dixon v. International Bhd. of Police
    Officers..994
Dixon v. Superior Court Scientific Resource
    Surveys, Inc. 984, 985
Doan v. City of Bismarck................281, 292
Dobrovolny v. Ford Motor Co. 803
Dobson v. La. Power & Light Co. 229, 231
Doca v. Marina Mercante Nicaraguense,
    S.A..859
Dockery v. World of Mirth Shows,
    Inc. 451
Dodson v. Allstate Ins. Co. 954
Dodson v. S.D. Dep't of Human
    Servs. 227, 384
Doe 1 ex rel. Doe 1 v. Roman Catholic
    Diocese of Nashville 242, 712
Doe 67C v. Archdiocese of
    Milwaukee 1135
Doe A. v. Coffee County Board of
    Educ. 647
Doe Parents No. 1 v. State Dep't of
    Educ. 265, 268, 621, 647, 716
Doe v. American Nat'l Red Cross 434
Doe v. Andujar 217
Doe v. Archdiocese of Cincinnati.............439
Doe v. Archdiocese of Milwaukee............439
Doe v. Arts...725, 727
Doe v. Baxter Healthcare Corp. 329
Doe v. Bishop of Charleston 438
Doe v. Cahill...971
Doe v. City of Chicago...............................754
Doe v. Claiborne County, Tennessee.......650
Doe v. Colligan 688
Doe v. Corporation of President of Church
    of Jesus Christ of Latter-Day
    Saints 708, 709
Doe v. Dilling..................................391, 1118
Doe v. Doe..1052
Doe v. Dominion Bank of
    Washington...............................283, 645
Doe v. Evans..456
Doe v. Forrest......................................758, 762
Doe v. Friendfinder Network, Inc. 1006
Doe v. Guthrie Clinic, Ltd. 531
Doe v. Liberatore...........................456, 1144
Doe v. Linder Const. Co..................362, 363

Doe v. Marion 248, 571
Doe v. Marlington Local School Dist. Board
    of Educ.. 564
Doe v. McKay...................................... 1057
Doe v. McMillan.................................... 581
Doe v. Methodist Hosp. 1018
Doe v. Miles Laboratories, Inc., Cutter
    Laboratories Div. 801
Doe v. Newbury Bible Church 761, 763
Doe v. Ortega-Piron............................. 241
Doe v. Pharmacia & Upjohn Co., Inc..... 209,
    680
Doe v. Phillips.................................... 578
Doe v. Rockdale Sch. Dist. No. 84.......... 449
Doe v. Roe 180, 1015
Doe v. Saint Francis Hosp. & Medical
    Center... 657
Doe v. Samaritan Counseling Ctr.......... 757,
    762
Doe v. State....................................... 219
Doe v. TCI Cablevision.........947, 1008, 1208
Doe v. Westfall Health Care Ctr.,
    Inc....................540, 543, 547, 677
Doe v. Zwelling 1052
Doehring v. Wagner 145, 147
Doering v. WEA Ins. Group. 663
Doerner v. Swisher Int'l, Inc.................. 720
Doerr v. Movius 173
Dokman v. Cnty. of Hennepin 161
Dolan v. Galluzzo 511
Dolan v. United States Postal Serv. 562
Dolgencorp, Inc. v. Taylor 470
Dollarhide v. Gunstream........................ 690
Domagala v. Rolland 635
Dombey v. Phoenix Newspapers, Inc...... 990
Dombrowski v. Moore............................ 512
Dominant Semiconductors SDN. BHD. v.
    Osram GMBH 1091
Domingo v. T.K..................................... 513
Dominguez v. Manhattan & Bronx Surface
    Transit Operating Auth...................... 397
Donaca v. Curry Cnty........................ 207, 485
Donahue v. Ledgends, Inc. 411
Donaldson v. Indianapolis Pub. Transp.
    Corp. 243
Donaldson v. Maffucci 505, 509
Donato v. Moldow 972
Donchez v. Coors Brewing Co. 1209
Donigan v. Finn................................... 1191
Donner v. Arkwright-Boston Mfrs. Mut. Ins.
    Co... 793
Donner v. Kearse.................................. 888
Donovan v. Fiumara 959
Donovan v. Philip Morris USA, Inc. 334,
    851, 853, 854
Donovan v. Village of Ohio..................... 570
Doomes v. Best Transit Corp. 805
Dorais v. Paquin.................................. 234
Dore v. City of Fairbanks...................... 574
Dormu v. District of Columbia................ 58
Dorn v. Burlington N. Santa Fe R.R.
    Co.. 693

Dornak v. Lafayette General Hosp. 651
Dorr v. Big Creek Wood Products,
    Inc...464
Dorrin v. Union Elec. Co........................234
Dorson, In re Guardianship of..... 1145, 1146
Dorton v. Francisco...............................464
Dorwart v. Caraway................................3
Dos Santos v. Coleta 471
Doser v. Interstate Power Co. 448
Doss v. Jones.......................................938
Dotson v. Hammerman..........................505
Dougan v. Nunes....................................781
Doughty v. Turner Manufacturing
    Co..358
Douglas Labs. Corp. v. Copper Tan.......1195
Douglas v. Bergland..............................462
Douglas v. Delp...................................1183
Douglas v. Freeman 496, 510, 531
Douglas v. Humble Oil & Refining Co. 97
Douglass v. Dolan 779
Doundoulakis v. Town of Hempstead 787
Douthit v. Jones 73, 77
Dow Corning Corp., In re......................433
Dowdle Butane Gas Co. v. Moore.........1157,
    1159
Dowis v. Continental Elevator Co.,
    Inc...628, 629
Dowler v. Boczkowski 489
Dowling v. Bullen...............................1051
Downey v. Bob's Discount Furniture
    Holdings, Inc.....................................297
Downing v. Hyland Pharmacy.........496, 831
Dowty v. Riggs 713
Doyle v. Volkswagenwerk A.G. 844
Drabek v. Sabley.............................76, 78
Draghetti v. Chmielwski.........................976
Dragonas v. School Comm. of
    Melrose 980, 982
Drake v. Park Newspapers of Ne. Okla.,
    Inc. 954
Draper Mortuary v. Superior Court........642
DRD Pool Serv., Inc. v. Freed.................687
Dresser Indus. v. Lee 890
Driggers v. Locke 484
Driver v. Hice.....................................118
Druyan v. Jagger...................................1111
Du Lac v. Perma Trans Prods., Inc. 79
Dubay v. Irish 59
Dubbs v. Head Start, Inc. 63
Dubinsky v. Meermart.........................1078
Dubreil v. Witt 1171
Dubreuil, In re......................................514
Duchess v. Langston Corp.....................823
Ducote v. State, Dep't of Social and Health
    Services..571
Duda v. Phatty McGees 415, 417
Dudas v. Glenwood Golf Club, Inc. 639
Duffin v. Idaho Crop Improvement
    Ass'n..1087
Duffy v. Togher 472
Dugan v. Mittal Steel USA Inc........939, 998
Duggar v. Arredondo..............................402

Duggin v. Adams 1102, 1103
Dukes v. United States Healthcare,
  Inc. 536
Duling v. Bluefield Sanitarium, Inc. 529
Dumas v. Cooney 331
Dumas v. State 887
Dun & Bradstreet, Inc. v. Greenmoss
  Builders, Inc. 990, 995, 1001
Dunagan v. Upham 957
Duncan v. Cessna Aircraft Co. 838
Duncan v. Corbetta 284
Duncan v. Scottsdale Med. Imaging,
  Ltd. 169, 170, 175, 514
Duncavage v. Allen 353, 644
Dunleavy v. Miller 380
Dunn v. City of Milwaukie 160
Dunn v. Grand Canyon Airlines, Inc. 302
Dunphy v. Gregor 721
Duphily v. Delaware Elec. Co-op.,
  Inc. 243, 354, 369
Dupler v. Seubert 76
Duprey v. Shane 921
Duracraft Corp. v. Holmes Prods.
  Corp. 985, 986
Durban v. Guajardo 705
Duren v. Kunkel 780
Durham v. Guest 1040, 1042, 1047
Durkin v. Hansen 490
Durney v. St. Francis Hosp., Inc. 598
Duty v. East Coast Tender Serv., Inc. 253
Duvall v. Goldin 500
Dyer v. Maine Drilling & Blasting,
  Inc. 314, 787
Dyer v. Superior Court 603
Dyer v. Trachtman 499
Dykhoff v. Xcel Energy 915
Dymond Cab Co. v. Branson 450
Dzenutis v. Dzenutis 594
Dziubak v. Mott 1191
E.G., In re 172
E.I. du Pont de Nemours & Co. v.
  Christopher 1204
E.I. du Pont de Nemours Powder Co. v.
  Masland 1206
E.J. Strickland Constr., Inc. v. Department
  of Agriculture and Consumer Servs. of
  Florida 114
E.P. v. Riley 572
E.S.S. Entertainment 2000, Inc. v. Rock
  Star Videos, Inc. 1196
Eagle Motor Lines, Inc. v. Mitchell 654
Eagle-Picher Indus., Inc. v. Balbos 833
Eagle-Picher Indus., Inc. v. Cox..... 440, 441,
  725
Eaglesteon v. Guido 588
East Coast Novelty Co., Inc. v. City of New
  York 107
East Penn Mfg. Co. v. Pineda 833
East River S.S. Corp. v. Transamerica
  Delaval, Inc. 803, 1065, 1084, 1085
Eastern Steel Constructors, Inc. v. City of
  Salem 1073, 1082

Eastin v. Broomfield 861
Eastman v. R. Warehousing & Port
  Services, Inc. 774
Eastwood v. Horse Harbor Found.,
  Inc. 1084
Eastwood v. National Enquirer, Inc. 994,
  1020
Eaton v. Eaton 305
Eaton v. McLain 388, 389
Ebanks v. New York City Transit
  Auth. 307
EBC I, Inc. v. Goldman Sachs & Co. 1144
EBWS, LLC v. Britly Corp. 1073, 1087
Eckman v. Cooper Tire & Rubber
  Co. 938, 983
Economopoulos v. A.G. Pollard Co. 940
Ed Miller & Sons, Inc. v. Earl 1133
Eddy v. Virgin Islands Water & Power
  Auth. 56
Edelman v. Jordan 564
Edenshaw v. Safeway, Inc. 470
Edgewater Motels, Inc. v. Gatzke 758,
  760
Edgin v. Entergy Operations, Inc. 414
Edmonds v. Williamson 1166
Edmunds v. Copeland 467
Edson v. Barre Supervisory Union
  No. 61 647
Edward C. v. City of Albuquerque 422
Edwards v. Fogarty 697
Edwards v. Honeywell, Inc. 265
Edwards v. Lee's Adm'r 95
Edwards v. Lexington County Sheriff's
  Dept. 571, 572
Edwards v. National Audubon Soc'y,
  Inc. 946, 979
Edwards v. Travelers Ins. of Hartford,
  Conn. 1121, 1131
Egbert v. Nissan Motor Co. 840
Egede-Nissen v. Crystal Mountain,
  Inc. 467
Ehrgott v. City of New York 339
Eighth Judicial Dist. Court ex rel. County
  of Clark, State v. 975
Eight Thousand Eight Hundred and Fifty
  Dollars, United States v. 583
Eisel v. Board of Educ. of Montgomery
  County 646, 658
Eiseman v. State 649
Eiss v. Lillis 395, 528
Eklund v. Trost 221
Elam v. Kansas City S. Ry. Co. 441, 443
Eldeco, Inc. v. Charleston Cnty. Sch.
  Dist. 1095, 1100, 1104
Elden v. Sheldon 720
Eldridge v. Johndrow 1100, 1101
Elgin v. Bartlett 719
Eli Investments, LLC v. Silver Slipper
  Casino Venture, LLC 364
Elkerson v. North Jersey Blood Ctr. 281
Elkins v. Ferencz.................................... 528
Ellinwood v. Cohen 605

Elliot, State v. 151
Elliott v. Brunswick Corp. 835
Elliott v. Callan 258
Elliott v. City of New York 244, 468
Elliott v. Denton & Denton 116
Elliott v. Roach 980
Elliott v. Videan 1185
Ellis County State Bank v. Keever 294
Ellis v. Alabama Power Co. 93
Ellis v. Estate of Ellis 436, 592
Ellis v. Price 1000, 1052
Ellis v. Wellons 1044
Ellsworth v. Sherne Lingerie, Inc. 839
Elmer Buchta Trucking, Inc. v. Stanley. 689
Elvis Presley Enterprises, Inc. v.
 Capece 1196
Emanuel v. Great Falls Sch. Dist. 265
Emberton v. GMRI, Inc. 438, 439
Emerich v. Phila. Ctr. for Human Dev.
 Inc. 501, 659
Emerick v. Mutual Benefit Life Ins.
 Co. 111
Emerson v. Magendantz 680, 682
Emery v. State 161
Emo v. Milbank Mut. Ins. Co. 980
Empire Cas. Co. v. St. Paul Fire & Marine
 Ins. Co. 676
Encinias v. Whitener Law Firm,
 P.A. 1173
Enders v. District of Columbia 73
Endorf v. Bohlender 511, 527
Endres v. Endres 58, 177
Engalla v. Permanente Med. Group,
 Inc. 1116, 1130
Engel v. CBS, Inc. 1041, 1111
Engler v. Gulf Interstate Engineering,
 Inc. 757
English v. General Elec. Co. 442
Ennabe v. Manosa 665, 666
Ennett v. Cumberland Cnty. Bd. of
 Educ. 708, 724
Ensminger v. Burton 110, 115
Entrekin v. Internal Medicine Associates of
 Dothan, P.A. 538
Entriken v. Motor Coach Federal Credit
 Union 116
Environmental Network Corp. v. Goodman
 Weiss Miller, LLP 1174, 1175
Eppendorf-Netheler-Hinz GMBH v. Ritter
 GMBH 1201
Equilon Enters., LLC v. Consumer Cause,
 Inc. 985, 986
Equitania Ins. Co. v. Slone & Garrett,
 P.S.C. 1171
Equity Group Ltd. v. Painewebber
 Incorporated 111
Erbrich Products Co., Inc. v. Wills 740
Erdelyi v. Lott 438
Ereth v. Cascade County 1190
ERI Consulting Eng'rs, Inc. v.
 Swinnea 1146

Eric M. v. Cajon Valley Union School
 Dist. 646
Erick Bowman Remedy Co. v. Jensen
 Salsbery Labs., Inc. 961
Ericksen, Arbuthnot, McCarthy, Kearney &
 Walsh, Inc. v. 100 Oak St. 1137
Erickson v. Jones St. Publishers,
 LLC 957
Erickson v. Kongsli 256
Erickson v. U-Haul Int'l 719, 720
Erie R.R. v. Tompkins 46, 476
Ernest F. Loewer, Jr. Farms, Inc. v.
 National Bank of Arkansas 128
Ervin v. American Guardian Life Assurance
 Co. 499
ESCA Corp. v. KPMG Peat
 Marwick 1131
Escola v. Coca Cola Bottling Co. of
 Fresno 22, 301
Eskin v. Bartee 716, 717
Espinal v. Melville Snow Contractors,
 Inc. 630
Espinoza v. Schulenburg 366, 611
Espinoza v. Thomas 68, 71
Ess v. Eskaton Props., Inc. 718
Estelle v. Gamble 584, 621, 645
Estep v. Mike Ferrell Ford Lincoln-
 Mercury, Inc. 407, 408, 844
Estiverne, Estate of Desir ex rel. v.
 Vertus 639
Etherton v. Doe 70
Ethyl Corp. v. Johnson 265
Etkind v. Suarez 679, 680
eToll, Inc. v. Elias/Savion Adver.,
 Inc. 1079
Ettlinger v. Trustees of Randolph-Macon
 Coll. 597
ETW Corp. v. Jireh Publ'g, Inc. 1006
Euclid, Ohio, Village of v. Ambler Realty
 Co. 739
Eugene, City of v. McDermed 914
Evans v. City of Bakersfield 137
Evans v. Dayton Hudson 720
Evans v. Dean Witter Reynolds, Inc. 1153
Evans v. Lorillard Tobacco Co. 809, 833
Evans v. State 876
Evard v. Southern California Edison 769
Evridge v. American Honda Motor
 Co. 829
Ewing v. Northridge Hospital Medical
 Center 659
Excavation Technologies, Inc. v. Columbia
 Gas Co. of Pa. 1062, 1068, 1069, 1071,
 1126
Excel Constr., Inc. v. HKM Eng'g,
 Inc. 1126
Exner v. Sherman Power Constr. Co. 787
Express Scripts, Inc., PBM Litig.,
 In re. 1144
Exxon Co., U.S.A. v. Sofec, Inc. 371, 373,
 374, 391
Exxon Mobil Corp. v. Albright 726

Exxon Mobil Corp. v. Kinder Morgan
   Operating L.P. 121
Exxon Shipping Co. v. Baker 863, 864,
   867, 870, 872
Ezell v. Cockrell...................... 564, 571, 574
Ezzell v. Miranne............................... 399
Ezzo, Champion ex rel. v. Dunfee.......... 651
F.A. v. W.J.F. 973
F.F.P. Operating Partners, L.P. v.
   Duenez....................................... 899, 900
F.G. v. MacDonell....................... 181, 455
Fabricor, Inc. v. E.I. DuPont de Nemours &
   Co... 1102
Fabrikant v. French 582
Fackrell v. Marshall 759
Faegre & Benson LLP v. Purdy............ 1006
Fager v. Hundt 594
Fahrendorff v. North Homes, Inc. 756
Faile v. South Carolina Dep't of Juvenile
   Justice 576, 579
Fair Oaks Hosp. v. Pocrass 73
Fair Price Med. Supply Corp. v. Travelers
   Indem. Co.. 927
Fairbanks, City of v. Rice........................ 959
Fairchild v. Glenhaven Funeral Servs. 16
Fairchild v. The California Stage Co. 447
Fairfax Hosp. v. Curtis 723
Faiveley Transport Malmo AB v. Wabtec
   Corp. 1204
Falada v. Trinity Industries, Inc. 844
Falcone v. Perry.................................... 857
Falk v. Sadler 1179
Falline v. GNLV Corp. 921
Falls v. Scott 768
Famology.Com Inc. v. Perot Systems
   Corp. 111
Fancher v. Fagella................................ 736
Fandrey ex rel. Connell v. American Family
   Mut. Ins. Co. 3, 340
Fantozzi v. Sandusky Cement Prods.
   Corp. 852
Farabaugh v. Pennsylvania Turnpike
   Comm'n 604
Farias v. Mr. Heater, Inc. 830
Farley v. Engelken 861
Farley v. Sartin 671
Farm Bureau Ins. v. Phillips 234, 236
Farm Bureau Mut. Ins. Co. of Ark., Inc. v.
   Henley 58, 87
Farm Bureau v. Cully's Motorcross
   Park 1027
Farmer v. B & G Food Enters., Inc.605, 607,
   609
Farmer v. Brennan............................ 60, 584
Farmers Educ. & Coop. Union of Am. v.
   WDAY, Inc. 965
Farmers Ins. Exchange v. State 160
Farnham v. Bombardier, Inc. 835
Farr v. NC Machinery Co........................ 352
Farrar v. Hobby 582
Farwell v. Boston & Worcester R.R. 911
Farwell v. Keaton 621

Faul v. Jelco, Inc. 758
Faust v. Albertson................................. 296
Faverty v. McDonald's Restaurants of
   Oregon, Inc. 637
Favreau v. Miller 491
Faya v. Almaraz 726
Fazzolari v. Portland School Dist.
   No. 1J... 647
Fearing v. Bucher 762
Federal Deposit Insurance Corp. v.
   Meyer... 551
Federal Ins. Co. I.C. v. Banco de
   Ponce.. 124
Federal Ins. Co. v. Lazzara Yachts of N.
   Am., Inc.. 1084
Fedorczyk v. Caribbean Cruise Lines,
   Ltd... 297, 316
Feeley v. Baer..................................... 519
Fehrman v. Smirl.................................. 302
Feiereisen v. Newpage Corp................... 915
Fein v. Permanente Med. Group 496, 875
Feld v. Borkowski 240, 425
Felder v. Physiotherapy Assocs.............. 852
Feldman v. Allegheny Airlines, Inc......... 859
Feldman v. Feldman............................ 1050
Feldman v. Gogos................................. 427
Feller v. First Interstate Bancsystem,
   Inc. 714
Fellner v. Tri-Union Seafoods, LLC 844
Fellows v. National Enquirer, Inc. 1021
Felsen v. Sol Cafe Mfg. Corp. 1104
Feltch v. General Rental Co. 720
Feltmeier v. Feltmeier 435
Felton v. Lovett 494, 514, 517, 519
FEMA Trailer Formaldehyde Products
   Liability Litigation (Mississippi
   Plaintiffs), In re 552
Fennell v. Southern Md. Hosp. Ctr.,
   Inc. 331
Ferdon v. Wisconsin Patients Comp.
   Fund.. 875
Ferebee v. Chevron Chem. Co. 833
Feres v. United States 558, 561
Ferguson v. City of Chicago.................. 1035
Ferguson v. Lieff, Cabraser, Heimann &
   Bernstein, LLP 1185
Fermino v. Fedco.......................... 922, 923
Fernandez v. Kozar............................... 697
Fernandez v. Romo 592
Fernandez v. Walgreen Hastings Co...... 716,
   719
Ferrara v. Galluchio....................... 725, 856
Ferreira v. D'Asaro 784
Ferrell v. Baxter.......................... 249, 251
Ferri v. Ackerman 581, 1191
Ferriter v. Daniel O'Connell's Sons,
   Inc. 719
Fetick v. American Cyanamid Co........... 728
FGA, Inc. v. Giglio.............................. 469
Fiacco v. Sigma Alpha Epsilon
   Fraternity 992
Fiala v. Rains 621

Ficek v. Morken 572
Field v. Boyer Co. 888
Field v. Empire Case Goods Co. 800
Field v. Mans 1131, 1132
Field v. Philadelphia Elec. Co. 67
Fielder v. Stonack 287
Fields v. Dailey 134
Fields v. Henrich 477
Fields v. Senior Citizens Ctr., Inc. 392
Fields v. State 140
Fieux v. Cardiovascular & Thoracic Clinic, P.C. 302
Fifield Manor v. Finston 1066
Fifth Club, Inc. v. Ramirez 764
Figueiredo-Torres v. Nickel 1052
Fike v. Peace 767
Fikes v. Furst 1096, 1098, 1100, 1101, 1104, 1109
Filip v. Block 1074
Finan v. Atria East Associates 469
Finch v. Christensen 217
Finch v. Inspectech, LLC 414
Finck v. City of Tea 947, 960
Finderne Mgmt. Co., Inc. v. Barrett 1138
Fine Host Corp. Sec. Litig. 1125
Fink v. City of New York 223
Finnegan ex rel. Skoglind v. Wis. Patients Comp. Fund 716
Fiocco v. Carver 760
Fiorenzano v. Lima 720
Fire Ins. Exch. v. Diehl 233
Fireman's Fund Ins. Co. v. SEC Donohue, Inc. 1081
First Arkansas Bank & Trust, Trustee v. Gill Elrod Ragon Owen & Sherman, P.A. 1175
First Assembly of God, Inc. v. Tex. Utils. Elec. Co. 218
First Fla. Bank, N.A. v. Max Mitchell & Co. 1135
First Interstate Bank of Gallup v. Foutz 1140
First Midwest Bank v. Stewart Title Guar. Co. 1074, 1086
First Nat'l Bank and Trust Corp. v. American Eurocopter Corp. 832
First Nat'l Bank of Ariz. v. Dupree 233, 234
First Nat'l Bank of Dwight v. Regent Sports Corp. 829
First Nat'l Bank of Pulaski, Tenn. v. Thomas 862
First Valley Bank of Los Fresnos v. Martin 1028, 1033
First Wyo. Bank, Casper v. Mudge 1098
Firth v. Scherzberg 742
Fischer v. Unipac Serv. Corp. 964
Fisher Bros. Sales, Inc. v. United States 554
Fisher v. Big Y Foods, Inc. 469
Fisher v. Carrousel Motor Hotel, Inc. 68
Fisher v. Kahler 1125

Fisher v. San Pedro Peninsula Hosp. 710
Fisher v. Swift Transp. Co. 347, 348
Fisher v. Townsends, Inc. 764, 765, 766
Fishman v. Brooks 1169
Fisk v. City of Kirkland 566, 574
Fitch v. Valentine 1051
Fitts v. Arms 510
Fitzmaurice v. Flynn 509
Fitzpatrick v. Natter 296, 518
Flagler Company v. Savage 467
Flagstaff Affordable Housing Ltd. P'ship v. Design Alliance, Inc. 1062, 1070, 1086, 1112
Flagstaff, City of v. Atchison, Topeka & Santa Fe Ry. 745
Flake v. Greensboro News Co. 1005
Flamm v. American Ass'n of Univ. Women 996
Flamm, King v. 504
Flanagan v. Flanagan 1010
Flanagan v. McLane 973
Flatley v. Mauro 986
Flatt v. Kantak 517
Flax v. DaimlerChrysler Corp. 724, 862
Flax v. Schertler 1171
Fleckner v. Dionne 371
Fleetwood Enters., Inc. v. Progressive N. Ins. Co. 803, 1065
Fleetwood Retail Corp. of New Mexico v. LeDoux 1028, 1040, 1047
Fleishman v. Eli Lilly & Co. 435
Fletcher v. City of Independence 734
Fletcher v. Dorchester Mutual Ins. Co 1157
Fletcher v. South Peninsula Hosp. 771
Flint Hills Rural Elec. Coop. Ass'n v. Federated Rural Elec. Ins. Corp. 864
Flizack v. Good News Home for Women, Inc. 707
Flood Litigation, In re 787
Florence v. Goldberg 286, 287, 571, 624
Florenzano v. Olson 1121
Flores v. Cameron County, Tex. 588
Flores v. Exprezit! Stores 98-Georgia, LLC 662
Florida Dep't of Corr. v. Abril 722
Florida Dep't of Health & Rehab. Servs. v. S.A.P. 438, 439
Florida Evergreen Foliage v. E.I. DuPont De Nemours & Co. 968
Florida Farm Bureau Casualty Ins. Co. v. Patterson 126
Florida Publishing Co. v. Fletcher 169
Florida Star v. B.J.F. 1018
Florida v. Jones 153
Flower v. Adam 192
Flowers v. Carville 1019
Flowers v. District of Columbia 683
Flowers v. Rock Creek Terrace Ltd. P'ship 607, 609, 610, 613
Flugge v. Flugge 1040
Flynn v. United States 557

Fochtman v. Honolulu Police and Fire
Departments 623
Foddrill v. Crane 296, 326
Foggia v. Des Moines Bowl-O-Mat,
Inc. 323
Foldi v. Jeffries 594
Foley v. Argosy Gaming Co. 1041
Foley v. Harris 743
Foley v. Polaroid Corp. 922
Folz v. State 723
Fontaine v. Roman Catholic Church of
Archdiocese of New Orleans 180
Fontenot v. Patterson Ins. 894
Food Lion, Inc. v. Capital Cities/ABC,
Inc. 177
Food Pageant, Inc. v. Consol. Edison Co.,
Inc. 240
Foot and Reynolds v. Wiswall 193
Foot v. Card 1050
Foote v. Albany Med. Ctr. Hosp. 681
Foote v. Simek 341
Foradori v. Harris 855
Ford Motor Co. v. Boomer 832
Ford Motor Co. v. Gibson 832
Ford Motor Co. v. Reed 811
Ford Motor Co. v. Rushford 827, 828
Ford Motor Credit Co. v. Byrd 116
Ford Motor Credit Co. v. Hickey Ford Sales,
Inc. 1026
Ford v. Revlon, Inc. 69, 72, 710
Ford v. Trident Fisheries Co. 318
Fordham v. Oldroyd 605
Foreign Car Ctr., Inc. v. Essex Process Serv.
Inc. 115, 125
Foreman v. AS Mid-America, Inc. 1122
Foreman v. Callahan 924
Foremost Farms USA Co-op. v.
Performance Process, Inc. 1082
Foremost Ins. Co. v. Parham 1131
Forest Laboratories, Inc. v. Pillsbury
Co. 1205
Foretich v. Capital Cities/ABC, Inc. 975
Forma Scientific, Inc. v. Biosera, Inc. 823
Formento v. Encanto Bus. Park 1136
Forminio v. City of New York 452
Forrester v. White 578, 967
Forsythe v. Clark USA, Inc. 204
Fort Smith, City of v. Brooks 917
Fortin v. The Roman Catholic Bishop of
Portland 456
Foshee v. Southern Finance & Thrift
Corp. 1034
Foss v. Kincade 239, 280, 345, 474, 477
Foss v. Kincaid 280
Fossett v. Davis 1108
Foster v. Churchill 944, 1096
Foster v. City of Keyser 307, 788
Foster v. Costco Wholesale Corp. 471
Foster v. Preston Mill Co. 792
Fotos v. Firemen's Ins. Co. of Washington,
D.C. 117, 118
Fouldes v. Willoughby 105

Four R Cattle Co. v. Mullins 1121
Fowle v. Fowle 1041
Fowler v. Key System Transit Lines 286
Fowler v. United States 552, 580
Fox v. City & Cty. of San Francisco 213,
226
Fox v. Ethicon Endo-Surgery, Inc. 430
Fox v. Ford Motor Co. 840
Fox v. Smith 513
Fox v. Warner-Quinlan Asphalt Co. 144
Fox v. White 1167
Fox v. Wills 1179
Fraguglia v. Sala 132
Frain v. State Farm Ins. Co. 654
Francis v. Gallo 966
Franco v. Bunyard 252
Franklin Corp. v. Tedford 240
Franklin Grove Corp. v. Drexel 1069,
1083
Franklin v. Hill 1056
Franks v. Independent Prod. Co.,
Inc. 605, 774
Fraser v. Park Newspapers of St. Lawrence
Inc. 957
Frazier ex rel. Frazier v. Norton 172, 233
Frazier v. Commonwealth 221
Fred Siegel Co., L.P.A. v. Arter &
Hadden 1095, 1096, 1097, 1104
Frederick v. Philadelphia Rapid Transit
Co. 460, 461
Fredericks v. Castora 231
Freeman & Mills, Inc. v. Belcher Oil
Co. 1146
Freeman v. Davidson 689
Freeman v. Grain Processing Corp. 733
Freeway Park Buildings, Inc. v. Western
States Wholesale Supply 149
Freightliner Corp. v. Myrick 846
Freihofer v. Hearst Corp. 1007,
1018, 1111
French Energy, Inc. v. Alexander 1128
French v. Jadon, Inc. 959
French v. Sunburst Properties 462
French-Tex Cleaners, Inc. v. Cafaro
Co. 128
Fresco v. 157 East 72nd Street
Condominium 267
Fresno Traction Co. v. Atchison, T. & S. F.
Ry. 245
Frey v. Kouf 56, 58, 61
Friederichs v. Huebner 400
Friedman v. C & S Car Servs. 859
Friedman v. Dozorc 1037, 1041, 1176
Friedman v. Friedman 1054
Friedman v. Merck & Co. 727
Friedrich v. Fetterman & Assocs.,
P.A. 317
Frieler v. Carlson Marketing Group,
Inc. 757, 761, 762
Friend v. Cove Methodist Church,
Inc. 599

Friends For All Children, Inc. v. Lockheed Aircraft Corp. 854
Friends of Animals, Inc. v. Associated Fur Mfrs., Inc. 993
Friends of Yelverton, Inc. v. 163rd Street Improvement Council, Inc. 150
Frinzi v. Hanson 943, 944, 948
Frisch, Matter of Estate of 172
Friske v. Hogan 1175
Friter v. Iolab Corp. 514
Fritts v. McKinne 395
Froelich v. Adair 1011
Frohs v. Greene 430
Fromson v. State 1111
Frontier Ins. Co. v. Blaty 693
Frost v. Allred 249, 251, 258
Frost v. Salter Path Fire & Rescue 914
Frugis v. Bracigliano 898, 899, 900
Fruit v. Schreiner 756
Fruiterman v. Granata 678
Fry v. Carter 221
Frye v. Clark County 574
Fu v. State 209, 214
Fuchsgruber v. Custom Accessories, Inc. 803, 835, 885
Fuentes v. Shevin 127
Fuerschbach v. Southwest Airlines Co. 58, 73, 74, 164
Fujimoto v. Au 411
Fuller Family Holdings, LLC v. Northern Trust Co. 1160
Fuller v. Local Union No. 106, United Broth. of Carpenters and Joiners of America 1043
Fuller v. Standard Stations, Inc. 654
Fuller v. Tucker 431
Fulmer v. Timber Inn Restaurant and Lounge, Inc. 473, 663
Fultz v. Delhaize Am., Inc. 292
Fuqua v. Aetna Cas. & Sur. Co. 852
Furman v. Rural Elec. Co. 215
Furstein v. Hill 463
Furumizo, United States v. 690
Fyssakis v. Knight Equipment Corp. 829
G.D. v. Kenny 955
G.J. Leasing Co., Inc. v. Union Elec. Co. 783, 788, 789
Gabaldon v. Jay-Bi Property Mgmt., Inc. 716
Gaboury v. Ireland Road Grace Brethern, Inc. 460
Gadsden, Ex parte City of 1031
Gaertner v. Holcka 408
Gagan v. Yast 976
Gagnon v. State 570
Gaidys, United States v. 94, 562
Gaines v. Comanche Cnty. Med. Hosp. 512, 539
Gaita v. Laurel Grove Cemetery Co. 466
Galaxy Cable, Inc. v. Davis 862
Galindo v. TMT Transp., Inc. 226
Galindo v. Town of Clarkstown 484

Gallagher v. H.V. Pierhomes, LLC 787
Gallara v. Koskovich 364
Gallo v. Alitalia-Linee Aeree Italiane-Societa per Azioni 960
Gallo, People v. 744
Galloway v. State 249, 414
Galvao v. G.R. Robert Const. Co. 773
Galveston, H. & S.A. Ry. v. Zantzinger 398
Galvez v. Frields 677, 678
Gamble v. Dollar Gen. Corp. 711
Ganim v. Smith & Wesson Corp. 1066
Gannon, Borns ex rel. v. Voss 781
Ganz v. United States Cycling Fed'n 287
Garback v. Lossing 1008
Garcia v. City of New York 647
Garcia v. City of South Tucson 610
Garcia v. Hargrove 251
Garcia v. Kozlov, Seaton, Romanini & Brooks, P.C. 1174
Garcia v. Lifemark Hospitals of Fla. 497
Garcia v. Sanchez 95
Garcia v. Sumrall 779
Garcia v. Whitaker 1036
Gardner v. National Bulk Carriers, Inc. 328, 621
Garhart v. Columbia/Healthone, LLC 875
Garland v. Roy 1183
Garnes v. Fleming Landfill, Inc. 865
Garnot v. Johnson 299
Garnsey v. Morbark Indus., Inc. 817, 824
Garofolo v. Fairview Park 1013
Garr v. City of Ottumwa 317
Garratt v. Dailey 56, 68, 82
Garreans v. City of Omaha 479
Garrison v. Deschutes County 564
Garrison v. Sun Printing & Publ'g Ass'n 999
Gartrell v. Department of Corr. 916
Garvin, Guardianship of v. Tupelo Furniture Market, Inc. 654
Garweth Corp. v. Boston Edison Co. 1067
Gaspard v. Beadle 708
Gaston v. Viclo Realty Co. 293
Gates of the Mountains Lakeshore Homes, Inc., United States v. 93
Gates v. Discovery Commc'ns, Inc. 1005, 1017
Gates v. Navy 399
Gates v. Richardson 723
Gateway Foam Insulators, Inc. v. Jokerst Paving & Contracting, Inc. 858
Gath v. M/A-Com, Inc. 1157, 1158
Gattis v. Kilgo 975, 980
Gau v. Smitty's Super Valu, Inc. 155
Gaubert, United States v. 554, 555, 556
Gaudio v. Ford Motor Co. 408
Gaudreau v. Clinton Irrigation Dist. 268
Gaulding v. Celotex Corp. 329
Gautschi v. Maisel 976
Gauvin v. Clark 424

Gavin W. v. YMCA of Metro. Los
    Angeles... 413
Gawloski v. Miller Brewing Co. 841
Gaylor v. Jeffco..................................... 1188
Gaytan v. Wal-Mart 764
Gazette, Inc. v. Harris................. 952, 1000
Gazo v. City of Stamford 628, 630, 766
Gebhardt v. O'Rourke 1188
Geddes v. Daughters of Charity of St.
    Vincent de Paul, Inc. 74
Geddes v. Mill Creek Country Club,
    Inc.. 419
Geernaert v. Mitchell 1134
Geier v. American Honda Motor Co. 846
General Elec. Co. v. Moritz............. 471, 604
General Elec. Co. v. Sargent & Lundy ... 974
General Motors Corp. v. Alumi-Bunk,
    Inc.. 1078
General Motors Corp. v. Saenz.............. 829
General Motors Corp. v. Sanchez ... 836, 837
General Motors Corp. v. Wolhar..... 373, 841
General Refractories Co. v. Fireman's Fund
    Ins. Co. 1042, 1043, 1044, 1045
Genereux v. Am. Beryllia Corp.............. 430
Gennari v. Weichert Co. Realtors........ 1130,
    1131
Genrich, Estate of v. OHIC Ins. Co. 697
Gentry v. Craycraft 425, 426
Genzel v. Halvorson 63
George F. Hillenbrand, Inc. v. Insurance
    Co. of North America........................ 1037
George v. Estate of Baker 450
George v. University of Idaho................. 648
Georgia Pacific, LLC v. Farrar 826
Gerdau Ameristeel, Inc. v. Ratliff........... 430
Gerill Corp. v. Jack L. Hargrove Builders,
    Inc.. 1140
Gertz v. Robert Welch, Inc. 46, 990
Getchell v. Lodge 247
Getchell v. Rogers Jewelry..................... 469
Get-N-Go, Inc. v. Markins..................... 417
Ghassemieh v. Scafer 59
Giacalone v. Housing Authority of Town of
    Wallingford 656
Giacona v. Tapley................................. 475
Giancarlo v. Karabanowski..................... 260
Giant Food, Inc. v. Mitchell 268
Giardina v. Bennett............................... 670
Gibb v. Stetson 606
Gibson v. Abbott................................... 969
Gibson v. Capano................................. 1128
Gibson v. County of Washoe, Nevada..... 355
Gibson v. Garcia 360
Gibson v. Gibson........................ 594, 1117
Gibson v. Regions Financial Corp......... 1046
Gibson v. State 1030
Giddings & Lewis, Inc. v. Industrial Risk
    Insurers.. 803
Giese v. NCNB Texas Forney Banking
    Center 152
Giggers v. Memphis Hous. Auth........... 204,
    205, 569

Gignilliat v. Gignilliat, Savitz & Bettis,
    LLP 1006
Gilbert v. Miodovnik 498
Gilbert v. Sykes...................................1091
Gilbert Wheeler, Inc. v. Enbridge Piplelines
    (East Texas), L.P. 97
Gilchrist v. City of Troy 422
Giles v. City of New Haven....................307
Giles v. General Motors Acceptance
    Corp.................... 1154, 1156, 1157
Giles v. Hill Lewis Marce.....................1045
Gilhooley v. Star Mkt. Co., Inc. 268
Gillespie, Application of...........................96
Gilliam v. Roche Biomedical Labs.,
    Inc...725
Gillikin v. Bell....................................954
Gillmor v. Salt Lake City......................161
Gilmer v. Ellington 636
Gilmore v. Acme Taxi Co. 763
Gilmore v. Shell Oil Co. 346
Gilmore v. Walgreen Co.........................472
Gilson v. Drees Bros...............................418
Gilson v. Metropolitan Opera..........285, 618
Gina Chin & Assoc. v. First Union
    Bank...757
Ginsberg v. Wineman 490
Gipson v. Kasey......................204, 205, 207,
    211, 212, 244
Giraldo v. California Dep't of Corrections
    and Rehabilitation..............................645
Giron v. Koktavy 1172
Gist v. Macon County Sheriff's Dept.......978
Giuliani v. Guiler.................................719
Giunta v. Delta Intern. Machinery 815
Givens v. Mullikin................................1046
Gladhart v. Oregon Vineyard Supply
    Co. 847
Gladon v. Greater Cleveland Regional
    Transit Auth......................... 460, 467
Glamann v. St. Paul Fire & Marine Ins.
    Co. 1184
Glamorgan Coal Company, Limited, and
    Others v. South Wales Miners'
    Federation and Others.......................1095
Glanzer v. Shepard 1124, 1125
Glaskox v. Glaskox................................593
Glass v. Hazen Confectionery Co. 911
Glaze v. Larsen 1187, 1190
Gleason v. Peters 571
Gleason v. Smolinski..............................708
Gleeson v. Virginia Midland Ry. Co........448
Gleitman v. Cosgrove.............................678
Glidden v. Szybiak................................106
Glittenberg v. Doughboy Recreational
    Industries 827
Glona v. American Guarantee & Liab. Ins.
    Co. 695
Glotzbach v. Froman.............................1159
Glover v. Boy Scouts of America 757
Glover v. Callahan 172
Glover v. Jackson State University........322,
    363

Gmurzynska v. Hutton.......................... 1200
Gobin v. Globe Pub. Co................. 996, 1001
Godbehere v. Phoenix Newspapers,
  Inc.. 1021
Goddard v. Farmers Ins. Co. of Or. 869
Godesky v. Provo City Corp. 376
Godfrey v. Iverson 36
Godwin v. Memorial Medical Center...... 532
Goff v. Clarke.................................... 62, 64
Goff v. Elmo Greer & Sons Constr. Co.,
  Inc.. 870
Gohari v. Darvish 975, 976
Goldberg v. Florida Power & Light
  Co.............................. 338, 353, 365
Goldberg v. Horowitz.............................. 505
Golden Peanut Co., LLC, In re 694
Golden, State ex rel. v. Kaufman.......... 1052
Goldizen v. Grant County Nursing
  Home 686
Goldnamer v. O'Brien............................. 183
Goldstein v. Levy 301
Goldstein v. Lustig 1179
Goldstein v. Sabella.............................. 1038
Golen v. Union Corp., U.C.O.-M.B.A.,
  Inc... 742, 744
Golla v. General Motors Corp. 847
Goller v. White....................................... 594
Gomez v. Superior Court......... 447, 448, 450
Gompper v. Visz, Inc. 1119
Gonsalves v. Nissan Motor Corp. in Haw.,
  Ltd. 943
Gonzales v. Mascarenas 670
Gonzalez v. City of Elgin........................ 585
Gonzalez v. Poplawsky............................ 314
Gonzalez v. Sessom 952
Gooch v. Bethel A.M.E. Church 631
Gooden v. City of Talladega 270, 575
Gooden v. Coors Technical Ceramic
  Co.. 914
Goodfellow v. Coggburn 236
Gooding v. University Hosp. Bldg.,
  Inc... 331
Goodrich v. Blair 225
Goodrich v. Long Island R.R. Co..... 707, 715
Goodwin v. Jackson 475
Goodyear Tire & Rubber Co. v. Hughes
  Supply, Inc. 303
Gorab v. Zook.. 516
Gordon v. Bank of N.Y. Mellon Corp. 709
Gordon v. Eastern Ry. Supply, Inc. 401
Gordon v. Sanders 768, 769
Gordon v. Villegas 74
Gordy, Matter of 172, 174
Gore v. People's Sav. Bank............. 257, 492
Gore v. Rains & Block 1183
Gorman v. Abbott Labs. 330
Gorman v. Sabo 749
Gorski v. Smith.......................... 1146, 1178
Gortarez v. Smitty's Super Valu, Inc..... 133,
  137, 151, 153, 154, 156
Gosden v. Louis 957, 960

Gosewisch v. American Honda Motor
  Co. 833
Gosnell Dev. Corp. of Ariz., In re 1077
Goss v. Allen.. 236
Gossels v. Fleet Nat'l Bank 1123, 1154
Gossett v. Jackson.................................... 214
Gossner v. Utah Power & Light 789
Gottschalk v. Benson 1202, 1203
Goudrealt v. Kleeman............................. 314
Gouge v. Central Illinois Public Service
  Co. 487
Gouin v. Gouin 72
Gould v. American Family Mut. Ins.
  Co. 420
Gourley v. Nebraska Methodist Health Sys.,
  Inc. 875
Gouse v. Cassel 163
Gouveia v. Phillips 514
Governmental Liability from Operation of
  Zoo 782
Grabenstein v. Sunsted 139
Graber v. City of Ankeny........................ 569
Graber v. City of Peoria 734
Grace v. Kumalaa 450
Gracey v. Eaker...................................... 1143
Graeff v. Baptist Temple of
  Springfield 855
Graff v. Motta.. 1093
Graff v. Robert M. Swendra Agency,
  Inc. 1074
Grager v. Schudar 178, 708
Gragg v. Calandra.................................... 514
Graham v. Connor............................ 583, 584
Graham v. Keuchel 353, 676
Graham v. Sheriff v. Logan County 178
Grambling, Godoy ex rel. v. E.I. DuPont de
  Nemours and Co. 809, 821
Gramlich v. Wurst 144, 146
Grammer v. John J. Kane Regional
  Centers-Glen Hazel...................... 545, 583
Grand Aerie Fraternal Order of Eagles v.
  Carneyhan 658
Grannum v. Berard................................. 171
Grant v. Allen... 158
Grant v. American Nat'l Red Cross......... 331
Grant v. Nihill....................................... 416
Grant v. Reader's Digest Ass'n, Inc........ 946
Grant v. South Roxana Dad's Club 474
Grant v. Thornton.................................. 244
Grantham v. Vanderzyl 711
Graubard Mollen Dannett & Horowitz v.
  Moskovitz.. 1176
Gravel v. United States 968
Graves v. Estabrook........................ 717, 721
Graves, Estate of v. City of
  Circleville.. 241 571
Gray v. Badger Mining Corp. 828, 829
Gray v. Manitowoc Co., Inc..................... 814
Gray v. State 1030
Gray v. Westinghouse Elec. Corp. 743
Grayson v. Wofsey, Rosen, Kweskin and
  Kuriansky 1182

Great American E & S Ins. Co. v.
  Quintairos, Prieto, Wood & Boyer,
  P.A. 1166
Great Atlantic & Pacific Tea Co. v.
  Paul 153
Great Coastal Express, Inc. v.
  Ellington.. 973
Great Escape, Inc. v. Union City Body Co.,
  Inc.. 1108
Great Lakes Higher Education Corp. v.
  Austin Bank of Chicago.................... 1152
Great Sw. Fire Ins. Co. v. CNA Ins.
  Cos. 1112
Greater Richmond Transit Co. v.
  Wilkerson 447
Greaves v. Galchutt................................ 415
Greco v. Sumner Tavern, Inc. 638
Green Acres Trust v. London 966, 977,
  981
Green Bay Packaging, Inc. v. Preferred
  Packaging, Inc........................ 1037, 1092
Green, In re Estate of.......................... 1144
Green v. Alpharma 313
Green v. Bittner.................................... 692
Green v. CBS Inc. 980, 1013
Green v. Edmands Co............................ 835
Green v. Ford Motor Co................. 407, 840
Green v. General Motors Corp. 859
Green v. General Petroleum Corp. 88,
  787
Green v. Lewis Truck Lines................... 435
Green v. Mid Dakota Clinic 419
Green v. N.B.S...................................... 873
Green v. Racing Ass'n of Cent. Iowa.... 1095,
  1097, 1104, 1105
Green v. Smith & Nephew AHP, Inc. 803,
  825
Green v. Spinning......................... 735, 742
Green v. Superior Court......................... 491
Green v. Walker. 499
Greenbelt Coop. Publ'g Ass'n v.
  Bresler..................................... 977, 989
Greenberg v. Giddings 214
Greenberg v. Perkins............................. 499
Greenberg v. Wolfberg 1041
Greenberg, Trager & Herbst, LLP v. HSBC
  Bank USA 1130
Greene v. Tinker.................................. 960
Greenman v. Yuba Power Prods.,
  Inc. 801, 1070
Greenmoss Builders, Inc. v. Dun &
  Bradstreet, Inc................................. 938
Greenpeace, Inc. v. Dow Chemical Co. 91
Greensleeves, Inc. v. Smiley 1096, 1098
Greenwich Citizens Comm., Inc. v. Counties
  of Warren and Washington Indus. Dev.
  Agency 1032
Gregoire v. City of Oak Harbor.............. 395
Gregor v. Argenot Great Central Ins.
  Co. 579
Gregory v. Carey.................................. 856
Gregory v. Clive................................... 572

Gregory v. Cott................................ 226, 420
Gregory v. Hawkins 1172
Gregory v. Johnson 477
Gregory's Inc. v. Haan 974
Gresham v. Taylor 778
Grey's Ex'r v. Mobile Trade Co.............. 252
Greycas, Inc. v. Proud 279, 394, 1131,
  1170
Greyhound Lines, Inc. v. Cobb County,
  Ga... 882
Gribben v. Wal-Mart Stores, Inc. 1157
Griebler v. Doughboy Recreational, Inc. .. 470
Griego v. Wilson................................... 139
Griesenbeck v. Walker............................ 663
Griesi v. Atlantic Gen. Hosp. Corp. 209,
  1125
Griffin v. Moseley................................. 516
Griffis v. Wheeler................................. 696
Griglione v. Martin 244
Grimes v. Kennedy Krieger Inst.,
  Inc. 174, 244, 252, 623
Grimm v. Ariz. Bd. of Pardons &
  Paroles 241, 576
Grimshaw v. Ford Motor Co. 276, 818
Grisham v. Philip Morris U.S.A., Inc...... 431
Griva v. Davison................................. 1169
Grivas v. Grivas.................................. 594
Groch v. General Motors Corp................. 848
Grodin v. Grodin.................................. 675
Groenevelt Transport Efficiency, Inc. v.
  Lubecore Intern., Inc....................... 1201
Grolean v. Bjornson Oil Co. 471
Groob v. KeyBank 1143
Groshek v. Trewin........................... 869, 870
Gross v. Capital Elec. Line Builders,
  Inc. 86, 189
Gross v. Lyons..................................... 880
Gross v. Sussex Inc. 1121, 1132
Grosso v. Monfalcone, Inc...................... 119
Grotts v. Zahner................................... 717
Grove v. PeaceHealth St. Joseph's
  Hospital 530
Grover v. Eli Lilly & Co. 676
Groves v. Taylor 716, 717
Grubbs v. Barbourville Family Health Ctr.,
  P.S.C. 679
Grube v. Daun....................... 787, 788, 789
Grube v. Union Pac. R.R....................... 715
Gruenberg v. Aetna Ins. Co. 1147
Grunwald v. Bronkesh........................... 430
Grynberg v. Questar Pipeline Co. 122,
  1078, 1156
Grzanka v. Pfeifer................................ 819
GTE Sw., Inc. v. Bruce......................... 706
Guaranty Residential Lending, Inc. v.
  International Mortgage Ctr., Inc...... 1074,
  1075
Guarascio v. Drake Associates Inc. 821
Gubbins v. Hurson 304
Guccione v. Hustler Magazine, Inc. 956
Guess v. Sharp Mfg. Co. of Am............. 917
Guest v. McLaverty.............................. 1181

Guillory v. Interstate Gas Station 915
Guinan v. Famous Players-Lasky
    Corp. 249
Guinn v. Murray 1181
Guldy v. Pyramid Corp. 283
Gulfstream Aerospace Servs. Corp. v.
    United States Aviation Underwriters,
    Inc. 1078, 1085
Gulycz v. Stop and Shop Companies 470
Gunderson v. Harrington 919
Gunkel v. Renovations, Inc. 804
Gunnell v. Arizona Public Service
    Co. 375, 376
Gunsberg v. Roseland Corp. 960
Gus' Catering, Inc. v. Menusoft Sys. 1079
Gustafson v. Payless Drug Stores
    Northwest, Inc. 1029
Guste v. M/V Testbank, Louisiana ex
    rel.v. 1068
Guth v. Freeland 704, 729
Gutierrez de Martinez v. Drug Enforcement
    Admin. 759, 760
Gutierrez de Martinez v. Lamagno 580
Guzman v. County of Monterey 564
Gypsum Carrier, Inc. v. Handelsman 859
H. Russell Taylor's Fire Prevention Serv.,
    Inc. v. Coca Cola Bottling Corp. 128
H.J., Inc. v. International Telephone &
    Telegraph Corp. 111, 1151
H.R. Moch Co. v. Rensselaer Water
    Co. 619, 628
H.R.B. v. J.L.G. 457
H.R.H. Metals, Inc. v. Miller 415
Haas, State v. 137, 141
Habco v. L & B Oilfield Serv., Inc. 882
Haberer v. Rice 1185
Habershaw v. Michaels Stores, Inc. 293,
    294, 297
Hac v. University of Haw. 707
Hack v. Gillespie 607
Hackbart v. Cincinnati Bengals, Inc. 424
Haddix v. Playtex Family Products
    Corp. 813
Haddock v. City of New York 658
Hadfield v. Gilchrist 119
Hafer v. Melo 586
Haff v. Hettich 887
Haft v. Lone Palm Hotel 244, 245, 327
Hagan v. Coca-Cola Bottling Co. 722
Hagans v. Franklin County Sheriff's
    Office 584
Hagberg v. California Fed. Bank FSB 79,
    966
Hagen v. Faherty 438
Hagenow v. Schmidt 219, 259
Hager v. City of Devils Lake 749
Hagerty v. L & L Marine Servs., Inc. 334,
    440, 854
Hagler v. Coastal Farm Holdings,
    Inc. 304
Hagler v. Proctor & Gamble Mfg. Co. 983
Hailey v. Otis Elevator Co. 301

Hailstone v. Martinez 982
Hairston v. Alexander Tank and Equipment
    Co. 370
Hairston v. General Pipeline Const.,
    Inc. 248
Halberstadt v. New York Life Ins.
    Co. 1034
Hale v. Beckstead 419, 471, 603
Hale v. Brown 346, 371
Hale v. George A. Hormel & Co. 1123
Hale v. Groce 1175
Hale v. Ostrow 316, 318, 484
Hale v. Ward County 745
Haley v. Casa Del Rey Homeowners
    Ass'n 941
Hall v. Bed Bath & Beyond, Inc. 1200
Hall v. Bergman 724
Hall v. Board of Supervisors Southern
    University 648
Hall v. Chicago & Nw. Ry. Co. 861
Hall v. Dartmouth Hitchcock Med.
    Ctr. 679, 683
Hall v. Lovell Regency Homes Ltd.
    P'ship 1140
Hall v. Polk 745, 746
Hall v. Post 1018
Hall v. Rogers 992
Hall v. United Parcel Serv. of Am.,
    Inc. 936
Hall, Estate of v. Akron Gen. Med.
    Ctr. 301
Halliday v. Sturm, Ruger & Co., Inc. 840
Halper v. Jewish Family & Children's Serv.
    of Greater Philadelphia 678
Halpern v. Wheeldon 423
Halpert v. Rosenthal 1128, 1129, 1132
Halpin v. Schultz 857
Halvorsen v. Ford Motor Co. 651
Halvorson v. Voeller 406, 407, 408
Hamberger v. Eastman 1008
Hamburger v. Cornell University 529
Hames v. Cravens 1119
Hamill v. Pawtucket Mut. Ins. Co. 1068,
    1087
Hamilton Development Co. v. Broad Rock
    Club, Inc. 98
Hamilton v. Asbestos Corp. 441
Hamilton v. Bares 516
Hamilton v. Beretta U.S.A. Corp. 653
Hamilton v. Lake Charles Am. Press,
    Inc. 956
Hamilton v. Oppen 385
Hamlet at Willow Creek Development Co.,
    LLC v. Northeast Land Development
    Corp. 111
Hamm v. United States 758
Hamman v. County of Maricopa 576, 658
Hammerlind v. Clear Lake Star Factory
    Skydiver's Club 449
Hammerstein v. Jean Development
    West 349, 355
Hammock v. Red Gold, Inc. 361

Hammond v. Bechtel Inc. 770
Hammond v. North American Asbestos
    Corp. 806
Hampton v. North Carolina Pulp Co. 746,
    1068
Hanauer v. Coscia 134, 136
Hancock v. Bryan County Bd. of
    Educ. 450
Hancock-Underwood v. Knight 221, 224
Hand v. Howell, Sarto & Howell 1172
Handa v. Munn 510
Handleman v. Cox 467
Handler Corp. v. Tlapechco 293, 604
Handy v. Nejam 460, 467
Hanford Nuclear Reservation Litig.,
    In re 313
Hankla v. Postell 512
Hanks v. Entergy Corp. 39
Hanks v. Powder Ridge Restaurant
    Corp. 6, 409
Hanlon v. Davis 989
Hannaford Bros. Co. Customer Data Sec.
    Breach Litig., In re 700
Hannah v. Heeter 1158, 1159,
    1160, 1161
Hanneman v. Downer 1075
Hannemann v. Boyson 514
Hannex Corp. v. GMI, Inc. 1108
Hannon v. Hayes-Bickford Lunch Sys.,
    Inc. 603
Hans v. Louisiana 564
Hansen v. Abrasive Eng'g & Mfg.,
    Inc. 283, 817
Hansen v. Anderson, Wilmarth & Van Der
    Maaten 882, 1172
Hansen v. Baxter Healthcare Corp. 830
Hansen v. Board of Trustees of Hamilton
    Southeastern School Corp. 761
Hansen v. City of Pocatello 307
Hanson v. Binder 388
Hanson v. Singsen 432
Happel v. Wal-Mart Stores, Inc. 206, 268,
    496
Haralson v. Fisher Surveying, Inc. 688,
    863
Harbeson v. Parke-Davis, Inc. 677, 681
Hardee v. Bio-Medical Applications of
    South Carolina, Inc. 501, 653, 660
Harder v. F.C. Clinton, Inc. 301, 306, 539
Hardin v. Caldwell 866
Hardingham v. United Counseling Service
    of Bennington 618
Hardt v. Reliance Standard Life Ins.
    Co. 924
Hardwicke v. Am. Boychoir Sch. 599
Hardy v. LaBelle's Distrib. Co. 76, 166
Hardy v. Monsanto Enviro-Chem Sys.
    Inc. 394
Hardy v. Vial 1037
Hargrove v. McGinley 219
Harkins v. Win Corp. 147
Harlfinger v. Martin 434

Harlin v. Sears Roebuck & Co. 474
Harlingen, City of v. Estate of
    Sharboneau 1142
Harlow v. Chin 528
Harlow v. Connelly 398
Harlow v. Fitzgerald 577
Harmon v. Washburn 381
Harnish v. Children's Hosp. Medical
    Center 517, 522
Harnish v. Herald-Mail Co. 956
Harold L. Martin Distributing Co., Ex
    parte 470
Harold McLaughlin Reliable Truck Brokers,
    Inc. v. Cox 1026
Harpending v. Meyer 129
Harper v. Baptist Medical Center—
    Princeton 531
Harper v. Kampschaefer 143, 146, 147
Harper v. McDonald 583
Harper v. Robinson 782
Harradon v. Schlamadinger 469
Harrell v. Louis Smith Mem'l Hosp. 598
Harrigfeld v. Hancock 1175
Harrington v. Brooks Drugs, Inc. 719
Harrinton v. Costello 430
Harris v. Bornhorst 1095, 1097
Harris v. Forklift Systems, Inc. 63
Harris v. Groth 506, 507
Harris v. Jones 431, 711
Harris v. Kissling 1184
Harris v. Kreutzer 499
Harris v. Miller 775
Harris v. Raymond 505
Harris v. Roderick 362
Harris v. State, Dep't of Corr. 922
Harris v. Suniga 1075, 1085
Harris v. Uebelhoer 224
Harris v. Westin Mgmt. Co. East 914
Harris-Fields v. Syze 609
Harrison v. Binnion 314, 318
Harrison v. Loyal Protective Life Ins.
    Co. 688
Harrison v. Middlesex Water Co. 483
Harrison v. NetCentric Corp. 1096, 1106
Harrison v. Springdale Water & Sewer
    Com'n 1036
Harrison v. United States 517
Harrison v. Wisdom 159
Harry Stoller and Co. v. City of
    Lowell 574
Hart v. Child's Nursing Home Co.,
    Inc. 727
Hart v. E.P. Dutton & Co. 1002
Hart v. Electronic Arts, Inc. 1008, 1207
Hart v. Shastri Narayan Swaroop,
    Inc. 608
Hart-Albin Co. v. McLees Inc. 839
Harte-Hanks Communications, Inc. v.
    Connaughton 1039
Hartford Accident & Indem. Co. v.
    Cardillo 914
Hartford Financial Corp. v. Burns 114

Hartford v. State Bar of California......... 116
Hartford v. Womens Services 745
Hartley v. Oidtman 137
Hartley v. Waldbaum, Inc..................... 470
Hartman v. Hartman 594, 595
Hartman v. Keri 1091
Hartman v. Moore 582
Hartwig v. Oregon Trail Eye Clinic........ 726
Harvey v. Metro. Utils. Dist. of
    Omaha... 305
Harvey v. Mid-Coast Hosp. 395
Harvey v. Strickland 182, 514
Harvey v. Washington............................ 320
Harwood Pharmacal Co. v. National Broad.
    Co.. 953
Haseman v. Orman 767, 768, 778
Haslam's Case 914
Hassan v. Deutsche Bank A.G. 1104
Hassan v. Mercy Am. River Hosp. 975
Hassan v. Stafford................................ 452
Hasson v. Hale..................................... 232
Hastings v. Mechalske 603
Hastings v. Sauve................................. 779
Hatahley v. United States...................... 562
Hatch v. Davis 712, 713, 1043
Hatch v. State Farm Fire & Cas. Co. 710
Hatch v. Town of Middletown 1013
Hatfield v. Health Mgmt. Assocs. of W.
    Va. 1112
Hatfill v. New York Times Co........ 936, 944,
    993
Hatton, State v. 137
Haudrich v. Howmedica, Inc.................. 853
Hauf v. Life Extension Foundation 1208
Haugen v. BioLife Plasma Services........ 304
Havana Cent. NY2 LLC v. Lunney's Pub,
    Inc. 1101
Haver v. Hinson.................................... 256
Hawaii Med. Ass'n v. Hawaii Med. Serv.
    Ass'n, Inc. 1079, 1100
Hawke v. Maus....................................... 87
Hawkins v. Harris................................. 578
Hawkins v. Hawkins 71
Hawkins v. Peart.................................. 414
Hawkins v. Scituate Oil Co., Inc............ 714
Haworth v. Feigon.......................... 983, 984
Hayes v. Camel..................................... 515
Hayes v. Decker.................................... 513
Hayes v. Price 383, 396
Hayes v. Smith 946
Haymon v. Pettit 486
Haynes v. Alfred A. Knopf, Inc. 1013,
    1022
Hays v. Miller 783
Hayward v. Cleveland Clinic Found...... 701,
    710
Haywood v. Drown 582
Hazine v. Montgomery Elevator Co....... 435,
    848
Head v. Head 1137
Health Call of Detroit v. Atrium Home &
    Health Care Servs., Inc. 1096

Health Trust, Inc. v. Cantrell.......... 529, 531
Healthcare Ctrs. of Texas, Inc. v.
    Rigby.. 540
Healthone v. Rodriguez 265, 498
Heard v. City of New York............ 626, 1123
Hearndon v. Graham 439
Hearst Corp. v. Skeen........................... 995
Heartland Academy Community Church v.
    Waddle.. 582
Heastie v. Roberts................... 298, 302, 307
Heath v. La Mariana Apartments......... 259,
    721
Heath v. Montana Mun. Ins. Auth......... 914
Heath v. Palmer...................... 1079, 1087
Heck v. Humphrey.............. 582, 1033, 1187
Heck, Estate of v. Stoffer 343
Heckler v. Campbell............................. 924
Hector v. Metro Centers, Inc. 87, 170
Hedgepeth v. Whitman Walker
    Clinic... 714
Hegel v. McMahon 716, 722, 723
Hegyes v. Unjian Enters., Inc................. 676
Hein v. Acuity 1147
Heiner v. K-Mart Corp.......................... 893
Heiner v. Moretuzzo............................. 727
Heinrich v. Sweet........................... 420, 509
Heinz v. Heinz..................................... 798
Heiser, Estate of v. Islamic Republic of
    Iran 717
Heldreth v. Marrs 718
Helena Chem. Co. v. Uribe 966
Helena Labs. Corp. v. Snyder............... 1052
Helfend v. Southern Cal. Rapid Transit
    Dist. 859
Hellar v. Bianco................................... 941
Helling v. Carey 506, 507
Hellriegel v. Tholl 63, 164
Hellums v. Raber 328
Helms v. Carmel High Sch. Vocational
    Bldg. Trades Corp. 605
Helms v. Helms................................... 1167
Helsel v. Noellesch 1051
Hembree v. State 357
Hemenway v. Presbyterian Hosp.
    Ass'n.. 599
Hemmings v. Pelham Wood Ltd. Liability
    Partnership.............................. 644, 645
Henderson v. MeadWestvaco Corp.......... 697
Henderson v. Security National
    Bank.. 152
Henderson v. Taylor............................. 450
Hendrick v. ABC Ins. Co...................... 1182
Hendricks v. Broderick 425
Hendrickson v. Genesis Health Venture,
    Inc. 537
Henley v. Dillard Department Stores ...1208
Hennessey v. Coastal Eagle Point Oil
    Co. 1012
Hennessey v. Pyne 396
Hennessey v. Restaurant Assocs.,
    Inc. 1159

Hennig v. Alltel Commc'ns, Inc. 1009, 1014

Hennigan v. Nantasket Boat Line, Inc. 449, 450

Henningsen v. Bloomfield Motors, Inc. 800

Henrich v. Libertyville High School 646

Henricksen v. State 714

Henry Hope X-Ray Products, Inc. v. Marron Carrel, Inc. 1205

Henry v. Deen 1025

Henry v. Dow Chem. Co. 854

Henry v. Mutual of Omaha Ins. Co. 686

Henry v. National Union Fire Ins. Co. ... 852

Henry v. Superior Court 887

Hensley v. Jackson County 566

Hensley v. Montgomery County 484

Henson v. Klein 218, 382

Hepps v. Philadelphia Newspapers, Inc. 938

Herber v. Johns-Manville Corp. 312, 334

Herberg v. Swartz 453

Herbst v. Wuennenberg 76

Hern v. Safeco Ins. Co. of Ill. 692, 693

Hernandez v. City of Pomona 162

Hernandez v. Hillsides, Inc. 708, 1009

Hernandez v. K-Mart Corp. 163

Hernandez v. Tokai Corp. 813, 815

Hernandez, Estate of v. Arizona Board of Regents 664

Hernandez-Gomez v. Leonardo (Volkswagen of America, Inc.) 846

Herr v. Wheeler 220

Herrera v. Quality Pontiac 363

Herrington v. Deloris Gaulden 625

Herrmann v. Newark Morning Ledger Co. 945, 949

Herron v. Anigbo 429, 432

Herron v. Hollis 279

Herron v. Tribune Publ'g Co., Inc. 978

Hersh v. County of Morris 914

Hershey v. Hershey 1056, 1057

Hertel v. Sullivan 180

Hertog v. City of Seattle 316, 576, 651

Hertz v. Luzenac Group 1204

Herzfeld v. Herzfeld 594

Herzog v. Yuill 1190

Hess v. Chase Manhattan Bank, USA, N.A. 1137

Hesse v. McClintic 207, 219

Hester v. Bandy 768, 769

Hetzel v. United States 556

Hewes v. Wolfe 1025

Hewitt v. Rice 1042

Hewlett v. George 593

Heyd v. Chicago Title Ins. Co. 1074

Heyman v. Gable, Gotwals, Mock, Schwabe, Kihle, Gabarino 1178

Heynen v. Fairbanks 489

Hibbard v. Secretary of Health & Human Servs. 929

Hickey v. Zezulka 372, 374, 395

Hickle v. Whitney Farms, Inc. 654

Hickman v. . Group Health Plan, Inc. 679

Higginbotham v. Public Serv. Comm'n of Md. 938

Higgins Invs., Inc. v. Sturgill 326

Higgins v. Butcher 685

Higgins v. E. Valley Sch. Dist. 227

Higgins v. Karp 1167

High Country Fashions, Inc. v. Marlenna Fashions, Inc. 1002

Highland Indus. Park, Inc. v. BEI Defense Sys. Co. 431

Highview North Apartments v. County of Ramsey 741

Hilario v. Reardon 1188

Hiles v. Episcopal Diocese of Mass. 970

Hill v. Alderman of City of Charlotte 568

Hill v. Carlstrom 1039

Hill v. City of Lincoln 294

Hill v. Fairfield Nursing & Rehabilitation Center, LLC 496

Hill v. McKinley 1010

Hill v. Mills 681

Hill v. National Collegiate Athletic Ass'n 1012

Hill v. Sparks 231

Hill v. Thompson 305

Hillrichs v. Avco Corp. 841

Hillsborough Cnty. Hosp. Authority v. Coffaro 526

Himsel, Estate of v. State 774

Hincks v. Walton Ranch Co. 292

Hines v. Davidowitz 442

Hines v. Garrett 448, 451

Hinish v. Meier & Frank Co., Inc. 1006, 1020

Hinkie v. United States 561, 674

Hinkle v. Cornwell Quality Tool Co. 124

Hinman v. Pacific Air Lines Transport 94

Hinman v. Westinghouse Elec. Co. 758

Hinsdale v. Orange County Publ'ns, Inc. 964

Hirpa v. IHC Hosps., Inc. 524

Hirsch v. S.C. Johnson & Son, Inc. 1208

Hirst v. Inverness Hotel Corp. 296

Hislop v. Salt River Project Agric. Improvement & Power Dist. 716, 718

Hitachi Chem. Electro-Products, Inc. v. Burley 673

Hite v. Brown 621, 720

Hitson v. Simms 1030

Hixon v. Buchberger 1056

Hizey v. Carpenter 1169

Hobart v. Shin 395

Hobson v. American Cast Iron Pipe Co. 1119

Hobson, State v. 137

Hocking v. City of Dodgeville 736

Hodge v. Craig 1116

Hodge v. Osteopathic Gen. Hosp. of R.I. 599

Hodgeden v. Hubbard 151

Hodges v. Gibson Prods. Co. 1032
Hodges v. Yarian 611
Hodgson v. Minnesota 172
Hoery v. United States 98
Hofer v. Gap, Inc. 303
Hofer v. Meyer 477
Hofflander v. St. Catherine's Hosp.,
    Inc.. 227
Hoffman v. Capital Cities/ABC, Inc. 1207
Hoffman v. Jones 384, 386
Hoffman v. Planters Gin Co................... 464
Hoffman v. Union Elec. Co. 269
Hoffman v. Unterberg 1153
Hoffman-LaRoche Inc. v. Mason............ 830
Hoffnagle v. McDonald's Corp. 766
Hogan v. New York Times Co. 996
Hogan v. Tavzel 176
Hogan v. Winder 955
Hogle v. Hall 674
Hohe v. San Diego Unified Sch. Dist. 414
Hoines v. Barney's Club, Inc................ 1035
Hojnowski v. Vans Skate Park 223, 414
Holcomb v. Colonial Assocs., LLC 780
Holcombe v. NationsBanc Fin. Servs.
    Corp. 297
Holdenville, City of v. Kiser 99
Holger v. Irish 279
Hollander v. Days Inn Motel.................. 452
Hollander v. Smith & Smith 450
Holleman v. Aiken 963
Holliday v. Jones 1189
Hollingshed v. Levine............................. 921
Hollingsworth v. Schminkey 349
Hollock v. Erie Ins. Exchange.............. 1147
Holloway v. Wachovia Bank & Trust
    Co... 79
Holmes v. Amerex Rent-A-Car 1158,
    1159, 1160, 1161
Holmes v. Elliott..................................... 510
Holmes v. Grubman 1123
Holmes v. Levine 339
Holodook v. Spencer 138, 594
Holsten v. Massey.................................... 572
Holton v. Memorial Hosp. 333
Holtzscheiter v. Tomson Newspapers,
    Inc.. 962
Holzheimer v. Johannsen....................... 464
Homac Corporation v. Sun Oil Co. 356
Home Pride Foods, Inc. v. Johnson....... 1206
Home Star Bank and Financial Services v.
    Emergency Care and Health
    Organization, Ltd. 523
Homer v. Long 713
Honda Motor Co. Ltd. v. Oberg.............. 867
Honda of America Mfg., Inc. v.
    Norman 822
Hondroulis v. Schuhmacher.................... 518
Hood, Commonwealth v. 157
Hoofnel v. Segal 170
Hook v. Trevino 1182, 1186
Hooker v. Dep't of Transportation 770
Hoopes v. Hammargren 1143

Hoover v. Broome....................................466
Hoover v. Williamson......................498, 500
Hopfauf v. Hieb 519
Hopkins v. Bonvicino 584
Hopkins v. Miss. Valley Gas Co. 217
Hopkins v. O'Connor................................939
Hopkins v. Silber.....................................528
Hopp & Flesch, LLC v. Backstreet........1169
Hoppe IV v. Hoppe III.............................594
Hopper v. Swinnerton 246
Horak v. Biris...713
Horizon/CMS Healthcare Corp. v.
    Auld............................538, 541, 863
Hormel Foods Corp. v. Jim Henson
    Productions..1196
Horn v. Citizens Hosp.............................434
Horn v. Fadal Machinery Centers,
    LLC..841
Horn v. Wooster 1163, 1175
Hornback v. Archdiocese of
    Milwaukee 658
Horne v. Patton...........................1014, 1015
Horne v. TGM Assocs., L.P. 117
Horne v. Vic Potamkin Chevrolet,
    Inc. 655
Horning v. Penrose Plumbing & Heating
    Inc. 433
Hornstein v. Wolf...................................1037
Horodyskyj v. Karanian...........................914
Horst v. Deere & Co. 801
Horstmeyer v. Golden Eagle
    Fireworks..253
Horton v. Goldminer's Daughter.............435
Horton v. Hinely.............................58, 233
Horton v. Tyree 1130, 1132
Horvath v. Ish 424
Hose v. Winn-Dixie Montgomery, Inc. 466
Hosein v. Checker Taxi Co., Inc. 766
Hough v. Mooningham.............................863
Houghum v. Valley Mem'l Homes.........1009
House v. Armour of America, Inc. 813
Houseman v. Publicaciones Paso del Norte,
    S.A. DE C.V. 952
Housing Auth. of City of Rolla v.
    Kimmel 305
Houston Lighting and Power Co. v.
    Sue...86
Houston v. Kinder-Care Learning Centers,
    Inc. 164, 173
Hout v. Johnson 258
Howard Frank, M.D., P.C. v. Superior
    Court..719
Howard v. Antilla....................................980
Howard v. Chimps, Inc. 241, 410
Howard v. Dorr Woolen Co. 1148
Howard v. East Texas Baptist Univ........479
Howard v. S. Baltimore Gen. Hosp. 597
Howard v. Univ. of Med. & Dentistry of
    New Jersey 515
Howard v. Zimmer, Inc.............................252
Howell v. Cahoon 220
Howell v. Howell 1053

Howland v. Balma 922
Howle v. PYA/Monarch, Inc. 225
Howlett v. Rose 582
Hoye v. Hoye 1051
Hoyt Props., Inc. v. Productions Res. Group,
    LLC 1132
Hoyt v. Cooks 584
Hoyt v. Rosenberg 234
HPI Health Care Servs., Inc. v. Mt. Vernon
    Hosp., Inc. 1097
Hubbard v. Beatty & Hyde, Inc. 1041
Hubbard v. Boelt 606, 610
Hubbard-Hall Chemical Co. v.
    Silverman 829
Hudak v. Georgy 670
Huddleston v. Union Rural Elec.
    Ass'n 767
Hudgens v. Prosper, Inc. 54
Hudson v. Courtesy Motors, Inc. 462
Hudson v. Gaitan 478
Hudson v. Janesville Conservation
    Club 783
Hudson v. McMillian 584
Hudson v. Old Guard Ins. 234, 259
Hudson-Connor v. Putney 233, 236
Huebner ex rel. Lane v. Koelfgren 236
Huffman v. Poore 1119
Hughes v. Doe 756
Hughes v. Lord Advocate 357
Hughes v. Massey-Ferguson, Inc. 843
Hughes v. Pair 708, 710
Hughes v. PeaceHealth 695, 875
Hughes v. United States 557
Hull v. Baran Telecom, Inc. 604
Hull v. Bishop-Stoddard Cafeteria 466
Hulse v. First Am. Title Co. of Crook
    County 1074
Human Rights Comm'n v. LaBrie,
    Inc. 710
Humes v. Clinton 830
Hummel v. Reiss 678
Humphers v. First Interstate Bank of
    Or. 1015
Humphreys v. Humphreys 791
Humphries v. Detch 1188
Hunnicutt v. Sewell 1179
Hunt ex rel. DeSombre v. State, Dep't of
    Safety & Homeland Sec., Div. of Del.
    State Police 707
Hunt v. Chang 1051
Hunt v. Statee Dep't of Safety & Homeland
    Sec. 64
Hunt, Henson ex rel. v. Intern. Paper
    Co. 476
Hunter v. Bryant 585
Hunter v. Dep't of Transp. & Dev. 281
Huntingdon Life Sciences, Inc. v. Stop
    Huntingdon Animal Cruelty USA,
    Inc. 985
Hupp v. Sasser 940, 944
Hurd v. Williamsburg County 287
Hurley v. Heart Physicians, P.C. 831

Huron Tool & Eng'g Co. v. Precision
    Consulting Servs., Inc. 1077, 1078,
    1084
Hurst v. East Coast Hockey League,
    Inc. 422
Husband v. Dubose 284
Husker News Co. v. Mahaska State
    Bank 128
Huskey v. Smith 669
Huss v. Gayden 432
Hustler Magazine v. Falwell 710, 936
Huston v. Konieczny 329, 664
Hutcherson v. City of Phoenix 572, 625,
    880
Hutchins v. Schwartz 407
Hutchinson v. Proxmire 581, 968
Hutchison v. Luddy 393, 862, 863
Hutchison v. Ross 111
Hutton v. Davis 697
HY Cite Corp. v. Badbusinessbureau.Com,
    LLC 972
Hydro Investors, Inc. v. Trafalgar Power
    Inc. 1074
Hylazewski v. Wet 'N Wild, Inc. 466
Hyler v. Garner 1128, 1130
Hymowitz v. Eli Lilly & Co. 328, 330
I.C.C. Metals v. Municipal Warehouse
    Co. 118
Iannacchino v. Ford Motor Co. 285
Ianotta v. Tishman Speyer Props.,
    Inc. 298
IDC Clambakes, Inc., In re 164
IDT Corp. v. Morgan Stanley Dean Witter
    & Co. 1145
Iemma v. Adventure RV Rentals,
    Inc. 114, 195
Iglehart v. Bd. of Cty. Comm'rs of Rogers
    County 205
Ikani v. Bennett 976, 980
Ilitzky v. Goodman 963
Illinois Bell Switching Station Litig.,
    In re 1069
Illinois Central R. v. White 463
Illinois v. Lidster 155
Imbler v. Pachtman 578, 582, 1025
Imig v. Beck 300
Imperial Distrib. Servs., Inc. v. Forrest .. 217
Incase Inc. v. Timex Corp. 1204
Indemnity Ins. Co. of N. Am. v. American
    Aviation, Inc. 1077, 1081, 1084, 1156
Independent Fire Ins. Co. v. Able Moving
    and Storage Co. 771
Independent Newspapers, Inc. v.
    Brodie 971
Indian Bayou Hunting Club, Inc. v.
    Taylor 91
Indian Towing Co. v. United States 552,
    554, 556, 559
Indiana Consol. Ins. Co. v. Mathew 269
Industrial Chem. & Fiberglass Corp. v.
    Chandler 689
Infant Fontaine, In re Estate of 696

Ingalls v. Standard Gypsum, LLC.......... 919
Ingham v. Luxor Cab Co. 450
Inglehart v. Board of County Com'rs of
   Rogers County.................................... 485
Ingraham v. Wright.............................. 139
Inmi-Etti v. Aluisi 123
Innes v. Howell Corp. 954
Insurance Co. of N. Am. v. Cease Elec.
   Inc.. 1065, 1087
Integrated Cash Management Services, Inc.
   v. Digital Transactions, Inc. 1204
Integrated Health Care Servs., Inc. v. Lang-
   Redway.. 527
Integrated Waste Services, Inc. v. Akzo
   Nobel Salt, Inc. 795
International Paper Co. v. Whilden...... 1148
International Sales & Serv., Inc. v. Austral
   Insulated Prods., Inc........................ 1104
International Strategies Group, Ltd. v.
   Greenberg Traurig, LLP......... 1166, 1176
International Union of Operating Eng'rs,
   Local 150 v. Lowe Excavating Co........ 873
Invest Cast, Inc. v. City of Blaine........... 574
Investors REIT One v. Jacobs................ 128
Iodice v. United States 500
Ioerger v. Halverson Constr. Co. 919
Ippolito v. Lennon................................. 1151
Ira S. Bushey & Sons, Inc. v. United
   States 756, 761
Irish v. Gimbel..................................... 433
Ironworkers Local Union 68 v. AstraZeneca
   Pharm., LP............................ 1119, 1140
Irvine v. Akron Beacon Journal............ 1012
Irvine v. Rare Feline Breeding Ctr.,
   Inc.. 782, 783
Irvine, Bennett ex rel. v. City of
   Philadelphia..................................... 649
Irwin v. Ashurst 967
Irwin v. Pacific Sw. Airlines................... 297
Isaacs v. Huntington Memorial Hosp..... 639
Israel v. Barnwell................................. 320
Ives v. Guilford Mills, Inc..................... 1105
Ives v. South Buffalo Ry. Co. 912
Ivy Manor Nursing Home, Inc. v.
   Brown.. 542
Ivy v. General Motors Acceptance
   Corp... 116
Iwai v. State..................................... 470, 472
Iwanski v. Gomes 180, 497
J. D. Cousins & Sons, Inc. v. Hartford
   Steam Boiler Inspection & Ins. 217
J. E. v. Beth Israel Hosp. 306
J. Smith Lanier & Co. v. Se. Forge,
   Inc. 700
J. v. Victory Tabernacle Baptist
   Church.............................. 456, 598, 657
J. Weingarten, Inc. v. Thompson............ 470
J.A.H. v. Wadle & Assocs. 503, 1057
J.M. v. Shell Oil Co............................... 766
J.T. Baggerly v. CSX Transp., Inc. 346,
   353, 357
Jablonowska v. Suther............................ 718

Jablonski v. Ford Motor Co. 844
Jackson Hole Mtn. Resort Corp. v.
   Rohrman 424
Jackson v. Axelrad.......... 229, 230, 231, 507
Jackson v. Bi-Lo Stores, Inc. 1103
Jackson v. Bumgardner 680, 682
Jackson v. City of Joliet......................... 619
Jackson v. City of Kansas City........ 572, 645
Jackson v. Columbus 982, 989
Jackson v. District of Columbia................ 61
Jackson v. General Motors Corp. 803,
   809, 812
Jackson v. Mateus................................. 781
Jackson v. McCuiston 236
Jackson v. Nestle-Beich, Inc............ 806, 808
Jackson v. PKM Corporation.................. 663
Jackson v. Post Props., Inc. 396
Jackson v. Power.......................... 530, 771
Jackson v. Scheible 487
Jackson v. Stanfield............................. 1103
Jackson v. Sun Oil Co. of Pa................... 707
Jackson v. United States 552, 560
Jackson, City of v. Spann 318
Jackson, In re Guardianship of 172
Jacob E. Decker & Sons, Inc. v.
   Capps 800
Jacobsen, Stark ex rel. v. Ford Motor
   Co. 838
Jacqueline R. v. Household of Faith Family
   Church, Inc. 180
Jacqueline S. v. City of New York 645
Jacques v. Childs Dining Hall Co...... 75, 153
Jacron Sales Co., Inc. v. Sindorf............. 995
Jaeger Baking Co. v. Kretschmann......... 914
Jaeger v. Evangelical Lutheran Holy Ghost
   Congregation 911
Jaffee v. Stone 1034
Jagger v. Mohawk Mountain Ski Area,
   Inc. 425
Jahn v. Hyundai Motor Co. 840
Jahner v. Jacob 132, 135
Jamar v. Patterson................................ 367
James G. v. Caserta 681, 682
James v. City of Douglas, Ga................. 1010
James v. Kelly Trucking Co.................... 657
Jamison v. Morris 766
Janelsins v. Button........................... 61, 167
Janicki v. Hospital of St. Raphael........... 729
Janis v. Nash Finch Co................... 466, 468
Jankee v. Clark Cty. 227
Janusauskas v. Fichman 517
Jarboe v. Board of County Comn'rs of
   Sedgwick County............................... 568
Jarmie v. Troncale 500
Jarrett v. Woodward Bros., Inc. 384
Jarrow Formulas, Inc. v. LaMarche.....1039,
   1047
Jarvis v. Ford Motor Co. 824
Jaskoviak v. Gruver........................ 515, 517
Jass v. Prudential Health Care Plan,
   Inc... 536
Jaworski v. Kiernan....................... 425, 426

Jay v. Moog Auto., Inc. 417, 836
Jaynes v. Centura Health Corp. 1148
Jean W. v. Commonwealth 572
Jeanes v. Bank of America, N.A. 1181
Jedrziewski v. Smith 898
Jeewarat v. Warner Bros. Entertainment,
     Inc. 759
Jefferies v. Bush 97
Jefferson County Commonwealth Attorney's
     Office v. Kaplan 888
Jefferson County School District R-1 v.
     Gilbert 627
Jeffres v. Countryside Homes of Lincoln,
     Inc. 157
Jeffries v. Potomac Development
     Corp. 464
Jelly v. Dabney 133
Jenco v. Islamic Republic of Iran 712
Jenkins v. Pensacola Health Trust,
     Inc. 697
Jennifer C. v. Los Angeles Unified School
     Dist. 647
Jennings v. Badgett 498
Jennison v. Providence St. Vincent Medical
     Ctr. 772
Jensen v. American Suzuki Motor
     Corp. 840
Jensen v. Anderson County Dep't of Social
     Services 634
Jensen, Thunder Hawk ex rel. v. Union
     Pacific R. Co. 477
Jerista v. Murray 1157
Jernigan v. Ham 123
Jerry's Enterprises, Inc. v. Larkin,
     Hoffman, Daly & Lindgren, Ltd. 1170,
     1171, 1173
Jesse v. Lindsley 411
JetBlue Airways Corp. Privacy Litigation,
     In re 106
Jeter v. Mayo Clinic Ariz. 671, 714
Jews For Jesus, Inc. v. Rapp 944, 950,
     1020
Jilani v. Jilani 594
Jimenez v. Sears, Roebuck & Co. 836, 842
Jivan v. Economy Inn & Suites 915
Jividen v. Law 780, 781
Jocelyn Canyon, Inc. v. Lentjes 1127
Joe Dickerson & Assocs., LLC v.
     Dittmar 1007, 1008
Johannesen v. New York City Dep't of
     Hous. Pres. & Dev. 916, 917
Johansen v. Makita U.S.A., Inc. 836
John B. v. Super. Ct. 188, 205, 269, 592
John Doe 1. v. Archdiocese of
     Milwaukee 436
John Hancock Mut. Life Ins. Co. v.
     Banerji 700
John Q. Hammons, Inc. v. Poletis 452,
     453
John R. Sand & Gravel Co. v. United
     States 429

John R. v. Oakland Unified School
     Dist. 647
Johnson & Johnson Corp., State ex rel. v.
     Karl 831
Johnson & Johnson v. Superior
     Court 862
Johnson County Sheriff's Posse, Inc. v.
     Endsley 490
Johnson ex rel. Johnson v. Young Men's
     Christian Ass'n of Great Falls 217
Johnson ex rel. Johnson, Estate of v.
     Badger Acquisition Of Tampa LLC 246
Johnson Insulation, Commonwealth v. ... 801
Johnson v. Allen 1009
Johnson v. American Standard, Inc. 831
Johnson v. Babcock 1188
Johnson v. Bollinger 71, 961
Johnson v. BP Chems., Inc. 922
Johnson v. Brooks 71
Johnson v. City of Milwaukee 273
Johnson v. Dallas Independent School
     Dist. 650
Johnson v. Ford Motor Co. 841, 866
Johnson v. Garnand 258
Johnson v. Hale 710
Johnson v. Halloran 1191
Johnson v. Healy 1127
Johnson v. Hillcrest Health Ctr., Inc. 353,
     529
Johnson v. Investment Co. of the South,
     LLC 462
Johnson v. Jamaica Hosp. 715
Johnson v. Johnson 117, 439
Johnson v. K-Mart Corp. 1013
Johnson v. K-Mart Enterprises, Inc. 155
Johnson v. Kosmos Portland Cement
     Co. 359
Johnson v. KTBS, Inc. 954
Johnson v. Lambotte 226
Johnson v. LeBonheur Children's Medical
     Ctr. 756
Johnson v. Luhman 1056
Johnson v. Manhattan & Bronx Surface
     Transit Operating Auth. 690, 861
Johnson v. Marks 1190
Johnson v. Matthew J. Batchelder
     Co. 382
Johnson v. Niagara Mach. & Tool
     Works 841
Johnson v. Omondi 523
Johnson v. Pankratz 83
Johnson v. Paynesville Farmers Union
     Co-op. Oil Co. 92
Johnson v. Pettigrew 474, 475
Johnson v. Ramsey County 61, 62, 83
Johnson v. Reiger 1143
Johnson v. Rental Unif. Serv. of Greenville,
     S.C., Inc. 921
Johnson v. Robbinsdale Indep. Sch. Dist.
     No. 281 992
Johnson v. Rockwell Automation, Inc. ... 889
Johnson v. Rogers 862

Johnson v. Ruark Obstetrics & Gynecology Assocs., P.A. 714, 722, 732
Johnson v. Scandia Associates, Inc. 492
Johnson v. Short....................................... 467
Johnson v. Southwestern Newspapers Corp.. 952
Johnson v. State 569, 576, 723
Johnson v. Stewart............................... 1009
Johnson v. Superior Court 677
Johnson v. United States 563
Johnson v. University Health Servs., Inc... 1122
Johnson v. University Hosps. of Cleveland 681
Johnson v. Wal-Mart Stores, Inc. 372
Johnson v. Weast................................... 1027
Johnson v. Weedman..................... 113, 114
Johnson v. Wysocki 1121
Johnson v. Yates...................................... 295
Johnson, In re Estate of 694
Johnson, State v. 134, 429
Johnson, United States v. 559, 560
Johnstone v. City of Albuquerque.......... 635
Jojo's Rests., Inc. v. McFadden 327
Jolly v. Eli Lilly & Co. 431
Jones & Laughlin Steel Corp. v. Pfeifer... 859
Jones Food Co., Inc. v. Shipman 604
Jones Motor Co., Inc. v. Holtkamp, Liese, Beckemeier & Childress, P.C. 1173
Jones v. Ahlberg 368
Jones v. Bennett 299
Jones v. Blair... 259
Jones v. Bland 453
Jones v. Brookshire Grocery Co............. 217
Jones v. City of Chicago 753, 1028
Jones v. Crawforth 889
Jones v. DCH Health Care Authority..... 112
Jones v. Dressel 410, 449
Jones v. Hansen...................................... 463
Jones v. HealthSouth Treasure Valley Hosp. 772
Jones v. Imperial Palace of Mississippi, LLC... 469
Jones v. Malinowski 682
Jones v. Mid-Atlantic Funding Co. 239
Jones v. NordicTrack, Inc. 821
Jones v. Owings...................................... 331
Jones v. Porretta 506
Jones v. State... 969
Jones v. Three Rivers Mgmt. Corp. 423
Jones v. United States 560
Jones v. Warner.................................... 1032
Jones v. Westernaires 600
Jordan v. Bailey.................................... 1030
Jordan v. Bogner 509
Jordan v. Commissioner of Soc. Sec. 924
Jordan v. Holt...................................... 1145
Jordan v. Jewel Food Stores, Inc. 1207
Jordan v. Jordan.................................... 318
Jordan v. Western Farmers Elec. Co-op.. 921

Jorgensen v. Colorado Rural Props., LLC 1078
Jorgensen v. Meade Johnson Lab., Inc. 676
Jorgenson v. Vener...........................504, 508
Joseph E. Seagram & Sons, Inc. v. McGuire 841
Joseph v. Bozzuto Mgmt. Co...................245
Joseph v. Scranton Times L.P. 953
Joseph v. State 372, 395
Joshi v. Providence Health Sys. of Or. Corp..322, 331
Jost v. Dairyland Power Coop. 738, 740, 741
Jourdain v. Dineen................................1139
Joyce v. General Motors Corp. 1203
Joyce v. State, Dep't of Corrections.........285
JP Morgan Trust Co. Nat'l Ass'n v. Mid-America Pipeline Co. 1146
Juarez v. Wavecrest Management Team Ltd..259, 489
Juchniewcz v. Bridgeport Hosp..............390
Judy v. Hanford Envtl. Health Found...499
Juhnke v. Evangelical Lutheran Good Samaritan Soc'y..........................538, 539
Juman v. Louise Wise Servs...................728
Junior Food Stores, Inc. v. Rice............1026
Junius Constr. Co. v. Cohen 1120, 1135
Jupin v. Kask 205, 212, 343, 744
Jurado v. Western Gear Works 835, 838, 839, 840
Jutzi-Johnson v. United States 265, 372
K & K Mgmt., Inc. v. Lee.......................1105
K.A.C. v. Benson 726
K.D. v. Bozarth..............................578, 1024
K.G. v. R.T.R. 706
K.M. v. Ala. Dep't of Youth Servs............705
Kaatz v. State.................................386, 387
KACT, Inc. v. Rubin 1094, 1102
Kaelin v. Globe Commc'ns Corp..............951
Kahn v. East Side Union High Sch. Dist...426
Kahn v. James Burton Company 476
Kahn v. Morse & Mobray.......................1183
Kahn v. Quintana 123
Kaho'ohanohano v. Department of Human Servs. 245
Kaiser Aluminum & Chem. Corp. v. Marshland Dredging Co....................1067
Kaiser v. Cook...283
Kaiser v. Suburban Transp. Sys. 500
Kalafut v. Gruver....................................670
Kalata v. Anheuser-Busch Cos., Inc........250
Kalina v. Fletcher 1025
Kallio v. Ford Motor Co. 821
Kallstrom v. United States......................717
Kambat v. St. Francis Hosp. 301, 307
Kambury v. DaimlerChrysler Corp.........848
Kamelgard v. Macura 940
Kaminer v. Canas 434
Kaminski v. Metal & Wire Prods. Co......921, 922

Kamla v. Space Needle Corp.................. 605
Kananen v. Alfred I. DuPont Inst. of
  Nemours Found. 497
Kane v. Lamothe 204, 618
Kane v. Quigley 1057
Kane, Kane & Kritzer, Inc. v.
  Altagen... 1185
Kann v. Kann..................................... 1145
Kansas State Bank & Trust Co. v.
  Specialized Transp. Servs., Inc. 896
Kant v. Altayar.................................... 84
Kanzler v. Renner.......................... 709, 710
Kaplan v. Mamelak 169
Karaduman v. Newsday, Inc.................. 980
Karage v. First Advantage Corp..... 941, 950
Karas v. Strevell........................... 424, 426
Karczmit v. State.................................. 406
Kardos v. Harrison 505
Karlsson v. Ford Motor Co..................... 803
Karraker v. Rent-A-Center, Inc........... 1014
Kash v. Jewish Home and Infirmary of
  Rochester, N.Y., Inc. 546
Kassama v. Magat................................. 677
Kassel v. Gannett Co., Inc..................... 991
Kassouf v. Lee Bros., Inc....................... 836
Kastner v. Toombs................................ 774
Katapodis v. Brooklyn Spectator 944
Kathleen K. v. Robert B. 176
Katko v. Briney 143, 144
Kaufman v. Fisher................................. 302
Kavadas v. Lorenzen 898
Kavanagh v. Trustees of Boston
  Univ.. 757
Keans v. Bottiarelli 404, 528
Kearney v. Philip Morris, Inc. 820
Kearns v. McNeill Brothers Moving and
  Storage Company............................. 118
Kearns, United States v........................ 1146
Keck v. Jackson 715, 718, 722
Keck v. Keck 1124
Keebler v. Winfield Carraway Hosp. 504,
  509
Keel v. Banach..................................... 681
Keenan v. Hill...................................... 253
Keesecker v. G.M. McKelvey Co. 101
Keffe v. Milwaukee & St. Paul Ry. 476
Kehoe v. New York Tribune.................. 1003
Kehoe v. Saltarelli.............................. 1166
Keller v. City of Spokane 486
Keller v. DeLong 225
Keller v. Kiedinger 367
Kellermann v. McDonough 346
Kelley Kar Company v. Maryland Casualty
  Co.. 124
Kelley v. Bonney............................ 966, 992
Kelley v. Callahan 924
Kelley v. Centennial Contractors
  Enters. 720
Kelley v. LaForce 110
Kelley v. Middle Tennessee Emergency
  Physicians, P.C. 497
Kelley v. Story County Sheriff................. 161

Kelley v. Tanoos 973, 976, 981
Kellos v. Sawilowsky.............................1168
Kelly v. Borough of Carlisle....................586
Kelly v. Brigham & Women's Hosp. 729
Kelly v. Daro 968
Kelly v. Golden 1111
Kelly v. Henry Muhs Co. 257
Kelly v. Stop and Shop, Inc. 469
Kelly, Estate of v. Falin 663
Kelso v. McGowan 1148
Kemezy v. Peters.........................863, 865
Kemp v. American Tel. & Tel. Co...........869
Kemper v. Builder's Square....................292
Kemper v. Gordon 332
Kempf v. Magida 1171
Kempner v. Schulte 854
Ken Cowden Chevrolet, Inc. v. Corts.....483
Ken Hood Constr. Co. v. Pacific Coast
  Constr., Inc. 857
Kenet v. Bailey....................................1153
Kennan v. Checker Taxi Co., Inc.........82, 83
Kennedy v. Flo-Tronics, Inc...................1133
Kennedy v. Ill. Cent. R.R. Co.................693
Kennedy v. Parrott................................170
Kennedy v. Sheriff of E. Baton
  Rouge 963, 973, 983, 984, 995
Kennedy v. Western Sizzlin Corp............766
Kennelly v. Burgess 221
Kennerly v. Shell Oil Co. 769
Kenney v. Barna 93
Kenney v. Kroger Co.............................470
Kenney v. Liston 859
Kenney v. Wal-Mart Stores, Inc. 936,
  1001
Kennis v. Mercy Hosp. Medical
  Center 515
Kenny v. Southeastern Pennsylvania
  Transportation Authority 452
Kensington Dev. Corp. v. Israel 1042
Kent v. Gulf States Utils. Co. 788
Kent v. United of Omaha Life Ins.
  Co. 1143
Kenton v. Hyatt Hotels Corp...........855, 856
Kentucky Fried Chicken of California, Inc.
  v. Superior Court................................643
Kentucky v. Graham.............................584
Kenyon v. Abel 116, 122
Keogh v. W.R. Grasle, Inc......................827
Keohane v. Stewart.......................941, 951
Keomaka v. Zakaib 522, 523
Kerans v. Porter Paint Co. 710, 917
Kerby v. Hal Roach Studios, Inc. 1007
Kerman v. City of New York 82
Kermarec v. Compagnie Generale
  Transatlantique...................................478
Kern v. Palmer Coll. of Chiropractic.....1100
Kernan v. American Dredging Co. 244,
  247
Kerns v. Sealy 298
Kerr v. Corning Glass Works 811
Kessel v. Leavitt..............1053, 1054, 1055
Kessler v. Mortenson 476

Keyser v. Phillips Petroleum Co. 783
Keystone Elec. Mfg. Co. v. City of Des
    Moines 365
Khalifa v. Shannon 1053, 1056
Khan v. Parsons Global Servs., Ltd. 914
Khan v. Singh 300
Khawar v. Globe Int'l, Inc. 979
Kibble v. Weeks Dredging & Constr.
    Co. 720
Kibler v. Northern Inyo County Local Hosp.
    Dist. 985
Kiesau v. Bantz 941, 998, 1115
Kik v. Sbraccia 720
Kilduff v. Adams, Inc. 1119
Killam v. Texas Oil & Gas Corp. 95
Killebrew v. Abbott Labs 861
Killebrew v. Sun Trust Banks, Inc. 188
Killough v. Jahandarfard 693
Kilpatrick v. Bryant 331
Kim v. Budget Rent A Car Systems,
    Inc. 341
Kimber v. Young 1120, 1122
Kimberlin v. DeLong 295
Kimberlin v. PM Transport 217, 253, 295
Kimberly S.M. v. Bradford Central
    School 647
Kimble v. Carey 240, 382
Kimble v. Land Concepts, Inc. 870
Kimbrell v. Kimbrell 1179
Kimco Development Corp. v. Michael D's
    Carpet Outlets 836
Kime v. Hobbs 764
Kimes v. Grosser 857
Kimmell v. Schaefer 1125
Kinder v. Fantasy Coachworks, Ltd. 309
Kindsfather, In re, Estate of 1119
King v. Allred 232
King v. Casad 234
King v. Kayak Mfg. Corp 419, 422
King v. Lens Creek Ltd. P'ship 767
King's Daughters & Sons Circle No. Two of
    Greenville v. Delta Reg'l Med.
    Ctr. 1112
Kings Creations Ltd. v. Conde Nast Publ'ns
    Inc. 1114
Kingstown Mobile Home Park v.
    Strashnick 1032, 1041
Kinney v. Barnes 1003
Kinsman Transit Co., Petition of 351, 363
Kinsman v. Unocal Corp. 604
Kinzel v. Discovery Drilling, Inc. 1104
Kirch v. Liberty Media Corp. 943,
    952, 1096
Kircher v. City of Jamestown 574, 626
Kirchner v. Crystal 595
Kirchner v. Shooters on the Water,
    Inc. 663
Kirk v. Koch 1050
Kirk v. Michael Reese Hosp. and Med.
    Ctr. 502, 660
Kirkland v. Blaine County Med. Ctr. 875

Kirkland v. Tamplin 1094, 1100,
    1104, 1109
Kirlin v. Halverson 762
Kirsch v. Duryea 1177
Kirschbaum v. McLaurin Parking Co. 113
Kirton v. Fields 173, 414
Kitowski v. United States 561
Kituskie v. Corbman 1185
Kivland v. Columbia Orthopaedic Group,
    LLP 333, 372
Kizer v. Harper 250, 253
Kjerstad v. Ravellette Pubs., Inc. 707
Klasch v. Walgreen Co. 830, 831
Klawonn v. Mitchell 861
Klecan v. Countrywide Home Loans,
    Inc. 1071
Klein v. Gutman 128
Klein v. Klein 592
Klein v. Pyrodyne Corp. 787, 793
Klein v. United States 480
Kleinschmidt v. Morrow 1026
Klentzman v. Brady 994
Kliebenstein v. Iowa Conference of the
    United Methodist Church 981
Kline v. 1500 Massachusetts Ave. Apt.
    Corp. 287, 644
Kline v. Ansell 1050
Kline v. Burns 491
Klobnak v. Wildwood Hills, Inc. 485, 779
Klooster v. North Iowa State Bank 116
Klump v. Duffus 1185
Klutman v. Sioux Falls Storm 383
Klutschkowski v. PeaceHealth 875
KM, LM ex rel. v. United States 563
K-Mart Corp. v. Gipson 300
K-Mart Corp. v. Herring 914
K-Mart Corp. v. Kyles 1026
K-Mart Corp. v. Washington 154, 155
Knapp v. Stanford 221
Knieper v. United States 1129
Knierim v. Izzo 711, 712
Knight v. City of Missoula 100
Knight v. Jewett 419, 420, 424, 425
Knight v. Schneider Nat'l Carriers,
    Inc. 606
Knighten v. Sam's Parking Valet 655
Knitz v. Minster Mach. Co 807, 815, 816
Knott Corp. v. Furman 454
Knoxville Optical Supply, Inc. v.
    Thomas 224
Knudsen v. Jensen 1128
Koapke v. Kerfendal 513
Kobrin v. Gastfriend 985
Koch v. Norris Pub. Power Dist. 305
Kocher v. Getz 405
Kocontes v. McQuaid 967
Kodiak Island Borough v. Exxon
    Corp. 745, 1076
Koepnick v. Sears Roebuck & Co. 106
Koestler v. Pollard 1052
Koffman v. Garnett 70
Kohl v. City of Phoenix 569

Kohn v. Schiappa.................................. 1183
Kolbe v. State................................. 500, 570
Koll v. Manatt's Transp. Co. 249
Kollar v. Martin........................ 1092, 1096
Koll-Irvine Center Property Owners Ass'n
   v. County of Orange 744
Kolstad v. American Dental Ass'n 862
Kolstad v. Rankin 743
Komlodi v. Picciano 373
Konikoff v. Prudential Ins. Co. of
   Am. 975, 976
Kopalchick v. Catholic Diocese of
   Richmond 439
Kopczynski v. Barger 474
Kopera v. Moschella 327
Kopka v. Bell Telephone Co. of Pa........... 87,
   101
Korando v. Uniroyal Goodrich Tire
   Co.................................... 338, 839
Kordis v. Kordis................................. 128
Kordus v. Montes................................ 436
Korea Supply Co. v. Lockheed Martin
   Corp. 1091, 1094, 1106, 1107
Kornegay v. Thompson........................... 129
Koruba v. American Honda Motor
   Co.. 828
Kossler v. Crisanti 1033
Kotecki v. Cyclops Welding Corp........... 919
Kovach v. Caligor Midwest 318
Kovacic v. Villarreal 585
Kowalski v. Gratopp...................... 612, 613
Kowalski v. Rose Drugs of Dardanelle,
   Inc....................................... 830
Kowalski v. St. Francis Hosp. & Health
   Ctrs....................................... 77
Kowalsky v. Conreco Co., Inc.......... 603, 605
Kozicki v. Dragon 363
Kraemer v. Harding 1102, 1103
Krahmer v. Christie's Inc..................... 1124
Krahn v. Kinney 1190, 1191
Krajewski v. Bourque........................... 610
Krajewski v. Enderes Tool Co.............. 836
Kramer Serv., Inc. v. Wilkins 313
Kramer v. Chabot............................... 1140
Kramer v. Petroleum Helicopters,
   Inc....................................... 303
Kramer v. Thompson........................... 1002
Kratze v. Independent Order of Oddfellows,
   Garden City Lodge No. 11 100
Krause v. U.S. Truck Co., Inc. 612
Krauss v. Champaign News Gazette,
   Inc....................................... 979
Krauth v. Geller 605, 607
Kreidt v. Burlington N. R.R. 218, 221
Kreski v. Modern Wholesale Elec. Supply
   Co.. 607
Kreuzer v. George Washington
   Univ. 1105
Krieg v. Massey 615
Krinsky v. Doe 6............................... 971
Krishnan v. Sepulveda 670
Krochalis v. Insurance Co. of N. Am. 74

Kroh v. Kroh.................................. 982
Krombein v. Gali Serv. Indus. 230
Kronemeyer, Estate of v. Meinig.....688, 697
Krouse v. Graham.............................. 692
Krueger v. Austad.......................991, 992
Krueger v. Lewis............................. 968
Krug v. Krug................................. 1167
KTRK Television v. Felder 980
Kubera v. Barnes & Noble Booksellers,
   Inc. 302
Kubrick, United States v. 430, 431
Kuhns v. Brugger............................. 367
Kumar v. Hall 435
Kumho Tire Co., Ltd. v. Carmichael....... 293
Kunsler ex rel. Kunsler v. Int'l House of
   Pancakes, Inc............................. 712
Kunz v. Allen............................... 1005
Kunz v. Utah Power & Light Co. 93
Kunzie v. City of Olivette 570
Kuo Feng Corp. v. Ma........................ 1121
Kuper v. Lincoln-Union Elec. Co............. 735
Kurns v. Railroad Friction Products
   Corp...................................... 845
Kuwik v. Starmark Star Mktg. & Admin.,
   Inc. 982
Kwansy v. United States 903
L & W Engineering Co., Inc. v. Hogan....164
L.A. Fitness Int'l, LLC v. Mayer 283
L.A.C. v. Ward Parkway Shopping Ctr.
   Co.....................................630, 640
L.D.G., Inc. v. Robinson 1171
L.G., L.W. ex rel. v. Toms River Regional
   Schools Board of Educ..................... 647
L.L. Bean, Inc. v. Drake Publishers,
   Inc. 1198
L.S. Ayres & Co. v. Hicks................... 619
La Sota v. Philadelphia Transp. Co. 452
Label Systems Corp. v.
   Aghamohammadi............................ 1037
Labonte v. Hutchins & Wheeler............. 865
Laboratory Corp. of Am. v. Hood............ 678
Labovitz v. Feinberg 1189
Lachenmaier v. First Bank Sys., Inc.....1105
Lacher v. Superior Court.................... 1125
Lackman v. Rousselle 887
Lackner v. LaCroix 1040
LaCount v. Hensel Phelps Const. Co. 768
Laeroc Waikiki Parkside, LLC v. K.S.K.
   (Oahu) Ltd. P'ship 410, 1146
LaFage v. Jani.............................. 685
LaFaso v. LaFaso............................ 351
Lafayette Par. Sch. Bd. v. Cormier ex rel.
   Cormier...............................233, 234
Lahm v. Farrington 203
Laird v. Nelms.............................. 553
Lake Panorama Servicing Corp. v. Central
   Iowa Energy Coop. 1109
Lake Philgas Service v. Valley Bank &
   Trust Co. 116
Lake v. D & L Langley Trucking, Inc. 385
Lake v. McCollum 503
Lake v. Wal-Mart Stores, Inc. 1020, 1021

Lakeview Blvd. Condo. Ass'n v. Apartment Sales Corp. 434
Lakey v. Puget Sound Energy, Inc. 742
Lakube v. Cohen....................................... 414
LaLonde v. Eissner.................................. 578
Lam v. Global Med. Sys., Inc. 498
LaMantia v. Redisi............................... 1027
Lamare v. Basbanes............................. 1176
Lamb v. State 71, 306
Lambert v. Holmberg............................ 96, 99
Lambert v. Sears, Roebuck & Co. 1032, 1033
Lambert v. Shearer 528
Lambertson v. Cincinnati Corp. 919
Lambertson v. United States.................. 552
Lambrecht v. Estate of Kaczmarczyk.... 299, 304, 305
Lambrecht v. Schreyer............................ 398
Lamke v. Futorian Corp.......................... 813
LaMon v. City of Westport...................... 940
Lamp v. Reynolds............................ 343, 390
Lamson v. American Axe & Tool Co. 416
LAN/STV v. Martin K. Eby Constr. Co.. 804, 1061
Lancaster v. Schilling Motors, Inc........ 1140
Lancaster v. Stevens 1189
Lancaster, City of v. Chambers 579
Lance Productions, Inc. v. Commerce Union Bank 126
Lance v. Wyeth 798
Land v. Yamaha Motor Corp. 434
Landeros v. Flood 571
Landers v. East Tex. Salt Water Disposal Co.. 321, 322
Landham v. Lewis Galoob Toys, Inc..... 1208
Landis v. Hearthmark, LLC 596, 841
Landmark Medical Center v. Gauthier.. 172
Landon v. Kroll Laboratory Specialists, Inc. 624, 628
Landreneau v. Fruge............................... 396
Landry v. Bellanger...................... 163, 399
Landry v. Hilton Head Plantation Property Owners Ass'n 466
Landskroner v. Landskroner 1095
Lane v. Atchison Heritage Conference Center, Inc. 482
Lane v. Gilbert Const. Co...................... 464
Lane v. Groetz 466
Lane v. Industrial Comm'n of Ariz........ 915
Lane v. MPG Newspapers............... 991, 992
Lane v. Schilling 943
Lane v. W.J. Curry & Sons 94, 95
Lang v. Holly Hill Motel, Inc. 244, 246
Lang v. Wonnenberg 365
Langan v. Bellinger................................ 738
Langan v. Valicopters, Inc. 788
Lange v. Fisher Real Estate Dev. Corp.. 157
Langemo v. Montana Rail Link, Inc....... 412
Langer v. Becker 1104, 1105
Langeslag v. KYMN, Inc. 709

Langner v. Simpson 439
Lanz v. Pearson..................................... 365
LaPlace v. Briere...................................113
LaPorte v. Associated Indeps., Inc. 709
Lappe and Associates, Inc. v. Palmen....111, 1152
Lara v. Thomas 941, 999
Larchick v. Diocese of Great Falls-Billings 381
Largey v. Rothman 517
Largosa v. Ford Motor Co. 486
Larini v. Biomass Industries, Inc............481
Larkin v. Marceau 736
Larmore v. Crown Point Iron Co. 145
Larrimore v. American Nat'l Ins. Co.......254
Larsen Chelsey Realty Co. v. Larsen...1094
Larsen v. Banner Health Sys. 700, 714, 730
Larson & Larson, P.A. v. TSE Indus., Inc. 431, 438, 1181
Larson v. Dunn 1054
Larson v. Johns-Manville Sales Corp..431
Larson-Murphy v. Steiner 485
LaSalle Nat'l Leasing Corp. v. Lyndecon, LLC 1146
Lascurain v. City of Newark............704, 711
Laster v. Norfolk S. Ry. Co. 239, 477
Latzel v. Bartek.............................353, 369
Laudermilk v. Carpenter.........................462
Lauer v. City of New York 570
Laurel v. Prince.....................................726
Laurence v. Sollitto...............................1187
Laurie Marie M. v. Jeffrey T.M. 64
LaVallee v. Vermont Motor Inns, Inc......283
LaVine v. Clear Creek Skiing Corp.........231
Lawnwood Med. Ctr., Inc. v. Sadow.......960, 1001
Lawrence v. Beverly Manor.....................694
Lawrence v. Grinde.................................938
Lawrence v. Meloni 117
Lawrence v. State 108
Laws v. Griep 719
Lawson v. Atwood...................................695
Lawson v. Kroger Co. 1027, 1028, 1032
Lawson v. Mitsubishi Motor Sales of America, Inc................................810, 1157
Layden v. Plante 411
Lazenby v. Mark's Constr., Inc...............608
Lazy Seven Coal Sales, Inc. v. Stone & Hinds, P.C...1168
Leach v. Leach 592
Leach v. Shapiro 182
Lead Paint Litigation, In re....................746
Leaf River Forest Products, Inc. v. Harrison...765
Leame v. Bray 192
Leang v. Jersey City Bd. of Educ. 1011
Learning Curve Toys, Inc. v. Playwood Toys, Inc....................................1204, 1205

Leather Manufacturers' Nat'l Bank v. Merchants' Nat'l Bank...................... 1154

Leatherman v. Tarrant County Narcotics Intelligence and Coordination Unit 586

Leavitt v. Brockton Hospital, Inc........... 346, 354, 608

Leavitt v. Glick Realty Corp. 491

Leavitt v. Twin County Rental Co.......... 489

LeClaire v. Commercial Siding and Maintenance Co. 653

Leder v. Spiegel 1168

Ledvina v. Cerasani 966, 974

Lee Lewis Const., Inc. v. Harrison 356, 770

Lee v. Chicago Transit Authority 460, 462

Lee v. City of New York 499

Lee v. Crookston Coca-Cola Bottling Co... 806, 811

Lee v. Gaufin 428, 434, 435

Lee v. GNLV Corp. 269

Lee v. Hartwig....................................... 217

Lee v. Kiku Restaurant.......................... 401

Lee v. Konrad 85

Lee v. Luigi, Inc............................. 606, 609

Lee v. Mitchell 1043

Lee v. State Farm Mut. Ins. Co. 722

Lee v. Stewart.. 101

Lees v. Lobosco 612

Lees v. Sea Breeze Health Care Ctr., Inc.. 709

Lefemine v. Wideman.............................. 582

LeFiell Mfg. Co. v. Superior Court 919

LeFlore v. Reflections of Tulsa, Inc. 1140

Lega Siciliana Social Club, Inc. v. St. Germaine... 953

Legg v. Chopra....................................... 511

Lehmuth v. Long Beach Unified Sch. Dist.. 233

Leibreich v. A.J. Refrigeration, Inc. 368

Leichtamer v. American Motors Corp. ... 807

Leichtman v. WLW Jacor Commc'ns, Inc.. 67, 68

Leiendecker v. Asian Women United of Minnesota 1047

Leiken v. Wilson..................................... 259

Leiner v. First Wythe Ave. Serv. Station, Inc... 794

Leitinger v. DBart, Inc.......................... 859

LeJeune v. Rayne Branch Hosp............. 505

Leleux v. United States.......................... 563

Lemmerman v. Fealk 439

Lemon v. Edwards.................................. 484

Lemon v. Harlem Globetrotters Int'l, Inc.. 1006

Lenard v. Dilley...................................... 221

Lennon v. Metro. Life Ins....................... 242

Lentino v. Fringe Emp. Plans, Inc........ 1169

Lenz Hardware, Inc. v. Wilson 948

Leo Publications, Inc. v. Reid.............. 1206

Leo v. Hillman 715

Leonard, Estate of v. Swift.................... 1179

Leonard v. Behrens.................. 420, 425, 426

Leonard v. Dorsey & Whitney, LLP 1175, 1176

Leonard v. John Crane, Inc. 720

Leonard v. State....................... 501, 502, 576

Leonard v. Walthall 1183

Leonardo v. Sley Sys. Garages, Inc. 961

Leordeanu v. American Protection Ins. Co. 914

LePage v. Horne.......................... 229, 303

Lepucki v. Lake County Sheriff's Dep't... 259

Lerner Shops of Nevada, Inc. v. Marin.. 154

Leroy Fibre Co. v. Chicago, Milwaukee & St. Paul Ry. Co. 396, 740, 794

LeRoy v. Allen, Yurasek & Merklin 1175

Lester v. Buchanen 1027, 1028

Lestina v. West Bend Mut. Ins. Co. 426

Lev v. Beverly Enterprises—Massachusetts, Inc. 637

Levaquin Products Liability Litigation, In re 833

Level 3 Commc'ns, LLC v. Liebert Corp... 1126

Levey v. Yamaha Motor Corp................. 828

Levi v. Southwest La. Elec. Membership Coop. 271, 276

Levin, Middlebrooks, Mabie, Thomas, Mayes & Mitchell, P.A. v. United States Fire Ins. Co. 967

Levine v. Chemical Bank....................... 611

Levine v. Peoples Broadcasting Corp...... 760

Levine v. Russell Blaine Co. 285

Levy v. Gandone...................................... 973

Levy v. Louisiana 695

Lewellen v. Franklin.............................. 875

Lewis Operating Corp. v. Super. Ct. 413

Lewis v. American Cyanamid Co. 826

Lewis v. B & R Corp.............................. 254

Lewis v. Coffing Hoist Div., Duff-Norton Co. 805

Lewis v. Cowen..................................... 1148

Lewis v. Equitable Life Assurance Soc'y of the U.S. 943

Lewis v. Gilmore 919

Lewis v. Hiatt.. 694

Lewis v. Lead Indus. Ass'n, Inc.............. 329

Lewis v. Miller....................................... 59

Lewis v. Puget Sound Power & Light Co. 396

Lewis v. White...................................... 1031

Lexmark Intern., Inc. v. Static Control Components, Inc...................... 1200, 1208

Li v. Yellow Cab Co. of Cal. 386

Libby v. Eighth Judicial Dist. Court....... 432

Liberman v. Gelstein 961, 982, 984

Liberty Bank of Seattle, Inc. v. Henderson... 969

Liberty Lobby, Inc. v. Anderson 955

Liberty Mut. Ins. Co. v. Steadman.......... 708

Liberty Nat'l Life Ins. Co. v. Weldon.......637

Liberty Northwest Ins. Co. v. Spudnik Equipment Co. 811
Liberty v. State Dep't of Transp. 481
Library of Congress v. Shaw 551
Lickteig v. Alderson, Ondov, Leonard & Sween 1183
Lickteig v. Kolar 54, 594
Lieberman v. Employers Ins. of Wausau 1167
Lieberman v. Powers.............................. 781
Lifson v. City of Syracuse........................ 220
Liggett v. Young 1168
Lightfoot v. School Administrative Dist. No. 35 564
Lillie v. Thompson 650
Limbaugh v. Coffee Med. Ctr......... 538, 540, 543
Limited Stores, Inc. v. Wilson-Robinson.................................... 76
Limone v. United States 562, 1027
Lincoln Elec. Co. v. McLemore............... 431
Lincoln v. Clark Freight Lines, Inc 295
Lindholm v. Brant 124
Lindquist v. City of Jersey City Fire Dep't 918
Lindsay Mfg. Co. v. Universal Surety Co.. 429
Lindsey v. E & E Automotive & Tire Service, Inc................................. 629
Lindstrom v. City of Corry 575
Linegar v. Armour of America, Inc........ 813, 818
Lingenfelter v. Astrue 924
Lingle v. Dion 253
Lingo v. Lingo 1146
Lininger v. Eisenbaum........................... 678
Link v. Wabash Co. 1164
Linscott v. Foy 1047
Linthicum v. Nationwide Life Ins. Co. ... 862
Lions Eye Bank of Tex. v. Perry 729
Lipham v. Federated Dep't Stores, Inc....................................... 464
Lipman v. Atlantic Coast Line R.R......... 703
Lippay v. Christos 1033
Lips v. Scottsdale Healthcare Corp. 1070, 1159
Lipson v. Superior Court of Orange County (Berger) 605, 609, 610
Liriano v. Hobart Corp.................... 326, 828
Lisa M. v. Henry Mayo Newhall Mem. Hosp. 761, 762
Littau v. Midwest Commodities, Inc. ... 1136
Little Rock Newspapers, Inc. v. Dodrill 936, 1001
Little Rock Newspapers, Inc. v. Fitzhugh.................................. 951
Little Rock, City of v. Cameron 200
Little v. Chesser 1102
Little v. Gibbs.................................... 1153
Little v. Liquid Air Corp. 292
Littlefield v. Schaefer........................... 411
Liu v. Allen 250

Livingston v. Adams 193, 194
Livingstone v. North Belle Vernon Borough...................................1036
Livsey v. Salt Lake County...................1013
LLMD of Mich., Inc. v. Jackson-Cross Co. 1024, 1074
Lloyd v. General Motors Corp. 803, 1086
Lloyd v. Sugarloaf Mtn. Corp. 413
Local Joint Exec. Bd. of Las Vegas, Culinary Workers Union, Local No. 226 v. Stern 1063
Locke v. Ford....................................452
Locke, United States v...........................442
Lockett v. Bi-State Transit Auth.............657
Lockhart v. Airco Heating & Cooling, Inc......................................624
Lockton v. O'Rourke............................1181
Lockwood v. Commissioner Soc. Sec. Admin. 924
Lodge v. Arett Sales Corp. 340, 347
Lodl v. Progressive Northern Ins. Co......574
Loe v. Lenhardt..................................788
Loeb v. Rasmussen...........................232, 244
Loevsky v. Carter................................232
Loftus v. Dehail..............................352, 362
Loge v. United States.......................553, 555
Logerquist v. Danforth 439
Logsdon v. Isco Co...............................915
Logusak v. City of Togiak, Estate of 579
Lokey v. Breuner.................................624
Lolley v. Charter Woods Hosp. Inc..........164
Lomando v. United States 552
Lombard v. Colorado Outdoor Educ. Center, Inc. 471
Lombard v. United States 561
Lombardo v. Doyle, Dane & Bernbach, Inc. 1209
Long Beach, City of v. Bozek 954
Long v. Daly 254
Long v. Hacker 775
Long v. Patterson 615
Longbehn v. Schoenrock 942, 999, 1002
Loosli v. City of Salem 1068, 1124
Lopatkovich v. City of Tiffin............253, 483
Lopes v. Farmer.................................1035
Lopez v. Arizona Water Co., Inc.............630
Lopez v. Baca 254
Lopez v. No Kit. Realty Co......................392
Lopez v. Southern California Rapid Transit Dist.......................................452
Lopez v. Superior Court.........................490
Lord v. Lovett....................................332
Lord, State v......................................140
Lorenz v. Air Illinois, Inc. 689
Lorenzetti, United States v. 920
Lorenzo v. Wirth..................................10
Los Angeles Airways, Inc. v. Davis 1105
Los Angeles Police Dep't v. United Reporting Publ'g Co. 1018
Losee v. Buchanan 785
Losee v. Clute....................................799
Lotring v. Philbrook.............................1051

Lott v. Levitt... 941
Lough v. BNSF Ry. Co.......................... 313
Lough v. Rolla Women's Clinic, Inc........ 209
Loughry v. Lincoln First Bank 863
Louis Vuitton Malletier S.A. v. Haute
   Diggity Dog, LLC 1196
Louisiana State Bar Association v.
   Hinrichs.. 112
Louisiana, State of ex rel. Guste v. M/V
   Testbank 746, 1067, 1071, 1082
Louisville & J. Ferry Co. v. Nolan 451
Louisville Gas & Elec. Co. v.
   Roberson... 628
Louk v. Isuzu Motors, Inc. 382
Lourim v. Swensen................................. 762
Love v. Walker 509
Lovejoy v. AT&T Corp.......................... 1130
Lovelace Med. Ctr. v. Mendez......... 396, 682
Lovelace v. Anderson............................. 759
Lovelace v. City of Shelby 572
Lovely v. United States........................... 560
Lovett v. Hobbs...................................... 192
Lower Commerce Ins. Inc. v. Halliday ... 745
Lowery v. Echostar Satellite Corp......... 265,
   267, 390
Lowney v. Knott 117
Lownsbury v. VanBuren 498
Loyd v. Herrington 769
Lozano v. Lozano.................................. 1054
Lozoya v. Sanchez................................. 721
LPP Mortg., Ltd. v. Marcin, Inc............ 1111
Lubecki v. City of New York 896, 903
Lubin v. Johnson 1116
Lucas v. Hamm.......................... 1170, 1175
Lucas v. Hesperia Golf & Country
   Club 244
Lucero v. Holbrook 204, 343
Luchejko v. City of Hoboken 483
Luciano v. Olsten Corp........................... 874
Lucky 7, LLC v. THT Realty, LLC 1135
Lugo v. Ameritech Corp., Inc. 471
Lugtu v. Cal. Highway Patrol........ 214, 292,
   366, 619
Lulay v. Parvin...................................... 653
Lumbermens Mut. Cas. Co. v.
   Thornton 206, 1125
Lumley v. Gye 1094, 1099
Luna v. Vela... 423
Lunceford v. Peachtree Cas. Ins. Co....... 864
Lunda v. Matthews 86
Lundy v. Adamar of New Jersey, Inc. 621
Lunsford v. Board of Educ. of Prince
   George's County................................... 646
Luoni v. Berube 468
Lurgio v. Commonwealth Edison Co. 609,
   610
Lusby v. Lusby.. 593
Luther v. City of Winner......................... 472
Lutheran Hosps. & Homes Soc'y of Am. v.
   Yepsen.. 599
Luthringer v. Moore 788
Lutz v. Watson.. 957

Lutzkovitz v. Murray 225
Lybrand v. Trask.............................. 708, 709
Lynch v. City of Alhambra.................... 1036
Lynch v. McQueen 1112
Lynch v. Rosenthal................................ 392
Lynch v. Scheininger 406, 676
Lyon v. Barrett....................................... 919
Lyon v. Carey 763
Lyon v. Ranger III.................................. 884
Lyons v. Grether 531
Lyons v. Midnight Sun Transp. Servs.,
   Inc. 221, 382
Lyons v. Nichols 989
Lyons v. Vaughan Reg'l Med. Ctr.,
   LLC 720
Lytle v. Bexar County, Tex. 162
M & D, Inc. v. McConkey...................... 1129
M.A. v. United States....................... 207, 680
M.G. v. Time Warner, Inc............ 1016, 1019
M.H. v. Caritas Family Servs................. 728
M.W. v. Dep't of Soc. & Health Servs...... 248
M/V DG Harmony, In re 787
Ma v. City & Cty. of San Francisco........ 209,
   210
Mabry, Sias ex rel. v. Wal-Mart Stores,
   Inc. 596
Mabus v. St. James Episcopal
   Church 454, 455, 1143
MacBoyle v. City of Parma 1035
MacDonald v. Clinger 1015
MacDonald v. Ortho Pharmaceutical
   Corp.. 829
MacDonald v. Riggs 951, 959
MacDonald v. Thomas M. Cooley Law
   Sch.. 1136
MacDougald v. Garber........................... 856
MacElree v. Philadelphia Newspapers,
   Inc. 946, 951
MacFawn v. Kresler.............................. 1034
MacGregor v. Walker...................... 203, 624
MacGuire v. Elometa Corp. 126
Machado v. City of Hartford................... 266
Macia v. Microsoft Corp........................ 1114
Macias v. Saberhagen Holdings, Inc. 825
Macias v. State of California 831
Mack Trucks, Inc. v. Tackett................... 890
Mack v. Carmack 671, 686
Mack v. County of Rockland................... 917
Mackintosh v. Carter 1056
MacPherson v. Buick Motor Co. 800,
   1070
Macy v. New York World-Telegram
   Corp.. 1000
Madden v. C & K Barbecue Carryout,
   Inc. 639
Mader v. United States........................... 551
Madison Ave. Gourmet Foods, Inc. v.
   Finlandia Ctr., Inc........... 209, 1067, 1070
Madison v. Ducktown Sulphur, Copper &
   Iron Co. 748
Madison v. Frazier 997
Madlem v. Arko..................................... 1180

Madrid v. Lincoln Cnty. Med. Ctr. 726
Maggard v. Conagra Foods, Inc. 612
Maglioli v. J.P. Noonan Transp., Inc. 219
Magna Trust Co. v. Illinois Cent. R.R. ... 401
Magnuson v. Billmayer 141
Magnuson v. O'Dea 1053
Magnusson v. New York Times Co. 957
Mahan v. New Hampshire Dep't of
  Administrative Services 569
Mahan v. State 224
Mahon v. Heim.. 236
Mahoney v. Carus Chem. Co., Inc. 610,
  613
Mahoney v. Nebraska Methodist
  Hosp. 859
Mahowald v. Minnesota Gas Co. 787, 789
Maiden v. Rozwood.................................. 579
Maison de France v. Mais Oui!,Inc......... 962
Majca v. Beekil 726
Majestic Realty Associates, Inc. v. Toti
  Contracting Co...................................... 768
Major v. United States 561
Makas v. Hillhaven, Inc. 547
Malaney v. Hannaford Bros. Co.............. 469
Malatesta v. Lowry................................. 462
Malcolm v. Evenflo Co., Inc............ 289, 805,
  844, 870
Maldanado, In re Estate of 694
Maldonado v. Sinai Med. Group, Inc. 855
Maldonado v. Southern Pac. Transp.
  Co... 620
Malen v. MTD Products, Inc. 840
Malley v. Briggs........................... 585, 1029
Malmberg v. Lopez................................. 293
Malolepszy v. State 352
Maloney v. Stone 115
Malouf v. Dallas Athletic Country
  Club 87
Maltman v. Sauer.................. 609, 610, 612
Manchack v. Willamette Indus., Inc....... 249
Mandel v. Geloso 735
Mandel v. The Boston Phoenix, Inc. 991
Mandel, Resnik & Kaiser, P.C. v. E.I.
  Electronics, Inc. 1177
Maneely v. General Motors Corp........... 827,
  828
Maness v. Gordon.................................... 439
Mangieri v. Prime Hospitality Corp. 453
Mangold v. Ind. Dep't of Nat'l Res......... 383
Mangum, City of v. Brownlee 783
Manley v. Sherer..................................... 327
Mann v. Cincinnati Enquirer................ 1021
Manning v. Grimsley.................... 80, 81, 82
Manning v. Michael................................ 136
Manno v. McIntosh.................................. 279
Manor Care, Inc. v. Douglas 544
Mansfield v. Circle K. Corp. 214, 251
Manske v. Workforce Safety & Ins. 918
Mansur v. Ford Motor Co............... 809, 812
Mansur v. Podhurst Orseck, P.A. 1166
Mantooth v. Richards.......................... 1054
Manuel v. Wilka 1025

Manufacturers Trust Co. v. Nelson.........111
Manufacturing Research Corp. v. Greenlee
  Tool Co...1103
Maples Lanes, Inc. v. New Media
  Corp..977, 981
Marble v. Chapin 940, 945
Marcel v. Placid Oil Co. 861
Marchant v. Cook....................................1122
Marchbanks v. Borum 61
Marchetti v. Kalish 425
Marcil v. Kells 958
Marcinczyk v. State of N.J. Police Training
  Comm'n..414
Marciniak v. Lundborg 682, 683
Marcone v. Penthouse Int'l Magazine for
  Men 956
Marcotte v. Timberlane/Hampstead Sch.
  Dist..693
Marcum v. Bowdens..................................664
Marcus Bros. Textiles, Inc. v. Price
  Waterhouse, LLP..................................1130
Marcus v. Liebman 177
Maresh v. State..368
Marin Tug & Barge, Inc. v. Westport
  Petroleum, Inc. 1095, 1100
Marioenzi v. DiPonte, Inc. 478
Mark v. King Broad. Co............................979
Mark v. Seattle Times 938
Mark v. State ex rel. Dep't of Fish and
  Wildlife 740
Markarian v. Simonian.............................489
Markle v. Hacienda Mexican
  Restaurant...468
Markowitz v. Helen Homes of Kendall
  Corp...469
Marks v. St. Luke's Episcopal Hosp........527
Markwell v. Whinery's Real Estate,
  Inc. 447
Marlene F. v. Affiliated Psychiatric Med.
  Clinic, Inc..713
Marley v. Providence Journal Co. 954
Marmet Health Care Center, Inc. v.
  Brown..538
Marple v. Sears, Roebuck & Co. 381
Marquay v. Eno...............246, 248, 251, 571
Marquis v. State Farm Fire & Cas.
  Co. 657
Marriage of Cutler, In re 1119
Marrogi v. Howard......................1024, 1074
Marsh v. Colby 167
Marsh v. Tilley Steel Co. 774
Marshak v. Marshak...............................1055
Marshall v. Burger King Corp........205, 207,
  208, 209, 638
Marshall v. Montgomery County Children
  Services Bd. 649
Marshall v. Nugent................353, 366, 371
Marshall v. Yale Podiatry Group 511
Marsingill v. O'Malley 293, 504, 520
Marston v. Minneapolis Clinic of Psychiatry
  and Neurology 757, 762
Marten's Chevrolet, Inc. v. Seney 1122

Martignetti v. Haigh-Farr Inc. 901
Martin & Martin, Inc. v. Bradley Enters.,
 Inc... 1128
Martin County Coal Corp. v. Universal
 Underwriters Ins. Co........................... 414
Martin Luther King, Jr., Center for Social
 Change, Inc. v. American Heritage
 Products, Inc. 1208, 1209
Martin v. Abbott Labs. 330
Martin v. Altman.................................... 253
Martin v. Atlantic Coast Line R.R.
 Co.. 691
Martin v. Brady 577
Martin v. Chicago Transit Authority...... 450
Martin v. Christman 780
Martin v. Cincinnati Gas and Elec.
 Co. 485, 652
Martin v. City of Albany 1028, 1033
Martin v. City of Gadsden...................... 482
Martin v. City of Washington, Mo. 466
Martin v. Clements 1180
Martin v. Estrella........................... 132, 135
Martin v. Hacker 828
Martin v. Heinold Commodities, Inc. ... 1135
Martin v. Herzog 243, 247
Martin v. Houck 75
Martin v. Keeley & Sons, Inc. 1161
Martin v. Lancaster Battery Co., Inc. 921
Martin v. Little, Brown and Co. 1203
Martin v. Marciano................................. 664
Martin v. Naik 696
Martin v. Northwest Washington Legal
 Services 1184
Martin v. Ohio Cnty. Hosp. Corp.... 719, 720
Martin v. Rankin Circle Apartments 492
Martin v. Reynolds Metals Co. 89, 90,
 736, 1113
Martin v. Roy... 957
Martin v. United States 893
Martin v. Yeoham................................... 132
Martin v. Ziherl 402
Martin, In re 174
Martinelli v. Bridgeport Roman Catholic
 Diocesan Corp. 180, 455
Martinez v. California 3
Martinez v. City of Schenectady 1034
Martinez v. Indus. Comm'n of Ariz......... 916
Martinez v. Lewis................................... 499
Martinez v. Maruszczak......................... 569
Martinez v. New York City Transit
 Auth... 295
Martinez v. Robledo............................... 857
Martinez v. The Port Authority of New York
 and New Jersey................................. 1026
Martinez v. Woodmar IV Condo.
 Homeowners Ass'n...................... 208, 643
Martino v. Wal-Mart Stores, Inc. 1160
Martishius v. Carolco Studios, Inc. 382
Marvin Lumber & Cedar Co. v. PPG Indus.,
 Inc... 1080
Marx v. Huron Little Rock 453
Mary M. v. City of Los Angeles 543, 753

Maryland Cas. Co. v. Baker..................... 763
Masaki v. General Motors Corp. 719
Mason v. City of Mt. Sterling 475, 477
Mason v. Sportsman's Pub 761
Masquat v. Maguire................................ 519
Massengale v. Pitts................................ 720
Massengill v. Yuma County.................... 570
Massey v. ConAgra Foods, Inc.............. 808
Masson v. New Yorker Magazine,
 Inc. 956, 995
Masterson v. Stambuck 599
Mastland, Inc. v. Evans Furniture,
 Inc... 233
Mathias v. Accor Econ. Lodging, Inc........ 17,
 865
Mathias v. Denver Union Terminal Ry.
 Co. 467
Mathis v. Cannon................................939, 1003
Mathis v. Daly...................................... 994
Mathis v. Exxon Corp. 739
Mathis v. Massachusetts Elec. Co........... 477
Matkovic v. Shell Oil Co. 793
Matsumoto v. Matsumoto.....................1054
Matsuyama v. Birnbaum................. 294, 333
Mattco Forge, Inc. v. Arthur Young &
 Co. 1074
Mattel, Inc. v. MCA Records, Inc. 1196,
 1198
Matthews v. Blue Cross and Blue Shield of
 Michigan 1027, 1030, 1032
Matthews v. Remington Arms Co.,
 Inc. 839
Matthies v. Mastromonaco 519, 520
Matthiessen v. Vanech........................... 399
Mattingly v. Sheldon Jackson Coll.........1076
Mattox v. Life Care Centers of America,
 Inc. 512, 539
Mattox v. State Dep't of Corrections.......645
Matzan v. Eastman Kodak Co...............1151
Maunz v. Perales................................... 395
Maurer v. Speedway, LLC...................... 255
Mauro v. Raymark Indus., Inc. 334
Mavrikidis v. Petullo....................... 764, 767
Mavrogenis, Lester ex rel. v. Hall 660
Maybee v. Jacobs Motor Co., Inc. 1135
Mayberry, State v. 690, 691
Maye v. Yappen.................................... 95
Mayfield v. Acme Barrel Co.................. 1158
Mayfield-Brown v. Sayegh..................... 597
Mayflower Indus. v. Thor Corp. 1041
Mayhue v. Sparkman............................. 332
Mayle v. Ohio Dep't of Rehab. &
 Corr. 244, 245
Mayor and Aldermen of Knoxville,
 State v... 159
Mayor of Savannah v. Mulligan 159
Mazda Motor Corp. v. Lindahl 840
Mazon v. Krafchick 1175
Mazzacano v. Estate of Kinnerman 662
MBank El Paso v. Sanchez............. 151, 769
Mbarika v. Board of Supervisors of La.
 State Univ.. 941

McAfee v. Cole 439
McAlister v. Carl 856
McAllen, City of v. De La Garza 486
McAllister v. Ha 679
McAllister, Estate of v. United States 559
McAuley v. Int'l Bus. Mach. Corp. 1125
McBride v. Bennett 575
McBride v. General Motors Corp. 867
McBride v. New Braunfels Herald-Zeitung 956
McCabe v. American Honda Motor Co. 812
McCabe, United States v. 171
McCain v. Florida Power Corp. 338
McCall v. Owens 116
McCall, Estate of ex rel. v. United States 526, 875
McCamey v. District of Columbia Dep't of Employment Servs. 916
McCandless v. State 83
McCann v. Wal-Mart Stores, Inc. 75
McCart v. Muir 899
McCarthy v. Olin Corp. 805
McCarthy v. Volkswagen of America, Inc. 172
McCartney v. Pawtucket Mut. Ins. 224
McCarty v. Phesant Run, Inc. 276, 281
McCathern v. Toyota Motor Corp. 809
McCay v. Philadelphia Elec. Co. 390
McClellan v. Health Maintenance Organization of Pa. 535
McClenahan v. Cooley 363
McClinton v. Delta Pride Catfish, Inc. 1032
McClinton v. White 691
McClosky v. Martin 1068
McClung v. Delta Square Ltd. P'ship 641
McClure v. Johnson 449
McCollum v. D'Arcy 439
McColm-Traska v. Baker 1165, 1172, 1174
McComish v. DeSoi 283
McConkey v. Aon Corp. 728, 1139
McConnell v. Cosco 829
McConnell v. Hunt Sports Enters. 1091
McConnell v. Williams 774, 775
McCord v. Bailey 1190
McCormick v. Carrier 247
McCormick v. Kopmann 690
McCourt v. Abernathy 694
McCoy v. Feinman 1180, 1182
McCoy v. Taylor Tire Co. 135
McCracken v. O.B. Sloan 64, 67
McCracken v. Walls-Kaufman 180
McCraney v. Flanagan 70
McCrystal v. Trumbull Mem'l Hosp. 393
McCullough v. Antolini 583
McCullough v. Visiting Nurse Serv. of S. Me., Inc. 950
McCune v. Neitzel 941, 947, 959
McCurcheon v. Moran 992

McCutchen v. McCutchen 1050
McDaniel v. Gile 180
McDaniel, In re 1156
McDermott v. Reynolds 1051
McDonald v. Hampton Training School for Nurses 764, 765
McDonald v. Haskins 583
McDonald v. Mass. Gen. Hosp. 597
McDonald v. Price 690
McDonald v. Smith 984
McDonald's Corp. v. Ogborn 75
McDougald v. Perry 302, 305
McDougall v. Lamm 714
McEachern v. Black 1035
McEvoy v. Group Health Co-op of Eau Claire 535
McFadden v. Haritatos 828
McFarland v. Bruno Mach. Corp. 823
McFarland v. Kahn 280
McFarlane v. City of Niagara Falls 747
MCG Health, Inc. v. Casey 498
McGanty v. Staudenraus 1106
McGarry v. Sax 422
McGathey v. Brookwood Health Services, Inc. 509
McGee v. A C & S, Inc. 693
McGee v. McGee 593
McGettigan v. National Bank of Washington 476, 477
McGill, Estate of v. Albrecht 548
McGonigal v. Gearhart Indus., Inc. 305
McGowan v. Estate of Wright 692
McGrath v. SNH Dev., Inc. 411, 412
McGrath v. State Dep't of Pub. Safety 917
McGregor v. Barton Sand & Gravel, Inc. 97
McGregor v. Marini 233
McGuire v. Hodges 244, 246
McHaffie v. Bunch 900
MCI Sales and Service, Inc. v. Hinton 846
McIntire v. Lee 1170
McIntyre v. Balentine 478
McKay v. Wilderness Dev't, LLC 700
McKay's Family Dodge v. Hardrives 405
McKee v. Laurion 948, 997
McKellips v. Saint Francis Hosp., Inc. 333
McKenna v. Wolkswagenwerk Aktiengesellschaft 366
McKenney, In re, Estate of 1122, 1128
McKennon v. Nashville Banner Pub. Co. 1035, 1101
McKenzie v. Egge 489
McKenzie v. Hawai'i Permanente Med. Group, Inc. 500, 535, 659
McKenzie v. S K Hand Tool Corp. 810
McKinley v. Flaherty 118
McKinney v. Okoye 966, 1025, 1027
McKinsey v. Wade 143, 144
McKinstry v. Valley Obstetrics-Gynecology Clinic 670
McKnight v. Dean 1170, 1174, 1175

McKnight, State v. 675
McKown v. Wal-Mart Stores, Inc............ 764
McLain v. Mariner Health Care, Inc. 545
McLain v. Schweiker 924
McLane v. Northwest Natural Gas.
  Co. 788
McLaughlin v. Chicago, M., St. P. & P. Ry.
  Co. 853
McLaughlin v. Sullivan 372
McLaughlin v. Sy...................................... 505
McLaughlin v. Williams 1119
McLean v. City of New York 571
McLean v. Colf.. 150
McLean v. Kirby Co., a Div. of Scott Fetzer
  Co. 363, 768
McLeod v. Grant County School Dist. No.
  128 .... 646, 647
McMackin v. Johnson County Healthcare
  Ctr. 333
McMahon v. Bergeson 732
McMahon v. N.Y., N.H. & H.R. Co. 232,
  393
McMillan v. City of New York 853
McMillan v. Durant.................................. 530
McMillan v. Mahoney..................... 328, 329
McMullen v. Ohio State Univ. Hosp....... 860
McNair v. Jones 780
McNamara v. Honeyman 394, 401
McNeil Nutritionals, LLC v. Heartland
  Sweeteners, LLC................................. 1199
McNulty v. City of New York 501, 661
McPherson v. McPherson........................ 177
McPherson v. Tamiami Trail Tours,
  Inc. 452
McQuade v. Draw Tite, Inc. 919
McQuaig v. Tarrant.................................. 264
McQuay v. Guntharp..................... 709, 710
McQuirk v. Donnelley 970
McQuitty v. Spangler 520
McRae v. Group Health Plan, Inc........... 430
McSurely v. McClellan 1012
McSwane v. Bloomington Hosp. &
  Healthcare Sys............................ 380, 638
McVicar v. W.R. Arthur & Co. 461
McWhirt v. Heavey................................ 1174
McWilliams v. Parham............................ 286
Mead v. Legacy Health System 498
Meade v. Cedarapids, Inc............ 1116, 1135
Meador v. Cabinet for Human
  Resources 650
Meadors v. Still................................ 430, 439
Meadowcraft Indus., Inc. 605
Meadows v. Blake.................................... 687
Meadows v. Union Carbide Corp. 436
Mealy v. B-Mobile, Inc. 721
Meaney v. Loew's Hotels, Inc................. 957
Mecca v. Shang...................................... 1124
Medasys Acquisition Corp. v. SDMS,
  P.C. 1140
Media Gen., Inc. v. Tomlin.................... 1122
Medical Informatics Eng'g, Inc. v.
  Orthopaedics Ne., P.C. 966

Medical Lab. Mgmt. Consultants v.
  American Broad. Cos., Inc. 1009, 1092
Medtronic, Inc., Sprint Fidelis Leads
  Products Liability Litigation, In re 846
Medtronic, Inv. v. Lohr 847
Medved v. Glenn 439
Meier ex rel. Meier v. Champ's Sport Bar &
  Grill, Inc... 251
Meier v. D'Ambose 489
Meiers v. Fred Koch Brewery................. 606
Meinhard v. Salmon................... 1144, 1145
Meinze v. Holmes................................... 498
Meistrich v. Casino Arena Attractions,
  Inc. 418
Mel Foster Co. Properties, Inc. v. American
  Oil Co. 98, 100, 735
Meland v. Youngberg 1136
Melin-Schilling v. Imm 753, 760
Melville v. Southward 511
Melvin v. Reid 1017
Memorial Hosp. of S. Bend, Inc. v.
  Scott 223
Memphis Light, Gas and Water Div. v.
  Goss 486
Memphis Publ'g Co. v. Nichols 995
Mendelowitz v. Neisner 145
Mendillo v. Bd. of Educ. of E.
  Haddam 719
Menefee v. Columbia Broad. Sys.,
  Inc. 1114
Mengwasser v. Anthony Kempker
  Trucking, Inc. 352
Mensink v. American Grain 468
Meracle v. Children's Serv. Soc'y of
  Wis. 678, 681
Merando v. United States........................ 557
Mercer Mut. Ins. Co. v. Proudman.......... 813
Mercer v. Cosley...................................... 963
Mercer v. Vanderbilt Univ., Inc....... 395, 528
Merck & Co., Inc. v. Garza 313
Merenoff v. Merenoff............................... 592
Meritor Sav. Bank, FSB v. Vinson 709
Merrell Dow Pharms., Inc. v. Havner 674
Merriam v. McConnell............................. 483
Merryweather v. Nixan 881
Mertsaris v. 73rd Corp............................ 220
Mesman v. Crane Pro Services, Div. of
  Konecranes, Inc. 820
Messerschmidt v. Millender 585
Messina v. Matarasso 63
Mest v. Cabot Corp. 97
Methodist Manor of Waukesha, Inc. v.
  Martin.. 1153
Metlife Auto & Home v. Joe Basic
  Chevrolet, Inc. 1160
Metromedia Co. v. WCBM Maryland,
  Inc. 87
Metro-North Commuter R.R. Co. v.
  Buckley 312, 854
Metropolitan Property and Cas. Ins. Co. v.
  Deere and Co. 810
Mettes v. Quinn...................................... 1179

Metz v. United States............................. 562
Metzgar v. Playskool, Inc. 819
Mexicali Rose v. Superior Court 808
Meyer v. Burger King Corp............ 673, 919
Meyer v. Fluor Corp. 854
Meyer v. Mulligan 1166
Meyer v. Wagner 1169, 1170
Meyers v. Epstein 514
Meyers v. Livingston, Adler, Pulda,
    Meiklejohn and Kelly, P.C................ 1163
Meyers v. Wal-Mart Stores, East,
    Inc.. 855
Meyerson v. Prime Realty Svcs.,
    LLC... 1018
Miami Herald Pub. Co. v. Tornillo........ 1004
Miami Herald Publishing Co. v.
    Kendall 765
Micari v. Mann 175, 178
Miccolis v. Amica Mut. Ins. Co. 670
Michael E. Greene, P.A. v. Leasing
    Associates, Inc.................................. 1177
Michael L., Weatherford ex rel. v.
    State 650
Michael v. Alestree................................. 192
Michael v. Cole 866
Michaud v. Great N. Nekoosa Corp........ 716
Michel v. Melgren................................... 164
Michels v. Sklavos 1180
Mickel v. Wilson 675
Middlebrooks v. Curtis Publ'g Co. 952
Midland Oil Co. v. Thigpen.................... 769
Midler v. Ford Motor Co............. 1006, 1208
Mid-States Plastics, Inc. v. Estate of
    Bryant 757
Midwest Home Distributor, Inc. v. Domco
    Indus. Ltd. 1140
Miele v. United States............................ 563
Mieske v. Bartell Drug Co....................... 106
Miessner v. All Dakota Ins. Assocs.,
    Inc.. 1031
Migliori v. Airborne Freight Corp..... 17, 717
Mignone v. Fieldcrest Mills..................... 613
Mikell v. School Admin. Unit No. 33..... 646,
    708
Mikolajczyk v. Ford Motor Co........ 803, 809,
    821
Mikula v. Duliba............................ 216, 218
Miles v. Apex Marine Corp. 686, 687, 692
Miles v. Naval Aviation Museum Found.,
    Inc. 555
Mileski v. Long Island R.R..................... 855
Miley v. Landry 732
Military Highway Water Supply Corp. v.
    Morin 486
Milk v. Federal Home Loan Mortg.
    Corp... 701
Milkovich v. Lorain Journal.......... 997, 1001
Millennium Equity Holdings, LLC v.
    Mahlowitz 700, 852
Miller ex rel. Miller v. Dacus 513, 674
Miller v. Armstrong World Industries,
    Inc.. 441

Miller v. Bahmmuller 352, 362
Miller v. Brass Rail Tavern, Inc......511, 513
Miller v. Brooks...........................592, 1010
Miller v. David Grace, Inc 265
Miller v. East Baton Rouge Parish Sheriff's
    Dept..1030
Miller v. Ensco, Inc................................921
Miller v. Evangeline Parish Police
    Jury..294
Miller v. General Motors Corp. 146
Miller v. HCA, Inc...................................174
Miller v. Johnson 875
Miller v. Kirk...670
Miller v. Lambert 769
Miller v. Levering Regional Health Care
    Center, LLC.....................................544
Miller v. Lockport Realty Group,
    Inc..1104
Miller v. McDonald's Corp.......................773
Miller v. Monsen 1056
Miller v. Mooney 1166, 1176
Miller v. National Broadcasting Co...........87
Miller v. Rhode Island Hosp. 182, 514
Miller v. State 648
Miller v. Westcor Ltd. P'ship 767, 769
Miller v. Willbanks 711
Millington v. Kuba 711
Millington v. Se. Elevator Co., Inc. 719
Milliun v. New Milfort Hospital..............512
Mills County State Bank v. Roure 1046
Mills v. C.H.I.L.D., Inc...........................1096
Mills v. City of Overland Park................661
Mills v. Giant of Maryland, LLC 827
Milwaukee & St. P. R. Co. v. Kellogg......346
Milwaukee Metro. Sewerage Dist. v. City of
    Milwaukee 736, 737
Mims v. Boland 61, 171
Miner v. Long Island Lighting Co. 289
Miniken v. Carr......................................467
Minnesota Fire & Cas. Ins. Co. v. Paper
    Recycling of La Crosse 481
Minnich v. Med-Waste, Inc.....................608
Minn-Kota Ag Products, Inc. v.
    Carlson..1172
Minns v. United States 562
Mintz v. Blue Cross of California 535
Miraliakbari v. Pennicooke.......................75
Mirand v. City of New York.............621, 647
Miranda v. Said....................................1183
Mireles v. Broderick....................303, 307
Mirjavadi v. Vakilzadeh 213, 214
Misany v. United States 1112
Misenheimer v. Burris...........................1051
Miskew v. Hess 1039, 1040
Mississippi Baptist Hosp. v. Holmes.......597
Mississippi Dep't of Pub. Safety v.
    Durn...264
Mississippi State Fed'n of Colored Women's
    Club Housing for Elderly in Clinton, Inc.
    v. L.R..715
Missner v. Clifford 940
Missouri Pac. R.R. Co. v. Limmer 443

Missouri Pac. R.R. Co. v. Maxwell 692
Mitchell v. Bearden 743
Mitchell v. Cedar Rapids Cmty. Sch.
    Dist. 327, 354
Mitchell v. Clark County Sch. Dist. 915
Mitchell v. Folmar & Assoc., LLP 1032
Mitchell v. Gonzales 322
Mitchell v. Griffin Television, LLC 989,
    999, 1001
Mitchell v. Hastings & Koch Enters.,
    Inc. 900
Mitchell v. Rochester Ry. Co. 721, 722
Mitchell v. Sanborn 919
Mitchell v. Volkswagenwerk AG 840
Mitchell v. W. T. Grant Co. 127
Mitchell, Jr. v. Fortis Ins. Co. 869, 870
Miyamoto v. Lum 369
Mobil Chem. Co. v. Bell........................ 301
Mobil Oil Corp. v. Bransford 773
Mobil Oil Corp. v. Thorn 1146
Mobile & O.R. R. v. Zimmern 748
Mobile Gas Serv. Corp. v. Robinson 214,
    223, 281
Mobile OB-GYN, P.C. v. Baggett 674
Mobilisa, Inc. v. Doe 971
Mobley ex rel. Mobley v. King 674
Mochen v. State 226
Mock v. Polley..................................... 68
Mody v. Ctr. for Women's Health,
    P.C. 503
Moeller v. Hauser 530
Moen v. Hanson 670
Moglia v. McNeil Co. 491
Mohoff v. Northrup King & Co. 119
Mohr v. Commonwealth......................... 432
Mohr v. Grant 941
Mohr v. Grantham............................... 332
Mohr v. Williams 63, 83, 169
Moix-McNutt v. Brown.......................... 1180
Moldowan v. City of Warren 583, 587
Molien v. Kaiser Found. Hosps. 1117
Molina v. Merritt & Furman Ins. Agency,
    Inc. 700
Molina, Colon ex rel. v. BIC USA,
    Inc. 822
Moll v. Abbott Labs. 431, 435
Molloy v. Meier 500, 679
Molnar v. Star-Ledger 978
Monaco v. United States 561, 674
Mondelli v. United States 561, 674
Monell v. City of New York 753
Monell v. Dep't of Social Services of the City
    of New York...............89, 583, 586, 587
Monessen Sw. Ry. Co. v. Morgan........... 859
Monge v. Beebe Rubber Co. 1147
Monitor Patriot Co. v. Roy 994
Monk v. Temple George Associates,
    LLC.. 639, 642
Monks v. City of Rancho Palos
    Verdes.. 742
Monroe v. Pape 89, 583

Monsanto Chem. Co. v. Perfect Fit Products
    Mfg. Co.. 1197
Monsanto Co. v. Reed 841
Montalvo v. Borkovec............................ 514
Montalvo v. Lapez................................ 693
Montano v. Land Title Guarantee
    Co. 1152
Montas v. JJC Constr. Corp. 292
Montecalvo v. Mandarelli 1042
Montes v. Indian Cliffs Ranch, Inc.......... 466
Montgomery Health Care Facility, Inc. v.
    Ballard 538
Montgomery v. Bazaz-Sehgal 514
Montgomery v. Devoid.................... 112, 113
Montgomery v. Midkiff.......................... 448
Montgomery v. Montgomery................... 1207
Montgomery Ward v. Wilson 1033
Montoya v. Bebensee 1057
Moody v. Delta Western, Inc. 605, 606
Moody v. Smith 1153
Moon v. Guardian Postacute Servs.,
    Inc. 717
Mooney v. Frazier 1191
Moor v. Licciardello.............................. 135
Moore v. Berkeley County School
    Dist. 648
Moore v. Burlington N. R.R. 217
Moore v. Chicago Park Dist.................... 482
Moore v. City of Detroit 80
Moore v. Evans 1033
Moore v. Ford Motor Co. 827
Moore v. Hartley Motors, Inc................. 410,
    411, 412
Moore v. Kitsmiller 225
Moore v. Memorial Hospital of
    Gulfport 496
Moore v. Mobile Infirmary Ass'n............ 875
Moore v. Myers.................................... 367
Moore v. P.W. Publ'g Co. 946
Moore v. Regents of the Univ. of Cal....... 112
Moore v. Waller................................... 410
Moore v. Warren 600
Moore-McCormack Lines, Inc. v.
    Richardson...................................... 689
Moores v. Greenberg 1170, 1175, 1185
Moorman Mfg. Co. v. National Tank
    Co. 803, 1065
Morales v. N.J. Acad. of Aquatic
    Sciences.. 597
Morales v. Sociedad Espanola de Auxilio
    Mutuo y Beneficencia......................... 532
Morales v. Town of Johnston........... 253, 570
Moran v. Atha Trucking 219
Moran v. Beyer.................................... 593
Moran v. Selig 175
Moransais v. Heathman 1074
Morden v. Continental AG.............. 798, 894
Moreno v. Hanford Sentinel, Inc. 1013
Morgan & Pottinger, Attorneys, P.S.C. v.
    Botts.. 966
Morgan State Univ. v. Walker................ 416
Morgan v. Braasch 279

Morgan v. Children's Hosp. 301, 303
Morgan v. City of Ruleville 567
Morgan v. Greenwaldt 170
Morgan v. Hudnell................................. 778
Morgan v. Kooistra............................... 938
Morgan v. Marquis 780
Morgan v. Scott.................287, 404, 721, 889
Morgan v. State 419
Morgan, Estates of v. Fairfield Family
    Counseling Center 360, 502, 576
Morguson v. 3M Co................................. 831
Moriarty v. Garden Sanctuary Church of
    God 431
Morin v. Bell Court Condominium
    Ass'n 464
Morin v. Traveler's Restat Motel, Inc..... 453
Morrell, United States v. 554
Morris v. Anderson County..................... 570
Morris v. De La Torre............. 466, 467, 640
Morris v. Farley Enterprises, Inc. 366
Morris v. Leaf 241
Morris v. Margulis................................ 1189
Morris v. National Western Life Ins.
    Co. 1156
Morris v. Platt 80
Morris v. Savoy............................ 874, 875
Morris v. Thomson................................. 508
Morris v. United States...................... 1129
Morris v. Wal-Mart Stores, Inc. 299, 469
Morris v. Yogi Bear's Jellystone Park Camp
    Resort 398
Morrison v. Goff................................... 1190
Morrison v. Northwest Nazarene
    Univ... 411
Morrow v. First Interstate Bank of
    Oregon.. 106
Morsani v. Major League Baseball....... 1097
Morse Bros., Inc. v. Webster 1047
Morse v. Goduti 280, 473
Morse v. Ripken 950
Morson v. Superior Court....................... 812
Mortgage Specialists, Inc. v. Davey....... 111,
    1106, 1205
Mortgage Specialists, Inc. v. Implode-
    Explode Heavy Indus., Inc. 971
Morway v. Trombly 579
Mosby v. Moore 566, 575
Moscatello v. Univ. of Medicine and
    Dentistry of New Jersey.................... 1172
Moseley v. V Secret Catalogue, Inc. 1197,
    1198
Moseng v. Frey 713
Moses v. Diocese of Colorado 181, 456
Moses v. Providence Hosp. and Medical
    Centers, Inc... 532
Moses, Estate of Moses ex rel. v. Sw. Va.
    Transit Mgmt. Co. 382, 390
Moss v. Crosman Corp. 805, 814
Moss v. Parr Waddoups Brown Gee &
    Loveless.................................... 967, 1025
Mostert v. CBL & Associates 466
Moteberg v. Johnson 855

Motyka v. City of Amsterdam 574
Moulton v. Puopolo, Estate of.................919
Moulton v. Rival Co. 807
Mount Juneau Enters., Inc. v. Juneau
    Empire 996
Mount Pleasant Independent Sch. Dist. v.
    Estate of Lindburg 449, 450
Mountain States Tel. & Tel. Co. v. Horn
    Tower Const. Co. 105
Moure v. Raeuchle 517, 518, 519
Moyer v. Phillips 688, 954
Moyer v. United Dominion Industries,
    Inc. 841
Moyera v. Quality Pork Int'l....................912
Mozzochi v. Beck....................................1025
MP TotalCare Services, Inc. v.
    Mattimoe..1204
Mrozek v. Intra Financial Corp.............1191
Mrozka v. Archdiocese of St. Paul &
    Minneapolis 180
Mt. Healthy City Sch. Dist. Bd. of Educ. v.
    Doyle 1032, 1101
Mt. Zion State Bank & Trust v.
    Consolidated Communications, Inc......477
MTW Inv. Co. v. Alcovy Properties,
    Inc. 1026
Mueller v. McMillian Warner Ins. Co. 623
Mueller v. Tepler.....................................721
Muick v. Glenayre Elecs. 1010
Mulchanock v. Whitehall Cement Mfg.
    Co. 88
Mulhern v. Catholic Health
    Initiatives 386, 395
Mull v. Kerstetter 608
Mullins v. Parkview Hosp. 65, 68
Mullins v. Pine Manor College 648
Mullins v. Tanksleary..............................915
Mullis v. United States Bankruptcy Court
    for Dist. of Nevada..............................581
Mulready v. University Research
    Corp..914
Mummert v. Alizadeh 697
Mundy v. Pirie-Slaughter Motor Co........253
Munich v. Skagit Emergency
    Communication Center.................570, 572
Muniz v. Flohern, Inc..............................657
Muniz, United States v. 556, 559, 563
Munzi v. Kennedy 489
Murphy v. Allstate Ins. Co. 542
Murphy v. Boston Herald, Inc. 942, 946,
    972, 989, 1000
Murphy v. Edmonds.................................875
Murphy v. Hendrix 491
Murphy v. I.S.K. Con. of New England,
    Inc. 1053
Murphy v. Implicito 700
Murphy v. Internal Revenue Serv...........861
Murphy v. Islamic Republic of Iran 709,
    712
Murphy v. Lord Thompson Manor,
    Inc. 731

Murphy v. North Am. River Runners, Inc..................410
Murphy v. Smith.................. 437, 1181
Murray v. Chi. Youth Ctr.................. 398
Murray v. Developmental Servs. of Sullivan County, Inc.................. 1157
Murray v. Farmers Ins. Co. 810
Murray v. Motorola, Inc. 720
Murray v. Plainfield Rescue Squad 577
Murray v. South Carolina R.R. 417
Murray v. UNMC Physicians.................. 509
Murrey v. United States 332
Murtha v. Cahalan.................. 430
Muse v. Page.................. 223
Muslow v. A.G. Edwards & Sons, Inc. 71
Muthukumarana v. Montgomery Cnty.................. 626
Mutual of Omaha Ins. Co. v. Novak 1198
Mutual Pharmaceutical Co. v. Bartlett.................. 846
Muzikowski v. Paramount Pictures Corp.................. 941
MV Transportation v. Allgeier.................. 754
Myers & Chapman, Inc. v. Thomas G. Evans, Inc. 1122
Myers v. Boleman.................. 415
Myers v. Cty. of Lake 227
Myers v. Lashley 1055, 1057
Myers v. Moore.................. 305
Myers v. Pickering Firm, Inc. 1003
Myers v. United States.................. 555
Myhaver v. Knutson.................. 221
Mylar v. Wilkinson.................. 1188
Myrick v. Barron 1009
Myrick v. Bishop.................. 91
Myrlak v. Port Authority of New York and New Jersey.................. 810
Myszkowski v. Penn Stroud Hotel, Inc.................. 766
NAACP v. Claiborne Hardware Co. 1105
Nabors Drilling, U.S.A., Inc. v. Escoto 637, 657
Nabozny v. Barnhill 424
Naccash v. Burger 681
Nadeau v. Costley.................. 449
Nagy v. McBurney.................. 1038
Nallan v. Helmsley-Spear, Inc. 638, 639
Nalwa v. Cedar Fair, L.P. 447, 448
Namislo v. Akzo Chems., Inc. 673
Nampa Charter Sch., Inc. v. DeLaPaz ... 953
Narkeeta Timber Co., Inc. v. Jenkins..... 903
Nash v. Hendricks.................. 1170, 1173
Nash v. Keene Publ'g Corp. 992
Nash v. Port Auth. of N.Y. & N.J. 894, 898
Nassa v. Hook-SupeRx, Inc............. 922, 960
Nassar v. Concordia Rod and Gun Club, Inc.................. 1032
Nasser v. Parker.................. 501
Nassr v. Commonwealth 737
National Airlines, Inc. v. Stiles.................. 691

National Cas. Co. v. Northern Trust Bank of Fla..................675
National City Bank, Indiana v. Shortridge.................. 1042, 1044
National Convenience Stores, Inc. v. Fantauzzi.................. 755
National Emp't Serv. Corp. v. Olsten Staffing Serv., Inc.................. 1098
National Found. for Cancer Research, Inc. v. Council of Better Bus. Bureraus, Inc.................. 993
National Garment Co. v. City of Paris, Missouri.................. 147
National Labor Relations Board v. Calkins.................. 85
National Ref. Co. v. Benzo Gas Motor Fuel Co.................. 953
National Steel Service Ctr. Inc. v. Gibbons 787
National Union Fire Ins. Co. of Pittsburgh, Pa. v. Wuerth.................. 754
National Union Fire Ins. v. United States.................. 556
Nationwide Mut. Ins. Co. v. Barton Solvents Inc.................. 832
Navarette v. United States.................. 557
Navellier v. Sletten 985
Nazar v. Branham 775
Nazeri v. Missouri Valley Coll........ 939, 946, 962, 1109
Neace v. Laimans.................. 305
Neade v. Portes 535
Neal v. Neal.................. 175
Neal v. Shiels, Inc. 234
Neal v. Wilkes 482
Nealis v. Baird 670
Near v. State of Minn. 1003
Nearing v. Weaver 570
Nebraska Innkeepers, Inc. v. Pittsburgh-Des Moines Corp. 1067
Neely v. Coffey 95, 96
Neely v. Wilson 955
Neff v. Bud Lewis, Co. 1131
Neibarger v. Universal Coops., Inc. 804, 1065
Neilan v. Braun.................. 91
Neilsen v. Beck.................. 437
Nelson v. American Red Cross 697
Nelson v. Anderson Lumber Co............ 1068, 1070
Nelson v. Carroll 65
Nelson v. City of Rupert 476
Nelson v. Dolan.................. 687, 692
Nelson v. Driscoll 245
Nelson v. Freeland 466
Nelson v. Ponsness-Warren Idgas Enters.................. 916
Nelson v. Salt Lake City.................. 625
Nelson v. Winnebago Indus., Inc............ 922
Nero v. Kansas State University............. 648
Nesler v. Fisher & Co., Inc. 1037, 1099
Nestorowich v. Ricotta.................. 221

Nesvig v. Nesvig 1169
Nettleton v. Stogsdill............................ 1164
Nettleton v. Thompson.................... 245, 259
Network Automation, Inc. v. Advanced
    Systems Concepts, Inc....................... 1196
Networkip, LLC v. Spread Enters.,
    Inc.. 1104
Neumann v. Indus. Sound Eng'g,
    Inc... 1038, 1039
Neurotron Inc. v. Medical Serv. Ass'n of Pa.,
    Inc.. 1114
Neustadt, United States v....................... 562
Nevada Yellow Cab Corp. v. Eighth Judicial
    Dist. Court ex rel. County of Clark ... 1167
New Destiny Treatment Ctr., Inc. v.
    Wheeler 1167
New Hampshire Div. of Human Servs. v.
    Allard.. 437
New Hampshire Fish & Game Dep't v.
    Bacon.. 225
New Times, Inc. v. Isaacks.............. 949, 995
New York Cent. R. v. Northern Indiana
    Public Service Co. 773
New York Cent. R. v. Wyatt.................... 468
New York City Asbestos Litigation,
    In re 485
New York State Elec. & Gas Corp. v.
    Westinghouse Elec. Corp.................. 1080
New York Stock Exchange, Inc. v. New
    York, New York Hotel, LLC 1197
New York Times Co. v. Connor.............. 995
New York Times Co. v. Sullivan.... 937, 952,
    953, 986, 987, 989, 994, 1003
New York, City of v.
    Smokes-Spirits.com 744
New York, City of, United States v. 912
New York, State of v. Shore Realty
    Corp.....................733, 737, 740, 743
Newbury v. Virgin 126
Newell v. Field Enters., Inc. 978
Newhall Land & Farming Co. v. Superior
    Court (Mobil Oil Corporation)............. 745
Newing v. Cheatham.............................. 302
Newlin v. New England Tel. & Tel.
    Co... 1067
Newman v. Cole....................................... 594
Newton, Town of v. Rumery................. 1035
Newton v. South Carolina Public Railways
    Com'n 370
Nguyen v. United States......................... 563
Niagara Mohawk Power Corp. v. Chevron
    U.S.A., Inc. 885
Nicholas v. Mynster................................ 511
Nichols v. Land Transport Corp. 761
Nichols v. Mid-Continent Pipe Line
    Co.. 734, 1068
Nichols v. St. Luke Center of Hyde
    Park 545
Nichols v. Sukaro Kennels 714, 858
Nicholson v. Hugh Chatham Mem. Hosp.,
    Inc. 719
Nicholson v. United Pac. Ins. Co. 1146

Nickerson, Commonwealth v...........171, 173
Nicoletti v. Westcor, Inc......................467
Nida v. American Rock Crusher Co. 92
Niece v. Elmview Group Home........540, 646
Nielsen v. Adams 1120, 1122
Nielson v. Flashberg 1119
Niemiera v. Schneider 513
Nienstedt v. Wetzel..............................1044
Niese v. City of Alexandria.....................574
Nims v. Harrison...................................709
Nisivoccia v. Glass Gardens, Inc. 469
Niskanen v. Giant Eagle, Inc. 383
Nixon v. Fitzgerald 581, 585
Nixon v. Halpin.....................................151
Nixon v. Harris.....................................778
Nixon v. Mr. Property Management
    Co...638
Nobl Park, LLC of Vancouver v. Shell Oil
    Co...1086
Noble v. Lamoni Prods...........................916
Noble v. Noble 61
Noble v. Ternyik 578
Nocula v. UGS Corp.............................1091
Noell v. Angle......................................1036
Noffke v. Bakke....................................424
Noguchi v. Nakamura...............................74
Nolan v. Weil-McLain............................315
Nold, Nold ex rel v. Binyon......498, 512, 519
Noll v. Harrisburg Area YMCA.............433
Nommensen v. American Cont'l Ins........221
Noonan v. Staples, Inc. 955
Nora Beverages, Inc. v. Perrier Group of
    America, Inc.......................................1201
Norfolk & W. Ry. v. Ayers 700, 701,
    725, 882
Norfolk & W. Ry. v. Liepelt 861
Norfolk S. Ry. Co. v. Sorrell....................374
Norfolk S. Ry. v. Shanklin 442
Norgard v. Brushwellman, Inc. 430
Norin v. Sheldt Mfg. Co. 1041
Norman v. Borison..........................966, 967
Norman v. Brown, Todd & Heyburn.....1129
Norman v. Greenland Drilling Co. 93
Normand v. City of New Orleans............783
Norris v. Bell Hellicopter-Textron,
    Inc. 437
North Am. Galvanizing & Coatings, Inc. v.
    Lake River Co., Inc.............................885
North Am. Medical Corp. v. Axiom
    Worldwide, Inc...........................1196, 1201
North Carolina v. Tennessee Valley
    Authority 744
North Georgia Finishing, Inc. v. Di-Chem,
    Inc. 127
North Pacific Ins. Co. v. Stucky 719
Northeast Bank of Lewiston and Auburn v.
    Murphy 109, 116
Northeastern Pharm. & Chem. Co., United
    States v. 197
Northern Indiana Pub. Serv. Co. v.
    Vesey..748
Northington v. Jackson............................72

Northland Wheels Roller Skating Center,
Inc. v. Detroit Free Press, Inc. 977
Northrop v. Piper.................................... 1137
Northwest, Inc. v. Ginsberg 442
Norton v. Glenn 979
Norton v. MacFarlane 1050
Nostrame v. Santiago............................ 1096
Nova Southeastern University, Inc. v.
Gross 648
Novak Heating & Air Conditioning v.
Carrier Corp.. 308
Novak v. Capital Management &
Development Corp. 639
Novick v. Becker 1041
Nowatske v. Osterloh 221
Nucor Corp. v. Kilman 463
Nunez v. Carrabba's Italian Grill,
Inc.. 663, 665
Nunez v. Professional Transit Management
of Tucson, Inc. 448
Nunez v. Spino.. 464
NXIVM Corp. v. Ross Institute............. 1200
NYCAL Corp. v. KPMG Peat Marwick
LLP. 1135
Nygard, Inc. v. Uusi-Keerttula 985
O.L. v. R.L. 627
O'Banner v. McDonald's Corp......... 766, 773
O'Brien v. Alexander 1034, 1041
O'Brien v. Bruscato 402
O'Brien v. Cunard S.S. Co...................... 166
O'Brien v. People ex rel. Kellogg
Switchboard & Supply Co. 1094
O'Brien v. Synnott.................................. 515
O'Bryan v. Hedgespeth 861
O'Connell v. Chasdi................................ 919
O'Connor v. Altus 487
O'Connor v. Burningham 992
O'Connor v. Diocese of Honolulu 970
O'Dee v. Tri-County Metropolitan Transp.
Dist. of Oregon 450
O'Donnell v. Elgin, J. & E. Ry. 260
O'Gara v. Ferrante 572
O'Guin v. Bingham County............. 254, 460
O'Hara v. Western Seven Trees Corp..... 644
O'Keeffe v. Snyder.................. 110, 123, 129
O'Leary v. Coenen 479
O'Neal Ford, Inc. v. Davie.................... 1140
O'Neil v. Schuckardt............................. 1050
O'Neill v. Dunham................................. 248
O'Neill v. Tichy..................................... 1181
O'Neill v. Windshire-Copeland Assocs.,
L.P. 385
O'Phelan v. Loy...................................... 707
O'Sullivan v. Shaw 471
O'Toole v. Carr....................................... 756
O'Toole v. Denihan 571
O'Toole v. Franklin............................... 1037
O'Toole v. Greenberg.............................. 681
O'Toole v. United States........................ 557
Oakes v. Patel....................................... 1178
Oakland Raders v. Oakland-Alameda
County Colisuem, Inc. 1137
Oats v. Nissan Motor Corp. 848
Ocean National Bank of Kennebunk v.
Diment 115
Oceanside, City of v. Superior Court.......612
Ochoa v. Vered 774
Ochs v. Borrelli 682, 683
OCM Principal Opportunities Fund v. CIBC
World Mkts. Corp..............................1135
Oddo v. Presser 1051
Odegard v. Finne....................................180
Odenthal v. Minn. Conference of Seventh
Day Adventists 1052
Oehler v. Humana Inc. 531
Office One, Inc. v. Lopez 985
Offshore Rental Co. v. Continental
Oil Co..1069
Ogden v. J.M. Steel Erecting, Inc............889
Ogle v. Barnes 193
Ogle v. Caterpillar Tractor Co.........847, 848
Ogle v. Hocker.......................................946
Ogletree v. Navistar Intern. Transp.
Corp................................814, 815, 826, 835
Ogwo v. Taylor 608
Ohio Acad. of Trial Lawyers v.
Steward..............................435, 902, 903
Ohio v. Akron Center for Reproductive
Health 172
Okin v. Village of Cornwall-on-Hudson
Police Dept...588
Ola v. YMCA of S. Hampton Roads,
Inc. 239, 597
Old Harbor Native Corp. v. Afognak Joint
Venture 1135
Old Island Fumigation, Inc. v. Barbee....788
Olinger v. Univ. Med. Ctr. 220
Oliver v. Cleveland Indians Baseball Co.
Ltd. P'ship...873
Oliver v. Morgan 692
Olivo v. Owens-Illinois, Inc. 485, 603, 635
Olsen v. Hooley 439
Olson v. 3M Company..............................976
Olson v. Ford Motor Co...........................408
Olson v. Fraase 1168, 1169
Olson v. Parchen 396
Olson v. Prosoco, Inc. 826
Olson v. Ratzel..............................251, 253
Olson v. Red Cedar Clinic...........1013, 1014
Olson v. Shumaker Trucking & Excavating
Contractors, Inc...................................246
Olson v. Walgreen Co...............................394
Olson v. Wrenshall..................................497
Olson, United States v.....................553, 559
Omega Chemical Co., Inc. v. United Seeds,
Inc. 743
Omega Envtl., Inc. v. Gilbarco, Inc. 1091
Onderko v. Richmond Mfg. Co.................836
Ondovchik Family Ltd. P'ship v. Agency of
Transp..86
One Industries, LLC v. Jim O'Neal
Distributing, Inc. 1196
One Nat'l Bank v. Pope............688, 690, 693

One Thousand Fleet Ltd. P'ship v. Guerriero... 1040
Onita Pac. Corp. v. Bronson.................. 1123
Ontai v. Straub Clinic and Hosp., Inc.. 815, 824
Oosterhous v. Short............................... 1179
Oparaugo v. Watts.................................. 942
Orca Communications Unlimited, LLC v. Noder... 1205
Orfield v. International Harvester Co... 814
Orleans, United States v......................... 551
Ornelas v. Randolph............................... 482
Ornstein v. N.Y.C. Health & Hosp. Corp.. 725
Orr v. First Nat'l Stores, Inc.......... 466, 474
Orr v. Pacific Southwest Airlines 451
Ortberg v. Goldman Sachs Group........... 708
Ortega v. City of New York.................. 1159, 1160, 1161
Ortega v. Flaim......................... 488, 489, 491
Ortega v. K-Mart Corp. 313, 470
Ortego v. Hickerson................................ 992
Orthopedic Equip. Co. v. Eutsler............ 817
Orzel v. Scott Drug Co............................ 403
Osborn v. Bank of United States 550
Osborn v. Haley....................................... 581
Osborn v. Irwin Mem. Blood Bank 504
Osborn v. Mason County......................... 570
Osborn v. Mission Ready Mix 472
Osborne v. Adams........................... 771, 772
Osborne v. Keeney............... 722, 724, 1173
Osborne v. Lyles 759
Osborne v. Twin Town Bowl, Inc. 341
OSI, Inc. v. United States 553
Osorio v. One World Technologies Inc... 821
Ostergren v. Cuccinelli.......................... 1018
Osterman v. Peters................................. 475
Ostrowski v. Azzara 405
Otani v. Broudy 688
Otero v. Jordon Restaurant Enters. 768, 770
Otis Elevator Co. v. Melott 282
Ott v. Smith 1177
Otten v. Schutt 982
Ouachita Wilderness Inst., Inc. v. Mergen 599
Ouellette v. Carde 382
Ovando v. County of Los Angeles 1186, 1189
Overseas Tankship (U.K.), Ltd. v. Morts Dock & Engineering Co., Limited (The Wagon Mound)................................... 347
Overstreet v. Gibson Product Co. of Del Rio 782
Overton v. Grillo.................................... 427
Owen v. City of Independence 160, 586
Owens Corning Fiberglass Corp. v. Cobb.. 889
Owens Corning Fiberglass Corp. v. Parrish 878

Owens Corning v. R.J. Reynolds Tobacco Co. 351
Owens v. Allis-Chalmers Corp. 819
Owens v. DeKalb Med. Ctr., Inc.............538
Owens v. Redd..469
Owens-Illinois, Inc. v. Wells...................433
Owens-Illinois, Inc. v. Zenobia 862
Oyster Bay, Town of v. Lizzo Indus., Inc...98
Ozaki v. Association of Apartment Owners of Discovery Bay...............................896
P & A Construction, Inc. v. Hackensack Water Co..91
P.F. Jurgs & Co. v. O'Brien 107, 110
P.L. v. Aubert..763
P.V. ex. rel. T.V. v. Camp Jaycee 597
P.W. and R.W. v. Kansas Dep't of Social and Rehabilitation Services 571
Paccar Financial Corp. v. Howard 114
Pace v. State...253
Pacelli Bros. Transp., Inc. v. Pacelli......1135
Pacht v. Morris..620
Pacific Mut. Life Ins. Co. v. Haslip 867, 868
Pacific Nw. Shooting Park Ass'n v. City of Sequim 1090, 1097
Pacificare of Oklahoma, Inc. v. Burrage...536
Padilla v. Kentucky................................1186
Padilla v. Rodas............................279, 474
Padwa v. Hadley 1051
Page v. United States 436
Pagelsdorf v. Safeco Ins. Co. of America..491
Paige K.B. v. Molepske 1179
Paiz v. State Farm Fire & Cas. Co..........240
Palandjian v. Foster.......................504, 506
Palazzo v. Alves........ 1037, 1041, 1044, 1047
Palka v. Servicemaster Management Services Corp.......................................630
Pallares v. Seinar........................1028, 1033
Palma v. United States Industrial Fasteners, Inc..363
Palmer Dev. Corp. v. Gordon.................1040
Palmer Ford, Inc. v. Wood 1031, 1032, 1044
Palmer v. Arkansas Council on Econ. Educ., RPL..1097
Palmer v. Intermed, Inc.........................542
Palmer v. Ted Stevens Honda, Inc..........866
Palmer v. United States 482
Palmetto Linen Serv., Inc. v. U.N.X., Inc. 1081, 1084, 1085
Palsgraf v. Long Island R.R...........340, 344, 345, 348, 360, 1067
Pamela L. v. Farmer...............................657
Pamela P. v. Frank S. 1118
Pan American Petroleum Corporation v. Long 111
Panagakos v. Walsh......................620, 663
Pancake House, Inc. v. Redmond 1164
Pannell v. Reynolds 1036

Pannu v. Land Rover North America, Inc. 825
Panzino v. City of Phoenix 1164
Papa John's Intern., Inc. v. McCoy 1028
Papa v. City of New York 1026
Papadopoulos v. Target Corp. 470
Papatheofanis v. Allen 1133
Paradigm Ins. Co. v. Langerman Law Offices, P.A. 1167, 1168, 1175
Paragon Family Restaurant v. Bartolini 639, 894
Paraskevaides v. Four Seasons Washington 452
Parish v. Jumpking, Inc. 821
Parker Bldg. Servs. Co., Inc. v. Lightsey ex rel. Lightsey 245
Parker v. Barefoot 738
Parker v. Freilich 772
Parker v. Highland Park, Inc. 473
Parker v. Learn Skills Corp. 1097
Parker v. Rogers 462, 464
Parks v. LaFace Records 1195, 1196, 1207
Parks v. Neuf 1043, 1045
Parkulo v. West Virginia Board of Probation and Parole 576
Parlato v. Connecticut Transit 452
Parli v. Reed 1029
Parnell v. Peak Oilfield Serv. Co. 318
Parrish v. Marquis 1039
Parsons v. Crown Disposal Co. 265, 270
Parsons v. Ford Motor Co. 811
Parsons v. Jow 371
Partin v. Merchants & Farmers Bank ... 917
Parvi v. City of Kingston 73
Parvin v. Dean 670
Pasco ex rel. Pasco v. Knoblauch 162
Passarello v. Grumbine 506
Passovoy v. Nordstrom, Inc. 142
Passwaters v. General Motors Corp. 817
Patch v. Hillerich & Bradsby Co. 417, 826
Patch, State v. 140
Pate v. Threlkel 500
Paterek v. Petersen & Ibold 1185
Patterson Enters. Inc. v. Johnson........... 419
Patterson v. Blair 761
Patterson v. Indiana Newspapers, Inc. 722
Patterson v. T.L. Wallace Construction, Inc. 764
Patton v. Hutchinson Wil-Rich Mfg. Co. 434
Patton v. TIC United Corp. 875
Paul F., In re 132
Paul v. Davis 936, 969, 1020
Paul v. Gordon 1171
Paul v. Luigi's, Inc. 609
Paul v. Providence Health System— Oregon 714
Paul v. Sherburne 1038
Paul v. Smith, Gambrell & Russell 1177
Pauley v. Circleville 482

Paulino v. QHG of Springdale, Inc. 531
Paulson v. Andicoechea 627
Paulus v. Bob Lynch Ford, Inc. 1038
Pavlick v. Pavlick 594
Pavlou v. City of N.Y. 390
Pawlowski v. American Family Mutual Ins. Co. 781
Paxson Trust I, In re 1146
Paxton v. Woodward 946
Payne v. Galen Hosp. Corp. 921
Payne v. Gardner 839
Payne v. United States 471
Payton v. United States 554
Paz v. Brush Engineered Materials, Inc. 722, 854
Paz v. State of California 628
Peace v. Conway 1109
Peagler v. Phoenix Newspapers, Inc. 995
Pearce v. Courier-Journal 978
Pearce v. L.J. Earnest, Inc. 97
Pearce v. Utah Athletic Found. 409, 410
Pearson v. Callahan 585
Pearson v. Dodd 112, 1015
Pearson v. Tippmann Pneumatics, Inc. 339
Pecan Shoppe of Springfield, Missouri, Inc. v. Tri-State Motor Transit Co. 792
Pechan v. Dynapro, Inc. 56
Peck v. Serio 329
Peck v. Tribune Co. 944
Peck, In re 945, 1000
Peckham v. Hirshfeld 1114
Pecoraro v. M & T Bank Corp. 129
Pedroza v. Bryant 287, 529
Peeler v. Hughes & Luce 1186, 1187, 1188
Pegg v. Gray 88, 778
Pegram v. Herdrich 536
Pehle v. Farm Bureau Life Ins. Co., Inc. 619
Pelaez v. Seide 571
Pellegrini v. Winter 1041
Pelletier v. Fort Kent Golf Club 387
Pelletier v. Sordona/Skanska Const. Co. 769
Pembaur v. City of Cincinnati 586, 587
Pemberton v. Dharmani 524
Pendergrast v. Aiken 93
Peneschi v. National Steel Corp. 795
Penland v. Redwood Sanitary Sewer Serv. Dist. 735, 739
Penn Harris Madison Sch. Corp. v. Howard 397
Pennfield Corp. v. Meadow Valley Elec., Inc. 329
Pennsylvania Glass Sand Corp. v. Caterpillar Tractor Co. 1085
Pennsylvania R. Co. v. City of Pittsburgh 88
Pensacola Motor Sales, Inc. v. Daphne Auto. 959
Penunuri v. Sundance Partners, Ltd. 414

People Express Airlines, Inc. v. Consolidated Rail Corp....... 1076
Pepper v. Star Equip., Ltd. 889, 890, 891
PepsiCo, Inc. v. Redmond...... 1206
Perdieu v. Blackstone Family Practice Center, Inc. 513, 527, 539
Perez v. Las Vegas Med. Ctr.... 333
Perez v. Lopez...... 372
Perez v. McConkey 416, 418, 421
Perez v. Van Groningen & Sons, Inc. 758
Perez v. Wyeth Laboratories Inc...... 831
Perin v. Hayne...... 509
Perius v. Nodak Mut. Ins. Co.... 331
Perkins v. Entergy Corp...... 313
Perkins v. Howard...... 523
Perkins v. Northeastern Log Homes 435
Perkins v. Wilkinson Sword, Inc..... 813, 816
Perna v. Pirozzi 514
Perodeau v. City of Hartford...... 714
Perri v. Furama Rest., Inc. 279
Perricone v. DiBartolo...... 236
Perrine v. E.I. du Pont de Nemours & Co...... 854, 870
Perry v. Rochester Lime Co. 362
Perry v. Shaw 169, 527
Perry v. Williamson...... 462
Perry-Rogers v. Obasaju 715, 731
Persinger v. Step by Step Infant Dev. Ctr....... 305
Person v. Children's Hospital National Medical Center...... 140
Peschke v. Carroll Coll....... 295
Pestco, Inc. v. Associated Products, Inc....... 111
Petco Animal Supplies v. Schuster...... 714
Pete v. Youngblood 298
Petefish ex rel. v. Dawe...... 220
Peters v. Calhoun County Com'n...... 369
Peters v. Forster...... 1070
Peters v. Hospital Auth. of Elbert Cnty....... 670
Peters v. Menard, Inc. 383, 402
Peters v. Saft 898
Peterson v. Balach...... 478
Peterson v. Eichhorn...... 292
Peterson v. Pittman...... 890
Peterson v. Sorlien 41
Peterson v. Summit Fitness, Inc..... 466
Peterson v. Superior Court 492
Peterson v. Worthen Bank & Trust Co....... 1045
Petolicchio v. Santa Cruz County Fair and Rodeo Ass'n, Inc....... 662
Petrell v. Shaw 181
Petrillo v. Bachenberg...... 1176
Petrove v. Fernandez 781
Petrovich v. Share Health Plan of Illinois, Inc....... 534, 535
Pettengill v. Booth Newspapers, Inc. 942
Pettry v. Rapid City Area Sch. Dist........ 417
Pexa v. Auto Owners Ins. Co. 854

PF Chang's v. Industrial Comm'n of Ariz....... 915
Pfannenstiel v. Osborne Publ'g Co....... 1022
Pfau v. Comair Holdings, Inc. 691
Pfenning v. Lineman...... 426
Pfister v. Shusta...... 425, 426
Phan Son Van v. Pena 361
Phelps v. Firebird Raceway, Inc...... 409, 421
Philadelphia Newspapers, Inc. v. Hepps...... 938, 955, 996
Philip Morris U.S.A. v. Williams..... 871, 872
Philip Morris, Inc. v. Emerson 612, 862
Phillips 66 Co. v. Lofton...... 432
Phillips v. Clancy...... 1170
Phillips v. Community Ins. Corp...... 583
Phillips v. Evening Star Newspapers Co....... 978
Phillips v. Frey...... 1203
Phillips v. Fujitec Am., Inc....... 383
Phillips v. Restaurant Mgmt. of Carolina, L.P....... 761
Phillips v. Seward 383
Phillips v. Smalley Maint. Servs., Inc...... 72, 1012
Phillips v. Sun Oil Co....... 87
Phillips v. Town of Many...... 97
Phillips v. Town of West Springfield....... 809
Phillips v. United States...... 381, 681
Phinney v. Boston Elevated Ry. Co....... 630
Phoenix Newspapers, Inc. v. Choisser 978, 979
Picard v. Barry Pontiac-Buick, Inc...... 68
Picher v. Roman Catholic Bishop of Portland 598, 599
Pickering v. Pickering...... 1050
Pickle v. Page 1053
Pierce v. ALSC Architects, P.S....... 244, 468
Pierce v. Cook...... 1169, 1184
Pierce v. Physicians Ins. Co. of Wis., Inc....... 693, 730
Pierson v. Ray 578
Pietrangelo v. Wilmer Cutler Pickering Hale & Dorr, LLP...... 1172
Piggott v. Miller 176, 1056
Pike v. Eubank...... 294
Pike v. Frank G. Hough Co....... 814
Pike v. Mullikin...... 1185
Pikersgill v. City of New York...... 305
Pikulski v. Waterbury Hosp. Health Ctr....... 860
Pile v. City of Brandenburg...... 246
Pilgrim's Pride Corp. v. Smoak 295
Pinchera v. Allstate Ins. Co....... 1204
Pine Island Farmers Coop v. Erstad & Reimer, P.A....... 1167
Pineda v. City of Houston...... 588
Pinellas Park, City of v. Brown....... 161, 575
Piner v. Superior Court 880
Pinewood Homes, Inc. v. Harris...... 1091
Pinkham, Estate of v. Cargill, Inc....... 808, 811
Pino v. United States...... 670

Pinsonneault v. Merchants & Farmers
    Bank & Trust Co. 641
Pinter Constr. Co. v. Frisby 912
Pinter v. American Family Mut. Ins.
    Co. 612
Pioneer Commercial Funding Corp. v.
    American Financial Mortgage
    Corp. 1156
Pioneer Hi-Bred Intern. v. Holden
    Foundation Seeds, Inc. 1205
Pioneer Investment Services Co. v.
    Brunswick Assocs. Ltd. P'ship 1165
Pioneer Res. Corp. v. Nami Res. Co.,
    LLC 1130
Pipitone v. Biomatrix, Inc. 513
Pippen v. NBCUniversal Media, LLC 960
Pirraglia v. Novell, Inc. 1119
Piscatelli v. Van Smith 977
Piselli v. 75th St. Med. 437
Pitre v. Opelousas Gen. Hosp. 682
Pittman v. Western Eng'g Co., Inc. 919
Pittsburgh Construction Co. v.
    Griffith 1156
Pittsburgh, C. C. & St. L. Ry. v.
    Kinney 414
Pittway Corp. v. Collins 338, 342
Pixley v. Pro-Pak Indus., Inc. 922
Pizel v. Zuspann 1170, 1177, 1180, 1182
Pizza Hut of Am., Inc. v. Keefe 673
Pizza Hut, Inc. v. Papa John's Intern.,
    Inc. 1200
Placek v. City of Sterling Heights 386
Planned Parenthood of the
    Columbia/Willamette, Inc. v. American
    Coal. of Life Activists 73, 709, 1015
Plant v. Wilbur 410, 411
Platzer v. Mammoth Mountain Ski
    Area 450
Playboy Enterprises, Inc. v. Welles 1194
Pleas v. City of Seattle 1098, 1103
Pleasants v. Alliance Corp. 221
Pleiss v. Barnes 381
Pletan v. Gaines 575
PLIVA, Inc. v. Mensing 846
Ploof v. Putnam 157
Plotnik v. Meihaus 709
Plourde Sand & Gravel v. JGI E.,
    Inc. 1068, 1071, 1078, 1087, 1126
Plumb v. Richmond Light & R.R. 448
Plumley v. Landmark Chevrolet, Inc. ... 945,
    954, 1000
Plummer v. Center Psychiatrists,
    Ltd. 758, 761, 762
Plummer v. United States 312
Plunkett v. Brooklyn Heights R.R. 223
Pocatello Auto Color, Inc. v. Akzo Coatings,
    Inc. 293
Podias v. Mairs 617, 621, 622
Podolsky v. Alma Energy Corp. 1044
Poelstra v. Basin Elec. Power Co-op 289
Poff v. Hayes 105
Poffenbarger v. Merit Energy Co. 97

Pohl v. County of Furnas 566
Polakoff v. Turner 250
Polando v. Vizzini 142
Pole Realty Co. v. Sorrells 491
Polemis and Furness, Withy & Co., Ltd., In
    re Arbitration Between 350
Poleski v. Polish Am. Publ'g Co. 1000
Politte v. Politte 1054, 1055
Polk County v. Dodson 1187
Pollard v. E.I. DuPont De Nemours,
    Inc. 707
Pollard v. Goldsmith 511
Pollmann v. Belle Plaine Livestock Auction,
    Inc. 1125
Polmatier v. Russ 58, 68
Polston v. Boomershine Pontiac-GMC
    Truck, Inc. 840
POM Wonderful LLC v. Coca-Cola
    Co. 1199
Pomer v. Schoolman 280
Pomeroy v. Little League Baseball of
    Collingswood 597
Pond v. Leslein 260
Ponder v. Angel Animal Hosp., Inc. 311
Ponder v. Fulton-DeKalb Hosp.
    Auth. 598
Pontiac School Dist. v. Miller, Canfield,
    Paddock & Stone 1178
Ponticas v. K.M.S. Investments 657
Pontier v. Wolfson 427
Poolaw v. Mercantel 585
Poole v. City of Rolling Meadows 400
Poole v. Coakley & Williams Constr.,
    Inc. 417, 431
Poole v. Copland, Inc. 732
Pooshs v. Philip Morris USA, Inc. 441
Pope v. Motel 6 .... 973, 983
Porcari v. Gannett Satellite Info. Network,
    Inc. 992
Portales Nat'l Bank v. Ribble 1111
Portee v. Jaffee 716
Porter v. Crawford & Co. 1111
Porter v. Delmarva Power & Light
    Co. 477
Porter v. Harshfield 761
Porterfield v. Brinegar 305
Portland, City of v. Berry 124
Porto v. Carlyle Plaza, Inc. 462
Portwood v. Copper Valley Elec. Ass'n,
    Inc. 693, 694
Posas v. Horton 219, 220
Poskus v. Lombardo's of Randolph,
    Inc. 340, 362, 363
Post Publ'g Co. v. Moloney 954
Post v. Mendel 967
Potochnick v. Perry 219
Potter v. Chicago Pneumatic Tool
    Co. 809, 821
Potter v. Department of Labor &
    Indus. 917
Potter v. Firestone Tire & Rubber Co. 18,
    287, 726, 863

Potter v. Washington State Patrol.......... 126
Potthast v. Metro-North R.R........... 307, 308
Poulos v. Poulos..................................... 1050
Poulston v. Rock 962
Pounders v. Trinity Court Nursing
   Home.................................... 73, 76, 77
Powell v. Associated Counsel for the
   Accused..................................... 1189
Powell v. Catholic Medical Ctr. 505
Power v. Arlington Hospital Ass'n......... 532
Powerhouse Motorsports Grp., Inc. v.
   Yamaha Motor Corp. 402
Powers v. Carvalho.................................. 973
Powers v. Gastineau................................ 947
Powers v. Hamilton Public Defenders
   Com'n... 340
Poyner v. Loftus...................................... 225
Poznanski v. Horvath............................. 781
Prah v. Maretti.. 739
Prahl v. Brosamle..................................... 86
Pratcher v. Methodist Healthcare Memphis
   Hosps.. 427
Pratico v. Portland Terminal Co............. 249
Pratt v. Nelson............................... 966, 980
Pratt v. Prodata, Inc................... 1100, 1101
Praus v. Mack... 249
Prempro Products Liab. Litigation,
   In re.................................... 827, 832, 834
President and Directors of Georgetown
   College v. Hughes 598, 599
President and Directors of Georgetown
   College, Inc., Application of................ 175
Presley's Estate v. Russen 1208, 1209
Preston v. Keith...................................... 403
Prete v. Cray... 777
Prewitt v. Branham 115
Price v. Blood Bank of Del., Inc. 252
Price v. City of Seattle........................ 69, 87
Price v. Divita 512
Price v. Howard 921
Price v. Kitsap Transit 233
Price v. Price 591, 592
Price v. State... 728
Price-Cornelison v. Brooks...................... 588
Pridgen v. Boston Housing Authority 461
Priebe v. Nelson...................................... 613
Prignano v. Prignano 296
Prill v. Marrone 372
Prima Paint v. Flood & Conklin 1137
Prime v. Beta Gamma Chapter of Pi Kappa
   Alpha... 661
Primiani v. Federal Ins. Co................... 1114
Prince George's Cnty. v. Longtin 79
Prince v. Atchison, Topeka & Santa Fe Ry.
   Co.. 760
Prince v. St. Francis-St.George Hosp.,
   Inc.. 1011
Pringle v. Valdez 407
Prior v. White 167
Priority Finishing Corp. v. LAL Const. Co.,
   Inc.. 108
Pritchard v. Mabrey 485

Pritchard v. Veterans Cab Co................. 236
Procter & Gamble Distributing Co. v.
   Lawrence American Field Warehousing
   Corp... 118
Proctor v. Washington Metro. Area Transit
   Auth... 720
Production Credit Assn of Madison v.
   Nowatzski.................................... 109
Professional Real Estate Investors, Inc. v.
   Columbia Pictures Indus., Inc. 984,
   1036, 1092
Progressive Halcyon Ins. Co. v.
   Philippi...................................... 919
Prokop v. Cannon........................... 965, 966
Prokop v. Hoch 1037
Prospect St. Tenants Ass'n v. Sheva
   Gardens, Inc.................................. 84
Prosser v. Kennedy Enterprises, Inc....... 573
Providence Health Center v. Dowell...... 373
Providence Hospital, Inc. v. Willis 530
Provoncha v. Vermont Motocross
   Ass'n...................................... 411, 413
Prozeralik v. Capital Cities Commc'ns,
   Inc. 999, 1001
Pruneyard Shopping Ctr. v. Robins 1004
Prunty v. Schwantes.............................. 687
Pryal v. Mardesich................................. 214
Pryzbowski v. United States Healthcare,
   Inc.. 536
Psychiatric Solutions, Inc. v. Palit 527
PTI Assocs., LLC v. Carolina Int'l Sales Co.,
   Inc... 1083
Public Serv. Co. of Colo. v. Van Wyk....... 736
Public Serv. Co. of Okla. v. Allen 427
Public Serv. Elec. & Gas Co. v. Federal
   Power Com'n................................. 119
Public Service Co. of Colorado v. Van
   Wyk... 92
Publications Intern., Ltd. v. Landoll,
   Inc. 1202, 1203
Puchalski v. Sch. Dist. Of Springfield.....947
Puckett v. Mt. Carmel Regional Medical
   Center 338, 342, 365, 369
Puckrein v. ATI Transport, Inc. 770
Pugh's IGA, Inc. v. Super Food Servs.,
   Inc. 1117
Pugiese v. Superior Court....................... 435
Pugsley v. Privette 170
Pulawa v. GTE Hawaiian Tel................. 267
Pullen v. West 793
Purdy v. Fleming.................................... 456
Purtill v. Hess 504, 509
Purtle v. Shelton 216, 236
Purvis v. Grant Parish Sch. Bd. 388
Pusey v. Bator.. 767
Pustejovsky v. Rapid-American Corp...... 441
Pyne v. Witmer....................... 758, 759, 760
QORE, Inc. v. Bradford Bldg. Co............. 384
Qualitex Co. v. Jacobson Products
   Co. 1194, 1201
Qualls v. United States Elevator
   Corp... 309

Quartana v. Utterback 950
Queen Ins. v. Hammond 233
Queen v. Carey 593
Quelimane Co., Inc. v. Stewart Title Guar.
    Co. 1096, 1107
Quereshi v. Ahmed 474
Quern v. Jordan 564
Quick v. Samp 1178
Quigley v. Wilson Line of Mass. 452
Quinby v. Plumsteadville Family Practice,
    Inc. 299, 300, 307
Quinn v. Thomas 1014
Quinonez v. Andersen 690
Quintana-Ruiz v. Hyundai Motor
    Corp. 822, 824
Quintero v. Rodgers 688
Quiroz v. Seventh Ave. Ctr. 246
Qwest Services Corp. v. Blood 862, 863
R & R Associates of Hampton, In re 1171
R.A.P. v. B.J.P. 1118
R.E.R. v. J.G. 1051
R.J. Reynolds Tobacco Co. v. Webb 855
R.J. v. Humana of Fla., Inc. 727
R.J.D. v. Vaughan Clinic, P.C. 173
R.K. v. St. Mary's Medical Center,
    Inc. 527
Raas v. State 572
Rabideau v. City of Racine 707, 714, 717
Rachou v. Cornerstone Village Inc. 537
Radiology Services, P.C. v. Hall 1168,
    1173
Radioshack Corp. v. ComSmart, Inc. 1132
Rae, Estate of v. Murphy 241
Raess v. Doescher 72, 82
Rafferty v. Scurry 1182
Raglin v. HMO Illinois, Inc. 535
Ragnone v. Portland School Dist.
    No. 1J 464
Railway Exp. Agency, Inc. v.
    Brabham 350
Rainier's Dairies v. Raritan Valley
    Farms 1025
Rains v. Bend of the River 244, 251, 372
Rains v. Superior Court (The Center
    Foundation) 176
Rajeev Sindhwani, M.D., PLLC v. Coe
    Business Service, Inc. 107
Rakestraw v. General Dynamics Land Sys.,
    Inc. 916
Rakowski v. Sarb 570
Raleigh v. Performance Plumbing and
    Heating, Inc. 657
Rallis v. Demoulas Super Mkts., Inc. 265,
    266
Ramirez v. Nelson 254
Ramirez v. Plough, Inc. 281, 289, 829
Ramsey v. Beavers 724
Ramunno v. Cawley 949, 951
Ranard v. O'Neil 258
Rancho Niguel Ass'n v. Ahmanson Devs.,
    Inc. 882

Rancho Viejo, LLC v. Tres Amigos Viejos,
    LLC 89
Randall v. Benton 314, 512
Randi W. v. Muroc Joint Unified Sch.
    Dist. 636, 647, 1117
Rando v. Anco Insulations Inc. 295
Randolph v. ING Life Ins. & Ann.
    Co. 1014
Ranells v. City of Cleveland 566
Ranes v. Adams Lab., Inc. 313, 314
Ranger Ins. Co. v. Pierce Cty. 204
Ransom v. City of Garden City 280, 655
Rantz v. Kaufman 1188, 1190
Rappaport v. Nichols 662
Raritan River Steel Co. v. Cherry, Bekaert
    & Holland 1135
Rascher v. Friend 341, 374, 382
Rasmussen v. Bennett 976
Rasmussen v. State Farm Mut. Auto. Ins.
    Co. 349
Ratcliff v. Barnes 958
Rathje v. Mercy Hosp. 430, 431
Rausch v. Pocatello Lumber Co., Inc. 899
Ravnikar v. Bogojavlensky 960
Rawlinson v. Cheyenne Bd. of Pub.
    Utils. 431
Ray Bell Constr. Co. v. King 914
Ray v. American Nat'l Red Cross 281,
    507
Ray v. BIC Corp. 812, 815, 825
Rayeski v. Gunstock Area/Gunstock Area
    Comm'n 423
Raymaker v. American Family Mut. Ins.
    Co. 248
Raymen v. United Senior Ass'n,
    Inc. 1007, 1008
Read v. Scott Fetzer Co. 768
Reader's Digest Ass'n v. Super. Ct. 993
Ready v. United/Goedecke Servs.,
    Inc. 888
Ream v. Keen 88
Reardon v. Boston Elevated Ry. Co. 450
Reardon v. Larkin 189, 199
Reardon v. Windswept Farm, LLC. 413
Reavis v. Slominski 171
Receivables Purchasing Co., Inc. v.
    Engineering & Prof'l Servs., Inc. 1121
Reda v. Sincaban 1131
Reddell v. Johnson 427
Redwing v. Catholic Bishop for Diocese of
    Memphis 438, 439
Reed v. Bojarski 499
Reed v. Hamilton 110
Reed v. King 744
Reed v. Melnick 964
Reed v. Mitchell & Timbanard, P.C. 1183
Reed v. Phillips 244
Reedy v. Evanson 711
Rees v. State, Dep't of Health &
    Welfare 634
Reese v. Danforth 1191
Reeser v. Weaver Bros., Inc. 749

Reeves v. Hanlon 1099, 1109
Refrigeration Indus., Inc. v.
   Nemmers... 1135
Regan v. Stromberg................................ 352
Regenstreif v. Phelps...................... 218, 219
Regester v. County of Chester 626
Regions Bank & Trust v. Stone County
   Skilled Nursing Facility, Inc. 539, 543,
   646
Register v. Wilmington Medical Center,
   Inc.. 530, 531
Rehabilitative Care System of America v.
   Davis 496
Rehberg v. Paulk 578
Reichardt v. Flynn.......................... 966, 974
Reicheneder v. Skaggs Drug Center....... 166
Reicheneker v. Reicheneker................... 463
Reichert v. Atler 893
Reid v. Spadone Mach. Co...................... 839
Reilly v. Anderson 885, 898
Reilly v. Dynamic Exploration, Inc........ 839
Reilly v. Spiegelhalter 462
Reilly v. United States 723
Rein v. Benchmark Construction Co. 541,
   631
Reinen, Estate of v. Northern Ariz.
   Orthopedics, Ltd. 410
Reis v. Volvo Cars of North America 798
Reisner v. Regents of Univ. of Cal. 500,
   660
Rejent v. Liberation Publ'ns, Inc. 946
Reliable Transfer Co., United
   States v.. 384, 386
Reliance Ins. Co. v. Shenandoah S.,
   Inc. 1114
Religious Technology Center v.
   F.A.C.T.NET, Inc............................... 1205
Remet Corp. v. City of Chicago 573, 574
Remmenga v. Selk................................... 231
Remsburg v. Docusearch, Inc................. 188
Remy v. MacDonald 208, 675
Renfro v. Adkins..................................... 280
Rennenger v. Pacesetter Co. 609
Renown Health, Inc. v. Vanderford 530
Rensch v. Riddle's Diamonds of Rapid City,
   Inc.. 117
Renslow v. Mennonite Hosp............ 500, 676
Rent-A-Center, West, Inc. v. Jackson..... 694
Rentz v. Brown 286
Republic Tobacco Co. v. North Atl. Trading
   Co., Inc. 978, 998
RepublicBank Dallas, N.A. v. First Wis.
   Nat'l Bank of Milwaukee................... 1136
Reserve Mooring, Inc. v. American
   Commercial Barge Line, LLC 1070
Resolution Trust Corp. v. Ferri............. 1165
Resource Bankshares Corp. v. St. Paul
   Mercury Ins. Co. 1012
Revell v. Hoffman.................................. 992
Reynolds Metals Co. v. Yturbide 301, 326
Reynolds v. CB Sports Bar, Inc. 639
Reynolds v. Clarke............................ 28, 190
Reynolds v. Kansas Dep't of Trans.......... 568
Reynolds v. Pardee & Curtin Lumber
   Co. 87
Reynolds v. Pegler................................... 975
Reynolds v. Texas & Pac. Ry. Co............. 326
RGR, LLC v. Settle 381
Rhee v. Highland Dev. Corp. 1134
Rhine v. Duluth, M & I R.R............. 285, 286
Rhine v. Haley...................................... 1172
Rhodes v. Illinois Cent. Gulf R.R. 284,
   287, 461
Rhue v. Dawson 1145
Rice v. Collins Commc'n, Inc. 209, 630
Rice v. Santa Fe Elevator Corp. 442
Richard Swaebe, Inc. v. Sears World Trade,
   Inc. 1080
Richard v. A. Waldman & Sons, Inc..... 1127,
   1129
Richard v. Hall...................................... 760
Richard v. Louisiana Extended Care Ctrs.,
   Inc. 540, 548
Richards v. Badger Mut. Ins. Co. 881, 885
Richards v. Broadview Heights Harborside
   Healthcare 539, 541
Richards v. Richards............................... 411
Richards v. United States........................ 552
Richardson v. Children's Hosp. 721
Richardson v. City of St. Louis 566
Richardson v. Fairbanks N. Star
   Borough.. 858
Richardson v. Hennly 67, 68
Richardson v. Sara Lee Corp................. 1161
Richey v. Brookshire Grocery Co.......... 1024,
   1030, 1032
Richland Sch. Dist. v. Mabton Sch.
   Dist.. 1123
Richmond Metro. Auth. v. McDevitt Street
   Bovis, Inc. 1119
Richmond v. Nodland............................. 982
Richmond v. Southwire Co. 976
Richmond v. State................................. 1034
Ricketts v. City of Columbia, Mo............ 588
Rickey v. Chicago Transit Auth. 715, 722
Rickrode v. Wistinghausen..................... 793
Riddle v. Golden Isles Broad., LLC 959
Riddle v. Perry 968
Ridenour v. Boehringer Ingelheim Pharms.,
   Inc. 432
Rider v. Speaker..................................... 392
Ridgway v. Yenny................................... 417
Ridings v. Ralph M. Parsons Co. 889, 890,
   920
Ridley v. Safety Kleen Corp............. 249, 405
Riedisser v. Nelson................................. 521
Riegel v. Medtronic, Inc. 847
Ries v. National R.R. Passenger
   Corp... 249
Rife v. D. T. Corner, Inc......................... 156
Rigazio v. Archdiocese of Louisville 439
Riggins v. Mauriello, D.O. 221
Right v. Breen 189, 311, 851
Riley v. American Honda Motor Co........ 832

Riley v. Becton Dickinson Vascular Access,
   Inc... 818, 820
Riley v. Harr 1016
Rinehart v. Morton Bldgs., Inc. 1123
Rinehart v. Western Local School Dist. Bd.
   of Educ.. 139
Rinella, In re 180
Ringier America, Inc. v. Enviro-Technics,
   Ltd. 1042
Rino v. Mead 1169
Rise v. United States 504
Rison v. Air Filter Sys., Inc..................... 917
Rissler & McMurry Co. v. Sheridan Area
   Water Supply Joint Powers Bd. 1081,
   1084
Ritchie v. Glidden Co..................... 268, 274
Rite Aid Corp. v. Levy-Gray.................. 831
Riter v. Keokuk Electro-Metals Co......... 748
Rittenour v. Gibson 463, 488
Ritter v. Stanton.................................... 855
Rivera v. Nelson Realty, LLC 489
Rivera v. Philadelphia Theological
   Seminary of St. Charles Borromeo,
   Inc.. 852
Rivera-Emerling v. M. Fortunoff of
   Westbury Corp..................................... 308
Riviello v. Waldron 758
Rizzuto v. Davidson Ladders, Inc. 4, 1158
Roach v. Harper................................... 1008
Roach v. Jimmy D. Enters., Ltd.............. 694
Robak v. United States 681, 683
Robb v. Chagrin Lagoons Yacht Club,
   Inc.. 1041, 1044
Robbins v. City of Wichita............... 221, 575
Robbins v. Hamburger Home for
   Girls.. 1053
Roberson v. Provident House.......... 540, 542
Robert S. Weiss & Assocs., Inc. v.
   Wiederlight 1097
Roberts v. Chimileski........1169, 1171, 1173
Roberts v. Federal Express Corp. 1030, 1031
Roberts v. Fisher 234
Roberts v. Galen of Virginia, Inc. 532
Roberts v. Healy 1172
Roberts v. Indiana Gas & Water Co. 284,
   286
Roberts v. NASCO Equip. Co., Inc. 604
Roberts v. Ohio Permanente Med. Group,
   Inc.. 333
Roberts v. Sentry Life Ins. 1039
Roberts v. Stop & Go, Inc...................... 654
Roberts v. Vaughn................................. 611
Roberts v. Weber & Sons, Co. 485
Roberts v. Williamson 719
Robie v. Lillis.................................. 738, 742
Robin Bay Assocs., LLC v. Merrill Lynch &
   Co.. 1079, 1085
Robins Dry Dock & Repair Co. v.
   Flint.. 1062, 1066
Robinson Helicopter Co., Inc. v. Dana
   Corp....................................... 1077, 1084
Robinson v. Bates 244, 248

Robinson v. Benton 1175
Robinson v. Charleston Area Med. Ctr.,
   Inc...875
Robinson v. City of Detroit 575
Robinson v. District of Columbia.............397
Robinson v. Greeley & Hansen...............852
Robinson v. Lindsay...............................236
Robinson v. Matt Mary Moran, Inc.........661
Robinson v. Okla. Nephrology Associates,
   Inc...504
Robinson v. St. John's Med. Ctr.,
   Joplin 505
Robinson v. Vivirito 213
Robinson v. Washington Metro. Transit
   Auth. 317
Robles v. Severyn 474
Robles v. Shoreside Petroleum, Inc.........825
Roboserve, Ltd. v. Tom's Foods, Inc. 1206
Roby v. McKesson Corp. 869
Rocci v. Ecole Secondaire Macdonald-
   Cartier 961
Rocha v. Faltys......................................616
Rochon v. State 575
Rock v. Antoine's, Inc............................156
Rock-Ola Mfg. Corp. v. Music & Television
   Corp...121
Rockweit v. Senecal 350
Rocky Mountain Thrift Stores, Inc. v. Salt
   Lake City Corp. 365
Rodenburg v. Fargo-Moorhead Young Men's
   Christian Ass'n 893, 896
Rodgers v. Colby's Ol' Place, Inc......901, 902
Rodgers v. W.T. Grant Co. 1031
Rodrigue v. Copeland.......................734, 735
Rodrigue v. Rodrigue 490
Rodriguez v. Clark 512
Rodriguez v. Del Sol Shopping Ctr.
   Assocs...422
Rodriguez v. New Orleans Pub. Serv.,
   Inc. 452
Rodriguez v. Pino 182
Rodriguez v. Primadonna Co., LLC 371
Roe v. Gelineau 427
Roe v. Quality Transp. Servs.................1012
Roe v. Wade...678
Rogers v. Allis-Chalmers Mfg. Co. 760
Rogers v. Hill 1035
Rogers v. Loews L'Enfant Plaza Hotel......61
Rogers v. T. J. Samson Community
   Hosp...514
Rohde v. Smiths Medical 810, 826, 831
Rolf v. Tri State Motor Transit Co. 719
Roller v. Roller 593
Rollins v. Phillips...................................703
Rollins v. Wackenhut Services, Inc.........372
Roma v. United States.....................605, 607
Romain v. Frankenmuth Mut. Ins.
   Co. 203, 889
Roman Catholic Church of the Archdiocese
   of New Orleans v. Louisiana Gas Serv.
   Co. 857

Roman Catholic Diocese of Covington v. Secter.. 894
Roman v. Estate of Gobbo 224
Rome v. Flower Memorial Hosp.............. 527
Romero v. Brenes..................................... 300
Romine v. Village of Irving 266
Rong Yao Zhou v. Jennifer Mall Restaurant, Inc.. 243, 251
Rorvig v. Douglas 1113
Rosa v. Dunkin' Donuts of Passaic 609
Rosa v. Taser Intern., Inc........................ 825
Rosales v. Stewart 656
Rosane v. Senger 529
Rosby, United States v. 1132, 1137
Rose Nulman Park Foundation v. Four Twenty Corp................................... 96, 100
Rose v. Chaikin........................ 735, 739, 741
Rose v. Jaques 39
Rose v. Provo City.................................... 486
Rosebush v. United States 569
Rosefield v. Rosefield............................ 1055
Rosell v. Central W. Motor Stages, Inc.. 900
Rosemont v. Marshall 539, 544
Rosenberg v. American Bowling Cong. 970
Rosenberg v. Helinski 967, 977, 978, 979
Rosenberg v. Otis Elevator Co. 309, 629
Rosenblit v. Zimmerman..................... 1158
Rosenbloom v. Flygare............................ 82
Rosenbloom v. Metromedia, Inc............. 988
Rosengren v. City of Seattle........... 484, 485
Rosenthal v. Great Western Fin. Sec. Corp. 1137
Ross Laboratories, Div. of Abbott Laboratories v. Thies.......... 807, 827, 829
Ross Neely Sys., Inc. v. Occidental Fire & Cas. Co. of N.C. 864
Ross v. A Betterway Rent-A-Car, Inc. 857
Ross v. Glaser 367
Ross v. Housing Auth. of Baltimore City 314
Ross v. Louise Wise Servs., Inc.............. 862
Ross v. Nutt 346, 363
Ross v. Wright 1097
Rosser v. Smith.. 224
Rossi v. DelDuca...................................... 157
Roth v. Norfalco LLC.............................. 442
Rothstein v. Carriere............................. 1031
Rothstein v. Orange Grove Ctr., Inc....... 719
Rothstein v. Snowbird Corp. 414
Rotkiewicz v. Sadowsky 992
Roton Barrier, Inc. v. Stanley Works 1204, 1205
Rouch v. Enquirer & News of Battle Creek, Mich.. 956
Rougeau v. Hyundai Motor Am. 408
Rountree v. Boise Baseball, LLC 419
Rousseau v. K.N. Constr., Inc. 1083
Roux v. Pflueger 1020
Rowe v. Barrup....................................... 111
Rowe v. Bennett........................... 713, 1052

Rowe v. Munye.................................355, 356
Rowe v. Sisters of the Pallottine Missionary Soc'y 395, 889
Rowe v. State Bank of Lombard......643, 644
Rowe, Munstermann ex rel. v. Alegant Health-Immanuel Medical Center.......659
Rowell v. Holt......................................1189
Rowland v. Christian.....................209, 478
Royal Indem. Co. v. Pittsfield Elec. Co. 687
Royce v. Hoening................... 1039, 1041
Rozhon v. Triangle Publ'ns...................1007
Rozny v. Marnul................. 1071, 1075, 1135
Rubeck v. Huffman 693
Rubesa v. Bull Run Jumpers, LLC 1078
Rubin v. Green 966
Rubin v. Johnson...................................252
Rubino v. Utah Canning Co....................848
Rubio v. Davis......................................853
Ruckelshaus v. Monsanto Co....... 1204, 1206
Rucker v. Wynn......................................150
Rudeck v. Wright 774
Ruder & Finn, Inc. v. Seaboard Surety Co. 964
Rudes v. Gottschalk 251, 252, 258
Rudisill v. Ford Motor Co. 922
Rudloe v. Karl 970
Rudolph v. Shayne, Dachs, Stanisci, Corker & Sauer...1183
Ruffing v. Ada County Paramedics........608, 609
Ruffin-Steinback v. dePasse..................1207
Rufo v. Bastian-Blessing Co. 848
Ruiz v, Podolsky 720
Ruiz v. Forman......................................158
Ruiz v. Mero 608, 609, 610
Ruiz v. Podolsky 694
Ruiz v. Varan.......................................1026
Ruiz v. Walgreen Co...............................302
Rule v. Cheeseman.................................509
Rumbauskas v. Cantor 1012
Runyon v. Reid......................................372
Rush v. Plains Tp....................................475
Rushford v. New Yorker Magazine, Inc. 977
Rushing v. Kansas City Southern Ry. Co. 739
Russ v. Western Union Tel. Co...............726
Russell v. Ingersoll-Rand Co. 697
Russell v. Mathis...................................382
Russell v. Men of Devon 565
Russell v. Noullet..................................759
Russell v. Western Union Tel. Co..........1079
Russell-Vaughn Ford, Inc. v. Rouse........118
Russin v. Wesson 956
Russo Farms, Inc. v. Vineland Bd. of Educ. 405
Russo v. Griffin 1168
Russo v. Sutton 1049, 1051
Russo v. White.......................................711
Rust International Corp. v. Greystone Power Corp. 629

Rust v. Reyer 665
Rutherford v. State................................. 721
Rutland v. Mullen................................. 1109
Rutz, United States ex rel. v. Levy 1034
Ryals v. United States Steel Corp. 459,
    460, 461
Ryan v. City of Emmetsburg.................. 100
Ryan v. KDI Sylvan Pools, Inc............... 819
Ryan v. Roman Catholic Bishop of
    Providence...................................... 439
Ryan v. State 570
Ryburn v. Huff....................................... 585
Rydde v. Morris 1176
Ryder v. Mitchell 1057
S.A. Empresa de Viacao Aerea Rio
    Grandense, United States v. 554, 555
S.A.V. v. K.G.V. 188, 592
S.B. v. Saint James Sch. 1021
S.K. Whitty & Co. v. Laurence L. Lambert
    & Assocs. 214
S.W. v. Spring Lake Park School Dist. No.
    16... 569
S.W. v. Towers Boat Club, Inc. 475
S/M Industries, Inc. v. Hapag-Lloyd
    A.G.. 117
Saab Auto. AB v. General Motors
    Co. 1108
Saab v. Massachusetts CVS Pharmacy,
    LLC 919
Saari v. Winter Sports, Inc. 481
Saarinen v. Kerr 221, 241, 575
Sabeta v. Baptist Hosp. of Miami,
    Inc.. 1066
Sabia v. State.............................. 570, 625
Sabolik v. HGG Chestnut Lake Ltd.
    P'ship... 258
Sacco v. High Country Indep. Press,
    Inc. 723, 724
Sachs v. Chiat.. 787
Sacramento, County of v. Lewis 588
Saden v. Kirby.. 323
Saelzler v. Advanced Group 400 ..... 327, 638
Safeway Managing Gen. Agency, Inc. v.
    Clark & Gamble............................... 1124
Safeway Stores, Inc. v. Nest-Kart.......... 891
Safford Unified School Dist. No. 1 v.
    Redding 585
Saglioccolo v. Eagle Ins. Co. 1102
Sahara Gaming Corp. v. Culinary Workers
    Union Local 226 978
Saher v. Norton Simon Museum of Art as
    Pasadena 129
Saint Petersburg Coca-Cola Bottling Co. v.
    Cuccinello... 101
Saiz v. Belen Sch. Dist. 767
Salehoo Group, Ltd. v. ABC Co.............. 971
Sales v. Kecoughtan Housing Co.,
    Ltd. 1132
Salica v. Tucson Heart Hosp.-Carondelet,
    LLC 327
Salinetro v. Nystrom 319

Salisbury Livestock Co. v. Colorado Central
    Credit Union.......................................152
Sallee v. GTE South, Inc.......... 607, 608, 610
Sallee v. Stewart 482
Salley v. Childs 1183
Salt River Project Agric. Improvement &
    Power Dist. v. Westinghouse Elec.
    Corp...1086
Salter v. Deaconess Family Medicine
    Center 512
Saltis v. A.B.B. Daimler Benz 451
Samples v. Florida Birth-Related
    Neurological Injury Comp. Ass'n 875
Sampson v. Contillo 530
Sampson v. MacDougall 664, 665
Samson v. Saginaw Professional Bldg.,
    Inc. 643, 645
Samuel v. Hepworth, Nungester & Lezamiz,
    Inc..1171
Samuels v. Southern Baptist Hosp. 543
San Antonio, City of v. Pollock 160
San Diego Gas & Elec. Co. v. Superior
    Court...92, 733
San Francisco Arts & Athletics, Inc. v.
    United States Olympic
    Committee 1198
Sanatass v. Consolidated Investing
    Co. 260, 769
Sanchez v. Coxon 578, 968
Sanchez v. J. Barron Rice, Inc...............284
Sanchez v. Medicorp Health Sys. 764, 770
Sanchez v. Schindler....................690, 693
Sanchez-Scott v. Alza Pharm. 1011
Sandborg v. Blue Earth Cty. 227, 395
Sandella v. Dick Corp. 231
Sander v. Alexander Richardson
    Investments 120
Sanders v. Ahmed 875
Sanders v. American Broad. Cos.,
    Inc. 1010
Sanders v. Casa View Baptist
    Church 455
Sanders v. Walden 224
Sanderson v. Indiana Soft Water Servs.,
    Inc. 1115
Sands ex rel. Sands v. Green.................434
Sands v. Living Word Fellowship.........1042,
    1043, 1046
Sansonni v. Jefferson Par. Sch. Bd. 216
Santa Barbara, City of v. Super. Ct. 410
Santana Prods. Inc. v. Bobrick Washroom
    Equip. Inc. 1107
Santiago v. First Student, Inc. 264
Santiago v. Phoenix Newspapers,
    Inc. 765, 766
Santos v. United States 551
Sapko v. State 914
Sapp v. Ford Motor Co...........................1084
Sarasota Fishing Co. v. J.M. Martinac &
    Co. 1085
Sarkissian v. Benjamin..........................1179
Sarvis v. Vermont State Colleges..........1135

Satterfield v. Breeding Insulation
  Co.. 210, 485, 635
Saucier v. Biloxi Regional Medical
  Center.. 464
Saucier v. Katz 585, 586
Saucier v. McDonald's Restaurants of
  Mont. 69
Sauder Custom Fabrication, Inc. v.
  Boyd.. 814
Saunders Sys. Birmingham Co. v.
  Adams.. 329
Saunders v. Bd. of Dirs., WHYY-TV....... 944
Saunders v. VanPelt............................... 945
Savage Indus. v. Duke............................ 233
Savage v. Boies 710
Savage v. Flagler Company 467
Save Charleston Foundation v.
  Murray 1152
Sawlani v. Mills...................................... 333
Sawyer v. Bailey 720
Sawyer v. Bank of Am. 700
Sawyer v. Comerci................................... 381
Sawyer v. Food Lion, Inc......................... 249
Saxena v. Goffney................................... 181
Scaccia v. Dayton Newspapers, Inc. 992
Scafidi v. Seiler............................... 332, 333
Schaaf v. Highfield 1130
Schaefer v. American Family Mut. Ins.
  Co.. 691
Schaerrer v. Stewart's Plaza Pharmacy,
  Inc. 831
Schafer v. American Cyanamid Co. 929
Schafer v. JLC Food Systems, Inc. 806,
  808, 810
Schafer v. Time, Inc................................ 957
Schanafelt v. Seaboard Fin. Co................ 75
Scheele v. Dustin..............709, 714, 717, 858
Scheffler v. Adams & Reese, LLP 1143,
  1175
Scheidt v. Denney.................................... 394
Schekall, Estate of, Broad ex rel. v. Randy
  Bauer Ins. Agency, Inc., ... 1074
Schelling v. Humphrey............................ 657
Schermerhorn v. Rosenberg............ 947, 951
Scheuerman v. Scharfenberg................. 143
Scheufele v. Newman 140
Schick v. Ferolito.................................... 241
Schieffer v. Catholic Archdiocese of
  Omaha....................164, 167, 180, 457
Schiele v. Hobart Corp. 430
Schilf v. Eli Lilly & Co. 833
Schirmer v. Mt. Auburn Obstetrics &
  Gynecological Assocs., Inc. 681
Schlanger v. Doe..................................... 308
Schlegel v. Ottumwa Courier........ 962, 1001
Schleier v. Kaiser Found. Health Plan of
  the Mid-Atlantic States, Inc....... 534, 535,
  859
Schloendorff v. Society of New York
  Hosp. 514
Schlossman's, Inc. v. Niewinski............ 1121
Schlup v. Auburn Needleworks, Inc. 916

Schmeck v. City of Shawnee.................... 628
Schmidt v. Coogan 1173, 1185
Schmidt v. Gibbs..................................... 300
Schmidt v. HTG, Inc. 576
Schmit v. Klumpyan 1044
Schmitz v. Smentowski........................... 1111
Schnathorst v. Williams 1031, 1032,
  1033, 1036
Schneider Nat'l Carriers, Inc. v.
  Bates 749
Schnellmann v. Roettger 1138
Schoen v. Washington Post 961, 999
Schoenfeld v. Quamme 560
Schooley v. Pinch's Deli Market, Inc....... 662
Schork v. Huber 680, 681
Schovanec v. Archdiocese of Okla.
  City.. 239
Schrader v. Eli Lilly & Co................ 976, 984
Schroeder v. Auto Driveaway
  Co. 118, 126
Schroeder v. St. Louis County 568
Schroeder v. Weighall 526
Schultz v. Roman Catholic Archdiocese of
  Newark 180
Schultz v. Boy Scouts of Am., Inc........... 597
Schultz v. Consumers Power Co.............. 217
Schulz v. City of Brentwood 566
Schuman v. Greenbelt Homes, Inc......... 312
Schumann v. McGinn 132
Schuoler, In re....................................... 1011
Schupmann v. Empire Fire & Marine Ins.
  Co.. 957
Schuster v. Altenberg 501, 576
Schuster v. City of New York 572
Schwarz v. Philip Morris Inc. 871
Schweizer v. Mulvehill........................... 1174
Schwennen v. Abell................................. 890
Schwinn v. Perkins 147, 149
Sciarrotta v. Global Spectrum 422
Scifres v. Kraft 464
Scott ex rel. Scott v. Iverson................... 218
Scott v. Archon Group, L.P. 465
Scott v. County of Los Angeles 898
Scott v. Garfield 491, 492, 859
Scott v. Greenville Pharmacy 372
Scott v. Harris 161
Scott v. Harrison.................................... 961
Scott v. Kass.. 295
Scott v. Matlack, Inc. 249, 251, 252, 281
Scott v. Rayhrer..................................... 329
Scott v. Robertson 295
Scott v. Shepherd 192
Scott v. Villegas..................................... 241
Scott v. Watson 342
Scottsdale Ins. Co. v. Cendejas............... 889
Scribner v. Summers 96, 735
Scroggins v. Bill Furst Florist &
  Greenhouse, Inc.................................. 1013
Scruggs, Millette, Bozeman & Dent, P.A. v.
  Merkel & Cocke, P.A. 1098
Scurti v. City of New York..............268, 478

Scutti Enters., LLC. v. Park Place Entm't
   Corp. 1109
SDV/ACCI, Inc. v. AT & T Corp. 952, 980
Seale v. Gramercy Pictures 1207
Seals v. County of Morris 487
Seaman's Direct Buying Serv. Inc. v.
   Standard Oil Co. of Cal. 1146
Searfoss v. Johnson & Johnson Co. 312
Sears v. Morrison 349
Sears, Roebuck & Co. v. Hartley 854
Sears, Roebuck & Co. v. Huang 594
Sears, Roebuck & Co. v. Stiffel Co. 1203
Sears, Roebuck and Co. v. Harris 839
Seaton v. TripAdvisor, LLC 938
Seavey v. Preble 159
Sebra v. Wentworth 98
Second Judicial District Court, County of
   Washoe, State v. 578
Seebold v. Prison Health Services,
   Inc. 660
Seegmiller v. KSL, Inc. 996
Seeholzer v. Kellstone, Inc. 462
Seeley v. New York Tel. Co. 309
Seely v. White Motor Co. 803, 804, 1077
Seevers v. Potter 1190
Sega v. State 482
Seide v. State 572, 575
Seisinger v. Siebel 512
Seitzinger v. Trans-Lux Corp. 869
Self v. Exec. Comm. Ga. Baptist Convention
   of Ga., Inc. 505
Self v. General Motors Corp. 818
Selle v. Tozser 862, 1096
Selmeczki v. New Mexico Dep't of
   Corrections 62, 68
Selvin v. DMC Regency Residence,
   Ltd. 542
Selwyn v. Ward 784, 785
Seminole Tribe of Fla. v. Times Publ'g Co.,
   Inc. 1099
Semon v. Royal Indemn. Co. 449
Senator Linie Gmbh & Co. Kg v. Sunway
   Line, Inc. 787
Seneris v. Haas 530
Senna v. Florimont 938
September 11 Litig., In re 363, 656, 928
Sergent v. City of Charleston 269, 575
Serio v. Merrell, Inc. 264
Serio-US Indus., Inc. v. Plastic Recovery
   Techs. Corp. 1092
Seropian v. Forman 948
Serra Chevrolet, Inc. v. Edwards Chevrolet,
   Inc. 1097
Setliff v. Akins 981
Settles v. Redstone Development
   Corp. 491
Seventh Regiment Fund, Inc.,
   State v. 117, 128
Sewell v. Brookbank 992
Seybert v. Cominco Alaska
   Exploration 1122

Shaari v. Harvard Student Agencies,
   Inc. 955
Shadday v. Omni Hotels Management
   Corp. 8
Shaeffer v. Poellnitz 107
Shalala v. Whitecotton 930
Shamberg, Johnson & Bergman, Chtd. v.
   Oliver 1168
Shamhart v. Morrison Cafeteria Co. 745
Shaner v. Tucson Airport Auth. Inc. 327
Shannahan v. Gigray 1038
Shantigar Found. v. Bear Mountain
   Builders 408, 888
Sharif-Munir-Davidson Dev. Corp. v.
   Bell 1042
Sharkey v. Prescott 1181
Sharma v. Vinmar Int'l, Ltd. 1145
Sharon v. City of Newton 173, 414
Sharp v. Town of Highland 345
Sharpe v. Peter Pan Bus Lines, Inc. 639
Shaw v. C.B. & E., Inc. 765
Shaw v. Jendzejec 670
Shay v. Walters 945
Shea v. Esensten 527
Shearer, United States v. 559, 560
Shearin v. Lloyd 429
Shebester v. Triple Crown Insurers 1151,
   1156
Sheehan v. Roche Bros. Supermarkets,
   Inc. 223, 469
Sheehan v. Weaver 719
Sheeley v. Mem. Hosp. 509
Sheffer v. Carolina Forge Co. 760
Shehyn v. United States 152
Shelcusky v. Garjulio 834
Sheldon Appel Co. v. Albert &
   Oliker 1024, 1025, 1030, 1038
Shell Oil Co. v. Khan 605
Shelton v. DeWitte 670
Shelton v. Kentucky Easter Seals Soc.,
   Inc. 471
Shelton v. State 568
Shemenski v. Chapiesky 712
Shen v. Leo A. Daly Co. 74
Shepard v. Capitol Foundry of Virginia,
   Inc. 693
Shepard v. Schurz Commc'ns, Inc. 980,
   996, 997
Shepherd v. Washington County 576, 635
Sheppard-Mobley v. King 730
Sheridan v. United States 563
Sherman v. Almeida 578
Sherrill v. Souder 436
Sherry v. East Suburban Football
   League 424
Sherwin-Williams Co. v. First Louisiana
   Const., Inc. 1183
Sheward, State v. 875
Shields v. Cape Fox Corp. 400
Shilkret v. Annapolis Emergency Hospital
   Ass'n 529
Shillington v. K-Mart Corp. 973

Shinaul, Estate of v. State Dep't of Soc. & Health Servs. 1117
Shine v. Vega.. 182
Shinholster v. Annapolis Hosp. 393, 528
Shipler v. General Motors Corp...... 819, 834
Shipman v. Kruck.................................... 437
Shirley v. Freunscht............................. 957
Shoemake v. Ferrer............................. 1182
Shoemaker v. Kingsbury................. 449, 450
Shoemaker v. Selnes 1031
Sholberg v. Truman............................. 744
Shooshanian v. Wagner......................... 803
Shore v. Town of Stonington.................. 573
Shorter v. Drury 410, 419
Shorter v. Shelton................................. 148
Shortnacy v. N. Atlanta Internal Medicine, P.C... 502
Show v. Ford Motor Co.......................... 809
Shuette v. Beazer Homes Holdings Corp. 405
Shugar v. Guill 66
Shuler v. Garrett 58, 515
Shull v. Reid 681
Shulman v. Group W Prods., Inc. 1007, 1012, 1016
Shump v. First Continental-Robinwood Associates... 488
Shumsky v. Eisenstein......... 436, 437, 1181
Shute v. Shute 1041
Sibbing v. Cave 342, 369
Sides v. St. Anthony's Med. Ctr..... 303, 306, 308
Sidis v. F-R Publ'g Corp. 1015
Siebeking v. Ford................................... 692
Siegel v. Ridgewells, Inc......................... 715
Siegler v. Kuhlman......................... 787, 788
Sieniarecki v. State 537
Sierra Fria Corp. v. Donald J. Evans, P.C... 1177
Sigal Constr. Corp. v. Stanbury...... 975, 999
Siglow v. Smart 410
Sigmund v. Starwood Urban Retail VI, LLC.. 641
Sigrist v. Love....................................... 256
Silberg v. Anderson 1025
Silva v. Southwest Fla. Blood Bank, Inc.. 434
Silva v. Union Pacific R.R. Co................ 473
Silver Falls Timber Co. v. Eastern & Western Lumber Co........................... 356
Silver v. Silver 47
Silverman v. Progressive Broad., Inc. ... 940, 945
Simeonoff v. Hiner.............................. 391
Simmerer v. Dabbas.............................. 680
Simmers v. Bentley Const. Co. 367
Simmons v. Comfort Suites Hotel.......... 916
Simmons v. Frazier 419
Simmons v. Pacor, Inc............ 312, 334, 723
Simmons v. Tuomey Regional Medical Center.. 530
Simmons v. United States...................... 179

Simms v. Seaman.................................. 968
Simon & Schuster, Inc. v. Members of the N.Y. State Crime Victims Bd............. 1002
Simon v. Drake Constr. Co. 496
Simon v. Navon 1044
Simon v. Wyeth Pharmaceuticals, Inc. 830
Simon's Feed Store, Inc. v. Leslein 285
Simonson v. White 221
Simpkins v. CSX Transp., Inc. 652
Simpson Strong-Tie Co., Inc. v. Stewart, Estes & Donnell.................. 940, 965, 966
Simpson v. Big Bear Stores Co............... 639
Simpson v. Boyd................................... 244
Simpson v. Kollasch......... 735, 737, 743, 748
Simpson v. Laytart 1043
Simpson v. Mars Inc. 940, 955
Sims v. Huntington............................... 279
Sinai v. Polinger Co. 231
Sinclair v. Merck & Co.................... 805, 854
Sindle v. New York City Transit Auth. 74, 78, 80
Singer v. Marx....................................... 79
Singleton v. Jackson 462, 467
Singleton, State v................................. 172
Sinka v. Northern Commercial Co. 848
Sinkler v. Kneale.................................. 669
Sinn v. Burd 723, 731
Sioux City & Pacific R.R. v. Stout 476
Sipple v. Chronicle Publ'g Co. 1016
Siragusa v. Swedish Hosp. 417
Sisson v. Lhowe.................................... 697
Sisters of Providence in Wash. v. A.A. Pain Clinic, Inc.. 1098
Sitzes v. Anchor Motor Freight, Inc........ 883
Siverson v. Weber 302
Skaggs v. Senior Servs. of Cent. Ill., Inc. 890
Skaskiw v. Vermont Agency of Agric. 973
Skees v. United States.................... 560, 561
Skelton v. Chicago Transit Auth. 451
Skinner v. Ogallala Pub. Sch. Dist. No. 1..382, 462
Skinner v. Railway Labor Executives' Ass'n.. 1012
Skinner v. South Carolina Dep't of Transp.. 483
Skinner v. Square D Co. 342
Skinner v. Vacaville Unified School Dist.. 647
Sklar v. Beth Israel Deaconess Med. Ctr. 1100
Skrtich v. Thornton.............................. 585
Slack v. Farmers Ins. Exch.................... 892
Slager v. HWA Corp.............................. 394
Slaney v. Ranger Ins. Co. 1039
Slater v. Baker 192
Slater v. Clarke 578
Slaton v. Vansickle 717
Slaughter v. Friedman......................... 945
Slavin v. Plumbers & Steamfitters Local 29... 462

Slawek v. Stroh.............. 175, 675
Sletten v. Ramsey County...................... 567
Slisze v. Stanley-Bostich 821
Slone v. General Motors Corp. 840
Slovensky v. Friedman........................ 1175
Small v. Fritz Cos., Inc.............. 1123, 1129
Small v. Howard................................ 508
Small v. McKennan Hosp...................... 687
Smaxwell v. Bayard.............................. 468
Smethers v. Campion 509, 510
SMI Owen Steel Co., Inc. v. Marsh USA,
  Inc.. 1087
Smialek v. Begay.................................... 704
Smit v. Anderson 618
Smith Mar., Inc. v. L/B Kaitlyn
  Eymard.. 1079
Smith v. Aaron 284
Smith v. Andrews 36
Smith v. Anonymous Joint Enter. 938
Smith v. Arbaugh's Restaurant, Inc....... 478
Smith v. Borello.................... 670, 730
Smith v. Burdette.................................. 551
Smith v. Calvary Christian Church 163
Smith v. Cap Concrete 91
Smith v. Carbide & Chemicals Corp. 96,
  749
Smith v. Chapman................................. 232
Smith v. Cote 678, 681
Smith v. Crown-Zellerbach, Inc. 480
Smith v. Cumberland County Agricultural
  Soc'y... 638
Smith v. Daily Mail Publ'g Co. 1018
Smith v. Delery...................................... 141
Smith v. Delta Tau Delta, Inc................. 766
Smith v. Department of Ins. 875
Smith v. Des Moines Pub. Sch. 972, 981
Smith v. Durden 944
Smith v. Eli Lilly & Co. 330
Smith v. Finch 265
Smith v. Fisher 511
Smith v. Foodmaker, Inc......................... 773
Smith v. Ford Motor Co...................... 1108
Smith v. Gore.................... 682, 683
Smith v. Haynesworth, Marioin, McKay &
  Geurard... 1168
Smith v. HCA Health Servs. of N.H. 720
Smith v. Holley..................................... 970
Smith v. Holmes 594
Smith v. Huntsville Times Co., Inc......... 947
Smith v. IMG Worldwide, Inc. 960
Smith v. Ingersoll-Rand Co............. 693, 835
Smith v. Jalbert 782, 783
Smith v. Jeppsen 860
Smith v. John Deere Company 152
Smith v. Keller Ladder Co. 822
Smith v. Knowles................................... 512
Smith v. Lockheed Propulsion Co........... 787
Smith v. Louisiana Farm Bureau........... 687
Smith v. Minster Mach. Co. 827
Smith v. Officers & Dirs. of Kart-N-Karry,
  Inc.. 603
Smith v. Otis Elevator Co. 453

Smith v. Owen.......................................259
Smith v. Parrott 332
Smith v. Paslode Corp. 434
Smith v. Pate...87
Smith v. Pavlovich 497, 512
Smith v. Pust..1052
Smith v. Smith 836
Smith v. Stasco Milling Co. 748
Smith v. State 334
Smith v. Stewart 939, 963
Smith v. Stone..87
Smith v. Toney 715, 717
Smith v. Town of Greenwich 881, 885,
  886
Smith v. United States 467
Smith v. VonCannon.....................165, 167
Smith v. Wade......................................3
Smith v. Wallowa County 735
Smith v. Wal-Mart Stores, Inc. 252, 469
Smith v. Welch 498, 706
Smith v. YMCA of Benton Harbor/St.
  Joseph..173
Smith, In re 1003
Smith, People v. 138
Smith, United States v. 581
Smith-Hunter v. Harvey........................1034
Smithwick v. Hall & Upson Co................390
Snead v. Society for Prevention of Cruelty
  to Animals of Pennsylvania 114
Snelson v. Kamm..................................512
Snepp v. United States 1002
Sniadach v. Family Finance Corp. of Bay
  View 127
Snouffer v. Snouffer...............................67
Snow v. City of Columbia 86
Snyder v. Am. Ass'n of Blood Banks 599
Snyder v. Baumecker.............................1189
Snyder v. Boy Scouts of Am., Inc............439
Snyder v. Icard, Merrill, Cullis, Timm,
  Furen and Ginsburg, P.A. 1046
Snyder v. Injured Patients & Families
  Comp. Fund 297
Snyder v. Lovercheck.............................1136
Snyder v. Michael's Stores, Inc. 673, 919
Snyder v. Phelps 710
Snyder v. United States..........................560
Sobanski v. Donahue 609
Sodergren v. Johns Hopkins Univ. Applied
  Physics Lab...966
Softel, Inc. v. Dragon Medical and Scientific
  Communications, Inc...........................1204
Sokolowski v. Medi Mart, Inc..................470
Solaia Tech., LLC. v. Specialty Publ'g
  Co. 979, 981
Solanki v. Ervin 390
Solano v. Playgirl, Inc.................1019, 1020
Soldano v. O'Daniels 616, 617
Soler v. Castmaster, Div. of H.P.M.
  Corp...818, 822
Solers, Inc. v. Doe..................................971
Sollami v. Eaton....................................828
Sollin v. Wangler...................................386

Solomon v. Shuell 349
Sommer v. Federal Signal Corp............. 803
Son v. Ashland Cmty. Healthcare
    Servs... 393, 395
Sonoran Desert Investigations v.
    Miller.. 402, 403
Sopha v. Owens-Corning Fiberglas
    Corp. 441
Soproni v. Polygon Apartment
    Partners 815
Sorensen v. Jarvis 251
Sorichetti v. City of New York 570, 656
Sorkin v. Lee....................................... 683
Sorrells v. M.Y.B. Hospitality Ventures of
    Asheville.. 398
Sosa v. Alvarez-Machain...................... 562
Soto v. Flores 588
Soto v. New York City Transit
    Authority.................................. 375, 376
Souci v. William C. Smith & Co............ 1068
Soule v. General Motors Corp. 809, 812
South Arkansas Petroleum Co. v.
    Schiesser 1036, 1043
South Carolina Ins. Co. v. James C. Greene
    and Co. 755
South Cent. Reg'l Med. Ctr. v.
    Pickering 726
South Dakota Dep't of Health v.
    Heim 159
South Port Marine, LLC v. Gulf Oil Ltd.
    P'ship 1076
South Shore Baseball, LLC v.
    DeJesus 422
South v. Maryland................................. 574
South v. National Railroad Passenger
    Corp. 619
Southern Alaska Carpenters Health & Sec.
    Trust Fund v. Jones............................ 894
Southern Baptist Hosp. of Fla., Inc. v.
    Welker... 999
Southers v. City of Farmington 572, 575,
    579
Southwestern Bell Tel. Co. v.
    Delanney 1080
Southwestern Bell Tel. Co. v. M.H. Burton
    Construction Co. 105
Southwestern Pub. Serv. Co. v. Artesia
    Alfalfa Growers' Ass'n 413
Sowers v. Forest Hills Subdivision 733,
    735, 739, 748
Sowinski v. Walker....................... 244, 401
Spahn v. Julian Messner, Inc. 1007
Spahn v. Town of Port Royal.......... 397, 415
Spangler v. Bechtel 670, 714
Spangler v. Kranco, Inc......................... 814
Spann v. Shuqualak Lumber Co., Inc. ... 318
Spano v. Perini Corp. 784
Spar v. Cha 517
Spar v. Pacific Bell 100
Sparks v. Ala. Power Co......................... 398
Spates v. Dameron Hospital Ass'n 112
Spaulding v. Cameron............................ 100

Spaur v. Owens-Corning Fiberglas
    Corp...324
Speakers of Sport, Inc. v. ProServ,
    Inc. 1102, 1108
Specialty Beverages, LLC v. Pabst Brewing
    Co. 1117
Specialty Mills, Inc. v. Citizens State
    Bank..1041
Speck v. Finegold 681
Speed Boat Leasing, Inc. v. Elmer 451
Speed v. Scott 960
Speer v. Dealy 1052
Spelina v. Sporry...................................150
Spellens v. Spellens 1046
Spence v. Flynt.....................................996
Spence v. Funk 958
Spencer v. A-1 Crane Serv., Inc..............861
Spencer v. Barber..................................1170
Spencer v. Burglass 1039
Spencer v. Goodill 515, 520, 521
Spencer v. McClure................................326
Spencer v. Time Warner Cable................917
Spengler v. ADT Security Services,
    Inc. 624
Sperl v. C.H. Robinson Worldwide,
    Inc. 764
Spier v. Barker 406, 407
Spilker v. City of Lincoln 434
Spirit Ridge Mineral Springs, LLC v.
    Franklin County.................................748
Spivey v. Battaglia...........................58, 66
Splendorio v. Bilray Demolition Co........347,
    789
Sports Imaging of Ariz., LLC v. 1993 CKC
    Trust 1083
Spragg v. Shuster...........................394, 401
Spratley v. State Farm Mut. Auto. Ins.
    Co. 1167
Sprietsma v. Mercury Marine, a Div. of
    Brunswick Corp..................................846
Spring Valley Estates, Inc. v.
    Cunningham.......................................91
Springer v. Bohling................................396
Springer v. City and County of
    Denver 551
Springfield Hydroelectric Co. v.
    Copp..1079
Springhill Hospitals, Inc. v.
    Larrimore..496
Sprouse v. Clay Commc'ns, Inc. 951
Spur Feeding Co. v. Fernandez..............478
Spur Industries, Inc. v. Del E. Webb
    Development Co. 740, 748
St. Benedict's Dev. Co. v. St. Benedict's
    Hosp..1104
St. Germain v. Husqvarna Corp..............815
St. James Condominium Ass'n v.
    Lokey...572
St. Joseph Hosp. v. Corbetta Constr. Co.,
    Inc. 1135
St. Joseph's Hosp. & Med. Ctr. v. Reserve
    Life Ins. Co. 1123

St. Louis, City of v. Benjamin Moore & Co. 315, 330
St. Luke's Episcopal Hospital v. Agbor 529
St. Malachy Roman Catholic Congretation of Geneseo v. Ingram 1176
St. Michelle v. Catania 763
St. Onge v. MacDonald 715, 717
St. Paul Fire & Marine Ins. Co. v. Russo Bros., Inc. 1129
Staab v. Diocese of St. Cloud 887
Stachniewicz v. Mar-Cam Corp. 251, 253
Stacy v. Jedco Constr., Inc. 226, 227
Stacy v. Rederiet Otto Danielsen, A.S. 715
Stacy v. Shapiro 462, 467
Staelens v. Dobert 340, 361, 366, 371
Stafford v. Borden 254
Stafford v. Shultz 454
Stahl v. St. Elizabeth Med. Ctr. 1044
Stahlecker v. Ford Motor Co. 213, 364, 805
Stalberg v. Western Title Ins. Co. 438
Staley v. Northern Utah Healthcare Corp. 531
Stallings v. Black and Decker (United States), Inc. 822
Stallman v. Youngquist 675
Stalter v. State 77
Standard Havens Products, Inc. v. Benitez 373
Stanley v. Luse 1117
Stanley v. McCarver 499, 628
Stanley, United States v. 559, 560, 561
Stanski v. Ezersky 1174
Stanton v. Lackawanna Energy, Ltd. 480
Stanton v. Schultz 1191
Stanton v. Sims 585
Stanton v. University of Maine System 638, 648
Staples v. CBL & Assocs., Inc. 212
Staples v. Duell 484
Star Bank, N.A. v. Laker 152
Star Transport, Inc. v. Byard 349
Star, Inc. v. Ford Motor Co. 798
Starcher v. Byrne 775
Starkenburg v. State 687
Starrh and Starrh Cotton Growers v. Aera Energy LLC 97, 98
State Farm Fire & Cas. Co. v. Municipality of Anchorage 305
State Farm Ins. Cos. v. Premier Manufactured Sys., Inc. 884, 891
State Farm Mut. Auto. Ins. Co. v. Campbell 869, 872
State Farm Mut. Auto. Ins. Co. v. Lucas 314
State Press Co. v. Willett 946
State Rubbish Collectors Ass'n v. Siliznoff 71, 84, 706
Lead Industries Ass'n, Inc., State v. 746

State, Dep't of Corrections v. Cowles 576, 634
State, Dep't of Environmental Protection v. Ventron 788
States v. Lourdes Hosp. 303
Steaks Unlimited, Inc. v. Deaner 993
Stebbins v. North Adams Trust Co. 1154
Stecks v. Young 965
Steel Creek Development Corp. v. James 93
Steele v. City of Houston 161
Steele v. Holiday Inns, Inc. 233
Steele v. Kerrigan 896, 899
Stegman v. Professional & Bus. Men's Life Ins. Co. 1136
Stehlik v. Rhoads 426
Stehno v. Sprint Spectrum, L.P. 1102, 1107
Steichen v. Talcott Properties, LLC 472
Steiger v. Burroughs 171
Steigman v. Outrigger Enterprises, Inc. 473
Stein, Hinkle, Dawe & Assocs., Inc. v. Continental Cas. Co. 700
Steinauer v. Sarpy County 854
Steinberg v. Irwin Operating Co. 453
Steinbuch v. Cutler 1014, 1019
Steiner Corp. v. Johnson & Higgins of Cal. 1132
Steinhauser v. Hertz Corp. 732
Steinson v. Heath 190
Stencel Aero Eng'g Corp. v. United States 559
Stephano v. News Group Publications, Inc. 1207, 1209
Stephen K. v. Roni L. 1118
Stephenson v. Air Products & Chemicals, Inc. 360
Stephenson v. Universal Metrics, Inc. 209
Stern v. Doe 1005, 1009
Sternhagen v. Dow Co. 801
Stevens v. Bispham 1186
Stevens v. Iowa Newspapers, Inc. 948
Stevens v. New York City Transit Auth. 895
Stevens v. Novartis Pharms. Corp. 437
Stevens v. Redwing 1054, 1056
Stevens v. Stevens 593, 1057
Stevens v. Tillman 946, 948
Stevens, United States v. 205, 206, 217
Stevensen v. Goodson 734
Stevenson Real Estate Servs., Inc. v. CB Richard Ellis Real Estate Servs., Inc. 1102
Stevenson v. E.I. DuPont de Nemours & Co. 736
Stevenson v. East Ohio Gas Co. 373
Steward v. State 568
Stewart Title Guar. Co. v. American Abstract & Title Co. 1097
Stewart Title Guar. Co. v. Dude 1130
Stewart v. Bernstein 545

Stewart v. Federated Dep't Stores, Inc... 294

Stewart v. Gibson Prods. Co. of Natchitoches Par. 223

Stewart v. Manhattan & Bronx Surface Transit Operating Auth....................... 232

Stewart v. Motts 206, 213, 215, 216, 217, 218

Stewart v. Walker................................. 1056

Stienbaugh v. Payless Drug Store, Inc.. 154

Stiff v. Eastern Illinois Area of Special Educ... 646

Still v. Cunningham 1136

Stillwater Condo. Ass'n v. Town of Salem... 1124

Stinnett v. Buchele........................... 280, 613

Stockett v. Tolin 62, 75, 82, 83

Stoddart v. Pocatello School Dist. No. L25... 647

Stodola v. Grunwald Mechanical Contractors, Inc. 356

Stokes v. State ex rel. Mont. Dep't of Transp. 1098

Stone Mountain Mem'l Ass'n v. Herrington 479

Stone v. Proctor 496

Stone v. Smith, Kline & French Laboratories.. 830

Stone v. Wall.. 1054

Stone v. Williamson.............................. 332

Stone v. York Haven Power Co.............. 483

Stop & Shop Cos., Inc. v. Fisher 1067

Storjohn v. Fay 225, 258

Storm v. Storm 1091

Storms v. Action Wis., Inc., In re.... 938, 962

Stowe v. Smith 1175

Strahin v. Cleavenger 885, 898, 1111

Strain v. Christians............................... 400

Strait v. Crary 236

Stratford Theater, Inc. v. Town of Stratford.. 749

Straub v. City of Scottsbluff................... 913

Straube v. Larson 1098, 1107

Strawn v. Canuso 744

Streeter v. Executive Jet Mgmt., Inc.. 1055

Strever, Estate of v. Cline.............. 362, 655

Strickland v. University of Scranton...................................... 1028, 1029

Strickland v. Washington 1186

Stringer v. Minnesota Vikings Football Club, LLC... 919

Strode v. Gleason.................................. 1057

Stromberg v. Moore 1154

Stromberger v. 3M Co. 1121

Stroop v. Day 781

Stropes v. Heritage House Childrens Ctr. of Shelbyville, Inc. 543, 763

Stroud v. Arthur Andersen & Co. 1132

Stroud v. Denny's Rest., Inc................... 864

Strubhart v. Perry Memorial Hospital Trust Authority 657

Structure Bldg. Corp. v. Abella 1092

Strunk v. Zoltanski.......................... 656, 780

Stuard v. Jorgenson............................... 429

Stuart v. W. Union Tel. Co. 703

Stubbs v. City of Rochester.................... 315

Stubbs v. United States 561

Student Loan Fund of Idaho, Inc. v. Duerner.. 946, 964

Stukuls v. State..................................... 969

Stump v. Ashland, Inc. 711

Stumpf v. Nye 295

Sturbridge Partners, Ltd. v. Walker....... 640

Sturm v. Peoples Trust & Sav. Bank 1123

Suburban Hosp., Inc. v. Kirson 921

Suder v. Whiteford, Taylor & Preston, LLP 1174

Suggs v. Carroll..................................... 85

Sullivan v. Baptist Mem'l Hosp....... 938, 943

Sullivan v. Conway 967

Sullivan v. Dunham 785, 791

Sullivan v. Durham................................ 89

Sullivan v. Fairmont Homes, Inc. 219

Sullivan v. Pulitzer Broad. Co. 1021

Sullivan v. Snyder.................................. 299

Sullivan v. Zebley.................................. 924

Sullivan-Coughlin v. Palos Country Club, Inc.. 420

Sullivant v. City of Oklahoma City......... 161

Sullo v. Greenberg 498

Sulton v. HealthSouth Corp. 866

Sumblin v. Craven Cnty. Hosp. Corp........ 69

Summerfield v. Superior Court 670

Summers v. Baptist Medical Center Arkadelphia... 532

Summers v. Tice.................................... 328

Sun Valley v. Rosholt, Robertson & Tucker... 1170

Sunday v. Stratton Corp.................. 420, 423

Sundberg v. Keller Ladder 807

Sundeen v. Kroger 1031

Sunderlin v. Bradstreet.......................... 964

Sundowner, Inc. v. King 742

Sunridge Dev. Corp. v. RB&G Eng'g, Inc. 1069, 1077

Sunshine Custom Paints & Body, Inc. v. South Douglas Highway Water & Sewer Dist.. 1102

Superior Const. Co. v. Elmo 749

Suppressed v. Suppressed 180

Suprise v. Dekock.................................. 742

Surette v. Islamic Republic of Iran 720, 876

Surina v. Lucey 1053

Surocco v. Geary................................... 159

Sutherland v. Saint Francis Hospital, Inc.. 466

Sutton v. Tacoma Sch. Dist. No. 10.......... 64

Suzuki Motor Corp. v. Consumers Union of U.S., Inc...................................... 1114, 1115

Swain v. Tillett..................................... 783

Swan v. Boardwalk Regency Corp. 1021
Swan v. I.P., Inc................................ 832
Swan v. Matthews 1190
Swanigan v. American Nat'l Red
    Cross.. 434
Sweeney v. Bettendorf............................ 320
Sweeney v. City of Bettendorf......... 411, 414
Sweeney v. F.W. Woolworth Co. 155
Sweeney v. Preston................................ 676
Swenson v. Waseca Mut. Ins. Co. ... 524, 623
Swindell v. J.A. Tobin Const. Co. 286
Swipies v. Kofka 582
Swope v. Columbian Chems. Co. 67
Sydnes v. United States 554
Sydney v. MacFadden Newspaper Publ'g
    Corp. 951
Sylvan R. Shemitz Designs, Inc. v. Newark
    Corp. 801
Sylvia v. Gobeille 669
Syndicate Sales, Inc. v. Hampshire Paper
    Corp. 1197
Synygy, Inc. v. Scott-Levin, Inc. 962, 998
T. & E. Indus. Inc. v. Safety Light
    Corp. 788
T.R. v. Boy Scouts of Am. 430
T.W.M. Custom Framing v. Industrial
    Comm'n 916
Taber v. Maine......................... 559, 560, 561
Table Steaks v. First Premier
    Banks 1108
Taboada v. Daly Seven, Inc..... 452, 620, 639
Tabor v. Scobee..................................... 174
Tacket v. General Motors Corp............... 941
Tackett v. State Farm Fire & Cas.
    Ins... 240
Tadros v. City of Omaha 264
Tafoya v. Rael 764
Taft v. Ball, Ball & Brosamer, Inc. 86
Taggart v. Drake Univ. 708
Tagle v. Jakob............................... 206, 473
Tait v. Wahl, ... 687
Taj Mahal Travel, Inc. v. Delta Airlines,
    Inc.. 957
Takashi Kataoka v. May Dep't Stores
    Co.. 451
Talcott v. National Exhibition Co. 78
Talent Tree Personnel Servs. v.
    Fleenor 863
Talkington v. Atria Reclamelucifers
    Fabrieken BV....................................... 813
Tall v. Board of School Comn'rs of
    Baltimore City 763
Talley v. Danek Med., Inc. 251
Talmadge v. Smith 79
Tamas v. Dep't of Social & Health
    Servs.. 583
Tamiami Gun Shop v. Klein 401
Tamko Roofing Prods., Inc. v. Smith Eng'g
    Co.. 1112
Tamposi Assocs., Inc. v. Star Mkt. Co.,
    Inc... 1093
Tanja H. v. Regents of Univ. of Cal. 649

Tanksley v. ProSoft Automation, Inc. 841
Tanner v. Hartog.............................. 670, 722
Tapp v. Owensboro Medical Health System,
    Inc. 512
Tappen v. Ager 1037
Tarasoff v. Regents of Univ. of Cal......... 208,
    501, 576
Tarbell Administrator, Inc. v. City of
    Concord 733, 737
Tarleton v. Arnstein & Lehr.................. 1178
Tarlton v. Kaufman 741, 742
Tarr v. Bob Ciasulli's Mack Auto Mall,
    Inc. 873
Tashman v. Gibbs 515, 516, 522
Tate v. City of Grand Rapids.................. 781
Tatera v. FMC Corp.............................. 918
Tatman v. Cordingly.............................. 135
Tatro v. Lehouiller 148
Tatum v. Schering Corp......................... 689
Tatur v. Solsrud 948
Taus v. Loftus...................... ......982, 1015
Tayar v. Camelback Ski Corp., Inc. 410
Taygeta Corp. v. Varian Assocs.,
    Inc. 432, 735
Taylor v. Barnes................................... 746
Taylor v. Beard 719
Taylor v. Cutler.................................... 676
Taylor v. Gilmartin 77
Taylor v. Johnston 61, 62, 175
Taylor v. Keefe 1056
Taylor v. McNichols 124
Taylor v. Mississippian Ry., Inc. 460
Taylor v. Riley 1176
Taylor v. Smith 500
Taylor v. Super Discount Market,
    Inc. 74, 154, 155
Taylor v. Vencor, Inc............................. 541
TBG Ins. Servs. Corp. v. Super. Ct. 1009
TCW/Camil Holding LLC v. Fox Horan &
    Camerini, LLP 1178
Tebo v. Havlik 859
Tech Plus, Inc. v. Ansel......................... 947
Ted's Master Service, Inc. v. Farina
    Brothers Co... 788
Tedesco v. Connors................................ 571
Tedla v. Ellman..................................... 259
Tedrick v. Community Resource Center,
    Inc. 659
Teeter v. Missouri Highway & Transp.
    Comm'n... 696
Tegman v. Accident & Med. Investigations,
    Inc. 896
Tel Oil Co. v. City of Schenectady 364
Telthorster v. Tennell 579
Temple Community Hospital v. Super.
    Ct... 1159, 1161
Ten Broeck Dupont, Inc. v. Brooks.......... 163
Tenamee v. Schmukler 1190
Tennant v. Marion Health Care
    Foundation, Inc. 505
Tennant v. Shoppers Food Warehouse Md.
    Corp..472

Tennaro v. Ryder Sys., Inc. 922
Tennessee v. Garner............................... 135
Tenney v. Atlantic Associates................. 362
Tennison v. City and County of San
    Francisco 583
Tenzer v. Superscope........................... 1136
Teper v. Weiss 1152
Teply v. Lincoln 260
Terbush v. United States 556
Terracon Consultants W., Inc. v. Mandalay
    Resort Group................................... 1126
Terrell v. Hester 140
Terry v. Ohio...................................... 155
Terry v. Panek 1140
Terwilliger v. Hennepin County 568, 569
Terwilliger v. Wands 961
Teschendorf v. State Farm Ins. Cos. 6
Teton County Sheriff's Dept., Board of
    County Comm'rs of Teton County ex rel.
    v. Bassett................................ 892, 896
Tetrault v. Mahoney, Hawkes &
    Goldings 708
Tetrick v. Frashure 407
Tetro v. Town of Stratford............... 346, 368
Tetuan v. A.H. Robins Co....................... 863
Texas & Pac. Ry. v. Behymer.......... 281, 282
Texas Beef Cattle Co. v. Green 1041
Texas Beef Group v. Winfrey 936
Texas Dep't of Health v. Rocha.............. 970
Texas Health Enters., Inc. v. Geisler 541,
    544
Texas Home Management, Inc. v.
    Peavy.. 659
Texas Utilities Elec. Co. v. Timmons...... 477
Thakkar v. St. Ives Country Club........... 104
Thames Shipyard and Repair Co. v. United
    States 629
Thapar v. Zezulka................................ 501
Thayer v. Boston................................. 160
The Exxon Valdez, In re........................ 746
The Mogul S.S. Co., Ltd. v. McGregor, Gow,
    & Co. 1095, 1101
The T.J. Hooper...................... 281, 282, 283
Theer v. Philip Carey Co........................ 835
Theofel v. Farey-Jones 177
Therrien, State v. 1178
Thibeault v. Larson 678, 680
Thierrien v. Target Corp. 853
Thing v. La Chusa................................ 718
Thiry v. Armstrong World Indus. 866
Thom v. Bristol-Myers Squibb Co........... 832
Thoma v. Cracker Barrel Old Country
    Store, Inc. 469
Thoma v. Hickel.................................. 579
Thomas v. Bedford............................... 139
Thomas v. Bethea............... 1170, 1173, 1185
Thomas v. Checker Cab Co. 766
Thomas v. City of Richmond 577
Thomas v. Commerford.......................... 243
Thomas v. E-Z Mart Stores, Inc............. 468
Thomas v. Hilburn 567
Thomas v. Inman 236

Thomas v. Jacksonville Television,
    Inc. 940, 944
Thomas v. Marion County 156
Thomas v. McKeever's Enters. Inc..........322
Thomas v. Newman 217
Thomas v. Panco Mgmt. of Md., LLC.....415,
    417
Thomas v. Siddiqui 1050
Thomas v. Telegraph Publ'g Co......955, 956,
    978, 981, 989
Thomas v. Uzoka.................................689
Thomas v. Winchester 800
Thompson v. Bernard G. Janowitz Constr.
    Corp...919
Thompson v. County of Alameda 576, 659
Thompson v. Estate of Petroff 688, 954
Thompson v. Harris 1031
Thompson v. Hi Tech Motor Sports,
    Inc. 410, 412
Thompson v. Kaczinski............212, 316, 338
Thompson v. KFB Ins. Co..................695, 861
Thompson v. Kyo-Ya Co., Ltd. 481
Thompson v. Lied Animal Shelter..........717,
    727
Thompson v. Michael............................383
Thompson v. Mindis Metals, Inc. 789
Thompson v. National R.R. Passenger
    Corp...856
Thompson v. Nebraska Mobile Homes
    Corp...803
Thompson v. Newark Housing
    Authority 569
Thompson v. Sun City Cmty. Hosp.,
    Inc. 326, 332
Thompson v. Tuggle 320
Thomson v. Littlefield..........................219
Thorn v. Mercy Mem'l Hosp. Corp. 690
Thornhill v. Wilson 74
Thornton v. Garcini......................700, 711
Thornton v. Lees..................................224
Thrift v. Hubbard................................1025
Thrifty Rent-A-Car v. Jeffrey 1032
Thropp v. Bache Halsey Stuart Shields,
    Inc. 287
Tiara Condo. Ass'n, Inc. v. Marsh &
    McLennan Cos., Inc.................1062, 1156
Tibbetts v. Dairyland Ins........................403
Tichenor v. Santillo..............................720
Tidwell v. Winn-Dixie, Inc..............973, 974
Tiegs v. Watts....................................733
Tierney v. St. Michael's Med. Ctr............306
Tietsworth v. Harley-Davidson, Inc......1080
Tiffany (NJ) Inc. v. eBay, Inc. 1194
TIG Ins. Co. v. Giffin Winning Cohen &
    Bodewes, P.C. 1172
Tigges, In re Marriage of 1010
Tiller v. Atlantic Coast Line R.R............421
Tim Torres Enterprises, Inc. v.
    Linscott..1201
Timberwalk Apartments, Partners, Inc. v.
    Cain..645
Time, Inc. v. Firestone.................706, 1000

Time, Inc. v. Hill.................................... 1021

Times Mirror Magazines v. Las Vegas
Sports News 1197

Timpte Industries, Inc. v. Gish...... 818, 819, 820

Tincani v. Inland Empire Zoological
Soc'y... 465

Tincher v. Omega Flex, Inc.................... 809

Tingley v. Harrison 1180

Tippett v. United States........................ 557

Tipton v. Town of Tabor 573

Tisdale v. Pruitt................................... 519

Tissicino v. Peterson............................... 655

Titan Am., LLC v. Riverton Inv.
Corp...........................965, 984, 1036, 1092

TJX Cos. Retail Sec. Breach Litig.,
In re.. 1126

TMJ Implants, Inc. v. Aetna, Inc.......... 1114

Tobacco Litig., In re............................... 871

Tobe v. City of Santa Ana 157

Tober v. Graco Children's Products,
Inc.. 839

Tobias v. Sports Club, Inc. 663

Tobin v. Norwood Country Club, Inc....... 662

Today Homes, Inc. v. Williams 1144

Todd v. Mass Transit Admin. 448, 452

Todd v. Societe Bic................................. 813

Toffoloni v. LFP Publ'g Group, LLC 1007, 1209

Togstad v. Vesely, Otto, Miller &
Keefe.................................1166, 1184, 1186

Toker v. Pollak...................................... 974

Tolbert v. Duckworth 221

Toler v. Sud-Chemie, Inc........................ 976

Tom's Foods, Inc. v. Carn 1108

Tomeo v. Thomas Whitesell Constr.
Co.. 56, 921

Tomey v. Dyson 225

Tomfohr v. Mayo Found. 394, 401

Tomlinson v. Wilson & Toomer Fertilizer
Co.. 229

Tommy Hilfiger Licensing, Inc. v. Nature
Labs, LLC... 1196

Tommy L. Griffin Plumbing & Heating Co.
v. Jordan, Jones & Goulding, Inc...... 1073

Tonelli v. Bd. of Educ. of Twp. of
Wycoff... 597

Toney v. Chester Cnty. Hosp. 730

Too Much Media, LLC v. Hale 958, 959, 971

Toogood v. Rogal................................... 302

Toogood v. Spyring 973

Torchik v. Boyce 610

Torian v. Ashford................................... 1030

Torres v. City of Los Angeles 221

Torres v. Damicis.................................... 570

Torres v. El Paso Elec. Co. 376

Torres v. North Am. Van Lines, Inc. 863

Torres v. State 256

Torrington Co. v. Stutzman 631, 806

Toth v. Cmty. Hosp. at Glen
Cove.. 231, 507

Totsky v. Riteway Bus Serv., Inc. 219

Toure v. Avis Rent A Car Sys., Inc..........926

Tower v. Glover.....................................1191

Towle v. St. Albans Publ'g Co., Inc. 957

Townsend v. Felthousen 1132

Townsend v. Jones 231

Townsend v. Legere...............................382

Toyota Motor Corp. v. Gregory................821

Traffix Devices, Inc. v. Marketing Displays,
Inc. 1202

Trager v. Thor 780, 781

Trahan-Laroche v. Lockheed Sanders,
Inc. 657

Trail v. Boys & Girls Clubs of Nw.
Ind...941

Trammel v. Bradberry 611

Tran v. General Motors Acceptance
Corp..97

Tran v. Toyota Motor Corp. 809

Tranchina v. Arcinas 1044

TransCare Maryland, Inc. v. Murray......524

Trans-Gulf Corp. v. Performance Aircraft
Servs, Inc...1087

Transport Ins. Co. v. Faircloth 1133

Tranum v. Broadway 959

Traudt v. Potomac Elec. Power Co. 768

Trau-Med of Am., Inc. v. Allstate Ins.
Co. 967

Travelers Indem. Co. of Am. v.
Jarrells...920

Travelers Indem. Co. v. Dammann &
Co. 804

Travelers Ins. Co. v. Smith.....................704

Traver Lakes Cmty. Maintenance Ass'n v.
Douglas Co...89

Travers v. Spidell..................................1136

Travis Lumber Co. v. Deichman 857

Travis v. Alcon Labs., Inc. 708, 709

Travis v. City of Mesquite 339, 363

Travis v. Ziter..439

Traxler v. Varady..................................182

Trentecosta v. Beck..........................942, 977

Trevino v. Flash Cab Co. 451

Trevino v. MacSports, Inc......................1006

Trevino v. Ortega 1157

Trevino v. United States.........................552

Triangle Publ'ns, Inc. v. Chumley...........942

Triangle Publ'ns, Inc. v. Rohrlich.........1197

Trickett v. Ochs 739

Tri-County Investment Group, Ltd. v.
Southern States, Inc............................749

Tri-G, Inc. v. Burke, Bosselman &
Weaver......................................858, 1163

Trindle v. Wheeler 508

Triple E, Inc. v. Hendrix and Dail,
Inc. 807

Triple Elkhorn Min. Co. v. Anderson........95

Tripp v. United States 1006

Tri-State Hospital Supply Corp. v. United
States...1025

Tri-State Wholesale Associated Grocers,
Inc. v. Barrera 349

Tritchler v. West Virginia Newspaper Pub. Co. 1031
Trobaugh v. Sondag 1187, 1190
Trombetta v. Conkling 717
Tropeano v. Atlantic Monthly Co. 1007
Trotter v. Callens 365
Troup v. Fischer Steel Corp. 890
Troupe v. McAuley 511
Trout v. Sec'y of Navy 551
Troutman v. Facetglas, Inc. 1148
Troy, Town of v. Cheshire R.R. 99
Trujeque v. Service Merchandise Co. 305, 308, 309
Trull v. Volkswagen of America, Inc. 841
Truman v. Griese 568
Truman v. Montana Eleventh Judicial Dist. Ct. 889
Truman v. Thomas 520
Trustees of Univ. of D.C. v. Vossoughi 125, 126, 403
Trytko v. Hubbell, Inc. 1138, 1140
TSC Indus., Inc. v. Northway, Inc. 827
Tucci v. District of Columbia 737
Tucker v. Duncan 1034
Tucker v. Fischbein 946
Tucker v. Lombardo 216, 218, 415
Tucker v. Philadelphia Daily News 946
Tucson Elec. Power Co. v. Dooley-Jones & Assocs., Inc. 882
Tucson, City of v. Wondergem 693
Tufo v. Township of Old Bridge 395, 405
Tuite v. Corbitt 944
Tulkku v. Mackworth Rees Div. of Avis Indus., Inc. 393, 394
Tuman v. Genesis Assocs. 1057
Tunkl v. Regents of the Univ. of Cal. 412
Turbo Systems AG v. Turbousa, Inc. 1204
Turcotte v. Fell 419, 420, 424
Turf Lawnmower Repair, Inc. v. Bergen Record Corp. 984
Turley v. ISG Lackawanna, Inc. 701
Turnbull v. LaRose 1140
Turner Constr. Co. v. Scales 435
Turner v. Anderson 1178
Turner v. Big Lake Oil Co. 785, 789
Turner v. Bucher 654
Turner v. Davis 314
Turner v. General Motors Corp. 840
Turner v. Jordan 896
Turner v. KTRK Television, Inc. 950
Turner v. Mandalay Sports Entm't, LLC 421
Turner v. Ohio Bell Tel. Co. 487
Turner v. Welliver 976
Turpin v. Merrell Dow Pharms., Inc. 276, 296, 313, 673
Turpin v. Sortini 677
Tuskeegee, Ex parte City of 567
Tweedy v. Wright Ford Sales, Inc. 817
Twigg v. Hercules Corp. 1012
Two Pesos, Inc. v. Taco Cabana, Inc. 1199, 1201, 1203

TXI Operations, L.P. v. Perry 468
TXO Prod. Corp. v. Alliance Res. Corp. 866, 868
Ty Inc. v. Perryman 1198
Tyne v. Time Warner Entertainment Co., L.P. 1207
Tyrone Pac. Intern., Inc. v. MV Eurychili 111
Tyrrell v. Investment Associates, Inc. 483
Tyson Foods v. Con Agra, Inc. 1204
Tzolis v. Wolff 1153
UAW-GM Human Res. Ctr. v. KSL Recreation Corp. 1137
Uddin v. Embassy Suites Hotel 475
Uebelacker v. Paula Allen Holdings, Inc. 946
U-Haul Int'l, Inc. v. Waldrip 240
Uhl v. Columbia Broad. Sys., Inc. 1019
Uhler v. Doak 1180
Ultramares Corp. v. Touche 1072, 1121
Umansky v. ABC Ins. Co. 569
Umble v. Sandy McKie and Sons, Inc. 655
Underberg v. Southern Alarm, Inc. 456, 657
Underwood-Gary v. Mathews 881
Union Bank of Cal., N.A. v. Copeland Lumber Yards, Inc. 697
Union Carbide & Carbon Corp. v. Stapleton 651
Union Carbide Corp. v. Industrial Comm'n 918
Union Elec. Co., State ex rel. v. Dolan 603
Union Oil Co. v. Oppen 746, 1068
Union Pac. R.R. v. Burke 120
Union Park Mem. Chapel v. Hutt 629
Union Traction Co. of Indiana v. Berry 448
Uniroyal Goodrich Tire Co. v. Martinez 826
United Auto. Workers v. Johnson Controls, Inc. 673
United Blood Servs. v. Quintana 215, 497
United Concrete & Constr., Inc. v. Red-D-Mix Concrete, Inc. 1133
United Ins. Co. of Am. v. Murphy 940, 962, 998
United Leasing Corp. v. Thrift Ins. Corp. 1152
United States Dep't of Justice v. Reporters Comm. for Freedom of the Press 1009
United States Healthcare, Inc. v. Blue Cross of Greater Philadelphia 1114
United Zinc & Chemical Co. v. Britt 476
Universal Coops., Inc. v. AAC Flying Serv., Inc. 255
University of Alaska v. Shanti 478
University of Ariz. Health Scis. Ctr. v. Superior Court 682
University of Maryland Medical System Corp. v. Waldt 518
University of Miami v. Echarte 875

University of Notre Dame Du Lac v.
    Twentieth Century-Fox Film
    Corp. 1007
University of Pittsburgh v.
    Townsend 1127
University of Va. Health Servs. Found. v.
    Morris 597
Unzicker v. Kraft Food Ingredients
    Corp. 890
Uranga v. Federated Publ'ns Inc. 706,
    1017, 1018
Urban v. Grasser 480
Urban v. Wait's Supermarket, Inc. 280,
    472
Urie v. Thompson 430
Vacanti v. Master Electronics Corp. 139
Vahdat v. Holland 219, 221
Vahila v. Hall 1188
Valadez v. Emmis Commc'ns 706, 707
Valentine v. On Target, Inc. 655
Valentine v. Pioneer Chlor Alkali Co.,
    Inc. 787, 788
Valiant Ins. v. City of LaFayette 217
Valkilzaden, State v. 1055
Valley Baptist Med. Ctr. v. Stradley 540
Valley Development Co. v. Weeks 97
Vallinet v. Eskew 484
Vallinoto v. DiSandro 711, 1172
Valspar Refinish, Inc. v. Gaylord's,
    Inc. 1123
Van Beeck v. Sabine Towing Co. 689
Van Brunt v. Stoddard 889
Van Buren v. Pima Cmty. Coll. Dist. ... 1125
Van Dam v. Gay 1180
Van de Kamp v. Goldstein 1025
Van Der Stok v. Van Voorhees 1136
Van Deusen v. Norton Co. 806, 811
Van Eaton v. Fink 966, 975
Van Fossen v. MidAmerican Energy
    Co. 485
Van Gaasbeck v. Webatuck Cent. Sch. Dist.,
    No. 1 .... 400, 401
Van Gundy v. Wilson 961
Van Hook v. Anderson 279, 301
Van Houten v. Pritchard 778, 780
Van Lare v. Vogt, Inc. 804
Van Polen v. Wisch 1189
Van Sickle Constr. Co. v. Wachovia
    Commercial Mortg., Inc. 1126, 1135
Van Sickle v. Hallmark & Assocs.,
    Inc. 1091, 1098
Van v. Grand Casinos of Mississippi,
    Inc. 1030, 1032
Vancherie v. Siperly 140
Vandagriff v. J.C. Penney Co. 450
Vandemark v. McDonald's Corp. 766
Vanderbeek v. Vernon Corp. 1153
Vandermay v. Clayton 1169
Vandersluis v. Weil 1036
Vandervelden v. Victoria 60
Vanderwater v. Hatch 305
Vandeventer v. Vandeventer 121

Vanover v. Kansas City Life Ins. Co. 962
Vanvooren v. Astin 679
Varela ex rel. Nelson v. St. Elizabeth's
    Hosp. of Chicago, Inc. 246
Varner v. District of Columbia 570
Vasa v. Compass Medical, P.C. 519
Vascular Solutions, Inc. v. Marine Polymer
    Technologies, Inc. 1199
Vasquez v. Wal-Mart Stores, Inc. 293
Vassallo v. Baxter Healthcare Corp. 825
Vastano v. Algeier 1181
Vaughan v. Miller Bros. 782
Vaughn v. First Transit, Inc. 753
Vaughn v. Mississippi Baptist Medical
    Center 512
Vaughn v. Missouri Public Service Co. 98
Vaughn v. Nissan Motor Corporation in
    U.S.A., Inc. 356
Vaughn v. Nw. Airlines, Inc. 393
Vaughn v. Ruoff 177
Vautour v. Body Masters Sports Industries,
    Inc. 821
Vazquez v. Reeves 1025
Vazquez, Estate of v. Hepner 491, 492
Vazquez-Filippetti v. Banco Popular de
    Puerto Rico 216
Veazey v. Elmwood Plantation Associates,
    Ltd. 644
Veeco Instruments, Inc. v. Candido 114,
    126
Veeder v. Kennedy 1051
Vega v. Eastern Courtyard Assocs. 244, 245,
    468
Veilleux v. National Broad. Co. 706
Velarde v. Illinois Cent. R.R. Co. 855
Velazquez v. City of Hialeah 585
Velazquez v. Jiminez 523
Velsicol Chem. Corp. v. Rowe 322
Vendetto v. Sonat Offshore Drilling
    Co. 394
Vendrella v. Astriab Family Limited
    Partnership 780
Venuto v. Carella, Byrne, Bain, Gilfillan,
    Cecchi & Stewart, P.C. 1041
Venuto v. Owens-Corning Fiberglas
    Corp. 746
Verchot v. General Motors Corp. 1158
Verdier v. Verdier 594
Verdoljak v. Mosinee Paper Corp. 481
Vergara v. Doan 505, 509
Vern J. Oja Assocs. v. Washington Park
    Towers, Inc. 787
Verspyck v. Franco 1036
Verstraelen v. Kellog 75
VF Corp. v. Wrexham Aviation
    Corp. 1121, 1127
Vickery v. Ballentine 693
Vicnire v. Ford Motor Credit Co. 711
Vietnamese Fishermen's Ass'n v. Knights of
    the Ku Klux Klan 71
Vigil v. Franklin 3
Vilas v. Steavenson 374

Vilcinskas v. Johnson 496
Villazon v. Prudential Health Care Plan, Inc. 535, 536
Villines v. Tomerlin 135
Vincent v. Alden-Park Strathmoor, Inc. 863
Vincent v. Fairbanks Mem'l Hosp. 322
Vincent v. Lake Erie Transportation Co. 158
Vincent v. Stinehour 193
Viner v. Sweet 322, 1173
Vines v. Branch 107, 125
Vinson v. Linn-Mar Cmty. Sch. Dist. 999
Violette v. Smith and Nephew Dyonics, Inc. 817
Viox v. Weinberg 527
Virden v. Betts and Beer Const. Co. 341
Virginia Elec. & Power Co. v. Cogbill 916
Virginia, Ex parte 578
Vitale v. Henchey 64, 514
Vitanza v. Upjohn Co. 803, 832
Vitello v. Captain Bills Restaurant 808
Vito v. Inman 1102
Vito v. North Medical Family Physicians, P.C. 504
Vizetelly v. Mudie's Select Library, Ltd. 942
Vodopest v. MacGregor 409, 411, 413
Voelbel v. Town of Bridgewater 578
Vogel v. Grant-Lafayette Elec. Co-op. ... 735, 737
Vogt v. Murraywood Swim and Racquet Club 462, 463, 466
Voilas v. General Motors Corp. 1116
Volpe v. Gallagher 369, 485
Volpe v. IKO Industries, Ltd. 822
Von der Heide v. Com., Dep't of Transp. 374
Voorhees v. Guyan Mach. Co. 1092, 1104
Voris v. Molinaro 720
Vortex Fishing Sys., Inc. v. Foss 714
Voss v. Black & Decker Mfg. Co. 815
Vossen v. Astrue 924
Voyles v. Sandia Mortgage Corp. 955
Vredenburg v. Sedgwick CMS 916
Vredeveld v. Clark 407
Vreeland v. Ferrer 441
Vultaggio v. Yasko 968
W. R. Grimshaw Co. v. Nevil C. Withrow Co. 1149
W.E. Stephens Mfg. Co. v. Goldberg 118
W.J.A. v. D.A. 990, 998
Waddell v. New River Co. 463
Wadler v. City of New York 605, 610, 611
Wagenblast v. Odessa Sch. Dist. No. 105–157–166J 413
Wagenmann v. Adams 1183, 1186, 1189
Waggoner v. City of Woodburn 482
Waggoner v. Troutman Oil Co., Inc. 611
Wagner v. Clark Equipment Co. 844
Wagner v. International Ry. 348
Wagner v. Miskin 966

Wagner v. Smith 594, 595
Wagner v. State 64
Wagon Mound II, Overseas Tankship (U.K.), Ltd. v. Miller Steamship Co. 348
Wait v. Travelers Indem. Co. 914, 915
Waite v. Waite 592
Waits v. Frito-Lay, Inc. 1208
Wakulich v. Mraz 627, 663
Wald v. Grainger 855
Walderbach v. Archdiocese of Dubuque, Inc. 764
Waldman v. Levine 1170
Waldon v. Marshall 190
Walk v. Ring 438, 439
Walker Rogge, Inc. v. Chelsea Title & Guaranty Co. 1074
Walker v. Brown 858
Walker v. City of Huntsville 707
Walker v. Cronin 1094
Walker v. General Elec. Co. 810
Walker v. Grand Cent. Sanitation, Inc. 962, 998
Walker v. Kelly 60
Walker v. Kiousis 989
Walker v. Mart 677
Walker v. Medtronic, Inc. 847
Walker v. Percy 1118
Walker v. Rinck 676
Walker v. Spokane, Portland & Seattle Ry. 397
Wall v. Stout 506
Wallace v. City of Atlantic City 161
Wallace v. Dean 569
Wallace v. Ohio Dep't of Commerce 252, 572
Wallace v. Stringer 75
Waller v. Smith 462
Walling v. Allstate Ins. Co. 531
Walls v. Oxford Management Co. 644
Wal-Mart Stores, Inc. v. Alexander 719
Wal-Mart Stores, Inc. v. Bathe 155
Wal-Mart Stores, Inc. v. Blackford 1035
Wal-Mart Stores, Inc. v. Cockrell 155
Wal-Mart Stores, Inc. v. Crossgrove 860
Wal-Mart Stores, Inc. v. Johnson 1157
Wal-Mart Stores, Inc. v. Lee 1019
Wal-Mart Stores, Inc. v. Lerma 474
Wal-Mart Stores, Inc. v. Mitchell 154
Wal-Mart Stores, Inc. v. Reinholtz 915
Wal-Mart Stores, Inc. v. Samara Bros. 1195, 1199, 1201, 1203
Wal-Mart Stores, Inc. v. Spates 265, 470
Wal-Mart Stores, Inc. v. Sturges, III 1098, 1100, 1102, 1103, 1109
Wal-Mart Stores, Inc. v. Wright 287
Walsh v. Johnston 96
Walski v. Tiesenga 296, 503
Walston v. Monumental Life Ins. Co. 1140
Walter v. Wal-Mart Stores, Inc. 394
Walters v. Rinker 497
Walton v. Tull 884

Wampler v. Higgins................................ 995
Wangsness v. Builders Cashway, Inc..... 835
Wankier v. Crown Equip. Corp.............. 821
Wanner v. Getter Trucking.................... 283
Ward One Democrats, Inc. v.
  Woodland 1195
Ward v. Forrester Day Care, Inc. ... 305, 544
Ward v. K-Mart Corp. 280, 367
Ward v. Mount Calvary Lutheran
  Church... 302
Ware v. City of Chicago........................ 570
Ware v. Timmons 753
Ware v. Ware.. 1143
Warner Fruehauf Trailer Co. v.
  Boston...................................... 815, 820
Warner v. McCaughan 687
Warner v. Simmons...................... 470, 471
Warren v. Williams 1166
Warsham v. James Muscatello, Inc....... 384
Wartnick v. Moss & Barnett................. 1170
Waschak v. Moffat................................ 737
Washburn v. Klara...................... 181, 515
Washburn v. Lavoie.............................. 974
Washington & G. R. Co. v. Hickey.......... 357
Washington Metro. Area Transit Auth. v.
  Jeanty... 1111
Washington Metro. Area Transit Auth. v.
  Reading 448
Washington Mut. Bank v. Houston
  Windcrest West Rd. I, L.P................. 1140
Washington State Physicians Ins. Exch. &
  Ass'n v. Fisons Corp. 1083
Washington Suburban Sanitary Comm'n v.
  CAE-Link Corp. 737
Washington v. City of Georgetown 1013
Washington v. Davis 587
Wassell v. Adams 278, 385
Wasson v. Schubert 1116
Waste Mgmt. of Tex., Inc. v. Texas Disposal
  Sys. Landfill, Inc...................... 953, 1000
Water Pik, Inc. v. Med-Systems, Inc. ... 1196
Waters v. Biesecker............................. 566
Waters v. Dennis Simmons Lumber
  Co... 91
Waterson v. General Motors Corp. 405,
  407
Waterton v. Linden Motor Inc. 239
Watkins v. Fromm................................ 436
Watson v. Brown 148
Watson v. Kentucky & Indiana Bridge &
  Railroad Co. 362
Watson v. Navistar Int'l Transp.
  Corp.. 281
Watt v. Longsdon................................. 975
Watts v. Smith.............................. 352, 881
Waugh v. Traxler........................... 250, 259
Wausau Tile, Inc. v. County Concrete
  Corp.. 1081
Wawanesa Mutual Insurance Co. v.
  Matlock... 101
Wayment v. Clear Channel Broad.,
  Inc.. 981, 993

Weaver v. Brush....................................774
Weaver v. Lentz 394, 400
Weaver v. Ward.....................................193
Weaver, Ex Parte 918
Webb v. Call Publ'g Co..........................1003
Webb v. City and Borough of Sitka 478
Webb v. Jarvis.......................................503
Webb v. Navistar Intern. Transp.
  Corp..837
Webb v. Omni Block, Inc. 296
Webb v. Virginia-Carolina Chemical
  Co..99, 100
Webbier v. Thoroughbred Racing Protective
  Bureau, Inc...71
Weber v. Lancaster Newspapers, Inc......981
Webster v. City of Houston.....................583
Webster v. Culbertson 462
Wegner v. Milwaukee Mutual Ins.
  Co..161
Weidenfeller v. Star & Garter 896
Weigel v. Broad 588
Weigel v. Lee 693
Weigel v. SPX Corp. 820
Weil v. Seltzer 691
Weinhold v. Wolff............. 738, 739, 741, 749
Weinstein v. Prudential Prop. & Cas. Ins.
  Co..870
Weir v. Citcorp Nat'l Servs., Inc.............964
Weirich v. Weirich................................1054
Weiss v. Bal 220
Weiss v. Hodge 894
Weiss v. Rojanasathit 504
Weitz v. Green.............................857, 958
Weitzmann v. A.L. Barber Asphalt
  Co..144
Welch v. Southland Corp. 880
Welge v. Planters Lifesavers Co......806, 811
Weller v. American Broad. Cos., Inc. 948
Wells Fargo Bank v. Arizona Laborers,
  Teamsters & Cement Masons Local No.
  395 Pension Trust Fund....................1099
Wells v. Schuster-Hax Nat'l Bank 1117
Wells v. Tallahassee Mem'l Reg'l Med. Ctr.,
  Inc..889
Welsh Mfg., Div. of Textron, Inc. v.
  Pinkerton's, Inc. 657
Welsh v. Todd...............................741, 742
Wendt v. Host Intern., Inc. 1209
Werne v. Exec. Women's Golf Ass'n 205,
  473
Werner v. Varner, Stafford & Seaman,
  P.A...502
Wesche v. Mecosta Cnty. Rd.
  Comm'n..720
Wessman v. Scandrett 285
West of England Shipowner's Mut. Prot. &
  Indem. Ass'n, United States v. 197
West Town Plaza Assocs. v. Wal-Mart
  Stores, Inc..96
West v. Atkins 582
West v. East Tennessee Pioneer Oil
  Co..654

West v. King's Dep't Store, Inc. 82
West v. Western Cas. & Sur. Co. 863
West Virginia CWP Fund v. Stacy 929
Westbrook v. City of Jackson 574
Westbrook v. Penley 986
Westby v. Gorsuch 1125
Westchester Media v. PRL USA
　Holdings, Inc. 1196
Western Fiberglass, Inc. v. Kirton,
　McConkie and Bushnell 1177
Western Forms, Inc. 1204
Western Idaho Production Credit Ass'n v.
　Simplot Feed Lots, Inc. 123
Western Mass. Blasting Corp. v.
　Metropolitan & Cas. Ins. Co. 1069
Western Techs., Inc. v. Sverdrup & Parcel,
　Inc. 1114
Westfall v. Erwin 580
Westfield Dev. Co. v. Rifle Inv.
　Assocs. 1104
Weston v. Kim's Dollar Store 847
Wexler v. Hecht 511
WFND, LLC v. Fargo Marc, LLC 391
Whalen v. Connelly 1041
Whalen v. On-Deck, Inc. 864
Wheelden v. Lowell 152
Wheeler v. White 1177
Whipple v. American Fork Irrigation
　Co. 475
Whisnant v. United States 555, 557
Whitcomb v. Hearst Corp. 1003
Whitcomb v. Huffington 1056
White Lighting Co. v. Wolfson 1043,
　1044, 1045
White Plains Coat & Apron Co., Inc. v.
　Cintas Corp. 1098, 1103, 1104, 1105
White v. Blue Cross & Blue Shield of Mass.,
　Inc. 943
White v. Brommer 707
White v. Drivas 118
White v. Edmond 609, 613
White v. Ford Motor Co. 863, 873
White v. Fraternal Order of Police 949
White v. Georgia Power Co. 280
White v. Leimbach 518, 521
White v. Morris 137
White v. Muniz 42, 65
White v. Revco Discount Drug Centers,
　Inc. 759
White v. Samsung Electronics America,
　Inc. 1208
White v. State 605, 606, 609
White v. Taylor Distrib. Co. 219
White v. University of Idaho 64, 67
White v. Wilkerson 960
White v. Wyeth 1130
White, State v. 142
Whitefield v. Stewart 783
Whiteheart v. Waller 1178
Whitehurst v. Showtime Networks,
　Inc. 1007
Whitley v. Andersen 61, 62

Whitlock v. Smith 399
Whitlow v. Board of Educ. of Kanawha
　County 433, 435
Whitlow v. Seaboard Air Line R.R.
　Co. 605
Whitner v. State 675
Whitt v. Silverman 213, 484
Whittaker v. Sandford 77
Whittaker v. Stangvick 93
Whitten v. Cox 156
Wickens v. Oakwood Healthcare Sys. 334
Wickliffe v. Sunrise Hospital, Inc. 529
Widell v. Holy Trinity Catholic
　Church 599
Widmyer v. Southeast Skyways, Inc. 302
Wieghmink v. Harrington 284
Wiegmann, State v. 137
Wiehagen v. Borough of North
　Braddock 567
Wiener v. Southcoast Childcare Centers,
　Inc. 363, 364, 641
Wiersma v. Maple Leaf Farms 671
Wieseler v. Sisters of Mercy Health
　Corp. 466
Wightman v. Consolidated Rail Corp. 399
Wilber v. Owens-Corning Fiberglass
　Corp. 441
Wilcox v. Plummer's Executors 1180
Wilcox v. Vermeulen 692
Wild Wild West Social Club, Inc., Ex
　parte 361
Wilden v. Neumann 470
Wilder v. Gardner 68
Wilder v. Johnson Publ'g Co., Inc. 946,
　948
Wildstein v. New York Post Corp. 949
Wiles v. Webb 221
Wiley v. County of San Diego 1186, 1188
Wiley v. General Motors Acceptance
　Corp. 116
Wiley v. Redd 609
Wilhoit v. WCSC, Inc. 962
Wilke v. Woodhouse Ford, Inc. 365
Wilkin Elevator v. Bennett State
　Bank 1104
Wilkins v. City of Haverhill 480
Wilkins v. Marshalltown Medical and
　Surgical Center 530, 770
Wilkinson v. United States 107, 708
Wilkinson v. Vesey 516, 519
Will v. Michigan Dep't of State Police 586
Willan v. Columbia County 1014
Williams Elec. Games, Inc. v.
　Garrity 1145, 1146
Williams ex rel. Raymond v. Wal-Mart
　Stores East, L.P. 244, 361
Williams Ford, Inc. v. Hartford Courant
　Co. 1131
Williams v. BASF Catalysts LLC 1158
Williams v. Bashman 1184
Williams v. Davis 484, 485
Williams v. District Court 962

Williams v. Eight Judicial Dist. Court of State, ex rel. County of Clark.............. 512
Williams v. Gannett Satellite Information Network, Inc. 952
Williams v. Goodwin 778, 779
Williams v. Hays 226
Williams v. Kearbey 58
Williams v. Kenney 966
Williams v. KFC Nat'l Mgmt. Co. 304, 309
Williams v. Lucy Webb Hayes Nat'l Training Sch. for Deaconesses and Missionaries 512
Williams v. Manchester 334, 671, 686
Williams v. Maulis............................... 1181
Williams v. Mayor & City Council of Baltimore 572
Williams v. Medical Coll. of Pa. 429
Williams v. Philip Morris Inc.................. 873
Williams v. Polgar 1124
Williams v. River Lakes Ranch Development Corporation 101
Williams v. Southern Calif. Gas Co. 615
Williams v. State Dep't of Revenue 917
Williams v. Tharp.................................. 980
Williams v. Thude 893
Williams v. Tysinger 781
Williams v. United States 552
Williams v. University Med. Ctr. of S. Nev. 1112
Williamson ex rel. Lipper Convertibles, L.P. v. PriceWaterhouse Coopers LLP 436
Williamson v. Amrani 512
Williamson v. Bennett............................ 732
Williamson v. Hosp. Serv. Dist. No. 1 of Jefferson.. 527
Williamson v. Mazda Motor of America, Inc.. 846
Williamson v. Smith............................... 418
Williamson v. Waldman 726
Williard v. Parsons Hill P'ship 492, 1141
Willing v. Mazzocone............................ 1003
Willis v. Foster..................................... 859
Willis v. Gami Golden Glades, LLC........ 722
Willis v. Manning 294
Willis v. Midland Finance Co.................. 118
Willis v. Parker..................................... 1046
Willis v. Westerfield 218, 219, 403
Willis v. Wu 677
Willner, People v. 134
Willow Inn, Inc. v. Public Serv. Mut. Ins. Co.. 871
Wilschinsky v. Medina 500
Wilson v. Amoco Corp. 744
Wilson v. Arkansas................................ 142
Wilson v. Bernet...................... 1024, 1055
Wilson v. City of Decatur 781
Wilson v. City of Eagan.......................... 230
Wilson v. El-Daief.................................. 432
Wilson v. Freitas 1014, 1020
Wilson v. Interlake Steel Co. 89, 90

Wilson v. Kansas State University 481
Wilson v. Kotzebue................................. 227
Wilson v. Kuenzi 679
Wilson v. Layne.................................... 1010
Wilson v. Lindamood Farms, Inc. 416
Wilson v. Meyer..................................... 981
Wilson v. Price...................................... 582
Wilson v. Sears, Roebuck & Co. 723
Wilson v. Seiter 584
Wilson v. Sibert.................................... 219
Wilson v. State Farm Ins....................... 915
Wilson v. Vukasin 401
Wilson, Estate of Massad ex rel. v. Granzow... 663
Winbun v. Moore................................... 431
Winding River Village Condo. Ass'n, Inc. v. Barnett.. 696
Windsong Enterprises, Inc. v. Upton 1097
Winfrey v. GGP Ala Moana LLC............. 306
Winn v. Gilroy 595
Winn v. Inman 132
Winniczek v. Nagelberg 1188
Winschel v. Brown 353, 402
Winter v. Brenner Tank, Inc. 810
Winter v. DC Comics.................. 1207, 1208
Winters v. Wright 302
Wippert v. Burlington Northern Inc. 153
Wirth v. Ehly.. 480
Wiseman v. Hallahan 626
Witherell v. Weimer............................... 511
Witmat Development Corp. v. Dickison 486
Witthauer v. Burkhart Roentgen, Inc. 841
Witthoeft, Estate of v. Kiskaddon 660
Wittorf v. City of New York..................... 566
Witzke v. City of Bismarck............ 966, 1024
WJLA-TV v. Levin 1021
Wojciechowicz v. United States............... 552
Wolf v. Wolf 1053, 1054, 1055
Wolfe v. Baube 398
Wolfe v. City of Wheeling 624
Wolfe v. Schaefer.................... 1010, 1013
Wolfinger v. Cheche 1039
Wolicki-Gables v. Arrow Intern., Inc. 846
Wollen v. DePaul Health Ctr.................. 332
Wolski v. Wandel 1168, 1171, 1174
Wood v. General Motors Corp. 846
Wood v. Groh.. 217
Wood v. Hustler Magazine, Inc. 1022
Wood v. McGrath, North, Ullin & Kratz, P.C..1170
Wood v. Mercedes-Benz of Oklahoma City... 472
Wood v. Mobil Chem. Co........................ 854
Wood v. Neuman 708
Wood v. Old Trapper Taxi 828
Wood v. RIH Acquisitions MS II, LLC 470
Wood v. University of Utah Med. Ctr. 679
Wood v. Wayman 693
Wood v. Wood 1054

Wood v. Wyeth-Ayerst Labs................... 854
Woodall v. Avalon Care Center-Federal
  Way, LLC 694
Woodard v. Custer................................... 511
Woodfield v. Providence Hosp................ 970
Woodman v. Kera, LLC........................... 414
Woodmen of the World, United No. 3 v.
  Jordan 749
Woodruff v. Gitlow................................. 499
Woodruff v. Tomlin............................... 1170
Woods v. Burlington N. & Santa Fe
  Ry. 247
Woods v. City of Warren 610
Woods v. Cole................................ 885, 898
Woods v. Lancet..................................... 669
Woods v. Schmitt................................... 438
Woods v. Town of Marion...................... 566
Woods-Leber v. Hyatt Hotels of Puerto Rico,
  Inc.. 782
Woodty v. West's Lamplighter Motels.... 453
Woolley v. Henderson 515, 516
Woolsey v. Nat'l Transp. Safety Bd. 449
World Trade Ctr. Bombing Litig.,
  In re... 894
World Trade Ctr. Lower Manhattan
  Disaster Site Litig., In re............. 431, 604
World Wide Prosthetic Supply, Inc. v.
  Mikulsky 1205
Worsham v. Nix..................................... 1172
Worthy v. Collagen Corp. 847
Wright v. Bachmurski........................... 942
Wright v. Brooke Group Ltd. 799,
  802, 809
Wright v. Brown 254
Wright v. Coleman 606
Wright v. Ford Motor Co. 844
Wright v. Grove Sun Newspaper Co.,
  Inc.. 193, 978
Wright v. Masonite Corp........................ 737
Wright v. Midwest Old Settlers and
  Threshers Assn. 449
Wright v. N.Y. City Transit Auth. 391
Wright v. United States 303
Wright v. Williams 1169
Wulf v. Kunnath 63
Wuterich v. Murtha......................... 580, 581
Wyant v. Crouse 101
Wyatt v. McDermott.............................. 1055
Wyatt v. Wehmueller 1042
Wyeth v. Levine...................... 441, 442, 845
Wyke v. Polk County School Board 589,
  649
Wyoming Workers' Comp. Div. v.
  Harris.. 916
Wyso v. Full Moon Tide, LLC 483
Wysocki v. Reed..................................... 329
Wyszomierski v. Siracusa 518
Y.H. Invs., Inc. v. Godales...................... 890
Yacubian v. United States 1033
Yaklevich v. Kemp, Schaeffer & Rowe Co.,
  L.P.A..................................... 1043, 1046
Yamaha Motor Co., U.S.A. v. Arnoult 828

Yancey v. Maestri 227
Yania v. Bigan..............................615, 616
Yarbro v. Hilton Hotels Corp................434
Yarbro, Ltd. v. Missoula Fed. Credit
  Union 128
Yarelli v. Goff.......................................581
Yath v. Fairview Clinics, N.P. 1014
Yauger v. Skiing Enters., Inc. 411, 412
Ybarra v. Spangard........................306, 309
Yeager v. Cingular Wireless LLC.........1007
Yeager v. Hurt.......................................157
Yeakey v. Hearst Commc'ns, Inc............994
Yerkes v. Asberry...................................400
Yeung v. Maric 1021
Yoder v. Cotton.......................................55
Yohe v. Nugent......................................978
Yommer v. McKenzie 788
Yonaty v. Mincolla 946
Yoneda v. Tom.......................................420
York v. Rush-Presbyterian-St. Luke's
  Medical Ctr...............................772, 773
York v. Story.......................................1010
Yorke v. Novant Health, Inc...................304
Yost v. Miner...232
Young v. First United Bank of
  Bellevue 955
Young v. Flood......................................260
Young v. Harrison.................................147
Young v. Melrose Granite Co. 916
Young v. Paxton.............................463, 464
Young v. Salt Lake City School Dist......647
Young v. Sherwin-Williams Co. 610
Young v. The Morning Journal 979
Young v. U-Haul Co. of D.C...................246
Young v. United States...........................556
Young, People v.....................................137
Youngberg v. Romeo 646, 649
Youngbey v. March 586
Yount v. Deibert............................326, 880
Yount v. Johnson...................................425
Youssoupoff v. Metro-Goldwyn-Mayer
  Pictures, Ltd..947
Yovino v. Big Bubba's BBQ, LLC 717
Yowell v. Piper Aircraft Corp. 687, 691,
  856
Yukon Equip. v. Fireman's Fund Ins.
  Co. 787, 792
Zacchini v. Scripps-Howard Broad.
  Co. 1008, 1208
Zacher v. Budd Co.................................289
Zafft v. Eli Lilly & Co............................330
Zager v. Dimilia 857
Zak v. Zifferblatt...................................527
Zamos v. Stroud 1037, 1176
Zamstein v. Marvasti.............................1057
Zanakis-Pico v. Cutter Dodge, Inc.........1139
Zaninovich v. American Airlines, Inc......859
Zapata v. Burns.....................................434
Zaputil v. Cowgill..................................560
Zarcone v. Perry....................................866
Zaslow v. Kroenert.......................105, 114
Zastrow v. Journal Commc'ns, Inc. 1144

Zatuchni v. Secretary of Health & Human
  Servs... 929
Zaza v. Marquess and Nell, Inc. 340
Zechman v. Merrill Lynch, Pierce, Fenner &
  Smith, Inc... 1021
Zehr v. Haugen....................................... 682
Zelenko v. Gimbel Bros. 623
Zelig v. County of Los Angeles................ 564
Zell v. Meek 715
Zellmer v. Zellmer 593, 594
Zeni v. Anderson..................................... 251
Zenith Ins. Co. v. Cozen O'Connor....... 1166,
  1176
Zeno v. Pine Plains Cent. School Dist. ... 647
Zeran v. America Online, Inc.................. 971
Zerby v. Warren....................................... 401
Zero Wholesale Gas Co., Inc. v.
  Stroud.. 787
Zeroulis v. Hamilton Am. Legion
  Assocs. 398, 400
Ziarko v. Soo Line R.R............................ 242
Ziegler v. City of Millbrook 574
Zielinski v. Kotsoris................................ 436
Zielinski, Matter of Estate of 172
Zima v. North Colonie Central School
  District 626
Zimmerman v. Dane Cnty....................... 717
Zimmerman v. Firstier Bank.................. 129
Zinda v. Louisiana Pac. Corp. 981
Ziobron v. Crawford............................... 1025
Zipkin v. Freeman 179
Zipusch v. LA Workout, Inc. 411
Zirkle v. Winkler 765
Zivich v.. 414
Zoeller v. American Fam. Mut. Ins.
  Co... 962
Zok v. Collins 1171
Zoppo v. Homestead Ins. Co.................. 1147
Zsigo v. Hurley Medical Ctr. 758, 761
Zuchowicz v. United States..... 326, 329, 521
Zuther v. Schild 463
Zwiren v. Thompson............................... 343

Index

References are to page numbers, including footnotes. If the topic continues or resumes on immediately succeeding pages, the reference is to the page on which discussion begins.

ABNORMALLY DANGEROUS ACTIVITIES
See STRICT LIABILITY

ABSOLUTE LIABILITY
See STRICT LIABILITY

ABUSE OF PROCESS
Generally, 1042
act after process requirement, 1045
coercive use of process for improper purpose, 1044
damages, 1025, 1043
excessive attachment, 1044
public entities, 562
punitive damages, 1026
SLAPP suits, 1046
wrongful lis pendens, 1044

ACT OF GOD
meaning and effects, 364

ACTS AND OMISSIONS
See also NON-ACTION
act defined, 68
civil rights torts, 588, 649
no-duty-to-rescue rule, 615
omission embedded in act, 618

ACTUAL CAUSE
See FACTUAL CAUSE

ADMINISTRATIVE PROCEEDINGS
defamation privileges in, 966
malicious prosecution based upon, 1037

ADMIRALTY AND MARITIME TORTS
constitutional allocation of jurisdiction in, 192
employer liability for maintenance and cure, 911
invitee, licensee, trespasser categories rejected in, 478
wrongful death, 685, 686

ADVERSE POSSESSION
trespass action to protect, 91

AFFIRMATIVE DEFENSES
burden of proof, 294
effect and meaning, 40

AGENCY
See VICARIOUS LIABILITY

AIDING, ABETTING, PROCURING OR RISKING OTHERS' TORTS
battery, causing another to commit, 68
false imprisonment, causing others to commit, 73
interference with family, 1054
malicious prosecution, instigation of, 1027
negligently causing another's battery, FTCA immunity, 563
negligently risking another's intentional tort, apportionment, 895
duty, 633
scope of liability (proximate cause), 361
negligently risking another's negligent tort, proximate cause, 365
procuring another's tort, 68
trespass to land, causing another's, 86

AIRCRAFT
See AVIATION

ALCOHOL AND SUBSTANCES OF ABUSE
See also DUTY TO PROTECT FROM THIRD PERSONS AND FROM SELF-HARM
Civil Damage Acts or Dram Shop Statutes, 661
drug testing in employment, 1012
illegal sales, negligence per se, 244
providers,
    alcohol, duty to protect from intoxicated patron, 661
    alcohol, duty to drinking patron, 662
    alcohol, proximate cause of drinker-caused injury, 362, 371
    illegal drugs, duties of, 664
social hosts providing, duties of, 663

ALIENATION OF AFFECTIONS
abolition of the tort, 1050
alternative claims, 1051
child or parent, 1056
interference with marital relationship, 1049

ANIMALS
abnormally dangerous domestic, 779
dangerous,
    personal injury, 779
    proximate cause limits on strict liability, 792
dogs,
    releasing foxhounds, trespass, 88
    standard of care for owner, 217
domestic, 779
escaping from land, 485
harm to without reduction in value, 311
killing in defense of property, 139
landlord's liability for tenant's, 656
livestock,
    fencing-out rule, 778
    highways, on, 779
    trespassing; strict liability, 778
wild; strict liability of keepers, 782

APPORTIONMENT OF LIABILITY
>See also COMPARATIVE FAULT OR
>>RESPONSIBILITY;
>>CONTRIBUTION;
>>INDEMNITY

>Generally, 877

appeals claiming errors in apportionment, 895
avoidable consequences as causal apportionment, 403
causal vs. fault apportionment, 389, 878
"comparative responsibility," 891
conduct subject to apportionment, 891
contribution, 882
defendant risking intentional harm by another, 895
defendant under duty to protect plaintiff from another's negligence, 898
defendants, between, 877
distinct or divisible injuries, 315
hybrid systems, 902
immune and non-party tortfeasors,
>generally, 888
>employers, 890
>non-parties' fault compared, 889
>statutory provisions, 888
>strategies involving, 888
indemnity, 882
indivisible injury,
>comparative fault apportionment, 406
>joint and several liability, 878, 881
intentional torts, comparison to negligence, 893, 895
joint and several liability,
>generally, 878
>contribution, 882
>criticisms, 883
>current status of, 881
>for economic damages only, 879
>indemnity, 882
>traditional rules, 881
>with reallocation, 879, 901
market share liability, 330
negligence, comparison to intentional tort, 893, 895
overview, 877
policy choices, 880
protecting plaintiff from another's negligence, 898
reckless or intentional tortious conduct,
>apportionment of, 891
risking intentional harm by another, 895
Restatement (Third) of Apportionment approach, 891
several liability,
>generally, 879
>effects of adopting, 886
>joint and several "exceptions," 885
>modern trend towards, 884
tortious conduct and parties included, 884
standards of apportionment, 893
strict liability, apportionment of, 891
threshold percentages, use of, 902
type of tort or type of damages variations, 903
workers' compensation,
>employer and tortfeasor, 919

multiple employers, 918

ARREST
>See also CIVIL RIGHTS; OFFICERS

civil rights claims, 583
defined, 155
police officers, by, without a warrant, 156
private persons, by, 155
privilege,
>defeating defense of property privilege, 141
>exceeding, 156
probable cause, 156
self-defense against, 136
warrant, 156
without a warrant, 156

ARSON
firefighter's claim against wanton fire-setter, 610
foreseeability of arson or fire, 364
gasoline container in violation of statute, 254

ASBESTOS
abnormal danger strict liability rejected, 788
emotional harm from exposure, 725
exposure and factual cause, 315
mass tort claims, 11, 905
products liability,
>design defects, 806
>supplier's duty to warn employers, 832
statute of limitations, discovery rule, 847

ASSAULT
>Generally, 69

apprehension of imminent touching, 70
battery, connection to, 69
civil rights analogue, 583
conditional threats, 72
consent and, 69
crime and, 72
damages, 70, 82
defense of property, threat of deadly force, 140
elements of simple assault, 69
emotional distress and, 72
examples, 70
fear vs. apprehension of contact, 70
federal governmental immunity, 562
imminence of threat, 71
intent, 70
prisoner claim for under Eighth Amendment, 584
public entities, 562
reasonableness of apprehension, 71
self-defense by, 132
stalking, 73
terminology, 69
words alone, 71

ASSUMPTION OF RISK
>See also CONTRACTUAL
>>LIMITATIONS ON LIABILITY

>Generally, 409

abnormally dangerous activities, 793
abolishing doctrine of, 415, 418, 421
animals, 793
bailees, 413
bar to recovery; traditional rule, 409, 414
caregivers and, 413

carriers and public utilities; contractual
    limitations on liability, 413
children, by, 415
coming to the nuisance, 740
comparative fault,
        merging, 418
        version of, 415, 420
consent,
        as, 409, 415, 419
        barring recovery, as, 415
        implied, 415
        relieving defendant of a duty in
            comparative fault regime, 415
contractual limitations on liability, 409
contributory negligence connection, 415
defamation, public figures, 987, 992
duty of defendant limited by, 416
employment risks, 416
express,
        generally, 409
        ambiguities in contract, 411
        bargaining power, role of, 412
        broad clauses, 411
        clarity of, requirements for, 411
        conspicuous language requirement, 411
        contractual limitations, 410
        effect to bar claim, 409
        employment context, 413
        gross negligence and recklessness, 410
        parental waivers of child's claim, 414
        public policy limitations, 412
        recreational activities, 410, 413
        scope of release, 411
        statutes, 414
fellow servant rule, 417, 912
firefighters, 605
human research or experimentation, 413
hunters, 425
implied; generally, 414
intentional torts, 410, 424
jaywalker, Prosser's, 418
knowledge of risk requirement, 417
landowners, 416
medical malpractice, consent to negligence, 412
no-duty, as, 416, 418, 420
no-negligence, as, 416, 418, 420
primary, 420
products liability, 413, 835
Restatement Third, abolition of implied form in,
    415
schools, 413
scope of the assumption, 409, 411
secondary, 420
sports,
        generally, 422
        consent and parties' expectations, 425
        duty of care, 422
        inherent risks, 422
        intentional harms, 424
        participants, 423
        policy, limitations based on, 425
        recklessness standard, 424
        risks assumed, 423
        spectators, 422
strict liability cases, in, 793

voluntariness requirement, 417

ATTACHMENT
See WRONGFUL ATTACHMENT OR LEVY

ATTORNEY'S FEES
American rule, 43
parties pay own, 43
wrongful civil litigation, 1039

ATTORNEYS
See LEGAL MALPRACTICE

ATTRACTIVE NUISANCE
foreseeability, role of, 476
general rule, 475
harmful potential, 477
origin of rule, 475
"reason to know" standard, 476
recreational use statutes, under, 480
risk-utility balancing, 477

AUTOMOBILES
blackouts or the like while driving, 224
children driving, standard of care, 236
intoxication and, 232
negligence per se, 243
stop, look, and listen rule, 10

AUTONOMY
battery law protecting, 62
consent rules and, 168, 173, 181
emotional harm claims and, 681
informed consent, 513
mother's liability for prenatal injury to fetus,
        and, 674
privacy and, 1005
right to reject medical treatment, 514
transferred intent and, 81
wrongful birth or pregnancy and, 677

AVIATION
emergency doctrine and, 218
overflights, nuisance or trespass, 94, 734
wrongful death claims, 686

AVOIDABLE CONSEQUENCES
causal apportionment rule, as, 403
comparative fault and, 403
seatbelts, failure to use, 406
wrongful birth, life, or pregnancy cases, 682

BAD FAITH
absolute privilege not destroyed by, 578
breach of contract, tort liability, 1089
conversion, 110, 113, 115
deliberate indifference standard, civil rights
        cases, 584
Eighth Amendment claims, prison official's good
        faith, 584
Fourth Amendment, officer's good faith
        irrelevant, 583
qualified immunity destroyed by, 579

BAILMENT
bailee's burden of proof upon non-return, 118
contractual limits on liability, 413
conversion by bailees, 115, 116, 118, 120, 1154
duties of bailees, 117, 191

BATTERY
> Generally, 60

act required, 68

autonomy rights protected, 62

bodily contact, 67

civil rights analogue, 583

consent, 63, 163, 167

damages, 61

direct vs. indirect harm, 61

disease communicated, as, 176

dual vs. single intent, 64

duty to protect from others, 69

elements, 60

extended liability for, 80

extension of plaintiff's body, touching an, 68

federal governmental immunity, 562

Fourth Amendment civil rights claims compared, 583

harmful or offensive touching, 61, 62, 81

inaction vs. "act," 68

informed consent and, 181, 514

intent; connection to consent, 63

intent required, 60, 63

intent to touch vs. intent to harm, 64

medical procedure not consented to, 61, 181

necessity privilege, 158

negligent, a solecism, 61

negligently permitting another's, government immunity, 563

offensive touching, 61, 62, 75

poisons administered, 67

policy, 62

privilege, discipline of children, 138

protecting a third person, 137

public entities, 562

purposeful intent, 64

right to refuse medical treatment, 62

seduction and, 176

single vs. dual intent, 64

self-defense against, 136

smoke, bodily contact by, 67

social usage, 61

strict liability or not, 65

substantial certainty intent, 64

tobacco smoking, 67

touch, causing other persons or objects to, 68

touching required, 64

touchings consistent with social usages, 61

transferred intent in, 80

trespass lineage, 61

***BIVENS* ACTION**
civil rights claim against federal employee, 581

BONA FIDE PURCHASER
conversion, 110, 115

BOND
conversion, subject of, 111

provisional remedies, replevin, 127

provisional remedies, wrongful civil litigation compared, 1041

BOYCOTT
free speech and, 1105

interference with contract, 1105

BRAINWASHING
false imprisonment and, 77

BROWN V. KENDALL
fault standard adopted, 29, 777

modern negligence law, role in, 194

BUILDERS AND CONTRACTORS
> See also INDEPENDENT CONTRACTORS

governmental immunity shared, 580

repair or dangerous condition, risks assumed, 603

responsibility for safety shifted to, 604

statute of repose, 433

BURDEN OF PROOF
> Generally, 293

affirmative defenses, 40, 294

burden of persuasion or production, 294

circumstantial evidence, 295

civil rights immunity, 585

clear and convincing evidence, 294, 989, 992, 994

defamation,
> constitutional burden of proof, 994
> privilege, 980
> truth or falsity, 954, 996

directed verdict and, 292

effect and meaning generally, 39, 293

elements, proving, and, 293

immunity, civil rights cases, 585

importance of, 40

interference with contract, 1095

interference with opportunity, 1107

meaning of term, 39, 293

negligence cases generally, 39

preponderance of evidence, 39, 294

prima facie case and, 39

products liability, 816, 822, 824

punitive damages, 862

qualified immunity, civil rights cases, 585

significance of, 40

sufficiency of evidence, generally, 292

weight or standard of persuasion, 294

BUSINESS OPPORTUNITIES
See INTERFERENCE WITH CONTRACTS OR
> OPPORTUNITIES

CAPACITY
See MENTAL DISABILITY

CARETAKERS AND CUSTODIANS
> See also FIDUCIARIES and particular
> > topics such as NURSING HOMES;
> > SCHOOLS

civil rights; duty to protect, when, 649

duty to,
> act affirmatively, 621
> protect from third persons, 645
> protect those in care from their own fault, 394

false imprisonment by, 77

foster homes, public entity's responsibility for, 649

jailer,
> duty to protect prisoner, 645
> duty to provide medical attention, 621

res ipsa loquitur, medical malpractice, 302, 303, 305, 309
vicarious liability of, 763

CARRIERS
See COMMON CARRIERS

CARROLL TOWING FORMULA
Generally, 271
costs and benefits on common scale, 273
criticizing and supporting, 275
economic justifications, 275
foreseeability and, 271
incentives, 276
jury interpretation of, 279
justifications and limits, 275
moral interpretation, 277
net burden to defendant, 273
precautions against unknown risk, 278
probability and average, 274
product defects generally, 814
reasonable expectations of safety, 279
risk-utility formula stated, 271
supporting and criticizing, 275
third persons, precautions for, 272
unworkable in some cases, 277

CATTLE
See ANIMALS; STRICT LIABILITY

CAUSE IN FACT
See FACTUAL CAUSE

CERTAINTY
test of intent, 56

CHARITIES
duty generally, 596
immunity,
	churches, 597
	general principle of, 596
	history, 596
	hospitals, 529, 597
	modification and rejection of, 598
	rationales, 597
	remnants of, 599
	risk-utility weighing distinguished, 596
individual good deeds, immunity or not, 600
volunteers, protection of, 600

CHILD ABUSE
See also CHILDREN; FAMILY
duty to investigate reports of, 634
negligence claim for, objective standard, 228
parental privilege to discipline and, 138
reporting statutes, 647

CHILDREN
See also CHILD ABUSE; FAMILY
abducting, enticing, or harboring, 1053
adult standard of care applied, when, 236
adult's failure to provide vehicle restraints, 408
assumption of risk by, 415
attracted to street vendor, 656
care owed to, 217
child custody; interference with, 1053
clergy sexual abuse, 180

consent, mature minors' consent to medical procedure, 172
consent, sexual relations, 172
darting out, danger to be avoided, 217
discipline, subject to, 138
fire-setting; standard of care, 236
fire, appreciation of danger, 229
incapacity generally, 171
infancy negating required intent, 58
infancy no defense, 58
intentional torts of, 58
invitees or licensees on land, as, 473
liability in tort generally, 58
limitation of actions, 331, 436
parents' consent for, 173
parents' duty to rescue, 621
rule of sevens, 233
sexual abuse; statute of limitations, 439
sexual relations, minor's consent to, 172
standard of care,
	adult standard, 236
	child standard, 233
statute of limitations for child sexual abuse claims, 439
statutes, violation of, 258
statutory rape, 172
trespass to land by, 87
trespassing, landowner's responsibility to, 475
violation of statute, effect, 233

CIVIL DAMAGE ACTS
See ALCOHOL AND SUBSTANCES OF ABUSE

CIVIL RIGHTS CLAIMS
Generally, 582
absolute immunity, 585
clearly established right requirement, immunity, 585
color of state law requirement, 582
common-law torts compared, 583
constitutional bases for, 582
context; civil rights violations as torts, 582
defamation, no action for, 969
deliberate indifference, 588
due process of law, 583
duty to protect, 649
Eighth Amendment (cruel and unusual punishment), 583, 584
equal protection of the laws, 583
excessive force, Fourth Amendment, 583
failure to act and, 585
federal right required, 583
foster homes, public entity's responsibility, 649
Fourteenth Amendment, 583
Fourth Amendment, 583
immunities, 584, 585
intentional torts, 583
malicious prosecution and, 1024
perjured testimony, no civil rights claim for, 1024
policy or custom requirement, state and local entities, 586
prisoners and persons in custody, 584, 621, 645
privacy, intrusion, 1010
public entities or officers liability, 582, 584, 586
qualified immunity, 584, 585
Section 1983 actions, 582

seizure of person, Fourth Amendment, 583
state and local entities, against, 586
state and local officials, against, 584
suicide, 589

COLLATERAL SOURCE RULE
Generally, 859
abolition of, 860
rationales for, 860

COMMERCIAL LOSS RULE
See ECONOMIC OR COMMERCIAL HARM;
UNFAIR COMPETITION; and particular
torts such as MISREPRESENTATION

COMMON CARRIERS
amusement vs. carriage distinction, 450
category, who is included, 448, 449
contractual limitations on liability, 413
defined, 449
delay, proximate cause, 350, 354
duty,
civility, 703
highest care, 447
protect passengers from external risks, 451
protect passengers from their disabilities,
448
protect passengers from third persons, 451
protect passengers' property, 191
rescue passenger, 620
general duty of highest care, 447
historical duties, 191
innkeepers as, 453
passenger, who counts as, 451
private carriers distinguished, 449
proximate cause, 354
receiving goods for transport not conversion, 115
rejecting expanded duty, 448
scope of liability, 354
standard of care owed passengers, 447
Warsaw Convention, 447
who counts as a common carrier, 448
who counts as a passenger, 451

COMMON LAW
American reception, 29
analysis, method of, 30
civil codes compared, 29
definition of, 3
history, 27
precedent and, 30
primary source of tort law, 3
reception of English common law, 29, 192
state law, as, 44
writs, generally, 27

**COMPARATIVE FAULT (INCLUDING
CONTRIBUTORY NEGLIGENCE)**
Generally, 379
affirmative defense, as, 379
all-or-nothing judgments after comparative fault,
389
apportionment standards, 893
assumption of risk and, merging, 418
attorneys, comparative fault of client, 1177
avoidable consequences and, 403, 404, 406
Butterfield rule, 379

calculating awards,
assigning shares of fault or responsibility,
386
avoidable consequences, 404, 406
comparing risks, 386
comparing non-party fault, 888
excluding justified and irrelevant risks, 387
immunity of some parties, 888
multiple actor cases, 877
caretakers and custodians; comparative fault no
defense, 394
causally related fault compared, 389
children, standard of care, 233
comparative fault,
comparing conduct, not state of mind, 388
development, 384
intentional torts and, 897
factors bearing on comparison of fault, 388
FELA cases, 384
modern approaches to, 384
modified, 385
pure, 385
comparative responsibility, 389
comparing cause vs. comparing fault, 389
comparing responsibility, 389, 894
comparing unjustified risks, 386
contribution and, 882
contributory negligence,
discovered peril exception, 397
exceptions to traditional bar effect, 397
intentional torts, 398
last clear chance exception, 397
traditional rule of, 379
custom as evidence of plaintiff fault, 394
defendant not negligent, 389
discovered peril, 397
duty,
plaintiff no-duty rules, 391
plaintiff self-care duty, 381plaintiff's own
fault, to protect against, 394, 400
seatbelts, to use or not, 406
employer's workers' compensation immunity and,
890
exceptions to rule charging plaintiff with, 397
factors in estimating, 388
factual cause, 382, 390
foreseeability, 264
fraud, fiduciary breach, no defense, 391, 1131
history of, 379, 384
illegal acts of plaintiff, 401
immune persons, comparing fault of, 888
intentional torts,
compared or not, 398, 895
traditional no-reduction rule, 398
intoxicated persons, 232
joint and several liability,
contribution among tortfeasors, 882
effect upon, 886
judge and jury, 382
last clear chance, 397
legal malpractice, 1177
limited capacity, plaintiff's, 392
medical malpractice, patient's fault, 393, 527
mental disabilities, 225, 383

misrepresentation, justifiable reliance distinguished, 1131
modified systems, 385
multiple actors causing harm, generally, 877
negligence parallels, 381
negligence rules applicable, 214, 381
negligence/contributory negligence distinctions, 383
nonparty fault, compared or not, 888
no negligence of defendant distinguished, 389
open and obvious danger; distinguishing other doctrines, 472
parallel analysis of plaintiff and defendant fault, 381
party and non-party fault comparisons, 888
plaintiff fault, defendant's duty to protect plaintiff from, 394
plaintiff no-duty rules, 391
plaintiff's duty of self-care, 381
plaintiff's illegal acts, 401
pre-injury precautions to minimize effect of injury, 405
products liability claims generally, 834
proximate cause,
 parallel treatment of plaintiff and defendant, 382
 plaintiff's conduct as sole, 373, 390
 plaintiff's conduct not, 374, 390
pure and modified systems of, 385
reasonable person standard and, 381
rescue, 381
risk allocated solely to defendant, when, 391
risk-utility approach in, 381
scope of liability,
 parallel treatment of plaintiff and defendant, 382
 plaintiff's conduct as sole proximate cause, 390
 plaintiff's conduct not within scope of liability, 390
seatbelts, failure to use, 405, 406
standard of care applied to plaintiff, 214, 226, 381
state of mind, 388
statutes, 385, 400, 403
strict liability, 793, 891
superior knowledge or experience, defendant's, 392
superseding cause, plaintiff's fault as, 373
terminology problem, 380
traditional exceptions to contributory negligence bar, 397
willful, wanton, or reckless torts, 397, 896
wrongful death, 696

COMPENSATION SYSTEMS
alternatives or supplements to tort liability, 24, 910
Keeton-O'Connell Plan, 925
National Childhood Vaccine Act, 929
no-fault auto insurance, 925
social security disability, 922
workers' compensation, 911

COMPLIANCE WITH STATUTE
admissible as evidence, 289
defense rejected generally, 289
exceptional cases, 289
federal preemption and, 443

CONDEMNATION
See TAKING OF PROPERTY FOR PUBLIC USE

CONSENT
Generally, 163
abuse of power or position, obtained by, 165, 178
act, consent to, as consent to consequences, 164, 170
actual vs. apparent, 165
actual vs. subjective, 165
affirmative defense, 163
attorney's sexual relations with client, 180
automatic termination of, 171
barring intentional tort claim, summary, 164
battery cases, 63, 163, 176
best interests standard, 174
burden of proof, 163
capacity to, appearance of, 171, 173
clergy's sexual activities, effect of, 180
children, by, 172
coercion, by, 177
collateral mistakes, 176
conditional, 169
conduct expressing, 165
consequences, consent to act a consent to, 164, 170
conversion, as defense to, 112, 115, 164
counselors and psychotherapists, 179
crime, to, effect, 165, 183
defamation, absolute defense, 970
determining scope of, 169
doctor's sexual relations with patient, 179
duress or coercion, effect on, 165, 177
economic threats, 177
effect of, 163
emergency rules, 182
employment setting, 178
exceeding, 169
false imprisonment claims, 164, 168
fiduciary duties, effect on, 179
fraud, induced by, 175
general principles, 163
implication of by conduct, 165
implication of by custom, 167
incapacity and, 164, 171, 173
informed consent, 165, 181, 495, 513, 535
 see also INFORMED CONSENT, this Index
lawyer's sexual relations with client, 180
job threats, 179
manifestation,
 generally, 165
 implied by conduct, 166
 implied by custom, 167
 mistake, relation to, 175
 rationale for protection, 167
media deception inducing, 177
medical battery, 181
mentally incompetent persons, 174
minors, by, 172
mistake,
 effect, 165, 175, 181

ignorance distinguished, 181
negating tortiousness of act, 164
objective manifestation sufficient, 164, 165
on behalf of another, 173
parents' or guardian's on behalf of minor or
    incompetent, 173
physical threats, 177
power to revoke, 170
prima facie case, effect on, 163
psychotherapists and counselors, 179
revocation, power of, 170
scope, 164, 169
silence, by, 167
single act evidencing, 167
social custom bearing on, 167
subjective uncommunicated consent, 168
substituted, 164, 174
termination of, 164
trespass to land, mistake, 177
unforeseeable consequences included, 164, 169
unmanifested, 168
withholding consent, limits on, 173
vaccination case example, 166

CONSORTIUM, LOSS OF
    Generally, 718
contemporary claims of, 719
derivation of claim, 718
derivative nature of claim, 720
emotional distress, species of, 718, 721
grandchildren and grandparents, 719
history, 718
limitations on claim for, 719
persons entitled, 719
unmarried cohabitants, 720
zone of danger rules inapplicable, 721

CONSTITUTIONAL DEFENSES
defamation generally, 986, 994, 996

CONSTITUTIONAL TORTS
See CIVIL RIGHTS

CONTRACTS OR UNDERTAKINGS
    See also ASSUMPTION OF RISK;
        CONTRACTUAL LIMITATIONS ON
        LIABILITY; DUTY;
        INTERFERENCE WITH
        CONTRACT OR OPPORTUNITIES;
        BAD FAITH
bad faith breach; tort action for generally, 1089
contract-tort comparisons or distinctions, 7, 623
implicit undertakings,
    beginning to assist or rescue, 622
    colleges, promises or representations, by,
        648
    duty to act created by, 622, 623
    employer's, 650
    gratuitous, 628
    landlord's; protection from others, 643
    medical services,497
    third persons, to, 627
landlord's contract to repair, effect, 489
legal malpractice claims, tort or contract, 1163
promissory estoppel creating duty to act, 628

**CONTRACTUAL LIMITATIONS ON
LIABILITY**
    See also ASSUMPTION OF RISK, express;
        SHIFTING RESPONSIBILITY
assuming risk by contract, 409, 410
bailees, carriers and public utilities, 413
construction against drafter, 411
employers, 413
misrepresentation cases, 1136
policy constraints on express limitation, 412
public policy limitations on, 412
schools, releases demanded by, 413
shifting responsibility by, 409
third persons' duties unaffected, 604

CONTRIBUTION
    See also APPORTIONMENT OF
        LIABILITY; INDEMNITY
apportionment among tortfeasors, 882
history, 882
immune co-defendant, 890
indemnity compared, 882
intentional tortfeasors denied, 882
joint and several liability system, in, 882
tortfeasor vs. workers' compensation employer,
    919

CONTRIBUTORY NEGLIGENCE
See COMPARATIVE FAULT

CONVERSION
    Generally, 107
accounts, 1153
acquiring possession, 115
action on the case for trover, 104
agent's act, 110, 115
alteration of goods, 114
alternatives, 108
bailees, 115, 116, 118, 120, 1154
banks, 1154
basic case of, 107
benefit to defendant not required for liability, 110
body cells, 112
bona fide purchasers generally, 110, 122
checks and money, 124
civil rights analogue, 583
consent of plaintiff negating, 112, 115, 164
consequential damages, 126
contracts affecting claim for, 1155
creditors, 115
damages, generally, 125
dead bodies, 112
defense of property by converting a chattel, 139
definition, 112
demand and refusal, 117
destruction, alteration or damage, 114
dispossession, by, 113
documents evidencing a right, 107, 111
dominion required, 109, 112
economic interests, 1151
economic loss rule, 120
examples, 107
extended liability for, 115
factors in determining, 112
forced sale, as, 107, 110, 112
good faith, 110, 113, 122

good faith of agent, 115
historical development, 103
intangibles, 107, 110, 1151
intent required, 109
lien asserted not conversion, 115
loss-of-use damages, 126
malicious prosecution alternative, 113
methods of committing, 113
misdelivery, by, 115
mistake, 110
modern expansion of claim for, 111
money, checks, and credits, 111, 124, 1153
negotiable instruments, 111, 1153
nominal damages, 126
nondelivery, by, 117
officer's seizing wrong property, 114
option to sue in tort or in contract, 120
other torts and, 108
possession as basis for claim, 108, 111
pre-trial seizure of property, 127
property issues vs. tort issues, 108
property subject to conversion, 110, 1151
punitive damages, 126
purchaser from thief as converter, 110
real property excluded, 111
recovery of chattel remedy, 127
recovery of later price increase, 125
remedies, 125
replevin, 127
Restatement test for, 112
Restitution, 125
sale or disposal, by, 115
secured transactions, 109
seriousness of dispossession, 114
statute of limitations, 127
substantial interference required, 108
tangible property requirement, 110, 1151
tort issues in, 109
towing vehicles as, 110, 114
transferring possession, 115
trespass damages, recovery of, 125
trespass to land compared, 110
Trover writ and, 107
UCC and, 109, 122, 123, 125, 127
use or interference, 114
warehouseman, by, 115
withholding possession, 117
wrongful levy, 115, 1153

CORRECTIVE JUSTICE
tort law, in, 17

CREDITORS
    See also WRONGFUL ATTACHMENT OR
        LEVY
abuse of process by, 1045
conversion, 109, 115
harassing debtor, emotional distress action, 708
misrepresentation to, by borrower's attorney,
    1176
repossession of goods by, 115, 151, 768
wrongful death recovery of debtor not subject to
    claims of, 694

CRIME
consent to, effect, 183

duty to protect others from, generally, 633
tort and distinguished, 6

CRIMINAL CONVERSATION
    Generally, 1049
alternative claims, 1051

CRUEL AND UNUSUAL PUNISHMENT
civil rights actions, 584

CUSTODY
affirmative care owed those in, 645
civil rights, significance of, 649
compulsory school attendance and, 648, 650
contributory negligence, custodian's duty to
        protect against, 394
duty to those in, 584
foster home liability, 649
interference with parental custody of a child,
    1053
medical aid for those in, 621
negligent release of one in custody, 575
noncustodial parent's limited rights, 1054
property in bailee's custody, 191
property lost or damaged in official custody, 156
removing children from parental custody, 138

CUSTOM
    Generally, 281
ambiguities in characterizing custom, 285
battery, touchings consistent with social usage,
        63
consent implied from, 167
constraints on use of, 284
customary violation of statute, 284
duty, affecting, 283
entering transactions in light of custom, 288
evidence of reasonable care, 281
feasibility, customary practice tending to show,
        282
foreseeability, customary practice tending to
        show, 282
legal malpractice, standard of care, 1168
limitations on use of, 284
livestock trespass or rights affected by, 778
medical standard of care set by, 503
non-safety customs, 285
private standards as "customs," 287
providing more care, custom of, 284
reasonable care, evidence of, 281
uniform practice, 286
varied uses as evidence in negligence analysis,
        282
violation of statute, customary, 284
shield, as, 283
sword, as, 283
transactions in light of custom, 288

DAMAGES
    Generally, 851
abuse of process, 1025
adjusting for inflation, 859
battery, 82
benefits rule, 859
caps, 695, 873, 874
collateral source rule, 859
comparable awards, pain and suffering, 855

defamation, 998
defined, 851
earning or earning capacity lost, 852
element of negligence claim, 851
elements of recoverable damages, 852
emotional distress; stand-alone damages, 699
enjoyment of life lost, 856
future losses; fixing a loss period, 858
hedonic damages, 856
inflation adjustments, 859
intentional torts to the person, 82
interference with contracts and opportunities, 1092
legal malpractice, 1182, 1189
loss of enjoyment of life, 856
lost earnings and earning capacity, 852
malicious prosecution, 1025, 1027
medical and other expenses, 853
medical monitoring, 854
mental or physical pain, 854
misrepresentation cases, 1137
negligence cases, required in, 311
nuisance, 748
pain and suffering,
    generally, 854
    caps on awards, 873
    comparable awards considered, 855
    forms of suffering included, 855
    survival actions, 687
parasitic damages, 699
personal injury; compensatory damages;
    elements, 852
present value adjustment, 859
presumed, defamation cases, 998
property harms, 856
punitive,
    generally, 861
    aggregate punishment, 867
    amount, 865
    basis for award, 861
    bifurcation of trial, 865
    burden of proof, 862
    caps on, 873
    comparable penalties, 871
    constitutional restrictions, 867
    conversion of chattels, 126
    criticism of, 864
    defamation, 1001
    deterrence, goal of, 863, 872
    excessive awards, prohibition of, 868
    extraterritoriality, 870
    factors in determining amount, 865
    intentional tort cases, 80
    legal malpractice, 1184
    purposes, 863
    ratio rules, 866, 869
    reallocation of, 876
    tort reform statutes and, 873, 876
    trespass to land, 98
    wealth evidence, 865, 866
    wrongful death, 812
reduction of future loss to present value, 859
survival actions, in, 687
taxation of compensatory awards, no, 861
tax savings, 861

tort reform, 873
trespass,
    generally, 96
    continuing vs. permanent, 98
trespass to land, nominal, 96
trespassory torts, recovery without harm, 26, 82
writ of case, damages required, 26
wrongful birth, life, or pregnancy, 680
wrongful civil litigation, 1025, 1041
wrongful death; nonpecuniary loss, 691

DEAD BODIES
conversion and, 112
emotional distress at handling of, 703, 729

DEADLY FORCE
criminal statutes affecting, spring guns, 146
defense of property, 140
self-defense, 131, 133

DEATH
    See also WRONGFUL DEATH
defamation of the dead, 954
right of publicity after, 1209

DECEIT
See MISREPRESENTATION

DEFAMATION
    Generally, 936
abuse of qualified privilege, 980
ambiguity,
    judge and jury, 948
    libel per quod, 962
bigotry, 946, 947
burden of proof,
    clear and convincing standard, 989, 994
    common law, 938
    truth or falsity, 954, 996
civil rights actions, none for, 969
clear and convincing evidence, 989, 994
common law, constitutional impact, 939
communication, types of, 940
Communications Decency Act, 970
consent to, 970
constitutional rules,
    generally, 986
    actual damages, when required, 987, 989, 990
    bases for, 987
    clear and convincing evidence, 989, 994
    fault requirements generally, 987
    fault tests and proof, 987, 988, 990, 994
    issues of no public concern, 990
    negligence or some fault requirement, 986, 990, 995
    opinion, 996
    provably false statement requirement, 987, 996
    public figures, who are, 992
    public issues, private plaintiffs, 990
    public official defined, 991
    punitive damages restriction, 990
    SLAPP suits, relation to, 990
    truth or falsity, burden of proof, 996
context, 950, 957
corporations, of, 953

criminal libel, 937, 954
criminal offense, imputation of, 959
damages,
    actual damages, 987, 998
    elements of, 999
    emotional harm without reputational loss, 1000
    libel-proof plaintiffs, 1002
    pecuniary loss, 961
    plaintiff's bad reputation affecting, 956, 1002
    presumed, 998
    punitive, 1001
debts unpaid, imputation, 945
deceased persons, of, 954
defamatory content required, 943
discrimination cases, in, 976
distributors distinguished from publishers, 942
electronic communications, 958, 970
elements,
    common law, 938
    constitutional, 939
employer references, consent, 970
employer retaliation for imputation of discrimination, 976
employer's defamatory discharge, 943
excessive publication, 980
executive branch business, 968
extrinsic evidence,
    identifying plaintiff, 951
    libel per quod, 962
    meaning shown by, 949
failure to check information, 995
fair comment, 977, 989
false light privacy and, 1018
Federal Tort Claims Act, claims excluded, 969
free speech; petitioning activity, 984
government entities as plaintiffs, 953
group defamation, 952
history, 936
immunity for internet service providers, 965, 970
implied falsehood from true statements, 957
improper purpose, 981
inaccuracy in reporting public proceedings, 981
incompatibility with trade, business etc., imputation of, 959
injunctions, 1002
injurious falsehood distinguished, 1114
insanity, 947
interference with contract and, 1105
internet, on, 942, 965, 970
internet content providers, 971
internet service providers, 965, 970
judge and jury, 948
judicial and quasi-judicial proceedings, 965
jury, defamatory content, 944
knowing or reckless falsehood, proof of, 994
legislative business, 965, 968
libel,
    oral communication with knowledge that it will be written, 958
    per se, 962
    per quod, 962
    slander distinguished, 958
libel-proof plaintiffs, 1002

libel-slander distinction, abolishing, 961
libraries, news dealers, 942
literal words and implications, 957
loathsome disease, imputation of, 959
lying, imputation of, 946
malice at common law, 981
meaning of publication, judge and jury, 948
motive,
    effect on privilege, 981
    mixed, 982
name-calling, 947
negligence and other fault, when required, 987, 988, 990, 995
negligence claims and, 936
negligent publication, 941
neutral reportage, 979
newsworthiness, 979
non-defamatory falsehoods, 947
of and concerning requirement, 951
opinion,
    generally, 996
    implying provably false statements, 997
    literally true statements, 957
    not provably false, when, 997
other torts and, 936
Peter Zenger's Case, 937
pleadings, report of defamatory, 978
police officers as public officials, 992
political affiliation, 948
presumptions, common law, 938
privacy claims and, 936
private persons plaintiffs generally, 990
privilege,
    absolute, 965
    common interest privilege, 975
    consent to publication, 970
    constitutional impact on common law, 982
    loss of qualified privilege, 980
    neutral reportage, 979
    perjury, 966
    pleadings, report of, 978
    publication to public official, 973
    qualified generally, 972
professional incompetence, imputation of, 945
public figures,
    generally, 987, 992
    all-purpose, 993
    entities as, 993
    limited-purpose, 993
    who are, 992
public interest privilege, 973
public officials,
    generally, 987
    who are, 991
publication,
    disseminators vs. publishers, 942
    failure to remove, 941
    intent and negligence, 941
    intent to publish vs. intent to defame, 942
    repeaters, 942
    requirement of, 940
    self-publication, 943
    third person required, 940, 943
punitive damages, 1001
qualified privilege, inaccuracy of report, 981

racism, imputation of, 946
reference to the plaintiff required, 951
repetition, liability for, 943
report of public proceedings, 977
reputation of plaintiff already bad, 1002
reputational harm, semi-exclusive law of, 936
restitution, 1002
retraction statutes, 1003
rhetorical hyperbole, 997
ridicule, 947
right of reply, 1004
right-thinking people, 944
scope, 936
sedition act, 937
self-interest privilege, 974
self-publication, 943
slander,
        generally, 958
        per se, 959
        special damages requirement, 961
slander-libel distinction, abolishing, 961
Star Chamber, 937
strict liability at common law, 938
survival, 954
teachers as public officials, 992
telephone and telegraph companies, 942
trademark disparagement, 1197
truth or falsity,
    burden of proof,
        common law, 954
        constitutional rules, 955, 996
    evidence, 956
    literal truth, embedded falsity, 957
    opinions or value judgments, 997
    substantial truth defense, 955
    true statements implying falsehoods, 957
unnamed plaintiffs, 952
"veggie libel laws, " 953
workers' compensation and, 921
Zenger's case, 937

DEFENSE OF PROPERTY
    Generally, 139
battery, conversion, or trespass in, 139
deadly force, 140
dwelling place, deadly force in defense of, 142
intruder's superior privilege, 141
least force effective, 141
means used including chains and pits, 146
merchants' privilege to detain for investigation,
    153
mistake in, 141
negligence law and, 146
others' property, 142
reasonable appearances, 141
reasonable force limit, 140
recovery of property distinguished, 140, 147
spring guns or traps, 142
statute authorizing deadly force, 140
third persons injured in, 142

DETERRENCE
goal in tort law, 15, 23
insurance and, 47

DETINUE
writ of, conversion and, 104

DIGNITARY TORTS
    See also ECONOMIC OR
        COMMERCIAL HARM and
        particular topics such as
        DEFAMATION; EMOTIONAL
        DISTRESS; PRIVACY
Generally, 931
economic torts, overlap with, 931
physical harm torts distinguished, 931

DISABILITY
    See also MENTAL DISABILITY OR
        INCAPACITY
care owed to persons with, 400
pregnancy, job discrimination forbidden, 673
seizures, standard of care of one subject to, 224
sexual torts against disabled; vicarious liability
    for, 763
standard of care, physical disability, 223
statute of limitations; tolling for, 436

DISCIPLINE
corporal punishment, 139
military, rationale for immunity, 559
parents, privilege to discipline children, 138
schools and teachers, privilege to discipline
    students, 139

DISCLAIMERS
See CONTRACTUAL LIMITATIONS ON
    LIABILITY

DISCRIMINATION
    See also EMPLOYMENT AND
        EMPLOYERS
defamation by charging, 976
emergency medical treatment, 531
emotional distress inflicted by, 710
employment, 710
pregnancy, job discrimination, 673
sexual discrimination, duty to prevent, 647

DISEASE
destruction of property to prevent spread of, 159
fear of, emotional harm, 725
medical monitoring damages awards, 854
negligent spread of sexually transmitted disease
    to spouse, 592
physician's duty to protect from spread, 660
property damaged to prevent spread of, 159
spread of, proximate cause, 366
surgeon's duty to disclose, 519
workers' compensation, 917

DISPARAGEMENT
See INJURIOUS FALSEHOOD

DOGS
See ANIMALS

DOMESTIC RELATIONS
See FAMILY

DRAM SHOP STATUTES
See ALCOHOL AND SUBSTANCES OF ABUSE

DRUGS
See ALCOHOL AND SUBSTANCES OF ABUSE

DUE PROCESS OF LAW
civil rights claim, 583
damage caps, constitutionality, 874
Fourteenth Amendment provisions, 159
negligence insufficient to show, 587
ousting possessor without hearing, 150
persons in custody, 645
placement in dangerous foster home, 649
pre-trial seizure of property, 127
privacy invasion as denial of, 1010
process values generally, 16
public records sealed, due process issue, 1017, 1018
punitive damages limits, 867
self-help repossession as denial of, 150
statutes of repose, constitutionality, 331
substantive, 583

DURESS OR COERCION
consent, effect on, 177
false imprisonment by, 75

DUTY TO ACT
See NON-ACTION, LIMITING LIABILITY FOR; DUTY TO PROTECT FROM THIRD PERSONS; DUTY

DUTY TO PROTECT FROM THIRD PERSONS AND SELF-HARM
Generally, 633
alcohol providers, duty to protect from patrons, 661
children attracted to street vendor, 656
civil rights liability, 649
colleges-students, 648
control over chattel creating, 655
criminal attacks, against, 638
defendant's relation to dangerous person creating, 651
employer-employee, 650
foreseeability of crime, 639
hospital-patient, 646
illegal drugs provider, 664
landlord-tenant, 643
landowner-visitor, 638
negligent entrustment, 653
no duty generally, 633
parent-child, 638, 646
physician's duty to non-patients, 660
prisoner escaping, 656
relationship between defendant and dangerous person creating, 651
relationship between defendant and plaintiff creating, 637
schools-students, 646
therapist, dangerous patients, 658

DUTY
Generally, 203
affirmative duty to act, see NON-ACTION, this Index
assumed; emotional distress cases, 728
assumption of risk as expression of no-duty rules, 416
breach distinguished, 205, 206, 207
common carriers, 447
comparative fault,
        duty issues under, 389
        plaintiff's duty of self-care inapplicable, when, 392
created by law independent of contract, 623
custom, 281
existence of duty, 203, 208
expanded,
        common carriers, 447
        fiduciaries, 454
        innkeepers, 452
factors in recognizing, 208
fetus, to, 674
fiduciaries, duty to protect from others, 455
foreseeability and, 211
general standard, as, 206
health care providers, see MEDICAL MALPRACTICE, this Index
innkeepers, 452
judge and jury issues, 198, 204, 210, 211
landowners, see LANDOWNERS AND OCCUPIERS, this Index
limited or special duties, 445
no duty to protect generally, 633
obligation to act in accordance with standard, as, 206
parent to child, 621
parents to fetus, 674
particularizing, trespass on the Case, 191
plaintiff's duty of self-care, 382
process issues, 209
professional risk-takers, to, 605
protect another against her own fault, 400
proximate cause and, 343, 344
reasonable care standard of, 213
relationship of parties, action on the case, 191
relationship with danger, 651
relationship with plaintiff, 637
requirement of, 203
rescue, relationship basis for, 620
rule of law, not standard of care, 198
school to student, 621
sports participants, limited, 422
standard or measure of duty, 198
vague standards of, criticism of, 209

EASEMENTS
trespass action unavailable to protect, 91

ECONOMIC ANALYSIS
approach to tort law, 21, 23
nuisance cases, 749
risk-utility formula in negligence cases, 271

ECONOMIC OR COMMERCIAL HARM
        See also particular economic torts such as INTERFERENCE WITH CONTRACTS OR OPPORTUNITIES
dignitary torts, overlap with, 931
economic loss rule, see ECONOMIC LOSS RULE, this Index
misrepresentation, 1117, 1126
nuisance generally, 733
physical harm torts distinguished, 931

products liability, 803
proximate cause, 373
public nuisance causing, 746
stand-alone economic harm claims, generally,
    931, 933, 1059
unfair competition, generally, 1193

ECONOMIC LOSS RULE
    Generally, 803, 933, 1059
categories of economic torts, 1063
communication of harmful information, 1064
consumer contracts and, 1084
contracting parties and, 1061, 1077
contractual exclusions of liability and, 1077
dignitary torts and, 931
economic loss as damages vs. economic tort, 1060
effect on negligence claims, 1061
exceptions, 1073, 1083
expansions, 1088
independent tort duty and, 1084
intentional torts and, 1088
legal malpractice claims unaffected by, 1087
misappropriation of intangible values, 1064
negligent economic loss and, 1061
policies behind, 1071, 1080
products liability, 803, 1085
professional malpractice actions, 1087
privity and, 1070
rejecting the rule, 1076
risk allocation and, 1082
scope of rules, 803, 1083
services, negligently provided, 1087
specific torts, 1060
strangers and, 1061, 1065
sudden calamitous event, 1085
supplying defective chattels, services, or
    property, 1065
transferred loss, 1074
statutes, 1076

EGGSHELL SKULL RULE
See THIN SKULL RULE

EIGHTH AMENDMENT
civil rights actions, 584

EMERGENCY
    See also NECESSITY
doctrine; reasonable person's conduct in, 218
emergency vehicles, care owed, 221
jury instructions, 220
medical,
    hospital's duty to screen, 531
    physicians' immunity in, 221, 523
negligence, acts in, 218, 223
physician or surgeon, foreseeable complication
    not, 220
privilege to act for a person's benefit without
    consent, 182
statutes, emergency vehicles, 221

EMINENT DOMAIN
See TAKING OF PROPERTY FOR PUBLIC USE

EMOTIONAL DISTRESS
    Generally, 699
abolishing restrictive rules for claiming, 723

AIDS; exposure to generally, 725
alienation of affections and, 1051, 1057
assault and, 72
assumed duty to protect plaintiff from, 728
bystander injury, 711, 714
cancer fears, 725
carriers and innkeepers, 703
consortium loss, generally, 718
criticism of allowing claims for, 700
damages, as element in another tort, 699
damages, difficulty in estimating, 701
damages resulting from battery, 82
dead bodies mishandled, 703, 729
defamation, 1001
direct victims, 721, 728
discrimination inflicting, 710
duty assumed by defendant to protect against,
    728
false imprisonment and, 82
fear of future harm, 725
fright or shock pattern, 721
genuineness, concern about, 701
historical development of claim for, 703
idiosyncratic reaction, 82 , 731
independent duty to protect against, 728
information supplied to the plaintiff causing, 726
intentional infliction of,
        generally, 705
    abuse of power, 708
    artful pleading, 705
    case by case adjudication of claims for, 706
    common characteristics of claims for, 707
    discrimination or words inflicting, 710
    duplicative damage awards, 705
    elements, 706
    extreme and outrageous conduct, 707
    inequality of parties and, 709
    intent to distress third persons, 711
    markers of outrage, 708
    overlapping with other tort claims, 705
    outrage and its characteristics, 708
    physical impact, 711
    physical manifestation or symptoms, 710
    repeated misconduct, 708
    Restatement rule, 706
    severe distress requirement, 710
    symptoms, 710
    third person as target, 711
    vulnerable plaintiffs, 708
legal malpractice cases, in, 1184, 1189
loss of consortium, 718
mitigation, in cases of, 702
negligent infliction of,
        generally, 713
    bystanders, 714
    doctor-patient relationship, in, 729
    duty to protect emotional well-being,
        independent, 728
    fear of future harm, 725
    foreseeability test, 724
    information, erroneous, causing, 726
    impact requirement, 722
    limitations on claims, generally, 713
    misdiagnosis cases, 727
    misrepresentation and, 728

physical manifestation requirement, 722
physical risks, absence of, 728
products warnings and, 727
relationships, role of, 716
restrictive rules, abolishing, 723
risks to another, causing, 714
sensitive plaintiffs, 731
severe distress requirement, 714, 723
zone of danger rule, 715
nuisance causing fear, 743
other torts and, 705
outrageousness defined, 707
parasitic damages, 699
proximate cause, 373, 732
religious freedom and, 710
Restatement rules on, 704, 706
risks to others causing, 711, 714
sensitive plaintiffs, 731
severe distress requirement, 710, 714, 723
sexual harassment inflicting, 710
stand-alone distress claims, nature of, 700
strict products liability claims for, 805
telegraphic messages, 726
therapists, 713
thin skull rule, 732
third persons,
    close relationship rule, 716
    contemporaneous and sensory awareness
        rule, 716
    distress or harm to, causing plaintiff's
        distress, 711
    presence requirement, 712
toxic exposure,
        generally, 725
    actual exposure vs. fear, 726
    AIDS exposure, 725
    environmental exposure, 726
    fear vs. actual exposure, 726
transferred intent rejected, 711
trespass to chattels, 124
trespassory torts and, 82
undertakings and, 713
vulnerable plaintiffs, 708
words inflicting, 710
wrongful birth, life, or pregnancy, 681
wrongful death, 692
wrongful litigation rules circumvented by claim
    of, 1037
zone of danger rule, 714

EMPLOYERS AND EMPLOYMENT
assumption of risk by employees, 416
common law liability of employer to employee,
    911
contractual limitations on liability to employee,
    414
defamation,
    employee charging discrimination, 976
    employer's references to prospective
        employer, 970
    defamatory discharge and self-publication,
        943
discrimination, emotional distress, 710
duties to workers and contractors, 603
duty to protect employee, 650
duty to rescue employee, 621

emotional distress claim and sexual harassment,
    710
employer's immunity; comparative fault effects,
    890
fellow servant rule, 417, 912
immunity of employer under workers'
    compensation, 918
manufacturer's product warnings to employer,
    832
negligent hiring, retention, or supervision, 657
negligent misrepresentations by, 1125
railroads; FELA liability to employees, 911
shifting responsibility to contractor, 603

ENTERPRISE LIABILITY
abnormally dangerous activities, 790
risk distribution argument generally, 14, 17
strict products liability rationale, 801
vicarious liability, basis for, 755
workers' compensation plans as, 911

ENVIRONMENTAL HARM
joint and several liability retained for, 885
private nuisance action, 735
public nuisance, 744
trespass damage, 97

EQUAL PROTECTION OF LAW
civil rights claim, 583
damages caps, constitutionality, 874
negligence insufficient to show, 587
statutes of repose, constitutionality, 331
wrongful death, excluding illegitimate children or
    parents, 695

ESTOPPEL
agency by, 530, 770
legal malpractice, 1190
limitation of actions, discovery rule
        distinguished, 429
reliance upon gratuitous promises, 628
to plead statute of limitations, 438

EVIDENCE
        See also RES IPSA LOQUITUR
admissibility and weight generally, 296
circumstantial evidence, 295
custom, of, generally, 281
expert testimony,
        circumstantial evidence and, 2965
        constraints on, 296, 817
        medical malpractice, 509
        res ipsa loquitur basis established by, 297,
            303
        ultimate issue of negligence, 296
inferences,
        cause in fact, 326
        of fact, 295
        res ipsa loquitur permitting, 297
judge's role in determining sufficiency, 36
presumptions, 300
spoliation,
        factual causation in claim for, 1161
        intentional, by a non-party, 1159
        intentional, by a party, 1157
        negligent, 1160
        presumption of causation in action for, 1161

res ipsa loquitur and, 1157
sufficiency, judge's role in determining, 292

EXCUSE
justification distinguished, 41
statutory violation, negligence per se and, 257

EXPLOSIVES
nondelegable duty as to, 767
storage, nuisance, 743
strict liability, 784, 787
trespass to land caused by, 88

**EXTENDED LIABILITY OR TRANSFERRED
    INTENT**
        Generally, 79, 101
assault, 80
battery, 80, 81, 101, 115
conversion, 115
criminal law connection, 80
emotional harm, rejected for, 84, 711
false imprisonment, 80
intent privileged or non-tortious, inappropriate
    when, 80
pros and cons, 80
purposeful infliction, 80
trespass to land, 101, 115

FACTUAL CAUSE
        See also APPORTIONMENT OF
            RESPONSIBILITY; DAMAGES
        Generally, 312
actual harm, connecting to, 324
alternative causation, 327
but-for test of,
        generally, 317
        aggregating conduct of multiple actors, 324
        alternatives to, 321
        counterfactual, as, 319
        hypothetical alternative must be
            considered, 319
        multiple tortfeasors, 321, 324
        specific negligence as key to, 325
        substantial factor test contrasted, 321
causal apportionment, 389
comparative causation, 389
comparative fault and, 382
connecting negligence and harm, 324
defendant's acts combine with other causes to
    inflict harm, 321
duplicative causation, 322
element in negligence case generally, 312
evidence and inferences of causation, 326
indivisible injury, 321
inferences and evidence of causation, 326
issue, 313, 315
lawyering strategy, 325
liberal inferences of, 326
lost chance of recovery, 331
market share liability substituted for, 330
multiple causes, 318, 321
negligent act or omission affecting cause in fact
    issue, 324
preemptive causation, 323
preexisting conditions, 331
proof, 324, 327
proportional causation, 330

proximate cause distinguished, 316, 342
res ipsa loquitur and, 297
scope of liability distinguished, 316, 342
specific negligence as key to but-for test, 325
spoliation of evidence cases, 1161
strategy, claiming "right" act of negligence, 325
substantial factor test of, 321
terminology of, 316, 342
Wright's Test, 324

FALSE ADVERTISING
Generally, 1198

FALSE ARREST
See FALSE IMPRISONMENT

FALSE IMPRISONMENT
        See also ARREST; CIVIL RIGHTS
        Generally, 73
arrest under a warrant, 156
arrest without a warrant, 156
awareness of confinement, 73
civil rights analogue, 78, 583
confinement,
        meaning, 74
        methods, 74
        threats and duress, by, 75
        undue influence and, 77
consent defeating claim, 73, 164
custodians, 77
damages, 82
defense of property, as means of, 140
duration of, 73
duty to release from confinement, 77
elements of, 73
emotional harm and, 78
false arrest distinguished, 73
federal governmental immunity, 562
Fourth Amendment civil rights claims, 583
innocently causing confinement, 78
instigation of imprisonment by others, 73
length of time, 73
malicious prosecution compared, 78, 1026
merchant's detention of suspected shoplifter, 153
motive irrelevant, 73
negligence and, 78
other torts and, 78
probable cause for arrest without a warrant, 156
public entities, 562
punitive damages, 83
relationship between parties, 78
self-defense against, 131, 136
submission to legal authority, 75
Taiwan, "confinement" in, 74
threats and duress, 75
transferred intent, 79
undue influence, 77

FAMILY
        See also CHILDREN; CONSORTIUM;
            PRENATAL INJURY; WRONGFUL
            BIRTH, LIFE OR PREGNANCY
abduction or enticement, 1050
aiding or abetting interference with, 1054
alienation of affections,
        parent's or child's, 1056
        tort of, 1049

child custody; interference with, 1053
children, seduction of, 1056
criminal conversation; tort of, 1049
domestic violence, 588, 593
duties within, 594
duty to act affirmatively for protection of
    members, 621
duty to protect others from, 652
fetal genetic problems, informed consent rights of
    parents, 520
fetus; duty to, 674
immunity of family members,
      generally, 591
    spousal, 591
    parental, 593
interference with family relationships, history,
    1049
malicious prosecution, family law court
    displacing tort, 1037
Married Women's Property Acts, 591
military negligence; service member's family
    claims, 561
parent consenting to treatment for child, 173
parental immunity, 593
parental privilege to discipline children, 138
parents' duty to child, 594
seduction of minor child, 1056
spousal immunity; traditional rule of, 591
therapist's interference with, 1057

FAULT OF THE PLAINTIFF
See COMPARATIVE NEGLIGENCE

FEDERAL EMPLOYERS LIABILITY ACT
See FELA

FEDERAL TORT CLAIMS ACT
See GOVERNMENT ENTITIES

FELA (FEDERAL EMPLOYERS LIABILITY ACT)
assumption of risk defense abolished by, 417
cause of action created by, 247
pure comparative negligence system under, 384, 386
railroad liability to employees under, 911
wrongful death, 686

FELLOW SERVANT RULE
assumption of risk, 417
workers' compensation, 912

FETUS
    See also WRONGFUL BIRTH, LIFE, OR
      PREGNANCY
death claims, 670
doctor's failure to provide genetic information,
    emotional harm, 727
duties to, 674
genetic damages, informed consent rights of
    parent, 520
mother's right to terminate pregnancy, 677
preconception injury, 675
toxic exposure at mother's workplace, 919
toxic injuries to, 672
viability at injury, 670

workers' compensation to mother, effect on claim
    for fetal injury, 919

FIDUCIARIES
attorneys,
      generally, 1164
    comparative fault of client, 1177
comparative fault defense rejected, 1131
consent to violation of duty, 179
constructive trust against, 1138
doctors, 516
duty of disclosure, 1135
employees as; trade secrets, 1206
lawyers, 1164, 1177
misrepresentation,
    negligent, 1125
    nondisclosure or silence, 1135
    opinion statements, 1132
physicians, 516
punitive damages against, 863
statute of limitations affected by status as, 439
therapists as, 179

FIRE
children setting, standard of care, 236
child's appreciation of danger, 233, 474
failure to protect from, immunity of municipality,
    570
property damaged to prevent spread of, 159
proximate cause, 356
strict liability rejected, 777
trespass to land, innocent fire caused, 101

FIREARMS
See WEAPONS

**FIREFIGHTERS AND FIREFIGHTERS'
    RULE**
barring claims, 605
employers, suits against, 613
extension beyond landowners, 606
general rule, 605
intentional or reckless acts, 610
landowner cases, 606
persons covered by, 605, 611
private employers, 612
products manufacturers and, 613
public building inspectors, 611
rationales, 607
rejections and limitations, 608
risks covered by, 608
volunteer and off-duty officers, 611

FIRST AMENDMENT
See DEFAMATION; FREE SPEECH

FORCIBLE ENTRY AND DETAINER
statutes, 91
tort liability for, 148

FORESEEABILITY
See DUTY; NEGLIGENCE; SCOPE OF
    LIABILITY (PROXIMATE CAUSE)

FRAUD
See MISREPRESENTATION

FREE SPEECH
defamation; constitutional rules, 986
emotional distress inflicted by words alone, 710
interference with contracts or opportunities, 1105
petitioning activity, 984
privacy,
    appropriation of identity, 1005
    appropriation of personality, 1005
    false light, 1019
    private facts in public records, 1017
private facts publicity; claims by public figures,
    1014
SLAPP suits, 984, 1046
social and political boycotts, 1105
trademark, satire or comment, 1196

GAMES AND SPORTS
See ASSUMPTION OF RISK; INTERFERENCE
    WITH CONTRACTS OR
    OPPORTUNITIES

GARNISHMENT
constitutional limitations on, 127
wrongful civil litigation, 1041

GAS OR ELECTRICITY
care required, 217
nuisance, stray voltage, 735
strict liability as abnormal danger rejected, 787

GOOD SAMARITAN STATUTES
charitable immunity and, 600
medical emergencies generally, 523

GOVERNMENT COMPENSATION FUNDS
    Generally, 927
9/11 Victim Compensation Fund, 692, 927
tax-created funds, 929

GOVERNMENT CONTRACTOR DEFENSE
immunity of, federal, 580

**GOVERNMENT ENTITIES, OFFICERS AND
    EMPLOYEES**
        See also CIVIL RIGHTS; OFFICERS;
            POLICE
    Generally, 549
agents, officers and employees, liability of,
    federal, 580
        Bivens action, 581
        Constitution, direct action under,
            581, 582
        executive officers, 581
        immunity under FTCA, 580
        judicial officers, 581
        legislative officers and employees,
            581
        President, immunity of, 581
    state and local,
            generally, 576
        civil rights claims, 582, 584
        executive officers, 578
        indemnity of employees, 576
        judicial and quasi-judicial functions,
            577
        legislative-branch officials, 578
        ministerial vs. discretionary
            decisions, 579

Bivens action, 581
civil rights claims against federal government,
    553
civil rights; municipalities; policy or custom
    requirement, 586
conversion, liability for, 114
defamation, plaintiff in suit for, 562, 953
discretionary immunity,
    criticisms of broad "policy" formulations,
        558
    expansive reading of, 557
    federal, 553
    operational-planning distinction, 554
    professional or scientific decisions, 556
    state and local entities, 568
federal, civil rights liability, 582
FTCA,
    battery claims, 562
    defamation claims excluded, 562, 969
    discretionary immunity, 553
    Feres rule, 558
    history, 551
    intentional torts, 562
    law governing, 551, 552
    operational-planning distinction, 554
    private person liability comparable, 552
    procedural requirements, 551
    statute of limitations, 551
    statutory exceptions to liability, 562
high speed police chases, 574
history of sovereign immunity, 549
human experimentation, service members, 561
military torts; generally, 558
municipal immunity,
    generally, 550, 565
    common-law rule, 565
    discretionary immunity, 568
    governmental vs. proprietary test, 566
    historical basis, 550
    statutory structures, 567
municipalities; civil rights liabilities, 586
parole of dangerous person, 575
police and fire protection, excluding liability for,
    574
police chases, 574
police power, contrasted with taking, 159
public duty doctrine, 569
public necessity, intentional damage to property,
    158
release of dangerous persons from custody, 575
sovereign immunity generally, 549
state and local entities,
    abolition of immunities, 550, 563
    civil rights claims against, 586
    discretionary immunity; conscious choice,
        569
    discretionary immunity generally, 568
    employee right of indemnity, 567
    governmental vs. proprietary functions, 566
    immunity generally, 550, 565
    immunity retained, 565
    insurance as waiver, 567
    local, common law rule of immunity, 565
    911 operators, 572
    nonfeasance and public duty, 570

planning vs. operational decisions, 569
police and fire protection, 574
procedural and remedial limitations on
liability, 565
property, negligently maintained, 566
public duty doctrine, 569
release of dangerous persons, 575
road maintenance, 566
statutory structures and duties, 567, 570
traditional immunity, states, 563
state and local officers and employees, 576
states; civil rights liabilities rejected, 586
statutes imposing duties on the public at large,
253, 570
taking of property, just compensation required,
159
traditional immunities and their passing, 549

GUARDIANS
incompetent patients, appointment for, 174
standards for deciding on behalf of incapacitated
person, 174

HAND FORMULA
See CARROLL TOWING FORMULA

HAZARDOUS WASTES
See also POISONS; TOXIC TORTS
deeply removed from surface, 96
government's immunity for delegating disposal to
others, 554
percolating liquids,
strict liability, 785, 789
trespass or nuisance, 95
public nuisance, 746
statutory regulation generally, 45
stigma nuisance, 743
trespassers, trap for, 146

HEALTH CARE PROVIDERS
See also HOSPITALS; INFORMED
CONSENT; MANAGED CARE
ORGANIZATIONS; MEDICAL
MALPRACTICE; THERAPISTS
Generally, 493
duty to non-patients, 660
emergency affecting consent of patient, 182
emergency doctrine, applicability of, 220
EMTALA and, 531
ERISA preemption of claims, 536
HMOs, 533
hospitals, 529
informed consent rules, 181, 495, 513, 535
See also INFORMED CONSENT, this
Index
malicious prosecution suits against lawyers, by,
1037
managed care organizations, 533
nursing homes, 537, 538, 542, 544
pharmacists relying on prescribing physician to
warn, 831
products liability, prescription drugs, 830
sexual activity with patient, effect of patient
consent, 179

**HEALTH MAINTENANCE
ORGANIZATIONS**
See MANAGED CARE ORGANIZATIONS

HIGH-SPEED POLICE CHASES
immunity of public entity vs. negligence analysis,
574
not a benefit for which public must pay costs, 161
scope of liability (proximate cause), 367

HISTORY
common law in America, 190, 192
common law writs, 27
conversion, development of, 91
defamation, 936
development of tort law, 27
fault principle adopted generally, 193
negligence actions, 190
negligence development after 1850, 195
oath-helpers, trial by, 104
products liability, 799
railroads' role in developing negligence law, 194,
195
Trespass and Case writs, 190

HOSPITALS
See also HEALTH CARE PROVIDERS;
INFORMED CONSENT; MANAGED
CARE ORGANIZATIONS; MEDICAL
MALPRACTICE
captain of the ship doctrine, 774
common-law responsibilities of, 529
"corporate negligence," 530
duty of reasonable care, 529
duty to accept patient for screening in
emergency, 531
ERISA preemption, 536
false imprisonment by, 74
HMOs, 533
immunities, 529, 597
managed care organizations, 533
mandatory screening and treatment, 531
ostensible agency, 530
patient dumping, 531
physicians as independent contractors, 530
practice of medicine by, 529
standard of care, 529
vicarious liability, 530

HUSBAND AND WIFE
See FAMILY

ICE AND SNOW
known danger, no reliance upon defendant's care,
625
landowner causing accumulations, duty of care,
485
natural accumulations, no duty of care, 483
obvious danger, 470
public entity immunity, 565
statutory duty to remove, public duty doctrine,
253
undertaking to third person, 627
unforeseeable, impossible to comply with rules of
the road, 259

ILLEGALITY
consent to illegal act, effect, 183
participation in illegal act barring claim, 144,
    183, 401
warrant fair on its face, privilege to execute, 156

IMMUNITIES
apportionment of liability and, 888
charities, 596
civil rights; state and local officers or entities,
    584, 586
comparative fault, calculation, 888
defamation, absolute privileges, 965
employer's immunity under workers'
    compensation statutes, 918
excuses distinguished, 42
good-deed immunity under statutes, 600
health care providers, good Samaritan statutes,
    523
hospitals, 529, 597
judicial, 1024
legal malpractice cases, 1178, 1191
legislative, 578, 584, 965, 968
lis pendens, filing, for, 1042
litigation participants generally, 1024
malicious prosecution, 1024
no-duty rules compared, 42
parental immunity, 593
privilege compared, 41
privilege distinguished, 593
public entities generally, 549
public officers or employees, 576
spousal, 591

INCAPACITY
adults, tests of, 171
consent, 164, 171
consent on behalf of person under an incapacity,
    173
determining capacity, 171
effects in giving consent, 171
judicial determination re civil commitment, 171
mental limitations distinguished, 172
minors, 172
standards applied in consenting for another, 173

INDEMNITY
        See also CONTRIBUTION
employer vicariously liable, indemnity vs.
    employee, 754
public officers, for, 576
traditional forms, 882

INDEPENDENT CONTRACTORS
        See also VICARIOUS LIABILITY
apparent authority or estoppel, 770
borrowed servants, 773
defined, 764
employer's vicarious liability for, 764
franchises, 765
non-delegable duties, 766
nuisance created by, employer's liability, 768
workers' compensation, contractors as employees,
    912

INDIVISIBLE INJURY
causal and fault apportionment of liability, 327,
    878
comparative fault apportionment, 406, 878
joint and several liability for, 327, 878, 881

INDUCING BREACH OF CONTRACT
See INTERFERENCE WITH CONTRACTS OR
    OPPORTUNITIES

INFANTS
See CHILDREN

INFORMED CONSENT
        Generally, 495, 513
autonomy and, 513
battery vs. negligence approaches, 514
causation requirements, 520
contributory fault of patient, 522
disclosure required; generally, 516
duress, 514
duty, who owes, 513
elements of claim, 515
expert testimony, 517
human experiments, military, 561
immaterial items, 518
information to be disclosed, 518
manner of disclosure, 520
material risk defined, 519
materiality standard of disclosure, 516, 518
medical standard of disclosure, 516, 518
mistake in giving consent generally, 181
negligence in performing procedure
    distinguished, 515
objective and subjective rules of causation, 521
patient entitlement to information, 513
probability of success, disclosure of, 519
refusal of treatment, 514
standards of disclosure, generally, 516
subjective and objective rules of causation, 521
therapeutic exception, 517
what must be disclosed, 518

INJUNCTIONS
compensated injunction, 748
defamation, 1002
effect of, 851
forbidding torts or ordering repair, 851
nuisance, 747
trade secret rights, 1204
trademark rights, 1205
trespass to land, 96
wrongful civil litigation, 1041

INJURIOUS FALSEHOOD
        See also INTERFERENCE WITH
            CONTRACTS OR
            OPPORTUNITIES
        Generally, 1113
defamation, relation to, 1114
elements, 1115
false advertising, trademark act, 1198
interests protected, 1113
malicious prosecution and, 1042
trademark tarnishment, 1197

INNKEEPERS
as "common carrier, " 453
duty of civility, emotional harm claims, 703
duty to protect guest from third persons, 454
duty to rescue guest, 620
general duty, 452
loss of guest's property, 191
protecting guests from third persons, 454
static conditions on property, 453
strict liability for property loss, 191

INSANITY
See MENTAL DISABILITY

INSURANCE
intended torts, coverage, 179
liability insurance generally, 47, 925
no-fault auto insurance, 925

INTELLECTUAL PROPERTY
See TRADE SECRETS; TRADEMARKS;
    UNFAIR COMPETITION

INTENT
    Generally, 55
battery, requirement of, 60
categorizing conduct as negligent or intentional,
    59
certainty test, 56, 88
children; capacity for, 58
conversion cases, 109
defined, 55
different person intended as victim, 79
different tort intended, 79
due process and equal protection claims, 583
Eighth Amendment civil rights claims, 584
evidence of, objective, 57
Fourth Amendment claims, 583
harm, intent to not required in trespass, 87
incapacity and, 58
interference with contracts or opportunities
    generally, 1089
meaning of, 55
mentally disabled persons, capacity for, 58
misrepresentation, 1120
motive distinguished, 57
negligence and, 58
non-tortious, 55
purpose test, 56
recklessness compared, 59
specificity of, 56
state of mind showing, 55
subjective quality of, 57
substantial certainty,
    risk distinguished, 200
    test of intent, 56, 707
third person intended victim, 79
transferred intent, 79, 101, 711
trespass to chattels, 105
trespass to land, 86
wantonness compared, 59

**INTENTIONAL INFLICTION OF
    EMOTIONAL DISTRESS**
See EMOTIONAL DISTRESS

INTENTIONAL TORTS
    See also particular torts such as ASSAULT
chattels, to, generally, 91
children's, 58
damages generally, 82
emotional distress, intentional infliction of, 705
extended liability for, 79
FTCA exclusion of specified torts, 562
land, to, generally, 85
negligence and, 187, 266
negligence distinguished, 200
negligently risking others', see AIDING,
    ABETTING, this Index
person, to, generally, 53
purposeful infliction of bodily harm claim, 55
real property, to, generally, 85
Restatement Third umbrella liability approach,
    54
transferred intent, 79
workers' compensation, exclusive remedy
    exception, 921

**INTERFERENCE WITH CONTRACTS OR
    OPPORTUNITIES**
    See also INJURIOUS FALSEHOOD
        and particular methods of
        interference such as
        DEFAMATION
    Generally, 1089
advising breach, privilege, 1105
agents, interference by, 1105
alienation of affections and, 1051, 1057
burden of proof, 1095, 1107
circumventing wrongful litigation rules by claim
    of, 1037
damages, 1092
defendant's financial interest as justification,
    1104
element of damages in some other tort, 1091
elements, 1095
factors in determining wrongfulness, 1098
federal governmental immunity, 562
free speech, 1105
history, 1093
inducing breach, 1089
intent required, 1099
interference by,
    boycott or refusal to deal, by, 1105
    breach of contract, 1102
    coercive threats, by, 1106
    competition, by, 1103
    exercising a right, 1104
    giving truthful information, 1105
knowledge of contract required, 1096
malice as meaning intent, 1099
marriage contracts, 1103
motives,
    contract interference cases, 1101
    mixed, 1101
    opportunity cases, 1108
negligent interference, 1112
opportunities,
    improper means, 1108
    litigation; spoliation of evidence, 1110
    motive, 1108
    non-contractual generally, 1107

noncommercial, 1110
plaintiff's performance, interference with, 1105
prima facie tort, as, 1110
privilege,
> generally, 1103
> advising breach, 1105
> agent's, 1105
> competition; opportunity cases, 1103
> marriage contracts, 1103
> protection of self or others by interfering, 1104

prospects, see Opportunities, this topic
public entities, 562
remedies, generally, 1092
truth, privilege to interfere by stating, 1105
wrongfulness required,
> generally, 1094, 1099
> factors in determining wrongfulness, 1098
> means and motive, 1100
> privileged or justified conduct, 1103

INTERFERENCE WITH FAMILY
See FAMILY

INTERNET PROVIDERS
defamation, privilege, 942, 970

INTERVENING CAUSE
See SCOPE OF LIABILITY (PROXIMATE CAUSE)

INTOXICATED PERSONS
alcohol providers, liability for injuries caused by, 661
arrest, no duty to, 656
automobile accidents, involved in most, 661
automobile owner's duty to recover keys from, 653
contributory negligence of, 232
driving as willful or wanton misconduct 59
duty to, 394, 663
negligence; standard of care and, 226, 231
negligent entrustment of land or chattels to, 653
standard of care, 226, 231
superseding cause or not, 364
violation of statute driving while intoxicated, 232
weapons sold to, 655

JAILERS
duty of custodians generally, 645
duty to furnish medical aid, 621
duty to prevent prisoner's suicide, 395
duty to release prisoner, 77

JOINT AND SEVERAL LIABILITY
> See also APPORTIONMENT OF LIABILITY; COMPARATIVE FAULT; FACTUAL CAUSE; CONTRIBUTION; INDEMNITY

Generally, 878
abolishing or modifying, 881, 884
concert of action, 881
contribution among tortfeasors, 882
criticisms, 883
current status of, 881
for economic damages only, 879

immune and nonparty tortfeasors, 888
indemnity, 882
indivisible injury rule, 881
market share distinguished, 330
meanings, 878
several liability systems compared, 884
tortfeasor who risks another's intentional tort, 895
traditional rules, 881
vicarious liability, 882
with reallocation, 879, 901
workers' compensation system compared, 918

JOINT ENTERPRISE
vicarious liability of joint enterprisers, 753

JUDGES
> See also JUDICIAL AND LEGAL PROCESS
absolute immunity, 577, 965

JUDICIAL AND LEGAL PROCESS
adjudication of tort cases, generally, 33
adversary system, 34
attorney's fees, 43
burden of proof, concept of, 39
community values and jury's role, 37
defamation, jury role in, 944, 948
duty determinations, judge and jury, 204, 211, 292
expense of trial, 34
judge's role, generally, 35, 291
jury's role, see JURY, this Index
justification for acts done under legal process, 156
preponderance of the evidence proof standard, 39
prima facie case, 38
process values affecting tort rules generally, 15
process values supporting objective rules, 227
remedies, 43
sources of evidence, 39
strategy; judge-jury roles and, 37
sufficiency of evidence, 36, 292

JURY
community values and, 37
credibility determinations, 36
criticisms of, 37
evaluator of evidence, 36
fact-evaluation role, 36
judicial roles compared, 35, 292
negligence cases, roles in, 291
roles in negligence cases, 291
strategic impact of, 37

JURY INSTRUCTIONS
care commensurate with danger, 216
child standard of care, 233
emergency doctrine, 220
medical malpractice, 505
mere happening, 221
reasonable person standard of care, 215
res ipsa loquitur, 300
superior knowledge, 230
unavoidable accident, 221

JUSTIFICATION
    See also ARREST; DEFENSE OF
        PROPERTY; PRIVILEGE; SELF-
        DEFENSE
excuse distinguished, 41
immunities and privileges compared, 41
interference with contract or opportunity, 1094,
    1103
legal process, 156

LANDLORD AND TENANT
conditions of premises, liability for, 488
criminal attacks, duty to protect against, 643
duty to control dangerous tenant, 656
forcible entry and detainer, 148
repossessing land from holdover tenant or others,
    91, 148
warranty of habitability, 491

LANDOWNERS OR OCCUPIERS
    See also DEFENSE OF PROPERTY;
        LANDLORD AND TENANT;
        NUISANCE; TRESPASS
abnormally dangerous activities; strict liability to
    persons on land, 786
abolishing categories generally, 478
activities on the land causing harm outside, 485
animals escaping, 485
attractive nuisance, 476, 480
children on the land, 473
classification of entrants,
    abolishing, 478
    children, 473
    invitees, 465
    licensees, 462
    trespassers, 460, 478
duty,
    intoxicated persons, 472
    invitees, 468
    firefighters, 605
    licensees, 463
    persons outside the land, 483
    persons straying from highway, 486
    protection of visitors from others, 638
    purchasers, 487
    rescue of invitee, 620
    trespassers, generally, 460
    trespassers who are discovered, 460
    trespassers who are foreseeable, 461
    trespassers who are trapped, 461
firefighters, 605
flagrant trespassers, lesser duty owed to, 478
household members sharing immunity, 459
invitees,
    classification, 465
    duty to, 468
    obvious dangers and, 470
    recreational use statutes, under, 479
licensees,
    activities on the land, 464
    classification, 462
    condition on the land, 463
    recreational use statutes, under, 479
natural conditions on the land, 483
naturally occurring snow or ice, 483
obvious dangers, 470

police officers, no duty to, 605
reasonable care standard for, 478
recreational use statutes, 4 79
Restatement Third approach, 478
slip and fall cases, 469
snow and ice,
    activities causing accumulation, 485
    removal from adjoining walks, 253
trees falling, 484
trespassers, 460, 478
trespassing children, 475
utility poles, 486
vegetation affecting highway safety, 484
vendors, 487

LAST CLEAR CHANCE
See COMPARATIVE FAULT

LATERAL AND SUBJACENT SUPPORT
strict liability, 777

LEGAL MALPRACTICE
    Generally, 1163
adversaries, no duty to, 1176
agency law and, 1164
attorney's fees, 1185
breach of duty, 1169
breach of fiduciary duty distinguished, 1164
case within a case,
    generally, 1173
    damages, collectability and settlement,
        1184
causation, 1172
client-lawyer relationship, establishing, 1165
codes of ethics, effect on claim, 1168
collectability, proof of, 1185
comparative fault, 1177
conflicts of interest, 1176
continuous representation rule, 1181
contract or tort claim for, 1164
contributory negligence, 1177
criminal malpractice,
    generally, 1186
    actual innocence requirement, 1188
    collateral estoppel, 1190
    court-appointed attorneys, 1191
    emotional distress recovery in, 1189
    exoneration requirement, 1187
    post-conviction relief requirement, 1187
    special rules for, 1187
damages,
    generally, 1182
    attorney's fees, 1185
    collectability, proof of, 1185
    emotional harm, 1183, 1189
    punitive, 1184
damages; case within a case, 1184
disciplinary proceedings distinguished, 1164
duty, 1165
economic loss rule not affecting action for, 1087
elements, 1165
entities, representation of, 1167
error of judgment rule, 1170
ethics rules, effect on standard, 1168
expert testimony requirement, 1169, 1171
factual cause, 1172

failure to read documents, client's, 1177
fiduciary duties, 1164
geographical limits on standard of care, 1168
immunities, 1178, 1187, 1191
in pari delicto, 1178
insured persons, representation of, 1167
intended beneficiaries, liability to, 1175
lawyer-client relationship, establishing, 1165
liability to non-clients, 1175
negligent misrepresentation theory, 1126
no duty to adversaries, 1176
non-clients, liability to, 1175
privity rule, 1175
proximate cause, 1172
public defenders, immunities, 1191
quasi-judicial immunity, 1179
remedies generally, 1182, 1189
scope of risk, 1172
settlements and, 1174
specialists, standard, 1168
standard of care, 1168
statute of limitations,
            generally, 1179
      continuous representation rule, 1181
      occurrence rule, 1179
      time-of-harm rule, 1180
third party beneficiaries, duty to, 1175
third-party fee payors, 1167
third persons, liability to or not, 1175
unsettled law, 1171

LEGISLATORS
absolute immunity, 578, 584, 965, 968

LENDER LIABILITY
See CREDITORS

LIABILITY INSURANCE
covering negligence, excluding intentional torts,
      179
no-fault auto insurance compared, 925
sovereign immunity, effect on, 567
tort law and, generally, 47, 925

LIBEL AND SLANDER
See DEFAMATION

LIENS
      See also INJURIOUS FALSEHOOD; LIS
            PENDENS; WRONGFUL
            ATTACHMENT OR LEVY
conversion, 115
excessive, liability for, 1042
legal malpractice, failure to file, 1170

LIS PENDENS
      See also WRONGFUL ATTACHMENT OR
            LEVY
wrongful civil litigation, 1042
wrongful use of, abuse of process as, 1044

LOSS OF A CHANCE
      See also SPOLIATION OF EVIDENCE
amount of recovery, 333
denial of liability, 331
diagnosis or treatment causing, 331
improbable chance of survival, generally, 331

increased risk creating duty, distinguished from,
      625
increased risk of future harm, 334
liability for all harm, 332
liability for value of the chance, 332
medical malpractice cases, 331
preexisting harm, 331
rescuer's liability for withdrawing aid, 622
scope of liability for increased risk, 331

MALICE
absence of probable cause for prosecution
            proving, 1028, 1033
as improper purpose, required for malicious
            prosecution claim, 1032
defamation,
            constitutional malice as knowing, reckless
                  falsehood, 994
            qualified privileged destroyed by, 969, 981
ill-will or improper purpose as, 965
interference with contract,
            intent as malice, 1094, 1099
            mixed motives, 1101
            proving motive by proving, 1100
malicious prosecution cases, 1032
nuisance; spite fences, 741
punitive damages, basis for claiming, 861

MALICIOUS PROSECUTION
            See also ABUSE OF PROCESS;
                  WRONGFUL ATTACHMENT
                  OR LEVY; WRONGFUL CIVIL
                  LITIGATION
            Generally, 1026
advice of counsel, 1029, 1036
damages, 1025, 1027
double jeopardy, termination of first action on
            grounds of, 1034
elements, 1026
false imprisonment compared, 78, 1026
falsity of complaint requirement, 1027
favorable termination requirement, 1033
federal governmental immunity, 562
guilt in fact as a defense, 1035
immunities, 1024
instigation of proceeding requirement, 1027
malice requirement, 1032
mixed motives in prosecuting, 1032
perjury not actionable as, 1024
policies, 1023
probable cause, 1028, 1032
public entities, 562
punitive damages, 1026
reasonable doubt, 1028
release of civil claim in exchange for
            abandonment of prosecution, 1035
statute of limitations, 1035

MANAGED CARE ORGANIZATIONS
cost containment devices creating risks, 535
ERISA preemption, 536
HMOs, 533
incentives, 536
independent-provider model, 534
informed consent, 535
liability of, 534

limitations on care provided by, 533
negligent hiring, 535
preemption of tort claims under ERISA, 536
staff model, 534
types of, 533
utilization review, 533
vicarious liability of, 534

MARITIME LAW
federal admiralty jurisdiction, 192
seaman injured, rights under, 911

MARKET SHARE LIABILITY
factual cause, substitute for, 330

MASTER AND SERVANT
See EMPLOYMENT AND EMPLOYERS;
    VICARIOUS LIABILITY

MEDICAL MALPRACTICE
    See also HEALTH CARE
        PROVIDERS; HOSPITALS;
        INFORMED CONSENT;
        MANAGED CARE
        ORGANIZATIONS
    Generally, 493
abandonment of patient, 531
assumption of risk, policy limits on, 412
battery, relation to informed consent, 515
blood suppliers protected under malpractice
    statutes, 331
captain of the ship doctrine, 774
causation, informed consent cases, 520
comparative fault of patient, 527
consent, parents' consent for minors, 173
contributory negligence of patient, 527
"corporate negligence" of hospitals, 530
defenses, 523
disclosure, standards of, 516
doctor-patient relationship, 497
duties to non-patients, 500
duty, generally, 497
duty to refer, 504
emergency, 220, 221, 495, 523
EMTALA statute, 531
ERISA preemption, employee benefits programs,
    536
expert testimony, 494, 509, 512, 517
geographical community, standard, 508
good Samaritan statutes, 523
HMOs, 529, 533
hospitals, responsibilities of, 529
informed consent, 181, 495, 513, 535
locality rule, 494, 508
loss of a small chance of more favorable outcome,
    331
"malpractice crisis" statutes, 524
managed care organizations, 529, 533
mandatory screening at hospitals, 531
mature minor's consent to medical procedure, 172
medical exams on behalf of third persons, 499
military, 560, 561
negligence action, as, 494
negligence unrelated to diagnosis, treatment, 527
non-patients, duties to, 500
nurses, 512
nursing homes, 537, 538, 542, 544

outpatients, duty to, 502
patient dumping, 531
patient's contributory negligence, 527
professional peer standard, 503
professional status, significance of, 495
reasonable care standard, 506
referral, duty of, 504
res ipsa loquitur, 302, 303, 305, 309
risk-utility weighing in, 506
rules in summary, 494
school of practice, standards, 509
specialists, standard, 508
standard of care,
    expert testimony required, 509
    geographical community, 508
    good Samaritan statutes, 523
    jury instructions, 505
    medical custom, 503
    professional-peer standard, 503
    reasonable person standard distinguished,
        506
    specialists, 508
    traditional, 503
state or national standard, 508
statute of limitations,
    continuing treatment, 436
    repose statutes, 433
statutes limiting liability, 524
therapists, sexual behavior with consenting
    patient, 179
third party retaining doctor for patient, 499
traditional medical standard of care, 503

MEMORY
false memory implanted, 1057
forgetfulness and the standard of care, 229
repressed memory, statute of limitations and,
    439

**MENTAL DISABILITY OR LEGAL
    INCAPACITY**
    See also DISABILITY
capacity for intent, 58
children, legal capacity, 58, 233
civil law, 227
consent affected by, 164, 171, 173
contributory negligence of mentally impaired,
    226
defendant's duty to deal with plaintiff's
    incapacity, 400
effect in determining negligence or comparative
    fault, 392
intoxicated persons, 231
liability of persons suffering, 58, 225
not a defense generally, 58
proceedings to determine, wrongful civil
    litigation, 1041
standard of care of mentally impaired, 226
statute of limitations,
    discovery rule, objective test, 430
    psychological impediments to suit, 436
    tolling for, 436
tests of, 171
undue influence, 77

MILITARY TORTS
See also GOVERNMENT ENTITIES
civilian negligence, 560
combat activities, immunity for, 558
families of service members, claims by, 561
Federal Torts Claims Act, 558
Feres rule, 558
foreign countries, claims arising in, 558
human experimentation, 561
"incident to service" test for immunity, 558
military discipline, 559

MINING
trespass to land by, 95

MINORS
See CHILDREN; FAMILY

MISREPRESENTATION
Generally, 1113
bargain context of, 1115
commercial loss rule, 1126
comparative fault, 1131
concealment as, 1135
conscious ignorance of facts, 1121
constructive fraud, 1117
contractual limitations on liability, 1136
damages,
    innocent misrepresentation, 1141
    intentional misrepresentation, 1138
    market based measures, 1138
    negligent misrepresentation, 1138
    rescission-equivalent, 1140
damages vs. rescission, 1117
describing fact vs. describing a tort, 1117
disclaimers, 1136
disgorgement of defendant's profits, 1138
duty of reasonable care in making, 1125
duty to correct, 1120
elements of the tort, 1118
exculpatory clauses, 1136
federal governmental immunity, 562
fiduciaries' duties, 1125
half-truth, 1120
innocent, 1127
intent required, 1120
intent to deceive, 1122
investigation by plaintiff, 1132
justifiable reliance,
    comparative fault issue distinguished, 1131
    investigation not required, 1132
    rule requiring, 1130
materiality requirement, 1119, 1128
negating consent, 175
negligence; relevance of, 1121
negligent, liability for, 1123
nondisclosure, 1135
opinion,
    approximation, as, 1133
    judgment or taste, as, 1133
    law, and prediction statements, generally, 1132
    statement of value or quality, 1134
prediction statements, 1132
privity not required, 1134
public entities, 562

reckless, defined, 1120
reformation, 1137
reliance,
    investigation by the plaintiff, 1132
    required, 1129
rescission,
        generally, 1138
    mistake, 1128
risking injury or property damage; distinguished, 1123
scienter required, 1120
statute of limitations, fraudulent concealment and, 438
strict liability,
    innocent misrepresentation, 1127
    rescission cases, 1128
third persons, negligent representations reaching, 1134
warranty and, 1127
workers' compensation and, 921

MISTAKE
appearances controlling in self-defense, 135
collateral mistake, 176
consent induced by, 175
conversion, no defense to, 110
defense of property, 141, 153
ignorance distinguished, 181
nature of transaction, 176
negating required intent, 42
not a defense generally, 42
protecting others from attack, 137
recapture of chattels, in, 151
self-defense, in, 135
trespass to land, no defense, 87

MITIGATION OF DAMAGES
See AVOIDABLE CONSEQUENCES

MOTION TO DISMISS
procedure defining tort issue, 34

MOTIVE
See also BAD FAITH; INTENT; MALICE
Generally, 57
abuse of process, required, 1235
affecting scope of absolute privilege, 1179
conversion cases, 110
defamation, 981
false imprisonment without privilege, irrelevant, 73
hospital's screening duty independent of, 531
intent distinguished, 57
interference with contract etc.,
    competitive motive, 1103
    exercising contract right, 1105
    role in liability, 1090, 1099, 1102, 1104, 1105
malicious prosecution, required, 1032
mixed motives, 757, 761, 1101
privacy, newsworthiness privilege held dependent upon, 1016
punitive damages, basis for, 861, 1001
vicarious liability, affecting, 757, 761

MUNICIPAL CORPORATIONS
See GOVERNMENT ENTITIES

NECESSITY
defense to intentional tort, as, 157
private, privilege to use another's land or
chattels, 157
privilege of, defeating defense of property
privilege, 141
public, privilege to affect property of others, 158
public, takings by public entities, constitutional
considerations, 159

NEGLIGENCE
See also particular elements of the case
such as DUTY; FACTUAL CAUSE
and SCOPE OF LIABILITY
(PROXIMATE CAUSE); and see also
particular settings such as
HOSPITALS, LANDOWNERS,
LEGAL MALPRACTICE, MEDICAL
MALPRACTICE, and PRODUCTS
LIABILITY
Generally, 185
ability or prowess special to the actor, 225
acceptable risks, 267
actual harm requirement, 311
affirmative defenses, generally, 198
amount of care/standard of care distinguished,
216
animals; dangerous, 780
assumption of risk negating, 420
background, common law, 190
balancing, see risk-utility assessment, this topic
blind persons, standard of care, 223
burden of proof, 293
care commensurate with danger standard, 216,
220
Case, Trespass on the, writ, 191
causing loss of a small chance of survival, 331
characteristics of the negligence case,
actual harm requirement, 189
bodily harm and property damage, 189
damages allowable, 189
elements of claim, 197
fault, role of, 187
fault principle developed, 193
jury roles, 189
open-ended claims, 188
personal injury and property damage, 189
prima facie case elements, 197
specific conduct rule, 188
varied negligence claims, 187
children,
adult standard of care, 236
anticipating negligence of, 217
rule of sevens, 233
standard of care, 233
violation of statute; effect, 233
circumstances,
considered, 216
effect of, 216
circumstantial evidence, 295
communication, 188
conduct,
intoxication cases, 231

specific physical act or omission, 263
state of mind distinguished, 200
contributory negligence judged similarly, 214
cost-benefit assessment, see risk-utility
assessment, this topic
credibility of witnesses, 36
custom, see CUSTOM, this Index
damages required, 311
defamation cases, in, 987, 990, 995
defendant's business practices evidence of
feasible precautions, 282
defendant's internal rules showing foreseeability
of harm, 282
defense of property, relationship, 146
defined as breach of duty, 198
defined as risk, 198, 200
disease communicated, as, 176
duty; breach distinguished, 198, 205
elements of the case, 197
emergency, 218, 223
evaluating conduct, methods or principles for,
215
evaluating fact, jury's role, 297
evidence,
circumstantial generally, 295
forms of, 295
inferences, 297
presumptions, 300
expert testimony, 296
extraordinary care in special danger, meaning,
217
fault, as one type of, 187
federal preemption, 441
foreseeability of harm, 264
forgetfulness and memory, 229
gas or electricity, care required, 217
general principle of liability, as, 193
gross negligence, 239
history and development, 190
instructions, 220, 229, 233
intent compared and distinguished, 57
intentional conduct creating risks, 200
intentional torts and, 187, 266
intoxicated persons, 226, 231
jury roles generally, 35, 189, 291
knowledge, 229
livestock on highways, 779
medical malpractice; see MEDICAL
MALPRACTICE
memory, 229
mental disability, 225
negligence per se, see *per se*, this topic
negligent entrustment, 367, 653
negligent hiring, retention, or supervision, 657
objective standard,
generally, 213
mental capacity, 225
subjective elements in, 222
per se,
generally, 243
children violating statute, 258
class of persons test, 255
duty, and, 245
evidence of negligence alternative, 249
examples of statutes, 243

excused violation of statute, 257
federal statutes, effect, 244, 252
intoxicated driving, 232
judicial borrowing and, 251
ordinary negligence, relation to, 245
OSHA regulations, 249
private right of action distinguished, 247
proximate cause, 256
public duty doctrine and, 253
rationales, 250
scope of risk, 256
statutory violations as, 243
strict liability or excused violation, 260
traffic violations, 243, 247
type of harm test, 253
unsuitable statutes, 252
physical disability sudden or unforeseeable, 224
Pied Piper cases, 656
police chases, 574
preconception tort, 675
preemption, federal, 441
presumptions, 300
probability of harm expressed as foreseeability, 265
proving negligence claims, 291
reasonable person,
    characteristics, 222, 223, 225
    knowledge, memory and skill of, 229
    mental capacity, 225
    physical characteristics, 223
    standard, see standard of care, this topic
reasonableness evaluations; risks and utilities considered, 268
reckless, willful or wanton misconduct, 240
releasing dangerous person, 575
res ipsa loquitur; see RES IPSA LOQUITUR, this Index
risk, 198, 229
risk-utility assessment,
    Carroll Towing formula, 271
    common scale, 273
    comparing dollar costs, 270
    criticism and support for, 275
    custom and, 282
    discounting harm to reflect probability, 274
    economic interpretation, 271
    factors in, 268
    illustration of, 269
    Learned Hand's formula, 271
    moral interpretation, 277
    practices showing precaution feasible, 282
    probability of harm, relevance, 265, 274
    safety precaution as a burden to defendant, 271
    structured approach to, 271
    utility of defendant's conduct, 268, 270
risking torts of others, 563, 634, 661, 895, 898
rules of the road, violating, 243
scope of negligence claims in tort system, 187
slip-and-fall, 469
snow and ice removal, 253
specific act or omission, 188, 263, 324
standard of care,
    amount of precaution distinguished, 216
    carriers' duty to passengers, 447

characteristics of reasonable people, 222
children, 233
circumstances alter cases, 222
commensurate care rule, 216
contributory negligence, 214, 226
custom evidence of, 281
dangerous instrumentalities, 216
defined, 213
emergency, actions in, 218
extraordinary care expressions, 217
formulations of, 214
generality of standard, 213
heightened danger, 216
intoxication, 226, 231
invariant with danger, 216
jury instructions on, 215
knowledge or memory, 229
mental capacity and disabilities, 225
negligence and contributory negligence, 214
non-technical usages of the term, 215
objective and subjective components, 195, 213, 222
ordinary, 213
particular "classes" of person, 214
physical characteristics and disabilities, 223
professionals generally, 230, 495
reasonable person standard,
    as default standard, 213
    breach distinguished, 216
    custom, and, 281
    displaced by specific rules, 243
    generality of, 213
    negligence per se and, 243
risk, relation to, 215
specific standards distinguished, 214, 243
superior knowledge, and, 231
terminology, 215
special danger, 216
superior knowledge or skill, 230
unchanging, 216
state of mind,
    comparative fault, 388
    insufficient to show, 200
statute violation, see *per se*, this topic
statutes; tort law effects of, 3, 30, 243
stop, look, listen rule, 10
strict liability,
    history relating to, 193
    pockets of, 197
subjective elements in, 222
summary judgment, 35
swimming pool operators, care owed, 217
terminology, risky conduct vs. type of case, 197
toxic substances, care required, 217
unavoidable accident, 218
unreasonable risk, as, 264
weapons, care required, 216

NEGLIGENT ENTRUSTMENT
liability for, 653
proximate cause, 367

NEGLIGENT HIRING, RETENTION, OR SUPERVISION
employer's liability, 657

vicarious liability distinguished, 754

NEGOTIABLE INSTRUMENTS
conversion of, 111

NO-FAULT AUTOMOBILE INSURANCE
        Generally, 925
adoption, 926
criticisms, 927

NOISE
causing accident, 270
nuisance as, 735, 742
trespass to land, not actionable as, 92

NOMINAL DAMAGES
trespass to land, 96

NON-ACTION, LIMITING LIABILITY FOR
        See also ACTS AND OMISSIONS;
                DUTY TO PROTECT
        Generally, 615
affirmative acts, distinguishing, 618
assuming duty by undertaking or promise, 623,
        631
bad Samaritan statutes, 617
beginning to assist as trigger of duty, 616, 622
causing harm as trigger of duty, 616
characterizing conduct, 618
creating risks as trigger of duty, 616
criminal statutes requiring action, 618
criticisms of general rule, 616, 617
beginning to assist or rescue, 622
        innocently harming or creating risk of
                harm, 619
        undertaking or promise, 623
exceptions, 616
general rule of no duty, 615, 618
good Samaritan statutes, 623
increased risk, undertaking and, 625
innocently harming or creating risk of harm, 619
moral blame and, 616
policy considerations, 630
promise as trigger of duty, 616
reliance, undertaking and, 625, 629
rescue, beginning to, as trigger of duty, 622
scope of rule protecting non-action, 618
social hosts serving alcohol and, 620
special relationships creating duty,
        generally, 616
        between plaintiff and defendant, 620
undertaking creating duty, generally, 623
        action as undertaking, 625
        contemporary rules, 628
        increased risk, 625
        non-performance increasing risk, 628
        reliance, 625, 629
        scope of duty created, 624, 631
        third persons, undertaking creating duty
                to, 627

NON-DELEGABLE DUTY
See VICARIOUS LIABILITY

NONFEASANCE
See NON-ACTION, LIMITING LIABILITY FOR

NUISANCE
abatement, 747
abnormal danger and, 784
absolute nuisance, 733
accommodation vs. rights, 734, 736
aircraft overflights, 94, 734
anticipated harm, 743
balancing harm and utility, 740
coming to the nuisance, 740
damages,
        generally, 748
        measured to provide incentives, 750
defenses, coming to the nuisance, 740
dignitary vs. economic tort, 931
fear of future harm, 743
gravity of harm, 740
independent contractor creating, 768
injunction,
        generally, 747
        compensated injunction, 748
intentional, 738
legislative declarations distinguished, 734
negligent, 736
neighborhood character, 738
noise and smoke, 92
obstruction of public ways, 745
owner's failure to abate another's, 737
per accidens and per se, 733
permanent, 748
personal injury, 746, 749
possessory rights distinguished, 91
preemption or displacement by other laws, 733
priority in time, 740
private,
        aesthetic nuisances, 742
        character of neighborhood, 738
        coming to the nuisance, 740
        defined, 734
        examples, 735
        fear of future harm, 743
        gravity of harm, 740
        intent, negligence, strict liability, 736
        magnitude, frequency, duration exceeding
                norms, 739
        non-invasive activities or conditions, 742
        unreasonable invasion required, 738
        utility of defendant's activity, 741
Prosser's jungle, 733
public,
        abutting owners, 745
        defined, 744
        personal injury, 746
        public waters, 746
        standing to sue, 745
remedies generally, 747
scope of nuisance law, 733
sensitive persons or uses, 735
smoke and noise, 92
strict liability, 737
surface waters causing, 92
temporary, 749
trespass and, 89, 93, 734, 735
underground liquids, 93
utility of defendant's activity, existence of
        nuisance and remedy, 747

vicarious responsibility for, 737
zoning, effect, 739

NURSING HOMES AND RESIDENTIAL FACILITIES
Generally, 537
abuse of residents, 540
common-law claims against, 542
elder abuse and, 537
false imprisonment by, 74
management decisions causing harm, 541
medical errors in, 539
neglect of residents, 541
negligent hiring, retention and supervision, 543
premises conditions, 541
protecting residents from employees, negligence in, 543
staff members, suits against, 542
standard of care, 538, 540
statutes and regulations,
    conflicts between medical malpractice and nursing home statutes, 547
    federal, 544
    state, 546
statutory claims against, 544
types of injuries caused in, 537
understaffing, 543
vicarious liability, 542

OCCUPIER'S LIABILITY
See LANDOWNERS OR OCCUPIERS

OFFICERS
See also ARREST; CIVIL RIGHTS; POLICE; GOVERNMENT ENTITIES
absolute immunity, judicial and legislative, 584
arrest under warrant, 156
arrest without a warrant, 156
civil rights, federal immunity, 584
conversion of chattels by, 114
custody of property, duty of protection, 156
federal, immunity, 580
liability for harm to seized goods, 156
parole officers' duty, 656
state and local,
    civil rights liabilities of, 584
    immunity, 576
    public indemnity for, 576
trespass to land by permitting others to enter, 86
warrants, executing, justification, 156

OMISSIONS
See ACTS AND OMISSIONS; NON-ACTION

OPEN AND OBVIOUS DANGER
comparative fault vs. no-negligence analysis, 389, 472
landowners warning duty and, 470
plaintiff's foreseeable encounter with, 470
products liability,
    consumer expectations test and, 812
    warning duty, 827

OUTRAGE
See EMOTIONAL DISTRESS

PARENT AND CHILD
See CHILDREN; FAMILY

PAROLE OF PRISONERS
discretionary immunity, 554
duty to supervise parolees, 656

PATENTS
preemption, role, effect on trademark protection, 1202

PERCOLATION OR MIGRATION OF LIQUIDS
nuisance, 735, 95, 740
strict liability, 785, 788
subsurface, trespass to land, 93, 95

PERJURY
no tort claim for, 966, 1024
spoliation of evidence distinguished, 1025

PERSONALITY OR PERFORMANCE RIGHTS
publicity, right of, 1005, 1206

PHYSICIANS AND SURGEONS
See HEALTH CARE PROVIDERS; MEDICAL MALPRACTICE; MANAGED CARE ORGANIZATIONS

PLAINTIFF NEGLIGENCE
See COMPARATIVE NEGLIGENCE

POISONS
See also HAZARDOUS WASTES
abnormally dangerous activities, 788
battery by, 67
crop dusting, inherent danger, 767
defense of property by, 146
insecticides, federal preemption, 845
products, warnings by pictographs, 829
statute, class of harm protected against, 254

POLICE
See also ARREST; CIVIL RIGHTS; OFFICERS
civil rights liabilities, 584
defamation of; officer as public official, 992
duty voluntarily assumed, 625
emotional distress inflicted by, 708
failure to train, 587
firefighters' rule applied to, 605
high-speed chases, 161, 367, 574
land damaged by law enforcement activity, 160
malicious prosecution, liability for, 1027
promise of protection, 625
victim treatment, emotional distress, 708

POLLUTION
See HAZARDOUS WASTES; NUISANCE; TOXIC TORTS

POSSESSION
conversion, basis of suit for, 108
land, rights of protected, 91
trespass to chattels, basis of suit for, 106

PRECONCEPTION NEGLIGENCE
Generally, 675

PREEMPTION
compliance with statute and, 441, 844

credit reporting, 946
effect on tort law, 45, 441
ERISA preemption, medical malpractice claims, 536
express, 442
federal laws ousting state laws, 45, 441
forms, 442
implied, 442
patent laws preempting state-granted protections, 1202
products liability, 443, 830, 844, 845
railroad cases, 442
Supremacy Clause, as source of, 45, 442

PREMISES LIABILITY
See LANDOWNERS OR OCCUPIERS

PRENATAL AND BIRTH-RELATED INJURY
Generally, 669
abortion, 671, 677
damages, special rules for, 680
liability for negligently inflicting, 675
mitigation of damages, 682
parental responsibility for, 675
parent's duty to fetus, 675
preconception negligence, 675
prenatal injury generally, 669
products liability for, 674
toxic injury, 672
viability, 670
workers' compensation and, 673, 919
wrongful birth, conception or life, 677
wrongful death of fetus or unborn child, 670

PREPONDERANCE OF THE EVIDENCE
See also BURDEN OF PROOF; PROCEDURE
loss of an unlikely chance, 331
meaning, 39

PRIMA FACIE CASE
affirmative defenses distinguished, 40
meaning, 39

PRIMA FACIE TORT
concept of, 1110
limitations, 1111

PRINCIPAL AND AGENT
See also EMPLOYERS AND EMPLOYMENT; INDEPENDENT CONTRACTORS; VICARIOUS LIABILITY
agent's privilege to advise principal to breach contract, 1105
agent's storage, purchase, or sale for principal as conversion, 115
client-lawyer relationship, 1164
guardian consenting to treatment for ward, 174
parent consenting to treatment on behalf of child, 173

PRISONS AND PRISONERS
custodian's duty to protect prisoner, 645
Eighth Amendment, 584
escape of prisoner, duty to protect from, 656
medical attention required, 584, 621
suicide of one in custody, 395

PRIVACY
Generally, 1005
appropriation of plaintiff's identity,
    generally, 1005, 1206
    dignitary vs. property right, 1006
    First Amendment and, 1008
    intent, 1007
    newsworthiness, 1007
biography, 1007
civil rights, intrusion, 1010
confidential client information, lawyer's duties, 1164
data privacy, 1009
false light,
    generally, 1019
    constitutional constraints, 1021
    defamation, and, 1019
    elements, 1019
    overlap with other torts, 1020
    rejecting the tort, 1020
gays and lesbians, outing, 1016
history, 1005
intrusion upon seclusion,
    generally, 1008
    data privacy, 1009
    emotional distress, 1011
    employee privacy rights, 1012
    expectation of privacy, 1009, 1010
    free speech concerns, 1012
    overlap with other torts, 1011
private facts publicity,
    constitutional limits on claim, 1014, 1018
    constitutional limitations as to public, 1014, 1017
    generally, 1013
    newsworthiness, 1015
    rejecting the tort, 1018
    wrongfully obtained information, 1015
public records,
    generally, 1017
    excluding public access to, 1018
seller's intrusion in repossessing goods, 152
types of, 1005

PRIVILEGE
See also CONSENT; IMMUNITIES; and particular topics such as DEFAMATION
Generally, 40
absolute, 1179, 1191
abuse of, destruction by, 980
arrest under warrant, 156
arrest without a warrant, 156
defamation, absolute, 965
defamation, qualified privileges generally, 972
defense of a third person, 137
defenses other than privilege, 41
discipline, 138
entry upon land, 152
executive branch business, 968
immunities compared and distinguished, 41, 593
interference with contract or opportunity, 1103
judicial proceedings,
    defamation, 965

lawyers, 1179, 1181
justification vs. excuse, 41
lis pendens as absolutely privileged, 1042
merchant's detention of suspected shoplifter, 153
necessity, 157
parental discipline, 594
protection of others, 137
public necessity, 158
qualified or conditional, 972
recapture of chattels, 150, 152
recovery of or reentry upon land, 147
rights distinguished, 41
schools, discipline of children, 138
self-defense, 131
teachers, discipline of children, 138
third person unintentionally injured in exercise
    of, 142

PRIVITY
    See also AIDING AND ABETTING;
        SCOPE OF LIABILITY
        (PROXIMATE CAUSE); THIRD
        PERSONS
legal malpractice, 1175
misrepresentation, not required, 1134
requirement in early products liability cases, 799

PROBABLE CAUSE
    See also ARREST; MALICIOUS
        PROSECUTION
arrest, 156
civil rights claims, in, 584
defined, arrest cases, 156
malicious prosecution, 1028
meaning generally, 156
required to sustain arrest without warrant, 156

PROCEDURE
    See also BURDEN OF PROOF;
        EVIDENCE; JUDICIAL AND
        LEGAL PROCESS
adversary presentation, 34
affirmative defenses, 40
burden of proof, 39
judge's rulings on admission or exclusion of
    evidence, 293
motions and rulings defining tort issues, 34
new trial, power of judge to grant, 292
preponderance of evidence or probability, 39
prima facie case, 38
summary judgment, 35
trials and appeals, 33

PROCESS RIGHTS
See ABUSE OF PROCESS; JUDICIAL AND
    LEGAL PROCESS; MALICIOUS
    PROSECUTION

PROCESS VALUES
See JUDICIAL AND LEGAL PROCESS

PRODUCTS LIABILITY
    Generally, 797
alteration of product, 838
alternative causation, 329
assumption of risk, 835

birth control prescriptions and devices, warnings
    due, 831
breach of warranty theory, 798
burden of proof,
    design defects; shifting, 824
    reasonable alternative design, 816, 820
    risk-utility test generally, 816
causation,
    proximate cause or superseding cause, 841
    required element, 805
    warning cases, 832
circumstantial evidence,
    design defects, 819
    manufacturing defects, 810
commercial distributors covered, 804
comparative causation, 838
comparative fault,
    apples and oranges argument, 838
    classifications of plaintiff-fault, 834
    defense generally, 834
    misuse, 842
    reduction of damages for, 834
    safety devices, 837
compliance with statute, 844
consumer expectations,
    open and obvious danger and test of, 812
    problems with test, 812
    Restatement 3d rejecting test, 808
    test of defect, 808
crashworthiness, 840
defect,
    design, generally, 806
    manufacturing, 806
    marketing, 807
    misuse negating, 838
    negligence and, 805
    requirement of, 804
    types of, 805
design defect,
    burden of proof, 824
    consumer expectations test for, 808
    defined, 806
    evidence of risks and utilities, 817
    expert testimony, 817, 822
    foreseeability requirement, 819
    negligence test, 816
    reasonable alternative design,
        alternative to proof of, 824
        evidence of, 822
        expert testimony, 822
        judicial support, 820
        objections to, 821
        requirement, 816, 820
        what counts as, 823
    risk-utility test for, 814, 816
    warning not a remedy, when, 826
economic harm, 803
economic loss rule, 803
employment, products sold for use in, 832
English-only warnings, 829
enhanced injury resulting from defect, 840
expert testimony required or not, 817
fetal injury, causal issues, 674
firefighters' rule and, 613
foreseeability requirement, 819

heeding presumption, 832
historical development, 799
industry standards, scientifically unknowable
        risk distinguished, 842
learned intermediary rule, 830
manufacturing defect;
                generally, 806
        causation, proving, 811
        proving, 810
mass inoculations, warnings due, 831
misrepresentation theories, 799
misuse,
        comparative fault, as, 842
        crashworthiness, 840
        defect issue, bearing on, 838
        foreseeable, 839
        meanings of term, 838
        superseding cause, as, 841
modification, 838
negligence, as theory, 798
negligence; privity rule abolished, 800
negligence vs. strict liability,
        burden of proof distinctions, 824
        risk-utility test, 816
        warning defects and, 825
open and obvious dangers,
        consumer expectations and, 812
        design cases, 820
        risks and utilities, 820
        warnings and, 827
pharmacists, 831
plaintiff's failure to discover product defect, 836
preemption of state law, 844
prescription drugs,
        warnings, 830
privity, 799
proving design defects,
        burden of proof, shifts in, 824
        expert testimony, 817
        reasonable alternative design, 820
        risk-utility test, 814, 816
        shifting burden of proof, 824
proving manufacturing defects, 810
proximate cause; superseding cause, 841
rationales for strict liability, 801
reasonable alternative design, 820
Restatement Second § 402A, 804, 808
Restatement Third (Products Liability),
        comparative fault, 835
        consumer expectation test under, 808
        design defects; reasonable alternative
                design, 816, 820
        risk-utility test under, 815
risk-utility test,
        cash costs of safety under, 817
        cost in increased risks to others under, 818
        cost of lost productive utility under, 818
        defect determined by, 814
        evidence under, 817
        negligence and, 816
        reasonable alternative design, 816, 820
        warnings, 826
scope of field, 797
scope of risk, 834
sophisticated users, 831

statutes of limitation, 433, 847
statutory defenses, 842
strict liability,
        decline of, 802
        development of, 801
        rationales for, 801
strict liability vs. negligence,
        burden of proof distinctions, 816, 824
        warning defects and, 825
subsequent remedial measures, 823
substitute products, relevance, 822
superseding cause, misuse, alteration as, 841
theories of, 797
unknowable risks, statutes, 842
warnings,
        adequacy, 828
        causation requirement, 832
        content and expression, 828
        employer as sophisticated purchaser, 832
        employer-purchasers, 832
        English-only warnings, 829
        failure to read, content vs. display
                adequacy, 833
        foreseeability of risks, 826
        form, location or display, 829
        heeding presumption, 832
        information defects and, 807
        learned intermediary rule, 830
        negligence vs. strict liability, 825
        open and obvious dangers, 827
        required, when, 826
        risk-utility analysis, 826
        role of, 826
        scope of risk or proximate cause, 834
        statutes prescribing, 830
        strict liability vs. negligence, 825
        sophisticated users, 830
warranty,
        implied; development of, 800
        privity rule abolished, 800
        theories associated with contract, 798

PROFESSIONAL RISK–TAKERS
See FIREFIGHTERS AND FIREFIGHTER'S
        RULE

PROMISSORY ESTOPPEL
reliance upon gratuitous promises, 628

PROPORTIONAL CAUSATION
See LOSS OF A CHANCE

PROTECTION FROM THIRD PERSONS
See DUTY TO PROTECT FROM THIRD
        PERSONS AND FROM SELF-HARM

PROXIMATE CAUSE
See SCOPE OF LIABILITY

**PURPOSEFUL INFLICTION OF BODILY
        HARM**
Restatement Third creation of claim for, 54
scope of tort, 55
umbrella liability for intentional physical harm
        approach, 54
unresolved issues with tort, 55

SCOPE OF LIABILITY (PROXIMATE CAUSE)
See also FACTUAL CAUSE
Generally 337
abnormally dangerous activities, 792
Act of God, 364
aggravation of existing injury, 356
alcohol providers, 362, 371, 371
animals, strict liability limitations, 792
basis of rule,
  corollary to negligence rules, 340
  practical concerns, 339
  principled limitations, 271
breach of duty, relation to, 342
carrier delay cases, 350
class of harm, statute violation, 254
class of persons foreseeably at risk, 348
comparative fault, 382
continuous sequence test of, 346
criminal intervening acts, 361
direct-cause pattern and foreseeable harms, 346
direct harm; liability for unforeseeable but direct injury, 350
distance and time, remoteness of, 360
duty, relation to,
  generally, 343
  intervening criminal act, 352
  limiting liability using, 343
  Palsgraf case, 344
  scope of duty, 205
  vs. proximate cause debate, 344
economic harm, 373
emotional harm, 373, 732
extended liability for intentional torts, 79, 101
extent of harm, 355
fact-specific determination, 344
factual cause distinguished, 316, 342
factual cause, relation to, 342
fire, 356
force of nature, 364
foreseeability,
  class of persons, 348
  extent of harm, 355
  forces of nature, 364
  intervening acts, 353, 359
  intervening cause and manner of harm rules, 359
  manner of harm, 356
  manner of harm integral part of risk, 358
  negligence vs. proximate cause foreseeability, 342
  precise manner of injury, 356
  rescuers, 348
  risk and, 354, 357
  terminology, 354
  test of,
    generally, 339, 341, 346
    rejected when, 350
  type of harm, 347
formal tests of, 345
high-speed chases, 367
injury in attempt to escape defendant's negligence, 366
injury remote in time or distance, 360
interests at risk, 349

intervening acts,
  aggravated and second injury, 368
  criminal acts, 361
  defined, 339, 351
  foreseeability of, 339, 365, 369
  general rule, 361, 365
  intentional acts, 361
  manner of harm rules, 359
  negligent entrustment, 367
  negligent risk of, 361, 365
  no-duty rules and, 364, 371
  police chase cases, 367
  scope of risk analysis, 365
  strict liability cases, 792
  superseding cause, 339, 361, 369
  termination of risk, 370
intervening forces of nature, 364, 366
intoxication without outward conduct, 232
joint and several liability alternative, 375
judge and jury, 343
jury instruction defining, 346
keys in the car, 342, 363
limited functions of rules, 341
manner of harm, 356, 359
multiple proximate causes, 339
natural and continuous sequence, 346
negligence and, 340, 342
negligence creating risk of intervening cause, 366
negligent entrustment, 367
patterns and formal tests,
  direct cause, 346, 350
  intervening cause, 345, 351
plaintiff's fault, 373, 382
police chases, 367
policy concern of, 339, 344
products liability, 841
pseudo-proximate cause issues, 342
reasons for, 339
remoteness expression of, 360
rescue doctrine, 350
rescuers, 348, 350
risk and foreseeability, 342
risk created by negligence, limiting liability to, 337
risk limited to specific manner of harm, 356
risk of intervening acts, 365
static conditions, 366
strict liability for abnormally dangerous activities, 792
substantial factor test of, 346
suicide, 371
superseding cause,
  generally, 339, 351
  abolishing analysis of, 376
  comparative fault and, 376
  foreseeability of intervening act, 339
  intervening act as, 339, 369
  intervening force of nature, 364
  plaintiff's act as, 373
susceptible plaintiff, 350, 355
termination of the risk, 370
thin skull rule,
  generally, 355, 355
  emotional distress cases, 732
time and distance, remoteness of, 360

transferred intent in intentional tort cases, 79
unforeseeable harms, liability for, 350

PUBLIC DUTY DOCTRINE
See also GOVERNMENT ENTITIES,
OFFICERS AND EMPLOYEES
public entities under, 569
statutory violation irrelevant in tort law under,
253

PUBLIC ENTITIES
See GOVERNMENT ENTITIES, OFFICERS
AND EMPLOYEES

PUBLIC RECORDS
privacy, 1017

PUBLICITY, RIGHT OF
Generally, 1005, 1206
death, after, 1209
descendability, 1209
dignitary tort vs. property right, 1006
newsworthiness, 1007

PUNITIVE DAMAGES
See DAMAGES

PURPOSE
test of intent, 56

RAILROADS
See also COMMON CARRIERS
attractive nuisance rule, origin, 475
child injured by railroad auger, 477
child injured on railroad turntable, 475
comparative negligence under FELA, 386
Federal Employers Liability Act, 386, 911
last clear chance cases, 397
role in developing negligence law, 195
turntable doctrine, 475

RECAPTURE OF CHATTELS
See REPOSSESSION OF PROPERTY

RECKLESSNESS
See WILLFUL, WANTON, OR RECKLESS
MISCONDUCT

RECREATIONAL USE STATUTES
Generally, 479
charitable immunity and, 600

RELEASE
See also ASSUMPTION OF RISK;
CONTRACTUAL LIMITATIONS ON
LIABILITY
contribution rights and, 882
effect on claims against other tortfeasors, 886
malicious prosecution, 1035
wrongful death claim barred by inter vivos
release, 697

RELIGIOUS FREEDOM
religious doctrine inflicting emotional distress,
710

REMEDIES
See also DAMAGES; INJUNCTIONS;
RESTITUTION
attorney's fees, 43

constructive trust, see RESTITUTION, this
Index
damages generally, 851
defamation generally, 998
forcible entry and detainer statutes, 148
interference with contract, 1092
legal malpractice, 1182, 1189
misrepresentation, 1137
nuisance, 747
peaceable repossession of chattel, 151
provisional remedies, 1041
rescission, see RESTITUTION, this Index
restitution, effect of, 851
retraction or reply, defamation cases, 1003
trespass to land generally, 96

REPLEVIN
distraint or distress cases, 104
officer's execution of writ, liabilities, 156
origins, 104
recovery of converted chattel, 127

REPOSSESSION OF PROPERTY
breach of peace by, conversion, 116
chattels,
generally, 150
entering another's land for, 152
fraudulent taking, 151
fresh pursuit, 150
seller's forcible repossession, liability, 151
seller's intrusion on private quarters, 152
commercial landowners repossessing, 149
defense of property distinguished, 147
forcible entry on land by rightful owner, policy,
149
forcible repossession, tort liability for, 147
land, forcible repossession prohibited, 147

RES IPSA LOQUITUR
Generally, 297
alternative explanations and, 303
attributing fault to defendant, 306
caretaker cases, 305
circumstantial evidence, 298
common knowledge or experience, 301
control of instrumentality, putative requirement
of, 307, 308
core rule, 297
custodian cases, 305
estimating probabilities of negligence, 301
examples of, 298
expert testimony, 297, 303
illustrations, 304
inappropriate uses of, 299
inferences permitted, required or unpermitted,
299
judge and jury roles, 299
jury instructions, 300
leading example, 298
limiting rules in summary, 298
meaning, 297
medical malpractice cases, in, 302, 303, 305, 309
mere happening insufficient to prove negligence,
221, 297
multiple actors, 309
non-reciprocal risks and, 306

plaintiff participates in events causing injury, 298

pleading in the alternative, 304

probability of unknown acts of negligence, estimating, 303

probability that defendant, not another, was responsible, 306

procedural effect, 299

rear-end collisions, 299

rebuttal evidence, 300

risk of judicial error, 304

shifting burden of persuasion, 300

specific conduct requirement, relation to, 298

spoliation of evidence and, 1157

superior access to evidence by defendant, 298

tangible instruments of harm known, 304

unknown instrument of harm, 305

RESCISSION

incapacity where tort remedy equivalent to, 171

misrepresentation, for, 1128

RESPONDEAT SUPERIOR

See VICARIOUS LIABILITY

RESTITUTION

constructive trust, 1138

defamation, 1002

fraud, remedy for, 1138

gains from tort disgorged, 851

rescission-equivalent damages for misrepresentation, 1140

rescission, fraud, 1117

rescission, innocent misrepresentation, 1128

trespass to land cases, 96

RIGHT IN PERSONALITY

See also PRIVACY; UNFAIR COMPETITION

Generally, 1005, 1206

RIGHT OF PRIVACY

See PRIVACY

RISK-UTILITY ANALYSIS

See CARROLL TOWING FORMULA

SCHOOLS

See also GOVERNMENT ENTITIES, OFFICERS AND EMPLOYEES

colleges, duty to protect students, 648

compulsory schooling, custodian's status or not, 646, 648

contractual limitations on liability, 413

discipline of children, privilege, 139

duty to protect or rescue student, 621, 645

sexual harassment of students, duty to prevent, 647

suicide of student, civil rights, 588

teacher misconduct; vicarious liability for, 763

SEAMEN

maintenance and cure, 911

ship's duty to rescue, 621

wrongful death, Jones Act, 686

SEARCHES AND SEIZURES

See also ARREST; CIVIL RIGHTS; OFFICERS

drug testing, 1012

excessive force, 156

Fourth Amendment civil rights claims generally, 583

intrusive invasion of privacy, 1008

SEATBELTS AND PROTECTIVE DEVICES

airbags, federal preemption, 846

comparative fault in failing to use, 406

duty to use, arguments, 406

evidence of non-use, admissibility, 407, 840

products liability, buyer's removal of safety features, 841

statutes excluding evidence of non-use, 408

SELF-DEFENSE

Generally, 131

assault as means of, 131, 132

assault, defense to claim of, 131, 136

battery, defense to claim of, 131, 136

burden of proof, 132

criminal-law rules compared, 133, 134

deadly force, 131, 133

defense of another person, 137

excess force, liability for, 132

facts known to defendant, analysis based on, 135

false imprisonment, against, 131, 136

general rule, 131

imminent harm requirement, 132

intentional tort liability, effect on, 131

mistake in, 136

objective judgment of appearances, 135

offensive batteries, against, 136

physical harms, against, 136

provocation by words, not grounds for, 136

reasonable force, 132

retreat, when required, 133

subjective perceptions of threat, 135

timing of the use of force, 132

types of harm appropriate for, 136

unjustified use of force, liability for, 135

unlawful arrest, against, 136

unreasonable force, liability for using, 132, 133

words, against, 136

SELF-HELP

privilege, 136

repossession of chattels, 150, 151

repossession of land, 147

SHIFTING RESPONSIBILITY

implied consent, by, 414

intervening actors, to, 371

third persons' duties unaffected, 604

to employer to pass on product warnings, 832

SLANDER

See DEFAMATION

SLANDER OF TITLE

See INJURIOUS FALSEHOOD

SLAPP SUITS

defamation and, 984

wrongful litigation alternatives, 1046

SOCIAL SECURITY DISABILITY
compensation for serious injury, 922
grids and listings, 924

SOVEREIGN IMMUNITY
See IMMUNITIES; GOVERNMENT ENTITIES,
    OFFICERS AND EMPLOYEES

SPOLIATION OF EVIDENCE
factual causation in claim for, 1161
intentional, by a non-party, 1159
intentional, by a party, 1157
interference with litigation, as, 1110
negligent, 1160
presumption of causation in action for, 1161

SPORTS
     See also ASSUMPTION OF RISK
assumption of risk and, generally, 422
duty of participants, 422
inherent risks, defining, 422
intentional harms, risks assumed, 424
negligence, risk of, assumed, 423
spectators, 422
sports enterprises, duty of, 422

SPOUSES
See FAMILY

SPRING GUNS
defense of property, 142

STANDARD OF CARE
See DUTY; NEGLIGENCE

STATUTE OF LIMITATIONS
     Generally, 427
accrual of claim,
    act vs. harm, 429
    continuing negligence, 435
    discovery rule, 429
    starting the clock, 429
accrued claims, latent harm, 439
administrative prerequisites, tolling for, 437
affirmative defense, as, 427
architects, engineers, builders, 433
bar to recovery generally, 427
burden of proof, 427
childhood sexual abuse, 439
children,
    repose statutes barring, 435
    tolling for, 436
continuing negligence, 435
continuous representation rule; legal malpractice,
    1181
discovery rule,
     generally, 429
    constitutionality, 430
    defendant's connection discovered, 431
    facts that must be discovered, 430
    fiduciary's silence, 439
    issues of fact, 432
    legal malpractice, 1180
    medical malpractice, 430
    objective test, 432
    repressed memory, 439
    statutory variations, 432
    toxic tort cases, 431

two distinct injuries, 431
undiscovered injury, 429
equitable tolling, 438
Federal Tort Claims Act, 430
flexible application by courts, 429
fraudulent concealment, 438
grace periods, 436
judicial or "equitable" tolling, 438
laches distinguished, 428
land improvements claims, 433
latent harm, 439
legal malpractice, 437, 1179
malicious prosecution, 1035
medical malpractice; repose statutes, 433
mentally disabled persons, tolling for, 436
occurrence rule in legal malpractice, 1179
postponed accrual; tolling distinguished, 437
products liability, 847
rationales, 428
repose, statutes of,
     generally, 432
    affected groups, 433
    constitutionality, 434
    construction of statutes, 433
    effects, 331
    extreme cases, 331
    minors, 435
    trigger dates, 433
repressed memory and, 439
time of harm accrual in legal malpractice, 1180
tolling, 436
waiver, 427
wrongful civil litigation, 1040
wrongful death, 696

STATUTES GENERALLY
effects in tort law generally, 3, 30, 243
federal,
    preempting state law, 441
    state tort actions, in, 252
limitation, statutes of, generally, 427
preemption, federal, 441
private right of action, 246
public duty doctrine, 253
strict liability for violation of, 260
violation; children, by, effect, 233
violation negligence per se, 232, 243
violation of as evidence of negligence only, 249

STRICT LIABILITY
     See also PRODUCTS LIABILITY;
         VICARIOUS LIABILITY
abnormally dangerous activities,
    American development, 785
    common activities excluded, 786
    contemporary cases, 786
    English background, 784
    high risk requirement, 785
    intervening acts, 792
    rationales for, 789
animals,
    dangerous; proximate cause limits on strict
        liability, 792
    domestic animals abnormally dangerous,
        779
    livestock,

personal injury from, 778
trespassing, 778
wild, 782
assumption of risk, 793
comparative fault, 793, 891
defamation, 938
defined, 777
Dram Shop Statutes, 663, 665
electricity or gas, 787
erosion after 1850, 29, 777
explosives and high energy activities, 787
fault system, after adoption of, 195
flooding, 93
government entities, 553
impoundments, 789
lateral and subjacent support, 777
misrepresentation,
generally, 1127
damages limits, 1140
non-natural use of land, 785
nuisance and, 784, 737
poisons or toxic materials, 788
proximate cause limitations, 792
Restatement's many factors, 785
Rylands v. Fletcher rule, 784
shifting to fault principle, 193
storage of explosives or the like, 787
trespass form of action, in, 29
trespassory torts, 190
violation of statute and, 260
workers' compensation imposing, 912

SUBSEQUENT REPAIRS
evidence, 823

SUBSTANCE ABUSE
See ALCOHOL AND SUBSTANCES OF ABUSE

SUBSTANTIAL CERTAINTY
test of intent, 56

SUICIDE
civil rights, school's duty, 588, 650
jailer's duty to prevent prisoner's, 645
school's duty to prevent student's, 646

SUMMARY JUDGMENT
procedure defining tort issue, 35

SUPERSEDING CAUSE
See SCOPE OF LIABILITY (PROXIMATE
CAUSE)

SURFACE WATERS
trespass or nuisance discharge of, 92

SURVIVAL ACTIONS
See WRONGFUL DEATH

SWIMMING
care owed swimmers, 217

TAKING OF PROPERTY FOR PUBLIC USE
public necessity compared, 159

THERAPISTS
alienating child's affections, 1057
alienation of spousal affections, 1052
duty to protect from dangerous patient, 658

emotional harm, causing, 730
failure to warn of dangerous patient, 576
fiduciaries, as, 179
governmental immunity for actions of, 568
sexual activity with patient, consent, 179
sexual relations with plaintiff's spouse, 713
vicarious liability for torts of, 762

THIN SKULL RULE
emotional distress claims, applied to, 732
proximate cause, 355

THIRD PERSONS
See also AIDING, ABETTING,
PROCURING OR RISKING
OTHERS' TORTS; DUTY TO
PROTECT FROM THIRD PERSONS
AND FROM SELF-HARM; SCOPE
OF LIABILITY (PROXIMATE
CAUSE)
burden of defendant's risky conduct to, 272
causing trespass by, 86
comparative fault, comparing fault of third
person, 888
duty to protect from generally, 633
emotional distress of, 711
legal malpractice affecting, 1167, 1175
misrepresentation relied upon by, 1134
physician's duty to protect from patient, 660
privilege to protect from attack, 137
therapist's duty to protect from patient, 658
transferred intent, 79
undertaking creating a duty to, 627
utility of defendant's risky conduct to, 270
workers' compensation exclusive remedy, no bar
to actions against, 918

TOBACCO
battery from tobacco smoke, 67
federal preemption of claims under labeling act,
845
products liability; consumer knowledge of
unhealthy quality, 813

TORT REFORM
criticisms of tort system, 905
damages, statutes affecting, 873
immunities for individuals, 601
joint and several liability, abolishing or
modifying, 881, 883, 884
medical malpractice statutes, 524

TORTIOUS INTERFERENCE
See INTERFERENCE WITH CONTRACTS OR
OPPORTUNITIES

TORTS, INTRODUCING
See also particular torts and areas of torts
adversary approach to disputes, 34
aims of tort law, 4, 15
alternative compensation systems, 24, 905
background conditions of tort law, 43
basis of liability for, 4
coherence of tort law, 12
common law,
basis of tort law, 3
writs of Trespass and Case, 27

common law as state law, 44
common law methods of analysis, 30
community standards, generally, 21
compensation aims, 21
contracts, and, generally, 7
corrective justice and, 17
crime distinguished, 6
criticisms, 905
definining, 1
deterrence and, 23
disputes about evaluation of facts, 33
disputes of fact and law, 33
distributive justice and, 18
economic analysis and, 23
fault basis of liability generally, 5, 19
federal aspects of, 44
fundamental operating conceptions, 38
history, methods and procedures of tort law, 27
insurance, 47
judge, jury and community values, 35
judges' choices in, 19
jury, role of, 37
justice aims of, generally, 15, 19
liability insurance, 47
morality or corrective justice and, 15
nonreciprocal risks, generally, 20
non-tort alternative systems, 910
personal injury law, and, 11
policy or utility and, 18
precedent and other sources, 30
process values in, 25
property rights and, 9
regulatory control and, 10
risk distribution and, generally, 21
rule formulation, 26
rules of, nature, 31
sources of tort law, 30, 44
statutes generally, 30
strict liability generally, 5, 20, 28
trials and appeals, 33
types of interests protected generally, 5
uncertainty in law of, 31
writs, common law, 27

TOXIC TORTS
    See also HAZARDOUS WASTES;
        NUISANCE; STRICT LIABILITY
care commensurate with risks required, 217
emotional distress from exposure to toxins, 725
fetal injury; generally, 672
limitation of actions, discovery rule, 431
military, 561
nuisance from toxic contamination, 743
statute of limitations; latent harm, 439
stigma nuisance resulting from contamination of
    nearby land, 743

TRADE LIBEL
See INJURIOUS FALSEHOOD

TRADE SECRETS
breach of confidence, 1203
losing rights in, 1205

TRADEMARKS
    Generally, 1194
dilution, 1197

disparagement of, defamation rules governing,
    1196
distinctiveness lost, 1195
free speech; parody, satire, comment, 1196
functional features unprotected, 1201
generic terms, 1195
infringement, 1193
parody, satire, comment; free speech, 1196
patent law and, 1202
protected marks, names, configurations, 1194
sponsorship confusion, 1196
tarnishment, 1197
trade dress or product design, 1201

TRANSFERRED INTENT
See EXTENDED LIABILITY OR
    TRANSFERRED INTENT

TRAPS
defense of property, 142

TRESPASS
    See also particular forms of trespass, below
meanings, 85
nuisance distinguished, 735
privacy comparisons, 1011
strict liability under old writ of, 190
writ as distinct from modern tort, 86

TRESPASS FORM OF ACTION
characteristics, 25, 103

TRESPASS ON THE CASE
characteristics, 25
indirect harms, 190
nature of, 25
relationship of parties in, 191
trover developing from, 104

TRESPASS TO CHATTELS
    Generally, 105
commercial calls, unwanted, 106
consent defeating claim, 164
consequential damages, 106
conversion compared, 107
defense of property by, 139
development of claim for, 103
direct vs. indirect interference, 105
economic loss rule and, 106
elements, 105
harm or dispossession required, 105, 106
history, 103
intent required, 105
possession, 105
types of cognizable harm, 106
using plaintiff's information as, 106

TRESPASS TO LAND
            See also PREMISES LIABILITY
    Generally, 85
abnormally dangerous activities and, 88
above the surface, 93
adverse possessor's suit for, 91
airspace, 93
attractive nuisance, 476
below the surface, 95
bullets, by, 93
causing another's trespass, 86

children, by, 87, 475
civil rights analogue, 583
consent to, 85, 164, 177
continuing vs. completed or permanent, 98
damages generally, 96
direct entry requirement, 92
door-to-door salesman, implied consent to, 167
easement, 91
elements, 85
emotional distress damages, 97
encroaching buildings, removal of, 96
entry unintended, 87
environmental damage, repair costs, 97
explosives causing, 88
extended liability for, 101
flooding, 93
footings projecting underground, by, 95
forcible entry and detainer statutes, 91
fox hunt example, 88
golf balls, by, 87
harm without intent, 87
injunctions, 96
innocent trespassers, 87, 88
intangibles, interference by, 90, 92
intent required, 86
interests protected, 89, 90
intrusion required, 92
lateral support withdrawn, 92
law enforcement activities damaging land, 160
loss-of-use damages, 97
media trespass, 177
microscopic particles, nuisance vs. trespass, 92
mining as, 95
mistake as to ownership, 87
negligent but unintended harm, 87
noise, 92
nominal damages, 96
nuisance and, 89, 93, 94 92
overflights by aircraft, 94
owner's action, 91
percolating liquids, 92, 95
permanent, continuing, or temporary, 98
physical integrity of land protected, 91
pollution; beneath surface as, 95
pollution; smoke, 92
possessory rights protected, 90
privileged entry generally, 152
public necessity permitting damage or
        destruction, 158
punitive damages, 98
refusing to leave, 85
remedies, 96
remote intrusions, 95
rental value damages, 96
repossession by ousted owner, 147
reversionary interest, owner's, 91
rights vs. accommodation, 89
riparian flooding, 93
salesman at door, consent implied, 167
seller exceeding privilege to repossess goods, 152
smoke, pollution, 92
statute of limitations, 91
strict liability, 88
subsiding soil, not trespassory, 92
substantial certainty rule, 88

subsurface, 95
surface waters, by, 92
tangible entry requirement, 92
temporary vs. permanent, 98
tenant's suit against trespasser, 91
terminology, 85
transferred intent, 91, 101
tree limbs or roots, by, 94, 95
trespassing chattels, privilege to remove, 139
underground intrusions, 93
underground pollution, 93
utility lines, by, 93
waters and liquids, 92
writ, 86
wrongful possessor's suit against owner, 91

TRESPASSERS
defending property against, 139, 142

TROVER
        See also CONVERSION
writ of, 104

UNAVOIDABLE ACCIDENT
historical significance of term, 193
jury instructions on, 221

UNDUE INFLUENCE
false imprisonment, confinement by, 77
malicious prosecution, instigating another's by,
        1027

UNFAIR COMPETITION
        See also RIGHTS IN PERSONALITY;
                TRADE SECRETS;
                TRADEMARKS
        Generally, 1193
ideas as such unprotected, 1203

UNJUST ENRICHMENT
See RESTITUTION

USE AND ENJOYMENT
nuisance interfering with, 734
possessory rights distinguished, 89

VACCINES
governmental liability, negligent licensing, 555
National Childhood Vaccine Injury Act, 929

VALUE OF A CHANCE
See LOSS OF A CHANCE

VICARIOUS LIABILITY
        See also INDEPENDENT
                CONTRACTORS; PRINCIPAL
                AND AGENT
        Generally, 753
aiding or abetting a tort, 937
apparent agency or estoppel, 770
borrowed servants, 773
captain of the ship doctrine, 774
caretakers and custodians, 762, 763
children, 757
churches, 763
clergy misconduct; vicarious liability for, 762
concert of action or conspiracy, 753
estoppel, agency by, 770
family, 757

fault, role of, 754
franchisees and licensees, 765
frolic and detour, 759
going and coming rule, 758
hospitals; borrowed servant, captain of the ship, 774
indemnity in favor of employer, 754
independent contractors, 764
intentional torts of employee, 761
joint and several liability, 882
joint enterprise liability, 753
legal malpractice, agency law and, 1164
managed care organizations, 534
motive of employee, 757, 761
non-delegable duty doctrine, 766
non-work related tasks, 760
nuisance created by another, 737
parents, for torts of children, 757
partners' liability, 753
personal acts of employee, 760
primary liability distinguished, 754
rationales, 755
reentry into employment, 760
schools; teacher misconduct, 763
scope of employment, 757, 758
terms defined, 753
therapists, 762

WAGER OF LAW
detinue, oath-helpers, 104

WARRANTY
See also PRODUCTS LIABILITY
privity requirement loosened, 800
products liability theory, 798
representations as, economic torts, 1127

WATERS
nuisance, public, 746
surface water, trespass or nuisance, 92

WEAPONS
children using, child standard of care, 236
gun control statutes, negligence per se, 244
hunting, risks of negligence not assumed, 425
negligent entrustment; scope of liability (proximate cause), 366
noise from, nuisance, 743
reasonable person standard of care, 216
selling to intoxicated persons, 655
trespass by firing across land, 94

WESTFALL ACT
federal employee immunity, 580

WILLFUL, WANTON, OR RECKLESS MISCONDUCT
comparative fault and, 397, 896
constitutional requirements in defamation cases, 987
constitutional requirements in false light privacy cases, 1021
defined, 59
discretionary immunity destroyed by, 579
duties under recreational use statutes, 479
duty to licensee, 463
duty to trespassers, 460

emergency vehicles standard, 575
emotional distress resulting, 707
exception to public duty doctrine immunity, 571
firefighter's rule, exception to, 610
good Samaritan statutes limiting liability, 523
intervening reckless acts and strict liability, 792
intoxicated driving as, 59
legal malpractice standard in criminal cases, 1187
parental liability for child's, 652
public duty doctrine not protecting, 571
punitive damages, 861
social host serving alcohol, 663
traps for trespassers, 146

WITNESSES
perjury, no tort action for, 966, 1024

WORKERS' COMPENSATION
Generally, 911
accidental injury requirement, 915
allocation of liability, effects on, by, 890
apportionment of responsibility, employer and tortfeasor, 918
benefits, 912
characteristic provisions, 912
emotional or "mental" injury, 916
employer immunity barring tort claim, effect on allocation, 890
employer liability for tort, 920
employer's immunity and comparative fault, 890
exclusive remedy,
    effect of barring tort claim, 918
    exceptions to, 920
    fetal injury and, 673
external event, 916
fetal injury and, 673
historical development, 911
injury arising in course of and out of employment, 914
intentional torts under, 915, 921
multiple employers', apportionment of liability for, 918
occupational disease, 917
preexisting conditions, 916
structure of systems, 912

WRITS
attachment, garnishment and other judicial process, 1043
common law, 29, 103
detinue, 104
officer's privilege to execute facially fair writs, 156
replevin, 127
trespass, 25, 86, 103
trespass de bonis asportatis, 104
trespass on the case, 29, 104
trespass on the case for trover, 104
trespass quare clausem fregit, 86
trespass strict liability for animals, 778
trover, 104

WRONGDOERS
denying recovery to, 144

WRONGFUL ATTACHMENT OR LEVY
    See also LIS PENDENS
abuse of process by, 1043
conversion by, 1153

**WRONGFUL BIRTH, LIFE, OR
    PREGNANCY**
        See also PRENATAL AND BIRTH-
            RELATED INJURY
    Generally, 677
damages, 681
damages rules restricting claims for, 680
emotional harm, 682

WRONGFUL CIVIL LITIGATION
        See also ABUSE OF PROCESS,
            MALICIOUS PROSECUTION;
            LIS PENDENS; WRONGFUL
            ATTACHMENT OR LEVY
    Generally, 1036
counterclaims for, 1040, 1047
damages, 1025, 1041
elements, 1036
loss in first trial, effect of, 1039
probable cause, 1038
punitive damages, 1026
special grievance or injury requirement, 1041
statute of limitations, 1040

WRONGFUL DEATH
    Generally, 685
adoption of statutes, 685
arbitration clauses, 694
common law rules against recovery, 685
comparative fault, 696
damages,
        caps on, 695
        combined measures of, 691
        decedents not earning or contributing, 690
        forms of evidence, 689
        loss of inheritance rule, 691
        loss to dependents rule, 689
        loss to estate rule, 690
        non-pecuniary losses, 691
        pecuniary loss, 688
        punitive, 693
        statutes, 691
emotional distress, 691
negligence and, 686
plaintiffs, 694
prenatal injury causing, 670
prior judgments, 697
procedure, 694
punitive damages, 693
release during decedent's life, 697
statutes of limitation, 696
statutory actions for, 686
survival actions,
        actions that survive or do not, 688
        damages, 687
        defamation excluded, 954
        defenses, 696
        derivative nature of, 696
        distinguished, 686
        nature and purpose, 687
        scope, 687

statute of limitations, 696
surviving the tortfeasor's death, 688

ZONING
nuisance, effect in claims for, 739